Sports Illustrated

2000

Sports
Almanac

By the Editors of Sports Illustrated

Sports Illustrated
2000
Sports
Almanac

Total/*Sports Illustrated* and *Sports Illustrated* are registered
trademarks of Time Inc. Used under license.

For information about permission to reproduce
selections from this book, please write to:
Permissions
Total/*Sports Illustrated*
100 Enterprise Dr.
Kingston, NY 12401

First Edition
ISBN 1-892129-14-0

Sports Illustrated 2000 Sports Almanac was prepared by
Bishop Books of New York City.

Sports Illustrated Editorial Director for Books: Joe Marshall
Sports Illustrated Director of Development: Stanley Weil

Cover photography credits (clockwise from upper left):
Brandi Chastain: John W. McDonough
David Cone: Chuck Solomon
John Elway: John Biever

Back cover photography credits (clockwise from upper right):
Wayne Gretzky: David E. Klutho
Tiger Woods: Bob Martin
Tim Duncan: John Biever

Title page photography credit: Simon Bruty

10 9 8 7 6 5 4 3 2 1
COM
PRINTED IN THE UNITED STATES OF AMERICA

CONTENTS

SOURCES

In compiling the *Sports Illustrated 1999 Sports Almanac*, the editors would again like to thank the staff of the *Sports Illustrated* library for its invaluable assistance. They would also like to extend their gratitude to the media relations offices of the following organizations for their help in providing information and materials relating to their sports: Major League Baseball; the Canadian Football League; the National Football League; the National Collegiate Athletic Association; the National Basketball Association; the National Hockey League; the Association of Tennis Professionals; the World Tennis Association; the U.S. Tennis Association; the U.S. Golf Association; the Ladies Professional Golf Association; the Professional Golfers Association; National Thoroughbred Racing Association; the U.S. Trotting Association; the Breeders' Cup; Churchill Downs; the New York Racing Association, Inc.; the Maryland Jockey Club; Championship Auto Racing Teams; the National Hot Rod Association; the International Motor Sports Association; the National Association for Stock Car Auto Racing; the Professional Bowlers Association; the Ladies Professional Bowlers Tour; the American Professional Soccer League; the National Professional Soccer League; the *Fédération Internationale de Football Association*; the U.S. Soccer Federation; the U.S. Olympic Committee; USA Track & Field; U.S. Swimming; U.S. Diving; U.S. Skiing; U.S. Skating; the U.S. Chess Federation; U.S. Curling; the Iditarod Trail Committee; the International Game Fish Association; the U.S. Gymnastics Federation; U.S. Handball Association; the Lacrosse Foundation; the American Power Boat Association; the Hydroplane Racing Association; the Professional Rodeo Cowboys Association; U.S. Rowing; the American Softball Association; the U.S. Speed Skating Association; U.S. Rugby Football Union; the Triathlon Federation USA; the National Archery Association; USA Wrestling; the U.S. Squash Racquets Association; the U.S. Polo Association; ABC Sports and the U.S. Volleyball Association.

The following sources were consulted in gathering information:

Baseball   *The Baseball Encyclopedia*, Macmillan Publishing Co., 1990; *Total Baseball*, Viking Penguin, 1995; *Baseballistics*, St. Martin's Press, 1990; *The Book of Baseball Records*, Seymour Siwoff, publisher, 1991; *The Complete Baseball Record Book*, The Sporting News Publishing Co., 1992; *The Sporting News Baseball Guide*, The Sporting News Publishing Co., 1996; *The Sporting News Official Baseball Register*, The Sporting News Publishing Co., 1996; *National League Green Book—1994*, The Sporting News Publishing Co., 1993; *American League Red Book—1994*, The Sporting News Publishing Co., 1993; *The Scouting Report: 1996,* Harper Perennial, 1996.

Pro Football   *The Official 1997 National Football League Record & Fact Book*, The National Football League, 1997; *The Official National Football League Encyclopedia*, New American Library, 1990; *The Sporting News Football Guide*, The Sporting News Publishing Co., 1996; *The Sporting News Football Register*, The Sporting News Publishing Co., 1996; *The 1993 National Football League Record & Fact Book,* Workman Publishing, 1993; *The Football Encyclopedia,* David Neft and Richard Cohen, St. Martin's Press, 1991.

College Football   *1997 NCAA Football*, The National Collegiate Athletic Association, 1997.

Pro Basketball   *The Official NBA Basketball Encyclopedia*, Villard Books, 1994; *The Sporting News Official NBA Guide*, The Sporting News Publishing Co., 1996; *The Sporting News Official NBA Register*, The Sporting News Publishing Co., 1996.

College Basketball   *1997 NCAA Basketball*, The National Collegiate Athletic Association, 1996.

Hockey *The National Hockey League Official Guide & Record Book 1997–98*, The National Hockey League, 1997; *The Sporting News Complete Hockey Book,* The Sporting News Publishing Co., 1993; *The Complete Encyclopedia of Hockey,* Visible Ink Press, 1993.

Tennis *1997 Official USTA Tennis Yearbook*, H.O. Zimman, Inc., 1997; *IBM/ATP Tour 1997 Player Guide*, Association of Tennis Professionals, 1997; *1997 Corel WTA Tour Media Guide*, Corel WTA Tour, 1997.

Golf *PGA Tour Book 1997*, PGA Tour Creative Services, 1997; *LPGA 1997 Player Guide*, LPGA Communications Department, 1997; *Senior PGA Tour Book 1997*, PGA Tour Creative Services, 1997; *USGA Yearbook 1997*, U.S. Golf Association, 1997.

Boxing *The Ring 1986–87 Record Book and Boxing Encyclopedia*, The Ring Publishing Corp., 1987. (To subscribe to *The Ring* magazine, write to P.O. Box 768, Rockville Centre, New York 11571-9905; or call (516) 678-7464); *Computer Boxing Update*, Ralph Citro, Inc., 1992; Bob Yalen, boxing statistician at ESPN.

Horse Racing *The American Racing Manual 1994*, Daily Racing Form, Inc., 1994; *1994 Directory and Record Book*, The Thoroughbred Racing Association, 1994; *The Trotting and Pacing Guide 1994*, United States Trotting Association, 1994; *Breeders' Cup 1993 Statistics*, Breeders' Cup Limited, 1993; *NYRA Media Guide 1993*, The New York Racing Association, 1994; *The 120th Kentucky Derby Media Guide, 1994*, Churchill Downs Public Relations Dept., 1994; *The 120th Preakness Press Guide, 1994*, Maryland Jockey Club, 1994; *Harness Racing News,* Harness Racing Communications.

Motor Sports *The Official NASCAR Yearbook and Press Guide 1997*, UMI Publications, Inc., 1997; *1994 Indianapolis 500 Media Fact Book*, Indy 500 Publications, 1994; *IMSA Yearbook 1995 Season Review*, International Motor Sports Association, 1995; *1994 Winston Drag Racing Series Media Guide*, Sports Marketing Enterprises, 1994.

Bowling *1994 Professional Bowlers Association Press, Radio and Television Guide*, Professional Bowlers Association, Inc., 1994; *The Professional Women's Bowling Association Tour Guide 1997*.

Soccer *Rothmans Football Yearbook 1993–94*, Headline Book Publishing, 1993; *American Professional Soccer League 1992 Media Guide*, APSL Media Relations Department, 1992; The *European Football Yearbook*, Facer Publications Limited, 1988; *Soccer America,* Burling Communications; Dan Goldstein, editor of *Football Europe.*

NCAA Sports *1997–98 National Collegiate Championships*, The National Collegiate Athletic Association, 1998; *1993–94 National Directory of College Athletics,* Collegiate Directories Inc., 1993.

Olympics *The Complete Book of the Olympics,* Little, Brown and Co., 1991; *The Complete Book of the Summer Olympics,* Little, Brown and Co., 1996

Track and Field *American Athletics Annual 1996*, The Athletics Congress/USA, 1996.

Swimming *6th World Swimming Championships Media Guide*, The World Swimming Championships Organizing Committee, 1991.

Skiing *U.S. Ski Team 1994 Media Guide / USSA Directory*, U.S. Ski Association, 1993; *Ski Racing Annual Competition Guide 1993–94*, Ski Racing International, 1993; *Ski Magazine's Encyclopedia of Skiing*, Harper & Row, 1974; *Caffe Lavazza Ski World Cup Press Kit*, Biorama, 1991.

The Year in Sports

The world champion
U.S. women's
soccer team

Out With a Bang

The 20th century ended with a rousing year in sports, which showed no signs of relinquishing center stage in our culture

BY MERRELL NODEN

WHATEVER ELSE the past 100 years have been—the American Century or the Age of Anxiety—they have also been, without doubt, the Century of Sport. One hundred years ago, when only the rich could afford to play games, when the modern Olympics were just four years old and there was no World Series, no Super Bowl, no Stanley, World or Ryder Cups, it would have been difficult to foresee the amount of money, time and interest we now invest in sports. They are the numbing year-round sound track to our lives. Forget religion: In the 20th century sports became the opiate of the masses.

Numerologists have been predicting weird things for the end of the millennium—weirder even than Dennis Rodman—and sure enough its penultimate year closed with some eye-catching images: U.S. soccer player Brandi Chastain ripping off her jersey in celebration at the Women's World Cup to reveal the black sports bra underneath; Spain's Sergio Gar-cia first running, then leaping into a scissors kick as he followed his miracle shot up the 16th fairway at the PGA Championship; and poor Jean Van de Velde of France looking more bewildered than Inspector Clouseau as he rolled up his pants legs and stepped into the Barry Burn at Carnoustie on the final hole of the British Open he let get away.

And speaking of things Gallic, it was impossible this year not to feel a strong sense of déjà vu: The Broncos repeated as Super Bowl champions, the Yankees as World Series winners, the Houston Comets as WNBA champs and Sammy Sosa and Mark McGwire once more slugged their way past 40, 50 and 60 home runs. Never mind Bill and Hillary: Sosa and McGwire were 1999's power couple, but this was a year big moments came from unlikely quarters: Chastain and her teammates galvanized the nation, and Lance Armstrong provided the year's miracle by winning the Tour de France only 34 months after being diagnosed with testicular cancer and hear-

BEN CURTIS/PRESS ASSOCIATION

Van de Velde did his best Clouseau impression at the British Open.

ing that he had a 50-50 chance of survival.

We also saw some of our heroes choking back sweet tears, for, as we bid farewell to a year and a century, we also had to say goodbye to a Rushmore of superb athletes, three men and a woman who have dominated their sports for the past decade. Among them Michael Jordan, John Elway, Wayne Gretzky and Steffi Graf have won six NBA titles, two Super Bowls, four Stanley Cups and 22 Grand Slam tennis titles.

But more important in a year sullied by a "millionaires versus billionaires pissing con-

test" in the NBA, as Jayson Williams so aptly described it, and a vote-buying scandal that shamed the Olympics, those four will be remembered for performing with transcendent grace. Though all of them could have hung on longer, and earned many millions of dollars for doing so, they chose to heed A.E. Housman's advice and "slipped betimes away," leaving us with indelible memories of their glorious peaks and not their decline. All will be sorely missed.

A bit more perplexing was the case of Detroit Lions running back Barry Sanders, who shocked the NFL by announcing his retirement while on vacation during the off-season. Sanders, reportedly miffed by the

Magnificent 7: Elway was one of several legends to retire in 1999.

dominating inside, the Spurs won 46 of their final 53 games, including four of five from the upstart New York Knicks in the NBA Finals.

Pro football found its newest star in Minnesota's super-speedy wide receiver, Randy Moss. Coming into the league after 19 teams passed him by in the draft because they were worried about his checkered past, Moss rewarded the Vikings' faith in him. Not only did he catch 17 touchdown passes, he also bolstered the confidence of veteran quarterback Randall Cunningham, who paced the league with a 106.0 passer rating and led the Vikings to an NFL-record 556 points and a 15–1 record, best in the league. But the Vikes' dream season ended in the NFC finals when kicker Gary Anderson, who had made a record 40 field goals in a row, missed a 39-yarder and Minnesota lost to the Atlanta Falcons 30–27 in overtime.

The Falcons, though, turned out to be no match for Elway and the Broncos in the Super Bowl. Denver lost only two games in the regular season as Terrell Davis became the fourth rusher to gain over 2,000 yards in a season, finishing with 2,008. In the Super Bowl the Broncos dominated Atlanta, and Elway made his final game one of his best, completing 18 of 29 passes for 336 yards and a TD. Davis carried 25 times for 102 yards, his seventh straight 100-yard playoff game, and the Broncos' defense intercepted three of Chris Chandler's passes. The final score was 34–19, but it really wasn't that close.

Blooming from the cracked concrete tennis courts of Compton, Calif., came the Williams sisters, Venus and Serena, whose dad, Richard, has groomed them to be both powerful and poised. Most observers had expected 19-year-old Venus to beat her sister to a Grand Slam title, but at the U.S. Open it was 17-year-old Serena who defeated

Lions' repeated failure to advance beyond the first round of the playoffs, retired at age 31, needing just 1,457 yards to surpass Walter Payton as the NFL's career rushing leader. There was a strong suspicion that Sanders would pop up elsewhere, but as of November he hadn't made a move.

But as we also learned in 1999, the sports world abhors a vacuum. For every superstar who bowed out, there seemed to be a fresh-faced kid ready to take his or her place, many hailing from unexpected places. Into the huge void left by Jordan stepped unassuming, efficient Tim Duncan, a former swimmer from St. Croix. Whereas Jordan lashed the Bulls with his fiery need to win, Duncan, 23, provided leadership of a quieter kind while leading the San Antonio Spurs to the NBA title. His line for the year read: 21.7 points and 11.4 rebounds per game, plus one reputation resurrected as he so perfectly complemented his oft-maligned frontcourt mate, David Robinson, that Robinson too came into his own and won the title he'd been seeking throughout his 10-year NBA career. With the two big men defending champ Lindsay Davenport and then No. 1–ranked Martina Hingis to claim the title. Serena was the first African-American woman to win a Grand Slam title since Althea Gibson won at Forest Hills in 1958.

Everyone assumed that staid old golf had already uncovered its future in that fist-pumping multiracial kid with the fierce nickname. But in 19-year-old Garcia of Spain, golf found an even younger star than Tiger Woods. Garcia won the Irish Open on July 4 and threw a scare into Woods at the PGA Championship a month later. In a sport full of grim-faced men who "play" while looking as though they were being led to their execution, Garcia's boyish exuberance was a welcome change.

If Garcia's giddy little gallop had a rival for Image of the Year it came in the Rose Bowl, on July 10, when Chastain ripped off her jersey as she fell to her knees to celebrate the penalty-kick goal that gave the U.S. women a 5–4 shootout win over China in the Women's World Cup soccer final. Though Chastain's moment in the spotlight will long be remembered, and striker Mia Hamm was the U.S. team's media darling, it was 33-year-old Michelle Akers who provided its unyielding heart. Akers defied age, injuries and chronic fatigue syndrome to marshal the U.S. midfield. Akers had to watch the shootout from the locker room with an IV in each arm. Completely spent, she had left the game late in regulation after a nasty collision.

Akers was not the only impossibly tough woman we saw in 1999. Ludmila Engquist, a 100-meter hurdler from Sweden, learned that she had cancer in March, had a mastectomy in April and then won the bronze medal at the world championships in August, between her fifth and sixth chemotherapy treatments. Not so lucky was Houston Comet guard Kim Perrot, who struggled against cancer all season before succumbing on Aug. 19, shortly before her team won its third straight WNBA title.

Cancer was also the backdrop for the most amazing comeback of the year, which is saying something in a year that featured not only Engquist but Andre Agassi, the U.S. Ryder Cup team and Manchester United, which rallied for two goals deep into stoppage time to beat Bayern Munich 2–1 and "do the treble," sweeping the FA Cup, the Premier League championship and the Champions League title all in the same year.

Cyclist Armstrong was diagnosed with advanced testicular cancer on Oct. 2, 1996. One of his testicles was removed the following day, but Armstrong soon learned that the cancer had spread to his lungs and brain. Armstrong chose a relatively risky drug called ifosfamide because it would give him a better chance of cycling again. On July 3 he won the Tour's prologue. That by itself was amazing, but three weeks later Armstrong rode down the Champs-Elysées as just the second U.S. rider to win the Tour de France.

The most incredible and inspiring story of the year, right? Well, cycling is so rife with drug use, the cloud hanging over the Tour after last year's drug scandal was so dark, that Armstrong's victory was greeted by at least as much skepticism as amazement. The French press was particularly suspicious of his accomplishment.

The year's greatest scandal involved the Olympics. It started when someone leaked to KTVX television a letter from the Salt Lake Organizing Committee's Dave Johnson to the daughter of Rene Essomba, the since-deceased IOC member from Cameroon, informing her that the accompanying check for $10,000 would be her last. The letter, it turned out, was a fake, but the information it contained was true, and as the story unraveled so did any notion that the Olympics were a purely selfless and noble undertaking. Votes, it seems, have been auctioned off by almost every city bidding to host the Olympics for anything from cash and expensive trips to sexual favors and even a history post at Brigham Young University.

As a direct result of these revelations, 10 IOC members either resigned or were expelled; major sponsors such as John Hancock and Johnson & Johnson pulled out; and Juan Antonio Samaranch, the

SHARP

few of the right calls in 1999. They furthered the sport's longstanding reputation for scandal and controversy. The biggest fight of the year, a heavyweight title unification bout between WBA and IBF champ Evander Holyfield and WBC champ Lennox Lewis on March 13, was judged to be a draw, a staggering miscarriage of justice since everyone this side of Don King saw clearly that the taller, younger Lewis had dominated Holyfield. Somehow judge Eugenia Williams scored the fight 115–113 for Holyfield. So egregious was this judgment that the three sanctioning bodies, which customarily can't agree on anything, ordered a rematch within six months. Far less egregious, but almost as anticlimactic, was September's welterweight showdown between boxing's Golden Boy, Oscar De La Hoya, and Felix Trinidad. De La Hoya dominated the first eight rounds but mysteriously eased off in the final four rounds and lost for the first time in 32 professional fights.

One of golf's golden boys, David Duval, won four times before the Masters and entered the record books with a final-round 59 at the Bob Hope Classic. Duval's win at the Players Championship vaulted him past Woods to the No. 1 spot in the World Rankings, but the year went downhill from there for Duval, as he failed to win again.

Paul Lawrie of Scotland won the British Open, though it's nowhere near as simple as that. Contested at rugged Carnoustie with its ribbon-thin fairways and knee-high roughs, the British Open was the toughest major tournament in years. Garcia shot an opening round 89 while first-day leader Rodney Pampling blew up to a second-round 86 and failed to make the cut. The Open seemed to have found its improbable winner in Van de Velde, who stepped onto

reactionary and stubborn IOC head, was under increasing pressure to resign.

Controversy touched the NHL, too, as a great Stanley Cup final ended on a sour note. At 54:51 of overtime in the sixth game, Brett Hull of the Dallas Stars shoveled the puck past Buffalo Sabres goalie Dominik Hasek and into the goal. Pandemonium broke loose on the ice. But replays showed that Hull's left skate was in the crease when the puck was not. The replay was so conclusive that when he saw it back in the locker room, Hasek began to suit up again, sure that the goal would not be allowed to stand. But it did. Referring to an earlier "clarification" of the rule that permits a player to stay inside the crease as long as he controls the puck, the NHL ruled the goal legitimate, a decision sure to embitter Buffalo fans for years. "What the heck is the NHL going to do?" asked Buffalo captain Michael Peca. "Open the floodgates by making the right call?"

The overseers of boxing, as usual, made

the 18th tee needing just a double-bogey 6 to win.

But on that final hole poor Van de Velde suffered a slow-motion breakdown, hitting his second shot into the greenside bleachers, from which it bounced back into the heavy rough. From there he chunked it into the burn. After wading down into the water, with the intention of hitting it out, Van de Velde decided to drop behind the burn, in the heavy rough, whence he hacked it into the bunker. He got up and down brilliantly, though for a triple bogey and a playoff instead of the British Open title. Lawrie, who'd started the day 10 strokes back, won the playoff easily. Van de Velde may have lost the only major he's likely to get a shot at, but he won universal admiration for his good humor and grace in the face of extraordinary disaster.

Woods dominated the rest of the year, regaining his No. 1 ranking and claiming the PGA title. He led the heavily favored U.S. team to the Ryder Cup at the Country Club in Brookline, Mass, where the U.S. overcame a seemingly insurmountable 10–6 deficit by winning 8 ½ of a possible 12 points in Sunday's singles matches. Justin Leonard clinched the Cup by draining a 45-foot putt on the 17th hole to guarantee at least half a point in his match against José María Olazábal.

That precipitated a giddy celebration, with players, captain Ben Crenshaw and even players' wives dancing around the green. Olazábal, waiting to attempt a 20-foot putt that could have tied the match, looked on in amazement. Though he did not blame the Americans when he missed, Olazábal and his teammates spoke bitterly of

the treatment they received in Boston, especially the insults directed at Colin Montgomerie, whose 70-year-old father left Sunday's match disgusted by the boorish behavior toward his son. One can only hope that the tone of this year's Cup doesn't set the standard for the future.

The ever temperamental world of tennis was the scene of both comebacks and debuts. In the championship match at the French Open, Hingis appeared to self-destruct in the face of both the jeering Roland Garros fans and Graf, who coolly won what would be the last major title of her great career. Hingis's problems continued at Wimbledon, where she lost in the first round. Also winning in Paris was Agassi, who had not won a Grand Slam title since the 1995 Australian Open. Agassi, who in April entered divorce proceedings with actress Brooke Shields, his wife of two years, also defeated Todd Martin to win the U.S. Open and soon after began a public romance with Graf.

Track and field had a banner year, with

TOM DIPACE

The Big Unit was huge for Arizona, going 17–9 with 364 strikeouts and a 2.48 ERA.

Johnson, who already owned the 200 world record, added the 400 in Seville.

records falling in the 100, 400, mile and decathlon. Hicham El Guerrouj of Morocco broke the world record in the mile, running 3:43.13 in Rome, but the bigger surprise was 20-year-old Noah Ngeny of Kenya, who finished second, .27 behind him. Still, the year's best action came in the sprints, where Maurice Greene spent the summer making sub-10-second 100s look routine. Greene smashed the world record with a 9.79 and then backed it up by overcoming a bad start to clock 9.80 at the World Championships, where he also won the 200 and anchored the winning 4 x 100 relay.

Michael Johnson provided the other great highlight at the world championships, when after years of coming close, he finally broke Butch Reynolds's 11-year-old record for the 400. Johnson, who had endured insinuations that he was ducking Greene when he claimed injury earlier in the season, ran 43.18 in Seville to set up a dream 200 with Greene next year.

The baseball season was a collection of milestones. Not only did both McGwire and Sosa top 60 homers again, but McGwire climbed past the 500-homer mark, and Tony Gwynn and Wade Boggs became the 22nd and 23rd players, respectively, to amass 3,000 hits. David Cone pitched a perfect game against the Montreal Expos, and both Randy Johnson and Pedro Martinez topped 300 strikeouts for the season. The National League wild card berth came down to a one-game playoff, between the Mets and the Reds (the Mets won 5–0), and the Arizona Diamondbacks won the NL West in only their second year of existence.

So it's on to Sydney and the first Olympics of the 21st century. Those sports-mad Aussies have already found their great Olympic hope in Ian Thorpe, a 16-year-old swimmer with size-16 feet, known to his teammates as the Thorpedo. At August's Pan Pacific championships in Sydney, Thorpe shaved a few tenths off the world 200-meter freestyle record, anchored Australia's winning 4 x 100 free relay that handed the U.S. its first defeat at a major meet and blasted countryman Kieren Perkins's world record in the 400-meter free. Many experts ranked that as one of the greatest swims of all time, though almost as impressive was Thorpe's decision to donate the $16,000 he won for setting the first world record in the Olympic pool to a local children's cancer charity. Swimmers, you know, don't make quite as much money as, say, NBA players or Ryder Cup golfers.

As we peer into the next century, we must ask what is to become of the badly tarnished Olympic ideal—indeed, what is to become of sports in general? They aren't about to disappear, and right now it's hard to imagine their ever assuming a smaller place in our world. How will they be shaped and changed by the struggle between winning at all costs and winning with fairness and integrity? How will more and more money mutate them? Oh, for the young legs of Sergio Garcia, to take a running leap and see what lies ahead!

compiled by Jeff Labrecque and Ward Calhoun

Baseball

Oct 23—Davey Johnson, whose .575 career winning percentage is the highest of any active manager, is named manager of the Los Angeles Dodgers.

Oct 26—Catcher Mike Piazza signs a record seven-year, $91 million contract to remain with the New York Mets. Two days later, the Mets re-sign ace Al Leiter to a four-year, $32 million deal.

Nov 2—American League umpire Don Denkinger, a 40-year veteran known for an infamous call in Game 6 of the 1985 World Series, announces his retirement effective Dec. 31. Denkinger called the Royals' Jorge Orta safe at first base, although replays showed that Orta was out. The call helped Kansas City win that game against St. Louis to tie the Series before winning Game 7 for the championship.

Nov 3—San Diego voters approve a proposition to move the Padres from Qualcomm Stadium, which the team shares with the NFL's Chargers, to a downtown ballpark.

Nov 6—The Yankees re-sign World Series MVP

RONALD C. MODRA

Scott Brosius to a three-year, $15.75 million contract.

Nov 8—Mets G.M. Steve Phillips takes a leave of absence amid the threat of a sexual harassment lawsuit. Frank Cashen, the Mets' G.M. from 1980 to '92, replaces him on an interim basis. Phillips returns on Nov. 16.

Nov 9—Cubs pitcher Kerry Wood, who tied a major league record with 20 strikeouts on May 6, narrowly defeats Colorado first baseman Todd Helton, 128–119, for NL Rookie of the Year. Wood had a 13–6 record and was third in the NL in strikeouts with 233.

Nov 10—Right fielder Ben Grieve of the Athletics is voted AL Rookie of the Year. Grieve batted .288 and led AL rookies in hits, homers, runs, doubles and RBIs.

Nov 10—The Braves trade 16–game winner Denny Neagle, outfielder Michael Tucker and prospect Robby Bell to the Reds for Gold Glove second baseman Bret Boone and pitcher Mike Remlinger.

Nov 11—Houston's Larry Dierker, who led the Astros to an 18-game improvement to finish with the third-most wins in the majors and the NL Central Division title, is named NL Manager of the Year.

Nov 12—Receiving 23 of 28 first-place votes, Joe Torre of the Yankees is named AL Manager of the Year.

Nov 15—Free agent Ken Caminiti, who helped the Padres reach the 1998 World Series, signs a two-year contract for $9.5 million with the Astros.

Nov 15—Sammy Sosa is named MVP of the U.S.-Japan all-star tour, won by the Americans five games to two. Sosa hit three homers during the series.

Nov 16—Toronto's Roger Clemens, who went 20–6 with a 2.65 ERA and 271 strikeouts, wins his record fifth Cy Young award, his second in a row.

Nov 17—Atlanta's Tom Glavine wins his second NL Cy Young award. San Diego reliever Trevor Hoffman finishes a close second in the voting.

Nov 18—Juan Gonzalez of Texas, who batted .318 with 45 home runs, 110 runs and 157 RBIs, wins his second AL MVP award in three years.

Nov 19—Chicago's Sammy Sosa defeats Mark McGwire in the NL MVP vote, 438–272. Sosa

After sizzling in Toronto, Clemens joined the Yanks and cooled off, going 14–10.

receives 30 first-place votes to McGwire's two.

Nov 23—Brian Jordan, a free-agent outfielder with the Cardinals last season, signs a $40 million, five-year deal with the Braves.

Nov 24—The Indians sign second baseman Roberto Alomar to a four-year contract. He will join his brother, catcher Sandy Alomar Jr.

Nov 30—The Diamondbacks sign lefthander Randy Johnson to a four-year, $52.4 million contract.

Dec 1—The Orioles sign outfielder Albert Belle to a five-year, $65 million contract, but lose first baseman Rafael Palmeiro when he signs with the Rangers for $45 million over five seasons.

Dec 1—The Dodgers send catcher Charles Johnson and outfielder Roger Cedeño to the Mets for catcher Todd Hundley and a prospect; the Mets then deal Johnson to the Orioles for reliever Armando Benitez.

Dec 9—Miami native Jose Canseco signs a contract with the Devil Rays for three years worth up to $16.4 million with incentives.

Dec 10—Red Sox reliever Dennis Eckersley, third on the alltime list for career saves (390),

retires after 24 years in the major leagues.

Dec 11—Yankees Hall of Famer Joe DiMaggio, 84, lapses into a coma while battling pneumonia in a Hollywood, Fla., hospital.

Dec 12—The Dodgers hand pitcher Kevin Brown the richest contract in baseball history: seven years, $105 million.

Dec 14—The Expos draft Heisman Trophy–winning running back Ricky Williams from the Phillies organization with the fourth overall pick of the annual Rule 5 draft.

Jan 5, 1999—After a 14-year feud, Yankees Hall of Famer Yogi Berra accepts George Steinbrenner's apology for the unprofessional manner in which Berra was fired as New York manager in 1985, and ends his official boycott of Yankee Stadium.

Jan 5—Nolan Ryan, George Brett, and Robin Yount are elected to Cooperstown, marking the first time since 1936 that three players are elected in their first year of eligibility.

Jan 12—Mark McGwire's 70th home-run ball is sold to an anonymous bidder at auction for $3.05 million.

Jan 18—Joe DiMaggio returns home after a 99-day stay in a Florida hospital.

Jan 18—An employee is injured when part of the new roof over Montreal's Olympic Stadium caves in as a result of snow. Montreal had received about 50 inches of snow during the previous two weeks.

Jan 24—Twins righthander Bob Tewksbury retires after 13 seasons. He leaves with a 110–102 career record and a 3.92 ERA for six major league teams.

Jan 24—While watching a television report on NBC, Joe DiMaggio is surprised to hear that he has passed away. NBC corrects the erroneous report 20 minutes later and offers DiMaggio an apology.

Jan 27—Major League Baseball announces that players who are not on teams' 40-man rosters will be allowed to play in Olympic qualifying in 1999 and in the 2000 Games in Sydney, Australia.

Jan 27—Lefthander Sterling Hitchcock, the MVP of the 1998 NL Championship Series, re-signs with the Padres for three years, $15.5 million.

Jan 29—Orioles lefthander Jimmy

The great Gwynn rapped out career hit No. 3,000.

JOHN IACONO

Key, who won 186 games in 15 major league seasons, retires at age 37. The five-time All-Star won the clinching games of the 1992 and 1996 World Series.

Feb 2—The Padres trade outfielder Greg Vaughn and pinch hitter Mark Sweeney to the Reds for outfielder Reggie Sanders and two minor league prospects.

Feb 3—Astros reliever Billy Wagner, who earned only $280,000 in 1998, re-signs for $10.3 million over the next three seasons.

Feb 5—In honor of the 25th anniversary of his 715th home run, Major League Baseball announces that a new award for the best hitter in each league—to be determined by a formula including hits, home runs and RBIs—will be named for Hank Aaron.

Feb 7—Indians righthander Dennis Martinez, the winningest Latin American pitcher in history (245–193), retires after 22 seasons in the major leagues.

Feb 15—After 32 years, the Reds lift their ban on facial hair after newly-acquired outfielder Greg Vaughn lobbies to keep his goatee.

Feb 17—After a one-year comeback, Blue Jays righthander Dave Stieb retires for the second time. His career record was 175–134, and included the franchise's only no-hitter.

Feb 18—Five-time Cy Young award winner Roger Clemens is traded from the Blue Jays to the Yankees in exchange for David Wells, Graeme Lloyd, and Homer Bush.

Feb 18—Braves first baseman Andres Galarraga is diagnosed with lymphoma and will miss the entire 1999 season.

Feb 22—Astros outfielder Moises Alou, third in the 1998 MVP voting, learns that he will miss the 1999 season with a torn ACL in his left knee.

March 2—Former NL MVP first baseman Orlando Cepeda, Negro League pitcher "Smokey Joe" Williams, AL umpire Nestor Chylak, and manager Frank Selee are named to the Baseball Hall of Fame by the Veterans Committee.

March 4—The Rockies re-sign rightfielder Larry Walker to a six-year, $75 million contract.

March 8—Joe DiMaggio, 84, passes away at his home in Florida.

March 8—Trevor Hoffman becomes the richest relief pitcher in baseball history when he re-signs with the Padres for four years and $32 million.

March 10—Yankees manager Joe Torre is diagnosed with prostate cancer and hands the reigns of the defending champions over to Don Zimmer.

March 16—The Cubs announce that 1998 NL Rookie of the Year Kerry Wood will miss all of 1999 with a torn ligament in his right elbow.

March 17—The Blue Jays fire manager Tim Johnson after Johnson admits he lied about serving in Vietnam with the Marine Corps.

March 28—The Orioles defeat the Cuban national team, 3–2, in Havana. It is the first time in 40 years that a major league team has visited the communist island.

April 4—Colorado defeats San Diego, 8–2, in Monterrey, Mexico, in the first season opener played outside the U.S. or Canada.

April 7—Cal Ripken, who voluntarily ended his consecutive game streak in 1998, misses a start because of an injury for the first time in his career.

April 14—Yankees' outfielder Darryl Strawberry is charged with possession of cocaine and soliciting a prostitute in Tampa, Fla.

April 14—Devil Rays slugger Jose Canseco becomes the 28th player in history, and the first to be born outside the U.S., to hit 400 home runs.

April 14—Mets reliever John Franco gets the save in a 4–1 win over the Marlins to become the second pitcher in baseball history with 400 career saves.

April 20—Controversial Reds' owner Marge Schott agrees to sell her interest in the team for $67 million.

May 3—In a rematch in Baltimore, Cuba hammers the Orioles, 12–6.

May 18—Pedro Martinez strikes out 11 Yankees and the Red Sox win, 6–3, in Joe Torre's return to the Yankees dugout after cancer surgery.

June 6—The Mets beat Roger Clemens and the Yankees, 7–2, ending Clemens's AL-record winning streak at 20.

June 13—Houston manager Larry Dierker collapses in the dugout with a seizure during the eighth inning of the Astros game with the Padres. The game is suspended with Houston leading 4–1.

June 25—Cardinals pitcher Jose Jimenez outduels Randy Johnson and no-hits the Diamondbacks, 1–0.

June 27—Ken Griffey Jr. hits a home run as the Mariners beat the Rangers, 5–2, in the final game played at the Kingdome.

July 12—Mark McGwire hits 13 first-round home runs at the All-Star Home Run Derby in Boston, but Ken Griffey Jr. wins the title for the second straight year.

July 13—MVP Pedro Martinez whiffs five National Leaguers in two innings of work and the AL wins its third straight All-Star Game, 4–1.

July 14—Fifty-seven of 68 major league umpires threaten to resign on Sept. 2 rather than accept a series of reforms and restructuring of their labor agreement.

July 14—Three construction workers are killed when a 567-foot crane collapses in Milwaukee's

Miller Park, which is scheduled to open in 2001.

July 18—Yankees righthander David Cone tosses the 14th perfect game in major league history in New York's 6–0 win over the Expos.

July 26—The Major League Umpires Association sues for the right to withdraw its mass resignations set for Sept. 2.

Aug 5—Cardinals first baseman Mark McGwire becomes the 16th player with 500 or more career home runs when he launches Nos. 500 and 501 against the Padres.

Aug 6—With a first-inning single against the Expos, Padres rightfielder Tony Gwynn becomes the 22nd player to amass 3,000 career hits.

Aug 7—Devil Rays' third baseman Wade Boggs belts a home run to become the 23rd player with 3,000 career hits and the first player to reach the milestone on a home run.

Aug 17—Orioles' reliever Jesse Orosco pitches in his 1,072nd game, a major league record.

Aug 22—Mark McGwire becomes the first player to reach 50 home runs in four consecutive seasons after bashing blasts Nos. 50 and 51 of the season against the New York Mets.

Sept 2—Orioles shortstop Cal Ripken Jr. becomes the 29th member of the 400-home run club with a third-inning shot against the Devil Rays.

Sept 11—Twins lefthander Eric Milton strikes out 13 Angels and records the third no-hitter of the season, as Minnesota wins 7–0.

Sept 15—In an effort to centralize league functions in the office of the commissioner, Major League Baseball owners vote unanimously to eliminate the positions of American and National League presidents.

Sept 18—Cubs rightfielder Sammy Sosa smacks his 60th home run of the season against the Brewers, becoming the first player in history to reach the 60-home run barrier twice.

Sept 24—In only their second season of existence, the Diamondbacks clinch the NL West crown and a trip to the playoffs with an 11–3 win against the Giants.

Sept 27—Detroit defeats the Royals 8–2 in the final home game at Tiger Stadium, which opened in 1912.

Oct 3—Mark McGwire hits his 65th home run and Sammy Sosa connects for his 63rd, as the Cardinals defeat the Cubs 9–5 in a rain-shortened season finale.

Oct 3—The Mets beat the Pirates on a wild pitch in the ninth inning, and the Reds defeat the Brewers to tie for the NL wild card with identical 96–66 records.

Oct 4—Mets lefthander Al Leiter tosses a complete-game two-hitter, and New York defeats the Reds in Cincinnati, 5–0, in a one-game playoff. The win gives the Mets their first postseason appearance since 1988.

Oct 9—Backup Todd Pratt, playing for injured Mets catcher Mike Piazza, slams a 10th-inning home run to beat the Diamondbacks 4–3 in Game 4 of the NL Division Series. The victory eliminates the Diamondbacks and propels the Mets to their first NLCS since 1988.

Oct 11—Held out of the starting lineup because of an ailing back, Pedro Martinez comes out of the bullpen to pitch six no-hit innings, and the Red Sox beat the Indians in Game 5 of their AL Division Series, 12–8. The victory eliminates the Indians, who won the first two games of the series but were outscored 44–18 in the final three Red Sox wins.

Oct 17—Robin Ventura connects for a 15th-inning grand slam-turned-single, and the Mets beat the Braves 4–3 in Game 5, the longest postseason game in baseball history (5:46). After the Braves score a go-ahead run in the top of the 15th, the Mets load the bases in the bottom of the inning. Todd Pratt earns a walk to tie the game before Ventura connects on his blast over the right-centerfield wall. Before he can reach second base, however, Ventura is mobbed by his teammates, and thus his home run is ruled a single and only the winning run counts.

Oct 18—ALCS MVP Orlando Hernandez wins his second game of the series and the Yankees advance to their second straight World Series with a 6–1 victory over the Red Sox in Game 5.

Oct 19—Kenny Rogers walks in the winning run in the 11th inning of Game 6 and the Braves advance to their fifth World Series of the decade. The Mets, who trailed 3–0 in the series, and 5–0 in this game, are only two outs from forcing a Game 7 when Ozzie Guillen drives in the tying run in the bottom of the 10th inning. Braves' catcher Eddie Perez, who hits .500 with two home runs and five RBIs, is named the NLCS MVP.

Oct 26—Yankees leftfielder Chad Curtis belts two home runs, including the game-winner, a solo shot in the bottom of the tenth inning, to propel New York to a 6–5 win over Atlanta in Game 3 of the World Series. The Yankees, who hit four home runs in the game, now have a commanding 3–0 series lead.

Oct 27—Roger Clemens scatters four hits over 7⅔ innings and Series MVP Mariano Rivera nails down his second save (to go with one victory) as the Yankees defeat the Braves 4–1 and claim their third World Series title in four years and their league-leading 25th championship overall. The Cardinals and the A's are second on the alltime list, with nine World Series victories each.

JOHN IACONO

Finding a worthy opponent was a tougher challenge for Jones (left) than Lou Del Valle (right).

Oct 19, 1998—Out of the ring for 16 months for biting Evander Holyfield's ears during a championship fight, Mike Tyson regains his Nevada boxing license after a 4–1 decision by the Nevada State Athletic Commission.

Oct 24—Olympic middleweight gold medalist David Reid is bloodied and hits the deck twice but wins a 12-round unanimous decision against James Coker in Atlantic City to boost his record to 11–0. In Düsseldorf, Germany, Sven Ottke upsets Charles Brewer in a split decision to take Brewer's super middleweight title.

Oct 27—Japanese super bantamweight Ken Katagiri dies of a brain injury suffered when he was knocked out in the ninth round by Fusaaki Takenaga on Oct. 12.

Oct 27—Mike Tyson is sued by a Las Vegas policeman who claims that the heavyweight struck him during the postfight melee after his June 28, 1997, rematch with Evander Holyfield.

Oct 31—At "Fright Night" in Atlantic City, WBO featherweight champion Naseem Hamed (31–0) wins an easy 12-round unanimous decision over Wayne McCullough.

Nov 3—The Nov. 21 Oscar De La Hoya–Ike Quartey fight is postponed. De La Hoya, the welterweight champion, needs stiches to close a cut on his left eyelid suffered while sparring. He will be unable to spar for three weeks and the fight is rescheduled for Feb. 13.

Nov 6—After a three-year hiatus, Thomas (Hit Man) Hearns, who won seven world titles in the welterweight, middleweight and light heavyweight divisions, knocks out Jay (Swamp Man) Snyder 88 seconds into their cruiserweight bout in Detroit. Snyder, 37, a maintenance supervisor at a manufacturing plant, has been knocked out in the first round three times in 1998. The 40-year-old Hearns improves his record to 58-4-1.

Dec 1—Mike Tyson pleads no contest to assaulting two motorists after a minor car accident in Maryland in August 1998.

Dec 21—Referee Mills Lane, who disqualified Mike Tyson for biting Evander Holyfield in 1997, retires to pursue opportunities in television.

Jan 9—Light heavyweight champion Roy Jones Jr. defends his title with an easy second-round knockout of No. 1 contender and New York cop Rick Frazier.

Jan 16—Mike Tyson knocks out Francois Botha of South Africa, who was leading on all cards, in the fifth round.

Feb 5—Mike Tyson is sentenced to two years in jail with a year suspended after he pleads no contest to two counts of misdemeanor assault.

Feb 13—Oscar De La Hoya gets up from a sixth-round knockdown to outpoint Ike Quartey and retain his WBC welterweight title.

Feb 20—IBF welterweight champion Felix Trinidad wins an easy 12-round decision against Pernell Whitaker.

March 6—David Reid wins the WBA super welterweight title from France's Laurent Boudouani with a unanimous decision in Atlantic City.

March 13—Lennox Lewis dominates Evander Holyfield in their heavyweight title unification fight at Madison Square Garden, but the judges rule the bout a draw.

May 24—Mike Tyson is released from a Maryland jail after serving 3½ months for misdemeanor assault.

June 5—Roy Jones Jr. adds the IBF crown to his WBA and WBC light heavyweight titles with an easy decision over Reggie Johnson.

Sept 18—Undefeated Felix Trinidad earns a disputed decision against Oscar De La Hoya in their welterweight title unification bout in Las Vegas.

Oct 23—Mike Tyson drops Orlin Norris with a punch after the bell ending the first round of their heavyweight fight in Las Vegas. Tyson is penalized two points and Norris is unable to answer the bell for the second round. The fight is ruled a no contest and Tyson's $10 million purse is withheld pending inquiry.

College Basketball

JOHN W. MCDONOUGH

After 26 seasons, 596 wins and one national title, Thompson decided to leave Georgetown.

Nov 11—No. 7 Temple, led by Rasheed Brokenbourough's 15 points, overcomes a 16-point deficit to beat Wake Forest 59–48 in the championship of the Coaches vs. Cancer tournament at Madison Square Garden.

Nov 15—In women's hoops, No. 5 Purdue stuns three-time defending national champion and No. 1-ranked Tennessee with a 78–68 win, snapping the Lady Vols' 46-game winning streak.

Nov 17—Virginia Tech's women's team upsets No. 4 Duke, 72–70, at the Blue Devils' home opener.

Oct 27, 1998—CBS, the NCAA and DirecTV announce a one-year agreement that allows the satellite television provider to offer subscribers CBS-produced telecasts of out-of-market NCAA tournament games on a pay-per-view basis.

Nov 2—Kentucky coach Tubby Smith announces the suspensions of Myron Anthony, Ryan Hogan and Jamaal Magloire for misdeeds off the court. They will miss the first two regular-season games.

Nov 5—The NCAA strips the Cincinnati men's basketball team of three scholarships and puts the program on two years' probation, citing a lack of institutional control and breach of ethical conduct in its recruiting practices.

Nov 18—LSU is banned from the 1999 NCAA tournament because of illicit cash payments and other infractions involving player Lester Earl.

Nov 19—No. 9 Tennessee is upset by Miami (OH) 68–62. Miami's Wally Szczerbiak scores 34 points and sinks a turnaround jump shot to save the RedHawks after they let a 12-point lead slip away.

Dec 8—Iowa defeats No. 10 Kansas 85–81 to snap the Jayhawks' 62-game home winning streak.

Jan 4, 1999—Fresno State defeats No. 17 New Mexico 86–80 to give head coach Jerry Tarkanian his 700th career victory.

Jan 8—Georgetown head coach John Thompson

resigns after more than 26 seasons as the Hoyas' head coach. Under his reign, the Hoyas won a national championship and 596 wins against 239 losses.

Jan 10—No. 2 Tennessee ends top-ranked Connecticut's 54-game home-court winning streak, as the Lady Vols win 92–81.

Jan 14—The top-ranked Lady Vols of Tennessee rip undefeated No. 4 Georgia 102–69.

Jan 20—No. 6 Auburn, one of only two undefeated men's teams remaining, falls to Kentucky, 72–62.

Jan 24—St. John's guard Bootsy Thornton scores 40 points but No. 2 Duke hangs on to beat the No. 10 Red Storm in overtime, 92–88.

Feb 1—Playing without leading scorer Richard Hamilton and leading rebounder Jake Voskuhl, No. 1 and undefeated Connecticut falls to No. 16 Syracuse, 59–42.

Feb 9—Princeton overcomes a 27-point deficit to stun Penn, 50–49.

Feb 14—Chamique Holdsclaw scores 19 points during a 71–63 win against No. 21 Auburn to become Tennessee's alltime career scoring leader (2,803 points).

Feb 17—Men's No. 1 Duke routs Florida State 85–59 for its 21st straight win, and clinches its sixth ACC regular-season title of the 1990s.

Feb 18—Chamique Holdsclaw, who helped Tennessee to a perfect 39–0 record and a third consecutive NCAA title in 1998, is awarded the 1998 Sullivan Award, given annually to the nation's top amateur athlete.

Feb 21—No. 24 LSU stuns the Lady Vols, 72–69, ending Tennessee's 31-game SEC winning streak.

Feb 27—No. 1 Duke overwhelms in-state rival North Carolina 81–61 to become only the eighth team in ACC history to finish the men's conference season undefeated.

March 9—Notre Dame men's head coach John McLeod resigns after failing to lead the Irish to the NCAA tournament in his eight seasons. McLeod was 106–124 overall and 14–16 in 1998–99.

March 10—The *St. Paul Pioneer Press* reports the Minnesota's men's basketball program is facing possible NCAA sanctions for rampant academic fraud.

March 11—For the first time since 1980, North Carolina loses in the first round of the NCAA Tournament. The third-seeded Tar Heels fall to Weber State 76–74. In the West Regional, Minnesota, facing NCAA sanctions over academic fraud, suspends four of its players before losing 75–63 to Gonzaga.

March 13—St. John's hands Indiana its worst NCAA tournament loss since 1940, 86–61.

March 14—Tenth-seeded Miami (OH) stuns second-seeded Utah 66–58 as Wally Szczerbiak, who scored 43 points in the RedHawks first-round win against Washington, contributes 24 points, seven rebounds, and five assists.

March 18—Former NBA star Mark Price returns to his alma mater, Georgia Tech, as an assistant coach to Bobby Cremins.

March 22—Duke's women's team joins its men's team in the Final Four by beating Tennessee 69–63 ending Chamique Holdsclaw's spectacular collegiate career and the Lady Vols' hopes for a four-peat.

March 22—Former Indiana All-American Steve Alford accepts Iowa's head coaching position after the school chooses not to renew Tom Davis's contract. Alford led Southwest Missouri State to the Sweet 16 and a 22–11 mark in 1998–99.

March 28—Purdue survives a horrible first half to beat Duke, 62–45, and claim the NCAA women's championship. It is the final game for Purdue head coach Carolyn Peck, who has signed to coach the Orlando Miracle of the WNBA.

March 29—Connecticut, behind Richard Hamilton's 27 points, defeats heavily favored Duke 77–74 to win its first NCAA men's championship.

March 30—Kansas assistant and former North Carolina player Matt Doherty takes over the head coaching job at Notre Dame.

March 30—Sidney Moncrief, who led Arkansas to the 1978 Final Four and later starred in the NBA, is named head coach at Arkansas–Little Rock.

March 31—Jim Harrick, who won a championship at UCLA and led Rhode Island to the NCAA Tournament, is named head coach at Georgia.

April 1—Missouri head coach Norm Stewart, whose 731 wins rank seventh in NCAA history, retires after 32 seasons.

April 7—Missouri names Quin Snyder, the top assistant at Duke for the last four seasons, its new head coach.

April 13—Khalid El-Amin, the sophomore point guard who helped Connecticut to a national championship, is charged with marijuana possession in Hartford, Conn.

April 14—Luke Recker, who averaged 16.1 points a game as a sophomore for Indiana, announces his intentions to transfer. He becomes the third starter in the last two years to leave the Hoosiers.

June 25—Clem Haskins, under pressure from allegations of academic fraud, agrees to a buyout of his current contract and steps down as head coach at Minnesota.

June 30—Purdue's men's team receives two years of probation for NCAA violations.

July 10—Luke Recker, a recent transfer to Arizona from Indiana, is injured in a car accident in Colorado that kills one and injures four others.

July 24—Dan Monson, who led Gonzaga to a 25–6 record and the Elite Eight of the 1999

NCAA tournament, is hired to coach at Minnesota.

Oct 12—Indiana coach Bobby Knight accidentally wounds a friend with a shotgun blast while hunting grouse in Wisconsin. He is later cited for failing to report the accident and hunting without a license.

Oct 26—Minnesota bans its men's basketball team from competing in the 2000 postseason as a result of alleged academic violations.

College Football

DOUGLAS C. PIZAC/AP

The pundits who pegged Idaho as the worst in Division I-A had another thing coming.

Oct 23, 1998—Auburn coach Terry Bowden resigns amid speculation that he will be fired. Auburn (1–5) is off to its worst season in 52 years.

Oct 24—Heisman hopeful Ricky Williams becomes the leading scorer in Division I-A history with 428 career points after scoring two TDs in the last 2:03 of Texas's 30–20 win against Baylor. Other records fall in small-college football: Emporia State (KS) running back Brian Shay gains 213 yards against Central Missouri State to become college football's career rushing leader with 6,428 yards; tailback Jerry Azumah of New Hampshire becomes the alltime leading rusher (5,436 yards) and scorer (370 points) among non-kickers in Division I-AA; and Georgia Southern fullback Adrian Peterson rushes for five

touchdowns, giving him 20 for the season, a I-AA record for a freshman. Lastly, Susquehanna (PA) scores 61 points, an NCAA record for a losing team, in a double-overtime loss to Juniata (PA), which scores 62.

Oct 26—UCLA (6–0), ranked second behind Ohio State (7–0) in both the coaches' and writers' polls, tops the Bowl Championship Series standings. Ohio State is second in the BCS standings.

Oct 31—Ricky Williams rushes for 150 yards as Texas upsets No. 7 Nebraska 20–16, ending the Cornhuskers' 47-game home winning streak. In Division I-AA, Eastern Washington's Bashir Levingston sets a record by returning three kickoffs (84, 90 and 92 yards) for touchdowns in a 31–25 win against Sacramento State.

Nov 2—Auburn coach Bill Oliver, who replaced Terry Bowden after Bowden's Oct. 23 resignation, fires offensive coordinator Rodney Allison.

Nov 7—Top-ranked Ohio State is upset by Michigan State 28–24, all but ruining the Buckeyes' chances for the national title. Ohio State (8–1) plummets to eighth in the BCS; Tennessee (8–0) and UCLA (8–0) hold the top two spots.

Nov 9—Florida State announces that 26-year-old starting quarterback Chris Wenke will have neck surgery and miss the rest of the season after injuries suffered during the Seminoles' 45–14 win against Virginia on Nov. 7.

Nov 22—Oklahoma fires coach John Blake after the team's worst three-year stretch (12–22) in school history.

Nov 23—Hayden Fry, who coached Iowa to 14 bowl games in 20 seasons, retires. In Columbia, South Carolina (1–10) fires coach Brad Scott.

Nov 27—Ricky Williams of Texas rushes for 259 yards during the Longhorns' 26–24 upset of No. 6 Texas A&M, breaking Tony Dorsett's alltime Division I-A rushing record. Williams finishes with 6,279 yards and also holds career records for all-purpose yards (7,206), touchdowns (75) and points (452).

Nov 28—Donovan McNabb throws for two touchdowns and rushes for three more as Syracuse destroys Miami (FL) 66–13 to win the Big East title.

Dec 3—Clemson names Tommy Bowden, who led Tulane to the Conference USA title and an undefeated season in 1998, as its new coach.

Dec 3—Four former Northwestern football players are indicted on federal perjury charges related to point shaving in 1993 and '94.

Dec 3—John Robinson, who coached Southern California and the NFL's Los Angeles Rams, is named the new head coach at perennial doormat UNLV.

Dec 4—Lou Holtz, who won a national championship at Notre Dame after the 1988 season, is named head coach at South Carolina after spending two years as a television analyst.

Dec 5—The final BCS rankings are thrown for a loop when Miami upsets UCLA 49–45 and Texas A&M shocks Kansas State in the Big 12 Championship game 36–33. Tennessee comes from behind to nip Mississippi State 24–14 in the SEC title game, and idle Florida State moves up in the rankings to sneak into the national championship game.

Dec 12—Texas running back Ricky Williams, the NCAA's alltime leading rusher, wins the Heisman Trophy. He beats out four quarterbacks in the voting: Kansas State's Michael Bishop, UCLA's Cade McNown, Kentucky's Tim Couch, and Syracuse's Donovan McNabb.

Dec 19—North Carolina kicks off the bowl schedule with a 20–13 victory against San Diego State in the Las Vegas Bowl, a game marred by 45-mph winds that wobble the goalposts and create mini-sandstorms.

Dec 19—Massachusetts running back Marcel Shipp rushes for a title-game record 244 yards and three touchdowns and the Minutemen surprise No. 1-seeded Georgia Southern, 55–43, to win the NCAA Division I-AA championship.

Dec 25—Colorado outguns No. 21 Oregon, 51–43, in the Aloha Bowl.

Dec 26—No. 23 Missouri wins its first bowl game in 17 years with a 34–31 defeat of West Virginia in the Insight.com Bowl.

Dec 29—No. 24 Virginia Tech slams Alabama, 38–7, in the inaugural Music City Bowl in Nashville. Miami (FL) and North Carolina State combine for nearly 1,100 yards of offense in the Micron PC Bowl, but the Hurricanes crush the Wolfpack, 46–23. In the Alamo Bowl, unranked Purdue hands No. 4 Kansas State its second straight loss, 37–34.

Dec 29—One month after receiving a vote of confidence from the school's athletic director, Washington head coach Jim Lambright is fired after the Huskies lose to Air Force in the Oahu Bowl.

Dec 30—Picked as the worst team in Division I-A football by some publications during the preseason, 17-point underdog Idaho caps a remarkable 9–3 season with a 42–35 win against Southern Miss in the Humanitarian Bowl. In the Holiday Bowl, No. 5 Arizona edges No. 14 Nebraska 23–20 handing the Cornhuskers their first four-loss season since 1968.

Dec 31—Tenth-ranked Tulane generates more than 500 yards of offense and defeats BYU 41–27 in the Liberty Bowl to finish the season with a perfect 12–0 record. In the Peach Bowl, No. 19 Georgia overcomes a 21–0 deficit to beat No. 13 Virginia 35–33.

Jan 1, 1999—No. 22 Penn State grounds quarterback Tim Couch and the Kentucky passing game in the Outback Bowl and ruins the Wildcats' first New Year's Day appearance since 1952 with a 26–14 win. In the Gator Bowl, No. 12 Georgia Tech holds off No. 17 Notre Dame 35–28. No. 15 Michigan wins its 10th game in its last 11 with a 45–31 Florida Citrus Bowl victory against No. 11 Arkansas. Heisman Trophy–winner Ricky Williams rushes for 203 yards and helps No. 20 Texas beat No. 25 Mississippi State 38–11 in the Cotton Bowl. Ron Dayne rushes for 246 yards and four touchdowns as No. 9 Wisconsin defeats No. 6 UCLA 38–31 in the Rose Bowl. In the Sugar Bowl, No. 3 Ohio State (11–1) finishes a near-perfect season with a 24–14 victory over No. 8 Texas A&M.

Jan 2—No. 7 Florida reaches 10 victories for the sixth consecutive season, defeating No. 18 Syracuse 31–10 in the Orange Bowl.

Jan 4—Top-ranked Tennessee, a 5½ point-underdog nonetheless, finishes 13–0 and claims its first national championship since 1951 with a 23–16 victory over No. 2 Florida State in the Fiesta Bowl.

Jan 11—Washington lures coach Rick Neuheisel away from Colorado with a seven-year contract worth $1.5 million per year.

Jan 12—Dennis Erickson, who won two national championships as head coach of Miami (FL), is named coach of Oregon State, a team with 28 straight losing seasons.

Jan 20—Northwestern coach Gary Barnett resigns to take the head coaching job at Colorado.

March 24—Wisconsin is placed on two years' probation for widespread, unauthorized spending of money from its booster club.

Aug 13—UCLA suspends running back Keith Brown and safety Eric Whitfield for two games for allegedly using handicap parking permits illegally, bringing the number of UCLA players who will miss games because of the violations to 11.

Aug 28—The college football season kicks off as preseason No. 1 Florida State hammers Louisiana Tech 41–7 and No. 4 Penn State turns heads with a 41–7 victory over No. 3 Arizona. Rejuvenated No. 12 Miami (FL) beats No. 9 Ohio State, 23–12.

Sept 11—Hawaii quarterback Dan Robinson passes for 452 yards and four touchdowns and the Rainbows end a 19-game losing streak with a 31–27 victory over Eastern Illinois.

Sept 18—No. 4 Florida extends its 30-game home winning streak with a 23–21 victory against No. 2 Tennessee. The loss ends Tennessee's 14-game winning streak.

Golf

Oct 11, 1998—Defending champ David Duval wins his fourth tournament of the year, firing a 16-under 268 to claim the Michelob Championship. In LPGA play Kelly Robbins surpasses the $3 million mark in career earnings with a four-stroke victory at the Tournament of Champions.

Nov 1—The U.S. LPGA team defeats Japan 24–12 in the Nichirei International tournament at Ina, Japan.

Nov 1—The PGA Tour season closes when Hal Sutton birdies to beat Vijay Singh in a playoff to win The Tour Championship and earn a spot in the Presidents Cup. David Duval, who finishes eighth, clinches the money title ($2,591,031) and the Vardon Trophy for lowest scoring average (69.13).

Nov 8—Hale Irwin makes up two strokes on third-round leader Gil Morgan to win the Senior Tour Championship. He wins his seventh title of the year and breaks the Senior Tour season records for earnings ($2,861,945) and scoring (68.59).

Nov 15—In his first event since undergoing shoulder surgery in April 1998, Greg Norman teams with Steve Elkington to win the Shark Shootout in a playoff in Thousand Oaks, Calif.

Nov 23—Augusta National Golf Club announces three new qualification parameters for next year's tournament. The three new qualifications call for the winner of the Players Championship to receive a three-year exemption, along with the top 50 in the World Golf Rankings for the previous calendar year, and the top 50 in the world rankings four weeks prior to the Masters.

Dec 6—Nick Price rolls in a 10-foot birdie putt on the fifth playoff hole to beat Tiger Woods and win his third Million Dollar Challenge in Sun City, South Africa.

Dec 13—The International Team wins its first Presidents Cup, slamming the U.S. 20½–11½ at Royal Melbourne Golf Club in Australia.

Jan 24, 1999—David Duval ties the PGA Tour's alltime single-round low of 59 and rallies from seven shots down to win the Bob Hope Classic in La Quinta, Calif. It is Duval's ninth win in his last 28 official starts.

Jan 27—Jack Nicklaus has hip-replacement surgery in Boston, forcing him to miss April's Masters for the first time in 40 years.

Jan 31—Hale Irwin, shut out during the first day of play, wins two holes totaling $230,000 to claim his first Senior Skins Game. At the Phoenix Open, Rocco Mediate holds off final-round charges from Justin Leonard and Tiger Woods for his first win since 1993. A spectator who is heckling Woods is detained by police after they discover he is carrying a handgun on the course.

Feb 7—Bruce Fleisher wins the Royal Caribbean Classic and joins Arnold Palmer, Jack Nicklaus, Gary Player and George Archer as the only golfers to win their first event on the Senior Tour.

Feb 28—No. 24-seed Jeff Maggert defeats No. 50 Andrew Magee 1-up to claim the $1 million prize at the inaugural World Match Play Championship in Carlsbad, Calif.

March 8—Tiger Woods announces that he has parted company with caddie Mike (Fluff) Cowan after 2½ years and seven PGA Tour victories.

March 14—Broadcaster Gary McCord defeats John Jacobs on the fifth playoff hole at the Toshiba Senior Classic for his first Senior PGA Tour win.

March 28—David Duval wins The Players Championship in Ponte Vedra Beach, Fla., for his third victory of 1999, and replaces Tiger Woods as the world's top-ranked player. At the Dinah Shore in Rancho Mirage, Calif., Dottie Pepper wins with a tournament-record 19-under 269.

April 4—David Duval wins the BellSouth Classic in Duluth, Ga., by three strokes to break the single-season earnings record ($2,598,300).

April 11—José María Olazábal makes two clutch putts at the 16th and 17th holes, and holds off Davis Love III and Greg Norman to win his second Masters championship.

May 13—Gene Sarazen, one of only four men to have won all four majors, dies at age 97.

June 6—At Old Waverly Golf Club in Mississippi, Juli Inkster shoots the lowest score in relation to par (-16, 272) in the 54-year history of the U.S. Open to win her fourth major.

June 20—One year after narrowly losing to Lee Janzen, Payne Stewart outduels Phil Mickelson at Pinehurst No. 2 in North Carolina to win his second U.S. Open championship. He is the only golfer to break par at the tournament.

June 27—Hale Irwin matches the Senior Players Championship record (267) to win the third major of the season by seven strokes. In Wilmington, Del., Juli Inkster becomes only the second player in history to win the modern career LPGA Grand Slam with a four-stroke victory over Liselotte Neumann at the LPGA Championship.

July 4—Spanish teenage sensation Sergio Garcia wins his first professional title with a three-stroke victory at the Irish Open.

July 18—Native son Paul Lawrie, who begins the day 10 strokes behind the leader, wins the 128th British Open in Carnoustie, Scotland. Frenchman Jean Van de Velde has a three-stroke lead after 71 holes, but triple-bogeys the 72nd to force a four-hole playoff with Lawrie and Justin Leonard. Lawrie completes the greatest comeback in major championship history when he wins the playoff by three strokes.

Aug 1—Karrie Webb wins her first major, the du Maurier Classic, and breaks the LPGA's season record for earnings with $1,254,051.

Aug 2—In a prime-time made-for-television match-play duel between the world's two top golfers, Tiger Woods edges David Duval 2 & 1 at Sherwood Country Club in Thousand Oaks, Calif.

Aug 15—Tiger Woods holds off Sergio Garcia to win his second major, the PGA Championship at Medinah Country Club, by one stroke. In Woburn, England, Sherri Steinhauer wins her second straight Women's British Open, becoming the first woman to repeat since Debbie Massey in 1980–81.

Aug 29—Tiger Woods becomes the youngest player to win five tournaments in one year since Jack Nicklaus in 1963 and the first golfer to top $4 million in one year with a one-stroke victory at the NEC Invitational in Akron, Ohio.

Sept 26—Justin Leonard sinks a 45-foot putt on the 17th hole that—after José María Olazábal's subsequent miss of a 20-foot putt—assures Leonard a half-point and clinches the Ryder Cup for the United States. The putt caps a miraculous comeback by the U.S., which trailed by four points heading into Sunday's play.

Oct 24—Casey Martin ties for 37th at the Nike Tour championship but earns his PGA Tour card for 2000 by finishing 14th on the year-end money list.

Hockey

Nov 2, 1998—The Ontario Hockey League bans Windsor Spitfires forward Jeff Kugel for life from the OHL for leaving the bench and punching an Owen Sound Platers player on Oct. 25. It is one of the harshest penalties handed out in junior hockey history.

Nov 4—Dominik Hasek becomes the winningest goalie in Buffalo Sabres history with his 157th career win, a 4–2 defeat of the Bruins.

Nov 6—The Kings lose Rob Blake, winner of the 1997 Norris Trophy as the NHL's top defenseman, for 15 games when an MRI exam discovers that he broke his foot as a result of getting hit by a puck in an Oct. 30 game.

Nov 7—John Cullen, attempting a comeback after missing last season while fighting cancer, scores twice and has five assists for the Cleveland Lumberjacks of the IHL.

Nov 9—Olaf Kolzig, who led the Capitals to the 1998 Stanley Cup finals, signs a four-year, $12 million extension.

Nov 11—Steve Yzerman's goal and assist during the Red Wings' 6–2 defeat of the Blues moves him past Bryan Trottier into 10th place on the alltime career points list with 1,426.

Nov 14—Brett Hull of the Stars gets his 1,000th point in a 3–1 win against the Bruins. He and his Hall-of-Fame father, Bobby (1,170 points), are the first father-son combination with 1,000 points each.

Nov 16—Former Quebec Nordiques stars Peter Stastny and Michel Goulet are inducted into the

NHL Hall of Fame, along with Roy Conacher, broadcaster Howie Meeker, sportswriter Yvon Pedneault and pioneer Athol Murray.

Nov 16—The Montreal Canadiens trade defensemen Dave Manson and Brad Brown and goaltender Jocelyn Thibault to Chicago for goalie Jeff Hackett and defensemen Eric Weinrich and Alain Nasreddine.

Nov 19—Mike Keenan coaches the Canucks to a 5–0 win over the Avalanche for his 500th career victory, tying Toe Blake for fifth on the alltime list.

Nov 23—Kings enforcer Matt Johnson is suspended 12 games for sucker-punching Jeff Beukeboom of the Rangers on Nov. 19. Johnson will forfeit $95,121.96 in salary.

Dec 19—Ray Bourque has three assists to move past Gordie Howe into third place on the alltime NHL assist list with 1,052 as the Bruins beat the Red Wings 4–1.

Jan 2, 1999—Brian Bellows of the Capitals records his 999th and 1,000th career points during a 5–2 win against the Maple Leafs.

Jan 4—The NHL fines the St. Louis Blues $1.5 million, takes away a first-round pick and imposes other sanctions for a 1994 tampering incident involving Devils' defenseman Scott Stevens.

Jan 7—Kings' left wing Luc Robitaille becomes the 27th member of the 500-goal club with his 22nd goal of the season during a game against the Sabres.

Jan 9—The Maple Leafs send backup goaltender Felix Potvin to the Islanders for 1996–97 rookie-of-the-year defenseman Bryan Berard.

Jan 17—The Canucks send hold-out superstar Pavel Bure, defensemen Bret Hedican and Brad Ference, and a third-round pick to the Panthers for defenseman Ed Jovanovski, goalie Kevin Weekes, centers Dave Gagner and Mike Brown and a first-round pick.

Jan 24—The North American team defeats the World team, 8–6, in the NHL All-Star Game in Tampa. Wayne Gretzky scores a goal and has two assists to win his third All-Star Game MVP award.

Jan 24—Mike Keenan, who has won a Stanley Cup and 506 games during his 14 years as an NHL

Bruins lifer Bourque eclipsed Howe on the career assists list.

coach, is fired by the Canucks and replaced by Marc Crawford.

Feb 13—After 68 years, Toronto's Maple Leaf Gardens hosts its final NHL game. The Blackhawks, who also beat the Maple Leafs in the arena's inaugural game in 1931, beat the Leafs 6–2.

March 3—Red Wings center Sergei Fedorov is suspended for five games and fined $386,178 for a tomahawk-style slash to the neck of the Islanders' Zdeno Chara.

March 23—On the eve of the NHL trade deadline, the Red Wings acquire defensemen Chris Chelios and Ulf Samuelsson, winger Wendel Clark and goalkeeper Bill Ranford in four separate deals.

March 28—Colorado's Patrick Roy becomes the NHL's alltime winningest goalie after a 7–2 victory against the Kings. His 407 regular-season victories, combined with his 99 playoff wins, give him one more win than Jacques Plante (505).

Hockey (Cont.)

March 29—Wayne Gretzky scores his 1,072nd goal as a pro, surpassing Gordie Howe's mark of career professional goals, including regular season and playoffs from both the NHL and WHA.

April 2—Flyers' center Eric Lindros is rushed to a Nashville hospital with a collapsed lung. He will miss the rest of the season.

April 18—The Penguins edge the Rangers 2–1 in overtime in the final home game for retiring Ranger Wayne Gretzky. Gretzky has an assist and soaks in a series of curtain calls and standing ovations during postgame ceremonies at Madison Square Garden.

May 4—The eighth-seeded Penguins stun the top-seeded Devils 4–2 in the seventh game of their first-round playoff series. It is the second consecutive year that New Jersey has been eliminated in the first round.

June 19—Brett Hull scores a controversial game-winner at 14:51 of the third overtime period of Game 6, and the Stars win their first Stanley Cup. Replays show that Hull's foot is in the crease when he knocks the puck, which is out of the crease, past Buffalo Sabres goalkeeper Dominik Hasek, but the goal stands. Stars center Joe Nieuwendyk, who had six game-winning goals in the playoffs, wins the Conn Smythe Trophy as the postseason MVP.

June 21—The NHL board of governors votes to eliminate the use of instant replay to determine crease violations, and introduces four skaters a side in regular-season overtime.

June 23—Wayne Gretzky becomes the 10th player elected to the Hockey Hall of Fame without the usual three-year waiting period. He is joined by NHL referee Andy Van Hellemond and "builder" Ian (Scotty) Morrison.

June 24—Penguins legend Mario Lemieux is awarded ownership of the Pittsburgh franchise by the NHL. Former teammate Jaromir Jagr of the Penguins wins his first Hart Trophy as the league's MVP. Jagr led the NHL with 127 points. Sabres goaltender Dominik Hasek, who won the last two Hart Trophys, wins his fifth Vezina Trophy as the league's top goalie.

July 29—Sabres goalkeeper Dominik Hasek announces that he will retire after the 1999–00 season in order to return with his family to the Czech Republic.

Aug 12—Devils center Rob Carpenter, the first U.S.-born player to have a 50-goal season, retires to become an assistant coach for the Albany River Rats.

Sept 1—Right wing Dino Ciccarelli of the Florida Panthers, the league's ninth leading alltime goal scorer, announces his retirement after 19 years in the NHL.

Oct 2—Ducks defenseman Ruslan Salei sends Stars center Mike Modano headfirst into the boards. Modano leaves the ice on a stretcher with a mild concussion, broken nose and strained neck. Salei is suspended by the NHL for 10 games.

Horse Racing

Oct 25, 1998—Belmont Park's season closes with Incurable Optimist winning wire-to-wire in the Pilgrim Stakes and Bele Cherie taking the lead in the stretch to win the Miss Grillo.

Oct 29—The U.S. Postal Service announces that Secretariat's likeness will appear on a commemorative stamp in the fall of 1999.

Nov 7—Pat Day rides Awesome Again to an upset victory in the Breeders' Cup Classic at Churchill Downs, beating 1997 Kentucky Derby winner Silver Charm by ¾ of a length. Skip Away finishes a disappointing sixth, four lengths behind, and fails to break Cigar's alltime earnings record.

Nov 14—Muscles Yankee locks up 3-year-old Colt Trotter of the Year honors by winning the Breeders Crown 3-year-old Colt and Gelding Trot championship at Colonial Downs in Providence Forge, Va.

Dec 20—Meiner Love edges Taiki Shuttle to win the 32nd Sprinters' Stakes at Nakayama Racecourse in Funabashi, Japan.

Dec 21—Moni Maker, a 5-year-old mare who earned $1,128,959 in 1998, is named Harness Horse of the Year.

Dec 28—Russell Baze rides three winners at Golden Gate Fields in Albany, Calif., to reach the 400-win mark for the seventh straight year. He is the only jockey to win 400 races in a season more than three times.

Jan 12, 1999—Escena, winner of the 1998 Breeders' Cup Distaff, is sold for a broodmare record $3.25 million at Keeneland, near Lexington, Ky.

Feb 7—Eddie Delahoussaye becomes the 14th jockey in North American horse racing history with 6,000 wins after he rides Sweetcakesanshakes to victory at Santa Anita Park in California.

Feb 22—Man o' War is named Horse of the Century by *The Blood-Horse* magazine, followed by Secretariat, Citation, Kelson and Count Fleet.

April 8—Julie Krone, racing's most successful female jockey, announces her retirement after 18 years and more than 3,500 victories.

BILL FRAKES

Lukas's charmed year with Charismatic ended sadly at the Belmont.

as recently as February, wins the Preakness Stakes at Pimlico Racetrack in Baltimore.

June 5—Charismatic's Triple Crown dreams come to a terrible end at Belmont Park. The Derby and Preakness winner finishes third behind Lemon Drop Kid and Vision and Verse, but breaks down after the finish line with a fractured leg. He survives, but his racing career is finished.

June 12—Silver Charm, the 1997 Kentucky Derby and Preakness winner, retires after finishing fourth in a stakes race at Churchill Downs. The 5-year-old won 12 of 24 starts and $6,944,369 in his career.

Sept 14—Dave Gall, who with 7,389 career wins trails only three other jockeys on the career victory list, announces his retirement.

May 1—Jockey Chris Antley and 31–1 longshot Charismatic, trained by D. Wayne Lukas, hold off Menifee and Cat Thief to win the 125th Kentucky Derby by a neck.

May 15—For the third consecutive year, a horse wins the first two legs of the Triple Crown as Charismatic, who was placed in a claiming race

Motor Sports

Nov 1, 1998—Jeff Gordon clinches his third Winston Cup title in four years and wins the AC Delco 400 in Rockingham, NC. He is the seventh driver to win three NASCAR season crowns.

Nov 1—Bobby Rahal finishes 11th in the final race of his career, the CART Marlboro 500 at California Speedway. It is also the final CART race for Alex Zanardi, who is moving to Formula One. On the Grand Prix circuit, Mika Hakkinen of Finland wins the season-ending Japanese Grand Prix to secure his first Formula One championship with 100 points.

Nov 2—Gary Scelzi sets a NHRA Top Fuel national speed record at 326.44 mph in the second round of eliminations en route to winning the Matco Tools SuperNationals at Houston Raceway Park. In the Funny Car competition, Cruz Pedegron sets a national elapsed-time record of 4.807 seconds.

Nov 8—Jeff Gordon wins his 13th NASCAR race of the season, the NAPA 500, tying Richard Petty for the modern-day record for wins in a season.

Nov 15—Dale Earnhardt Jr. clinches the NASCAR Grand National Title at the Miami 300, to become NASCAR's first third-generation champion. On the drag-racing circuit, John Force wins his eighth NHRA Funny Car championship in nine years.

Nov 19—Arie Luyendyk announces that he will retire after competing in the next Indianapolis 500, a race he has won twice.

Jan 31, 1999—Bruce Leitzinger drives Rob Dyson's Riley & Scott Mark III across the finish line to win the Rolex 24 endurance race at Daytona Speedway. Three drivers steer the car through 708 laps—2,520.54 miles—at an average speed of 104.9 mph.

Feb 14—Two-time defending Winston Cup champion Jeff Gordon wins his second Daytona 500, holding off defending champ Dale Earnhardt.

Feb 20—Jeff Burton begins the race from the 30th position, but still wins the Grand National Alltel 200 at North Carolina Speedway in Rockingham.

April 22—Crew chief Harry Hyde and drivers Gordon Johncock, Alain Prost, Wendell Scott and Louise Smith are named to the International Motorsports Hall of Fame.

May 1—Three people are killed and eight hurt when debris from a three-car wreck flies into the stands during the VisionAire 500 IRL event in Concord, NC.

May 15—Juan Montoya becomes the first CART rookie to win three races in a row after finishing first at the Rio 200.

May 31—Kenny Brack, the 1998 IRL champion, wins the 1999 Indianapolis 500.

June 13—In only its second year of competition, BMW wins the 67th 24 Hours of LeMans race.

July 11—Michael Schumacher, who is leading the current Formula One season along with Mika Hakkinen, breaks his right leg in two places after crashing at the British Grand Prix. David Coulthard wins the race to rejoin the title chase.

July 25—Tony Kanaan of Brazil surges into the lead on the last lap to win the U.S. 500 at Michigan Speedway.

Aug 10—NASCAR suspends crew members Mike Culbertson of Derrike Cope's team and Ray Labbe from Terry Labonte's team for life after investigating their roles in the racial taunting of David Scott, an African American member of Jeremy Mayfield's team, during a July 9 NASCAR event at Loudon, N.H.

Aug 16—Jeff Gordon seizes his record fifth consecutive win on a road course, taking the Frontier at the Glen at Watkins Glen International.

Sept 5—In Vancouver, Juan Montoya, 23, takes the Molson Indy to win his third race in a row and become the first CART rookie to win seven races in a season. Montoya is the series leader with four races to go. In NASCAR, Jeff Burton wins the rain-shortened Southern 500 and Ernie Irvan announces his retirement.

Sept 27—Formula One legend Jackie Stewart wins for the first time as an owner when Johnny Herbert drives his Stewart-Ford to victory at the European Grand Prix in Nurburgring, Germany. Mika Hakkinen finishes fifth in the race to take the season lead by two points.

Oct 17—Mika Hakkinen all but locks up the F/1 season title after Eddie Irvine and Michael Schumacher, who finished first and second, are disqualified from the Malaysian Grand Prix for technical violations, and Hakkinen is awarded first place. In CART, Scotland's Dario Franchitti overtakes Juan Montoya in the season points race with one race remaining by winning the Gold Coast Indy 300 in Surfers Paradise, Australia. Dale Jarrett, who is assured of winning the NASCAR season title, finishes second at the Winston 500 in Talladega, Ala., behind Dale Earnhardt, who wins his third race of the year.

Oct 26, 1998—Dennis Swanson, former ABC Sports president, is named co-chairman of NBC's Olympics with NBC Sports chairman Dick Ebersol.

Oct 28—A Houston judge approves an agreement between U.S. Olympic gymnast Dominique Moceanu and her parents to allow her to be declared a legal adult. The 17-year-old, who plans to compete in the 2000 Sydney Games, ran away from home on Oct. 17 and filed a lawsuit alleging that her father squandered money she's earned since age 10.

Nov 4—USA Softball names Ralph Raymond coach of the U.S. Women's softball team in the 2000 Olympics. Raymond, 76, led the United States to softball's first gold medal in the 1996 Games and has a 74–0 record in international play.

Nov 5—China, preparing to send more than 800 athletes to Thailand for the Asian Games, announces that random drug tests will be given to athletes in track and field, swimming and cycling. At the 1994 Asian Games 11 Chinese athletes, including seven swimmers, failed drug tests.

Nov 5—Led by two goals and an assist from former NHLer Neal Broten, the United States defeats Kazakhstan 3–0 in the qualification tournament in Klagenfurt, Austria. The win, combined with an earlier defeat of Estonia and a 2–0 win against Austria on Nov. 8, keeps the U.S. team in the elite A Pool of the World Championships, a prelude to the 2002 Olympics.

Nov 6—The doping panel of swimming's international federation, FINA, suspends U.S. swimmer Gary Hall Jr. for three months but deducts time he spent during a provisional ban immediately after a positive marijuana test on May 15. That sanction was lifted on Aug. 11, so the suspension is effectively for time served.

Nov 9—Veteran college coaches Mark Schubert of Southern California and Richard Quick of Stanford are named as coaches of the U.S. men's and women's swim teams, respectively, at the 2000 Olympics.

Dec 5—While reporting on the alleged bribery scandal involving Salt Lake City officials and members of the International Olympic Committee, who vote to select the host cities of the Games, *The Salt Lake Tribune* reveals that IOC president Juan Antonio Samaranch received at least two Browning firearms from the Salt Lake bid committee. IOC members are prohibited from accepting gifts worth more than $150. The weapons, a shotgun and a rifle, are valued at more than $1,000.

Dec 29—International Olympic Committee (IOC) vice president Dick Pound of Canada arrives in Salt Lake City to begin the IOC's investigation of alleged bribery surrounding the city's bid to host the 2002 Olympics. Four panels—the IOC, the U.S. Olympic Committee, a Salt Lake Organizing Committee ethics panel and the U.S. Justice Department—are looking into the alleged scandal.

Jan 8, 1999—Following a month full of embarrassing revelations that members of the

Salt Lake Organizing Committee (SLOC) gave gifts, medical and educational expenses and cash payments to members of the IOC in hopes of securing the 2002 Winter Olympics for Salt Lake, SLOC president Frank Joklik and vice president Dave Johnson submit their resignations. Joklik acknowledges that one payment exceeded $70,000.

Jan 11—Further repercussions from the scandal in Salt Lake City, which has quickly become the worst in Olympics history: Salt Lake City mayor Deedee Corradini, who is an SLOC member, abruptly announces she will not seek another term in office; Rene Paquet, who spearheaded Quebec City's bid to host the 2002 Games, states that he is considering suing the IOC; IOC vice president Anita DeFrantz announces that there will be expulsions and/or resignations of IOC members in the coming days; and on Jan 12, the investigation of bribery extends to Sydney's bid for the 2000 Games.

Jan 20—Utah Attorney General Jan Graham announces that the state will begin an investigation of the SLOC bribery scandal, bringing to five the number of inquiries into the matter. The IOC releases the names of eight of its members who have been implicated in the affair.

Feb 9—The Salt Lake Organizing Committee releases its ethics panel's report on the Olympic bid scandal. The inquiry names 10 IOC members allegedly involved in wrongdoing; added to the 14 members the IOC itself had implicated in January, the total number of IOC members accused of malfeasance is 24. The IOC has 110 members worldwide.

March 1—Reserving its sharpest rebuke for the IOC, the United States Olympic Committee (USOC) releases its findings on the Salt Lake Scandal. Less detailed than the Salt Lake and IOC reports, the USOC inquiry doesn't assign blame to specific individuals but concludes that the IOC "gravely damaged the credibility of the Olympic movement" by fostering an environment in which corruption could flourish.

March 12—The IOC issues strong warnings to, but does not expel, two of its top members, executive board member Un Yong Kim of South Korea and former Australian Olympic canoeist Phil Coles.

March 17—Concluding the punishment phase of its investigation with a hearing in Lausanne, the IOC expels six of its members for their roles in the Salt Lake scandal. Ten IOC members have either resigned or been expelled since the allegations came to light.

March 30—Juan Antonio Samaranch, the president of the International Olympic Committee who recently requested that people address him as His Excellency, declines to appear before a U.S. Senate Commerce Committee investigating the IOC bribery scandal.

March 31—Officials for the 2000 Sydney Summer Olympics announce that they will adjust the schedule of the track and field events so that U.S. sprinter Marion Jones can attempt to become the first woman to win five gold medals in a single Games. Jones is seeking gold medals in the 100- and 200-meter dashes, the long jump, and the 4 x 100- and 4 x 400-meter relays.

April 1—John Smith of Oklahoma State and Greg Strobel of Lehigh are named co-coaches of the U.S. freestyle wrestling team for the 2000 Games in Sydney.

April 6—Citing a rash of injuries, including torn calf muscles in both legs and a rotator cuff problem in his right shoulder, U.S. diver Mark Lenzi announces he will abandon his attempt to return to the sport and qualify for the Sydney Games. Lenzi, 30, won a gold medal in the 3-meter springboard in Barcelona in 1992 and a bronze medal in Atlanta in '96.

April 7—Wrestling legend Dan Gable is added to the coaching staff of the 2000 Olympic U.S. freestyle wrestling team.

April 19—Citing the recent Salt Lake bribery scandal, John Hancock Financial Services announces that it will withdraw its Olympic sponsorship following the 2000 Games in Sydney.

May 25—Duke's Elton Brand and Miami of Ohio's Wally Szczerbiak are added to the U.S. basketball team that will begin Olympic qualifying in June. They are the only collegians on the NBA-dominated roster.

June 5—Jeff Blatnick, who overcame Hodgkin's disease to win a gold medal in Greco-Roman wrestling at the 1984 Olympics in Los Angeles, is inducted into the National Wrestling Hall of Fame in Stillwater, Okla.

July 5—Rockets coach Rudy Tomjanovich steps down as coach of the U.S. Olympic basketball team, citing medical reasons. Larry Brown of the Philadelphia 76ers will replace him.

Aug 29—Jason Gatson, 19, one of the top two gymnasts on the U.S. Olympic team, suffers a torn anterior cruciate ligament during competition at the U.S. nationals in Sacramento. He hopes to return for the Sydney Olympics.

Sept 2—Sydney officials announce that the track and field schedule for the 2000 Games will be altered to create a one-day break between the semifinals and finals of events 400 meters or longer and a two-day respite for events 3,000 meters or longer. The IOC must approve the changes.

The Bulls began their rebuilding process by drafting Brand (42).

MANNY MILLAN

Oct 27, 1998—The New Jersey Nets agree to keep playing basketball at the Meadowlands sports complex through the 2007–08 season.

Oct 28—The American Basketball League names Philadelphia Rage guard-forward Teresa Edwards, a two-time all-ABL selection and the only four-time Olympian in U.S. basketball history, to its board of directors.

Oct 28—After several hours of fruitless negotiations between NBA owners and the players union, the league cancels all games through Nov. 30, leaving an average of 69 scheduled games per team. (A normal season is 82 games.) The players have lost $200 million in salary so far.

Oct 28—The NBA unanimously approves the sale of the New Jersey Nets, reportedly worth $150 million, to a group of state businessmen who are considering moving the team to Newark.

Nov 3—On what was supposed to be the start of the NBA regular season, the labor dispute reaches its 127th day, with no end in sight. The only pro basketball scheduled to take place this week is the women's ABL, which opens on Nov. 5.

Nov 5—WNBA players vote 56–24 to form a union and have the NBA Players Association represent them. In Hartford, Conn., the ABL opens its season as the New England Blizzard defeats the Philadelphia Rage 72–63.

Nov 12—Wizards forward Juwan Howard is awarded more than $100,000 in a judgment against Melissa Reed, whom he sued for character defamation. In April Reed accused Howard and then-teammate Chris Webber of sexually assaulting her at a party at Howard's home. Howard says he will donate the award to the Washington, D.C., Rape Crisis Center.

Nov 17—The NBA cancels the 1999 Jam Session scheduled for Feb. 11–14, and hints that the All-Star Game may be next. The earliest start date for the endangered regular season is Dec. 21.

Nov 18—Brian Alger, coach of the two-time ABL champion Columbus (Ohio) Quest, becomes the first coach to leave the league for its rival, the WNBA. At the end of the ABL season he will join the WNBA's expansion team in Minnesota.

Nov 24—The NBA informs NBC Sports that its two Christmas games have been canceled, bringing the number of games wiped out by the 147-day lockout to 358. The network plans to show the movie *It's A Wonderful Life* on Christmas night instead.

Dec 7—The WNBA's expansion franchise in Minnesota unveils its logo and name, the Lynx. The following week, the Orlando expansion franchise, the Miracle, does the same.

Dec 8—NBA commissioner David Stern announces that the league's All-Star weekend, scheduled for Feb. 12–14 in Philadelphia, will be canceled due to the labor dispute.

Dec 22—One-third of the way through its third season, the American Basketball League, a circuit for women, folds. Though the league had attracted the cream of U.S. women players, it could not compete with the marketing muscle of the NBA-backed WNBA.

Dec 23—Commissioner David Stern announces that if there is no collective bargaining agreement by Jan. 7, 1999, the 1998–99 season will be canceled.

Jan 4, 1999—The No. 1 pick in the '98 NBA draft, Michael Olowokandi, decides to sign with Italian club Kinder Bologna but retains the option to return to the U.S. if the lockout ends. The Los Angeles Clippers hold his NBA rights.

Jan 6—Two days before the NBA's "drop dead" date for canceling the season, union head Billy Hunter and commissioner David Stern engage in an all-night negotiating session. They emerge the following day and announce that they've reached an agreement to end the lockout. The deal, which most observers agree is a victory for the owners, makes the NBA the only major professional sports league in the U.S. with a maximum salary.

Jan 7—Though it has not finalized the schedule, the NBA announces that its lockout-truncated

1998–99 season will consist of 50 games, with teams tipping off on Feb. 5.

Jan 13—Arguably the greatest player in NBA history, 35-year-old Michael Jordan, who led the Chicago Bulls to six NBA titles, won five MVP awards and 10 scoring titles, announces his retirement. In his last game, on June 14, 1998, he scored 45 points and hit the winning bucket with 5.2 seconds left to deliver the Bulls to an 87–86 win over Utah in the decisive Game 6 of the NBA finals.

Jan 19—The New York Knicks and the Houston Rockets each trade for marquee players as New York deals guard John Starks and forwards Terry Cummings and Chris Mills to the Golden State Warriors for guard Latrell Sprewell, and Houston sends center Roy Rogers and a conditional draft pick to the Chicago Bulls for forward Scottie Pippen.

Feb 2—The Charlotte Hornets, who have already lost their top scorer, Glen Rice, for several weeks to an elbow injury, learn that they will be without their leading rebounder, Anthony Mason, for the entire season after Mason ruptures his biceps tendon in practice.

Feb 5—The NBA season finally tips off, and if opening-weekend turnouts are any indication, the fans have forgiven the league for its protracted labor dispute. Sellout crowds pack Madison Square Garden, where the Knicks lose their second straight game, 83–79 to Miami, and the Forum in Inglewood, Calif., where actor Jack Nicholson is in his customary courtside to see the Lakers down the Rockets, 99–91. In Salt Lake City, the previous year's title contestants, Chicago and Utah, meet, but the rematch is no contest as the Bulls, bereft of Michael Jordan, Scottie Pippen and Dennis Rodman, fall 104–96.

Feb 8—The lockout appears to have had no ill effect on Grant Hill's game: The Detroit star scores a career-high 46 points, including the winning free-throws in the final seconds, in the Pistons' 106–103 victory over Washington.

Feb 9—After only two games with his new team, recent Knicks acquisition Latrell Sprewell suffers a stress fracture in his right heel and will miss three to six weeks.

Feb 12—Four-time All-Star guard and career free-throw percentage leader (.904) Mark Price announces his retirement.

Feb 17—The Sacramento Kings defeat Seattle 109–106 in overtime to hand the SuperSonics, the league's last unbeaten team, their first loss of the season after six games.

Feb 22—Point guard Kim Perrot, who has helped lead the Houston Comets to the first two WNBA titles, announces that she has been diagnosed with cancer.

Feb 23—Dennis Rodman, the former Bulls forward who has been inactive this season, signs a contract with the Los Angeles Lakers. The following day the Lakers announce that coach Del Harris has been dismissed. Harris will be replaced by former Laker Kurt Rambis on Feb. 26.

March 1—The Knicks' Latrell Sprewell, out since Feb. 9 with a stress fracture in his right heel, is cleared by doctors to return to practice.

March 10—In a five-player deal, the Lakers acquire ace shooting guard Glen Rice, forward J.R. Reid and guard B.J. Armstrong from Charlotte in exchange for guard Eddie Jones and forward Elden Campbell. Rice is recovering from elbow surgery and has yet to play this season.

March 13—Dennis Rodman goes AWOL from the Los Angeles Lakers, and later contacts the team to say he needs to take care of some "personal problems." He returns to the team on March 21.

March 11—The Minnesota Timberwolves deal point guard Stephon Marbury, who will be a free agent at the end of the season, to the New Jersey Nets in a labyrinthine three-team trade. The transaction involves eight players and one draft pick and brings point guard Terrell Brandon to the Timberwolves from Milwaukee.

March 15—Following a 102–76 loss to the Miami Heat which drops them to 3–17, the New Jersey Nets fire coach John Calipari. Former assistant Don Casey is named interim coach.

April 10—The Chicago Bulls lose to Miami 82–49 at the United Center to set an NBA record for the lowest score by a team since the inception of the shot clock in 1954–55. In his 13-year career with the Bulls, Michael Jordan scored more than 50 points in a game 38 times.

April 16—The Lakers release Dennis Rodman after a troubled, 23-game dalliance with the forward, who averaged 11.2 rebounds per game for the team.

April 17—The Nets' 90–85 victory over Atlanta—only their sixth win in 30 games—turns out to be a Pyrrhic one as Jayson Williams, New Jersey's leading rebounder, goes down with a broken leg in the final minute and is lost for the season.

April 21—Ernie Grunfeld, the Knicks G.M. who acquired Latrell Sprewell and Marcus Camby, is demoted. The Knicks are 21–21 and have lost four games in a row.

May 1—Philadelphia clinches its first playoff berth since 1991 with a 103–96 victory over Toronto.

May 4—Versatile Tennessee star Chamique Holdsclaw is the first pick of the WNBA draft, going to the Washington Mystics.

May 10—Orlando Magic guard Darrell Armstrong, who averaged career highs in points (13.8), assists (6.7), rebounds (3.6) and steals (2.16), wins the NBA Sixth Man award. Ten days later Armstrong is named the NBA's Most

Improved Player, becoming the first player ever to win both awards.

May 16—The Knicks and the 76ers score first-round playoff upsets as Philadelphia beats Orlando 101-91 to win their series in four games and New York eliminates the Heat 78–77 on Allan Houston's last-second shot in Game 5. In Utah, the upstart Sacramento Kings push the Jazz to the limit before falling 99–92 in overtime in Game 5, while in Los Angeles the Lakers dispatch Houston in four games.

May 23—Tim Duncan scores 33 points to lead San Antonio to a 118–107 win over the Lakers in Inglewood, Calif., and a four-game sweep of their conference semifinal series.

May 24—New York continues to surprise in the playoffs, routing Atlanta 79–66 at Madison Square Garden to complete a four-game sweep of the Hawks. The Knicks will meet the Pacers, who swept Philadelphia, in the Eastern Conference finals. In Orlando, Magic coach Chuck Daly retires.

May 26—Following a season in which he led his team in scoring (18.3 ppg) and to the brink of the playoffs, Toronto's high-flying Vince Carter is named Rookie of the Year.

May 27—Joining the Spurs in the Western Conference finals are the Trailblazers, who eliminate defending conference champs Utah with a 92–80 victory in Game 6 in Portland.

June 2—With the Eastern Conference finals series tied at one game apiece, the Knicks lose center Patrick Ewing for the rest of the year. Ewing, who has limped through much of the season, is diagnosed with a partially torn left Achilles' tendon.

June 3—Karl Malone, who scored 23.8 points a game for the Jazz, is named league MVP.

June 5—After sinking a three-pointer as he is fouled by Indiana's Antonio Davis, Larry Johnson drains the free-throw to complete a four-point play with 5.7 seconds remaining and drive the Knicks to a 92–91 victory over the Pacers in Game 3 of the Eastern Conference finals in New York.

June 6—With a 94–80 rout in Portland, the San Antonio Spurs sweep the Trailblazers and advance to the first NBA Finals in franchise history. Center David Robinson leads the way with 20 points and 10 rebounds.

June 7—Former NBA star Doc Rivers signs a four-year, $8 million contract to coach Orlando.

June 10—The WNBA season tips off as the league's No.-1 draft pick, Chamique Holdsclaw, debuts for the Mystics. Holdsclaw scores 18 points in Washington's 83–73 loss to the Charlotte Sting. In Houston, the two-time defending champion Comets rout the expansion Orlando Miracle 77–63.

June 12—Led by guard Allan Houston's 32 points, the Knicks defeat Indiana 90–82 to eliminate the Pacers in six games and become the first No. 8 seed ever to advance to the NBA Finals.

June 16—The Los Angeles Lakers announce that they have signed former Bulls coach Phil Jackson to replace interim coach Kurt Rambis.

June 16—San Antonio cruises to an 89–77 victory over New York in Game 1 of the NBA Finals. Tim Duncan scores 33 points and grabs 16 rebounds to lead the Spurs.

June 26—The low-post combination of Tim Duncan and David Robinson is too much for New York to handle without big man Patrick Ewing, and San Antonio wins the NBA title in five games. Though the Knicks steal Game 3, 89–81, the Spurs win Games 4 and 5 in New York and Duncan, who scores 31 points in the 78–77 title-clinching victory, is named series MVP.

June 29—At the 1999 NBA draft, former Duke star Elton Brand goes No. 1, to the Bulls, and former Maryland guard Steve Francis is the second pick, taken by Vancouver.

July 18—Former Bulls assistant coach Tex Winter, architect of the vaunted "triangle offense," departs Chicago to join Phil Jackson's coaching staff in Los Angeles.

Aug 2—Atlanta trades guards Steve Smith and Ed Gray to Portland for guards Isaiah Rider and Jim Jackson. Three days later Orlando sends guard Anfernee Hardaway to Phoenix for forward Danny Manning and two draft picks.

Aug 3—NBA Hall of Famer Isiah Thomas purchases the Continental Basketball Association for $10 million. Thomas hopes to establish affiliations between CBA and NBA teams for player development.

Aug 16—The Spur's Sean Elliott undergoes a successful kidney-transplant operation in San Antonio.

Sept 4—With 2.4 seconds remaining in Game 2 of the WNBA Finals, New York Liberty point guard Teresa Weatherspoon launches a shot from behind halfcourt and makes it as the buzzer sounds. The three-pointer gives the Liberty a 68–67 victory over the Houson Comets and sends the WNBA Finals to a deciding third game.

Sept 5—Dedicating the victory to their former point guard Kim Perrot, who died of cancer on Aug. 19, the Houston Comets defeat the New York Liberty 59–47 to clinch their third consecutive WNBA championship, two games to one. The Comets are the only champion the three-year old league has known.

Sept 14—Dan Issel, who played for the Nuggets and is the franchise's current G.M., signs a three-year contract to coach Denver. It will be his second stint as Denver's coach.

Oct 13, 1998—The San Diego Chargers fire coach Kevin Gilbride, replacing him for the interim with offensive coordinator June Jones.

Oct 18—The 49ers, 18-point favorites, avoid one of the biggest upsets of the season when they rally from a 21–0 deficit to beat the Colts 43–31. Quarterback Steve Young is sacked five times and suffers nausea at halftime from a stomach illness yet throws for two touchdowns, rushes for two more and sets an NFL record with his sixth consecutive 300-yard passing game.

Oct 25—Several NFL records are broken or tied as Jerry Rice catches four passes in the 49ers' 28–10 win over St. Louis for a record 184th consecutive game with at least one reception; Rice also becomes the first player to top 17,000 career receiving yards; at Mile High Stadium in Denver, Broncos kicker Jason Elam boots a 63-yard field goal to tie Tom Dempsey's record of Nov. 8, 1970;

Coach Chris Palmer (center) led the Browns back to the NFL.

in the same game, Denver's Terrell Davis joins O.J. Simpson and Jim Brown as the only running backs to rush for more than 1,000 yards after only seven games; and at Giants Stadium, 44-year-old Steve DeBerg of the Falcons' becomes the oldest quarterback to start an NFL game as he completes 9 of 20 passes for 117 yards and one interception in a 28–3 loss to the Jets.

Oct 27—Former Giants linebacker Lawrence Taylor enters drug rehabilitation following his arrest on Oct. 19 on crack cocaine charges.

Oct 28—The NFL owners vote to reinstate the Cleveland Browns to their old AFC Central division when the franchise returns to the league in 1999.

Oct 28—Rams rookie linebacker Leonard Little is charged with involuntary manslaughter for his involvement in a fatal drunk-driving accident on Oct. 19.

Nov 1—Randall Cunningham completes 18 of his first 20 passes for 269 yards, but cannot stop Tampa Bay from handing the Vikings their first loss of the season after seven victories, 27–24. In Green Bay, Niners quarterback Steve Young sets two NFL records but is unable to lead his team past the Packers, who win 36–22. Young and receiver Jerry Rice hook up on a record 80th scoring pass, and Young also scores his 41st rushing touchdown, a record for quarterbacks.

Nov 3—Saints quarterback Kerry Collins, cut in October by the Panthers after telling the team that he had lost his desire to play, is charged with driving while impaired in Charlotte, N.C.

Nov 8—The Vikings' top two quarterbacks, Randall Cunningham and Brad Johnson, are injured in Minnesota's 31–24 victory against the Saints. In only the second matchup between Heisman Trophy–winning quarterbacks, Vinny Testaverde throws for 258 yards and three TDs as the Jets defeat Doug Flutie and the Bills 34–12. The Broncos (9–0) remain the NFL's only undefeated team by rolling over San Diego 27–10, despite quarterback John Elway's sitting out most of the game with sore ribs.

Nov 12—Colts fullback Craig Heyward undergoes surgery to remove a benign tumor from the base of his skull that was pressing on the optic nerve in his right eye, causing blurred vision.

Nov 14—The Tennessee Oilers announce that the team will be known as the Titans next season. Titans was the original nickname of the New York Jets in the old American Football League.

Nov 15—The Jets' Aaron Glenn returns a field goal attempt by Indianapolis kicker Mike Vanderjagt 104 yards for a TD, breaking a 27-year-old record. In Atlanta, the Falcons upset the 49ers 31–19 to take a one-game lead in the NFC West.

Nov 16—Quarterback Bubby Brister, subbing for the injured John Elway, runs 38 yards for a

DAVID LIAM KYLE

touchdown, and halfback Terrell Davis has his eighth 100-yard rushing game as the 10–0 Broncos crush the Chiefs 30–7 in Kansas City. The game's end is marred by five personal fouls during Denver's last drive, three of them by Chiefs linebacker Derrick Thomas, who will is later suspended for one game without pay by his team.

Nov 19—Patroits owner Robert Karft announces that the team will relocate to Hartford, Conn., before the 2001–02 season.

Nov 22—In the CFL, Mark McLoughlin's 35-yard field goal on the final play gives the Calgary Stampeders a thrilling 26–24 win over the Hamilton Tiger-Cats in the Grey Cup.

Nov 29—The Broncos become the fourth team in NFL history to start 12–0 after a 31–16 win over the Chargers in San Diego. In Miami, quarterback Dan Marino becomes the first player to throw 400 career touchdown passes with the second of his three TD passes during a 30–10 victory over the Saints.

Dec 6—The call for the use of instant replay as an officiating tool goes up again as the Jets edge the Seahawks in Seattle on a controversial late touchdown by quarterback Vinny Testaverde. Replays clearly show that Testaverde, who was running a quarterback sneak with 20 seconds remaining in the game, was stopped short of the goal line, but head linesman Earnie Frantz rules the play a touchdown, handing the Jets (9–4) a 32–31 victory that keeps them in a tie for first in the AFC East with Miami. The Seahawks drop to 6–7, their playoff hopes all but gone.

Dec 13—The New York Giants (6–8), who had not beaten a winning team all season, knock off the Broncos 20–16 to hand Denver (13–1) its first loss of the season and prevent the Broncos from equaling the 14–0 regular-season record of the 1972 Miami Dolphins, who finished that year 17–0 after winning Super Bowl VII. In the Vikings' 38–28 victory over Baltimore, Minnesota kicker Gary Anderson kicks six field goals on six attempts to run his streak of consecutive field goals to 34, an NFL record.

Dec 14—Atlanta coach Dan Reeves undergoes successful quadruple bypass surgery. He is expected to return to the Falcons sideline for the playoffs.

Dec 15—State representatives in Connecticut approve the construction, at taxpayers' expense, of a $375 million stadium in downtown Hartford, clearing the way for the New England Patriots to move from Foxboro, Mass., to Hartford.

Dec 13—Peyton Manning breaks Charlie Conerly's 50-year-old rookie record of 22 TD passes in a season with his 23rd of the year in the third quarter of the Colts' 39–26 win over Cincinnati. With 210 passing yards in the game, Manning also becomes the first rookie

quarterback to pass for more than 3,000 yards in a season. He finishes the year with 3,739.

Dec 20—The playoff picture begins to come into focus as the Falcons clinch their first NFC West title in 19 years with a 24–17 comeback victory over Detroit, and in Foxboro, the Patriots score twice in the final eight minutes to upset San Francisco 24–21 and clinch an AFC wild-card spot after Tennessee falls to playoff-bound Green Bay 30–22. Buffalo (9–6) becomes the fifth team ever to qualify for the playoffs after starting the season 0–3 when it backs into a wild-card berth despite losing to the Jets at home, 17–10.

Dec 27—The Arizona Cardinals clinch the final NFC playoff berth, and the franchise's first since 1982, with a dramatic 16–13 win at home over San Diego. Cardinals kicker Chris Jacke boots a 52-yard field goal with one second remaining to provide the winning margin and end the league's longest playoff drought.

Dec 27—Needing 170 yards to become the fourth NFL runner to rush for 2,000 yards in a season, Denver's Terrell Davis gains 178 in the Broncos' 28–21 win over Seattle.

Dec 28—On the day after the conclusion of the regular season, five NFL head coaches are dismissed within hours of one another. The newly unemployed and their former teams are Dom Capers (Carolina), Dennis Erickson (Seattle) Ted Marchibroda (Baltimore), Ray Rhodes (Philadelphia), and Dave Wannstedt (Chicago).

Jan 2, 1999—The wild-card weekend kicks off as the Dolphins hold on to defeat Buffalo 24–17 in Miami, and in Dallas, Arizona upends the Cowboys 20–7. The following day the Jaguars roll over the Patriots 25-10 at home and the 49ers, on a sensational, last-second 25-yard touchdown catch in traffic by Terrell Owens, knock off Green Bay 30–27 in San Francisco. Packers defensive end Reggie White announces his retirement following the game.

Jan 10—And then there were four: the divisional playoffs pare the Super Bowl contenders down to Denver, which routs Miami 38–3, the Jets, 34–24 winners over Jacksonville, the Falcons, who squeak by San Francisco 20–18, and Minnesota, which cruises past Arizona 41–21.

Jan 17—The Atlanta Falcons advance to the Super Bowl for the first time in franchise history as they edge the Vikings 30–27 in overtime in Minnesota. Vikings kicker Gary Anderson, who made a record 40 consecutive field goals in 1998–99, misses from 39 yards late in the game. The Falcons will meet defending champion Denver, which beats the Jets 23–10 in the AFC title game, in Super Bowl XXXIII.

Jan 27—Vikings quarterback Randall Cunningham, who passed for 3,704 yards and 34 touchdowns during the regular-season record, is named NFL Player of the Year.

Jan 30—On the eve of the Super Bowl, Falcons safety Eugene Robinson—the recipient, earlier that day, of Athletes in Action's Bart Starr Award for high moral character—is arrested in Miami and charged with soliciting oral sex from an undercover police officer.

Jan 31—In what turns out to be the last game of his career, Denver quarterback John Elway runs for one touchdown, passes for another and racks up 336 passing yards to lead the Broncos to their second straight Super Bowl triumph, a 34–19 drubbing of Atlanta. Falcons quarterback Chris Chandler throws three interceptions in the second half and Morten Andersen misses a 26-yard field goal as Atlanta falls behind 31–6 after three quarters. Elway is named MVP of the game.

Feb 1—Five former NFL stars are elected to the Hall of Fame's class of 1999: running back Eric Dickerson, who gained a record 2,105 yards with the Rams in 1984; Lawrence Taylor, a fearsome linebacker who led the Giants to two Super Bowl titles; Ozzie Newsome, a tight end who had 662 career receptions for the Browns; Billy Shaw, a dominant offensive guard with the Bills in the 1960s; and Tom Mack, a bruising guard for the Rams.

Feb 2—Former Chicago Bears running back Walter Payton, the NFL's alltime leader in career rushing yards, announces that he has a rare, incurable liver disease called primary sclerosing cholangitis.

Feb 7—The AFC defeats the NFC 23–10 in the Pro Bowl. Receiver Keyshawn Johnson, who makes seven catches for 87 yards, and cornerback Ty Law, who returns an interception 67 yards for a touchdown, are named co-MVPs.

Feb 15—Shortly after losing quarterback Trent Green as a free agent to St. Louis, the Redskins trade three draft picks for former Vikings starting QB Brad Johnson.

Feb 15—Former Lions guard Mike Utley, who was paralyzed in a Nov. 17, 1991 game, makes good on his vow to walk again, taking three steps in a Phoenix hotel conference room.

Davis, who rushed for 2,008 yards in '98, tore knee ligaments in '99.

March 16—The NFL levies a $1 million fine against 49ers owner Eddie DeBartolo for "conduct detrimental to the league" in the wake of DeBartolo's pleading no contest to federal extortion charges stemming from his attempt to secure a casino license in Louisiana.

March 17—At the winter meetings in Phoenix, NFL owners vote to bring back the use of instant replay as an officiating tool. The motion, which will be enacted on a one-year basis, passes by a 28–3 vote.

April 17—For the second year in a row, the top two selections in the NFL draft are quarterbacks as the Cleveland Browns select Kentucky's Tim Couch with the No. 1 pick, and the Philadelphia Eagles take Doncvan McNabb of Syracuse with the second choice. The Saints trade six 1999 draft picks and two 2000 selections to the Redskins for the right to draft Texas running back Ricky Williams with the fifth selection.

May 2—After 16 seasons, two Super Bowl victories and 51,475 passing yards, Denver quarterback John Elway announces his retirement.

May 6—Former Cowboys lineman Mark Tuinei dies of a heroin overdose in Plano, TX.

May 24—Patriots owner Robert Kraft announces that the team will not move to Hartford after all, but remain in Foxboro, with plans for a new $225 million stadium, funded partly by taxpayers and partly by the NFL, going forward.

May 25—NFL owners unanimously approve the sale of the Washington Redskins to a group headed by communications executive Daniel Snyder for a record $800 million.

June 4—Leon Lett, a defensive lineman for the Dallas Cowboys, is suspended indefinitely by the NFL after he violates the league's substance abuse policy for the third time in his eight-year career.

July 16—Defensive end Charles Haley, 35, rejoins the 49ers, signing a four-year deal. Haley has won five Super Bowl rings in his 11-year career, more than any other player. Ten days later the Niners sign former NFL back Lawrence Phillips, who led the World League in rushing over the summer, to a two-year contract.

July 28—One of the top backs in NFL history, who at age 31 is only 1,457 yards short of Walter Payton's career rushing record, Barry Sanders of the Detroit Lions announces his retirement.

Aug 11—Falcons running back Jamal Anderson ends his 14 day holdout and re-signs with Atlanta for five years and $32 million, including a $7.5 million signing bonus.

Sept 12—The 1999–00 NFL season kicks off as the Cleveland Browns return to the league after a three-year absence, only to be routed by Pittsburgh 43–0 in their new stadium alongside Lake Erie. The Jets receive an even tougher blow at Giants Stadium when quarterback Vinny Testaverde ruptures his Achilles tendon during a 30–28 loss to New England and is lost for the year. In Nashville, the Tennessee Titans open their new home, the Adelphia Coliseum, with a 36–35 win over Cincinnati, and in the weekend's most exciting game, the Cowboys rally from a 21-point fourth-quarter deficit to defeat Washington in overtime 41–35.

Sept 20—The previous season's Super Bowl participants, Atlanta and Denver, begin the new year 0–2 as the Broncos fall to Kansas City 26–10 on Sunday, and the Falcons lose to Dallas 24–7 on Monday night. Atlanta, whose quarterback Chris Chandler is already out with an injury, loses running back Jamal Anderson for the year when he tears ligaments in his knee during the loss.

Oct 3—The Jets and the Broncos, who met in the AFC title game the previous year, square off in Denver under entirely different circumstances as both teams, reeling from the loss of key players, are 0–3. The Jets win 21–13, and the news gets worse for Denver, which loses running back Terrell Davis for the season to torn knee ligaments.

Oct 17—Parity is the order of the day in the young NFL season as the St. Louis Rams, of all teams, are the league's only unbeatens after six weeks. Led by former Arena League star Kurt Warner at quarterback, the Rams go to 5–0 with a 41–13 thrashing of Atlanta. No other NFC team has a record better than 3–2. In the AFC the Jaguars defeat Cleveland 24–7 to remain tied with Tennessee (5–1), a 24–21 winner over the Saints, atop the central division.

Soccer

Oct 25, 1998—D.C. United's reign atop MLS comes to a close at the Rose Bowl as the expansion Chicago Fire upsets the two-time defending champions 2–0 in MLS Cup '98. Game MVP Peter Nowak assists on both first-half goals, by Jerzy Podbronzy and Diego Gutierrez.

Oct 28—D.C. United coach Bruce Arena is named coach of the U.S. men's national team. Arena will coach D.C. through the Interamerican Cup, which concludes on Dec. 5.

Oct 28—Goalie Walter Zenga returns to the New England Revolution as a player-coach, the first in MLS history. Zenga played for the Revolution in 1997 and retired, but returned to coach the final six games of the 1998 season.

Oct 30—The Chicago Fire joins D.C. United as the only teams to win the MLS title and the U.S. Open Cup in the same year when it defeats Columbus 2–1 in overtime of the Open Cup final at Soldier Field. Chicago will compete in the 1999 CONCACAF Cup-Winners Cup against club champions from Central America and Mexico.

Nov 2—Former U.S. national team coach Bora Milutonovic is hired to coach the New York/New Jersey MetroStars.

Nov 6—The Bruce Arena–coached U.S. national team debuts with a 0–0 tie against Australia in San Jose.

Nov 14—D.C. United is beaten by Brazilian power Vasco da Gama in the opening game of the Interamerican Cup, a two-game, total-goals series to crown the top club team in the Western Hemisphere.

Dec 2—D.C. United hires former Tampa Bay and New England coach Thomas Rongen to replace Bruce Arena.

Dec 5—Behind a 34th minute goal by midfielder Tony Sanneh and a 77th minute strike by defender Eddie Pope, D.C. United shocks Vasco da Gama of Brazil 2–0 to win the Interamerican Cup. The victory gives D.C. a 2–1 total-goals triumph and bragging rights as the best club team in the Western Hemisphere.

Jan 28, 1999—The MetroStars trade defender Alexi Lalas and goalkeeper Tony Meola to the Kansas City Wizards in exchange for midfielder Mark Chung and goalie Mike Amman. New York/New Jersey also deals defender Diego Sonora to D.C. United in a three-team deal with San Jose involving draft picks.

Jan 30—Michelle Akers scores the 100th international goal of her career as the U.S. women blank Portugal 6–0 in Fort Lauderdale, Fla.

Feb 1—France's Zinedine Zidane, who scored two goals in his country's 3–0 win over Brazil in the 1998 World Cup Final, is named FIFA World Player of the Year.

Feb 2—D.C. United trades midfielder John Harkes to New England for two draft picks.

Feb 6—Bruce Arena's third game as U.S. national team coach is a stunner: the Americans rout Germany 3–0 in Jacksonville, Fla.

Feb 23—MLS commissioner Doug Logan announces that Sunil Gulati, the deputy commissioner of MLS whose duties included player acquisitions, has been dismissed.

March 10—Eric Wynalda undergoes surgery on a torn knee ligament he suffered while playing for Leon in the Mexican first division. He will be out for six months.

March 15—Mexico downs the U.S. 2–1 in San Diego to win the four-team U.S. Cup for the third year in a row.

March 17—Kansas City Wizards goalkeeper and U.S. international Tony Meola tears an anterior cruciate knee ligament in practice and will miss the upcoming MLS season.

March 18—Julie Foudy and Kristine Lilly score as the U.S. women down Norway 2–1 in the semifinals of the Algarve Cup in Portugal. The U.S. falls to China 2–1 in the finals two days later.

March 20—MLS Year Four kicks off as defending champ Chicago topples San Jose 3–1, D.C. United routs Tampa Bay 5–2, the MetroStars and Los Angeles win shootouts over Miami and Colorado, respectively; and the Dallas Burn scorches Kansas City 4–0.

April 14—Ron Newman resigns as coach of the 0–4 Kansas City Wizards. Former U.S. national team coach Bob Gansler replaces him.

April 22—Tisha Venturini scores in stoppage time to give the U.S. women a 2–1 victory over China in a Women's World Cup tuneup in Hershey, Pa. China will avenge the defeat by the same score three days later at Giants Stadium.

April 22—Former UCLA coach Sigi Schmid replaces Octavio Zambrano as coach of the L.A. Galaxy.

May 8—The Wizards halt their MLS-record 10 game losing streak (stretching from the previous season) with a 3–1 win over Los Angeles.

May 15—A standing-room only crowd of more than 24,485 attends the opening of Columbus Crew Stadium in Columbus, Ohio, to see the home team blank New England 2–0. The brand-new, soccer-only facility, built by Crew investor-operator Lamar Hunt for $28.5 million, is viewed by many as a sign of the future in MLS.

May 22—Mia Hamm becomes the alltime leading international goal scorer, notching her 108th career goal in the United States's 3–0 win over Brazil.

May 26—In an astounding reversal of fortune, Manchester United scores two goals in less than four minutes of stoppage time to stun Bayern Munich 2–1 in the European Cup final. The victory completes a rare triple by United, which also won the English Premier League and the F.A. Cup.

June 13—Joe-Max Moore scores in the 88th minute to give the U.S. a 1–0 shocker over Argentina in Washington, D.C.

June 19—The third Women's World Cup opens at Giants Stadium as 78,972 fans watch the U.S. blank Denmark 3–0 on goals by Mia Hamm, Julie Foudy and Kristine Lilly. In other games, China beats Sweden 2–1, Brazil routs Mexico 7–1 and Japan and Canada play to a 1–1 draw.

June 24—After giving up a goal in the second minute, the U.S. women's team settles down and methodically dismantles Nigeria, winning 7–1 before 65,080 fans at Soldier Field in Chicago.

June 26—China completes an undefeated run through the group-play phase of the Women's World Cup with a 3–1 win over Australia. China has outscored its three opponents 12–2.

June 27—The U.S. shuts out North Korea 3–0 in Foxboro, Mass., to advance to the quarterfinals of the Women's World Cup.

July 1—In front of 54,642 fans—inlcuding President Clinton and his family—at Jack Kent Cooke Stadium in Landover, Md., the U.S. overcomes deficits of 1–0 and 2–1 to defeat Germany 3–2 and advance to the semifinals of the Women's World Cup. Tiffeny Millbrett, Brandi Chastain and Joy Fawcett score the U.S. goals.

July 4—The Women's World Cup Final is set as the U.S. edges Brazil 2–0 in Palo Alto, Calif., to advance to the title match, where it will meet China, which routed Norway 5–0 in Foxboro, Mass.

July 10—After 120 hard-fought minutes of scoreless play, the U.S. and China go to penalty kicks to settle the Women's World Cup Final. Briana Scurry stops China's third shooter, Liu Ying, and the U.S. makes all five of its attempts, including Brandi Chastain's dramatic clincher in the fifth round, to win the Cup.

July 30—At the FIFA Confederations Cup in Guadalajara, Mexico, the U.S. blanks Germany for the second time in 1999, downing the erstwhile world power 2–0 on goals by Ben Olsen and Joe-Max Moore. The victory sends the U.S., which has beaten New Zealand 2-1 and fallen to Brazil 1–0, into the semifinals of the tournament, where it will meet Mexico.

Aug 3—Paul Bravo and Brian McBride score as

Soccer (Cont.)

the U.S., which lost 1–0 in overtime to Mexico in the semifinals, defeats Saudi Arabia 2–0 to claim third place at the Confederations Cup.

Aug 10—Major League Soccer introduces former NFL executive Don Garber as its new commissioner. Garber replaces Doug Logan, who was dismissed a week earlier.

Sept 12—The MetroStars win for the first time since May 15, surprising the Columbus Crew 2–1 to end their MLS-record 12-game losing streak.

Sept 14—The Rochester Rhinos of the (second division) A-League upset Colorado of MLS 2–0 in the final of the U.S. Open Cup in Columbus, Ohio. The Rhinos are the first non-MLS team to win the tournament since the league formed in 1996.

Oct 16—The MLS playoff series kick off with hosts D.C. United blanking Miami 2–0 and Tampa Bay losing 2–0 to the Crew in Columbus. In the West, Dallas defeats Chicago 2–1 at the Cotton Bowl and Los Angeles routs Colorado 3–0 in the Rose Bowl.

Oct 24—MLS decides three of its final four as D.C. United advances past the Fusion with a shootout win in Miami, and the Galaxy eliminates the Rapids with a 2–0 victory in Denver. They join

PHIL COALE/AP

Arena breathed new life into the U.S. men's national team, which went 7-3-2 in 1999.

Columbus, 2–0 winners in Tampa Bay on Oct. 22., in the semis. The Chicago-Dallas series is tied 1–1.

Tennis

Oct 25, 1998—Andre Agassi, ranked No. 141 a year ago, climbs to No. 5 with a 6–2, 3–6, 6–3 win over Jan Kroslak in the Czech Indoor final. The victory gives Agassi his fifth title of the year and a tour-best 65 match victories, earning him a berth in the ATP Tour Championships in November.

Nov 8—Steffi Graf returns to action after a two-month absence because of wrist surgery, and reaches the final of the Leipzig Open. She defeats Nathalie Tauziat for her 105th career title and earns $79,000 to increase her career winnings to $20,445,842, which breaks Martina Navratilova's record for earnings by a female athlete.

Nov 12—Venus Williams, No. 5 in the world, withdraws from the season-ending Chase Championships because of a knee injury.

Nov 15—Francisco Clavet defeats Younes El Aynaoui 6–2, 6–4 in the Chevrolet Cup final. Marcelo Rios, who could have unseated Pete Sampras from the No. 1 ranking by winning the tournament, loses in the quarterfinals.

Nov 23—In the finals of the season-ending Chase Championships at Madison Square Garden, Martina Hingis defeats Lindsay Davenport 7–5, 6–4, 4–6, 6–2. Reaching the final, however, is enough for Davenport to hold on to the No. 1 ranking.

Nov 28—Despite losing to Spain's Alex Corretja 4–6, 6–3, 7–6 (7-3) in the semifinals of the

season-ending ATP Tour World Championships, Pete Sampras retains the No. 1 ranking for a record sixth consecutive year. The following day Corretja defeats countryman Carlos Moya 3–6, 3–6, 7–5, 6–3, 7–5, in the finals.

Dec 5—With a 4–1 pasting of Italy in Milan, Sweden becomes the first nation since the U.S. in 1970 to repeat as Davis Cup champion.

Dec 22—The International Tennis Federation announces that Petr Korda tested positive for steroids during Wimbledon the previous July. Korda will forfeit the 199 rankings points and $94,529 he had earned for reaching the quarterfinals.

Jan 4, 1999—World No. 1 Pete Sampras announces that he will skip the first month of the new season, which includes the Australian Open, to rest and regroup.

Jan 30—Martina Hingis wins the Australian Open for the third consecutive year, rolling over Amelie Mauresmo 6–2, 6–3 in the final in Melbourne. The following day, Yevgeny Kafelnikov defeats Thomas Enqvist 4–6, 6–0, 6–3, 7–6 (7-1) to win the men's title.

Feb 7—Martina Hingis reclaims the No. 1 ranking, bumping Lindsay Davenport from the top spot by taking the Pan Pacific Open in Tokyo with a 6–2, 6–1 win over Amanda Coetzer in the final.

Feb 28—Venus and Serena Williams become

the first siblings to win WTA Tour titles in the same week as Venus defeats Amanda Coetzer 6–4, 6–0 in the final of the IGA Classic in Oklahoma City and Serena edges Amelie Mauresmo 6–2, 3–6, 7–6 (7–4) to win the Gaz de France in Paris, her first pro title.

March 13—Two weeks after winning her first tournament as a pro, Serena Williams wins her second, surprising Steffi Graf 6–3, 3–6, 7–5 in the final of the Evert Cup in Indian Wells, Calif.

March 28—Venus Williams defeats her sister Serena 6–1,4–6, 6–4 in the finals of the Lipton Championships in Key Biscayne, Fla. It is the first time siblings have met in a WTA Tour final. In the men's final one day earlier Richard Krajicek downed unseeded Sebastien Grosjean 4–6, 6–1, 6–2, 7–5.

April 4—Slovakia eliminates defending champion Sweden 3–2 in Davis Cup play.

May 27—Pete Sampras is bounced out of the French Open, the only Grand Slam tournament he has never won, in the second round, losing to No. 99 Andrei Medvedev 5–7, 6–1, 6–4, 6–3.

June 5—Calling it the "biggest win" of her career, Steffi Graf becomes the first woman in the Open era to defeat the top three ranked players in the world at the same event, defeating world No. 2 Lindsay Davenport, No. 3 Monica Seles, and No. 1 Martina Hingis en route to the French Open title, the 22nd Grand Slam of her career. Graf beats Hingis 4–6, 7–5, 6–2 in the final.

June 6—Serena and Venus Williams defeat Martina Hingis and Anna Kournikova 6–3, 6–7 (2-7), 8–6 in the French Open women's doubles final to become the second team of sisters to win a Grand Slam doubles title. Grace and Ellen Roosevelt, who won the U.S. Nationals in 1890, were the first.

June 6—The men's French Open title goes to the resurgent Andre Agassi—who was ranked 141st in the world 21 months earlier—as he rallies to defeat Andrei Medvedev 1–6, 2–6, 6–4, 6–3, 6–4 in the final. With the victory Agassi joins Don Budge, Rod Laver, Fred Perry and Roy Emerson as the only men to win all four Grand Slams.

Graf won her 22nd Grand Slam, at the French Open, then retired.

June 13—After seizing his first title of the year with a 6–7 (1-7), 6–4, 7–6 (7-4) win over Tim Henman in the final of the Queen's Club grass-court tournament in London, Pete Sampras reclaims the No. 1 ranking.

June 16—The Czech Republic's Petr Korda, 31, who is battling the International Tennis Federation over his punishment for a positive steroids test during the 1998 Wimbledon, announces that he will retire. In a Wimbledon tuneup tournament the day before his announcement, Korda lost 3–6, 7–6, 6–4 to world No. 590 Danny Sapsford of England.

June 22—Jelena Dokic, a 16-year-old qualifier from Australia who is ranked 129th in the world, eliminates No. 1 seed Martina Hingis 6–2, 6–0 in the first round of Wimbledon.

July 4—Unleashing 17 aces, Pete Sampras steamrolls Andre Agassi—who was trying to become the first man since Bjorn Borg in 1980 to win the French Open and Wimbledon in the same year—6–3, 6–4, 7–5 in the Wimbledon final. It is Sampras's sixth Wimbledon triumph and his 12th career Grand Slam title, which ties him with Roy Emerson for the alltime lead.

July 4—Lindsay Davenport completes a dominating run through Wimbledon without losing a set, defeating Steffi Graf 6–4, 7–5 in the final.

July 10—John McEnroe is inducted into the International Tennis Hall of Fame.

July 18—Australia defeats the U.S. 4–1 in a quarterfinal Davis Cup tie in Chestnut Hill, Mass. The following week Venus and Serena Williams have a hand in all four victories during the U.S.'s 4–1 triumph over Italy in the Fed Cup semifinals.

Aug 8—Martina Hingis regains the No. 1 ranking and wins her first title since May with a 6–4, 6–0 rout of Venus Williams in the final of the TIG Classic in San Diego.

Aug 13—Citing a loss of motivation and saying "I have done everything I wanted to do in tennis", Steffi Graf, 30, announces her retirement. The 1999 French Open champion and '99 Wimbledon finalist, Graf won 22 Grand Slam titles, second only to Margaret Smith Court, in her legendary career.

Aug 30—On the first day of the U.S. Open Richard Williams, the father of Venus and Serena Williams, predicts that the two sisters will meet in the women's singles final. Venus opens with a 6–1, 6–2 victory over Tatiana Poutchek of Belarus.

Aug 31—Pete Sampras withdraws from the U.S. Open with a herniated disk.

Sept 9—The Williams sisters fall one round short of fulfilling their father's prophesy as Venus loses 1–6, 6–4, 3–6 to Martina Hingis in the U.S. Open semifinals. Serena, however, defeats Lindsay Davenport 6–4, 1–6, 6–4 and advances to the final.

Sept 11—Serena Williams knocks off top-ranked Martina Hingis 6–3, 7–6 (7-4) to win the first

Grand Slam of her career and become the first African-American woman since Althea Gibson in 1958 to win a Grand Slam singles title.

Sept 12—In a grueling U.S. Open men's final that lasts three hours and 23 minutes, Andre Agassi wins his second Grand Slam of 1999, outlasting Todd Martin 6–4, 6–7 (5-7), 6–7 (2-7), 6–3, 6–2.

Sept 19—The U.S. routs Russia 4–1 to win the Fed Cup in Stanford, Calif.

Oct 10—Martina Hingis goes home with $520,000 and a new Porsche after defeating Mary Pierce 6–4, 6–1 in the final of the Porsche Grand Prix in Filderstadt, Germany.

Oct 17—Venus Williams wins the Swisscom Challenge in Zurich, defeating Martina Hingis 6–3, 6–4 in the final.

Other Sports

Oct 25, 1998—The World Cup skiing season begins with Austria, led by Hermann Maier, taking the top four places in the men's giant slalom at Soelden, Austria. A day earlier, Andrine Flemmen becomes the first Norwegian woman to win a giant slalom race, defeating Austria's Alexandra Meissnitzer and Italian Olympic champ Deborah Compagnoni.

Nov 1—In the event's second-closest finish ever, Kenya's John Kagwe survives a three-man duel in the final three miles to win his second straight New York City marathon, in 2 hours, 8 minutes, 45 seconds. His countryman Joseph Chebet finishes three seconds later. Kagwe runs the last mile in 4:30, the race's fastest. Franca Fiacconi, who finished third in 1997, becomes the first Italian to win the women's race, finishing in 2:25:17.

Nov 1—Alberto Tomba, the skier whose career included three Olympic gold medals, two silvers and 50 World Cup wins, announces his retirement.

Nov 4—Erren O'Leary hooks a 732-pound blue Marlin to claim the $535,380 first prize at the Bisbee's Black & Blue Marlin Jackpot Tournament off Cabo San Lucas, Mexico.

Nov 9—Tony Roventini becomes the second bowler and first left-hander to bowl an American Bowling Congress–approved 900 series, rolling a trio of 300 games during a regional tournament in Greensfield, Wis.

Nov 23—At Rim Rock Farm in Lawrence, Kans., Arkansas wins a record ninth NCAA Division I Cross Country title. Villanova wins the women's crown, the Pennsylvania school's seventh.

Dec 13—At the National Finals Rodeo in Las Vegas, Ty Murray of Stephenville, Tex., wins a record seventh world all-around title, his first since 1994.

Dec 20—Long Beach State completes a perfect 36–0 season with a 3–2 win over Penn State in the NCAA Division I women's volleyball championship.

Dec 21—The home team dominates the World Cup Super-G at Patscherkofel, Austria, in unprecedented fashion, seizing the top nine places in the event. Hermann Maier is the winner.

Jan 17, 1999—Benjamin Raich of Austria, a rookie on the World Cup circuit, wins his third men's slalom of the year, clocking 1:41.40 in Wengen, Switzerland.

Feb 2—Lasse Kjus of Norway and Hermann Maier of Austria make skiing history by tying for first in the downhill at the World Alpine Ski Championships in Beaver Creek, Colo. Both men finish in 1:14.53, 0.01 ahead of bronze medal winner Hans Knauss of Norway.

Feb 13—In Salt Lake City, Michelle Kwan wins the U.S. figure skating title, the third of her career. Thirteen-year-old Naomi Nari Nam finishes second. Michael Weiss, who narrowly missed winning in 1997 and '98, takes the men's competition.

Feb 17—Susie O'Neill of Australia breaks American Mary T. Meagher's 18-year-old short-course record in the 200-meter butterfly, clocking 2:05.37 in Malmo, Sweden.

March 14—With a blazing second run of 59.82, Norway's Lasse Kjus vaults from 15th place to seventh place in the giant slalom at Sierra Nevada, Spain. The season-ending effort is good enough to hold off his countryman Kjetil Andre Aamodt by 23 points for the overall title. Alexandra Meissnitzer is the women's downhill and overall season champ.

March 17—Doug Swingley of Lincoln, Mont., wins the Iditarod Trail Sled Dog Race, crossing the finish line in Nome, Alaska, with a time of 9 days, 14 hours, 31 minutes.

March 20—Iowa wins the NCAA Division I wrestling title for the fifth year in a row, outpointing Minnesota 100.5–98.5. The Hawkeyes have won 17 of the last 25 national titles.

March 26—Russia sweeps the world figure skating championships as Alexei Yagudin wins the men's title, Maria Butyrskaya wins the women's, Elena Berezhnaya and Anton Sikharulidze take the pairs competition and Anjelika Krylova and Oleg Ovsyannikov win the dance.

March 28—In Belfast, Kenya's Paul Tergat holds off countryman Patrick Ivuti to win his record fifth consecutive World Cross Country Championship, covering the 7.5 mile course in 38:28.

April 19—Joseph Chebet of Kenya wins the Boston Marathon in 2:09:52. Ethiopia's Fatuma Roba becomes the second runner (after Uta Pippig of Germany) to win the women's race three straight times, finishing first in 2:23:25.

May 8—Brigham Young defeats Long Beach State for the NCAA Division I men's volleyball title.

May 31—Virginia wins its first NCAA men's Division I lacrosse title since 1972, downing Syracuse 12–10 in the final.

MARK THOMPSON/ALLSPORT

June 7—In London, a three-man Court of Arbitration for Sport rejects Irish swimmer Michelle Smith de Bruin's appeal of her four-year suspension by swimming's governing body for tampering with a urine sample. De Bruin announces her retirement the next day.

June 16—U.S. sprinter Maurice Greene shatters the world record in the 100-meter dash, clocking 9.79 in Athens.

July 7—Morocco's Hicham El Guerrouj runs 3:43.13 in Rome to lower the world record in the mile by 1.26 seconds.

July 25—Lance Armstrong of the U.S., who was diagnosed with testicular cancer in October 1996 and underwent two operations and 12 weeks of chemotherapy, wins the 2,300-mile Tour de France, cycling's most prestigious event.

Aug 22—Australia's Ian Thorpe, 16, knocks almost two seconds off the 400-meter freestyle world record, clocking 3:41.83 at the Pan Pacific championships in Sydney. The following day Jenny Thompson of the U.S. breaks countrywoman Mary T. Meagher's 100-yard butterfly mark of 57.93, set in 1981. Thompson clocks 57.88. There are 12 world records set at the meet, including one more by Thorpe, in the 200 free, and three by American backstroker Lenny Krayzelburg.

Aug 25—Marion Jones, the U.S. sprinter who had come to the world championships in Seville hoping to win four individual gold medals, sees her quest end bitterly as she finishes third in the long jump on Aug. 23rd and then pulls up in the 200 meter semifinal with back spasms.

Aug 26—Michael Johnson of the U.S., who already owns the world record in the 200 meters, breaks the 400-meter world record with a time of 43.18 at the world championships in Seville.

Aug 29—Osaka, Japan, blanks Phenix City, Ala., 5–0 to win the Little League World Series.

Sept 2—U.S. sprinter Marion Jones, who suffered back spasms at the world championships, withdraws from a meet in Brussels, and announces she will sit out the rest of the season to recuperate.

Sept 7—Hicham El Guerrouj sets his third world record of the year, finishing the 2,000 meters at the ISTAF meet in Berlin in 4:44.79 to shave more than three seconds off the previous record. Guerrouj earlier broke records in the mile and 1,500 meters

Oct 16—At the world championships in Tianjin, China, U.S. gymnast Blaine Wilson establishes himself as a medal contender for the 2000 Olympics by finishing fourth in the all-around. Wilson misses the bronze medal by .001. Russia dominates the event, winning six of the 11 individual events.

El Guerrouj dropped three world records— and the jaws of all those who watched.

Baseball

The World Series
champion New York
Yankees

Team of the Century

Team of the Decade? The Yankees claimed a bigger place in history when they won their 25th title

BY MARK BECHTEL

THE 1998 BASEBALL season, with Mark McGwire, Sammy Sosa and, later, the New York Yankees, chasing history on a nightly basis, went a long way toward putting to rest any residual ill will fans might have had after the strike of 1994.

People came to the park in record numbers, media attention was at an alltime high and the sport once again became an accepted water cooler topic. As incredible as the season was, though, it presented a bit of a problem as the calendar turned to 1999: Just what could baseball do for an encore?

As it turned out, the grand old game adopted an if-it-ain't-broke-don't-fix-it mentality. Big Mac and Sosa reprised their Homeric quest, and the Yankees, just as they did in '98, finished the season by sweeping an overwhelmed National League team—in this case, the Atlanta Braves—in the World Series.

The 1999 season, though, was anything but a retread. In fact, if success were measured in bitten nails, one could argue that it

was the best season in recent memory. As excellent as the Yankees were—they lost only one game in the postseason and seemed incapable of making a mistake—it was the other New York team that provided some of the fall's most memorable moments.

Behind brash manager Bobby Valentine, who had fans raving about him one day and ranting about him the next, the Mets returned to the postseason for the first time since 1988. They did so only after blowing a four-game lead in the wild-card race with 12 to play, then recovering to sweep a three-game series from the Pirates and beat the Reds in a one-game playoff. After the Mets beat Arizona in the Division Series on a walk-off home run by journeyman catcher Todd Pratt, it seemed a Subway Series was destined to materialize.

It wasn't, of course, because the Braves knocked the Mets out in the NL Championship Series. But in those six games, fans got a reminder of just how suspenseful baseball can be. The Braves took the first game 4–2, a score that in this series was

Chad Curtis hit two homers in Game 3, including the game-winner in the 10th.

V.J. LOVERO

something of a blowout. Atlanta then won each of the next two games by one run to take a commanding 3-0 lead in the series.

Then things got interesting. In Game 4, the Mets blew a 1–0 lead in the 8th when Rick Reed gave up back-to-back solo homers to Brian Jordan and Ryan Klesko. Braves closer John Rocker, a cocky, overadrenalized lefty who just happened to be nearly unhittable, came in to protect that lead. Rocker showed he could talk the talk by telling Shea Stadium fans who heckled him to, "go to hell. They're a tired act." He also showed he could walk the walk by saving two of the Braves first three wins. The Mets finally got to him when John Olerud smacked a two-out, two-run single off him in the bottom of the 8th in Game 4, and the Mets stayed alive for another day.

That day would prove to be one of the longest and most fascinating in baseball history. The teams were tied at 2–2 after the fourth inning, and the score stayed there until 12 pitchers later when the Braves pushed across a run in the top of the 15th. In the bottom half of the frame, the Mets tied it back up when Pratt drew a bases loaded walk from Kevin McGlinchy. The next hitter, Robin Ventura, lined a pitch over the rightfield wall for what would have been a game-winning grand slam if Pratt and his teammates hadn't mobbed Ventura near second base, turning his clout into a game-winning single. Somewhere Tug McGraw was smiling.

As wild as the five-hour, 46-minute marathon was, it wasn't nearly as exciting as Game 6, in which both teams' bats, which had been more or less silent up to

that point, came to life. The Mets came back from a 5–0 deficit to take leads of 8–7 and 9–8, but the Braves answered and finally won when Kenny Rogers walked Andruw Jones with the bases loaded in the bottom of the 11th.

Had the Mets been able to beat the Braves, it would have set up the first Subway Series since 1956, because the Yankees blew through the AL playoffs. They swept the Rangers in the first round for the third year in a row, setting up a showdown with the Red Sox, who came from two games down to beat the Indians in the first round, outslugging Cleveland 23–6 in a memorable Game 4.

It was the first time the Yanks and Sox had met in the postseason, and it quickly became the hottest ticket in New England. One fan, a Massachusetts physician, paid $12,000 for four tickets to the Pedro Martinez–Roger Clemens showdown in Game 3 at Fenway Park. The Sox won that game, but lost the other four, ensuring that their streak of World Series futility would extend to the end of the century.

The Fall Classic was supposed to be a matchup of the Braves great pitching and

DAMIAN STROHMEYER

his pitching elbow, putting his future in question.

The rash of health woes continued after the end of spring training. On June 13, Houston Astros manager Larry Dierker suffered a grand mal seizure during a game against San Diego. He was taken from the field in an ambulance and rushed to the hospital. Two days later he had brain surgery. He missed a month, during which the Astros (already playing without their best run producer, Moises Alou, who was out for the season after falling off a treadmill in February and injuring his knee) struggled to a 13–14 record.

Over the long haul, though, the Astros, like the Braves and the Yankees, fared well in the face of adversity. Chipper Jones made up for Galarraga's loss by having one of the finest seasons ever by a switch-hitter. Working with hitting coach Don Baylor, he improved his power stroke from the right side of the plate. The adjustment yielded huge numbers: 45 homers, 110 RBIs, a .319 batting average and 126 walks. Even more impressive was Jones's performance in the clutch. In late September the New York Mets came to Atlanta for a three-game series, trailing the Braves by one game in the National League East. Jones hit game-winning homers in two of the three games, and the Braves all but wrapped up their eighth straight division crown. When the Braves visited New York a week later, Jones also displayed a potent tongue. When asked if he felt sorry for Mets fans after the Braves had once again taken two of three from New York, he said, "No. I guess they can all go put on their Yankees stuff now."

Yankees paraphernalia remained a hot commodity as the defending champs welcomed Torre back on May 18 and cruised to their second straight AL East title, with

the Yankees great bats, but New York pitching ended up dominating the series. Starters Orlando Hernandez, David Cone and Roger Clemens allowed a combined six hits in 21⅔ innings, and Atlanta never stood a chance. The Yankees' 25th World Championship had to be one of their most satisfying, coming as it did in a season in which they, like their opponents, found themselves staring adversity squarely in the face.

The first sign that the 1999 regular season wasn't going to be as charmed as its feel-good predecessor came on Feb. 18, when the Braves announced that first baseman Andres Galarraga, the team's top run-producer and one of its most popular players, would miss the season due to a cancerous tumor in his back. Three weeks later, Yankees manager Joe Torre left the team after receiving a diagnosis of prostate cancer on the same day that Darryl Strawberry made his return to the Yankee clubhouse following colon cancer surgery in October 1998. A week after that, one of 1998's brightest stars, the Chicago Cubs' Kerry Wood, had season-ending surgery on a slightly new cast of characters. In spring training, general manager Brian Cashman received an offer from his counterpart in Toronto, Gord Ash, that, Cashman said, "made my knees buckle." Ash offered five-time Cy Young Award winner Roger Clemens in exchange for the heart and soul of the '98 world champs, pitcher David Wells, along with second baseman Homer Bush and reliever Graeme Lloyd. Cashman took him up on it. It was a gutsy move, tinkering with his chemistry to upgrade his rotation, and in the end, the Blue Jays may have gotten the better deal. Clemens went just 14–10 in pinstripes, and his ERA of 4.60 was nearly two runs higher than his '98 average. Wells won 17 games for Toronto, while Bush batted .320 and stole 32 bases and Lloyd appeared in 74 games with a 3.63 ERA. But Clemens's shortcomings were made up for by Orlando Hernandez. In his first full season El Duque led the Bombers with 17 wins and established himself as a bona fide ace.

Unlike in 1998, the Yankees actually had to check the standings every once in a while this season. Boston stayed within shouting distance of New York throughout the year, thanks to the right arm of Pedro Martinez. The Dominican Dandy dominated the American League, winning 23 games and striking out 10 or more hitters in 19 of his 29 starts. After Martinez beat the Yankees with a one-hitter in which he struck out 17 batters and didn't walk one, New York pitcher David Cone said, "It may have been the best performance I've ever seen. He had three dominating pitches: an overpowering fastball, a knee-buckling curve and a parachute changeup. I don't think I've ever seen anyone with all three." Cone's praise was all the more impressive given the fact that two months earlier, on July 18, he had thrown a perfect game against the Montreal Expos.

As amazing as Martinez was, though, one could argue that his wasn't the best season by a major league pitcher in '99. After signing a four-year, $52.4 million contract with the Diamondbacks, Randy Johnson paid immediate dividends. He made a run at Nolan Ryan's modern record of 383 strikeouts in a season and came up just 19 short. He won 17 games but easily could have won half a dozen more. In one five-game stretch Johnson allowed five earned runs and struck out 62 in 40 innings, and had an 0–4 record to show for it. The Big Unit was the biggest acquisition made by Arizona owner Jerry Colangelo, who opened up his checkbook and bought himself a contender for Christmas. He added six free agents over the winter, at a cost of $118.9 million. The investment paid a healthy return, as the D-backs won 100 games and waltzed to the NL West crown. They lost to the wild-card Mets in the Division Series, but the Diamondbacks were easily the most successful second-year expansion team ever.

Not every big spender fared as well. Baltimore, which had a payroll of $78 million, finished under .500 for the second straight year. A collection of aching and aging vets (like Cal Ripken Jr., who took his first career trip to the disabled list) and underachieving superstars (like Albert Belle, who incurred the wrath of team brass by repeatedly failing to hustle despite a $13 million salary), the Orioles were nonetheless spared from having to wear the label of Baseball's Biggest Disappointment. That tag stuck squarely on the backs of the Los Angeles Dodgers, whose payroll topped $79 million and who finished with 77 wins. The Dodgers' miserable campaign brought smiles to the faces of many NL front-office types, who were put off by the brashness of new G.M. Kevin Malone, who talked about a Los Angeles–New York World Series before the season began. Malone's boldest stroke was the acquisition of pitcher Kevin Brown for a mind-boggling $105 million over seven years. Brown was available because his former employers, the Padres, were unable to come up with the cash to bring him back. Financial woes saw San Diego also bid adieu to Steve Finley (free agent to Arizona), Ken Caminiti (free agent to Houston) and Greg Vaughn (traded to Cincinnati), making the Padres the second consecutive National League champs (Florida was the other) to fall from

time, so we were very fortunate. Obviously it took our timetable of 2003 and pushed it up about four years."

The Reds weren't the only small-market performers to thrive. The A's made a strong run at the AL wild card, thanks largely to the fine pitching of midseason call-up Tim Hudson. Pittsburgh's Brian Giles hit 39 home runs in his first season as a regular. Philadelphia's Bobby Abreu finished third in the NL batting race, won by Colorado's Larry Walker (.379). And Montreal's Vladimir Guerrero smacked 42 home runs despite being the only threat in the Expos' lineup.

Of course, in the era of Mac and Sammy, 42 home runs is almost small potatoes. The dynamic duo who made 1998 so memorable, were, incredibly, at it again in '99. Mark McGwire and Sammy Sosa became the first players ever to eclipse 60 home runs in a season two years in a row. McGwire, who holds the record of 70, belted 65, and Sosa smashed 63. They didn't receive half as much attention as in '98, but their peers took notice. "That they're doing it this year is extremely impressive, more so than last year," Cubs first baseman Mark Grace said. "It's probably taken for granted because it's not new news anymore. ... But I'm looking at it as a player. I consider myself an expert on the game. And I know it's even more impressive because it's unbelievable to do it again."

Grace was talking about Sosa and McGwire, but he could have been talking about baseball in general. The 1998 season was a tough act to follow, but as the '99 season ended the sport had given its fans a whole new collection of memories and moments to savor.

As encores go, it was pretty impressive.

grace in the interests of fiscal unburdening.

Vaughn clubbed 45 home runs for the Reds, who were an example of a team that spent wisely and got considerable bang for its buck. After opening the decade with a World Series title, Cincinnati spent most of the 1990s languishing in small-marketville, and there was no reason to expect anything else in 1999. But G.M. Jim Bowden assembled a competitive group—including sweet-swinging first baseman Sean Casey, whom manager Jack McKeon likened to Tony Gwynn—that earned only a combined $35 million but kept pace with the Astros in the NL Central all year. The Reds lost the division on the season's last day, but their 96 wins were good enough to land them in a one-game playoff with the Mets for the NL wild-card berth. The Mets won behind Al Leiter's two-hitter, but the Reds' season showed that with all of the spending going on, it is still possible to blend intelligent front office moves with homegrown talent and remain competitive. "They just developed earlier than we thought they would," Bowden said. "We thought some would develop this year, some next. What happened was that they all developed at one

Final Standings

National League

EASTERN DIVISION

Team	Won	Lost	Pct	GB	Home	Away
Atlanta	103	59	.636	—	56–25	47–34
†*New York	97	66	.595	6½	49–32	48–34
Philadelphia	77	85	.475	26	41–40	36–45
Montreal	68	94	.420	35	35–46	33–48
Florida	64	98	.395	39	35–45	29–53

CENTRAL DIVISION

Team	Won	Lost	Pct	GB	Home	Away
Houston	97	65	.599	—	50–32	47–33
*Cincinnati	96	67	.588	1½	45–37·	51–30
Pittsburgh	78	83	.484	18½	45–36	33–47
St. Louis	75	86	.466	21½	38–42	37–44
Milwaukee	74	87	.460	22½	32–47	42–39
Chicago	67	95	.414	30	34–48	33–48

WESTERN DIVISION

Team	Won	Lost	Pct	GB	Home	Away
Arizona	100	62	.617	—	52–29	48–33
San Francisco	86	76	.531	14	49–32	37–44
Los Angeles	77	85	.475	23	37–44	40–41
San Diego	74	88	.457	26	46–35	28–53
Colorado	72	90	.444	28	39–42	33–48

†Wild-card team. *Played one-game playoff.

American League

EASTERN DIVISION

Team	Won	Lost	Pct	GB	Home	Away
New York	98	64	.605	—	48–33	50–31
†Boston	94	68	.580	4	49–32	45–36
Toronto	84	78	.515	14	40–41	44–37
Baltimore	78	84	.481	20	41–40	37–44
Tampa Bay	69	93	.426	29	33–48	36–45

CENTRAL DIVISION

Team	Won	Lost	Pct	GB	Home	Away
Cleveland	97	65	.599	—	47–34	50–31
Chicago	75	86	.466	21½	38–42	37–44
Detroit	69	92	.429	27½	38–43	31–49
Kansas City	64	97	.398	32½	33–47	31–50
Minnesota	63	97	.394	33	31–50	32–47

WESTERN DIVISION

Team	Won	Lost	Pct	GB	Home	Away
Texas	95	67	.586	—	51–30	44–37
Oakland	87	75	.537	8	52–29	35–46
Seattle	79	83	.488	16	43–38	36–45
Anaheim	70	92	.432	25	37–44	33–48

1999 Playoffs

National League Divisional Playoffs

Oct 5 ....Houston 6 at Atlanta 1
Oct 6 ....Houston 1 at Atlanta 5

Oct 8 ....Atlanta 5 at Houston 3.(12 innings)
Oct 9 ....Atlanta 7 at Houston 5

(Atlanta won series 3–1.)

Oct 5 ....New York 8 at Arizona 4
Oct 6 ....New York 1 at Arizona 7

Oct 8 ....Arizona 2 at New York 9
Oct 9 ....Arizona 3 at New York 4 (10 innings)

(New York won series 3–1.)

National League Championship Series

Oct 12 ....New York 2 at Atlanta 4
Oct 13 ....New York 3 at Atlanta 4
Oct 15 ....Atlanta 1 at New York 0

Oct 16 ....Atlanta 2 at New York 3
Oct 17 ....Atlanta 3 at New York 4 (15 innings)
Oct 19 ....New York 9 at Atlanta 10 (11 innings)

(Atlanta won series 4–2.)

GAME 1

New York	0	0	0	1	0	0	0	0	1	—2
Atlanta	1	0	0	0	1	1	0	1	x	—4

WP—Maddux. **LP**—Yoshii. **Save**—Rocker.
E—New York: Henderson, Olerud; Atlanta: Williams, C. Jones. **LOB**—New York 6, Atlanta 9. **2B**—New York: Cedeno, Alfonzo (2); Atlanta: Perez, Weiss. **HR**—Atlanta: Perez. **SB**—Atlanta: Williams, C. Jones, Weiss. **CS**—New York: Cedeno. **GIDP**—Atlanta: A. Jones. **T**—3:09. **A**—44,172.
Recap: Atlanta catcher Eddie Perez hit a solo home run in the sixth inning and light-hitting shortstop Walt Weiss collected three hits as the Braves defeated the Mets for the 10th time in 13 meetings this season.

GAME 2

New York	0	1	0	0	1	0	0	1	0	—3
Atlanta	0	0	0	0	0	4	0	0	x	—4

GAME 2 (CONT.)

WP—Millwood. **LP**—Rogers. **Save**—Smoltz.
E—New York: Alfonzo; Atlanta: C. Jones. **LOB**—New York 5, Atlanta 6. **2B**—New York: Alfonzo. **HR**—New York: Mora; Atlanta: Jordan, Perez. **Sac**—New York: Rogers. **CS**—Atlanta: Williams, A. Jones. **GIDP**—Atlanta: Williams 2. **T**—2:42. **A**—44,624.
Recap: Brian Jordan and Eddie Perez connected for two two-run home runs in the sixth inning and John Rocker and John Smoltz shut down the Mets in the 8th and 9th innings to preserve the win.

GAME 3

Atlanta	1	0	0	0	0	0	0	0	0	—1
New York	0	0	0	0	0	0	0	0	0	—0

WP—Glavine. **LP**—Leiter. **Save**—Rocker.
E—Atlanta: Weiss; New York: Leiter, Piazza. **LOB**—Atlanta 4, New York 8. **SB**—Atlanta: Boone, Williams. **CS**—New York: Dunston.

National League Championship Series *(Cont.)*

GAME 3 *(CONT.)*

CS—New York: Dunston. **Sac**—Atlanta: Glavine. **GIDP**—New York: Olerud. **T**—3:04. **A**—55,911.
Recap: The Braves took advantage of two first-inning Met errors to score the game's only run, and Tom Glavine pitched seven scoreless innings to give Atlanta a 3–0 lead in the series.

GAME 4

Atlanta	0	0	0		0	0	0		0	2	0	—2
New York	0	0	0		0	0	1		0	2	x	—3

WP—Wendell. **LP**—Remlinger. **S**—Benitez.
LOB—Atlanta 0, New York 3. **HR**—Atlanta: Jordan, Klesko; New York: Olerud. **SB**—New York: Cedeno 2, Mora. **CS**—Atlanta: Boone. **T**—2:20. **A**—55,872.
Recap: John Olerud drove in all three New York runs with a sixth-inning solo home run and an eighth-inning single, as the Mets avoided elimination.

GAME 5

Atlanta	0 0 0 2 0 0 0 0 0 0 0 0 1	—3
New York	2 0 0 0 0 0 0 0 0 0 0 0 2	—4

WP—Dotel. **LP**—McGlinchy.
E—Atlanta: Klesko 2; New York: Olerud. **LOB**—Atlanta 19, New York 12. **2B**—Atlanta: Perez, Boone, C. Jones 2, Williams, Weiss; New York: Hamilton. **3B**—Atlanta: Lockhart. **HR**—New York: Olerud. **SB**—Atlanta: Nixon, Battle, Weiss; New York: Agbayani, Dunston.

GAME 5 *(CONT.)*

CS—Atlanta: Klesko. **Sac**—Atlanta: A. Jones; New York: Alfonzo. **GIDP**—Atlanta: Weiss; New York: Ordonez, Ventura. **T**—5:46. **A**—55,723.
Recap: Robin Ventura's walk-off grand slam-turned-single won this 15-inning classic and sent the series back to Atlanta with the Braves leading 3–2. Ventura was mobbed by his teammates near second base, making his blast one of the longest singles in history.

GAME 6

New York	0	0	0		0	0	3		4	1	0		1	0	—11
Atlanta	5	0	0		0	0	2		0	1	0		1	1	—10

WP—Springer. **LP**—Rogers.
E—New York: Piazza 2; Atlanta: Hunter. **LOB**—New York 8, Atlanta 9. **2B**—New York: Alfonzo, Ventura, Franco, Henderson; Atlanta: Williams. **HR**—New York—Piazza. **SB**—New York—Henderson, Mora; Atlanta: Boone, Williams, C. Jones 2, Hunter, Nixon.. **CS**—New York: Agbayani. **Sac**—New York: Ordonez, Piazza, Pratt; Atlanta: Perez, Weiss, Boone, Hunter. **GIDP**—Atlanta: Weiss. **T**—4:25. **A**—52,335.
Recap: The Braves squandered leads of 5–0 and 7–3 and trailed in the 8th and 10th innings. But Kenny Rogers walked Andruw Jones in the 11th to force in the game-winning run and send the Braves to their fifth World Series of the 1990s.

American League Divisional Playoffs

Oct 5 ....Texas 0 at New York 8
Oct 7 ....Texas 1 at New York 3
Oct 9 ....New York 3 at Texas 0

(New York won series 3–0.)

Oct 6 ....Boston 2 at Cleveland 3
Oct 7 ....Boston 1 at Cleveland 11
Oct 9 ....Cleveland 3 at Boston 9
Oct 10 ....Cleveland 7 at Boston 23
Oct 11 ....Boston 12 at Cleveland 8

(Boston won series 3–2)

American League Championship Series

Oct 13 ....Boston 3 at New York 4 (10 innings)
Oct 14 ....Boston 2 at New York 3
Oct 16 ....New York 1 at Boston 13
Oct 17 ....New York 9 at Boston 2
Oct 18 ....New York 6 at Boston 1

(New York won series 4–1.)

GAME 1

Boston	2	1	0		0	0	0		0	0	0		0	—3
New York	0	2	0		0	0	0		1	0	0		1	—4

WP—Rivera. **LP**—Beck.
E—Boston: Varitek, Garciaparra 2; New York: Jeter. **LOB**—Boston 6, New York 9. **2B**—Boston: Valentine; New York: Jeter. **3B**—New York: Brosius. **HR**—New York: Brosius, Williams. **SB**—Boston: Lewis; New York: Williams. **CS**—Boston: Lewis. **Sac**—New York: Knoblauch. **GIDP**—Boston: Daubach. **T**—3:39. **A**—57,181.
Recap: Orlando Hernandez settled down after a rough start to pitch eight solid innings, and Bernie Williams led off the 10th with a home run to center field to beat the Red Sox. Last year's World Series MVP, Scott Brosius, tripled and homered for New York.

GAME 2

Boston	0	0	0		0	2	0		0	0	0	—2
New York	0	0	0		1	0	0		2	0	x	—3

WP—Cone. **LP**—R. Martinez. **Save**—Rivera.
LOB—Boston 13, New York 8. **2B**—Boston: Varitek, O'Leary; New York: Knoblauch. **3B**—Boston: Varitek. **HR**—Boston: Garciaparra; New York: Martinez. **SB**—Boston: Offerman; New York: Knoblauch. **CS**—New York: Ledee. **Sac**—Boston: Varitek; New York: Brosius. **T**—3:46. **A**—57,180.
Recap: Rightfielder Paul O'Neill, playing with a broken rib, singled home the winning run in the 7th inning, and closer Mariano Rivera flirted with disaster in the 9th before nailing down the save. The win gave the Yankees a record-tying 12 straight victories in the postseason, dating back to last year's ALCS.

American League Championship Series (Cont.)

GAME 3

New York	0 0 0	0 0 0	0 1 0	—1
Boston	2 2 2	0 2 1	4 0 x	—13

WP—P. Martinez. **LP**—Clemens.
E—New York: Knoblauch, Posada, Ledee; Boston: Garciaparra. **LOB**—New York 6, Boston 10. **2B**—Boston: Nixon 2, Garciaparra, Daubach, Lewis, O'Leary. **3B**—Boston: Offerman. **HR**—New York: Brosius; Boston: Valentin, Daubach, Garciaparra. **GIDP**—Boston: Stanley, Buford. **T**—3:14. **A**—33,190.
Recap: Pedro Martinez pitched seven innings of two-hit ball and fanned 12 Yankees as Boston roughed up ex-Red Sox Roger Clemens (2 IP, 5 ER). Third baseman John Valentin homered and drove in five runs for a Boston offense that produced 21 hits.

GAME 4

New York	0 1 0	2 0 0	0 0 6	—9
Boston	0 1 1	0 0 0	0 0 0	—2

WP—Pettitte. **LP**—Saberhagen. **S**—Rivera.
E—Boston: Garciaparra, Saberhagen, Offerman, Lewis. **LOB**—New York 8, Boston 5. **2B**—New York: Martinez, Williams; Boston: Huskey, Valentin, O'Leary. **HR**—New York: Strawberry, Ledee. **SB**—Boston: Buford. **GIDP**—Boston: Varitek, Offerman, Valentin. **T**—3:39. **A**—33,586.
Recap: Ricky Ledee's pinch-hit grand slam capped a six-run ninth inning that gave the Yankees a 9–2

GAME 4 (CONT.)

victory. New York starter Andy Pettitte scattered eight hits in eight-plus innings of work and Mariano Rivera earned his second save of the series.

GAME 5

New York	2 0 0	0 0 0	2 0 2	—6
Boston	0 0 0	0 0 0	0 1 0	—1

WP—Hernandez. **LP**—Mercker. **Save**—Mendoza.
E—New York: Jeter; Boston: Stanley, Offerman. **LOB**— New York 11, Boston 11. **2B**—Boston: Garciaparra; New York: Jeter; Boston: Varitek. **SB**—New York: Curtis; Boston: Garciaparra. **CS**—New York: Martinez. **T**—4:09. **A**—33,589.
Recap: ALCS MVP Orlando Hernandez struck out nine Red Sox in seven innings of work and shortstop Derek Jeter provided him with all the offense he needed with a first-inning home run. The victory gave the Yankees their 36th American League pennant and their third trip to the World Series in the last four years.

Composite Box Scores

National League Championship Series

NEW YORK

BATTING	AB	R	H	HR	RBI	Avg
Cedeno	12	2	6	0	1	.500
Pratt	2	0	1	0	3	.500
M. Franco	2	1	1	0	0	.500
Mora	14	3	6	1	2	.429
Hamilton	15	0	6	0	2	.400
Bonilla	3	0	1	0	0	.333
Olerud	27	4	8	2	6	.296
Alfonzo	27	2	6	0	1	.222
Henderson	23	2	4	0	0	.174
Piazza	24	1	4	1	4	.167
Agbayani	7	2	1	0	0	.143
Dunston	7	2	1	0	0	.143
Ventura	25	2	3	0	1	.120
Ordonez	24	0	1	0	0	.042
6 others	11	0	0	0	0	.000
Totals	225	21	49	4	21	.218

PITCHING	G	IP	H	BB	SO	ERA
Hershiser	2	4⅓	1	3	5	0.00
Cook	3	1⅓	1	2	1	0.00
Benitez	5	6⅔	3	2	9	1.35
Mahomes	3	6⅓	4	3	3	1.42
Reed	1	7	3	0	5	2.57
Dotel	1	3	4	2	5	3.00
J. Franco	3	2⅔	3	1	3	3.38
Yoshii	2	7⅔	9	3	4	4.70
Wendell	5	5⅔	2	4	5	4.76
Rogers	3	7⅔	11	7	2	5.87
Leiter	2	7	5	4	5	6.43
Totals	6	60	46	31	47	3.45

ATLANTA

BATTING	AB	R	H	HR	RBI	Avg
E. Perez	20	2	10	2	5	.500
Hernandez	2	0	1	0	2	.500
Lockhart	5	0	2	0	1	.400
Guillen	3	0	1	0	1	.333
Weiss	21	2	6	0	1	.286
C. Jones	19	3	5	0	1	.263
Jordan	25	3	5	2	5	.250
A. Jones	23	5	5	0	1	.217
Boone	22	2	4	0	1	.182
Williams	28	4	5	0	1	.179
Klesko	8	1	1	1	1	.125
Hunter	10	1	1	0	2	.100
Battle	2	0	0	0	0	.000
Fabregas	2	0	0	0	0	.000
Myers	2	0	0	0	0	.000
6 others	14	1	0	0	0	.000
Totals	206	24	46	5	22	.223

PITCHING	G	IP	H	BB	SO	ERA
Glavine	1	7	7	1	8	0.00
Rocker	6	6⅔	3	2	9	0.00
Mulholland	2	2⅔	1	1	2	0.00
Springer	2	2	0	1	1	0.00
Maddux	2	14	12	1	7	1.93
Remlinger	5	5⅔	3	3	4	3.18
Millwood	2	12⅔	13	1	9	3.55
Smoltz	3	8⅔	8	0	8	6.23
McGlinchy	1	1	2	4	1	18.00
Totals	6	60⅓	49	14	49	2.69

American League Championship Series

BOSTON

BATTING	AB	R	H	HR	RBI	Avg
Offerman	24	4	11	0	2	.458
Garciaparra	20	2	8	2	5	.400
Buford	5	1	2	0	0	.400
O'Leary	20	2	7	0	1	.350
Valentin	23	3	8	1	5	.348
Nixon	14	2	4	0	0	.286
Stanley	18	1	4	0	1	.222
Varitek	20	1	4	1	1	.200
Huskey	5	1	1	0	0	.200
Daubach	17	2	3	1	3	.176
Lewis	17	2	2	0	1	.118
Hatteberg	1	0	0	0	0	.000
Merloni	0	0	0	0	0	—
Sadler	0	0	0	0	0	—
Totals	184	21	54	5	19	.293

PITCHING	G	IP	H	BB	SO	ERA
P. Martinez	1	7	2	2	12	0.00
Cormier	4	3⅔	3	3	4	0.00
Rapp	1	1	0	1	0	0.00
Lowe	3	6⅓	6	2	7	1.42
Saberhagen	1	6	5	1	5	1.50
R. Martinez	1	6⅔	6	3	5	4.05
Mercker	2	7⅔	12	4	5	4.70
Garces	2	3	3	1	2	12.00
Gordon	3	2	3	1	3	13.50
Beck	2	⅔	2	0	1	27.00
Totals	5	44	42	18	44	3.68

NEW YORK

BATTING	AB	R	H	HR	RBI	Avg
Jeter	20	3	7	1	3	.350
Knoblauch	18	3	6	0	1	.333
Strawberry	6	1	2	1	1	.333
O'Neill	21	2	6	0	1	.286
Martinez	19	3	5	1	3	.263
Williams	20	3	5	1	2	.250
Girardi	8	0	2	0	0	.250
Ledee	8	2	2	1	4	.250
Brosius	18	3	4	2	3	.222
Spencer	9	1	1	0	0	.111
Posada	10	1	1	1	2	.100
Davis	11	0	1	0	1	.091
Curtis	6	1	0	0	0	.000
Bellinger	1	0	0	0	0	.000
Sojo	1	0	0	0	0	.000
Totals	176	23	42	8	21	.239

PITCHING	G	IP	H	BB	SO	ERA
Rivera	3	4⅔	5	0	3	0.00
Mendoza	2	2⅓	0	0	2	0.00
Watson	3	1	2	2	1	0.00
Nelson	2	⅔	0	0	0	0.00
Stanton	3	⅓	1	1	0	0.00
Hernandez	2	15	12	6	13	1.80
Pettitte	1	7⅓	8	1	5	2.45
Cone	1	7	7	3	9	2.57
Irabu	1	4⅔	13	0	3	13.50
Clemens	1	2	6	2	2	22.50
Totals	5	45	54	15	38	3.80

1999 World Series

Oct 23 ....New York 4 at Atlanta 1
Oct 24 ....New York 7 at Atlanta 2
Oct 26 ....Atlanta 5 at New York 6 (10 innings)
Oct 27 ....Atlanta 1 at New York 4

(New York won series 4–0.)

GAME 1

New York	0	0	0	0	0	0	4	0	—4
Atlanta	0	0	0	1	0	0	0	0	—1

WP—Hernandez. **LP**—Maddux. **S**—Rivera.
E—Atlanta: Hunter 2. **LOB**—New York 7, Atlanta 4.
HR—Atlanta: C.Jones. **SB**—New York: Jeter;
Williams. **CS**—New York: Jeter; Atlanta: C. Jones.
Sac—New York: Hernandez, Knoblauch. **GIDP**—
New York: Posada.
T—2:57. **A**—51,342.
Recap: Orlando Hernandez and Greg Maddux
dueled for seven innings, but two eighth-inning errors
led to four Yankee runs and New York took Game 1,
4–1. Hernandez allowed only one hit, a fourth inning
home run by Chipper Jones, and struck out 10
Braves. Maddux cruised into the eighth until Brian
Hunter, a defensive replacement at first base,
committed two errors that led to Yankees runs. Last
year's World Series' MVP Scott Brosius ripped three
singles for New York.

GAME 2

New York	3	0	2	1	1	0	0	0	0	—7
Atlanta	0	0	0	0	0	0	0	0	2	—2

WP—Cone. **LP**—Millwood.
E—New York: Cone; Atlanta: Guillen. **LOB**—New
York 11, Atlanta 7. **2B**—New York: Ledee, Jeter,
Brosius; Atlanta: Boone. **SB**—New York: Knoblauch.
Sac—New York: Girardi. **GIDP**—New York: Williams;
Atlanta: Guillen, A. Jones, Williams.
T—3:14. **A**—51,226.
Recap: Atlanta manager Bobby Cox's strategy to load
his lineup with lefties to face Yankee starter David Cone
backfired, as the Braves managed only one hit through
seven innings and fell behind in the series, 2–0. Braves'
starter Kevin Millwood, Atlanta's top pitcher all year,
failed to escape the third inning after allowing eight hits
and five runs. The Yankees finished with 14 hits as they
won their 10th World Series game, in a row.

GAME 3

Atlanta	1	0	3	1	0	0	0	0	0	—5
New York	1	0	0	0	1	0	1	2	0	1	—6

WP—Rivera. **LP**—Remlinger.
E—Atlanta: Jordan. **LOB**—Atlanta 9, New York 2.
2B—Atlanta: Boone 3, J. Hernandez; New York: Knoblauch. **3B**—Atlanta: Williams. **HR**—New York: Curtis 2, Martinez, Knoblauch. **SB**—Atlanta: J. Hernandez. **CS**—Atlanta: Boone, Nixon. **GIDP**—Atlanta: Jordan; New York: O'Neill.
T—3:16. **A**—56,794.
Recap: Chad Curtis, New York's platoon outfielder who hit only five home runs all season, hit two home runs, including the game-winner in the bottom of the 10th, as the Yankees won their 11th straight World Series game. The Braves, who had been handcuffed by Yankee pitching in Atlanta, knocked around Andy Pettitte for 10 hits and five runs in less that four innings of work. But the bullpen of Jason Grimsley, Jeff Nelson and Mariano Rivera shut down the Braves for the final six innings while the Yankees crept back into the game, one home run at a time. Chuck Knoblauch's two-run home run off Tom Glavine in the eighth evened the score at five to set up Curtis' late-inning heroics.

GAME 4

Atlanta	0	0	0	0	0	0	0	1	0	—1
New York	0	0	3	0	0	0	0	1	x	—4

WP—Clemens. **LP**—Smoltz. **Save**—Rivera.
LOB—Atlanta 5, New York 7. **2B**—New York: Posada. **HR**—New York: Leyritz. **SB**—New York, Jeter 2. **GIDP**—Atlanta: Perez.
T—2:58. **A**—56,752.
Recap: Team of the year. Team of the decade. Team of the century. The New York Yankees defeated Atlanta 4–1 to sweep its second consecutive World Series and win the franchise's 25th championship. Roger Clemens, who struggled at times during the regular season, saved his best for last, pitching 7⅔ strong innings before handing the game over to the Yankee bullpen. World Series MVP Mariano Rivera finished the job, nailing down his second save of the series and fifth of his career. He trails only Rollie Fingers (6) on the all-time World Series save list. Atlanta starter John Smoltz, matched Clemens pitch for pitch, except in the third inning, when New York put three runs across. He struck out 11 Yankees in seven innings of work. After Atlanta chased Clemens and ruined the shutout in the top of the eighth, Yankee pinch hitter Jim Leyritz answered with a solo home run in the bottom of the inning that cemented New York's lead. Dating back to 1996, the Yankees have won three championships and an amazing 12 World Series games in a row.

1999 World Series Composite Box Score

ATLANTA

BATTING	AB	R	H	HR	RBI	Avg
Boone	13	1	7	0	3	.538
Nixon	2	0	1	0	0	.500
Myers	6	0	2	0	1	.333
Hunter	4	0	1	0	0	.250
C. Jones	13	2	3	1	2	.231
Weiss	9	1	2	0	0	.222
Hernandez	5	0	1	0	2	.200
Williams	17	2	3	0	0	.176
Klesko	12	0	2	0	0	.167
Lockhart	7	1	1	0	0	.143
Perez	8	0	1	0	0	.125
A. Jones	13	1	1	0	0	.077
Jordan	13	1	1	0	1	.077
Guillen	5	0	0	0	0	.000
Fabregas	1	0	0	0	0	.000
Battle	0	0	0	0	0	—
Others	2	0	0	0	0	.000
Totals	130	9	26	1	9	.200

PITCHING	G	IP	H	BB	SO	ERA
Rocker	2	3	2	2	4	0.00
Springer	2	2⅓	1	0	1	0.00
McGlinchy	1	2	2	1	2	0.00
Maddux	1	7	5	3	5	2.57
Smoltz	1	7	6	3	11	3.86
Glavine	1	7	7	0	3	5.14
Mulholland	2	3⅔	5	1	3	7.36
Remlinger	2	1	1	1	0	9.00
Millwood	1	2	8	2	2	18.00
Totals	4	35	37	13	31	4.37

NEW YORK

BATTING	AB	R	H	HR	RBI	Avg
Leyritz	1	1	1	1	1	1.000
Brosius	16	2	6	0	1	.375
Jeter	17	4	6	0	1	.353
Curtis	6	3	2	2	2	.333
Strawberry	3	0	1	0	0	.333
Knoblauch	16	5	5	1	3	.313
Girardi	7	1	2	0	0	.286
Martinez	15	3	4	1	5	.267
Posada	8	0	2	0	1	.250
Williams	13	2	3	0	0	.231
O'Neill	15	0	3	0	4	.200
Ledee	10	0	2	0	1	.200
Davis	4	0	0	0	0	.000
Sojo	0	0	0	0	0	—
Others	6	0	0	0	0	.000
Totals	137	21	37	5	20	.270

PITCHING	G	IP	H	BB	SO	ERA
Cone	1	7	1	5	4	0.00
Rivera	3	4⅔	3	1	3	0.00
Nelson	4	2⅔	2	1	3	0.00
Grimsley	1	2⅓	2	2	0	0.00
Stanton	1	⅓	0	0	1	0.00
Clemens	1	7⅔	4	2	4	1.17
Hernandez	1	7	1	2	10	1.29
Mendoza	1	1⅔	3	1	0	10.80
Pettitte	1	3⅔	10	1	1	12.27
Totals	4	37	26	15	26	2.19

1999 Individual Leaders

National League Batting

BATTING AVERAGE

Larry Walker, Col .... .379
Luis Gonzalez, Ariz............ .336
Bobby Abreu, Phil............ .335
Sean Casey, Cin............... .332
Jeff Cirillo, Mil .... .326
Mark Grudzielanek, LA ...... .326
Carl Everett, Hou .... .325
Doug Glanville, Phil .... .325
Todd Helton, Col............... .320
Chipper Jones, Atl .... .319

HITS

Luis Gonzalez, Ariz............206
Doug Glanville, Phil 204
Jeff Cirillo, Mil 198
Sean Casey, Cin 197
Vladimir Guerrero, Mtl........193
Neifi Perez, Col 193
Edgardo Alfonzo, NY 191
Matt Williams, Ariz 190
Craig Biggio, Hou 188
Todd Helton, Col.................185

DOUBLES

Craig Biggio, Hou 56
Luis Gonzalez, Ariz...............45
Jose Vidro, Mtl 45
Mark Grace, Chi 44
Geoff Jenkins, Mil 43

TRIPLES

Bobby Abreu, Phil...............11
Neifi Perez, Col 11
Tony Womack, Ariz................10
Steve Finley, Ariz 10
Mike Carmeron, Cin................9
Mark Kotsay, Fla 9

HOME RUNS

Mark McGwire, StL 65
Sammy Sosa, Chi 63
Chipper Jones, Atl.................45
Greg Vaughn, Cin 45
Jeff Bagwell, Hou...................42
Vladimir Guerrero, Mtl............42
Mike Piazza, NY 40
Brian Giles, Pitt 39
Jay Bell, Ariz 38
Larry Walker, Col 37

RUNS SCORED

Jeff Bagwell, Hou.................143
Jay Bell, Ariz 132
Craig Biggio, Hou 123
Edgardo Alfonzo, NY 123
Bobby Abreu, Phil.................118
Mark McGwire, StL 118
Chipper Jones, Atl 116
Sammy Sosa, Chi 114
Todd Helton, Col...................114
Luis Gonzalez, Ariz...............112

TOTAL BASES

Sammy Sosa, Chi 397
Vladimir Guerrero, Mtl..........366
Mark McGwire, StL 363
Chipper Jones, Atl 359
Todd Helton, Col...................339

STOLEN BASES

Tony Womack, Ariz.................72
Roger Cedeno, NY 66
Eric Young, LA.......................51
Luis Castillo, Fla....................50
Pokey Reese, Cin 38
Mike Cameron, Cin 38

RUNS BATTED IN

Mark McGwire, StL 147
Matt Williams, Ariz 142
Sammy Sosa, Chi 141
Dante Bichette, Col...............133
Vladimir Guerrero, Mtl..........131
Jeff Bagwell, Hou..................126
Mike Piazza, NY....................124
Robin Ventura, NY 120
Greg Vaughn, Cin.................118
Three tied with 115.

SLUGGING PERCENTAGE

Larry Walker, Col .... .710
Mark McGwire, StL .... .697
Sammy Sosa, Chi .... .635
Chipper Jones, Atl............... .633
Brian Giles, Pitt .... .614

ON-BASE PERCENTAGE

Larry Walker, Col .... .458
Jeff Bagwell, Hou................. .454
Bobby Abreu, Phil............... .446
Chipper Jones, Atl................ .441
John Olerud, NY .... .428

BASES ON BALLS

Jeff Bagwell, Hou.................149
Mark McGwire, StL 133
Chipper Jones, Atl 126
John Olerud, NY 125
Bobby Abreu, Phil................109

National League Pitching

EARNED RUN AVERAGE

Randy Johnson, Ariz..........2.48
Kevin Millwood, Atl 2.68
Mike Hampton, Hou............2.90
Kevin Brown, LA 3.00
John Smoltz, Atl..................3.19
Todd Ritchie, Pitt 3.49
Curt Schilling, Phil...............3.54
Greg Maddux, Atl 3.57
Jose Lima, Hou 3.58
Omar Daal, Ariz 3.65

SAVES

Ugueth Urbina, Mtl 41
Trevor Hoffman, SD 40
Billy Wagner, Hou 39
John Rocker, Atl.....................38
Bob Wickman, Mil..................37
Robb Nen, Fla.........................37
Jeff Shaw, LA.........................34
Matt Mantei, Ariz....................32
Dave Veras, Col......................31
Danny Graves, Cin 27

WINS

Mike Hampton, Hou..............22
Jose Lima, Hou......................21
Greg Maddux, Atl 19
Kent Bottenfield, StL..............18
Kevin Millwood, Atl 18
Kevin Brown, LA.....................18
Russ Ortiz, SF 18
Randy Johnson, Ariz..............17
Pedro Astacio, Col.................17
Three tied with 16.

GAMES PITCHED

Steve Kline, Mtl 82
Turk Wendell, NY 80
Scott Sullivan, Cin.................79
Anthony Telford, Mtl..............79
Armando Benitez, NY 77

INNINGS PITCHED

Randy Johnson, Ariz 271⅔
Kevin Brown, LA.................252⅓
Jose Lima, Hou...................246½
Mike Hampton, Hou............239
Tom Glavine, Atl 234

STRIKEOUTS

Randy Johnson, Ariz............364
Kevin Brown, LA...................221
Pedro Astacio, Col................210
Kevin Millwood, Atl 205
Shane Reynolds, Hou...........197
Sterling Hitchcock, SD.........194
Jose Lima, Hou.....................187
Jon Lieber, Chi 186
Mike Hampton, Hou..............177
Chan Ho Park, LA 174

COMPLETE GAMES

Randy Johnson, Ariz..............12
Curt Schilling, Phil...................8
Pedro Astacio, Col...................7
Kevin Brown, LA 5
Four tied with four.

SHUTOUTS

Andy Ashby, SD 3
Six tied with two.

American League Batting

BATTING AVERAGE

Nomar Garciaparra, Bos ... .357
Derek Jeter, NY .... .349
Bernie Williams, NY .... .342
Edgar Martinez, Sea .... .337
Manny Ramirez, Clev......... .333
Omar Vizquel, Clev........... .333
Ivan Rodriguez, Tex.......... .332
Tony Fernandez, Tor.......... .328
Juan Gonzalez, Tex.......... .326
Rafael Palmeiro, Tex......... .324

HITS

Derek Jeter, NY 219
B.J. Suhroff, Balt..................207
Bernie Williams, NY 202
Randy Velarde, Ana-Oak.....200
Ivan Rodriguez, Tex.............199
Joe Randa, KC 197
Carlos Beltran, KC 194
Omar Vizquel, Clev..............191
Nomar Garciaparra, Bos 190
Shawn Green, Tor................190

DOUBLES

Shawn Green, Tor..................45
Jermaine Dye, KC..................44
Mike Sweeney, KC.................44
Nomar Garciaparra, Bos 42
Three tied with 41.

TRIPLES

Jose Offerman, Bos...............11
Johnny Damon, KC..................9
Carlos Febles, KC...................9
Derek Jeter, NY 9
Four tied with eight.

HOME RUNS

Ken Griffey Jr., Sea...............48
Rafael Palmeiro, Tex.............47
Carlos Delgado, Tor 44
Manny Ramirez, Clev............44
Shawn Green, Tor.................42
Alex Rodriguez, Sea.............42
Juan Gonzalez, Tex..............39
Dean Palmer, Det.................38
Matt Stairs, Oak 38
Albert Belle, Balt..................37

RUNS SCORED

Roberto Alomar, Clev 138
Shawn Green, Tor................134
Derek Jeter, NY 134
Manny Ramirez, Clev...........131
Ken Griffey Jr., Sea.............123
Chuck Knoblauch, NY 120
Bernie Williams, NY 116
Ivan Rodriguez, Tex.............116
Jason Giambi, Oak...............115
Juan Gonzalez, Tex.............114

TOTAL BASES

Shawn Green, Tor................361
Rafael Palmeiro, Tex............356
Ken Griffey Jr., Sea.............349
Derek Jeter, NY 346
Manny Ramirez, Clev...........346

STOLEN BASES

Brian L. Hunter, Sea 44
Omar Vizquel, Clev...............42
Tom Goodwin, Tex.................39
Roberto Alomar, Clev 37
Shannon Stewart, Tor 37

RUNS BATTED IN

Manny Ramirez, Clev...........165
Rafael Palmeiro, Tex............148
Carlos Delgado, Tor 134
Ken Griffey Jr., Sea.............134
Juan Gonzalez, Tex..............128
Jason Giambi, Oak...............123
Shawn Green, Tor................123
Roberto Alomar, Clev 120
Jermaine Dye, KC................119
Albert Belle, Balt..................117
Maglio Ordonez, Chi............117

SLUGGING PERCENTAGE

Manny Ramirez, Clev............ .663
Rafael Palmeiro, Tex.......... .630
Nomar Garciaparra, Bos ... .603
Juan Gonzalez, Tex........... .601
Shawn Green, Tor.............. .588

ON-BASE PERCENTAGE

Edgar Martinez, Sea.......... .447
Manny Ramirez, Clev.......... .442
Derek Jeter, NY .... .438
Bernie Williams, NY .... .435
Tony Fernandez, Tor.......... .427

BASES ON BALLS

Jim Thome, Clev 127
Jason Giambe, Oak.............105
Albert Belle, Balt..................101
John Jaha, Oak....................101
Bernie Williams, NY 100

American League Pitching

EARNED RUN AVERAGE

Pedro Martinez, Bos 2.07
David Cone, NY 3.44
Mike Mussina, Balt..............3.50
Brad Radke, Minn...............3.75
Jose Rosado, KC.................3.85
Jamie Moyer, Sea................3.87
Bartolo Colon, Clev.............3.95
Mike Sirotka, Chi.................4.00
Freddie An. Garcia, Sea.....4.07
Orlando Hernandez, NY 4.12

SAVES

Mariano Rivera, NY...............45
Roberto Hernandez, TB........43
John Wetteland, Tex.............43
Mike Jackson, Clev...............39
Jose Mesa, Sea 33
Billy Koch, Tor......................31
Troy Percival, Ana................31
Todd Jones, Det...................30
Bob Howry, Chi.....................28
Mike Timlin, Balt...................27

WINS

Pedro Martinez, Bos 23
Bartolo Colon, Clev...............18
Mike Mussina, Balt................18
Aaron Sele, Tex 18
Charles Nagy, Clev...............17
Orlando Hernandez, NY 17
Freddie An. Garcia, Sea........17
David Wells, Tor....................17
Kevin Appier, KC-Oak 16
Three tied with 15.

GAMES PITCHED

Buddy Groom, Oak................76
Bob Wells, Minn....................76
Mike Trombley, Minn 75
Graeme Lloyd, Tor.................74
Derek Lowe, Bos 74

INNINGS PITCHED

David Wells, Tor 231⅔
Scott Erickson, Balt 230⅓
Jamie Moyer, Sea 228
Dave Burba, Clev 220
Rick Helling, Tex................219⅓

STRIKEOUTS

Pedro Martinez, Bos 313
Chuck Finley, Ana................200
Aaron Sele, Tex 186
David Cone, NY 177
Dave Burba, Clev 174
Mike Mussina, Balt...............172
Freddie An. Garcia, Sea 170
David Wells, Tor...................169
Roger Clemens, NY 163
Eric Milton, Minn 163

COMPLETE GAMES

David Wells, Tor......................7
Scott Erickson, Balt.................6
Sidney Ponson, Balt.................6
Pedro Martinez, Bos 5
Jose Rosado, KC.....................5
Eric Milton, Minn 5

SHUTOUTS

Scott Erickson, Balt.................3
Brian Moehler, Det...................2
Eric Milton, Minn.....................2
Aaron Sele, Tex 2
Bobby Witt, TB........................2

1999 Team Statistics

National League

TEAM BATTING	BA	AB	R	H	TB	2B	3B	HR	RBI	SB	BB	SO
Colorado	.288	5717	906	1644	2696	305	39	223	863	70	508	863
New York	.279	5572	853	1553	2421	297	14	181	814	150	717	994
Arizona	.277	5658	908	1566	2595	289	46	216	865	137	588	1045
Philadelphia	.275	5598	841	1539	2412	302	44	161	797	125	631	1081
Milwaukee	.273	5582	815	1524	2378	299	30	165	777	81	658	1065
Cincinnati	.272	5649	865	1536	2549	312	37	209	820	164	569	1125
San Francisco	.271	5563	872	1507	2414	307	18	188	828	109	696	1028
Houston	.267	5485	823	1463	2306	293	23	168	784	166	728	1138
Atlanta	.266	5569	840	1481	2427	309	23	197	791	148	608	962
Los Angeles	.266	5567	793	1480	2340	253	23	187	761	167	594	1030
Montreal	.265	5559	718	1473	2376	320	47	163	680	70	438	939
Florida	.263	5578	691	1465	2203	266	44	128	655	92	479	1145
St. Louis	.262	5570	809	1461	2371	274	27	194	763	134	613	1202
Pittsburgh	.259	5468	775	1417	2292	282	40	171	735	112	573	1197
Chicago	.257	5482	747	1411	2303	255	35	189	717	60	571	1170
San Diego	.252	5394	710	1360	2119	256	22	153	671	174	631	1169

TEAM PITCHING	ERA	W	L	Sho	CG	SV	Inn	H	R	ER	BB	SO
Atlanta	3.63	103	59	9	9	45	1471	1398	661	593	507	1197
Arizona	3.77	100	62	9	16	42	1467⅓	1387	676	615	543	1198
Houston	3.83	97	65	8	12	48	1458⅔	1485	675	620	478	1204
Cincinnati	3.98	96	67	11	6	55	1462	1309	711	647	636	1081
New York	4.27	97	66	7	5	49	1456⅔	1372	711	691	617	1172
Pittsburgh	4.33	78	83	3	8	34	1433⅓	1444	782	689	633	1083
Los Angeles	4.45	77	85	6	8	37	1453	1438	787	718	594	1077
San Diego	4.47	74	88	6	5	43	1420⅓	1454	781	705	529	1078
Montreal	4.69	68	94	4	6	44	1434⅓	1505	853	748	572	1043
San Francisco	4.71	86	76	3	6	42	1456⅓	1486	831	762	655	1076
St. Louis	4.74	75	86	3	5	38	1445⅓	1519	838	761	667	1025
Florida	4.90	64	98	5	6	33	1435⅔	1560	852	781	655	943
Philadelphia	4.92	77	85	6	11	32	1438⅓	1494	846	787	627	1030
Milwaukee	5.07	74	87	5	2	40	1442⅔	1618	886	813	616	987
Chicago	5.27	67	95	6	11	32	1430⅔	1619	920	837	529	980
Colorado	6.01	72	90	2	12	33	1429	1700	1028	955	737	1032

American League

TEAM BATTING	BA	AB	R	H	TB	2B	3B	HR	RBI	SB	BB	SO
Texas	.293	5651	945	1653	2705	304	29	230	897	111	611	937
Cleveland	.289	5634	1009	1629	2629	309	32	209	960	147	743	1099
Kansas City	.282	5624	856	1584	2435	294	52	151	800	127	535	932
New York	.282	5568	900	1568	2521	302	36	193	855	104	718	978
Toronto	.280	5642	883	1580	2581	337	14	212	856	119	578	1077
Baltimore	.279	5637	851	1572	2522	299	21	203	804	107	615	890
Boston	.278	5579	836	1551	2497	334	42	176	808	67	597	929
Chicago	.277	5644	777	1563	2421	298	37	162	742	110	499	810
Tampa Bay	.274	5586	772	1531	2296	272	29	145	728	73	544	1042
Seattle	.269	5572	859	1499	2536	263	21	244	825	130	610	1095
Minnesota	.264	5495	686	1450	2110	285	30	105	643	118	500	978
Detroit	.261	5481	747	1433	2426	289	34	212	704	108	458	1049
Oakland	.259	5519	893	1430	2462	287	20	235	845	70	770	1129
Anaheim	.256	5494	711	1404	2170	248	22	158	673	71	511	1022

TEAM PITCHING	ERA	W	L	Sho	CG	SV	Inn	H	R	ER	BB	SO
Boston	4.00	94	68	12	6	50	1436⅔	1396	718	638	469	1131
New York	4.13	98	64	10	6	50	1439⅔	1402	731	661	581	1111
Oakland	4.69	87	75	5	6	48	1438⅓	1537	846	750	569	967
Baltimore	4.77	78	84	11	17	33	1435	1468	815	760	647	983
Anaheim	4.79	70	92	7	4	37	1431⅓	1472	826	762	624	877
Cleveland	4.89	97	65	6	3	46	1450⅓	1503	860	788	634	1120
Chicago	4.92	75	86	3	6	39	1438⅓	1608	870	786	596	968
Toronto	4.92	84	78	9	14	39	1439	1582	862	787	575	1009
Minnesota	5.00	63	97	8	13	34	1423⅓	1591	845	791	487	927
Tampa Bay	5.06	69	93	5	6	45	1433	1606	913	805	695	1055
Texas	5.07	95	67	9	6	47	1436⅓	1626	859	809	509	979
Detroit	5.17	69	92	6	4	33	1421	1528	882	817	583	976
Seattle	5.24	79	83	6	7	40	1433⅔	1613	905	834	684	980
Kansas City	5.35	64	97	3	11	29	1420⅔	1607	921	844	643	831

Arizona Diamondbacks

BATTING	BA	G	AB	R	H	TB	2B	3B	HR	RBI	SB	BB	SO
Gonzalez, Luis	.336	153	614	112	206	337	45	4	26	111	9	66	63
Durazo, Erubiel	.329	52	155	31	51	92	4	2	11	30	1	26	43
Harris, Lenny	.310	110	187	17	58	74	13	0	1	20	2	6	7
Williams, Matt	.303	154	627	98	190	336	37	2	35	142	2	41	93
Gilkey, Bernard	.294	94	204	28	60	102	16	1	8	39	2	29	42
Bell, Jay	.289	151	589	132	170	328	32	6	38	112	7	82	132
Womack, Tony	.277	144	614	111	170	227	25	10	4	41	72	52	68
Miller, Damian	.270	86	296	35	80	132	19	0	11	47	0	19	78
Finley, Steve	.264	156	590	100	156	310	32	10	34	103	8	63	94
Fox, Andy	.255	99	274	34	70	104	12	2	26	33	4	33	61
Lee, Travis	.237	120	375	57	89	136	16	2	9	50	17	58	50
Stinnett, Kelly	.232	88	284	36	66	121	13	0	14	38	2	24	83

PITCHING	ERA	W	L	G	GS	CG	SV	INN	H	R	ER	BB	SO
Johnson, Randy	2.48	17	9	35	35	12	0	271⅔	207	86	75	70	364
Swindell, Greg	2.51	4	0	63	0	0	1	64⅔	54	19	18	21	51
Mantei, Matt	2.76	1	3	32	0	0	32	65⅓	44	21	20	44	99
Daal, Omar	3.65	16	9	32	32	2	0	214⅔	188	92	87	79	148
Olson, Gregg	3.71	9	4	61	0	0	14	60⅔	54	28	25	25	45
Stottlemyre, Todd	4.09	6	3	17	17	0	0	101⅓	106	51	46	40	74
Reynoso, Armando	4.37	10	6	31	27	0	0	167	178	90	81	67	79
Anderson, Brian	4.57	8	2	31	19	2	1	130	144	69	66	28	75
Benes, Andy	4.81	13	12	33	32	0	0	198⅓	216	117	106	82	141

Atlanta Braves

BATTING	BA	G	AB	R	H	TB	2B	3B	HR	RBI	SB	BB	SO
Jones, Chipper	.319	157	567	116	181	359	41	1	45	110	25	126	94
Lopez, Javy	.317	65	246	34	78	131	18	1	11	45	0	20	41
Simon, Randall	.317	90	218	26	69	100	16	0	5	25	2	17	25
Klesko, Ryan	.297	133	404	55	120	215	28	2	21	80	5	53	69
Jordan, Brian	.283	153	576	100	163	268	28	4	23	115	13	51	81
Jones, Andruw	.275	162	592	97	163	286	35	5	26	84	24	76	103
Williams, Gerald	.275	143	422	76	116	193	24	1	17	68	19	33	67
Hernandez, Jose	.266	147	508	79	135	216	20	2	19	62	11	52	145
Boone, Bret	.252	152	608	102	153	253	38	1	20	63	14	47	112
Perez, Eddie	.249	104	309	30	77	115	17	0	7	30	0	17	40
Hunter, Brian	.249	114	181	28	45	77	12	1	6	30	0	31	40
Guillen, Ozzie	.241	92	232	21	56	75	16	0	1	20	4	15	17
Weiss, Walt	.226	110	279	38	63	90	13	4	2	29	7	35	48

PITCHING	ERA	W	L	G	GS	CG	SV	INN	H	R	ER	BB	SO
Remlinger, Mike	2.37	10	1	73	0	0	1	83⅔	66	24	22	35	81
Rocker, John	2.49	4	5	74	0	0	38	72⅓	47	24	20	37	104
Millwood, Kevin	2.68	18	7	33	33	2	0	228	168	80	68	59	205
McGlinchy, Kevin	2.82	7	3	64	0	0	0	70⅓	66	25	22	30	67
Smoltz, John	3.19	11	8	29	29	1	0	186⅓	168	70	66	40	156
Seanez, Rudy	3.35	6	1	56	0	0	3	532/3	47	21	20	21	41
Maddux, Greg	3.57	19	9	33	33	4	0	219⅓	258	103	87	37	136
Glavine, Tom	4.12	14	11	35	35	2	0	234	259	115	107	83	138
Mulholland, Terry	4.39	10	8	42	24	0	1	170⅓	201	95	83	45	83
Bergman, Sean	5.21	5	6	25	16	2	0	105⅓	135	62	61	29	44

Chicago Cubs

BATTING	BA	G	AB	R	H	TB	2B	3B	HR	RBI	SB	BB	SO
Grace, Mark	.309	161	593	107	183	285	44	5	16	91	3	83	44
Rodriguez, Henry	.304	130	447	72	136	243	29	0	26	87	2	56	113
Hill, Glenallen	.300	99	253	43	76	147	9	1	20	55	5	22	61
Sosa, Sammy	.288	162	625	114	180	397	24	2	63	141	7	78	171
Alexander, Manny	.271	90	177	17	48	63	11	2	0	15	4	10	38
Johnson, Lance	.260	95	335	46	87	113	11	6	1	21	13	37	20
Reed, Jeff	.258	103	256	29	66	95	16	2	3	28	1	45	58
Santiago, Benito	.249	109	350	28	87	132	18	3	7	36	1	32	71
Morandini, Mickey	.241	144	456	60	110	150	18	5	4	37	6	48	61
Blauser, Jeff	.240	104	200	41	48	84	5	2	9	26	2	26	52
Houston, Tyler	.233	100	249	26	58	96	9	1	9	27	1	28	67
Gaetti, Gary	.204	113	280	22	57	95	9	1	9	46	0	21	51
Andrews, Shane	.195	117	348	41	68	128	12	0	16	51	1	50	109

National League Team-by-Team Statistical Leaders *(Cont.)*

Chicago Cubs *(Cont.)*

PITCHING	ERA	W	L	G	GS	CG	SV	INN	H	R	ER	BB	SO
Ayala, Bobby	3.51	1	7	66	0	0	0	82	71	43	32	39	79
Adams, Terry	4.02	6	3	52	0	0	13	65	60	33	29	28	57
Lieber, Jon	4.07	10	11	31	31	3	0	203⅓	226	107	92	46	186
Myers, Rodney L.	4.38	3	1	46	0	0	0	63⅔	71	34	31	25	41
Tapani, Kevin	4.83	6	12	23	23	1	0	136	151	81	73	33	73
Farnsworth, Kyle	5.05	5	9	27	21	1	0	130	140	80	73	52	70
Sanders, Scott	5.52	4	7	67	6	0	2	104⅓	112	69	64	53	89
Lorraine, Andrew	5.55	2	5	11	11	2	0	61⅔	71	42	38	22	40
Trachsel, Steve	5.56	8	18	34	34	4	0	205⅔	226	133	127	64	149
Serafini, Dan	6.93	3	2	42	4	0	1	62⅓	86	51	48	32	17

Cincinnati Reds

BATTING	BA	G	AB	R	H	TB	2B	3B	HR	RBI	SB	BB	SO
Casey, Sean	.332	151	594	103	197	320	42	3	25	99	0	61	88
Taubensee, Eddie	.311	126	424	58	132	221	22	2	21	87	0	30	67
Young, Dmitri	.300	127	373	63	112	188	30	2	14	56	3	30	71
Larkin, Barry	.293	161	583	108	171	245	30	4	12	75	30	93	57
Reese, Pokey	.285	149	585	85	167	244	37	5	10	52	38	35	81
Boone, Aaron	.280	139	472	56	132	210	26	5	14	72	17	30	79
Hammonds, Jeffrey	.279	123	262	43	73	137	13	0	17	41	3	27	64
Cameron, Mike	.256	146	542	93	139	254	34	9	21	66	38	80	145
Lewis, Mark	.254	88	173	18	44	78	16	0	6	28	0	7	24
Tucker, Michael	.253	133	296	55	75	126	8	5	11	44	11	37	81
Vaughn, Greg	.245	153	550	104	135	294	20	2	45	118	15	85	137

PITCHING	ERA	W	L	G	GS	CG	SV	INN	H	R	ER	BB	SO
Williamson, Scott	2.41	12	7	62	0	0	19	93⅓	54	29	25	43	107
Sullivan, Scott	3.01	5	4	79	0	0	3	113⅔	88	41	38	47	78
Guzman, Juan	3.03	6	3	12	12	1	0	77⅓	70	33	26	21	60
Graves, Danny	3.08	8	7	75	0	0	27	111	90	42	38	49	69
Parris, Steve	3.50	11	4	22	21	2	0	128⅔	124	59	50	52	86
Harnisch, Pete	3.68	16	10	33	33	2	0	198⅓	190	86	81	57	120
Reyes, Dennis	3.79	2	2	65	1	0	2	61⅔	53	30	26	39	72
Villone, Ron	4.23	9	7	29	22	0	2	142⅔	114	70	67	73	97
Neagle, Denny	4.27	9	5	20	19	0	0	111⅔	95	54	53	40	76
White, Gabe	4.43	1	2	50	0	0	0	61	68	31	30	14	61
Tomko, Bret	4.92	5	7	33	26	1	0	172	175	103	94	60	132
Avery, Steve	5.16	6	7	19	19	0	0	96	75	62	55	78	51

Colorado Rockies

BATTING	BA	G	AB	R	H	TB	2B	3B	HR	RBI	SB	BB	SO
Walker, Larry	.379	127	438	108	166	311	26	4	37	115	11	57	52
Shumpert, Terry	.347	92	262	58	91	153	26	3	10	37	14	31	41
Helton, Todd	.320	159	578	114	185	339	39	5	35	113	7	68	77
Bichette, Dante	.298	151	593	104	177	321	38	2	34	133	6	54	84
Echevarria, Angel	.293	102	191	28	56	96	7	0	11	35	1	17	34
Perez, Neifi	.280	157	690	108	193	278	27	11	12	70	13	28	54
Castilla, Vinny	.275	158	615	83	169	294	24	1	33	102	2	53	75
Abbott, Kurt	.273	96	286	41	78	123	17	2	8	41	3	16	69
Barry, Jeff	.268	74	168	19	45	76	16	0	5	26	0	19	29
Blanco, Henry	.232	88	263	30	61	97	12	3	6	28	1	34	38
McRae, Brian	.224	103	321	36	72	115	14	1	9	37	2	41	64

PITCHING	ERA	W	L	G	GS	CG	SV	INN	H	R	ER	BB	SO
DiPoto, Jerry	4.26	4	5	63	0	0	1	86⅔	91	44	41	44	69
Wright, Jamey	4.87	4	3	16	16	0	0	94⅓	110	52	51	54	49
Astacio, Pedro	5.04	17	11	34	34	7	0	232	258	140	130	75	210
Leskanic, Curt	5.08	6	2	63	0	0	0	85	87	54	48	49	77
Veres, Dave	5.14	4	8	73	0	0	31	77	88	46	44	37	71
Bohanon, Brian	6.20	12	12	33	33	3	0	197⅓	236	146	136	92	120
Jones, Bobby	6.33	6	10	30	20	0	0	112⅓	132	91	79	77	74
Kile, Darryl	6.61	8	13	32	32	1	0	190⅔	225	150	140	109	116
Thomson, John	8.04	1	10	14	13	1	0	62⅔	85	62	56	36	34
DeJean, Mike	8.41	2	4	56	0	0	0	61	83	61	57	32	31

Florida Marlins

BATTING	BA	G	AB	R	H	TB	2B	3B	HR	RBI	SB	BB	SO
Floyd, Cliff	.303	69	251	37	76	130	19	1	11	49	5	30	47
Castillo, Luis	.302	128	487	76	147	178	23	4	0	28	50	67	85
Redmond, Mike	.302	84	242	22	73	85	9	0	1	27	0	26	34
Aven, Bruce	.289	137	381	57	110	169	19	2	12	70	3	44	82
Bautista, Danny	.288	70	205	32	59	86	10	1	5	24	3	4	30
Berg, Dave	.286	109	304	42	87	116	18	1	3	25	2	27	59
Millar, Kevin	.285	105	351	48	100	152	17	4	9	67	1	40	64
Wilson, Preston	.280	149	482	67	135	242	21	4	26	71	11	46	156
Gonzalez, Alex	.277	136	560	81	155	241	28	8	14	59	3	15	113
Kotsay, Mark	.271	148	495	57	134	199	23	9	8	50	7	29	50
Orie, Kevin	.254	77	240	26	61	95	16	0	6	29	1	22	43
Lowell, Mike	.253	97	308	32	78	129	15	0	12	47	0	26	69
Dunwoody, Todd	.220	64	186	20	41	59	6	3	2	20	3	12	41
Lee, Derrek	.206	70	218	21	45	71	9	1	5	20	2	17	70

PITCHING	ERA	W	L	G	GS	CG	SV	INN	H	R	ER	BB	SO
Alfonseca, Antonio	3.24	4	5	73	0	0	21	77⅔	79	28	28	29	46
Fernandez, Alex	3.38	7	8	24	24	1	0	141	135	60	53	41	91
Looper, Braden	3.80	3	3	72	0	0	0	83	96	43	35	31	50
Nunez, Vladimir	4.06	7	10	44	12	0	1	108⅓	95	63	49	54	86
Dempster, Ryan	4.71	7	8	25	25	0	0	147	146	77	77	93	126
Springer, Dennis	4.86	6	16	38	29	3	1	196⅓	231	121	106	64	83
Meadows, Brian	5.60	11	15	31	31	0	0	178¾	214	117	111	57	72
Edmondson, Brian	5.84	5	8	68	0	0	1	94	106	65	61	44	58
Sanchez, Jesus	6.01	5	7	59	10	0	0	76⅓	84	53	51	60	62

Houston Astros

BATTING	BA	G	AB	R	H	TB	2B	3B	HR	RBI	SB	BB	SO
Everett, Carl	.325	123	464	86	151	265	33	3	25	108	27	50	94
Bagwell, Jeff	.304	162	562	143	171	332	35	0	42	126	30	149	127
Biggio, Craig	.294	160	639	123	188	292	56	0	16	73	28	88	107
Spiers, Bill	.288	127	393	56	113	153	18	5	4	39	10	47	45
Caminiti, Ken	.286	78	273	45	78	130	11	1	13	56	6	46	58
Javier, Stan	.285	132	397	61	113	145	19	2	3	34	16	38	63
Eusebio, Tony	.272	103	323	31	88	115	15	0	4	33	0	40	67
Gutierrez, Ricky	.261	85	268	33	70	90	7	5	1	25	2	37	45
Bako, Paul	.256	73	215	16	55	77	14	1	2	17	1	26	57
Bogar, Tim	.239	106	309	44	74	106	16	2	4	31	3	38	52
Bell, Derek	.236	128	509	61	120	178	22	0	12	66	18	50	129
Hidalgo, Richard	.227	108	383	49	87	161	25	2	15	56	8	56	73

PITCHING	ERA	W	L	G	GS	CG	SV	INN	H	R	ER	BB	SO
Wagner, Billy	1.57	4	1	66	0	0	39	74⅔	35	14	13	23	124
Hampton, Mike	2.90	22	4	34	34	3	0	239	206	86	77	101	177
Elarton, Scott	3.48	9	5	42	15	0	1	124	111	55	48	43	121
Lima, Jose	3.58	21	10	35	35	3	0	246⅓	256	108	98	44	187
Reynolds, Shane	3.85	16	14	35	35	4	0	231¾	250	108	99	37	197
Powell, Jay	4.32	5	4	67	0	0	4	75	82	38	36	40	77
Williams, Brian	4.41	2	1	50	0	0	0	67⅓	69	35	33	35	53
Holt, Chris	4.66	5	13	32	26	0	1	164	193	92	85	57	115
Miller, Trevor	5.07	3	2	47	0	0	1	49⅔	58	29	28	29	37

Los Angeles Dodgers

BATTING	BA	G	AB	R	H	TB	2B	3B	HR	RBI	SB	BB	SO
Grudzielanek, Mark	.326	123	488	72	159	213	23	5	7	46	6	31	65
Karros, Eric	.304	153	578	74	176	318	40	0	34	112	8	53	119
Sheffield, Gary	.301	152	549	103	165	287	20	0	34	101	11	101	64
Hollandsworth, Todd	.284	92	261	39	74	117	12	2	9	32	5	24	61
Young, Eric	.281	119	456	73	128	162	24	2	2	41	51	63	26
Beltre, Carlos	.275	152	538	84	148	230	27	5	15	67	18	61	105
White, Devon	.268	134	474	60	127	193	20	2	14	68	19	39	88
Mondesi, Raul	.253	159	601	98	152	290	29	5	33	99	36	71	134
Vizcaino, Jose	.252	94	266	27	67	79	9	0	1	29	2	20	23
Counsell, Craig	.218	87	174	24	38	45	7	0	0	11	1	14	24
Hundley, Todd	.207	114	376	49	78	164	14	0	24	55	3	44	113

Los Angeles Dodgers *(Cont.)*

PITCHING	ERA	W	L	G	GS	CG	SV	INN	H	R	ER	BB	SO
Shaw, Jeff	2.78	2	4	64	0	0	34	68	64	25	21	15	43
Brown, Kevin	3.00	18	9	35	35	5	0	252⅓	210	99	84	59	221
Mills, Alan	3.73	3	4	68	0	0	0	72⅓	70	33	30	43	49
Maddux, Mike	3.77	1	1	53	0	0	0	59⅔	63	26	25	22	45
Valdez, Ismael	3.98	9	14	32	32	2	0	203⅓	213	97	90	58	143
Borbon, Pedro	4.09	4	3	70	0	0	1	50⅔	39	23	23	29	33
Masaoka, Onan	4.32	2	4	54	0	0	1	66⅔	55	33	32	47	61
Dreifort, Darren	4.79	13	13	30	29	1	0	178⅔	177	105	95	76	140
Park, Chan Ho	5.23	13	11	33	33	0	0	194⅓	208	120	113	100	174
Arnold, Jamie	5.48	2	4	36	3	0	1	69	81	50	42	34	26
Perez, Carlos	7.43	2	10	17	16	0	0	89⅔	116	77	74	39	40

Milwaukee Brewers

BATTING	BA	G	AB	R	H	TB	2B	3B	HR	RBI	SB	BB	SO
Cirillo, Jeff	.326	157	607	98	198	280	35	1	15	88	7	75	83
Jenkins, Geoff	.313	135	447	70	140	252	43	3	21	82	5	35	87
Nilsson, Dave	.309	115	343	56	106	190	19	1	21	62	1	53	64
Ochoa, Alex	.300	119	277	47	83	129	16	3	8	40	6	45	43
Belliard, Ronnie	.295	124	457	60	135	196	29	4	8	58	4	64	59
Loretta, Mark	.290	153	587	93	170	229	34	5	5	67	4	52	59
Burnitz, Jeromy	.270	130	467	87	126	262	33	2	33	103	7	91	124
Grissom, Marquis	.267	154	603	92	161	250	27	1	20	83	24	49	109
Vina, Fernando	.266	37	154	17	41	51	7	0	1	16	5	14	6
Banks, Brian	.242	105	219	34	53	77	7	1	5	22	6	25	59
Berry, Sean	.228	106	259	26	59	78	11	1	2	23	0	17	50
Valentin, Jose	.227	89	256	45	58	107	9	5	10	38	3	48	52

PITCHING	ERA	W	L	G	GS	CG	SV	INN	H	R	ER	BB	SO
Wickman, Bob	3.39	3	8	71	0	0	37	74⅓	75	31	28	38	60
Woodard, Steve	4.52	11	8	31	29	2	0	185	219	101	93	36	119
Nomo, Hideo	4.54	12	8	28	28	0	0	176⅓	173	96	89	78	161
Peterson, Kyle	4.56	4	7	17	12	0	0	77	87	46	39	25	34
Weathers, Dave	4.65	7	4	63	0	0	2	93	102	49	48	38	54
Karl, Scott	4.78	11	11	33	33	0	0	197⅔	246	121	105	69	74
Plunk, Eric	5.02	4	4	68	0	0	0	75⅓	71	44	42	43	63
Roque, Rafael	5.34	1	6	43	9	0	0	84⅓	96	52	50	42	66
Pulsipher, Bill	5.98	5	6	19	16	0	0	87⅓	100	65	58	36	42
Bere, Jason	6.08	5	0	17	14	0	0	66⅔	79	52	45	50	47
Abbott, Jim	6.91	2	8	20	15	0	0	82	110	71	63	42	37
Eldred, Cal	7.79	2	8	20	15	0	0	82	101	75	71	46	60

Montreal Expos

BATTING	BA	G	AB	R	H	TB	2B	3B	HR	RBI	SB	BB	SO
Guerrero, Vladimir	.316	160	610	102	193	366	37	5	42	131	14	55	62
White, Rondell	.312	138	539	83	168	272	26	6	22	64	10	32	85
Vidro, Jose	.304	140	494	67	150	235	45	2	12	59	0	29	51
Barrett, Michael	.293	126	433	53	127	189	32	3	8	52	0	32	39
Guerrero, Wilton	.292	132	315	42	92	127	15	7	2	31	7	13	38
Fullmer, Brad	.277	100	347	38	96	161	34	2	9	47	2	22	35
Merced, Orlando	.268	93	194	25	52	90	12	1	8	26	2	26	27
Widger, Chris	.264	124	383	42	101	169	24	1	14	56	1	28	86
Cabrera, Orlando	.254	104	382	48	97	154	23	5	8	39	2	18	38
Martinez, Manny	.245	137	331	48	81	113	12	7	2	26	19	17	51
Mordecai, Mike	.235	109	226	29	53	82	10	2	5	25	2	20	31

PITCHING	ERA	W	L	G	GS	CG	SV	INN	H	R	ER	BB	SO
Mota, Guillermo	2.93	2	4	51	0	0	0	55⅓	54	24	18	25	27
Urbina, Ugueth	3.69	6	6	71	0	0	41	75⅔	59	35	31	36	100
Kline, Steve	3.75	7	4	82	0	0	0	69⅔	56	32	29	33	69
Telford, Anthony	3.94	5	4	79	0	0	2	96	112	52	42	38	69
Thurman, Mike	4.05	7	11	29	27	0	0	146⅔	140	84	66	52	85
Hermanson, Dustin	4.20	9	14	34	34	0	0	216⅓	225	110	101	69	145
Powell, Jeremy	4.73	4	8	17	17	0	0	97	113	60	51	44	44
Batista, Miguel	4.88	8	7	39	17	2	1	134⅓	146	88	73	58	95
Vazquez, Javier	5.00	9	8	26	26	3	0	154⅔	154	98	86	52	113
Pavano, Carl	5.63	6	8	19	18	1	0	104	117	66	65	35	70

New York Mets

BATTING	BA	G	AB	R	H	TB	2B	3B	HR	RBI	SB	BB	SO
Dunston, Shawon	.321	104	243	35	78	110	11	3	5	41	10	2	39
Henderson, Rickey	.315	121	438	89	138	204	30	0	12	42	37	82	82
Hamilton, Daryl	.315	146	505	82	159	213	19	4	9	45	6	57	39
Cedeno, Roger	.313	155	453	90	142	185	23	4	4	36	66	60	100
Alfonzo, Edgardo	.304	158	628	123	191	315	41	1	27	108	9	85	85
Piazza, Mike	.303	141	534	100	162	307	25	0	40	124	2	51	70
Ventura, Robin	.301	161	588	88	177	311	38	0	32	120	1	74	109
Olerud, John	.298	162	581	107	173	269	39	0	19	96	3	125	66
Pratt, Todd	.293	71	140	18	41	54	4	0	3	21	2	15	32
Agbayani, Benny	.286	101	276	42	79	145	18	3	14	42	6	32	60
Ordonez, Rey	.258	154	520	49	134	165	24	2	1	60	8	49	59
Franco, Matt	.235	122	132	18	31	48	5	0	4	21	0	28	21
Bonilla, Bobby	.160	60	119	12	19	36	5	0	4	18	0	19	16

PITCHING	ERA	W	L	G	GS	CG	SV	INN	H	R	ER	BB	SO
Benitez, Armando	1.85	4	3	77	0	0	22	78	40	17	16	41	128
Franco, John	2.88	0	2	46	0	0	19	40⅔	40	14	13	19	41
Wendell, Turk	3.05	5	4	80	0	0	3	85⅔	80	31	29	37	77
Mahomes, Pat	3.68	8	0	39	0	0	0	63⅔	44	26	26	37	51
Cook, Dennis	3.86	10	5	71	0	0	3	63	50	27	27	27	68
Rogers, Kenny	4.03	5	1	12	12	2	0	76	71	35	34	28	58
Leiter, Al	4.23	13	12	32	32	1	0	213	209	107	100	93	162
Yoshii, Masato	4.40	12	8	31	29	1	0	174	168	86	85	58	105
Hershiser, Orel	4.58	13	12	32	32	0	0	179	175	92	91	77	89
Reed, Rick	4.58	11	5	26	26	1	0	149⅓	163	77	76	47	104
Dotel, Octavio	5.38	8	3	19	14	0	0	85⅓	69	52	51	49	85

Philadelphia Phillies

BATTING	BA	G	AB	R	H	TB	2B	3B	HR	RBI	SB	BB	SO
Abreu, Bobby	.335	152	546	118	183	300	35	11	20	93	27	109	113
Glanville, Doug	.325	150	628	101	204	287	38	6	11	73	34	48	82
Arias, Alex	.303	118	347	43	105	139	20	1	4	48	2	36	31
Lieberthal, Mike	.300	145	510	84	153	281	33	1	31	96	0	44	86
Jordan, Kevin	.285	120	347	36	99	134	17	3	4	51	0	24	34
Brogna, Rico	.278	157	619	90	172	281	29	4	24	102	8	54	132
Sefcik, Kevin	.278	111	209	28	58	82	15	3	1	11	9	29	24
Rolen, Scott	.268	112	421	74	113	221	28	1	26	77	12	67	114
Ducey, Rob	.261	104	188	29	49	87	10	2	8	33	2	38	57
Gant, Ron	.260	138	516	107	134	222	27	5	17	77	13	85	112
Anderson, Marlon	.252	129	452	48	114	163	26	4	5	54	13	24	61
Relaford, Desi	.242	65	211	31	51	69	11	2	1	26	4	19	34

PITCHING	ERA	W	L	G	GS	CG	SV	INN	H	R	ER	BB	SO
Montgomery, Steve	3.34	1	5	53	0	0	3	64⅔	54	25	24	31	55
Schilling, Curt	3.54	15	6	24	24	8	0	180½	159	74	71	44	152
Gomes, Wayne	4.26	5	5	73	0	0	19	74	70	38	35	56	58
Person, Robert	4.27	10	5	31	22	0	0	137	130	72	65	70	127
Schrenk, Steve	4.29	1	3	32	2	0	1	50⅓	41	24	24	14	36
Byrd, Paul	4.60	15	11	32	32	1	0	199⅔	205	119	102	70	106
Loewer, Carlton	5.12	2	6	20	13	2	0	89⅔	100	54	51	26	48
Wolf, Randy	5.55	6	9	22	21	0	0	121¾	126	78	75	67	116
Ogea, Chad	5.63	6	12	36	28	0	0	168	192	110	105	61	77
Telemaco, Amaury	5.77	4	0	49	0	0	0	53	52	34	34	26	43
Grace, Mike	7.69	1	4	27	5	0	0	55	80	48	47	30	28

National League Team-by-Team Statistical Leaders *(Cont.)*

Pittsburgh Pirates

BATTING	BA	G	AB	R	H	TB	2B	3B	HR	RBI	SB	BB	SO
Kendall, Jason	.332	78	280	61	93	143	20	3	8	41	22	38	32
Giles, Brian	.315	141	521	109	164	320	33	3	39	115	6	95	80
Young, Kevin	.298	156	584	103	174	305	41	6	26	106	22	75	124
Morris, Warren	.288	147	511	65	147	218	20	3	15	73	3	59	88
Martin, Al	.277	143	541	97	150	274	36	8	24	63	20	49	119
Brown, Adrian	.270	116	226	34	61	82	5	2	4	17	5	33	39
Sprague, Ed	.267	137	490	71	131	228	27	2	22	81	3	50	93
Benjamin, Mike	.247	110	368	42	91	134	26	7	1	37	10	20	90
Brown, Brant	.232	130	341	49	79	153	20	3	16	58	3	22	114
Nunez, Abraham	.220	90	259	25	57	65	8	0	0	17	9	28	54
Oliver, Joe	.201	45	134	10	27	38	8	0	1	13	2	10	33
Osik, Keith	.186	66	167	12	31	42	3	1	2	13	0	11	30

PITCHING	ERA	W	L	G	GS	CG	SV	INN	H	R	ER	BB	SO
Sauerbeck, Scott	2.00	4	1	65	0	0	2	67⅔	53	19	15	38	55
Clontz, Brad	2.74	1	3	56	0	0	2	49⅓	49	21	15	24	40
Ritchie, Todd	3.49	15	9	28	26	2	0	172⅔	169	79	67	54	107
Benson, Kris	4.07	11	14	31	31	2	0	196⅔	184	105	89	83	139
Schmidt, Jason	4.19	13	11	33	33	2	0	212⅔	219	110	99	85	148
Wilkins, Marc	4.24	2	3	46	0	0	0	51	49	28	24	26	44
Cordova, Francisco	4.43	8	10	27	27	2	0	160⅔	166	83	79	59	98
Williams, Mike	5.09	3	4	58	0	0	23	58⅓	63	36	33	37	76
Schourek, Pete	5.34	4	7	30	17	0	0	113	128	75	67	49	94
Silva, Jose	5.73	2	8	34	12	0	4	97⅓	108	70	62	39	77
Peters, Chris	6.59	5	4	19	11	0	0	71	98	59	52	27	46

St. Louis Cardinals

BATTING	BA	G	AB	R	H	TB	2B	3B	HR	RBI	SB	BB	SO
Lankford, Ray	.306	122	422	77	129	208	32	1	15	63	14	49	110
Tatis, Fernando	.298	149	537	104	160	297	31	2	34	107	21	82	128
Howard, Thomas	.292	98	195	16	57	85	10	0	6	28	1	17	26
Paquette, Craig	.287	48	157	21	45	81	6	0	10	37	1	6	38
McGwire, Mark	.278	153	521	118	145	363	21	1	65	147	0	133	141
Polanco, Placido	.277	88	220	24	61	79	9	3	1	19	1	15	24
Renteria, Edgar	.275	154	585	92	161	234	36	2	11	63	37	53	82
McEwing, Joe	.275	152	513	65	141	204	28	4	9	44	7	41	87
Castillo, Alberto	.263	93	255	21	67	87	8	0	4	31	0	24	48
Bragg, Darren	.260	93	273	38	71	103	12	1	6	26	3	44	67
Davis, Eric	.257	58	191	27	49	77	9	2	5	30	5	30	49
McGee, Willie	.251	132	271	25	68	75	7	0	0	20	7	17	60
Drew, J.D.	.242	104	368	72	89	156	16	6	13	39	19	50	77
Marrero, Eli	.192	114	317	32	61	94	13	1	6	34	11	18	56

PITCHING	ERA	W	L	G	GS	CG	SV	INN	H	R	ER	BB	SO
Slocumb, Heathcliff	2.36	3	2	40	0	0	2	53⅓	49	16	14	30	48
Bottenfield, Kent	3.97	18	7	31	31	0	0	190⅓	197	91	84	89	124
Croushore, Rick	4.14	3	7	59	0	0	3	71⅔	68	42	33	43	88
Stephenson, Garrett	4.22	6	3	18	12	0	0	85⅓	90	43	40	29	59
Oliver, Darren	4.26	9	9	30	30	2	0	196⅓	197	96	93	74	119
Mohler, Mike	4.38	1	1	48	0	0	1	49⅓	47	26	24	23	31
Painter, Lance	4.83	4	5	56	4	0	1	63⅓	63	37	34	25	56
Bottalico, Ricky	4.91	3	7	68	0	0	20	73⅓	83	45	40	49	66
Mercker, Kent	5.12	6	5	25	18	0	0	103⅔	125	73	59	51	64
Luebbers, Larry	5.12	3	3	8	8	1	0	45⅔	46	27	26	16	16
Aybar, Manny	5.47	4	5	65	1	0	3	97	104	67	59	36	74
Jiminez, Jose	5.85	6	8	29	28	2	0	163	173	114	106	71	113
Acevedo, Juan	5.89	6	8	50	12	0	4	102⅓	115	71	67	48	52

National League Team-by-Team Statistical Leaders (*Cont.*)

San Diego Padres

BATTING	BA	G	AB	R	H	TB	2B	3B	HR	RBI	SB	BB	SO
Gwynn, Tony	.338	111	411	59	139	196	27	0	10	62	7	29	14
Sanders, Reggie	.285	133	478	92	136	252	24	7	26	72	36	65	108
Veras, Quilvio	.280	132	475	95	133	180	25	2	6	41	30	65	88
Magadan, Dave	.274	116	248	20	68	88	12	1	2	30	1	45	36
Vander Wal, John	.272	132	246	26	67	103	18	0	6	41	2	37	59
Nevin, Phil	.269	128	383	52	103	202	27	0	24	85	1	51	82
Owens, Eric	.266	149	440	55	117	172	22	3	9	61	33	38	50
Gomez, Chris	.252	76	234	20	59	72	8	1	1	15	1	27	49
Joyner, Wally	.248	110	323	34	80	113	14	2	5	43	0	58	54
Davis, Ben	.244	76	266	29	65	96	14	1	5	30	2	25	70
Arias, George	.244	55	164	20	40	69	8	0	7	20	0	6	54
Leyritz, Jim	.239	50	134	17	32	61	5	0	8	21	0	15	37
Jackson, Damian	.224	133	388	56	87	138	20	2	9	39	34	53	105
Rivera, Rueben	.195	147	411	65	80	167	16	1	23	48	18	55	143

PITCHING	ERA	W	L	G	GS	CG	SV	INN	H	R	ER	BB	SO
Hoffman, Trevor	2.14	2	3	64	0	0	40	67⅓	48	23	16	15	73
Wall, Donne	3.07	7	4	55	0	0	0	70⅓	58	31	24	23	53
Boehringer, Brian	3.24	6	5	33	11	0	0	94⅓	97	38	34	23	53
Reyes, Carlos	3.72	2	4	65	0	0	1	77⅓	76	38	32	24	57
Ashby, Andy	3.80	14	10	31	31	4	0	206	204	95	87	54	132
Hitchcock, Sterling	4.11	12	14	33	33	0	0	208⅓	213	106	102	73	137
Miceli, Dan	4.46	4	5	66	0	0	2	68⅔	67	39	34	36	59
Clement, Matt	4.48	10	12	31	31	0	0	180⅔	190	106	90	86	135
Murray, Heath	5.76	0	4	22	8	0	0	50	60	33	32	26	25
Carlyle, Buddy	5.97	1	3	7	7	0	0	37⅔	36	28	25	17	29

San Francisco Giants

BATTING	BA	G	AB	R	H	TB	2B	3B	HR	RBI	SB	BB	SO
Rios, Armando	.327	72	150	32	49	79	9	0	7	29	7	24	35
Mayne, Brent	.301	117	322	39	97	135	32	0	2	39	2	43	65
Benard, Marvin	.290	149	562	100	163	257	36	5	16	64	27	55	97
Mueller, Bill	.290	116	414	61	120	150	24	0	2	36	4	65	52
Kent, Jeff	.290	138	511	86	148	261	40	2	23	101	13	61	112
Burks, Ellis	.282	120	390	73	110	222	19	0	31	96	7	69	86
Aurilia, Rich	.281	152	558	68	157	248	23	1	22	80	2	43	71
Snow, J.T.	.274	161	570	93	156	257	25	2	24	98	0	86	121
Servais, Scott	.273	69	198	21	54	79	10	0	5	21	0	13	31
Martinez, Ramon	.264	61	144	21	38	59	6	0	5	19	1	14	17
Bonds, Barry	.262	102	355	91	93	219	20	2	34	83	15	73	62
Santangelo, F.P.	.260	113	254	49	66	98	17	3	3	26	12	53	54
Hayes, Charlie	.205	95	264	33	54	83	9	1	6	48	3	33	41

PITCHING	ERA	W	L	G	GS	CG	SV	INN	H	R	ER	BB	SO
Johnstone, John	2.60	4	6	62	0	0	3	65⅔	48	24	19	20	56
Embree, Alan	3.38	3	2	68	0	0	0	58⅔	42	22	22	26	53
Rodriguez, Felix	3.80	2	3	47	0	0	0	66⅓	67	32	28	29	55
Ortiz, Russ	3.81	18	9	33	33	3	0	207⅔	189	109	88	125	164
Nen, Robb	3.98	3	8	72	0	0	37	72⅓	79	36	32	27	77
Nathan, Joe	4.18	7	4	19	14	0	0	90⅓	84	45	42	46	54
Spradlin, Jerry	4.19	3	1	59	0	0	0	58	59	31	27	29	52
Hernandez, Livan	4.64	8	12	30	30	2	0	199⅔	227	110	103	76	144
Estes, Shawn	4.92	11	11	32	32	1	0	203	209	121	111	112	159
Rodriguez, Rich	5.24	3	0	62	0	0	0	56⅔	60	33	33	28	44
Rueter, Kirk	5.41	15	10	33	33	1	0	184⅔	219	118	11	55	94
Brock, Chris	5.48	6	8	19	19	0	0	106⅔	124	69	65	41	76
Tavarez, Julian	5.93	2	0	47	0	0	0	54⅔	65	38	36	25	33
Gardner, Mark	6.47	5	11	29	21	1	0	139	142	103	100	57	86

Anaheim Angels

BATTING	BA	G	AB	R	H	TB	2B	3B	HR	RBI	SB	BB	SO
Anderson, Garret	.303	157	629	88	188	291	36	2	21	80	3	34	81
Vaughn, Mo	.281	139	524	63	147	266	20	0	33	108	0	54	127
Palmeiro, Orlando	.278	109	317	46	88	105	12	1	1	23	5	39	30
Salmon, Tim	.266	98	353	60	94	173	24	2	17	69	4	63	82
Huson, Jeff	.262	97	225	21	59	68	7	1	0	18	10	16	27
Molina, Ben	.257	31	101	8	26	34	5	0	1	10	0	6	6
Erstad, Darin	.253	142	585	84	148	219	22	5	13	53	13	47	101
Edmonds, Jim	.250	55	204	34	51	87	17	2	5	23	5	28	45
Greene, Todd	.243	97	321	36	78	140	20	0	14	42	1	12	63
Walbeck, Matt	.240	107	288	26	69	88	8	1	3	22	2	26	46
Glaus, Troy	.240	154	551	85	132	248	29	1	29	79	5	71	143
DiSarcina, Gary	.229	81	271	32	62	74	7	1	1	29	5	15	32
Sheets, Andy	.197	87	244	22	48	67	10	0	3	29	1	14	59
Durrington, Trent	.180	43	122	14	22	24	2	0	0	2	4	9	28

PITCHING	ERA	W	L	G	GS	CG	SV	INN	H	R	ER	BB	SO
Magnante, Mike	3.38	5	2	53	0	0	0	69⅓	68	30	26	29	44
Levine, Al	3.39	1	1	50	1	0	0	85	76	40	32	29	37
Petkovsek, Mark	3.47	10	4	64	0	0	1	83	85	37	32	21	43
Percival, Troy	3.79	4	6	60	0	0	31	57	38	24	24	22	58
Finley, Chuck	4.43	12	11	33	33	1	0	213⅓	197	117	105	94	200
Hill, Ken	4.77	4	11	26	22	0	0	128⅓	129	72	68	76	76
Hasegawa, Shigetoshi	4.91	4	6	64	1	0	2	77	80	45	42	34	44
Fyhrie, Mike	5.05	0	4	16	7	0	0	51⅔	61	32	29	21	26
Washburn, Jarrod	5.25	4	5	16	10	0	0	61⅔	61	36	36	26	39
Sparks, Steve	5.42	5	11	28	26	0	0	147⅔	165	101	89	82	73
Schoeneweis, Scott	5.49	1	1	31	0	0	0	39⅓	47	27	24	14	22
Ortiz, Ramon	6.52	2	3	9	9	0	0	48⅓	50	35	35	25	44
Belcher, Tim	6.73	6	8	24	24	0	0	132½	168	104	99	46	52

Baltimore Orioles

BATTING	BA	G	AB	R	H	TB	2B	3B	HR	RBI	SB	BB	SO
Ripken, Cal Jr.	.340	86	332	51	113	194	27	0	18	57	0	13	31
Surhoff, B.J.	.308	162	673	104	207	331	38	1	28	107	5	43	78
Clark, Will	.303	77	251	40	76	121	15	0	10	29	2	38	42
Belle, Albert	.297	161	610	108	181	330	36	1	37	117	17	101	82
Conine, Jeff	.291	139	444	54	129	201	31	1	13	75	0	30	40
Anderson, Brady	.282	150	564	109	159	269	28	5	24	81	36	96	105
Amaral, Rich	.277	91	137	21	38	48	8	1	0	11	9	15	20
Bordick, Mike	.277	160	631	93	175	254	35	7	10	77	14	54	102
Hairston, Jerry	.269	50	175	26	47	73	12	1	4	17	9	11	24
DeShields, Delino	.264	96	330	46	87	120	11	2	6	34	11	37	52
Johnson, Charles	.251	135	426	58	107	176	19	1	16	54	0	55	107
Reboulet, Jeff	.162	99	154	25	25	29	4	0	0	4	1	33	29

PITCHING	ERA	W	L	G	GS	CG	SV	INN	H	R	ER	BB	SO
Mussina, Mike	3.50	18	7	31	31	4	0	203⅓	207	88	79	52	172
Timlin, Mike	3.57	3	9	62	0	0	27	63	51	30	25	23	50
Guzman, Juan	4.18	5	9	21	21	1	0	122⅔	124	63	57	65	95
Corsi, Jim	4.34	1	3	36	0	0	0	37⅓	40	19	18	20	22
Johns, Doug	4.47	6	4	32	5	0	0	86⅔	81	45	43	25	50
Ponson, Sidney	4.71	12	12	32	32	6	0	210	227	118	110	80	112
Erickson, Scott	4.81	15	12	34	34	6	0	230⅔	244	127	123	99	106
Kamieniecki, Scott	4.95	2	4	43	3	0	2	56⅓	52	32	31	29	39
Rhodes, Arthur	5.43	3	4	43	0	0	3	53	43	37	32	45	59
Johnson, Jason	5.46	8	7	22	21	0	0	115⅓	120	74	70	55	71
Linton, Doug	5.95	1	4	14	8	0	0	59	69	41	39	25	32
Bones, Ricky	5.98	0	3	30	2	0	0	43⅔	59	29	29	19	26

Boston Red Sox

BATTING	BA	G	AB	R	H	TB	2B	3B	HR	RBI	SB	BB	SO
Garciaparra, Nomar...	.357	135	532	103	190	321	42	4	27	104	14	51	39
Daubach, Brian..........	.294	110	381	61	112	214	33	3	21	73	0	36	92
Offerman, Jose..........	.294	149	586	107	172	255	37	11	8	69	18	96	79
Veras, Wilton..............	.288	36	118	14	34	47	5	1	2	13	0	5	14
Huskey, Butch.............	.282	119	386	62	109	190	15	0	22	77	3	34	65
Stanley, Mike..............	.281	136	427	59	120	199	22	0	19	72	0	70	94
O'Leary, Troy..............	.280	157	596	84	167	295	36	4	28	103	1	56	91
Jefferson, Reggie.......	.277	83	206	21	57	87	13	1	5	17	0	17	55
Nixon, Trot.................	.270	124	381	67	103	180	22	5	15	52	3	53	75
Varitek, Jason............	.269	144	483	70	130	233	39	2	20	76	1	46	85
Merloni, Lou	.254	43	126	18	32	42	7	0	1	13	0	8	16
Valentin, John............	.253	113	450	58	114	179	27	1	12	70	0	40	68
Buford, Damon............	.242	91	297	39	72	109	15	2	6	38	9	21	74
Lewis, Darren	.240	135	470	63	113	145	14	6	2	40	16	45	52

PITCHING	ERA	W	L	G	GS	CG	SV	INN	H	R	ER	BB	SO
Garces, Rich	1.55	5	1	30	0	0	2	40⅔	25	9	7	18	33
Martinez, Pedro...........	2.07	23	4	31	29	5	0	213⅓	160	56	49	37	313
Lowe, Derek	2.63	6	3	74	0	0	15	109⅓	84	35	32	25	80
Saberhagen, Bret........	2.95	10	6	22	22	0	0	119	122	43	39	11	81
Cormier, Rheal	3.69	2	0	60	0	0	0	63⅓	61	34	26	18	39
Wasdin, John	4.12	8	3	45	0	0	2	74⅓	66	38	34	18	57
Rapp, Pat	4.12	6	7	37	26	0	0	146⅓	147	78	67	69	90
Florie, Bryce	4.65	4	1	41	5	0	0	81⅓	94	50	42	35	65
Rose, Brian.................	4.87	7	6	22	18	0	0	98	112	59	53	29	51
Wakefield, Tim............	5.08	6	11	49	17	0	15	140	146	93	79	72	104
Portugal, Mark............	5.51	7	12	31	27	1	0	150⅓	179	100	92	41	79
Gordon, Tom	5.60	0	2	21	0	0	11	17⅞	17	11	11	12	24
Guthrie, Mark	5.83	1	1	46	0	0	2	46⅓	50	32	30	20	36

Chicago White Sox

BATTING	BA	G	AB	R	H	TB	2B	3B	HR	RBI	SB	BB	SO
Thomas, Frank	.305	135	486	74	148	229	36	0	15	77	3	87	66
Ordonez, Magglio	.301	157	624	100	188	318	34	3	30	117	13	47	64
Singleton, Chris..........	.300	133	496	72	149	243	31	6	17	72	20	22	45
Fordryce, Brook	.297	105	333	36	99	153	25	1	9	49	2	21	48
Durham, Ray	.296	153	612	109	181	266	30	8	13	60	34	73	105
Konerko, Paul.............	.294	142	513	71	151	262	31	4	24	81	1	45	68
Lee, Carlos.................	.293	127	492	66	144	228	32	2	16	84	4	13	72
Jackson, Darrin...........	.275	73	149	22	41	64	9	1	4	16	4	3	20
Norton, Greg	.255	132	436	62	111	185	26	0	16	50	4	69	93
Caruso, Mike	.250	136	529	60	132	157	11	4	2	35	12	20	36
Wilson, Craig..............	.238	98	252	28	60	82	8	1	4	26	1	23	22
Johnson, Mark.............	.227	73	207	27	47	70	11	0	4	16	3	36	58

PITCHING	ERA	W	L	G	GS	CG	SV	INN	H	R	ER	BB	SO
Foulke, Keith	2.22	3	3	67	0	0	9	105⅓	72	28	26	21	123
Howry, Bob	3.59	5	3	69	0	0	28	67⅔	58	34	27	38	80
Lowe, Sean	3.67	4	1	64	0	0	0	95⅓	90	39	39	46	62
Simas, Bill..................	3.75	6	3	70	0	0	2	72	73	36	30	32	41
Sirotka, Mike...............	4.00	11	13	32	32	3	0	209	236	108	93	57	125
Wells, Kip	4.04	4	1	7	7	0	0	35⅓	33	17	16	15	29
Baldwin, James...........	5.10	12	13	35	33	1	0	199⅓	219	119	113	81	123
Parque, Jim	5.13	9	15	31	30	1	0	173⅓	210	111	99	79	111
Castillo, Carlos	5.71	2	2	18	2	0	0	41	45	26	26	14	23
Navarro, Jaime............	6.09	8	13	32	27	0	0	159⅓	206	126	108	71	74
Snyder, John	6.68	9	12	25	25	1	0	129⅓	167	103	96	49	67
Ward, Bryan	7.55	0	1	40	0	0	0	39⅓	63	36	33	11	35

American League Team-by-Team Statistical Leaders *(Cont.)*

Cleveland Indians

BATTING	BA	G	AB	R	H	TB	2B	3B	HR	RBI	SB	BB	SO
Ramirez, Manny	.333	147	522	131	174	346	34	3	44	165	2	96	131
Vizquel, Omar	.333	144	574	112	191	250	36	4	5	66	42	65	50
Alomar, Roberto	.323	159	563	138	182	300	40	3	24	120	37	99	96
Baines, Harold	.312	135	430	62	134	229	18	1	25	103	1	54	48
Alomar, Sandy	.307	37	137	19	42	73	13	0	6	25	0	4	23
Lofton, Kenny	.301	120	465	110	140	201	28	6	7	39	25	79	84
Cordero, Wil	.299	54	194	35	58	97	15	0	8	32	2	15	37
Justice, David	.287	133	429	75	123	204	18	0	21	88	1	94	90
Diaz, Einar	.281	119	392	43	110	142	21	1	3	32	11	23	41
Thome, Jim	.277	146	494	101	137	267	27	2	33	108	0	127	171
Wilson, Enrique	.262	113	332	41	87	117	22	1	2	24	5	25	41
Sexson, Richie	.255	134	479	72	122	246	17	7	31	116	3	34	117
Fryman, Travis	.255	85	322	45	82	132	16	2	10	48	2	25	57
Roberts, David	.238	41	143	26	34	44	4	0	2	12	11	9	16

PITCHING	ERA	W	L	G	GS	CG	SV	INN	H	R	ER	BB	SO
Karsay, Steve	2.97	10	2	50	3	0	1	78⅔	71	29	26	30	68
Shuey, Paul	3.53	8	5	72	0	0	6	81⅔	68	37	32	40	103
Colon, Bartolo	3.95	18	5	32	32	1	0	205	185	97	90	76	161
Jackson, Mike	4.06	3	4	72	0	0	39	68⅔	60	32	31	26	55
Reed, Steve	4.23	3	2	63	0	0	0	61⅔	69	33	29	20	44
Burba, Dave	4.25	15	9	34	34	1	0	220	211	113	104	96	174
Nagy, Charles	4.95	17	11	33	32	1	0	202	238	120	111	59	126
Langston, Mark	5.25	1	2	25	5	0	0	61⅔	69	40	36	29	43
Wright, Jaret	6.06	8	10	26	26	0	0	133⅔	144	99	90	77	91
Gooden, Dwight	6.26	3	4	26	22	0	0	115	127	90	80	67	88
Candiottie, Tom	7.32	4	6	18	13	0	0	71⅓	86	64	58	30	41

Detroit Tigers

BATTING	BA	G	AB	R	H	TB	2B	3B	HR	RBI	SB	BB	SO
Polonia, Luis	.324	87	333	46	108	175	21	8	10	32	17	16	32
Cruz, Deivi	.284	155	518	64	147	221	35	0	13	58	1	12	57
Clark, Tony	.280	143	536	74	150	272	29	0	31	99	2	64	133
Catalanotto, Frank	.276	100	286	41	79	131	19	0	11	35	3	15	49
Ausmus, Brad	.275	127	458	62	126	190	25	6	9	54	12	51	71
Easley, Damion	.266	151	549	83	146	238	30	1	20	65	11	51	124
Palmer, Dean	.263	150	560	92	147	290	25	2	38	100	3	57	153
Encarnacion, Juan	.255	132	509	62	130	229	30	6	19	74	33	14	113
Kapler, Gabe	.245	130	416	60	102	186	22	4	18	49	11	42	74
Garcia, Karim	.240	96	288	38	69	127	10	3	14	32	2	20	67
Higginson, Bobby	.239	107	377	51	90	144	18	0	12	46	4	64	66
Jefferies, Greg	.200	70	205	22	41	67	8	0	6	18	3	13	11

PITCHING	ERA	W	L	G	GS	CG	SV	INN	H	R	ER	BB	SO
Brocail, Doug	2.52	4	4	70	0	0	2	82	60	23	23	25	78
Jones, Todd	3.80	4	4	65	0	0	30	66⅓	64	30	28	35	64
Nitkowski, C.J.	4.30	4	5	68	7	0	0	81⅔	63	44	39	45	66
Mlicki, Dave	4.60	14	12	31	31	2	0	191⅔	209	108	98	70	119
Moehler, Brian	5.04	10	16	32	32	2	0	196⅓	229	116	110	59	106
Thompson, Justin	5.11	9	11	24	24	0	0	142⅔	152	85	81	59	83
Weaver, Jeff	5.55	9	12	30	29	0	0	163⅔	176	104	101	56	114
Cruz, Nelson	5.67	2	5	29	6	0	0	66⅔	74	44	42	23	46
Anderson, Matt	5.68	2	1	37	0	0	0	38	33	27	24	35	32
Borkowski, Dave	6.10	2	6	17	12	0	0	76⅔	86	58	52	40	50
Kida, Masao	6.26	1	0	49	0	0	1	64⅔	73	48	45	30	50
Blair, Willie	6.85	3	11	39	16	0	0	134	169	107	102	44	82

Kansas City Royals

BATTING	BA	G	AB	R	H	TB	2B	3B	HR	RBI	SB	BB	SO
Sweeney, Mike	.322	150	575	101	185	299	44	2	22	102	6	54	48
Randa, Joe	.314	156	628	92	197	297	36	8	16	84	5	50	80
Damon, Johnny	.307	145	583	101	179	278	39	9	14	77	36	67	50
Dye, Jermaine	.294	158	608	96	179	320	44	8	27	119	2	58	119
Sanchez, Rey	.294	134	479	66	141	177	18	6	2	56	11	22	48
Beltran, Carlos	.293	156	663	112	194	301	27	7	22	108	27	46	123
Giambi, Jeremy	.285	90	288	34	82	106	13	1	3	34	0	40	67
Pose, Scott	.285	86	137	27	39	42	3	0	0	12	6	21	22
Holbert, Ray	.280	34	100	14	28	31	3	0	0	5	7	8	20
Febles, Carlos	.256	123	453	71	116	186	22	9	10	53	20	47	91
Sutton, Larry	.225	43	102	14	23	35	6	0	2	15	1	13	17
Kreuter, Chad	.225	107	324	31	73	103	15	0	5	35	0	34	65
Spehr, Tim	.206	60	155	26	32	66	7	0	9	26	1	22	47

PITCHING	ERA	W	L	G	GS	CG	SV	INN	H	R	ER	BB	SO
Santiago, Jose	3.42	3	4	34	0	0	2	47⅓	46	23	18	14	15
Rosado, Jose	3.85	10	14	33	33	5	0	208	197	103	89	72	141
Morman, Alvin	4.05	2	4	49	0	0	1	53⅓	66	27	24	23	31
Mathews, T.J.	4.38	2	1	24	1	0	1	39	44	21	19	17	19
Suppan, Jeff	4.53	10	12	32	32	4	0	208⅔	222	113	105	62	103
Stein, Blake	4.56	1	2	13	12	0	0	73	65	38	37	47	47
Rigby, Brad	5.06	4	6	49	0	0	0	83⅔	102	51	47	31	36
Witasick, Jay	5.57	9	12	32	28	1	0	158⅓	191	108	98	83	102
Service, Scott	6.09	5	5	68	0	0	8	75⅓	87	51	51	42	68
Whisenant, Matt	6.35	4	4	48	0	0	1	39⅔	40	28	28	26	27
Suzuki, Mac	6.79	2	5	38	13	0	0	110	124	92	83	64	68
Montgomery, Jeff	6.84	1	4	49	0	0	12	51⅓	72	40	39	21	27
Fussell, Chris	7.39	0	5	17	8	0	2	56	72	51	46	36	37

Minnesota Twins

BATTING	BA	G	AB	R	H	TB	2B	3B	HR	RBI	SB	BB	SO
Koskie, Corey	.310	117	342	42	106	160	21	0	11	58	4	40	72
Jones, Jacque	.289	95	322	54	93	148	24	2	9	44	3	17	63
Cordova, Marty	.285	124	425	62	121	197	28	3	14	70	13	48	96
Steinbach, Terry	.284	101	338	35	96	132	16	4	4	42	2	38	54
Walker, Todd	.279	143	531	62	148	211	37	4	6	46	18	52	83
Allen, Chad	.277	137	481	69	133	190	21	3	10	46	14	37	89
Hocking, Denny	.267	136	386	47	103	146	18	2	7	41	11	22	54
Coomer, Ron	.263	127	467	53	123	198	25	1	16	65	2	30	69
Lawton, Matt	.259	118	406	58	105	144	18	0	7	54	26	57	42
Hunter, Torii	.255	135	384	52	98	146	17	2	9	35	10	26	72
Gates, Brent	.255	110	306	40	78	104	13	2	3	38	1	34	56
Valentin, Javier	.248	78	218	22	54	83	12	1	5	28	0	22	39
Mientkiewicz, Doug	.229	118	327	34	75	108	21	3	2	32	1	43	51
Guzman, Cristian	.226	131	420	47	95	116	12	3	1	26	9	22	90

PITCHING	ERA	W	L	G	GS	CG	SV	INN	H	R	ER	BB	SO
Miller, Travis	2.72	2	2	52	0	0	0	49⅔	55	19	15	16	40
Radke, Brad	3.75	12	14	33	33	4	0	218⅔	239	97	91	44	121
Wells, Bob	3.81	8	3	76	0	0	1	87⅓	79	41	37	28	44
Trombley, Mike	4.33	2	8	75	0	0	24	87⅓	93	42	42	28	82
Mays, Joseph	4.37	6	11	49	20	2	0	171	179	92	83	67	115
Milton, Eric	4.49	7	11	34	34	5	0	206⅓	190	111	103	63	163
Guardado, Eddie	4.50	2	5	63	0	0	2	48	37	24	24	25	60
Carrasco, Hector	4.96	2	3	39	0	0	1	49	48	29	27	18	35
Perkins, Dan	6.54	1	7	29	12	0	0	86⅔	117	69	63	43	44
Hawkins, LaTroy	6.66	10	14	33	33	1	0	174⅓	238	136	129	60	103
Lincoln, Mike	6.84	3	10	18	15	0	0	76⅓	102	59	58	26	27
Sampson, Ben	8.11	3	2	30	4	0	0	71	107	65	64	34	56

New York Yankees

BATTING

	BA	G	AB	R	H	TB	2B	3B	HR	RBI	SB	BB	SO
Jeter, Derek	.349	158	627	134	219	346	37	9	24	102	19	91	116
Williams, Bernie	.342	158	591	116	202	317	28	6	25	115	9	100	95
Knoblauch, Chuck	.292	150	603	120	176	274	36	4	18	68	28	83	57
O'Neill, Paul	.285	153	597	70	170	274	39	4	19	110	11	66	89
Ledee, Ricky	.276	88	250	45	69	119	13	5	9	40	4	28	73
Davis, Chili	.269	146	476	59	128	212	25	1	19	78	4	73	100
Martinez, Tino	.263	159	589	95	155	270	27	2	28	105	3	69	86
Curtis, Chad	.262	96	195	37	51	72	6	0	5	24	8	43	35
Sojo, Luis	.252	49	127	20	32	44	6	0	2	16	1	4	17
Brosius, Scott	.247	133	473	64	117	196	26	1	17	71	9	39	74
Posada, Jorge	.245	112	379	50	93	152	19	2	12	57	1	53	91
Giradi, Joe	.239	65	209	23	50	74	16	1	2	27	3	10	26
Spencer, Shane	.234	71	205	25	48	80	8	0	8	20	0	18	51

PITCHING

	ERA	W	L	G	GS	CG	SV	INN	H	R	ER	BB	SO
Rivera, Mariano	1.83	4	3	66	0	0	45	69	43	15	14	18	52
Watson, Alan	2.89	4	1	24	0	0	0	37⅓	36	17	12	13	32
Cone, David	3.44	12	9	31	31	1	0	193⅔	164	84	74	90	177
Grimsley, Jason	3.60	7	2	55	0	0	1	75	66	39	30	40	49
Hernandez, Orlando	4.12	17	9	33	33	2	0	214⅓	187	108	98	87	157
Nelson, Jeff	4.15	2	1	39	0	0	1	30½	27	14	14	22	35
Mendoza, Ramiro	4.29	9	9	53	6	0	3	123⅔	141	68	59	27	80
Stanton, Mike	4.33	2	2	73	1	0	0	62⅓	71	30	30	18	59
Naulty, Dan	4.38	1	0	33	0	0	0	49¼	40	24	24	22	25
Clemens, Roger	4.60	14	10	30	30	1	0	187⅔	185	101	96	90	163
Pettitte, Andy	4.70	14	11	31	31	0	0	191⅓	216	105	100	89	121
Irabu, Hideki	4.84	11	7	32	27	2	0	169⅓	180	98	91	46	133

Oakland Athletics

BATTING

	BA	G	AB	R	H	TB	2B	3B	HR	RBI	SB	BB	SO
Velarde, Randy	.317	156	631	105	200	287	25	7	16	76	24	70	98
Giambi, Jason	.315	158	575	115	181	318	36	1	33	123	1	105	106
Hernandez, Ramon	.279	40	136	13	38	54	7	0	3	21	1	18	11
Jaha, John	.276	142	457	93	126	254	23	0	35	111	2	101	129
Saenz, Olmedo	.275	97	255	41	70	121	18	0	11	41	1	22	47
Grieve, Ben	.265	148	486	80	129	234	21	0	28	86	4	63	108
Stairs, Matt	.258	146	531	94	137	283	26	3	38	102	2	89	124
Tejada, Miguel	.251	159	593	93	149	253	33	4	21	84	8	57	94
Chavez, Eric	.247	115	356	47	88	152	21	2	13	50	1	46	56
Phillips, Tony	.244	106	406	76	99	176	24	4	15	49	11	71	94
Macfarlane, Mike	.243	81	226	24	55	84	17	0	4	31	0	13	52
Spiezio, Scott	.243	89	247	31	60	108	24	0	8	33	0	29	36
Hinch, A.J.	.215	76	205	26	44	71	4	1	7	24	6	11	41
Christenson, Ryan	.209	106	268	41	56	82	12	1	4	24	7	38	58
McDonald, Jason	.209	100	187	26	39	52	2	1	3	8	6	25	48

PITCHING

	ERA	W	L	G	GS	CG	SV	INN	H	R	ER	BB	SO
Hudson, Tim	3.23	11	2	21	21	1	0	136⅓	121	56	49	62	132
Jones, Doug	3.55	5	5	70	0	0	10	104	106	43	41	24	63
Mathews, T.J.	3.81	9	5	50	0	0	3	59	46	28	25	20	42
Taylor, Billy	3.98	1	5	43	0	0	26	43	48	23	19	14	38
Worrell, Tim	4.15	2	2	53	0	0	0	69⅓	69	38	32	34	62
Olivares, Omar	4.16	15	11	32	32	4	0	205⅔	217	105	95	81	85
Rogers, Kenny	4.30	5	3	19	19	3	0	119⅓	135	66	57	41	68
Heredia, Gil	4.81	13	8	33	33	1	0	200⅓	228	119	107	34	117
Groom, Buddy	5.09	3	2	76	0	0	0	46	48	29	26	18	32
Appier, Kevin	5.17	16	14	34	34	1	0	209	230	131	120	84	131
Oquist, Mike	5.37	9	10	28	24	0	0	140⅔	158	86	84	64	89
Haynes, Jimmy	6.34	7	12	30	25	0	0	142	158	112	100	80	93

Seattle Mariners

BATTING	BA	G	AB	R	H	TB	2B	3B	HR	RBI	SB	BB	SO
Martinez, Edgar	.337	142	502	86	169	278	35	1	24	86	7	97	99
Lampkin, Tom	.291	76	206	29	60	102	11	2	9	34	1	13	32
Griffey, Ken Jr.	.285	160	606	123	173	349	26	3	48	134	24	91	108
Rodriguez, Alex	.285	129	502	110	143	294	25	0	42	111	21	56	109
Bell, David	.268	157	597	92	160	258	31	2	21	78	7	58	90
Wilson, Dan	.266	123	414	46	110	158	23	2	7	38	5	29	83
Ibanez, Raul	.258	87	209	23	54	88	7	0	9	27	5	17	32
Davis, Russ	.245	124	432	55	106	188	17	1	21	59	3	32	111
Mabry, John	.244	87	262	34	64	105	14	0	9	33	2	20	60
Hunter, Brian L.	.232	139	539	79	125	162	13	6	4	34	44	37	91
Buhner, Jay	.222	87	266	37	59	112	11	0	14	38	0	69	100

PITCHING	ERA	W	L	G	GS	CG	SV	INN	H	R	ER	BB	SO
Abbott, Paul	3.10	6	2	25	7	0	0	72⅔	50	31	25	32	68
Moyer, Jamie	3.87	14	8	32	32	4	0	228	235	108	98	48	137
Paniagua, Jose	4.06	6	11	59	0	0	3	77⅔	75	37	35	52	74
Garcia, Freddie	4.07	17	8	33	33	2	0	201⅓	205	96	91	90	170
Halama, John	4.22	11	10	38	24	1	0	179	193	88	84	56	105
Davey, Tom	4.71	2	1	45	0	0	1	65	62	41	34	40	59
Meche, Gil	4.73	8	4	16	15	0	0	85⅓	73	48	45	57	47
Mesa, Jose	4.98	3	6	68	0	0	33	68⅔	84	42	38	40	42
Rodriguez, Frank	5.65	2	4	28	5	0	3	73⅓	94	47	46	30	47
Cloude, Ken	7.96	4	4	31	6	0	1	72⅓	106	67	64	46	35
Hinchliffe, Brett	8.80	0	4	11	4	0	0	30⅔	41	31	30	21	14

Tampa Bay Devil Rays

BATTING	BA	G	AB	R	H	TB	2B	3B	HR	RBI	SB	BB	SO
McGriff, Fred	.310	144	529	75	164	292	30	1	32	104	1	86	107
DiFelice, Mike	.307	51	179	21	55	84	11	0	6	27	0	8	23
Boggs, Wade	.301	90	292	40	88	110	14	1	2	29	1	38	23
Stocker, Kevin	.299	79	254	39	76	94	11	2	1	27	9	24	41
Cairo, Miguel	.295	120	465	61	137	171	15	5	3	36	22	24	46
Trammell, Bubba	.290	82	283	49	82	143	19	0	14	39	0	43	37
Martinez, Dave	.284	143	514	79	146	199	25	5	6	66	13	60	76
Canseco, Jose	.279	113	430	75	120	242	18	1	34	95	3	58	135
Flaherty, John	.278	117	446	53	124	185	19	0	14	71	0	19	64
Winn, Randy	.267	79	303	44	81	111	16	4	2	24	9	17	63
Ledesma, Aaron	.265	93	294	32	78	93	15	0	0	30	1	14	35
Lowery, Terrell	.259	66	185	25	48	71	15	1	2	17	0	19	53
Perry, Herbert	.254	66	209	29	53	83	10	1	6	32	0	16	42
Sorrento, Paul	.235	99	294	40	69	118	14	1	11	42	1	49	101
Smith, Bobby	.181	68	199	18	36	51	4	1	3	19	4	16	64

PITCHING	ERA	W	L	G	GS	CG	SV	INN	H	R	ER	BB	SO
Hernandez, Roberto	3.07	2	3	72	0	0	43	73⅓	68	27	25	33	69
Duvall, Mike	4.05	1	1	40	0	0	0	40	46	21	18	27	18
White, Rick	4.08	5	3	63	1	0	0	108	132	56	49	38	81
Alvarez, Wilson	4.22	9	9	28	28	1	0	160	159	92	75	79	128
Charlton, Norm	4.44	2	3	42	0	0	0	50⅔	49	29	25	36	45
Rupe, Ryan	4.55	8	9	24	24	0	0	142⅓	136	81	72	57	97
Lopez, Albie	4.64	3	2	51	0	0	1	64	66	40	33	24	37
Arrojo, Rolando	5.18	7	12	24	24	2	0	140⅔	162	84	81	60	107
Eiland, Dave	5.60	4	8	21	15	0	0	80⅓	98	59	50	27	53
Rekar, Bryan	5.80	6	6	27	12	0	0	94⅔	121	68	61	41	55
Witt, Bobby	5.84	7	15	32	32	3	0	180⅓	213	130	117	96	123
Yan, Esteban	5.90	3	4	50	1	0	0	61	77	41	40	32	46

American League Team-by-Team Statistical Leaders *(Cont.)*

Texas Rangers

BATTING	BA	G	AB	R	H	TB	2B	3B	HR	RBI	SB	BB	SO
Rodriguez, Ivan	.332	144	600	116	199	335	29	1	35	113	25	24	64
Gonzalez, Juan	.326	144	562	114	183	338	36	1	39	128	3	51	105
Palmeiro, Rafael	.324	158	565	96	183	356	30	1	47	148	2	97	69
Greer, Rusty	.300	147	556	107	167	274	41	3	20	101	2	96	67
Kelly, Roberto	.300	87	290	41	87	130	17	1	8	37	6	21	57
Zeile, Todd	.293	156	588	80	172	287	41	1	24	98	1	56	94
Clayton, Royce	.288	133	465	69	134	207	21	5	14	52	8	39	100
Stevens, Lee	.282	146	517	76	146	251	31	1	24	81	2	52	132
McLemore, Mark	.274	144	566	105	155	207	20	7	6	45	16	83	79
Goodwin, Tom	.259	109	405	63	105	138	12	6	3	33	39	40	61
Mateo, Ruben	.238	32	122	16	29	55	9	1	5	18	3	4	28
Alicea, Luis	.201	68	164	33	33	52	10	0	3	17	2	28	32

PITCHING	ERA	W	L	G	GS	CG	SV	INN	H	R	ER	BB	SO
Zimmerman, Jeff	2.36	9	3	65	0	0	3	87⅔	50	24	23	23	67
Venafro, Michael	3.29	3	2	65	0	0	0	68⅓	63	29	25	22	37
Crabtree, Tim	3.46	5	1	68	0	0	0	65	71	26	25	18	54
Wetteland, John	3.68	4	4	62	0	0	43	66	67	30	27	19	60
Munoz, Mike	3.93	2	1	56	0	0	1	52⅔	52	24	23	18	27
Loaiza, Esteban	4.56	9	5	30	15	0	0	120⅓	128	65	61	40	77
Sele, Aaron	4.79	18	9	33	33	2	0	205	244	115	109	70	186
Helling, Rick	4.84	13	11	35	35	3	0	219⅓	228	127	118	85	131
Burkett, John	5.62	9	8	30	25	0	0	147⅓	184	95	92	46	96
Patterson, Danny	5.67	2	0	53	0	0	0	60⅓	77	38	38	19	43
Morgan, Mike	6.24	13	10	34	25	1	0	140	184	108	97	48	61
Fassero, Jeff	7.20	5	14	37	27	0	0	156⅓	208	135	125	83	114
Glynn, Ryan	7.24	2	4	13	10	0	0	54⅔	71	46	44	35	39
Clark, Mark	8.60	3	7	15	15	0	0	74⅓	103	73	71	34	44

Toronto Blue Jays

BATTING	BA	G	AB	R	H	TB	2B	3B	HR	RBI	SB	BB	SO
Fernandez, Tony	.328	142	485	73	159	218	41	0	6	75	6	77	62
Bush, Homer	.320	128	485	69	155	204	26	4	5	55	32	21	82
Green, Shawn	.309	153	614	134	190	361	45	0	42	123	20	66	117
Stewart, Shannon	.304	145	608	102	185	250	28	2	11	67	37	59	83
Segui, David	.298	121	440	57	131	206	27	3	14	52	1	40	60
Gonzalez, Alex	.292	38	154	22	45	64	13	0	2	12	4	16	23
Fletcher, Darrin	.291	115	412	48	120	200	26	0	18	80	0	26	47
Batista, Tony	.285	98	375	61	107	212	25	1	26	79	2	22	79
Delgado, Carlos	.272	152	573	113	156	327	39	0	44	134	1	86	141
Cruz, Jose Jr.	.241	106	349	63	84	151	19	3	14	45	14	64	91
Otanez, Willis	.237	71	207	28	49	81	11	0	7	24	0	15	46
Brumfield, Jacob	.235	62	170	25	40	60	8	3	2	19	1	19	39
Matheny, Mike	.215	57	163	16	35	50	6	0	3	17	0	12	37
Greene, Willie	.204	81	226	22	46	89	7	0	12	41	0	20	56

PITCHING	ERA	W	L	G	GS	CG	SV	INN	H	R	ER	BB	SO
Quantrill, Paul	3.33	3	2	41	0	0	0	48⅔	53	19	18	17	28
Koch, Billy	3.39	0	5	56	0	0	31	63⅔	55	26	24	30	57
Frascatore, John	3.41	7	1	33	0	0	1	37	42	16	14	9	22
Lloyd, Graeme	3.63	5	3	74	0	0	3	72	68	36	29	23	47
Halladay, Roy	3.92	8	7	36	18	1	1	149⅓	156	76	65	79	82
Carpenter, Chris	4.38	9	8	24	24	4	0	150	177	81	73	48	106
Spoljaric, Paul	4.65	2	2	37	2	0	0	62	62	41	32	32	63
Hentgen, Pat	4.79	11	12	34	34	1	0	199	225	115	106	65	118
Wells, David	4.82	17	10	34	34	7	0	231⅔	246	132	124	62	169
Escobar, Kelvim	5.49	14	11	33	30	1	0	174	203	118	110	81	129
Munro, Peter	6.02	0	2	31	2	0	0	55⅓	70	38	37	23	38
Hamilton, Joey	6.52	7	8	22	18	0	0	98	118	73	71	39	56

FOR THE RECORD·Year by Year

The World Series

Results

1903 ....Boston (A) 5, Pittsburgh (N) 3
1904 ....No series
1905 ....New York (N) 4, Philadelphia (A) 1
1906 ....Chicago (A) 4, Chicago (N) 2
1907 ....Chicago (N) 4, Detroit (A) 0; 1 tie
1908 ....Chicago (N) 4, Detroit (A) 1
1909 ....Pittsburgh (N) 4, Detroit (A) 3
1910 ....Philadelphia (A) 4, Chicago (N) 1
1911 ....Philadelphia (A) 4, New York (N) 2
1912 ....Boston (A) 4, New York (N) 3; 1 tie
1913 ....Philadelphia (A) 4, New York (N) 1
1914 ....Boston (N) 4, Philadelphia (A) 0
1915 ....Boston (A) 4, Philadelphia (N) 1
1916 ....Boston (A) 4, Brooklyn (N) 1
1917 ....Chicago (A) 4, New York (N) 2
1918 ....Boston (A) 4, Chicago (N) 2
1919 ....Cincinnati (N) 5, Chicago (A) 3
1920 ....Cleveland (A) 5, Brooklyn (N) 2
1921 ....New York (N) 5, New York (A) 3
1922 ....New York (N) 4, New York (A) 0; 1 tie
1923 ....New York (A) 4, New York (N) 2
1924 ....Washington (A) 4, New York (N) 3
1925 ....Pittsburgh (N) 4, Washington (A) 3
1926 ....St. Louis (N) 4, New York (A) 3
1927 ....New York (A) 4, Pittsburgh (N) 0
1928 ....New York (A) 4, St. Louis (N) 0
1929 ....Philadelphia (A) 4, Chicago (N) 1
1930 ....Philadelphia (A) 4, St. Louis (N) 2
1931 ....St. Louis (N) 4, Philadelphia (A) 3
1932 ....New York (A) 4, Chicago (N) 0
1933 ....New York (N) 4, Washington (A) 1
1934 ....St. Louis (N) 4, Detroit (A) 3
1935 ....Detroit (A) 4, Chicago (N) 2
1936 ....New York (A) 4, New York (N) 2
1937 ....New York (A) 4, New York (N) 1
1938 ....New York (A) 4, Chicago (N) 0
1939 ....New York (A) 4, Cincinnati (N) 0
1940 ....Cincinnati (N) 4, Detroit (A) 3
1941 ....New York (A) 4, Brooklyn (N) 1
1942 ....St. Louis (N) 4, New York (A) 1
1943 ....New York (A) 4, St. Louis (N) 1
1944 ....St. Louis (N) 4, St. Louis (A) 2
1945 ....Detroit (A) 4, Chicago (N) 3
1946 ....St. Louis (N) 4, Boston (A) 3
1947 ....New York (A) 4, Brooklyn (N) 3
1948 ....Cleveland (A) 4, Boston (N) 2
1949 ....New York (A) 4, Brooklyn (N) 1
1950 ....New York (A) 4, Philadelphia (N) 0
1951 ....New York (A) 4, New York (N) 2

1952 ....New York (A) 4, Brooklyn (N) 3
1953 ....New York (A) 4, Brooklyn (N) 2
1954 ....New York (N) 4, Cleveland (A) 0
1955 ....Brooklyn (N) 4, New York (A) 3
1956 ....New York (A) 4, Brooklyn (N) 3
1957 ....Milwaukee (N) 4, New York (A) 3
1958 ....New York (A) 4, Milwaukee (N) 3
1959 ....Los Angeles (N) 4, Chicago (A) 2
1960 ....Pittsburgh (N) 4, New York (A) 3
1961 ....New York (A) 4, Cincinnati (N) 1
1962 ....New York (A) 4, San Francisco (N) 3
1963 ....Los Angeles (N) 4, New York (A) 0
1964 ....St. Louis (N) 4, New York (A) 3
1965 ....Los Angeles (N) 4, Minnesota (A) 3
1966 ....Baltimore (A) 4, Los Angeles (N) 0
1967 ....St. Louis (N) 4, Boston (A) 3
1968 ....Detroit (A) 4, St. Louis (N) 3
1969 ....New York (N) 4, Baltimore (A) 1
1970 ....Baltimore (A) 4, Cincinnati (N) 1
1971 ....Pittsburgh (N) 4, Baltimore (A) 3
1972 ....Oakland (A) 4, Cincinnati (N) 3
1973 ....Oakland (A) 4, New York (N) 3
1974 ....Oakland (A) 4, Los Angeles (N) 1
1975 ....Cincinnati (N) 4, Boston (A) 3
1976 ....Cincinnati (N) 4, New York (A) 0
1977 ....New York (A) 4, Los Angeles (N) 2
1978 ....New York (A) 4, Los Angeles (N) 2
1979 ....Pittsburgh (N) 4, Baltimore (A) 3
1980 ....Philadelphia (N) 4, Kansas City (A) 2
1981 ....Los Angeles (N) 4, New York (A) 2
1982 ....St. Louis (N) 4, Milwaukee (A) 3
1983 ....Baltimore (A) 4, Philadelphia (N) 1
1984 ....Detroit (A) 4, San Diego (N) 1
1985 ....Kansas City (A) 4, St. Louis (N) 3
1986 ....New York (N) 4, Boston (A) 3
1987 ....Minnesota (A) 4, St. Louis (N) 3
1988 ....Los Angeles (N) 4, Oakland (A) 1
1989 ....Oakland (A) 4, San Francisco (N) 0
1990 ....Cincinnati (N) 4, Oakland (A) 0
1991 ....Minnesota (A) 4, Atlanta (N) 3
1992 ....Toronto (A) 4, Atlanta (N) 2
1993 ....Toronto (A) 4, Philadelphia (N) 2
1994 ....Series canceled due to players' strike.
1995 ....Atlanta (N) 4, Cleveland (A) 2
1996 ....New York (A) 4, Atlanta (N) 2
1997 ....Florida (N) 4, Cleveland (A) 3
1998 ....New York (A) 4, San Diego (N) 0
1999 ....New York (A) 4, Atlanta (N) 0

Most Valuable Players

1955	Johnny Podres, Bklyn
1956	Don Larsen, NY (A)
1957	Lew Burdette, Mil
1958	Bob Turley, NY (A)
1959	Larry Sherry, LA
1960	Bobby Richardson, NY (A)
1961	Whitey Ford, NY (A)
1962	Ralph Terry, NY (A)
1963	Sandy Koufax, LA
1964	Bob Gibson, StL
1965	Sandy Koufax, LA
1966	Frank Robinson, Balt
1967	Bob Gibson, StL
1968	Mickey Lolich, Det
1969	Donn Clendenon, NY (N)
1970	Brooks Robinson, Balt
1971	Roberto Clemente, Pitt
1972	Gene Tenace, Oak
1973	Reggie Jackson, Oak
1974	Rollie Fingers, Oak
1975	Pete Rose, Cin
1976	Johnny Bench, Cin
1977	Reggie Jackson, NY (A)

1978	Bucky Dent, NY (A)
1979	Willie Stargell, Pitt
1980	Mike Schmidt, Phil
1981	Ron Cey, Steve Yeager, Pedro Guerrero, LA
1982	Darrell Porter, StL
1983	Rick Dempsey, Balt
1984	Alan Trammell, Det
1985	Bret Saberhagen, KC
1986	Ray Knight, NY (N)
1987	Frank Viola, Minn
1988	Orel Hershiser, LA
1989	Dave Stewart, Oak
1990	Jose Rijo, Cin
1991	Jack Morris, Minn
1992	Pat Borders, Tor
1993	Paul Molitor, Tor
1994	Series canceled due to strike
1995	Tom Glavine, Atl
1996	John Wetteland, NY (A)
1997	Livan Hernandez, Fla
1998	Scott Brosius, NY (A)
1999	Mariano Rivera, NY (A)

Career Batting Leaders (Minimum 50 at bats)

GAMES

Yogi Berra	75
Mickey Mantle	65
Elston Howard	54
Hank Bauer	53
Gil McDougald	53
Phil Rizzuto	52
Joe DiMaggio	51
Frankie Frisch	50
Pee Wee Reese	44
Roger Maris	41
Babe Ruth	41

AT BATS

Yogi Berra	259
Mickey Mantle	230
Joe DiMaggio	199
Frankie Frisch	197
Gil McDougald	190
Hank Bauer	188
Phil Rizzuto	183
Elston Howard	171
Pee Wee Reese	169
Roger Maris	152

HITS

Yogi Berra	71
Mickey Mantle	59
Frankie Frisch	58
Joe DiMaggio	54
Pee Wee Reese	46
Hank Bauer	46
Phil Rizzuto	45
Gil McDougald	45
Lou Gehrig	43
Eddie Collins	42
Babe Ruth	42
Elston Howard	42

BATTING AVERAGE

Pepper Martin	.418
Paul Molitor	.418
Lou Brock	.391
Marquis Grissom	.390
Thurman Munson	.373
George Brett	.373
Hank Aaron	.364
Frank Baker	.363
Roberto Clemente	.362
Lou Gehrig	.361

HOME RUNS

Mickey Mantle	18
Babe Ruth	15
Yogi Berra	12
Duke Snider	11
Reggie Jackson	10
Lou Gehrig	10
Frank Robinson	8
Bill Skowron	8
Joe DiMaggio	8
Goose Goslin	7
Hank Bauer	7
Gil McDougald	7

RUNS BATTED IN

Mickey Mantle	40
Yogi Berra	39
Lou Gehrig	35
Babe Ruth	33
Joe DiMaggio	30
Bill Skowron	29
Duke Snider	26
Reggie Jackson	24
Bill Dickey	24
Hank Bauer	24
Gil McDougald	24

RUNS

Mickey Mantle	42
Yogi Berra	41
Babe Ruth	37
Lou Gehrig	30
Joe DiMaggio	27
Roger Maris	26
Elston Howard	25
Gil McDougald	23
Jackie Robinson	22
Gene Woodling	21
Reggie Jackson	21
Duke Snider	21
Phil Rizzuto	21
Hank Bauer	21

STOLEN BASES

Lou Brock	14
Eddie Collins	14
Frank Chance	10
Davey Lopes	10
Phil Rizzuto	10
Honus Wagner	9
Frankie Frisch	9
Johnny Evers	8
Pepper Martin	7
Joe Morgan	7
Rickey Henderson	7

TOTAL BASES

Mickey Mantle	123
Yogi Berra	117
Babe Ruth	96
Lou Gehrig	87
Joe DiMaggio	84
Duke Snider	79
Hank Bauer	75
Reggie Jackson	74
Frankie Frisch	74
Gil McDougald	72

Career Batting Leaders *(Cont.)*

SLUGGING AVERAGE		STRIKEOUTS	
Reggie Jackson	.755	Mickey Mantle	54
Babe Ruth	.744	Elston Howard	37
Lou Gehrig	.731	Duke Snider	33
Al Simmons	.658	Babe Ruth	30
Lou Brock	.655	Gil McDougald	29
Paul Molitor	.636	Bill Skowron	26
Pepper Martin	.636	Hank Bauer	25
Hank Greenberg	.624	Reggie Jackson	24
Charlie Keller	.611	Bob Meusel	24
Jimmie Foxx	.609	Frank Robinson	23
Dave Henderson	.606	George Kelly	23
		Tony Kubek	23
		Joe DiMaggio	23

Career Pitching Leaders

GAMES		LOSSES		COMPLETE GAMES	
Whitey Ford	22	Whitey Ford	8	Christy Mathewson	10
Rollie Fingers	16	Eddie Plank	5	Chief Bender	9
Allie Reynolds	15	Schoolboy Rowe	5	Bob Gibson	8
Bob Turley	15	Joe Bush	5	Red Ruffing	7
Clay Carroll	14	Rube Marquard	5	Whitey Ford	7
Clem Labine	13	Christy Mathewson	5	George Mullin	6
Waite Hoyt	12			Eddie Plank	6
Catfish Hunter	12			Art Nehf	6
Art Nehf	12	**SAVES**		Waite Hoyt	6
Paul Derringer	11	Rollie Fingers	6		
Carl Erskine	11	Mariano Rivera	5		
Rube Marquard	11	Allie Reynolds	4	**STRIKEOUTS**	
Christy Mathewson	11	Johnny Murphy	4	Whitey Ford	94
Vic Raschi	11	John Wetteland	4	Bob Gibson	92
		Roy Face	3	Allie Reynolds	62
INNINGS PITCHED		Herb Pennock	3	Sandy Koufax	61
Whitey Ford	146	Kent Tekulve	3	Red Ruffing	61
Christy Mathewson	101⅔	Firpo Marberry	3	Chief Bender	59
Red Ruffing	85⅔	Will McEnaney	3	George Earnshaw	56
Chief Bender	85	Todd Worrell	3	John Smoltz	52
Waite Hoyt	83⅔	Tug McGraw	3	Waite Hoyt	49
Bob Gibson	81			Christy Mathewson	48
Art Nehf	79	***EARNED RUN AVERAGE**			
Allie Reynolds	77	Jack Billingham	.36	**BASES ON BALLS**	
Jim Palmer	65	Harry Brecheen	.83	Whitey Ford	34
Catfish Hunter	63	Babe Ruth	.87	Allie Reynolds	32
		Sherry Smith	.89	Art Nehf	32
WINS		Sandy Koufax	.95	Jim Palmer	31
Whitey Ford	10	Hippo Vaughn	1.00	Bob Turley	29
Bob Gibson	7	Monte Pearson	1.01	Paul Derringer	27
Red Ruffing	7	Christy Mathewson	1.15	Red Ruffing	27
Allie Reynolds	7	Babe Adams	1.29	Don Gullett	26
Lefty Gomez	6	Eddie Plank	1.32	Burleigh Grimes	26
Chief Bender	6			Vic Raschi	25
Waite Hoyt	6	**SHUTOUTS**			
Jack Coombs	5	Christy Mathewson	4		
Three Finger Brown	5	Three Finger Brown	3		
Herb Pennock	5	Whitey Ford	3		
Christy Mathewson	5	Bill Hallahan	2		
Vic Raschi	5	Lew Burdette	2		
Catfish Hunter	5	Bill Dinneen	2		
		Sandy Koufax	2		
		Allie Reynolds	2		
		Art Nehf	2		
		Bob Gibson	2		

*Minimum 25 innings pitched.

Alltime Team Rankings (by championships)

Team	W	L	Appearances	Pct.	Most Recent	Last Championship
New York Yankees	25	11	36	.694	1999	1999
Phil/K.C./Oakland Athletics	9	5	14	.643	1990	1989
St. Louis Cardinals	9	6	15	.600	1987	1982
Brooklyn/L.A. Dodgers	6	12	18	.333	1988	1988
Pittsburgh Pirates	5	2	7	.714	1979	1979
Cincinnati Reds	5	4	9	.556	1990	1990
Boston Red Sox	5	4	9	.556	1986	1918
New York/San Francisco Giants	5	11	16	.313	1989	1954
Detroit Tigers	4	5	9	.444	1984	1984
Washington/Minnesota Twins	3	3	6	.500	1991	1991
St. Louis/Baltimore Orioles	3	4	7	.429	1983	1983
Boston/Milwaukee/Atlanta Braves	3	6	9	.333	1999	1995
Toronto Blue Jays	2	0	2	1.000	1993	1993
New York Mets	2	1	3	.667	1986	1986
Chicago White Sox	2	2	4	.500	1959	1917
Cleveland Indians	2	3	5	.400	1997	1948
Chicago Cubs	2	8	10	.200	1945	1908
Florida Marlins	1	0	1	1.000	1997	1997
Kansas City Royals	1	1	2	.500	1985	1985
Philadelphia Phillies	1	4	5	.200	1993	1980
Seattle/Milwaukee Brewers	0	1	1	.000	1982	—
San Diego Padres	0	2	2	.000	1998	—

League Championship Series

National League

1969	New York (E) 3, Atlanta (W) 0
1970	Cincinnati (W) 3, Pittsburgh (E) 0
1971	Pittsburgh (E) 3, San Francisco (W) 1
1972	Cincinnati (W) 3, Pittsburgh (E) 2
1973	New York (E) 3, Cincinnati (W) 2
1974	Los Angeles (W) 3, Pittsburgh (E) 1
1975	Cincinnati (W) 3, Pittsburgh (E) 0
1976	Cincinnati (W) 3, Philadelphia (E) 0
1977	Los Angeles (W) 3, Philadelphia (E) 1
1978	Los Angeles (W) 3, Philadelphia (E) 1
1979	Pittsburgh (E) 3, Cincinnati (W) 0
1980	Philadelphia (E) 3, Houston (W) 2
1981	Los Angeles (W) 3, Montreal (E) 2
1982	St. Louis (E) 3, Atlanta (W) 0
1983	Philadelphia (E) 3, Los Angeles (W) 1
1984	San Diego (W) 3, Chicago (E) 2
1985	St. Louis (E) 4, Los Angeles (W) 2
1986	New York (E) 4, Houston (W) 2
1987	St. Louis (E) 4, San Francisco (W) 3
1988	Los Angeles (W) 4, New York (E) 3
1989	San Francisco (W) 4, Chicago (E) 1
1990	Cincinnati (W) 4, Pittsburgh (E) 2
1991	Atlanta (W) 4, Pittsburgh (E) 3
1992	Atlanta (W) 4, Pittsburgh (E) 3
1993	Philadelphia (E) 4, Atlanta (W) 2
1994	Playoffs canceled due to players' strike.
1995	Atlanta (E) 4, Cincinnati (C) 0
1996	Atlanta (E) 4, St. Louis (C) 3
1997	Florida (wc) 4, Atlanta (E) 2
1998	San Diego (W) 4, Atlanta (E) 2
1999	Atlanta (E) 4, New York (wc) 2

American League

1969	Baltimore (E) 3, Minnesota (W) 0
1970	Baltimore (E) 3, Minnesota (W) 0
1971	Baltimore (E) 3, Oakland (W) 0
1972	Oakland (W) 3, Detroit (E) 2
1973	Oakland (W) 3, Baltimore (E) 2
1974	Oakland (W) 3, Baltimore (E) 1
1975	Boston (E) 3, Oakland (W) 0
1976	New York (E) 3, Kansas City (W) 2
1977	New York (E) 3, Kansas City (W) 2
1978	New York (E) 3, Kansas City (W) 1
1979	Baltimore (E) 3, California (W) 1
1980	Kansas City (W) 3, New York (E) 0
1981	New York (E) 3, Oakland (W) 0
1982	Milwaukee (E) 3, California (W) 2
1983	Baltimore (E) 3, Chicago (W) 1
1984	Detroit (E) 3, Kansas City (W) 0
1985	Kansas City (W) 4, Toronto (E) 3
1986	Boston (E) 4, California (W) 3
1987	Minnesota (W) 4, Detroit (E) 1
1988	Oakland (W) 4, Boston (E) 0
1989	Oakland (W) 4, Toronto (E) 1
1990	Oakland (W) 4, Boston (E) 0
1991	Minnesota (W) 4, Toronto (E) 1
1992	Toronto (E) 4, Oakland (W) 2
1993	Toronto (E) 4, Chicago (W) 2
1994	Playoffs canceled due to players' strike.
1995	Cleveland (C) 4, Seattle (W) 2
1996	New York (E) 4, Baltimore (wc) 1
1997	Cleveland (C) 4, Baltimore (E) 2
1998	New York (E) 4, Cleveland (C) 2
1999	New York (E) 4, Boston (wc) 1

NLCS Most Valuable Player

1977........Dusty Baker, LA	1985........Ozzie Smith, StL	1992........John Smoltz, Atl
1978........Steve Garvey, LA	1986........Mike Scott, Hou	1993........Curt Schilling, Phil
1979........Willie Stargell, Pitt	1987........Jeffrey Leonard, SF	1994........Playoffs canceled
1980........Manny Trillo, Phil	1988........Orel Hershiser, LA	1995........Mike Devereaux, Atl
1981........Burt Hooton, LA	1989........Will Clark, SF	1996........Javier Lopez, Atl
1982........Darrell Porter, StL	1990........Randy Myers, Cin	1997........Livan Hernandez, Fla
1983........Gary Matthews, Phil	Rob Dibble, Cin	1998........Sterling Hitchcock, SD
1984........Steve Garvey, SD	1991........Steve Avery, Atl	1999........Eddie Perez, Atl

ALCS Most Valuable Player

1980........Frank White, KC	1987........Gary Gaetti, Minn	1994........Playoffs canceled
1981........Graig Nettles, NY	1988........Dennis Eckersley, Oak	1995........Orel Hershiser, Clev
1982........Fred Lynn, Calif	1989........Rickey Henderson, Oak	1996........Bernie Williams, NY
1983........Mike Boddicker, Balt	1990........Dave Stewart, Oak	1997........Marquis Grissom, Clev
1984........Kirk Gibson, Det	1991........Kirby Puckett, Minn	1998........David Wells, NY
1985........George Brett, KC	1992........Roberto Alomar, Tor	1999........Orlando Hernandez, NY
1986........Marty Barrett, Bos	1993........Dave Stewart, Tor	

Divisional Playoffs

National League

1995 ....Atlanta (E) 3, Colorado (wc) 1
Cincinnati (C) 3, Los Angeles (W) 0
1996 ....St. Louis (C) 3, San Diego (W) 0
Atlanta (E) 3, Los Angeles (wc) 0
1997 ....Atlanta (E) 3, Houston (C) 0
Florida (wc) 3, San Francisco (W) 0
1998 ....San Diego (W) 3, Houston (C) 1
Atlanta (E) 3, Chicago (wc) 0
1999 ....Atlanta (E) 3, Houston (C) 1
New York (wc) 3, Arizona (W) 1

American League

1995 ....Cleveland (C) 3, Boston (E) 0
Seattle (W) 3, New York (wc) 2
1996 ....Baltimore (wc) 3, Cleveland (C) 1
New York (E) 3, Texas (W) 1
1997 ....Baltimore (E) 3, Seattle (W) 1
Cleveland (C) 3, New York (wc) 2
1998 ....New York (E) 3, Texas (W) 0
Cleveland (C) 3, Boston (wc) 1
1999 ....New York (E) 3, Texas (W) 1
Boston (wc) 3, Cleveland (C) 2

The All Star Game

Results

Date	Winner	Score	Site	Date	Winner	Score	Site
7-6-33	American	4–2	Comiskey Park, Chi	7-8-58	American	4–3	Memorial Stadium, Balt
7-10-34	American	9–7	Polo Grounds, NY	7-7-59	National	5–4	Forbes Field, Pitt
7-8-35	American	4–1	Municipal Stadium, Clev	8-3-59	American	5–3	Memorial Coliseum, LA
7-7-36	National	4–3	Braves Field, Bos	7-11-60	National	5–3	Municipal Stadium, KC
7-7-37	American	8–3	Griffith Stadium, Wash	7-13-60	National	6–0	Yankee Stadium, NY
7-6-38	National	4–1	Crosley Field, Cin	7-11-61	National	5–4	Candlestick Park, SF
7-11-39	American	3–1	Yankee Stadium, NY	7-31-61	Tie*	1–1	Fenway Park, Bos
7-10-40	National	4–0	Sportsman's Park, StL	7-10-62	National	3–1	D.C. Stadium, Wash
7-8-41	American	7–5	Briggs Stadium, Det	7-30-62	American	9–4	Wrigley Field, Chi
7-6-42	American	3–1	Polo Grounds, NY	7-9-63	National	5–3	Municipal Stadium, Clev
7-13-43	American	5–3	Shibe Park, Phil	7-7-64	National	7–4	Shea Stadium, NY
7-11-44	National	7–1	Forbes Field, Pitt	7-13-65	National	6–5	Metropolitan Stadium, Minn
1945 ....No game due to wartime travel restrictions.							
7-9-46	American	12–0	Fenway Park, Bos	7-12-66	National	2–1	Busch Stadium, StL
7-8-47	American	2–1	Wrigley Field, Chi	7-11-67	National	2–1	Anaheim Stadium, Cal
7-13-48	American	5–2	Sportsman's Park, StL	7-9-68	National	1–0	Astrodome, Hou
7-12-49	American	11–7	Ebbets Field, Bklyn	7-23-69	National	9–3	R.F.K. Memorial Stadium, Wash
7-11-50	National	4–3	Comiskey Park, Chi				
7-10-51	National	8–3	Briggs Stadium, Det	7-14-70	National	5–4	Riverfront Stadium, Cin
7-8-52	National	3–2	Shibe Park, Phil	7-13-71	American	6–4	Tiger Stadium, Det
7-14-53	National	5–1	Crosley Field, Cin	7-25-72	National	4–3	Atlanta Stadium, Atl
7-13-54	American	11–9	Municipal Stadium, Clev	7-24-73	National	7–1	Royals Stadium, KC
7-12-55	National	6–5	County Stadium, Mil	7-23-74	National	7–2	Three Rivers Stadium, Pitt
7-10-56	National	7–3	Griffith Stadium, Wash	7-15-75	National	6–3	County Stadium, Mil
7-9-57	American	6–5	Busch Stadium, StL	7-13-76	National	7–1	Veterans Stadium, Phil

*Game called because of rain after 9 innings.

Results (Cont.)

Date	Winner	Score	Site	Date	Winner	Score	Site
7-19-77	National	7–5	Yankee Stadium, NY	7-11-89	American	5–3	Anaheim Stadium, Cal
7-11-78	National	7–3	Jack Murphy Stadium, SD	7-10-90	American	2–0	Wrigley Field, Chi
7-17-79	National	7–6	Kingdome, Sea	7-9-91	American	4–2	SkyDome, Tor
7-8-80	National	4–2	Dodger Stadium, LA	7-14-92	American	13–6	Jack Murphy Stadium, SD
8-9-81	National	5–4	Municipal Stadium, Clev	7-13-93	American	9–3	Camden Yards, Balt
7-13-82	National	4–1	Olympic Stadium, Mtl	7-12-94	National	8–7	Three Rivers Stadium, Pitt
7-6-83	American	13–3	Comiskey Park, Chi	7-11-95	National	3–2	The Ballpark in
7-10-84	National	3–1	Candlestick Park, SF				Arlington, Tex
7-16-85	National	6–1	Metrodome, Minn	7-9-96	National	6–0	Veterans Stadium, Phil
7-15-86	American	3–2	Astrodome, Hou	7-8-97	American	3–1	Jacobs Field, Clev
7-14-87	National	2–0	Oakland Coliseum, Oak	7-7-98	American	13–8	Coors Field, Col
7-12-88	American	2–1	Riverfront Stadium, Cin	7-13-99	American	4–1	Fenway Park, Bos

Most Valuable Players

1962	Maury Wills, LA	NL	1975	Bill Madlock, Chi	NL	1988	Terry Steinbach, Oak	AL
	Leon Wagner, LA	AL		Jon Matlack, NY	NL	1989	Bo Jackson, KC	AL
1963	Willie Mays, SF	NL	1976	George Foster, Cin	NL	1990	Julio Franco, Tex	AL
1964	Johnny Callison, Phil	NL	1977	Don Sutton, LA	NL	1991	Cal Ripken Jr, Balt	AL
1965	Juan Marichal, SF	NL	1978	Steve Garvey, LA	NL	1992	Ken Griffey Jr, Sea	AL
1966	Brooks Robinson, Balt	AL	1979	Dave Parker, Pitt	NL	1993	Kirby Puckett, Minn	AL
1967	Tony Perez, Cin	NL	1980	Ken Griffey, Cin	NL	1994	Fred McGriff, Atl	NL
1968	Willie Mays, SF	NL	1981	Gary Carter, Mtl	NL	1995	Jeff Conine, Fla	NL
1969	Willie McCovey, SF	NL	1982	Dave Concepcion, Cin	NL	1996	Mike Piazza, LA	NL
1970	Carl Yastrzemski, Bos	AL	1983	Fred Lynn, Calif	AL	1997	Sandy Alomar, Clev	AL
1971	Frank Robinson, Balt	AL	1984	Gary Carter, Mtl	NL	1998	Roberto Alomar, Balt	AL
1972	Joe Morgan, Cin	NL	1985	LaMarr Hoyt, SD	NL	1999	Pedro Martinez, Bos	AL
1973	Bobby Bonds, SF	NL	1986	Roger Clemens, Bos	AL			
1974	Steve Garvey, LA	NL	1987	Tim Raines, Mtl	NL			

The Regular Season

Most Valuable Players

NATIONAL LEAGUE

Year	Name and Team	Position	Noteworthy
1911	Wildfire Schulte, Chi	Outfield	21 HR†, 121 RBI†, .300
1912	*Larry Doyle, NY	Second base	10 HR, 90 RBI, .330
1913	Jake Daubert, Bklyn	First base	52 RBI, .350†
1914	*Johnny Evers, Bos	Second base	F.A. .976†, .279
1915–23	No selection		
1924	Dazzy Vance, Bklyn	Pitcher	28†–6, 2.16 ERA†, 262 K†
1925	Rogers Hornsby, StL	Second base, Manager	39 HR†, 143 RBI†, .403†
1926	*Bob O'Farrell, StL	Catcher	7 HR, 68 RBI, .293
1927	*Paul Waner, Pitt	Outfield	237 hits†, 131 RBI†, .380†
1928	*Jim Bottomley, StL	First base	31 HR†, 136 RBI†, .325
1929	*Rogers Hornsby, Chi	Second base	39 HR, 149 RBI, 156 runs†, .380
1930	No selection		
1931	*Frankie Frisch, StL	Second base	4 HR, 82 RBI, 28 SB†, .311
1932	Chuck Klein, Phil	Outfield	38 HR†, 137 RBI, 226 hits†, .348
1933	*Carl Hubbell, NY	Pitcher	23†–12, 1.66 ERA†, 10 SO†
1934	*Dizzy Dean, StL	Pitcher	30†–7, 2.66 ERA, 195 K†
1935	*Gabby Hartnett, Chi	Catcher	13 HR, 91 RBI, .344
1936	*Carl Hubbell, NY	Pitcher	26†–6, 2.31 ERA†
1937	Joe Medwick, StL	Outfield	31 HR‡, 154 RBI†, 111 runs†, .374†
1938	Ernie Lombardi, Cin	Catcher	19 HR, 95 RBI, .342†
1939	*Bucky Walters, Cin	Pitcher	27†–11, 2.29 ERA†, 137 K‡
1940	*Frank McCormick, Cin	First base	19 HR, 127 RBI, 191 hits†, .309
1941	*Dolph Camilli, Bklyn	First base	34 HR†, 120 RBI†, .285
1942	*Mort Cooper, StL	Pitcher	22†–7, 1.78 ERA†, 10 SO†
1943	*Stan Musial, StL	Outfield	13 HR, 81 RBI, 220 hits†, .357†

*Played for pennant or, after 1968, division winner. †Led league. ‡Tied for league lead.

Most Valuable Players (Cont.)
NATIONAL LEAGUE (Cont.)

Year	Name and Team	Position	Noteworthy
1944	*Marty Marion, StL	Shortstop	F.A. .972†, 63 RBI
1945	*Phil Cavarretta, Chi	First base	6 HR, 97 RBI, .355†
1946	*Stan Musial, StL	First base, Outfield	103 RBI, 124 runs†, 228 hits†, .365†
1947	Bob Elliott, Bos	Third base	22 HR, 113 RBI, .317
1948	Stan Musial, StL	Outfield	39 HR, 131 RBI†, .376†
1949	*Jackie Robinson, Bklyn	Second base	16 HR, 124 RBI, 37 SB†, .342†
1950	*Jim Konstanty, Phil	Pitcher	16–7, 22 saves†, 2.66 ERA
1951	Roy Campanella, Bklyn	Catcher	33 HR, 108 RBI, .325
1952	Hank Sauer, Chi	Outfield	37 HR‡, 121 RBI†, .270
1953	*Roy Campanella, Bklyn	Catcher	41 HR, 142 RBI†, .312
1954	*Willie Mays, NY	Outfield	41 HR, 110 RBI, 13 3B†, .345†
1955	*Roy Campanella, Bklyn	Catcher	32 HR, 107 RBI, .318
1956	*Don Newcombe, Bklyn	Pitcher	27†–7, 3.06 ERA
1957	*Hank Aaron, Mil	Outfield	44 HR†, 132 RBI†, .322
1958	Ernie Banks, Chi	Shortstop	47 HR†, 129 RBI†, .313
1959	Ernie Banks, Chi	Shortstop	45 HR†, 143 RBI†, .304
1960	*Dick Groat, Pitt	Shortstop	2 HR, 50 RBI, .325†
1961	*Frank Robinson, Cin	Outfield	37 HR, 124 RBI, .323
1962	Maury Wills, LA	Shortstop	104 SB†, 208 hits, .299, GG
1963	*Sandy Koufax, LA	Pitcher	25‡–5, 1.88 ERA†, 306 K†
1964	*Ken Boyer, StL	Third Base	24 HR, 119 RBI†, .295
1965	Willie Mays, SF	Outfield	52 HR†, 112 RBI, .317, GG
1966	Roberto Clemente, Pitt	Outfield	29 HR, 119 RBI, 202 hits, .317, GG
1967	*Orlando Cepeda, StL	First base	25 HR, 111 RBI†, .325
1968	*Bob Gibson, StL	Pitcher	22–9, 1.12 ERA†, 268 K†, 13 SO†, GG
1969	Willie McCovey, SF	First base	45 HR†, 126 RBI†, .320
1970	*Johnny Bench, Cin	Catcher	45 HR†, 148 RBI†, .293, GG
1971	Joe Torre, StL	Third base	24 HR, 137 RBI†, .363†
1972	*Johnny Bench, Cin	Catcher	40 HR†, 125 RBI†, .270, GG
1973	*Pete Rose, Cin	Outfield	5 HR, 64 RBI, .338†, 230 hits†
1974	*Steve Garvey, LA	First base	21 HR, 111 RBI, 200 hits, .312, GG
1975	*Joe Morgan, Cin	Second base	17 HR, 94 RBI, 67 SB, .327, GG
1976	*Joe Morgan, Cin	Second base	27 HR, 111 RBI, 60 SB, .320, GG
1977	George Foster, Cin	Outfield	52 HR†, 149 RBI†, .320
1978	Dave Parker, Pitt	Outfield	30 HR, 117 RBI, .334†, GG
1979	Keith Hernandez, StL	First base	11 HR, 105 RBI, 210 hits, .344†, GG
	*Willie Stargell, Pitt	First base	32 HR, 82 RBI, .281
1980	*Mike Schmidt, Phil	Third base	48 HR†, 121 RBI†, .286, GG
1981	Mike Schmidt, Phil	Third base	31 HR†, 91 RBI†, 78 runs†, .316, GG
1982	*Dale Murphy, Atl	Outfield	36 HR, 109 RBI‡, .281, GG
1983	Dale Murphy, Atl	Outfield	36 HR, 121 RBI†, .302, GG
1984	*Ryne Sandberg, Chi	Second base	19 HR, 84 RBI, 114 runs†, .314, GG
1985	*Willie McGee, StL	Outfield	10 HR, 82 RBI, 18 3B†, .353†, GG
1986	Mike Schmidt, Phil	Third base	37 HR†, 119 RBI†, .290, GG
1987	Andre Dawson, Chi	Outfield	49 HR†, 137 RBI†, .287, GG
1988	*Kirk Gibson, LA	Outfield	25 HR, 76 RBI, 106 runs, .290
1989	*Kevin Mitchell, SF	Outfield	47 HR†, 125 RBI†, .291
1990	*Barry Bonds, Pitt	Outfield	33 HR, 114 RBI, .301
1991	*Terry Pendleton, Atl	Third base	23 HR, 86 RBI, .319†
1992	Barry Bonds, SF	Outfield	34 HR, 103 RBI, .311
1993	Barry Bonds, SF	Outfield	46 HR†, 123 RBI†, .336
1994	Jeff Bagwell, Hou	First base	39 HR, 116 RBI†, .368
1995	*Barry Larkin, Cin	Shortstop	15 HR, 66 RBI, 51 SB, .319
1996	*Ken Caminiti, SD	Third base	40 HR, 130 RBI, .326
1997	Larry Walker, Col	Outfield	49 HR†, 130 RBI, .452 OBA†, .366, GG
1998	Sammy Sosa, Chi	Outfield	66 HR, 158 RBI†, 134 runs†, 416 TB†, .308

*Played for pennant or, after 1968, division winner. †Led league. ‡Tied for league lead.

Most Valuable Players *(Cont.)*

AMERICAN LEAGUE

Year	Name and Team	Position	Noteworthy
1911	Ty Cobb, Det	Outfield	8 HR, 144 RBI†, 24 3B†, .420†
1912	*Tris Speaker, Bos	Outfield	10 HR‡, 98 RBI, 53 2B†, .383
1913	Walter Johnson, Wash	Pitcher	36†–7, 1.09 ERA†, 11 SO†, 243 K†
1914	*Eddie Collins, Phil	Second base	2 HR, 85 RBI, 122 runs†, .344
1915-21	No selection		
1922	George Sisler, StL	First base	8 HR, 105 RBI, 246 hits†, .420†
1923	*Babe Ruth, NY	Outfield	41 HR†, 131 RBI, .393
1924	*Walter Johnson, Wash	Pitcher	23†–7, 2.72 ERA†, 158 K†
1925	*Roger Peckinpaugh, Wash	Shortstop	4 HR, 64 RBI, .294
1926	George Burns, Clev	First base	114 RBI, 216 hits†, 64 2B†, .358
1927	*Lou Gehrig, NY	First base	47 HR, 175 RBI†, 52 2B†, .373
1928	Mickey Cochrane, Phil	Catcher	10 HR, 57 RBI, .293
1929	No selection		
1930	No selection		
1931	*Lefty Grove, Phil	Pitcher	31†–4, 2.06 ERA†, 175 K†
1932	Jimmie Foxx, Phil	First base	58 HR†, 169 RBI†, 151 runs†, .364
1933	Jimmie Foxx, Phil	First base	48 HR†, 163 RBI†, .356†
1934	*Mickey Cochrane, Det	Catcher	2 HR, 76 RBI, .320
1935	*Hank Greenberg, Det	First base	36 HR‡, 170 RBI†, 203 hits, .328
1936	*Lou Gehrig, NY	First base	49 HR†, 152 RBI, 167 runs†, .354
1937	Charlie Gehringer, Det	Second base	14 HR, 96 RBI, 133 runs, .371†
1938	Jimmie Foxx, Bos	First base	50 HR, 175 RBI†, .349†
1939	*Joe DiMaggio, NY	Outfield	30 HR, 126 RBI, .381†
1940	*Hank Greenberg, Det	Outfield	41 HR†, 150 RBI†, 50 2B†, .340
1941	*Joe DiMaggio, NY	Outfield	30 HR, 125 RBI†, .357
1942	*Joe Gordon, NY	Second base	18 HR, 103 RBI, .322
1943	*Spud Chandler, NY	Pitcher	20†–4, 1.64 ERA†, 5 SO‡
1944	Hal Newhouser, Det	Pitcher	29†–9, 2.22 ERA†, 187 K†
1945	*Hal Newhouser, Det	Pitcher	25†–9, 1.81 ERA†, 8 SO†, 212 K†
1946	*Ted Williams, Bos	Outfield	38 HR, 123 RBI, 142 runs†, .342
1947	*Joe DiMaggio, NY	Outfield	20 HR, 97 RBI, .315
1948	*Lou Boudreau, Clev	Shortstop	18 HR, 106 RBI, .355
1949	Ted Williams, Bos	Outfield	43 HR†, 159 RBI‡, 150 runs†, .343
1950	*Phil Rizzuto, NY	Shortstop	125 runs, 200 hits, .324
1951	*Yogi Berra, NY	Catcher	27 HR, 88 RBI, .294
1952	Bobby Shantz, Phil	Pitcher	24†–7, 2.48 ERA
1953	Al Rosen, Clev	Third base	43 HR†, 145 RBI†, 115 runs†, .336
1954	Yogi Berra, NY	Catcher	22 HR, 125 RBI, .307
1955	*Yogi Berra, NY	Catcher	27 HR, 108 RBI, .272
1956	*Mickey Mantle, NY	Outfield	52 HR†, 130 RBI†, 132 runs†, .353†
1957	*Mickey Mantle, NY	Outfield	34 HR, 94 RBI, 121 runs†, .365
1958	Jackie Jensen, Bos	Outfield	35 HR, 122 RBI†, .286
1959	*Nellie Fox, Chi	Second base	2 HR, 70 RBI, .306, GG
1960	*Roger Maris, NY	Outfield	39 HR, 112 RBI†, .283, GG
1961	*Roger Maris, NY	Outfield	61 HR†, 142 RBI†, .269
1962	*Mickey Mantle, NY	Outfield	30 HR, 89 RBI, .321, GG
1963	*Elston Howard, NY	Catcher	28 HR, 85 RBI, .287, GG
1964	Brooks Robinson, Balt	Third base	28 HR, 118 RBI†, .317, GG
1965	*Zoilo Versalles, Minn	Shortstop	126 runs†, 45 2B‡, 12 3B†, GG
1966	*Frank Robinson, Balt	Outfield	49 HR†, 122 RBI†, 122 runs†, .316†
1967	*Carl Yastrzemski, Bos	Outfield	44 HR‡, 121 RBI†, 112 runs†, .326†, GG
1968	*Denny McLain, Det	Pitcher	31†–6, 1.96 ERA, 280 K
1969	*Harmon Killebrew, Minn	Third base, First base	49 HR†, 140 RBI†, .276
1970	*Boog Powell, Balt	First base	35 HR, 114 RBI, .297
1971	*Vida Blue, Oak	Pitcher	24–8, 1.82 ERA†, 8 SO†, 301 K
1972	Dick Allen, Chi	First base	37 HR†, 113 RBI†, .308
1973	*Reggie Jackson, Oak	Outfield	32 HR†, 117 RBI†, 99 runs†, .293
1974	Jeff Burroughs, Tex	Outfield	25 HR, 118 RBI†, .301
1975	*Fred Lynn, Bos	Outfield	21 HR, 105 RBI, 103 runs†, .331, GG
1976	*Thurman Munson, NY	Catcher	17 HR, 105 RBI, .302
1977	Rod Carew, Minn	First base	100 RBI, 128 runs†, 239 hits†, .388†
1978	Jim Rice, Bos	Outfield, DH	46 HR†, 139 RBI†, 213 hits†, .315
1979	*Don Baylor, Calif	Outfield, DH	36 HR, 139 RBI†, 120 runs†, .296
1980	*George Brett, KC	Third base	24 HR, 118 RBI, .390†

Most Valuable Players (Cont.)
AMERICAN LEAGUE (Cont.)

Year	Name and Team	Position	Noteworthy
1981	*Rollie Fingers, Mil	Pitcher	6–3, 28 saves†, 1.04 ERA
1982	*Robin Yount, Mil	Shortstop	29 HR, 114 RBI, 210 hits†, .331, GG
1983	*Cal Ripken, Balt	Shortstop	27 HR, 102 RBI, 121 runs†, 211 hits†, .318
1984	*Willie Hernandez, Det	Pitcher	9–3, 32 saves, 1.92 ERA
1985	Don Mattingly, NY	First base	35 HR, 145 RBI†, 48 2B†, .324, GG
1986	*Roger Clemens, Bos	Pitcher	24†–4, 2.48 ERA†, 238 K
1987	George Bell, Tor	Outfield	47 HR, 134 RBI†, .308
1988	*Jose Canseco, Oak	Outfield	42 HR†, 124 RBI†, 40 SB, .307
1989	Robin Yount, Mil	Outfield	21 HR, 103 RBI, 101 runs, .318
1990	*Rickey Henderson, Oak	Outfield	28 HR, 119 runs†, 65 SB†, .325
1991	Cal Ripken Jr., Balt	Shortstop	34 HR, 114 RBI, .323
1992	Dennis Eckersley, Oak	Pitcher	7–1, 1.91 ERA, 51 saves
1993	Frank Thomas, Chi	First base	41 HR, 128 RBI, .317
1994	Frank Thomas, Chi	First base	38 HR, 101 RBI, .353
1995	*Mo Vaughn, Bos	First base	39 HR, 126 RBI, .300
1996	*Juan Gonzalez, Tex	Outfield	47 HR, 144 RBI, .314
1997	*Ken Griffey Jr., Sea	Outfield	56 HR†, 125 runs†, 393 TB†, 147 RBI†, .304
1998	*Juan Gonzalez, Tex	Outfield	45 HR, 157 RBI†, 50 2B†, .318

*Played for pennant or, after 1968, division winner. †Led league. ‡Tied for league lead.

Notes: 2B=doubles; 3B=triples; F.A.=fielding average; GG=won Gold Glove, award begun in 1957; K=strikeouts; SO=shutouts; SB=stolen bases; TB=total bases.

Rookies of the Year

NATIONAL LEAGUE

1947*	Jackie Robinson, Bklyn (1B)
1948*	Alvin Dark, Bos (SS)
1949	Don Newcombe, Bklyn (P)
1950	Sam Jethroe, Bos (OF)
1951	Willie Mays, NY (OF)
1952	Joe Black, Bklyn (P)
1953	Junior Gilliam, Bklyn (2B)
1954	Wally Moon, StL (OF)
1955	Bill Virdon, StL (OF)
1956	Frank Robinson, Cin (OF)
1957	Jack Sanford, Phil (P)
1958	Orlando Cepeda, SF (1B)
1959	Willie McCovey, SF (1B)
1960	Frank Howard, LA (OF)
1961	Billy Williams, Chi (OF)
1962	Ken Hubbs, Chi (2B)
1963	Pete Rose, Cin (2B)
1964	Dick Allen, Phil (3B)
1965	Jim Lefebvre, LA (2B)
1966	Tommy Helms, Cin (2B)
1967	Tom Seaver, NY (P)
1968	Johnny Bench, Cin (C)
1969	Ted Sizemore, LA (2B)
1970	Carl Morton, Mtl(P)
1971	Earl Williams, Atl (C)
1972	Jon Matlack, NY (P)
1973	Gary Matthews, SF (OF)
1974	Bake McBride, StL (OF)
1975	John Montefusco, SF (P)
1976	Pat Zachry, Cin (P)
	Butch Metzger, SD (P)
1977	Andre Dawson, Mtl (OF)
1978	Bob Horner, Atl (3B)
1979	Rick Sutcliffe, LA (P)
1980	Steve Howe, LA (P)
1981	Fernando Valenzuela, LA (P)
1982	Steve Sax, LA (2B)

AMERICAN LEAGUE

1949	Roy Sievers, StL (OF)
1950	Walt Dropo, Bos (1B)
1951	Gil McDougald, NY (3B)
1952	Harry Byrd, Phil (P)
1953	Harvey Kuenn, Det (SS)
1954	Bob Grim, NY (P)
1955	Herb Score, Clev (P)
1956	Luis Aparicio, Chi (SS)
1957	Tony Kubek, NY (OF, SS)
1958	Albie Pearson, Wash (OF)
1959	Bob Allison, Wash (OF)
1960	Ron Hansen, Balt (SS)
1961	Don Schwall, Bos (P)
1962	Tom Tresh, NY (SS)
1963	Gary Peters, Chi (P)
1964	Tony Oliva, Minn (OF)
1965	Curt Blefary, Balt (OF)
1966	Tommie Agee, Chi (OF)
1967	Rod Carew, Minn (2B)
1968	Stan Bahnsen, NY (P)
1969	Lou Piniella, KC (OF)
1970	Thurman Munson, NY (C)
1971	Chris Chambliss, Clev (1B)
1972	Carlton Fisk, Bos (C)
1973	Al Bumbry, Balt (OF)
1974	Mike Hargrove, Tex (1B)
1975	Fred Lynn, Bos (OF)
1976	Mark Fidrych, Det (P)
1977	Eddie Murray, Balt (DH)
1978	Lou Whitaker, Det (2B)
1979	Alfredo Griffin, Tor (SS)
	John Castino, Minn (3B)
1980	Joe Charboneau, Clev (OF)
1981	Dave Righetti, NY (P)
1982	Cal Ripken, Balt (SS)
1983	Ron Kittle, Chi (OF)
1984	Alvin Davis, Sea (1B)

*Just one selection for both leagues.

Rookies of the Year (Cont.)

NATIONAL LEAGUE (Cont.)	AMERICAN LEAGUE (Cont.)
1983 ....Darryl Strawberry, NY (OF)	1985 ....Ozzie Guillen, Chi (SS)
1984 ....Dwight Gooden, NY (P)	1986 ....Jose Canseco, Oak (OF)
1985 ....Vince Coleman, StL (OF)	1987 ....Mark McGwire, Oak (1B)
1986 ....Todd Worrell, StL (P)	1988 ....Walt Weiss, Oak (SS)
1987 ....Benito Santiago, SD (C)	1989 ....Gregg Olson, Balt (P)
1988 ....Chris Sabo, Cin (3B)	1990 ....Sandy Alomar Jr., Clev (C)
1989 ....Jerome Walton, Chi (OF)	1991 ....Chuck Knoblauch, Minn (2B)
1990 ....Dave Justice, Atl (OF)	1992 ....Pat Listach, Mil (SS)
1991 ....Jeff Bagwell, Hou (3B)	1993 ....Tim Salmon, Calif (OF)
1992 ....Eric Karros, LA (1B)	1994 ....Bob Hamelin, Minn (DH)
1993 ....Mike Piazza, LA (C)	1995 ....Marty Cordova, Minn (OF)
1994 ....Raul Mondesi, LA (OF)	1996 ....Derek Jeter, NY (SS)
1995 ....Hideo Nomo, LA (P)	1997 ....Nomar Garciaparra, Bos (SS)
1996 ....Todd Hollandsworth, LA (OF)	1998 ....Ben Grieve, Oak (OF)
1997 ....Scott Rolen, Phil (3B)	
1998 ....Kerry Wood, Chi (P)	

Cy Young Award

Year	W-L	Sv	ERA	Year	W-L	Sv	ERA
1956....*Don Newcombe, Bklyn (NL)	27–7	0	3.06	1962....Don Drysdale, LA (NL)	25–9	1	2.83
1957....Warren Spahn, Mil (NL)	21–11	3	2.69	1963....*Sandy Koufax, LA (NL)	25–5	0	1.88
1958....Bob Turley, NY (AL)	21–7	1	2.97	1964....Dean Chance, LA (AL)	20–9	4	1.65
1959....Early Wynn, Chi (AL)	22–10	0	3.17	1965....Sandy Koufax, LA (NL)	26–8	2	2.04
1960....Vernon Law, Pitt (NL)	20–9	0	3.08	1966....Sandy Koufax, LA (NL)	27–9	0	1.73
1961....Whitey Ford, NY (AL)	25–4	0	3.21				

NATIONAL LEAGUE

Year	W–L	Sv	ERA
1967.....Mike McCormick, SF	22–10	0	2.85
1968.....*Bob Gibson, StL	22–9	0	1.12
1969.....Tom Seaver, NY	25–7	0	2.21
1970.....Bob Gibson, StL	23–7	0	3.12
1971.....Ferguson Jenkins, Chi	24–13	0	2.77
1972.....Steve Carlton, Phil	27–10	0	1.97
1973.....Tom Seaver, NY	19–10	0	2.08
1974.....Mike Marshall, LA	15–12	21	2.42
1975.....Tom Seaver, NY	22–9	0	2.38
1976.....Randy Jones, SD	22–14	0	2.74
1977.....Steve Carlton, Phil	23–10	0	2.64
1978.....Gaylord Perry, SD	21–6	0	2.72
1979.....Bruce Sutter, Chi	6–6	37	2.23
1980.....Steve Carlton, Phil	24–9	0	2.34
1981.....Fernando Valenzuela, LA	13–7	0	2.48
1982.....Steve Carlton, Phil	23–11	0	3.10
1983.....John Denny, Phil	19–6	0	2.37
1984.....†Rick Sutcliffe, Chi	16–1	0	2.69
1985.....Dwight Gooden, NY	24–4	0	1.53
1986.....Mike Scott, Hou	18–10	0	2.22
1987.....Steve Bedrosian, Phil	5–3	40	2.83
1988.....Orel Hershiser, LA	23–8	1	2.26
1989.....Mark Davis, SD	4–3	44	1.85
1990.....Doug Drabek, Pitt	22–6	0	2.76
1991.....Tom Glavine, Atl	20–11	0	2.55
1992.....Greg Maddux, Chi	20–11	0	2.18
1993.....Greg Maddux, Atl	20–10	0	2.36
1994.....Greg Maddux, Atl	16–6	0	1.56
1995.....Greg Maddux, Atl	19–2	0	1.63
1996.....John Smoltz, Atl	24–8	0	2.94
1997.....Pedro Martinez, Mtl	17–8	0	1.90
1998.....Tom Glavine, Atl	20–6	0	2.47

AMERICAN LEAGUE

Year	W–L	Sv	ERA
1967.....Jim Lonborg, Bos	22–9	0	3.16
1968.....*Denny McLain, Det	31–6	0	1.96
1969.....Denny McLain, Det	24–9	0	2.80
.............Mike Cuellar, Balt	23–11	0	2.38
1970.....Jim Perry, Minn	24–12	0	3.03
1971.....*Vida Blue, Oak	24–8	0	1.82
1972.....Gaylord Perry, Clev	24–16	1	1.92
1973.....Jim Palmer, Balt	22–9	1	2.40
1974.....Catfish Hunter, Oak	25–12	0	2.49
1975.....Jim Palmer, Balt	23–11	1	2.09
1976.....Jim Palmer, Balt	22–13	0	2.51
1977.....Sparky Lyle, NY	13–5	26	2.17
1978.....Ron Guidry, NY	25–3	0	1.74
1979.....Mike Flanagan, Balt	23–9	0	3.08
1980.....Steve Stone, Balt	25–7	0	3.23
1981.....*Rollie Fingers, Mil	6–3	28	1.04
1982.....Pete Vuckovich, Mil	18–6	0	3.34
1983.....LaMarr Hoyt, Chi	24–10	0	3.66
1984.....*Willie Hernandez, Det	9–3	32	1.92
1985.....Bret Saberhagen, KC	20–6	0	2.87
1986.....*Roger Clemens, Bos	24–4	0	2.48
1987.....Roger Clemens, Bos	20–9	0	2.97
1988.....Frank Viola, Minn	24–7	0	2.64
1989.....Bret Saberhagen, KC	23–6	0	2.16
1990.....Bob Welch, Oak	27–6	0	2.95
1991.....Roger Clemens, Bos	18–10	0	2.62
1992.....*Dennis Eckersley, Oak	7–1	51	1.91
1993.....Jack McDowell, Chi	22–10	0	3.37
1994.....David Cone, KC	16–4	0	2.94
1995.....Randy Johnson, Sea	18–2	0	2.48
1996.....Pat Hentgen, Tor	20–10	0	3.22
1997.....Roger Clemens, Tor	21–7	0	2.05
1998.....Roger Clemens, Tor	20–6	0	2.65

*Pitchers who won- the MVP and Cy Young awards in the same season.

†NL games only. Sutcliffe pitched 15 games with Cleveland before being traded to the Cubs.

Career Individual Batting

GAMES

Pete Rose	3562
Carl Yastrzemski	3308
Hank Aaron	3298
Ty Cobb	3035
Stan Musial	3026
Eddie Murray	3026
Willie Mays	2992
Dave Winfield	2973
Rusty Staub	2951
Brooks Robinson	2896
Robin Yount	2856
Al Kaline	2834
Eddie Collins	2826
Reggie Jackson	2820
Frank Robinson	2808
Honus Wagner	2792
*Cal Ripken Jr.	2790
Tris Speaker	2789
Tony Perez	2777
*Rickey Henderson	2733

AT BATS

Pete Rose	14053
Hank Aaron	12364
Carl Yastrzemski	11988
Ty Cobb	11434
Eddie Murray	11336
Robin Yount	11008
Dave Winfield	11003
Stan Musial	10972
Willie Mays	10881
Paul Molitor	10835
*Cal Ripken Jr.	10765
Brooks Robinson	10654
Honus Wagner	10430
George Brett	10349
Lou Brock	10332
Luis Aparicio	10230
Tris Speaker	10195
Al Kaline	10116
Rabbit Maranville	10078
Frank Robinson	10006

HOME RUNS

Hank Aaron	755
Babe Ruth	714
Willie Mays	660
Frank Robinson	586
Harmon Killebrew	573
Reggie Jackson	563
Mike Schmidt	548
Mickey Mantle	536
Jimmie Foxx	534
*Mark McGwire	522
Ted Williams	521
Willie McCovey	521
Eddie Mathews	512
Ernie Banks	512
Mel Ott	511
Eddie Murray	504
Lou Gehrig	493
Willie Stargell	475
Stan Musial	475
Dave Winfield	465

HITS

Pete Rose	4256
Ty Cobb	4189
Hank Aaron	3771
Stan Musial	3630
Tris Speaker	3514
Carl Yastrzemski	3419
Honus Wagner	3415
Paul Molitor	3319
Eddie Collins	3312
Willie Mays	3283
Eddie Murray	3255
Nap Lajoie	3242
George Brett	3154
Paul Waner	3152
Robin Yount	3142
Dave Winfield	3110
*Tony Gwynn	3067
Rod Carew	3053
Lou Brock	3023
Al Kaline	3007

BATTING AVERAGE

Ty Cobb	.366
Rogers Hornsby	.358
Joe Jackson	.356
Ed Delahanty	.346
Tris Speaker	.345
Ted Williams	.344
Billy Hamilton	.344
Dan Brouthers	.342
Babe Ruth	.342
Harry Heilmann	.342
Pete Browning	.341
Willie Keeler	.341
Bill Terry	.341
George Sisler	.340
Lou Gehrig	.340
*Tony Gwynn	.339
Jesse Burkett	.338
Nap Lajoie	.338
Riggs Stephenson	.336
Al Simmons	.334

RUNS

Ty Cobb	2246
Babe Ruth	2174
Hank Aaron	2174
Pete Rose	2165
*Rickey Henderson	2103
Willie Mays	2062
Stan Musial	1949
Lou Gehrig	1888
Tris Speaker	1882
Mel Ott	1859
Frank Robinson	1829
Eddie Collins	1821
Carl Yastrzemski	1816
Ted Williams	1798
Paul Molitor	1782
Charlie Gehringer	1774
Jimmie Foxx	1751
Honus Wagner	1736
Jesse Burkett	1720
Cap Anson	1719
Willie Keeler	1719

DOUBLES

Tris Speaker	792
Pete Rose	746
Stan Musial	725
Ty Cobb	724
George Brett	665
Nap Lajoie	657
Carl Yastrzemski	646
Honus Wagner	640
Hank Aaron	624
Paul Waner	605
Paul Molitor	605
Robin Yount	583
*Wade Boggs	578
Charlie Gehringer	574
*Cal Ripken Jr.	571
Eddie Murray	560
Harry Heilmann	542
Rogers Hornsby	541
Joe Medwick	540
Dave Winfield	540

TRIPLES

Sam Crawford	309
Ty Cobb	295
Honus Wagner	252
Jake Beckley	243
Roger Connor	233
Tris Speaker	222
Fred Clarke	220
Dan Brouthers	205
Joe Kelley	194
Paul Waner	191
Bid McPhee	188
Eddie Collins	186
Ed Delahanty	185
Sam Rice	184
Jesse Burkett	182
Edd Roush	182
Ed Konetchy	181
Buck Ewing	178
Rabbit Maranville	177
Stan Musial	177

BASES ON BALLS

Babe Ruth	2056
Ted Williams	2019
*Rickey Henderson	1972
Joe Morgan	1865
Carl Yastrzemski	1845
Mickey Mantle	1733
Mel Ott	1708
Eddie Yost	1614
Darrell Evans	1605
Stan Musial	1599
Pete Rose	1566
Harmon Killebrew	1559
Lou Gehrig	1508
Mike Schmidt	1507
Eddie Collins	1499
Willie Mays	1464
Jimmie Foxx	1452
Eddie Mathews	1444
*Barry Bonds	1430
Frank Robinson	1420

* Active

Career Individual Batting (Cont.)

RUNS BATTED IN

Hank Aaron	2297
Babe Ruth	2213
Lou Gehrig	1995
Stan Musial	1951
Ty Cobb	1937
Jimmie Foxx	1922
Eddie Murray	1917
Willie Mays	1903
Cap Anson	1879
Mel Ott	1860
Carl Yastrzemski	1844
Ted Williams	1839
Dave Winfield	1833
Al Simmons	1827
Frank Robinson	1812
Honus Wagner	1732
Reggie Jackson	1702
Tony Perez	1652
Ernie Banks	1636
Goose Goslin	1609

SLUGGING AVERAGE

Babe Ruth	.690
Ted Williams	.634
Lou Gehrig	.632
Jimmie Foxx	.609
Hank Greenberg	.605
*Mark McGwire	.587
Joe DiMaggio	.579
Rogers Hornsby	.577
*Mike Piazza	.575
*Albert Belle	.573
*Frank Thomas	.573
*Juan Gonzalez	.572
*Ken Griffey Jr.	.569
*Larry Walker	.567
Johnny Mize	.562
Stan Musial	.559
*Barry Bonds	.559
Willie Mays	.557
Mickey Mantle	.557
Hank Aaron	.555

STOLEN BASES

*Rickey Henderson	1334
Lou Brock	938
Billy Hamilton	912
Ty Cobb	892
*Tim Raines	807
Vince Coleman	752
Eddie Collins	744
Arlie Latham	739
Max Carey	738
Honus Wagner	722
Joe Morgan	689
Willie Wilson	668
Tom Brown	657
Bert Campaneris	649
George Davis	616
Dummy Hoy	594
*Otis Nixon	620
Maury Wills	586
George Van Haltren	583
Ozzie Smith	580

PINCH HITS

Manny Mota	150
Smoky Burgess	145
Greg Gross	143
Jose Morales	123
Jerry Lynch	116
Red Lucas	114
Steve Braun	113
Terry Crowley	108
Denny Walling	108
Gates Brown	107
Mike Lum	103
Jim Dwyer	102
Rusty Staub	100
Larry Biittner	95
Vic Davalillo	95
Gerald Perry	95
Jerry Hairston	94
Dave Philley	93
Joel Youngblood	93
Jay Johnstone	92

TOTAL BASES

Hank Aaron	6856
Stan Musial	6134
Willie Mays	6066
Ty Cobb	5854
Babe Ruth	5793
Pete Rose	5752
Carl Yastrzemski	5539
Eddie Murray	5397
Frank Robinson	5373
Dave Winfield	5221
Tris Speaker	5101
Lou Gehrig	5060
George Brett	5044
Mel Ott	5041
Jimmie Foxx	4956
Ted Williams	4884
Honus Wagner	4862
*Cal Ripken Jr.	4856
Paul Molitor	4854
Al Kaline	4852

STRIKEOUTS

Reggie Jackson	2597
Willie Stargell	1936
Mike Schmidt	1883
Tony Perez	1867
Dave Kingman	1816
*Jose Canseco	1765
Bobby Bonds	1757
Dale Murphy	1748
Lou Brock	1730
Mickey Mantle	1710
Harmon Killebrew	1699
*Chili Davis	1698
Dwight Evans	1697
Dave Winfield	1686
*Andres Galarraga	1615
*Gary Gaetti	1599
Lee May	1570
Dick Allen	1556
Willie McCovey	1550
Dave Parker	1537

The 30–30 Club (30 HR, 30 SB in single season)

Year		HR	SB	Year		HR	SB
1922	Kenny Williams, StL	39	37	1991	Ron Gant, Atl	32	34
1956	Willie Mays, NYG	36	40	1991	Howard Johnson, NYM	38	30
1957	Willie Mays, NYG	35	38	1992	Barry Bonds, Pitt	34	39
1963	Hank Aaron, Mil	44	31	1993	Sammy Sosa, ChiC	33	36
1969	Bobby Bonds, SF	32	45	1995	Barry Bonds, SF	33	31
1970	Tommy Harper, Mil	31	38	1995	Sammy Sosa, ChiC	36	34
1973	Bobby Bonds, SF	39	43	1996	Barry Bonds, SF	42	40
1975	Bobby Bonds, NYY	32	30	1996	Ellis Burks, Col	40	32
1977	Bobby Bonds, Cal	37	41	1996	Barry Larkin, Cin	33	36
1978	Bobby Bonds, Chi/Tex	31	43	1996	Dante Bichette, Col	31	31
1983	Dale Murphy, Atl	36	30	1997	Larry Walker, Col	49	33
1987	Joe Carter, Clev	32	31	1997	Jeff Bagwell, Hou	43	31
1987	Eric Davis, Cin	37	50	1997	Raul Mondesi, LA	30	32
1987	Darryl Strawberry, NYM	39	36	1997	Barry Bonds, SF	40	37
1987	Howard Johnson, NYM	36	32	1998	Alex Rodriguez, Sea	42	46
1988	Jose Canseco, Oak	42	40	1998	Shawn Green, Tor	35	35
1989	Howard Johnson, NYM	36	41	1999	Jeff Bagwell, Hou	42	30
1990	Ron Gant, Atl	32	33	1999	Raul Mondesi, LA	33	36
1990	Barry Bonds, Pitt	33	52				

Career Individual Pitching

GAMES

*Jesse Orosco	1090
Dennis Eckersley	1071
Hoyt Wilhelm	1070
Kent Tekulve	1050
Lee Smith	1022
Goose Gossage	1002
Lindy McDaniel	987
Rollie Fingers	944
Gene Garber	931
Cy Young	906
Sparky Lyle	899
Jim Kaat	898
*Paul Assenmacher	884
Jeff Reardon	880
*John Franco	878
Don McMahon	874
Phil Niekro	864
Charlie Hough	858
Roy Face	848
Tug McGraw	824

INNINGS PITCHED

Cy Young	7356.2
Pud Galvin	5941.1
Walter Johnson	5914.2
Phil Niekro	5404.1
Nolan Ryan	5386.0
Gaylord Perry	5350.1
Don Sutton	5282.1
Warren Spahn	5243.2
Steve Carlton	5217.1
Grover Alexander	5190.0
Kid Nichols	5056.1
Tim Keefe	5047.1
Bert Blyleven	4970.0
Mickey Welch	4802.0
Tom Seaver	4782.2
Christy Mathewson	4780.2
Tommy John	4710.1
Robin Roberts	4688.2
Early Wynn	4564.0
John Clarkson	4536.1

WINS

Cy Young	511
Walter Johnson	417
Grover Alexander	373
Christy Mathewson	373
Warren Spahn	363
Kid Nichols	361
Pud Galvin	360
Tim Keefe	342
Steve Carlton	329
John Clarkson	328
Eddie Plank	326
Nolan Ryan	324
Don Sutton	324
Phil Niekro	318
Gaylord Perry	314
Tom Seaver	311
Charley Radbourn	309
Mickey Welch	307
Lefty Grove	300
Early Wynn	300

LOSSES

Cy Young	316
Pud Galvin	308
Nolan Ryan	292
Walter Johnson	279
Phil Niekro	274
Gaylord Perry	265
Don Sutton	256
Jack Powell	254
Eppa Rixey	251
Bert Blyleven	250
Robin Roberts	245
Warren Spahn	245
Steve Carlton	244
Early Wynn	244
Jim Kaat	237
Frank Tanana	236
Gus Weyhing	232
Tommy John	231
Bob Friend	230
Ted Lyons	230

WINNING PERCENTAGE

Dave Foutz	.690
Whitey Ford	.690
Bob Caruthers	.688
Lefty Grove	.680
*Mike Mussina	.673
Vic Raschi	.667
Larry Corcoran	.665
Christy Mathewson	.665
Sam Leever	.660
Sal Maglie	.657
Sandy Koufax	.655
Johnny Allen	.654
Ron Guidry	.651
Lefty Gomez	.649
John Clarkson	.648
*Roger Clemens	.648
Three Finger Brown	.648
*Randy Johnson	.645
Dizzy Dean	.644
Pete Alexander	.642

SAVES

Lee Smith	478
*John Franco	416
Dennis Eckersley	390
Jeff Reardon	367
Randy Myers	347
Rollie Fingers	341
Tom Henke	311
Goose Gossage	310
*Jeff Montgomery	304
*Doug Jones	301
Bruce Sutter	300
*John Wetteland	296
*Rick Aguilera	289
*Rod Beck	260
Dave Righetti	252
Todd Worrell	252
Dan Quisenberry	244
Sparky Lyle	238
*Roberto Hernandez	234
*Trevor Hoffman	228

EARNED RUN AVERAGE

Ed Walsh	1.82
Addie Joss	1.89
Three Finger Brown	2.06
John Ward	2.10
Christy Mathewson	2.13
Rube Waddell	2.16
Walter Johnson	2.17
Orval Overall	2.23
Tommy Bond	2.25
Ed Reulbach	2.28
Will White	2.28
Jim Scott	2.30
Eddie Plank	2.35
Larry Corcoran	2.36
Eddie Cicotte	2.38
Ed Killian	2.38
George McQuillan	2.38
Doc White	2.39
Nap Rucker	2.42
Terry Larkin	2.43
Jim McCormick	2.43
Jeff Tesreau	2.43

SHUTOUTS

Walter Johnson	110
Grover Alexander	90
Christy Mathewson	79
Cy Young	76
Eddie Plank	69
Warren Spahn	63
Nolan Ryan	61
Tom Seaver	61
Bert Blyleven	60
Don Sutton	58
Pud Galvin	57
Ed Walsh	57
Bob Gibson	56
Three Finger Brown	55
Steve Carlton	55
Jim Palmer	53
Gaylord Perry	53
Juan Marichal	52
Rube Waddell	50
Vic Willis	50

COMPLETE GAMES

Cy Young	749
Pud Galvin	639
Tim Keefe	554
Walter Johnson	531
Kid Nichols	531
Mickey Welch	525
Charley Radbourn	489
John Clarkson	485
Tony Mullane	468
Jim McCormick	466
Gus Weyhing	448
Grover Alexander	437
Christy Mathewson	434
Jack Powell	422
Eddie Plank	410
Will White	394
Amos Rusie	392
Vic Willis	388
Warren Spahn	382
Jim Whitney	377

* Active

Career Individual Pitching (Cont.)

STRIKEOUTS		BASES ON BALLS	
Nolan Ryan	5714	Nolan Ryan	2795
Steve Carlton	4136	Steve Carlton	1833
Bert Blyleven	3701	Phil Niekro	1809
Tom Seaver	3640	Early Wynn	1775
Don Sutton	3574	Bob Feller	1764
Gaylord Perry	3534	Bobo Newsom	1732
Walter Johnson	3509	Amos Rusie	1704
Phil Niekro	3342	Charlie Hough	1665
*Roger Clemens	3316	Gus Weyhing	1566
Ferguson Jenkins	3192	Red Ruffing	1541
Bob Gibson	3117	Bump Hadley	1442
Jim Bunning	2855	Warren Spahn	1434
Mickey Lolich	2832	Earl Whitehill	1431
Cy Young	2803	Tony Mullane	1408
Frank Tanana	2773	Sad Sam Jones	1396
*Randy Johnson	2693	Jack Morris	1390
Warren Spahn	2583	Tom Seaver	1390
Bob Feller	2581	Gaylord Perry	1379
Jerry Koosman	2556	Mike Torrez	1371
Tim Keefe	2543	Walter Johnson	1363

Alltime Winningest Managers

CAREER

	W	L	Pct	Yrs		W	L	Pct	Yrs
Connie Mack	3755	3967	.486	53	*Tony LaRussa	1662	1532	.520	21
John McGraw	2810	1987	.586	33	Ralph Houk	1627	1539	.514	20
Sparky Anderson	2238	1855	.547	26	Fred Clarke	1609	1189	.575	19
Bucky Harris	2168	2228	.493	29	Dick Williams	1592	1474	.519	21
Joe McCarthy	2155	1346	.616	24	Tommy Lasorda	1589	1434	.526	20
Walter Alston	2063	1634	.558	23	*Bobby Cox	1576	1242	.559	18
Leo Durocher	2015	1717	.540	24	Earl Weaver	1506	1080	.582	17
Casey Stengel	1942	1868	.510	25	Clark Griffith	1491	1367	.522	20
Gene Mauch	1907	2044	.483	26	Miller Huggins	1431	1149	.555	17
Bill McKechnie	1904	1737	.523	25	Al Lopez	1412	1012	.583	17

REGULAR SEASON

	W	L	Pct	Yrs		W	L	Pct	Yrs
Connie Mack	3731	3948	.486	53	*Tony LaRussa	1639	1511	.520	21
John McGraw	2784	1959	.587	33	Ralph Houk	1619	1531	.514	20
Sparky Anderson	2194	1834	.545	26	Fred Clarke	1602	1181	.576	19
Bucky Harris	2157	2218	.493	29	Dick Williams	1571	1451	.520	21
Joe McCarthy	2125	1333	.615	24	Tommy Lasorda	1558	1404	.526	20
Walter Alston	2040	1613	.558	23	*Bobby Cox	1521	1204	.558	18
Leo Durocher	2008	1709	.540	24	Clark Griffith	1491	1367	.522	20
Casey Stengel	1905	1842	.508	25	Earl Weaver	1480	1060	.583	17
Gene Mauch	1902	2037	.483	26	Miller Huggins	1413	1134	.555	17
Bill McKechnie	1896	1723	.524	25	Al Lopez	1410	1004	.584	17

WORLD SERIES

	W	L	T	Pct	App	WS		W	L	T	Pct	App	WS
Casey Stengel	37	26	0	.587	10	7	Bucky Harris	11	10	0	.524	3	2
Joe McCarthy	30	13	0	.698	9	7	Billy Southworth	11	11	0	.500	4	2
John McGraw	26	28	2	.482	9	2	Earl Weaver	11	13	0	.458	4	1
Connie Mack	24	19	0	.558	8	5	*Bobby Cox	11	18	0	.379	5	1
Walter Alston	20	20	0	.500	7	4	Whitey Herzog	10	11	0	.476	3	1
Miller Huggins	18	15	1	.544	6	3	Bill Carrigan	8	2	0	.800	2	2
Sparky Anderson	16	12	0	.571	5	3	Cito Gaston	8	4	0	.667	2	2
*Joe Torre	12	2	0	.857	3	3	Danny Murtaugh	8	6	0	.571	2	2
Tommy Lasorda	12	11	0	.522	4	2	*Tom Kelly	8	6	0	.571	2	2
Dick Williams	12	14	0	.462	4	2	Ralph Houk	8	8	0	.500	3	2
Frank Chance	11	9	1	.548	4	2	Bill McKechnie	8	14	0	.364	4	2

* Active

Individual Batting (Single Season)

HITS

George Sisler, 1920............257
Lefty O'Doul, 1929..............254
Bill Terry, 1930....................254
Al Simmons, 1925................253
Rogers Hornsby, 1922.........250
Chuck Klein, 1930 250
Ty Cobb, 1911.....................248
George Sisler, 1922.............246
Heinie Manush, 1928...........241
Babe Herman, 1930 241

BATTING AVERAGE

Hugh Duffy, 1894............... .440
Tip O'Neill, 1887 .... .435
Ross Barnes, 1876 .... .429
Nap Lajoie, 1901 .... .426
Willie Keeler, 1897 .... .424
Rogers Hornsby, 1924....... .424
George Sisler, 1922........... .420
Ty Cobb, 1911................... .420
Fred Dunlap, 1884............. .412
Ed Delahanty, 1899 .... .410

DOUBLES

Earl Webb, 1931 67
George Burns, 1926 64
Joe Medwick, 1936...............64
Hank Greenberg, 1934.........63
Paul Waner, 1932 62
Charlie Gehringer, 1936 60
Tris Speaker, 1923...............59
Chuck Klein, 1930 59
Billy Herman, 1936 57
Billy Herman, 1935 57

TOTAL BASES

Babe Ruth, 1921..................457
Rogers Hornsby, 1922.........450
Lou Gehrig, 1927.................447
Chuck Klein, 1930 445
Jimmie Foxx, 1932..............438
Stan Musial, 1948 429
Hack Wilson, 1930...............423
Chuck Klein, 1932 420
Lou Gehrig, 1930.................419
Joe DiMaggio, 1937 418

TRIPLES

Chief Wilson, 1912................36
Dave Orr, 1886 31
Heinie Reitz, 1894.................31
Perry Werden, 1893..............29
Harry Davis, 1897 28
George Davis, 1893...............27
Sam Thompson, 1894............27
Jimmy Williams, 1899 27
John Reilly, 1890 26
George Treadway, 1894.........26
Joe Jackson, 1912.................26
Sam Crawford, 1914..............26
Kiki Cuyler, 1925...................26

HOME RUNS

Mark McGwire, 1998 70
Sammy Sosa, 1998................66
Mark McGwire, 1999 65
Sammy Sosa, 1999................63
Roger Maris, 1961.................61
Babe Ruth, 1927...................60
Babe Ruth, 1921...................59
Jimmie Foxx, 1932................58
Hank Greenberg, 1938..........58
Mark McGwire, 1997 58

RUNS BATTED IN

Hack Wilson, 1930...............190
Lou Gehrig, 1931.................184
Hank Greenberg, 1937.........183
Lou Gehrig, 1927.................175
Jimmie Foxx, 1938...............175
Lou Gehrig, 1930.................174
Babe Ruth, 1921..................171
Chuck Klein, 1930 170
Hank Greenberg, 1935.........170
Jimmie Foxx, 1932...............169

STRIKEOUTS

Bobby Bonds, 1970.............189
Bobby Bonds, 1969.............187
Rob Deer, 1987 186
Pete Incaviglia, 1986 185
Cecil Fielder, 1990...............182
Mike Schmidt, 1975.............180
Rob Deer, 1986 179
Dave Nicholson, 1963 175
Gorman Thomas, 1979.........175
Jose Canseco, 1986.............175
Rob Deer, 1991 175
Jay Buhner, 1997.................175

RUNS

Billy Hamilton, 1894.............192
Tom Brown, 1891.................177
Babe Ruth, 1921..................177
Tip O'Neill, 1887 167
Lou Gehrig, 1936.................167
Billy Hamilton, 1895.............166
Willie Keeler, 1894...............165
Joe Kelley, 1894 165
Arlie Latham, 1887...............163
Babe Ruth, 1928..................163
Lou Gehrig, 1931.................163

STOLEN BASES

Hugh Nicol, 1887.................138
Rickey Henderson, 1982.....130
Arlie Latham, 1887...............129
Lou Brock, 1974 118
Charlie Comiskey, 1887.......117
John Ward, 1887 111
Billy Hamilton, 1889.........1..111
Billy Hamilton, 1891.............111
Vince Coleman, 1985 110
Arlie Latham, 1888...............109
Vince Coleman, 1987 109

BASES ON BALLS

Babe Ruth, 1923..................170
Ted Williams, 1947...............162
Ted Williams, 1949 162
Mark McGwire, 1998 162
Ted Williams, 1946...............156
Eddie Yost, 1956 151
Eddie Joost, 1949.................149
Jeff Bagwell, 1999................149
Babe Ruth, 1920..................148
Eddie Stanky, 1945..............148
Jimmy Wynn, 1969...............148

SLUGGING AVERAGE

Babe Ruth, 1920................ .847
Babe Ruth, 1921................ .846
Babe Ruth, 1927................ .772
Lou Gehrig, 1927................ .765
Babe Ruth, 1923................ .764
Rogers Hornsby, 1925........ .756
Mark McGwire, 1998 .... .752
Jeff Bagwell, 1994.............. .750
Jimmie Foxx, 1932............. .749
Babe Ruth, 1924................ .739

Individual Pitching (Single Season)

GAMES

Mike Marshall, 1974.............106
Kent Tekulve, 1979................94
Mike Marshall, 1973..............92
Kent Tekulve, 1978................91
Wayne Granger, 1969 90
Mike Marshall, 1979..............90
Kent Tekulve, 1987................90
Mark Eichhorn, 1987.............89
Wilbur Wood, 1968 88
Mike Myers, 1997.................88

GAMES STARTED

Will White, 1879 75
Jim Galvin, 1883.....................75
Jim McCormick, 1880.............74
Charley Radbourn, 1884 73
Guy Hecker, 1884..................73
Jim Galvin, 1884....................72
John Clarkson, 1889..............72
Bill Hutchison, 1892...............71
John Clarkson, 1885..............70
Matt Kilroy, 1887...................69

INNINGS PITCHED

Will White, 1878 ....680.0
Charley Radbourn, 1884....678.2
Guy Hecker, 1884...............670.2
Jim McCormick, 1880.......657.2
Jim Galvin, 1883................656.1
Jim Galvin, 1884................636.1
Charley Radbourn, 1883....632.1
Bill Hutchison, 1892..........627.0
John Clarkson, 1885..........623.0
Jim Devlin, 1876 ....622.0

WINS

Charley Radbourn, 1884 59
John Clarkson, 1885..............53
Guy Hecker, 1884..................52
John Clarkson, 1889..............49
Charley Radbourn, 1883 48
Charlie Buffinton, 1884 48
Al Spalding, 1876 47
John Ward, 1879 47
Jim Galvin, 1883....................46
Jim Galvin, 1884....................46
Matt Kilroy, 1887...................46

LOSSES

John Coleman, 1883..............48
Will White, 1880 42
Larry McKeon, 1884 41
George Bradley, 1879............40
Jim McCormick, 1879...........40
Henry Porter, 1888.................37
Kid Carsey, 1891...................37
George Cobb, 1892...............37
Stump Weidman, 1886 36
Bill Hutchison, 1892..............36

WINNING PERCENTAGE

Roy Face, 1959.....................947
Johnny Allen, 1937 938
Greg Maddux, 1995 905
Randy Johnson, 1995............900
Ron Guidry, 1978...............893
Freddie Fitzsimmons, 1940....889
Lefty Grove, 1931 886
Bob Stanley, 1978................882
Preacher Roe, 1951...........880
Fred Goldsmith, 1880 875
Tom Seaver, 1981...............875

SAVES

Bobby Thigpen, 1990............57
Randy Myers, 1993................53
Trevor Hoffman, 1998............53
Dennis Eckersley, 1992........51
Rod Beck, 1998 51
Dennis Eckersley, 1990 48
Rod Beck, 1993 48
Jeff Shaw, 1998.....................48
Lee Smith, 1991....................47
Lee Smith, 1993....................46
Dave Righetti, 1986 46
Bryan Harvey, 1991...............46
Jose Mesa, 1995 46
Tom Gordon, 1998.................46

EARNED RUN AVERAGE

Tim Keefe, 1880..................0.86
Dutch Leonard, 1914...........0.96
Three Finger Brown, 1906....1.04
Bob Gibson, 1968................1.12
Christy Mathewson, 1909 ...1.14
Walter Johnson, 1913.........1.14
Jack Pfiester, 1907 ....1.15
Addie Joss, 1908.................1.16
Carl Lundgren, 1907............1.17
Denny Driscoll, 1882 ....1.21

SHUTOUTS

George Bradley, 1876 16
Grover Alexander, 1916 16
Jack Coombs, 1910...............13
Bob Gibson, 1968..................13
Jim Galvin, 1884....................12
Ed Morris, 1886 12
Grover Alexander, 1915 12
Tommy Bond, 1879 11
Charley Radbourn, 1884 11
Dave Foutz, 1886..................11
Christy Mathewson, 1908 11
Ed Walsh, 1908.....................11
Walter Johnson, 1913............11
Sandy Koufax, 1963 11
Dean Chance, 1964...............11

COMPLETE GAMES

Will White, 1879 75
Charley Radbourn, 1884 73
Jim McCormick, 1880.............72
Jim Galvin, 1883....................72
Guy Hecker, 1884..................72
Jim Galvin, 1884....................71
Tim Keefe, 1883....................68
John Clarkson, 1885..............68
John Clarkson, 1889..............68
Bill Hutchison, 1892..............67

STRIKEOUTS

Matt Kilroy, 1886..................513
Toad Ramsey, 1886..............499
Hugh Daily, 1884.................483
Dupee Shaw, 1884................451
Charley Radbourn, 1884 441
Charlie Buffinton, 1884 417
Guy Hecker, 1884................385
Nolan Ryan, 1973 383
Sandy Koufax, 1965 382
Bill Sweeney, 1884...............374

BASES ON BALLS

Amos Rusie, 1890.................289
Mark Baldwin, 1889..............274
Amos Rusie, 1892.................267
Amos Rusie, 1891.................262
Mark Baldwin, 1890..............249
Jack Stivetts, 1891................232
Mark Baldwin, 1891..............227
Phil Knell, 1891.....................226
Bob Barr, 1890 219
Amos Rusie 1893.................218

Manager of the Year

NATIONAL LEAGUE		AMERICAN LEAGUE	
1983	Tommy Lasorda, LA	1983	Tony La Russa, Chi
1984	Jim Frey, Chi	1984	Sparky Anderson, Det
1985	Whitey Herzog, StL	1985	Bobby Cox, Tor
1986	Hal Lanier, Hou	1986	John McNamara, Bos
1987	Buck Rodgers, Mtl	1987	Sparky Anderson, Det
1988	Tommy Lasorda, LA	1988	Tony La Russa, Oak
1989	Don Zimmer, Chi	1989	Frank Robinson, Balt
1990	Jim Leyland, Pitt	1990	Jeff Torborg, Chi
1991	Bobby Cox, Atl	1991	Tom Kelly, Minn
1992	Jim Leyland, Pitt	1992	Tony La Russa, Oak
1993	Dusty Baker, SF	1993	Gene Lamont, Chi
1994	Felipe Alou, Mtl	1994	Buck Showalter, NY
1995	Don Baylor, Col	1995	Lou Piniella, Sea
1996	Bruce Bochy, SD	1996	Joe Torre, NY
1997	Dusty Baker, SF		Johnny Oates, Tex
1998	Larry Dierker, Hou	1997	Davey Johnson, Balt
		1998	Joe Torre, NY

Individual Batting (Single Game)

MOST RUNS

7 .... Guy Hecker, Lou   Aug 15, 1886

MOST HITS

7 .... Wilbert Robinson, Balt   June 10, 1892
Rennie Stennett, Pitt   Sept 16, 1975

MOST HOME RUNS

4 .... Bobby Lowe, Bos (N)   May 30, 1894
Ed Delahanty, Phil   July 13, 1896
Lou Gehrig, NY (A)   June 3, 1932
Gil Hodges, Bklyn   Aug 31, 1950
Joe Adcock, Mil (N)   July 31, 1954
Rocky Colavito, Clev   June 10, 1959
Willie Mays, SF   April 30, 1961
Bob Horner, Atl   July 6, 1986
Mark Whiten, StL   Sept 7, 1993

MOST GRAND SLAMS

2 .... Tony Lazzeri, NY (A)   May 24, 1936
Jim Tabor, Bos (A)   July 4, 1939
Rudy York, Bos (A)   July 27, 1946
Jim Gentile, Balt   May 9, 1961
Tony Cloninger, Atl   July 3, 1966
Jim Northrup, Det   June 24, 1968
Frank Robinson, Balt   June 26, 1970
Robin Ventura, Chi (A) Sept 4, 1995
Fernando Tatis, StL   Apr 23, 1999
N. Garciaparra, Bos   May 10, 1999

MOST RBI

12 ..... Jim Bottomley, StL   Sept 16, 1924
Mark Whiten, StL   Sept 7, 1993

Individual Batting (Single Inning)

MOST RUNS

3 .... Tommy Burns, Chi (N)   Sept 6, 1883, 7th inning
Ned Williamson, Chi (N) Sept 6, 1883, 7th inning
Sammy White, Bos (A)   June 18, 1953,
7th inning

MOST HITS

3 .... Tommy Burns, Chi (N)   Sept 6, 1883, 7th inning
Fred Pfeiffer, Chi (N)   Sept 6, 1883, 7th inning
Ned Williamson, Chi (N) Sept 6, 1883, 7th inning
Gene Stephens, Bos (A) June 18, 1953,
7th inning

MOST RBI

8 .... Fernando Tatis, StL   Apr 23, 1999   3rd inning

Note: All single-game hitting records for nine-inning game.

Individual Pitching (Single Game)

MOST INNINGS PITCHED

26 .....Leon Cadore, Bklyn	May 1, 1920, tie 1–1
Joe Oeschger, Bos (N)	May 1, 1920, tie 1–1

MOST RUNS ALLOWED

24 .....Al Travers, Det   May 18, 1912

MOST HITS ALLOWED

36 .....Jack Wadsworth, Lou   Aug 17, 1894

MOST STRIKEOUTS

20 .....Roger Clemens, Bos (A)	April 29, 1986
20 .....Roger Clemens, Bos (A)	Sept 18, 1996
20 .....Kerry Wood, Chi (N)	May 6, 1998

MOST WALKS ALLOWED

16 .....Bill George, NY (N)	May 30, 1887
George Van Haltren, Chi (N)	June 27, 1887
Henry Gruber, Clev	Apr 19, 1890
Bruno Haas, Phil (A)	June 2, 1915

MOST WILD PITCHES

6 .......J.R. Richard, Hou	April 10, 1979
Phil Niekro, Atl	Aug 14, 1979
Bill Gullickson, Mtl	April 10, 1982

Individual Pitching (Single Inning)

MOST RUNS ALLOWED

13 .....Lefty O'Doul, Bos (A)   July 7, 1923

MOST WALKS ALLOWED

8 ....Dolly Gray, Wash   Aug 28, 1909

MOST WILD PITCHES

4 ....Walter Johnson, Wash	Sept 21, 1914
Phil Niekro, Atl	Aug 14, 1979

Miscellaneous

LONGEST GAME, BY INNINGS

26 .....Brooklyn 1, Boston 1   May 1, 1920

LONGEST NINE-INNING GAME, BY TIME

4:21...New York 13, Baltimore 10   April 30, 1996

Baseball Hall of Fame

Players

Name	Position	Career	Selected	Name	Position	Career	Selected
Hank Aaron	OF	1954–76	1982	Frank Chance	1B	1898–1914	1946
Grover Alexander	P	1911–30	1938	Oscar Charleston*	OF		1976
Cap Anson	1B	1876–97	1939	Jack Chesbro	P	1899–1909	1946
Luis Aparicio	SS	1956–73	1984	Fred Clarke	OF	1894–1915	1945
Luke Appling	SS	1930–50	1964	John Clarkson	P	1882–94	1963
Richie Ashburn	OF	1948–62	1995	Roberto Clemente	OF	1955–72	1973
Earl Averill	OF	1929–41	1975	Ty Cobb	OF	1905–28	1936
Frank Baker	3B	1908–22	1955	Mickey Cochrane	C	1925–37	1947
Dave Bancroft	SS	1915–30	1971	Eddie Collins	2B	1906–30	1939
Ernie Banks	SS-1B	1953–71	1977	Jimmy Collins	3B	1895–1908	1945
Jake Beckley	1B	1888–1907	1971	Earle Combs	OF	1924–35	1970
Cool Papa Bell*	OF		1974	Roger Connor	1B	1880–97	1976
Johnny Bench	C	1967–83	1989	Stan Coveleski	P	1912–28	1969
Chief Bender	P	1903–25	1953	Sam Crawford	OF	1899–1917	1957
Yogi Berra	C	1946–65	1972	Joe Cronin	SS	1926–45	1956
Jim Bottomley	1B	1922–37	1974	Candy Cummings	P	1872–77	1939
Lou Boudreau	SS	1938–52	1970	Kiki Cuyler	OF	1921–38	1968
Roger Bresnahan	C	1897–1915	1945	Ray Dandridge*	3B		1987
George Brett	3B	1973–93	1999	George Davis	SS	1890–1909	1998
Lou Brock	OF	1961–79	1985	Leon Day*	P		1995
Dan Brouthers	1B	1879–1904	1945	Dizzy Dean	P	1930–47	1953
Three Finger Brown	P	1903–16	1949	Ed Delahanty	OF	1888–1903	1945
Jim Bunning	P	1955–1971	1996	Bill Dickey	C	1928–46	1954
Jesse Burkett	OF	1890–1905	1946	Martin Dihigo*	P-OF		1977
Roy Campanella	C	1948–57	1969	Joe DiMaggio	OF	1936–51	1955
Rod Carew	1B-2B	1967–85	1991	Larry Doby	OF	1947–59	1998
Max Carey	OF	1910–29	1961	Bobby Doerr	2B	1937–51	1986
Steve Carlton	P	1965–88	1994	Don Drysdale	P	1956–69	1984
Orlando Cepeda	1B	1958–74	1999	Hugh Duffy	OF	1888–1906	1945

Note: Career dates indicate first and last appearances in the majors.

*Elected on the basis of his career in the Negro leagues.

Players (Cont.)

	Position	Career	Selected		Position	Career	Selected
Johnny Evers	2B	1902–29	1939	Christy Mathewson	P	1900–16	1936
Buck Ewing	C	1880–97	1946	Willie Mays	OF	1951–73	1979
Red Faber	P	1914–33	1964	Tommy McCarthy	OF	1884–96	1946
Bob Feller	P	1936–56	1962	Willie McCovey	1B	1959–80	1986
Rick Ferrell	C	1929–47	1984	Joe McGinnity	P	1899–1908	1946
Rollie Fingers	P	1968–85	1992	Joe Medwick	OF	1932–48	1968
Elmer Flick	OF	1898–1910	1963	Johnny Mize	1B	1936–53	1981
Whitey Ford	P	1950–67	1974	Joe Morgan	2B	1963–84	1990
Bill Foster*	P		1996	Stan Musial	OF-1B	1941–63	1969
Nellie Fox	2B	1947–65	1997	Hal Newhouser	P	1939–55	1992
Jimmie Foxx	1B	1925–45	1951	Kid Nichols	P	1890–1906	1949
Frankie Frisch	2B	1919–37	1947	Phil Niekro	P	1964–87	1997
Pud Galvin	P	1879–92	1965	Jim O'Rourke	OF	1876–1904	1945
Lou Gehrig	1B	1923–39	1939	Mel Ott	OF	1926–47	1951
Charlie Gehringer	2B	1924–42	1949	Satchel Paige*	P	1948–65	1971
Bob Gibson	P	1959–75	1981	Jim Palmer	P	1965–84	1990
Josh Gibson*	C		1972	Herb Pennock	P	1912–34	1948
Lefty Gomez	P	1930–43	1972	Gaylord Perry	P	1962–83	1991
Goose Goslin	OF	1921–38	1968	Eddie Plank	P	1901–17	1946
Hank Greenberg	1B	1930–47	1956	Charley Radbourn	P	1880–91	1939
Burleigh Grimes	P	1916–34	1964	Pee Wee Reese	SS	1940–58	1984
Lefty Grove	P	1925–41	1947	Sam Rice	OF	1915–35	1963
Chick Hafey	OF	1924–37	1971	Eppa Rixey	P	1912–33	1963
Jesse Haines	P	1918–37	1970	Phil Rizzuto	SS	1941–56	1994
Billy Hamilton	OF	1888–1901	1961	Robin Roberts	P	1948–66	1976
Gabby Hartnett	C	1922–41	1955	Brooks Robinson	3B	1955–77	1983
Harry Heilmann	OF	1914–32	1952	Frank Robinson	OF	1956–76	1982
Billy Herman	2B	1931–47	1975	Jackie Robinson	2B	1947–56	1962
Harry Hooper	OF	1909–25	1971	Joe (Bullet) Rogan*	P		1998
Rogers Hornsby	2B	1915–37	1942	Edd Roush	OF	1913–31	1962
Waite Hoyt	P	1918–38	1969	Red Ruffing	P	1924–47	1967
Carl Hubbell	P	1928–43	1947	Amos Rusie	P	1889–1901	1977
Catfish Hunter	P	1965–79	1987	Babe Ruth	OF	1914–35	1936
Monte Irvin*	OF	1949–56	1973	Nolan Ryan	P	1966–93	1999
Reggie Jackson	OF	1967–87	1993	Ray Schalk	C	1912–29	1955
Travis Jackson	SS	1922–36	1982	Mike Schmidt	3B	1972–89	1995
Ferguson Jenkins	P	1965–83	1991	Red Schoendienst	2B	1945–63	1989
Hugh Jennings	SS	1891–1918	1945	Tom Seaver	P	1967–86	1992
Judy Johnson*	3B		1975	Joe Sewell	SS	1920–33	1977
Walter Johnson	P	1907–27	1936	Al Simmons	OF	1924–44	1953
Addie Joss	P	1902–10	1978	George Sisler	1B	1915–30	1939
Al Kaline	OF	1953–74	1980	Enos Slaughter	OF	1938–59	1985
Tim Keefe	P	1880–93	1964	Duke Snider	OF	1947–64	1980
Willie Keeler	OF	1892–1910	1939	Warren Spahn	P	1942–65	1973
George Kell	3B	1943–57	1983	Al Spalding	P	1871–78	1939
Joe Kelley	OF	1891–1908	1971	Tris Speaker	OF	1907–28	1937
George Kelly	1B	1915–32	1973	Willie Stargell	OF-1B	1962–82	1988
King Kelly	C	1878–93	1945	Don Sutton	P	1966–88	1998
Harmon Killebrew	1B-3B	1954–75	1984	Bill Terry	1B	1923–36	1954
Ralph Kiner	OF	1946–55	1975	Sam Thompson	OF	1885–1906	1974
Chuck Klein	OF	1928–44	1980	Joe Tinker	SS	1902–16	1946
Sandy Koufax	P	1955–66	1972	Pie Traynor	3B	1920–37	1948
Nap Lajoie	2B	1896–1916	1937	Dazzy Vance	P	1915–35	1955
Tony Lazzeri	2B	1926–39	1991	Arky Vaughan	SS	1932–48	1985
Bob Lemon	P	1941–58	1976	Rube Waddell	P	1897–1910	1946
Buck Leonard*	1B		1977	Honus Wagner	SS	1897–1917	1936
Fred Lindstrom	3B	1924–36	1976	Bobby Wallace	SS	1894–1918	1953
Pop Lloyd*	SS-1B		1977	Ed Walsh	P	1904–17	1946
Ernie Lombardi	C	1931–47	1986	Lloyd Waner	OF	1927–45	1967
Ted Lyons	P	1923–46	1955	Paul Waner	OF	1926–45	1952
Mickey Mantle	OF	1951–68	1974	John Ward	2B-P	1878–94	1964
Heinie Manush	OF	1923–39	1964	Mickey Welch	P	1880–92	1973
Rabbit Maranville	SS-2B	1912–35	1954	Willie Wells*	SS	1924–49	1997
Juan Marichal	P	1960–75	1983	Zach Wheat	OF	1909–27	1959
Rube Marquard	P	1908–25	1971	Hoyt Wilhelm	P	1952–72	1985
Eddie Mathews	3B	1952–68	1978	Billy Williams	OF	1959–76	1987

Players *(Cont.)*

	Position	Career	Selected
Ted Williams	OF	1939–60	1966
Vic Willis	P	1898–1910	1995
Hack Wilson	OF	1923–34	1979
Early Wynn	P	1939–63	1972
Carl Yastrzemski	OF	1961–83	1989
Cy Young	P	1890–1911	1937
Ross Youngs	OF	1917–26	1972
Robin Yount	SS	1974–93	1999

Umpires

	Year Selected
Al Barlick	1989
Nestor Chylak	1999
Jocko Conlan	1974
Tom Connolly	1953
Billy Evans	1973
Cal Hubbard	1976
Bill Klem	1953
Bill McGowan	1992

Pioneers/Executives

	Year Selected
Ed Barrow (manager-executive)	1953
Morgan Bulkeley (executive)	1937
Alexander Cartwright (executive)	1938
Henry Chadwick (writer-executive)	1938
Happy Chandler (commissioner)	1982
Charles Comiskey (manager-executive)	1939
Rube Foster (player–manager-executive)	1981
Ford Frick (commissioner-executive)	1970
Warren Giles (executive)	1979

Pioneers/Executives *(Cont.)*

	Year Selected
Will Harridge (executive)	1972
William Hulbert (executive)	1995
Ban Johnson (executive)	1937
Kenesaw M. Landis (commissioner)	1944
Larry MacPhail (executive)	1978
Lee MacPhail Jr (executive)	1998
Branch Rickey (manager–executive)	1967
Al Spalding (player–executive)	1939
Bill Veeck (owner)	1991
George Weiss (executive)	1971
George Wright (player–manager)	1937
Harry Wright (player–manager–executive)	1953
Tom Yawkey (executive)	1980

Managers

	Years Managed	Year Selected
Walt Alston	1954–76	1983
Leo Durocher	1939–73	1994
Clark Griffith	1901–20	1946
Bucky Harris	1924–56	1975
Ned Hanlon	1899–1907	1996
Miller Huggins	1913–29	1964
Tom Lasorda	1977–96	1997
Al Lopez	1951–69	1977
Connie Mack	1894–1950	1937
Joe McCarthy	1926–50	1957
John McGraw	1899–1932	1937
Bill McKechnie	1915–46	1962
Wilbert Robinson	1902–31	1945
Frank Selee	1890–1905	1999
Casey Stengel	1934–65	1966
Earl Weaver	1968–82, 85–86	1996

Notable Achievements

No-Hit Games, 9 Innings or More

NATIONAL LEAGUE

Date	Pitcher and Game	Date	Pitcher and Game
1876......July 15	George Bradley, StL vs Hart 2–0	1893......Aug 16	Bill Hawke, Balt vs Wash 5–0
1880......June 12	John Richmond, Wor vs Clev 1–0 (perfect game)	1897......Sept 18	Cy Young, Clev vs Cin 6–0
June 17	Monte Ward, Prov vs Buff 5–0 (perfect game)	1898......Apr 22	Ted Breitenstein, Cin vs Pitt 11–0
		Apr 22	Jim Hughes, Balt vs Bos 8–0
Aug 19	Larry Corcoran, Chi vs Bos 6–0	July 8	Frank Donahue, Phil vs Bos 5–0
Aug 20	Pud Galvin, Buff at Wor 1–0	Aug 21	Walter Thornton, Chi vs Bklyn 2–0
1882......Sept 20	Larry Corcoran, Chi vs Wor 5–0	1899......May 25	Deacon Phillippe, Lou vs NY 7–0
Sept 22	Tim Lovett, Bklyn vs NY 4–0	Aug 7	Vic Willis, Bos vs Wash 7–1
1883......July 25	Hoss Radbourn, Prov at Clev 8–0	1900......July 12	Noodles Hahn, Cin vs Phil 4–0
Sept 13	Hugh Daily, Clev at Phil 1–0	1901......July 15	Christy Mathewson, NY at StL 5–0
1884......June 27	Larry Corcoran, Chi vs Prov 6–0	1903......Sept 18	Chick Fraser, Phil at Chi 10–0
Aug 4	Pud Galvin, Buff at Det 18–0	1904......June 11	Bob Wicker, Chi at NY 1–0 (hit in 10th; won in 12th)
1885......July 27	John Clarkson, Chi at Prov 4–0	1905......June 13	Christy Mathewson, NY at Chi 1–0
Aug 29	Charles Ferguson, Phil vs Prov 1–0	1906......May 1	John Lush, Phil at Bklyn 6–0
1891......July 31	Amos Rusie, NY vs Bklyn 6–0	July 20	Mal Eason, Bklyn at StL 2–0
June 22	Tom Lovett, Bklyn vs NY 4–0	Aug 1	Harry McIntire, Bklyn vs Pitt 0–1 (hit in 11th; lost in 13th)
1892......Aug 6	Jack Stivetts, Bos vs Bklyn 11–0	1907......May 8	Frank Pfeffer, Bos vs Cin 6–0
Aug 22	Alex Sanders, Lou vs Balt 6–2	Sept 20	Nick Maddox, Pitt vs Bklyn 2–1
Oct 15	Bumpus Jones, Cin vs Pitt 7–1 (first major league game)		

No-Hit Games, 9 Innings or More *(Cont.)*

NATIONAL LEAGUE *(Cont.)*

Date	Pitcher and Game	Date	Pitcher and Game
1908......July 4	George Wiltse, NY vs Phil 1–0 (10 innings)	1967......June 18	Don Wilson, Hou vs Atl 2–0
Sept 5	Nap Rucker, Bklyn vs Bos 6–0	1968......July 29	George Culver, Cin at Phil 6–1
1909......Apr 15	Leon Ames, NY vs Bklyn 0–3 (hit in 10th; lost in 13th)	Sept 17	Gaylord Perry, SF vs StL 1–0
		Sept 18	Ray Washburn, StL at SF 2–0
1912......Sept 6	Jeff Tesreau, NY at Phil 3–0	1969......Apr 17	Bill Stoneman, Mtl at Phil 7–0
1914......Sept 9	George Davis, Bos vs Phil 7–0	Apr 30	Jim Maloney, Cin vs Hou 10–0
1915......Apr 15	Rube Marquard, NY vs Bklyn 2–0	May 1	Don Wilson, Hou at Cin 4–0
Aug 31	Jimmy Lavender, Chi at NY 2–0	Aug 19	Ken Holtzman, Chi vs Atl 3–0
1916......June 16	Tom Hughes, Bos vs Pitt 2–0	Sept 20	Bob Moose, Pitt at NY 4–0
1917......May 2	Jim Vaughn, Chi vs Cin 0–1 (hit in 10th; lost in 10th)	1970......June 12	Dock Ellis, Pitt at SD 2–0
		July 20	Bill Singer, LA vs Phil 5–0
May 2	Fred Toney, Cin at Chi 1–0 (10 innings)	1971......June 3	Ken Holtzman, Chi at Cin 1–0
		June 23	Rick Wise, Phil at Cin 4–0
1919......May 11	Hod Eller, Cin vs StL 6–0	Aug 14	Bob Gibson, StL at Pitt 11–0
1922......May 7	Jesse Barnes, NY vs Phil 6–0	1972......Apr 16	Burt Hooton, Chi vs Phil 4–0
1924......July 17	Jesse Haines, StL vs Bos 5–0	Sept 2	Milt Pappas, Chi vs SD 8–0
1925......Sept 13	Dazzy Vance, Bklyn vs Phil 10–1	Oct 2	Bill Stoneman, Mtl vs NY 7–0
1929......May 8	Carl Hubbell, NY vs Pitt 11–0	1973......Aug 5	Phil Niekro, Atl vs SD 9–0
1934......Sept 21	Paul Dean, StL vs Bklyn 3–0	1975......Aug 24	Ed Halicki, SF vs NY 6–0
1938......June 11	Johnny Vander Meer, Cin vs Bos 3–0	1976......July 9	Larry Dierker, Hou vs Mtl 6–0
		Aug 9	John Candelaria, Pitt vs LA 2–0
June 15	Johnny Vander Meer, Cin at Bklyn 6–0	Sept 29	John Mtlefusco, SF at Atl 9–0
1940......Apr 30	Tex Carleton, Bklyn at Cin, 3–0	1978......Apr 16	Bob Forsch, StL vs Phil 5–0
1941......Aug 30	Lon Warneke, StL at Cin 2–0	June 16	Tom Seaver, Cin vs StL 4–0
1944......Apr 27	Jim Tobin, Bos vs Bklyn 2–0	1979......Apr 7	Ken Forsch, Hou vs Atl 6–0
May 15	Clyde Shoun, Cin vs Bos 1–0	1980......June 27	Jerry Reuss, LA at SF 8–0
1946......Apr 23	Ed Head, Bklyn vs Bos 5–0	1981......May 10	Charlie Lea, Mtl vs SF 4–0
1947......June 18	Ewell Blackwell, Cin vs Bos 6–0	Sept 26	Nolan Ryan, Hou vs LA 5–0
1948......Sept 9	Rex Barney, Bklyn at NY 2–0	1983......Sept 26	Bob Forsch, StL vs Mtl 3–0
1950......Aug 11	Vern Bickford, Bos vs Bklyn 7–0	1986......Sept 25	Mike Scott, Hou vs SF 2–0
1951......May 6	Cliff Chambers, Pitt at Bos 3–0	1988......Sept 16	Tom Browning, Cin vs LA 1–0 (perfect game)
1952......June 19	Carl Erskine, Bklyn vs Chi 5–0		
1954......June 12	Jim Wilson, Mil vs Phil 2–0	1990 June 29	Fernando Valenzuela, LA vs StL 6–0
1955......May 12	Sam Jones, Chi vs Pitt 4–0		
1956......May 12	Carl Erskine, Bklyn vs NY 3–0	1990 ......Aug 15	Terry Mulholland, Phil vs SF 6–0
Sept 25	Sal Maglie, Bklyn vs Phil 5–0	1991......May 23	Tommy Greene, Phil at Mtl 2–0
1959......May 26	Harvey Haddix, Pitt at Mil 0–1 (hit in 13th; lost in 13th)	July 26	Mark Gardner, Mtl at LA 0–1 (hit in 10th, lost in 10th)
1960......May 15	Don Cardwell, Chi vs StL 4–0	July 28	Dennis Martinez, Mtl at LA 2–0 (perfect game)
Aug 18	Lew Burdette, Mil vs Phil 1–0		
Sept 16	Warren Spahn, Mil vs Phil 4–0	Sept 11	Kent Mercker (6), Mark Wohlers (2), and Alejandro Pena (1), Atl at SD 1–0
1961......Apr 28	Warren Spahn, Mil vs SF 1–0		
1962......June 30	Sandy Koufax, LA vs NY 5–0	1992......Aug 17	Kevin Gross, LA vs SF 2–0
1963......May 11	Sandy Koufax, LA vs SF 8–0	1993......Sept 8	Darryl Kile, Hou vs NY 7–1
May 17	Don Nottebart, Hou vs Phil 4–1	1994......Apr 8	Kent Mercker, Atl vs LA 6–0
June 15	Juan Marichal, SF vs Hou 1–0	1995......June 3	Pedro Martinez, Mtl vs SD 1–0 (perfect through 9, hit in 10th)
1964......Apr 23	Ken Johnson, Hou vs Cin 0–1		
June 4	Sandy Koufax, LA at Phil 3–0	July 14	Ramon Martinez, LA vs Fla 7–0
June 21	Jim Bunning, Phil at NY 6–0 (perfect game)	1996......May 11	Al Leiter, Fla vs Colorado 11–0
		Sept 17	Hideo Nomo, LA at Colorado 9–0
1965......June 14	Jim Maloney, Cin vs NY 0–1 (hit in 11th; lost in 11th)	1997......June 10	Kevin Brown, Fla vs SF 9–0
		July 12	Francisco Cordova (9) and Ricardo Rincon (1), Pittsburgh vs Colorado 3–0
Aug 19	Jim Maloney, Cin at Chi 1–0 (10 innings)		
Sept 9	Sandy Koufax, LA vs Chi 1–0 (perfect game)	1999......June 25	Jose Jimenez, StL at Ariz 1–0

Note: Includes the games struck from the official record book on September 4, 1991, when baseball's committee on statistical accuracy voted to define no-hitters as games of 9 innings or more that end with a team getting no hits.

No-Hit Games, 9 Innings or More *(Cont.)*

AMERICAN LEAGUE

Date	Pitcher and Game
1901......May 9	Earl Moore, Clev vs Chi 2–4 (hit in 10th; lost in 10th)
1902......Sept 20	Jimmy Callahan, Chi vs Det 3–0
1904......May 5	Cy Young, Bos vs Phil 3–0 (perfect game)
Aug 17	Jesse Tannehill, Bos at Chi 6–0
1905......July 22	Weldon Henley, Phil at StL 6–0
Sept 6	Frank Smith, Chi at Det 15–0
Sept 27	Bill Dinneen, Bos vs Chi 2–0
1908......June 30	Cy Young, Bos at NY 8–0
Sept 18	Bob Rhoades, Clev vs Bos 2–1
Sept 20	Frank Smith, Chi vs Phil 1–0
1908......Oct 2	Addie Joss, Clev vs Chi 1–0 (perfect game)
1910......Apr 20	Addie Joss, Clev at Chi 1–0
May 12	Chief Bender, Phil vs Clev 4–0
Aug 30	Tom Hughes, NY vs Clev 0–5 (hit in 10th; lost in 11th)
1911......July 29	Joe Wood, Bos vs StL 5–0
Aug 27	Ed Walsh, Chi vs Bos 5–0
1912......July 4	George Mullin, Det vs StL 7–0
Aug 30	Earl Hamilton, StL at Det 5–1
1914......May 14	Jim Scott, Chi at Wash 0–1 (hit in 10th; lost in 10th)
May 31	Joe Benz, Chi vs Clev 6–1
1916......June 21	George Foster, Bos vs NY 2–0
Aug 26	Joe Bush, Phil vs Clev 5–0
Aug 30	Dutch Leonard, Bos vs StL 4–0
1917......Apr 14	Ed Cicotte, Chi at StL 11–0
Apr 24	George Mogridge, NY at Bos 2–1
May 5	Ernie Koob, StL vs Chi 1–0
May 6	Bob Groom, StL vs Chi 3–0
June 23	Ernie Shore, Bos vs Wash 4–0 (perfect game)
1918......June 3	Dutch Leonard, Bos at Det 5–0
1919......Sept 10	Ray Caldwell, Clev at NY 3–0
1920......July 1	Walter Johnson, Wash at Bos 1–0
1922......Apr 30	Charlie Robertson, Chi at Det 2–0 (perfect game)
1923......Sept 4	Sam Jones, NY at Phil 2–0
Sept 7	Howard Ehmke, Bos at Phil 4–0
1926......Aug 21	Ted Lyons, Chi at Bos 6–0
1931......Apr 29	Wes Ferrell, Clev vs StL 9–0
Aug 8	Bob Burke, Wash vs Bos 5–0
1934......Sept 18	Bobo Newsom, StL vs Bos 1–2 (hit in 10th; lost in 10th)
1935......Aug 31	Vern Kennedy, Chi vs Clev 5–0
1937......June 1	Bill Dietrich, Chi vs StL 8–0
1938......Aug 27	Mtle Pearson, NY vs Clev 13–0
1940......Apr 16	Bob Feller, Clev at Chi 1–0 (opening day)
1945......Sept 9	Dick Fowler, Phil vs StL 1–0
1946......Apr 30	Bob Feller, Clev at NY 1–0
1947......July 10	Don Black, Clev vs Phil 3–0
Sep 3	Bill McCahan, Phil vs Wash 3–0
1948......June 30	Bob Lemon, Clev at Det 2–0
1951......July 1	Bob Feller, Clev vs Det 2–1
July 12	Allie Reynolds, NY at Clev 1–0
Sept 28	Allie Reynolds, NY vs Bos 8–0
1952......May 15	Virgil Trucks, Det vs Wash 1–0
Aug 25	Virgil Trucks, Det at NY 1–0
1953......May 6	Bobo Holloman, StL vs Phil 6–0 (first major league start)

Date	Pitcher and Game
1956......July 14	Mel Parnell, Bos vs Chi 4–0
1966......Oct 8	Don Larsen, NY (A) vs Bklyn (N) 2–0 (World Series) (perfect game)
1957......Aug 20	Bob Keegan, Chi vs Wash 6–0
1958......July 20	Jim Bunning, Det at Bos 3–0
Sept 20	Hoyt Wilhelm, Balt vs NY 1–0
1962......May 5	Bo Belinsky, LA vs Balt 2–0
June 26	Earl Wilson, Bos vs LA 2–0
Aug 1	Bill Monbouquette, Bos at Chi 1–0
Aug 26	Jack Kralick, Minn vs KC 1–0
1965......Sept 16	Dave Morehead, Bos vs Clev 2–0
1966......June 10	Sonny Siebert, Clev vs Wash 2–0
1967......Apr 30	Steve Barber (8⅔) and Stu Miller (⅓), Balt vs Det 1–2
Aug 25	Dean Chance, Minn at Clev 2–1
Sept 10	Joel Horlen, Chi vs Det 6–0
1968......Apr 27	Tom Phoebus, Balt vs Bos 6–0
May 8	Catfish Hunter, Oak vs Minn 4–0 (perfect game)
1969......Aug 13	Jim Palmer, Balt vs Oak 8–0
1970......July 3	Clyde Wright, Cal vs Oak 4–0
Sept 21	Vida Blue, Oak vs Minn 6–0
1973......Apr 27	Steve Busby, KC at Det 3–0
May 15	Nolan Ryan, Cal at KC 3–0
July 15	Nolan Ryan, Cal at Det 6–0
July 30	Jim Bibby, Tex at Oak 6–0
1974......June 19	Steve Busby, KC at Mil 2–0
July 19	Dick Bosman, Clev vs Oak 4–0
Sept 28	Nolan Ryan, Cal vs Minn 4–0
1975......June 1	Nolan Ryan, Cal vs Balt 1–0
Sept 28	Vida Blue (5), Glenn Abbott and Paul Lindblad (1), Rollie Fingers (2), Oak vs Cal 5–0
1976......July 28	John Odom (5) and Francisco Barrios (4), Chi at Oak 2–1
1977......May 14	Jim Colborn, KC vs Tex 6–0
May 30	Dennis Eckersley, Clev vs Cal 1–0
Sept 22	Bert Blyleven, Tex at Cal 6–0
1981......May 15	Len Barker, Clev vs Tor 3–0 (perfect game)
1983......July 4	Dave Righetti, NY vs Bos 4–0
Sept 29	Mike Warren, Oak vs Chi 3–0
1984......Apr 7	Jack Morris, Det at Chi 4–0
Sept 30	Mike Witt, Cal at Tex 1–0 (perfect game)
1986......Sept 19	Joe Cowley, Chi at Cal 7–1
1987......Apr 15	Juan Nieves, Mil at Balt 7–0
1990......Apr 11	Mark Langston (7), Mike Witt (2), Cal vs Sea 1–0
June 2	Randy Johnson, Sea vs Det 2–0
June 11	Nolan Ryan, Tex at Oak 5–0
June 29	Dave Stewart, Oak at Tor 5–0
1990......July 1	Andy Hawkins, NY at Chi 0–4 (pitched 8 innings of 9–inning game)
Sept 2	Dave Stieb, Tor at Clev 3–0
1991......May 1	Nolan Ryan, Tex vs Tor 3–0
July 13	Bob Milacki (6), Mike Flanagan (1), Mark Williamson (1), and Gregg Olson (1), Balt at Oak 2–0
Aug 11	Wilson Alvarez, Chi at Balt 7–0
Aug 26	Bret Saberhagen, KC vs Chi 7–0

No-Hit Games, 9 Innings or More *(Cont.)*

AMERICAN LEAGUE *(CONT.)*

Date	Pitcher and Game	Date	Pitcher and Game
1993......Apr 22	Chris Bosio, Sea vs Bos 7–0	1998......May 17	David Wells, NY vs Minn 4–0
Sept 4	Jim Abbott, NY vs Clev 4–0		(perfect game)
1994......Apr 27	Scott Erickson, Minn vs Mil 6–0	1999......July 18	David Cone, NY vs Mtl 6–0
July 28	Kenny Rogers, Texas vs Cal 4–0		(perfect game)
	(perfect game)	Sept 11	Eric Milton, Minn vs Ana 7–0
1996......May 14	Dwight Gooden, NY vs Sea 2–0		

Longest Hitting Streaks

NATIONAL LEAGUE

Player and Team	Year	G
Willie Keeler, Balt	1897	44
Pete Rose, Cin	1978	44
Bill Dahlen, Chi	1894	42
Tommy Holmes, Bos	1945	37
Billy Hamilton, Phil	1894	36
Fred Clarke, Lou	1895	35
Benito Santiago, SD	1987	34
George Davis, NY	1893	33
Rogers Hornsby, StL	1922	32
Ed Delahanty, Phil	1899	31
Willie Davis, LA	1969	31
Rico Carty, Atl	1970	31
Vladimir Guerrero, Mtl	1999	31

AMERICAN LEAGUE

Player and Team	Year	G
Joe DiMaggio, NY	1941	56
George Sisler, StL	1922	41
Ty Cobb, Det	1911	40
Paul Molitor, Mil	1987	39
Ty Cobb, Det	1917	35
Ty Cobb, Det	1912	34
George Sisler, StL	1925	34
John Stone, Det	1930	34
George McQuinn, StL	1938	34
Dom DiMaggio, Bos	1949	34
Hal Chase, NY	1907	33
Heinie Manush, Wash	1933	33
Nap Lajoie, Clev	1906	31
Sam Rice, Wash	1924	31
Ken Landreaux, Minn	1980	31

Triple Crown Hitters

NATIONAL LEAGUE

Player and Team	Year	HR	RBI	BA
Paul Hines, Prov	1878	4	50	.358
Hugh Duffy, Bos	1894	18	145	.438
Heinie Zimmerman*, Chi	1912	14	103	.372
Rogers Hornsby, StL	1922	42	152	.401
	1925	39	143	.403
Chuck Klein, Phil	1933	28	120	.368
Joe Medwick, StL	1937	31	154	.374

AMERICAN LEAGUE

Player and Team	Year	HR	RBI	BA
Nap Lajoie, Phil	1901	14	125	.422
Ty Cobb, Det	1909	9	115	.377
Jimmie Foxx, Phil	1933	48	163	.356
Lou Gehrig, NY	1934	49	165	.363
Ted Williams, Bos	1942	36	137	.356
	1947	32	114	.343
Mickey Mantle, NY	1956	52	130	.353
Frank Robinson, Balt	1966	49	122	.316
Carl Yastrzemski, Bos	1967	44	121	.326

*Zimmerman ranked first in RBIs as calculated by Ernie Lanigan, but only third as calculated by Information Concepts Inc.

THEY SAID IT

Brian Meadows, Marlins pitcher, on making contact with a fourth-inning Randy Johnson fastball: "I started swinging in the second inning."

Triple Crown Pitchers

NATIONAL LEAGUE

Player and Team	Year	W	L	SO	ERA
Tommy Bond, Bos	1877	40	17	170	2.11
Hoss Radbourn, Prov	1884	60	12	441	1.38
Tim Keefe, NY	1888	35	12	333	1.74
John Clarkson, Bos	1889	49	19	284	2.73
Amos Rusie, NY	1894	36	13	195	2.78
Christy Mathewson, NY	1905	31	8	206	1.27
	1908	37	11	259	1.43
Grover Alexander, Phil	1915	31	10	241	1.22
	1916	33	12	167	1.55
	1917	30	13	201	1.86
Hippo Vaughn, Chi	1918	22	10	148	1.74
Grover Alexander, Chi	1920	27	14	173	1.91
Dazzy Vance, Bklyn	1924	28	6	262	2.16
Bucky Walters, Cin	1939	27	11	137	2.29
Sandy Koufax, LA	1963	25	5	306	1.88
	1965	26	8	382	2.04
	1966	27	9	317	1.73
Steve Carlton, Phil	1972	27	10	310	1.97
Dwight Gooden, NY	1985	24	4	268	1.53

AMERICAN LEAGUE

Player and Team	Year	W	L	SO	ERA
Cy Young, Bos	1901	33	10	158	1.62
Rube Waddell, Phil	1905	26	11	287	1.48
Walter Johnson, Wash	1913	36	7	303	1.09
	1918	23	13	162	1.27
	1924	23	7	158	2.72
Lefty Grove, Phil	1930	28	5	209	2.54
	1931	31	4	175	2.06
Lefty Gomez, NY	1934	26	5	158	2.33
	1937	21	11	194	2.33
Hal Newhouser, Det	1945	25	9	212	1.81
Roger Clemens, Tor	1997	21	7	292	2.05
	1998	20	6	271	2.64
Pedro Martinez, Bos	1999	23	4	313	2.07

Consecutive Games Played, 500 or More Games

Cal Ripken Jr.	2,632	Frank McCormick	652
Lou Gehrig	2,130	Sandy Alomar Sr.	648
Everett Scott	1,307	Eddie Brown	618
Steve Garvey	1,207	Roy McMillan	585
Billy Williams	1,117	George Pinckney	577
Joe Sewell	1,103	Steve Brodie	574
Stan Musial	895	Aaron Ward	565
Eddie Yost	829	Candy LaChance	540
Gus Suhr	822	Buck Freeman	535
Nellie Fox	798	Fred Luderus	533
Pete Rose	745	Clyde Milan	511
Dale Murphy	740	Charlie Gehringer	511
Richie Ashburn	730	Vada Pinson	508
Ernie Banks	717	Tony Cuccinello	504
Earl Averill	673	Charlie Gehringer	504
Pete Rose	678	Omar Moreno	503

Unassisted Triple Plays

Player and Team	Date	Pos	Opp	Opp Batter
Neal Ball, Clev	7-19-09	SS	Bos	Amby McConnell
Bill Wambsganss, Clev	10-10-20	2B	Bklyn	Clarence Mitchell
George Burns, Bos	9-14-23	1B	Clev	Frank Brower
Ernie Padgett, Bos	10-6-23	SS	Phil	Walter Holke
Glenn Wright, Pitt	5-7-25	SS	StL	Jim Bottomley
Jimmy Cooney, Chi	5-30-27	SS	Pitt	Paul Waner
Johnny Neun, Det	5-31-27	1B	Clev	Homer Summa
Ron Hansen, Wash	7-30-68	SS	Clev	Joe Azcue
Mickey Morandini, Phil	9-20-92	2B	Pitt	Jeff King
John Valentin, Bos	7-15-94	SS	Minn	Marc Newfield

National League

Pennant Winners

Year	Team	Manager	W	L	Pct	GA
1900	Brooklyn	Ned Hanlon	82	54	.603	4½
1901	Pittsburgh	Fred Clarke	90	49	.647	7½
1902	Pittsburgh	Fred Clarke	103	36	.741	27½
1903	Pittsburgh	Fred Clarke	91	49	.650	6½
1904	New York	John McGraw	106	47	.693	13
1905	New York	John McGraw	105	48	.686	9
1906	Chicago	Frank Chance	116	36	.763	20
1907	Chicago	Frank Chance	107	45	.704	17
1908	Chicago	Frank Chance	99	55	.643	1
1909	Pittsburgh	Fred Clarke	110	42	.724	6½
1910	Chicago	Frank Chance	104	50	.675	13
1911	New York	John McGraw	99	54	.647	7½
1912	New York	John McGraw	103	48	.682	10
1913	New York	John McGraw	101	51	.664	12½
1914	Boston	George Stallings	94	59	.614	10½
1915	Philadelphia	Pat Moran	90	62	.592	7
1916	Brooklyn	Wilbert Robinson	94	60	.610	2½
1917	New York	John McGraw	98	56	.636	10
1918	Chicago	Fred Mitchell	84	45	.651	10½
1919	Cincinnati	Pat Moran	96	44	.686	9
1920	Brooklyn	Wilbert Robinson	93	61	.604	7
1921	New York	John McGraw	94	59	.614	4
1922	New York	John McGraw	93	61	.604	7
1923	New York	John McGraw	95	58	.621	4½
1924	New York	John McGraw	93	60	.608	1½
1925	Pittsburgh	Bill McKechnie	95	58	.621	8½
1926	St. Louis	Rogers Hornsby	89	65	.578	2
1927	Pittsburgh	Donie Bush	94	60	.610	1½
1928	St. Louis	Bill McKechnie	95	59	.617	2
1929	Chicago	Joe McCarthy	98	54	.645	10½
1930	St. Louis	Gabby Street	92	62	.597	2
1931	St. Louis	Gabby Street	101	53	.656	13
1932	Chicago	Charlie Grimm	90	64	.584	4
1933	New York	Bill Terry	91	61	.599	5
1934	St. Louis	Frankie Frisch	95	58	.621	2
1935	Chicago	Charlie Grimm	100	54	.649	4
1936	New York	Bill Terry	92	62	.597	5
1937	New York	Bill Terry	95	57	.625	3
1938	Chicago	Gabby Hartnett	89	63	.586	2
1939	Cincinnati	Bill McKechnie	97	57	.630	4½
1940	Cincinnati	Bill McKechnie	100	53	.654	12
1941	Brooklyn	Leo Durocher	100	54	.649	2½
1942	St. Louis	Billy Southworth	106	48	.688	2
1943	St. Louis	Billy Southworth	105	49	.682	18
1944	St. Louis	Billy Southworth	105	49	.682	14½
1945	Chicago	Charlie Grimm	98	56	.636	3
1946	St. Louis*	Eddie Dyer	98	58	.628	2
1947	Brooklyn	Burt Shotton	94	60	.610	5
1948	Boston	Billy Southworth	91	62	.595	6½
1949	Brooklyn	Burt Shotton	97	57	.630	1
1950	Philadelphia	Eddie Sawyer	91	63	.591	2
1951	New York†	Leo Durocher	98	59	.624	1
1952	Brooklyn	Chuck Dressen	96	57	.627	4½
1953	Brooklyn	Chuck Dressen	105	49	.682	13
1954	New York	Leo Durocher	97	57	.630	5
1955	Brooklyn	Walt Alston	98	55	.641	13½
1956	Brooklyn	Walt Alston	93	61	.604	1
1957	Milwaukee	Fred Haney	95	59	.617	8
1958	Milwaukee	Fred Haney	92	62	.597	8
1959	Los Angeles‡	Walt Alston	88	68	.564	2
1960	Pittsburgh	Danny Murtaugh	95	59	.617	7
1961	Cincinnati	Fred Hutchinson	93	61	.604	4
1962	San Francisco#	Al Dark	103	62	.624	1
1963	Los Angeles	Walt Alston	99	63	.611	6
1964	St. Louis	Johnny Keane	93	69	.574	1

Pennant Winners (Cont.)

Year	Team	Manager	W	L	Pct	GA
1965	Los Angeles	Walt Alston	97	65	.599	2
1966	Los Angeles	Walt Alston	95	67	.586	1½
1967	St. Louis	Red Schoendienst	101	60	.627	10½
1968	St. Louis	Red Schoendienst	97	65	.599	9
1969	New York (E)††	Gil Hodges	100	62	.617	8
1970	Cincinnati (W)††	Sparky Anderson	102	60	.630	14½
1971	Pittsburgh (E)††	Danny Murtaugh	97	65	.599	7
1972	Cincinnati (W)††	Sparky Anderson	95	59	.617	10½
1973	New York (E)††	Yogi Berra	82	79	.509	1½
1974	Los Angeles (W)††	Walt Alston	102	60	.630	4
1975	Cincinnati (W)††	Sparky Anderson	108	54	.667	20
1976	Cincinnati (W)††	Sparky Anderson	102	60	.630	10
1977	Los Angeles (W)††	Tommy Lasorda	98	64	.605	10
1978	Los Angeles (W)††	Tommy Lasorda	95	67	.586	2½
1979	Pittsburgh (E)††	Chuck Tanner	98	64	.605	2
1980	Philadelphia (E)††	Dallas Green	91	71	.562	1
1981	Los Angeles (W)††	Tommy Lasorda	63	47	.573	**
1982	St. Louis (E)††	Whitey Herzog	92	70	.568	3
1983	Philadelphia (E)††	Pat Corrales/ Paul Owens	90	72	.556	6
1984	San Diego (W)††	Dick Williams	92	70	.568	12
1985	St. Louis (E)††	Whitey Herzog	101	61	.623	3
1986	New York (E)††	Dave Johnson	108	54	.667	21½
1987	St. Louis (E)††	Whitey Herzog	95	67	.586	3
1988	Los Angeles (W)††	Tommy Lasorda	94	67	.584	7
1989	San Francisco (W)††	Roger Craig	92	70	.568	3
1990	Cincinnati (W)††	Lou Piniella	91	71	.562	5
1991	Atlanta (W)††	Bobby Cox	94	68	.580	1
1992	Atlanta (W)††	Bobby Cox	98	64	.605	8
1993	Philadelphia (E)††	Jim Fregosi	97	65	.599	3
1994	Season ended Aug. 11 due to players' strike.					
1995	Atlanta (E)††	Bobby Cox	90	54	.625	21
1996	Atlanta (E)††	Bobby Cox	96	66	.593	8
1997	Florida (wc)††	Jim Leyland	92	70	.568	—
1998	San Diego (W)††	Bruce Bochy	98	64	.605	9½
1999	Atlanta Braves (E)††	Bobby Cox	103	59	.636	6½

*Defeated Brooklyn, two games to none, in playoff for pennant. †Defeated Brooklyn, two games to one, in playoff for pennant. ‡Defeated Milwaukee, two games to none, in playoff for pennant. #Defeated Los Angeles, two games to one, in playoff for pennant. ††Won Championship Series. **First half 36–21; second half 27–26, in season split by strike; defeated Houston in playoff for Western Division title.

Witch Hitter

Without knowing it, Cal Ripken Jr. provided the last laugh in the 1999 movie hit of the summer. Near the end of *The Blair Witch Project*, which is set in a Maryland woods during the summer of 1994, doomed sound technician Mike shouts, "Two thousand, one hundred and thirty consecutive games, and Cal Ripken is king! Cal Ripken is king, and I'm not gonna see it because I'm gonna be stuck in the woods." The line was an ad lib by Michael Williams, who like the other two actors in the film improvised most of his dialogue during shooting in '97. "Michael and I are huge baseball fans," says *Blair Witch* codirector Eduardo Sanchez. "We agreed that mentioning Ripken would add authenticity."

"My character's consecutive-days-lived streak was in jeopardy, so I went for gallows humor," says Williams, a lifelong Yanks fan whose reference to Ripken's breaking Lou Gehrig's consecutive-games mark delighted Orioles fan Sanchez.

"When we started this project we just hoped it'd go to video," Sanchez says of his $35,000 film, which has grossed more than $100 million. "We never imagined Cal might actually see it."

So will he? "I'm curious because they mention my name," says Ripken, "so I probably will see it—if my wife wants to go."

—John Walters

Leading Batsmen

Year	Player and Team	BA	Year	Player and Team	BA
1900	Honus Wagner, Pitt	.381	1951	Stan Musial, StL	.355
1901	Jesse Burkett, StL	.382	1952	Stan Musial, StL	.336
1902	Ginger Beaumtl, Pitt	.357	1953	Carl Furillo, Bklyn	.344
1903	Honus Wagner, Pitt	.355	1954	Willie Mays, NY	.345
1904	Honus Wagner, Pitt	.349	1955	Richie Ashburn, Phil	.338
1905	Cy Seymour, Cin	.377	1956	Hank Aaron, Mil	.328
1906	Honus Wagner, Pitt	.339	1957	Stan Musial, StL	.351
1907	Honus Wagner, Pitt	.350	1958	Richie Ashburn, Phil	.350
1908	Honus Wagner, Pitt	.354	1959	Hank Aaron, Mil	.355
1909	Honus Wagner, Pitt	.339	1960	Dick Groat, Pitt	.325
1910	Sherry Magee, Phil	.331	1961	Roberto Clemente, Pitt	.351
1911	Honus Wagner, Pitt	.334	1962	Tommy Davis, LA	.346
1912	Heinie Zimmerman, Chi	.372	1963	Tommy Davis, LA	.326
1913	Jake Daubert, Bklyn	.350	1964	Roberto Clemente, Pitt	.339
1914	Jake Daubert, Bklyn	.329	1965	Roberto Clemente, Pitt	.329
1915	Larry Doyle, NY	.320	1966	Matty Alou, Pitt	.342
1916	Hal Chase, Cin	.339	1967	Roberto Clemente, Pitt	.357
1917	Edd Roush, Cin	.341	1968	Pete Rose, Cin	.335
1918	Zach Wheat, Bklyn	.335	1969	Pete Rose, Cin	.348
1919	Edd Roush, Cin	.321	1970	Rico Carty, Atl	.366
1920	Rogers Hornsby, StL	.370	1971	Joe Torre, StL	.363
1921	Rogers Hornsby, StL	.397	1972	Billy Williams, Chi	.333
1922	Rogers Hornsby, StL	.401	1973	Pete Rose, Cin	.338
1923	Rogers Hornsby, StL	.384	1974	Ralph Garr, Atl	.353
1924	Rogers Hornsby, StL	.424	1975	Bill Madlock, Chi	.354
1925	Rogers Hornsby, StL	.403	1976	Bill Madlock, Chi	.339
1926	Bubbles Hargrave, Cin	.353	1977	Dave Parker, Pitt	.338
1927	Paul Waner, Pitt	.380	1978	Dave Parker, Pitt	.334
1928	Rogers Hornsby, Bos	.387	1979	Keith Hernandez, StL	.344
1929	Lefty O'Doul, Phil	.398	1980	Bill Buckner, Chi	.324
1930	Bill Terry, NY	.401	1981	Bill Madlock, Pitt	.341
1931	Chick Hafey, StL	.349	1982	Al Oliver, Mtl	.331
1932	Lefty O'Doul, Bklyn	.368	1983	Bill Madlock, Pitt	.323
1933	Chuck Klein, Phil	.368	1984	Tony Gwynn, SD	.351
1934	Paul Waner, Pitt	.362	1985	Willie McGee, StL	.353
1935	Arky Vaughan, Pitt	.385	1986	Tim Raines, Mtl	.334
1936	Paul Waner, Pitt	.373	1987	Tony Gwynn, SD	.370
1937	Joe Medwick, StL	.374	1988	Tony Gwynn, SD	.313
1938	Ernie Lombardi, Cin	.342	1989	Tony Gwynn, SD	.336
1939	Johnny Mize, StL	.349	1990	Willie McGee, StL	.335
1940	Debs Garms, Pitt	.355	1991	Terry Pendleton, Atl	.319
1941	Pete Reiser, Bklyn	.343	1992	Gary Sheffield, SD	.330
1942	Ernie Lombardi, Bos	.330	1993	Andres Galarraga, Col	.370
1943	Stan Musial, StL	.357	1994	Tony Gwynn, SD	.394
1944	Dixie Walker, Bklyn	.357	1995	Tony Gwynn, SD	.368
1945	Phil Cavarretta, Chi	.355	1996	Tony Gwynn, SD	.353
1946	Stan Musial, StL	.365	1997	Tony Gwynn, SD	.372
1947	Harry Walker, StL-Phil	.363	1998	Larry Walker, Col	.363
1948	Stan Musial, StL	.376	1999	Larry Walker, Col	.379
1949	Jackie Robinson, Bklyn	.342			
1950	Stan Musial, StL	.346			

Leaders in Runs Scored

Year	Player and Team	Runs	Year	Player and Team	Runs
1900	Roy Thomas, Phil	131	1952	Stan Musial, StL	105
1901	Jesse Burkett, StL	139		Solly Hemus, StL	105
1902	Honus Wagner, Pitt	105	1953	Duke Snider, Bklyn	132
1903	Ginger Beaumont, Pitt	137	1954	Stan Musial, StL	120
1904	George Browne, NY	99		Duke Snider, Bklyn	120
1905	Mike Donlin, NY	124	1955	Duke Snider, Bklyn	126
1906	Honus Wagner, Pitt	103	1956	Frank Robinson, Cin	122
	Frank Chance, Chi	103	1957	Hank Aaron, Mil	118
1907	Spike Shannon, NY	104	1958	Willie Mays, SF	121
1908	Fred Tenney, NY	101	1959	Vada Pinson, Cin	131
1909	Tommy Leach, Pitt	126	1960	Bill Bruton, Mil	112
1910	Sherry Magee, Phil	110	1961	Willie Mays, SF	129
1911	Jimmy Sheckard, Chi	121	1962	Frank Robinson, Cin	134
1912	Bob Bescher, Cin	120	1963	Hank Aaron, Mil	121
1913	Tommy Leach, Chi	99	1964	Dick Allen, Phil	125
	Max Carey, Pitt	99	1965	Tommy Harper, Cin	126
1914	George Burns, NY	100	1966	Felipe Alou, Atl	122
1915	Gavvy Cravath, Phil	89	1967	Hank Aaron, Atl	113
1916	George Burns, NY	105		Lou Brock, StL	113
1917	George Burns, NY	103	1968	Glenn Beckert, Chi	98
1918	Heinie Groh, Cin	88	1969	Bobby Bonds, SF	120
1919	George Burns, NY	86		Pete Rose, Cin	120
1920	George Burns, NY	115	1970	Billy Williams, Chi	137
1921	Rogers Hornsby, StL	131	1971	Lou Brock, StL	126
1922	Rogers Hornsby, StL	141	1972	Joe Morgan, Cin	122
1923	Ross Youngs, NY	121	1973	Bobby Bonds, SF	131
1924	Frankie Frisch, NY	121	1974	Pete Rose, Cin	110
	Rogers Hornsby, StL	121	1975	Pete Rose, Cin	112
1925	Kiki Cuyler, Pitt	144	1976	Pete Rose, Cin	130
1926	Kiki Cuyler, Pitt	113	1977	George Foster, Cin	124
1927	Lloyd Waner, Pitt	133	1978	Ivan DeJesus, Chi	104
	Rogers Hornsby, NY	133	1979	Keith Hernandez, StL	116
1928	Paul Waner, Pitt	142	1980	Keith Hernandez, StL	111
1929	Rogers Hornsby, Chi	156	1981	Mike Schmidt, Phil	78
1930	Chuck Klein, Phil	158	1982	Lonnie Smith, StL	120
1931	Bill Terry, NY	121	1983	Tim Raines, Mtl	133
	Chuck Klein, Phil	121	1984	Ryne Sandberg, Chi	114
1932	Chuck Klein, Phil	152	1985	Dale Murphy, Atl	118
1933	Pepper Martin, StL	122	1986	Von Hayes, Phil	107
1934	Paul Waner, Pitt	122		Tony Gwynn, SD	107
1935	Augie Galan, Chi	133	1987	Tim Raines, Mtl	123
1936	Arky Vaughan, Pitt	122	1988	Brett Butler, SF	109
1937	Joe Medwick, StL	111	1989	Howard Johnson, NY	104
1938	Mel Ott, NY	116		Will Clark, SF	104
1939	Billy Werber, Cin	115		Ryne Sandberg, Chi	104
1940	Arky Vaughan, Pitt	113	1990	Ryne Sandberg, Chi	116
1941	Pete Reiser, Bklyn	117	1991	Brett Butler, LA	112
1942	Mel Ott, NY	118	1992	Barry Bonds, Pitt	109
1943	Arky Vaughan, Bklyn	112	1993	Lenny Dykstra, Phil	143
1944	Bill Nicholson, Chi	116	1994	Jeff Bagwell, Hou	104
1945	Eddie Stanky, Bklyn	128	1995	Craig Biggio, Hou	123
1946	Stan Musial, StL	124	1996	Ellis Burks, Col	142
1947	Johnny Mize, NY	137	1997	Craig Biggio, Hou	146
1948	Stan Musial, StL	135	1998	Sammy Sosa, Chi	134
1949	Pee Wee Reese, Bklyn	132	1999	Jeff Bagwell, Hou	143
1950	Earl Torgeson, Bos	120			
1951	Stan Musial, StL	124			
	Ralph Kiner, Pitt	124			

Leaders in Hits

Year	Player and Team	Hits	Year	Player and Team	Hits
1900	Willie Keeler, Bklyn	208	1953	Richie Ashburn, Phil	205
1901	Jesse Burkett, StL	228	1954	Don Mueller, NY	212
1902	Ginger Beaumont, Pitt	194	1955	Ted Kluszewski, Cin	192
1903	Ginger Beaumont, Pitt	209	1956	Hank Aaron, Mil	200
1904	Ginger Beaumont, Pitt	185	1957	Red Schoendienst, NY-Mil	200
1905	Cy Seymour, Cin	219	1958	Richie Ashburn, Phil	215
1906	Harry Steinfeldt, Chi	176	1959	Hank Aaron, Mil	223
1907	Ginger Beaumont, Bos	187	1960	Willie Mays, SF	190
1908	Honus Wagner, Pitt	201	1961	Vada Pinson, Cin	208
1909	Larry Doyle, NY	172	1962	Tommy Davis, LA	230
1910	Honus Wagner, Pitt	178	1963	Vada Pinson, Cin	204
	Bobby Byrne, Pitt	178	1964	Roberto Clemente, Pitt	211
1911	Doc Miller, Bos	192		Curt Flood, StL	211
1912	Heinie Zimmerman, Chi	207	1965	Pete Rose, Cin	209
1913	Gavvy Cravath, Phil	179	1966	Felipe Alou, Atl	218
1914	Sherry Magee, Phil	171	1967	Roberto Clemente, Pitt	209
1915	Larry Doyle, NY	189	1968	Felipe Alou, Atl	210
1916	Hal Chase, Cin	184		Pete Rose, Cin	210
1917	Heinie Groh, Cin	182	1969	Matty Alou, Pitt	231
1918	Charlie Hollocher, Chi	161	1970	Pete Rose, Cin	205
1919	Ivy Olson, Bklyn	164		Billy Williams, Chi	205
1920	Rogers Hornsby, StL	218	1971	Joe Torre, StL	230
1921	Rogers Hornsby, StL	235	1972	Pete Rose, Cin	198
1922	Rogers Hornsby, StL	250	1973	Pete Rose, Cin	230
1923	Frankie Frisch, NY	223	1974	Ralph Garr, Atl	214
1924	Rogers Hornsby, StL	227	1975	Dave Cash, Phil	213
1925	Jim Bottomley, StL	227	1976	Pete Rose, Cin	215
1926	Eddie Brown, Bos	201	1977	Dave Parker, Pitt	215
1927	Paul Waner, Pitt	237	1978	Steve Garvey, LA	202
1928	Freddy Lindstrom, NY	231	1979	Garry Templeton, StL	211
1929	Lefty O'Doul, Phil	254	1980	Steve Garvey, LA	200
1930	Bill Terry, NY	254	1981	Pete Rose, Phil	140
1931	Lloyd Waner, Pitt	214	1982	Al Oliver, Mtl	204
1932	Chuck Klein, Phil	226	1983	Jose Cruz, Hou	189
1933	Chuck Klein, Phil	223		Andre Dawson, Mtl	189
1934	Paul Waner, Pitt	217	1984	Tony Gwynn, SD	213
1935	Billy Herman, Chi	227	1985	Willie McGee, StL	216
1936	Joe Medwick, StL	223	1986	Tony Gwynn, SD	211
1937	Joe Medwick, StL	237	1987	Tony Gwynn, SD	218
1938	Frank McCormick, Cin	209	1988	Andres Galarraga, Mtl	184
1939	Frank McCormick, Cin	209	1989	Tony Gwynn, SD	203
1940	Stan Hack, Chi	191	1990	Brett Butler, SF	192
	Frank McCormick, Cin	191		Lenny Dykstra, Phil	192
1941	Stan Hack, Chi	186	1991	Terry Pendleton, Atl	187
1942	Enos Slaughter, StL	188	1992	Terry Pendleton, Atl	199
1943	Stan Musial, StL	220		Andy Van Slyke, Pitt	199
1944	Stan Musial, StL	197	1993	Lenny Dykstra, Phil	194
	Phil Cavarretta, Chi	197	1994	Tony Gwynn, SD	165
1945	Tommy Holmes, Bos	224	1995	Dante Bichette, Col	197
1946	Stan Musial, StL	228		Tony Gwynn, SD	197
1947	Tommy Holmes, Bos	191	1996	Lance Johnson, NY	227
1948	Stan Musial, StL	230	1997	Tony Gwynn, SD	220
1949	Stan Musial, StL	207	1998	Dante Bichette, Col	219
1950	Duke Snider, Bklyn	199	1999	Luis Gonzalez, Ariz	206
1951	Richie Ashburn, Phil	221			
1952	Stan Musial, StL	194			

Home Run Leaders

Year	Player and Team	HR	Year	Player and Team	HR
1900	Herman Long, Bos	12	1948	Ralph Kiner, Pitt	40
1901	Sam Crawford, Cin	16		Johnny Mize, NY	40
1902	Tommy Leach, Pitt	6	1949	Ralph Kiner, Pitt	54
1903	Jimmy Sheckard, Bklyn	9	1950	Ralph Kiner, Pitt	47
1904	Harry Lumley, Bklyn	9	1951	Ralph Kiner, Pitt	42
1905	Fred Odwell, Cin	9	1952	Ralph Kiner, Pitt	37
1906	Tim Jordan, Bklyn	12		Hank Sauer, Chi	37
1907	Dave Brain, Bos	10	1953	Eddie Mathews, Mil	47
1908	Tim Jordan, Bklyn	12	1954	Ted Kluszewski, Cin	49
1909	Red Murray, NY	7	1955	Willie Mays, NY	51
1910	Fred Beck, Bos	10	1956	Duke Snider, Bklyn	43
	Wildfire Schulte, Chi	10	1957	Hank Aaron, Mil	44
1911	Wildfire Schulte, Chi	21	1958	Ernie Banks, Chi	47
1912	Heinie Zimmerman, Cin	14	1959	Eddie Mathews, Mil	46
1913	Gavvy Cravath, Phil	19	1960	Ernie Banks, Chi	41
1914	Gavvy Cravath, Phil	19	1961	Orlando Cepeda, SF	46
1915	Gavvy Cravath, Phil	24	1962	Willie Mays, SF	49
1916	Dave Robertson, NY	12	1963	Hank Aaron, Mil	44
	Cy Williams, Chi	12		Willie McCovey, SF	44
1917	Dave Robertson, NY	12	1964	Willie Mays, SF	47
	Gavvy Cravath, Phil	12	1965	Willie Mays, SF	52
1918	Gavvy Cravath, Phil	8	1966	Hank Aaron, Atl	44
1919	Gavvy Cravath, Phil	12	1967	Hank Aaron, Atl	39
1920	Cy Williams, Phil	15	1968	Willie McCovey, SF	36
1921	George Kelly, NY	23	1969	Willie McCovey, SF	45
1922	Rogers Hornsby, StL	42	1970	Johnny Bench, Cin	45
1923	Cy Williams, Phil	41	1971	Willie Stargell, Pitt	48
1924	Jack Fournier, Bklyn	27	1972	Johnny Bench, Cin	40
1925	Rogers Hornsby, StL	39	1973	Willie Stargell, Pitt	44
1926	Hack Wilson, Chi	21	1974	Mike Schmidt, Phil	36
1927	Hack Wilson, Chi	30	1975	Mike Schmidt, Phil	38
	Cy Williams, Phil	30	1976	Mike Schmidt, Phil	38
1928	Hack Wilson, Chi	31	1977	George Foster, Cin	52
	Jim Bottomley, StL	31	1978	George Foster, Cin	40
1929	Chuck Klein, Phil	43	1979	Dave Kingman, Chi	48
1930	Hack Wilson, Chi	56	1980	Mike Schmidt, Phil	48
1931	Chuck Klein, Phil	31	1981	Mike Schmidt, Phil	31
1932	Chuck Klein, Phil	38	1982	Dave Kingman, NY	37
	Mel Ott, NY	38	1983	Mike Schmidt, Phil	40
1933	Chuck Klein, Phil	28	1984	Dale Murphy, Atl	36
1934	Ripper Collins, StL	35		Mike Schmidt, Phil	36
	Mel Ott, NY	35	1985	Dale Murphy, Atl	37
1935	Wally Berger, Bos	34	1986	Mike Schmidt, Phil	37
1936	Mel Ott, NY	33	1987	Andre Dawson, Chi	49
1937	Mel Ott, NY	31	1988	Darryl Strawberry, NY	39
	Joe Medwick, StL	31	1989	Kevin Mitchell, SF	47
1938	Mel Ott, NY	36	1990	Ryne Sandberg, Chi	40
1939	Johnny Mize, StL	28	1991	Howard Johnson, NY	38
1940	Johnny Mize, StL	43	1992	Fred McGriff, SD	35
1941	Dolph Camilli, Bklyn	34	1993	Barry Bonds, SF	46
1942	Mel Ott, NY	30	1994	Matt Williams, SF	43
1943	Bill Nicholson, Chi	29	1995	Dante Bichette, Col	40
1944	Bill Nicholson, Chi	33	1996	Andres Galarraga, Col	47
1945	Tommy Holmes, Bos	28	1997	Larry Walker, Col	49
1946	Ralph Kiner, Pitt	23	1998	Mark McGwire, StL	70
1947	Ralph Kiner, Pitt	51	1999	Mark McGwire, StL	65
	Johnny Mize, NY	51			

Runs Batted In Leaders

Year	Player and Team	RBI	Year	Player and Team	RBI
1900	Elmer Flick, Phil	110	1950	Del Ennis, Phil	126
1901	Honus Wagner, Pitt	126	1951	Monte Irvin, NY	121
1902	Honus Wagner, Pitt	91	1952	Hank Sauer, Chi	121
1903	Sam Mertes, NY	104	1953	Roy Campanella, Bklyn	142
1904	Bill Dahlen, NY	80	1954	Ted Kluszewski, Cin	141
1905	Cy Seymour, Cin	121	1955	Duke Snider, Bklyn	136
1906	Jim Nealon, Pitt	83	1956	Stan Musial, StL	109
	Harry Steinfeldt, Chi	83	1957	Hank Aaron, Mil	132
1907	Sherry Magee, Phil	85	1958	Ernie Banks, Chi	129
1908	Honus Wagner, Pitt	109	1959	Ernie Banks, Chi	143
1909	Honus Wagner, Pitt	100	1960	Hank Aaron, Mil	126
1910	Sherry Magee, Phil	123	1961	Orlando Cepeda, SF	142
1911	Wildfire Schulte, Chi	121	1962	Tommy Davis, LA	153
1912	Heinie Zimmerman, Chi	103	1963	Hank Aaron, Mil	130
1913	Gavvy Cravath, Phil	128	1964	Ken Boyer, StL	119
1914	Sherry Magee, Phil	103	1965	Deron Johnson, Cin	130
1915	Gavvy Cravath, Phil	115	1966	Hank Aaron, Atl	127
1916	Heinie Zimmerman, Chi-NY	83	1967	Orlando Cepeda, StL	111
1917	Heinie Zimmerman, NY	102	1968	Willie McCovey, SF	105
1918	Sherry Magee, Phil	76	1969	Willie McCovey, SF	126
1919	Hi Myers, Bklyn	73	1970	Johnny Bench, Cin	148
1920	George Kelly, NY	94	1971	Joe Torre, StL	137
	Rogers Hornsby, StL	94	1972	Johnny Bench, Cin	125
1921	Rogers Hornsby, StL	126	1973	Willie Stargell, Pitt	119
1922	Rogers Hornsby, StL	152	1974	Johnny Bench, Cin	129
1923	Irish Meusel, NY	125	1975	Greg Luzinski, Phil	120
1924	George Kelly, NY	136	1976	George Foster, Cin	121
1925	Rogers Hornsby, StL	143	1977	George Foster, Cin	149
1926	Jim Bottomley, StL	120	1978	George Foster, Cin	120
1927	Paul Waner, Pitt	131	1979	Dave Winfield, SD	118
1928	Jim Bottomley, StL	136	1980	Mike Schmidt, Phil	121
1929	Hack Wilson, Chi	159	1981	Mike Schmidt, Phil	91
1930	Hack Wilson, Chi	190	1982	Dale Murphy, Atl	109
1931	Chuck Klein, Phil	121		Al Oliver, Mtl	109
1932	Don Hurst, Phil	143	1983	Dale Murphy, Atl	121
1933	Chuck Klein, Phil	120	1984	Gary Carter, Mtl	106
1934	Mel Ott, NY	135		Mike Schmidt, Phil	106
1935	Wally Berger, Bos	130	1985	Dave Parker, Cin	125
1936	Joe Medwick, StL	138	1986	Mike Schmidt, Phil	119
1937	Joe Medwick, StL	154	1987	Andre Dawson, Chi	137
1938	Joe Medwick, StL	122	1988	Will Clark, SF	109
1939	Frank McCormick, Cin	128	1989	Kevin Mitchell, SF	125
1940	Johnny Mize, StL	137	1990	Matt Williams, SF	122
1941	Dolph Camilli, Bklyn	120	1991	Howard Johnson, NY	117
1942	Johnny Mize, NY	110	1992	Darren Daulton, Phil	109
1943	Bill Nicholson, Chi	128	1993	Barry Bonds, SF	123
1944	Bill Nicholson, Chi	122	1994	Jeff Bagwell, Hou	116
1945	Dixie Walker, Bklyn	124	1995	Dante Bichette, Col	128
1946	Enos Slaughter, StL	130	1996	Andres Galarraga, Col	150
1947	Johnny Mize, NY	138	1997	Andres Galarraga, Col	140
1948	Stan Musial, StL	131	1998	Sammy Sosa, Chi	158
1949	Ralph Kiner, Pitt	127	1999	Mark McGwire, StL	147

Leading Base Stealers

Year	Player and Team	SB	Year	Player and Team	SB
1900	George Van Haltren, NY	45	1948	Richie Ashburn, Phil	32
	Patsy Donovan, StL	45	1949	Jackie Robinson, Bklyn	37
1901	Honus Wagner, Pitt	48	1950	Sam Jethroe, Bos	35
1902	Honus Wagner, Pitt	43	1951	Sam Jethroe, Bos	35
1903	Jimmy Sheckard, Bklyn	67	1952	Pee Wee Reese, Bklyn	30
	Frank Chance, Chi	67	1953	Bill Bruton, Mil	26
1904	Honus Wagner, Pitt	53	1954	Bill Bruton, Mil	34
1905	Billy Maloney, Chi	59	1955	Bill Bruton, Mil	35
	Art Devlin, NY	59	1956	Willie Mays, NY	40
1906	Frank Chance, Chi	57	1957	Willie Mays, NY	38
1907	Honus Wagner, Pitt	61	1958	Willie Mays, SF	31
1908	Honus Wagner, Pitt	53	1959	Willie Mays, SF	27
1909	Bob Bescher, Cin	54	1960	Maury Wills, LA	50
1910	Bob Bescher, Cin	70	1961	Maury Wills, LA	35
1911	Bob Bescher, Cin	80	1962	Maury Wills, LA	104
1912	Bob Bescher, Cin	67	1963	Maury Wills, LA	40
1913	Max Carey, Pitt	61	1964	Maury Wills, LA	53
1914	George Burns, NY	62	1965	Maury Wills, LA	94
1915	Max Carey, Pitt	36	1966	Lou Brock, StL	74
1916	Max Carey, Pitt	63	1967	Lou Brock, StL	52
1917	Max Carey, Pitt	46	1968	Lou Brock, StL	62
1918	Max Carey, Pitt	58	1969	Lou Brock, StL	53
1919	George Burns, NY	40	1970	Bobby Tolan, Cin	57
1920	Max Carey, Pitt	52	1971	Lou Brock, StL	64
1921	Frankie Frisch, NY	49	1972	Lou Brock, StL	63
1922	Max Carey, Pitt	51	1973	Lou Brock, StL	70
1923	Max Carey, Pitt	51	1974	Lou Brock, StL	118
1924	Max Carey, Pitt	49	1975	Davey Lopes, LA	77
1925	Max Carey, Pitt	46	1976	Davey Lopes, LA	63
1926	Kiki Cuyler, Pitt	35	1977	Frank Taveras, Pitt	70
1927	Frankie Frisch, StL	48	1978	Omar Moreno, Pitt	71
1928	Kiki Cuyler, Chi	37	1979	Omar Moreno, Pitt	77
1929	Kiki Cuyler, Chi	43	1980	Ron LeFlore, Mtl	97
1930	Kiki Cuyler, Chi	37	1981	Tim Raines, Mtl	71
1931	Frankie Frisch, StL	28	1982	Tim Raines, Mtl	78
1932	Chuck Klein, Phil	20	1983	Tim Raines, Mtl	90
1933	Pepper Martin, StL	26	1984	Tim Raines, Mtl	75
1934	Pepper Martin, StL	23	1985	Vince Coleman, StL	110
1935	Augie Galan, Chi	22	1986	Vince Coleman, StL	107
1936	Pepper Martin, StL	23	1987	Vince Coleman, StL	109
1937	Augie Galan, Chi	23	1988	Vince Coleman, StL	81
1938	Stan Hack, Chi	16	1989	Vince Coleman, StL	65
1939	Stan Hack, Chi	17	1990	Vince Coleman, StL	77
	Lee Handley, Pitt	17	1991	Marquis Grissom, Mtl	76
1940	Lonny Frey, Cin	22	1992	Marquis Grissom, Mtl	78
1941	Danny Murtaugh, Phil	18	1993	Chuck Carr, Flor	58
1942	Pete Reiser, Bklyn	20	1994	Craig Biggio, Hou	39
1943	Arky Vaughan, Bklyn	20	1995	Quilvio Veras, Fla	56
1944	Johnny Barrett, Pitt	28	1996	Eric Young, Col	53
1945	Red Schoendienst, StL	26	1997	Tony Womack, Pitt	60
1946	Pete Reiser, Bklyn	34	1998	Tony Womack, Pitt	58
1947	Jackie Robinson, Bklyn	29	1999	Tony Womack, Ariz	72

Leading Pitchers—Winning Percentage

Year	Pitcher and Team	W	L	Pct	Year	Pitcher and Team	W	L	Pct
1900	Jesse Tannehill, Pitt	20	6	.769	1951	Preacher Roe, Bklyn	22	3	.880
1901	Jack Chesbro, Pitt	21	10	.677	1952	Hoyt Wilhelm, NY	15	3	.833
1902	Jack Chesbro, Pitt	28	6	.824	1953	Carl Erskine, Bklyn	20	6	.769
1903	Sam Leever, Pitt	25	7	.781	1954	Johnny Antonelli, NY	21	7	.750
1904	Joe McGinnity, NY	35	8	.814	1955	Don Newcombe, Bklyn	20	5	.800
1905	Sam Leever, Pitt	20	5	.800	1956	Don Newcombe, Bklyn	27	7	.794
1906	Ed Reulbach, Chi	19	4	.826	1957	Bob Buhl, Mil	18	7	.720
1907	Ed Reulbach, Chi	17	4	.810	1958	Warren Spahn, Mil	22	11	.667
1908	Ed Reulbach, Chi	24	7	.774		Lew Burdette, Mil	20	10	.667
1909	Christy Mathewson, NY	25	6	.806	1959	Roy Face, Pitt	18	1	.947
	Howie Camnitz, Pitt	25	6	.806	1960	Ernie Broglio, StL	21	9	.700
1910	King Cole, Chi	20	4	.833	1961	Johnny Podres, LA	18	5	.783
1911	Rube Marquard, NY	24	7	.774	1962	Bob Purkey, Cin	23	5	.821
1912	Claude Hendrix, Pitt	24	9	.727	1963	Ron Perranoski, LA	16	3	.842
1913	Bert Humphries, Chi	16	4	.800	1964	Sandy Koufax, LA	19	5	.792
1914	Bill James, Bos	26	7	.788	1965	Sandy Koufax, LA	26	8	.765
1915	Grover Alexander, Phil	31	10	.756	1966	Juan Marichal, SF	25	6	.806
1916	Tom Hughes, Bos	16	3	.842	1967	Dick Hughes, StL	16	6	.727
1917	Ferdie Schupp, NY	21	7	.750	1968	Steve Blass, Pitt	18	6	.750
1918	Claude Hendrix, Chi	19	7	.731	1969	Tom Seaver, NY	25	7	.781
1919	Dutch Ruether, Cin	19	6	.760	1970	Bob Gibson, StL	23	7	.767
1920	Burleigh Grimes, Bklyn	23	11	.676	1971	Don Gullett, Cin	16	6	.727
1921	Bill Doak, StL	15	6	.714	1972	Gary Nolan, Cin	15	5	.750
1922	Pete Donohue, Cin	18	9	.667	1973	Tommy John, LA	16	7	.696
1923	Dolf Luque, Cin	27	8	.771	1974	Andy Messersmith, LA	20	6	.769
1924	Emil Yde, Pitt	16	3	.842	1975	Don Gullett, Cin	15	4	.789
1925	Bill Sherdel, StL	15	6	.714	1976	Steve Carlton, Phil	20	7	.741
1926	Ray Kremer, Pitt	20	6	.769	1977	John Candelaria, Pitt	20	5	.800
1927	Larry Benton, Bos-NY	17	7	.708	1978	Gaylord Perry, SD	21	6	.778
1928	Larry Benton, NY	25	9	.735	1979	Tom Seaver, Cin	16	6	.727
1929	Charlie Root, Chi	19	6	.760	1980	Jim Bibby, Pitt	19	6	.760
1930	Freddie Fitzsimmons, NY	19	7	.731	1981*	Tom Seaver, Cin	14	2	.875
1931	Paul Derringer, StL	18	8	.692	1982	Phil Niekro, Atl	17	4	.810
1932	Lon Warneke, Chi	22	6	.786	1983	John Denny, Phil	19	6	.760
1933	Ben Cantwell, Bos	20	10	.667	1984	Rick Sutcliffe, Chi	16	1	.941
1934	Dizzy Dean, StL	30	7	.811	1985	Orel Hershiser, LA	19	3	.864
1935	Bill Lee, Chi	20	6	.769	1986	Bob Ojeda, NY	18	5	.783
1936	Carl Hubbell, NY	26	6	.813	1987	Dwight Gooden, NY	15	7	.682
1937	Carl Hubbell, NY	22	8	.733	1988	David Cone, NY	20	3	.870
1938	Bill Lee, Chi	22	9	.710	1989	Mike Bielecki, Chi	18	7	.720
1939	Paul Derringer, Cin	25	7	.781	1990	Doug Drabeck, Pitt	22	6	.786
1940	Freddie Fitzsimmons, Bklyn	16	2	.889	1991	John Smiley, Pitt	20	8	.714
1941	Elmer Riddle, Cin	19	4	.826		Jose Rijo, Cin	15	6	.714
1942	Larry French, Bklyn	15	4	.789	1992	Bob Tewksbury, StL	16	5	.762
1943	Mort Cooper, StL	21	8	.724	1993	Tom Glavine, Atl	22	6	.786
1944	Ted Wilks, StL	17	4	.810	1994	Ken Hill, Mtl	16	5	.762
1945	Harry Brecheen, StL	15	4	.789	1995	Greg Maddux, Atl	19	2	.905
1946	Murray Dickson, StL	15	6	.714	1996	John Smoltz, Atl	24	8	.750
1947	Larry Jansen, NY	21	5	.808	1997	Denny Neagle, Atl	20	5	.800
1948	Harry Brecheen, StL	20	7	.741	1998	John Smoltz, Atl	17	3	.850
1949	Preacher Roe, Bklyn	15	6	.714	1999	Mike Hampton, Hou	22	4	.846
1950	Sal Maglie, NY	18	4	.818					

*1981 percentages based on 10 or more victories. Note: Percentages based on 15 or more victories in all other years.

Leading Pitchers—Earned-Run Average

Year	Player and Team	ERA	Year	Player and Team	ERA
1900	Rube Waddell, Pitt	2.37	1951	Chet Nichols, Bos	2.88
1901	Jesse Tannehill, Pitt	2.18	1952	Hoyt Wilhelm, NY	2.43
1902	Jack Taylor, Chi	1.33	1953	Warren Spahn, Mil	2.10
1903	Sam Leever, Pitt	2.06	1954	Johnny Antonelli, NY	2.29
1904	Joe McGinnity, NY	1.61	1955	Bob Friend, Pitt	2.84
1905	Christy Mathewson, NY	1.27	1956	Lew Burdette, Mil	2.71
1906	Three Finger Brown, Chi	1.04	1957	Johnny Podres, Bklyn	2.66
1907	Jack Pfiester, Chi	1.15	1958	Stu Miller, SF	2.47
1908	Christy Mathewson, NY	1.43	1959	Sam Jones, SF	2.82
1909	Christy Mathewson, NY	1.14	1960	Mike McCormick, SF	2.70
1910	George McQuillan, Phil	1.60	1961	Warren Spahn, Mil	3.01
1911	Christy Mathewson, NY	1.99	1962	Sandy Koufax, LA	2.54
1912	Jeff Tesreau, NY	1.96	1963	Sandy Koufax, LA	1.88
1913	Christy Mathewson, NY	2.06	1964	Sandy Koufax, LA	1.74
1914	Bill Doak, StL	1.72	1965	Sandy Koufax, LA	2.04
1915	Grover Alexander, Phil	1.22	1966	Sandy Koufax, LA	1.73
1916	Grover Alexander, Phil	1.55	1967	Phil Niekro, Atl	1.87
1917	Grover Alexander, Phil	1.83	1968	Bob Gibson, StL	1.12
1918	Hippo Vaughn, Chi	1.74	1969	Juan Marichal, SF	2.10
1919	Grover Alexander, Chi	1.72	1970	Tom Seaver, NY	2.81
1920	Grover Alexander, Chi	1.91	1971	Tom Seaver, NY	1.76
1921	Bill Doak, StL	2.58	1972	Steve Carlton, Phil	1.98
1922	Rosy Ryan, NY	3.00	1973	Tom Seaver, NY	2.08
1923	Dolf Luque, Cin	1.93	1974	Buzz Capra, Atl	2.28
1924	Dazzy Vance, Bklyn	2.16	1975	Randy Jones, SD	2.24
1925	Dolf Luque, Cin	2.63	1976	John Denny, StL	2.52
1926	Ray Kremer, Pitt	2.61	1977	John Candelaria, Pitt	2.34
1927	Ray Kremer, Pitt	2.47	1978	Craig Swan, NY	2.43
1928	Dazzy Vance, Bklyn	2.09	1979	J.R. Richard, Hou	2.71
1929	Bill Walker, NY	3.08	1980	Don Sutton, LA	2.21
1930	Dazzy Vance, Bklyn	2.61	1981	Nolan Ryan, Hou	1.69
1931	Bill Walker, NY	2.26	1982	Steve Rogers, Mtl	2.40
1932	Lon Warneke, Chi	2.37	1983	Atlee Hammaker, SF	2.25
1933	Carl Hubbell, NY	1.66	1984	Alejandro Pena, LA	2.48
1934	Carl Hubbell, NY	2.30	1985	Dwight Gooden, NY	1.53
1935	Cy Blanton, Pitt	2.59	1986	Mike Scott, Hou	2.22
1936	Carl Hubbell, NY	2.31	1987	Nolan Ryan, Hou	2.76
1937	Jim Turner, Bos	2.38	1988	Joe Magrane, StL	2.18
1938	Bill Lee, Chi	2.66	1989	Scott Garrelts, SF	2.28
1939	Bucky Walters, Cin	2.29	1990	Danny Darwin, Hou	2.21
1940	Bucky Walters, Cin	2.48	1991	Dennis Martinez, Mtl	2.39
1941	Elmer Riddle, Cin	2.24	1992	Bill Swift, SF	2.08
1942	Mort Cooper, StL	1.77	1993	Greg Maddux, Atl	2.36
1943	Howie Pollet, StL	1.75	1994	Greg Maddux, Atl	1.56
1944	Ed Heusser, Cin	2.38	1995	Greg Maddux, Atl	1.63
1945	Hank Borowy, Chi	2.14	1996	Kevin Brown, Fla	1.89
1946	Howie Pollet, StL	2.10	1997	Pedro Martinez, Mtl	1.90
1947	Warren Spahn, Bos	2.33	1998	Greg Maddux, Atl	1.98
1948	Harry Brecheen, StL	2.24	1999	Randy Johnson, Ariz	2.48
1949	Dave Koslo, NY	2.50			
1950	Jim Hearn, StL-NY	2.49			

Note: Based on 10 complete games through 1950, then 154 innings until National League expanded in 1962, when it became 162 innings. In strike-shortened 1981, one inning per game required.

Leading Pitchers—Strikeouts

Year	Player and Team	SO	Year	Player and Team	SO
1900	Rube Waddell, Pitt	133	1950	Warren Spahn, Bos	191
1901	Noodles Hahn, Cin	233	1951	Warren Spahn, Bos	164
1902	Vic Willis, Bos	226		Don Newcombe, Bklyn	164
1903	Christy Mathewson, NY	267	1952	Warren Spahn, Bos	183
1904	Christy Mathewson, NY	212	1953	Robin Roberts, Phil	198
1905	Christy Mathewson, NY	206	1954	Robin Roberts, Phil	185
1906	Fred Beebe, Chi-StL	171	1955	Sam Jones, Chi	198
1907	Christy Mathewson, NY	178	1956	Sam Jones, Chi	176
1908	Christy Mathewson, NY	259	1957	Jack Sanford, Phil	188
1909	Orval Overall, Chi	205	1958	Sam Jones, StL	225
1910	Christy Mathewson, NY	190	1959	Don Drysdale, LA	242
1911	Rube Marquard, NY	237	1960	Don Drysdale, LA	246
1912	Grover Alexander, Phil	195	1961	Sandy Koufax, LA	269
1913	Tom Seaton, Phil	168	1962	Don Drysdale, LA	232
1914	Grover Alexander, Phil	214	1963	Sandy Koufax, LA	306
1915	Grover Alexander, Phil	241	1964	Bob Veale, Pitt	250
1916	Grover Alexander, Phil	167	1965	Sandy Koufax, LA	382
1917	Grover Alexander, Phil	200	1966	Sandy Koufax, LA	317
1918	Hippo Vaughn, Chi	148	1967	Jim Bunning, Phil	253
1919	Hippo Vaughn, Chi	141	1968	Bob Gibson, StL	268
1920	Grover Alexander, Chi	173	1969	Ferguson Jenkins, Chi	273
1921	Burleigh Grimes, Bklyn	136	1970	Tom Seaver, NY	283
1922	Dazzy Vance, Bklyn	134	1971	Tom Seaver, NY	289
1923	Dazzy Vance, Bklyn	197	1972	Steve Carlton, Phil	310
1924	Dazzy Vance, Bklyn	262	1973	Tom Seaver, NY	251
1925	Dazzy Vance, Bklyn	221	1974	Steve Carlton, Phil	240
1926	Dazzy Vance, Bklyn	140	1975	Tom Seaver, NY	243
1927	Dazzy Vance, Bklyn	184	1976	Tom Seaver, NY	235
1928	Dazzy Vance, Bklyn	200	1977	Phil Niekro, Atl	262
1929	Pat Malone, Chi	166	1978	J.R. Richard, Hou	303
1930	Bill Hallahan, StL	177	1979	J.R. Richard, Hou	313
1931	Bill Hallahan, StL	159	1980	Steve Carlton, Phil	286
1932	Dizzy Dean, StL	191	1981	Fernando Valenzuela, LA	180
1933	Dizzy Dean, StL	199	1982	Steve Carlton, Phil	286
1934	Dizzy Dean, StL	195	1983	Steve Carlton, Phil	275
1935	Dizzy Dean, StL	182	1984	Dwight Gooden, NY	276
1936	Van Lingle Mungo, Bklyn	238	1985	Dwight Gooden, NY	268
1937	Carl Hubbell, NY	159	1986	Mike Scott, Hou	306
1938	Clay Bryant, Chi	135	1987	Nolan Ryan, Hou	270
1939	Claude Passeau, Phil-Chi	137	1988	Nolan Ryan, Hou	228
	Bucky Walters, Cin	137	1989	Jose DeLeon, StL	201
1940	Kirby Higbe, Phil	137	1990	David Cone, NY	233
1941	Johnny Vander Meer, Cin	202	1991	David Cone, NY	241
1942	Johnny Vander Meer, Cin	186	1992	John Smoltz, Atl	215
1943	Johnny Vander Meer, Cin	174	1993	Jose Rijo, Cin	227
1944	Bill Voiselle, NY	161	1994	Andy Benes, SD	189
1945	Preacher Roe, Pitt	148	1995	Hideo Nomo, LA	236
1946	Johnny Schmitz, Chi	135	1996	John Smoltz, Atl	276
1947	Ewell Blackwell, Cin	193	1997	Curt Schilling, Phil	319
1948	Harry Brecheen, StL	149	1998	Curt Schilling, Phil	300
1949	Warren Spahn, Bos	151	1999	Randy Johnson, Ariz	364

Leading Pitchers—Saves

Year	Player and Team	SV	Year	Player and Team	SV
1947	Hugh Casey, Bklyn	18	1974	Mike Marshall, LA	21
1948	Harry Gumpert, Cin	17	1975	Al Hrabosky, StL	22
1949	Ted Wilks, StL	9		Rawly Eastwick, Cin	22
1950	Jim Konstanty, Phil	22	1976	Rawly Eastwick, Cin	26
1951	Ted Wilks, StL, Pitt	13	1977	Rollie Fingers, SD	35
1952	Al Brazle, StL	16	1978	Rollie Fingers, SD	37
1953	Al Brazle, StL	18	1979	Bruce Sutter, Chi	37
1954	Jim Hughes, Bklyn	24	1980	Bruce Sutter, Chi	28
1955	Jack Meyer, Phil	16	1981	Bruce Sutter, StL	25
1956	Clem Labine, Bklyn	19	1982	Bruce Sutter, StL	36
1957	Clem Labine, Bklyn	17	1983	Lee Smith, Chi	29
1958	Roy Face, Pitt	20	1984	Bruce Sutter, StL	45
1959	Lindy McDaniel, StL	15	1985	Jeff Reardon, Mtl	41
	Don McMahon, Mil	15	1986	Todd Worrell, StL	36
1960	Lindy McDaniel, StL	26	1987	Steve Bedrosian, Phil	40
1961	Stu Miller, SF	17	1988	John Franco, Cin	39
	Roy Face, Pitt	17	1989	Mark Davis, SD	44
1962	Roy Face, Pitt	28	1990	John Franco, NY	33
1963	Lindy McDaniel, Chi	22	1991	Lee Smith, StL	47
1964	Hal Woodeshick, Hou	23	1992	Lee Smith, StL	42
1965	Ted Abernathy, Chi	31	1993	Randy Myers, Chi	53
1966	Phil Regan, LA	21	1994	John Franco, NY	30
1967	Ted Abernathy, Cin	28	1995	Randy Myers, Chi	38
1968	Phil Regan, Chi, LA	25	1996	Jeff Brantley, Cin	44
1969	Fred Gladding, Hou	29		Todd Worrell, LA	44
1970	Wayne Granger, Cin	35	1997	Jeff Shaw, Cin	42
1971	Dave Giusti, Pitt	30	1998	Trevor Hoffman, SD	53
1972	Clay Carroll, Cin	37	1999	Ugueth Urbina, Mtl	41
1973	Mike Marshall, Mtl	13			

The Sad Case of Peter and Paul

Five days after he started the Mets' 1997 opener, Pete Harnisch told manager Bobby Valentine that he couldn't go back out there. Harnisch was anxious and unable to sleep, effects he thought were caused by ending a 13-year chewing tobacco habit. Later, though, Harnisch learned he was suffering from depression. The 1991 National League All-Star went on the disabled list for four months while undergoing treatment.

According to Harnisch, Valentine had accused him of being "afraid to pitch," a cruel charge in light of more recent events. In fact Harnisch showed immense courage in fighting a disease that now threatens to tear his family apart.

Harnisch got his career back on track in 1998, going 14–7 for the Reds. He also became a spokesman for the company that makes Paxil, an antidepressant he took for six months, and told *The New York Times* that his ordeal proved that "you can get through this thing, you can get your life and your personality back." Pete's older brother Paul, however, might never get his life back.

Paul Harnisch, 39, was an assistant district attorney for Orange County, N.Y. In 1990 doctors told him he had bipolar disorder, or manic depression—such disorders tend to run in families. The Harnisch family was rocked on June 26, 1999, when Paul, wearing only a pair of panty hose, drove his car down a bicycle trail on which newlyweds Ed and Tammi Quirk were rollerblading. Harnisch's car missed Tammie but struck Ed with such force that his head and torso crashed through the windshield and into the passenger seat. Paul drove on for about 500 yards with Quirk's body beside him, then pulled over. He told bystanders he needed help, walked into town, stole a car and drove around Chester, N.Y., until police stopped him. Paul told them he was on a top secret mission. The following month he was charged with grand larceny and second-degree murder.

At a July 15, 1999, hearing attended by Pete, Judge Joseph West released Paul on $125,000 bail with the stipulation that he be held in a mental ward with an electronic monitor on his ankle. William Tendy, Paul's lawyer, planned a defense based on his client's psychiatric problems. The court may well consider Paul's case in light of his family history, including Pete's depression.

Pete didn't want to add to his family's sorrow by talking about his brother. Instead as he struggled to deal with Paul's troubles he took the ball every fifth day, went out and did his job. He finished the '99 season at 16–10, with a 3.68 ERA, 11th best in the league, for a surprising Reds club that lost to the Mets in a one-game playoff for the National League wild card berth.

Pennant Winners

Year	Team	Manager	W	L	Pct	GA
1901	Chicago	Clark Griffith	83	53	.610	4
1902	Philadelphia	Connie Mack	83	53	.610	5
1903	Boston	Jimmy Collins	91	47	.659	14½
1904	Boston	Jimmy Collins	95	59	.617	1½
1905	Philadelphia	Connie Mack	92	56	.622	2
1906	Chicago	Fielder Jones	93	58	.616	3
1907	Detroit	Hughie Jennings	92	58	.613	1½
1908	Detroit	Hughie Jennings	90	63	.588	½
1909	Detroit	Hughie Jennings	98	54	.645	3½
1910	Philadelphia	Connie Mack	102	48	.680	14½
1911	Philadelphia	Connie Mack	101	50	.669	13½
1912	Boston	Jake Stahl	105	47	.691	14
1913	Philadelphia	Connie Mack	96	57	.627	6½
1914	Philadelphia	Connie Mack	99	53	.651	8½
1915	Boston	Bill Carrigan	101	50	.669	2½
1916	Boston	Bill Carrigan	91	63	.591	2
1917	Chicago	Pants Rowland	100	54	.649	9
1918	Boston	Ed Barrow	75	51	.595	2½
1919	Chicago	Kid Gleason	88	52	.629	3½
1920	Cleveland	Tris Speaker	98	56	.636	2
1921	New York	Miller Huggins	98	55	.641	4½
1922	New York	Miller Huggins	94	60	.610	1
1923	New York	Miller Huggins	98	54	.645	16
1924	Washington	Bucky Harris	92	62	.597	2
1925	Washington	Bucky Harris	96	55	.636	8½
1926	New York	Miller Huggins	91	63	.591	3
1927	New York	Miller Huggins	110	44	.714	19
1928	New York	Miller Huggins	101	53	.656	2½
1929	Philadelphia	Connie Mack	104	46	.693	18
1930	Philadelphia	Connie Mack	102	52	.662	8
1931	Philadelphia	Connie Mack	107	45	.704	13½
1932	New York	Joe McCarthy	107	47	.695	13
1933	Washington	Joe Cronin	99	53	.651	7
1934	Detroit	Mickey Cochrane	101	53	.656	7
1935	Detroit	Mickey Cochrane	93	58	.616	3
1936	New York	Joe McCarthy	102	51	.667	19½
1937	New York	Joe McCarthy	102	52	.662	13
1938	New York	Joe McCarthy	99	53	.651	9½
1939	New York	Joe McCarthy	106	45	.702	17
1940	Detroit	Del Baker	90	64	.584	1
1941	New York	Joe McCarthy	101	53	.656	17
1942	New York	Joe McCarthy	103	51	.669	9
1943	New York	Joe McCarthy	98	56	.636	13½
1944	St. Louis	Luke Sewell	89	65	.578	1
1945	Detroit	Steve O'Neill	88	65	.575	1½
1946	Boston	Joe Cronin	104	50	.675	12
1947	New York	Bucky Harris	97	57	.630	12
1948	Cleveland†	Lou Boudreau	97	58	.626	1
1949	New York	Casey Stengel	97	57	.630	1
1950	New York	Casey Stengel	98	56	.636	3
1951	New York	Casey Stengel	98	56	.636	5
1952	New York	Casey Stengel	95	59	.617	2
1953	New York	Casey Stengel	99	52	.656	8½
1954	Cleveland	Al Lopez	111	43	.721	8
1955	New York	Casey Stengel	96	58	.623	3
1956	New York	Casey Stengel	97	57	.630	9
1957	New York	Casey Stengel	98	56	.636	8
1958	New York	Casey Stengel	92	62	.597	10
1959	Chicago	Al Lopez	94	60	.610	5
1960	New York	Casey Stengel	97	57	.630	8
1961	New York	Ralph Houk	109	53	.673	8
1962	New York	Ralph Houk	96	66	.593	5
1963	New York	Ralph Houk	104	57	.646	10½
1964	New York	Yogi Berra	99	63	.611	1
1965	Minnesota	Sam Mele	102	60	.630	7
1966	Baltimore	Hank Bauer	97	63	.606	9

Pennant Winners (Cont.)

Year	Team	Manager	W	L	Pct	GA
1967	Boston	Dick Williams	92	70	.568	1
1968	Detroit	Mayo Smith	103	59	.636	12
1969	Baltimore (E)‡	Earl Weaver	109	53	.673	19
1970	Baltimore (E)‡	Earl Weaver	108	54	.667	15
1971	Baltimore (E)‡	Earl Weaver	101	57	.639	12
1972	Oakland (W)‡	Dick Williams	93	62	.600	5½
1973	Oakland (W)‡	Dick Williams	94	68	.580	6
1974	Oakland (W)‡	Al Dark	90	72	.556	5
1975	Boston (E)‡	Darrell Johnson	95	65	.594	4½
1976	New York (E)‡	Billy Martin	97	62	.610	10½
1977	New York (E)‡	Billy Martin	100	62	.617	2½
1978	New York (E)†‡	Billy Martin, Bob Lemon	100	63	.613	1
1979	Baltimore (E)‡	Earl Weaver	102	57	.642	8
1980	Kansas City (W)‡	Jim Frey	97	65	.599	14
1981	New York (E)‡	Gene Michael, Bob Lemon	59	48	.551	#
1982	Milwaukee (E)‡	Buck Rodgers, Harvey Kuenn	95	67	.586	1
1983	Baltimore (E)‡	Joe Altobelli	98	64	.605	6
1984	Detroit (E)‡	Sparky Anderson	104	58	.642	15
1985	Kansas City (W)‡	Dick Howser	91	71	.562	1
1986	Boston (E)‡	John McNamara	95	66	.590	5½
1987	Minnesota (W)‡	Tom Kelly	85	77	.525	2
1988	Oakland (W)‡	Tony La Russa	104	58	.642	13
1989	Oakland (W)‡	Tony La Russa	99	63	.611	7
1990	Oakland (W)‡	Tony La Russa	103	59	.636	9
1991	Minnesota (W)‡	Tom Kelly	95	67	.586	8
1992	Toronto‡	Cito Gaston	96	66	.593	4
1993	Toronto‡	Cito Gaston	95	67	.586	7
1994	Season ended Aug. 11 due to players' strike					
1995	Cleveland (C)‡	Mike Hargrove	100	44	.694	30
1996	New York (E)‡	Joe Torre	92	70	.568	4
1997	Cleveland (C)‡	Mike Hargrove	86	75	.534	6
1998	New York (E)‡	Joe Torre	114	48	.704	22
1999	New York (E)‡	Joe Torre	98	64	.605	4

†Defeated Boston in one-game playoff. ‡Won championship series.
#First half 34–22; second 25–26, in season split by strike; defeated Milwaukee in playoff for Eastern Divison title.

Leading Batsmen

Year	Player and Team	BA	Year	Player and Team	BA
1901	Nap Lajoie, Phil	.422	1924	Babe Ruth, NY	.378
1902	Ed Delahanty, Wash	.376	1925	Harry Heilmann, Det	.393
1903	Nap Lajoie, Clev	.355	1926	Heinie Manush, Det	.378
1904	Nap Lajoie, Clev	.381	1927	Harry Heilmann, Det	.398
1905	Elmer Flick, Clev	.306	1928	Goose Goslin, Wash	.379
1906	George Stone, StL	.358	1929	Lew Fonseca, Clev	.369
1907	Ty Cobb, Det	.350	1930	Al Simmons, Phil	.381
1908	Ty Cobb, Det	.324	1931	Al Simmons, Phil	.390
1909	Ty Cobb, Det	.377	1932	Dale Alexander, Det-Bos	.367
1910	Nap Lajoie, Clev*	.383	1933	Jimmie Foxx, Phil	.356
1911	Ty Cobb, Det	.420	1934	Lou Gehrig, NY	.363
1912	Ty Cobb, Det	.410	1935	Buddy Myer, Wash	.349
1913	Ty Cobb, Det	.390	1936	Luke Appling, Chi	.388
1914	Ty Cobb, Det	.368	1937	Charlie Gehringer, Det	.371
1915	Ty Cobb, Det	.369	1938	Jimmie Foxx, Bos	.349
1916	Tris Speaker, Clev	.386	1939	Joe DiMaggio, NY	.381
1917	Ty Cobb, Det	.383	1940	Joe DiMaggio, NY	.352
1918	Ty Cobb, Det	.382	1941	Ted Williams, Bos	.406
1919	Ty Cobb, Det	.384	1942	Ted Williams, Bos	.356
1920	George Sisler, StL	.407	1943	Luke Appling, Chi	.328
1921	Harry Heilmann, Det	.394	1944	Lou Boudreau, Clev	.327
1922	George Sisler, StL	.420	1945	Snuffy Stirnweiss, NY	.309
1923	Harry Heilmann, Det	.403	1946	Mickey Vernon, Wash	.353

*League president Ban Johnson declared Ty Cobb batting champion with a .385 average, beating Lajoie's .384. However, subsequent research has led to the revision of Lajoie's average to .383 and Cobb's to .382.

Leading Batsmen (Cont.)

Year	Player and Team	BA	Year	Player and Team	BA
1947	Ted Williams, Bos	.343	1974	Rod Carew, Minn	.364
1948	Ted Williams, Bos	.369	1975	Rod Carew, Minn	.359
1949	George Kell, Det	.343	1976	George Brett, KC	.333
1950	Billy Goodman, Bos	.354	1977	Rod Carew, Minn	.388
1951	Ferris Fain, Phil	.344	1978	Rod Carew, Minn	.333
1952	Ferris Fain, Phil	.327	1979	Fred Lynn, Bos	.333
1953	Mickey Vernon, Wash	.337	1980	George Brett, KC	.390
1954	Bobby Avila, Clev	.341	1981	Carney Lansford, Bos	.336
1955	Al Kaline, Det	.340	1982	Willie Wilson, KC	.332
1956	Mickey Mantle, NY	.353	1983	Wade Boggs, Bos	.361
1957	Ted Williams, Bos	.388	1984	Don Mattingly, NY	.343
1958	Ted Williams, Bos	.328	1985	Wade Boggs, Bos	.368
1959	Harvey Kuenn, Det	.353	1986	Wade Boggs, Bos	.357
1960	Pete Runnels, Bos	.320	1987	Wade Boggs, Bos	.363
1961	Norm Cash, Det	.361	1988	Wade Boggs, Bos	.366
1962	Pete Runnels, Bos	.326	1989	Kirby Puckett, Minn	.339
1963	Carl Yastrzemski, Bos	.321	1990	George Brett, KC	.329
1964	Tony Oliva, Minn	.323	1991	Julio Franco, Tex	.341
1965	Tony Oliva, Minn	.321	1992	Edgar Martinez, Sea	.343
1966	Frank Robinson, Balt	.316	1993	John Olerud, Tor	.363
1967	Carl Yastrzemski, Bos	.326	1994	Paul O'Neill, NY	.359
1968	Carl Yastrzemski, Bos	.301	1995	Edgar Martinez, Sea	.356
1969	Rod Carew, Minn	.332	1996	Alex Rodriguez, Sea	.358
1970	Alex Johnson, Cal	.329	1997	Frank Thomas, Chi	.347
1971	Tony Oliva, Minn	.337	1998	Bernie Williams, NY	.339
1972	Rod Carew, Minn	.318	1999	Nomar Garciaparra, Bos	.357
1973	Rod Carew, Minn	.350			

Leaders in Runs Scored

Year	Player and Team	Runs	Year	Player and Team	Runs
1901	Nap Lajoie, Phil	145	1937	Joe DiMaggio, NY	151
1902	Dave Fultz, Phil	110	1938	Hank Greenberg, Det	144
1903	Patsy Dougherty, Bos	108	1939	Red Rolfe, NY	139
1904	Patsy Dougherty, Bos-NY	113	1940	Ted Williams, Bos	134
1905	Harry Davis, Phil	92	1941	Ted Williams, Bos	135
1906	Elmer Flick, Clev	98	1942	Ted Williams, Bos	141
1907	Sam Crawford, Det	102	1943	George Case, Wash	102
1908	Matty McIntyre, Det	105	1944	Snuffy Stirnweiss, NY	125
1909	Ty Cobb, Det	116	1945	Snuffy Stirnweiss, NY	107
1910	Ty Cobb, Det	106	1946	Ted Williams, Bos	142
1911	Ty Cobb, Det	147	1947	Ted Williams, Bos	125
1912	Eddie Collins, Phil	137	1948	Tommy Henrich, NY	138
1913	Eddie Collins, Phil	125	1949	Ted Williams, Bos	150
1914	Eddie Collins, Phil	122	1950	Dom DiMaggio, Bos	131
1915	Ty Cobb, Det	144	1951	Dom DiMaggio, Bos	113
1916	Ty Cobb, Det	113	1952	Larry Doby, Clev	104
1917	Donie Bush, Det	112	1953	Al Rosen, Clev	115
1918	Ray Chapman, Clev	84	1954	Mickey Mantle, NY	129
1919	Babe Ruth, Bos	103	1955	Al Smith, Clev	123
1920	Babe Ruth, NY	158	1956	Mickey Mantle, NY	132
1921	Babe Ruth, NY	177	1957	Mickey Mantle, NY	121
1922	George Sisler, StL	134	1958	Mickey Mantle, NY	127
1923	Babe Ruth, NY	151	1959	Eddie Yost, Det	115
1924	Babe Ruth, NY	143	1960	Mickey Mantle, NY	119
1925	Johnny Mostil, Chi	135	1961	Mickey Mantle, NY	132
1926	Babe Ruth, NY	139		Roger Maris, NY	132
1927	Babe Ruth, NY	158	1962	Albie Pearson, LA	115
1928	Babe Ruth, NY	163	1963	Bob Allison, Minn	99
1929	Charlie Gehringer, Det	131	1964	Tony Oliva, Minn	109
1930	Al Simmons, Phil	152	1965	Zoilo Versalles, Minn	126
1931	Lou Gehrig, NY	163	1966	Frank Robinson, Balt	122
1932	Jimmie Foxx, Phil	151	1967	Carl Yastrzemski, Bos	112
1933	Lou Gehrig, NY	138	1968	Dick McAuliffe, Det	95
1934	Charlie Gehringer, Det	134	1969	Reggie Jackson, Oak	123
1935	Lou Gehrig, NY	125	1970	Carl Yastrzemski, Bos	125
1936	Lou Gehrig, NY	167	1971	Don Buford, Balt	99

Leaders in Runs Scored *(Cont.)*

Year	Player and Team	Runs	Year	Player and Team	Runs
1972	Bobby Murcer, NY	102	1987	Paul Molitor, Mil	114
1973	Reggie Jackson, Oak	99	1988	Wade Boggs, Bos	128
1974	Carl Yastrzemski, Bos	93	1989	Rickey Henderson, NY-Oak	113
1975	Fred Lynn, Bos	103		Wade Boggs, Bos	113
1976	Roy White, NY	104	1990	Rickey Henderson, Oak	119
1977	Rod Carew, Minn	128	1991	Paul Molitor, Mil	133
1978	Ron LeFlore, Det	126	1992	Tony Phillips, Det	114
1979	Don Baylor, Cal	120	1993	Rafael Palmeiro, Tex	124
1980	Willie Wilson, KC	133	1994	Frank Thomas, Chi	106
1981	Rickey Henderson, Oak	89	1995	Albert Belle, Clev	121
1982	Paul Molitor, Mil	136		Edgar Martinez, Sea	121
1983	Cal Ripken, Balt	121	1996	Alex Rodriguez, Sea	141
1984	Dwight Evans, Bos	121	1997	Ken Griffey Jr., Sea	125
1985	Rickey Henderson, NY	146	1998	Derek Jeter, NY	127
1986	Rickey Henderson, NY	130	1999	Roberto Alomar, Clev	138

Leaders in Hits

Year	Player and Team	Hits	Year	Player and Team	Hits
1901	Nap Lajoie, Phil	229	1943	Dick Wakefield, Det	200
1902	Piano Legs Hickman, Bos-Clev	194	1944	Snuffy Stirnweiss, NY	205
1903	Patsy Dougherty, Bos	195	1945	Snuffy Stirnweiss, NY	195
1904	Nap Lajoie, Clev	211	1946	Johnny Pesky, Bos	208
1905	George Stone, StL	187	1947	Johnny Pesky, Bos	207
1906	Nap Lajoie, Clev	214	1948	Bob Dillinger, StL	207
1907	Ty Cobb, Det	212	1949	Dale Mitchell, Clev	203
1908	Ty Cobb, Det	188	1950	George Kell, Det	218
1909	Ty Cobb, Det	216	1951	George Kell, Det	191
1910	Nap Lajoie, Clev	227	1952	Nellie Fox, Chi	192
1911	Ty Cobb, Det	248	1953	Harvey Kuenn, Det	209
1912	Ty Cobb, Det	227	1954	Nellie Fox, Chi	201
1913	Joe Jackson, Clev	197		Harvey Kuenn, Det	201
1914	Tris Speaker, Bos	193	1955	Al Kaline, Det	200
1915	Ty Cobb, Det	208	1956	Harvey Kuenn, Det	196
1916	Tris Speaker, Clev	211	1957	Nellie Fox, Chi	196
1917	Ty Cobb, Det	225	1958	Nellie Fox, Chi	187
1918	George Burns, Phil	178	1959	Harvey Kuenn, Det	198
1919	Ty Cobb, Det	191	1960	Minnie Minoso, Chi	184
	Bobby Veach, Det	191	1961	Norm Cash, Det	193
1920	George Sisler, StL	257	1962	Bobby Richardson, NY	209
1921	Harry Heilmann, Det	237	1963	Carl Yastrzemski, Bos	183
1922	George Sisler, StL	246	1964	Tony Oliva, Minn	217
1923	Charlie Jamieson, Clev	222	1965	Tony Oliva, Minn	185
1924	Sam Rice, Wash	216	1966	Tony Oliva, Minn	191
1925	Al Simmons, Phil	253	1967	Carl Yastrzemski, Bos	189
1926	George Burns, Clev	216	1968	Bert Campaneris, Oak	177
	Sam Rice, Wash	216	1969	Tony Oliva, Minn	197
1927	Earle Combs, NY	231	1970	Tony Oliva, Minn	204
1928	Heinie Manush, StL	241	1971	Cesar Tovar, Minn	204
1929	Dale Alexander, Det	215	1972	Joe Rudi, Oak	181
	Charlie Gehringer, Det	215	1973	Rod Carew, Minn	203
1930	Johnny Hodapp, Clev	225	1974	Rod Carew, Minn	218
1931	Lou Gehrig, NY	211	1975	George Brett, KC	195
1932	Al Simmons, Phil	216	1976	George Brett, KC	215
1933	Heinie Manush, Wash	221	1977	Rod Carew, Minn	239
1934	Charlie Gehringer, Det	214	1978	Jim Rice, Bos	213
1935	Joe Vosmik, Clev	216	1979	George Brett, KC	212
1936	Earl Averill, Clev	232	1980	Willie Wilson, KC	230
1937	Beau Bell, StL	218	1981	Rickey Henderson, Oak	135
1938	Joe Vosmik, Bos	201	1982	Robin Yount, Mil	210
1939	Red Rolfe, NY	213	1983	Cal Ripken, Balt	211
1940	Rip Radcliff, StL	200	1984	Don Mattingly, NY	207
	Barney McCosky, Det	200	1985	Wade Boggs, Bos	240
	Doc Cramer, Bos	200	1986	Don Mattingly, NY	238
1941	Cecil Travis, Wash	218	1987	Kirby Puckett, Minn	207
1942	Johnny Pesky, Bos	205		Kevin Seitzer, KC	207

Leaders in Hits (Cont.)

Year	Player and Team	Hits	Year	Player and Team	Hits
1988	Kirby Puckett, Minn	234	1994	Kenny Lofton, Clev	160
1989	Kirby Puckett, Minn	215	1995	Lance Johnson, Chi	186
1990	Rafael Palmeiro, Tex	191	1996	Paul Molitor, Minn	225
1991	Paul Molitor, Mil	216	1997	Nomar Garciaparra, Bos	209
1992	Kirby Puckett, Minn	210	1998	Alex Rodriguez, Sea	213
1993	Paul Molitor, Tor	211	1999	Derek Jeter, NY	219

Home Run Leaders

Year	Player and Team	HR	Year	Player and Team	HR
1901	Nap Lajoie, Phil	13	1953	Al Rosen, Clev	43
1902	Socks Seybold, Phil	16	1954	Larry Doby, Clev	32
1903	Buck Freeman, Bos	13	1955	Mickey Mantle, NY	37
1904	Harry Davis, Phil	10	1956	Mickey Mantle, NY	52
1905	Harry Davis, Phil	8	1957	Roy Sievers, Wash	42
1906	Harry Davis, Phil	12	1958	Mickey Mantle, NY	42
1907	Harry Davis, Phil	8	1959	Rocky Colavito, Clev	42
1908	Sam Crawford, Det	7		Harmon Killebrew, Wash	42
1909	Ty Cobb, Det	9	1960	Mickey Mantle, NY	40
1910	Jake Stahl, Bos	10	1961	Roger Maris, NY	61
1911	Frank Baker, Phil	9	1962	Harmon Killebrew, Minn	48
1912	Frank Baker, Phil	10	1963	Harmon Killebrew, Minn	45
	Tris Speaker, Bos	10	1964	Harmon Killebrew, Minn	49
1913	Frank Baker, Phil	13	1965	Tony Conigliaro, Bos	32
1914	Frank Baker, Phil	9	1966	Frank Robinson, Balt	49
1915	Braggo Roth, Chi-Clev	7	1967	Harmon Killebrew, Minn	44
1916	Wally Pipp, NY	12		Carl Yastrzemski, Bos	44
1917	Wally Pipp, NY	9	1968	Frank Howard, Wash	44
1918	Babe Ruth, Bos	11	1969	Harmon Killebrew, Minn	49
	Tilly Walker, Phil	11	1970	Frank Howard, Wash	44
1919	Babe Ruth, Bos	29	1971	Bill Melton, Chi	33
1920	Babe Ruth, NY	54	1972	Dick Allen, Chi	37
1921	Babe Ruth, NY	59	1973	Reggie Jackson, Oak	32
1922	Ken Williams, StL	39	1974	Dick Allen, Chi	32
1923	Babe Ruth, NY	41	1975	Reggie Jackson, Oak	36
1924	Babe Ruth, NY	46		George Scott, Mil	36
1925	Bob Meusel, NY	33	1976	Graig Nettles, NY	32
1926	Babe Ruth, NY	47	1977	Jim Rice, Bos	39
1927	Babe Ruth, NY	60	1978	Jim Rice, Bos	46
1928	Babe Ruth, NY	54	1979	Gorman Thomas, Mil	45
1929	Babe Ruth, NY	46	1980	Reggie Jackson, NY	41
1930	Babe Ruth, NY	49		Ben Oglivie, Mil	41
1931	Babe Ruth, NY	46	1981	Tony Armas, Oak	22
	Lou Gehrig, NY	46	1981	Dwight Evans, Bos	22
1932	Jimmie Foxx, Phil	58		Bobby Grich, Cal	22
1933	Jimmie Foxx, Phil	48		Eddie Murray, Balt	22
1934	Lou Gehrig, NY	49	1982	Reggie Jackson, Cal	39
1935	Jimmie Foxx, Phil	36		Gorman Thomas, Mil	39
	Hank Greenberg, Det	36	1983	Jim Rice, Bos	39
1936	Lou Gehrig, NY	49	1984	Tony Armas, Bos	43
1937	Joe DiMaggio, NY	46	1985	Darrell Evans, Det	40
1938	Hank Greenberg, Det	58	1986	Jesse Barfield, Tor	40
1939	Jimmie Foxx, Bos	35	1987	Mark McGwire, Oak	49
1940	Hank Greenberg, Det	41	1988	Jose Canseco, Oak	42
1941	Ted Williams, Bos	37	1989	Fred McGriff, Tor	36
1942	Ted Williams, Bos	36	1990	Cecil Fielder, Det	51
1943	Rudy York, Det	34	1991	Jose Canseco, Oak	44
1944	Nick Etten, NY	22		Cecil Fielder, Det	44
1945	Vern Stephens, StL	24	1992	Juan Gonzalez, Tex	43
1946	Hank Greenberg, Det	44	1993	Juan Gonzalez, Tex	46
1947	Ted Williams, Bos	32	1994	Ken Griffey Jr., Sea	40
1948	Joe DiMaggio, NY	39	1995	Albert Belle, Clev	50
1949	Ted Williams, Bos	43	1996	Mark McGwire, Oak	52
1950	Al Rosen, Clev	37	1997	Ken Griffey Jr., Sea	56
1951	Gus Zernial, Chi-Phil	33	1998	Ken Griffey Jr., Sea	56
1952	Larry Doby, Clev	32	1999	Ken Griffey Jr., Sea	48

Runs Batted In Leaders

Year	Player and Team	RBI	Year	Player and Team	RBI
1907	Ty Cobb, Det	116	1953	Al Rosen, Clev	145
1908	Ty Cobb, Det	108	1954	Larry Doby, Clev	126
1909	Ty Cobb, Det	107	1955	Ray Boone, Det	116
1910	Sam Crawford, Det	120		Jackie Jensen, Bos	116
1911	Ty Cobb, Det	144	1956	Mickey Mantle, NY	130
1912	Frank Baker, Phil	133	1957	Roy Sievers, Wash	114
1913	Frank Baker, Phil	126	1958	Jackie Jensen, Bos	122
1914	Sam Crawford, Det	104	1959	Jackie Jensen, Bos	112
1915	Sam Crawford, Det	112	1960	Roger Maris, NY	112
	Bobby Veach, Det	112	1961	Roger Maris, NY	142
1916	Del Pratt, StL	103	1962	Harmon Killebrew, Minn	126
1917	Bobby Veach, Det	103	1963	Dick Stuart, Bos	118
1918	Bobby Veach, Det	78	1964	Brooks Robinson, Balt	118
1919	Babe Ruth, Bos	114	1965	Rocky Colavito, Clev	108
1920	Babe Ruth, NY	137	1966	Frank Robinson, Balt	122
1921	Babe Ruth, NY	171	1967	Carl Yastrzemski, Bos	121
1922	Ken Williams, StL	155	1968	Ken Harrelson, Bos	109
1923	Babe Ruth, NY	131	1969	Harmon Killebrew, Minn	140
1924	Goose Goslin, Wash	129	1970	Frank Howard, Wash	126
1925	Bob Meusel, NY	138	1971	Harmon Killebrew, Minn	119
1926	Babe Ruth, NY	145	1972	Dick Allen, Chi	113
1927	Lou Gehrig, NY	175	1973	Reggie Jackson, Oak	117
1928	Babe Ruth, NY	142	1974	Jeff Burroughs, Tex	118
	Lou Gehrig, NY	142	1975	George Scott, Mil	109
1929	Al Simmons, Phil	157	1976	Lee May, Balt	109
1930	Lou Gehrig, NY	174	1977	Larry Hisle, Minn	119
1931	Lou Gehrig, NY	184	1978	Jim Rice, Bos	139
1932	Jimmie Foxx, Phil	169	1979	Don Baylor, Cal	139
1933	Jimmie Foxx, Phil	163	1980	Cecil Cooper, Mil	122
1934	Lou Gehrig, NY	165	1981	Eddie Murray, Balt	78
1935	Hank Greenberg, Det	170	1982	Hal McRae, KC	133
1936	Hal Trosky, Clev	162	1983	Cecil Cooper, Mil	126
1937	Hank Greenberg, Det	183		Jim Rice, Bos	126
1938	Jimmie Foxx, Bos	175	1984	Tony Armas, Bos	123
1939	Ted Williams, Bos	145	1985	Don Mattingly, NY	145
1940	Hank Greenberg, Det	150	1986	Joe Carter, Clev	121
1941	Joe DiMaggio, NY	125	1987	George Bell, Tor	134
1942	Ted Williams, Bos	137	1988	Jose Canseco, Oak	124
1943	Rudy York, Det	118	1989	Ruben Sierra, Tex	119
1944	Vern Stephens, StL	109	1990	Cecil Fielder, Det	132
1945	Nick Etten, NY	111	1991	Cecil Fielder, Det	133
1946	Hank Greenberg, Det	127	1992	Cecil Fielder, Det	124
1947	Ted Williams, Bos	114	1993	Albert Belle, Clev	129
1948	Joe DiMaggio, NY	155	1994	Kirby Puckett, Minn	112
1949	Ted Williams, Bos	159	1995	Albert Belle, Clev	126
	Vern Stephens, Bos	159		Mo Vaughn, Bos	126
1950	Walt Dropo, Bos	144	1996	Albert Belle, Clev	148
	Vern Stephens, Bos	144	1997	Ken Griffey Jr., Sea	147
1951	Gus Zernial, Chi-Phil	129	1998	Juan Gonzales, Tex	157
1952	Al Rosen, Clev	105	1999	Manny Ramirez, Clev	165

Note: Runs Batted In not compiled before 1907; officially adopted in 1920.

Leading Base Stealers

Year	Player and Team	SB	Year	Player and Team	SB
1901	Frank Isbell, Chi	48	1911	Ty Cobb, Det	83
1902	Topsy Hartsel, Phil	54	1912	Clyde Milan, Wash	88
1903	Harry Bay, Clev	46	1913	Clyde Milan, Wash	75
1904	Elmer Flick, Clev	42	1914	Fritz Maisel, NY	74
	Harry Bay, Clev	42	1915	Ty Cobb, Det	96
1905	Danny Hoffman, Phil	46	1916	Ty Cobb, Det	68
1906	Elmer Flick, Clev	39	1917	Ty Cobb, Det	55
	John Anderson, Wash	39	1918	George Sisler, StL	45
1907	Ty Cobb, Det	49	1919	Eddie Collins, Chi	33
1908	Patsy Dougherty, Chi	47	1920	Sam Rice, Wash	63
1909	Ty Cobb, Det	76	1921	George Sisler, StL	35
1910	Eddie Collins, Phil	81	1922	George Sisler, StL	51

Leading Base Stealers (Cont.)

Year	Player and Team	SB	Year	Player and Team	SB
1923	Eddie Collins, Chi	49	1961	Luis Aparicio, Chi	53
1924	Eddie Collins, Chi	42	1962	Luis Aparicio, Chi	31
1925	John Mostil, Chi	43	1963	Luis Aparicio, Balt	40
1926	John Mostil, Chi	35	1964	Luis Aparicio, Balt	57
1927	George Sisler, StL	27	1965	Bert Campaneris, KC	51
1928	Buddy Myer, Bos	30	1966	Bert Campaneris, KC	52
1929	Charlie Gehringer, Det	27	1967	Bert Campaneris, KC	55
1930	Marty McManus, Det	23	1968	Bert Campaneris, Oak	62
1931	Ben Chapman, NY	61	1969	Tommy Harper, Sea	73
1932	Ben Chapman, NY	38	1970	Bert Campaneris, Oak	42
1933	Ben Chapman, NY	27	1971	Amos Otis, KC	52
1934	Bill Werber, Bos	40	1972	Bert Campaneris, Oak	52
1935	Bill Werber, Bos	29	1973	Tommy Harper, Bos	54
1936	Lyn Lary, StL	37	1974	Bill North, Oak	54
1937	Bill Werber, Phil	35	1975	Mickey Rivers, Cal	70
	Ben Chapman, Wash-Bos	35	1976	Bill North, Oak	75
1938	Frank Crosetti, NY	27	1977	Freddie Patek, KC	53
1939	George Case, Wash	51	1978	Ron LeFlore, Det	68
1940	George Case, Wash	35	1979	Willie Wilson, KC	83
1941	George Case, Wash	33	1980	Rickey Henderson, Oak	100
1942	George Case, Wash	44	1981	Rickey Henderson, Oak	56
1943	George Case, Wash	61	1982	Rickey Henderson, Oak	130
1944	Snuffy Stirnweiss, NY	55	1983	Rickey Henderson, Oak	108
1945	Snuffy Stirnweiss, NY	33	1984	Rickey Henderson, Oak	66
1946	George Case, Clev	28	1985	Rickey Henderson, NY	80
1947	Bob Dillinger, StL	34	1986	Rickey Henderson, NY	87
1948	Bob Dillinger, StL	28	1987	Harold Reynolds, Sea	60
1949	Bob Dillinger, StL	20	1988	Rickey Henderson, NY	93
1950	Dom DiMaggio, Bos	15	1989	Rickey Henderson, NY-Oak	77
1951	Minnie Minoso, Clev-Chi	31	1990	Rickey Henderson, Oak	65
1952	Minnie Minoso, Chi	22	1991	Rickey Henderson, Oak	58
1953	Minnie Minoso, Chi	25	1992	Kenny Lofton, Clev	66
1954	Jackie Jensen, Bos	22	1993	Kenny Lofton, Clev	70
1955	Jim Rivera, Chi	25	1994	Kenny Lofton, Clev	60
1956	Luis Aparicio, Chi	21	1995	Kenny Lofton, Clev	54
1957	Luis Aparicio, Chi	28	1996	Kenny Lofton, Clev	75
1958	Luis Aparicio, Chi	29	1997	Brian Hunter, Det	74
1959	Luis Aparicio, Chi	56	1998	Rickey Henderson, Oak	66
1960	Luis Aparicio, Chi	51	1999	Brian Hunter, Sea	44

Leading Pitchers—Winning Percentage

Year	Pitcher and Team	W	L	Pct	Year	Pitcher and Team	W	L	Pct
1901	Clark Griffith, Chi	24	7	.774	1924	Walter Johnson, Wash	23	7	.767
1902	Bill Bernhard, Phil-Clev	18	5	.783	1925	Stan Coveleski, Wash	20	5	.800
1903	Earl Moore, Clev	22	7	.759	1926	George Uhle, Clev	27	11	.711
1904	Jack Chesbro, NY	41	12	.774	1927	Waite Hoyt, NY	22	7	.759
1905	Jess Tannehill, Bos	22	9	.710	1928	General Crowder, StL	21	5	.808
1906	Eddie Plank, Phil	19	6	.760	1929	Lefty Grove, Phil	20	6	.769
1907	Wild Bill Donovan, Det	25	4	.862	1930	Lefty Grove, Phil	28	5	.848
1908	Ed Walsh, Chi	40	15	.727	1931	Lefty Grove, Phil	31	4	.886
1909	George Mullin, Det	29	8	.784	1932	Johnny Allen, NY	17	4	.810
1910	Chief Bender, Phil	23	5	.821	1933	Lefty Grove, Phil	24	8	.750
1911	Chief Bender, Phil	17	5	.773	1934	Lefty Gomez, NY	26	5	.839
1912	Smoky Joe Wood, Bos	34	5	.872	1935	Eldon Auker, Det	18	7	.720
1913	Walter Johnson, Wash	36	7	.837	1936	Monte Pearson, NY	19	7	.731
1914	Chief Bender, Phil	17	3	.850	1937	Johnny Allen, Clev	15	1	.938
1915	Smoky Joe Wood, Bos	15	5	.750	1938	Red Ruffing, NY	21	7	.750
1916	Eddie Cicotte, Chi	15	7	.682	1939	Lefty Grove, Bos	15	4	.789
1917	Reb Russell, Chi	15	5	.750	1940	Schoolboy Rowe, Det	16	3	.842
1918	Sad Sam Jones, Bos	16	5	.762	1941	Lefty Gomez, NY	15	5	.750
1919	Eddie Cicotte, Chi	29	7	.806	1942	Ernie Bonham, NY	21	5	.808
1920	Jim Bagby, Clev	31	12	.721	1943	Spud Chandler, NY	20	4	.833
1921	Carl Mays, NY	27	9	.750	1944	Tex Hughson, Bos	18	5	.783
1922	Joe Bush, NY	26	7	.788	1945	Hal Newhouser, Det	25	9	.735
1923	Herb Pennock, NY	19	6	.760	1946	Boo Ferriss, Bos	25	6	.806

Leading Pitchers—Winning Percentage (Cont.)

Year	Pitcher and Team	W	L	Pct	Year	Pitcher and Team	W	L	Pct
1947	Allie Reynolds, NY	19	8	.704	1974	Mike Cuellar, Balt	22	10	.688
1948	Jack Kramer, Bos	18	5	.783	1975	Mike Torrez, Balt	20	9	.690
1949	Ellis Kinder, Bos	23	6	.793	1976	Bill Campbell, Minn	17	5	.773
1950	Vic Raschi, NY	21	8	.724	1977	Paul Splittorff, KC	16	6	.727
1951	Bob Feller, Clev	22	8	.733	1978	Ron Guidry, NY	25	3	.893
1952	Bobby Shantz, Phil	24	7	.774	1979	Mike Caldwell, Mil	16	6	.727
1953	Ed Lopat, NY	16	4	.800	1980	Steve Stone, Balt	25	7	.781
1954	Sandy Consuegra, Chi	16	3	.842	1981*	Pete Vuckovich, Mil	14	4	.778
1955	Tommy Byrne, NY	16	5	.762	1982	Pete Vuckovich, Mil	18	6	.750
1956	Whitey Ford, NY	19	6	.760		Jim Palmer, Balt	15	5	.750
1957	Dick Donovan, Chi	16	6	.727	1983	Richard Dotson, Chi	22	7	.759
	Tom Sturdivant, NY	16	6	.727	1984	Doyle Alexander, Tor	17	6	.739
1958	Bob Turley, NY	21	7	.750	1985	Ron Guidry, NY	22	6	.786
1959	Bob Shaw, Chi	18	6	.750	1986	Roger Clemens, Bos	24	4	.857
1960	Jim Perry, Clev	18	10	.643	1987	Roger Clemens, Bos	20	9	.690
1961	Whitey Ford, NY	25	4	.862	1988	Frank Viola, Minn	24	7	.774
1962	Ray Herbert, Chi	20	9	.690	1989	Bret Saberhagen, KC	23	6	.793
1963	Whitey Ford, NY	24	7	.774	1990	Bob Welch, Oak	27	6	.818
1964	Wally Bunker, Balt	19	5	.792	1991	Scott Erickson, Minn	20	8	.714
1965	Mudcat Grant, Minn	21	7	.750	1992	Mike Mussina, Balt	18	5	.783
1966	Sonny Siebert, Clev	16	8	.667	1993	Jimmy Key, NY	18	6	.750
1967	Joel Horlen, Chi	19	7	.731	1994	Jimmy Key, NY	17	4	.810
1968	Denny McLain, Det	31	6	.838	1995	Randy Johnson, Sea	18	2	.900
1969	Jim Palmer, Balt	16	4	.800	1996	Charles Nagy, Clev	17	5	.773
1970	Mike Cuellar, Balt	24	8	.750	1997	Randy Johnson, Sea	20	4	.833
1971	Dave McNally, Balt	21	5	.808	1998	David Wells, NY	18	4	.818
1972	Catfish Hunter, Oak	21	7	.750	1999	Pedro Martinez, Bos	23	4	.852
1973	Catfish Hunter, Oak	21	5	.808					

*1981 percentages based on 10 or more victories. Note: Percentages based on 15 or more victories in all other years.

Leading Pitchers—Earned-Run Average

Year	Player and Team	ERA	Year	Player and Team	ERA
1913	Walter Johnson, Wash	1.14	1946	Hal Newhouser, Det	1.94
1914	Dutch Leonard, Bos	1.01	1947	Spud Chandler, NY	2.46
1915	Smoky Joe Wood, Bos	1.49	1948	Gene Bearden, Clev	2.43
1916	Babe Ruth, Bos	1.75	1949	Mel Parnell, Bos	2.78
1917	Eddie Cicotte, Chi	1.53	1950	Early Wynn, Clev	3.20
1918	Walter Johnson, Wash	1.27	1951	Saul Rogovin, Det-Chi	2.78
1919	Walter Johnson, Wash	1.49	1952	Allie Reynolds, NY	2.07
1920	Bob Shawkey, NY	2.46	1953	Ed Lopat, NY	2.43
1921	Red Faber, Chi	2.47	1954	Mike Garcia, Clev	2.64
1922	Red Faber, Chi	2.80	1955	Billy Pierce, Chi	1.97
1923	Stan Coveleski, Clev	2.76	1956	Whitey Ford, NY	2.47
1924	Walter Johnson, Wash	2.72	1957	Bobby Shantz, NY	2.45
1925	Stan Coveleski, Wash	2.84	1958	Whitey Ford, NY	2.01
1926	Lefty Grove, Phil	2.51	1959	Hoyt Wilhelm, Balt	2.19
1927	Wilcy Moore, NY#	2.28	1960	Frank Baumann, Chi	2.68
1928	Garland Braxton, Wash	2.52	1961	Dick Donovan, Wash	2.40
1929	Lefty Grove, Phil	2.81	1962	Hank Aguirre, Det	2.21
1930	Lefty Grove, Phil	2.54	1963	Gary Peters, Chi	2.33
1931	Lefty Grove, Phil	2.06	1964	Dean Chance, LA	1.65
1932	Lefty Grove, Phil	2.84	1965	Sam McDowell, Clev	2.18
1933	Monte Pearson, Clev	2.33	1966	Gary Peters, Chi	1.98
1934	Lefty Gomez, NY	2.33	1967	Joe Horlen, Chi	2.06
1935	Lefty Grove, Bos	2.70	1968	Luis Tiant, Clev	1.60
1936	Lefty Grove, Bos	2.81	1969	Dick Bosman, Wash	2.19
1937	Lefty Gomez, NY	2.33	1970	Diego Segui, Oak	2.56
1938	Lefty Grove, Bos	3.07	1971	Vida Blue, Oak	1.82
1939	Lefty Grove, Bos	2.54	1972	Luis Tiant, Bos	1.91
1940	Bob Feller, Clev†	2.62	1973	Jim Palmer, Balt	2.40
1941	Thornton Lee, Chi	2.37	1974	Catfish Hunter, Oak	2.49
1942	Ted Lyons, Chi	2.10	1975	Jim Palmer, Balt	2.09
1943	Spud Chandler, NY	1.64	1976	Mark Fidrych, Det	2.34
1944	Dizzy Trout, Det	2.12	1977	Frank Tanana, Cal	2.54
1945	Hal Newhouser, Det	1.81	1978	Ron Guidry, NY	1.74

Leading Pitchers—Earned-Run Average *(Cont.)*

Year	Player and Team	ERA	Year	Player and Team	ERA
1979	Ron Guidry, NY	2.78	1990	Roger Clemens, Bos	1.93
1980	Rudy May, NY	2.47	1991	Roger Clemens, Bos	2.62
1981	Steve McCatty, Oak	2.32	1992	Roger Clemens, Bos	2.41
1982	Rick Sutcliffe, Clev	2.96	1993	Kevin Appier, KC	2.56
1983	Rick Honeycutt, Tex	2.42	1994	Steve Ontiveros, Oak	2.65
1984	Mike Boddicker, Balt	2.79	1995	Randy Johnson, Sea	2.48
1985	Dave Stieb, Tor	2.48	1996	Juan Guzman, Tor	2.93
1986	Roger Clemens, Bos	2.48	1997	Roger Clemens, Tor	2.05
1987	Jimmy Key, Tor	2.76	1998	Roger Clemens, Tor	2.64
1988	Allan Anderson, Minn	2.45	1999	Pedro Martinez, Bos	2.07
1989	Bret Saberhagen, KC	2.16			

Note: Based on 10 complete games through 1950, then, 154 innings until the American League expanded in 1961, when it became 162 innings. In strike-shortened 1981, one inning per game required. Earned runs not tabulated in American League prior to 1913.

#Wilcy Moore pitched only six complete games—he started 12—in 1927, but was recognized as leader because of 213 innings pitched. †Ernie Bonham, New York, had 1.91 ERA and 10 complete games in 1940, but appeared in only 12 games and 99 innings, and Bob Feller was recognized as leader.

Leading Pitchers—Strikeouts

Year	Player and Team	SO	Year	Player and Team	SO
1901	Cy Young, Bos	159	1947	Bob Feller, Clev	196
1902	Rube Waddell, Phil	210	1948	Bob Feller, Clev	164
1903	Rube Waddell, Phil	301	1949	Virgil Trucks, Det	153
1904	Rube Waddell, Phil	349	1950	Bob Lemon, Clev	170
1905	Rube Waddell, Phil	286	1951	Vic Raschi, NY	164
1906	Rube Waddell, Phil	203	1952	Allie Reynolds, NY	160
1907	Rube Waddell, Phil	226	1953	Billy Pierce, Chi	186
1908	Ed Walsh, Chi	269	1954	Bob Turley, Balt	185
1909	Frank Smith, Chi	177	1955	Herb Score, Clev	245
1910	Walter Johnson, Wash	313	1956	Herb Score, Clev	263
1911	Ed Walsh, Chi	255	1957	Early Wynn, Clev	184
1912	Walter Johnson, Wash	303	1958	Early Wynn, Chi	179
1913	Walter Johnson, Wash	243	1959	Jim Bunning, Det	201
1914	Walter Johnson, Wash	225	1960	Jim Bunning, Det	201
1915	Walter Johnson, Wash	203	1961	Camilo Pascual, Minn	221
1916	Walter Johnson, Wash	228	1962	Camilo Pascual, Minn	206
1917	Walter Johnson, Wash	188	1963	Camilo Pascual, Minn	202
1918	Walter Johnson, Wash	162	1964	Al Downing, NY	217
1919	Walter Johnson, Wash	147	1965	Sam McDowell, Clev	325
1920	Stan Coveleski, Clev	133	1966	Sam McDowell, Clev	225
1921	Walter Johnson, Wash	143	1967	Jim Lonborg, Bos	246
1922	Urban Shocker, StL	149	1968	Sam McDowell, Clev	283
1923	Walter Johnson, Wash	130	1969	Sam McDowell, Clev	279
1924	Walter Johnson, Wash	158	1970	Sam McDowell, Clev	304
1925	Lefty Grove, Phil	116	1971	Mickey Lolich, Det	308
1926	Lefty Grove, Phil	194	1972	Nolan Ryan, Cal	329
1927	Lefty Grove, Phil	174	1973	Nolan Ryan, Cal	383
1928	Lefty Grove, Phil	183	1974	Nolan Ryan, Cal	367
1929	Lefty Grove, Phil	170	1975	Frank Tanana, Cal	269
1930	Lefty Grove, Phil	209	1976	Nolan Ryan, Cal	327
1931	Lefty Grove, Phil	175	1977	Nolan Ryan, Cal	341
1932	Red Ruffing, NY	190	1978	Nolan Ryan, Cal	260
1933	Lefty Gomez, NY	163	1979	Nolan Ryan, Cal	223
1934	Lefty Gomez, NY	158	1980	Len Barker, Clev	187
1935	Tommy Bridges, Det	163	1981	Len Barker, Clev	127
1936	Tommy Bridges, Det	175	1982	Floyd Bannister, Sea	209
1937	Lefty Gomez, NY	194	1983	Jack Morris, Det	232
1938	Bob Feller, Clev	240	1984	Mark Langston, Sea	204
1939	Bob Feller, Clev	246	1985	Bert Blyleven, Clev-Minn	206
1940	Bob Feller, Clev	261	1986	Mark Langston, Sea	245
1941	Bob Feller, Clev	260	1987	Mark Langston, Sea	262
1942	Bobo Newsom, Wash		1988	Roger Clemens, Bos	291
	Tex Hughson, Bos	113	1989	Nolan Ryan, Tex	301
1943	Allie Reynolds, Clev	151	1990	Nolan Ryan, Tex	232
1944	Hal Newhouser, Det	187	1991	Roger Clemens, Bos	241
1945	Hal Newhouser, Det	212	1992	Randy Johnson, Sea	241
1946	Bob Feller, Clev	348	1993	Randy Johnson, Sea	308

Leading Pitchers—Strikeouts *(Cont.)*

Year	Player and Team	SO	Year	Player and Team	SO
1994	Randy Johnson, Sea	204	1997	Roger Clemens, Tor	292
1995	Randy Johnson, Sea	294	1998	Roger Clemens, Tor	271
1996	Roger Clemens, Bos	257	1999	Pedro Martinez, Bos	313

Leading Pitchers—Saves

Year	Player and Team	SV	Year	Player and Team	SV
1947	Joe Page, NY	17	1974	Terry Forster, Chi	24
1948	Russ Christopher, Clev	17	1975	Goose Gossage, Chi	26
1949	Joe Page, NY	29	1976	Sparky Lyle, NY	23
1950	Mickey Harris, Wash	15	1977	Bill Campbell, Bos	31
1951	Ellis Kinder, Bos	14	1978	Goose Gossage, NY	27
1952	Harry Dorish, Chi	11	1979	Mike Marshall, Minn	32
1953	Ellis Kinder, Bos	27	1980	Dan Quisenberry, KC	33
1954	Johnny Sain, NY	22	1981	Rollie Fingers, Mil	28
1955	Ray Narleski, Clev	19	1982	Dan Quisenberry, KC	35
1956	George Zuverink, Bal	16	1983	Dan Quisenberry, KC	35
1957	Bob Grim, NY	19	1984	Dan Quisenberry, KC	44
1958	Ryne Duren, NY	20	1985	Dan Quisenberry, KC	37
1959	Turk Lown, Chi	15	1986	Dave Righetti, NY	46
1960	Mike Fornieles, Bos	14	1987	Tom Henke, Tor	34
	Johnny Klippstein, Clev	14	1988	Dennis Eckersley, Oak	45
1961	Luis Arroyo, NY	29	1989	Jeff Russell, Tex	38
1962	Dick Radatz, Bos	24	1990	Bobby Thigpen, Chi	57
1963	Stu Miller, Bal	27	1991	Bryan Harvey, Cal	46
1964	Dick Radatz, Bos	29	1992	Dennis Eckersley, Oak	51
1965	Ron Kline, Wash	29	1993	Jeff Montgomery, KC	45
1966	Jack Aker, KC	32		Duane Ward, Tor	45
1967	Minnie Rojas, Cal	27	1994	Lee Smith, Bal	33
1968	Al Worthington, Minn	18	1995	Jose Mesa, Clev	46
1969	Ron Perranoski, Minn	31	1996	John Wetteland, NY	43
1970	Ron Perranoski, Minn	34	1997	Randy Myers, Balt	45
1971	Ken Sanders, Mil	31	1998	Tom Gordon, Bos	46
1972	Sparky Lyle, NY	35	1999	Mariano Rivera, NY	45
1973	John Hiller, Det	38			

The Commissioners of Baseball

Kenesaw Mountain Landis — Elected November 12, 1920. Served until his death on November 25, 1944.

Happy Chandler — Elected April 24, 1945. Served until July 15, 1951.

Ford Frick — Elected September 20, 1951. Served until November 16, 1965.

William Eckert — Elected November 17, 1965. Served until December 20, 1968.

Bowie Kuhn — Elected February 8, 1969. Served until September 30, 1984.

Peter Ueberroth — Elected March 3, 1984. Took office October 1, 1984. Served through March 31, 1989.

A. Bartlett Giamatti — Elected September 8, 1988. Took office April 1, 1989. Served until his death on September 1, 1989.

Francis Vincent Jr. — Appointed Acting Commissioner September 2, 1989. Elected Commissioner September 13, 1989. Served through September 7, 1992.

Allan H. (Bud) Selig — Elected chairman of the executive council and given the powers of interim commissioner on September 9, 1992. Unanimously elected Commissioner July 9, 1998.

Pro Football

John Elway of the Super Bowl champion Broncos

Bronco Brilliance

In a season that saw new stars emerge and old ones reappear, John Elway and Denver once again outshined them all

BY DAVID FLEMING

WHEN THE moment arrived, Denver owner Pat Bowlen gave the go-ahead for his players and staff to open the tiny ring boxes in front of them. An extended series of "ooohs" and "ahhhs" followed. At a banquet in early June 1999, the Broncos received their lasting reward for conquering the NFL for a second year in a row. With 4.04 carats and weighing in at 2.3 ounces—"My shoulder is starting to hurt already," joked wide receiver Ed McCaffrey—Denver's new Super Bowl XXXIII rings are decorated with 120 diamonds, including six across the top to represent the team's six trips to the Super Bowl. The rings have mini Lombardi Trophies on the sides and a pair of Bronco heads on the crest with Australian orange diamonds for eyes. In a word, the Broncos' new baubles are stunning (or stunningly ostentatious, depending on your point of view).

Denver's season was just as brilliant, a dominating 17–2 run full of gems like the one quarterback John Elway delivered at the Super Bowl in Miami. In what would turn out to be the final game of the 38-year-old quarterback's Hall of Fame career, Elway completed 18 of 29 passes for 336 yards, passed for a touchdown and ran for a another and was named MVP of the Super Bowl as the Broncos breezed past the Atlanta Falcons 34–19. "I never thought it could get any better than last year," Elway said in the locker room after the game. "But just look at this scene."

Elway, who retired in April 1999 as only the second quarterback with more than 50,000 career passing yards, was motivated for one last big game by the Falcons' pregame focus on Denver running back Terrell Davis. "All week long all the Falcons talked about was stopping our running game," Elway said. "I knew they were saying, Make Elway beat us.' My thought was, Good, let's go. I was so motivated, it wasn't even funny."

So too were several other Broncos—diamonds in the rough?—who spurred the convincing Super Bowl victory. Wideout Rod

Smith, a practice-squad player in '94 who carries a one-dollar food stamp in his wallet to remind him of less fortunate times, caught five passes in the big game for 152 yards and a touchdown. The Denver D, led by cornerback Darrien Gordon (two interceptions), forced four turnovers. Bit players made big plays all season long for Denver. In Week 8, kicker Jason Elam tied Tom Dempsey's 28-year-old record for the longest field goal with a 63-yard boot against Jacksonville. Backup quarterback Bubby Brister was 4–0 as a starter when Elway went down with injuries in September and November.

Of course, there was also Davis, a former sixth-round draft pick who rushed for 2,008 yards in the regular season to become only the fourth runner in history to break the 2,000-yard barrier. Davis gained 102 yards on 25 carries in Super Bowl XXXIII for his record seventh-straight 100-yard playoff game.

In 50 years, though, when the Broncos' rings have lost some of their luster and the gaudy numbers they produced have faded from memory, historians will reexamine Denver's back-to-back Super Bowl wins and find that coach Mike Shanahan was the team's real star. His astute guidance and revolutionary seal-blocking scheme sent the Broncos bucking into history. Shanahan's system flies in the face of NFL convention by using smaller, quicker blockers who work defenders sideways, instead of north and south—sealing them off the way opponents are contained by a pick in basketball. Davis can then choose the best hole. Several teams have begun to copy the system. And why not? Shanahan is now one of only five coaches to have won back-to-back Super Bowls. His players have nicknamed him the Mastermind. "Without Mike we're in disarray," says Denver's voluble tight end Shannon Sharpe. "We're 8–8, 9–7, even with John. Mike's the reason we're two-time Super Bowl champs."

In stark contrast to the Broncos' cool, calculated efficiency, was the harum-scarum style of the Atlanta Falcons, a team that had never been to the Super Bowl and had gone 3–13 just two seasons earlier. The Falcons slipped past Minnesota 30–27 in overtime in

DAMIAN STROHMEYER

Shanahan became only the fifth coach to win back-to-back Super Bowls.

the NFC Championship Game after Vikings kicker Gary Anderson missed a 39-yard field goal that would have iced it for his team with 2:11 remaining. Before the critical miss Anderson had made an NFL-record 40 consecutive field goals. "It feels like a miracle," said Falcons cornerback Ray Buchanan. "This team was dirt. People stepped on us and wiped their feet on the doormat. Now we feel like a bunch of Michael Jordans. You can't kill us."

The Dirty Birds' immortality would last only two more weeks, during which time Buchanan's antics continued unabated. On Super Bowl media day he wore a dog collar. Prior to the game he guaranteed an Atlanta victory. Yet by game time Buchanan seemed like the most sane guy on the Falcons' bench. Head coach Dan Reeves returned to the sidelines less than a month after undergoing quadruple-bypass surgery. In the week leading up to the game,

PETER READ MILLER

the Super Bowl was a near-perfect 125.0, Chandler threw three interceptions in the Falcons' loss on Super Sunday. But the journeyman who had played for five teams in nine years produced the best season of his career while guiding the Falcons to the NFC title. He was one of the many retreads and rookies who flourished in 1998.

Under the direction of veteran quarterback Randall Cunningham—who sat out the 1996 season and spent the year laying marble in Las Vegas, working on his hands and knees, 12 hours a day—the Minnesota offense set an NFL record for points in a season with 556. Cunningham says his time away from the game put his life into perspective and gave him a state of grace and peace that transferred onto the field.

The Vikings' addition of sensational rookie wide receiver Randy Moss may have contributed to Cunningham's peace of mind on the field as well, but whatever the reason, he was certainly a changed man in 1998. He led the NFL with a passer rating of 106.0.

In the AFC, erstwhile washed-up quarterback Vinny Testaverde topped all passers with a 101.6 rating for the Jets. Before joining New York, Testaverde had led the Cleveland Browns and the Baltimore Ravens to a combined record of 25-36-1. In his first full season as a Jets starter, he led the team to a 12–4 record and its first division title since the AFL-NFL merger. After knocking off Jacksonville 34–24 in the playoffs, the Jets advanced to the AFC title game against Denver. Though they lost 23–10, their rejuvenated quarterback played the game of his life, completing 31 of 56 passes for 356 yards.

Reeves—who once coached Elway in Denver, where Shanahan was on his staff—accused Elway and Shanahan of conspiring to get him fired from the Broncos. On the eve of the game, just hours after accepting the Bart Starr Award honoring NFL players with high moral character, Atlanta's defensive leader and free safety Eugene Robinson was arrested for soliciting oral sex from an undercover Miami police officer. Late in the game, after he had missed a tackle near the Denver sideline that sprung a 39-yard gain by Davis, some of the Broncos said to Robinson, "You look a little tired, Eugene. Up late last night?"

Falcons quarterback Chris Chandler fared only slightly better than Robinson during the biggest game of his career. Although his passer rating in the six games leading up to

The 35-year-old Testaverde says faith in coach Bill Parcells has allowed him to relax and play with confidence. He also got a little help from his friends in the black-and-white striped shirts, who had a rough go of it in important games in '98. Against the Seahawks in Week 14, Testaverde was awarded a game-winning touchdown even though cameras clearly showed he never broke the plane of the end zone. This was perhaps the most egregious in a seasonlong series of blown calls in big games that inspired NFL owners to reinstate the use of instant replay for the 1999 season.

Like Testaverde, quarterback Doug Flutie got a confidence boost in 1998. The former Canadian Football League MVP who was considered too small (5'10") and too old (36) to play in the NFL stepped in for the injured Rob Johnson and led the Bills on an improbable run to the playoffs, where they bowed to Miami 24–17 in the wild-card round. Buffalo was one of four AFC East teams to make the playoffs, and that competitive division was a prime example of how the league's power balance has shifted to the AFC. The conference now has an edge in talent and, following a 13-year run by the NFC, has won the last two Super Bowls.

Sharing the spotlight with Flutie and the rest of the old fogies in 1998 were a group of rookies and youngsters who seemed poised for NFL greatness. Indianapolis quarterback Peyton Manning, the No. 1 pick in the draft, had a superb rookie season, throwing for 3,739 yards and 26 TDs. His quarterbacking contemporary, Ryan Leaf, on the other hand, struggled mightily in his rookie season with the San Diego Chargers. He and Manning had been the top two picks in the 1998 NFL draft—only the third time in league history that a pair of QBs had gone first—but they traveled in opposite directions from there. Leaf's 39.0 passer rating, by far the worst in the league, all but short-circuited the Chargers' No. 1–ranked defense. He had problems off the field as well and was eventually benched.

A third rookie quarterback, Charlie Batch, emerged from relative anonymity at Eastern Michigan to perform well for the Detroit Lions. Batch threw 11 touchdown passes in 12 games, including a 98-yarder—the longest pass of the season—to Johnnie Morton on Oct. 4 against the Bears.

The Bears and the Lions are two of the league's most venerable franchises, and in 1999, they will be rejoined in the NFL by another famous Rust Belt team, the Cleveland Browns. The Browns will return to the league after a three-year hiatus caused by former owner Art Modell's moving the team to Baltimore. As the result of a compromise negotiated by commissioner Paul Tagliabue, the Browns

DAMIAN STROHMEYER

The 35-year-old Testaverde (16) produced the best season of his career.

JOHN BIEVER

Manning (center) lived up to his billing and gave Indianapolis fans hope for the future.

franchise's first playoff win in 52 years. Yes, five decades. "December 28, 1947," said Arizona owner Bill Bidwill, who was a water boy for the Chicago Cardinals at the time. "We beat the Eagles 28–21 on a frozen field at Comiskey Park."

Just about every other momentous occasion in 1998 seemed to involve Vikings rookie Moss. Skipped over in the draft by 19 teams worried about his checkered past, Moss was finally selected by the Vikings as the 21st pick overall. A 6'4" human pogo stick with 4.34 speed in the 40-yard dash, Moss went on to catch 69 passes for 1,313 yards and an NFC-best 17 TDs.

After the Vikings had wrenched control of the NFC's top division away from the Packers with a 28–14 win in Week 12, quarterback Brett Favre sought out Moss on the field and told him, "You're a great player." That might have been an understatement. Moss, the runaway rookie of the year, was the most dangerous element of Minnesota's potent offense.

Since former car salesman Red McCombs bought the Vikings after the 1997 season and started throwing his Texas-sized personality around the Twin Cities, the Vikings have only lost two games, exhibition and playoffs included. If the Vikes can rebound from the NFC title game loss to Atlanta, they are the odds-on favorite to challenge Denver in 1999.

Of course, the Broncos have other plans. With Bubby Brister calling the signals instead of the great Elway, Denver hopes to add a third gold-and-diamond-studded keepsake—the NFL's very expensive version of brass knuckles. No team has ever done it before. "I look forward to next February," said Bowlen. "Hopefully we'll be designing rings for a team that just made history by winning three Super Bowls in a row."

will resume play in their familiar brown-and-orange uniforms, and with their team records and history intact. On Sept. 12, 1999, when the countdown wristwatches that folks in Cleveland will have been wearing for almost 1,000 days finally expire, and longtime rival Pittsburgh comes to town to face the Browns in their brand-new stadium on the shores of Lake Erie, all will seem right with the football world once again.

It may take the revived Browns a few seasons to reach the playoffs, but Cleveland fans hope the wait won't be as long as it was for the Arizona Cardinals, who made it to the NFL postseason dance in '98 for the first time in 16 years, ending the league's longest playoff drought. They did so on the slithery back of the game's best young quarterback, Jake (the Snake) Plummer. With just one full season under his belt as a starter, Plummer has already engineered nine fourth-quarter comebacks, including a 16–13 win over the Chargers in the season finale that put the Cards in the playoffs. "You know, it's actually good to be a Cardinal," said Arizona lineman Lomas Brown. Stranger words have rarely been spoken this decade in the NFL.

In the wild-card game Plummer and the 'Zona defense pounded out a 20–7 win over Dallas, a team that had beaten the Cardinals in 16 of their last 17 meetings. It was the

1998 NFL Final Standings

American Football Conference

EASTERN DIVISION

	W	L	T	Pct	Pts	OP
NY Jets	12	4	0	.750	416	266
†Miami	10	6	0	.625	321	265
†Buffalo	10	6	0	.625	400	333
†New England	9	7	0	.563	337	329
Indianapolis	3	13	0	.188	310	444

CENTRAL DIVISION

	W	L	T	Pct	Pts	OP
Jacksonville	11	5	0	.688	392	338
Tennessee	8	8	0	.500	330	320
Pittsburgh	7	9	0	.438	263	303
Baltimore	6	10	0	.375	270	334
Cincinnati	3	13	0	.188	268	452

WESTERN DIVISION

	W	L	T	Pct	Pts	OP
Denver	14	2	0	.875	501	309
Oakland	8	8	0	.500	288	356
Seattle	8	8	0	.500	372	310
Kansas City	7	9	0	.438	327	363
San Diego	5	11	0	.313	241	342

† Wild-card team.

National Football Conference

EASTERN DIVISION

	W	L	T	Pct	Pts	OP
Dallas	10	6	0	.625	381	275
†Arizona	9	7	0	.563	325	378
NY Giants	8	8	0	.500	287	309
Washington	6	10	0	.375	319	421
Philadelphia	3	13	0	.188	161	344

CENTRAL DIVISION

	W	L	T	Pct	Pts	OP
Minnesota	15	1	0	.938	556	296
†Green Bay	11	5	0	.688	408	319
Tampa Bay	8	8	0	.500	314	295
Detroit	5	11	0	.313	306	378
Chicago	4	12	0	.250	276	368

WESTERN DIVISION

	W	L	T	Pct	Pts	OP
Atlanta	14	2	0	.875	375	265
†San Francisco	12	4	0	.750	479	328
New Orleans	6	10	0	.375	305	359
Carolina	4	12	0	.250	336	413
St. Louis	4	12	0	.250	285	378

1998–99 NFL Playoffs

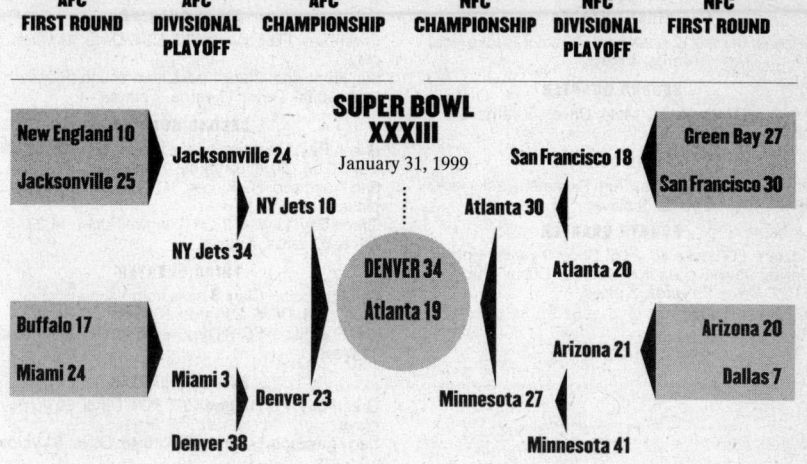

AFC FIRST ROUND	AFC DIVISIONAL PLAYOFF	AFC CHAMPIONSHIP		NFC CHAMPIONSHIP	NFC DIVISIONAL PLAYOFF	NFC FIRST ROUND

SUPER BOWL XXXIII
January 31, 1999

New England 10
Jacksonville 25

Jacksonville 24

NY Jets 10

NY Jets 34

Buffalo 17
Miami 24

Miami 3

Denver 23

Denver 38

DENVER 34
Atlanta 19

Green Bay 27
San Francisco 30

San Francisco 18

Atlanta 30

Atlanta 20

Arizona 21

Arizona 20
Dallas 7

Minnesota 27

Minnesota 41

NFL Playoff Box Scores

AFC Wild-card Games

New England	0	0	7	3—10
Jacksonville	6	6	0	13—25

FIRST QUARTER

Jacksonville: FG Hollis 35, 6:03. Drive: 22 yards, 8 plays.
Jacksonville: FG Hollis 24, 12:59. Drive: 60 yards, 8 plays.

SECOND QUARTER

Jacksonville: Taylor 13 run (two-point conversion failed), 9:02. Drive: 68 yards, 9 plays.

THIRD QUARTER

New England: Edwards 1 run (Vinatieri kick), 10:33. Drive: 85 yards, 17 plays.

FOURTH QUARTER

New England: FG Vinatieri 27, 0:12. Drive: 45 yards, 8 plays.
Jacksonville: Smith 37 pass from Brunell (Hollis kick), 2:36. Drive: 70 yards, 6 plays.
Jacksonville: FG Hollis 34, 9:08. Drive: 9 yards, 4 plays.
Jacksonville: FG Hollis 21, 13:16. Drive: 17 yards, 7 plays.
A: 71,139; T: 3:22.

Buffalo	0	7	7	3—17
Miami	3	3	8	10—24

FIRST QUARTER

Miami: FG Mare 31, 8:53. Drive: 57 yards, 16 plays.

SECOND QUARTER

Miami: FG Mare 40, 4:24. Drive: 66 yards, 11 plays.
Buffalo: Thomas 1 run (Christie kick), 6:06. Drive: 42 yards, 3 plays.

THIRD QUARTER

Miami: Abdul-Jabbar 3 run (Pritchett run for two-point conversion), 12:28. Drive: 52 yards, 12 plays.
Buffalo: Moulds 32 pass from Flutie (Christie kick) 14:12. Drive: 81 yards, 4 plays.

FOURTH QUARTER

Miami: FG Mare 23, 5:15. Drive: 77 yards, 11 plays.
Miami: Thomas 11 pass from Marino (Mare kick), 11:18. Drive: 50 yards, 8 plays.
Buffalo: FG Christie 33, 13:27. Drive: 65 yards, 7 plays.
A: 72,698; T: 3:17.

NFC Wild-card Games

Arizona	7	3	7	3—20
Dallas	0	0	0	7— 7

FIRST QUARTER

Arizona: Murrell 12 pass from Plummer (Jacke kick), 12:13. Drive: 73 yards, 4 plays.

SECOND QUARTER

Arizona: FG Jacke 37, 14:41. Drive: 43 yards, 8 plays.

THIRD QUARTER

Arizona: Centers 3 pass from Plummer (Jacke kick), 1:16. Drive: 80 yards, 3 plays.

FOURTH QUARTER

Arizona: FG Jacke 46, 2:05. Drive: 9 yards, 4 plays.
Dallas: Davis 6 pass from Aikman (Cunningham kick), 11:27. Drive: 25 yards, 5 plays.
A: 62,969; T: 3:10.

Green Bay	3	14	0	10—27
San Francisco	7	3	10	10—30

FIRST QUARTER

Green Bay: FG Longwell 23, 5:34. Drive: 48 yards, 10 plays.
San Francisco: Clark 1 pass from Young (Richey kick), 10:50. Drive: 19 yards, 3 plays.

SECOND QUARTER

Green Bay: Freeman 2 pass from Favre (Longwell kick), 0:04. Drive: 62 yards, 9 plays.
San Francisco: FG Richey 34, 8:07. Drive: 37 yards, 8 plays.
Green Bay: Levens 2 run (Longwell kick), 14:29. Drive: 83 yards, 7 plays.

THIRD QUARTER

San Francisco: Clark 8 pass from Young (Richey kick), 5:58. Drive: 33 yards, 5 plays.
San Francisco: FG Richey 48, 12:48. Drive: 48 yards, 11 plays.

FOURTH QUARTER

Green Bay: FG Longwell 37, 3:09. Drive: 60 yards, 11 plays.
San Francisco: FG Richey 40, 8:48. Drive: 51 yards, 10 plays.
Green Bay: Freeman 15 pass from Favre (Longwell kick), 13:04. Drive: 89 yards, 9 plays.
San Francisco: Owens 25 pass from Young (Richey kick), 14:57. Drive: 76 yards, 9 plays.
A: 66,506; T: 3:05.

AFC Divisional Games

Miami	0	3	0	0 —3
Denver	14	7	3	14—38

FIRST QUARTER

Denver: Davis 1 run (Elam kick), 9:05. Drive: 92 yards, 14 plays.
Denver: Davis 20 run (Elam kick), 13:58. Drive: 66 yards, 4 plays.

SECOND QUARTER

Miami: FG Mare 22, 4:53. Drive: 76 yards, 11 plays.
Denver: Loville 11 run (Elam kick), 10:21. Drive: 87 yards, 11 plays.

THIRD QUARTER

Denver: FG Elam 32, 3:08. Drive: 66 yards, 5 plays.

FOURTH QUARTER

Denver: Smith 28 pass from Elway (Elam kick), 1:37. Drive: 52 yards, 5 plays.
Denver: Smith 79 fumble return (Elam kick), 5:11.
A: 75,729; T: 2:48.

Jacksonville	0	7	7	10—24
NY Jets	7	10	14	3—34

FIRST QUARTER

New York: Johnson 21 pass from Testaverde (Hall kick), 4:34. Drive: 70 yards, 7 plays.

SECOND QUARTER

New York: FG Hall 52, 4:25. Drive: 59 yards, 13 plays.
New York: Johnson 10 run (Hall kick), 14:27. Drive 65 yards, 11 plays.
Jacksonville: Smith 52 pass from Brunell (Hollis kick), 15:00. Drive: 63 yards, 3 plays.

THIRD QUARTER

New York: Martin 1 run (Hall kick), 5:47. Drive: 40 yards, 7 plays.
Jacksonville: McCardell 3 pass from Brunell (Hollis kick), 6:52. Drive: 4 yards, 4 plays.
New York: Martin 1 run (Hall kick), 12:44. Drive: 70 yards, 9 plays.

FOURTH QUARTER

Jacksonville: Smith 19 pass from Brunell (Hollis kick), 5:02. Drive: 64 yards, 8 plays.
Jacksonville: FG Hollis 37, 8:22. Drive: 22 yards, 7 plays.
New York: FG Hall 30, 14:35.
A: 78,817; T: 3:07.

NFC Divisional Games

Arizona	0	7	7	7—21
Minnesota	7	17	10	7—41

FIRST QUARTER

Minnesota: Hoard 1 run, (Anderson kick), 7:20. Drive: 80 yards, 13 plays.

SECOND QUARTER

Minnesota: Glover 15 pass from Cunningham (Anderson kick), 2:15. Drive: 62 yards, 4 plays.
Minnesota: FG Anderson 34, 3:36.
Arizona: Bates 1 run (Jacke kick), 11:28. Drive: 80 yards, 13 plays.
Minnesota: Hoard 16 pass from Cunningham (Anderson kick), 14:36. Drive: 74 yards, 8 plays.

THIRD QUARTER

Arizona: Bates 1 run (Jacke kick), 7:35. Drive: 80 yards, 14 plays.
Minnesota: FG Anderson 20, 11:01. Drive: 54 yards, 6 plays.
Minnesota: Moss 2 pass from Cunningham (Anderson kick), 13:29. Drive: 10 yards, 3 plays.

FOURTH QUARTER

Arizona: Bates 1 run (Jacke kick), 3:15. Drive: 25 yards, 8 plays.
Minnesota: Hoard 6 run (Anderson kick), 10:27. Drive: 73 yards, 12 plays.
A: 63,760; T: 3:08.

San Francisco	0	10	0	8—18
Atlanta	7	7	3	3—20

FIRST QUARTER

Atlanta: Anderson 2 run (Andersen kick), 8:35. Drive: 38 yards, 6 plays.

SECOND QUARTER

Atlanta: Anderson 34 run (Andersen kick), 11:48. Drive: 82 yards, 7 plays.
San Francisco: Rice 17 pass from Young (Richey kick), 13:50. Drive: 80 yards, 9 plays.
San Francisco: FG Richey 36, 14:59. Drive: 18 yards, 5 plays.

THIRD QUARTER

Atlanta: FG Andersen 29, 13:44. Drive: 9 yards, 6 plays.

FOURTH QUARTER

Atlanta: FG Andersen 32, 4:27. Drive: 21 yards, 7 plays.
San Francisco: Young 8 run (Clark pass from Detmer for two-point conversion), 12:03. Drive: 87 yards, 13 plays.
A: 70,262; T: 2:57.

AFC Championship

NY Jets	0	3	7	0—10
Denver	0	0	20	3—23

SECOND QUARTER

New York: FG Hall 32, 15:00. Drive: 46 yards, 6 plays.

THIRD QUARTER

New York: Martin 1 run (Hall kick), 3:04. Drive: 68 yards, 11 plays.
Denver: Griffith 11 pass from Elway (Elam kick), 4:42. Drive: 64 yards, 3 plays.
Denver: FG Elam 44, 6:37. Drive: 5 yards, 4 plays.
Denver: FG Elam 48, 12:02. Drive: 27 yards, 8 plays.
Denver: Davis 31 run (Elam kick), 14:42. Drive: 38 yards, 3 plays.

FOURTH QUARTER

Denver: FG Elam 35, 11:20. Drive: 1 yard, 4 plays.
A:75,482; T: 3:16.

NFC Championship

Atlanta	7	7	3	10	3—30
Minnesota	7	13	0	7	0—27

FIRST QUARTER

Atlanta: Anderson 5 pass from Chandler (Andersen kick), 6:39. Drive: 76 yards, 12 plays.
Minnesota: Moss 31 pass from Cunningham (Anderson kick), 9:27. Drive: 80 yards, 5 plays.

SECOND QUARTER

Minnesota: FG Anderson 29, 5:08. Drive: 49 yards, 12 plays.
Minnesota: Cunningham 1 run (Anderson kick), 9:07. Drive: 33 yards, 6 plays.
Minnesota: FG Anderson 35, 12:15. Drive: 39 yards, 5 plays.
Atlanta: Mathis 14 pass from Chandler (Andersen kick), 14:04. Drive: 14 yards, 1 play.

THIRD QUARTER

Atlanta: FG Andersen 27, 9:24. Drive: 62 yards, 10 plays.

FOURTH QUARTER

Minnesota: Hatchette 5 pass from Cunningham (Anderson kick), 1:19. Drive: 82 yards, 15 plays.
Atlanta: FG Andersen 24, 3:58. Drive: 73 yards, 7 plays.
Atlanta: Mathis 16 pass from Chandler (Andersen kick), 14:11. Drive: 71 yards, 8 plays.

OVERTIME

Atlanta: FG Andersen 38, 11:52. Drive: 70 yards, 10 plays.
A: 64,060; T: 3:43.

Super Bowl Box Score

Denver	7	10	0	17—34
Atlanta	3	3	0	13—19

FIRST QUARTER

Atlanta: FG Andersen 32, 5:25. Drive: 48 yards, 10 plays. Key plays: Anderson 13 run; Crockett 25 interference penalty. **Atlanta 3–0.**
Denver: Griffith 1 run (Elam kick), 11:05. Drive: 80 yards, 10 plays. Key plays: Sharpe 12 pass from Elway; R. Smith 41 pass from Elway. **Denver 7–3.**

SECOND QUARTER

Denver: FG Elam 26, 5:43. Drive: 63 yards, 11 plays. Key plays: Smith 18 pass from Elway; Davis 13 run. **Denver 10–3.**
Denver: Smith 80 pass from Elway (Elam kick), 10:06. Drive: 80 yards, 1 play. **Denver 17–3.**
Atlanta: FG Andersen 28, 12:35. Drive: 38 yards, 7 plays. Key plays: Dwight 42 kickoff return; Martin 23 pass from Chandler. **Denver 17–6.**

FOURTH QUARTER

Denver: Griffith 1 run (Elam kick), 0:04. Drive: 24 yards, 5 plays. Key plays: Gordon 58 interception return; McCaffrey 15 pass from Elway. **Denver 24–6.**
Denver: Elway 3 run (Elam kick), 3:40. Drive: 48 yards, 3 plays. Key plays: Gordon 50 interception return; Davis 39 pass from Elway. **Denver 31–6.**
Atlanta: Dwight 94 kickoff return (Andersen kick), 3:59. **Denver 31–13.**
Denver: FG Elam 35, 7:52. Drive: 36 yards, 7 plays. Key plays: Chamberlain fields onside kick; McCaffrey 25 pass from Elway. **Denver 34–13.**
Atlanta: Mathis 3 pass from Chandler (two-point conversion failed), 12:56. Drive: 76 yards, 16 plays. Key plays: Martin 17 pass from Chandler; Mathis 10 pass from Chandler. **Denver 34–19.**
A: 74,803; T: 3:18.

Team Statistics

	Denver	Atlanta
FIRST DOWNS	22	21
Rushing	8	8
Passing	14	12
Penalty	0	1
THIRD DOWN EFF	6–13	5–11
FOURTH DOWN EFF	0–1	1–2
TOTAL NET YARDS	457	337
Total plays	65	60
Avg gain	7.0	5.6
NET YARDS RUSHING	121	131
Rushes	36	23
Avg per rush	3.4	5.7
NET YARDS PASSING	336	206
Completed–Att	18–29	19–35
Yards per pass	11.6	5.6
Sacked–yards lost	0–0	2–13
Had intercepted	1	3
PUNTS–Avg	4–35.5	4–36.5
TOTAL RETURN YARDS	180	228
Punt returns	0–0	0–0
Kickoff returns	3–44	7–227
Interceptions	3–136	1–1
PENALTIES–Yds	4–61	0–0
FUMBLES–Lost	0–0	1–1
TIME OF POSSESSION	31:23	28:37

Passing

DENVER

	Comp	Att	Yds	Int	TD
Elway	18	29	336	1	1

ATLANTA

	Comp	Att	Yds	Int	TD
Chandler	19	35	219	3	1

Rushing

DENVER

	No.	Yds	Lg	TD
Davis	25	102	15	0
Griffith	4	9	4	2
Loville	2	8	6	0
Elway	3	2	3	1
R. Smith	1	1	1	0
Brister	1	-1	-1	0

ATLANTA

	No.	Yds	Lg	TD
Anderson	18	96	15	0
Chandler	4	30	12	0
Dwight	1	5	5	0

Receiving

DENVER

	No.	Yds	Lg	TD
R. Smith	5	152	t80	1
McCaffrey	5	72	25	0
Chamberlain	3	29	13	0
Davis	2	50	39	0
Sharpe	2	26	14	0
Griffith	1	7	7	0

ATLANTA

	No.	Yds	Lg	TD
Mathis	7	85	30	1
Martin	5	79	23	0
Anderson	3	16	9	0
Harris	2	21	13	0
Santiago	1	13	13	0
Kozlowski	1	5	5	0

Defense

DENVER

	Tck	Ast	Int	Sack
Crockett	5	0	0	0
Atwater	4	3	0	0
Cadrez	4	4	0	0
Romanowski	4	1	0	1
Gordon	2	1	2	0
Tanuvasa	2	1	0	0
Williams	2	0	0	0
Braxton	1	1	0	0
Coghill	1	0	0	0
Hasselbach	1	1	0	0
D. Johnson	1	0	1	0
Mobley	1	2	0	1
Traylor	1	2	0	0
Washington	1	0	0	0

ATLANTA

	Tck	Ast	Int	Sack
White	9	1	0	0
Dronett	6	1	0	0
Robinson	6	0	0	0
Tuggle	5	0	0	0
Bennett	4	0	0	0
Bradford	4	2	1	0
Hall	3	1	0	0
Fuller	2	0	0	0
Brooking	1	0	0	0
Buchanan	1	2	0	0
Edwards	1	0	0	0
Smith	1	1	0	0
Crockett	0	2	0	0

1998 Associated Press All-Pro Team

OFFENSE

Randy Moss, Minnesota	Wide Receiver
Antonio Freeman, Green Bay	Wide Receiver
Shannon Sharpe, Denver	Tight End
Tony Boselli, Jacksonville	Tackle
Larry Allen, Dallas	Tackle
Randall McDaniel, Minnesota	Guard
Bruce Matthews, Tennessee	Guard
Dermontti Dawson, Pittsburgh	Center
Randall Cunningham, Minnesota	Quarterback
Terrell Davis, Denver	Running Back
Jamal Anderson, Atlanta	Running Back
Mike Alstott, Tampa Bay	Fullback

DEFENSE

Reggie White, Green Bay	Defensive End
Michael Strahan, NY Giants	Defensive End
John Randle, Minnesota	Tackle
Darrell Russell, Oakland	Tackle
Chad Brown, Seattle	Outside Linebacker
Mo Lewis, NY Jets	Outside Linebacker
Junior Seau, San Diego	Inside Linebacker
Zach Thomas, Miami	Inside Linebacker
Ty Law, New England	Cornerback
Deion Sanders, Dallas	Cornerback
Rodney Harrison, San Diego	Safety
LeRoy Butler, Green Bay	Safety

SPECIALISTS

Gary Anderson, Minnesota	Kicker
Craig Hentrich, Tennessee	Punter
Jermaine Lewis, Baltimore	Kick Returner

1998 AFC Team-by-Team Results

BALTIMORE RAVENS (6–10)			BUFFALO BILLS (10–6)			CINCINNATI BENGALS (3–13)		
13	PITTSBURGH	20	14	at San Diego	16	14	TENNESSEE	23
24	at NY Jets	10	7	at Miami	13	34	at Detroit (OT)	28
10	at Jacksonville	24	33	ST. LOUIS	34	6	GREEN BAY	13
31	CINCINNATI	24		OPEN DATE		24	at Baltimore	31
	OPEN DATE		26	SAN FRANCISCO	21		OPEN DATE	
8	TENNESSEE	12	31	at Indianapolis	24	25	PITTSBURGH	20
6	at Pittsburgh	16	17	JACKSONVILLE	16	14	at Tennessee	44
10	at Green Bay	28	30	at Carolina	14	10	at Oakland	27
19	JACKSONVILLE	45	30	MIAMI	24	26	DENVER	33
13	OAKLAND	10	12	at NY Jets	34	11	at Jacksonville	24
13	at San Diego	14	13	NEW ENGLAND	10	3	at Minnesota	24
20	at Cincinnati	13	34	INDIANAPOLIS	11	13	BALTIMORE	20
38	INDIANAPOLIS	31	21	at New England	25	17	JACKSONVILLE	34
14	at Tennessee	16	33	at Cincinnati	20	20	BUFFALO	33
28	MINNESOTA	38	44	OAKLAND	21	26	at Indianapolis	39
3	at Chicago	24	10	NY JETS	17	25	at Pittsburgh	24
19	DETROIT	10	45	at New Orleans	33	0	TAMPA BAY	35
270		334	400		333	268		452

DENVER BRONCOS (14–2)

27	NEW ENGLAND	21
42	DALLAS	23
34	at Oakland	17
38	at Washington	16
41	PHILADELPHIA	16
21	at Seattle	16
	OPEN DATE	
37	JACKSONVILLE	24
33	at Cincinnati	26
27	SAN DIEGO	10
30	at Kansas City	7
40	OAKLAND	14
31	at San Diego	16
35	KANSAS CITY	31
16	at NY Giants	20
21	at Miami	31
28	SEATTLE	21
501		**309**

INDIANAPOLIS COLTS (3–13)

15	MIAMI	24
6	at New England	29
6	at NY Jets	44
13	NEW ORLEANS (OT)	19
17	SAN DIEGO	12
24	BUFFALO	31
31	at San Francisco	34
	OPEN DATE	
16	NEW ENGLAND	21
14	at Miami	27
24	NY JETS	23
11	at Buffalo	34
31	at Baltimore	38
21	at Atlanta	28
39	CINCINNATI	26
23	at Seattle	27
19	CAROLINA	27
310		**444**

JACKSONVILLE JAGUARS (11–5)

24	at Chicago	23
21	KANSAS CITY	16
24	BALTIMORE	10
27	at Tennessee	22
	OPEN DATE	
28	MIAMI	21
16	at Buffalo	17
24	at Denver	37
45	at Baltimore	19
24	CINCINNATI	11
29	TAMPA BAY	24
15	at Pittsburgh	30
34	at Cincinnati	17
37	DETROIT	22
13	TENNESSEE	16
10	at Minnesota	50
21	PITTSBURGH	3
392		**338**

KANSAS CITY CHIEFS (7–9)

28	OAKLAND	8
16	at Jacksonville	21
23	SAN DIEGO	7
24	at Philadelphia	21
17	SEATTLE	6
10	at New England	40
	OPEN DATE	
13	PITTSBURGH	20
17	NY JETS	20
12	at Seattle	24
7	DENVER	30
37	at San Diego	38
34	ARIZONA	24
31	at Denver	35
20	DALLAS	17
7	at NY Giants	28
31	at Oakland	24
327		**363**

MIAMI DOLPHINS (10–6)

24	at Indianapolis	15
13	BUFFALO	7
21	PITTSBURGH	0
	OPEN DATE	
9	at NY Jets	20
21	at Jacksonville	28
14	ST. LOUIS	0
12	NEW ENGLAND (OT)	9
24	at Buffalo	30
27	INDIANAPOLIS	14
13	at Carolina	9
23	at New England	26
30	NEW ORLEANS	10
27	at Oakland	17
16	NY JETS	21
31	DENVER	21
16	at Atlanta	38
321		**265**

NEW ENGLAND PATRIOTS (9–7)

21	at Denver	27
29	INDIANAPOLIS	6
27	TENNESSEE	16
	OPEN DATE	
30	at New Orleans	27
40	KANSAS CITY	10
14	NY JETS	24
9	at Miami (OT)	12
21	at Indianapolis	16
10	ATLANTA	41
10	at Buffalo	13
26	MIAMI	23
25	BUFFALO	21
23	at Pittsburgh	9
18	at St. Louis	32
24	SAN FRANCISCO	21
10	at NY Jets	31
337		**329**

NEW YORK JETS (12–4)

30	at San Francisco (OT)	36
10	BALTIMORE	24
44	INDIANAPOLIS	6
	OPEN DATE	
20	MIAMI	9
10	at St. Louis	30
24	at New England	14
28	ATLANTA	3
20	at Kansas City	17
34	BUFFALO	12
23	at Indianapolis	24
24	at Tennessee	3
48	CAROLINA	21
32	SEATTLE	31
21	at Miami	16
17	at Buffalo	10
31	NEW ENGLAND	10
416		**266**

OAKLAND RAIDERS (8–8)

8	at Kansas City	28
20	NY GIANTS	17
17	DENVER	34
13	at Dallas	12
23	at Arizona	20
7	SAN DIEGO	6
	OPEN DATE	
27	CINCINNATI	10
31	at Seattle	18
10	at Baltimore	13
20	SEATTLE	17
14	at Denver	40
19	WASHINGTON	29
17	MIAMI	27
21	at Buffalo	44
17	at San Diego	10
24	KANSAS CITY	31
288		**356**

PITTSBURGH STEELERS (7–9)

20	at Baltimore	13
17	CHICAGO	12
0	at Miami	21
13	SEATTLE	10
	OPEN DATE	
20	at Cincinnati	25
16	BALTIMORE	6
20	at Kansas City	13
31	TENNESSEE	41
27	GREEN BAY	20
14	at Tennessee	23
30	JACKSONVILLE	15
16	at Detroit (OT)	19
9	NEW ENGLAND	23
3	at Tampa Bay	16
24	CINCINNATI	25
3	at Jacksonville	21
263		**303**

SAN DIEGO CHARGERS (5–11)

16	BUFFALO	14
13	at Tennessee	7
7	at Kansas City	23
16	NY GIANTS	34
12	at Indianapolis	17
6	at Oakland	7
13	PHILADELPHIA	10
20	SEATTLE	27
	OPEN DATE	
10	at Denver	27
14	BALTIMORE	13
38	KANSAS CITY	37
16	DENVER	31
20	at Washington	24
17	at Seattle	38
10	OAKLAND	17
13	at Arizona	16
241		**342**

SEATTLE SEAHAWKS (8–8)

38	at Philadelphia	0
33	ARIZONA	14
24	WASHINGTON	14
10	at Pittsburgh	13
6	at Kansas City	17
16	DENVER	21
	OPEN DATE	
27	at San Diego	20
18	OAKLAND	31
24	KANSAS CITY	12
17	at Oakland	20
22	at Dallas	30
20	TENNESSEE	18
31	at NY Jets	32
38	SAN DIEGO	17
27	INDIANAPOLIS	23
21	at Denver	28
372		**310**

TENNESSEE OILERS (8–8)

23	at Cincinnati	14
7	SAN DIEGO	13
16	at New England	27
22	JACKSONVILLE	27
	OPEN DATE	
12	at Baltimore	8
44	CINCINNATI	14
20	CHICAGO	23
41	at Pittsburgh	31
31	at Tampa Bay	22
23	PITTSBURGH	14
3	NY JETS	24
18	at Seattle	20
16	BALTIMORE	14
16	at Jacksonville	13
22	at Green Bay	30
16	MINNESOTA	26
330		**320**

ARIZONA CARDINALS (9–7)

10	at Dallas	38
14	at Seattle	33
17	PHILADELPHIA	3
20	at St. Louis	17
20	OAKLAND	23
20	CHICAGO	7
7	at NY Giants	34
	OPEN DATE	
17	at Detroit	15
29	WASHINGTON	27
28	DALLAS	35
45	at Washington	42
24	at Kansas City	34
19	NY GIANTS	23
20	at Philadelphia	17
19	NEW ORLEANS	17
16	SAN DIEGO	13
325		**378**

ATLANTA FALCONS (14–2)

19	at Carolina	14
17	PHILADELPHIA	12
	OPEN DATE	
20	at San Francisco	31
51	CAROLINA	23
34	at NY Giants	20
31	NEW ORLEANS	23
3	at NY Jets	28
37	ST. LOUIS	15
41	at New England	10
31	SAN FRANCISCO	19
20	CHICAGO	13
21	at St. Louis	10
28	INDIANAPOLIS	21
27	at New Orleans	17
24	at Detroit	17
38	MIAMI	16
442		**289**

CAROLINA PANTHERS (4–12)

14	ATLANTA	19
14	at New Orleans	19
	OPEN DATE	
30	GREEN BAY	37
23	at Atlanta	51
20	at Dallas	27
13	at Tampa Bay	16
14	BUFFALO	30
31	NEW ORLEANS	17
23	at San Francisco	25
9	MIAMI	13
24	at St. Louis	20
21	at NY Jets	48
28	SAN FRANCISCO	31
25	WASHINGTON	28
20	ST. LOUIS	13
27	at Indianapolis	19
336		**413**

CHICAGO BEARS (4–12)

23	JACKSONVILLE	24
12	at Pittsburgh	17
15	at Tampa Bay	27
28	MINNESOTA	31
31	DETROIT	27
7	at Arizona	20
13	DALLAS	12
23	at Tennessee	20
	OPEN DATE	
13	ST. LOUIS	20
3	at Detroit	26
13	at Atlanta	20
17	TAMPA BAY	31
22	at Minnesota	48
20	at Green Bay	26
24	BALTIMORE	3
13	GREEN BAY	16
276		**368**

DALLAS COWBOYS (10–6)

38	ARIZONA	13
23	at Denver	42
31	at NY Giants	7
12	OAKLAND	13
31	at Washington	10
27	CAROLINA	20
12	at Chicago	13
	OPEN DATE	
34	at Philadelphia	0
16	NY GIANTS	6
35	at Arizona	28
30	SEATTLE	22
36	MINNESOTA	46
3	at New Orleans	22
17	at Kansas City	20
13	PHILADELPHIA	9
23	WASHINGTON	7
381		**275**

DETROIT LIONS (5–11)

19	at Green Bay	38
28	CINCINNATI	34
6	at Minnesota	29
27	TAMPA BAY	6
27	at Chicago	31
	OPEN DATE	
27	GREEN BAY	20
13	MINNESOTA	34
15	ARIZONA	17
9	at Philadelphia	10
26	CHICAGO	3
28	at Tampa Bay	25
19	PITTSBURGH (OT)	16
22	at Jacksonville	37
13	at San Francisco	35
17	ATLANTA	24
10	at Baltimore	19
306		**378**

GREEN BAY PACKERS (11-5)

38	DETROIT	19
23	TAMPA BAY	15
13	at Cincinnati	6
37	at Carolina	30
24	MINNESOTA	37
	OPEN DATE	
20	at Detroit	27
28	BALTIMORE	10
36	SAN FRANCISCO	22
20	at Pittsburgh	27
37	at NY Giants	3
14	at Minnesota	28
24	PHILADELPHIA	16
22	at Tampa Bay	24
26	CHICAGO	20
30	TENNESSEE	22
16	at Chicago	13
408		319

MINNESOTA VIKINGS (15-1)

31	TAMPA BAY	7
38	at St. Louis	31
29	DETROIT	6
31	at Chicago	28
37	at Green Bay	24
	OPEN DATE	
41	WASHINGTON	7
34	at Detroit	13
24	at Tampa Bay	27
31	NEW ORLEANS	24
24	CINCINNATI	3
28	GREEN BAY	14
46	at Dallas	36
48	CHICAGO	22
38	at Baltimore	28
50	JACKSONVILLE	10
26	at Tennessee	16
556		296

NEW ORLEANS SAINTS (6-10)

24	at St. Louis	17
19	CAROLINA	14
	OPEN DATE	
19	at Indianapolis (OT)	13
27	NEW ENGLAND	30
0	SAN FRANCISCO	31
23	at Atlanta	31
9	TAMPA BAY	3
17	at Carolina	31
24	at Minnesota	31
24	ST. LOUIS	3
20	at San Francisco	31
10	at Miami	30
22	DALLAS	3
17	ATLANTA	27
17	at Arizona	19
33	BUFFALO	45
305		359

NEW YORK GIANTS (8-8)

31	WASHINGTON	24
17	at Oakland	20
7	DALLAS	31
34	at San Diego	16
3	at Tampa Bay	20
20	ATLANTA	34
34	ARIZONA	7
	OPEN DATE	
14	at Washington	21
6	at Dallas	16
3	GREEN BAY	37
20	PHILADELPHIA	0
7	at San Francisco	31
23	at Arizona	19
20	DENVER	16
28	KANSAS CITY	7
20	at Philadelphia	10
287		309

PHILADELPHIA EAGLES (3-13)

0	SEATTLE	38
12	at Atlanta	17
3	at Arizona	17
21	KANSAS CITY	24
16	at Denver	41
17	WASHINGTON	12
10	at San Diego	13
	OPEN DATE	
0	DALLAS	34
10	DETROIT	9
3	at Washington	28
0	at NY Giants	20
16	at Green Bay	24
17	ST. LOUIS	14
17	ARIZONA	20
9	at Dallas	13
10	NY GIANTS	20
161		344

ST. LOUIS RAMS (4-12)

17	NEW ORLEANS	24
31	MINNESOTA	38
34	at Buffalo	33
17	ARIZONA	20
	OPEN DATE	
30	NY JETS	10
0	at Miami	14
10	SAN FRANCISCO	28
15	at Atlanta	37
20	at Chicago	12
3	at New Orleans	24
20	CAROLINA	24
10	ATLANTA	21
14	at Philadelphia	17
32	NEW ENGLAND	18
13	at Carolina	20
19	at San Francisco	38
285		378

SAN FRANCISCO 49ERS (12-4)

36	NY JETS (OT)	30
45	at Washington	10
	OPEN DATE	
31	ATLANTA	20
21	at Buffalo	26
31	at New Orleans	0
34	INDIANAPOLIS	31
28	at St. Louis	10
22	at Green Bay	36
25	CAROLINA	23
19	at Atlanta	31
31	NEW ORLEANS	20
31	NY GIANTS	7
31	at Carolina	28
35	DETROIT	13
21	at New England	24
38	ST. LOUIS	19
479		328

TAMPA BAY BUCCANEERS (8-8)

7	at Minnesota	31
15	at Green Bay	23
27	CHICAGO	15
6	at Detroit	27
20	NY GIANTS	3
	OPEN DATE	
16	CAROLINA	13
3	at New Orleans	9
27	MINNESOTA	24
22	TENNESSEE	31
24	at Jacksonville	29
25	DETROIT	28
31	at Chicago	17
24	GREEN BAY	22
16	PITTSBURGH	3
16	at Washington	20
35	at Cincinnati	0
314		295

WASHINGTON REDSKINS (6-10)

24	at NY Giants	31
10	SAN FRANCISCO	45
14	at Seattle	24
16	DENVER	38
10	DALLAS	31
12	at Philadelphia	17
7	at Minnesota	41
	OPEN DATE	
21	NY GIANTS	14
27	at Arizona	29
28	PHILADELPHIA	3
42	ARIZONA	45
29	at Oakland	19
24	SAN DIEGO	20
28	at Carolina	25
20	TAMPA BAY	16
7	at Dallas	23
319		421

American Football Conference
Scoring

TOUCHDOWNS	TD	Rush	Rec	Ret	Pts	KICKING	PAT	FG	Lg	Pts
Davis, Den	23	21	2	0	138	Christie, Buff	41/41	33/41	52	140
Taylor, Jax	17	14	3	0	102	Del Greco, Tenn	28/28	36/39	48	136
Edwards, NE	12	9	3	0	72	Elam, Den	58/58	23/27	63	127
Galloway, Sea	12	0	10	2	72	Vinatieri, NE	32/32	31/39	55	127
Johnson, NYJ	11	1	10	0	66	Hall, NYJ	45/46	25/35	54	120
Faulk, Ind	10	6	4	0	60	Stoyanovich, KC	34/34	27/32	53	115
McCaffrey, Den	10	0	10	0	62	Hollis, Jax	45/45	21/26	47	108
Sharpe, Den	10	0	10	0	60	Vanderjagt, Ind	23/23	27/31	53	104
Brown, Oak	9	0	9	0	54	Johnson, Pitt	21/21	26/31	49	99
Martin, NYJ	9	8	1	0	54	Mare, Mia	33/34	22/27	48	99
						Peterson, Sea	41/41	19/24	51	98

Passing

	Att	Comp	Pct Comp	Yds	Avg Gain	TD	Pct TD	Int	Pct Int	Lg	Rating Pts
Testaverde, NYJ	421	259	61.5	3256	7.70	29	6.9	7	1.7	t82	101.6
Elway, Den	356	210	59.0	2806	7.90	22	6.2	10	2.8	58	93.0
O'Donnell, Cin	343	212	61.8	2216	6.50	15	4.4	4	1.2	t76	90.2
Brunell, Jax	354	208	58.8	2601	7.40	20	5.6	9	2.5	t78	89.9
Flutie, Buff	354	202	57.1	2711	7.70	20	5.6	11	3.1	t84	87.4
Bledsoe, NE	481	263	54.7	3633	7.60	20	4.2	14	2.9	t86	80.9
Gannon, KC	354	206	58.2	2305	6.50	10	2.8	6	1.7	t80	80.1
McNair, Tenn	492	289	58.7	3228	6.60	15	3.0	10	2.0	47	80.1
Marino, Mia	537	310	57.7	3497	6.50	23	4.3	15	2.8	t61	80.0
Moon, Sea	258	145	56.2	1632	6.30	11	4.3	8	3.1	45	76.6

Pass Receiving

RECEPTIONS	No.	Yds	Avg	Lg	TD	YARDS	Yds	No.	Avg	Lg	TD
McDuffie, Mia	90	1050	11.7	t61	7	Moulds, Buff	1368	67	20.4	t84	9
Faulk, Ind	86	908	10.6	t78	4	R. Smith, Den	1222	86	14.2	58	6
R. Smith, Den	86	1222	14.2	58	6	J. Smith, Jax	1182	78	15.2	t72	8
Johnson, NYJ	83	1131	13.6	t41	10	Johnson, NYJ	1131	83	13.6	t41	10
Pickens, Cin	82	1023	12.5	t67	5	Chrebet, NYJ	1083	75	14.4	t63	8
T. Brown, Oak	81	1012	12.5	49	9	McCaffrey, Den	1053	64	16.5	48	10
J. Smith, Jax	78	1182	15.2	t72	8	McDuffie, Mia	1050	90	11.7	t61	7
Chrebet, NYJ	75	1083	14.4	t63	8	Galloway, Sea	1047	65	16.1	t81	10
Wycheck, Tenn	70	768	11.0	38	2	Pickens, Cin	1023	82	12.5	t67	5
Coates, NE	67	668	10.0	33	6	T. Brown, Oak	1012	81	12.5	49	9
Moulds, Buff	67	1368	20.4	t84	9						

Rushing / Total Yards from Scrimmage

	Att	Yds	Avg	Lg	TD	Total Yards from Scrimmage	Total	Rush	Rec
Davis, Den	392	2008	5.1	70	21	Faulk, Ind	2227	1319	908
Faulk, Ind	324	1319	4.1	t68	6	Davis, Den	2225	2008	217
George, Tenn	348	1298	3.7	t37	5	Martin, NYJ	1652	1287	365
Martin, NYJ	369	1287	3.5	t60	8	Taylor, Jax	1644	1223	421
Watters, Sea	319	1239	3.9	t39	9	Watters, Sea	1612	1239	373
Taylor, Jax	264	1223	4.6	t77	14	George, Tenn	1604	1294	310
Bettis, Pitt	316	1185	3.8	42	3	Edwards, NE	1446	1115	331
Dillon, Cin	262	1130	4.3	66	4	Moulds, Buff	1368	0	1368
A. Smith, Buff	300	1124	3.7	30	8	Dillon, Cin	1308	1130	178
Edwards, NE	291	1115	3.8	53	9	R. Smith, Den	1285	63	1222
Holmes, Balt	233	1008	4.3	56	7	Bettis, Pitt	1275	1185	90

Interceptions

	No.	Yds	Lg	TD
Law, NE	9	133	t59	1
Buckley, Mia	8	157	67	1
Madison, Mia	8	114	35	0
Springs, Sea	7	142	t56	2
Five tied with six.				

Sacks

Sinclair, Sea	16.5
McCrary, Balt	14.5
Thomas, KC	12.0
Gildon, Pitt	11.0
Johnstone, Oak	11.0
Armstrong, Mia	10.5

American Football Conference *(Cont.)*

Punting

	No.	Yds	Avg	Net Avg	TB	In 20	Lg	Blk	Ret	Ret Yds
Hentrich, Tenn	69	3258	47.2	39.2	11	18	71	0	34	332
Rouen, Den	66	3097	46.9	37.6	10	14	76	1	43	381
Gardocki, Ind	79	3583	45.4	37.1	10	23	62	0	42	451
Barker, Jax	85	3824	45.0	38.5	11	28	65	0	40	332
Johnson, Cin	69	3083	44.7	35.6	8	14	69	1	31	428

Punt Returns

	No.	Yds	Avg	Lg	TD
Barlow, Jax	43	555	12.9	t85	1
J. Lewis, Balt	32	405	12.7	t87	2
Buckley, Mia	29	354	12.2	35	0
Rachal, SD	32	387	12.1	56	0
Howard, Oak	45	541	12.0	t75	2

Kickoff Returns

	No.	Yds	Avg	Lg	TD
Harris, Balt	35	965	27.6	t95	1
Broussard, Sea	29	781	26.9	t90	1
Hebron, Den	46	1216	26.4	t95	1
Mack, Cin	45	1165	25.9	t97	1
Avery, Mia	43	1085	25.2	55	0

National Football Conference

Scoring

TOUCHDOWNS	TD	Rush	Rec	Ret	Pts
Moss, Minn	17	0	17	0	106
Anderson, Atl	16	14	2	0	98
Owens, SF	15	1	14	0	92
Smith, Dall	15	13	2	0	90
Freeman, GB	14	0	14	0	86
Carter, Minn	12	0	12	0	72
Mathis, Atl	11	0	11	0	66
Hoard, Minn	10	9	1	0	60
Murrell, Ariz	10	8	2	0	60
Alstott, TB	9	8	1	0	54

KICKING	PAT	FG	Lg	Pts
Anderson, Minn	59/59	35/35	53	164
Longwell, GB	41/43	29/33	45	128
Cunningham, Dall	40/40	29/35	54	127
Andersen, Atl	51/52	23/28	53	120
Hanson, Det	27/29	29/33	51	114
Richey, SF	49/51	18/27	46	103
Daluiso, NYG	32/32	21/27	51	95
Husted, TB	29/30	21/28	52	92
Kasay, Car	35/37	19/26	56	92
Brien, NO	31/31	20/22	56	91

Passing

	Att	Comp	Pct Comp	Yds	Avg Gain	TD	Pct TD	Int	Pct Int	Lg	Rating Pts
Cunningham, Minn	425	259	60.9	3704	8.70	34	8.0	10	2.4	t67	106.0
S. Young, SF	517	322	62.3	4170	8.10	36	7.0	12	2.3	t81	101.1
Chandler, Atl	327	190	58.1	3154	9.70	25	7.6	12	3.7	t78	100.9
Aikman, Dall	315	187	59.4	2330	7.40	12	3.8	5	1.6	t67	88.5
Beuerlein, Car	343	216	63.0	2613	7.60	17	5.0	12	3.5	t68	88.2
Favre, GB	551	347	63.0	4212	7.60	31	5.6	23	4.2	t84	87.8
Batch, Det	303	173	57.1	2178	7.20	11	3.6	6	2.0	t98	83.5
Kramer, Chi	250	151	60.4	1823	7.30	9	3.6	7	2.8	t79	83.1
T. Green, Wash	509	278	54.6	3441	6.80	23	4.5	11	2.2	t75	81.8

Pass Receiving

RECEPTIONS	No.	Yds	Avg	Lg	TD
Sanders, Ariz	89	1145	12.9	42	3
Freeman, GB	84	1424	17.0	t84	14
Moore, Det	82	983	12.0	36	5
Rice, SF	82	1157	14.1	t75	9
Carter, Minn	78	1011	13.0	t54	12
Irvin, Dall	74	1057	14.3	51	1
Centers, Ariz	69	559	8.1	54	2
Ismail, Car	69	1024	14.8	62	8
Morton, Det	69	1028	14.9	t98	2
Moss, Minn	69	1313	19.0	t61	17

YARDS	Yds	No.	Avg	Lg	TD
Freeman, GB	1424	84	17.0	t84	14
Moss, Minn	1313	69	19.0	t61	17
Martin, Atl	1181	66	17.9	62	6
Rice, SF	1157	82	14.1	t75	9
Sanders, Ariz	1145	89	12.9	42	3
Mathis, Atl	1136	64	17.8	t78	11
Owens, SF	1097	67	16.4	t79	14
Irvin, Dall	1057	74	14.3	51	1
Morton, Det	1028	69	14.9	t98	2
Ismail, Car	1024	69	14.8	62	8

National Football Conference (Cont.)

Rushing

	Att	Yds	Avg	Lg	TD
Anderson, Atl	410	1846	4.5	48	14
Hearst, SF	310	1570	5.1	t96	7
Sanders, Det	343	1491	4.3	t73	4
E. Smith, Dall	319	1332	4.2	32	13
R. Smith, Minn	249	1187	4.8	t74	6
Staley, Phil	258	1065	4.1	t64	5
Brown, NYG	247	1063	4.3	45	5
Murrell, Ariz	274	1042	3.8	32	8
Dunn, TB	245	1026	4.2	50	2
Alstott, TB	215	846	3.9	37	8

Total Yards from Scrimmage

	Total	Rush	Rec
Anderson, Atl	2165	1846	319
Hearst, SF	2105	1570	535
Sanders, Det	1780	1491	289
E. Smith, Dall	1507	1332	175
Staley, Phil	1497	1065	432
R. Smith, Minn	1478	1187	291
Freeman, GB	1429	5	1424
Dunn, TB	1370	1026	344
Moss, Minn	1317	4	1313
Murrell, Ariz	1211	1042	169

Interceptions

	No.	Yds	Lg	TD
Lassiter, Ariz	8	80	29	0
Buchanan, Atl	7	102	34	0
Hitchcock, Minn	7	242	t79	3
Knight, NO	6	171	t91	2

Six tied with five.

Sacks

White, GB	16.0
Doleman, SF	15.0
Greene, Car	15.0
Strahan, NYG	15.0
Douglas, Phil	12.5
Barker, SF	12.0

Punting

	No.	Yds	Avg	Net Avg	TB	In 20	Lg	Blk	Ret	Ret Yds
Royals, NO	88	4017	45.6	36.0	10	26	64	0	52	649
Maynard, NYG	101	4566	45.2	37.8	8	30	63	0	53	587
Berger, Minn	55	2458	44.7	37.0	5	17	67	0	27	325
Tuten, StL	95	4202	44.2	35.3	10	16	64	0	58	652
Turk, Wash	93	4103	44.1	39.0	9	33	69	1	31	260
Jett, Det	66	2892	43.8	36.0	6	17	60	0	38	390

Punt Returns

	No.	Yds	Avg	Lg	TD
Sanders, Dall	24	375	15.6	t69	2
Green, TB	30	453	15.1	t95	1
Hastings, NO	22	307	14.0	76	0
Milburn, Chi	25	291	11.6	t93	1
Mitchell, Wash	44	506	11.5	47	0

Kickoff Returns

	No.	Yds	Avg	Lg	TD
Fair, Det	51	1428	28.0	t105	2
Dwight, Atl	36	973	27.0	t93	1
Preston, GB	57	1497	26.3	t101	2
Bates, Car	59	1480	25.1	t99	1
Milburn, Chi	62	1550	25.0	t94	2

1998 NFL Team Leaders

AFC Total Offense

	Total Yds	Yds Rush	Yds Pass	Time of Poss	Avg Pts/Game
Denver	6092	2468	3624	32:08	31.3
NY Jets	5715	1879	3836	32:17	26.0
Buffalo	5541	2161	3380	32:26	25.0
Tennessee	5261	1970	3291	31:41	20.6
Jacksonville	5214	2102	3112	28:59	24.5
New England	5140	1480	3660	28:34	21.1
Indianapolis	5116	1486	3630	27:47	19.4
Miami	4930	1535	3395	32:10	20.1
Cincinnati	4824	1639	3185	28:31	16.8
Oakland	4815	1727	3088	28:51	18.0
Kansas City	4808	1548	3260	29:53	20.4
Seattle	4626	1626	3000	27:05	23.3
San Diego	4592	1728	2864	31:17	15.1
Pittsburgh	4586	2034	2552	30:20	16.4
Baltimore	4498	1629	2869	28:04	16.8

AFC Total Defense

	Opp Total Yds	Opp Yds Rush	Opp Yds Pass	Avg PA/Game
San Diego	4208	1140	3068	21.4
Miami	4435	1511	2924	16.6
Oakland	4550	1674	2876	22.3
Buffalo	4691	1493	3198	20.8
NY Jets	4699	1659	3040	16.6
Kansas City	4854	1869	2985	22.7
Denver	4935	1287	3648	19.3
Pittsburgh	4963	1642	3321	18.9
Tennessee	5121	1610	3511	20.0
New England	5182	1547	3635	20.6
Baltimore	5297	1705	3592	20.9
Jacksonville	5559	2000	3559	21.1
Seattle	5689	1999	3690	19.4
Cincinnati	5763	2612	3159	28.3
Indianapolis	5836	2570	3266	27.8

1998 NFL Team Leaders (Cont.)

NFC Total Offense

	Total Yds	Yds Rush	Yds Pass	Time of Poss	Avg Pts/Game
San Francisco	6800	2544	4256	31:52	29.9
Minnesota	6264	1936	4328	29:58	34.7
Green Bay	5636	1526	4110	31:37	25.5
Atlanta	5487	2101	3386	33:10	27.6
Dallas	5450	2014	3436	31:50	23.8
Arizona	5109	1627	3482	29:15	20.3
Detroit	5085	1955	3130	29:22	19.1
Washington	5010	1685	3325	28:34	19.9
Carolina	4780	1458	3322	28:10	21.0
Chicago	4766	1713	3053	29:26	17.2
Tampa Bay	4754	2148	2606	31:58	19.6
St. Louis	4472	1385	3087	28:59	17.8
New Orleans	4463	1325	3138	28:03	19.1
NY Giants	4455	1889	2566	28:21	17.9
Philadelphia	4188	1775	2413	29:24	10.0

NFC Total Defense

	Opp Total Yds	Opp Yds Rush	Opp Yds Pass	Avg PA/Game
Tampa Bay	4345	1583	2762	18.4
Green Bay	4507	1442	3065	19.9
Atlanta	4734	1203	3531	18.1
St. Louis	4880	2049	2831	23.6
Minnesota	5066	1614	3452	18.5
Chicago	5103	1875	3228	23.0
Detroit	5117	2102	3015	23.6
Philadelphia	5136	2416	2720	21.5
Dallas	5164	1619	3545	17.2
NY Giants	5171	2004	3167	19.3
Arizona	5265	1989	3276	23.6
San Francisco	5343	1610	3733	20.5
Washington	5354	2436	2918	26.3
New Orleans	5668	1700	3968	22.4
Carolina	5842	2133	3709	25.8

Takeaways/Giveaways

American Football Conference

	Takeaways Int	Fum	Total	Giveaways Int	Fum	Total	Net Diff
Buffalo	18	13	31	14	6	20	11
Denver	19	11	30	14	6	20	10
Jacksonville	13	17	30	12	8	20	10
Miami	29	7	36	16	12	28	8
Seattle	24	18	42	18	16	34	8
New England	24	7	31	17	7	24	7
NY Jets	21	9	30	13	11	24	6
Kansas City	13	20	33	18	14	32	1
Tennessee	12	7	19	10	9	19	0
Cincinnati	13	7	20	10	12	22	-2
Pittsburgh	16	13	29	20	12	32	-3
Baltimore	17	6	23	15	15	30	-7
Oakland	21	14	35	25	18	43	-8
Indianapolis	8	11	19	28	5	33	-14
San Diego	20	7	27	34	17	51	-24

National Football Conference

	Takeaways Int	Fum	Total	Giveaways Int	Fum	Total	Net Diff
Atlanta	19	25	44	15	9	24	20
Minnesota	19	15	34	16	4	20	14
Dallas	14	12	26	8	7	15	11
Arizona	20	19	39	20	16	36	3
San Francisco	21	12	33	15	15	30	3
NY Giants	19	7	26	15	9	24	2
New Orleans	21	11	32	19	14	33	-1
Carolina	19	14	33	18	17	35	-2
Detroit	12	9	21	13	12	25	-4
Tampa Bay	12	14	26	18	13	31	-5
Chicago	14	14	28	13	21	34	-6
Washington	13	8	21	14	15	29	-8
Philadelphia	9	8	17	18	8	26	-9
St. Louis	6	17	23	18	15	33	-10
Green Bay	13	10	23	23	11	34	-11

Conference Rankings

American Football Conference

	Offense Total	Rush	Pass	Defense Total	Rush	Pass
Baltimore	15	10	13	11	6	4
Buffalo	3	2	6	4	13	9
Cincinnati	9	9	9	14	1	10
Denver	1	1	4	7	14	2
Indianapolis	7	14	3	15	2	8
Jacksonville	5	3	10	12	3	5
Kansas City	11	12	8	6	5	13
Miami	8	13	5	2	12	14
New England	6	15	2	10	11	3
NY Jets	2	6	1	5	8	12
Oakland	10	8	11	3	7	15
Pittsburgh	14	4	15	8	9	7
San Diego	13	7	14	1	15	11
Seattle	12	11	12	13	4	1
Tennessee	4	5	7	9	10	6

National Football Conference

	Offense Total	Rush	Pass	Defense Total	Rush	Pass
Arizona	10	11	4	11	7	7
Atlanta	12	3	6	3	15	5
Carolina	7	13	8	15	3	3
Chicago	6	9	12	6	8	8
Dallas	11	4	5	9	10	4
Detroit	9	5	10	7	4	11
Green Bay	13	12	3	2	14	10
Minnesota	14	6	1	5	11	6
New Orleans	3	15	9	14	9	1
NY Giants	2	7	14	10	6	9
Philadelphia	1	8	15	8	2	15
St. Louis	4	14	11	4	5	13
San Francisco	15	1	2	12	12	2
Tampa Bay	5	2	13	1	13	14
Washington	8	10	7	13	1	12

Baltimore Ravens

SCORING	Rush	TD Rec	Ret	PAT	FG	S	Pts
Stover	0	0	0	24/24	21/28	0	87
J. Lewis	0	6	2	0/0	0/0	0	48
Holmes	7	0	0	0/0	0/0	0	42
Turner	0	5	0	0/0	0/0	0	34

RUSHING	No.	Yds	Avg	Lg	TD
Holmes	233	1008	4.3	56	7
Rhett	44	180	4.1	46	0
Harbaugh	39	172	4.4	15	0

PASSING	Att	Comp	Pct Comp	Yds	Avg Gain	TD	Int	Rating Pts
Harbaugh	293	164	56.0	1839	6.28	12	11	72.9
Zeier	181	107	59.1	1312	7.25	4	3	82.0

RECEIVING	No.	Yds	Avg	Lg	TD
Holmes	43	260	6.0	25	0
J. Lewis	41	784	19.1	t73	6
M. Jackson	38	477	12.6	53	0
Green	34	422	12.4	56	1
Turner	32	512	13.0	t66	5
Potts	30	168	5.6	18	2

INTERCEPTIONS: Woodson, 6

PUNTING	No.	Yds	Avg	Net Avg	TB	In 20	Lg	Blk
K. Rich's'n	90	3948	43.9	38.3	7	25	67	2

SACKS: McCrary, 14.5

Buffalo Bills

SCORING	Rush	TD Rec	Ret	PAT	FG	S	Pts
Christie	0	0	0	41/41	33/41	0	140
Moulds	0	9	0	0/0	0/0	0	54
A. Smith	8	0	0	0/0	0/0	0	48
Riemersma	0	6	0	0/0	0/0	0	36
Reed	0	5	0	0/0	0/0	0	30

RUSHING	No.	Yds	Avg	Lg	TD
A. Smith	300	1124	3.7	30	8
Thomas	93	381	4.1	t17	2
Flutie	48	248	5.2	23	1
Linton	45	195	4.3	20	1

PASSING	Att	Comp	Pct Comp	Yds	Avg Gain	TD	Int	Rating Pts
Flutie	354	202	57.1	2711	7.66	20	11	87.4
R. Johnsn	107	67	62.6	910	8.50	8	3	102.9

RECEIVING	No.	Yds	Avg	Lg	TD
Moulds	67	1368	20.4	t84	9
Reed	63	795	12.6	t67	5
K. Williams	29	392	13.5	55	1
Thomas	26	220	8.5	26	1
Riemersma	25	288	11.5	28	6
Early	19	217	11.4	37	1

INTERCEPTIONS: Schulz, 6

PUNTING	No.	Yds	Avg	Net Avg	TB	In 20	Lg	Blk
Mohr	69	2882	41.8	33.2	11	18	57	0

SACKS: B. Smith, 10

Cincinnati Bengals

SCORING	Rush	TD Rec	Ret	PAT	FG	S	Pts
Pelfrey	0	0	0	21/21	19/27	0	78
Scott	0	7	0	0/0	0/0	0	42
Pickens	0	5	0	0/0	0/0	0	32
Dillon	4	1	0	0/0	0/0	0	30
Gibson	0	3	1	0/0	0/0	0	24

RUSHING	No.	Yds	Avg	Lg	TD
Dillon	262	1130	4.3	66	4
Bennett	77	243	3.2	17	2

PASSING	Att	Comp	Pct Comp	Yds	Avg Gain	TD	Int	Rating Pts
O'Donnell	343	212	61.8	2216	6.46	15	4	90.2
Blake	93	51	54.8	739	7.95	3	3	78.2
Justin	63	34	54.0	426	6.76	1	3	60.7

RECEIVING	No.	Yds	Avg	Lg	TD
Pickens	82	1023	12.5	67t	5
Scott	51	817	16.0	70t	7
Dillon	28	178	6.4	41	1

INTERCEPTIONS: Shade and Hawkins, 3

PUNTING	No.	Yds	Avg	Net Avg	TB	In 20	Lg	Blk
Costello	10	495	49.5	32.7	3	0	73	1
Johnson	69	3083	44.7	35.6	8	14	69	1

SACKS: Wilson, 6

Denver Broncos

SCORING	Rush	TD Rec	Ret	PAT	FG	S	Pts
Davis	21	2	0	0/0	0/0	0	138
Elam	0	0	0	58/58	23/27	0	127
McCaffrey	0	10	0	0/0	0/0	0	62
Sharpe	0	10	0	0/0	0/0	0	60
R. Smith	0	6	1	0/0	0/0	0	42

RUSHING	No.	Yds	Avg	Lg	TD
Davis	392	2008	5.1	70	21
Loville	53	161	3.0	12	2

PASSING	Att	Comp	Pct Comp	Yds	Avg Gain	TD	Int	Rating Pts
Elway	356	210	59.0	2806	7.88	22	10	93.0
Brister	131	78	59.5	986	7.53	10	3	99.0

RECEIVING	No.	Yds	Avg	Lg	TD
R. Smith	86	1222	14.2	58	6
McCaffrey	64	1053	16.5	48	10
Sharpe	64	768	12.0	38t	10
Davis	25	217	8.7	35	2
Green	16	194	12.1	50	1

INTERCEPTIONS: Gordon, 4

PUNTING	No.	Yds	Avg	Net Avg	TB	In 20	Lg	Blk
Rouen	66	3097	46.9	37.6	10	14	76	1

SACKS: Pryce and Tanuvasa, 8.5

Indianapolis Colts

SCORING	Rush	TD Rec	Ret	PAT	FG	S	Pts
Vanderjagt	0	0	0	23/23	27/31	0	104
Faulk	6	4	0	0/0	0/0	0	60
Harrison	0	7	0	0/0	0/0	0	44
Small	0	7	0	0/0	0/0	0	42
Pollard	0	4	0	0/0	0/0	0	28

RUSHING	No.	Yds	Avg	Lg	TD
Faulk	324	1319	4.1	t68	6
Manning	15	62	4.1	15	0
Warren	25	61	2.4	14	1
Elias	8	24	3.0	8	0
Heyward	6	15	2.5	8	0

PASSING	Att	Comp	Pct Comp	Yds	Avg Gain	TD	Int	Rating Pts
Manning	575	326	56.7	3739	6.50	26	28	71.2
Small	1	0	0.0	0	0.00	0	0	39.6

RECEIVING	No.	Yds	Avg	Lg	TD
Faulk	86	908	10.6	t78	4
Harrison	59	776	13.2	t61	7
Pathon	50	511	10.2	45	1
Small	45	681	15.1	53	7
Dilger	31	303	9.8	27	1

INTERCEPTIONS: Eight tied with one.

PUNTING	No.	Yds	Avg	Net Avg	TB	In 20	Lg	Blk
Gardocki	79	3583	45.4	37.1	10	23	62	0

SACKS: E. Johnson, 8

Jacksonville Jaguars

SCORING	Rush	TD Rec	Ret	PAT	FG	S	Pts
Hollis	0	0	0	45/45	21/26	0	108
F. Taylor	14	3	0	0/0	0/0	0	102
J. Smith	0	8	0	0/0	0/0	0	48
McCardell	0	6	0	0/0	0/0	0	38

RUSHING	No.	Yds	Avg	Lg	TD
F. Taylor	264	1223	4.6	77	14
Stewart	53	217	4.1	30	2
Brunell	49	192	3.9	18	0

PASSING	Att	Comp	Pct Comp	Yds	Avg Gain	TD	Int	Rating Pts
Brunell	354	208	58.8	2601	7.35	20	9	89.9
Quinn	64	34	53.1	387	6.05	2	3	62.4
Martin	45	27	60.0	355	7.89	2	0	99.8

RECEIVING	No.	Yds	Avg	Lg	TD
J. Smith	78	1182	15.2	t72	8
McCardell	64	892	13.9	t67	6
F. Taylor	44	421	9.6	t78	3
Mitchell	38	363	9.6	38	2
Barlow	11	168	15.3	31	0

INTERCEPTIONS: Beasley and Hudson, 3

PUNTING	No.	Yds	Avg	Net Avg	TB	In 20	Lg	Blk
Barker	85	3824	45.0	38.5	11	28	65	0

SACKS: Smeenge, 7.5

Kansas City Chiefs

SCORING	Rush	TD Rec	Ret	PAT	FG	S	Pts
Stoyanovich	0	0	0	34/34	27/32	0	115
Morris	8	0	0	0/0	0/0	0	48
Bennett	5	1	0	0/0	0/0	0	36
Rison	0	5	0	0/0	0/0	0	30
Alexander	0	4	0	0/0	0/0	0	24

RUSHING	No.	Yds	Avg	Lg	TD
Bennett	148	527	3.6	26	5
Morris	124	505	4.1	30	11
Anders	58	230	4.0	20	1
Gannon	44	168	3.8	21	3

PASSING	Att	Comp	Pct Comp	Yds	Avg Gain	TD	Int	Rating Pts
Gannon	354	206	58.2	2305	6.51	10	6	80.1
Grbac	188	98	52.1	1142	6.07	5	12	53.1

RECEIVING	No.	Yds	Avg	Lg	TD
Anders	64	462	7.2	29	2
Gonzalez	59	621	10.5	32	2
Alexander	54	992	18.4	65	4
Rison	40	542	13.6	t80	5
Lockett	19	281	14.8	38	0

INTERCEPTIONS: Hasty, 4

PUNTING	No.	Yds	Avg	Net Avg	TB	In 20	Lg	Blk
Aguiar	75	3226	43.0	34.4	5	20	59	1

SACKS: Thomas, 12

Miami Dolphins

SCORING	Rush	TD Rec	Ret	PAT	FG	S	Pts
Mare	0	0	0	33/34	22/27	0	99
McDuffie	0	7	0	0/0	0/0	0	42
Gadsden	0	7	0	0/0	0/0	0	42
Abdul-Jabbar	6	0	0	0/0	0/0	0	36
L. Thomas	0	5	0	0/0	0/0	0	30

RUSHING	No.	Yds	Avg	Lg	TD
Abdul-Jabbar	270	960	3.6	45	6
Avery	143	503	3.5	44	2

PASSING	Att	Comp	Pct Comp	Yds	Avg Gain	TD	Int	Rating Pts
Marino	537	310	57.7	3497	6.51	23	15	80.0

RECEIVING	No.	Yds	Avg	Lg	TD
McDuffie	90	1050	11.7	t61	7
Gadsden	48	713	14.9	50	7
L. Thomas	43	603	14.0	t56	5
Drayton	30	334	11.1	35	3
Perry	25	255	10.2	46	0
Parmalee	21	221	10.5	23	0
Abdul-Jabbar	21	102	4.9	18	0

INTERCEPTIONS: Buckley and Madison, 8

PUNTING	No.	Yds	Avg	Net Avg	TB	In 20	Lg	Blk
Wilmsm'r.	93	3949	57.0	42.5	13	23	57	1

SACKS: Armstrong, 10.5

New England Patriots

SCORING

		TD					
SCORING	Rush	Rec	Ret	PAT	FG	S	Pts
Vinatieri	0	0	0	33/33	31/39	0	125
Edwards	9	3	0	0/0	0/0	0	72
Coates	0	6	0	0/0	0/0	0	36
Glenn	0	3	0	0/0	0/0	0	18
Simmons	0	3	0	0/0	0/0	0	18

RUSHING

RUSHING	No.	Yds	Avg	Lg	TD
Edwards	291	1115	3.8	53	9
S. Shaw	48	236	4.9	71	0
Cullors	18	48	2.7	15	0

PASSING

PASSING	Att	Comp	Pct Comp	Yds	Avg Gain	TD	Int	Rating Pts
Bledsoe	481	263	54.7	3633	7.55	20	14	80.9

RECEIVING

RECEIVING	No.	Yds	Avg	Lg	TD
Coates	67	668	10.0	33	6
Glenn	50	792	15.8	t86	3
Edwards	35	331	9.5	46	3
Jefferson	34	771	22.7	t61	2
Simmons	23	474	20.6	t63	3
Brown	23	346	15.0	52	1

INTERCEPTIONS: Law, 9

PUNTING	No.	Yds	Avg	Net Avg	TB	In 20	Lg	Blk
Tupa	74	3294	44.5	35.4	9	13	64	0

SACKS: Thomas, 6.5

New York Jets

SCORING

		TD					
SCORING	Rush	Rec	Ret	PAT	FG	S	Pts
Hall	0	0	0	45/46	25/35	0	120
K. Johnson	1	10	0	0/0	0/0	0	66
Martin	8	1	0	0/0	0/0	0	54
Chrebet	0	8	0	0/0	0/0	0	48
Brady	0	5	0	0/0	0/0	0	30

RUSHING

RUSHING	No.	Yds	Avg	Lg	TD
Martin	369	1287	3.5	t60	8
L. Johnson	41	185	4.5	40	2
Sowell	40	164	4.1	33	0

PASSING

PASSING	Att	Comp	Pct Comp	Yds	Avg Gain	TD	Int	Rating Pts
Testaverde	421	259	61.5	3256	7.73	29	7	101.6
Foley	108	58	53.7	749	6.94	4	6	64.9

RECEIVING

RECEIVING	No.	Yds	Avg	Lg	TD
K. Johnson	83	1131	13.6	t41	10
Chrebet	75	1083	14.4	t63	8
Martin	43	365	8.5	23	1
Brady	30	315	10.5	35	5
Byars	26	258	9.9	29	3

INTERCEPTIONS: Glenn, 6

PUNTING	No.	Yds	Avg	Net Avg	TB	In 20	Lg	Blk
B. Hansen	31	1233	39.8	32.7	2	26	62	0

SACKS: Lewis, 7

Oakland Raiders

SCORING

		TD					
SCORING	Rush	Rec	Ret	PAT	FG	S	Pts
Davis	0	0	0	31/31	17/27	0	82
T. Brown	0	9	0	0/0	0/0	0	54
Jett	0	6	0	0/0	0/0	0	36
Dudley	0	5	0	0/0	0/0	0	32
H. Williams	2	0	0	0/0	0/0	0	12
Howard	0	0	2	0/0	0/0	0	12

RUSHING

RUSHING	No.	Yds	Avg	Lg	TD
Kaufman	217	921	4.2	t80	2
H. Williams	128	496	3.9	t25	2
Jordan	47	159	3.4	23	1
Hollas	29	120	4.1	14	1

PASSING

PASSING	Att	Comp	Pct Comp	Yds	Avg Gain	TD	Int	Rating Pts
Hollas	260	135	51.9	1754	6.75	10	16	60.6

RECEIVING

RECEIVING	No.	Yds	Avg	Lg	TD
T. Brown	81	1012	12.5	49	9
Jett	45	882	19.6	t75	6
Dudley	36	549	15.3	32	5
Ritchie	29	225	7.8	31	0
H. Williams	26	173	6.7	15	0

INTERCEPTIONS: Two tied with five.

PUNTING	No.	Yds	Avg	Net Avg	TB	In 20	Lg	Blk
Araguz	98	4256	43.4	33.4	10	29	64	0

SACKS: Johnstone, 11

Pittsburgh Steelers

SCORING

		TD					
SCORING	Rush	Rec	Ret	PAT	FG	S	Pts
N. Johnson	0	0	0	21/21	26/31	0	99
C. Johnson	0	7	0	0/0	0/0	0	46
Bettis	3	0	0	0/0	0/0	0	18
Fu'-Ma'afala	2	1	0	0/0	0/0	0	18
Stewart	2	0	0	0/0	0/0	0	12

RUSHING

RUSHING	No.	Yds	Avg	Lg	TD
Bettis	316	1185	3.8	42	3
Stewart	81	406	5.0	56	2
Huntley	55	242	4.4	48	1
McAfee	18	111	6.2	14	0

PASSING

PASSING	Att	Comp	Pct Comp	Yds	Avg Gain	TD	Int	Rating Pts
Stewart	458	252	55.0	2560	5.59	11	18	62.9
Tomczak	30	21	70.0	204	6.80	2	2	83.2

RECEIVING

RECEIVING	No.	Yds	Avg	Lg	TD
Hawkins	66	751	11.4	53	1
C. Johnson	65	815	12.5	t55	7
Blackwell	32	297	9.3	t24	1
Bruener	19	157	8.3	20	2
Bettis	16	90	5.6	26	0

INTERCEPTIONS: Washington, 5

PUNTING	No.	Yds	Avg	Net Avg	TB	In 20	Lg	Blk
Miller	81	3530	43.6	36.8	12	34	73	0

SACKS: Gildon, 11

San Diego Chargers

SCORING	Rush	TD Rec	Ret	PAT	FG	S	Pts
Carney	0	0	0	19/19	26/30	0	97
Fletcher	5	0	0	0/0	0/0	0	30
Means	5	0	0	0/0	0/0	0	30
F. Jones	3	0	0	0/0	0/0	0	20
C. Jones	3	0	0	0/0	0/0	0	18

RUSHING	No.	Yds	Avg	Lg	TD
Means	212	883	4.2	t72	5
Fletcher	153	543	3.5	21	5
Stephens	35	122	3.5	12	1

PASSING	Att	Comp	Pct Comp	Yds	Avg Gain	TD	Int	Rating Pts
Whelihan	320	149	46.6	1803	5.63	8	19	48.0
Leaf	245	111	45.3	1289	5.26	2	15	39.0

RECEIVING	No.	Yds	Avg	Lg	TD
F. Jones	57	602	10.6	28	3
C. Jones	46	699	15.2	56	3
Still	43	605	14.1	67	2
Ricks	30	450	15.0	t39	2
Fletcher	30	188	6.3	22	0

INTERCEPTIONS: G. Jackson 6

PUNTING	No.	Yds	Avg	Net Avg	TB	In 20	Lg	Blk
Bennett	95	4174	43.9	36.8	8	27	65	0

SACKS: Hand, 6

He's Elvis in Name Only

In November 1998 *People* named Chiefs quarterback Elvis Grbac its sexiest athlete of the year. The news stunned his teammates. "Was that the Braille edition?" one player wondered.

Seattle Seahawks

SCORING	Rush	TD Rec	Ret	PAT	FG	S	Pts
Peterson	0	0	0	41/41	19/24	0	98
Galloway	0	10	2	0/0	0/0	0	72
Watters	9	0	0	0/0	0/0	0	56
Pritchard	0	3	0	0/0	0/0	0	20
Springs	0	0	3	0/0	0/0	0	18

RUSHING	No.	Yds	Avg	Lg	TD
Watters	319	1239	3.9	t39	9
Green	35	209	6.0	64	1
Kitna	20	67	3.4	21	1

PASSING	Att	Comp	Pct Comp	Yds	Avg Gain	TD	Int	Rating Pts
Moon	258	145	56.2	1632	6.33	11	8	76.6
Kitna	172	98	57.0	1177	6.84	7	8	72.3

RECEIVING	No.	Yds	Avg	Lg	TD
Galloway	65	1047	16.1	t81	10
Pritchard	58	742	12.8	t50	3
Watters	52	373	7.2	24	0
Fauria	37	377	10.2	25	2

INTERCEPTIONS: Springs, 7

PUNTING	No.	Yds	Avg	Net Avg	TB	In 20	Lg	Blk
Feagles	81	3570	44.1	36.5	12	27	59	0

SACKS: Sinclair, 16.5

Tennessee Oilers

SCORING	Rush	TD Rec	Ret	PAT	FG	S	Pts
Del Greco	0	0	0	28/28	36/39	0	136
E. George	5	1	0	0/0	0/0	0	38
McNair	4	0	0	0/0	0/0	0	24
Thigpen	0	3	0	0/0	0/0	0	18
Mason	0	3	0	0/0	0/0	0	18

RUSHING	No.	Yds	Avg	Lg	TD
E. George	348	1294	3.7	t37	5
McNair	77	559	7.3	t71	4
Thomas	24	100	4.2	21	2

PASSING	Att	Comp	Pct Comp	Yds	Avg Gain	TD	Int	Rating Pts
McNair	492	289	58.7	3228	6.56	15	10	80.1

RECEIVING	No.	Yds	Avg	Lg	TD
Wycheck	70	768	11.0	38	2
Harris	43	412	9.6	32	2
Thigpen	38	493	13.0	55	3
E. George	37	310	8.4	29	1
Davis	32	461	14.4	38	3
Mason	25	333	13.3	47	3

INTERCEPTIONS: Lewis, 4

PUNTING	No.	Yds	Avg	Net Avg	TB	In 20	Lg	Blk
Hentrich	69	3528	47.2	39.2	11	18	71	0

SACKS: Marts, 4

1998 NFC Team-by-Team Statistical Leaders

Arizona Cardinals

SCORING	TD Rush	Rec	Ret	PAT	FG	S	Pts
Nedney	0	0	0	30/30	13/19	0	69
Murrell	8	2	0	0/0	0/0	0	60
Bates	6	0	0	0/0	0/0	0	36
Jacke	0	0	0	6/6	10/14	0	36
Rob Moore	0	5	0	0/0	0/0	0	30
McWilliams	0	4	0	0/0	0/0	0	24

RUSHING	No.	Yds	Avg	Lg	TD
Murrell	274	1042	3.8	32	8
Plummer	51	217	4.3	27	4
Bates	60	165	2.8	15	6

PASSING	Att	Comp	Pct Comp	Yds	Avg Gain	TD	Int	Rating Pts
Plummer	547	324	59.2	3737	6.83	17	20	75.0

RECEIVING	No.	Yds	Avg	Lg	TD
Sanders	89	1145	12.9	42	3
Centers	69	559	8.1	54	2
Rob Moore	67	982	14.7	57	5
Metcalf	31	324	40.5	29	0
McWilliams	26	284	10.9	26	4
Gedney	22	271	12.3	32	1

INTERCEPTIONS: Lassiter, 8

PUNTING	No.	Yds	Avg	Net Avg	TB	In 20	Lg	Blk
Player	81	3378	41.7	35.9	6	12	67	1

SACKS: Rice, 10

Atlanta Falcons

SCORING	TD Rush	Rec	Ret	PAT	FG	S	Pts
Andersen	0	0	0	51/52	23/28	0	120
J. Anderson	14	2	0	0/0	0/0	0	98
Mathis	0	11	0	0/0	0/0	0	66
Martin	0	6	0	0/0	0/0	0	36
Santiago	0	5	0	0/0	0/0	0	30
Christian	2	1	0	0/0	0/0	0	18

RUSHING	No.	Yds	Avg	Lg	TD
J. Anderson	410	1846	4.5	48	14
Chandler	36	121	3.4	19	2
Oxendine	18	50	2.8	21	0

PASSING	Att	Comp	Pct Comp	Yds	Avg Gain	TD	Int	Rating Pts
Chandler	327	190	58.1	3154	9.65	25	12	100.9
DeBerg	59	80	50.8	369	6.25	3	1	80.4

RECEIVING	No.	Yds	Avg	Lg	TD
Martin	66	1181	17.9	62	6
Mathis	64	1136	17.8	t78	11
Santiago	27	428	15.9	t62	5
J. Anderson	27	319	11.8	27	2
Christian	19	214	11.3	39	1

INTERCEPTIONS: Buchanan, 7

PUNTING	No.	Yds	Avg	Net Avg	TB	In 20	Lg	Blk
Stryzinski	74	2963	40.0	36.6	7	25	55	0

SACKS: Archambeau, 10

Carolina Panthers

SCORING	TD Rush	Rec	Ret	PAT	FG	S	Pts
Kasay	0	0	0	35/37	19/26	0	92
Ismail	0	8	0	0/0	0/0	0	48
Muhammad	0	6	0	0/0	0/0	0	38
Walls	0	5	0	0/0	0/0	0	30
Lane	5	0	0	0/0	0/0	0	30

RUSHING	No.	Yds	Avg	Lg	TD
Lane	205	717	3.5	31	5
Biakabutuka	101	427	4.2	41	3
Johnson	36	135	3.8	21	0

PASSING	Att	Comp	Pct Comp	Yds	Avg Gain	TD	Int	Rating Pts
Beuerlein	343	216	63.0	2613	7.62	17	12	88.2
Collins	162	76	46.9	1011	6.24	8	5	70.8

RECEIVING	No.	Yds	Avg	Lg	TD
Ismail	69	1024	14.8	62	8
Muhammad	68	941	13.8	t72	6
Walls	49	506	10.3	30	5
Johnson	27	242	9.0	t38	1
Floyd	24	123	5.1	20	1
Carrier	19	301	15.8	42	2

INTERCEPTIONS: E. Davis, 5

PUNTING	No.	Yds	Avg	Net Avg	TB	In 20	Lg	Blk
Walter	77	3131	40.7	38.1	5	20	59	0

SACKS: Greene, 15

Chicago Bears

SCORING	TD Rush	Rec	Ret	PAT	FG	S	Pts
Jaeger	0	0	0	27/28	21/26	0	90
Engram	0	5	0	0/0	0/0	0	30
Penn	0	3	0	0/0	0/0	0	20
Milburn	0	0	3	0/0	0/0	0	18
Conway	0	3	0	0/0	0/0	0	18
J. Allen	1	1	0	0/0	0/0	0	12

RUSHING	No.	Yds	Avg	Lg	TD
Bennett	173	611	3.5	43	2
Enis	133	497	3.7	29	0

PASSING	Att	Comp	Pct Comp	Yds	Avg Gain	TD	Int	Rating Pts
Kramer	250	151	60.4	1823	7.29	9	7	83.1
Stenstrom	196	112	57.1	1252	6.39	4	6	70.4

RECEIVING	No.	Yds	Avg	Lg	TD
Engram	64	987	15.4	t79	5
Conway	54	733	13.6	47	3
Penn	31	448	14.5	37	3
Bennett	28	209	7.5	31	0
Hallock	25	166	6.6	16	0

INTERCEPTIONS: W. Harris, 4

PUNTING	No.	Yds	Avg	Net Avg	TB	In 20	Lg	Blk
Horan	64	2643	41.3	35.4	4	12	57	0

SACKS: Flanigan, 8.5

Dallas Cowboys

SCORING

SCORING	TD Rush	Rec	Ret	PAT	FG	S	Pts
Cunningham	0	0	0	40/40	29/35	0	127
E. Smith	13	2	0	0/0	0/0	0	90
Warren	4	1	0	0/0	0/0	0	30
Mills	0	4	0	0/0	0/0	0	24
Sanders	0	3	0	0/0	0/0	0	18

RUSHING

RUSHING	No.	Yds	Avg	Lg	TD
E. Smith	319	1332	4.2	32	13
Warren	59	291	4.9	49	4
S. Williams	64	220	3.4	24	1

PASSING

PASSING	Att	Comp	Pct Comp	Yds	Avg Gain	TD	Int	Rating Pts
Aikman	315	187	59.4	2330	7.40	12	5	88.5
Garrett	158	91	57.6	1206	7.63	5	3	84.5

RECEIVING

RECEIVING	No.	Yds	Avg	Lg	TD
Irvin	74	1057	14.3	51	1
B. Davis	39	691	17.7	t80	3
Mills	28	479	17.1	t43	4
E. Smith	27	175	6.5	24	2
LaFleur	20	176	8.8	24	2
Jeffers	18	330	18.3	t67	2

INTERCEPTIONS: Sanders, 5

PUNTING

PUNTING	No.	Yds	Avg	Net Avg	TB	In 20	Lg	Blk
Gowin	77	3342	43.4	36.6	14	31	65	1

SACKS: Pittman, 6

Detroit Lions

SCORING

SCORING	TD Rush	Rec	Ret	PAT	FG	S	Pts
Hanson	0	0	0	27/29	29/33	0	114
Vardell	6	1	0	0/0	0/0	0	42
Moore	0	5	0	0/0	0/0	0	30
Sanders	4	0	0	0/0	0/0	0	24
Crowell	0	3	0	0/0	0/0	0	18

RUSHING

RUSHING	No.	Yds	Avg	Lg	TD
Sanders	343	1491	4.3	t73	4
Batch	41	229	5.6	17	1
Rivers	19	102	5.4	t36	1

PASSING

PASSING	Att	Comp	Pct Comp	Yds	Avg Gain	TD	Int	Rating Pts
Batch	303	173	57.1	2178	7.19	11	6	83.5
Reich	110	63	57.3	768	6.98	5	4	78.9

RECEIVING

RECEIVING	No.	Yds	Avg	Lg	TD
Moore	82	963	12.0	36	5
Morton	69	1028	14.9	t98	2
Sanders	37	289	7.8	44	0
Crowell	25	464	18.6	t68	3
Rasby	15	119	7.9	17	1

INTERCEPTIONS: Westbrook, 3

PUNTING

PUNTING	No.	Yds	Avg	Net Avg	TB	In 20	Lg	Blk
Jett	66	2892	43.8	36.0	6	17	60	0

SACKS: Porcher, 11.5

Green Bay Packers

SCORING

SCORING	TD Rush	Rec	Ret	PAT	FG	S	Pts
Longwell	0	0	0	41/43	29/33	0	128
Freeman	0	14	0	0/0	0/0	0	86
T. Davis	0	7	0	0/0	0/0	0	42
Chmura	0	4	0	0/0	0/0	0	24
Preston	0	0	3	0/0	0/0	0	18

RUSHING

RUSHING	No.	Yds	Avg	Lg	TD
Holmes	93	386	4.2	43	1
Levens	115	378	3.3	50	1
Jervey	83	325	3.9	16	1
R. Harris	79	228	2.9	14	1

PASSING

PASSING	Att	Comp	Pct Comp	Yds	Avg Gain	TD	Int	Rating Pts
Favre	551	347	63.0	4212	7.64	31	23	87.8

RECEIVING

RECEIVING	No.	Yds	Avg	Lg	TD
Freeman	84	1424	17.0	t84	14
Chmura	47	554	11.8	t25	4
Henderson	37	241	6.5	15	1
Schroeder	31	452	14.6	46	1
Brooks	31	420	13.5	t30	3

INTERCEPTIONS: T. Williams, 5

PUNTING

PUNTING	No.	Yds	Avg	Net Avg	TB	In 20	Lg	Blk
Landeta	65	2788	42.9	37.1	7	30	72	0

SACKS: White, 16

Minnesota Vikings

SCORING

SCORING	TD Rush	Rec	Ret	PAT	FG	S	Pts
Anderson	0	0	0	59/59	35/35	0	164
R. Moss	0	17	0	0/0	0/0	0	106
Carter	0	12	0	0/0	0/0	0	72
Hoard	9	1	0	0/0	0/0	0	60
R. Smith	6	2	0	0/0	0/0	0	48
Glover	0	5	0	0/0	0/0	0	30

RUSHING

RUSHING	No.	Yds	Avg	Lg	TD
R. Smith	249	1187	4.8	t74	6
Hoard	115	479	4.2	t50	9
Cunningham	32	132	4.1	22	1
Evans	23	67	2.9	12	1

PASSING

PASSING	Att	Comp	Pct Comp	Yds	Avg Gain	TD	Int	Rating Pts
Cunningh'm	425	259	60.9	3704	8.72	34	10	106.0
Johnson	101	65	64.4	747	7.40	7	5	89.0

RECEIVING

RECEIVING	No.	Yds	Avg	Lg	TD
Carter	78	1011	13.0	t54	12
R. Moss	69	1313	19.0	t61	17
Glover	35	522	14.9	36	5
J. Reed	34	474	14.9	t56	4
R. Smith	28	291	10.4	t67	2

INTERCEPTIONS: Hitchcock, 7

PUNTING

PUNTING	No.	Yds	Avg	Net Avg	TB	In 20	Lg	Blk
Berger	50	2458	44.7	37.0	5	17	67	0

SACKS: Randle, 10.5

New Orleans Saints

SCORING

SCORING	Rush	TD Rec	Ret	PAT	FG	S	Pts
Brien	0	0	0	31/31	20/22	0	91
Cleeland	0	6	0	0/0	0/0	0	36
Craver	2	2	1	0/0	0/0	0	30
L. Smith	1	2	0	0/0	0/0	0	18
Bech	0	3	0	0/0	0/0	0	18
Hastings	0	3	0	0/0	0/0	0	18
Knight	0	0	2	0/0	0/0	0	12

RUSHING

RUSHING	No.	Yds	Avg	Lg	TD
L. Smith	138	457	3.3	33	1
Craver	45	180	4.0	25	2

PASSING

PASSING	Att	Comp	Pct Comp	Yds	Avg Gain	TD	Int	Rating Pts
Tolliver	198	110	55.6	1427	7.21	8	4	83.5
Collins	191	94	49.2	1202	6.29	4	10	54.5

RECEIVING

RECEIVING	No.	Yds	Avg	Lg	TD
Cleeland	54	684	12.7	53	6
Dawkins	53	823	15.5	t64	1
Hastings	35	455	13.0	t89	3
Craver	33	214	6.5	49	2
Poole	24	509	21.2	t82	2

INTERCEPTIONS: Knight, 6

PUNTING

PUNTING	No.	Yds	Avg	Net Avg	TB	In 20	Lg	Blk
Royals	88	4017	45.6	36.0	10	26	64	0

SACKS: Glover, 10

New York Giants

SCORING

SCORING	Rush	TD Rec	Ret	PAT	FG	S	Pts
Daluiso	0	0	0	32/32	21/27	0	95
Calloway	0	6	0	0/0	0/0	0	36
Brown	5	0	0	0/0	0/0	0	30
Toomer	0	5	0	0/0	0/0	0	30
Way	3	1	0	0/0	0/0	0	24

RUSHING

RUSHING	No.	Yds	Avg	Lg	TD
Brown	247	1063	4.3	45	5
Way	113	432	3.8	21	3
Barber	52	166	3.2	23	0

PASSING

PASSING	Att	Comp	Pct Comp	Yds	Avg Gain	TD	Int	Rating Pts
Kanell	299	160	53.5	1603	5.36	11	10	67.3
Graham	205	105	51.2	1219	5.95	7	5	70.8

RECEIVING

RECEIVING	No.	Yds	Avg	Lg	TD
Calloway	62	812	13.1	36	6
Hilliard	51	715	14.0	50	2
Barber	42	348	8.3	t87	3
Way	31	131	4.2	16	1

INTERCEPTIONS: Ellsworth, 5

PUNTING

PUNTING	No.	Yds	Avg	Net Avg	TB	In 20	Lg	Blk
Maynard	101	4566	45.2	37.8	8	33	63	0

SACKS: Strahan, 15

Philadelphia Eagles

SCORING

SCORING	Rush	TD Rec	Ret	PAT	FG	S	Pts
Boniol	0	0	0	15/17	14/21	0	57
Staley	5	1	0	0/0	0/0	0	36
Garner	4	0	0	0/0	0/0	0	24
Graham	0	2	0	0/0	0/0	0	12
Fryar	0	2	0	0/0	0/0	0	12

RUSHING

RUSHING	No.	Yds	Avg	Lg	TD
Staley	258	1065	4.1	t64	5
Garner	96	381	4.0	40	4

PASSING

PASSING	Att	Comp	Pct Comp	Yds	Avg Gain	TD	Int	Rating Pts
Hoying	224	114	50.9	961	4.29	0	9	45.6
Detmer	181	97	53.6	1011	5.59	5	5	67.7
Peete	129	71	55.0	758	5.88	2	4	64.7

RECEIVING

RECEIVING	No.	Yds	Avg	Lg	TD
Staley	57	432	7.6	33	1
Fryar	48	556	11.6	t61	2
Graham	47	600	12.8	45	2
Turner	34	232	6.8	18	0
Solomon	21	198	9.4	20	1

INTERCEPTIONS: Dawkins, 2

PUNTING

PUNTING	No.	Yds	Avg	Net Avg	TB	In 20	Lg	Blk
Hutton	104	4339	41.7	34.9	10	21	61	0

SACKS: Douglas, 12.5

St. Louis Rams

SCORING

SCORING	Rush	TD Rec	Ret	PAT	FG	S	Pts
Wilkins	0	0	0	25/26	20/26	0	85
Lee	2	2	0	0	0	0	26
G. Hill	4	0	0	0/0	0/0	0	24
Banks	3	0	0	0/0	0/0	0	20

RUSHING

RUSHING	No.	Yds	Avg	Lg	TD
Henley	88	313	3.6	22	3
Holcombe	98	230	2.3	12	2
Lee	44	175	4.0	38	2
G. Hill	40	240	6.0	46	4

PASSING

PASSING	Att	Comp	Pct Comp	Yds	Avg Gain	TD	Int	Rating Pts
Banks	408	241	59.1	2535	6.21	7	14	68.6
Bono	136	69	50.7	807	5.93	5	4	69.1

RECEIVING

RECEIVING	No.	Yds	Avg	Lg	TD
Lee	64	667	10.4	44	2
Proehl	60	771	12.9	47	3
Henley	35	252	7.2	43	0
Bruce	32	457	14.3	t80	1

INTERCEPTIONS: Lyght, 3

PUNTING

PUNTING	No.	Yds	Avg	Net Avg	TB	In 20	Lg	Blk
Tuten	95	4202	44.2	35.3	10	16	64	0

SACKS: Carter, 12

San Francisco 49ers

SCORING

SCORING	Rush	Rec	Ret	PAT	FG	S	Pts
Richey	0	0	0	49/51	18/27	0	103
Owens	1	14	0	0/0	0/0	0	92
Rice	0	9	0	0/0	0/0	0	58
Hearst	7	2	0	0/0	0/0	0	56
Stokes	0	8	0	0/0	0/0	0	48
S. Young	6	0	0	0/0	0/0	0	36

RUSHING

RUSHING	No.	Yds	Avg	Lg	TD
Hearst	310	1570	5.1	t96	7
S. Young	70	454	6.5	24	6
Kirby	48	258	5.4	t31	3

PASSING

PASSING	Att	Comp	Pct Comp	Yds	Avg Gain	TD	Int	Rating Pts
S. Young	517	322	62.3	4170	8.07	36	12	101.1
Detmer	38	24	63.2	312	8.21	4	3	91.1

RECEIVING

RECEIVING	No.	Yds	Avg	Lg	TD
Rice	82	1157	14.1	t75	9
Owens	67	1097	16.4	t79	14
Stokes	63	770	12.2	t33	8
Hearst	39	535	13.7	t81	2
Smith	25	266	10.6	t25	5
Edwards	22	218	9.9	t47	2

INTERCEPTIONS: Walker, 4

PUNTING

PUNTING	No.	Yds	Avg	Net Avg	TB	In 20	Lg	Blk
Roby	60	2511	41.9	34.3	6	14	66	0
Howard	9	324	36.0	32.8	1	2	45	0

SACKS: Doleman, 15

Say It Again?

The NFL hyped the 1998–99 playoffs with with a slam-bang TV ad featuring gridiron mayhem and a pounding rendition of Edwin Starr's 1970 hit *War*. But the ad turned the song's message on its head. Starr's anthem is scathingly antiwar, down to the refrain that the NFL spot conveniently left out: *War ... what is it good for? Absolutely nothin'!*

Good god, y'all! Let's hope the NFL doesn't get its hands on *Give Peace a Chance*.

Tampa Bay Buccaneers

SCORING

SCORING	Rush	Rec	Ret	PAT	FG	S	Pts
Husted	0	0	0	29/30	21/28	0	92
Alstott	8	1	0	0/0	0/0	0	54
Anthony	0	7	0	0/0	0/0	0	44
Moore	0	4	0	0/0	0/0	0	24
Green	0	2	1	0/0	0/0	0	18
Dilfer	2	0	0	0/0	0/0	0	12

RUSHING

RUSHING	No.	Yds	Avg	Lg	TD
Dunn	245	1026	4.2	50	2
Alstott	215	846	3.9	37	8
Dilfer	40	141	3.5	17	2

PASSING

PASSING	Att	Comp	Pct Comp	Yds	Avg Gain	TD	Int	Rating Pts
Dilfer	429	225	52.4	2729	6.36	21	15	74.0

RECEIVING

RECEIVING	No.	Yds	Avg	Lg	TD
Anthony	51	708	13.9	t79	7
Dunn	34	344	7.8	31	0
Emanuel	41	636	15.5	t62	2
Moore	24	255	10.6	t44	4
Alstott	22	155	6.9	26	1

INTERCEPTIONS: Mincy, 4

PUNTING

PUNTING	No.	Yds	Avg	Net Avg	TB	In 20	Lg	Blk
Barnhardt	81	3340	41.2	35.3	9	19	55	0

SACKS: Culpepper, 9

Washington Redskins

SCORING

SCORING	Rush	Rec	Ret	PAT	FG	S	Pts
Blanchard	0	0	0	30/31	11/17	0	63
Shepherd	1	8	0	0/0	0/0	0	56
Hicks	8	0	0	0/0	0/0	0	48
Westbrook	0	6	0	0/0	0/0	0	36

RUSHING

RUSHING	No.	Yds	Avg	Lg	TD
Allen	148	700	4.7	45	2
Hicks	122	433	3.5	28	8
Mitchell	39	208	5.3	22	2

PASSING

PASSING	Att	Comp	Pct Comp	Yds	Avg Gain	TD	Int	Rating Pts
T. Green	509	278	54.6	3441	6.76	23	11	81.8
Frerotte	54	25	46.3	283	5.24	1	3	45.5

RECEIVING

RECEIVING	No.	Yds	Avg	Lg	TD
Westbrook	44	736	16.7	t75	6
Mitchell	44	306	7.0	24	0
Shepherd	43	712	16.6	t43	8
S. Alexander	37	383	10.4	33	4
Connell	28	451	16.1	61	2

INTERCEPTIONS: L. Evans, 3

PUNTING

PUNTING	No.	Yds	Avg	Net Avg	TB	In 20	Lg	Blk
M. Turk	93	4103	44.1	39	9	33	69	1

SACKS: Wilkinson, 7.5

1999 NFL Draft

First two rounds of the 64th annual NFL Draft held April 17–18 in New York City.

First Round

Team	Selection	Position
1. Cleveland	Tim Couch, Kentucky	QB
2. Philadelphia	Donovan McNabb, Syracuse	QB
3. Cincinnati	Akili Smith, Oregon	QB
4. Indianapolis	Edgerrin James, Miami	RB
5. New Orleans	Ricky Williams, Texas	RB
6. St. Louis	Torry Holt, NC State	WR
7. Washington	Champ Bailey, Georgia	DB
8. Arizona	David Boston, Ohio St	WR
9. Detroit	Chris Claiborne, Southern Cal	LB
10. Baltimore	Chris McAlister, Arizona	DB
11. Minnesota	Daunte Culpepper, Cent. Fla.	QB
12. Chicago	Cade McNown, UCLA	QB
13. Pittsburgh	Troy Edwards, Louisiana Tech	WR
14. Kansas City	John Tait, Brigham Young	OT
15. Tampa Bay	Anthony McFarland, Louisiana St	DT
16. Tennessee	Jevon Kearse, Florida	DE
17. New England	Damien Woody, Boston College	C
18. Oakland	Matt Stinchcomb, Georgia	OT
19. NY Giants	Luke Petitgout, Notre Dame	OT
20. Dallas	Ebenezer Ekuban, N Carolina	DE
21. Arizona	L.J. Shelton, Eastern Michigan	OT
22. Seattle	Lamar King, Saginaw Valley	DE
23. Buffalo	Antoine Winfield, Ohio St	CB
24. San Francisco	Reggie McGrew, Florida	DT
25. Green Bay	Antwan Edwards, Clemson	S
26. Jacksonville	Fernando Bryant, Alabama	CB
27. Detroit	Aaron Gibson, Wisconsin	OT
28. New England	Andy Katzenmoyer, Ohio St	LB
29. Minnesota	Dimitrius Underwood, Michigan St	DE
30. Atlanta	Patrick Kerney, Virginia	DE
31. Denver	Al Wilson, Tennessee	LB

Second Round

Team	Selection	Position
32. Cleveland	Kevin Johnson, Syracuse	WR
33. Cincinnati	Charles Fisher, W Virginia	DB
34. Carolina	Chris Terry, Georgia	OT
35. Philadelphia	Barry Gardener, Northwestern	LB
36. Indianapolis	Mike Peterson, Florida	LB
37. Washington	John Jansen, Michigan	OT
38. Carolina	Mike Rucker, Nebraska	DE
39. Miami	James Johnson, Mississippi St	RB
40. Oakland	Tony Bryant, Florida St	DT
41. St. Louis	Dre Bly, N Carolina	CB
42. Atlanta	Reggy Kelly, Mississippi St	TE
43. Miami	Rob Konrad, Syracuse	FB
44. Minnesota	Jim Kleinsasser, N Dakota	TE
45. Cleveland	Rahim Abdullah, Clemson	LB
46. New England	Kevin Faulk, Louisiana St	RB
47. Green Bay	Fred Vinson, Vanderbilt	CB
48. Chicago	Russell Davis, N Carolina	DT
49. NY Giants	Joe Montgomery, Ohio St	RB
50. Tampa Bay	Shaun King, Tulane	QB
51. Arizona	Jonny Rutledge, Florida	LB
52. Tennessee	John Thornton, W Virginia	DT
53. Buffalo	Peerless Price, Tennessee	WR
54. Kansas City	Mike Cloud, Boston College	RB
55. Dallas	Solomon Page, W Virginia	OT
56. Jacksonville	Larry Smith, Florida St	DT
57. NY Jets	Randy Thomas, Mississippi St	OG
58. Denver	Montae Reagor, Texas Tech	DE
59. Pittsburgh	Scott Shields, Weber St	S
60. San Diego	Jermaine Fazande, Oklahoma	FB
61. Denver	Leonard Friedman, Duke	OG

Lost in Translation

A brochure touting the first American Football World Cup, an amateur tournament held in the summer of 1999 in Palermo, features this rundown on first downs and touchdowns: "If a team go beyond the 10 yards, it gains another four chances to advance further and so on until the crossing of the goal line and the consequent attainment of the touch down (goal) which is worth 6 points and gives the right of a 1 point transformation (kicking the ball between two posts) or a 2 point transformation (with a manoeuvre)." *Capisce?*

1999 NFL Europe†

Final Standings

	W	L	T	Pct	Pts/Tm	Pts/Opp
Barcelona*	7	3	0	.700	263	246
Frankfurt*	6	4	0	.600	239	223
Rhein	6	4	0	.600	286	149
Amsterdam	4	6	0	.400	236	243
Scotland	4	6	0	.400	270	298
Berlin	3	7	0	.300	173	308

*Clinched World Bowl '99 berth.

1999 World Bowl

June 27, 1999, in Dusseldorf

Frankfurt Galaxy	3	14	7	14—39
Barcelona Dragons	10	0	7	7—24

FIRST QUARTER

Barcelona: FG Angoy 38, 7:50.
Frankfurt: FG Kleinmann 25, 3:19.
Barcelona: Phillips 4 run (Angoy kick), 0:21.

SECOND QUARTER

Frankfurt: McCullough 11 pass from Barnes (Kleinmann kick), 12:40.
Frankfurt: McCullough 32 pass from Barnes (Kleinmann kick), 7:26.

THIRD QUARTER

Barcelona: Finneran 5 pass from Bouman (Angoy kick), 10:10.
Frankfurt: Ingoglia 3 run (Kleinmann kick), 6:31.

FOURTH QUARTER

Frankfurt: Bailey 8 pass from Delhomme (Kleinmann kick), 12:26.
Barcelona: Grier 2 run (Angoy kick), 8:58.
Frankfurt: McCullough 7 pass from Barnes (Kleinmann kick), 3:18.
A: 39,643.

NFL Europe Individual Leaders

PASSING

	Att	Comp	Pct Comp	Yds	Avg Gain	TD	Pct TD	Int	Pct Int	Lg	Rating Pts
J. Arellanes, Rhein	151	80	53.0	1325	8.77	15	9.9	4	2.6	t96	104.9
J. Delhomme, Frankfurt	202	136	67.3	1410	6.98	12	5.9	5	2.5	47	96.8
D. Craig, Scotland	339	198	58.4	2932	8.65	21	6.2	12	3.5	t86	92.7
P. Barnes, Frankfurt	164	94	57.3	1468	8.95	12	7.3	8	4.9	t73	91.2
T. Bouman, Barcelona	324	170	52.5	2296	7.09	16	4.9	11	3.4	71	77.7

RECEIVING

RECEPTIONS	No.	Yds	Avg	Lg	TD	YARDS	Yds	No.	Avg	Lg	TD
M. Bailey, Frankfurt	63	850	13.5	t51	8	D. Sellers, Scotland	931	58	16.1	71	7
D. Sellers, Scotland	58	931	16.1	71	7	A. McCullough, Frank.	883	48	18.4	t73	10
B. Finneran, Barcelona	54	844	15.6	t67	8	M. Bailey, Frankfurt	850	63	13.5	t51	8
A. McCullough, Frankfurt	48	883	18.4	t73	10	B. Finneran, Barc.	844	54	15.6	t67	8
Y. Murphy, Scotland	45	752	16.7	t75	4	Y. Murphy, Scotland	752	45	16.7	t75	4

RUSHING

	Att	Yds	Avg	Lg	TD
L. Phillips, Barcelona	194	1021	5.3	t72	14
K. Bynum, Rhein	194	960	4.9	51	5
D. Clark, Rhein	104	521	5.0	t29	3
D. Thompson, Amst.	114	503	4.4	62	3
E. Watson, Berlin	117	503	4.3	33	3

Other Statistical Leaders

Points (TDs)	L. Phillips, Barcelona	84
Points (Kicking)	M. Burgsmuller, Rhein	68
Yards from Scrimmage	L. Phillips, Barcelona	1268
Interceptions	G. Williams, Amsterdam	6
Sacks	T. Williams, Rhein	9.0
Punting Avg.	C. Dolan, Scotland	46.0
Punt Return Avg.	L. Ryans, Rhein	12.0
Kickoff Return Avg.	J. Kidd, Amsterdam	26.6

†Formerly World League of American Football.

1998 Canadian Football League

EASTERN DIVISION

	W	L	T	Pts	Pct	PF	PA
Hamilton	12	5	1	25	.706	503	351
Montreal	12	5	1	25	.706	470	435
Toronto	9	9	0	18	.500	452	410
Winnipeg	3	15	0	6	.167	399	588

WESTERN DIVISION

	W	L	T	Pts	Pct	PF	PA
Calgary	12	6	0	24	.667	558	397
Edmonton	9	9	0	18	.500	396	450
British Columbia	9	9	0	18	.500	394	427
Saskatchewan	5	13	0	10	.278	411	525

Regular Season Statistical Leaders

Points (TDs)	Kelvin Anderson, Calgary	96
Points (Kicking)	Terry Baker, Montreal	203
Yards (Rushing)	Michael Pringle, Montreal	2064
Yards (Passing)	Kerwin Bell, Toronto	4983
Yards (Receiving)	Derrell Mitchell, Toronto	2004
Receptions	Derrell Mitchell, Toronto	160

1998 Playoff Results

DIVISION SEMIFINALS

East: MONTREAL 41, Toronto 28
West: EDMONTON 40, British Columbia 33

DIVISION FINALS

East: HAMILTON 22, Montreal 20
West: CALGARY 33, Edmonton 10

1998 Grey Cup Championship

Nov. 22, 1998, at Winnipeg Stadium, Winnipeg

Hamilton Tiger-Cats	3	13	2	6—24
Calgary Stampeders	4	6	7	9—26

A: 34,157.

Two-Point Perversion

Halfway into the second quarter of the Jan. 3, 1999, wild-card game between Jacksonville and New England, the Jaguars scored a touchdown to take a 12–0 lead over the Patriots. Jacksonville coach Tom Coughlin ordered his offense to stay on the field for a two-point conversion instead of settling for a point after. Question of the week: What's up with that? NFL teams succeeded on just 41 of 105 two-point tries in the '98 season, a conversion rate of 39%. Jacksonville had been 1 for 2 on the year. Meanwhile, Jaguars kicker Mike Hollis had gone 45 for 45 on PATs.

Clearly, Coughlin figured that if the Jags got two, they'd be a full two touchdowns ahead. But with 36 minutes left to play, why spurn an automatic point for a less than even chance at two?

As it turned out, the Patriots stopped running back Fred Taylor at the three-yard line. The score stayed 12–0, and when New England later closed the gap to 12–10, it looked like Coughlin's first-half decision might cost his team the game. The fact that Jacksonville went on to win 25–10 doesn't mean that his choice made sense.

Considering what a conservative lot NFL coaches are, it's amazing how reckless they can be about going for two. On Oct. 18, 1998, in Chicago, Chan Gailey had his Cowboys try a two-point conversion after a touchdown put them up 12–7 in the third quarter. Dallas failed; the Bears kicked two field goals and won 13–12. Bill Parcells made questionable two-point calls in Jets wins over the Panthers on Nov. 29, 1998, and the Seahawks the next week. Jimmy Johnson went to the other extreme: After Miami went 0 for 3 on two-pointers earlier in the '98 season, Johnson had his Dolphins kick a useless PAT while trailing Parcells's Jets 14–9 with 6:25 left in their AFC showdown. Fittingly, Miami lost.

Coaches are crazy to go for two except in extreme situations or when the call is a no-brainer. A two-point conversion before the fourth quarter, for instance, is almost always a bad idea. Unless you're getting blown out or a late touchdown puts you ahead by a single point, going for two is probably pointless.

The Super Bowl

Results

Date	Winner (Share)	Loser (Share)	Score	Site (Attendance)
I 1-15-67	Green Bay ($15,000)	Kansas City ($7,500)	35–10	Los Angeles (61,946)
II 1-14-68	Green Bay ($15,000)	Oakland ($7,500)	33–14	Miami (75,546)
III 1-12-69	NY Jets ($15,000)	Baltimore ($7,500)	16–7	Miami (75,389)
IV 1-11-70	Kansas City ($15,000)	Minnesota ($7,500)	23–7	New Orleans (80,562)
V 1-17-71	Baltimore ($15,000)	Dallas ($7,500)	16–13	Miami (79,204)
VI 1-16-72	Dallas ($15,000)	Miami ($7,500)	24–3	New Orleans (81,023)
VII 1-14-73	Miami ($15,000)	Washington ($7,500)	14–7	Los Angeles (90,182)
VIII 1-13-74	Miami ($15,000)	Minnesota ($7,500)	24–7	Houston (71,882)
IX 1-12-75	Pittsburgh ($15,000)	Minnesota ($7,500)	16–6	New Orleans (80,997)
X 1-18-76	Pittsburgh ($15,000)	Dallas ($7,500)	21–17	Miami (80,187)
XI 1-9-77	Oakland ($15,000)	Minnesota ($7,500)	32–14	Pasadena (103,438)
XII 1-15-78	Dallas ($18,000)	Denver ($9,000)	27–10	New Orleans (75,583)
XIII 1-21-79	Pittsburgh ($18,000)	Dallas ($9,000)	35–31	Miami (79,484)
XIV 1-20-80	Pittsburgh ($18,000)	Los Angeles ($9,000)	31–19	Pasadena (103,985)
XV 1-25-81	Oakland ($18,000)	Philadelphia ($9,000)	27–10	New Orleans (76,135)
XVI 1-24-82	San Francisco ($18,000)	Cincinnati ($9,000)	26–21	Pontiac, MI (81,270)
XVII 1-30-83	Washington ($36,000)	Miami ($18,000)	27–17	Pasadena (103,667)
XVIII 1-22-84	LA Raiders ($36,000)	Washington ($18,000)	38–9	Tampa (72,920)
XIX 1-20-85	San Francisco ($36,000)	Miami ($18,000)	38–16	Stanford (84,059)
XX 1-26-86	Chicago ($36,000)	New England ($18,000)	46–10	New Orleans (73,818)
XXI 1-25-87	NY Giants ($36,000)	Denver ($18,000)	39–20	Pasadena (101,063)
XXII 1-31-88	Washington ($36,000)	Denver ($18,000)	42–10	San Diego (73,302)
XXIII 1-22-89	San Francisco ($36,000)	Cincinnati ($18,000)	20–16	Miami (75,129)
XXIV 1-28-90	San Francisco ($36,000)	Denver ($18,000)	55–10	New Orleans (72,919)
XXV 1-27-91	NY Giants ($36,000)	Buffalo ($18,000)	20–19	Tampa (73,813)
XXVI 1-26-92	Washington ($36,000)	Buffalo ($18,000)	37–24	Minneapolis (63,130)
XXVII 1-31-93	Dallas ($36,000)	Buffalo ($18,000)	52–17	Pasadena (98,374)
XXVIII 1-30-94	Dallas ($38,000)	Buffalo ($23,500)	30–13	Atlanta (72,817)
XXIX 1-29-95	San Francisco ($42,000)	San Diego ($26,000)	49–26	Miami (74,107)
XXX 1-28-96	Dallas ($42,000)	Pittsburgh ($27,000)	27–17	Tempe, AZ (76,347)
XXXI 1-26-97	Green Bay ($48,000)	New England ($29,000)	35–21	New Orleans (72,301)
XXXII 1-25-98	Denver ($48,000)	Green Bay ($27,500)	31–24	San Diego (68,912)
XXXIII 1-31-99	Denver ($53,000)	Atlanta ($32,500)	34–19	Miami (74,803)

Most Valuable Players

Super Bowl	Player/ Team	Position
I	Bart Starr, GB	QB
II	Bart Starr, GB	QB
III	Joe Namath, NYJ	QB
IV	Len Dawson, KC	QB
V	Chuck Howley, Dall	LB
VI	Roger Staubach, Dall	QB
VII	Jake Scott, Mia	S
VIII	Larry Csonka, Mia	RB
IX	Franco Harris, Pitt	RB
X	Lynn Swann, Pitt	WR
XI	Fred Biletnikoff, Oak	WR
XII	Randy White, Dall	DT
	Harvey Martin, Dall	DE
XIII	Terry Bradshaw, Pitt	QB
XIV	Terry Bradshaw, Pitt	QB
XV	Jim Plunkett, Oak	QB
XVI	Joe Montana, SF	QB
XVII	John Riggins, Wash	RB
XVIII	Marcus Allen, Rai	RB
XIX	Joe Montana, SF	QB
XX	Richard Dent, Chi	DE
XXI	Phil Simms, NYG	QB
XXII	Doug Williams, Wash	QB
XXIII	Jerry Rice, SF	WR
XXIV	Joe Montana, SF	QB

Super Bowl	Player/ Team	Position
XXV	Ottis Anderson, NYG	RB
XXVI	Mark Rypien, Wash	QB
XXVII	Troy Aikman, Dall	QB
XXVIII	Emmitt Smith, Dall	RB
XXIX	Steve Young, SF	QB
XXX	Larry Brown, Dall	DB
XXXI	Desmond Howard, GB	KR
XXXII	Terrell Davis, Den	RB
XXXIII	John Elway, Den	QB

Composite Standings

	W	L	Pct	Pts	Opp Pts
San Francisco 49ers	5	0	1.000	188	89
New York Giants	2	0	1.000	59	39
Chicago Bears	1	0	1.000	46	10
New York Jets	1	0	1.000	16	7
Pittsburgh Steelers	4	1	.800	120	100
Green Bay Packers	3	1	.750	127	76
Oakland/LA Raiders	3	1	.750	111	66
Dallas Cowboys	5	3	.625	221	132
Washington Redskins	3	2	.600	122	103
Baltimore Colts	1	1	.500	23	29
Kansas City Chiefs	1	1	.500	33	42
Miami Dolphins	2	3	.400	74	103
Denver Broncos	2	4	.333	115	206
Los Angeles Rams	0	1	.000	19	31
Philadelphia Eagles	0	1	.000	10	27
San Diego Chargers	0	1	.000	26	49
Atlanta Falcons	0	1	.000	19	34
Cincinnati Bengals	0	2	.000	37	46
New England Patriots	0	2	.000	31	81
Buffalo Bills	0	4	.000	73	139
Minnesota Vikings	0	4	.000	34	95

Career Leaders
Passing

	GP	Att	Comp	Pct Comp	Yds	Avg Gain	TD	Pct TD	Int	Pct Int	Lg	Rating Pts
Joe Montana, SF	4	122	83	68.0	1142	9.36	11	9.0	0	0.0	44	127.8
Jim Plunkett, Rai	2	46	29	63.0	433	9.41	4	8.7	0	0.0	t80	122.8
Terry Bradshaw, Pitt	4	84	49	58.3	932	11.10	9	10.7	4	4.8	t75	112.8
Troy Aikman, Dall	3	80	56	70.0	689	8.61	5	6.3	1	1.3	t56	111.9
Bart Starr, GB	2	47	29	61.7	452	9.62	3	6.4	1	2.1	t62	106.0
Brett Favre, GB	2	69	39	56.5	502	7.28	5	7.2	1	1.4	t81	97.7
Roger Staubach, Dall	4	98	61	62.2	734	7.49	8	8.2	4	4.1	t45	95.4
Len Dawson, KC	2	44	28	63.6	353	8.02	2	4.5	2	4.5	t46	84.8
Bob Griese, Mia	3	41	26	63.4	295	7.20	1	2.4	2	4.9	t28	72.7
Dan Marino, Mia	1	50	29	58.0	318	6.36	1	2.0	2	4.0	30	66.9

Note: Minimum 40 attempts.

Rushing

	GP	Yds	Att	Avg	Lg	TD
Franco Harris, Pitt	4	354	101	3.5	25	4
Larry Csonka, Mia	3	297	57	5.2	9	2
Emmitt Smith, Dall	3	289	70	4.1	38	5
Terrell Davis, Den	2	259	75	4.1	15	3
John Riggins, Wash	2	230	64	3.6	43	2
Timmy Smith, Wash	1	204	22	9.3	58	2
Thurman Thomas, Buff	4	204	52	3.9	31	4
Roger Craig, SF	3	198	52	3.8	18	2
Marcus Allen, Rai	1	191	20	9.6	t74	2
Tony Dorsett, Dall	2	162	31	5.2	29	1

Receiving

	GP	No.	Yds	Avg	Lg	TD
Jerry Rice, SF	3	28	512	18.3	t44	7
Andre Reed, Buff	4	27	323	11.9	40	0
Roger Craig, SF	3	20	212	10.6	40	2
Thurman Thomas, Buff	4	20	144	7.2	24	0
Tom Novacek, Dall	3	17	178	10.5	23	2
Lynn Swann, Pitt	4	16	364	22.8	t64	3
Michael Irvin, Dall	3	16	256	16.0	25	2
Chuck Foreman, Minn	3	15	139	9.3	26	0
Cliff Branch, Rai	3	14	181	12.9	50	3
Preston Pearson, Balt-Pitt-Dall	5	12	105	8.8	14	0
Don Beebe, Buff-GB	5	12	171	14.3	43	2
Kenneth Davis, Buff	4	12	72	6.0	19	0
Antonio Freeman, GB	2	12	231	19.3	t81	3

Stadium Ahoy!

In 1997 the Academy of Architecture, Arts and Sciences in Los Angeles gave architects a field goal: Design a football stadium that could lure the NFL back to L.A. Shih-Fu Peng and Roisin Heneghan won first prize with Bigfoot, an 80,000-seat floating facility complete with helipads, a parking lot and mall space for anchor stores like Barnes & Noble. The proposed field, which the architects say could ride piggy back on a supertanker moored at the end of Santa Monica Pier, would be ideal for today's fickle franchises. "Should the team be sold, the stadium could go along with it," says Peng. A club Bigfooting it out of L.A. might wind up in Florida, circled by tailgators.

Single-Game Leaders

Scoring

	Pts
Roger Craig: XIX, San Francisco vs Miami (1 R, 2 P)	18
Jerry Rice: XXIV, San Francisco vs Denver (3 P); XXIX, SF vs San Diego (3 P)	18
Ricky Watters: XXIX, San Francisco vs San Diego (1 R, 2 P)	18
Terrell Davis: XXXII, Denver vs Green Bay (3 R)	18

Rushing Yards

	Yds
Timmy Smith: XXII, Washington vs Denver	204
Marcus Allen: XVIII, LA Raiders vs Washington	191
John Riggins: XVII, Washington vs Miami	166
Franco Harris: IX, Pittsburgh vs Minnesota	158
Terrell Davis: XXXII, Denver vs Green Bay	157
Larry Csonka: VIII, Miami vs Minnesota	145
Clarence Davis: XI, Oakland vs Minnesota	137
Thurman Thomas: XXV, Buffalo vs NY Giants	135
Emmitt Smith: XXVIII, Dallas vs Buffalo	132
Matt Snell: III, New York Jets vs Baltimore Colts	121

Receptions

	No.
Dan Ross: XVI, Cincinnati vs San Francisco	11
Jerry Rice: XXIII, San Francisco vs Cincinnati	11
Tony Nathan: XIX, Miami vs San Francisco	10
Jerry Rice: XXIX, San Francisco vs San Diego	10
Andre Hastings: XXX, Pittsburgh vs Dallas	10
Ricky Sanders: XXII, Washington vs Denver	9
Antonio Freeman: XXXII, Green Bay vs Denver	9
Six tied with eight.	

Touchdown Passes

	No.
Steve Young: XXIX, San Francisco vs San Diego	6
Joe Montana: XXIV, San Francisco vs Denver	5
Terry Bradshaw: XIII, Pittsburgh vs Dallas	4
Doug Williams: XXII, Washington vs Denver	4
Troy Aikman: XXVII, Dallas vs Buffalo	4
Five tied with three.	

Receiving Yards

	Yds
Jerry Rice: XXIII, San Francisco vs Cincinnati	215
Ricky Sanders: XXII, Washington vs Denver	193
Lynn Swann: X, Pittsburgh vs Dallas	161
Andre Reed: XXVII, Buffalo vs Dallas	152
Rod Smith: XXXIII, Denver vs Atlanta	152
Jerry Rice: XXIX, San Francisco vs San Diego	149
Jerry Rice: XXIV, San Francisco vs Denver	148
Max McGee: I, Green Bay vs Kansas City	138
George Sauer: III, NY Jets vs Baltimore	133

Passing Yards

	Yds
Joe Montana: XXIII, San Francisco vs Cincinnati	357
Doug Williams: XXII, Washington vs Denver	340
John Elway: XXXIII, Denver vs Atlanta	336
Joe Montana: XIX, San Francisco vs Miami	331
Steve Young: XXIX, San Francisco vs San Diego	325
Terry Bradshaw: XIII, Pittsburgh vs Dallas	318
Dan Marino: XIX, Miami vs San Francisco	318
Terry Bradshaw: XIV, Pittsburgh vs LA Rams	309
John Elway: XXI, Denver vs NY Giants	304

NFL Playoff History

1933
NFL championship Chicago Bears 23, NY Giants 21

1934
NFL championship NY Giants 30, Chicago Bears 13

1935
NFL championship Detroit 26, NY Giants 7

1936
NFL championship Green Bay 21, Boston 6

1937
NFL championship Washington 28, Chicago Bears 21

1938
NFL championship NY Giants 23, Green Bay 17

1939
NFL championship Green Bay 27, NY Giants 0

1940
NFL championship Chicago Bears 73, Washington 0

1941
W. div. playoff   Chicago Bears 33, Green Bay 14
NFL championship Chicago Bears 37, NY Giants 9

1942
NFL championship Washington 14, Chicago Bears 6

1943
E. div. playoff   Washington 28, NY Giants 0
NFL championship Chicago Bears 41, Washington 21

1944
NFL championship Green Bay 14, NY Giants 7

1945
NFL championship Cleveland 15, Washington 14

1946
NFL championship Chicago Bears 24, NY Giants 14

1947
E. div. playoff   Philadelphia 21, Pittsburgh 0
NFL championship Chi Cardinals 28, Philadelphia 21

1948
NFL championship Philadelphia 7, Chi Cardinals 0

1949
NFL championship Philadelphia 14, Los Angeles 0

1950
Am. Conf. playoff Cleveland 8, NY Giants 3
Nat. Conf. playoff Los Angeles 24, Chicago Bears 14
NFL championship Cleveland 30, Los Angeles 28

1951
NFL championship Los Angeles 24, Cleveland 17

1952

Nat. Conf. playoff	Detroit 31, Los Angeles 21
NFL championship	Detroit 17, Cleveland 7

1953

NFL championship	Detroit 17, Cleveland 16

1954

NFL championship	Cleveland 56, Detroit 10

1955

NFL championship	Cleveland 38, Los Angeles 14

1956

NFL championship	NY Giants 47, Chicago Bears 7

1957

W. Conf. playoff	Detroit 31, San Francisco 27
NFL championship	Detroit 59, Cleveland 14

1958

E. Conf. playoff	NY Giants 10, Cleveland 0
NFL championship	Baltimore 23, NY Giants 17

1959

NFL championship	Baltimore 31, NY Giants 16

1960

NFL championship	Philadelphia 17, Green Bay 13
AFL championship	Houston 24, LA Chargers 16

1961

NFL championship	Green Bay 37, NY Giants 0
AFL championship	Houston 10, San Diego 3

1962

NFL championship	Green Bay 16, NY Giants 7
AFL championship	Dallas Texans 20, Houston 17

1963

NFL championship	Chicago 14, NY Giants 10
AFL E. div. playoff	Boston 26, Buffalo 8
AFL championship	San Diego 51, Boston 10

1964

NFL championship	Cleveland 27, Baltimore 0
AFL championship	Buffalo 20, San Diego 7

1965

NFL W. Conf. playoff	Green Bay 13, Baltimore 10
NFL championship	Green Bay 23, Cleveland 12
AFL championship	Buffalo 23, San Diego 0

1966

NFL championship	Green Bay 34, Dallas 27
AFL championship	Kansas City 31, Buffalo 7

1967

NFL E. Conf. championship	Dallas 52, Cleveland 14
NFL W. Conf. championship	Green Bay 28, Los Angeles 7
NFL championship	Green Bay 21, Dallas 17
AFL championship	Oakland 40, Houston 7

1968

NFL E. Conf. championship	Cleveland 31, Dallas 20
NFL W. Conf. championship	Baltimore 24, Minnesota 14
NFL championship	Baltimore 34, Cleveland 0

1968 *(Cont.)*

AFL W. div. playoff	Oakland 41, Kansas City 6
AFL championship	NY Jets 27, Oakland 23

1969

NFL E. Conf. championship	Cleveland 38, Dallas 14
NFL W. Conf. championship	Minnesota 23, Los Angeles 20
NFL championship	Minnesota 27, Cleveland 7
AFL div. playoffs	Kansas City 13, NY Jets 6
	Oakland 56, Houston 7
AFL championship	Kansas City 17, Oakland 7

1970

AFC div. playoffs	Baltimore 17, Cincinnati 0
	Oakland 21, Miami 14
AFC championship	Baltimore 27, Oakland 17
NFC div. playoffs	Dallas 5, Detroit 0
	San Francisco 17, Minnesota 14
NFC championship	Dallas 17, San Francisco 10

1971

AFC div. playoffs	Miami 27, Kansas City 24
	Baltimore 20, Cleveland 3
AFC championship	Miami 21, Baltimore 0
NFC div. playoffs	Dallas 20, Minnesota 12
	San Francisco 24, Washington 20
NFC championship	Dallas 14, San Francisco 3

1972

AFC div. playoffs	Pittsburgh 13, Oakland 7
	Miami 20, Cleveland 14
AFC championship	Miami 21, Pittsburgh 17
NFC div. playoffs	Dallas 30, San Francisco 28
	Washington 16, Green Bay 3
NFC championship	Washington 26, Dallas 3

1973

AFC div. playoffs	Oakland 33, Pittsburgh 14
	Miami 34, Cincinnati 16
AFC championship	Miami 27, Oakland 10
NFC div. playoffs	Minnesota 27, Washington 20
	Dallas 27, Los Angeles 16
NFC championship	Minnesota 27, Dallas 10

1974

AFC div. playoffs	Oakland 28, Miami 26
	Pittsburgh 32, Buffalo 14
AFC championship	Pittsburgh 24, Oakland 13
NFC div. playoffs	Minnesota 30, St Louis 14
	Los Angeles 19, Washington 10
NFC championship	Minnesota 14, Los Angeles 10

1975

AFC div. playoffs	Pittsburgh 28, Baltimore 10
	Oakland 31, Cincinnati 28
AFC championship	Pittsburgh 16, Oakland 10
NFC div. playoffs	Los Angeles 35, St Louis 23
	Dallas 17, Minnesota 14
NFC championship	Dallas 37, Los Angeles 7

1976

AFC div. playoffs	Oakland 24, New England 21
	Pittsburgh 40, Baltimore 14
AFC championship	Oakland 24, Pittsburgh 7
NFC div. playoffs	Minnesota 35, Washington 20
	Los Angeles 14, Dallas 12
NFC championship	Minnesota 24, Los Angeles 13

1977

AFC div. playoffs	Denver 34, Pittsburgh 21
	Oakland 37, Baltimore 31
AFC championship	Denver 20, Oakland 17
NFC div. playoffs	Dallas 37, Chicago 7
	Minnesota 14, Los Angeles 7
NFC championship	Dallas 23, Minnesota 6

1978

AFC 1st-rd. playoff	Houston 17, Miami 9
AFC div. playoffs	Houston 31, New England 14
	Pittsburgh 33, Denver 10
AFC championship	Pittsburgh 34, Houston 5
NFC 1st-rd. playoff	Atlanta 14, Philadelphia 13
NFC div. playoffs	Dallas 27, Atlanta 20
	Los Angeles 34, Minnesota 10
NFC championship	Dallas 28, Los Angeles 0

1979

AFC 1st-rd. playoff	Houston 13, Denver 7
AFC div. playoffs	Houston 17, San Diego 14
	Pittsburgh 34, Miami 14
AFC championship	Pittsburgh 27, Houston 13
NFC 1st-rd. playoff	Philadelphia 27, Chicago 17
NFC div. playoffs	Tampa Bay 24, Philadelphia 17
	Los Angeles 21, Dallas 19
NFC championship	Los Angeles 9, Tampa Bay 0

1980

AFC 1st-rd. playoff	Oakland 27, Houston 7
AFC div. playoffs	San Diego 20, Buffalo 14
	Oakland 14, Cleveland 12
AFC championship	Oakland 34, San Diego 27
NFC 1st-rd. playoff	Dallas 34, Los Angeles 13
NFC div. playoffs	Philadelphia 31, Minnesota 16
	Dallas 30, Atlanta 27
NFC championship	Philadelphia 20, Dallas 7

1981

AFC 1st-rd. playoff	Buffalo 31, NY Jets 27
AFC div. playoffs	San Diego 41, Miami 38
	Cincinnati 28, Buffalo 21
AFC championship	Cincinnati 27, San Diego 7
NFC 1st-rd. playoff	NY Giants 27, Philadelphia 21
NFC div. playoffs	Dallas 38, Tampa Bay 0
	San Francisco 38, NY Giants 24
NFC championship	San Francisco 28, Dallas 27

1982

AFC 1st-rd. playoffs	Miami 28, New England 13
	LA Raiders 27, Cleveland 10
	NY Jets 44, Cincinnati 17
	San Diego 31, Pittsburgh 28
AFC div. playoffs	NY Jets 17, LA Raiders 14
	Miami 34, San Diego 13
AFC championship	Miami 14, NY Jets 0
NFC 1st-rd. playoffs	Washington 31, Detroit 7
	Green Bay 41, St Louis 16
	Minnesota 30, Atlanta 24
	Dallas 30, Tampa Bay 17
NFC div. playoffs	Washington 21, Minnesota 7
	Dallas 37, Green Bay 26
NFC championship	Washington 31, Dallas 17

1983

AFC 1st-rd. playoff	Seattle 31, Denver 7
AFC div. playoffs	Seattle 27, Miami 20
	LA Raiders 38, Pittsburgh 10
AFC championship	LA Raiders 30, Seattle 14
NFC 1st-rd. playoff	LA Rams 24, Dallas 17

1983 *(Cont.)*

NFC div. playoffs	San Francisco 24, Detroit 23
	Washington 51, LA Rams 7
NFC championship	Washington 24, San Francisco 21

1984

AFC 1st-rd. playoff	Seattle 13, LA Raiders 7
AFC div. playoffs	Miami 31, Seattle 10
	Pittsburgh 24, Denver 17
AFC championship	Miami 45, Pittsburgh 28
NFC 1st-rd. playoff	NY Giants 16, LA Rams 13
NFC div. playoffs	San Francisco 21, NY Giants 10
	Chicago 23, Washington 19
NFC championship	San Francisco 23, Chicago 0

1985

AFC 1st-rd. playoff	New England 26, NY Jets 14
AFC div. playoffs	Miami 24, Cleveland 21
	New England 27, LA Raiders 20
AFC championship	New England 31, Miami 14
NFC 1st-rd. playoff	NY Giants 17, San Francisco 3
NFC div. playoffs	LA Rams 20, Dallas 0
	Chicago 21, NY Giants 0
NFC championship	Chicago 24, LA Rams 0

1986

AFC 1st-rd. playoff	NY Jets 35, Kansas City 15
AFC div. playoffs	Cleveland 23, NY Jets 20
	Denver 22, New England 17
AFC championship	Denver 23, Cleveland 20
NFC 1st-rd. playoff	Washington 19, LA Rams 7
NFC div playoffs	Washington 27, Chicago 13
	NY Giants 49, San Francisco 3
NFC championship	NY Giants 17, Washington 0

1987

AFC 1st-rd. playoff	Houston 23, Seattle 20
AFC div. playoffs	Cleveland 38, Indianapolis 21
	Denver 34, Houston 10
AFC championship	Denver 38, Cleveland 33
NFC 1st-rd. playoff	Minnesota 44, New Orleans 10
NFC div playoffs	Minnesota 36, San Francisco 24
	Washington 21, Chicago 17
NFC championship	Washington 17, Minnesota 10

1988

AFC 1st-rd. playoff	Houston 24, Cleveland 23
AFC div. playoffs	Cincinnati 21, Seattle 13
	Buffalo 17, Houston 10
AFC championship	Cincinnati 21, Buffalo 10
NFC 1st-rd. playoff	Minnesota 28, LA Rams 17
NFC div. playoffs	Chicago 20, Philadelphia 12
	San Francisco 34, Minnesota 9
NFC championship	San Francisco 28, Chicago 3

1989

AFC 1st-rd. playoff	Pittsburgh 26, Houston 23
AFC div. playoffs	Cleveland 34, Buffalo 30
	Denver 24, Pittsburgh 23
AFC championship	Denver 37, Cleveland 21
NFC 1st-rd. playoff	LA Rams 21, Philadelphia 7
NFC div. playoffs	LA Rams 19, NY Giants 13
	San Francisco 41, Minnesota 13
NFC championship	San Francisco 30, LA Rams 3

1990

AFC 1st-rd. playoffs	Miami 17, Kansas City 16
	Cincinnati 41, Houston 14
AFC div. playoffs	Buffalo 44, Miami 34
	LA Raiders 20, Cincinnati 10
AFC championship	Buffalo 51, LA Raiders 3
NFC 1st-rd. playoffs	Chicago 16, New Orleans 6

1990 *(Cont.)*

NFC 1st-rd playoffs	Washington 20, Philadelphia 6
NFC div. playoffs	NY Giants 31, Chicago 3
	San Francisco 28, Washington 10
NFC championship	NY Giants 15, San Francisco 13

1991

AFC 1st-rd. playoffs	Houston 17, NY Jets 10
	Kansas City 10, LA Raiders 6
AFC div. playoffs	Denver 26, Houston 24
	Buffalo 37, Kansas City 14
AFC championship	Buffalo 10, Denver 7
NFC 1st-rd. playoffs	Atlanta 27, New Orleans 20
	Dallas 17, Chicago 13
NFC div. playoffs	Washington 24, Atlanta 7
	Detroit 38, Dallas 6
NFC championship	Washington 41, Detroit 10

1992

AFC 1st-rd. playoffs	San Diego 17, Kansas City 0
	Buffalo 41, Houston 38 (OT)
AFC div. playoffs	Buffalo 24, Pittsburgh 3
	Miami 31, San Diego 0
AFC championship	Buffalo 29, Miami 10
NFC 1st-rd. playoffs	Washington 24, Minnesota 7
	Philadelphia 36, New Orleans 20
NFC div. playoffs	San Francisco 20, Washington 13
	Dallas 34, Philadelphia 10
NFC championship	Dallas 30, San Francisco 20

1993

AFC 1st-rd. playoffs	LA Raiders 42, Denver 24
	Kansas City 27, Pittsburgh 24 (OT)
AFC div. playoffs	Buffalo 29, LA Raiders 23
	Kansas City 28, Houston 20
AFC championship	Buffalo 30, Kansas City 13
NFC 1st-rd. playoffs	NY Giants 17, Minnesota 10
	Green Bay 28, Detroit 24
NFC div. playoffs	San Francisco 44, NY Giants 3
	Dallas 27, Green Bay 17
NFC championship	Dallas 38, San Francisco 21

1994

AFC 1st-rd. playoffs	Miami 27, Kansas City 17
	Cleveland 20, New England 13
AFC div. playoffs	San Diego 22, Miami 21
	Pittsburgh 29, Cleveland 9
AFC championship	San Diego 17, Pittsburgh 13
NFC 1st-rd. playoffs	Green Bay 16, Detroit 12
	Chicago 35, Minnesota 18
NFC div. playoffs	Dallas 35, Green Bay 9
	San Francisco 44, Chicago 15
NFC championship	San Francisco 38, Dallas 28

1995

AFC 1st-rd. playoffs	Buffalo 37, Miami 22
	Indianapolis 35, San Diego 20
AFC div. playoffs	Pittsburgh 40, Buffalo 21
	Indianapolis 10, Kansas City 7
AFC championship	Pittsburgh 20, Indianapolis 16
NFC 1st-rd. playoffs	Philadelphia 58, Detroit 37
	Green Bay 37, Atlanta 20
NFC div. playoffs	Dallas 30, Philadelphia 11
	Green Bay 27, San Francisco 17
NFC championship	Dallas 38, Green Bay 27

1996

AFC 1st-rd. playoffs	Jacksonville 30, Buffalo 27
	Pittsburgh 42, Indianapolis 14
AFC div. playoffs	Jacksonville 30, Denver 27
	New England 28, Pittsburgh 3
AFC championship	New England 20, Jacksonville 6

1996 *(Cont.)*

NFC 1st-rd. playoffs	Dallas 40, Minnesota 15
	San Francisco 14, Philadelphia 0
NFC div. playoffs	Green Bay 35, San Francisco 14
	Carolina 26, Dallas 17
NFC championship	Green Bay 30, Carolina 13

1997

AFC 1st-rd. playoffs	Denver 42, Jacksonville 17
	New England 17, Miami 3
AFC div. playoffs	Denver 14, Kansas City 10
	Pittsburgh 7, New England 6
AFC championship	Denver 24, Pittsburgh 21
NFC 1st-rd. playoffs	Minnesota 23, NY Giants 22
	Tampa Bay 20, Detroit 10
NFC div. playoffs	Green Bay 21, Tampa Bay 7
	San Francisco 38, Minnesota 22
NFC championship	Green Bay 23, San Francisco 10

1998

AFC 1st-rd. playoffs	Miami 24, Buffalo 17
	Jacksonville 25, New England 10
AFC div. playoffs	Denver 38, Miami 3
	NY Jets 34, Jacksonville 24
AFC championship	Denver 23, NY Jets 10
NFC 1st-rd. playoffs	Arizona 20, Dallas 7
	San Francisco 30, Green Bay 27
NFC div. playoffs	Atlanta 20, San Francisco 18
	Minnesota 41, Arizona 21
NFC championship	Atlanta 30, Minnesota 27 (OT)

Tossing Out The Toss

The brouhaha that followed the disputed coin toss at the start of overtime during the 1998 Thanksgiving Day game between the Detroit Lions and the Pittsburgh Steelers showed that even the flip's basic instruction—"Call it in the air!"—can lead to confusion. That makes a 1998 proposal by Micron Electronics, title sponsor of the Micron PC Bowl (formerly the Carquest and the Blockbuster bowls), more sensible than it appeared on first glance. In the spirit of its New Rules, New Tools marketing campaign, Micron proposed replacing the pregame coin toss with a rock-paper-scissors showdown.

Now, just to make sure that everyone—are you listening, Jerome Bettis and referee Phil Luckett?—is on the same page: Rocks beats scissors, scissors beats paper....

Alltime NFL Individual Statistical Leaders

Career Leaders

Scoring

	Yrs	TD	FG	PAT	Pts
George Blanda	26	9	335	943	2002
†Gary Anderson	17	0	420	585	1855
†Morten Andersen	17	0	401	558	1761
Nick Lowery	18	0	383	562	1711
Jan Stenerud	19	0	373	580	1699
†Norm Johnson	17	0	348	613	1657
Eddie Murray	17	0	325	498	1473
Pat Leahy	18	0	304	558	1470
Jim Turner	16	1	304	521	1439
Matt Bahr	17	0	300	522	1422
Mark Moseley	16	0	300	482	1382
Jim Bakken	17	0	282	534	1380
Fred Cox	15	0	282	519	1365
†Al Del Greco	15	0	299	464	1360
Lou Groza	17	1	234	641	1349
Jim Breech	14	0	243	517	1246
Chris Bahr	14	0	241	490	1213
Kevin Butler	13	0	265	426	1208
Gino Cappelletti	11	42	176	350	1130
Ray Wersching	15	0	222	456	1122

Cappelletti's total includes four two-point conversions.

Rushing

	Yrs	Att	Yds	Avg	Lg	TD
Walter Payton	13	3,838	16,726	4.4	76	110
†Barry Sanders	10	3,062	15,269	5.0	85	99
Eric Dickerson	11	2,996	13,259	4.4	85	90
Tony Dorsett	12	2,936	12,739	4.3	99	77
†Emmitt Smith	9	2,914	12,566	4.8	75	125
Jim Brown	9	2,359	12,312	5.2	80	106
Marcus Allen	16	3,022	12,243	4.1	61	123
Franco Harris	13	2,949	12,120	4.1	75	91
†Thurman Thomas	11	2,813	11,786	4.2	80	65
John Riggins	14	2,916	11,352	3.9	66	104
O.J. Simpson	11	2,404	11,236	4.7	94	61
Ottis Anderson	14	2,562	10,273	4.0	76	81
Earl Campbell	8	2,187	9,407	4.3	81	74
Jim Taylor	10	1,941	8,597	4.4	84	83
Joe Perry	14	1,737	8,378	4.8	78	53
Earnest Byner	14	2,095	8,261	3.9	54	56
Herschel Walker	12	1,954	8,225	4.2	91	61
Roger Craig	11	1,991	8,189	4.1	71	56
Gerald Riggs	10	1,989	8,188	4.1	58	69
Larry Csonka	11	1,891	8,081	4.3	54	64

Touchdowns

	Yrs	Rush	Pass Rec	Ret	Total TD
†Jerry Rice	14	10	164	1	175
Marcus Allen	16	123	21	1	145
†Emmitt Smith	9	125	9	0	134
Jim Brown	9	106	20	0	126
Walter Payton	13	110	15	0	125
John Riggins	14	104	12	0	116
Lenny Moore	12	63	48	2	113
†Barry Sanders	10	99	10	0	109
Don Hutson	11	3	99	3	105
Steve Largent	14	1	100	0	101
Franco Harris	13	91	9	0	100
Eric Dickerson	11	90	6	0	96
Jim Taylor	10	83	10	0	93
Tony Dorsett	12	77	13	1	91
Bobby Mitchell	11	18	65	8	91
Leroy Kelly	10	74	13	3	90
Charley Taylor	13	11	79	0	90
Don Maynard	15	0	88	0	88
Lance Alworth	11	2	85	0	87
Ottis Anderson	14	81	5	0	86
Paul Warfield	13	1	85	0	86

Combined Yards Gained

	Yrs	Total	Rush	Rec	Int Ret	Punt Ret	Kickoff Ret	Fum Ret
Walter Payton	13	21,803	16,726	4,538	0	0	539	0
†Barry Sanders	10	18,308	15,269	2,921	0	0	118	0
Herschel Walker	12	18,168	8,225	4,859	0	0	5,084	0
Marcus Allen	16	17,562	12,243	5,325	0	0	0	-6
†Jerry Rice	14	17,075	614	17,612	0	0	6	0
Tony Dorsett	12	16,326	12,739	3,554	0	0	0	33
†Thurman Thomas	11	16,090	11,786	4,304	0	0	0	0
†Henry Ellard	16	15,603	50	13,748	0	1,527	364	0
Jim Brown	9	15,459	12,312	2,499	0	0	648	0
Eric Dickerson	11	15,411	13,259	2,137	0	0	0	15
James Brooks	12	14,910	7,962	3,621	0	565	2,762	0
Franco Harris	13	14,622	12,120	2,287	0	0	233	-18
O.J. Simpson	11	14,368	11,236	2,142	0	0	990	0
James Lofton	16	14,277	246	14,004	0	0	0	27
Bobby Mitchell	11	14,078	2,735	7,954	0	699	2,690	0
John Riggins	14	13,435	11,352	2,090	0	0	0	-7
Steve Largent	14	13,396	83	13,089	0	68	156	0
Ottis Anderson	14	13,364	10,273	3,062	0	0	0	29
Drew Hill	14	13,337	19	9,831	0	22	3,460	5
Greg Pruitt	12	13,262	5,672	3,069	0	2,007	2,514	0

† Active player.

Career Leaders (Cont.)

Passing

PASSING EFFICIENCY*

	Yrs	Att	Comp	Pct Comp	Yds	Avg Gain	TD	Pct TD	Int	Pct Int	Rating Pts
†Steve Young	14	4,065	2,622	64.5	32,678	8.04	229	5.6	103	2.5	97.5
Joe Montana	15	5,391	3,409	63.2	40,551	7.52	273	5.1	139	2.6	92.3
†Brett Favre	8	3,757	2,318	61.7	26,803	7.13	213	5.6	118	3.1	89.0
†Dan Marino	16	7,989	4,763	4,763	58,913	7.37	408	5.1	226	2.8	87.7
†Mark Brunell	5	1,719	1,038	60.3	12,512	7.28	72	4.2	43	2.5	86.3
Jim Kelly	11	4,779	2,874	60.1	35,467	7.42	237	5.0	175	3.7	84.3
Roger Staubach	11	2,958	1,685	57.0	22,700	7.67	153	5.2	109	3.7	83.4
Neil Lomax	8	3,153	1,817	57.6	22,771	7.22	136	4.3	90	2.9	82.7
Sonny Jurgensen	18	4,262	2,433	57.1	32,224	7.56	255	6.0	189	4.4	82.6
Len Dawson	19	3,741	2,136	57.1	28,711	7.67	239	6.4	183	4.9	82.6
†Troy Aikman	10	4,011	2,479	61.8	28,346	7.06	141	3.5	115	2.8	82.8
Bernie Kosar	12	3,365	1,994	59.3	23,301	6.93	124	3.7	87	2.6	81.9
Ken Anderson	16	4,475	2,654	59.3	32,838	7.34	197	4.4	160	3.6	81.9
Danny White	13	2,950	1,761	59.7	21,959	7.44	155	5.3	132	4.5	81.7
†Randall Cunningham	13	3,875	2,177	56.2	27,082	6.99	190	4.9	119	3.1	81.6
†Dave Krieg	19	5,311	3,105	58.5	38,147	7.18	261	4.9	199	3.7	81.4
Boomer Esiason	14	5,205	2,969	57.0	37,920	7.29	247	4.7	181	3.5	81.1
†Warren Moon	15	6,786	3,972	58.5	49,097	7.24	290	4.3	232	3.4	81.0
†Jeff Hostetler	13	2,338	1,357	58.0	16,430	7.03	94	4.0	71	3.0	80.5
Bart Starr	16	3,149	2,020	57.4	24,718	7.85	152	4.8	138	4.4	80.5

*1,500 or more attempts. The passer ratings are based on performance standards established for completion percentage, interception percentage, touchdown percentage and average gain. Passers are allocated points according to how their marks compare with those standards.

YARDS

	Yrs	Att	Comp	Pct Comp	Yds		Yrs	Att	Comp	Pct Comp	Yds
†Dan Marino	16	7,989	4,763	58.5	58,913	Jim Everett	12	4,923	2,841	57.7	34,837
†John Elway	16	7,250	4,123	56.9	51,475	Jim Hart	19	5,076	2,593	51.1	34,665
†Warren Moon	15	6,786	3,972	58.5	49,097	†Steve DeBerg	17	4,746	2,924	61.6	34,241
Fran Tarkenton	18	6,467	3,686	57.0	47,003	John Hadl	16	4,687	2,363	50.4	33,503
Dan Fouts	15	5,604	3,297	58.8	43,040	Phil Simms	14	4,647	2,576	55.4	33,462
Joe Montana	15	5,391	3,409	63.2	40,551	Ken Anderson	16	4,475	2,654	59.3	32,838
Johnny Unitas	18	5,186	2,830	54.6	40,239	Sonny Jurgensen	18	4,262	2,433	57.1	32,224
†Dave Krieg	19	5,311	3,105	58.5	38,147	John Brodie	17	4,491	2,469	55.0	31,548
Boomer Esiason	14	5,205	2,969	57.0	37,920	Norm Snead	15	4,353	2,276	52.3	30,797
Jim Kelly	11	4,779	2,874	60.1	35,467	Joe Ferguson	18	4,519	2,369	52.4	29,817

TOUCHDOWNS

	No.		No.		No.
†Dan Marino	408	John Hadl	244	Jim Everett	203
Fran Tarkenton	342	Len Dawson	239	Phil Simms	199
†John Elway	300	Jim Kelly	237	Ken Anderson	197
Johnny Unitas	290	George Blanda	236	Joe Ferguson	196
†Warren Moon	290	†Steve Young	229	Bobby Layne	196
Joe Montana	273	John Brodie	214	Norm Snead	196
†Dave Krieg	261	†Brett Favre	213	†Steve DeBerg	196
Sonny Jurgensen	255	Terry Bradshaw	212	Ken Stabler	194
Dan Fouts	254	Y.A. Tittle	212	Bob Griese	192
Boomer Esiason	247	Jim Hart	209	†Randall Cunningham	190

† Active player.

Career Leaders (Cont.)

Receiving

RECEPTIONS

	Yrs	No.	Yds	Avg	Lg	TD		Yrs	No.	Yds	Avg	Lg	TD
†Jerry Rice	14	1139	17,612	15.5	96	164	Gary Clark	11	699	10,856	15.5	84	65
Art Monk	16	940	12,721	13.5	79	68	†Andre Rison	10	681	9,381	13.8	80	78
†Andre Reed	14	889	12,559	14.1	83	85	†Tim Brown	11	680	9,600	14.1	80	69
†Cris Carter	12	834	10,447	12.5	80	111	Ozzie Newsome	13	662	7,980	12.1	74	47
Steve Largent	14	819	13,089	16.0	74	100	Charley Taylor	13	649	9,110	14.0	88	79
†Henry Ellard	16	812	13,749	16.9	81	65	Drew Hill	14	634	9,831	15.5	81	60
†Irving Fryar	15	784	11,427	15.3	80	77	Don Maynard	15	633	11,834	18.7	87	88
James Lofton	16	764	14,004	18.3	80	75	Raymond Berry	13	631	9,275	14.7	70	68
Charlie Joiner	18	750	12,146	16.2	87	65	†Keith Byars	13	610	5,661	9.2	60	32
†Michael Irvin	11	740	11,737	15.9	87	62	†Herman Moore	8	610	8,467	13.9	93	57

YARDS

	No.		No.		No.
†Jerry Rice	17,612	Don Maynard	11,834	Lance Alworth	10,266
James Lofton	14,004	†Michael Irvin	11,737	Drew Hill	9,831
†Henry Ellard	13,749	†Irving Fryar	11,427	†Tim Brown	9,600
Steve Largent	13,089	Gary Clark	10,856	†Andre Rison	9,381
Art Monk	12,721	Stanley Morgan	10,716	Raymond Berry	9,275
†Andre Reed	12,559	†Cris Carter	10,447	Anthony Miller	9,148
Charlie Joiner	12,146	Harold Jackson	10,372		

Sacks

†Reggie White	192.5	†Chris Doleman	142.5
†Bruce Smith	164.0	Richard Dent	137.5
†Kevin Greene	148.0		

Note: Officially compiled since 1982.

Interceptions

	Yrs	No.	Yds	Avg	Lg	TD
Paul Krause	16	81	1185	14.6	81	3
Emlen Tunnell	14	79	1282	16.2	55	4
Dick (Night Train) Lane	14	68	1207	17.8	80	5
Ken Riley	15	65	596	9.2	66	5
Ronnie Lott	14	63	730	11.3	83	5

Punting

	Yrs	No.	Yds	Avg	Lg	Blk
Sammy Baugh	16	338	15,245	45.1	85	9
Tommy Davis	11	511	22,833	44.7	82	2
Yale Lary	11	503	22,279	44.3	74	4
Bob Scarpitto	8	283	12,408	43.8	87	4
Horace Gillom	7	385	16,872	43.8	80	5
Jerry Norton	11	358	15,671	43.8	78	2

Note: 250 or more punts.

Punt Returns

	Yrs	No.	Yds	Avg	Lg	TD
†Darrien Gordon	5	137	1786	13.0	90	3
George McAfee	8	112	1431	12.8	74	2
Jack Christiansen	8	85	1084	12.8	89	8
Claude Gibson	5	110	1381	12.6	85	3
†Jermaine Lewis	3	96	1181	12.3	89	4

Note: 75 or more returns.

Kickoff Returns

	Yrs	No.	Yds	Avg	Lg	TD
Gale Sayers	7	91	2781	30.6	103	6
Lynn Chandnois	7	92	2720	29.6	93	3
Abe Woodson	9	193	5538	28.7	105	5
Claude (Buddy) Young	6	90	2514	27.9	104	2
Travis Williams	5	102	2801	27.5	105	6

Note: 75 or more returns.

† Active player.

Rhodes Can't Catch a Break

In late 1998 Nicolas Perillo, an inmate at the Gander Hill Correctional Institute in Wilmington, Del., testified against his fellow inmate Thomas Capano, who was on trial for murder. When Perillo appeared on the witness stand, Jack O'Donnell, Capano's attorney, suggested Perillo had struck a deal to get out of prison early in exchange for his testimony, saying, "Well, if you were giving information about the defensive line of the Philadelphia Eagles, do you think prosecutors would have cut you a deal?"

"No," Perillo said. "But I would say, 'Get rid of Ray Rhodes.' "

Single-Season Leaders
Scoring

POINTS

	Year	TD	PAT	FG	Pts
Paul Hornung, GB	1960	15	41	15	176
Gary Anderson, Minn	1998	0	59	35	164
Mark Moseley, Wash	1983	0	62	33	161
Gino Cappelletti, Bos	1964	7	38	25	155
Emmitt Smith, Dall	1995	25	0	0	150
Chip Lohmiller, Wash	1991	0	56	31	149
Gino Cappelletti, Bos	1961	8	48	17	147
Paul Hornung, GB	1961	10	41	15	146
Jim Turner, NYJ	1968	0	43	34	145
John Kasay, Car	1996	0	34	37	145
John Riggins, Wash	1983	24	0	0	144
Kevin Butler, Chi	1985	0	51	31	144

Note: Cappelletti's 1964 total includes a two-point conversion.

TOUCHDOWNS

	Year	Rush	Rec	Ret	Total
Emmitt Smith, Dall	1995	25	0	0	25
John Riggins, Wash	1983	24	0	0	24
O.J. Simpson, Buff	1975	16	7	0	23
Jerry Rice, SF	1987	1	22	0	23
Terrell Davis, Den	1998	21	2	0	23
Gale Sayers, Chi	1965	14	6	2	22
Emmitt Smith, Dall	1994	21	1	0	22

FIELD GOALS

	Year	Att	No.
John Kasay, Car	1996	45	37
Cary Blanchard, Ind	1996	40	36
Al Del Greco, Tenn	1998	39	36
Gary Anderson, Minn	1998	35	35
Jeff Jaeger, LA Raiders	1993	44	35
Ali Haji-Sheikh, NYG	1983	42	35
Jim Turner, NYJ	1968	46	34
Jason Hanson, Det	1993	43	34
Fuad Reveiz, Minn	1994	39	34
Norm Johnson, Pitt	1995	41	34
Richie Cunningham, Dall	1997	37	34

Rushing

YARDS GAINED

	Year	Att	Yds	Avg
Eric Dickerson, LA Rams	1984	379	2105	5.6
Barry Sanders, Det	1997	335	2053	6.1
Terrell Davis, Den	1998	392	2008	5.1
O.J. Simpson, Buff	1973	332	2003	6.0
Earl Campbell, Hou	1980	373	1934	5.2
Jim Brown, Clev	1963	291	1883	6.4
Barry Sanders, Det	1994	331	1883	5.7
Walter Payton, Chi	1977	339	1852	5.5
Jamal Anderson, Atl	1998	410	1846	4.5
Eric Dickerson, LA Rams	1986	404	1821	4.5
O.J. Simpson, Buff	1975	329	1817	5.5
Eric Dickerson, LA Rams	1983	390	1808	4.6

AVERAGE GAIN

	Year	Avg
Beattie Feathers, Chi	1934	8.44
Randall Cunningham, Phil	1990	7.98
Bobby Douglass, Chi	1972	6.87

Minimum 100 attempts.

TOUCHDOWNS

	Year	No.
Emmitt Smith, Dall	1995	25
John Riggins, Wash	1983	24
Emmitt Smith, Dall	1994	21
Joe Morris, NYG	1985	21
Terry Allen, Wash	1996	21
Terrell Davis, Den	1998	21

Passing

YARDS GAINED

	Year	Att	Comp	Pct	Yds
Dan Marino, Mia	1984	564	362	64.2	5084
Dan Fouts, SD	1981	609	360	59.1	4802
Dan Marino, Mia	1986	623	378	60.7	4746
Dan Fouts, SD	1980	589	348	59.1	4715
Warren Moon, Hou	1991	655	404	61.7	4690
Warren Moon, Hou	1990	584	362	62.0	4689
Neil Lomax, StL Cards	1984	560	345	61.6	4614
Drew Bledsoe, NE	1994	691	400	57.9	4555
Lynn Dickey, GB	1983	484	289	59.7	4458
Dan Marino, Mia	1994	615	385	62.6	4453

PASSER RATING

	Year	Rat.
Steve Young, SF	1994	112.8
Joe Montana, SF	1989	112.4
Milt Plum, Clev	1960	110.4
Sammy Baugh, Wash	1945	109.9
Dan Marino, Mia	1984	108.9

TOUCHDOWNS

	Year	No.
Dan Marino, Mia	1984	48
Dan Marino, Mia	1986	44
Brett Favre, GB	1995	38
George Blanda, Hou	1961	36
Y.A. Tittle, NYG	1963	36
Steve Young, SF	1998	36

Single-Season Leaders *(Cont.)*

Receiving

RECEPTIONS

	Year	No.	Yds
Herman Moore, Det	1995	123	1686
Cris Carter, Minn	1994	122	1256
Jerry Rice, SF	1995	122	1848
Cris Carter, Minn	1995	122	1371
Isaac Bruce, StL Rams	1995	119	1781
Sterling Sharpe, GB	1993	112	1274
Jerry Rice, SF	1994	112	1499
Terance Mathis, Atl	1994	111	1342
Michael Irvin, Dall	1995	111	1603
Sterling Sharpe, GB	1992	108	1461
Brett Perriman, Det	1995	108	1488
Jerry Rice, SF	1996	108	1254

YARDS GAINED

	Year	Yds
Jerry Rice, SF	1995	1848
Isaac Bruce, StL Rams	1995	1781
Charley Hennigan, Hou	1961	1746
Herman Moore, Det	1995	1686
Michael Irvin, Dall	1995	1603

TOUCHDOWNS

	Year	No.
Jerry Rice, SF	1987	22
Mark Clayton, Mia	1984	18
Sterling Sharpe, GB	1994	18

Six tied with 17.

All-Purpose Yards

	Year	Run	Rec	Ret	Total
Lionel James, SD	1985	516	1027	992	2535
Terry Metcalf, StL Cards	1975	816	378	1268	2462
Mack Herron, NE	1974	824	474	1146	2444
Gale Sayers, Chi	1966	1231	447	762	2440
Timmy Brown, Phil	1963	841	487	1100	2428
Barry Sanders, Det	1997	2053	305	0	2358
Tim Brown, LA Rai	1988	50	725	1542	2317
Marcus Allen, LA Rai	1985	1759	555	-6	2308
Timmy Brown, Phil	1962	545	849	912	2306
Gale Sayers, Chi	1965	867	507	898	2272
Eric Dickerson, LA Rams	1984	2105	139	15	2259
O.J. Simpson, Buff	1975	1817	426	0	2243

Punting

	Year	No.	Yds	Avg
Sammy Baugh, Wash	1940	35	1799	51.4
Yale Lary, Det	1963	35	1713	48.9
Sammy Baugh, Wash	1941	30	1462	48.7
Yale Lary, Det	1961	52	2516	48.4
Sammy Baugh, Wash	1942	37	1783	48.2

Sacks

	Year	No.
Mark Gastineau, NYJ	1984	22
Reggie White, Phil	1987	21
Chris Doleman, Minn	1989	21
Lawrence Taylor, NYG	1986	20.5

Interceptions

	Year	No.
Dick (Night Train) Lane, LA Rams	1952	14
Dan Sandifer, Wash	1948	13
Spec Sanders, NY Yanks	1950	13
Lester Hayes, Oak	1980	13

Nine tied with 12.

Kickoff Returns

	Year	Avg
Travis Williams, GB	1967	41.1
Gale Sayers, Chi	1967	37.7
Ollie Matson, Chi Cards	1958	35.5
Jim Duncan, Balt Colts	1970	35.4
Lynn Chandnois, Pitt	1952	35.2

Punt Returns

	Year	Avg
Herb Rich, Balt Colts	1950	23.0
Jack Christiansen, Det	1952	21.5
Dick Christy, NY Titans	1961	21.3
Bob Hayes, Dall	1968	20.8

Single-Game Leaders

Scoring

POINTS

	Date	Pts
Ernie Nevers, Chi Cards vs Chi	11-28-29	40
Dub Jones, Clev vs Chi	11-25-51	36
Gale Sayers, Chi vs SF	12-12-65	36
Paul Hornung, GB vs Balt Colts	10-8-61	33

On Thanksgiving Day, 1929, Nevers scored all the Cardinals' points on six rushing TDs and four PATs. The Cards defeated Red Grange and the Bears, 40-6. Jones and Sayers each rushed for four touchdowns and scored two more on returns in their teams' victories. Hornung scored four touchdowns and kicked 6 PATs and a field goal in a 45-7 win over the Colts.

FIELD GOALS

	Date	No.
Jim Bakken, StL Cards vs Pitt	9-24-67	7
Rich Karlis, Minn vs LA Rams	11-5-89	7
Chris Boniol, Dall vs GB	11-18-96	7

Fourteen players tied with 6 FGs each.

Bakken was 7 for 9, Karlis and Boniol 7 for 7.

Single-Game Leaders (Cont.)

Scoring (Cont.)

TOUCHDOWNS

	Date	No.
Ernie Nevers, Chi Cards vs Chi	11-28-29	6
Dub Jones, Clev vs Chi	11-25-51	6
Gale Sayers, Chi vs SF	12-12-65	6
Bob Shaw, Chi Cards vs Balt Colts	10-2-50	5
Jim Brown, Clev vs Balt Colts	11-1-59	5
Abner Haynes, Dall Texans vs Oak	11-26-61	5
Billy Cannon, Hou vs NY Titans	12-10-61	5
Cookie Gilchrist, Buff vs NYJ	12-8-63	5
Paul Hornung, GB vs Balt Colts	12-12-65	5
Kellen Winslow, SD vs Oak	11-22-81	5
Jerry Rice, SF vs Atl	10-14-90	5
James Stewart, Jax vs Phil	10-12-97	5

Rushing

YARDS GAINED

	Date	Yds
Walter Payton, Chi vs Minn	11-20-77	275
O.J. Simpson, Buff vs Det	11-25-76	273
O.J. Simpson, Buff vs NE	9-16-73	250
Willie Ellison, LA Rams vs NO	12-5-71	247
Corey Dillon, Cin vs Tenn	12-4-97	246

CARRIES

	Date	No.
Jamie Morris, Wash vs Cin	12-17-88	45
Butch Woolfolk, NYG vs Phil	11-20-83	43
James Wilder, TB vs GB	9-30-84	43
James Wilder, TB vs Pitt	10-30-83	42
Franco Harris, Pitt vs Cin	10-17-76	41
Gerald Riggs, Atl vs LA Rams	11-17-85	41

TOUCHDOWNS

	Date	No.
Ernie Nevers, Chi Cards vs Chi	11-28-29	6
Jim Brown, Clev vs Balt Colts	11-1-59	5
Cookie Gilchrist, Buff vs NYJ	12-8-63	5
James Stewart, Jax vs Phil	10-12-97	5

Passing

YARDS GAINED

	Date	Yds
N. Van Brocklin, LA Rams vs NY Yanks	9-28-51	554
Warren Moon, Hou vs KC	12-16-90	527
Boomer Esiason, Ariz vs Wash	11-10-96	522
Dan Marino, Mia vs NYJ	10-23-88	521
Phil Simms, NYG vs Cin	10-13-85	513

COMPLETIONS

	Date	No.
Drew Bledsoe, NE vs Minn	11-13-94	45
Richard Todd, NYJ vs SF	9-21-80	42
Warren Moon, Hou vs Dall	11-10-91	41
Ken Anderson, Cin vs SD	12-20-82	40
Phil Simms, NYG vs Cin	10-13-85	40
Vinny Testaverde, NYJ vs Sea	12-6-98	42

TOUCHDOWNS

	Date	No.
Sid Luckman, Chi vs NYG	11-14-43	7
Adrian Burk, Phil vs Wash	10-17-54	7
George Blanda, Hou vs NY Titans	11-19-61	7
Y. A. Tittle, NYG vs Wash	10-28-62	7
Joe Kapp, Minn vs Balt Colts	9-28-69	7

Receiving

YARDS GAINED

	Date	Yds
Flipper Anderson, LA Rams vs NO	11-26-89	336
Stephone Paige, KC vs SD	12-22-85	309
Jim Benton, Clev vs Det	11-22-45	303
Cloyce Box, Det vs Balt Colts	12-3-50	302
Jerry Rice, SF vs Minn	12-18-95	289

RECEPTIONS

	Date	No.
Tom Fears, LA Rams vs GB	12-3-50	18
Clark Gaines, NYJ vs SF	9-21-80	17
Sonny Randle, StL Cards vs NYG	11-4-62	16
Jerry Rice, SF vs LA Rams	11-20-94	16
Keenan McCardell, Jax vs StL Rams	10-20-96	16
Rickey Young, Minn vs NE	12-16-79	15
William Andrews, Atl vs Pitt	11-15-81	15
Andre Reed, Buff vs GB	11-20-94	15
Isaac Bruce, StL Rams vs Mia	12-24-95	15

Single-Game Leaders (Cont.)

Receiving (Cont.)

TOUCHDOWNS

	Date	No.
Bob Shaw, Chi Cards vs Balt Colts	10-2-50	5
Kellen Winslow, SD vs Oak	11-22-81	5
Jerry Rice, SF vs Atl	10-14-90	5

All-Purpose Yards

	Date	Yds
Glyn Milburn, Den vs Sea	12-10-95	404
Billy Cannon, Hou vs NY Titans	12-10-61	373
Tyrone Hughes, NO vs LA Rams	10-23-94	347
Lionel James, SD vs LA Rai	11-10-85	345
Timmy Brown, Phil vs St.L Cards	12-16-62	341

Longest Plays

RUSHING	Opponent	Year	Yds
Tony Dorsett, Dall	Minn	1983	99
Andy Uram, GB	Chi Cards	1939	97
Bob Gage, Pitt	Chi	1949	97
Jim Spitval, Balt Colts	GB	1950	96
Bob Hoernschemeyer, Det	NY Yanks	1950	96
Garrison Hearst, SF	NYJ	1998	96

PASSING	Opponent	Year	Yds
Frank Filchock to Andy Farkas, Wash	Pitt	1939	99
George Izo to Bobby Mitchell, Wash	Clev	1963	99
Karl Sweetan to Pat Studstill, Det	Balt Colts	1966	99
Sonny Jurgensen to Gerry Allen, Wash	Chi	1968	99
Jim Plunkett to Cliff Branch, LA Rai	Wash	1983	99
Ron Jaworski to Mike Quick, Phil	Atl	1985	99
Stan Humphries to Tony Martin, SD	Sea	1994	99
Brett Favre to Robert Brooks, GB	Chi	1995	99

FIELD GOALS	Opponent	Year	Yds
Tom Dempsey, NO	Det	1970	63
Jason Elam, Den	Jax	1998	63
Steve Cox, Clev	Cin	1984	60
Morten Andersen, NO	Chi	1991	60

PUNTS	Opponent	Year	Yds
Steve O'Neal, NYJ	Den	1969	98
Joe Lintzenich, Chi	NYG	1931	94
Shawn McCarthy, NE	Buff	1991	93
Randall Cunningham, Phil	NYG	1989	91

INTERCEPTION RETURNS	Opponent	Year	Yds
Vencie Glenn, SD	Den	1987	103
Louis Oliver, Mia	Buff	1992	103
Six players tied at 102.			

KICKOFF RETURNS	Opponent	Year	Yds
Al Carmichael, GB	Chi	1956	106
Noland Smith, KC	Den	1967	106
Roy Green, StL Cards	Dall	1979	106

PUNT RETURNS	Opponent	Year	Yds
Robert Bailey, LA Rams	NO	1994	103
Gil LeFebvre, Cin	Brooklyn	1933	98
Charlie West, Minn	Wash	1968	98
Dennis Morgan, Dall	StL Cards	1974	98
Terance Mathis, NYJ	Dall	1990	98

Two-Sport Star

Mark Rodenhauser, the Pittsburgh Steelers' long snapper, can hike a football through a basketball hoop. He says he averages 60% from half-court and 20% from full court. Rodenhauser developed this Stupid Snapper Trick during the bitter winters in his native Chicago, when he was often forced to take his football into his high school's gym. "I couldn't shoot a basketball, so I figured I might as well bend over and do it," he says.
Has Shaq tried this?

Rushing

Year	Player, Team	Att.	Yards	Avg.	TD	Year	Player, Team	Att.	Yards	Avg.	TD
1932	Cliff Battles, Bos	148	576	3.9	3	1971	Floyd Little, Den, AFC	284	1133	4.0	6
1933	Jim Musick, Bos	173	809	4.7	5		John Brockington,				
1934	Beattie Feathers,						GB, NFC	216	1105	5.1	4
	Chi	101	1004	9.9	8	1972	O.J. Simpson, Buff, AFC	292	1251	4.3	6
1935	Doug Russell,						Larry Brown, Wash, NFC	285	1216	4.3	8
	Chi Cards	140	499	3.6	0	1973	O.J. Simpson, Buff, AFC	332	2003	6.0	12
1936	Alphonse Leemans, NY	206	830	4.0	2		John Brockington,				
1937	Cliff Battles, Wash	216	874	4.0	5		GB, NFC	265	1144	4.3	3
1938	Byron White, Pitt	152	567	3.7	4	1974	Otis Armstrong,				
1939	Bill Osmanski,						Den, AFC	263	1407	5.3	9
	Chi	121	699	5.8	7		Lawrence McCutcheon,				
1940	Byron White, Det	146	514	3.5	5		LA, NFC	236	1109	4.7	3
1941	Clarence Manders,					1975	O.J. Simpson, Buff, AFC	329	1817	5.5	16
	Bklyn	111	486	4.4	5		Jim Otis, StL, NFC	269	1076	4.0	5
1942	Bill Dudley, Pitt	162	696	4.3	5	1976	O.J. Simpson, Buff, AFC	290	1503	5.2	8
1943	Bill Paschal, NY	147	572	3.9	10		Walter Payton, Chi, NFC	311	1390	4.5	13
1944	Bill Paschal, NY	196	737	3.8	9	1977	Walter Payton, Chi, NFC	339	1852	5.5	14
1945	Steve Van Buren, Phil	143	832	5.8	15		Mark van Eeghen,				
1946	Bill Dudley, Pitt	146	604	4.1	3		Oak, AFC	324	1273	3.9	7
1947	Steve Van Buren, Phil	217	1008	4.6	13	1978	Earl Campbell, Hou, AFC	302	1450	4.8	13
1948	Steve Van Buren, Phil	201	945	4.7	10		Walter Payton, Chi, NFC	333	1395	4.2	11
1949	Steve Van Buren, Phil	263	1146	4.4	11	1979	Earl Campbell, Hou, AFC	368	1697	4.6	19
1950	Marion Motley, Clev	140	810	5.8	3		Walter Payton, Chi, NFC	369	1610	4.4	14
1951	Eddie Price, NY	271	971	3.6	7	1980	Earl Campbell, Hou, AFC	373	1934	5.2	13
1952	Dan Towler, LA	156	894	5.7	10		Walter Payton, Chi, NFC	317	1460	4.6	6
1953	Joe Perry, SF	192	1018	5.3	10	1981	George Rogers,				
1954	Joe Perry, SF	173	1049	6.1	8		NO, NFC	378	1674	4.4	13
1955	Alan Ameche, Balt	213	961	4.5	9		Earl Campbell, Hou, AFC	361	1376	3.8	10
1956	Rick Casares,					1982	Freeman McNeil,				
	Chi	234	1126	4.8	12		NY Jets, AFC	151	786	5.2	6
1957	Jim Brown, Clev	202	942	4.7	9		Tony Dorsett, Dall, NFC	177	745	4.2	5
1958	Jim Brown, Clev	257	1527	5.9	17	1983	Eric Dickerson,				
1959	Jim Brown, Clev	290	1329	4.6	14		LA Rams, NFC	390	1808	4.6	18
1960	Jim Brown, Clev, NFL	215	1257	5.8	9		Curt Warner, Sea, AFC	335	1449	4.3	13
	Abner Haynes,					1984	Eric Dickerson,				
	Dall Texans, AFL	156	875	5.6	9		LA Rams, NFC	379	2105	5.6	14
1961	Jim Brown, Clev, NFL	305	1408	4.6	8		Earnest Jackson,				
	Billy Cannon, Hou, AFL	200	948	4.7	6		SD, AFC	296	1179	4.0	8
1962	Jim Taylor, GB, NFL	272	1474	5.4	19	1985	Marcus Allen,				
	Cookie Gilchrist,						LA Raiders, AFC	380	1759	4.6	11
	Buff, AFL	214	1096	5.1	13		Gerald Riggs, Atl, NFC	397	1719	4.3	10
1963	Jim Brown, Clev, NFL	291	1863	6.4	12	1986	Eric Dickerson,				
	Clem Daniels, Oak, AFL	215	1099	5.1	3		LA Rams, NFC	404	1821	4.5	11
1964	Jim Brown, Clev, NFL	280	1446	5.2	7		Curt Warner, Sea, AFC	319	1481	4.6	13
	Cookie Gilchrist,					1987	Charles White,				
	Buff, AFL	230	981	4.3	6		LA Rams, NFC	324	1374	4.2	11
1965	Jim Brown, Clev, NFL	289	1544	5.3	17		Eric Dickerson, Ind, AFC	223	1011	4.5	5
	Paul Lowe, SD, AFL	222	1121	5.0	7	1988	Eric Dickerson, Ind, AFC	388	1659	4.3	14
1966	Jim Nance, Bos, AFL	299	1458	4.9	11		Herschel Walker,				
	Gale Sayers, Chi, NFL	229	1231	5.4	8		Dall, NFC	361	1514	4.2	5
1967	Jim Nance, Bos, AFL	269	1216	4.5	7	1989	Christian Okoye,				
	Leroy Kelly, Clev, NFL	235	1205	5.1	11		KC, AFC	370	1480	4.0	12
1968	Leroy Kelly, Clev, NFL	248	1239	5.0	16		Barry Sanders, Det, NFC	280	1470	5.3	14
	Paul Robinson, Cin, AFL	238	1023	4.3	8	1990	Barry Sanders, Det, NFC	255	1304	5.1	13
1969	Gale Sayers, Chi, NFL	236	1032	4.4	8		Thurman Thomas,				
	Dickie Post, SD, AFL	182	873	4.8	6		Buff, AFC	271	1297	4.8	11
1970	Larry Brown, Wash, NFC	237	1125	4.7	5	1991	Emmitt Smith, Dall, NFC	365	1563	4.3	12
	Floyd Little, Den, AFC	209	901	4.3	3		Thurman Thomas,				
							Buff, AFC	288	1407	4.9	7

Rushing *(Cont.)*

Year	Player, Team	Att.	Yards	Avg.	TD
1992	Emmitt Smith, Dall, NFC	373	1713	4.6	18
	Barry Foster, Pitt, AFC	390	1690	4.3	11
1993	Emmitt Smith, Dall, NFC	283	1486	5.3	9
	Thurman Thomas, Buff, AFC	355	1315	3.7	6
1994	Barry Sanders, Det, NFC	331	1883	5.7	7
	Chris Warren, Sea, AFC	333	1545	4.6	9
1995	Emmitt Smith, Dall, NFC	377	1773	4.7	25
	Curtis Martin, NE, AFC	368	1487	4.0	14
1996	Barry Sanders, Det, NFC	307	1553	5.1	11
	Terrell Davis, Den, AFC	345	1538	4.5	13
1997	Barry Sanders, Det, NFC	335	2053	6.1	11
	Terrell Davis, Den, AFC	369	1730	4.7	15
1998	Terrell Davis, Den, AFC	392	2008	5.1	21
	Jamal Anderson, Atl, NFC	410	1846	4.5	14

Passing*

Year	Player, Team	Att.	Comp	Yards	TD	Int
1932	Arnie Herber, GB	101	37	639	9	9
1933	Harry Newman, NY	136	53	973	11	17
1934	Arnie Herber, GB	115	42	799	8	12
1935	Ed Danowski, NY	113	57	794	10	9
1936	Arnie Herber, GB	173	77	1239	11	13
1937	Sammy Baugh, Wash	171	81	1127	8	14
1938	Ed Danowski, NY	129	70	848	7	8
1939	Parker Hall, Clev	208	106	1227	9	13
1940	Sammy Baugh, Wash	177	111	1367	12	10
1941	Cecil Isbell, GB	206	117	1479	15	11
1942	Cecil Isbell, GB	268	146	2021	24	14
1943	Sammy Baugh, Wash	239	133	1754	23	19
1944	Frank Filchock, Wash	147	84	1139	13	9
1945	Sammy Baugh, Wash	182	128	1669	11	4
	Sid Luckman, Chi	217	117	1725	14	10
1946	Bob Waterfield, LA	251	127	1747	18	17
1947	Sammy Baugh, Wash	354	210	2938	25	15
1948	Tommy Thompson, Phil	246	141	1965	25	11
1949	Sammy Baugh, Wash	255	145	1903	18	14
1950	Norm Van Brocklin, LA	233	127	2061	18	14
1951	Bob Waterfield, LA	176	88	1566	13	10
1952	Norm Van Brocklin, LA	205	113	1736	14	17
1953	Otto Graham, Clev	258	167	2722	11	9
1954	Norm Van Brocklin, LA	260	139	2637	13	21
1955	Otto Graham, Clev	185	98	1721	15	8
1956	Ed Brown, Chi	168	96	1667	11	12
1957	Tommy O'Connell, Clev	110	63	1229	9	8
1958	Eddie LeBaron, Wash	145	79	1365	11	10
1959	Charlie Conerly, NY	194	113	1706	14	4
1960	Milt Plum, Clev, NFL	250	151	2297	21	5
	Jack Kemp, LA, AFL	406	211	3018	20	25
1961	George Blanda, Hou, AFL	362	187	3330	36	22
	Milt Plum, Clev, NFL	302	177	2416	18	10
1962	Len Dawson, Dall, AFL	310	189	2759	29	17
	Bart Starr, GB, NFL	285	178	2438	12	9
1963	Y.A. Tittle, NY, NFL	367	221	3145	36	14
	Tobin Rote, SD, AFL	286	170	2510	20	17
1964	Len Dawson, KC, AFL	354	199	2879	30	18
	Bart Starr, GB, NFL	272	163	2144	15	4
1965	Rudy Bukich, Chi, NFL	312	176	2641	20	9
	John Hadl, SD, AFL	348	174	2798	20	21
1966	Bart Starr, GB, NFL	251	156	2257	14	3
	Len Dawson, KC, AFL	284	159	2527	26	10
1967	Sonny Jurgensen, Wash, NFL	508	288	3747	31	16
	Daryle Lamonica, Oakland, AFL	425	220	3228	30	20
1968	Len Dawson, KC, AFL	224	131	2109	17	9
	Earl Morrall, Balt, NFL	317	182	2909	26	17
1969	Sonny Jurgensen, Wash, NFL	442	274	3102	22	15
	Greg Cook, Cin, AFL	197	106	1854	15	11
1970	John Brodie, SF, NFC	378	223	2941	24	10
	Daryle Lamonica, Oak, AFC	356	179	2516	22	15
1971	Roger Staubach, Dall, NFC	211	126	1882	15	4
	Bob Griese, Mia, AFC	263	145	2089	19	9
1972	Norm Snead, NY, NFC	325	196	2307	17	12
	Earl Morrall, Mia, AFC	150	83	1360	11	7
1973	Roger Staubach, Dall, NFC	286	179	2428	23	15
	Ken Stabler, Oak, AFC	260	163	1997	14	10
1974	Ken Anderson, Cin, AFC	328	213	2667	18	10
	Sonny Jurgensen, Wash, NFC	167	107	1185	11	5
1975	Ken Anderson, Cin, AFC	377	228	3169	21	11
	Fran Tarkenton, Minn, NFC	425	273	2994	25	13
1976	Ken Stabler, Oak, AFC	291	194	2737	27	17
	James Harris, LA, NFC	158	91	1460	8	6
1977	Bob Griese, Mia, AFC	307	180	2252	22	13
	Roger Staubach, Dall, NFC	361	210	2620	18	9
1978	Roger Staubach, Dall, NFC	413	231	3190	25	16
	Terry Bradshaw, Pitt, AFC	368	207	2915	28	20
1979	Roger Staubach, Dall, NFC	461	267	3586	27	11
	Dan Fouts, SD, AFC	530	332	4082	24	24
1980	Brian Sipe, Clev, AFC	554	337	4132	30	14
	Ron Jaworski, Phi, NFC	451	257	3529	27	12
1981	Ken Anderson, Cin, AFC	479	300	3754	29	10
	Joe Montana, SF, NFC	488	311	3565	19	12
1982	Ken Anderson, Cin, AFC	309	218	2495	12	9
	Joe Theismann, Wash, NFC	252	161	2033	13	9
1983	Steve Bartkowski, Atl, NFC	432	274	3167	22	5
	Dan Marino, Mia AFC	296	173	2210	20	6
1984	Dan Marino, Mia, AFC	564	362	5084	48	17
	Joe Montana, SF, NFC	432	279	3630	28	10
1985	Ken O'Brien, NY, AFC	488	297	3888	25	8
	Joe Montana, SF, NFC	494	303	3653	27	13

Passing *(Cont.)*

Year	Player, Team	Att.	Comp	Yards	TD	Int
1986	Tommy Kramer,					
	Minn, NFC	372	208	3000	24	10
	Dan Marino, Mia, AFC	623	378	4746	44	23
1987	Joe Montana, SF, NFC	398	266	3054	31	13
	Bernie Kosar,					
	Clev, AFC	389	241	3033	22	9
1988	Boomer Esiason,					
	Cin, AFC	388	223	3572	28	14
	Wade Wilson,					
	Minn, NFC	332	204	2746	15	9
1989	Joe Montana, SF, NFC	386	271	3521	26	8
	Boomer Esiason,					
	Cin, AFC	455	258	3525	28	11
1990	Jim Kelly, Buffalo, AFC	346	219	2829	24	9
	Phil Simms, NY, NFC	311	184	2284	15	4
1991	Steve Young, SF, NFC	279	180	2517	17	8
	Jim Kelly, Buff, AFC	474	304	3844	33	17

Year	Player, Team	Att.	Comp	Yards	TD	Int
1992	Steve Young, SF, NFC	402	268	3465	25	7
	Warren Moon,					
	Hou, AFC	346	224	2521	18	12
1993	Steve Young, SF, NFC	462	314	4023	29	16
	John Elway, Den, AFC	551	348	4030	25	10
1994	Steve Young, SF, NFC	461	324	3969	35	10
	Dan Marino, Mia, AFC	615	385	4453	30	17
1995	Brett Favre, GB, NFC	570	359	4413	38	13
	Jeff Blake, Cin, AFC	567	326	3822	28	17
1996	Vinny Testaverde,					
	Balt, AFC	549	325	4177	33	19
	Brett Favre, GB, NFC	543	325	3899	39	13
1997	Steve Young, SF, NFC	356	241	3029	19	6
	Mark Brunell, Jax, AFC	435	264	3281	18	7
1998	Randall Cunningham,					
	Minn, NFC	425	259	3704	34	10
	Vinny Testaverde,					
	NYJ, AFC	421	259	3256	29	7

*Since 1973, the annual passing leaders have been determined by a passer rating system that compares individual performances to a fixed performance standard.

Pass Receiving*

Year	Player, Team	No.	Yds	Avg	TD
1932	Ray Flaherty, NY	21	350	16.7	3
1933	John Kelly, Brooklyn	22	246	11.2	3
1934	Joe Carter, Phil	16	238	14.9	4
	Morris Badgro, NY	16	206	12.9	1
1935	Tod Goodwin, NY	26	432	16.6	4
1936	Don Hutson, GB	34	536	15.8	8
1937	Don Hutson, GB	41	552	13.5	7
1938	Gaynell Tinsley, Chi Cards	41	516	12.6	1
1939	Don Hutson, GB	34	846	24.9	6
1940	Don Looney, Phil	58	707	12.2	4
1941	Don Hutson, GB	58	738	12.7	10
1942	Don Hutson, GB	74	1211	16.4	17
1943	Don Hutson, GB	47	776	16.5	11
1944	Don Hutson, GB	58	866	14.9	9
1945	Don Hutson, GB	47	834	17.7	9
1946	Jim Benton, LA	63	981	15.6	6
1947	Jim Keane, Chi	64	910	14.2	10
1948	Tom Fears, LA	51	698	13.7	4
1949	Tom Fears, LA	77	1013	13.2	9
1950	Tom Fears, LA	84	1116	13.3	7
1951	Elroy Hirsch, LA	66	1495	22.7	17
1952	Mac Speedie, Clev	62	911	14.7	5
1953	Pete Pihos, Phil	63	1049	16.7	10
1954	Pete Pihos, Phil	60	872	14.5	10
	Billy Wilson, SF	60	830	13.8	5
1955	Pete Pihos, Phil	62	864	13.9	7
1956	Billy Wilson, SF	60	889	14.8	5
1957	Billy Wilson, SF	52	757	14.6	6
1958	Raymond Berry, Balt	56	794	14.2	9
	Pete Retzlaff, Phil	56	766	13.7	2
1959	Raymond Berry, Balt	66	959	14.5	14
1960	Lionel Taylor, Den, AFL	92	1235	13.4	12
	Raymond Berry, Balt, NFL	74	1298	17.5	10
1961	Lionel Taylor, Den, AFL	100	1176	11.8	4
	Jim Phillips, LA, NFL	78	1092	14.0	5
1962	Lionel Taylor, Den, AFL	77	908	11.8	4
	Bobby Mitchell,				
	Wash, NFL	72	1384	19.2	11

Year	Player, Team	No.	Yds	Avg	TD
1963	Lionel Taylor, Den, AFL	78	1101	14.1	10
	Bobby Joe Conrad,				
	St. Louis, NFL	73	967	13.2	10
1964	Charley Hennigan,				
	Houston, AFL	101	1546	15.3	8
	Johnny Morris, Chi, NFL	93	1200	12.9	10
1965	Lionel Taylor, Den, AFL	85	1131	13.3	6
	Dave Parks, SF, NFL	80	1344	16.8	12
1966	Lance Alworth, SD, AFL	73	1383	18.9	13
	Charley Taylor, Wash, NFL	72	1119	15.5	12
1967	George Sauer, NY, AFL	75	1189	15.9	6
	Charley Taylor, Wash, NFL	70	990	14.1	9
1968	Clifton McNeil, SF, NFL	71	994	14.0	7
	Lance Alworth, SD, AFL	68	1312	19.3	10
1969	Dan Abramowicz,				
	NO, NFL	73	1015	13.9	7
	Lance Alworth, SD, AFL	64	1003	15.7	4
1970	Dick Gordon, Chi, NFC	71	1026	14.5	13
	Marlin Briscoe, Buff, AFC	57	1036	18.2	8
1971	Fred Biletnikoff, Oak, AFC	61	929	15.2	9
	Bob Tucker, NY, NFC	59	791	13.4	4
1972	Harold Jackson,				
	Phil, NFC	62	1048	16.9	4
	Fred Biletnikoff, Oak, AFC	58	802	13.8	7
1973	Harold Carmichael,				
	Phil, NFC	67	1116	16.7	9
	Fred Willis, Hou, AFC	57	371	6.5	1
1974	Lydell Mitchell, Balt, AFC	72	544	7.6	2
	Charles Young,				
	Phil, NFC	63	696	11.0	3
1975	Chuck Foreman,				
	Minn, NFC	73	691	9.5	9
	Reggie Rucker,				
	Clev, AFC	60	770	12.8	3
	Lydell Mitchell, Balt, AFC	60	544	9.1	4
1976	MacArthur Lane,				
	KC, AFC	66	686	10.4	1
	Drew Pearson, Dall, NFC	58	806	13.9	6

*Most catches.

Pass Receiving (Cont.)

Year	Player, Team	No.	Yds	Avg	TD
1977	Lydell Mitchell, Balt, AFC	71	620	8.7	4
	Ahmad Rashad, Minn, NFC	51	681	13.4	2
1978	Rickey Young, Minn, NFC	88	704	8.0	5
	Steve Largent, Sea, AFC	71	1168	16.5	8
1979	Joe Washington, Balt, AFC	82	750	9.1	3
	Ahmad Rashad, Minn, NFC	80	1156	14.5	9
1980	Kellen Winslow, SD, AFC	89	1290	14.5	9
	Earl Cooper, SF, NFC	83	567	6.8	4
1981	Kellen Winslow, SD, AFC	88	1075	12.2	10
	Dwight Clark, SF, NFC	85	1105	13.0	4
1982	Dwight Clark, SF, NFC	60	913	15.2	5
	Kellen Winslow, SD, AFC	54	721	13.4	6
1983	Todd Christensen, LA, AFC	92	1247	13.6	12
	Roy Green, StL, NFC	78	1227	15.7	14
	Charlie Brown, Wash, NFC	78	1225	15.7	8
	Earnest Gray, NY, NFC	78	1139	14.6	5
1984	Art Monk, Wash, NFC	106	1372	12.9	7
	Ozzie Newsome, Clev, AFC	89	1001	11.2	5
1985	Roger Craig, SF, NFC	92	1016	11.0	6
	Lionel James, SD, AFC	86	1027	11.9	6
1986	Todd Christensen, LA Rai, AFC	95	1153	12.1	8
	Jerry Rice, SF, NFC	86	1570	18.3	15
1987	J.T. Smith, StL Card, NFC	91	1117	12.3	8
	Al Toon, NY, AFC	68	976	14.4	5
1988	Al Toon, NY, AFC	93	1067	11.5	5
	Henry Ellard, LA Rams, NFC	86	1414	16.4	10
1989	Sterling Sharpe, GB, NFC	90	1423	15.8	12
	Andre Reed, Buff, AFC	88	1312	14.9	9
1990	Jerry Rice, SF, NFC	100	1502	15.0	13
	Haywood Jeffires, Hou, AFC	74	1048	14.2	8
	Drew Hill, Hou, AFC	74	1019	13.8	5
1991	Haywood Jeffires, Hou, AFC	100	1181	11.8	7
	Michael Irvin, Dall, NFC	93	1523	16.4	8
1992	Sterling Sharpe, GB, NFC	108	1461	13.5	13
	Haywood Jeffires, Hou, AFC	90	913	10.1	9
1993	Sterling Sharpe, GB, NFC	112	1274	11.4	11
	Reggie Langhorne, Ind, AFC	85	1038	12.2	3
1994	Cris Carter, Minn, NFC	122	1256	10.3	7
	Ben Coates, NE, AFC	96	1174	12.2	7
1995	Herman Moore, Det, NFC	123	1686	13.7	14
	Carl Pickens, Cin, AFC	99	1234	12.5	17
1996	Jerry Rice, SF, NFC	108	1254	11.6	8
	Carl Pickens, Cin, AFC	100	1180	11.8	12
1997	Herman Moore, Det, NFC	104	1293	12.4	8
	Tim Brown, Oak, AFC	104	1408	13.5	5
1998	Frank Sanders, Ariz, NFC	89	1145	12.9	3
	O.J. McDuffie, Mia, AFC	90	1050	11.7	7

Some Welcome Coachspeak

In the summer of 1995, when Marv Levy, then the Buffalo Bills's coach, learned he had prostate cancer, his mind raced through the standard checklist of the cancer sufferer—rage, denial, despair—before he remembered Len Dawson. Levy knew Dawson, a Hall of Fame quarterback for the Chiefs and a prostate survivor, from Levy's coaching days in Kansas City. He telephoned Dawson, and they spoke at length about a cancer that will afflict one in five American men their lifetimes. Ten days later Dawson called back to share some further thoughts. "The talks were tremendously helpful to me," said Levy, who had his prostate removed in October 1995. "I was fortunate enough to get through the surgery and, remembering how meaningful the support ... had been, I wanted to try to do something positive."

Levy, who retired from coaching after the '97 season, has become a one-man support group, spending hours each week in his Bills office, phoning or writing letters to other men with prostate cancer. There is nothing formal about his work—it is simply heartfelt. Prostate cancer and its treatment can affect sexual and urinary functions, so it's sometimes a difficult subject to broach. "Often I get a call from someone asking me to speak to his father, who is too embarrassed to call me himself," said the 73-year-old Levy, who splits time between Buffalo and his hometown of Chicago. "I'm happy to make those calls."

"Marv was unbelievable with me," said Ian MacDonald, whose prostate cancer was diagnosed in September 1997. MacDonald, a sportswriter for *The Gazette* in Montreal, met Levy in the '70s when Levy coached the Alouettes of the Canadian Football League. "I called him up," said MacDonald. "I said, 'Listen, I don't want to bother you....' I mean, it was the middle of the season. He had enough bloody things to do. But we spoke once a week. If I didn't call him, he would call me."

Levy's doctors say he is healthy and shows no signs that the cancer has returned. He has a checkup every six months and continues to spread the word. He doesn't add anything startling to the national conversation about prostate cancer—men over 50 should have annual screenings; early detection is critical—but sometimes it takes the right messenger to get the message across.

Scoring

Year	Player, Team	TD	FG	PAT	TP
1932	Earl Clark, Portsmouth	6	3	10	55
1933	Ken Strong, NY	6	5	13	64
	Glenn Presnell, Ports	6	6	10	64
1934	Jack Manders, Chi	3	10	31	79
1935	Earl Clark, Det	6	1	16	55
1936	Earl Clark, Det	7	4	19	73
1937	Jack Manders, Chi	5	18	15	69
1938	Clarke Hinkle, GB	7	3	7	58
1939	Andy Farkas, Wash	11	0	2	68
1940	Don Hutson, GB	7	0	15	57
1941	Don Hutson, GB	12	1	20	95
1942	Don Hutson, GB	17	1	33	138
1943	Don Hutson, GB	12	3	36	117
1944	Don Hutson, GB	9	0	31	85
1945	Steve Van Buren, Phil	18	0	2	110
1946	Ted Fritsch, GB	10	9	13	100
1947	Pat Harder, Chicago Cards	7	7	39	102
1948	Pat Harder, Chicago Cards	6	7	53	110
1949	Pat Harder, Chicago Cards	8	3	45	102
	Gene Roberts, NY	17	0	0	102
1950	Doak Walker, Det	11	8	38	128
1951	Elroy Hirsch, LA	17	0	0	102
1952	Gordy Soltau, SF	7	6	34	94
1953	Gordy Soltau, SF	6	10	48	114
1954	Bobby Walston, Phil	11	4	36	114
1955	Doak Walker, Det	7	9	27	96
1956	Bobby Layne, Det	5	12	33	99
1957	Sam Baker, Wash	1	14	29	77
	Lou Groza, Clev	0	15	32	77
1958	Jim Brown, Clev	18	0	0	108
1959	Paul Hornung, GB	7	7	31	94
1960	Paul Hornung, GB, NFL	15	15	41	176
	Gene Mingo, Den, AFL	6	18	33	123
1961	Gino Cappelletti, Bos, AFL	8	17	48	147
	Paul Hornung, GB, NFL	10	15	41	146
1962	Gene Mingo, Den, AFL	4	27	32	137
	Jim Taylor, GB, NFL	19	0	0	114
1963	Gino Cappelletti, Bos, AFL	2	22	35	113
	Don Chandler, NY, NFL	0	18	52	106
1964	Gino Cappelletti, Bos, AFL	7	25	36	155
	Lenny Moore, Balt, NFL	20	0	0	120
1965	Gale Sayers, Chi, NFL	22	0	0	132
	Gino Cappelletti, Bos, AFL	9	17	27	132
1966	Gino Cappelletti, Bos, AFL	6	16	35	119
	Bruce Gossett, LA, NFL	0	28	29	113
1967	Jim Bakken, StL, NFL	0	27	36	117
	George Blanda, Oak, AFL	0	20	56	116
1968	Jim Turner, NY, AFL	0	34	43	145
	Leroy Kelly, Clev, NFL	20	0	0	120
1969	Jim Turner, NY, AFL	0	32	33	129
	Fred Cox, Minn, NFL	0	26	43	121
1970	Fred Cox, Minn, NFC	0	30	35	125
	Jan Stenerud, KC, AFC	0	30	26	116
1971	Garo Yepremian, Mia, AFC	0	28	33	117
	Curt Knight, Wash, NFC	0	29	27	114
1972	Chester Marcol, GB, NFC	0	33	29	128
	Bobby Howfield, NY AFC	0	27	40	121
1973	David Ray, LA, NFC	0	30	40	130
	Roy Gerela, Pitt, AFC	0	29	36	123
1974	Chester Marcol, GB, NFC	0	25	19	94
	Roy Gerela, Pitt, AFC	0	20	33	93
1975	O.J. Simpson, Buff, AFC	23	0	0	138
	Chuck Foreman, Minn, NFC	22	0	0	132
1976	Toni Linhart, Balt, AFC	0	20	49	109
	Mark Moseley, Wash, NFC	0	22	31	97
1977	Errol Mann, Oak, AFC	0	20	39	99
	Walter Payton, Chi, NFC	16	0	0	96
1978	Frank Corral, LA, NFC	0	29	31	118
	Pat Leahy, NY, AFC	0	22	41	107
1979	John Smith, NE, AFC	0	23	46	115
	Mark Moseley, Wash, NFC	0	25	39	114
1980	John Smith, NE, AFC	0	26	51	129
	Ed Murray, Det, NFC	0	27	35	116
1981	Ed Murray, Det, NFC	0	25	46	121
	Rafael Septien, Dall, NFC	0	27	40	121
	Jim Breech, Cin, AFC	0	22	49	115
	Nick Lowery, KC, AFC	0	26	37	115
1982	Marcus Allen, LA, AFC	14	0	0	84
	Wendell Tyler, LA, NFC	13	0	0	78
1983	Mark Moseley, Wash, NFC	0	33	62	161
	Gary Anderson, Pitt, AFC	0	27	38	119
1984	Ray Wersching, SF, NFC	0	25	56	131
	Gary Anderson, Pitt, AFC	0	24	45	117
1985	Kevin Butler, Chi, NFC	0	31	51	144
	Gary Anderson, Pitt, AFC	0	33	40	139
1986	Tony Franklin, NE, AFC	0	32	44	140
	Kevin Butler, Chi, NFC	0	28	36	120
1987	Jerry Rice, SF, NFC	23	0	0	138
	Jim Breech, Cin, AFC	0	24	25	97
1988	Scott Norwood, Buff, AFC	0	32	33	129
	Mike Cofer, SF, NFC	0	27	40	121
1989	Mike Cofer, SF, NFC	0	29	49	136
	David Treadwell, Den, AFC	0	27	39	120
1990	Nick Lowery, KC, AFC	0	34	37	139
	Chip Lohmiller, Wash, NFC	0	30	41	131
1991	Chip Lohmiller, Wash, NFC	0	31	56	149
	Pete Stoyanovich, Mia, AFC	0	31	28	121
1992	Pete Stoyanovich, Mia, AFC	0	30	34	124
	Morten Anderson, NO, NFC	0	29	33	120
	Chip Lohmiller, Wash, NFC	0	30	30	120
1993	Jeff Jaeger, Rai, AFC	0	35	27	132
	Jason Hanson, Det, NFC	0	34	28	130
1994	John Carney, SD, AFC	0	34	33	135
	Fuad Reveiz, Minn, NFC	0	34	30	132
	Emmitt Smith, Dall, NFC	22	0	0	132
1995	Emmitt Smith, Dall, NFC	25	0	0	150
	Norm Johnson, Pitt, AFC	0	34	39	141
1996	John Kasay, Car, NFC	0	37	34	145
	Cary Blanchard, Ind, AFC	0	36	27	135
1997	Richie Cunningham, Dall, NFC	0	34	24	126
	Mike Hollis, Jax, AFC	0	41	31	134
1998	Gary Anderson, Minn, NFC	0	35	59	164
	Steve Christie, Buff, AFC	0	33	41	140

Pro Bowl Alltime Results

Date	Result	Date	Result	Date	Result
1-15-39	NY Giants 13, Pro All-Stars 10	1-13-63	AFL West 21, East 14	1-17-77	AFC 24, NFC 14
1-14-40	Green Bay 16, NFL All-Stars 7	1-13-63	NFL East 30, West 20	1-23-78	NFC 14, AFC 13
12-29-40	Chi Bears 28, NFL All-Stars 14	1-12-64	NFL West 31, East 17	1-29-79	NFC 13, AFC 7
1-4-42	Chi Bears 35, NFL All-Stars 24	1-19-64	AFL West 27, East 24	1-27-80	NFC 37, AFC 27
12-27-42	NFL All-Stars 17, Washington 14	1-10-65	NFL West 34, East 14	2-1-81	NFC 21, AFC 7
1-14-51	A Conf 28, N Conf 27	1-16-65	AFL West 38, East 14	1-31-82	AFC 16, NFC 13
1-12-52	N Conf 30, A Conf 13	1-15-66	AFL All-Stars 30, Buffalo 19	2-6-83	NFC 20, AFC 19
1-10-53	N Conf 27, A Conf 7	1-15-66	NFL East 36, West 7	1-29-84	NFC 45, AFC 3
1-17-54	East 20, West 9	1-21-67	AFL East 30, West 23	1-27-85	AFC 22, NFC 14
1-16-55	West 26, East 19	1-22-67	NFL East 20, West 10	2-2-86	NFC 28, AFC 24
1-15-56	East 31, West 30	1-21-68	AFL East 25, West 24	2-1-87	AFC 10, NFC 6
1-13-57	West 19, East 10	1-21-68	NFL West 38, East 20	2-7-88	AFC 15, NFC 6
1-12-58	West 26, East 7	1-19-69	AFL West 38, East 25	1-29-89	NFC 34, AFC 3
1-11-59	East 28, West 21	1-19-69	NFL West 10, East 7	2-4-90	NFC 27, AFC 21
1-17-60	West 38, East 21	1-17-70	AFL West 26, East 3	2-3-91	AFC 23, NFC 21
1-15-61	West 35, East 31	1-18-70	NFL West 16, East 13	2-2-92	NFC 21, AFC 15
1-7-62	AFL West 47, East 27	1-24-71	NFC 27, AFC 6	2-7-93	AFC 23, NFC 20
1-14-62	NFL West 31, East 30	1-23-72	AFC 26, NFC 13	2-6-94	NFC 17, AFC 3
		1-21-73	AFC 33, NFC 28	2-5-95	AFC 41, NFC 13
		1-20-74	AFC 15, NFC 13	2-4-96	NFC 20, AFC 13
		1-20-75	NFC 17, AFC 10	2-2-97	AFC 26, NFC 23
		1-26-76	NFC 23, AFC 20	2-1-98	AFC 29, NFC 24
				2-7-99	AFC 23, NFC 10

Chicago All-Star Game Results

Date	Result (Attendance)	Date	Result (Attendance)
8-31-34	Chi Bears 0, All-Stars 0 (79,432)	8-10-56	Cleveland 26, All-Stars 0 (75,000)
8-29-35	Chi Bears 5, All-Stars 0 (77,450)	8-9-57	NY Giants 22, All-Stars 12 (75,000)
9-3-36	All-Stars 7, Detroit 7 (76,000)	8-15-58	All-Stars 35, Detroit 19 (70,000)
9-1-37	All-Stars 6, Green Bay 0 (84,560)	8-14-59	Baltimore 29, All-Stars 0 (70,000)
8-31-38	All-Stars 28, Washington 16 (74,250)	8-12-60	Baltimore 32, All-Stars 7 (70,000)
8-30-39	NY Giants 9, All-Stars 0 (81,456)	8-4-61	Philadelphia 28, All-Stars 14 (66,000)
8-29-40	Green Bay 45, All-Stars 28 (84,567)	8-3-62	Green Bay 42, All-Stars 20 (65,000)
8-28-41	Chi Bears 37, All-Stars 13 (98,203)	8-2-63	All-Stars 20, Green Bay 17 (65,000)
8-28-42	Chi Bears 21, All-Stars 0 (101,100)	8-7-64	Chicago 28, All-Stars 17 (65,000)
8-25-43	All-Stars 27, Washington 7 (48,471)	8-6-65	Cleveland 24, All-Stars 16 (68,000)
8-30-44	Chi Bears 24, All-Stars 21 (48,769)	8-5-66	Green Bay 38, All-Stars 0 (72,000)
8-30-45	Green Bay 19, All-Stars 7 (92,753)	8-4-67	Green Bay 27, All-Stars 0 (70,934)
8-23-46	All-Stars 16, Los Angeles 0 (97,380)	8-2-68	Green Bay 34, All-Stars 17 (69,917)
8-22-47	All-Stars 16, Chi Bears 0 (105,840)	8-1-69	NY Jets 26, All-Stars 24 (74,208)
8-20-48	Chi Cardinals 28, All-Stars 0 (101,220)	7-31-70	Kansas City 24, All-Stars 3 (69,940)
8-12-49	Philadelphia 38, All-Stars 0 (93,780)	7-30-71	Baltimore 24, All-Stars 17 (52,289)
8-11-50	All-Stars 17, Philadelphia 7 (88,885)	7-28-72	Dallas 20, All-Stars 7 (54,162)
8-17-51	Cleveland 33, All-Stars 0 (92,180)	7-27-73	Miami 14, All-Stars 3 (54,103)
8-15-52	Los Angeles 10, All-Stars 7 (88,316)	1974	No game
8-14-53	Detroit 24, All-Stars 10 (93,818)	8-1-75	Pittsburgh 21, All-Stars 14 (54,103)
8-13-54	Detroit 31, All-Stars 6 (93,470)	7-23-76	Pittsburgh 24, All-Stars 0 (52,895)
8-12-55	All-Stars 30, Cleveland 27 (75,000)		

Those Hoarsey Broncos

In advance of his team's 1998 game with bitter rival Kansas City, ever loquacious Denver tight end Shannon Sharpe refused to talk to the media. That, plus coach Mike Shanahan's dislike of the league's injury-reporting system, led the Broncos to add the following to last week's injury report: "TE Shannon Sharpe (laryngitis) probable."

Alltime Winningest NFL Coaches

Most Career Wins

Coach	Yrs	Teams	Regular Season				Career			
			W	L	T	Pct	W	L	T	Pct
Don Shula 33		Colts, Dolphins	328	156	6	.676	347	173	6	.665
George Halas..........40		Bears	318	148	31	.671	324	151	31	.671
Tom Landry 29		Cowboys	250	162	6	.605	270	178	6	.601
Curly Lambeau 33		Packers, Cardinals, Redskins	226	132	22	.624	229	134	22	.623
Chuck Noll 23		Steelers	193	148	1	.566	209	156	1	.572
Chuck Knox 22		Rams, Bills, Seahawks	186	147	1	.558	193	158	1	.550
†Dan Reeves 18		Broncos, Giants, Falcons	162	117	1	.580	172	125	1	.579
Paul Brown.............21		Browns, Bengals	166	100	6	.621	170	108	6	.609
Bud Grant 18		Vikings	158	96	5	.620	168	108	5	.607
Marv Levy 17		Chiefs, Bills	143	112	0	.561	154	120	0	.562
Steve Owen............23		Giants	151	100	17	.595	153	108	17	.581
†M. Schottenheimer...15		Browns, Chiefs	145	85	1	.630	150	96	1	.607
†Bill Parcells 14		Giants, Patriots, Jets	130	92	1	.583	141	98	1	.590
Joe Gibbs 12		Redskins	124	60	0	.674	140	65	0	.683
Hank Stram 17		Chiefs, Saints	131	97	10	.571	136	100	10	.573
Weeb Ewbank........20		Colts, Jets	130	129	7	.502	134	130	7	.507
†Mike Ditka 13		Bears, Saints	118	82	0	.590	124	88	0	.585
Sid Gillman............18		Rams, Chargers, Oilers	122	99	7	.550	123	104	7	.541
George Allen...........12		Rams, Redskins	116	47	5	.705	118	54	5	.681
Don Coryell 14		Cardinals, Chargers	111	83	1	.572	114	89	1	.561
†Active coach.										

Top Winning Percentages

	W	L	T	Pct		W	L	T	Pct
George Seifert................108	108	35	0	.755	George Halas.................324	324	151	31	.671
Vince Lombardi..............105	105	35	6	.740	Don Shula.......................347	347	173	6	.665
John Madden 112	112	39	7	.731	Curly Lambeau................229	229	134	22	.623
Joe Gibbs 140	140	65	0	.683	Bill Walsh.......................102	102	63	1	.617
George Allen 118	118	54	5	.681	Paul Brown 170	170	108	6	.609

Note: Minimum 100 victories.

Alltime Number-One Draft Choices

Year	Team	Selection	Position
1936 ....Philadelphia		Jay Berwanger, Chicago	HB
1937 ....Philadelphia		Sam Francis, Nebraska	FB
1938 ....Cleveland		Corbett Davis, Indiana	FB
1939 ....Chicago Cardinals		Ki Aldrich, Texas Christian	C
1940 ....Chicago Cardinals		George Cafego, Tennessee	HB
1941 ....Chicago Bears		Tom Harmon, Michigan	HB
1942 ....Pittsburgh		Bill Dudley, Virginia	HB
1943 ....Detroit		Frank Sinkwich, Georgia	HB
1944 ....Boston		Angelo Bertelli, Notre Dame	QB
1945 ....Chicago Cardinals		Charley Trippi, Georgia	HB
1946 ....Boston		Frank Dancewicz, Notre Dame	QB
1947 ....Chicago Bears		Bob Fenimore, Oklahoma A&M	HB
1948 ....Washington		Harry Gilmer, Alabama	QB
1949 ....Philadelphia		Chuck Bednarik, Pennsylvania	C
1950 ....Detroit		Leon Hart, Notre Dame	E
1951 ....New York Giants		Kyle Rote, Southern Methodist	HB
1952 ....Los Angeles		Bill Wade, Vanderbilt	QB
1953 ....San Francisco		Harry Babcock, Georgia	E
1954 ....Cleveland		Bobby Garrett, Stanford	QB
1955 ....Baltimore		George Shaw, Oregon	QB
1956 ....Pittsburgh		Gary Glick, Colorado A&M	DB
1957 ....Green Bay		Paul Hornung, Notre Dame	HB
1958 ....Chicago Cardinals		King Hill, Rice	QB

Alltime Number-One Draft Choices (Cont.)

Year	Team	Selection	Position
1959	Green Bay	Randy Duncan, Iowa	QB
1960	Los Angeles	Billy Cannon, Louisiana State	RB
1961	Minnesota	Tommy Mason, Tulane	RB
	Buffalo (AFL)	Ken Rice, Auburn	G
1968	Minnesota	Ron Yary, Southern California	T
1969	Buffalo (AFL)	O.J. Simpson, Southern California	RB
1970	Pittsburgh	Terry Bradshaw, Louisiana Tech	QB
1971	New England	Jim Plunkett, Stanford	QB
1972	Buffalo	Walt Patulski, Notre Dame	DE
1973	Houston	John Matuszak, Tampa	DE
1974	Dallas	Ed Jones, Tennessee State	DE
1975	Atlanta	Steve Bartkowski, California	QB
1976	Tampa Bay	Lee Roy Selmon, Oklahoma	DE
1977	Tampa Bay	Ricky Bell, Southern California	RB
1978	Houston	Earl Campbell, Texas	RB
1979	Buffalo	Tom Cousineau, Ohio State	LB
1980	Detroit	Billy Sims, Oklahoma	RB
1981	New Orleans	George Rogers, South Carolina	RB
1982	New England	Kenneth Sims, Texas	DT
1983	Baltimore	John Elway, Stanford	QB
1984	New England	Irving Fryar, Nebraska	WR
1985	Buffalo	Bruce Smith, Virginia Tech	DE
1986	Tampa Bay	Bo Jackson, Auburn	RB
1987	Tampa Bay	Vinny Testaverde, Miami (FL)	QB
1988	Atlanta	Aundray Bruce, Auburn	LB
1989	Dallas	Troy Aikman, UCLA	QB
1990	Indianapolis	Jeff George, Illinois	QB
1991	Dallas	Russell Maryland, Miami (FL)	DT
1992	Indianapolis	Steve Emtman, Washington	DT
1993	New England	Drew Bledsoe, Washington State	QB
1994	Cincinnati	Dan Wilkinson, Ohio State	DT
1995	Cincinnati	Ki-Jana Carter, Penn State	RB
1996	New York Jets	Keyshawn Johnson, Southern California	WR
1997	St Louis	Orlando Pace, Ohio State	OT
1998	Indianapolis	Peyton Manning, Tennessee	QB
1999	Cleveland	Tim Couch, Kentucky	QB

From 1947 through 1958, the first selection in the draft was a bonus pick, awarded to the winner of a random draw. That club, in turn, forfeited its last-round draft choice. The winner of the bonus choice was eliminated from future draws. The system was abolished after 1958, by which time all clubs had received a bonus choice.

Members of the Pro Football Hall of Fame

Herb Adderley
Lance Alworth
Doug Atkins
Morris (Red) Badgro
Lem Barney
Cliff Battles
Sammy Baugh
Chuck Bednarik
Bert Bell
Bobby Bell
Raymond Berry
Charles W. Bidwill, Sr.
Fred Biletnikoff
George Blanda
Mel Blount
Terry Bradshaw
Jim Brown
Paul Brown
Roosevelt Brown
Willie Brown
Buck Buchanan
Dick Butkus
Earl Campbell
Tony Canadeo

Joe Carr
Guy Chamberlin
Jack Christiansen
Earl (Dutch) Clark
George Connor
Jimmy Conzelman
Lou Creekmur
Larry Csonka
Al Davis
Willie Davis
Len Dawson
Eric Dickerson
Dan Dierdorf
Mike Ditka
Art Donovan
Tony Dorsett
John (Paddy) Driscoll
Bill Dudley
Albert Glen (Turk) Edwards
Weeb Ewbank
Tom Fears
Jim Finks
Ray Flaherty
Len Ford

Dan Fortmann
Dan Fouts
Frank Gatski
Bill George
Joe Gibbs
Frank Gifford
Sid Gillman
Otto Graham
Harold (Red) Grange
Bud Grant
Joe Greene
Forrest Gregg
Bob Griese
Lou Groza
Joe Guyon
George Halas
Jack Ham
John Hannah
Franco Harris
Mike Haynes
Ed Healey
Mel Hein
Ted Hendricks
Wilbur (Pete) Henry

Arnie Herber
Bill Hewitt
Clarke Hinkle
Elroy (Crazylegs) Hirsch
Paul Hornung
Ken Houston
Cal Hubbard
Sam Huff
Lamar Hunt
Don Hutson
Jimmy Johnson
John Henry Johnson
Charlie Joiner
David (Deacon) Jones
Stan Jones
Henry Jordan
Sonny Jurgensen
Leroy Kelly
Walt Kiesling
Frank (Bruiser) Kinard
Paul Krause
Earl (Curly) Lambeau
Jack Lambert
Tom Landry
Dick (Night Train) Lane
Jim Langer
Willie Lanier
Steve Largent
Yale Lary
Dante Lavelli
Bobby Layne
Alphonse (Tuffy) Leemans
Bob Lilly
Larry Little
Vince Lombardi
Sid Luckman
William Roy (Link) Lyman
Tom Mack
John Mackey
Tim Mara
Wellington Mara
Gino Marchetti
George Preston Marshall

Ollie Matson
Don Maynard
George McAfee
Mike McCormack
Tommy McDonald
Hugh McElhenny
Johnny (Blood) McNally
Mike Michalske
Wayne Millner
Bobby Mitchell
Ron Mix
Lenny Moore
Marion Motley
Anthony Munoz
George Musso
Bronko Nagurski
Joe Namath
Earle (Greasy) Neale
Ernie Nevers
Ozzie Newsome
Ray Nitschke
Chuck Noll
Leo Nomellini
Merlin Olsen
Jim Otto
Steve Owen
Alan Page
Clarence (Ace) Parker
Jim Parker
Walter Payton
Joe Perry
Pete Pihos
Hugh (Shorty) Ray
Dan Reeves
Mel Renfro
John Riggins
Jim Ringo
Andy Robustelli
Art Rooney
Pete Rozelle
Bob St. Clair
Gale Sayers
Joe Schmidt

Tex Schramm
Lee Roy Selmon
Billy Shaw
Art Shell
Don Shula
O.J. Simpson
Mike Singletary
Jackie Smith
Bart Starr
Roger Staubach
Ernie Stautner
Jan Stenerud
Dwight Stephenson
Ken Strong
Joe Stydahar
Fran Tarkenton
Charley Taylor
Jim Taylor
Lawrence Taylor
Jim Thorpe
Y.A. Tittle
George Trafton
Charley Trippi
Emlen Tunnell
Clyde (Bulldog) Turner
Johnny Unitas
Gene Upshaw
Norm Van Brocklin
Steve Van Buren
Doak Walker
Bill Walsh
Paul Warfield
Bob Waterfield
Mike Webster
Arnie Weinmeister
Randy White
Bill Willis
Larry Wilson
Kellen Winslow
Alex Wojciechowicz
Willie Wood

Canadian Football League Grey Cup

Year	Results	Site	Attendance
1909	U of Toronto 26, Parkdale 6	Toronto	3,807
1910	U of Toronto 16, Hamilton Tigers 7	Hamilton	12,000
1911	U of Toronto 14, Toronto 7	Toronto	13,687
1912	Hamilton Alerts 11, Toronto 4	Hamilton	5,337
1913	Hamilton Tigers 44, Parkdale 2	Hamilton	2,100
1914	Toronto 14, U of Toronto 2	Toronto	10,500
1915	Hamilton Tigers 13, Toronto RAA 7	Toronto	2,808
1916-19	No game		
1920	U of Toronto 16, Toronto 3	Toronto	10,088
1921	Toronto 23, Edmonton 0	Toronto	9,558
1922	Queen's U 13, Edmonton 1	Kingston	4,700
1923	Queen's U 54, Regina 0	Toronto	8,629
1924	Queen's U 11, Balmy Beach 3	Toronto	5,978
1925	Ottawa Senators 24, Winnipeg 1	Ottawa	6,900
1926	Ottawa Senators 10, Toronto U 7	Toronto	8,276
1927	Balmy Beach 9, Hamilton Tigers 6	Toronto	13,676
1928	Hamilton Tigers 30, Regina 0	Hamilton	4,767
1929	Hamilton Tigers 14, Regina 3	Hamilton	1,906
1930	Balmy Beach 11, Regina 6	Toronto	3,914
1931	Montreal AAA 22, Regina 0	Montreal	5,112
1932	Hamilton Tigers 25, Regina 6	Hamilton	4,806
1933	Toronto 4, Sarnia 3	Sarnia	2,751
1934	Sarnia 20, Regina 12	Toronto	8,900
1935	Winnipeg 18, Hamilton Tigers 12	Hamilton	6,405
1936	Sarnia 26, Ottawa RR 20	Toronto	5,883
1937	Toronto 4, Winnipeg 3	Toronto	11,522
1938	Toronto 30, Winnipeg 7	Toronto	18,778
1939	Winnipeg 8, Ottawa 7	Ottawa	11,738
1940	Ottawa 12, Balmy Beach 5	Ottawa	1,700
1940	Ottawa 8, Balmy Beach 2	Toronto	4,998
1941	Winnipeg 18, Ottawa 16	Toronto	19,065
1942	Toronto RCAF 8, Winnipeg RCAF 5	Toronto	12,455
1943	Hamilton F Wild 23, Winnipeg RCAF 14	Toronto	16,423
1944	Montreal St H-D Navy 7, Hamilton F Wild 6	Hamilton	3,871
1945	Toronto 35, Winnipeg 0	Toronto	18,660
1946	Toronto 28, Winnipeg 6	Toronto	18,960
1947	Toronto 10, Winnipeg 9	Toronto	18,885
1948	Calgary 12, Ottawa 7	Toronto	20,013
1949	Montreal Als 28, Calgary 15	Toronto	20,087
1950	Toronto 13, Winnipeg 0	Toronto	27,101
1951	Ottawa 21, Saskatchewan 14	Toronto	27,341
1952	Toronto 21, Edmonton 11	Toronto	27,391
1953	Hamilton Ticats 12, Winnipeg 6	Toronto	27,313
1954	Edmonton 26, Montreal 25	Toronto	27,321
1955	Edmonton 34, Montreal 19	Vancouver	39,417
1956	Edmonton 50, Montreal 27	Toronto	27,425
1957	Hamilton 32, Winnipeg 7	Toronto	27,051
1958	Winnipeg 35, Hamilton 28	Vancouver	36,567
1959	Winnipeg 21, Hamilton 7	Toronto	33,133
1960	Ottawa 16, Edmonton 6	Vancouver	38,102
1961	Winnipeg 21, Hamilton 14	Toronto	32,651
1962	Winnipeg 28, Hamilton 27	Toronto	32,655
1963	Hamilton 21, British Columbia 10	Vancouver	36,545
1964	British Columbia 34, Hamilton 24	Toronto	32,655
1965	Hamilton 22, Winnipeg 16	Toronto	32,655
1966	Saskatchewan 29, Ottawa 14	Vancouver	36,553
1967	Hamilton 24, Saskatchewan 1	Ottawa	31,358
1968	Ottawa 24, Calgary 21	Toronto	32,655
1969	Ottawa 29, Saskatchewan 11	Montreal	33,172
1970	Montreal 23, Calgary 10	Toronto	32,669
1971	Calgary 14, Toronto 11	Vancouver	34,484
1972	Hamilton 13, Saskatchewan 10	Hamilton	33,993
1973	Ottawa 22, Edmonton 18	Toronto	36,653
1974	Montreal 20, Edmonton 7	Vancouver	34,450
1975	Edmonton 9, Montreal 8	Calgary	32,454

Canadian Football League Grey Cup *(Cont.)*

Year	Results	Site	Attendance
1976	Ottawa 23, Saskatchewan 20	Toronto	53,467
1977	Montreal 41, Edmonton 6	Montreal	68,318
1978	Edmonton 20, Montreal 13	Toronto	54,695
1979	Edmonton 17, Montreal 9	Montreal	65,113
1980	Edmonton 48, Hamilton 10	Toronto	54,661
1981	Edmonton 26, Ottawa 23	Montreal	52,478
1982	Edmonton 32, Toronto 16	Toronto	54,741
1983	Toronto 18, British Columbia 17	Vancouver	59,345
1984	Winnipeg 47, Hamilton 17	Edmonton	60,081
1985	British Columbia 37, Hamilton 24	Montreal	56,723
1986	Hamilton 39, Edmonton 15	Vancouver	59,621
1987	Edmonton 38, Toronto 36	Vancouver	59,478
1988	Winnipeg 22, British Columbia 21	Ottawa	50,604
1989	Saskatchewan 43, Hamilton 40	Toronto	54,088
1990	Winnipeg 50, Edmonton 11	Vancouver	46,968
1991	Toronto 36, Calgary 21	Winnipeg	51,985
1992	Calgary 24, Winnipeg 10	Toronto	45,863
1993	Edmonton 33, Winnipeg 23	Calgary	50,035
1994	British Columbia 26, Baltimore 23	Vancouver	55,097
1995	Baltimore 37, Calgary 20	Regina, Saskatchewan	52,564
1996	Toronto 43, Edmonton 37	Hamilton, Ontario	38,595
1997	Toronto 47, Saskatchewan 23	Edmonton	60,431
1998	Calgary 26, Hamilton 24	Winnipeg	34,157

In 1909, Earl Grey, the Governor-General of Canada, donated a trophy for the Rugby Football Championship of Canada. The trophy, which subsequently became known as the Grey Cup, was originally open only to teams registered with the Canada Rugby Union. Since 1954, it has been awarded to the winner of the Canadian Football League's championship game.

AMERICAN FOOTBALL LEAGUE I

Year	Champion	Record
1926	Philadelphia Quakers	7-2

AMERICAN FOOTBALL LEAGUE II

Year	Champion	Record
1936	Boston Shamrocks	8-3
1937	LA Bulldogs	8-0

AMERICAN FOOTBALL LEAGUE III

Year	Champion	Record
1940	Columbus Bullies	8-1-1
1941	Columbus Bullies	5-1-2

ALL-AMERICAN FOOTBALL CONFERENCE

Year	Championship Game
1946	Cleveland 14, NY Yankees 9
1947	Cleveland 14, NY Yankees 3
1948	Cleveland 49, Buffalo 7
1949	Cleveland 21, San Francisco 7

WORLD FOOTBALL LEAGUE

Year	World Bowl Championship
1974	Birmingham 22, Florida 21
1975	Disbanded midseason

UNITED STATES FOOTBALL LEAGUE

Year	Championship Game
1983	Michigan 24, Philadelphia 22, at Denver
1984	Philadelphia 23, Arizona 3, at Tampa
1985	Baltimore 28, Oakland 24, at East Rutherford

NFL EUROPE

Year	Champion	Record
1992	Sacramento	8-2-0
1995	Frankfurt	6-4-0
1996	Scotland	7-3-0
1997	Barcelona	5-5-0
1998	Rhein	7-3-0
1999	Frankfurt	6-4-0

Known as World League of American Football until 1998.

College Football

Heisman Trophy winner Ricky Williams of Texas

Lucky Thirteen

With talent, team chemistry and more than a little good fortune, Tennessee won the national title and a school-record 13 games

BY DAVID FLEMING

IT WAS ONE of those moments in sports where time seemed to stand still. With less than two minutes to play and the No. 1–ranked Tennessee Volunteers trailing Arkansas 24–22, the 106,365 rain-soaked fans inside Neyland Stadium stood together in stunned silence. Razorbacks quarterback Clint Stoerner leaned over center and prepared to run the clock out on the game and on the Vols' chance at a national title. Stoerner took the snap cleanly, but as he rolled out on a naked bootleg he stumbled, and when he reached down to the turf to try to regain his balance, somehow he left the ball behind. Then, for a split second, before anyone realized what had happened, the ball sat there all alone on the muddy grass near the 43-yard line— placed perfectly with its strings up as if delivered from above.

At once the vacuum seal around the stadium seemed to lift. The crowd roared, defensive tackle Billy Ratliff pounced on the ball. Five plays later the Vols scored to win the game 28–24 and remain unbeaten.

Afterward junior quarterback Tee Martin stood on the field and pointed to the heavens with his finger, as if to say thanks. "I wouldn't call it a miracle," said a stern Phil Fulmer, the Vols' coach. "How about dramatic?"

To win a school-record 13 games in 1998–99, a second straight SEC title and Tennessee's first national championship in 47 years, the resilient and unselfish Vols blended leaders with overachievers. "This year's team had a bunch of guys all pulling together with great chemistry," said former Vols quarterback Peyton Manning, who was the No. 1 pick, by Indianapolis, in the 1998 NFL draft. "We had good teams and good guys, but I'm not sure that we ever had chemistry like this team has. They deserve this."

Indeed they did, but en route to their miraculous season, the Vols were also blessed with splendid fortune. Some teams are touched by destiny. This one was led by the hand. "They've had so many breaks," said Kentucky coach Hal Mumme before his team was pounded 59–21 by Tennessee. "It's

PETER READ MILLER

like Tennessee is touched by Divine Providence or something."

Perhaps God isn't a Notre Dame fan after all. At least he didn't appear to be in 1998. No, in '98 the big guy upstairs was dressed in orange and pulling hard for Tennessee. In a season-opening 34–33 win at Syracuse, the Vols' game-winning drive was kept alive by a dubious fourth-down pass interference call. Two weeks later the Vols narrowly escaped losing to Florida for the sixth time in a row with a 20–17 overtime win. The Gators passed for more than 400 yards but fumbled the ball four times. In the overtime Tennessee kicker Jeff Hall nailed a 41-yard field goal on the first possession and then watched as Florida's Collins Cooper sent the Gators' 32-yard get-even attempt wide left. Fans stormed the field and yanked down the goalposts to celebrate the Vols' finally getting the Gator off their collective back.

Then came the Arkansas game. "Destiny, luck, something," said Tennessee linebacker Raynoch Thompson, describing his team's knack for landing on its feet in '98. Still, nobody in college football wins a national title without a lot of talent to go with its luck. Despite losing 11 players to the NFL and adopting a No Stars theme in 1998—they broke huddles in practice by bellowing "One, two, three … underdogs!"—the Vols had plenty of talent. So much that deep into the '98 season the No Stars theme seemed a bit inappropriate. When running back Jamal Lewis went down against Auburn with an injured right knee, sophomores Travis Henry and Travis Stephens shared the load and helped the Vols average an SEC-best 211.3 yards per game rushing. Martin overcame a shaky start (a combined 16 for 46 against Syracuse and Florida) to etch a place of his own in the NCAA and Tennessee record books

alongside Manning. In a win over South Carolina, Martin completed 23 straight passes against the not-so-Gamecocks and finished with a 95.8 completion percentage—both NCAA records.

On the receiving end of most of Martin's passes was the team's biggest nonstar star, the sinewy senior wideout Peerless Price. Trailing Mississippi State 14–10 in the fourth quarter of the SEC championship game, Price caught a 41-yard touchdown pass that brought the Vols back from the brink for the fourth time in 12 games. He finished the season with 920 yards receiving, 10 touchdowns and 61 catches, an amazing 45 (74%) of them for first downs. "Peerless was always a

Unkind Sirr: Parker dashed Kansas State's title hopes in the Big 12 championship game.

really good receiver," said Fulmer. "But this year he's made more big plays than anyone we've had here in some time." At a place nicknamed Wide Receiver U, that's saying something.

The Vols added a decisive ingredient to their mix of talent in '98: a never-say-die leader in All-America middle linebacker Al Wilson. "For the last few years we've been relying on a few people to win games for us," said Wilson. "It was time for us to become a team." A ferocious tackler, Wilson took ownership of the team last season, during halftime of the 1997 SEC championship game. With the Vols trailing Auburn 20–10, Wilson went on an impassioned rampage, challenging everyone from the coaches to the team's stars. By the end of his speech there were tears streaming down his cheeks. "I'll remember that forever," said Price. "Someday I'll tell my kids about how he was crying." An inspired Tennessee team came back to win 30–29. And although Wilson would struggle with injuries in 1998, the Vols had found their post-Peyton leader and, more importantly, the emotional catalyst who would carry them to the pinnacle of college football.

The Vols' journey to the top concluded with a 23–16 victory over Florida State in the Fiesta Bowl, which gave them a 13–0 record and an undisputed claim to the national title. Price, who was named MVP of the game, was peerless once again. He caught four passes for 199 yards and one touchdown against a Florida State defense ranked No. 1 in the country and nicknamed the D-molition Crew. With nine minutes to play in the sloppy penalty- and turnover-marred game, Price and Martin hooked up on a pretty, 79-yard rainbow to ice Tennessee's win. (The Vols' defense, for its part, held Price's rival, Florida State's All-America wideout Peter Warrick, to one catch for seven yards.) "So many times we needed to make something special happen, and we always did," said Wilson after the game, his eyes filled with tears of joy this time. "Always." Maybe Martin put it best when he said, simply, "It's our turn, that's all."

That the Vols would win the national title by surviving a rather topsy-turvy game, and season, only seemed fitting in a college football season filled with more twists and turns than a basket of curly fries. For starters, the arcane formulas behind the (yet again) revised Bowl Championship Series (BCS) rankings set an appropriately baffled tone for the season. And teams behaved accordingly. Co–defending national champion Michigan started 0–2, and their partners in glory, Nebraska, lost an unheard of four games; Temple, 0–26 alltime in Big East road games and a 35½-point underdog against Virginia Tech, beat the Hokies 28–24; Prairie View A&M snapped its NCAA-record 80-game losing streak; and N.C. State, led by its opportunistic defense, pulled off a monumental upset by beating Florida State 24–7 on Sept. 12.

Seminoles coach Bobby Bowden called the loss one of the most disappointing of his career, and it began a rather trying spell for his family. In October his son Terry resigned under booster pressure as the head coach at Auburn. Bobby's second son, Tommy, led Tulane to an 11–0 record and then announced, before the Green Wave's season had concluded, that he had accepted the head coaching job at Clemson.

While Tommy assembled his staff at Clemson, the Bowden patriarch sat at home on Dec. 5 and watched two crucial games on television while downing handfuls of Chips Ahoy cookies dipped in peanut butter. To Bowden's utter amazement, UCLA and Kansas State, both previously unbeaten, lost, catapulting FSU to the No. 2 ranking and a trip to Tempe, Ariz.

That stunning day marked the second time UCLA had been beaten by a Hurricane. The Bruins had been scheduled to play Miami in September, but Hurricane Georges intruded. To assuage the BCS mathematicians, the game was rescheduled rather than canceled, and thus on Dec. 5 UCLA fell from the ranks of the undefeated. Actually they plummeted, giving up 689 yards (299 of them to tailback Edgerrin James) in a 49–45 loss to Miami.

Midway through the second quarter of the day's other significant tilt, the Big 12 championship game in St. Louis, second-ranked Kansas State led Texas A&M 17–3. The public address announcer relayed the UCLA score, and Wildcats fans erupted, envisioning a berth in the national title game for K-State. But the celebration didn't last long. In the waning moments of the game a shell-shocked Kansas State had its dream crushed by a gimpy running back. Aggie senior Sirr Parker, who had been ineffective most of the season while nursing a bad hamstring, tied the game with 65 seconds to play on a nine-yard touchdown catch and a two-point conversion. Parker then gave the Aggies a 36–33 victory in the second overtime when he turned a quick slant into a 32-yard score.

Understandably, by the time Florida State athletic director Dave Hart visited Bowden at home that night, the 69-year-old coach, who has won 10 or more games in each of the last 12 seasons, was so giddy all he could say was, "I can't hardly believe it."

That was a phrase folks in college football repeated often in 1998. How else would one respond to the departure of Iowa coaching legend Hayden Fry, who stepped down after 20 years with the Hawkeyes, or the return of Lou Holtz, hired by lowly South Carolina after two years away from the game? Or the record-setting 65-yard field goal by Kansas State's Martin Gramatica on Sept. 12; or Louisiana Tech's Troy Edwards torching Nebraska for an NCAA-record 405 receiving yards; or Division III Linfield College's

BOB ROSATO

from Michigan to 2-9-1. "It's hard to win all of your games," said Cooper. "I know that as well as anyone."

The only other part of the game to follow a discernible pattern was the consistently brilliant play of Heisman Trophy winner Ricky Williams. The senior running back from Texas ran his career rushing yard total to 6,279 to break Tony Dorsett's 22-year-old NCAA Division I-A record. Like Price's poise or Kentucky quarterback Tim Couch's arm, Williams's raw, explosive power was truly something to behold. "The best, by far," said Oklahoma defensive coordinator Rex Ryan. "You hold your breath when [Williams] has the football; you're scared to death."

After Williams plowed over Nebraska for 150 yards in Texas's 20–16 upset, ending the Cornhuskers' 47-game home field winning streak, fans in Lincoln chanted his name as a tribute. Nebraska defensive coordinator Charlie McBride shook his head and said, "That guy is something special. The two best backs we've ever played against are Barry Sanders and Ricky Williams." The latter finished his career with 20 Division I-A records, including career touchdowns (75) and all-purpose yards (7,206).

We specify the division because, technically, after last year Emporia State's Brian Shay is the most prolific collegiate runner of all time. While playing Division II ball in Kansas, Shay, a 5'9", 220-pound back, set records for all divisions with 9,301 all-purpose yards, 6,958 yards rushing and 88 touchdowns. "If you have heart and determination," said Shay, "anything is possible."

Never was that statement more true than in college football's unpredictable 1998 season.

record-breaking 43rd consecutive winning season. Whoa, Nellie! Even longtime announcer Keith Jackson weirded out in '98, flip-flopping on plans to retire after 32 years in the ABC booth.

There was also Notre Dame's revival, Northwestern's regression and Wisconsin's Rose Bowl renascence. (The Badgers downed UCLA 38–31 in Pasadena.) Perhaps the only predictable thing that happened in '98 was Ohio State's seemingly annual fall from grace. This year it was a 28–24 loss to 28-point underdog Michigan State that undid the Buckeyes. The loss marked the fifth time in the last six years that a team from Michigan spoiled the Buckeyes' shot at a national title, and it dropped coach John Cooper's record in November against teams

Final Polls

Associated Press

#		Record	Pts	Head Coach	SI Preseason Rank
1.	Tennessee (70)	13–0	1750	Phillip Fulmer	9
2.	Ohio St	11–1	1673	John Cooper	1
3.	Florida St	11–2	1574	Bobby Bowden	2
4.	Arizona	12–1	1535	Dick Tomey	—
5.	Florida	10–2	1463	Steve Spurrier	4
6.	Wisconsin	11–1	1427	Barry Alvarez	—
7.	Tulane	12–0	1252	Tommy Bowden	—
8.	UCLA	10–2	1123	Bob Toledo	6
9.	Georgia Tech	10–2	1122	George O'Leary	—
10.	Kansas St	11–2	1086	Bill Snyder	3
11.	Texas A&M*	11–3	1071	R. C. Slocum	21
12.	Michigan	10–3	1052	Lloyd Carr	8
13.	Air Force	12–1	980	Fisher DeBerry	—
14.	Georgia	9–3	785	Jim Donnan	20
15.	Texas	9–3	740	Mack Brown	—
16.	Arkansas	9–3	621	Houston Nutt	—
17.	Penn St	9–3	619	Joe Paterno	14
18.	Virginia	9–3	544	George Welsh	—
19.	Nebraska	9–4	454	Frank Solich	5
20.	Miami (FL)	9–3	426	Butch Davis	19
21.	Missouri	8–4	335	Larry Smith	16
22.	Notre Dame	9–3	315	Bob Davie	25
23.	Virginia Tech	9–3	256	Frank Beamer	—
24.	Purdue	9–4	236	Joe Tiller	—
25.	Syracuse	8–4	161	Paul Pasqualoni	11

*Forfeited 28–7 win against Louisiana Tech for using an ineligible player

Note: As voted by a panel of 70 sportswriters and broadcasters following bowl games (1st-place votes in parentheses).

USA Today/ESPN

#		Pts	Prev Rank	#		Pts	Prev Rank
1.	Tennessee (62)	1550	1	14.	Georgia	677	19
2.	Ohio St	1473	3	15.	Penn St	640	20
3.	Florida St	1376	2	16.	Texas	577	22
4.	Arizona	1347	6	17.	Arkansas	566	11
5.	Wisconsin	1289	8	18.	Virginia	485	12
6.	Florida	1282	7	19.	Virginia Tech	471	24
7.	Tulane	1117	10	20.	Nebraska	321	16
8.	UCLA	998	5	21.	Miami (FL)	291	—
9.	Kansas St	991	4	22.	Notre Dame	256	18
10.	Air Force	971	13	23.	Purdue	233	—
11.	Georgia Tech	932	14	24.	Syracuse	192	17
12.	Michigan	863	15	25.	Missouri	171	—
13.	Texas A&M	839	9				

Note: As voted by a panel of 62 Division I-A head coaches; 25 points for 1st, 24 for 2nd, etc. (1st-place votes in parentheses).

Bowls and Playoffs

NCAA Division I-A Bowl Results

Date	Bowl	Result	Payout/Team ($)	Attendance
12-19-98	Las Vegas	N Carolina 20, San Diego St 13	800,000	21,514
12-23-98	Motor City	Marshall 48, Louisville 29	750,000	44,598
12-25-98	Aloha	Colorado 51, Oregon 43	750,000	43,340
12-25-98	Oahu	Air Force 45, Washington 25	750,000	49,385
12-26-98	Insight.com	Missouri 34, W Virginia 31	750,000	36,147
12-29-98	Music City	Virginia Tech 38, Alabama 7	750,000	16,131
12-29-98	Micron PC	Miami (FL) 46, N Carolina St 23	750,000	28,262
12-29-98	Alamo	Purdue 37, Kansas St 34	1.1 million	50,761

NCAA Division I-A Bowl Results *(Cont.)*

Date	Bowl	Result	Payout/Team ($)	Attendance
12-30-98	Humanitarian	Idaho 42, Southern Mississippi 35	750,000	19,664
12-30-98	Holiday	Arizona 23, Nebraska 20	1.8 million	65,106
12-31-98	Liberty	Tulane 41, Brigham Young 27	1.1 million	52,192
12-31-98	Sun	Texas Christian 28, Southern Cal 19	1 million	46,612
12-31-98	Peach	Georgia 35, Virginia 33	1.5 million	72,876
12-31-98	Independence	Mississippi 35, Texas Tech 18	1 million	46,862
1-1-99	Outback	Penn St 26, Kentucky 14	1.8 million	66,005
1-1-99	Cotton	Texas 38, Mississippi St 11	2.5 million	72,611
1-1-99	Gator	Georgia Tech 35, Notre Dame 28	1.4 million	70,791
1-1-99	Citrus	Michigan 45, Arkansas 31	3.75 million	63,584
1-1-99	Rose	Wisconsin 38, UCLA 31	11-13 million	93,872
1-1-99	Sugar	Ohio St 24, Texas A&M 14	11-13 million	76,503
1-2-99	Orange	Florida 31, Syracuse 10	11-13 million	67,919
1-4-99	Fiesta	Tennessee 23, Florida St 16	11-13 million	84,470

NCAA Division I-AA Championship Boxscore

Massachusetts	**21**	**17**	**0**	**17—55**
Georgia Southern	**7**	**14**	**12**	**10—43**

FIRST QUARTER
UMass: Shipp 25 run (Cherry kick), 12:56.
UMass: Ayi 9 fum return (Cherry kick), 8:29.
GSU: Hill 40 run (Chambers kick), 7:25.
UMass: Zullo 7 pass from Holston (Cherry kick), 5:04.

SECOND QUARTER
UMass: FG Cherry 22, 14:56.
GSU: Joyner 6 pass from Hill (Chambers kick), 10:54.
UMass: Bankhead 1 run (Cherry kick), 7:17.
UMass: Shipp 4 run (Cherry kick), 4:09.
GSU: Peterson 1 run (Chambers kick), 2:09.

THIRD QUARTER
GSU: Peterson 5 run (kick failed), 8:54.
GSU: Hill 2 run (run failed), 0:41.

FOURTH QUARTER
UMass: Quinlan 2 run (Cherry kick), 13:42.
UMass: Shipp 2 run (Cherry kick), 11:51.
GSU: FG Chambers 38, 8:39.
UMass: FG Cherry 25, 2:21.
GSU: Revere 29 run (Chambers kick), 1:04.

	Mass	GA Southern
First downs	23	26
Rushing yardage	51–303	65–457
Passing yardage	159	138
Return yardage	6–105	9–169
Passes (comp-att-int)	18-26-0	10-21-1
Punts (no.–avg)	4-51.0	1-35.0
Fumbles (no.–lost)	3–2	6–6
Penalties (no.–yards)	6–45	5–51

Att: 17,501

Small College Championship Summaries

NCAA DIVISION II

First round: Carson-Newman 30, W Georgia 20; Fort Valley St 21, Delta St 14; Slippery Rock 37, Grand Valley St 14; Shepherd 9, Indiana (PA) 6; NW Missouri St 28, Nebraska-Omaha 14; Northern Colorado 52, N Dakota 24; Central OK 21, Chadron St 19; Texas A&M-Kingsville 54, UC Davis 21.

Quarterfinals: Carson-Newman 34, Fort Valley St 31 OT; Slippery Rock 31, Shepherd 20; NW Missouri St 42, Northern Colorado 17; Texas A&M-Kingsville 24, Central OK 21 [ot].

Semifinals: Carson-Newman 47, Slippery Rock 21; NW Missouri St 49, Texas A&M-Kingsville 34.

Championship: 12-12-98 Florence, AL

Carson-Newman	6	0	0	0— 6
NW Missouri St	0	17	7	0—24

NCAA DIVISION III

First round: Mt Union 21, Albion 19; Wittenberg 13, Millikin 10; Lycoming 49, Catholic 14; Trinity (TX) 30, Western Maryland 20; WI-Eau Claire 28, Central Iowa 21; St. John's 33, Pacific Lutheran 20; Buffalo St 38, Springfield (MA) 35; Rowan 26, College of New Jersey 2.

Quarterfinals: Mt Union 21, Wittenberg 3; Trinity (TX) 37, Lycoming 21; WI-Eau Claire 10, St. John's 7; Rowan 19, Buffalo St 17.

Semifinals: Mtt Union 34, Trinity (TX) 29; Rowan 22, WI-Eau Claire 19.

Championship: 12-12-98 Salem, VA

Mount Union	7	9	15	13—44
Rowan	14	0	10	0—24

NAIA PLAYOFFS

First round: Olivet Nazarene (IL) 32, Hastings (NE) 26; Georgetown (KY) 46, Malone (OH) 41; Sioux Falls (SD) 29, Mary (ND) 25; Southwestern (KS) 12, Lindenwood (MO) 10; Tri-State (IN) 33, Benedictine (KS) 28; Huron (SD) 61, Jamestown (ND) 19; Central Wash 41, Rocky Mountain (MT) 38; Azusa Pacific (CA) 31, Taylor (IN) 28.

Quarterfinals: Tri-State 37, Georgetown 23; Olivet Nazarene 37, Sioux Falls 34; Huron 52, Southwestern 6; Azusa Pacific 35, Central Washington 28.

Semifinals: Olivet Nazarene 33, Tri-State 28; Azusa Pacific 26, Huron 24.

Championship: 12-19-98 Hardin County, TN

Olivet Nazarene	7	7	0	0—14
Azusa Pacific	0	7	0	10—17

Awards

Heisman Memorial Trophy

Player, School	Class	Pos	1st	2nd	3rd	Total
Ricky Williams, Texas	Sr	RB	714	91	31	2355
Michael Bishop, Kansas St	Sr	QB	41	250	169	792
Cade McNown, UCLA	Sr	QB	28	217	178	696
Tim Couch, Kentucky	Sr	QB	26	153	143	527
Donovan McNabb, Syracuse	Sr	QB	13	54	85	232
Daunte Culpepper, C Florida	Sr	QB	5	11	30	67
Champ Bailey, Georgia	Jr	CB/WR	6	8	21	55
Torry Holt, N Carolina St	Sr	WR	2	8	22	44
Joe Germaine, Ohio St	Sr	QB	2	11	15	43
Shaun King, Tulane	Sr	QB	1	11	13	38

Note: Former Heisman winners and the media vote, with ballots allowing for three names (3 points for 1st, 2 for 2nd, 1 for 3rd).

Offensive Players of the Year

Maxwell Award (Player)..............................Ricky Williams, Texas, RB
Walter Camp Player of the Year (Back) .....Ricky Williams, Texas, RB
Davey O'Brien Award (QB) ....Michael Bishop, Kansas St, QB
Doak Walker Award (RB) ....Ricky Williams, Texas, RB

Other Awards

Biletnikoff Award (WR) ....Troy Edwards, Louisiana Tech, WR
Vince Lombardi/Rotary Award (Lineman)...Dat Nguyen, Texas A&M, LB
Outland Trophy (Interior lineman) ....Kris Farris, UCLA, OL
Butkus Award (Linebacker)........................Chris Claiborne, Southern Cal, LB
Jim Thorpe Award (Defensive back)..........Antoine Winfield, Ohio St, CB
Sporting News Player of the Year ....Ricky Williams, Texas, RB
Walter Payton Award (Div I-AA Player) ......Jerry Azumah, New Hampshire, RB
Harlon Hill Trophy (Div II Player) ....Brian Shay, Emporia St, RB

Coaches' Awards

Walter Camp Award ....Bill Snyder, Kansas St
Eddie Robinson Award (Div I-AA)..............Paul Johnson, Georgia Southern
Bobby Dodd Award ....Bill Snyder, Kansas St
Bear Bryant Award ....Bill Snyder, Kansas St

AFCA COACHES OF THE YEAR

Division I-A ....Phillip Fulmer, Tennessee
Division I-AA...Mark Whipple, Massachusetts
Division II and NAIA Division I....................Mel Tjeerdsma, Northwest Missouri St
Division III and NAIA Division II..................Larry Kehres, Mount Union

Football Writers Association of America All-America Team

OFFENSE

David Boston, Ohio St, Jr ....Wide receiver
Troy Edwards, Louisiana Tech, Sr ......Wide receiver
Torry Holt, N Carolina St, Sr ....Wide receiver
Ben Adams, Texas, Jr ....OL
Kris Farris, UCLA, Sr ....OL
Aaron Gibson, Wisconsin, Sr ....OL
Jason Whitaker, Florida St, Jr..............OL
Craig Page, Georgia Tech, Sr.............Center
Tim Couch, Kentucky, Sr......................Quarterback
Ricky Williams, Texas, Sr ....Running back
Mike Cloud, Boston College, Sr ....Running back
Sebastian Janikowski, Florida St, So...Placekicker
David Allen, Kansas St, Jr...................Kick returner

DEFENSE

Tom Burke, Wisconsin, Sr ....DL
Patrick Kerney, Virginia, Sr..................DL
Montae Reagor, Texas Tech, Sr..........DL
Chris Claiborne, Southern Cal, Sr ....Linebacker
Jeff Kelly, Kansas St, Sr ....Linebacker
Dat Nguyen, Texas A&M, Sr ....Linebacker
Al Wilson, Tennessee, Sr.....................Linebacker
Champ Bailey, Georgia, Jr...................Defensive back
Chris McAlister, Arizona, Sr ....Defensive back
Anthony Poindexter, Virginia, Sr..........Defensive back
Antoine Winfield, Ohio St, Sr ....Defensive back
Joe Kristosik, Nevada, Sr ....Punter

Division I-A

ATLANTIC COAST CONFERENCE

	Conference		Full Season		
	W	L	W	L	Pct
Florida St	7	1	11	2	.846
Georgia Tech	7	1	10	2	.833
Virginia	6	2	9	3	.750
N Carolina St	5	3	7	5	.583
N Carolina	5	3	7	5	.583
Duke	2	6	4	7	.364
Wake Forest	2	6	3	8	.273
Clemson	1	7	3	8	.273
Maryland	1	7	3	8	.273

BIG EAST CONFERENCE

	Conference		Full Season		
	W	L	W	L	Pct
Syracuse	6	1	8	4	.667
Miami (FL)	5	2	9	3	.750
Virginia Tech	5	2	9	3	.750
W Virginia	5	2	8	4	.667
Boston College	3	4	4	7	.634
Rutgers	2	5	5	6	.455
Temple	2	5	2	9	.182
Pittsburgh	0	7	2	9	.182

BIG TEN CONFERENCE

	Conference		Full Season		
	W	L	W	L	Pct
Ohio St	7	1	11	1	.917
Wisconsin	7	1	11	1	.917
Michigan	7	1	10	3	.769
Purdue	6	2	9	4	.692
Penn St	5	3	9	3	.750
Michigan St	4	4	6	6	.500
Minnesota	2	6	5	6	.455
Indiana	2	6	4	7	.366
Illinois	2	6	3	8	.273
Iowa	2	6	3	8	.273
Northwestern	0	8	3	9	.250

BIG 12 CONFERENCE

	Conference		Full Season		
NORTH	W	L	W	L	Pct
*Kansas St	8	0	11	2	.846
Nebraska	5	3	9	4	.692
Missouri	5	3	8	4	.667
Colorado	4	4	8	4	.667
Kansas	1	7	4	7	.364
Iowa St	1	7	3	8	.273
SOUTH					
*Texas A&M	7	1	11	3	.786
Texas	6	2	9	3	.750
Texas Tech	4	4	7	5	.583
Oklahoma	3	5	5	6	.455
Oklahoma St	3	5	5	6	.455
Baylor	1	7	2	9	.182

*Full season record includes Big 12 Championship Game in which Texas A&M defeated Kansas St 36–33, on Dec. 5.

BIG WEST CONFERENCE

	Conference		Full Season		
	W	L	W	L	Pct
Idaho	4	1	9	3	.750
Nevada	3	2	6	5	.727
N Texas	3	2	3	8	.273
Boise St	2	3	6	5	.545
Utah St	2	3	3	8	.272
New Mexico St	1	4	3	8	.273

Division I-A *(Cont.)*

CONFERENCE USA

	Conference		Full Season		
	W	L	W	L	Pct
Tulane	6	0	12	0	1.000
Southern Mississippi	5	1	7	5	.583
Louisville	4	2	7	5	.583
E Carolina	3	3	6	5	.545
Army	2	4	2	8	.273
Houston	2	4	3	8	.273
Cincinnati	1	5	2	9	.182
Memphis	1	5	2	9	.182

MID-AMERICAN ATHLETIC CONFERENCE

	Conference		Full Season		
EAST	W	L	W	L	Pct
*Marshall	7	1	12	1	.923
Miami (OH)	7	1	10	1	.909
Bowling Green	5	3	5	6	.455
Ohio	5	3	5	6	.455
Akron	3	6	4	7	.364
Kent	0	8	0	11	.000
WEST					
*Toledo	6	2	7	5	.583
Western Michigan	5	3	7	4	.636
Central Michigan	5	3	6	5	.545
Eastern Michigan	3	6	3	8	.273
Northern Illinois	2	6	2	9	.182
Ball State	1	7	1	10	.100

*Full season record includes MAC Championship Game in which Marshall defeated Toledo 23–17, on Dec. 4.

PACIFIC-10 CONFERENCE

	Conference		Full Season		
	W	L	W	L	Pct
UCLA	8	0	10	2	.833
Arizona	7	1	12	1	.923
Oregon	5	3	8	4	.667
Southern Cal	5	3	8	4	.667
Washington	4	4	6	6	.500
Arizona St	4	4	5	6	.455
California	3	5	5	6	.455
Oregon St	2	6	5	6	.455
Stanford	2	6	3	8	.273
Washington St	0	8	3	8	.273

SOUTHEASTERN CONFERENCE

	Conference		Full Season		
EAST	W	L	W	L	Pct
*Tennessee	8	0	13	0	1.000
Florida	7	1	10	2	.833
Georgia	6	2	9	3	.750
Kentucky	4	4	7	5	.583
Vanderbilt	1	7	2	9	.182
S Carolina	0	8	1	10	.100
WEST					
Arkansas	6	2	9	3	.750
*Mississippi St	6	2	8	5	.615
Alabama	4	4	7	5	.583
Mississippi	3	5	6	5	.545
Louisiana St	2	6	4	7	.364
Auburn	1	7	3	8	.273

*Full season record includes SEC Championship Game in which Tennessee defeated Mississippi St 24–14, on Dec. 5.

Division I-A *(Cont.)*

WESTERN ATHLETIC CONFERENCE

	Conference		Full Season		
PACIFIC	W	L	W	L	Pct
San Diego St	7	1	7	5	.583
*Brigham Young	7	1	9	5	.643
Utah	5	3	7	4	.636
Fresno St	5	3	5	6	.455
San Jose St	3	5	4	8	.333
Texas-El Paso	3	5	3	8	.272
New Mexico	1	7	3	9	.250
Hawaii	0	8	0	12	.000
MOUNTAIN					
*Air Force	7	1	12	1	.923
Wyoming	6	2	8	3	.727
Colorado St	5	3	7	4	.636
Rice	5	3	6	5	.545
Texas Christian	4	4	7	5	.583
Southern Methodist	4	4	6	5	.545
Tulsa	2	6	4	7	.571
UNLV	0	8	2	9	.182

*Full season record includes WAC Championship Game in which Air Force defeated Brigham Young 20–13, on Dec. 5.

INDEPENDENTS

	Full Season		
	W	L	Pct
Central Florida	9	2	.818
Notre Dame	9	3	.750
Louisiana	6	6	.500
NW Louisiana	5	6	.455
Alabama-Birmingham	4	7	.364
Arkansas St	4	8	.333
Navy	3	8	.273
SW Louisiana	2	9	.182

Division I-AA

ATLANTIC 10

	Conference		Full Season		
NEW ENGLAND	W	L	W	L	Pct
Connecticut	6	2	10	3	.770
Massachusetts	6	2	12	3	.800
Maine	3	5	6	5	.545
New Hampshire	3	5	4	7	.364
Rhode Island	2	6	3	8	.273
MID ATLANTIC					
Richmond	7	1	9	3	.750
Delaware	4	4	7	4	.636
William & Mary	4	4	7	4	.636
Villanova	4	4	6	5	.545
Northeastern	3	5	5	6	.455
James Madison	2	6	3	8	.273

BIG SKY CONFERENCE

	Conference		Full Season		
	W	L	W	L	Pct
Montana	6	2	8	4	.667
Cal St-Northridge	5	3	7	4	.636
Montana St	5	3	7	4	.636
Weber St	4	4	6	5	.545
Eastern Washington	4	4	5	6	.455
Portland St	4	4	5	6	.455
Northern Arizona	3	5	6	5	.545
Cal St-Sacramento	3	5	5	6	.455
Idaho St	2	6	3	8	.273

Division I-AA *(Cont.)*

GATEWAY COLLEGIATE ATHLETIC CONFERENCE

	Conference		Full Season		
	W	L	W	L	Pct
Western Illinois	5	1	11	2	.846
Illinois St	4	2	8	4	.667
Northern Iowa	3	3	7	4	.636
Youngstown St	3	3	6	5	.455
SW Missouri St	3	3	5	6	.273
Indiana St	2	4	5	6	.273
Southern Illinois	1	5	3	8	.182

IVY GROUP

	Conference		Full Season		
	W	L	W	L	Pct
Pennsylvania	6	1	8	2	.800
Brown	5	2	7	3	.700
Yale	5	2	6	4	.600
Princeton	4	3	5	5	.500
Columbia	3	4	4	6	.400
Harvard	3	4	4	6	.400
Cornell	1	6	4	6	.400
Dartmouth	1	6	2	8	.200

METRO ATLANTIC ATHLETIC CONFERENCE

	Conference		Full Season		
	W	L	W	L	Pct
Fairfield	6	1	9	2	.818
Georgetown	6	1	9	2	.818
Duquesne	5	2	8	3	.727
Marist	5	2	7	3	.700
St. John's	3	4	6	5	.545
Canisius	2	5	3	7	.300
Siena	1	6	4	6	.400
Iona	0	0	4	6	.400
St. Peter's	0	7	0	10	.000

MID-EASTERN ATHLETIC LEAGUE

	Conference		Full Season		
	W	L	W	L	Pct
Florida A&M	7	1	11	2	.846
Hampton	7	1	9	3	.750
Bethune-Cookman	6	2	8	2	.800
N Carolina A&T	5	3	8	3	.727
Howard	5	3	7	4	.636
S Carolina St	3	5	5	6	.455
Norfolk St	2	6	2	9	.182
Morgan St	1	7	1	10	.091
Delaware St	0	8	0	11	.000

PIONEER FOOTBALL LEAGUE

	Conference		Full Season		
	W	L	W	L	Pct
Drake	4	0	7	3	.700
Dayton	3	1	6	4	.600
Valparaiso	2	2	5	6	.455
Butler	1	3	4	6	.400
San Diego	0	4	2	8	.200

SOUTHERN CONFERENCE

	Conference		Full Season		
	W	L	W	L	Pct
Georgia Southern	8	0	14	1	.933
Appalachian St	6	2	10	3	.770
Western Carolina	5	3	6	5	.545
TN-Chattanooga	4	4	5	6	.454
The Citadel	4	4	5	6	.454
Furman	3	5	5	6	.454
E Tennessee St	3	5	4	7	.364
Wofford	3	5	4	7	.364
Virginia Military	0	8	1	10	.091

Division I-AA (Cont.)

SOUTHLAND CONFERENCE

	Conference		Full Season		
	W	L	W	L	Pct
Northwestern St	6	1	11	2	.846
McNeese St	5	2	9	3	.750
Troy St	5	2	8	4	.667
Jacksonville St	4	3	7	4	.636
Nicholls St	3	4	4	7	.363
SW Texas St	2	5	4	7	.363
Stephen F. Austin	2	5	3	8	.273
Sam Houston St	1	6	3	8	.273

SOUTHWESTERN

	Conference		Full Season		
	W	L	W	L	Pct
Southern	8	0	8	3	.727
Jackson St	7	1	7	4	.636
Arkansas-Pine Bluff	6	2	8	3	.727
Texas Southern	4	4	6	5	.545
Grambling	4	4	5	6	.455
Alabama St	3	5	5	6	.455
Alcorn St	3	5	5	6	.455
Mississippi Valley St	1	7	1	10	.091
*Alabama A&M	0	0	5	6	.455
Prairie View A&M	0	8	1	10	.091

*Alabama A&M was not eligible for the league title.

INDEPENDENTS

	Full Season		
	W	L	Pct
Morehead St	9	2	.818
Davidson	8	2	.800
Hofstra	8	3	.727
S Florida	8	3	.727
Western Kentucky	7	4	.636
Samford	6	5	.545
Elon	5	6	.455
Liberty	5	6	.455
Southern Utah	5	6	.455
Jacksonville	4	5	.444
Austin Peay	4	7	.364
Buffalo	4	7	.364
La Salle	3	6	.333
Cal Poly-San Luis Obispo	3	8	.273
Charleston Southern	3	8	.273
St. Mary's	2	8	.200

Division I-A

SCORING

	Class	GP	TD	XP	FG	Pts	Pts/Game
Troy Edwards, Louisiana Tech	Sr	12	31	2	0	188	15.67
Ricky Williams, Texas	Sr	11	28	0	0	168	15.27
Martin Gramatica, Kansas St	Jr	11	0	69	22	135	11.25
Travis Prentice, Miami (OH)	Jr	11	20	0	0	120	10.91
Leroy Collins, Louisville	Sr	11	19	2	0	116	10.55
Edgerrin James, Miami (FL)	Jr	11	19	0	0	114	10.36
Sebastian Janikowski, Florida St	So	12	0	42	27	123	10.25
Nathan Villegas, Oregon	Sr	11	0	52	20	112	10.18
Devin West, Missouri	Sr	11	18	0	0	108	9.82
Shayne Graham, Virginia Tech	Jr	11	0	37	22	103	9.36
Kevin Faulk, Louisiana St	Sr	11	17	0	0	102	9.27

FIELD GOALS

	Class	GP	FGA	FG	Pct	FG/Game
Sebastian Janikowski, Florida St	So	12	32	27	.844	2.25
Brad Bohn, Utah St	Sr	11	28	24	.857	2.18
Paul Edinger, Michigan St	Sr	12	26	22	.846	2.00
Shayne Graham, Virginia Tech	Jr	12	32	22	.688	2.00
Derek Franz, Colorado St	Sr	11	26	21	.808	1.91
Martin Gramatica, Kansas St	Sr	11	31	22	.710	1.83
Nathan Villegas, Oregon	Sr	11	22	20	.909	1.82
Travis Forney, Penn St	Jr	11	29	20	.690	1.82

TOTAL OFFENSE

			Rushing		Passing		Total Offense			
	Class	GP	Car	Net	Att	Yds	Yds	Yds/Play	TDR*	Yds/Game
Tim Rattay, Louisiana Tech	Jr	12	43	-78	559	4943	4865	8.04	47	405.42
Chris Redman, Louisville	Sr	10	40	-33	473	4041	4009	7.81	31	400.90
Daunte Culpepper, C Florida	Sr	11	141	463	402	3690	4153	7.65	40	377.55
Tim Couch, Kentucky	Sr	11	64	-124	553	4275	4151	6.73	37	377.36
David Neill, Nevada	Fr	9	65	102	344	3249	3351	8.20	31	372.33
Shaun King, Tulane	Sr	11	140	532	328	3232	3764	8.04	46	342.18
Drew Brees, Purdue	So	12	59	168	516	3753	3921	6.82	39	326.75
Akili Smith, Oregon	Sr	11	74	182	325	3308	3490	8.75	37	317.27
Cade McNown, UCLA	Sr	11	63	167	338	3130	3297	8.54	26	299.73
Michael Bishop, Kansas St	Sr	12	177	748	295	2844	3592	6.90	37	299.33
Tim Lester, Western Mich	Sr	11	70	-49	406	3311	3262	6.85	23	296.55
Jamie Barnette, N Carolina St	Jr	11	83	13	377	3169	3182	6.92	21	289.27

*Touchdowns responsible for are TDs scored and passed for.

RUSHING

	Class	GP	Car	Yds	Avg	TD	Yds/Game
Ricky Williams, Texas	Sr	11	361	2124	5.9	28	193.09
Travis Prentice, Miami (OH)	Jr	11	365	1787	4.9	20	162.45
Mike Cloud, Boston College	Sr	11	308	1726	5.6	14	156.91
Ricky Williams, Texas Tech	So	11	306	1582	5.2	13	143.82
Devin West, Missouri	Sr	11	283	1578	5.6	18	143.45
Amos Zereoue, W Virginia	Jr	10	261	1430	5.5	13	143.00
Denvis Manns, New Mexico St	Sr	11	269	1469	5.5	6	133.55
Edgerrin James, Miami (FL)	Jr	11	242	1416	5.9	17	128.73
Ron Dayne, Wisconsin	Jr	10	268	1279	4.8	11	127.90
Steve Hoofkin, Ohio	Sr	11	273	1315	4.8	11	119.55

Division I-A *(Cont.)*

PASSING EFFICIENCY

	Class	GP	Att	Comp	Pct Comp	Yds	Yds/Att	TD	Int	Rating Pts
Shaun King, Tulane	Sr	11	328	223	67.99	3232	9.85	36	6	183.3
Akili Smith, Oregon	Sr	11	325	191	58.77	3307	10.18	30	7	170.4
Daunte Culpepper, C Florida	Sr	11	402	296	73.63	3690	9.18	28	7	170.2
Tim Rattay, Louisiana Tech	Jr	12	559	380	67.98	4943	8.84	46	13	164.8
David Neill, Nevada	Fr	9	344	199	57.85	3249	9.44	29	9	159.8
Michael Bishop, Kansas St	Sr	11	295	164	55.59	2844	9.64	23	4	159.6
Donovan McNabb, Syracuse	Sr	11	251	157	62.55	2134	8.50	22	5	158.9
Marc Bulger, W Virginia	Jr	11	369	240	65.04	3178	8.61	27	8	157.2
Cade McNown, UCLA	Sr	11	323	188	58.20	3130	9.69	23	10	156.9
Joe Germaine, Ohio St	Sr	11	346	209	60.40	3108	8.98	24	7	154.7

Note: Minimum 15 attempts per game.

RECEPTIONS PER GAME

	Class	GP	No.	Yds	TD	R/Game
Troy Edwards, Louisiana Tech	Sr	12	140	1996	27	11.67
Dameane Douglas, California	Sr	11	100	1150	4	9.09
Geoff Noisy, Nevada	Sr	11	94	1405	6	8.55
Arnold Jackson, Louisville	Sr	11	90	1165	10	8.18
Torry Holt, N Carolina St	Sr	11	88	1604	10	8.00
Siaha Burley, Central Florida	Sr	11	88	1142	8	8.00

RECEIVING YARDS PER GAME

	Class	GP	No.	Yds	TD	Yds/Game
Troy Edwards, Louisiana Tech	Sr	12	140	1996	27	166.33
Torry Holt, N Carolina St	Sr	11	88	1604	10	145.82
Geoff Noisy, Nevada	Sr	11	94	1405	6	127.73
Travis McGriff, Florida	Sr	11	70	1357	10	123.36
David Boston, Ohio St	Jr	11	74	1330	13	120.91

ALL-PURPOSE RUNNERS

	Class	GP	Rush	Rec	PR	KOR	Yds	Yds/Game
Troy Edwards, Louisiana Tech	Sr	12	227	1996	235	326	2784	232.00
Ricky Williams, Texas	Sr	11	2124	262	0	0	2386	216.91
Kevin Faulk, Louisiana St	Sr	11	1279	287	265	278	2109	191.73
Torry Holt, N Carolina St	Sr	11	102	1604	273	0	1979	179.91
Jaime Kimbrough, Fresno St	Sr	11	1168	391	0	393	1952	177.45

INTERCEPTIONS

	Class	GP	No.	Yds	TD	Int/Game
Jamar Fletcher, Wisconsin	So	9	6	99	2	.67
Pat Dennis, NE Louisiana	So	11	7	196	2	.64
Lloyd Harrison, N Carolina St	Jr	11	7	51	0	.64
Hank Poteat, Pittsburgh	Jr	10	6	53	0	.60
Wade Perkins, Missouri	Sr	11	6	129	1	.55
David Macklin, Penn St	Jr	11	6	120	1	.55
Tim Smith, Stanford	Jr	11	6	69	0	.55

PUNTING

	Class	No.	Avg
Joe Kristosik, UNLV	Sr	76	46.17
Josh Bidwell, Oregon	Sr	47	45.81
Stephen Baker, Arizona St	Fr	56	45.73
Dave Zastudil, Ohio	Fr	50	45.32
Bill Lafleur, Nebraska	Jr	52	44.94

Note: Minimum of 3.6 per game.

PUNT RETURNS

	Class	No.	Yds	TD	Avg
David Allen, Kansas St	Jr	33	730	4	22.12
D. Gourdine, San Diego St	Jr	16	294	2	18.38
Nick Davis, Wisconsin	Fr	27	424	2	15.70
David Boston, Ohio St	Jr	18	268	1	14.89
Payton Williams, Fresno St	Jr	24	343	1	14.29

Note: Minimum 1.2 per game.

Division I-A (Cont.)

KICKOFF RETURNS

	Class	No.	Yds	TD	Avg
Broderick McGrew, N Texas	Jr	18	587	1	32.61
Dee Moronkola, Washington St	Sr	16	504	2	31.50
Kevin Johnson, Syracuse	Sr	23	690	2	30.00
Tim Alexander Oregon St	Sr	27	799	1	29.59
Craig Yeast, Kentucky	Sr	14	410	1	29.29

Note: Minimum of 1.2 per game.

Division I-A Single-Game Highs

RUSHING AND PASSING

Rushing and passing plays: 84—Drew Brees, Purdue, Oct 10 (vs Wisconsin).
Rushing and passing yards: 582—David Neill, Nevada, Oct 10 (vs New Mexico St).
Rushing plays: 49—Eric Flowers, Central Michigan, Oct 10 (vs Eastern Michigan).
Net rushing yards: 350—Ricky Williams, Texas, Oct 3 (vs Iowa St).
Passes attempted: 83—Drew Brees, Purdue, Oct 10 (vs Wisconsin).
Passes completed: 55—Drew Brees, Purdue, Oct 10 (vs Wisconsin).
Passing yards: 611—David Neill, Nevada, Oct 10 (vs New Mexico St).

RECEIVING AND RETURNS

Passes caught: 18—Randall Lane, Purdue, Oct 10 (vs Wisconsin).
Receiving yards: 405—Troy Edwards, Louisiana Tech, Aug 29 (vs Nebraska).
Punt return yards: 189—Damone Williams, Marshall Oct 10 (vs Ohio).
Kickoff return yards: 211—Dee Moronkole, Washington St, Oct 10 (vs Oregon).

Division I-AA

SCORING

	Class	GP	TD	XP	FG	Pts	Pts/Game
Brian Westbrook, Villanova	Sr	11	26	4	0	160	14.55
Adrian Peterson, Georgia Southern	Fr	11	26	0	0	156	14.18
Chris Reed, Monmouth	Sr	10	22	0	0	132	13.20
Jerry Azumah, New Hampshire	Sr	11	23	2	0	140	12.73
Jessie Burton, McNeese St	Fr	9	19	0	0	114	12.67

FIELD GOALS

	Class	GP	FGA	FG	Pct	FG/Game
Mike Goldstein, N Arizona	Sr	11	23	16	.696	1.45
Scott Sheilds, Weber St	Sr	11	23	16	.696	1.45
Bill Gramatica, S Florida	So	11	24	16	.667	1.45
Chad Johnson, Hofstra	Jr	11	27	16	.593	1.45
Joe Lopez, W Illinios	So	11	28	16	.571	1.45

TOTAL OFFENSE

			Rushing				Passing		Total Offense			
	Class	GP	Car	Gain	Loss	Net	Att	Yds	Yds	Yds/Play	TDR*	Yds/Game
Patrick Bonner, Fla A&M	Sr	11	62	227	132	95	426	3479	3568	7.31	38	324.36
James Perry, Brown	Jr	10	23	20	83	-63	444	3165	3102	6.64	23	310.20
Ryan Vena, Colgate	Fr	10	177	953	217	736	230	2298	3034	7.46	27	303.40
Brian Ah Yat, Montana	Sr	10	49	157	165	-8	386	2952	2944	6.77	30	294.40
Ted White, Howard	Sr	11	50	138	186	-48	383	3253	3215	7.42	32	292.27

*Touchdowns responsible for are TDs scored and passed for.

RUSHING

	Class	GP	Car	Yds	Avg	TD	Yds/Game
Charles Roberts, Cal St–Sacramento	So	11	386	2260	5.9	19	205.45
Jerry Azumah, New Hampshire	Sr	11	342	2195	6.4	22	199.55
Marcel Shipp, Massachusetts	So	11	319	1949	6.1	13	177.18
Adrian Peterson, Georgia Southern	Fr	11	257	1932	7.5	25	175.64
Karlton Carpenter, Southern Illinois	Jr	11	323	1892	5.9	16	172.00

Division I-AA *(Cont.)*

PASSING EFFICIENCY

	Class	GP	Att	Comp	Pct Comp	Yds	Yds/Att	TD	Int	Rating Pts
Jim Blanchard, Portland St	So	11	169	112	66.27	1512	8.95	14	1	167.6
Matt Nagy, Delaware	So	11	298	182	61.07	2916	9.79	20	12	157.4
Chad Barnhardt, S Florida	Sr	11	193	114	59.07	1776	9.20	17	9	156.1
Patrick Bonner, Florida A&M	Sr	11	426	265	62.21	3473	8.15	37	7	156.1
Ryan Vena, Colgate	Jr	11	230	134	58.26	2298	10.00	16	11	155.6

Note: Minimum 15 attempts per game.

RECEPTIONS PER GAME

	Class	GP	No.	Yds	TD	R/Game
Jacquay Nunnally, Florida A&M	So	11	93	1316	12	8.45
Sean Morey, Brown	Sr	10	83	1023	10	8.30
Eddie Conti, Delaware	Sr	11	91	1712	10	8.27
Brian Westbrook, Villanova	So	11	89	1144	15	8.09
Mike Furrey, Northern Iowa	Jr	11	86	1074	10	7.82

RECEIVING YARDS PER GAME

	Class	GP	No.	Yds	TD	Yds/Game
Eddie Conti, Delaware	Sr	11	91	1712	10	155.64
Jacquay Nunnally, Florida A&M	So	11	93	1316	12	119.64
Corey Hill, Colgate	Sr	11	71	1287	11	117.00
Rondel Menendez, Eastern Kentucky	Sr	9	52	1032	11	114.67
Sylvester Morris, Jackson St	Jr	11	62	1258	17	114.36

ALL-PURPOSE RUNNERS

	Class	GP	Rush	Rec	PR	KOR	Yds*	Yds/Game
Brian Westbrook, Villanova	So	11	1046	1144	192	644	3026	275.09
Jerry Azumah, New Hampshire	Sr	11	2195	218	5	308	2726	247.82
Charles Roberts, Cal St-Sacremento	So	11	2260	79	0	91	2430	220.91
Eddie Conti, Delaware	Sr	11	-2	1712	156	502	2368	215.27
Marcel Shipp, Massachusetts	So	11	1949	288	0	100	2337	212.45

*Includes interception return yards.

INTERCEPTIONS

	Class	GP	No.	Yds	TD	Int/Game
Ken Krapf, St. John's (NY)	Jr	11	9	144	2	.82
Eric Kenesie, Valparaiso	Jr	11	9	88	0	.82
Clif Henry, Davidson	Sr	10	7	145	0	.70
Eric Sloan, Troy St	Jr	11	7	137	1	.64
Ron Iannotti, Rhode Island	Sr	11	7	131	0	.64

PUNTING

	Class	No.	Avg
Chad Stanley, Stephen F. Austin	Sr	58	46.60
Matt Bushart, Southern	Jr	50	45.20
Ken Hinsley, Western Carolina	Sr	57	44.49
Mike Leach, William & Mary	Jr	45	44.38
Ryan Klaus, Sam Houston St	Sr	72	44.19

Note: Minimum 3.6 per game.

Division II

SCORING

	Class	GP	TD	XP	FG	Pts	Pts/Game
Brian Shay, Emporia St	Sr	11	29	2	0	176	16.0
Rashaan Dumas, Southern Conn St	Jr	10	25	0	0	150	15.0
Carlton Jones, Livingstone	Fr	10	23	2	0	140	14.0
Kavin Gailliard, American Int'l	Jr	10	22	2	0	134	13.4
Tyrone Morgan, Northern St	So	11	24	2	0	146	13.3

FIELD GOALS

	Class	GP	FGA	FG	Pct	FG/Game
Jason Williams, Southern Arkansas	So	10	24	20	83.3	2.00
Doc Proctor, Ferris St	Jr	11	27	19	70.4	1.73
Josh Barcus, Pittsburg St	Sr	10	20	16	80.0	1.60
Matt Gross, Catawba	Fr	10	21	16	76.2	1.60
Brett Gorden, S Dakota St	Sr	11	22	14	63.6	1.27

TOTAL OFFENSE

	Class	GP	Yds	Yds/Game
Mike Mitros, West Chester	Jr	11	3478	316.2
Jeff Fox, Grand Valley St	Sr	11	3472	315.6
Drew Folmar, Millersville	So	10	2970	297.0
Matt Kissell, Mercyhurst	Sr	10	2876	287.6
Kevin Daft, UC-Davis	Sr	11	3148	286.2

RUSHING

	Class	GP	Car	Yds	TD	Yds/Game
Brian Shay, Emporia St	Sr	10	293	2265	29	205.9
Kavin Gailliard, American Int'l	Jr	11	269	1971	23	179.2
Damian Beane, Shepherd	Jr	10	299	1775	17	177.5
Josh Ranek, S Dakota St	Fr	11	302	1881	13	171.0
Tyrone Morgan, Northern St	So	11	318	1838	22	167.1

PASSING EFFICIENCY

	Class	GP	Att	Comp	Pct Comp	Yds	TD	Int	Rating Pts
Sleepie Tollie, Northwood	Fr	9	148	80	54.0	1862	18	7	190.4
Corte McGuffey, Northern Colorado	Jr	11	299	189	63.2	2547	32	4	167.4
Drew Folmar, Millersville	So	10	334	220	65.8	3039	30	12	164.8
Eric Hannah, Western St	Sr	10	278	161	57.9	2313	25	8	151.7
Jeff Fox, Grand Valley St	Sr	11	394	236	59.9	3260	30	7	150.9

Note: Minimum 15 attempts per game.

RECEPTIONS PER GAME

	Class	GP	No.	Yds	TD	Rec/Game
Kevin Ingram, West Chester	Jr	11	115	1673	21	10.5
Damon Thompson, Virginia St	So	10	88	1330	13	8.8
Damien Hoffman, MN-Morris	So	10	85	850	7	8.5
Desmond Thornton, Virginia St	Jr	10	79	825	1	7.9
Alvin Slaughter, Clarion	Sr	11	85	1369	13	7.7

RECEIVING YARDS PER GAME

	Class	GP	No.	Yds	TD	Yds/Game
Kevin Ingram, West Chester	Jr	11	115	1673	21	152.1
Damon Thompson, Virginia St	So	10	88	1330	13	133.0
Ben Clampitt, Western Washington	Jr	10	74	1288	10	128.8
John South, Adams St	Jr	9	62	1151	9	127.9
Alvin Slaughter, Clarion	Sr	11	85	1369	13	124.5

Division II (Cont.)

INTERCEPTIONS

	Class	GP	No.	Yds	Int/Game
Jermel Johnson, Fayetteville St	Sr	10	9	95	.9
Roderick Williams, Bowie St	Jr	9	8	47	.9
Shavarez Thompson, Livingstone	Fr	8	7	48	.9
Johnnie Jones, Central Okla	Jr	11	9	162	.8
Che Bryant, Tuskegee	Jr	10	8	98	.8

PUNTING

	Class	No.	Avg
Jason Van Dyke, Adams St	Sr	59	46.2
Brian Moorman, Pittsburg St	Sr	38	45.6
Jason Gross, California (PA)	Fr	50	44.6
Jeff Works, Ouachita Baptist	Jr	54	44.1
Tom O'Brien, S Dakota St	Sr	42	44.0

Note: Minimum 3.6 per game.

Division III

SCORING

	Class	GP	TD	XP	FG	Pts	Pts/Game
R.J. Bowers, Grove City	So	10	34	2	0	206	20.6
Guy Leman, Simpson	Sr	10	33	0	0	198	19.8
Trevor Shannon, Wartburg	Sr	10	26	6	0	162	16.2
Scott Pingel, Westminster (MO)	Jr	10	26	6	0	162	16.2
Jamie Lee, MacMurray	Sr	10	26	4	0	160	16.0

FIELD GOALS

	Class	GP	FGA	FG	Pct	FG/Game
Michael Padgett, Bridgewater (VA)	Sr	10	23	13	56.5	1.30
David Vitatoe, John Carroll	Jr	10	16	13	81.3	1.30
Martin Hlinka, Augsburg	Sr	10	18	12	66.7	1.20
Kevin Bowser, Allegheny	Sr	10	19	12	63.2	1.20
Steve Morat, Union (NY)	Fr	9	12	10	83.3	1.11

TOTAL OFFENSE

	Class	GP	Yds	Yds/Game
Justin Peery, Westminster (MO)	Jr	10	4651	465.1
Chris Stormer, Hanover	Sr	10	3467	346.7
Troy Dougherty, Grinnell	Jr	10	3296	329.6
Matt Bunyan, WI-Stout	Sr	10	3143	314.3
Mike Burton, Trinity (TX)	Jr	10	3002	300.2

RUSHING

	Class	GP	Car	Yds	TD	Yds/Game
R.J. Bowers, Grove City	So	10	229	2283	34	228.3
Krishaun Gilmore, Rensselaer	Sr	9	228	1670	22	185.6
Jamie Lee, MacMurray	Sr	10	252	1818	25	181.8
Guy Leman, Simpson	Sr	10	333	1788	31	178.8
Casey Donaldson, Wittenberg	So	10	234	1639	21	163.9

PASSING EFFICIENCY

	Class	GP	Att	Comp	Pct Comp	Yds	TD	Int	Rating Pts
Troy Dougherty, Grinnell	Jr	10	293	198	67.5	3310	36	5	199.6
Ty Grovesteen, WI-Whitewater	Sr	9	180	103	57.2	2074	22	5	188.8
Matt Wheeler, Wartburg	Jr	9	227	152	66.9	2150	23	9	172.0
Geoff Helmlinger, Baldwin-Wallace	Sr	10	268	171	63.8	2518	27	7	170.8
Gary Smeck, Mt. Union	So	10	282	188	66.6	2717	23	9	168.1

Note: Minimum 15 attempts per game.

Division III (Cont.)

RECEPTIONS PER GAME

	Class	GP	No.	Yds	TD	Rec/Game
Scott Pingel, Westminster (MO)	Jr	10	130	2157	26	13.0
Scott Hvistendahl, Augsburg	Sr	10	112	1860	15	11.2
Mike Hunter, Catholic	Jr	10	87	1279	12	8.7
Tarrik Wilson, Hanover	Jr	10	85	1013	15	8.5
Richard Wemer, Grinnell	Sr	10	83	1150	13	8.3

RECEIVING YARDS PER GAME

	Class	GP	No.	Yds	TD	Yds/Game
Scott Pingel, Westminster (MO)	Jr	10	130	2157	26	215.7
Scott Hvistendahl, Augsburg	Sr	10	112	1860	15	186.0
Dave Snider, Grinnell	Sr	10	63	1383	21	138.3
Mike Hunter, Catholic	Jr	10	87	1279	12	127.9
Jon May, WI-Oshkosh	Sr	10	58	1230	16	123.0

INTERCEPTIONS

	Class	GP	No.	Yds	Int/Game
Mike Cotton, Mass-Dartmouth	Jr	10	11	206	1.1
Kevin Fahey, Wesleyan-Illinois	Sr	9	9	124	1.0
Eric Feest, Concordia-WI	Fr	10	9	50	.9
J. Blomenberg, Rose-Hulman	So	10	9	9	.9

PUNTING

	Class	No.	Avg
Chris Morehouse, Albright	Jr	52	43.2
Robert Andrews, Mississippi College	Sr	47	41.9
Mark Kevern, Cal Lutheran	Jr	40	41.9
Mario Acosta, Chapman	Sr	59	41.5
Matt Mahaffey, Wooster	Jr	39	41.2

Note: Minimum 3.6 per game.

1998 NCAA Division I-A Team Leaders

Offense

SCORING

	GP	Pts	Avg
Kansas St	12	576	48.0
Tulane	11	499	45.4
Syracuse	11	468	42.5
Louisiana Tech	12	493	41.1
UCLA	11	445	40.5
Louisville	11	444	40.4
Oregon	11	430	39.1
Kentucky	11	417	37.9
Ohio St	11	406	36.9
Miami (FL)	11	402	36.5

RUSHING

	GP	Car	Yds	Avg	TD	Yds/Game
Army	11	610	3232	5.3	25	293.8
Ohio	11	680	3044	4.5	27	276.7
Air Force	12	648	3201	5.0	39	266.8
Navy	11	580	2874	5.0	25	261.3
Rice	11	624	2829	4.5	25	257.2
Nebraska	12	636	3045	4.8	37	253.8
New Mexico St	11	579	2790	4.8	18	253.6
Texas Christian	11	542	2630	4.9	21	239.1
Missouri	11	546	2552	4.7	28	232.0
Syracuse	11	521	2512	4.8	34	228.4

TOTAL OFFENSE

	GP	Plays	Yds	Avg	TD*	Yds/Game
Louisville	11	883	6156	6.9	62	559.64
Louisiana Tech	12	894	6479	7.2	66	539.92
Kentucky	11	911	5876	6.7	50	534.18
Tulane	11	816	5578	6.5	64	507.09
Nevada	11	869	5577	6.4	49	507.00
Ohio St	11	853	5539	6.5	46	503.55
Central Florida	11	789	5365	6.8	50	487.73
UCLA	11	785	5309	6.8	56	482.64
Kansas St	12	887	5742	6.5	65	478.50
Oregon	11	785	5260	6.7	49	478.18

*Defensive and special teams TDs not included.

Offense *(Cont.)*

PASSING

	GP	Att	Comp	Yds	Pct Comp	Yds/Att	TD	Int	Yds/Game
Louisiana Tech	12	600	402	5185	67.0	8.6	48	13	432.1
Kentucky	11	574	414	4534	72.1	7.9	39	16	412.2
Louisville	11	515	338	4498	65.6	8.7	33	15	408.9
Nevada	11	458	265	3992	57.9	8.7	32	18	362.9
Florida	11	417	238	3807	57.1	9.1	35	15	346.1
Central Florida	11	411	302	3771	73.5	9.2	29	7	342.8
Purdue	12	541	352	3978	65.1	7.4	40	17	331.5
Stanford	11	513	263	3516	51.3	6.9	22	8	319.6
Western Michigan	11	409	238	3414	54.2	8.4	24	16	310.4
North Carolina St.	11	405	210	3401	51.9	8.4	20	11	309.2

Single-Game Highs

Points scored: 77—Louisiana Tech, Sept 19 (vs SW Louisiana).
Net rushing yards: 515—Navy, Oct 17 (vs Colgate).
Passing yards: 615—Louisville, Nov 14 (vs E Carolina).
Rushing and passing yards: 770—Louisiana Tech, Sept 19 (vs SW Louisiana).
Fewest rushing and passing yards allowed: 44—Kansas St, Oct 31 (vs Kansas).

Defense

SCORING

	GP	Pts	Avg
Wisconsin	11	112	10.2
Florida St	12	138	11.5
Ohio St	11	130	11.8
Miami (OH)	11	142	12.9
Virginia Tech	11	142	12.9
Kansas St	12	160	13.3
Air Force	12	160	13.3
Florida	11	155	14.1
Tennessee	12	173	14.4
Texas A&M	13	190	14.6

TOTAL DEFENSE

	GP	Plays	Yds	Avg	Yds/Game
Florida St	12	747	2570	3.4	214.8
Ohio St	11	762	2835	3.7	257.7
Kansas St	12	759	3220	4.2	268.3
Wisconsin	11	714	2973	4.2	270.3
Brigham Young	13	830	3561	4.3	273.9
Oklahoma	11	694	3067	4.4	278.8
Virginia Tech	11	710	3134	4.4	284.9
Texas Tech	11	710	3135	4.4	285.0
Florida	11	773	3153	4.1	286.6
Texas A&M	13	871	3761	4.3	289.3

RUSHING

	GP	Car	Yds	Avg	TD	Yds/Game
Ohio St	11	348	741	2.1	5	67.4
Florida St	12	412	958	2.3	5	79.8
Wisconsin	11	377	986	2.6	4	89.6
Florida	11	393	998	2.5	6	90.7
Brigham Young	13	444	1186	2.7	12	91.2
Tennessee	12	420	1127	2.7	5	93.9
Arkansas	11	390	1050	2.7	6	95.5
Penn St	11	407	1070	2.6	7	97.3
Utah	11	344	1071	3.1	9	97.4
Kansas St	12	433	1179	2.7	3	98.3

TURNOVER MARGIN

		Turnovers Gained			Turnovers Lost			Margin/
	GP	Fum	Int	Total	Fum	Int	Total	Game
Wisconsin	11	13	18	31	4	5	9	2.00
NE Louisiana	11	21	18	39	12	11	23	1.45
UCLA	11	21	12	33	6	11	17	1.45
Air Force	12	14	16	30	7	6	13	1.42
Tulane	11	12	14	26	5	6	11	1.36
Tennessee	12	17	16	33	10	7	17	1.33
Texas A&M	13	16	15	31	10	5	15	1.23
Syracuse	11	13	11	24	5	6	11	1.18

PASSING EFFICIENCY

	GP	Att	Comp	Yds	Pct Comp	Yds/Att	TD	Pct TD	Int	Pct Int	Rating Pts
Florida St	12	335	138	1620	41.19	4.84	9	2.68	18	5.37	79.90
Ohio St	11	414	197	2094	47.59	5.06	7	1.69	17	4.11	87.40
Southern Cal	12	455	225	2248	50.56	4.94	14	3.07	24	5.27	90.60
Colorado	11	290	138	1633	47.59	5.63	4	1.38	11	3.79	91.90
Miami (OH)	11	298	142	1659	47.65	5.57	6	2.01	13	4.36	92.30
Wisconsin	11	337	182	1987	54.00	5.90	5	1.48	18	5.34	97.70
Florida	11	380	197	2155	51.84	5.67	9	2.37	13	3.42	100.5
Penn St	11	362	188	2170	51.93	5.99	9	2.49	17	4.70	101.1
Kansas St	12	326	141	2041	43.25	6.26	15	4.60	16	4.91	101.2
Michigan St	12	385	188	2298	48.83	5.97	11	2.86	13	3.38	101.6

FOR THE RECORD·Year by Year

National Champions

Year	Champion	Record	Bowl Game	Head Coach
1883	Yale	8-0-0	No bowl	Ray Tompkins (Captain)
1884	Yale	9-0-0	No bowl	Eugene L. Richards (Captain)
1885	Princeton	9-0-0	No bowl	Charles DeCamp (Captain)
1886	Yale	9-0-1	No bowl	Robert N. Corwin (Captain)
1887	Yale	9-0-0	No bowl	Harry W. Beecher (Captain)
1888	Yale	13-0-0	No bowl	Walter Camp
1889	Princeton	10-0-0	No bowl	Edgar Poe (Captain)
1890	Harvard	11-0-0	No bowl	George A. Stewart/George C. Adams
1891	Yale	13-0-0	No bowl	Walter Camp
1892	Yale	13-0-0	No bowl	Walter Camp
1893	Princeton	11-0-0	No bowl	Tom Trenchard (Captain)
1894	Yale	16-0-0	No bowl	William C. Rhodes
1895	Pennsylvania	14-0-0	No bowl	George Woodruff
1896	Princeton	10-0-1	No bowl	Garrett Cochran
1897	Pennsylvania	15-0-0	No bowl	George Woodruff
1898	Harvard	11-0-0	No bowl	W. Cameron Forbes
1899	Harvard	10-0-1	No bowl	Benjamin H. Dibblee
1900	Yale	12-0-0	No bowl	Malcolm McBride
1901	Michigan	11-0-0	Won Rose	Fielding Yost
1902	Michigan	11-0-0	No bowl	Fielding Yost
1903	Princeton	11-0-0	No bowl	Art Hillebrand
1904	Pennsylvania	12-0-0	No bowl	Carl Williams
1905	Chicago	11-0-0	No bowl	Amos Alonzo Stagg
1906	Princeton	9-0-1	No bowl	Bill Roper
1907	Yale	9-0-1	No bowl	Bill Knox
1908	Pennsylvania	11-0-1	No bowl	Sol Metzger
1909	Yale	10-0-0	No bowl	Howard Jones
1910	Harvard	8-0-1	No bowl	Percy Houghton
1911	Princeton	8-0-2	No bowl	Bill Roper
1912	Harvard	9-0-0	No bowl	Percy Houghton
1913	Harvard	9-0-0	No bowl	Percy Houghton
1914	Army	9-0-0	No bowl	Charley Daly
1915	Cornell	9-0-0	No bowl	Al Sharpe
1916	Pittsburgh	8-0-0	No bowl	Pop Warner
1917	Georgia Tech	9-0-0	No bowl	John Heisman
1918	Pittsburgh	4-1-0	No bowl	Pop Warner
1919	Harvard	9-0-1	Won Rose	Bob Fisher
1920	California	9-0-0	Won Rose	Andy Smith
1921	Cornell	8-0-0	No bowl	Gil Dobie
1922	Cornell	8-0-0	No bowl	Gil Dobie
1923	Illinois	8-0-0	No bowl	Bob Zuppke
1924	Notre Dame	10-0-0	Won Rose	Knute Rockne
1925	Alabama (H)	10-0-0	Won Rose	Wallace Wade
	Dartmouth (D)	8-0-0	No bowl	Jesse Hawley
1926	Alabama (H)	9-0-1	Tied Rose	Wallace Wade
	Stanford (D)(H)	10-0-1	Tied Rose	Pop Warner
1927	Illinois	7-0-1	No bowl	Bob Zuppke
1928	Georgia Tech (H)	10-0-0	Won Rose	Bill Alexander
	Southern Cal (D)	9-0-1	No bowl	Howard Jones
1929	Notre Dame	9-0-0	No bowl	Knute Rockne
1930	Notre Dame	10-0-0	No bowl	Knute Rockne
1931	Southern Cal	10-1-0	Won Rose	Howard Jones
1932	Southern Cal (H)	10-0-0	Won Rose	Howard Jones
	Michigan (D)	8-0-0	No bowl	Harry Kipke
1933	Michigan	7-0-1	No bowl	Harry Kipke
1934	Minnesota	8-0-0	No bowl	Bernie Bierman
1935	Minnesota (H)	8-0-0	No bowl	Bernie Bierman
	Southern Methodist (D)	12-1-0	Lost Rose	Matty Bell
1936	Minnesota	7-1-0	No bowl	Bernie Bierman
1937	Pittsburgh	9-0-1	No bowl	Jock Sutherland
1938	Texas Christian (AP)	11-0-0	Won Sugar	Dutch Meyer
	Notre Dame (D)	8-1-0	No bowl	Elmer Layden
1939	Southern Cal (D)	8-0-2	Won Rose	Howard Jones
	Texas A&M (AP)	11-0-0	Won Sugar	Homer Norton
1940	Minnesota	8-0-0	No bowl	Bernie Bierman
1941	Minnesota	8-0-0	No bowl	Bernie Bierman
1942	Ohio St	9-1-0	No bowl	Paul Brown

Year	Champion	Record	Bowl Game	Head Coach
1943	Notre Dame	9-1-0	No bowl	Frank Leahy
1944	Army	9-0-0	No bowl	Red Blaik
1945	Army	9-0-0	No bowl	Red Blaik
1946	Notre Dame	8-0-1	No bowl	Frank Leahy
1947	Notre Dame	9-0-0	No bowl	Frank Leahy
	Michigan*	10-0-0	Won Rose	Fritz Crisler
1948	Michigan	9-0-0	No bowl	Bennie Oosterbaan
1949	Notre Dame	10-0-0	No bowl	Frank Leahy
1950	Oklahoma	10-1-0	Lost Sugar	Bud Wilkinson
1951	Tennessee	10-1-0	Lost Sugar	Bob Neyland
1952	Michigan St	9-0-0	No bowl	Biggie Munn
1953	Maryland	10-1-0	Lost Orange	Jim Tatum
1954	Ohio St	10-0-0	Won Rose	Woody Hayes
	UCLA (UPI)	9-0-0	No bowl	Red Sanders
1955	Oklahoma	11-0-0	Won Orange	Bud Wilkinson
1956	Oklahoma	10-0-0	No bowl	Bud Wilkinson
1957	Auburn	10-0-0	No bowl	Shug Jordan
	Ohio St (UPI)	9-1-0	Won Rose	Woody Hayes
1958	Louisiana St	11-0-0	Won Sugar	Paul Dietzel
1959	Syracuse	11-0-0	Won Cotton	Ben Schwartzwalder
1960	Minnesota	8-2-0	Lost Rose	Murray Warmath
1961	Alabama	11-0-0	Won Sugar	Bear Bryant
1962	Southern Cal	11-0-0	Won Rose	John McKay
1963	Texas	11-0-0	Won Cotton	Darrell Royal
1964	Alabama	10-1-0	Lost Orange	Bear Bryant
1965	Alabama	9-1-1	Won Orange	Bear Bryant
	Michigan St (UPI)	10-1-0	Lost Rose	Duffy Daugherty
1966	Notre Dame	9-0-1	No bowl	Ara Parseghian
1967	Southern Cal	10-1-0	Won Rose	John McKay
1968	Ohio St	10-0-0	Won Rose	Woody Hayes
1969	Texas	11-0-0	Won Cotton	Darrell Royal
1970	Nebraska	11-0-1	Won Orange	Bob Devaney
	Texas (UPI)	10-1-0	Lost Cotton	Darrell Royal
1971	Nebraska	13-0-0	Won Orange	Bob Devaney
1972	Southern Cal	12-0-0	Won Rose	John McKay
1973	Notre Dame	11-0-0	Won Sugar	Ara Parseghian
	Alabama (UPI)	11-1-0	Lost Sugar	Bear Bryant
1974	Oklahoma	11-0-0	No bowl	Barry Switzer
	Southern Cal (UPI)	10-1-1	Won Rose	John McKay
1975	Oklahoma	11-1-0	Won Orange	Barry Switzer
1976	Pittsburgh	12-0-0	Won Sugar	Johnny Majors
1977	Notre Dame	11-1-0	Won Cotton	Dan Devine
1978	Alabama	11-1-0	Won Sugar	Bear Bryant
	Southern Cal (UPI)	12-1-0	Won Rose	John Robinson
1979	Alabama	12-0-0	Won Sugar	Bear Bryant
1980	Georgia	12-0-0	Won Sugar	Vince Dooley
1981	Clemson	12-0-0	Won Orange	Danny Ford
1982	Penn St	11-1-0	Won Sugar	Joe Paterno
1983	Miami (FL)	11-1-0	Won Orange	Howard Schnellenberger
1984	Brigham Young	13-0-0	Won Holiday	LaVell Edwards
1985	Oklahoma	11-1-0	Won Orange	Barry Switzer
1986	Penn St	12-0-0	Won Fiesta	Joe Paterno
1987	Miami (FL)	12-0-0	Won Orange	Jimmy Johnson
1988	Notre Dame	12-0-0	Won Fiesta	Lou Holtz
1989	Miami (FL)	11-1-0	Won Sugar	Dennis Erickson
1990	Colorado	11-1-1	Won Orange	Bill McCartney
	Georgia Tech (UPI)	11-0-1	Won Citrus	Bobby Ross
1991	Miami (FL)	12-0-0	Won Orange	Dennis Erickson
	Washington (CNN)	12-0-0	Won Rose	Don James
1992	Alabama	13-0-0	Won Sugar	Gene Stallings
1993	Florida St	12-1-0	Won Orange	Bobby Bowden
1994	Nebraska	13-0-0	Won Orange	Tom Osborne
1995	Nebraska	12-0-0	Won Fiesta	Tom Osborne
†1996	Florida	12–1	Won Sugar	Steve Spurrier

Year	Champion	Record	Bowl Game	Head Coach
1997	Michigan	12–0	Won Rose	Lloyd Carr
	Nebraska (ESPN)	13–0	Won Orange	Tom Osborne
1998	Tennessee	13–0	Won Fiesta	Phillip Fulmer

*The AP, which had voted Notre Dame No. 1, took a second vote, giving the national title to Michigan after its 49–0 win over Southern Cal in the Rose Bowl.   Note: Selectors: Helms Athletic Foundation (H) 1883–1935, The Dickinson System (D) 1924–40, The Associated Press (AP) 1936–present, United Press International (UPI) 1958–90, *USA Today*/CNN (CNN) 1991–96, and *USA Today*/ESPN (ESPN) 1997–present. †In 1996 the NCAA introduced overtime to break ties.

Results of Major Bowl Games

Rose Bowl

1-1-02	Michigan 49, Stanford 0
1-1-16	Washington St 14, Brown 0
1-1-17	Oregon 14, Pennsylvania 0
1-1-18	Mare Island 19, Camp Lewis 7
1-1-19	Great Lakes 17, Mare Island 0
1-1-20	Harvard 7, Oregon 6
1-1-21	California 28, Ohio St 0
1-2-22	Washington & Jefferson 0, California 0
1-1-23	Southern Cal 14, Penn St 3
1-1-24	Navy 14, Washington 14
1-1-25	Notre Dame 27, Stanford 10
1-1-26	Alabama 20, Washington 19
1-1-27	Alabama 7, Stanford 7
1-2-28	Stanford 7, Pittsburgh 6
1-1-29	Georgia Tech 8, California 7
1-1-30	Southern Cal 47, Pittsburgh 14
1-1-31	Alabama 24, Washington St 0
1-1-32	Southern Cal 21, Tulane 12
1-2-33	Southern Cal 35, Pittsburgh 0
1-1-34	Columbia 7, Stanford 0
1-1-35	Alabama 29, Stanford 13
1-1-36	Stanford 7, Southern Methodist 0
1-1-37	Pittsburgh 21, Washington 0
1-1-38	California 13, Alabama 0
1-2-39	Southern Cal 7, Duke 3
1-1-40	Southern Cal 14, Tennessee 0
1-1-41	Stanford 21, Nebraska 13
1-1-42	Oregon St 20, Duke 16
1-1-43	Georgia 9, UCLA 0
1-1-44	Southern Cal 29, Washington 0
1-1-45	Southern Cal 25, Tennessee 0
1-1-46	Alabama 34, Southern Cal 14
1-1-47	Illinois 45, UCLA 14
1-1-48	Michigan 49, Southern Cal 0
1-1-49	Northwestern 20, California 14
1-2-50	Ohio St 17, California 14
1-1-51	Michigan 14, California 6
1-1-52	Illinois 40, Stanford 7
1-1-53	Southern Cal 7, Wisconsin 0
1-1-54	Michigan St 28, UCLA 20
1-1-55	Ohio St 20, Southern Cal 7
1-2-56	Michigan St 17, UCLA 14
1-1-57	Iowa 35, Oregon St 19
1-1-58	Ohio St 10, Oregon 7
1-1-59	Iowa 38, California 12
1-1-60	Washington 44, Wisconsin 8
1-2-61	Washington 17, Minnesota 7
1-1-62	Minnesota 21, UCLA 3
1-1-63	Southern Cal 42, Wisconsin 37
1-1-64	Illinois 17, Washington 7
1-1-65	Michigan 34, Oregon St 7
1-1-66	UCLA 14, Michigan St 12
1-2-67	Purdue 14, Southern Cal 13
1-1-68	Southern Cal 14, Indiana 3
1-1-69	Ohio St 27, Southern Cal 16
1-1-70	Southern Cal 10, Michigan 3
1-1-71	Stanford 27, Ohio St 17
1-1-72	Stanford 13, Michigan 12
1-1-73	Southern Cal 42, Ohio St 17
1-1-74	Ohio St 42, Southern Cal 21
1-1-75	Southern Cal 18, Ohio St 17
1-1-76	UCLA 23, Ohio St 10
1-1-77	Southern Cal 14, Michigan 6
1-2-78	Washington 27, Michigan 20
1-1-79	Southern Cal 17, Michigan 10
1-1-80	Southern Cal 17, Ohio St 16
1-1-81	Michigan 23, Washington 6
1-1-82	Washington 28, Iowa 0
1-1-83	UCLA 24, Michigan 14
1-2-84	UCLA 45, Illinois 9
1-1-85	Southern Cal 20, Ohio St 17
1-1-86	UCLA 45, Iowa 28
1-1-87	Arizona St 22, Michigan 15
1-1-88	Michigan St 20, Southern Cal 17
1-2-89	Michigan 22, Southern Cal 14
1-1-90	Southern Cal 17, Michigan 10
1-1-91	Washington 46, Iowa 34
1-1-92	Washington 34, Michigan 14
1-1-93	Michigan 38, Washington 31
1-1-94	Wisconsin 21, UCLA 16
1-2-95	Penn St 38, Oregon 20
1-1-96	Southern Cal 41, Northwestern 32
1-1-97	Ohio St 20, Arizona St 17
1-1-98	Michigan 21, Washington St 16
1-1-99	Wisconsin 38, UCLA 31

City: Pasadena. Stadium: Rose Bowl, capacity 102,083.

Playing Sites: Tournament Park (1902, 1916-22), Rose Bowl (1923-41, since 1943), Duke Stadium, Durham, NC (1942).

Orange Bowl

1-1-35	Bucknell 26, Miami (FL) 0
1-1-36	Catholic 20, Mississippi 19
1-1-37	Duquesne 13, Mississippi St 12
1-1-38	Auburn 6, Michigan St 0
1-2-39	Tennessee 17, Oklahoma 0
1-1-40	Georgia Tech 21, Missouri 7

Note: The Fiesta, Orange and Sugar Bowls constitute the Bowl Alliance, formed in 1995. The Alliance holds six berths: one each for the champions of the SEC, Big 12, Big East and ACC, and two at-large, one of which is guaranteed to Notre Dame if it is ranked in the top 10 in one of the two final regular-season polls. Of the six teams, the two highest-ranked go to the Fiesta Bowl in 1996, the Sugar Bowl in 1997, and the Orange Bowl in 1998. The champions of the Big Ten and Pac-10 go to the Rose Bowl, which will join the alliance after the 1998 season. Once these four matches have been set conferences may place the remaining qualified teams in the other bowls. Teams that have won at least six games against Division I-A teams qualify.

Orange Bowl *(Cont.)*

1-1-41 ....Mississippi St 14, Georgetown 7
1-1-42 ....Georgia 40, Texas Christian 26
1-1-43 ....Alabama 37, Boston College 21
1-1-44 ....Louisiana St 19, Texas A&M 14
1-1-45 ....Tulsa 26, Georgia Tech 12
1-1-46 ....Miami (FL) 13, Holy Cross 6
1-1-47 ....Rice 8, Tennessee 0
1-1-48 ....Georgia Tech 20, Kansas 14
1-1-49 ....Texas 41, Georgia 28
1-2-50 ....Santa Clara 21, Kentucky 13
1-1-51 ....Clemson 15, Miami (FL) 14
1-1-52 ....Georgia Tech 17, Baylor 14
1-1-53 ....Alabama 61, Syracuse 6
1-1-54 ....Oklahoma 7, Maryland 0
1-1-55 ....Duke 34, Nebraska 7
1-2-56 ....Oklahoma 20, Maryland 6
1-1-57 ....Colorado 27, Clemson 21
1-1-58 ....Oklahoma 48, Duke 21
1-1-59 ....Oklahoma 21, Syracuse 6
1-1-60 ....Georgia 14, Missouri 0
1-2-61 ....Missouri 21, Navy 14
1-1-62 ....Louisiana St 25, Colorado 7
1-1-63 ....Alabama 17, Oklahoma 0
1-1-64 ....Nebraska 13, Auburn 7
1-1-65 ....Texas 21, Alabama 17
1-1-66 ....Alabama 39, Nebraska 28
1-2-67 ....Florida 27, Georgia Tech 12
1-1-68 ....Oklahoma 26, Tennessee 24
1-1-69 ....Penn St 15, Kansas 14
1-1-70 ....Penn St 10, Missouri 3
1-1-71 ....Nebraska 17, Louisiana St 12
1-1-72 ....Nebraska 38, Alabama 6
1-1-73 ....Nebraska 40, Notre Dame 6
1-1-74 ....Penn St 16, Louisiana St 9
1-1-75 ....Notre Dame 13, Alabama 11
1-1-76 ....Oklahoma 14, Michigan 6
1-1-77 ....Ohio St 27, Colorado 10
1-2-78 ....Arkansas 31, Oklahoma 6
1-1-79 ....Oklahoma 31, Nebraska 24
1-1-80 ....Oklahoma 24, Florida St 7
1-1-81 ....Oklahoma 18, Florida St 17
1-1-82 ....Clemson 22, Nebraska 15
1-1-83 ....Nebraska 21, Louisiana St 20
1-2-84 ....Miami (FL) 31, Nebraska 30
1-1-85 ....Washington 28, Oklahoma 17
1-1-86 ....Oklahoma 25, Penn St 10
1-1-87 ....Oklahoma 42, Arkansas 8
1-1-88 ....Miami (FL) 20, Oklahoma 14
1-2-89 ....Miami (FL) 23, Nebraska 3
1-1-90 ....Notre Dame 21, Colorado 6
1-1-91 ....Colorado 10, Notre Dame 9
1-1-92 ....Miami (FL) 22, Nebraska 0
1-1-93 ....Florida St 27, Nebraska 14
1-1-94 ....Florida St 18, Nebraska 16
1-1-95 ....Nebraska 24, Miami (FL) 17
1-1-96 ....Florida St 31, Notre Dame 26
12-31-96 ....Nebraska 41, Virginia Tech 21
1-2-98 ....Nebraska 42, Tennessee 17
1-2-99 ....Florida 31, Syracuse 10

City: Miami. Stadium: Pro Player Stadium, capacity 75,192.
Playing Sites: Orange Bowl (1935-96), Pro Player Stadium
(since 1996).

Sugar Bowl

1-1-35 ....Tulane 20, Temple 14
1-1-36 ....Texas Christian 3, Louisiana St 2
1-1-37 ....Santa Clara 21, Louisiana St 14
1-1-38 ....Santa Clara 6, Louisiana St 0
1-2-39 ....Texas Christian 15, Carnegie Tech 7
1-1-40 ....Texas A&M 14, Tulane 13
1-1-41 ....Boston Col 19, Tennessee 13
1-1-42 ....Fordham 2, Missouri 0
1-1-43 ....Tennessee 14, Tulsa 7
1-1-44 ....Georgia Tech 20, Tulsa 18
1-1-45 ....Duke 29, Alabama 26
1-1-46 ....Oklahoma St 33, St Mary's (CA) 13
1-1-47 ....Georgia 20, N Carolina 10
1-1-48 ....Texas 27, Alabama 7
1-1-49 ....Oklahoma 14, N Carolina 6
1-2-50 ....Oklahoma 35, Louisiana St 0
1-1-51 ....Kentucky 13, Oklahoma 7
1-1-52 ....Maryland 28, Tennessee 13
1-1-53 ....Georgia Tech 24, Mississippi 7
1-1-54 ....Georgia Tech 42, W Virginia 19
1-1-55 ....Navy 21, Mississippi 0
1-2-56 ....Georgia Tech 7, Pittsburgh 0
1-1-57 ....Baylor 13, Tennessee 7
1-1-58 ....Mississippi 39, Texas 7
1-1-59 ....Louisiana St 7, Clemson 0
1-1-60 ....Mississippi 21, Louisiana St 0
1-2-61 ....Mississippi 14, Rice 6
1-1-62 ....Alabama 10, Arkansas 3
1-1-63 ....Mississippi 17, Arkansas 13
1-1-64 ....Alabama 12, Mississippi 7
1-1-65 ....Louisiana St 13, Syracuse 10
1-1-66 ....Missouri 20, Florida 18
1-2-67 ....Alabama 34, Nebraska 7
1-1-68 ....Louisiana St 20, Wyoming 13
1-1-69 ....Arkansas 16, Georgia 2
1-1-70 ....Mississippi 27, Arkansas 22
1-1-71 ....Tennessee 34, Air Force 13
1-1-72 ....Oklahoma 40, Auburn 22
12-31-72 ....Oklahoma 14, Penn St 0
12-31-73 ....Notre Dame 24, Alabama 23
12-31-74 ....Nebraska 13, Florida 10
12-31-75 ....Alabama 13, Penn St 6
1-1-77 ....Pittsburgh 27, Georgia 3
1-2-78 ....Alabama 35, Ohio St 6
1-1-79 ....Alabama 14, Penn St 7
1-1-80 ....Alabama 24, Arkansas 9
1-1-81 ....Georgia 17, Notre Dame 10
1-1-82 ....Pittsburgh 24, Georgia 20
1-1-83 ....Penn St 27, Georgia 23
1-2-84 ....Auburn 9, Michigan 7
1-1-85 ....Nebraska 28, Louisiana St 10
1-1-86 ....Tennessee 35, Miami (FL) 7
1-1-87 ....Nebraska 30, Louisiana St 15
1-1-88 ....Syracuse 16, Auburn 16
1-2-89 ....Florida St 13, Auburn 7
1-1-90 ....Miami (FL) 33, Alabama 25
1-1-91 ....Tennessee 23, Virginia 22
1-1-92 ....Notre Dame 39, Florida 28
1-1-93 ....Alabama 34, Miami (FL) 13
1-1-94 ....Florida 41, West Virginia 7
1-2-95 ....Florida St 23, Florida 17
12-31-95 ....Virginia Tech 28, Texas 10
1-2-97 ....Florida 52, Florida St 20

Sugar Bowl *(Cont.)*

1-1-98 ....Florida St 31, Ohio St 14
1-1-99 ....Ohio St 24, Texas A&M 14

City: New Orleans. Stadium: Louisiana Superdome, capacity 76,791.

Playing Sites: Tulane Stadium (1935–74), Louisiana Superdome (since 1975).

Cotton Bowl

1-1-37 ....Texas Christian 16, Marquette 6
1-1-38 ....Rice 28, Colorado 14
1-2-39 ....St. Mary's (CA) 20, Texas Tech 13
1-1-40 ....Clemson 6, Boston Col 3
1-1-41 ....Texas A&M 13, Fordham 12
1-1-42 ....Alabama 29, Texas A&M 21
1-1-43 ....Texas 14, Georgia Tech 7
1-1-44 ....Texas 7, Randolph Field 7
1-1-45 ....Oklahoma St 34, Texas Christian 0
1-1-46 ....Texas 40, Missouri 27
1-1-47 ....Arkansas 0, Louisiana St 0
1-1-48 ....SMU 13, Penn St 13
1-1-49 ....SMU 21, Oregon 13
1-2-50 ....:Rice 27, N Carolina 13
1-1-51 ....Tennessee 20, Texas 14
1-1-52 ....Kentucky 20, Texas Christian 7
1-1-53 ....Texas 16, Tennessee 0
1-1-54 ....Rice 28, Alabama 6
1-1-55 ....Georgia Tech 14, Arkansas 6
1-2-56 ....Mississippi 14, Texas Christian 13
1-1-57 ....Texas Christian 28, Syracuse 27
1-1-58 ....Navy 20, Rice 7
1-1-59 ....Texas Christian 0, Air Force 0
1-1-60 ....Syracuse 23, Texas 14
1-2-61 ....Duke 7, Arkansas 6
1-1-62 ....Texas 12, Mississippi 7
1-1-63 ....Louisiana St 13, Texas 0
1-1-64 ....Texas 28, Navy 6
1-1-65 ....Arkansas 10, Nebraska 7
1-1-66 ....Louisiana St 14, Arkansas 7
12-31-66 ....Georgia 24, SMU 9
1-1-68 ....Texas A&M 20, Alabama 16
1-1-69 ....Texas 36, Tennessee 13
1-1-70 ....Texas 21, Notre Dame 17
1-1-71 ....Notre Dame 24, Texas 11
1-1-72 ....Penn St 30, Texas 6
1-1-73 ....Texas 17, Alabama 13
1-1-74 ....Nebraska 19, Texas 3
1-1-75 ....Penn St 41, Baylor 20
1-1-76 ....Arkansas 31, Georgia 10
1-1-77 ....Houston 30, Maryland 21
1-2-78 ....Notre Dame 38, Texas 10
1-1-79 ....Notre Dame 35, Houston 34
1-1-80 ....Houston 17, Nebraska 14
1-1-81 ....Alabama 30, Baylor 2
1-1-82 ....Texas 14, Alabama 12
1-1-83 ....SMU 7, Pittsburgh 3
1-2-84 ....Georgia 10, Texas 9
1-1-85 ....Boston Col 45, Houston 28
1-1-86 ....Texas A&M 36, Auburn 16
1-1-87 ....Ohio St 28, Texas A&M 12
1-1-88 ....Texas A&M 35, Notre Dame 10
1-2-89 ....UCLA 17, Arkansas 3
1-1-90 ....Tennessee 31, Arkansas 27
1-1-91 ....Miami (FL) 46, Texas 3
1-1-92 ....Florida St 10, Texas A&M 2
1-1-93 ....Notre Dame 28, Texas A&M 3
1-1-94 ....Notre Dame 24, Texas A&M 21

Cotton Bowl *(Cont.)*

1-2-95 ....Southern Cal 55, Texas Tech 14
1-1-96 ....Colorado 38, Oregon 6
1-1-97 ....Brigham Young 19, Kansas St 15
1-1-98 ....UCLA 29, Texas A&M 23
1-1-99 ....Texas 38, Mississippi St 11

City: Dallas. Stadium: Cotton Bowl, capacity 68,252.

Sun Bowl

1-1-36 ....Hardin-Simmons 14, New Mexico St 14
1-1-37 ....Hardin-Simmons 34, UTEP 6
1-1-38 ....W Virginia 7, Texas Tech 6
1-2-39 ....Utah 26, New Mexico 0
1-1-40 ....Catholic 0, Arizona St 0
1-1-41 ....Case Reserve 26, Arizona St 13
1-1-42 ....Tulsa 6, Texas Tech 0
1-1-43 ....2nd Air Force 13, Hardin-Simmons 7
1-1-44 ....Southwestern (TX) 7, New Mexico 0
1-1-45 ....Southwestern (TX) 35, New Mexico 0
1-1-46 ....New Mexico 34, Denver 24
1-1-47 ....Cincinnati 18, Virginia Tech 6
1-1-48 ....Miami (OH) 13, Texas Tech 12
1-1-49 ....:W Virginia 21, UTEP 12
1-2-50 ....UTEP 33, Georgetown 20
1-1-51 ....West Texas St 14, Cincinnati 13
1-1-52 ....Texas Tech 25, Pacific 14
1-1-53 ....Pacific 26, Southern Miss 7
1-1-54 ....UTEP 37, Southern Miss 14
1-1-55 ....UTEP 47, Florida St 20
1-2-56 ....Wyoming 21, Texas Tech 14
1-1-57 ....George Washington 13, UTEP 0
1-1-58 ....Louisville 34, Drake 20
12-31-58 ....Wyoming 14, Hardin-Simmons 6
12-31-59 ....New Mexico St 28, N Texas 8
12-31-60 ....New Mexico St 20, Utah St 13
12-30-61 ....Villanova 17, Wichita St 9
12-31-62 ....W Texas St 15, Ohio 14
12-31-63 ....Oregon 21, SMU 14
12-26-64 ....Georgia 7, Texas Tech 0
12-31-65 ....UTEP 13, Texas Christian 12
12-24-66 ....Wyoming 28, Florida St 20
12-30-67 ....UTEP 14, Mississippi 7
12-28-68 ....Auburn 34, Arizona 10
12-20-69 ....Nebraska 45, Georgia 6
12-19-70 ....Georgia Tech 17, Texas Tech 9
12-18-71 ....Louisiana St 33, Iowa St 15
12-30-72 ....N Carolina 32, Texas Tech 28
12-29-73 ....Missouri 34, Auburn 17
12-28-74 ....Mississippi St 26, N Carolina 24
12-26-75 ....Pittsburgh 33, Kansas 19
1-2-77 ....Texas A&M 37, Florida 14
12-31-77 ....Stanford 24, Louisiana St 14
12-23-78 ....Texas 42, Maryland 0
12-22-79 ....Washington 14, Texas 7
12-27-80 ....Nebraska 31, Mississippi St 17
12-26-81 ....Oklahoma 40, Houston 14
12-25-82 ....N Carolina 26, Texas 10
12-24-83 ....Alabama 28, SMU 7
12-22-84 ....Maryland 28, Tennessee 27
12-28-85 ....Georgia 13, Arizona 13
12-25-86 ....Alabama 28, Washington 6
12-25-87 ....Oklahoma St 35, W Virginia 33
12-24-88 ....Alabama 29, Army 28
12-30-89 ....Pittsburgh 31, Texas A&M 28
12-31-90 ....Michigan St 17, Southern Cal 16
12-31-91 ....UCLA 6, Illinois 3
12-31-92 ....Baylor 20, Arizona 15

Sun Bowl *(Cont.)*

12-24-93 ....Oklahoma 41, Texas Tech 10
12-30-94 ....Texas 35, N Carolina 31
12-29-95 ....Iowa 38, Washington 18
12-31-96 ....Stanford 38, Michigan St 0
12-31-97 ....Arizona St 17, Iowa 7
12-31-98 ....Texas Christian 28, Southern Cal 19

City: El Paso. Stadium: Sun Bowl, capacity 52,000.

Name Changes: Sun Bowl (1936–86; 94–), John Hancock Sun Bowl (1987–88), John Hancock Bowl (1989–93).

Playing Sites: Kidd Field (1936–62), Sun Bowl (since 1963).

Gator Bowl

1-1-46 ....Wake Forest 26, S Carolina 14
1-1-47 ....Oklahoma 34, N Carolina St 13
1-1-48 ....Maryland 20, Georgia 20
1-1-49 ....Clemson 24, Missouri 23
1-2-50 ....Maryland 20, Missouri 7
1-1-51 ....Wyoming 20, Washington & Lee 7
1-1-52 ....Miami (FL) 14, Clemson 0
1-1-53 ....Florida 14, Tulsa 13
1-1-54 ....Texas Tech 35, Auburn 13
12-31-54 ....Auburn 33, Baylor 13
12-31-55 ....Vanderbilt 25, Auburn 13
12-29-56 ....Georgia Tech 21, Pittsburgh 14
12-28-57 ....Tennessee 3, Texas A&M 0
12-27-58 ....Mississippi 7, Florida 3
1-2-60 ....Arkansas 14, Georgia Tech 7
12-31-60 ....Florida 13, Baylor 12
12-30-61 ....Penn St 30, Georgia Tech 15
12-29-62 ....Florida 17, Penn St 7
12-28-63 ....N Carolina 35, Air Force 0
1-2-65 ....Florida St 36, Oklahoma 19
12-31-65 ....Georgia Tech 31, Texas Tech 21
12-31-66 ....Tennessee 18, Syracuse 12
12-30-67 ....Penn St 17, Florida St 17
12-28-68 ....Missouri 35, Alabama 10
12-27-69 ....Florida 14, Tennessee 13
1-2-71 ....Auburn 35, Mississippi 28
12-31-71 ....Georgia 7, N Carolina 3
12-30-72 ....Auburn 24, Colorado 3
12-29-73 ....Texas Tech 28, Tennessee 19
12-30-74 ....Auburn 27, Texas 3
12-29-75 ....Maryland 13, Florida 0
12-27-76 ....Notre Dame 20, Penn St 9
12-30-77 ....Pittsburgh 34, Clemson 3
12-29-78 ....Clemson 17, Ohio St 15
12-28-79 ....N Carolina 17, Michigan 15
12-29-80 ....Pittsburgh 37, S Carolina 9
12-28-81 ....N Carolina 31, Arkansas 27
12-30-82 ....Florida St 31, W Virginia 12
12-30-83 ....Florida 14, Iowa 6
12-28-84 ....Oklahoma St 21, S Carolina 14
12-30-85 ....Florida St 34, Oklahoma St 23
12-27-86 ....Clemson 27, Stanford 21
12-31-87 ....Louisiana St 30, S Carolina 13
1-1-89 ....Georgia 34, Michigan St 27
12-30-89 ....Clemson 27, W Virginia 7
1-1-91 ....Michigan 35, Mississippi 3
12-29-91 ....Oklahoma 48, Virginia 14
12-31-92 ....Florida 27, N Carolina St 10
12-31-93 ....Alabama 24, North Carolina 10
12-30-94 ....Tennessee 45, Virginia Tech 23
1-1-96 ....Syracuse 41, Clemson 0
1-1-97 ....N Carolina 20, W Virginia 13
1-1-98 ....N Carolina 42, Viginia Tech 13
1-1-99 ....Georgia Tech 35, Notre Dame 28

City: Jacksonville, FL. Stadium: Jacksonville Municipal Stadium, capacity 73,000.

Florida Citrus Bowl

1-1-47 ....Catawba 31, Maryville (TN) 6
1-1-48 ....Catawba 7, Marshall 0
1-1-49 ....Murray St 21, Sul Ross St 21
1-2-50 ....St Vincent 7, Emory & Henry 6
1-1-51 ....Morris Harvey 35, Emory & Henry 14
1-1-52 ....Stetson 35, Arkansas St 20
1-1-53 ....E Texas St 33, Tennessee Tech 0
1-1-54 ....E Texas St 7, Arkansas St 7
1-1-55 ....NE-Omaha 7, Eastern Kentucky 6
1-2-56 ....Juniata 6, Missouri Valley 6
1-1-57 ....W Texas St 20, Southern Miss 13
1-1-58 ....E Texas St 10, Southern Miss 9
12-27-58 ....E Texas St 26, Missouri Valley 7
1-1-60 ....Middle Tennessee St 21, Presbyterian 12
12-30-60 ....Citadel 27, Tennessee Tech 0
12-29-61 ....Lamar 21, Middle Tennessee St 14
12-22-62 ....Houston 49, Miami (OH) 21
12-28-63 ....Western Kentucky 27, Coast Guard 0
12-12-64 ....E Carolina 14, Massachusetts 13
12-11-65 ....E Carolina 31, Maine 0
12-10-66 ....Morgan St 14, West Chester 6
12-16-67 ....TN-Martin 25, West Chester 8
12-27-68 ....Richmond 49, Ohio 42
12-26-69 ....Toledo 56, Davidson 33
12-28-70 ....Toledo 40, William & Mary 12
12-28-71 ....Toledo 28, Richmond 3
12-29-72 ....Tampa 21, Kent St 18
12-22-73 ....Miami (OH) 16, Florida 7
12-21-74 ....Miami (OH) 21, Georgia 10
12-20-75 ....Miami (OH) 20, S Carolina 7
12-18-76 ....Oklahoma St 49, Brigham Young 21
12-23-77 ....Florida St 40, Texas Tech 17
12-23-78 ....N Carolina St 30, Pittsburgh 17
12-22-79 ....Louisiana St 34, Wake Forest 10
12-20-80 ....Florida 35, Maryland 20
12-19-81 ....Missouri 19, Southern Miss 17
12-18-82 ....Auburn 33, Boston Col 26
12-17-83 ....Tennessee 30, Maryland 23
12-22-84 ....Georgia 17, Florida St 17
12-28-85 ....Ohio St 10, Brigham Young 7
1-1-87 ....Auburn 16, Southern Cal 7
1-1-88 ....Clemson 35, Penn St 10
1-2-89 ....Clemson 13, Oklahoma 6
1-1-90 ....Illinois 31, Virginia 21
1-1-91 ....Georgia Tech 45, Nebraska 21
1-1-92 ....California 37, Clemson 13
1-1-93 ....Georgia 21, Ohio State 14
1-1-94 ....Penn State 31, Tennessee 13
1-2-95 ....Alabama 24, Ohio St 17
1-1-96 ....Tennessee 20, Ohio St 14
1-1-97 ....Tennessee 48, Northwestern 28
1-1-98 ....Florida 21, Penn St 6
1-1-99 ....Michigan 45, Arkansas 31

City: Orlando, FL. Stadium: Florida Citrus Bowl, capacity 72,000.

Name Change: Tangerine Bowl (1947–82).

Playing Sites: Tangerine Bowl (1947–72, 1974–82); Florida Field, Gainesville (1973); Orlando Stadium (1983–85); Florida Citrus Bowl-Orlando (since 1986). Tangerine Bowl, Orlando Stadium and Florida Citrus Bowl-Orlando are identical site.

Liberty Bowl

12-19-59 ....Penn St 7, Alabama 0
12-17-60 ....Penn St 41, Oregon 12
12-16-61 ....Syracuse 15, Miami (FL) 14
12-15-62 ....Oregon St 6, Villanova 0

Liberty Bowl (Cont.)

12-21-63 ....Mississippi St 16, N Carolina St 12
12-19-64 ....Utah 32, W Virginia 6
12-18-65 ....Mississippi 13, Auburn 7
12-10-66 ....Miami (FL) 14, Virginia Tech 7
12-16-67 ....N Carolina St 14, Georgia 7
12-14-68 ....Mississippi 34, Virginia Tech 17
12-13-69 ....Colorado 47, Alabama 33
12-12-70 ....Tulane 17, Colorado 3
12-20-71 ....Tennessee 14, Arkansas 13
12-18-72 ....Georgia Tech 31, Iowa St 30
12-17-73 ....N Carolina St 31, Kansas 18
12-16-74 ....Tennessee 7, Maryland 3
12-22-75 ....Southern Cal 20, Texas A&M 0
12-20-76 ....Alabama 36, UCLA 6
12-19-77 ....Nebraska 21, N Carolina 17
12-23-78 ....Missouri 20, Louisiana St 15
12-22-79 ....Penn St 9, Tulane 6
12-27-80 ....Purdue 28, Missouri 25
12-30-81 ....Ohio St 31, Navy 28
12-29-82 ....Alabama 21, Illinois 15
12-29-83 ....Notre Dame 19, Boston Col 18
12-27-84 ....Auburn 21, Arkansas 15
12-27-85 ....Baylor 21, Louisiana St 7
12-29-86 ....Tennessee 21, Minnesota 14
12-29-87 ....Georgia 20, Arkansas 17
12-28-88 ....Indiana 34, S Carolina 10
12-28-89 ....Mississippi 42, Air Force 29
12-27-90 ....Air Force 23, Ohio St 11
12-29-91 ....Air Force 38, Mississippi St 15
12-31-92 ....Mississippi 13, Air Force 0
12-28-93 ....Louisville 18, Michigan St 7
12-31-94 ....Illinois 30, E Carolina 0
12-30-95 ....East Carolina 19, Stanford 13
12-27-96 ....Syracuse 30, Houston 17
12-31-97 ....Southern Mississippi 41, Pittsburgh 7
12-31-98 ....Tulane 41, Brigham Young 27

City: Memphis (since 1965). Stadium: Liberty Bowl Memorial Stadium, capacity 62,380.

Playing Sites: Philadelphia (Municipal Stadium, 1959–63), Atlantic City (Convention Center, 1964).

Bluebonnet Bowl

12-19-59 ....Clemson 23, Texas Christian 7
12-17-60 ....Texas 3, Alabama 3
12-16-61 ....Kansas 33, Rice 7
12-22-62 ....Missouri 14, Georgia Tech 10
12-21-63 ....Baylor 14, LSU 7
12-19-64 ....Tulsa 14, Mississippi 7
12-18-65 ....Tennessee 27, Tulsa 6
12-17-66 ....Texas 19, Mississippi 0
12-23-67 ....Colorado 31, Miami (FL) 21
12-31-68 ....SMU 28, Oklahoma 27
12-31-69 ....Houston 36, Auburn 7
12-31-70 ....Alabama 24, Oklahoma 24
12-31-71 ....Colorado 29, Houston 17
12-30-72 ....Tennessee 24, Louisiana St 17
12-29-73 ....Houston 47, Tulane 7
12-23-74 ....N Carolina St 31, Houston 31
12-27-75 ....Texas 38, Colorado 21
12-31-76 ....Nebraska 27, Texas Tech 24
12-31-77 ....Southern Cal 47, Texas A&M 28
12-31-78 ....Stanford 25, Georgia 22
12-31-79 ....Purdue 27, Tennessee 22
12-31-80 ....N Carolina 16, Texas 7
12-31-81 ....Michigan 33, UCLA 14
12-31-82 ....Arkansas 28, Florida 24
12-31-83 ....Oklahoma St 24, Baylor 14

Bluebonnet Bowl (Cont.)

12-31-84 ....W Virginia 31, Texas Christian 14
12-31-85 ....Air Force 24, Texas 16
12-31-86 ....Baylor 21, Colorado 9
12-31-87 ....Texas 32, Pittsburgh 27

City: Houston. Playing sites: Rice Stadium (1959–67; 1985–86), Astrodome (1968–84, 1987).

Name change: Astro-Bluebonnet Bowl (1968–76). Bowl was discontinued after 1987.

Peach Bowl

12-30-68 ....Louisiana St 31, Florida St 27
12-30-69 ....W Virginia 14, S Carolina 3
12-30-70 ....Arizona St 48, N Carolina 26
12-30-71 ....Mississippi 41, Georgia Tech 18
12-29-72 ....N Carolina St 49, W Virginia 13
12-28-73 ....Georgia 17, Maryland 16
12-28-74 ....Vanderbilt 6, Texas Tech 6
12-31-75 ....W Virginia 13, N Carolina St 10
12-31-76 ....Kentucky 21, N Carolina 0
12-31-77 ....N Carolina St 24, Iowa St 14
12-25-78 ....Purdue 41, Georgia Tech 21
12-31-79 ....Baylor 24, Clemson 18
1-2-81 ....Miami (FL) 20, Virginia Tech 10
12-31-81 ....W Virginia 26, Florida 6
12-31-82 ....Iowa 28, Tennessee 22
12-30-83 ....Florida St 28, N Carolina 3
12-31-84 ....Virginia 27, Purdue 24
12-31-85 ....Army 31, Illinois 29
12-31-86 ....Virginia Tech 25, N Carolina St 24
1-2-88 ....Tennessee 27, Indiana 22
12-31-88 ....N Carolina St 28, Iowa 23
12-30-89 ....Syracuse 19, Georgia 18
12-29-90 ....Auburn 27, Indiana 23
1-1-92 ....E Carolina 37, N Carolina St 34
1-2-93 ....North Carolina 21, Mississippi St 17
12-31-93 ....Clemson 14, Kentucky 13
1-1-95 ....N Carolina St 28, Mississippi St 24
12-30-95 ....Virginia 34, Georgia 27
12-28-96 ....Louisiana St 10, Clemson 7
1-2-98 ....Auburn 21, Clemson 17
12-31-98 ....Georgia 35, Virginia 33

City: Atlanta. Stadium: Georgia Dome, capacity 71,228.
Playing Sites: Grant Field (1968–70), Atlanta-Fulton County Stadium (1971–92), Georgia Dome (since 1993).

Fiesta Bowl

12-27-71 ....Arizona St 45, Florida St 38
12-23-72 ....Arizona St 49, Missouri 35
12-21-73 ....Arizona St 28, Pittsburgh 7
12-28-74 ....Oklahoma St 16, Brigham Young 6
12-26-75 ....Arizona St 17, Nebraska 14
12-25-76 ....Oklahoma 41, Wyoming 7
12-25-77 ....Penn St 42, Arizona St 30
12-25-78 ....Arkansas 10, UCLA 10
12-25-79 ....Pittsburgh 16, Arizona 10
12-26-80 ....Penn St 31, Ohio St 19
1-1-82 ....Penn St 26, Southern Cal 10
1-1-83 ....Arizona St 32, Oklahoma 21
1-2-84 ....Ohio St 28, Pittsburgh 23
1-1-85 ....UCLA 39, Miami (FL) 37
1-1-86 ....Michigan 27, Nebraska 23
1-2-87 ....Penn St 14, Miami (FL) 10
1-1-88 ....Florida St 31, Nebraska 28
1-2-89 ....Notre Dame 34, W Virginia 21
1-1-90 ....Florida St 41, Nebraska 17
1-1-91 ....Louisville 34, Alabama 7
1-1-92 ....Penn St 42, Tennessee 17

Fiesta Bowl *(Cont.)*

1-1-93 ....Syracuse 26, Colorado 22
1-1-94 ....Arizona 29, Miami (FL) 0
1-2-95 ....Colorado 41, Notre Dame 24
1-2-96 ....Nebraska 62, Florida 24
1-1-97 ....Penn St 38, Texas 15
12-31-97 ....Kansas St 35, Syracuse 18
1-4-99 ....Tennessee 23, Florida St 16

City: Tempe, AZ. Stadium: Sun Devil Stadium, capacity 73,656.

Independence Bowl

12-13-76 ....McNeese St 20, Tulsa 16
12-17-77 ....Louisiana Tech 24, Louisville 14
12-16-78 ....E Carolina 35, Louisiana Tech 13
12-15-79 ....Syracuse 31, McNeese St 7
12-13-80 ....Southern Miss 16, McNeese St 14
12-12-81 ....Texas A&M 33, Oklahoma St 16
12-11-82 ....Wisconsin 14, Kansas St 3
12-10-83 ....Air Force 9, Mississippi 3
12-15-84 ....Air Force 23, Virginia Tech 7
12-21-85 ....Minnesota 20, Clemson 13
12-20-86 ....Mississippi 20, Texas Tech 17
12-19-87 ....Washington 24, Tulane 12
12-23-88 ....Southern Miss 38, UTEP 18
12-16-89 ....Oregon 27, Tulsa 24
12-15-90 ....Louisiana Tech 34, Maryland 34
12-29-91 ....Georgia 24, Arkansas 15
12-31-92 ....Wake Forest 39, Oregon 35
12-31-93 ....Virginia Tech 45, Indiana 20
12-28-94 ....Virginia 20, Texas Christian 10
12-29-95 ....Louisiana St 45, Michigan St 26
12-31-96 ....Auburn 32, Army 29
12-28-97 ....Louisiana St 27, Notre Dame 9
12-31-98 ....Mississippi 35, Texas Tech 18

City: Shreveport, LA. Stadium: Independence Stadium, capacity 50,832.

All-American Bowl

12-22-77 ....Maryland 17, Minnesota 7
12-20-78 ....Texas A&M 28, Iowa St 12
12-29-79 ....Missouri 24, S Carolina 14
12-27-80 ....Arkansas 34, Tulane 15
12-31-81 ....Mississippi St 10, Kansas 0
12-31-82 ....Air Force 36, Vanderbilt 28
12-22-83 ....W Virginia 20, Kentucky 16
12-29-84 ....Kentucky 20, Wisconsin 19
12-31-85 ....Georgia Tech 17, Michigan St 14
12-31-86 ....Florida St 27, Indiana 13
12-22-87 ....Virginia 22, Brigham Young 16
12-29-88 ....Florida 14, Illinois 10
12-28-89 ....Texas Tech 49, Duke 21
12-28-90 ....N Carolina St 31, S Mississippi 27

City: Birmingham, AL. Stadium: Legion Field.
Name Change: Hall of Fame Classic (1977–84). Bowl was discontinued after 1990.

Holiday Bowl

12-22-78 ....Navy 23, Brigham Young 16
12-21-79 ....Indiana 38, Brigham Young 37
12-19-80 ....Brigham Young 46, SMU 45
12-18-81 ....Brigham Young 38, Washington St 36
12-17-82 ....Ohio St 47, Brigham Young 17
12-23-83 ....Brigham Young 21, Missouri 17
12-21-84 ....Brigham Young 24, Michigan 17
12-22-85 ....Arkansas 18, Arizona St 17
12-30-86 ....Iowa 39, San Diego St 38

Holiday Bowl *(Cont.)*

12-30-87 ....Iowa 20, Wyoming 19
12-30-88 ....Oklahoma St 62, Wyoming 14
12-29-89 ....Penn St 50, Brigham Young 39
12-29-90 ....Texas A&M 65, Brigham Young 14
12-30-91 ....Iowa 13, Brigham Young 13
12-30-92 ....Hawaii 27, Illinois 17
12-30-93 ....Ohio St 28, Brigham Young 21
12-30-94 ....Michigan 24, Colorado St 14
12-29-95 ....Kansas St 54, Colorado St 21
12-30-96 ....Colorado 33, Washington 21
12-29-97 ....Colorado St 35, Missouri 24
12-30-98 ....Arizona 23, Nebraska 20

City: San Diego. Stadium: San Diego Jack Murphy Stadium, capacity 60,000.

Las Vegas Bowl

12-19-81 ....Toledo 27, San Jose St 25
12-18-82 ....Fresno St 29, Bowling Green 28
12-17-83 ....Northern Illinois 20, Cal St-Fullerton 13
12-15-84 ....UNLV 30, Toledo 13*
12-14-85 ....Fresno St 51, Bowling Green 7
12-13-86 ....San Jose St 37, Miami (OH) 7
12-12-87 ....Eastern Michigan 30, San Jose St 27
12-10-88 ....Fresno St 35, Western Michigan 30
12-9-89 ....Fresno St 27, Ball St 6
12-8-90 ....San Jose St 48, Central Michigan 24
12-14-91 ....Bowling Green 28, Fresno St 21
12-18-92 ....Bowling Green 35, Nevada 34
12-17-93 ....Utah St 42, Ball St 33
12-15-94 ....UNLV 52, Central Michigan 24
12-14-95 ....Toledo 40, Nevada 37
12-19-96 ....Nevada 18, Ball St 15
12-19-97 ....Oregon 41, Air Force 13
12-19-98 ....N Carolina 20, San Diego St 13

* Toledo won later by forfeit.

City: Las Vegas (since 1992). Stadium: Sam Boyd Silver Bowl Stadium, capacity 32,000.

Name change: California Bowl (1981–91).

Playing sites: Fresno, CA (Bulldog Stadium, 1981–91), Las Vegas.

Aloha Bowl

12-25-82 ....Washington 21, Maryland 20
12-26-83 ....Penn St 13, Washington 10
12-29-84 ....SMU 27, Notre Dame 20
12-28-85 ....Alabama 24, Southern Cal 3
12-27-86 ....Arizona 30, N Carolina 21
12-25-87 ....UCLA 20, Florida 16
12-25-88 ....Washington St 24, Houston 22
12-25-89 ....Michigan St 33, Hawaii 13
12-25-90 ....Syracuse 28, Arizona 0
12-25-91 ....Georgia Tech 18, Stanford 17
12-25-92 ....Kansas 23, Brigham Young 20
12-25-93 ....Colorado 41, Fresno St 30
12-25-94 ....Boston College 12, Kansas St 7
12-25-95 ....Kansas 51, UCLA 30
12-25-96 ....Navy 42, California 38
12-25-97 ....Washington 51, Michigan St 23
12-25-98 ....Colorado 51, Oregon 43

City: Honolulu. Stadium: Aloha Stadium, capacity 50,000.

Freedom Bowl

12-16-84 ....Iowa 55, Texas 17
12-30-85 ....Washington 20, Colorado 17
12-30-86 ....UCLA 31, Brigham Young 10
12-30-87 ....Arizona St 33, Air Force 28
12-29-88 ....Brigham Young 20, Colorado 17
12-30-89 ....Washington 34, Florida 7
12-29-90 ....Colorado St 32, Oregon 31
12-30-91 ....Tulsa 28, San Diego St 17
12-29-92 ....Fresno St 24, Southern Cal 7
12-30-93 ....Southern Cal 28, Utah 21
12-29-94 ....Utah 16, Arizona 13

City: Anaheim. Stadium: Anaheim Stadium. Bowl was discontinued after 1994.

Outback Bowl

12-23-86 ....Boston College 27, Georgia 24
1-2-88 ....Michigan 28, Alabama 24
1-2-89 ....Syracuse 23, Louisiana St 10
1-1-90 ....Auburn 31, Ohio St 14
1-1-91 ....Clemson 30, Illinois 0
1-1-92 ....Syracuse 24, Ohio St 17
1-1-93 ....Tennessee 38, Boston College 23
1-1-94 ....Michigan 42, N Carolina St 7
1-2-95 ....Wisconsin 34, Duke 20
1-1-96 ....Penn St 43, Auburn 14
1-1-97 ....Alabama 17, Michigan 14
1-1-98 ....Georgia 33, Wisconsin 6
1-1-99 ....Penn St 26, Kentucky 14

Name change: Hall of Fame Bowl (1986–95).

Insight.com Bowl

12-31-89 ....Arizona 17, N Carolina St 10
12-31-90 ....California 17, Wyoming 15
12-31-91 ....Indiana 24, Baylor 0
12-29-92 ....Washington St 31, Utah 28
12-29-93 ....Kansas St 52, Wyoming 17
12-29-94 ....Brigham Young 31, Oklahoma 6

Insight.com Bowl *(Cont.)*

12-27-95 ....Texas Tech 55, Air Force 41
12-27-96 ....Wisconsin 38, Utah 10
12-27-97 ....Arizona 20, New Mexico 14
12-26-98 ....Missouri 34, W Virginia 31

City: Tucson. Stadium: Arizona Stadium, capacity 56,167.
Name change: Copper Bowl 1989–97.

Micron PC Bowl

12-28-90 ....Florida St 24, Penn St 17
12-28-91 ....Alabama 30, Colorado 25
1-1-93 ....Stanford 24, Penn St 3
1-1-94 ....Boston College 31, Virginia 13
1-2-95 ....S Carolina 24, W Virginia 21
12-30-95 ....N Carolina 20, Arkansas 10
12-27-96 ....Miami (FL) 31, Virginia 21
12-29-97 ....Georgia Tech 35, West Virginia 30
12-29-98 ....Miami (FL) 46, N Carolina St 23

City: Miami. Stadium: Pro Player Stadium, capacity 75,192.
Name Changes: Blockbuster Bowl (1990–93), Carquest
Bowl (1994–97).

Alamo Bowl

12-31-93 ....California 37, Iowa 3
12-31-94 ....Washington St 10, Baylor 3
12-28-95 ....Texas A&M 22, Michigan 20
12-29-96 ....Iowa 27, Texas Tech 0
12-30-97 ....Purdue 33, Oklahoma St 20
12-29-98 ....Purdue 37, Kansas St 34

City: San Antonio, TX. Stadium: Alamodome, capacity
65,000.

Sportsmane of the Year: Pita Elisara

Ricky Williams's locks were dread-fully stylish and Dennis Rodman's coifs continued to captivate, but for sheer unshorn elegance no athlete in 1998 surpassed Indiana's Pita Elisara, a 6' 5", 296-pound tackle from American Samoa. Elisara became a cult hero in Bloomington in the fall of '98, not just for his work on the offensive line but also for the frizzy ponytail that trailed out behind his helmet and often obscured the name on his jersey. The hirsute Hoosier got an occasional trim but hadn't had a full-fledged cut in three years.

According to Elisara, only once in the '98 season did an opponent try to tug his massive 'do—while Elisara was blocking on a field goal attempt against Cincinnati. (No penalty was called.) Otherwise, he said, "everybody was cool with it." Even his parents don't mind his long hair, Elisara said, "as long as I'm away from home."

1936

		Record	Coach
1.	Minnesota	7-1-0	Bernie Bierman
2.	Louisiana St	9-0-1	Bernie Moore
3.	Pittsburgh	7-1-1	Jack Sutherland
4.	Alabama	8-0-1	Frank Thomas
5.	Washington	7-1-1	Jimmy Phelan
6.	Santa Clara	7-1-0	Buck Shaw
7.	Northwestern	7-1-0	Pappy Waldorf
8.	Notre Dame	6-2-1	Elmer Layden
9.	Nebraska	7-2-0	Dana X. Bible
10.	Pennsylvania	7-1-0	Harvey Harman
11.	Duke	9-1-0	Wallace Wade
12.	Yale	7-1-0	Ducky Pond
13.	Dartmouth	7-1-1	Red Blaik
14.	Duquesne	7-2-0	John Smith
15.	Fordham	5-1-2	Jim Crowley
16.	Texas Christian	8-2-2	Dutch Meyer
17.	Tennessee	6-2-2	Bob Neyland
18.	Arkansas	7-3-0	Fred Thomsen
19.	Navy	6-3-0	Tom Hamilton
20.	Marquette	7-1-0	Frank Murray

1937

		Record	Coach
1.	Pittsburgh	9-0-1	Jack Sutherland
2.	California	9-0-1	Stub Allison
3.	Fordham	7-0-1	Jim Crowley
4.	Alabama	9-0-0	Frank Thomas
5.	Minnesota	6-2-0	Bernie Bierman
6.	Villanova	8-0-1	Clipper Smith
7.	Dartmouth	7-0-2	Red Blaik
8.	Louisiana St	9-1-0	Bernie Moore
9.	Notre Dame	6-2-1	Elmer Layden
	Santa Clara	8-0-0	Buck Shaw
11.	Nebraska	6-1-2	Biff Jones
12.	Yale	6-1-1	Ducky Pond
13.	Ohio St	6-2-0	Francis Schmidt
14.	Holy Cross	8-0-2	Eddie Anderson
	Arkansas	6-2-2	Fred Thomsen
16.	Texas Christian	4-2-2	Dutch Meyer
17.	Colorado	8-0-0	Bunnie Oakes
18.	Rice	5-3-2	Jimmy Kitts
19.	N Carolina	7-1-1	Ray Wolf
20.	Duke	7-2-1	Wallace Wade

1938

		Record	Coach
1.	Texas Christian	10-0-0	Dutch Meyer
2.	Tennessee	10-0-0	Bob Neyland
3.	Duke	9-0-0	Wallace Wade
4.	Oklahoma	10-0-0	Tom Stidham
5.	#Notre Dame	8-1-0	Elmer Layden
6.	Carnegie Tech	7-1-0	Bill Kern
7.	Southern Cal	8-2-0	Howard Jones
8.	Pittsburgh	8-2-0	Jack Sutherland
9.	Holy Cross	8-1-0	Eddie Anderson
10.	Minnesota	6-2-0	Bernie Bierman
11.	Texas Tech	10-0-0	Pete Cawthon
12.	Cornell	5-1-1	Carl Snavely
13.	Alabama	7-1-1	Frank Thomas
14.	California	10-1-0	Stub Allison
15.	Fordham	6-1-2	Jim Crowley
16.	Michigan	6-1-1	Fritz Crisler
17.	Northwestern	4-2-2	Pappy Waldorf

1938 (Cont.)

		Record	Coach
18.	Villanova	8-0-1	Clipper Smith
19.	Tulane	7-2-1	Red Dawson
20.	Dartmouth	7-2-0	Red Blaik

#Selected No. 1 by the Dickinson System.

1939

		Record	Coach
1.	Texas A&M	10-0-0	Homer Norton
2.	Tennessee	10-0-0	Bob Neyland
3.	#Southern Cal	7-0-2	Howard Jones
4.	Cornell	8-0-0	Carl Snavely
5.	Tulane	8-0-1	Red Dawson
6.	Missouri	8-1-0	Don Faurot
7.	UCLA	6-0-4	Babe Horrell
8.	Duke	8-1-0	Wallace Wade
9.	Iowa	6-1-1	Eddie Anderson
10.	Duquesne	8-0-1	Buff Donelli
11.	Boston College	9-1-0	Frank Leahy
12.	Clemson	8-1-0	Jess Neely
13.	Notre Dame	7-2-0	Elmer Layden
14.	Santa Clara	5-1-3	Buck Shaw
15.	Ohio St	6-2-0	Francis Schmidt
16.	Georgia Tech	7-2-0	Bill Alexander
17.	Fordham	6-2-0	Jim Crowley
18.	Nebraska	7-1-1	Biff Jones
19.	Oklahoma	6-2-1	Tom Stidham
20.	Michigan	6-2-0	Fritz Crisler

#Selected No. 1 by the Dickinson System.

1940

		Record	Coach
1.	Minnesota	8-0-0	Bernie Bierman
2.	Stanford	9-0-0	C. Shaughnessy
3.	Michigan	7-1-0	Fritz Crisler
4.	Tennessee	10-0-0	Bob Neyland
5.	Boston College	10-0-0	Frank Leahy
6.	Texas A&M	8-1-0	Homer Norton
7.	Nebraska	8-1-0	Biff Jones
8.	Northwestern	6-2-0	Pappy Waldorf
9.	Mississippi St	9-0-1	Allyn McKeen
10.	Washington	7-2-0	Jimmy Phelan
11.	Santa Clara	6-1-1	Buck Shaw
12.	Fordham	7-1-0	Jim Crowley
13.	Georgetown	8-1-0	Jack Hagerty
14.	Pennsylvania	6-1-1	George Munger
15.	Cornell	6-2-0	Carl Snavely
16.	SMU	8-1-1	Matty Bell
17.	Hard.-Simmons	9-0-0	Abe Woodson
18.	Duke	7-2-0	Wallace Wade
19.	Lafayette	9-0-0	Hooks Mylin
20.	—		

Only 19 teams selected.

1941

		Record	Coach
1.	Minnesota	8-0-0	Bernie Bierman
2.	Duke	9-0-0	Wallace Wade
3.	Notre Dame	8-0-1	Frank Leahy
4.	Texas	8-1-1	Dana X. Bible
5.	Michigan	6-1-1	Fritz Crisler
6.	Fordham	7-1-0	Jim Crowley
7.	Missouri	8-1-0	Don Faurot
8.	Duquesne	8-0-0	Buff Donelli
9.	Texas A&M	9-1-0	Homer Norton
10.	Navy	7-1-1	Swede Larson
11.	Northwestern	5-3-0	Pappy Waldorf
12.	Oregon St	7-2-0	Lon Stiner
13.	Ohio St	6-1-1	Paul Brown
14.	Georgia	8-1-1	Wally Butts
15.	Pennsylvania	7-1-1	George Munger
16.	Mississippi St	8-1-1	Allyn McKeen
17.	Mississippi	6-2-1	Harry Mehre
18.	Tennessee	8-2-0	John Barnhill
19.	Washington St	6-4-0	Babe Hollingbery
20.	Alabama	8-2-0	Frank Thomas

1942

		Record	Coach
1.	Ohio St	9-1-0	Paul Brown
2.	Georgia	10-1-0	Wally Butts
3.	Wisconsin	8-1-1	H. Stuhldreher
4.	Tulsa	10-0-0	Henry Frnka
5.	Georgia Tech	9-1-0	Bill Alexander
6.	Notre Dame	7-2-2	Frank Leahy
7.	Tennessee	8-1-1	John Barnhill
8.	Boston College	8-1-0	Denny Myers
9.	Michigan	7-3-0	Fritz Crisler
10.	Alabama	7-3-0	Frank Thomas
11.	Texas	8-2-0	Dana X. Bible
12.	Stanford	6-4-0	Marchie Schwartz
13.	UCLA	7-3-0	Babe Horrell
14.	William & Mary	9-1-1	Carl Voyles
15.	Santa Clara	7-2-0	Buck Shaw
16.	Auburn	6-4-1	Jack Meagher
17.	Washington St	6-2-2	Babe Hollingbery
18.	Mississippi St	8-2-0	Allyn McKeen
19.	Minnesota	5-4-0	George Hauser
	Holy Cross	5-4-1	Ank Scanlon
	Penn St	6-1-1	Bob Higgins

1943

		Record	Coach
1.	Notre Dame	9-1-0	Frank Leahy
2.	Iowa Pre-Flight	9-1-0	Don Faurot
3.	Michigan	8-1-0	Fritz Crisler
4.	Navy	8-1-0	Billick Whelchel
5.	Purdue	9-0-0	Elmer Burnham
6.	Great Lakes	10-2-0	Tony Hinkle
7.	Duke	8-1-0	Eddie Cameron
8.	Del Monte P-F	7-1-0	Bill Kern
9.	Northwestern	6-2-0	Pappy Waldorf
10.	March Field	9-1-0	Paul Schissler
11.	Army	7-2-1	Red Blaik
12.	Washington	4-0-0	Ralph Welch
13.	Georgia Tech	7-3-0	Bill Alexander

1943 *(Cont.)*

		Record	Coach
14.	Texas	7-1-0	Dana X. Bible
15.	Tulsa	6-0-1	Henry Frnka
16.	Dartmouth	6-1-0	Earl Brown
17.	Bainbridge NTS	7-0-0	Joe Maniaci
18.	Colorado College	7-0-0	Hal White
19.	Pacific	7-2-0	Amos A. Stagg
20.	Pennsylvania	6-2-1	George Munger

1944

		Record	Coach
1.	Army	9-0-0	Red Blaik
2.	Ohio St	9-0-0	Carroll Widdoes
3.	Randolph Field	11-0-0	Frank Tritico
4.	Navy	6-3-0	Oscar Hagberg
5.	Bainbridge NTS	9-0-0	Joe Maniaci
6.	Iowa Pre-Flight	10-1-0	Jack Meagher
7.	Southern Cal	7-0-2	Jeff Cravath
8.	Michigan	8-2-0	Fritz Crisler
9.	Notre Dame	8-2-0	Ed McKeever
10.	March Field	7-1-2	Paul Schissler
11.	Duke	5-4-0	Eddie Cameron
12.	Tennessee	8-0-1	John Barnhill
13.	Georgia Tech	8-2-0	Bill Alexander
	Norman P-F	6-0-0	John Gregg
15.	Illinois	5-4-1	Ray Eliot
16.	El Toro Marines	8-1-0	Dick Hanley
17.	Great Lakes	9-2-1	Paul Brown
18.	Fort Pierce	9-0-0	Hamp Pool
19.	St. Mary's P-F	4-4-0	Jules Sikes
20.	2nd Air Force	7-2-1	Bill Reese

1945

		Record	Coach
1.	Army	9-0-0	Red Blaik
2.	Alabama	9-0-0	Frank Thomas
3.	Navy	7-1-1	Oscar Hagberg
4.	Indiana	9-0-1	Bo McMillan
5.	Oklahoma A&M	8-0-0	Jim Lookabaugh
6.	Michigan	7-3-0	Fritz Crisler
7.	St. Mary's (CA)	7-1-0	Jimmy Phelan
8.	Pennsylvania	6-2-0	George Munger
9.	Notre Dame	7-2-1	Hugh Devore
10.	Texas	9-1-0	Dana X. Bible
11.	Southern Cal	7-3-0	Jeff Cravath
12.	Ohio St	7-2-0	Carroll Widdoes
13.	Duke	6-2-0	Eddie Cameron
14.	Tennessee	8-1-0	John Barnhill
15.	Louisiana St	7-2-0	Bernie Moore
16.	Holy Cross	8-1-0	John DeGrosa
17.	Tulsa	8-2-0	Henry Frnka
18.	Georgia	8-2-0	Wally Butts
19.	Wake Forest	4-3-1	Peahead Walker
20.	Columbia	8-1-0	Lou Little

1946

		Record	Coach
1.	Notre Dame	8-0-1	Frank Leahy
2.	Army	9-0-1	Red Blaik
3.	Georgia	10-0-0	Wally Butts
4.	UCLA	10-0-0	B. LaBrucherie

Note: Except where indicated with an asterisk, the polls from 1936 through 1964 were taken before the bowl games and those from 1965 through the present were taken after the bowl games.

1946 *(Cont.)*

		Record	Coach
5.	Illinois	7-2-0	Ray Eliot
6.	Michigan	6-2-1	Fritz Crisler
7.	Tennessee	9-1-0	Bob Neyland
8.	Louisiana St	9-1-0	Bernie Moore
9.	N Carolina	8-1-1	Carl Snavely
10.	Rice	8-2-0	Jess Neely
11.	Georgia Tech	8-2-0	Bobby Dodd12.
	Yale	7-1-1	Howard Odell
13.	Pennsylvania	6-2-0	George Munger
14.	Oklahoma	7-3-0	Jim Tatum
15.	Texas	8-2-0	Dana X. Bible
16.	Arkansas	6-3-1	John Barnhill
17.	Tulsa	9-1-0	J.O. Brothers
18.	N Carolina St	8-2-0	Beattie Feathers
19.	Delaware	9-0-0	Bill Murray
20.	Indiana	6-3-0	Bo McMillan

1947

		Record	Coach
1.	Notre Dame	9-0-0	Frank Leahy
2.	#Michigan	9-0-1	Fritz Crisler
3.	SMU	9-0-1	Matty Bell
4.	Penn St	9-0-0	Bob Higgins
5.	Texas	9-1-0	Blair Cherry
6.	Alabama	8-2-0	Red Drew
7.	Pennsylvania	7-0-1	George Munger
8.	Southern Cal	7-1-1	Jeff Cravath
9.	N Carolina	8-2-0	Carl Snavely
10.	Georgia Tech	9-1-0	Bobby Dodd
11.	Army	5-2-2	Red Blaik
12.	Kansas	8-0-2	George Sauer
13.	Mississippi	8-2-0	Johnny Vaught
14.	William & Mary	9-1-0	Rube McCray
15.	California	9-1-0	Pappy Waldorf
16.	Oklahoma	7-2-1	Bud Wilkinson
17.	N Carolina St	5-3-1	Beattie Feathers
18.	Rice	6-3-1	Jess Neely
19.	Duke	4-3-2	Wallace Wade
20.	Columbia	7-2-0	Lou Little

#The AP, which had voted Notre Dame No. 1 before the bowl games, took a second vote, giving the title to Michigan after its 49-0 win over Southern Cal in the Rose Bowl.

1948

		Record	Coach
1.	Michigan	9-0-0	Bennie Oosterbaan
2.	Notre Dame	9-0-1	Frank Leahy
3.	N Carolina	9-0-1	Carl Snavely
4.	California	10-0-0	Pappy Waldorf
5.	Oklahoma	9-1-0	Bud Wilkinson
6.	Army	8-0-1	Red Blaik
7.	Northwestern	7-2-0	Bob Voigts
8.	Georgia	9-1-0	Wally Butts
9.	Oregon	9-1-0	Jim Aiken
10.	SMU	8-1-1	Matty Bell
11.	Clemson	10-0-0	Frank Howard
12.	Vanderbilt	8-2-1	Red Sanders
13.	Tulane	9-1-0	Henry Frnka
14.	Michigan St	6-2-2	Biggie Munn
15.	Mississippi	8-1-0	Johnny Vaught
16.	Minnesota	7-2-0	Bernie Bierman
17.	William & Mary	6-2-2	Rube McCray
18.	Penn St	7-1-1	Bob Higgins
19.	Cornell	8-1-0	Lefty James
20.	Wake Forest	6-3-0	Peahead Walker

1949

		Record	Coach
1.	Notre Dame	10-0-0	Frank Leahy
2.	Oklahoma	10-0-0	Bud Wilkinson
3.	California	10-0-0	Pappy Waldorf
4.	Army	9-0-0	Red Blaik
5.	Rice	9-1-0	Jess Neely
6.	Ohio St	6-1-2	Wes Fesler
7.	Michigan	6-2-1	Bennie Oosterbaan
8.	Minnesota	7-2-0	Bernie Bierman
9.	Louisiana St	8-2-0	Gaynell Tinsley
10.	Pacific	11-0-0	Larry Siemering
11.	Kentucky	9-2-0	Bear Bryant
12.	Cornell	8-1-0	Lefty James
13.	Villanova	8-1-0	Jim Leonard
14.	Maryland	8-1-0	Jim Tatum
15.	Santa Clara	7-2-1	Len Casanova
16.	N Carolina	7-3-0	Carl Snavely
17.	Tennessee	7-2-1	Bob Neyland
18.	Princeton	6-3-0	Charlie Caldwell
19.	Michigan St	6-3-0	Biggie Munn
20.	Missouri	7-3-0	Don Faurot
	Baylor	8-2-0	Bob Woodruff

1950

		Record	Coach
1.	Oklahoma	10-0-0	Bud Wilkinson
2.	Army	8-1-0	Red Blaik
3.	Texas	9-1-0	Blair Cherry
4.	Tennessee	10-1-0	Bob Neyland
5.	California	9-0-1	Pappy Waldorf
6.	Princeton	9-0-0	Charlie Caldwell
7.	Kentucky	10-1-0	Bear Bryant
8.	Michigan St	8-1-0	Biggie Munn
9.	Michigan	5-3-1	Bennie Oosterhaan
10.	Clemson	8-0-1	Frank Howard
11.	Washington	8-2-0	Howard Odell
12.	Wyoming	9-0-0	Bowden Wyatt
13.	Illinois	7-2-0	Ray Eliot
14.	Ohio St	6-3-0	Wes Fesler
15.	Miami (FL)	9-0-1	Andy Gustafson
16.	Alabama	9-2-0	Red Drew
17.	Nebraska	6-2-1	Bill Glassford
18.	Wash & Lee	8-2-0	George Barclay
19.	Tulsa	9-1-1	J.O. Brothers
20.	Tulane	6-2-1	Henry Frnka

1951

		Record	Coach
1.	Tennessee	10-0-0	Bob Neyland
2.	Michigan St	9-0-0	Biggie Munn
3.	Maryland	9-0-0	Jim Tatum
4.	Illinois	8-0-1	Ray Eliot
5.	Georgia Tech	10-0-1	Bobby Dodd
6.	Princeton	9-0-0	Charlie Caldwell
7.	Stanford	9-1-0	Chuck Taylor
8.	Wisconsin	7-1-1	Ivy Williamson
9.	Baylor	8-1-1	George Sauer
10.	Oklahoma	8-2-0	Bud Wilkinson
11.	Texas Christian	6-4-0	Dutch Meyer
12.	California	8-2-0	Pappy Waldorf
13.	Virginia	8-1-0	Art Guepe
14.	San Francisco	9-0-0	Joe Kuharich
15.	Kentucky	7-4-0	Bear Bryant
16.	Boston Univ	6-4-0	Buff Donelli
17.	UCLA	5-3-1	Red Sanders
18.	Washington St	7-3-0	Forest Evashevski

1951 (Cont.)

		Record	Coach
19.	Holy Cross	8-2-0	Eddie Anderson
20.	Clemson	7-2-0	Frank Howard

1952

		Record	Coach
1.	Michigan St	9-0-0	Biggie Munn
2.	Georgia Tech	11-0-0	Bobby Dodd
3.	Notre Dame	7-2-1	Frank Leahy
4.	Oklahoma	8-1-1	Bud Wilkinson
5.	Southern Cal	9-1-0	Jess Hill
6.	UCLA	8-1-0	Red Sanders
7.	Mississippi	8-0-2	Johnny Vaught
8.	Tennessee	8-1-1	Bob Neyland
9.	Alabama	9-2-0	Red Drew
10.	Texas	8-2-0	Ed Price
11.	Wisconsin	6-2-1	Ivy Williamson
12.	Tulsa	8-1-1	J.O. Brothers
13.	Maryland	7-2-0	Jim Tatum
14.	Syracuse	7-2-0	Ben Schwartzwalder
15.	Florida	7-3-0	Bob Woodruff
16.	Duke	8-2-0	Bill Murray
17.	Ohio St	6-3-0	Woody Hayes
18.	Purdue	4-3-2	Stu Holcomb
19.	Princeton	8-1-0	Charlie Caldwell
20.	Kentucky	5-4-2	Bear Bryant

1953

		Record	Coach
1.	Maryland	10-0-0	Jim Tatum
2.	Notre Dame	9-0-1	Frank Leahy
3.	Michigan St	8-1-0	Biggie Munn
4.	Oklahoma	8-1-1	Bud Wilkinson
5.	Rice	8-2-0	Jess Neely
6.	UCLA	8-1-0	Red Sanders
7.	Illinois	7-1-1	Ray Eliot
8.	Georgia Tech	8-2-1	Bobby Dodd
9.	Iowa	5-3-1	Forest Evashevski
10.	West Virginia	8-1-0	Art Lewis
11.	Texas	7-3-0	Ed Price
12.	Texas Tech	10-1-0	DeWitt Weaver
13.	Alabama	6-2-3	Red Drew
14.	Army	7-1-1	Red Blaik
15.	Wisconsin	6-2-1	Ivy Williamson
16.	Kentucky	7-2-1	Bear Bryant
17.	Auburn	7-2-1	Shug Jordan
18.	Duke	7-2-1	Bill Murray
19.	Stanford	6-3-1	Chuck Taylor
20.	Michigan	6-3-0	Bennie Oosterbaan

1954

		Record	Coach
1.	Ohio St	9-0-0	Woody Hayes
2.	#UCLA	9-0-0	Red Sanders
3.	Oklahoma	10-0-0	Bud Wilkinson
4.	Notre Dame	9-1-0	Terry Brennan
5.	Navy	7-2-0	Eddie Erdelatz
6.	Mississippi	9-1-0	Johnny Vaught
7.	Army	7-2-0	Red Blaik
8.	Maryland	7-2-1	Jim Tatum
9.	Wisconsin	7-2-0	Ivy Williamson
10.	Arkansas	8-2-0	Bowden Wyatt
11.	Miami (FL)	8-1-0	Andy Gustafson
12.	West Virginia	8-1-0	Art Lewis
13.	Auburn	7-3-0	Shug Jordan

1954 (Cont.)

		Record	Coach
14.	Duke	7-2-1	Bill Murray
15.	Michigan	6-3-0	Bennie Oosterbaan
16.	Virginia Tech	8-0-1	Frank Moseley
17.	Southern Cal	8-3-0	Jess Hill
18.	Baylor	7-3-0	George Sauer
19.	Rice	7-3-0	Jess Neely
20.	Penn St	7-2-0	Rip Engle

#Selected No. 1 by UP.

1955

		Record	Coach
1.	Oklahoma	10-0-0	Bud Wilkinson
2.	Michigan St	8-1-0	Duffy Daugherty
3.	Maryland	10-0-0	Jim Tatum
4.	UCLA	9-1-0	Red Sanders
5.	Ohio St	7-2-0	Woody Hayes
6.	Texas Christian	9-1-0	Abe Martin
7.	Georgia Tech	8-1-1	Bobby Dodd
8.	Auburn	8-1-1	Shug Jordan
9.	Notre Dame	8-2-0	Terry Brennan
10.	Mississippi	9-1-0	Johnny Vaught
11.	Pittsburgh	7-3-0	John Michelosen
12.	Michigan	7-2-0	Bennie Oosterbaan
13.	Southern Cal	6-4-0	Jess Hill
14.	Miami (FL)	6-3-0	Andy Gustafson
15.	Miami (OH)	9-0-0	Ara Parseghian
16.	Stanford	6-3-1	Chuck Taylor
17.	Texas A&M	7-2-1	Bear Bryant
18.	Navy	6-2-1	Eddie Erdelatz
19.	West Virginia	8-2-0	Art Lewis
20.	Army	6-3-0	Red Blaik

1956

		Record	Coach
1.	Oklahoma	10-0-0	Bud Wilkinson
2.	Tennessee	10-0-0	Bowden Wyatt
3.	Iowa	8-1-0	Forest Evashevski
4.	Georgia Tech	9-1-0	Bobby Dodd
5.	Texas A&M	9-0-1	Bear Bryant
6.	Miami (FL)	8-1-1	Andy Gustafson
7.	Michigan	7-2-0	Bennie Oosterbaan
8.	Syracuse	7-1-0	Ben Schwartzwalder
9.	Michigan St	7-2-0	Duffy Daugherty
10.	Oregon St	7-2-1	Tommy Prothro
11.	Baylor	8-2-0	Sam Boyd
12.	Minnesota	6-1-2	Murray Warmath
13.	Pittsburgh	7-2-1	John Michelosen
14.	Texas Christian	7-3-0	Abe Martin
15.	Ohio St	6-3-0	Woody Hayes
16.	Navy	6-1-2	Eddie Erdelatz
17.	Geo Washington	7-1-1	Gene Sherman
18.	Southern Cal	8-2-0	Jess Hill
19.	Clemson	7-1-2	Frank Howard
20.	Colorado	7-2-1	Dallas Ward
	Penn St	6-2-1	Rip Engle

1957

		Record	Coach
1.	Auburn	10-0-0	Shug Jordan
2.	#Ohio St	8-1-0	Woody Hayes
3.	Michigan St	8-1-0	Duffy Daugherty
4.	Oklahoma	9-1-0	Bud Wilkinson
5.	Navy	8-1-1	Eddie Erdelatz
6.	Iowa	7-1-1	Forest Evashevski
7.	Mississippi	8-1-1	Johnny Vaught
8.	Rice	7-3-0	Jess Neely
9.	Texas A&M	8-2-0	Bear Bryant
10.	Notre Dame	7-3-0	Terry Brennan
11.	Texas	6-3-1	Darrell Royal
12.	Arizona St	10-0-0	Dan Devine
13.	Tennessee	7-3-0	Bowden Wyatt
14.	Mississippi St	6-2-1	Wade Walker
15.	N Carolina St	7-1-2	Earle Edwards
16.	Duke	6-2-2	Bill Murray
17.	Florida	6-2-1	Bob Woodruff
18.	Army	7-2-0	Red Blaik
19.	Wisconsin	6-3-0	Milt Brunt
20.	VMI	9-0-1	John McKenna

#Selected No. 1 by UP.

1958

		Record	Coach
1.	Louisiana St	10-0-0	Paul Dietzel
2.	Iowa	7-1-1	Forest Evashevski
3.	Army	8-0-1	Red Blaik
4.	Auburn	9-0-1	Shug Jordan
5.	Oklahoma	9-1-0	Bud Wilkinson
6.	Air Force	9-0-1	Ben Martin
7.	Wisconsin	7-1-1	Milt Bruhn
8.	Ohio St	6-1-2	Woody Hayes
9.	Syracuse	8-1-0	Ben Schwartzwalder
10.	Texas Christian	8-2-0	Abe Martin
11.	Mississippi	8-2-0	Johnny Vaught
12.	Clemson	8-2-0	Frank Howard
13.	Purdue	6-1-2	Jack Mollenkopf
14.	Florida	6-3-1	Bob Woodruff
15.	S Carolina	7-3-0	Warren Giese
16.	California	7-3-0	Pete Elliott
17.	Notre Dame	6-4-0	Terry Brennan
18.	SMU	6-4-0	Bill Meek
19.	Oklahoma St	7-3-0	Cliff Speegle
20.	Rutgers	8-1-0	John Stiegman

1959

		Record	Coach
1.	Syracuse	10-0-0	Ben Schwartzwalder
2.	Mississippi	9-1-0	Johnny Vaught
3.	Louisiana St	9-1-0	Paul Dietzel
4.	Texas	9-1-0	Darrell Royal
5.	Georgia	9-1-0	Wally Butts
6.	Wisconsin	7-2-0	Milt Bruhn
7.	Texas Christian	8-2-0	Abe Martin
8.	Washington	9-1-0	Jim Owens
9.	Arkansas	8-2-0	Frank Broyles
10.	Alabama	7-1-2	Bear Bryant
11.	Clemson	8-2-0	Frank Howard

1959 (Cont.)

		Record	Coach
12.	Penn St	8-2-0	Rip Engle
13.	Illinois	5-3-1	Ray Eliot
14.	Southern Cal	8-2-0	Don Clark
15.	Oklahoma	7-3-0	Bud Wilkinson
16.	Wyoming	9-1-0	Bob Devaney
17.	Notre Dame	5-5-0	Joe Kuharich
18.	Missouri	6-4-0	Dan Devine
19.	Florida	5-4-1	Bob Woodruff
20.	Pittsburgh	6-4-0	John Michelosen

1960

		Record	Coach
1.	Minnesota	8-1-0	Murray Warmath
2.	Mississippi	9-0-1	Johnny Vaught
3.	Iowa	8-1-0	Forest Evashevski
4.	Navy	9-1-0	Wayne Hardin
5.	Missouri	9-1-0	Dan Devine
6.	Washington	9-1-0	Jim Owens
7.	Arkansas	8-2-0	Frank Broyles
8.	Ohio St	7-2-0	Woody Hayes
9.	Alabama	8-1-1	Bear Bryant
10.	Duke	7-3-0	Bill Murray
11.	Kansas	7-2-1	Jack Mitchell
12.	Baylor	8-2-0	John Bridgers
13.	Auburn	8-2-0	Shug Jordan
14.	Yale	9-0-0	Jordan Oliver
15.	Michigan St	6-2-1	Duffy Daugherty
16.	Penn St	6-3-0	Rip Engle
17.	New Mexico St	10-0-0	Warren Woodson
18.	Florida	8-2-0	Ray Graves
19.	Syracuse	7-2-0	Ben Schwartzwalder
	Purdue	4-4-1	Jack Mollenkopf

1961

		Record	Coach
1.	Alabama	10-0-0	Bear Bryant
2.	Ohio St	8-0-1	Woody Hayes
3.	Texas	9-1-0	Darrell Royal
4.	Louisiana St	9-1-0	Paul Dietzel
5.	Mississippi	9-1-0	Johnny Vaught
6.	Minnesota	7-2-0	Murray Warmath
7.	Colorado	9-1-0	Sonny Grandelius
8.	Michigan St	7-2-0	Duffy Daugherty
9.	Arkansas	8-2-0	Frank Broyles
10.	Utah St	9-0-1	John Ralston
11.	Missouri	7-2-1	Dan Devine
12.	Purdue	6-3-0	Jack Mollenkopf
13.	Georgia Tech	7-3-0	Bobby Dodd
14.	Syracuse	7-3-0	Ben Schwartzwalder
15.	Rutgers	9-0-0	John Bateman
16.	UCLA	7-3-0	Bill Barnes
17.	Rice	7-3-0	Jess Neely
	Penn St	7-3-0	Rip Engle
	Arizona	8-1-1	Jim LaRue
20.	Duke	7-3-0	Bill Murray

1962

		Record	Coach
1.	Southern Cal	10-0-0	John McKay
2.	Wisconsin	8-1-0	Milt Bruhn
3.	Mississippi	9-0-0	Johnny Vaught
4.	Texas	9-0-1	Darrell Royal
5.	Alabama	9-1-0	Bear Bryant
6.	Arkansas	9-1-0	Frank Broyles
7.	Louisiana St	8-1-1	Charlie McClendon
8.	Oklahoma	8-2-0	Bud Wilkinson
9.	Penn St	9-1-0	Rip Engle
10.	Minnesota	6-2-1	Murray Warmath

11-20: UPI

		Record	Coach
11.	Georgia Tech	7-2-1	Bobby Dodd
12.	Missouri	7-1-2	Dan Devine
13.	Ohio St	6-3-0	Woody Hayes
14.	Duke	8-2-0	Bill Murray
	Washington	7-1-2	Jim Owens
16.	Northwestern	7-2-0	Ara Parseghian
	Oregon St	8-2-0	Tommy Prothro
18.	Arizona St	7-2-1	Frank Kush
	Miami (FL)	7-3-0	Andy Gustafson
	Illinois	2-7-0	Pete Elliott

1963

		Record	Coach
1.	Texas	10-0-0	Darrell Royal
2.	Navy	9-1-0	Wayne Hardin
3.	Illinois	7-1-1	Pete Elliott
4.	Pittsburgh	9-1-0	John Michelosen
5.	Auburn	9-1-0	Shug Jordan
6.	Nebraska	9-1-0	Bob Devaney
7.	Mississippi	7-0-2	Johnny Vaught
8.	Alabama	8-2-0	Bear Bryant
9.	Oklahoma	8-2-0	Bud Wilkinson
10.	Michigan St	6-2-1	Duffy Daugherty

11-20: UPI

		Record	Coach
11.	Mississippi St	6-2-2	Paul Davis
12.	Syracuse	8-2-0	Ben Schwartzwalder
13.	Arizona St	8-1-0	Frank Kush
14.	Memphis St	9-0-1	Billy J. Murphy
15.	Washington	6-4-0	Jim Owens
16.	Penn St	7-3-0	Rip Engle
	Southern Cal	7-3-0	John McKay
	Missouri	7-3-0	Dan Devine
19.	N Carolina	8-2-0	Jim Hickey
20.	Baylor	7-3-0	John Bridgers

1964

		Record	Coach
1.	Alabama	10-0-0	Bear Bryant
2.	Arkansas	10-0-0	Frank Broyles
3.	Notre Dame	9-1-0	Ara Parseghian
4.	Michigan	8-1-0	Bump Elliott
5.	Texas	9-1-0	Darrell Royal
6.	Nebraska	9-1-0	Bob Devaney
7.	Louisiana St	7-2-1	Charlie McClendon
8.	Oregon St	8-2-0	Tommy Prothro
9.	Ohio St	7-2-0	Woody Hayes
10.	Southern Cal	7-3-0	John McKay

1964 *(Cont.)*

		Record	Coach

11–20: UPI

		Record	Coach
11.	Florida St	8-1-1	Bill Peterson
12.	Syracuse	7-3-0	Ben Schwartzwalder
13.	Princeton	9-0-0	Dick Colman
14.	Penn St	6-4-0	Rip Engle
	Utah	8-2-0	Ray Nagel
16.	Illinois	6-3-0	Pete Elliott
	New Mexico	9-2-0	Bill Weeks
18.	Tulsa	8-2-0	Glenn Dobbs
19.	Missouri	6-3-1	Dan Devine
20.	Mississippi	5-4-1	Johnny Vaught
	Michigan St	4-5-1	Duffy Daugherty

1965

		Record	Coach
1.	Alabama	9-1-1	Bear Bryant
2.	#Michigan St	10-1-0	Duffy Daugherty
3.	Arkansas	10-1-0	Frank Broyles
4.	UCLA	8-2-1	Tommy Prothro
5.	Nebraska	10-1-0	Bob Devaney
6.	Missouri	8-2-1	Dan Devine
7.	Tennessee	8-1-2	Doug Dickey
8.	Louisiana St	8-3-0	Charlie McClendon
9.	Notre Dame	7-2-1	Ara Parseghian
10.	Southern Cal	7-2-1	John McKay

11-20: UPI

		Record	Coach
11.	Texas Tech	8-2-0	J.T. King
12.	Ohio St	7-2-0	Woody Hayes
13.	Florida	7-3-0	Ray Graves
14.	Purdue	7-2-1	Jack Mollenkopf
15.	Georgia	6-4-0	Vince Dooley
16.	Tulsa	8-2-0	Glenn Dobbs
17.	Mississippi	6-4-0	Johnny Vaught
18.	Kentucky	6-4-0	Charlie Bradshaw
19	Syracuse	7-3-0	Ben Schwartzwalder
20.	Colorado	6-2-2	Eddie Crowder

#Selected No. 1 by UPI.

1966*

		Record	Coach
1.	Notre Dame	9-0-1	Ara Parseghian
2.	Michigan St	9-0-1	Duffy Daugherty
3.	Alabama	10-0-0	Bear Bryant
4.	Georgia	9-1-0	Vince Dooley
5.	UCLA	9-1-0	Tommy Prothro
6.	Nebraska	9-1-0	Bob Devaney
7.	Purdue	8-2-0	Jack Mollenkopf
8.	Georgia Tech	9-1-0	Bobby Dodd
9.	Miami (FL)	7-2-1	Charlie Tate
10.	SMU	8-2-0	Hayden Fry

11-20: UPI

		Record	Coach
11.	Florida	8-2-0	Ray Graves
12.	Mississippi	8-2-0	Johnny Vaught
13.	Arkansas	8-2-0	Frank Broyles
14.	Tennessee	7-3-0	Doug Dickey
15.	Wyoming	9-1-0	Lloyd Eaton
16.	Syracuse	8-2-0	Ben Schwartzwalder
17.	Houston	8-2-0	Bill Yeoman
18.	Southern Cal	7-3-0	John McKay
19.	Oregon St	7-3-0	Dee Andros
20.	Virginia Tech	8-1-1	Jerry Claiborne

Note: Except where indicated with an asterisk, the polls from 1936 through 1964 were taken before the bowl games and those from 1965 through the present were taken after the bowl games. Additionally, the AP ranked only ten teams in its polls from 1962–67; positions 11–20 from those years are from the UPI poll.

1967*

		Record	Coach
1.	Southern Cal	9-1-0	John McKay
2.	Tennessee	9-1-0	Doug Dickey
3.	Oklahoma	9-1-0	Chuck Fairbanks
4.	Indiana	9-1-0	John Pont
5.	Notre Dame	8-2-0	Ara Parseghian
6.	Wyoming	10-0-0	Lloyd Eaton
7.	Oregon St.	7-2-1	Dee Andros
8.	Alabama	8-1-1	Bear Bryant
9.	Purdue	8-2-0	Jack Mollenkopf
10.	Penn St.	8-2-0	Joe Paterno

11-20: UPI†

		Record	Coach
11.	UCLA	7-2-1	Tommy Prothro
12.	Syracuse	8-2-0	Ben Schwartzwalder
13.	Colorado	8-2-0	Eddie Crowder
14.	Minnesota	8-2-0	Murray Warmath
15.	Florida St.	7-2-1	Bill Peterson
16.	Miami (FL)	7-3-0	Charlie Tate
17.	N Carolina St.	8-2-0	Earle Edwards
18.	Georgia	7-3-0	Vince Dooley
19.	Houston	9-2-0	Bill Yeoman
20.	Arizona St.	8-2-0	Frank Kush

†UPI ranked Penn St 11th and did not rank Alabama, which was on probation.

1968

		Record	Coach
1.	Ohio St	10-0-0	Woody Hayes
2.	Penn St.	11-0-0	Joe Paterno
3.	Texas	9-1-1	Darrell Royal
4.	Southern Cal	9-1-1	John McKay
5.	Notre Dame	7-2-1	Ara Parseghian
6.	Arkansas	10-1-0	Frank Broyles
7.	Kansas	9-2-0	Pepper Rodgers
8.	Georgia	8-1-2	Vince Dooley
9.	Missouri	8-3-0	Dan Devine
10.	Purdue	8-2-0	Jack Mollenkopf
11.	Oklahoma	7-4-0	Chuck Fairbanks
12.	Michigan	8-2-0	Bump Elliott
13.	Tennessee	8-2-1	Doug Dickey
14.	SMU	8-3-0	Hayden Fry
15.	Oregon St.	7-3-0	Dee Andros
16.	Auburn	7-4-0	Shug Jordan
17.	Alabama	8-3-0	Bear Bryant
18.	Houston	6-2-2	Bill Yeoman
19.	Louisiana St	8-3-0	Charlie McClendon
20.	Ohio	10-1-0	Bill Hess

1969

		Record	Coach
1.	Texas	11-0-0	Darrell Royal
2.	Penn St.	11-0-0	Joe Paterno
3.	Southern Cal	10-0-1	John McKay
4.	Ohio St	8-1-0	Woody Hayes
5.	Notre Dame	8-2-1	Ara Parseghian
6.	Missouri	9-2-0	Dan Devine
7.	Arkansas	9-2-0	Frank Broyles
8.	Mississippi	8-3-0	Johnny Vaught
9.	Michigan	8-3-0	Bo Schembechler
10.	Louisiana St	9-1-0	Charlie McClendon

1969 (Cont.)

		Record	Coach
11.	Nebraska	9-2-0	Bob Devaney
12.	Houston	9-2-0	Bill Yeoman
13.	UCLA	8-1-1	Tommy Prothro
14.	Florida	9-1-1	Ray Graves
15.	Tennessee	9-2-0	Doug Dickey
16.	Colorado	8-3-0	Eddie Crowder
17.	West Virginia	10-0-1	Jim Carlen
18.	Purdue	8-2-0	Jack Mollenkopf
19.	Stanford	7-2-1	John Ralston
20.	Auburn	8-3-0	Shug Jordan

1970

		Record	Coach
1.	Nebraska	11-0-1	Bob Devaney
2.	Notre Dame	10-1-0	Ara Parseghian
3.	#Texas	10-1-0	Darrell Royal
4.	Tennessee	11-0-1	Bill Battle
5.	Ohio St	9-1-0	Woody Hayes
6.	Arizona St.	11-0-0	Frank Kush
7.	Louisiana St	9-3-0	Charlie McClendon
8.	Stanford	9-3-0	John Ralston
9.	Michigan	9-1-0	Bo Schembechler
10.	Auburn	9-2-0	Shug Jordan
11.	Arkansas	9-2-0	Frank Broyles
12.	Toledo	12-0-0	Frank Lauterbur
13.	Georgia Tech	9-3-0	Bud Carson
14.	Dartmouth	9-0-0	Bob Blackman
15.	Southern Cal	6-4-1	John McKay
16.	Air Force	9-3-0	Ben Martin
17.	Tulane	8-4-0	Jim Pittman
18.	Penn St	7-3-0	Joe Paterno
19.	Houston	8-3-0	Bill Yeoman
20.	Oklahoma	7-4-1	Chuck Fairbanks
	Mississippi	7-4-0	Johnny Vaught

#Selected No. 1 by UPI.

1971

		Record	Coach
1.	Nebraska	13-0-0	Bob Devaney
2.	Oklahoma	11-1-0	Chuck Fairbanks
3.	Colorado	10-2-0	Eddie Crowder
4.	Alabama	11-1-0	Bear Bryant
5.	Penn St.	11-1-0	Joe Paterno
6.	Michigan	11-1-0	Bo Schembechler
7.	Georgia	11-1-0	Vince Dooley
8.	Arizona St.	11-1-0	Frank Kush
9.	Tennessee	10-2-0	Bill Battle
10.	Stanford	9-3-0	John Ralston
11.	Louisiana St	9-3-0	Charlie McClendon
12.	Auburn	9-2-0	Shug Jordan
13.	Notre Dame	8-2-0	Ara Parseghian
14.	Toledo	12-0-0	John Murphy
15.	Mississippi	10-2-0	Billy Kinard
16.	Arkansas	8-3-1	Frank Broyles
17.	Houston	9-3-0	Bill Yeoman
18.	Texas	8-3-0	Darrell Royal
19.	Washington	8-3-0	Jim Owens
20.	Southern Cal	6-4-1	John McKay

Note: Except where indicated with an asterisk, the polls from 1936 through 1964 were taken before the bowl games and those from 1965 through the present were taken after the bowl games. Additionally, the AP ranked only ten teams in its polls from 1962–67; positions 11–20 from those years are from the UPI poll.

1972

		Record	Coach
1.	Southern Cal	12-0-0	John McKay
2.	Oklahoma	11-1-0	Chuck Fairbanks
3.	Texas	10-1-0	Darrell Royal
4.	Nebraska	9-2-1	Bob Devaney
5.	Auburn	10-1-0	Shug Jordan
6.	Michigan	10-1-0	Bo Schembechler
7.	Alabama	10-2-0	Bear Bryant
8.	Tennessee	10-2-0	Bill Battle
9.	Ohio St	9-2-0	Woody Hayes
10.	Penn St	10-2-0	Joe Paterno
11.	Louisiana St	9-2-1	Charlie McClendon
12.	N Carolina	11-1-0	Bill Dooley
13.	Arizona St	10-2-0	Frank Kush
14.	Notre Dame	8-3-0	Ara Parseghian
15.	UCLA	8-3-0	Pepper Rodgers
16.	Colorado	8-4-0	Eddie Crowder
17.	N Carolina St	8-3-1	Lou Holtz
18.	Louisville	9-1-0	Lee Corso
19.	Washington St	7-4-0	Jim Sweeney
20.	Georgia Tech	7-4-1	Bill Fulcher

1973

		Record	Coach
1.	Notre Dame	11-0-0	Ara Parseghian
2.	Ohio St	10-0-1	Woody Hayes
3.	Oklahoma	10-0-1	Barry Switzer
4.	#Alabama	11-1-0	Bear Bryant
5.	Penn St	12-0-0	Joe Paterno
6.	Michigan	10-0-1	Bo Schembechler
7.	Nebraska	9-2-1	Tom Osborne
8.	Southern Cal	9-2-1	John McKay
9.	Arizona St	11-1-0	Frank Kush
	Houston	11-1-0	Bill Yeoman
11.	Texas Tech	11-1-0	Jim Carlen
12.	UCLA	9-2-0	Pepper Rodgers
13.	Louisiana St	9-3-0	Charlie McClendon
14.	Texas	8-3-0	Darrell Royal
15.	Miami (OH)	11-0-0	Bill Mallory
16.	N Carolina St	9-3-0	Lou Holtz
17.	Missouri	8-4-0	Al Onofrio
18.	Kansas	7-4-1	Don Fambrough
19.	Tennessee	8-4-0	Bill Battle
20.	Maryland	8-4-0	Jerry Claiborne
	Tulane	9-3-0	Bennie Ellender

#Selected No. 1 by UPI.

1974

		Record	Coach
1.	Oklahoma	11-0-0	Barry Switzer
2.	#Southern Cal	10-1-1	John McKay
3.	Michigan	10-1-0	Bo Schembechler
4.	Ohio St	10-2-0	Woody Hayes
5.	Alabama	11-1-0	Bear Bryant
6.	Notre Dame	10-2-0	Ara Parseghian
7.	Penn St	10-2-0	Joe Paterno
8.	Auburn	10-2-0	Shug Jordan
9.	Nebraska	9-3-0	Tom Osborne
10.	Miami (OH)	10-0-1	Dick Crum
11.	N Carolina St	9-2-1	Lou Holtz
12.	Michigan St	7-3-1	Denny Stolz

1974 (Cont.)

		Record	Coach
13.	Maryland	8-4-0	Jerry Claiborne
14.	Baylor	8-4-0	Grant Teaff
15.	Florida	8-4-0	Doug Dickey
16.	Texas A&M	8-3-0	Emory Ballard
17.	Mississippi St	9-3-0	Bob Tyler
	Texas	8-4-0	Darrell Royal
19.	Houston	8-3-1	Bill Yeoman
20.	Tennessee	7-3-2	Bill Battle

#Selected No. 1 by UPI.

1975

		Record	Coach
1.	Oklahoma	11-1-0	Barry Switzer
2.	Arizona St	12-0-0	Frank Kush
3.	Alabama	11-1-0	Bear Bryant
4.	Ohio St	11-1-0	Woody Hayes
5.	UCLA	9-2-1	Dick Vermeil
6.	Texas	10-2-0	Darrell Royal
7.	Arkansas	10-2-0	Frank Broyles
8.	Michigan	8-2-2	Bo Schembechler
9.	Nebraska	10-2-0	Tom Osborne
10.	Penn St	9-3-0	Joe Paterno
11.	Texas A&M	10-2-0	Emory Bellard
12.	Miami (OH)	11-1-0	Dick Crum
13.	Maryland	9-2-1	Jerry Claiborne
14.	California	8-3-0	Mike White
15.	Pittsburgh	8-4-0	Johnny Majors
16.	Colorado	9-3-0	Bill Mallory
17.	Southern Cal	8-4-0	John McKay
18.	Arizona	9-2-0	Jim Young
19.	Georgia	9-3-0	Vince Dooley
20.	West Virginia	9-3-0	Bobby Bowden

1976

		Record	Coach
1.	Pittsburgh	12-0-0	Johnny Majors
2.	Southern Cal	11-1-0	John Robinson
3.	Michigan	10-2-0	Bo Schembechler
4.	Houston	10-2-0	Bill Yeoman
5.	Oklahoma	9-2-1	Barry Switzer
6.	Ohio St	9-2-1	Woody Hayes
7.	Texas A&M	10-2-0	Emory Bellard
8.	Maryland	11-1-0	Jerry Claiborne
9.	Nebraska	9-3-1	Tom Osborne
10.	Georgia	10-2-0	Vince Dooley
11.	Alabama	9-3-0	Bear Bryant
12.	Notre Dame	9-3-0	Dan Devine
13.	Texas Tech	10-2-0	Steve Sloan
14.	Oklahoma St	9-3-0	Jim Stanley
15.	UCLA	9-2-1	Terry Donahue
16.	Colorado	8-4-0	Bill Mallory
17.	Rutgers	11-0-0	Frank Burns
18.	Kentucky	9-3-0	Fran Curci
19.	Iowa St	8-3-0	Earle Bruce
20.	Mississippi St	9-2-0	Bob Tyler

1977

		Record	Coach
1.	Notre Dame	11-1-0	Dan Devine
2.	Alabama	11-1-0	Bear Bryant
3.	Arkansas	11-1-0	Lou Holtz
4.	Texas	11-1-0	Fred Akers
5.	Penn St.	11-1-0	Joe Paterno
6.	Kentucky	10-1-0	Fran Curci
7.	Oklahoma	10-2-0	Barry Switzer
8.	Pittsburgh	9-2-1	Jackie Sherrill
9.	Michigan	10-2-0	Bo Schembechler
10.	Washington	10-2-0	Don James
11.	Ohio St.	9-3-0	Woody Hayes
12.	Nebraska	9-3-0	Tom Osborne
13.	Southern Cal	8-4-0	John Robinson
14.	Florida St.	10-2-0	Bobby Bowden
15.	Stanford	9-3-0	Bill Walsh
16.	San Diego St.	10-1-0	Claude Gilbert
17.	N Carolina	8-3-1	Bill Dooley
18.	Arizona St.	9-3-0	Frank Kush
19.	Clemson	8-3-1	Charley Pell
20.	Brigham Young	9-2-0	LaVell Edwards

1978

		Record	Coach
1.	Alabama	11-1-0	Bear Bryant
2.	#Southern Cal	12-1-0	John Robinson
3.	Oklahoma	11-1-0	Barry Switzer
4.	Penn St.	11-1-0	Joe Paterno
5.	Michigan	10-2-0	Bo Schembechler
6.	Clemson	11-1-0	Charley Pell
7.	Notre Dame	9-3-0	Dan Devine
8.	Nebraska	9-3-0	Tom Osborne
9.	Texas	9-3-0	Fred Akers
10.	Houston	9-3-0	Bill Yeoman
11.	Arkansas	9-2-1	Lou Holtz
12.	Michigan St.	8-3-0	Darryl Rogers
13.	Purdue	9-2-1	Jim Young
14.	UCLA	8-3-1	Terry Donahue
15.	Missouri	8-4-0	Warren Powers
16.	Georgia	9-2-1	Vince Dooley
17.	Stanford	8-4-0	Bill Walsh
18.	N Carolina St.	9-3-0	Bo Rein
19.	Texas A&M	8-4-0	Emory Bellard (4-2) Tom Wilson (4-2)
20.	Maryland	9-3-0	Jerry Claiborne

#Selected No. 1 by UPI.

1979

		Record	Coach
1.	Alabama	12-0-0	Bear Bryant
2.	Southern Cal	11-0-1	John Robinson
3.	Oklahoma	11-1-0	Barry Switzer
4.	Ohio St.	11-1-0	Earle Bruce
5.	Houston	11-1-0	Bill Yeoman
6.	Florida St.	11-1-0	Bobby Bowden
7.	Pittsburgh	11-1-0	Jackie Sherrill
8.	Arkansas	10-2-0	Lou Holtz
9.	Nebraska	10-2-0	Tom Osborne
10.	Purdue	10-2-0	Jim Young
11.	Washington	10-1-0	Don James
12.	Texas	9-3-0	Fred Akers
13.	Brigham Young	11-1-0	LaVell Edwards
14.	Baylor	8-4-0	Grant Teaff
15.	N Carolina	8-3-1	Dick Crum
16.	Auburn	8-3-0	Doug Barfield
17.	Temple	10-2-0	Wayne Hardin

1979 (Cont.)

		Record	Coach
18.	Michigan	8-4-0	Bo Schembechler
19.	Indiana	8-4-0	Lee Corso
20.	Penn St.	8-4-0	Joe Paterno

1980

		Record	Coach
1.	Georgia	12-0-0	Vince Dooley
2.	Pittsburgh	11-1-0	Jackie Sherrill
3.	Oklahoma	10-2-0	Barry Switzer
4.	Michigan	10-2-0	Bo Schembechler
5.	Florida St.	10-2-0	Bobby Bowden
6.	Alabama	10-2-0	Bear Bryant
7.	Nebraska	10-2-0	Tom Osborne
8.	Penn St.	10-2-0	Joe Paterno
9.	Notre Dame	9-2-1	Dan Devine
10.	N Carolina	11-1-0	Dick Crum
11.	Southern Cal	8-2-1	John Robinson
12.	Brigham Young	12-1-0	LaVell Edwards
13.	UCLA	9-2-0	Terry Donahue
14.	Baylor	10-2-0	Grant Teaff
15.	Ohio St.	9-3-0	Earle Bruce
16.	Washington	9-3-0	Don James
17.	Purdue	9-3-0	Jim Young
18.	Miami (FL)	9-3-0	H. Schnellenberger
19.	Mississippi St.	9-3-0	Emory Bellard
20.	SMU	8-4-0	Ron Meyer

1981

		Record	Coach
1.	Clemson	12-0-0	Danny Ford
2.	Texas	10-1-1	Fred Akers
3.	Penn St.	10-2-0	Joe Paterno
4.	Pittsburgh	11-1-0	Jackie Sherrill
5.	SMU	10-1-0	Ron Meyer
6.	Georgia	10-2-0	Vince Dooley
7.	Alabama	9-2-1	Bear Bryant
8.	Miami (FL)	9-2-0	H. Schnellenberger
9.	N Carolina	10-2-0	Dick Crum
10.	Washington	10-2-0	Don James
11.	Nebraska	9-3-0	Tom Osborne
12.	Michigan	9-3-0	Bo Schembechler
13.	Brigham Young	11-2-0	LaVell Edwards
14.	Southern Cal	9-3-0	John Robinson
15.	Ohio St.	9-3-0	Earle Bruce
16.	Arizona St.	9-2-0	Darryl Rogers
17.	West Virginia	9-3-0	Don Nehlen
18.	Iowa	8-4-0	Hayden Fry
19.	Missouri	8-4-0	Warren Powers
20.	Oklahoma	7-4-1	Barry Switzer

1982

		Record	Coach
1.	Penn St.	11-1-0	Joe Paterno
2.	SMU	11-0-1	Bobby Collins
3.	Nebraska	12-1-0	Tom Osborne
4.	Georgia	11-1-0	Vince Dooley
5.	UCLA	10-1-1	Terry Donahue
6.	Arizona St.	10-2-0	Darryl Rogers
7.	Washington	10-2-0	Don James
8.	Clemson	9-1-1	Danny Ford
9.	Arkansas	9-2-1	Lou Holtz
10.	Pittsburgh	9-3-0	Foge Fazio
11.	Louisiana St.	8-3-1	Jerry Stovall
12.	Ohio St.	9-3-0	Earle Bruce

1982 *(Cont.)*

		Record	Coach
13.	Florida St	9-3-0	Bobby Bowden
14.	Auburn	9-3-0	Pat Dye
15.	Southern Cal	8-3-0	John Robinson
16.	Oklahoma	8-4-0	Barry Switzer
17.	Texas	9-3-0	Fred Akers
18.	N Carolina	8-4-0	Dick Crum
19.	West Virginia	9-3-0	Don Nehlen
20.	Maryland	8-4-0	Bobby Ross

1983

		Record	Coach
1.	Miami (FL)	11-1-0	H. Schnellenberger
2.	Nebraska	12-1-0	Tom Osborne
3.	Auburn	11-1-0	Pat Dye
4.	Georgia	10-1-1	Vince Dooley
5.	Texas	11-1-0	Fred Akers
6.	Florida	9-2-1	Charlie Pell
7.	Brigham Young	11-1-0	LaVell Edwards
8.	Michigan	9-3-0	Bo Schembechler
9.	Ohio St	9-3-0	Earle Bruce
10.	Illinois	10-2-0	Mike White
11.	Clemson	9-1-1	Danny Ford
12.	SMU	10-2-0	Bobby Collins
13.	Air Force	10-2-0	Ken Hatfield
14.	Iowa	9-3-0	Hayden Fry
15.	Alabama	8-4-0	Ray Perkins
16.	West Virginia	9-3-0	Don Nehlen
17.	UCLA	7-4-1	Terry Donahue
18.	Pittsburgh	8-3-1	Foge Fazio
19.	Boston College	9-3-0	Jack Bicknell
20.	E Carolina	8-3-0	Ed Emory

1984

		Record	Coach
1.	Brigham Young	13-0-0	LaVell Edwards
2.	Washington	11-1-0	Don James
3.	Florida	9-1-1	Chas Pell (0-1-1)
			Galen Hall (9-0)
4.	Nebraska	10-2-0	Tom Osborne
5.	Boston College	10-2-0	Jack Bicknell
6.	Oklahoma	9-2-1	Barry Switzer
7.	Oklahoma St	10-2-0	Pat Jones
8.	SMU	10-2-0	Bobby Collins
9.	UCLA	9-3-0	Terry Donahue
10.	Southern Cal	9-3-0	Ted Tollner
11.	South Carolina	10-2-0	Joe Morrison
12.	Maryland	9-3-0	Bobby Ross
13.	Ohio St	9-3-0	Earle Bruce
14.	Auburn	9-4-0	Pat Dye
15.	Louisiana St	8-3-1	Bill Arnsparger
16.	Iowa	8-4-1	Hayden Fry
17.	Florida St	7-3-2	Bobby Bowden
18.	Miami (FL)	8-5-0	Jimmy Johnson
19.	Kentucky	9-3-0	Jerry Claiborne
20.	Virginia	8-2-2	George Welsh

1985

		Record	Coach
1.	Oklahoma	11-1-0	Barry Switzer
2.	Michigan	10-1-1	Bo Schembechler
3.	Penn St	11-1-0	Joe Paterno
4.	Tennessee	9-1-2	Johnny Majors
5.	Florida	9-1-1	Galen Hall
6.	Texas A&M	10-2-0	Jackie Sherrill
7.	UCLA	9-2-1	Terry Donahue
8.	Air Force	12-1-0	Fisher DeBerry

1985 *(Cont.)*

		Record	Coach
9.	Miami (FL)	10-2-0	Jimmy Johnson
10.	Iowa	10-2-0	Hayden Fry
11.	Nebraska	9-3-0	Tom Osborne
12.	Arkansas	10-2-0	Ken Hatfield
13.	Alabama	9-2-1	Ray Perkins
14.	Ohio St	9-3-0	Earle Bruce
15.	Florida St	9-3-0	Bobby Bowden
16.	Brigham Young	11-3-0	LaVell Edwards
17.	Baylor	9-3-0	Grant Teaff
18.	Maryland	9-3-0	Bobby Ross
19.	Georgia Tech	9-2-1	Bill Curry
20.	Louisiana St	9-2-1	Bill Arnsparger

1986

		Record	Coach
1.	Penn St	12-0-0	Joe Paterno
2.	Miami (FL)	11-1-0	Jimmy Johnson
3.	Oklahoma	11-1-0	Barry Switzer
4.	Arizona St	10-1-1	John Cooper
5.	Nebraska	10-2-0	Tom Osborne
6.	Auburn	10-2-0	Pat Dye
7.	Ohio St	10-3-0	Earle Bruce
8.	Michigan	11-2-0	Bo Schembechler
9.	Alabama	10-3-0	Ray Perkins
10.	Louisiana St	9-3-0	Bill Arnsparger
11.	Arizona	9-3-0	Larry Smith
12.	Baylor	9-3-0	Grant Teaff
13.	Texas A&M	9-3-0	Jackie Sherrill
14.	UCLA	8-3-1	Terry Donahue
15.	Arkansas	9-3-0	Ken Hatfield
16.	Iowa	9-3-0	Hayden Fry
17.	Clemson	8-2-2	Danny Ford
18.	Washington	8-3-1	Don James
19.	Boston College	9-3-0	Jack Bicknell
20.	Virginia Tech	9-2-1	Bill Dooley

1987

		Record	Coach
1.	Miami (FL)	12-0-0	Jimmy Johnson
2.	Florida St	11-1-0	Bobby Bowden
3.	Oklahoma	11-1-0	Barry Switzer
4.	Syracuse	11-0-1	Dick MacPherson
5.	Louisiana St	10-1-1	Mike Archer
6.	Nebraska	10-2-0	Tom Osborne
7.	Auburn	9-1-2	Pat Dye
8.	Michigan St	9-2-1	George Perles
9.	UCLA	10-2-0	Terry Donahue
10.	Texas A&M	10-2-0	Jackie Sherrill
11.	Oklahoma St	10-2-0	Pat Jones
12.	Clemson	10-2-0	Danny Ford
13.	Georgia	9-3-0	Vince Dooley
14.	Tennessee	10-2-1	Johnny Majors
15.	S Carolina	8-4-0	Joe Morrison
16.	Iowa	10-3-0	Hayden Fry
17.	Notre Dame	8-4-0	Lou Holtz
18.	Southern Cal	8-4-0	Larry Smith
19.	Michigan	8-4-0	Bo Schembechler
20.	Arizona St	7-4-1	John Cooper

1988

		Record	Coach
1.	Notre Dame	12-0-0	Lou Holtz
2.	Miami (FL)	11-1-0	Jimmy Johnson
3.	Florida St	11-1-0	Bobby Bowden
4.	Michigan	9-2-1	Bo Schembechler
5.	West Virginia	11-1-0	Don Nehlen
6.	UCLA	10-2-0	Terry Donahue
7.	Southern Cal	10-2-0	Larry Smith
8.	Auburn	10-2-0	Pat Dye
9.	Clemson	10-2-0	Danny Ford
10.	Nebraska	11-2-0	Tom Osborne
11.	Oklahoma St	10-2-0	Pat Jones
12.	Arkansas	10-2-0	Ken Hatfield
13.	Syracuse	10-2-0	Dick MacPherson
14.	Oklahoma	9-3-0	Barry Switzer
15.	Georgia	9-3-0	Vince Dooley
16.	Washington St	9-3-0	Dennis Erickson
17.	Alabama	9-3-0	Bill Curry
18.	Houston	9-3-0	Jack Pardee
19.	Louisiana St	8-4-0	Mike Archer
20.	Indiana	8-3-1	Bill Mallory

†1989

		Record	Coach
1.	Miami (FL)	11-1-0	Dennis Erickson
2.	Notre Dame	12-1-0	Lou Holtz
3.	Florida St	10-2-0	Bobby Bowden
4.	Colorado	11-1-0	Bill McCartney
5.	Tennessee	11-1-0	Johnny Majors
6.	Auburn	10-2-0	Pat Dye
7.	Michigan	10-2-0	Bo Schembechler
8.	Southern Cal	9-2-1	Larry Smith
9.	Alabama	10-2-0	Bill Curry
10.	Illinois	10-2-0	John Mackovic
11.	Nebraska	10-2-0	Tom Osborne
12.	Clemson	10-2-0	Danny Ford
13.	Arkansas	10-2-0	Ken Hatfield
14.	Houston	9-2-0	Jack Pardee
15.	Penn St	8-3-1	Joe Paterno
16.	Michigan St	8-4-0	George Perles
17.	Pittsburgh	8-3-1	Mike Gottfried
18.	Virginia	10-3-0	George Welsh
19.	Texas Tech	9-3-0	Spike Dykes
20.	Texas A&M	8-4-0	R.C. Slocum
21.	West Virginia	8-3-1	Don Nehlen
22.	Brigham Young	10-3-0	LaVell Edwards
23.	Washington	8-4-0	Don James
24.	Ohio St	8-4-0	John Cooper
25.	Arizona	8-4-0	Dick Tomey

1990

		Record	Coach
1.	Colorado	11-1-1	Bill McCartney
2.	#Georgia Tech	11-0-1	Bobby Ross
3.	Miami (FL)	10-2-0	Dennis Erickson
4.	Florida St	10-2-0	Bobby Bowden
5.	Washington	10-2-0	Don James
6.	Notre Dame	9-3-0	Lou Holtz
7.	Michigan	9-3-0	Gary Moeller
8.	Tennessee	9-2-2	Johnny Majors
9.	Clemson	10-2-0	Ken Hatfield
10.	Houston	10-1-0	John Jenkins
11.	Penn St	9-3-0	Joe Paterno
12.	Texas	10-2-0	David McWilliams

1990 *(Cont.)*

		Record	Coach
13.	Florida	9-2-0	Steve Spurrier
14.	Louisville	10-1-1	H. Schnellenberger
15.	Texas A&M	9-3-1	R.C. Slocum
16.	Michigan St	8-3-1	George Perles
17.	Oklahoma	8-3-0	Gary Gibbs
18.	Iowa	8-4-0	Hayden Fry
19.	Auburn	8-3-1	Pat Dye
20.	Southern Cal	8-4-1	Larry Smith
21.	Mississippi	9-3-0	Billy Brewer
22.	Brigham Young	10-3-0	LaVell Edwards
23.	Virginia	8-4-0	George Wells
24.	Nebraska	9-3-0	Tom Osborne
25.	Illinois	8-4-0	John Mackovic

#Selected No. 1 by UPI.

1991

		Record	Coach
1.	Miami (FL)	12-0-0	Dennis Erickson
2.	#Washington	12-0-0	Don James
3.	Penn St	11-2-0	Joe Paterno
4.	Florida St	11-2-0	Bobby Bowden
5.	Alabama	11-1-0	Gene Stallings
6.	Michigan	10-2-0	Gary Moeller
7.	Florida	10-2-0	Steve Spurrier
8.	California	10-2-0	Bruce Snyder
9.	E Carolina	11-1-0	Bill Lewis
10.	Iowa	10-1-1	Hayden Fry
11.	Syracuse	10-2-0	Paul Pasqualoni
12.	Texas A&M	10-2-0	R.C. Slocum
13.	Notre Dame	10-3-0	Lou Holtz
14.	Tennessee	9-3-0	Johnny Majors
15.	Nebraska	9-2-1	Tom Osborne
16.	Oklahoma	9-3-0	Gary Gibbs
17.	Georgia	9-3-0	Ray Goff
18.	Clemson	9-2-1	Ken Hatfield
19.	UCLA	9-3-0	Terry Donahue
20.	Colorado	8-3-1	Bill McCartney
21.	Tulsa	10-2-0	David Rader
22.	Stanford	8-4-0	Dennis Green
23.	Brigham Young	8-3-2	LaVell Edwards
24.	N Carolina St	9-3-0	Dick Sheridan
25.	Air Force	10-3-0	Fisher DeBerry

#Selected No. 1 by *USA Today*/ CNN.

1992

		Record	Coach
1.	Alabama	13-0-0	Gene Stallings
2.	Florida St	11-1-0	Bobby Bowden
3.	Miami	11-1-0	Dennis Erickson
4.	Notre Dame	10-1-1	Lou Holtz
5.	Michigan	9-0-3	Gary Moeller
6.	Syracuse	10-2-0	Paul Pasqualoni
7.	Texas A&M	12-1-0	R.C. Slocum
8.	Georgia	10-2-0	Ray Goff
9.	Stanford	10-3-0	Bill Walsh
10.	Florida	9-4-0	Steve Spurrier
11.	Washington	9-3-0	Don James
12.	Tennessee	9-3-0	Johnny Majors
13.	Colorado	9-2-1	Bill McCartney
14.	Nebraska	9-3-0	Tom Osborne
15.	Washington St	9-3-0	Mike Price
16.	Mississippi	9-3-0	Billy Brewer
17.	N Carolina St	9-3-1	Dick Sheridan
18.	Ohio St	8-3-1	John Cooper
19.	N Carolina	9-3-0	Mack Brown
20.	Hawaii	11-2-0	Bob Wagner

1992 (Cont.)

	Record	Coach
21. Boston College	8-3-1	Tom Coughlin
22. Kansas	8-4-0	Glen Mason
23. Mississippi St	7-5-0	Jackie Sherrill
24. Fresno St	9-4-0	Jim Sweeney
25. Wake Forest	8-4-0	Bill Dooley

1993

	Record	Coach
1. Florida St	12-1-0	Bobby Bowden
2. Notre Dame	11-1-0	Lou Holtz
3. Nebraska	11-1-0	Tom Osborne
4. Auburn	11-0-0	Terry Bowden
5. Florida	11-2-0	Steve Spurrier
6. Wisconsin	10-1-1	Barry Alvarez
7. West Virginia	11-1-0	Don Nehlen
8. Penn St	10-2-0	Joe Paterno
9. Texas A&M	10-2-0	R.C. Slocum
10. Arizona	10-2-0	Dick Tomey
11. Ohio St	10-1-1	John Cooper
12. Tennessee	9-2-1	Phil Fulmer
13. Boston College	9-3-0	Tom Coughlin
14. Alabama	9-3-1	Gene Stallings
15. Miami	9-3-0	Dennis Erickson
16. Colorado	8-3-1	Bill McCartney
17. Oklahoma	9-3-0	Gary Gibbs
18. UCLA	8-4-0	Terry Donahue
19. N Carolina	10-3-0	Mack Brown
20. Kansas St	9-2-1	Bill Snyder
21. Michigan	8-4-0	Gary Moeller
22. Virginia Tech	9-3-0	Frank Beamer
23. Clemson	9-3-0	Ken Hatfield
24. Louisville	9-3-0	H. Schnellenberger
25. California	9-4-0	Keith Gilbertson

1994

	Record	Coach
1. Nebraska	13-0-0	Tom Osborne
2. Penn St	12-0-0	Joe Paterno
3. Colorado	11-1-0	Bill McCartney
4. Florida St	10-1-1	Bobby Bowden
5. Alabama	12-1-0	Gene Stallings
6. Miami (FL)	10-2-0	Dennis Erickson
7. Florida	10-2-1	Steve Spurrier
8. Texas A&M	10-0-1	R.C. Slocum
9. Auburn	9-1-1	Terry Bowden
10. Utah	10-2-0	Ron McBride
11. Oregon	9-4-0	Rich Brooks
12. Michigan	8-4-0	Gary Moeller
13. Southern Cal	8-3-1	John Robinson
14. Ohio St	9-4-0	John Cooper
15. Virginia	9-3-0	George Welsh
16. Colorado St	10-2-0	Sonny Lubick
17. N Carolina St	9-3-0	Mike O'Cain
18. Brigham Young	10-3-0	LaVell Edwards
19. Kansas St	9-3-0	Bill Snyder
20. Arizona	8-4-0	Dick Tomey
21. Washington St	8-4-0	Mike Price
22. Tennessee	8-4-0	Phillip Fulmer
23. Boston College	7-4-1	Dan Henning
24. Mississippi St	8-4-0	Jackie Sherrill
25. Texas	8-4-0	John Mackovic

1995

	Record	Coach
1. Nebraska	12-0-0	Tom Osborne
2. Florida	12-1-0	Steve Spurrier
3. Tennessee	11-1-0	Phillip Fulmer
4. Florida St	10-2-0	Bobby Bowden
5. Colorado	10-2-0	Rick Neuheisel
6. Ohio St	11-2-0	John Cooper
7. Kansas St	10-2-0	Bill Snyder
8. Northwestern	10-2-0	Gary Barnett
9. Kansas	10-2-0	Glen Mason
10. Virginia Tech	10-2-0	Frank Beamer
11. Notre Dame	9-3-0	Lou Holtz
12. Southern Cal	9-2-1	John Robinson
13. Penn St	9-3-0	Joe Paterno
14. Texas	10-2-1	John Mackovic
15. Texas A&M	9-3-0	S.C. Slocum
16. Virginia	9-4-0	George Welsh
17. Michigan	9-4-0	Lloyd Carr
18. Oregon	9-3-0	Mike Bellotti
19. Syracuse	9-3-0	Paul Pasqualoni
20. Miami (FL)	8-3-0	Butch Davis
21. Alabama	8-3-0	Gene Stallings
22. Auburn	8-4-0	Terry Bowden
23. Texas Tech	9-3-0	Spike Dykes
24. Toledo	11-0-1	Gary Pinkel
25. Iowa	8-4-0	Hayden Fry

1996

	Record*	Coach
1. Florida	12–1	Steve Spurrier
2. Ohio St	11–1	John Cooper
3. Florida St	11–1	Bobby Bowden
4. Arizona St	11–1	Bruce Snyder
5. Brigham Young	14–1	LaVell Edwards
6. Nebraska	11–2	Tom Osborne
7. Penn St	11–2	Joe Paterno
8. Colorado	10–2	Rick Neuheisel
9. Tennessee	10–2	Phillip Fulmer
10. North Carolina	10–2	Mack Brown
11. Alabama	10–3	Gene Stallings
12. Louisiana St	10–2	Gerry DiNardo
13. Virginia Tech	10–2	Frank Beamer
14. Miami (FL)	9–3	Butch Davis
15. Northwestern	9–3	Gary Barnett
16. Washington	9–3	Jim Lambright
17. Kansas St	9–3	Bill Snyder
18. Iowa	9–3	Hayden Fry
19. Notre Dame	8–3	Lou Holtz
20. Michigan	8–4	Lloyd Carr
21. Syracuse	9–3	Paul Pasqualoni
22. Wyoming	10–2	Joe Tiller
23. Texas	8–5	John Mackovic
24. Auburn	8–4	Terry Bowden
25. Army	10–2	Bob Sutton

†In 1989 the Associated Press expanded its final poll to 25 teams.
*In 1996 the NCAA introduced overtime to break ties.

1997

		Record	Coach
1.	Michigan	12–0	Lloyd Carr
2.	Nebraska	13–0	Tom Osborne
3.	Florida St	11–1	Bobby Bowden
4.	Florida	10–2	Steve Spurrier
5.	UCLA	10–2	Bob Toledo
6.	N Carolina	11–1	Mack Brown
7.	Tennessee	11–2	Phillip Fulmer
8.	Kansas St	11–1	Bill Snyder
9.	Washington St	10–2	Mike Price
10.	Georgia	10–2	Jim Donnan
11.	Auburn	10–3	Terry Bowden
12.	Ohio St	10–3	John Cooper
13.	Louisiana St	9–3	Gerry DiNardo
14.	Arizona St	8–3	Bruce Snyder
15.	Purdue	9–3	Joe Tiller
16.	Penn St	9–3	Joe Paterno
17.	Colorado St	11–2	Sonny Lubick
18.	Washington	8–4	Jim Lambright
19.	Southern Mississippi	9–3	Jeff Bower
20.	Texas A&M	9–4	R. C. Slocum
21.	Syracuse	9–4	Paul Pasqualoni
22.	Mississippi	8–4	Tommy Tuberville
23.	Missouri	7–5	Larry Smith
24.	Oklahoma St	8–4	Bob Simmons
25.	Georgia Tech	7–5	George O'Leary

1998

		Record	Coach
1.	Tennessee	13–0	Phillip Fulmer
2.	Ohio St	11–1	John Cooper
3.	Florida St	11–2	Bobby Bowden
4.	Arizona	12–1	Dick Tomey
5.	Florida	10–2	Steve Spurrier
6.	Wisconsin	11–1	Barry Alvarez
7.	Tulane	12–0	Tommy Bowden
8.	UCLA	10–2	Bob Toledo
9.	Georgia Tech	10–2	George O'Leary
10.	Kansas St	11–2	Bill Snyder
11.	Texas A&M	11–3	R.C. Slocum
12.	Michigan	10–3	Lloyd Carr
13.	Air Force	12–1	Fisher DeBerry
14.	Georgia	9–3	Jim Donnan
15.	Texas	9–3	Mack Brown
16.	Arkansas	9–3	Houston Nutt
17.	Penn St	9–3	Joe Paterno
18.	Virginia	9–3	George Welsh
19.	Nebraska	9–4	Frank Solich
20.	Miami (FL)	9–3	Butch Davis
21.	Missouri	8–4	Larry Smith
22.	Notre Dame	9–3	Bob Davie
23.	Virginia Tech	9–3	Frank Beamer
24.	Purdue	9–4	Joe Tiller
25.	Syracuse	8–4	Paul Pasqualoni

Space Case

Anyone who saw UCLA lose to Miami 49–45 in December 1998 might call the Bruins' defense pass-challenged, but porousness is not recognized as a handicap under the Americans with Disabilities Act. That's why 14 current and former UCLA football players—including guard Oscar Cabrera, fullback Durell Price and linebackers Ryan Neece and Tony White, all starters in '98—are in trouble with the law. In July 1999 Los Angeles city attorney Jim Hahan filed criminal charges against the players, accusing them of submitting false applications for handicapped-parking permits. According to Hahn's office the players' applications claimed bogus disabilities and bore the signatures of nonexistent doctors. The *Los Angeles Times* reported that one player cited Bell's palsy, a condition that typically causes temporary facial paralysis, as his handicap. Another used "bad knees" as his reason for needing to use special parking spaces.

The players could face six months in jail and fines of $1,000 each. "I am embarrassed and disappointed for the young men who were involved," said UCLA coach Bob Toledo. "Those individuals will be disciplined by me."

NCAA Divisional Championships

Division I-AA

Year	Winner	Runner-Up	Score
1978	Florida A&M	Massachusetts	35–28
1979	Eastern Kentucky	Lehigh	30–7
1980	Boise St	Eastern Kentucky	31–29
1981	Idaho St	Eastern Kentucky	34–23
1982	Eastern Kentucky	Delaware	17–14
1983	Southern Illinois	Western Carolina	43–7
1984	Montana St	Louisiana Tech	19–6
1985	Georgia Southern	Furman	44–42
1986	Georgia Southern	Arkansas St	48–21
1987	NE Louisiana	Marshall	43–42
1988	Furman	Georgia Southern	17–12
1989	Georgia Southern	SF Austin St	37–34
1990	Georgia Southern	NV-Reno	36–13
1991	Youngstown St	Marshall	25–17
1992	Marshall	Youngstown St	31–28
1993	Youngstown St	Marshall	17–5
1994	Youngstown St	Boise St	28–14
1995	Montana	Marshall	22–20
1996	Marshall	Montana	49–29
1997	Youngstown St	McNesse St	10–9
1998	Massachusetts	Georgia Southern	55–43

Division II

Year	Winner	Runner-Up	Score
1973	Louisiana Tech	Western Kentucky	34–0
1974	Central Michigan	Delaware	54–14
1975	Northern Michigan	Western Kentucky	16–14
1976	Montana St	Akron	24–13
1977	Lehigh	Jacksonville St	33–0
1978	Eastern Illinois	Delaware	10–9
1979	Delaware	Youngstown St	38–21
1980	Cal Poly SLO	Eastern Illinois	21–13
1981	SW Texas St	N Dakota St	42–13
1982	SW Texas St	UC-Davis	34–9
1983	N Dakota St	Central St (OH)	41–21
1984	Troy St	N Dakota St	18–17
1985	N Dakota St	N Alabama	35–7
1986	N Dakota St	S Dakota	27–7
1987	Troy St	Portland St	31–17
1988	N Dakota St	Portland St	35–21
1989	Mississippi College	Jacksonville St	3–0
1990	N Dakota St	Indiana (PA)	51–11
1991	Pittsburg St	Jacksonville St	23–6
1992	Jacksonville St	Pittsburg St	17–13
1993	N Alabama	Indiana (PA)	41–34
1994	N Alabama	Texas A&M-Kingsville	16–10
1995	N Alabama	Pittsburg St	27–7
1996	Northern Colorado	Carson-Newman	23–14
1997	Northern Colorado	New Haven	51–0
1998	NW Missouri St	Carson-Newman	24–6

Division III

Year	Winner	Runner-Up	Score
1973	Wittenberg	Juniata	41–0
1974	Central (IA)	Ithaca	10–8
1975	Wittenberg	Ithaca	28–0
1976	St John's (MN)	Towson St	31–28
1977	Widener	Wabash	39–36
1978	Baldwin-Wallace	Wittenberg	24–10
1979	Ithaca	Wittenberg	14–10
1980	Dayton	Ithaca	63–0
1981	Widener	Dayton	17–10
1982	W Georgia	Augustana (IL)	14–0
1983	Augustana (IL)	Union (NY)	21–17
1984	Augustana (IL)	Central (IA)	21–12
1985	Augustana (IL)	Ithaca	20–7
1986	Augustana (IL)	Salisbury St	31–3
1987	Wagner	Dayton	19–3

Division III *(Cont.)*

Year	Winner	Runner-Up	Score
1988	Ithaca	Central (IA)	39–24
1989	Dayton	Union (NY)	17–7
1990	Allegheny	Lycoming	21–14 (OT)
1991	Ithaca	Dayton	34–20
1992	WI-LaCrosse	Washington & Jefferson	16–12
1993	Mount Union	Rowan	34–24
1994	Albion	Washington & Jefferson	38–15
1995	WI-LaCrosse	Rowan	36–7
1996	Mount Union	Rowan	56–24
1997	Mount Union	Lycoming	61–12
1998	Mount Union	Rowan	44–24

NAIA Divisional Championships†

Division I

Year	Winner	Runner-Up	Score
1956	St Joseph's (IN)/ Montana St		0–0
1957	Pittsburg St (KS)	Hillsdale (MI)	27–26
1958	NE Oklahoma	Northern Arizona	19–13
1959	Texas A&I	Lenoir-Rhyne (NC)	20–7
1960	Lenoir-Rhyne (NC)	Humboldt St (CA)	15–14
1961	Pittsburg St (KS)	Linfield (OR)	12–7
1962	Central St (OK)	Lenoir-Rhyne (NC)	28–13
1963	St John's (MN)	Prairie View (TX)	33–27
1964	Concordia-Moorhead/ Sam Houston		7–7
1965	St John's (MN)	Linfield (OR)	33–0
1966	Waynesburg (PA)	WI-Whitewater	42–21
1967	Fairmont St (WV)	Eastern Washington	28–21
1968	Troy St (MI)	Texas A&I	43–35
1969	Texas A&I	Concordia-Moorhead (MN)	32–7
1970	Texas A&I	Wofford (SC)	48–7
1971	Livingston (AL)	Arkansas Tech	14–12
1972	E Texas St	Carson-Newman (TN)	21–18
1973	Abilene Christian	Elon (NC)	42–14
1974	Texas A&I	Henderson St (AR)	34–23
1975	Texas A&I	Salem (WV)	37–0
1976	Texas A&I	Central Arkansas	26–0
1977	Abilene Christian	SW Oklahoma	24–7
1978	Angelo St (TX)	Elon (NC)	34–14
1979	Texas A&I	Central St (OK)	20–14
1980	Elon (NC)	NE Oklahoma	17–10
1981	Elon (NC)	Pittsburg St	3–0
1982	Central St (OK)	Mesa (CO)	14–11
1983	Carson-Newman (TN)	Mesa (CO)	36–28
1984	Carson-Newman (TN)/ Central Arkansas		19–19
1985	Central Arkansas/ Hillsdale (MI)		10–10
1986	Carson-Newman (TN)	Cameron (OK)	17–0
1987	Cameron (OK)	Carson-Newman (TN)	30–2
1988	Carson-Newman (TN)	Adams St (CO)	56–21
1989	Carson-Newman (TN)	Emporia St (KS)	34–20
1990	Central St (OH)	Mesa St (CO)	38–16
1991	Central Arkansas	Central St (OH)	19–16
1992	Central St (OH)	Gardner-Webb (NC)	19–16
1993	East Central (OK)	Glenville St (WV)	49–35
1994	Northeastern St (OK)	Arkansas-Pine Bluff	13–12
1995	Central St (OH)	Northeastern St (OK)	37–7
1996	SW Oklahoma St	Montana Tech	33–31
1997	Findlay (OH)	Willamette (OR)	14–7
1998	Azusa Pacific	Olivet Nazarene	17–14

† In 1997 the NAIA consolidated its two divisions into one.

Division II

Year	Winner	Runner-Up	Score
1970	Westminster (PA)	Anderson (IN)	21–16
1971	California Lutheran	Westminster (PA)	30–14
1972	Missouri Southern	Northwestern (IA)	21–14
1973	Northwestern (IA)	Glenville St (WV)	10–3
1974	Texas Lutheran	Missouri Valley	42–0
1975	Texas Lutheran	California Lutheran	34–8
1976	Westminster (PA)	Redlands (CA)	20–13
1977	Westminster (PA)	California Lutheran	17–9
1978	Concordia-Moorhead (MN)	Findlay (OH)	7–0
1979	Findlay (OH)	Northwestern (IA)	51–6
1980	Pacific Lutheran	Wilmington (OH)	38–10
1981	Austin Coll./ Conc.-Moorhead (MN)		24–24
1982	Linfield (OR)	William Jewell (MO)	33–15
1983	Northwestern (IA)	Pacific Lutheran	25–21
1984	Linfield (OR)	Northwestern (IA)	33–22
1985	WI-La Crosse	Pacific Lutheran	24–7
1986	Linfield (OR)	Baker (KS)	17–0
1987	Pacific Lutheran	WI-Stevens Point*	16–16
1988	Westminster (PA)	WI-La Crosse	21–14
1989	Westminster (PA)	WI-La Crosse	51–30
1990	Peru St (NE)	Westminster (PA)	17–7
1991	Georgetown (KY)	Pacific Lutheran	28–20
1992	Findlay (OH)	Linfield (OR)	26–13
1993	Pacific Lutheran (WA)	Westminster (PA)	50–20
1994	Westminster (PA)	Pacific Lutheran	27–7
1995	Findlay (OH)/ Central Washington		21–21
1996	Sioux Falls (SD)	Western Washington	47–25

*Forfeited 1987 season due to use of an ineligible player.   †In 1997 the NAIA consolidated its two divisions into one.

Awards

Heisman Memorial Trophy

Awarded to the best college player by the Downtown Athletic Club of New York City. The trophy is named after John W. Heisman, who coached Georgia Tech to the national championship in 1917 and later served as DAC athletic director.

Year	Winner, College, Position	Winner's Season Statistics	Runner-Up, College
1935	Jay Berwanger, Chicago, HB	Rush: 119 Yds: 577 TD: 6	Monk Meyer, Army
1936	Larry Kelley, Yale, E	Rec: 17 Yds: 372 TD: 6	Sam Francis, Nebraska
1937	Clint Frank, Yale, HB	Rush: 157 Yds: 667 TD: 11	Byron White, Colorado
1938	†Davey O'Brien, Texas Christian, QB	Att/Comp: 194/110 Yds: 1733 TD: 19	Marshall Goldberg, Pittsburgh
1939	Nile Kinnick, Iowa, HB	Rush: 106 Yds: 374 TD: 5	Tom Harmon, Michigan
1940	Tom Harmon, Michigan, HB	Rush: 191 Yds: 852 TD: 16	John Kimbrough, Texas A&M
1941	†Bruce Smith, Minnesota, HB	Rush: 98 Yds: 480 TD: 6	Angelo Bertelli, Notre Dame
1942	Frank Sinkwich, Georgia, HB	Att/Comp: 166/84 Yds: 1392 TD: 10	Paul Governali, Columbia
1943	Angelo Bertelli, Notre Dame, QB	Att/Comp: 36/25 Yds: 511 TD: 10	Bob Odell, Pennsylvania
1944	Les Horvath, Ohio State, QB	Rush: 163 Yds: 924 TD: 12	Glenn Davis, Army
1945	*†Doc Blanchard, Army, FB	Rush: 101 Yds: 718 TD: 13	Glenn Davis, Army
1946	Glenn Davis, Army, HB	Rush: 123 Yds: 712 TD: 7	Charley Trippi, Georgia
1947	†John Lujack, Notre Dame, QB	Att/Comp: 109/61 Yds: 777 TD: 9	Bob Chappius, Michigan
1948	*Doak Walker, Southern Methodist, HB	Rush: 108 Yds: 532 TD: 8	Charlie Justice, N Carolina
1949	†Leon Hart, Notre Dame, E	Rec: 19 Yds: 257 TD: 5	Charlie Justice, N Carolina
1950	*Vic Janowicz, Ohio St, HB	Att/Comp: 77/32 Yds: 561 TD: 12	Kyle Rote, Southern Methodist
1951	Dick Kazmaier, Princeton, HB	Rush: 149 Yds: 861 TD: 9	Hank Lauricella, Tennessee
1952	Billy Vessels, Oklahoma, HB	Rush: 167 Yds: 1072 TD: 17	Jack Scarbath, Maryland
1953	John Lattner, Notre Dame, HB	Rush: 134 Yds: 651 TD: 6	Paul Giel, Minnesota
1954	Alan Ameche, Wisconsin, FB	Rush: 146 Yds: 641 TD: 9	Kurt Burris, Oklahoma
1955	Howard Cassady, Ohio St, HB	Rush: 161 Yds: 958 TD: 15	Jim Swink, Texas Christian
1956	Paul Hornung, Notre Dame, QB	Att/Comp: 111/59 Yds: 917 TD: 3	Johnny Majors, Tennessee
1957	John David Crow, Texas A&M, HB	Rush: 129 Yds: 562 TD: 10	Alex Karras, Iowa
1958	Pete Dawkins, Army, HB	Rush: 78 Yds: 428 TD: 6	Randy Duncan, Iowa

Heisman Memorial Trophy (Cont.)

Year	Winner, College, Position	Winner's Season Statistics	Runner-Up, College
1959	Billy Cannon, Louisiana St, HB	Rush: 139 Yds: 598 TD: 6	Rich Lucas, Penn St
1960	Joe Bellino, Navy, HB	Rush: 168 Yds: 834 TD: 18	Tom Brown, Minnesota
1961	Ernie Davis, Syracuse, HB	Rush: 150 Yds: 823 TD: 15	Bob Ferguson, Ohio St
1962	Terry Baker, Oregon St, QB	Att/Comp: 203/112 Yds: 1738 TD: 15	Jerry Stovall, Louisiana St
1963	*Roger Staubach, Navy, QB	Att/Comp: 161/107 Yds: 1474 TD: 7	Billy Lothridge, Georgia Tech
1964	John Huarte, Notre Dame, QB	Att/Comp: 205/114 Yds: 2062 TD: 16	Jerry Rhome, Tulsa
1965	Mike Garrett, Southern Cal, HB	Rush: 267 Yds: 1440 TD: 16	Howard Twilley, Tulsa
1966	Steve Spurrier, Florida, QB	Att/Comp: 291/179 Yds: 2012 TD: 16	Bob Griese, Purdue
1967	Gary Beban, UCLA, QB	Att/Comp: 156/87 Yds: 1359 TD: 8	O.J. Simpson, Southern Cal
1968	O.J. Simpson, Southern Cal, HB	Rush: 383 Yds: 1880 TD: 23	Leroy Keyes, Purdue
1969	Steve Owens, Oklahoma, FB	Rush: 358 Yds: 1523 TD: 23	Mike Phipps, Purdue
1970	Jim Plunkett, Stanford, QB	Att/Comp: 358/191 Yds: 2715 TD: 18	Joe Theismann, Notre Dame
1971	Pat Sullivan, Auburn, QB	Att/Comp: 281/162 Yds: 2012 TD: 20	Ed Marinaro, Cornell
1972	Johnny Rodgers, Nebraska, FL	Rec: 55 Yds: 942 TD: 17	Greg Pruitt, Oklahoma
1973	John Cappelletti, Penn St, HB	Rush: 286 Yds: 1522 TD: 17	John Hicks, Ohio St
1974	*Archie Griffin, Ohio St, HB	Rush: 256 Yds: 1695 TD: 12	Anthony Davis, Southern Cal
1975	Archie Griffin, Ohio St, HB	Rush: 262 Yds: 1450 TD: 4	Chuck Muncie, California
1976	†Tony Dorsett, Pittsburgh, HB	Rush: 370 Yds: 2150 TD: 23	Ricky Bell, Southern Cal
1977	Earl Campbell, Texas, FB	Rush: 267 Yds: 1744 TD: 19	Terry Miller, Oklahoma St
1978	*Billy Sims, Oklahoma, HB	Rush: 231 Yds: 1762 TD: 20	Chuck Fusina, Penn St
1979	Charles White, Southern Cal, HB	Rush: 332 Yds: 1803 TD: 19	Billy Sims, Oklahoma
1980	George Rogers, S Carolina, HB	Rush: 324 Yds: 1894 TD: 14	Hugh Green, Pittsburgh
1981	Marcus Allen, Southern Cal, HB	Rush: 433 Yds: 2427 TD: 23	Herschel Walker, Georgia
1982	*Herschel Walker, Georgia, HB	Rush: 335 Yds: 1752 TD: 17	John Elway, Stanford
1983	Mike Rozier, Nebraska, HB	Rush: 275 Yds: 2148 TD: 29	Steve Young, Brigham Young
1984	Doug Flutie, Boston College, QB	Att/Comp: 396/233 Yds: 3454 TD: 27	Keith Byars, Ohio St
1985	Bo Jackson, Auburn, HB	Rush: 278 Yds: 1786 TD: 17	Chuck Long, Iowa
1986	Vinny Testaverde, Miami (FL), QB	Att/Comp: 276/175 Yds: 2557 TD: 26	Paul Palmer, Temple
1987	Tim Brown, Notre Dame, WR	Rec: 39 Yds: 846 TD: 7	Don McPherson, Syracuse
1988	*Barry Sanders, Oklahoma St, RB	Rush: 344 Yds: 2628 TD: 39	Rodney Peete, Southern Cal
1989	*Andre Ware, Houston, QB	Att/Comp: 578/365 Yds: 4699 TD: 46	Anthony Thompson, Indiana
1990	*Ty Detmer, Brigham Young, QB	Att/Comp: 562/361 Yds: 5188 TD: 41	Raghib Ismail, Notre Dame
1991	*Desmond Howard, Michigan, WR	Rec: 61 Yds: 950 TD: 23	Casey Weldon, Florida St
1992	Gino Torretta, Miami (FL), QB	Att/Comp: 402/228 Yds: 3060 TD: 19	Marshall Faulk, San Diego St
1993	†Charlie Ward, Florida St, QB	Att/Comp: 380/264 Yds: 3032 TD: 27	Heath Shuler, Tennessee
1994	Rashaan Salaam, Colorado, RB	Rush: 298 Yds: 2055 TD: 24	Ki-Jana Carter, Penn St
1995	Eddie George, Ohio State, RB	Rush: 303 Yds: 1826 TD: 23	Tommie Frazier, Nebraska
1996	†Danny Wuerffel, Florida, QB	Att/Comp: 360/207 Yds: 3625 TD: 39	Troy Davis, Iowa St
1997	†Charles Woodson, Michigan, CB/ WR	7 interceptions; Rec: 11 Yds: 231 TD: 4	Peyton Manning, Tennessee
1998	Ricky Williams, Texas, RB	Rush: 361 Yds: 2124 TD: 28	Michael Bishop, Kansas St

*Juniors (all others seniors). †Winners who played for national championship teams the same year.

Note: Former Heisman winners and national media cast votes, with ballots allowing for three names (3 points for first, 2 for second and 1 for third).

Awards (Cont.)

Maxwell Award

Given to the nation's outstanding college football player by the Maxwell Football Club of Philadelphia.

Year	Player, College, Position	Year	Player, College, Position
1937	Clint Frank, Yale, HB	1969	Mike Reid, Penn St, DT
1938	Davey O'Brien, Texas Christian, QB	1970	Jim Plunkett, Stanford, QB
1939	Nile Kinnick, Iowa, HB	1971	Ed Marinaro, Cornell, RB
1940	Tom Harmon, Michigan, HB	1972	Brad Van Pelt, Michigan St, DB
1941	Bill Dudley, Virginia, HB	1973	John Cappelletti, Penn St, RB
1942	Paul Governali, Columbia, QB	1974	Steve Joachim, Temple, QB
1943	Bob Odell, Pennsylvania, HB	1975	Archie Griffin, Ohio St, RB
1944	Glenn Davis, Army, HB	1976	Tony Dorsett, Pittsburgh, RB
1945	Doc Blanchard, Army, FB	1977	Ross Browner, Notre Dame, DE
1946	Charley Trippi, Georgia, HB	1978	Chuck Fusina, Penn St, QB
1947	Doak Walker, Southern Meth, HB	1979	Charles White, Southern Cal, RB
1948	Chuck Bednarik, Pennsylvania, C	1980	Hugh Green, Pittsburgh, DE
1949	Leon Hart, Notre Dame, E	1980	Hugh Green, Pittsburgh, DE
1950	Reds Bagnell, Pennsylvania, HB	1981	Marcus Allen, Southern Cal, RB
1951	Dick Kazmaier, Princeton, HB	1982	Herschel Walker, Georgia, RB
1952	John Lattner, Notre Dame, HB	1983	Mike Rozier, Nebraska, RB
1953	John Lattner, Notre Dame, HB	1984	Doug Flutie, Boston College, QB
1954	Ron Beagle, Navy, E	1985	Chuck Long, Iowa, QB
1955	Howard Cassady, Ohio St, HB	1986	Vinny Testaverde, Miami (FL), QB
1956	Tommy McDonald, Oklahoma, HB	1987	Don McPherson, Syracuse, QB
1957	Bob Reifsnyder, Navy, T	1988	Barry Sanders, Oklahoma St, RB
1958	Pete Dawkins, Army, HB	1989	Anthony Thompson, Indiana, RB
1959	Rich Lucas, Penn St, QB	1990	Ty Detmer, Brigham Young, QB
1960	Joe Bellino, Navy, HB	1991	Desmond Howard, Michigan, WR
1961	Bob Ferguson, Ohio St, FB	1992	Gino Torretta, Miami (FL), QB
1962	Terry Baker, Oregon St, QB	1993	Charlie Ward, Florida St, QB
1963	Roger Staubach, Navy, QB	1994	Kerry Collins, Penn St, QB
1964	Glenn Ressler, Penn St, C	1995	Eddie George, Ohio St, RB
1965	Tommy Nobis, Texas, LB	1996	Danny Wuerffel, Florida, QB
1966	Jim Lynch, Notre Dame, LB	1997	Peyton Manning, Tennessee, QB
1967	Gary Beban, UCLA, QB	1998	Ricky Williams, Texas, RB
1968	O.J. Simpson, Southern Cal, RB		

Davey O'Brien National Quarterback Award

Given to the top quarterback in the nation by the Davey O'Brien Educational and Charitable Trust of Fort Worth. Named for Texas Christian Hall of Fame quarterback Davey O'Brien (1936-38).

Year	Player, College	Year	Player, College
1981	Jim McMahon, Brigham Young	1990	Ty Detmer, Brigham Young
1982	Todd Blackledge, Penn St	1991	Ty Detmer, Brigham Young
1983	Steve Young, Brigham Young	1992	Gino Torretta, Miami (FL)
1984	Doug Flutie, Boston College	1993	Charlie Ward, Florida St
1985	Chuck Long, Iowa	1994	Kerry Collins, Penn St
1986	Vinny Testaverde, Miami (FL)	1995	Danny Wuerffel, Florida
1987	Don McPherson, Syracuse	1996	Danny Wuerffel, Florida
1988	Troy Aikman, UCLA	1997	Peyton Manning, Tennessee
1989	Andre Ware, Houston	1998	Michael Bishop, Kansas St

Note: Originally known as the Davey O'Brien Memorial Trophy, honoring the outstanding football player in the Southwest as follows: 1977—Earl Campbell, Texas, RB; 1978—Billy Sims, Oklahoma, RB; 1979—Mike Singletary, Baylor, LB; 1980—Mike Singletary, Baylor, LB.

Vince Lombardi/Rotary Award

Given to the outstanding college lineman of the year, the award is sponsored by the Rotary Club of Houston.

Year	Player, College, Position	Year	Player, College, Position
1970	Jim Stillwagon, Ohio St, MG	1984	Tony Degrate, Texas, DT
1971	Walt Patulski, Notre Dame, DE	1985	Tony Casillas, Oklahoma, NG
1972	Rich Glover, Nebraska, MG	1986	Cornelius Bennett, Alabama, LB
1973	John Hicks, Ohio St, OT	1987	Chris Spielman, Ohio St, LB
1974	Randy White, Maryland, DT	1988	Tracy Rocker, Auburn, DT
1975	Lee Roy Selmon, Oklahoma, DT	1989	Percy Snow, Michigan St, LB
1976	Wilson Whitley, Houston, DT	1990	Chris Zorich, Notre Dame, NG
1977	Ross Browner, Notre Dame, DE	1991	Steve Emtman, Washington, DT
1978	Bruce Clark, Penn St, DT	1992	Marvin Jones, Florida St, LB
1979	Brad Budde, Southern Cal, G	1993	Aaron Taylor, Notre Dame, OT
1980	Hugh Green, Pittsburgh, DE	1994	Warren Sapp, Miami (FL), DT
1981	Kenneth Sims, Texas, DT	1995	Orlando Pace, Ohio St, OT
1982	Dave Rimington, Nebraska, C	1996	Orlando Pace, Ohio St, OT
1983	Dean Steinkuhler, Nebraska, G	1997	Grant Wistrom, Nebraska, DE
		1998	Dat Nguyen, Texas A&M, LB

Outland Trophy

Given to the outstanding interior lineman, selected by the Football Writers Association of America.

Year	Player, College, Position	Year	Player, College, Position
1946	George Connor, Notre Dame, T	1973	John Hicks, Ohio St, OT
1947	Joe Steffy, Army, G	1974	Randy White, Maryland, DE
1948	Bill Fischer, Notre Dame, G	1975	Lee Roy Selmon, Oklahoma, DT
1949	Ed Bagdon, Michigan St, G	1976	*Ross Browner, Notre Dame, DE
1950	Bob Gain, Kentucky, T	1977	Brad Shearer, Texas, DT
1951	Jim Weatherall, Oklahoma, T	1978	Greg Roberts, Oklahoma, G
1952	Dick Modzelewski, Maryland, T	1979	Jim Ritcher, N Carolina St, C
1953	J.D. Roberts, Oklahoma, G	1980	Mark May, Pittsburgh, OT
1954	Bill Brooks, Arkansas, G	1981	*Dave Rimington, Nebraska, C
1955	Calvin Jones, Iowa, G	1982	Dave Rimington, Nebraska, C
1956	Jim Parker, Ohio St, G	1983	Dean Steinkuhler, Nebraska, G
1957	Alex Karras, Iowa, T	1984	Bruce Smith, Virginia Tech, DT
1958	Zeke Smith, Auburn, G	1985	Mike Ruth, Boston Col, NG
1959	Mike McGee, Duke, T	1986	Jason Buck, Brigham Young, DT
1960	Tom Brown, Minnesota, G	1987	Chad Hennings, Air Force, DT
1961	Merlin Olsen, Utah St, T	1988	Tracy Rocker, Auburn, DT
1962	Bobby Bell, Minnesota, T	1989	Mohammed Elewonibi, Brigham Young, G
1963	Scott Appleton, Texas, T	1990	Russell Maryland, Miami (FL), DT
1964	Steve DeLong, Tennessee, T	1991	*Steve Emtman, Washington, DT
1965	Tommy Nobis, Texas, G	1992	Will Shields, Nebraska, G
1966	Loyd Phillips, Arkansas, T	1993	Rob Waldrop, Arizona, NG
1967	Ron Yary, Southern Cal, T	1994	Zach Wiegert, Nebraska, G
1968	Bill Stanfill, Georgia, T	1995	Jonathan Ogden, UCLA, OT
1969	Mike Reid, Penn St, DT	1996	*Orlando Pace, Ohio St, OT
1970	Jim Stillwagon, Ohio St, MG	1997	Aaron Taylor, Nebraska, G
1971	Larry Jacobson, Nebraska, DT	1998	Kris Farris, UCLA, OL
1972	Rich Glover, Nebraska, MG		

*Juniors (all others seniors).

Butkus Award

Given to the top collegiate linebacker, the award was established by the Downtown Athletic Club of Orlando and named for college Hall of Famer Dick Butkus of Illinois.

Year	Player, College	Year	Player, College
1985	Brian Bosworth, Oklahoma	1992	Marvin Jones, Florida St
1986	Brian Bosworth, Oklahoma	1993	Trev Alberts, Nebraska
1987	Paul McGowan, Florida St	1994	Dana Howard, Illinois
1988	Derrick Thomas, Alabama	1995	Kevin Hardy, Illinois
1989	Percy Snow, Michigan St	1996	Matt Russell, Colorado
1990	Alfred Williams, Colorado	1997	Andy Katzenmoyer, Ohio St
1991	Erick Anderson, Michigan	1998	Chris Claiborne, Southern Cal

Jim Thorpe Award

Given to the best defensive back of the year, the award is presented by the Jim Thorpe Athletic Club of Oklahoma City.

Year	Player, College	Year	Player, College
1986	Thomas Everett, Baylor	1992	Deon Figures, Colorado
1987	Bennie Blades, Miami (FL)	1993	Antonio Langham, Alabama
	Rickey Dixon, Oklahoma	1994	Chris Hudson, Colorado
1988	Deion Sanders, Florida St	1995	Greg Myers, Colorado St
1989	Mark Carrier, Southern Cal	1996	Lawrence Wright, Florida
1990	Darryl Lewis, Arizona	1997	Charles Woodson, Michigan
1991	Terrell Buckley, Florida St	1998	Antoine Winfield, Ohio St

Walter Payton Player of the Year Award

Given to the top Division I-AA player as voted by Division I-AA sports information directors. Sponsored by Sports Network.

Year	Player, College, Position	Year	Player, College, Position
1987	Kenny Gamble, Colgate, RB	1993	Doug Nussmeier, Idaho, QB
1988	Dave Meggett, Towson St, RB	1994	Steve McNair, Alcorn St, QB
1989	John Friesz, Idaho, QB	1995	Dave Dickenson, Montana, QB
1990	Walter Dean, Grambling, RB	1996	Archie Amerson, Northern Arizona, RB
1991	Jamie Martin, Weber St, QB	1997	Brian Finneran, Villanova, WR
1992	Michael Payton, Marshall, QB	1998	Jerry Azumah, New Hampshire, RB

The Harlon Hill Trophy

Given to the outstanding NCAA Division II college football player, the award is sponsored by the National Harlon Hill Awards Committee, Florence, AL.

Year	Player, College, Position	Year	Player, College, Position
1986	Jeff Bentrim, N Dakota St, QB	1993	Roger Graham, New Haven, RB
1987	Johnny Bailey, Texas A&I, RB	1994	Chris Hatcher, Valdosta St, QB
1988	Johnny Bailey, Texas A&I, RB	1995	Ronald McKinnon, N Alabama, LB
1989	Johnny Bailey, Texas A&I, RB	1996	Jarrett Anderson, Truman St, RB
1990	Chris Simdorn, N Dakota St, QB	1997	Irvin Sigler, Bloomsburg, RB
1991	Ronnie West, Pittsburg St, WR	1998	Brian Shay, Emporia St, RB
1992	Ronald Moore, Pittsburg St, RB		

NCAA Division I-A Individual Records

Career

SCORING

Most Points Scored: 452 — Ricky Williams, Texas, 1995–98
Most Points Scored per Game: 12.1 — Marshall Faulk, San Diego St, 1991-93
Most Touchdowns Scored: 75 — Ricky Williams, Texas, 1995–98
Most Touchdowns Scored per Game: 2.0 — Marshall Faulk, San Diego St, 1991-93
Most Touchdowns Scored, Rushing: 72 — Ricky Williams, Texas, 1995–98
Most Touchdowns Scored, Passing: 121 — Ty Detmer, Brigham Young, 1988-91
Most Touchdowns Scored, Receiving: 50 — Troy Edwards, Louisiana Tech, 1996–98
Most Touchdowns Scored, Interception Returns: 5 — Ken Thomas, San Jose St, 1979-82; Jackie Walker, Tennessee, 1969-71
Most Touchdowns Scored, Punt Returns: 7 — Johnny Rodgers, Nebraska, 1970-72; Jack Mitchell, Oklahoma, 1946-48
Most Touchdowns Scored, Kickoff Returns: 6 — Anthony Davis, Southern Cal, 1972-74

TOTAL OFFENSE

Most Plays: 1795 — Ty Detmer, Brigham Young, 1988-91
Most Plays per Game: 48.5 — Doug Gaynor, Long Beach St, 1984-85
Most Yards Gained: 14,665 — Ty Detmer, Brigham Young, 1988-91 (15,031 passing, -366 rushing)
Most Yards Gained per Game: 320.9 — Chris Vargas, Nevada, 1992-93
Most 300+ Yard Games: 33 —Ty Detmer, Brigham Young, 1988-91

RUSHING

Most Rushes: 1,215 — Steve Bartalo, Colorado St, 1983-86 (4813 yds)
Most Rushes per Game: 34.0 — Ed Marinaro, Cornell, 1969-71
Most Yards Gained: 6,279 — Ricky Williams, Texas, 1995–98
Most Yards Gained per Game: 174.6 — Ed Marinaro, Cornell, 1969-71
Most 100+ Yard Games: 33 — Tony Dorsett, Pittsburgh, 1973-76; Archie Griffin, Ohio St, 1972-75
Most 200+ Yard Games: 11 — Marcus Allen, Southern Cal, 1978-81; Ricky Williams, Texas, 1995–98

PASSING

Highest Passing Efficiency Rating: 163.6 — Danny Wuerffel, Florida, 1993-96 (1,170 attempts, 708 completions, 42 interceptions, 10,875 yards, 114 touchdown passes)
Most Passes Attempted: 1,530 — Ty Detmer, Brigham Young, 1988-91
Most Passes Attempted per Game: 39.6 — Mike Perez, San Jose St, 1986-87
Most Passes Completed: 958 — Ty Detmer, Brigham Young, 1988-91
Most Passes Completed per Game: 27.4 — Tim Couch, Kentucky, 1996–98
*Highest Completion Percentage: 67.1 — Tim Couch, Kentucky, 1996–98
Most Yards Gained: 15,031 — Ty Detmer, Brigham Young, 1988-91
Most Yards Gained per Game: 326.8 — Ty Detmer, Brigham Young, 1988-91

*Minimum 1100 attempts.

RECEIVING

Most Passes Caught: 295— Geoff Noisy, Nevada, 1995–98
Most Passes Caught per Game: 10.5 — Emmanuel Hazard, Houston, 1989-90
Most Yards Gained: 4,518 — Marcus Harris, Wyoming, 1993-96
Most Yards Gained per Game: 140.9 — Alex Van Dyke, Nevada, 1994-95
Highest Average Gain per Reception: 25.7 — Wesley Walker, California, 1973-75

Career *(Cont.)*

ALL-PURPOSE RUNNING

Most Plays: 1347 — Steve Bartalo, Colorado St, 1983-86 (1215 rushes, 132 receptions)
Most Yards Gained: 7206 — Ricky Williams, Texas, 1995–98 (6279 rushing, 927 receiving)
Most Yards Gained per Game: 237.8 — Ryan Benjamin, Pacific, 1990–92
Highest Average Gain per Play: 17.4 — Anthony Carter, Michigan, 1979–82

INTERCEPTIONS

Most Passes Intercepted: 29 — Al Brosky, Illinois, 1950–52
Most Passes Intercepted per Game: 1.1 — Al Brosky, Illinois, 1950–52
Most Yards on Interception Returns: 501 — Terrell Buckley, Florida St, 1989–91
Highest Average Gain per Interception: 26.5 — Tom Pridemore, W Virginia, 1975–77

SPECIAL TEAMS

Highest Punt Return Average: 23.6 — Jack Mitchell, Oklahoma, 1946-48
Highest Kickoff Return Average: 36.2 — Forrest Hall, San Francisco, 1946-47
Highest Average Yards per Punt: 46.3 — Todd Sauerbrun, West Virginia, 1991-94

Single Season

SCORING

Most Points Scored: 234 — Barry Sanders, Oklahoma St, 1988
Most Points Scored per Game: 21.27 — Barry Sanders, Oklahoma St, 1988
Most Touchdowns Scored: 39 — Barry Sanders, Oklahoma St, 1988
Most Touchdowns Scored, Rushing: 37 — Barry Sanders, Oklahoma St, 1988
Most Touchdowns Scored, Passing: 54 — David Klingler, Houston, 1990
Most Touchdowns Scored, Receiving: 27 — Troy Edwards, Louisiana Tech, 1998
Most Touchdowns Scored, Interception Returns: 3 — by many players
Most Touchdowns Scored, Punt Returns:
4 — David Allen, Kansas St, 1998; Quinton Spotwood, Syracuse, 1997; Tinker Keck, Cincinnati, 1997; James Henry, Southern Miss, 1987; Golden Richards, Brigham Young, 1971; Cliff Branch, Colorado, 1971
Most Touchdowns Scored, Kickoff Returns:
3 — Leland McElroy, Texas A&M, 1993; Terance Mathis, New Mexico, 1989; Willie Gault, Tennessee, 1980; Anthony Davis, Southern Cal, 1974; Stan Brown, Purdue, 1970; Forrest Hall, San Francisco, 1946

TOTAL OFFENSE

Most Plays: 704 — David Klingler, Houston, 1990
Most Yards Gained: 5,221 — David Klingler, Houston, 1990
Most Yards Gained per Game: 474.6 — David Klingler, Houston, 1990
Most 300+ Yard Games: 12 — Ty Detmer, Brigham Young, 1990

RUSHING

Most Rushes: 403 — Marcus Allen, Southern Cal, 1981
Most Rushes per Game: 39.6 — Ed Marinaro, Cornell, 1971
Most Yards Gained: 2628 — Barry Sanders, Oklahoma St, 1988
Most Yards Gained per Game: 238.9 — Barry Sanders, Oklahoma St, 1988
Most 100+ Yard Games: 11 — By 14 players, most recently Ahman Green, Nebraska, 1997

PASSING

Highest Passing Efficiency Rating: 183.3 — Shaun King, Tulane, 1998 (328 attempts, 223 completions, 6 interceptions, 3232 yards, 36 TD passes)
Most Passes Attempted: 643 — David Klingler, Houston, 1990
Most Passes Attempted per Game: 58.5 — David Klingler, Houston, 1990
Most Passes Completed: 400 — Tim Couch, Kentucky, 1998
Most Passes Completed per Game: 36.4 — Daunte Culpepper, Central Florida, 1998
Highest Completion Percentage: 73.6 — Daunte Culpepper, Central Florida, 1998
Most Yards Gained: (12 games) 5188 — Ty Detmer, Brigham Young, 1990; (11 games) 5140 — David Klingler, Houston, 1990
Most Yards Gained per Game: 467.3 — David Klingler, Houston, 1990

RECEIVING

Most Passes Caught: 142 — Emmanuel Hazard, Houston, 1989
Most Passes Caught per Game: 13.4 — Howard Twilley, Tulsa, 1965
Most Yards Gained: 1996 — Troy Edwards, Louisiana Tech, 1998
Most Yards Gained per Game: 177.9 — Howard Twilley, Tulsa, 1965
Highest Average Gain per Reception: 27.9 — Elmo Wright, Houston, 1968 (min. 30 receptions)

ALL-PURPOSE RUNNING

Most Plays: 432 — Marcus Allen, Southern Cal, 1981
Most Yards Gained: 3250 — Barry Sanders, Oklahoma St, 1988
Most Yards Gained per Game: 295.5 — Barry Sanders, Oklahoma St, 1988
Highest Average Gain per Play: 18.5 — Henry Bailey, UNLV, 1992

NCAA Division I-A Individual Records (Cont.)

Single Season (Cont.)

INTERCEPTIONS

Most Passes Intercepted: 14 — Al Worley, Washington, 1968
Most Yards on Interception Returns: 302 — Charles Phillips, Southern Cal, 1974
Highest Average Gain per Interception: 50.6 — Norm Thompson, Utah, 1969

SPECIAL TEAMS

Highest Punt Return Average: 25.9 — Bill Blackstock, Tennessee, 1951
Highest Kickoff Return Average: 40.1 — Paul Allen, Brigham Young, 1961
Highest Average Yards per Punt: 50.3 — Chad Kessler, Louisiana St, 1997

Single Game

SCORING

Most Points Scored: 48 — Howard Griffith, Illinois, 1990 (vs Southern Illinois)
Most Field Goals: 7 — Dale Klein, Nebraska, 1985 (vs Missouri); Mike Prindle, Western Michigan, 1984 (vs Marshall)
Most Extra Points (Kick): 13 — Derek Mahoney, Fresno St, 1991 (vs New Mexico); Terry Leiweke, Houston, 1968 (vs Tulsa)
Most Extra Points (2-Pts): 6 — Jim Pilot, New Mexico St, 1961 (vs Hardin-Simmons)

TOTAL OFFENSE

Most Yards Gained: 732 — David Klingler, Houston, 1990 (vs Arizona St)

RUSHING

Most Yards Gained: 396 — Tony Sands, Kansas, 1991 (vs Missouri)
Most Touchdowns Rushed: 8 — Howard Griffith, Illinois, 1990 (vs Southern Illinois)

PASSING

Most Passes Completed: 55 — Rusty LaRue, Wake Forest, 1995 (vs Duke); Drew Brees, Purdue, 1998 (vs Wisconsin)
Most Yards Gained: 716 — David Klingler, Houston, 1990 (vs Arizona St)
Most Touchdowns Passed: 11 — David Klingler, Houston, 1990 [vs Eastern Washington (I-AA)]

RECEIVING

Most Passes Caught: 23 — Randy Gatewood, UNLV, 1994 (vs Idaho)
Most Yards Gained: 405 — Troy Edwards, Louisiana Tech, 1998 (vs Nebraska)
Most Touchdown Catches: 6 — Tim Delaney, San Diego St, 1969 (vs New Mexico St)

NCAA Division I-AA Individual Records

Career

SCORING

Most Points Scored: 418 — Jerry Azumah, New Hampshire, 1995–98
Most Touchdowns Scored: 69 — Jerry Azumah, New Hampshire, 1995–98
Most Touchdowns Scored, Rushing: 60 — Jerry Azumah, New Hampshire, 1995–98
Most Touchdowns Scored, Passing: 139 — Willie Totten, Mississippi Valley, 1982–85
Most Touchdowns Scored, Receiving: 50 — Jerry Rice, Mississippi Valley, 1981–84

RUSHING

Most Rushes: 1,044 — Jerry Azumah, New Hampshire, 1995–98
Most Rushes per Game: 38.2 — Arnold Mickens, Butler, 1994–95
Most Yards Gained: 6,193 — Jerry Azumah, New Hampshire, 1995–98
Most Yards Gained per Game: 151.0 — Jerry Azumah, New Hampshire, 1995–98

PASSING

Highest Passing Efficiency Rating: 170.8 — Shawn Knight, William & Mary, 1991–94
Most Passes Attempted: 1,680 — Steve McNair, Alcorn St, 1991–94
Most Passes Completed: 934 — Jamie Martin, Weber St, 1989–92
Most Passes Completed per Game: 25.1 — Aaron Flowers, Cal St-Northridge, 1996–97
Highest Completion Percentage: 67.3 — Dave Dickenson, Montana, 1992–95
Most Yards Gained: 14,496 — Steve McNair, Alcorn St, 1991–94
Most Yards Gained per Game: 350 — Neil Lomax, Portland St, 1978–80

RECEIVING

Most Passes Caught: 301 — Jerry Rice, Mississippi Valley, 1981–84
Most Yards Gained: 4,693 — Jerry Rice, Mississippi Valley, 1981–84
Most Yards Gained per Game: 114.5 — Jerry Rice, Mississippi Valley, 1981–84
Highest Average Gain per Reception: 24.3 — John Taylor, Delaware St, 1982–85

Single Season

SCORING

Most Points Scored: 170 — Geoff Mitchell, Weber St, 1991
Most Touchdowns Scored: 28 — Geoff Mitchell, Weber St, 1991
Most Touchdowns Scored, Rushing: 25 — Adrian Peterson, Ga Southern, 1998; Archie Amerson, Northern Arizona, 1996
Most Touchdowns Scored, Passing: 56 — Willie Totten, Mississippi Valley, 1984
Most Touchdowns Scored, Receiving: 27 — Jerry Rice, Mississippi Valley, 1984

RUSHING

Most Rushes: 409 — Arnold Mickens, Butler, 1994
Most Rushes per Game: 40.9 — Arnold Mickens, Butler, 1994
Most Yards Gained: 2,260 — Charles Roberts, Cal St-Sacramento, 1998
Most Yards Gained per Game: 225.5 — Arnold Mickens, Butler, 1994

PASSING

Highest Passing Efficiency Rating: 204.6 — Shawn Knight, William & Mary, 1993
Most Passes Attempted: 530 — Steve McNair, Alcorn St, 1994
Most Passes Completed: 324 — Willie Totten, Mississippi Valley, 1984
Most Passes Completed per Game: 32.4 — Willie Totten, Mississippi Valley, 1984
Highest Completion Percentage: 70.6 — Giovanni Carmazzi, Hofstra, 1997
Most Yards Gained: 4,863 — Steve McNair, Alcorn St, 1994
Most Yards Gained per Game: 455.7 — Willie Totten, Mississippi Valley, 1984

RECEIVING

Most Passes Caught: 115 — Brian Forster, Rhode Island, 1985
Most Yards Gained: 1,712 — Eddie Conti, Delaware, 1998
Most Yards Gained per Game: 168.2 — Jerry Rice, Mississippi Valley, 1984
Highest Average Gain per Reception: 28.9 — Mikhael Ricks, Stephen F. Austin, 1997; (min. 35 receptions)

Single Game

SCORING

Most Points Scored: 42 — Jesse Burton, McNeese St, 1998 (vs Southern Utah); Archie Amerson, Northern Arizona, 1996 (vs Weber St)
Most Field Goals: 8 — Goran Lingmerth, Northern Arizona, 1986 (vs Idaho)

RUSHING

Most Yards Gained: 379 — Reggie Green, Siena, 1996 (vs St John's [NY])
Most Touchdowns Rushed: 7 — Archie Amerson, Northern Arizona, 1996 (vs Weber St)

PASSING

Most Passes Completed: 48 — Clayton Millis, Cal St-Northridge, 1995 (vs St Mary's [CA])
Most Yards Gained: 649 — Steve McNair, Alcorn St, 1994 (vs Southern-BR)
Most Touchdowns Passed: 9 — Willie Totten, Mississippi Valley, 1984 (vs Kentucky St)

RECEIVING

Most Passes Caught: 24 — Jerry Rice, Mississippi Valley, 1983 (vs Southern-BR)
Most Yards Gained: 370 — Michael Lerch, Princeton, 1991 (vs Brown)
Most Touchdown Catches: 5 — Five players, most recently by Sylvester Morris, Jackson St, 1998 (vs Grambling)

NCAA Division II Individual Records

Career

SCORING

Most Points Scored: 544 — Brian Shay, Emporia St, 1995–98
Most Touchdowns Scored: 88 — Brian Shay, Emporia St 1995–98
Most Touchdowns Scored, Rushing: 81 — Brian Shay, Emporia St, 1995–98
Most Touchdowns Scored, Passing: 116 — Chris Hatcher, Valdosta St, 1991–94
Most Touchdowns Scored, Receiving: 53 — Carlos Ferralls, Glenville St, 1994–97

RUSHING

Most Rushes: 1,072 — Bernie Peeters, Luther, 1968–71
Most Rushes per Game: 29.8 — Bernie Peeters, Luther, 1968–71
Most Yards Gained: 6,958 — Brian Shay, Emporia St, 1995–98
Most Yards Gained per Game: 183.4 — Anthony Gray, Western NM, 1997–98

Career (Cont.)

PASSING

Highest Passing Efficiency Rating: 167.0 — Wilkie Perez, Glenville St, 1997–98
Most Passes Attempted: 1,719 — Bob McLaughlin, Lock Haven, 1992–95
Most Passes Completed: 1,001 — Chris Hatcher, Valdosta St, 1991–94
Most Passes Completed per Game: 25.7 — Chris Hatcher, Valdosta St, 1991–94
Highest Completion Percentage: 69.6 — Chris Peterson, UC-Davis, 1985–86
Most Yards Gained: 10,878 — Chris Hatcher, Valdosta St, 1991–94
Most Yards Gained per Game: 312.1 — Grady Benton, West Texas A&M, 1994–95

RECEIVING

Most Passes Caught: 282 — Carlos Ferralls, Glenville St, 1994–97
Most Yards Gained: 4,468 — James Roe, Norfolk St, 1992–95
Most Yards Gained per Game: 160.8 — Chris George, Glenville St, 1993–94
Highest Average Gain per Reception: 22.8 — Tyrone Johnson, Western St (CO), 1990–93

Single Season

SCORING

Most Points Scored: 198 — Brian Shay, Emporia St, 1997
Most Touchdowns Scored: 32 — Brian Shay, Emporia St, 1997
Most Touchdowns Scored, Rushing: 29 — Brian Shay, Emporia St, 1997 and 1998
Most Touchdowns Scored, Passing: 50 — Chris Hatcher, Valdosta St, 1994
Most Touchdowns Scored, Receiving: 21 — Kevin Ingram, West Chester, 1998; Chris Perry, Adams St, 1995

RUSHING

Most Rushes: 385 — Joe Gough, Wayne St (MI), 1994
Most Rushes per Game: 38.6 — Mark Perkins, Hobart, 1968
Most Yards Gained: 2,265 — Brian Shay, Emporia St, 1998
Most Yards Gained per Game: 222.0 — Anthony Gray, Western New Mexico, 1997

PASSING

Highest Passing Efficiency Rating: 210.1 — Boyd Crawford, College of Idaho, 1953
Most Passes Attempted: 544 — Lance Funderburk, Valdosta St, 1995
Most Passes Completed: 356 — Lance Funderburk, Valdosta St, 1995
Most Passes Completed per Game: 32.4 — Lance Funderburk, Valdosta St, 1995
Highest Completion Percentage: 74.7 — Chris Hatcher, Valdosta St, 1994
Most Yards Gained: 4,189 — Wilkie Perez, Glenville St, 1997
Most Yards Gained per Game: 393.4 — Grady Benton, W Texas A&M, 1994

RECEIVING

Most Passes Caught: 119 — Brad Bailey, W Texas A&M, 1994
Most Yards Gained: 1,876 — Chris George, Glenville St, 1993
Most Yards Gained per Game: 187.6 — Chris George, Glenville St, 1993
Highest Average Gain per Reception: 32.5 — Tyrone Johnson, Western St, 1991 (min. 30 receptions)

Single Game

SCORING

Most Points Scored: 48 — Paul Zaeske, N Park, 1968 (vs N Central); Junior Wolf, Panhandle St, 1958 (vs St Mary [KS])
Most Field Goals: 6 — Steve Huff, Central Missouri St, 1985 (vs SE Missouri St)

RUSHING

Most Yards Gained: 403 — Rob Davidson, Fairmont St, 1998 (vs Concord)
Most Touchdowns Rushed: 8 — Junior Wolf, Panhandle St, 1958 (vs St Mary [KS])

PASSING

Most Passes Completed: 56 — Jarrod DeGeorgia, Wayne St (NE), 1996 (vs Drake)
Most Yards Gained: 642 — Wilkie Perez, Glenville St, 1997, (vs Concord)
Most Touchdowns Passed: 10 — Bruce Swanson, N Park, 1968 (vs N Central)

RECEIVING

Most Passes Caught: 23 — Chris George, Glenville St, 1994 (vs W VA Wesleyan); Barry Wagner, Alabama A&M, 1989 (vs Clark Atlanta)
Most Yards Gained: 401 — Kevin Ingram, West Chester, 1998 (vs Clarion)
Most Touchdown Catches: 8 — Paul Zaeske, N Park, 1968 (vs N Central)

NCAA Division III Individual Records

Career

SCORING

Most Points Scored: 528 — Carey Bender, Coe, 1991–94
Most Touchdowns Scored: 86 — Carey Bender, Coe, 1991–94
Most Touchdowns Scored, Rushing: 76 — Joe Dudek, Plymouth St, 1982–85
Most Touchdowns Scored, Passing: 141 — Bill Borchert, Mt Union, 1994–97
Most Touchdowns Scored, Receiving: 55 — Chris Bisaillon, Illinois Wesleyan, 1989–92

RUSHING

Most Rushes: 1,112 — Mike Birosak, Dickinson, 1986–89
Most Rushes per Game: 32.7 — Chris Sizemore, Bridgewater (VA), 1972–74
Most Yards Gained: 6,125 — Carey Bender, Coe, 1991–94
Most Yards Gained per Game: 175.1 — Ricky Gales, Simpson, 1988–89

PASSING

Highest Passing Efficiency Rating: 194.2 — Bill Borchert, Mt Union, 1994–97
Most Passes Attempted: 1,696 — Kirk Baumgartner, WI-Stevens Point, 1986–89
Most Passes Completed: 883 — Kirk Baumgartner, WI-Stevens Point, 1986–89
Most Passes Completed per Game: 24.9 — Keith Bishop, Illinois Wesleyan, 1981, Wheaton (IL), 1983–85
Highest Completion Percentage: 66.5 — Bill Borchert, Mt Union (OH) 1994–97
Most Yards Gained: 13,028 — Kirk Baumgartner, WI-Stevens Point, 1986–89
Most Yards Gained per Game: 317.8 — Kirk Baumgartner, WI-Stevens Point, 1986–89

RECEIVING

Most Passes Caught: 300 — Scott Pingel, Westminster (MO), 1996–98
Most Yards Gained: 4,697 — Scott Hvistendahl, Augsburg, 1995–98
Most Yards Gained per Game: 113.9 — Jeff Clay, Catholic, 1994–97
Highest Average Gain per Reception: 22.9 — Kirk Aikens, Hartwick, 1995–98

Single Season

SCORING

Most Points Scored: 206 — R. J. Bowers, Grove City, 1998
Most Points Scored per Game: 20.8 — James Regan, Pomona-Pitzer, 1997
Most Touchdowns Scored: 34 — R. J. Bowers, Grove City, 1998
Most Touchdowns Scored, Rushing: 34 — R. J. Bowers, Grove City, 1998
Most Touchdowns Scored, Passing: 51 — Justin Peery, Westminster (MO), 1998
Most Touchdowns Scored, Receiving: 26 — Scott Pingel, Westminster (MO), 1998

RUSHING

Most Rushes: 380 — Mike Birosak, Dickinson, 1989
Most Rushes per Game: 38.0 — Mike Birosak, Dickinson, 1989
Most Yards Gained: 2,385 — Dante Brown, Marietta, 1996

PASSING

Highest Passing Efficiency Rating: 225.0 — Mike Simpson, Eureka, 1994
Most Passes Attempted: 527 — Kirk Baumgartner, WI-Stevens Point, 1988
Most Passes Completed: 283 — Justin Peery, Westminster (MO), 1998
Most Passes Completed per Game: 31.9 — Justin Peery, Westminster (MO), 1998
Highest Completion Percentage: 73.4 — Mike Simpson, Eureka, 1994
Most Yards Gained: 4,501 — Justin Peery, Westminster (MO), 1998
Most Yards Gained per Game: 450.1 — Justin Peery, Westminster (MO), 1998

RECEIVING

Most Passes Caught: 130 — Scott Pingel, Westminster (MO), 1998
Most Yards Gained: 2,157 — Scott Pingel, Westminster, (MO), 1998
Most Yards Gained per Game: 215.7 — Scott Pingel, Westminster, (MO), 1998
Highest Average Gain per Reception: 26.9 — Marty Redlawsk, Concordia (IL), 1985

Single Game

SCORING

Most Field Goals: 6 — Jim Hever, Rhodes, 1984 (vs Millsaps)

PASSING

Most Passes Completed: 50 — Justin Peery, Westminster (MO), 1998 (vs MacMurray); Tim Lynch, Hofstra, 1991 (vs Fordham)
Most Yards Gained: 619 — Justin Peery, Westminster (MO), 1998 (vs MacMurray)
Most Touchdowns Passed: 9 — Joe Zarlinga, Ohio Northern, 1998 (vs Capital)

RUSHING

Most Yards Gained: 441 — Dante Brown, Marietta, 1996 (vs Baldwin-Wallace)
Most Touchdowns Rushed: 8 — Carey Bender, Coe, 1994 (vs Beloit)

RECEIVING

Most Passes Caught: 23 — Sean Munroe, Mass-Boston, 1992 (vs Mass-Maritime)
Most Yards Gained: 395 — Scott Pingel, Westminster (MO), 1998 (vs Bethel, Tenn.)
Most Touchdown Catches: 7 — Matt Perceval, Wesleyan (Conn), 1998 (vs Middlebury)

Career

Scoring

POINTS (KICKERS)

	Years	Pts
Roman Anderson, Houston	1988–91	423
Carlos Huerta, Miami (FL)	1988–91	397
Jason Elam, Hawaii	1988–92	395
Derek Schmidt, Florida St	1984–87	393
Kris Brown, Nebraska	1995–98	388

POINTS (NON-KICKERS)

	Years	Pts
Ricky Williams, Texas	1995–98	452
Anthony Thompson, Indiana	1986–89	394
Marshall Faulk, San Diego St.	1991–93	376
Tony Dorsett, Pittsburgh	1973–76	356
Glenn Davis, Army	1943–46	354
Troy Edwards, Lousiana Tech	1996–98	344

POINTS PER GAME (NON-KICKERS)

	Years	Pts/Game
Marshall Faulk, San Diego St.	1991–93	12.1
Ed Marinaro, Cornell	1969–71	11.8
Bill Burnett, Arkansas	1968–70	11.3
Steve Owens, Oklahoma	1967–69	11.2
Eddie Talboom, Wyoming	1948–50	10.8

Total Offense

YARDS GAINED

	Years	Yds
Ty Detmer, Brigham Young	1988–91	14,665
Doug Flutie, Boston Col	1981–84	11,317
Peyton Manning, Tennessee	1994–97	11,020
Eric Zeier, Georgia	1991–94	10,841
Alex Van Pelt, Pittsburgh	1989–92	10,814

YARDS PER GAME

	Years	Yds/Game
Chris Vargas, Nevada	1992–93	320.9
Ty Detmer, Brigham Young	1988–91	318.8
Duante Culpepper, C Florida	1996–98	313.5
Mike Perez, San Jose St	1986–87	309.1
Josh Wallwork, Wyoming	1995–96	307.0
Doug Gaynor, Long Beach St	1984–85	305.0

Rushing

YARDS GAINED

	Years	Yds
Ricky Williams, Texas	1995–98	6,279
Tony Dorsett, Pittsburgh	1973–76	6,082
Charles White, Southern Cal	1976–79	5,598
Herschel Walker, Georgia	1980–82	5,259
Archie Griffin, Ohio St	1972–75	5,177

YARDS PER GAME

	Years	Yds/Game
Ed Marinaro, Cornell	1969–71	174.6
O.J. Simpson, Southern Cal	1967–68	164.4
Herschel Walker, Georgia	1980–82	159.4
LeShon Johnson, N Illinois	1992–93	150.6
Marshall Faulk, San Diego St	1991–93	148.0

TOUCHDOWNS RUSHING

	Years	TD
Ricky Williams, Texas	1995–98	72
Anthony Thompson, Indiana	1986–89	64
Marshall Faulk, San Diego St	1991–93	57
Travis Prentice, Miami (OH)	1996–98	56
Steve Owens, Oklahoma	1967–69	56
Tony Dorsett, Pittsburgh	1973–76	55
Pete Johnson, Ohio St	1973–76	51

Passing

PASSING EFFICIENCY

	Years	Rating
Danny Wuerffel, Florida	1993–96	163.6
Ty Detmer, Brigham Young	1988–91	162.7
Steve Sarkisian, Brigham Young	1995–96	162.0
Billy Blanton, San Diego St	1993–96	157.1
Jim McMahon, Brigham Young	1977–78, 80–81	156.9

Note: Minimum 500 completions.

YARDS GAINED

	Years	Yds
Ty Detmer, Brigham Young	1988–91	15,031
Todd Santos, San Diego St.	1984–87	11,425
Peyton Manning, Tennessee	1994–97	11,201
Eric Zeier, Georgia	1991–94	11,153
Alex Van Pelt, Pittsburgh	1989–92	10,913

Note: Minimum 500 completions.

COMPLETIONS

	Years	Comp
Ty Detmer, Brigham Young	1988–91	958
Todd Santos, San Diego St.	1984–87	910
Brian McClure, Bowling Green	1982–85	900
Eric Wilhelm, Oregon St	1989–92	870
Peyton Manning, Tennessee	1994–97	863

Note: Minimum 500 completions.

TOUCHDOWNS PASSING

	Years	TD
Ty Detmer, Brigham Young	1988–91	121
Danny Wuerffel, Florida	1993–96	114
David Klingler, Houston	1988–91	92
Peyton Manning, Tennessee	1994–97	89
Troy Kopp, Pacific	1989–92	87

Receiving

CATCHES

	Years	No.
Geoff Noisy, Nevada	1995–98	295
Troy Edwards, Louisiana Tech	1996–98	280
Aaron Turner, Pacific	1989–92	266
Chad Mackey, Louisiana Tech	1993–96	264
Terance Mathis, New Mexico	1985–87, 89	263

CATCHES PER GAME

	Years	No./Game
Emmanuel Hazard, Houston	1989–90	10.5
Alex Van Dyke, Nevada	1994–95	10.3
Howard Twilley, Tulsa	1963–65	10.0
Jason Phillips, Houston	1987–88	9.4
Troy Edwards, Louisiana Tech	1996–98	8.2
Bryan Reeves, Nevada	1992–93	8.2

YARDS GAINED

	Years	Yds
Marcus Harris, Wyoming	1993–96	4,518
Ryan Yarborough, Wyoming	1990–93	4,357
Troy Edwards, Louisiana Tech	1996–98	4,352
Aaron Turner, Pacific	1989–92	4,345
Terance Mathis, New Mexico	1985–87, 89	4,254

TOUCHDOWN CATCHES

	Years	TD
Troy Edwards, Louisiana Tech	1996–98	50
Aaron Turner, Pacific	1989–92	43
Ryan Yarborough, Wyoming	1990–93	42
Marcus Harris, Wyoming	1993–96	38
Clarkston Hines, Duke	1986–89	38

Career (Cont.)

All-Purpose Running

YARDS GAINED	Years	Yds
Ricky Williams, Texas	1996–98	7206
Napoleon McCallum, Navy	1981–85	7172
Darrin Nelson, Stanford	1977–78, 80–81	6885
Kevin Faulk, Louisiana St	1995–98	6833
Terance Mathis, New Mexico	1985–87, 89	6691
Tony Dorsett, Pittsburgh	1973–76	6615
Paul Palmer, Temple	1983–86	6609

YARDS PER GAME	Years	Yds/Game
Ryan Benjamin, Pacific	1990–92	237.8
Sheldon Canley, San Jose St	1988–90	205.8
Howard Stevens, Louisville	1971–72	193.7
O.J. Simpson, Southern Cal	1967–68	192.9
Alex Van Dyke, Nevada	1994–95	188.5

Interceptions

PLAYER/SCHOOL	Years	Int
Al Brosky, Illinois	1950–52	29
John Provost, Holy Cross	1972–74	27
Martin Bayless, Bowling Green	1980–83	27
Tom Curtis, Michigan	1967–69	25
Tony Thurman, Boston Col	1981–84	25
Tracy Saul, Texas Tech	1989–92	25

Punting Average

PLAYER/SCHOOL	Years	Avg
Todd Sauerbrun, W Virginia	1991–94	46.3
Reggie Roby, Iowa	1979–82	45.6
Greg Montgomery, Michigan St	1985–87	45.4
Tom Tupa, Ohio St	1984–87	45.2
Barry Helton, Colorado	1984–87	44.9

Note: At least 150 punts kicked.

Punt Return Average

PLAYER/SCHOOL	Years	Avg
Jack Mitchell, Oklahoma	1946–48	23.6
Gene Gibson, Cincinnati	1949–50	20.5
Eddie Macon, Pacific	1949–51	18.9
Jackie Robinson, UCLA	1939–40	18.8
Mike Fuller, Auburn	1972–74	17.7
Bobby Dillon, Texas	1949–51	17.7

Note: At least 1.2 punt returns per game.

Kickoff Return Average

PLAYER/SCHOOL	Years	Avg
Anthony Davis, Southern Cal	1972–74	35.1
Eric Booth, Southern Miss	1994–97	32.4
Overton Curtis, Utah St	1957–58	31.0
Fred Montgomery, New Mexico St	1991–92	30.5
Altie Taylor, Utah St	1966–68	29.3
Stan Brown, Purdue	1968–70	28.8

Note: At least 1.2 kickoff returns per game. Min. 30 returns.

Single Season

Scoring

POINTS	Year	Pts
Barry Sanders, Oklahoma St	1988	234
Troy Edwards, Louisiana Tech	1998	188
Mike Rozier, Nebraska	1983	174
Lydell Mitchell, Penn St	1971	174
Ricky Williams, Texas	1998	168

FIELD GOALS	Year	FG
John Lee, UCLA	1984	29
Paul Woodside, W Virginia	1982	28
Luis Zendejas, Arizona St	1983	28
Fuad Reveiz, Tennessee	1982	27

Four tied with 25.

All-Purpose Running

YARDS GAINED	Year	Yds
Barry Sanders, Oklahoma St	1988	3250
Ryan Benjamin, Pacific	1991	2995
Mike Pringle, Fullerton St	1989	2690
Paul Palmer, Temple	1986	2633
Ryan Benjamin, Pacific	1992	2597

All-Purpose Running (Cont.)

YARDS PER GAME	Year	Yds/Game
Barry Sanders, Oklahoma St	1988	295.5
Ryan Benjamin, Pacific	1991	249.6
Byron (Whizzer) White, Colorado	1937	246.3
Mike Pringle, Fullerton St	1989	244.6
Paul Palmer, Temple	1986	239.4

Total Offense

YARDS GAINED	Year	Yds
David Klingler, Houston	1990	5221
Ty Detmer, Brigham Young	1990	5022
Tim Rattay, Louisiana Tech	1998	4840
Andre Ware, Houston	1989	4661
Jim McMahon, Brigham Young	1980	4627
Ty Detmer, Brigham Young	1989	4433

YARDS PER GAME	Year	Yds/Game
David Klingler, Houston	1990	474.6
Andre Ware, Houston	1989	423.7
Ty Detmer, Brigham Young	1990	418.5
Tim Rattay, Louisiana Tech	1998	403.3

Single Season *(Cont.)*

Rushing

YARDS GAINED	Year	Yds
Barry Sanders, Oklahoma St	1988	2628
Marcus Allen, Southern Cal	1981	2342
Troy Davis, Iowa St	1996	2185
Mike Rozier, Nebraska	1983	2148
Ricky Williams, Texas	1998	2124

YARDS PER GAME	Year	Yds/Game
Barry Sanders, Oklahoma St	1988	238.9
Marcus Allen, Southern Cal	1981	212.9
Ed Marinaro, Cornell	1971	209.0
Troy Davis, Iowa St	1996	198.6
Ricky Williams, Texas	1998	193.1

TOUCHDOWNS RUSHING	Year	TD
Barry Sanders, Oklahoma St	1988	37
Mike Rozier, Nebraska	1983	29
Ricky Williams, Texas	1998	27

Four tied with 24

Passing

PASSING EFFICIENCY	Year	Rating
Shaun King, Tulane	1998	183.3
Danny Wuerffel, Florida	1995	178.4
Jim McMahon, Brigham Young	1980	176.9
Ty Detmer, Brigham Young	1989	175.6
Steve Sarkisian, Brigham Young	1996	173.6

Passing *(Cont.)*

YARDS GAINED	Year	Yds
Ty Detmer, Brigham Young	1990	5188
David Klingler, Houston	1990	5140
Andre Ware, Houston	1989	4699
Tim Rattay, Louisiana Tech	1998	4943
Jim McMahon, Brigham Young	1980	4571

COMPLETIONS	Year	Att	Comp
David Klingler, Houston	1990	643	374
Andre Ware, Houston	1989	578	365
Tim Couch, Kentucky	1997	547	363
Ty Detmer, Brigham Young	1990	562	361
Tim Rattay, Louisiana Tech	1998	559	380
Tim Couch, Kentucky	1998	553	400

TOUCHDOWNS PASSING	Year	TD
David Klingler, Houston	1990	54
Jim McMahon, Brigham Young	1980	47
Andre Ware, Houston	1989	46
Tim Rattay, Louisiana Tech	1998	46
Ty Detmer, Brigham Young	1990	41

Receiving

CATCHES	Year	GP	No.
Emmanuel Hazard, Houston	1989	11	142
Troy Edwards, Louisiana Tech	1998	12	140
Howard Twilley, Tulsa	1965	10	134
Alex Van Dyke, Nevada	1995	11	129
Damond Wilkins, Nevada	1996	11	114

YARDS GAINED	Year	Yds
Troy Edwards, Louisiana Tech	1998	1996
Alex Van Dyke, Nevada	1995	1854
Howard Twilley, Tulsa	1965	1779
Troy Edwards, Louisiana Tech	1997	1707
Emmanuel Hazard, Houston	1989	1689

CATCHES PER GAME	Year	No.	No./Game
Howard Twilley, Tulsa	1965	134	13.4
Emmanuel Hazard, Houston	1989	142	12.9
Troy Edwards, Louisiana Tech	1998	140	11.7
Alex Van Dyke, Nevada	1995	129	11.7
Damond Wilkins, Nevada	1996	114	10.4

TOUCHDOWN CATCHES	Year	TD
Troy Edwards, Louisiana Tech	1998	27
Randy Moss, Marshall	1997	25
Emmanuel Hazard, Houston	1989	22
Desmond Howard, Michigan	1991	19

Five tied with 18

Single Game

Scoring

POINTS	Opponent	Year	Pts
Howard Griffith, Illinois	Southern Illinois	1990	48
Marshall Faùlk, San Diego St	Pacific	1991	44
Jim Brown, Syracuse	Colgate	1956	43
Showboat Boykin, Mississippi	Mississippi St	1951	42
Fred Wendt, UTEP*	New Mexico St	1948	42

*UTEP was Texas Mines in 1948.

FIELD GOALS	Opponent	Year	FG
Dale Klein, Nebraska	Missouri	1985	7
Mike Prindle, Western Michigan	Marshall	1984	7

Note: Klein's distances were 32-22-43-44-29-43-43.
Prindle's distances were 32-44-42-23-48-41-27.

Single Game *(Cont.)*

Total Offense

YARDS GAINED	Opponent	Year	Yds
David Klingler, Houston ...Arizona St		1990	732
Matt Vogler, Texas Christian	Houston	1990	696
David Klingler, Houston ...Texas Christian		1990	625
Scott Mitchell, Utah	Air Force	1988	625
Jimmy Klingler, Houston...Rice		1992	612

Passing

YARDS GAINED	Opponent	Year	Yds
David Klingler, Houston ...Arizona St		1990	716
Matt Vogler, Texas Christian	Houston	1990	690
Scott Mitchell, Utah	Air Force	1988	631
Jeremy Leach, New Mexico	Utah	1989	622
Dave Wilson, Illinois	Ohio St	1980	621

COMPLETIONS	Opponent	Year	Comp
Drew Brees, Purdue	Wisconsin	1998	55
Rusty LaRue, Wake Forest	Duke	1995	55
Rusty LaRue, Wake Forest	NC St	1995	50
David Klingler, Houston	SMU	1990	48
Tim Couch, Kentucky	Arkansas	1998	47

TOUCHDOWNS PASSING	Opponent	Year	TD
David Klingler, Houston	E. Wash	1990	11

Note: Klingler's TD passes were 5-48-29-7-3-7-40-10-7-8-51.

Rushing

YARDS GAINED	Opponent	Year	Yds
Tony Sands, Kansas	Missouri	1991	396
Marshall Faulk, San Diego St	Pacific	1991	386
Troy Davis, Iowa St	Missouri	1996	378
Anthony Thompson, Indiana	Wisconsin	1989	377
Mike Pringle, California St-Fullerton	New Mex St	1989	357
Rueben Mayes, Washington St	Oregon	1984	357

TOUCHDOWNS RUSHING	Opponent	Year	TD
Howard Griffith, Illinois	Southern Illinois	1990	8

Note: Griffith's TD runs were 5-51-7-41-5-18-5-3.

Receiving

CATCHES	Opponent	Year	No.
Randy Gatewood, UNLV	Idaho	1994	23
Jay Miller, Brigham Young	New Mexico	1973	22
Troy Edwards, Lou Tech	Nebraska	1998	21
Rick Eber, Tulsa	Idaho St	1967	20
Emmanuel Hazard, Hou	Texas Christian	1989	19
Emmanuel Hazard, Hou	Texas	1989	19
Ron Fair, Arizona St	Washington St	1989	19

YARDS GAINED	Opponent	Year	Yds
Troy Edwards,Louisiana Teck	Nebraska	1998	405
Randy Gatewood, UNLV	Idaho	1994	363
Chuck Hughes, UTEP*	N Texas St	1965	349
Rick Eber, Tulsa	Idaho St	1967	322
Harry Wood, Tulsa	Idaho St	1967	318

*UTEP was Texas Western in 1965.

TOUCHDOWN CATCHES	Opponent	Year	TD
Tim Delaney, San Diego St	New Mexico St	1969	6

Note: Delaney's TD catches were 2-22-34-31-30-9.

Longest Plays *(since 1941)*

PASSING	Opponent	Year	Yds
Fred Owens to Jack Ford, Portland	St Mary's (CA)	1947	99
Bo Burris to Warren McVea, Houston	Washington St	1966	99
Colin Clapton to Eddie Jenkins, Holy Cross	Boston U	1970	99
Terry Peel to Robert Ford, Houston	Syracuse	1970	99
Terry Peel to Robert Ford, Houston	San Diego St	1972	99
Cris Collinsworth to Derrick Gaffney, Florida	Rice	1977	99
Scott Ankrom to James Maness, Texas Christian	Rice	1984	99
Gino Toretta to Horace Copeland, Miami	Arkansas	1991	99
John Paci to Thomas Lewis, Indiana	Penn St	1993	99
Troy DeGar to Wes Caswell, Tulsa	Oklahoma	1996	99

RUSHING	Opponent	Year	Yds
Gale Sayers, Kansas	Nebraska	1963	99
Max Anderson, Arizona St	Wyoming	1967	99
Ralph Thompson, W Texas St	Wichita St	1970	99
Kelsey Finch, Tennessee	Florida	1977	99

FIELD GOALS	Opponent	Year	Yds
Steve Little, Arkansas	Texas	1977	67
Russell Erxleben, Texas	Rice	1977	67
Joe Williams, Wichita St	Southern IL	1978	67
Martin Gramatica, Kansas St	Northern IL	1998	65
Tony Franklin, Texas A&M	Baylor	1976	65
Tony Franklin, Texas A&M	Baylor	1976	64

PUNTS	Opponent	Year	Yds
Pat Brady, Nevada*	Loyola (CA)	1950	99
George O'Brien, Wisconsin	Iowa	1952	96
John Hadl, Kansas	Oklahoma	1959	94
Carl Knox, Texas Christian	Oklahoma St	1947	94
Preston Johnson, SMU	Pittsburgh	1940	94

*Nevada was Nevada-Reno in 1950.

DIVISION I-A WINNINGEST TEAMS
Alltime Winning Percentage

	Yrs	W	L	T	Pct	GP	Bowl Record
Notre Dame	110	762	230	42	.757	1,034	13-10-0
Michigan	119	785	257	36	.745	1,066	14-15-0
Alabama	104	724	265	43	.724	1,032	28-18-3
Ohio St	109	709	277	53	.706	1,039	14-17-0
Oklahoma	104	682	273	53	.706	1,008	20-11-1
Texas	106	725	294	33	.705	1,052	18-18-2
Nebraska	109	731	296	40	.704	1,067	18-19-0
Southern Cal	106	667	274	54	.698	995	25-14-0
Penn St	112	723	302	41	.698	1,066	22-11-2
Tennessee	102	690	285	52	.697	1,027	22-17-0
Florida St	52	369	182	17	.659	568	16-9-2
Boise St	31	231	224	2	.653	357	0-0-0
Washington	109	599	330	50	.638	979	13-11-1
Central Michigan	98	506	285	36	.635	827	0-2-0
Miami (OH)	110	584	323	44	.634	951	5-2-0
Louisiana St	105	607	348	47	.632	1002	14-16-1
Arizona St	86	478	278	24	.631	780	10-6-1
Army	109	613	356	51	.630	1,020	2-2-0
Georgia	105	624	354	54	.630	1,032	17-14-3
Auburn	106	596	355	47	.625	998	14-10-2
Colorado	109	600	363	36	.618	999	10-12-0
Miami (FL)	72	452	277	19	.615	748	12-11-0
Florida	92	545	340	40	.608	925	12-13-0
Texas A&M	104	594	376	48	.604	1018	12-12-0
Syracuse	109	625	403	49	.603	1075	10-8-1

Note: Includes bowl games.

Alltime Victories

Michigan	785	
Notre Dame	762	
Nebraska	731	
Texas	725	
Alabama	724	
Penn St	723	
Ohio St	709	
Tennessee	690	
Oklahoma	682	
Southern Cal	667	
Syracuse	625	
Georgia	624	
Army	613	
Louisiana St	607	
Colorado	600	
Washington	599	
Auburn	596	
Texas A&M	594	
W Virginia	592	
N Carolina	590	
Pittsburgh	584	
Miami (OH)	584	
Georgia Tech	583	
Arkansas	580	
Navy	573	
Minnesota	573	
Virginia Tech	557	
Clemson	556	
California	551	
Rutgers	546	

NUMBER ONE VS NUMBER TWO

The No. 1 and No. 2 teams, according to the Associated Press Poll, have met 32 times, including 12 bowl games, since the poll's inception in 1936. The No. 1 teams have a 19-11-2 record in these matchups. Notre Dame (4-3-2) has played in nine of the games.

Date	Results	Stadium
10-9-43	No. 1 Notre Dame 35, No. 2 Michigan 12	Michigan (Ann Arbor)
11-20-43	No. 1 Notre Dame 14, No. 2 Iowa Pre-Flight 13	Notre Dame (South Bend)
12-2-44	No. 1 Army 23, No. 2 Navy 7	Municipal (Baltimore)
11-10-45	No. 1 Army 48, No. 2 Notre Dame 0	Yankee (New York)
12-1-45	No. 1 Army 32, No. 2 Navy 13	Municipal (Philadelphia)
11-9-46	No. 1 Army 0, No. 2 Notre Dame 0	Yankee (New York)
1-1-63	No. 1 Southern Cal 42, No. 2 Wisconsin 37 (Rose Bowl)	Rose Bowl (Pasadena)
10-12-63	No. 2 Texas 28, No. 1 Oklahoma 7	Cotton Bowl (Dallas)
1-1-64	No. 1 Texas 28, No. 2 Navy 6 (Cotton Bowl)	Cotton Bowl (Dallas)
11-19-66	No. 1 Notre Dame 10, No. 2 Michigan St 10	Spartan (East Lansing)
9-28-68	No. 1 Purdue 37, No. 2 Notre Dame 22	Notre Dame (South Bend)
1-1-69	No. 1 Ohio St 27, No. 2 Southern Cal 16 (Rose Bowl)	Rose Bowl (Pasadena)
12-6-69	No. 1 Texas 15, No. 2 Arkansas 14	Razorback (Fayetteville)
11-25-71	No. 1 Nebraska 35, No. 2 Oklahoma 31	Owen Field (Norman)
1-1-72	No. 1 Nebraska 38, No. 2 Alabama 6 (Orange Bowl)	Orange Bowl (Miami)
1-1-79	No. 2 Alabama 14, No. 1 Penn St 7 (Sugar Bowl)	Sugar Bowl (New Orleans)
9-26-81	No. 1 Southern Cal 28, No. 2 Oklahoma 24	Coliseum (Los Angeles)
1-1-83	No. 2 Penn St 27, No. 1 Georgia 23 (Sugar Bowl)	Sugar Bowl (New Orleans)

NUMBER ONE VS NUMBER TWO *(Cont.)*

Date	Results	Stadium
10-19-85	No. 1 Iowa 12, No. 2 Michigan 10	Kinnick (Iowa City)
9-27-86	No. 2 Miami (FL) 28, No. 1 Oklahoma 16	Orange Bowl (Miami)
1-2-87	No. 2 Penn St 14, No. 1 Miami (FL) 10 (Fiesta Bowl)	Sun Devil (Tempe)
11-21-87	No. 2 Oklahoma 17, No. 1 Nebraska 7	Memorial (Lincoln)
1-1-88	No. 2 Miami (FL) 20, No. 1 Oklahoma 14 (Orange Bowl)	Orange Bowl (Miami)
11-26-88	No. 1 Notre Dame 27, No. 2 Southern Cal 10	Coliseum (Los Angeles)
9-16-89	No. 1 Notre Dame 24, No. 2 Michigan 19	Michigan (Ann Arbor)
11-16-91	No. 2 Miami (FL) 17, No. 1 Florida St 16	Campbell (Tallahassee)
1-1-93	No. 2 Alabama 34, No. 1 Miami (FL) 13 (Sugar Bowl)	Superdome (New Orleans)
11-13-93	No. 2 Notre Dame 31, No. 1 Florida St 24	Notre Dame (South Bend)
1-1-94	No. 1 Florida St 18, No. 2 Nebraska 16 (Orange Bowl)	Orange Bowl (Miami)
1-2-96	No. 1 Nebraska 62, No. 2 Florida 24 (Fiesta Bowl)	Sun Devil (Tempe)
11-30-96	No. 2 Florida St 24, No. 1 Florida 21	Campbell (Tallahassee)
1-4-99	No. 1 Tennessee 23, No. 2 Florida St 16 (Fiesta Bowl)	Sun Devil (Tempe)

LONGEST DIVISION I-A WINNING STREAKS

Wins	Team	Yrs	Ended by	Score
47	Oklahoma	1953-57	Notre Dame	7–0
39	Washington	1908-14	Oregon St	0–0
37	Yale	1890-93	Princeton	6–0
37	Yale	1887-89	Princeton	10–0
35	Toledo	1969-71	Tampa	21–0
34	Pennsylvania	1894-96	Lafayette	6–4
31	Oklahoma	1948-50	Kentucky	13–7
31	Pittsburgh	1914-18	Cleveland Naval Reserve	10–9
31	Pennsylvania	1896-98	Harvard	10–0
30	Texas	1968-70	Notre Dame	24–11
29	Miami (FL)	1990-93	Alabama	34–13
29	Michigan	1901-03	Minnesota	6–6

LONGEST DIVISION I-A UNBEATEN STREAKS

No.	W	T	Team	Yrs	Ended by	Score
63	59	4	Washington	1907-17	California	27–0
56	55	1	Michigan	1901-05	Chicago	2–0
50	46	4	California	1920-25	Olympic Club	15–0
48	47	1	Oklahoma	1953-57	Notre Dame	7–0
48	47	1	Yale	1885-89	Princeton	10–0
47	42	5	Yale	1879-85	Princeton	6–5
44	42	2	Yale	1894-96	Princeton	24–6
42	39	3	Yale	1904-08	Harvard	4–0
39	37	2	Notre Dame	1946-50	Purdue	28–14
37	36	1	Oklahoma	1972-75	Kansas	23–3
37	37	0	Yale	1890-93	Princeton	6–0
35	35	0	Toledo	1969-71	Tampa	21–0
35	34	1	Minnesota	1903-05	Wisconsin	16–12
34	33	1	Nebraska	1912-16	Kansas	7–3
34	34	0	Pennsylvania	1894-96	Lafayette	6–4
34	32	2	Princeton	1884-87	Harvard	12–0
34	29	5	Princeton	1877-82	Harvard	1–0
33	30	3	Tennessee	1926-30	Alabama	18–6
33	31	2	Georgia Tech	1914-18	Pittsburgh	32–0
33	30	3	Harvard	1911-15	Cornell	10–0
32	31	1	Nebraska	1969-71	UCLA	20–17
32	30	2	Army	1944-47	Columbia	21–20
32	31	1	Harvard	1898-1900	Yale	28–0
31	30	1	Alabama	1991-93	Louisiana St	17–13
31	30	1	Penn St	1967-70	Colorado	41–13
31	30	1	San Diego St	1967-70	Long Beach St	27–11
31	29	2	Georgia Tech	1950-53	Notre Dame	27–14
31	31	0	Oklahoma	1948-50	Kentucky	13–7
31	31	0	Pittsburgh	1919-22	Cleveland Naval	10–9
31	31	0	Pennsylvania	1896-98	Harvard	10–0

Note: Includes bowl games.

Notable Achievements (Cont.)

LONGEST DIVISION I-A LOSING STREAKS

Losses		Seasons	Ended Against	Score
34	Northwestern	1979-82	Northern Illinois	31–6
28	Virginia	1958-61	William & Mary	21–6
28	Kansas St	1945-48	Arkansas St	37–6
27	New Mexico St	1988-90	Cal St-Fullerton	43-9
27	Eastern Michigan	1980-82	Kent St	9–7

MOST-PLAYED DIVISION I-A RIVALRIES

GP	Opponents (Series Leader Listed First)	Record	First Game
108	Minnesota-Wisconsin	57-43-8	1890
107	Missouri-Kansas	50-48-9	1891
105	Nebraska-Kansas	81-21-3	1892
105	Texas-Texas A&M	67-33-5	1894
103	Baylor-Texas Christian*	49-47-7	1899
103	Miami (OH)-Cincinnati	55-41-7	1888
103	N Carolina-Virginia	55-44-4	1892
102	Auburn-Georgia	48-46-8	1892
102	Oregon-Oregon St	51-41-10	1894
101	Purdue-Indiana	61-34-6	1891
101	Stanford-California	51-39-11	1892

GP	Opponents (Series Leader Listed First)	Record	First Game
99	Army-Navy	48-44-7	1890
96	Utah-Utah St	63-29-4	1892
96	Clemson-S Carolina	57-35-4	1896
96	Kansas-Kansas St	61-30-5	1902
95	Oklahoma-Kansas	62-27-6	1903
95	N Carolina-Wake Forest	64-29-2	1888
95	Michigan-Ohio St	54-35-6	1897
95	Mississippi-Miss St	54-35-6	1901

*Have not met since 1996.

NCAA Coaches' Records

ALLTIME WINNINGEST DIVISION I-A COACHES

Coach (Alma Mater)	Colleges Coached	Yrs	W	L	T	Pct
Knute Rockne (Notre Dame '14)†	Notre Dame 1918–30	13	105	12	5	.881
Frank W. Leahy (Notre Dame '31)†	Boston Col 1939–40; Notre Dame 1941–43, 1946–53	13	107	13	9	.864
George W. Woodruff (Yale 1889)†	Pennsylvania 1892–01; Illinois 1903; Carlisle 1905	12	142	25	2	.846
Barry Switzer (Arkansas '60)	Oklahoma 1973–88	16	157	29	4	.837
Tom Osborne (Hastings '59)†	Nebraska 1973–98	25	255	49	3	.836
Percy D. Haughton (Harvard 1899)†	Cornell 1899–1900; Harvard 1908–16; Columbia 1923–24	13	96	17	6	.832
Bob Neyland (Army '16)†	Tennessee 1926–34, 1936–40, 1946–52	21	173	31	12	.829
Fielding (Hurry Up) Yost (W Virginia 1895)†	Ohio Wesleyan 1897; Nebraska 1898; Kansas 1899; Stanford 1900; Michigan 1901–23, 1925–26	29	196	36	12	.828
Bud Wilkinson (Minnesota '37)†	Oklahoma 1947–63	17	145	29	4	.826
Jock Sutherland (Pittsburgh '18)†	Lafayette 1919–23; Pittsburgh 1924–38	20	144	28	14	.812
Bob Devaney (Alma, MI '39)†	Wyoming 1957–61; Nebraska 1962–72	16	136	30	7	.806
Frank W. Thomas (Notre Dame '23)†	Tenn.-Chattanooga 1925–28; Alabama 1931–42, 1944–46	19	141	33	9	.795
Joe Paterno (Brown '50)*	Penn St 1966–present	33	307	80	3	.791
Henry L. Williams (Yale 1891)†	Army 1891; Minnesota 1900–21	23	141	34	12	.786
Gil Dobie (Minnesota '02)†	N Dakota St 1906–07; Washington 1908-16; Navy 1917–19; Cornell 1920–35; Boston College 1936–38	33	180	45	15	.781
Steve Spurrier (Florida '67)*	Duke 1987–89; Florida 1990–present	12	113	31	2	.781

*Active coach. †Hall of Fame member.
Note: Minimum 10 years as head coach at Division I institutions; record at four-year colleges only; bowl games included; ties computed as half won, half lost.

ALLTIME WINNINGEST DIVISION I-A COACHES (Cont.)

By Victories

	Yrs	W	L	T	Pct		Yrs	W	L	T	Pct
Paul (Bear) Bryant	38	323	85	17	.780	Bo Schembechler	27	234	65	8	.775
Glenn (Pop) Warner	44	319	106	32	.733	Hayden Fry	37	232	178	10	.564
Amos Alonzo Stagg	57	314	199	35	.605	*Lou Holtz	27	216	95	7	.690
*Joe Paterno	33	307	80	3	.791	Jess Neely	40	207	176	19	.539
*Bobby Bowden	33	292	85	4	.772	Warren Woodson	31	203	95	14	.673
Tom Osborne	25	255	49	3	.836	Vince Dooley	25	201	77	10	.715
*LaVell Edwards	27	243	90	3	.728	Eddie Anderson	39	201	128	15	.606
Woody Hayes	33	238	72	10	.759	*Active coach.					

Most Bowl Victories

	W	L	T		W	L	T
*Joe Paterno	19	9	1	Barry Switzer	8	5	0
*Bobby Bowden	16	5	1	Darrell Royal	8	7	1
Paul (Bear) Bryant	15	12	2	Vince Dooley	8	10	2
Jim Wacker	13	2	0	John Robinson	7	1	0
Tom Osborne	12	13	0	Bob Devaney	7	3	0
Don James	10	5	0	Dan Devine	7	3	0
*Lou Holtz	10	8	2	Earle Bruce	7	5	0
John Vaught	10	8	0	Charlie McClendon	7	6	0
Bobby Dodd	9	4	0	*Hayden Fry	7	9	1
Johnny Majors	9	7	0	*LaVell Edwards	7	10	1
Terry Donahue	8	4	1	Pat Dye	7	2	1

*Active coach.

WINNINGEST ACTIVE DIVISION I-A COACHES
By Percentage

						Bowls		
Coach, College	Yrs	W	L	T	Pct#	W	L	T
Phillip Fulmer, Tennessee	7	67	11	0	.859	5	2	0
Joe Paterno, Penn St	33	307	80	3	.791	19	9	1
Steve Spurrier, Florida	12	113	31	2	.781	5	4	0
Bobby Bowden, Florida St	33	292	85	4	.772	16	5	1
R. C. Slocum, Texas A&M	10	94	28	2	.766	2	6	0
John Robinson, UNLV	12	104	35	4	.741	7	1	0
Dennis Erickson, Oregon St	13	113	40	1	.737	*5	5	0
LaVell Edwards, Brigham Young	27	243	91	3	.726	7	13	1
Paul Pasqualoni, Syracuse	13	102	43	1	.702	*4	3	0
John Cooper, Ohio St	22	178	74	6	.702	5	8	0

#Bowl games included in overall record.   Ties computed as half win, half loss.   *Includes record in NCAA and/or NAIA championships.

Note: Minimum five years as Division I-A head coach; record at four-year colleges only.

Smashing Success

Miami coach Butch Davis was so distraught when the Hurricanes led woeful Rutgers by only 13–3 at the half of their 1998 game that he put his fist through a blackboard in the locker room. Miami outscored the Scarlet Knights 40–14 in the second half to win 53–17. Said Davis of his display, "I think we had a good meeting."

WINNINGEST ACTIVE DIVISION I-A COACHES *(Cont.)*
By Victories

Joe Paterno, Penn St	307
Bobby Bowden, Florida St	292
LaVell Edwards, Brigham Young	243
Lou Holtz, S Carolina	216
Don Nehlen, W Virginia	191
John Cooper, Ohio St	178
George Welsh, Virginia	176
Jackie Sherrill, Mississippi St	154
Dick Tomey, Arizona	147
Ken Hatfield, Rice	139

WINNINGEST ACTIVE DIVISION I-AA COACHES
By Percentage

Coach, College	Yrs	W	L	T	Pct*
Mike Kelly, Dayton	18	171	32	1	.841
Al Bagnoli, Pennsylvania	17	138	36	0	.793
Pete Richardson, Southern	11	96	30	1	.760
Larry Blakeney, Troy St	8	71	25	1	.737
Walt Hamelin, Wagner	18	136	51	2	.725
Roy Kidd, Eastern Kentucky	35	286	108	8	.721
Tubby Raymond, Delaware	33	277	107	3	.720
Joe Gardi, Hofstra	9	70	27	2	.717
Greg Gattuso, Duquesne	6	45	18	0	.714
Billy Joe, Florida A&M	25	195	78	4	.711

*Playoff games included.

Note: Minimum five years as a Division I-A and/or Division I-AA head coach; record at four-year colleges only.

By Victories

Roy Kidd, Eastern Kentucky	286
Tubby Raymond, Delaware	277
Billy Joe, Florida A&M	195
Ron Randleman, Sam Houston St	178
Mike Kelly, Dayton	171
Willie Jeffries, S Carolina St	166
Bill Hayes, N Carolina A&T	164
Al Bagnoli, Pennsylvania	138
Walt Hamelin, Wagner	136
Bob Ricca, St. John's (N.Y.)	133

WINNINGEST ACTIVE DIVISION II COACHES
By Percentage

Coach, College	Yrs	W	L	T	Pct*
Chuck Broyles, Pittsburg St	9	93	16	2	.847
Ken Sparks, Carson-Newman	19	184	45	2	.801
Peter Yetten, Bentley	11	80	23	1	.774
Jerry Kill, Emporia St	5	38	14	0	.731
Brian Kelly, Grand Valley St	8	65	24	2	.725
Randy Avery, Saginaw Valley	5	36	14	0	.720
Danny Hale, Bloomsburg	11	85	33	1	.718
Gene Nicholson, Westminster (PA)	8	64	25	2	.714
Gene Carpenter, Millersville	30	205	83	6	.707
Frank Cignetti, Indiana (PA)	17	140	58	1	.706

*Ties computed as half win, half loss. Playoff games included.

Note: Minimum five years as a college head coach; record at four-year colleges only.

By Victories

Ron Harms, Texas A&M-Kingsville*	214
Gene Carpenter, Millersville	205
Ken Sparks, Carson-Newman	184
Willard Bailey, Virginia Union	175
Bud Elliott, Eastern New Mexico	165
Claire Boroff, NE-Kearney	162
Hampton Smith, Albany St. (GA)	150
Dennis Douds, E Stroudsburg	145
Frank Cignetti, Indiana (PA)	140
Gary Howard, Central Oklahoma	139

*Formerly Texas A&I.

WINNINGEST ACTIVE DIVISION III
By Percentage

Coach, College	Yrs	W	L	T	Pct*
Larry Kehres, Mt Union	13	138	16	3	.889
Dick Farley, Williams	12	81	12	3	.859
Tom Clark, Catholic	5	41	8	1	.830
Tim Coen, Salve Regina	6	46	10	0	.821
K.C. Keeler, Rowan	6	58	15	1	.791
John Luckhardt, Washington & Jefferson	17	137	37	2	.784
Roger Harring, WI-La Crosse	30	254	71	7	.776
John Gagliardi, St John's (MN)	50	353	105	11	.764
Bob Packard, Baldwin-Wallace	18	138	42	2	.764
Tony DeCarlo, John Carroll	12	90	27	4	.760

*Ties computed as half won, half lost. Playoff games included.

Note: Minimum five years as a college head coach; record at four-year colleges only.

By Victories

John Gagliardi, St John's (MN)	353	Don Miller, Trinity (CT)	174
Frosty Westering, Pacific Lutheran	264	Peter Mazzaferro, Bri'water (MA)	170
Roger Harring, WI-La Crosse	254	Tom Gilburg, Franklin & Marshall	153
Jim Christopherson, Concordia-M'head	207	Eric Hamilton, College of New Jersey	139
Frank Girardi, Lycoming	202	Larry Kehres, Mt Union	138

NAIA Coaches' Records

WINNINGEST ACTIVE NAIA COACHES
By Percentage

Coach, College	Yrs	W	L	T	Pct*
Ted Kessinger, Bethany (KS)	23	185	44	1	.807
Hank Biesiot, Dickinson St (ND)	23	162	58	1	.735
Geno DeMarco, Geneva (PA)	6	45	18	0	.714
Carl Poelker, McKendree (IL)	16	105	50	1	.676
Bob Young, Sioux Falls (SD)	16	113	57	3	.662
Monty Lewis, Southwestern (KS)	6	40	21	0	.656
Vic Wallace, Lambuth (TN)	18	123	65	4	.651
Larry Wilcox, Benedictine (KS)	20	132	74	0	.641
Bill Ramseyer, Virginia's College at Wise	27	161	90	4	.639

*Playoff games included.

Note: Minimum five years as a collegiate head coach and includes record against four-year institutions only.

By Victories

Ted Kessinger, Bethany (KS)	185	Kevin Donley, St. Francis (IN)	117
Hank Biesiot, Dickinson St (ND)	162	Bob Young, Sioux Falls (SD)	113
Bill Ramseyer, Virginia's College at Wise	161	Jim Dennison, Walsh (OH)	106
Larry Wilcox, Benedictine (KS)	132	Carl Poelker, McKendree (IL)	105
Vic Wallace, Lambuth (TN)	123	Dennis Gorsline, Martin Luther College (MN)	92

Pro Basketball

David Robinson
of the NBA champion
San Antonio Spurs

San Antonio Rose

The Spurs and their classy big men provided a welcome, sweet-smelling touch in an uneven, lockout-marred season

BY MARTY BURNS

IN THE END it was only fitting that the NBA title would end up in San Antonio, home of the Alamo. For rarely has a pro sports league faced a threat as big as Texas, like the NBA did in 1998–99. From the 191-day lockout that forced the cancellation of regular-season games for the first time in league history to the retirement of Michael Jordan and the breakup of the wildly popular Chicago Bulls, the NBA withstood a fusillade on par with the one faced by Davy Crockett and his band.

Fortunately for NBA commissioner David Stern & Co., the Spurs were there to provide a positive ending to the league's annus horribilis. Led by Finals MVP Tim Duncan, San Antonio held off the upstart New York Knicks in five games to claim the first NBA title in the franchise's 23-year history. It wasn't simply that the Spurs, the first former ABA team to win a crown, had waited so long. More important for a league concerned about its image, they were seen as nice guys off the court. "Critics used to say we were too soft," said veteran center David Robinson of the team's choir-boy image. "Well, we've proved that you don't have to talk a lot of trash to be successful."

With their Twin Towers—the 7'0" Duncan and the 7'1" Robinson—patrolling the paint against a Knicks team playing without injured center Patrick Ewing, the Spurs were unstoppable in the Finals. San Antonio took Game 1 at the Alamodome, 89–77, behind Duncan's 33 points and 16 rebounds, and followed with an 80–67 victory in Game 2, in which Duncan and Robinson combined for nine blocked shots and helped hold New York to 32.9% field goal shooting. Showing the resilience that made them the first No. 8 seed to reach the NBA Finals, the Knicks refused to fold and claimed Game 3, 89–81, at Madison Square Garden. But San Antonio bounced back with a 96–89 victory in Game 4, fueled by Duncan's 28 points and 18 rebounds, and then overcame a 35-point outburst from Knicks guard Latrell Sprewell in Game 5 to clinch the title with a thrilling 78–77 triumph. The game's final play per-

Not so fast: Duncan (21) blocked Bryant's path to the title of best young talent.

fectly symbolized the series: With 2.1 seconds left on the clock, Sprewell caught an inbounds pass under the basket but was swarmed by Duncan and Robinson and wound up trying a turnaround jumper at the horn that didn't even hit the rim. "Their size was the ultimate difference," Sprewell said. "We just didn't have an answer for them."

San Antonio's brilliant 15–2 postseason run, which included a record 12 straight victories, put an impressive cap on a season seemingly cursed from the start. The trouble began on July 1, 1998, with the NBA's decision to lock out its 348 players in hopes of forcing a new collective bargaining agreement, one that featured protections against runaway salaries such as the six-year, $126 million deal signed in '98 by Minnesota Timberwolves forward Kevin Garnett. The NBA ultimately got its wish, but it came at a steep price. The lockout stretched all the way to Jan. 6, forcing a halt to all league business—including player transactions—as well as the cancellation of training camps, the exhibition season, the All-Star Game in Philadelphia and a combined 464 games of the regular season before play resumed on Feb. 5 with the start of an abbreviated 50-game schedule.

Fan reaction during the dispute was predictable. Unable to fathom why owners and

DAVID E. KLUTHO

called it quits at a press conference on the United Center floor. Calling it "the perfect time to walk away from the game," Jordan smiled and fought back tears as his No. 23 Bulls jersey was again raised to the rafters (as it had been after his first retirement, in '93). Concerned about a possible backlash after the lockout and Jordan's departure, the NBA began a campaign to win back fans. It required each team to host one free scrimmage and one free exhibition, and to sell 500 $10 tickets at every game. The players agreed to do their part, standing at arena turnstiles before the exhibitions and greeting all who entered. The fan-friendly efforts failed to sway everyone, however. At a Toronto Raptors–Boston Celtics game in the FleetCenter, a fan strode onto the floor and flung a pile of dollar bills at the players.

players couldn't agree on how to divide the spoils of their $1.7 billion–a–year operation, many expressed disgust at both parties and vowed not to watch if and when NBA play resumed. An ESPN Internet poll in November '98, revealed that 63% of sports fans said they wouldn't care if the season was canceled. When the players' association organized a made–for–pay TV all-star game Dec. 19 at the 12,000-seat Atlantic City Convention Center, only 9,526 people showed up, and even fewer around the nation seemed to notice.

Making matters worse for the NBA was the impending retirement of the 35-year-old Jordan, the game's greatest player. Though his departure had been forecast as far back as the end of the '98 season, Jordan vowed to wait until after the lockout was over before making his decision. On Jan. 13, seven days after the labor dispute was settled, he

When the season tipped off in February, several players looked out of shape and the action was ragged, a predictable development after such a long layoff and a relatively brief training camp. Soon, however, emerging stars such as Philadelphia 76ers guard Allen Iverson, Sacramento Kings rookie point guard Jason Williams and Raptors rookie forward Vince Carter were bringing fans back to the arena—and out of their seats—with their superior skills and unique flair. Iverson, who had switched from point guard to shooting guard, won the scoring title and led the surprising Sixers to a first-round playoff upset of the Orlando Magic. Williams, a ball handling wizard with Pete Maravich–style razzle-dazzle, paired up with rejuvenated forward Chris Webber to generate a hoops revival in Sacramento. Carter's high-flying dunks became a staple of the nightly sports highlights, and the former North Carolina Tar Heel won the Rookie of the Year award. Meanwhile, poised second-year pro Duncan led the Spurs to a tie for the best record in the league while finishing third in a tight race for regular season MVP, behind Utah Jazz forward Karl Malone and Heat center Alonzo Mourning.

Ironically, another player who generated fan interest was Sprewell, the poster child for misbehavior, who had been suspended for most of the '98 season after attacking his coach with the Golden State Warriors, P.J. Carlesimo. Acquired by the Knicks before the season in a trade that sent popular guard John Starks and forwards Terry Cummings and Chris Mills to the Warriors, Sprewell got off to a slow start in New York. But he silenced his critics by playing his best basketball down the stretch and sparking the Knicks, who finished the regular season at 27–23 and barely made the playoffs, to a scintillating playoff run to the Finals. With his braided hairstyle and his intense mien Sprewell still looked the same, but off the court, he seemed to be a changed man. Making the most of his second chance, he dealt patiently with media and fans and avoided any overt signs of anger. At the end Knicks superfan Spike Lee was wearing a No. 8 Sprewell jersey to games, and Madison Square Garden fans were chanting his name. Even on the road, he was sometimes cheered by small groups of supporters.

Along with his image, Sprewell turned around the fortunes of his team. On April 21, New York's record stood at 21–21, Ewing was hobbled by a sore left Achilles tendon and G.M. Ernie Grunfeld had just been demoted. Amid speculation that coach Jeff Van Gundy would be fired next—one New York tabloid ran a back-page photo of Van Gundy under the headline DEAD VAN WALKING—the Knicks suddenly caught fire, winning six of their final eight games to make the playoffs. New York then stunned the top-seeded Miami Heat—eliminating their hated rivals in Game 5 on a buzzer-beater by guard Allan Houston—swept the Atlanta Hawks and upset the heavily favored Pacers to reach the Finals for the first time since '94.

The Broadway revival was bizarre even by New York standards. It was Grunfeld, after all, who had acquired the two main catalysts for the surge—Sprewell and forward Marcus Camby (who had arrived in a trade for popular forward Charles Oakley)—with the vision of transforming the Knicks into a younger, more athletic team. Yet it was Van Gundy, initially resistant to the roster changes, who came off as a sympathetic figure, especially after it was established during the Atlanta series that Madison Square Garden president Dave Checketts had met secretly with former Bulls coach Phil Jackson to inquire about Jackson's interest in coaching the Knicks. Van Gundy heard his name chanted by Garden fans during playoff games, and he was ultimately rewarded with a two-year, $8 million contract extension after the season.

In contrast to events in New York, the Los Angeles Lakers could not seem to do anything right. With their all-star core of Shaquille O'Neal, Kobe Bryant and Eddie Jones, the Lakers entered '99 as title contenders. But after a 6–6 start, L.A. signed controversial former Bulls forward Dennis Rodman for, of all things, veteran leadership, and fired coach Del Harris and replaced him with rookie coach Kurt Rambis. They then acquired all-star Glen Rice from the Charlotte Hornets for Jones and big man Elden Campbell. The moves brought together the league's most dominant center, its premier shooter and its seven-time rebounding king, and looked on paper to all but guarantee a title for the Lakers in their final season at the Forum. (They will move to the Staples Center in 1999.) But the flamboyant Rodman proved divisive from the start. He toed the line for his first nine games, all Lakers victories, but then suddenly bolted for four games for personal reasons. When he came back he dressed apart from the Lakers, missed practices and struggled against the better power forwards in the game. His disruptive 51-day stint ended when he was fired for showing up late to yet another practice. The Lakers never had time to develop chemistry in the shortened season and were swept by the

No choke: Sprewell returned in style, leading the No. 8–seed Knicks to the Finals.

Spurs in the second round of the playoffs. Rambis was fired shortly after and replaced by Jackson, who signed a five-year, $30 million deal.

Despite the lockout and its ill effects, the NBA managed—like Sprewell and Van Gundy—to survive. Average attendance stayed pretty much the same. TV ratings slumped slightly, but not as much as league officials feared given Jordan's departure. The settlement with the players, meanwhile, was hailed as a slam dunk for NBA higher-ups. The agreement set $14 million as the maximum salary a player with 10 seasons or more experience may receive in the first year of a new contract, $11 million for a player with seven-to-nine seasons and $9 million for a player with six seasons or less. With that, Stern had made the NBA the only one of the four major professional sports leagues to have a maximum salary, and he had rendered agents unable to drive bidding wars for their clients into the stratosphere. He also made it possible for teams to hold on to their draft choices for five years—two years longer than under the past agreement—before those players become unrestricted free agents. In return, the NBA's main concession was to raise minimum salaries for rookies to $287,500 and for vets to $350,000–$1 million, depending on experience.

With its financial house in order, the league began looking for ways to improve the product. Concerned about a continued decline in offense that saw teams score a modern-era low of 91.6 points per game, the league convened a 16-member committee to consider rules changes that would reverse the trend and bring open-court basketball back into vogue. Some possible modifications included simplifying the illegal defense rules, limiting physical contact on players cutting through the lane and barring players from possessing the ball for more than five seconds at a time. Flat TV ratings in the Finals were also a concern, as was the increasing number of players making the jump directly from high school to the NBA.

At the other end of the pro sports spectrum, the WNBA, which is owned by the NBA, was at a critical juncture in its third season of operation. Though it boasted leaguewide average attendance of close to 10,000 a game and had successfully forced the rival ABL out of business, the WNBA struggled to gain a foothold in the public consciousness, and its TV ratings were low compared to other sports.

By far the NBA's biggest worry, however, was simply getting fans to put the lockout behind and rekindle their love affair with the pro game. That's why the Spurs' march to the title was so important. In Duncan and Robinson, San Antonio featured two of the game's biggest stars, and gentlemen. The rest of the cast—Avery Johnson, Mario Elie, Sean Elliott, Jaren Jackson and Steve Kerr—played with heart and determination while seeming to enjoy their moment in the spotlight. After a long, hard season of acrimony, the Spurs' triumph seemed to make everyone, at least those outside New York, feel good. It also made for a succinct motto to sum up the NBA in '98–99: Remember the Alamodome. Forget everything else.

FOR THE RECORD·1998–1999

NBA Final Standings

Eastern Conference

ATLANTIC DIVISION

Team	W	L	Pct	GB
Miami	33	17	.660	—
Orlando	33	17	.660	—
Philadelphia	28	22	.560	5
New York	27	23	.540	6
Boston	19	31	.380	14
Washington	18	32	.360	15
New Jersey	16	34	.320	17

CENTRAL DIVISION

Team	W	L	Pct	GB
Indiana	33	17	.660	—
Atlanta	31	19	.620	2
Detroit	29	21	.580	4
Milwaukee	28	22	.560	5
Charlotte	26	24	.520	7
Toronto	23	27	.460	10
Cleveland	22	28	.440	11
Chicago	13	37	.260	20

Western Conference

MIDWEST DIVISION

Team	W	L	Pct	GB
San Antonio	37	13	.740	—
Utah	37	13	.740	—
Houston	31	19	.620	6
Minnesota	25	25	.500	12
Dallas	19	31	.380	18
Denver	14	36	.280	23
Vancouver	8	42	.160	29

PACIFIC DIVISION

Team	W	L	Pct	GB
Portland	35	15	.700	—
LA Lakers	31	19	.620	4
Sacramento	27	23	.540	8
Phoenix	27	23	.540	8
Seattle	25	25	.500	10
Golden State	21	29	.420	14
LA Clippers	9	41	.180	26

1999 NBA Playoffs

EASTERN CONFERENCE

1st ROUND · SEMIFINALS · FINALS

Miami
New York — New York (3–2)
Detroit
Atlanta — Atlanta (3–2)
New York (4–0)
Orlando
Philadelphia — Philadelphia (3–1)
New York (4–2)
Milwaukee
Indiana — Indiana (3–0)
Indiana (4–0)

NBA FINALS

SAN ANTONIO (4–1)

WESTERN CONFERENCE

FINALS · SEMIFINALS · 1st ROUND

San Antonio (3–1)
San Antonio (4–0)
LA Lakers (3–1)
San Antonio (4–0)
Sacramento
Portland (4–2)
Utah (3–2)
Portland (3–0)

San Antonio
Minnesota
LA Lakers
Houston
Utah
Sacramento
Portland
Phoenix

1999 NBA Playoff Results

Eastern Conference First Round

May 8	New York	95	at Miami	75
May 10	New York	73	at Miami	83
May 12	Miami	73	at New York	97
May 14	Miami	87	at New York	72
May 16	New York	78	at Miami	77

New York won series 3–2.

May 9	Milwaukee	88	at Indiana	110
May 11	Milwaukee	107	at Indiana	108*
May 13	Indiana	99	at Milwaukee	91

Indiana won series 3–0.

May 9	Philadelphia	104	at Orlando	90
May 11	Philadelphia	68	at Orlando	79
May 13	Orlando	85	at Philadelphia	97
May 15	Orlando	91	at Philadelphia	101

Philadelphia won series 3–1.

May 8	Detroit	70	at Atlanta	90
May 10	Detroit	69	at Atlanta	89
May 12	Atlanta	63	at Detroit	79
May 14	Atlanta	82	at Detroit	103
May 16	Detroit	75	at Atlanta	87

Atlanta won series 3–2.

Western Conference First Round

May 9	Minnesota	86	at San Antonio	99
May 11	Minnesota	80	at San Antonio	71
May 13	San Antonio	85	at Minnesota	71
May 15	San Antonio	92	at Minnesota	85

San Antonio won series 3–1.

May 8	Phoenix	85	at Portland	95
May 10	Phoenix	99	at Portland	110
May 12	Portland	103	at Phoenix	93

Portland won series 3–0.

May 8	Sacramento	87	at Utah	117
May 10	Sacramento	101	at Utah	90
May 12	Utah	81	at Sacramento	84*
May 14	Utah	90	at Sacramento	89
May 16	Sacramento	92	at Utah	99*

Utah won series 3–2.

May 9	Houston	100	at LA Lakers	101
May 11	Houston	98	at LA Lakers	110
May 13	LA Lakers	88	at Houston	102
May 15	LA Lakers	98	at Houston	88

LA Lakers won series 3–1.

Eastern Conference Semifinals

May 17	Philadelphia	90	at Indiana	94
May 19	Philadelphia	82	at Indiana	85
May 21	Indiana	97	at Philadelphia	86
May 23	Indiana	89	at Philadelphia	86

Indiana won series 4–0.

May 18	New York	100	at Atlanta	92
May 20	New York	77	at Atlanta	70
May 23	Atlanta	78	at New York	90
May 24	Atlanta	66	at New York	79

New York won series 4–0.

Western Conference Semifinals

May 17	LA Lakers	81	at San Antonio	87
May 19	LA Lakers	76	at San Antonio	79
May 22	San Antonio	103	at LA Lakers	91
May 23	San Antonio	118	at LA Lakers	107

San Antonio won series 4–0.

May 18	Portland	83	at Utah	93
May 20	Portland	84	at Utah	81
May 22	Utah	87	at Portland	97
May 23	Utah	75	at Portland	81
May 25	Portland	71	at Utah	88
May 27	Utah	80	at Portland	92

Portland won series 4–2.

Eastern Conference Finals

May 30	New York	93	at Indiana	90
June 1	New York	86	at Indiana	88
June 5	Indiana	91	at New York	92
June 7	Indiana	90	at New York	78
June 9	New York	101	at Indiana	94
June 11	Indiana	82	at New York	90

New York won series 4–2.

Western Conference Finals

May 29	Portland	76	at San Antonio	80
May 31	Portland	85	at San Antonio	86
June 4	San Antonio	85	at Portland	63
June 6	San Antonio	94	at Portland	80

San Antonio won series 4–0.

Finals

June 16	New York	77	at San Antonio	89
June 18	New York	67	at San Antonio	80
June 21	San Antonio	81	at New York	89
June 23	San Antonio	96	at New York	89
June 25	San Antonio	78	at New York	77

San Antonio won series 4–1.

*Overtime game.

NBA Finals Composite Box Score

NEW YORK KNICKS

Player	GP	Field Goals		3-Pt FG		Free Throws		Rebounds		A	Stl	TO	BS	Avg	Hi
		FGM	Pct	FGM	FGA	FTM	Pct	Off	Total						
Sprewell	5	48	41.0	2	7	32	84.2	6	33	13	7	14	1	26.0	35
Houston	5	41	42.7	2	12	24	92.3	2	16	17	2	13	0	21.6	34
Camby	5	21	50.0	0	0	6	75.0	13	39	1	3	2	10	9.6	20
Johnson	5	14	28.6	2	18	8	61.5	6	24	7	6	8	1	7.6	16
Ward	5	12	46.1	4	12	1	50.0	6	16	18	13	7	2	5.8	11
Thomas	5	11	34.4	0	0	6	60.0	13	38	2	6	1	0	5.6	13
Childs	5	5	22.7	1	5	1	50.0	1	6	11	2	8	0	2.4	4
Dudley	5	2	25.0	0	0	2	33.3	2	19	1	1	5	3	1.2	2
Williams	2	0	0.0	0	0	0	—	0	0	0	0	0	0	0.0	0
Brunson	1	0	—	0	0	0	—	0	0	0	0	0	0	0.0	0
Total	5	154	39.2	11	54	80	76.2	49	244	70	40	63	17	79.8	89

SAN ANTONIO SPURS

Player	GP	Field Goals		3-Pt FG		Free Throws		Rebounds		A	Stl	TO	BS	Avg	Hi
		FGM	Pct	FGM	FGA	FTM	Pct	Off	Total						
Duncan	5	51	53.7	0	2	35	79.5	14	70	12	5	17	11	27.4	33
Robinson	5	25	42.4	0	0	33	68.7	14	59	12	5	8	15	16.6	25
Elie	5	17	44.7	4	13	20	87.0	2	20	12	6	8	0	11.6	18
Johnson	5	20	50.0	0	1	6	60.0	2	13	36	3	20	0	9.2	14
Elliot	5	14	33.3	5	18	7	63.6	4	15	15	4	6	1	8.0	14
Jackson	5	12	32.4	9	24	0	—	1	7	5	5	9	0	6.6	17
Daniels	4	4	80.0	2	2	0	—	0	2	4	1	2	0	2.5	8
Kerr	5	4	40.0	1	2	0	0.0	2	5	2	0	2	0	1.8	5
Rose	5	2	20.0	0	0	2	50.0	3	12	2	3	5	2	1.2	2
Kersey	2	1	100.0	0	0	0	—	0	0	0	0	0	0	1.0	2
King	2	0	—	0	0	0	—	0	0	0	0	0	0	0.0	0
Total	5	150	44.5	21	62	103	73.0	42	245	100	32	81	29	84.8	96

NBA Finals Box Scores

Game 1

NEW YORK 77

NEW YORK	Min	FG M–A	FT M–A	Reb O–T	A	PF	S	TO	TP
Johnson	21	3–4	3–4	0–1	1	5	0	2	5
Sprewell	46	9–24	0–0	1–7	2	2	0	6	19
Dudley	24	0–3	2–6	1–5	0	3	0	4	2
Houston	43	7–17	5–5	0–2	3	3	0	2	19
Ward	24	3–6	0–0	0–4	3	1	0	0	7
Thomas	31	5–11	3–4	7–16	0	4	4	0	13
Camby	23	5–8	0–0	3–6	0	5	1	0	10
Childs	26	1–8	0–0	1–2	3	4	2	1	2
Williams	2	0–1	0–0	0–0	0	0	0	0	0
Totals	240	31–81	13–19	13–43	12	27	7	15	77

Percentages: FG—.383, FT—.684. 3-pt goals: 2–8, .250 (Sprewell 1–2, Houston 0–2, Ward 1–3, Childs 0–1). Team rebounds: 13. Blocked shots: 6 (Ward 2, Dudley 2, Camby, Johnson).

SAN ANTONIO 89

S ANTONIO	Min	FG M–A	FT M–A	Reb O–T	A	PF	S	TO	TP
Duncan	44	13–21	7–10	3–16	2	3	2	1	33
Elliott	29	3–6	0–0	0–3	3	2	2	2	7
Robinson	37	3–10	7–12	0–9	7	3	3	3	13
Elie	38	3–7	3–4	0–4	3	1	1	1	9
Johnson	38	2–3	2–4	0–2	8	0	0	3	6
Jackson	25	6–13	0–0	1–2	2	4	1	4	17
Rose	15	1–3	0–0	0–1	0	4	0	0	2
Kerr	9	0–2	0–1	0–0	0	0	0	0	0
Kersey	2	0–0	0–0	0–0	0	1	0	0	0
Daniels	3	1–2	0–0	0–0	0	0	0	0	2
Totals	240	32–67	19–31	4–37	25	18	9	14	89

Percentages: FG—.478, FT—.613. 3-pt goals: 6–15, .400 (Elliott 1–2, Elie 0–2, Jackson 5–10, Kerr 0–1). Team rebounds: 10. Blocked shots: 6 (Robinson 3, Duncan 2, Rose).
A: 39,514. Officials: Salvatore, Evans, Javie.

Game 2

NEW YORK 67

NEW YORK	Min	FG M–A	FT M–A	Reb O–T	A	PF	S	TO	TP
Johnson	43	2–12	0–1	2–6	1	3	3	1	5
Sprewell	40	8–22	10–10	1–7	1	1	1	1	26
Dudley	13	0–2	0–0	1–6	0	2	1	0	0
Houston	43	9–20	1–1	0–2	2	1	0	3	19
Ward	23	2–3	0–0	3–3	3	2	3	2	5
Thomas	20	1–6	0–0	0–7	0	5	1	0	2
Camby	32	3–9	0–0	3–11	0	6	2	1	6
Childs	26	2–8	0–0	0–1	1	5	0	2	4
Totals	240	27–82	11–12	10–43	8	25	11	13	67

Percentages: FG—.329, FT—.917. 3-pt goals: 2–14, .143 (Johnson 1–7, Sprewell 0–2, Houston 0–2, Ward 1–1, Childs 0–2). Team rebounds: 6. Blocked shots: 4 (Camby 3, Sprewell).

SAN ANTONIO 80

S ANTONIO	Min	FG M–A	FT M–A	Reb O–T	A	PF	S	TO	TP
Duncan	45	9–17	7–9	5–15	3	0	0	4	25
Elliott	38	4–12	1–5	0–3	1	3	0	2	10
Robinson	34	5–8	6–9	0–11	4	4	0	0	16
Elie	37	4–10	7–8	0–4	2	2	1	2	15
Johnson	35	3–8	2–2	0–3	5	2	1	2	8
Jackson	22	1–5	0–0	0–1	0	0	1	0	3
Rose	15	0–1	1–2	0–2	1	2	2	1	1
Kerr	12	1–2	0–0	0–2	1	0	0	1	2
Daniels	1	0–0	0–0	0–0	1	0	0	0	0
King	1	0–0	0–0	0–0	0	0	0	0	0
Totals	240	27–63	24–35	5–41	18	13	5	14	80

Percentages: FG—.429, FT—.686. 3-pt goals: 2–12, .167 (Elliott 1–4, Elie 0–3, Jackson 1–5). Team rebounds: 13. Blocked shots: 9 (Robinson 5, Duncan 4). A: 39,554. Officials: J. Crawford, Kersey, D. Crawford.

Game 3

SAN ANTONIO 81

S ANTONIO	Min	FG M–A	FT M–A	Reb O–T	A	PF	S	TO	TP
Duncan	47	8–16	4–4	3–12	2	3	3	5	20
Elliott	38	3–9	0–0	0–1	2	2	1	1	7
Robinson	39	6–12	13–17	1–10	1	3	0	2	25
Johnson	39	5–9	0–0	2–4	4	3	1	6	10
Elie	26	2–6	1–1	0–0	1	5	0	1	6
Daniels	16	3–3	0–0	0–1	3	2	1	2	8
Kerr	14	2–4	0–0	2–2	0	3	0	1	5
Jackson	10	0–3	0–0	0–0	2	4	0	1	0
Rose	10	0–3	0–0	2–6	0	2	0	1	0
King	1	0–0	0–0	0–0	0	0	0	0	0
Totals	240	29–65	18–22	10–36	15	27	6	20	81

Percentages: FG—.446, FT—.818. 3-pt goals: 5–13, .385 (Duncan 0–1, Elliott 1–5, Elie 1–3, Daniels 2–2, Kerr 1–1, Jackson 0–1). Team rebounds: 8. Blocked shots: 3 (Robinson 2, Duncan).

NEW YORK 89

NEW YORK	Min	FG M–A	FT M–A	Reb O–T	A	PF	S	TO	TP
Sprewell	46	9–22	6–10	1–5	5	1	2	2	24
Johnson	43	6–16	3–4	2–5	1	3	1	2	16
Camby	16	2–4	1–2	2–4	0	6	0	0	5
Houston	45	10–24	12–12	1–3	4	0	0	0	34
Ward	31	1–4	0–0	1–2	2	2	4	2	2
Childs	22	1–2	1–2	0–3	3	4	0	2	4
Dudley	19	1–2	0–0	0–4	1	3	0	1	2
Thomas	17	1–4	0–0	5–10	1	4	1	1	2
Brunson	1	0–0	0–0	0–0	0	0	0	0	0
Totals	240	31–78	23–30	12–36	17	23	8	10	89

Percentages: FG—.397, FT—.767. 3-pt goals: 4–13, .308 (Sprewell 0–1, Johnson 1–5, Houston 2–4, Ward 0–2, Childs 1–1). Team rebounds: 14. Blocked shots: 4 (Camby 3, Dudley). A: 19,763. Officials: Bavetta, Hollins, Nunn.

Game 4

SAN ANTONIO 96

S ANTONIO	Min	FG M–A	FT M–A	Reb O–T	A	PF	S	TO	TP
Duncan	47	9–19	10–12	3–18	3	4	0	5	28
Elliott	40	4–11	4–4	0–2	4	3	1	1	14
Robinson	36	6–15	2–2	9–17	0	5	0	1	14
Elie	39	6–9	5–6	1–6	4	4	2	3	18
Johnson	44	6–10	2–4	0–2	10	3	1	3	14
Kerr	4	1–1	0–0	0–0	1	0	0	0	2
Rose	13	1–2	0–0	1–3	0	2	0	2	2
Jackson	15	1–7	0–0	0–1	1	4	1	2	2
Kersey	2	1–1	0–0	0–0	0	0	0	0	2
Totals	240	35–75	23–28	14–49	23	25	5	17	96

Percentages: FG—.467, FT—.821. 3-pt goals: 3–9, .333 (Elliott 2–5, Elie 1–2, Jackson 0–2). Team rebounds: 6. Blocked shots: 9 (Robinson 4, Duncan 3, Elliott, Rose).

NEW YORK 89

NEW YORK	Min	FG M–A	FT M–A	Reb O–T	A	PF	S	TO	TP
Johnson	37	2–8	1–2	1–6	0	6	0	3	5
Sprewell	46	9–22	8–8	1–4	3	2	2	2	26
Camby	37	8–15	4–5	5–13	0	4	0	0	20
Houston	46	7–18	6–7	0–2	3	3	0	4	20
Ward	41	4–9	1–2	2–4	8	3	4	1	11
Thomas	19	2–7	1–4	1–2	1	5	0	0	5
Childs	7	0–0	0–0	0–0	0	0	0	1	0
Dudley	7	1–1	0–0	0–3	0	2	0	0	2
Totals	240	33–80	21–28	10–34	15	25	6	11	89

Percentages: FG—.413, FT—.750. 3-pt goals: 2–10, .200 (Johnson 0–3, Sprewell 0–1, Houston 0–1, Ward 2–5). Team rebounds: 10. Blocked shots: 2 (Camby 2). A: 19,763. Officials: Evans, Garretson, Mathis.

Game 5

SAN ANTONIO 78

S ANTONIO	Min	FG M–A	FT M–A	Reb O–T	A	PF	S	TO	TP
Duncan	46	12–22	7–9	0–9	2	2	0	2	31
Elliott	36	0–4	2–2	4–6	5	4	0	0	2
Robinson	39	5–14	5–8	4–12	0	1	2	2	15
Elie	35	2–6	4–4	1–6	3	2	2	1	10
Johnson	40	4–10	0–0	0–2	9	3	0	6	8
Jackson	24	4–9	0–0	0–3	0	1	2	2	11
Rose	11	0–1	1–2	0–0	1	3	1	1	1
Kerr	5	0–1	0–0	0–1	0	0	0	0	0
Daniels	4	0–0	0–0	0–1	0	1	0	0	0
Totals	240	27–67	19–25	9–40	20	17	7	16	78

Percentages: FG—.403, FT—.760. 3-pt goals: 5–13, .385 (Duncan 0–1, Elliott 0–2, Elie 2–3, Johnson 0–1, Jackson 3–6). Team rebounds: 5. Blocked shots: 2 (Duncan, Robinson).

NEW YORK 77

NEW YORK	Min	FG M–A	FT M–A	Reb O–T	A	PF	S	TO	TP
Johnson	41	3–10	1–2	1–6	4	5	2	0	7
Sprewell	43	13–27	8–10	2–10	2	1	2	3	35
Camby	27	3–6	1–1	0–5	1	4	0	1	7
Houston	45	8–17	0–1	1–7	5	2	2	4	16
Ward	26	2–4	0–0	0–3	2	1	2	2	4
Thomas	18	2–4	2–2	0–3	0	5	0	0	6
Dudley	15	0–0	0–0	0–1	0	4	0	0	0
Childs	24	1–4	0–0	0–0	4	1	0	2	2
Williams	1	0–0	0–0	0–0	0	0	0	0	0
Totals	240	32–72	12–16	4–35	18	23	8	14	77

Percentages: FG—.444, FT—.750. 3-pt goals: 1–9, .111 (Johnson 0–3, Sprewell 1–1, Houston 0–3, Ward 0–1, Childs 0–1). Team rebounds: 10. Blocked shots: 1 (Camby).

A: 19,763. Officials: J. Crawford, Javie, Salvatore.

NBA Awards

All-NBA Teams

FIRST TEAM	SECOND TEAM	THIRD TEAM
G Allen Iverson, Philadelphia	Gary Payton, Seattle	Kobe Bryant, LA Lakers
G Jason Kidd, Phoenix	Tim Hardaway, Miami	John Stockton, Utah
C Alonzo Mourning, Miami	Shaquille O'Neal, LA Lakers	Hakeem Olajuwon, Houston
F Karl Malone, Utah	Chris Webber, Sacramento	Kevin Garnett, Minnesota
F Tim Duncan, San Antonio	Grant Hill, Detroit	Antonio McDyess, Denver

NBA All-Defensive Teams

FIRST TEAM	SECOND TEAM
G Gary Payton, Seattle	Mookie Blaylock, Atlanta
G Jason Kidd, Phoenix	Eddie Jones, Charlotte
C Alonzo Mourning, Miami	Dikembe Mutombo, Atlanta
F Tim Duncan, San Antonio	PJ Brown, Miami
F Scottie Pippen, Houston	Theo Ratliff, Philadelphia
F Karl Malone, Utah	

All-Rookie Teams
(Chosen Without Regard to Position)

FIRST TEAM	SECOND TEAM
Vince Carter, Toronto	Michael Dickerson, Houston
Paul Pierce, Boston	Cuttino Mobley, Houston
Jason Williams, Sacramento	Michael Doleac, Orlando
Mike Bibby, Vancouver	Michael Olowokandi, LA Clippers
Matt Harpring, Orlando	Antawn Jamison, Golden State

NBA Individual Leaders

Scoring

	GP	Pts	Avg
Allen Iverson, Phil	48	1284	26.8
Shaquille O'Neal, LA Lakers	49	1289	26.3
Karl Malone, Utah	49	1164	23.8
Shareef Abdur-Rahim, Van	50	1152	23.0
Keith Van Horn, NJ	42	916	21.8
Tim Duncan, SA	50	1084	21.7
Gary Payton, Sea	50	1084	21.7
Stephon Marbury, NJ	49	1044	21.3
Antonio McDyess, Den	50	1061	21.2
Grant Hill, Det	50	1053	21.1

Assists

	GP	Assists	Avg
Jason Kidd, Phoe	50	539	10.8
Rod Strickland, Wash	44	434	9.9
Stephon Marbury, NJ	49	437	8.9
Gary Payton, Sea	50	436	8.7
Terrell Brandon, Minn	36	309	8.6
Mark Jackson, Ind	49	386	7.9
Brevin Knight, Clev	39	302	7.7
John Stockton, Utah	50	374	7.5
Avery Johnson, SA	50	369	7.4
Nick Van Exel, Den	50	368	7.4

Free-Throw Percentage

	FTA	FTM	Pct
Reggie Miller, Ind	247	226	.915
Chauncy Billups, Den	172	157	.913
Darrell Armstrong, Orl	178	161	.904
Ray Allen, Mil	195	176	.903
Hersey Hawkins, Sea	132	119	.902
Jeff Hornacek, Utah	140	125	.893
Chris Mullin, Ind	92	80	.870
Glenn Robinson, Mil	161	140	.870
Mario Elie, SA	119	103	.866
Eric Piatkowski, LA Clippers	102	88	.863

Steals

	GP	Steals	Avg
Kendall Gill, NJ	50	134	2.68
Eddie Jones, Char	50	125	2.50
Allen Iverson, Phil	48	110	2.29
Jason Kidd, Phoe	50	114	2.28
Doug Christie, Tor	50	113	2.26
Anfernee Hardaway, Orl	50	111	2.22
Gary Payton, Sea	50	109	2.18
Darrell Armstrong, Orl	50	108	2.16
Eric Snow, Phil	48	100	2.08
Mookie Blaylock, Atl	48	99	2.06

Rebounds

	GP	Reb	Avg
Chris Webber, Sac	42	545	13.0
Charles Barkley, Hou	42	516	12.3
Dikembe Mutombo, Atl	50	610	12.2
Danny Fortson, Den	50	581	11.6
Tim Duncan, SA	50	571	11.4
Alonzo Mourning, Mia	46	507	11.0
Antonio McDyess, Den	50	537	10.7
Shaquille O'Neal, LA Lakers	49	525	10.7
Kevin Garnett, Minn	47	489	10.4
Vlade Divac, Sac	50	501	10.0
David Robinson, SA	49	492	10.0

Field-Goal Percentage

	FGA	FGM	Pct
Shaquille O'Neal, LA Lakers	885	510	.576
Otis Thorpe, Wash	440	240	.545
Hakeem Olajuwon, Hou	725	373	.514
Alonzo Mourning, Mia	634	324	.511
David Robinson, SA	527	268	.509
Rasheed Wallace, Port	476	242	.508
Bison Dele, Det	431	216	.501
Tim Duncan, SA	845	418	.495
Danny Fortson, Den	386	191	.495
Vitaly Potapenko, Bos	412	204	.495

Three-Point Field-Goal Percentage

	FGA	FGM	Pct
Dell Curry, Char	145	69	.476
Chris Mullin, Ind	157	73	.465
Hubert Davis, Dall	144	65	.451
Walt Williams, Port	144	63	.438
Michael Dickerson, Hou	164	71	.433
Dale Ellis, Sea	217	94	.433
Jeff Hornacek, Utah	81	34	.420
Clifford Robinson, Phoe	139	58	.417
George McCloud, Phoe	166	69	.416
Jud Buechler, Det	148	61	.412
Paul Pierce, Bos	204	84	.412

Blocked Shots

	GP	BS	Avg
Alonzo Mourning, Mia	46	180	3.91
Shawn Bradley, Dall	49	159	3.24
Theo Ratliff, Phil	50	149	2.98
Dikembe Mutombo, Atl	50	147	2.94
Greg Ostertag, Utah	48	131	2.73
Patrick Ewing, NY	38	100	2.63
Tim Duncan, SA	50	126	2.52
Hakeem Olajuwon, Hou	50	123	2.46
David Robinson, SA	49	119	2.43
Antonio McDyess, Den	50	115	2.30

NBA Team Statistics

Offense

Team	Field Goals FGM	Pct	3-Pt Field Goals 3FGM	Pct	Free Throws FTM	Pct	Rebounds Off	Total	A	Stl	Scoring Avg
Sacramento	1918	44.5	290	30.8	883	68.3	706	2279	1129	444	100.2
LA Lakers	1841	46.8	241	35.2	1027	68.3	619	2101	1095	389	99.0
Phoenix	1797	44.9	261	37.2	924	76.0	598	2016	1249	444	95.6
Seattle	1756	44.2	309	34.4	922	68.1	676	2098	1087	393	94.9
Portland	1747	44.2	246	36.4	1002	74.3	646	2216	1073	411	94.8
Indiana	1731	44.8	294	36.8	977	79.6	574	2026	1005	316	94.7
Houston	1755	46.2	336	36.8	865	72.9	536	2075	1058	386	94.2
Denver	1681	42.1	302	32.8	1010	76.2	647	2039	969	376	93.5
Utah	1684	46.5	140	36.1	1158	76.7	555	2063	1204	398	93.3
Boston	1816	43.6	273	36.0	745	69.2	680	2138	1073	453	93.0
Minnesota	1838	42.5	122	29.8	849	74.3	754	2146	1218	426	92.9
Charlotte	1671	44.9	268	36.5	1034	74.7	480	1973	1110	443	92.9
San Antonio	1740	45.6	172	33.0	988	69.8	614	2198	1101	421	92.8
Milwaukee	1753	45.9	231	37.3	847	73.3	570	1939	1030	442	91.7
Dallas	1749	43.4	202	33.9	881	72.8	645	2123	921	352	91.6
New Jersey	1691	40.6	225	33.1	962	76.9	715	2152	923	491	91.4
Washington	1768	44.5	179	30.9	845	70.5	595	1998	1064	393	91.2
Toronto	1660	42.1	226	34.1	1011	76.0	712	2159	1036	439	91.1
LA Clippers	1711	42.7	214	32.0	883	72.1	665	1958	820	424	90.4
Detroit	1660	44.7	248	36.5	950	74.0	605	2017	1009	444	90.4
Philadelphia	1656	42.6	98	26.4	1073	72.2	729	2157	934	542	89.7
Orlando	1687	42.8	223	33.0	876	70.0	688	2133	1067	496	89.5
Miami	1616	45.3	289	35.9	928	73.5	503	2016	1019	327	89.0
Vancouver	1643	42.8	148	32.7	1009	71.7	650	2009	964	420	88.9
Golden State	1730	41.5	162	28.7	794	67.6	816	2375	1037	414	88.3
Cleveland	1562	43.9	182	34.1	1016	74.9	472	1788	1093	452	86.4
New York	1610	43.5	208	35.3	892	73.2	551	2061	963	395	86.4
Atlanta	1539	40.9	197	30.6	1040	73.1	676	2175	782	346	86.3
Chicago	1539	40.1	177	28.9	840	70.9	573	1967	1017	436	81.9

Defense (Opponent's Statistics)

Team	Field Goals FGM	Pct	3-Pt Field Goals 3FGM	Pct	Free Throws FTM	Pct	Rebounds Off	Total	Stl	Scoring Avg	Diff
Atlanta	1598	41.3	190	30.0	784	72.9	581	1950	379	83.4	+2.9
Miami	1565	41.1	211	34.8	860	73.7	619	1961	387	84.0	+5.0
San Antonio	1631	40.2	170	30.4	805	70.1	696	2102	437	84.7	+8.1
New York	1528	40.3	234	35.3	979	73.3	616	2042	425	85.4	+1.0
Utah	1595	41.3	214	32.1	936	72.1	635	1929	431	86.8	+6.5
Orlando	1708	44.3	230	34.5	697	70.7	595	2019	468	86.9	+2.6
Detroit	1585	43.6	236	34.6	941	71.5	548	1926	424	86.9	+3.5
Philadelphia	1599	42.3	241	33.7	941	73.1	619	2021	435	87.6	+2.1
Cleveland	1597	43.6	236	35.0	978	74.3	591	1996	392	88.2	-1.8
Portland	1644	41.7	220	31.8	916	72.5	616	2004	411	88.5	+6.3
Milwaukee	1600	42.7	272	33.4	1029	75.2	657	2055	399	90.0	+1.7
Golden State	1617	42.0	193	33.6	1114	72.8	656	2159	400	90.8	-2.5
Indiana	1706	43.4	206	32.5	928	75.6	626	2052	357	90.9	+3.8
Chicago	1723	45.5	208	34.0	914	73.3	551	2119	444	91.4	-9.5
Houston	1793	43.4	230	35.7	779	73.4	664	2055	441	91.9	+2.3
Minnesota	1680	43.9	213	32.6	1055	71.8	591	2154	363	92.6	+0.3
Toronto	1694	43.9	255	37.2	996	72.8	614	2007	446	92.8	-1.7
Charlotte	1739	43.4	212	33.3	959	73.4	655	2146	443	93.0	-0.1
Phoenix	1772	45.0	272	36.0	850	69.4	614	2120	410	93.3	+2.3
Washington	1705	44.6	218	35.2	1044	73.6	617	2134	402	93.4	-2.2
Dallas	1815	45.0	216	31.5	855	71.7	660	2179	361	94.0	-2.4
Boston	1725	44.3	175	31.2	1118	74.2	642	2186	461	94.9	-1.9
New Jersey	1796	45.3	223	34.1	943	72.7	624	2205	395	95.2	-3.8
Seattle	1838	45.7	264	34.5	857	72.2	652	2098	399	95.9	-1.0
LA Lakers	1759	44.1	217	33.2	1064	70.9	628	2031	408	96.0	+3.0
Vancouver	1813	46.3	229	35.1	1021	72.9	673	2129	490	97.5	-8.6
LA Clippers	1830	47.4	222	35.4	1078	74.6	640	2146	419	99.2	-8.8
Denver	1885	46.9	237	37.0	997	74.5	620	2122	396	100.1	-6.6
Sacramento	2009	44.6	219	33.6	793	71.2	750	2348	490	100.6	-0.4

Atlanta Hawks

Player	GP	Min	Field Goals		3-Pt FG		Free Throws		Rebounds		A	Stl	TO	BS	Avg
			FGM	Pct	FGA	FGM	FTM	Pct	Off	Total					
Smith	36	1314	217	40.2	139	47	191	84.9	50	151	118	36	99	11	18.7
Blaylock	48	1763	247	37.9	251	77	69	75.8	45	224	278	99	115	9	13.3
Henderson	38	1142	187	44.2	1	0	100	67.1	100	250	28	33	58	19	12.5
Mutombo	50	1829	173	51.2	0	0	195	68.4	192	610	57	16	94	147	10.8
Ellis	20	539	80	42.1	5	1	43	70.5	25	109	18	8	34	7	10.2
Long	50	1380	151	42.1	18	3	184	78.3	100	296	53	57	74	16	9.8
Corbin	47	1066	131	39.1	119	38	52	65.0	37	145	43	31	43	7	7.5
Crawford	42	784	110	43.1	33	11	57	81.4	37	90	24	10	48	13	6.9
Johnson	49	885	91	40.4	19	5	57	69.5	16	75	107	35	65	7	5.0
Gray	30	337	53	29.1	42	12	28	75.7	7	28	12	12	29	1	4.9
McLeod	34	348	62	38.0	10	1	37	82.2	12	50	14	2	23	1	4.8
Sheppard	18	185	15	38.5	7	2	8	61.5	6	22	16	3	7	0	2.2
West	49	499	22	37.3	0	0	16	35.6	49	125	13	4	17	22	1.2
Hawks	**50**	**12075**	**1539**	**40.9**	**644**	**197**	**1040**	**73.1**	**676**	**2175**	**782**	**346**	**706**	**260**	**86.3**
Opponents	**50**	**12075**	**1598**	**41.3**	**634**	**190**	**784**	**72.9**	**581**	**1950**	**895**	**379**	**630**	**243**	**83.4**

Boston Celtics

Player	GP	Min	Field Goals		3-Pt FG		Free Throws		Rebounds		A	Stl	TO	BS	Avg
			FGM	Pct	FGA	FGM	FTM	Pct	Off	Total					
Walker	42	1549	303	41.2	176	65	113	55.9	106	359	130	63	119	28	18.7
Mercer	41	1551	305	43.1	30	5	83	79.0	37	155	104	67	89	12	17.0
Pierce	48	1632	284	43.9	204	84	139	71.3	117	309	115	82	113	50	16.5
Anderson	34	1010	161	45.1	24	6	84	83.2	24	103	193	33	71	2	12.1
Potapenko	50	1394	204	49.5	1	0	91	58.7	114	332	75	35	100	36	10.0
Barros	50	1156	168	45.3	160	64	64	87.7	16	105	208	52	88	5	9.3
Battie	50	1121	147	51.9	3	0	41	67.2	96	300	53	29	45	71	6.7
McCarty	32	659	64	36.2	50	13	40	70.2	36	115	40	24	40	13	5.7
D. Jones	24	344	43	36.1	62	25	14	82.4	6	44	42	13	17	0	5.2
Minor	44	765	85	41.7	28	8	36	75.0	31	117	50	20	38	6	4.9
P. Jones	18	206	20	39.2	1	0	14	82.4	28	52	15	5	7	0	3.0
Bowen	30	494	26	28.0	26	7	11	45.8	15	52	28	21	13	9	2.3
Riley	35	337	28	51.9	0	0	22	71.0	36	99	13	9	26	26	2.2
Garnett	24	205	15	29.4	23	6	15	75.0	3	21	18	5	12	1	2.1
Celtics	**50**	**12150**	**1816**	**43.6**	**758**	**273**	**745**	**69.2**	**680**	**2138**	**1073**	**453**	**777**	**255**	**93.0**
Opponents	**50**	**12150**	**1725**	**44.3**	**561**	**175**	**1118**	**74.2**	**642**	**2186**	**1018**	**461**	**791**	**253**	**94.9**

Charlotte Hornets

Player	GP	Min	Field Goals		3-Pt FG		Free Throws		Rebounds		A	Stl	TO	BS	Avg
			FGM	Pct	FGA	FGM	FTM	Pct	Off	Total					
Jones	50	1881	260	43.7	142	48	212	78.2	50	194	186	125	93	58	15.6
Phills	43	1574	215	43.3	172	68	115	68.5	39	174	149	60	92	25	14.3
Wesley	50	1848	243	44.6	170	61	159	83.2	23	161	322	100	142	10	14.1
Coleman	37	1178	168	41.4	33	7	143	75.3	76	328	78	24	90	42	13.1
Campbell	49	1459	222	47.7	1	0	172	63.9	126	397	69	39	80	73	12.6
Brown	48	1192	176	47.2	40	15	40	67.8	36	174	57	16	38	19	8.5
Miller	38	469	78	56.5	2	1	81	79.4	35	117	22	9	32	18	6.3
Person	50	990	112	38.8	157	55	24	75.0	17	132	60	20	41	8	6.1
Recasner	44	708	82	44.6	60	24	34	87.2	20	77	91	17	58	1	5.0
Davis	46	557	81	40.5	12	2	45	76.3	40	84	58	30	54	7	4.5
Shackleford	32	367	44	48.9	0	0	19	65.5	41	129	13	5	27	13	3.3
Beck	24	180	18	46.2	1	1	8	53.3	6	28	20	9	13	2	1.9
Hornets	**50**	**12150**	**1671**	**44.9**	**735**	**268**	**1034**	**74.7**	**480**	**1973**	**1110**	**443**	**760**	**247**	**92.9**
Opponents	**50**	**12150**	**1739**	**43.4**	**637**	**212**	**959**	**73.4**	**655**	**2146**	**1092**	**443**	**728**	**232**	**93.0**

Chicago Bulls

Player	GP	Min	Field Goals		3-Pt FG		Free Throws		Rebounds		A	Stl	TO	BS	Avg
			FGM	Pct	FGA	FGM	FTM	Pct	Off	Total					
Kukoc	44	1654	315	42.0	137	39	159	74.0	65	310	235	49	121	11	18.8
Harper	35	1107	147	37.7	85	27	71	70.3	49	180	115	60	65	35	11.2
Barry	37	1181	141	39.6	172	52	78	77.2	39	144	116	42	72	11	11.1
Simpkins	50	1448	150	46.3	1	0	156	64.5	110	339	65	36	72	13	9.1
Bryant	45	1204	168	48.3	1	0	71	64.5	92	232	48	34	68	16	9.0
Brown	39	1139	132	41.4	10	0	78	75.7	27	132	149	68	80	8	8.8
David	50	902	109	44.9	1	0	90	81.1	70	173	40	23	48	17	6.2
LaRue	43	732	78	35.9	89	30	17	100.0	9	56	63	33	34	3	4.7
Carr	42	624	71	32.9	30	5	24	75.0	8	49	66	21	46	7	4.1
Lang	21	386	32	32.3	0	0	16	69.6	33	93	13	5	17	12	3.8
Benjamin	31	320	44	37.6	14	3	27	67.5	15	40	10	11	21	8	3.8
Wennington	38	451	62	34.8	1	1	18	81.8	20	79	18	13	17	12	3.8
Jones	29	476	39	31.7	61	19	11	50.0	9	42	41	18	29	5	3.7
Booth	39	432	49	32.5	10	1	21	50.0	25	93	38	22	39	11	3.1
Bulls	**50**	**12075**	**1539**	**40.1**	**612**	**177**	**840**	**70.9**	**573**	**1967**	**1017**	**436**	**730**	**169**	**81.9**
Opponents	**50**	**12075**	**1723**	**45.5**	**612**	**208**	**914**	**73.3**	**551**	**2119**	**1099**	**444**	**753**	**285**	**91.4**

Cleveland Cavaliers

Player	GP	Min	Field Goals		3-Pt FG		Free Throws		Rebounds		A	Stl	TO	BS	Avg
			FGM	Pct	FGA	FGM	FTM	Pct	Off	Total					
Kemp	42	1475	277	48.2	2	1	307	78.9	131	388	101	48	127	45	20.5
Ilgauskas	5	171	29	50.9	0	0	18	60.0	17	44	4	4	9	7	15.2
Person	45	1342	198	45.3	200	75	32	60.4	19	142	80	37	41	16	11.2
Anderson	38	978	125	39.8	69	21	138	83.6	20	109	145	48	82	4	10.8
Knight	39	1186	134	42.5	5	0	105	74.5	16	131	302	70	105	7	9.6
Henderson	50	1517	189	41.7	12	2	74	81.3	45	197	113	58	97	24	9.1
DeClercq	47	1102	138	50.0	0	0	95	67.4	104	255	31	50	54	29	7.9
Ferry	50	1058	141	47.6	97	38	29	87.9	16	102	53	23	39	10	7.0
Newman	50	949	106	42.2	61	23	68	81.0	15	75	41	28	41	12	6.1
Butler	31	418	67	48.2	29	11	23	71.9	13	44	22	15	29	4	5.4
Sura	50	841	70	33.3	45	9	65	63.1	21	102	152	46	67	14	4.3
Boykins	22	221	30	38.0	18	3	2	66.7	7	17	33	6	20	0	3.0
Blount	34	530	36	36.0	1	0	28	51.9	58	151	12	19	21	16	2.9
Stack	18	199	14	37.8	0	0	19	95.0	19	34	5	2	9	11	2.6
Cavs	**50**	**12050**	**1562**	**43.9**	**534**	**182**	**1016**	**74.9**	**472**	**1788**	**1093**	**452**	**738**	**203**	**86.4**
Opponents	**50**	**12050**	**1597**	**43.6**	**675**	**236**	**978**	**74.3**	**591**	**1996**	**1056**	**392**	**790**	**282**	**88.2**

Dallas Mavericks

Player	GP	Min	Field Goals		3-Pt FG		Free Throws		Rebounds		A	Stl	TO	BS	Avg
			FGM	Pct	FGA	FGM	FTM	Pct	Off	Total					
Finley	50	2051	389	44.4	136	45	186	82.3	69	263	218	66	107	15	20.2
Trent	45	1362	287	47.7	5	0	145	61.7	127	351	77	29	66	23	16.0
Ceballos	13	352	59	42.1	28	11	34	69.4	23	85	12	7	28	5	12.5
Davis	50	1378	174	43.8	144	65	44	88.0	3	86	89	21	57	3	9.1
Pack	25	468	75	43.1	4	0	72	81.8	9	36	81	20	49	1	8.9
Bradley	49	1294	167	48.0	4	0	86	74.8	130	392	40	35	56	159	8.6
Nowitzki	47	958	136	40.5	68	14	99	77.3	41	162	47	29	73	27	8.2
Nash	40	1269	114	36.3	131	49	38	82.6	32	114	219	37	83	2	7.9
Strickland	33	567	89	40.3	59	18	53	81.5	12	83	64	40	36	2	7.5
Walker	39	568	88	46.3	1	0	53	54.1	46	143	6	9	37	16	5.9
Green	50	924	108	42.2	8	0	30	57.7	82	228	25	28	19	8	4.9
Anstey	41	470	50	36.0	7	0	34	70.8	35	97	27	18	26	13	3.3
Williams	25	403	11	33.3	0	0	7	70.0	36	83	15	13	18	13	1.2
Mavericks	**50**	**12075**	**1749**	**43.4**	**595**	**202**	**881**	**72.8**	**645**	**2123**	**921**	**352**	**651**	**292**	**91.6**
Opponents	**50**	**12075**	**1815**	**45.0**	**686**	**216**	**855**	**71.7**	**660**	**2179**	**1073**	**361**	**663**	**244**	**94.0**

Denver Nuggets

Player	GP	Min	Field Goals		3-Pt FG		Free Throws		Rebounds		A	Stl	TO	BS	Avg
			FGM	Pct	FGA	FGM	FTM	Pct	Off	Total					
McDyess	50	1937	415	47.1	9	1	230	68.0	168	537	82	73	138	115	21.2
Van Exel	50	1802	306	39.8	234	72	142	81.1	14	113	368	40	121	3	16.5
Billups	45	1488	191	38.6	235	85	157	91.3	24	96	173	58	98	14	13.9
LaFrentz	12	387	59	45.7	31	12	36	75.0	33	91	8	9	9	17	13.8
Fortson	50	1417	191	49.5	3	0	168	72.7	210	581	32	31	77	22	11.0
E. Williams	38	780	80	36.5	26	6	111	79.9	34	81	37	27	49	8	7.3
Alexander	36	778	97	37.3	105	30	37	84.1	7	74	119	35	69	5	7.3
Stith	46	1194	114	39.3	106	31	61	85.9	30	107	82	28	45	15	7.0
Taylor	36	724	82	41.4	68	26	17	73.9	30	101	24	28	34	17	5.8
Washington	38	761	73	39.7	97	37	22	68.8	35	89	30	25	34	18	5.4
Clark	28	409	36	45.0	1	0	21	56.8	36	96	10	10	21	31	3.3
Herrera	28	307	30	39.5	1	0	5	45.5	25	62	4	12	16	7	2.3
Nuggets	**50**	**12025**	**1681**	**42.1**	**922**	**302**	**1010**	**76.2**	**647**	**2039**	**969**	**376**	**713**	**275**	**93.5**
Opponents	**50**	**12025**	**1885**	**46.9**	**640**	**237**	**997**	**74.5**	**620**	**2122**	**1175**	**396**	**667**	**274**	**100.1**

Detroit Pistons

Player	GP	Min	Field Goals		3-Pt FG		Free Throws		Rebounds		A	Stl	TO	BS	Avg
			FGM	Pct	FGA	FGM	FTM	Pct	Off	Total					
Hill	50	1852	384	47.9	14	0	285	75.2	65	355	300	80	184	27	21.1
Stackhouse	42	1188	181	37.1	126	35	210	85.0	26	107	118	34	121	19	14.5
Hunter	49	1755	228	43.5	153	59	67	75.3	26	168	193	86	92	8	11.9
Dumars	38	1116	144	41.1	221	89	51	83.6	12	68	134	23	53	2	11.3
Dele	49	1177	216	50.1	1	0	81	68.6	92	272	71	38	111	40	10.5
Laettner	16	337	38	35.8	3	1	44	77.2	21	54	24	15	19	12	7.6
Williams	50	1154	124	50.0	0	0	107	67.3	158	349	23	63	41	7	7.1
Buechler	50	1056	100	41.7	148	61	13	72.2	29	133	57	37	21	13	5.5
Reid	47	935	97	55.7	0	0	48	60.8	66	170	33	27	36	43	5.1
Vaught	37	481	59	38.1	1	0	9	64.3	36	146	11	15	17	6	3.4
O'Bannon	18	165	24	42.9	1	0	8	100.0	18	34	12	2	8	3	3.1
Reeves	11	112	8	38.1	3	1	6	57.1	3	7	11	4	7	0	2.3
Montross	46	577	42	52.5	1	0	11	34.4	45	139	14	12	16	27	2.1
Pistons	**50**	**12050**	**1660**	**44.7**	**679**	**248**	**950**	**74.0**	**605**	**2017**	**1009**	**444**	**738**	**208**	**90.4**
Opponents	**50**	**12050**	**1585**	**43.6**	**682**	**236**	**941**	**71.5**	**548**	**1926**	**1043**	**424**	**750**	**225**	**86.9**

Golden State Warriors

Player	GP	Min	Field Goals		3-Pt FG		Free Throws		Rebounds		A	Stl	TO	BS	Avg
			FGM	Pct	FGA	FGM	FTM	Pct	Off	Total					
Starks	50	1686	269	37.0	269	78	74	74.0	33	163	235	69	83	5	13.8
Marshall	48	1250	208	42.1	26	72	88	72.7	115	342	66	47	80	37	11.0
Mills	47	1395	186	41.1	115	32	79	82.3	49	237	103	39	58	14	10.3
Jamison	47	1058	178	45.2	10	3	90	58.8	131	301	34	38	68	16	9.6
Coles	48	1272	183	44.2	25	6	83	82.2	21	117	222	45	82	11	9.5
Cummings	50	1011	186	43.9	1	1	81	71.1	95	255	58	46	58	10	9.1
Dampier	50	1414	161	38.9	0	0	120	58.8	164	382	54	26	92	58	8.8
Caffey	35	876	123	44.4	1	0	62	63.3	79	205	18	24	75	9	8.8
Delk	36	630	92	36.4	66	16	46	64.8	11	54	95	16	45	6	6.8
Bogues	36	714	76	49.4	6	0	31	86.1	16	73	134	43	47	1	5.1
Foyle	44	614	52	43.0	0	0	25	49.0	79	194	18	15	31	43	2.9
Spencer	26	159	15	45.5	0	0	12	46.2	18	46	0	5	9	10	1.6
Warriors	**50**	**12125**	**1730**	**41.5**	**565**	**162**	**794**	**67.6**	**816**	**2375**	**1037**	**414**	**729**	**221**	**88.3**
Opponents	**50**	**12125**	**1617**	**42.0**	**575**	**193**	**1114**	**72.8**	**656**	**2159**	**1023**	**400**	**705**	**304**	**90.8**

Houston Rockets

Player	GP	Min	Field Goals		3-Pt FG		Free Throws		Rebounds		A	Stl	TO	BS	Avg
			FGM	Pct	FGA	FGM	FTM	Pct	Off	Total					
Olajuwon	50	1784	373	51.4	13	4	195	71.7	106	477	88	82	139	123	18.9
Barkley	42	1526	240	47.8	25	4	192	71.9	167	516	192	43	100	13	16.1
Pippen	50	2011	261	43.2	212	72	132	72.1	63	323	293	98	159	37	14.5
Dickerson	50	1558	215	46.5	164	71	46	63.9	26	83	95	27	66	11	10.9
Mack	44	1083	167	43.5	219	87	51	87.9	14	95	55	35	33	4	10.7
Mobley	49	1456	172	42.5	148	53	90	81.8	22	111	121	44	79	23	9.9
Harrington	41	903	156	51.3	0	0	88	72.1	72	246	15	6	61	25	9.8
Price	40	806	100	48.3	112	46	46	75.4	18	78	113	33	65	1	7.3
Drew	34	441	47	36.4	49	16	8	100.0	3	32	52	12	31	4	3.5
Bullard	41	413	43	37.7	62	24	7	70.0	9	42	18	13	14	4	2.9
Carr	18	152	21	40.4	1	0	5	71.4	9	31	9	1	9	10	2.6
Miller	29	249	28	46.7	1	0	14	63.6	26	67	7	7	9	5	2.4
Maloney	15	186	5	17.9	15	1	10	90.9	2	10	21	4	14	0	1.4
Rockets	**50**	**12075**	**1755**	**46.2**	**914**	**336**	**865**	**72.9**	**536**	**2075**	**1058**	**386**	**770**	**260**	**94.2**
Opponents	**50**	**12075**	**1793**	**43.4**	**645**	**230**	**779**	**73.4**	**664**	**2055**	**1034**	**441**	**631**	**245**	**91.9**

Indiana Pacers

Player	GP	Min	Field Goals		3-Pt FG		Free Throws		Rebounds		A	Stl	TO	BS	Avg
			FGM	Pct	FGA	FGM	FTM	Pct	Off	Total					
Miller	50	1787	294	43.8	275	106	226	91.5	25	135	112	37	76	9	18.4
Smits	49	1271	310	49.0	2	0	108	81.8	73	275	52	18	75	52	14.9
Rose	49	1238	200	40.3	65	17	125	79.1	34	154	93	50	72	15	11.1
Mullin	50	1179	177	47.7	157	73	80	87.0	25	160	81	47	60	13	10.1
A. Davis	49	1271	164	47.1	0	0	135	70.3	116	344	33	22	50	42	9.4
D. Davis	50	1374	161	53.3	0	0	76	61.8	155	416	22	20	43	57	8.0
Jackson	49	1382	138	41.9	103	32	65	82.3	33	184	386	42	99	3	7.6
Best	49	1043	127	41.6	59	22	70	84.3	19	80	169	42	62	4	7.1
Perkins	48	789	80	40.0	90	35	43	71.7	36	138	25	15	22	14	5.0
McKey	13	244	23	44.2	1	0	14	82.4	18	41	13	12	12	4	4.6
Croshere	27	249	32	42.7	29	8	20	87.0	16	45	10	7	23	8	3.4
Harrington	21	160	18	32.1	5	0	9	60.0	20	39	5	4	11	2	2.1
Pacers	**50**	**12100**	**1731**	**44.8**	**799**	**294**	**977**	**79.6**	**574**	**2026**	**1005**	**316**	**609**	**223**	**94.7**
Opponents	**50**	**12100**	**1706**	**43.4**	**634**	**206**	**928**	**75.6**	**626**	**2052**	**955**	**357**	**623**	**238**	**90.9**

Los Angeles Clippers

Player	GP	Min	Field Goals		3-Pt FG		Free Throws		Rebounds		A	Stl	TO	BS	Avg
			FGM	Pct	FGA	FGM	FTM	Pct	Off	Total					
Taylor	46	1505	311	46.1	6	1	150	72.8	100	242	67	16	120	29	16.8
Murray	50	1317	226	39.1	103	34	126	80.3	59	195	61	58	99	20	12.2
Piatkowski	49	1242	180	43.2	165	65	88	86.3	39	140	53	44	53	6	10.5
Nesby	50	1288	182	44.9	96	35	104	78.2	57	175	82	77	53	20	10.1
Olowokandi	45	1279	172	43.1	0	0	57	48.3	120	357	25	27	85	55	8.9
Douglas	30	842	96	43.8	11	0	55	63.2	16	58	124	27	61	3	8.2
Martin	37	941	102	36.7	106	31	61	80.3	5	48	144	43	67	4	8.0
Rogers	47	968	131	44.1	63	18	68	67.3	65	179	77	47	66	22	7.4
Hudson	25	524	60	40.0	47	15	34	89.5	15	55	92	11	38	2	6.8
Wright	48	1135	119	45.8	1	0	81	69.2	142	361	33	26	48	36	6.6
Skinner	21	258	33	46.5	0	0	20	60.6	20	53	1	10	19	13	4.1
Smith	23	317	35	36.1	33	7	21	43.8	7	24	13	17	20	14	3.7
Clippers	**50**	**12125**	**1711**	**42.7**	**668**	**214**	**883**	**72.1**	**665**	**1958**	**820**	**424**	**760**	**236**	**90.4**
Opponents	**50**	**12125**	**1830**	**47.4**	**627**	**222**	**1078**	**74.6**	**640**	**2146**	**1101**	**419**	**764**	**289**	**99.2**

Los Angeles Lakers

Player	GP	Min	Field Goals		3-Pt FG		Free Throws		Rebounds		A	Stl	TO	BS	Avg
			FGM	Pct	FGA	FGM	FTM	Pct	Off	Total					
O'Neal	49	1705	510	57.6	1	0	269	54.0	187	525	114	36	122	82	26.3
Bryant	50	1896	362	46.5	101	27	245	83.9	53	264	190	72	157	50	19.9
Rice	27	985	171	43.2	135	53	77	85.6	9	99	71	17	45	6	17.5
Reid	41	1029	132	47.7	1	0	105	76.6	45	212	48	37	51	10	9.0
Fox	44	944	148	44.8	95	32	66	74.2	26	89	89	28	56	10	9.0
Harper	45	1120	120	41.2	117	43	26	81.3	13	67	187	44	52	4	6.9
Fisher	50	1131	99	37.6	97	38	60	75.9	21	91	197	61	77	1	5.9
Lue	15	188	28	43.1	16	7	12	57.1	2	6	25	5	11	0	5.0
Horry	38	744	67	45.9	45	20	34	73.9	56	152	56	36	49	39	4.9
Knight	37	525	67	51.5	1	0	22	75.9	34	128	31	21	35	27	4.2
Rooks	36	315	32	40.5	2	0	34	70.8	33	72	9	2	21	9	2.7
Patterson	24	144	21	41.2	6	1	22	71.0	17	30	2	5	12	3	2.7
Rodman	23	657	16	34.8	2	0	17	43.6	62	258	30	10	31	12	2.1
Lakers	50	12050	1841	46.8	685	241	1027	68.3	619	2101	1095	389	741	287	99.0
Opponents	50	12050	1759	44.1	653	217	1064	70.9	628	2031	1062	408	685	196	96.0

Miami Heat

Player	GP	Min	Field Goals		3-Pt FG		Free Throws		Rebounds		A	Stl	TO	BS	Avg
			FGM	Pct	FGA	FGM	FTM	Pct	Off	Total					
Mourning	46	1753	324	51.1	2	0	276	65.2	166	507	74	34	139	180	20.1
Hardaway	48	1772	301	40.0	311	112	121	81.2	15	152	352	57	131	6	17.4
Mashburn	24	855	134	45.1	30	13	75	72.1	24	146	75	20	60	3	14.8
Brown	50	1311	229	48.0	0	0	113	77.4	115	346	66	46	69	48	11.4
Porter	50	1365	172	46.5	141	58	123	83.1	13	140	146	48	74	11	10.5
Weatherspoon	49	1040	141	53.4	0	0	115	80.4	72	243	34	28	61	17	8.1
Majerle	50	1624	118	39.6	203	68	33	71.7	21	208	150	38	55	7	7.0
Lenard	12	190	31	39.2	35	12	8	72.7	4	16	10	3	7	1	6.8
Strickland	32	357	50	49.5	1	0	19	73.1	26	78	9	7	13	8	3.7
Edwards	24	283	32	44.4	10	4	9	69.2	7	33	30	17	21	5	3.2
Walters	33	506	35	36.8	38	12	19	82.6	10	50	58	10	32	3	3.1
Causwell	19	137	20	57.1	0	0	4	33.3	14	35	2	0	18	11	2.3
Askins	33	415	20	32.3	29	8	5	62.5	10	44	10	17	13	3	1.6
Heat	50	12025	1616	45.3	804	289	928	73.5	503	2016	1019	327	707	304	89.0
Opponents	50	12025	1565	41.1	606	211	860	73.7	619	1961	853	387	643	188	84.0

Milwaukee Bucks

Player	GP	Min	Field Goals		3-Pt FG		Free Throws		Rebounds		A	Stl	TO	BS	Avg
			FGM	Pct	FGA	FGM	FTM	Pct	Off	Total					
Robinson	47	1579	347	45.9	79	31	140	87.0	73	276	100	46	106	41	18.4
R. Allen	50	1719	303	45.0	208	74	176	90.3	57	212	178	53	122	7	17.1
Cassell	8	199	39	41.9	10	2	47	94.0	5	15	36	9	20	0	15.9
D. Curry	42	864	163	48.5	145	69	28	82.4	18	85	48	36	45	3	10.1
Gilliam	34	668	101	45.3	1	0	79	78.2	33	126	19	22	36	12	8.3
Thomas	50	812	132	47.3	68	21	73	65.2	49	126	46	26	46	12	7.2
Workman	29	815	73	42.9	47	17	37	78.7	14	102	172	32	63	1	6.9
Del Negro	48	1093	114	42.2	30	13	40	80.0	14	102	174	33	55	3	5.9
Gatling	48	775	117	44.2	8	1	37	39.8	52	179	32	32	62	10	5.7
Traylor	49	786	108	53.7	1	0	43	53.8	80	182	38	44	42	44	5.3
Johnson	50	1027	96	50.8	0	0	64	61.0	120	320	19	29	47	57	5.1
M. Curry	50	1146	90	43.7	15	1	63	79.7	19	108	78	42	37	7	4.9
Bucks	50	12050	1753	45.9	619	231	847	73.3	570	1939	1030	442	693	202	91.7
Opponents	50	12050	1600	42.7	814	272	1029	75.2	657	2055	1018	399	786	194	90.0

Minnesota Timberwolves

Player	GP	Min	Field Goals		3-Pt FG		Free Throws		Rebounds		A	Stl	TO	BS	Avg
			FGM	Pct	FGA	FGM	FTM	Pct	Off	Total					
Garnett	47	1780	414	46.0	14	4	145	70.4	166	489	202	78	135	83	20.8
Brandon	36	1217	212	41.8	47	12	65	83.3	27	134	309	63	74	10	13.9
Smith	43	1418	223	42.7	3	0	142	75.5	154	354	68	32	66	66	13.7
Mitchell	50	1344	213	40.8	38	9	126	76.4	55	182	98	35	34	16	11.2
Peeler	28	810	103	37.9	114	34	30	73.2	30	84	78	35	38	6	9.6
Sealy	31	731	95	41.1	23	6	55	90.2	23	92	36	30	33	5	8.1
Jackson	50	941	141	40.5	27	10	61	77.2	43	135	167	39	75	3	7.1
Scott	36	738	87	40.8	97	37	23	74.2	8	58	40	15	19	3	6.5
Robinson	31	506	67	36.2	74	21	28	68.3	18	62	56	22	44	8	5.9
Garrett	49	1054	116	50.2	0	0	38	74.5	99	257	28	30	29	45	5.5
Hammonds	49	716	82	45.8	0	0	48	64.0	54	136	20	8	32	7	4.3
Patterson	35	284	43	44.3	5	0	28	77.8	30	65	15	19	22	7	3.3
Curley	35	372	29	40.3	5	1	19	86.4	20	51	14	17	10	9	2.2
Evans	16	145	13	29.5	13	4	4	100.0	6	19	15	5	2	3	2.1
Jordan	27	296	15	27.8	0	0	21	55.3	27	59	41	12	14	5	1.9
T'wolves	**50**	**12025**	**1838**	**42.5**	**410**	**122**	**849**	**74.3**	**754**	**2146**	**1218**	**426**	**629**	**272**	**92.9**
Opponents	**50**	**12025**	**1680**	**43.9**	**654**	**213**	**1055**	**71.8**	**591**	**2154**	**1114**	**363**	**795**	**262**	**92.6**

New Jersey Nets

Player	GP	Min	Field Goals		3-Pt FG		Free Throws		Rebounds		A	Stl	TO	BS	Avg
			FGM	Pct	FGA	FGM	FTM	Pct	Off	Total					
Van Horn	42	1576	322	42.8	53	16	256	85.9	114	358	65	43	133	53	21.8
Marbury	49	1895	378	42.8	197	66	222	79.9	37	142	437	59	164	8	21.3
Kittles	46	1570	227	37.0	158	50	88	77.2	52	191	116	79	66	26	12.9
Gill	50	1606	236	39.8	17	2	114	68.3	61	244	123	134	71	26	11.8
Williams	30	1020	97	44.5	2	0	48	56.5	147	360	33	24	46	60	8.1
Murdock	15	401	45	39.5	22	8	21	80.8	3	35	66	22	29	2	7.9
Burrell	32	706	75	36.1	72	28	34	81.0	32	119	45	40	23	11	6.6
Feick	28	852	67	50.0	0	0	43	71.7	112	288	24	25	34	18	6.3
Hendrickson	22	399	39	44.3	1	0	42	84.0	27	68	13	12	15	1	5.5
Harris	36	602	73	40.3	50	11	36	75.0	21	67	31	18	18	7	5.4
Carr	39	445	76	37.1	75	28	27	67.5	23	71	23	8	28	2	5.3
Perry	35	290	37	37.9	24	10	10	71.4	7	34	47	20	34	0	2.8
McIlvaine	22	269	22	43.1	0	0	4	66.7	31	54	2	9	13	32	2.2
Nets	**50**	**12050**	**1691**	**40.6**	**679**	**225**	**962**	**76.9**	**715**	**2152**	**923**	**491**	**710**	**273**	**91.4**
Opponents	**50**	**12050**	**1796**	**45.3**	**654**	**223**	**943**	**72.7**	**624**	**2205**	**968**	**395**	**780**	**326**	**95.2**

New York Knicks

Player	GP	Min	Field Goals		3-Pt FG		Free Throws		Rebounds		A	Stl	TO	BS	Avg
			FGM	Pct	FGA	FGM	FTM	Pct	Off	Total					
Ewing	38	1300	247	43.5	2	0	163	70.6	74	377	43	30	99	100	17.3
Sprewell	37	1233	215	41.5	77	21	155	81.2	41	156	91	46	79	2	16.4
Houston	50	1815	294	41.8	140	57	168	86.2	20	152	137	35	130	9	16.3
Johnson	49	1639	210	45.9	92	33	134	81.7	91	284	119	34	89	10	12.0
Thomas	50	1182	170	46.2	1	0	66	61.1	82	286	55	45	73	17	8.1
Ward	50	1556	135	40.4	149	53	55	70.5	23	172	271	103	131	8	7.6
Camby	46	945	136	52.1	0	0	57	55.3	102	253	12	29	39	74	7.2
Childs	48	1297	114	42.7	94	36	64	82.1	18	133	193	44	85	1	6.8
Dudley	46	685	48	44.0	0	0	19	47.5	79	193	7	13	24	38	2.5
Davis	8	21	7	41.2	0	0	3	50.0	9	11	3	0	1	0	2.1
Williams	6	34	4	50.0	0	0	2	100.0	3	6	0	0	2	2	1.7
Brunson	17	95	6	28.6	5	0	5	27.8	3	10	19	9	12	0	1.0
Wingate	20	92	7	43.8	0	0	0	—	3	8	5	4	6	0	0.7
Knicks	**50**	**12100**	**1610**	**43.5**	**589**	**208**	**892**	**73.2**	**551**	**2061**	**963**	**395**	**775**	**262**	**86.4**
Opponents	**50**	**12100**	**1528**	**40.3**	**662**	**234**	**979**	**73.3**	**616**	**2042**	**923**	**425**	**726**	**215**	**85.4**

Orlando Magic

Player	GP	Min	Field Goals		3-Pt FG		Free Throws		Rebounds		A	Stl	TO	BS	Avg
			FGM	Pct	FGA	FGM	FTM	Pct	Off	Total					
Hardaway	50	1944	301	42.0	140	40	149	70.6	74	284	266	111	150	23	15.8
Anderson	47	1581	253	39.5	277	96	99	61.1	51	277	91	64	83	15	14.9
D. Armstrong	50	1502	230	44.1	189	69	161	90.4	53	180	335	108	158	4	13.8
Austin	49	1259	185	40.8	7	2	105	66.9	83	237	89	47	114	35	9.7
Grant	50	1660	198	43.4	2	0	47	67.1	117	351	90	46	44	60	8.9
Harpring	50	1114	148	46.3	25	10	102	71.3	88	214	45	30	73	6	8.2
Outlaw	31	851	84	54.5	3	0	35	43.2	54	167	56	40	58	43	6.5
Doleac	49	780	125	46.8	0	0	54	67.5	66	148	20	19	26	17	6.2
Strong	44	695	76	42.2	2	0	71	71.7	66	161	17	15	37	7	5.1
D. Wilkins	27	252	50	37.9	19	5	29	69.0	30	71	16	4	23	1	5.0
B. Armstrong	32	358	40	45.5	15	7	18	85.7	2	39	61	12	25	0	3.3
Magic	**50**	**12050**	**1687**	**42.8**	**675**	**223**	**876**	**70.0**	**688**	**2133**	**1067**	**496**	**798**	**213**	**89.5**
Opponents	**50**	**12050**	**1708**	**44.3**	**667**	**230**	**697**	**70.7**	**595**	**2019**	**1039**	**468**	**828**	**239**	**86.9**

Philadelphia 76ers

Player	GP	Min	Field Goals		3-Pt FG		Free Throws		Rebounds		A	Stl	TO	BS	Avg
			FGM	Pct	FGA	FGM	FTM	Pct	Off	Total					
Iverson	48	1990	435	41.2	199	58	356	75.1	66	236	223	110	167	7	26.8
Geiger	50	1540	266	47.9	5	1	141	79.7	137	362	58	39	101	40	13.5
Ratliff	50	1627	197	47.0	0	0	166	72.5	139	407	30	45	92	149	11.2
Hughes	50	988	170	41.1	52	8	107	70.9	83	189	77	44	68	14	9.1
Snow	48	1716	149	42.8	21	5	110	73.3	25	162	301	100	111	1	8.6
Hill	38	1104	122	45.5	0	0	81	54.0	115	287	35	34	59	16	8.6
Lynch	43	1315	147	42.1	23	9	53	63.1	110	279	76	85	79	22	8.3
McKie	50	959	95	40.1	31	6	44	71.0	27	140	100	63	57	3	4.8
Overton	24	244	36	42.9	7	2	18	90.0	7	21	23	5	20	1	3.8
Grant	47	798	62	36.9	6	1	21	72.4	36	110	23	20	21	16	3.1
76ers	**50**	**12150**	**1656**	**42.6**	**371**	**98**	**1073**	**72.2**	**729**	**2157**	**934**	**542**	**781**	**271**	**89.7**
Opponents	**50**	**12150**	**1599**	**42.3**	**716**	**241**	**941**	**73.1**	**619**	**2021**	**999**	**435**	**856**	**263**	**87.6**

Phoenix Suns

Player	GP	Min	Field Goals		3-Pt FG		Free Throws		Rebounds		A	Stl	TO	BS	Avg
			FGM	Pct	FGA	FGM	FTM	Pct	Off	Total					
Gugliotta	43	1563	277	48.3	7	2	173	79.4	131	381	121	59	88	21	17.0
Kidd	50	2060	310	44.4	123	45	181	75.7	87	339	539	114	150	19	16.9
Robinson	50	1740	299	47.5	139	58	163	69.7	69	227	128	75	88	59	16.4
Chapman	38	1183	165	35.9	151	53	76	83.5	12	104	109	34	54	9	12.1
Manning	50	1184	187	48.4	9	1	78	69.6	62	219	113	36	69	38	9.1
McCloud	48	1245	142	43.8	166	69	75	82.6	34	162	79	45	49	14	8.9
Longley	39	933	140	48.3	0	0	59	77.6	59	221	45	23	53	21	8.7
Garrity	39	538	85	50.0	18	7	40	71.4	26	75	18	8	20	3	5.6
Morris	44	535	64	43.0	56	16	40	87.0	54	121	23	16	21	11	4.2
Bailey	27	249	34	39.5	5	1	9	69.2	24	54	13	9	11	2	2.9
Brown	33	236	33	37.1	10	3	11	78.6	5	22	31	5	22	1	2.4
Kleine	31	374	30	40.5	2	0	8	66.7	27	67	12	8	10	1	2.2
Suns	**50**	**12050**	**1797**	**44.9**	**702**	**261**	**924**	**76.0**	**598**	**2016**	**1249**	**444**	**653**	**200**	**95.6**
Opponents	**50**	**12050**	**1772**	**45.0**	**755**	**272**	**850**	**69.4**	**614**	**2120**	**1064**	**410**	**779**	**205**	**93.3**

Portland Trail Blazers

Player	GP	Min	FGM	Pct	FGA	FGM	FTM	Pct	Off	Total	A	Stl	TO	BS	Avg
			Field Goals		3-Pt FG		Free Throws		Rebounds						
Rider	47	1385	249	41.2	111	42	111	75.5	59	196	104	25	95	9	13.9
Wallace	49	1414	242	50.8	31	13	131	73.2	57	241	60	48	80	54	12.8
Stoudamire	50	1673	249	39.6	142	44	89	73.0	41	167	312	49	110	4	12.6
Sabonis	50	1349	232	48.5	24	7	135	77.1	88	393	119	34	85	63	12.1
B. Grant	48	1525	183	47.9	0	0	184	81.4	173	470	67	21	96	34	11.5
Williams	48	1044	147	42.4	144	63	89	83.2	36	143	80	37	63	28	9.3
Jackson	49	1175	152	41.1	90	25	85	84.2	36	159	128	43	82	6	8.4
Anthony	50	806	104	41.4	125	49	62	69.7	14	63	100	66	55	3	6.4
Augmon	48	874	78	44.8	2	0	52	68.4	47	125	58	57	30	18	4.3
Cato	43	546	58	45.0	1	1	34	50.7	49	150	19	23	27	56	3.5
O'Neal	35	310	36	43.4	1	0	18	51.4	42	97	13	4	14	14	2.6
Trail Blazers	50	12175	1747	44.2	675	246	1002	74.3	646	2216	1073	411	744	290	94.8
Opponents	50	12175	1644	41.7	691	220	916	72.5	616	2004	962	411	755	244	88.5

Sacramento Kings

Player	GP	Min	FGM	Pct	FGA	FGM	FTM	Pct	Off	Total	A	Stl	TO	BS	Avg
			Field Goals		3-Pt FG		Free Throws		Rebounds						
Webber	42	1719	378	48.6	34	4	79	45.4	149	545	173	60	148	89	20.0
Divac	50	1761	262	47.0	43	11	179	70.2	140	501	215	44	131	51	14.3
Williamson	50	1374	269	48.5	5	1	120	63.8	85	206	66	30	75	8	13.2
Williams	50	1805	231	37.4	323	100	79	75.2	14	153	299	95	143	1	12.8
Maxwell	46	1007	164	39.0	231	80	84	73.7	13	85	76	30	67	3	10.7
Abdul-Wahad	49	1205	177	43.5	21	6	94	69.1	72	186	50	50	70	16	9.3
Funderburke	47	936	167	55.9	5	1	85	70.8	101	222	30	22	52	23	8.9
Stojakovic	48	1025	141	37.8	178	57	63	85.1	43	143	72	41	53	7	8.4
Pollard	16	259	33	54.1	0	0	16	69.6	38	82	4	8	5	18	5.1
Barry	43	736	59	42.8	79	24	71	84.5	25	96	112	53	47	5	5.0
Hawkins	24	203	14	35.0	19	5	3	100.0	10	25	27	3	13	1	1.5
Kings	50	12200	1918	44.5	943	290	883	68.3	706	2279	1129	444	824	232	100.2
Opponents	50	12200	2009	44.6	652	219	793	71.2	750	2348	1165	490	759	221	100.6

San Antonio Spurs

Player	GP	Min	FGM	Pct	FGA	FGM	FTM	Pct	Off	Total	A	Stl	TO	BS	Avg
			Field Goals		3-Pt FG		Free Throws		Rebounds						
Duncan	50	1963	418	49.5	7	1	247	69.0	159	571	121	45	146	126	21.7
Robinson	49	1554	268	50.9	1	0	239	65.8	148	492	103	69	108	119	15.8
Elliott	50	1509	208	41.0	119	39	106	75.7	35	213	117	26	71	17	11.2
Johnson	50	1672	218	47.3	12	1	50	56.8	22	118	369	51	112	11	9.7
Elie	47	1291	156	47.1	107	40	103	86.6	36	137	89	46	61	12	9.7
Jackson	47	861	108	38.0	147	53	32	82.1	21	99	49	41	37	9	6.4
Rose	47	608	93	46.3	1	0	98	67.1	90	182	29	40	56	22	6.0
Daniels	47	614	83	45.4	17	5	49	75.4	13	54	106	30	44	6	4.7
Kerr	44	734	68	39.1	80	25	31	88.6	6	44	49	23	22	3	4.4
Kersey	45	699	68	34.0	14	3	6	42.9	42	130	41	37	30	14	3.2
Perdue	37	445	38	63.3	0	0	14	53.8	33	138	18	9	22	10	2.4
Spurs	50	12075	1740	45.6	521	172	988	69.8	614	2198	1101	421	717	351	92.8
Opponents	50	12075	1631	40.2	559	170	805	70.1	696	2102	941	437	695	243	84.7

Seattle SuperSonics

Player	GP	Min	Field Goals		3-Pt FG		Free Throws		Rebounds		A	Stl	TO	BS	Avg
			FGM	Pct	FGA	FGM	FTM	Pct	Off	Total					
Payton	50	2008	401	43.4	281	83	199	72.1	62	244	436	109	154	12	21.7
Schrempf	50	1765	259	47.2	86	34	200	82.3	77	370	184	41	103	26	15.0
Baker	34	1162	198	45.3	3	0	72	45.0	86	211	56	32	76	34	13.8
MacLean	17	365	63	39.6	33	9	50	62.5	18	65	16	5	25	5	10.9
Hawkins	50	1644	171	41.9	180	55	119	90.2	51	201	123	80	80	18	10.3
Ellis	48	1232	174	44.1	217	94	53	75.7	25	115	38	25	45	3	10.3
Owens	21	451	65	39.4	11	5	28	80.0	35	80	38	12	33	4	7.8
Polynice	48	1481	169	47.2	1	1	29	30.9	184	425	43	20	49	30	7.7
Crotty	27	382	51	41.1	36	14	43	86.0	8	31	63	11	33	0	5.9
Stepania	23	313	53	42.4	3	0	21	52.5	27	75	12	10	32	23	5.5
McCoy	26	331	56	73.7	0	0	21	50.0	27	79	4	11	10	20	5.1
Williams	40	458	52	42.3	1	0	54	73.0	54	128	22	14	30	24	4.0
Norris	12	140	13	32.5	15	6	6	37.5	4	20	24	7	16	0	3.2
Lewis	20	145	19	36.5	6	1	8	57.1	13	25	4	8	20	1	2.4
Barry	17	183	10	31.3	24	8	9	69.2	3	20	29	7	12	1	2.2
SuperSonics	**50**	**12100**	**1756**	**44.2**	**899**	**309**	**922**	**68.1**	**676**	**2098**	**1087**	**393**	**721**	**201**	**94.9**
Opponents	**50**	**12100**	**1838**	**45.7**	**765**	**264**	**857**	**72.2**	**652**	**2098**	**1111**	**399**	**705**	**224**	**95.9**

Toronto Raptors

Player	GP	Min	Field Goals		3-Pt FG		Free Throws		Rebounds		A	Stl	TO	BS	Avg
			FGM	Pct	FGA	FGM	FTM	Pct	Off	Total					
Carter	50	1760	345	45.0	66	19	204	76.1	94	283	149	55	110	77	18.3
Christie	50	1768	252	38.8	161	49	207	84.1	59	207	187	113	119	26	15.2
Willis	42	1216	187	41.8	2	0	130	83.9	109	350	67	28	86	28	12.0
Brown	49	1377	187	37.8	349	135	40	72.7	15	103	143	56	80	8	11.2
McGrady	49	1106	168	43.6	35	8	114	72.6	120	278	113	52	80	66	9.3
Wallace	48	812	153	43.2	0	0	105	70.0	54	171	46	12	70	43	8.6
Oakley	50	1633	140	42.8	5	1	67	80.7	96	374	168	46	96	21	7.0
A. Williams	50	1051	95	40.1	42	14	44	84.6	19	82	130	51	56	12	5.0
Thomas	39	593	71	57.7	1	0	27	56.3	65	134	15	17	21	9	4.3
Slater	30	263	31	38.3	0	0	53	62.4	36	70	5	3	25	3	3.8
Stewart	42	394	22	41.5	0	0	17	68.0	43	99	5	4	12	28	1.5
Raptors	**50**	**12075**	**1660**	**42.1**	**662**	**226**	**1011**	**76.0**	**712**	**2159**	**1036**	**439**	**767**	**321**	**91.1**
Opponents	**50**	**12075**	**1694**	**43.9**	**686**	**255**	**996**	**72.8**	**614**	**2007**	**1095**	**446**	**735**	**258**	**92.8**

Utah Jazz

Player	GP	Min	Field Goals		3-Pt FG		Free Throws		Rebounds		A	Stl	TO	BS	Avg
			FGM	Pct	FGA	FGM	FTM	Pct	Off	Total					
Malone	49	1832	393	49.3	1	0	378	78.8	107	463	201	62	162	28	23.8
Russell	50	1770	217	46.4	147	52	136	79.5	65	266	74	76	76	15	12.4
Hornacek	48	1435	214	47.7	81	34	125	89.3	33	160	192	52	82	14	12.2
Stockton	50	1410	200	48.8	50	16	137	81.1	31	146	374	81	110	13	11.1
Anderson	50	1072	162	44.6	41	14	89	71.2	49	132	56	39	66	10	8.5
Eisley	50	1038	140	44.6	50	21	67	83.8	12	94	185	30	109	2	7.4
Ostertag	48	1340	99	47.6	0	0	75	62.0	105	348	23	12	45	131	5.7
Bailey	43	543	78	44.6	2	0	25	73.5	36	94	26	9	27	28	4.2
Keefe	44	642	56	45.2	4	0	62	69.7	51	142	28	16	33	12	4.0
Fuller	42	462	56	45.2	0	0	30	60.0	28	101	6	6	27	14	3.4
Foster	42	458	52	37.7	4	1	13	61.9	28	83	25	6	24	8	2.8
Jazz	**50**	**12175**	**1684**	**46.5**	**388**	**140**	**1158**	**76.7**	**555**	**2063**	**1204**	**398**	**786**	**276**	**93.3**
Opponents	**50**	**12175**	**1595**	**41.3**	**666**	**214**	**936**	**72.1**	**635**	**1929**	**904**	**431**	**714**	**264**	**86.8**

Vancouver Grizzlies

Player	GP	Min	Field Goals		3-Pt FG		Free Throws		Rebounds		A	Stl	TO	BS	Avg
			FGM	Pct	FGA	FGM	FTM	Pct	Off	Total					
Abdur-Rahim	50	2021	386	43.2	36	11	369	84.1	114	374	172	69	186	55	23.0
Bibby	50	1758	260	43.0	74	15	127	75.1	30	136	325	78	146	5	13.2
Massenburg	43	1143	189	48.7	2	0	103	66.5	83	257	23	26	64	39	11.2
Reeves	25	702	102	40.6	1	0	67	57.8	50	138	37	13	47	8	10.8
Lopez	47	1218	169	44.6	44	12	87	64.4	69	166	62	49	82	14	9.3
West	14	294	31	47.7	2	0	19	76.0	5	25	19	16	12	7	5.8
Parks	48	1118	118	42.9	1	0	30	54.5	75	243	36	28	49	28	5.5
Smith	48	1098	77	53.5	1	0	76	59.4	135	350	48	46	60	18	4.8
Wheat	46	590	73	37.8	60	22	40	72.7	11	45	102	26	48	2	4.5
Chilcutt	46	697	63	36.6	68	26	14	82.4	29	117	30	22	28	12	3.6
Rhodes	13	156	13	25.0	7	1	16	64.0	9	17	11	5	20	2	3.3
Henderson	30	331	35	36.5	5	2	25	55.6	20	47	22	9	18	4	3.2
Dehere	26	291	31	36.5	39	16	5	71.4	7	24	27	7	16	3	3.2
Grizzlies	**50**	**12175**	**1643**	**42.8**	**453**	**148**	**1009**	**71.7**	**650**	**2009**	**964**	**420**	**807**	**199**	**88.9**
Opponents	**50**	**12175**	**1813**	**46.3**	**653**	**229**	**1021**	**72.9**	**673**	**2129**	**1189**	**490**	**756**	**328**	**97.5**

Washington Wizards

Player	GP	Min	Field Goals		3-Pt FG		Free Throws		Rebounds		A	Stl	TO	BS	Avg
			FGM	Pct	FGA	FGM	FTM	Pct	Off	Total					
Richmond	50	1912	331	41.2	221	70	251	85.7	30	172	122	64	136	10	19.7
Howard	36	1430	286	47.4	3	0	110	75.3	90	293	107	42	95	14	18.9
Strickland	44	1632	251	41.6	42	12	176	74.6	56	212	434	76	142	5	15.7
Thorpe	49	1539	240	54.5	2	0	74	69.8	96	334	101	42	88	19	11.3
Cheaney	50	1266	172	41.4	37	8	33	49.3	33	141	73	39	42	16	7.7
Murray	36	653	83	35.0	103	33	34	81.0	18	81	27	21	29	6	6.5
Wallace	46	1231	115	57.8	0	0	47	35.6	137	384	18	50	36	90	6.0
Whitney	39	441	64	41.0	95	32	27	87.1	8	47	69	18	36	2	4.8
Jackson	27	271	46	42.6	7	1	21	65.6	30	54	8	3	26	11	4.2
Legler	30	377	51	44.3	35	14	3	50.0	8	40	21	4	14	3	4.0
McInnis	35	427	50	37.3	35	9	21	75.0	9	21	73	19	30	1	3.7
Davis	37	578	49	53.3	0	0	28	73.7	50	139	10	11	16	3	3.4
White	20	191	17	53.1	0	0	15	42.9	23	58	1	3	16	11	2.5
Wizards	**50**	**12050**	**1768**	**44.5**	**580**	**179**	**845**	**70.5**	**595**	**1998**	**1064**	**393**	**708**	**193**	**91.2**
Opponents	**50**	**12050**	**1705**	**44.6**	**619**	**218**	**1044**	**73.6**	**617**	**2134**	**1079**	**402**	**750**	**212**	**93.4**

1999 NBA Draft

The 1999 NBA Draft was held on June 30 in Washington, D.C.

First Round

1. Elton Brand, Chicago
2. Steve Francis, Vancouver
3. Baron Davis, Charlotte
4. Lamar Odom, LA Clippers
5. Jonathan Bender, Toronto
6. Wally Szczerbiak, Minnesota
7. Richard Hamilton, Washington
8. Andre Miller, Cleveland
9. Shawn Marion, Phoenix
10. Jason Terry, Atlanta
11. Trajan Langdon, Cleveland
12. Aleksandar Radojevic, Toronto
13. Corey Maggette, Seattle (to Orlando)
14. William Avery, Minnesota
15. Frederic Weis, New York
16. Ron Artest, Chicago
17. Cal Bowdler, Atlanta
18. James Posey, Denver
19. Quincy Lewis, Utah
20. Dion Glover, Atlanta
21. Jeff Foster, Golden State (to Indiana)
22. Kenny Thomas, Houston
23. Devean George, LA Lakers
24. Andrei Kirilenko, Utah
25. Tim James, Miami
26. Vonteego Cummings, Indiana (to Golden State)
27. Jumaine Jones, Atlanta (to Philadelphia)
28. Scott Padgett, Utah
29. Leon Smith, San Antonio (to Dallas)

Second Round

30. John Celestand, LA Lakers
31. Rico Hill, LA Clippers
32. Michael Ruffin, Chicago
33. Chris Herrin, Denver
34. Evan Eschmeyer, New Jersey
35. Calvin Booth, Washington
36. Wang Zhi-Zhi, Dallas
37. Obinna Ekezie, Vancouver
38. Laron Profit, Orlando
39. A.J. Bramlett, Cleveland
40. Gordon Giricek, Dallas (to San Antonio)
41. Francisco Elson, Denver
42. Louis Bullock, Minnesota (to Orlando)
43. Lee Nailon, Charlotte
44. Tyrone Washington, Houston
45. Ryan Robertson, Sacramento
46. J.R. Koch, New York
47. Todd MacCulloch, Philadelphia
48. Galen Young, Milwaukee
49. Lari Ketner, Chicago
50. Venson Hamilton, Houston
51. Antwain Smith, Vancouver
52. Roberto Bergersen, Atlanta (to Portland)
53. Rodney Buford, Miami
54. Melvin Levett, Detroit
55. Kris Clack, Boston
56. Tim Young, Golden State
57. Emmanuel Ginobili, Golden State
58. Eddie Lucas, Utah

Women's National Basketball Association

Final Standings

EASTERN CONFERENCE

Team	W	L	Pct	GB
†New York	18	14	.563	—
*Detroit	15	17	.469	3
*Charlotte	15	17	.469	3
Orlando	15	17	.469	3
Washington	12	20	.375	6
Cleveland	7	25	.219	11

WESTERN CONFERENCE

Team	W	L	Pct	GB
†Houston	26	6	.813	—
*Los Angeles	20	12	.625	6
*Sacramento	19	13	.594	7
Minnesota	15	17	.469	11
Phoenix	15	17	.469	11
Utah	15	17	.469	11

†Clinched conference title.   *Clinched playoff berth

1999 Playoffs

FIRST ROUND

Aug 24 .... Charlotte   60   at Detroit   54   Aug. 24 ...... Sacramento 58   at Los Angeles 71

EASTERN CONFERENCE FINALS

Aug 27 .... New York   67   at Charlotte   78
Aug 29 ...... Charlotte   70   at New York   74
Aug 30 .... Charlotte   54   at New York   69

New York won series 2–1

WESTERN CONFERENCE FINALS

Aug. 26 ...... Houston   60   at Los Angeles 75
Aug. 29 ...... Los Angeles 55   at Houston   83
Aug. 30 ...... Los Angeles 62   at Houston   72

Houston won series 2–1

WNBA CHAMPIONSHIP

Sept 2 .... Houston   73   at New York   60
Sept 4 .... New York   68   at Houston   67
Sept 5 .... New York   47   at Houston   59

A League of Their Own

After the Lakers traded him to the Hornets in March 1999, Eddie Jones lifted his average from 13.6 to 17, raised his shooting percentage from 42.3 to to 44.6 and went from 23rd in the league in steals to second. So then why did Nike dock him $300,000 on his endorsement deal? Because Jones had also gone from the top of the company's marketing ladder to the bottom.

As a Laker, Jones played for what Nike calls a Group A team, one of the marquee franchises at the top of a three-tiered system the comany uses to assess the marketing value of NBA players. (The Bulls, Celtics, Heat and Knicks are the others.) His deal with Nike, which became public as part of a lawsuit he filed against his former agent, paid him $950,000 a year as long as he remained with a Group A team, but that sum automatically dropped to $650,000 when he was dealt to small-market Charlotte, one of the 19 league cities that lacks even the modest Group B status of Atlanta, Detroit, Houston, Philadelphia and Seattle. Still, Jones can probably get by on what his shoe deal and roughly $2.2 million Hornets contract will pay him next season, and he's in good company: Tim Duncan and David Robinson play for a Group C team, too.

NBA Champions

Season	Winner	Series	Runner-Up	Winning Coach	Finals MVP
1946–47	Philadelphia	4–1	Chicago	Eddie Gottlieb	—
1947–48	Baltimore	4–2	Philadelphia	Buddy Jeannette	—
1948–49	Minneapolis	4–2	Washington	John Kundla	—
1949–50	Minneapolis	4–2	Syracuse	John Kundla	—
1950–51	Rochester	4–3	New York	Les Harrison	—
1951–52	Minneapolis	4–3	New York	John Kundla	—
1952–53	Minneapolis	4–1	New York	John Kundla	—
1953–54	Minneapolis	4–3	Syracuse	John Kundla	—
1954–55	Syracuse	4–3	Ft Wayne	Al Cervi	—
1955–56	Philadelphia	4–1	Ft Wayne	George Senesky	—
1956–57	Boston	4–3	St Louis	Red Auerbach	—
1957–58	St Louis	4–2	Boston	Alex Hannum	—
1958–59	Boston	4–0	Minneapolis	Red Auerbach	—
1959–60	Boston	4–3	St Louis	Red Auerbach	—
1960–61	Boston	4–1	St Louis	Red Auerbach	—
1961–62	Boston	4–3	LA Lakers	Red Auerbach	—
1962–63	Boston	4–2	LA Lakers	Red Auerbach	—
1963–64	Boston	4–1	San Francisco	Red Auerbach	—
1964–65	Boston	4–1	LA Lakers	Red Auerbach	—
1965–66	Boston	4–3	LA Lakers	Red Auerbach	—
1966–67	Philadelphia	4–2	San Francisco	Alex Hannum	—
1967–68	Boston	4–2	LA Lakers	Bill Russell	—
1968–69	Boston	4–3	LA Lakers	Bill Russell	Jerry West, LA
1969–70	New York	4–3	LA Lakers	Red Holzman	Willis Reed, NY
1970–71	Milwaukee	4–0	Baltimore	Larry Costello	Kareem Abdul-Jabbar, Mil
1971–72	LA Lakers	4–1	New York	Bill Sharman	Wilt Chamberlain, LA
1972–73	New York	4–1	LA Lakers	Red Holzman	Willis Reed, NY
1973–74	Boston	4–3	Milwaukee	Tommy Heinsohn	John Havlicek, Bos
1974–75	Golden State	4–0	Washington	Al Attles	Rick Barry, GS
1975–76	Boston	4–2	Phoenix	Tommy Heinsohn	JoJo White, Bos
1976–77	Portland	4–2	Philadelphia	Jack Ramsay	Bill Walton, Port
1977–78	Washington	4–3	Seattle	Dick Motta	Wes Unseld, Wash
1978–79	Seattle	4–1	Washington	Lenny Wilkens	Dennis Johnson, Sea
1979–80	LA Lakers	4–2	Philadelphia	Paul Westhead	Magic Johnson, LA
1980–81	Boston	4–2	Houston	Bill Fitch	Cedric Maxwell, Bos
1981–82	LA Lakers	4–2	Philadelphia	Pat Riley	Magic Johnson, LA
1982–83	Philadelphia	4–0	LA Lakers	Billy Cunningham	Moses Malone, Phil
1983–84	Boston	4–3	LA Lakers	K.C. Jones	Larry Bird, Bos
1984–85	LA Lakers	4–2	Boston	Pat Riley	Kareem Abdul-Jabbar, LA
1985–86	Boston	4–2	Houston	K.C. Jones	Larry Bird, Bos
1986–87	LA Lakers	4–2	Boston	Pat Riley	Magic Johnson, LA
1987–88	LA Lakers	4–3	Detroit	Pat Riley	James Worthy, LA
1988–89	Detroit	4–0	LA Lakers	Chuck Daly	Joe Dumars, Det
1989–90	Detroit	4–1	Portland	Chuck Daly	Isiah Thomas, Det
1990–91	Chicago	4–1	LA Lakers	Phil Jackson	Michael Jordan, Chi
1991–92	Chicago	4–2	Portland	Phil Jackson	Michael Jordan, Chi
1992–93	Chicago	4–2	Phoenix	Phil Jackson	Michael Jordan, Chi
1993–94	Houston	4–3	New York	Rudy Tomjanovich	Hakeem Olajuwon, Hou
1994–95	Houston	4–0	Orlando	Rudy Tomjanovich	Hakeem Olajuwon, Hou
1995–96	Chicago	4–2	Seattle	Phil Jackson	Michael Jordan, Chi
1996–97	Chicago	4–2	Utah	Phil Jackson	Michael Jordan, Chi
1997–98	Chicago	4–2	Utah	Phil Jackson	Michael Jordan, Chi
1998–99	San Antonio	4–1	New York	Gregg Popovich	Tim Duncan, SA

NBA Awards

Most Valuable Player: Maurice Podoloff Trophy

Season	Player, Team	GP	Field Goals		3-Pt FG		Free Throws		Rebounds		A	Stl	BS	Avg
			FGM	Pct	FGM	Pct	FTM	Pct	Off	Total				
1955–56	Bob Pettit, StL	72	646	42.9	–	–	557	73.6	–	1,164	189	–	–	25.7
1956–57	Bob Cousy, Bos	64	478	37.8	–	–	363	82.1	–	309	478	–	–	20.6
1957–58	Bill Russell, Bos	69	456	44.2	–	–	230	51.9	–	1,564	202	–	–	16.6
1958–59	Bob Pettit, StL	72	719	43.8	–	–	667	75.9	–	1,182	221	–	–	29.2
1959–60	Wilt Chamberlain, Phil	72	1,065	46.1	–	–	577	58.2	–	1,941	168	–	–	37.6
1960–61	Bill Russell, Bos	78	532	42.6	–	–	258	55.0	–	1,868	264	–	–	16.9
1961–62	Bill Russell, Bos	76	575	45.7	–	–	286	59.5	–	1,891	341	–	–	18.9
1962–63	Bill Russell, Bos	78	511	43.2	–	–	287	55.5	–	1,843	348	–	–	16.8
1963–64	Oscar Robertson, Cin	79	840	48.3	–	–	800	85.3	–	783	868	–	–	31.4
1964–65	Bill Russell, Bos	78	429	43.8	–	–	244	57.3	–	1,878	410	–	–	14.1
1965–66	Wilt Chamberlain, Phil	79	1,074	54.0	–	–	501	51.3	–	1,943	414	–	–	33.5
1966–67	Wilt Chamberlain, Phil	81	785	68.3	–	–	386	44.1	–	1,957	630	–	–	24.1
1967–68	Wilt Chamberlain, Phil	82	819	59.5	–	–	354	38.0	–	1,952	702	–	–	24.3
1968–69	Wes Unseld, Balt	82	427	47.6	–	–	277	60.5	–	1,491	213	–	–	13.8
1969–70	Willis Reed, NY	81	702	50.7	–	–	351	75.6	–	1,126	161	–	–	21.7
1970–71	Kareem Abdul-Jabbar, Mil	82	1,063	57.7	–	–	470	69.0	–	1,311	272	–	–	31.7
1971–72	Kareem Abdul-Jabbar, Mil	81	1,159	57.4	–	–	504	68.9	–	1,346	370	–	–	34.8
1972–73	Dave Cowens, Bos	82	740	45.2	–	–	204	77.9	–	1,329	333	–	–	20.5
1973–74	Kareem Abdul-Jabbar, Mil	81	948	53.9	–	–	295	70.2	287	1,178	386	112	283	27.0
1974–75	Bob McAdoo, Buff	82	1,095	51.2	–	–	641	80.5	307	1,155	179	92	174	34.5
1975–76	Kareem Abdul-Jabbar, LA	82	914	52.9	–	–	447	70.3	272	1,383	413	119	338	27.7
1976–77	Kareem Abdul-Jabbar, LA	82	888	57.9	–	–	376	70.1	266	1,090	319	101	261	26.2
1977–78	Bill Walton, Port	58	460	52.2	–	–	177	72.0	118	766	291	60	146	18.9
1978–79	Moses Malone, Hou	82	716	54.0	–	–	599	73.9	587	1,444	147	79	119	24.8
1979–80	Kareem Abdul-Jabbar, LA	82	835	60.4	0	00.0	364	76.5	190	886	371	81	280	24.8
1980–81	Julius Erving, Phil	82	794	52.1	4	22.2	422	78.7	244	657	364	173	147	24.6
1981–82	Moses Malone, Hou	81	945	51.9	0	00.0	630	76.2	558	1,188	142	76	125	31.1
1982–83	Moses Malone, Phil	78	654	50.1	0	00.0	600	76.1	445	1,194	101	89	157	24.5
1983–84	Larry Bird, Bos	79	758	49.2	18	24.7	374	88.8	181	796	520	144	69	24.2
1984–85	Larry Bird, Bos	80	918	52.2	56	42.7	403	88.2	164	842	531	129	98	28.7
1985–86	Larry Bird, Bos	82	796	49.6	82	42.3	441	89.6	190	805	557	166	51	25.8
1986–87	Magic Johnson, LA Lakers	80	683	52.2	8	20.5	535	84.8	122	504	977	138	36	23.9
1987–88	Michael Jordan, Chi	82	1,069	53.5	7	13.2	723	84.1	139	449	485	259	131	35.0
1988–89	Magic Johnson, LA Lakers	77	579	50.9	59	31.4	513	91.1	111	607	988	138	22	22.5
1989–90	Magic Johnson, LA Lakers	79	546	48.0	106	38.4	567	89.0	128	522	907	132	34	22.3
1990–91	Michael Jordan, Chi	82	990	53.9	29	31.2	571	85.1	118	492	453	223	83	31.5
1991–92	Michael Jordan; Chi	80	943	51.9	27	27.0	491	83.2	91	511	489	182	75	30.1
1992–93	Charles Barkley, Phoe	76	716	52.0	67	30.5	445	76.5	237	928	385	119	74	25.6
1993–94	Hakeem Olajuwon, Hou	80	894	52.8	8	42.1	388	71.6	229	955	287	128	297	27.3
1994–95	David Robinson, SA	81	788	53.0	6	30.0	656	77.4	234	877	236	134	262	27.6
1995–96	Michael Jordan, Chi	82	916	49.5	111	42.7	548	83.4	148	543	352	180	42	30.4
1996–97	Karl Malone, Utah	82	864	55.0	0	00.0	521	75.5	193	809	368	113	48	27.4
1997–98	Michael Jordan, Chi	82	881	46.5	30	23.8	565	78.4	130	475	283	141	45	28.7
1998–99	Karl Malone, Utah	49	393	49.3	0	00.0	378	78.8	107	463	201	62	28	23.8

Coach of the Year: Arnold "Red" Auerbach Trophy

1962–63...Harry Gallatin, StL
1963–64...Alex Hannum, SF
1964–65...Red Auerbach, Bos
1965–66...Dolph Schayes, Phil
1966–67...Johnny Kerr, Chi
1967–68...Richie Guerin, StL
1968–69...Gene Shue, Balt
1969–70...Red Holzman, NY
1970–71...Dick Motta, Chi
1971–72...Bill Sharman, LA
1972–73...Tom Heinsohn, Bos
1973–74...Ray Scott, Det
1974–75...Phil Johnson, KC-Oma

1975–76...Bill Fitch, Clev
1976–77...Tom Nissalke, Hou
1977–78...Hubie Brown, Atl
1978–79...Cotton Fitzsimmons, KC
1979–80...Bill Fitch, Bos
1980–81...Jack McKinney, Ind
1981–82...Gene Shue, Wash
1982–83...Don Nelson, Mil
1983–84...Frank Layden, Utah
1984–85...Don Nelson, Mil
1985–86...Mike Fratello, Atl
1986–87...Mike Schuler, Port
1987–88...Doug Moe, Den

1988–89...Cotton Fitzsimmons, Phoe
1989–90...Pat Riley, LA Lakers
1990–91...Don Chaney, Hou
1991–92...Don Nelson, GS
1992–93...Pat Riley, NY
1993–94...Lenny Wilkens, Atl
1994–95...Del Harris, LA Lakers
1995–96...Phil Jackson, Chi
1996–97...Pat Riley, Mia
1997–98...Larry Bird, Ind
1998–99...Mike Dunleavy, Port

Note: Award named after Auerbach in 1986.

Rookie of the Year: Eddie Gottlieb Trophy

1952–53...Don Meineke, FW
1953–54...Ray Felix, Balt
1954–55...Bob Pettit, Mil
1955–56...Maurice Stokes, Roch
1956–57...Tom Heinsohn, Bos
1957–58...Woody Sauldsberry, Phil
1958–59...Elgin Baylor, Minn
1959–60...Wilt Chamberlain, Phil
1960–61...Oscar Robertson, Cin
1961–62...Walt Bellamy, Chi
1962–63...Terry Dischinger, Chi
1963–64...Jerry Lucas, Cin
1964–65...Willis Reed, NY
1965–66...Rick Barry, SF
1966–67...Dave Bing, Det
1967–68...Earl Monroe, Balt
1968–69...Wes Unseld, Balt

1969–70...K. Abdul-Jabbar, Mil
1970–71...Dave Cowens, Bos
         Geoff Petrie, Port
1971–72...Sidney Wicks, Port
1972–73...Bob McAdoo, Buff
1973–74...Ernie DiGregorio, Buff
1974–75...Keith Wilkes, GS
1975–76...Alvan Adams, Phoe
1976–77...Adrian Dantley, Buff
1977–78...Walter Davis, Phoe
1978–79...Phil Ford, KC
1979–80...Larry Bird, Bos
1980–81...Darrell Griffith, Utah
1981–82...Buck Williams, NJ
1982–83...Terry Cummings, SD
1983–84...Ralph Sampson, Hou
1984–85...Michael Jordan, Chi

1985–86...Patrick Ewing, NY
1986–87...Chuck Person, Ind
1987–88...Mark Jackson, NY
1988–89...Mitch Richmond, GS
1989–90...David Robinson, SA
1990–91...Derrick Coleman, NJ
1991–92...Larry Johnson, Char
1992–93...Shaquille O'Neal, Orl
1993–94...Chris Webber, GS
1994–95...Jason Kidd, Dal
         Grant Hill, Det
1995–96...Damon Stoudamire, Tor
1996–97...Allen Iverson, Phil
1997–98...Tim Duncan, SA
1998–99...Vince Carter, Tor

Defensive Player of the Year

1982–83...Sidney Moncrief, Mil
1983–84...Sidney Moncrief, Mil
1984–85...Mark Eaton, Utah
1985–86...Alvin Robertson, SA
1986–87...Michael Cooper, LA
         Lakers

1987–88...Michael Jordan, Chi
1988–89...Mark Eaton, Utah
1989–90...Dennis Rodman, Det
1990–91...Dennis Rodman, Det
1991–92...David Robinson, SA
1992–93...Hakeem Olajuwon, Hou

1993–94...Hakeem Olajuwon, Hou
1994–95...Dikembe Mutombo, Den
1995–96...Gary Payton, Sea
1996–97...Dikembe Mutombo, Den
1997–98...Dikembe Mutombo, Atl
1998–99...Alonzo Mourning, Mia

Sixth Man Award

1982–83...Bobby Jones, Phil
1983–84...Kevin McHale, Bos
1984–85...Kevin McHale, Bos
1985–86...Bill Walton, Bos
1986–87...Ricky Pierce, Mil
1987–88...Roy Tarpley, Dall

1988–89...Eddie Johnson, Phoe
1989–90...Ricky Pierce, Mil
1990–91...Detlef Schrempf, Ind
1991–92...Detlef Schrempf, Ind
1992–93...Cliff Robinson, Port
1993–94...Dell Curry, Char

1994–95...Anthony Mason, NY
1995–96...Tony Kukoc, Chi
1996–97...John Starks, NY
1997–98...Danny Manning, Phoe
1998–99...Darrell Armstrong, Orl

J. Walter Kennedy Citizenship Award

1974–75...Wes Unseld, Wash
1975–76...Slick Watts, Sea
1976–77...Dave Bing, Wash
1977–78...Bob Lanier, Det
1978–79...Calvin Murphy, Hou
1979–80...Austin Carr, Clev
1980–81...Mike Glenn, NY
1981–82...Kent Benson, Det
1982–83...Julius Erving, Phil
1983–84...Frank Layden, Utah

1984–85...Dan Issel, Den
1985–86...Michael Cooper, LA
         Lakers
         Rory Sparrow, NY
1986–87...Isiah Thomas, Det
1987–88...Alex English, Den
1988–89...Thurl Bailey, Utah
1989–90...Glenn Rivers, Atl
1990–91...Kevin Johnson, Phoe

1991–92...Magic Johnson, LA
         Lakers
1992–93...Terry Porter, Port
1993–94...Joe Dumars, Det
1994–95...Joe O'Toole, Atl
1995–96...Chris Dudley, Port
1996–97...P.J. Brown, Mia
1997–98...Steve Smith, Atl
1998–99...Brian Grant, Port

Most Improved Player

1985–86...Alvin Robertson, SA
1986–87...Dale Ellis, Sea
1987–88...Kevin Duckworth, Port
1988–89...Kevin Johnson, Phoe
1989–90...Rony Seikaly, Mia

1990–91...Scott Skiles, Orl
1991–92...Pervis Ellison, Wash
1992–93...Chris Jackson, Den
1993–94...Don MacLean, Wash
1994–95...Dana Barros, Phil

1995–96...Gheorghe Muresan,
         Wash
1996–97...Isaac Austin, Mia
1997–98...Alan Henderson, Atl
1998–99...Darrell Armstrong, Orl

Executive of the Year

1972–73...Joe Axelson, KC-Oma
1973–74...Eddie Donovan, Buff
1974–75...Dick Vertlieb, GS
1975–76...Jerry Colangelo, Phoe
1976–77...Ray Patterson, Hou
1977–78...Angelo Drossos, SA
1978–79...Bob Ferry, Wash
1979–80...Red Auerbach, Bos
1980–81...Jerry Colangelo, Phoe
1981–82...Bob Ferry, Wash

1982–83...Zollie Volchok, Sea
1983–84...Frank Layden, Utah
1984–85...Vince Boryla, Den
1985–86...Stan Kasten, Atl
1986–87...Stan Kasten, Atl
1987–88...Jerry Krause, Chi
1988–89...Jerry Colangelo, Phoe
1989–90...Bob Bass, SA
1990–91...Bucky Buckwalter, Port
1991–92...Wayne Embry, Clev

1992–93...Jerry Colangelo, Phoe
1993–94...Bob Whitsitt, Sea
1994–95...Jerry West, LA Lakers
1995–96...Jerry Krause, Chi
1996–97...Bob Bass, Char
1997–98...Wayne Embry, Clev
1998–99...Geoff Petrie, Sac

Sponsored by *The Sporting News.*

Scoring

MOST POINTS, CAREER

	Pts	Avg
Kareem Abdul-Jabbar	38,387	24.6
Wilt Chamberlain	31,419	30.1
Michael Jordan	29,277	31.5
Karl Malone	28,946	26.1
Moses Malone	27,409	20.6
Elvin Hayes	27,313	21.0
Oscar Robertson	26,710	25.7
Dominique Wilkins	26,669	24.8
John Havlicek	26,395	20.8
Alex English	25,613	21.5

MOST POINTS, SEASON

Wilt Chamberlain, Phil	4,029	1961–62
Wilt Chamberlain, SF	3,586	1962–63
Michael Jordan, Chi	3,041	1986–87
Wilt Chamberlain, Phil	3,033	1960–61
Wilt Chamberlain, SF	2,948	1963–64
Michael Jordan, Chi	2,868	1987–88
Bob McAdoo, Buff	2,831	1974–75
Rick Barry, SF	2,775	1966–67
Michael Jordan, Chi	2,753	1989–90
Elgin Baylor, LA	2,719	1962–63

HIGHEST SCORING AVERAGE, CAREER

Michael Jordan	31.5	930 games
Wilt Chamberlain	30.1	1,045 games
Elgin Baylor	27.4	846 games
Shaquille O'Neal	27.1	455 games
Jerry West	27.0	932 games
Bob Pettit	26.4	792 games
George Gervin	26.2	791 games
Karl Malone	26.1	1,110 games
Oscar Robertson	25.7	1,040 games
Dominique Wilkins	24.8	1,074 games

HIGHEST SCORING AVERAGE, SEASON

Wilt Chamberlain, Phil	50.4	1961–62
Wilt Chamberlain, SF	44.8	1962–63
Wilt Chamberlain, Phil	38.4	1960–61
Wilt Chamberlain, Phil	37.6	1959–60
Michael Jordan, Chi	37.1	1986–87
Wilt Chamberlain, SF	36.9	1963–64
Rick Barry, SF	35.6	1966–67
Michael Jordan, Chi	35.0	1987–88
Elgin Baylor, LA	34.8	1960–61

Note: Minimum 70 games.

MOST POINTS, GAME

Player, Team		Opp	Date
100	Wilt Chamberlain, Phil	NY	3/2/62
78	Wilt Chamberlain, Phil	LA	12/8/61
73	Wilt Chamberlain, Phil	Chi	1/13/62
73	Wilt Chamberlain, SF	NY	11/16/62
73	David Thompson, Den	Det	4/9/78
72	Wilt Chamberlain, SF	LA	11/3/62
71	David Robinson, SA	LAC	4/24/94
71	Elgin Baylor, LA	NY	11/15/60
70	Wilt Chamberlain, SF	Syr	3/10/63
69	Michael Jordan, Chi	Clev	3/28/90

Field-Goal Percentage

Highest FG Percentage, Career: .599—Artis Gilmore
Highest Field-Goal Percentage, Season: .727—Wilt Chamberlain, LA Lakers, 1972–73 (426/586)

Free Throws

HIGHEST FREE-THROW PERCENTAGE, CAREER

Mark Price	.904
Rick Barry	.900
Calvin Murphy	.892
Scott Skiles	.889
Larry Bird	.886

Note: Minimum 1200 free throws made.

HIGHEST FREE-THROW PERCENTAGE, SEASON

Calvin Murphy, Hou	.958	1980–81
Mahmoud Abdul-Rauf, Den	.956	1993–94
Mark Price, Clev	.948	1992–93
Mark Price, Clev	.947	1991–92
Rick Barry, Hou	.946	1978–79

MOST FREE THROWS MADE, CAREER

	No.	Yrs	Pct
Moses Malone	8,531	19	.769
Oscar Robertson	7,694	14	.838
Karl Malone	7,511	14	.730
Jerry West	7,160	14	.814
Dolph Schayes	6,979	16	.844

Three-Point Field Goals

Most Three-Point Field-Goals, Career: 1,702—Reggie Miller

Highest Three-Point Field-Goal Percentage, Career: .463—Steve Kerr

Most Three-Point Field Goals, Season: 267—Dennis Scott, Orl, 1995–96

Highest Three-Point Field-Goal Percentage, Season: .524—Steve Kerr, Chi, 1994–95

Most Three-Point Field Goals, Game: 11—Dennis Scott, Orlando vs Atlanta, 4/18/96

Note: First year of shot: 1979–80.

Steals

Most Steals, Career: 2,701—John Stockton

Most Steals, Season: 301—Alvin Robertson, San Antonio, 1985–86

Most Steals, Game: 11—Kendall Gill, New Jersey vs Miami, 4/3/99; Larry Kenon, San Antonio vs Kansas City, 12/26/76

Rebounds

MOST REBOUNDS, CAREER

	No.	Yrs	Avg
Wilt Chamberlain	23,924	14	22.9
Bill Russell	21,620	13	22.5
Kareem Abdul-Jabbar	17,440	20	11.4
Elvin Hayes	16,279	16	12.5
Moses Malone	16,212	19	12.2
Robert Parish	14,715	21	9.1
Nate Thurmond	14,464	14	15.0
Walt Bellamy	14,241	14	13.7
Wes Unseld	13,769	13	14.0
Jerry Lucas	12,942	11	15.6

Rebounds *(Cont.)*

MOST REBOUNDS, SEASON

Wilt Chamberlain, Phil	2,149	1960–61
Wilt Chamberlain, Phil	2,052	1961–62
Wilt Chamberlain, Phil	1,957	1966–67
Wilt Chamberlain, Phil	1,952	1967–68
Wilt Chamberlain, SF	1,946	1962–63
Wilt Chamberlain, Phil	1,943	1965–66
Wilt Chamberlain, Phil	1,941	1959–60
Bill Russell, Bos	1,930	1963–64
Bill Russell, Bos	1,878	1964–65
Bill Russell, Bos	1,868	1960–61

MOST REBOUNDS, GAME

	Player, Team	Opp	Date
55	Wilt Chamberlain, Phi	Bos	11/24/60
51	Bill Russell, Bos	Syr	2/5/60
49	Bill Russell, Bos	Phi	11/16/57
49	Bill Russell, Bos	Det	3/11/65
45	Wilt Chamberlain, Phil	Syr	2/6/60
45	Wilt Chamberlain, Phil	LA	1/21/61

Assists

MOST ASSISTS, CAREER

John Stockton	13,087
Magic Johnson	10,141
Oscar Robertson	9,887
Isiah Thomas	9,061
Mark Jackson	7,924

Assists *(Cont.)*

MOST ASSISTS, SEASON

John Stockton, Utah	1,164	1990–91
John Stockton, Utah	1,134	1989–90
John Stockton, Utah	1,128	1987–88
John Stockton, Utah	1,126	1991–92
Isiah Thomas, Det	1,123	1984–85

MOST ASSISTS, GAME: 30—Scott Skiles, Orlando vs Denver, 12/30/90

Blocked Shots

MOST BLOCKED SHOTS, CAREER

Hakeem Olajuwon	3,582
Kareem Abdul-Jabbar	3,189
Mark Eaton	3,064
Patrick Ewing	2,674
Wayne (Tree) Rollins	2,542

MOST BLOCKED SHOTS, SEASON

Mark Eaton, Utah	456	1984–85
Manute Bol, Wash	397	1985–86
Elmore Smith, LA	393	1973–74

MOST BLOCKED SHOTS, GAME: 17—Elmore Smith, LA Lakers vs Portland, 10/28/73

Scoring

MOST POINTS, CAREER

	Pts	Yrs	Avg
Michael Jordan	5,987	13	33.4
Kareem Abdul-Jabbar	5,762	18	24.3
Jerry West	4,457	13	29.1
Karl Malone	3,931	14	26.9
Larry Bird	3,897	12	23.8
John Havlicek	3,776	13	22.0
Hakeem Olajuwon	3,727	14	27.0
Magic Johnson	3,701	13	19.5
Elgin Baylor	3,623	12	27.0
Wilt Chamberlain	3,607	13	22.5

*HIGHEST SCORING AVERAGE, CAREER

	Avg	Games
Michael Jordan	33.4	179
Jerry West	29.1	153
Elgin Baylor	27.0	134
George Gervin	27.0	59
Shaquille O'Neal	26.7	58
Hakeem Olajuwon	26.6	136
Karl Malone	26.6	137
Bob Pettit	25.5	88
Dominique Wilkins	25.4	55
Rick Barry	24.8	74

*Minimum of 25 games.

Scoring *(Cont.)*

MOST POINTS, GAME

	Player, Team	Opp	Date
†63	Michael Jordan, Chi	Bos	4/20/86
61	Elgin Baylor, LA	Bos	4/14/62
56	Wilt Chamberlain, Phil	Syr	3/22/62
56	Michael Jordan, Chi	Mia	4/29/92
56	Charles Barkley, Phoe	GS	5/4/94
55	Rick Barry, SF	Phil	4/18/67
55	Michael Jordan, Chi	Clev	5/1/88
55	Michael Jordan, Chi	Phoe	4/16/95
55	Michael Jordan, Chi	Wash	4/27/97

†Double overtime game.

Rebounds

MOST REBOUNDS, CAREER

	No.	Yrs	Avg
Bill Russell	4,104	13	24.9
Wilt Chamberlain	3,913	13	24.5
Kareem Abdul-Jabbar	2,481	18	10.5
Wes Unseld	1,777	12	14.9
Robert Parish	1,765	16	9.6

MOST REBOUNDS, GAME

	Player, Team	Opp	Date
41	Wilt Chamberlain, Phil	Bos	4/5/67
40	Bill Russell, Bos	Phil	3/23/58
40	Bill Russell, Bos	StL	3/29/60
*40	Bill Russell, Bos	LA	4/18/62

Three tied at 39.
*Overtime game.

Assists

MOST ASSISTS, CAREER

	No.	Games
Magic Johnson	2,346	190
John Stockton	1,613	158
Larry Bird	1,062	164
Dennis Johnson	1,006	180
Isiah Thomas	987	111

MOST ASSISTS, GAME

	Player, Team	Opp	Date
24	Magic Johnson, LA	Pho	5/15/84
24	John Stockton, Utah	LAL	5/17/88
23	Magic Johnson, LA	Port	5/3/85
22	Doc Rivers, Atl	Bos	5/16/88
Four tied at 21.			

Games played

Kareem Abdul-Jabbar	237
Danny Ainge	193
Magic Johnson	190
Robert Parish	184
Byron Scott	183

Appearances

Kareem Abdul-Jabbar	18
Robert Parish	16
Dolph Schayes	16
Clyde Drexler	15
John Stockton	15
Paul Silas	14
Buck Williams	14
Karl Malone	14

NBA Season Leaders

Scoring

1946–47	Joe Fulks, Phil	1389	1973–74	Bob McAdoo, Buff	30.6
1947–48	Max Zaslofsky, Chi	1007	1974–75	Bob McAdoo, Buff	34.5
1948–49	George Mikan, Minn	1698	1975–76	Bob McAdoo, Buff	31.1
1949–50	George Mikan, Minn	1865	1976–77	Pete Maravich, NO	31.1
1950–51	Paul Arizin, Phil	1932	1977–78	George Gervin, SA	27.2
1951–52	Paul Arizin, Phil	1674	1978–79	George Gervin, SA	29.6
1952–53	Neil Johnston, Phil	1564	1979–80	George Gervin, SA	33.1
1953–54	Neil Johnston, Phil	1759	1980–81	Adrian Dantley, Utah	30.7
1954–55	Neil Johnston, Phil	1631	1981–82	George Gervin, SA	32.3
1955–56	Bob Pettit, StL	1849	1982–83	Alex English, Den	28.4
1956–57	Paul Arizin, Phil	1817	1983–84	Adrian Dantley, Utah	30.6
1957–58	George Yardley, Det	2001	1984–85	Bernard King, NY	32.9
1958–59	Bob Pettit, StL	2105	1985–86	Dominique Wilkins, Atl	30.3
1959–60	Wilt Chamberlain, Phil	2707	1986–87	Michael Jordan, Chi	37.1
1960–61	Wilt Chamberlain, Phil	3033	1987–88	Michael Jordan, Chi	35.0
1961–62	Wilt Chamberlain, Phil	4029	1988–89	Michael Jordan, Chi	32.5
1962–63	Wilt Chamberlain, SF	3586	1989–90	Michael Jordan, Chi	33.6
1963–64	Wilt Chamberlain, SF	2948	1990–91	Michael Jordan, Chi	31.5
1964–65	Wilt Chamberlain, SF-Phil	2534	1991–92	Michael Jordan, Chi	30.1
1965–66	Wilt Chamberlain, Phil	2649	1992–93	Michael Jordan, Chi	32.6
1966–67	Rick Barry, SF	2775	1993–94	David Robinson, SA	29.8
1967–68	Dave Bing, Det	2142	1994–95	Shaquille O'Neal, Orl	29.3
1968–69	Elvin Hayes, SD	2327	1995–96	Michael Jordan, Chi	30.4
1969–70	Jerry West, LA	*31.2	1996–97	Michael Jordan, Chi	29.6
1970–71	Kareem Abdul-Jabbar, Mil	31.7	1997–98	Michael Jordan, Chi	28.7
1971–72	Kareem Abdul-Jabbar, Mil	34.8	1998–99	Allen Iverson, Phil	26.8
1972–73	Nate Archibald, KC-Oma	34.0			

*Based on per game average since 1969–70.

Rebounding

1950–51	Dolph Schayes, Syr	1080	1961–62	Wilt Chamberlain, Phil	2052
1951–52	Larry Foust, FW	880	1962–63	Wilt Chamberlain, SF	1946
	Mel Hutchins, Mil	880	1963–64	Bill Russell, Bos	1930
1952–53	George Mikan, Minn	1007	1964–65	Bill Russell, Bos	1878
1953–54	Harry Gallatin, NY	1098	1965–66	Wilt Chamberlain, Phil	1943
1954–55	Neil Johnston, Phil	1085	1966–67	Wilt Chamberlain, Phil	1957
1955–56	Bob Pettit, StL	1164	1967–68	Wilt Chamberlain, Phil	1952
1956–57	Maurice Stokes, Roch	1256	1968–69	Wilt Chamberlain, LA	1712
1957–58	Bill Russell, Bos	1564	1969–70	Elvin Hayes, SD	*16.9
1958–59	Bill Russell, Bos	1612	1970–71	Wilt Chamberlain, LA	18.2
1959–60	Wilt Chamberlain, Phil	1941	1971–72	Wilt Chamberlain, LA	19.2
1960–61	Wilt Chamberlain, Phil	2149	1972–73	Wilt Chamberlain, LA	18.6

Rebounding (Cont.)

1973–74	Elvin Hayes, Capital	18.1	1986–87	Charles Barkley, Phil	14.6
1974–75	Wes Unseld, Wash	14.8	1987–88	Michael Cage, LA Clippers	13.0
1975–76	Kareem Abdul-Jabbar, LA	16.9	1988–89	Hakeem Olajuwon, Hou	13.5
1976–77	Bill Walton, Port	14.4	1989–90	Hakeem Olajuwon, Hou	14.0
1977–78	Len Robinson, NO	15.7	1990–91	David Robinson, SA	13.0
1978–79	Moses Malone, Hou	17.6	1991–92	Dennis Rodman, Det	18.7
1979–80	Swen Nater, SD	15.0	1992–93	Dennis Rodman, Det	18.3
1980–81	Moses Malone, Hou	14.8	1993–94	Dennis Rodman, SA	17.3
1981–82	Moses Malone, Hou	14.7	1994–95	Dennis Rodman, SA	16.8
1982–83	Moses Malone, Phil	15.3	1995–96	Dennis Rodman, Chi	14.9
1983–84	Moses Malone, Phil	13.4	1996–97	Dennis Rodman, Chi	16.1
1984–85	Moses Malone, Phil	13.1	1997–98	Dennis Rodman, Chi	15.0
1985–86	Bill Laimbeer, Det	13.1	1998–99	Chris Webber, Sac	13.0

*Based on per game average since 1969–70.

Assists

1946–47	Ernie Calverly, Prov	202	1973–74	Ernie DiGregorio, Buff	8.2
1947–48	Howie Dallmar, Phil	120	1974–75	Kevin Porter, Wash	8.0
1948–49	Bob Davies, Roch	321	1975–76	Don Watts, Sea	8.1
1949–50	Dick McGuire, NY	386	1976–77	Don Buse, Ind	8.5
1950–51	Andy Phillip, Phil	414	1977–78	Kevin Porter, NJ-Det	10.2
1951–52	Andy Phillip, Phil	539	1978–79	Kevin Porter, Det	13.4
1952–53	Bob Cousy, Bos	547	1979–80	Micheal Richardson, NY	10.1
1953–54	Bob Cousy, Bos	578	1980–81	Kevin Porter, Wash	9.1
1954–55	Bob Cousy, Bos	557	1981–82	Johnny Moore, SA	9.6
1955–56	Bob Cousy, Bos	642	1982–83	Magic Johnson, LA	10.5
1956–57	Bob Cousy, Bos	478	1983–84	Magic Johnson, LA	13.1
1957–58	Bob Cousy, Bos	463	1984–85	Isiah Thomas, Det	13.9
1958–59	Bob Cousy, Bos	557	1985–86	Magic Johnson, LA Lakers	12.6
1959–60	Bob Cousy, Bos	715	1986–87	Magic Johnson, LA Lakers	12.2
1960–61	Oscar Robertson, Cin	690	1987–88	John Stockton, Utah	13.8
1961–62	Oscar Robertson, Cin	899	1988–89	John Stockton, Utah	13.6
1962–63	Guy Rodgers, SF	825	1989–90	John Stockton, Utah	14.5
1963–64	Oscar Robertson, Cin	868	1990–91	John Stockton, Utah	14.2
1964–65	Oscar Robertson, Cin	861	1991–92	John Stockton, Utah	13.7
1965–66	Oscar Robertson, Cin	847	1992–93	John Stockton, Utah	12.0
1966–67	Guy Rodgers, Chi	908	1993–94	John Stockton, Utah	12.6
1967–68	Wilt Chamberlain, Phil	702	1994–95	John Stockton, Utah	12.3
1968–69	Oscar Robertson, Cin	772	1995–96	John Stockton, Utah	11.2
1969–70	Len Wilkens, Sea	*9.1	1996–97	Mark Jackson, Ind	11.4
1970–71	Norm Van Lier, Cin	10.1	1997–98	Rod Strickland, Wash	10.1
1971–72	Jerry West, LA	9.7	1998–99	Jason Kidd, Phoe	10.8
1972–73	Nate Archibald, KC-Oma	11.4			

*Based on per game average since 1969–70.

Field-Goal Percentage

1946–47	Bob Feerick, Wash	40.1	1965–66	Wilt Chamberlain, Phil	54.0
1947–48	Bob Feerick, Wash	34.0	1966–67	Wilt Chamberlain, Phil	68.3
1948–49	Arnie Risen, Roch	42.3	1967–68	Wilt Chamberlain, Phil	59.5
1949–50	Alex Groza, Ind	47.8	1968–69	Wilt Chamberlain, LA	58.3
1950–51	Alex Groza, Ind	47.0	1969–70	Johnny Green, Cin	55.9
1951–52	Paul Arizin, Phil	44.8	1970–71	Johnny Green, Cin	58.7
1952–53	Neil Johnston, Phil	45.2	1971–72	Wilt Chamberlain, LA	64.9
1953–54	Ed Macauley, Bos	48.6	1972–73	Wilt Chamberlain, LA	72.7
1954–55	Larry Foust, FW	48.7	1973–74	Bob McAdoo, Buff	54.7
1955–56	Neil Johnston, Phil	45.7	1974–75	Don Nelson, Bos	53.9
1956–57	Neil Johnston, Phil	44.7	1975–76	Wes Unseld, Wash	56.1
1957–58	Jack Twyman, Cin	45.2	1976–77	Kareem Abdul-Jabbar, LA	57.9
1958–59	Ken Sears, NY	49.0	1977–78	Bobby Jones, Den	57.8
1959–60	Ken Sears, NY	47.7	1978–79	Cedric Maxwell, Bos	58.4
1960–61	Wilt Chamberlain, Phil	50.9	1979–80	Cedric Maxwell, Bos	60.9
1961–62	Walt Bellamy, Chi	51.9	1980–81	Artis Gilmore, Chi	67.0
1962–63	Wilt Chamberlain, SF	52.8	1981–82	Artis Gilmore, Chi	65.2
1963–64	Jerry Lucas, Cin	52.7	1982–83	Artis Gilmore, SA	62.6
1964–65	Wilt Chamberlain, SF-Phil	51.0	1983–84	Artis Gilmore, SA	63.1

Field-Goal Percentage *(Cont.)*

1984–85	James Donaldson, LA Clippers	63.7	1992–93	Cedric Ceballos, Phoe	57.6
1985–86	Steve Johnson, SA	63.2	1993–94	Shaquille O'Neal, Orl	59.9
1986–87	Kevin McHale, Bos	60.4	1994–95	Chris Gatling, GS	63.3
1987–88	Kevin McHale, Bos	60.4	1995–96	Gheorghe Muresan, Wash	58.4
1988–89	Dennis Rodman, Det	59.5	1996–97	Gheorghe Muresan, Wash	60.4
1989–90	Mark West, Phoe	62.5	1997–98	Shaquille O'Neal, LA Lakers	58.4
1990–91	Buck Williams, Port	60.2	1998–99	Shaquille O'Neal, LA Lakers	57.6
1991–92	Buck Williams, Port	60.4			

Free-Throw Percentage

1946–47	Fred Scolari, Wash	81.1	1973–74	Ernie DiGregorio, Buff	90.2
1947–48	Bob Feerick, Wash	78.8	1974–75	Rick Barry, GS	90.4
1948–49	Bob Feerick, Wash	85.9	1975–76	Rick Barry, GS	92.3
1949–50	Max Zaslofsky, Chi	84.3	1976–77	Ernie DiGregorio, Buff	94.5
1950–51	Joe Fulks, Phil	85.5	1977–78	Rick Barry, GS	92.4
1951–52	Bob Wanzer, Roch	90.4	1978–79	Rick Barry, Hou	94.7
1952–53	Bill Sharman, Bos	85.0	1979–80	Rick Barry, Hou	93.5
1953–54	Bill Sharman, Bos	84.4	1980–81	Calvin Murphy, Hou	95.8
1954–55	Bill Sharman, Bos	89.7	1981–82	Kyle Macy, Phoe	89.9
1955–56	Bill Sharman, Bos	86.7	1982–83	Calvin Murphy, Hou	92.0
1956–57	Bill Sharman, Bos	90.5	1983–84	Larry Bird, Bos	88.8
1957–58	Dolph Schayes, Syr	90.4	1984–85	Kyle Macy, Phoe	90.7
1958–59	Bill Sharman, Bos	93.2	1985–86	Larry Bird, Bos	89.6
1959–60	Dolph Schayes, Syr	89.2	1986–87	Larry Bird, Bos	91.0
1960–61	Bill Sharman, Bos	92.1	1987–88	Jack Sikma, Mil	92.2
1961–62	Dolph Schayes, Syr	89.6	1988–89	Magic Johnson, LA Lakers	91.1
1962–63	Larry Costello, Syr	88.1	1989–90	Larry Bird, Bos	93.0
1963–64	Oscar Robertson, Cin	85.3	1990–91	Reggie Miller, Ind	91.8
1964–65	Larry Costello, Phil	87.7	1991–92	Mark Price, Clev	94.7
1965–66	Larry Siegfried, Bos	88.1	1992–93	Mark Price, Clev	94.8
1966–67	Adrian Smith, Cin	90.3	1993–94	Mahmoud Abdul-Rauf, Den	95.6
1967–68	Oscar Robertson, Cin	87.3	1994–95	Spud Webb, Sac	93.4
1968–69	Larry Siegfried, Bos	86.4	1995–96	Mahmoud Abdul-Rauf, Den	93.0
1969–70	Flynn Robinson, Mil	89.8	1996–97	Mark Price, GS	90.6
1970–71	Chet Walker, Chi	85.9	1997–98	Chris Mullin, Ind	93.9
1971–72	Jack Marin, Balt	89.4	1998–99	Reggie Miller, Ind	91.5
1972–73	Rick Barry, GS	90.2			

Three-Point Field-Goal Percentage

1979–80	Fred Brown, Sea	44.3	1989–90	Steve Kerr, Clev	50.7
1980–81	Brian Taylor, SD	38.3	1990–91	Jim Les, Sac	46.1
1981–82	Campy Russell, NY	43.9	1991–92	Dana Barros, Sea	44.6
1982–83	Mike Dunleavy, SA	34.5	1992–93	B.J. Armstrong, Chi	45.3
1983–84	Darrell Griffith, Utah	36.1	1993–94	Tracy Murray, Por	45.9
1984–85	Byron Scott, LA Lakers	43.3	1994–95	Steve Kerr, Chi	52.4
1985–86	Craig Hodges, Mil	45.1	1995–96	Tim Legler, Wash	52.2
1986–87	Kiki Vandeweghe, Por	48.1	1996–97	Kevin Gamble, Sac	48.2
1987–88	Craig Hodges, Mil-Phoe	49.1	1997–98	Dale Ellis, Sea	46.0
1988–89	Jon Sundvold, Mia	52.2	1998–99	Dell Curry, Char	47.6

Steals

1973–74	Larry Steele, Por	2.68	1986–87	Alvin Robertson, SA	3.21
1974–75	Rick Barry, GS	2.85	1987–88	Michael Jordan, Chi	3.16
1975–76	Don Watts, Sea	3.18	1988–89	John Stockton, Utah	3.21
1976–77	Don Buse, Ind	3.47	1989–90	Michael Jordan, Chi	2.77
1977–78	Ron Lee, Phoe	2.74	1990–91	Alvin Robertson, Mil	3.04
1978–79	M.L. Carr, Det	2.46	1991–92	John Stockton, Utah	2.98
1979–80	Micheal Richardson, NY	3.23	1992–93	Michael Jordan, Chi	2.83
1980–81	Magic Johnson, LA	3.43	1993–94	Nate McMillan, Sea	2.96
1981–82	Magic Johnson, LA	2.67	1994–95	Scottie Pippen, Chi	2.94
1982–83	Micheal Richardson, GS-NJ	2.84	1995–96	Gary Payton, Sea	2.85
1983–84	Rickey Green, Utah	2.65	1996–97	Mookie Blaylock, Atl	2.72
1984–85	Micheal Richardson, NJ	2.96	1997–98	Mookie Blaylock, Atl	2.61
1985–86	Alvin Robertson, SA	3.67	1998–99	Kendall Gill, NJ	2.68

Blocked Shots

1973–74	Elmore Smith, LA	4.85	1986–87	Mark Eaton, Utah	4.06
1974–75	Kareem Abdul-Jabbar, Mil	3.26	1987–88	Mark Eaton, Utah	3.71
1975–76	Kareem Abdul-Jabbar, LA	4.12	1988–89	Manute Bol, GS	4.31
1976–77	Bill Walton, Port	3.25	1989–90	Hakeem Olajuwon, Hou	4.59
1977–78	George Johnson, NJ	3.38	1990–91	Hakeem Olajuwon, Hou	3.95
1978–79	Kareem Abdul-Jabbar, LA	3.95	1991–92	David Robinson, SA	4.49
1979–80	Kareem Abdul-Jabbar, LA	3.41	1992–93	Hakeem Olajuwon, Hou	4.17
1980–81	George Johnson, SA	3.39	1993–94	Dikembe Mutombo, Den	4.10
1981–82	George Johnson, SA	3.12	1994–95	Dikembe Mutombo, Den	3.91
1982–83	Wayne Rollins, Atl	4.29	1995–96	Dikembe Mutombo, Den	4.49
1983–84	Mark Eaton, Utah	4.28	1996–97	Shawn Bradley, NJ	3.40
1984–85	Mark Eaton, Utah	5.56	1997–98	Marcus Camby, Tor	3.65
1985–86	Manute Bol, Wash	4.96	1998–99	Alonzo Mourning, Mia	3.91

NBA All-Star Game Results

Year	Result	Site	Winning Coach	Most Valuable Player
1951	East 111, West 94	Boston	Joe Lapchick	Ed Macauley, Bos
1952	East 108, West 91	Boston	Al Cervi	Paul Arizin, Phil
1953	West 79, East 75	Ft Wayne	John Kundla	George Mikan, Minn
1954	East 98, West 93 (OT)	New York	Joe Lapchick	Bob Cousy, Bos
1955	East 100, West 91	New York	Al Cervi	Bill Sharman, Bos
1956	West 108, East 94	Rochester	Charley Eckman	Bob Pettit, StL
1957	East 109, West 97	Boston	Red Auerbach	Bob Cousy, Bos
1958	East 130, West 118	St Louis	Red Auerbach	Bob Pettit, StL
1959	West 124, East 108	Detroit	Ed Macauley	Bob Pettit, StL
				Elgin Baylor, Minn
1960	East 125, West 115	Philadelphia	Red Auerbach	Wilt Chamberlain, Phil
1961	West 153, East 131	Syracuse	Paul Seymour	Oscar Robertson, Cin
1962	West 150, East 130	St Louis	Fred Schaus	Bob Pettit, StL
1963	East 115, West 108	Los Angeles	Red Auerbach	Bill Russell, Bos
1964	East 111, West 107	Boston	Red Auerbach	Oscar Robertson, Cin
1965	East 124, West 123	St Louis	Red Auerbach	Jerry Lucas, Cin
1966	East 137, West 94	Cincinnati	Red Auerbach	Adrian Smith, Cin
1967	West 135, East 120	San Francisco	Fred Schaus	Rick Barry, SF
1968	East 144, West 124	New York	Alex Hannum	Hal Greer, Phil
1969	East 123, West 112	Baltimore	Gene Shue	Oscar Robertson, Cin
1970	East 142, West 135	Philadelphia	Red Holzman	Willis Reed, NY
1971	West 108, East 107	San Diego	Larry Costello	Lenny Wilkens, Sea
1972	West 112, East 110	Los Angeles	Bill Sharman	Jerry West, LA
1973	East 104, West 84	Chicago	Tom Heinsohn	Dave Cowens, Bos
1974	West 134, East 123	Seattle	Larry Costello	Bob Lanier, Det
1975	East 108, West 102	Phoenix	K.C. Jones	Walt Frazier, NY
1976	East 123, West 109	Philadelphia	Tom Heinsohn	Dave Bing, Wash
1977	West 125, East 124	Milwaukee	Larry Brown	Julius Erving, Phil
1978	East 133, West 125	Atlanta	Billy Cunningham	Randy Smith, Buff
1979	West 134, East 129	Detroit	Lenny Wilkens	David Thompson, Den
1980	East 144, West 135 (OT)	Washington	Billy Cunningham	George Gervin, SA
1981	East 123, West 120	Cleveland	Billy Cunningham	Nate Archibald, Bos
1982	East 120, West 118	New Jersey	Bill Fitch	Larry Bird, Bos
1983	East 132, West 123	Los Angeles	Billy Cunningham	Julius Erving, Phil
1984	East 154, West 145 (OT)	Denver	K.C. Jones	Isiah Thomas, Det
1985	West 140, East 129	Indiana	Pat Riley	Ralph Sampson, Hou
1986	East 139, West 132	Dallas	K.C. Jones	Isiah Thomas, Det
1987	West 154, East 149 (OT)	Seattle	Pat Riley	Tom Chambers, Sea
1988	East 138, West 133	Chicago	Mike Fratello	Michael Jordan, Chi
1989	West 143, East 134	Houston	Pat Riley	Karl Malone, Utah
1990	East 130, West 113	Miami	Chuck Daly	Magic Johnson, LA Lakers
1991	East 116, West 114	Charlotte	Chris Ford	Charles Barkley, Phil
1992	West 153, East 113	Orlando	Don Nelson	Magic Johnson, LA Lakers
1993	West 135, East 132	Salt Lake City	Paul Westphal	Karl Malone, Utah
				John Stockton, Utah
1994	East 127, West 118	Minneapolis	Lenny Wilkens	Scottie Pippen, Chi
1995	West 139, East 112	Phoenix	Paul Westphal	Mitch Richmond, Sac
1996	East 129, West 118	San Antonio	Phil Jackson	Michael Jordan, Chi
1997	East 132, West 120	Cleveland	Doug Collins	Glen Rice, Char
1998	East 135, West 114	New York	Larry Bird	Michael Jordan, Chi
1999	Cancelled due to lockout.			

Members of the Basketball Hall of Fame

Contributors

Senda Abbott (1984)
Forest C. (Phog) Allen (1959)
Clair F. Bee (1967)
Walter A. Brown (1965)
John W. Bunn (1964)
Bob Douglas (1971)
Al Duer (1981)
Wayne Embry (1999)
Clifford Fagan (1983)
Harry A. Fisher (1973)
Larry Fleisher (1991)
Edward Gottlieb (1971)
Luther H. Gulick (1959)
Lester Harrison (1979)
Ferenc Hepp (1980)
Edward J. Hickox (1959)

Paul D. (Tony) Hinkle (1965)
Ned Irish (1964)
R. William Jones (1964)
J. Walter Kennedy (1980)
Emil S. Liston (1974)
John B. McLendon (1978)
Bill Mokray (1965)
Ralph Morgan (1959)
Frank Morgenweck (1962)
James Naismith (1959)
Peter F. Newell (1978)
John J. O'Brien (1961)
Larry O'Brien (1991)
Harold G. Olsen (1959)
Maurice Podoloff (1973)
H. V. Porter (1960)

William A. Reid (1963)
Elmer Ripley (1972)
Lynn W. St. John (1962)
Abe Saperstein (1970)
Arthur A. Schabinger (1961)
Amos Alonzo Stagg (1959)
Boris Stankovic (1991)
Edward Steitz (1983)
Chuck Taylor (1968)
Oswald Tower (1959)
Arthur L. Trester (1961)
Clifford Wells (1971)
Lou Wilke (1982)
Fred Zollner (1999)

Players

Kareem Abdul-Jabbar (1995)
Nate (Tiny) Archibald (1991)
Paul J. Arizin (1977)
Thomas B. Barlow (1980)
Rick Barry (1987)
Elgin Baylor (1976)
John Beckman (1972)
Walt Bellamy (1993)
Sergei Belov (1992)
Dave Bing (1990)
Larry Bird (1998)
Carol Blazejowski (1994)
Bennie Borgmann (1961)
Bill Bradley (1982)
Joseph Brennan (1974)
Al Cervi (1984)
Wilt Chamberlain (1978)
Charles (Tarzan) Cooper (1976)
Kresimir Cosic (1996)
Bob Cousy (1970)
Dave Cowens (1991)
Joan Crawford (1997)
Billy Cunningham (1986)
Denise Curry (1997)
Bob Davies (1969)
Forrest S. DeBernardi (1961)
Dave DeBusschere (1982)
H.G. (Dutch) Dehnert (1968)
Anne Donovan (1995)
Paul Endacott (1971)
Alex English (1997)
Julius Erving (1993)
Harold (Bud) Foster (1964)
Walter (Clyde) Frazier (1987)
Max (Marty) Friedman (1971)
Joe Fulks (1977)
Lauren (Laddie) Gale (1976)
Harry (the Horse) Gallatin (1991)
William Gates (1989)

George Gervin (1996)
Tom Gola (1975)
Gail Goodrich (1996)
Hal Greer (1981)
Robert (Ace) Gruenig (1963)
Clifford O. Hagan (1977)
Victor Hanson (1960)
John Havlicek (1983)
Connie Hawkins (1992)
Elvin Hayes (1990)
Marques Haynes (1998)
Tom Heinsohn (1986)
Nat Holman (1964)
Robert J. Houbregs (1987)
Bailey Howell (1997)
Chuck Hyatt (1959)
Dan Issel (1993)
Harry (Buddy) Jeannette (1994)
William C. Johnson (1976)
D. Neil Johnston (1990)
K.C. Jones (1989)
Sam Jones (1983)
Edward (Moose) Krause (1975)
Bob Kurland (1961)
Bob Lanier (1992)
Joe Lapchick (1966)
Nancy Lieberman-Cline (1996)
Clyde Lovellette (1988)
Jerry Lucas (1979)
Angelo (Hank) Luisetti (1959)
C. Edward Macauley (1960)
Peter P. Maravich (1987)
Slater Martin (1981)
Branch McCracken (1960)
Jack McCracken (1962)
Bobby McDermott (1988)
Dick McGuire (1993)
Kevin McHale (1999)
Ann Meyers (1993)

George L. Mikan (1959)
Vern Mikkelsen (1995)
Cheryl Miller (1995)
Earl Monroe (1990)
Calvin Murphy (1993)
Charles (Stretch) Murphy (1960)
H. O. (Pat) Page (1962)
Bob Pettit (1970)
Andy Phillip (1961)
Jim Pollard (1977)
Frank Ramsey (1981)
Willis Reed (1981)
Arnie Risen (1998)
Oscar Robertson (1979)
John S. Roosma (1961)
Bill Russell (1974)
John (Honey) Russell (1964)
Adolph Schayes (1972)
Ernest J. Schmidt (1973)
John J. Schommer (1959)
Barney Sedran (1962)
Uljana Semjonova (1993)
Bill Sharman (1975)
Christian Steinmetz (1961)
Lusia Harris Stewart (1992)
David Thompson (1996)
John A. (Cat) Thompson (1962)
Nate Thurmond (1984)
Jack Twyman (1982)
Wes Unseld (1988)
Robert (Fuzzy) Vandivier (1974)
Edward A. Wachter (1961)
Bill Walton (1993)
Robert F. Wanzer (1987)
Jerry West (1979)
Nera White (1992)
Lenny Wilkens (1989)
John R. Wooden (1960)
George (Bird) Yardley (1996)

Coaches

Harold Anderson (1984)
Red Auerbach (1968)
Sam Barry (1978)
Ernest A. Blood (1960)
Howard G. Cann (1967)
H. Clifford Carlson (1959)

Lou Carnesecca (1992)
Ben Carnevale (1969)
Pete Carril (1997)
Everett Case (1981)
Jody Conradt (1998)
Denny Crum (1994)

Chuck Daly (1994)
Everett S. Dean (1966)
Antonio Diaz-Miguel (1997)
Edgar A. Diddle (1971)
Bruce Drake (1972)
Clarence Gaines (1981)

Note: Year of election in parentheses.

Coaches *(Cont.)*

Jack Gardner (1983)
Amory T. (Slats) Gill (1967)
Aleksandr Gomelsky (1995)
Alex Hannum (1998)
Marv Harshman (1984)
Don Haskins (1997)
Edgar S. Hickey (1978)
Howard A. Hobson (1965)
Red Holzman (1986)
Hank Iba (1968)
Alvin F. (Doggie) Julian (1967)
Frank W. Keaney (1960)
George E. Keogan (1961)
Bob Knight (1991)

John Kundla (1995)
Ward L. Lambert (1960)
Harry Litwack (1975)
Kenneth D. Loeffler (1964)
A.C. (Dutch) Lonborg (1972)
Arad A. McCutchan (1980)
Al McGuire (1992)
Frank McGuire (1976)
Walter E. Meanwell (1959)
Raymond J. Meyer (1978)
Ralph Miller (1988)
Billie Moore (1999)
Aleksandar Nikolic (1998)
Jack Ramsay (1992)

Cesare Rubini (1994)
Adolph F. Rupp (1968)
Leonard D. Sachs (1961)
Everett F. Shelton (1979)
Dean Smith (1982)
Fred R. Taylor (1985)
Bertha Teague (1984)
John Thompson (1999)
Margaret Wade (1984)
Stanley H. Watts (1985)
Lenny Wilkens (1998)
John R. Wooden (1972)
Phil Woolpert (1992)

Referees

James E. Enright (1978)
George T. Hepbron (1960)
George Hoyt (1961)
Matthew P. Kennedy (1959)
Lloyd Leith (1982)
Zigmund J. Mihalik (1985)

John P. Nucatola (1977)
Ernest C. Quigley (1961)
J. Dallas Shirley (1979)
Earl Strom (1995)
David Tobey (1961)
David H. Walsh (1961)

Teams

Buffalo Germans (1961)
First Team (1959)
Original Celtics (1959)
Renaissance (1963)

ABA Champions

Year	Champion	Series	Loser	Winning Coach
1968	Pittsburgh Pipers	4–3	New Orleans Bucs	Vince Cazetta
1969	Oakland Oaks	4–1	Indiana Pacers	Alex Hannum
1970	Indiana Pacers	4–2	Los Angeles Stars	Bob Leonard
1971	Utah Stars	4–3	Kentucky Colonels	Bill Sharman
1972	Indiana Pacers	4–2	New York Nets	Bob Leonard
1973	Indiana Pacers	4–3	Kentucky Colonels	Bob Leonard
1974	New York Nets	4–1	Utah Stars	Kevin Loughery
1975	Kentucky Colonels	4–1	Indiana Pacers	Hubie Brown
1976	New York Nets	4–2	Denver Nuggets	Kevin Loughery

ABA Postseason Awards

Most Valuable Player

1967–68	Connie Hawkins, Pitt
1968–69	Mel Daniels, Ind
1969–70	Spencer Haywood, Den
1970–71	Mel Daniels, Ind
1971–72	Artis Gilmore, Ken
1972–73	Billy Cunningham, Car
1973–74	Julius Erving, NY
1974–75	Julius Erving, NY
	George McGinnis, Ind
1975–76	Julius Erving, NY

Rookie of the Year

1967–68	Mel Daniels, Minn
1968–69	Warren Armstrong, Oak
1969–70	Spencer Haywood, Den
1970–71	Charlie Scott, Vir
	Dan Issel, Ken
1971–72	Artis Gilmore, Ken
1972–73	Brian Taylor, NY
1973–74	Swen Nater, SA
1974–75	Marvin Barnes, StL
1975–76	David Thompson, Den

Coach of the Year

1967–68	Vince Cazetta, Pitt
1968–69	Alex Hannum, Oak
1969–70	Bill Sharman, LA
	Joe Belmont, Den
1970–71	Al Bianchi, Vir
1971–72	Tom Nissalke, Dall
1972–73	Larry Brown, Car
1973–74	Babe McCarthy, Ken
	Joe Mullaney, Utah
1974–75	Larry Brown, Den
1975–76	Larry Brown, Den

ABA Season Leaders

Scoring

		GP	Pts	Avg
1967–68	Connie Hawkins, Pitt	70	1875	26.8
1968–69	Rick Barry, Oak	35	1190	34.0
1969–70	Spencer Haywood, Den	84	2519	30.0
1970–71	Dan Issel, Ken	83	2480	29.4
1971–72	Charlie Scott, Vir	73	2524	34.6
1972–73	Julius Erving, Vir	71	2268	31.9
1973–74	Julius Erving, NY	84	2299	27.4
1974–75	George McGinnis, Ind	79	2353	29.8
1975–76	Julius Erving, NY	84	2462	29.3

Rebounds

1967–68	Mel Daniels, Minn	15.6
1968–69	Mel Daniels, Ind	16.5
1969–70	Spencer Haywood, Den	19.5
1970–71	Mel Daniels, Ind	18.0
1971–72	Artis Gilmore, Ken	17.8
1972–73	Artis Gilmore, Ken	17.5
1973–74	Artis Gilmore, Ken	18.3
1974–75	Swen Nater, SA	16.4
1975–76	Artis Gilmore, Ken	15.5

Assists

1967–68	Larry Brown, NO	6.5
1968–69	Larry Brown, Oak	7.1
1969–70	Larry Brown, Wash	7.1
1970–71	Bill Melchionni, NY	8.3
1971–72	Bill Melchionni, NY	8.4
1972–73	Bill Melchionni, NY	7.5
1973–74	Al Smith, Den	8.2
1974–75	Mack Calvin, Den	7.7
1975–76	Don Buse, Ind	8.2

Steals

1973–74	Ted McClain, Car	2.98
1974–75	Brian Taylor, NY	2.80
1975–76	Don Buse, Ind	4.12

Blocked Shots

1973–74	Caldwell Jones, SD	4.00
1974–75	Caldwell Jones, SD	3.24
1975–76	Billy Paultz, SA	3.05

World Championship of Basketball

Year	Winner	Runner-Up	Score	Site
1950	Argentina	United States	†	Rio de Janeiro
1954	United States	Brazil	†	Rio de Janeiro
1959	Brazil	United States	†	Santiago, Chile
1963	Brazil	Yugoslavia	†	Rio de Janeiro
1967	Soviet Union	Yugoslavia	†	Montevideo, Uruguay
1970	Yugoslavia	Brazil	†	Ljubljana, Yugoslavia
1974	Soviet Union	Yugoslavia	†	San Juan
1978	Yugoslavia	Soviet Union	82–81 (OT)	Manila
1982	Soviet Union	United States	95–94	Cali, Colombia
1986	United States	Soviet Union	87–85	Madrid
1990	Yugoslavia	Soviet Union	92–75	Buenos Aires
1994*	United States	Russia	137–91	Toronto
1998	Yugoslavia	Russia	64–62	Athens

*U.S. professionals began competing in 1994. In 1998, the NBA labor dispute resulted in a boycott of the World Championship by NBA stars; the U.S. roster was filled by members of the CBA and European professional leagues and college players.
†Result determined by overall record in final round of competition.

THEY SAID IT

Malik Rose, San Antonio Spurs forward, claiming the lockout forced him to move back into his mother's house and share a room with his eight-year-old brother: "This is it. I sleep on Rugrats pillowcases."

College
Basketball

Endangered Species

Unexpected champions Connecticut and Purdue offered evidence that college basketball dynasties may soon be extinct

BY B.J. SCHECTER

PERHAPS University of Connecticut coach Jim Calhoun has had more talented teams, groups that have exhibited more grace, possessed prettier jump shots or won with more ease. Just maybe several of those teams could have—and in a case or two perhaps should have—won national championships. But they didn't. Indeed, prior to this season UConn had never even made it to the Final Four, a fact Calhoun has worn like a scarlet letter in the state of Connecticut, where his team has a following equivalent to that of a professional franchise. So how did this year's Connecticut team create Husky mania? By not only clawing and scraping to the Final Four, but topping it off by beating seemingly invincible Duke in the championship game. To accomplish this feat the Huskies needed a player who personified their coach, someone who had the same type of leadership abilities, a bit of a chip on his shoulder and a desire to win that matched the fiery 56-year-old Calhoun's. UConn found that person in the most unlikely of places: the body of a pudgy, 5'10", 205-pound point guard named Khalid El-Amin.

To understand how badly UConn needed someone like El-Amin to come along you have to go back to April 1997, the day that El-Amin arrived in Storrs for his recruiting trip. After touring the campus El-Amin played in a pickup game with UConn players at Gampel Pavilion. El-Amin immediately took over, yelling at his teammates if they were out of position, ordering them to set screens and pick up their intensity. After one player missed a few shots El-Amin turned to him and said, "If you keep missing, I won't pass you the ball anymore." What did the rest of the Huskies think of the high-schooler's chutzpah? "We loved it," says Ricky Moore, the point guard at the time, who moved to shooting guard when El-Amin arrived. "Khalid had exactly the type of poise and leadership abilities that we needed."

He had the confidence, too. Whether he was taking the last shot or proclaiming his own importance to the team, El-Amin's message was loud and clear: Follow me. During the summer of 1998, while on an exhibition tour in Israel, El-Amin and his

The unlikely looking El-Amin (42) got the Huskies over the hump in '99.

JOHN W. MCDONOUGH

teammates were treated to a camel ride in the desert. While his peers shied away from the camels for fear of being bitten or spat on, El-Amin ran up and jumped on one of the dromedaries. Not surprisingly, the rest of the team followed suit. El-Amin wasn't UConn's best player in 1998–99—All-America forward Richard Hamilton was—but there is no question that the Huskies would not have won a national title without him.

When asked before the championship game why the Huskies had never made it to the Final Four before, El-Amin said, "I've said it before and I'll say it again. All this team was missing to win the national championship was a player of my stature and capability." And having talked the talk, El-Amin walked the walk. Every time he stepped on the floor—in practice or in games—El-Amin let his opposition know they were in for a war. Few observers gave the Huskies much of a chance against 37–1 Duke in the NCAA finals, but El-Amin knew the matter would be settled by the players on the court, not the analysts in the TV studios. Fittingly, it was his two free throws with five seconds remaining that sealed the Huskies 77–74 victory.

El-Amin was the poster boy for an NCAA tournament that embraced the little guy and showed that small schools from little-known conferences can play with the big boys. The Missouri Valley Conference received as many bids (three) as the ACC, and Gonzaga, a small Jesuit school located in Spokane—and previously known for

being the alma mater of Bing Crosby and John Stockton—made it all the way to the West Regional final, where it nearly knocked off UConn. Weber State's Harold Arceneaux scored 36 points in a 76–74 first-round upset of North Carolina, sending the Tar Heels out of the tournament in the first round for the first time in 19 years.

All in all, eight double-digit seeds advanced to the second round. A record five made it to the Sweet 16, and the aforementioned Gonzaga, a 10 seed, wore the glass slipper all the way to the Elite Eight. After beating Minnesota, Stanford and Florida the Zags proved that a team's number of national television appearances (Gonzaga had none entering the NCAA tournament.) is not necessarily the measure of its ability. The NCAAs provided many intriguing story lines, from Wally World—Miami of Ohio's Wally Szczerbiak, who propelled the RedHawks into the Sweet 16 by scoring a combined 67 points

Gee, Wally: The talented Szczerbiak (32) took Miami of Ohio to the Sweet 16.

and grabbing 19 rebounds in wins over Washington and Utah—to Oklahoma, which not only advanced to the second round for the first time in nine years, but also inspired the name of a newborn baby. After the Sooners hit 10 three-pointers in a 61–60 first-round upset of Arizona, Oklahoma assistant coach Ray Lopes persuaded his wife to change the name of their infant son from Marcus to Trey.

But when the tournament reached St. Petersburg, the clock struck midnight on the Cinderellas, and the Final Four looked more like the regular season—with the big powers hogging the headlines—than the frenzied, upset-laden first two weeks of the tournament. The Big Ten received a record-tying seven bids to the Big Dance and sent two teams, Michigan State and Ohio State, to the Final Four. They were joined by Duke and UConn, the only two schools to hold the No. 1 ranking in 1998–99. There were three No. 1 seeds and No. 4 Ohio State, which, like UConn, rode the back of a 5' 10" point guard. That was Scoonie Penn, who helped turn the Buckeyes from an 8–22 team in 1997–98 to a national semifinalist after transferring to Columbus from Boston College along with former Eagle coach, Jim O'Brien.

Many of the top stories in 1998–99 revolved around coaches. On the day of its first-round NCAA tournament game, Minnesota was plunged into scandal when a former academic counselor alleged that with the full knowledge of Gopher coach Clem Haskins she wrote over 400 papers and homework assignments for several current and former Minnesota players. Although Haskins denied knowledge of any wrongdoing, stories about the scandal dominated the offseason, and the school bought out the remainder of Haskins's contract in late June.

Iowa's Tom Davis wasn't fortunate enough to receive a financial settlement. Even though he averaged more than 20 wins a year in his 13 seasons, Davis was told by Hawkeyes athletic director Bob Bowlsby that his contract wouldn't be renewed after the season. The exiting coach refused to utter a negative word about his dismissal or the man who executed it, and his players rallied around him, snapping Kansas's 62-game home winning streak in December and making it to the West Regional semifinal. In January legendary Georgetown coach John Thompson resigned after 27 years, citing personal reasons. Another legendary—or notorious, depending on your point of view—coach,

Jerry Tarkanian, just kept going, ushering in the New Year with his 700th career victory as his Fresno State Bulldogs defeated New Mexico 86–80.

Coach Cliff Ellis helped bring unaccustomed college basketball joy back to Auburn, which hadn't been to the NCAA tournament since 1988. The Tigers won the SEC title, something they'd accomplished once in the previous 67 years, and they went from unranked in the preseason to No. 2 in the nation in February. They lost 72–64 to Ohio State in the South Regional semifinal, but by that time fans were already saying, on a sign in downtown Auburn, AUBURN, BASKETBALL CAPITAL OF THE SOUTH.

While the Tigers were a huge surprise, and the Big Ten was clearly the power conference in 1998–99, the basketball capital of the South, and the nation, was in Durham, N.C. Until the final, Duke was unquestionably the team of the year. The Blue Devils sailed through the regular season and turned the usually fiercely competitive ACC into a one-horse race. Duke led the nation in scoring margin (25.9 points) and points per game (92.9), and held opponents to a 38.8 field-goal percentage, while hitting 51.8% of its own shots. Duke had all the elements—a bruising yet mobile center in All-America Elton Brand; a team leader and deadly three-point shooter in Trajan Langdon; a versatile point guard in William Avery; and a pair of often overlooked forwards in Chris Carrawell and Shane Battier, who would have been stars on most other teams. Duke's sixth man, for god's sake, freshman Corey Maggette, was a first-round NBA draft choice when he decided to leave school in April. He averaged 10.6 points per game while playing only 18 minutes per game.

The Blue Devils' lone regular-season loss was a last-second defeat to Cincinnati in the Great Alaskan Shootout in November. Since that game coach Mike Krzyzewski's team was remarkably focused and efficient, often leaving opponents scratching their heads and wondering, How do you beat a team with no apparent weakness?

It was the same question women's teams had been asking about Tennessee for the previous three years. The Vols entered 1998–99 as the three-time defending national champions and featured Chamique Holdsclaw, the best player in the nation. Tennessee was untouchable in 1997–98—streamrolling to a 39–0 record en route to the national title—and with Holdsclaw back for her final season and a new crop of high school All-Americas, a fourth consecutive national championship appeared to be a foregone conclusion.

Like the Duke men, the Tennessee women lost their No. 1 ranking in November. The Vols had their 40-game winning streak snapped by fifth-ranked Purdue, 78–68, in West Lafayette, Ind. This seemed to come as a relief to Tennessee coach Pat Summitt, who had been critical of her team's intensity during the preseason. "I've known this was coming," Summitt said. "The contrast in the past three weeks has been frustrating." But the loss was merely a bump in the road for Tennessee. The Vols resumed their winning ways and sent a clear message with a 92–81 victory over top-ranked Connecticut in January in Storrs, Conn. Its contents? That the road to the national title still went through Knoxville.

Meanwhile, playing in the shadow of the Blue Devils men, the Duke women were quietly having the best season in school history. They cruised through the ACC with a 15–1 record, their only loss coming to Clemson. But unlike their male counterparts, who were picked as national championship favorites from the start, the Duke women seemed unlikely to reach the Final Four. When the tournament pairings came out, the likelihood shrank further: mighty Tennessee was in the East region with the Blue Devils.

On March 22, one day after the Duke men completed the inevitable, the Duke women pulled off the impossible. Before a partisan crowd in Greensboro, N.C., the Blue Devils shocked Tennessee 69–63 in the East Regional final. It was one of the biggest upsets in women's tournament his-

Figgs (5) scored 18 second-half points to lead Purdue past Duke in the women's final.

came alive in the second half, scoring 18 points. With four minutes left, Figgs's back-courtmate, White-McCarty, sprained her ankle and had to leave the game. Figgs made all six of her free throws and set the tone for the Boilermakers down the stretch as they made 15 of 17 free throws in the final 3:49. "From the moment Steph went down, it was like six against five out there," said Purdue assistant Kerry Cremeans. "Ukari was not going to let us lose."

Figgs may not have been the go-to player all season, but she was a quality veteran who did what she had to do to help her team win. The same can be said of UConn's Moore. When El-Amin came in Moore sacrificed his offense and became one of the best defensive players in the country. Yet when the Huskies needed it, Moore brought tenacity and killer instinct—not to mention fine offensive skills. His versatility and toughness proved to be the difference in the final against Duke. He scored 13 points in the first half and opened up the floor for Hamilton and El-Amin, but it was his defensive stop that won the game. With 15 seconds remaining and the Huskies leading 75–74, Duke went to its leader, Trajan Langdon. "I heard Coach K yelling to Trajan, 'Go get the ball and take him!'" said Moore. "Him against me. I started smiling because I knew he wasn't going to score that basket." Langdon didn't; Moore stuck to him and forced a traveling call.

As Duke and Tennessee will attest, dynasties are difficult to sustain in this era of college basketball. The Blue Devils did go to five Final Fours in the 1990s and won two titles, but they couldn't win with what seemed to be their most talented team of the five. The Vols won three straight titles but fell short in the great Holdsclaw's senior year, when they were stocked as ever with stars. Calhoun and Connecticut may not repeat in 2000, but they proved that they could win the big one—and that it takes more than talent.

tory, and it occasioned only the second time that a school had sent both its men's and women's teams to the Final Four. Joining Duke in the women's semifinals were Purdue, Georgia and Louisiana Tech.

Duke and Purdue advanced, creating an interesting subplot for the final: Duke's stars, center Michelle VanGorp and guard Nicole Erickson, began their careers at Purdue along with Boilermakers guards Stephanie White-McCarty and Ukari Figgs. After Purdue coach Lin Dunn was fired in 1996, VanGorp and Erickson transferred to Duke. According to Erickson, a Duke-Purdue final was "destiny" after the Blue Devils knocked off Tennessee. "I've been thinking about that since I left Purdue three years ago," she said.

There hadn't been a women's final without Summitt's stare or Holdsclaw's glare in four years, but Purdue and Figgs proved more than adequate replacements. After the lowest-scoring half in championship-game history Duke took a 22–17 lead into the locker room. Figgs had been held scoreless in the first 20 minutes, but she

NCAA Championship Game Box Score

Connecticut 77

CONNECTICUT	Min	FG M–A	FT M–A	Reb O–T	A	PF	TP
Freeman	32	3–6	0–0	5–8	0	1	6
Hamilton	38	10–22	5–6	4–7	3	1	27
Voskuhl	28	1–1	0–0	0–3	2	3	2
Moore	37	6–10	0–1	0–8	2	4	13
El-Amin	22	5–12	2–4	3–4	4	3	12
Wane	8	2–2	0–0	0–0	0	4	4
Mouring	17	3–4	0–1	0–3	0	1	6
Saunders	11	1–3	2–4	0–3	0	3	4
Jones	6	1–1	1–2	0–2	0	0	3
Klaiber	1	0–0	0–0	0–0	0	0	0
Totals	200	32–61	10–18	12–38	11	20	77

Percentages: FG—.525, FT—.556. 3-pt goals: 3–8, .375 (Hamilton 2–4, Moore 1–1, El-Amin 0–2, Mouring 0–1). Team rebounds: 3. Blocked shots: 6 (Freeman 3, Voskuhl 2, Mouring). Turnovers: 16 (El-Amin 6, Freeman 3, Moore 3, Mouring 2, Jones, Saunders). Steals: 4 (Hamilton 2, Moore, Wane).

Duke 74

DUKE	Min	FG M–A	FT M–A	Reb O–T	A	PF	TP
Carrawell	31	3–7	3–4	0–4	2	4	9
Battier	33	2–7	1–2	3–4	2	3	6
Brand	38	5–8	5–8	2–13	0	3	15
Avery	36	3–12	4–4	2–4	5	4	11
Langdon	38	7–15	6–7	0–1	1	2	25
James	6	0–0	0–0	0–1	0	0	0
Maggette	11	3–7	2–2	0–0	0	2	8
Burgess	7	0–0	0–0	0–0	0	1	0
Totals	200	23–56	21–27	7–27	10	19	74

Percentages: FG—.411, FT—.778. 3-pt goals: 7–19, .368 (Carrawell 0–2, Battier 1–3, Avery 1–3, Langdon 5–10, Maggette 0–1). Team rebounds: 4. Blocked shots: 4 (Carrawell 2, Brand 2). Turnovers: 19 (Carrawell 4, Brand 3, Langdon 2, Maggette 2, Avery). Steals: 6 (Langdon 3, Brand 2, Carrawell).

Halftime: Duke 39, Connecticut 37. A: 41,340.
Officials: Higgins, Boudreaux, Thornley.

Final AP Top 25

Poll taken before NCAA Tournament.

1. Duke	32–1	
2. Michigan St	29–4	
3. Connecticut	28–2	
4. Auburn	27–3	
5. Maryland	26–5	
6. Utah	27–4	
7. Stanford	25–6	
8. Kentucky	25–8	
9. St. John's	25–8	
10. Miami (FL)	22–6	
11. Cincinnati	26–5	
12. Arizona	22–6	
13. N Carolina	24–9	
14. Ohio St	23–8	
15. UCLA	22–8	
16. College of Charleston	28–2	
17. Arkansas	22–10	
18. Wisconsin	22–9	
19. Indiana	22–10	
20. Tennessee	20–8	
21. Iowa	18–9	
22. Kansas	22–9	
23. Florida	20–8	
24. UNC-Charlotte	22–10	
25. New Mexico	24–8	

National Invitation Tournament Scores

First round: Xavier 86, Toledo 84; N Carolina St 92, Providence 86; Princeton 54, Georgetown 47; Wake Forest 73, Alabama 57; Nebraska 68, UNLV 55; Texas Christian 72, Kansas St 71; Clemson 77, Georgia 57; Old Dominion 70, Seton Hall 56; Rutgers 58, Hofstra 45; Butler 51, Bradley 50; Colorado 65, Pepperdine 61; Colorado St 69, Mississippi St 56; Wyoming 81, Southern Cal 77; California 79, Fresno St 71; DePaul 69, Northwestern 64; Oregon 67, Georgia Tech 64.
Second round: Xavier 87, Wake Forest 76; Princeton 61, N Carolina St 58; Texas Christian 101, Nebraska 89; Butler 75, Old Dominion 62; Oregon 93, Wyoming 72; Clemson 78, Rutgers 68; California 58, DePaul 57; Colorado St 86, Colorado 76.
Third round: Xavier 65, Princeton 58; Oregon 77, Texas Christian 68; Clemson 89, Butler 69; California 71, Colorado St 62.
Semifinals: Clemson 79, Xavier 76; California 85, Oregon 69.
Championship: California 61, Clemson 60.
Consolation game: Xavier 106, Oregon 75.

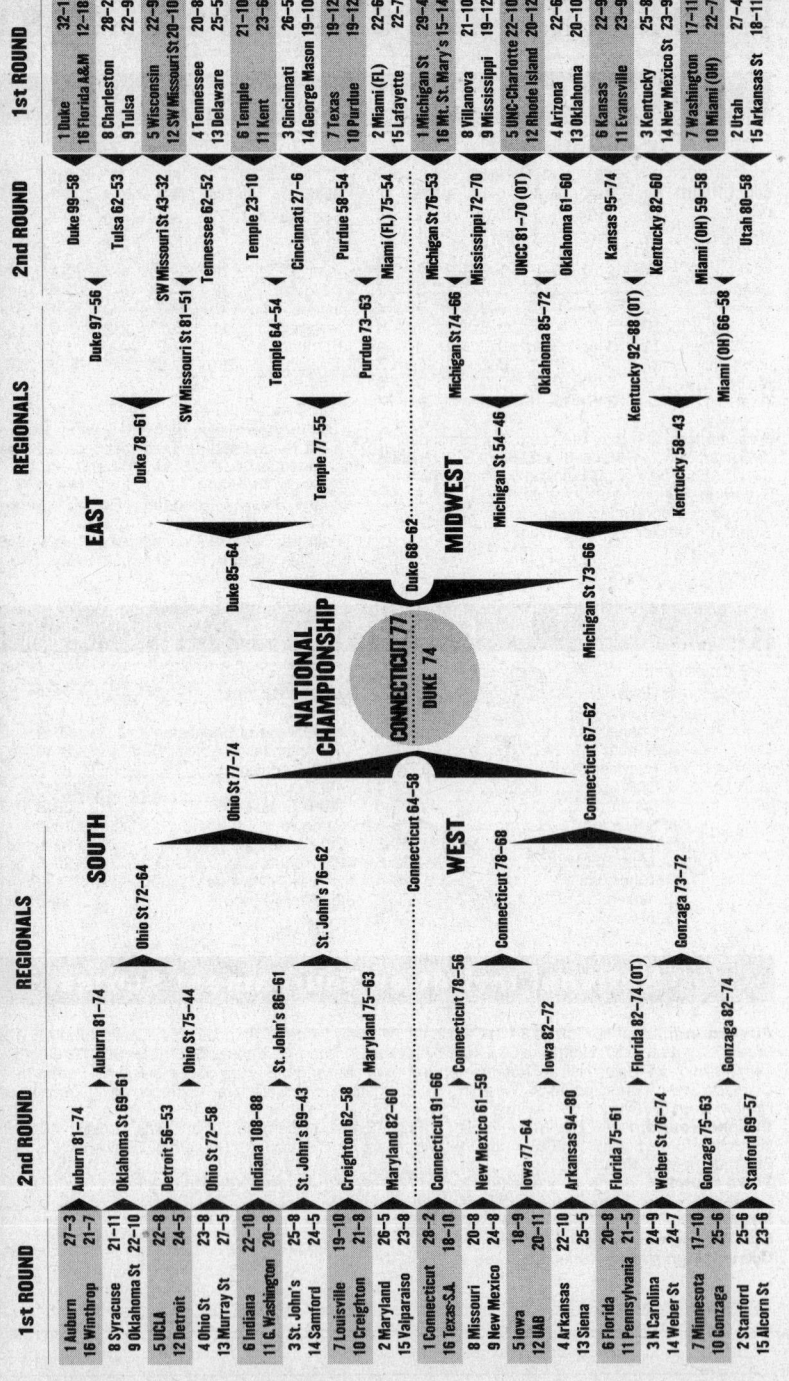

1st ROUND

Seed	Team	Record
1	Duke	32-1
16	Florida A&M	12-18
8	Charleston	28-2
9	Tulsa	22-9
5	Wisconsin	22-9
12	SW Missouri St	20-10
4	Tennessee	20-8
13	Delaware	25-5
6	Temple	21-10
11	Kent	23-6
3	Cincinnati	26-5
14	George Mason	19-10
7	Texas	19-12
10	Purdue	19-12
2	Miami (FL)	22-6
15	Lafayette	22-7
1	Michigan St	29-4
16	Mt. St. Mary's	15-14
8	Villanova	21-10
9	Mississippi	19-12
5	UNC-Charlotte	22-10
12	Rhode Island	20-12
4	Arizona	22-6
13	Oklahoma	20-10
6	Kansas	22-9
11	Evansville	23-9
3	Kentucky	25-8
14	New Mexico St	23-9
7	Washington	17-11
10	Miami (OH)	22-7
2	Utah	27-4
15	Arkansas St	18-11

2nd ROUND

- Duke 99-58
- Tulsa 62-53
- SW Missouri St 43-32
- Tennessee 62-52
- Temple 23-10
- Cincinnati 27-6
- Purdue 58-54
- Miami (FL) 75-54
- Michigan St 76-53
- Mississippi 72-70
- UNCC 81-70 (OT)
- Oklahoma 61-60
- Kansas 95-74
- Kentucky 82-60
- Miami (OH) 59-58
- Utah 80-58

REGIONALS

EAST

- Duke 97-56
- SW Missouri St 81-51
- Temple 64-54
- Cincinnati 27-6
- Duke 78-61
- Temple 77-55
- Duke 85-64

MIDWEST

- Michigan St 74-66
- Oklahoma 85-72
- Kentucky 92-88 (OT)
- Michigan St 54-46
- Kentucky 58-43
- Michigan St 73-66

NATIONAL CHAMPIONSHIP

- Duke 68-62
- **CONNECTICUT 77**
- **DUKE 74**
- Connecticut 64-58

SOUTH

- Ohio St 77-74
- St. John's 76-62
- Ohio St 72-64
- Ohio St 75-44
- St. John's 86-61
- Maryland 75-63

WEST

- Connecticut 78-68
- Iowa 82-72
- Florida 82-74 (OT)
- Gonzaga 73-72
- Connecticut 78-56
- Gonzaga 82-74
- Connecticut 67-62

2nd ROUND

- Auburn 81-74
- Oklahoma St 69-61
- Detroit 56-53
- Ohio St 72-58
- Indiana 108-88
- St. John's 69-43
- Creighton 62-58
- Maryland 82-60
- Connecticut 91-66
- New Mexico 61-59
- Iowa 77-64
- Arkansas 94-80
- Florida 75-61
- Weber St 76-74
- Gonzaga 75-63
- Stanford 69-57

1st ROUND

Seed	Team	Record
1	Auburn	27-3
16	Winthrop	21-7
8	Syracuse	21-11
9	Oklahoma St	22-10
5	UCLA	22-8
12	Detroit	24-5
4	Ohio St	23-8
13	Murray St	27-5
6	Indiana	22-10
11	G. Washington	20-8
3	St. John's	25-8
14	Samford	24-5
7	Louisville	19-10
10	Creighton	21-8
2	Maryland	26-5
15	Valparaiso	23-8
1	Connecticut	28-2
16	Texas-S.A.	18-10
8	Missouri	20-8
9	New Mexico	24-8
5	Iowa	18-9
12	UAB	20-11
4	Arkansas	22-10
13	Siena	25-5
6	Florida	20-8
11	Pennsylvania	21-5
3	N Carolina	24-9
14	Weber St	24-7
7	Minnesota	17-10
10	Gonzaga	25-6
2	Stanford	25-6
15	Alcorn St	23-6

NCAA Men's Division I Conference Standings

America East

	Conference			All Games		
	W	L	Pct	W	L	Pct
†Delaware	15	3	.833	25	6	.806
Drexel	15	3	.833	20	9	.690
Hofstra	14	4	.778	22	10	.688
Maine	13	5	.722	19	9	.679
Hartford	9	9	.500	11	16	.407
Vermont	7	11	.389	11	16	.407
Northeastern	6	12	.333	10	18	.357
Boston University	5	13	.278	9	18	.333
Towson	4	14	.222	6	22	.214
New Hampshire	2	16	.111	4	23	.148

Atlantic Coast

	Conference			All Games		
	W	L	Pct	W	L	Pct
†Duke	16	0	1.000	37	2	.949
Maryland	13	3	.813	28	6	.824
N Carolina	10	6	.625	24	10	.706
Wake Forest	7	9	.438	17	14	.548
N Carolina St	6	10	.375	19	14	.576
Georgia Tech	6	10	.375	15	16	.484
Clemson	5	11	.313	20	15	.571
Florida St	5	11	.313	13	17	.433
Virginia	4	12	.250	14	16	.467

Atlantic 10

	Conference			All Games		
EAST	W	L	Pct	W	L	Pct
Temple	13	3	.813	24	11	.686
†Rhode Island	10	6	.625	20	13	.606
Massachusetts	9	7	.562	14	16	.467
St. Bonaventure	8	8	.500	14	15	.483
Fordham	5	11	.313	12	15	.444
St. Joseph's	5	11	.313	12	18	.400
WEST						
George Washington	13	3	.813	20	9	.690
Xavier	12	4	.750	25	11	.694
La Salle	8	8	.500	13	15	.464
Virginia Tech	7	9	.438	13	15	.464
Dayton	5	11	.313	11	17	.393
Duquesne	1	15	.063	5	23	.179

Big East

	Conference			All Games		
	W	L	Pct	W	L	Pct
†Connecticut	16	2	.889	34	2	.944
Miami (FL)	15	3	.833	23	7	.767
St. John's	14	4	.778	28	9	.757
Villanova	10	8	.556	21	11	.656
Syracuse	10	8	.556	21	12	.636
Rutgers	9	9	.500	19	13	.594
Providence	9	9	.500	16	14	.533
Seton Hall	8	10	.444	15	15	.500
Notre Dame	8	10	.444	14	16	.467
Georgetown	6	12	.333	15	16	.484
Pittsburgh	5	13	.278	14	16	.467
W Virginia	4	14	.222	10	19	.345
Boston College	3	15	.167	6	21	.222

Big Sky

	Conference			All Games		
	W	L	Pct	W	L	Pct
†Weber St	13	3	.813	25	8	.758
Northern Arizona	12	4	.750	21	8	.724
Portland St	9	7	.563	17	11	.607
Cal St-Northridge	9	7	.563	17	12	.586
Montana St	9	7	.563	16	13	.552
Eastern Washington	7	9	.438	10	17	.370
Montana	6	10	.375	13	14	.481
Idaho St	4	12	.250	6	20	.231
Cal St-Sacramento	3	13	.188	3	23	.115

Big South

	Conference			All Games		
	W	L	Pct	W	L	Pct
†Winthrop	9	1	.900	21	8	.724
Radford	8	2	.800	20	8	.714
UNC-Asheville	5	5	.500	11	18	.379
Charleston So.	4	6	.400	12	16	.429
Coastal Carolina	4	6	.400	7	20	.259
Liberty	0	10	.000	4	23	.148

Big Ten

	Conference			All Games		
	W	L	Pct	W	L	Pct
†Michigan St	15	1	.938	33	5	.868
Ohio St	12	4	.750	27	9	.750
Indiana	9	7	.563	23	11	.676
Wisconsin	9	7	.563	22	10	.688
Iowa	9	7	.563	20	10	.667
Minnesota	8	8	.500	17	11	.607
Purdue	7	9	.438	21	13	.618
Northwestern	6	10	.400	15	14	.517
Michigan	5	11	.313	12	19	.387
Penn St	5	11	.313	13	14	.482
Illinois	3	13	.188	14	18	.336

Big 12

	Conference			All Games		
	W	L	Pct	W	L	Pct
Texas	13	3	.813	19	13	.594
Missouri	11	5	.688	20	9	.690
†Kansas	11	5	.688	23	10	.697
Oklahoma	11	5	.688	22	11	.667
Oklahoma St	10	6	.625	23	11	.676
Nebraska	10	6	.625	20	13	.606
Kansas St	7	9	.438	20	13	.606
Colorado	7	9	.438	18	15	.545
Iowa St	6	10	.375	15	15	.500
Texas A&M	5	11	.312	12	15	.444
Texas Tech	5	11	.312	13	17	.433
Baylor	0	16	.000	6	24	.200

†Conference tourney winner.
Note: Standings based on regular-season conference play only; overall records include all tournament play.

Big West

EAST	Conference			All Games		
	W	L	Pct	W	L	Pct
Boise St	12	4	.750	21	8	.724
†New Mexico St	12	4	.750	23	10	.697
Idaho	11	5	.688	16	11	.593
Utah St	8	8	.500	15	13	.536
Nevada	4	12	.250	8	18	.308
N Texas	4	12	.250	4	22	.154
WEST						
UC-Santa Barbara	12	4	.750	15	13	.536
Long Beach St	9	7	.563	13	15	.464
Pacific	9	7	.563	14	13	.519
Cal St-Fullerton	7	9	.438	13	14	.481
Cal Poly	6	10	.375	11	16	.407
UC-Irvine	2	14	.125	6	20	.231

Colonial Athletic

	Conference			All Games		
	W	L	Pct	W	L	Pct
†George Mason	13	3	.813	19	11	.633
Old Dominion	11	5	.688	25	8	.758
Richmond	10	6	.625	15	12	.556
James Madison	9	7	.563	16	11	.593
UNC-Wilmington	9	7	.563	11	17	.393
VA Commonwealth	8	8	.500	15	16	.484
E Carolina	7	9	.438	13	14	.481
William & Mary	3	13	.188	8	19	.296
American	2	14	.125	7	21	.250

Conference USA

AMERICAN	Conference			All Games		
	W	L	Pct	W	L	Pct
Cincinnati	12	4	.750	27	6	.818
Louisville	11	5	.688	19	11	.633
†UNC-Charlotte	10	6	.625	23	11	.676
DePaul	10	6	.625	18	13	.581
St. Louis	8	8	.500	15	16	.484
Marquette	6	10	.375	14	15	.483
NATIONAL						
AL-Birmingham	10	6	.625	20	12	.625
S Florida	6	10	.375	14	14	.500
Southern Miss	6	10	.375	14	16	.467
Memphis	6	10	.375	13	15	.464
Tulane	6	10	.375	12	15	.444
Houston	5	11	.313	10	17	.370

Ivy League

	Conference			All Games		
	W	L	Pct	W	L	Pct
Pennsylvania	13	1	.929	21	6	.778
Princeton	11	3	.786	22	8	.733
Dartmouth	10	4	.714	14	12	.538
Harvard	7	7	.500	13	13	.500
Cornell	6	8	.429	11	15	.423
Columbia	5	9	.357	10	16	.385
Brown	2	12	.143	4	22	.154
Yale	2	12	.143	4	22	.154

Metro Atlantic Athletic

	Conference			All Games		
	W	L	Pct	W	L	Pct
†Siena	13	5	.722	25	6	.806
Niagara	13	5	.722	17	12	.586
Iona	12	6	.667	16	14	.533
Canisius	11	7	.611	15	12	.556
St. Peter's	10	8	.556	14	15	.483
Marist	8	10	.444	16	12	.571
Rider	7	11	.389	12	16	.429
Fairfield	7	11	.389	12	15	.444
Loyola (MD)	6	12	.333	13	15	.464
Manhattan	3	15	.167	5	22	.185

Mid-American

EAST	Conference			All Games		
	W	L	Pct	W	L	Pct
Miami (OH)	15	3	.833	24	8	.750
†Kent	13	5	.722	23	7	.767
Akron	12	6	.667	18	9	.667
Ohio	12	6	.667	18	10	.643
Bowling Green	12	6	.667	18	10	.643
Marshall	11	7	.611	16	11	.593
Buffalo	1	17	.056	5	24	.172
WEST						
Toledo	11	7	.611	19	9	.679
Ball St	10	8	.556	16	11	.593
Central Michigan	7	11	.389	10	16	.385
Western Michigan	6	12	.333	11	15	.423
Eastern Michigan	5	13	.278	5	20	.200
Northern Illinois	2	16	.111	6	20	.231

Mid-Continent

	Conference			All Games		
	W	L	Pct	W	L	Pct
†Valparaiso	10	4	.714	23	9	.719
Oral Roberts	10	4	.714	17	11	.607
Western Illinois	9	5	.643	16	12	.571
Youngstown St	9	5	.643	14	14	.500
Southern Utah	6	8	.429	13	17	.433
IU/PUI	6	8	.429	11	16	.407
MO-Kansas City	3	11	.214	8	22	.267
Chicago St	3	11	.214	3	24	.111
Oakland	—	—	—	12	15	.444

Mid-Eastern Athletic

	Conference			All Games		
	W	L	Pct	W	L	Pct
S Carolina St	14	4	.778	17	12	.586
Coppin St	14	4	.778	15	14	.517
Morgan St	12	6	.667	14	14	.500
Norfolk St	11	7	.611	15	12	.556
Bethune-Cookman	10	9	.526	11	16	.407
N Carolina A&T St	9	9	.500	13	15	.464
Hampton	8	10	.444	8	19	.296
†Florida A&M	8	11	.421	12	19	.387
MD-Eastern Shore	7	11	.389	10	17	.370
Delaware St	5	13	.278	8	19	.296
Howard	2	16	.111	2	25	.074

†Conference tourney winner.

Midwestern Collegiate

	Conference			All Games		
	W	L	Pct	W	L	Pct
†Detroit	12	2	.857	25	6	.806
Butler	11	3	.786	22	10	.688
WI-Green Bay	9	5	.643	20	11	.645
Loyola (IL)	7	7	.500	9	18	.333
Cleveland St	6	8	.429	14	14	.500
WI-Milwaukee	5	9	.357	8	19	.296
Wright St	4	10	.286	9	18	.333
IL-Chicago	2	12	.143	7	21	.250

Missouri Valley

	Conference			All Games		
	W	L	Pct	W	L	Pct
Evansville	13	5	.722	23	10	.697
†Creighton	11	7	.611	22	9	.710
SW Missouri St	11	7	.611	22	11	.667
Bradley	11	7	.611	17	12	.586
Indiana St	10	8	.556	15	12	.556
Southern Illinois	10	8	.556	15	12	.556
Illinois St	7	11	.389	16	15	.516
Wichita St	6	12	.333	13	17	.433
Northern Iowa	6	12	.333	9	18	.333
Drake	5	13	.278	10	17	.370

Northeast

	Conference			All Games		
	W	L	Pct	W	L	Pct
MD-Balt. County	17	3	.850	19	9	.679
St. Francis (NY)	16	4	.800	20	8	.714
Robert Morris	12	8	.600	15	12	.556
Central Conn. St	11	9	.550	19	13	.594
Long Island	10	10	.500	10	17	.370
†Mount St. Mary's	10	10	.500	15	15	.500
Fairleigh Dickinson	9	11	.450	12	16	.429
Wagner	7	13	.350	9	18	.333
St. Francis (PA)	7	13	.350	9	17	.346
Quinnipiac	6	14	.300	9	18	.333
Monmouth	5	15	.250	5	21	.192

Ohio Valley

	Conference			All Games		
	W	L	Pct	W	L	Pct
†Murray St	16	2	.889	27	6	.818
SE Missouri	15	3	.833	20	9	.690
Morehead St	9	9	.500	13	15	.464
Tennessee St	9	9	.500	12	15	.444
Austin Peay	9	9	.500	11	16	.408
Middle Tennessee	9	9	.500	12	19	.387
Eastern Illinois	8	10	.444	13	16	.448
Tennessee Tech	8	10	.444	12	15	.444
Tennessee–Martin	5	13	.278	8	18	.308
Eastern Kentucky	2	16	.111	3	23	.115

Pacific-10

	Conference			All Games		
	W	L	Pct	W	L	Pct
Stanford	15	3	.833	26	7	.788
Arizona	13	5	.722	22	7	.759
UCLA	12	6	.667	22	9	.710
Washington	10	8	.556	17	12	.586
California	8	10	.444	22	11	.667
Oregon	8	10	.444	19	13	.594
Southern Cal	7	11	.389	15	13	.536
Oregon St	7	11	.389	13	14	.481
Arizona St	6	12	.333	14	16	.467
Washington St	4	14	.222	10	19	.345

Patriot League

	Conference			All Games		
	W	L	Pct	W	L	Pct
†Lafayette	10	2	.833	22	8	.733
Navy	9	3	.750	20	7	.741
Bucknell	9	3	.750	16	13	.552
Colgate	7	5	.583	14	14	.500
Army	4	8	.333	8	19	.296
Holy Cross	3	9	.250	7	20	.259
Lehigh	0	12	.000	6	22	.214

Southeastern

	Conference			All Games		
EAST	W	L	Pct	W	L	Pct
Tennessee	12	4	.750	21	9	.700
†Kentucky	11	5	.688	28	9	.757
Florida	10	6	.625	22	9	.710
Georgia	6	10	.375	15	15	.500
Vanderbilt	5	11	.313	14	15	.483
S Carolina	3	13	.188	8	21	.276
WEST						
Auburn	14	2	.875	29	4	.879
Arkansas	9	7	.563	23	11	.676
Mississippi	8	8	.500	20	13	.606
Mississippi St	8	8	.500	20	13	.606
Alabama	6	10	.375	17	15	.531
Louisiana St	4	12	.250	12	15	.444

Southern

	Conference			All Games		
NORTH	W	L	Pct	W	L	Pct
Appalachian St	13	3	.813	21	8	.724
Davidson	11	5	.688	16	11	.593
E Tennessee St	9	7	.563	17	11	.607
VMI	9	7	.563	12	15	.444
UNC-Greensboro	5	11	.313	7	20	.259
Western Carolina	2	14	.125	8	21	.276
SOUTH						
†Coll. of Charleston	16	0	1.000	28	2	.933
Chattanooga	9	7	.563	16	12	.571
Wofford	8	8	.500	11	16	.407
Georgia Southern	6	10	.375	11	17	.393
Furman	5	11	.313	12	16	.428
Citadel	3	13	.188	9	18	.333

†Conference tourney winner.

Southland

	Conference			All Games		
	W	L	Pct	W	L	Pct
SW Texas St	13	5	.722	19	9	.679
†TX-San Antonio	12	6	.667	18	11	.620
Nicholls St	12	6	.667	14	15	.483
NE Louisiana	12	6	.667	13	14	.481
Lamar	11	7	.611	17	11	.607
McNeese St	11	7	.611	13	15	.464
Northwestern St	8	10	.444	11	15	.423
TX-Arlington	8	10	.444	10	16	.385
San Houston St	7	11	.389	10	16	.385
Southeastern LA	3	15	.167	6	20	.231
Stephen F. Austin	2	16	.111	4	22	.154

Southwestern Athletic

	Conference			All Games		
	W	L	Pct	W	L	Pct
†Alcorn St	14	2	.875	23	7	.767
Southern	13	3	.813	21	7	.750
Jackson St	11	5	.688	16	12	.571
Mississippi Valley	10	6	.625	14	13	.519
Alabama St	8	8	.500	11	16	.407
Texas Southern	6	10	.375	8	19	.296
Grambling	5	11	.313	6	21	.222
Prairie View	4	12	.250	6	21	.222
AR-Pine Bluff	1	15	.063	3	24	.111

Sun Belt

	Conference			All Games		
	W	L	Pct	W	L	Pct
Louisiana Tech	10	4	.714	19	9	.679
†Arkansas St	9	5	.643	18	12	.600
Florida International	7	7	.500	13	16	.448
Southwestern LA	7	7	.500	13	16	.448
Western Kentucky	7	7	.500	13	16	.448
S Alabama	6	8	.429	11	16	.407
New Orleans	5	9	.357	14	16	.467
AR-Little Rock	5	9	.357	12	15	.444

Trans America Athletic

	Conference			All Games		
	W	L	Pct	W	L	Pct
†Samford	15	1	.938	24	6	.800
Central Florida	13	3	.813	19	10	.655
Georgia St	11	5	.688	17	13	.567
Stetson	10	6	.625	14	13	.519
Centenary	9	7	.563	14	14	.500
Jacksonville	7	9	.438	12	15	.444
Troy St	6	10	.375	9	18	.333
Campbell	6	10	.375	9	18	.333
Mercer	5	11	.313	8	18	.308
Florida Atlantic	3	13	.188	6	20	.231
Jacksonville St	3	13	.188	8	18	.308

West Coast

	Conference			All Games		
	W	L	Pct	W	L	Pct
†Gonzaga	12	2	.857	28	7	.800
Pepperdine	9	5	.643	19	13	.594
San Diego	9	5	.643	18	9	.667
Santa Clara	8	6	.571	14	15	.483
Loyola Marymount	6	8	.429	11	16	.407
St. Mary's	5	9	.357	13	18	.419
San Francisco	4	10	.286	12	17	.414
Portland	3	11	.214	9	18	.333

Western Athletic

	Conference			All Games		
	W	L	Pct	W	L	Pct
PACIFIC						
†Utah	14	0	1.000	28	5	.848
New Mexico	9	5	.643	25	9	.735
Fresno St	9	5	.643	21	12	.636
UTEP	8	6	.571	16	12	.571
Brigham Young	6	8	.429	12	16	.429
San Jose St	5	9	.357	12	16	.429
Hawaii	3	11	.214	6	20	.231
San Diego St	2	12	.143	4	22	.154
MOUNTAIN						
UNLV	9	5	.643	16	13	.552
Tulsa	9	5	.643	23	10	.697
Rice	8	6	.571	18	10	.643
Texas Christian	7	7	.500	21	11	.656
Southern Methodist	7	7	.500	15	15	.500
Colorado St	7	7	.500	19	11	.633
Wyoming	7	7	.500	18	10	.643
Air Force	2	12	.143	10	16	.385

Independents

	All Games		
	W	L	Pct
Belmont	14	13	.519
Denver	10	17	.370
TX-Pan American	5	22	.185

†Conference tourney winner.

Scoring

	Class	GP	Field Goals			3-Pt FG		Free Throws			Reb	Pts	Avg
			FGA	FG	Pct	FGA	FG	FTA	FT	Pct			
Alvin Young, Niagara	Sr	29	535	253	47.3	160	65	199	157	78.9	167	728	25.1
Ray Minlend, St. Francis (NY)	Sr	28	452	210	46.5	121	31	305	229	75.1	95	680	24.3
Wally Szczerbiak, Miami (OH)	Sr	32	517	270	52.2	177	63	207	172	83.1	272	775	24.2
Brian Merriweather, TX-Pan American	So	27	586	239	40.8	272	110	58	53	91.4	72	641	23.7
Damian Woolfolk, Norfolk St	Jr	27	487	237	48.7	131	46	145	115	79.3	111	635	23.5
Quincy Lewis, Minnesota	Sr	27	495	226	45.7	133	53	148	120	81.1	160	625	23.1
Jason Hartman, Portland St	Sr	28	434	198	45.6	209	79	202	164	81.2	156	639	22.8
Lee Nailon, Texas Christian	Sr	31	524	266	50.8	15	4	239	171	71.5	288	707	22.8
Maurice Evans, Wichita St	So	28	458	211	46.1	164	69	178	141	79.2	130	632	22.6
Harold Arceneaux, Weber St	Jr	32	521	266	51.1	103	34	194	147	75.8	193	713	22.3
Roberto Bergerson, Boise St	Sr	29	467	224	48.0	179	71	146	125	85.6	116	644	22.2
Robert Johnson, Rice	Sr	28	440	191	43.4	230	83	209	152	72.7	120	617	22.0
Jamel Thomas, Providence	Sr	30	532	225	42.3	183	58	203	153	75.4	217	661	22.0
Jason Terry, Arizona	Sr	29	472	209	44.3	191	76	168	141	83.9	97	635	21.9
Damon Arnette, Florida Atlantic	Sr	24	373	176	47.2	116	46	182	127	69.8	197	525	21.9
Kevin Martin, UNC-Asheville	Sr	29	447	215	48.1	86	30	234	174	74.4	164	634	21.9
Jason Rowe, Loyola (MD)	Jr	28	428	216	50.5	161	58	155	122	78.7	136	612	21.9
Mike Pegues, Delaware	Jr	31	491	243	49.5	6	2	239	187	78.2	224	675	21.8
Richard Hamilton, Connecticut	Jr	34	557	247	44.3	196	68	204	170	83.3	163	732	21.5
Courtney Alexander, Fresno St	Jr	32	563	264	46.9	158	50	140	106	75.7	121	684	21.4
Faragi Phillips, Mississippi Valley St	Sr	24	450	172	38.2	180	69	115	89	77.4	126	502	20.9
Fred Warrick, Coppin St	Sr	29	512	195	38.1	254	98	160	117	73.1	145	605	20.9
Nate Holmstadt, Montana St	Sr	29	438	237	54.1	36	9	163	119	73.0	229	602	20.8
Louis Bullock, Michigan	Sr	31	476	195	41.0	199	75	206	178	86.4	127	643	20.7
Shawnta Rogers, George Wash.	Sr	29	503	195	38.8	238	86	144	125	86.8	116	601	20.7
Keion Brooks, Wright St	Sr	27	494	208	42.1	91	26	160	117	73.1	151	559	20.7
Marcus Wilson, Evansville	Sr	33	422	216	51.2	182	85	184	165	89.7	100	682	20.7
George Gervin Jr, Houston	Jr	27	418	177	42.3	155	62	177	140	79.1	113	556	20.6
Ugo Edezue, Wyoming	So	28	435	206	47.4	4	1	271	162	59.8	208	575	20.5
Monroe Pippins, Florida A&M	Jr	31	528	209	39.6	228	71	203	147	72.4	206	636	20.5

FIELD-GOAL PERCENTAGE

	Class	GP	FGA	FG	Pct
Todd MacCulloch, Washington	Sr	29	317	210	66.2
Quincy Gause, Georgia St	Sr	23	221	144	65.2
Ryan Moss, AR-Little Rock	Sr	24	210	135	64.3
Elton Brand, Duke	So	39	411	255	62.0
Damous Anderson, Florida St	Jr	23	190	115	60.5
Charles Gosa, New Mexico St	Sr	33	329	199	60.5
David Tompkins, Yale	Sr	26	275	165	60.0
Bud Eley, SE Missouri St	Sr	29	286	170	59.4
J.R. Van Hoose, Marshall	Fr	27	251	149	59.4
Evan Eschmeyer, Northwestern	Sr	29	308	180	58.4

Note: Minimum 5 made per game.

FREE-THROW PERCENTAGE

	Class	GP	FTA	FT	Pct
Lonnie Cooper, Louisiana Tech	Sr	25	76	70	92.1
Haywood Eaddy, Loyola Marymount	Sr	21	88	79	89.8
Marcus Wilson, Evansville	Sr	33	184	165	89.7
Jermel President, Charleston	Sr	31	105	94	89.5
Arthur Lee, Stanford	Sr	33	158	140	88.6
Matt Sundblad, Lamar	Sr	28	95	84	88.4
Rayford Young, Texas Tech	Jr	25	114	100	87.7
Brandon Welsch, Robert Morris	Jr	27	81	71	87.7
Brian Earl, Princeton	Sr	30	88	77	87.5
Mike DeRocckis, Drexel	Sr	29	88	77	87.5

Note: Minimum 2.5 made per game.

REBOUNDS

	Class	GP	Reb	Avg
Ian McGinnis, Dartmouth	So	26	317	12.2
Todd MacCulloch, Washington	Sr	29	345	11.9
Jeff Foster, SW Texas St	Sr	28	316	11.3
Chris Mihm, Texas	So	32	351	11.0
K'Zell Wesson, La Salle	Sr	28	301	10.8
Bud Eley, SE Missouri St	Sr	29	310	10.7
Quentin Richardson, DePaul	Fr	31	327	10.5
Michael Ruffin, Tulsa	Sr	33	342	10.4
Derek Hood, Arkansas	Sr	34	349	10.3
Eric Dow, Denver	Sr	27	276	10.2

ASSISTS

	Class	GP	A	Avg
Doug Gottlieb, Oklahoma St	Jr	34	299	8.8
Chico Fletcher, Arkansas St	Jr	30	250	8.3
Ali Ton, Davidson	Sr	25	190	7.6
Ed Cota, N Carolina	Jr	32	238	7.4
Chris Herron, Fresno St	Sr	25	181	7.2
Mateen Cleaves, Michigan St	Jr	38	274	7.2
Prince Fowler, Texas Christian	Sr	32	226	7.1
Devan Clark, Southern	So	28	194	6.9
Shawnta Rogers, George Wash.	Sr	29	196	6.8
Tim Hill, Harvard	Sr	26	172	6.6

*Includes games played in tournaments.

THREE-POINT FIELD-GOAL PERCENTAGE

	Class	GP	FGA	FG	Pct
Rodney Thomas, IU/PUI	Jr	26	113	59	52.2
Ross Land, Northern Arizona	Jr	29	163	83	50.9
Brian Grawer, Missouri	So	29	129	64	49.6
Ryan Borowicz, WI-Green Bay	Sr	31	159	78	49.1
Alan Puckett, Citadel	Fr	27	113	55	48.7
Kevin Worley, Canisius	Sr	27	111	54	48.6
Scott Thomason, Pacific (CA)	Sr	27	111	54	48.6
Tim Heskett, Oklahoma	So	32	167	79	47.3
Nathan Jameson, UNC-Greens.	So	27	119	56	47.1
Keith Greene, TX-Arlington	Jr	26	139	65	46.8

Note: Minimum 1.5 made per game.

THREE-POINT FIELD GOALS MADE PER GAME

	Class	GP	FG	Avg
Brian Merriweather, TX-Pan Am	So	27	110	4.1
Shannon Taylor, Eastern Wash	Sr	27	103	3.8
Alan Barksdale, AR-Little Rock	Jr	25	95	3.8
Josh Heard, Tennessee Tech	Jr	27	98	3.6
Fred Warrick, Coppin St	Sr	29	98	3.4
Clay McKnight, Pacific (CA)	Jr	27	90	3.3
Leslie Ballard, Radford	Sr	28	92	3.3
Greg Buth, Dartmouth	So	26	83	3.2
Jan-Michael Thomas, Washington St.	Jr	28	89	3.2
Jamie Roberts, Tennessee St	So	25	78	3.1

BLOCKED SHOTS

	Class	GP	BS	Avg
Tarvis Williams, Hampton	Jr	27	135	5.0
Henry Jordan, Miss Valley St	So	27	108	4.0
Etan Thomas, Syracuse	Jr	33	131	4.0
Wojciech Myrda, NE Louisiana	Fr	27	96	3.6
Calvin Booth, Penn St	Sr	27	95	3.5
Alvin Jones, Georgie Tech	So	31	107	3.5
Frantz Pierre-Louis, Wagner	Sr	27	84	3.1
Kris Hunter, Virginia	Jr	29	88	3.0
John Bennett, Delaware	Sr	31	93	3.0
Joel Przybilla, Minnesota	Fr	28	84	3.0

STEALS

	Class	GP	S	Avg
Shawnta Rogers, George Wash.	Sr	29	103	3.6
Tim Winn, St. Bonaventure	Jr	23	81	3.5
Jason Rowe, Loyola (MD)	Jr	28	95	3.4
John Linehan, Providence	So	30	98	3.3
Cookie Belcher, Nebraska	Jr	32	102	3.2
Damon Arnette, Florida Atlantic	So	24	76	3.2
Pepe Sanchez, Temple	Jr	33	101	3.1
Jason Hart, Syracuse	Jr	33	101	3.1
Gene Nabors, Robert Morris	Jr	27	82	3.0
Skip Victor, Navy	Sr	27	80	3.0

Single-Game Highs

POINTS

44 ....Lee Nailon, Texas Christian, Dec 30 (vs Gonzaga)
44 ....Alvin Young, Niagara, Feb 8 (vs Siena)
43 ....Wally Szczerbiak, Miami (OH), Mar 12 (vs Washington)

REBOUNDS

24 ....Darren Phillips, Fairfield, Dec 5 (vs Loyola [MD])
22 ....Lee Nailon, Texas Christian, Jan 11 (vs Southern Methodist)
22 ....Troy Mack, Wichita St, Jan 18 (vs SW Missouri St)

ASSISTS

18 ....Doug Gottlieb, Oklahoma St, Dec 1 (vs Florida Atlantic)
17 ....Chico Fletcher, Arkansas St, Nov 23 (vs Texas Christian)
17 ....Jermaine Johnson, TX-Arlington, Dec 28 (vs Sam Houston St)

THREE-POINT FIELD GOALS

10 ....Pat Bradley, Arkansas, Dec 30 (vs N Texas)

Fifteen tied with nine.

STEALS

12 ....Richard Duncan, Middle Tennessee St, Feb 20 (vs Eastern
Kentucky)
10 ....Dionte Harvey, Southern, Nov 23 (vs Prairie View)
10 ....Aaron Bates, Southern, Dec 5 (vs Southeastern Louisiana)
10 ....Ivan Wagner, Texas, Feb 3 (vs Texas A&M)

BLOCKED SHOTS

12 ....Tarvis Williams, Hampton, Jan 9 (vs N Carolina A&T)
11 ....Stromile Swift, Louisiana St, Feb 10 (vs Alabama)
10 ....Tarvis Williams, Hampton, Nov 14 (vs Maine)
10 ....Joel Przybilla, Minnesota, Dec 4 (vs Fresno St)
10 ....Bud Eley, SE Missouri St, Jan 4 (vs Morehead St)

SCORING OFFENSE

	GP	W	L	Pts	Avg		GP	W	L	Pts	Avg
Duke	39	37	2	3581	91.8	Southern	28	21	7	2372	84.7
Texas Christian	32	21	11	2776	86.8	Maryland	34	28	6	2873	84.5
Siena	31	25	6	2686	86.6	Arizona	29	22	7	2383	82.2
Norfolk St	27	15	12	2330	86.3	Cal St-Northridge	29	17	12	2378	82.0
Cal Poly SLO	27	11	16	2293	84.9	Wyoming	28	18	10	2286	81.6

SCORING DEFENSE

	GP	W	L	Pts	Avg		GP	W	L	Pts	Avg
Princeton	30	22	8	1581	52.7	Northwestern	29	15	14	1655	57.1
Wisconsin	32	22	10	1766	55.2	Temple	35	24	11	2048	58.5
Detroit	31	25	6	1713	55.3	College of Charleston	31	28	3	1834	59.2
Utah	33	28	5	1827	55.4	Michigan St	38	33	5	2262	59.5
WI-Green Bay	31	20	11	1736	56.0	Butler	32	22	10	1921	60.0

SCORING MARGIN

	Off	Def	Mar		Off	Def	Mar
Duke	91.8	67.2	24.7	College of Charleston	72.8	59.2	13.7
Auburn	81.2	61.6	19.6	St. John's (NY)	79.0	65.4	13.6
Maryland	84.5	66.4	18.1	Gonzaga	78.4	65.1	13.2
Connecticut	77.3	61.3	15.9	Cincinnati	73.9	61.2	12.7
Utah	71.3	55.4	15.9	Kentucky	75.4	62.7	12.7

FIELD-GOAL PERCENTAGE

	FGA	FG	Pct		FGA	FG	Pct
Northern Arizona	1497	783	52.3	Samford	1487	729	49.0
Duke	2422	1244	51.4	College of Charleston	1702	830	48.8
Evansville	1739	879	50.5	Montana St	1688	821	48.6
Maryland	2108	1044	49.5	Oral Roberts	1625	782	48.1
Texas Christian	2050	1006	49.1	Loyola (MD)	1642	790	48.1

FIELD-GOAL PERCENTAGE DEFENSE

	FGA	FG	Pct		FGA	FG	Pct
Kansas St	1963	729	37.1	Navy	1519	575	37.9
Detroit	1583	590	37.3	Rice	1599	606	37.9
Northwestern	1548	577	37.3	Stanford	1894	719	38.0
SW Texas St	1601	597	37.3	Kentucky	2162	823	38.1
Old Dominion	2116	797	37.7	Cincinnati	1841	703	38.2

FREE-THROW PERCENTAGE

	FTA	FT	Pct		FTA	FT	Pct
Siena	854	672	78.7	Detroit	553	416	75.2
Evansville	667	515	77.2	Michigan	640	481	75.2
Western Michigan	568	435	76.6	Northern Arizona	571	429	75.1
Miami (OH)	570	436	76.5	New Mexico	707	531	75.1
Robert Morris	594	452	76.1	Akron	692	519	75.0

Arkansas State Assist Man

It's hard to find Chico Fletcher. He plays for little Arkansas State in the overlooked Sun Belt Conference and he stands just 5'5½". His opponents tend to discover him the hard way. As Fletcher was scoring 13 points and dishing out a school-record 17 assists at Texas Christian on Nov. 23, 1998, Horned Frogs coach Billy Tubbs screeched at his point guard, Prince Fowler, "I don't care what you do—trip him, kick him in the shins, do anything, just get that little guy out of the game."

Three years ago Fletcher went to Arkansas State on a football scholarship, but after redshirting his freshman season, he made the basketball team as a walk-on point guard. He started the final 20 games of the 1996–97 season and led the Sun Belt with an average of 6.3 assists. Fletcher, whose first name derives from his mother's favorite sit-com, Chico and the Man, quit football in '97. He then set an Arkansas State record with 240 assists and became the first sophomore since '83 to win the Sun Belt player of the year award. In 1998–99, he led the Indians to a second-place finish in the conference, and ranked second in the nation in assists (8.3 apg), reaffirming once and for all that Chico is the man.

THREE-POINT FIELD GOALS MADE PER GAME

	GP	FG	Avg		GP	FG	Avg
Cal Poly SLO	27	255	9.4	Eastern Washington	27	241	8.9
Florida	31	289	9.3	Arkansas	34	296	8.7
Samford	30	278	9.3	St. Mary's	31	267	8.6
Air Force	26	233	9.0	Creighton	31	263	8.5
Portland St	28	250	8.9	Troy St	27	229	8.5

THREE-POINT FIELD-GOAL PERCENTAGE

	GP	FGA	FG	Pct		GP	FGA	FG	Pct
Northern Arizona	29	591	254	43.0	IL-Chicago	28	460	192	41.7
Utah St	33	324	139	42.9	Western Michigan	29	511	509	40.9
Pennsylvania	29	526	223	42.4	Stanford	35	642	262	40.8
Harvard	26	448	188	42.0	Gonzaga	34	678	274	40.4
Michigan	34	621	260	41.9	New Mexico	32	748	301	40.2

Note: Minimum 3.0 made per game.

NCAA Women's Championship Game Box Score

Duke 45

Duke	Min	FG M-A	FT M-A	Reb O-T	A	PF	TP
Browne	31	2–13	1–2	5–9	0	2	5
Schweitzer	18	0–3	0–0	0–4	1	3	0
VanGorp	32	7–10	1–2	2–5	0	4	15
Howard	35	3–9	0–0	0–3	2	2	9
Erickson	37	3–9	0–0	0–2	4	5	8
Parent	21	2–3	2–2	2–5	4	3	6
Rice	20	1–5	0–0	1–8	0	3	2
Black	1	0–0	0–0	0–0	0	0	0
Gingrich	5	0–5	0–0	0–0	1	1	0
Totals	200	18–55	4–6	10–36	12	23	45

Percentages: FG—.327, FT—.667. 3-pt goals: 5–21, .238 (Browne 0–1, Schweitzer 0–1, VanGorp 0–1, Howard 3–6, Erickson 2–6, Rice 0–4, Gingrich 0-2). Team rebounds: 2. Blocked shots: 2 (VanGorp, Rice). Turnovers: 20 (Schweitzer 6, Howard 4, Browne 3, Rice 3, Erickson 2, VanGorp 2) Steals: 2 (Rice, VanGorp).

Purdue 62

Purdue	Min	FG M-A	FT M-A	Reb O-T	A	PF	TP
White-McCarty	36	6–17	0–1	0–1	2	3	12
Duhart	37	2–3	1–2	2–5	2	3	5
Cooper	36	5–9	3–6	2–7	0	3	13
Figgs	40	5–15	8–9	0–3	1	1	18
Douglas	36	3–9	6–8	2–5	2	3	13
Crawford	4	0–0	0–0	0–0	0	1	0
Young	3	0–2	0–0	1–2	0	0	0
Komara	8	0–0	1–2	0–2	1	0	1
Totals	200	21–55	19–28	7–25	8	14	62

Percentages: FG—.382, FT—.679. 3-pt goals: 1–13, .077 (White-McCarty 0–4, Figgs 0–5, Douglas 1–3, Young 0–1). Team rebounds: 8. Blocked shots: 3 (Duhart, Cooper, Douglas). Turnovers: 8 (Figgs 5, Douglas 2, White-McCarty). Steals: 7 (Figgs 3, Duhart 2, Douglas, White-McCarty).

Halftime: Duke 22, Purdue 17.
A: 17,773. Officials: Trammell, Barlow, Dahlem.

Hokie Happy Ending

Virginia Tech forward Michelle Hollister had great expectations for the 1996–97 season, but she never expected to be expecting. In October '96, just after the Hokies finished preseason workouts, Hollister learned that she was pregnant. She left the team and withdrew from school. The next summer, Hollister married former Virginia Tech football player Billy Houseright and gave birth to their daughter, Jordan (named after you know who). Without their top scorer and rebounder from 1995–96, Virginia Tech went 10–21.

Inspired by Sheryl Swoopes, who starred for the WNBA's Houston Comets in 1997 after delivering a son named Jordan, the postpartum Houseright lost 50 pounds and returned to the court just six months after her daughter's birth. As a junior in 1997–98 she helped lead Virginia Tech to its first Atlantic 10 tournament title. In 1998–99, with Houseright jug-gling motherhood, schoolwork and her role as the Hokies' third-leading scorer and rebounder (8.9 points, 4.0 rebounds per game), Virginia Tech finished the regular season 25–1 and ranked a best-ever ninth in the nation.

A program that averaged just 764 fans a game two seasons ago drew 8,079 to its season-ending 66–64 win over George Washington. Houseright had seven points, four rebounds and four steals in her last home performance, and little Jordan was on hand to see it.

"When I left school to have a baby, I felt terrible abandoning my team," Houseright said. "I owed it to them to come back. It's been a strange journey, but how many kids can say they saw their mom play college basketball? This is one helluva way for a mother to go out."

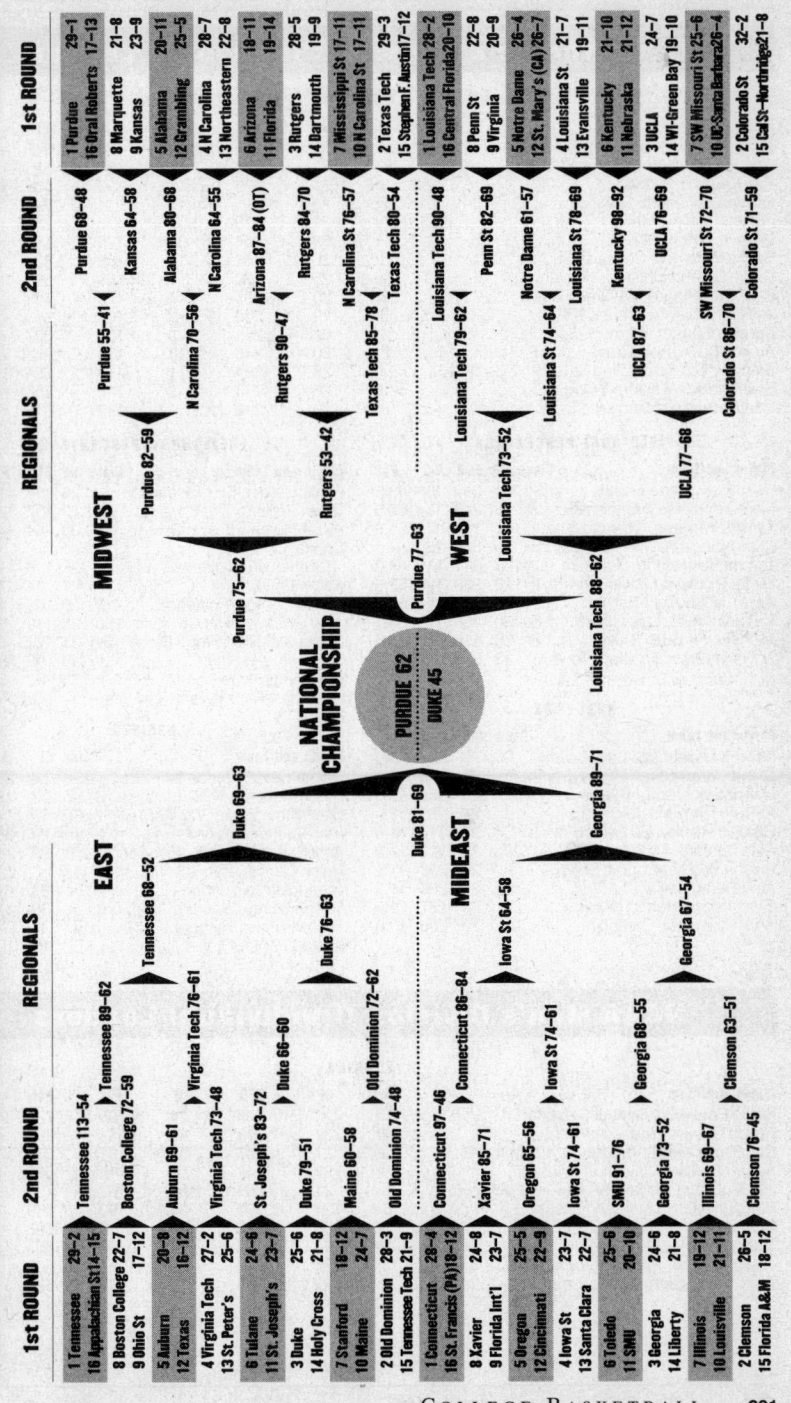

1999 NCAA Basketball Women's Division I Tournament

NCAA Women's Division I Individual Leaders

SCORING

Player and Team	Class	GP	TFG	3FG	FT	Pts	Avg
Tamika Whitmore, Memphis	Sr	32	325	30	163	843	26.3
Jackie Stiles, SW Missouri St	So	32	288	66	181	823	25.7
Kim Knuth, Toledo	Sr	31	270	49	199	788	25.4
Kristina Behnfeldt, Marshall	Sr	26	195	17	214	621	23.9
Jamie Cassidy, Maine	Jr	31	278	7	175	738	23.8
Linda Froelich, UNLV	Fr	28	251	30	125	657	23.5
Becky Hammon, Colorado St	Sr	36	261	114	188	824	22.9
Diana Caramonico, Pennsylvania	So	26	220	1	149	590	22.7
Chari Nordgaard, WI-Green Bay	Sr	29	235	7	176	653	22.5
Jess Zinobile, St. Francis (PA)	Jr	29	232	5	184	653	22.5
Karalyn Church, Vermont	Jr	28	251	2	123	627	22.4
Amy O'Brien, Holy Cross	Jr	29	246	18	133	643	22.2
Summer Erb, N Carolina St	Jr	29	254	1	115	624	21.5
Leah Aldrich, Eastern Illinois	Jr	26	216	12	112	556	21.4
Lisa Baswell, Jacksonville St	Jr	29	210	9	189	618	21.3

FIELD-GOAL PERCENTAGE

Player and Team	Class	GP	FGA	FG	Pct
Ruth Riley, Notre Dame	So	31	290	198	68.3
Meredith Morse, Manhattan	Jr	28	249	164	65.9
Tamika Williams, Connecticut	Fr	33	263	173	65.8
Chari Nordgaard, WI-Green Bay	Sr	29	363	235	64.7
Tammi Blackstone, Drake	Jr	31	341	219	64.2
Jamie Thomatis, Middle Tenn. St.	Fr	26	238	149	62.6
Amy Kieckbusch, Ball St	Sr	26	344	214	62.2
DeTrina White, Louisiana St	Sr	30	256	159	62.1
Michele VanGorp, Duke	Sr	36	416	258	62.0
Amanda Wilson, Louisiana Tech	Sr	33	389	241	62.0

Note: Minimum 5 made per game.

REBOUNDS

Player and Team	Class	GP	Reb	Avg
Monica Logan, MD-Balt. County	Sr	27	364	13.5
Diana Caramonico, Pennsylvania	So	26	333	12.8
Malveata Johnson, N Carolina A&T	So	28	353	12.6
AuBree Hamilton, Miami (OH)	Jr	24	285	11.9
Carolyn Harvey, St. Francis (NY)	Sr	27	314	11.6
Kate Sanford, Charleston So.	Jr	28	323	11.5
Kiesha Brooks, Coppin St	So	26	298	11.5
Amy Herrig, Iowa	Sc	27	306	11.3
Elise James, Robert Morris	Jr	26	287	11.0
April Cromartie, Campbell	Fr	28	306	10.9

FREE-THROW PERCENTAGE

Player and Team	Class	GP	FTA	FT	Pct
Paula Corder, SE Missouri St	Jr	28	118	111	94.1
Dawn Zerman, Kent	Jr	29	137	122	89.1
Alissa Murphy, Boston College	Jr	30	164	146	89.0
Crystal Carpenter, Charleston Southern	Sr	28	126	112	88.9
Karen Shutz, Iona	Jr	27	84	74	88.1
Kristin Hepton, Portland	Sr	28	105	92	87.6
Amy Sutton, Texas Christian	So	28	113	99	87.6
Sheila McMillen, Notre Dame	Sr	31	101	88	87.1
Sarah Hurrle, Butler	Sr	28	92	80	87.0
Niele Ivey, Notre Dame	Jr	28	92	80	87.0

Note: Minimum 2.5 made per game.

ASSISTS

Player and Team	Class	GP	A	Avg
Dalma Ivanyi, Florida Int'l	Sr	30	265	8.8
Nikki Kremer, Xavier	Sr	32	275	8.6
Lisa Witherspoon, Virginia Tech	Sr	30	246	8.2
Amy Vachon, Maine	Jr	29	234	8.1
Amy Sheiron, Sam Houston St	Sr	27	215	8.0
Helen Darling, Penn St	Jr	30	226	7.5
Brandi McCain, Florida	Fr	33	246	7.5
Milena Flores, Stanford	Jr	30	219	7.3
Tasha Pointer, Rutgers	So	33	226	6.8
Kristen Pool, UNLV	Sr	28	191	6.8

NCAA Men's Division II Individual Leaders

SCORING

Player and Team	Class	GP	TFG	3FG	FT	Pts	Avg
Eddie Robinson, Central Oklahoma	Sr	26	305	24	95	729	28.0
Ajamu Gaines, Charleston (WV)	Jr	31	278	83	161	800	25.8
Cory Dumphord, Kentucky St	Jr	27	247	38	137	669	24.8
Robert Conley, Clayton St	Sr	27	247	28	142	664	24.6
Jeff McBroon, Seattle Pacific	Sr	31	266	120	102	754	24.3
Rodney Dean, Central Arkansas	Sr	24	191	94	93	569	23.7
Curtis Pass, W Georgia	Sr	28	227	94	110	658	23.5
Titus Warmsley, Montana St-Billings	Sr	28	172	77	236	657	23.5
Justin Walther, Pitt-Johnstown	Jr	26	210	22	164	606	23.3
Terry Clark, Glenville St	Sr	27	234	15	145	628	23.3

REBOUNDS

Player and Team	Class	GP	Reb	Avg
Antonio Garcia, KY Wesleyan	Sr	37	540	14.6
Jermaine Thomas, TX A&M-Comm.	Jr	28	341	12.2
Damon Reed, St. Rose	Jr	32	383	12.0
Kristian Pipkins, Southeastern Oklahoma	Sr	27	318	11.8
John Tomsich, Le Moyne	Sr	26	305	11.7
Malik Richardson, Concordia (NY)	Sr	26	303	11.7
Earl Ike, Montevallo	Jr	26	297	11.4
Latif McMorrin, NJIT	Jr	30	338	11.3
Steve Shannon, Mansfield	Jr	26	280	10.8
Sam Randolph, Columbia Union	Sr	27	286	10.6

ASSISTS

Player and Team	Class	GP	A	Avg
Shawn Brown, Merrimack	Jr	27	223	8.3
Shannon Lee, Hawaii Pacific	Sr	29	229	7.9
Michael Hamelin, W Texas A&M	Sr	29	217	7.5
Jamie Stevens, Montana St-Billings	Sr	28	207	7.4
Adam Kaufman, Edinboro	So	28	203	7.3
Brandon Manning, TX A&M-Comm.	Jr	28	201	7.2
Kevin Moyer, Le Moyne	Jr	27	179	6.6
Andy Niedzwiecki, Assumption	Jr	29	190	6.6
Marvin Moore, Catawba	Sr	30	196	6.5
Donald Johnson, Franklin Pierce	So	29	189	6.5

FIELD-GOAL PERCENTAGE

Player and Team	Class	GP	FGA	FG	Pct
DaVonn Harp, Kutztown St	Sr	27	205	140	68.3
Nick Jenkins, MO Western St	Sr	29	274	183	66.8
Javares Anderson, Tuskegee	Jr	25	216	141	65.3
Antonio Garcia, KY Wesleyan	Sr	37	397	255	64.2
Leighton Nash, Southern Indiana	Sr	24	271	165	60.9
Jason Burgess, Cheyney	Sr	25	221	134	60.6
Jermaine Thomas, TX A&M-Comm.	Jr	28	314	190	60.5
Kyle Lindsay, Oakland City	Sr	29	248	150	60.5
Shaun Kunz, Western St	Sr	24	232	140	60.3
Jeff Boinski, Michigan Tech	Sr	29	371	222	59.8

Note: Minimum 5 made per game.

FREE-THROW PERCENTAGE

Player and Team	Class	GP	FTA	FT	Pct
Travis Starns, Colorado Mines	Sr	26	93	87	93.5
Brandon Palmer, Florida Tech	Sr	27	84	77	91.7
T.J. Trimboli, Southern Connecticut St	Jr	28	125	114	91.2
Hunter Berg, N Dakota	Sr	27	120	108	90.0
Jay Tipton, Cal St-Stanislaus	So	29	93	83	89.2
Louie Moore, Slippery Rock	Jr	24	92	82	89.1
Nate White, Augustana (SD)	Jr	30	89	79	88.8
Joe Meade, West Chester	Jr	29	148	128	86.5
Mudumango Lee, St. Paul's	Sr	24	81	70	86.4
Forrest Witt, St. Cloud St	Fr	27	88	76	86.4

Note: Minimum 2.5 made per game.

NCAA Women's Division II Individual Leaders

SCORING

Player and Team	Class	GP	TFG	3FG	FT	Pts	Avg
Angie Hupfer, St. Joe's (IN)	Jr	27	316	35	160	827	30.6
Darcy Stracke, NE-Kearney	Jr	28	246	36	151	679	24.3
Gulsah Akkaya, Lynn	Sr	27	221	53	147	642	23.8
Teresa Jones-Benson, E Central	Sr	28	229	37	138	633	22.6
Heather Kearney, Slippery Rock	Sr	24	201	1	135	538	22.4
Elizabeth Ramsey, Indianapolis	So	25	198	9	129	534	21.4
Sindiate Davis, Shaw	Jr	21	164	48	70	446	21.2
Jurgita Kausaite, Emporia St	Sr	32	256	34	128	674	21.1
Angie Williams, Barry	Jr	27	226	0	108	560	20.7
Tanisha Rickman, W Florida	Sr	28	196	50	138	580	20.7

REBOUNDS

Player and Team	Class	GP	Reb	Avg
Heather Corby, California (PA)	Sr	27	366	13.6
Heather Kearney, Slippery Rock	Sr	24	307	12.8
Tracy Sprolden, Valdosta St	So	28	347	12.4
Tiffany Johnson, Newberry	Jr	27	334	12.4
Katearia Smith, Cheyney	Jr	24	289	12.0
Loarie Hanna, W Virginia Tech	Jr	25	298	11.9
Ashley Totedo, Shippensburg	Sr	31	369	11.9
Angie Hupfer, St. Joe's (IN)	Jr	27	319	11.8
LaKisha Phifer, St. Paul's	Jr	25	291	11.6
Sharon Kukal, NJIT	Sr	27	309	11.4

ASSISTS

Player and Team	Class	GP	A	Avg
Rima Petronyte, Kennesaw St	Jr	31	263	8.5
Jennifer Perine, Emporia St	Jr	33	271	8.2
Sarah Ferland, St. Michael's	Sr	27	221	8.2
Kelly Parker, Central Oklahoma	Sr	26	199	7.7
Latisha Martin, Oakland	Fr	27	186	6.9
LaShawn Mincey, Columbus St	So	32	214	6.7
Liz Blanchard, Concordia (NY)	Sr	25	166	6.6
Carrie Roys, Ferris St	Jr	28	184	6.6
Cissely Hunter, Belmont Abbey	Jr	30	193	6.4
Jaime Pudenz, N Dakota	Jr	32	205	6.4

FIELD-GOAL PERCENTAGE

Player and Team	Class	GP	FGA	FG	Pct
Staci Elder, W Alabama	Jr	24	259	172	66.4
Temeshia Dawkins, Wingate	So	29	262	169	64.5
Kelly Easton, W Liberty St	Jr	26	267	172	64.4
Jackie Bucher, Abilene Christian	Jr	31	371	235	63.3
Stacy Nelson, MN-Duluth	Sr	29	385	243	63.1
Serita Gauldin, N Alabama	Jr	27	327	203	62.1
Shari Grady, SW Baptist	Jr	28	263	160	60.8
Michelle Cottrell, Northern KY	Fr	33	360	219	60.8
Marloss Roetgerink, Incarnate Word	So	30	276	167	60.5
Angie Williams, Barry	Jr	27	374	226	60.4

Note: Minimum 5 made per game.

FREE-THROW PERCENTAGE

Player and Team	Class	GP	FTA	FT	Pct
Briana Abrahamsen, Western Washington	So	30	93	85	91.4
Kylie Nabors, Incarnate Word	So	30	130	117	90.0
Tara Macciocco, Lock Haven	Sr	22	70	63	90.0
Erin Walker, Bemidji St	Jr	27	77	69	89.6
Melissa Burke, Chadron St	So	27	83	74	89.2
Andrea Schreier, SW St	So	25	137	122	89.1
Taneisha Lenon, Christian Bros	Jr	26	77	68	88.3
Reagan Housch, Columbus St	Sr	32	109	95	87.2
Jill Razor, Rollins	So	30	185	161	87.0
Khelli Mullen, Arkansas Tech	Sr	38	124	107	86.3

Note: Minimum 2.5 made per game.

NCAA Men's Division III Individual Leaders

SCORING

Player and Team	Class	GP	TFG	3FG	FT	Pts	Avg
Jeff Clement, Grinnell	Sr	22	217	166	121	721	32.8
Darrel Lewis, Lincoln (PA)	Sr	24	249	81	121	700	29.2
Devean George, Augsburg	Sr	28	281	45	163	770	27.5
Mike Kmiec, Babson	Jr	25	237	48	161	683	27.3
Carl Howell, St. Joseph's (ME)	Sr	29	289	55	136	769	26.5
Eric Joldersma, Bethel (MN)	Sr	23	219	37	134	609	26.5
Andy Panko, Lebanon Valley	Sr	28	232	44	220	728	26.0
Mike Schantz, Hamilton	Sr	27	246	3	205	700	25.9
Sean Harrington, UMass-Boston	Sr	25	237	18	135	627	25.1
Christian Morgia, Austin	Sr	26	243	48	89	623	24.0

REBOUNDS

Player and Team	Class	GP	Reb	Avg
Anthony Peeples, Montclair St	Sr	24	345	14.4
Mike Schantz, Hamilton	Sr	27	336	12.4
Rich Williamson, Thiel	Sr	25	307	12.3
Adam Doll, Simpson	Sr	27	323	12.0
Kevin Rutherford, Lycoming	Sr	25	294	11.8
Jon Schmiegal, Hamilton	Sr	21	244	11.6
Juahmal Sturgeon, William Penn	So	22	254	11.5
Devean George, Augsburg	Sr	28	317	11.3
Mark Wadams, Brockport St	Jr	23	255	11.1
Lonnie Walker, Alvernia	Sr	25	276	11.0

ASSISTS

Player and Team	Class	GP	A	Avg
Tim Kelly, Pacific Lutheran	Jr	25	214	8.6
Brian Nigro, Mt. St. Vincent	Jr	25	198	7.9
Matt Lucero, Austin	So	26	201	7.7
Shaka Smart, Kenyon	Sr	25	184	7.4
Greg Dunne, Nazareth	Jr	26	191	7.3
Eric Prendeville, Salisbury St	Sr	26	178	6.8
John Cali, Staten Island	Sr	28	187	6.7
Brandon Moersch, Carleton	Jr	24	156	6.5
Jermel Mayo, Montclair St	So	23	148	6.4
Daniel Martinez, McMurry	Jr	22	141	6.4

FIELD-GOAL PERCENTAGE

Player and Team	Class	GP	FGA	FG	Pct
Jason Nickerson, Virginia Wesleyan	Sr	26	363	242	66.7
Kevin Rutherford, Lycoming	Sr	25	222	145	65.3
Ryan Abraham, Western New England	Jr	25	280	181	64.6
Rene Guzman, Southwestern	Sr	24	189	122	64.6
Tim Czarnecki, Albion	Jr	27	219	141	64.4
Ben Jones, Ozarks (AR)	Sr	24	281	180	64.1
Quincy Longacre, E Mennonite	Jr	25	213	136	63.8
Ike Kirch, Thomas More	Sr	23	267	170	63.7
Josh Johnson, St. Norbert	Sr	24	241	151	62.7
Brian Trudman, McMurry	Sr	25	246	154	62.6

Note: Minimum 5 made per game.

FREE-THROW PERCENTAGE

Player and Team	Class	GP	FTA	FT	Pct
Ryan Eklund, WI-La Crosse	Sr	26	87	80	92.0
Brad Clark, WI-Oshkosh	Jr	26	166	152	91.6
Thad Peck, Wartburg	Sr	22	73	66	90.4
Joel Kauffman, E Mennonite	So	25	124	112	90.3
Seth Stapleton, Alma	Jr	23	71	64	90.1
Greg Dunne, Nazareth	Jr	26	97	87	89.7
Greg Adams, Wash. (MD)	So	27	158	141	89.2
Dave Jannuzzi, Wilkes	Jr	29	135	120	88.9
Merrill Brunson, WI-Platteville	Jr	32	158	140	88.6
Michael Crateley, Grove City	Sr	25	79	70	88.6

Note: Minimum 2.5 made per game.

NCAA Women's Division III Individual Leaders

SCORING

Player and Team	Class	GP	TFG	3FG	FT	Pts	Avg
Ronda Jo Miller, Gallaudet	Jr	30	337	6	110	790	26.3
Angela Ensley, Cedar Crest	Jr	25	232	51	98	613	24.5
Anna Celaya, Occidental	Sr	25	212	50	129	603	24.1
Tara Carleton, Randolph-Macon	Jr	25	201	7	178	587	23.5
Tiffany Pope, Medgar Evers	Fr	25	235	23	91	584	23.4
Natalie Whitewood, Sul Ross St.	Jr	22	176	24	115	491	22.3
Kristen Venne, Susquehanna	Sr	27	219	1	140	579	21.4
Missy Johnson, WI-River Falls	Sr	26	199	0	158	556	21.4
Joanne Polakoski, King's (PA)	Jr	24	199	7	107	512	21.3
Jeanne Waznak, Delaware Valley	Jr	27	201	56	115	573	21.2

REBOUNDS

Player and Team	Class	GP	Reb	Avg
Nicole Kilgannon, Notre Dame (MD)	Sr	23	359	15.6
Heather Kile, Swarthmore	Fr	24	355	14.8
Helen Libby, Hood	Sr	20	283	14.1
Heather Stewart, New Rochelle	Jr	26	366	14.1
Nicole Cruz, Lehman	Jr	22	309	14.0
Andreen Gilpin, UMass-Boston	Fr	24	328	13.7
Jeannette Jackson, Wesleyan (GA)	Sr	24	328	13.7
Ronda Jo Miller, Gallaudet	Jr	30	407	13.6
Jasmine Sanchez, New Paltz St	Sr	24	311	13.0
Erica Pearson, St. Mary's (MD)	Sr	28	351	12.5

FIELD-GOAL PERCENTAGE

Player and Team	Class	GP	FGA	FG	Pct
Karyn Kern, Susquehanna	Jr	27	260	169	65.0
Laura Wendorff, St. Benedict	Jr	30	319	205	64.3
Rachel Lachecki, WI-Oshkosh	Sr	29	253	157	62.1
Jayme Anderson, WI-Eau Claire	So	28	345	213	61.7
Val Duncan, Greenville	Jr	25	280	170	60.7
Kristen Schmaelzle, Westfield St	Sr	26	256	154	60.2
Renee Zando, Randolph-Macon	Jr	28	271	162	59.8
Ann Terpstra, Adrian	Jr	25	260	155	59.6
Jen Zabek, Eastern Conn. St	Sr	26	319	189	59.2
Melissa Posse, Cabrini	Sr	27	299	175	58.5

Note: Minimum 5 made per game.

ASSISTS

Player and Team	Class	GP	A	Avg
Amy Cooke, Salisbury St	Sr	26	218	8.4
Alisa DiBonaventura, Delaware Valley	So	27	194	7.2
Colleen McCrave, Bates	Sr	24	169	7.0
Kara Grishkat, Otterbein	So	25	176	7.0
P.J. McTigue, Geneseo St	Sr	28	186	6.6
Allison McKinney, Austin	Sr	27	178	6.6
Wendy Coleman, Albertus Magnus	Jr	26	170	6.5
Kaylyn Charriere, Willamette	Sr	25	163	6.5
Tosha Crass, Maryville (TN)	So	25	155	6.2
Janine Mazzie, Salve Regina	Jr	23	142	6.2

FREE-THROW PERCENTAGE

Player and Team	Class	GP	FTA	FT	Pct
Amanda Waterbury, Muhlenberg	Sr	26	103	91	88.3
Helen Dinan, Regis	Fr	26	94	83	88.3
Kim Rooney, Widener	Jr	24	101	89	88.1
Angela Osborn, Bridgewater	So	28	86	75	87.2
Kelly Morrison, DePauw	Sr	27	90	78	86.7
Martha Vest, Illinois College	Sr	24	126	109	86.5
Delilah Whisenhunt, Dallas	Jr	25	131	113	86.3
Molly Quinn, Trinity (TX)	So	25	86	74	86.0
Shera Wolf, Ohio Northern	Jr	25	107	91	86.0
Whitney Elmore, Hendrix	Jr	25	75	64	85.3

Note: Minimum 2.5 made per game.

Impeach Baskets

Illinois Republican Henry Hyde, chairman of the House Judiciary Committee, led the team of prosecutors in the impeachment trial of President Clinton. Fifty-six years earlier, as a backup center at Georgetown, Hyde did battle with another titan—George Mikan of DePaul—in the NCAA Final Four.

"March 25, 1943—I can still feel the excitement of playing in Madison Square Garden," Hyde says of the '43 semifinal in which the Hoyas beat Mikan's Blue Demons 53–49. A 6'3" string bean, Hyde started the second half after John Mahnken fouled out trying to stop the 6'10½" Mikan. Hyde held Mikan to a single second-half point, mostly by shoving and elbowing him. "I know I will spend a lot of time in purgatory for what I did to Mikan in that game," said Hyde, whose lone basket of the tournament came that day. The Hoyas lost to Wyoming 46–34 in the final.

In January 1999, Hyde said he would "obviously" prefer watching basketball to "having to deal with the present situation" in Washington—by which he did not mean the '98–99 Hoyas' sub-.500 record.

NCAA Men's Division I Championship Results

NCAA Final Four Results

Year	Winner	Score	Runner-up	Third Place	Fourth Place	Winning Coach
1939	Oregon	46–33	Ohio St	*Oklahoma	*Villanova	Howard Hobson
1940	Indiana	60–42	Kansas	*Duquesne	*Southern Cal	Branch McCracken
1941	Wisconsin	39–34	Washington St	*Pittsburgh	*Arkansas	Harold Foster
1942	Stanford	53–38	Dartmouth	*Colorado	*Kentucky	Everett Dean
1943	Wyoming	46–34	Georgetown	*Texas	*DePaul	Everett Shelton
1944	Utah	42–40 (OT)	Dartmouth	*Iowa St	*Ohio St	Vadal Peterson
1945	Oklahoma St	49–45	NYU	*Arkansas	*Ohio St	Hank Iba
1946	Oklahoma St	43–40	N Carolina	Ohio St	California	Hank Iba
1947	Holy Cross	58–47	Oklahoma	Texas	CCNY	Alvin Julian
1948	Kentucky	58–42	Baylor	Holy Cross	Kansas St	Adolph Rupp
1949	Kentucky	46–36	Oklahoma St	Illinois	Oregon St	Adolph Rupp
1950	CCNY	71–68	Bradley	N Carolina St	Baylor	Nat Holman
1951	Kentucky	68–58	Kansas St	Illinois	Oklahoma St	Adolph Rupp
1952	Kansas	80–63	St. John's (NY)	Illinois	Santa Clara	Forrest Allen
1953	Indiana	69–68	Kansas	Washington	Louisiana St	Branch McCracken
1954	La Salle	92–76	Bradley	Penn St	Southern Cal	Kenneth Loeffler
1955	San Francisco	77–63	La Salle	Colorado	Iowa	Phil Woolpert
1956	San Francisco	83–71	Iowa	Temple	Southern Meth	Phil Woolpert
1957	N Carolina	54–53 (3OT)	Kansas	San Francisco	Michigan St	Frank McGuire
1958	Kentucky	84–72	Seattle	Temple	Kansas St	Adolph Rupp
1959	California	71–70	W Virginia	Cincinnati	Louisville	Pete Newell
1960	Ohio St	75–55	California	Cincinnati	NYU	Fred Taylor
1961	Cincinnati	70–65 (OT)	Ohio St	Vacated‡	Utah	Edwin Jucker
1962	Cincinnati	71–59	Ohio St	Wake Forest	UCLA	Edwin Jucker
1963	Loyola (IL)	60–58 (OT)	Cincinnati	Duke	Oregon St	George Ireland
1964	UCLA	98–83	Duke	Michigan	Kansas St	John Wooden
1965	UCLA	91–80	Michigan	Princeton	Wichita St	John Wooden
1966	UTEP	72–65	Kentucky	Duke	Utah	Don Haskins
1967	UCLA	79–64	Dayton	Houston	N Carolina	John Wooden
1968	UCLA	78–55	N Carolina	Ohio St	Houston	John Wooden
1969	UCLA	92–72	Purdue	Drake	N Carolina	John Wooden
1970	UCLA	80–69	Jacksonville	New Mexico St	St. Bonaventure	John Wooden
1971	UCLA	68–62	Vacated‡	Vacated‡	Kansas	John Wooden
1972	UCLA	81–76	Florida St	N Carolina	Louisville	John Wooden
1973	UCLA	87–66	Memphis St	Indiana	Providence	John Wooden
1974	N Carolina St	76–64	Marquette	UCLA	Kansas	Norm Sloan
1975	UCLA	92–85	Kentucky	Louisville	Syracuse	John Wooden
1976	Indiana	86–68	Michigan	UCLA	Rutgers	Bob Knight
1977	Marquette	67–59	N Carolina	UNLV	NC-Charlotte	Al McGuire
1978	Kentucky	94–88	Duke	Arkansas	Notre Dame	Joe Hall
1979	Michigan St	75–64	Indiana St	DePaul	Penn	Jud Heathcote
1980	Louisville	59–54	Vacated‡	Purdue	Iowa	Denny Crum
1981	Indiana	63–50	N Carolina	Virginia	Louisiana St	Bob Knight
1982	N Carolina	63–62	Georgetown	*Houston	*Louisville	Dean Smith
1983	N Carolina St	54–52	Houston	*Georgia	*Louisville	Jim Valvano
1984	Georgetown	84–75	Houston	*Kentucky	*Virginia	John Thompson
1985	Villanova	66–64	Georgetown	St. John's (NY)	Vacated‡	Rollie Massimino
1986	Louisville	72–69	Duke	*Kansas	*Louisiana St	Denny Crum
1987	Indiana	74–73	Syracuse	*UNLV	*Providence	Bob Knight
1988	Kansas	83–79	Oklahoma	*Arizona	*Duke	Larry Brown
1989	Michigan	80–79 (OT)	Seton Hall	*Duke	*Illinois	Steve Fisher
1990	UNLV	103–73	Duke	*Arkansas	*Georgia Tech	Jerry Tarkanian
1991	Duke	72–65	Kansas	*UNLV	*N Carolina	Mike Krzyzewski
1992	Duke	71–51	Michigan	*Cincinnati	*Indiana	Mike Krzyzewski
1993	N Carolina	77–71	Michigan	*Kansas	*Kentucky	Dean Smith
1994	Arkansas	76–72	Duke	*Arizona	*Florida	Nolan Richardson
1995	UCLA	89–78	Arkansas	*N Carolina	*Oklahoma St	Jim Harrick
1996	Kentucky	76–67	Syracuse	Vacated‡	Mississippi St	Rick Pitino
1997	Arizona	84–79 (OT)	Kentucky	*Minnesota	*N Carolina	Lute Olson
1998	Kentucky	78–69	Utah	*Stanford	*N Carolina	Tubby Smith
1999	Connecticut	77–74	Duke	*Michigan St	*Ohio St	Jim Calhoun

*Tied for third place. ‡Student-athletes representing St. Joseph's (PA) in 1961, Villanova in 1971, Western Kentucky in 1971, UCLA in 1980, Memphis State in 1985 and Massachusetts in 1996 were declared ineligible subsequent to the tournament. Under NCAA rules, the teams' and ineligible student-athletes' records were deleted, and the teams' places in the standings were vacated.

NCAA Final Four MVPs

Year	Winner, School	GP	Field Goals		3-Pt FG		Free Throws		Reb	A	Stl	BS	Avg
			FGM	Pct	FGA	FGM	FTM	Pct					
1939	None selected												
1940	Marv Huffman, Indiana	2	7	—	—	—	4		—	—	—	—	9.0
1941	John Kotz, Wisconsin	2	8	—	—	—	6	—	—	—	—	—	11.0
1942	Howard Dallmar, Stanford	2	8	—	—	—	4	66.7	—	—	—	—	10.0
1943	Ken Sailors, Wyoming	2	10	—	—	—	8	72.7	—	—	—	—	14.0
1944	Arnie Ferrin, Utah	2	11	—	—	—	6	—	—	—	—	—	14.0
1945	Bob Kurland, Oklahoma St	2	16	—	—	—	5	—	—	—	—	—	18.5
1946	Bob Kurland, Oklahoma St	2	21	—	—	—	10	66.7	—	—	—	—	26.0
1947	George Kaftan, Holy Cross	2	18	—	—	—	12	70.6	—	—	—	—	24.0
1948	Alex Groza, Kentucky	2	16	—	—	—	5	—	—	—	—	—	18.5
1949	Alex Groza, Kentucky	2	19	—	—	—	14	—	—	—	—	—	26.0
1950	Irwin Dambrot, CCNY	2	12	42.9	—	—	4	50.0	—	—	—	—	14.0
1951	None selected												
1952	Clyde Lovellette, Kansas	2	24	—	—	—	18	—	—	—	—	—	33.0
1953	*B.H. Horn, Kansas	2	17	—	—	—	17	—	—	—	—	—	25.5
1954	Tom Gola, La Salle	2	12	—	—	—	14	—	—	—	—	—	19.0
1955	Bill Russell, San Francisco	2	19	—	—	—	9	—	—	—	—	—	23.5
1956	*Hal Lear, Temple	2	32	—	—	—	16	—	—	—	—	—	40.0
1957	*Wilt Chamberlain, Kansas	2	18	51.4	—	—	19	70.4	25	—	—	—	32.5
1958	*Elgin Baylor, Seattle	2	18	34.0	—	—	12	75.0	41	—	—	—	24.0
1959	*Jerry West, West Virginia	2	22	66.7	—	—	22	68.8	25	—	—	—	33.0
1960	Jerry Lucas, Ohio State	2	16	66.7	—	—	3	100.0	23	—	—	—	17.5
1961	*Jerry Lucas, Ohio State	2	20	71.4	—	—	16	94.1	25	—	—	—	28.0
1962	Paul Hogue, Cincinnati	2	23	63.9	—	—	12	63.2	38	—	—	—	29.0
1963	Art Heyman, Duke	2	18	41.0	—	—	15	68.2	19	—	—	—	25.5
1964	Walt Hazzard, UCLA	2	11	55.0	—	—	8	66.7	10	—	—	—	15.0
1965	*Bill Bradley, Princeton	2	34	63.0	—	—	19	95.0	24	—	—	—	43.5
1966	*Jerry Chambers, Utah	2	25	53.2	—	—	20	83.3	35	—	—	—	35.0
1967	Lew Alcindor, UCLA	2	14	60.9	—	—	11	45.8	38	—	—	—	19.5
1968	Lew Alcindor, UCLA	2	22	62.9	—	—	9	90.0	34	—	—	—	26.5
1969	Lew Alcindor, UCLA	2	23	67.7	—	—	16	64.0	41	—	—	—	31.0
1970	Sidney Wicks, UCLA	2	15	71.4	—	—	9	60.0	34	—	—	—	19.5
1971	*†Howard Porter, Villanova	2	20	48.8	—	—	7	77.8	24	—	—	—	23.5
1972	Bill Walton, UCLA	2	20	69.0	—	—	17	73.9	41	—	—	—	28.5
1973	Bill Walton, UCLA	2	28	82.4	—	—	2	40.0	30	—	—	—	29.0
1974	David Thompson, NC State	2	19	51.4	—	—	11	78.6	17	—	—	—	24.5
1975	Richard Washington, UCLA	2	23	54.8	—	—	8	72.7	20	—	—	—	27.0
1976	Kent Benson, Indiana	2	17	50.0	—	—	7	63.6	18	—	—	—	20.5
1977	Butch Lee, Marquette	2	11	34.4	—	—	8	100.0	6	2	1	1	15.0
1978	Jack Givens, Kentucky	2	28	65.1	—	—	8	66.7	17	4	1	3	32.0
1979	Earvin Johnson, Michigan St	2	17	68.0	—	—	19	86.4	17	3	0	2	26.5
1980	Darrell Griffith, Louisville	2	23	62.2	—	—	11	68.8	7	15	0	2	28.5
1981	Isiah Thomas, Indiana	2	14	56.0	—	—	9	81.8	4	9	3	4	18.5
1982	James Worthy, N Carolina	2	20	74.1	—	—	2	28.6	8	9	0	4	21.0
1983	*Akeem Olajuwon, Houston	2	16	55.2	—	—	9	64.3	40	3	2	5	20.5
1984	Patrick Ewing, Georgetown	2	8	57.1	—	—	2	100.0	18	1	1	15	9.0
1985	Ed Pinckney, Villanova	2	8	57.1	—	—	12	75.0	15	6	3	0	14.0
1986	Pervis Ellison, Louisville	2	15	60.0	—	—	6	75.0	24	2	3	1	18.0
1987	Keith Smart, Indiana	2	14	63.6	1	0	7	77.8	7	7	0	2	17.5
1988	Danny Manning, Kansas	2	25	55.6	1	0	6	66.7	17	4	8	9	28.0
1989	Glen Rice, Michigan	2	24	49.0	16	7	4	100.0	16	1	0	3	29.5
1990	Anderson Hunt, UNLV	2	19	61.3	16	9	2	50.0	4	9	1	1	24.5
1991	Christian Laettner, Duke	2	12	54.5	1	1	21	91.3	17	2	1	2	23.0
1992	Bobby Hurley, Duke	2	10	41.7	12	7	8	80.0	3	11	0	3	17.5
1993	Donald Williams, N Carolina	2	15	65.2	14	10	10	100.0	4	2	2	0	25.0
1994	Corliss Williamson, Arkansas	2	21	50.0	0	0	10	71.4	21	8	4	3	26.0
1995	Ed O'Bannon, UCLA	2	16	45.7	8	3	10	76.9	25	3	7	1	22.5
1996	Tony Delk, Kentucky	2	15	41.7	16	8	6	54.6	9	2	3	2	22.0
1997	Miles Simon, Arizona	2	17	45.9	10	3	17	77.3	8	6	0	1	27.0
1998	Jeff Sheppard, Kentucky	2	16	55.2	10	4	7	77.8	10	7	4	0	21.5
1999	Richard Hamilton, Connecticut	2	20	51.3	7	3	8	72.7	12	4	2	1	25.5

*Not a member of the championship-winning team.   †Record later vacated.

Best NCAA Tournament Single-Game Scoring Performances

Player and Team	Year	Round	FG	3FG	FT	TP
Austin Carr, Notre Dame vs Ohio	1970	1st	25	—	11	61
Bill Bradley, Princeton vs Wichita St	1965	C*	22	—	14	58
Oscar Robertson, Cincinnati vs Arkansas	1958	C	21	—	14	56
Austin Carr, Notre Dame vs Kentucky	1970	2nd	22	—	8	52
Austin Carr, Notre Dame vs Texas Christian	1971	1st	20	—	12	52
David Robinson, Navy vs Michigan	1987	1st	22	0	6	50
Elvin Hayes, Houston vs Loyola (IL)	1968	1st	20	—	9	49
Hal Lear, Temple vs SMU	1956	C*	17	—	14	48
Austin Carr, Notre Dame vs Houston	1971	C	17	—	13	47
Dave Corzine, DePaul vs Louisville	1978	2nd	18	—	10	46

C=regional third place; C*=third-place game.

NIT Championship Results

Year	Winner	Score	Runner-up	Year	Winner	Score	Runner-up
1938	Temple	60–36	Colorado	1969	Temple	89–76	Boston College
1939	Long Island U	44–32	Loyola (IL)	1970	Marquette	65–53	St. John's (NY)
1940	Colorado	51–40	Duquesne	1971	N Carolina	84–66	Georgia Tech
1941	Long Island U	56–42	Ohio U	1972	Maryland	100–69	Niagara
1942	W Virginia	47–45	W Kentucky	1973	Virginia Tech	92–91 (OT)	Notre Dame
1943	St. John's (NY)	48–27	Toledo	1974	Purdue	97–81	Utah
1944	St. John's (NY)	47–39	DePaul	1975	Princeton	80–69	Providence
1945	DePaul	71–54	Bowling Green	1976	Kentucky	71–67	NC-Charlotte
1946	Kentucky	46–45	Rhode Island	1977	St. Bonaventure	94–91	Houston
1947	Utah	49–45	Kentucky	1978	Texas	101–93	N Carolina St
1948	St. Louis	65–52	NYU	1979	Indiana	53–52	Purdue
1949	San Francisco	48–47	Loyola (IL)	1980	Virginia	58–55	Minnesota
1950	CCNY	69–61	Bradley	1981	Tulsa	86–84 (OT)	Syracuse
1951	BYU	62–43	Dayton	1982	Bradley	67–58	Purdue
1952	La Salle	75–64	Dayton	1983	Fresno St	69–60	DePaul
1953	Seton Hall	58–46	St. John's (NY)	1984	Michigan	83–63	Notre Dame
1954	Holy Cross	71–62	Duquesne	1985	UCLA	65–62	Indiana
1955	Duquesne	70–58	Dayton	1986	Ohio St	73–63	Wyoming
1956	Louisville	93–80	Dayton	1987	Southern Miss	84–80	La Salle
1957	Bradley	84–83	Memphis St	1988	Connecticut	72–67	Ohio St
1958	Xavier (OH)	78–74 (OT)	Dayton	1989	St. John's (NY)	73–65	St. Louis
1959	St. John's (NY)	76–71 (OT)	Bradley	1990	Vanderbilt	74–72	St. Louis
1960	Bradley	88–72	Providence	1991	Stanford	78–72	Oklahoma
1961	Providence	62–59	St. Louis	1992	Virginia	81–76	Notre Dame
1962	Dayton	73–67	St. John's (NY)	1993	Minnesota	62–61	Georgetown
1963	Providence	81–66	Canisius	1994	Villanova	80–73	Vanderbilt
1964	Bradley	86–54	New Mexico	1995	Virginia Tech	65–64 (OT)	Marquette
1965	St. John's (NY)	55–51	Villanova	1996	Nebraska	60–56	St. Joseph's
1966	BYU	97–84	NYU	1997	Michigan	82–73	Florida St
1967	Southern Illinois	71–56	Marquette	1998	Minnesota	79–72	Penn St
1968	Dayton	61–48	Kansas	1999	California	61–60	Clemson

NCAA Men's Division I Season Leaders

Scoring Average

Year	Player and Team	Ht	Class	GP	FG	3FG	FT	Pts	Avg
1948	Murray Wier, Iowa	5-9	Sr	19	152	—	95	399	21.0
1949	Tony Lavelli, Yale	6-3	Sr	30	228	—	215	671	22.4
1950	Paul Arizin, Villanova	6-3	Sr	29	260	—	215	735	25.3
1951	Bill Mlkvy, Temple	6-4	Sr	25	303	—	125	731	29.2
1952	Clyde Lovellette, Kansas	6-9	Sr	28	315	—	165	795	28.4
1953	Frank Selvy, Furman	6-3	Jr	25	272	—	194	738	29.5
1954	Frank Selvy, Furman	6-3	Sr	29	427	—	355	1209	41.7
1955	Darrell Floyd, Furman	6-1	Jr	25	344	—	209	897	35.9
1956	Darrell Floyd, Furman	6-1	Sr	28	339	—	268	946	33.8
1957	Grady Wallace, S Carolina	6-4	Sr	29	336	—	234	906	31.2
1958	Oscar Robertson, Cincinnati	6-5	So	28	352	—	280	984	35.1
1959	Oscar Robertson, Cincinnati	6-5	Jr	30	331	—	316	978	32.6
1960	Oscar Robertson, Cincinnati	6-5	Sr	30	369	—	273	1011	33.7
1961	Frank Burgess, Gonzaga	6-1	Sr	26	304	—	234	842	32.4
1962	Billy McGill, Utah	6-9	Sr	26	394	—	221	1009	38.8

Scoring Average *(Cont.)*

Year	Player and Team	Ht	Class	GP	FG	3FG	FT	Pts	Avg
1963	Nick Werkman, Seton Hall	6-3	Jr	22	221	—	208	650	29.5
1964	Howard Komives, Bowling Green	6-1	Sr	23	292	—	260	844	36.7
1965	Rick Barry, Miami (FL)	6-7	Sr	26	340	—	293	973	37.4
1966	Dave Schellhase, Purdue	6-4	Sr	24	284	—	213	781	32.5
1967	Jim Walker, Providence	6-3	Sr	28	323	—	205	851	30.4
1968	Pete Maravich, Louisiana St	6-5	So	26	432	—	274	1138	43.8
1969	Pete Maravich, Louisiana St	6-5	Jr	26	433	—	282	1148	44.2
1970	Pete Maravich, Louisiana St	6-5	Sr	31	522	—	337	1381	44.5
1971	Johnny Neumann, Mississippi	6-6	So	23	366	—	191	923	40.1
1972	Dwight Lamar, Southwestern Louisiana	6-1	Jr	29	429	—	196	1054	36.3
1973	William Averitt, Pepperdine	6-1	Sr	25	352	—	144	848	33.9
1974	Larry Fogle, Canisius	6-5	So	25	326	—	183	835	33.4
1975	Bob McCurdy, Richmond	6-7	Sr	26	321	—	213	855	32.9
1976	Marshall Rodgers, TX-Pan American	6-2	Sr	25	361	—	197	919	36.8
1977	Freeman Williams, Portland St	6-4	Jr	26	417	—	176	1010	38.8
1978	Freeman Williams, Portland St	6-4	Sr	27	410	—	149	969	35.9
1979	Lawrence Butler, Idaho St	6-3	Sr	27	310	—	192	812	30.1
1980	Tony Murphy, Southern-BR	6-3	Sr	29	377	—	178	932	32.1
1981	Zam Fredrick, S Carolina	6-2	Sr	27	300	—	181	781	28.9
1982	Harry Kelly, Texas Southern	6-7	Jr	29	336	—	190	862	29.7
1983	Harry Kelly, Texas Southern	6-7	Sr	29	333	—	169	835	28.8
1984	Joe Jakubick, Akron	6-5	Sr	27	304	—	206	814	30.1
1985	Xavier McDaniel, Wichita St	6-8	Sr	31	351	—	142	844	27.2
1986	Terrance Bailey, Wagner	6-2	Jr	29	321	—	212	854	29.4
1987	Kevin Houston, Army	5-11	Sr	29	311	63	268	953	32.9
1988	Hersey Hawkins, Bradley	6-3	Sr	31	377	87	284	1125	36.3
1989	Hank Gathers, Loyola Marymount	6-7	Jr	31	419	0	177	1015	32.7
1990	Bo Kimble, Loyola Marymount	6-5	Sr	32	404	92	231	1131	35.3
1991	Kevin Bradshaw, U.S. Int'l	6-6	Sr	28	358	60	278	1054	37.6
1992	Brett Roberts, Morehead St	6-8	Sr	29	278	66	193	815	28.1
1993	Greg Guy, TX-Pan American	6-1	Jr	19	189	67	111	556	29.3
1994	Glenn Robinson, Purdue	6-8	Jr	34	368	79	215	1030	30.3
1995	Kurt Thomas, Texas Christian	6-9	Sr	27	288	3	202	781	28.9
1996	Kevin Granger, Texas Southern	6-3	Sr	24	194	30	230	648	27.0
1997	Charles Jones, LIU-Brooklyn	6-3	Jr	30	338	109	118	903	30.1
1998	Charles Jones, LIU-Brooklyn	6-3	Sr	30	326	116	101	869	29.0
1999	Alvin Young, Niagara	6-3	Sr	29	253	65	157	728	25.1

Rebounds

Year	Player and Team	Ht	Class	GP	Reb	Avg
1951	Ernie Beck, Pennsylvania	6-4	So	27	556	20.6
1952	Bill Hannon, Army	6-3	So	17	355	20.9
1953	Ed Conlin, Fordham	6-5	So	26	612	23.5
1954	Art Quimby, Connecticut	6-5	Jr	26	588	22.6
1955	Charlie Slack, Marshall	6-5	Jr	21	538	25.6
1956	Joe Holup, George Washington	6-6	Sr	26	604	†.256
1957	Elgin Baylor, Seattle	6-6	Jr	25	508	†.235
1958	Alex Ellis, Niagara	6-5	Sr	25	536	†.262
1959	Leroy Wright, Pacific	6-8	Jr	26	652	†.238
1960	Leroy Wright, Pacific	6-8	Sr	17	380	†.234
1961	Jerry Lucas, Ohio St	6-8	Jr	27	470	†.198
1962	Jerry Lucas, Ohio St	6-8	Sr	28	499	†.211
1963	Paul Silas, Creighton	6-7	Sr	27	557	20.6
1964	Bob Pelkington, Xavier (OH)	6-7	Sr	26	567	21.8
1965	Toby Kimball, Connecticut	6-8	Sr	23	483	21.0
1966	Jim Ware, Oklahoma City	6-8	Sr	29	607	20.9
1967	Dick Cunningham, Murray St	6-10	Jr	22	479	21.8
1968	Neal Walk, Florida	6-10	Jr	25	494	19.8
1969	Spencer Haywood, Detroit	6-8	So	22	472	21.5
1970	Artis Gilmore, Jacksonville	7-2	Jr	28	621	22.2
1971	Artis Gilmore, Jacksonville	7-2	Sr	26	603	23.2
1972	Kermit Washington, American	6-8	Jr	23	455	19.8
1973	Kermit Washington, American	6-8	Sr	22	439	20.0
1974	Marvin Barnes, Providence	6-9	Sr	32	597	18.7
1975	John Irving, Hofstra	6-9	So	21	323	15.4
1976	Sam Pellom, Buffalo	6-8	So	26	420	16.2
1977	Glenn Mosley, Seton Hall	6-8	Sr	29	473	16.3
1978	Ken Williams, N Texas St	6-7	Sr	28	411	14.7
1979	Monti Davis, Tennessee St	6-7	Jr	26	421	16.2
1980	Larry Smith, Alcorn St	6-8	Sr	26	392	15.1

†From 1956–1962, title was based on highest individual recoveries out of total by both teams in all games.

Rebounds *(Cont.)*

Year	Player and Team	Ht	Class	GP	Reb	Avg
1981	Darryl Watson, Miss Valley	6-7	Sr	27	379	14.0
1982	LaSalle Thompson, Texas	6-10	Jr	27	365	13.5
1983	Xavier McDaniel, Wichita St	6-7	So	28	403	14.4
1984	Akeem Olajuwon, Houston	7-0	Jr	37	500	13.5
1985	Xavier McDaniel, Wichita St	6-8	Sr	31	460	14.8
1986	David Robinson, Navy	6-11	Jr	35	455	13.0
1987	Jerome Lane, Pittsburgh	6-6	So	33	444	13.5
1988	Kenny Miller, Loyola (IL)	6-9	Fr	29	395	13.6
1989	Hank Gathers, Loyola (CA)	6-7	Jr	31	426	13.7
1990	Anthony Bonner, St. Louis	6-8	Sr	33	456	13.8
1991	Shaquille O'Neal, Louisiana St	7-1	So	28	411	14.7
1992	Popeye Jones, Murray St	6-8	Sr	30	431	14.4
1993	Warren Kidd, Middle Tenn St	6-9	Sr	26	386	14.8
1994	Jerome Lambert, Baylor	6-8	Jr	24	355	14.8
1995	Kurt Thomas, Texas Christian	6-9	Sr	27	393	14.6
1996	Marcus Mann, Mississippi Valley	6-8	Sr	29	394	13.6
1997	Tim Duncan, Wake Forest	6-11	Sr	31	457	14.7
1998	Ryan Perryman, Dayton	6-7	Sr	33	412	12.5
1999	Ian McGinnis, Dartmouth	6-8	So	26	317	12.2

Assists

Year	Player and Team	Class	GP	A	Avg
1984	Craig Lathen, IL-Chicago	Jr	29	274	9.45
1985	Rob Weingard, Hofstra	Sr	24	228	9.50
1986	Mark Jackson, St. John's (NY)	Jr	36	328	9.11
1987	Avery Johnson, Southern-BR	Jr	31	333	10.74
1988	Avery Johnson, Southern-BR	Sr	30	399	13.30
1989	Glenn Williams, Holy Cross	Sr	28	278	9.93
1990	Todd Lehmann, Drexel	Sr	28	260	9.29
1991	Chris Corchiani, N Carolina St	Sr	31	299	9.65
1992	Van Usher, Tennessee Tech	Sr	29	254	8.76
1993	Sam Crawford, New Mex St	Sr	34	310	9.12
1994	Jason Kidd, California	So	30	272	9.06
1995	Nelson Haggerty, Baylor	Sr	28	284	10.10
1996	Raimonds Miglinieks, UC-Irvine	Sr	27	230	8.52
1997	Kenny Mitchell, Dartmouth	Sr	26	203	7.81
1998	Ahlon Lewis, Arizona St	Sr	32	294	9.19
1999	Doug Gottlieb, Oklahoma St	Jr	34	299	8.79

Blocked Shots

Year	Player and Team	Class	GP	BS	Avg
1986	David Robinson, Navy	Jr	35	207	5.91
1987	David Robinson, Navy	Sr	32	144	4.50
1988	Rodney Blake, St. Joseph's (PA)	Sr	29	116	4.00
1989	Alonzo Mourning, Georgetown	Fr	34	169	4.97
1990	Kenny Green, Rhode Island	Sr	26	124	4.77
1991	Shawn Bradley, Brigham Young	Fr	34	177	5.21
1992	Shaquille O'Neal, Louisiana St	Jr	30	157	5.23
1993	Theo Ratliff, Wyoming	Jr	28	124	4.43
1994	Grady Livingston, Howard	Jr	26	115	4.42
1995	Keith Closs, Central Conn St	Fr	26	139	5.35
1996	Keith Closs, Central Conn St	So	28	178	6.36
1997	Adonal Foyle, Colgate	Jr	28	180	6.43
1998	Jerome James, Florida A&M	Sr	27	125	4.63
1999	Tarvis Williams, Hampton	Jr	27	135	5.00

Steals

Year	Player and Team	Class	GP	S	Avg
1986	Darron Brittman, Chicago St	Sr	28	139	4.96
1987	Tony Fairley, Charleston Sou	Sr	28	114	4.07
1988	Aldwin Ware, Florida A&M	Sr	29	142	4.90
1989	Kenny Robertson, Cleveland St	Jr	28	111	3.96
1990	Ronn McMahon, E Washington	Sr	29	130	4.48
1991	Van Usher, Tennessee Tech	Jr	28	104	3.71
1992	Victor Snipes, NE Illinois	So	25	86	3.44
1993	Jason Kidd, California	Fr	29	110	3.80
1994	Shawn Griggs, SW Louisiana	Sr	30	120	4.00
1995	Roderick Anderson, Texas	Sr	30	101	3.37
1996	Pointer Williams, McNeese St	Sr	27	118	4.37
1997	Joel Hoover, MD-Eastern Shore	Fr	28	90	3.21
1998	Bonzi Wells, Ball St	Sr	29	103	3.55
1999	Shawnta Rogers, George Wash	Sr	29	103	3.55

Single Game Records

SCORING HIGHS VS DIVISION I OPPONENT

Pts	Player and Team vs Opponent	Date
72	Kevin Bradshaw, U.S. Int'l vs Loyola Marymount	1-5-91
69	Pete Maravich, Louisiana St vs Alabama	2-7-70
68	Calvin Murphy, Niagara vs Syracuse	12-7-68
66	Jay Handlan, Washington & Lee vs Furman	2-17-51
66	Pete Maravich, Louisiana St vs Tulane	2-10-69
66	Anthony Roberts, Oral Roberts vs N Carolina A&T	2-19-77
65	Anthony Roberts, Oral Roberts vs Oregon	3-9-77
65	Scott Haffner, Evansville vs Dayton	2-18-89
64	Pete Maravich, Louisiana St vs Kentucky	2-21-70
63	Johnny Neumann, Mississippi vs Louisiana St	1-30-71
63	Hersey Hawkins, Bradley vs Detroit	2-22-88

SCORING HIGHS VS NON-DIVISION I OPPONENT

Pts	Player and Team vs Opponent	Date
100	Frank Selvy, Furman vs Newberry	2-13-54
85	Paul Arizin, Villanova vs Philadelphia NAMC	2-12-49
81	Freeman Williams, Portland St vs Rocky Mountain	2-3-78
73	Bill Mlkvy, Temple vs Wilkes	3-3-51
71	Freeman Williams, Portland St vs Southern Oregon	2-9-77

REBOUNDING HIGHS BEFORE 1973

Reb	Player and Team vs Opponent	Date
51	Bill Chambers, William & Mary vs Virginia	2-14-53
43	Charlie Slack, Marshall vs Morris Harvey	1-12-54
42	Tom Heinsohn, Holy Cross vs Boston College	3-1-55
40	Art Quimby, Connecticut vs Boston U	1-11-55
39	Maurice Stokes, St. Francis (PA) vs John Carroll	1-28-55
39	Dave DeBusschere, Detroit vs Central Michigan	1-30-60
39	Keith Swagerty, Pacific vs UC-Santa Barbara	3-5-65

REBOUNDING HIGHS SINCE 1973*

Reb	Player and Team vs Opponent	Date
34	David Vaughn, Oral Roberts vs Brandeis	1-8-73
33	Robert Parish, Centenary vs Southern Miss	1-22-73
32	Jervaughn Scales, Southern-BR vs Grambling	2-7-94
32	Durand Macklin, Louisiana St vs Tulane	11-26-76
31	Jim Bradley, Northern Illinois vs WI-Milwaukee	2-19-73
31	Calvin Natt, NE Louisiana vs Georgia Southern	12-29-76

ASSISTS

A	Player and Team vs Opponent	Date
22	Tony Fairley, Baptist vs Armstrong St	2-9-87
22	Avery Johnson, Southern-BR vs Texas Southern	1-25-88
22	Sherman Douglas, Syracuse vs Providence	1-28-89
21	Mark Wade, UNLV vs Navy	12-29-86
21	Kelvin Scarborough, New Mexico vs Hawaii	2-13-87
21	Anthony Manuel, Bradley vs UC-Irvine	12-19-87
21	Avery Johnson, Southern-BR vs Alabama St	1-16-88

STEALS

S	Player and Team vs Opponent	Date
13	Mookie Blaylock, Oklahoma vs Centenary	12-12-87
13	Mookie Blaylock, Oklahoma vs Loyola Marymount	12-17-88
12	Kenny Robertson, Cleveland St vs Wagner	12-3-88
12	Terry Evans, Oklahoma vs Florida A&M	1-27-93
12	Richard Duncan, Middle Tenn St vs Eastern Kentucky	2-20-99

Nine tied with 11, most recently Philip Huler, Fla. Atlantic vs Campbell, 1-18-97.

*Freshmen became eligible for varsity play in 1973.

Single Game Records *(Cont.)*

BLOCKED SHOTS

BS	Player and Team vs Opponent	Date
14	David Robinson, Navy vs NC-Wilmington	1-4-86
14	Shawn Bradley, Brigham Young vs Eastern Kentucky	12-7-90
14	Roy Rogers, Alabama vs Georgia	2-10-96
13	Kevin Roberson, Vermont vs New Hampshire	1-9-92
13	Jim McIlvaine, Marquette vs Northeastern (IL)	12-9-92
13	Keith Closs, Central Conn. St vs St. Francis (PA)	12-21-94

Single Season Records

POINTS

Player and Team	Year	GP	FG	3FG	FT	Pts
Pete Maravich, Louisiana St	1970	31	522	—	337	1381
Elvin Hayes, Houston	1968	33	519	—	176	1214
Frank Selvy, Furman	1954	29	427	—	355	1209
Pete Maravich, Louisiana St	1969	26	433	—	282	1148
Pete Maravich, Louisiana St	1968	26	432	—	274	1138
Bo Kimble, Loyola Marymount	1990	32	404	92	231	1131
Hersey Hawkins, Bradley	1988	31	377	87	284	1125
Austin Carr, Notre Dame	1970	29	444	—	218	1106
Austin Carr, Notre Dame	1971	29	430	—	241	1101
Otis Birdsong, Houston	1977	36	452	—	186	1090

SCORING AVERAGE

Player and Team	Year	GP	FG	3FG	FT	Pts
Pete Maravich, Louisiana St	1970	31	522	337	1381	44.5
Pete Maravich, Louisiana St	1969	26	433	282	1148	44.2
Pete Maravich, Louisiana St	1968	26	432	274	1138	43.8
Frank Selvy, Furman	1954	29	427	355	1209	41.7
Johnny Neumann, Mississippi	1971	23	366	191	923	40.1
Freeman Williams, Portland St	1977	26	417	176	1010	38.8
Billy McGill, Utah	1962	26	394	221	1009	38.8
Calvin Murphy, Niagara	1968	24	337	242	916	38.2
Austin Carr, Notre Dame	1970	29	444	218	1106	38.1
Austin Carr, Notre Dame	1971	29	430	241	1101	38.0

REBOUNDS

Player and Team	Year	GP	Reb	Player and Team	Year	GP	Reb
Walt Dukes, Seton Hall	1953	33	734	Artis Gilmore, Jacksonville	1970	28	621
Leroy Wright, Pacific	1959	26	652	Tom Gola, La Salle	1955	31	618
Tom Gola, La Salle	1954	30	652	Ed Conlin, Fordham	1953	26	612
Charlie Tyra, Louisville	1956	29	645	Art Quimby, Connecticut	1955	25	611
Paul Silas, Creighton	1964	29	631	Bill Russell, San Francisco	1956	29	609
Elvin Hayes, Houston	1968	33	624	Jim Ware, Oklahoma City	1966	29	607

REBOUND AVERAGE BEFORE 1973

Player and Team	Year	GP	Reb	Avg
Charlie Slack, Marshall	1955	21	538	25.6
Leroy Wright, Pacific	1959	26	652	25.1
Art Quimby, Connecticut	1955	25	611	24.4
Charlie Slack, Marshall	1956	22	520	23.6
Ed Conlin, Fordham	1953	26	612	23.5

REBOUND AVERAGE SINCE 1973*

Player and Team	Year	GP	Reb	Avg
Kermit Washington, American	1973	22	439	20.0
Marvin Barnes, Providence	1973	30	571	19.0
Marvin Barnes, Providence	1974	32	597	18.7
Pete Padgett, NV-Reno	1973	26	462	17.8
Jim Bradley, Northern Illinois	1973	24	426	17.8

*Freshmen became eligible for varsity play in 1973.

Single Season Records (Cont.)

ASSISTS

Player and Team	Year	GP	A	Player and Team	Year	GP	A
Mark Wade, UNLV	1987	38	406	Sherman Douglas, Syracuse	1989	38	326
Avery Johnson, Southern-BR	1988	30	399	Sam Crawford, New Mex. St	1993	34	310
Anthony Manuel, Bradley	1988	31	373	Greg Anthony, UNLV	1991	35	310
Avery Johnson, Southern-BR	1987	31	333	Reid Gettys, Houston	1984	37	309
Mark Jackson, St. John's (NY)	1986	32	328	Carl Golston, Loyola (IL)	1985	33	305

ASSIST AVERAGE

Player and Team	Year	GP	A	Avg	Player and Team	Year	GP	A	Avg
Avery Johnson, Southern-BR	1988	30	399	13.3	Chris Corchiani, N Carolina St	1991	31	299	9.6
Anthony Manuel, Bradley	1988	31	373	12.0	Tony Fairley, Charleston So.*	1987	28	270	9.6
Avery Johnson, Southern-BR	1987	31	333	10.7	Tyrone Bogues, Wake Forest	1987	29	276	9.5
Mark Wade, UNLV	1987	38	406	10.7	Ron Weingard, Hofstra	1985	24	228	9.5
Nelson Haggerty, Baylor	1995	28	284	10.1	Craig Neal, Georgia Tech	1988	32	303	9.5

*Formerly Baptist.

FIELD-GOAL PERCENTAGE

Player and Team	Year	GP	FG	FGA	Pct
Steve Johnson, Oregon St	1981	28	235	315	74.6
Dwayne Davis, Florida	1989	33	179	248	72.2
Keith Walker, Utica	1985	27	154	216	71.3
Steve Johnson, Oregon St	1980	30	211	297	71.0
Oliver Miller, Arkansas	1991	38	254	361	70.4
Alan Williams, Princeton	1987	25	163	232	70.3
Mark McNamara, California	1982	27	231	329	70.2
Warren Kidd, Middle Tennessee St	1991	30	173	247	70.0
Pete Freeman, Akron	1991	28	175	250	70.0
Joe Senser, West Chester	1977	25	130	186	69.9

Based on qualifiers for annual championship.

FREE-THROW PERCENTAGE

Player and Team	Year	GP	FT	FTA	Pct
Craig Collins, Penn St	1985	27	94	98	95.9
Rod Foster, UCLA	1982	27	95	100	95.0
Danny Basile, Marist	1994	27	84	89	94.4
Carlos Gibson, Marshall	1978	28	84	89	94.4
Jim Barton, Dartmouth	1986	26	65	69	94.2
Jack Moore, Nebraska	1982	27	123	131	93.9
Dandrea Evans, Troy St	1994	27	72	77	93.5
Rob Robbins, New Mexico	1990	34	101	108	93.5
Tommy Boyer, Arkansas	1962	23	125	134	93.3
Damon Goodwin, Dayton	1986	30	95	102	93.1

Based on qualifiers for annual championship.

THREE-POINT FIELD-GOAL PERCENTAGE

Player and Team	Year	GP	3FG	3FGA	Pct
Glenn Tropf, Holy Cross	1988	29	52	82	63.4
Sean Wightman, Western Michigan	1992	30	48	76	63.2
Keith Jennings, E Tennessee St	1991	33	84	142	59.2
Dave Calloway, Monmouth (NJ)	1989	28	48	82	58.5
Steve Kerr, Arizona	1988	38	114	199	57.3
Reginald Jones, Prairie View	1987	28	64	112	57.1
Jim Cantamessa, Siena	1998	29	66	117	56.4
Joel Tribelhorn, Colorado St	1989	33	76	135	56.3
Mike Joseph, Bucknell	1988	28	65	116	56.0
Brian Jackson, Evansville	1995	27	53	95	55.8

Based on qualifiers for annual championship.

Single Season Records *(Cont.)*

STEALS

Player and Team	Year	GP	S
Mookie Blaylock, Oklahoma	1988	39	150
Aldwin Ware, Florida A&M	1988	29	142
Darron Brittman, Chicago St	1986	28	139
Nadav Henefeld, Connecticut	1990	37	138
Mookie Blaylock, Oklahoma	1989	35	131

BLOCKED SHOTS

Player and Team	Year	GP	BS
David Robinson, Navy	1986	35	207
Adonal Foyle, Colgate	1997	28	180
Keith Closs, Central Conn St	1996	28	178
Shawn Bradley, BYU	1991	34	177
Alonzo Mourning, Georgetown	1989	34	169

STEAL AVERAGE

Player and Team	Year	GP	S	Avg
Darron Brittman, Chicago St	1986	28	139	4.96
Aldwin Ware, Florida A&M	1988	29	142	4.90
Ronn McMahon, E Washington	1990	29	130	4.48
Pointer Williams, McNeese St	1996	27	118	4.37
Jim Paguaga, St Francis (NY)	1986	28	120	4.29

BLOCKED-SHOT AVERAGE

Player and Team	Year	GP	BS	Avg
Adonal Foyle, Colgate	1997	28	180	6.43
Keith Closs, Central Conn St	1996	28	178	6.36
David Robinson, Navy	1986	35	207	5.91
Adonal Foyle, Colgate	1996	29	165	5.69
Keith Closs, Central Conn St	1995	26	139	5.34

Career Records

POINTS

Player and Team	Ht	Final Year	GP	FG	3FG*	FT	Pts
Pete Maravich, Louisiana St	6-5	1970	83	1387	—	893	3667
Freeman Williams, Portland St	6-4	1978	106	1369	—	511	3249
Lionel Simmons, La Salle	6-7	1990	131	1244	56	673	3217
Alphonso Ford, Mississippi Valley	6-2	1993	109	1121	333	590	3165
Harry Kelly, Texas Southern	6-7	1983	110	1234	—	598	3066
Hersey Hawkins, Bradley	6-3	1988	125	1100	118	690	3008
Oscar Robertson, Cincinnati	6-5	1960	88	1052	—	869	2973
Danny Manning, Kansas	6-10	1988	147	1216	10	509	2951
Alfredrick Hughes, Loyola (IL)	6-5	1985	120	1226	—	462	2914
Elvin Hayes, Houston	6-8	1968	93	1215	—	454	2884
Larry Bird, Indiana St	6-9	1979	94	1154	—	542	2850
Otis Birdsong, Houston	6-4	1977	116	1176	—	480	2832
Kevin Bradshaw, Bethune-Cookman, U.S. Int'l	6-6	1991	111	1027	132	618	2804
Allan Houston, Tennessee	6-6	1993	128	902	346	651	2801
Hank Gathers, Southern Cal, Loyola Marymount	6-7	1990	117	1127	0	469	2723
Reggie Lewis, Northeastern	6-7	1987	122	1043	30 (1)	592	2708
Daren Queenan, Lehigh	6-5	1988	118	1024	29	626	2703
Byron Larkin, Xavier (OH)	6-3	1988	121	1022	51	601	2696
David Robinson, Navy	7-1	1987	127	1032	1	604	2669
Wayman Tisdale, Oklahoma	6-9	1985	104	1077	—	507	2661

*Listed is the number of three-pointers scored since it became the national rule in 1987; the number in the parentheses is number scored prior to 1987—these counted as three points in the game but counted as two-pointers in the national rankings. The three-pointers in the parentheses are not included in total points.

SCORING AVERAGE

Player and Team	Final Year	GP	FG	FT	Pts	Avg
Pete Maravich, Louisiana St	1968	83	1387	893	3667	44.2
Austin Carr, Notre Dame	1971	74	1017	526	2560	34.6
Oscar Robertson, Cincinnati	1960	88	1052	869	2973	33.8
Calvin Murphy, Niagara	1970	77	947	654	2548	33.1
Dwight Lamar, Southwestern Louisiana	1973	57	768	326	1862	32.7
Frank Selvy, Furman	1954	78	922	694	2538	32.5
Rick Mount, Purdue	1970	72	910	503	2323	32.3
Darrell Floyd, Furman	1956	71	868	545	2281	32.1
Nick Werkman, Seton Hall	1964	71	812	649	2273	32.0
Willie Humes, Idaho St	1971	48	565	380	1510	31.5
William Averitt, Pepperdine	1973	49	615	311	1541	31.4
Elgin Baylor, Coll. of Idaho, Seattle	1958	80	956	588	2500	31.3
Elvin Hayes, Houston	1968	93	1215	454	2884	31.0
Freeman Williams, Portland St	1978	106	1369	511	3249	30.7
Larry Bird, Indiana St	1979	94	1154	542	2850	30.3

Career Records (Cont.)

REBOUNDS BEFORE 1973

Player and Team	Final Year	GP	Reb
Tom Gola, La Salle	1955	118	2201
Joe Holup, George Washington	1956	104	2030
Charlie Slack, Marshall	1956	88	1916
Ed Conlin, Fordham	1955	102	1884
Dickie Hemric, Wake Forest	1955	104	1802

REBOUNDS SINCE 1973*

Player and Team	Final Year	GP	Reb
Tim Duncan, Wake Forest	1997	128	1570
Derrick Coleman, Syracuse	1990	143	1537
Malik Rose, Drexel	1996	120	1514
Ralph Sampson, Virginia	1983	132	1511
Pete Padgett, NV-Reno	1976	104	1464

ASSISTS

Player and Team	Final Year	GP	A
Bobby Hurley, Duke	1993	140	1076
Chris Corchiani, N Carolina St	1991	124	1038
Keith Jennings, E Tennessee St	1991	127	983
Sherman Douglas, Syracuse	1989	138	960
Tony Miller, Marquette	1995	123	956

FIELD-GOAL PERCENTAGE

Player and Team	Final Year	FG	FGA	Pct
Ricky Nedd, Appalachian St	1994	412	597	69.0
Stephen Scheffler, Purdue	1990	408	596	68.5
Steve Johnson, Oregon St	1981	828	1222	67.8
Murray Brown, Florida St	1980	566	847	66.8
Lee Campbell, SW Missouri St	1990	411	618	66.5

Note: Minimum 400 field goals.

FREE-THROW PERCENTAGE

Player and Team	Final Year	FT	FTA	Pct
Greg Starrick, Kentucky; Southern Illinois	1972	341	375	90.9
Jack Moore, Nebraska	1982	446	495	90.1
Steve Henson, Kansas St	1990	361	401	90.0
Steve Alford, Indiana	1987	535	596	89.8
Bob Lloyd, Rutgers	1967	543	605	89.8

Note: Minimum 300 free throws.

*Freshmen became eligible for varsity play in 1973.

The Vandy Plan

Will academic scandals like the one at Minnesota (SI, June 14, 1999) spur reform in college sports? Big Ten commissioner Jim Delany hopes so. In late June 1999, a 29-member NCAA committee weighed two measures that Delany recommended for men's Division I basketball—making freshman ineligible and giving schools with high graduation rates an extra scholarship. "I hope the committee is bold and does what's right for the game," says Delany.

The SEC was backing an idea introduced by Vanderbilt athletic director Todd Turner. Under Turner's plan a university could no longer reassign the scholarships of athletes who permanently lose their academic eligibility. If a basketball player flunked out as a freshman, for instance, his school could not use his scholarship again until after his class graduated. Turner's proposal didn't get much support from other SEC athletic directors, but academics all over the conference supported the idea. In May '99 the SEC presidents endorsed it by a 9–0 vote. Florida and Tennessee didn't show up for the vote; Arkansas abstained.

The Vandy plan was being reviewed by the NCAA's panel on academic eligibility. "If you value educating student-athletes, you should favor this," said Turner, who developed the idea with Vanderbilt chancellor Joe B. Wyatt. "Presidents, chancellors and faculty will have a hard time arguing against it."

Career Records (Cont.)

THREE-POINT FIELD GOALS MADE

Player and Team	Final Year	GP	3FG
Curtis Staples, Virginia	1998	122	413
Keith Veney, Lamar; Marshall	1997	111	409
Doug Day, Radford	1993	117	401
Ronnie Schmitz, MO-Kansas City	1993	112	378
Mark Alberts, Akron	1993	103	375

THREE-POINT FIELD-GOAL PERCENTAGE

Player and Team	Final Year	3FG	3FGA	Pct
Tony Bennett, WI-Green Bay	1992	290	584	49.7
Keith Jennings, E Tennessee St	1991	223	452	49.3
Kirk Manns, Michigan St	1990	212	446	47.5
Tim Locum, Wisconsin	1991	227	481	47.2
David Olson, Eastern Illinois	1992	262	562	46.6

Note: Minimum 200 3-point field goals.

STEALS

Player and Team	Final Year	GP	S
Eric Murdock, Providence	1991	117	376
Bonzi Wells, Ball St	1998	116	347
Gerald Walker, San Francisco	1996	111	344
Johnny Rhodes, Maryland	1996	122	344
Michael Anderson, Drexel	1988	115	341
Kenny Robertson, New Mexico; Clev. St	1990	119	341

BLOCKED SHOTS

Player and Team	Final Year	GP	BS
Adonal Foyle, Colgate	1997	87	492
Tim Duncan, Wake Forest	1997	128	481
Alonzo Mourning, Georgetown	1992	120	453
Lorenzo Coleman, Tennessee Tech	1997	113	437
Calvin Booth, Penn St	1999	114	428

NCAA Men's Division I Team Leaders

Division I Team Alltime Wins

Team	First Year	Yrs	W	L	T
Kentucky	1903	96	1748	538	1
N Carolina	1911	89	1733	609	0
Kansas	1899	101	1688	724	0
Duke	1906	94	1585	755	0
St. John's (NY)	1908	92	1582	715	0
Temple	1895	103	1520	824	0
Syracuse	1901	98	1498	704	0
Pennsylvania	1897	99	1475	838	2
Oregon St	1902	98	1469	999	0
Indiana	1901	99	1453	778	0
UCLA	1920	80	1445	621	0
Notre Dame	1898	94	1441	792	1
Princeton	1901	99	1408	851	0
Utah	1909	91	1404	737	0
Purdue	1897	101	1404	771	0

Note: Minimum of 25 years in Division I.

Division I Alltime Winning Percentage

Team	First Year	Yrs	W	L	T	Pct
Kentucky	1903	96	1748	538	1	.765
N Carolina	1911	89	1733	609	0	.740
UNLV	1959	41	847	320	0	.726
Kansas	1899	101	1688	724	0	.700
UCLA	1920	80	1445	621	0	.699
St. John's (NY)	1908	92	1582	715	0	.689
Syracuse	1901	98	1498	704	0	.680
Duke	1906	94	1585	755	0	.677
Western Kentucky	1915	80	1379	685	0	.668
Arkansas	1924	76	1315	682	0	.658
Utah	1909	91	1404	737	0	.656
Indiana	1901	99	1453	778	0	.651
Louisville	1912	85	1356	727	0	.651
Temple	1895	103	1520	824	0	.648
DePaul	1924	76	1200	654	0	.647

Note: Minimum of 25 years in Division I.

NCAA Men's Division I Winning Streaks

Longest—Full Season

Team	Games	Years	Ended by
UCLA	88	1971–74	Notre Dame (71–70)
San Francisco	60	1955–57	Illinois (62–33)
UCLA	47	1966–68	Houston (71–69)
UNLV	45	1990–91	Duke (79–77)
Texas	44	1913–17	Rice (24–18)
Seton Hall	43	1939–41	LIU-Brooklyn (49–26)
LIU-Brooklyn	43	1935–37	Stanford (45–31)
UCLA	41	1968–69	Southern Cal (46–44)
Marquette	39	1970–71	Ohio St (60–59)
Cincinnati	37	1962–63	Wichita St (65–64)
N Carolina	37	1957–58	W Virginia (75–64)

Longest—Regular Season

Team	Games	Years	Ended by
UCLA	76	1971–74	Notre Dame (71–70)
Indiana	57	1975–77	Toledo (59–57)
Marquette	56	1970–72	Detroit (70–49)
Kentucky	54	1952–55	Georgia Tech (59–58)
San Francisco	51	1955–57	Illinois (62–33)
Pennsylvania	48	1970–72	Temple (57–52)
Ohio State	47	1960–62	Wisconsin (86–67)
Texas	44	1913–17	Rice (24–18)
UCLA	43	1966–68	Houston (71–69)
LIU-Brooklyn	43	1935–37	Stanford (45–31)
Seton Hall	42	1939–41	LIU-Brooklyn (49–26)

Longest—Home Court

Team	Games	Years
Kentucky	129	1943–55
St. Bonaventure	99	1948–61
UCLA	98	1970–76
Cincinnati	86	1957–64
Marquette	81	1967–73
Arizona	81	1945–51

Team	Games	Years
Lamar	80	1978–84
Long Beach St	75	1968–74
UNLV	72	1974–78
Arizona	71	1987–92
Cincinnati	68	1972–78
Western Kentucky	67	1949–55

NCAA Men's Division I Winningest Coaches

Active Coaches

WINS

Coach and Team	W
James Phelan, Mt. St. Mary's (MD)	800
Bob Knight, Indiana	743
Don Haskins, UTEP	719
Lefty Driesell, Georgia St	716
Jerry Tarkanian, Fresno St	709
Lou Henson, New Mexico St	704
Denny Crum, Louisville	644
Eddie Sutton, Oklahoma St	632
John Chaney, Temple	605
Lute Olson, Arizona	586

Note: Minimum 5 years as a Division I head coach; includes record at 4-year colleges only.

WINNING PERCENTAGE

Coach and Team	Yrs	W	L	Pct
Jerry Tarkanian, Fresno St	28	709	170	.807
Roy Williams, Kansas	11	305	74	.805
John Kresse, Coll. of Charleston	19	469	115	.803
Rick Majerus, Utah	15	337	116	.744
Jim Boeheim, Syracuse	23	549	193	.740
John Chaney, Temple	27	605	219	.734
Nolan Richardson, Arkansas	19	456	166	.733
Lute Olson, Arizona	26	586	213	.733
Bob Huggins, Cincinnati	18	415	154	.729
Bob Knight, Indiana	34	743	281	.726

Note: Minimum 5 years as a Division I head coach; includes record at 4-year colleges only.

Alltime Winningest Men's Division I Coaches

WINS

Coach (Team)	W
Dean Smith (N Carolina)	879
Adolph Rupp (Kentucky)	876
Hank Iba (NW Missouri St, Colorado, Oklahoma St)	767
Ed Diddle (Western Kentucky)	759
Phog Allen (Baker, Kansas, Haskell, Central Missouri St, Kansas)	746
Bob Knight (Army, Indiana)	743
Norm Stewart (Northern Iowa, Missouri)	731
Ray Meyer (DePaul)	724
Don Haskins (UTEP)	719
Lefty Driesell (Davidson, Maryland, James Madison, Georgia St)	716
Jerry Tarkanian (Long Beach St, UNLV, Fresno St)	709
Lou Henson (Hardin-Simmons, New Mexico St, Illinois)	704
John Wooden (Indiana St, UCLA)	664
Ralph Miller (Wichita St, Iowa, Oregon St)	657
Marv Harshman (Pacific Lutheran, Washington St, Washington)	654

Note: Minimum 10 head coaching seasons in Division I.

Alltime Winningest Men's Division I Coaches (Cont.)

WINNING PERCENTAGE

Coach (Team, Years)	Yrs	W	L	Pct
Clair Bee (Rider 29–31, LIU-Brooklyn 32–45, 46–51)	21	412	87	.826
Adolph Rupp (Kentucky 31–72)	41	876	190	.822
Jerry Tarkanian (Long Beach St 69–73, UNLV 74–92, Fresno St 95–)	28	709	170	.807
Roy Williams (Kansas 89–)	11	305	74	.805
John Wooden (Indiana St 47–48, UCLA 49–75)	29	664	162	.804
Dean Smith (N Carolina 62–97)	36	879	254	.776
Harry Fisher (Columbia 07–16, Army 22–23, 25)	13	147	44	.770
Frank Keaney (Rhode Island 21–48)	27	387	117	.768
George Keogan (St. Louis 16, Allegheny 19, Valparaiso 20–21, Notre Dame 24–43)	24	385	117	.767
Jack Ramsay (St. Joseph's [PA] 56–66)	11	231	71	.765
Vic Bubas (Duke 60–69)	10	213	67	.761
Charles (Chick) Davies (Duquesne 25–43, 47–48)	21	314	106	.748
Ray Mears (Wittenberg 57–62, Tennessee 63–77)	21	399	135	.747
Rick Majerus (Marquette 84–86, Ball St 88–89, Utah 90–)	15	337	116	.744
Jim Boeheim (Syracuse 77–)	23	549	193	.740
Al McGuire (Belmont Abbey 58–64, Marquette 65–77)	20	405	143	.739
Rick Pitino (Boston 79–83, Providence 86–87, Kentucky 90–97)	15	352	124	.739
Phog Allen (Baker 06–08, Kansas 08–09, Haskell 09, Cent MO St 13–19, Kansas 20–56)	48	746	264	.739
Everett Case (N Carolina St 47–64)	18	376	133	.739
John Chaney (Cheyney 73–82, Temple 83–)	27	605	219	.734

Note: Minimum 10 head coaching seasons in Division I.

NCAA Women's Division I Championship Results

Year	Winner	Score	Runner-up	Winning Coach
1982	Louisiana Tech	76–62	Cheyney	Sonja Hogg
1983	Southern Cal	69–67	Louisiana Tech	Linda Sharp
1984	Southern Cal	72–61	Tennessee	Linda Sharp
1985	Old Dominion	70–65	Georgia	Marianne Stanley
1986	Texas	97–81	Southern Cal	Jody Conradt
1987	Tennessee	67–44	Louisiana Tech	Pat Summitt
1988	Louisiana Tech	56–54	Auburn	Leon Barmore
1989	Tennessee	76–60	Auburn	Pat Summitt
1990	Stanford	88–81	Auburn	Tara VanDerveer
1991	Tennessee	70–67 (OT)	Virginia	Pat Summitt
1992	Stanford	78–62	Western Kentucky	Tara VanDerveer
1993	Texas Tech	84–82	Ohio State	Marsha Sharp
1994	N Carolina	60–59	Louisiana Tech	Sylvia Hatchell
1995	Connecticut	70–64	Tennessee	Geno Auriemma
1996	Tennessee	83–65	Georgia	Pat Summitt
1997	Tennessee	68–59	Old Dominion	Pat Summitt
1998	Tennessee	93–75	Louisiana Tech	Pat Summitt
1999	Purdue	62–45	Duke	Carolyn Peck

NCAA Women's Division I Alltime Individual Leaders

Single-Game Records

SCORING HIGHS

Pts	Player and Team vs Opponent	Year
60	Cindy Brown, Long Beach St vs San Jose St	1987
58	Kim Perrot, SW Louisiana vs SE Louisiana	1990
58	Lorri Bauman, Drake vs SW Missouri St	1984
55	Patricia Hoskins, Mississippi Valley vs Southern-BR	1989
55	Patricia Hoskins, Mississippi Valley vs Alabama St	1989
54	Anjinea Hopson, Grambling vs Jackson St	1994
54	Mary Lowry, Baylor vs Texas	1994
54	Wanda Ford, Drake vs SW Missouri St	1986
53	Felisha Edwards, NE Louisiana vs Southern Mississippi	1991
53	Chris Starr, NV-Reno vs Cal St-Sacramento	1983
53	Sheryl Swoopes, Texas Tech vs Texas	1993

Single-Game Records *(Cont.)*

REBOUNDING HIGHS

Reb	Player and Team vs Opponent	Year
40	Deborah Temple, Delta St vs AL-Birmingham	1983
37	Rosina Pearson, Bethune-Cookman vs Florida Memorial	1985
33	Maureen Formico, Pepperdine vs Loyola (CA)	1985
31	Darlene Beale, Howard vs S Carolina St	1987
30	Cindy Bonforte, Wagner vs Queens (NY)	1983
30	Kayone Hankins, New Orleans vs. Nicholls St	1994
29	Wanda Ford, Drake vs Eastern Illinois	1985
29	Gail Norris, Alabama St vs Texas Southern	1992
29	Joy Kellogg, Oklahoma City vs Oklahoma Christian	1984
29	Joy Kellogg, Oklahoma City vs UTEP	1984

ASSISTS

A	Player and Team vs Opponent	Year
23	Michelle Burden, Kent St vs Ball St	1991
22	Shawn Monday, Tennessee Tech vs Morehead St	1988
22	Veronica Pettry, Loyola (IL) vs Detroit	1989
22	Tine Freil, Pacific vs Wichita St	1991
21	Tine Freil, Pacific vs Fresno St	1992
21	Amy Bauer, Wisconsin vs Detroit	1989
21	Neacole Hall, Alabama St vs Southern-BR	1989

Five tied with 20.

POINTS

Season Records

Player and Team	Year	GP	FG	3FG	FT	Pts
Cindy Brown, Long Beach St	1987	35	362	—	250	974
Genia Miller, Cal St-Fullerton	1991	33	376	0	217	969
Sheryl Swoopes, Texas Tech	1993	34	356	32	211	955
Andrea Congreaves, Mercer	1992	28	353	77	142	925
Wanda Ford, Drake	1986	30	390	—	139	919
Chamique Holdsclaw, Tennessee	1998	39	370	9	166	915
Barbara Kennedy, Clemson	1982	31	392	—	124	908
Patricia Hoskins, Mississippi Valley	1989	27	345	13	205	908
LaTaunya Pollard, Long Beach St	1983	31	376	—	155	907
Tina Hutchinson, San Diego St	1984	30	383	—	132	898

SEASON SCORING AVERAGE

Player and Team	Year	GP	FG	3FG	FT	Pts	Avg
Patricia Hoskins, Mississippi Valley	1989	27	345	13	205	908	33.6
Andrea Congreaves, Mercer	1992	28	353	77	142	925	33.0
Deborah Temple, Delta St	1984	28	373	—	127	873	31.2
Andrea Congreaves, Mercer	1993	26	302	51	150	805	31.0
Wanda Ford, Drake	1986	30	390	—	139	919	30.6
Anucha Browne, Northwestern	1985	28	341	—	173	855	30.5
LeChandra LeDay, Grambling	1988	28	334	36	146	850	30.4
Kim Perrot, Southwestern Louisiana	1990	28	308	95	128	839	30.0
Tina Hutchinson, San Diego St	1984	30	383	—	132	898	29.9
Jan Jensen, Drake	1991	30	358	6	166	888	29.6
Genia Miller, Cal St-Fullerton	1991	33	376	0	217	969	29.4
Barbara Kennedy, Clemson	1982	31	392	—	124	908	29.3
LaTaunya Pollard, Long Beach St	1983	31	376	—	155	907	29.3
Lisa McMullen, Alabama St	1991	28	285	126	119	815	29.1
Tresa Spaulding, BYU	1987	28	347	—	116	810	28.9
Hope Linthicum, Central Conn. St	1987	23	282	—	101	665	28.9

Season Records *(Cont.)*

REBOUNDS

Player and Team	Year	GP	Reb	Player and Team	Year	GP	Reb
Wanda Ford, Drake	1985	30	534	Rosina Pearson, Beth.-Cookman	1985	26	480
Wanda Ford, Drake	1986	30	506	Patricia Hoskins, Miss Valley	1987	28	476
Anne Donovan, Old Dominion	1983	35	504	Cheryl Miller, Southern Cal	1985	30	474
Darlene Jones, Miss Valley	1983	31	487	Darlene Beale, Howard	1987	29	459
Melanie Simpson, Okla. City	1982	37	481	Olivia Bradley, W Virginia	1985	30	458

REBOUND AVERAGE

Player and Team	Year	GP	Reb	Avg
Rosina Pearson, Bethune-Cookman	1985	26	480	18.5
Wanda Ford, Drake	1985	30	534	17.8
Katie Beck, E Tennessee St	1988	25	441	17.6
DeShawne Blocker, E Tenn. St	1994	26	450	17.3
Patricia Hoskins, Mississippi Valley	1987	28	476	17.0
Wanda Ford, Drake	1986	30	506	16.9
Patricia Hoskins, Mississippi Valley	1989	27	440	16.3
Joy Kellogg, Oklahoma City	1984	23	373	16.2
Deborah Mitchell, Mississippi Coll.	1983	28	447	16.0

FIELD-GOAL PERCENTAGE

Player and Team	Year	GP	FG	FGA	Pct
Myndee Larsen, Southern Utah	1998	28	249	344	72.4
Deneka Knowles, Southeastern La.	1996	26	199	276	72.1
Barbara Farris, Tulane	1998	27	151	210	71.9
Renay Adams, Tennessee Tech	1991	30	185	258	71.7
Regina Days, Georgia Southern	1986	27	234	332	70.5
Kim Wood, WI-Green Bay	1994	27	188	271	69.4
Kelly Lyons, Old Dominion	1990	31	308	444	69.4
Alisha Hill, Howard	1995	28	194	281	69.0
Ruth Riley, Notre Dame	1999	31	198	290	68.3
Trina Roberts, Georgia Southern	1982	31	189	277	68.2
Lidiya Varbanova, Boise St	1991	22	128	188	68.1

Based on qualifiers for annual championship.

FREE-THROW PERCENTAGE

Player and Team	Year	GP	FT	FTA	Pct
Ginny Doyle, Richmond	1992	29	96	101	95.0
Paula Corder, SE Missouri St	1999	28	111	118	94.1
Linda Cyborski, Delaware	1991	29	74	79	93.7
Jennifer Howard, N Carolina St	1994	27	118	127	92.9
Keely Feeman, Cincinnati	1986	30	76	82	92.7
Amy Slowikowski, Kent St	1989	27	112	121	92.6
Lea Ann Parsley, Marshall	1990	28	96	104	92.3
Chris Starr, NV-Reno	1986	25	119	129	92.2
DeAnn Craft, Central Florida	1987	24	94	102	92.2

Based on qualifiers for annual championship.

Career Records

POINTS

Player and Team	Yrs	GP	Pts
Patricia Hoskins, Mississippi Valley 1985–89	110	3122
Lorri Bauman, Drake 1981–84	120	3115
Chamique Holdsclaw, Tennessee 1995–99	148	3025
Cheryl Miller, Southern Cal..........................1983–86	128	3018
Cindy Blodgett, Maine...................................1994–98	118	3005
Valorie Whiteside, Appalachian St 1984–88	116	2944
Joyce Walker, Louisiana St 1981–84	117	2906
Sandra Hodge, New Orleans 1981–84	107	2860
Andrea Congreaves, Mercer.......................1989–93	108	2796
Karen Pelphrey, Marshall 1983–86	114	2746
Cindy Brown, Long Beach St 1983–87	128	2696

SCORING AVERAGE

Player and Team	Yrs	GP	FG	3FG	FT	Pts	Avg
Patricia Hoskins, Mississippi Valley.......1985–89	110	1196	24	706	3122	28.4
Sandra Hodge, New Orleans 1981–84	107	1194	—	472	2860	26.7
Lorri Bauman, Drake.............................1981–84	120	1104	—	907	3115	26.0
Andrea Congreaves, Mercer 1989–93	108	1107	153	429	2796	25.9
Cindy Blodgett, Maine 1994–98	118	1055	219	676	3005	25.5
Valorie Whiteside, Appalachian St 1984–88	116	1153	0	638	2944	25.4
Joyce Walker, Louisiana St...................1981–84	117	1259	—	388	2906	24.8
Tarcha Hollis, Grambling......................1988–91	85	904	3	247	2058	24.2
Korie Hlede, Duquesne 1994–98	109	1045	162	379	2631	24.1
Karen Pelphrey, Marshall 1983–86	114	1175	—	396	2746	24.1
Erma Jones, Bethune-Cookman............1982–84	87	961	—	173	2095	24.1

NCAA Men's Division II Championship Results

Year	Winner	Score	Runner-up	Third Place	Fourth Place
1957 ......Wheaton (IL)	89–65	Kentucky Wesleyan	Mount St Mary's (MD)	Cal St-Los Angeles
1958 ......S Dakota	75–53	St. Michael's	Evansville	Wheaton (IL)
1959 ......Evansville	83–67	SW Missouri St	N Carolina A&T	Cal St-Los Angeles
1960 ......Evansville	90–69	Chapman	Kentucky Wesleyan	Cornell College
1961 ....Wittenberg	42–38	SE Missouri St .	S Dakota St	Mount St Mary's (MD)
1962 ......Mount St Mary's (MD)	58–57 (OT)	Cal St-Sacramento	Southern Illinois	Nebraska Wesleyan
1963 ......S Dakota St	44–42	Wittenberg	Oglethorpe	Southern Illinois
1964 ......Evansville	72–59	Akron	N Carolina A&T	Northern Iowa
1965 ......Evansville	85–82 (OT)	Southern Illinois	N Dakota	St Michael's
1966 ......Kentucky Wesleyan	54–51	Southern Illinois	Akron	N Dakota
1967 ......Winston-Salem	77–74	SW Missouri St	Kentucky Wesleyan	Illinois St
1968 ......Kentucky Wesleyan	63–52	Indiana St	Trinity (TX)	Ashland
1969 ......Kentucky Wesleyan	75–71	SW Missouri St	†Vacated	Ashland
1970 ......Philadelphia Textile	76–65	Tennessee St	UC-Riverside	Buffalo St
1971 ......Evansville	97–82	Old Dominion	†Vacated	Kentucky Wesleyan
1972 ......Roanoke	84–72	Akron	Tennessee St	Eastern Mich
1973 ......Kentucky Wesleyan	78–76 (OT)	Tennessee St	Assumption	Brockport St
1974 ......Morgan St	67–52	SW Missouri St	Assumption	New Orleans
1975 ......Old Dominion	76–74	New Orleans	Assumption	TN-Chattanooga
1976 ......Puget Sound	83–74	TN-Chattanooga	Eastern Illinois	Old Dominion
1977 ......TN-Chattanooga	71–62	Randolph-Macon	N Alabama	Sacred Heart
1978 ......Cheyney	47–40	WI-Green Bay	Eastern Illinois	Central Florida
1979 ......N Alabama	64–50	WI-Green Bay	Cheyney	Bridgeport
1980 ......Virginia Union	80–74	New York Tech	Florida Southern	N Alabama
1981 ......Florida Southern	73–68	Mount St Mary's (MD)	Cal Poly-SLO	WI-Green Bay
1982 ......District of Columbia	73–63	Florida Southern	Kentucky Wesleyan	Cal St-Bakersfield
1983 ......Wright St	92–73	District of Columbia	*Cal St-Bakersfield	*Morningside
1984 ......Central Missouri St	81–77	St. Augustine's	*Kentucky Wesleyan	*N Alabama
1985........Jacksonville St	74–73	S Dakota St	*Kentucky Wesleyan	*Mount St. Mary's (MD)
1986 ......Sacred Heart	93–87	SE Missouri St	*Cheyney	*Florida Southern
1987 ......Kentucky Wesleyan	92–74	Gannon	*Delta St	*Eastern Montana
1988 ......Lowell	75–72	AK-Anchorage	Florida Southern	Troy St

*Indicates tied for third. †Student-athletes representing American International in 1969 and Southwestern Louisiana in 1971 were declared ineligible subsequent to the tournament. Under NCAA rules, the teams' and ineligible student-athletes' records were deleted, and the teams' places in the final standings were vacated.

Year	Winner	Score	Runner-up	Third Place	Fourth Place
1989	N Carolina Central	73–46	SE Missouri St	UC-Riverside	Jacksonville St
1990	Kentucky Wesleyan	93–79	Cal St-Bakersfield	N Dakota	Morehouse
1991	N Alabama	79–72	Bridgeport (CT)	*Cal St-Bakersfield	*Virginia Union
1992	Virginia Union	100–75	Bridgeport (CT)	*Cal St-Bakersfield	*California (PA)
1993	Cal St-Bakersfield	85–72	Troy St (AL)	*New Hampshire Coll	*Wayne St (MI)
1994	Cal St-Bakersfield	92–86	Southern Indiana	*New Hampshire Coll	*Washburn
1995	Southern Indiana	71–63	UC-Riverside	*Norfolk St	*Indiana (PA)
1996	Fort Hays St	70–63	Northern Kentucky	*California (PA)	*Virginia Union
1997	Cal St-Bakersfield	57–56	Northern Kentucky	*Lynn	*Salem-Teikyo
1998	UC-Davis	83–77	Kentucky Wesleyan	*St. Rose	*Virginia Union
1999	Kentucky Wesleyan	75–60	Metropolitan St	*Truman St	*Florida Southern

NCAA Men's Division II Alltime Individual Leaders

SINGLE-GAME SCORING HIGHS

Pts	Player and Team vs Opponent	Date
113	Bevo Francis, Rio Grande vs Hillsdale	1954
84	Bevo Francis, Rio Grande vs Alliance	1954
82	Bevo Francis, Rio Grande vs Bluffton	1954
80	Paul Crissman, Southern Cal Col vs Pacific Christian	1966
77	William English, Winston-Salem vs Fayetteville St	1968

Season Records

SCORING AVERAGE

Player and Team	Year	GP	FG	FT	Pts	Avg
Bevo Francis, Rio Grande	1954	27	444	367	1255	46.5
Earl Glass, Mississippi Industrial	1963	19	322	171	815	42.9
Earl Monroe, Winston-Salem	1967	32	509	311	1329	41.5
John Rinka, Kenyon	1970	23	354	234	942	41.0
Willie Shaw, Lane	1964	18	303	121	727	40.4

REBOUND AVERAGE

Player and Team	Year	GP	Reb	Avg
Tom Hart, Middlebury	1956	21	620	29.5
Tom Hart, Middlebury	1955	22	649	29.5
Frank Stronczek, American Int'l	1966	26	717	27.6
R.C. Owens, College of Idaho	1954	25	677	27.1
Maurice Stokes, St Francis (PA)	1954	26	689	26.5

ASSISTS

Player and Team	Year	GP	A
Steve Ray, Bridgeport	1989	32	400
Steve Ray, Bridgeport	1990	33	385
Tony Smith, Pfeiffer	1992	35	349
Jim Ferrer, Bentley	1989	31	309
Rob Paternostro, New Hamp. Coll.	1995	33	309

ASSIST AVERAGE

Player and Team	Year	GP	A	Avg
Steve Ray, Bridgeport	1989	32	400	12.5
Steve Ray, Bridgeport	1990	33	385	11.7
Demetri Beekman, Assumption	1993	23	264	11.5
Ernest Jenkins, NM Highlands	1995	27	291	10.8
Brian Gregory, Oakland	1989	28	300	10.7

FIELD-GOAL PERCENTAGE

Player and Team	Year	Pct
Todd Linder, Tampa	1987	75.2
Maurice Stafford, N Alabama	1984	75.0
Matthew Cornegay, Tuskegee	1982	74.8
Brian Moten, W Georgia	1992	73.4
Ed Phillips, Alabama A&M	1968	73.3

FREE-THROW PERCENTAGE

Player and Team	Year	Pct
Paul Cluxton, Northern Kentucky	1997	100.0
Tomas Rimkus, Pace	1997	95.6
Billy Newton, Morgan St	1976	94.4
Kent Andrews, McNeese St	1968	94.4
Mike Sanders, Northern Colorado	1987	94.3

Career Records

POINTS

Player and Team	Yrs	Pts
Travis Grant, Kentucky St	1969–72	4045
Bob Hopkins, Grambling	1953–56	3759
Tony Smith, Pfeiffer	1989–92	3350
Earnest Lee, Clark Atlanta	1984–87	3298
Joe Miller, Alderson-Broaddus	1954–57	3294

Career Records *(Cont.)*

CAREER SCORING AVERAGE

Player and Team	Yrs	GP	Pts	Avg
Travis Grant, Kentucky St	1969–72	121	4045	33.4
John Rinka, Kenyon	1967–70	99	3251	32.8
Florindo Vieira, Quinnipiac	1954–57	69	2263	32.8
Willie Shaw, Lane	1961–64	76	2379	31.3
Mike Davis, Virginia Union	1966–69	89	2758	31.0

REBOUND AVERAGE

Player and Team	Yrs	GP	Reb	Avg
Tom Hart, Middlebury	1953, 55–56	63	1738	27.6
Maurice Stokes, St. Francis (PA)	1953–55	72	1812	25.2
Frank Stronczek, American Int'l	1965–67	62	1549	25.0
Bill Thieben, Hofstra	1954–56	76	1837	24.2
Hank Brown, Lowell Tech	1965–67	49	1129	23.0

ASSISTS

Player and Team	Yrs	A
Demetri Beekman, Assumption	1990–93	1044
Rob Paternostro, New Hamp. Coll.	1992–95	919
Gallagher Driscoll, St. Rose	1989–92	878
Tony Smith, Pfeiffer	1989–92	828
Jamie Stevens, Montana St-Billings	1996–99	805

ASSIST AVERAGE

Player and Team	Yrs	GP	A	Avg
Steve Ray, Bridgeport	1989–90	65	785	12.1
Demetri Beekman, Assumption	1990–93	119	1044	8.8
Ernest Jenkins, NM Highlands	1992–95	84	699	8.3
Mark Benson, Texas A&I	1989–91	86	674	7.8
Pat Madden, Jacksonville St	1989–91	88	688	7.8

Note: Minimum 550 Assists.

FIELD-GOAL PERCENTAGE

Player and Team	Yrs	Pct
Todd Linder, Tampa	1984–87	70.8
Tom Schurfranz, Bellarmine	1989–92	70.2
Chad Scott, California (PA)	1991–94	70.0
Ed Phillips, Alabama, A&M	1968–71	68.9
Ulysses Hackett, SC-Spartanburg	1990–92	67.9

Note: Minimum 400 FGM.

FREE-THROW PERCENTAGE

Player and Team	Yrs	Pct
Paul Cluxton, Northern Kentucky	1994–97	93.5
Kent Andrews, McNeese St	1967–69	91.6
Jon Hagen, Mankato St	1963–65	90.0
Dave Reynolds, Davis & Elkins	1986–89	89.3
Michael Shue, Lock Haven	1994–97	88.5

Note: Minimum 250 FTM.

NCAA Men's Division III Championship Results

Year	Winner	Score	Runner-up	Third Place	Fourth Place
1975	LeMoyne-Owen	57–54	Glassboro St	Augustana (IL)	Brockport St
1976	Scranton	60–57	Wittenberg	Augustana (IL)	Plattsburgh St
1977	Wittenberg	79–66	Oneonta St	Scranton	Hamline
1978	North Park	69–57	Widener	Albion	Stony Brook
1979	North Park	66–62	Potsdam St	Franklin & Marshall	Centre
1980	North Park	83–76	Upsala	Wittenberg	Longwood
1981	Potsdam St	67–65 (OT)	Augustana (IL)	Ursinus	Otterbein
1982	Wabash	83–62	Potsdam St	Brooklyn	Cal St-Stanislaus
1983	Scranton	64–63	Wittenberg	Roanoke	WI-Whitewater
1984	WI-Whitewater	103–86	Clark (MA)	DePauw	Upsala
1985	North Park	72–71	Potsdam St	Nebraska Wesleyan	Widener
1986	Potsdam St	76–73	LeMoyne-Owen	Nebraska Wesleyan	Jersey City St
1987	North Park	106–100	Clark (MA)	Wittenberg	Stockton St
1988	Ohio Wesleyan	92–70	Scranton	Nebraska Wesleyan	Hartwick
1989	WI-Whitewater	94–86	Trenton St	Southern Maine	Centre
1990	Rochester	43–42	DePauw	Washington (MD)	Calvin
1991	WI-Platteville	81–74	Franklin & Marshall	Otterbein	Ramapo (NJ)
1992	Calvin	62–49	Rochester	WI-Platteville	Jersey City St
1993	Ohio Northern	71–68	Augustana	Mass-Dartmouth	Rowan
1994	Lebanon Valley Coll	66–59 (OT)	New York University	Wittenberg	St Thomas (MN)
1995	WI-Platteville	69–55	Manchester	Rowan	Trinity (CT)
1996	Rowan	100–93	Hope (MI)	Illinois Wesleyan	Franklin & Marshall
1997	Illinois Wesleyan	89–86	Nebraska Wesleyan	Williams	Alvernia
1998	WI-Platteville	69–56	Hope (MI)	Williams	Wilkes
1999	WI-Platteville	76–75 (2 OT)	Hampden-Sydney	William Paterson	Connecticut Coll.

SINGLE-GAME SCORING HIGHS

Pts	Player and Team vs Opponent	Year
77	Jeff Clement, Grinnell vs Illinois College	1998
69	Steve Diekmann, Grinnell vs Simpson	1995
63	Joe DeRoche, Thomas vs St. Joseph's (ME)	1988
62	Shannon Lilly, Bishop vs Southwest Assembly of God	1983
61	Steve Honderd, Calvin vs Kalamazoo	1993
61	Dana Wilson, Husson vs Ricker	1974

Season Records

SCORING AVERAGE

Player and Team	Year	GP	FG	FT	Pts	Avg
Steve Diekmann, Grinnell	1995	20	223	162	745	37.3
Rickey Sutton, Lyndon St	1976	14	207	93	507	36.2
Shannon Lilly, Bishop	1983	26	345	218	908	34.9
Dana Wilson, Husson	1974	20	288	122	698	34.9
Rickey Sutton, Lyndon St	1977	16	223	112	558	34.9

REBOUND AVERAGE

Player and Team	Year	GP	Reb	Avg
Joe Manley, Bowie St	1976	29	579	20.0
Fred Petty, New Hampshire College	1974	22	436	19.8
Larry Williams, Pratt	1977	24	457	19.0
Charles Greer, Thomas	1977	17	318	18.7
Larry Parker, Plattsburgh St	1975	23	430	18.7

ASSISTS

Player and Team	Year	GP	A
Robert James, Kean	1989	29	391
Ricky Spicer, WI-Whitewater	1989	31	295
Joe Marcotte, New Jersey Tech	1995	30	292
Andre Bolton, Chris. Newport	1996	30	289
Ron Torgalski, Hamilton	1989	26	275

ASSIST AVERAGE

Player and Team	Year	GP	A	Avg
Robert James, Kean	1989	29	391	13.5
Albert Kirchner, Mt. St. Vincent	1990	24	267	11.1
Ron Torgalski, Hamilton	1989	26	275	10.6
Louis Adams, Rust	1989	22	227	10.3
Eric Johnson, Coe	1991	24	238	9.9

FIELD-GOAL PERCENTAGE

Player and Team	Year	Pct
Travis Weiss, St. John's (MN)	1994	76.6
Pete Metzelaars, Wabash	1982	75.3
Tony Rychlec, Mass. Maritime	1981	74.9
Tony Rychlec, Mass. Maritime	1982	73.1
Russ Newnan, Menlo	1991	73.0

FREE-THROW PERCENTAGE

Player and Team	Year	Pct
Chanse Young, Manchester	1998	95.6
Andy Enfield, Johns Hopkins	1991	95.3
Chris Carideo, Widener	1992	95.2
Yudi Teichman, Yeshiva	1989	95.2
Brett Davis, WI-Oshkosh	1998	94.7

Career Records

POINTS

Player and Team	Yrs	Pts
Andre Foreman, Salisbury St	1989–92	2940
Lamont Strothers, Chris. Newport	1988–91	2709
Matt Hancock, Colby	1987–90	2678
Scott Fitch, Geneseo St	1990–94	2634
Greg Grant, Trenton St	1987–89	2611

CAREER SCORING AVERAGE

Player and Team	Yrs	GP	Avg
Dwain Govan, Bishop	1974–75	55	32.8
Dave Russell, Shepherd	1974–75	60	30.6
Rickey Sutton, Lyndon St	1976–79	80	29.7
John Atkins, Knoxville	1976–78	70	28.7
Steve Peknik, Windham	1974–77	76	27.6

REBOUND AVERAGE

Player and Team	Yrs	GP	Reb	Avg
Larry Parker, Plattsburgh St	1975–78	85	1482	17.4
Charles Greer, Thomas	1975–77	58	926	16.0
Willie Parr, LeMoyne-Owen	1974–76	76	1182	15.6
Michael Smith, Hamilton	1989–92	107	1632	15.2
Dave Kufeld, Yeshiva	1977–80	81	1222	15.1
Ed Owens, Hampden-Sydney	1977–80	77	1160	15.1

ASSIST AVERAGE

Player and Team	Yrs	Avg
Phil Dixon, Shenandoah	1993–96	8.6
Steve Artis, Chris. Newport	1990–93	8.1
David Genovese, Mt. St. Vincent	1992–95	7.5
Kevin Root, Eureka	1989–91	7.1
Dennis Jacobi, Bowdoin	1989–92	7.1

Hockey

DAVID E. KLUTHO

Derian Hatcher and the
Stanley Cup champion
Dallas Stars.

Crease Is The Word

A controversial goal overshadowed one of the best finals in years and stirred great debate over that blue semicircle in front of the net

BY DAVID FLEMING

THE DALLAS STARS' Brett Hull has always been one of the most vociferous players in hockey, so perhaps it was appropriate that he scored the goal that will most likely be talked about and debated from now until kingdom come. It came late—very late—in Game 6 of the Stanley Cup finals inside Buffalo's Marine Midland Arena. In the second-longest finals game ever, the Stars and the Buffalo Sabres were tied 1–1 three-quarters of the way through the third extra period, when Hull gathered the rebound of his shot and pushed it past the sprawled form of Sabres goalie Dominik Hasek. The goal, which came after 54:51 of overtime, gave the Stars' a 2–1 win and the NHL its first Stanley Cup champion from the southern United States.

Or did it? Replays showed clearly that Hull's left skate was in the crease when the puck was not, a no-no according to the NHL rule book. Hull took a close-range shot, Hasek stopped it, the puck left the crease for an instant, and Hull, with one foot still in the crease, corralled it and fired it into the net. According to a March 25 directive by NHL senior vice president Colin Campbell, an attacking player may stay in the blue-painted area in front of the net as long as he maintains control of the puck. Director of officiating Bryan Lewis and two other replay officials watched the goal on tape while the Stars began their wild on-ice celebration and concluded that because Hull was, in their view, kicking the puck back to his stick he was still in control of it and therefore within the rules. The goal was allowed. It was a liberal interpretation to say the least.

"The NHL's just trying to cover its ass," said Buffalo forward Joe Juneau. Hasek, whose team had risen from the No. 7 seed in the Eastern Conference to battle for the Stanley Cup, was so convinced the goal would be disallowed when he saw it on television in the locker room that he pulled his jersey back on and prepared to resume play. Later he said the goal judge must have been either asleep or in the men's room. "Everybody is going to remember this as the Stanley Cup that was never won," said Juneau.

They won't remember it that way in Dallas, Joe, but the controversy was a shame, because it overshadowed one of the best finals in recent history. Despite all the rules tweaking the league has done to increase scoring and offense—a smaller crease, more space behind the net, extra referees—the Stars and the Sabres revitalized the game with suffocating defense, courageous effort, genuine nastiness and splendid goaltending.

Dallas goalkeeper Ed Belfour finished with a 1.69 goals-against average and a .930 save percentage but was beaten out for the Conn Smythe Trophy as the postseason MVP by teammate Joe Nieuwendyk, who tied an NHL record with six game-winning goals in the playoffs. Largely due to the play of Hasek and Belfour, the two teams combined to score just 22 goals, which was the lowest in a six-game final since 1947. In 430

En route to his fifth Vezina Trophy, the indomitable Hasek led seventh-seeded Buffalo to the Stanley Cup finals.

minutes of hockey, there were only a pair of two-goal leads, and they lasted fewer than five minutes combined.

It was an epic, physical series, played with fervor and savvy, and it effectively erased the memory of four consecutive years of Stanley Cup sweeps.

"This series did a lot for hockey but maybe not in the way the league intended," said Buffalo general manager Darcy Regier. "We've been doing everything the past few years to get more offense. This wasn't an offensive series. If you equate offense with excitement, you might not have liked seeing the two teams with the lowest goals-against averages during the season go at it. But for the fans who've been around the game, they understood this was about character. This was about the soul of the game."

That part of the game took a blow in

1998–99 when Wayne Gretzky, the sport's alltime leading scorer and its great ambassador, said goodbye in April after an incredible 20-year NHL career (see sidebar). It was fitting that in Gretzky's final game at Madison Square Garden, Pittsburgh Penguins right wing Jaromir Jagr scored the game-winner in overtime.

After the game the two players hugged, and Gretzky, passing the torch, later called Jagr the "best young player in the game." Jagr finished the season with 44 goals and 83 assists, which placed him 20 points ahead of the Mighty Ducks' Teemu Selanne in the scoring race—the largest winning margin since 1991, when Gretzky

Goodbye to the Great One

On April 18, 1999, Wayne Gretzky glided around the ice inside Madison Square Garden one last time. After a thunderous 15-minute ovation he stepped between the boards, out of the spotlight's glare and into retirement, closing a glorious 20-year NHL career that ranks with the most impressive and influential of all time, in any sport.

PAUL J. BERESWILL

Gretzky won four Stanley Cups with the Oilers.

The 1999 retirements of Michael Jordan, John Elway and Barry Sanders notwithstanding, Gretzky's departure leaves the biggest void. To comprehend No. 99's impact on the record books requires an ability to think beyond the normal parameters of the sport. His off years are career years for most NHL players. Gretzky won four Stanley Cups and nine Hart (MVP) Trophies, he played in 18 NHL All-Star Games and holds 61 NHL records, many of which, like his 92 goals in an 80-game season (1981–82), or his 51-game scoring streak (1983–84), are all but untouchable. Between 1981 and '87 he averaged 203 points a season. No other hockey player has ever scored 200 points in a season. There's more. You could take back every single one of his goals and he would still lead the league in career scoring on the strength of his 1,963 assists. Paul Coffey is second on the assists list. He trails Gretzky by, oh, 861.

On that afternoon in the Big Apple, Gretzky recorded the 2,857th, and final,

point of his career with an assist on a power-play goal by Brian Leetch in the second period. A satisfying ending, for it was Gretzky's unselfish, and uncanny, passing ability that defines him as a player and as a person. "Ten years from now they won't even talk about my goal scoring," said the 38-year-old Gretzky. "It'll just be my passing."

As with all the greats, the game seemed to slow down for Gretzky. He knew where every player on the ice was at any given moment and always seemed to provide the perfect pass or a quick and deadly accurate shot at the perfect time. He perfected the "spinorama" move as a way of separating from defenders by peeling off toward the beat Hull by 32 points. Gretzky was the only player to outscore Jagr in the '90s, with 878 points to Jagr's 862. "When I'm feeling good," says Jagr, "I can do anything on the ice I want."

The 27-year-old Czech led the Penguins into the postseason during a year of financial strife for the franchise. Chicago Blackhawks assistant coach Denis Savard called Jagr "the best player in the game by a million miles."

Following in Jagr's starry slipstream are players like Anaheim's Paul Kariya and the Flyers' Eric Lindros. Kariya reemerged to average 1.23 points per game in 1998–99 after missing most of last season with contract problems and a nasty concussion.

boards after breaking into the offensive zone. Another Gretzky signature was his use of the area behind the net. Indeed, the back of the net became his "office." Stationed there, he'd score wraparound goals or make pinpoint passes to teammates in the slot or—with another maneuver he invented—bank the puck off the backs of dumbfounded goalies and into the goal.

In tribute to Gretzky the Rangers painted a 99 on the ice behind both nets for his final game. "Gretzky sees a picture out there that no one else sees," said Boston general manager Harry Sinden. "It's difficult to describe because I've never seen the game he's looking at."

And beyond his incomparable abilities on the ice, Gretzky was a superb representative for his sport. At his core he was always an unassuming small-town kid who had been taught the sport's fundamentals, just like most players, by his dad in the backyard of their home in Brantford, Ont. "He was the highest profile player in the league his entire career, and I don't think he ever made a mistake," said Sinden. "When your best player is like that, it has an effect on everyone in the game. Not just the young guys. Even a person like me. I don't think Wayne Gretzky ever did anything that wasn't for the betterment of the game."

Gretzky's artistry and class transformed and raised the profile of a sport that, when he entered the league in 1979, was dominated by teams like the Philadelphia Flyers' Broad Street Bullies, who empha-

sized brawn over brains, fighting over finesse. When Gretzky was traded from Edmonton to L.A. in a blockbuster deal in 1988, all of Canada lamented the loss. With four Cups between 1983 and '88, the Oilers had become one of the decade's sports dynasties. "He was our best reason for living here," said a newspaper columnist in Edmonton.

The rest of the league saw the trade as a glorious opportunity. Hockey had never succeeded in a warm-weather market or as a national television draw. In fact, the Kings were the only team in California at the time. Eleven years later there are three franchises in the state, eight in warm-weather cities and a lucrative new TV contract for the league.

Gretzky took the Kings to the Stanley Cup finals in 1993 after scoring a hat trick in Game 7 of the conference finals, a performance he calls the finest of his career. It would be his last deep run into the playoffs. He was traded to St. Louis in 1996 and then to New York, where in 1999 Gretzky missed 12 games with a protruding disk in his neck. He would return to lead the team in scoring, but while he was away from the game Gretzky realized it was time to say goodbye.

To honor him after his final game, the Hockey Hall of Fame waived the three-year waiting period for nomination, and the NHL retired Gretzky's No. 99 leaguewide. It was a fitting, singular honor for an athlete and icon who will forever be known as the Great One.

LOU CAPOZZOLA

Despite all the youthful stars in the league, when the March 23 trading deadline approached, Detroit Red Wings G.M. Ken Holland went on a six-hour trading binge for veterans that brought the struggling two-time defending Stanley Cup champions back into the playoff picture. When it was over, he had dealt six draft choices and two role players for 37-year-old Chicago defenseman Chris Chelios, Rangers defenseman Ulf Samuelson, Tampa Bay left wing Wendel Clark and his teammate, goalie Bill Ranford. Before the trade Detroit was a long shot for a threepeat; afterward they had leapfrogged over the Stars as favorites to win the Western Conference.

The Wings flew into the playoffs and won their first six games, sweeping the Mighty Ducks and seizing the first two games on the road against their bitter rivals, the Avalanche. Then those old legs seemed to hit the wall, and the Red Wings' scorers ran into an even stronger barrier: the near perfect goaltending of Colorado's Patrick Roy. In a stunning change of momentum, Colorado won three games on Detroit's ice—which hadn't been done in a single series in Hockeytown since 1966—and took the series in six games.

But the Avalanche melted in Dallas in the next round. The Stars beat Colorado in a tense seven-game series and then slipped past Buffalo and into the record, and rule, books. Less than 48 hours after Dallas had secured the final Cup of the millennium, the NHL's board of governors changed the crease rule, making plays like Hull's Cup-winning goal ineligible for video review.

Lindros was also bothered by injuries, including a near-fatal punctured lung, but he still scored 40 goals and passed off for 53 assists in the 71 games he played.

Around the rest of the league, young, talented players seemed to come in pairs. Rookie Marian Hossa, 20, and former first-round draft pick Alexei Yashin, 25, turned the Ottawa Senators from league doormat into Northeast Division champs. The Senators were the second seed in the Eastern Conference playoffs but were rudely awakened from their dream season by Buffalo, which swept Ottawa in the first round. Nineteen ninety-seven first-round draft picks Sergei Samsonov and Joe Thornton boosted the Boston Bruins to the second round of the playoffs, and in Colorado the Avalanche won another division title and made it to one game shy of the Stanley Cup finals thanks, in part, to the play of rookie forwards Chris Drury and Milan Hejduk. The pair combined for 92 points in the regular season and scored five game-winning goals in the Av's first eight postseason victories. Hejduk led all rookies with 48 points (14 goals and 34 assists) during the regular season, and the hard-checking Drury, the former pitcher who won a Little League World Series title with Trumbull, Conn., in 1989, scored 20 goals and won the Calder Trophy as rookie of the year.

FOR THE RECORD·1998–1999

NHL Final Standings

Eastern Conference

NORTHEAST DIVISION

	GP	W	L	T	GF	GA	Pts
Ottawa	82	44	23	15	239	179	103
Toronto	82	45	30	7	268	231	97
Boston	82	39	30	13	214	181	91
Buffalo	82	37	28	17	207	175	91
Montreal	82	32	39	11	184	209	75

ATLANTIC DIVISION

	GP	W	L	T	GF	GA	Pts
New Jersey	82	47	24	11	248	196	105
Philadelphia	82	37	26	19	231	196	93
Pittsburgh	82	38	30	14	242	225	90
NY Rangers	82	33	38	11	217	227	77
NY Islanders	82	24	48	10	194	244	58

SOUTHEAST DIVISION

	GP	W	L	T	GF	GA	Pts
Carolina	82	34	30	18	210	202	86
Florida	82	30	34	18	210	228	78
Washington	82	31	45	6	200	218	68
Tampa Bay	82	19	54	9	179	292	47

Western Conference

CENTRAL DIVISION

	GP	W	L	T	GF	GA	Pts
Detroit	82	43	32	7	245	202	93
St. Louis	82	37	32	13	237	209	87
Chicago	82	29	41	12	202	248	70
Nashville	82	28	47	7	190	261	63

PACIFIC DIVISION

	GP	W	L	T	GF	GA	Pts
Dallas	82	51	19	12	236	168	114
Phoenix	82	39	31	12	205	197	90
Anaheim	82	35	34	13	215	206	83
San Jose	82	31	33	18	196	191	80
Los Angeles	82	32	45	5	189	222	69

NORTHWEST DIVISION

	GP	W	L	T	GF	GA	Pts
Colorado	82	44	28	10	239	205	98
Edmonton	82	33	37	12	230	226	78
Calgary	82	30	40	12	211	234	72
Vancouver	82	23	47	12	192	258	58

1999 Stanley Cup Playoffs

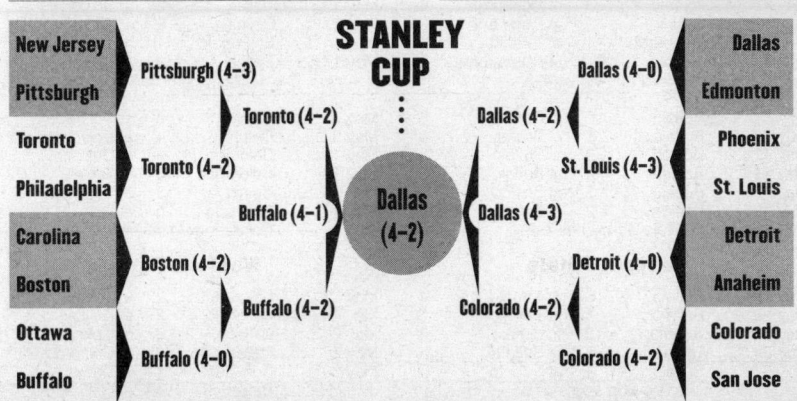

Stanley Cup Playoff Results

Conference Quarterfinals

EASTERN CONFERENCE

April 22	Pittsburgh	1	at New Jersey	3
April 24	Pittsburgh	4	at New Jersey	1
April 25	New Jersey	2	at Pittsburgh	4
April 27	New Jersey	4	at Pittsburgh	2

April 30	Pittsburgh	3	at New Jersey	4
May 2	New Jersey	2	at Pittsburgh	3
May 4	Pittsburgh	4	at New Jersey	2

Pittsburgh won series 4–3.

Conference Quarterfinals (Cont.)

EASTERN CONFERENCE (Cont.)

April 21	Buffalo	2	at Ottawa	1	April 22	Boston	2	at Carolina	0
April 23	Buffalo	3	at Ottawa	2†	April 24	Boston	*2	at Carolina	3*
April 25	Ottawa	0	at Buffalo	3	April 26	Carolina	3	at Boston	2
April 27	Ottawa	3	at Buffalo	4	April 28	Carolina	1	at Boston	4
					April 30	Boston	4	at Carolina	3†
					May 2	Carolina	0	at Boston	2

Buffalo won series 4–0.   Boston won series 4–2.

April 22	Philadelphia	3	at Toronto	0	April 30	Philadelphia	1	at Toronto	2*
April 24	Philadelphia	1	at Toronto	2	May 2	Toronto	1	at Philadelphia	0
April 26	Toronto	2	at Philadelphia	1					
April 28	Toronto	2	at Philadelphia	5					

Toronto won series 4–2.

WESTERN CONFERENCE

April 21	Edmonton	1	at Dallas	2	April 21	Anaheim	3	at Detroit	5
April 23	Edmonton	2	at Dallas	3	April 23	Anaheim	1	at Detroit	5
April 25	Dallas	3	at Edmonton	2	April 25	Detroit	4	at Anaheim	2
April 27	Dallas	3	at Edmonton	2#	April 27	Detroit	3	at Anaheim	0

Dallas won series 4–0.   Detroit won series 4–0.

April 24	San Jose	1	at Colorado	3	April 22	St. Louis	3	at Phoenix	1
April 26	San Jose	1	at Colorado	2*	April 24	St. Louis	3	at Phoenix	4*
April 28	Colorado	2	at San Jose	4	April 25	Phoenix	5	at St. Louis	4
April 30	Colorado	3	at San Jose	7	April 27	Phoenix	2	at St. Louis	1
May 1	San Jose	2	at Colorado	6	April 30	St. Louis	3	at Phoenix	1*
May 3	Colorado	3	at San Jose	2*	May 2	Phoenix	3	at St. Louis	5
					May 4	St. Louis	1	at Phoenix	0

Colorado won series 4–2.   St. Louis won series 4–3.

Conference Semifinals

EASTERN CONFERENCE

May 7	Pittsburgh	2	at Toronto	0	May 6	St. Louis	0	at Dallas	3
May 9	Pittsburgh	2	at Toronto	4	May 8	St. Louis	4	at Dallas	5*
May 11	Toronto	3	at Pittsburgh	4	May 10	Dallas	2	at St. Louis	3*
May 13	Toronto	3	at Pittsburgh	2*	May 12	Dallas	2	at St. Louis	3*
May 15	Pittsburgh	1	at Toronto	4	May 15	St. Louis	1	at Dallas	3
May 17	Toronto	4	at Pittsburgh	3*	May 17	Dallas	2	at St. Louis	1*

Toronto won series 4–2.   Dallas won series 4–2.

May 6	Buffalo	2	at Boston	4	May 7	Detroit	3	at Colorado	2*
May 9	Buffalo	3	at Boston	1	May 9	Detroit	4	at Colorado	0
May 12	Boston	2	at Buffalo	3	May 11	Colorado	5	at Detroit	3
May 14	Boston	0	at Buffalo	3	May 13	Colorado	6	at Detroit	2
May 16	Buffalo	3	at Boston	5	May 16	Detroit	3	at Colorado	0
May 18	Boston	2	at Buffalo	3	May 18	Colorado	5	at Detroit	2

Buffalo won series 4–2.   Colorado won series 4–2.

Eastern Finals   ### Western Finals

May 23	Buffalo	5	at Toronto	4	May 22	Colorado	2	at Dallas	1
May 25	Buffalo	3	at Toronto	6	May 24	Colorado	2	at Dallas	4
May 27	Toronto	2	at Buffalo	4	May 26	Dallas	3	at Colorado	0
May 29	Toronto	2	at Buffalo	5	May 28	Dallas	2	at Colorado	3*
May 31	Buffalo	4	at Toronto	2	May 30	Colorado	7	at Dallas	5
					June 1	Dallas	4	at Colorado	1
					June 4	Colorado	1	at Dallas	4

Buffalo won series 4–1.   Dallas won series 4–3.

Stanley Cup Finals

June 8	Buffalo	3	at Dallas	2*	June 17	Buffalo	0	at Dallas	2
June 10	Buffalo	2	at Dallas	4	June 19	Dallas	2	at Buffalo	1#
June 12	Dallas	2	at Buffalo	1					
June 15	Dallas	1	at Buffalo	2					

Dallas won series 4–2.

*Overtime game. †Double overtime game. # Triple overtime game.

Stanley Cup Championship Box Scores

Game 1

```
Buffalo ............0    0    2    1—3
Dallas..............1    0    1    0—2
```

FIRST PERIOD

Scoring: 1, Dall, Hull 6 (power play) (Modano, Lehtinen), 10:17. Penalties: Zubov, Dall (roughing), 6:36; Satan, Buff (boarding), 8:18; Patrick, Buff (double high-sticking minor), 12:46; Ward, Buff (interference), 19:11.

SECOND PERIOD

Scoring: None. Penalties: Varada, Buff (goalie interference), 4:53; Zhitnik, Buff (interference), 7:07; Ward, Buff (roughing), 9:34; Ludwig, Dall (hooking), 12:21; Matvichuk, Dall (interference), 16:33.

THIRD PERIOD

Scoring: 2, Buff, Barnes 5 (Juneau, Smehlik), 8:33. 3, Buff, Primeau 3 (power play) (Zhitnik, Smehlik), 13:37. 4, Dall, Lehtinen 8 (Modano, Zubov), 19:11. Penalties: Sydor, Dall (tripping), 12:10; McKee, Buff (charging), 14:17.

OVERTIME

Scoring: 5, Buff, Woolley 4 (Brown), 15:30. Penalties: Zhitnik, Buff (hooking), 6:41; Sanderson, Buff (boarding), 9:06.

Shots on goal: Buff—5-4-10-5—24. Dall—11-12-7-7—37. Power-play opportunities: Buff 0-of-4; Dall 1-of-10. Goalies: Buff, Hasek (37 shots, 35 saves), Dall, Belfour (24 shots, 21 saves). A: 17,001.
Referee: Gregson, McCreary. Linesmen: Scapinello, Sharrers.

Game 2

```
Buffalo ............0    1    1—2
Dallas..............0    1    3—4
```

FIRST PERIOD

Scoring: None. Penalties: Skrudland, Dall (charging), 12:25; Zhitnik, Buff (boarding), 15:31; Modano, Dall (tripping), 20:00; Hatcher, Dall (roughing), 20:00; Nieuwendyk, Dall (fighting major), 20:00; Zhitnik, Buff (cross checking), 20:00; Smehlik, Buff (roughing), 20:00; B. Holzinger, Buff (fighting major), 20:00.

SECOND PERIOD

Scoring: 1, Buff, Peca 5 (power play) (Woolley, Satan), 7:22. 2, Dall, Langenbrunner 10 (Matvichuk, Nieuwendyk), 18:26. Penalties: Sydor, Dall (hooking), 5:41; Woolley, Buff (interference), 9:19; Varada, Buff (obst tripping), 13:14; Zhitnik, Buff (tripping), 20:00.

THIRD PERIOD

Scoring: 3, Dall, Ludwig 1 (Skrudland), 4:25. 4. Buff, Zhitnik 4 (power play) (unassisted), 5:36. 5. Dall, Hull 7 (Hrkac, Chambers), 17:10. 6, Dall, Hatcher 1 (empty net), 19:34. Penalties: Sydor, Dall (high sticking), 4:50; Varada, Buff (high sticking), 10:32; Zhitnik, Buff (hooking), 11:48; Hatcher, Dall (high sticking), 17:31.

Shots on goal: Buff—7-10-4—21. Dall—5-7-19—31. Power-play opportunities: Buff 2-of-4; Dall 0-of-6. Goalies: Buff, Hasek (30 shots, 27 saves), Dall, Belfour (21 shots, 19 saves). A: 17,001.
Referee: Fraser, Marouelli. Linesmen: Broseker, Collins.

Game 3

```
Dallas..............0    1    1—2
Buffalo ............0    1    0—1
```

FIRST PERIOD

Scoring: None. Penalties: Ludwig, Dall (interference), 7:45; Chambers, Dall (roughing), 7:45; Rasmussen, Buff (roughing), 7:45; Matvichuk, Dall (roughing), 9:43; Skrudland, Dall (slashing), 18:13; Hatcher, Dall (roughing), 18:46.

SECOND PERIOD

Scoring: 1, Buff, Barnes 6 (Smehlik, B. Holzinger), 7:51. 2, Dall, Nieuwendyk 10 (Reid, Langenbrunner), 15:33. Penalties: Zhitnik, Buff (interference), 3:38; Modano, Dall (obstr tripping), 9:54; Modano, Dall (slashing), 12:21; B. Holzinger, Buff (high sticking), 19:09; Modano, Dall (interference), 19:23.

THIRD PERIOD

Scoring: 3, Dall, Nieuwendyk 11 (Langenbrunner, Reid), 9:35. Penalties: Hrkac, Dall (tripping), 17:38.

Shots on goal: Dall—8-13-8—29. Buff—3-6-3—12. Power-play opportunities: Dall 0-of-2; Buff 0-of-8. Goalies: Dall, Belfour (12 shots, 11 saves), Buff, Hasek (29 shots, 27 saves). A: 18,595.
Referee: Gregson, Koharski. Linesmen: Scapinello, Sharrers.

Game 4

```
Dallas..............1    0    0—1
Buffalo ............1    1    0—2
```

FIRST PERIOD

Scoring: 1, Buff, Sanderson 4 (unassisted), 8:09. 2, Dall, Lehtinen 9 (power play) (Modano, Hatcher), 10:14. Penalties: Matvichuk, Dall (roughing), 3:48; Primeau, Buff (charging), 9:32; Woolley, Buff (holding), 19:05.

SECOND PERIOD

Scoring: 3, Buff, D Ward 7 (unassisted), 7:37 Penalties: Verbeek, Buff (interference), 0:21; Ludwig, Dall (interference), 11:07; Skrudland, Dall (roughing), 14:49; B Holzinger, Buff (boarding), 16:44; Hatcher, Dall (roughing), 20:00; Verbeek, Dall (roughing), 20:00; Hasek, Buff (roughing), 20:00; Zhitnik, Buff (roughing), 20:00.

THIRD PERIOD

Scoring: None. Penalties: Nieuwendyk, Dall (hooking), 1:06; Langenbrunner, Dall (slashing), 20:00; Reid, Dall (roughing), 20:00; R Warrener, Buff (roughing), 20:00; D Ward, Buff (double roughing minor).

Shots on goal: Dall—9-9-13—31. Buff—7-9-2—18. Power-play opportunities: Dall 1-of-3; Buff 0-of-5. Goalies: Dall, Belfour (18 shots, 16 saves), Buff, Hasek (31 shots, 30 saves). A: 18,595.
Referee: Marouelli, McCreary. Linesmen: Collins, Broseker.

Game 5

```
Buffalo ............0      0      0——0
Dallas...............0      1      1——2
```

FIRST PERIOD

Scoring: None. Penalties: Ludwig, Dall (obstr tripping), 2:08.

SECOND PERIOD

Scoring: 1, Dall, Sydor 3 (power play) (Modano, Zubov), 2:23. Penalties: Brown, Buff (interference), 1:42; Woolley, Buff (obstr holding), 3:31; Langenbrunner, Dall (roughing), 7:44.

THIRD PERIOD

Scoring: 2, Dall, Verbeek 3 (Matvichuk, Modano),

15:21. Penalties: Sydor, Dall (roughing), 8:21; Primeau, Buff (roughing), 8:21; R Warrener, Buff (slashing), 16:31; Zhitnik, Buff (elbowing), 17:27; Nieuwendyk, Dall (roughing), 17:27; Skrudland, Dall (obstr tripping), 19:29; R Warrener (roughing), 20:00; Hatcher, Dall (roughing), 20:00.

Shots on goal: Buff—9-5-9—23. Dall—8-7-6—21. Power-play opportunities: Buff 0-of-3; Dall 1-of-3. Goalies: Buff, Hasek (21 shots, 19 saves); Dall, Belfour (23 shots, 23 saves). A: 17,001.
Referee: Fraser, Koharsky. Linesmen: Scapinello, Sharrers.

Game 6

```
Dallas ............1    0    0    0    0    1——2
Buffalo...........0    1    0    0    0    0——1
```

FIRST PERIOD

Scoring: 1, Dall, Lehtinen 10 (Modano, Ludwig), 8:09.

SECOND PERIOD

Scoring: 2, Buff, Barnes 7 (Primeau, Zhitnik). Penalties: Sanderson, Buff (interference), 5:19; Ludwig, Dall (interference), 10:49; Hogue, Dall (tripping), 14:28; Peca, Buff (slashing), 19:27.

THIRD PERIOD

Scoring: None.

THIRD OVERTIME

Scoring: 3, Dall, Hull 8 (Lehtinen, Modano), 14:51.

Shots on goal: Dall—5-11-10-4-13-7—50. Buff—11-15-6-6-12-4—54. Power-play opportunities: Dall 0-of-2; Buff 0-for-2. Goalies: Dall, Belfour (54 shots, 53 saves); Buff, Hasek (50 shots, 48 saves). A: 18,595.
Referee: Gregson, McCreary. Linesmen: Broseker, Collins.

Individual Playoff Leaders

Scoring

POINTS

Player and Team	GP	G	A	Pts	+/–	PM
Peter Forsberg, Col 19		8	16	24	7	31
Mike Modano, Dall 23		5	18	23	6	16
Joe Nieuwendyk, Dall....23		11	10	21	7	19
Joe Sakic, Col 19		6	13	19	-2	8
J. Langenbrunner, Dall..23		10	7	17	7	16
Theoren Fleury, Col 18		5	12	17	-2	20
Mats Sundin, Tor...........17		8	8	16	2	16
Brett Hull, Dall..............22		8	7	15	3	4
Martin Straka, Pitt 13		6	9	15	0	6
Jason Woolley, Buff 21		4	11	15	0	10
Alexei Zhitnik, Buff........21		4	11	15	-6	52
Claude Lemieux, Col.....19		3	11	14	5	26

Player and Team	GP	G	A	Pts	+/–	PM
Jere Lehtinen, Dall.........23		10	3	13	8	2
Steve Yzerman, Det.......10		9	4	13	6	0
Curtis Brown, Buff..........21		7	6	13	3	10
Michael Peca, Buff 21		5	8	13	1	18
Pierre Turgeon, StL........13		4	9	13	5	6
Sergei Zubov, Dall 23		1	12	13	13	4
Adam Deadmarsh, Col....19		8	4	12	2	20
Dixon Ward, Buff............21		7	5	12	6	32
Milan Hejduk, Col 16		6	6	12	3	4
Sergei Berezin, Tor 17		6	6	12	0	4
Jaromir Jagr, Pitt.............9		5	7	12	1	16
Alexei Kovalev, Pitt 10		5	7	12	0	14

GOALS

Player and Team	GP	G
Joe Nieuwendyk, Dall 23		11
J. Langenbrunner, Dall....23		10
Jere Lehtinen, Dall 23		10
Steve Yzerman, Det 10		9
Mats Sundin, Tor 17		8
Adam Deadmarsh, Col ...19		8
Peter Forsberg, Col.........19		8

POWER PLAY GOALS

Player and Team	GP	PP
Steve Yzerman, Det 10		4
Stu Barnes, Buff 21		4
Alexei Zhitnik, Buff 21		4
J. Langenbrunner, Dall....23		4
Nine tied with three.		

ASSISTS

Player and Team	GP	A
Mike Modano, Dall 23		18
Peter Forsberg, Col.........19		16
Joe Sakic, Col 19		13
Theoren Fleury, Col 18		12
Sergei Zubov, Dall...........23		12

GAME-WINNING GOALS

Player and Team	GP	GW
Joe Nieuwendyk, Dall 23		6
Chris Drury, Col...............19		4
Four tied with three.		

SHORT-HANDED GOALS

Player and Team	GP	SH
Vincent Damphousse, SJ...6		2
Dixon Ward, Buff..............21		2
Eight tied with one.		

PLUS/MINUS

Player and Team	GP	+/–
Sergei Zubov, Dall...........23		13
Jay McKee, Buff...............21		13
Rhett Warrener, Buff 20		12
Daniil Markov, Tor............17		9
Three tied with eight.		

Individual Playoff Leaders (Cont.)

Goaltending (Minimum 420 minutes)

GOALS AGAINST AVERAGE

Player and Team	GP	Mins	GA	Avg
Ed Belfour, Dall	23	1527	43	1.69
Dominik Hasek, Buff	19	1200	36	1.80
Byron Dafoe, Bos	12	767	26	2.03
Grant Fuhr, StL	13	790	31	2.35
Nikolai Khabibulin, Phoe	7	449	18	2.41

SAVE PERCENTAGE

Player and Team	GP	Mins	GA	SA	Pct	W	L
Dominik Hasek, Buff	19	1200	36	587	.939	13	6
Ed Belfour, Dall	23	1527	43	617	.930	16	7
Nikolai Khabibulin, Phoe	7	449	18	236	.924	3	4
Byron Dafoe, Bos	12	767	26	330	.921	6	6
Patrick Roy, Col	19	1173	52	650	.920	11	8

NHL Awards

Award	Player and Team
Hart Trophy (MVP)	Jaromir Jagr, Pitt
Calder Trophy (top rookie)	Chris Drury, Col
Vezina Trophy (top goaltender)	Dominik Hasek, Buff
Norris Trophy (top defenseman)	Al MacInnis, StL
Lady Byng Trophy (for gentlemanly play)	Wayne Gretzky, NYR
Adams Award (top coach)	Jacques Martin, Ott

Award	Player and Team
Selke Trophy (top defensive forward)	Jere Lehtinen, Dall
Jennings Trophy (goaltender on club allowing fewest goals)	Ed Belfour, Dall / Roman Turek, Dall
Conn Smythe Trophy (playoff MVP)	Joe Nieuwendyk, Dall

NHL Individual Leaders

Scoring

POINTS

Player and Team	GP	G	A	Pts	+/–	PM
Jaromir Jagr, Pitt	81	44	83	127	17	66
Teemu Selanne, Ana	75	47	60	107	18	30
Paul Kariya, Ana	82	39	62	101	17	40
Peter Forsberg, Col	78	30	67	97	27	108
Joe Sakic, Col	73	41	55	96	23	29
Alexei Yashin, Ott	82	44	50	94	16	54
Eric Lindros, Phil	71	40	53	93	35	120
Theoren Fleury, Col	75	40	53	93	26	86
John LeClair, Phil	76	43	47	90	36	30
Pavol Demitra, StL	82	37	52	89	13	16
Martin Straka, Pitt	80	35	48	83	12	26
Mats Sundin, Tor	82	31	52	83	22	58
Mike Modano, Dall	77	34	47	81	29	44
Jason Allison, Bos	82	23	53	76	5	68
Tony Amonte, Chi	82	44	31	75	0	60
Luc Robitaille, LA	82	39	35	74	-1	54
Steve Yzerman, Det	80	29	45	74	8	42
Rod Brind'Amour, Phil	82	24	50	74	3	47
Steve Thomas, Tor	78	28	45	73	26	33
Petr Sykora, NJ	80	29	43	72	16	22

GOALS

Player and Team	GP	G
Teemu Selanne, Ana	75	47
Jaromir Jagr, Pitt	81	44
Alexei Yashin, Ott	82	44
Tony Amonte, Chi	82	44
John LeClair, Phil	76	43

GAME-WINNING GOALS

Player and Team	GP	GW
Brett Hull, Dall	60	11
Pavol Demitra, StL	82	10
Six tied with eight.		

SHORT-HANDED GOALS

Player and Team	GP	SHG
Joe Sakic, Col	73	5
Brian Rolston, NJ	82	5
Scott Pellerin, StL	80	5
Four tied with four.		

ASSISTS

Player and Team	GP	A
Jaromir Jagr, Pitt	81	83
Peter Forsberg, Col	78	67
Paul Kariya, Ana	82	62
Teemu Selanne, Ana	75	60
Joe Sakic, Col	73	55

POWER PLAY GOALS

Player and Team	GP	PP
Teemu Selanne, Ana	75	25
Alexei Yashin, Ott	82	19
Adrian Aucoin, Van	82	18
John LeClair, Phil	76	16
Three tied with 15.		

PLUS/MINUS

Player and Team	GP	+/–
A. Karpovtsev, Tor	58	39
John LeClair, Phil	76	36
Eric Lindros, Phil	71	35
Al MacInnis, StL	82	33
Magnus Arvedson, Ott	80	33

Goaltending (Minimum 25 games)

GOALS AGAINST AVERAGE

Player and Team	GP	Mins	GA	Avg
Ron Tugnutt, Ott	43	2509	75	1.79
Dominik Hasek, Buff	64	3817	119	1.87
Ed Belfour, Dall	61	3536	117	1.99
Byron Dafoe, Bos	68	4001	133	1.99
Roman Turek, Dall	26	1383	48	2.08
Nikolai Khabibulin, Phoe	63	3658	130	2.13
J. Vanbiesbrouck, Phil	62	3711	135	2.18

SAVE PERCENTAGE

Player and Team	GP	GA	SA	Pct	W	L	T
Dominik Hasek, Buff	64	119	1876	.937	30	18	14
Byron Dafoe, Bos	68	133	1803	.926	32	23	11
Ron Tugnutt, Ott	43	75	1005	.925	22	10	8
N. Khabibulin, Phoe	63	130	1681	.923	32	23	7
Arturs Irbe, Car	62	135	1753	.923	27	20	12
Guy Hebert, Ana	69	166	2115	.922	31	29	9
Steve Shields, SJ	37	80	1011	.921	15	11	8

Goaltending (Cont.)

WINS

Player and Team	GP	Mins	W	L	T
Martin Brodeur, NJ	70	4241	39	21	10
Ed Belfour, Dall	61	3538	35	15	9
Curtis Joseph, Tor	67	4002	35	24	7
Chris Osgood, Det	63	3675	34	25	4
Patrick Roy, Col	61	3644	32	19	8
Nikolai Khabibulin, Phoe	63	3658	32	23	7
Byron Dafoe, Bos	68	4001	32	23	11

SHUTOUTS

Player and Team	GP	Mins	SO	W	L	T
Byron Dafoe, Bos	68	4001	10	32	23	11
Dominik Hasek, Buff	64	3817	9	30	18	14
Nikolai Khabibulin, Phoe	63	3658	8	32	23	7
Garth Snow, Van	65	3502	6	20	32	8
Arturs Irbe, Car	62	3644	6	27	20	12
Guy Hebert, Ana	69	4083	6	31	29	9
J. Vanbiesbrouck, Phil	62	3711	6	27	18	15

NHL Team-by-Team Statistical Leaders

Anaheim Mighty Ducks

SCORING

Player	GP	G	A	Pts	+/-	PM
Teemu Selanne, R	75	47	60	107	18	30
Paul Kariya, L	82	39	62	101	17	40
Steve Rucchin, C	69	23	39	62	11	22
Fredrik Olausson, D	74	16	40	56	17	30
Marty McInnis, L	81	19	35	54	-15	42
Tomas Sandstrom, R	58	15	17	32	-5	42
Travis Green, C	79	13	17	30	-7	81
Matt Cullen, C	75	11	14	25	-12	47
Ruslan Salei, D	74	2	14	16	1	65
Ted Drury, C	75	5	6	11	2	83
Jim McKenzie, L	73	5	4	9	-18	99
Jeff Nielsen, R	80	5	4	9	-12	34
*Johan Davidsson, C	64	3	5	8	-9	14
Jason Marshall, D	72	1	7	8	-5	142
*Antti Aalto, C	73	3	5	8	-12	24
Kevin Haller, D	82	1	6	7	-1	122
*Pascal Trepanier, D	45	2	4	6	0	48
*Mike Crowley, D	20	2	3	5	-10	16
Pavel Trnka, D	63	0	4	4	-6	60
Jamie Pushor, D	70	1	2	3	-20	112
Stu Grimson, L	73	3	0	3	0	158

GOALTENDING

Player	GP	Mins	Avg	W	L	T	SO
Guy Hebert	69	4083	2.42	31	29	9	6
Dominic Roussel	18	884	2.51	4	5	4	1
Team total	82	4990	2.48	35	34	13	7

*Rookie.

Boston Bruins

SCORING

Player	GP	G	A	Pts	+/-	PM
Jason Allison, C	82	23	53	76	5	68
Dmitri Khristich, R	79	29	42	71	11	48
Ray Bourque, D	81	10	47	57	-7	34
Sergei Samsonov, L	79	25	26	51	-6	18
Joe Thornton, C	81	16	25	41	3	69
Anson Carter, C	55	24	16	40	7	22
Steve Heinze, R	73	22	18	40	7	30
Kyle McLaren, D	52	6	18	24	1	48
Rob Dimaio, R	71	7	14	21	-14	95
Darren Van Impe, D	60	5	15	20	-5	66
Per Axelsson, R	77	7	10	17	-14	18
Peter Ferraro	46	6	8	14	10	44
Grant Ledyard, D	47	4	8	12	-8	33
Don Sweeney, D	81	2	10	12	14	64
Tim Taylor, C	49	4	7	11	-10	55
Hal Gill, D	80	3	7	10	-10	63
*Shawn Bates, C	33	5	4	9	3	2
Chris Taylor, C	37	3	5	8	-3	12
*Cameron Mann, R	33	5	2	7	0	17
Ken Belanger, L	54	2	5	7	-1	182
Landon Wilson, R	22	3	3	6	0	17
Mattias Timander, D	22	0	6	6	4	10
Dave Ellett, D	54	0	6	6	11	25
Ken Baumgartner, L	69	1	3	4	-6	119
*Antti Laaksonen, L	11	1	2	3	-1	2

GOALTENDING

Player	GP	Mins	Avg	W	L	T	SO
Byron Dafoe	68	4001	1.99	32	23	11	10
Rob Tallas	17	985	2.62	7	7	2	1
Team total	82	5001	2.17	39	30	13	11

THEY SAID IT

Roger Neilson, Flyers coach, on allowing his players to spend a four-day break in New Orleans: "I was a little worried about the drinking, but they assured me they would be drinking anywhere they went."

Buffalo Sabres

SCORING

Player	GP	G	A	Pts	+/-	PM
Miroslav Satan, L	81	40	26	66	24	44
Mike Peca, C	82	27	29	56	7	81
Michael Grosek, L	76	20	30	50	21	102
Curtis Brown, L	78	16	31	47	23	56
Dixon Ward, R	78	20	24	44	10	44
Joe Juneau, C	72	15	28	43	-4	22
Jason Woolley, D	80	10	33	43	16	62
Stu Barnes, C	81	20	16	36	-11	30
Brian Holzinger, C	81	17	17	34	2	45
Alexei Zhitnik, D	81	7	26	33	-6	96
Vaclav Varada, R	72	7	24	31	11	61
Geoff Sanderson, L	75	12	18	30	8	22
Darryl Shannon, D	71	3	12	15	28	52
Richard Smehlik, D	72	3	11	14	-9	44
Wayne Primeau, C	67	5	8	13	-6	38
*Erik Rasmussen, C	42	3	7	10	6	37
James Patrick, D	45	1	7	8	12	16
Rhett Warrener, D	61	1	7	8	2	84
Jay McKee, D	72	0	6	6	20	75
Randy Cunneyworth, L	14	2	2	4	1	0
Rob Ray, R	76	0	4	4	-2	261
Paul Kruse, L	43	3	0	3	0	114
*J-Luc Grand-Pierre, D	16	0	1	1	0	17

GOALTENDING

Player	GP	Mins	Avg	W	L	T	SO
Dominik Hasek	64	3817	1.87	30	18	14	9
Martin Biron	6	281	2.14	1	2	1	0
Dwayne Roloson	18	911	2.77	6	8	2	1
Team total	82	5020	2.09	37	28	17	10

Calgary Flames

SCORING

Player	GP	G	A	Pts	+/-	PM
Cory Stillman, C	76	27	30	57	7	38
Phil Housley, D	79	11	43	54	14	52
Valeri Bure, R	80	26	27	53	0	22
Jarome Iginla, R	82	28	23	51	1	58
Andrew Cassels, C	70	12	25	37	-12	18
Derek Morris, D	71	7	27	34	4	73
Rene Corbett, L	73	13	18	31	1	68
Jeff Shantz, C	76	13	17	30	14	44
Jason Wiemer, L	78	8	13	21	-12	177
*Clarke Wilm, C	78	10	8	18	11	53
Andrei Nazarov, R	62	7	9	16	-4	73
Steve Smith, D	69	1	14	15	-3	80
Steve Dubinsky, C	62	4	10	14	-7	14
Cale Hulse, D	73	3	9	12	-8	117
Hnat Domenichelli, C	23	5	5	10	-4	11
Todd Simpson, D	73	2	8	10	18	151
Ed Ward, R	68	3	5	8	-4	67
*Denis Gauthier, D	55	3	4	7	3	68
Dave Roche, L	36	3	3	6	-1	44
Tommy Albelin, D	60	1	5	6	-11	8
Greg Pankewicz, R	18	0	3	3	0	20
Tom Chorske, R	26	0	3	3	-8	8
Bob Bassen, L	41	1	2	3	-13	35
*Martin St. Louis, C	13	1	1	2	-2	10
Eric Charron, D	12	0	1	1	-6	14
*Rico Fata, R	20	0	1	1	0	4
*Wade Belak, D	31	0	1	1	1	94

GOALTENDING

Player	GP	Mins	Avg	W	L	T	SO
Fred Brathwaite	28	1663	2.45	11	9	7	1
Tyler Moss	11	550	2.51	3	7	0	0
Ken Wregget	27	1590	2.53	10	12	4	1
J.S. Giguere	15	860	3.21	6	7	1	0
Andrei Trefilov	5	186	4.84	0	4	0	0
*Tyrone Garner	3	139	5.18	0	2	0	0
Team total	82	4990	2.81	30	40	12	2

Carolina Hurricanes

SCORING

Player	GP	G	A	Pts	+/-	PM
Keith Primeau, C	78	30	32	62	8	75
Sami Kapanen, R	81	24	35	59	-1	10
Ray Sheppard, R	74	25	33	58	4	16
Ron Francis, C	82	21	31	52	-2	34
Gary Roberts, L	77	14	28	42	2	178
Andrei Kovalenko, L	74	19	21	40	-6	32
Jeff O'Neill, C	75	16	15	31	3	66
Martin Gelinas, L	76	13	15	28	3	67
Robert Kron, R	75	9	16	25	-13	10
Glen Wesley, D	74	7	17	24	14	44
Paul Ranheim, L	78	9	10	19	4	39
Jon Battaglia, L	60	7	11	18	7	22
Kevin Dineen, R	67	8	10	18	5	97
Kent Manderville, C	81	5	11	16	9	38
Nolan Pratt, D	61	1	14	15	15	95
Paul Coffey, D	54	2	12	14	-7	28
Marek Malik, D	52	2	9	11	-6	36
Sean Hill, D	54	0	10	10	9	48
Steve Chiasson, D	28	1	8	9	7	16
Curtis Leschyshyn, D	65	2	7	9	-1	50
*Steven Halko, D	20	0	3	3	5	24
Dave Karpa, D	33	0	2	2	1	55
*Mike Rucinski, D	15	0	1	1	1	8
*Craig MacDonald, C	11	0	0	0	0	0

GOALTENDING

Player	GP	Mins	Avg	W	L	T	SO
Arturs Irbe	62	3643	2.22	27	20	12	6
Trevor Kidd	25	1358	2.70	7	10	6	2
Team total	82	5022	2.41	34	30	18	8

*Rookie.

Chicago Blackhawks

SCORING

Player	GP	G	A	Pts	+/−	PM
Tony Amonte, R	82	44	31	75	0	60
Alexei Zhamnov, C	76	20	41	61	-10	50
Doug Gilmour, C	72	16	40	56	-16	56
Boris Mironov, D	75	11	38	49	13	131
Eric Daze, L	72	22	20	42	-13	22
Dean McAmmond, L	77	10	20	30	8	38
Ed Olczyk, R	61	10	15	25	-3	29
Dave Manson, D	75	6	17	23	1	155
Bob Probert, L	78	7	14	21	-1	206
Anders Eriksson, D	72	2	18	20	11	34
*J.P. Dumont, R	25	9	6	15	7	10
Doug Zmolek, D	62	0	14	14	1	102
*Todd White, C	35	5	8	13	-1	20
Reid Simpson, L	53	5	4	9	2	145
Josef Marha, C	32	2	6	8	1	4
J.Y. Leroux, L	40	3	5	8	-7	21
*Brad Brown, D	66	1	7	8	-4	205
Chris Murray, R	42	1	6	7	-2	79
*Bryan Muir, D	54	1	4	5	1	50
Jamie Allison, D	39	2	2	4	0	62
Mark Janssens, C	60	1	0	1	-11	65

GOALTENDING

Player	GP	Mins	Avg	W	L	T	SO
Jocelyn Thibault	62	3544	2.69	24	30	7	5
Mark Fitzpatrick	27	1403	2.74	6	8	6	0
Team total	82	4989	2.98	29	41	12	4

Colorado Avalanche

SCORING

Player	GP	G	A	Pts	+/−	PM
Peter Forsberg, C	78	30	67	97	27	108
Joe Sakic, C	73	41	55	96	23	29
Theoren Fleury, R	75	40	53	93	26	86
Claude Lemieux, R	82	27	24	51	0	102
Adam Deadmarsh, R	66	22	27	49	-2	99
*Milan Hejduk, R	82	14	34	48	8	26
Valeri Kamensky, L	65	14	30	44	1	28
*Chris Drury, C	79	20	24	44	9	62
Sandis Ozolinsh, D	39	7	25	32	10	22
Adam Foote, D	64	5	16	21	20	92
Sylvain Lefebvre, D	76	2	18	20	18	48
Shean Donovan, R	68	7	12	19	4	37
Aaron Miller, D	76	5	13	18	3	42
Stephane Yelle, C	72	8	7	15	-8	40
Alexei Gusarov, D	54	3	10	13	12	24
Dale Hunter, C	62	2	9	11	-7	119
Shjon Podein, L	55	3	6	9	-5	24
Eric Messier, D	31	4	2	6	0	14
Jeff Odgers, R	75	2	3	5	-3	259
Greg de Vries, D	73	1	3	4	-7	64
Jon Klemm, D	39	1	2	3	4	31
Cam Russell, D	42	1	2	3	-4	94
Warren Rychel, L	28	0	2	2	3	63

GOALTENDING

Player	GP	Mins	Avg	W	L	T	SO
Patrick Roy	61	3648	2.29	32	19	8	5
Marc Denis	4	217	2.49	1	1	0	0
Craig Billington	21	1086	2.87	11	8	1	0
Team total	82	4974	2.47	44	28	10	5

Dallas Stars

SCORING

Player	GP	G	A	Pts	+/−	PM
Mike Modano, C	77	34	47	81	29	44
Brett Hull, L	60	32	26	58	19	30
Joe Nieuwendyk, C	67	28	27	55	11	34
Jere Lehtinen, R	74	20	32	52	29	18
Sergei Zubov, D	81	10	41	51	9	20
Jamie Langenbrunner, C	75	12	33	45	10	62
Pat Verbeek, R	78	17	17	34	11	133
Grant Marshall, R	82	13	18	31	1	85
Derian Hatcher, D	80	9	21	30	21	102
Benoit Hogue, L	74	12	17	29	-10	54
Mike Keane, R	81	6	23	29	-2	62
Tony Hrkac, C	69	13	14	27	2	26
Derek Plante, C	51	6	14	20	4	16
Guy Carbonneau, C	74	4	12	16	-3	31
Richard Matvichuck, D	61	3	9	12	23	51
Shawn Chambers, D	61	2	9	11	6	18
Craig Ludwig, D	80	2	6	8	5	87
Brian Skrudland, C	40	4	1	5	2	33
*Brad Lukowich, D	14	1	2	3	3	19
Brent Severyn, L	30	1	2	3	-2	50

GOALTENDING

Player	GP	Mins	Avg	W	L	T	SO
Ed Belfour	61	3536	1.99	35	15	9	5
Manny Fernandez	1	60	2.00	0	1	0	0
Roman Turek	26	1382	2.08	16	3	3	1
Team total	82	4986	2.02	51	19	12	6

*Rookie.

Detroit Red Wings

SCORING

Player	GP	G	A	Pts	+/−	PM
Steve Yzerman, C	80	29	45	74	8	42
Igor Larionov, C	75	14	49	63	13	48
Sergei Fedorov, C	77	26	37	63	9	66
Vyacheslav Kozlov, L	79	29	29	58	10	45
Brendan Shanahan, L	81	31	27	58	2	123
Nicklas Lidstrom, D	81	14	43	57	14	14
Larry Murphy, D	80	10	42	52	21	42
Wendel Clark, L	77	32	16	48	-24	37
Darren McCarty, R	69	14	26	40	10	108
Chris Chelios, D	75	9	27	36	1	93
Tomas Holmstrom, L	82	13	21	34	-11	69
Martin LaPointe, R	77	16	13	29	7	141
Doug Brown, R	80	9	19	28	5	42
Kris Draper, C	80	4	14	18	2	79
Kirk Maltby, L	53	8	6	14	-6	34
Mathieu Dandenault, R	75	4	10	14	17	59
*Stacy Roest, C	59	4	8	12	-7	14
Ulf Samuelsson, D	71	4	8	12	5	99
Aaron Ward, D	60	3	8	11	-5	52
Jamie Macoun, D	69	1	10	11	-1	36
Todd Gill, D	51	4	5	9	-10	27
Joey Kocur, R	39	2	5	7	0	87

GOALTENDING

Player	GP	Mins	Avg	W	L	T	S
Norm Maracle	16	821	2.27	6	5	2	0
Chris Osgood	63	3691	2.42	34	25	4	3
Bill Ranford	36	1812	3.64	6	18	4	1
Team total	82	4962	2.44	43	32	7	3

Edmonton Oilers

SCORING

Player	GP	G	A	Pts	+/−	PM
Bill Guerin, R	80	30	34	64	7	133
Josef Beranek, L	66	19	30	49	6	23
Mike Grier, R	82	20	24	44	5	54
Pat Falloon, R	82	17	23	40	-4	20
Rem Murray, L	78	21	18	39	4	20
Doug Weight, C	43	6	31	37	-8	12
Todd Marchant, L	82	14	22	36	3	65
Alexander Selivanov, R	72	14	19	33	-8	42
Roman Hamrlik, D	75	8	24	32	9	70
Ryan Smythe, L	71	13	18	31	0	62
Janne Niinimaa, D	81	4	24	28	7	88
Chad Kilger, C	77	15	12	27	-4	34
*Tom Poti, D	73	5	16	21	10	42
Ethan Moreau, L	80	10	11	21	-3	92
Jason Smith, D	72	3	12	15	-9	51
Boyd Devereaux, C	61	6	8	14	2	23
Christian Laflamme, D	73	2	12	14	-3	70
Daniel Cleary, L	35	4	5	9	-1	24
Kelly Buchberger, R	52	4	4	8	-6	68
*Sean Brown, D	51	0	7	7	1	188
Todd Reirden, D	17	2	3	5	-1	20
*Georges Laraque, D	39	3	2	5	-1	57
Marty McSorley, D	46	2	3	5	-5	101
Frank Musil, D	39	0	3	3	0	34
Craig Millar, D	24	0	2	2	-6	19

GOALTENDING

Player	GP	Mins	Avg	W	L	T	SO
Tommy Salo	64	3717	2.57	25	28	9	5
Bob Essensa	39	2091	2.75	12	14	6	0
Steve Passmore	6	352	2.82	1	4	1	0
Team total	82	4997	2.71	33	37	12	3

Florida Panthers

SCORING

Player	GP	G	A	Pts	+/−	PM
Ray Whitney, L	81	26	38	64	-3	18
Viktor Kozlov, C	65	16	35	51	13	24
Rob Niedermayer, C	82	18	33	51	-13	50
Scott Mellanby, R	67	18	27	45	5	85
Radek Dvorak, L	82	19	24	43	7	29
*Mark Parrish, R	73	24	13	37	-6	25
Robert Svehla, D	80	8	29	37	-13	83
Bill Lindsay, L	75	12	15	27	-1	92
*Oleg Kvasha, L	68	12	13	25	5	45
Bret Hedican, D	67	5	18	23	5	51
Johan Garpenlov, L	64	8	9	17	-9	42
Pavel Bure, R	11	13	3	16	3	4
*Jaroslav Spacek, D	63	3	12	15	15	28
Kirk Muller, C	82	4	11	15	-11	49
Terry Carkner, D	62	2	9	11	0	54
Paul Laus, D	75	1	9	10	-1	218
*Peter Worrell, L	62	4	5	9	0	258
*Dan Boyle, D	22	3	5	8	0	6
Dino Ciccarelli, R	14	6	1	7	-1	27
Gord Murphy, D	51	0	7	7	4	16
Alex Hicks, L	55	0	7	7	-5	62
Mike Wilson, D	34	1	2	3	12	47
Chris Wells, C	20	0	2	2	-4	31
*Peter Ratchuk, D	24	1	1	2	-1	10

GOALTENDING

Player	GP	Mins	Avg	W	L	T	SO
Sean Burke	59	3402	2.66	21	24	14	3
Kirk McLean	30	1597	2.74	9	10	4	2
Team total	82	4996	2.73	33	38	11	5

Los Angeles Kings

SCORING

Player	GP	G	A	Pts	+/−	PM	Player	GP	G	A	Pts	+/−	PM
Luc Robitaille, L	82	39	35	74	-1	54	Philippe Boucher, D	45	2	6	8	-12	32
Donald Audette, R	49	18	18	36	7	51	Mattias Norstrom, D	78	2	5	7	-10	36
Rob Blake, D	62	12	23	35	-7	128	Sandy Moger, R	42	3	2	5	-9	26
Jozef Stumpel, C	64	13	21	34	-18	10	*Josh Green, L	27	1	3	4	-5	8
Glen Murray, R	61	16	15	31	-14	36	*Mark Visheau, D	28	1	3	4	-7	107
Ray Ferraro, C	65	13	18	31	0	59	Sean Pronger, D	29	0	4	4	-1	8
Vladimir Tsyplakov, L	69	11	12	23	-7	32	Nathan Lafayette, C	33	2	2	4	0	35
*Olli Jokinen, C	66	9	12	21	-10	44	Matt Johnson, L	49	2	1	3	-5	131
Russ Courtnall, R	57	6	13	19	-9	19	Steve McKenna, L	20	1	0	1	-3	36
Craig Johnson, L	69	7	12	19	-12	32							
*Pavel Rosa, R	29	4	12	16	0	6							
Garry Galley, D	60	4	12	16	-9	30							

GOALTENDING

Player	GP	Mins	Avg	W	L	T	SO
Jamie Storr	28	1525	2.40	12	12	2	4
Stephane Fiset	42	2403	2.60	18	21	1	3
*Manny Legace	17	899	2.60	2	9	2	0
*Ryan Bach	3	108	4.44	0	3	0	0
Team total	82	4960	2.69	32	45	5	8

Los Angeles Kings scoring continued:

Player	GP	G	A	Pts	+/−	PM
Doug Bodger, D	65	3	11	14	1	34
Sean O'Donnell, D	80	1	13	14	1	186
Ian Laperriere, C	72	3	10	13	-5	138
Brandon Convery, C	15	2	7	9	4	12
Dave Babych, D	41	2	6	8	-2	22

* Rookie.

Montreal Canadiens

SCORING

Player	GP	G	A	Pts	+/–	PM
Saku Koivu, L	65	14	30	44	-7	38
Vladimir Malakhov, D	62	13	21	34	-7	77
Martin Rucinsky, L	73	17	17	34	-25	50
Shayne Corson, L	63	12	20	32	-10	147
Benoit Brunet, L	60	14	17	31	-1	31
Turner Stevenson, R	69	10	17	27	6	88
Stephane Quintal, D	82	8	19	27	-23	84
Brian Savage, L	54	16	10	26	-14	20
Patrick Poulin, L	81	8	17	25	6	21
Sergei Zholtok, C	70	7	15	22	-12	6
Eric Weinrich, D	80	7	15	22	-25	89
Jonas Hoglund, L	74	8	10	18	-5	16
Danius Zubrus, R	80	6	10	16	-8	29
Jason Dawe, R	59	6	8	14	0	22
Patrice Brisebois, D	54	3	9	12	-8	28
Igor Ulanov, D	76	3	9	12	-3	109
Scott Thornton, C	47	7	4	11	-2	87
Scott Lachance, D	76	2	9	11	-21	41
Craig Rivet, D	66	2	8	10	-3	66
Brett Clark, D	61	2	2	4	-3	16
*Matt Higgins, C	25	1	0	1	-2	0

GOALTENDING

Player	GP	Mins	Avg	W	L	T	SO
*Frederic Chabot	11	430	2.23	1	3	0	0
Jeff Hackett	63	3616	2.49	26	26	10	5
Jose Theodore	18	913	3.29	4	12	0	1
Team total	82	4988	2.51	32	39	11	7

Nashville Predators

SCORING

Player	GP	G	A	Pts	+/–	PM
Cliff Ronning, C	79	20	40	60	-3	42
Greg Johnson, C	68	16	34	50	-8	24
Sergei Krivokrasov, R	70	25	23	48	-5	42
Scott Walker, C	71	15	25	40	0	103
Sebastien Bordeleau, C	72	16	24	40	-14	26
Tom Fitzgerald, R	80	13	19	32	-18	48
Patrick Kjellberg, R	71	11	20	31	-13	24
Andrew Brunette, L	77	11	20	31	-10	26
Jamie Heward, R	63	6	12	18	-24	44
Vitali Yachmenev, R	55	7	10	17	-10	10
Drake Berehowsky, D	74	2	15	17	-9	140
Denny Lambert, L	76	5	11	16	-3	218
Joel Bouchard, D	64	4	11	15	-10	60
John Slaney, D	46	2	12	14	-12	14
Bob Boughner, D	79	3	10	13	-6	137
*Kimmo Timonen, D	50	4	8	12	-4	30
Jan Vopat, D	55	5	6	11	0	28
Ville Peltonen, L	14	5	5	10	1	2
Darren Turcotte, C	40	5	5	9	-11	16
Robert Valicevic, R	19	4	2	6	4	2
*Mark Mowers, R	30	0	6	6	-4	4
*Patrick Cote, L	70	1	2	3	-7	242

GOALTENDING

Player	GP	Mins	Avg	W	L	T	SO
Tomas Vokoun	37	1954	2.95	12	18	4	1
Mike Dunham	44	2472	3.08	16	23	3	1
Eric Fichaud	9	447	3.22	0	6	0	0
*Chris Mason	3	69	5.22	0	0	0	0
Team total	82	4964	3.15	28	47	7	2

New Jersey Devils

SCORING

Player	GP	G	A	Pts	+/–	PM
Petr Sykora, C	80	29	43	72	16	22
Bobby Holik, C	78	27	37	64	16	119
Brian Rolston, L	82	24	33	57	11	14
Jason Arnott, C	74	27	27	54	10	79
Patrik Elias, R	74	17	33	50	19	34
Scott Niedermayer, D	72	11	35	46	16	26
*Brendan Morrison, C	76	13	33	46	-4	18
Randy McKay, R	70	17	20	37	10	143
Lyle Odelein, D	70	5	26	31	6	114
Dave Andreychuk, L	52	15	13	28	1	20
*Vadim Sharifijanov, R	53	11	16	27	11	28
Jay Pandolpho, L	70	14	13	27	3	10
Scott Stevens, D	75	5	22	27	29	64
Denis Pederson, C	76	11	12	23	-10	66
Sergei Nemchinov, C	77	12	8	20	-13	28
Sergei Brylin, C	47	5	10	15	8	28
Krzysztof Oliwa, L	64	5	7	12	4	240
Kevin Dean, D	62	1	10	11	4	22
Ken Daneyko, D	82	2	9	11	27	63
Bob Carpenter, C	56	2	8	10	-3	36
Brad Bombardir, D	56	1	7	8	-4	16
Sheldon Souray, D	70	1	7	8	5	110

GOALTENDING

Player	GP	Mins	Avg	W	L	T	SO
Martin Brodeur	70	4239	2.29	39	21	10	4
Chris Terreri	12	726	2.48	8	3	1	1
Team total	82	4986	2.36	47	24	11	5

New York Islanders

SCORING

Player	GP	G	A	Pts	+/–	PM
Zigmund Palffy, R	50	22	28	50	-6	34
Trevor Linden, C	82	18	29	47	-14	32
Bryan Smolinski, C	82	16	24	40	-7	49
Mariusz Czerkawski, C	78	21	17	38	-10	14
Claude Lapointe, C	82	14	23	37	-19	62
Mark Lawrence, R	60	14	16	30	-8	38
Craig Janney, C	56	5	22	27	-15	14
Kenny Jonsson, D	63	8	18	26	-18	34
Mats Lindgren, C	60	10	15	25	6	24
*Mike Watt, L	75	8	17	25	-2	12
Barry Richter, D	72	6	18	24	-4	34
*Eric Brewer, D	63	5	6	11	-14	32
Brad Isbister, R	32	4	4	8	1	46
*Zdeno Chara, D	59	2	6	8	-8	83
David Harlock, D	70	2	6	8	-16	68
Gino Odjick, L	23	4	3	7	-2	133
Kip Miller, C	33	1	5	6	-5	13
Richard Pilon, D	52	0	4	4	-8	88
Ted Crowley, D	13	1	2	3	-1	2
Joe Sacco, R	73	3	0	3	-24	45
*Vladimir Orszagh, R	12	1	0	1	2	6

GOALTENDING

Player	GP	Mins	Avg	W	L	T	SO
Marcel Cousineau	6	293	2.87	0	4	0	0
Wade Flaherty	19	1048	3.03	5	11	2	0
Felix Potvin	16	905	3.71	5	9	1	0
Team total	82	4990	2.93	24	48	10	5

New York Rangers

SCORING

Player	GP	G	A	Pts	+/-	PM
Wayne Gretzky, C	70	9	53	62	-23	14
John MacLean, R	82	28	27	55	5	46
Brian Leetch, D	82	13	42	55	-7	42
Adam Graves, L	82	38	15	53	-12	47
Petr Nedved, C	56	20	27	47	-6	50
Marc Savard, C	70	9	36	45	-7	38
Kevin Stevens, L	81	23	20	43	-10	64
Niklas Sundstrom, R	81	13	30	43	-2	20
Mike Knuble, R	82	15	20	35	-7	26
Mathieu Schneider, D	75	10	24	34	-19	71
Todd Harvey, R	37	11	17	28	-1	72
*Manny Malhotra, C	73	8	8	16	-2	13
Mike Maneluk, R	45	6	9	15	5	20
Brent Fedyk, R	67	4	6	10	-11	30
Jeff Beukeboom, D	45	0	9	9	-2	60
Kevin Brown, R	12	4	2	6	-2	0
Scott Fraser, C	28	2	4	6	-12	14
Chris Tamer, D	63	1	5	6	-14	124
Peter Popovic, D	68	1	4	5	-12	40
*Richard Brennan, D	24	1	3	4	-4	23
*Ruman Ndur, D	39	1	3	4	-1	62
Eric Lacroix, L	64	2	2	4	-12	18
Esa Tikkanen, L	32	0	3	3	-5	38

GOALTENDING

Player	GP	Mins	Avg	W	L	T	SO
Mike Richter	68	3878	2.63	27	30	8	4
Dan Cloutier	22	1097	2.68	6	8	3	0
Team total	82	4996	2.73	33	38	11	4

Ottawa Senators

SCORING

Player	GP	G	A	Pts	+/-	PM
Alexei Yashin, C	82	44	50	94	16	54
Shawn McEachern, L	77	31	25	56	8	46
Andreas Dackell, R	77	15	35	50	9	30
Magnus Arvedson, L	80	21	26	47	33	50
Nelson Emerson, R	65	13	24	37	8	51
Andreas Johansson, R	69	21	16	37	1	34
Vaclav Prospal, C	79	10	26	36	8	58
Jason York, D	79	4	31	35	17	48
Daniel Alfredsson, R	58	11	22	33	8	14
Radek Bonk, C	81	16	16	32	15	48
*Marian Hossa, R	60	15	15	30	18	37
Wade Redden, D	72	8	21	29	7	54
Ted Donato, L	82	11	16	27	-8	41
Igor Kravchuk, D	79	4	21	25	14	32
*Sami Salo, D	61	7	12	19	20	24
Shaun Van Allen, C	79	6	11	17	3	30
Janne Laukkanen, D	50	1	11	12	18	40
Bruce Gardiner, C	59	4	8	12	6	43
*Patrick Traverse, D	46	1	9	10	10	12
Lance Pitlick, D	50	3	6	9	7	33
Steve Martins, C	36	4	3	7	4	10

GOALTENDING

Player	GP	Mins	Avg	W	L	T	SO
Ron Tugnutt	43	2508	1.79	22	10	8	3
Damian Rhodes	45	2480	2.44	22	13	7	3
Team total	82	4999	2.15	44	23	15	6

* Rookie.

Philadelphia Flyers

SCORING

Player	GP	G	A	Pts	+/-	PM
Eric Lindros, C	71	40	53	93	35	120
John LeClair, L	76	43	47	90	36	30
Rod Brind'Amour, L	82	24	50	74	3	47
Mark Recchi, R	71	16	37	53	-7	34
Keith Jones, R	78	20	33	53	23	98
Eric Desjardins, D	68	15	36	51	18	38
Daniel McGillis, D	78	8	37	45	16	61
Mikael Renberg, R	66	15	23	38	5	18
Daymond Langkow, C	78	14	19	33	-8	39
Steve Duchesne, D	71	6	24	30	-6	24
Valeri Zelepukin, R	74	16	9	25	0	48
Chris Therien, D	74	3	15	18	16	48
Jody Hull, R	72	3	11	14	-2	12
Sandy McCarthy, L	80	5	8	13	-24	160
*Dmitri Tertyshny, D	62	2	8	10	-1	30
Marc Bureau, C	71	4	6	10	-2	10
Craig Berube, L	77	5	4	9	-10	194
Karl Dykhuis, D	78	4	5	9	-23	50
Mikael Andersson, L	47	2	4	6	-7	4
Luke Richardson, D	78	0	6	6	-3	106
Adam Burt, D	68	0	4	4	4	60
Roman Vopat, L	54	0	3	3	-7	90

GOALTENDING

Player	GP	Mins	Avg	W	L	T	SO
J. Vanbiesbrouck	62	3712	2.18	27	18	15	6
Ron Hextall	23	1235	2.53	10	7	4	0
J-Marc Pelletier	1	60	5.00	0	1	0	0
Team total	82	5025	2.34	37	26	19	7

Phoenix Coyotes

SCORING

Player	GP	G	A	Pts	+/-	PM
Jeremy Roenick, C	78	24	48	72	7	130
Robert Reichel, C	83	26	43	69	-13	54
Keith Tkachuk, L	68	36	32	68	22	151
Rick Tocchet, R	81	26	30	56	5	147
Greg Adams, L	75	19	24	43	-1	26
Teppo Numminen, D	82	10	30	40	3	30
Dallas Drake, C	53	9	22	31	17	65
Jyrki Lumme, D	60	7	21	28	5	34
Oleg Tverdovsky, D	82	7	18	25	11	32
Juha Ylonen, C	59	6	17	23	18	20
*Daniel Briere, C	64	8	14	22	-3	30
Shane Doan, R	79	6	16	22	-5	54
Bob Corkum, C	77	9	10	19	-9	17
Mike Stapleton, C	76	9	9	18	-6	34
Keith Carney, D	82	2	14	16	15	62
Deron Quint, D	60	5	8	13	-10	20
J.J. Daigneault, D	70	2	9	11	-12	70
Jim Cummins, R	55	1	7	8	3	190
Mike Sullivan, L	63	2	4	6	-11	24

GOALTENDING

Player	GP	Mins	Avg	W	L	T	SO
N. Khabibulin	63	3657	2.13	32	23	7	8
M. Shtalenkov	38	2063	2.62	13	19	4	3
Jim Waite	16	898	2.74	6	5	4	1
*Robert Esche	3	130	3.23	0	1	0	0
Scott Langkow	1	35	5.14	0	0	0	0
Team total	82	4985	2.37	39	31	12	9

Pittsburgh Penguins

SCORING

Player	GP	G	A	Pts	+/–	PM
Jaromir Jagr, R	81	44	83	127	17	66
Martin Straka, C	80	35	48	83	12	26
German Titov, L	72	11	45	56	18	34
Alexei Kovalev, C	77	23	30	53	2	49
Robert Lang, C	72	21	23	44	-10	24
Kip Miller, C	77	19	23	42	1	22
*Jan Hrdina, C	82	13	29	42	-2	40
Kevin Hatcher, D	66	11	27	38	11	24
Rob Brown, R	58	13	11	24	-15	16
Brad Werenka, D	81	6	18	24	17	93
Jiri Slegr, D	63	3	20	23	13	86
Matthew Barnaby, R	62	6	16	22	-12	177
Alexei Morozov, R	67	9	10	19	5	14
Dan Kesa, R	67	2	8	10	-9	27
Bobby Dollas, D	70	2	8	10	-3	60
Ian Moran, R	62	4	5	9	1	37
*Maxim Galanov, D	51	4	3	7	-8	14
Jeff Serowik, D	26	0	6	6	-4	16
Darius Kasparaitis, D	48	1	4	5	12	70
*Martin Sonnenberg, L	44	1	1	2	-2	19
Victor Ignatjev, D	11	0	1	1	-3	6

GOALTENDING

Player	GP	Mins	Avg	W	L	T	SO
*J-Sebastien Aubin	17	756	2.22	4	3	6	2
Tom Barrasso	43	2306	2.55	19	16	3	4
Peter Skudra	37	1914	2.79	15	11	5	3
Team total	82	5011	2.69	38	30	14	9

St. Louis Blues

SCORING

Player	GP	G	A	Pts	+/–	PM
Pavol Demitra, L	82	37	52	89	13	16
Pierre Turgeon, C	67	31	34	65	4	36
Al MacInnis, D	82	20	42	62	33	70
Scott Young, R	75	24	28	52	8	27
Chris Pronger, D	67	13	33	46	3	113
Scott Pellerin, R	80	20	21	41	1	42
Craig Conroy, C	69	14	25	39	14	38
Mike Eastwood, C	82	9	21	30	6	36
Pascal Rheaume, L	60	9	18	27	10	24
Terry Yake, R	60	9	18	27	-9	34
Jim Campbell, R	55	4	21	25	-8	41
Michel Picard, L	45	11	11	22	5	16
Blair Atcheynum, R	65	10	8	18	-8	18
*Lubos Bartecko, R	32	5	11	16	4	6
*Michal Handzus, C	66	4	12	16	-9	30
Ricard Persson, D	54	1	12	13	4	94
Geoff Courtnall, L	24	5	7	12	2	28
*Marty Reasoner, C	22	3	7	10	2	8
Kelly Chase, R	45	3	7	10	2	143
*Jamal Mayers, C	34	4	5	9	-3	40
Tony Twist, L	63	2	6	8	0	149
Jamie Rivers, D	76	2	5	7	-3	47
Bryan Helmer, D	40	0	4	4	5	42
Jeff Finley, D	32	1	2	3	11	20
Chris McAlpine, D	51	1	1	2	-10	50
Marc Bergevin, D	52	1	1	2	-14	99

GOALTENDING

Player	GP	Mins	Avg	W	L	T	SO
*Brent Johnson	6	286	2.10	3	2	0	0
Jamie McLennan	33	1763	2.38	13	14	4	3
Grant Fuhr	39	2193	2.44	16	11	8	2
Rich Parent	10	519	2.54	4	3	1	1
Jim Carey	4	202	3.86	1	2	0	0
Team total	82	4989	2.51	37	32	13	6

San Jose Sharks

SCORING

Player	GP	G	A	Pts	+/–	PM
Jeff Friesen, L	78	22	35	57	3	42
Vincent Damphousse, C	77	19	30	49	-4	50
Joe Murphy, R	76	25	23	48	10	73
Owen Nolan, R	78	19	26	45	16	129
Patrick Marleau, C	81	21	24	45	10	24
Mike Ricci, L	82	13	26	39	1	68
Marco Sturm, C	78	16	22	38	7	52
Bill Houlder, D	76	9	23	32	8	40
Alexander Korolyuk, C	55	12	18	30	3	26
Stephane Matteau, L	68	8	15	23	2	73
Jeff Norton, D	72	4	18	22	2	44
Ronnie Stern, R	78	7	9	16	-3	158
Dave Lowry, L	61	6	9	15	-5	24
Murray Craven, L	43	4	10	14	-3	18
Mike Rathje, D	82	5	9	14	15	36
Marcus Ragnarsson, D	74	0	13	13	7	66
Tony Granato, L	35	6	6	12	4	54
Bob Rouse, D	70	0	11	11	0	44
Ron Sutter, C	57	2	7	9	-2	22
Bryan Marchment, D	59	2	6	8	-7	101
Stephen Guolla, L	14	2	2	4	3	6
Andrei Zyuzin, D	25	3	1	4	5	38
*Andy Sutton, D	31	0	3	3	-4	65
Bernie Nicholls, C	10	0	2	2	-4	4
Jarrod Skalde, C	17	1	1	2	-6	4
Shawn Burr, L	18	0	1	1	-3	29
Brantt Myhres, R	30	1	0	1	-2	116

GOALTENDING

Player	GP	Mins	Avg	W	L	T	SO
*Sean Gauthier	1	3	0.00	0	0	0	0
Steve Shields	37	2162	2.22	15	11	8	4
Mike Vernon	49	2831	2.27	16	22	10	4
Team total	82	5016	2.28	31	33	18	8

* Rookie.

Tampa Bay Lightning

SCORING

Player	GP	G	A	Pts	+/–	PM
Darcy Tucker, C	82	21	22	43	-34	176
Chris Gratton, C	78	8	26	34	-28	143
Stephane Richer, L	64	12	21	33	-10	22
*Vincent Lecavalier, C	82	13	15	28	-19	23
Petr Svoboda, D	59	5	18	23	1	81
*Pavel Kubina, D	68	9	12	21	-33	80
Colin Forbes, R	80	12	8	20	-5	61
Rob Zamuner, L	58	8	11	19	-15	24
Cory Cross, D	67	2	16	18	-25	92
Alexandre Daigle, R	63	9	8	17	-13	4
Jassen Cullimore, D	78	5	12	17	-22	81
Michael Nylander, C	33	4	10	14	-9	8
Mike Sillinger, R	79	8	5	13	-29	36
*Sergey Gusev, D	36	1	7	8	-3	16
David Wilkie, D	46	1	7	8	-19	69
Robert Petrovicky, C	28	3	4	7	-8	6
Mike McBain, D	37	0	6	6	-11	14
Kjell Samuelsson, D	46	1	4	5	-6	38
Steve Kelly, D	34	1	3	4	-15	27
Michal Sykora, D	10	1	2	3	-7	0
Brent Peterson, L	20	2	1	3	-2	0
Drew Bannister, D	21	1	2	3	-4	24
Jason Bonsignore, C	23	0	3	3	-4	8
Andrei Skopintsev, D	19	1	1	2	1	10
Paul Ysebaert, L	10	0	1	1	-5	2

GOALTENDING

Player	GP	Mins	Avg	W	L	T	SO
Zac Bierk	1	59	2.03	0	1	0	0
Daren Puppa	13	691	2.87	5	6	1	2
Kevin Hodson	9	413	2.91	2	3	1	0
Derek Wilkinson	5	253	3.08	1	3	1	0
Corey Schwab	40	2146	3.52	8	25	3	0
Team total	82	4974	3.52	19	54	9	4

Toronto Maple Leafs

SCORING

Player	GP	G	A	Pts	+/–	PM
Mats Sundin, C	82	31	52	83	22	58
Steve Thomas, L	78	28	45	73	26	33
Sergei Berezin, R	76	37	22	59	16	12
Derek King, L	81	24	28	52	15	20
Igor Korolev, C	66	13	34	47	11	46
Mike Johnson, R	79	20	24	44	13	35
Yanic Perreault, C	76	17	25	42	7	42
Steve Sullivan, C	63	20	20	40	12	28
Bryan Berard, D	69	9	25	34	1	48
Fredrik Modin, L	67	16	15	31	14	35
Garry Valk, L	77	8	21	29	8	53
Sylvain Cote, D	79	5	24	29	22	58
A. Karpovtsev, D	58	3	25	28	39	52
Dimitri Yushkevich, D	78	6	22	28	25	88
Alyn McCauley, C	39	9	15	24	7	2
*Tomas Kaberle, D	57	4	18	22	3	12
Tie Domi, R	72	8	14	22	5	198
Todd Warriner, L	53	9	10	19	-6	28
Daniil Markov, D	57	4	8	12	5	47
Yannick Tremblay, D	35	2	7	9	0	16
*Ladislav Kohn, R	16	1	3	4	1	4
Chris McAllister, D	48	1	3	4	-3	102
Kris King, L	67	2	2	4	-16	105
Dallas Eakins, D	18	0	2	2	3	24

GOALTENDING

Player	GP	Mins	Avg	W	L	T	SO
Curtis Joseph	67	4001	2.56	35	24	7	3
Glenn Healy	9	546	2.97	6	3	0	0
Jeff Reese	2	106	4.53	1	1	0	0
Team total	82	4972	2.79	45	30	7	3

Vancouver Canucks

SCORING

Player	GP	G	A	Pts	+/–	PM
Markus Naslund, L	80	36	30	66	-13	74
Mark Messier, C	59	13	35	48	-12	33
Alexander Mogilny, R	59	14	31	45	0	58
*Bill Muckalt, R	73	16	20	36	-9	98
Mattias Ohlund, D	74	9	26	35	-19	83
Adrian Aucoin, D	82	23	11	34	-14	77
Dave Gagner, C	69	6	22	28	-16	63
Ed Jovanovski, D	72	5	22	27	-9	126
Dave Scatchard, C	82	13	13	26	-12	40
Bryan McCabe, D	69	7	14	21	-11	120
Donald Brashear, L	82	8	10	18	-25	209
Brad May, L	66	6	11	17	-14	102
Todd Bertuzzi, L	32	8	8	16	-6	44
Harry York, C	56	7	9	16	-6	44
Peter Zezel, C	41	6	8	14	5	16
Trent Klatt, R	75	4	10	14	-3	12

Player	GP	G	A	Pts	+/–	PM
Darby Hendrickson, C	62	4	5	9	-19	52
*Peter Schaefer, L	25	4	4	8	-1	8
Murray Baron, D	81	2	6	8	-23	115
*Josh Holden, C	30	2	4	6	-10	10
Bert Robertsson, D	39	2	2	4	-7	13
Jason Strudwick, D	65	0	3	3	-19	114
Dana Murzyn, D	12	0	2	2	1	21
*Matt Cooke, C	30	0	2	2	-12	27
Steve Staios, D	57	0	2	2	-12	54

GOALTENDING

Player	GP	Mins	Avg	W	L	T	SO
Garth Snow	65	3501	2.93	20	31	8	6
Corey Hirsch	20	919	3.13	3	8	3	1
Kevin Weekes	11	532	3.83	0	8	1	0
Team total	82	4981	3.11	23	47	12	7

* Rookie.

Washington Capitals

SCORING

Player	GP	G	A	Pts	+/-	PM	Player	GP	G	A	Pts	+/-	PM
Peter Bondra, R	66	31	24	55	-1	56	Brendan Witt, D	54	2	5	7	-6	87
Adam Oates, C	59	12	41	53	-1	22	Kelly Miller, L	62	2	5	7	-5	29
Brian Bellows, L	76	17	19	36	-12	36	Jeff Toms, L	21	1	5	6	0	2
Andre Nikolishin, C	73	8	27	35	0	28	Mark Tinordi, D	48	0	6	6	-6	108
Sergei Gonchar, D	53	21	10	31	1	57	Mike Eagles, L	52	4	2	6	-5	50
James Black, C	75	16	14	30	5	14	Trevor Halverson, L	17	0	4	4	-5	28
Calle Johansson, D	67	8	21	29	10	22	*Matthew Herr, C	30	2	2	4	-7	8
Steve Konowalchuk, C	45	12	12	24	0	26	Enrico Ciccone, D	59	3	1	4	-8	127
Jan Bulis, C	38	7	16	23	3	6							
Ken Klee, D	78	7	13	20	-9	80							

GOALTENDING

Player	GP	G	A	Pts	+/-	PM	Player	GP	Mins	Avg	W	L	T	SO
Richard Zednik, L	49	9	8	17	-6	50	*Mike Rosati	1	28	0.00	1	0	0	0
Dmitri Mironov, D	46	2	14	16	-5	80	Rick Tabaracci	23	1193	2.51	4	12	3	2
Jaroslav Svejkovsky, L	25	6	8	14	-2	12	Olaf Kolzig	64	3586	2.58	26	31	3	4
Michal Pivonka, C	36	5	6	11	-6	12	*Martin Brochu	2	120	3.00	0	2	0	0
Chris Simon, L	23	3	7	10	-4	48	Team total	82	4959	2.64	31	45	6	6
Joe Reekie, D	73	0	10	10	12	68								
*Benoit Gratton, C	16	4	3	7	-1	16								

* Rookie.

1999 NHL Draft

First Round

The opening round of the 1999 NHL draft was held on June 26 in Boston.

Team	Selection	Position	Team	Selection	Position
1.....Atlanta	Patrik Stefan	C	15...Phoenix	Scott Kelman	C
2.....Vancouver	Daniel Sedin	L	16...Carolina	David Tanabe	D
3.....Vancouver	Henrik Sedin	C	17...St. Louis	Barret Jackman	D
4.....NY Rangers	Pavel Brendl	R	18...Pittsburgh	Konstantin Koltsov	L/R
5.....NY Islanders	Tim Connolly	C	19...Phoenix	Kiril Safronov	D
6.....Nashville	Brian Finley	G	20...Buffalo	Barrett Heisten	L
7.....Washington	Kris Beech	C	21...Boston	Nick Boynton	D
8.....NY Islanders	Taylor Pyatt	L	22...Philadelphia	Maxime Ouellet	G
9.....NY Rangers	Jamie Lundmark	C	23...Chicago	Steve McCarthy	D
10...NY Islanders	Branislav Mezei	D	24...Toronto	Luca Cereda	C
11...Calgary	Oleg Saprykin	C/L	25...Colorado	Mikhail Kuleshov	L
12...Florida	Denis Shvidki	R	26...Ottawa	Martin Havlak	C
13...Edmonton	Jani Rita	L/R	27...New Jersey	Ari Ahonen	G
14...San Jose	Jeff Jillson	D	28...NY Islanders	Kristian Kudroc	D

Slap Shtick

Harpo, Chico and Groucho. Moe, Larry and Curly. Alvin, Simon and Theodore. On the evolutionary ladder of comic threesomes, the bottom rung has long been occupied by Jeff, Steve and Dave, the hard-checking, high-sticking Hanson brothers of the 1977 hockey film *Slap Shot*. Eyes obscured by taped-up glasses, fists swathed in knuckle-dusting tinfoil, these geeky goons had a motto: "Old-time hockey!"

In the two decades since the release of *Slap Shot*, the Hanson brothers have become cult heroes to several generations of hockey fans. When video clips of them are shown on pro scoreboards, *Slap*-happy spectators chant the characters' lines by heart. The object of this adulation is a trio of career bush leaguers who together played all of 85 games in the NHL. Today the Hansons—brothers Jeff and Steve Carlson and buddy Dave Hanson—

work as an electrician, a truck driver and a manager of a sports complex, respectively. But they're still creating mayhem at rinks around the country....

In 1993, when Steve was coaching in the Central Hockey League, Jeff and Dave joined him for a ceremonial puck drop. They sold out the 9,500-seat arena. Dave, then the general manager of the New York Islanders' farm team in Troy, N.Y., figured the trio could make an appearance with his team, too. The Hansons showed up in their Chiefs uniforms [from the film] and packed the house."We wondered if anyone would remember us," says Steve. "Once we saw the response, it was like, Wow!"

Before long, Bud Ice put the Hansons in a TV commercial and sent them on an 80-city tour. Three years later they're stll at it.

—Franz Lidz

The Stanley Cup

Awarded annually to the team that wins the NHL's best-of-seven final-round playoffs. The Stanley Cup is the oldest trophy competed for by professional athletes in North America. It was donated in 1893 by Frederick Arthur, Lord Stanley of Preston.

Results

WINNERS PRIOR TO FORMATION OF NHL IN 1917

1892–93.....Montreal A.A.A.	1900–01.....Winnipeg Victorias	1907–08.....Montreal Wanderers
1893–94.....Montreal A.A.A.	1901–02.....Winnipeg Victorias (Jan)	1908–09.....Ottawa Senators
1894–95.....Montreal Victorias	1901–02.....Montreal A.A.A. (Mar)	1909–10.....Montreal Wanderers
1895–96.....Winnipeg Victorias (Feb)	1902–03.....Montreal A.A.A. (Feb)	1910–11.....Ottawa Senators
1895–96.....Montreal Victorias (Dec)	1902–03.....Ottawa Silver Seven (Mar)	1911–12.....Quebec Bulldogs
1896–97.....Montreal Victorias	1903–04.....Ottawa Silver Seven	1912–13.....Quebec Bulldogs
1897–98.....Montreal Victorias	1904–05.....Ottawa Silver Seven	1913–14.....Toronto Blueshirts
1898–99.....Montreal Victorias (Feb)	1905–06.....Ottawa Silver Seven (Feb)	1914–15.....Vancouver Millionaires
1898–99.....Montreal Shamrocks (Mar)	1905–06.....Montreal Wanderers (Mar)	1915–16.....Montreal Canadiens
1899–1900...Montreal Shamrocks	1906–07.....Kenora Thistles (Jan)	1916–17.....Seattle Metropolitans
	1906–07.....Montreal Wanderers (Mar)	

NHL WINNERS AND FINALISTS

Season	Champion	Finalist	GP in Final
1917–18	Toronto Arenas	Vancouver Millionaires	5
1918–19	No decision*	No decision*	5
1919–20	Ottawa Senators	Seattle Metropolitans	5
1920–21	Ottawa Senators	Vancouver Millionaires	5
1921–22	Toronto St. Pats	Vancouver Millionaires	5
1922–23	Ottawa Senators	Vancouver Maroons, Edmonton Eskimos	2, 4
1923–24	Montreal Canadiens	Vancouver Maroons, Calgary Tigers	2, 2
1924–25	Victoria Cougars	Montreal Canadiens	4
1925–26	Montreal Maroons	Victoria Cougars	4
1926–27	Ottawa Senators	Boston Bruins	4
1927–28	New York Rangers	Montreal Maroons	5
1928–29	Boston Bruins	New York Rangers	2
1929–30	Montreal Canadiens	Boston Bruins	2
1930–31	Montreal Canadiens	Chicago Blackhawks	5
1931–32	Toronto Maple Leafs	New York Rangers	3
1932–33	New York Rangers	Toronto Maple Leafs	4
1933–34	Chicago Blackhawks	Detroit Red Wings	4
1934–35	Montreal Maroons	Toronto Maple Leafs	3
1935–36	Detroit Red Wings	Toronto Maple Leafs	4
1936–37	Detroit Red Wings	New York Rangers	5
1937–38	Chicago Blackhawks	Toronto Maple Leafs	4
1938–39	Boston Bruins	Toronto Maple Leafs	5
1939–40	New York Rangers	Toronto Maple Leafs	6
1940–41	Boston Bruins	Detroit Red Wings	4
1941–42	Toronto Maple Leafs	Detroit Red Wings	7
1942–43	Detroit Red Wings	Boston Bruins	4
1943–44	Montreal Canadiens	Chicago Blackhawks	4
1944–45	Toronto Maple Leafs	Detroit Red Wings	7
1945–46	Montreal Canadiens	Boston Bruins	5
1946–47	Toronto Maple Leafs	Montreal Canadiens	6
1947–48	Toronto Maple Leafs	Detroit Red Wings	4
1948–49	Toronto Maple Leafs	Detroit Red Wings	4
1949–50	Detroit Red Wings	New York Rangers	7
1950–51	Toronto Maple Leafs	Montreal Canadiens	5
1951–52	Detroit Red Wings	Montreal Canadiens	4
1952–53	Montreal Canadiens	Boston Bruins	5
1953–54	Detroit Red Wings	Montreal Canadiens	7
1954–55	Detroit Red Wings	Montreal Canadiens	7
1955–56	Montreal Canadiens	Detroit Red Wings	5
1956–57	Montreal Canadiens	Boston Bruins	5
1957–58	Montreal Canadiens	Boston Bruins	6
1958–59	Montreal Canadiens	Toronto Maple Leafs	5
1959–60	Montreal Canadiens	Toronto Maple Leafs	4
1960–61	Chicago Blackhawks	Detroit Red Wings	6

NHL WINNERS AND FINALISTS (Cont.)

Season	Champion	Finalist	GP in Final
1961–62	Toronto Maple Leafs	Chicago Blackhawks	6
1962–63	Toronto Maple Leafs	Detroit Red Wings	5
1963–64	Toronto Maple Leafs	Detroit Red Wings	7
1964–65	Montreal Canadiens	Chicago Blackhawks	7
1965–66	Montreal Canadiens	Detroit Red Wings	6
1966–67	Toronto Maple Leafs	Montreal Canadiens	6
1967–68	Montreal Canadiens	St. Louis Blues	4
1968–69	Montreal Canadiens	St. Louis Blues	4
1969–70	Boston Bruins	St. Louis Blues	4
1970–71	Montreal Canadiens	Chicago Blackhawks	7
1971–72	Boston Bruins	New York Rangers	6
1972–73	Montreal Canadiens	Chicago Blackhawks	6
1973–74	Philadelphia Flyers	Boston Bruins	6
1974–75	Philadelphia Flyers	Buffalo Sabres	6
1975–76	Montreal Canadiens	Philadelphia Flyers	4
1976–77	Montreal Canadiens	Boston Bruins	4
1977–78	Montreal Canadiens	Boston Bruins	6
1978–79	Montreal Canadiens	New York Rangers	5
1979–80	New York Islanders	Philadelphia Flyers	6
1980–81	New York Islanders	Minnesota North Stars	5
1981–82	New York Islanders	Vancouver Canucks	4
1982–83	New York Islanders	Edmonton Oilers	4
1983–84	Edmonton Oilers	New York Islanders	5
1984–85	Edmonton Oilers	Philadelphia Flyers	5
1985–86	Montreal Canadiens	Calgary Flames	6
1986–87	Edmonton Oilers	Philadelphia Flyers	7
1987–88	Edmonton Oilers	Boston Bruins	4
1988–89	Calgary Flames	Montreal Canadiens	6
1989–90	Edmonton Oilers	Boston Bruins	5
1990–91	Pittsburgh Penguins	Minnesota North Stars	6
1991–92	Pittsburgh Penguins	Chicago Blackhawks	4
1992–93	Montreal Canadiens	Los Angeles Kings	5
1993–94	New York Rangers	Vancouver Canucks	7
1994–95	New Jersey Devils	Detroit Red Wings	4
1995–96	Colorado Avalanche	Florida Panthers	4
1996–97	Detroit Red Wings	Philadelphia Flyers	4
1997–98	Detroit Red Wings	Washington Capitals	4
1998–99	Dallas Stars	Buffalo Sabres	6

*In 1919 the Montreal Canadiens traveled to meet Seattle, the PCHL champions. After 5 games had been played—the teams were tied at 2 wins and 1 tie—the series was called off by the local Department of Health because of the influenza epidemic and the death of Canadian defenseman Joe Hall from influenza.

Conn Smythe Trophy

Awarded to the Most Valuable Player of the Stanley Cup playoffs, as selected by the Professional Hockey Writers Association. The trophy is named after the former coach, general manager, president and owner of the Toronto Maple Leafs.

1965	Jean Beliveau, Mtl	1983	Bill Smith, NYI
1966	Roger Crozier, Det	1984	Mark Messier, Edm
1967	Dave Keon, Tor	1985	Wayne Gretzky, Edm
1968	Glenn Hall, StL	1986	Patrick Roy, Mtl
1969	Serge Savard, Mtl	1987	Ron Hextall, Phil
1970	Bobby Orr, Bos	1988	Wayne Gretzky, Edm
1971	Ken Dryden, Mtl	1989	Al MacInnis, Cgy
1972	Bobby Orr, Bos	1990	Bill Ranford, Edm
1973	Yvan Cournoyer, Mtl	1991	Mario Lemieux, Pitt
1974	Bernie Parent, Phil	1992	Mario Lemieux, Pitt
1975	Bernie Parent, Phil	1993	Patrick Roy, Mtl
1976	Reggie Leach, Phil	1994	Brian Leetch, NYR
1977	Guy Lafleur, Mtl	1995	Claude Lemieux, NJ
1978	Larry Robinson, Mtl	1996	Joe Sakic, Col
1979	Bob Gainey, Mtl	1997	Mike Vernon, Det
1980	Bryan Trottier, NYI	1998	Steve Yzerman, Det
1981	Butch Goring, NYI	1999	Joe Nieuwendyk, Dall
1982	Mike Bossy, NYI		

Alltime Stanley Cup Playoff Leaders

Points

	Yrs	GP	G	A	Pts		Yrs	GP	G	A	Pts
Wayne Gretzky, four teams	17	208	122	260	382	*Ray Bourque, Bos	19	180	37	124	161
*Mark Messier, Edm, NYR	17	236	109	186	295	Mike Bossy, NYI	10	129	85	75	160
Jari Kurri, four teams	15	200	106	127	233	Gordie Howe, Det, Hart	20	157	68	92	160
Glenn Anderson, four teams	15	225	93	121	214	Bobby Smith, Minn, Mtl	13	184	64	96	160
*Paul Coffey, six teams	16	198	59	137	196	Mario Lemieux, Pitt	7	89	70	85	155
Bryan Trottier, NYI, Pitt	17	221	71	113	184	Stan Mikita, Chi	18	155	59	91	150
Jean Beliveau, Mtl	17	162	79	97	176	*Steve Yzerman, Det	14	145	61	87	148
Denis Savard, Chi, Mtl	16	169	66	109	175	Brian Propp, Phil, Bos, Minn	13	160	64	84	148
*Doug Gilmour, four teams	14	152	54	117	171	*Claude Lemieux, Mtl, NJ, Col	14	198	76	71	147
Denis Potvin, NYI	14	185	56	108	164	*Larry Murphy, six teams	18	200	35	111	146

*Active player.

Goals

	Yrs	GP	G
Wayne Gretzky, four teams	17	208	122
*Mark Messier, Edm, NYR	17	236	109
Jari Kurri, five teams	15	200	106
Glenn Anderson, four teams	15	225	93
Mike Bossy, NYI	10	129	85
Maurice Richard, Mtl	15	133	82
Jean Beliveau, Mtl	17	162	79
*Brett Hull, Cgy, StL, Dall	14	130	77
*Claude Lemieux, Mtl, NJ, Col	14	198	76
*Dino Ciccarelli, five teams	14	141	73

*Active player.

Assists

	Yrs	GP	A
Wayne Gretzky, four teams	17	208	260
*Mark Messier, Edm, NYR	17	236	186
*Paul Coffey, six teams	16	198	137
Jari Kurri, five teams	15	196	127
*Ray Bourque, Bos	19	180	124
Glenn Anderson, four teams	15	225	121
*Doug Gilmour, four teams	14	152	117
Larry Robinson, Mtl, LA	20	227	116
Bryan Trottier, NYI, Pitt	17	221	113
*Larry Murphy, six teams	18	200	111

*Active player.

Goaltending

WINS	W	L	Pct
*Patrick Roy, Mtl, Col	110	67	.621
*Grant Fuhr, five teams	92	50	.648
Billy Smith, LA, NYI	88	36	.710
Ken Dryden, Mtl	80	32	.714
*Mike Vernon, Cgy, Det, SJ	77	52	.597
Jacques Plante, five teams	71	37	.657
Andy Moog, four teams	68	57	.544
*Ed Belfour, Chi, SJ, Dall	61	42	.592
Tom Barrasso, Buff, Pitt	59	50	.596
Turk Broda, Tor	58	42	.580

*Active player.

SHUTOUTS	GP	W	SO
Clint Benedict, Ott, Mtl M	48	25	15
Jacques Plante, five teams	112	71	14
Turk Broda, Tor	101	58	13
Terry Sawchuk, five teams	106	54	12
*Patrick Roy, Mtl, Col	177	110	12

GOALS AGAINST AVG	Avg
George Hainsworth, Mtl, Tor	1.93
*Martin Brodeur, NJ	1.95
Turk Broda, Tor	1.98
*Dominik Hasek, Chi, Buff	2.06
*Chris Osgood, Det	2.16

Note: At least 50 games played.

Alltime Stanley Cup Standings

TEAM	W	L	Pct	TEAM	W	L	Pct
Montreal	381	249	.605	Colorado**	75	70	.517
Boston	236	252	.484	Calgary*	69	87	.442
Detroit	228	211	.519	Washington	64	73	.467
Toronto	219	238	.479	New Jersey†	57	53	.518
Chicago	187	214	.467	Los Angeles	55	91	.376
NY Rangers	183	195	.484	Vancouver	54	70	.435
Philadelphia	147	133	.525	Phoenix††	26	55	.321
Edmonton	130	78	.625	Carolina§	20	35	.364
NY Islanders	128	90	.587	San Jose	15	22	.405
St. Louis	117	142	.452	Florida	13	14	.481
Dallas#	115	112	.507	Ottawa	8	14	.364
Pittsburgh	94	85	.525	Anaheim	4	11	.267
Buffalo	91	100	.476	Tampa Bay	2	4	.333

*Atlanta Flames 1972–80. †Colorado Rockies 1976–82. #Minnesota North Stars 1967–93. **Quebec Nordiques 1979–95. ††Winnipeg Jets 1979–96. §Hartford Whalers 1979–97. Note: Teams ranked by playoff victories.

Stanley Cup Coaching Records

Coach	Team	Yrs	Series	Series W	Series L	Games	Games W	Games L	Games T	Cups	Pct
Glen Sather	Edm	10	27	21	6	*126	89	37	0	4	.706
Toe Blake	Mtl	13	23	18	5	119	82	37	0	8	.689
†Scott Bowman	Five teams	25	61	44	17	315	200	115	0	8	.635
Hap Day	Tor	9	14	10	4	80	49	31	0	5	.613
Jacques Lemaire	Mtl, NJ	6	15	10	5	83	49	34	0	1	.590
Al Arbour	StL, NYI	16	42	30	12	209	123	86	0	4	.589
Mike Keenan	five teams	11	28	18	10	160	91	69	0	1	.569
Fred Shero	Phil, NYR	8	21	15	6	108	61	47	0	2	.565
Jacques Demers	Que, StL, Det, Mtl	9	19	11	8	104	57	47	0	1	.548
Bob Johnson	Cgy, Pitt	6	14	9	5	76	41	35	0	1	.539

*Does not include suspended game, May 24, 1988. †Active coach.
Note: Coaches ranked by winning percentage. Minimum: 65 games.

The 10 Longest Overtime Games

Date	Result	OT	Scorer	Series	Series Winner
3-24-36	Det 1 vs Mtl M 0	116:30	Mud Bruneteau	SF	Det
4-3-33	Tor 1 vs Bos 0	104:46	Ken Doraty	SF	Tor
4-24-96	Pitt 3 vs Wash 2	79:15	Petr Nedved	CQF	Pitt
3-23-43	Tor 3 vs Det 2	70:18	Jack McLean	SF	Det
3-28-30	Mtl 2 vs NYR 1	68:52	Gus Rivers	SF	Mtl
4-18-87	NYI 3 vs Wash 2	68:47	Pat LaFontaine	DSF	NYI
4-27-94	Buff 1 vs NJ 0	65:43	Dave Hannan	CQF	NJ
3-27-51	Mtl 3 vs Det 2	61:09	Maurice Richard	SF	Mtl
3-27-38	NYA 3 vs NYR 2	60:40	Lorne Carr	QF	NYA
3-26-32	NYR 4 vs Mtl 3	59:32	Fred Cook	SF	NYR

NHL Awards

Hart Memorial Trophy

Awarded annually "to the player adjudged to be the most valuable to his team." The original trophy was donated by Dr. David A. Hart, father of Cecil Hart, former manager-coach of the Montreal Canadiens. In the decade of the 1980s Wayne Gretzky won the award nine of 10 times.

Year	Winner	Key Statistics	Runner-Up
1924	Frank Nighbor, Ott	10 goals, 3 assists in 20 games	Sprague Cleghorn, Mtl
1925	Billy Burch, Ham	20 goals, 4 assists in 27 games	Howie Morenz, Mtl
1926	Nels Stewart, Mtl M	42 points in 36 games	Sprague Cleghorn, Mtl
1927	Herb Gardiner, Mtl	12 points in 44 games as defenseman	Bill Cook, NYR
1928	Howie Morenz, Mtl	33 goals, 18 assists	Roy Worters, Pitt
1929	Roy Worters, NYA	1.21 goals against, 13 shutouts	Ace Bailey, Tor
1930	Nels Stewart, Mtl M	39 goals, 16 assists	Lionel Hitchman, Bos
1931	Howie Morenz, Mtl	28 goals, 23 assists	Eddie Shore, Bos
1932	Howie Morenz, Mtl	24 goals, 25 assists	Ching Johnson, NYR
1933	Eddie Shore, Bos	27 assists in 48 games as defenseman	Bill Cook, NYR
1934	Aurel Joliat, Mtl	27 points	Lionel Conacher, Chi
1935	Eddie Shore, Bos	26 assists in 48 games as defenseman	Charlie Conacher, Tor
1936	Eddie Shore, Bos	16 assists in 46 games as defenseman	Hooley Smith, Mtl M
1937	Babe Siebert, Mtl	28 points	Lionel Conacher, Mtl M
1938	Eddie Shore, Bos	17 points in 47 games as defenseman	Paul Thompson, Chi
1939	Toe Blake, Mtl	led NHL in points (47)	Syl Apps, Tor
1940	Ebbie Goodfellow, Det	28 points	Syl Apps, Tor
1941	Bill Cowley, Bos	led NHL in assists (45) and points (62)	Dit Clapper, Bos
1942	Tom Anderson, Bos	41 points	Syl Apps, Tor
1943	Bill Cowley, Bos	led NHL in assists (45)	Doug Bentley, Chi
1944	Babe Pratt, Tor	57 points in 50 games	Bill Cowley, Bos
1945	Elmer Lach, Mtl	led NHL in assists (54) and points (80)	Maurice Richard, Mtl
1946	Max Bentley, Chi	61 points in 47 games	Gaye Stewart, Tor
1947	Maurice Richard, Mtl	led NHL in goals (45); 26 assists	Milt Schmidt, Bos
1948	Buddy O'Connor, NYR	60 points in 60 games	Frank Brimsek, Bos
1949	Sid Abel, Det	28 goals, 26 assists	Bill Durnan, Mtl

Hart Memorial Trophy (Cont.)

Year	Winner	Key Statistics	Runner-Up
1950	Charlie Rayner, NYR	6 shutouts	Ted Kennedy, Tor
1951	Milt Schmidt, Bos	61 points in 62 games	Maurice Richard, Mtl
1952	Gordie Howe, Det	led NHL in goals (47) and points (86)	Elmer Lach, Mtl
1953	Gordie Howe, Det	led NHL in goals (49) and points (95)	Al Rollins, Chi
1954	Al Rollins, Chi	5 shutouts	Red Kelly, Det
1955	Ted Kennedy, Tor	52 points	Harry Lumley, Tor
1956	Jean Beliveau, Mtl	led NHL in goals (47) and points (88)	Tod Sloan, Tor
1957	Gordie Howe, Det	led NHL in goals (44) and points (89)	Jean Beliveau, Mtl
1959	Andy Bathgate, NYR	74 points in 70 games	Gordie Howe, Det
1960	Gordie Howe, Det	45 assists, 73 points	Bobby Hull, Chi
1961	Bernie Geoffrion, Mtl	50 goals, 95 points	Johnny Bower, Tor
1962	Jacques Plante, Mtl	42 wins, 2.37 goals against avg.	Doug Harvey, NYR
1963	Gordie Howe, Det	47 assists, 73 points	Stan Mikita, Chi
1964	Jean Beliveau, Mtl	50 assists, 78 points	Bobby Hull, Chi
1965	Bobby Hull, Chi	39 goals, 32 assists	Norm Ullman, Det
1966	Bobby Hull, Chi	led NHL in goals (54) and points (97)	Jean Beliveau, Mtl
1967	Stan Mikita, Chi	led NHL in assists (62) and points (97)	Ed Giacomin, NYR
1968	Stan Mikita, Chi	40 goals, 47 assists	Jean Beliveau, Mtl
1969	Phil Esposito, Bos	led NHL in assists (77) and points (126)	Jean Beliveau, Mtl
1970	Bobby Orr, Bos	led NHL in assists (87) and points (120)	Tony Esposito, Chi
1971	Bobby Orr, Bos	102 assists, 139 points	Tony Esposito, Chi
1972	Bobby Orr, Bos	80 assists, 117 points	Ken Dryden, Mtl
1973	Bobby Clarke, Phil	67 assists, 104 points	Phil Esposito, Bos
1974	Phil Esposito, Bos	led NHL in goals (68) and points (145)	Bernie Parent, Phil
1975	Bobby Clarke, Phil	89 assists, 116 points	Rogatien Vachon, LA
1976	Bobby Clarke, Phil	89 assists, 119 points	Denis Potvin, NYI
1977	Guy Lafleur, Mtl	led NHL in assists (80) and points (136)	Bobby Clarke, Phil
1978	Guy Lafleur, Mtl	led NHL in goals (60) and points (132)	Bryan Trottier, NYI
1979	Bryan Trottier, NYI	led NHL in assists (87) and points (134)	Guy Lafleur, Mtl
1980	Wayne Gretzky, Edm	51 goals, 86 assists	Marcel Dionne, LA
1981	Wayne Gretzky, Edm	led NHL in assists (109) and points (164)	Mike Liut, StL
1982	Wayne Gretzky, Edm	NHL-record 92 goals and 212 points	Bryan Trottier, NYI
1983	Wayne Gretzky, Edm	led NHL in goals (71) and points (196)	Pete Peeters, Bos
1984	Wayne Gretzky, Edm	led NHL in goals (87) and points (205)	Rod Langway, Wash
1985	Wayne Gretzky, Edm	led NHL in goals (73) and points (208)	Dale Hawerchuk, Winn
1986	Wayne Gretzky, Edm	NHL-record 163 assists and 215 points	Mario Lemieux, Pitt
1987	Wayne Gretzky, Edm	led NHL in assists (121) and points (183)	Ray Bourque, Bos
1988	Mario Lemieux, Pitt	led NHL in goals (70) and points (168)	Grant Fuhr, Edm
1989	Wayne Gretzky, LA	114 assists, 168 points	Mario Lemieux, Pitt
1990	Mark Messier, Edm	84 assists, 129 points	Ray Bourque, Bos
1991	Brett Hull, StL	led NHL in goals (86); 131 points	Wayne Gretzky, LA
1992	Mark Messier, NYR	72 assists, 107 points	Patrick Roy, Mtl
1993	Mario Lemieux, Pitt	69 goals, 91 assists in 60 games	Doug Gilmour, Tor
1994	Sergei Fedorov, Det	56 goals, 64 assists	Dominik Hasek, Buff
1995	Eric Lindros, Phil	29 goals, 41 assists in 46 games	Jaromir Jagr, Pitt
1996	Mario Lemieux, Pitt	led NHL in goals (69) and points (161)	Mark Messier, NYR
1997	Dominik Hasek, Buff	5 shutouts, 2.27 goals against	Paul Kariya, Ana
1998	Dominik Hasek, Buff	13 shutouts, 2.09 goals against	Jaromir Jagr, Pitt
1999	Jaromir Jagr, Pitt	44 goals, 127 points	Alexei Yashin, Ott

Up Close and Personal

Devils coach Robbie Ftorek believes in having strong relationships with his players, which is why he hand-delivers their biweekly paychecks—a task more commonly performed in the NHL by an in-house courier or the U.S. mail. While Ftorek typically uses the payday encounters to ask about a player's family or engage in banter, his presence with the booty imparts a sense of accountability. "Sometimes a guy will say, 'Jeez, I feel guilty taking it this week,'" Ftorek says.

Not that he encourages such thoughts. "Robbie likes to look you in the eye to see if you feel you deserve it, but he's always friendly and positive," says defenseman Sheldon Souray. "And he's never given me a blank check. Knock on wood, though—the season isn't over."

Art Ross Trophy

Awarded annually "to the player who leads the league in scoring points at the end of the regular season." The trophy was presented to the NHL in 1947 by Arthur Howie Ross, former manager-coach of the Boston Bruins. The tie-breakers, in order, are as follows: (1) player with most goals, (2) player with fewer games played, (3) player scoring first goal of the season. Bobby Orr is the only defenseman in NHL history to win this trophy, and he won it twice (1970 and 1975).

Year	Winner	Pts	Year	Winner	Pts
1919	Newsy Lalonde, Mtl	44	1959	Dickie Moore, Mtl	96
1920	Joe Malone, Que	30	1960	Bobby Hull, Chi	81
1921	Newsy Lalonde, Mtl	48	1961	Bernie Geoffrion, Mtl	95
1922	Punch Broadbent, Ott	41	1962	Bobby Hull, Chi	84
1923	Babe Dye, Tor	46	1963	Gordie Howe, Det	86
1924	Cy Denneny, Ott	37	1964	Stan Mikita, Chi	89
1925	Babe Dye, Tor	23	1965	Stan Mikita, Chi	87
1926	Nels Stewart, Mtl M	44	1966	Bobby Hull, Chi	97
1927	Bill Cook, NYR	42	1967	Stan Mikita, Chi	97
1928	Howie Morenz, Mtl	37	1968	Stan Mikita, Chi	87
1929	Ace Bailey, Tor	51	1969	Phil Esposito, Bos	126
1930	Cooney Weiland, Bos	32	1970	Bobby Orr, Bos	120
1931	Howie Morenz, Mtl	73	1971	Phil Esposito, Bos	152
1932	Harvey Jackson, Tor	51	1972	Phil Esposito, Bos	133
1933	Bill Cook, NYR	53	1973	Phil Esposito, Bos	130
1934	Charlie Conacher, Tor	50	1974	Phil Esposito, Bos	145
1935	Charlie Conacher, Tor	57	1975	Bobby Orr, Bos	135
1936	Sweeney Schriner, NYA	45	1976	Guy Lafleur, Mtl	125
1937	Sweeney Schriner, NYA	46	1977	Guy Lafleur, Mtl	136
1938	Gordie Drillon, Tor	52	1978	Guy Lafleur, Mtl	132
1939	Toe Blake, Mtl	47	1979	Bryan Trottier, NYI	134
1940	Milt Schmidt, Bos	52	1980	Marcel Dionne, LA	137
1941	Bill Cowley, Bos	62	1981	Wayne Gretzky, Edm	164
1942	Bryan Hextall, NYR	56	1982	Wayne Gretzky, Edm	212
1943	Doug Bentley, Chi	73	1983	Wayne Gretzky, Edm	196
1944	Herb Cain, Bos	82	1984	Wayne Gretzky, Edm	205
1945	Elmer Lach, Mtl	80	1985	Wayne Gretzky, Edm	208
1946	Max Bentley, Chi	61	1986	Wayne Gretzky, Edm	215
1947	*Max Bentley, Chi	72	1987	Wayne Gretzky, Edm	183
1948	Elmer Lach, Mtl	61	1988	Mario Lemieux, Pitt	168
1949	Roy Conacher, Chi	68	1989	Mario Lemieux, Pitt	199
1950	Ted Lindsay, Det	78	1990	Wayne Gretzky, LA	142
1951	Gordie Howe, Det	86	1991	Wayne Gretzky, LA	163
1952	Gordie Howe, Det	86	1992	Mario Lemieux, Pitt	131
1953	Gordie Howe, Det	95	1993	Mario Lemieux, Pitt	160
1954	Gordie Howe, Det	81	1994	Wayne Gretzky, LA	130
1955	Bernie Geoffrion, Mtl	75	1995	Jaromir Jagr, Pitt	70
1956	Jean Beliveau, Mtl	88	1996	Mario Lemieux, Pitt	161
1957	Gordie Howe, Det	89	1997	Mario Lemieux, Pitt	122
1958	Dickie Moore, Mtl	84	1998	Jaromir Jagr, Pitt	102
			1999	Jaromir Jagr, Pitt	127

Note: Listing includes scoring leaders prior to inception of Art Ross Trophy in 1947–48.

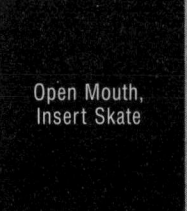

Open Mouth, Insert Skate

According to several San Jose Sharks players, during a January 1999 game New Jersey Devils defenseman Scott Stevens called San Jose enforcer Brantt Myhres a "drunk" and told him to "have another beer." Only two months earlier the 24-year-old Myhres completed six weeks of treatment for alcohol dependency, his second rehab stint in a year. Stevens didn't deny his verbal attack but downplayed it by saying it came "in the heat of battle."

That's no excuse. Stevens's words were all the more offensive given that his longtime teammate Ken Daneyko spent seven weeks in an alcohol treatment center last season and recently counseled Myhres on staying sober.

We can't endorse Myhres's vigilante plans—he said that when the Devils and the Sharks played again, he "hopes we get a lead, so I can go after him"—but when Myhres says that Stevens is "an idiot," we have to agree.

Lady Byng Memorial Trophy

Awarded annually "to the player adjudged to have exhibited the best type of sportsmanship and gentlemanly conduct combined with a high standard of playing ability." Lady Byng, who first presented the trophy in 1925, was the wife of Canada's Governor-General. She donated a second trophy in 1936 after the first was given permanently to Frank Boucher of the New York Rangers, who won it seven times in eight seasons. Stan Mikita, one of the league's most penalized players during his early years in the NHL, won the trophy twice late in his career (1967 and 1968).

1925..........Frank Nighbor, Ott	1963..........Dave Keon, Tor
1926..........Frank Nighbor, Ott	1964..........Ken Wharram, Chi
1927..........Billy Burch, NYA	1965..........Bobby Hull, Chi
1928..........Frank Boucher, NYR	1966..........Alex Delvecchio, Det
1929..........Frank Boucher, NYR	1967..........Stan Mikita, Chi
1930..........Frank Boucher, NYR	1968..........Stan Mikita, Chi
1931..........Frank Boucher, NYR	1969..........Alex Delvecchio, Det
1932..........Joe Primeau, Tor	1970..........Phil Goyette, StL
1933..........Frank Boucher, NYR	1971..........John Bucyk, Bos
1934..........Frank Boucher, NYR	1972..........Jean Ratelle, NYR
1935..........Frank Boucher, NYR	1973..........Gilbert Perreault, Buff
1936..........Doc Romnes, Chi	1974..........John Bucyk, Bos
1937..........Marty Barry, Det	1975..........Marcel Dionne, Det
1938..........Gordie Drillon, Tor	1976..........Jean Ratelle, NYR-Bos
1939..........Clint Smith, NYR	1977..........Marcel Dionne, LA
1940..........Bobby Bauer, Bos	1978..........Butch Goring, LA
1941..........Bobby Bauer, Bos	1979..........Bob MacMillan, Atl
1942..........Syl Apps, Tor	1980..........Wayne Gretzky, Edm
1943..........Max Bentley, Chi	1981..........Rick Kehoe, Pitt
1944..........Clint Smith, Chi	1982..........Rick Middleton, Bos
1945..........Billy Mosienko, Chi	1983..........Mike Bossy, NYI
1946..........Toe Blake, Mtl	1984..........Mike Bossy, NYI
1947..........Bobby Bauer, Bos	1985..........Jari Kurri, Edm
1948..........Buddy O'Connor, NYR	1986..........Mike Bossy, NYI
1949..........Bill Quackenbush, Det	1987..........Joe Mullen, Cgy
1950..........Edgar Laprade, NYR	1988..........Mats Naslund, Mtl
1951..........Red Kelly, Det	1989..........Joe Mullen, Cgy
1952..........Sid Smith, Tor	1990..........Brett Hull, StL
1953..........Red Kelly, Det	1991..........Wayne Gretzky, LA
1954..........Red Kelly, Det	1992..........Wayne Gretzky, LA
1955..........Sid Smith, Tor	1993..........Pierre Turgeon, NYI
1956..........Earl Reibel, Det	1994..........Wayne Gretzky, LA
1957..........Andy Hebenton, NYR	1995..........Ron Francis, Pitt
1958..........Camille Henry, NYR	1996..........Paul Kariya, Ana
1959..........Alex Delvecchio, Det	1997..........Paul Kariya, Ana
1960..........Don McKenney, Bos	1998..........Ron Francis, Pitt
1961..........Red Kelly, Tor	1999..........Wayne Gretzky, NYR
1962..........Dave Keon, Tor	

A Legacy That Endures

The measure of Gordie Howe is not his six scoring titles, six Hart Trophies and four Stanley Cups, but that nothing he has done since those six scoring titles, six Hart Trophies and four Stanley Cups has diminished him. Since leaving the Red Wings in 1971, Howe has been, more or less, a novelty act: Mr. Hockey turned carny barker. Sometimes there was a touch of nobility to Howe's quixotic restlessness, as when he unretired in 1973 to fulfill his desire to play with his sons Mark and Marty. Sometimes there was a sense of wonderment, as when he made it back to the NHL in 1979 at the age of 51 as a member of the Hartford Whalers. And sometimes there was the whiff of shamelessness, as when he took a single shift with the minor league Detroit Vipers in 1997 at 69, thus becoming the first person to play professional hockey in six decades.

Nevertheless, Howe has always followed his muses. If the rest of hockey had a problem with that, tough. He once did some front-office work in Hartford but was never cut out to be anyone's Vice President for Handshaking. He had to be Gordie.

James Norris Memorial Trophy

Awarded annually "to the defense player who demonstrates throughout the season the greatest all-around ability in the position." James Norris was the former owner-president of the Detroit Red Wings. Bobby Orr holds the record for most consecutive times winning the award (eight, 1968–1975).

1954 ......Red Kelly, Det	1970 ......Bobby Orr, Bos	1986 ......Paul Coffey, Edm
1955 ......Doug Harvey, Mtl	1971 ......Bobby Orr, Bos	1987 ......Ray Bourque, Bos
1956 ......Doug Harvey, Mtl	1972 ......Bobby Orr, Bos	1988 ......Ray Bourque, Bos
1957 ......Doug Harvey, Mtl	1973 ......Bobby Orr, Bos	1989 ......Chris Chelios, Mtl
1958 ......Doug Harvey, Mtl	1974 ......Bobby Orr, Bos	1990 ......Ray Bourque, Bos
1959 ......Tom Johnson, Mtl	1975 ......Bobby Orr, Bos	1991 ......Ray Bourque, Bos
1960 ......Doug Harvey, Mtl	1976 ......Denis Potvin, NYI	1992 ......Brian Leetch, NYR
1961 ......Doug Harvey, Mtl	1977 ......Larry Robinson, Mtl	1993 ......Chris Chelios, Chi
1962 ......Doug Harvey, NYR	1978 ......Denis Potvin, NYI	1994 ......Ray Bourque, Bos
1963 ......Pierre Pilote, Chi	1979 ......Denis Potvin, NYI	1995 ......Paul Coffey, Det
1964 ......Pierre Pilote, Chi	1980 ......Larry Robinson, Mtl	1996 ......Chris Chelios, Chi
1965 ......Pierre Pilote, Chi	1981 ......Randy Carlyle, Pitt	1997 ......Brian Leetch, NYR
1966 ......Jacques Laperriere, Mtl	1982 ......Doug Wilson, Chi	1998 ......Rob Blake, LA
1967 ......Harry Howell, NYR	1983 ......Rod Langway, Wash	1999 ......Al MacInnis, StL
1968 ......Bobby Orr, Bos	1984 ......Rod Langway, Wash	
1969 ......Bobby Orr, Bos	1985 ......Paul Coffey, Edm	

Calder Memorial Trophy

Awarded annually "to the player selected as the most proficient in his first year of competition in the National Hockey League." Frank Calder was a former NHL president. Sergei Makarov, who won the award in 1989–90, was the oldest recipient of the trophy, at 31. Players are no longer eligible for the award if they are 26 or older as of September 15th of the season in question.

1933 ......Carl Voss, Det	1956 ......Glenn Hall, Det	1979 ......Bobby Smith, Minn
1934 ......Russ Blinko, Mtl M	1957 ......Larry Regan, Bos	1980 ......Ray Bourque, Bos
1935 ......Dave Schriner, NYA	1958 ......Frank Mahovlich, Tor	1981 ......Peter Stastny, Que
1936 ......Mike Karakas, Chi	1959 ......Ralph Backstrom, Mtl	1982 ......Dale Hawerchuk, Winn
1937 ......Syl Apps, Tor	1960 ......Bill Hay, Chi	1983 ......Steve Larmer, Chi
1938 ......Cully Dahlstrom, Chi	1961 ......Dave Keon, Tor	1984 ......Tom Barrasso, Buff
1939 ......Frank Brimsek, Bos	1962 ......Bobby Rousseau, Mtl	1985 ......Mario Lemieux, Pitt
1940 ......Kilby MacDonald, NYR	1963 ......Kent Douglas, Tor	1986 ......Gary Suter, Cgy
1941 ......Johnny Quilty, Mtl	1964 ......Jacques Laperriere, Mtl	1987 ......Luc Robitaille, LA
1942 ......Grant Warwick, NYR	1965 ......Roger Crozier, Det	1988 ......Joe Nieuwendyk, Cgy
1943 ......Gaye Stewart, Tor	1966 ......Brit Selby, Tor	1989 ......Brian Leetch, NYR
1944 ......Gus Bodnar, Tor	1967 ......Bobby Orr, Bos	1990 ......Sergei Makarov, Cgy
1945 ......Frank McCool, Tor	1968 ......Derek Sanderson, Bos	1991 ......Ed Belfour, Chi
1946 ......Edgar Laprade, NYR	1969 ......Danny Grant, Minn	1992 ......Pavel Bure, Van
1947 ......Howie Meeker, Tor	1970 ......Tony Esposito, Chi	1993 ......Teemu Selanne, Winn
1948 ......Jim McFadden, Det	1971 ......Gilbert Perreault, Buff	1994 ......Martin Brodeur, NJ
1949 ......Pentti Lund, NYR	1972 ......Ken Dryden, Mtl	1995 ......Peter Forsberg, Que
1950 ......Jack Gelineau, Bos	1973 ......Steve Vickers, NYR	1996 ......Daniel Alfredsson, Ott
1951 ......Terry Sawchuk, Det	1974 ......Denis Potvin, NYI	1997 ......Bryan Berard, NYI
1952 ......Bernie Geoffrion, Mtl	1975 ......Eric Vail, Atl	1998 ......Sergei Samsonov, Bos
1953 ......Gump Worsley, NYR	1976 ......Bryan Trottier, NYI	1999 ......Chris Drury, Col
1954 ......Camille Henry, NYR	1977 ......Willi Plett, Atl	
1955 ......Ed Litzenberger, Chi	1978 ......Mike Bossy, NYI	

Vezina Trophy

Awarded annually "to the goalkeeper adjudged to be the best at his position." The trophy is named after Georges Vezina, an outstanding goalie for the Montreal Canadiens who collapsed during a game on November 28, 1925, and died four months later of tuberculosis. The general managers of the NHL teams vote on the award.

1927 ....George Hainsworth, Mtl	1956 ....Jacques Plante, Mtl	1978 ....Ken Dryden, Mtl
1928 ....George Hainsworth, Mtl	1957 ....Jacques Plante, Mtl	Michel Larocque, Mtl
1929 ....George Hainsworth, Mtl	1958 ....Jacques Plante, Mtl	1979 ....Ken Dryden, Mtl
1930 ....Tiny Thompson, Bos	1959 ....Jacques Plante, Mtl	Michel Larocque, Mtl
1931 ....Roy Worters, NYA	1960 ....Jacques Plante, Mtl	1980 ....Bob Sauve, Buff
1932 ....Charlie Gardiner, Chi	1961 ....Johnny Bower, Tor	Don Edwards, Buff
1933 ....Tiny Thompson, Bos	1962 ....Jacques Plante, Mtl	1981 ....Richard Sevigny, Mtl
1934 ....Charlie Gardiner, Chi	1963 ....Glenn Hall, Chi	Denis Herron, Mtl
1935 ....Lorne Chabot, Chi	1964 ....Charlie Hodge, Mtl	Michel Larocque, Mtl
1936 ....Tiny Thompson, Bos	1965 ....Terry Sawchuk, Tor	1982 ....Billy Smith, NYI
1937 ....Normie Smith, Det	Johnny Bower, Tor	1983 ....Pete Peeters, Bos
1938 ....Tiny Thompson, Bos	1966 ....Gump Worsley, Mtl	1984 ....Tom Barrasso, Buff
1939 ....Frank Brimsek, Bos	Charlie Hodge, Mtl	1985 ....Pelle Lindbergh, Phil
1940 ....Dave Kerr, NYR	1967 ....Glenn Hall, Chi	1986 ....John Vanbiesbrouck,
1941 ....Turk Broda, Tor	Rogie Vachon, Mtl	NYR
1942 ....Frank Brimsek, Bos	1969 ....Jacques Plante, StL	1987 ....Ron Hextall, Phil
1943 ....Johnny Mowers, Det	Glenn Hall, StL	1988 ....Grant Fuhr, Edm
1944 ....Bill Durnan, Mtl	1970 ....Tony Esposito, Chi	1989 ....Patrick Roy, Mtl
1945 ....Bill Durnan, Mtl	1971 ....Ed Giacomin, NYR	1990 ....Patrick Roy, Mtl
1946 ....Bill Durnan, Mtl	Gilles Villemure, NYR	1991 ....Ed Belfour, Chi
1947 ....Bill Durnan, Mtl	1972 ....Tony Esposito, Chi	1992 ....Patrick Roy, Mtl
1948 ....Turk Broda, Tor	Gary Smith, Chi	1993 ....Ed Belfour, Chi
1949 ....Bill Durnan, Mtl	1973 ....Ken Dryden, Mtl	1994 ....Dominik Hasek, Buff
1950 ....Bill Durnan, Mtl	1974 ....Bernie Parent, Phil	1995 ....Dominik Hasek, Buff
1951 ....Al Rollins, Tor	Tony Esposito, Chi	1996 ....Jim Carey, Wash
1952 ....Terry Sawchuk, Det	1975 ....Bernie Parent, Phil	1997 ....Dominik Hasek, Buff
1953 ....Terry Sawchuk, Det	1976 ....Ken Dryden, Mtl	1998 ....Dominik Hasek, Buff
1954 ....Harry Lumley, Tor	1977 ....Ken Dryden, Mtl	1999 ....Dominik Hasek, Buff
1955 ....Terry Sawchuk, Det	Michel Larocque, Mtl	

Selke Trophy

Awarded annually "to the forward who best excels in the defensive aspects of the game." The trophy is named after Frank J. Selke, the architect of the Montreal Canadians dynasty that won five consecutive Stanley Cups in the late '50s. The winner is selected by a vote of the Professional Hockey Writers Association

1978........Bob Gainey, Mtl	1986........Troy Murray, Chi	1994........Sergei Fedorov, Det
1979........Bob Gainey, Mtl	1987........Dave Poulin, Phil	1995........Ron Francis, Pitt
1980........Bob Gainey, Mtl	1988........Guy Carbonneau, Mtl	1996........Sergei Fedorov, Det
1981........Bob Gainey, Mtl	1989........Guy Carbonneau, Mtl	1997........Michael Peca, Buff
1982........Steve Kasper, Bos	1990........Rick Meagher, StL	1998........Jere Lehtinen, Dall
1983........Bobby Clarke, Phil	1991........Dirk Graham, Chi	1999........Jere Lehtinen, Dall
1984........Doug Jarvis, Wash	1992........Guy Carbonneau, Mtl	
1985........Craig Ramsay, Buff	1993........Doug Gilmour, Tor	

News of the Beak

Bruins forward Rob DiMaio has the NHL's most spectacular schnozz. Lumpy and brightly scarred at its bridge, the DiMaio proboscis possesses an angular inconsistency that would befuddle a geometrician. The nose has been broken more than a dozen times in DiMaio's 11-year career because he fearlessly sticks it into any scrum and, as he points out, "at my height [5'10"], I'm at elbow level for a lot of guys."

The mishaps have done nothing to inhibit DiMaio's scrappy style, but residual scar tissue has caused him to have difficulty breathing. To help alleviate that, he underwent surgery in which a piece of his skull was grafted into his nose. Still, the 31-year-old DiMaio broke his nose several more times last season. Not long ago, DiMaio vowed that when he retires, he'll have his nose repaired once and for all. "I'm going to get it fixed up nice," he said. "That'll be the only good thing about not playing anymore."

Adams Award

Awarded annually "to the NHL coach adjudged to have contributed the most to his team's success." The trophy is named in honor of Jack Adams, longtime coach and general manager of the Detroit Red Wings. The winner is selected by a vote of the National Hockey League Broadcasters' Association.

1974 .....Fred Shero, Phil	1983 .....Orval Tessier, Chi	1992 .....Pat Quinn, Van
1975 .....Bob Pulford, LA	1984 .....Bryan Murray, Wash	1993 .....Pat Burns, Tor
1976 .....Don Cherry, Bos	1985 .....Mike Keenan, Phil	1994 .....Jacques Lemaire, NJ
1977 .....Scott Bowman, Mtl	1986 .....Glen Sather, Edm	1995 .....Marc Crawford, Que
1978 .....Bobby Kromm, Det	1987 .....Jacques Demers, Det	1996 .....Scotty Bowman, Det
1979 .....Al Arbour, NYI	1988 .....Jacques Demers, Det	1997 .....Ted Nolan, Buff
1980 .....Pat Quinn, Phil	1989 .....Pat Burns, Mtl	1998 .....Pat Burns, Bos
1981 .....Red Berenson, StL	1990 .....Bob Murdoch, Winn	1999 .....Jacques Martin, Ott
1982 .....Tom Watt, Winn	1991 .....Brian Sutter, StL	

Career Records

Alltime Point Leaders

	Player	Yrs	GP	G	A	Pts	Pts/game
1.	*Wayne Gretzky, Edm, LA, StL, NYR	20	1487	894	1963	2857	1.921
2.	Gordie Howe, Det, Hart	26	1767	801	1049	1850	1.047
3.	Marcel Dionne, Det, LA, NYR	18	1348	731	1040	1771	1.314
4.	*Mark Messier, Edm, NYR, Van	20	1413	610	1050	1660	1.175
5.	Phil Esposito, Chi, Bos, NYR	18	1282	717	873	1590	1.240
6.	Mario Lemieux, Pitt	12	745	613	881	1494	2.005
7.	*Paul Coffey, Edm, Pitt, LA, Det, Hart, Phil	19	1322	385	1102	1487	1.125
8.	*Ron Francis, Hart, Pitt	18	1329	449	1037	1486	1.118
9.	*Steve Yzerman, Det	16	1178	592	891	1483	1.259
10.	*Ray Bourque, Bos	20	1453	385	1083	1468	1.010
11.	Stan Mikita, Chi	22	1394	541	926	1467	1.052
12.	Bryan Trottier, NYI, Pitt	18	1279	524	901	1425	1.114
13.	Dale Hawerchuk, Winn, Buff, StL, Phil	16	1188	518	891	1409	1.186
14.	Jari Kurri, Edm, LA, NYR, Ana, Col	17	1251	601	797	1397	1.118
15.	John Bucyk, Det, Bos	23	1540	556	813	1369	.889

*Active in 1998–99.

Alltime Goal-Scoring Leaders

	Player	Yrs	GP	G	G/game
1.	*Wayne Gretzky, Edm, LA, StL, NYR	20	1487	894	.601
2.	Gordie Howe, Det, Hart	26	1767	801	.453
3.	Marcel Dionne, Det, LA, NYR	18	1348	731	.542
4.	Phil Esposito, Chi, Bos, NYR	18	1282	717	.559
5.	Mike Gartner, Wash, Minn, NYR, Tor, Phoe	19	1432	708	.494
6.	Mario Lemieux, Pitt	12	745	613	.823
7.	Bobby Hull, Chi, Winn, Hart	16	1063	610	.574
8.	*Mark Messier, Edm, NYR, Van	20	1413	610	.432
9.	*Dino Ciccarelli, Minn, Wash, Det, TB, Fla	19	1232	608	.494
10.	Jari Kurri, Edm, LA, NYR, Ana, Col	17	1251	601	.480

*Active in 1998–99.

Alltime Assist Leaders

	Player	Yrs	GP	A	A/game
1.	Wayne Gretzky, Edm, LA, StL	20	1487	1963	1.320
2.	*Paul Coffey, Edm, Pitt, LA, Det, Hart, Phil	19	1322	1102	.834
3.	*Ray Bourque, Bos	20	1453	1083	.745
4.	*Mark Messier, Edm, NYR, Van	20	1413	1050	.743
5.	Gordie Howe, Det, Hart	26	1767	1049	.594
6.	Marcel Dionne, Det, LA, NYR	18	1348	1040	.771
7.	*Ron Francis, Hart, Pitt	18	1329	1037	.780
8.	Stan Mikita, Chi	22	1394	926	.664
9.	Bryan Trottier, NYI, Pitt	18	1279	901	.704
10.	Dale Hawerchuk, Winn, Buff, StL, Phil	16	1188	891	.750
	*Steve Yzerman, Det	16	1178	891	.756

*Active player.

Alltime Penalty Minutes Leaders

	Player	Yrs	GP	PIM	Min/game
1.	Dave Williams, Tor, Van, Det, LA, Hart	14	962	3966	4.12
2.	*Dale Hunter, Que, Wash, Col	19	1407	3565	2.53
3.	*Marty McSorley, Pitt, Edm, LA, NYR, SJ	16	934	3319	3.55
4.	Tim Hunter, Calg, Que, Van, SJ	16	815	3146	3.86
5.	Chris Nilan, Mtl, NYR, Bos	13	688	3043	4.42
6.	*Bob Probert, Det, Chi	13	726	2907	4.00
7.	*Rick Tocchet, Phil, Pitt, LA, Bos, Wash, Phoe	15	990	2771	2.80
8.	*Pat Verbeek, NJ, Hart, NYR, Dall	17	1225	2665	2.18
9.	*Craig Berube, Phil, Tor, Cgy, Wash	13	796	2651	3.33
10.	*Dave Manson, Chi, Edm, Winn, Phoe, Mtl	13	919	2604	2.83

*Active player.

Twilight of the Goons

Rocky Thompson is only 21, but he's old-school, definitely old-school. The long-haired, snaggle-toothed son of a pulp-mill worker, Thompson used the chops that made him a Saskatchewan Gloden Gloves champ to win a spot on the Flames' roster during the 1997–98 season. He played in only 12 games all year. After sparring in the summer of '98 in a Calgary fight club and engaging in several on-ice bouts during the '98–99 preseason, Thompson was spotted limping around the Flames' locker room before the season opener sporting a purplish forehead and a split upper lip. Asked to assess his hockey skills, he paused and said, "My skating is a weaker part of my game."

For all his bare-knuckle appeal, Thompson didn't get into a game before being sent to the minors in October '98—another reminder of how hard life is for good-hit, no-skate players in today's NHL. Thanks to a crackdown on brawling and an influx of finesse-oriented Europeans, the NHL's fights-per-game average dropped from 2.1 in 1987–88 to 1.2 in '98–99. Listen to Nick Fotiu, a former Police Athletic League boxing champ who bludgeoned his way through a 13-year NHL career that ended in '89. "The way hockey is now, guys can't just fight," said Fotiu, now a minor league coach. "They also have to be able to play."

Good teams, such as Ottawa and Philadelphia, did without a facebreaker in '98–99, and the Red Wings stayed atop their division without the services of injured cudgeler Joe Kocur. In the 1980s the Wings built a team and an ad campaign around Kocur and fellow hit man Bob Probert: the Bruise Brothers. "They beat a lot of people up and helped sell a lot of tickets," said Detroit president Jim Devellano. "You couldn't market that today, which is good—we're not the WWF."

Goaltending Records

ALLTIME WIN LEADERS

Goaltender	W	L	T	Pct
Terry Sawchuk, five teams 447	330	173	.562
Jacques Plante, five teams 434	246	147	.614
Tony Esposito, Mtl, Chi................423	306	152	.566
*Patrick Roy, Mtl, Col...................412	243	95	.613
Glenn Hall, Det, Chi, StL..............407	327	163	.545
*Grant Fuhr, five teams 398	282	112	.573
Andy Moog, Edm, Bos, Dall, Mtl...372	209	88	.622
Rogie Vachon, Mtl, LA, Det, Bos...355	291	127	.541
*Mike Vernon, Cgy, Det, SJ.........347	223	83	.595
*Tom Barrasso, Buff, Pitt 345	248	79	.572

*Active player.

ACTIVE GOALTENDING LEADERS

Goaltender	W	L	T	Pct
Chris Osgood, Det........................166	77	34	.661
Martin Brodeur, NJ........................201	105	57	.632
Patrick Roy, Mtl, Col......................412	243	95	.613
Ed Belfour, Chi, SJ, Dall................276	174	75	.597
Mike Vernon, Cgy, Det...................347	223	83	.595
Grant Fuhr, five teams 398	282	112	.573
Tom Barrasso, Buff, Pitt 345	248	79	.572
Ron Hextall, Phil, Que, NYI...........296	214	69	.571
Dominik Hasek, Chi, Buff...............195	140	62	.571
Mike Richter, NYR.........................230	174	57	.561

Note: Ranked by winning percentage; minimum 250 games played.

ALLTIME SHUTOUT LEADERS

Goaltender	Team	Yrs	GP	SO
Terry Sawchuk...................Det, Bos, Tor, LA, NYR	21	971	103
George Hainsworth ....Mtl, Tor	11	465	94
Glenn Hall......................Det, Chi, StL	18	906	84
Jacques Plante.................Mtl, NYR, StL, Tor, Bos	18	837	82
Tiny Thompson.................Bos, Det	12	553	81
Alex Connell ....Ott, Det, NYA, Mtl M	12	417	81
Tony Esposito ....Mtl, Chi	16	886	76
Lorne Chabot ....NYR, Tor, Mtl, Chi, Mtl M, NYA	11	411	73
Harry Lumley ....Det, NYR, Chi, Tor, Bos	16	804	71
Roy Worters......................Pitt Pir, NYA, *Mtl	12	484	66

*Played 1 game for Canadiens in 1929–30, not a shutout.

ALLTIME GOALS AGAINST AVERAGE LEADERS (PRE-1950)

Goaltender	Team	Yrs	GP	GA	GAA
George Hainsworth ....Mtl, Tor	11	465	937	1.91
Alex Connell ....Ott, Det, NYA, Mtl M	12	417	830	1.91
Chuck Gardiner.................Chi	7	316	664	2.02
Lorne Chabot ....NYR, Tor, Mtl, Chi, Mtl M, NYA	11	411	861	2.04
Tiny Thompson.................Bos, Det	12	553	1183	2.08

ALLTIME GOALS AGAINST AVERAGE LEADERS (POST-1950)

Goaltender	Team	Yrs	GP	GA	GAA
*Martin Brodeur ....NJ	7	375	789	2.19
Ken Dryden ....Mtl	8	397	870	2.24
*Dominik Hasek.................Chi, Buff	9	414	901	2.26
*Chris Osgood..................Det	6	284	647	2.35
Jacques Plante.................Mtl, NYR, StL, Tor, Bos	18	837	1965	2.38

*Active player

Note: Minimum 250 games played. Goals against average equals goals against per 60 minutes played.

Coaching Records

Coach	Team	Seasons	W	L	T	Pct
Scott Bowman.............five teams	1967–87, 91–	1100	515	285	.654
Toe Blake ....Mtl	1955–68	500	255	159	.634
Glen Sather.................Edm	1979–89, 93–94	464	268	110	.616
Fred Shero ....Phil, NYR	1971–81	390	225	119	.612
Pat Burns ....Mtl, Tor, Bos	1988–	385	271	109	.575
Mike Keenan ....five teams	1984–1999	506	360	115	.574
Emile Francis ....NYR, StL	1965–77, 81–83	388	273	117	.574
Billy Reay ....Tor, Chi	1957–59, 63–77	542	385	175	.571
Terry Murray................Wash, Phil, Fla	1989-	311	232	76	.564
Bryan Murray ....Wash, Det, Fla	1981–98	484	368	123	.559

Note: Minimum 600 regular-season games. Ranked by percentage.

Single-Season Records

Goals

Player	Season	GP	G	Player	Season	GP	G
Wayne Gretzky, Edm	1981–82	80	92	Wayne Gretzky, Edm	1982–83	80	71
Wayne Gretzky, Edm	1983–84	74	87	Brett Hull, StL	1991–92	73	70
Brett Hull, StL	1990–91	78	86	Mario Lemieux, Pitt	1987–88	77	70
Mario Lemieux, Pitt	1988–89	76	85	Bernie Nicholls, LA	1988–89	79	70
Alexander Mogilny, Buff	1992–93	77	76	Mario Lemieux, Pitt	1992–93	60	69
Phil Esposito, Bos	1970–71	78	76	Mario Lemieux, Pitt	1995–96	70	69
Teemu Selanne, Winn	1992–93	84	76	Mike Bossy, NYI	1978–79	80	69
Wayne Gretzky, Edm	1984–85	80	73	Phil Esposito, Bos	1973–74	78	68
Brett Hull, StL	1989–90	80	72	Jari Kurri, Edm	1985–86	78	68
Jari Kurri, Edm	1984–85	73	71	Mike Bossy, NYI	1980–81	79	68

Assists

Player	Season	GP	A	Player	Season	GP	A
Wayne Gretzky, Edm	1985–86	80	163	Wayne Gretzky, LA	1989–90	73	102
Wayne Gretzky, Edm	1984–85	80	135	Bobby Orr, Bos	1970–71	78	102
Wayne Gretzky, Edm	1982–83	80	125	Mario Lemieux, Pitt	1987–88	77	98
Wayne Gretzky, LA	1990–91	78	122	Adam Oates, Bos	1992–93	84	97
Wayne Gretzky, Edm	1986–87	79	121	Doug Gilmour, Tor	1992–93	83	95
Wayne Gretzky, Edm	1981–82	80	120	Pat LaFontaine, Buff	1992–93	84	95
Wayne Gretzky, Edm	1983–84	74	118	Mario Lemieux, Pitt	1985–86	79	93
Mario Lemieux, Pitt	1988–89	76	114	Peter Stastny, Que	1981–82	80	93
Wayne Gretzky, LA	1988–89	78	114	Wayne Gretzky, LA	1993–94	81	92
Wayne Gretzky, Edm	1987–88	64	109	Mario Lemieux, Pitt	1995–96	70	92
Wayne Gretzky, Edm	1980–81	80	109	Ron Francis, Pitt	1995–96	77	92

Points

Player	Season	G	A	Pts	Player	Season	G	A	Pts
Wayne Gretzky, Edm	1985–86	52	163	215	Wayne Gretzky, LA	1990–91	41	122	163
Wayne Gretzky, Edm	1981–82	92	120	212	Mario Lemieux, Pitt	1995–96	69	92	161
Wayne Gretzky, Edm	1984–85	73	135	208	Mario Lemieux, Pitt	1992–93	69	91	160
Wayne Gretzky, Edm	1983–84	87	118	205	Steve Yzerman, Det	1988–89	65	90	155
Mario Lemieux, Pitt	1988–89	85	114	199	Phil Esposito, Bos	1970–71	76	76	152
Wayne Gretzky, Edm	1982–83	71	125	196	Bernie Nicholls, LA	1988–89	70	80	150
Wayne Gretzky, Edm	1986–87	62	121	183	Wayne Gretzky, Edm	1987–88	40	109	149
Mario Lemieux, Pitt	1987–88	70	98	168	Pat LaFontaine, Buff	1992–93	53	95	148
Wayne Gretzky, LA	1988–89	54	114	168	Mike Bossy, NYI	1981–82	64	83	147
Wayne Gretzky, Edm	1980–81	55	109	164	Phil Esposito, Bos	1973–74	68	77	145

Points per Game

Player	Season	GP	Pts	Avg	Player	Season	GP	Pts	Avg
Wayne Gretzky, Edm	1983–84	74	205	2.77	Mario Lemieux, Pitt	1987–88	77	168	2.18
Wayne Gretzky, Edm	1985–86	80	215	2.69	Wayne Gretzky, LA	1988–89	78	168	2.15
Mario Lemieux, Pitt	1992–93	60	160	2.67	Wayne Gretzky, LA	1990–91	78	163	2.09
Wayne Gretzky, Edm	1981–82	80	212	2.65	Mario Lemieux, Pitt	1989–90	59	123	2.08
Mario Lemieux, Pitt	1988–89	76	199	2.62	Wayne Gretzky, Edm	1980–81	80	164	2.05
Wayne Gretzky, Edm	1984–85	80	208	2.60	Mario Lemieux, Pitt	1991–92	64	131	2.05
Wayne Gretzky, Edm	1982–83	80	196	2.45	Bill Cowley, Bos	1943–44	36	71	1.97
Wayne Gretzky, Edm	1987–88	64	149	2.33	Phil Esposito, Bos	1970–71	78	152	1.95
Wayne Gretzky, Edm	1986–87	79	183	2.32	Wayne Gretzky, LA	1989–90	73	142	1.95
Mario Lemieux, Pitt	1995–96	70	161	2.30	Steve Yzerman, Det	1988–89	80	155	1.94

Note: Minimum 50 points in one season.

Goals per Game

Player	Season	GP	G	Avg
Joe Malone, Mtl	1917–18	20	44	2.20
Cy Denneny, Ott	1917–18	22	36	1.64
Newsy Lalonde, Mtl	1917–18	14	23	1.64
Joe Malone, Que	1919–20	24	39	1.63
Newsy Lalonde, Mtl	1919–20	23	36	1.57
Joe Malone, Ham	1920–21	20	30	1.50
Babe Dye, Ham-Tor	1920–21	24	35	1.46
Cy Denneny, Ott	1920–21	24	34	1.42
Reg Noble, Tor	1917–18	20	28	1.40
Newsy Lalonde, Mtl	1920–21	24	33	1.38

Note: Minimum 20 goals in one season.

Assists per Game

Player	Season	GP	A	Avg
Wayne Gretzky, Edm	1985–86	80	163	2.04
Wayne Gretzky, Edm	1987–88	64	109	1.70
Wayne Gretzky, Edm	1984–85	80	135	1.69
Wayne Gretzky, Edm	1983–84	74	118	1.59
Wayne Gretzky, Edm	1982–83	80	125	1.56
Wayne Gretzky, LA	1990–91	78	122	1.56
Wayne Gretzky, Edm	1986–87	79	121	1.53
Mario Lemieux, Pitt	1992–93	60	91	1.52
Wayne Gretzky, Edm	1981–82	80	120	1.50
Mario Lemieux, Pitt	1988–89	76	114	1.50

Note: Minimum 35 assists in one season.

Shutout Leaders

	Season	SO	Length of Schedule
George Hainsworth, Mtl	1928–29	22	44
Alex Connell, Ott	1925–26	15	36
Alex Connell, Ott	1927–28	15	44
Hal Winkler, Bos	1927–28	15	44
Tony Esposito, Chi	1969–70	15	76
George Hainsworth, Mtl	1926–27	14	44
Clint Benedict, Mtl M	1926–27	13	44
Alex Connell, Ott	1926–27	13	44
George Hainsworth, Mtl	1927–28	13	44
John Roach, NYR	1928–29	13	44
Roy Worters, NYA	1928–29	13	44
Harry Lumley, Tor	1953–54	13	70
Dominik Hasek, Buff	1997–98	13	82
Tiny Thompson, Bos	1928–29	12	44
Lorne Chabot, Tor	1928–29	12	44
Chuck Gardiner, Chi	1930–31	12	44
Terry Sawchuk, Det	1951–52	12	70
Terry Sawchuk, Det	1953–54	12	70
Terry Sawchuk, Det	1954–55	12	70
Glenn Hall, Det	1955–56	12	70
Bernie Parent, Phil	1973–74	12	78
Bernie Parent, Phil	1974–75	12	80

	Season	SO	Length of Schedule
Lorne Chabot, NYR	1927–28	11	44
Harry Holmes, Det	1927–28	11	44
Clint Benedict, Mtl M	1928–29	11	44
Joe Miller, Pitt Pirates	1928–29	11	44
Tiny Thompson, Bos	1932–33	11	48
Terry Sawchuck, Det	1950–51	11	70
Lorne Chabot, NYR	1926–27	10	44
Roy Worters, Pitt Pirates	1927–28	10	44
Clarence Dolson, Det	1928–29	10	44
John Roach, Det	1932–33	10	48
Chuck Gardiner, Chi	1933–34	10	48
Tiny Thompson, Bos	1935–36	10	48
Frank Brimsek, Bos	1938–39	10	48
Bill Durnan, Mtl	1948–49	10	60
Gerry McNeil, Mtl	1952–53	10	70
Harry Lumley, Tor	1952–53	10	70
Tony Esposito, Chi	1973–74	10	78
Ken Dryden, Mtl	1976–77	10	80
Martin Brodeur, NJ	1996–97	10	82
Martin Brodeur, NJ	1997–98	10	82
Byron Dafoe, Bos	1998–99	10	82

Wins

	Season	Record
Bernie Parent, Phil	1973–74	47-13-12
Bernie Parent, Phil	1974–75	44-14-9
Terry Sawchuk, Det	1950–51	44-13-13
Terry Sawchuk, Det	1951–52	44-14-12
Tom Barasso, Pitt	1992–93	43-14-5
Ed Belfour, Chi	1990–91	43-19-7
Martin Brodeur, NJ	1997–98	43-17-8
Jacques Plante, Mtl	1955–56	42-12-10
Jacques Plante, Mtl	1961–62	42-14-14
Ken Dryden, Mtl	1975–76	42-10-8
Mike Richter, NYR	1993–94	42-12-6

Goals Against Average

(PRE-1950)

	Season	GP	GAA
George Hainsworth, Mtl	1928–29	44	0.92
George Hainsworth, Mtl	1927–-28	44	1.05
Alex Connell, Ott	1925–26	36	1.12
Tiny Thompson, Bos	1928–29	44	1.18
Roy Worters, NYA	1928–29	38	1.21

(POST-1950)

	Season	GP	GAA
Al Rollins, Tor	1950–51	40	1.7744
Tony Esposito, Chi	1971–72	48	1.7698
Ron Tugnutt, Ott	1998–99	43	1.7943
Jacques Plante, Mtl	1955–56	64	1.8594
Harry Lumley, Tor	1953–54	69	1.8551
Dominik Hasek, Buff	1998–99	64	1.8706
Martin Brodeur, NJ	1996–97	67	1.8759
Ed Belfour, Dall	1997–98	61	1.8766

Single-Game Records

Goals

	Date	G
Joe Malone, Que vs Tor	1-31-20	7
Newsy Lalonde, Mtl vs Tor	1-10-20	6
Joe Malone, Que vs Ott	3-10-20	6
Corb Denneny, Tor vs Ham	1-26-21	6
Cy Denneny, Ott vs Ham	3-7-21	6
Syd Howe, Det vs NYR	2-3-44	6
Red Berenson, StL vs Phil	11-7-68	6
Darryl Sittler, Tor vs Bos	2-7-76	6

Assists

	Date	A
Billy Taylor, Det vs Chi	3-16-47	7
Wayne Gretzky, Edm vs Wash	2-15-80	7
Wayne Gretzky, Edm vs Chi	12-11-85	7
Wayne Gretzky, Edm vs Que	2-14-86	7

Note: 19 tied with 6.

Points

	Date	G	A	Pts
Darryl Sittler, Tor vs Bos	2-7-76	6	4	10
Maurice Richard, Mtl vs Det	12-28-44	5	3	8
Bert Olmstead, Mtl vs Chi	1-9-54	4	4	8
Tom Bladon, Phil vs Clev	12-11-77	4	4	8
Bryan Trottier, NYI vs NYR	12-23-78	5	3	8
Peter Stastny, Que vs Wash	2-22-81	4	4	8
Anton Stastny, Que vs Wash	2-22-81	3	5	8
Wayne Gretzky, Edm vs NJ	11-19-83	3	5	8
Wayne Gretzky, Edm vs Minn	1-4-84	4	4	8
Paul Coffey, Edm vs Det	3-14-86	2	6	8
Mario Lemieux, Pitt vs StL	10-15-88	2	6	8
Bernie Nicholls, LA vs Tor	12-1-88	2	6	8
Mario Lemieux, Pitt vs NJ	12-31-88	5	3	8

NHL Season Leaders

Points

Season	Player and Club	Pts	Season	Player and Club	Pts
1917–18	Joe Malone, Mtl	44	1952–53	Gordie Howe, Det	95
1918–19	Newsy Lalonde, Mtl	30	1953–54	Gordie Howe, Det	81
1919–20	Joe Malone, Que	48	1954–55	Bernie Geoffrion, Mtl	75
1920–21	Newsy Lalonde, Mtl	41	1955–56	Jean Beliveau, Mtl	88
1921–22	Punch Broadbent, Ott	46	1956–57	Gordie Howe, Det	89
1922–23	Babe Dye, Tor	37	1957–58	Dickie Moore, Mtl	84
1923–24	Cy Denneny, Ott	23	1958–59	Dickie Moore, Mtl	96
1924–25	Babe Dye, Tor	44	1959–60	Bobby Hull, Chi	81
1925–26	Nels Stewart, Mtl M	42	1960–61	Bernie Geoffrion, Mtl	95
1926–27	Bill Cook, NY	37	1961–62	Andy Bathgate, NY	84
1927–28	Howie Morenz, Mtl	51		Bobby Hull, Chi	84
1928–29	Ace Bailey, Tor	32	1962–63	Gordie Howe, Det	86
1929–30	Cooney Weiland, Bos	73	1963–64	Stan Mikita, Chi	89
1930–31	Howie Morenz, Mtl	51	1964–65	Stan Mikita, Chi	87
1931–32	Harvey Jackson, Tor	53	1965–66	Bobby Hull, Chi	97
1932–33	Bill Cook, NY	50	1966–67	Stan Mikita, Chi	97
1933–34	Charlie Conacher, Tor	52	1967–68	Stan Mikita, Chi	87
1934–35	Charlie Conacher, Tor	57	1968–69	Phil Esposito, Bos	126
1935–36	Sweeney Schriner, NYA	45	1969–70	Bobby Orr, Bos	120
1936–37	Sweeney Schriner, NYA	46	1970–71	Phil Esposito, Bos	152
1937–38	Gord Drillon, Tor	52	1971–72	Phil Esposito, Bos	133
1938–39	Hector Blake, Mtl	47	1972–73	Phil Esposito, Bos	130
1939–40	Milt Schmidt, Bos	52	1973–74	Phil Esposito, Bos	145
1940–41	Bill Cowley, Bos	62	1974–75	Bobby Orr, Bos	135
1941–42	Bryan Hextall, NY	54	1975–76	Guy Lafleur, Mtl	125
1942–43	Doug Bentley, Chi	73	1976–77	Guy Lafleur, Mtl	136
1943–44	Herb Cain, Bos	82	1977–78	Guy Lafleur, Mtl	132
1944–45	Elmer Lach, Mtl	80	1978–79	Bryan Trottier, NYI	134
1945–46	Max Bentley, Chi	61	1979–80	Marcel Dionne, LA	137
1946–47	Max Bentley, Chi	72		Wayne Gretzky, Edm	137
1947–48	Elmer Lach, Mtl	61	1980–81	Wayne Gretzky, Edm	164
1948–49	Roy Conacher, Chi	68	1981–82	Wayne Gretzky, Edm	212
1949–50	Ted Lindsay, Det	78	1982–83	Wayne Gretzky, Edm	196
1950–51	Gordie Howe, Det	86	1983–84	Wayne Gretzky, Edm	205
1951–52	Gordie Howe, Det	86	1984–85	Wayne Gretzky, Edm	208

Points (Cont.)

Season	Player and Club	Pts	Season	Player and Club	Pts
1985–86	Wayne Gretzky, Edm	215	1992–93	Mario Lemieux, Pitt	160
1986–87	Wayne Gretzky, Edm	183	1993–94	Wayne Gretzky, LA	130
1987–88	Mario Lemieux, Pitt	168	1994–95	Jaromir Jagr, Pitt	70
1988–89	Mario Lemieux, Pitt	199	1995–96	Mario Lemieux, Pitt	161
1989–90	Wayne Gretzky, LA	142	1996–97	Mario Lemieux, Pitt	122
1990–91	Wayne Gretzky, LA	163	1997–98	Jaromir Jagr, Pitt	102
1991–92	Mario Lemieux, Pitt	131	1998–99	Jaromir Jagr, Pitt	127

Goals

Season	Player and Club	G	Season	Player and Club	G
1917–18	Joe Malone, Mtl	44	1958–59	Jean Beliveau, Mtl	45
1918–19	Odie Cleghorn, Mtl	23	1959–60	Bobby Hull, Chi	39
1919–20	Joe Malone, Que	39		Bronco Horvath, Bos	39
1920–21	Babe Dye, Ham-Tor	35	1960–61	Bernie Geoffrion, Mtl	50
1921–22	Punch Broadbent, Ott	32	1961–62	Bobby Hull, Chi	50
1922–23	Babe Dye, Tor	26	1962–63	Gordie Howe, Det	38
1923–24	Cy Denneny, Ott	22	1963–64	Bobby Hull, Chi	43
1924–25	Babe Dye, Tor	38	1964–65	Norm Ullman, Det	42
1925–26	Nels Stewart, Mtl	34	1965–66	Bobby Hull, Chi	54
1926–27	Bill Cook, NY	33	1966–67	Bobby Hull, Chi	52
1927–28	Howie Morenz, Mtl	33	1967–68	Bobby Hull, Chi	44
1928–29	Ace Bailey, Tor	22	1968–69	Bobby Hull, Chi	58
1929–30	Cooney Weiland, Bos	43	1969–70	Phil Esposito, Bos	43
1930–31	Bill Cook, NY	30	1970–71	Phil Esposito, Bos	76
1931–32	Charlie Conacher, Tor	34	1971–72	Phil Esposito, Bos	66
	Bill Cook, NY	34	1972–73	Phil Esposito, Bos	55
1932–33	Bill Cook, NY	28	1973–74	Phil Esposito, Bos	68
1933–34	Charlie Conacher, Tor	32	1974–75	Phil Esposito, Bos	61
1934–35	Charlie Conacher, Tor	36	1975–76	Guy Lafleur, Mtl	56
1935–36	Charlie Conacher, Tor	23	1976–77	Steve Shutt, Mtl	60
	Bill Thoms, Tor	23	1977–78	Guy Lafleur, Mtl	60
1936–37	Larry Aurie, Det	23	1978–79	Mike Bossy, NYI	69
	Nels Stewart, Bos-NYA	23	1979–80	Charlie Simmer, LA	56
1937–38	Gord Drill, Tor	26		Blaine Stoughton, Hart	56
1938–39	Roy Conacher, Bos	26	1980–81	Mike Bossy, NYI	68
1939–40	Bryan Hextall, NY	24	1981–82	Wayne Gretzky, Edm	92
1940–41	Bryan Hextall, NY	26	1982–83	Wayne Gretzky, Edm	71
1941–42	Lynn Patrick, NY	32	1983–84	Wayne Gretzky, Edm	87
1942–43	Doug Bentley, Chi	43	1984–85	Wayne Gretzky, Edm	73
1943–44	Doug Bentley, Chi	38	1985–86	Jari Kurri, Edm	68
1944–45	Maurice Richard, Mtl	50	1986–87	Wayne Gretzky, Edm	62
1945–46	Gaye Stewart, Tor	37	1987–88	Mario Lemieux, Pitt	70
1946–47	Maurice Richard, Mtl	50	1988–89	Mario Lemieux, Pitt	85
1947–48	Ted Lindsay, Det	33	1989–90	Brett Hull, StL	72
1948–49	Sid Abel, Det	28	1990–91	Brett Hull, StL	78
1949–50	Maurice Richard, Mtl	43	1991–92	Brett Hull, StL	70
1950–51	Gordie Howe, Det	43	1992–93	Alexander Mogilny, Buff	76
1951–52	Gordie Howe, Det	47		Teemu Selanne, Winn	76
1952–53	Gordie Howe, Det	49	1993–94	Pavel Bure, Van	60
1953–54	Maurice Richard, Mtl	37	1994–95	Peter Bondra, Wash	34
1954–55	Bernie Geoffrion, Mtl	38	1995–96	Mario Lemieux, Pitt	69
	Maurice Richard, Mtl	38	1996–97	Keith Tkachuk, Phoe	52
1955–56	Jean Beliveau, Mtl	47	1997–98	Teemu Selanne, Ana	52
1957–58	Dickie Moore, Mtl	36		Peter Bondra, Wash	52
1956–57	Gordie Howe, Det	44	1998–99	Teemu Selanne, Ana	47

Assists

Season	Player and Club	A	Season	Player and Club	A
1917–18	statistic not kept		1961–62	Andy Bathgate, NY	56
1918–19	Newsy Lalonde, Mtl	9	1962–63	Henri Richard, Mtl	50
1919–20	Corbett Denneny, Tor	12	1963–64	Andy Bathgate, NY-Tor	58
1920–21	Louis Berlinquette, Mtl	9	1964–65	Stan Mikita, Chi	59
1921–22	Punch Broadbench, Ott	14	1965–66	Stan Mikita, Chi	48
1922–23	Babe Dye, Tor	11		Bobby Rousseau, Mtl	48
1923–24	Billy Boucher, Mtl	6		Jean Beliveau, Mtl	48
1924–25	Cy Denneny, Ott	15	1966–67	Stan Mikita, Chi	62
1925–26	Cy Denneny, Ott	12	1967–68	Phil Esposito, Bos	49
1926–27	Dick Irvin, Chi	18	1968–69	Phil Esposito, Bos	77
1927–28	Howie Morenz, Mtl	18	1969–70	Bobby Orr, Bos	87
1928–29	Frank Boucher, NY	16	1970–71	Bobby Orr, Bos	102
1929–30	Frank Boucher, NY	36	1971–72	Bobby Orr, Bos	80
1930–31	Joe Primeau, Tor	36	1972–73	Phil Esposito, Bos	75
1931–32	Joe Primeau, Tor	37	1973–74	Bobby Orr, Bos	89
1932–33	Frank Boucher, NY	28	1974–75	Bobby Clarke, Phil	89
1933–34	Joe Primeau, Tor	32		Bobby Orr, Bos	89
1934–35	Art Chapman, NYA	28	1975–76	Bobby Clarke, Phil	89
1935–36	Art Chapman, NYA	28	1976–77	Guy Lafleur, Mtl	80
1936–37	Syl Apps, Tor	29	1977–78	Bryan Trottier, NYI	77
1937–38	Syl Apps, Tor	29	1978–79	Bryan Trottier, NYI	87
1938–39	Bill Cowley, Bos	34	1979–80	Wayne Gretzky, Edm	86
1939–40	Milt Schmidt, Bos	30	1980–81	Wayne Gretzky, Edm	109
1940–41	Bill Cowley, Bos	45	1981–82	Wayne Gretzky, Edm	120
1941–42	Phil Watson, NY	37	1982–83	Wayne Gretzky, Edm	125
1942–43	Bill Cowley, Bos	45	1983–84	Wayne Gretzky, Edm	118
1943–44	Clint Smith, Chi	49	1984–85	Wayne Gretzky, Edm	135
1944–45	Elmer Lach, Mtl	54	1985–86	Wayne Gretzky, Edm	163
1945–46	Elmer Lach, Mtl	34	1986–87	Wayne Gretzky, Edm	121
1946–47	Billy Taylor, Det	46	1987–88	Wayne Gretzky, Edm	109
1947–48	Doug Bentley, Chi	37	1988–89	Wayne Gretzky, LA	114
1948–49	Doug Bentley, Chi	43		Mario Lemieux, Pitt	114
1949–50	Ted Lindsay, Det	55	1989–90	Wayne Gretzky, LA	102
1950–51	Gordie Howe, Det	43	1990–91	Wayne Gretzky, LA	122
	Ted Kennedy, Tor	43	1991–92	Wayne Gretzky, LA	90
1951–52	Elmer Lach, Mtl	50	1992–93	Adam Oates, Bos	97
1952–53	Gordie Howe, Det	46	1993–94	Wayne Gretzky, LA	92
1953–54	Gordie Howe, Det	48	1994–95	Ron Francis, Pitt	48
1954–55	Bert Olmstead, Mtl	48	1995–96	Mario Lemieux, Pitt	92
1955–56	Bert Olmstead, Mtl	56		Ron Francis, Pitt	92
1956–57	Ted Lindsay, Det	55	1996–97	Mario Lemieux, Pitt	72
1957–58	Henri Richard, Mtl	52	1997–98	Jaromir Jagr, Pitt	67
1958–59	Dickie Moore, Mtl	55		Wayne Gretzky, NYR	67
1959–60	Bobby Hull, Chi	42	1998–99	Jaromir Jagr, Pitt	83
1960–61	Jean Beliveau, Mtl	58			

Dog Bites Man, Man Stops Puck

Your typical NHL goalie is a big, brash millionaire who sports a mask painted with fangs and answers to nicknames like Dominator and Cujo. Then there's quiet little Arturs Irbe of the Carolina Hurricanes, who works for a base salary of $550,000, peers out of a white mask marked only by a small Hurricane swirl and whose moniker, Archie, wouldn't even be intimidating at Riverdale High. But after another solid year where he helped the Hurricanes into the playoffs, he is starting to register on fans' radar even though, at 5'8", he's among the NHL's shortest players.

In 1993–94 Irbe played a then NHL record 4,412 minutes for the San Jose Sharks and carried the team to the seventh game of the Western Conference semifinals. A cool customer from Latvia, he could have been describing both his persona and his results when he said in '94 that he'd been playing "like wall." Soon after that season, however, he was bitten by his Newfoundland dog. The bite severed an artery in his right hand, and Irbe struggled with nerve damage even after it healed. San Jose let him depart as a free agent in 1996. He caught on with Dallas in 1996–97 and played sporadically for Vancouver in 1998.

When he signed with the Hurricanes in September 1998, Irbe was expected to back up Trevor Kidd, who stands 6'3" and has all the swagger of his surnamesake, Billy the. But after Kidd allowed seven goals in the first 3½ periods of the season, Irbe took over. Teammates say his easy manner sets the tone for Carolina's buttoned-down style. In fact, Irbe may be the only NHL star who takes a sewing kit on road trips. He's the guy you'll see quietly mending his gear in the visitor's locker room.

"He's playing great, and he saves us money in equipment repair," said Hurricanes coach Paul Maurice. "The guy's a bargain."

Goals Against Average

Season	Goaltender and Club	GP	Min	GA	SO	Avg
1917–18	Georges Vezina, Mtl	21	1282	84	1	3.93
1918–19	Clint Benedict, Ott	18	1113	53	2	2.86
1919–20	Clint Benedict, Ott	24	1444	64	5	2.66
1920–21	Clint Benedict, Ott	24	1457	75	2	3.09
1921–22	Clint Benedict, Ott	24	1508	84	2	3.34
1922–23	Clint Benedict, Ott	24	1478	54	4	2.19
1923–24	Georges Vezina, Mtl	24	1459	48	3	1.97
1924–25	Georges Vezina, Mtl	30	1860	56	5	1.81
1925–26	Alex Connell, Ott	36	2251	42	15	1.12
1926–27	Clint Benedict, Mtl M	43	2748	65	13	1.42
1927–28	George Hainsworth, Mtl	44	2730	48	13	1.05
1928–29	George Hainsworth, Mtl	44	2800	43	22	0.92
1929–30	Tiny Thompson, Bos	44	2680	98	3	2.19
1930–31	Roy Worters, NYA	44	2760	74	8	1.61
1931–32	Chuck Gardiner, Chi	48	2989	92	4	1.85
1932–33	Tiny Thompson, Bos	48	3000	88	11	1.76
1933–34	Wilf Cude, Det-Mtl	30	1920	47	5	1.47
1934–35	Lorne Chabot, Chi	48	2940	88	8	1.80
1935–36	Tiny Thompson, Bos	48	2930	82	10	1.68
1936–37	Normie Smith, Det	48	2980	102	6	2.05
1937–38	Tiny Thompson, Bos	48	2970	89	7	1.80
1938–39	Frank Brimsek, Bos	43	2610	68	10	1.56
1939–40	Dave Kerr, NYR	48	3000	77	8	1.54
1940–41	Turk Broda, Tor	48	2970	99	5	2.00
1941–42	Frank Brimsek, Bos	47	2930	115	3	2.35
1942–43	Johnny Mowers, Det	50	3010	124	6	2.47
1943–44	Bill Durnan, Mtl	50	3000	109	2	2.18
1944–45	Bill Durnan, Mtl	50	3000	121	1	2.42
1945–46	Bill Durnan, Mtl	40	2400	104	4	2.60
1946–47	Bill Durnan, Mtl	60	3600	138	4	2.30
1947–48	Turk Broda, Tor	60	3600	143	5	2.38
1948–49	Bill Durnan, Mtl	60	3600	126	10	2.10
1949–50	Bill Durnan, Mtl	64	3840	141	8	2.20
1950–51	Al Rollins, Tor	40	2367	70	5	1.77
1951–52	Terry Sawchuk, Det	70	4200	133	12	1.90
1952–53	Terry Sawchuk, Det	63	3780	120	9	1.90
1953–54	Harry Lumley, Tor	69	4140	128	13	1.86
1954–55	Harry Lumley, Tor	69	4140	134	8	1.94
	Terry Sawchuk, Det	68	4060	132	12	1.94
1955–56	Jacques Plante, Mtl	64	3840	119	7	1.86
1956–57	Jacques Plante, Mtl	61	3660	123	9	2.02
1957–58	Jacques Plante, Mtl	57	3386	119	9	2.11
1958–59	Jacques Plante, Mtl	67	4000	144	9	2.16
1959–60	Jacques Plante, Mtl	69	4140	175	3	2.54
1960–61	Johnny Bower, Tor	58	3480	145	2	2.50
1961–62	Jacques Plante, Mtl	70	4200	166	4	2.37
1962–63	Jacques Plante, Mtl	56	3320	138	5	2.49
1963–64	Johnny Bower, Tor	51	3009	106	5	2.11
1964–65	Johnny Bower, Tor	34	2040	81	3	2.38
1965–66	Johnny Bower, Tor	35	1998	75	3	2.25
1966–67	Glenn Hall, Chi	32	1664	66	2	2.38
1967–68	Gump Worsley, Mtl	40	2213	73	6	1.98
1968–69	Jacques Plante, StL	37	2139	70	5	1.96
1969–70	Ernie Wakely, StL	30	1651	58	4	2.11
1970–71	Jacques Plante, Tor	40	2329	73	4	1.88
1971–72	Tony Esposito, Chi	48	2780	82	9	1.77
1972–73	Ken Dryden, Mtl	54	3165	119	6	2.26
1973–74	Bernie Parent, Phil	73	4314	136	12	1.89
1974–75	Bernie Parent, Phil	68	4041	137	12	2.03
1975–76	Ken Dryden, Mtl	62	3580	121	8	2.03
1976–77	Michael Larocque, Mtl	26	1525	53	4	2.09
1977–78	Ken Dryden, Mtl	52	3071	105	5	2.05
1978–79	Ken Dryden, Mtl	47	2814	108	5	2.30

Goals Against Average (Cont.)

Season	Goaltender and Club	GP	Min	GA	SO	Avg
1979–80	Bob Sauve, Buff	32	1880	74	4	2.36
1980–81	Richard Sevigny, Mtl	33	1777	71	2	2.40
1981–82	Denis Herron, Mtl	27	1547	68	3	2.64
1982–83	Pete Peeters, Bos	62	3611	142	8	2.36
1983–84	Pat Riggin, Wash	41	2299	102	4	2.66
1984–85	Tom Barrasso, Buff	54	3248	144	5	2.66
1985–86	Bob Froese, Phil	51	2728	116	5	2.55
1986–87	Brian Hayward, Mtl	37	2178	102	1	2.81
1987–88	Pete Peeters, Wash	35	1896	88	2	2.78
1988–89	Patrick Roy, Mtl	48	2744	113	4	2.47
1989–90	Patrick Roy, Mtl	54	3173	134	3	2.53
	Mike Liut, Hart-Wash	37	2161	91	4	2.53
1990–91	Ed Belfour, Chi	74	4127	170	4	2.47
1991–92	Patrick Roy, Mtl	67	3935	155	5	2.36
1992–93	*Felix Potvin, Tor	48	2781	116	2	2.50
1993–94	Dominik Hasek, Buff	58	3358	109	7	1.95
1994–95	Dominik Hasek, Buff	41	2416	85	5	2.11
1995–96	Ron Hextall, Phil	53	3102	112	4	2.17
	Chris Osgood, Det	50	2933	106	5	2.17
1996–97	Martin Brodeur, NJ	67	3838	120	10	1.88
1997–98	Ed Belfour, Dall	61	3581	112	9	1.88
1998–99	Ron Tugnutt, Ott	43	2508	75	3	1.79

*Rookie.

Penalty Minutes

Season	Player and Club	GP	PIM	Season	Player and Club	GP	PIM
1918–19	Joe Hall, Mtl	17	85	1959–60	Carl Brewer, Tor	67	150
1919–20	Cully Wilson, Tor	23	79	1960–61	Pierre Pilote, Chi	70	165
1920–21	Bert Corbeau, Mtl	24	86	1961–62	Lou Fontinato, Mtl	54	167
1921–22	Sprague Cleghorn, Mtl	24	63	1962–63	Howie Young, Det	64	273
1922–23	Billy Boucher, Mtl	24	52	1963–64	Vic Hadfield, NYR	69	151
1923–24	Bert Corbeau, Tor	24	55	1964–65	Carl Brewer, Tor	70	177
1924–25	Billy Boucher, Mtl	30	92	1965–66	Reggie Fleming, Bos-NYR	69	166
1925–26	Bert Corbeau, Tor	36	121	1966–67	John Ferguson, Mtl	67	177
1926–27	Nels Stewart, Mtl M	44	133	1967–68	Barclay Plager, StL	49	153
1927–28	Eddie Shore, Bos	44	165	1968–69	Forbes Kennedy, Phil-Tor	77	219
1928–29	Red Dutton, Mtl M	44	139	1969–70	Keith Magnuson, Chi	76	213
1929–30	Joe Lamb, Ott	44	119	1970–71	Keith Magnuson, Chi	76	291
1930–31	Harvey Rockburn, Det	42	118	1971–72	Brian Watson, Pitt	75	212
1931–32	Red Dutton, NYA	47	107	1972–73	Dave Schultz, Phil	76	259
1932–33	Red Horner, Tor	48	144	1973–74	Dave Schultz, Phil	73	348
1933–34	Red Horner, Tor	42	126	1974–75	Dave Schultz, Phil	76	472
1934–35	Red Horner, Tor	46	125	1975–76	Steve Durbano, Pitt-KC	69	370
1935–36	Red Horner, Tor	43	167	1976–77	Dave Williams, Tor	77	338
1936–37	Red Horner, Tor	48	124	1977–78	Dave Schultz, LA-Pitt	74	405
1937–38	Red Horner, Tor	47	82	1978–79	Dave Williams, Tor	77	298
1938–39	Red Horner, Tor	48	85	1979–80	Jimmy Mann, Winn	72	287
1939–40	Red Horner, Tor	30	87	1980–81	Dave Williams, Van	77	343
1940–41	Jimmy Orlando, Det	48	99	1981–82	Paul Baxter, Pitt	76	409
1941–42	Jimmy Orlando, Det	48	81	1982–83	Randy Holt, Wash	70	275
1942–43	Jimmy Orlando, Det	40	89	1983–84	Chris Nilan, Mtl	76	338
1943–44	Mike McMahon, Mtl	42	98	1984–85	Chris Nilan, Mtl	77	358
1944–45	Pat Egan, Bos	48	86	1985–86	Joey Kocur, Det	59	377
1945–46	Jack Stewart, Det	47	73	1986–87	Tim Hunter, Cgy	73	361
1946–47	Gus Mortson, Tor	60	133	1987–88	Bob Probert, Det	74	398
1947–48	Bill Barilko, Tor	57	147	1988–89	Tim Hunter, Cgy	75	375
1948–49	Bill Ezinicki, Tor	52	145	1989–90	Basil McRae, Minn	66	351
1949–50	Bill Ezinicki, Tor	67	144	1990–91	Bob Ray, Buff	66	350
1950–51	Gus Mortson, Tor	60	142	1991–92	Mike Peluso, Chi	63	408
1951–52	Gus Kyle, Bos	69	127	1992–93	Marty McSorley, LA	81	399
1952–53	Maurice Richard, Mtl	70	112	1993–94	Tie Domi, Winn	81	347
1953–54	Gus Mortson, Chi	68	132	1994–95	Enrico Ciccone, TB	41	225
1954–55	Fern Flaman, Bos	70	150	1995–96	Matthew Barnaby, Buff	73	335
1955–56	Lou Fontinato, NYR	70	202	1996–97	Gino Odjick, Van	70	371
1956–57	Gus Mortson, Chi	70	147	1997–98	Donald Brashear, Van	77	372
1957–58	Lou Fontinato, NYR	70	152	1998–99	Rob Ray, Buff	76	261
1958–59	Ted Lindsay, Chi	70	184				

NHL All-Star Game

First played in 1947, this game was scheduled before the start of the regular season and used to match the defending Stanley Cup Champions against a squad made up of the league All-stars from other teams. In 1966 the games were moved to mid-season, although there was no game that year. The format changed to a conference versus conference showdown in 1969.

Results

Year	Site	Score	MVP	Attendance
1947	Toronto	All-Stars 4, Toronto 3	None named	14,169
1948	Chicago	All-Stars 3, Toronto 1	None named	12,794
1949	Toronto	All-Stars 3, Toronto 1	None named	13,541
1950	Detroit	Detroit 7, All-Stars 1	None named	9,166
1951	Toronto	1st team 2, 2nd team 2	None named	11,469
1952	Detroit	1st team 1, 2nd team 1	None named	10,680
1953	Montreal	All-Stars 3, Montreal 1	None named	14,153
1954	Detroit	All-Stars 2, Detroit 2	None named	10,689
1955	Detroit	Detroit 3, All-Stars 1	None named	10,111
1956	Montreal	All-Stars 1, Montreal 1	None named	13,095
1957	Montreal	All-Stars 5, Montreal 3	None named	13,003
1958	Montreal	Montreal 6, All-Stars 3	None named	13,989
1959	Montreal	Montreal 6, All-Stars 1	None named	13,818
1960	Montreal	All-Stars 2, Montreal 1	None named	13,949
1961	Chicago	All-Stars 3, Chicago 1	None named	14,534
1962	Toronto	Toronto 4, All-Stars 1	Eddie Shack, Tor	14,236
1963	Toronto	All-Stars 3, Toronto 3	Frank Mahovlich, Tor	14,034
1964	Toronto	All-Stars 3, Toronto 2	Jean Beliveau, Mtl	14,232
1965	Montreal	All-Stars 5, Montreal 2	Gordie Howe, Det	13,529
1967	Montreal	Montreal 3, All-Stars 0	Henri Richard, Mtl	14,284
1968	Toronto	Toronto 4, All-Stars 3	Bruce Gamble, Tor	15,753
1969	Montreal	East 3, West 3	Frank Mahovlich, Det	16,260
1970	St Louis	East 4, West 1	Bobby Hull, Chi	16,587
1971	Boston	West 2, East 1	Bobby Hull, Chi	14,790
1972	Minnesota	East 3, West 2	Bobby Orr, Bos	15,423
1973	NY Rangers	East 5, West 4	Greg Polis, Pitt	16,986
1974	Chicago	West 6, East 4	Garry Unger, StL	16,426
1975	Montreal	Wales 7, Campbell 1	Syl Apps Jr, Pitt	16,080
1976	Philadelphia	Wales 7, Campbell 5	Pete Mahovlich, Mtl	16,436
1977	Vancouver	Wales 4, Campbell 3	Rick Martin, Buff	15,607
1978	Buffalo	Wales 3, Campbell 2 (OT)	Billy Smith, NYI	16,433
1980	Detroit	Wales 6, Campbell 3	Reg Leach, Phil	21,002
1981	Los Angeles	Campbell 4, Wales 1	Mike Liut, StL	15,761
1982	Washington	Wales 4, Campbell 2	Mike Bossy, NYI	18,130
1983	NY Islanders	Campbell 9, Wales 3	Wayne Gretzky, Edm	15,230
1984	NJ Devils	Wales 7, Campbell 6	Don Maloney, NYR	18,939
1985	Calgary	Wales 6, Campbell 4	Mario Lemieux, Pitt	16,825
1986	Hartford	Wales 4, Campbell 3 (OT)	Grant Fuhr, Edm	15,100
1988	St Louis	Wales 6, Campbell 5 (OT)	Mario Lemieux, Pitt	17,878
1989	Edmonton	Campbell 9, Wales 5	Wayne Gretzky, LA	17,503
1990	Pittsburgh	Wales 12, Campbell 7	Mario Lemieux, Pitt	16,236
1991	Chicago	Campbell 11, Wales 5	Vince Damphousse, Tor	18,472
1992	Philadelphia	Campbell 10, Wales 6	Brett Hull, StL	17,380
1993	Montreal	Wales 16, Campbell 6	Mike Gartner, NYR	17,137
1994	NY Rangers	East 9, West 8	Mike Richter, NYR	18,200
1996	Boston	East 5, West 4	Ray Bourque, Bos	17,565
1997	San Jose	East 11, West 7	Mark Recchi, Mtl	17,565
1998	Vancouver	North America 8, World 7	Teemu Selanne, Ana (World)	18,422
1999	Tampa Bay	North America 8, World 6	Wayne Gretzky, NYR (N America)	19,758

Note: The Challenge Cup, a series between the NHL All-Stars and the Soviet Union, was played instead of the All-Star Game in 1979. Eight years later, Rendez-Vous '87, a two-game series matching the Soviet Union and the NHL All-Stars, replaced the All-Star Game. The 1995 NHL All-Star game was cancelled due to a labor dispute. The 1998 NHL All-Star game, billed as a preview to the 1998 Winter Olympics in Nagano, Japan, matched North Amercian–born All-Stars and All-Stars born elsewhere.

Hockey Hall of Fame

Located in Toronto, the Hockey Hall of Fame was officially opened on August 26, 1961. The current chairman is William C. Hay. There are, at present, 306 members of the Hockey Hall of Fame—209 players, 84 "builders," and 14 on-ice officials. (One member, Alan Eagleson, resigned from the Hall 3-25-98.) To be eligible, player and referee/linesman candidates should have been out of the game for three years, but the Hall's Board of Directors can make exceptions.

Players

Sid Abel (1969)
Jack Adams (1959)
Charles (Syl) Apps (1961)
George Armstrong (1975)
Irvine (Ace) Bailey (1975)
Donald H. (Dan) Bain (1945)
Hobey Baker (1945)
Bill Barber (1990)
Marty Barry (1965)
Andy Bathgate (1978)
Bobby Bauer (1996)
Jean Beliveau (1972)
Clint Benedict (1965)
Douglas Bentley (1964)
Max Bentley (1966)
Hector (Toe) Blake (1966)
Leo Boivin (1986)
Dickie Boon (1952)
Mike Bossy (1991)
Emile (Butch) Bouchard (1966)
Frank Boucher (1958)
George (Buck) Boucher (1960)
Johnny Bower (1976)
Russell Bowie (1945)
Frank Brimsek (1966)
Harry L. (Punch) Broadbent (1962)
Walter (Turk) Broda (1967)
John Bucyk (1981)
Billy Burch (1974)
Harry Cameron (1962)
Gerry Cheevers (1985)
Francis (King) Clancy (1958)
Aubrey (Dit) Clapper (1947)
Bobby Clarke (1987)
Sprague Cleghorn (1958)
Neil Colville (1967)
Charlie Conacher (1961)
Lionel Conacher (1994)
Roy Conacher (1998)
Alex Connell (1958)
Bill Cook (1952)
Fred (Bun) Cook (1995)
Arthur Coulter (1974)
Yvan Cournoyer (1982)
Bill Cowley (1968)
Samuel (Rusty) Crawford (1962)
Jack Darragh (1962)
Allan M. (Scotty) Davidson (1950)
Clarence (Hap) Day (1961)
Alex Delvecchio (1977)
Cy Denneny (1959)
Marcel Dionne (1992)
Gordie Drillon (1975)
Charles Drinkwater (1950)

Ken Dryden (1983)
Woody Dumart (1992)
Thomas Dunderdale (1974)
Bill Durnan (1964)
Mervyn A. (Red) Dutton (1958)
Cecil (Babe) Dye (1970)
Phil Esposito (1984)
Tony Esposito (1988)
Arthur F. Farrell (1965)
Ferdinand (Fern) Flaman (1990)
Frank Foyston (1958)
Frank Frederickson (1958)
Bill Gadsby (1970)
Bob Gainey (1992)
Chuck Gardiner (1945)
Herb Gardiner (1958)
Jimmy Gardner (1962)
Bernie (Boom Boom) Geoffrion (1972)
Eddie Gerard (1945)
Ed Giacomin (1987)
Rod Gilbert (1982)
Hamilton (Billy) Gilmour (1962)
Frank (Moose) Goheen (1952)
Ebenezer R. (Ebbie) Goodfellow (1963)
Michel Goulet (1998)
Mike Grant (1950)
Wilfred (Shorty) Green (1962)
Wayne Gretzky (1999)
Si Griffis (1950)
George Hainsworth (1961)
Glenn Hall (1975)
Joe Hall (1961)
Doug Harvey (1973)
George Hay (1958)
William (Riley) Hern (1962)
Bryan Hextall (1969)
Harry (Hap) Holmes (1972)
Tom Hooper (1962)
George (Red) Horner (1965)
Miles (Tim) Horton (1977)
Gordie Howe (1972)
Syd Howe (1965)
Harry Howell (1979)
Bobby Hull (1983)
John (Bouse) Hutton (1962)
Harry M. Hyland (1962)
James (Dick) Irvin (1958)
Harvey (Busher) Jackson (1971)
Ernest (Moose) Johnson (1952)
Ivan (Ching) Johnson (1958)
Tom Johnson (1970)
Aurel Joliat (1947)
Gordon (Duke) Keats (1958)

Leonard (Red) Kelly (1969)
Ted (Teeder) Kennedy (1966)
Dave Keon (1986)
Elmer Lach (1966)
Guy Lafleur (1988)
Edouard (Newsy) Lalonde (1950)
Jacques Laperriere (1987)
Guy LaPointe (1993)
Edgar Laprade (1993)
Reed Larson (1996)
Jean (Jack) Laviolette (1962)
Hugh Lehman (1958)
Jacques Lemaire (1984)
Mario Lemieux (1997)
Percy LeSueur (1961)
Herbert A. Lewis (1989)
Ted Lindsay (1966)
Harry Lumley (1980)
Lanny McDonald (1992)
Frank McGee (1945)
Billy McGimsie (1962)
George McNamara (1958)
Duncan (Mickey) MacKay (1952)
Frank Mahovlich (1981)
Joe Malone (1950)
Sylvio Mantha (1960)
Jack Marshall (1965)
Fred G. (Steamer) Maxwell (1962)
Stan Mikita (1983)
Dicky Moore (1974)
Patrick (Paddy) Moran (1958)
Howie Morenz (1945)
Billy Mosienko (1965)
Frank Nighbor (1947)
Reg Noble (1962)
Herbert (Buddy) O'Connor (1988)
Harry Oliver (1967)
Bert Olmstead (1985)
Bobby Orr (1979)
Bernie Parent (1984)
Brad Park (1988)
Lester Patrick (1947)
Lynn Patrick (1980)
Gilbert Perreault (1990)
Tommy Phillips (1945)
Pierre Pilote (1975)
Didier (Pit) Pitre (1962)
Jacques Plante (1978)
Denis Potvin (1991)
Walter (Babe) Pratt (1966)
Joe Primeau (1963)
Marcel Pronovost (1978)
Bob Pulford (1991)
Harvey Pulford (1945)

Hockey Hall of Fame (Cont.)

Players (Cont.)

Hubert (Bill) Quackenbush (1976)
Frank Rankin (1961)
Jean Ratelle (1985)
Claude (Chuck) Rayner (1973)
Kenneth Reardon (1966)
Henri Richard (1979)
Maurice (Rocket) Richard (1961)
George Richardson (1950)
Gordon Roberts (1971)
Larry Robinson (1995)
Art Ross (1945)
Blair Russel (1965)
Ernest Russell (1965)
Jack Ruttan (1962)
Borje Salming (1996)
Serge Savard (1986)
Terry Sawchuk (1971)
Fred Scanlan (1965)
Milt Schmidt (1961)
Dave (Sweeney) Schriner (1962)
Earl Seibert (1963)
Oliver Seibert (1961)
Eddie Shore (1947)
Steve Shutt (1993)
Albert C. (Babe) Siebert (1964)
Harold (Bullet Joe) Simpson (1962)
Daryl Sittler (1989)
Alfred E. Smith (1962)
Billy Smith (1993)
Clint Smith (1991)
Reginald (Hooley) Smith (1972)
Thomas Smith (1973)
Allan Stanley (1981)
Russell (Barney) Stanley
   (1962)
Peter Stastny (1998)
John (Black Jack) Stewart
   (1964)
Nels Stewart (1962)
Bruce Stuart (1961)
Hod Stuart (1945)
Frederic (Cyclone) (O.B.E.)
   Taylor (1947)
Cecil R. (Tiny) Thompson
   (1959)
Vladislav Tretiak (1989)
Harry J. Trihey (1950)
Bryan Trottier (1997)
Norm Ullman (1982)
Georges Vezina (1945)
Jack Walker (1960)
Marty Walsh (1962)
Harry Watson (1994)
Harry E. Watson (1962)
Ralph (Cooney) Weiland (1971)
Harry Westwick (1962)
Fred Whitcroft (1962)
Gordon (Phat) Wilson (1962)
Lorne (Gump) Worsley (1980)
Roy Worters (1969)

Builders

Charles Adams (1960)
Weston W. Adams (1972)
Thomas (Frank) Ahearn (1962)
John (Bunny) Ahearne (1977)
Montagu Allan (C.V.O.) (1945)
Keith Allen (1992)
Al Arbour (1996)
Harold Ballard (1977)
David Bauer (1989)
John Bickell (1978)
Scott Bowman (1991)
George V. Brown (1961)
Walter A. Brown (1962)
Frank Buckland (1975)
Jack Butterfield (1980)
Frank Calder (1947)
Angus D. Campbell (1964)
Clarence Campbell (1966)
Joe Cattarinich (1977)
Bob Cole (1996)
Joseph (Leo) Dandurand (1963)
Francis Dilio (1964)
George S. Dudley (1958)
James A. Dunn (1968)
Robert Alan Eagleson (1989–98*)
Sergio Gambucci (1996)
Emile Francis (1982)
Jack Gibson (1976)
Tommy Gorman (1963)
Frank Griffiths (1993)
William Hanley (1986)
Charles Hay (1974)
James C. Hendy (1968)
Foster Hewitt (1965)
William Hewitt (1947)
Fred J. Hume (1962)
George (Punch) Imlach (1984)
Tommy Ivan (1974)
William M. Jennings (1975)
Bob Johnson (1992)
Gordon W. Juckes (1979)
John Kilpatrick (1960)
Seymour Knox III (1993)
George Leader (1969)
Robert LeBel (1970)
Thomas F. Lockhart (1965)
Paul Loicq (1961)
Frederic McLaughlin (1963)
John Mariucci (1985)
Frank Mathers (1992)
John (Jake) Milford (1984)
Hartland Molson (1973)
Scotty Morrison (1999)
Mngr. Athol (Pere) Murray (1998)
Francis Nelson (1947)
Bruce A. Norris (1969)
James Norris, Sr. (1958)
James D. Norris (1962)
William M. Northey (1947)
John O'Brien (1962)

Builders (Cont.)

Brian O'Neill (1994)
Fred Page (1993)
Craig Patrick (1996)
Frank Patrick (1958)
Allan W. Pickard (1958)
Rudy Pilous (1985)
Norman (Bud) Poile (1990)
Samuel Pollock (1978)
Donat Raymond (1958)
John Robertson (1947)
Claude C. Robinson (1947)
Philip D. Ross (1976)
Gunther Sabetzki (1995)
Glen Sather (1997)
Frank J. Selke (1960)
Harry Sinden (1983)
Frank D. Smith (1962)
Conn Smythe (1958)
Edward M. Snider (1988)
Lord Stanley of Preston
   (G.C.B.) (1945)
James T. Sutherland (1947)
Anatoli V. Tarasov (1974)
Bill Torrey (1995)
Lloyd Turner (1958)
William Tutt (1978)
Carl Potter Voss (1974)
Fred C. Waghorn (1961)
Arthur Wirtz (1971)
Bill Wirtz (1976)
John A. Ziegler, Jr. (1987)

Referees/Linesmen

Neil Armstrong (1991)
John Ashley (1981)
William L. Chadwick (1964)
John D'Amico (1993)
Chaucer Elliott (1961)
George Hayes (1988)
Robert W. Hewitson (1963)
Fred J. (Mickey) Ion (1961)
Matt Pavelich (1987)
Mike Rodden (1962)
J. Cooper Smeaton (1961)
Roy (Red) Storey (1967)
Frank Udvari (1973)
Andy van Hellemond (1999)

Note: Year of election to the Hall of Fame is in parentheses after the member's name.
*Eagleson resigned from Hall March 25, 1998.

Tennis

French and U.S. Open
champion Andre Agassi

Ebb and Flow

In a season of extremes, tennis's profile rose and fell along with the fortunes of its brightest stars

BY B.J. SCHECTER

THE TIDES of tennis can shift in an instant. One minute the game seems like it's ready to disappear from the sporting landscape, swallowed by a wave of anonymous players; the next it shoots back to the forefront, buttressed by compelling stories and exciting new rivalries. In 1999 we shunted back and forth between these extremes. We had everything from Pete Sampras the no-show at the Australian Open to Pete Sampras the legendarily dominant champion at Wimbledon; Andre Agassi the has-been to Andre Agassi the remarkable French and U.S. Open champion; Serena Williams the lesser-known younger sister of Venus Williams to Serena Williams the surprising first of the two to win a Grand Slam title; and Martina Hingis the brat to, well, Martina Hingis the brat.

But, oh, Serena. For years she had been better known as the Williams sister who was pretty good but not quite at the level of Venus. The pair became the first sister act to meet in a professional-level tournament final in 115 years when they both advanced to the title match at the Lipton Championships in March. Venus won 6–1, 4–6, 6–4, but the sisters' voluble father, Richard, along with a few observers, had long contended that Serena would be the better player. Most tennis fans just brushed it off as hype. Venus had a higher ranking, more experience and more poise. Surely she would be the first to win a Grand Slam.

Throughout 1999 the Williams sisters arranged their schedules so that they would play in different tournaments whenever possible. On Feb. 28 they won titles on the same day: Venus took the IGA Superthrift in Oklahoma City, and Serena won the Open Gaz de France in Paris. They avoided one another in the draws of the first three Grand Slams of the year but were on a crash course in the U.S. Open. Before the tournament began Richard declared that there would be an all-Williams final. People mostly chuckled and accused him of seeking more publicity; Hingis called him a big mouth. But he was nearly right.

On Friday, Sept. 10, the sisters played

Serena surprised many—her father not among them—by becoming the first of the Williams sisters to win a Slam.

back-to-back semifinal matches in what was the most exhilarating day of the year in tennis. First, after waiting out a five-hour rain delay, Serena displayed power and patience while dispatching defending champion Lindsay Davenport 6–4, 1–6, 6–4. Then Venus and Hingis battled like two heavyweights going toe to toe. Hingis escaped with a three-set victory. After watching her sister fall to the top-ranked player in the world, Serena retreated to the practice courts. "She's outside practicing?" a dumbfounded Hingis said when she heard the news.

The next day, with Venus watching from the family box with a hood over her head, Serena outwilled and over-powered Hingis 6–3, 7–6 (7–4) to become the first African-American woman since Althea Gibson (1958) to win a Grand Slam singles title and the first African-American to do so since Arthur Ashe in 1975. Off the court Venus and Serena are best friends, but Venus was sullen and could barely clap as she watched her sister accept the championship trophy. "She thinks since she's the oldest, she should have been the first, that maybe she should have been tougher," said their mother, Oracene. "That's something they've thought about all their lives: Meeting in the final, two sisters. She feels she let everybody down."

Venus hardly let anyone down in 1999; Serena simply stole the spotlight. She possesses a better forehand, covers more of the court and has a better second serve than her sister. She reeled off 16 consecutive wins during the year, a streak that was broken when she lost to Venus in the Lipton final. Richard Williams's prediction may not have come true this time, but the Williams sisters showed that there may be many all-Williams Grand Slam finals in the future.

If Serena was a star born on tour this year, then Agassi was a star reborn. Yes, he made a mini-comeback ·in 1998, but as '99

approached it appeared his best days were behind him. He was inconsistent, often out of shape and out of focus. Then in January, Agassi told his personal trainer he was ready to do whatever it took to get back to a championship level. Agassi worked harder than ever, training at his home in Las Vegas and enduring the 112° heat while repeatedly running up a 320-yard hill he called Magic Mountain. For a man who had sunk as low as 141st in the rankings, Agassi came full circle in '99, winning the French Open, the U.S. Open and losing in the final of Wimbledon.

He was just what the men's tour needed. Before the French Open, Yevgeny Kafelnikov was crowned the No. 1 player in the world and then lost six straight first-round matches. After one lackluster defeat he said, "I don't really care how I play in Hamburg, Rome, whatever." The next day, former No. 1 Marcelo Ríos declared the

ATP tour "pretty boring" and said, "There's nothing to do. They don't do anything to make it fun." A stronger and fitter-than-ever Agassi completed stage 1 of his comeback with an emotional victory over Andrei Medvedev to win the French Open and become the fifth man—and the first since Rod Laver—to win all four slams in his career.

On July 4, fittingly enough, Agassi met Pete Sampras in an all-American Wimbledon final. Throughout the tournament, Agassi and Sampras dressed at nearby lockers but never discussed their seemingly imminent meeting. The day before the final Agassi turned to Sampras and said, "When I was 141 in the world, you didn't think you would ever have to go to sleep at night thinking about me, huh?"

But Sampras had little trouble with Agassi on this day, overpowering him in a three-set victory to earn his record-tying 12th Grand Slam title. If Sampras hadn't withdrawn with a back injury prior to the tournament, the pair may well have met again in the U.S. Open final. As it happened, Agassi overcame an improved Todd Martin in the final, 6–4, 6–7, 6–7, 6–3, 6–2, and was once again the top player in the world.

The women's game was characterized by a frothy combination of power tennis and soap opera drama. At the Australian Open unseeded 19-year-old Amelie Mauresmo of France reached the final—where she lost to Hingis in straight sets—but drew more attention by coming out of the closet and going out of her way to be openly affectionate with her girlfriend. The muscular Mauresmo surprised Davenport in the semifinal with her overwhelming power, which prompted Davenport to say she thought she was playing a guy. The budding controversy picked up more momentum when Hingis weighed in. "Everyone makes her own choices, but you don't have to show everything you do," Hingis said. "They are hugging and kissing all the time, and I'm just, 'O.K., there's a limit.' "

It was Hingis's turn to be at the center of the storm when she played Steffi Graf in the French Open final. She lost her cool several times when calls didn't go her way and at one point marched around the net to Graf's baseline to point out a ball mark. "I've never seen that before," said Graf, who won the match for her 22nd Grand Slam title. "Everybody knows you're never supposed to do that." Then in a childish temper tantrum, Hingis sat in her seat pouting before returning to play after a point penalty. Hingis wasn't done. After the match she bolted to the locker room and refused to return for the awards ceremony until her mother dragged her out. But Hingis's display couldn't mar the final major victory for the great Graf, who would announce her retirement before the U.S. Open.

Eighteen-year-old Alexandra Stevenson of the U.S. made history at the All England Club, becoming the first woman qualifier to make the semifinals. But as was the norm on the women's tour in 1999, she didn't do so without controversy. First, her mother, Samantha, made waves, winning a dispute with Wimbledon over prize money and then describing the tour as full of racist attitudes and claiming Alexandra needed protection from hazing by other women. A few days later the *Fort Lauderdale Sun Sentinel* broke a story claiming that basketball Hall of Famer Julius Erving was listed as the father on Stevenson's birth certificate. Erving, who later confirmed the story, said he met Samantha Stevenson while he was playing for the Philadelphia 76ers and she was a sportswriter covering the team.

But soap operas and controversies couldn't overshadow the exciting style of tennis the women's game offered. The rangy, powerful Davenport won Wimbledon and emerged as one of the top two players in the world. Serena and Venus Williams brought power to a new level and in less than three years have injected new energy into the sport. CBS's rating for the U.S. Open women's final increased by 100%, and the Williams sisters, Davenport and Hingis signaled a bright future for the sport. Providing thrills both on and off the court, those four, along with Agassi, made sure that '99 finished at high tide.

FOR THE RECORD·1998−1999

1999 Grand Slam Champions

Australian Open
Men's Singles

	Winner	Finalist	Score
Quarterfinals	Nicolas Lapentti	Karol Kucera (7)	7–6 (7–4), 6–7 (6–8), 6–2, 0–6, 8–6
	Thomas Enqvist	Marc Rosset	6–3, 6–4, 6–4
	Yevgeny Kafelnikov (10)	Todd Martin (15)	6–2, 7–6 (7–1), 6–2
	Tommy Haas	Vincent Spadea	7–6 (7–5), 7–5, 6–3
Semifinals	Thomas Enqvist	Nicolas Lapentti	6–3, 7–5, 6–1
	Yevgeny Kafelnikov	Tommy Haas	6–3, 6–4, 7–5
Final	Yevgeny Kafelnikov	Thomas Enqvist	4–6, 6–0, 6–3, 7–6 (7–1)

Women's Singles

	Winner	Finalist	Score
Quarterfinals	Lindsay Davenport (1)	Venus Williams (5)	6–4, 6–0
	Amelie Mauresmo	Dominique Van Roost (11)	6–3, 7–6 (7–3)
	Martina Hingis (2)	Mary Pierce (7)	6–3, 6–4
	Monica Seles (6)	Steffi Graf (10)	7–5, 6–1
Semifinals	Amelie Mauresmo	Lindsay Davenport	4–6, 7–5, 7–5
	Martina Hingis	Monica Seles	6–2, 6–4
Final	Martina Hingis	Amelie Mauresmo	6–2, 6–3

Doubles

	Winner	Finalist	Score
Men's Final	Jonas Bjorkman/ Patrick Rafter (5)	Mahesh Bhupathi/ Leander Paes (1)	6–3, 4–6, 6–4, 6–7 (10–12), 6–4
Women's Final	Martina Hingis/ Anna Kournikova (3)	Lindsay Davenport/ Natasha Zvereva (1)	7–5, 6–3
Mixed Final	David Adams/ Mariaan de Swardt	Max Mirnyi/ Serena Williams	6–4, 4–6, 7–6 (7–5)

French Open
Men's Singles

	Winner	Finalist	Score
Quarterfinals	Andre Agassi (13)	Marcelo Filippini	6–2, 6–2, 6–0
	Dominik Hrbaty	Marcelo Rios (9)	7–6 (7–4), 6–2, 6–7 (6–8), 6–3
	Fernando Meligeni	Alex Corretja (6)	6–2, 6–2, 6–0
	Andrei Medvedev	Gustavo Kuerten (8)	7–5, 6–4, 6–4
Semifinals	Andrei Medvedev	Fernando Meligeni	7–5, 3–6, 6–4, 7–6
	Andre Agassi	Dominik Hrbaty	6–4, 7–6 (8–6), 3–6, 6–4
Final	Andre Agassi	Andrei Medvedev	1–6, 2–6, 6–4, 6–3, 6–4

Women's Singles

	Winner	Finalist	Score
Quarterfinals	Arantxa Sánchez Vicario (7)	Sylvia Plischke	6–2, 6–4
	Martina Hingis (1)	Barbara Schwartz	6–2, 6–2
	Steffi Graf (6)	Lindsay Davenport (2)	6–1, 6–7 (5–7), 6–3
	Monica Seles (3)	Conchita Martinez	6–1, 6–4
Semifinals	Martina Hingis	Arantxa Sánchez Vicario	6–3, 6–2
	Steffi Graf	Monica Seles	6–7, 6–3, 6–4
Final	Steffi Graf	Martina Hingis	4–6, 7–5, 6–2

Note: Seedings in parentheses.

French Open *(Cont.)*

Doubles

	Winner	Finalist	Score
Men's Final	Mahesh Bhupathi/ Leander Paes (1)	Goran Ivanisevic/ Jeff Tarango	6–2, 7–5
Women's Final	Serena Williams/ Venus Williams (9)	Martina Hingis/ Anna Kournikova (2)	6–3, 6–7 (2–7), 8–6
Mixed Final	Katarina Srebotnik/ Piet Norval	Larisa Neiland/ Rick Leach (6)	6–3, 3–6, 6–3

Wimbledon

Men's Singles

	Winner	Finalist	Score
Quarterfinals	Pete Sampras (1)	Mark Philippoussis (7)	4–6, 2–1 retired
	Tim Henman (6)	Cedric Pioline	6–4, 6–2, 4–6, 6–3
	Andre Agassi (4)	Gustavo Kuerten (11)	6–3, 6–4, 6–4
	Patrick Rafter (2)	Todd Martin (8)	6–3, 6–7, 7–6 (7–5), 7–6 (7–3)
Semifinals	Pete Sampras	Tim Henman	3–6, 6–4, 6–3, 6–4
	Andre Agassi	Patrick Rafter	7–5, 7–6 (7–5), 6–2
Final	Pete Sampras	Andre Agassi	6–3, 6–4, 7–5

Women's Singles

	Winner	Finalist	Score
Quarterfinals	Steffi Graf (2)	Venus Williams (6)	6–2, 3–6, 6–4
	Lindsay Davenport (3)	Jana Novotna (5)	6–3, 6–4
	Alexandra Stevenson	Jelena Dokic	6–3, 1–6, 6–3
	Mirjana Lucic	Nathalie Tauziat	4–6, 6–4, 7–5
Semifinals	Lindsay Davenport	Alexandra Stevenson	6–1, 6–1
	Steffi Graf	Mirjana Lucic	6–7 (3–7), 6–4, 6–3
Final	Lindsay Davenport	Steffi Graf	6–4, 7–5

Doubles

	Winner	Finalist	Score
Men's Final	Mahesh Bhupathi/ Leander Paes (1)	Paul Haarhuis/ Jared Palmer (8)	6–7 (10–12), 6–3, 6–4, 7–6 (7–4)
Women's Final	Lindsay Davenport/ Corina Morariu (7)	Mariaan De Swardt/ Elena Tatarkova (9)	6–4, 6–4
Mixed Final	Leander Paes/ Lisa Raymond (1)	Jonas Bjorkman/ Anna Kournikova (3)	6–4, 3–6, 6–3

U.S. Open

Men's Singles

	Winner	Finalist	Score
Quarterfinals	Andre Agassi (2)	Nicolas Escude	7–6 (7–3), 6–3, 6–4
	Yevgeny Kafelnikov (3)	Richard Krajicek (12)	7–6 (7–0), 7–6 (7–4), 3–6, 1–6, 7–6 (7–5)
	Todd Martin (7)	Slava Dosedel	6–3, 5–7, 6–4, 6–4
	Cedric Pioline	Gustavo Kuerten (5)	4–6, 7–6 (8–6), 7–6 (16–14), 7–6 (10–8)
Semifinals	Andre Agassi	Yevgeny Kafelnikov	1–6, 6–3, 6–3, 6–3
	Todd Martin	Cedric Pioline	6–4, 6–1, 6–2
Final	Andre Agassi	Todd Martin	6–4, 6–7 (5–7), 6–7 (2–7), 6–3, 6–2

Note: Seedings in parentheses.

U.S. Open *(Cont.)*
Women's Singles

	Winner	Finalist	Score
Quarterfinals	Martina Hingis (1)	Anke Huber	6–2, 6–0
	Venus Williams (3)	Barbara Schett (12)	6–4, 6–3
	Serena Williams (7)	Monica Seles (4)	4–6, 6–3, 6–2
	Lindsay Davenport (2)	Mary Pierce (5)	6–2, 3–6, 7–5
Semifinals	Martina Hingis	Venus Williams	6–1, 4–6, 6–3
	Serena Williams	Lindsay Davenport	6–4, 1–6, 6–4
Final	Serena Williams	Martina Hingis	6–3, 7–6 (7–4)

Doubles

	Winner	Finalist	Score
Men's Final	Sebastian Lareau/ Alex O'Brien (11)	Mahesh Bhupathi/ Leander Paes (1)	7–6 (9–7), 6–4
Women's Final	Serena Williams/ Venus Williams (5)	Chanda Rubin/ Sandrine Testud	4–6, 6–1, 6–4
Mixed Final	Ai Sugiyama/ Mahesh Bhupathi (2)	Kimberly Po/ Donald Johnson	6–4, 6–4

Major Tournament Results

Men's Tour (late 1998)

Date	Tournament	Site	Winner	Finalist	Score
Oct 5–11	Swiss Indoors	Basel, Switzerland	Tim Henman	Andre Agassi	6–4, 6–3, 3–6, 6–4
Oct 5–11	Shanghai Open	Shanghai	Michael Chang	Goran Ivanisevic	4–6, 6–1, 6–2
Oct 12–18	CA Tennis Trophy	Vienna	Pete Sampras	Karol Kucera	6–3, 7–6 (7–3), 6–1
Oct 12–18	Heineken Open	Singapore	Marcelo Rios	Mark Woodforde	6–4, 6–2
Oct 19–25	Grand Prix de Tennis	Lyon, France	Alex Corretja	Tommy Haas	2–6, 7–6 (8–6), 6–1
Oct 19–26	Czech Indoors	Ostrava, Czech Republic	Andre Agassi	Jan Kroslak	6–2, 3–6, 6–3
Oct 26–Nov 1	Eurocard Open	Stuttgart, Germany	Richard Krajicek	Y. Kafelnikov	6–4, 6–3, 6–3
Nov 2–8	Paris Open	Paris	Greg Rusedski	Pete Sampras	6–4, 7–6 (7–4), 6–3
Nov 9–15	Stockholm Open	Stockholm	Todd Martin	T. Johansson	6–3, 6–4, 6–4
Nov 9–15	Kremlin Cup	Moscow	Y. Kafelnikov	Goran Ivanisevic	7–6 (7–2), 7–6 (7–5)
Nov 23–29	ATP Tour Championship	Hannover, Germany	Alex Corretja	Carlos Moya	3–6, 3–6, 7–5, 6–3 7–5

Men's Tour (Through September 27, 1999)

Date	Tournament	Site	Winner	Finalist	Score
Jan 4–10	Qatar Open	Doha, Qatar	Rainer Schuttler	Tim Henman	6–4, 5–7, 6–1
Jan 18–31	Australian Open	Melbourne	Y. Kafelnikov	Thomas Enqvist	4–6, 6–0, 6–3, 7–6 (7–1)
Feb 1–7	Marseille Open	Marseille, France	Fabrice Santoro	Arnaud Clement	6–3, 4–6, 6–4
Feb 8–14	Dubai Open	Dubai, UAE	Jerome Golmard	Nicolas Kiefer	6–4, 6–2
Feb 15–21	ABN/Amro Tournament	Rotterdam, Amsterdam	Y. Kafelnikov	Tim Henman	6–2, 7–6 (7–3)
Feb 15–21	Kroger St. Jude	Memphis	Tommy Haas	Jim Courier	6–4, 6–1
Feb 22–28	Guardian Direct Cup	London	Richard Krajicek	Greg Rusedski	7–6 (8–6), 6–7 (7–5) 7–5
Mar 8–14	Champions Cup	Indian Wells, California	M. Philippoussis	Carlos Moya	5–7, 6–4, 6–4, 4–6, 6–2
Mar 15–20	Lipton Championships	Key Biscayne, Florida	Richard Krajicek	S. Grosjean	4–6, 6–1, 6–2, 7–5
Apr 5–11	Estoril Open	Estoril, Portugal	Albert Costa	Todd Martin	7–6 (7–4), 2–6, 6–3
Apr 12–18	Japan Open	Tokyo	Nicolas Kiefer	Wayne Ferreira	7–6 (7–5), 7–5

Men's Tour (Through September 27, 1999) (Cont.)

Date	Tournament	Site	Winner	Finalist	Score
Apr 12–18	Open Seat Godo	Barcelona	Felix Mantilla	Karim Alami	7–6 (7–2), 6–3, 6–3
Apr 19–25	Monte Carlo Open	Monte Carlo	Gustavo Kuerten	Marcelo Rios	6–4, 2–1 retired
Apr 26–May 2	BMW Open	Munich	Franco Squillari	Andrei Pavel	6–4, 6–3
May 3–9	German Open	Hamburg	Marcelo Rios	Mariano Zabaleta	6–7 (5–7), 7–5, 5–7, 7–6 (7–5), 6–2
May 10–16	Italian Open	Rome	Gustavo Kuerten	Patrick Rafter	6–4, 7–5, 7–6 (8–6)
May 24–June 6	French Open	Paris	Andre Agassi	Andrei Medvedev	1–6, 2–6, 6–4, 6–3, 6–4
June 7–13	Gerry Weber Open	Halle, Germany	Nicolas Kiefer	Nicklas Kulti	6–3, 6–2
June 7–13	Stella Artois Cup	London	Pete Sampras	Tim Henman	6–7 (1–7), 6–4, 7–6 (7–4)
June 21–July 4	Wimbledon	Wimbledon	Pete Sampras	Andre Agassi	6–3, 6–4, 7–5
July 5–11	Swiss Open	Gstaad, Switzerland	Albert Costa	Nicolas Lapentti	7–6 (7–4), 6–3, 6–4
July 19–25	Mercedes Cup	Stuttgart, Germany	Magnus Norman	Tommy Haas	6–7 (6–8), 4–6, 7–6 (9–7), 6–0, 6–3
July 26–Aug 1	Generali Open	Kitzbuhel, Austria	Albert Costa	Fernando Vicente	7–5, 6–2, 6–7 (5–7), 7–6 (7–4)
Aug 2–8	du Maurier Open	Montreal	T. Johansson	Y. Kafelnikov	1–6, 6–3, 6–3
Aug 9–15	ATP Championship	Cincinnati	Pete Sampras	Patrick Rafter	7–6 (9–7), 6–3
Aug 16–22	RCA Championships	Indianapolis	Nicolas Lapentti	Vincent Spadea	4–6, 6–4, 6–4
Aug 16–22	Legg Mason Classic	Washington, DC	Andre Agassi	Y. Kafelnikov	7–6 (7–3), 6–1
Aug 30–Sep 12	U.S. Open	New York City	Andre Agassi	Todd Martin	6–4, 6–7 (5–7), 6–7 (2–7), 6–3, 6–2

Women's Tour (Late 1998)

Date	Tournament	Site	Winner	Finalist	Score
Oct 12–18	European Indoors	Zurich	L. Davenport	Venus Williams	7–5, 6–3
Oct 19–25	Ladies Kremlin Cup	Moscow	Mary Pierce	Monica Seles	7–6 (7–2), 6–3
Nov 1–8	Sparkassen Cup	Leipzig, Germany	Steffi Graf	Nathalie Tauziat	6–3, 6–4
Nov 9–15	Advanta Champ'ships	Philadelphia	Steffi Graf	L. Davenport	4–6, 6–3, 6–4
Nov 16–22	Chase Champ'ships	New York	Martina Hingis	L. Davenport	7–5, 6–4, 4–6, 6–2

Women's Tour (Through September 24, 1999)

Date	Tournament	Site	Winner	Finalist	Score
Jan 11–17	adidas International	Sydney	L. Davenport	Martina Hingis	6–4, 6–3
Jan 18–31	Australian Open	Melbourne	Martina Hingis	Amelie Mauresmo	6–2, 6–3
Feb 1–7	Pan Pacific Open	Tokyo	Martina Hingis	Amanda Coetzer	6–2, 6–1
Feb 15–21	Faber Grand Prix	Hannover, Germany	Jana Novotna	Venus Williams	6–4, 6–4
Feb 22–28	Open Gaz de France	Paris	Serena Williams	Amelie Mauresmo	6–2, 3–6, 7–6 (7–4)
Mar 1–14	Evert Cup	Indian Wells, California	Serena Williams	Steffi Graf	6–3, 3–6, 7–5
Mar 15–28	Lipton Championships	Key Biscayne, Florida	Venus Williams	Serena Williams	6–1, 4–6, 6–4
Mar 29–Apr 4	Family Circle Cup	Hilton Head, S Carolina	Martina Hingis	Anna Kournikova	6–4, 6–3
Apr 5–11	Bausch & Lomb Championships	Amelia Island, Florida	Monica Seles	R. Dragomir	6–2, 6–3
Apr 26–May 2	Betty Barclay Cup	Hamburg	Venus Williams	Mary Pierce	6–0, 6–3
May 3–9	Italian Open	Rome	Venus Williams	Mary Pierce	6–4, 6–2
May 10–16	German Open	Berlin	Martina Hingis	J. Halard-Decugis	6–0, 6–1
May 17–23	Int'l de Strasbourg	Strasbourg, France	Jennifer Capriati	Elena Likhovtseva	6–1, 6–3
May 24–June 6	French Open	Paris	Steffi Graf	Martina Hingis	4–6, 7–5, 6–2
June 14–20	Direct Line Champ'ships	Eastbourne, England	N. Zvereva	Nathalie Tauziat	0–6, 7–5, 6–3
June 22–July 4	Wimbledon	Wimbledon	L. Davenport	Steffi Graf	6–4, 7–5

Women's Tour (Through September 24, 1999) (Cont.)

Date	Tournament	Site	Winner	Finalist	Score
July 26–Aug 1	Bank of the W Classic	Stanford, California	L. Davenport	Venus Williams	7–6 (7–1), 6–2
Aug 2–8	TIG Tennis Classic	San Diego	Martina Hingis	Venus Williams	6–4, 6–0
Aug 9–15	Acura Classic	Los Angeles	Serena Williams	J. Halard-Decugis	6–1, 6–4
Aug 16–22	du Maurier Open	Montreal	Martina Hingis	Monica Seles	6–4, 6–4
Aug 23–29	Pilot Pen Int'l	New Haven,CT	Venus Williams	L. Davenport	6–2, 7–5
Aug 30–Sep 12	U.S. Open	New York City	Serena Williams	Martina Hingis	6–3, 7–6 (7–4)

1998 Singles Leaders

Men

Rank	Player	Tournament Wins	Match Record	Earnings ($)
1.	Pete Sampras	4	61–17	3,931,497
2.	Marcelo Rios	7	68–17	3,420,054
3.	Alex Corretja	5	57–21	2,702,569
4.	Patrick Rafter	6	60–21	2,867,017
5.	Carlos Moya	2	49–28	2,572,553
6.	Andre Agassi	5	68–18	1,836,233
7.	Tim Henman	2	59–29	1,448,770
8.	Karol Kucera	2	53–29	1,402,557
9.	Greg Rusedski	2	53–22	1,860,437
10.	Richard Krajicek	2	45–15	1,219,624
11.	Yevgeny Kafelnikov	3	57–29	2,543,077
12.	Goran Ivanisevic	1	44–28	1,541,177
13.	Petr Korda	2	34–21	1,387,393
14.	Albert Costa	2	47–25	1,013,446
15.	Mark Philippoussis	1	33–20	1,272,620
16.	Todd Martin	2	44–21	771,943
17.	Thomas Johansson	0	45–31	667,858
18.	Cedric Pioline	0	41–29	808,688
19.	Jan Siemerink	2	41–25	638,990
20.	Felix Mantilla	1	42–26	823,916

Note: Compiled by the ATP Tour.

Women

Rank	Player	Tournament Wins	Match Record	Earnings ($)
1.	Lindsay Davenport	6	69–15	2,697,788
2	Martina Hingis	5	67–13	3,175,631
3	Jana Novotna	4	51–16	2,039,912
4	Arantxa Sanchez-Vicario	2	48–20	1,505,964
5	Venus Williams	3	53–13	1,712,246
6	Monica Seles	2	46–13	1,000,514
7	Mary Pierce	4	35–12	662,237
8	Conchita Martinez	2	40–21	859,417
9	Steffi Graf	3	33–9	537,577
10	Nathalie Tauziat	0	42–24	990,224
11	Patty Schnyder	5	56–22	901,828
12	Dominique Van Roost	1	47–26	440,324
13	Anna Kournikova	0	40–19	526,633
14	Sandrine Testud	1	52–27	477,795
15	Irina Spirlea	1	36–25	530,988
16	Natasha Zvereva	0	36–22	931,945
17	Amanda Coetzer	1	32–23	534,948
18	Ai Sugiyama	2	37–21	354,950
19	Silvia Farina	0	42–26	291,186
20	Serena Williams	0	29–11	310,211

Note: Compiled by the Women's Tennis Association (WTA).

Love, American Style

What with Andre Agassi loudly cheering on Jim Courier during his second-round victory at Wimbledon in 1999 and Pete Sampras declaring that Courier's Davis Cup heroics over England in April '99 had rekindled his own motivation, things have gotten unusually harmonious at the top of U.S. men's tennis. Sampras's addition to the Davis Cup squad as a doubles player for the July '99 tie against Australia in Boston caused no grumbling, and singles stalwart Todd Martin volunteered to step aside should captain Tom Gullikson want Sampras to play singles. "There's a lot of love in the air," Sampras said facetiously. "I feel a love."

That kind of camaraderie has long been a hallmark of the Australian program. But not in 1999. Aussie singles player Mark Philippoussis has had a fractious history with coaches John Newcombe and Tony Roche over his lack of commitment to Davis Cup, and Philippoussis's relationships with fellow singles player Pat Rafter and the doubles team of Todd Woodbridge and Mark Woodforde are cool at best.

"We don't go to movies or dinner, but we see each other and say hello," said Philippoussis after his second-round win over Woodforde at Wimbledon in '99. "But there's no real friends on the tour, even if you are Australian. I've got my friends and my life, and that's all I'm worried about."

1998 Davis Cup World Group Final

Sweden def. Italy 4–1, Dec. 4–6 in Milan, Italy
>   Magnus Norman (SWE) def. Andrea Gaudenzi (ITA), 6–7 (9–11), 7–6 (7–0), 4–6, 6–3, 6-6 ret.
>   Magnus Gustafsson (SWE) def. Davide Sanguinetti (ITA), 6–1, 6–4, 6–0
>   Jonas Bjorkman and Nicklas Kulti (SWE) def. Davide Sanguinetti and Diego Nargiso (ITA), 7–6 (7–1), 6–1, 6–3
>   Magnus Gustafsson (SWE) def. Gianluca Pozzi (ITA), 6–4, 6–2
>   Diego Nargiso (ITA) def. Magnus Norman (SWE), 6–2, 6–3

1999 Davis Cup World Group Tournament

FIRST ROUND

United States def. Great Britain, 3–2
Slovakia def. Sweden, 3–2
Russia def. Germany, 3–2
Australia def. Zimbabwe, 4–1
France def. Netherlands, 4–1
Brazil def. Spain, 3–2
Belgium def. Czech Republic, 3–2
Switzerland def. Italy, 3–2

QUARTERFINAL ROUND

Australia def. United States, 4–1
Russia def. Slovakia, 3–2
France def. Brazil, 3–2
Belgium def. Switzerland, 3–2

SEMIFINALS

Australia def. Russia 4–1
>   Wayne Arthurs (AUS) def. Yevgeny Kafelnikov (RUS) 6–2, 6–7 (4–7), 6–2, 6–0
>   Lleyton Hewitt (AUS) def. Marat Safin (RUS) 7–6 (7–0), 6–2, 4–6, 6–3
>   Yevgeny Kafelnikov/Andrei Olhovskiy (RUS) def. Mark Woodforde/Sandon Stolle (AUS) 6–1, 6–4, 4–6, 4–6, 8–6
>   Lleyton Hewitt (AUS) def. Yevgeny Kafelnikov (RUS) 6–4, 7–5, 6–2
>   Wayne Arthurs (AUS) def. Marat Safin (RUS) 6–3, 6–2

France def. Belgium 4–1
>   Sebastien Grosjean (FRA) def. Xavier Malisse (BEL), 7–5, 6–2, 7–6 (7–3)
>   Cedric Pioline (FRA) def. Filip Dewulf (BEL), 6–3, 5–7, 3–6, 6–3, 6–2
>   Olivier Delaitre/Fabrice Santoro (FRA) def. Xavier Malisse/Christophe Van Garsse (BEL), 6–3, 6–3, 6–3
>   Christophe Van Garsse (BEL) def. Cedric Pioline (FRA) 6–3, 6–4
>   Fabrice Santoro (FRA) def. Christophe Rochus (BEL) 7–5, 6–4

FINAL: France versus Australia to be held Dec. 3–5, in Nice, France.

1999 Federation Cup World Group Tournament

FIRST ROUND

Italy def. Spain, 3–2
United States def. Croatia, 5–0
Russia def. France, 3–2
Slovakia def. Switzerland, 5–0

SEMIFINALS

United States def. Italy, 4–1
>   Venus Williams (USA) def. Rita Grande (ITA), 6–2, 6–3
>   Silvia Farina (ITA) def. Monica Seles (USA), 6–4, 4–6, 6–4
>   Venus Williams/Serena Williams (USA) def. Andriana Serra-Zanetti/Tathiana Garbin (ITA), 6–2, 6–2
>   Venus Williams (USA) def. Silvia Farina (ITA), 6–1, 6–1
>   Serena Williams (USA) def. Rita Grande (ITA), 6–1, 6–1

Russia def. Slovakia, 3–2
>   Elena Likhovtseva (RUS) def. Ludmila Cervanova (SLO), 7–5, 6–7 (5–7), 6–3
>   Karina Habsudova (SLO) def. Tatyana Panova (RUS), 7–6 (7–5), 6–1
>   Ludmila Cervanova/Daniela Hantuchova (SLO) def. Elena Makarova/Elena Dementieva (RUS), 7–5, 7–6 (7–5)
>   Elena Likhovtseva (RUS) def. Karina Habsudova (SLO) 3–6, 6–4, 6–2
>   Tatyana Panova (RUS) def. Ludmila Cervanova (SLO) 6–4, 6–4

FINAL

United States def. Russia 4–1, Sept. 18–19 in Palo Alto, California
>   Venus Williams (USA) def. Elena Likhovtseva (RUS), 6–3, 6–4
>   Lindsay Davenport (USA) def. Elena Dementieva (RUS), 6–4, 6–0
>   Serena Williams/Venus Williams (USA) def. Elena Dementieva/Elena Makarova (RUS), 6–2, 6–1
>   Lindsay Davenport (USA) def. Elena Likhovtseva (RUS) 6–4, 6–4
>   Elena Dementieva (RUS) def. Venus Williams (USA), 1–6, 6–3, 7–6 (7–5)

Grand Slam Tournaments

MEN
Australian Championships

Year	Winner	Finalist	Score
1905	Rodney Heath	A. H. Curtis	4–6, 6–3, 6–4, 6–4
1906	Tony Wilding	H. A. Parker	6–0, 6–4, 6–4
1907	Horace M. Rice	H. A. Parker	6–3, 6–4, 6–4
1908	Fred Alexander	A. W. Dunlop	3–6, 3–6, 6–0, 6–2, 6–3
1909	Tony Wilding	E. F. Parker	6–1, 7–5, 6–2
1910	Rodney Heath	Horace M. Rice	6–4, 6–3, 6–2
1911	Norman Brookes	Horace M. Rice	6–1, 6–2, 6–3
1912	J. Cecil Parke	A. E. Beamish	3–6, 6–3, 1–6, 6–1, 7–5
1913	E. F. Parker	H. A. Parker	2–6, 6–1, 6–2, 6–3
1914	Pat O'Hara Wood	G. L. Patterson	6–4, 6–3, 5–7, 6–1
1915	Francis G. Lowe	Horace M. Rice	4–6, 6–1, 6–1, 6–4
1916–18	No tournament		
1919	A. R. F. Kingscote	E. O. Pockley	6–4, 6–0, 6–3
1920	Pat O'Hara Wood	Ron Thomas	6–3, 4–6, 6–8, 6–1, 6–3
1921	Rhys H. Gemmell	A. Hedeman	7–5, 6–1, 6–4
1922	Pat O'Hara Wood	Gerald Patterson	6–0, 3–6, 3–6, 6–3, 6–2
1923	Pat O'Hara Wood	C. B. St John	6–1, 6–1, 6–3
1924	James Anderson	R. E. Schlesinger	6–3, 6–4, 3–6, 5–7, 6–3
1925	James Anderson	Gerald Patterson	11–9, 2–6, 6–2, 6–3
1926	John Hawkes	J. Willard	6–1, 6–3, 6–1
1927	Gerald Patterson	John Hawkes	3–6, 6–4, 3–6, 18–16, 6–3
1928	Jean Borotra	R. O. Cummings	6–4, 6–1, 4–6, 5–7, 6–3
1929	John C. Gregory	R. E. Schlesinger	6–2, 6–2, 5–7, 7–5
1930	Gar Moon	Harry C. Hopman	6–3, 6–1, 6–3
1931	Jack Crawford	Harry C. Hopman	6–4, 6–2, 2–6, 6–1
1932	Jack Crawford	Harry C. Hopman	4–6, 6–3, 3–6, 6–3, 6–1
1933	Jack Crawford	Keith Gledhill	2–6, 7–5, 6–3, 6–2
1934	Fred Perry	Jack Crawford	6–3, 7–5, 6–1
1935	Jack Crawford	Fred Perry	2–6, 6–4, 6–4, 6–4
1936	Adrian Quist	Jack Crawford	6–2, 6–3, 4–6, 3–6, 9–7
1937	Vivian B. McGrath	John Bromwich	6–3, 1–6, 6–0, 2–6, 6–1
1938	Don Budge	John Bromwich	6–4, 6–2, 6–1
1939	John Bromwich	Adrian Quist	6–4, 6–1, 6–3
1940	Adrian Quist	Jack Crawford	6–3, 6–1, 6–2
1941–45	No tournament		
1946	John Bromwich	Dinny Pails	5–7, 6–3, 7–5, 3–6, 6–2
1947	Dinny Pails	John Bromwich	4–6, 6–4, 3–6, 7–5, 8–6
1948	Adrian Quist	John Bromwich	6–4, 3–6, 6–3, 2–6, 6–3
1949	Frank Sedgman	Ken McGregor	6–3, 6–3, 6–2
1950	Frank Sedgman	Ken McGregor	6–3, 6–4, 4–6, 6–1
1951	Richard Savitt	Ken McGregor	6–3, 2–6, 6–3, 6–1
1952	Ken McGregor	Frank Sedgman	7–5, 12–10, 2–6, 6–2
1953	Ken Rosewall	Mervyn Rose	6–0, 6–3, 6–4
1954	Mervyn Rose	Rex Hartwig	6–2, 0–6, 6–4, 6–2
1955	Ken Rosewall	Lew Hoad	9–7, 6–4, 6–4
1956	Lew Hoad	Ken Rosewall	6–4, 3–6, 6–4, 7–5
1957	Ashley Cooper	Neale Fraser	6–3, 9–11, 6–4, 6–2
1958	Ashley Cooper	Mal Anderson	7–5, 6–3, 6–4
1959	Alex Olmedo	Neale Fraser	6–1, 6–2, 3–6, 6–3
1960	Rod Laver	Neale Fraser	5–7, 3–6, 6–3, 8–6, 8–6
1961	Roy Emerson	Rod Laver	1–6, 6–3, 7–5, 6–4
1962	Rod Laver	Roy Emerson	8–6, 0–6, 6–4, 6–4
1963	Roy Emerson	Ken Fletcher	6–3, 6–3, 6–1
1964	Roy Emerson	Fred Stolle	6–3, 6–4, 6–2
1965	Roy Emerson	Fred Stolle	7–9, 2–6, 6–4, 7–5, 6–1
1966	Roy Emerson	Arthur Ashe	6–4, 6–8, 6–2, 6–3
1967	Roy Emerson	Arthur Ashe	6–4, 6–1, 6–1
1968	Bill Bowrey	Juan Gisbert	7–5, 2–6, 9–7, 6–4
1969*	Rod Laver	Andres Gimeno	6–3, 6–4, 7–5

*Became Open (amateur and professional) in 1969.

MEN (Cont.)

Australian Championships (Cont.)

Year	Winner	Finalist	Score
1970	Arthur Ashe	Dick Crealy	6–4, 9–7, 6–2
1971	Ken Rosewall	Arthur Ashe	6–1, 7–5, 6–3
1972	Ken Rosewall	Mal Anderson	7–6, 6–3, 7–5
1973	John Newcombe	Onny Parun	6–3, 6–7, 7–5, 6–1
1974	Jimmy Connors	Phil Dent	7–6, 6–4, 4–6, 6–3
1975	John Newcombe	Jimmy Connors	7–5, 3–6, 6–4, 7–5
1976	Mark Edmondson	John Newcombe	6–7, 6–3, 7–6, 6–1
1977 (Jan)	Roscoe Tanner	Guillermo Vilas	6–3, 6–3, 6–3
1977 (Dec)	Vitas Gerulaitis	John Lloyd	6–3, 7–6, 5–7, 3–6, 6–2
1978	Guillermo Vilas	John Marks	6–4, 6–4, 3–6, 6–3
1979	Guillermo Vilas	John Sadri	7–6, 6–3, 6–2
1980	Brian Teacher	Kim Warwick	7–5, 7–6, 6–3
1981	Johan Kriek	Steve Denton	6–2, 7–6, 6–7, 6–4
1982	Johan Kriek	Steve Denton	6–3, 6–3, 6–2
1983	Mats Wilander	Ivan Lendl	6–1, 6–4, 6–4
1984	Mats Wilander	Kevin Curren	6–7, 6–4, 7–6, 6–2
1985 (Dec)	Stefan Edberg	Mats Wilander	6–4, 6–3, 6–3
1987 (Jan)	Stefan Edberg	Pat Cash	6–3, 6–4, 3–6, 5–7, 6–3
1988	Mats Wilander	Pat Cash	6–3, 6–7, 3–6, 6–1, 8–6
1989	Ivan Lendl	Miloslav Mecir	6–2, 6–2, 6–2
1990	Ivan Lendl	Stefan Edberg	4–6, 7–6, 5–2, ret.
1991	Boris Becker	Ivan Lendl	1–6, 6–4, 6–4, 6–4
1992	Jim Courier	Stefan Edberg	6–3, 3–6, 6–4, 6–2
1993	Jim Courier	Stefan Edberg	6–2, 6–1, 2–6, 7–5
1994	Pete Sampras	Todd Martin	7–6, 6–4, 6–4
1995	Andre Agassi	Pete Sampras	4–6, 6–1, 7–6, 6–4
1996	Boris Becker	Michael Chang	6–2, 6–4, 2–6, 6–2
1997	Pete Sampras	Carlos Moya	6–2, 6–3, 6–3
1998	Petr Korda	Marcelo Rios	6–2, 6–2, 6–2
1999	Yevgeny Kafelnikov	Thomas Enqvist	4–6, 6–0, 6–3, 7–6

French Championships

Year	Winner	Finalist	Score
1925†	Rene Lacoste	Jean Borotra	7–5, 6–1, 6–4
1926	Henri Cochet	Rene Lacoste	6–2, 6–4, 6–3
1927	Rene Lacoste	Bill Tilden	6–4, 4–6, 5–7, 6–3, 11–9
1928	Henri Cochet	Rene Lacoste	5–7, 6–3, 6–1, 6–3
1929	Rene Lacoste	Jean Borotra	6–3, 2–6, 6–0, 2–6, 8–6
1930	Henri Cochet	Bill Tilden	3–6, 8–6, 6–3, 6–1
1931	Jean Borotra	Claude Boussus	2–6, 6–4, 7–5, 6–4
1932	Henri Cochet	Giorgio de Stefani	6–0, 6–4, 4–6, 6–3
1933	Jack Crawford	Henri Cochet	8–6, 6–1, 6–3
1934	Gottfried von Cramm	Jack Crawford	6–4, 7–9, 3–6, 7–5, 6–3
1935	Fred Perry	Gottfried von Cramm	6–3, 3–6, 6–1, 6–3
1936	Gottfried von Cramm	Fred Perry	6–0, 2–6, 6–2, 2–6, 6–0
1937	Henner Henkel	Henry Austin	6–1, 6–4, 6–3
1938	Don Budge	Roderick Menzel	6–3, 6–2, 6–4
1939	Don McNeill	Bobby Riggs	7–5, 6–0, 6–3
1940	No tournament		
1941‡	Bernard Destremau	n/a	n/a
1942‡	Bernard Destremau	n/a	n/a
1943‡	Yvon Petra	n/a	n/a
1944‡	Yvon Petra	n/a	n/a
1945‡	Yvon Petra	Bernard Destremau	7–5, 6–4, 6–2
1946	Marcel Bernard	Jaroslav Drobny	3–6, 2–6, 6–1, 6–4, 6–3
1947	Joseph Asboth	Eric Sturgess	8–6, 7–5, 6–4
1948	Frank Parker	Jaroslav Drobny	6–4, 7–5, 5–7, 8–6
1949	Frank Parker	Budge Patty	6–3, 1–6, 6–1, 6–4
1950	Budge Patty	Jaroslav Drobny	6–1, 6–2, 3–6, 5–7, 7–5
1951	Jaroslav Drobny	Eric Sturgess	6–3, 6–3, 6–3
1952	Jaroslav Drobny	Frank Sedgman	6–2, 6–0, 3–6, 6–4
1953	Ken Rosewall	Vic Seixas	6–3, 6–4, 1–6, 6–2

MEN *(Cont.)*
French Championships *(Cont.)*

Year	Winner	Finalist	Score
1954	Tony Trabert	Arthur Larsen	6–4, 7–5, 6–1
1955	Tony Trabert	Sven Davidson	2–6, 6–1, 6–4, 6–2
1956	Lew Hoad	Sven Davidson	6–4, 8–6, 6–3
1957	Sven Davidson	Herbie Flam	6–3, 6–4, 6–4
1958	Mervyn Rose	Luis Ayala	6–3, 6–4, 6–4
1959	Nicola Pietrangeli	Ian Vermaak	3–6, 6–3, 6–4, 6–1
1960	Nicola Pietrangeli	Luis Ayala	3–6, 6–3, 6–4, 4–6, 6–3
1961	Manuel Santana	Nicola Pietrangeli	4–6, 6–1, 3–6, 6–0, 6–2
1962	Rod Laver	Roy Emerson	3–6, 2–6, 6–3, 9–7, 6–2
1963	Roy Emerson	Pierre Darmon	3–6, 6–1, 6–4, 6–4
1964	Manuel Santana	Nicola Pietrangeli	6–3, 6–1, 4–6, 7–5
1965	Fred Stolle	Tony Roche	3–6, 6–0, 6–2, 6–3
1966	Tony Roche	Istvan Gulyas	6–1, 6–4, 7–5
1967	Roy Emerson	Tony Roche	6–1, 6–4, 2–6, 6–2
1968*	Ken Rosewall	Rod Laver	6–3, 6–1, 2–6, 6–2
1969	Rod Laver	Ken Rosewall	6–4, 6–3, 6–4
1970	Jan Kodes	Zeljko Franulovic	6–2, 6–4, 6–0
1971	Jan Kodes	Ilie Nastase	8–6, 6–2, 2–6, 7–5
1972	Andres Gimeno	Patrick Proisy	4–6, 6–3, 6–1, 6–1
1973	Ilie Nastase	Nikki Pilic	6–3, 6–3, 6–0
1974	Bjorn Borg	Manuel Orantes	6–7, 6–0, 6–1, 6–1
1975	Bjorn Borg	Guillermo Vilas	6–2, 6–3, 6–4
1976	Adriano Panatta	Harold Solomon	6–1, 6–4, 4–6, 7–6
1977	Guillermo Vilas	Brian Gottfried	6–0, 6–3, 6–0
1978	Bjorn Borg	Guillermo Vilas	6–1, 6–1, 6–3
1979	Bjorn Borg	Victor Pecci	6–3, 6–1, 6–7, 6–4
1980	Bjorn Borg	Vitas Gerulaitis	6–4, 6–1, 6–2
1981	Bjorn Borg	Ivan Lendl	6–1, 4–6, 6–2, 3–6, 6–1
1982	Mats Wilander	Guillermo Vilas	1–6, 7–6, 6–0, 6–4
1983	Yannick Noah	Mats Wilander	6–2, 7–5, 7–6
1984	Ivan Lendl	John McEnroe	3–6, 2–6, 6–4, 7–5, 7–5
1985	Mats Wilander	Ivan Lendl	3–6, 6–4, 6–2, 6–2
1986	Ivan Lendl	Mikael Pernfors	6–3, 6–2, 6–4
1987	Ivan Lendl	Mats Wilander	7–5, 6–2, 3–6, 7–6
1988	Mats Wilander	Henri Leconte	7–5, 6–2, 6–1
1989	Michael Chang	Stefan Edberg	6–1, 3–6, 4–6, 6–4, 6–2
1990	Andres Gomez	Andre Agassi	6–3, 2–6, 6–4, 6–4
1991	Jim Courier	Andre Agassi	3–6, 6–4, 2–6, 6–1, 6–4
1992	Jim Courier	Petr Korda	7–5, 6–2, 6–1
1993	Sergi Bruguera	Jim Courier	6–4, 2–6, 6–2, 3–6, 6–3
1994	Sergi Bruguera	Alberto Berasategui	6–3, 7–5, 2–6, 6–1
1995	Thomas Muster	Michael Chang	7–5, 6–2, 6–4
1996	Yevgeny Kafelnikov	Michael Stich	7–6, 7–5, 7–6
1997	Gustavo Kuerten	Sergi Bruguera	6–3, 6–4, 6–2
1998	Carlos Moya	Alex Corretja	6–3, 7–5, 6–3
1999	Andre Agassi	Andrei Medvedev	1–6, 2–6, 6–4, 6–3, 6–4

*Became Open (amateur and professional) in 1968 but closed to contract professionals in 1972.

†1925 was the first year that entries were accepted from all countries.
‡From 1941 to 1945 the event was called Tournoi de France and was closed to all foreigners.

Wimbledon Championships

Year	Winner	Finalist	Score
1877	Spencer W. Gore	William C. Marshall	6–1, 6–2, 6–4
1878	P. Frank Hadow	Spencer W. Gore	7–5, 6–1, 9–7
1879	John T. Hartley	V. St Leger Gould	6–2, 6–4, 6–2
1880	John T. Hartley	Herbert F. Lawford	6–0, 6–2, 2–6, 6–3
1881	William Renshaw	John T. Hartley	6–0, 6–2, 6–1
1882	William Renshaw	Ernest Renshaw	6–1, 2–6, 4–6, 6–2, 6–2
1883	William Renshaw	Ernest Renshaw	2–6, 6–3, 6–3, 4–6, 6–3
1884	William Renshaw	Herbert F. Lawford	6–0, 6–4, 9–7
1885	William Renshaw	Herbert F. Lawford	7–5, 6–2, 4–6, 7–5

MEN *(Cont.)*

Wimbledon Championship *(Cont.)*

Year	Winner	Finalist	Score
1886	William Renshaw	Herbert F. Lawford	6–0, 5–7, 6–3, 6–4
1887	Herbert F. Lawford	Ernest Renshaw	1–6, 6–3, 3–6, 6–4, 6–4
1888	Ernest Renshaw	Herbert F. Lawford	6–3, 7–5, 6–0
1889	William Renshaw	Ernest Renshaw	6–4, 6–1, 3–6, 6–0
1890	William J. Hamilton	William Renshaw	6–8, 6–2, 3–6, 6–1, 6–1
1891	Wilfred Baddeley	Joshua Pim	6–4, 1–6, 7–5, 6–0
1892	Wilfred Baddeley	Joshua Pim	4–6, 6–3, 6–3, 6–2
1893	Joshua Pim	Wilfred Baddeley	3–6, 6–1, 6–3, 6–2
1894	Joshua Pim	Wilfred Baddeley	10–8, 6–2, 8–6
1895	Wilfred Baddeley	Wilberforce V. Eaves	4–6, 2–6, 8–6, 6–2, 6–3
1896	Harold S. Mahoney	Wilfred Baddeley	6–2, 6–8, 5–7, 8–6, 6–3
1897	Reggie F. Doherty	Harold S. Mahoney	6–4, 6–4, 6–3
1898	Reggie F. Doherty	H. Laurie Doherty	6–3, 6–3, 2–6, 5–7, 6–1
1899	Reggie F. Doherty	Arthur W. Gore	1–6, 4–6, 6–2, 6–3, 6–3
1900	Reggie F. Doherty	Sidney H. Smith	6–8, 6–3, 6–1, 6–2
1901	Arthur W. Gore	Reggie F. Doherty	4–6, 7–5, 6–4, 6–4
1902	H. Laurie Doherty	Arthur W. Gore	6–4, 6–3, 3–6, 6–0
1903	H. Laurie Doherty	Frank L. Riseley	7–5, 6–3, 6–0
1904	H. Laurie Doherty	Frank L. Riseley	6–1, 7–5, 8–6
1905	H. Laurie Doherty	Norman E. Brookes	8–6, 6–2, 6–4
1906	H. Laurie Doherty	Frank L. Riseley	6–4, 4–6, 6–2, 6–3
1907	Norman E. Brookes	Arthur W. Gore	6–4, 6–2, 6–2
1908	Arthur W. Gore	H. Roper Barrett	6–3, 6–2, 4–6, 3–6, 6–4
1909	Arthur W. Gore	M. J. G. Ritchie	6–8, 1–6, 6–2, 6–2, 6–2
1910	Anthony F. Wilding	Arthur W. Gore	6–4, 7–5, 4–6, 6–2
1911	Anthony F. Wilding	H. Roper Barrett	6–4, 4–6, 2–6, 6–2 ret
1912	Anthony F. Wilding	Arthur W. Gore	6–4, 6–4, 4–6, 6–4
1913	Anthony F. Wilding	Maurice E. McLoughlin	8–6, 6–3, 10–8
1914	Norman E. Brookes	Anthony F. Wilding	6–4, 6–4, 7–5
1915–18	No tournament		
1919	Gerald L. Patterson	Norman E. Brookes	6–3, 7–5, 6–2
1920	Bill Tilden	Gerald L. Patterson	2–6, 6–3, 6–2, 6–4
1921	Bill Tilden	Brian I. C. Norton	4–6, 2–6, 6–1, 6–0, 7–5
1922	Gerald L. Patterson	Randolph Lycett	6–3, 6–4, 6–2
1923	Bill Johnston	Francis T. Hunter	6–0, 6–3, 6–1
1924	Jean Borotra	Rene Lacoste	6–1, 3–6, 6–1, 3–6, 6–4
1925	Rene Lacoste	Jean Borotra	6–3, 6–3, 4–6, 8–6
1926	Jean Borotra	Howard Kinsey	8–6, 6–1, 6–3
1927	Henri Cochet	Jean Borotra	4–6, 4–6, 6–3, 6–4, 7–5
1928	Rene Lacoste	Henri Cochet	6–1, 4–6, 6–4, 6–2
1929	Henri Cochet	Jean Borotra	6–4, 6–3, 6–4
1930	Bill Tilden	Wilmer Allison	6–3, 9–7, 6–4
1931	Sidney B. Wood Jr	Francis X. Shields	walkover
1932	Ellsworth Vines	Henry Austin	6–4, 6–2, 6–0
1933	Jack Crawford	Ellsworth Vines	4–6, 11–9, 6–2, 2–6, 6–4
1934	Fred Perry	Jack Crawford	6–3, 6–0, 7–5
1935	Fred Perry	Gottfried von Cramm	6–2, 6–4, 6–4
1936	Fred Perry	Gottfried von Cramm	6–1, 6–1, 6–0
1937	Don Budge	Gottfried von Cramm	6–3, 6–4, 6–2
1938	Don Budge	Henry Austin	6–1, 6–0, 6–3
1939	Bobby Riggs	Elwood Cooke	2–6, 8–6, 3–6, 6–3, 6–2
1940–45	No tournament		
1946	Yvon Petra	Geoff E. Brown	6–2, 6–4, 7–9, 5–7, 6–4
1947	Jack Kramer	Tom P. Brown	6–1, 6–3, 6–2
1948	Bob Falkenburg	John Bromwich	7–5, 0–6, 6–2, 3–6, 7–5
1949	Ted Schroeder	Jaroslav Drobny	3–6, 6–0, 6–3, 4–6, 6–4
1950	Budge Patty	Frank Sedgman	6–1, 8–10, 6–2, 6–3
1951	Dick Savitt	Ken McGregor	6–4, 6–4, 6–4
1952	Frank Sedgman	Jaroslav Drobny	4–6, 6–3, 6–2, 6–3
1953	Vic Seixas	Kurt Nielsen	9–7, 6–3, 6–4
1954	Jaroslav Drobny	Ken Rosewall	13–11, 4–6, 6–2, 9–7
1955	Tony Trabert	Kurt Nielsen	6–3, 7–5, 6–1
1956	Lew Hoad	Ken Rosewall	6–2, 4–6, 7–5, 6–4
1957	Lew Hoad	Ashley Cooper	6–2, 6–1, 6–2

MEN (Cont.)
Wimbledon Championships (Cont.)

Year	Winner	Finalist	Score
1958	Ashley Cooper	Neale Fraser	3–6, 6–3, 6–4, 13–11
1959	Alex Olmedo	Rod Laver	6–4, 6–3, 6–4
1960	Neale Fraser	Rod Laver	6–4, 3–6, 9–7, 7–5
1961	Rod Laver	Chuck McKinley	6–3, 6–1, 6–4
1962	Rod Laver	Martin Mulligan	6–2, 6–2, 6–1
1963	Chuck McKinley	Fred Stolle	9–7, 6–1, 6–4
1964	Roy Emerson	Fred Stolle	6–4, 12–10, 4–6, 6–3
1965	Roy Emerson	Fred Stolle	6–2, 6–4, 6–4
1966	Manuel Santana	Dennis Ralston	6–4, 11–9, 6–4
1967	John Newcombe	Wilhelm Bungert	6–3, 6–1, 6–1
1968*	Rod Laver	Tony Roche	6–3, 6–4, 6–2
1969	Rod Laver	John Newcombe	6–4, 5–7, 6–4, 6–4
1970	John Newcombe	Ken Rosewall	5–7, 6–3, 6–2, 3–6, 6–1
1971	John Newcombe	Stan Smith	6–3, 5–7, 2–6, 6–4, 6–4
1972	Stan Smith	Ilie Nastase	4–6, 6–3, 6–3, 4–6, 7–5
1973	Jan Kodes	Alex Metreveli	6–1, 9–8, 6–3
1974	Jimmy Connors	Ken Rosewall	6–1, 6–1, 6–4
1975	Arthur Ashe	Jimmy Connors	6–1, 6–1, 5–7, 6–4
1976	Bjorn Borg	Ilie Nastase	6–4, 6–2, 9–7
1977	Bjorn Borg	Jimmy Connors	3–6, 6–2, 6–1, 5–7, 6–4
1978	Bjorn Borg	Jimmy Connors	6–2, 6–2, 6–3
1979	Bjorn Borg	Roscoe Tanner	6–7, 6–1, 3–6, 6–3, 6–4
1980	Bjorn Borg	John McEnroe	1–6, 7–5, 6–3, 6–7, 8–6
1981	John McEnroe	Bjorn Borg	4–6, 7–6, 7–6, 6–4
1982	Jimmy Connors	John McEnroe	3–6, 6–3, 6–7, 7–6, 6–4
1983	John McEnroe	Chris Lewis	6–2, 6–2, 6–2
1984	John McEnroe	Jimmy Connors	6–1, 6–1, 6–2
1985	Boris Becker	Kevin Curren	6–3, 6–7, 7–6, 6–4
1986	Boris Becker	Ivan Lendl	6–4, 6–3, 7–5
1987	Pat Cash	Ivan Lendl	7–6, 6–2, 7–5
1988	Stefan Edberg	Boris Becker	4–6, 7–6, 6–4, 6–2
1989	Boris Becker	Stefan Edberg	6–0, 7–6, 6–4
1990	Stefan Edberg	Boris Becker	6–2, 6–2, 3–6, 3–6, 6–4
1991	Michael Stich	Boris Becker	6–4, 7–6, 6–4
1992	Andre Agassi	Goran Ivanisevic	6–7, 6–4, 6–4, 1–6, 6–4
1993	Pete Sampras	Jim Courier	7–6, 7–6, 3–6, 6–3
1994	Pete Sampras	Goran Ivanisevic	7–6, 7–6, 6–0
1995	Pete Sampras	Boris Becker	6–7, 6–2, 6–4, 6–2
1996	Richard Krajicek	MaliVai Washington	6–3, 6–4, 6–3
1997	Pete Sampras	Cedric Pioline	6–4, 6–2, 6–4
1998	Pete Sampras	Goran Ivanisevic	6–7, 7–6, 6–4, 3–6, 6–2
1999	Pete Sampras	Andre Agassi	6–3, 6–4, 7–5

*Became Open (amateur and professional) in 1968 but closed to contract professionals in 1972.

Note: Prior to 1922 the tournament was run on a challenge-round system. The previous year's winner "stood out" of an All Comers event, which produced a challenger to play him for the title.

United States Championships

Year	Winner	Finalist	Score
1881	Richard D. Sears	W.E. Glyn	6–0, 6–3, 6–2
1882	Richard D. Sears	C.M. Clark	6–1, 6–4, 6–0
1883	Richard D. Sears	James Dwight	6–2, 6–0, 9–7
1884	Richard D. Sears	H.A. Taylor	6–0, 1–6, 6–0, 6–2
1885	Richard D. Sears	G.M. Brinley	6–3, 4–6, 6–0, 6–3
1886	Richard D. Sears	R.L. Beeckman	4–6, 6–1, 6–3, 6–4
1887	Richard D. Sears	H.W. Slocum Jr	6–1, 6–3, 6–2
1888‡	H. W. Slocum Jr	H.A. Taylor	6–4, 6–1, 6–0
1889	H. W. Slocum Jr	Q.A. Shaw	6–3, 6–1, 4–6, 6–2
1890	Oliver S. Campbell	H.W. Slocum Jr	6–2, 4–6, 6–3, 6–1
1891	Oliver S. Campbell	Clarence Hobart	2–6, 7–5, 7–9, 6–1, 6–2
1892	Oliver S. Campbell	Frederick H. Hovey	7–5, 3–6, 6–3, 7–5
1893‡	Robert D. Wrenn	Frederick H. Hovey	6–4, 3–6, 6–4, 6–4
1894	Robert D. Wrenn	M.F. Goodbody	6–8, 6–1, 6–4, 6–4
1895	Frederick H. Hovey	Robert D. Wrenn	6–3, 6–2, 6–4
1896	Robert D. Wrenn	Frederick H. Hovey	7–5, 3–6, 6–0, 1–6, 6–1

MEN *(Cont.)*

United States Championships *(Cont.)*

Year	Winner	Finalist	Score
1897	Robert D. Wrenn	Wilberforce V. Eaves	4–6, 8–6, 6–3, 2–6, 6–2
1898‡	Malcolm D. Whitman	Dwight F. Davis	3–6, 6–2, 6–2, 6–1
1899	Malcolm D. Whitman	J. Parmly Paret	6–1, 6–2, 3–6, 7–5
1900	Malcolm D. Whitman	William A. Larned	6–4, 1–6, 6–2, 6–2
1901‡	William A. Larned	Beals C. Wright	6–2, 6–8, 6–4, 6–4
1902	William A. Larned	Reggie F. Doherty	4–6, 6–2, 6–4, 8–6
1903	H. Laurie Doherty	William A. Larned	6–0, 6–3, 10–8
1904‡	Holcombe Ward	William J. Clothier	10–8, 6–4, 9–7
1905	Beals C. Wright	Holcombe Ward	6–2, 6–1, 11–9
1906	William J. Clothier	Beals C. Wright	6–3, 6–0, 6–4
1907‡	William A. Larned	Robert LeRoy	6–2, 6–2, 6–4
1908	William A. Larned	Beals C. Wright	6–1, 6–2, 8–6
1909	William A. Larned	William J. Clothier	6–1, 6–2, 5–7, 1–6, 6–1
1910	William A. Larned	Thomas C. Bundy	6–1, 5–7, 6–0, 6–8, 6–1
1911	William A. Larned	Maurice E. McLoughlin	6–4, 6–4, 6–2
1912†	Maurice E. McLoughlin	Bill Johnson	3–6, 2–6, 6–2, 6–4, 6–2
1913	Maurice E. McLoughlin	Richard N. Williams	6–4, 5–7, 6–3, 6–1
1914	Richard N. Williams	Maurice E. McLoughlin	6–3, 8–6, 10–8
1915	Bill Johnston	Maurice E. McLoughlin	1–6, 6–0, 7–5, 10–8
1916	Richard N. Williams	Bill Johnston	4–6, 6–4, 0–6, 6–2, 6–4
1917#	R.L. Murray	N. W. Niles	5–7, 8–6, 6–3, 6–3
1918	R.L. Murray	Bill Tilden	6–3, 6–1, 7–5
1919	Bill Johnston	Bill Tilden	6–4, 6–4, 6–3
1920	Bill Tilden	Bill Johnston	6–1, 1–6, 7–5, 5–7, 6–3
1921	Bill Tilden	Wallace F. Johnson	6–1, 6–3, 6–1
1922	Bill Tilden	Bill Johnston	4–6, 3–6, 6–2, 6–3, 6–4
1923	Bill Tilden	Bill Johnston	6–4, 6–1, 6–4
1924	Bill Tilden	Bill Johnston	6–1, 9–7, 6–2
1925	Bill Tilden	Bill Johnston	4–6, 11–9, 6–3, 4–6, 6–3
1926	Rene Lacoste	Jean Borotra	6–4, 6–0, 6–4
1927	Rene Lacoste	Bill Tilden	11–9, 6–3, 11–9
1928	Henri Cochet	Francis T. Hunter	4–6, 6–4, 3–6, 7–5, 6–3
1929	Bill Tilden	Francis T. Hunter	3–6, 6–3, 4–6, 6–2, 6–4
1930	John H. Doeg	Francis X. Shields	10–8, 1–6, 6–4, 16–14
1931	Ellsworth Vines	George M. Lott Jr	7–9, 6–3, 9–7, 7–5
1932	Ellsworth Vines	Henri Cochet	6–4, 6–4, 6–4
1933	Fred Perry	Jack Crawford	6–3, 11–13, 4–6, 6–0, 6–1
1934	Fred Perry	Wilmer L. Allison	6–4, 6–3, 1–6, 8+6
1935	Wilmer L. Allison	Sidney B. Wood Jr	6–2, 6–2, 6–3
1936	Fred Perry	Don Budge	2–6, 6–2, 8–6, 1–6, 10–8
1937	Don Budge	Gottfried von Cramm	6–1, 7–9, 6–1, 3–6, 6–1
1938	Don Budge	Gene Mako	6–3, 6–8, 6–2, 6–1
1939	Bobby Riggs	Welby Van Horn	6–4, 6–2, 6–4
1940	Don McNeill	Bobby Riggs	4–6, 6–8, 6–3, 6–3, 7–5
1941	Bobby Riggs	Francis Kovacs II	5–7, 6–1, 6–3, 6–3
1942	Ted Schroeder	Frank Parker	8–6, 7–5, 3–6, 4–6, 6–2
1943	Joseph R. Hunt	Jack Kramer	6–3, 6–8, 10–8, 6–0
1944	Frank Parker	William F. Talbert	6–4, 3–6, 6–3, 6–3
1945	Frank Parker	William F. Talbert	14–12, 6–1, 6–2
1946	Jack Kramer	Tom P. Brown	9–7, 6–3, 6–0
1947	Jack Kramer	Frank Parker	4–6, 2–6, 6–1, 6–0, 6–3
1948	Pancho Gonzales	Eric W. Sturgess	6–2, 6–3, 14–12
1949	Pancho Gonzales	Ted Schroeder	16–18, 2–6, 6–1, 6–2, 6–4
1950	Arthur Larsen	Herbie Flam	6–3, 4–6, 5–7, 6–4, 6–3
1951	Frank Sedgman	Vic Seixas	6–4, 6–1, 6–1
1952	Frank Sedgman	Gardnar Mulloy	6–1, 6–2, 6–3
1953	Tony Trabert	Vic Seixas	6–3, 6–2, 6–3
1954	Vic Seixas	Rex Hartwig	3–6, 6–2, 6–4, 6–4
1955	Tony Trabert	Ken Rosewall	9–7, 6–3, 6–3
1956	Ken Rosewall	Lew Hoad	4–6, 6–2, 6–3, 6–3
1957	Mal Anderson	Ashley J. Cooper	10–8, 7–5, 6–4
1958	Ashley J. Cooper	Mal Anderson	6–2, 3–6, 4–6, 10–8, 8–6
1959	Neale Fraser	Alex Olmedo	6–3, 5–7, 6–2, 6–4

MEN (Cont.)
United States Championships (Cont.)

Year	Winner	Finalist	Score
1960	Neale Fraser	Rod Laver	6–4, 6–4, 9–7
1961	Roy Emerson	Rod Laver	7–5, 6–3, 6–2
1962	Rod Laver	Roy Emerson	6–2, 6–4, 5–7, 6–4
1963	Rafael Osuna	Frank Froehling III	7–5, 6–4, 6–2
1964	Roy Emerson	Fred Stolle	6–4, 6–2, 6–4
1965	Manuel Santana	Cliff Drysdale	6–2, 7–9, 7–5, 6–1
1966	Fred Stolle	John Newcombe	4–6, 12–10, 6–3, 6–4
1967	John Newcombe	Clark Graebner	6–4, 6–4, 8–6
1968*	Arthur Ashe	Tom Okker	14–12, 5–7, 6–3, 3–6, 6–3
1968**	Arthur Ashe	Bob Lutz	4–6, 6–3, 8–10, 6–0, 6–4
1969	Rod Laver	Tony Roche	7–9, 6–1, 6–3, 6–2
1969**	Stan Smith	Bob Lutz	9–7, 6–3, 6–1
1970	Ken Rosewall	Tony Roche	2–6, 6–4, 7–6, 6–3
1971	Stan Smith	Jan Kodes	3–6, 6–3, 6–2, 7–6
1972	Ilie Nastase	Arthur Ashe	3–6, 6–3, 6–7, 6–4, 6–3
1973	John Newcombe	Jan Kodes	6–4, 1–6, 4–6, 6–2, 6–3
1974	Jimmy Connors	Ken Rosewall	6–1, 6–0, 6–1
1975	Manuel Orantes	Jimmy Connors	6–4, 6–3, 6–3
1976	Jimmy Connors	Bjorn Borg	6–4, 3–6, 7–6, 6–4
1977	Guillermo Vilas	Jimmy Connors	2–6, 6–3, 7–6, 6–0
1978	Jimmy Connors	Bjorn Borg	6–4, 6–2, 6–2
1979	John McEnroe	Vitas Gerulaitis	7–5, 6–3, 6–3
1980	John McEnroe	Bjorn Borg	7–6, 6–1, 6–7, 5–7, 6–4
1981	John McEnroe	Bjorn Borg	4–6, 6–2, 6–4, 6–3
1982	Jimmy Connors	Ivan Lendl	6–3, 6–2, 4–6, 6–4
1983	Jimmy Connors	Ivan Lendl	6–3, 6–7, 7–5, 6–0
1984	John McEnroe	Ivan Lendl	6–3, 6–4, 6–1
1985	Ivan Lendl	John McEnroe	7–6, 6–3, 6–4
1986	Ivan Lendl	Miloslav Mecir	6–4, 6–2, 6–0
1987	Ivan Lendl	Mats Wilander	6–7, 6–0, 7–6, 6–4
1988	Mats Wilander	Ivan Lendl	6–4, 4–6, 6–3, 5–7, 6–4
1989	Boris Becker	Ivan Lendl	7–6, 1–6, 6–3, 7–6
1990	Pete Sampras	Andre Agassi	6–4, 6–3, 6–2
1991	Stefan Edberg	Jim Courier	6–2, 6–4, 6–0
1992	Stefan Edberg	Pete Sampras	3–6, 6–4, 7–6, 6–2
1993	Pete Sampras	Cedric Pioline	6–4, 6–4, 6–3
1994	Andre Agassi	Michael Stich	6–1, 7–6, 7–5
1995	Pete Sampras	Andre Agassi	6–4, 6–3, 4–6, 7–5
1996	Pete Sampras	Michael Chang	6–1, 6–4, 7–6
1997	Patrick Rafter	Greg Rusedski	6–3, 6–2, 4–6, 7–5
1998	Patrick Rafter	Mark Philippoussis	6–3, 3–6, 6–2, 6–0
1999	Andre Agassi	Todd Martin	6–4, 6–7, 6–7, 6–3, 6–2

‡No challenge round played.

*Became Open (amateur and professional) in 1968.

†Challenge round abolished; #National Patriotic Tournament. **Amateur event held.

WOMEN
Australian Championships

Year	Winner	Finalist	Score
1922	Margaret Molesworth	Esna Boyd	6–3, 10–8
1923	Margaret Molesworth	Esna Boyd	6–1, 7–5
1924	Sylvia Lance	Esna Boyd	6–3, 3–6, 6–4
1925	Daphne Akhurst	Esna Boyd	1–6, 8–6, 6–4
1926	Daphne Akhurst	Esna Boyd	6–1, 6–3
1927	Esna Boyd	Sylvia Harper	5–7, 6–1, 6–2
1928	Daphne Akhurst	Esna Boyd	7–5, 6–2
1929	Daphne Akhurst	Louise Bickerton	6–1, 5–7, 6–2
1930	Daphne Akhurst	Sylvia Harper	10–8, 2–6, 7–5
1931	Coral Buttsworth	Margorie Crawford	1–6, 6–3, 6–4
1932	Coral Buttsworth	Kathrine Le Messurier	9–7, 6–4
1933	Joan Hartigan	Coral Buttsworth	6–4, 6–3

WOMEN *(Cont.)*
Australian Championships *(Cont.)*

Year	Winner	Finalist	Score
1934	Joan Hartigan	Margaret Molesworth	6–1, 6–4
1935	Dorothy Round	Nancye Wynne Bolton	1–6, 6–1, 6–3
1936	Joan Hartigan	Nancye Wynne Bolton	6–4, 6–4
1937	Nancye Wynne Bolton	Emily Westacott	6–3, 5–7, 6–4
1938	Dorothy Bundy	D. Stevenson	6–3, 6–2
1939	Emily Westacott	Nell Hopman	6–1, 6–2
1940	Nancye Wynne Bolton	Thelma Coyne	5–7, 6–4, 6–0
1941–45	No tournament		
1946	Nancye Wynne Bolton	Joyce Fitch	6–4, 6–4
1947	Nancye Wynne Bolton	Nell Hopman	6–3, 6–2
1948	Nancye Wynne Bolton	Marie Toomey	6–3, 6–1
1949	Doris Hart	Nancye Wynne Bolton	6–3, 6–4
1950	Louise Brough	Doris Hart	6–4, 3–6, 6–4
1951	Nancye Wynne Bolton	Thelma Long	6–1, 7–5
1952	Thelma Long	H. Angwin	6–2, 6–3
1953	Maureen Connolly	Julia Sampson	6–3, 6–2
1954	Thelma Long	J. Staley	6–3, 6–4
1955	Beryl Penrose	Thelma Long	6–4, 6–3
1956	Mary Carter	Thelma Long	3–6, 6–2, 9–7
1957	Shirley Fry	Althea Gibson	6–3, 6–4
1958	Angela Mortimer	Lorraine Coghlan	6–3, 6–4
1959	Mary Carter-Reitano	Renee Schuurman	6–2, 6–3
1960	Margaret Smith	Jan Lehane	7–5, 6–2
1961	Margaret Smith	Jan Lehane	6–1, 6–4
1962	Margaret Smith	Jan Lehane	6–0, 6–2
1963	Margaret Smith	Jan Lehane	6–2, 6–2
1964	Margaret Smith	Lesley Turner	6–3, 6–2
1965	Margaret Smith	Maria Bueno	5–7, 6–4, 5–2 ret.
1966	Margaret Smith	Nancy Richey	Default
1967	Nancy Richey	Lesley Turner	6–1, 6–4
1968	Billie Jean King	Margaret Smith	6–1, 6–2
1969*	Margaret Smith Court	Billie Jean King	6–4, 6–1
1970	Margaret Smith Court	Kerry Melville Reid	6–3, 6–1
1971	Margaret Smith Court	Evonne Goolagong	2–6, 7–6, 7–5
1972	Virginia Wade	Evonne Goolagong	6–4, 6–4
1973	Margaret Smith Court	Evonne Goolagong	6–4, 7–5
1974	Evonne Goolagong	Chris Evert	7–6, 4–6, 6–0
1975	Evonne Goolagong	Martina Navratilova	6–3, 6–2
1976	Evonne Goolagong Cawley	Renata Tomanova	6–2, 6–2
1977 (Jan)	Kerry Melville Reid	Dianne Balestrat	7–5, 6–2
1977 (Dec)	Evonne Goolagong Cawley	Helen Gourlay	6–3, 6–0
1978	Chris O'Neil	Betsy Nagelsen	6–3, 7–6
1979	Barbara Jordan	Sharon Walsh	6–3, 6–3
1980	Hana Mandlikova	Wendy Turnbull	6–0, 7–5
1981	Martina Navratilova	Chris Evert Lloyd	6–7, 6–4, 7–5
1982	Chris Evert Lloyd	Martina Navratilova	6–3, 2–6, 6–3
1983	Martina Navratilova	Kathy Jordan	6–2, 7–6
1984	Chris Evert Lloyd	Helena Sukova	6–7, 6–1, 6–3
1985 (Dec)	Martina Navratilova	Chris Evert Lloyd	6–2, 4–6, 6–2
1987 (Jan)	Hana Mandlikova	Martina Navratilova	7–5, 7–6
1988	Steffi Graf	Chris Evert	6–1, 7–6
1989	Steffi Graf	Helena Sukova	6–4, 6–4
1990	Steffi Graf	Mary Joe Fernandez	6–3, 6–4
1991	Monica Seles	Jana Novotna	5–7, 6–3, 6–1
1992	Monica Seles	Mary Joe Fernandez	6–2, 6–3
1993	Monica Seles	Steffi Graf	4–6, 6–3, 6–2
1994	Steffi Graf	Arantxa Sánchez Vicario	6–0, 6–2
1995	Mary Pierce	Arantxa Sánchez Vicario	6–3, 6–2
1996	Monica Seles	Anke Huber	6–4, 6–1
1997	Martina Hingis	Mary Pierce	6–2, 6–2
1998	Martina Hingis	Conchita Martinez	6–3, 6–3
1999	Martina Hingis	Amelie Mauresmo	6–2, 6–3

*Became Open (amateur and professional) in 1969.

WOMEN (Cont.)
French Championships

Year	Winner	Finalist	Score
1925†	Suzanne Lenglen	Kathleen McKane	6–1, 6–2
1926	Suzanne Lenglen	Mary K. Browne	6–1, 6–0
1927	Kea Bouman	Irene Peacock	6–2, 6–4
1928	Helen Wills	Eileen Bennett	6–1, 6–2
1929	Helen Wills	Simone Mathieu	6–3, 6–4
1930	Helen Wills Moody	Helen Jacobs	6–2, 6–1
1931	Cilly Aussem	Betty Nuthall	8–6, 6–1
1932	Helen Wills Moody	Simone Mathieu	7–5, 6–1
1933	Margaret Scriven	Simone Mathieu	6–2, 4–6, 6–4
1934	Margaret Scriven	Helen Jacobs	7–5, 4–6, 6–1
1935	Hilde Sperling	Simone Mathieu	6–2, 6–1
1936	Hilde Sperling	Simone Mathieu	6–3, 6–4
1937	Hilde Sperling	Simone Mathieu	6–2, 6–4
1938	Simone Mathieu	Nelly Landry	6–0, 6–3
1939	Simone Mathieu	Jadwiga Jedrzejowska	6–3, 8–6
1940–45	No tournament		
1946	Margaret Osborne	Pauline Betz	1–6, 8–6, 7–5
1947	Patricia Todd	Doris Hart	6–3, 3–6, 6–4
1948	Nelly Landry	Shirley Fry	6–2, 0–6, 6–0
1949	Margaret Osborne duPont	Nelly Adamson	7–5, 6–2
1950	Doris Hart	Patricia Todd	6–4, 4–6, 6–2
1951	Shirley Fry	Doris Hart	6–3, 3–6, 6–3
1952	Doris Hart	Shirley Fry	6–4, 6–4
1953	Maureen Connolly	Doris Hart	6–2, 6–4
1954	Maureen Connolly	Ginette Bucaille	6–4, 6–1
1955	Angela Mortimer	Dorothy Knode	2–6, 7–5, 10–8
1956	Althea Gibson	Angela Mortimer	6–0, 12–10
1957	Shirley Bloomer	Dorothy Knode	6–1, 6–3
1958	Zsuzsi Kormoczi	Shirley Bloomer	6–4, 1–6, 6–2
1959	Christine Truman	Zsuzsi Kormoczi	6–4, 7–5
1960	Darlene Hard	Yola Ramirez	6–3, 6–4
1961	Ann Haydon	Yola Ramirez	6–2, 6–1
1962	Margaret Smith	Lesley Turner	6–3, 3–6, 7–5
1963	Lesley Turner	Ann Haydon Jones	2–6, 6–3, 7–5
1964	Margaret Smith	Maria Bueno	5–7, 6–1, 6–2
1965	Lesley Turner	Margaret Smith	6–3, 6–4
1966	Ann Jones	Nancy Richey	6–3, 6–1
1967	Francoise Durr	Lesley Turner	4–6, 6–3, 6–4
1968*	Nancy Richey	Ann Jones	5–7, 6–4, 6–1
1969	Margaret Smith Court	Ann Jones	6–1, 4–6, 6–3
1970	Margaret Smith Court	Helga Niessen	6–2, 6–4
1971	Evonne Goolagong	Helen Gourlay	6–3, 7–5
1972	Billie Jean King	Evonne Goolagong	6–3, 6–3
1973	Margaret Smith Court	Chris Evert	6–7, 7–6, 6–4
1974	Chris Evert	Olga Morozova	6–1, 6–2
1975	Chris Evert	Martina Navratilova	2–6, 6–2, 6–1
1976	Sue Barker	Renata Tomanova	6–2, 0–6, 6–2
1977	Mima Jausovec	Florenza Mihai	6–2, 6–7, 6–1
1978	Virginia Ruzici	Mima Jausovec	6–2, 6–2
1979	Chris Evert Lloyd	Wendy Turnbull	6–2, 6–0
1980	Chris Evert Lloyd	Virginia Ruzici	6–0, 6–3
1981	Hana Mandlikova	Sylvia Hanika	6–2, 6–4
1982	Martina Navratilova	Andrea Jaeger	7–6, 6–1
1983	Chris Evert Lloyd	Mima Jausovec	6–1, 6–2
1984	Martina Navratilova	Chris Evert Lloyd	6–3, 6–1
1985	Chris Evert Lloyd	Martina Navratilova	6–3, 6–7, 7–5
1986	Chris Evert Lloyd	Martina Navratilova	2–6, 6–3, 6–3
1987	Steffi Graf	Martina Navratilova	6–4, 4–6, 8–6
1988	Steffi Graf	Natalia Zvereva	6–0, 6–0
1989	Arantxa Sánchez Vicario	Steffi Graf	7–6, 3–6, 7–5
1990	Monica Seles	Steffi Graf	7–6, 6–4
1991†	Monica Seles	Arantxa Sánchez Vicario	6–3, 6–4
1992	Monica Seles	Steffi Graf	6–2, 3–6, 10–8

WOMEN *(Cont.)*
French Championships *(Cont.)*

Year	Winner	Finalist	Score
1993	Steffi Graf	Mary Joe Fernandez	4–6, 6–2, 6–4
1994	Arantxa Sánchez Vicario	Mary Pierce	6–4, 6–4
1995	Steffi Graf	Arantxa Sánchez Vicario	7–5, 4–6, 6–0
1996	Steffi Graf	Arantxa Sánchez Vicario	6–3, 6–7 (4–7), 10–8
1997	Iva Majoli	Martina Hingis	6–4, 6–2
1998	Arantxa Sánchez Vicario	Monica Seles	7–6 (7–5), 0–6, 6–2
1999	Steffi Graf	Martina Hingis	4–6, 7–5, 6–2

†1925 was the first year that entries were accepted from all countries.

*Became Open (amateur and professional) in 1968 but closed to contract professionals in 1972.

Wimbledon Championships

Year	Winner	Finalist	Score
1884	Maud Watson	Lilian Watson	6–8, 6–3, 6–3
1885	Maud Watson	Blanche Bingley	6–1, 7–5
1886	Blanche Bingley	Maud Watson	6–3, 6–3
1887	Charlotte Dod	Blanche Bingley	6–2, 6–0
1888	Charlotte Dod	Blanche Bingley Hillyard	6–3, 6–3
1889	Blanche Bingley Hillyard	n/a	n/a
1890	Lena Rice	n/a	n/a
1891	Charlotte Dod	n/a	n/a
1892	Charlotte Dod	Blanche Bingley Hillyard	6–1, 6–1
1893	Charlotte Dod	Blanche Bingley Hillyard	6–8, 6–1, 6–4
1894	Blanche Bingley Hillyard	n/a	n/a
1895	Charlotte Cooper	n/a	
1896	Charlotte Cooper	Mrs. W. H. Pickering	6–2, 6–3
1897	Blanche Bingley Hillyard	Charlotte Cooper	5–7, 7–5, 6–2
1898	Charlotte Cooper	n/a	n/a
1899	Blanche Bingley Hillyard	Charlotte Cooper	6–2, 6–3
1900	Blanche Bingley Hillyard	Charlotte Cooper	4–6, 6–4, 6–4
1901	Charlotte Cooper Sterry	Blanche Bingley Hillyard	6–2, 6–2
1902	Muriel Robb	Charlotte Cooper Sterry	7–5, 6–1
1903	Dorothea Douglass	n/a	n/a
1904	Dorothea Douglass	Charlotte Cooper Sterry	6–0, 6–3
1905	May Sutton	Dorothea Douglass	6–3, 6–4
1906	Dorothea Douglass	May Sutton	6–3, 9–7
1907	May Sutton	Dorothea Douglass Lambert Chambers	6–1, 6–4
1908	Charlotte Cooper Sterry	n/a	n/a
1909	Dora Boothby	n/a	n/a
1910	Dorothea Douglass Lambert Chambers	Dora Boothby	6–2, 6–2
1911	Dorothea Douglass Lambert Chambers	Dora Boothby	6–0, 6–0
1912	Ethel Larcombe	n/a	n/a
1913	Dorothea Douglass Lambert Chambers		
1914	Dorothea Douglass Lambert Chambers	Ethel Larcombe	7–5, 6–4
1915–18	No tournament		
1919	Suzanne Lenglen	Dorothea Douglass Lambert Chambers	10–8, 4–6, 9–7
1920	Suzanne Lenglen	Dorothea Douglass Lambert Chambers	6–3, 6–0
1921	Suzanne Lenglen	Elizabeth Ryan	6–2, 6–0
1922	Suzanne Lenglen	Molla Mallory	6–2, 6–0
1923	Suzanne Lenglen	Kathleen McKane	6–2, 6–2
1924	Kathleen McKane	Helen Wills	4–6, 6–4, 6–2
1925	Suzanne Lenglen	Joan Fry	6–2, 6–0
1926	Kathleen McKane Godfree	Lili de Alvarez	6–2, 4–6, 6–3
1927	Helen Wills	Lili de Alvarez	6–2, 6–4
1928	Helen Wills	Lili de Alvarez	6–2, 6–3
1929	Helen Wills	Helen Jacobs	6–1, 6–2

WOMEN (Cont.)

Wimbledon Championships (Cont.)

Year	Winner	Finalist	Score
1930	Helen Wills Moody	Elizabeth Ryan	6–2, 6–2
1931	Cilly Aussem	Hilde Kranwinkel	7–5, 7–5
1932	Helen Wills Moody	Helen Jacobs	6–3, 6–1
1933	Helen Wills Moody	Dorothy Round	6–4, 6–8, 6–3
1934	Dorothy Round	Helen Jacobs	6–2, 5–7, 6–3
1935	Helen Wills Moody	Helen Jacobs	6–3, 3–6, 7–5
1936	Helen Jacobs	Hilde Kranwinkel Sperling	6–2, 4–6, 7–5
1937	Dorothy Round	Jadwiga Jedrzejowska	6–2, 2–6, 7–5
1938	Helen Wills Moody	Helen Jacobs	6–4, 6–0
1939	Alice Marble	Kay Stammers	6–2, 6–0
1940–45	No tournament		
1946	Pauline Betz	Louise Brough	6–2, 6–4
1947	Margaret Osborne	Doris Hart	6–2, 6–4
1948	Louise Brough	Doris Hart	6–3, 8–6
1949	Louise Brough	Margaret Osborne duPont	10–8, 1–6, 10–8
1950	Louise Brough	Margaret Osborne duPont	6–1, 3–6, 6–1
1951	Doris Hart	Shirley Fry	6–1, 6–0
1952	Maureen Connolly	Louise Brough	6–4, 6–3
1953	Maureen Connolly	Doris Hart	8–6, 7–5
1954	Maureen Connolly	Louise Brough	6–2, 7–5
1955	Louise Brough	Beverly Fleitz	7–5, 8–6
1956	Shirley Fry	Angela Buxton	6–3, 6–1
1957	Althea Gibson	Darlene Hard	6–3, 6–2
1958	Althea Gibson	Angela Mortimer	8–6, 6–2
1959	Maria Bueno	Darlene Hard	6–4, 6–3
1960	Maria Bueno	Sandra Reynolds	8–6, 6–0
1961	Angela Mortimer	Christine Truman	4–6, 6–4, 7–5
1962	Karen Hantze Susman	Vera Sukova	6–4, 6–4
1963	Margaret Smith	Billie Jean Moffitt	6–3, 6–4
1964	Maria Bueno	Margaret Smith	6–4, 7–9, 6–3
1965	Margaret Smith	Maria Bueno	6–4, 7–5
1966	Billie Jean King	Maria Bueno	6–3, 3–6, 6–1
1967	Billie Jean King	Ann Haydon Jones	6–3, 6–4
1968*	Billie Jean King	Judy Tegart	9–7, 7–5
1969	Ann Haydon Jones	Billie Jean King	3–6, 6–3, 6–2
1970	Margaret Smith Court	Billie Jean King	14–12, 11–9
1971	Evonne Goolagong	Margaret Smith Court	6–4, 6–1
1972	Billie Jean King	Evonne Goolagong	6–3, 6–3
1973	Billie Jean King	Chris Evert	6–0, 7–5
1974	Chris Evert	Olga Morozova	6–0, 6–4
1975	Billie Jean King	Evonne Goolagong Cawley	6–0, 6–1
1976	Chris Evert	Evonne Goolagong Cawley	6–3, 4–6, 8–6
1977	Virginia Wade	Betty Stove	4–6, 6–3, 6–1
1978	Martina Navratilova	Chris Evert	2–6, 6–4, 7–5
1979	Martina Navratilova	Chris Evert Lloyd	6–4, 6–4
1980	Evonne Goolagong Cawley	Chris Evert Lloyd	6–1, 7–6
1981	Chris Evert Lloyd	Hana Mandlikova	6–2, 6–2
1982	Martina Navratilova	Chris Evert Lloyd	6–1, 3–6, 6–2
1983	Martina Navratilova	Andrea Jaeger	6–0, 6–3
1984	Martina Navratilova	Chris Evert Lloyd	7–6, 6–2
1985	Martina Navratilova	Chris Evert Lloyd	4–6, 6–3, 6–2
1986	Martina Navratilova	Hana Mandlikova	7–6, 6–3
1987	Martina Navratilova	Steffi Graf	7–5, 6–3
1988	Steffi Graf	Martina Navratilova	5–7, 6–2, 6–1
1989	Steffi Graf	Martina Navratilova	6–2, 6–7, 6–1
1990	Martina Navratilova	Zina Garrison	6–4, 6–1
1991	Steffi Graf	Gabriela Sabatini	6–4, 3–6, 8–6
1992	Steffi Graf	Monica Seles	6–2, 6–1
1993	Steffi Graf	Jana Novotna	7–6, 1–6, 6–4
1994	Conchita Martinez	Martina Navratilova	6–4, 3–6, 6–3
1995	Steffi Graf	Arantxa Sánchez Vicario	4–6, 6–1, 7–5
1996	Steffi Graf	Arantxa Sánchez Vicario	6–3, 7–5
1997	Martina Hingis	Jana Novotna	2–6, 6–3, 6–3

WOMEN *(Cont.)*

Wimbledon Championships *(Cont.)*

Year	Winner	Finalist	Score
1998	Jana Novotna	Nathalie Tauziat	6–4, 7–6
1999	Lindsay Davenport	Steffi Graf	6–4, 7–5

*Became Open (amateur and professional) in 1968 but closed to contract professionals in 1972.

Note: Prior to 1922 the tournament was run on a challenge-round system. The previous year's winner "stood out" of an All Comers event, which produced a challenger to play her for the title.

United States Championships

Year	Winner	Finalist	Score
1887	Ellen Hansell	Laura Knight	6–1, 6–0
1888	Bertha L. Townsend	Ellen Hansell	6–3, 6–5
1889	Bertha L. Townsend	Louise Voorhes	7–5, 6–2
1890	Ellen C. Roosevelt	Bertha L. Townsend	6–2, 6–2
1891	Mabel Cahill	Ellen C. Roosevelt	6–4, 6–1, 4–6, 6–3
1892	Mabel Cahill	Elisabeth Moore	5–7, 6–3, 6–4, 4–6, 6–2
1893	Aline Terry	Alice Schultze	6–1, 6–3
1894	Helen Hellwig	Aline Terry	7–5, 3–6, 6–0, 3–6, 6–3
1895	Juliette Atkinson	Helen Hellwig	6–4, 6–2, 6–1
1896	Elisabeth Moore	Juliette Atkinson	6–4, 4–6, 6–2, 6–2
1897	Juliette Atkinson	Elisabeth Moore	6–3, 6–3, 4–6, 3–6, 6–3
1898	Juliette Atkinson	Marion Jones	6–3, 5–7, 6–4, 2–6, 7–5
1899	Marion Jones	Maud Banks	6–1, 6–1, 7–5
1900	Myrtle McAteer	Edith Parker	6–2, 6–2, 6–0
1901	Elisabeth Moore	Myrtle McAteer	6–4, 3–6, 7–5, 2–6, 6–2
1902**	Marion Jones	Elisabeth Moore	6–1, 1–0, ret.
1903	Elisabeth Moore	Marion Jones	7–5, 8–6
1904	May Sutton	Elisabeth Moore	6–1, 6–2
1905	Elisabeth Moore	Helen Homans	6–4, 5–7, 6–1
1906	Helen Homans	Maud Barger-Wallach	6–4, 6–3
1907	Evelyn Sears	Carrie Neely	6–3, 6–2
1908	Maud Barger–Wallach	Evelyn Sears	6–3, 1–6, 6–3
1909	Hazel Hotchkiss	Maud Barger–Wallach	6–0, 6–1
1910	Hazel Hotchkiss	Louise Hammond	6–4, 6–2
1911	Hazel Hotchkiss	Florence Sutton	8–10, 6–1, 9–7
1912†	Mary K. Browne	Eleanora Sears	6–4, 6–2
1913	Mary K. Browne	Dorothy Green	6–2, 7–5
1914	Mary K. Browne	Marie Wagner	6–2, 1–6, 6–1
1915	Molla Bjurstedt	Hazel Hotchkiss Wightman	4–6, 6–2, 6–0
1916	Molla Bjurstedt	Louise Hammond Raymond	6–0, 6–1
1917‡	Molla Bjurstedt	Marion Vanderhoef	4–6, 6–0, 6–2
1918	Molla Bjurstedt	Eleanor Goss	6–4, 6–3
1919	Hazel Hotchkiss Wightman	Marion Zinderstein	6–1, 6–2
1920	Molla Bjurstedt Mallory	Marion Zinderstein	6–3, 6–1
1921	Molla Bjurstedt Mallory	Mary K. Browne	4–6, 6–4, 6–2
1922	Molla Bjurstedt Mallory	Helen Wills	6–3, 6–1
1923	Helen Wills	Molla Bjurstedt Mallory	6–2, 6–1
1924	Helen Wills	Molla Bjurstedt Mallory	6–1, 6–3
1925	Helen Wills	Kathleen McKane	3–6, 6–0, 6–2
1926	Molla Bjurstedt Mallory	Elizabeth Ryan	4–6, 6–4, 9–7
1927	Helen Wills	Betty Nuthall	6–1, 6–4
1928	Helen Wills	Helen Jacobs	6–2, 6–1
1929	Helen Wills	Phoebe Holcroft Watson	6–4, 6–2
1930	Betty Nuthall	Anna McCune Harper	6–1, 6–4
1931	Helen Wills Moody	Eileen Whittingstall	6–4, 6–1
1932	Helen Jacobs	Carolin Babcock	6–2, 6–2
1933	Helen Jacobs	Helen Wills Moody	8–6, 3–6, 3–0, ret.
1934	Helen Jacobs	Sarah Palfrey	6–1, 6–4
1935	Helen Jacobs	Sarah Palfrey Fabyan	6–2, 6–4
1936	Alice Marble	Helen Jacobs	4–6, 6–3, 6–2
1937	Anita Lizane	Jadwiga Jedrzejowska	6–4, 6–2
1938	Alice Marble	Nancye Wynne	6–0, 6–3
1939	Alice Marble	Helen Jacobs	6–0, 8–10, 6–4
1940	Alice Marble	Helen Jacobs	6–2, 6–3
1941	Sarah Palfrey Cooke	Pauline Betz	7–5, 6–2

WOMEN *(Cont.)*
United States Championships *(Cont.)*

Year	Winner	Finalist	Score
1942	Pauline Betz	Louise Brough	4–6, 6–1, 6–4
1943	Pauline Betz	Louise Brough	6–3, 5–7, 6–3
1944	Pauline Betz	Margaret Osborne	6–3, 8–6
1945	Sarah Palfrey Cooke	Pauline Betz	3–6, 8–6, 6–4
1946	Pauline Betz	Patricia Canning	11–9, 6–3
1947	Louise Brough	Margaret Osborne	8–6, 4–6, 6–1
1948	Margaret Osborne duPont	Louise Brough	4–6, 6–4, 15–13
1949	Margaret Osborne duPont	Doris Hart	6–4, 6–1
1950	Margaret Osborne duPont	Doris Hart	6–4, 6–3
1951	Maureen Connolly	Shirley Fry	6–3, 1–6, 6–4
1952	Maureen Connolly	Doris Hart	6–3, 7–5
1953	Maureen Connolly	Doris Hart	6–2, 6–4
1954	Doris Hart	Louise Brough	6–8, 6–1, 8–6
1955	Doris Hart	Patricia Ward	6–4, 6–2
1956	Shirley Fry	Althea Gibson	6–3, 6–4
1957	Althea Gibson	Louise Brough	6–3, 6–2
1958	Althea Gibson	Darlene Hard	3–6, 6–1, 6–2
1959	Maria Bueno	Christine Truman	6–1, 6–4
1960	Darlene Hard	Maria Bueno	6–4, 10–12, 6–4
1961	Darlene Hard	Ann Haydon	6–3, 6–4
1962	Margaret Smith	Darlene Hard	9–7, 6–4
1963	Maria Bueno	Margaret Smith	7–5, 6–4
1964	Maria Bueno	Carole Graebner	6–1, 6–0
1965	Margaret Smith	Billie Jean Moffitt	8–6, 7–5
1966	Maria Bueno	Nancy Richey	6–3, 6–1
1967	Billie Jean King	Ann Haydon Jones	11–9, 6–4
1968*	Virginia Wade	Billie Jean King	6–4, 6–4
1968#	Margaret Smith Court	Maria Bueno	6–2, 6–2
1969	Margaret Smith Court	Nancy Richey	6–2, 6–2
1969#	Margaret Smith Court	Virginia Wade	4–6, 6–3, 6–0
1970	Margaret Smith Court	Rosie Casals	6–2, 2–6, 6–1
1971	Billie Jean King	Rosie Casals	6–4, 7–6
1972	Billie Jean King	Kerry Melville	6–3, 7–5
1973	Margaret Smith Court	Evonne Goolagong	7–6, 5–7, 6–2
1974	Billie Jean King	Evonne Goolagong	3–6, 6–3, 7–5
1975	Chris Evert	Evonne Goolagong Cawley	5–7, 6–4, 6–2
1976	Chris Evert	Evonne Goolagong Cawley	6–3, 6–0
1977	Chris Evert	Wendy Turnbull	7–6, 6–2
1978	Chris Evert	Pam Shriver	7–6, 6–4
1979	Tracy Austin	Chris Evert Lloyd	6–4, 6–3
1980	Chris Evert Lloyd	Hana Mandlikova	5–7, 6–1, 6–1
1981	Tracy Austin	Martina Navratilova	1–6, 7–6, 7–6
1982	Chris Evert Lloyd	Hana Mandlikova	6–3, 6–1
1983	Martina Navratilova	Chris Evert Lloyd	6–1, 6–3
1984	Martina Navratilova	Chris Evert Lloyd	4–6, 6–4, 6–4
1985	Hana Mandlikova	Martina Navratilova	7–6, 1–6, 7–6
1986	Martina Navratilova	Helena Sukova	6–3, 6–2
1987	Martina Navratilova	Steffi Graf	7–6, 6–1
1988	Steffi Graf	Gabriela Sabatini	6–3, 3–6, 6–1
1989	Steffi Graf	Martina Navratilova	3–6, 6–4, 6–2
1990	Gabriela Sabatini	Steffi Graf	6–2, 7–6
1991	Monica Seles	Martina Narvatilova	7–6, 6–1
1992	Monica Seles	Arantxa Sánchez Vicario	6–3, 6–2
1993	Steffi Graf	Helena Sukova	6–3, 6–3
1994	Arantxa Sánchez Vicario	Steffi Graf	1–6, 7–6, 6–4
1995	Steffi Graf	Monica Seles	7–6, 0–6, 6–3
1996	Steffi Graf	Monica Seles	7–5, 7–4
1997	Martina Hingis	Venus Williams	6–0, 6–4
1998	Lindsay Davenport	Martina Hingis	6–3, 7–5
1999	Serena Williams	Martina Hingis	6–3, 7–6

**Five-set final abolished; †Challenge round abolished.

*Became Open (amateur and professional) in 1968.

‡National Patriotic Tournament; #Amateur event held.

Singles

Don Budge, 1938
Maureen Connolly, 1953
Rod Laver, 1962, 1969
Margaret Smith Court, 1970
Steffi Graf, 1988

Doubles

Frank Sedgman and Ken McGregor, 1951
Martina Navratilova and Pam Shriver, 1984
Maria Bueno and two partners: Christine Truman
(Australian), Darlene Hard (French, Wimbledon
and U.S. Championships), 1960
Martina Hingis and two partners: Mirjana Lucic
(Australian), Jana Novotna (French, Wimbledon
and U.S. Championships), 1998

Mixed Doubles

Margaret Smith and Ken Fletcher, 1963
Owen Davidson and two partners: Lesley Turner
(Australian), Billie Jean King (French, Wimbledon
and U.S. Championships), 1967

Alltime Grand Slam Champions

MEN

Player	Aus. S-D-M	French S-D-M	Wim. S-D-M	U.S. S-D-M	Total
Roy Emerson	6-3-0	2-6-0	2-3-0	2-4-0	28
John Newcombe	2-5-0	0-3-0	3-6-0	2-3-1	25
Frank Sedgman	2-2-2	0-2-2	1-3-2	2-2-2	22
Bill Tilden	†	0-0-1	3-1-0	7-5-4	21
Rod Laver	3-4-0	2-1-1	4-1-2	2-0-0	20
John Bromwich	2-8-1	0-0-0	0-2-2	0-3-1	19
Jean Borotra	1-1-1	1-5-2	2-3-1	0-0-1	18
Fred Stolle	0-3-1	1-2-0	0-2-3	1-3-2	18
Ken Rosewall	4-3-0	2-2-0	0-2-0	2-2-1	18
Neale Fraser	0-3-1	0-3-0	1-2-0	2-3-3	18
Adrian Quist	3-10-0	0-1-0	0-2-0	0-1-0	17
John McEnroe	0-0-0	0-0-1	3-4-0	4-5-0	17
Jack Crawford	4-4-3	1-1-1	1-1-1	0-0-0	17

†Did not compete.

WOMEN

Player	Aus. S-D-M	French S-D-M	Wim. S-D-M	U.S. S-D-M	Total
Margaret Smith Court	11-8-2	5-4-4	3-2-5	5-5-8	62
Martina Navratilova	3-8-0	2-7-2	9-7-3	4-9-2	56
Billie Jean King	1-0-1	1-1-2	6-10-4	4-5-4	39
Doris Hart	1-1-2	2-5-3	1-4-5	2-4-5	35
Helen Wills Moody	†	4-2-0	8-3-1	7-4-2	31
Louise Brough	1-1-0	0-3-0	4-5-4	1-8-3	30**
Margaret Osborne duPont	†	2-3-0	1-5-1	3-8-6	29**
Elizabeth Ryan	†	0-4-0	0-12-7	0-1-2	26
*Steffi Graf	4-0-0	6-0-0	7-1-0	5-0-0	23
Pam Shriver	0-7-0	0-4-1	0-5-0	0-5-0	22
Chris Evert	2-0-0	7-2-0	3-1-0	6-0-0	21
Darlene Hard	†	1-3-2	0-4-3	2-6-0	21
Suzanne Lenglen	†	2-2-2#	6-6-3	0-0-0	21
Nancye Wynne Bolton	6-10-4	0-0-0	0-0-0	0-0-0	20
Maria Bueno	0-1-0	0-1-1	3-5-0	4-4-0	19
Thelma Coyne Long	2-12-4	0-0-1	0-0-0	0-0-0	19

*Active player. †Did not compete.
#Suzanne Lenglen also won four singles titles at the French Championships before 1925, when competition was first opened to entries from all nations
**From 1940–45, with competition in the U.S. Championships thinned due to wartime constraints, Louise Brough Clapp also won four doubles titles (1942–45) and one mixed doubles title (1942); and Margaret Osborne duPont won five doubles titles (1941–45) and three mixed doubles titles (1943–45).

Alltime Grand Slam Singles Champions

MEN

Player	Aus.	French	Wim.	U.S.	Total
Roy Emerson 6		2	2	2	12
*Pete Sampras.................2		0	6	4	12
Bjorn Borg 0		6	5	0	11
Rod Laver 3		2	4	2	11
Bill Tilden ....†		0	3	7	10
Jimmy Connors.................1		0	2	5	8
Ivan Lendl.........................2		3	0	3	8
Fred Perry.........................1		1	3	3	8
Ken Rosewall 4		2	0	2	8
Henri Cochet ....†		4	2	1	7
Rene Lacoste ....†		3	2	2	7
Bill Larned ....†		†	0	7	7
John McEnroe 0		0	3	4	7
John Newcombe 2		0	3	2	7
Willie Renshaw ....†		†	7	†	7
Dick Sears ....†		†	0	7	7

*Active player. †Did not compete.

WOMEN

Player	Aus.	French	Wim.	U.S.	Total
Margaret Smith Court 11		5	3	5	24
*Steffi Graf 4		6	7	5	22
Helen Wills Moody.............†		4	8	7	19
Chris Evert 2		7	3	6	18
Martina Navratilova...........3		2	9	4	18
Billie Jean King 1		1	6	4	12
Maureen Connolly 1		2	3	3	9
*Monica Seles...................4		3	0	2	9
Suzanne Lenglen..............†		2#	6	0	8
Molla Bjurstedt Mallory ......†		†	0	8	8
Maria Bueno 0		0	3	4	7
Evonne Goolagong...........4		1	2	0	7
Dorothea D.L. Chambers ..†		†	7	0	7
Nancye Wynne Bolton 6		0	0	0	6
Louise Brough 1		0	4	1	6
Margaret Osborne duPont...†		2	1	3	6
Doris Hart 1		2	1	2	6
Blanche Bingley Hillyard ...†		†	6	†	6

*Active player. †Did not compete.
#Suzanne Lenglen also won four singles titles at the French Championships before 1925, when competition was first opened to entries from all nations.

Hugh, Idiot

In the process of hyping his summer 1999 movie, *Mickey Blue Eyes*, British actor Hugh Grant talked to *USA Today* in late August about many things, including his hair. (File that under More Information Than We Need to Know.) Mr. Elizabeth Hurley told the newspaper that a few years earlier he got his wavy locks shorn, with disastrous results. 'Unfortunately I looked like a butch lesbian," said Grant. "It was supposed to be spiky and Brad Pitt–y. But I looked like a female Wimbledon champion."

Given Grant's past, which includes a 1995 conviction in Los Angeles on two counts of "participating in a lewd act," one would think he'd choose his words more carefully. Grant would not comment on his *USA Today* remark, but his publicist, Robert Garlock, said, "The question was asked and answered with tongue firmly planted in cheek." As for a possible apology, Garlock said, "Hugh"s a comedian. Anyone would take his answer with a sense of humor, just as with all the quotes in that story."

Female Wimbledon champions and women tennis players in general aren't likely to consider Grant much of a comedian. And should he venture near the locker room during Wimbledon 2000 he may find a title for his next film: *Four Weddings and Another Funeral*.

National Team Competition

Davis Cup

Started in 1900 as the International Lawn Tennis Challenge Trophy by America's Dwight Davis, the runner-up in the 1898 U.S. Championships. A Davis Cup meeting between two countries is known as a tie and is a three-day event consisting of two singles matches, followed by one doubles match and then two more singles matches. The United States boasts the greatest number of wins (31), followed by Australia (20).

Year	Winner	Finalist	Site	Score
1900	United States	Great Britain	Boston	3–0
1901	No tournament			
1902	United States	Great Britain	New York	3–2
1903	Great Britain	United States	Boston	4–1
1904	Great Britain	Belgium	Wimbledon	5–0
1905	Great Britain	United States	Wimbledon	5–0
1906	Great Britain	United States	Wimbledon	5–0
1907	Australasia	Great Britain	Wimbledon	3–2
1908	Australasia	United States	Melbourne	3–2
1909	Australasia	United States	Sydney	5–0
1910	No tournament			
1911	Australasia	United States	Christchurch, NZ	5–0
1912	Great Britain	Australasia	Melbourne	3–2
1913	United States	Great Britain	Wimbledon	3–2
1914	Australasia	United States	New York	3–2
1915–18	No tournament			
1919	Australasia	Great Britain	Sydney	4–1
1920	United States	Australasia	Auckland, NZ	5–0
1921	United States	Japan	New York	5–0
1922	United States	Australasia	New York	4–1
1923	United States	Australasia	New York	4–1
1924	United States	Australia	Philadelphia	5–0
1925	United States	France	Philadelphia	5–0
1926	United States	France	Philadelphia	4–1
1927	France	United States	Philadelphia	3–2
1928	France	United States	Paris	4–1
1929	France	United States	Paris	3–2
1930	France	United States	Paris	4–1
1931	France	Great Britain	Paris	3–2
1932	France	United States	Paris	3–2
1933	Great Britain	France	Paris	3–2
1934	Great Britain	United States	Wimbledon	4–1
1935	Great Britain	United States	Wimbledon	5–0
1936	Great Britain	Australia	Wimbledon	3–2
1937	United States	Great Britain	Wimbledon	4–1
1938	United States	Australia	Philadelphia	3–2
1939	Australia	United States	Philadelphia	3–2
1940–45	No tournament			
1946	United States	Australia	Melbourne	5–0
1947	United States	Australia	New York	4–1
1948	United States	Australia	New York	5–0
1949	United States	Australia	New York	4–1
1950	Australia	United States	New York	4–1
1951	Australia	United States	Sydney	3–2
1952	Australia	United States	Adelaide	4–1
1953	Australia	United States	Melbourne	3–2
1954	United States	Australia	Sydney	3–2
1955	Australia	United States	New York	5–0
1956	Australia	United States	Adelaide	5–0
1957	Australia	United States	Melbourne	3–2
1958	United States	Australia	Brisbane	3–2
1959	Australia	United States	New York	3–2
1960	Australia	Italy	Sydney	4–1
1961	Australia	Italy	Melbourne	5–0
1962	Australia	Mexico	Brisbane	5–0
1963	United States	Australia	Adelaide	3–2
1964	Australia	United States	Cleveland	3–2
1965	Australia	Spain	Sydney	4–1
1966	Australia	India	Melbourne	4–1
1967	Australia	Spain	Brisbane	4–1
1968	United States	Australia	Adelaide	4–1

Davis Cup *(Cont.)*

Year	Winner	Finalist	Site	Score
1969	United States	Romania	Cleveland	5–0
1970	United States	West Germany	Cleveland	5–0
1971	United States	Romania	Charlotte, NC	3–2
1972	United States	Romania	Bucharest	3–2
1973	Australia	United States	Cleveland	5–0
1974	South Africa	India	*	walkover
1975	Sweden	Czechoslovakia	Stockholm	3–2
1976	Italy	Chile	Santiago	4–1
1977	Australia	Italy	Sydney	3–1
1978	United States	Great Britain	Palm Springs	4–1
1979	United States	Italy	San Francisco	5–0
1980	Czechoslovakia	Italy	Prague	4–1
1981	United States	Argentina	Cincinnati, Ohio	3–1
1982	United States	France	Grenoble	4–1
1983	Australia	Sweden	Melbourne	3–2
1984	Sweden	United States	Göteborg, Sweden	4–1
1985	Sweden	West Germany	Munich	3–2
1986	Australia	Sweden	Melbourne	3–2
1987	Sweden	India	Göteborg, Sweden	5–0
1988	West Germany	Sweden	Göteborg, Sweden	4–1
1989	West Germany	Sweden	Stuttgart	3–2
1990	United States	Australia	St. Petersburg	3–2
1991	France	United States	Lyon	3–1
1992	United States	Switzerland	Fort Worth, TX	3–1
1993	Germany	Australia	Dusseldorf	4–1
1994	Sweden	Russia	Moscow	4–1
1995	United States	Russia	Moscow	3–2
1996	France	Sweden	Malmö, Sweden	3–2
1997	Sweden	United States	Göteborg, Sweden	5–0
1998	Sweden	Italy	Milan, Italy	4–1

*India refused to play the final in protest over South Africa's governmental policy of apartheid.
Note: Prior to 1972 the challenge-round system was in effect, with the previous year's winner "standing out" of the competition until the finals. A straight 16-nation tournament has been held since 1981.

Federation Cup

The Federation Cup was started in 1963 by the International Lawn Tennis Federation (now the ITF). Until 1991 all entrants gathered at one site at one time for a tournament that was concluded within one week. Since 1995 the Fed Cup, as it is now called, has been contested in three rounds by a World Group of eight nations. A meeting between two countries now consists of five matches: four singles and one doubles. The United States has the most wins (15), followed by Australia (7).

Year	Winner	Finalist	Site	Score
1963	United States	Australia	London	2–1
1964	Australia	United States	Philadelphia	2–1
1965	Australia	United States	Melbourne	2–1
1966	United States	West Germany	Turin	3–0
1967	United States	Great Britain	West Berlin	2–0
1968	Australia	Netherlands	Paris	3–0
1969	United States	Australia	Athens	2–1
1970	Australia	Great Britain	Freiburg	3–0
1971	Australia	Great Britain	Perth	3–0
1972	South Africa	Great Britain	Johannesburg	2–1
1973	Australia	South Africa	Bad Homburg	3–0
1974	Australia	United States	Naples	2–1
1975	Czechoslovakia	Australia	Aix-en-Provence	3–0
1976	United States	Australia	Philadelphia	2–1
1977	United States	Australia	Eastbourne, UK	2–1
1978	United States	Australia	Melbourne	2–1
1979	United States	Australia	Madrid	3–0
1980	United States	Australia	West Berlin	3–0
1981	United States	Great Britain	Nagoya	3–0
1982	United States	West Germany	Santa Clara	3–0
1983	Czechoslovakia	West Germany	Zurich	2–1
1984	Czechoslovakia	Australia	Sao Paulo	2–1
1985	Czechoslovakia	United States	Tokyo	2–1

Federation Cup *(Cont.)*

Year	Winner	Finalist	Site	Score
1986	United States	Czechoslovakia	Prague	3–0
1987	West Germany	United States	Vancouver	2–1
1988	Czechoslovakia	USSR	Melbourne	2–1
1989	United States	Spain	Tokyo	3–0
1990	United States	USSR	Atlanta	2–1
1991	Spain	United States	Nottingham	2–1
1992	Germany	Spain	Frankfurt	2–1
1993	Spain	Australia	Frankfurt	3–0
1994	Spain	United States	Frankfurt	3–0
1995	Spain	United States	Valencia, Spain	3–2
1996	United States	Spain	Atlantic City	5–0
1997	France	Netherlands	Hertogenbosch, Neth.	4–1
1998	Spain	Switzerland	Geneva	3–2
1999	United States	Russia	Palo Alto, California	4–1

Rankings

ATP Computer Year-End Top 10
MEN

1973
1. Ilie Nastase
2. John Newcombe
3. Jimmy Connors
4. Tom Okker
5. Stan Smith
6. Ken Rosewall
7. Manuel Orantes
8. Rod Laver
9. Jan Kodes
10. Arthur Ashe

1974
1. Jimmy Connors
2. John Newcombe
3. Bjorn Borg
4. Rod Laver
5. Guillermo Vilas
6. Tom Okker
7. Arthur Ashe
8. Ken Rosewall
9. Stan Smith
10. Ilie Nastase

1975
1. Jimmy Connors
2. Guillermo Vilas
3. Bjorn Borg
4. Arthur Ashe
5. Manuel Orantes
6. Ken Rosewall
7. Ilie Nastase
8. John Alexander
9. Roscoe Tanner
10. Rod Laver

1976
1. Jimmy Connors
2. Bjorn Borg
3. Ilie Nastase
4. Manuel Orantes
5. Raul Ramirez
6. Guillermo Vilas
7. Adriano Panatta
8. Harold Solomon
9. Eddie Dibbs
10. Brian Gottfried

1977
1. Jimmy Connors
2. Guillermo Vilas
3. Bjorn Borg
4. Vitas Gerulaitis
5. Brian Gottfried
6. Eddie Dibbs
7. Manuel Orantes
8. Raul Ramirez
9. Ilie Nastase
10. Dick Stockton

1978
1. Jimmy Connors
2. Bjorn Borg
3. Guillermo Vilas
4. John McEnroe
5. Vitas Gerulaitis
6. Eddie Dibbs
7. Brian Gottfried
8. Raul Ramirez
9. Harold Solomon
10. Corrado Barazzutti

1979
1. Bjorn Borg
2. Jimmy Connors
3. John McEnroe
4. Vitas Gerulaitis
5. Roscoe Tanner
6. Guillermo Vilas
7. Arthur Ashe
8. Harold Solomon
9. Jose Higueras
10. Eddie Dibbs

1980
1. Bjorn Borg
2. John McEnroe
3. Jimmy Connors
4. Gene Mayer
5. Guillermo Vilas
6. Ivan Lendl
7. Harold Solomon
8. Jose–Luis Clerc
9. Vitas Gerulaitis
10. Eliot Teltscher

1981
1. John McEnroe
2. Ivan Lendl
3. Jimmy Connors
4. Bjorn Borg
5. Jose–Luis Clerc
6. Guillermo Vilas
7. Gene Mayer
8. Eliot Teltscher
9. Vitas Gerulaitis
10. Peter McNamara

ATP Computer Year-End Top 10
MEN *(CONT.)*

1982

1....John McEnroe
2....Jimmy Connors
3....Ivan Lendl
4....Guillermo Vilas
5....Vitas Gerulaitis
6....Jose–Luis Clerc
7....Mats Wilander
8....Gene Mayer
9....Yannick Noah
10..Peter McNamara

1983

1....John McEnroe
2....Ivan Lendl
3....Jimmy Connors
4....Mats Wilander
5....Yannick Noah
6....Jimmy Arias
7....Jose Higueras
8....Jose–Luis Clerc
9....Kevin Curren
10..Gene Mayer

1984

1....John McEnroe
2....Jimmy Connors
3....Ivan Lendl
4....Mats Wilander
5....Andres Gomez
6....Anders Jarryd
7....Henrik Sundstrom
8....Pat Cash
9....Eliot Teltscher
10..Yannick Noah

1985

1....Ivan Lendl
2....John McEnroe
3....Mats Wilander
4....Jimmy Connors
5....Stefan Edberg
6....Boris Becker
7....Yannick Noah
8....Anders Jarryd
9....Miloslav Mecir
10..Kevin Curren

1986

1....Ivan Lendl
2....Boris Becker
3....Mats Wilander
4....Yannick Noah
5....Stefan Edberg
6....Henri Leconte
7....Joakim Nystrom
8....Jimmy Connors
9....Miloslav Mecir
10..Andres Gomez

1987

1....Ivan Lendl
2....Stefan Edberg
3....Mats Wilander
4....Jimmy Connors
5....Boris Becker
6....Miloslav Mecir
7....Pat Cash
8....Yannick Noah
9....Tim Mayotte
10..John McEnroe

1988

1....Mats Wilander
2....Ivan Lendl
3....Andre Agassi
4....Boris Becker
5....Stefan Edberg
6....Kent Carlsson
7....Jimmy Connors
8....Jakob Hlasek
9....Henri Leconte
10...Tim Mayotte

1989

1....Ivan Lendl
2....Boris Becker
3....Stefan Edberg
4....John McEnroe
5....Michael Chang
6....Brad Gilbert
7....Andre Agassi
8....Aaron Krickstein
9....Alberto Mancini
10...Jay Berger

1990

1....Stefan Edberg
2....Boris Becker
3....Ivan Lendl
4....Andre Agassi
5....Pete Sampras
6....Andres Gomez
7....Thomas Muster
8....Emilio Sanchez
9....Goran Ivanisevic
10...Brad Gilbert

1991

1....Stefan Edberg
2....Jim Courier
3....Boris Becker
4....Michael Stich
5....Ivan Lendl
6....Pete Sampras
7....Guy Forget
8....Karel Novacek
9....Petr Korda
10...Andre Agassi

1992

1....Jim Courier
2....Stefan Edberg
3....Pete Sampras
4....Goran Ivanisevic
5....Boris Becker
6....Michael Chang
7....Petr Korda
8....Ivan Lendl
9....Andre Agassi
10...Richard Krajicek

1993

1....Pete Sampras
2....Michael Stich
3....Jim Courier
4....Sergi Bruguera
5....Stefan Edberg
6....Andrei Medvedev
7....Goran Ivanisevic
8....Michael Chang
9....Thomas Muster
10...Cedric Pioline

1994

1....Pete Sampras
2....Andre Agassi
3....Boris Becker
4....Sergi Bruguera
5....Goran Ivanisevic
6....Michael Chang
7....Stefan Edberg
8....Alberto Berasategui
9....Michael Stich
10...Todd Martin

1995

1....Pete Sampras
2....Andre Agassi
3....Thomas Muster
4....Boris Becker
5....Michael Chang
6....Yevgeny Kafelnikov
7....Thomas Enqvist
8....Jim Courier
9....Wayne Ferreira
10...Goran Ivanisevic

1996

1....Pete Sampras
2....Michael Chang
3....Yevgeny Kafelnikov
4....Goran Ivanisevic
5....Thomas Muster
6....Boris Becker
7....Richard Krajicek
8....Andre Agassi
9....Thomas Enqvist
10...Wayne Ferreira

ATP Computer Year-End Top 10
MEN (CONT.)

1997
1 ....Pete Sampras
2 ....Patrick Rafter
3 ....Michael Chang
4 ....Jonas Bjorkman
5 ....Yevgeny Kafelnikov
6 ....Greg Rusedski
7 ....Carlos Moya
8 ....Sergei Bruguera
9 ....Thomas Muster
10...Marcelo Ríos

1998
1. ...Pete Sampras
2. ...Marcelo Rios
3. ...Alex Corretja
4. ...Patrick Rafter
5. ...Carlos Moya
6. ...Andre Agassi
7. ...Tim Henman
8. ...Karol Kucera
9. ..Greg Rusedski
10...Richard Krajicek

WTA Computer Year-End Top 10
WOMEN

1973
1 ....Margaret Smith
        Court
2 ....Billie Jean King
3 ....Evonne Goolagong
4 ....Chris Evert
5 ....Rosie Casals
6 ....Virginia Wade
7 ....Kerry Reid
8 ....Nancy Gunter
9 ....Julie Heldman
10...Helga Masthoff

1974
1 ....Billie Jean King
2 ....Evonne Goolagong
3 ....Chris Evert
4 ....Virginia Wade
5 ....Julie Heldman
6 ....Rosie Casals
7 ....Kerry Reid
8 ....Olga Morozova
9 ....Lesley Hunt
10...Francoise Durr

1975
1 ....Chris Evert
2 ....Billie Jean King
3 ....Evonne Goolagong
        Cawley
4 ....Martina Navratilova
5 ....Virginia Wade
6 ....Margaret Smith
        Court
7 ....Olga Morozova
8 ....Nancy Gunter
9 ....Francoise Durr
10...Rosie Casals

1976
1 ....Chris Evert
2 ....Evonne Goolagong
        Cawley
3 ....Virginia Wade
4 ....Martina Navratilova
5 ....Sue Barker
6 ....Betty Stove
7 ....Dianne Balestrat
8 ....Mima Jausovec
9 ....Rosie Casals
10...Francoise Durr

1977
1 ....Chris Evert
2 ....Billie Jean King
3 ....Martina Navratilova
4 ....Virginia Wade
5 ....Sue Barker
6 ....Rosie Casals
7 ....Betty Stove
8 ....Dianne Balestrat
9 ....Wendy Turnbull
10...Kerry Reid

1978
1 ....Martina Navratilova
2 ....Chris Evert
3 ....Evonne Goolagong
        Cawley
4 ....Virginia Wade
5 ....Billie Jean King
6 ....Tracy Austin
7 ....Wendy Turnbull
8 ....Kerry Reid
9 ....Betty Stove
10...Dianne Balestrat

1979
1 ....Martina Navratilova
2 ....Chris Evert Lloyd
3 ....Tracy Austin
4 ....Evonne Goolagong
        Cawley
5 ....Billie Jean King
6 ....Dianne Balestrat
7 ....Wendy Turnbull
8 ....Virginia Wade
9 ....Kerry Reid
10...Sue Barker

1980
1 ....Chris Evert Lloyd
2 ....Tracy Austin
3 ....Martina Navratilova
4 ....Hana Mandlikova
5 ....Evonne Goolagong
        Cawley
6 ....Billie Jean King
7 ....Andrea Jaeger
8 ....Wendy Turnbull
9 ....Pam Shriver
10...Greer Stevens

1981
1 ....Chris Evert Lloyd
2 ....Tracy Austin
3 ....Martina Navratilova
4 ....Andrea Jaeger
5 ....Hana Mandlikova
6 ....Sylvia Hanika
7 ....Pam Shriver
8 ....Wendy Turnbull
9 ....Bettina Bunge
10...Barbara Potter

1982
1 ....Martina Navratilova
2 ....Chris Evert Lloyd
3 ....Andrea Jaeger
4 ....Tracy Austin
5 ....Wendy Turnbull
6 ....Pam Shriver
7 ....Hana Mandlikova
8 ....Barbara Potter
9 ....Bettina Bunge
10...Sylvia Hanika

1983
1 ....Martina Navratilova
2 ....Chris Evert Lloyd
3 ....Andrea Jaeger
4 ....Pam Shriver
5 ....Sylvia Hanika
6 ....Jo Durie
7 ....Bettina Bunge
8 ....Wendy Turnbull
9 ....Tracy Austin
10...Zina Garrison

1984
1 ....Martina Navratilova
2 ....Chris Evert Lloyd
3 ....Hana Mandlikova
4 ....Pam Shriver
5 ....Wendy Turnbull
6 ....Manuela Maleeva
7 ....Helena Sukova
8 ....Claudia Kohde-
        Kilsch
9 ....Zina Garrison
10...Kathy Jordan

WTA Computer Year-End Top 10 *(Cont.)*

WOMEN *(CONT.)*

1985
1 ....Martina Navratilova
2 ....Chris Evert Lloyd
3 ....Hana Mandlikova
4 ....Pam Shriver
5 ....Claudia Kohde-
    Kilsch
6 ....Steffi Graf
7 ....Manuela Maleeva
8 ....Zina Garrison
9 ....Helena Sukova
10...Bonnie Gadusek

1986
1 ....Martina Navratilova
2 ....Chris Evert Lloyd
3 ....Pam Shriver
4 ....Hana Mandlikova
5 ....Helena Sukova
6 ....Pam Shriver
7 ....Claudia Kohde-
    Kilsch
8 ....Manuela Maleeva
9 ....Kathy Rinaldi
10...Gabriela Sabatini

1987
1 ....Steffi Graf
2 ....Martina Navratilova
3 ....Chris Evert
4 ....Pam Shriver
5 ....Hana Mandlikova
6 ....Gabriela Sabatini
7 ....Helena Sukova
8 ....Manuela Maleeva
9 ....Zina Garrison
10...Claudia Kohde-
    Kilsch

1988
1 ....Steffi Graf
2 ....Martina Navratilova
3 ....Chris Evert
4 ....Gabriela Sabatini
5 ....Pam Shriver
6 ....Manuela Maleeva-
    Fragniere
7 ....Natalia Zvereva
8 ....Helena Sukova
9 ....Zina Garrison
10...Barbara Potter

1989
1 ....Steffi Graf
2 ....Martina Navratilova
3 ....Gabriela Sabatini
4 ....Zina Garrison
5 ....Arantxa Sánchez
    Vicario
6 ....Monica Seles
7 ....Conchita Martinez
8 ....Helena Sukova
9 ....Manuela Maleeva-
    Fragniere
10...*Chris Evert

1990
1 ....Steffi Graf
2 ....Monica Seles
3 ....Martina Navratilova
4 ....Mary Joe Fernandez
5 ....Gabriela Sabatini
6 ....Katerina Maleeva
7 ....Arantxa Sánchez
    Vicario
8 ....Jennifer Capriati
9 ....Manuela Maleeva-
    Fragniere
10...Zina Garrison

1991
1 ....Monica Seles
2 ....Steffi Graf
3 ....Gabriela Sabatini
4 ....Martina Navratilova
5 ....Arantxa Sánchez
    Vicario
6 ....Jennifer Capriati
7 ....Jana Novotna
8 ....Mary Joe Fernandez
9 ....Conchita Martinez
10..Manuela Maleeva-
    Fragniere

1992
1 ....Monica Seles
2 ....Steffi Graf
3 ....Gabriela Sabatini
4 ....Arantxa Sánchez
    Vicario
5 ....Martina Navratilova
6 ....Mary Joe Fernandez
7 ....Jennifer Capriati
8 ....Conchita Martinez
9 ....Manuela Maleeva-
    Fragniere
10..Jana Novotna

1993
1 ....Steffi Graf
2 ....Arantxa Sánchez
    Vicario
3 ....Martina Navratilova
4 ....Conchita Martinez
5 ....Gabriela Sabatini
6 ....Jana Novotna
7 ....Mary Joe Fernandez
8 ....Monica Seles
9 ....Jennifer Capriati
10..Anke Huber

1994
1 ....Steffi Graf
2 ....Arantxa Sánchez
    Vicario
3 ....Conchita Martinez
4 ....Jana Novotna
5 ....Mary Pierce
6 ....Lindsay Davenport
7 ....Gabriela Sabatini
8 ....Martina Navratilova
9 ....Kimiko Date
10..Natasha Zvereva

1995
1 ....Steffi Graf (co-No. 1)
1 ....Monica Seles
    (co-No. 1)
2 ...Conchita Martinez
3 ....Arantxa Sánchez
    Vicario
4 ....Kimiko Date
5 ....Mary Pierce
6 ....Magdalena Maleeva
7 ....Gabriela Sabatini
8 ....Mary Joe Fernandez
9 ....Iva Majoli
10..Anke Huber

1996
1 ....Steffi Graf
2 ....Monica Seles
3 ....Jana Novotna
4 ....Lindsay Davenport
5 ....Martina Hingis
6 ....Stephanie de Ville
7 ....Tamarine
    Tanasugarn
8 ....Anke Huber
9 ....Conchita Martinez
10..Julie Halard-
    Decugis

1997
1 ....Martina Hingis
2 ....Jana Novotna
3 ....Lindsay Davenport
4 ....Amanda Coetzer
5 ....Monica Seles
6 ....Iva Majoli
7 ....Mary Pierce
8 ....Irina Spirlea
9 ....Arantxa Sánchez
    Vicario
10...Mary Joe Fernandez

1998
1 ....Lindsay Davenport
2 ....Martina Hingis
2 ....Jana Novotna
4 ....Arantxa Sánchez
    Vicario
5 ....Venus Williams
6 ....Monica Seles
7 ....Mary Pierce
8 ....Conchita Martinez
9 ....Steffi Graf
10...Nathalie Tauziat

*When Chris Evert announced her retirement at the 1989 United States Open, she was ranked fourth in the world. That was her last official series tournament.

Prize Money

Top 25 Men's Career Prize Money Leaders

Note: From arrival of Open tennis in 1968 through September 27, 1999.

	Earnings ($)
Pete Sampras	37,393,411
Boris Becker	25,079,186
Ivan Lendl	21,262,417
Stefan Edberg	20,630,941
Goran Ivanisevic	18,105,269
Michael Chang	17,748,288
Andre Agassi	17,238,144
Jim Courier	13,894,363
Yevgeny Kafelnikov	13,586,506
Michael Stich	12,616,650
John McEnroe	12,539,622
Thomas Muster	12,224,410
Sergi Bruguera	11,268,285
Petr Korda	10,447,665
Richard Krajicek	8,930,360
Jimmy Connors	8,641,040
Mats Wilander	7,976,256
Mark Woodforde	7,797,574
Todd Woodbridge	7,162,584
Marcelo Rios	7,053,050
Wayne Ferreira	6,894,706
Jonas Bjorkman	6,849,462
Paul Haarhuis	6,838,717
Todd Martin	6,497,816
Alex Corretja	6,049,202

Top 25 Women's Career Prize Money Leaders

Note: From arrival of Open tennis in 1968 through September 27, 1999.

	Earnings ($)
Steffi Graf	21,839,777
Martina Navratilova	20,344,061
Arantxa Sánchez Vicario	14,615,863
Monica Seles	11,655,320
Jana Novotna	11,113,834
Martina Hingis	10,535,676
Chris Evert	8,896,195
Gabriela Sabatini	8,785,850
Lindsay Davenport	8,416,052
Conchita Martinez	8,157,233
Natasha Zvereva	7,411,595
Helena Sukova	6,391,245
Pam Shriver	5,460,566
Mary Joe Fernandez	5,252,571
Gigi Fernandez	4,681,906
Zina Garrison	4,590,816
Mary Pierce	4,513,293
Nathalie Tauziat	4,432,806
Larisa Neiland	3,991,444
Venus Williams	3,694,654
Iva Majoli	3,464,778
Lori McNeil	3,399,932
Anke Huber	3,392,342
Hana Mandlikova	3,340,959
Manuela Maleeva-Fragniere	3,244,811

All Chauvinist Tennis Club

Ah, tradition. There's nothing to beat the All England Club: tennis whites, grass courts, the bow to the royal box, the insufferable sexism. It's astonishing, but here at century's end sit the lords of Wimbledon, still harrumphing at the idea of equal pay for men and women and dreaming of the days when women knew their place. In late June '99 Chris Gorringe, the chief executive of the All England Club, set the tournament back a few decades when he justified paying the women's champion $72,000 less than the men's winner by saying that otherwise "we wouldn't have so much to spend on the petunias." *Petunias?*

Britain's No. 1 player, Tim Henman, citing the disparity between purses on the men's and women's tours, advised the women to leave the Grand Slams alone and called them "greedy" for having the gall even to raise the issue. After Henman took a sound thrashing in the British press, Jim Courier begged to be asked about the topic so he could chime in on Henman's side. "Everything he said is true," Courier said.

Not content to let the matter rest, the All England Club issued a press release noting that the prize money on the men's tour is 50% more than on the women's and pointing out that the four women semifinalists at Wimbledon in 1998—Martina Hingis, Jana Novotna, Nathalie Tauziat and Natasha Zvereva—took home more prize money during that tournament than the men's semifinalists, Henman, Goran Ivanisevic, Richard Krajicek and Pete Sampras. What the release didn't mention is that Wimbledon has virtually never followed the example of the pro tours when setting policies. Nor did the release acknowledge that those four women also played doubles at Wimbledon in '98, while the four men didn't.

So the All England Club proved itself not only cheap, sanctimonious and chauvinistic, but deceitful too. All for the sake of relative pocket change.

Open Era Overall Wins

Men's Career Leaders—Singles Titles Won

The top tournament-winning men from the institution of Open tennis in 1968 through September 27, 1999.

	W		W
Jimmy Connors	109	Andre Agassi	43
Ivan Lendl	94	Stefan Edberg	41
John McEnroe	77	Stan Smith	39
Bjorn Borg	62	Michael Chang	33
Guillermo Vilas	62	Arthur Ashe	33
Pete Sampras	60	Mats Wilander	33
Ilie Nastase	57	John Newcombe	32
Boris Becker	49	Manuel Orantes	32
Rod Laver	47	Ken Rosewall	32
Thomas Muster	44	Tom Okker	31

Women's Career Leaders—Singles Titles Won

The top tournament-winning women from the institution of Open tennis in 1968 through September 22, 1999.

	W		W
Martina Navratilova	167	Hana Mandlikova	27
Chris Evert	157	Gabriela Sabatini	27
Steffi Graf	108	Arantxa Sánchez Vicario	27
Evonne Goolagong Cawley	88	Martina Hingis	25
Margaret Smith Court	79	Nancy Richey	25
Billie Jean King	67	Jana Novotna	24
Virginia Wade	55	Lindsay Davenport	23
Monica Seles	44	Kerry Melville Reid	22
Conchita Martinez	31	Sue Barker	21
Tracy Austin	29	Pam Shriver	21

Annual ATP/WTA Champions

Men—ATP Tour World Championship

Year	Player	Year	Player
1970	Stan Smith	1985	John McEnroe
1971	Ilie Nastase	1986 (Jan)	Ivan Lendl
1972	Ilie Nastase	1986 (Dec)	Ivan Lendl
1973	Ilie Nastase	1987	Ivan Lendl
1974	Guillermo Vilas	1988	Boris Becker
1975	Ilie Nastase	1989	Stefan Edberg
1976	Manuel Orantes	1990	Andre Agassi
1977	Not held	1991	Pete Sampras
1978	Jimmy Connors	1992	Boris Becker
1979	John McEnroe	1993	Michael Stich
1980	Bjorn Borg	1994	Pete Sampras
1981	Bjorn Borg	1995	Boris Becker
1982	Ivan Lendl	1996	Pete Sampras
1983	Ivan Lendl	1997	Pete Sampras
1984	John McEnroe	1998	Alex Corretja

Note: Event held twice in 1986. *Since 1984 the final has been best-of-five sets.

Women—WTA Tour Championship

Year	Player	Year	Player
1972	Chris Evert	1986 (Mar)	Martina Navratilova
1973	Chris Evert	1986 (Nov)	Martina Navratilova
1974	Evonne Goolagong	1987	Steffi Graf
1975	Chris Evert	1988	Gabriela Sabatini
1976	Evonne Goolagong Cawley	1989	Steffi Graf
1977	Chris Evert	1990	Monica Seles
1978	Martina Navratilova	1991	Monica Seles
1979	Martina Navratilova	1992	Monica Seles
1980	Tracy Austin	1993	Steffi Graf
1981	Martina Navratilova	1994	Gabriela Sabatini
1982	Sylvia Hanika	1995	Steffi Graf
1983	Martina Navratilova	1996	Steffi Graf
1984*	Martina Navratilova	1997	Jana Novotna
1985	Martina Navratilova	1998	Martina Hingis

Viele Plays Trump Card

Befitting a man whose threshold for shame is so high that he names skyscrapers in his honor, Donald Trump issued a press release in the first week of September '99 to announce that he was in the tennis agent business, never mind that his lone client has yet to play a pro match. T Management Group, as Trump's agency is called, will represent Monique Viele, a 14-year-old prodigy who had been with IMG since she was nine and her parents sent the omnipotent management firm a videotape of her whacking balls.

Monique's father, Rick, says that Team Viele hired Trump in part because IMG "dragged its feet" in pressuring the WTA tour to suspend its age-eligibility rules and allow Monique to embark on her pro career. Rick and his wife, Bernadette, had long vowed to sue the WTA if Monique wasn't allowed to turn pro by the 1999 U.S. Open. The Vieles never filed, and when they finagled a minor relaxation of the rules to permit a 14-year-old to receive one wild-card entry to a tour event, Rick says, he signed a waiver against bringing legal action against the WTA. "We were disappointed that IMG didn't do more to help us," says Rick. "Monique's dream was to debut at the U.S. Open, and it's a shame she didn't get the opportunity."

The Vieles say that another reason they divorced themselves from IMG—which represents scores of tennis players, including defending U.S. Open women's champ Lindsay Davenport—was the agency's neglect of Monique's offcourt talents. "We didn't think IMG took her singing, her acting and her modeling seriously enough," agrees Monique's coach, Rick Macci. "With Trump and his capabilities, there's a lot more synergy and opportunity."

Viele's former IMG agent, Tony Godsick, replies, "Monique has a ton of potential, but the tennis has to come first."

All eyes will be on Monique when she makes her pro debut at the Toyota Princess Cup in Tokyo in late September '99, two weeks before her 15th birthday. While a legion of experts who have seen her practice predict that she will be a star, others point out that she hasn't played a sanctioned match in more than a year. "With all the publicity they've tried to drum up for her," says one former top women's player, "she ought to be the best thing since sliced bread."

Says Macci, "She's going to be the first tennis player to sing the national anthem before a match and then go out and win the tournament. You just wait."

—L. Jon Wertheim

Pauline Betz Addie (1965)
George T. Adee (1964)
Fred B. Alexander (1961)
Wilmer L. Allison (1963)
Manuel Alonso (1977)
Arthur Ashe (1985)
Juliette Atkinson (1974)
H.W. Bunny Austin (1997)
Tracy Austin (1992)
Lawrence A. Baker Sr. (1975)
Maud Barger–Wallach (1958)
Angela Mortimer Barrett (1993)
Karl Behr (1969)
Bjorn Borg (1987)
Jean Borotra (1976)
Lesley Turner Bowrey (1997)
Maureen Connolly Brinker(1968)
John Bromwich (1984)
Norman Everard Brookes (1977)
Mary K. Browne (1957)
Jacques Brugnon (1976)
J. Donald Budge (1964)
Maria E. Bueno (1978)
May Sutton Bundy (1956)
Mabel E. Cahill (1976)
Rosie Casals (1996)
Oliver S. Campbell (1955)
Malcolm Chace (1961)
Dorothea Douglass
  Chambers (1981)
Philippe Chatrier (1992)
Louise Brough Clapp (1967)
Clarence Clark (1983)
Joseph S. Clark (1955)
William J. Clothier (1956)
Henri Cochet (1976)
Arthur W. (Bud) Collins Jr. (1994)
Jimmy Connors (1998)
Ashley Cooper (1991)
Margaret Smith Court (1979)
Gottfried von Cramm (1977)
Jack Crawford (1979)
Joseph F. Cullman III (1990)
Allison Danzig (1968)
Sarah Palfrey Danzig (1963)
Herman David (1998)
Dwight F. Davis (1956)
Charlotte Dod (1983)
John H. Doeg (1962)
Lawrence Doherty (1980)
Reginald Doherty (1980)
Jaroslav Drobny (1983)
Margaret Osborne duPont
  (1967)

James Dwight (1955)
Roy Emerson (1982)
Pierre Etchebaster (1978)
Chris Evert (1995)
Robert Falkenburg (1974)
Neale Fraser (1984)
Shirley Fry-Irvin (1970)
Charles S. Garland (1969)
Althea Gibson (1971)
Kathleen McKane Godfree
  (1978)
Richard A. Gonzales (1968)
Evonne Goolagong Cawley
  (1988)
Bryan M. Grant Jr. (1972)
David Gray (1985)
Clarence Griffin (1970)
King Gustaf V of Sweden
  (1980)
Harold H. Hackett (1961)
Ellen Forde Hansell (1965)
Darlene R. Hard (1973)
Doris J. Hart (1969)
Gladys M. Heldman (1979)
W.E. (Slew) Hester Jr. (1981)
Bob Hewitt (1992)
Lew Hoad (1980)
Harry Hopman (1978)
Fred Hovey (1974)
Joseph R. Hunt (1966)
Lamar Hunt (1993)
Francis T. Hunter (1961)
Helen Hull Jacobs (1962)
William Johnston (1958)
Ann Haydon Jones (1985)
Perry Jones (1970)
Billie Jean King (1987)
Jan Kodes (1990)
John A. Kramer (1968)
Rene Lacoste (1976)
Al Laney (1979)
William A. Larned (1956)
Arthur D. Larsen (1969)
Rod G. Laver (1981)
Suzanne Lenglen (1978)
Dorothy Round Little (1986)
George M. Lott Jr. (1964)
Gene Mako (1973)
Molla Bjurstedt Mallory (1958)
Hana Mandlikova (1994)
Alice Marble (1964)
Alastair B. Martin (1973)
Dan Maskell (1996)
William McChesney Martin (1982)

John McEnroe (1999)
Ken McGregor (1999)
Chuck McKinley (1986)
Maurice McLoughlin (1957)
Frew McMillan (1992)
W. Donald McNeill (1965)
Elisabeth H. Moore (1971)
Gardnar Mulloy (1972)
R. Lindley Murray (1958)
Julian S. Myrick (1963)
Ilie Nastase (1991)
John D. Newcombe (1986)
Arthur C. Nielsen Sr (1971)
Alex Olmedo (1987)
Rafael Osuna (1979)
Mary Ewing Outerbridge (1981)
Frank A. Parker (1966)
Gerald Patterson (1989)
Budge Patty (1977)
Theodore R. Pell (1966)
Fred Perry (1975)
Tom Pettitt (1982)
Nicola Pietrangeli (1986)
Adrian Quist (1984)
Dennis Ralston (1987)
Ernest Renshaw (1983)
William Renshaw (1983)
Vincent Richards (1961)
Bobby Riggs (1967)
Helen Wills Moody Roark
  (1959)
Anthony D. Roche (1986)
Ellen C. Roosevelt (1975)
Ken Rosewall (1980)
Elizabeth Ryan (1972)
Manuel Santana (1984)
Richard Savitt (1976)
Frederick R. Schroeder (1966)
Eleonora Sears (1968)
Richard D. Sears (1955)
Frank Sedgman (1979)
Pancho Segura (1984)
Vic Seixas Jr. (1971)
Francis X. Shields (1964)
Betty Nuthall Shoemaker (1977)
Henry W. Slocum Jr. (1955)
Stan Smith (1987)
Fred Stolle (1985)
William F. Talbert (1967)
Bill Tilden (1959)
Lance Tingay (1982)
Ted Tinling (1986)
Bertha Townsend Toulmin
  (1974)

Tony Trabert (1970)
James H. Van Alen (1965)
John Van Ryn (1963)
Guillermo Vilas (1991)
Ellsworth Vines (1962)
Virginia Wade (1989)
Marie Wagner (1969)

Holcombe Ward (1956)
Watson Washburn (1965)
Malcolm D. Whitman (1955)
Hazel Hotchkiss Wightman
   (1957)
Anthony Wilding (1978)
Richard Norris Williams II

   (1957)
Major Walter Clopton Wingfield
   (1997)
Sidney B. Wood (1964)
Robert D. Wrenn (1955)
Beals C. Wright (1956)

Note: Years in parentheses are dates of induction.

You Call This a Tennis Mom?

Lindsay Davenport has the most clueless mom in pro tennis. Ann Davenport doesn't coach her daughter, manage her daughter or represent her daughter. She doesn't order her daughter's clothes, lunch or boyfriends. She doesn't write her daughter's letters, speeches or checks. What kind of caring tennis parent doesn't have at least one restraining order against her?

Lindsay may have been among the favorites to win the 1999 U.S. Open women's singles title, but her mom sure wasn't acting like it. Most tennis parents are on their offspring like Dr. Dentons. Where was Ann? Not in the locker room or the press room. She watched Lindsay play a match early in the tournament, didn't scream advice once, clapped happily when Lindsay won and then went back to her hotel. "We might talk tonight," Ann said, "but she's awfully busy."

Uh, hello? Last year Justin Gimelstob's dad almost got in a fistfight with Andre Agassi's coach, Brad Gilbert. Has Ann ever thrown a haymaker at Steffi Graf's coach? In 1999 Richard Williams announced that he wanted his daughter Venus to retire at 22. When's the last time Ann Davenport made a crucial life decision for Lindsay? No wonder Ann works full time as president of the Southern California Volleyball Association. She doesn't have the sense to live off her daughter!

Longtime tennis writers could no more pick Ann Davenport out of a crowd than J.D. Salinger. She has been to only one Grand Slam venue—the '99 U.S. Open. Ever! Lindsay *won* Wimbledon in '99, but was Ann there? No! She was busy with her own life. The nerve!

Superstar Martina Hingis recently dismissed her coach–racket stringer–agent–mom, Melanie Molitor, then took her back five weeks later, explaining, "We kind of complete each other." What's Ann thinking, bringing up a daughter who's already complete?

Ann's not Lindsay's psychiatrist, masseuse or publicist. She's not her valet, chauffeur or accountant. She's not her crutch, salvation or guru. All she is is her mother. In a way, she's not even that. "I think we're more like sisters," says Lindsay, 23, who lives with Ann, 57, in Newport Beach, Calif. "We have so much fun together."

Fun? Tennis parents do not have *fun*.

...Ann doesn't use her daughter as an ATM, the way Jennifer Capriati's dad reportedly did. She doesn't use her daughter as a punching bag, the way Mirjana Lucic's dad allegedly did. She doesn't need to be banned from the circuit and court-ordered to stay away from her daughter, the way Mary Pierce's dad was.

"I just always wanted Lindsay to make her own decisions and her own mistakes," says Ann. "It's her life, and it's her career. I just stayed with her until she got up on her own two feet."

In 1996 Lindsay moved back in with her mom, but only because she really needed somebody. Not Lindsay. Ann. She and her husband of 28 years, Wink, were divorcing. Lindsay came back just to get her mom up on her own two feet.

Now they're closer than freckles on a redhead. O.K., sometimes Ann will say, "You really need to wear something a little more form-fitting," and Lindsay will break down and do it. She lost 30 pounds over three years, with her mother's help, and Ann says, "I think she should show it off." Sometimes she'll go off on dates, leaving her housemate alone for the evening, but Lindsay can handle it.

Maybe it's a coincidence, but ever since Lindsay got her terrific new roomie, her tennis has been terrific. In '96 she was ranked No. 9 in the world. Before the '99 U.S. Open she'd won two of the last four Grand Slam tournaments and was ranked No. 2. Ann, naturally, was here at the U.S. Open to guide her. Not on the court. "Bloomingdale's," says Ann, laughing.

Every now and then a woman—not a girl—shows up on top of tennis. When it happens, it's usually because she was given the chance to become one.

—Rick Reilly

Golf

**Ryder Cup hero
Justin Leonard of the
United States**

Golf Goes Global

With ballooning purses, a lucrative TV contract and an expanded international schedule, golf hit the big time in 1999

BY RICK LIPSEY

PGA TOUR commissioner Tim Finchem is not the most demonstrative soul in the world, but he allowed himself a smile during the season-opening Mercedes Championships as he watched David Duval wrap up his nine-shot victory. "This," said Finchem, "is the start of a new era."

The commissioner was anticipating the Tour's bewildering new prosperity. Total purses would reach $132 million in 1999, up 40% from '98. The World tour had finally come to fruition, with three World championship events on the '99 schedule. There was also the budding rivalry between Duval and Tiger Woods.

How was Finchem to know that by year's end those spoils would seem like ancient history? That in 1999 the Tour would be transformed into an international juggernaut, with many of the problems that come with the spotlight: zillionaire players complaining that they don't get paid enough; unruly, beer-swigging fans; controversies being debated on *The New York Times* Op-Ed page?

After jump-starting the year at the Mercedes, Duval won again two weeks later at the Bob Hope Desert Classic. He stormed from five shots back on Sunday with a 59, the third in Tour history, and a round that included 11 birdies, no bogeys and an eagle at the 543-yard par-5 18th hole.

The victory gave Duval nine wins in his last 28 starts and pushed him over $1 million for the young season, but he was still No. 2 in the rankings behind Woods. Duval and Woods had never battled down the stretch in a Tour event or been paired together for even a single round, but that didn't stop the media from anointing these whiz kids the Gen Y2K version of Jack 'n' Arnie. The subjects, however, feigned indifference. "It takes two people [going head-to-head] to create a rivalry, doesn't it?" asked Duval.

Maybe, maybe not. Three weeks after the Hope, Woods played at the Buick Invitational with an intensity he hadn't displayed in a long time, apparently fired up to reclaim bragging rights as the best player on earth. He sealed his first Tour victory in nine

ROBERT BECK

Nearly two years after embarking on a complete overhaul of his swing, Woods was playing better than ever.

months with a final-round 65. Winning was particularly sweet for Woods, as it proved to him that the major swing overhaul he had been working on for almost two years was now bearing fruit.

Neither Duval nor Woods were factors at the first World Championship event in late February, the Andersen Consulting Match Play at La Costa, which had the top 64 players in the World Ranking. But big Nielsen ratings and so many hits to PGATOUR.com that the site was constantly crashing proved that match play between the world's best players is a good idea, even if the format's fickle nature yields an Andrew Magee vs. Jeff Maggert final. Maggert won with a 20-foot chip on the second hole of sudden-death and took home the biggest paycheck ($1 million) in Tour history.

In the spring Duval won the Players Championship and the BellSouth Classic to head into the Masters as the runaway favorite and the No. 1–ranked player in the world. Change is usually glacial at Augusta, but for this Masters the club made several major alterations to the course. They grew rough for the first time in the tournament's 63-year history, planted a small forest of 35-foot pine trees to the right of the fairway at the par-5 15th hole and added 25 yards to the 2nd and 17th holes. Suddenly Woods's 1997 record score of 270 looked invincible, and players were shaking in their spikes. José María Olazábal used his magical short game to win his second Masters, with a 280, two strokes ahead of Davis Love III and three ahead of Greg Norman.

Olazábal's countryman, 19-year-old Sergio Garcia, made a scintillating Tour debut at the Byron Nelson Classic in May. He shot a personal-best 62 in the first round, ended up tied for third and endeared himself to the fans with his playful smile and go-for-broke attitude. His rookie season—during which he became an appealing foil for Woods as well as the youngest player to

compete at the Ryder Cup—was full of spectacular feats, the most memorable being his final-round charge at the PGA Championship. He valiantly battled back to challenge Woods for the title but Woods drained a clutch 8-foot putt for par at 17 on Sunday to hold him off and win the second major of his career.

The rest of the season belonged to Woods, who regained the No. 1 ranking after winning the PGA and the NEC Invitational, to two vicious courses and to the Ryder Cup. The courses were Pinehurst and Carnoustie, which hosted the U.S. and British Opens, respectively, and made the pros look like Gerald Ford.

At Pinehurst, curvaceous greens surrounded by closely shaved chipping areas maddened the players and sent scores into the stratosphere. Payne Stewart won the war of attrition by one shot over Phil Mickelson. Stewart put on a short-game clinic down the stretch, capped off by a 15-foot par putt at the 72nd hole to win with a one-under 279.

The carnage was worse at Carnoustie, where winner Paul Lawrie, a Scotsman from nearby Aberdeen, shot a six-over-par 290, the highest winning score in a major since Jack Nicklaus won the '72 U.S. Open with a 290.

JIM GUND

unsportsmanlike behavior (UNITED SLOBS OF AMERICA barked England's daily *The Mirror*). One person who emerged relatively unscathed, though, was U.S. captain Ben Crenshaw, who had brought the Ryder Cup back to the U.S. for the first time since 1993. "I don't know how these things happen," Crenshaw said. "It's mystical to me."

Kind of like Juli Inkster's Zenlike transformation from a 39-year-old mother of two with thoughts of retirement into the 17th member of the LPGA Hall of Fame. After winning twice early in the season, Inkster won two majors in June, the U.S. Open, and the LPGA Championship. Suddenly, thanks to a change in the LPGA Hall requirements, Inkster was only one point away from gaining entry. She got that point in late September, winning the LPGA Golf Championship in Portland. During a raucous celebration at the 18th green, Inkster said, "I never dreamed I could get seven points [needed for induction] in such a short time." Still, in mid-October Inskter was second on the LPGA money list to Karrie Webb, the most dominant golfer on the planet in 1999. Webb, 24, had won six titles, including her first major, the du Maurier, and had four seconds and four thirds. She had made the top 10 in 20 of her 23 starts.

But Lawrie should not have gone home with the claret jug. It should have gone to France's Jean Van de Velde, who led through 71 holes but made the biggest 72nd hole blunder in championship golf history. Needing only a double-bogey 6 to win, Van de Velde made a 7 and tumbled into a playoff with Lawrie and Justin Leonard.

Van de Velde's collapse was unparalleled, but in September at the Ryder Cup in Brookline, Mass., players from Europe let another one get away. After two days Europe held a 10–6 lead over the U.S. team, whose patriotic image was marred by several players grumbling about not being paid substantially for the event. But the U.S. put its complaints aside and stormed back on Sunday to win the first six singles matches. Then Leonard clinched the victory with a 45-foot birdie putt on the 17th hole in his match against Olazábal. U.S. players and wives stormed onto the green to celebrate the triumph, but their joy was premature because Olazábal still had a 20-foot birdie putt that could have tied the hole. Had he drained it and then won the 18th hole, Olazábal would have won the match, and the Euros still could have won the cup. But Olazabal missed the putt and Europe lost 14½ to 13½.

The European players and media blasted the American players and spectators for their

So what was the most amazing happening in 1999, when golf went prime time and became a major player in the sports world? The rancorous Ryder Cup? Garcia's rise? Inkster's run to the Hall? No, the most astounding feat was accomplished by Tyler Cundith, 34, of Overland Park, Kans. On July 20, Cundith made a hole-in-one on a par-5, the 488-yard 6th hole at Oak Country Golf Course. He drove 325 yards over trees on the left; his ball hit the dried-out and doglegged fairway and ran 100 yards into the cup. The shot was eight yards short of the record for an ace, held by Shaun Lynch of England. "If I hadn't hit it, I wouldn't believe it either," said Cundith. "I never dreamed anything this amazing could happen."

Wait till next year.

Men's Majors

The Masters
**Augusta National GC; Augusta, GA
(par 72; 6,925 yds) April 8–11**

Player	Score	Earnings ($)
José María Olazábal	70-66-73-71—280	720,000
Davis Love III	69-72-70-71—282	432,600
Greg Norman	71-68-71-73—283	272,600
Bob Estes	71-72-69-72—284	176,000
Steve Pate	71-75-65-73—284	176,000
David Duval	71-74-70-70—285	125,200
Carlos Franco	72-72-68-73—285	125,200
Phil Mickelson	74-69-71-71—285	125,200
Nick Price	69-72-72-72—285	125,200
Lee Westwood	75-71-68-71—285	125,200
Steve Elkington	72-70-71-74—287	92,000
Bernhard Langer	76-66-72-73—287	92,000
Colin Montgomerie	70-72-71-74—287	92,000
Jim Furyk	72-73-70-73—288	70,000
Lee Janzen	70-69-73-76—288	70,000
Brandt Jobe	72-71-74-71—288	70,000
Ian Woosnam	71-74-71-72—288	70,000
Tiger Woods	72-72-70-75—289	52,160
Scott McCarron	69-68-76-76—289	52,160
Justin Leonard	70-72-73-74—289	52,160
Bill Glasson	72-70-73-74—289	52,160
Brandell Chamblee	69-73-75-72—289	52,160

U.S. Open
**Pinehurst Resort & CC; Pinehurst, NC
(par 70; 7,175 yds) June 17–20**

Player	Score	Earnings ($)
Payne Stewart	68-69-72-70—279	625,000
Phil Mickelson	67-70-73-70—280	370,000
Tiger Woods	68-71-72-70—281	196,792
Vijay Singh	69-70-73-69—281	196,792
Steve Stricker	70-73-69-73—285	130,655
Tim Herron	69-72-70-75—286	116,935
David Duval	67-70-75-75—287	96,260
Jeff Maggert	71-69-74-73—287	96,260
Hal Sutton	69-70-76-72—287	96,260
Darren Clarke	73-70-74-71—288	78,863
Billy Mayfair	67-72-74-75—288	78,863
Paul Goydos	67-74-74-74—289	67,347
Davis Love III	70-73-74-72—289	67,347
Paul Azinger	72-72-75-70—289	67,347
Colin Montgomerie	72-72-74-72—290	58,215
Justin Leonard	69-75-73-73—290	58,215
John Huston	71-69-75-76—291	46,756
Scott Verplank	72-73-72-74—291	46,756
Dudley Hart	73-73-76-69—291	46,756
Jim Furyk	69-73-77-72—291	46,756
Jay Haas	74-72-73-72—291	46,756
Jesper Parnevik	71-71-76-73—291	46,756

British Open
**Carnoustie GC; Carnoustie, Scotland
(par 71; 7,316 yds) July 15–18**

Player	Score	Earnings ($)
†Paul Lawrie	73-74-76-67—290	577,500
Justin Leonard	73-74-71-72—290	305,250
Jean Van de Velde	75-68-70-77—290	305,250
Angel Cabrera	75-69-77-70—291	165,000
Craig Parry	76-75-67-73—291	165,000
Greg Norman	76-70-75-72—293	115,500
Tiger Woods	74-72-74-74—294	82,500
Davis Love III	74-74-77-69—294	82,500
David Frost	80-69-71-74—294	82,500
Scott Dunlap	72-77-76-70—295	57,420
Jim Furyk	78-71-76-70—295	57,420
Retief Goosen	76-75-73-71—295	57,420
Jesper Parnevik	74-71-78-72—295	57,420
Hal Sutton	73-78-72-72—295	57,420
Colin Montgomerie	74-76-72-74—296	42,900
Tsuyoshi Yoneyama	77-74-73-72—296	42,900
Scott Verplank	80-74-73-69—296	42,900
Lee Westwood	76-75-74-72—297	33,825
Costantino Rocca	81-69-74-73—297	33,825
Patrik Sjoland	74-72-77-74—297	33,825
Andrew Coltart	74-74-72-77—297	33,825
Bernhard Langer	72-77-73-75—297	33,825
Frank Nobilo	76-76-70-75—297	33,825

† Won four-hole playoff

PGA Championship
**Medinah CC, Medinah, IL
(par 72; 7,401 yds) August 12–15**

Player	Score	Earnings ($)
Tiger Woods	70-67-68-72—277	630,000
Sergio Garcia	66-73-68-71—278	378,000
Stewart Cink	69-70-68-73—280	203,000
Jay Haas	68-67-75-70—280	203,000
Nick Price	70-71-69-71—281	129,000
Bob Estes	71-70-72-69—282	112,000
Colin Montgomerie	72-70-70-70—282	112,000
Steve Pate	72-70-73-69—284	96,500
Jim Furyk	71-70-69-74—284	96,500
David Duval	70-71-72-72—285	72,167
Corey Pavin	69-74-71-71—285	72,167
Chris Perry	70-73-71-71—285	72,167
Miguel Jimenez	70-70-75-70—285	72,167
Jesper Parnevik	72-70-73-70—285	72,167
Mike Weir	68-68-69-80—285	72,167
Gabriel Hjertstedt	72-70-73-72—287	48,600
Mark Brooks	70-73-70-74—287	48,600
Brandt Jobe	69-74-69-75—287	48,600
Greg Turner	73-69-70-75—287	48,600
Lee Westwood	70-68-74-75—287	48,600

Men's Tour Results

Late 1998 PGA Tour Events

Tournament	Final Round	Winner	Score/ Under Par	Earnings ($)
Las Vegas Invitational	Oct 18	Jim Furyk	335/–25	360,000
National Car Rental Classic	Oct 25	John Huston	272/–16	360,000
The Tour Championship	Nov 1	Hal Sutton*	274/–6	720,000
Sarazen World Open Championship**	Nov 10	Dudley Hart	272/–16	360,000
Shark Shootout**	Nov 15	Steve Elkington/Greg Norman	189/–27	160,000 each
JC Penney Classic**	Dec 6	Meg Mallon/Steve Pate	255/–29	218,750 each

1999 PGA Tour Events

Tournament	Final Round	Winner	Score/ Under Par	Earnings ($)
Mercedes Championships	Jan 10	David Duval	266/–26	468,000
Sony Open	Jan 17	Jeff Sluman	271/–9	468,000
Bob Hope Classic	Jan 24	David Duval	334/–26	540,000
Phoenix Open	Jan 31	Rocco Mediate	273/–11	540,000
Pebble Beach National Pro-Am#	Feb 7	Payne Stewart	206/–10	504,000
Buick Invitational	Feb 14	Tiger Woods	266/–22	486,000
Nissan Open	Feb 21	Ernie Els	270/–14	504,000
Tucson Open	Feb 28	Gabriel Hjertstedt*	276/–12	495,000
Match Play Championship	Feb 28	Jeff Maggert†		1,000,000
Doral-Ryder Open	Mar 7	Steve Elkington	275/–13	540,000
Honda Classic	Mar 14	Vijay Singh	277/–11	468,000
Bay Hill Invitational	Mar 21	Tim Herron*	274/–14	486,000
The Players Championship	Mar 28	David Duval	285/–3	900,000
BellSouth Classic	Apr 4	David Duval	270/–18	450,000
The Masters	Apr 11	José-María Olazábal	280/–8	720,000
MCI Classic	Apr 18	Glen Day*	274/–10	450,000
Greater Greensboro Classic	Apr 25	Jesper Parnevik	265/–23	468,000
Houston Open	May 2	Stuart Appleby	279/–9	450,000
Compaq Classic	May 9	Carlos Franco	269/–19	468,000
Byron Nelson Classic	May 16	Loren Roberts*	262/–18	540,000
The Colonial	May 23	Olin Browne	272/–8	504,000
Kemper Open	May 30	Rich Beem	274/–10	450,000
The Memorial	June 6	Tiger Woods	273/–15	459,000
St. Jude Classic	June 14	Ted Tryba	265/–19	450,000
U.S. Open	June 20	Payne Stewart	279/–1	625,000
Buick Classic	June 27	Duffy Waldorf*	276/–8	450,000
Western Open	July 4	Tiger Woods	273/–15	450,000
Greater Milwaukee Open	July 11	Carlos Franco	264/–20	414,000
British Open	July 18	Paul Lawrie*	290/+6	577,500
John Deere Classic	July 25	J.L. Lewis*	261/–19	360,000
Greater Hartford Open	Aug 1	Brent Geiberger	262/–18	450,000
Buick Open	Aug 8	Tom Pernice Jr.	270/–18	432,000
PGA Championship	Aug 15	Tiger Woods	277/–11	630,000
Sprint International	Aug 22	David Toms	47‡	468,000
World Golf Championships NEC Invit.	Aug 29	Tiger Woods	270/–10	1,000,000
Reno-Tahoe Open	Aug 29	Notah Begay	274/–14	495,000
Air Canada Championship	Sep 5	Mike Weir	266/–18	450,000
Canadian Open	Sept 12	Hal Sutton	275/–13	450,000
B.C. Open	Sept 20	Brad Faxon*	273/–15	288,000
Texas Open	Sept 26	Duffy Waldorf*	270/–18	360,000
Buick Challenge	Oct 3	David Toms	271/–17	324,000
Michelob Championship	Oct 10	Notah Begay*	274/–10	450,000
Las Vegas Invitational	Oct 17	Jim Furyk	331/–29	450,000

* Won sudden-death playoff. †Won on the second extra hole of match play. # Tournament shortened by rain. ‡ Revised Stableford scoring.
** Not an official event.

Nabisco Dinah Shore
Mission Hills CC; Rancho Mirage, CA
(par 72; 6,460 yds) March 25–28

Player	Score	Earnings ($)
Dottie Pepper	70-66-67-66—269	150,000
Meg Mallon	66-69-71-69—275	93,093
Karrie Webb	73-71-70-66—280	67,933
Kelly Robbins	69-73-67-72—281	52,837
Charlotta Sörenstam	72-68-76-66—282	42,772
Juli Inkster	72-66-71-74—283	35,224
Catriona Matthew	72-73-69-70—284	26,502
Janice Moodie	69-68-75-72—284	26,502
Annika Sörenstam	70-73-71-70—284	26,502
Helen Alfredsson	69-71-73-72—285	19,289
Maria Hjorth	77-68-68-72—285	19,289
Sherri Steinhauer	70-72-72-71—285	19,289
Pat Bradley	73-69-72-72—286	13,712
Mayumi Hirase	70-72-69-75—286	13,712
Rosie Jones	73-70-73-70—286	13,712
Cindy McCurdy	70-74-69-73—286	13,712
Se Ri Pak	73-69-69-75—286	13,712
Michele Redman	71-74-69-72—286	13,712
Kris Tschetter	68-70-73-75—286	13,712
Maggie Will	72-71-73-70—286	13,712

LPGA Championship
DuPont Country Club; Wilmington, DE
(par 71; 6,376 yds) June 24–27

Player	Score	Earnings ($)
Juli Inkster	68-66-69-65—268	210,000
Liselotte Neumann	67-67-70-68—272	130,330
Mardi Lunn	68-74-65-66—273	84,538
Nancy Scranton	69-68-66-70—273	84,538
Rosie Jones	64-72-68-70—274	54,596
Cristie Kerr	70-64-69-71—274	54,596
Emilee Klein	72-68-67-48—275	35,224
Jill McGill	70-69-68-68—275	35,224
Laura Davies	65-71-71-68—275	35,224
Se Ri Pak	68-69-67-71—275	35,224
Mayumi Hirase	70-73-68-65—276	23,487
Sara Sanders	70-68-68-70—276	23,487
Tammie Green	68-70-68-70—276	23,487
Jenny Lidback	67-67-72-70—276	23,487
Meg Mallon	70-71-63-72—276	23,487
Annika Sörenstam	73-68-68-68—277	18,415
Susie Redman	70-68-70-69—277	18,415
Jan Stephenson	69-69-69-70—277	18,415
Dottie Pepper	71-72-68-67—278	16,301
Sherri Steinhauer	74-69-65-70—278	16,301
Hiromi Kobayashi	70-67-71-70—278	16,301

U.S. Women's Open
Old Waverly GC; West Point, MS
(par 72; 6,433 yds) June 3–6

Player	Score	Earnings ($)
Juli Inkster	65-69-67-71—272	315,000
Sherri Turner	69-69-68-71—277	185,000
Kelli Kuehne	64-71-70-74—279	118,227
Lorie Kane	70-64-71-75—280	82,399
Meg Mallon	70-70-69-72—281	62,938
Karin Koch	72-69-68-72—281	62,938
Karrie Webb	70-70-68-74—282	53,132
Helen Dobson	71-70-73-69—283	45,244
Maria Hjorth	73-69-70-71—283	45,244
Catriona Matthew	69-68-74-72—283	45,244
Grace Park*	70-67-73-73—283	
Helen Alfredsson	72-68-70-74—284	37,666
Becky Iverson	72-64-73-75—284	37,666
Michele Redman	72-71-75-67—285	32,390
Se Ri Pak	68-70-74-73—285	32,390
Dottie Pepper	68-69-72-76—285	32,390
Liselotte Neumann	73-71-69-73—286	27,422
A.J. Eathorne	69-71-75-71—286	27,422
Catrin Nilsmark	69-71-70-76—286	27,422
Cindy McCurdy	72-72-74-69—287	21,832
Leta Lindley	72-72-73-70—287	21,832
Sophie Gustafson	72-72-70-73—287	21,832
Donna Andrews	69-71-72-75—287	21,832
Akiko Fukushima	69-70-71-77—287	21,832

du Maurier Classic
Priddis Greens Golf & CC; Calgary, Alberta
(par 72; 6,415 yds) July 29–August 1

Player	Score	Earnings ($)
Karrie Webb	73-72-66-66—277	180,000
Laura Davies	72-66-69-72—279	111,711
Julie Inkster	68-69-74-69—280	81,519
Dawn Coe-Jones	72-65-72-74—283	63,404
Catriona Matthew	68-70-72-74—284	51,326
Maggie Will	74-69-74-68—285	36,431
Mi Hyun Kim	78-69-69-69—285	36,431
Lorie Kane	70-72-73-70—285	36,431
Carin Koch	71-71-73-71—286	24,486
Sherri Turner	72-72-70-72—286	24,486
Jill McGill	72-71-71-72—286	24,486
Rosie Jones	67-74-72-73—286	24,486
Dina Ammaccapane	73-70-73-71—287	18,177
Se Ri Pak	75-71-68-73—287	18,177
Beth Daniel	72-70-72-73—287	18,177
Michele Redman	70-72-72-73—287	18,177
Maria Hjorth	72-72-73-71—288	15,157
Mhairi McKay	73-69-74-72—288	15,157
Cristie Kerr	71-71-70-76—288	15,157
Helen Dobson	75-74-72-68—289	13,346
Wendy Ward	73-72-75-69—289	13,346
Tammie Green	73-74-71-71—289	13,346

* Amateur.

Women's Tour Results

Late 1998 LPGA Tour Events

Tournament	Final Round	Winner	Score/ Under Par	Earnings ($)
World Championship of Women's Golf	Oct 25	Juli Inkster	275/–13	137,000
Japan Classic	Nov 8	Hiromi Kobayashi*	205/–11	120,000
LPGA Tour Championship	Nov 22	Laura Davies	277/–11	215,000
JC Penney Classic**	Dec 6	Meg Mallon/Steve Pate	255/–29	218,750 each

1999 LPGA Tour Events

Tournament	Final Round	Winner	Score/ Under Par	Earnings ($)
The Inaugural	Jan 17	Kelly Robbins	205/–11	82,500
Naples LPGA Memorial	Jan 24	Meg Mallon	272/–16	112,500
LPGA Office Depot	Jan 30	Karrie Webb	278/–10	101,250
Valley of the Stars Championship	Feb 14	Catrin Nilsmark*	204/–12	97,500
Hawaiian Ladies Open	Feb 20	Alison Nicholas	209/–7	97,500
Australian Ladies Masters	Feb 28	Karrie Webb	262/–26	112,500
Welch's/Circle K Championship	Mar 14	Juli Inkster	273/–15	93,750
Standard Register PING	Mar 21	Karrie Webb	274/–14	127,500
Nabisco Dinah Shore	Mar 28	Dottie Pepper	269/–19	150,000
Longs Drugs Challenge	Apr 4	Juli Inkster	280/–8	90,000
Chick-fil-A Charity Championship	Apr 25	Rachel Hetherington*	204/–12	120,000
Myrtle Beach Classic#	May 2	Rachel Hetherington	137/–7	101,250
Titleholders Championship	May 10	Karrie Webb	271/–17	135,000
Sara Lee Classic	May 16	Meg Mallon	199/–17	112,500
Philips Invitational	May 23	Akiko Fukushima	267/–13	120,000
Corning Classic	May 30	Kelli Kuehne	278/–10	112,500
U.S. Women's Open	June 6	Juli Inkster	272/–16	315,000
Rochester International	June 13	Karrie Webb	280/–8	150,000
ShopRite Classic	June 20	Se Ri Pak	198/–15	150,000
LPGA Championship	June 27	Juli Inkster	268/–16	210,000
Jamie Farr Classic	July 4	Se Ri Pak*	276/–8	135,000
Michelob Light Classic	July 11	Annika Sörenstam*	278/–10	120,000
Big Apple Classic	July 18	Sherri Steinhauer*	273/–11	127,500
Giant Eagle Classic	July 25	Jackie Gallagher-Smith	199/–17	150,000
du Maurier Classic	Aug 1	Karrie Webb	277/–11	180,000
areaWEB.COM Challenge	Aug 8	Mardi Lunn	275/–13	120,000
Women's British Open	Aug 15	Sherri Steinhauer	283/–9	160,000
Firstar LPGA Classic	Aug 22	Rosie Jones*	207/–9	97,500
Oldsmobile Classic	Aug 29	Dottie Pepper	270/–18	105,000
Rail Classic	Sept 6	Mi Hyun Kim	204/–12	116,250
World Championship of Golf	Sept 12	Se Ri Pak	280/–8	150,000
SAFECO Classic	Sept 19	Maria Hjorth	271/–17	97,500
Safeway LPGA Championship	Sept 26	Juli Inkster	207/–9	120,000
New Albany Golf Classic	Oct 3	Annika Sörenstam	269/–19	150,000
Betsy King Classic	Oct 10	Mi Hyun Kim	280/–8	108,750
AFLAC Tournament of Champions	Oct 17	Akiko Fukushima	279/–9	122,000

* Won sudden-death playoff. #Shortened due to rain. **Not an official event

Captain Ben's History Lesson

Take a burgundy suitcase and get it stickered by customs in 30 countries and you have the look of what the American team wore for the final day of competition at the Ryder Cup. Dreamed up by U.S. captain Ben Crenshaw and designed by Jeff Rose & Co., the short-sleeve top featured black-and-white photos of six victorious U.S. squads. A BBC wag dubbed it the Pizza Shirt.

"We got responses from people who thought it was the ugliest thing they'd ever seen, and from people who thought it was the most unique thing they'd ever seen," said Preston Piermattei, partner and executive vice-president of sales and marketing for Jeff Rose. "Actually it's a piece of art more than a golf shirt."

Indeed it was a piece of something. Under PGA rules, Jeff Rose was not allowed to sell apparel it designed for the team before the match ended. But because the shirt received so much airtime in the U.S.'s victory, the company was considering putting it on the shelves in the weeks following the event. The price Jeff Rose was considering: $160.
—Gene Menez

Senior Men's Tour Results

Late 1998 Senior Tour Events

Tournament	Final Round	Winner	Score/ Under Par	Earnings ($)
Raley's Gold Rush Classic	Oct 18	Dana Quigley	203/–13	150,000
Kaanapali Classic	Oct 25	Jay Sigel	201/–12	150,000
Pacific Bell Senior Classic	Nov 1	Joe Inman	202/–11	165,000
Senior Tour Championship	Nov 8	Hale Irwin	274/–14	347,000

1999 Senior Tour Events

Tournament	Final Round	Winner	Score/ Under Par	Earnings ($)
MasterCard Championship	Jan 24	John Jacobs	203/–13	185,000
Senior Skins Game**	Jan 31	Hale Irwin	7 skins	230,000
Royal Caribbean Classic	Feb 7	Bruce Fleisher	205/–8	150,000
American Express Invitational	Feb 14	Bruce Fleisher	203/–13	180,000
GTE Classic	Feb 21	Larry Nelson	205/–8	180,000
ACE Group Classic	Feb 28	Allen Doyle	203/–13	180,000
Senior Slam**	Mar 3	Gil Morgan	132/–12	300,000
Toshiba Classic	Mar 14	Gary McCord*	279/–9	180,000
Legends of Golf**	Mar 21	Gil Morgan/Hubert Green	194/–22	158,000 each
Emerald Coast Classic	Mar 28	Bob Duval	200/–10	165,000
The Tradition#	April 4	Graham Marsh	136/–8	225,000
PGA Seniors Championship	April 18	Allen Doyle	274/–14	315,000
Home Depot Invitational	April 25	Bruce Fleisher	205/–11	180,000
Bruno's Memorial Classic	May 2	Larry Nelson	205/–11	180,000
Nationwide Championship	May 9	Hale Irwin	206/–10	210,000
Las Vegas Senior Classic	May 16	Vincente Fernandez	274/–13	210,000
Bell Atlantic Classic	May 23	Tom Jenkins*	206/–10	165,000
Boone Valley Classic	May 30	Hale Irwin	203/–13	210,000
Cadillac NFL Golf Classic	June 6	Allen Doyle*	204/–12	165,000
BellSouth Senior Classic	June 13	Bruce Fleisher	200/–16	210,000
Southwestern Bell Dominion	June 20	John Mahaffey*	204/–12	165,000
Senior Players Championship	June 27	Hale Irwin	267/–21	300,000
State Farm Classic	July 4	Christy O'Connor Jr.	198/–18	195,000
U.S. Senior Open	July 11	Dave Eichelberger	281/–7	315,000
Ameritech Senior Open	July 18	Hale Irwin	206/–10	195,000
Burnet Senior Classic	July 25	Hale Irwin	201/–15	225,000
Utah Showdown	Aug 1	Dave Eichelberger*	197/–19	202,500
Lightpath Long Island Classic	Aug 8	Bruce Fleisher	206/–10	180,000
Foremost Insurance Championship	Aug 15	Christy O'Connor Jr.	205/–11	150,000
BankBoston Classic	Aug 22	Tom McGinnis*	205/–11	180,000
Canada Senior Open	Aug 29	Jim Ahern*	272/–16	202,500
TD Waterhouse Championship	Sep 5	Allen Doyle	198/–18	180,000
Comfort Classic	Sep 12	Gil Morgan	201/–15	180,000
Bank One Championship	Sep 19	Tom Watson	196/–20	195,000
Kroger Senior Classic	Sep 26	Gil Morgan	198/–12	210,000
Vantage Championship	Oct 3	Fred Gibson	195/–15	225,000
The Transamerica	Oct 10	Bruce Fleisher	199/–17	165,000
Raley's Gold Rush Classic	Oct 17	David Graham	199/–17	165,000

*Won sudden-death playoff. #Shortened due to rain. **Not an official event.

U.S. Amateur Results

Tournament	Final Round	Winner	Score	Runner-Up
Women's Amateur Public Links	June 27	Jody Niemann	1 up	Sue Billek-Nyhus
Men's Amateur Public Links	July 17	Hunter Haas	4 & 3	Michael Kirk
Boys' Junior Amateur	July 31	Hunter Mahan	4 & 2	Camilo Villegas
Girls' Junior Amateur	Aug 7	Aree Wongluekiet	2 up	Nancy Abiecunas
Women's Amateur	Aug 14	Dorothy Delasin	4 & 3	Jimin Kang
Men's Amateur	Aug 22	David Gossett	9 & 8	Sung Yoon Kim
Senior Men	Oct 7	Bill Ploeger	3 & 2	Gary Menzel
Senior Women	Sept 19	Carol Semple Thompson	1st extra hole	Cecilia Mourgue D'Algue
Men's Mid-Amateur	Sept 30	Danny Green	2 & 1	Jerry Courville
Women's Mid-Amateur	Oct 7	Alissa Herron	1 up	Leland Beckel

International Results

Tournament	Final Round	Winner	Score	Runner-Up
Walker Cup	Sept 12	GB/Ireland	15–9	United States
Ryder Cup	Sept 26	United States	14½ – 13½	Europe

PGA Tour Final 1998 Money Leaders

Name	Events	Best Finish	Scoring Average*	Money ($)
David Duval	23	1 (4)	69.13	2,591,031
Vijay Singh	26	1 (2)	69.85	2,238,998
Jim Furyk	28	1	69.50	2,054,334
Tiger Woods	20	1	69.21	1,841,117
Hal Sutton	30	1 (2)	70.05	1,838,740
Phil Mickelson	24	1 (2)	70.28	1,837,246
Mark O'Meara	19	1 (2)	69.63	1,786,699
Justin Leonard	28	1	70.12	1,671,823
Fred Couples	17	1 (2)	69.87	1,650,389
John Huston	25	1 (2)	69.65	1,544,110

*Adjusted for average score of field in each tournament entered.

LPGA Tour Final 1998 Money Leaders

Name	Events	Best Finish	Scoring Average	Money ($)
Annika Sörenstam	21	1 (4)	69.99	1,092,748
Se Ri Pak	27	1 (4)	71.41	872,170
Donna Andrews	24	1	70.69	715,428
Karrie Webb	23	1 (2)	70.52	704,477
Liselotte Neumann	21	1 (2)	71.15	665,069
Juli Inkster	25	1	70.78	656,012
Brandie Burton	26	1	71.15	652,084
Pat Hurst	26	1	71.20	612,329
Meg Mallon	28	1	70.58	593,458
Dottie Pepper	25	2 (3)	70.46	539,792

Senior Tour Final 1998 Money Leaders

Name	Events	Finish	Average	Money ($)
Hale Irwin	22	1 (7)	68.59	2,861,945
Gil Morgan	25	1 (6)	69.46	2,179,047
Larry Nelson	23	1 (3)	69.87	1,442,476
Jay Sigel	32	1 (2)	70.55	1,403,912
Hugh Baiocchi	35	1 (2)	70.86	1,183,958
Jim Colbert	32	1	70.84	1,122,413
Dana Quigley	38	1 (2)	70.94	1,103,882
Bruce Summerhays	37	1	71.17	1,098,942
Isao Aoki	22	1	70.54	1,042,200
Dave Stockton	27	2 (2)	70.49	1,040,524

Impeaching the Presidents

It's not surprising that David Duval provoked outrage when he cried that the PGA of America was exploiting the U.S. Ryder Cup team. Duval and Tiger Woods, who joined in grousing that the $5,000 stipend allotted to Ryder competitors was too meager, were correct in noting that the PGA reaps $17 million or more in net revenue from the Cup. But Duval, Woods and some other members of the 12-man team that played Europe's best at The Country Club in Brookline, Mass., Sept. 24–26, 1999, seemed to forget that the PGA is a nonprofit organization that uses Cup proceeds to run events for lesser lights and to support various golf-related charities.

Facing charges of greed, Duval claimed that he'd been misunderstood, that what he really wanted the money for was his own charities. Woods said that was also true in his case. But as Brad Faxon pointed out, Woods and Duval, who had already won a combined $6.4 million as of August 15, hardly needed such help if they wanted to give to charity.

So what was really the issue here? "The reason this [controversy] is occurring is the Presidents Cup," said Payne Stewart, laying the blame on the Ryder wannabe event hatched by PGA Tour commissioner Tim Finchem in 1994. With the Presidents Cup, which matches a U.S. team against a squad of foreign pros from anywhere but Europe, filling even years and the Ryder odd—and with both events requiring the U.S. players to glad-hand corporate heavies—top pros must now go through the whole tired exercise every 12 months instead of every 24. Woods hints that this is part of his objection when he wearily says, "It's pros on parade."

In fact, two biennial international team matches are one too many. The 1998 Presidents Cup, held in Melbourne, roused so little interest—partly because the time difference between Australia and the U.S. made it inconvenient to watch on TV—that even the U.S. players seemed drowsy, losing 20½ to 11½ to a team featuring the likes of Vijay Singh and Steve Elkington, players who could be seen on the Tour every week.

Stewart worried that, burdened with two international team events, the top golfers would start opting out of the Ryder Cup, as the top U.S. tennis players do with the Davis Cup. The answer was not to funnel the Ryder proceeds through the players. This was never about philanthropy. The answer was to recognize the Presidents Cup for the clutter it is and get rid of it.

—*Cameron Morfit*

Men's Golf

THE MAJOR TOURNAMENTS

The Masters

Year	Winner	Score	Runner-Up	Year	Winner	Score	Runner-Up
1934	Horton Smith	284	Craig Wood	1971	Charles Coody	279	Johnny Miller
1935	Gene Sarazen* (144)	282	Craig Wood (149)				Jack Nicklaus
	(only 36-hole playoff)			1972	Jack Nicklaus	286	Bruce Crampton
1936	Horton Smith	285	Harry Cooper				Bobby Mitchell
1937	Byron Nelson	283	Ralph Guldahl				Tom Weiskopf
1938	Henry Picard	285	Ralph Guldahl	1973	Tommy Aaron	283	J.C. Snead
			Harry Cooper	1974	Gary Player	278	Tom Weiskopf
1939	Ralph Guldahl	279	Sam Snead				Dave Stockton
1940	Jimmy Demaret	280	Lloyd Mangrum	1975	Jack Nicklaus	276	Johnny Miller
1941	Craig Wood	280	Byron Nelson				Tom Weiskopf
1942	Byron Nelson* (69)	280	Ben Hogan (70)	1976	Ray Floyd	271	Ben Crenshaw
1943–45	No tournament			1977	Tom Watson	276	Jack Nicklaus
1946	Herman Keiser	282	Ben Hogan	1978	Gary Player	277	Hubert Green
1947	Jimmy Demaret	281	Byron Nelson				Rod Funseth
			Frank Stranahan				Tom Watson
1948	Claude Harmon	279	Cary Middlecoff	1979	Fuzzy Zoeller* (4–3)†	280	Ed Sneed (4–4)
1949	Sam Snead	282	Johnny Bulla				Tom Watson (4–4)
			Lloyd Mangrum	1980	Seve Ballesteros	275	Gibby Gilbert
1950	Jimmy Demaret	283	Jim Ferrier				Jack Newton
1951	Ben Hogan	280	Skee Riegel	1981	Tom Watson	280	Johnny Miller
1952	Sam Snead	286	Jack Burke Jr				Jack Nicklaus
1953	Ben Hogan	274	Ed Oliver Jr	1982	Craig Stadler* (4)	284	Dan Pohl (5)
1954	Sam Snead* (70)	289	Ben Hogan (71)	1983	Seve Ballesteros	280	Ben Crenshaw
1955	Cary Middlecoff	279	Ben Hogan				Tom Kite
1956	Jack Burke Jr.	289	Ken Venturi	1984	Ben Crenshaw	277	Tom Watson
1957	Doug Ford	282	Sam Snead	1985	Bernhard Langer	282	Curtis Strange
1958	Arnold Palmer	284	Doug Ford				Seve Ballesteros
			Fred Hawkins				Ray Floyd
1959	Art Wall Jr.	284	Cary Middlecoff	1986	Jack Nicklaus	279	Greg Norman
1960	Arnold Palmer	282	Ken Venturi				Tom Kite
1961	Gary Player	280	Charles R. Coe	1987	Larry Mize* (4–3)	285	Seve Ballesteros (5)
			Arnold Palmer				Greg Norman (4–4)
1962	Arnold Palmer* (68)	280	Gary Player (71)	1988	Sandy Lyle	281	Mark Calcavecchia
			D. Finsterwald (77)	1989	Nick Faldo* (5–3)	283	Scott Hoch (5–4)
1963	Jack Nicklaus	286	Tony Lema	1990	Nick Faldo* (4–4)	278	Ray Floyd (4–x)
1964	Arnold Palmer	276	Dave Marr	1991	Ian Woosnam	277	José María Olazábal
			Jack Nicklaus	1992	Fred Couples	275	Ray Floyd
1965	Jack Nicklaus	271	Arnold Palmer	1993	Bernhard Langer	277	Chip Beck
			Gary Player	1994	José María Olazábal	279	Tom Lehman
1966	Jack Nicklaus* (70)	288	Tommy Jacobs (72)	1995	Ben Crenshaw	274	Davis Love III
			Gay Brewer Jr. (78)	1996	Nick Faldo	276	Greg Norman
1967	Gay Brewer Jr.	280	Bobby Nichols	1997	Tiger Woods	270	Tom Kite
1968	Bob Goalby	277	Roberto DeVicenzo	1998	Mark O'Meara	279	David Duval
1969	George Archer	281	Billy Casper				Fred Couples
			George Knudson	1999	José María Olazábal	280	Davis Love III
			Tom Weiskopf				
1970	Billy Casper* (69)	279	Gene Littler (74)				

*Winner in playoff. Playoff scores are in parentheses. †Playoff cut from 18 holes to sudden death.
Note: Played at Augusta National Golf Club, Augusta, GA.

United States Open Championship

Year	Winner	Score	Runner-Up	Site
1895	Horace Rawlins	†173	Willie Dunn	Newport GC, Newport, RI
1896	James Foulis	†152	Horace Rawlins	Shinnecock Hills GC, Southampton, NY
1897	Joe Lloyd	†162	Willie Anderson	Chicago GC, Wheaton, IL
1898	Fred Herd	328	Alex Smith	Myopia Hunt Club, Hamilton, MA
1899	Willie Smith	315	George Low Val Fitzjohn W.H. Way	Baltimore CC, Baltimore
1900	Harry Vardon	313	John H. Taylor	Chicago GC, Wheaton, IL
1901	Willie Anderson* (85)	331	Alex Smith (86)	Myopia Hunt Club, Hamilton, MA
1902	Laurie Auchterlonie	307	Stewart Gardner	Garden City GC, Garden City, NY
1903	Willie Anderson* (82)	307	David Brown (84)	Baltusrol GC, Springfield, NJ
1904	Willie Anderson	303	Gil Nicholls	Glen View Club, Golf, IL
1905	Willie Anderson	314	Alex Smith	Myopia Hunt Club, Hamilton, MA
1906	Alex Smith	295	Willie Smith	Onwentsia Club, Lake Forest, IL
1907	Alex Ross	302	Gil Nicholls	Philadelphia Cricket Club, Chestnut Hill, PA
1908	Fred McLeod* (77)	322	Willie Smith (83)	Myopia Hunt Club, Hamilton, MA
1909	George Sargent	290	Tom McNamara	Englewood GC, Englewood, NJ
1910	Alex Smith* (71)	298	John McDermott (75) Macdonald Smith (77)	Philadelphia Cricket Club, Chestnut Hill, PA
1911	John McDermott* (80)	307	Mike Brady (82) George Simpson (85)	Chicago GC, Wheaton, IL
1912	John McDermott	294	Tom McNamara	CC of Buffalo, Buffalo
1913	Francis Ouimet* (72)	304	Harry Vardon (77) Edward Ray (78)	The Country Club, Brookline, MA
1914	Walter Hagen	290	Chick Evans	Midlothian CC, Blue Island, IL
1915	Jerry Travers	297	Tom McNamara	Baltusrol GC, Springfield, NJ
1916	Chick Evans	286	Jock Hutchison	Minikahda Club, Minneapolis
1917–18	No tournament			
1919	Walter Hagen* (77)	301	Mike Brady (78)	Brae Burn CC, West Newton, MA
1920	Edward Ray	295	Harry Vardon Jack Burke Leo Diegel Jock Hutchison	Inverness CC, Toledo
1921	Jim Barnes	289	Walter Hagen Fred McLeod	Columbia CC, Chevy Chase, MD
1922	Gene Sarazen	288	John L. Black Bobby Jones	Skokie CC, Glencoe, IL
1923	Bobby Jones* (76)	296	Bobby Cruickshank (78)	Inwood CC, Inwood, NY
1924	Cyril Walker	297	Bobby Jones	Oakland Hills CC, Birmingham, MI
1925	W. MacFarlane* (75–72)	291	Bobby Jones (75–73)	Worcester CC, Worcester, MA
1926	Bobby Jones	293	Joe Turnesa	Scioto CC, Columbus, OH
1927	Tommy Armour* (76)	301	Harry Cooper (79)	Oakmont CC, Oakmont, PA
1928	Johnny Farrell* (143)	294	Bobby Jones (144)	Olympia Fields CC, Matteson, IL
1929	Bobby Jones* (141)	294	Al Espinosa (164)	Winged Foot GC, Mamaroneck, NY
1930	Bobby Jones	287	Macdonald Smith	Interlachen CC, Hopkins, MN
1931	Billy Burke* (149–148)	292	George Von Elm (149–149)	Inverness Club, Toledo
1932	Gene Sarazen	286	Phil Perkins Bobby Cruickshank	Fresh Meadows CC, Flushing, NY
1933	Johnny Goodman	287	Ralph Guldahl	North Shore CC, Glenview, IL
1934	Olin Dutra	293	Gene Sarazen	Merion Cricket Club, Ardmore, PA
1935	Sam Parks Jr.	299	Jimmy Thompson	Oakmont CC, Oakmont, PA
1936	Tony Manero	282	Harry Cooper	Baltusrol GC (Upper Course), Springfield, NJ
1937	Ralph Guldahl	281	Sam Snead	Oakland Hills CC, Birmingham, MI
1938	Ralph Guldahl	284	Dick Metz	Cherry Hills CC, Denver, CO
1939	Byron Nelson* (68–70)	284	Craig Wood (68–73) Denny Shute (76)	Philadelphia CC, Philadelphia
1940	Lawson Little* (70)	287	Gene Sarazen (73)	Canterbury GC, Cleveland
1941	Craig Wood	284	Denny Shute	Colonial Club, Fort Worth
1942–45	No tournament			
1946	Lloyd Mangrum* (72–72)	284	Vic Ghezzi (72–73) Byron Nelson (72–73)	Canterbury GC, Cleveland

United States Open Championship (Cont.)

Year	Winner	Score	Runner-Up	Site
1947	Lew Worsham* (69)	282	Sam Snead (70)	St. Louis CC, Clayton, MO
1948	Ben Hogan	276	Jimmy Demaret	Riviera CC, Los Angeles
1949	Cary Middlecoff	286	Sam Snead Clayton Heafner	Medinah CC, Medinah, IL
1950	Ben Hogan* (69)	287	Lloyd Mangrum (73) George Fazio (75)	Merion GC, Ardmore, PA
1951	Ben Hogan	287	Clayton Heafner	Oakland Hills CC, Birmingham, MI
1952	Julius Boros	281	Ed Oliver	Northwood CC, Dallas
1953	Ben Hogan	283	Sam Snead	Oakmont CC, Oakmont, PA
1954	Ed Furgol	284	Gene Littler	Baltusrol GC (Lower Course), Springfield, NJ
1955	Jack Fleck* (69)	287	Ben Hogan (72)	Olympic Club (Lake Course), San Francisco
1956	Cary Middlecoff	281	Ben Hogan Julius Boros	Oak Hill CC, Rochester, NY
1957	Dick Mayer* (72)	282	Cary Middlecoff (79)	Inverness Club, Toledo
1958	Tommy Bolt	283	Gary Player	Southern Hills CC, Tulsa
1959	Billy Casper	282	Bob Rosburg	Winged Foot GC, Mamaroneck, NY
1960	Arnold Palmer	280	Jack Nicklaus	Cherry Hills CC, Denver
1961	Gene Littler	281	Bob Goalby Doug Sanders	Oakland Hills CC, Birmingham, MI
1962	Jack Nicklaus* (71)	283	Arnold Palmer (74)	Oakmont CC, Oakmont, PA
1963	Julius Boros* (70)	293	Jacky Cupit (73) Arnold Palmer (76)	The Country Club, Brookline, MA
1964	Ken Venturi	278	Tommy Jacobs	Congressional CC, Bethesda, MD
1965	Gary Player* (71)	282	Kel Nagle (74)	Bellerive CC, St. Louis
1966	Billy Casper* (69)	278	Arnold Palmer (73)	Olympic Club (Lake Course), San Francisco
1967	Jack Nicklaus	275	Arnold Palmer	Baltusrol GC (Lower Course), Springfield, NJ
1968	Lee Trevino	275	Jack Nicklaus	Oak Hill CC, Rochester, NY
1969	Orville Moody	281	Deane Beman Al Geiberger Bob Rosburg	Champions GC (Cypress Creek Course), Houston
1970	Tony Jacklin	281	Dave Hill	Hazeltine GC, Chaska, MN
1971	Lee Trevino* (68)	280	Jack Nicklaus (71)	Merion GC (East Course), Ardmore, PA
1972	Jack Nicklaus	290	Bruce Crampton	Pebble Beach GL, Pebble Beach, CA
1973	Johnny Miller	279	John Schlee	Oakmont CC, Oakmont, PA
1974	Hale Irwin	287	Forrest Fezler	Winged Foot GC, Mamaroneck, NY
1975	Lou Graham* (71)	287	John Mahaffey (73)	Medinah CC, Medinah, IL
1976	Jerry Pate	277	Tom Weiskopf Al Geiberger	Atlanta Athletic Club, Duluth, GA
1977	Hubert Green	278	Lou Graham	Southern Hills CC, Tulsa
1978	Andy North	285	Dave Stockton J.C. Snead	Cherry Hills CC, Denver
1979	Hale Irwin	284	Gary Player Jerry Pate	Inverness Club, Toledo
1980	Jack Nicklaus	272	Isao Aoki	Baltusrol GC (Lower Course), Springfield, NJ
1981	David Graham	273	George Burns Bill Rogers	Merion GC, Ardmore, PA
1982	Tom Watson	282	Jack Nicklaus	Pebble Beach GL, Pebble Beach, CA
1983	Larry Nelson	280	Tom Watson	Oakmont CC, Oakmont, PA
1984	Fuzzy Zoeller* (67)	276	Greg Norman (75)	Winged Foot GC, Mamaroneck, NY
1985	Andy North	279	Dave Barr T.C. Chen Denis Watson	Oakland Hills CC, Birmingham, MI
1986	Ray Floyd	279	Lanny Wadkins Chip Beck	Shinnecock Hills GC, Southampton, NY
1987	Scott Simpson	277	Tom Watson	Olympic Club (Lake Course), San Francisco
1988	Curtis Strange* (71)	278	Nick Faldo (75)	The Country Club, Brookline, MA
1989	Curtis Strange	278	Chip Beck Mark McCumber Ian Woosnam	Oak Hill CC, Rochester, NY
1990	Hale Irwin* (74) (3)	280	Mike Donald (74) (4)	Medinah CC, Medinah, IL
1991	Payne Stewart (75)	282	Scott Simpson (77)	Hazeltine GC, Chaska, MN
1992	Tom Kite	285	Jeff Sluman	Pebble Beach GL, Pebble Beach, CA
1993	Lee Janzen	272	Payne Stewart	Baltusrol GC, Springfield, NJ

U.S. Open (Cont.)

Year	Winner	Score	Runner-Up	Site
1994	Ernie Els*	279	Loren Roberts	Oakmont CC, Oakmont, PA
			Colin Montgomerie	
1995	Corey Pavin	280	Greg Norman	Shinnecock Hills GC, Southampton, NY
1996	Steve Jones	278	Davis Love III	Oakland Hills CC, Birmingham, MI
			Tom Lehman	
1997	Ernie Els	276	Colin Montgomerie	Congressional CC, Bethesda, MD
1998	Lee Janzen	280	Payne Stewart	The Olympic Club, San Francisco, CA
1999	Payne Stewart	279	Phil Mickelson	Pinehurst Resort and CC, Pinehurst, NC

*Winner in playoff. Playoff scores are in parentheses. The 1990 playoff went to one hole of sudden death after an 18-hole playoff. In the 1994 playoff, Montgomerie was eliminated after 18 playoff holes, and Els beat Roberts on the 20th.
†Before 1898, 36 holes. From 1898 on, 72 holes.

British Open

Year	Winner	Score	Runner-Up	Site
1860†	Willie Park	174	Tom Morris Sr.	Prestwick, Scotland
1861‡	Tom Morris Sr.	163	Willie Park	Prestwick, Scotland
1862	Tom Morris Sr.	163	Willie Park	Prestwick, Scotland
1863	Willie Park	168	Tom Morris Sr.	Prestwick, Scotland
1864	Tom Morris, Sr.	160	Andrew Strath	Prestwick, Scotland
1865	Andrew Strath	162	Willie Park	Prestwick, Scotland
1866	Willie Park	169	David Park	Prestwick, Scotland
1867	Tom Morris Sr.	170	Willie Park	Prestwick, Scotland
1868	Tom Morris Jr.	154	Tom Morris Sr.	Prestwick, Scotland
1869	Tom Morris Jr.	157	Tom Morris Sr.	Prestwick, Scotland
1870	Tom Morris Jr.	149	David Strath	Prestwick, Scotland
			Bob Kirk	
1871	No tournament			
1872	Tom Morris Jr.	166	David Strath	Prestwick, Scotland
1873	Tom Kidd	179	Jamie Anderson	St. Andrews, Scotland
1874	Mungo Park	159	No record	Musselburgh, Scotland
1875	Willie Park	166	Bob Martin	Prestwick, Scotland
1876	Bob Martin#	176	David Strath	St. Andrews, Scotland
1877	Jamie Anderson	160	Bob Pringle	Musselburgh, Scotland
1878	Jamie Anderson	157	Robert Kirk	Prestwick, Scotland
1879	Jamie Anderson	169	Andrew Kirkaldy	St. Andrews, Scotland
			James Allan	
1880	Robert Ferguson	162	No record	Musselburgh, Scotland
1881	Robert Ferguson	170	Jamie Anderson	Prestwick, Scotland
1882	Robert Ferguson	171	Willie Fernie	St. Andrews, Scotland
1883	Willie Fernie*	159	Robert Ferguson	Musselburgh, Scotland
1884	Jack Simpson	160	Douglas Rolland	Prestwick, Scotland
			Willie Fernie	
1885	Bob Martin	171	Archie Simpson	St. Andrews, Scotland
1886	David Brown	157	Willie Campbell	Musselburgh, Scotland
1887	Willie Park, Jr.	161	Bob Martin	Prestwick, Scotland
1888	Jack Burns	171	Bernard Sayers	St. Andrews, Scotland
			David Anderson	
1889	Willie Park Jr.* (158)	155	Andrew Kirkaldy (163)	Musselburgh, Scotland
1890	John Ball	164	Willie Fernie	Prestwick, Scotland
1891	Hugh Kirkaldy	166	Andrew Kirkaldy	St. Andrews, Scotland
			Willie Fernie	
1892	Harold Hilton	**305	John Ball	Muirfield, Scotland
			Hugh Kirkaldy	
1893	William Auchterlonie	322	John E. Laidlay	Prestwick, Scotland
1894	John H. Taylor	326	Douglas Rolland	Royal St. George's, England
1895	John H. Taylor	322	Alexander Herd	St. Andrews, Scotland
1896	Harry Vardon* (157)	316	John H. Taylor (161)	Muirfield, Scotland
1897	Harold Hilton	314	James Braid	Hoylake, England
1898	Harry Vardon	307	Willie Park Jr.	Prestwick, Scotland
1899	Harry Vardon	310	Jack White	Royal St. George's, England
1900	John H. Taylor	309	Harry Vardon	St. Andrews, Scotland
1901	James Braid	309	Harry Vardon	Muirfield, Scotland
1902	Alexander Herd	307	Harry Vardon	Hoylake, England

British Open (Cont.)

Year	Winner	Score	Runner-Up	Site
1903	Harry Vardon	300	Tom Vardon	Prestwick, Scotland
1904	Jack White	296	John H. Taylor	Royal St. George's, England
1905	James Braid	318	John H. Taylor	St. Andrews, Scotland
			Rolland Jones	
1906	James Braid	300	John H. Taylor	Muirfield, Scotland
1907	Arnaud Massy	312	John H. Taylor	Hoylake, England
1908	James Braid	291	Tom Ball	Prestwick, Scotland
1909	John H. Taylor	295	James Braid	Deal, England
			Tom Ball	
1910	James Braid	299	Alexander Herd	St. Andrews, Scotland
1911	Harry Vardon	303	Arnaud Massy	Royal St. George's, England
1912	Ted Ray	295	Harry Vardon	Muirfield, Scotland
1913	John H. Taylor	304	Ted Ray	Hoylake, England
1914	Harry Vardon	306	John H. Taylor	Prestwick, Scotland
1915–19	No tournament			
1920	George Duncan	303	Alexander Herd	Deal, England
1921	Jock Hutchison* (150)	296	Roger Wethered (159)	St. Andrews, Scotland
1922	Walter Hagen	300	George Duncan	Royal St. George's, England
			Jim Barnes	
1923	Arthur G. Havers	295	Walter Hagen	Troon, Scotland
1924	Walter Hagen	301	Ernest Whitcombe	Hoylake, England
1925	Jim Barnes	300	Archie Compston	Prestwick, Scotland
			Ted Ray	
1926	Bobby Jones	291	Al Watrous	Royal Lytham & St. Anne's, England
1927	Bobby Jones	285	Aubrey Boomer	St. Andrews, Scotland
1928	Walter Hagen	292	Gene Sarazen	Royal St. George's, England
1929	Walter Hagen	292	Johnny Farrell	Muirfield, Scotland
1930	Bobby Jones	291	Macdonald Smith	Hoylake, England
			Leo Diegel	
1931	Tommy Armour	296	Jose Jurado	Carnoustie, Scotland
1932	Gene Sarazen	283	Macdonald Smith	Prince's, England
1933	Denny Shute* (149)	292	Craig Wood (154)	St. Andrews, Scotland
1934	Henry Cotton	283	Sidney F. Brews	Royal St. George's, England
1935	Alfred Perry	283	Alfred Padgham	Muirfield, Scotland
1936	Alfred Padgham	287	James Adams	Hoylake, England
1937	Henry Cotton	290	Reginald A. Whitcombe	Carnoustie, Scotland
1938	Reginald A. Whitcombe	295	James Adams	Royal St. George's, England
1939	Richard Burton	290	Johnny Bulla	St. Andrews, Scotland
1940–45	No tournament			
1946	Sam Snead	290	Bobby Locke	St. Andrews, Scotland
			Johnny Bulla	
1947	Fred Daly	293	Reginald W. Horne	Hoylake, England
			Frank Stranahan	
1948	Henry Cotton	294	Fred Daly	Muirfield, Scotland
1949	Bobby Locke* (135)	283	Harry Bradshaw (147)	Royal St. George's, England
1950	Bobby Locke	279	Roberto DeVicenzo	Troon, Scotland
1951	Max Faulkner	285	Tony Cerda	Portrush, Ireland
1952	Bobby Locke	287	Peter Thomson	Royal Lytham & St. Anne's, England
1953	Ben Hogan	282	Frank Stranahan	Carnoustie, Scotland
			Dai Rees	
			Peter Thomson	
			Tony Cerda	
1954	Peter Thomson	283	Sidney S. Scott	Royal Birkdale, England
			Dai Rees	
			Bobby Locke	
1955	Peter Thomson	281	John Fallon	St. Andrews, Scotland
1956	Peter Thomson	286	Flory Van Donck	Hoylake, England
1957	Bobby Locke	279	Peter Thomson	St. Andrews, Scotland
1958	Peter Thomson* (139)	278	Dave Thomas (143)	Royal Lytham & St. Anne's, England
1959	Gary Player	284	Fred Bullock	Muirfield, Scotland
			Flory Van Donck	
1960	Kel Nagle	278	Arnold Palmer	St. Andrews, Scotland

British Open (Cont.)

Year	Winner	Score	Runner-Up	Site
1961	Arnold Palmer	284	Dai Rees	Royal Birkdale, England
1962	Arnold Palmer	276	Kel Nagle	Troon, Scotland
1963	Bob Charles* (140)	277	Phil Rodgers (148)	Royal Lytham & St. Anne's, England
1964	Tony Lema	279	Jack Nicklaus	St. Andrews, Scotland
1965	Peter Thomson	285	Brian Huggett	Southport, England
			Christy O'Connor	
1966	Jack Nicklaus	282	Doug Sanders	Muirfield, Scotland
			Dave Thomas	
1967	Robert DeVicenzo	278	Jack Nicklaus	Hoylake, England
1968	Gary Player	289	Jack Nicklaus	Carnoustie, Scotland
			Bob Charles	
1969	Tony Jacklin	280	Bob Charles	Royal Lytham & St. Anne's, England
1970	Jack Nicklaus* (72)	283	Doug Sanders (73)	St. Andrews, Scotland
1971	Lee Trevino	278	Lu Liang Huan	Royal Birkdale, England
1972	Lee Trevino	278	Jack Nicklaus	Muirfield, Scotland
1973	Tom Weiskopf	276	Johnny Miller	Troon, Scotland
1974	Gary Player	282	Peter Oosterhuis	Royal Lytham & St. Anne's, England
1975	Tom Watson* (71)	279	Jack Newton (72)	Carnoustie, Scotland
1976	Johnny Miller	279	Jack Nicklaus	Royal Birkdale, England
			Seve Ballesteros	
1977	Tom Watson	268	Jack Nicklaus	Turnberry, Scotland
1978	Jack Nicklaus	281	Ben Crenshaw	St. Andrews, Scotland
			Tom Kite	
			Ray Floyd	
			Simon Owen	
1979	Seve Ballesteros	283	Ben Crenshaw	Royal Lytham & St. Anne's, England
			Jack Nicklaus	
1980	Tom Watson	271	Lee Trevino	Muirfield, Scotland
1981	Bill Rogers	276	Bernhard Langer	Royal St. George's, England
1982	Tom Watson	284	Nick Price	Troon, Scotland
			Peter Oosterhuis	
1983	Tom Watson	275	Andy Bean	Royal Birkdale, England
1984	Seve Ballesteros	276	Tom Watson	St. Andrews, Scotland
			Bernhard Langer	
1985	Sandy Lyle	282	Payne Stewart	Royal St. George's, England
1986	Greg Norman	280	Gordon Brand	Turnberry, Scotland
1987	Nick Faldo	279	Paul Azinger	Muirfield, Scotland
			Rodger Davis	
1988	Seve Ballesteros	273	Nick Price	Royal Lytham & St. Anne's, England
1989††	Mark Calcavecchia* (4-3-3-3)	275	Wayne Grady (4-4-4-4)	Troon, Scotland
			Greg Norman (3-3-4-x)	
1990	Nick Faldo	270	Payne Stewart	St. Andrews, Scotland
			Mark McNulty	
1991	Ian Baker-Finch	272	Mike Harwood	Royal Birkdale, England
1992	Nick Faldo	272	John Cook	Muirfield, Scotland
1993	Greg Norman	267	Nick Faldo	Royal St. George's, England
1994	Nick Price	268	Jesper Parnevik	Turnberry, Scotland
1995	John Daly* (4-3-4-4)	282	C. Rocca (5-4-7-3)	St. Andrews, Scotland
1996	Tom Lehman	271	Mark McCumber	Royal Lytham & St. Anne's, England
			Ernie Els	
1997	Justin Leonard	272	Jesper Parnevik	Troon, Scotland
			Darren Clarke	
1998	Mark O'Meara* (4-4-5-4)	280	Brian Watts (5-4-5-5)	Southport, England
1999	Paul Lawrie* (5-4-3-3)	290	Jean Van de Velde (6-4-3-5)	Carnoustie GC, Carnoustie,
			Justin Leonard (5-4-4-5)	Scotland

*Winner in playoff. Playoff scores are in parentheses. †The first event was open only to professional golfers.
‡The second annual open was open to amateurs and pros. #Tied, but refused playoff.
**Championship extended from 36 to 72 holes. ††Playoff cut from 18 holes to 4 holes.

PGA Championship

Year	Winner	Score	Runner-Up	Site
1916	Jim Barnes	1 up	Jock Hutchison	Siwanoy CC, Bronxville, NY
1917–18	No tournament			
1919	Jim Barnes	6 & 5	Fred McLeod	Engineers CC, Roslyn, NY
1920	Jock Hutchison	1 up	J. Douglas Edgar	Flossmoor CC, Flossmoor, IL
1921	Walter Hagen	3 & 2	Jim Barnes	Inwood CC, Far Rockaway, NY
1922	Gene Sarazen	4 & 3	Emmet French	Oakmont CC, Oakmont, PA
1923	Gene Sarazen	1 up 38 holes	Walter Hagen	Pelham CC, Pelham, NY
1924	Walter Hagen	2 up	Jim Barnes	French Lick CC, French Lick, IN
1925	Walter Hagen	6 & 5	William Mehlhorn	Olympia Fields CC, Olympia Fields, IL
1926	Walter Hagen	5 & 3	Leo Diegel	Salisbury GC, Westbury, NY
1927	Walter Hagen	1 up	Joe Turnesa	Cedar Crest CC, Dallas
1928	Leo Diegel	6 & 5	Al Espinosa	Five Farms CC, Baltimore
1929	Leo Diegel	6 & 4	Johnny Farrell	Hillcrest CC, Los Angeles
1930	Tommy Armour	1 up	Gene Sarazen	Fresh Meadow CC, Flushing, NY
1931	Tom Creavy	2 & 1	Denny Shute	Wannamoisett CC, Rumford, RI
1932	Olin Dutra	4 & 3	Frank Walsh	Keller GC, St. Paul
1933	Gene Sarazen	5 & 4	Willie Goggin	Blue Mound CC, Milwaukee
1934	Paul Runyan	1 up	Craig Wood	Park CC, Williamsville, NY
1935	Johnny Revolta	5 & 4 38 holes	Tommy Armour	Twin Hills CC, Oklahoma City
1936	Denny Shute	3 & 2	Jimmy Thomson	Pinehurst CC, Pinehurst, NC
1937	Denny Shute	1 up 37 holes	Harold McSpaden	Pittsburgh FC, Aspinwall, PA
1938	Paul Runyan	8 & 7	Sam Snead	Shawnee CC, Shawnee-on-Delaware, PA
1939	Henry Picard	1 up 37 holes	Byron Nelson	Pomonok CC, Flushing, NY
1940	Byron Nelson	1 up	Sam Snead	Hershey CC, Hershey, PA
1941	Vic Ghezzi	1 up 38 holes	Byron Nelson	Cherry Hills CC, Denver
1942	Sam Snead	2 & 1	Jim Turnesa	Seaview CC, Atlantic City
1943	No tournament			
1944	Bob Hamilton	1 up	Byron Nelson	Manito G & CC, Spokane, WA
1945	Byron Nelson	4 & 3	Sam Byrd	Morraine CC, Dayton
1946	Ben Hogan	6 & 4	Ed Oliver	Portland GC, Portland, OR
1947	Jim Ferrier	2 & 1	Chick Harbert	Plum Hollow CC, Detroit
1948	Ben Hogan	7 & 6	Mike Turnesa	Norwood Hills CC, St. Louis
1949	Sam Snead	3 & 2	Johnny Palmer	Hermitage CC, Richmond
1950	Chandler Harper	4 & 3	Henry Williams Jr.	Scioto CC, Columbus, OH
1951	Sam Snead	7 & 6	Walter Burkemo	Oakmont CC, Oakmont, PA
1952	Jim Turnesa	1 up	Chick Harbert	Big Spring CC, Louisville
1953	Walter Burkemo	2 & 1	Felice Torza	Birmingham CC, Birmingham, MI
1954	Chick Harbert	4 & 3	Walter Burkemo	Keller GC, St. Paul
1955	Doug Ford	4 & 3	Cary Middlecoff	Meadowbrook CC, Detroit
1956	Jack Burke	3 & 2	Ted Kroll	Blue Hill CC, Boston
1957	Lionel Hebert	2 & 1	Dow Finsterwald	Miami Valley CC, Dayton
1958	Dow Finsterwald	276	Billy Casper	Llanerch CC, Havertown, PA
1959	Bob Rosburg	277	Jerry Barber Doug Sanders	Minneapolis GC, St. Louis Park, MN
1960	Jay Hebert	281	Jim Ferrier	Firestone CC, Akron
1961	Jerry Barber* (67)	277	Don January (68)	Olympia Fields CC, Olympia Fields, IL
1962	Gary Player	278	Bob Goalby	Aronimink GC, Newton Square, PA
1963	Jack Nicklaus	279	Dave Ragan Jr.	Dallas Athletic Club, Dallas
1964	Bobby Nichols	271	Jack Nicklaus Arnold Palmer	Columbus CC, Columbus, OH
1965	Dave Marr	280	Billy Casper Jack Nicklaus	Laurel Valley CC, Ligonier, PA
1966	Al Geiberger	280	Dudley Wysong	Firestone CC, Akron
1967	Don January* (69)	281	Don Massengale (71)	Columbine CC, Littleton, CO
1968	Julius Boros	281	Bob Charles Arnold Palmer	Pecan Valley CC, San Antonio
1969	Ray Floyd	276	Gary Player	NCR CC, Dayton
1970	Dave Stockton	279	Arnold Palmer Bob Murphy	Southern Hills CC, Tulsa

PGA Championship *(Cont.)*

Year	Winner	Score	Runner-Up	Site
1971	Jack Nicklaus	281	Billy Casper	PGA Nat'l GC, Palm Beach Gardens, FL
1972	Gary Player	281	Tommy Aaron	Oakland Hills CC, Birmingham, MI
			Jim Jamieson	
1973	Jack Nicklaus	277	Bruce Crampton	Canterbury GC, Cleveland
1974	Lee Trevino	276	Jack Nicklaus	Tanglewood GC, Winston-Salem, NC
1975	Jack Nicklaus	276	Bruce Crampton	Firestone CC, Akron
1976	Dave Stockton	281	Ray Floyd	Congressional CC, Bethesda, MD
			Don January	
1977†	Lanny Wadkins* (4-4-4)	282	Gene Littler (4-4-5)	Pebble Beach GL, Pebble Beach, CA
1978	John Mahaffey* (4–3)	276	Jerry Pate (4–4)	Oakmont CC, Oakmont, PA
			Tom Watson (4–5)	
1979	David Graham* (4-4-2)	272	Ben Crenshaw (4-4-4)	Oakland Hills CC, Birmingham, MI
1980	Jack Nicklaus	274	Andy Bean	Oak Hill CC, Rochester, NY
1981	Larry Nelson	273	Fuzzy Zoeller	Atlanta Athletic Club, Duluth, GA
1982	Raymond Floyd	272	Lanny Wadkins	Southern Hills CC, Tulsa
1983	Hal Sutton	274	Jack Nicklaus	Riviera CC, Pacific Palisades, CA
1984	Lee Trevino	273	Gary Player	Shoal Creek, Birmingham, AL
			Lanny Wadkins	
1985	Hubert Green	278	Lee Trevino	Cherry Hills CC, Denver
1986	Bob Tway	276	Greg Norman	Inverness CC, Toledo
1987	Larry Nelson* (4)	287	Lanny Wadkins (5)	PGA Natl GC, Palm Beach Gardens, FL
1988	Jeff Sluman	272	Paul Azinger	Oak Tree GC, Edmond, OK
1989	Payne Stewart	276	Mike Reid	Kemper Lakes GC, Hawthorn Woods, IL
1990	Wayne Grady	282	Fred Couples	Shoal Creek, Birmingham, AL
1991	John Daly	276	Bruce Lietzke	Crooked Stick GC, Carmel, IN
1992	Nick Price	278	Jim Gallagher Jr.	Bellerive CC, St. Louis
1993	Paul Azinger* (4–4)	272	Greg Norman (4–5)	Inverness CC, Toledo, OH
1994	Nick Price	269	Corey Pavin	Southern Hills CC, Tulsa, OK
1995	Steve Elkington* (3)	267	Colin Montgomerie (4)	Riviera CC, Pacific Palisades, CA
1996	Mark Brooks* (3)	277	Kenny Perry (x)	Valhalla GC, Louisville, KY
1997	Davis Love III	269	Justin Leonard	Winged Foot GC, Mamaroneck, NY
1998	Vijay Singh	271	Steve Stricker	Sahalee CC, Redmond, WA
1999	Tiger Woods	277	Sergio Garcia	Medinah CC, Medinah, IL

*Winner in playoff. Playoff scores are in parentheses. †Playoff changed from 18 holes to sudden death.

Alltime Major Championship Winners

	Masters	U.S. Open	British Open	PGA Champ.	U.S. Amateur	British Amateur	Total
†Jack Nicklaus	6	4	3	5	2	0	20
Bobby Jones	0	4	3	0	5	1	13
Walter Hagen	0	2	4	5	0	0	11
Ben Hogan	2	4	1	2	0	0	9
†Gary Player	3	1	3	2	0	0	9
John Ball	0	0	1	0	0	8	9
†Arnold Palmer	4	1	2	0	1	0	8
*Tom Watson	2	1	5	0	0	0	8
Harold Hilton	0	0	2	0	1	4	7
Gene Sarazen	1	2	1	3	0	0	7
Sam Snead	3	0	1	3	0	0	7
Harry Vardon	0	1	6	0	0	0	7

*Active PGA player. †Active Senior PGA player.

Alltime Multiple Professional Major Winners

MASTERS

Jack Nicklaus	6
Arnold Palmer	4
Jimmy Demaret	3
Nick Faldo	3
Gary Player	3
Sam Snead	3
Seve Ballesteros	2
Ben Crenshaw	2
Ben Hogan	2
Bernhard Langer	2
Byron Nelson	2
José Maria Olazábal	2
Horton Smith	2
Tom Watson	2

U.S. OPEN

Willie Anderson	4
Ben Hogan	4
Bobby Jones	4
Jack Nicklaus	4

U.S. OPEN *(Cont.)*

Hale Irwin	3
Julius Boros	2
Billy Casper	2
Ernie Els	2
Ralph Guldahl	2
Walter Hagen	2
Lee Janzen	2
John McDermott	2
Cary Middlecoff	2
Andy North	2
Gene Sarazen	2
Alex Smith	2
Payne Stewart	2
Curtis Strange	2
Lee Trevino	2

BRITISH OPEN

Harry Vardon	6
James Braid	5
J.H. Taylor	5

BRITISH OPEN *(Cont.)*

Peter Thomson	5
Tom Watson	5
Walter Hagen	4
Bobby Locke	4
Tom Morris Sr	4
Tom Morris Jr	4
Willie Park	4
Jamie Anderson	3
Seve Ballesteros	3
Henry Cotton	3
Nick Faldo	3
Robert Ferguson	3
Bobby Jones	3
Jack Nicklaus	3
Gary Player	3
Harold Hilton	2
Bob Martin	2
Greg Norman	2
Arnold Palmer	2
Willie Park Jr.	2
Lee Trevino	2

PGA CHAMPIONSHIP

Walter Hagen	5
Jack Nicklaus	5
Gene Sarazen	3
Sam Snead	3
Jim Barnes	2
Leo Diegel	2
Raymond Floyd	2
Ben Hogan	2
Byron Nelson	2
Larry Nelson	2
Gary Player	2
Paul Runyan	2
Denny Shute	2
Dave Stockton	2
Lee Trevino	2

THE PGA TOUR

Most Career Wins

	Wins		Wins		Wins
Sam Snead	81	Billy Casper	51	Tom Watson	34
Jack Nicklaus	70	Walter Hagen	40	Horton Smith	32
Ben Hogan	63	Cary Middlecoff	40	Harry Cooper	31
Arnold Palmer	60	Gene Sarazen	38	Jimmy Demaret	31
Byron Nelson	52	Lloyd Mangrum	36	Leo Diegel	30

Season Money Leaders

		Earnings ($)			Earnings ($)			Earnings ($)
1934	Paul Runyan	6,767.00	1956	Ted Kroll	72,835.83	1978	Tom Watson	362,428.93
1935	Johnny Revolta	9,543.00	1957	Dick Mayer	65,835.00	1979	Tom Watson	462,636.00
1936	Horton Smith	7,682.00	1958	Arnold Palmer	42,607.50	1980	Tom Watson	530,808.33
1937	Harry Cooper	14,138.69	1959	Art Wall	53,167.60	1981	Tom Kite	375,698.84
1938	Sam Snead	19,534.49	1960	Arnold Palmer	75,262.85	1982	Craig Stadler	446,462.00
1939	Henry Picard	10,303.00	1961	Gary Player	64,540.45	1983	Hal Sutton	426,668.00
1940	Ben Hogan	10,655.00	1962	Arnold Palmer	81,448.33	1984	Tom Watson	476,260.00
1941	Ben Hogan	18,358.00	1963	Arnold Palmer	128,230.00	1985	Curtis Strange	542,321.00
1942	Ben Hogan	13,143.00	1964	Jack Nicklaus	113,284.50	1986	Greg Norman	653,296.00
1943	No statistics compiled		1965	Jack Nicklaus	140,752.14	1987	Curtis Strange	925,941.00
1944	Byron Nelson*	37,967.69	1966	Billy Casper	121,944.92	1988	Curtis Strange	1,147,644.00
1945	Byron Nelson*	63,335.66	1967	Jack Nicklaus	188,998.08	1989	Tom Kite	1,395,278.00
1946	Ben Hogan	42,556.16	1968	Billy Casper	205,168.67	1990	Greg Norman	1,165,477.00
1947	Jimmy Demaret	27,936.83	1969	Frank Beard	164,707.11	1991	Corey Pavin	979,430.00
1948	Ben Hogan	32,112.00	1970	Lee Trevino	157,037.63	1992	Fred Couples	1,344,188.00
1949	Sam Snead	31,593.83	1971	Jack Nicklaus	244,490.50	1993	Nick Price	1,478,557.00
1950	Sam Snead	35,758.83	1972	Jack Nicklaus	320,542.26	1994	Nick Price	1,499,927.00
1951	Lloyd Mangrum	26,088.83	1973	Jack Nicklaus	308,362.10	1995	Greg Norman	1,654,959.00
1952	Julius Boros	37,032.97	1974	Johnny Miller	353,021.59	1996	Tom Lehman	1,780,159.00
1953	Lew Worsham	34,002.00	1975	Jack Nicklaus	298,149.17	1997	Tiger Woods	2,066,833.00
1954	Bob Toski	65,819.81	1976	Jack Nicklaus	266,438.57	1998	David Duval	2,591,031.00
1955	Julius Boros	63,121.55	1977	Tom Watson	310,653.16			

* War bonds. Note: Total money listed from 1968 through 1974. Official money listed from 1975 on.

Career Money Leaders*

	Earnings ($)			Earnings ($)			Earnings ($)
1.	Greg Norman	12,507,322	18. Steve Elkington	8,023,038	35. Lanny Wadkins	6,351,306
2.	Davis Love III	11,877,463	19. Tom Lehman	7,961,912	36. Steve Pate	6,319,645
3.	Payne Stewart	11,737,008	20. John Cook	7,817,220	37. Bruce Lietzke	6,316,759
4.	Fred Couples	11,305,069	21. Craig Stadler	7,675,059	38. Chip Beck	6,135,688
5.	Mark O'Meara	11,162,269	22. Jeff Sluman	7,626,418	39. Billy Mayfair	6,057,999
6.	Nick Price	11,118,570	23. Jay Haas	7,602,960	40. Fred Funk	6,010,656
7.	Tom Kite	10,533,102	24. Curtis Strange	7,339,850	41. Larry Mize	6,000,563
8.	Scott Hoch	10,122,745	25. Lee Janzen	7,332,488	42. Hale Irwin	5,981,800
9.	David Duval	9,944,747	26. Jeff Maggert	7,295,965	43. Scott Simpson	5,838,933
10.	Mark Calcavecchia	9,670,706	27. Loren Roberts	7,211,300	44. Ernie Els	5,825,524
11.	Tom Watson	9,425,272	28. Ben Crenshaw	7,075,996	45. Andrew Magee	5,794,951
12.	Tiger Woods	8,965,128	29. Justin Leonard	6,897,692	46. Fuzzy Zoeller	5,760,263
13.	Hal Sutton	8,885,472	30. John Huston	6,822,082	47. Mark Brooks	5,719,393
14.	Corey Pavin	8,852,303	31. Jim Furyk	6,816,140	48. Jack Nicklaus	5,696,747
15.	Phil Mickelson	8,564,408	32. David Frost	6,810,267	49. Peter Jacobsen	5,582,489
16.	Paul Azinger	8,553,127	33. Brad Faxon	6,782,223	50. Bill Glasson	5,381,022
17	Vijay Singh	8,202,456	34. Bob Tway	6,669,380		

*Through 10/17/99.

Year by Year Statistical Leaders

SCORING AVERAGE

1980	Lee Trevino	69.73
1981	Tom Kite	69.80
1982	Tom Kite	70.21
1983	Raymond Floyd	70.61
1984	Calvin Peete	70.56
1985	Don Pooley	70.36
1986	Scott Hoch	70.08
1987	David Frost	70.09
1988	Greg Norman	69.38
1989	Payne Stewart	69.485†
1990	Greg Norman	69.10
1991	Fred Couples	69.59
1992	Fred Couples	69.38
1993	Greg Norman	68.90
1994	Greg Norman	68.81
1995	Greg Norman	69.06
1996	Tom Lehman	69.32
1997	Nick Price	68.98
1998	David Duval	69.13

Note: Scoring average per round, with adjustments made at each round for the field's course scoring average.

DRIVING DISTANCE

		Yds
1980	Dan Pohl	274.3
1981	Dan Pohl	280.1
1982	Bill Calfee	275.3
1983	John McComish	277.4
1984	Bill Glasson	276.5
1985	Andy Bean	278.2
1986	Davis Love III	285.7
1987	John McComish	283.9
1988	Steve Thomas	284.6
1989	Ed Humenik	280.9
1990	Tom Purtzer	279.6

DRIVING DISTANCE (Cont.)

1991	John Daly	288.9
1992	John Daly	283.4
1993	John Daly	288.9
1994	Davis Love III	283.8
1995	John Daly	289.0
1996	John Daly	288.8
1997	John Daly	302.0
1998	John Daly	299.4

Note: Average computed by charting distance of two tee shots on a predetermined par-four or par-five hole (one on front nine, one on back nine).

DRIVING ACCURACY

1980	Mike Reid	79.5
1981	Calvin Peete	81.9
1982	Calvin Peete	84.6
1983	Calvin Peete	81.3
1984	Calvin Peete	77.5
1985	Calvin Peete	80.6
1986	Calvin Peete	81.7
1987	Calvin Peete	83.0
1988	Calvin Peete	82.5
1989	Calvin Peete	82.6
1990	Calvin Peete	83.7
1991	Hale Irwin	78.3
1992	Doug Tewell	82.3
1993	Doug Tewell	82.5
1994	David Edwards	81.6
1995	Fred Funk	81.3
1996	Fred Funk	78.7
1997	Allen Doyle	80.8
1998	Bruce Fleisher	81.4

Note: Percentage of fairways hit on number of par-four and par-five holes played; par-three holes excluded.

GREENS IN REGULATION

1980	Jack Nicklaus	72.1
1981	Calvin Peete	73.1
1982	Calvin Peete	72.4
1983	Calvin Peete	71.4
1984	Andy Bean	72.1
1985	John Mahaffey	71.9
1986	John Mahaffey	72.0
1987	Gil Morgan	73.3
1988	John Adams	73.9
1989	Bruce Lietzke	72.6
1990	Doug Tewell	70.9
1991	Bruce Lietzke	73.3
1992	Tim Simpson	74.0
1993	Fuzzy Zoeller	73.6
1994	Bill Glasson	73.0
1995	Lenny Clements	72.3
1996	Fred Couples	71.8
	Mark O'Meara	71.8
1997	Tom Lehman	72.7
1998	Hal Sutton	71.3

Note: Average of greens reached in regulation out of total holes played; hole is considered hit in regulation if any part of the ball rests on the putting surface in two shots less than the hole's par—a par-5 hit in two shots is one green in regulation.

PUTTING

1980	Jerry Pate	28.81
1981	Alan Tapie	28.70
1982	Ben Crenshaw	28.65
1983	Morris Hatalsky	27.96
1984	Gary McCord	28.57
1985	Craig Stadler	28.627†
1986	Greg Norman	1.736
1987	Ben Crenshaw	1.743

† Number had to be carried to extra decimal place to determine winner.

Year by Year Statistical Leaders *(Cont.)*

PUTTING *(Cont.)*

1988 ....Don Pooley	1.729	1992 ....Mark O'Meara	1.731	1996 ....Brad Faxon	1.709
1989 ....Steve Jones	1.734	1993 ....David Frost	1.739	1997 ....Don Pooley	1.718
1990 ....Larry Rinker	1.7467†	1994 ....Loren Roberts	1.737	1998 ....Rick Fehr	1.722
1991 ....Jay Don Blake	1.7326†	1995 ....Jim Furyk	1.708		

Note: Average number of putts taken on greens reached in regulation; prior to 1986, based on average number of putts per 18 holes.

ALL-AROUND

1987 ....Dan Pohl	170	1991 ....Scott Hoch	283	1995 ....Justin Leonard	323
1988 ....Payne Stewart	170	1992 ....Fred Couples	256	1996 ....Fred Couples	214
1989 ....Paul Azinger	250	1993 ....Gil Morgan	252	1997 ....Bill Glasson	282
1990 ....Paul Azinger	162	1994 ....Bob Estes	227	1998 ....John Huston	151

Note: Sum of the places of standing from the other seven statistical categories; the player with the number closest to zero leads.

SAND SAVES

1980 ....Bob Eastwood	65.4	1987 ....Paul Azinger	63.2	1994 ....Corey Pavin	65.4
1981 ....Tom Watson	60.1	1988 ....Greg Powers	63.5	1995 ....Billy Mayfair	68.6
1982 ....Isao Aoki	60.2	1989 ....Mike Sullivan	66.0	1996 ....Gary Rusnak	64.0
1983 ....Isao Aoki	62.3	1990 ....Paul Azinger	67.2	1997 ....Bob Estes	70.3
1984 ....Peter Oosterhuis	64.7	1991 ....Ben Crenshaw	64.9	1998 ....Keith Fergus	71.0
1985 ....Tom Purtzer	60.8	1992 ....Mitch Adcock	66.9		
1986 ....Paul Azinger	63.8	1993 ....Ken Green	64.4		

Note: Percentage of up-and-down efforts from greenside sand traps only—fairway bunkers excluded.

PAR BREAKERS

1980 ....Tom Watson	.213	1984 ....Craig Stadler	.220	1988 ....Ken Green	.236
1981 ....Bruce Lietzke	.225	1985 ....Craig Stadler	.218	1989 ....Greg Norman	.224
1982 ....Tom Kite	.2154†	1986 ....Greg Norman	.248	1990 ....Greg Norman	.219
1983 ....Tom Watson	.211	1987 ....Mark Calcavecchia	.221		

Note: Average based on total birdies and eagles scored out of total holes played. Discontinued as an official category after 1990.

EAGLES

1980 ....Dave Eichelberger	16	1986 ....Joey Sindelar	16	1993 ....Davis Love III	15
1981 ....Bruce Lietzke	12	1987 ....Phil Blackmar	20	1994 ....Davis Love III	18
1982 ....Tom Weiskopf	10	1988 ....Ken Green	21	1995 ....Kelly Gibson	16
J.C. Snead	10	1989 ....Lon Hinkle	14	1996 ....Tom Watson	97.2
Andy Bean	10	Duffy Waldorf	14	1997 ....Tiger Woods	104.1
1983 ....Chip Beck	15	1990 ....Paul Azinger	14	1998 ....Davis Love III	83.3
1984 ....Gary Hallberg	15	1991 ....Andy Bean	15		
1985 ....Larry Rinker	14	1992 ....Dan Forsman	18		

Note: Total of eagles scored 1980–1995. Since 1996 winner determined by number of holes played per eagle.

BIRDIES

1980 ....Andy Bean	388	1987 ....Dan Forsman	409	1994 ....Brad Bryant	397
1981 ....Vance Heafner	388	1988 ....Dan Forsman	465	1995 ....Steve Lowery	410
1982 ....Andy Bean	392	1989 ....Ted Schulz	415	1996 ....Fred Couples	4.20
1983 ....Hal Sutton	399	1990 ....Mike Donald	401	1997 ....Tiger Woods	4.25
1984 ....Mark O'Meara	419	1991 ....Scott Hoch	446	1998 ....David Duval	4.29
1985 ....Joey Sindelar	411	1992 ....Jeff Sluman	417		
1986 ....Joey Sindelar	415	1993 ....John Huston	426		

Note: Total of birdies scored 1980–95. Since 1996, winner determined by average number of birdies per round.

PGA Player of the Year Award

1948 ....Ben Hogan	1965 ....Dave Marr	1982 ....Tom Watson
1949 ....Sam Snead	1966 ....Billy Casper	1983 ....Hal Sutton
1950 ....Ben Hogan	1967 ....Jack Nicklaus	1984 ....Tom Watson
1951 ....Ben Hogan	1968 ....Not awarded	1985 ....Lanny Wadkins
1952 ....Julius Boros	1969 ....Orville Moody	1986 ....Bob Tway
1953 ....Ben Hogan	1970 ....Billy Casper	1987 ....Paul Azinger
1954 ....Ed Furgol	1971 ....Lee Trevino	1988 ....Curtis Strange
1955 ....Doug Ford	1972 ....Jack Nicklaus	1989 ....Tom Kite
1956 ....Jack Burke	1973 ....Jack Nicklaus	1990 ....Wayne Levi
1957 ....Dick Mayer	1974 ....Johnny Miller	1991 ....Fred Couples
1958 ....Dow Finsterwald	1975 ....Jack Nicklaus	1992 ....Fred Couples
1959 ....Art Wall	1976 ....Jack Nicklaus	1993 ....Nick Price
1960 ....Arnold Palmer	1977 ....Tom Watson	1994 ....Nick Price
1961 ....Jerry Barber	1978 ....Tom Watson	1995 ....Greg Norman
1962 ....Arnold Palmer	1979 ....Tom Watson	1996 ....Tom Lehman
1963 ....Julius Boros	1980 ....Tom Watson	1997 ....Tiger Woods
1964 ....Ken Venturi	1981 ....Bill Rogers	1998 ....David Duval

Vardon Trophy: Scoring Average

Year	Winner	Avg	Year	Winner	Avg	Year	Winner	Avg
1937	Harry Cooper	*500	1961	Arnold Palmer	69.85	1981	Tom Kite	69.80
1938	Sam Snead	520	1962	Arnold Palmer	70.27	1982	Tom Kite	70.21
1939	Byron Nelson	473	1963	Billy Casper	70.58	1983	Raymond Floyd	70.61
1940	Ben Hogan	423	1964	Arnold Palmer	70.01	1984	Calvin Peete	70.56
1941	Ben Hogan	494	1965	Billy Casper	70.85	1985	Don Pooley	70.36
1942–46	No award		1966	Billy Casper	70.27	1986	Scott Hoch	70.08
1947	Jimmy Demaret	69.90	1967	Arnold Palmer	70.18	1987	Don Pohl	70.25
1948	Ben Hogan	69.30	1968	Billy Casper	69.82	1988	Chip Beck	69.46
1949	Sam Snead	69.37	1969	Dave Hill	70.34	1989	Greg Norman	69.49
1950	Sam Snead	69.23	1970	Lee Trevino	70.64	1990	Greg Norman	69.10
1951	Lloyd Mangrum	70.05	1971	Lee Trevino	70.27	1991	Fred Couples	69.59
1952	Jack Burke	70.54	1972	Lee Trevino	70.89	1992	Fred Couples	69.38
1953	Lloyd Mangrum	70.22	1973	Bruce Crampton	70.57	1993	Nick Price	69.11
1954	E.J. Harrison	70.41	1974	Lee Trevino	70.53	1994	Greg Norman	68.81
1955	Sam Snead	69.86	1975	Bruce Crampton	70.51	1995	Steve Elkington	69.62
1956	Cary Middlecoff	70.35	1976	Don January	70.56	1996	Tom Lehman	69.32
1957	Dow Finsterwald	70.30	1977	Tom Watson	70.32	1997	Nick Price	68.98
1958	Bob Rosburg	70.11	1978	Tom Watson	70.16	1998	David Duval	69.13
1959	Art Wall	70.35	1979	Tom Watson	70.27			
1960	Billy Casper	69.95	1980	Lee Trevino	69.73			

*Point system used, 1937–41.
Note: As of 1988, based on minimum of 60 rounds per year. Adjusted for average score of field in tournaments entered.

Alltime PGA Tour Records*

Scoring

90 HOLES
325—(67-67-64-65-62) by Tom Kite, at four courses, Indian Hills, CA, in winning the 1993 Bob Hope Classic (35 under par).

72 HOLES
257—(60-68-64-65) by Mike Souchak, at Brackenridge Park GC, San Antonio, to win 1955 Texas Open (27 under par).
260—(63-65-66-66) by John Huston, at Waialae CC, Honolulu, at the 1998 Hawaiian Open (28 under par).

54 HOLES, OPENING ROUNDS
189—(64-62-63) by John Cook, at the TPC at Southwind, Memphis, TN, en route to winning the 1996 St. Jude Classic.

54 HOLES, CONSECUTIVE ROUNDS
189—(63-63-63) by Chandler Harper in the last three rounds to win the 1954 Texas Open at Brackenridge Park GC, San Antonio.
189—(64-62-63) by John Cook, at the TPC at Southwind, Memphis, TN, in the first three rounds of the 1996 St. Jude Classic.

Alltime PGA Tour Records *(Cont.)**

Scoring *(Cont.)*

36 HOLES, OPENING ROUNDS

126—(64-62) by Tommy Bolt, at Cavalier Yacht & CC, Virginia Beach, VA, in 1954 Virginia Beach Open.

126—(64–62) by Paul Azinger, at Oak Hills CC, San Antonio, in the 1989 Texas Open.

126—(64–62) by John Cook, at the TPC at Southwind, Memphis, TN, in the 1996 St. Jude Classic.

126—(64–62) by Rick Fehr, at the Las Vegas Hilton CC/TPC at Summerlin, Las Vegas, in the 1996 Las Vegas Invitational.

126—(62–64) by Steve Jones, at the TPC, Scottsdale, AR in the 1997 Phoenix Open.

126—(63–63) by David Frost at the TPC at Southwind,Memphis, TN, in the 1999 Fedex St. Jude Classic.

36 HOLES, CONSECUTIVE ROUNDS

125—(64–61) by Gay Brewer in the middle rounds of the 1967 Pensacola Open, which he won, at Pensacola CC, Pensacola, FL.

125—(63–62) by Ron Streck in the last two rounds to win the 1978 Texas Open at Oak Hills CC, San Antonio.

125—(62–63) by Blaine McCallister in the middle two rounds in winning the 1988 Hardee's Golf Classic at Oakwood CC, Coal Valley, IL.

125—(62–63) by John Cook, in the middle two rounds in winning the 1996 St. Jude Classic at the TPC at Southwind, Memphis, TN.

125—(62–63) by John Cook, in the fourth and fifth rounds in winning the 1997 Bob Hope Chrysler Classic at Indian Wells CC, Indian Hills, CA.

18 HOLES

59—by Al Geiberger, at Colonial Country Club, Memphis, in second round in winning the 1977 Memphis Classic.

59—by Chip Beck, at Sunrise Golf Club, Las Vegas, in third round of the 1991 Las Vegas Invitational.

59—by David Duval on the Palmer Course at PGA West, La Quinta, CA, in the fifth round of the 1999 Bob Hope Chrysler Classic.

9 HOLES

27—by Mike Souchak, at Brackenridge Park GC, San Antonio, on par-35 second nine of first round in the 1955 Texas Open.

27—by Andy North at En-Joie GC, Endicott, NY, on par-34 second nine of first round in the 1975 BC Open.

MOST CONSECUTIVE ROUNDS UNDER 70

19—Byron Nelson in 1945.

MOST BIRDIES IN A ROW

8—Bob Goalby at Pasadena GC, St. Petersburg, FL, during fourth round in winning the 1961 St Petersburg Open.

8—Fuzzy Zoeller, at Oakwood CC, Coal Valley, IL, during first round of 1976 Quad Cities Open.

8—Dewey Arnette, Warwick Hills GC, Grand Blanc, MI, during first round of the 1987 Buick Open.

MOST BIRDIES IN A ROW TO WIN

5—Jack Nicklaus to win 1978 Jackie Gleason Inverrary Classic (last 5 holes).

Wins

MOST CONSECUTIVE YEARS WINNING AT LEAST ONE TOURNAMENT

17—Jack Nicklaus, 1962–78.

17—Arnold Palmer, 1955–71.

16—Billy Casper, 1956–71.

MOST CONSECUTIVE WINS

11—Byron Nelson, from Miami Four Ball, March 8–11, 1945, through Canadian Open, August 2–4, 1945.

MOST WINS IN A SINGLE EVENT

8—Sam Snead, Greater Greensboro Open, 1938, 1946, 1949, 1950, 1955, 1956, 1960, and 1965.

MOST CONSECUTIVE WINS IN A SINGLE EVENT

4—Walter Hagen, PGA Championships, 1924-27.

4—Gene Sarazen, Miami Open, 1926, (schedule change) 1928–30.

MOST WINS IN A CALENDAR YEAR

18—Byron Nelson, 1945

MOST YEARS BETWEEN WINS

15 yrs, 5 mos—Butch Baird, 1961–76.

MOST YEARS FROM FIRST WIN TO LAST

28 yrs, 11 mos, 20 days—Raymond Floyd, 1963–92.

YOUNGEST WINNERS

19 yrs, 10 mos—John McDermott, 1911 US Open.

OLDEST WINNER

52 yrs, 10 mos—Sam Snead, 1965 Greater Greensboro Open.

WIDEST WINNING MARGIN: STROKES

16—Bobby Locke, 1948 Chicago Victory National Championship.

Putting

FEWEST PUTTS, ONE ROUND

18—Andy North, at Kingsmill GC, in second round of 1990 Anheuser Busch Golf Classic.

18—Kenny Knox, at Harbour Town GL, in first round of 1989 MCI Heritage Classic.

18—Mike McGee, at Colonial CC, in first round of 1987 Federal Express St. Jude Classic.

18—Sam Trahan, at Whitemarsh Valley CC, in final round of 1979 IVB Philadelphia Golf Classic.

18—Jim McGovern, at TPC at Southwind, in second round of 1992 Federal Express St. Jude Classic.

FEWEST PUTTS, FOUR ROUNDS

93—Kenny Knox, in 1989 MCI Heritage Classic at Harbour Town GL.

*Through 10/11/98.

THE MAJOR TOURNAMENTS
LPGA Championship

Year	Winner	Score	Runner-Up	Site
1955	Beverly Hanson† (4 and 3)	220	Louise Suggs	Orchard Ridge CC, Ft Wayne, IN
1956	Marlene Hagge*	291	Patty Berg	Forest Lake CC, Detroit
1957	Louise Suggs	285	Wiffi Smith	Churchill Valley CC, Pittsburgh
1958	Mickey Wright	288	Fay Crocker	Churchill Valley CC, Pittsburgh
1959	Betsy Rawls	288	Patty Berg	Sheraton Hotel CC, French Lick, IN
1960	Mickey Wright	292	Louise Suggs	Sheraton Hotel CC, French Lick, IN
1961	Mickey Wright	287	Louise Suggs	Stardust CC, Las Vegas
1962	Judy Kimball	282	Shirley Spork	Stardust CC, Las Vegas
1963	Mickey Wright	294	Mary Lena Faulk Mary Mills Louise Suggs	Stardust CC, Las Vegas
1964	Mary Mills	278	Mickey Wright	Stardust CC, Las Vegas
1965	Sandra Haynie	279	Clifford A. Creed	Stardust CC, Las Vegas
1966	Gloria Ehret	282	Mickey Wright	Stardust CC, Las Vegas
1967	Kathy Whitworth	284	Shirley Englehorn	Pleasant Valley CC, Sutton, MA
1968	Sandra Post* (68)	294	Kathy Whitworth (75)	Pleasant Valley CC, Sutton, MA
1969	Betsy Rawls	293	Susie Berning Carol Mann	Concord GC, Kiameshia Lake, NY
1970	Shirley Englehorn* (74)	285	Kathy Whitworth (78)	Pleasant Valley CC, Sutton, MA
1971	Kathy Whitworth	288	Kathy Ahern	Pleasant Valley CC, Sutton, MA
1972	Kathy Ahern	293	Jane Blalock	Pleasant Valley CC, Sutton, MA
1973	Mary Mills	288	Betty Burfeindt	Pleasant Valley CC, Sutton, MA
1974	Sandra Haynie	288	JoAnne Carner	Pleasant Valley CC, Sutton, MA
1975	Kathy Whitworth	288	Sandra Haynie	Pine Ridge GC, Baltimore
1976	Betty Burfeindt	287	Judy Rankin	Pine Ridge GC, Baltimore
1977	Chako Higuchi	279	Pat Bradley Sandra Post Judy Rankin	Bay Tree Golf Plantation, N. Myrtle Beach, SC
1978	Nancy Lopez	275	Amy Alcott	Jack Nicklaus GC, Kings Island, OH
1979	Donna Caponi	279	Jerilyn Britz	Jack Nicklaus GC, Kings Island, OH
1980	Sally Little	285	Jane Blalock	Jack Nicklaus GC, Kings Island, OH
1981	Donna Caponi	280	Jerilyn Britz Pat Meyers	Jack Nicklaus GC, Kings Island, OH
1982	Jan Stephenson	279	JoAnne Carner	Jack Nicklaus GC, Kings Island, OH
1983	Patty Sheehan	279	Sandra Haynie	Jack Nicklaus GC, Kings Island, OH
1984	Patty Sheehan	272	Beth Daniel Pat Bradley	Jack Nicklaus GC, Kings Island, OH
1985	Nancy Lopez	273	Alice Miller	Jack Nicklaus GC, Kings Island, OH
1986	Pat Bradley	277	Patty Sheehan	Jack Nicklaus GC, Kings Island, OH
1987	Jane Geddes	275	Betsy King	Jack Nicklaus GC, Kings Island, OH
1988	Sherri Turner	281	Amy Alcott	Jack Nicklaus GC, Kings Island, OH
1989	Nancy Lopez	274	Ayako Okamoto	Jack Nicklaus GC, Kings Island, OH
1990	Beth Daniel	280	Rosie Jones	Bethesda CC, Bethesda, MD
1991	Meg Mallon	274	Pat Bradley Ayako Okamoto	Bethesda CC, Bethesda, MD
1992	Betsy King	267	Karen Noble	Bethesda CC, Bethesda, MD
1993	Patty Sheehan	275	Lauri Merten	Bethesda CC, Bethesda, MD
1994	Laura Davies	279	Alice Ritzman	DuPont CC, Wilmington, DE
1995	Kelly Robbins	274	Laura Davies	DuPont CC, Wilmington, DE
1996	Laura Davies	213†	Julie Piers	DuPont CC, Wilmington, DE
1997	Chris Johnson*	281	Leta Lindley	DuPont CC, Wilmington, DE
1998	Se Ri Pak	273	Donna Andrews	DuPont CC, Wilmington, DE
1999	Juli Inkster	268	Liselotte Neumann	DuPont CC, Wilmington, DE

*Won in playoff. Playoff scores are in parentheses. 1956 and 1997 were sudden death; 1968 and 1970 were 18-hole playoffs. †Won match play final. #Shortened due to rain.

U.S. Women's Open

Year	Winner	Score	Runner-Up	Site
1946	Patty Berg	5 & 4	Betty Jameson	Spokane CC, Spokane, WA
1947	Betty Jameson	295	Sally Sessions	Starmount Forest CC, Greensboro, NC
			Polly Riley	
1948	Babe Zaharias	300	Betty Hicks	Atlantic City CC, Northfield, NJ
1949	Louise Suggs	291	Babe Zaharias	Prince George's G & CC, Landover, MD
1950	Babe Zaharias	291	Betsy Rawls	Rolling Hills CC, Wichita, KS
1951	Betsy Rawls	293	Louise Suggs	Druid Hills GC, Atlanta
1952	Louise Suggs	284	Marlene Bauer	Bala GC, Philadelphia
			Betty Jameson	
1953	Betsy Rawls* (71)	302	Jackie Pung (77)	CC of Rochester, Rochester, NY
1954	Babe Zaharias	291	Betty Hicks	Salem CC, Peabody, MA
1955	Fay Crocker	299	Mary Lena Faulk	Wichita CC, Wichita, KS
			Louise Suggs	
1956	Kathy Cornelius* (75)	302	Barbara McIntire (82)	Northland CC, Duluth, MN
1957	Betsy Rawls	299	Patty Berg	Winged Foot GC, Mamaroneck, NY
1958	Mickey Wright	290	Louise Suggs	Forest Lake CC, Detroit
1959	Mickey Wright	287	Louise Suggs	Churchill Valley CC, Pittsburgh
1960	Betsy Rawls	292	Joyce Ziske	Worcester CC, Worcester, MA
1961	Mickey Wright	293	Betsy Rawls	Baltusrol GC (Lower Course), Springfield, NJ
1962	Murle Breer	301	Jo Ann Prentice	Dunes GC, Myrtle Beach, SC
			Ruth Jessen	
1963	Mary Mills	289	Sandra Haynie	Kenwood CC, Cincinnati
			Louise Suggs	
1964	Mickey Wright* (70)	290	Ruth Jessen (72)	San Diego CC, Chula Vista, CA
1965	Carol Mann	290	Kathy Cornelius	Atlantic City CC, Northfield, NJ
1966	Sandra Spuzich	297	Carol Mann	Hazeltine Natl GC, Chaska, MN
1967	Catherine LaCoste	294	Susie Berning	Hot Springs GC (Cascades Course),
			Beth Stone	Hot Springs, VA
1968	Susie Berning	289	Mickey Wright	Moslem Springs GC, Fleetwood, PA
1969	Donna Caponi	294	Peggy Wilson	Scenic Hills CC, Pensacola, FL
1970	Donna Caponi	287	Sandra Haynie	Muskogee CC, Muskogee, OK
			Sandra Spuzich	
1971	JoAnne Carner	288	Kathy Whitworth	Kahkwa CC, Erie, PA
1972	Susie Berning	299	Kathy Ahern	Winged Foot GC, Mamaroneck, NY
			Pam Barnett	
			Judy Rankin	
1973	Susie Berning	290	Gloria Ehret	CC of Rochester, Rochester, NY
			Shelley Hamlin	
1974	Sandra Haynie	295	Carol Mann	La Grange CC, La Grange, IL
			Beth Stone	
1975	Sandra Palmer	295	JoAnne Carner	Atlantic City CC, Northfield, NJ
			Sandra Post	
			Nancy Lopez	
1976	JoAnne Carner* (76)	292	Sandra Palmer (78)	Rolling Green CC, Springfield, PA
1977	Hollis Stacy	292	Nancy Lopez	Hazeltine Natl GC, Chaska, MN
1978	Hollis Stacy	289	JoAnne Carner	CC of Indianapolis, Indianapolis
			Sally Little	
1979	Jerilyn Britz	284	Debbie Massey	Brooklawn CC, Fairfield, CT
			Sandra Palmer	
1980	Amy Alcott	280	Hollis Stacy	Richland CC, Nashville
1981	Pat Bradley	279	Beth Daniel	La Grange CC, La Grange, IL
1982	Janet Anderson	283	Beth Daniel	Del Paso CC, Sacramento
			Sandra Haynie	
			Donna White	
			JoAnne Carner	
1983	Jan Stephenson	290	JoAnne Carner	Cedar Ridge CC, Tulsa
			Patty Sheehan	
1984	Hollis Stacy	290	Rosie Jones	Salem CC, Peabody, MA
1985	Kathy Baker	280	Judy Dickinson	Baltusrol GC (Upper Course), Springfield, NJ
1986	Jane Geddes* (71)	287	Sally Little (73)	NCR GC, Dayton
1987	Laura Davies* (71)	285	Ayako Okamoto (73)	Plainfield CC, Plainfield, NJ
			JoAnne Carner (74)	
1988	Liselotte Neumann	277	Patty Sheehan	Baltimore CC, Baltimore
1989	Betsy King	278	Nancy Lopez	Indianwood G & CC, Lake Orion, MI
1990	Betsy King	284	Patty Sheehan	Atlanta Athletic Club, Duluth, GA
1991	Meg Mallon	283	Pat Bradley	Colonial Club, Fort Worth

U.S. Women's Open (Cont.)

Year	Winner	Score	Runner-Up	Site
1992	Patty Sheehan* (72)	280	Juli Inkster	Oakmont CC, Oakmont, PA
1993	Lauri Merten	280	Donna Andrew	Crooked Stick, Carmel, IN
			Helen Alfredsson	
1994	Patty Sheehan	277	Tammie Green	Indianwood G & CC, Lake Orion, MI
1995	Annika Sörenstam	278	Meg Mallon	The Broadmoor GC, Colorado Springs, CO
1996	Annika Sörenstam	272	Kris Tschetter	Pine Needles GC, Southern Pines, NC
1997	Alison Nicholas	274	Nancy Lopez	Pumpkin Ridge CC, North Plains, OR
1998	Se Ri Pak†	290	Jenny Chuasiriporn	Blackwolf Run Golf Resort, Kohler, WI
1999	Juli Inkster	272	Sherri Turner	Old Waverly GC, West Point, MS

* Winner in playoff; 18-hole playoff scores are in parentheses.
† Winner on second hole of sudden death after 18-hole playoff ended in a tie.

Dinah Shore

Year	Winner	Score	Runner-Up	Year	Winner	Score	Runner-Up
1972	Jane Blalock	213	Carol Mann	1987	Betsy King*	283	Patty Sheehan
			Judy Rankin	1988	Amy Alcott	274	Colleen Walker
1973	Mickey Wright	284	Joyce Kazmierski	1989	Juli Inkster	279	Tammie Green
1974	Jo Ann Prentice*	289	Jane Blalock				JoAnne Carner
			Sandra Haynie	1990	Betsy King	283	Kathy Postlewait
1975	Sandra Palmer	283	Kathy McMullen				Shirley Furlong
1976	Judy Rankin	285	Betty Burfeindt	1991	Amy Alcott	273	Dottie Mochrie
1977	Kathy Whitworth	289	JoAnne Carner	1992	Dottie Mochrie*	279	Juli Inkster
			Sally Little	1993	Helen Alfredsson	284	Amy Benz
1978	Sandra Post*	283	Penny Pulz				Tina Barrett
1979	Sandra Post	276	Nancy Lopez				Betsy King
1980	Donna Caponi	275	Amy Alcott	1994	Donna Andrews	276	Laura Davies
1981	Nancy Lopez	277	Carolyn Hill	1995	Nanci Bowen	285	Susie Redman
1982	Sally Little	278	Hollis Stacy	1996	Patti Sheehan	281	Kelly Robbins
			Sandra Haynie				Meg Mallon
1983	Amy Alcott	282	Beth Daniel				Annika Sörenstam
			Kathy Whitworth	1997	Betsy King	276	Kris Tschetter
1984	Juli Inkster*	280	Pat Bradley	1998	Pat Hurst	281	Helen Dobson
1985	Alice Miller	275	Jan Stephenson	1999	Dottie Pepper	269	Meg Mallon
1986	Pat Bradley	280	Val Skinner				

*Winner in sudden-death playoff.
Note: Designated fourth major in 1983.
Played at Mission Hills CC, Rancho Mirage, CA.

du Maurier Classic

Year	Winner	Score	Runner-Up	Site
1973	Jocelyne Bourassa*	214	Sandra Haynie	Montreal GC, Montreal
			Judy Rankin	
1974	Carole Jo Callison	208	JoAnne Carner	Candiac GC, Montreal
1975	JoAnne Carner*	214	Carol Mann	St. George's CC, Toronto
1976	Donna Caponi*	212	Judy Rankin	Cedar Brae G & CC, Toronto
1977	Judy Rankin	214	Pat Meyers	Lachute G & CC, Montreal
			Sandra Palmer	
1978	JoAnne Carner	278	Hollis Stacy	St. George's CC, Toronto
1979	Amy Alcott	285	Nancy Lopez	Richelieu Valley CC, Montreal
1980	Pat Bradley	277	JoAnne Carner	St. George's CC, Toronto
1981	Jan Stephenson	278	Nancy Lopez	Summerlea CC, Dorion, Quebec
			Pat Bradley	
1982	Sandra Haynie	280	Beth Daniel	St. George's CC, Toronto
1983	Hollis Stacy	277	JoAnne Carner	Beaconsfield GC, Montreal
			Alice Miller	
1984	Juli Inkster	279	Ayako Okamoto	St. George's G & CC, Toronto
1985	Pat Bradley	278	Jane Geddes	Beaconsfield CC, Montreal
1986	Pat Bradley*	276	Ayako Okamoto	Board of Trade CC, Toronto
1987	Jody Rosenthal	272	Ayako Okamoto	Islesmere G & CC, Laval, Quebec
1988	Sally Little	279	Laura Davies	Vancouver GC, Coquitlam, British Columbia
1989	Tammie Green	279	Pat Bradley	Beaconsfield GC, Montreal
			Betsy King	
1990	Cathy Johnston	276	Patty Sheehan	Westmount G & CC, Kitchener, Ontario

du Maurier Classic *(Cont.)*

Year	Winner	Score	Runner-Up	Site
1991	Nancy Scranton	279	Debbie Massey	Vancouver GC, Coquitlam, British Columbia
1992	Sherri Steinhauer	277	Judy Dickinson	St. Charles CC, Winnipeg, Manitoba
1993	Brandie Burton	277	Betsy King	London Hunt and CC, London, Ontario
1994	Martha Nause	279	Michelle McGann	Ottawa Hunt and GC, Ottawa, Ont.
1995	Jenny Lidback	280	Liselotte Neumann	Beaconsfield GC, Pointe-Claire, Quebec
1996	Laura Davies	277	Nancy Lopez	Edmonton CC, Edmonton, Alberta
			Karrie Webb	
1997	Colleen Walker	278	Liselotte Neumann	Glen Abbey GC, Oakville, Ontario
1998	Brandie Burton	270	Annika Sörenstam	Essex G & CC, Windsor, Ontario
1999	Karrie Webb	277	Laura Davies	Priddis Greens G & CC, Calgary, Alberta

*Winner in sudden-death playoff.
Note: Designated third major in 1979.

Alltime Major Championship Winners

	LPGA	U.S. Open	Dinah Shore	du Maurier	#Titleholders	†Western	U.S. Am	British Am	Total
Patty Berg	0	1	0	0	7	7	1	0	16
Mickey Wright	4	4	0	0	2	3	0	0	13
Louise Suggs	1	2	0	0	4	4	1	1	13
Babe Zaharias	0	3	0	0	3	4	1	1	12
Betsy Rawls	2	4	0	0	0	2	0	0	8
*JoAnne Carner	0	2	0	0	0	0	5	0	7
*Juli Inkster	1	1	2	1	0	0	3	0	8
Kathy Whitworth	3	0	0	0	2	1	0	0	6
*Pat Bradley	1	1	1	3	0	0	0	0	6
*Patty Sheehan	3	2	1	0	0	0	0	0	6
Glenna Vare	0	0	0	0	0	0	6	0	6
*Betsy King	1	2	3	0	0	0	0	0	6

*Active LPGA player.
#Major from 1937–1972. †Major from 1937–1967.

Alltime Multiple Professional Major Winners

LPGA

Mickey Wright	4
Nancy Lopez	3
Patty Sheehan	3
Kathy Whitworth	3
Donna Caponi	2
Sandra Haynie	2
Mary Mills	2
Betsy Rawls	2
Laura Davies	2

U.S. OPEN

Betsy Rawls	4
Mickey Wright	4
Susie Maxwell Berning	3

U.S. OPEN *(Cont.)*

Hollis Stacy	3
Babe Zaharias	3
JoAnne Carner	2
Donna Caponi	2
Betsy King	2
Patty Sheehan	2
Louise Suggs	2
Annika Sorenstam	2

DINAH SHORE

Amy Alcott	3
Betsy King	3
Juli Inkster	2

DU MAURIER

Pat Bradley	3
Brandie Burton	2
JoAnne Carner	2

TITLEHOLDERS

Patty Berg	7
Louise Suggs	4
Babe Zaharias	3
Dorothy Kirby	2
Marilynn Smith	2
Kathy Whitworth	2
Mickey Wright	2

WESTERN OPEN

Patty Berg	7
Louise Suggs	4
Babe Zaharias	4
Mickey Wright	3
June Beebe	2
Opal Hill	2
Betty Jameson	2
Betsy Rawls	2

THE LPGA TOUR

Most Career Wins†

	Wins		Wins		Wins
Kathy Whitworth	88	JoAnne Carner	42	*Betsy King	31
Mickey Wright	82	Sandra Haynie	42	Babe Zaharias	31
Patty Berg	57	Carol Mann	38	Amy Alcott	29
Betsy Rawls	55	*Patty Sheehan	35	Jane Blalock	29
Louise Suggs	50	*Beth Daniel	32	Judy Rankin	26
*Nancy Lopez	48	*Pat Bradley	31		

*Active LPGA player. †Through 10/17/99.

Season Money Leaders

	Earnings ($)		Earnings ($)		Earnings ($)
1950...Babe Zaharias	14,800	1967...Kathy Whitworth	32,937	1984...Betsy King	266,771
1951...Babe Zaharias	15,087	1968...Kathy Whitworth	48,379	1985...Nancy Lopez	416,472
1952...Betsy Rawls	14,505	1969...Carol Mann	49,152	1986...Pat Bradley	492,021
1953...Louise Suggs	19,816	1970...Kathy Whitworth	30,235	1987...Ayako Okamoto	466,034
1954...Patty Berg	16,011	1971...Kathy Whitworth	41,181	1988...Sherri Turner	350,851
1955...Patty Berg	16,492	1972...Kathy Whitworth	65,063	1989...Betsy King	654,132
1956...Marlene Hagge	20,235	1973...Kathy Whitworth	82,864	1990...Beth Daniel	863,578
1957...Patty Berg	16,272	1974...JoAnne Carner	87,094	1991...Pat Bradley	763,118
1958...Beverly Hanson	12,639	1975...Sandra Palmer	76,374	1992...Dottie Mochrie	693,335
1959...Betsy Rawls	26,774	1976...Judy Rankin	150,734	1993...Betsy King	595,992
1960...Louise Suggs	16,892	1977...Judy Rankin	122,890	1994...Laura Davies	687,201
1961...Mickey Wright	22,236	1978...Nancy Lopez	189,814	1995...Annika Sörenstam	666,533
1962...Mickey Wright	21,641	1979...Nancy Lopez	197,489	1996...Karrie Webb	1,002,000
1963...Mickey Wright	31,269	1980...Beth Daniel	231,000	1997...Annika Sörenstam	1,236,789
1964...Mickey Wright	29,800	1981...Beth Daniel	206,998	1998...Annika Sörenstam	1,092,748
1965...Kathy Whitworth	28,658	1982...JoAnne Carner	310,400		
1966...Kathy Whitworth	33,517	1983...JoAnne Carner	291,404		

Career Money Leaders†

	Earnings ($)		Earnings ($)		Earnings ($)
1. Betsy King	6,425,999	11. Rosie Jones	4,224,012	22. Jan Stephenson	2,884,983
2. Beth Daniel	5,671,801	12. Karrie Webb	4,185,542	22. Brandie Burton	2,796,570
3. Pat Bradley	5,669,439	13. Liselotte Neumann	3,837,386	23. Colleen Walker	2,746,371
4. Patty Sheehan	5,479,064	14. Jane Geddes	3,583,834	24. Ayako Okamoto	2,743,175
5. Nancy Lopez	5,245,772	15. Kelly Robbins	3,541,544	25. Michelle McGann	2,629,431
6. Dottie Pepper	5,095,436	16. Amy Alcott	3,346,139	26. Donna Andrews	2,619,053
7. Juli Inkster	5,034,070	17. Tammie Green	3,326,823	27. D. Ammaccapane	2,555,584
8. Annika Sörenstam	4,779,398	18. Chris Johnson	3,229,084	28. Hollis Stacy	2,526,765
9. Laura Davies	4,494,398	19. Sherri Steinhauer	3,140,093	29. Deb Richard	2,445,242
10. Meg Mallon	4,310,678	20. JoAnne Carner	2,929,886	30. Dawn Coe-Jones	2,443,392

†Through 10/17/99.

LPGA Player of the Year

1966	Kathy Whitworth	1977	Judy Rankin	1988	Nancy Lopez
1967	Kathy Whitworth	1978	Nancy Lopez	1989	Betsy King
1968	Kathy Whitworth	1979	Nancy Lopez	1990	Beth Daniel
1969	Kathy Whitworth	1980	Beth Daniel	1991	Pat Bradley
1970	Sandra Haynie	1981	JoAnne Carner	1992	Dottie Mochrie
1971	Kathy Whitworth	1982	JoAnne Carner	1993	Betsy King
1972	Kathy Whitworth	1983	Patty Sheehan	1994	Beth Daniel
1973	Kathy Whitworth	1984	Betsy King	1995	Annika Sörenstam
1974	JoAnne Carner	1985	Nancy Lopez	1996	Laura Davies
1975	Sandra Palmer	1986	Pat Bradley	1997	Annika Sörenstam
1976	Judy Rankin	1987	Ayako Okamoto	1998	Annika Sörenstam

Vare Trophy: Best Scoring Average

Year	Player	Avg	Year	Player	Avg	Year	Player	Avg
1953	Patty Berg	75.00	1969	Kathy Whitworth	72.38	1985	Nancy Lopez	70.73
1954	Babe Zaharias	75.48	1970	Kathy Whitworth	72.26	1986	Pat Bradley	71.10
1955	Patty Berg	74.47	1971	Kathy Whitworth	72.88	1987	Betsy King	71.14
1956	Patty Berg	74.57	1972	Kathy Whitworth	72.38	1988	Colleen Walker	71.26
1957	Louise Suggs	74.64	1973	Judy Rankin	73.08	1989	Beth Daniel	70.38
1958	Beverly Hanson	74.92	1974	JoAnne Carner	72.87	1990	Beth Daniel	70.54
1959	Betsy Rawls	74.03	1975	JoAnne Carner	72.40	1991	Pat Bradley	70.76
1960	Mickey Wright	73.25	1976	Judy Rankin	72.25	1992	Dottie Mochrie	70.80
1961	Mickey Wright	73.55	1977	Judy Rankin	72.16	1993	Nancy Lopez	70.83
1962	Mickey Wright	73.67	1978	Nancy Lopez	71.76	1994	Beth Daniel	70.90
1963	Mickey Wright	72.81	1979	Nancy Lopez	71.20	1995	Annika Sörenstam	71.00
1964	Mickey Wright	72.46	1980	Amy Alcott	71.51	1996	Annika Sörenstam	70.47
1965	Kathy Whitworth	72.61	1981	JoAnne Carner	71.75	1997	Karrie Webb	70.00
1966	Kathy Whitworth	72.60	1982	JoAnne Carner	71.49	1998	Annika Sörenstam	69.99
1967	Kathy Whitworth	72.74	1983	JoAnne Carner	71.41			
1968	Carol Mann	72.04	1984	Patty Sheehan	71.40			

Alltime LPGA Tour Records†

Scoring

72 HOLES

261—(71-61-63-66) by Se Ri Pak to win at the Highland Meadows CC, Sylvania, OH, in the 1998 Jamie Farr Kroger Classic (23 under par).

54 HOLES

194—(63-67-64) by Karrie Webb to lead at the Royal Pines Resort, Ashmore, Goldcoast, Queensland, Australia, in the 1999 Australian Ladies Masters (22-under-par).

36 HOLES

128—(63-65) by Michelle McGann to lead at the Hermitage Golf Course, Old Hickory, TN, at the 1999 Sara Lee Classic (16-under par).

18 HOLES

61—by Se Ri Pak at Highland Meadows CC, Sylvania, OH, in the second round in winning 1998 Jamie Farr Kroger Classic (10 under par)

61—by Annika Sorenstam at Hermitage Golf Course, Old Hickory, TN, in the first round in leading the 1999 Sara Lee Classic (11-under par).

9 HOLES

28—by Mary Beth Zimmerman at Rail GC, 1984 Rail Charity Golf Classic, Springfield, IL (par 36). Zimmerman shot 64.

28—by Pat Bradley at Green Gables CC, Denver, 1984 Columbia Savings Classic (par 35). Bradley shot 65.

28—by Muffin Spencer-Devlin at Knollwood CC, Elmsford, NY, in winning the 1985 MasterCard International Pro-Am (par 35). Spencer-Devlin shot 64.

†Through 10/17/99.

Scoring (Cont.)

9 HOLES (CONT.)

28—by Peggy Kirsch at Squaw Creek CC, Vienna, OH, in the 1991 Phar-Mor (par 35).

28—by Renee Heiken at Highland Meadows CC, Sylvania, OH, in the 1996 Jamie Farr Kroger Classic (par 34).

MOST CONSECUTIVE ROUNDS UNDER 70

9—Beth Daniel, in 1990.

MOST BIRDIES IN A ROW

9—Beth Daniel at Onion Creek Club in Austin, TX, in the second round of the 1999 Philips Invitational. Daniel shot 62 (8-under par).

Wins

MOST CONSECUTIVE WINS IN SCHEDULED EVENTS

4—Mickey Wright, in 1962.
4—Mickey Wright, in 1963.
4—Kathy Whitworth, in 1969.

MOST CONSECUTIVE WINS IN ENTERED TOURNAMENTS

5—Nancy Lopez, in 1987.

MOST WINS IN A CALENDAR YEAR

13—Mickey Wright, in 1963.

WIDEST WINNING MARGIN, STROKES

14—Louise Suggs, 1949 US Women's Open.
14—Cindy Mackey, 1986 MasterCard Int'l Pro-Am.

Senior Golf

U.S. Senior Open

Year	Winner	Score	Runner-Up	Site
1980	Roberto DeVicenzo	285	William C. Campbell	Winged Foot GC, Mamaroneck, NY
1981	Arnold Palmer* (70)	289	Bob Stone (74)	Oakland Hills CC, Birmingham, MI
			Billy Casper (77)	
1982	Miller Barber	282	Gene Littler	Portland GC, Portland, OR
			Dan Sikes, Jr	
1983	Billy Casper* (75) (3)	288	Rod Funseth (75) (4)	Hazeltine GC, Chaska, MN
1984	Miller Barber	286	Arnold Palmer	Oak Hill CC, Rochester, NY
1985	Miller Barber	285	Roberto DeVicenzo	Edgewood Tahoe GC, Stateline, NV
1986	Dale Douglass	279	Gary Player	Scioto CC, Columbus, OH
1987	Gary Player	270	Doug Sanders	Brooklawn CC, Fairfield, CT
1988	Gary Player* (68)	288	Bob Charles (70)	Medinah CC, Medinah, IL
1989	Orville Moody	279	Frank Beard	Laurel Valley GC, Ligonier, PA
1990	Lee Trevino	275	Jack Nicklaus	Ridgewood CC, Paramus, NJ
1991	Jack Nicklaus (65)	282	Chi Chi Rodriguez (69)	Oakland Hills CC, Birmingham, MI
1992	Larry Laoretti	275	Jim Colbert	Saucon Valley CC, Bethlehem, PA
1993	Jack Nicklaus	278	Tom Weiskopf	Cherry Hills CC, Englewood, CO
1994	Simon Hobday	274	Jim Albus	Pinehurst Resort & CC, Pinehurst, NC
1995	Tom Weiskopf	275	Jack Nicklaus	Congressional CC, Bethesda, MD
1996	Dave Stockton	277	Hale Irwin	Canterbury GC, Beachwood, OH
1997	Graham Marsh	280	Hale Irwin	Olympia Fields CC, Olympia Fields, IL
1998	Hale Irwin	285	Vicente Fernandez	Riviera CC, Pacific Palisades, CA
1999	Dave Eichelberger	281	Ed Dougherty	Des Moines G & CC, Des Moines, IA

*Winner in playoff. Playoff scores are in parentheses. The 1983 playoff went to one hole of sudden death after an 18-hole playoff.

SENIOR TOUR

Season Money Leaders

	Earnings ($)		Earnings ($)		Earnings ($)
1980...Don January	44,100	1987...Chi Chi Rodriguez	509,145	1994...Dave Stockton	1,402,519
1981...Miller Barber	83,136	1988...Bob Charles	533,929	1995...Jim Colbert	1,444,386
1982...Miller Barber	106,890	1989...Bob Charles	725,887	1996...Jim Colbert	1,627,890
1983...Don January	237,571	1990...Lee Trevino	1,190,518	1997...Hale Irwin	2,449,420
1984...Don January	328,597	1991...Mike Hill	1,065,657	1998...Hale Irwin	2,861,945
1985...Peter Thomson	386,724	1992...Lee Trevino	1,027,002		
1986...Bruce Crampton	454,299	1993...Dave Stockton	1,175,944		

Career Money Leaders†

	Earnings ($)		Earnings ($)		Earnings ($)
1. Hale Irwin	9,542,075	11. Chi Chi Rodriguez	6,314,484	21. Tom Wargo	4,848,625
2. Jim Colbert	8,847,501	12. Dale Douglass	6,017,684	22. Bruce Crampton	4,652,684
3. Lee Trevino	8,622,830	13. Gil Morgan	5,939,029	23. Rocky Thompson	4,103,096
4. Dave Stockton	7,996,326	14. Bob Murphy	5,609,145	24. Bruce Summerhays	3,949,576
5. Bob Charles	7,995,030	15. Jay Sigel	5,524,990	25. Gibby Gilbert	3,945,255
6. George Archer	6,936,017	16. J.C. Snead	5,332,059	26. Miller Barber	3,939,453
7. Ray Floyd	6,860,604	17. Graham Marsh	5,150,786	27. Simon Hobday	3,863,534
8. Mike Hill	6,784,427	18. Gary Player	5,128,934	28. Kermit Zarley	3,833,226
9. Jim Dent	6,780,273	19. Al Geiberger	4,960,583	29. Harold Henning	3,729,815
10. Isao Aoki	6,506,860	20. Jim Albus	4,909,804	30. Charles Coody	3,655,826

Most Career Wins†

	Wins		Wins
Lee Trevino	28	Gary Player	19
Hale Irwin	25	Jim Colbert	19
Miller Barber	24	Mike Hill	18
Bob Charles	23	George Archer	18
Don January	22	Gil Morgan	15
Chi Chi Rodriguez	22	Dave Stockton	14
Bruce Crampton	20		

†Through 10/17/99.

MAJOR MEN'S AMATEUR CHAMPIONSHIPS
U.S. Amateur

Year	Winner	Score	Runner-Up	Site
1895	Charles B. Macdonald	12 & 11	Charles E. Sands	Newport GC, Newport, RI
1896	H.J. Whigham	8 & 7	J.G Thorp	Shinnecock Hills GC, Southampton, NY
1897	H.J. Whigham	8 & 6	W. Rossiter Betts	Chicago GC, Wheaton, IL
1898	Findlay S. Douglas	5 & 3	Walter B. Smith	Morris County GC, Morristown, NJ
1899	H.M. Harriman	3 & 2	Findlay S. Douglas	Onwentsia Club, Lake Forest, IL
1900	Walter Travis	2 up	Findlay S. Douglas	Garden City GC, Garden City, NY
1901	Walter Travis	5 & 4	Walter E. Egan	CC of Atlantic City, NJ
1902	Louis N. James	4 & 2	Eben M. Byers	Glen View Club, Golf, IL
1903	Walter Travis	5 & 4	Eben M. Byers	Nassau CC, Glen Cove, NY
1904	H. Chandler Egan	8 & 6	Fred Herreshoff	Baltusrol GC, Springfield, NJ
1905	H. Chandler Egan	6 & 5	D.E. Sawyer	Chicago GC, Wheaton, IL
1906	Eben M. Byers	2 up	George S. Lyon	Englewood GC, Englewood, NJ
1907	Jerry Travers	6 & 5	Archibald Graham	Euclid Club, Cleveland, OH
1908	Jerry Travers	8 & 7	Max H. Behr	Garden City GC, Garden City, NY
1909	Robert A. Gardner	4 & 3	H. Chandler Egan	Chicago GC, Wheaton, IL
1910	William C. Fownes Jr.	4 & 3	Warren K. Wood	The Country Club, Brookline, MA
1911	Harold Hilton	1 up	Fred Herreshoff	The Apawamis Club, Rye, NY
1912	Jerry Travers	7 & 6	Charles Evans Jr.	Chicago GC, Wheaton, IL
1913	Jerry Travers	5 & 4	John G. Anderson	Garden City GC, Garden City, NY
1914	Francis Ouimet	6 & 5	Jerry Travers	Ekwanok CC, Manchester, VT
1915	Robert A. Gardner	5 & 4	John G. Anderson	CC of Detroit, Grosse Pt. Farms, MI
1916	Chick Evans	4 & 3	Robert A. Gardner	Merion Cricket Club, Haverford, PA
1917–18	No tournament			
1919	S. Davidson Herron	5 & 4	Bobby Jones	Oakmont CC, Oakmont, PA
1920	Chick Evans	7 & 6	Francis Ouimet	Engineers' CC, Roslyn, NY
1921	Jesse P. Guilford	7 & 6	Robert A. Gardner	St. Louis CC, Clayton, MO
1922	Jess W. Sweetser	3 & 2	Chick Evans	The Country Club, Brookline, MA
1923	Max R. Marston	1 up	Jess W. Sweetser	Flossmoor CC, Flossmoor, IL
1924	Bobby Jones	9 & 8	George Von Elm	Merion Cricket Club, Ardmore, PA
1925	Bobby Jones	8 & 7	Watts Gunn	Oakmont CC, Oakmont, PA
1926	George Von Elm	2 & 1	Bobby Jones	Baltusrol GC, Springfield, NJ
1927	Bobby Jones	8 & 7	Chick Evans	Minikahda Club, Minneapolis
1928	Bobby Jones	10 & 9	T. Phillip Perkins	Brae Burn CC, West Newton, MA
1929	Harrison R. Johnston	4 & 3	Dr. O.F. Willing	Del Monte G & CC, Pebble Beach, CA
1930	Bobby Jones	8 & 7	Eugene V. Homans	Merion Cricket Club, Ardmore, PA
1931	Francis Ouimet	6 & 5	Jack Westland	Beverly CC, Chicago, IL
1932	C. Ross Somerville	2 & 1	John Goodman	Baltimore CC, Timonium, MD
1933	George T. Dunlap Jr.	6 & 5	Max R. Marston	Kenwood CC, Cincinnati, OH
1934	Lawson Little	8 & 7	David Goldman	The Country Club, Brookline, MA
1935	Lawson Little	4 & 2	Walter Emery	The Country Club, Cleveland, OH
1936	John W. Fischer	1 up	Jack McLean	Garden City GC, Garden City, NY
1937	John Goodman	2 up	Raymond E. Billows	Alderwood CC, Portland, OR
1938	William P. Turnesa	8 & 7	B. Patrick Abbott	Oakmont CC, Oakmont, PA
1939	Marvin H. Ward	7 & 5	Raymond E. Billows	North Shore CC, Glenview, IL
1940	Richard D. Chapman	11 & 9	W. McCullough Jr.	Winged Foot GC, Mamaroneck, NY
1941	Marvin H. Ward	4 & 3	B. Patrick Abbott	Omaha Field Club, Omaha, NE
1942–45	No tournament			
1946	Ted Bishop	1 up	Smiley L. Quick	Baltusrol GC, Springfield, NJ
1947	Skee Riegel	2 & 1	John W. Dawson	Del Monte G & CC, Pebble Beach, CA
1948	William P. Turnesa	2 & 1	Raymond E. Billows	Memphis CC, Memphis, TN
1949	Charles R. Coe	11 & 10	Rufus King	Oak Hill CC, Rochester, NY
1950	Sam Urzetta	1 up	Frank Stranahan	Minneapolis GC, Minneapolis, MN
1951	Billy Maxwell	4 & 3	Joseph F. Gagliardi	Saucon Valley CC, Bethlehem, PA
1952	Jack Westland	3 & 2	Al Mengert	Seattle GC, Seattle, WA
1953	Gene Littler	1 up	Dale Morey	Oklahoma City G & CC, Oklahoma City
1954	Arnold Palmer	1 up	Robert Sweeny	CC of Detroit, Grosse Pt. Farms, MI
1955	E. Harvie Ward Jr.	9 & 8	Wm. Hyndman III	CC of Virginia, Richmond, VA
1956	E. Harvie Ward Jr.	5 & 4	Charles Kocsis	Knollwood Club, Lake Forest, IL
1957	Hillman Robbins Jr.	5 & 4	Dr. Frank M. Taylor	The Country Club, Brookline, MA
1958	Charles R. Coe	5 & 4	Tommy Aaron	Olympic Club, San Francisco, CA
1959	Jack Nicklaus	1 up	Charles R. Coe	Broadmoor GC, Colorado Springs, CO
1960	Deane Beman	6 & 4	Robert W. Gardner	St. Louis CC, Clayton, MO
1961	Jack Nicklaus	8 & 6	H. Dudley Wysong	Pebble Beach GL, Pebble Beach, CA

U.S. Amateur (Cont.)

Year	Winner	Score	Runner-Up	Site
1962	Labron E. Harris Jr.	1 up	Downing Gray	Pinehurst CC, Pinehurst, NC
1963	Deane Beman	2 & 1	Richard H. Sikes	Wakonda Club, Des Moines, IA
1964	William C. Campbell	1 up	Edgar M. Tutwiler	Canterbury GC, Cleveland, OH
1965	Robert J. Murphy Jr.	291	Robert B. Dickson	Southern Hills, CC, Tulsa, OK
1966	Gary Cowan	285–75	Deane Beman	Merion GC, Ardmore, PA
1967	Robert B. Dickson	285	Marvin Giles III	Broadmoor GC, Colorado Springs, CO
1968	Bruce Fleisher	284	Marvin Giles III	Scioto CC, Columbus, OH
1969	Steven N. Melnyk	286	Marvin Giles III	Oakmont CC, Oakmont, PA
1970	Lanny Wadkins	279	Tom Kite	Waverley CC, Portland, OR
1971	Gary Cowan	280	Eddie Pearce	Wilmington CC, Wilmington DE
1972	Marvin Giles III	285	two tied	Charlotte CC, Charlotte, NC
1973	Craig Stadler	6 & 5	David Strawn	Inverness Club, Toledo, OH
1974	Jerry Pate	2 & 1	John P. Grace	Ridgewood CC, Ridgewood, NJ
1975	Fred Ridley	2 up	Keith Fergus	CC of Virginia, Richmond, VA
1976	Bill Sander	8 & 6	C. Parker Moore Jr.	Bel Air CC, Los Angeles, CA
1977	John Fought	9 & 8	Doug Fischesser	Aronimink GC, Newton Square, PA
1978	John Cook	5 & 4	Scott Hoch	Plainfield CC, Plainfield, NJ
1979	Mark O'Meara	8 & 7	John Cook	Canterbury GC, Cleveland, OH
1980	Hal Sutton	9 & 8	Bob Lewis	CC of North Carolina, Pinehurst, NC
1981	Nathaniel Crosby	1 up	Brian Lindley	Olympic Club, San Francisco, CA
1982	Jay Sigel	8 & 7	David Tolley	The Country Club, Brookline, MA
1983	Jay Sigel	8 & 7	Chris Perry	North Shore CC, Glenviedw IL
1984	Scott Verplank	4 & 3	Sam Randolph	Oak Tree GC, Edmond, OK
1985	Sam Randolph	1 up	Peter Persons	Montclair GC, West Orange, NJ
1986	Buddy Alexander	5 & 3	Chris Kite	Shoal Creek, Shoal Creek AL
1987	Bill Mayfair	4 & 3	Eric Rebmann	Jupiter Hills Club, Jupiter, FL
1988	Eric Meeks	7 & 6	Danny Yates	Va. Hot Springs G & CC, VA
1989	Chris Patton	3 & 1	Danny Green	Merion GC, Ardmore, PA
1990	Phil Mickelson	5 & 4	Manny Zerman	Cherry Hills CC, Englewood, CO
1991	Mitch Voges	7 & 6	Manny Zerman	The Honors Course, Ooltewah, TN
1992	Justin Leonard	8 & 7	Tom Scherrer	Muirfield Village GC, Dublin, OH
1993	John Harris	5 & 3	Danny Ellis	Champions GC, Houston, TX
1994	Tiger Woods	2 up	Trip Kuehne	TPC-Sawgrass, Ponte Vedre, FL
1995	Tiger Woods	2 up	Buddy Marucci	Newport Country Club, Newport, RI
1996	Tiger Woods	38 holes	Steve Scott	Pumpkin Ridge GC, Cornelius, OR
1997	Matthew Kuchar	2 & 1	Joel Kribel	Cog Hill G & CC, Lemont, IL
1998	Hank Kuehne	2 & 1	Tom McKnight	Oak Hill CC, Rochester, NY
1999	David Gossett	9 & 8	Sung Yoon Kim	Pebble Beach GL, Pebble Beach, CA

Note: All stroke play from 1965 to 1972.

U.S. Junior Amateur

1948...Dean Lind	1961...Charles McDowell	1974...David Nevatt	1987...Brett Quigley
1949...Gay Brewer	1962...Jim Wiechers	1975...Brett Mullin	1988...Jason Widener
1950...Mason Rudolph	1963...Gregg McHatton	1976...Madden Hatcher III	1989...David Duval
1951...Tommy Jacobs	1964...Johnny Miller	1977...Willie Wood Jr.	1990...Mathew Todd
1952...Don Bisplinghoff	1965...James Masserio	1978...Don Hurter	1991...Tiger Woods
1953...Rex Baxter	1966...Gary Sanders	1979...Jack Larkin	1992...Tiger Woods
1954...Foster Bradley	1967...John Crooks	1980...Eric Johnson	1993...Tiger Woods
1955...William Dunn	1968...Eddie Pearce	1981...Scott Erickson	1994...Terry Noe
1956...Harlan Stevenson	1969...Aly Trompas	1982...Rich Marik	1995...D. Scott Hailes
1957...Larry Beck	1970...Gary Koch	1983...Tim Straub	1996...Shane McMenamy
1958...Buddy Baker	1971...Mike Brannan	1984...Doug Martin	1997...Jason Allred
1959...Larry Lee	1972...Bob Byman	1985...Charles Rymer	1998...James Oh
1960...Bill Tindall	1973...Jack Renner	1986...Brian Montgomery	1999...Hunter Mahan

Note: Event is for amateur golfers younger than 18 years of age.

Mid-Amateur Championship

1981...Jim Holtgrieve	1986...Bill Loeffler	1991...Jim Stuart	1996...John Miller
1982...William Hoffer	1987...Jay Sigel	1992...Danny Yates	1997...Ken Bakst
1983...Jay Sigel	1988...David Eger	1993...Jeff Thomas	1998...John Miller
1984...Mike Podolak	1989...James Taylor	1994...Tim Jackson	1999...Danny Green
1985...Jay Sigel	1990...Jim Stuart	1995...Jerry Courville Jr.	

Note: Event is for amateur golfers at least 25 years of age.

British Amateur

1887	H. G. Hutchinson
1888	John Ball
1889	J.E. Laidlay
1890	John Ball
1891	J.E. Laidlay
1892	John Ball
1893	Peter Anderson
1894	John Ball
1895	L.M.B. Melville
1896	F.G. Tait
1897	A.J.T. Allan
1898	F.G. Tait
1899	John Ball
1900	H.H. Hilton
1901	H.H. Hilton
1902	C. Hutchings
1903	R. Maxwell
1904	W.J. Travis
1905	A.G. Barry
1906	James Robb
1907	John Ball
1908	E.A. Lassen
1909	R. Maxwell
1910	John Ball
1911	H.H. Hilton
1912	John Ball
1913	H.H. Hilton
1914	J.L.C. Jenkins
1915-19	not held
1920	C.J.H. Tolley
1921	W.I. Hunter
1922	E.W.E. Holderness
1923	R.H. Wethered
1924	E.W.E. Holderness
1925	R. Harris

1926	Jess Sweetser
1927	Dr. W. Tweddell
1928	T.P. Perkins
1929	C.J.H. Tolley
1930	Robert T. Jones Jr.
1931	E. Martin Smith
1932	J. DeForest
1933	M. Scott
1934	W. Lawson Little
1935	W. Lawson Little
1936	H. Thomson
1937	R. Sweeney Jr.
1938	C.R. Yates
1939	A.T. Kyle
1940-45	not held
1946	J. Bruen
1947	Willie D. Turnesa
1948	Frank R. Stranahan
1949	S.M. McReady
1950	Frank R. Stranahan
1951	Richard D. Chapman
1952	E.H. Ward
1953	J.B. Carr
1954	D.W. Bachli
1955	J.W. Conrad
1956	J.C. Beharrel
1957	R. Reid Jack
1958	J.B. Carr
1959	Deane Beman
1960	J.B. Carr
1961	M. Bonallack
1962	R. Davies
1963	M. Lunt
1964	C. Clark
1965	M. Bonallack

1966	C.R. Cole
1967	R. Dickson
1968	M. Bonallack
1969	M. Bonallack
1970	M. Bonallack
1971	Steve Melnyk
1972	Trevor Homer
1973	R. Siderowf
1974	Trevor Homer
1975	M. Giles
1976	R. Siderowf
1977	P. McEvoy
1978	P. McEvoy
1979	J. Sigel
1980	D. Evans
1981	P. Ploujoux
1982	M. Thompson
1983	A. Parkin
1984	J.M. Olazabal
1985	G. McGimpsey
1986	D. Curry
1987	P. Mayo
1988	C. Hardin
1989	S. Dodd
1990	R. Muntz
1991	G. Wolstenholme
1992	S. Dundas
1993	I. Pyman
1994	L. James
1995	G. Sherry
1996	W. Bladon
1997	C. Watson
1998	Sergio Garcia
1999	Graeme Storm

Amateur Public Links

1922	Edmund R. Held
1923	Richard J. Walsh
1924	Joseph Coble
1925	Raymond J. McAuliffe
1926	Lester Bolstad
1927	Carl F. Kauffmann
1928	Carl F. Kauffmann
1929	Carl F. Kauffmann
1930	Robert E. Wingate
1931	Charles Ferrera
1932	R.L. Miller
1933	Charles Ferrera
1934	David A. Mitchell
1935	Frank Strafaci
1936	B. Patrick Abbott
1937	Bruce N. McCormick
1938	Al Leach
1939	Andrew Szwedko
1940	Robert C. Clark
1941	William M. Welch Jr.
1942-45	not held
1946	Smiley L. Quick
1947	Wilfred Crossley
1948	Michael R. Ferentz
1949	Kenneth J. Towns

1950	Stanley Bielat
1951	Dave Stanley
1952	Omer L. Bogan
1953	Ted Richards Jr.
1954	Gene Andrews
1955	Sam D. Kocsis
1956	James H. Buxbaum
1957	Don Essig III
1958	Daniel D. Sikes Jr.
1959	William A. Wright
1960	Verne Callison
1961	Richard H. Sikes
1962	Richard H. Sikes
1963	Robert Lunn
1964	William McDonald
1965	Arne Dokka
1966	Lamont Kaser
1967	Verne Callison
1968	Gene Towry
1969	John M. Jackson Jr.
1970	Robert Risch
1971	Fred Haney
1972	Bob Allard
1973	Stan Stopa
1974	Charles Barenaba
1975	Randy Barenaba

1976	Eddie Mudd
1977	Jerry Vidovic
1978	Dean Prince
1979	Dennis Walsh
1980	Jodie Mudd
1981	Jodie Mudd
1982	Billy Tuten
1983	Billy Tuten
1984	Bill Malley
1985	Jim Sorenson
1986	Bill Mayfair
1987	Kevin Johnson
1988	Ralph Howe III
1989	Tim Hobby
1990	Michael Combs
1991	David Berganio Jr.
1992	Warren Schulte
1993	David Berganio Jr.
1994	Guy Yamamoto
1995	Chris Wollmann
1996	Tim Hogarth
1997	Tim Clark
1998	Trevor Immelman
1999	Hunter Haas

U.S. Senior Golf

1955 ....J. Wood Platt	1970 ....Gene Andrews	1985 ....Lewis W. Oehmig
1956 ....Frederick J. Wright	1971 ....Tom Draper	1986 ....Bo Williams
1957 ....J. Clark Espie	1972 ....Lewis W. Oehmig	1987 ....John Richardson
1958 ....Thomas C. Robbins	1973 ....William Hyndman III	1988 ....Clarence Moore
1959 ....J. Clark Espie	1974 ....Dale Morey	1989 ....Bo Williams
1960 ....Michael Cestone	1975 ....William F. Colm	1990 ....Jackie Cummings
1961 ....Dexter H. Daniels	1976 ....Lewis W. Oehmig	1991 ....Bill Bosshard
1962 ....Merrill L. Carlsmith	1977 ....Dale Morey	1992 ....Clarence Moore
1963 ....Merrill L. Carlsmith	1978 ..........K.K. Compton	1993 ....Joe Ungvary
1964 ....William D. Higgins	1979 ....William C. Campbell	1994 ....O. Gordon Brewer
1965 ....Robert B. Kiersky	1980 ....William C. Campbell	1995 ....James Stahl Jr.
1966 ....Dexter H. Daniels	1981 ....Ed Updegraff	1996 ....O. Gordon Brewer
1967 ....Ray Palmer	1982 ....Alton Duhon	1997 ....Cliff Cunningham
1968 ....Curtis Person Sr.	1983 ....William Hyndman III	1998 ....Bill Shean Jr.
1969 ....Curtis Person Sr.	1984 ....Bob Rawlins	1999 ....Bill Ploeger

Note: Event is for amateur golfers at least 55 years of age.

MAJOR WOMEN'S AMATEUR CHAMPIONSHIPS

U.S. Women's Amateur

Year	Winner	Score	Runner-Up	Site
1895 ....Mrs. Charles S. Brown		132	Nellie Sargent	Meadow Brook Club, Hempstead, NY
1896 ....Beatrix Hoyt		2 & 1	Mrs. Arthur Turnure	Morris Couty GC, Morristown, NJ
1897 ....Beatrix Hoyt		5 & 4	Nellie Sargent	Essex County Club, Manchester, MA
1898 ....Beatrix Hoyt		5 &3	Maude Wetmore	Ardsley Club, Ardsley-on-Hudson, NY
1899 ....Ruth Underhill		2 & 1	Margaret Fox	Philadelphia CC, Philadelphia, PA
1900 ....Frances C. Griscom		6 & 5	Margaret Curtis	Shinnecock Hills GC, Shinnecock Hills, NY
1901 ....Genevieve Hecker		5 & 3	Lucy Herron	Baltusrol GC, Springfield, NJ
1902 ....Genevieve Hecker		4 & 3	Louisa A. Wells	The Country Club, Brookline, MA
1903 ....Bessie Anthony		7 & 6	J. Anna Carpenter	Chicago GC, Wheaton, IL
1904 ....Georgianna M. Bishop		5 & 3	Mrs. E.F. Sanford	Merion Cricket Club, Haverford, PA
1905 ....Pauline Mackay		1 up	Margaret Curtis	Morris County GC, Convent, NJ
1906 ....Harriot S. Curtis		2 & 1	Mary B. Adams	Brae Burn CC, West Newton, MA
1907 ....Margaret Curtis		7 & 6	Harriot S. Curtis	Midlothian CC, Blue Island, IL
1908 ....Katherine C. Harley		6 & 5	Mrs. T.H. Polhemus	Chevy Chase Club, Chevy Chase, MD
1909 ....Dorothy I. Campbell		3 & 2	Nonna Barlow	Merion Cricket Club, Haverford, PA
1910 ....Dorothy I. Campbell		2 & 1	Mrs. G.M. Martin	Homewood CC, Flossmoor, IL
1911 ....Margaret Curtis		5 & 3	Lillian B. Hyde	Baltusrol GC, Springfield, NJ
1912 ....Margaret Curtis		3 & 2	Nonna Barlow	Essex County Club, Manchester, MA
1913 ....Gladys Ravenscroft		2 up	Marion Hollins	Wilmington CC, Wilmington, DE
1914 ....Katherine Harley		1 up	Elaine V. Rosenthal	Nassau CC, Glen Cove, NY
1915 ....Florence Vanderbeck		3 & 2	Margaret Gavin	Onwentsia Club, Lake Forest, IL
1916 ....Alexa Stirling		2 & 1	Mildred Caverly	Belmont Springs CC, Waverley, MA
1917–18 .....No tournament				
1919............Alexa Stirling		6 & 5	Margaret Gavin	Shawnee CC, Shawnee-on-Delaware, PA
1920 ....Alexa Stirling		5 & 4	Dorothy Campbell	Mayfield CC, Cleveland, OH
1921 ....Marion Hollins		5 & 4	Alexa Stirling	Hollywood GC, Deal, NJ
1922 ....Glenna Collett		5 & 4	Margaret Gavin	Greenbriar GC, White Sulphur Springs, WV
1923 ....Edith Cummings		3 & 2	Alexa Stirling	Westchester-Biltmore CC, Rye, NY
1924 ....Dorothy Campbell		7 & 6	Mary K. Browne	Rhode Island CC, Nyatt, RI
1925 ....Glenna Collett		9 & 8	Alexa Stirling	St. Louis CC, Clayton, MO
1926 ....Helen Stetson		3 & 1	Elizabeth Goss	Merion Cricket Club, Ardmore, PA
1927 ....Miiriam Burns Horn		5 & 4	Maureen Orcutt	Cherry Valley Club, Garden City, NY
1928 ....Glenna Collett		13 & 12	Virginia Van Wie	Va. Hot Springs G & TC, Hot Springs, VA
1929 ....Glenna Collett		4 & 3	Leona Pressler	Oakland Hills CC, Birmingham, MI
1930 ....Glenna Collett		6 & 5	Virginia Van Wie	Los Angeles CC, Beverly Hills, CA
1931 ....Helen Hicks		2 & 1	Glenna Collet Vare	CC of Buffalo, Williamsville, NY
1932 ....Virginia Van Wie		10 & 8	Glenna Collet Vare	Salem CC, Peabody, MA
1933 ....Virginia Van Wie		4 & 3	Helen Hicks	Exmoor CC, Highland Park, IL
1934 ....Virginia Van Wie		2 & 1	Dorothy Traung	Whitemarsh Valley CC, Chestnut Hill, PA
1935 ....Glenna Collett Vare		3 & 2	Patty Berg	Interlachen CC, Hopkins, MN
1936 ....Pamela Barton		4 & 3	Maureen Orcutt	Canoe Brook CC, Summit, NJ
1937 ....Estelle Lawson		7 & 6	Patty Berg	Memphis CC, Memphis, TN
1938 ....Patty Berg		6 & 5	Estelle Lawson	Westmoreland CC, Wilmette, IL

U.S. Women's Amateur (Cont.)

Year	Winner	Score	Runner-Up	Site
1939	Betty Jameson	3 & 2	Dorothy Kirby	Wee Burn Club, Darien, CT
1940	Betty Jameson	6 & 5	Jane S. Cothran	Del Monte G & CC, Pebble Beach, CA
1941	Elizabeth Hicks	5 & 3	Helen Sigel	The Country Club, Brookline, MA
1942–45	No tournament			
1946	Babe Zaharias	11 & 9	Clara Sherman	Southern Hills CC, Tulsa, OK
1947	Louise Suggs	2 up	Dorothy Kirby	Franklin Hills CC, Franklin, MI
1948	Grace S. Lenczyk	4 & 3	Helen Sigel	Del Monte G & CC, Pebble Beach, CA
1949	Dorothy Porter	3 & 2	Dorothy Kielty	Merion GC, Ardmore, PA
1950	Beverly Hanson	6 & 4	Mae Murray	Atlanta AC, Atlanta, GA
1951	Dorothy Kirby	2 & 1	Claire Doran	Town & CC, St. Paul, MN
1952	Jacqueline Pung	2 & 1	Shirley McFedters	Waverley CC, Portland, OR
1953	Mary Lena Faulk	3 & 2	Polly Riley	Rhode Island CC, West Barrington, RI
1954	Barbara Romack	4 & 2	Mickey Wright	Allegheny CC, Sewickley, PA
1955	Patricia A. Lesser	7 & 6	Jane Nelson	Myers Park CC, Charlotte, NC
1956	Marlene Stewart	2 & 1	JoAnne Gunderson	Meridian Hills CC, Indianapolis, IN
1957	JoAnne Gunderson	8 & 6	Ann Casey Johnstone	Del Paso CC, Sacramento, CA
1958	Anne Quast	3 & 2	Barbara Romack	Wee Burn CC, Darien, CT
1959	Barbara McIntire	4 & 3	Joanne Goodwin	Congressional CC, Washington, D.C.
1960	JoAnne Gunderson	6 & 5	Jean Ashley	Tulsa CC, Tulsa, OK
1961	Anne Quast Decker	14 & 13	Phyllis Preuss	Tacoma G & CC, Tacoma, WA
1962	JoAnne Gunderson	9 & 8	Anne Baker	CC of Rochester, Rochester, NY
1963	Anne Quast Decker	2 & 1	Peggy Conley	Taconic GC, Williamstown, MA
1964	Barbara McIntire	3 & 2	JoAnne Gunderson	Prairie Dunes CC, Hutchinson, KS
1965	Jean Ashley	5 & 4	Anne Quast Decker	Lakewood CC, Denver, CO
1966	JoAnne Gunderson	1 up	Marlene Stewart Streit	Sewickley Heights GC, Sewickley, PA
1967	Mary Lou Dill	5 & 4	Jean Ashley	Annandale GC, Pasadena, CA
1968	JoAnne Gunderson Carner	5 & 4	Anne Quast Decker	Birmingham CC, Birmingham, MI
1969	Catherine Lacoste	3 & 2	Shelley Hamling	Las Colinas CC, Irving, TX
1970	Martha Wilkinson	3 & 2	Cynthia Hall	Wee Burn CC, Darien, CT
1971	Laura Baugh	1 up	Beth Barry	Atlanta CC, Atlanta, GA
1972	Mary Budke	5 & 4	Cynthia Hill	St. Louis CC, St. Louis, MO
1973	Carol Semple	1 up	Anne Quast Decker	Montclair GC, Montclair, NJ
1974	Cynthia Hill	5 & 4	Carol Semple	Broadmoor GC, Seattle, WA
1975	Beth Daniel	3 & 2	Donna Horton	Brae Burn CC, West Newton, MA
1976	Donna Horton	2 & 1	Marianne Bretton	Del Paso CC, Sacramento, CA
1977	Beth Daniel	3 & 1	Cathy Sherk	Cincinnati CC, Cincinnati, OH
1978	Cathy Sherk	4 & 3	Judith Oliver	Sunnybrook GC, Plymouth Meeting, PA
1979	Carolyn Hill	7 & 6	Patty Sheehan	Memphis CC, Memphis, TN
1980	Juli Inkster	2 up	Patti Rizzo	Prairie Dunes CC, Hutchinson, KS
1981	Juli Inkster	1 up	Lindy Goggin	Waverley CC, Portland, OR
1982	Juli Inkster	4 & 3	Cathy Hanlon	Broadmoor GC, Colorado Springs, CO
1983	Joanne Pacillo	2 & 1	Sally Quinlan	Canoe Brook CC, Summit, NJ
1984	Deb Richard	1 up	Kimberly Williams	Broadmoor GC, Seattle, WA
1985	Michiko Hattori	5 & 4	Cheryl Stacy	Fox Chapel CC, Pittsburgh, PA
1986	Kay Cockerill	9 & 7	Kathleen McCarthy	Pasatiempo GC, Santa Cruz, CA
1987	Kay Cockerill	3 & 2	Tracy Kerdyk	Rhode Island CC, Barrington, RI
1988	Pearl Sinn	6 & 5	Karen Noble	Minikahda Club, Minneapolis, MN
1989	Vicki Goetze	4 & 3	Brandie Burton	Pinehurst CC (No. 2), Pinehurst, NC
1990	Pat Hurst	37 holes	Stephanie Davis	Canoe Brook CC, Summit, NJ
1991	Amy Fruhwirth	5 & 4	Heidi Voorhees	Prairie Dunes CC, Hutchinson, KN
1992	Vicki Goetz	1-up	Annika Sorensteam	Kemper Lakes GC, Hawthorne Hills, IL
1993	Jill McGill	1-up	Sarah Ingram	San Diego CC, Chula Vista, CA
1994	Wendy Ward	2 & 1	Jill McGill	The Homestead, Hot Springs, WV
1995	Kelli Kuehne	4 & 3	Anne-Marie Knight	The Country Club, Brookline, MA
1996	Kelli Kuehne	2 & 1	Marisa Baena	Firethorn GC, Lincoln, NE
1997	Silvia Cavalleri	5 & 4	Robin Burke	Brae Burn CC, West Newton, MA
1998	Grace Park	7 & 6	Jenny Chuasiriporn	Barton Hills CC, Ann Arbor, MI
1999	Dorothy Delasin	4 & 3	Jimin Kang	Biltmore Forest CC, Asheville, NC

U.S. Girls' Junior Amateur

1949 ....Marlene Bauer	1967 ....Elizabeth Story	1985 ....Dana Lofland
1950 ....Patricia Lesser	1968 ....Peggy Harmon	1986 ....Pat Hurst
1951 ....Arlene Brooks	1969 ....Hollis Stacy	1987 ....Michelle McGann
1952 ....Mickey Wright	1970 ....Hollis Stacy	1988 ....Jamille Jose
1953 ....Millie Meyerson	1971 ....Hollis Stacy	1989 ....Brandie Burton
1954 ....Margaret Smith	1972 ....Nancy Lopez	1990 ....Sandrine Mendiburu
1955 ....Carole Jo Kabler	1973 ....Amy Alcott	1991 ....Emilee Klein
1956 ....JoAnne Gunderson	1974 ....Nancy Lopez	1992 ....Jamie Koizumi
1957 ....Judy Eller	1975 ....Dayna Benson	1993 ....Kellee Booth
1958 ....Judy Eller	1976 ....Pilar Dorado	1962 ....Maureen Orcutt
1959 ....Judy Rand	1977 ....Althea Tome	1963 ....Sis Choate
1960 ....Carol Sorenson	1978 ....Lori Castillo	1994 ....Kelli Kuehne
1961 ....Mary Lowell	1979 ....Penny Hammel	1995 ....Marcy Newton
1962 ....Mary Lou Daniel	1980 ....Laurie Rinker	1996 ....Dorothy Delasin
1963 ....Janis Ferraris	1981 ....Kay Cornelius	1997 ....Beth Bauer
1964 ....Peggy Conley	1982 ....Heather Farr	1998 ....Leigh Anne Hardin
1965 ....Gail Sykes	1983 ....Kim Saiki	1999 ....Aree Wongluekiet
1966 ....Claudia Mayhew	1984 ....Cathy Mockett	

Women's British Amateur

1893 ....Lady Margaret Scott	1928 ....Miss N. Le Blan	1964 ....C. Sorenson
1894 ....Lady Margaret Scott	1929 ....Miss J. Wethered	1965 ....B. Varangot
1895 ....Lady Margaret Scott	1930 ....Miss D. Fishwick	1966 ....E. Chadwick
1896 ....Miss Pascoe	1931 ....Miss E. Wilson	1967 ....E. Chadwick
1897 ....Miss E.C. Orr	1932 ....Miss E. Wilson	1968 ....B. Varangot
1898 ....Miss L. Thomson	1933 ....Miss E. Wilson	1975 ....C. Lacoste
1899 ....Miss M. Hezlet	1934 ....Mrs. A.M. Holm	1976 ....D. Oxley
1900 ....Miss Adair	1935 ....Miss W. Morgan	1977 ....A. Uzielli
1901 ....Miss Graham	1936 ....Miss P. Barton	1978 ....E. Kennedy
1902 ....Miss M. Hezlet	1937 ....Miss J. Anderson	1979 ....M. Madill
1903 ....Miss Adair	1938 ....Mrs. A.M. Holm	1980 ....A. Quast
1904 ....Miss L. Dod	1939 ....Miss P. Barton	1981 ..............I.C. Robertson
1905 ....Miss B. Thompson	1940–45 ......not held	1982 ....K. Douglas
1906 ....Mrs. Kennon	1946 ..............G.W. Hetherington	1983 ....J. Thornhill
1907 ....Miss M. Hezlet	1947 ....B. Zaharias	1984 ....J. Rosenthal
1908 ....Miss M. Titterton	1948 ....L. Suggs	1985 ....L. Beman
1909 ....Miss D. Campbell	1949 ....F. Stephens	1986 ....M. McGuire
1910 ....Miss Grant Suttie	1950 ....Vicomtesse de Saint	1987 ....J. Collingham
1911 ....Miss D. Campbell	Sauveur	1988 ....J. Furby
1912 ....Miss G. Ravenscroft	1951 ..............P.J. MacCann	1989 ....H. Dobson
1913 ....Miss M. Dodd	1952 ....M. Paterson	1990 ....J. Hall
1914 ....Miss C. Leitch	1953 ....M. Stewart	1991 ....V. Michaud
1915–19 ......not held	1954 ....F. Stephens	1992 ....P. Pedersen
1920 ....Miss C. Leitch	1955 ....J. Valentine	1993 ....Catriona Lambert
1921 ....Miss C. Leitch	1956 ....M. Smith	1994 ....Emma Duggleby
1922 ....Miss J. Wethered	1957 ....P. Garvey	1995 ....Julie Hall
1923 ....Miss D. Chambers	1958 ....J. Valentine	1996 ....Kelli Kuehne
1924 ....Miss J. Wethered	1959 ....E. Price	1997 ....Alison Rose
1925 ....Miss J. Wethered	1960 ....B. McIntyre	1998 ....K. Rostron
1926 ....Miss C. Leitch	1961 ....M. Spearman	1999 ....Marine Monnet
1927 ....Miss Thion de la	1962 ....M. Spearman	
Chaume	1963 ....B. Varangot	

Women's Amateur Public Links

1977 ....Kelly Fuiks	1985 ....Danielle	1992 ....Amy Fruhwirth
1978 ....Kelly Fuiks	Ammaccapane	1993 ....Connie Masterson
1979 ....Lori Castillo	1986 ....Cindy Schreyer	1994 ....Jill McGill
1980 ....Lori Castillo	1987 ....Tracy Kerdyk	1995 ....Jo Jo Robertson
1981 ....Mary Enright	1988 ....Pearl Sinn	1996 ....Heather Graff
1982 ....Nancy Taylor	1989 ....Pearl Sinn	1997 ....Jo Jo Robertson
1983 ....Kelli Antolock	1990 ....Cathy Mockett	1998 ....Amy Spooner
1984 ....Heather Farr	1991 ....Tracy Hanson	1999 ....Jody Niemann

Amateur Golf *(Cont.)*

U.S. Senior Women's Amateur

1964 ....Loma Smith
1965 ....Loma Smith
1966 ....Maureen Orcutt
1967 ....Marge Mason
1968 ....Carolyn Cudone
1969 ....Carolyn Cudone
1970 ....Carolyn Cudone
1971 ....Carolyn Cudone
1972 ....Carolyn Cudone
1973 ....Gwen Hibbs
1974 ....Justine Cushing
1975 ....Alberta Bower
1976 ....Cecile H. Maclaurin
1977 ....Dorothy Porter
1978 ....Alice Dye
1979 ....Alice Dye
1980 ....Dorothy Porter
1981 ....Dorothy Porter
1982 ....Edean Ihlanfeldt
1983 ....Dorothy Porter
1984 ....Constance Guthrie
1985 ....Marlene Streit
1986 ....Connie Guthrie
1987 ....Anne Sander
1988 ....Lois Hodge
1989 ....Anne Sander
1990 ....Anne Sander
1991 ....Phyllis Preuss
1992 ....Rosemary Thompson
1993 ....Anne Sander
1994 ....Marlene Streit
1995 ....Jean Smith
1996 ....Gayle Borthwick
1997 ....Nancy Fitzgerald
1998 ....Gayle Borthwick
1999 ....C. Semple Thompson

Women's Mid-Amateur Championship

1987 ....Cindy Scholefield
1988 ....Martha Lang
1989 ....Robin Weiss
1990 ....Carol Semple Thompson
1991 ....Sarah LeBrun Ingram
1992 ....Marion Mamey-McInerney
1993 ....Sarah Ingram
1994 ....Sarah Ingram
1995 ....Ellen Port
1996 ....Ellen Port
1997 ....Carol Semple Thompson
1998 ....Virginia Derby Grimes
1999 ....Alissa Herron

International Golf

Ryder Cup Matches

Year	Results	Site
1927	United States 9½, Great Britain 2½	Worcester CC, Worcester, MA
1929	Great Britain 7, United States 5	Moortown GC, Leeds, England
1931	United States 9, Great Britain 3	Scioto CC, Columbus, OH
1933	Great Britain 6½, United States 5½	Southport and Ainsdale Courses, Southport, England
1935	United States 9, Great Britain 3	Ridgewood CC, Ridgewood, NJ
1937	United States 8, Great Britain 4	Southport and Ainsdale Courses, Southport, England
1939-1945	No tournament	
1947	United States 11, Great Britain 1	Portland GC, Portland, OR
1949	United States 7, Great Britain 5	Ganton GC, Scarborough, England
1951	United States 9½, Great Britain 2½	Pinehurst CC, Pinehurst, NC
1953	United States 6½, Great Britain 5½	Wentworth Club, Surrey, England
1955	United States 8, Great Britain 4	Thunderbird Ranch & CC, Palm Springs, CA
1957	Great Britain 7½, United States 4½	Lindrick GC, Yorkshire, England
1959	United States 8½, Great Britain 3½	Eldorado CC, Palm Desert, CA
1961	United States 14½, Great Britain 9½	Royal Lytham & St. Anne's GC, St Anne's-on-the-Sea, England
1963	United States 23, Great Britain 9	East Lake CC, Atlanta
1965	United States 19½, Great Britain 12½	Royal Birkdale GC, Southport, England
1967	United States 23½, Great Britain 8½	Champions GC, Houston
1969	United States 16, Great Britain 16	Royal Birkdale GC, Southport, England
1971	United States 18½, Great Britain 13½	Old Warson CC, St. Louis
1973	United States 19, Great Britain 13	Hon Co of Edinburgh Golfers, Muirfield, Scotland
1975	United States 21, Great Britain 11	Laurel Valley GC, Ligonier, PA
1977	United States 12½, Great Britain 7½	Royal Lytham & St. Anne's GC, St. Anne's-on-the-Sea, England
1979	United States 17, Europe 11	Greenbrier, White Sulphur Springs, WV
1981	United States 18½, Europe 9½	Walton Heath GC, Surrey, England
1983	United States 14½, Europe 13½	PGA National GC, Palm Beach Gardens, FL
1985	Europe 16½, United States 11½	Belfry GC, Sutton Coldfield, England
1987	Europe 15, United States 13	Muirfield GC, Dublin, OH
1989	Europe 14, United States 14	Belfry GC, Sutton Coldfield, England
1991	United States 14½, Europe 13½	Ocean Course, Kiawah Island, SC
1993	United States 15, Europe 13	Belfry GC, Sutton Coldfield, England
1995	Europe 14½, United States 13½	Oak Hill CC, Rochester, NY
1997	Europe 14½, United States 13½	Valderrama GC, Sotogrande, Spain
1999	United States 14½, Europe 13½	The Country Club, Brookline, MA

Team matches held every odd year between U.S. professionals and those of Great Britain/Europe (since 1979—prior to that it was U.S. vs G.B.). Team members selected on basis of finishes in PGA and European tour events.

Walker Cup Matches

Year	Results	Site
1922	United States 8, Great Britain 4	Nat. Golf Links of America, Southampton, NY
1923	United States 6, Great Britain 5	St. Andrews, Scotland
1924	United States 9, Great Britain 3	Garden City GC, Garden City, NY
1926	United States 6, Great Britain 5	St. Andrews, Scotland
1928	United States 11, Great Britain 1	Chicago GC, Wheaton, IL
1930	United States 10, Great Britain 2	Royal St. George GC, Sandwich, England
1932	United States 8, Great Britain 1	The Country Club, Brookline, MA
1934	United States 9, Great Britain 2	St. Andrews, Scotland
1936	United States 9, Great Britain 0	Pine Valley GC, Clementon, NJ
1938	Great Britain 7, United States 4	St. Andrews, Scotland
1940–46	No tournament	
1947	United States 8, Great Britain 4	St. Andrews, Scotland
1949	United States 10, Great Britain 2	Winged Foot GC, Mamaroneck, NY
1951	United States 6, Great Britain 3	Birkdale GC, Southport, England
1953	United States 9, Great Britain 3	The Kittansett Club, Marion, MA
1955	United States 10, Great Britain 2	St. Andrews, Scotland
1957	United States 8, Great Britain 3	Minikahda Club, Minneapolis, MN
1959	United States 9, Great Britain 3	Muirfield, Scotland
1961	United States 11, Great Britain 1	Seattle GC, Seattle, WA
1963	United States 12, Great Britain 8	Ailsa Course, Turnberry, Scotland
1965	Great Britain 11, United States 11	Baltimore CC, Five Farms, Baltimore, MD
1967	United States 13, Great Britain 7	Royal St. George's GC, Sandwich, England
1969	United States 10, Great Britain 8	Milwaukee CC, Milwaukee, WI
1971	Great Britain 13, United States 11	St. Andrews, Scotland
1973	United States 14, Great Britain 10	The Country Club, Brookline, MA
1975	United States 15½, Great Britain 8½	St. Andrews, Scotland
1977	United States 16, Great Britain 8	Shinnecock Hills GC, Southampton, NY
1979	United States 15½, Great Britain 8½	Muirfield, Scotland
1981	United States 15, Great Britain 9	Cypress Point Club, Pebble Beach, CA
1983	United States 13½, Great Britain 10½	Royal Liverpool GC, Hoylake, England
1985	United States 13, Great Britain 11	Pine Valley GC, Pine Valley, NJ
1987	United States 16½, Great Britain 7½	Sunningdale GC, Berkshire, England
1989	Great Britain 12½, United States 11½	Peachtree Golf Club, Atlanta, GA
1991	United States 14, Great Britain 10	Portmarnock GC, Dublin, Ireland
1993	United States 19, Great Britain 5	Interlachen CC, Edina, MN
1995	Great Britain/Ireland 14, United States 10	Royal Porthcawl, Porthcawl, Wales
1997	United States 18, Great Britain/Ireland 6	Quaker Ridge GC, Scarsdale, NY
1999	Great Britain/Ireland 15, United States 9	Nairn GC, Nairn, Scotland

Men's amateur team competition every other year between United States and Great Britain/Ireland. U.S. team members selected by USGA.

Solheim Cup Matches

Year	Results	Site
1990	United States 11½, Europe 4½	Lake Nona GC, Orlando, FL
1992	Europe 11½, United States 6½	Dalmahoy Hotel GC, Edinburgh
1994	United States 13, Europe 7	The Greenbriar, White Sulpher Springs, WV
1996	United States 17, Europe 11	Marriot St Pierre Hotel & CC, Chepstow, Wales
1998	United States 16, Europe 12	Muirfield Village GC, Dublin, OH

Team matches held every other year between U.S. professionals and those of Europe. Team members selected on basis of finishes in LPGA and European tour events.

Curtis Cup Matches

Year	Results	Site
1932	United States 5½, British Isles 3½	Wentworth GC, Wentworth, England
1934	United States 6½, British Isles 2½	Chevy Chase Club, Chevy Chase, MD
1936	United States 4½, British Isles 4½	King's Course, Gleneagles, Scotland
1938	United States 5½, British Isles 3½	Essex CC, Manchester, MA
1940–46	No tournament	
1948	United States 6½, British Isles 2½	Birkdale GC, Southport, England
1950	United States 7½, British Isles 1½	CC of Buffalo, Williamsville, NY
1952	British Isles 5, United States 4	Muirfield, Scotland
1954	United States 6, British Isles 3	Merion GC, Ardmore, PA
1956	British Isles 5, United States 4	Prince's GC, Sandwich Bay, England

Curtis Cup Matches (Cont.)

Year	Results	Site
1958	British Isles 4½, United States 4½	Brae Burn CC, West Newton, Mass.
1960	United States 6½, British Isles 2½	Lindrick GC, Worksop, England
1962	United States 8, British Isles 1	Broadmoor CG, Colorado Springs,CO
1964	United States 10½, British Isles 7½	Royal Porthcawl GC, Porthcawl, South Wales
1966	United States 13, British Isles 5	Va. Hot Springs G & TC, Hot Springs, VA
1968	United States 10½, British Isles 7½	Royal County Down GC, Newcastle, N. Ire.
1970	United States 11½, British Isles 6½	Brae Burn CC, West Newton, MA
1972	United States 10, British Isles 8	Western Gailes, Ayrshire, Scotland
1974	United States 13, British Isles 5	San Francisco GC, San Francisco, CA
1976	United States 11½, British Isles 6½	Royal Lytham & St. Anne's GC, England
1978	United States 12, British Isles 6	Apawamis Club, Rye, NY
1980	United States 13, British Isles 5	St. Pierre G & CC, Chepstow, Wales
1982	United States 14½, British Isles 3½	Denver CC, Denver, CO
1984	United States 9½, British Isles 8½	Muirfield, Scotland
1986	British Isles 13, United States 5	Prairie Dunes CC, Hutchinson, KS
1988	British Isles 11, United States 7	Royal St. George's GC, Sandwich, England
1990	United States 14, British Isles 4	Somerset Hills CC, Bernardsville, NJ
1992	Great Britain/Ireland 10, United States 8	Royal Liverpool GC, Hoylake, England
1994	Great Britain/Ireland 9, United States 9	The Honors Course, Ooltewah, TN
1996	Great Britain/Ireland 11½, United States 6½	Killarney Golf & Fishing Club, Killarney, Ireland
1998	United States 10, Great Britain/Ireland 8	The Minikahda Club, Minneapolis

Women's amateur team competition every other year between the United States and Great Britain/Ireland. U.S. team members selected by USGA.

Double-timing into History

On Jan. 11, 1999, when the LPGA announced in a players meeting in Orlando that it would ease the requirement to qualify for the Hall of Fame, Juli Inkster feverishly scrawled figures on a slip of paper. "Ooh, I only need six points," she said. In fact, Inkster later realized, she needed seven, which she figured would take a few good years to earn. Wrong again. When Inkster won by six strokes over Tina Barrett and Grace Park at the Safeway LPGA Golf Championship at Columbia Edgewater Country Club in Portland in September, earning her fifth title—including two majors—in '99, she qualified for the Hall, a plateau that had once seemed too lofty to even think about.

Before this season, Inkster's 17 victories, including three majors, left her 13 wins short of admission. "I knew I wasn't going to play long enough to get that many," says the 39-year-old mother of two. But the new rules, which among other changes doubled the value of a major, gave her hope, and Inkster responded with a huge '99, leading to a wild celebration in Portland.

Led by Nancy Lopez, three dozen of Inkster's peers, armed with eight bottles of champagne, greeted the 17th Hall member as she came off the final green. "It was nice not to have it drag on and to win right away," said the bubbly-soaked Inkster after several wet hugs. "I never dreamed I could get seven points in such a short time."

—Tim Hanson

Total Player Rankings

Introduction

As 1999 ends, many panels of experts are offering their lists of this century's greatest athletes. In the following 15 pages, the editors at Total Sports offer something slightly different. Instead of rating the top athletes based on personal opinion, analytical methods have been applied to provide an objective ranking of players in a variety of sports. The goal is a fair comparison of athletes from different eras. Some of these methods are more scientific or rigorous than others. Some have been around for many years, while others appear here for the first time in print. These rankings may spur more debate than they settle, but the editors will be content if they have shed light on some great, undeservedly obscure athletes.

Statistical research and ratings were provided by: Bob Bellotti, Bob Carroll, Dan Diamond, Sean Lahman, Pete Palmer and John Thorn.

Auto Racing

Stock Car Racing

Sanctioned by NASCAR since 1947. Ranking based on performance points system which awards points for top-six finishes.

	Driver	Career	Points	Wins	Championships
1............	Richard Petty	1958–1992	3645	200	7
2............	David Pearson	1960–1986	2045	105	3
3............	Bobby Allison	1961–1988	1993	84	1
4............	*Darrell Waltrip	1972–	1646	84	3
5............	Cale Yarborough	1957–1988	1559	83	3
6............	*Dale Earnhardt	1975–	1549	72	7
7............	Lee Petty	1949–1964	1269	54	3
8............	Buck Baker	1949–1976	1262	46	2
9............	Ned Jarrett	1953–1966	1044	50	2
10.........	*Rusty Wallace	1980–	959	50	1
11.........	Buddy Baker	1959–1984	916	19	0
12.........	*Mark Martin	1981–	880	30	0
13.........	Benny Parsons	1964–1988	866	21	1
14.........	*Bill Elliott	1976–	849	40	1
15.........	*Terry Labonte	1978–	835	23	2
16.........	Herb Thomas	1949–1962	796	48	2
17.........	Bobby Isaac	1961–1976	795	37	1
18.........	Junior Johnson	1953–1966	778	50	0
19.........	Jim Paschal	1949–1972	755	25	0
20.........	*Jeff Gordon	1992–	704	56	3

*Active in 1999. Includes races through 9/15/99.

Indy Car Racing

Sanctioned by the AAA from 1909–1954, USAC 1955–1978, CART 1979–1999. Ranking based on 5 points for winning the annual PPG Cup championship, 2 points for each race won, an additional 3 points for each win in the Indianapolis 500.

	Driver	Career	Points	Wins	Championships	Indy 500 Wins
1............	A.J. Foyt	1957–1992	181	67	7	4
2............	Mario Andretti	1964–1994	127	52	4	1
3............	Al Unser	1964–1993	105	39	3	4
4............	Bobby Unser	1962–1981	89	35	2	3
5............	Rick Mears	1976–1992	85	29	3	4
6............	*Michael Andretti	1983–	81	38	1	0
7............	*Al Unser Jr.	1982–	78	31	2	2
8............	Tommy Milton	1917–1925	69	23	2	2
9T.........	Ralph DePalma	1908–1936	68	24	2	1
9T.........	Johnny Rutherford	1962–1989	68	27	1	3
9T.........	Rodger Ward	1951–1966	68	26	2	2
12.........	Bobby Rahal	1982–1998	66	24	3	1
13.........	Jimmy Bryan	1953–1958	63	19	3	1
14.........	Earl Cooper	1912–1926	62	20	3	0
15.........	Gordon Johncock	1964–1992	61	25	1	2
16.........	Jimmy Murphy	1920–1924	58	19	2	1
17T........	Emerson Fittipaldi	1984–1996	55	22	1	2
17T........	Louie Meyer	1924–1939	55	12	3	3
19.........	Tony Bettenhausen	1946–1961	54	22	2	0
20.........	Ralph Mulford	1910–1919	51	17	2	0

*Active in 1999. Includes races through 9/15/99.

Auto Racing (Cont.)

Grand Prix Racing

Sanctioned by Formula One from 1950–1999. Ranking based on performance points system which awards points for top-six finishes.

	Driver	Career	Points	Wins	Championships	Country
1............	Alain Prost	1980–1993	798.5	51	4	France
2............	Ayrton Senna	1984–1994	614	41	3	Brazil
3............	*Michael Schumacher	1991–	558	35	2	Germany
4............	Nelson Piquet	1978–1991	485.5	23	3	Brazil
5............	Nigel Mansell	1980–1995	482	31	1	England
6............	Niki Lauda	1971–1985	420.5	25	3	Austria
7............	Gerhard Berger	1984–1997	385	10	0	Austria
8T.........	*Damon Hill	1992–	360	22	2	England
8T............	Jackie Stewart	1965–1973	360	27	3	Scotland
10..........	Carlos Reutemann	1972–1982	310	12	0	Argentina
11..........	Graham Hill	1958–1975	289	14	0	England
12T..........	Emerson Fittipaldi	1970–1980	281	14	2	Brazil
12T.........	Riccardo Patrese	1977–1993	281	6	0	Italy
14..........	*Mika Hakkinen	1991–	278	13	1	Finland
15..........	Juan Manuel Fangio	1950–1958	277.64	24	5	Argentina
16..........	Jim Clark	1960–1968	274	25	2	Scotland
17..........	Jack Brabham	1955–1970	261	14	3	Australia
18..........	Jody Scheckter	1972–1980	255	10	1	South Africa
19..........	Denny Hulme	1965–1974	248	8	1	New Zealand
20..........	*Jean Alesi	1989–	235	1	0	France

*Active in 1999. Includes races through 9/15/99.

Baseball

Total Player Ratings (TPR) are an estimate of the number of wins a player contributed based on batting, pitching, fielding and baserunning. Players who played primarily in the 19th century are excluded.

Top Players By Position

	Pitcher	TPR	Won	Lost	E.R.A.
1..	Walter Johnson	90.1	417	279	2.17
2..	Cy Young	79.8	511	316	2.63
3..	Grover Alexander	64.9	373	208	2.56
4..	Christy Mathewson	62.8	373	188	2.13
5..	Lefty Grove	61.2	300	141	3.06
6..	Kid Nichols	60.9	361	208	2.95
7..	*Greg Maddux	54.5	221	126	2.81
8..	*Roger Clemens	53.9	247	134	3.04
9..	Tom Seaver	48.2	311	205	2.86
10..	Warren Spahn	47.0	363	245	3.09
11..	Bob Gibson	44.0	251	174	2.91
12..	Ed Walsh	43.3	195	126	1.82
13..	Hal Newhouser	40.8	207	150	3.06
14..	Hoyt Wilhelm	39.7	143	122	2.52
15..	Carl Hubbell	39.2	253	154	2.98
16..	Whitey Ford	37.2	236	106	2.75
17..	Bob Lemon	36.9	207	128	3.23
18..	Ted Lyons	36.7	260	230	3.67
19..	Carl Mays	36.2	208	126	2.92
20..	Jim Palmer	35.5	268	152	2.86
21..	Phil Niekro	35.4	318	274	3.35
22..	Three Finger Brown	34.8	239	130	2.06
23..	Dizzy Trout	34.5	170	161	3.23
24..	Gaylord Perry	34.4	314	265	3.11
25..	Don Drysdale	34.0	209	166	2.95
26..	Steve Carlton	33.2	329	244	3.22
27..	Wes Ferrell	32.4	193	128	4.04
28..	Fergie Jenkins	30.9	284	226	3.34
29..	*John Franco	30.7	77	70	2.64
30..	Bert Blyleven	30.8	287	250	3.31

*Active in 1999. Total include 1999 regular season.

	Pitcher	TPR	Won	Lost	E.R.A.
31	Rich Gossage	29.5	124	107	3.01
32	Clark Griffith	29.0	237	146	3.31
33	Juan Marichal	28.9	243	142	2.89
34	Tommy Bridges	28.7	194	138	3.57
35	Bob Feller	28.5	266	162	3.25
36	*Kevin Brown	28.2	157	108	3.27
37	*Bret Saberhagen	27.7	166	115	3.33
38	Stan Coveleski	27.5	215	142	2.89
39	Dave Stieb	27.1	176	137	3.44
40T	Red Faber	27.0	254	213	3.15
40T	Eddie Plank	27.0	326	194	2.35
40T	Dazzy Vance	27.0	197	140	3.24
43	Red Ruffing	26.8	273	225	3.80
44	Dennis Eckersley	26.7	197	171	3.50
45	*Tom Glavine	27.2	187	116	3.38
46	Bucky Walters	26.4	198	160	3.30
47	Dolf Luque	26.3	194	179	3.24
48	Eddie Rommel	26.0	171	119	3.54
49T	Eppa Rixey	25.9	266	251	3.15
49T	Urban Shocker	25.9	187	117	3.17

	Catcher	TPR	Avg.	HR	RBI
1	Gabby Hartnett	40.1	.297	236	1179
2	Yogi Berra	36.2	.285	358	1430
3	Bill Dickey	35.4	.313	202	1209
4	*Mike Piazza	31.7	.328	240	768
5	Mickey Cochrane	31.4	.320	119	832
6	Gary Carter	29.6	.262	324	1225
7	Johnny Bench	24.3	.267	389	1376
8	Carlton Fisk	24.0	.269	376	1330
9	Roy Campanella	21.6	.276	242	856
10	Roger Bresnahan	19.8	.279	26	530

	1st Base	TPR	Avg.	HR	RBI
1	Lou Gehrig	65.7	.340	493	1995
2	Jimmie Foxx	54.3	.325	534	1922
3	*Jeff Bagwell	41.4	.304	263	961
4T	Willie McCovey	36.5	.270	521	1555
4T	*Frank Thomas	36.5	.320	301	1040
6	Johnny Mize	36.2	.312	359	1337
7	Dick Allen	35.3	.292	351	1119
8	*Mark McGwire	34.9	.265	522	1277
9	Keith Hernandez	34.4	.296	162	1071
10	Eddie Murray	34.1	.287	504	1917

	2nd Base	TPR	Avg.	HR	RBI
1	Nap Lajoie	94.1	.338	82	1599
2	Rogers Hornsby	81.2	.358	301	1584
3	Eddie Collins	69.8	.333	47	1300
4	Joe Morgan	56.3	.271	268	1133
5	Charlie Gehringer	44.4	.320	184	1427
6	Bobby Grich	44.0	.266	224	864
7T	Bobby Doerr	39.0	.288	223	1247
7T	Frankie Frisch	39.0	.316	105	1244
9	Bill Mazeroski	36.3	.260	138	853
10	*Craig Biggio	35.9	.292	152	706

	3rd Base	TPR	Avg.	HR	RBI
1	Mike Schmidt	78.4	.267	548	1595
2	Eddie Mathews	51.6	.271	512	1453
3	*Wade Boggs	43.3	.328	118	1014
4	Ron Santo	39.5	.277	342	1331
5	George Brett	39.0	.305	317	1595
6	Darrell Evans	34.7	.248	414	1354
7	Frank Baker	33.8	.307	96	987
8T	Heinie Groh	27.2	.292	26	566
8T	Stan Hack	27.2	.301	57	642
10	Jimmy Collins	23.1	.294	65	983

*Active in 1999. Total include 1999 regular season.

Baseball (Cont.)

	Shortstop	TPR	Avg.	HR	RBI
1	Honus Wagner	81.1	.327	101	1732
2	*Barry Larkin	43.3	.300	168	793
3	Robin Yount	43.1	.285	251	1406
4	Ozzie Smith	43.0	.262	28	793
5	Lou Boudreau	41.3	.295	68	789
6	Luke Appling	40.7	.310	45	1116
7	*Cal Ripken	40.6	.278	402	1571
8	Joe Cronin	39.4	.301	170	1424
9	Arky Vaughan	39.2	.318	96	926
10	Dave Bancroft	35.2	.279	32	591

	Left Field	TPR	Avg.	HR	RBI
1	Ted Williams	85.7	.344	521	1839
2	*Barry Bonds	82.8	.288	445	1299
3	*Rickey Henderson	81.2	.284	278	1020
4	Stan Musial	70.5	.331	475	1951
5	*Tim Raines	51.8	.295	168	964
6	Carl Yastrzemski	45.5	.285	452	1844
7	Joe Jackson	37.5	.356	54	785
8	Bob Johnson	35.6	.296	288	1283
9	*Albert Belle	34.6	.296	358	1136
10	Willie Stargell	32.8	.282	475	1540

	Center Field	TPR	Avg.	HR	RBI
1	Willie Mays	92.2	.302	660	1903
2	Ty Cobb	91.1	.366	117	1937
3	Tris Speaker	86.5	.345	117	1529
4	Mickey Mantle	76.1	.298	536	1509
5	Joe DiMaggio	46.9	.325	361	1537
6	*Ken Griffey Jr.	43.1	.299	398	1152
7	Richie Ashburn	30.2	.308	29	586
8	Kirby Puckett	29.1	.318	207	1085
9	Cesar Cedeno	28.3	.285	199	976
10	Lenny Dykstra	25.6	.285	81	404

	Right Field	TPR	Avg.	HR	RBI
1	Babe Ruth	124.8	.342	714	2213
2	Hank Aaron	89.8	.305	755	2297
3	Frank Robinson	69.0	.294	586	1812
4	Mel Ott	62.7	.304	511	1860
5	*Tony Gwynn	49.2	.339	133	1104
6	Al Kaline	44.6	.297	399	1583
7	Roberto Clemente	42.9	.317	240	1305
8	Reggie Jackson	42.8	.262	563	1702
9	Dave Winfield	38.6	.283	465	1833
10	Paul Waner	36.1	.333	113	1309

*Active in 1999. Total include 1999 regular season.

Basketball

Points Created (PC) evaluates overall performance. It adds the good things a player did (points, rebounds, assists, steals and blocked shots) and subtracts the bad things (missed field goals and free throws, turnovers and personal fouls). With Points Created, a player's statistics are pared down to a single number—the points a player "creates" through his overall play.

Based on the NBA's average points scored per possession, the system assigns a value to each statistical category. Because the average points per possession changes from year to year and decade to decade—for example, NBA teams averaged 74.6 points per 100 possessions in 1963–64 and 88.9 points in 1998–99—Points Created is a viable way to compare players from different eras.

Ppg = Points per game; Rpg = Rebounds per game; Apg = Assists per game; PC/min = Points Created per minute.

	Overall Players	Ppg	Rpg	Apg	PC/min
1	Wilt Chamberlain	30.1	22.9	4.4	.880
2	Magic Johnson	19.5	7.2	11.2	.794
3	David Robinson	24.4	11.5	3.0	.789
4	Michael Jordan	31.5	6.3	5.4	.786
5	Kareem Abdul-Jabbar	24.6	11.2	3.6	.782

*Active in 1998–1999.

Basketball (Cont.)

	Overall Players	Ppg	Rpg	Apg	PC/min
6	Bob Pettit	26.4	16.2	3.0	.781
7	Oscar Robertson	25.7	7.5	9.5	.777
8	Larry Bird	24.3	10.0	6.3	.765
9	Elgin Baylor	27.4	13.5	4.3	.745
10	*Hakeem Olajuwon	23.6	11.8	2.7	.739
11	*Charles Barkley	22.3	11.7	3.9	.735
12	Jerry West	27.0	5.8	6.7	.722
13	*Karl Malone	26.1	10.7	3.3	.715
14	†Julius Erving	24.2	8.5	4.2	.703
15	Paul Arizin	22.8	8.6	2.3	.693
16	Bob Lanier	20.1	10.1	3.1	.690
17	George Mikan	23.1	13.4	2.8	.687
18	†Artis Gilmore	18.8	12.3	1.4	.682
19T	Bill Russell	15.1	22.5	4.3	.681
19T	Dolph Schayes	18.5	12.1	3.1	.681
21	Moses Malone	20.6	12.2	1.4	.673
22	Jerry Lucas	17.0	15.6	3.3	.671
23	Bob McAdoo	22.1	9.4	2.3	.668
24	†Dan Issel	22.6	9.1	2.4	.667
25	*Patrick Ewing	23.3	10.4	2.1	.666
26	†Billy Cunningham	21.1	10.4	4.3	.664
27	†George McGinnis	20.2	11.0	3.7	.663
28	*John Stockton	13.4	2.7	11.1	.660
29	Walt Bellamy	20.1	13.7	2.4	.658
30	Mel Daniels	18.7	15.1	1.8	.654
31T	†Rick Barry	24.8	6.7	4.9	.653
31T	Bob Cousy	5.2	7.5	18.4	.653
33	†Cliff Hagan	17.7	6.6	3.2	.634
34T	Alvan Adams	14.1	7.0	4.1	.633
34T	Kevin Johnson	18.0	3.3	9.2	.633
36	Bailey Howell	18.7	9.9	2.0	.632
37	†George Gervin	26.2	4.6	2.8	.629
38	Clyde Drexler	20.4	6.1	5.6	.626
39	Willis Reed	18.7	12.9	1.8	.625
40	Larry Nance	17.1	8.0	2.6	.623
41T	Alex English	21.5	5.5	3.6	.622
41T	†Swen Nater	12.2	10.8	2.0	.622
43	Robert Parish	14.5	9.1	1.4	.620
44	Kevin McHale	17.9	7.3	1.7	.618
45	Dave Cowens	17.6	13.6	3.8	.615
46	†Connie Hawkins	18.3	8.8	3.8	.614
47	Adrian Dantley	24.3	5.7	3.0	.611
48	Tom Boerwinkle	7.2	9.0	3.2	.608
49	Marques Johnson	20.1	7.0	3.6	.605
50	John Drew	20.7	6.9	1.7	.604

	Forwards	Ppg	Rpg	Apg	PC/min
1	Bob Pettit	26.4	16.2	3.0	.781
2	Larry Bird	24.3	10.0	6.3	.765
3	Elgin Baylor	27.4	13.5	4.3	.745
4	*Charles Barkley	22.3	11.7	3.9	.735
5	*Karl Malone	26.1	10.7	3.3	.715
6	†Julius Erving	24.2	8.5	4.2	.703
7	Paul Arizin	22.8	8.6	2.3	.693
8	Dolph Schayes	18.5	12.1	3.1	.681
9	Jerry Lucas	17.0	15.6	3.3	.671
10	†Billy Cunningham	21.1	10.4	4.3	.664
11	†George McGinnis	20.2	11.0	3.7	.663
12	Mel Daniels	18.7	15.1	1.8	.654
13	†Rick Barry	24.8	6.7	4.9	.653
14	†Cliff Hagan	17.7	6.6	3.2	.634
15	Bailey Howell	18.7	9.9	2.0	.632
16	Willis Reed	18.7	12.9	1.8	.625
17	Larry Nance	17.1	8.0	2.6	.623
18	Alex English	21.5	5.5	3.6	.622
19	Kevin McHale	17.9	7.3	1.7	.618
20	†Connie Hawkins	18.3	8.8	3.8	.614

*Active in 1998–99. †Includes player's ABA statistics. Minimum 500 regular-season games.

Basketball (Cont.)

	Centers	Ppg	Rpg	Apg	PC/min
1	Wilt Chamberlain	30.1	22.9	4.4	.880
2	*David Robinson	24.4	11.5	3.0	.789
3	Kareem Abdul-Jabbar	24.6	11.2	3.6	.782
4	*Hakeem Olajuwon	23.6	11.8	2.7	.739
5	Bob Lanier	20.1	10.1	3.1	.690
6	George Mikan	23.1	13.4	2.8	.687
7	†Artis Gilmore	18.8	12.3	1.4	.682
8	Bill Russell	15.1	22.5	4.3	.681
9	Moses Malone	20.6	12.2	1.4	.673
10	Bob McAdoo	22.1	9.4	2.3	.668
11	†Dan Issel	22.6	9.1	2.4	.667
12	*Patrick Ewing	23.3	10.4	2.1	.666
13	Walt Bellamy	20.1	13.7	2.4	.658
14	Alvan Adams	14.1	7.0	4.1	.633
15	†Swen Nater	12.2	10.8	2.0	.622
16	Robert Parish	14.5	9.1	1.4	.620
17	Dave Cowens	17.6	13.6	3.8	.615
18	Tom Boerwinkle	7.2	9.0	3.2	.608
19	†Zelmo Beaty	17.1	10.9	1.5	.596
20	Wes Unseld	10.8	14.0	3.9	.586

	Guards	Ppg	Rpg	Apg	PC/min
1	Magic Johnson	19.5	7.2	11.2	.794
2	Michael Jordan	31.5	6.3	5.4	.786
3	Oscar Robertson	25.7	7.5	9.5	.777
4	Jerry West	27.0	5.8	6.7	.722
5	*John Stockton	13.4	2.7	11.1	.660
6	Bob Cousy	5.2	7.5	18.4	.653
7	Kevin Johnson	18.0	3.3	9.2	.633
8	†George Gervin	26.2	4.6	2.8	.629
9	Clyde Drexler	20.4	6.1	5.6	.626
10T	Walt Frazier	18.9	5.9	6.1	.590
10T	Paul Westphal	15.6	1.9	4.4	.590
12	Fat Lever	13.9	6.0	6.2	.581
13	Walter Davis	18.9	30.0	3.8	.579
14	Sam Jones	17.7	4.9	2.5	.577
15	Pete Maravich	24.2	4.2	5.4	.569
16	Richie Guerin	17.3	5.0	5.0	.565
17T	*Tim Hardaway	19.4	3.6	9.0	.560
17T	Ray Williams	15.5	3.6	5.8	.560
19T	Isiah Thomas	19.2	3.6	9.3	.552
19T	Lenny Wilkens	16.5	4.7	6.7	.552

*Active in 1998–99. †Includes player's ABA statistics. Minimum 500 regular-season games.

Boxing

Points awarded to lineal champions as follows: Years held the title times weighted record in title fights (plus one point for a win, plus a half point for a draw, minus one point for a loss, plus one). Does not include 19th century fighters or records in non-title fights.

	Heavyweights	Years	W	L	D	Points
1	Joe Louis	11.690	26	1	0	303.94
2	Larry Holmes	7.285	21	2	0	145.70
3	Muhammad Ali	7.247	22	3	0	144.94
4	Jim Jeffries	5.926	8	1	0	47.41
5	Joe Frazier	4.888	10	2	0	43.99
6	Jack Dempsey	7.222	6	2	0	36.11
7	Jack Johnson	6.301	5	1	1	34.66
8	Tommy Burns	2.838	11	1	0	31.22
9	Rocky Marciano	3.595	7	0	0	28.76
10	George Foreman	4.819	7	3	0	24.10

	Light Heavyweights	Years	W	L	D	Points
1.	Bob Foster	6.321	15	0	0	101.14
2.	Archie Moore	9.164	9	0	0	91.64
3.	Gus Lesnevich	7.159	6	1	0	42.95
4.	John Henry Lewis	3.668	5	0	0	22.01
5.	Michael Spinks	2.518	5	0	0	15.11

	Middleweights	Years	W	L	D	Points
1.	Carlos Monzon	6.732	14	0	0	100.98
2.	Marvin Hagler	6.526	13	1	1	88.10
3.	Tommy Ryan	6.932	3	0	0	27.73
4.	Mickey Walker	4.545	4	0	0	22.73
5.	Sugar Ray Robinson	5.018	8	5	0	20.07

	Welterweights	Years	W	L	D	Points
1.	Jose Napoles	6.137	15	2	0	85.92
2.	Henry Armstrong	2.351	21	2	0	47.01
3.	Emile Griffith	4.649	10	2	0	41.84
4.	Pernell Whitaker	4.107	8	1	1	34.91
5.	Jack Britton	4.805	6	2	0	24.03

	Lightweights	Years	W	L	D	Points
1.	Roberto Duran	6.608	13	0	0	92.52
2.	Benny Leonard	7.644	9	0	0	76.44
3.	Joe Brown	5.663	12	1	0	67.96
4.	Joe Gans	4.318	16	3	0	60.45
5.	Carlos Ortiz	5.605	11	2	0	56.05

	Featherweights	Years	W	L	D	Points
1.	Abe Attell	6.005	12	1	3	81.07
2.	Willie Pep	7.523	11	2	0	75.23
3.	Johnny Kilbane	11.285	6	2	3	73.35
4.	Sandy Saddler	6.668	5	1	0	33.34
5.	Vicente Saldivar	3.649	10	2	0	32.84

	Bantamweights	Years	W	L	D	Points
1.	Manuel Ortiz	7.482	21	2	0	149.64
2.	Panama Al Brown	5.959	12	1	0	71.51
3.	Eder Jofre	4.712	8	2	0	32.99
4.	Jeff Chandler	3.400	9	1	0	32.30
5.	Johnny Coulon	4.266	5	1	0	21.33

	Flyweights	Years	W	L	D	Points
1.	Miguel Canto Solis	5.693	15	1	1	88.24
2.	Yuri Arbachakov	5.395	10	1	0	53.95
3.	Sot Chitalda	5.504	11	3	1	52.29
4.	Pascual Perez	5.395	10	2	0	48.55
5.	Jimmy Wilde	7.348	5	1	0	36.74

Football

Two-Way Players (1920–49)

Players ranked based on years as All-Pro through 1998, with points given as follows:
C: 8 points for Consensus All-Pro from all teams selected; 1st: 5 points for First team All-Pro for any major all-pro team or pro bowl; 2nd: 3 points for Second team All-Pro for any major all-pro team.

Ends	C	1st	2nd	Total	Tackles	C	1st	2nd	Total
1. Don Hutson	7	2	2	72	1. Albert Wistert	5	2	1	53
2. Lavie Dilweg	5	2	1	53	2T. Turk Edwards	4	3	1	50
3. Bill Hewitt	4	2	0	42	2T. Bruiser Kinard	4	3	1	50
4T. Guy Chamberlin	3	1	0	29	4. Ed Healey	4	3	0	47
4T. Ray Flaherty	2	2	1	29	5. Cal Hubbard	5	1	0	45
4T. Red Badgro	3	1	0	29					

Two-Way Players (1920–49) *(Cont.)*

Guards	C	1st	2nd	Total
1...... Danny Fortmann	6	1	1	56
2...... Mike Michalske	6	1	0	53
3...... Riley Matheson	4	2	2	48
4...... Ox Emerson	4	2	0	42
5...... Ray Bray	3	2	0	34

Backs	C	1st	2nd	Total
1...... Paddy Driscoll	7	1	1	64
2...... Dutch Clark	6	0	0	48
3...... Clarke Hinkle	3	4	3	41
4T.... Ernie Nevers	5	0	0	40
4T.... Ken Strong	4	1	1	40

Centers	C	1st	2nd	Total
1...... Mel Hein	7	1	4	73
2...... Bulldog Turner	7	2	1	69
3...... George Trafton	3	2	1	37
4...... Nate Barrager	2	0	3	25

One-Way Players (1950–98)

Quarterbacks	C	1st	2nd	Total
1...... Otto Graham	9	1	0	77
2...... Johnny Unitas	5	6	0	70
3T.... Sammy Baugh	5	3	2	61
3T.... Fran Tarkenton	2	9	0	61
5...... *Dan Marino	3	6	0	54
6...... Sid Luckman	5	1	2	51
7...... *John Elway	1	8	0	48
8T.... Jack Kemp	2	6	0	46
8T.... Joe Montana	2	6	0	46
10.... *Warren Moon	0	9	0	45

Offensive Tackles	C	1st	2nd	Total
1...... Anthony Munoz	9	2	0	82
2...... Rosey Brown	8	2	1	77
3...... Ron Mix	9	0	0	72
4...... Jim Tyrer	7	3	0	71
5...... Forrest Gregg	6	4	0	68
6...... Lou Groza	5	4	2	66
7...... Lou Creekmur	6	3	0	63
8...... Ron Yary	7	1	0	61
9...... Bob Brown	6	1	1	56
10.... Art Shell	6	1	0	53

Running Backs	C	1st	2nd	Total
1...... Jim Brown	8	1	0	69
2...... *Barry Sanders	6	4	0	68
3...... Walter Payton	7	2	0	66
4...... Lenny Moore	5	3	0	65
5...... Ollie Matson	4	4	0	52
6...... Franco Harris	2	7	0	51
7...... Steve Van Buren	5	1	1	48
8T.... Frank Gifford	4	3	0	47
8T.... *Emmitt Smith	4	3	0	47
9T.... O. J. Simpson	5	1	0	45
9T.... Eric Dickerson	5	1	0	45

Offensive Guards	C	1st	2nd	Total
1...... John Hannah	9	1	1	80
2...... Bruce Matthews	7	4	0	76
3...... Tom Mack	7	3	0	71
4...... Jim Parker	7	2	0	66
5...... Gene Upshaw	5	5	0	65
6...... *Randall McDaniel	6	4	0	58
7...... Larry Little	5	2	1	53
8T.... Billy Shaw	4	4	0	52
8T.... *Steve Wisniewski	4	4	0	52
10T.. Ed Budde	2	7	0	51
10T.. Joe DeLamielleure	6	0	1	51
10T.. Mike Munchak	2	7	0	51

Receivers	C	1st	2nd	Total
1...... *Jerry Rice	8	4	0	84
2...... Paul Warfield	6	2	0	58
3...... Lance Alworth	7	0	0	56
4...... Pete Pihos	5	2	2	52
5T.... James Lofton	2	6	0	46
5T.... Charley Taylor	3	5	1	46
7T.... Steve Largent	1	5	4	45
7T.... Mac Speedie	5	1	0	45
9T.... Fred Biletnikoff	2	4	1	39
9T.... Dante Lavelli	3	3	2	39

Centers	C	1st	2nd	Total
1...... Jim Otto	12	1	0	101
2...... Jim Ringo	6	4	1	71
3...... Mike Webster	5	5	1	68
4...... Mick Tinglehoff	7	0	0	56
5...... *Dermonti Dawson	5	2	0	50
6...... Jim Langer	5	1	0	45
7...... Dwight Stephenson	5	0	0	40
8...... Ray Wietecha	1	6	0	38
9T.... Tom Banks	4	1	0	37
9T.... Frank Gatski	4	1	0	37
9T.... Jay Hilgenberg	2	5	0	37

Tight Ends	C	1st	2nd	Total
1...... *Shannon Sharpe	4	3	0	47
2T.... Fred Arbanas	3	3	0	39
2T.... Keith Jackson	3	3	0	39
4...... Mike Ditka	3	2	1	37
5T.... Kellen Winslow	3	2	0	34
5T.... John Mackey	3	2	0	34
7...... Ozzie Newsome	1	3	3	32
8T.... Todd Christensen	2	3	0	31
8T.... *Ben Coates	2	3	0	31
10.... Steve Jordan	0	6	0	30

Defensive Ends	C	1st	2nd	Total
1...... *Reggie White	9	4	0	92
2...... Gino Marchetti	7	4	0	76
3...... *Bruce Smith	6	5	0	73
4...... Carl Eller	6	2	1	61
5...... Andy Robustelli	3	6	2	60
6...... Jack Youngblood	6	2	0	58
7...... Deacon Jones	6	2	0	58
8T.... Doug Atkins	2	7	0	51
8T.... Claude Humphrey	4	2	3	51
10.... Howie Long	3	5	0	49

*Active in 1998.

One-Way Players (1950–98) *(Cont.)*

Defensive Tackles	C	1st	2nd	Total
1...... Merlin Olsen	7	7	0	91
2...... Joe Greene	9	2	0	82
3...... Alan Page	7	4	0	76
4T.... Bob Lilly	8	1	0	69
4T.... Randy White	8	1	0	69
6...... Leo Nomellini	5	4	2	66
7...... Bill Willis	5	3	0	55
8T.... George Connor	6	1	0	51
8T.... Alex Karras	4	2	3	51
10.... Buck Buchanan	4	3	1	50

Linebackers	C	1st	2nd	Total
1...... Lawrence Taylor	8	2	0	74
2...... Ted Hendricks	6	5	0	73
3...... Joe Schmidt	7	3	0	71
4...... Chuck Bednarik	7	2	1	69
5T.... Bill George	7	2	0	66
5T.... Jack Lambert	7	2	0	66
5T.... Mike Singletary	7	2	0	66
8...... Jack Ham	7	1	1	64
9...... Nick Buoniconti	6	3	0	63
10.... Bobby Bell	7	1	0	61
11.... Dick Butkus	6	2	0	58
12.... Larry Grantham	3	4	1	57
13.... *Junior Seau	5	3	0	55
14T.. Chuck Howley	4	4	0	52
14T.. Willie Lanier	4	4	0	52
16.... Maxie Baughan	2	7	0	51
17.... Robert Brazile	5	2	0	50
18.... Andy Russell	3	4	1	48
19.... Bill Bergey	5	1	1	48
20.... Mike Stratton	4	3	0	47

Defensive Backs	C	1st	2nd	Total
1...... Ken Houston	6	6	0	78
2...... Paul Krause	6	3	1	66
3T.... Willie Wood	5	5	0	65
3T.... Emlen Tunnell	5	5	0	65
3T.... Ronnie Lott	5	5	0	65
6...... Johnny Robinson	6	3	0	63
7...... Larry Wilson	6	2	0	58
8...... Dick Lane	4	5	0	57
9...... Mel Renfro	2	8	0	56
10.... *Deion Sanders	5	3	0	55
11.... Yale Lary	3	6	0	54
12T.. Willie Brown	6	1	0	53
12T.. Roger Wehrli	6	1	0	53
14.... Dave Grayson	4	3	1	50
15.... Herb Adderley	3	5	0	49
16T.. Cornell Green	4	3	0	47
16T.. *Rod Woodson	4	3	0	47
18.... Lemar Parrish	2	6	0	46
19.... *Steve Atwater	2	6	0	46
20.... Jack Christiansen	5	1	0	45

*Active in 1998.

Men

Based on PGA results from 1916–1999. Excludes events on the PGA Senior Tour. Point system based on 3 points for each tour win, 2 points for each second place, 1 point for each third place, and 10 bonus points for each major championship.

	Golfer	1st	2nd	3rd	Majors	Pts	Turned Pro
1.................	Jack Nicklaus	70	59	35	18	543	1961
2.................	Sam Snead	81	63	54	7	493	1934
3.................	Ben Hogan	63	46	30	9	401	1931
4.................	Arnold Palmer	60	42	29	7	363	1954
5.................	Byron Nelson	52	36	34	5	346	1932
6.................	Walter Hagen	40	23	19	11	295	1912
7.................	Billy Casper	51	36	24	3	279	1954
8.................	Gene Sarazen	37	30	31	7	272	1920
9.................	*Tom Watson	34	31	23	8	267	1971
10...............	Gary Player	21	33	22	9	241	1953
11...............	Cary Middlecoff	39	30	23	3	230	1947
12...............	Lee Trevino	27	34	21	6	230	1960
13...............	Jimmy Demaret	31	34	29	3	220	1927
14...............	Lloyd Mangrum	36	28	43	1	217	1929
15...............	Horton Smith	30	37	24	2	208	1926
16...............	Harry Cooper	30	37	26	0	190	1923
17...............	Gene Littler	29	34	20	1	185	1954
18...............	Leo Diegel	29	23	16	2	169	1916
19...............	Paul Runyan	28	20	24	2	168	1930

*Active in 1999. Results updated through 9/15/1999.

Golf (Cont.)

Men (Cont.)

20................	Ray Floyd	22	24	13	4	167	1961
21................	Hale Irwin	20	25	24	3	164	1968
22................	Johnny Farrell	22	26	35	1	163	1922
23................	Tommy Armour	24	23	12	3	160	1924
24................	Craig Wood	21	28	20	2	159	1920
25T..............	Tom Kite	19	29	22	1	147	1972
25T..............	*Greg Norman	18	31	11	2	147	1976

Women

Based on LPGA results from 1950–1999. Women's rankings based on three points for each tour win, one point for each second place finish, and three bonus points for each victory in a major championship.

	Golfer	1st	2nd	Majors	Pts
1...	Kathy Whitworth	96	99	7	408
2...	Mickey Wright	87	52	14	355
3...	Betsy Rawls	56	43	8	235
4...	Louise Suggs	49	49	11	229
5...	*Nancy Lopez	51	57	4	222
6...	*Joanne Carner	48	61	4	217
7...	Sandra Haynie	43	63	4	204
8...	Patty Berg	36	42	15	195
9...	*Pat Bradley	35	57	6	180
10...	*Patty Sheehan	36	35	6	161
11...	*Beth Daniel	36	46	1	157
12...	Carol Mann	38	33	2	153
13...	*Betsy King	33	33	6	150
14T.......................................	*Amy Alcott	30	26	5	131
14T.......................................	Donna Caponi	28	29	6	131
14T.......................................	Judy Rankin	28	41	2	131
17...	Jane Blalock	31	32	1	128
18...	Babe Didrikson Zaharias	27	11	10	122
19...	Marlene Bauer Hagge	25	37	1	115
20...	Sandra Palmer	26	26	3	113
21...	*Juli Inkster	24	15	5	102
22...	*Hollis Stacy	20	27	4	99
23...	Marilynn Smith	23	24	2	99
24...	*Laura Davies	19	22	4	91
25...	*Jan Stephenson	20	17	3	86

*Active in 1999. Results updated through 9/15/1999.

Hockey

NHL Players ranked by adjusted points, a method for normalizing statistics across different eras.

	Player	Adjusted Points	Goals	Assists	Points	First Season	Last Season
1.............	*Wayne Gretzky	2250	894	1963	2857	1979–80	1998–99
2.............	Gordie Howe	2225	801	1049	1850	1946–47	1979–80
3.............	Aurel Joliat	1713	270	190	460	1922–23	1937–38
4.............	Howie Morenz	1640	270	197	467	1923–24	1936–37
5.............	Cy Denneny	1506	246	85	331	1917–18	1928–29
6.............	Phil Esposito	1505	717	873	1590	1963–64	1980–81
7.............	Nels Stewart	1477	324	191	515	1925–26	1939–40
8.............	Stan Mikita	1468	541	926	1467	1958–59	1979–80
9.............	Alex Delvecchio	1428	456	825	1281	1950–51	1973–74
10...........	Marcel Dionne	1413	731	1040	1771	1971–72	1988–89
11...........	Jean Beliveau	1400	507	712	1219	1950–51	1970–71
12...........	John Bucyk	1389	556	813	1369	1955–56	1977–78
13...........	Frank Boucher	1377	160	263	423	1921–22	1943–44
14...........	*Mark Messier	1355	610	1050	1660	1979–80	1998–99
15...........	Maurice Richard	1320	544	421	965	1942–43	1959–60
16...........	Norm Ullman	1304	490	739	1229	1955–56	1974–75
17...........	Bobby Hull	1283	610	560	1170	1957–58	1979–80
18...........	Hooley Smith	1276	200	215	415	1924–25	1940–41
19...........	*Steve Yzerman	1233	592	891	1483	1983–84	1998–99
20...........	*Ron Francis	1224	449	1037	1486	1981–82	1998–99

*Active during 1998–99 season.

Hockey (Cont.)

	Player	Adjusted Points	Goals	Assists	Points	First Season	Last Season
21	Reg Noble	1211	167	97	264	1917–18	1932–33
22	Mario Lemieux	1175	613	881	1494	1984–85	1996–97
23	*Ray Bourque	1170	385	1083	1468	1979–80	1998–99
24T	Jean Ratelle	1168	491	776	1267	1960–61	1980–81
24T	Frank Nighbor	1168	137	92	229	1917–18	1929–30
26	Frank Mahovlich	1167	533	570	1103	1956–57	1973–74
27	*Paul Coffey	1161	385	1102	1487	1980–81	1998–99
28	Ted Lindsay	1134	379	472	851	1944–45	1964–65
29	King Clancy	1130	137	144	281	1921–22	1936–37
30	Henri Richard	1118	358	688	1046	1955–56	1974–75
31	Andy Bathgate	1109	349	624	973	1952–53	1970–71
32	Guy Lafleur	1105	560	793	1353	1971–72	1990–91
33	Bryan Trottier	1097	524	901	1425	1975–76	1993–94
34	Jari Kurri	1087	601	797	1398	1980–81	1997–98
35T	Dale Hawerchuk	1077	518	891	1409	1981–82	1996–97
35T	Gilbert Perreault	1077	512	814	1326	1970–71	1986–87
37	Mike Gartner	1075	708	627	1335	1979–80	1997–98
38	Bill Cook	1065	229	138	367	1926–27	1936–37
39	Babe Dye	1058	202	44	246	1919–20	1930–31
40	Dit Clapper	1029	228	246	474	1927–28	1947–48
41	Denis Savard	1023	473	865	1338	1980–81	1996–97
42	*Doug Gilmour	1012	397	835	1232	1983–84	1998–99
43	Harvey Jackson	1011	241	234	475	1929–30	1943–44
44	Bernie Geoffrion	1008	393	429	822	1950–51	1967–68
45	Bobby Clarke	1001	358	852	1210	1969–70	1983–84
46	Red Kelly	998	281	542	823	1947–48	1967–68
47	Rod Gilbert	994	406	615	1021	1960–61	1977–78
48	Syd Howe	988	237	291	528	1929–30	1945–46
49	*Dino Ciccarelli	985	608	592	1200	1980–81	1998–99
50	*Bernie Nicholls	981	475	734	1209	1981–82	1998–99
51	Dave Keon	975	396	590	986	1960–61	1981–82
52	George Boucher	969	120	81	201	1917–18	1933–34
53T	Dean Prentice	956	391	469	860	1952–53	1973–74
53T	*Dave Andreychuk	956	532	608	1140	1982–83	1998–99
55	Bun Cook	953	158	144	302	1926–27	1936–37
56	*Adam Oates	952	288	838	1126	1985–86	1998–99
57	*Brett Hull	941	586	459	1045	1985–86	1998–99
58	*Luc Robitaille	929	517	559	1076	1986–87	1998–99
59	Bill Cowley	928	195	353	548	1934–35	1946–47
60	*Larry Murphy	920	275	880	1155	1980–81	1998–99
61	Darryl Sittler	918	484	637	1121	1970–71	1984–85
62	Peter Stastny	913	450	789	1239	1980–81	1994–95
63T	Charlie Conacher	912	225	173	398	1929–30	1940–41
63T	Babe Siebert	912	140	156	296	1925–26	1938–39
65	Milt Schmidt	908	229	346	575	1936–37	1955–56
66	Marty Barry	894	195	192	387	1927–28	1939–40
67	Paul Thompson	889	153	179	332	1926–27	1939–40
68	Elmer Lach	885	215	408	623	1940–41	1953–54
69	*Joe Sakic	875	375	604	979	1988–89	1998–99
70T	*Pierre Turgeon	873	397	600	997	1987–88	1998–99
70T	*Michel Goulet	873	548	604	1152	1979–80	1993–94
72	*Phil Housley	869	302	773	1075	1982–83	1998–99
73	Mike Bossy	866	573	553	1126	1977–78	1986–87
74	*Al MacInnis	864	290	775	1065	1981–82	1998–99
75	Cooney Weiland	862	173	160	333	1928–29	1939–40
76	Toe Blake	858	235	292	527	1934–35	1947–48
77	Bobby Orr	853	270	645	915	1966–67	1978–79
78	Glenn Anderson	850	498	601	1099	1980–81	1995–96
79	Joe Mullen	846	502	561	1063	1979–80	1996–97
80	Bernie Federko	841	369	761	1130	1976–77	1989–90
81	Eddie Shore	839	105	179	284	1926–27	1939–40
82	Johnny Gottselig	838	176	195	371	1928–29	1945–46
83	Hec Kilrea	837	167	129	296	1925–26	1939–40
84	Yvan Cournoyer	834	428	435	863	1963–64	1978–79
85	Pat LaFontaine	827	468	545	1013	1983–84	1997–98
86	*Brian Bellows	825	485	537	1022	1982–83	1998–99
87T	*Pat Verbeek	822	478	487	965	1982–83	1998–99

*Active during 1998–99 season.

Player	Adjusted Points	Goals	Assists	Points	First Season	Last Season
87T......... *Jaromir Jagr	822	345	517	862	1990–91	1998–99
89.......... George Armstrong	819	296	417	713	1949–50	1970–71
90.......... Hap Day	817	86	116	202	1924–25	1937–38
91.......... Denis Potvin	811	310	742	1052	1973–74	1987–88
92.......... Dave Taylor	810	431	638	1069	1977–78	1993–94
93.......... Harry Broadbent	807	122	48	170	1918–19	1928–29
94.......... *Vincent Damphousse	804	347	582	929	1986–87	1998–99
95.......... Lanny McDonald	802	500	506	1006	1973–74	1988–89
96.......... *Dale Hunter	798	323	697	1020	1980–81	1998–99
97.......... Steve Larmer	794	441	571	1012	1980–81	1994–95
98.......... Doug Bentley	789	219	324	543	1939–40	1953–54
99.......... Mush March	787	153	230	383	1928–29	1944–45
100........ Max Bentley	782	245	299	544	1940–41	1953–54

Goaltender†	Points	Games	Wins	Losses	Ties	Shutouts
1............. Terry Sawchuk	1169	971	447	330	172	103
2............. Jacques Plante	1096	837	434	246	146	82
3............. Tony Esposito	1074	886	423	306	152	76
4............. Glenn Hall	1061	906	407	326	163	84
5............. *Patrick Roy	965	778	412	243	95	46
6............. *Grant Fuhr	933	845	398	282	112	25
7............. Rogie Vachon	888	795	355	291	127	51
8............. Harry Lumley	874	804	330	329	143	71
9............. Gump Worsley	863	861	335	352	150	43
10.......... Andy Moog	857	713	372	209	88	25
11.......... *John Vanbiesbrouck	806	779	333	303	105	35
12.......... *Tom Barrasso	803	708	345	248	79	34
13.......... *Mike Vernon	799	673	347	223	83	22
14.......... Turk Broda	767	629	302	224	101	62
15.......... Billy Smith	737	680	305	233	105	22
16.......... Ed Giacomin	729	610	289	208	97	54
17.......... Tiny Thompson	724	553	284	194	75	81
18.......... Bernie Parent	718	608	271	198	121	55
19.......... Dan Bouchard	712	655	286	232	113	27
20.......... Gilles Meloche	691	788	270	351	131	20
21.......... Mike Liut	687	663	294	271	74	25
22.......... *Ron Hextall	684	608	296	214	69	23
23.......... *Ed Belfour	672	550	276	174	75	45
24.......... George Hainsworth	660	465	246	145	74	94
25.......... Kelly Hrudey	646	677	271	265	88	16
26.......... Ken Dryden	636	397	258	57	74	46
27.......... Don Beaupre	628	667	268	277	75	17
28.......... Johnny Bower	627	552	250	195	90	37
29.......... Frank Brimsek	624	514	252	182	80	40
30.......... Curtis Joseph	608	524	248	196	61	51
31.......... Eddie Johnston	581	592	234	257	81	32
32.......... Glenn Resch	570	571	231	224	82	26
33T......... John Roach	564	492	219	204	68	58
33T......... Pete Peeters	564	489	246	155	51	21
35T......... Gerry Cheevers	560	418	230	102	74	26
35T......... *Bill Ranford	560	631	236	273	73	15
37.......... *Kirk McLean	549	567	230	244	67	22
38.......... Reggie Lemelin	547	507	236	162	63	12
39.......... *Mike Richter	539	492	230	174	57	22
40.......... Alex Connell	538	417	199	155	59	81
41.......... Lorne Chabot	537	411	201	148	62	73
42.......... Greg Millen	536	604	215	284	89	17
43T......... Bill Durnan	512	383	208	112	62	34
43T......... Roger Crozier	512	518	206	197	70	30
45.......... Don Edwards	506	459	208	155	74	16
46.......... Cesare Maniago	504	568	189	261	96	30
47.......... *Martin Brodeur	495	375	201	105	57	36
48.......... *Dominik Hasek	494	414	195	139	62	42
49.......... Dave Kerr	493	427	203	148	75	12
50.......... *Ken Wregget	482	546	211	238	51	9

†NHL goaltenders ranked by points, two points per win, one per tie, and one per shutout.

*Active during 1998–99 season.

Athletes are ranked by comparing the ratio of their Olympic scores to the world record (WR) for that event at the time. For track events, only times recorded in the medal rounds are included. Includes Summer Olympic Games from 1900–1996. All measurements of height and distance are given in feet and inches.

Men

100 Meters

	Athlete	Country	Olympics	Time	WR	Ratio
1	Bob Hayes	United States	Tokyo 1964	10.0	10.0	1.000
2	Jim Hines	United States	Mexico City 1968	9.95	9.90	.995
3	Carl Lewis	United States	Los Angeles 1984	9.99	9.93	.994
4	Carl Lewis	United States	Seoul 1988	9.92	9.83	.991
5	Jesse Owens	United States	Berlin 1936	10.3	10.2	.990

Note: Canadian Ben Johnson ran 9.79 in 1988, breaking the world record of 9.83, a ratio of 1.004. His medal was withdrawn by the IOC when he failed the post-race drug test.

1500 Meters

	Athlete	Country	Olympics	Time	WR	Ratio
1	Charles Bennett	Great Britain	Paris 1900	04:06.2	4:10.4	1.017
2	Henri Deloge	France	Paris 1900	04:06.6	4:10.4	1.015
3	John Bray	United States	Paris 1900	04:07.2	4:10.4	1.013
4	John Lovelock	New Zealand	Berlin 1936	03:47.8	3:48.8	1.004
5	Jim Lightbody	United States	St. Louis 1904	04:05.4	4:06.2	1.003

5000 Meters

	Athlete	Country	Olympics	Time	WR	Ratio
1	J. Kolehmainen	Finland	Stockholm 1912	14:36.6	15:01.2	1.028
2	Jean Bouin	France	Stockholm 1912	14:36.7	15:01.2	1.028
3	Vladimir Kuts	Soviet Union	Melbourne 1956	13:39.6	13:36.8	.997
4	Paavo Nurmi	Finland	Paris 1924	14:31.2	14:28.2	.997
5	Ville Ritola	Finland	Paris 1924	14:31.4	14:28.2.	996

Long Jump

	Athlete	Country	Olympics	Dist.	WR	Ratio
1	Bob Beamon	United States	Mexico City 1968	29-2½	27-4¾	1.066
2	Albert Gutterson	United States	Stockholm 1912	24-11¼	24-11¾	.999
3	Jesse Owens	United States	Berlin 1936	26-5½	26-8¼	.991
4	Ralph Boston	United States	Rome 1960	26-7¾	26-11¼	.989
5	Bo Roberson	United States	Rome 1960	26-7¼	26-11¼	.988

High Jump

	Athlete	Country	Olympics	Ht	WR	Ratio
1	Gerd Wessig	East Germany	Moscow 1980	7-8¾	7-8½	1.004
2	Charles Dumas	United States	Melbourne 1956	6-11½	7-0½	.986
3	Hennady Avdeyenko	Soviet Union	Seoul 1988	7-9¾	7-11½	.983
4	Dietmar Mogenburg	West Germany	Los Angeles 1984	7-8½	7-10	.983
5	Jacek Wszola	Poland	Moscow 1980	7-7	7-8½	.983

Pole Vault

	Athlete	Country	Olympics	Ht.	WR	Ratio
1	Frank Foss	United States	Antwerp 1920	13-5	13-2¼	1.017
2	W. Kozakiewicz	Poland	Moscow 1980	18-11½	18-11	1.002
3	Bob Seagren	United States	Mexico City 1968	17-8½	17-9	.998
4	Claus Schiprowski	West Germany	Mexico City 1968	17-8½	17-9	.998
5	Wolfgang Nordwig	East Germany	Mexico City 1968	17-8½	17-9	.998

Decathlon

Athlete	Country	Olympics	Score	WR	Ratio
1.......Jim Thorpe	United States	Stockholm 1912	8412	7414	1.135
2.......Hugo Wieslander	Sweden	Stockholm 1912	7724	7414	1.042
3.......Harold Osborn	United States	Paris 1924	7711	7482	1.031
4.......James Bausch	United States	Los Angeles 1932	8462	8255	1.025
5.......Bruce Jenner	United States	Montreal 1976	8618	8538	1.009

Women

100 Meters

Athlete	Country	Olympics	Time	WR	Ratio
1.......Wilma Rudolph	United States	Rome 1960	11.0	11.3	1.027
2.......Helen Stephens	United States	Berlin 1936	11.5	11.6	1.009
3.......Wyomia Tyus	United States	Mexico City 1968	11.08	11.1	1.002
4.......Renate Stecher	East Germany	Munich 1972	11.07	11.08	1.001
5.......Dorothy Hyman	Great Britain	Rome 1960	11.3	11.3	1.000

High Jump

Athlete	Country	Olympics	Ht.	WR	Ratio
1.......Jean Shiley	United States	Los Angeles 1932	5-5¼	5-3¾	1.023
2.......Babe Didrikson	United States	Los Angeles 1932	5-5¼	5-3¾	1.023
3.......Mildred McDaniel	United States	Melbourne 1956	5-9¼	5-8¾	1.006
4.......Ulrike Meyfarth	West Germany	Munich 1972	6-3½	6-3½	1.000
5.......Iolanda Balas	Romania	Tokyo 1964	6-2¾	6-3¼	.995

Long Jump

Athlete	Country	Olympics	Dist.	WR	Ratio
1.......Mary Rand	Great Britain	Tokyo 1964	22-2¼	21-11¾	1.009
2.......Viorica Viscopoleanu	Romania	Mexico City 1968	22-4½	22-2¼	1.009
3.......Elzbieta Krzesinska	Poland	Melbourne 1956	20-10	20-10	1.000
4.......Yvette Williams	New Zealand	Helsinki 1952	20-5¾	20-6¼	.998
5.......Tatiana Kolpakova	Soviet Union	Moscow 1980	23-2	23-3¾	.996

Javelin

Athlete	Country	Olympics	Dist.	WR	Ratio
1.......Mihaela Penes	Romania	Tokyo 1964	198-7	201-4¼	.986
2.......Ruth Fuchs	East Germany	Munich 1972	209-7	213-5½	.982
3.......Maria Colon	Cuba	Moscow 1980	224-5	229-10	.976
4.......Inese Janunzeme	Soviet Union	Melbourne 1956	176-8	182-0	.971
5.......Angela Nemeth	Hungary	Mexico City 1968	198-0	204-8¾	.967

Shot Put

Athlete	Country	Olympics	Dist.	WR	Ratio
1.......Margitta Gummel	East Germany	Mexico City 1968	64-4	61-11	1.039
2.......Nadezhda Chizhova	Soviet Union	Munich 1972	69-0	67-8¼	1.019
3.......Galina Zybina	Soviet Union	Helsinki 1952	50-1¾	49-10	1.006
4.......Ilona Slupianek	East Germany	Moscow 1980	73-6¼	73-8	.998
5.......Marita Lange	East Germany	Mexico City 1968	61-7½	61-11	.995

Tennis

Men

Rankings based on five points for each win in a Grand Slam singles event, and two points for finishing as runner-up. Includes all Grand Slam singles events from 1900–1999.

		Won	2nd	Pts	Career
1.	Rod Laver	11	6	67	1959–1979
2.	Roy Emerson	12	3	66	1959–1983
3.	Bjorn Borg	11	5	65	1972–1993
4.	*Pete Sampras	12	2	64	1988–
5.	Ivan Lendl	8	11	62	1978–1994
6.	Bill Tilden	10	5	60	1920–1930
7.	Ken Rosewall	8	8	56	1953–1980
8.	Jimmy Connors	8	7	54	1970–1996
9.	Fred Perry	8	2	44	1931–1936
10T.	John McEnroe	7	4	43	1977–1994
10T.	Mats Wilander	7	4	43	1980–1996
12.	Jack Crawford	6	6	42	1928–1937
13T.	Henri Cochet	7	3	41	1922–1933
13T.	John Newcombe	7	3	41	1963–1981
13T.	Rene Lacoste	7	3	41	1923–1928
16.	Stefan Edberg	6	5	40	1982–1996
17.	Bill Larned	7	2	39	1902–1912
18.	*Boris Becker	6	4	38	1983–
19.	*Andre Agassi	5	5	35	1985–
20T.	Jean Borotra	4	6	32	1922–1932
20T.	Don Budge	6	1	32	1935–1953
20T.	Laurence Doherty	6	1	32	1900–1906
20T.	Tony Wilding	6	1	32	1904–1914
24.	Frank Sedgman	5	3	31	1949–1974
25.	Arthur Ashe	4	4	28	1963–1979

Women

		Won	2nd	Pts	Career
1.	Margaret Smith Court	24	5	130	1960–1975
2.	*Steffi Graf	21	9	123	1982–
3.	Chris Evert	18	16	122	1971–1989
4.	Martina Navratilova	18	14	118	1973–1994
5.	Helen Wills Moody	19	3	101	1919–1938
6.	Billie Jean King	12	4	68	1963–1983
7.	Evonne Goolagong Cawley	7	11	57	1969–1985
8.	*Monica Seles	9	4	53	1988–
9.	Doris Hart	6	11	52	1942–1955
10T.	Helen Jacobs	5	11	47	1928–1940
10T.	Maria Bueno	7	6	47	1965–1977
12.	Louise Brough	6	8	46	1941–1957
13.	Maureen Connolly	9	0	45	1949–1954
14.	Suzanne Lenglen	8	0	40	1919–1926
15.	Margaret Osborne duPont	6	4	38	1941–1962
16.	*Arantxa Sanchez–Vicario	4	8	36	1986–
17.	*Martina Hingis	5	4	33	1994–
18.	Pauline Betz	5	3	31	1939–1947
19.	Althea Gibson	5	2	29	1950–1968
20T.	Hana Mandlikova	4	4	28	1978–1990
20T.	Shirley Fry	4	4	28	1941–1957
22T.	Dorothea Chambers	4	3	26	1903–1925
22T.	Molla Mallory	4	3	26	1915–1929
24T.	Alice Marble	5	0	25	1933–1941
24T.	Daphne Akhurst	5	0	25	1925–1931

*Active in 1999. Includes all events through 1999 U.S. Open.

PAGE 433 PHOTO CREDITS (clockwise from upper left): Richard Mackson (Jordan); Albert Watson (Montana); Neil Leifer (Ali); Baseball Hall of Fame Library (Ruth); Ronald C. Modra (Navratilova).

Boxing

IBF and WBC
welterweight champion
Felix Trinidad

Score One For Scandal

A mainstay of the fight game, controversy had a banner season in 1999, dogging the sport's every step

BY MARTY BURNS

THE USUAL cast of characters filled the boxing scene in 1999, from Mike Tyson and Evander Holyfield to Roy Jones Jr. and Oscar De La Hoya. But it wasn't any of those heavy punchers in baggy shorts who ultimately ruled. No, it was a rugged customer named Kid Controversy who dominated the sport all year, stalking it around the ring, throwing haymakers and eventually overshadowing everything else.

Whatever the occasion, from the Holyfield–Lennox Lewis heavyweight title bout to Tyson's return to prison to the De La Hoya–Felix Trinidad welterweight title fight, boxing just couldn't keep discord at bay. It swallowed up fighters, trainers, promoters and judges, leading to investigations, lawsuits, complaints—and, finally, questions about the integrity of the sport. Even by boxing's bottom-dwelling standards, it was bad.

The unseemliness began in March at the Holyfield-Lewis bout, the most heavily anticipated title scrape since the Holyfield-Tyson ear-biting fiasco two years earlier. Holyfield, 36, was the WBA and IBF champ, the proud warrior with the lion's heart who had twice toppled Iron Mike. Lewis, 33, was the 6'5", 245-pound Brit with the hunger to finally live up to his potential, which was as enormous as his frame. Two boxers with skill, courage and motivation going head-to-head in boxing's mecca, Madison Square Garden. It should have been the sport's finest hour.

Instead it was a mockery, thanks to some bizarre scoring by the fight's judges, who turned a fairly one-sided Lewis triumph into a draw. Lewis peppered Holyfield from the opening bell, drilling him with stiff jabs and a steady mix of rights and uppercuts. It was an honest beating that left little doubt as to the outcome. Lewis connected on 348 punches over 12 rounds; Holyfield connected on 130. Lewis nailed 65% of his power punches; Holyfield, 36%. Yet to the disbelief of nearly all who witnessed the bout, one judge had Lewis the winner by a 116–113 score, one ruled the fight a draw, and another scored it 115–113 for Holyfield, making the outcome a draw. When the decision was read, Lewis looked shocked. The Garden crowd, similarly stunned, booed lustily.

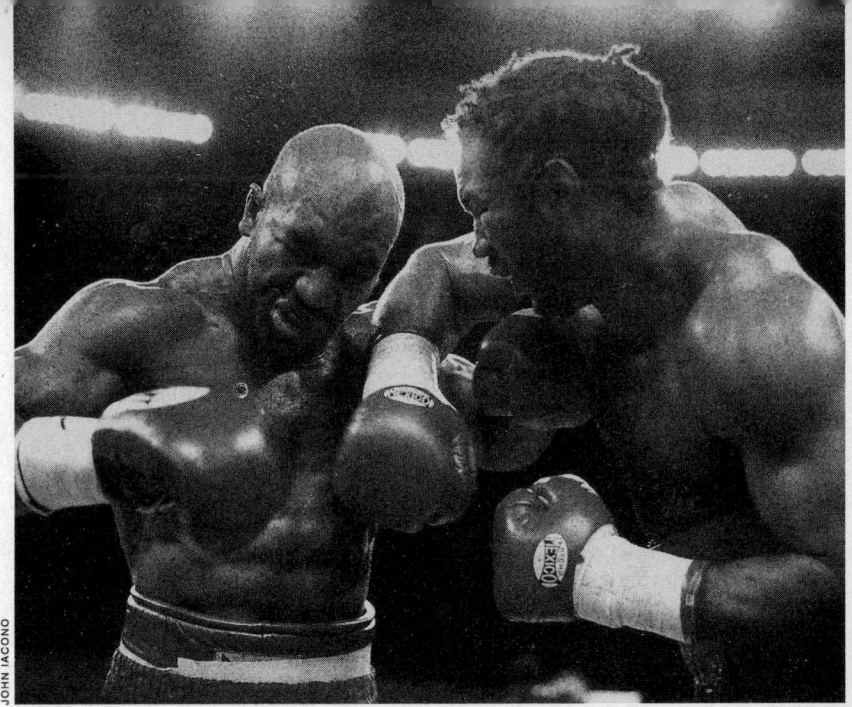

After Lewis (right) pummeled Holyfield at the Garden, the judges hammered him.

The attorney general of New York, the New York Athletic Commission and the New York state senate each launched investigations to determine whether there had been some kind of fix. Although no evidence was uncovered, the sport's credibility took a blow. Meanwhile, boxing's three major sanctioning bodies called for a rematch within six months, an event that because of the sport's usual politics would otherwise never have happened. About the only person who was happy with the result was promoter Don King, who had the rights to Holyfield's lucrative bouts. "What do you do when you have a dispute?" King asked. "You resolve it."

With Holyfield-Lewis II not scheduled to take place until November '99, boxing fans—those that remained—were in for a long summer. Making it all the more tedious was the absence of Tyson, still the sport's most compelling figure, who had gone to jail in Maryland in February after pleading no contest to assaulting two men during a traffic

accident in the summer of 1998. Tyson's lawyers, saying the state had promised not to give their client jail time in exchange for his plea, cried foul but to no avail. He was sentenced to a year in prison, with 60 additional days tacked on later by an Indiana judge for violating his parole for his 1991 rape conviction. As a result of his jail sentence, Tyson had to cancel an April 24 bout against an undetermined opponent. He was released from prison in May, but his next scheduled bout was not until November '99.

Too bad, because in his one '99 appearance before he went to jail, a fifth-round knockout of Francois Botha in January, Tyson had shown just enough of his old form to make fans take notice. He didn't box particularly well, but he did thrill the Las Vegas crowd by dropping Botha with a quick and devastating right that seemed to catch everyone by surprise. The punch barely traveled six inches, but it staggered Botha, causing him to reel around the ring, toppling and wobbling before finally sliding down the ropes to the canvas. It might not have been the most important knockdown of the year, but it was probably the most memorable.

The punch revived the Tyson mystique but proved little about his ability to execute the sweet science. After 19 months away from the sport, Tyson looked predictably rusty and one-dimensional, struggling so much that Botha won every round before he went lights out. What's more, Tyson, who earned $10 million for the bout, showed some of his old bad habits, cursing out a TV reporter a week before the fight and causing a mini brouhaha when he clamped down on Botha's arm during a clinch at the end of the first round. The two careered around the ring, tussling until arena security stepped in and separated them. When Tyson tried the arm-bending tactic again in the next round, he was penalized a point. Given that he had been ordered to undergo psychiatric testing, including anger-management counseling, to regain his boxing license after the infamous Holyfield episode, it was an inauspicious return to the ring.

With such dismal displays billed as the sport's main events, it was no surprise that fans gravitated to the long-awaited "Odd Couple" matchup between Oscar (De La Hoya) and Felix (Trinidad) like desert travelers approaching an oasis. Set for late September in (appropriately enough) Las Vegas, the bout turned out to be a mirage.

De La Hoya, the golden boy and WBC champ, was coming off impressive victories in his last two bouts. He won a split decision over Ike Quartey in February and stopped Oba Carr in the 11th round in May. Against Trinidad he hoped to silence the critics who said he was too cautious, and maybe a little soft. Trinidad, the under-promoted hard-hitter and IBF champ, came in riding a big win over Pernell (Sweet Pea) Whitaker and vowing to make the most of his opportunity.

It was one of the biggest nonheavy-weight fights ever, a megabout harkening back to the heydays of Sugar Ray Leonard and Thomas Hearns. De La Hoya would make a guaranteed $15 million, and Trinidad would pull in $8.5 million. But fans hoping to see two heavy punchers battle it out until the best man won were severely disappointed.

De La Hoya controlled the fight from the start, employing a dazzling but resolutely defensive style that kept Trinidad at bay. De La Hoya bloodied Trinidad's nose in the second round and generally neutralized his opponent's hard right hand. However, in the later stages, De La Hoya opted not to go for the kill; instead he danced around and gave by-example boxing instruction. It was a decision he'd later regret.

Apparently punishing De La Hoya for putting on a clinic instead of a slugfest, the judges awarded the 12-round decision to Trinidad. Again a controversial decision had marred a major boxing event, though the outrage was nothing compared with what followed the Holyfield-Lewis bout. Even De La Hoya's strongest supporters admitted their fighter had coasted through the last three rounds—Trinidad won all three on two of the judges' cards—giving away his lead.

The Holyfield-Lewis and De La Hoya–Trinidad disappointments formed sorry bookends for boxing in '99, but in the middle it wasn't all bad. Jones, who is pound-for-pound the best fighter in the sport, went undefeated, struggling only to find a worthy opponent. And the flamboyant featherweight Prince Naseem Hamed remained unbeaten, stopping Paul Ingle in the 11th round of their April title fight. Junior welterweight Sugar Shane Mosley (32–0), a sweet-natured solid citizen who until late in the year lived in his parents' garage, emerged as a major talent with box office appeal. Michael Grant (30–0, 21 KOs), a piano-playing 6'7" former basketball star at Cal State–Fullerton, led a trio of promising heavyweights that also included David Tua (33–1, 28 KOs) and Ike Ibeabuchi (20–0, 15 KOs). In women's boxing, Laila Ali—one of Muhammad Ali's daughters—made a successful pro debut.

But these positive stories weren't enough to save boxing in '99. In the end, Kid Controversy was just too tough. And no judges' ruling in the world could make it otherwise.

FOR THE RECORD·1998-1999

Current Champions

Division	Weight Limit	WBC Champion	WBA Champion	IBF Champion
Heavyweight	None	Lennox Lewis	Evander Holyfield	Evander Holyfield
Cruiserweight	190	Juan Carlos Gomez	Fabrice Tiozzo	Vassily Jirov
Light heavyweight	175	Roy Jones Jr	Roy Jones Jr	Roy Jones Jr
Super middleweight	168	Richie Woodhall	Byron Mitchell	Sven Ottke
Middleweight	160	Keith Holmes	William Joppy Jr	Bernard Hopkins
Junior middleweight	154	Javier Castillejo	David Reid	Fernando Vargas
Welterweight	147	Felix Trinidad	James Page	Felix Trinidad
Junior welterweight	140	Kostya Tszyu	Sharmba Mitchell	Terronn Millett
Lightweight	135	Steve Johnston	Stefano Zoff	Paul Spadafora
Junior lightweight	130	Floyd Mayweather	Lavka Sim	Roberto Garcia
Featherweight	126	Cesar Soto	Freddie Norwood	Manuel Medina
Junior featherweight	122	Erik Morales	Nestor Garza	Lehlohonolo Ledwaba
Bantamweight	118	Veerapol Sahaprom	Paulie Ayala	Tim Austin
Junior bantamweight	115	Cho In-Joo	Hideki Todaka	Mark Johnson
Flyweight	112	Manny Pacquiao	S. Kratchingdaeng	Irene Pacheco
Junior flyweight	108	Saman Sor Jaturong	Phichit Chor Siriwat	Ricardo Lopez
Strawweight	105	Ricardo Lopez	Ricardo Lopez	Zolani Petelo

Note: WBC = World Boxing Council; WBA = World Boxing Association; IBF = International Boxing Federation

Championship and Major Fights of 1998 and 1999

Abbreviations: WBC=World Boxing Council; WBA= World Boxing Association; IBF=International Boxing Federation; KO=knockout; TKO=technical knockout; Dec=decision; Split=split decision; Disq=disqualification.

Heavyweight

Date	Winner	Loser	Result	Title	Site
Mar 13	Lennox Lewis	Evander Holyfield	Draw	IBF/WBA/WBC	New York

Cruiserweight

Date	Winner	Loser	Result	Title	Site
Oct 3	Juan Carlos Gomez	Alexei Iliin	TKO 2	WBC	Augsburg, Germany
Oct 30	Arthur Williams	Imamu Mayfield	TKO 9	IBF	Biloxi, MS
Nov 14	Fabrice Tiozzo	Ezequiel Paixao	KO 2	WBA	Mont-de-Marsan, France
Dec 12	Juan Carlos Gomez	Rodney Gordon	TKO 2	WBC	Frankfurt, Germany
Mar 13	Juan Carlos Gomez	Marcelo Dominguez	Dec 12	WBC	Lubeck, Germany
June 5	Vassily Jirov	Arthur Williams	TKO 7	IBF	Biloxi, MS
July 17	Juan Carlos Gomez	Bruce Scott	TKO 6	WBC	Dusseldorf, Germany
Sept 18	Vassily Jirov	Dale Brown	KO 10	IBF	Las Vegas

Light Heavyweight

Date	Winner	Loser	Result	Title	Site
Nov 14	Roy Jones	Otis Grant	TKO 10	WBC/WBA	Mashantucket, CT
Dec 5	Richard Hall	Anthony Bigeni	TKO 3	interim WBA	Atlantic City
Jan 9	Roy Jones	Richard Frazier	TKO 2	WBC/WBA	Pensacola, FL
Feb 27	Reggie Johnson	Will Taylor	Dec 12	IBF	Miami
June 5	Roy Jones	Reggie Johnson	Dec 12	IBF/WBA/WBC	Biloxi, MS

Super Middleweight

Date	Winner	Loser	Result	Title	Site
Oct 24	Sven Ottke	Charles Brewer	Split 12	IBF	Dusseldorf, Germany
Feb 13	Richie Woodhall	Vincenzo Nardiello	TKO 6	WBC	Newcastle, England
Feb 27	Sven Ottke	Giovanni Nardiello	KO 3	IBF	Berlin
May 8	Sven Ottke	Gabriel Hernandez	Dec 12	IBF	Dusseldorf, Germany
June 12	Byron Mitchell	Frank Liles	TKO 11	WBA	Wilmington, MA
Sept 4	Sven Ottke	Thomas Tate	T-Dec 11	IBF	Magdeburg, Germany

Middleweight

Date	Winner	Loser	Result	Title	Site
Apr 24	Keith Holmes	Hassine Cherifi	TKO 7	WBC	Washington, DC
Feb 6	Bernard Hopkins	Robert Allen	TKO 7	IBF	Washington, DC
Feb 20	Julio Cesar Green	Darren Obah	TKO 9	interim WBA	New York
Sept 24	Keith Holmes	Andrew Council	Dec 12	WBC	Washington, DC
Sept 24	William Joppy Jr	Julio Cesar Green	TKO 7	WBA	Washington, DC

Junior Middleweight (Super Welterweight)

Date	Winner	Loser	Result	Title	Site
Nov 30	Laurent Boudouani	Terry Norris	TKO 9	WBA	Paris
Dec 12	Fernando Vargas	Yori Boy Campas	TKO 7	IBF	Atlantic City
Jan 30	F. Javier Castillejo	Keith Mullings	Dec 12	WBC	Leganes, Spain
Mar 6	David Reid	Laurent Boudouani	Dec 12	WBA	Atlantic City
Mar 13	Fernando Vargas	Howard Clarke	TKO 4	IBF	New York
May 14	F. Javier Castillejo	Humberto Arande	TKO 4	WBC	Leganes, Spain
July 16	David Reid	Kevin Kelly	Dec 12	WBA	Atlantic City
July 17	Fernando Vargas	Raul Marquez	TKO 11	IBF	Lake Tahoe, NV
Aug 28	David Reid	Keith Mullings	Dec 12	WBA	Las Vegas
Sept 10	F. Javier Castillejo	Paolo Roberto	TKO 7	WBC	Leganes, Spain

Welterweight

Date	Winner	Loser	Result	Title	Site
Oct 10	James Page	Andrei Pestriaev	KO 2	WBA	Paris
Dec 5	James Page	Jose Luis Lopez	Dec 12	WBA	Atlantic City
Feb 13	Oscar De La Hoya	Ike Quartey	Split 12	WBC	Las Vegas
Feb 20	Felix Trinidad	Pernell Whitaker	Dec 12	IBF	New York
Mar 13	James Page	Sam Garr	Dec 12	WBA	New York
May 22	Oscar De La Hoya	Oba Carr	TKO 11	WBC	Las Vegas
May 29	Felix Trinidad	Hugo Pineda	KO 4	IBF	San Juan, PR
July 24	James Page	Freddie Pendleton	TKO 11	WBA	Las Vegas
Sept 18	Felix Trinidad	Oscar De La Hoya	Dec 12	IBF/WBC	Las Vegas

Junior Welterweight (Super Lightweight)

Date	Winner	Loser	Result	Title	Site
Oct 10	Sharmba Mitchell	Khalid Rahilou	Dec 12	WBA	Paris
Nov 28	Kostya Tszyu	Diobelys Hurtado	TKO 5	WBC	Indio, CA
Jan 16	Zabdiel Judah	Wilfredo Negron	KO 4	interim IBF	Las Vegas
Feb 6	Sharmba Mitchell	Pedro Saiz	Dec 12	WBA	Washington, DC
Feb 20	Terronn Millett	Vincent Phillips	TKO 5	IBF	New York
Apr 24	Sharmba Mitchell	Reggie Green	Dec 12	WBA	Washington, DC
July 24	Terronn Millett	Virgil McClendon	TKO 12	IBF	Las Vegas
Aug 21	Kostya Tszyu	Miguel A. Gonzalez	TKO 10	WBC	Miami

Lightweight

Date	Winner	Loser	Result	Title	Site
Sept 22	Shane Mosley	Eduardo Morales	TKO 5	IBF	New York
Oct 30	Cesar Bazan	Mauro Lucero	Dec 12	WBC	Chihuahua, Mexico
Nov 14	Shane Mosley	Jesse James Leija	TKO 9	IBF	Mashantucket, CT
Jan 9	Shane Mosley	Golden Johnson	KO 7	IBF	Pensacola, FL
Jan 25	Jean-Baptiste Mendy	Alberto Sicurella	Dec 12	WBA	Paris
Feb 27	Steve Johnston	Cesar Bazan	Split 12	WBC	Miami
Apr 10	Julien Lorcy	Jean-Baptiste Mendy	TKO 6	WBA	Paris-Bercy, France
Apr 17	Shane Mosley	John Brown	TKO 8	IBF	Indio, CA
June 26	Steve Johnston	Aldo Rios	Dec 12	WBC	Las Vegas
Aug 7	Stefano Zoff	Julien Lorcy	Split 12	WBA	Le Cannet, France
Aug 14	Steve Johnston	Angel Manfredy	Dec 12	WBC	Ledyard, CT
Aug 20	Paul Spadafora	Israel Cardona	Dec 12	IBF	Chester, WV

Junior Lightweight (Super Featherweight)

Date	Winner	Loser	Result	Title	Site
Oct 3	Floyd Mayweather	Genaro Hernandez	TKO 8	WBC	Las Vegas
Oct 24	Roberto Garcia	Ramon Ledon	TKO 5	IBF	Atlantic City
Jan 16	Roberto Garcia	Juan Molina	Dec 12	IBF	Las Vegas
Feb 13	Takanori Hatakeyama	Saul Duran	Split Draw	WBA	Tokyo
Feb 17	Floyd Mayweather	Carlos Rios	Dec 12	WBC	Grand Rapids, MI
Feb 20	Antonio Hernandez	Justin Juuko	TKO 11	interim WBA	Ft. Worth, TX
May 22	Floyd Mayweather	Justin Juuko	KO 9	WBC	Las Vegas
June 19	Joel Casamayor	Antonio Hernandez	Dec 12	interim WBA	Miami
June 27	Lakva Sim	Takanori Hatekeyama	TKO 5	WBA	Tokyo
Sept 11	Floyd Mayweather	Carlos Gerena	TKO 7	WBC	Las Vegas

Featherweight

Date	Winner	Loser	Result	Title	Site
Oct 3	Antonio Cermeno	Genaro Rios	KO 4	WBA	Caracas, Venezuela
Nov 28	Luisito Espinosa	Kennedy McKinney	TKO 2	WBC	Indio, CA
Feb 5	Antonio Cermeno	Eddy Saenz	KO 2	WBA	Miami
Apr 16	Manuel Medina	Victor Polo	T-Dec 9	IBF	Las Vegas
May 15	Cesar Soto	Luisito Espinosa	Dec 12	WBC	El Paso, TX
May 29	Freddy Norwood	Antonio Cermeno	Split 12	WBA	San Juan, PR
Sept 11	Freddy Norwood	Juan Manuel Marquez	Dec 12	WBA	Las Vegas

Junior Featherweight (Super Bantamweight)

Date	Winner	Loser	Result	Title	Site
Oct 3	Carlos Barreto	Hector Acero-Sanchez	Dec 12	interim WBA	Caracas, Venezuela
Oct 31	Vuyani Bungu	Danny Romero	Dec 12	IBF	Atlantic City
Dec 12	Nestor Garza	Enrique Sanchez	Dec 12	WBA	Indio, CA
Feb 6	Vuyani Bungu	Victor Llerena	TKO 7	IBF	Hammanskraal, S. Africa
Feb 13	Erik Morales	Angel Chacon	KO 2	WBC	Las Vegas
May 8	Erik Morales	Juan Carlos Ramirez	TKO 9	WBC	Las Vegas
May 8	Nestor Garza	Carlos Barreto	TKO 8	WBA	Las Vegas
May 29	Lehlohonolo Ledwaba	John Johnson	Dec 12	IBF	Hammanskraal, S. Africa
July 31	Erik Morales	Reynante Jamile	TKO 6	WBC	Tijuana, Mexico
Sept 25	Lehlohonolo Ledwaba	Edison Valencia	TKO 5	IBF	Temecula, CA

Bantamweight

Date	Winner	Loser	Result	Title	Site
Dec 5	Johnny Tapia	Nana Yaw Konadu	Dec 12	WBA	Atlantic City
Dec 29	Veerapol Sahaprom	Joichiro Tatsuyoshi	KO 6	WBC	Osaka, Japan
Mar 27	Tim Austin	Sergio Aguila	KO 9	IBF	Miami
May 21	Veerapol Sahaprom	Mauro Blanc	TKO 5	WBC	Saraburi, Thailand
June 26	Paulie Ayala	Johnny Tapia	Dec 12	WBA	Las Vegas
Aug 29	Veerapol Sahaprom	Joichiro Tatsuyoshi	TKO 7	WBC	Osaka, Japan

Junior Bantamweight (Super Flyweight)

Date	Winner	Loser	Result	Title	Site
Dec 23	Jesus Rojas	Satoshi Iida	Dec 12	WBA	Nagoya, Japan
Jan 10	Cho In-Joo	Joel Luna Zarate	Dec 12	WBC	Seoul
Mar 28	Jesus Rojas	Hideki Todaka	T-Draw 4	WBA	Miyazaki, Japan
Apr 24	Mark Johnson	Ratanachai S. Voraphin	Dec 12	IBF	Washington, DC
May 29	Leo Gamez	Josue Camacho	TKO 8	interim WBA	San Juan, PR
June 13	Cho In-Joo	Pone Saengmorakot	KO 8	WBC	Seoul
July 31	Hideki Todaka	Jesus Rojas	Dec 12	WBA	Nahoya, Japan
Aug 13	Mark Johnson	Jorge Lacierva	T-Dec 9	IBF	Ledyard, CT
Sept 5	Cho In-Joo	Keiji Yamaguchi	Dec 12	WBC	Tokyo

Flyweight

Date	Winner	Loser	Result	Title	Site
Oct 3	Mauricio Pastrana	Jose Bonilla	Dec 12	interim WBA	Caracas, Venezuela
Dec 4	Manny Pacquiao	Chatchai Sasakul	KO 8	WBC	Phuttamonthon, Thailand
Mar 13	Leo Gamez	Hugo Soto	KO 3	WBA	New York
Apr 10	Irene Pacheco	Luis Cox	KO 9	IBF	Barranquilla, Columbia
Apr 24	Manny Pacquiao	Gabriel Mira	TKO 4	WBC	Quezon City, Phillipines
Sept 3	Sornpichai Pisnurachan	Leo Gamez	KO 8	WBA	Mukdahan, Thailand
Sept 17	Medgoen 3K-Battery	Manny Pacquiao	KO 3	WBC	Nakron Si Thammarat, Phillipines

Junior Flyweight

Date	Winner	Loser	Result	Title	Site
Oct 17	Phichit Chor Siriwat	Lee Tae-Kil	TKO 8	WBA	Bangkok
Nov 26	Saman Sorjaturong	Ladislao Vazquez	Dec 12	WBC	Pathum Thani, Thailand
Dec 18	Will Grigsby	Ratanapol S. Voraphin	Dec 12	IBF	Ft. Lauderdale, FL
Feb 20	Phichit Chor Siriwat	Joma Gamboa	Dec 12	WBA	Koh Samui, Thailand
Mar 6	Will Grigsby	Carmelo Caceres	Dec 12	IBF	Minneapolis, MN
Oct 2	Ricardo Lopez	Will Grigsby	Dec 12	IBF	Las Vegas

Strawweight (Mini Flyweight)

Date	Winner	Loser	Result	Title	Site
Nov 13	Ricardo Lopez	Rosendo Alvarez	Split 12	WBA	Las Vegas
Jan 30	Songkram Porpaoin	Ronnie Magramo	T-Dec 9	interim WBA	Pattaya, Thailand
May 4	Wandee Singwancha	Yasuo Tokimitsu	TKO 12	interim WBC	Kurashiki, Japan
May 29	Zolani Petelo	Eric Jamili	KO 1	IBF	Hammanskraal, S. Africa

The Judge Couldn't See

Jean Williams has a clear conscience. Williams, the judge who blew the March 1999 Holyfield-Lewis fight—and became known to sports fans by her full name, Eugenia, as well as nastier terms—conceded that Lennox Lewis won the pivotal fifth round, but said her view was obstructed. "I called what I saw," Williams said.

A $39,200-a-year clerk in Atlantic City's landlord-tenant relations office, Williams said she earned $5,100 for her night at the fights. She was amazed that by calling the fight 115–113 for Evander Holyfield she spurred a New York grand jury investigation and a state senate hearing into the bout. All the fuss was not only "very hurtful," she said, but nonsensical, too. Williams, 48, filed for bankruptcy in January, citing $33,000 in credit card debt, and says she'd never call attention to herself by fixing the prizefight of the year. "My office has been under the gun numerous times," she told SI, referring to city hall probes of the landlord-tenant office. "I'm not going to do anything illegal knowing they're watching me like a hawk."

In the aftermath of the bout she was pestered by strangers and by 4 a.m. calls from reporters. "You never know who's outside the door," said Williams, who hoped to be just Jean again soon. As for the bout that made her infamous, she sees Holyfield-Lewis more as a failure of fighters than of judges: "I've seen both of them box before, and I've seen them apply themselves more."

World Champions

Sanctioning bodies: the National Boxing Association (NBA), the New York State Athletic Commission (NY), the World Boxing Association (WBA), the World Boxing Council (WBC), and the International Boxing Federation (IBF).

Heavyweights
(Weight: Unlimited)

Champion	Reign	Champion	Reign	Champion	Reign
John L. Sullivan	1885–92	Sonny Liston	1962–64	Tim Witherspoon* WBA	1986
James J. Corbett	1892–97	Muhammad Ali	1964–70	Trevor Berbick* WBC	1986
Bob Fitzsimmons	1897–99	Ernie Terrell* WBA	1965–67	Mike Tyson* WBC	1986–87
James J. Jeffries	1899–1905†	Joe Frazier* NY	1968–70	James Bonecrusher	
Marvin Hart	1905–06	Jimmy Ellis* WBA	1968–70	Smith* WBA	1986–87
Tommy Burns	1906–08	Joe Frazier	1970–73	Tony Tucker* IBF	1987
Jack Johnson	1908–15	George Foreman	1973–74	Mike Tyson	1987–90
Jess Willard	1915–19	Muhammad Ali	1974–78	Buster Douglas	1990
Jack Dempsey	1919–26	Leon Spinks	1978	Evander Holyfield	1990–92
Gene Tunney	1926–28	Ken Norton* WBC	1978	Lennox Lewis* WBC	1993–95
Max Schmeling	1930–32	Larry Holmes* WBC	1978–80	Riddick Bowe	1992–93
Jack Sharkey	1932–33	Muhammad Ali	1978–79†	Evander Holyfield	1993–94
Primo Carnera	1933–34	John Tate* WBA	1979–80	Michael Moorer	1994
Max Baer	1934–35	Mike Weaver* WBA	1980–82	George Foreman	1994–95
James J. Braddock	1935–37	Larry Holmes	1980–85	Oliver McCall* WBC	1995
Joe Louis	1937–49†	Michael Dokes* WBA	1982–83	Frank Bruno* WBC	1995–96
Ezzard Charles	1949–51	Gerrie Coetzee* WBA	1983–84	Bruce Seldon* WBA	1995–96
Jersey Joe Walcott	1951–52	Tim Witherspoon* WBC	1984	Mike Tyson WBA	1996
Rocky Marciano	1952–56†	Pinklon Thomas* WBC	1984–86	Michael Moorer* IBF	1996–97
Ingemar Johansson	1959–60	Greg Page* WBA	1984–85	Lennox Lewis* WBC	1997–
Floyd Patterson	1960–62	Michael Spinks	1985–87	E. Holyfield WBA, IBF	1996–

Cruiserweights
(Weight Limit: 190 pounds)

Champion	Reign	Champion	Reign	Champion	Reign
Marvin Camel* WBC	1980	Ricky Parkey* IBF	1986–87	Alfred Cole* IBF	1992–96
Carlos De Leon* WBC	1980–82	E. Holyfield* WBA/IBF	1987–88	Orlin Norris* WBA	1993–95
Ossie Ocasio* WBA	1982–84	Evander Holyfield	1988†	Nate Miller* WBA	1995–97
S.T. Gordon* WBC	1982–83	Toufik Belbouli* WBA	1989	Marcelo	
Carlos De Leon* WBC	1983–85	Robert Daniels* WBA	1989–91	Dominguez* WBC	1996–98
Marvin Camel* IBF	1983–84	Carlos De Leon* WBC	1989–90	A. Washington* IBF	1996–97
Lee Roy Murphy* IBF	1984–86	Glenn McCrory* IBF	1989–90	Uriah Grant* IBF	1997
Piet Crous* WBA	1984–85	Jeff Lampkin* IBF	1990	Imamu Mayfield* IBF	1997–98
Alfonso Ratliff* WBC	1985	M. Duran* WBC	1990–91	Fabrice Tiozzo* WBA	1997–
Dwight Braxton* WBA	1985–86	Bobby Czyz* WBA	1991–92†	J.C. Gomez* WBC	1998–
Bernard Benton* WBC	1985–86	Anaclet Wamba* WBC	1991–95	Arthur Williams* IBF	1998–99
Carlos De Leon* WBC	1986–88	James Pritchard* IBF	1991	Vassily Jirov* IBF	1999–
Evander Holyfield* WBA	1986–88	James Warring* IBF	1991–92		

Note: Division called Junior Heavyweight by the WBA.

Light Heavyweights
(Weight Limit: 175 pounds)

Champion	Reign	Champion	Reign	Champion	Reign
Jack Root	1903	Maxie Rosenbloom	1930–34	Willie Pastrano	1963–65
George Gardner	1903	George Nichols* NBA	1932	Jose Torres	1965–66
Bob Fitzsimmons	1903–05	Bob Godwin* NBA	1933	Dick Tiger	1966–68
Philadelphia Jack		Bob Olin	1934–35	Bob Foster	1968–74†
O'Brien	1905–12†	John Henry Lewis	1935–38	Vicente Rondon* WBA	1971–72
Jack Dillon	1914–16	Melio Bettina	1939	John Conteh* WBC	1974–77
Battling Levinsky	1916–20	Billy Conn	1939–40†	Victor Galindez* WBA	1974–78
Georges Carpentier	1920–22	Anton Christoforidis	1941	Miguel A. Cuello* WBC	1977–78
Battling Siki	1922–23	Gus Lesnevich	1941–48	Mate Parlov* WBC	1978
Mike McTigue	1923–25	Freddie Mills	1948–50	Mike Rossman* WBA	1978–79
Paul Berlenbach	1925–26	Joey Maxim	1950–52	Marvin Johnson* WBC	1978–79
Jack Delaney	1926–27†	Archie Moore	1952–62†	Matthew Saad	
Jimmy Slattery* NBA	1927	Harold Johnson* NBA	1961	Muhammad* WBC	1979–81
Tommy Loughran	1927–29	Harold Johnson	1962–63	Marvin Johnson* WBA	1979–80

*Champion not generally recognized. †Champion retired or relinquished title.

Light Heavyweights *(Cont.)*

Champion	Reign	Champion	Reign	Champion	Reign
Eddie Mustapha Muhammad* WBA	1980–81	Leslie Stewart* WBA	1987	Iran Barkley* WBA	1992
Michael Spinks* WBA	1981–83	Virgil Hill* WBA	1987	Virgil Hill* WBA	1992–97
D. Muhammad		Pr Charles Williams* IBF	1987–93	Henry Maske* IBF	1993–96
Qawi* WBC	1981–83	Thomas Hearns* WBC	1987†	Mike McCallum* WBC	1994–95
Michael Spinks	1983–85†	Donny Lalonde* WBC	1987–88	Fabrice Tiozzo* WBC	1995–96
J. B. Williamson* WBC	1985–86	Sugar Ray Leonard* WBC	1988	Roy Jones WBC/WBA	1997–
Slobodan Kacar* IBF	1985–86	Dennis Andries* WBC	1989	William Guthrie* IBF	1997–98
Marvin Johnson* WBA	1986–87	Jeff Harding* WBC	1989–90	Reggie Johnson* IBF	1998–99
Dennis Andries* WBC	1986–87	Dennis Andries* WBC	1990–91	Roy Jones Jr	1999–
Bobby Czyz* IBF	1986–87	Thomas Hearns* WBA	1991–92		
		Jeff Harding* WBC	1991–94		

Super Middleweights
(Weight Limit: 168 pounds)

Champion	Reign	Champion	Reign	Champion	Reign
Murray Sutherland* IBF	1984	Mauro Galvano* WBC	1990–92	Roy Jones Jr* IBF	1994–96
Chong-Pal Park* IBF	1984–87	Victor Cordova* WBA	1991	Thulane Malinga* WBC	1996
Chong-Pal Park* WBA	1987–88	Darrin Van Horn* IBF	1991–92	V. Nardiello* WBC	1996
G. Rocchigiani* IBF	1988–89	Iran Barkley *WBA	1992	Robin Reid* WBC	1996–97
F. Obelmejias* WBA	1988–89	Nigel Benn* WBC	1992–96	Charles Brewer* IBF	1997–98
Ray Leonard* WBC	1988–90†	James Toney* IBF	1992–94	Thulane Malinga* WBC	1997–98
In-Chul Baek* WBA	1989–90	Michael Nunn* WBA	1992–94	Richie Woodhall* WBC	1998–
Lindell Holmes* IBF	1990–91	Steve Little* WBA	1994	Sven Ottke* IBF	1998–
C. Tiozzo* WBA	1990–91	Frank Liles* WBA	1994–99	Byron Mitchell* WBA	1999–

Middleweights
(Weight Limit: 160 pounds)

Champion	Reign	Champion	Reign	Champion	Reign
Jack Dempsey	1884–91	Marcel Cerdan	1948–49	Alan Minter	1980
Bob Fitzsimmons	1891–97	Jake La Motta	1949–51	Marvin Hagler	1980–87
Kid McCoy	1897–98	Sugar Ray Robinson	1951	Sugar Ray Leonard	1987
Tommy Ryan	1898–1907	Randy Turpin	1951	Frank Tate* IBF	1987–88
Stanley Ketchel	1908	Sugar Ray Robinson	1951–52	Sumbu Kalambay* WBA	1987–89
Billy Papke	1908	Bobo Olson	1953–55	Thomas Hearns* WBC	1987–88
Stanley Ketchel	1908–10	Sugar Ray Robinson	1955–57	Iran Barkley* WBC	1988–89
Frank Klaus	1913	Gene Fullmer	1957	Michael Nunn* IBF	1988–91
George Chip	1913–14	Sugar Ray Robinson	1957	Roberto Duran* WBC	1989–90
Al McCoy	1914–17	Carmen Basilio	1957–58	Mike McCallum* WBA	1989–91
Mike O'Dowd	1917–20	Sugar Ray Robinson	1958–60	Julian Jackson* WBC	1990–93
Johnny Wilson	1920–23	Gene Fullmer* NBA	1959–62	James Toney* IBF	1991–93
Harry Greb	1923–26	Paul Pender	1960–61	Reggie Johnson* WBA	1992–94
Tiger Flowers	1926	Terry Downes	1961–62	Roy Jones* IBF	1993–95†
Mickey Walker	1926–31†	Paul Pender	1962–63	G. McClellan* WBC	1993–95†
Gorilla Jones	1931–32	Dick Tiger* WBA	1962–63	Jorge Castro* WBA	1994–95
Marcel Thil	1932–37	Dick Tiger	1963	Shinji Takehara* WBA	1995–96
Fred Apostoli	1937–39	Joey Giardello	1963–65	Jullian Jackson* WBC	1995
Al Hostak* NBA	1938	Dick Tiger	1965–66	Quincy Taylor* WBC	1995–96
Solly Krieger* NBA	1938–39	Emile Griffith	1966–67	Bernard Hopkins* IBF	1995–
Al Hostak* NBA	1939–40	Nino Benvenuti	1967	Keith Holmes* WBC	1996–98
Ceferino Garcia	1939–40	Emile Griffith	1967–68	William Joppy Jr* WBA	1996–97
Ken Overlin	1940–41	Nino Benvenuti	1968–70	J.C. Green* WBA	1997
Tony Zale* NBA	1940–41	Carlos Monzon	1970–77†	William Joppy Jr.* WBA	1998–
Billy Soose	1941	Rodrigo Valdez* WBC	1974–76	Hassine Cherifi* WBC	1998–99
Tony Zale	1941–47	Rodrigo Valdez	1977–78	Keith Holmes* WBC	1999–
Rocky Graziano	1947–48	Hugo Corro	1978–79		
Tony Zale	1948	Vito Antuofermo	1979–80		

Junior Middleweights
(Weight Limit: 154 pounds)

Champion	Reign	Champion	Reign	Champion	Reign
Emile Griffith (EBU)	1962–63	Sandro Mazzinghi	1968	Miguel de Oliveira* WBC	1975–76
Dennis Moyer	1962–63	Freddie Little	1969–70	Jae-Do Yuh	1975–76
Ralph Dupas	1963	Carmelo Bossi	1970–71	Elisha Obed* WBC	1975–76
Sandro Mazzinghi	1963–65	Koichi Wajima	1971–74	Koichi Wajima	1976
Nino Benvenuti	1965–66	Oscar Albarado	1974–75	Jose Duran	1976
Ki-Soo Kim	1966–68	Koichi Wajima	1975	Eckhard Dagge* WBC	1976–77

*Champion not generally recognized. †Champion retired or relinquished title.

Junior Middleweights (Cont.)

Champion	Reign	Champion	Reign	Champion	Reign
Miguel Angel Castellini	1976–77	Buster Drayton* IBF	1986–87	Simon Brown* WBC	1994
Eddie Gazo	1977–78	Duane Thomas* WBC	1986–87	Terry Norris *WBC	1994–97
Rocky Mattioli* WBC	1977–79	Matthew Hilton* IBF	1987–88	Vincent Pettway* IBF	1994–95
Masashi Kudo	1978–79	Lupe Aquino* WBC	1987	Paul Vaden* IBF	1995
Maurice Hope* WBC	1979–81	Gianfranco Rosi* WBC	1987–88	Carl Daniels* WBA	1995
Ayub Kalule	1979–81	Julian Jackson* WBA	1987–90	Terry Norris WBC	1995–97
Wilfred Benitez* WBC	1981–82	Donald Curry* WBC	1988–89	Terry Norris IBF	1995–96
Sugar Ray Leonard	1981–82	Robert Hines* IBF	1988–89	L. Boudouani* WBA	1996–99
Tadashi Mihara* WBA	1981–82	Darrin Van Horn* IBF	1989	Raul Marquez* IBF	1997
Davey Moore* WBA	1982–83	Rene Jacquot* WBC	1989	Keith Mullings* WBC	1997–99
Thomas Hearns* WBC	1982–84	John Mugabi* WBC	1989–90	Yori Boy Campas* IBF	1997–98
Roberto Duran* WBA	1983–84	Gianfranco Rosi* IBF	1989–94	Fernando Vargas* IBF	1998–
Mark Medal* IBF	1984	Terry Norris* WBC	1990–94	F. Javier Castillejo* WBC	1999–
Thomas Hearns	1984–86	Gilbert Dele* WBA	1991	David Reid* WBA	1999–
Mike McCallum* WBA	1984–87	Vinny Pazienza* WBA	1991–92		
Carlos Santos* IBF	1984–86	Julio C. Vasquez* WBA	1992–95		

Note: Division called Super Welterweight by the WBC.

Welterweights
(Weight Limit: 147 pounds)

Champion	Reign	Champion	Reign	Champion	Reign
Paddy Duffy	1888–90	Jimmy McLarnin	1933–34	Pipino Cuevas* WBA	1976–80
Mysterious Billy Smith	1892–94	Barney Ross	1934	Wilfredo Benitez	1979
Tommy Ryan	1894–98	Jimmy McLarnin	1934–35	Sugar Ray Leonard	1979–80
Mysterious Billy Smith	1898–1900	Barney Ross	1935–38	Roberto Duran	1980
Rube Ferns	1900	Henry Armstrong	1938–40	Thomas Hearns* WBA	1980–81
Matty Matthews	1900–01	Fritzie Zivic	1940–41	Sugar Ray Leonard	1980–82
Rube Ferns	1901	Red Cochrane	1941–46	Donald Curry* WBA	1983–85
Joe Walcott	1901–04	Marty Servo	1946	Milton McCrory* WBC	1983–85
The Dixie Kid	1904–05	Sugar Ray Robinson	1946–51†	Donald Curry	1985–86
Honey Mellody	1906–07	Johnny Bratton	1951	Lloyd Honeyghan	1986–87
Twin Sullivan	1907–08	Kid Gavilan	1951–54	Jorge Vaca WBC	1987–88
Jimmy Gardner	1908	Johnny Saxton	1954–55	Lloyd Honeyghan WBC	1988–89
Jimmy Clabby	1910–11	Tony DeMarco	1955	Mark Breland* WBA	1987
Waldemar Holberg	1914	Carmen Basilio	1955–56	Marlon Starling* WBA	1987–88
Tom McCormick	1914	Johnny Saxton	1956	Tomas Molinares* WBA	1988–89
Matt Wells	1914–15	Carmen Basilio	1956–57	Simon Brown* IBF	1988–91
Mike Glover	1915	Virgil Akins	1958	Mark Breland* WBA	1989–90
Jack Britton	1915	Don Jordan	1958–60	Marlon Starling* WBC	1989–90
Ted "Kid" Lewis	1915–16	Kid Paret	1960–61	Aaron Davis* WBA	1990–91
Jack Britton	1916–17	Emile Griffith	1961	Maurice Blocker* WBC	1990–91
Ted "Kid" Lewis	1917–19	Kid Paret	1961–62	Meldrick Taylor* WBA	1991–92
Jack Britton	1919–22	Emile Griffith	1962–63	Simon Brown* WBC	1991
Mickey Walker	1922–26	Luis Rodriguez	1963	Buddy McGirt* WBC	1991–93
Pete Latzo	1926–27	Emile Griffith	1963–66	Felix Trinidad* IBF	1993–
Joe Dundee	1927–29	Curtis Cokes	1966–69	Pernell Whitaker WBC	1993–97
Jackie Fields	1929–30	Jose Napoles	1969–70	Crisanto Espana* WBA	1992–94
Young Jack Thompson	1930	Billy Backus	1970–71	Ike Quartey* WBA	1994–97†
Tommy Freeman	1930–31	Jose Napoles	1971–75	Oscar De La Hoya* WBC	1997–99
Young Jack Thompson	1931	Hedgemon Lewis* NY	1972–73	James Page* WBA	1998–
Lou Brouillard	1931–32	Angel Espada* WBA	1975–76	Felix Trinidad IBF, WBC	1999–
Jackie Fields	1932–33	John H. Stracey	1975–76		
Young Corbett III	1933	Carlos Palomino	1976–79		

Junior Welterweights
(Weight Limit: 140 pounds)

Champion	Reign	Champion	Reign	Champion	Reign
Pinkey Mitchell	1922–25	Battling Shaw	1933	Duilio Loi	1962–63
Red Herring	1925	Tony Canzoneri	1933	Roberto Cruz* WBA	1963
Mushy Callahan	1926–30	Barney Ross	1933–35	Eddie Perkins	1963–65
Jack (Kid) Berg	1930–31	Tippy Larkin	1946	Carlos Hernandez	1965–66
Tony Canzoneri	1931–32	Carlos Ortiz	1959–60	Sandro Lopopolo	1966–67
Johnny Jadick	1932–33	Duilio Loi	1960–62	Paul Fujii	1967–68
Sammy Fuller*	1932–33	Eddie Perkins	1962	Nicolino Loche	1968–72

*Champion not generally recognized. †Champion retired or relinquished title.

Junior Welterweights *(Cont.)*

Champion	Reign
Pedro Adigue* WBC	1968–70
Bruno Arcari* WBC	1970–74
Alfonso Frazer	1972
Antonio Cervantes	1972–76
Perico Fernandez* WBC	1974–75
S. Muangsurin* WBC	1975–76
Wilfred Benitez	1976–79
M. Velasquez* WBC	1976
S. Muangsurin* WBC	1976–78
A. Cervantes* WBA	1977–80
Sang-Hyun Kim* WBC	1978–80
Saoul Mamby* WBC	1980–82
Aaron Pryor* WBA	1980–83
Leroy Haley* WBC	1982–83
Aaron Pryor* IBF	1983–85
Bruce Curry* WBC	1983–84
Johnny Bumphus* WBA	1984
Bill Costello* WBC	1984–85
Gene Hatcher* WBA	1984–85

Champion	Reign
Ubaldo Sacco* WBA	1985–86
Lonnie Smith* WBC	1985–86
Patrizio Oliva* WBA	1986–87
Gary Hinton* IBF	1986
Rene Arredondo* WBC	1986
Tsuyoshi Hamada* WBC	1986–87
Joe Louis Manley* IBF	1986–87
Terry Marsh* IBF	1987
Juan Coggi* WBA	1987–90
Rene Arredondo* WBC	1987
R. Mayweather* WBC	1987–89
James McGirt* IBF	1988
Meldrick Taylor* IBF	1988–90
Julio César Chávez* WBC	1989–94
Julio César Chávez* IBF	1990–91
Loreto Garza* WBA	1990–91
Juan Coggi* WBA	1991
Edwin Rosario* WBA	1991–92
Rafael Pineda* IBF	1991–92

Champion	Reign
Akinobu Hiranaka* WBA	1992
Pernell Whitaker*† IBF	1992–93
Charles Murray* IBF	1993–94
Jake Rodriguez* IBF	1994–95
Juan Coggi* WBA	1993–94
Frankie Randall* WBC	1994
Frankie Randall* WBA	1994–96
Juan Coggi* WBA	1996
Julio César Chávez WBC	1994–96
Kostya Tszyu* IBF	1995–97
Frankie Randall* WBA	1996–97
Oscar De La Hoya WBC	1996–97†
Khalid Rahilou* WBA	1997–98
Vincent Phillips* IBF	1997–99
Sharmba Mitchell* WBA	1998–
Kostya Tszyu* WBC	1998–
Terronn Millett* IBF	1999–

Lightweights
(Weight Limit: 135 pounds)

Champion	Reign
Jack McAuliffe	1886–94
Kid Lavigne	1896–99
Frank Erne	1899–1902
Joe Gans	1902–04
Jimmy Britt	1904–05
Battling Nelson	1905–06
Joe Gans	1906–08
Battling Nelson	1908–10
Ad Wolgast	1910–12
Willie Ritchie	1912–14
Freddie Welsh	1915–17
Benny Leonard	1917–25†
Jimmy Goodrich	1925
Rocky Kansas	1925–26
Sammy Mandell	1926–30
Al Singer	1930
Tony Canzoneri	1930–33
Barney Ross	1933–35†
Tony Canzoneri	1935–36
Lou Ambers	1936–38
Henry Armstrong	1938–39
Lou Ambers	1939–40
Sammy Angott* NBA	1940–41
Lew Jenkins	1940–41
Sammy Angott	1941–42†
Beau Jack* NY	1942–43
Bob Montgomery* NY	1943
Sammy Angott* NBA	1943–44
Beau Jack* NY	1943–44
Bob Montgomery* NY	1944–47
Juan Zurita* NBA	1944–45
Ike Williams	1947–51
James Carter	1951–52

Champion	Reign
Lauro Salas	1952
James Carter	1952–54
Paddy DeMarco	1954
James Carter	1954–55
Wallace Smith	1955–56
Joe Brown	1956–62
Carlos Ortiz	1962–65
Ismael Laguna	1965
Carlos Ortiz	1965–68
Carlos Teo Cruz	1968–69
Mando Ramos	1969–70
Ismael Laguna	1970
Ken Buchanan	1970–72
Roberto Duran	1972–79†
Chango Carmona* WBC	1972
Rodolfo Gonzalez* WBC	1972–74
Ishimatsu Suzuki* WBC	1974–76
Estaban DeJesus* WBC	1976–78
Jim Watt* WBC	1979–81
Ernesto Espana* WBA	1979–80
Hilmer Kenty* WBA	1980–81
Sean O'Grady* WBA	1981
Claude Noel* WBA	1981
Alexis Arguello* WBC	1981–82
Arturo Frias* WBA	1981–82
Ray Mancini* WBA	1982–84
Alexis Arguello	1982–83
Edwin Rosario* WBC	1983–84
Choo Choo Brown* IBF	1984
L. Bramble* WBA	1984–86
Jose Luis Ramirez* WBC	1984–85
Harry Arroyo* IBF	1984–85
Jimmy Paul* IBF	1985–86

Champion	Reign
Hector Camacho* WBC	1985–86
Greg Haugen* IBF	1986–87
Edwin Rosario* WBA	1986–87
Julio César Chávez* WBA	1987–88
Jose Luis Ramirez* WBC	1987–88
Julio César Chávez	1988–89
Vinny Pazienza* IBF	1987–88
Greg Haugen* IBF	1988–89
P. Whitaker* WBC, IBF	1989–90
Edwin Rosario* WBA	1989–90
Juan Nazario* WBA	1990
P. Whitaker* WBA, WBC	1990–92
Pernell Whitaker* IBF	1991–92
Julio César Chávez* IBF	1990–91
Edwin Rosario* WBA	1991–92
Julio César Chávez* WBC	1990–92
Miguel Gonzalez* WBC	1992–95
Joey Gamache* WBA	1992–93
Dingaan Thobela* WBA	1993
Fred Pendleton* IBF	1993–94
Orzubek Nazarov* WBA	1993–98
Rafael Ruelas* IBF	1994–95
Phillip Holiday* IBF	1995–97
Jean B. Mendy* WBC	1996–97
Steve Johnston* WBC	1997–98
Shane Mosley* IBF	1997–99†
Jean B. Mendy* WBA	1998–99
Cesar Bazan* WBC	1998–99
Steve Johnston* WBC	1999–
Julien Lorcy* WBA	1999
Stefano Zoff* WBA	1999–
Paul Spadafora* IBF	1999–

*Champion not generally recognized. †Champion retired or relinquished title.

Junior Lightweights
(Weight Limit: 130 pounds)

Champion	Reign
Johnny Dundee	1921–23
Jack Bernstein	1923
Johnny Dundee	1923–24
Steve (Kid) Sullivan	1924–25
Mike Ballerino	1925
Tod Morgan	1925–29
Benny Bass	1929–31
Kid Chocolate	1931–33
Frankie Klick	1933–34
Sandy Saddler	1949–50
Harold Gomes	1959–60
Gabriel (Flash) Elorde	1960–67
Yoshiaki Numata	1967
Hiroshi Kobayashi	1967–71
Rene Barrientos* WBC	1969–70
Yoshiaki Numata* WBC	1970–71
Alfredo Marcano	1971–72
R. Arredondo* WBC	1971–74
Ben Villaflor	1972–73
Kuniaki Shibata	1973
Ben Villaflor	1973–76

Champion	Reign
Kuniaki Shibata* WBC	1974–75
Alfredo Escalera* WBC	1975–78
Samuel Serrano	1976–80
Alexis Arguello* WBC	1978–80
Yasutsune Uehara	1980–81
Rafael Limon* WBC	1980–81
C. Boza-Edwards* WBC	1981
Samuel Serrano	1981–83
R. Navarrete* WBC	1981–82
Rafael Limon* WBC	1982
Bobby Chacon* WBC	1982–83
Roger Mayweather	1983–84
Hector Camacho* WBC	1983–84
Rocky Lockridge	1984–85
Hwan-Kil Yuh* IBF	1984–85
Julio César Chávez* WBC	1984–87
Lester Ellis* IBF	1985
Wilfredo Gomez	1985–86
Barry Michael* IBF	1985–87
Alfredo Layne* WBA	1986
Brian Mitchell* WBA	1986–91

Champion	Reign
Rocky Lockridge* IBF	1987–88
Azumah Nelson* WBC	1988–94
Tony Lopez* IBF	1988–89
Juan Molina* IBF	1989–90
Tony Lopez* IBF	1990–91
Joey Gamache WBA	1991
Brian Mitchell* IBF	1991
Genaro Hernandez* WBA	1991–95
James Leija* WBC	1994
Juan Molina* IBF	1991–95
Gabriel Ruelas* WBC	1994–95
Eddie Hopson* IBF	1995
Tracy Patterson* IBF	1995
Azumah Nelson* WBC	1995–97
Choi Yong-Soo* WBA	1995–98
Arturo Gatti* IBF	1995–98†
Genaro Hernandez* WBC	1997–98
Roberto Garcia* IBF	1998–
Floyd Mayweather* WBC	1998–
T. Hatakeyama* WBA	1998–99
Lakva Sim* WBA	1999–

Featherweights
(Weight Limit: 126 pounds)

Champion	Reign
Torpedo Billy Murphy	1890
Young Griffo	1890–92
George Dixon	1892–97
Solly Smith	1897–98
Dave Sullivan	1898
George Dixon	1898–1900
Terry McGovern	1900–01
Young Corbett II	1901–04
Jimmy Britt	1904
Tommy Sullivan	1904–05
Abe Attell	1906–12
Johnny Kilbane	1912–23
Eugene Criqui	1923
Johnny Dundee	1923–24
"Kid" Kaplan	1925–26
Benny Bass	1927–28
Tony Canzoneri	1928
Andre Routis	1928–29
Battling Battalino	1929–32
Tommy Paul* NBA	1932–33
Kid Chocolate* NY	1932–33
Freddie Miller* NBA	1933–36
Mike Beloise* NY	1936–37
Petey Sarron* NBA	1936–37
Maurice Holtzer	1937–38
Henry Armstrong	1937–38
Joey Archibald* NY	1938–39
Leo Rodak* NBA	1938–39
Joey Archibald	1939–40
Petey Scalzo* NBA	1940–41
Harry Jeffra	1940–41
Joey Archibald	1941
Richie Lamos* NBA	1941

Champion	Reign
Chalky Wright	1941–42
Jackie Wilson* NBA	1941–43
Willie Pep	1942–48
Jackie Callura* NBA	1943
Phil Terranova* NBA	1943–44
Sal Bartolo* NBA	1944–46
Sandy Saddler	1948–49
Willie Pep	1949–50
Sandy Saddler	1950–57†
Kid Bassey	1957–59
Davey Moore	1959–63
Sugar Ramos	1963–64
Vicente Saldivar	1964–67†
Paul Rojas* WBA	1968
Jose Legra* WBC	1968–69
Shozo Saijyo* WBA	1968–71
J. Famechon* WBC	1969–70
Vicente Saldivar WBC	1970
Kuniaki Shibata WBC	1970–72
Antonio Gomez* WBA	1971–72
C. Sanchez WBC	1972
Ernesto Marcel* WBA	1972–74
Jose Legra WBC	1972–73
Eder Jofre WBC	1973–74
Ruben Olivares* WBA	1974
Bobby Chacon* WBC	1974–75
Alexis Arguello WBA	1974–76
Ruben Olivares* WBC	1975
Poison Kotey* WBC	1975–76
Danny Lopez WBC	1976–80
Rafael Ortega* WBA	1977
Cecilio Lastra* WBA	1977–78
Eusebio Pedroza* WBA	1978–85

Champion	Reign
S. Sanchez WBC	1980–82
Juan LaPorte* WBC	1982–84
Wilfredo Gomez* WBC	1984
Min-Keun Oh* IBF	1984–85
Azumah Nelson* WBC	1984–88
Barry McGuigan* WBA	1985–86
Ki Young Chung* IBF	1985–86
Steve Cruz* WBA	1986–87
Antonio Rivera* IBF	1986–88
A. Esparragoza* WBA	1987–91
Calvin Grove* IBF	1988
Jorge Paez* IBF	1988–91
Jeff Fenech* WBC	1988–90†
Marcos Villasana* WBC	1990–91
Paul Hodkinson* WBC	1991–93
Troy Dorsey* IBF	1991
Manuel Medina* IBF	1991–93
Yung Kyun Park* WBA	1991–93
Gregorio Vargas* WBC	1993
Tom Johnson* IBF	1993–97†
Eloy Rojas* WBA	1993–96
Kevin Kelley* WBC	1993–95
A. Gonzalez* WBC	1995
Manuel Medina* WBC	1995–95
Luisito Espinosa* WBC	1995–99
Wilfredo Vazquez* WBA	1996–98†
Hector Lizarraga* IBF	1997–98
Freddie Norwood* WBA	1998
Manuel Medina* IBF	1998–
Antonio Cermeno* WBA	1998–99
Cesar Soto* WBC	1999–
Freddie Norwood* WBA	1999–

Junior Featherweights
(Weight Limit: 122 pounds)

Champion	Reign
Jack (Kid) Wolfe*	1922–23
Carl Duane*	1923–24
Rigoberto Riasco* WBC	1976
Royal	
Kobayashi* WBC	1976
Dong-Kyun Yum* WBC	1976–77
Wilfredo Gomez* WBC	1977–83
Soo-Hwan Hong* WBA	1977–78
Ricardo Cardona* WBA	1978–80
Leo Randolph* WBA	1980
Sergio Palma* WBA	1980–82
Leonardo Cruz* WBA	1982–84
Jaime Garza* WBC	1983
Bobby Berna* IBF	1983–84
Loris Stecca* WBA	1984
Seung-Il Suh* IBF	1984–85
Victor Callejas* WBA	1984–86
Juan (Kid) Meza* WBC	1984–85

Champion	Reign
Ji-Won Kim* IBF	1985–86
Lupe Pintor* WBC	1985–86
Samart	
Payakaroon* WBC	1986–87
Seung-Hoon Lee* IBF	1987–88
Louie Espinoza* WBA	1987
Jeff Fenech* WBC	1987
Julio Gervacio* WBA	1987–88
Daniel Zaragoza* WBC	1988–90
Jose Sanabria* IBF	1988–89
Bernardo	
Pinango* WBA	1988
Juan Jose	
Estrada* WBA	1988–89
Fabrice Benichou* IBF	1989–90
Jesus Salud* WBA	1989–90
Welcome Ncita* IBF	1990–92
Paul Banke* WBC	1990

Champion	Reign
Luis Mendoza* WBA	1990–91
Rual Perez* WBA	1992
Pedro Decima* WBC	1990–91
K. Hatanaka* WBC	1991
Daniel Zaragoza* WBC	1991–92
Tracy Patterson* WBC	1992–94
Kennedy McKinney* IBF	1993–94
Wilfredo Vasquez* WBA	1992–95
Vuyani Bungu* IBF	1994–99†
H. Acero Sanchez* WBC	1994–95
Antonio Cermeno* WBA	1995–98†
Daniel Zaragoza* WBC	1995–97
Erik Morales* WBC	1997–
Enrique Sanchez* WBA	1998
Nestor Garza* WBA	1998–
L. Ledwaba* IBF	1999–

Bantamweights
(Weight Limit: 118 pounds)

Champion	Reign
Spider Kelly	1887
Hughey Boyle	1887–88
Spider Kelly	1889
Chappie Moran	1889–90
George Dixon	1890–91
Pedlar Palmer*	1895–99
Terry McGovern	1899–1900
Harry Harris	1901–02
Harry Forbes	1902–03
Frankie Neil	1903–04
Joe Bowker	1904–05
Jimmy Walsh	1905–06
Owen Moran	1907–08
Monte Attell*	1909–10
Frankie Conley	1910–11
Johnny Coulon	1911–14
Kid Williams	1914–17
Kewpie Ertle*	1915
Pete Herman	1917–20
Joe Lynch	1920–21
Pete Herman	1921
Johnny Buff	1921–22
Joe Lynch	1922–24
Abe Goldstein	1924
Cannonball Martin	1924–25
Phil Rosenberg	1925–27
Bud Taylor NBA	1927–28
Bushy Graham* NY	1928–29
Panama Al Brown	1929–35
Sixto Escobar* NBA	1934–35
Baltazar Sangchilli	1935–36
Lou Salica* NBA	1935
Sixto Escobar* NBA	1935–36
Tony Marino	1936
Sixto Escobar	1936–37
Harry Jeffra	1937–38†
Sixto Escobar	1938–39

Champion	Reign
Georgie Pace NBA	1939–40
Lou Salica	1940–42
Manuel Ortiz	1942–47
Harold Dade	1947
Manuel Ortiz	1947–50
Vic Toweel	1950–52
Jimmy Carruthers	1952–54†
Robert Cohen	1954–56
Paul Macias* NBA	1955–57
Mario D'Agata	1956–57
Alphonse Halimi	1957–59
Joe Becerra	1959–60†
Eder Jofre	1961–65
Fighting Harada	1965–68
Lionel Rose	1968–69
Ruben Olivares	1969–70
Chucho Castillo	1970–71
Ruben Olivares	1971–72
Rafael Herrera	1972
Enrique Pinder	1972–73
Romeo Anaya	1973
Rafael Herrera* WBC	1973–74
Soo-Hwan Hong	1974–75
Rodolfo Martinez* WBC	1974–76
Alfonso Zamora	1975–77
Carlos Zarate* WBC	1976–79
Jorge Lujan	1977–80
Lupe Pintor* WBC	1979–83
Julian Solis	1980
Jeff Chandler	1980–84
Albert Davila* WBC	1983–85
Richard Sandoval	1984–86
Satoshi Shingaki* IBF	1984–85
Jeff Fenech* IBF	1985
Daniel Zaragoza* WBC	1985
Miguel Lora* WBC	1985–88
Gaby Canizales	1986

Champion	Reign
Bernardo Pinango	1986–87
W. Vasquez* WBA	1987–88
Kevin Seabrooks* IBF	1987–88
Kaokor Galaxy* WBA	1988
Moon Sung-Kil* WBA	1988–89
Kaokor Galaxy* WBA	1989
Raul Perez* WBC	1988–91
O. Canizales* IBF	1988–95
Luisito Espinosa* WBA	1989–91
Israel Contreras* WBA	1991–92
Eddie Cook* WBA	1992–93
Greg Richardson* WBC	1991
J. Tatsuyoshi, WBC	1991–92
Victor Rabanales* WBC	1992–93
Jung-Il Byun* WBC	1993
Jorge Julio WBA	1993
Yasuei Yakushiji* WBC	1993–95
Junior Jones WBA*	1994
John M. Johnson* WBA	1994
D. Chuvatana*WBA	1994–95
V. Sahaprom* WBA	1995–96
W. McCullough* WBC	1995–96
Harold Mestre* IBF	1995
Mbulelo Botile* IBF	1995–97
Nana Yaw	
Konadu* WBA	1996–98
S. Singmanassak* WBC	1996–97
Tim Austin* IBF	1997–
J.Tatsuyoshi* WBC	1997–98
Johnny Tapia* WBA	1998–99
V. Sahaprom* WBC	1998–
Paulie Ayala* WBA	1999–

*Champion not generally recognized. †Champion retired or relinquished title.

Junior Bantamweights
(Weight Limit: 115 pounds)

Champion	Reign	Champion	Reign	Champion	Reign
Rafael Orono* WBC	1980–81	Santos Laciar* WBC	1987	Harold Grey* IBF	1994–95
Chul-Ho Kim* WBC	1981–82	Tae-Il Chang* IBF	1987	Alimi Goitia* WBA	1995–96
Gustavo Ballas* WBA	1981	Sugar Rojas* WBC	1987–88	Yokthai Sith-Oar* WBA	1996–97
Rafael Pedroza* WBA	1981–82	Ellyas Pical* IBF	1987–89	Carlos Salazar* IBF	1995–96
Jiro Watanabe* WBA	1982–84	Giberto Roman* WBC	1988–89	Harold Grey* IBF	1996
Rafael Orono* WBC	1982–83	Juan Polo Perez* IBF	1989–90	Danny Romero* IBF	1996–97
Payao Poontarat* WBC	1983–84	Nana Konadu* WBC	1989–90	Gerry Penalosa* WBC	1997–98
Joo-Do Chun* IBF	1983–85	Sung-Kil Moon* WBC	1990–93	Johnny Tapia* IBF	1997–99†
Jiro Watanabe	1984–86	Robert Quiroga* IBF	1990–93	Satoshi Iida* WBA	1997–98
Kaosai Galaxy* WBA	1984	Julio Borboa* IBF	1993–94	Cho In-Joo* WBC	1998–
Ellyas Pical* IBF	1985–86	Katsuya Onizuka* WBA	1993–94	Jesus Rojas* WBA	1998–99
Cesar Polanco* IBF	1986	Lee Hyung-Chul* WBA	1994–95	Mark Johnson* IBF	1999–
Gilberto Roman* WBC	1986–87	Jose Luis Bueno* WBC	1993–94	Hideki Todaka* WBA	1999–
Ellyas Pical* IBF	1986	Hiroshi Kawashima*WBC	1994–97		

Flyweights
(Weight Limit: 112 pounds)

Champion	Reign	Champion	Reign	Champion	Reign
Sid Smith	1913	B. Villacampo* WBA	1969–70	Hilario Zapate* WBA	1985–87
Bill Ladbury	1913–14	Chartchai Chionoi	1970	Chong-Kwan	
Percy Jones	1914	B. Chartvanchai* WBA	1970	Chung* IBF	1985–86
Joe Symonds	1914–16	Masao Ohba* WBA	1970–73	Bi-Won Chung* IBF	1986
Jimmy Wilde	1916–23	Erbito Salavarria	1970–73	Hi-Sup Shin* IBF	1986–87
Pancho Villa	1923–25	B. Gonzalez* WBA	1972	Dodie Penalosa* IBF	1987
Fidel LaBarba	1925–27†	V. Borkorsor* WBC	1972–73	Fidel Bassa* WBA	1987–89
Frenchy Belanger NBA	1927–28	Venice Borkorsor	1973	Choi-Chang Ho* IBF	1987–88
Izzy Schwartz NY	1927–29	Chartchai Chionoi* WBA	1973–74	Rolando Bohol* IBF	1988
Frankie Genaro NBA	1928–29	B. Gonzalez* WBA	1973–74	Yong-Kang Kim* WBC	1988–89
Spider Pladner NBA	1929	Shoji Oguma* WBC	1974–75	Duke McKenzie* IBF	1988–89
Frankie Genaro NBA	1929–31	S. Hanagata* WBA	1974–75	Sot Chitalada* WBC	1989–91
Midget Wolgast* NY	1930–35	Miguel Canto* WBC	1975–79	Dave McAuley* IBF	1989–92
Young Perez NBA	1931–32	Erbito Salavarria* WBA	1975–76	Jesus Rojas* WBA	1989–90
Jackie Brown NBA	1932–35	Alfonso Lopez* WBA	1976	Yul-Woo Lee* WBA	1990
Benny Lynch	1935–38	G. Espadas* WBA	1976–78	L. Tamakuma* WBA	1990–91
Small Montana* NY	1935–37	B. Gonzalez* WBA	1978–79	M. Kittikasem* WBC	1991–92
Peter Kane	1938–43	Chan-Hee Park* WBC	1979–80	Yuri Arbachakov* WBC	1992–97
Little Dado* NY	1938–40	Luis Ibarra* WBA	1979–80	Yong Kang Kim* WBA	1991–92
Jackie Paterson	1943–48	Tae-Shik Kim* WBA	1980	Rodolfo Blanco* IBF	1992–93
Rinty Monaghan	1948–50	Shoji Oguma* WBC	1980–81	P. Sithbangprachan* IBF	1993–95
Terry Allen	1950	Peter Mathebula* WBA	1980–81	David Griman* WBA	1992–94
Dado Marino	1950–52	Santos Laciar* WBA	1981	S.S. Ploenchit* WBA	1994–96
Yoshio Shirai	1953–54	Antonio Avelar* WBC	1981–82	Francisco Tejedor* IBF	1995
Pascual Perez	1954–60	Luis Ibarra* WBA	1981	Danny Romero* IBF	1995–96
Pone Kingpetch	1960–62	Juan Herrera* WBA	1981–82	Mark Johnson* IBF	1996–99†
Masahiko Harada	1962–63	P. Cardona* WBC	1982	Jose Bonilla* WBA	1996–98
Pone Kingpetch	1963	Santos Laciar* WBA	1982–85	Chatchai Sasakul* WBC	1997–98
Hiroyuki Ebihara	1963–64	Freddie Castillo* WBC	1982	Hugo Soto* WBA	1998–99
Pone Kingpetch	1964–65	E. Mercedes* WBC	1982–83	Manny Pacquiao* WBC	1998–99
Salvatore Burrini	1965–66	Charlie Magri* WBC	1983	Leo Gamez* WBA	1999
H. Accavallo* WBA	1966–68	Frank Cedeno* WBC	1983–84	Irene Pacheco* IBF	1999–
Walter McGowan	1966	Soon-Chun Kwon* IBF	1983–85	S. Pisnurachan* WBA	1999–
Chartchai Chionoi	1966–69	Koji Kobayashi* WBC	1984	M. 3K-Battery* WBC	1999–
Efren Torres	1969–70	Gabriel Bernal* WBC	1984		
Hiroyuki Ebihara* WBA	1969	Sot Chitalada* WBC	1984–88		

Junior Flyweights
(Weight Limit: 108 pounds)

Champion	Reign	Champion	Reign	Champion	Reign
Franco Udella* WBC	1975	Lupe Madera* WBA	1983–84	Hirokia Ioka* WBA	1991–92
Jaime Rios* WBA	1975–76	Dodie Penalosa* IBF	1983–86	Michael Carbajal, WBC	1993–94
Luis Estaba* WBC	1975–78	Francisco Quiroz* WBA	1984–85	Myung-Woo Yuh* WBA	1993
Juan Guzman* WBA	1976	Joey Olivo* WBA	1985	Leo Gamez* WBA	1993–95
Yoko Gushiken* WBA	1976–81	Myung-Woo Yuh* WBA	1985–91	H. Gonzalez* WBC, IBF	1994–95
Freddy Castillo* WBC	1978	Jum-Hwan Choi* IBF	1986–88	Choi Hi-Yong* WBA	1995–96
Netrnoi Vorasingh* WBC	1978	Tacy Macalos* IBF	1988–89	S. Sor Jaturong* WBC, IBF	1995–96
Sung-Jun Kim* WBC	1978–80	German Torres* WBC	1988–89	Carlos Murillo* WBA	1996
Shigeo Nakajima* WBC	1980	Yul-Woo Lee* WBC	1989	Keiji Yamaguchi* WBA	1996
Hilario Zapata* WBC	1980–82	Muangchai		Michael Carbajal* IBF	1996–97
Pedro Flores* WBA	1981	Kittikasem* IBF	1989–90	S. Sor Jaturong* WBC	1995–
Hwan-Jin Kim* WBA	1981	Humberto		Phichit Chor Siriwat* WBA	1996–
Katsuo Tokashiki* WBA	1981–83	Gonzalez* WBC	1989–90	Mauricio Pastrana* IBF	1997–98†
Amado Urzua* WBC	1982	Michael Carbajal* IBF	1990–94	Will Grigsby* IBF	1998–99
Tadashi Tomori* WBC	1982	R. Pascua* WBC	1990	Ricardo Lopez* IBF	1999–
Hilario Zapata* WBC	1982–83	M. C. Castro* WBC	1991		
Jung-Koo Chang* WBC	1983–88	H. Gonzalez* WBC	1991–93		

Strawweights
(Weight Limit: 105 pounds)

Champion	Reign	Champion	Reign	Champion	Reign
Franco Udella* WBC	1975	Amado Urzua* WBC	1982	M. Kittikasem* IBF	1989–90
Jaime Rios* WBA	1975–76	Tadashi Tomori* WBC	1982	H. Gonzalez* WBC	1989–90
Luis Estaba* WBC	1975–78	Hilario Zapata* WBC	1982–83	Michael Carbajal* IBF	1990
Juan Guzman* WBA	1976	Jung-Koo Chang* WBC	1983–88	Rolando Pascua* WBC	1990
Yoko Gushiken* WBA	1976–81	Lupe Madera* WBA	1983–84	M.C. Castro* WBC	1991
Freddy Castillo* WBC	1978	Dodie Penalosa* IBF	1983–86	Ricardo Lopez* WBC	1990–
Netrnoi Vorasingh* WBC	1978	Francisco Quiroz* WBA	1984–85	R.S. Voraphin* IBF	1992–97
Sung-Jun Kim* WBC	1978–80	Joey Olivo* WBA	1985	Chana Porpaoin* WBA	1993–95
Shigeo Nakajima* WBC	1980	Myung-Woo Yuh* WBA	1985–93	Rosendo Alvarez* WBA	1995–98
Hilario Zapata* WBC	1980–82	Jum-Hwan Choi* WBC	1986–88	Zolani Petelo* IBF	1997–
Pedro Flores* WBA	1981	Tacy Macalos* IBF	1988–89	Ricardo Lopez WBA, WBC	1998–
Hwan-Jin Kim* WBA	1981	German Torres* WBC	1988–89		
Katsuo Tokashiki* WBA	1981–83	Yul-Woo Lee* WBC	1989		

*Champion not generally recognized. †Champion retired or relinquished title.

Alltime Career Leaders

Total Bouts

Name	Years Active	Bouts	Name	Years Active	Bouts
Len Wickwar	1928–47	463	Maxie Rosenbloom	1923–39	299
Jack Britton	1905–30	350	Harry Greb	1913–26	298
Johnny Dundee	1910–32	333	Young Stribling	1921–33	286
Billy Bird	1920–48	318	Battling Levinsky	1910–29	282
George Marsden	1928–46	311	Ted (Kid) Lewis	1909–29	279

Note: Based on records in *The Ring Record Book* and *Boxing Encyclopedia*.

Most Knockouts

Name	Years Active	KOs	Name	Years Active	KOs
Archie Moore	1936–63	130	Sandy Saddler	1944–56	103
Young Stribling	1921–33	126	Sam Langford	1902–26	102
Billy Bird	1920–48	125	Henry Armstrong	1931–45	100
George Odwell	1930–45	114	Jimmy Wilde	1911–23	98
Sugar Ray Robinson	1940–65	110	Len Wickwar	1928–47	93

Note: Based on records in *The Ring Record Book* and *Boxing Encyclopedia*.

World Heavyweight Championship Fights

Date	Winner	Wgt	Loser	Wgt	Result	Site
Sept 7, 1892	James J. Corbett*	178	John L. Sullivan	212	KO 21	New Orleans
Jan 25, 1894	James J. Corbett	184	Charley Mitchell	158	KO 3	Jacksonville, FL
Mar 17, 1897	Bob Fitzsimmons*	167	James J. Corbett	183	KO 14	Carson City, NV
June 9, 1899	James J. Jeffries*	206	Bob Fitzsimmons	167	KO 11	Coney Island, NY
Nov 3, 1899	James J. Jeffries	215	Tom Sharkey	183	Ref 25	Coney Island, NY
Apr 6, 1900	James J. Jeffries	n/a	Jack Finnegan	n/a	KO 1	Detroit
May 11, 1900	James J. Jeffries	218	James J. Corbett	188	KO 23	Coney Island, NY
Nov 15, 1901	James J. Jeffries	211	Gus Ruhlin	194	TKO 6	San Francisco
July 25, 1902	James J. Jeffries	219	Bob Fitzsimmons	172	KO 8	San Francisco
Aug 14, 1903	James J. Jeffries	220	James J. Corbett	190	KO 10	San Francisco
Aug 25, 1904	James J. Jeffries	219	Jack Munroe	186	TKO 2	San Francisco
July 3, 1905	Marvin Hart*	190	Jack Root	171	KO 12	Reno
Feb 23, 1906	Tommy Burns*	180	Marvin Hart	188	Ref 20	Los Angeles
Oct 2, 1906	Tommy Burns	n/a	Jim Flynn	n/a	KO 15	Los Angeles
Nov 28, 1906	Tommy Burns	172	Jack O'Brien	163½	Draw 20	Los Angeles
May 8, 1907	Tommy Burns	180	Jack O'Brien	167	Ref 20	Los Angeles
Jul 4, 1907	Tommy Burns	181	Bill Squires	180	KO 1	Colma, CA
Dec 2, 1907	Tommy Burns	177	Gunner Moir	204	KO 10	London
Feb 10, 1908	Tommy Burns	n/a	Jack Palmer	n/a	KO 4	London
Mar 17, 1908	Tommy Burns	n/a	Jem Roche	n/a	KO 1	Dublin
Apr 18, 1908	Tommy Burns	n/a	Jewey Smith	n/a	KO 5	Paris
June 13, 1908	Tommy Burns	184	Bill Squires	183	KO 8	Paris
Aug 24, 1908	Tommy Burns	181	Bill Squires	184	KO 13	Sydney
Sept 2, 1908	Tommy Burns	183	Bill Lang	187	KO 6	Melbourne
Dec 26, 1908	Jack Johnson*	192	Tommy Burns	168	TKO 14	Sydney
Mar 10, 1909	Jack Johnson	n/a	Victor McLaglen	n/a	ND 6	Vancouver
May 19, 1909	Jack Johnson	205	Jack O'Brien	161	ND 6	Philadelphia
June 30, 1909	Jack Johnson	207	Tony Ross	214	ND 6	Pittsburgh
Sept 9, 1909	Jack Johnson	209	Al Kaufman	191	ND 10	San Francisco
Oct 16, 1909	Jack Johnson	205½	Stanley Ketchel	170¼	KO 12	Colma, CA
July 4, 1910	Jack Johnson	208	James J. Jeffries	227	KO 15	Reno
July 4, 1912	Jack Johnson	195½	Jim Flynn	175	TKO 9	Las Vegas
Dec 19, 1913	Jack Johnson	n/a	Jim Johnson	n/a	Draw 10	Paris
June 27, 1914	Jack Johnson	221	Frank Moran	203	Ref 20	Paris
Apr 5, 1915	Jess Willard*	230	Jack Johnson	205½	KO 26	Havana
Mar 25, 1916	Jess Willard	225	Frank Moran	203	ND 10	New York City
July 4, 1919	Jack Dempsey*	187	Jess Willard	245	TKO 4	Toledo, OH
Sept 6, 1920	Jack Dempsey	185	Billy Miske	187	KO 3	Benton Harbor, MI
Dec 14, 1920	Jack Dempsey	188¼	Bill Brennan	197	KO 12	New York City
July 2, 1921	Jack Dempsey	188	Georges Carpentier	172	KO 4	Jersey City
July 4, 1923	Jack Dempsey	188	Tommy Givvons	175½	Ref 15	Shelby, MT
Sept 14, 1923	Jack Dempsey	192½	Luis Firpo	216½	KO 2	New York City
Sept 23, 1926	Gene Tunney*	189½	Jack Dempsey	190	UD 10	Philadelphia
Sept 22, 1927	Gene Tunney	189½	Jack Dempsey	192½	UD 10	Chicago
July 26, 1928	Gene Tunney	192	Tom Heeney	203½	TKO 11	New York City
June 12, 1930	Max Schmeling*	188	Jack Sharkey	197	DQ 4	New York City
July 3, 1931	Max Schmeling	189	Young Stribling	186½	TKO 15	Cleveland
June 21, 1932	Jack Sharkey*	205	Max Schmeling	188	Split 15	Long Island City
June 29, 1933	Primo Carnera*	260½	Jack Sharkey	201	KO 6	Long Island City
Oct 22, 1933	Primo Carnera	259½	Paulino Uzcudun	229¼	UD 15	Rome
Mar 1, 1934	Primo Carnera	270	Tommy Loughran	184	UD 15	Miami
June 14, 1934	Max Baer*	209½	Primo Carnera	263¼	TKO 11	Long Island City
June 13, 1935	James J. Braddock*	193¾	Max Baer	209½	UD 15	Long Island City
June 22, 1937	Joe Louis	197¼	James J. Braddock	197	KO 8	Chicago
Aug 30, 1937	Joe Louis	197	Tommy Farr	204¼	UD 15	New York City
Feb 23, 1938	Joe Louis	200	Nathan Mann	193½	KO 3	New York City
Apr 1, 1938	Joe Louis	202½	Harry Thomas	196	KO 5	Chicago
June 22, 1938	Joe Louis	198¼	Max Schmeling	193	KO 1	New York City
Jan 25, 1939	Joe Louis	200¼	John Henry Lewis	180¾	KO 1	New York City
Apr 17, 1939	Joe Louis	201¼	Jack Roper	204¾	KO 1	Los Angeles
June 28, 1939	Joe Louis	200¾	Tony Galento	233¾	TKO 4	New York City
Sept 20, 1939	Joe Louis	200	Bob Pastor	183	KO 11	Detroit
Feb 9, 1940	Joe Louis	203	Arturo Godoy	202	Split 15	New York City
Mar 29, 1940	Joe Louis	201½	Johnny Paychek	187½	KO 2	New York City
June 20, 1940	Joe Louis	199	Arturo Godoy	201¼	TKO 8	New York City
Dec 16, 1940	Joe Louis	202¼	Al McCoy	180¾	TKO 6	Boston
Jan 31, 1941	Joe Louis	202½	Red Burman	188	KO 5	New York City

World Heavyweight Championship Fights (Cont.)

Date	Winner	Wgt	Loser	Wgt	Result	Site
Feb 17, 1941	Joe Louis	203½	Gus Dorazio	193½	KO 2	Philadelphia
Mar 21, 1941	Joe Louis	202	Abe Simon	254½	TKO 13	Detroit
Apr 8, 1941	Joe Louis	203½	Tony Musto	199½	TKO 9	St Louis
May 23, 1941	Joe Louis	201½	Buddy Baer	237½	DQ 7	Washington, DC
June 18, 1941	Joe Louis	199½	Billy Conn	174	KO 13	New York City
Sept 29, 1941	Joe Louis	202¼	Lou Nova	202½	TKO 6	New York City
Jan 9, 1942	Joe Louis	206¾	Buddy Baer	250	KO 1	New York City
Mar 27, 1942	Joe Louis	207½	Abe Simon	255½	KO 6	New York City
June 9, 1946	Joe Louis	207	Billy Conn	187	KO 8	New York City
Sept 18, 1946	Joe Louis	211	Tami Mauriello	198½	KO 1	New York City
Dec 5, 1947	Joe Louis	211½	Jersey Joe Walcott	194½	Split 15	New York City
June 25, 1948	Joe Louis	213½	Jersey Joe Walcott	194¾	KO 11	New York City
June 22, 1949	Ezzard Charles*	181¾	Jersey Joe Walcott	195½	UD 15	Chicago
Aug 10, 1949	Ezzard Charles	180	Gus Lesnevich	182	TKO 8	New York City
Oct 14, 1949	Ezzard Charles	182	Pat Valentino	188½	KO 8	San Francisco
Aug 15, 1950	Ezzard Charles	183¼	Freddie Beshore	184½	TKO 14	Buffalo
Sept 27, 1950	Ezzard Charles	184½	Joe Louis	218	UD 15	New York City
Dec 5, 1950	Ezzard Charles	185	Nick Barone	178½	KO 11	Cincinnati
Jan 12, 1951	Ezzard Charles	185	Lee Oma	193	TKO 10	New York City
Mar 7, 1951	Ezzard Charles	186	Jersey Joe Walcott	193	UD 15	Detroit
May 30, 1951	Ezzard Charles	182	Joey Maxim	181½	UD 15	Chicago
July 18, 1951	Jersey Joe Walcott*	194	Ezzard Charles	182	KO 7	Pittsburgh
June 5, 1952	Jersey Joe Walcott	196	Ezzard Charles	191½	UD 15	Philadelphia
Sept 23, 1952	Rocky Marciano*	184	Jersey Joe Walcott	196	KO 13	Philadelphia
May 15, 1953	Rocky Marciano	184½	Jersey Joe Walcott	197¾	KO 1	Chicago
Sept 24, 1953	Rocky Marciano	185	Roland LaStarza	184¾	TKO 11	New York City
June 17, 1954	Rocky Marciano	187½	Ezzard Charles	185½	UD 15	New York City
Sept 17, 1954	Rocky Marciano	187	Ezzard Charles	192½	KO 8	New York City
May 16, 1955	Rocky Marciano	189	Don Cockell	205	TKO 9	San Francisco
Sept 21, 1955	Rocky Marciano	188¼	Archie Moore	188	KO 9	New York City
Nov 30, 1956	Floyd Patterson*	182¼	Archie Moore	187¾	KO 5	Chicago
July 29, 1957	Floyd Patterson	184	Tommy Jackson	192½	TKO 10	New York City
Aug 22, 1957	Floyd Patterson	187¼	Pete Rademacher	202	KO 6	Seattle
Aug 18, 1958	Floyd Patterson	184½	Roy Harris	194	TKO 13	Los Angeles
May 1, 1959	Floyd Patterson	182½	Brian London	206	KO 11	Indianapolis
June 26, 1959	Ingemar Johansson*	196	Floyd Patterson	182	TKO 3	New York City
June 20, 1960	Floyd Patterson*	190	Ingemar Johansson	194¾	KO 5	New York City
Mar 13, 1961	Floyd Patterson	194¾	Ingemar Johansson	206½	KO 6	Miami Beach
Dec 4, 1961	Floyd Patterson	188½	Tom McNeeley	197	KO 4	Toronto
Sept 25, 1962	Sonny Liston*	214	Floyd Patterson	189	KO 1	Chicago
July 22, 1963	Sonny Liston	215	Floyd Patterson	194½	KO 1	Las Vegas
Feb 25, 1964	Cassius Clay	210½	Sonny Liston	218	TKO 7	Miami Beach
Mar 5, 1965	Ernie Terrell WBA*	199	Eddie Machen	192	UD 15	Chicago
May 25, 1965	Muhammad Ali	206	Sonny Liston	215¼	KO 1	Lewiston, ME
Nov 1, 1965	Ernie Terrell WBA*	206	George Chuvalo	209	UD 15	Toronto
Nov 22, 1965	Muhammad Ali	210	Floyd Patterson	196¾	TKO 12	Las Vegas
Mar 29, 1966	Muhammad Ali	214½	George Chuvalo	216	UD 15	Toronto
May 21, 1966	Muhammad Ali	201½	Henry Cooper	188	TKO 6	London
June 28, 1966	Ernie Terrell WBA*	209½	Doug Jones	187½	UD 15	Houston
Aug 6, 1966	Muhammad Ali	209½	Brian London	201½	KO 3	London
Sept 10, 1966	Muhammad Ali	203½	Karl Mildenberger	194¼	TKO 12	Frankfurt
Nov 14, 1966	Muhammad Ali	212¾	Cleveland Williams	210½	TKO 3	Houston
Feb 6, 1967	Muhammad Ali	212¼	Ernie Terrell WBA	212½	UD 15	Houston
Mar 22, 1967	Muhammad Ali	211½	Zora Folley	202½	KO 7	New York City
Mar 4, 1968	Joe Frazier*	204½	Buster Mathis	243½	TKO 11	New York City
Apr 27, 1968	Jimmy Ellis*	197	Jerry Quarry	195	Maj 15	Oakland
June 24, 1968	Joe Frazier NY*	203½	Manuel Ramos	208	TKO 2	New York City
Aug 14, 1968	Jimmy Ellis WBA*	198	Floyd Patterson	188	Ref 15	Stockholm
Dec 10, 1968	Joe Frazier NY*	203	Oscar Bonavena	207	UD 15	Philadelphia
Apr 22, 1969	Joe Frazier NY*	204½	Dave Zyglewicz	190½	KO 1	Houston
June 23, 1969	Joe Frazier NY*	203½	Jerry Quarry	198½	TKO 8	New York City
Feb 16, 1970	Joe Frazier NY*	205	Jimmy Ellis WBA	201	TKO 5	New York City
Nov 18, 1970	Joe Frazier*	209	Bob Foster	188	KO 2	Detroit
Mar 8, 1971	Joe Frazier*	205½	Muhammad Ali	215	UD 15	New York City
Jan 15, 1972	Joe Frazier	215½	Terry Daniels	195	TKO 4	New Orleans
May 26, 1972	Joe Frazier	217½	Ron Stander	218	TKO 5	Omaha
Jan 22, 1973	George Foreman*	217½	Joe Frazier	214	TKO 2	Kingston, Jam.

World Heavyweight Championship Fights (Cont.)

Date	Winner	Wgt	Loser	Wgt	Result	Site
Sept 1, 1973	George Foreman	219½	Jose Roman	196½	KO 1	Tokyo
Mar 26, 1974	George Foreman	224¼	Ken Norton	212¼	TKO 2	Caracas
Oct 30, 1974	Muhammad Ali*	216½	George Foreman	220	KO 8	Kinshasa, Zaire
Mar 24, 1975	Muhammad Ali	223½	Chuck Wepner	225	TKO 15	Cleveland
May 16, 1975	Muhammad Ali	224½	Ron Lyle	219	TKO 11	Las Vegas
July 1, 1975	Muhammad Ali	224½	Joe Bugner	230	UD 15	Kuala Lumpur, Malay.
Oct 1, 1975	Muhammad Ali	224½	Joe Frazier	215	TKO 15	Manila
Feb 20, 1976	Muhammad Ali	226	Jean Pierre Coopman	206	KO 5	San Juan
Apr 30, 1976	Muhammad Ali	230	Jimmy Young	209	UD 15	Landover, MD
May 24, 1976	Muhammad Ali	230	Richard Dunn	206½	TKO 5	Munich
Sept 28, 1976	Muhammad Ali	221	Ken Norton	217½	UD 15	New York City
May 16, 1977	Muhammad Ali	221¼	Alfredo Evangelista	209¼	UD 15	Landover, MD
Sept 29, 1977	Muhammad Ali	225	Earnie Shavers	211¼	UD 15	New York City
Feb 15, 1978	Leon Spinks*	197¼	Muhammad Ali	224¼	Split 15	Las Vegas
June 9, 1978	Larry Holmes*	209	Ken Norton WBC	220	Split 15	Las Vegas
Sept 15, 1978	Muhammad Ali*	221	Leon Spinks	201	UD 15	New Orleans
Nov 10, 1978	Larry Holmes WBC*	214	Alfredo Evangelista	208¼	KO 7	Las Vegas
Mar 23, 1979	Larry Holmes WBC*	214	Osvaldo Ocasio	207	TKO 7	Las Vegas
June 22, 1979	Larry Holmes WBC*	215	Mike Weaver	202	TKO 12	New York City
Sept 28, 1979	Larry Holmes WBC*	210	Earnie Shavers	211	TKO 11	Las Vegas
Oct 20, 1979	John Tate*	240	Gerrie Coetzee	222	UD 15	Pretoria
Feb 3, 1980	Larry Holmes WBC*	213½	Lorenzo Zanon	215	TKO 6	Las Vegas
Mar 31, 1980	Mike Weaver*	232	John Tate WBA	232	KO 15	Knoxville
Mar 31, 1980	Larry Holmes WBC*	211	Leroy Jones	254½	TKO 8	Las Vegas
July 7, 1980	Larry Holmes WBC*	214¼	Scott LeDoux	226	TKO 7	Minneapolis
Oct 2, 1980	Larry Holmes WBC*	211¼	Muhammad Ali	217½	TKO 11	Las Vegas
Oct 25, 1980	Mike Weaver WBA*	210	Gerrie Coetzee	226½	KO 13	Sun City, S.A.
Apr 11, 1981	Larry Holmes	215	Trevor Berbick	215½	UD 15	Las Vegas
June 12, 1981	Larry Holmes	212¼	Leon Spinks	200¼	TKO 3	Detroit
Oct 3, 1981	Mike Weaver WBA*	215	James Quick Tillis	209	UD 15	Rosemont, IL
Nov 6, 1981	Larry Holmes	213¼	Renaldo Snipes	215¾	TKO 11	Pittsburgh
June 11, 1982	Larry Holmes	212½	Gerry Cooney	225½	TKO 13	Las Vegas
Nov 26, 1982	Larry Holmes	217½	Tex Cobb	234¼	UD 15	Houston
Dec 10, 1982	Michael Dokes*	216	Mike Weaver WBA	209¾	TKO 1	Las Vegas
Mar 27, 1983	Larry Holmes	221	Lucien Rodriguez	209	UD 12	Scranton, PA
May 20, 1983	Michael Dokes WBA*	223	Mike Weaver	218½	Draw 15	Las Vegas
May 20, 1983	Larry Holmes	213	Tim Witherspoon	219½	Split 12	Las Vegas
Sept 10, 1983	Larry Holmes	223	Scott Frank	211¼	TKO 5	Atlantic City
Sept 23, 1983	Gerrie Coetzee*	215	Michael Dokes WBA	217	KO 10	Richfield, OH
Nov 25, 1983	Larry Holmes	219	Marvis Frazier	200	TKO 1	Las Vegas
Mar 9, 1984	Tim Witherspoon	220¼	Greg Page	239½	Maj 12	Las Vegas
Aug 31, 1984	Pinklon Thomas*	216	Tim Witherspoon WBC	217	Maj 12	Las Vegas
Nov 9, 1984	Larry Holmes IBF	221½	James Smith	227	TKO 12	Las Vegas
Dec 1, 1984	Greg Page*	236½	Gerrie Coetzee WBA	218	KO 8	Sun City, S.A.
Mar 15, 1985	Larry Holmes	223½	David Bey	233¼	TKO 10	Las Vegas
Apr 29, 1985	Tony Tubbs*	229	Greg Page WBA	239½	UD 15	Buffalo
May 20, 1985	Larry Holmes	224¼	Carl Williams	215	UD 15	Las Vegas
June 15, 1985	Pinklon Thomas*	220¼	Mike Weaver	221¼	KO 8	Las Vegas
Sept 21, 1985	Michael Spinks*	200	Larry Holmes IBF	221½	UD 15	Las Vegas
Jan 17, 1986	Tim Witherspoon	227	Tony Tubbs WBA	229	Maj 15	Atlanta
Mar 22, 1986	Trevor Berbick*	218½	Pinklon Thomas WBC	222¾	UD 15	Las Vegas
Apr 19, 1986	Michael Spinks	205	Larry Holmes	223	Split 15	Las Vegas
July 19, 1986	Tim Witherspoon*	234¾	Frank Bruno	228	TKO 11	Wembley, Eng.
Sept 6, 1986	Michael Spinks	201	Steffen Tangstad	214¾	TKO 4	Las Vegas
Nov 22, 1986	Mike Tyson*	221¼	Trevor Berbick WBC	218½	TKO 2	Las Vegas
Dec 12, 1986	James Smith*	228½	Tim Witherspoon WBA	233½	TKO 1	New York City
Mar 7, 1987	Mike Tyson WBC*	219	James Smith WBA	233	UD 12	Las Vegas
May 30, 1987	Mike Tyson*	218¾	Pinklon Thomas	217¾	TKO 6	Las Vegas
May 30, 1987	Tony Tucker	222¼	Buster Douglas	227¼	TKO 10	Las Vegas
June 15, 1987	Michael Spinks	208¾	Gerry Cooney	238	TKO 5	Atlantic City
Aug 1, 1987	Mike Tyson*	221	Tony Tucker IBF	221	UD 12	Las Vegas
Oct 16, 1987	Mike Tyson*	216	Tyrell Biggs	228¾	TKO 7	Atlantic City
Jan 22, 1988	Mike Tyson*	215¾	Larry Holmes	225¾	TKO 4	Atlantic City
Mar 20, 1988	Mike Tyson*	216¼	Tony Tubbs	238¼	KO 2	Tokyo
June 27, 1988	Mike Tyson*	218¼	Michael Spinks	212¼	KO 1	Atlantic City
Feb 25, 1989	Mike Tyson	218	Frank Bruno	228	TKO 5	Las Vegas
July 21, 1989	Mike Tyson	219¼	Carl Williams	218	TKO 1	Atlantic City

Date	Winner	Wgt	Loser	Wgt	Result	Site
Feb 10, 1990	Buster Douglas	231½	Mike Tyson	220½	KO 10	Tokyo
Oct 25, 1990	Evander Holyfield	208	Buster Douglas	246	KO 3	Las Vegas
Apr 19, 1991	Evander Holyfield	212	George Foreman	257	UD 12	Atlantic City
Nov 23, 1991	Evander Holyfield	210	Bert Cooper	215	TKO 7	Atlanta
June 19, 1992	Evander Holyfield	210	Larry Holmes	233	UD 12	Las Vegas
Nov 13, 1992	Riddick Bowe	235	Evander Holyfield	205	UD 12	Las Vegas
Feb 6, 1993	Riddick Bowe	243	Michael Dokes	244	KO 1	New York City
May 8, 1993	Lennox Lewis*	235	Tony Tucker	235	UD 12	Las Vegas
May 22, 1993	Riddick Bowe	244	Jesse Ferguson	224	KO 2	Washington, DC
Oct 2, 1993	Lennox Lewis*	229	Frank Bruno	233	KO 7	London
Nov 6, 1993	Evander Holyfield	217	Riddick Bowe	246	Split 12	Las Vegas
Apr 22, 1994	Michael Moorer	214	Evander Holyfield	214	Split 12	Las Vegas
May 6, 1994	Lennox Lewis*	235	Phil Jackson	218	TKO 8	Atlantic City
Nov 6, 1994	George Foreman	250	Michael Moorer	222	KO 10	Las Vegas
Mar 11, 1995	Riddick Bowe*	241	Herbie Hide	214	KO 6	Las Vegas
Apr 8, 1995	Oliver McCall*	231	Larry Holmes	236	UD 12	Las Vegas
Apr 8, 1995	Bruce Seldon*	236	Tony Tucker	243	TKO 7	Las Vegas
Apr 22, 1995	George Foreman	256	Axel Schulz	221	Split 12	Las Vegas
Jun 17, 1995	Riddick Bowe*	243	Jorge Luis Gonzalez	237	KO 6	Las Vegas
Aug 19, 1995	Bruce Seldon*	234	Joe Hipp	233	TKO 10	Las Vegas
Sept 2, 1995	Frank Bruno*	247¾	Oliver McCall	234¾	UD 12	London
Dec 9, 1995	Frans Botha*	237	Axel Shulz	223	Split 12	Stuttgart
Mar 16, 1996	Mike Tyson*	220	Frank Bruno	247	TKO 3	Las Vegas
June 22, 1996	Michael Moorer*	222¼	Axel Shulz	222¾	Split 12	Dortmund, Ger.
Sept 7, 1996	Mike Tyson	219	Bruce Seldon	229	TKO 1	Las Vegas
Nov 9, 1996	Evander Holyfied	215	Mike Tyson	222	TKO 11	Las Vegas
Feb 7, 1997	Lennox Lewis*	251	Oliver McCall	237	TKO 5	Las Vegas
June 28, 1997	Evander Holyfied	218	Mike Tyson	218	DQ 4	Las Vegas
Oct 4, 1997	Lennox Lewis*	244	Andrew Golota	244	TKO 1	Atlantic City
Nov 8, 1997	Evander Holyfield	214	Michael Moorer	223	TKO 8	Las Vegas
Mar 28, 1998	Lennox Lewis*	243	Shannon Briggs	228	TKO 5	Atlantic City
Mar 13, 1999	Evander Holyfield	215	Lennox Lewis	246	Draw 12	New York City

*Champion not generally recognized. KO=knockout; TKO=technical knockout; UD=unanimous decision; Split=split decision; Ref=referee's decision; DQ=disqualification; ND=no decision.

Sad End to a Long Fight

It would be a shame if Jerry Quarry were remembered only as another Great White Hope, a crowd-pleasing pug who took high-profile beatings from Muhammad Ali and Joe Frazier. Quarry was surprisingly fast, a hard hitter and a brilliant counterpuncher. His 53-9-4 record over 27 years as a pro included victories over Floyd Patterson and Ernie Shavers. In another era he might have worn a championship belt. He was also a warrior of tremendous heart—a quality that contributed to the darker side of his legacy.

Quarry, who died at 53 in Templeton, Calif., in January, had been hospitalized for six days with pneumonia. He'd then gone into cardiac arrest. His family allowed him to be removed from life support, but he was gone long before that. He had spent the final years of his life stumbling through a shadowy world of confusion and disability neurologists call dementia pugilistica. In the argot of the not-so-sweet science, he had been punch-drunk, his brain dying prematurely as a result of his taking so many blows to the head.

Quarry's plight had brought him back into the public eye in recent years. His was the classic tale of an aging fighter—a grim echo of his old foe Ali's struggles with Parkinson's syndrome. PEOPLE and CBS's 48 Hours showed Quarry, no longer able to live alone, being shaved and fed by his mother and his brother.

In 1983 the 37-year-old Quarry, then training for a comeback, was one of three fighters who underwent neurological testing for an SI story on brain damage in boxers. He showed no outward signs of dementia but performed poorly on several neuropsychological tests. A CAT scan that appeared with the article showed atrophy in Quarry's cortex as well as a cavum septum, a split in a crucial brain membrane. According to Ira Carson, the neurologist who performed the tests in '83 and has examined hundreds of boxers since, the latter condition is "the hallmark of what happens to these guys."

Carson recalled urging Quarry not to fight again. "He was living proof of what too many fights can do," said Carson. Yet Quarry fought three more times, including a final comeback bout in 1992, in which he was battered for six rounds by a club fighter for a purse of $1,050. "The damage is cumulative," said Carson. "The sooner you stop fighting, the better chance you have." Quarry never wanted to stop.

Ring Magazine Fighter and Fight of the Year

Year	Fighter	Year	Fighter	Year	Fighter
1928	Gene Tunney	1935	Barney Ross	1940	Billy Conn
1929	Tommy Loughran	1936	Joe Louis	1941	Joe Louis
1930	Max Schmeling	1937	Henry Armstrong	1942	Ray Robinson
1932	Jack Sharkey	1938	Joe Louis	1943	Fred Apostoli
1934	T. Canzoneri/B. Ross	1939	Joe Louis	1944	Beau Jack

Note: No award in 1933; no fight of the year named until 1945

Year	Fighter	Fight	Winner	Site
1945	Willie Pep	Rocky Graziano–Freddie Cochrane	Rocky Graziano	New York City
1946	Tony Zale	Tony Zale–Rocky Graziano	Tony Zale	New York City
1947	Gus Lesnevich	Rocky Graziano–Tony Zale	Rocky Graziano	Chicago
1948	Ike Williams	Marcel Cerdan–Tony Zale	Marcel Cerdan	Jersey City
1949	Ezzard Charles	Willie Pep–Sandy Saddler	Willie Pep	New York City
1950	Ezzard Charles	Jake LaMotta–Laurent Dauthuille	Jake LaMotta	Detroit
1951	Ray Robinson	Jersey Joe Walcott–Ezzard Charles	Jersey Joe Walcott	Pittsburgh
1952	Rocky Marciano	Rocky Marciano–Jersey Joe Walcott	Rocky Marciano	Philadelphia
1953	Carl Olson	Rocky Marciano–Roland LaStarza	Rocky Marciano	New York City
1954	Rocky Marciano	Rocky Marciano–Ezzard Charles	Rocky Marciano	New York City
1955	Rocky Marciano	Carmen Basilio–Tony DeMarco	Carmen Basilio	Boston
1956	Floyd Patterson	Carmen Basilio–Johnny Saxton	Carmen Basilio	Syracuse
1957	Carmen Basilio	Carmen Basilio–Ray Robinson	Carmen Basilio	New York City
1958	Ingemar Johansson	Ray Robinson–Carmen Basilio	Ray Robinson	Chicago
1959	Ingemar Johansson	Gene Fullmer–Carmen Basilio	Gene Fullmer	San Francisco
1960	Floyd Patterson	Floyd Patterson–Ingemar Johansson	Floyd Patterson	New York City
1961	Joe Brown	Joe Brown–Dave Charnley	Joe Brown	London
1962	Dick Tiger	Joey Giardello–Henry Hank	Joey Giardello	Philadelphia
1963	Cassius Clay	Cassius Clay–Doug Jones	Cassius Clay	New York City
1964	Emile Griffith	Cassius Clay–Sonny Liston	Cassius Clay	Miami Beach
1965	Dick Tiger	Floyd Patterson–George Chuvalo	Floyd Patterson	New York City
1966	No award	Jose Torres–Eddie Cotton	Jose Torres	Las Vegas
1967	Joe Frazier	Nino Benvenuti–Emile Griffith	Nino Benvenuti	New York City
1968	Nino Benvenuti	Dick Tiger–Frank DePaula	Dick Tiger	New York City
1969	Jose Napoles	Joe Frazier–Jerry Quarry	Joe Frazier	New York City
1970	Joe Frazier	Carlos Monzon–Nino Benvenuti	Carlos Monzon	Rome
1971	Joe Frazier	Joe Frazier–Muhammad Ali	Joe Frazier	New York City
1972	Muhammad Ali / Carlos Monzon	Bob Foster–Chris Finnegan	Bob Foster	London
1973	George Foreman	George Foreman–Joe Frazier	George Foreman	Kingston, Jam.
1974	Muhammad Ali	Muhammad Ali–George Foreman	Muhammad Ali	Kinshasa, Zaire
1975	Muhammad Ali	Muhammad Ali–Joe Frazier	Muhammad Ali	Manila
1976	George Foreman	George Foreman–Ron Lyle	George Foreman	Las Vegas
1977	Carlos Zarate	Joe Young–George Foreman	Joe Young	San Juan
1978	Muhammad Ali	Leon Spinks–Muhammad Ali	Leon Spinks	Las Vegas
1979	Ray Leonard	Danny Lopez–Tony Ayala	Danny Lopez	San Antonio
1980	Thomas Hearns	Saad Muhammad–Danny Lopez	Saad Muhammad	McAfee, NJ
1981	Ray Leonard / Salvador Sanchez	Ray Leonard–Tommy Hearns	Ray Leonard	Las Vegas
1982	Larry Holmes	Bobby Chacon–Rafael Limon	Bobby Chacon	Sacramento
1983	Marvin Hagler	Bobby Chacon–Cornelius Boza-Edwards	Bobby Chacon	Las Vegas
1984	Thomas Hearns	Jose Luis Ramirez–Edwin Rosario	Jose Luis Ramirez	San Juan
1985	Donald Curry / Marvin Hagler	Marvin Hagler–Tommy Hearns	Marvin Hagler	Las Vegas
1986	Mike Tyson	Stevie Cruz–Barry McGuigan	Stevie Cruz	Las Vegas
1987	Evander Holyfield	Ray Leonard–Marvin Hagler	Ray Leonard	Las Vegas
1988	Mike Tyson	Tony Lopez–Rocky Lockridge	Tony Lopez	Inglewood, CA
1989	Pernell Whitaker	Roberto Duran–Iran Barkley	Roberto Duran	Atlantic City
1990	Julio César Chávez	Julio César Chávez–Meldrick Taylor	Julio César Chávez	Las Vegas
1991	James Toney	Robert Quiroga–Kid Akeem Anifowoshe	Robert Quiroga	San Antonio
1992	Riddick Bowe	Riddick Bowe–Evander Holyfield	Riddick Bowe	Las Vegas
1993	Michael Carbajal	Michael Carbajal–Humberto Gonzalez	Michael Carbajal	Las Vegas
1994	Roy Jones	Jorge Castro–John David Jackson	Jorge Castro	Monterrey, Mex.
1995	Oscar De La Hoya	Saman Sor Jaturong–Chiquita Gonzalez	Saman Sor Jaturong	Inglewood, CA
1996	Evander Holyfield	Evander Holyfield–Mike Tyson	Evander Holyfield	Las Vegas
1997	Evander Holyfield	Arturo Gatti–Gabriel Ruelas	Arturo Gatti	Atlantic City
1998	Floyd Mayweather	Ivan Robinson–Arturo Gatti	Ivan Robinson	Atlantic City

U.S. Olympic Gold Medalists

LIGHT FLYWEIGHT
1984 ....Paul Gonzales

FLYWEIGHT
1904 ....George Finnegan
1920 ....Frank Di Gennara
1024 ....Fidel LaBarba
1952 ....Nathan Brooks
1976 ....Leo Randolph
1984 ....Steve McCrory

BANTAMWEIGHT
1904 ....Oliver Kirk
1988 ....Kennedy McKinney

FEATHERWEIGHT
1904 ....Oliver Kirk
1924 ....John Fields
1984 ....Meldrick Taylor

LIGHTWEIGHT
1904 ....Harry Spanger
1920 ....Samuel Mosberg
1968 ....Ronald W. Harris
1976 ....Howard Davis
1984 ....Pernell Whitaker
1992 ....Oscar De La Hoya

LIGHT WELTERWEIGHT
1952 ....Charles Adkins
1972 ....Ray Seales
1976 ....Ray Leonard
1984 ....Jerry Page

WELTERWEIGHT
1904 ....Albert Young
1932 ....Edward Flynn
1984 ....Mark Breland

LIGHT MIDDLEWEIGHT
1960 ....Wilbert McClure
1984 ....Frank Tate
1996 ....David Reid

MIDDLEWEIGHT
1904 ....Charles Mayer
1932 ....Carmen Bath
1952 ....Floyd Patterson
1960 ....Edward Crook
1976 ....Michael Spinks

LIGHT HEAVYWEIGHT
1920 ....Eddie Eagan
1952 ....Norvel Lee
1956 ....James Boyd
1960 ....Cassius Clay
1976 ....Leon Spinks
1988 ....Andrew Maynard

HEAVYWEIGHT
1984 ....Henry Tillman
1988 ....Ray Mercer

SUPER HEAVYWEIGHT
1904 ....Samuel Berger
1952 ....H. Edward Sanders
1956 ....T. Peter
............Rademacher
1964 ....Joe Frazier
1968 ....George Foreman
1984 ....Tyrell Biggs

He's a Knockout

The surprise of Vivienne Westwood's Fall/Winter 1999/2000 fashion show was former WBO super middleweight champ Chris Eubank of England, who vamped down the runway in a glittering ankle-length evening gown. This silvery number was one of the latest creations from Westwood, who expected dresses for men to be the next fad. Eubank, 34, who lost his title to Ireland's Steve Collins in '95, looked like more than a match for super-lightwaif Kate Moss as he styled to wild applause. All that was missing was a shout from Michael Buffer: "Let's get ready to rhumba!"

Horse Racing

Preakness winner
Charismatic, with Chris
Antley up

Carrying The Flag

The appropriately named Charismatic won legions of new fans for horse racing in '99

BY MARTY BURNS

THE SCENE was vivid and unforgettable: Charismatic, hobbled by a broken foreleg, standing nervously just beyond the finish line at the Belmont Stakes with his crestfallen jockey, Chris Antley, at his side. If there was one enduring image of horse racing in '99, this was it. For Charismatic's dramatic rise and fall in many ways symbolized the fortunes of the sport.

Charismatic, the former claimer who had gone on to surprising victories at the Kentucky Derby and the Preakness, entered the Belmont seeking to become the 12th thoroughbred in history—and the first since Affirmed in 1978—to win the Triple Crown. Like Silver Charm ('97) and Real Quiet ('98), two other thoroughbreds who went to Belmont with a shot at racing's most coveted prize, he came up just short. Leading with a quarter mile to go, Charismatic faded down the stretch and finished third behind winner Lemon Drop Kid and runner-up Vision and Verse.

Just as a Belmont crowd of 85,818 was absorbing its third Triple Crown near-miss in as many years, it received an additional disappointment. Sixty yards past the finish line Charismatic abruptly pulled up lame. As Antley leaped off the saddle and began cradling the chestnut's injured left leg, it was clear that the outcome of the race no longer mattered. Within minutes Charismatic was being led haltingly up the ramp of an equine ambulance as the crowd looked on in stunned silence. X-rays revealed that Charismatic had suffered not only a displaced lateral condylar fracture but also a fractured sesamoid bone in the ankle joint. His racing career was over. "We needed him. He was carrying the banner for our sport," trainer D. Wayne Lukas said after the race. "These Hollywood scripts don't always play out in racing."

Charismatic's rags-to-riches tale was certainly worthy of Tinseltown. A late bloomer who had run in a $62,500 claiming race in February, Charismatic shocked the racing world by winning the Derby as a 31–1 long shot. It was a thrilling triumph for the colt's owners, Bob and Beverly Lewis, who had enjoyed similar success with Silver Charm in '97, but few experts thought it would lead to anything else.

The Derby had been one of the roughest in years, with many of the favorites, such as

Both Antley and Charismatic were long shots before the season began.

General Challenge, Menifee and Cat Thief, crunched and clobbered around the track. Starting from way outside in the 16th position, Charismatic had benefited from a smooth ride. Two weeks later at the Preakness, Charismatic went off at a modest 8–1, behind four other horses. Showing the heart of his grandsire Secretariat, however, Charismatic proved the naysayers wrong once again by sweeping to the lead in the final turn and holding off Menifee to win by 1½ lengths.

Charismatic's rider, Antley, showed the same determination. Considered among the best jockeys in the world after leading Strike the Gold to victory in the '91 Kentucky Derby, Antley's career had plummeted in recent years, largely because of weight problems. After years of dieting, diuretics and endless hours in the hotbox, he finally gave up. He weighed 147 pounds when he left Del Mar in August '97 and returned home to Columbia, S.C., hoping to find another line of work. It wasn't long, however, before Antley began missing the sport. He found a no-carb diet that suited him and began running hundreds of miles on Columbia roads, past grocery stores and gas stations. Soon

locals were calling him Forrest Gump, but the hard work was paying off. By New Year's Day he was down to 125 pounds and back at Santa Anita. Convinced Antley could regain his form, Lukas gave him a call.

Lukas, after all, was attempting his own comeback of sorts. With a résumé that included 519 graded stakes winners, and three Derby champs, the trainer was a Hall of Famer and a living legend. Recently, however, he was overshadowed by rival Bob Baffert, who had won the Derby and the Preakness in 1997 and '98, with Silver Charm and Real Quiet. Like Antley, Lukas wanted badly to get back to the winner's circle. The pairing worked well. Lukas trained Charismatic hard, stoking a fire in the colt that had been dormant. On the track Antley rode him masterfully, weaving through a crowded field at the Derby and into the winner's circle. Thanks to Charismatic's thrilling chase for the Triple Crown, the Belmont set a new attendance record, and TV ratings for both the Belmont and the Preakness improved.

That's not to say horse racing had a bump-free ride in '99. In March, J.T. Lundy, a former president of Calumet Farm, the sport's top breeding stable, was arrested and charged with conspiracy, bank fraud and bribery in connection with an alleged scheme to acquire $50 million in loans to prop up the

Lemon Drop Kid (6) took the lead in the stretch and held on to win the Belmont by a head.

she had nothing left to prove and was "tired of getting hurt," the 4' 10½" Krone, who had broken her back, right kneecap, right ankle and both hands during her career, retired to her home in Colt's Neck, N.J. "I'm leaving with a smile on my face," she said.

It was against this backdrop that Charismatic rode out of the blue to give the sport a lift. But he wasn't the only horse to make big news. Lemon Drop Kid would add an impressive victory at the Travers to his Belmont triumph, and the filly Silverbulletday dominated the distaff competition like no other horse in recent memory. Those two and Behrens, the Oaklawn Handicap winner, were the prime challengers to Charismatic for Horse of the Year.

Unfortunately, Charismatic's breakdown was not the only one in 1999. In May, Free House, who had won the $1 million Santa Anita Handicap, injured himself at the Pimlico Special and was lost for the year. Real Quiet cracked a bone in his leg and was taken out for the year, followed by Victory Gallop, the '98 Belmont winner, who tore a ligament in his left foreleg and was retired, and Valhol, who had surgery to remove a bone chip from his left knee.

With so many of its top performers retired or on the shelf, thoroughbred racing needed reinforcements as 2000 approached. Fortunately a promising group of 2-year-olds, including More Than Ready, Forest Camp, Dixie Union and the filly Chilukki, were on the horizon. Additionally, jockey Laffit Pincay Jr. was nearing Willie Shoemaker's alltime record of 8,833 victories.

A fallen Triple Crown contender might have provided the enduring image of '99, but as the year ended it was clear that the sport of kings was still standing.

financially strapped Calumet. As part of its investigation, the FBI looked into the death of the champion stallion Alydar, who was put down at Calumet in November '90 after he had reportedly broken his leg by kicking his stall. When Calumet Farm pocketed $36.5 million in insurance money for Alydar's death, the biggest such payout in history, the FBI became suspicious that the prize horse, once the sport's greatest sire, might have been killed for insurance money. Lundy denied all the charges. His trial was scheduled to begin in November '99.

In April the racing world was stunned by the news that Arkansas officials were investigating Valhol's unlikely win in the $500,000 Arkansas Derby because the horse's jockey, Billy Patin, had carried a battery during the race. Known as a buzzer in some racing circles, the battery, when applied to a horse's neck, gives him a charge that could make him run faster. Shortly after Valhol, a 30–1 long shot, pulled off the upset, a maintenance man found the buzzer on the track, and race officials determined that Patin had carried it. Valhol's victory was overturned, and Patin was suspended for five years.

Sandwiched between those two sorry episodes was the retirement of Julie Krone, the sport's winningest female jockey. Krone, 35, finished her stellar 18-year career with 3,546 wins, including the '93 Belmont aboard Colonial Affair. Saying

THOROUGHBRED RACING

The Triple Crown

125th Kentucky Derby

May 1, 1999. Grade I, 3-year-olds; 8th race, Churchill Downs, Louisville. All 126 lbs. Distance: 1¼ miles. Stakes value: $1,186,200; Winner: $886,200 Second: $170,000; Third: $85,000; Fourth: $45,000. Track: Fast. Off: 5:29 p.m. Winner: Charismatic (B. c, Mar, by Summer Squall—Bali Babe, by Drone); Times: 0:23.52, 0:47.88, 1:12.52, 1:37.58, 2:03.29. Won: Driving. Breeder: William Farish and Parrish Hill Farm.

Horse	Finish-PP	Margin	Jockey/Owner
Charismatic	1–16	neck	Chris Antley/Robert and Beverly Lewis
Menifee	2–18	¾	Pat Day/Arthur B. Hancock III and James Stone
Cat Thief	3–10	1¼	Mike Smith/Overbrook Farm
Prime Timber	4–13	nose	D.R. Flores/Marie and Aaron Jones
Excellent Meeting	5–5	½	Kent Desormeaux/Golden Eagle Farm
Kimberlite Pipe	6–12	1¼	Robby Albarado/John Gunther and Prairie Star Racing
Worldly Manner	7–11	½	Jerry Bailey/Goldolphin Racing Inc.
K One King	8–9	1	Alex Solis/Madeleine and Allen Paulson
Lemon Drop Kid	9–19	neck	Jose Santos/Jeanne G. Vance
Answer Lively	10–7	½	Craig Perret/John A. Franks
General Challenge	11–14	¾	Gary Stevens/Golden Eagle Farm
Ecton Park	12–3	½	Robbie Davis/Mark Stanley
Desert Hero	13-6	1¼	Corey Nakatani/The Thoroughbred Corp.
Stephen Got Even	14–4	1½	Chris McCarron/Stephen Hilbert
Valhol	15–8	2	Willie Martinez/James Jackson
First American	16–15	2	Eddie Delahoussaye/T N T Stud
Adonis	17–1	4¾	Jorge Chavez/Paraneck Stable
Vicar	18–17	3¼	Shane Sellers/James Tafel
Three Ring	19–2	–	John Velazquez/Barry Schwartz

124th Preakness Stakes

May 15, 1999. Grade I, 3-year-olds; 10th race, Pimlico Race Course, Baltimore. All 126 lbs. Distance: 1³⁄₁₆ miles; Stakes value: $1,000,000; Winner: $650,000; Second: $200,000; Third: $100,000; Fourth: $50,000. Track: Fast. Off: 5:28 p.m. Winner: Charismatic (B. c, Mar, by Summer Squall—Bali Babe, by Drone); Times: 0:22.50, 0:45.27, 1:10.31, 1:35.24, 1:55.32. Won: Driving. Breeder: William Farish and Parrish Hill Farm.

Horse	Finish-PP	Margin	Jockey/Owner
Charismatic	1–6	1½	Chris Antley/Robert and Beverly Lewis
Menifee	2–5	head	Pat Day/Arthur B. Hancock III and James Stone
Badge	3–4	2½	Mike Luzzi/Michael Anchel
Stephen Got Even	4–11	3	Gary Stevens/Stephen Hilbert
Patience Game	5–8	½	Corey Nakatani/The Thoroughbred Corp.
Adonis	6–9	3¼	Jorge Chavez/Paraneck Stable
Cat Thief	7–3	¾	Mike Smith/Overbrook Farm
Kimberlite Pipe	8–2	8¼	Shane Sellers/John Gunther and Prairie Star Racing
Valhol	9–12	1	Edgar Prado/James Jackson
Vicar	10–13	5¾	Robby Albarado/James Tafel
Torrid Sand	11–1	9¾	Tim Doocy/Phyllis Lamberth Raines and Mike Langford
Worldly Manner	12–10	–	Jerry Bailey/Godolphin Racing Inc.
Excellent Meeting	13–7	–	Kent Desormeaux/Golden Eagle Farm

131st Belmont Stakes

June 5, 1999. Grade I, 3-year-olds; 9th race, Belmont Park, Elmont, NY. All 126 lbs. Distance: 1½ miles. Stakes purse: $1,000,000; Winner: $600,000; Second: $200,000; Third: $110,000; Fourth: $50,000; Fifth: $30,000. Track: Fast. Off: 5:29 p.m. Winner: Lemon Drop Kid (B. c, Mar, by Kingmambo—Charming Lassie, by Seattle Slew)Times: 0:23.79, 47.60, 1:12.8, 1:36.57, 2:01.90, 2:27.88. Won: Driving. Breeder: William Farish and WIlliam Kilroy.

Horse	Finish-PP	Margin	Jockey/Owner
Lemon Drop Kid	1–6	head	Jose Santos/Jeanne G. Vance
Vision and Verse	2–2	1½	Heberto Castillo/W.B. Lunsford
Charismatic	3–4	4¾	Chris Antley/Bob and Beverly Lewis
Best of Luck	4–12	½	Jean-Luc Samyn/Bohemia Stable
Stephen Got Even	5–11	3½	Shane Sellers/Stephen Hilbert
Patience Game	6–7	nose	Kent Desormeaux/The Thoroughbred Corp.
Silverbulletday	7–3	7½	Jerry Bailey/Mike Pegram
Menifee	8–10	3¼	Pat Day/Arthur B. Hancock III and James Stone
Pineaff	9–5	8	Sidney LeJeune/Joyce and Roy Monroe
Prime Directive	10–9	neck	Mike Smith/Noreen Carpenito
Teletable	11–1	2¾	John Velazquez/Robert Perez
Adonis	12–8	—	Jorge Chavez/Paraneck Stable

Major Stakes Races

Late 1998

Date	Race	Track	Distance	Winner	Jockey/Trainer	Purse ($)
Sept 19	Woodward Stakes	Belmont Park	1⅛ miles	Skip Away	Jerry Bailey/ H. Hine	500,000
Sept 25	Pegasus Handicap	Meadowlands	1⅛ miles	Tomorrows Cat	Joe Bravo M. Hennig	500,000
Sept 26	Kentucky Cup Classic Handicap	Turfway Park	1¹/₈ miles	SilverCharm/ Wild Rush	G. Stevens/P. Day B. Baffert/P. Byrne	492,500
Sept 27	Super Derby	Louisiana Downs	1¼ miles	Arch	Corey Nakatani/ F. Brothers	500,000
Oct 3	Flower Bowl Invitational Handicap	Belmont Park	1¼ miles	Auntie Mame	John Velazquez/ A. Penna, Jr.	400,000
Oct 4	Prix De L'Arc De Triomphe	Longchamp, France	1½ miles	Sagamix	Oliver Plesier/ A. Fabre	1,234,350
Oct 10	Queen Elizabeth II Challenge Cup	Keeneland	1⅛ miles	Tenski	Richard Migliore/ L. Rice	400,000
Oct. 10	Hawthorne Gold Cup	Hawthorne	1¼ miles	Awesome Again	Pat Day/ Patrick Byrne	400,000
Oct 10	The Jockey Club Gold Cup	Belmont Park	1¼ miles	Wagon Limit	Robbie Davis/ A. Jerkens	1,000,000
Oct 10	Turf Classic Invitational	Belmont Park	1½ miles	Buck's Boy	Shane Sellers/ N. Hickey	500,000
Oct 10	Moet Champagne Stakes	Belmont Park	1¹/₁₆ miles	The Groom Is Red	Corey Nakatani/ Nick Zito	400,000
Oct 10	Beldame Stakes	Belmont Park	1⅛ miles	Sharp Cat	Corey Nakatani/ W. Dollase	400,000
Oct 10	Frizette Stakes	Belmont Park	1¹/₁₆ miles	Confessional	Jerry Bailey/ William Mott	400,000
Oct 11	Alcibiades Stakes	Keeneland	1¹/₁₆ miles	Silverbullet-day	Gary Stevens/ Bob Baffert	454,800
Oct 16	Meadowlands Cup Handicap	Meadowlands	1⅛ miles	K.J.'s Appeal	John Velazquez/ F. Alexander	500,000
Oct 17	Spinster Stakes	Keeneland	1⅛ miles	Banshee Breeze	Robby Albarado/ C. Natzger	551,500
Oct 17	Goodwood Breeders' Cup Handicap	Santa Anita	1⅛ miles	Silver Charm	Gary Stevens/ Bob Baffert	446,000
Oct 18	Canadian International Stakes	Woodbine	1½ miles	Royal Anthem	Gary Stevens/ H. Cecil	1,050,000
Oct 18	Breeders' Futurity	Keeneland	1¹/₁₆ miles	Cat Thief	Pat Day/ D. Wayne Lukas	439,600
Oct 18	E.P. Taylor Stakes	Woodbine	1¼ miles	Zomaradah	Gary Stevens/ L. Cumani	456,000
Nov 7	Breeders' Cup Classic	Churchill Downs	1¼ miles	Awesome Again	Pat Day/ Patrick Byrne	4,689,920
Nov 7	Breeders' Cup Turf	Churchill Downs	1½miles	Buck's Boy	Shane Sellers/ N. Hickey	1,832,000
Nov 7	Breeders' Cup Sprint	Churchill Downs	6 furlongs	Reraise	Corey Nakatani/ C. Dollase	1,007,600
Nov 7	Breeders' Cup Mile	Churchill Downs	1 mile	Da Hoss	John Velazquez/ M. Dickinson	1,000,000
Nov 7	Breeders' Cup Juvenile Fillies	Churchill Downs	1¹/₁₆ miles	Silverbullet-day	Gary Stevens/ Bob Baffert	1,000,000
Nov 7	Breeders' Cup Distaff	Churchill Downs	1⅛ miles	Escena	Gary Stevens/ William Mott	1,832,000
Nov 7	Breeders' Cup Juvenile	Hollywood Park	1¹/₁₆ miles	Answer Lively	Jerry Bailey/ B. Barnett	1,000,000
Nov 8	Yellow Ribbon Stakes	Santa Anita Park	1¼ miles	Fiji	Kent Desormeaux/ N. Drysdale	500,000
Nov 27	Clark Handicap	Churchill Downs	1⅛ miles	Silver Charm	Gary Stevens/ Bob Baffert	444,800
Nov 28	Cigar Mile	Aqueduct	1 mile	Sir Bear	Jerry Bailey/ R. Zladje	300,000
Nov 29	Japan Cup	Tokyo Racecourse	1½miles	El Condor Pasa	Masayoshi Ebina/ Y. Ninomiya	2,849,902
Nov 29	Matriarch Stakes	Hollywood Park	1¼ miles	Squeak	Alex Solis/ B. Cecil	700,000
Nov 29	Hollywood Derby	Hollywood Park	1⅛ miles	Vergennes	John Velazquez/ M. Hennig	500,000

1999 (Through September 11)

Date	Race	Track	Distance	Winner	Jockey/Trainer	Purse ($)
Jan 30	Donn Handicap	Gulfstream Park	1⅛ miles	Puerto Madero	Kent Desormeaux/ Richard Mandella	500,000
Feb 27	Gulfstream Park Handicap	Gulfstream Park	1¼ miles	Behrens	Jorge Chavez/ H. Bond	350,000
Mar 6	Santa Anita Handicap	Santa Anita Park	1¼ miles	Free House	Chris McCarron/ P. Gonzalez	1,000,000
Mar 7	Santa Margarita Handicap	Santa Anita Park	1⅛ miles	Manistique	Gary Stevens/ J. Shirreffs	294,000
Mar 7	New Orleans Handicap	Fair Grounds	1⅛ miles	Precocity	Eddie Martin/ B. Barnett	534,000
Mar 8	Florida Derby	Gulfstream Park	1⅛ miles	Vicar	Shane Sellers/ C. Nafzger	750,000
Mar 13	Fair Grounds Oaks	Fair Grounds	1¹⁄₁₆ miles	Silverbullet-day	Gary Stevens/ Bob Baffert	372,900
Mar 14	Louisiana Derby	Fair Grounds	1¹⁄₁₆ miles	Kimberlite Pipe	Robby Albarado/ D. Steward	640,000
Mar 14	Santa Anita Oaks	Santa Anita Park	1¹⁄₁₆ miles	Excellent Meeting	Kent Desormeaux/ Bob Baffert	250,000
Mar 27	Gallery Furniture Com Stakes	Turfway Park	1⅛ miles	Stephen Got Even	Shane Sellers/ Nick Zito	750,000
Mar 28	Emirates Dubai World Cup	Nad Al Sheba	1¼ miles	Almutawakel	Richard Hills/ S. bin Suroor	5,000,000
Apr 3	Santa Anita Derby	Santa Anita Park	1⅛ miles	General Challenge	Gary Stevens/ Bob Baffert	750,000
Apr 3	Oaklawn Handicap	Oaklawn Park	1⅛ miles	Behrens	Jorge Chavez/ H.J. Bond	750,000
Apr 3	Ashland Stakes	Keeneland	1¹⁄₁₆ miles	Silverbullet-day	Jerry Bailey/ Bob Baffert	544,500
Apr 9	Apple Blossom Handicap	Oaklawn Park	1¹⁄₁₆ miles	Banshee Breeze	Jerry Bailey/ C. Nafzger	500,000
Apr 10	Arkansas Derby	Oaklawn Park	1⅛ miles	Valhol†	Brian Patin/ D. Keen	500,000
Apr 10	Bluegrass Stakes	Keeneland	1⅛ miles	Menifee	Pat Day/ E. Walden	750,000
Apr 10	Wood Memorial Stakes	Aqueduct	1⅛ miles	Adonis	Jorge Chavez/ Nick Zito	600,000
Apr 30	Kentucky Oaks	Churchill Downs	1⅛ miles	Silverbullet-day	Gary Stevens/ Bob Baffert	551,000
May 1	Kentucky Derby	Churchill Downs	1¼ miles	Charismatic	Chris Antley/ D. Wayne Lukas	1,186,200
May 8	Illinois Derby	Sportsman's Park	1⅛ miles	Vision and Verse	Herberto Castillo/ William Mott	500,000
May 15	The Preakness Stakes	Pimlico	1³⁄₁₆ miles	Charismatic	Chris Antley/ D. Wayne Lukas	1,000,000
May 29	Metropolitan Handicap	Belmont Park	1 mile	Sir Bear	John Velazquez/ R. Zladje	500,000
May 29	Massachusetts Handicap	Suffolk Downs	1⅛ miles	Behrens	Jorge Chavez/ J. Bond	600,000
May 31	Charles Whittingham Handicap	Hollywood Park	1¼ miles	River Bay	Alex Solis/ R. Frankel	400,000
May 31	Lone Star Park Handicap	Lone Star Park	1¹⁄₁₆ miles	Mocha Express	Marlon St. Julien/ T. Harder	303,300
June 5	Fleur De Lis Handicap	Churchill Downs	1⅛ miles	Banshee Breeze	Robby Albarado/ C. Nafzger	309,333
June 5	Belmont Stakes	Belmont Park	1½ miles	Lemon Drop Kid	Jose Santos/ F. Schulhofer	1,000,000
June 12	Stephen Foster Handicap	Churchill Downs	1⅛ miles	Victory Gallop	Jerry Bailey/ W.E. Walden	827,250
June 13	Shoemaker Breeders' Cup Mile	Hollywood Park	1 mile	Silic	Corey Nakatani/ J. Canani	447,000
June 26	Vanity Handicap	Hollywood Park	1⅛ miles	Manistique	Chris McCarron/ J. Shirreffs	400,000
June 27	Queen's Plate	Woodbine	1¼ miles	Woodcarver Bay	Mickey Walls/ M. Keough	500,000
June 27	Hollywood Gold Cup	Hollywood Park	1¼ miles	Real Quiet	Jerry Bailey/ Bob Baffert	1,000,000

1999 (Through September 11) *(Cont.)*

Date	Race	Track	Distance	Winner	Jockey/Trainer	Purse ($)
June 27	Irish Derby	The Curragh	1½ miles	Montjou	Cash Asmussen/ J. Hammond	959,108
July 5	Suburban Handicap	Belmont Park	1¼ miles	Behrens	Jorge Chavez/ J. Bond	400,000
July 18	Swaps Stakes	Hollywood Park	1⅛ miles	Cat Thief	Pat Day/ D. Wayne Lukas	490,000
July 18	Sunset Handicap	Hollywood Park	1½ miles	Plicok	David Flores/ R. McAnally	250,000
July 24	King George VI Queen Elizabeth	Ascot, England	1½ miles	Daylami	FrankieDettori/ S. bin Suroor	881,939
July 25	Delaware Handicap	Delaware Park	1¼ miles	Tap to Music	Pat Day/ J. Orseno	502,400
Aug 1	Whitney Handicap	Saratoga	1⅛ miles	Victory Gallop	Jerry Bailey/ W.E. Walden	600,000
Aug 8	Haskell Invitational	Monmouth Park	1⅛ miles	Menifee	Pat Day/ E. Walden	1,000,000
Aug 27	Personal Ensign Handicap	Saratoga	1¼ miles	Beautiful Pleasure	Jorge Chavez/ J. Ward	400,000
Aug 28	Travers Stakes	Saratoga	1¼ miles	Lemon Drop Kid	Jose Santos/ F. Schulhofer	1,000,000
Aug 29	Pacific Classic	Del Mar	1¼ miles	General Challenge	David Flores/ Bob Baffert	1,800,000
Sept 4	Ramona Handicap	Del Mar	1⅛ miles	Tuzla	David Flores/ Bob Baffert	400,000
Sept 6	Del Mar Derby	Del Mar	1⅛ miles	Val Royal	Corey Nakatani/ J. Canani	300,000
Sept 11	Man O' War	Belmont Park	1⅜ miles	Val's Prince	Jorge Chavez/ J. Bond	500,000

†Valhol was later disqualified.

1998 Statistical Leaders

Horses

Horse	Starts	1st	2nd	3rd	Purses ($)	Horse	Starts	1st	2nd	3rd	Purses ($)
Silver Charm	9	6	2	0	4,696,506	Buck's Boy	10	6	2	1	1,874,020
Awesome Again	6	6	0	0	3,845,990	Real Quiet	6	2	3	0	1,788,800
Skip Away	9	7	0	1	2,740,000	Coronado's Quest	11	5	2	0	1,739,950
Escena	9	5	3	0	2,032,425	Banshee Breeze	10	6	2	2	1,425,980
Victory Gallop	8	3	4	0	1,981,720	Silverbulletday	7	6	0	0	1,114,110

Jockeys

Jockey	Mounts	1st	2nd	3rd	Purses ($)	Win Pct	$ Pct*
Gary Stevens	869	178	145	122	19,358,840	.20	.51
Pat Day	1,237	278	199	211	17,380,569	.22	.55
Jerry Bailey	1,039	262	187	122	17,188,628	.25	.54
Kent Desormeaux	1,053	198	206	151	14,592,355	.18	.52
Corey Nakatani	974	211	175	159	13,437,003	.21	.55
Shane Sellers	1,286	262	191	161	12,887,304	.20	.47
Chris McCarron	728	156	121	84	10,815,559	.21	.49
John Velazquez	1,360	231	205	196	10,714,006	.16	.46
Alex Solis	1,057	166	178	146	10,587,417	.15	.46
Edgar Prado	1,969	470	377	285	9,921,241	.23	.57

*Percentage in the Money (1st, 2nd, and 3rd).

Trainers

Trainer	Starts	1st	2nd	3rd	Purses ($)	Win Pct	$ Pct*
Bob Baffert	538	139	91	80	15,000,870	.25	.57
William Mott	581	136	99	63	10,012,899	.23	.49
D. Wayne Lukas	599	103	89	68	7,248,847	.17	.43
Noll Drysdale	277	73	53	46	6,574,484	.26	.62
Jerry Hollendorfer	922	241	155	133	6,385,111	.26	.57
Richard Mandella	324	62	60	42	5,483,995	.19	.50
Patrick Byrne	91	35	11	11	5,253,707	.38	.62
W. Elliott Walden	441	75	71	66	5,082,727	.17	.48
Todd Pletcher	545	109	86	80	5,045,923	.20	.50
Claude McGaughey	294	62	48	51	5,001,211	.21	.54

*Percentage in the Money (1st, 2nd, and 3rd).

Owners

Owner	Starts	1st	2nd	3rd	Purses ($)
Stronach Stable	370	91	41	51	7,221,416
Robert and Beverly Lewis	129	31	17	16	5,776,914
Golden Eagle Farm	404	95	73	70	5,525,661
Allen E. Paulson	384	84	54	41	5,483,756
John Franks	715	123	104	77	5,145,343
Michael Pegram	106	30	17	17	4,023,643
Carolyn Hine	39	13	5	6	2,966,692
Robert and Bea Roberts	432	75	67	69	2,919,800
The Thoroughbred Corporation	126	32	20	16	2,846,751
Overbrook Farm	229	43	36	23	2,839,593

HARNESS RACING

Major Stakes Races

Late 1998

Date	Race	Location	Winner	Driver/Trainer	Purse ($)
Oct 30	Three Diamonds Pace Filly Trot	Garden State Park	Future Millbank	Michel Lachance/ Carl Conte, Jr.	493,700
Nov 14	BC Two-year-old Colt/Gelding Trot	Colonial Downs	CR Commando	Carl Allen/ Carl Allen	340,700
Nov 14	BC Two-year-old Filly Pace	Colonial Downs	Juliet's Fate	George Brennan/ Brett Pelling	431,800
Nov 14	BC Two-year-old Colt/Gelding Pace	Colonial Downs	Badlands Hanover	Ron Pierce/ Joe Holloway	502,000
Nov 14	BC Two-year-old Filly Trot	Colonial Downs	Musical Victory	Luc Ouellette/ Per Eriksson	328,200
Nov 14	BC Three-year-old Colt/Gelding Trot	Colonial Downs	Muscles Yankee	John Campbell/ Chuck Sylvester	480,000
Nov 14	BC Three-year-old Filly Trot	Colonial Downs	Lassie's Goal	Mark O'Mara/ Mark O'Mara	440,000
Nov 14	BC Three-year-old Filly Pace	Colonial Downs	Galleria	George Brennan/ Jim Campbell	480,000
Nov 14	BC Three-year-old Colt/Gelding Pace	Colonial Downs	Artiscape	Michel Lachance/ Bob McIntosh	440,000
Nov 28	Governor's Cup	Garden State Park	Island Fantasy	Michel Lachance/ Bob McIntosh	600,000

1999 (Through September 23)

Date	Race	Location	Winner	Driver/Trainer	Purse ($)
June 5	New Jersey Classic	Meadowlands	Art's Conquest	Michel Lachance Brett Pelling	500,000
June 26	North America Cup	Woodbine	The Panderosa	John Campbell/ Brett Pelling	1,000,000

Major Stakes Races *(Cont.)*

1999 (Through September 23) *(Cont.)*

Date	Race	Location	Winner	Driver/Trainer	Purse ($)
July 16	Beacon Course Trot	Meadowlands	CR Renegade	Rod Allen/ Carl Allen	430,000
July 17	Meadowlands Pace	Meadowlands	The Panderosa	John Campbell/ Brett Pelling	1,000,000
July 31	BC Three and up Open Trot	Meadowlands	Supergrit	Ron Pierce/ Carl Conte, Jr.	580,000
July 31	BC Three and up Mare Pace	Meadowlands	Shore By Five	Daniel Dube/ Bob McIntosh	282,500
July 31	BC Three and up Open Pace	Meadowlands	Red Bow Tie	Luc Ouellette/ Monti Gelrod	380,000
Aug 5	Sweetheart Pace	Meadowlands	Panything Goes	George Brennan/ Ivan Sugg	461,400
Aug 5	P. Haughton Memorial	Meadowlands	Smok'n Lantern	Berndt Lindstedt/ Jan Johnson	509,400
Aug 6	Woodrow Wilson	Meadowlands	Richness Hanover	Michel Lachance/ Bob McIntosh	600,000
Aug 7	Hambletonian	Meadowlands	Self Possessed	Michel Lachance/ Ron Gurfein	1,000,000
Aug 7	Hambletonian Oaks	Meadowlands	Oolong	John Campbell/ Frank Sheetz	500,000
Sept 23	Little Brown Jug	Delaware, OH	Blissfull Hall	Ron Pierce/ Benjamin Wallace	489,580

Major Races

The Hambletonian

Ran at The Meadowlands, East Rutherford, NJ, on August 7, 1999.

Horse	Driver	PP	¼	½	¾	Stretch-Margin	Finish-Margin
Self Possessed	Michel Lachance	4	2°	1°	1	1–2½	1-5½
Angus Hall	John Campbell	9	1°	2	2°	2–2½	2-5½
Enjoy Lavec	Luc Ouellette	7	6°	5	4	3–5½	3-5¾
Raffaello Ambrosio	Jack Moiseyev	10	8°	7	6°	4–7½	4-11½
Cherry Hills	Dave Palone	2	7	6	7°	5–10	5-14¼
Comets Tail	Berndt Lindstedt	5	9	8	8°	6–10¼	6-14½
Davanti	D.R. Ackerman	8	10	9	9	8–14¼	6-14½
Pearsall Hanover	Mickey McNichol	6	3	4	5	7–11¼	8-18¼
CR Renegade	Rod Allen	1	4	3	3	9–19¼	9-30
CR Commando	Carl Allen.	3	x5x	10	10	10–DIS	10-44

Times: 0:27.2, 0:55.3, 1:23.3, 1:51.3; Fast.

The Little Brown Jug

Ran at the Delaware County Fairgrounds, in Delaware, OH, on September 23, 1999.

Horse	Driver	PP	¼	½	¾	Stretch–Margin	Finish–Margin
Blissfull Hall	Ron Pierce	2	3	4	4°	1–2	1–1
Looking for Art	Eric Ledford	1	2	3	3	3–3	2–1
Mystical Shark	Jack Moiseyev	4	1	1°	1°	2–2	3–3¾
Royalflush Hanover	Luc Ouellette	3	4	2°	2°	4–4½	4–11

Time: 0:28.2, 0:57.3, 1:28.3, 1:55.3; Fast

Note: The 1999 Little Brown Jug was decided by a race off.

1998 Statistical Leaders

1998 Leading Moneywinners by Age, Sex and Gait

Division	Horse	Starts	1st	2nd	3rd	Earnings ($)
2-Year-Old Pacing Colts	Island Fantasy	17	10	2	2	799,919
2-Year-Old Pacing Fillies	Mattaroni	13	8	2	3	673,734
3-Year-Old Pacing Colts	Shady Character	20	10	3	2	1,070,569
3-Year-Old Pacing Fillies	Armbro Romance	18	13	2	1	784,595
Aged Pacing Horses	Red Bow Tie	30	17	4	2	839,137
Aged Pacing Mares	Jay's Table	31	13	6	2	380,590
2-Year-Old Trotting Colts	Starchip Enterprise	12	4	3	1	374,684
2-Year-Old Trotting Fillies	Rae	14	7	3	2	378,859
3-Year-Old Trotting Colts	Muscles Yankee	12	9	1	1	1,258,611
3-Year-Old Trotting Fillies	Fern	19	12	1	3	644,823
Aged Trotting Horses	Glorys Comet	31	13	7	4	720,100
Aged Trotting Mares	Moni Maker*	17	12	3	2	1,229,828

* Statistics include foreign start information

Drivers

Driver	Earnings ($)	Driver	Earnings ($)
John Campbell	10,768,771	Tony Morgan	5,777,534
Michel Lachance	9,926,239	Jack Moiseyev	5,647,414
Luc Ouellette	9,758,137	Cat Manzi	5,438,686
George Brennen	7,567,146	Steve Condren	4,590,460
Ron Pierce	5,927,575	Walter Case, Jr.	4,472,338

Feeling His Oats

Less than a month after Charismatic broke down in the Belmont Stakes, the muscular colt poked his head out of his stall in Barn 10 at Belmont Park and playfully nipped at trainer D. Wayne Lukas's fingers. "He's starting to get happy," said Lukas. "We'll have to keep him from playing too much."

For the first couple of months after his injury, playing was potentially hazardous to the health of the 1999 Kentucky Derby and Preakness winner. The broken left leg he suffered in the Belmont kept him confined to his stall for 60 days and while June 6 surgery to insert four screws into his fractured cannon bone was a success, the horse had to stay put until Lukas and veterinarians agreed that he was ready to start a walking program. "He's doing absolutely super," said Lukas. "He's an excellent patient."

A white support bandage on Charismatic's foreleg was the only evidence of his injury. The stitches from the operation were removed on June 18, and shortly thereafter he went off the anti-inflammatory medication phenylbutazone. Lukas's chief concern was how a horse as tightly wound as Charismatic —a colt who thrived on frequent strenous workouts—would handle spending his days in a 10-by-10-foot stall. "At least he's never alone," Lukas said, alluding to the round-the-clock watch his staff kept over Barn 10.

Charismatic was put up for sale to a breeding farm over the summer, but he stayed at Belmont until autumn. Then he headed to the breeding shed where he will spend his days trying to transmit some of the genes he inherited from his great-grandpa Secretariat to horses who might make a run for the Triple Crown in 2004.

FOR THE RECORD · Year by Year

THOROUGHBRED RACING

Kentucky Derby

Run at Churchill Downs, Louisville, KY, on the first Saturday in May.

Year	Winner (Margin)	Jockey	Second	Third	Time
1875	Aristides (1)	Oliver Lewis	Volcano	Verdigris	2:37¾
1876	Vagrant (2)	Bobby Swim	Creedmoor	Harry Hill	2:38¼
1877	Baden-Baden (2)	William Walker	Leonard	King William	2:38
1878	Day Star (2)	Jimmie Carter	Himyar	Leveler	2:37¼
1879	Lord Murphy (1)	Charlie Shauer	Falsetto	Strathmore	2:37
1880	Fonso (1)	George Lewis	Kimball	Bancroft	2:37½
1881	Hindoo (4)	Jimmy McLaughin	Lelex	Alfambra	2:40
1882	Apollo (½)	Babe Hurd	Runnymede	Bengal	2:40¼
1883	Leonatus (3)	Billy Donohue	Drake Carter	Lord Raglan	2:43
1884	Buchanan (2)	Isaac Murphy	Loftin	Audrain	2:40¼
1885	Joe Cotton (Neck)	Erskine Henderson	Bersan	Ten Booker	2:37¼
1886	Ben Ali (½)	Paul Duffy	Blue Wing	Free Knight	2:36½
1887	Montrose (2)	Isaac Lewis	Jim Gore	Jacobin	2:39¼
1888	MacBeth II (1)	George Covington	Gallifet	White	2:38¼
1889	Spokane (Nose)	Thomas Kiley	Proctor Knott	Once Again	2:34½
1890	Riley (2)	Isaac Murphy	Bill Letcher	Robespierre	2:45
1891	Kingman (1)	Isaac Murphy	Balgowan	High Tariff	2:52¼
1892	Azra (Nose)	Alonzo Clayton	Huron	Phil Dwyer	2:41½
1893	Lookout (5)	Eddie Kunze	Plutus	Boundless	2:39¼
1894	Chant (2)	Frank Goodale	Pearl Song	Sigurd	2:41
1895	Halma (3)	Soup Perkins	Basso	Laureate	2:37½
1896	Ben Brush (Nose)	Willie Simms	Ben Eder	Semper Ego	2:07¼
1897	Typhoon II (Head)	Buttons Garner	Ornament	Dr. Catlett	2:12½
1898	Plaudit (Neck)	Willie Simms	Lieber Karl	Isabey	2:09
1899	Manuel (2)	Fred Taral	Corsini	Mazo	2:12
1900	Lieut. Gibson (4)	Jimmy Boland	Florizar	Thrive	2:06¼
1901	His Eminence (2)	Jimmy Winkfield	Sannazarro	Driscoll	2:07¾
1902	Alan-a-Dale (Nose)	Jimmy Winkfield	Inventor	The Rival	2:08¾
1903	Judge Himes (¾)	Hal Booker	Early	Bourbon	2:09
1904	Elwood (½)	Frankie Prior	Ed Tierney	Brancas	2:08½
1905	Agile (3)	Jack Martin	Ram's Horn	Layson	2:10¾
1906	Sir Huon (2)	Roscoe Troxler	Lady Navarre	James Reddick	2:08⅘
1907	Pink Star (2)	Andy Minder	Zal	Ovelando	2:12⅗
1908	Stone Street (1)	Arthur Pickens	Sir Cleges	Dunvegan	2:15⅕
1909	Wintergreen (4)	Vincent Powers	Miami	Dr. Barkley	2:08⅕
1910	Donau (½)	Fred Herbert	Joe Morris	Fighting Bob	2:06⅖
1911	Meridian (¾)	George Archibald	Governor Gray	Colston	2:05
1912	Worth (Neck)	Carroll H. Schilling	Duval	Flamma	2:09⅖
1913	Donerail (½)	Roscoe Goose	Ten Point	Gowell	2:04⅘
1914	Old Rosebud (8)	John McCabe	Hodge	Bronzewing	2:03⅖
1915	Regret (2)	Joe Notter	Pebbles	Sharpshooter	2:05⅖
1916	George Smith (Neck)	Johnny Loftus	Star Hawk	Franklin	2:04
1917	Omar Khayyam (2)	Charles Borel	Ticket	Midway	2:04⅗
1918	Exterminator (1)	William Knapp	Escoba	Viva America	2:10⅘
1919	Sir Barton (5)	Johnny Loftus	Billy Kelly	Under Fire	2:09⅘
1920	Paul Jones (Head)	Ted Rice	Upset	On Watch	2:09
1921	Behave Yourself (Head)	Charles Thompson	Black Servant	Prudery	2:04⅕
1922	Morvich (½)	Albert Johnson	Bet Mosie	John Finn	2:04⅗
1923	Zev (1½)	Earl Sande	Martingale	Vigil	2:05⅖
1924	Black Gold (½)	John Mooney	Chilhowee	Beau Butler	2:05⅕
1925	Flying Ebony (1½)	Earl Sande	Captain Hal	Son of John	2:07⅗
1926	Bubbling Over (5)	Albert Johnson	Bagenbaggage	Rock Man	2:03⅗
1927	Whiskery (Head)	Linus McAtee	Osmond	Jock	2:06
1928	Reigh Count (3)	Chick Lang	Misstep	Toro	2:10⅖
1929	Clyde Van Dusen (2)	Linus McAtee	Naishapur	Panchio	2:10⅘
1930	Gallant Fox (2)	Earl Sande	Gallant Knight	Ned O.	2:07⅗
1931	Twenty Grand (4)	Charles Kurtsinger	Sweep All	Mate	2:01⅘
1932	Burgoo King (5)	Eugene James	Economic	Stepenfetchit	2:05⅕
1933	Brokers Tip (Nose)	Don Meade	Head Play	Charley O.	2:06⅘

Kentucky Derby *(Cont.)*

Year	Winner (Margin)	Jockey	Second	Third	Time
1934	Cavalcade (2½)	Mack Garner	Discovery	Agrarian	2:04
1935	Omaha (1½)	Willie Saunders	Roman Soldier	Whiskolo	2:05
1936	Bold Venture (Head)	Ira Hanford	Brevity	Indian Broom	2:03⅗
1937	War Admiral (1¾)	Charles Kurtsinger	Pompoon	Reaping Reward	2:03⅕
1938	Lawrin (1)	Eddie Arcaro	Dauber	Can't Wait	2:04⅘
1939	Johnstown (8)	James Stout	Challedon	Heather Broom	2:03⅖
1940	Gallahadion (1½)	Carroll Bierman	Bimelech	Dit	2:05
1941	Whirlaway (8)	Eddie Arcaro	Staretor	Market Wise	2:01⅖
1942	Shut Out (2½)	Wayne Wright	Alsab	Valdina Orphan	2:04⅖
1943	Count Fleet (3)	John Longden	Blue Swords	Slide Rule	2:04
1944	Pensive (4½)	Conn McCreary	Broadcloth	Stir Up	2:04⅕
1945	Hoop Jr. (6)	Eddie Arcaro	Pot o' Luck	Darby Dieppe	2:07
1946	Assault (8)	Warren Mehrtens	Spy Song	Hampden	2:06⅗
1947	Jet Pilot (Head)	Eric Guerin	Phalanx	Faultless	2:06⅘
1948	Citation (3½)	Eddie Arcaro	Coaltown	My Request	2:05⅖
1949	Ponder (3)	Steve Brooks	Capot	Palestinian	2:04⅕
1950	Middleground (1¼)	William Boland	Hill Prince	Mr. Trouble	2:01⅗
1951	Count Turf (4)	Conn McCreary	Royal Mustang	Ruhe	2:02⅗
1952	Hill Gail (2)	Eddie Arcaro	Sub Fleet	Blue Man	2:01⅗
1953	Dark Star (Head)	Hank Moreno	Native Dancer	Invigorator	2:02
1954	Determine (1½)	Ray York	Hasty Road	Hasseyampa	2:03
1955	Swaps (1½)	Bill Shoemaker	Nashua	Summer Tan	2:01⅘
1956	Needles (¾)	Dave Erb	Fabius	Come On Red	2:03⅖
1957	Iron Liege (Nose)	Bill Hartack	Gallant Man	Round Table	2:02⅕
1958	Tim Tam (½)	Ismael Valenzuela	Lincoln Road	Noureddin	2:05
1959	Tomy Lee (Nose)	Bill Shoemaker	Sword Dancer	First Landing	2:02⅕
1960	Venetian Way (3½)	Bill Hartack	Bally Ache	Victoria Park	2:02⅖
1961	Carry Back (¾)	John Sellers	Crozier	Bass Clef	2:04
1962	Decidedly (2¼)	Bill Hartack	Roman Line	Ridan	2:00⅖
1963	Chateaugay (1¼)	Braulio Baeza	Never Bend	Candy Spots	2:01⅘
1964	Northern Dancer (Neck)	Bill Hartack	Hill Rise	The Scoundrel	2:00
1965	Lucky Debonair (Neck)	Bill Shoemaker	Dapper Dan	Tom Rolfe	2:01⅕
1966	Kauai King (½)	Don Brumfield	Advocator	Blue Skyer	2:02
1967	Proud Clarion (1)	Bobby Ussery	Barbs Delight	Damascus	2:00⅗
1968	Forward Pass (Disq.)	Ismael Valenzuela	Francie's Hat	T.V. Commercial	2:02⅕
1969	Majestic Prince (Neck)	Bill Hartack	Arts and Letters	Dike	2:01⅘
1970	Dust Commander (5)	Mike Manganello	My Dad George	High Echelon	2:03⅖
1971	Canonero II (3¾)	Gustavo Avila	Jim French	Bold Reason	2:03⅕
1972	Riva Ridge (3¼)	Ron Turcotte	No Le Hace	Hold Your Peace	2:01⅘
1973	Secretariat (2½)	Ron Turcotte	Sham	Our Native	1:59⅖
1974	Cannonade (2¼)	Angel Cordero Jr.	Hudson County	Agitate	2:04
1975	Foolish Pleasure (1¾)	Jacinto Vasquez	Avatar	Diabolo	2:02
1976	Bold Forbes (1)	Angel Cordero Jr.	Honest Pleasure	Elocutionist	2:01⅗
1977	Seattle Slew (1¾)	Jean Cruguet	Run Dusty Run	Sanhedrin	2:02⅕
1978	Affirmed (1¼)	Steve Cauthen	Alydar	Believe It	2:01⅕
1979	Spectacular Bid (2¾)	Ronald J. Franklin	General Assembly	Golden Act	2:02⅖
1980	Genuine Risk (1)	Jacinto Vasquez	Rumbo	Jaklin Klugman	2:02
1981	Pleasant Colony (¾)	Jorge Velasquez	Woodchopper	Partez	2:02
1982	Gato Del Sol (2½)	Eddie Delahoussaye	Laser Light	Reinvested	2:02⅕
1983	Sunny's Halo (2)	Eddie Delahoussaye	Desert Wine	Caveat	2:02⅕
1984	Swale (3¼)	Laffit Pincay Jr.	Coax Me Chad	At the Threshold	2:02⅖
1985	Spend A Buck (5)	Angel Cordero Jr.	Stephan's Odyssey	Chief's Crown	2:00⅕
1986	Ferdinand (2¼)	Bill Shoemaker	Bold Arrangement	Broad Brush	2:02⅘
1987	Alysheba (¾)	Chris McCarron	Bet Twice	Avies Copy	2:03⅖
1988	Winning Colors (Neck)	Gary Stevens	Forty Niner	Risen Star	2:02⅕
1989	Sunday Silence (2½)	Pat Valenzuela	Easy Goer	Awe Inspiring	2:05
1990	Unbridled (3½)	Craig Perret	Summer Squall	Pleasant Tap	2:02
1991	Strike the Gold (1¾)	Chris Antley	Best Pal	Mane Minister	2:03
1992	Lil E. Tee (1)	Pat Day	Casual Lies	Dance Floor	2:03
1993	Sea Hero (2½)	Jerry Bailey	Prairie Bayou	Wild Gale	2:02⅖
1994	Go for Gin (2½)	Chris McCarron	Strodes Creek	Blumin Affair	2:03⅗
1995	Thunder Gulch (2¼)	Gary Stevens	Tejano Run	Timber Country	2:01⅕
1996	Grindstone (Nose)	Jerry Bailey	Cavonnier	Prince of Thieves	2:01
1997	Silver Charm (Head)	Gary Stevens	Captain Bodgit	Free House	2:02⅖
1998	Real Quiet (½)	Kent Desormeaux	Victory Gallop	Indian Charlie	2:02⅒
1999	Charismatic (Neck)	Chris Antley	Menifee	Cat Thief	2:03⅕

Note: Distance: 1½ miles (1875–95), 1¼ miles (1896–present).

Preakness

Run at Pimlico Race Course, Baltimore, Md., two weeks after the Kentucky Derby.

Year	Winner (Margin)	Jockey	Second	Third	Time
1873	Survivor (10)	G. Barbee	John Boulger	Artist	2:43
1874	Culpepper (¾)	W. Donohue	King Amadeus	Scratch	2:56½
1875	Tom Ochiltree (2)	L. Hughes	Viator	Bay Final	2:43½
1876	Shirley (4)	G. Barbee	Rappahannock	Algerine	2:44¾
1877	Cloverbrook (4)	C. Holloway	Bombast	Lucifer	2:45½
1878	Duke of Magenta (6)	C. Holloway	Bayard	Albert	2:41¾
1879	Harold (3)	L. Hughes	Jericho	Rochester	2:40½
1880	Grenada (¾)	L. Hughes	Oden	Emily F.	2:40½
1881	Saunterer (½)	T. Costello	Compensation	Baltic	2:40½
1882	Vanguard (Neck)	T. Costello	Heck	Col Watson	2:44½
1883*	Jacobus (4)	G. Barbee	Parnell		2:42½
1884*	Knight of Ellerslie (2)	S. Fisher	Welcher		2:39½
1885	Tecumseh (2)	Jim McLaughlin	Wickham	John C.	2:49
1886	The Bard (3)	S. Fisher	Eurus	Elkwood	2:45
1887	Dunboyne (1)	W. Donohue	Mahoney	Raymond	2:39½
1888	Refund (3)	F. Littlefield	Judge Murray	Glendale	2:49
1889*	Buddhist (8)	W. Anderson	Japhet	*	2:17½
1890*	Montague (3)	W. Martin	Philosophy	Barrister	2:36¾
1894	Assignee (3)	Fred Taral	Potentate	Ed Kearney	1:49¼
1895	Belmar (1)	Fred Taral	April Fool	Sue Kittie	1:50½
1896	Margrave (1)	H. Griffin	Hamilton II	Intermission	1:51
1897	Paul Kauvar (1½)	C. Thorpe	Elkins	On Deck	1:51¼
1898	Sly Fox (2)	C. W. Simms	The Huguenot	Nuto	1:49⅗
1899	Half Time (1)	R. Clawson	Filigrane	Lackland	1:47
1900	Hindus (Head)	H. Spencer	Sarmation	Ten Candles	1:48⅖
1901	The Parader (2)	F. Landry	Sadie S.	Dr. Barlow	1:47⅕
1902	Old England (Nose)	L. Jackson	Major Daingerfield	Namtor	1:45⅘
1903	Flocarline (½)	W. Gannon	Mackey Dwyer	Rightful	1:44⅘
1904	Bryn Mawr (1)	E. Hildebrand	Wotan	Dolly Spanker	1:44⅕
1905	Cairngorm (Head)	W. Davis	Kiamesha	Coy Maid	1:45⅘
1906	Whimsical (4)	Walter Miller	Content	Larabie	1:45
1907	Don Enrique (1)	G. Mountain	Ethon	Zambesi	1:45⅖
1908	Royal Tourist (4)	E. Dugan	Live Wire	Robert Cooper	1:46⅖
1909	Effendi (1)	Willie Doyle	Fashion Plate	Hilltop	1:39⅘
1910	Layminster (½)	R. Estep	Dalhousie	Sager	1:40⅗
1911	Watervale (1)	E. Dugan	Zeus	The Nigger	1:51
1912	Colonel Holloway (5)	C. Turner	Bwana Tumbo	Tipsand	1:56⅗
1913	Buskin (Neck)	J. Butwell	Kleburne	Barnegat	1:53⅖
1914	Holiday (¾)	A. Schuttinger	Brave Cunarder	Defendum	1:53⅘
1915	Rhine Maiden (1½)	Douglas Hoffman	Half Rock	Runes	1:58
1916	Damrosch (1½)	Linus McAtee	Greenwood	Achievement	1:54⅘
1917	Kalitan (2)	E. Haynes	Al M. Dick	Kentucky Boy	1:54⅖
1918*	War Cloud (¾)	Johnny Loftus	Sunny Slope	Lanius	1:53⅗
1918*	Jack Hare, Jr (2)	C. Peak	The Porter	Kate Bright	1:53⅖
1919	Sir Barton (4)	Johnny Loftus	Eternal	Sweep On	1:53
1920	Man o' War (1½)	Clarence Kummer	Upset	Wildair	1:51⅗
1921	Broomspun (¾)	F. Coltiletti	Polly Ann	Jeg	1:54⅕
1922	Pillory (Head)	L. Morris	Hea	June Grass	1:51⅗
1923	Vigil (1¼)	B. Marinelli	General Thatcher	Rialto	1:53⅗
1924	Nellie Morse (1½)	J. Merimee	Transmute	Mad Play	1:57⅕
1925	Coventry (4)	Clarence Kummer	Backbone	Almadel	1:59
1926	Display (Head)	J. Maiben	Blondin	Mars	1:59⅘
1927	Bostonian (½)	A. Abel	Sir Harry	Whiskery	2:01⅗
1928	Victorian (Nose)	Sonny Workman	Toro	Solace	2:00⅕
1929	Dr. Freeland (1)	Louis Schaefer	Minotaur	African	2:01⅗
1930	Gallant Fox (¾)	Earl Sande	Crack Brigade	Snowflake	2:00⅗
1931	Mate (1½)	G. Ellis	Twenty Grand	Ladder	1:59
1932	Burgoo King (Head)	E. James	Tick On	Boatswain	1:59⅘
1933	Head Play (4)	Charles Kurtsinger	Ladysman	Utopian	2:02
1934	High Quest (Nose)	R. Jones	Cavalcade	Discovery	1:58⅕
1935	Omaha (6)	Willie Saunders	Firethorn	Psychic Bid	1:58⅖
1936	Bold Venture (Nose)	George Woolf	Granville	Jean Bart	1:59
1937	War Admiral (Head)	Charles Kurtsinger	Pompoon	Flying Scot	1:58⅖
1938	Dauber (7)	M. Peters	Cravat	Menow	1:59⅘

Preakness (Cont.)

Year	Winner (Margin)	Jockey	Second	Third	Time
1939	Challedon (1¼)	George Seabo	Gilded Knight	Volitant	1:59⅘
1940	Bimelech (3)	F. A. Smith	Mioland	Gallahadion	1:58⅗
1941	Whirlaway (5½)	Eddie Arcaro	King Cole	Our Boots	1:58⅘
1942	Alsab (1)	B. James	Requested Sun Again	(dead heat for second)	1:57
1943	Count Fleet (8)	Johnny Longden	Blue Swords	Vincentive	1:57⅖
1944	Pensive (¾)	Conn McCreary	Platter	Stir Up	1:59⅕
1945	Polynesian (2½)	W. D. Wright	Hoop Jr.	Darby Dieppe	1:58⅘
1946	Assault (Neck)	Warren Mehrtens	Lord Boswell	Hampden	2:01⅖
1947	Faultless (1¼)	Doug Dodson	On Trust	Phalanx	1:59
1948	Citation (5½)	Eddie Arcaro	Vulcan's Forge	Boyard	2:02⅖
1949	Capot (Head)	Ted Atkinson	Palestinian	Noble Impulse	1:56
1950	Hill Prince (5)	Eddie Arcaro	Middleground	Dooley	1:59⅕
1951	Bold (7)	Eddie Arcaro	Counterpoint	Alerted	1:56⅖
1952	Blue Man (3½)	Conn McCreary	Jampol	One Count	1:57⅖
1953	Native Dancer (Neck)	Eric Guerin	Jamie K.	Royal Bay Gem	1:57⅘
1954	Hasty Road (Neck)	Johnny Adams	Correlation	Hasseyampa	1:57⅖
1955	Nashua (1)	Eddie Arcaro	Saratoga	Traffic Judge	1:54⅗
1956	Fabius (¾)	Bill Hartack	Needles	No Regrets	1:58⅖
1957	Bold Ruler (2)	Eddie Arcaro	Iron Liege	Inside Tract	1:56⅕
1958	Tim Tam (1½)	I. Valenzuela	Lincoln Road	Gone Fishin'	1:57⅕
1959	Royal Orbit (4)	William Harmatz	Sword Dancer	Dunce	1:57
1960	Bally Ache (4)	Bobby Ussery	Victoria Park	Celtic Ash	1:57⅗
1961	Carry Back (¾)	Johnny Sellers	Globemaster	Crozier	1:57⅗
1962	Greek Money (Nose)	John Rotz	Ridan	Roman Line	1:56⅕
1963	Candy Spots (3½)	Bill Shoemaker	Chateaugay	Never Bend	1:56⅕
1964	Northern Dancer (2¼)	Bill Hartack	The Scoundrel	Hill Rise	1:56⅘
1965	Tom Rolfe (Neck)	Ron Turcotte	Dapper Dan	Hail to All	1:56⅕
1966	Kauai King (1¾)	Don Brumfield	Stupendous	Amberoid	1:55⅖
1967	Damascus (2¼)	Bill Shoemaker	In Reality	Proud Clarion	1:55⅕
1968	Forward Pass (6)	I. Valenzuela	Out of the Way	Nodouble	1:56⅘
1969	Majestic Prince (Head)	Bill Hartack	Arts and Letters	Jay Ray	1:55⅗
1970	Personality (Neck)	Eddie Belmonte	My Dad George	Silent Screen	1:56⅕
1971	Canonero II (1½)	Gustavo Avila	Eastern Fleet	Jim French	1:54
1972	Bee Bee Bee (1¼)	Eldon Nelson	No Le Hace	Key to the Mint	1:55⅗
1973	Secretariat (2½)	Ron Turcotte	Sham	Our Native	1:54⅖
1974	Little Current (7)	Miguel Rivera	Neapolitan Way	Cannonade	1:54⅗
1975	Master Derby (1)	Darrel McHargue	Foolish Pleasure	Diabolo	1:56⅖
1976	Elocutionist (3)	John Lively	Play the Red	Bold Forbes	1:55
1977	Seattle Slew (1½)	Jean Cruguet	Iron Constitution	Run Dusty Run	1:54⅖
1978	Affirmed (Neck)	Steve Cauthen	Alydar	Believe It	1:54⅖
1979	Spectacular Bid (5½)	Ron Franklin	Golden Act	Screen King	1:54⅕
1980	Codex (4¾)	Angel Cordero Jr.	Genuine Risk	Colonel Moran	1:54⅕
1981	Pleasant Colony (1)	Jorge Velasquez	Bold Ego	Paristo	1:54⅗
1982	Aloma's Ruler (½)	Jack Kaenel	Linkage	Cut Away	1:55⅖
1983	Deputed Testamony (2¾)	Donald Miller Jr.	Desert Wine	High Honors	1:55⅖
1984	Gate Dancer (1½)	Angel Cordero Jr.	Play On	Fight Over	1:53⅗
1985	Tank's Prospect (Head)	Pat Day	Chief's Crown	Eternal Prince	1:53⅖
1986	Snow Chief (4)	Alex Solis	Ferdinand	Broad Brush	1:54⅘
1987	Alysheba (½)	Chris McCarron	Bet Twice	Cryptoclearance	1:55⅘
1988	Risen Star (1¼)	E. Delahoussaye	Brian's Time	Winning Colors	1:56⅕
1989	Sunday Silence (Nose)	Pat Valenzuela	Easy Goer	Rock Point	1:53⅘
1990	Summer Squall (2¼)	Pat Day	Unbridled	Mister Frisky	1:53⅗
1991	Hansel (Head)	Jerry Bailey	Corporate Report	Mane Minister	1:54
1992	Pine Bluff (¾)	Chris McCarron	Alydeed	Casual Lies	1:55⅗
1993	Prairie Bayou (½)	Mike Smith	Cherokee Run	El Bakan	1:56⅗
1994	Tabasco Cat (¾)	Pat Day	Go For Gin	Concern	1:56⅖
1995	Timber Country (½)	Pat Day	Oliver's Twist	Thunder Gulch	1:54⅖
1996	Louis Quatorze (3¼)	Pat Day	Skip Away	Editor's Note	1:53⅖
1997	Silver Charm (Head)	Gary Stevens	Free House	Captain Bodgit	1:54⅖
1998	Real Quiet (2¼)	Kent Desormeaux	Victory Gallop	Classic Cat	1:54⅗
1999	Charismatic (1½)	Chris Antley	Menifee	Badge	1:55⅕

*Preakness was a two-horse race in 1883, '84 and '89. It was not run 1891–1893; and in 1918, it was run in two divisions.

Note: Distance: 1½ miles (1873–88), 1¼ miles (1889), 1½ miles (1890), 1 1/16 miles (1894–1900), 1 mile and 70 yards (1901–1907), 1 1/16 miles (1908), 1 mile (1909–10), 1⅛ miles (1911–24), 1 3/16 miles (1925–present).

Belmont

Run at Belmont Park, Elmont, NY, three weeks after the Preakness Stakes. Held previously at two locations in the Bronx, NY: Jerome Park (1867–1889) and Morris Park (1890–1904).

Year	Winner (Margin)	Jockey	Second	Third	Time
1867	Ruthless (Head)	J. Gilpatrick	De Courcy	Rivoli	3:05
1868	General Duke (2)	R. Swim	Northumberland	Fannie Ludlow	3:02
1869	Fenian (Unknown)	C. Miller	Glenelg	Invercauld	3:04¼
1870	Kingfisher (½)	E. Brown	Foster	Midday	2:59½
1871	Harry Bassett (3)	W. Miller	Stockwood	By-the-Sea	2:56
1872	Joe Daniels (¾)	James Rowe	Meteor	Shylock	2:58¼
1873	Springbok (4)	James Rowe	Count d'Orsay	Strachino	3:01¾
1874	Saxon (Neck)	G. Barbee	Grinstead	Aaron Pennington	2:39½
1875	Calvin (2)	R. Swim	Aristides	Milner	2:40¼
1876	Algerine (Head)	W. Donahue	Fiddlestick	Barricade	2:40½
1877	Cloverbrook (1)	C. Holloway	Loiterer	Baden-Baden	2:46
1878	Duke of Magenta (2)	L. Hughes	Bramble	Sparta	2:43½
1879	Spendthrift (5)	S. Evans	Monitor	Jericho	2:42¾
1880	Grenada (½)	L. Hughes	Ferncliffe	Turenne	2:47
1881	Saunterer (Neck)	T. Costello	Eole	Baltic	2:47
1882	Forester (5)	James McLaughlin	Babcock	Wyoming	2:43
1883	George Kinney (2)	James McLaughlin	Trombone	Renegade	2:42½
1884	Panique (½)	James McLaughlin	Knight of Ellerslie	Himalaya	2:42
1885	Tyrant (3½)	Paul Duffy	St. Augustine	Tecumseh	2:43
1886	Inspector B (1)	James McLaughlin	The Bard	Linden	2:41
1887	Hanover (28-32)	James McLaughlin	Oneko		2:43½
1888	Sir Dixon (12)	James McLaughlin	Prince Royal		2:40¼
1889	Eric (Head)	W. Hayward	Diable	Zephyrus	2:47
1890	Burlington (1)	S. Barnes	Devotee	Padishah	2:07¾
1891	Foxford (Neck)	E. Garrison	Montana	Laurestan	2:08¾
1892	Patron (Unknown)	W. Hayward	Shellbark		2:17
1893	Comanche (Head)(21)	Willie Simms	Dr. Rice	Rainbow	1:53¼
1894	Henry of Navarre (2-4)	Willie Simms	Prig	Assignee	1:56½
1895	Belmar (Head)	Fred Taral	Counter Tenor	Nanki Pooh	2:11½
1896	Hastings (Neck)	H. Griffin	Handspring	Hamilton II	2:24½
1897	Scottish Chieftain (1)	J. Scherrer	On Deck	Octagon	2:23¼
1898	Bowling Brook (8)	P. Littlefield	Previous	Hamburg	2:32
1899	Jean Bereaud (Head)	R. R. Clawson	Half Time	Glengar	2:23
1900	Ildrim (Head)	N. Turner	Petrucio	Missionary	2:21½
1901	Commando (½)	H. Spencer	The Parader	All Green	2:21
1902	Masterman (2)	John Bullmann	Ranald	King Hanover	2:22½
1903	Africander (2)	John Bullmann	Whorler	Red Knight	2:23⅕
1904	Delhi (3½)	George Odom	Graziallo	Rapid Water	2:06⅗
1905	Tanya (1/2)	E. Hildebrand	Blandy	Hot Shot	2:08
1906	Burgomaster (4)	L. Lyne	The Quail	Accountant	2:20
1907	Peter Pan (1)	G. Mountain	Superman	Frank Gill	Unknown
1908	Colin (Head)	Joe Notter	Fair Play	King James	Unknown
1909	Joe Madden (8)	E. Dugan	Wise Mason	Donald MacDonald	2:21⅗
1910*	Sweep (6)	J. Butwell	Duke of Ormonde		2:22
1913	Prince Eugene (½)	Roscoe Troxler	Rock View	Flying Fairy	2:18
1914	Luke McLuke (8)	M. Buxton	Gainer	Charlestonian	2:20
1915	The Finn (4)	G. Byrne	Half Rock	Pebbles	2:18⅘
1916	Friar Rock (3)	E. Haynes	Spur	Churchill	2:22
1917	Hourless (10)	J. Butwell	Skeptic	Wonderful	2:17⅘
1918	Johren (2)	Frank Robinson	War Cloud	Cum Sah	2:20⅘
1919	Sir Barton (5)	Johnny Loftus	Sweep On	Natural Bridge	2:17⅖
1920	Man o' War (20)	Clarence Kummer	Donnacona		2:14⅕
1921	Grey Lag (3)	Earl Sande	Sporting Blood	Leonardo II	2:16⅘
1922	Pillory (2)	C. H. Miller	Snob II	Hea	2:18⅘
1923	Zev (1½)	Earl Sande	Chickvale	Rialto	2:19
1924	Mad Play (2)	Earl Sande	Mr. Mutt	Modest	2:18⅘
1925	American Flag (8)	Albert Johnson	Dangerous	Swope	2:16⅘
1926	Crusader (1)	Albert Johnson	Espino	Haste	2:32⅕
1927	Chance Shot (1½)	Earl Sande	Bois de Rose	Flambino	2:32⅖
1928	Vito (3)	Clarence Kummer	Genie	Diavolo	2:33⅕

Belmont (Cont.)

Year	Winner (Margin)	Jockey	Second	Third	Time
1929	Blue Larkspur (¾)	Mack Garner	African	Jack High	2:32⅘
1930	Gallant Fox (3)	Earl Sande	Whichone	Questionnaire	2:31⅗
1931	Twenty Grand (10)	Charles Kurtsinger	Sun Meadow	Jamestown	2:29⅗
1932	Faireno (1½)	T. Malley	Osculator	Flag Pole	2:32⅘
1933	Hurryoff (1½)	Mack Garner	Nimbus	Union	2:32⅗
1934	Peace Chance (6)	W. D. Wright	High Quest	Good Goods	2:29⅕
1935	Omaha (1½)	Willie Saunders	Firethorn	Rosemont	2:30⅗
1936	Granville (Nose)	James Stout	Mr. Bones	Hollyrood	2:30
1937	War Admiral (3)	Charles Kurtsinger	Sceneshifter	Vamoose	2:28⅗
1938	Pasteurized (Neck)	James Stout	Dauber	Cravat	2:29⅖
1939	Johnstown (5)	James Stout	Belay	Gilded Knight	2:29⅗
1940	Bimelech (¾)	F. A. Smith	Your Chance	Andy K	2:29⅗
1941	Whirlaway (2½)	Eddie Arcaro	Robert Morris	Yankee Chance	2:31
1942	Shut Out (2)	Eddie Arcaro	Alsab	Lochinvar	2:29⅕
1943	Count Fleet (25)	Johnny Longden	Fairy Manhurst	Deseronto	2:28⅕
1944	Bounding Home (½)	G. L. Smith	Pensive	Bull Dandy	2:32⅕
1945	Pavot (5)	Eddie Arcaro	Wildlife	Jeep	2:30⅕
1946	Assault (3)	Warren Mehrtens	Natchez	Cable	2:30⅘
1947	Phalanx (5)	R. Donoso	Tide Rips	Tailspin	2:29⅖
1948	Citation (8)	Eddie Arcaro	Better Self	Escadru	2:28⅕
1949	Capot (½)	Ted Atkinson	Ponder	Palestinian	2:30⅕
1950	Middleground (1)	William Boland	Lights Up	Mr. Trouble	2:28⅗
1951	Counterpoint (4)	D. Gorman	Battlefield	Battle Morn	2:29
1952	One Count (2½)	Eddie Arcaro	Blue Man	Armageddon	2:30⅕
1953	Native Dancer (Neck)	Eric Guerin	Jamie K.	Royal Bay Gem	2:38⅗
1954	High Gun (Neck)	Eric Guerin	Fisherman	Limelight	2:30⅘
1955	Nashua (9)	Eddie Arcaro	Blazing Count	Portersville	2:29
1956	Needles (Neck)	David Erb	Career Boy	Fabius	2:29⅘
1957	Gallant Man (8)	Bill Shoemaker	Inside Tract	Bold Ruler	2:26⅗
1958	Cavan (6)	Pete Anderson	Tim Tam	Flamingo	2:30⅕
1959	Sword Dancer (¾)	Bill Shoemaker	Bagdad	Royal Orbit	2:28⅖
1960	Celtic Ash (5½)	Bill Hartack	Venetian Way	Disperse	2:29⅗
1961	Sherluck (2¼)	Braulio Baeza	Globemaster	Guadalcanal	2:29⅕
1962	Jaipur (Nose)	Bill Shoemaker	Admiral's Voyage	Crimson Satan	2:28⅘
1963	Chateaugay (2½)	Braulio Baeza	Candy Spots	Choker	2:30⅕
1964	Quadrangle (2)	Manuel Ycaza	Roman Brother	Northern Dancer	2:28⅖
1965	Hail to All (Neck)	John Sellers	Tom Rolfe	First Family	2:28⅖
1966	Amberold (2½)	William Boland	Buffle	Advocator	2:29⅗
1967	Damascus (2½)	Bill Shoemaker	Cool Reception	Gentleman James	2:28⅘
1968	Stage Door Johnny (1¼)	Hellodoro Gustines	Forward Pass	Call Me Prince	2:27⅕
1969	Arts and Letters (5½)	Braulio Baeza	Majestic Prince	Dike	2:28⅘
1970	High Echelon (¾)	John L. Rotz	Needles N Pins	Naskra	2:34
1971	Pass Catcher (¾)	Walter Blum	Jim French	Bold Reason	2:30⅖
1972	Riva Ridge (7)	Ron Turcotte	Ruritania	Cloudy Dawn	2:28
1973	Secretariat (31)	Ron Turcotte	Twice a Prince	My Gallant	2:24
1974	Little Current (7)	Miguel A. Rivera	Jolly Johu	Cannonade	2:29⅕
1975	Avatar (Neck)	Bill Shoemaker	Foolish Pleasure	Master Derby	2:28⅕
1976	Bold Forbes (Neck)	Angel Cordero Jr.	McKenzie Bridge	Great Contractor	2:29
1977	Seattle Slew (4)	Jean Cruguet	Run Dusty Run	Sanhedrin	2:29⅗
1978	Affirmed (Head)	Steve Cauthen	Alydar	Darby Creek Road	2:26⅘
1979	Coastal (3¼)	Ruben Hernandez	Golden Act	Spectacular Bid	2:28⅗
1980	Temperence Hill (2)	Eddie Maple	Genuine Risk	Rockhill Native	2:29⅘
1981	Summing (Neck)	George Martens	Highland Blade	Pleasant Colony	2:29
1982	Conquistador Cielo (14½)	Laffit Pincay, Jr.	Gato Del Sol	Illuminate	2:28⅕
1983	Caveat (3½)	Laffit Pincay Jr.	Slew o'Gold	Barberstown	2:27⅘
1984	Swale (4)	Laffit Pincay Jr.	Pine Circle	Morning Bob	2:27⅕
1985	Creme Fraiche (½)	Eddie Maple	Stephan's Odyssey	Chief's Crown	2:27
1986	Danzig Connection (1¼)	Chris McCarron	Johns Treasure	Ferdinand	2:29⅘
1987	Bet Twice (14)	Craig Perret	Cryptoclearance	Gulch	2:28⅕
1988	Risen Star (14¾)	Eddie Delahoussaye	Kingpost	Brian's Time	2:26⅖
1989	Easy Goer (8)	Pat Day	Sunday Silence	Le Voyageur	2:26

Belmont (Cont.)

Year	Winner (Margin)	Jockey	Second	Third	Time
1990	Go and Go (8¼)	Michael Kinane	Thirty Six Red	Baron de Vaux	2:27⅕
1991	Hansel (Head)	Jerry Bailey	Strike the Gold	Mane Minister	2:28
1992	A.P. Indy (¾)	Eddie Delahoussaye	My Memoirs	Pine Bluff	2:26
1993	Colonial Affair (2¼)	Julie Krone	Kissin Kris	Wild Gale	2:29⅘
1994	Tabasco Cat (2)	Pat Day	Go For Gin	Strodes Creek	2:26⅘
1995	Thunder Gulch (2)	Gary Stevens	Star Standard	Citadeed	2:32
1996	Editor's Note (1)	Rene Douglas	Skip Away	My Flag	2:28⅘
1997	Touch Gold (¾)	Chris McCarron	Silver Charm	Free House	2:28⅘
1998	Victory Gallop (Nose)	Gary Stevens	Real Quiet	Thomas Jo	2:28⅘
1999	Lemon Drop Kid (Head)	Jose Santos	Vision and Verse	Charismatic	2:27⅘

*Belmont was a two-horse race in 1887, 88, 92, 1910 and '20; and was not held in 1911–1912.
Note: Distance: 1 mile 5 furlongs (1867–89), 1¼ miles (1890–1905), 1⅜ miles (1906–25), 1½ miles (1926–present).

Triple Crown Winners

Year	Horse	Jockey	Owner	Trainer
1919	Sir Barton	John Loftus	J. K. L. Ross	H. G. Bedwell
1930	Gallant Fox	Earle Sande	Belair Stud	James Fitzsimmons
1935	Omaha	William Saunders	Belair Stud	James Fitzsimmons
1937	War Admiral	Charles Kurtsinger	Samuel D. Riddle	George Conway
1941	Whirlaway	Eddie Arcaro	Calumet Farm	Ben Jones
1943	Count Fleet	John Longden	Mrs J. D. Hertz	Don Cameron
1946	Assault	Warren Mehrtens	King Ranch	Max Hirsch
1948	Citation	Eddie Arcaro	Calumet Farm	Jimmy Jones
1973	Secretariat	Ron Turcotte	Meadow Stable	Lucien Laurin
1977	Seattle Slew	Jean Cruguet	Karen L. Taylor	William H. Turner Jr.
1978	Affirmed	Steve Cauthen	Harbor View Farm	Laz Barrera

Awards

Horse of the Year

Year	Horse	Owner	Trainer	Breeder
1936	Granville	Belair Stud	James Fitzsimmons	Belair Stud
1937	War Admiral	Samuel D. Riddle	George Conway	Mrs. Samuel D. Riddle
1938	Seabiscuit	Charles S. Howard	Tom Smith	Wheatley Stable
1939	Challedon	William L. Brann	Louis J. Schaefer	Branncastle Farm
1940	Challedon	William L. Brann	Louis J. Schaefer	Branncastle Farm
1941	Whirlaway	Calumet Farm	Ben Jones	Calumet Farm
1942	Whirlaway	Calumet Farm	Ben Jones	Calumet Farm
1943	Count Fleet	Mrs. John D. Hertz	Don Cameron	Mrs. John D. Hertz
1944	Twilight Tear	Calumet Farm	Ben Jones	Calumet Farm
1945	Busher	Louis B. Mayer	George Odom	Idle Hour Stock Farm
1946	Assault	King Ranch	Max Hirsch	King Ranch
1947	Armed	Calumet Farm	Jimmy Jones	Calumet Farm
1948	Citation	Calumet Farm	Jimmy Jones	Calumet Farm
1949	Capot	Greentree Stable	John M. Gaver Sr.	Greentree Stable
1950	Hill Prince	C.T. Chenery	Casey Hayes	C.T. Chenery
1951	Counterpoint	C.V. Whitney	Syl Veitch	C.V. Whitney
1952	One Count	Mrs. W. M. Jeffords	O. White	W M. Jeffords
1953	Tom Fool	Greentree Stable	John M. Gaver Sr.	D.A. Headley
1954	Native Dancer	A.G. Vanderbilt	Bill Winfrey	A.G. Vanderbilt
1955	Nashua	Belair Stud	James Fitzsimmons	Belair Stud
1956	Swaps	Ellsworth-Galbreath	Mesh Tenney	R. Ellsworth
1957	Bold Ruler	Wheatley Stable	James Fitzsimmons	Wheatley Stable
1958	Round Table	Kerr Stables	Willy Molter	Claiborne Farm
1959	Sword Dancer	Brookmeade Stable	Elliott Burch	Brookmeade Stable
1960	Kelso	Bohemia Stable	C. Hanford	Mrs. R.C. duPont
1961	Kelso	Bohemia Stable	C. Hanford	Mrs. R.C. duPont
1962	Kelso	Bohemia Stable	C. Hanford	Mrs. R.C. duPont
1963	Kelso	Bohemia Stable	C. Hanford	Mrs. R.C. duPont
1964	Kelso	Bohemia Stable	C. Hanford	Mrs. R.C. duPont
1965	Roman Brother	Harbor View Stable	Burley Parke	Ocala Stud
1966	Buckpasser	Ogden Phipps	Eddie Neloy	Ogden Phipps
1967	Damascus	Mrs. E. W. Bancroft	Frank Y. Whiteley Jr.	Mrs. E. W. Bancroft

Horse of the Year (Cont.)

Year	Horse	Owner	Trainer	Breeder
1968	Dr. Fager	Tartan Stable	John A. Nerud	Tartan Farms
1969	Arts and Letters	Rokeby Stable	Elliott Burch	Paul Mellon
1970	Fort Marcy	Rokeby Stable	Elliott Burch	Paul Mellon
1971	Ack Ack	E.E. Fogelson	Charlie Whittingham	H.F. Guggenheim
1972	Secretariat	Meadow Stable	Lucien Laurin	Meadow Stud
1973	Secretariat	Meadow Stable	Lucien Laurin	Meadow Stud
1974	Forego	Lazy F Ranch	Sherrill W. Ward	Lazy F Ranch
1975	Forego	Lazy F Ranch	Sherrill W. Ward	Lazy F Ranch
1976	Forego	Lazy F Ranch	Frank Y. Whiteley Jr.	Lazy F Ranch
1977	Seattle Slew	Karen L. Taylor	Billy Turner Jr.	B.S. Castleman
1978	Affirmed	Harbor View Farm	Laz Barrera	Harbor View Farm
1979	Affirmed	Harbor View Farm	Laz Barrera	Harbor View Farm
1980	Spectacular Bid	Hawksworth Farm	Bud Delp	Mmes. Gilmore and Jason
1981	John Henry	Dotsam Stable	Ron McAnally and Lefty Nickerson	Golden Chance Farm
1982	Conquistador Cielo	H. de Kwiatkowski	Woody Stephens	L.E. Landoli
1983	All Along	Daniel Wildenstein	P.L. Biancone	Dayton
1984	John Henry	Dotsam Stable	Ron McAnally	Golden Chance Farm
1985	Spend a Buck	Hunter Farm	Cam Gambolati	Irish Hill Farm & R.W. Harper
1986	Lady's Secret	Mr. & Mrs. Eugene Klein	D. Wayne Lukas	R.H. Spreen
1987	Ferdinand	Mrs. H.B. Keck	Charlie Whittingham	H.B. Keck
1988	Alysheba	D. & P. Scharbauer	Jack Van Berg	Preston Madden
1989	Sunday Silence	Gaillard, Hancock, & Whittingham	Charlie Whittingham	Oak Cliff Thoroughbreds
1990	Criminal Type	Calumet Farm	D. Wayne Lukas	Calumet Farm
1991	Black Tie Affair	Jeffrey Sullivan	Ernie Poulos	Stephen D. Peskoff
1992	A.P. Indy	Tomonori Tsurumaki	Neil Drysdale	W.S. Farish & W.S. Kilroy
1993	Kotashaan	La Presle Farm	Richard Mandella	La Presle Farm
1994	Holy Bull	Jimmy Croll	Jimmy Croll	Pelican Stable
1995	Cigar	Allen E. Paulson	William Mott	Allen E. Paulson
1996	Cigar	Allen E. Paulson	William Mott	Allen E. Paulson
1997	Favorite Trick	Joseph LaCombe	William Mott	Mr. & Mrs. M.L. Wood
1998	Skip Away	Carolyn Hine	Hubert Hine	Anna Marie Barnhart

Note: From 1936 to 1970, the *Daily Racing Form* annually selected a "Horse of the Year." In 1971 the *Daily Racing Form*, with the Thoroughbred Racing Association and the National Turf Writers Association, jointly created the Eclipse Awards.

Eclipse Award Winners

	2-YEAR-OLD COLT		2-YEAR-OLD FILLY		3-YEAR-OLD COLT
1971	Riva Ridge	1971	Numbered Account	1971	Canonero II
1972	Secretariat	1972	La Prevoyante	1972	Key to the Mint
1973	Protagonist	1973	Talking Picture	1973	Secretariat
1974	Foolish Pleasure	1974	Ruffian	1974	Little Currant
1975	Honest Pleasure	1975	Dearly Precious	1975	Wajima
1976	Seattle Slew	1976	Sensational	1976	Bold Forbes
1977	Affirmed	1977	Lakeville Miss	1977	Seattle Slew
1978	Spectacular Bid	1978	Candy Eclair, It's in the Air	1978	Affirmed
1979	Rockhill Native	1979	Smart Angle	1979	Spectacular Bid
1980	Lord Avie	1980	Heavenly Cause	1980	Temperence Hill
1981	Deputy Minister	1981	Before Dawn	1981	Pleasant Colony
1982	Roving Boy	1982	Landaluce	1982	Conquistador Cielo
1983	Devil's Bag	1983	Althea	1983	Slew o' Gold
1984	Chief's Crown	1984	Outstandingly	1984	Swale
1985	Tasso	1985	Family Style	1985	Spend A Buck
1986	Capote	1986	Brave Raj	1986	Snow Chief
1987	Forty Niner	1987	Epitome	1987	Alysheba
1988	Easy Goer	1988	Open Mind	1988	Risen Star
1989	Rhythm	1989	Go for Wand	1989	Sunday Silence
1990	Fly So Free	1990	Meadow Star	1990	Unbridled
1991	Arazi	1991	Pleasant Stage	1991	Hansel
1992	Gilded Time	1992	Eliza	1992	A.P. Indy
1993	Dehere	1993	Phone Chatter	1993	Prairie Bayou
1994	Timber Country	1994	Flanders	1994	Holy Bull
1995	Maria's Mon	1995	Golden Attraction	1995	Thunder Gulch
1996	Boston Harbor	1996	Storm Song	1996	Skip Away
1997	Favorite Trick	1997	Countess Diana	1997	Silver Charm
1998	Answer Lively	1998	Silverbullettday	1998	Real Quiet

Eclipse Award Winners (Cont.)

3-YEAR-OLD FILLY

1971 ....Turkish Trousers
1972 ....Susan's Girl
1973 ....Desert Vixen
1974 ....Chris Evert
1975 ....Ruffian
1976 ....Revidere
1977 ....Our Mims
1978 ....Tempest Queen
1979 ....Davona Dale
1980 ....Genuine Risk
1981 ....Wayward Lass
1982 ....Christmas Past
1983 ....Heartlight No. One
1984 ....Life's Magic
1985 ....Mom's Command
1986 ....Tiffany Lass
1987 ....Sacahuista
1988 ....Winning Colors
1989 ....Open Mind
1990 ....Go for Wand
1991 ....Dance Smartly
1992 ....Saratoga Dew
1993 ....Hollywood Wildcat
1994 ....Heavenly Prize
1995 ....Serena's Song
1996 ....Yank's Music
1997 ....Ajina
1998 ....Banshee Breeze

OLDER COLT, HORSE OR GELDING

1971 .....Ack Ack (5)
1972 ....Autobiography (4)
1973 ....Riva Ridge (4)
1974 ....Forego (4)
1975 ....Forego (5)
1976 ....Forego (6)
1977 ....Forego (7)
1978 ....Seattle Slew (4)
1979 ....Affirmed (4)
1980 ....Spectacular Bid (4)
1981 ....John Henry (6)
1982 ....Lemhi Gold (4)
1983 ....Bates Motel (4)
1984 ....Slew o'Gold (4)
1985 ....Vanlandingham (4)
1986 ....Turkoman (4)
1987 ....Ferdinand (4)
1988 ....Alysheba (4)
1989 ....Blushing John (4)
1990 ....Criminal Type (5)
1991 ....Black Tie Affair (5)
1992 ....Pleasant Tap (5)
1993 ....Bertrando (4)
1994 ....The Wicked North (5)
1995 ....Cigar (5)
1996 ....Cigar (6)
1997 ....Skip Away (4)
1998 ....Skip Away (5)

OLDER FILLY OR MARE

1971 ....Shuvee (5)
1972 ....Typecast (6)
1973 ....Susan's Girl (4)
1974 ....Desert Vixen (4)
1975 ....Susan's Girl (6)
1976 ....Proud Delta (4)
1977 ....Cascapedia (4)
1978 ....Late Bloomer (4)

OLDER FILLY OR MARE (Cont.)

1979 ....Waya (5)
1980 .....Glorious Song (4)
1981 ....Relaxing (5)
1982 ....Track Robbery (6)
1983 ....Ambassador of Luck (4)
1984 ....Princess Rooney (4)
1985 ....Life's Magic (4)
1986 ....Lady's Secret (4)
1987 ....North Sider (5)
1988 ....Personal Ensign (4)
1989 .....Bayakoa (5)
1990 .....Bayakoa (6)
1991 .....Queena (5)
1992 .....Paseana (4)
1993 .....Paseana (6)
1994 .....Sky Beauty (4)
1995 ....Inside Information (4)
1996 ....Jewel Princess (4)
1997 .....Hidden Lake (4)
1998 .....Escena (5)

CHAMPION TURF HORSE

1971 .....Run the Gantlet (3)
1972 .....Cougar II (6)
1973 .....Secretariat (3)
1974 .....Dahlia (4)
1975 .....Snow Knight (4)
1976 .....Youth (3)
1977 .....Johnny D (3)
1978 .....Mac Diarmida (3)

CHAMPION MALE TURF HORSE

1979 .....Bowl Game (5)
1980 .....John Henry (5)
1981 .....John Henry (6)
1982 .....Perrault (5)
1983 .....John Henry (8)
1984 .....John Henry (9)
1985 .....Cozzene (4)
1986 .....Manila (3)
1987 .....Theatrical (5)
1988 .....Sunshine Forever (3)
1989 .....Steinlen (6)
1990 .....Itsallgreektome (3)
1991 .....Tight Spot (4)
1992 .....Sky Classic (5)
1993 .....Kotashaan (5)
1994 .....Paradise Creek (5)
1995 .....Northern Spur (4)
1996 .....Singspiel (4)
1997 .....Chief Bearhart (4)
1998 .....Buck's Boy (5)

CHAMPION FEMALE TURF HORSE

1979 .....Trillion (5)
1980 .....Just a Game II (4)
1981 .....De La Rose (3)
1982 .....April Run (4)
1983 .....All Along (4)
1984 .....Royal Heroine (4)
1985 .....Pebbles (4)
1986 .....Estrapade (6)
1987 .....Miesque (3)
1988 .....Miesque (4)
1989 .....Brown Bess (7)
1990 .....Laugh and Be Merry (5)
1991 .....Miss Alleged (4)
1992 .....Flawlessly (4)

CHAMPION FEMALE TURF HORSE (Cont.)

1993 .....Flawlessly (5)
1994 .....Hatoof (5)
1995 .....Possibly Perfect (5)
1996 .....Wandesta (5)
1997 .....Ryafan (3)
1998 .....Fiji (4)

STEEPLECHASE OR HURDLE HORSE

1971 .....Shadow Brook (7)
1972 .....Soothsayer (5)
1973 .....Athenian Idol (5)
1974 .....Gran Kan (8)
1975 .....Life's Illusion (4)
1976 .....Straight & True (6)
1977 .....Cafe Prince (7)
1978 .....Cafe Prince (8)
1979 .....Martie's Anger (4)
1980 .....Zaccio (4)
1981 .....Zaccio (5)
1982 .....Zaccio (6)
1983 .....Flatterer (4)
1984 .....Flatterer (5)
1985 .....Flatterer (6)
1986 .....Flatterer (7)
1987 .....Inlander (6)
1988 .....Jimmy Lorenzo (6)
1989 .....Highland Bud (4)
1990 .....Morley Street (7)
1991 .....Morley Street (8)
1992 .....Lonesome Glory (4)
1993 .....Lonesome Glory (5)
1994 .....Warm Spell (6)
1995 .....Lonesome Glory (7)
1996 .....Corregio (5)
1997 .....Lonesome Glory (9)
1998 .....Flat Top (5)

SPRINTER

1971 .....Ack Ack (5)
1972 .....Chou Croute (4)
1973 .....Shecky Greene (3)
1974 .....Forego (4)
1975 .....Gallant Bob (3)
1976 .....My Juliet (4)
1977 .....What a Summer (4)
1978 .....Dr. Patches (4)
              J.O. Tobin (4)
1979 .....Star de Naskra (4)
1980 .....Plugged Nickel (3)
1981 .....Guilty Conscience (5)
1982 .....Gold Beauty (3)
1983 .....Chinook Pass (4)
1984 .....Eillo (4)
1985 .....Precisionist (4)
1986 .....Smile (4)
1987 .....Groovy (4)
1988 .....Gulch (4)
1989 .....Safely Kept (3)
1990 .....Housebuster (3)
1991 .....Housebuster (4)
1992 .....Rubiano (5)
1993 .....Cardmania (7)
1994 .....Cherokee Run (4)
1995 .....Not Surprising (5)
1996 .....Lit de Justice (6)
1997 .....Smoke Glacken (3)
1998 .....Reraise (3)

Note: Number in parentheses is horse's age.

Eclipse Award Winners (Cont.)

OUTSTANDING OWNER

1971.....Mr. & Mrs. E. E. Fogleson
1974.....Dan Lasater
1975.....Dan Lasater
1976.....Dan Lasater
1977.....Maxwell Gluck
1978.....Harbor View Farm
1979.....Harbor View Farm
1980.....Mr. & Mrs. Bertram
1981.....Dotsam Stable
1982.....Viola Sommer
1983.....John Franks
1984.....John Franks
1985.....Mr. & Mrs. Eugene Klein
1986.....Mr. & Mrs. Eugene Klein
1987.....Mr. & Mrs. Eugene Klein
1988.....Ogden Phipps
1989.....Ogden Phipps
1990.....Frances Genter
1991.....Sam-Son Farm
1992.....Juddmonte Farms
1993.....John Franks
1994.....John Franks
1995.....Allen E. Paulson
1996.....Allen E. Paulson
1997.....Carolyn Hine
1998.....Frank Stronach

OUTSTANDING TRAINER

1971.....Charlie Whittingham
1972.....Lucien Laurin
1973.....H. Allen Jerkens
1974.....Sherrill Ward
1975.....Steve DiMauro
1976.....Lazaro Barrera
1977.....Lazaro Barrera
1978.....Lazaro Barrera
1979.....Lazaro Barrera
1980.....Bud Delp
1981.....Ron McAnally
1982.....Charlie Whittingham
1983.....Woody Stephens
1984.....Jack Van Berg
1985.....D. Wayne Lukas
1986.....D. Wayne Lukas
1987.....D. Wayne Lukas
1988.....Claude R. McGaughey III
1989.....Charlie Whittingham
1990.....Carl Nafzger
1991.....Ron McAnally
1992.....Ron McAnally
1993.....Bobby Frankel
1994.....D. Wayne Lukas
1995.....William Mott
1996.....William Mott
1997.....Bob Baffert
1998.....Bob Baffert

OUTSTANDING JOCKEY

1971.....Laffit Pincay Jr.
1972.....Braulio Baeza
1973.....Laffit Pincay Jr
1974.....Laffit Pincay Jr
1975.....Braulio Baeza
1976.....Sandy Hawley
1977.....Steve Cauthen
1978.....Darrel McHargue
1979.....Laffit Pincay Jr.
1980.....Chris McCarron
1981.....Bill Shoemaker
1982.....Angel Cordero Jr
1983.....Angel Cordero Jr
1984.....Pat Day
1985.....Laffit Pincay Jr
1986.....Pat Day
1987.....Pat Day
1988.....Jose Santos
1989.....Kent Desormeaux
1990.....Craig Perret
1991.....Pat Day
1992.....Kent Desormeaux
1993.....Mike Smith
1994.....Mike Smith
1995.....Jerry Bailey
1996.....Jerry Bailey
1997.....Jerry Bailey
1998.....Gary Stevens

OUTSTANDING APPRENTICE JOCKEY

1971.....Gene St. Leon
1972.....Thomas Wallis
1973.....Steve Valdez
1974.....Chris McCarron
1975.....Jimmy Edwards
1976.....George Martens
1977.....Steve Cauthen
1978.....Ron Franklin
1979.....Cash Asmussen
1980.....Frank Lovato Jr.
1981.....Richard Migliore
1982.....Alberto Delgado
1983.....Declan Murphy
1984.....Wesley Ward
1985.....Art Madrid Jr.
1986.....Allen Stacy
1987.....Kent Desormeaux
1988.....Steve Capanas
1989.....Michael Luzzi
1990.....Mark Johnston
1991.....Mickey Walls
1992.....Jesus A. Bracho
1993.....Juan Umana
1994.....Dale Beckner
1995.....Ramon Perez
1996.....Neil Pozansky
1997.....Phil Teator
　　　　　Roberto Rosado
1998.....Shaun Bridgmohan

OUTSTANDING BREEDER

1974.....John W. Galbreath
1975.....Fred W. Hooper
1976.....Nelson Bunker Hunt
1977.....Edward Plunket Taylor
1978.....Harbor View Farm
1979.....Claiborne Farm
1980.....Mrs. Henry D. Paxson
1981.....Golden Chance Farm
1982.....Fred W. Hooper
1983.....Edward Plunket Taylor
1984.....Claiborne Farm
1985.....Nelson Bunker Hunt
1986.....Paul Mellon
1987.....Nelson Bunker Hunt
1988.....Ogden Phipps
1989.....North Ridge Farm
1990.....Calumet Farm
1991.....John and Betty Mabee
1992.....William S. Farish III
1993.....Allen Paulson
1994.....William T. Young
1995.....Juddmonte Farms
1996.....Fansworth Farms
1997.....Golden Eagle Farm
1998.....John and Betty Mabee

AWARD OF MERIT

1976.....Jack J. Dreyfus
1977.....Steve Cauthen
1978.....Ogden Phipps
1979.....Frank E. Kilroe
1980.....John D. Schapiro
1981.....Bill Shoemaker
1984.....John Gaines
1985.....Keene Daingerfield
1986.....Herman Cohen
1987.....J. B. Faulconer
1988.....John Forsythe
1989.....Michael P. Sandler
1991.....Fred W. Hooper
1994.....Alfred G. Vanderbilt
1996.....Allen E. Paulson

SPECIAL AWARD

1971.....Robert J. Kleberg
1974.....Charles Hatton
1976.....Bill Shoemaker
1980.....John T. Landry
　　　　　Pierre E. Bellocq (Peb)
1984.....C. V. Whitney
1985.....Arlington Park
1987.....Anheuser-Busch
1988.....Edward J. DeBartolo Sr.
1989.....Richard Duchossois
1994.....John Longden
　　　　　Edward Arcaro
1998.....Oak Tree Racing
　　　　　Association

Note: Special Award and Award of Merit not presented annually. For long-term and/or outstanding service to the industry.

Breeders' Cup

Location: Hollywood Park (CA) 1984, '87, '97; Aqueduct Racetrack (NY) 1985; Santa Anita Park (CA) 1986, '93; Churchill Downs (KY) 1988, '91, '98; Gulfstream Park (FL) 1989, '92; Belmont Park (NY) 1990, '95; Woodbine (Toronto) 1996.

Juveniles

Year	Winner (Margin)	Jockey	Second	Third	Time
1984	Chief's Crown (¾)	Don MacBeth	Tank's Prospect	Spend a Buck	1:36⅕
1985	Tasso (Nose)	Laffit Pincay Jr.	Storm Cat	Scat Dancer	1:36⅕
1986	Capote (1¼)	Laffit Pincay Jr.	Qualify	Alysheba	1:43⅘
1987	Success Express (1¾)	Jose Santos	Regal Classic	Tejano	1:35⅕
1988	Is It True (1¼)	Laffit Pincay Jr.	Easy Goer	Tagel	1:46⅗
1989	Rhythm (2)	Craig Perret	Grand Canyon	Slavic	1:43⅗
1990	Fly So Free (3)	Jose Santos	Take Me Out	Lost Mountain	1:43⅖
1991	Arazi (4¾)	Pat Valenzuela	Bertrando	Snappy Landing	1:44⅗
1992	Gilded Time (¾)	Chris McCarron	It'sali'lknownfact	River Special	1:43⅖
1993	Brocco (5)	Gary Stevens	Blumin Affair	Tabasco Cat	1:42⅘
1994	Timber Country (½)	Pat Day	Eltish	Tejano Run	1:44⅖
1995	Unbridled's Song (Neck)	Mike Smith	Hennessy	Editor's Note	1:41⅗
1996	Boston Harbor (Neck)	Jerry Bailey	Acceptable	Ordway	1:43⅖
1997	Favorite Trick (5½)	Pat Day	Dawson's Legacy	Nationalore	1:41⅗
1998	Answer Lively (Head)	Jerry Bailey	Aly's Alley	Cat Thief	1:44

Note: One mile (1984–85, 87); $1\frac{1}{16}$ miles (1986 and since 1988).

Juvenile Fillies

Year	Winner (Margin)	Jockey	Second	Third	Time
1984	Outstandingly*	Walter Guerra	Dusty Heart	Fine Spirit	1:37⅘
1985	Twilight Ridge (1)	Jorge Velasquez	Family Style	Steal a Kiss	1:35⅘
1986	Brave Raj (5½)	Pat Valenzuela	Tappiano	Saros Brig	1:43⅕
1987	Epitome (Nose)	Pat Day	Jeanne Jones	Dream Team	1:36⅖
1988	Open Mind (1¾)	Angel Cordero Jr.	Darby Shuffle	Lea Lucinda	1:46⅗
1989	Go for Wand (2¾)	Randy Romero	Sweet Roberta	Stella Madrid	1:44⅕
1990	Meadow Star (5)	Jose Santos	Private Treasure	Dance Smartly	1:44
1991	Pleasant Stage (Neck)	Eddie Delahoussaye	La Spia	Cadillac Women	1:46⅖
1992	Eliza (1½)	Pat Valenzuela	Educated Risk	Boots 'n Jackie	1:42⅘
1993	Phone Chatter (Head)	Laffit Pincay	Sardula	Heavenly Prize	1:43
1994	Flanders (Head)	Pat Day	Serena's Song	Stormy Blues	1:45⅕
1995	My Flag (½)	Jerry Bailey	Cara Rafaela	Golden Attraction	1:42⅖
1996	Storm Song (4½)	Craig Perret	Love That Jazz	Critical Factor	1:43⅗
1997	Countess Diana (8½)	Shane Sellers	Career Collection	Primaly	1:42⅕
1998	Silverbulletday (1/2)	Gary Stevens	Excellent Meeting	Three Ring	1:43⅗

*In 1984, winner Fran's Valentine was disqualified for interference in the stretch and placed 10th.
Note: One mile (1984–85, 87); $1\frac{1}{16}$ miles (1986 and since 1988).

Sprint

Year	Winner (Margin)	Jockey	Second	Third	Time
1984	Eillo (Nose)	Craig Perret	Commemorate	Fighting Fit	1:10⅕
1985	Precisionist (¾)	Chris McCarron	Smile	Mt. Livermore	1:08⅖
1986	Smile (1¼)	Jacinto Vasquez	Pine Tree Lane	Bedside Promise	1:08⅖
1987	Very Subtle (4)	Pat Valenzuela	Groovy	Exclusive Enough	1:08⅘
1988	Gulch (¾)	Angel Cordero Jr	Play the King	Afleet	1:10⅖
1989	Dancing Spree (Neck)	Angel Cordero Jr	Safely Kept	Dispersal	1:09
1990	Safely Kept (Neck)	Craig Perret	Dayjur	Black Tie Affair	1:09⅗
1991	Sheikh Albadou (Neck)	Pat Eddery	Pleasant Tap	Robyn Dancer	1:09⅕
1992	Thirty Slews (Neck)	Eddie Delahoussaye	Meafara	Rubiano	1:08⅕
1993	Cardmania (Neck)	Eddie Delahoussaye	Meafara	Gilded Time	1:08⅗
1994	Cherokee Run (Head)	Mike Smith	Soviet Problem	Cardmania	1:09⅖
1995	Desert Stormer (Neck)	Kent Desormeaux	Mr. Greeley	Lit de Justice	1:09
1996	Lit de Justice (1¼)	Corey Nakatani	Paying Dues	Honour and Glory	1:08⅗
1997	Elmhurst (½)	Corey Nakatani	Hesabull	Bet on Sunshine	1:08
1998	Reraise (2)	Corey Nakatani	Grand Slam	Kona Gold	1:09

Note: Six furlongs (since 1984).

Breeders' Cup (*Cont.*)

Mile

Year	Winner (Margin)	Jockey	Second	Third	Time
1984	Royal Heroine (1½)	Fernando Toro	Star Choice	Cozzene	1:32⅗
1985	Cozzene (2¼)	Walter Guerra	Al Mamoon*	Shadeed	1:35
1986	Last Tycoon (Head)	Yves St-Martin	Palace Music	Fred Astaire	1:35⅕
1987	Miesque (3½)	Freddie Head	Show Dancer	Sonic Lady	1:32⅘
1988	Miesque (4)	Freddie Head	Steinlen	Simply Majestic	1:38⅗
1989	Steinlen (¾)	Jose Santos	Sabona	Most Welcome	1:37⅕
1990	Royal Academy (Neck)	Lester Piggott	Itsallgreektome	Priolo	1:35⅕
1991	Opening Verse (2¼)	Pat Valenzuela	Val de Bois	Star of Cozzene	1:37⅖
1992	Lure (3)	Mike Smith	Paradise Creek	Brief Truce	1:32⅘
1993	Lure (2¼)	Mike Smith	Ski Paradise	Fourstars Allstar	1:33⅖
1994	Barathea (Head)	Frankie Dettori	Johann Quatz	Unfinished Symph	1:34⅖
1995	Ridgewood Pearl (2)	John Murtagh	Fastness	Sayyedati	1:43⅗
1996	Da Hoss (1½)	Gary Stevens	Spinning World	Same Old Wish	1:35⅘
1997	Spinning World (2)	Cash Asmussen	Geri	Decorated Hero	1:32⅘
1998	Da Hoss (Head)	John Velazquez	Hawksley Hill	Labeeb	1:35⅕

*2nd place finisher Palace Music was disqualified for interference and placed 9th.

Distaff

Year	Winner (Margin)	Jockey	Second	Third	Time
1984	Princess Rooney (7)	Eddie Delahoussaye	Life's Magic	Adored	2:02⅖
1985	Life's Magic (6¼)	Angel Cordero Jr.	Lady's Secret	Dontstop Themusic	2:02
1986	Lady's Secret (2½)	Pat Day	Fran's Valentine	Outstandingly	2:01⅕
1987	Sacahuista (2¼)	Randy Romero	Clabber Girl	Oueee Bebe	2:02⅘
1988	Personal Ensign (Nose)	Randy Romero	Winning Colors	Goodbye Halo	1:52
1989	Bayakoa (1½)	Laffit Pincay Jr.	Gorgeous	Open Mind	1:47⅖
1990	Bayakoa (6¾)	Laffit Pincay Jr.	Colonial Waters	Valay Maid	1:49⅕
1991	Dance Smarty (½)	Pat Day	Versailles Treaty	Brought to Mind	1:50⅘
1992	Paseana (4)	Chris McCarron	Versailles Treaty	Magical Maiden	1:48
1993	Hollywood Wildcat (Nose)	Eddie Delahoussaye	Paseana	Re Toss	1:48⅕
1994	One Dreamer (Neck)	Gary Stevens	Heavenly Prize	Miss Dominique	1:50⅗
1995	Inside Information (13½)	Mike Smith	Heavenly Prize	Lakeway	1:46
1996	Jewel Princess (1½)	Corey Nakatani	Serena's Song	Different	1:48⅖
1997	Ajina (2)	Mike Smith	Sharp Cat	Escena	1:47⅕
1998	Escena (Nose)	Gary Stevens	Banshee Breeze	Keeper Hill	1:49⅘

Note: 1¼ miles (1984–87); 1⅛ miles (since 1988).

Turf

Year	Winner (Margin)	Jockey	Second	Third	Time
1984	Lashkari (Neck)	Yves St. Martin	All Along	Raami	2:25⅕
1985	Pebbles (Neck)	Pat Eddery	Strawberry Rd II	Mourjane	2:27
1986	Manila (Neck)	Jose Santos	Theatrical	Estrapade	2:25⅖
1987	Theatrical (½)	Pat Day	Trempolino	Village Star II	2:24⅖
1988	Great Communicator (½)	Ray Sibille	Sunshine Forever	Indian Skimmer	2:35⅕
1989	Prized (Head)	Eddie Delahoussaye	Sierra Roberta	Star Lift	2:28
1990	In the Wings (½)	Gary Stevens	With Approval	El Senor	2:29⅗
1991	Miss Alleged (2)	Eric Legrix	Itsallgreektome	Quest for Fame	2:30⅘
1992	Fraise (Nose)	Pat Valenzuela	Sky Classic	Quest For Fame	2:24
1993	Kotashaan (½)	Kent Desormeaux	Bien Bien	Luazar	2:25
1994	Tikkanen (1½)	Mike Smith	Hatoof	Paradise Creek	2:26⅖
1995	Northern Spur (Neck)	Chris McCarron	Freedom Cry	Carnegie	2:42
1996	Pilsudski (1¼)	Walter Swinburn	Singspiel	Swain	2:30⅕
1997	Chief Bearhart (¾)	Jose Santos	Borgia	Flag Down	2:23⅘
1998	Buck's Boy (1¼)	Shane Sellers	Yagli	Dushyantor	2:28⅗

Note: 1½ miles.

Breeders' Cup *(Cont.)*

Classic

Year	Winner (Margin)	Jockey	Second	Third	Time
1984	Wild Again (Head)	Pat Day	Slew o' Gold*	Gate Dancer	2:03⅖
1985	Proud Truth (Head)	Jorge Velasquez	Gate Dancer	Turkoman	2:00⅘
1986	Skywalker (1¼)	Laffit Pincay Jr.	Turkoman	Precisionist	2:00⅖
1987	Ferdinand (Nose)	Bill Shoemaker	Alysheba	Judge Angelucci	2:01⅖
1988	Alysheba (Nose)	Chris McCarron	Seeking the Gold	Waquoit	2:04⅘
1989	Sunday Silence (½)	Chris McCarron	Easy Goer	Blushing John	2:00⅕
1990	Unbridled (1)	Pat Day	Ibn Bey	Thirty Six Red	2:02⅕
1991	Black Tie Affair (1¼)	Jerry Bailey	Twilight Agenda	Unbridled	2:02⅘
1992	A.P. Indy (2)	Eddie Delahoussaye	Pleasant Tap	Jolypha	2:00⅕
1993	Arcangues (2)	Jerry Bailey	Bertrando	Kissin Kris	2:00⅘
1994	Concern (Neck)	Jerry Bailey	Tabasco Cat	Dramatic Gold	2:02⅖
1995	Cigar (2½)	Jerry Bailey	L'Carriere	Unaccounted For	1:59⅖
1996	Alphabet Soup (Nose)	Chris McCarron	Louis Quatorze	Cigar	2:01
1997	Skip Away (6)	Mike Smith	Deputy Commander	Dowty	1:59⅕
1998	Awesome Again (¾)	Pat Day	Silver Charm	Swain	2:02

*2nd place finisher Gate Dancer was disqualified for interference and placed 3rd.

Note: 1¼ miles.

England's Triple Crown Winners

England's Triple Crown consists of the Two Thousand Guineas, held at Newmarket; the Epsom Derby, held at Epsom Downs; and the St. Leger Stakes, held at Doncaster.

Year	Horse	Owner	Year	Horse	Owner
1853	West Australian	Mr. Bowes	1900	Diamond Jubilee	Prince of Wales
1865	Gladiateur	F. DeLagrange	1903	*Rock Sand	J. Miller
1866	Lord Lyon	R. Sutton	1915	Pommern	S. Joel
1886	*Ormonde	Duke of Westminster	1917	Gay Crusader	Mr. Fairie
1891	Common	†F. Johnstone	1918	Gainsborough	Lady James Douglas
1893	Isinglass	H. McCalmont	1935	*Bahram	Aga Khan
1897	Galtee More	J. Gubbins	1970	‡Nijinsky II	C. W. Engelhard
1899	Flying Fox	Duke of Westminster			

*Imported into United States. †Raced in name of Lord Alington in Two Thousand Guineas. ‡Canadian-bred.

Homestretch

When Julie Krone hung up her tack last spring, the curtain fell on one of horse racing's most spectacular careers. A 4'10½" daredevil, Krone—the top female rider of all time—was a fierce competitor who won over 3,500 races and more than $80 million in purses in her 18 years as a jockey. She was the third-leading rider in the U.S. in 1989 with 368 wins. Four years later she guided Colonial Affair to victory in the Belmont, becoming the only woman to win a Triple Crown race. Krone announced that she'd race for the final time at Lone Star Park in Grand Prairie, Texas. "It's not worth the physical torture anymore," said Krone, 35, who took a frightful spill at Saratoga in '93 and was shelved for nine months with a fractured right ankle that required two steel plates and 14 screws to rebuild. In her career she had also broken her back, right kneecap and both hands. "I don't need to get carried out on a stretcher," said the queen of the sport of kings. "I'm leaving with a smile on my face."

Horse—Money Won

Year	Horse	Age	Starts	1st	2nd	3rd	Winnings ($)
1919	Sir Barton	3	13	8	3	2	88,250
1920	Man o'War	3	11	11	0	0	166,140
1921	Morvich	2	11	11	0	0	115,234
1922	Pillory	3	7	4	1	1	95,654
1923	Zev	3	14	12	1	0	272,008
1924	Sarzen	3	12	8	1	1	95,640
1925	Pompey	2	10	7	2	0	121,630
1926	Crusader	3	15	9	4	0	166,033
1927	Anita Peabody	2	7	6	0	1	111,905
1928	High Strung	2	6	5	0	0	153,590
1929	Blue Larkspur	3	6	4	1	0	153,450
1930	Gallant Fox	3	10	9	1	0	308,275
1931	Gallant Flight	2	7	7	0	0	219,000
1932	Gusto	3	16	4	3	2	145,940
1933	Singing Wood	2	9	3	2	2	88,050
1934	Cavalcade	3	7	6	1	0	111,235
1935	Omaha	3	9	6	1	2	142,255
1936	Granville	3	11	7	3	0	110,295
1937	Seabiscuit	4	15	11	2	2	168,580
1938	Stagehand	3	15	8	2	3	189,710
1939	Challedon	3	15	9	2	3	184,535
1940	Bimelech	3	7	4	2	1	110,005
1941	Whirlaway	3	20	13	5	2	272,386
1942	Shut Out	3	12	8	2	0	238,872
1943	Count Fleet	3	6	6	0	0	174,055
1944	Pavot	2	8	8	0	0	179,040
1945	Busher	3	13	10	2	1	273,735
1946	Assault	3	15	8	2	3	424,195
1947	Armed	6	17	11	4	1	376,325
1948	Citation	3	20	19	1	0	709,470
1949	Ponder	3	21	9	5	2	321,825
1950	Noor	5	12	7	4	1	346,940
1951	Counterpoint	3	15	7	2	1	250,525
1952	Crafty Admiral	4	16	9	4	1	277,225
1953	Native Dancer	3	10	9	1	0	513,425
1954	Determine	3	15	10	3	2	328,700
1955	Nashua	3	12	10	1	1	752,550
1956	Needles	3	8	4	2	0	440,850
1957	Round Table	3	22	15	1	3	600,383
1958	Round Table	4	20	14	4	0	662,780
1959	Sword Dancer	3	13	8	4	0	537,004
1960	Bally Ache	3	15	10	3	1	445,045
1961	Carry Back	3	16	9	1	3	565,349
1962	Never Bend	2	10	7	1	2	402,969
1963	Candy Spots	3	12	7	2	1	604,481
1964	Gun Bow	4	16	8	4	2	580,100
1965	Buckpasser	2	11	9	1	0	568,096
1966	Buckpasser	3	14	13	1	0	669,078
1967	Damascus	3	16	12	3	1	817,941
1968	Forward Pass	3	13	7	2	0	546,674
1969	Arts and Letters	3	14	8	5	1	555,604
1970	Personality	3	18	8	2	1	444,049
1971	Riva Ridge	2	9	7	0	0	503,263
1972	Droll Role	4	19	7	3	4	471,633
1973	Secretariat	3	12	9	2	1	860,404
1974	Chris Evert	3	8	5	1	2	551,063
1975	Foolish Pleasure	3	11	5	4	1	716,278
1976	Forego	6	8	6	1	1	401,701
1977	Seattle Slew	3	7	6	0	1	641,370
1978	Affirmed	3	11	8	2	0	901,541
1979	Spectacular Bid	3	12	10	1	1	1,279,334
1980	Temperence Hill	3	17	8	3	1	1,130,452
1981	John Henry	6	10	8	0	0	1,798,030
1982	Perrault	5	8	4	1	2	1,197,400

Horse—Money Won (Cont.)

Year	Horse						Winnings ($)
1983	All Along	4	7	4	1	1	2,138,963
1984	Slew o'Gold	4	6	5	1	0	2,627,944
1985	Spend A Buck	3	7	5	1	1	3,552,704
1986	Snow Chief	3	9	6	1	1	1,875,200
1987	Alysheba	3	10	3	3	1	2,511,156
1988	Alysheba	4	9	7	1	0	3,808,600
1989	Sunday Silence	3	9	7	2	0	4,578,454
1990	Unbridled	3	11	4	3	2	3,718,149
1991	Dance Smartly	3	8	8	0	0	2,876,821
1992	A.P. Indy	3	7	5	0	1	2,622,560
1993	Kotashaan	3	10	6	3	0	2,619,014
1994	Paradise Creek	5	11	8	2	1	2,610,187
1995	Cigar	5	10	10	0	0	4,819,800
1996	Cigar	6	8	5	2	1	4,910,000
1997	Skip Away	4	11	4	5	2	4,089,000
1998	Silver Charm	4	9	6	2	0	4,696,506

Trainer—Money Won

Year	Trainer	Wins	Winnings ($)
1908	James Rowe, Sr.	50	284,335
1909	Sam Hildreth	73	123,942
1910	Sam Hildreth	84	148,010
1911	Sam Hildreth	67	49,418
1912	John F. Schorr	63	58,110
1913	James Rowe, Sr.	18	45,936
1914	R. C. Benson	45	59,315
1915	James Rowe, Sr.	19	75,596
1916	Sam Hildreth	39	70,950
1917	Sam Hildreth	23	61,698
1918	H. Guy Bedwell	53	80,296
1919	H. Guy Bedwell	63	208,728
1920	L. Feustal	22	186,087
1921	Sam Hildreth	85	262,768
1922	Sam Hildreth	74	247,014
1923	Sam Hildreth	75	392,124
1924	Sam Hildreth	77	255,608
1925	G. R. Tompkins	30	199,245
1926	Scott P. Harlan	21	205,681
1927	W. H. Bringloe	63	216,563
1928	John F. Schorr	65	258,425
1929	James Rowe, Jr.	25	314,881
1930	Sunny Jim Fitzsimmons	47	397,355
1931	Big Jim Healey	33	297,300
1932	Sunny Jim Fitzsimmons	68	266,650
1933	Humming Bob Smith	53	135,720
1934	Humming Bob Smith	43	249,938
1935	Bud Stotler	87	303,005
1936	Sunny Jim Fitzsimmons	42	193,415
1937	Robert McGarvey	46	209,925
1938	Earl Sande	15	226,495
1939	Sunny Jim Fitzsimmons	45	266,205
1940	Silent Tom Smith	14	269,200
1941	Plain Ben Jones	70	475,318
1942	John M. Gaver Sr.	48	406,547
1943	Plain Ben Jones	73	267,915
1944	Plain Ben Jones	60	601,660
1945	Silent Tom Smith	52	510,655
1946	Hirsch Jacobs	99	560,077
1947	Jimmy Jones	85	1,334,805
1948	Jimmy Jones	81	1,118,670
1949	Jimmy Jones	76	978,587
1950	Preston Burch	96	637,754
1951	John M. Gaver Sr.	42	616,392
1952	Plain Ben Jones	29	662,137
1953	Harry Trotsek	54	1,028,873
1954	Willie Molter	136	1,107,860
1955	Sunny Jim Fitzsimmons	66	1,270,055
1956	Willie Molter	142	1,227,402
1957	Jimmy Jones	70	1,150,910
1958	Willie Molter	69	1,116,544
1959	Willie Molter	71	847,290
1960	Hirsch Jacobs	97	748,349
1961	Jimmy Jones	62	759,856
1962	Mesh Tenney	58	1,099,474
1963	Mesh Tenney	40	860,703
1964	Bill Winfrey	61	1,350,534
1965	Hirsch Jacobs	91	1,331,628
1966	Eddie Neloy	93	2,456,250
1967	Eddie Neloy	72	1,776,089
1968	Eddie Neloy	52	1,233,101
1969	Elliott Burch	26	1,067,936
1970	Charlie Whittingham	82	1,302,354
1971	Charlie Whittingham	77	1,737,115
1972	Charlie Whittingham	79	1,734,020
1973	Charlie Whittingham	85	1,865,385
1974	Pancho Martin	166	2,408,419
1975	Charlie Whittingham	93	2,437,244
1976	Jack Van Berg	496	2,976,196
1977	Laz Barrera	127	2,715,848
1978	Laz Barrera	100	3,307,164
1979	Laz Barrera	98	3,608,517
1980	Laz Barrera	99	2,969,151
1981	Charlie Whittingham	74	3,993,300
1982	Charlie Whittingham	63	4,587,457
1983	D. Wayne Lukas	78	4,267,261
1984	D. Wayne Lukas	131	5,835,921
1985	D. Wayne Lukas	218	11,155,188
1986	D. Wayne Lukas	259	12,345,180
1987	D. Wayne Lukas	343	17,502,110
1988	D. Wayne Lukas	318	17,842,358
1989	D. Wayne Lukas	305	16,103,998
1990	D. Wayne Lukas	267	14,508,871
1991	D. Wayne Lukas	289	15,942,223
1992	D. Wayne Lukas	230	9,806,436
1993	Robert Frankel	79	8,883,252
1994	D. Wayne Lukas	147	9,247,457
1995	D. Wayne Lukas	194	12,842,865
1996	D. Wayne Lukas	192	15,966,344
1997	D. Wayne Lukas	175	10,338,957
1998	Bob Baffert	139	15,000,870

Jockey—Money Won

Year	Jockey	Mts	1st	2nd	3rd	Pct	Winnings ($)
1919	John Loftus	177	65	36	24	.37	252,707
1920	Clarence Kummer	353	87	79	48	.25	292,376
1921	Earl Sande	340	112	69	59	.33	263,043
1922	Albert Johnson	297	43	57	40	.14	345,054
1923	Earl Sande	430	122	89	79	.28	569,394
1924	Ivan Parke	844	205	175	121	.24	290,395
1925	Laverne Fator	315	81	54	44	.26	305,775
1926	Laverne Fator	511	143	90	86	.28	361,435
1927	Earl Sande	179	49	33	19	.27	277,877
1928	Pony McAtee	235	55	43	25	.23	301,295
1929	Mack Garner	274	57	39	33	.21	314,975
1930	Sonny Workman	571	152	88	79	.27	420,438
1931	Charles Kurtsinger	519	93	82	79	.18	392,095
1932	Sonny Workman	378	87	48	55	.23	385,070
1933	Robert Jones	471	63	57	70	.13	226,285
1934	Wayne D. Wright	919	174	154	114	.19	287,185
1935	Silvio Coucci	749	141	125	103	.19	319,760
1936	Wayne D. Wright	670	100	102	73	.15	264,000
1937	Charles Kurtsinger	765	120	94	106	.16	384,202
1938	Nick Wall	658	97	94	82	.15	385,161
1939	Basil James	904	191	165	105	.21	353,333
1940	Eddie Arcaro	783	132	143	112	.17	343,661
1941	Don Meade	1,164	210	185	158	.18	398,627
1942	Eddie Arcaro	687	123	97	89	.18	481,949
1943	John Longden	871	173	140	121	.20	573,276
1944	Ted Atkinson	1,539	287	231	213	.19	899,101
1945	John Longden	778	180	112	100	.23	981,977
1946	Ted Atkinson	1,377	233	213	173	.17	1,036,825
1947	Douglas Dodson	646	141	100	75	.22	1,429,949
1948	Eddie Arcaro	726	188	108	98	.26	1,686,230
1949	Steve Brooks	906	209	172	110	.23	1,316,817
1950	Eddie Arcaro	888	195	153	144	.22	1,410,160
1951	Bill Shoemaker	1,161	257	197	161	.22	1,329,890
1952	Eddie Arcaro	807	188	122	109	.23	1,859,591
1953	Bill Shoemaker	1,683	485	302	210	.29	1,784,187
1954	Bill Shoemaker	1,251	380	221	142	.30	1,876,760
1955	Eddie Arcaro	820	158	126	108	.19	1,864,796
1956	Bill Hartack	1,387	347	252	184	.25	2,343,955
1957	Bill Hartack	1,238	341	208	178	.28	3,060,501
1958	Bill Shoemaker	1,133	300	185	137	.26	2,961,693
1959	Bill Shoemaker	1,285	347	230	159	.27	2,843,133
1960	Bill Shoemaker	1,227	274	196	158	.22	2,123,961
1961	Bill Shoemaker	1,256	304	186	175	.24	2,690,819
1962	Bill Shoemaker	1,126	311	156	128	.28	2,916,844
1963	Bill Shoemaker	1,203	271	193	137	.22	2,526,925
1964	Bill Shoemaker	1,056	246	147	133	.23	2,649,553
1965	Braulio Baeza	1,245	270	200	201	.22	2,582,702
1966	Braulio Baeza	1,341	298	222	190	.22	2,951,022
1967	Braulio Baeza	1,064	256	184	127	.24	3,088,888
1968	Braulio Baeza	1,089	201	184	145	.18	2,835,108
1969	Jorge Velasquez	1,442	258	230	204	.18	2,542,315
1970	Laffit Pincay Jr.	1,328	269	208	187	.20	2,626,526
1971	Laffit Pincay Jr.	1,627	380	288	214	.23	3,784,377
1972	Laffit Pincay Jr.	1,388	289	215	205	.21	3,225,827
1973	Laffit Pincay Jr.	1,444	350	254	209	.24	4,093,492
1974	Laffit Pincay Jr.	1,278	341	227	180	.27	4,251,060
1975	Braulio Baeza	1,190	196	208	180	.16	3,674,398
1976	Angel Cordero Jr.	1,534	274	273	235	.18	4,709,500
1977	Steve Cauthen	2,075	487	345	304	.23	6,151,750
1978	Darrel McHargue	1,762	375	294	263	.21	6,188,353
1979	Laffit Pincay Jr.	1,708	420	302	261	.25	8,183,535
1980	Chris McCarron	1,964	405	318	282	.20	7,666,100
1981	Chris McCarron	1,494	326	251	207	.22	8,397,604
1982	Angel Cordero Jr.	1,838	397	338	227	.22	9,702,520
1983	Angel Cordero Jr.	1,792	362	296	237	.20	10,116,807
1984	Chris McCarron	1,565	356	276	218	.23	12,038,213

Jockey—Money Won *(Cont.)*

Year	Jockey	Mts	1st	2nd	3rd	Pct	Winnings ($)
1985	Laffit Pincay Jr.	1,409	289	246	183	.21	13,415,049
1986	Jose Santos	1,636	329	237	222	.20	11,329,297
1987	Jose Santos	1,639	305	268	208	.19	12,407,355
1988	Jose Santos	1,867	370	287	265	.20	14,877,298
1989	Jose Santos	1,459	285	238	220	.20	13,847,003
1990	Gary Stevens	1,504	283	245	202	.19	13,881,198
1991	Chris McCarron	1,440	265	228	206	.18	14,441,083
1992	Kent Desormeaux	1,568	361	260	208	.23	14,193,006
1993	Mike Smith	1,510	343	235	214	.23	14,008,148
1994	Mike Smith	1,484	317	250	196	.21	15,979,820
1995	Jerry Bailey	1,265	287	193	144	.23	16,308,230
1996	Jerry Bailey	1,187	298	189	165	.25	19,465,376
1997	Jerry Bailey	1,143	272	186	178	.26	18,260,553
1998	Gary Stevens	869	178	145	122	.20	19,358,840

Jockey—Races Won

Year	Jockey	Mts	1st	2nd	3rd	Pct
1895	J. Perkins	762	192	177	129	.25
1896	J. Scherrer	1,093	271	227	172	.24
1897	H. Martin	803	173	152	116	.21
1898	T. Burns	973	277	213	149	.28
1899	T. Burns	1,064	273	173	266	.26
1900	C. Mitchell	874	195	140	139	.23
1901	W. O'Connor	1,047	253	221	192	.24
1902	J. Ranch	1,069	276	205	181	.26
1903	G.C. Fuller	918	229	152	122	.25
1904	E. Hildebrand	1,169	297	230	171	.25
1905	D. Nicol	861	221	143	136	.26
1906	W. Miller	1,384	388	300	199	.28
1907	W. Miller	1,194	334	226	170	.28
1908	V. Powers	1,260	324	204	185	.26
1909	V. Powers	704	173	121	114	.25
1910	G. Garner	947	200	188	153	.20
1911	T. Koerner	813	162	133	112	.20
1912	P. Hill	967	168	141	129	.17
1913	M. Buxton	887	146	131	136	.16
1914	J. McTaggart	787	157	132	106	.20
1915	M. Garner	775	151	118	90	.19
1916	F. Robinson	791	178	131	124	.23
1917	W. Crump	803	151	140	101	.19
1918	F. Robinson	864	185	140	108	.21
1919	C. Robinson	896	190	140	126	.21
1920	J. Butwell	721	152	129	139	.21
1921	C. Lang	696	135	110	105	.19
1922	M. Fator	859	188	153	116	.22
1923	I. Parke	718	173	105	95	.24
1924	I. Parke	844	205	175	121	.24
1925	A. Mortensen	987	187	145	138	.19
1926	R. Jones	1,172	190	163	152	.16
1927	L. Hardy	1,130	207	192	151	.18
1928	J. Inzelone	1,052	155	152	135	.15
1929	M. Knight	871	149	132	133	.17
1930	H.R. Riley	861	177	145	123	.21
1931	H. Roble	1,174	173	173	155	.15
1932	J. Gilbert	1,050	212	144	160	.20
1933	J. Westrope	1,224	301	235	166	.25
1934	M. Peters	1,045	221	179	147	.21
1935	C. Stevenson	1,099	206	169	146	.19
1936	B. James	1,106	245	195	161	.22
1937	J. Adams	1,265	260	186	177	.21
1938	J. Longden	1,150	236	168	171	.21
1939	D. Meade	1,284	255	221	180	.20
1940	E. Dew	1,377	287	201	180	.21
1941	D. Meade	1,164	210	185	158	.18
1942	J. Adams	1,120	245	185	150	.22

Jockey—Races Won (Cont.)

Year	Jockey	Mts	1st	2nd	3rd	Pct
1943	J. Adams	1,069	228	159	171	.21
1944	T. Atkinson	1,539	287	231	213	.19
1945	J.D. Jessop	1,085	290	182	168	.27
1946	T. Atkinson	1,377	233	213	173	.17
1947	J. Longden	1,327	316	250	195	.24
1948	J. Longden	1,197	319	233	161	.27
1949	G. Glisson	1,347	270	217	181	.20
1950	W. Shoemaker	1,640	388	266	230	.24
1951	C. Burr	1,319	310	232	192	.24
1952	A. DeSpirito	1,482	390	247	212	.26
1953	W. Shoemaker	1,683	485	302	210	.29
1954	W. Shoemaker	1,251	380	221	142	.30
1955	W. Hartack	1,702	417	298	215	.25
1956	W. Hartack	1,387	347	252	184	.25
1957	W. Hartack	1,238	341	208	178	.28
1958	W. Shoemaker	1,133	300	185	137	.26
1959	W. Shoemaker	1,285	347	230	159	.27
1960	W. Hartack	1,402	307	247	190	.22
1961	J. Sellers	1,394	328	212	227	.24
1962	R. Ferraro	1,755	352	252	226	.20
1963	W. Blum	1,704	360	286	215	.21
1964	W. Blum	1,577	324	274	170	.21
1965	J. Davidson	1,582	319	228	190	.20
1966	A. Gomez	996	318	173	142	.32
1967	J. Velasquez	1,939	438	315	270	.23
1968	A. Cordero Jr.	1,662	345	278	219	.21
1969	L. Snyder	1,645	352	290	243	.21
1970	S. Hawley	1,908	452	313	265	.24
1971	L Pincay Jr.	1,627	380	288	214	.23
1972	S. Hawley	1,381	367	269	200	.27
1973	S. Hawley	1,925	515	336	292	.27
1974	C.J. McCarron	2,199	546	392	297	.25
1975	C.J. McCarron	2,194	458	389	305	.21
1976	S. Hawley	1,637	413	245	201	.25
1977	S. Cauthen	2,075	487	345	304	.23
1978	E. Delahoussaye	1,666	384	285	238	.23
1979	D. Gall	2,146	479	396	326	.22
1980	C.J. McCarron	1,964	405	318	282	.20
1981	D. Gall	1,917	376	305	297	.20
1982	Pat Day	1,870	399	326	255	.21
1983	Pat Day	1,725	454	321	251	.26
1984	Pat Day	1,694	399	296	259	.24
1985	C.W. Antley	2,335	469	371	288	.20
1986	Pat Day	1,417	429	246	202	.30
1987	Kent Desormeaux	2,207	450	370	294	.28
1988	Kent Desormeaux	1,897	474	295	276	.25
1989	Kent Desormeaux	2,312	598	385	309	.25
1990	Pat Day	1,421	364	265	222	.26
1991	Pat Day	1,405	430	256	213	.31
1992	Russell Baze	1,691	433	296	237	.25
1993	Russell Baze	1,579	410	297	225	.26
1994	Russell Baze	1,588	415	301	266	.26
1995	Russell Baze	1,531	445	310	232	.29
1996	Russell Baze	1,482	415	297	200	.28
1997	Edgar S. Prado	2,037	533	384	308	.26
1998	Edgar S. Prado	1,969	470	377	285	.23

Leading Jockeys—Career Records

Jockey	Years Riding	Mts	1st	2nd	3rd	Win Pct	Winnings ($)
Bill Shoemaker (1990)	42	40,350	8,833	6,136	4,987	.219	123,375,524
Laffit Pincay Jr	34	44,439	8,793	7,188	6,139	.198	205,538,142
Pat Day	27	34,542	7,561	5,857	4,904	.218	217,790,355
Dave Gall (1999)	41	41,775	7,396	6,525	6,131	.177	24,547,584
Angel Cordero (1992)	31	38,646	7,057	6,136	5,359	.183	164,561,227
Chris McCarron	25	32,632	6,822	5,397	4,468	.209	232,293,337
Jorge Velasquez (1998)	35	40,852	6,795	6,178	5,755	.166	125,544,379
Russell Baze	26	32,829	6,736	5,381	4,617	.205	95,631,797
Sandy Hawley (1998)	31	31,455	6,449	4,825	4,159	.205	88,681,292
Larry Snyder (1994)	35	35,681	6,388	5,030	3,440	.179	47,207,289
Carl Gambardella (1994)	39	39,018	6,349	5,953	5,353	.163	29,389,041
Earlie Fires	35	41,817	6,094	5,176	4,990	.146	75,692,395
Eddie Delahoussaye	30	36,950	6,061	5,350	5,216	.164	173,897,139
John Longden (1966)	40	32,413	6,032	4,914	4,273	.186	24,665,800
Jacinto Vasquez (1998)	38	37,390	5,231	4,721	4,513	.140	80,764,853
Ron Ardoin	27	29,884	4,926	4,049	3,526	.165	53,249,173
Eddie Arcaro (1961)	31	24,092	4,779	3,807	3,302	.198	30,039,543
Jerry Bailey	26	25,967	4,643	3,676	3,239	.179	178,271,483
Don Brumfield (1989)	37	33,223	4,573	4,076	3,758	.138	43,567,861
Gary Stevens	25	25,341	4,494	4,004	3,640	.177	184,843,056
Steve Brooks (1975)	34	30,330	4,451	4,219	3,658	.147	18,239,817
Eddie Maple (1998)	31	33,974	4,398	4,516	4,335	.129	105,338,573
Rick Wilson	28	21,976	4,396	3,772	3,079	.200	61,658,269
Walter Blum (1975)	22	28,673	4,382	3,913	3,350	.153	26,497,189

Note: Records go through October 6,1999, and include available statistics for races ridden in foreign countries. Figures in parentheses after jockey's name indicate last year in which he rode.

Leading jockeys courtesy of *The American Racing Manual*, a publication of Daily Racing Form, Inc.

Horse Power

Anyone seeking signs of life in horse racing needs look no further than 1999's Belmont Stakes. Sports fans everywhere, it seems, want to see a Triple Crown winner. Charismatic, the former claimer and 31–1 long-shot winner of the Kentucky Derby, was the 26th horse—and third in three years—to journey to New York with a shot at immortality, and even fans who think racing lacks charisma were asking, "Can he do it?"

Back when swing and cigars were in style, horse racing wasn't just the sport of kings. It was the king of sports. Then came the late 1950s, when racing's leaders made a mistake they're still paying for. Offered a chance to put their product on television every week, as the NFL and Major league baseball were doing, the thoroughbred industry's clubby, insular brain trust said no. If racing were on television, they reasoned, nobody would come to the track. The consequences of that decision are visible today in the sport's awful TV ratings and in attendance figures that have been tumbling for three decades. Competing forms of legal gambling also sped racing's fall into obscurity, and by the early '90s it was stuck somewhere between billiards and boxing on the sports barometer.

Things aren't much better now, but at least racing's kingpins have a plan. In an unprece-dented display of unity—and desperation—track owners and other prominent horsemen formed the National Thoroughbred Racing Association in 1998 to boost racing's profile, largely through aggressive advertising and expanded TV coverage. Their Go-Baby-Go ad campaign may be gathering steam: In New York, for instance, attendance was up in '98 for the first time in 17 years. With swing and stogies trendy again, who's to say horse racing won't be the third jewel in a Triple Crown of comebacks?

Fans who trek to the track might applaud what they find. In what other game can you make a dizzying array of legal bets and enjoy a thrilling two minutes of action 10 times a day? In the era of the $50 box seat, a day at the races is a bargain, too. For less than it costs to buy two beers and a hot dog at Yankee Stadium, a family of four can see a wall of horses turning for home near the Pacific surf at Del Mar or enjoy the grubbier charms of Pimlico, shoe-horned into a neighborhood overlooking downtown Baltimore. Better yet, you could spend a Saturday in June with 80,000 or so other railbirds at Belmont, the Taj Mahal of American racing, and maybe watch history unfold before your eyes.

—Mark Beech

HORSES

Ack Ack (1986, 1966)
Affectionately (1989, 1960)
Affirmed (1980, 1975)
All Along (1990, 1979)
Alsab (1976, 1939)
Alydar (1989, 1975)
Alysheba (1993, 1984)
American Eclipse (1970, 1814)
Armed (1963, 1941)
Artful (1956, 1902)
Arts and Letters (1994, 1966)
Assault (1964, 1943)
Battleship (1969, 1927)
Bayakoa (1998, 1984)
Bed o' Roses (1976, 1947)
Beldame (1956, 1901)
Ben Brush (1955, 1893)
Bewitch (1977, 1945)
Bimelech (1990, 1937)
Black Gold (1989, 1921)
Black Helen (1991, 1932)
Blue Larkspur (1957, 1926)
Bold 'n Determined (1997, 1977)
Bold Ruler (1973, 1954)
Bon Nouvel (1976, 1960)
Boston (1955, 1833)
Broomstick (1956, 1901)
Buckpasser (1970, 1963)
Busher (1964, 1942)
Bushranger (1967, 1930)
Cafe Prince (1985, 1970)
Carry Back (1975, 1958)
Cavalcade (1993, 1931)
Challedon (1977, 1936)
Chris Evert (1988, 1971)
Cicada (1967, 1959)
Citation (1959, 1945)
Coaltown (1983, 1945)
Colin (1956, 1905)
Commando (1956, 1898)
Count Fleet (1961, 1940)
Crusader (1995, 1923)
Dahlia (1981, 1970)
Damascus (1974, 1964)
Dark Mirage (1974, 1965)
Davona Dale (1985, 1976)
Desert Vixen (1979, 1970)
Devil Diver (1980, 1939)
Discovery (1969, 1931)
Domino (1955, 1891)
Dr. Fager (1971, 1964)
Easy Goer (1997, 1986)
Eight Thirty (1994, 1936)

Elkridge (1966, 1938)
Emperor of Norfolk (1988, 1885)
Equipoise (1957, 1928)
Exceller (1999, 1973)
Exterminator (1957, 1915)
Fairmount (1985, 1921)
Fair Play (1956, 1905)
Fashion (1980, 1837)
Firenze (1981, 1884)
Flatterer (1994, 1979)
Foolish Pleasure (1995, 1972)
Forego (1979, 1970)
Fort Marcy (1998, 1964)
Gallant Bloom (1977, 1966)
Gallant Fox (1957, 1927)
Gallant Man (1987, 1954)
Gallorette (1962, 1942)
Gamely (1980, 1964)
Genuine Risk (1986, 1977)
Go For Wand (1996, 1987)
Good and Plenty (1956, 1900)
Grandville (1997, 1933)
Grey Lag (1957, 1918)
Gun Bow (1999, 1960)
Hamburg (1986, 1895)
Hanover (1955, 1884)
Henry of Navarre (1985, 1891)
Hill Prince (1991, 1947)
Hindoo (1955, 1878)
Imp (1965, 1894)
Jay Trump (1971, 1957)
John Henry (1990, 1975)
Johnstown (1992, 1936)
Jolly Roger (1965, 1922)
Kelso (1967, 1957)
Kentucky (1983, 1861)
Kingston (1955, 1884)
Lady's Secret (1992, 1982)
La Prevoyante (1995, 1970)
L'Escargot (1977, 1963)
Lexington (1955, 1850)
Longfellow (1971, 1867)
Luke Blackburn (1956, 1877)
Majestic Prince (1988, 1966)
Man o' War (1957, 1917)
Miesque (1999, 1984)
Miss Woodford (1967, 1880)
Myrtlewood (1979, 1932)
Nashua (1965, 1952)
Native Dancer (1963, 1950)
Native Diver (1978, 1959)
Neji (1966, 1950)
Northern Dancer (1976, 1961)

Oedipus (1978, 1946)
Old Rosebud (1968, 1911)
Omaha (1965, 1932)
Pan Zareta (1972, 1910)
Parole (1984, 1873)
Personal Ensign (1993, 1984)
Peter Pan (1956, 1904)
Princess Doreen (1982, 1921)
Princess Rooney (1991, 1980)
Real Delight (1987, 1949)
Regret (1957, 1912)
Reigh Count (1978, 1923)
Riva Ridge (1998, 1969)
Roamer (1981, 1911)
Roseben (1956, 1901)
Round Table (1972, 1954)
Ruffian (1976, 1972)
Ruthless (1975, 1864)
Salvator (1955, 1886)
Sarazen (1957, 1921)
Seabiscuit (1958, 1933)
Searching (1978, 1952)
Seattle Slew (1981, 1974)
Secretariat (1974, 1970)
Shuvee (1975, 1966)
Silver Spoon (1978, 1956)
Sir Archy (1955, 1805)
Sir Barton (1957, 1916)
Slew o' Gold (1992, 1980)
Spectacular Bid (1982, 1976)
Stymie (1975, 1941)
Sun Beau (1996, 1925)
Sunday Silence (1996, 1986)
Susan's Girl (1976, 1969)
Swaps (1966, 1952)
Sword Dancer (1977, 1956)
Sysonby (1956, 1902)
Ta Wee (1994, 1967)
Ten Broeck (1982, 1872)
Tim Tam (1985, 1955)
Tom Fool (1960, 1949)
Top Flight (1966, 1929)
Tosmah (1984, 1961)
Twenty Grand (1957, 1928)
Twilight Tear (1963, 1941)
Two Lea (1982, 1946)
War Admiral (1958, 1934)
Whirlaway (1959, 1938)
Whisk Broom II (1979, 1907)
Zaccio (1990, 1976)
Zev (1983, 1920)

Note: Years of election and foaling in parentheses.

HARNESS RACING

Major Races

Hambletonian

Year	Winner	Driver	Year	Winner	Driver
1926	Guy McKinney	Nat Ray	1964	Ayres	J. Simpson Sr.
1927	Iosola's Worthy	Marvin Childs	1965	Egyptian Candor	Del Cameron
1928	Spenser	W. H. Leese	1966	Kerry Way	Frank Ervin
1929	Walter Dear	Walter Cox	1967	Speedy Streak	Del Cameron
1930	Hanover's Bertha	Tom Berry	1968	Nevele Pride	Stanley Dancer
1931	Calumet Butler	R. D. McMahon	1969	Lindy's Pride	H. Beissinger
1932	The Marchioness	William Caton	1970	Timothy T.	J. Simpson Jr.
1933	Mary Reynolds	Ben White	1971	Speedy Crown	H. Beissinger
1934	Lord Jim	Doc Parshall	1972	Super Bowl	Stanley Dancer
1935	Greyhound	Sep Palin	1973	Flirth	Ralph Baldwin
1936	Rosalind	Ben White	1974	Christopher T.	Bill Haughton
1937	Shirley Hanover	Henry Thomas	1975	Bonefish	Stanley Dancer
1938	McLin Hanover	Henry Thomas	1976	Steve Lobell	Bill Haughton
1939	Peter Astra	Doc Parshall	1977	Green Speed	Bill Haughton
1940	Spencer Scott	Fred Egan	1978	Speedy Somolli	H. Beissinger
1941	Bill Gallon	Lee Smith	1979	Legend Hanover	George Sholty
1942	The Ambassador	Ben White	1980	Burgomeister	Bill Haughton
1943	Volo Song	Ben White	1981	Shiaway St. Pat	Ray Remmen
1944	Yankee Maid	Henry Thomas	1982	Speed Bowl	Tom Haughton
1945	Titan Hanover	H. Pownall Sr.	1983	Duenna	Stanley Dancer
1946	Chestertown	Thomas Berry	1984	Historic Freight	Ben Webster
1947	Hoot Mon	Sep Palin	1985	Prakas	Bill O'Donnell
1948	Demon Hanover	Harrison Hoyt	1986	Nuclear Kosmos	Ulf Thoresen
1949	Miss Tilly	Fred Egan	1987	Mack Lobell	John Campbell
1950	Lusty Song	Del Miller	1988	Armbro Goal	John Campbell
1951	Mainliner	Guy Crippen	1989	Park Ave. Joe/ Probe*	R. Waples/B. Fahy
1952	Sharp Note	Bion Shively	1990	Harmonious	John Campbell
1953	Helicopter	Harry Harvey	1991	Giant Victory	Jack Moiseyev
1954	Newport Dream	Del Cameron	1992	Alf Palema	Mickey McNichol
1955	Scott Frost	Joe O'Brien	1993	American Winner	Ron Pierce
1956	The Intruder	Ned Bower	1994	Victory Dream	Michel Lachance
1957	Hickory Smoke	J. Simpson Sr.	1995	Tagliabue	John Campbell
1958	Emily's Pride	Flave Nipe	1996	Continentalvictory	Michel Lachance
1959	Diller Hanover	Frank Ervin	1997	Malabar Man	Mal Burroughs
1960	Blaze Hanover	Joe O'Brien	1998	Muscles Yankee	John Campbell
1961	Harlan Dean	James Arthur	1999	Self Possessed	Michel Lachance
1962	A. C.'s Viking	Sanders Russell			
1963	Speedy Scot	Ralph Baldwin			

*Park Avenue Joe and Probe dead-heated for win. Park Avenue finished first in the summary 2-1-1 to Probe's 1-9-1 finish.
Note: Run at 1 mile since 1947.

Tale of Whoa

Almost as memorable as Charismatic's victory in the Preakness (May 15, 1999) was a scene that unfolded earlier that afternoon at Pimlico. As more than 100,000 shocked spectators looked on, Lee Chang Ferrell, 22, of Bel Air, Md., walked onto the track and tried to take on a nine-horse field charging for the wire in the Maryland Breeders' Cup. Ferrell, who police said was drunk, scaled a seven-foot-high chain-link fence around the infield—unnoticed by the track's 1,000-person security force—then strolled across Pimlico's turf course and crawled under the rail to the main track. He strode toward the horses as they raced through the top of the stretch, then stood with his hands on his hips. Finally he took a boxers stance, side-stepped leader Yes It's True and stood directly in the path of Artax, a 1,000-pound colt. "I thought he was going to walk across the track," jockey Jorge Chavez said. "Then he turned and looked right at me. He was waiting for me." Ferrell took a wild overhand swing at Artax but hit Chavez in the back. After the horses thundered by, security guards shoved Ferrell to the ground. Police took him to Sinai Hospital for psychiatric evaluation, then charged him with first- and second-degree assault, reckless endangerment, disorderly conduct, trespassing and resisting arrest. The cops said Ferrell offered them a simple motive: "I was trying to kill myself."

Little Brown Jug

Year	Winner	Driver	Year	Winner	Driver
1946	Ensign Hanover	Wayne Smart	1973	Melvin's Woe	Joe O'Brien
1947	Forbes Chief	Del Cameron	1974	Armbro Omaha	Bill Haughton
1948	Knight Dream	Frank Safford	1975	Seatrain	Ben Webster
1949	Good Time	Frank Ervin	1976	Keystone Ore	Stanley Dancer
1950	Dudley Hanover	Del Miller	1977	Governor Skipper	John Chapman
1951	Tar Heel	Del Cameron	1978	Happy Escort	William Popfinger
1952	Meadow Rice	Wayne Smart	1979	Hot Hitter	Herve Filion
1953	Keystoner	Frank Ervin	1980	Niatross	Clint Galbraith
1954	Adios Harry	Morris MacDonald	1981	Fan Hanover	Glen Garnsey
1955	Quick Chief	Bill Haughton	1982	Merger	John Campbell
1956	Noble Adios	John Simpson Sr.	1983	Ralph Hanover	Ron Waples
1957	Torpid	John Simpso Sr.	1984	Colt Fortysix	Chris Boring
1958	Shadow Wave	Joe O'Brien	1985	Nihilator	Bill O'Donnell
1959	Adios Butler	Clint Hodgins	1986	Barberry Spur	Bill O'Donnell
1960	Bullet Hanover	John Simpson Sr.	1987	Jaguar Spur	Dick Stillings
1961	Henry T. Adios	Stanley Dancer	1988	B. J. Scoot	Michel Lachance
1962	Lehigh Hanover	Stanley Dancer	1989	Goalie Jeff	Michel Lachance
1963	Overtrick	John Patterson	1990	Beach Towel	Ray Remmen
1964	Vicar Hanover	Bill Haughton	1991	Precious Bunny	Jack Moiseye
1965	Bret Hanover	Frank Ervin	1992	Fake Left	Ron Waples
1966	Romeo Hanover	George Sholty	1993	Life Sign	John Campbell
1967	Best of All	James Hackett	1994	Magical Mike	Michel Lachance
1968	Rum Customer	Bill Haughton	1995	Nick's Fantasy	John Campbell
1969	Laverne Hanover	Bill Haughton	1996	Armbro Operative	Jack Moiseyev
1970	Most Happy Fella	Stanley Dancer	1997	Western Dreamer	Michel Lachance
1971	Nansemond	Herve Filion	1998	Shady Character	Ron Pierce
1972	Strike Out	Keith Waples	1999	Blissful Hall	Ron Pierce

Breeders' Crown

1984

Div	Winner	Driver
2PC	Dragon's Lair	Jeff Mallet
2PF	Amneris	John Campbell
3PC	Troublemaker	Bill O'Donnell
3PF	Naughty But Nice	Tommy Haughton
2TC	Workaholic	Berndt Lindstedt
2TF	Conifer	George Sholty
3TC	Baltic Speed	Jan Nordin
3TF	Fancy Crown	Bill O'Donnell

1985

Div	Winner	Driver
2PC	Robust Hanover	John Campbell
2PF	Caressable	Herve Filion
3PC	Nihilator	Bill O'Donnell
3PF	Stienam	Buddy Gilmour
2TC	Express Ride	John Campbell
2TF	JEF's Spice	Mickey McNichol
3TC	Prakas	John Campbell
3TF	Armbro Devona	Bill O'Donnell
AP	Division Street	Michel Lachance
AT	Sandy Bowl	John Campbell

1986

Div	Winner	Driver
2PC	Sunset Warrior	Bill Gale
2PF	Halcyon	Ray Remmen
3PC	Masquerade	Richard Silverman
3PF	Glow Softly	Ron Waples
2TC	Mack Lobell	John Campbell
2TF	Super Flora	Ron Waples
3TC	Sugarcane Hanover	Ron Waples
3TF	JEF's Spice	Bill O'Donnell
APM	Samshu Bluegrass	Michel Lachance
ATM	Grades Singing	Herve Filion
APH	Forrest Skipper	Lucien Fontaine
ATH	Nearly Perfect	Mickey McNichol

1987

Div	Winner	Driver
2PC	Camtastic	Bill O'Donnell
2PF	Leah Almahurst	Bill Fahy
3PC	Call For Rain	Clint Galbraith
3PF	Pacific	Tom Harmer
2TC	Defiant One	Howard Beissinger
2TF	Nan's Catch	Berndt Lindstedt
3TC	Mack Lobell	John Campbell
3TF	Armbro Fling	George Sholty
APM	Follow My Star	John Campbell
ATM	Grades Singing	Olle Goop
APH	Armbro Emerson	Walter Whelan
ATH	Sugarcane Hanover	Ron Waples

Note: 2=Two-year-old; T=Trotter; C=Colt; 3=Three-year-old; P=Pacer; F=Filly; A=Aged; H=Horse; M=Mare.

Breeders' Crown (Cont.)

1988

Div	Winner	Driver
2PC	Kentucky Spur	Dick Stillings
2PF	Central Park West	John Campbell
3PC	Camtastic	Bill O'Donnell
3PF	Sweet Reflection	Bill O'Donnell
2TC	Valley Victory	Bill O'Donnell
2TF	Peace Corps	John Campbell
3TC	Firm Tribute	Mark O'Mara
3TF	Nalda Hanover	Mickey McNichol
APM	Anniecrombie	Dave Magee
ATM	Armbro Flori	Larry Walker
APH	Call For Rain	Clint Galbraith
ATH	Mack Lobell	John Campbell

1989

Div	Winner	Driver
2PC	Till We Meet Again	Mickey McNichol
2PF	Town Pro	Doug Brown
3PC	Goalie Jeff	Michel Lachance
3PF	Cheery Hello	John Campbell
2TC	Royal Troubador	Carl Allen
2TF	Delphi's Lobell	Ron Waples
3TC	Esquire Spur	Dick Stillings
3TF	Pace Corps	John Campbell
APM	Armbro Feather	John Kopas
ATM	Grades Singing	Olle Goop
APH	Matt's Scooter	Michel Lachance
ATH	Delray Lobell	John Campbell

1990

Div	Winner	Driver
2PC	Artsplace	John Campbell
2PF	Miss Easy	John Campbell
3PC	Beach Towel	Ray Remmen
3PF	Town Pro	Doug Brown
2TC	Crysta's Best	Dick Richardson Jr.
2TF	Jean Bi	Jan Nordin
3TC	Embassy Lobell	Michel Lachance
3TF	Me Maggie	Berndt Lindstedt
APM	Caesar's Jackpot	Bill Fahy
ATM	Peace Corps	Stig Johansson
APH	Bay's Fella	Paul MacDonnell
ATH	No Sex Please	Ron Waples

1991

Div	Winner	Driver
2PC	Digger Almahurst	Doug Brown
2PF	Hazleton Kay	John Campbell
3PC	Three Wizzards	Bill Gale
3PF	Miss Easy	John Campbell
2TC	King Conch	Bill Gale
2TF	Armbro Keepsake	John Campbell
3TC	Giant Victory	Ron Pierce
3TF	Twelve Speed	Ron Waples
APM	Delinquent Account	Bill O'Donnell
ATM	Me Maggie	Berndt Lindstedt
APH	Camluck	Michel Lachance
ATH	Billyjojimbob	Paul MacDonnell

1992

Div	Winner	Driver
2PC	Village Jiffy	Ron Waples
2PF	Immortality	John Campbell
3PC	Kingsbridge	Roger Mayotte
3PF	So Fresh	John Campbell
2TC	Giant Chill	John Patterson Jr.
2TF	Winky's Goal	Cat Manzi
3TC	Baltic Striker	Michel Lachance
3TF	Imperfection	Michel Lachance

1992 (Cont.)

Div	Winner	Driver
APM	Shady Daisy	Ron Pierce
ATM	Peace Corps	Torbjorn Jansson
APH	Artsplace	John Campbell
ATH	No Sex Please	Ron Waples

1993

Div	Winner	Driver
2PC	Expensive Scooter	Jack Moiseyev
2PF	Electric Scooter	Mike Lachance
3PC	Life Sign	John Campbell
3PF	Immortality	John Campbell
2TC	Westgate Crown	John Campbell
2TF	Gleam	Jimmy Takter
3TC	Pine Chip	John Campbell
3TF	Expressway Hanover	Per Henriksen
APM	Swing Back	Kelly Sheppard
ATM	Lifetime Dream	Paul MacDonnell
APH	Staying Together	Bill O'Donnell
ATH	Earl	Chris Christoforou Jr.

1994

Div	Winner	Driver
2PC	Jenna's Beach Boy	Bill Fahy
2PF	Yankee Cashmere	Peter Wrenn
3PC	Magical Mike	Michel Lachance
3PF	Hardie Hanover	Tim Twaddle
2TC	Eager Seelster	Teddy Jacobs
2TF	Lookout Victory	John Patterson
3TC	Incredible Abe	Italo Tamborrino
3TF	Imageofa Clear Day	Bill O'Donnell
APM	Shady Daisy	Michel Lachance
ATM	Armbro Keepsake	Stig Johansson
APH	Village Jiffy	Paul MacDonnell
ATH	Pine Chip	John Campbell

1995

Div	Winner	Driver
2PC	John Street North	Jack Moiseyev
2PF	Paige Nicole Q	John Campbell
3PC	Jenna's Beach Boy	Bill Fahy
3PF	Headline Hanover	Doug Brown
2TC	Armbro Officer	Steve Condren
2TF	Continentalvictory	Michel Lachance
3TC	Abundance	Bill O'Donnell
3TF	Lookout Victory	Sonny Patterson
APM	Ellamony	Mike Saftic
ATM	CR Kay Suzie	Rod Allen
APH	Thatll Be Me	Roger Mayotte
ATH	Panifesto	Luc Ouellette

1996

Div	Winner	Driver
2PC	His Mattjesty	Doug Brown
2PF	Before Sunrise	Steve Condren
3PC	Armbro Operative	Michel Lachance
3PF	Mystical Maddy	Michel Lachance
2TC	Malabar Man	Mal Burroughs
2TF	Armbro Prowess	Jimmy Takter
3TC	Running Sea	Wally Hennessey
3TF	Personal Banner	Peter Wrenn
APM	She's A Great Lady	John Campbell
APH	Jenna's Beach Boy	Bill Fahy
AT	CR Kay Suzie	Rod Allen

Note: 2=Two-year-old; T=Trotter; C=Colt; 3=Three-year-old; P=Pacer; F=Filly; A=Aged; H=Horse; M=Mare.

Breeders' Crown (Cont.)

Div	1997 Winner	Driver	Div	1998 Winner	Driver
2PC	Artiscape	Michel Lachance	2PC	Badlands Hanover	Ron Pierce
2PF	Take Flight	Luc Ouellette	2PF	Juliet's Fate	George Brennan
3PC	Village Jasper	Paul McDonnell	3PC	Artiscape	Michel Lachance
3PF	Stienam's Place	Jack Moiseyev	3PF	Galleria	George Brennan
2TC	Catch As Catch Can	Wally Hennessey	2TC	CR Commando	Carl Allen
2TF	My Dolly	Wally Hennessey	2TF	Musical Victory	Luc Ouellette
3TC	Malabar Man	Malvern Burroughs	3TC	Muscles Yankee	John Campbell
3TF	No Nonsense Woman	Jim Doherty	3TF	Lassie's Goal	Mark O'Mara
APM	Jay's Table	John Campbell	APM	Shore By Five	Daniel Dube
APH	Red Bow Tie	Luc Ouellette	APH	Red Bow Tie	Luc Ouellette
AT	Moni Maker	Wally Hennessey	AT	Supergrit	Ron Pierce

Triple Crown Winners

Trotting

Trotting's Triple Crown consists of the Hambletonian (first run in 1926), the Kentucky Futurity (first run in 1893), and the Yonkers Trot (known as the Yonkers Futurity when it began in 1955).

Year	Horse	Owner	Breeder	Trainer & Driver
1955	Scott Frost	S.A. Camp Farms	Est of W.N. Reynolds	Joe O'Brien
1963	Speedy Scot	Castleton Farms	Castleton Farms	Ralph Baldwin
1964	Ayres	Charlotte Sheppard	Charlotte Sheppard	John Simpson Sr
1968	Nevele Pride	Nevele Acres & Lou Resnick	Mr & Mrs E.C. Quin	Stanley Dancer
1969	Lindy's Pride	Lindy Farm	Hanover Shoe Farms	Howard Beissinger
1972	Super Bowl	Rachel Dancer & Rose Hild Breeding Farm	Stoner Creek Stud	Stanley Dancer

Pacing

Pacing's Triple Crown consists of the Cane Pace (called the Cane Futurity when it began in 1955), the Little Brown Jug (first run in 1946), and the Messenger Stakes (first run in 1956).

Year	Horse	Owner	Breeder	Trainer/Driver
1959	Adios Butler	Paige West & Angelo Pellillo	R.C. Carpenter	Paige West/Clint Hodgins
1965	Bret Hanover	Richard Downing	Hanover Shoe Farms	Frank Ervin
1966	Romeo Hanover	Lucky Star Stables & Morton Finder	Hanover Shoe Farms	Jerry Silverman/ William Meyer (Cane) & George Sholty (Jug & Messenger)
1968	Rum Customer	Kennilworth Farms & L. C. Mancuso	Mr. & Mrs. R.C. Larkin	Bill Haughton
1970	Most Happy Fella	Egyptian Acres Stable	Stoner Creek Stud	Stanley Dancer
1980	Niatross	Niagara Acres, C. Galbraith & Niatross Stables	Niagara Acres	Clint Galbraith
1983	Ralph Hanover	Waples Stable, Pointsetta Stable, Grant's Direct Stable & P. J. Baugh	Hanover Shoe Farms	Stew Firlotte/Ron Waples
1997	Western Dreamer	Daniel and Matthew Daly and Patrick Daly Jr.	Kentuckiana Farms	Bill Robinson/Michel Lachance

Awards

Horse of the Year

Year	Horse	Gait	Owner	Year	Horse	Gait	Owner
1947	Victory Song	T	Castleton Farm	1954	Stenographer	T	Max Hempt
1948	Rodney	T	R.H. Johnston	1955	Scott Frost	T	S.A. Camp Farms
1949	Good Time	P	William Cane	1956	Scott Frost	T	S.A. Camp Farms
1950	Proximity	T	Ralph and Gordon Verhurst	1957	Torpid	P	Sherwood Farm
1951	Pronto Don	T	Hayes Fair Acres Stable	1958	Emily's Pride	T	Walnut Hall and Castleton Farms
1952	Good Time	P	William Cane	1959	Bye Bye Byrd	P	Mr. and Mrs. Rex Larkin
1953	Hi Lo's Forbes	P	Mr. and Mrs. Earl Wagner				

Horse of the Year (Cont.)

Year	Horse	Gait	Owner
1960	Adios Butler	P	Adios Butler Syndicate
1961	Adios Butler	P	Adios Butler Syndicate
1962	Su Mac Lad	T	I.W. Berkemeyer
1963	Speedy Scot	T	Castleton Farm
1964	Bret Hanover	P	Richard Downing
1965	Bret Hanover	P	Richard Downing
1966	Bret Hanover	P	Richard Downing
1967	Nevele Pride	T	Nevele Acres
1968	Nevele Pride	T	Nevele Acres, Louis Resnick
1969	Nevele Pride	T	Nevele Acres, Louis Resnick
1970	Fresh Yankee	T	Duncan MacDonald
1971	Albatross	P	Albatross Stable
1972	Albatross	P	Amicable Stable
1973	Sir Dalrae	P	A La Carte Racing Stable
1974	Delmonica Hanover	T	Delvin Miller, W. Arnold Hanger
1975	Savoir	T	Allwood Stable
1976	Keystone Ore	P	Mr. and Mrs. Stanley Dancer, Rose Hild Farms, Robert Jones
1977	Green Speed	T	Beverly Lloyds
1978	Abercrombie	P	Shirley Mitchell, L. Keith Bulen
1979	Niatross	P	Niagara Acres, Clint Galbraith
1980	Niatross	P	Niatross Syndicate, Niagara Acres, Clint Galbraith
1981	Fan Hanover	P	Dr. J. Glen Brown
1982	Cam Fella	P	Norm Clements, Norm Faulkner
1983	Cam Fella	P	JEF's Standardbred, Norm Clements, Norm Faulkner
1984	Fancy Crown	T	Fancy Crown Stable
1985	Nihilator	P	Wall Street-Nihilator Syndicate
1986	Forrest	P	Forrest L. Bartlett
1987	Mack Lobell	T	One More Time Stable and Fair Wind Farm
1988	Mack Lobell	T	John Erik Magnusson
1989	Matt's Scooter	P	Gordon and Illa Rumpel, Charles Jurasvinski
1990	Beach Towel	P	Uptown Stables
1991	Precious Bunny	P	R. Peter Heffering
1992	Artsplace	P	George Segal
1993	Staying Together	P	Robert Hamather
1994	Cam's Card Shark	P	Jeffrey S. Snyder
1995	CR Kay Suzie	T	Carl & Rod Allen Stable, Inc.
1996	Continental-victory	T	Continentalvictory Stables
1997	Malabar Man	T	Malvern Burroughs
1998	Moni Maker	T	Moni Maker Stable

Note: Balloting is conducted by the U.S Trotting Association for the U.S. Harness Writers Association.

Leading Drivers—Money Won

Year	Driver	Winnings ($)	Year	Driver	Winnings ($)
1946	Thomas Berry	121,933	1973	Herve Filion	2,233,303
1947	H.C. Fitzpatrick	133,675	1974	Herve Filion	3,474,315
1948	Ralph Baldwin	153,222	1975	Carmine Abbatiello	2,275,093
1949	Clint Hodgins	184,108	1976	Herve Filion	2,278,634
1950	Del Miller	306,813	1977	Herve Filion	2,551,058
1951	John Simpson Sr.	333,316	1978	Carmine Abbatiello	3,344,457
1952	Bill Haughton	311,728	1979	John Campbell	3,308,984
1953	Bill Haughton	374,527	1980	John Campbell	3,732,306
1954	Bill Haughton	415,577	1981	Bill O'Donnell	4,065,608
1955	Bill Haughton	599,455	1982	Bill O'Donnell	5,755,067
1956	Bill Haughton	572,945	1983	John Campbell	6,104,082
1957	Bill Haughton	586,950	1984	Bill O'Donnell	9,059,184
1958	Bill Haughton	816,659	1985	Bill O'Donnell	10,207,372
1959	Bill Haughton	771,435	1986	John Campbell	9,515,055
1960	Del Miller	567,282	1987	John Campbell	10,186,495
1961	Stanley Dancer	674,723	1988	John Campbell	11,148,565
1962	Stanley Dancer	760,343	1989	John Campbell	9,738,450
1963	Bill Haughton	790,086	1990	John Campbell	11,620,878
1964	Stanley Dancer	1,051,538	1991	Jack Moiseyev	9,568,468
1965	Bill Haughton	889,943	1992	John Campbell	8,202,108
1966	Stanley Dancer	1,218,403	1993	John Campbell	9,926,482
1967	Bill Haughton	1,305,773	1994	John Campbell	9,834,139
1968	Bill Haughton	1,654,463	1995	John Campbell	9,469,797
1969	Del Insko	1,635,463	1996	Michel Lachance	8,408,231
1970	Herve Filion	1,647,837	1997	Michel Lachance	9,215,388
1971	Herve Filion	1,915,945	1998	John Campbell	10,768,771
1972	Herve Filion	2,473,265			

Motor Sports

AL TIELEMANS

Back to The Pack

After his win at Daytona, defending NASCAR champ Jeff Gordon proved he was only human after all

BY MARK BECHTEL

THE QUESTION on everyone's mind heading into the 1999 auto racing season was, *What will Jeff Gordon do for an encore?* The 27-year-old wunderkind was coming off his second straight NASCAR season title, which he won in a points race so lopsided he could have run the last two races of 1998 backwards, just like he does in those Pepsi commercials, and still won the Cup handily. His near-perfect '98 season included 13 wins, which tied him with Richard Petty for the most victories in a season in NASCAR's modern era, and two $1 million bonuses in the Winston No Bull program. He won races on tracks new and old, long and short, round and road—a surface he was supposedly inadequate on. Stock car racing in 1998 was, in short, Jeff's world. Everyone else just drove in it.

So imagine the surprise around America's speedways when the answer to the foregoing question was, *Come back to the pack and watch everyone else compete for his title.*

Gordon's decline was all the more unexpected because after the season's first race, the Daytona 500, he looked even better than he had in '98. Conventional wisdom holds that in a superspeedway race, in which restrictor plates are used on the cars, you can't win without help, without aerodynamic boosts from other cars. Gordon quickly realized that his fellow drivers weren't exactly lining up to lend the legend-in-the-making a hand. So he adopted a me-against-the-world attitude and got downright chippy. Gordon is still—unfairly—considered soft by fans and, to a certain extent, by other drivers. Perhaps that's because he's not big, he's not gruff, he's not loud, and he appears to devote some attention to personal grooming. There was also the matter of his weeping following his first career win, at Charlotte in 1994. After his teary postrace press conference, he was razzed mercilessly by grizzled vets Dale Earnhardt and Rusty Wallace.

Those two would figure in his 1999 win at Daytona. After passing Earnhardt with 12 laps left to move into second place,

Gordon (24) made aggressive—some said dangerous—maneuvers to win at Daytona.

Gordon closed in on Wallace. With 10 laps to go, he darted low, going past Wallace but nearly ramming into the back of Ricky Rudd's lapped car at what Gordon said felt like "a thousand miles an hour." Gordon slid around Rudd and ahead of Wallace, narrowly avoiding contact, and held on to win.

His rivals left Daytona glumly. There was no reason to expect anything but a Gordon win a week later now that the guy in the best car was doing a pretty good Earnhardt imitation, driving like the ol' Intimidator himself. But 310 laps into the race at Rockingham, Gordon's Monte Carlo blew its engine. That mishap began a string of results that proved Gordon was, after all, mortal. He wrecked in Texas—"That's the hardest I've ever hit a wall, that's for sure," he said—and power steering problems consigned him to a 39th-place finish at the World 600 in Charlotte, a race Gordon had won in '97 and '98. Gordon's improbable spell of five finishes outside the top 30 in 12 races allowed a few other drivers to creep into the spotlight. Dale Jarrett was a model

of consistency, finishing in the top six in 14 straight races during the season and forging a hefty lead in the series points race. Jeff Burton showed he was ready to make the jump from very good driver to bona fide contender, winning two of the circuit's first five races. But Burton's biggest win came at the World 600, where despite the victory, he was upstaged by a couple of rookies.

Dale Earnhardt Jr., the 24-year-old 1998 Busch Series champion, made his debut with the big boys at Charlotte. He finished in 16th place, 10 spots behind his dad, but the old man had some kind words for his namesake afterward. "He told me I did a good job, that I stayed clean and out of trouble," said Junior, whose aw-shucks demeanor and good looks combined with his surname to make him an instant crowd favorite. The other rookie to make a splash at Charlotte that day was Tony Stewart. Earlier in the day the 28-year-old raced to a ninth-place finish at the Indianapolis 500. He then hopped on a jet and got to Charlotte in time to take the wheel of his Pontiac. All he had eaten during the day were two bagels, so a quarter of the way through his second race he tried to do what many of us do every day—steer with one hand and eat with the other. Turns out it's much more difficult to do when traveling 150 mph and wearing a helmet, so Stewart ended up throwing his chocolate nutrition bar out the window after two messy bites. Despite his empty stomach, Stewart finished fourth. Four months later he won at Richmond to become the first rookie to win a race since 1987 and all but wrap up the first top 10 points finish by a newcomer since 1980.

At Indy, Stewart watched a bizarre finish unfurl in front of him. Pole sitter and two-time Indy champ Arie Luyendyk, who was competing in his last race, spun out trying to lap a car with 82 laps to go, handing the lead to Greg Ray. Two laps later Ray crashed as he came out of the pits. Twenty-nine laps from the finish, Robbie Gordon, the only driver from the rival CART circuit to race at the Brickyard, took over the lead and held on to to it until running out of fuel with slightly more than a lap left. That made a winner out of Kenny Brack, who couldn't figure out a way to give up the lead in the 2.5 miles he held it. (Despite his gaffe Ray was the cream of the IRL crop in '99, winning three of five races down the stretch to build a formidable lead in the standings.)

After the race, in one of the fledgling IRL's least shining p.r. moments, Gordon bellowed, "Aw s---," on live television. Four months later Brickyard legend A.J. Foyt, the owner of Brack's car, announced that he will devote "99 percent" of his time next year to his newly formed NASCAR team, leaving his IRL team to languish without him.

The I-don't-want-it-you-take-it finish of the Indy 500 underscored the mediocre driving on the IRL circuit and had open-wheel aficionados clamoring for a resolution to the schism between CART and IRL, which has done significant damage to the sport in the past few years. A few weeks before the race Indianapolis Motor Speedway president and IRL founder Tony George held preliminary meetings with CART cofounder Roger Penske and NASCAR czar Bill France, who owns 10 tracks, to address the fundamental philo-sophical differences—most having to do with team budgets—between the circuits.

In CART, rookie Juan Montoya, a 23-year-old Colombian who took the place of two-time defending series champ Alex Zanardi on the Chip Ganassi Racing team, wasted little time making an impact. He got into a skirmish with Michael Andretti, and his car owner, Ganassi, reportedly later slapped the cigar out of the mouth of Andretti's car owner, Carl Haas. Such behavior was reminiscent of the flamboyant Zanardi, who was CART's best and most colorful driver. And Montoya resembled Zanardi on the track as well. He won his third start and built a large points lead as the season progressed.

Both the CART and IRL seasons were marred by fatal crashes. CART driver Gonzalo Rodriguez, a 27-year-old from Uruguay, was killed during practice for a race at California's Laguna Seca Raceway. And at the IRL's VisionAire 500 in Charlotte three fans were killed when debris from a crash hurtled into a grandstand.

There were notable comings and goings. After hitting the wall during practice at Michigan Speedway five years to the day after a crash at the same track nearly killed him, the popular Ernie Irvan decided to retire. Zanardi left CART for Formula One, where he struggled.

The F/1 title came down to Mika Hakkinen and British driver Eddie Irvine, who careered toward one of the tightest finishes the circuit has seen. Their down-to-the-wire denouement went largely unnoticed in America, but the sport might soon make inroads in the U.S. The Ford Motor Company announced that it would buy Jackie Stewart's team, making it the first U.S.-based manufacturer to own an F/1 team outright. And in September 2000, the U.S. Grand Prix will be run on a road course at the Indianapolis Motor Speedway.

For now, though, nothing is going to challenge NASCAR's supremacy at America's tracks. There's no question about that. In fact, the only question worth asking now is, *How will Jeff Gordon bounce back in 2000?*

Indy Racing League

Indianapolis 500

Results of the 83rd running of the Indianapolis 500 and third round of the 1999 Indy Racing League season. Held Sunday May 23, 1999, at the 2.5-mile Indianapolis Motor Speedway in Indianapolis, IN.
Distance, 500 miles; starters, 33; time of race, 3 hours, 15 minutes, 51.182 seconds; average speed, 153.176 mph; margin of victory, 6.562 seconds; caution flags, 8 for 42 laps; lead changes, 18 among 7 drivers.

TOP 10 FINISHERS

Pos	Driver (start pos.)	Chassis-Engine	Qual. Speed	Laps	Status
1	Kenny Brack (8)	Dallara-Aurora	222.659	200	running
2	Jeff Ward (14)	Dallara-Aurora	221.363	200	running
3	Billy Boat (3)	Dallara-Aurora	223.469	200	running
4	Robby Gordon (4)	Dallara-Aurora	223.066	200	running
5	Robby McGehee (27)	Dallara-Aurora	220.139	199	running
6	Robbie Buhl (32)	Dallara-Aurora	220.115	199	running
7	Buddy Lazier (22)	Dallara-Aurora	220.721	198	running
8	Robby Unser (17)	Dallara-Aurora	221.304	197	running
9	Tony Stewart (24)	Dallara-Aurora	220.653	196	running
10	Hideshi Matsuda (10)	Dallara-Aurora	222.065	196	running

1999 Indy Racing League Results

Date	Race	Winner (start pos.)	Chassis-Engine	Avg Speed
Jan 24	Transworld Indy 200	Eddie Cheever, Jr (13)	Dallara-Aurora	118.538
Mar 28	MCI WorldCom 200	Scott Goodyear (3)	G Force-Aurora	102.856
May 23	Indianapolis 500	Kenny Brack (8)	Dallara-Aurora	153.176
June12	Longhorn 500K	Scott Goodyear (8)	G Force-Aurora	151.177
June 27	Radison 200	Greg Ray (1)	Dallara-Aurora	134.111
July 17	Kobalt 500K	Scott Sharp (6)	Dallara-Aurora	141.546
Aug 1	MBNA Mid-Atlantic 200	Greg Ray (3)	Dallara-Aurora	114.258
Aug 29	Colorado Indy 200	Greg Ray (1)	Dallara-Aurora	135.450
Sept 26	Vegas.com 500K	Sam Schmidt (1)	G Force-Aurora	124.936

Note: Distances are in miles unless followed by K (kilometers).

1998 Final Championship Standings

Driver	Starts	Highest Finish	Pts
Kenny Brack	11	1	332
Davey Hamilton	11	2	292
Tony Stewart	11	1	289
Scott Sharp	11	1	272
Buddy Lazier	11	2	262

Championship Auto Racing Teams

U.S. 500

Results of the 4th running of the U.S. 500 and 12th round of the 1999 CART Series. Held Sunday, July 25, 1999, at the 2-mile Michigan International Speedway in Brooklyn, MI.
Distance, 500 miles; starters, 26; time of race, 2:41:12.362; average speed, 186.097 mph; margin of victory, .032 seconds; caution flags, four for 29 laps; lead changes, 30 among seven drivers.

TOP 10 FINISHERS

Pos	Driver (start pos.)	Car	Qual. Speed	Laps	Status
1	Tony Kanaan (11)	Reynard-Honda	227.029	250	running
2	Juan Montoya (3)	Reynard-Honda	229.321	250	running
3	Paul Tracy (8)	Reynard-Honda	227.790	250	running
4	Michael Andretti (4)	Swift-Ford	229.168	250	running
5	Dario Franchitti (9)	Reynard-Honda	227.790	250	running
6	Adrian Fernandez (2)	Reynard-Ford	229.438	250	running
7	Max Papis (6)	Reynard-Ford	228.231	250	running
8	Christian Fittipaldi (16)	Swift-Ford	225.996	250	running
9	Jimmy Vasser (1)	Reynard-Honda	229.606	249	running
10	Patrick Carpentier (12)	Reynard-Mercedes	226.922	248	running

1999 CART Championship Series Results (Through September 29)

Date	Event	Winner (start pos.)	Car	Avg Speed (mph)
Mar 21	Grand Prix of Miami	Greg Moore (1)	Reynard-Mercedes	136.671
Apr 10	Japan 500	Adrian Fernandez (4)	Reynard-Ford	176.195
Apr 18	Grand Prix of Long Beach	Juan Montoya (5)	Reynard-Honda	87.915
May 2	Nazareth Grand Prix	Juan Montoya (1)	Reynard-Honda	120.225
May 15	Rio 400	Juan Montoya (3)	Reynard-Honda	125.120
May 29	Motorola 300	Michael Andretti (11)	Swift-Ford	123.513
June 6	Miller Lite 225	Paul Tracy (6)	Reynard-Honda	128.029
June 20	Portland 200	Gil de Ferran (3)	Reynard-Honda	107.457
June 27	Grand Prix of Cleveland	Juan Montoya (1)	Reynard-Honda	93.931
July 11	Elkhart Lake 200	Christian Fittipaldi (4)	Swift-Ford	137.697
July 18	Indy Toronto	Dario Franchetti (2)	Reynard-Honda	85.897
July 25	U.S. 500	Tony Kanaan (11)	Reynard-Honda	186.097
Aug 8	Grand Prix of Detroit	Dario Franchetti (4)	Reynard-Honda	81.643
Aug 15	Mid-Ohio 200	Juan Montoya (8)	Reynard-Honda	109.606
Aug 22	Target Grand Prix	Juan Montoya (10)	Reynard-Honda	117.938
Sept 5	Indy Vancouver	Juan Montoya (1)	Reynard-Honda	65.279
Sept 12	Grand Prix of Monterey	Bryan Herta (1)	Reynard-Ford	101.924
Sept 26	Grand Prix of Houston	Paul Tracy (3)	Reynard-Honda	78.960

1998 Championship Standings

Driver	Starts	Wins	Pts
Alex Zanardi	19	7	285
Jimmy Vasser	19	3	169
Dario Franchitti	19	3	160
Adrian Fernandez	19	2	154
Greg Moore	19	2	140
Scott Pruett	19	0	121
Michael Andretti	19	1	112
Bryan Herta	19	1	97
Tony Kanaan	19	0	92
Bobby Rahal	19	0	82

National Association for Stock Car Auto Racing

Daytona 500

Results of the opening round of the 1999 Winston Cup series. Held Sunday, February 14, at the 2.5-mile high-banked Daytona International Speedway.

Distance, 500 miles; starters, 43; time of race, 3:05:42; average speed, 161.551 mph; margin of victory, 0.128 sec; caution flags, 4 for 20 laps; lead changes, 14 among 7 drivers.

TOP 10 FINISHERS

Pos	Driver (start pos.)	Car	Laps	Winnings ($)
1	Jeff Gordon (1)	Chevrolet	200	2,194,246
2	Dale Earnhardt (4)	Chevrolet	200	613,659
3	Kenny Irwin (41)	Ford	200	464,084
4	Mike Skinner (12)	Chevrolet	200	438,834
5	Michael Waltrip (13)	Chevrolet	200	290,596
6	Ken Schrader (7)	Chevrolet	200	240,731
7	Kyle Petty (24)	Pontiac	200	145,809
8	Rusty Wallace (10)	Ford	200	199,209
9	Chad Little (26)	Ford	200	142,884
10	Rick Mast (21)	Ford	200	164,096

Late 1998 Winston Cup Series Results

Date	Track/Distance	Winner (start pos.)	Car	Avg Speed	Winnings ($)
Oct 4	Charlotte 500	Mark Martin (2)	Ford	123.188	151,950
Oct 11	Talladega 500	Dale Jarrett (3)	Ford	159.317	110,125
Oct 17	Daytona 400	Jeff Gordon (8)	Chevrolet	144.549	184,325
Oct 25	Phoenix 500 K	Rusty Wallace (6)	Ford	108.211	78,005
Nov 1	N Carolina 400	Jeff Gordon (9)	Chevrolet	128.423	111,575
Nov 8	Atlanta 500	Jeff Gordon (21)	Chevrolet	114.915	164,450

Note: Distances are in miles unless followed by * (laps) or K (kilometers).

1999 Winston Cup Series Results (through September 29)

Date	Track/Distance	Winner (start pos.)	Car	Avg Speed	Winnings ($)
Feb 14	Daytona 500	Jeff Gordon (1)	Chevrolet	161.551	2,194,246
Feb 21	N Carolina 400	Mark Martin (5)	Ford	120.750	104,635
Mar 7	Las Vegas 400	Jeff Burton (19)	Ford	137.535	336,590
Mar 14	Atlanta 500	Jeff Gordon (8)	Chevrolet	143.296	117,650
Mar 21	Darlington 400	Jeff Burton (9)	Ford	121.294	161,900
Mar 28	Texas 500	Terry Labonte (4)	Chevrolet	144.276	376,840
Apr 11	Bristol 500*	Rusty Wallace (1)	Ford	93.366	92,435
Apr 18	Martinsville 500*	John Andretti (21)	Pontiac	75.653	113,275
Apr 25	Talladega 500	Dale Earnhardt (17)	Chevrolet	163.395	147,795
May 2	California 500	Jeff Gordon (5)	Chevrolet	150.890	155,890
May 15	Richmond 400*	Dale Jarrett (21)	Ford	100.102	169,715
May 30	World 600	Jeff Burton (2)	Ford	151.367	1,212,500
June 6	Dover Downs 400	Bobby Labonte (1)	Pontiac	120.603	144,820
June 13	Michigan 400	Dale Jarrett (6)	Ford	173.997	151,240
June 20	Pocono 500	Bobby Labonte (3)	Pontiac	118.898	151,110
June 27	Sears Point 350 K	Jeff Gordon (1)	Chevrolet	70.378	125,040
July 3	Daytona 400	Dale Jarrett (12)	Ford	169.213	164,965
July 11	New Hampshire 300*	Jeff Burton (38)	Ford	101.876	139,490
July 25	Pocono 500	Bobby Labonte (4)	Pontiac	116.982	139,385
Aug 7	Indianapolis 400	Dale Jarrett (4)	Ford	148.228	712,240
Aug 15	Watkins Glen 90*	Jeff Gordon (3)	Chevrolet	87.722	119,860
Aug 22	Michigan 400	Bobby Labonte (19)	Pontiac	144.332	121,320
Aug 28	Bristol 500*	Dale Earnhardt (26)	Chevrolet	91.276	89,880
Sept 5	Darlington 500	Jeff Burton (15)	Ford	100.816	1,148,170
Sept 11	Richmond 400	Tony Stewart (2)	Pontiac	104.006	135,160
Sept 19	New Hampshire 300*	Joe Nemechek (11)	Chevrolet	100.673	157,625
Sept 26	Dover Downs 400	Mark Martin (8)	Ford	127.434	115,710

Note: Distances are in miles unless followed by * (laps) or K (kilometers).

1998 Winston Cup Final Standings

Driver	Car	Starts	Wins	Pts
Jeff Gordon	Chevy	33	13	5,328
Mark Martin	Ford	33	7	4,964
Dale Jarrett	Ford	33	3	4,619
Rusty Wallace	Ford	33	1	4,501
Jeff Burton	Ford	33	2	4,415
Bobby Labonte	Pontiac	33	2	4,180
Jeremy Mayfield	Ford	33	1	4,157
Dale Earnhardt	Chevy	33	1	3,928
Terry Labonte	Chevy	33	1	3,901
Bobby Hamilton	Chevy	33	1	3,786

1998 Winston Cup Driver Winnings

Driver	Winnings ($)
Jeff Gordon	6,175,867
Dale Jarrett	3,368,735
Mark Martin	3,279,370
Bobby Labonte	2,648,970
Dale Earnhardt	2,611,100
Rusty Wallace	2,133,435
Jeff Burton	2,114,597
Jeremy Mayfield	1,970,521
Terry Labonte	1,838,415
Bobby Hamilton	1,789,180

Formula One Grand Prix Racing

1999 Formula One Results (Through September 29)

Date	Grand Prix	Winner	Car	Time
Mar 7	Australia	Eddie Irvine	McLaren-Mercedes	1:35:01.659
Apr 11	Brazil	Mika Hakkinen	McLaren-Mercedes	1:36:03.785
May 2	San Marino	Michael Schumacher	Ferrari	1:33:44.792
May 16	Monaco	Michael Schumacher	Ferrari	1:49:31.812
May 30	Spain	Mika Hakkinen	McLaren-Mercedes	1:34:13.665
June 13	Canada	Mika Hakkinen	McLaren-Mercedes	1:41:35.727
June 27	France	Heinz-Harald Frentzen	Jordan-Mugen Honda	1:58:24.343
July 11	Great Britain	David Coulthard	McLaren-Mercedes	1:32:30.144
July 25	Austria	Eddie Irvine	Ferrari	1:28:12.438
Aug 1	Germany	Eddie Irvine	Ferrari	1:21:58.594
Aug 15	Hungary	Mika Hakkinen	McLaren-Mercedes	1:46:23.536
Aug 29	Belgium	David Coulthard	McLaren-Mercedes	1:25:43.057
Sept 12	Italy	Heinz-Harald Frentzen	Jordan-Mugan Honda	1:17:02.928
Sept 26	European (Germany)	Johnny Herbert	Stewart-Ford	1:41:54.314

1998 World Championship Final Standings

Drivers compete in Grand Prix races for the title of World Driving Champion. Below are the top 10 results from the 1998 season. Points are awarded for places 1–6 as follows: 10-6-4-3-2-1.

Driver, Country	Starts	Wins	Car	Pts
Mika Hakkinen, Finland	16	8	McLaren-Mercedes	100
Michael Schumacher, Germany	16	6	Ferrari	86
David Coulthard, Great Britain	16	1	McLaren-Mercedes	56
Eddie Irvine, Great Britain	16	0	Ferrari	47
Jacques Villeneuve, Canada	16	0	Williams	21
Damon Hill, Great Britain	16	1	Jordan	20
Heinz-Harald Frentzen, Germany	16	0	Williams	17
Alexander Wurz, Austria	16	0	Benetton	17
Giancarlo Fisichella, Italy	16	0	Benetton	16
Ralf Schumacher, Germany	16	0	Jordan	14

Professional Sports Car Racing, Inc.

The 24 Hours of Daytona

Held at the Daytona International Speedway on January 30–31, the 24 Hours of Daytona annually serves as the opening round of United States Road Racing Championship's season.

Place	Drivers	Car (Class)	Distance
1	Elliott Forbes-Robinson, Butch Leitzinger, Andy Wallace	Riley & Scott Ford (CA)	708 laps (104.9 mph)
2	Massimiliano Angelelli, Didier de Radigues, Allan McNish, Wayne Taylor	Ferrari 333 SP (CA)	706 laps
3	Jim Matthews, Max Papis, Jimmy Vasser	Ferrari 333 SP (CA)	694 laps
4	Lilian Bryner, Enzo Calderari, Carl Rosenblad, Angelo Zadra	Ferrari 333 SP (CA)	679 laps
5	Henry Camferdam, Duncan Dayton, Eliseo Salazar, Scott Schubot	Riley & Scott Ford (CA)	643 laps

1999 American Le Mans Series—Prototype Class (Through September 30)

Date	Race	Winners	Car
Mar 20	12 Hours at Sebring	J.J. Lehto, Tom Kristensen, Jörg Müller	BMW
Apr 18	Grand Prix of Atlanta	Eric van de Poele, Domenico Schiattarella	Riley & Scott/Judd
June 27	Grand Prix of Mosport	Jan Magnussen, Johnny O'Connell	Panoz LMP/Ford
July 25	Grand Prix of Sonoma	J.J. Lehto, Steve Soper	BMW
Aug 1	Rose City Grand Prix	Eric Bernard, David Brabham	Panoz LMP/Ford
Sept 18	Petit Le Mans	David Brabham, Eric Bernard, Andy Wallace	Panoz LMP/Ford

1999 American Le Mans Series—GTS Class (Through September 30)

Date	Race	Winners	Car
Mar 20	12 Hours at Sebring	Martin Snow, Patrick Huisman, Melanie Snow	Porsche
Apr 18	Grand Prix of Atlanta	John O'Steen, Larry Schumacher	Porsche
June 27	Grand Prix of Mosport	Olivier Beretta, David Donohue	Dodge Viper
July 25	Grand Prix of Sonoma	Olivier Beretta, David Donohue	Dodge Viper
Aug 1	Rose City Grand Prix	David Donohue, Olivier Beretta	Dodge Viper
Sept 18	Petit Le Mans	Olivier Beretta, Karl Wendlinger, Marc Duez	Dodge Viper

1999 American Le Mans Series—GT Class (Through September 30)

Date	Race	Winners	Car
Mar 20	12 Hours at Sebring	Kelly Collins, Cort Wagner, Darryl Havens	Porsche
Apr 18	Grand Prix of Atlanta	Brian Cunningham, Johannes van Overbeek	BMW
June 27	Grand Prix of Mosport	Dirk Mueller, Cort Wagner	Porsche
July 25	Grand Prix of Sonoma	Hans Stuck, Boris Said	BMW
Aug 1	Rose City Grand Prix	Dirk Mueller, Cort Wagner	Porsche
Sept 18	Petit Le Mans	Dirk Mueller, Sascha Maassen, Cort Wagner	Porsche

1998 World SportsCar Championship Final Standings

Driver	Pts
Butch Leitzinger	173
Wayne Taylor	166
Eric van de Poele	155
James Weaver	126
Dorsey Schroeder	119
Didier Theys	110
Jim Downing	103
Jon Field	92
Elliott Forbes-Robinson	82
David Murray	72

24 Hours of Le Mans

Held at Le Mans, France, on June 12–13, 1999, the 24 Hours of Le Mans is the most prestigious international event in endurance racing.

Place	Drivers	Car	Laps
1	Yannick Dalmas, Joachim Winkelhock, Pierluigi Martini	BMW V12 LMR	365 (3,087.8 mi)
2	Ukyo Katayama, Keiichi Tsuchiya, Toshio Suzuki	Toyota GT1	364
3	Emmanuel Pirro, Franck Biela, Didier Theys	Audi R8R	360
4	Michele Alboreto, Rinaldo Cappello, Laurent Aiello	Audi R8R	346
5	Thomas Bscher, Bill Auberlen, Steve Soper	BMW V12 LM98	345
6	Alex Caffi, Andrea Montermini, Dominico Schiattarella	Courage C52	342
7	David Brabham, Eric Bernard, Butch Leitzinger	Panoz LMP	336
8	Didier Cottaz, Marc Goosens, Fredrik Ekblom	Nissan C52	334
9	Henri Pescarolo, Michel Ferte, Patrice Gay	Courage C50	327
10	Olivier Beretta, Karl Wendlinger, Dominique Dupuy	Chrysler Viper	325

National Hot Rod Association

1999 Results (Through September 27)

TOP FUEL

Date	Race, Site	Winner	Time	Speed
Feb 4–7	Winternationals, Pomona, CA	Mike Dunn	4.522	318.88
Feb 25–28	Arizona Nationals, Phoenix	Joe Amato	4.565	320.66
Mar 18–21	Mac Tools Gatornationals, Gainesville, FL	Mike Dunn	4.550	319.98
Apr 8–11	O'Reilly Nationals, Houston	Doug Herbert	4.657	309.56
Apr 22–25	Castrol Nationals, Dallas	Gary Scelzi	4.563	319.60
Apr 29–May 2	Pennzoil Nationals, Richmond, VA	Cory McClenathan	4.684	310.05
May 13–16	Southern Nationals, Atlanta	Gary Scelzi	4.698	307.23
May 20–23	Mopar Nationals, Englishtown, NJ	Joe Amato	4.614	313.58
June 3–6	Fram Route 66 Nationals, Chicago	Mike Dunn	4.702	316.67
June 10–13	Pontiac Nationals, Columbus, OH	Doub Herbert	4.696	313.00
June 24–27	Sears Nationals, Madison, IL	Gary Scelzi	4.602	312.13
July 15–18	Mile-High Nationals, Denver	Joe Amato	5.710	253.85
July 30–Aug 1	Northwest Nationals, Seattle	Joe Amato	4.704	306.95
Aug 6–8	Autolite Nationals, Sonoma, CA	Doug Kalitta	4.615	315.93
Aug 19–22	NHRA Nationals, Brainerd, MN	Larry Dixon	4.594	294.95
Sept 1–6	U.S. Nationals, Indianapolis	Joe Amato	4.529	324.20
Sept 16–19	Keystone Nationals, Reading, PA	Joe Amato	4.677	303.95

FUNNY CAR

Date	Race, Site	Winner	Time	Speed
Feb 4–7	Winternationals, Pomona, CA	Tony Pedregon	4.970	311.49
Feb 25–28	Arizona Nationals, Phoenix	John Force	4.843	317.87
Mar 18–21	Mac Tools Gatornationals, Gainesville, FL	John Force	4.819	311.92
Apr 8–11	O'Reilly Nationals, Houston	John Force	4.878	307.02
Apr 22–25	Castrol Nationals, Dallas	Tony Pedregon	4.982	309.70
Apr 29–May 2	Pennzoil Nationals, Richmond, VA	John Force	4.940	303.30
May 13–16	Southern Nationals, Atlanta	John Force	5.147	283.61

1999 Results (Through September 19) *(Cont.)*

FUNNY CAR *(CONT.)*

Date	Race, Site	Winner	Time	Speed
May 20–23	Mopar Nationals, Englishtown, NJ	John Force	4.878	309.34
June 3–6	Fram Route 66 Nationals, Chicago	Tom Wilkerson	5.970	239.06
June 10–13	Pontiac Nationals, Columbus, OH	Phil Burkart	5.163	280.89
June 24–27	Sears Nationals, Madison, IL	John Force	4.947	297.88
July 8–10	Winston Showdown, Bristol, TN	John Force	5.470	262.18
July 15–18	Mile-High Nationals, Denver	Tony Pedregon	5.209	279.96
July 30–Aug 1	Northwest Nationals, Seattle	Del Worsham	5.283	279.87
Aug 6–8	Autolite Nationals, Sonoma, CA	Whit Bazemore	4.963	301.74
Aug 19–22	NHRA Nationals, Brainerd, MN	John Force	4.929	313.80
Sept 1–6	U.S. Nationals, Indianapolis	Tommy Johnson	4.885	315.71
Sept 16–19	Keystone Nationals, Reading, PA	Tommy Johnson	5.108	281.51

PRO STOCK

Date	Race, Site	Winner	Time	Speed
Feb 4–7	Winternationals, Pomona, CA	Jeg Coughlin	6.969	198.52
Feb 25–28	Arizona Nationals, Phoenix	Kurt Johnson	6.970	197.97
Mar 18–21	Mac Tools Gatornationals, Gainesville, FL	Warren Johnson	6.971	199.37
Apr 8–11	O'Reilly Nationals, Houston	Kurt Johnson	6.969	199.14
Apr 22–25	Castrol Nationals, Dallas	Warren Johnson	6.945	198.85
Apr 29–May 2	Pennzoil Nationals, Richmond, VA	Allen Johnson	6.970	198.17
May 13–16	Southern Nationals, Atlanta	Warren Johnson	6.998	198.63
May 20–23	Mopar Nationals, Englishtown, NJ	Richie Stevens	6.959	198.00
June 3–6	Fram Route 66 Nationals, Chicago	Warren Johnson	6.987	198.06
June 10–13	Pontiac Nationals, Columbus, OH	Warren Johnson	7.008	197.57
June 24–27	Sears Nationals, Madison, IL	Jim Yates	7.018	195.85
July 8–10	Winston Showdown, Bristol, TN	Jeg Coughlin	7.004	196.85
July 15–18	Mile-High Nationals, Denver	Jeg Coughlin	7.267	188.67
July 30–Aug 1	Northwest Nationals, Seattle	Kurt Johnson	6.923	200.44
Aug 6–8	Autolite Nationals, Sonoma, CA	Jim Yates	6.982	197.48
Aug 19–22	NHRA Nationals, Brainerd, MN	Jeg Coughlin	7.063	194.60
Sept 1–6	U.S. Nationals, Indianapolis	Warren Johnson	6.920	199.82
Sept 16–19	Keystone Nationals, Reading, PA	Jeg Coughlin	6.936	198.80

1998 Standings

TOP FUEL

Driver	Wins	Pts
Gary Scelzi	6	1,781
Cory McClenathan	6	1,640
Joe Amato	4	1,522
Kenny Bernstein	5	1,385
Mike Dunn	0	1,344
Doug Kalitta	1	1,098
Larry Dixon Jr.	1	1,093
Jim Head	0	1,083
Bob Vandergriff Jr.	0	993
Bruce Sarver	0	957

FUNNY CAR

Driver	Wins	Pts
John Force	3	1,663
Ron Capps	5	1,528
Cruz Pedregon	5	1,445
Chuck Etchells	3	1,430
Whit Bazemore	1	1,281
Tony Pedregon	2	1,256
Tim Wilkerson	0	1,143
Dean Skuza	1	1,117
Al Hofmann	1	1,044
Del Worsham	0	905

PRO STOCK

Driver	Wins	Pts
Warren Johnson	9	1,973
Jeg Coughlin	4	1,533
Kurt Johnson	1	1,416
Jim Yates	1	1,390
Mark Osborne	2	1,066
Mike Thomas	1	977
Mike Edwards	1	975
Tom Martino	1	964
Richie Stevens	1	917
Mark Pawuk	0	819

Indianapolis 500

First held in 1911, the Indianapolis 500—200 laps of the 2.5-mile Indianapolis Motor Speedway Track (called the Brickyard in honor of its original pavement)—grew to become the most famous auto race in the world. Though the Memorial Day weekend event lost participants and prestige in the mid-1990s due to feuding in the world of U.S. open-wheel racing, it annually attracts crowds of over 100,000.

Year	Winner (Start Position)	Car	Avg MPH	Pole Winner	MPH
1911	Ray Harroun (28)	Marmon Wasp	74.590	Lewis Strang	Awarded pole
1912	Joe Dawson (7)	National	78.720	Gil Anderson	Drew pole
1913	Jules Goux (7)	Peugeot	75.930	Caleb Bragg	Drew pole
1914	Rene Thomas (15)	Delage	82.470	Jean Chassagne	Drew pole
1915	Ralph DePalma (2)	Mercedes	89.840	Howard Wilcox	98.90
1916	Dario Resta (4)	Peugeot	84.000	John Aitken	96.69
1917–18	No race				
1919	Howard Wilcox (2)	Peugeot	88.050	Rene Thomas	104.78
1920	Gaston Chevrolet (6)	Monroe	88.620	Ralph DePalma	99.15
1921	Tommy Milton (20)	Frontenac	89.620	Ralph DePalma	100.75
1922	Jimmy Murphy (1)	Murphy Special	94.480	Jimmy Murphy	100.50
1923	Tommy Milton (1)	H.C.S. Special	90.950	Tommy Milton	108.17
1924	L.L. Corum	Duesenberg Special	98.230	Jimmy Murphy	108.037
	Joe Boyer (21)				
1925	Peter DePaolo (2)	Duesenberg Special	101.130	Leon Duray	113.196
1926	Frank Lockhart (20)	Miller Special	95.904	Earl Cooper	111.735
1927	George Souders (22)	Duesenberg	97.545	Frank Lockhart	120.100
1928	Louis Meyer (13)	Miller Special	99.482	Leon Duray	122.391
1929	Ray Keech (6)	Simplex Piston Ring Special	97.585	Cliff Woodbury	120.599
1930	Billy Arnold (1)	Miller Hartz Special	100.448	Billy Arnold	113.268
1931	Louis Schneider (13)	Bowes Seal-Fast Special	96.629	Russ Snowberger	112.796
1932	Fred Frame (27)	Miller Hartz Special	104.144	Lou Moore	117.363
1933	Louis Meyer (6)	Tydol Special	104.162	Bill Cummings	118.524
1934	Bill Cummings (10)	Boyle Products Special	104.863	Kelly Petillo	119.329
1935	Kelly Petillo (22)	Gilmore Speedway Special	106.240	Rex Mays	120.736
1936	Louis Meyer (28)	Ring-Free Special	109.069	Rex Mays	119.664
1937	Wilbur Shaw (2)	Shaw-Gilmore Special	113.580	Bill Cummings	123.343
1938	Floyd Roberts (1)	Burd Piston Ring Special	117.200	Floyd Roberts	125.681
1939	Wilbur Shaw (3)	Boyle Special	115.035	Jimmy Snyder	130.138
1940	Wilbur Shaw (2)	Boyle Special	114.277	Rex Mays	127.850
1941	Floyd Davis	Noc-Out Hose Clamp Special	115.117	Mauri Rose	128.691
	Mauri Rose (17)				
1942–45	No race				
1946	George Robson (15)	Thorne Engineering Special	114.820	Cliff Bergere	126.471
1947	Mauri Rose (3)	Blue Crown Spark Plug Special	116.338	Ted Horn	126.564
1948	Mauri Rose (3)	Blue Crown Spark Plug Special	119.814	Rex Mays	130.577
1949	Bill Holland (4)	Blue Crown Spark Plug Special	121.327	Duke Nalon	132.939
1950	Johnnie Parsons (5)	Wynn's Friction Proofing	124.002	Walt Faulkner	134.343
1951	Lee Wallard (2)	Belanger Special	126.244	Duke Nalon	136.498
1952	Troy Ruttman (7)	Agajanian Special	128.922	Fred Agabashian	138.010
1953	Bill Vukovich (1)	Fuel Injection Special	128.740	Bill Vukovich	138.392
1954	Bill Vukovich (19)	Fuel Injection Special	130.840	Jack McGrath	141.033
1955	Bob Sweikert (14)	John Zink Special	128.209	Jerry Hoyt	140.045
1956	Pat Flaherty (1)	John Zink Special	128.490	Pat Flaherty	145.596
1957	Sam Hanks (13)	Belond Exhaust Special	135.601	Pat O'Connor	143.948
1958	Jim Bryan (7)	Belond AP Parts Special	133.791	Dick Rathmann	145.974
1959	Rodger Ward (6)	Leader Card 500 Roadster	135.857	Johnny Thomson	145.908
1960	Jim Rathmann (2)	Ken-Paul Special	138.767	Eddie Sachs	146.592
1961	A.J. Foyt (7)	Bowes Seal-Fast Special	139.130	Eddie Sachs	147.481
1962	Rodger Ward (2)	Leader Card 500 Roadster	140.293	Parnelli Jones	150.370
1963	Parnelli Jones (1)	Agajanian-Willard Special	143.137	Parnelli Jones	151.153
1964	A.J. Foyt (5)	Sheraton-Thompson Special	147.350	Jim Clark	158.828
1965	Jim Clark (2)	Lotus Ford	150.686	A.J. Foyt	161.233
1966	Graham Hill (15)	American Red Ball Special	144.317	Mario Andretti	165.899
1967	A.J. Foyt (4)	Sheraton-Thompson Special	151.207	Mario Andretti	168.982
1968	Bobby Unser (3)	Rislone Special	152.882	Joe Leonard	171.559
1969	Mario Andretti (2)	STP Oil Treatment Special	156.867	A.J. Foyt	170.568
1970	Al Unser (1)	Johnny Lightning 500 Special	155.749	Al Unser	170.221
1971	Al Unser (5)	Johnny Lightning Special	157.735	Peter Revson	178.696
1972	Mark Donohue (3)	Sunoco McLaren	162.962	Bobby Unser	195.940
1973	Gordon Johncock (11)	STP Double Oil Filters	159.036	Johnny Rutherford	198.413
1974	Johnny Rutherford (25)	McLaren	158.589	A.J. Foyt	191.632

Year	Winner (Start Position)	Car	Avg MPH	Pole Winner	MPH
1975	Bobby Unser (3)	Jorgensen Eagle	149.213	A.J. Foyt	193.976
1976	Johnny Rutherford (1)	Hy-Gain McLaren/Goodyear	148.725	Johnny Rutherford	188.957
1977	A.J. Foyt (4)	Gilmore Racing Team	161.331	Tom Sneva	198.884
1978	Al Unser (5)	FNCTC Chaparral Lola	161.361	Tom Sneva	202.156
1979	Rick Mears (1)	The Gould Charge	158.899	Rick Mears	193.736
1980	Johnny Rutherford (1)	Pennzoil Chaparral	142.862	Johnny Rutherford	192.256
1981	Bobby Unser (1)	Norton Spirit Penske PC-9B	139.084	Bobby Unser	200.546
1982	Gordon Johncock (5)	STP Oil Treatment	162.026	Rick Mears	207.004
1983	Tom Sneva (4)	Texaco Star	162.117	Teo Fabi	207.395
1984	Rick Mears (3)	Pennzoil Z-7	163.612	Tom Sneva	210.029
1985	Danny Sullivan (8)	Miller American Special	152.982	Pancho Carter	212.583
1986	Bobby Rahal (4)	Budweiser/Truesports/March	170.722	Rick Mears	216.828
1987	Al Unser (20)	Cummins Holset Turbo	162.175	Mario Andretti	215.390
1988	Rick Mears (1)	Penske-Chevrolet	144.809	Rick Mears	219.198
1989	Emerson Fittipaldi (3)	Penske-Chevrolet	167.581	Rick Mears	223.885
1990	Arie Luyendyk (3)	Domino's Pizza Chevrolet	185.981*	Emerson Fittipaldi	225.301
1991	Rick Mears (1)	Penske-Chevrolet	176.457	Rick Mears	224.113
1992	Al Unser Jr (12)	G92-Chevrolet	134.477	Roberto Guerrero	232.482
1993	Emerson Fittipaldi (9)	Penske-Chevrolet	157.207	Arie Luyendyk	223.967
1994	Al Unser Jr (1)	Penske-Mercedes	160.872	Al Unser Jr.	228.011
1995	Jacques Villeneuve (5)	Reynard-Ford	153.616	Scott Brayton	231.616
1996	Buddy Lazier (5)	Reynard-Ford	147.956	Tony Stewart	233.100†
1997	Arie Luyendyk (1)	G Force Aurora	145.827	Arie Luyendyk	231.468
1998	Eddie Cheever (17)	Dallara Aurora	145.155	Billy Boat	223.503
1999	Kenny Brack (8)	Dallara Aurora	153.176	Arie Luyendyk	225.179

*Track record, winning time. †Track record, qualifying time.

Indianapolis 500 Rookie of the Year Award

1952	Art Cross	1969	Mark Donohue*	1985	Arie Luyendyk*
1953	Jimmy Daywalt	1970	Donnie Allison	1986	Randy Lanier
1954	Larry Crockett	1971	Denny Zimmerman	1987	Fabrizio Barbazza
1955	Al Herman	1972	Mike Hiss	1988	Billy Vukovich III
1956	Bob Veith	1973	Graham McRae	1989	Bernard Jourdain
1957	Don Edmunds	1974	Pancho Carter		Scott Pruett
1958	George Amick	1975	Bill Puterbaugh	1990	Eddie Cheever*
1959	Bobby Grim	1976	Vern Schuppan	1991	Jeff Andretti
1960	Jim Hurtubise	1977	Jerry Sneva	1992	Lyn St. James
1961	Parnelli Jones*	1978	Rick Mears*	1993	Nigel Mansell
	Bobby Marshman		Larry Rice	1994	Jacques Villeneuve*
1962	Jimmy McElreath	1979	Howdy Holmes	1995	Gil de Ferran
1963	Jim Clark*	1980	Tim Richmond	1996	Tony Stewart
1964	Johnny White	1981	Josele Garza	1997	Jeff Ward
1965	Mario Andretti*	1982	Jim Hickman	1998	Steve Knapp
1966	Jackie Stewart	1983	Teo Fabi	1999	Robby McGehee
1967	Denis Hulme	1984	Michael Andretti		
1968	Billy Vukovich		Roberto Guerrero		

*Future winner of Indy 500.

CART Championship Series Champions

From 1909 to 1955, this championship was awarded by the American Automobile Association (AAA), and from 1956 to 1979 by the United States Auto Club (USAC). Since 1979, Championship Auto Racing Teams (CART) has conducted the championship. Known as PPG CART World Series until 1998.

1909	George Robertson	1920	Tommy Milton	1931	Louis Schneider
1910	Ray Harroun	1921	Tommy Milton	1932	Bob Carey
1911	Ralph Mulford	1922	Jimmy Murphy	1933	Louis Meyer
1912	Ralph DePalma	1923	Eddie Hearne	1934	Bill Cummings
1913	Earl Cooper	1924	Jimmy Murphy	1935	Kelly Petillo
1914	Ralph DePalma	1925	Peter DePaolo	1936	Mauri Rose
1915	Earl Cooper	1926	Harry Hartz	1937	Wilbur Shaw
1916	Dario Resta	1927	Peter DePaolo	1938	Floyd Roberts
1917	Earl Cooper	1928	Louis Meyer	1939	Wilbur Shaw
1918	Ralph Mulford	1929	Louis Meyer	1940	Rex Mays
1919	Howard Wilcox	1930	Billy Arnold	1941	Rex Mays

PPG CART World Series Champions (Cont.)

1942–45 ....No racing	1964 .............A.J. Foyt	1982 ....Rick Mears
1946 ....Ted Horn	1965 ....Mario Andretti	1983 ....Al Unser
1947 ....Ted Horn	1966 ....Mario Andretti	1984 ....Mario Andretti
1948 ....Ted Horn	1967 .............A.J. Foyt	1985 ....Al Unser
1949 ....Johnnie Parsons	1968 ....Bobby Unser	1986 ....Bobby Rahal
1950 ....Henry Banks	1969 ....Mario Andretti	1987 ....Bobby Rahal
1951 ....Tony Bettenhausen	1970 ....Al Unser	1988 ....Danny Sullivan
1952 ....Chuck Stevenson	1971 ....Joe Leonard	1989 ....Emerson Fittipaldi
1953 ....Sam Hanks	1972 ....Joe Leonard	1990 ....Al Unser Jr.
1954 ....Jimmy Bryan	1973 ....Roger McCluskey	1991 ....Michael Andretti
1955 ....Bob Sweikert	1974 ....Bobby Unser	1992 ....Bobby Rahal
1956 ....Jimmy Bryan	1975 .............A.J. Foyt	1993 ....Nigel Mansell
1957 ....Jimmy Bryan	1976 ....Gordon Johncock	1994 ....Al Unser Jr.
1958 ....Tony Bettenhausen	1977 ....Tom Sneva	1995 ....Jacques Villeneuve
1959 ....Rodger Ward	1978 ....Tom Sneva	1996 ....Jimmy Vasser
1960 .............A.J. Foyt	1979 .............A.J. Foyt	1997 ....Alex Zanardi
1961 .............A.J. Foyt	1979 ....Rick Mears	1998 ....Alex Zanardi
1962 ....Rodger Ward	1980 ....Johnny Rutherford	
1963 .............A.J. Foyt	1981 ....Rick Mears	

Alltime CART Leaders

WINS		WINNINGS ($)		POLE POSITIONS	
A.J. Foyt	67	*Al Unser Jr.	18,805,906	Mario Andretti	67
Mario Andretti	52	Bobby Rahal	16,344,008	A.J. Foyt	53
Al Unser	39	*Michael Andretti	15,886,869	Bobby Unser	49
*Michael Andretti	38	Emerson Fittipaldi	14,293,625	Rick Mears	40
Bobby Unser	35	Mario Andretti	11,552,154	*Michael Andretti	32
*Al Unser Jr.	31	Rick Mears	11,050,807	Al Unser	27
Rick Mears	29	*Jimmy Vasser	9,010,494	Johnny Rutherford	23
Johnny Rutherford	27	Danny Sullivan	8,884,126	Gordon Johncock	20
Rodger Ward	26	Arie Luyendyk	7,732,188	Rex Mays	19
Gordon Johncock	25	Raul Boesel	6,971,887	Danny Sullivan	19
Bobby Rahal	24	*Paul Tracy	6,872,278	Bobby Rahal	18
Ralph DePalma	24	Al Unser	6,740,843	Emerson Fittipaldi	17
Tommy Milton	23	Alex Zanardi	5,733,750	Tony Bettenhausen	14
Tony Bettenhausen	22	*Scott Pruett	5,422,644	Don Branson	14
Emerson Fittipaldi	22	A.J. Foyt	5,357,589	Tom Sneva	14
Earl Cooper	20	Teo Fabi	5,045,881	Parnelli Jones	12
Jimmy Bryan	19	Scott Brayton	4,807,274	*Paul Tracy	12
Jimmy Murphy	19	Scott Goodyear	4,579,451		
Ralph Mulford	17	Tom Sneva	4,392,993		
Danny Sullivan	17	Roberto Guerrero	4,275,163		

*Active driver. Note: Leaders through September 27, 1999.

National Association for Stock Car Auto Racing

Stock Car Racing's Major Events

Winston offers a $1 million bonus to any driver to win three of NASCAR's top four events in the same season. These races are the richest (Daytona 500), the fastest (Talladega 500), the longest (World 600 at Charlotte) and the oldest (Southern 500 at Darlington). These events form the backbone of NASCAR racing. Only four drivers, Lee Roy Yarbrough (1969), David Pearson (1976), Bill Elliott (1985) and Jeff Gordon (1997) have scored the three-track hat trick.

Daytona 500

Year	Winner	Car	Avg MPH	Pole Winner	MPH
1959	Lee Petty	Oldsmobile	135.520	Cotton Owens	143.198
1960	Junior Johnson	Chevrolet	124.740	Fireball Roberts	151.556
1961	Marvin Panch	Pontiac	149.601	Fireball Roberts	155.709
1962	Fireball Roberts	Pontiac	152.529	Fireball Roberts	156.995
1963	Tiny Lund	Ford	151.566	Johnny Rutherford	165.183
1964	Richard Petty	Plymouth	154.345	Paul Goldsmith	174.910
1965	Fred Lorenzen	Ford	141.539	Darel Dieringer	171.151
1966	Richard Petty	Plymouth	160.627	Richard Petty	175.165
1967	Mario Andretti	Ford	149.926	Curtis Turner	180.831
1968	Cale Yarborough	Mercury	143.251	Cale Yarborough	189.222
1969	Lee Roy Yarbrough	Ford	157.950	David Pearson	190.029

Daytona 500 (Cont.)

Year	Winner	Car	Avg MPH	Pole Winner	MPH
1970	Pete Hamilton	Plymouth	149.601	Cale Yarborough	194.015
1971	Richard Petty	Plymouth	144.462	A.J. Foyt	182.744
1972	A.J. Foyt	Mercury	161.550	Bobby Isaac	186.632
1973	Richard Petty	Dodge	157.205	Buddy Baker	185.662
1974	Richard Petty	Dodge	140.894	David Pearson	185.017
1975	Benny Parsons	Chevrolet	153.649	Donnie Allison	185.827
1976	David Pearson	Mercury	152.181	A.J. Foyt	185.943
1977	Cale Yarborough	Chevrolet	153.218	Donnie Allison	188.048
1978	Bobby Allison	Ford	159.730	Cale Yarborough	187.536
1979	Richard Petty	Oldsmobile	143.977	Buddy Baker	196.049
1980	Buddy Baker	Oldsmobile	177.602*	A.J. Foyt	195.020
1981	Richard Petty	Buick	169.651	Bobby Allison	194.624
1982	Bobby Allison	Buick	153.991	Benny Parsons	196.317
1983	Cale Yarborough	Pontiac	155.979	Ricky Rudd	198.864
1984	Cale Yarborough	Chevrolet	150.994	Cale Yarborough	201.848
1985	Bill Elliott	Ford	172.265	Bill Elliott	205.114
1986	Geoff Bodine	Chevrolet	148.124	Bill Elliott	205.039
1987	Bill Elliott	Ford	176.263	Bill Elliott	210.364†
1988	Bobby Allison	Buick	137.531	Ken Schrader	193.823
1989	Darrell Waltrip	Chevrolet	148.466	Ken Schrader	196.996
1990	Derrike Cope	Chevrolet	165.761	Ken Schrader	196.515
1991	Ernie Irvan	Chevrolet	148.148	Davey Allison	195.955
1992	Davey Allison	Ford	160.256	Sterling Marlin	192.213
1993	Dale Jarrett	Chevrolet	154.972	Kyle Petty	189.426
1994	Sterling Marlin	Chevrolet	156.931	Loy Allen Jr.	190.158
1995	Sterling Marlin	Chevrolet	141.710	Dale Jarrett	193.498
1996	Dale Jarrett	Ford	154.308	Dale Earnhardt	189.510
1997	Jeff Gordon	Chevrolet	148.295	Mike Skinner	189.813
1998	Dale Earnhardt	Chevrolet	172.712	Bobby Labonte	192.415
1999	Jeff Gordon	Chevrolet	161.551	Jeff Gordon	195.067

*Track record, winning time. †Track record, qualifying time. Note: The Daytona 500, held annually in February, now opens the NASCAR season with 200 laps around the high-banked Daytona International Speedway.

World 600

Year	Winner	Car	Avg MPH	Pole Winner
1960	Joe Lee Johnson	Chevrolet	107.752	J.L. Johnson
1961	David Pearson	Pontiac	111.634	Richard Petty
1962	Nelson Stacy	Ford	125.552	Fireball Roberts
1963	Fred Lorenzen	Ford	132.418	Junior Johnson
1964	Jim Paschal	Plymouth	125.772	Junior Johnson
1965	Fred Lorenzen	Ford	121.772	Fred Lorenzon
1966	Marvin Panch	Plymouth	135.042	Paul Goldsmith
1967	Jim Paschal	Plymouth	135.832	Cale Yarborough
1968	Buddy Baker	Dodge	104.207	Donnie Allison
1969	Lee Yarbrough	Mercury	134.631	Donnie Allison
1970	Donnie Allison	Ford	129.680	Bobby Isaac
1971	Bobby Allison	Mercury	140.442	Charlie Glotzbach
1972	Buddy Baker	Dodge	142.255	Bobby Allison
1973	Buddy Baker	Dodge	134.890	Buddy Baker
1974	David Pearson	Mercury	135.720	David Pearson
1975	Richard Petty	Dodge	145.327	David Pearson
1976	David Pearson	Mercury	137.352	David Pearson
1977	Richard Petty	Dodge	137.636	David Pearson
1978	Darrell Waltrip	Chevrolet	138.355	David Pearson
1979	Darrell Waltrip	Chevrolet	136.674	Neil Bonnet
1980	Benny Parsons	Chevrolet	119.265	Cale Yarborough
1981	Bobby Allison	Buick	129.326	Neil Bonnett
1982	Neil Bonnett	Ford	130.508	David Pearson
1983	Neil Bonnett	Chevrolet	140.406	Buddy Baker
1984	Bobby Allison	Buick	129.233	Harry Gant
1985	Darrell Waltrip	Chevrolet	141.807	Bill Elliott
1986	Dale Earnhardt	Chevrolet	140.406	Geoff Bodine
1987	Kyle Petty	Ford	131.483	Bill Elliott
1988	Darrell Waltrip	Chevrolet	124.460	Davey Allison
1989	Darrell Waltrip	Chevrolet	144.077	Alan Kulwicki
1990	Rusty Wallace	Pontiac	137.650	Ken Schrader
1991	Davey Allison	Ford	138.951	Mark Martin
1992	Dale Earnhardt	Chevrolet	132.980	Bill Elliott

World 600 *(Cont.)*

Year	Winner	Car	Avg MPH	Pole Winner
1993	Dale Earnhardt	Chevrolet	145.504	Ken Schrader
1994	Jeff Gordon	Chevrolet	139.445	Jeff Gordon
1995	Bobby Labonte	Chevrolet	151.952	Jeff Gordon
1996	Dale Jarrett	Ford	147.581	Jeff Gordon
1997	Jeff Gordon	Chevrolet	136.745	Jeff Gordon
1998	Jeff Gordon	Chevrolet	136.424	Jeff Gordon
1999	Jeff Burton	Ford	151.367	Bobby Labonte

Note: Held at the 1.5-mile high-banked Charlotte Motor Speedway on Memorial Day weekend.

Talladega 500

Year	Winner	Car	Avg MPH	Pole Winner	MPH
1969	Richard Brickhouse	Dodge	153.778	Charlie Glotzbach	199.466
1970	Pete Hamilton	Plymouth	158.517	Bobby Isaac	186.834
1971	Bobby Allison	Mercury	145.945	Davey Allison	187.323
1972	James Hylton	Mercury	148.728	Bobby Isaac	190.677
1973	Dick Brooks	Plymouth	145.454	Bobby Allison	187.064
1974	Richard Petty	Dodge	148.637	David Pearson	184.926
1975	Buddy Baker	Ford	130.892	Dave Marcis	191.340
1976	Dave Marcis	Dodge	157.547	Dave Marcis	190.651
1977	Davey Allison	Chevrolet	162.524	Benny Parsons	192.682
1978	Lennie Pond	Olds	174.700	Cale Yarborough	192.917
1979	Darrell Waltrip	Olds	161.229	Neil Bonnet	193.600
1980	Neil Bonnett	Mercury	166.894	Buddy Baker	198.545
1981	Ron Bouchard	Buick	156.737	Harry Gant	195.897
1982	Darrell Waltrip	Buick	168.157	Geoff Bodine	199.400
1983	Dale Earnhardt	Ford	170.611	Cale Yarborough	201.744
1984	Dale Earnhardt	Chevrolet	155.485	Cale Yarborough	202.474
1985	Cale Yarborough	Ford	148.772	Bill Elliott	207.578
1986	Bobby Hillin	Buick	151.552	Bill Elliott	209.005
1987	Bill Elliott	Ford	171.293	Bill Elliott	203.827
1988	Ken Schrader	Chevrolet	154.505	Darrell Waltrip	196.274
1989	Terry Labonte	Ford	157.354	Mark Martin	194.800
1990	Dale Earnhardt	Chevrolet	174.430	Dale Earnhardt	192.513
1991	Harry Gant	Olds	165.620	Sterling Marlin	192.085
1992	Ernie Irvan	Chevrolet	176.309	Sterling Marlin	190.586
1993	Dale Earnhardt	Chevrolet	153.858	Bill Elliott	192.397
1994	Jimmy Spencer	Ford	163.217	Dale Earnhardt	193.470
1995	Sterling Marlin	Chevrolet	173.188	Sterling Marlin	194.212
1996	Jeff Gordon	Chevrolet	133.387	Jeremy Mayfield	192.370
1997	Mark Martin	Ford	188.345	John Andretti	193.627
1998	Bobby Labonte	Pontiac	163.439	Bobby Labonte	195.728
1999	Dale Earnhardt	Chevrolet	163.395	Ken Schrader	197.765

Note: Held every spring at the 2.66-mile Talladega Superspeedway.

Southern 500

Year	Winner	Car	Avg MPH	Pole Winner
1950	Johnny Mantz	Plymouth	76.260	Wally Campbell
1951	Herb Thomas	Hudson	76.900	Marshall Teague
1952	Fonty Flock	Olds	74.510	Dick Rathman
1953	Buck Baker	Olds	92.780	Fonty Flock
1954	Herb Thomas	Hudson	94.930	Buck Baker
1955	Herb Thomas	Chevrolet	92.281	Tim Flock
1956	Curtis Turner	Ford	95.067	Buck Baker
1957	Speedy Thompson	Chevrolet	100.100	Paul Goldsmith
1958	Fireball Roberts	Chevrolet	102.590	Fireball Roberts
1959	Jim Reed	Chevrolet	111.836	Fireball Roberts
1960	Buck Baker	Pontiac	105.901	Cotton Owens
1961	Nelson Stacy	Ford	117.880	Fireball Roberts
1962	Larry Frank	Ford	117.965	Fireball Roberts
1963	Fireball Roberts	Ford	129.784	Fireball Roberts
1964	Buck Baker	Dodge	117.757	Richard Petty
1965	Ned Jarrett	Ford	115.924	Junior Johnson
1966	Darel Dieringer	Mercury	114.830	Lee Yarborough
1967	Richard Petty	Plymouth	131.933	David Pearson
1968	Cale Yarborough	Mercury	126.132	Charlie Glotzbach
1969	Lee Roy Yarbrough	Ford	105.612	Cale Yarborough

Southern 500 (Cont.)

Year	Winner	Car	Avg MPH	Pole Winner
1970	Buddy Baker	Dodge	128.817	David Pearson
1971	Bobby Allison	Mercury	131.398	Bobby Allison
1972	Bobby Allison	Chevrolet	128.124	David Pearson
1973	Cale Yarborough	Chevrolet	134.033	David Pearson
1974	Cale Yarborough	Chevrolet	111.075	Richard Petty
1975	Bobby Allison	Matador	116.825	David Pearson
1976	David Pearson	Mercury	120.534	David Pearson
1977	David Pearson	Mercury	106.797	Darrell Waltrip
1978	Cale Yarborough	Olds	116.828	David Pearson
1979	David Pearson	Chevrolet	126.259	Bobby Allison
1980	Terry Labonte	Chevrolet	115.210	Darrell Waltrip
1981	Neil Bonnett	Ford	126.410	Harry Gant
1982	Cale Yarborough	Buick	126.703	David Pearson
1983	Bobby Allison	Buick	123.343	Neil Bonnett
1984	Harry Gant	Chevrolet	128.270	Harry Gant
1985	Bill Elliott	Ford	121.254	Bill Elliott
1986	Tim Richmond	Chevrolet	121.068	Tim Richmond
1987	Dale Earnhardt	Chevrolet	115.520	Davey Allison
1988	Bill Elliott	Ford	128.297	Bill Elliott
1989	Dale Earnhardt	Chevrolet	135.462	Alan Kulwicki
1990	Dale Earnhardt	Chevrolet	123.141	Dale Earnhardt
1991	Harry Gant	Olds	133.508	Davey Allison
1992	Darrell Waltrip	Chevrolet	129.114	Sterling Marlin
1993	Mark Martin	Ford	137.932	Ken Schrader
1994	Bill Elliott	Ford	127.915	Geoff Bodine
1995	Jeff Gordon	Chevrolet	121.231	John Andretti
1996	Jeff Gordon	Chevrolet	135.757	Dale Jarrett
1997	Jeff Gordon	Chevrolet	121.149	Bobby Labonte
1998	Jeff Gordon	Chevrolet	139.031	Dale Jarrett
1999	Jeff Burton	Ford	100.816	Kenny Irwin

Note: Held at the 1.366-mile Darlington (SC) Raceway on Labor Day weekend.

Winston Cup NASCAR Champions

Year	Driver	Car	Wins	Poles	Winnings ($)
1949	Red Byron	Oldsmobile	2	0	5,800
1950	Bill Rexford	Oldsmobile	1	0	6,175
1951	Herb Thomas	Hudson	7	4	18,200
1952	Tim Flock	Hudson	8	4	20,210
1953	Herb Thomas	Hudson	11	10	27,300
1954	Lee Petty	Dodge	7	3	26,706
1955	Tim Flock	Chrysler	18	19	33,750
1956	Buck Baker	Chrysler	14	12	29,790
1957	Buck Baker	Chevrolet	10	5	24,712
1958	Lee Petty	Olds	7	4	20,600
1959	Lee Petty	Plymouth	10	2	45,570
1960	Rex White	Chevrolet	6	3	45,260
1961	Ned Jarrett	Chevrolet	1	4	27,285
1962	Joe Weatherly	Pontiac	9	6	56,110
1963	Joe Weatherly	Mercury	3	6	58,110
1964	Richard Petty	Plymouth	9	8	98,810
1965	Ned Jarrett	Ford	13	9	77,966
1966	David Pearson	Dodge	14	7	59,205
1967	Richard Petty	Plymouth	27	18	130,275
1968	David Pearson	Ford	16	12	118,824
1969	David Pearson	Ford	11	14	183,700
1970	Bobby Isaac	Dodge	11	13	121,470
1971	Richard Petty	Plymouth	21	9	309,225
1972	Richard Petty	Plymouth	8	3	227,015
1973	Benny Parsons	Chevrolet	1	0	114,345
1974	Richard Petty	Dodge	10	7	299,175
1975	Richard Petty	Dodge	13	3	378,865
1976	Cale Yarborough	Chevrolet	9	2	387,173
1977	Cale Yarborough	Chevrolet	9	3	477,499
1978	Cale Yarborough	Oldsmobile	10	8	530,751
1979	Richard Petty	Chevrolet	5	1	531,292

Winston Cup NASCAR Champions (Cont.)

Year	Driver	Car	Wins	Poles	Winnings ($)
1980	Dale Earnhardt	Chevrolet	5	0	588,926
1981	Darrell Waltrip	Buick	12	11	693,342
1982	Darrell Waltrip	Buick	12	7	873,118
1983	Bobby Allison	Buick	6	0	828,355
1984	Terry Labonte	Chevrolet	2	2	713,010
1985	Darrell Waltrip	Chevrolet	3	4	1,318,735
1986	Dale Earnhardt	Chevrolet	5	1	1,783,880
1987	Dale Earnhardt	Chevrolet	11	1	2,099,243
1988	Bill Elliott	Ford	6	6	1,574,639
1989	Rusty Wallace	Pontiac	6	4	2,247,950
1990	Dale Earnhardt	Chevrolet	9	4	3,083,056
1991	Dale Earnhardt	Chevrolet	4	0	2,396,685
1992	Alan Kulwicki	Ford	2	6	2,322,561
1993	Dale Earnhardt	Chevrolet	6	2	3,353,789
1994	Dale Earnhardt	Chevrolet	4	2	3,400,733
1995	Jeff Gordon	Chevrolet	7	8	4,347,343
1996	Terry Labonte	Chevrolet	2	4	4,030,648
1997	Jeff Gordon	Chevrolet	10	1	4,201,227
1998	Jeff Gordon	Chevrolet	13	7	6,175,867

Alltime NASCAR Leaders

WINS		WINNINGS ($)		POLE POSITIONS	
Richard Petty	200	*Dale Earnhardt	35,640,003	Richard Petty	126
David Pearson	105	*Jeff Gordon	30,705,097	David Pearson	113
Bobby Allison	84	*Mark Martin	20,987,784	Cale Yarborough	70
*Darrell Waltrip	84	*Terry Labonte	20,797,326	*Darrell Waltrip	59
Cale Yarborough	83	*Bill Elliott	20,774,999	Bobby Allison	57
*Dale Earnhardt	73	*Rusty Wallace	20,578,448	Bobby Isaac	51
Lee Petty	55	*Dale Jarrett	18,379,323	*Bill Elliott	49
Ned Jarrett	50	*Darrell Waltrip	18,054,538	Junior Johnson	47
Junior Johnson	50	*Ricky Rudd	16,367,296	Buck Baker	44
*Rusty Wallace	49	*Geoff Bodine	13,780,333	Buddy Baker	40
Herb Thomas	48	*Ken Schrader	13,538,631	Tim Flock	39
*Jeff Gordon	47	*Sterling Marlin	12,957,614	Herb Thomas	39
Buck Baker	46	*Bobby Labonte	11,739,845	*Mark Martin	38
*Bill Elliott	40	*Jeff Burton	11,687,595	*Geoff Bodine	37
Tim Flock	40	*Ernie Irvan	11,625,817	Rex White	35
				Fireball Roberts	35
				Ned Jarrett	35

*Active drivers. Note: NASCAR leaders through September 28, 1999.

Formula One Grand Prix Racing

World Driving Champions

Year	Winner	Car	Year	Winner	Car
1950	Guiseppe Farina, Italy	Alfa Romeo	1961	Phil Hill, United States	Ferrari
1951	Juan-Manuel Fangio, Argentina	Alfa Romeo	1962	Graham Hill, England	BRM
			1963	Jim Clark, Scotland	Lotus-Climax
1952	Alberto Ascari, Italy	Ferrari	1964	John Surtees, England	Ferrari
1953	Alberto Ascari, Italy	Ferrari	1965	Jim Clark, Scotland	Lotus-Climax
1954	Juan-Manuel Fangio, Argentina	Maserati/ Mercedes	1966	Jack Brabham, Australia	Brabham-Climax
			1967	Denis Hulme, New Zealand	Brabham-Repco
1955	Juan-Manuel Fangio, Argentina	Mercedes	1968	Graham Hill, England	Lotus-Ford
1956	Juan-Manuel Fangio, Argentina	Ferrari	1969	Jackie Stewart, Scotland	Matra-Ford
			1970	Jochen Rindt, Austria*	Lotus-Ford
1957	Juan-Manuel Fangio, Argentina	Maserati	1971	Jackie Stewart, Scotland	Tyrell-Ford
			1972	Emerson Fittipaldi, Brazil	Lotus-Ford
1958	Mike Hawthorne, England	Ferrari	1973	Jackie Stewart, Scotland	Tyrell-Ford
1959	Jack Brabham, Australia	Cooper-Climax	1974	Emerson Fittipaldi, Brazil	McLaren-Ford
1960	Jack Brabham, Australia	Cooper-Climax	1975	Niki Lauda, Austria	Ferrari

World Driving Champions *(Cont.)*

Year	Winner	Car	Year	Winner	Car
1976	James Hunt, England	McLaren-Ford	1988	Ayrton Senna, Brazil	McLaren-Honda
1977	Niki Lauda, Austria	Ferrari	1989	Alain Prost, France	McLaren-Honda
1978	Mario Andretti, U.S.	Lotus-Ford	1990	Ayrton Senna, Brazil	McLaren-Honda
1979	Jody Scheckter, S Africa	Ferrari	1991	Ayrton Senna, Brazil	McLaren-Honda
1980	Alan Jones, Australia	Williams-Ford	1992	Nigel Mansell, Britain	Williams-Renault
1981	Nelson Piquet, Brazil	Brabham-Ford	1993	Alain Prost, France	Williams-Renault
1982	Keke Rosberg, Finland	Williams-Ford	1994	Michael Schumacher, Ger	Benetton-Ford
1983	Nelson Piquet, Brazil	Brabham-BMW	1995	Michael Schumacher, Ger	Benetton-Renault
1984	Niki Lauda, Austria	McLaren-Porsche	1996	Damon Hill, Great Britain	Williams-Renault
1985	Alain Prost, France	McLaren-Porsche	1997	Jacques Villeneuve, Canada	Williams-Renault
1986	Alain Prost, France	McLaren-Porsche	1998	Mika Hakkinen, Finland	McLaren-Mercedes
1987	Nelson Piquet, Brazil	Williams-Honda			

Alltime Grand Prix Winners

Driver	Wins	Driver	Wins
Alain Prost, France	51	Jim Clark, Great Britain	25
Ayrton Senna, Brazil	41	Niki Lauda, Austria	25
*Michael Schumacher, Germany	35	Juan Manuel Fangio, Argentina	24
Nigel Mansell, Great Britain	31	Nelson Piquet, Brazil	23
Jackie Stewart, Great Britain	27	*Damon Hill, Great Britain	22

*Active driver. Note: Grand Prix winners through September 27, 1999.

Alltime Grand Prix Pole Winners

Driver	Poles	Driver	Poles
Ayrton Senna, Brazil	65	Niki Lauda, Austria	24
Alain Prost, France	33	Nelson Piquet, Brazil	24
Jim Clark, Great Britain	33	*Michael Schumacher, Germany	21
Nigel Mansell, Great Britain	32	*Mika Hakkinen, Finland	21
Juan Manuel Fangio, Argentina	29	*Damon Hill, Great Britain	20

*Active driver. Note: Pole winners through September 27, 1999.

Professional Sports Car Racing, Inc.

The 24 Hours of Daytona

Year	Winner	Car	Avg Speed	Distance
1962	Dan Gurney	Lotus 19-Class SP11	104.101 mph	3 hrs (312.42 mi)
1963	Pedro Rodriguez	Ferrari-Class 12	102.074 mph	3 hrs (308.61 mi)
1964	Pedro Rodriguez/Phil Hill	Ferrari 250 LM	98.230 mph	2,000 km
1965	Ken Miles/Lloyd Ruby	Ford	99.944 mph	2,000 km
1966	Ken Miles/Lloyd Ruby	Ford Mark II	108.020 mph	24 hrs (2,570.63 mi)
1967	Lorenzo Bandini/Chris Amon	Ferrari 330 P4	105.688 mph	24 hrs (2,537.46 mi)
1968	Vic Elford/Jochen Neerpasch	Porsche 907	106.697 mph	24 hrs (2,565.69 mi)
1969	Mark Donohue/Chuck Parsons	Chevy Lola	99.268 mph	24 hrs (2,383.75 mi)
1970	Pedro Rodriguez/Leo Kinnunen	Porsche 917	114.866 mph	24 hrs (2,758.44 mi)
1971	Pedro Rodriguez/Jackie Oliver	Porsche 917K	109.203 mph	24 hrs (2,621.28 mi)
1972*	Mario Andretti/Jacky Ickx	Ferrari 312/P	122.573 mph	6 hrs (738.24 mi)
1973	Peter Gregg/Hurley Haywood	Porsche Carrera	106.225 mph	24 hrs (2,552.7 mi)
1974	(No race)			
1975	Peter Gregg/Hurley Haywood	Porsche Carrera	108.531 mph	24 hrs (2,606.04 mi)
1976†	Peter Gregg/Brian Redman/ John Fitzpatrick	BMW CSL	104.040 mph	24 hrs (2,092.8 mi)
1977	John Graves/Hurley Haywood/ Dave Helmick	Porsche Carrera	108.801 mph	24 hrs (2,615 mi)
1978	Rolf Stommelen/ Antoine Hezemans/Peter Gregg	Porsche Turbo	108.743 mph	24 hrs (2,611.2 mi)
1979	Ted Field/Danny Ongais/ Hurley Haywood	Porsche Turbo	109.249 mph	24 hrs (2,626.56 mi)
1980	Volkert Meri/Rolf Stommelen/ Reinhold Joest	Porsche Turbo	114.303 mph	24 hrs

The 24 Hours of Daytona *(Cont.)*

Year	Winner	Car	Avg Speed	Distance
1981	Bob Garretson/Bobby Rahal/ Brian Redman	Porsche Turbo	113.153 mph	24 hrs
1982	John Paul Jr./John Paul Sr./ Rolf Stommelen	Porsche Turbo	114.794 mph	24 hrs
1983	Preston Henn/Bob Wollek/ Claude Ballot-Lena/A. J. Foyt	Porsche Turbo	98.781 mph	24 hrs
1984	Sarel van der Merwe/ Graham Duxbury/Tony Martin	Porsche March	103.119 mph	24 hrs (2,476.8 mi)
1985	A. J. Foyt/Bob Wollek/ Al Unser/Thierry Boutsen	Porsche 962	104.162 mph	24 hrs (2,502.68 mi)
1986	Al Holbert/Derek Bell/Al Unser Jr.	Porsche 962	105.484 mph	24 hrs (2,534.72 mi)
1987	Chip Robinson/Derek Bell/ Al Holbert/Al Unser Jr.	Porsche 962	111.599 mph	24 hrs (2,680.68 mi)
1988	Martin Brundle/John Nielsen/ Raul Boesel	Jaguar XJR-9	107.943 mph	24 hrs (2,591.68 mi)
1989	John Andretti/Derek Bell/ Bob Wollek	Porsche 962	92.009 mph	24 hrs (2,210.76 mi)
1990	Davy Jones/ Jan Lammers/ Andy Wallace	Jaguar XJR-12	112.857 mph	24 hrs (2,709.16 mi)
1991	Hurley Haywood/ John Winter/ Frank Jelinski/ Henri Pescarolo/ Bob Wollek	Porsche 962C	106.633 mph	24 hrs (2,559.64 mi)
1992	Massahiro Hasemi/ Kazuoyshi Hoshino/ Toshio Suzuki/ Anders Olofsson	Nissan R91CP	112.987 mph	24 hrs (2,712.72 mi)
1993	P.J. Jones/Mark Dismore/ Rocky Moran	Toyota Eagle MK III	103.537 mph	24 hrs (2,484.88 mi)
1994	Paul Gentilozzi/ Scott Pruett/ Butch Leitzinger/ Steve Millen	Nissan 300 ZX	104.80 mph	24 hrs (2,693.67 mi)
1995	Jurgen Lassig/ Christophe Buochut/ Giovanni Lavaggi/ Marco Werner	Porsche Spyder K8	102.28 mph	690 laps (2,456.4 mi)
1996	Wayne Taylor/ Scott Sharp/ Jim Pace	Oldsmobile Mark III	103.32 mph	697 laps (2,481.32 mi)
1997	Elliot Forbes/John Schneider/ Rob Dyson/John Paul Jr./ Butch Leitzinger/James Weaver/ Andy Wallace	Ford R & S MK III	102.292 mph	690 laps (2,456.4 mi)
1998	Arie Luyendyk/Didier Theys/ Mauro Baldi	Ferrari 333 SP	105.565 mph	711 laps (2,531.16 mi)
1999	Elliott Forbes-Robinson/Butch Leitzinger, Andy Wallace	Ford R & S MK III	104.9 mph	708 laps (2,520.48 mi)

*Race shortened due to fuel crisis. †Course lengthened from 3.81 miles to 3.84 miles.

World SportsCar Champions*

Year	Winner	Car	Year	Winner	Car
1978	Peter Gregg	Porsche 935	1989	Geoff Brabham	Nissan GTP
1979	Peter Gregg	Porsche 935	1990	Geoff Brabham	Nissan GTP
1980	John Fitzpatrick	Porsche 935	1991	Geoff Brabham	Nissan NPT
1981	Brian Redman	Chevy Lola	1992	Juan Fangio II	Toyota EGL MKIII
1982	John Paul Jr.	Chevy Lola	1993	Juan Fangio II	Toyota EGL MKIII
1983	Al Holbert	Chevy March	1994	Wayne Taylor	Mazda Kudzu
1984	Randy Lanier	Chevy March	1995	Fermin Velez	Ferrari 333 SP
1985	Al Holbert	Porsche 962	1996	Wayne Taylor	Mazda Kudzu
1986	Al Holbert	Porsche 962	1997	Butch Leitzinger	Ford R&S MKIII
1987	Chip Robinson	Porsche 962	1998	Butch Leitzinger	Ford R&S MKIII
1988	Geoff Brabham	Nissan GTP			

*1978–93 champions raced in the GT series, which in 1994 was replaced by the World SportsCar series. Beginning in 1999, racing was reclassified according to the American Le Mans Series. The Series is comprised of two different types of race cars divided into two categories and five separate classes. The Prototype category features open cockpit prototype World Sports Cars (WSC) and Le Mans Prototypes (LMP), as well as Grand Touring Prototype (GTP) class cars. The Grand Touring category features the Grand Touring S (GTS) class cars, formerly known as GT2, and Grand Touring (GT) cars, formerly known as GT3. Both classes feature purpose-built race cars with an emphasis on spectator car identification.

Alltime SportsCar Leaders

PROTOTYPE WINS (WORLD SPORTS CAR)

James Weaver	10
Butch Leitzinger	9
Gianpiero Moretti	6
Wayne Taylor	6
Fermin Velez	5
John Paul Jr.	5
Jeremy Dale	4
Andy Wallace	4
Andy Evans	3
Jim Pace	3
Max Papis	3
Eliseo Salazar	3
Antonio Hermann	3
Andrea Montermini	3

GTS AND GT WINS (SUPREME GT SERIES)

Al Holbert	49
Peter Gregg	41
Hurley Haywood	31
Geoff Brabham	26
Parker Johnstone	25
Jim Downing	23
Irv Hoerr	23
Jack Baldwin	22
Don Devendorf	22
Bob Earl	22
Tommy Riggins	22
Juan Fangio II	21
Roger Mandeville	21

Note: Leaders through September 21, 1999.

24 Hours of Le Mans

Year	Winning Drivers	Car
1923	André Lagache/René Léonard	Chenard & Walker
1924	John Duff/Francis Clement	Bentley
1925	Gérard de Courcelles/André Rossignol	La Lorraine
1926	Robert Bloch/André Rossignol	La Lorraine
1927	J. Dudley Benjafield/Sammy Davis	Bentley
1928	Woolf Barnato/Bernard Rubin	Bentley
1929	Woolf Barnato/Sir Henry Birkin	Bentley Speed 6
1930	Woolf Barnato/Glen Kidston	Bentley Speed 6
1931	Earl Howe/Sir Henry Birkin	Alfa Romeo 8C-2300 sc
1932	Raymond Sommer/Luigi Chinetti	Alfa Romeo 8C-2300 sc
1933	Raymond Sommer/Tazio Nuvolari	Alfa Romeo 8C-2300 sc
1934	Luigi Chinetti/Philippe Etancelin	Alfa Romeo 8C-2300 sc
1935	John Hindmarsh/Louis Fontés	Lagonda M45R
1936	Race cancelled	
1937	Jean-Pierre Wimille/Robert Benoist	Bugatti 57G sc
1938	Eugene Chaboud/Jean Tremoulet	Delahaye 135M
1939	Jean-Pierre Wimille/Pierre Veyron	Bugatti 57G sc
1940–48	Races cancelled	
1949	Luigi Chinetti/Lord Selsdon	Ferrari 166MM
1950	Louis Rosier/Jean-Louis Rosier	Talbot-Lago
1951	Peter Walker/Peter Whitehead	Jaguar C
1952	Hermann Lang/Fritz Reiss	Mercedes-Benz 300 SL
1953	Tony Rolt/Duncan Hamilton	Jaguar C
1954	Froilan Gonzales/Maurice Trintignant	Ferrari 375
1955	Mike Hawthorn/Ivor Bueb	Jaguar D
1956	Ron Flockhart/Ninian Sanderson	Jaguar D
1957	Ron Flockhart/Ivor Buab	Jaguar D
1958	Olivier Gendebien/Phil Hill	Ferrari 250 TR58
1959	Carroll Shelby/Roy Salvadori	Aston Martin DBR1
1960	Olivier Gendebien/Paul Frère	Ferrari 250 TR59/60
1961	Olivier Gendebien/Phil Hill	Ferrari 250 TR61
1962	Olivier Gendebien/Phil Hill	Ferrari 250P
1963	Lodovico Scarfiotti/Lorenzo Bandini	Ferrari 250P
1964	Jean Guichel/Nino Vaccarella	Ferrari 275P
1965	Jochen Rindt/Masten Gregory	Ferrari 250LM
1966	Chris Amon/Bruce McLaren	Ford Mk2
1967	Dan Gurney/A. J. Foyt	Ford Mk4
1968	Pedro Rodriguez/Lucien Bianchi	Ford GT40
1969	Jacky Ickx/Jackie Oliver	Ford GT40
1970	Hans Herrmann/Richard Attwood	Porsche 917
1971	Helmut Marko/Gijs van Lennep	Porsche 917
1972	Henri Pescarolo/Graham Hill	Matra-Simca MS670
1973	Henri Pescarolo/Gérard Larrousse	Matra-Simca MS670B

Year	Winning Drivers	Car
1974	Henri Pescarolo/Gérard Larrousse	Matra-Simca MS670B
1975	Jacky Ickx/Derek Bell	Mirage-Ford MB
1976	Jacky Ickx/Gijs van Lennep	Porsche 936
1977	Jacky Ickx/Jurgen Barth/Hurley Haywood	Porsche 936
1978	Jean-Pierre Jaussaud/Didier Pironi	Renault-Alpine A442
1979	Klaus Ludwig/Bill Whittington/Don Whittington	Porsche 935
1980	Jean-Pierre Jaussaud/Jean Rondeau	Rondeau-Ford M379B
1981	Jacky Ickx/Derek Bell	Porsche 936-81
1982	Jacky Ickx/Derek Bell	Porsche 956
1983	Vern Schuppan/Hurley Haywood/Al Holbert	Porsche 956-83
1984	Klaus Ludwig/Henri Pescarolo	Porsche 956B
1985	Klaus Ludwig/Paolo Barilla/John Winter	Porsche 956B
1986	Derek Bell/Hans-Joachim Stuck/Al Holbert	Porsche 962C
1987	Derek Bell/Hans-Joachim Stuck/Al Holbert	Porsche 962C
1988	Jan Lammers/Johnny Dumfries/Andy Wallace	Jaguar XJR9LM
1989	Jochen Mass/Manuel Reuter/Stanley Dickens	Sauber-Mercedes C9-88
1990	John Nielsen/Price Cobb/Martin Brundle	TWR Jaguar XJR-12
1991	Volker Weidler/Johnny Herbert/Bertrand Gachof	Mazda 787B
1992	Derek Warwick/Yannick Dalmas/Mark Blundell	Peugeot 905B
1993	Geoff Brabham/Christophe Bouchut/Eric Helary	Peugeot 905
1994	Yannick Dalmas/Hurley Haywood/Mauro Baldi	Porsche 962
1995	Yannick Dalmas/J.J. Lehto/Masanori Sekiya	McLaren BMW
1996	Manuel Reuter/Davy Jones/Alexander Wurz	TWR Porsche
1997	Michele Alboreto/Stefan Johansson/Tom Kristensen	TWR Porsche
1998	Alan McNish, Laurent Aiello, Stephane Ortelli	Porsche GT One
1999	Yannick Dalmas, Joachim Winkelhock, Pierluigi Martini	BMW V12 LMR

Breaking Up

Jeff Gordon has long known that one day he would lose Ray Evernham, the only crew chief he has had in eight seasons with the Hendrick Motorsports team and a man largely responsible for Gordon's three Winston Cup championships over the past four years. Gordon just never knew when Evernham would go or what would lure him away.

Though no official announcement about those particulars had been made by early October 1999, team owner Rick Hendrick tried to resolve Evernham's contract, which runs through 2006. The crew chief reportedly was poised to join a NASCAR effort being planned by automotove giant Daimler-Chrysler Corp. According to sources, Hendrick was considering granting his release with the stipulation that he not compete in NASCAR for a year and that he not hire any Hendrick employees.

Evernham is widely thought to have organizational and engineering talents far beyond his job description as a crew chief, which is why he might be chosen to help lead a NASCAR program at DaimlerChrysler Corp., the company born in 1998 of the merger of Chrysler Corp. and Daimler-Benz, parent company of Mercedes-Benz. Sources within the company say that an announcement about DaimlerChrysler's NASCAR plans would be made before the end of the year. The team would not begin to compete in Winston Cup before 2001. The Chrysler brands, Dodge and Plymouth, have been absent from NASCAR for 20 years. Chrysler enjoyed its last real success in NASCAR in the 1970s, when Richard Petty drove Chrysler cars to six Winston Cups.

If the deal materializes, there is a good chance that Evernham would have at his disposal the enormous technological resources of two British-based firms, Ilmor Engineering and Reynard, both of which have ties to DaimlerChrysler. Ilmor builds the engines that power the McLaren-Mercedes Formula One team, which features defending F/1 world champion Mika Hakkinen. Reynard builds the cars that have powered Target-Ganassi racing to three consecutive CART championships. Developing NASCAR engines would be a "complete departure from the direction we're going in at the moment," said Paul Ray, Ilmor's vice president of U.S. operations. But, he conceded, "It would be extremely interesting to take on a project like that."

Evernham apparently agrees.

Drag Racing: Milestone Performances

Top Fuel

ELAPSED TIME

Time (Sec.)	Driver	Date	Site
9.00	Jack Chrisman	Feb 18, 1961	Pomona, CA
8.97	Jack Chrisman	May 20, 1961	Empona, VA
7.96	Bobby Vodnick	May 16, 1964	Bayview, MD
6.97	Don Johnson	May 7, 1967	Carlsbad, CA
5.97	Mike Snively	Nov 17, 1972	Ontario, CA
5.78	Don Garlits	Nov 18, 1973	Ontario, CA
5.698	Gary Beck	Oct 10, 1975	Ontario, CA
5.573	Gary Beck	Oct 18, 1981	Irvine, CA
5.484	Gary Beck	Sept 6, 1982	Clermont, IN
5.391	Gary Beck	Oct 1, 1983	Fremont, CA
5.280	Darrell Gwynn	Sept 25, 1986	Ennis, TX
5.176	Darrell Gwynn	April 4, 1987	Ennis, TX
5.090	Joe Amato	Oct 1, 1987	Ennis, TX
4.990	Eddie Hill	April 9, 1988	Ennis, TX
4.881	Gary Ormsby	Sept 28, 1990	Topeka, KS
4.799	Cory McClenathan	Sept 19, 1992	Mohnton, PA
4.762	Cory McClenathan	Oct 3, 1993	Topeka, KS
4.690	Michael Brotherton	May 20, 1994	Englishtown, NJ
4.595	Joe Amato	July 5,1996	Topeka, KS
4.539	Joe Amato	Mar 21, 1998	Baytown, TX
4.525	Gary Scelzi	Oct 23, 1998	Ennis, TX
4.503	Mike Dunn	Feb 5, 1999	Pomona, CA
4.486	Larry Dixon	Apr 9, 1999	Houston

SPEED

MPH	Driver	Date	Site
180.36	Connie Kalitta	Sept 3, 1962	Indianapolis
190.26	Don Garlits	Sept 21, 1963	East Haddam, CT
201.34	Don Garlits	Aug 1, 1964	Great Meadows, NJ
211.26	Donny Milani	May 15, 1965	Sacramento, CA
223.32	Don Cook	Apr 24, 1965	Fremont, CA
230.17	James Warren	Apr 10, 1967	Fresno, CA
243.24	Don Garlits	March 18, 1973	Gainesville, FL
250.69	Don Garlits	Oct 11, 1975	Ontario, CA
260.11	Joe Amato	March 18, 1984	Gainesville, FL
272.56	Don Garlits	March 23, 1986	Gainesville, FL
282.13	Joe Amato	Sept 5, 1987	Clermont, IN
291.54	Connie Kalitta	Feb 11, 1989	Pomona, CA
301.70	Kenny Bernstein	March 20, 1992	Gainesville, FL
311.86	Kenny Bernstein	Oct 30, 1994	Pomona, CA
319.82	Joe Amato	Mar 21, 1998	Baytown, TX
323.50	Joe Amato	May 17, 1998	Englishtown, NJ
326.44	Gary Scelzi	Nov 2, 1998	Houston

All Things Not Being Equal

CART and the Indy Racing League appeared to be on the brink of unification in early August 1999 when negotiations were blown off track by Indianapolis Motor Speedway president and IRL founder Tony George, who said, "I don't think there's going to be any kind of unification for 2000. I think 2001 is questionable."

A sticking point is the implementation of an equivalency formula—essentially the mechanical handicapping of one league's engines—that would be necessary until the entities' vastly different sets of technical rules could be standardized. George said that he's against equivalency "absolutely. Period. That will not happen."

His statement was baffling because equivalency formulas have often been used in the Indy 500, so insiders on both sides think George was merely posturing in hopes of improving his leverage at the bargaining table. If he wasn't, major American open-wheel racing, which has been on life support with dwindling attendance and TV ratings since its civil war began in 1995, has virtually no chance of recovery.

Funny Car

ELAPSED TIME

Time (Sec.)	Driver	Date	Site
6.92	Leroy Goldstein	Sept 3, 1970	Clermont, IN
5.987	Don Prudhomme	Oct 12, 1975	Ontario, CA
5.868	Raymond Beadle	July 16, 1981	Englishtown, NJ
5.799	Tom Anderson	Sept 3, 1982	Clermont, IN
5.637	Don Prudhomme	Sept 4, 1982	Clermont, IN
5.588	Rick Johnson	Feb 3, 1985	Pomona, CA
5.425	Kenny Bernstein	Sept 26, 1986	Ennis, TX
5.397	Kenny Bernstein	April 5, 1987	Ennis, TX
5.255	Ed McCulloch	April 17, 1988	Ennis, TX
5.193	Don Prudhomme	March 2, 1989	Baytown, TX
5.077	Cruz Pedregon	Sept 20, 1992	Mohnton, PA
4.987	Chuck Etcholis	Oct 2, 1993	Topeka, KS
4.819	Cruz Pedregon	Mar 21, 1998	Baytown, TX
4.807	Cruz Pedregon	Nov 1, 1998	Houston
4.788	John Force	Apr 11, 1999	Houston

SPEED

MPH	Driver	Date	Site
200.44	Gene Snow	August, 1968	Houston, TX
250.00	Don Prudhomme	May 23, 1982	Baton Rouge, LA
260.11	Kenny Bernstein	March 18, 1984	Gainesville, FL
271.41	Kenny Bernstein	Aug 30, 1986	Indianapolis
280.72	Mike Dunn	Oct 2, 1987	Ennis, TX
290.13	Jim White	Oct 11, 1991	Ennis, TX
291.82	Jim White	Oct 25, 1991	Pomona, CA
300.40	Jim Epler	Oct 3, 1993	Topeka, KS
303.64	John Force	Sept 2, 1995	Indianapolis
308.74	John Force	Sept 28, 1997	Topeka, KS
317.46	John Force	Mar 21, 1998	Baytown, TX
323.89	John Force	May 17, 1998	Englishtown, NJ
324.05	John Force	Mar 19, 1999	Gainesville, FL

Pro Stock

ELAPSED TIME

Time (Sec.)	Driver	Date	Site
7.778	Lee Shepherd	March 12, 1982	Gainesville, FL
7.655	Lee Shepherd	Oct 1, 1982	Fremont, CA
7.557	Bob Glidden	Feb 2, 1985	Pomona, CA
7.497	Bob Glidden	Sep 13, 1985	Maple Grove, PA
7.377	Bob Glidden	Aug 28, 1986	Clermont, IN
7.294	Frank Sanchez	Oct 7, 1988	Baytown, TX
7.184	Darrell Alderman	Oct 12, 1990	Ennis, TX
7.099	Scott Geoffrion	Sept 19, 1992	Mohnton, PA
6.988	Kurt Johnson	May 20, 1994	Englishtown, NJ
6.873	Warren Johnson	Mar 14, 1998	Gainesville, FL
6.867	Warren Johnson	Oct 23, 1998	Ennis, TX
6.866	Warren Johnson	Mar 19, 1999	Gainesville, FL
6.840	Kurt Johnson	May 1, 1999	Dinwiddie, VA

Pro Stock (Cont.)

SPEED

MPH	Driver	Date	Site
181.08	Warren Johnson	Oct 1, 1982	Fremont, CA
190.07	Warren Johnson	Aug 29, 1986	Clermont, IN
191.32	Bob Glidden	Sep 4, 1987	Clermont, IN
192.18	Warren Johnson	Oct 13, 1990	Ennis, TX
193.21	Bob Glidden	July 28, 1991	Sonoma, CA
194.51	Warren Johnson	July 31, 1992	Sonoma, CA
195.99	Warren Johnson	May 21, 1993	Englishtown, NJ
196.24	Warren Johnson	Mar 19, 1993	Gainesville, FL
197.15	Warren Johnson	Apr 23, 1994	Commerce, GA
199.15	Warren Johnson	Mar 10, 1995	Baytown, TX
201.20	Warren Johnson	Mar 14, 1998	Gainesville, FL
201.34	Warren Johnson	Oct 23, 1998	Ennis, TX
201.37	Warren Johnson	Mar 19, 1999	Gainesville, FL
202.24	Warren Johnson	Apr 30,1999	Dinwiddie, VA

Alltime Drag Racing Leaders

NATIONAL EVENT WINS

Bob Glidden	85
*John Force	78
*Warren Johnson	78
*Kenny Bernstein	52
*Joe Amato	50
Don Prudhomme	49
David Schultz	43
Don Garlits	35
John Myers	33
Darrell Alderman	27

BEST WON-LOST RECORD (WINNING PCT)

*Matt Hines	127–20 (.864)
John Myers	268–69 (.795)
*David Schultz	306–88 (.777)
*Gary Scelzi	101–33 (.754)
*John Force	578–209 (.734)
*Jeg Coughlin	47–17 (.734)
*Warren Johnson	641–236 (.731)
Darrell Alderman	202–78 (.721)
*Angelle Seeling	70–29 (.707)
*Jim Yates	237–116 (.671)

*Active driver. Note: Leaders through September 30, 1999.

Stewart Does Indy, Charlotte

His face drained from color from dehydration and his legs too exhausted for him to stand, Tony Stewart stretched out on the black leather couch in the back of the Joe Gibbs Racing hauler and laughed about the only thing missing from his 13-hour Indy Car–Winston Cup driving adventure: a large pizza with everything. In May 1999, Stewart, a 28-year-old NASCAR rookie and former IRL points champion, became the first driver to complete the Indianapolis 500, which started at 11 a.m. EDT, and the World 600, which began seven hours and 15 minutes later, on the same day. (In 1994 John Andretti finished 10th in the 500 but didn't complete the 600 because of engine failure.) Stewart placed ninth at Indy and fourth at Lowe's Motor Speedway.

Because he had eaten only two minibagels all day, Stewart was so hungry around Lap 115 of the World 600 that he tried to drive with one hand while stuffing a chocolate nutrition bar under his helmet and into his mouth. He took two bites before chucking the bar out the window and onto the infield grass out of frustration.

"It's great to know that I have left a little mark in the record books for finishing both races," said Stewart, who was fifth in the Winston Cup point standing and on track to become the first rookie since 1980 to finish in the top 10. "We proved 1,100 miles can be done, but you better have a good day at both tracks."

In the end, Stewart's blistered hands steered two cars for 596 laps and through 2,384 left-hand turns in less than 12 hours. Over the previous month he made seven trips between Indianapolis and Charlotte. It's a feat he isn't eager to repeat. "One time was enough," said Stewart, yawning. "Right now I just want to go to sleep—and I'm not sure when I'll wake up."

Bowling

PWBA Player of the Year
Carol Gianotti-Block

Bowling In The Park

As part of an ongoing effort to raise its sagging profile, the PBA staged an outdoor tournament in New York City

BY MERRELL NODEN

BOWLERS, LIKE vampires, have always had a thing about sunlight. For years they have plied their trade in a twilight world of neon, smoke and brew.

But with signs abounding that the sport's profile is in decline (ABC ended its 36-year pact with the sport in 1997, and the Professional Bowlers Association concluded its two-year relationship with CBS by having to write the network a check in the high six figures to cover a shortfall), the PBA knew it was time to make a radical break with the past. On May 1 the PBA took its show out into the bright light of day—or at least what passes for it in New York City—by staging its first ever outdoor final. Held in Bryant Park, directly behind the city's venerable public library, the event was billed as the "New York City PBA Experience." On a sun-drenched Saturday afternoon, amid several thousand fans arrayed on bleachers around two specially constructed lanes, with more watching the proceedings on a Jumbotron video screen, pale-faced keglers squinted up at the sky, wondering, one supposed, who had turned on the lights and if it meant it was time to drink up and go home.

The initial confusion, however, was erased by a thrilling day of bowling. Eric Forkel of Tucson staged a furious comeback and survived a final frame in which Mark Mosayebi, needing only a spare to win, left a 6-7-10 split. "Fortunately I struck out," said Forkel, who won 243–231 to claim a first-place check worth $17,000. "Anything can happen in the 10th frame."

The fresh-air match was just one sign of the sport's determination to reinvent itself. Another came at the Columbia 300 Open in Austin, where the PBA used instant replay as an officiating tool for the first time, determining that Parker Bohn III's foot had broken the plane on a three-pin spare attempt in the fourth. Though he lost points there, Bohn won the tournament, beating Pete Weber 225–211. The popular southpaw also won the Empire State Open in April and the Showboat Invitational in June and finished

BOWLING, INC.

Three for III: Player of the Year candidate Bohn won tournaments in February, April and June.

split the year's two majors, as Barrette survived a three-way shootout in the first round of the WIBC Queens Open and went on to beat Dede Davidson 256–174 in the championship round to win her first major. Adler beat Lynda Barnes 213–195 to win bowling's U.S. Open for the third major title of her career.

Elsewhere the sport offered up its usual crew of intriguing heroes. Dave Wodka tied the PBA record for a six-game series, recording a 1,635 pinfall for a 272.5 average at the Brunswick Circuit Pro Bowling Classic in Wichita, Kans. Dale Eagle dominated the senior tour, notching a record-tying fourth title by early July. And in a remarkable display of perseverance and longevity, Joe Dean of Columbus, Ohio, who had bowled in leagues for 60 years but never recorded a perfect game in league play, rolled a 300 to become at 87 the oldest person to record a sanctioned 300 game. "I can usually tell how I'm going to do by how my legs feel," said Dean. "They were really feeling well that day."

second two times to make himself the favorite to succeed Walter Ray Williams Jr. as Player of the Year. Another worthy candidate was 1998 Rookie of the Year Chris Barnes, who in June briefly ended Williams's 3 1/2-year reign at the top of the computer rankings before Williams regained it with a win at the Tucson Open.

On the women's tour, parity ruled the day. In February, Carol Gianotti-Block of Perth, Australia, became the first non-American to be elected PWBA Player of the Year. She won two titles and made a record-tying 12 television finals in 1998. Gianotti-Block then faded, replaced by Leanne Barrette, the midseason ranking leader, and Kim Adler, the midseason earnings leader. That pair also

The sport's legs, recently unsteady, showed signs of strengthening in '99. To increase bowling's exposure, in the fall the PBA launched its Tour Challenge League, a 16-week national competition among four-bowler (men or women) teams that aimed "to reposition bowling as a challenging sport" in the words of PBA commissioner Mark Gerberich. Finally, the PBA announced that for the first time since Dwight D. Eisenhower was president it would not be appearing on network television. The PBA has signed instead with ESPN, which, the organization hopes, will lead bowling into a brighter future.

The Majors

MEN

1998 Brunswick World Tournament of Champions

CHAMPIONSHIP ROUND

Bowler	Games	Total	Earnings ($)
Bryan Goebel	1	245	60,000
Steve Hoskins	4	933	33,000
Walter Ray Williams Jr	1	216	24,000
Mike Miller	1	178	18,000
Mark Williams	1	174	12,000

Playoff Results: Hoskins def. Williams, 204–174; Hoskins def. Miller, 268–178; Hoskins def. Williams Jr, 226–216; Goebel def. Hoskins, 245–235.

Held at Incred-A-Bowl, Overland Park, KS, November 17–22, 1998.

1999 PBA National Championship

CHAMPIONSHIP ROUND

Bowler	Games	Total	Earnings ($)
Tim Criss	1	238	28,000
Dave Arnold	3	656	14,500
Chris Barnes	1	215	9,000
Danny Wiseman	2	420	7,000
Lonnie Waliczek	1	204	6,000

Playoff Results: Wiseman defeated Waliczek, 217–204; Arnold defeated Wiseman, 258–203; Arnold defeated Barnes, 237–215; Criss defeated Arnold, 238–161.

Held at Ducat's Imperial Lanes, Toledo, OH, February 21–27, 1999.

1999 ABC Masters

CHAMPIONSHIP ROUND

Bowler	Games	Total	Earnings ($)
Brian Boghosian	2	492	40,000
Parker Bohn III	1	231	24,000
Ricky Ward	1	169	16,000
Tom Baker	1	158	11,000

Playoff Results: Boghosian defeated Ward and Baker, 245–169–158; Boghosian defeated Bohn, 247–231.

Held at The OnCenter, Syracuse, NY, May 3–8, 1999.

Bayer/Brunswick Touring Players Championship

CHAMPIONSHIP ROUND

Bowler	Games	Total	Earnings ($)
Steve Hoskins	2	503	40,000
Parker Bohn III	1	183	21,000
Jason Couch	1	227	12,000
Robert Smith	1	207	9,000

Playoff Results: Hoskins defeated Couch and Smith, 257–227–207; Hoskins defeated Bohn, 246–183.

Held at Stonehedge Family Fun Center, Akron, OH, May 10–15, 1999.

MEN *(Cont.)*
1999 United States Open

CHAMPIONSHIP ROUND

Bowler	Games	Total	Earnings ($)
Bob Learn Jr	1	231	35,000
Jason Couch	2	455	20,000
Dave Arnold	1	184	14,000

Playoff Results: Couch defeated Arnold, 240–184; Learn defeated Couch, 231–215.

Held at Mohegan Sun, Uncasville, CT, July 25–August 1, 1999

WOMEN
1998 AMF Gold Cup

CHAMPIONSHIP ROUND

Bowler	Games	Total	Earnings ($)
Dana Miller-Mackie	1	278	28,000
Dede Davidson	2	425	15,000
Anne Marie Duggan	2	451	10,000
Carolyn Dorin-Ballard	2	455	8,000
Michelle Feldman	1	228	7,000

Playoff Results: Dorin-Ballard defeated Feldman, 233–228; Duggan defeated Dorin-Ballard, 235–222; Davidson defeated Duggan, 255–215; Miller-Mackie defeated Davidson, 278–170.

Held at AMF Hanover Lanes, Richmond, VA, October 11–15, 1998.

1998 Sam's Town Invitational

CHAMPIONSHIP ROUND

Bowler	Games	Total	Earnings ($)
Julie Gardner	4	961	35,000
Dede Davidson	1	226	18,500
Marianne DiRupo	1	203	10,700
Debbie Rinella	1	215	8,000
Anne Marie Duggan	1	208	7,000

Playoff Results: Gardner defeated Duggan, 233–208; Gardner defeated Rinella, 229–215; Gardner defeated DiRupo, 231–203; Gardner defeated Davidson, 268–226.

Held at Sam's Town Bowling Center, Las Vegas, November 14–21, 1998.

1999 WIBC Queens

CHAMPIONSHIP ROUND

Bowler	Games	Total	Earnings ($)
Leanne Barrette	4	1041	20,000
Dede Davidson	2	387	10,000
Brenda Norman	1	205	7,500
Dana Miller-Mackie	1	192	6,000
Tish Johnson	1	153	4,500

Playoff Results: Barrette defeated Miller-Mackie and Johnson, 238–192–153; Barrette defeated Norman, 278–205; Barrette defeated Davidson, 269–213; Barrette defeated Davidson, 256–174.

Held at All-Star Bowl, Indianapolis, May 15–21, 1999.

WOMEN (Cont.)

1999 United States Open

CHAMPIONSHIP ROUND

Bowler	Games	Total	Earnings ($)
Kim Adler	2	446	35,000
Lynda Barnes	1	195	20,000
Cara Honeychurch	1	214	14,000

Playoff Results: Adler defeated Honeychurch, 224–214; Adler defeated Barnes, 213–195.

Held at Mohegan Sun, Uncasville, CT, July 25–August 1, 1999.

PBA Tour Results

1998 Fall Tour

Date	Event	Winner	Earnings ($)	Runner-Up
Sept 17–20	Oronamin C Japan Cup	Parker Bohn III	50,000	Steve Jaros
Oct 3–7	National Finance Championship	Brian Voss	20,000	W.R. Williams, Jr
Oct 10–14	Brunswick Long Island Open	Walter Ray Williams, Jr	19,000	Robert Smith
Oct 17–21	Greater Rochester Open	Norm Duke	18,000	Steve Hoskins
Oct 24–28	Bay City Classic	Walter Ray Williams, Jr	18,000	Tommy Delutz, Jr
Oct 31–Nov 4	National Finance Challenge	Walter Ray Williams, Jr	20,000	Amleto Monacelli
Nov 7–11	Brunswick Circuit Pro Bowling Classic	Norm Duke	19,000	Ryan Shafer
Nov 17–22	Brunswick World Tournament of Champions	Bryan Goebel	60,000	Steve Hoskins
Dec 10–13	Phillip Morris Mixed Doubles	Steve Hoskins Kim Canady	40,000	Parker Bohn III Cheryl Daniels

1999 Winter Tour

Date	Event	Winner	Earnings ($)	Runner-Up
Jan 19–23	Albuquerque Open	Brian Himmler	17,000	Chris Barnes
Jan 26–30	Don Carter PBA Classic	Mike Miller	17,000	Dave Wodka
Feb 2–6	Columbia 300 Open	Parker Bohn III	22,000	Pete Weber
Feb 9–13	Chattanooga Open	Steve Jaros	17,000	Parker Bohn III
Feb 16–20	Flagship Open	Chris Barnes	17,000	Rudy Kasimakis
Feb 21–27	PBA National Championship	Tim Criss	28,000	Dave Arnold

1999 Spring/Summer Tour

Date	Event	Winner	Earnings ($)	Runner-Up
Apr 13–17	Empire State Open	Parker Bohn III	17,000	Rick Steelsmith
Apr 20–24	Brunswick Johnny Petraglia Open	Doug Kent	26,000	Rudy Kasimakis
Apr 27–May 1	Brunswick Long Island Open	Eric Forkel	17,000	Mark Mosayebi
May 3–8	ABC Masters	Brian Boghosian	40,000	Parker Bohn III
May 10–15	Bayer/Brunswick Touring Players Championship	Steve Hoskins	40,000	Parker Bohn III
May 25–29	PBA Oregon Open	Chris Barnes	17,000	Norm Duke
May 30–June 5	Showboat Invitational	Parker Bohn III	24,000	Amleto Monacelli
June 8–12	Tucson Open	Walter Ray Williams, Jr	17,000	David Ozio
June 13–20	National Bowling Stadium Open	Ricky Ward	24,000	Mike Miller
June 22–26	ACDelco All-Star Classic	Tommy Delutz, Jr	31,000	Tony Reyes
July 25–Aug 1	U.S. Open	Bob Learn, Jr	35,000	Jason Couch

1998–99 Senior Tour

Date	Event	Winner	Earnings ($)	Runner-Up
Sept 5–10	The Villages Senior Tournament of Champions	John Handegard	10,000	Pete Couture
Sept 6–10	The Villages Senior Open	Phil Barnes	7,000	Roger Tramp
Sept 13–17	Greater Sebring Senior Open	Ron Winger	8,000	Johnny Petraglia
Sept 20–24	Naples Senior Open	Pete Couture	8,000	Dave Soutar
Oct 4–8	Jackson Senior Open	Steve Neff	8,000	Gary Dickinson
Jan 4–9	ABC Senior Masters	Darrell Storkson	20,000	Dale Eagle
Jan 10–16	National Bowling Stadium National Senior Doubles	Johnny Petraglia Jason Hurd	34,000	Dale Eagle Paul Fleming
Jan 17–21	Lakewood Senior Open	Dale Eagle	7,500	John Hricsina
Mar 7–12	Senior World Open	Dale Eagle	18,000	Mike Durbin
Apr 10–15	Hartford Senior Open	Roger Workman	8,000	Gene Stus
June 6–10	Spokane Senior Open	Dale Eagle	9,000	Mike Pullin
June 12–18	Seattle Senior Open	Al Sanford	8,500	Dale Eagle
June 20–24	Portland Senior Open	Steve Neff	8,500	Pete Couture
June 27–July 1	Boise Senior Open	Barry Gurney	8,000	Dick Baker
July 4–8	Brentwood Senior Open	Dale Eagle	7,500	Gary Mage
July 11–17	Showboat Senior Open	Vince Range	15,000	Dick Baker

†PWBA Tour Results

1998 Fall Tour

Date	Event	Winner	Earnings ($)	Runner-Up
Sept 13–17	Visionary Bowling Product Classic	Marianne DiRupo	10,000	Liz Johnson
Sept 20–24	Track Triton TKO Open	Wendy Macpherson	11,000	C. Dorin-Ballard
Sept 26–30	Columbia 300 Delaware Open	Carol Gianotti-Block	11,000	A.M. Duggan
Oct 10–15	AMF Gold Cup	Dana Miller-Mackie	28,000	Dede Davidson
Oct 17–22	Brunswick Women's World Open	Carolyn Dorin-Ballard	25,000	Dede Davidson
Oct 30–Nov 8	Three Rivers Open	Carol Gianotti-Block	11,000	Kim Canady
Nov 14–21	Sam's Town Invitational	Julie Gardner	35,000	Dede Davidson
Dec 10–13	Phillip Morris Mixed Doubles	Steve Hoskins Kim Canady	40,000	Parker Bohn III Cheryl Daniels

1999 Winter Tour

Date	Event	Winner	Earnings ($)	Runner-Up
Feb 7–11	Greater Atlanta Open	Leanne Barrette	11,500	Kim Adler
Feb 14–18	Choo-Choo Classic	Lisa Bishop	6,200	W. Macpherson
Feb 21–25	Greater Jacksonville Classic	Carolyn Dorin-Ballard	4,200	M. Feldman
Feb 28–Mar 4	Greater Orlando Classic	Liz Johnson	3,500	Leanne Barrett

1999 Spring Tour

Date	Event	Winner	Earnings ($)	Runner-Up
May 2–5	Track KO Punch Doubles Tournament	Kim Canady Lynda Norry	22,000	M. DiRupo Kelly Kulick
May 8–12	Omaha Open	Lisa Wagner	11,500	Kim Canady
May 15–21	WIBC Queens	Leanne Barrette	20,000	Dede Davidson
May 22–27	St. Clair Classic	Wendy Macpherson	11,500	Leanne Barrette

1999 Summer Tour

Date	Event	Winner	Earnings ($)	Runner-Up
July 23–Aug 1	United States Open	Kim Adler	35,000	Lynda Barnes
Aug 1–5	Lady Ebonite Classic	Kim Adler	14,400	Leanne Barrette
Aug 8–12	Chattanooga Open	Lisa Wagner	14,400	Kim Adler
Aug 15–19	Greater Terre Haute Open	Jennifer Swanson	11,500	W. Macpherson
Aug 21–26	Hammer Players Championship	Lisa Bishop	16,000	Tish Johnson

†Known as LBPT until 1998.

PBA

MONEY LEADERS

Name	Titles	Tournaments	Earnings ($)
Walter Ray Williams Jr.	5	26	238,225
Parker Bohn III	4	23	191,780
Steve Hoskins	2	26	154,105
Tim Criss	1	26	133,796
Norm Duke	3	24	106,095

AVERAGE

Name	Games	Average
Walter Ray Williams Jr.	973	226.13
Parker Bohn III	671	222.56
Norm Duke	755	222.37
Tim Criss	868	221.85
Amleto Monacelli	732	221.32

Seniors

MONEY LEADERS

Name	Titles	Tournaments	Earnings ($)
Pete Couture	4	12	117,300
Gary Dickinson	1	12	60,950
Gene Stus	2	12	42,020
Mike Durbin	0	11	41,610
Ron Garr	0	10	40,215

AVERAGE

Name	Games	Average
Pete Couture	487	226.36
Johnny Petraglia	212	225.21
Gary Dickinson	534	225.09
Mike Durbin	439	224.00
Gene Stus	458	223.50

PWBA

MONEY LEADERS

Name	Titles	Tournaments	Earnings ($)
Carol Gianotti-Block	2	22	150,350
Aleta Sill	2	23	122,505
Dede Davidson	1	14	121,600
Carolyn Dorin-Ballard	2	22	118,478
Kim Adler	2	20	101,260

AVERAGE

Name	Games	Average
Dede Davidson	660	217.25
Carol Gianotti-Block	948	215.81
Carolyn Dorin-Ballard	912	214.89
Marianne DiRupo	806	214.17
Kim Adler	841	213.53

Men's Majors

BPAA United States Open

Year	Winner	Score	Runner-Up	Site
1942	John Crimmins	265.09–262.33	Joe Norris	Chicago
1943	Connie Schwoegler	not available	Frank Benkovic	Chicago
1944	Ned Day	315.21–298.21	Paul Krumske	Chicago
1945	Buddy Bomar	304.46–296.16	Joe Wilman	Chicago
1946	Joe Wilman	310.27–305.37	Therman Gibson	Chicago
1947	Andy Varipapa	314.16–308.04	Allie Brandt	Chicago
1948	Andy Varipapa	309.23–309.06	Joe Wilman	Chicago
1949	Connie Schwoegler	312.31–307.27	Andy Varipapa	Chicago
1950	Junie McMahon	318.37–307.17	Ralph Smith	Chicago
1951	Dick Hoover	305.29–304.07	Lee Jouglard	Chicago
1952	Junie McMahon	309.29–305.41	Bill Lillard	Chicago
1953	Don Carter	304.17–297.36	Ed Lubanski	Chicago
1954	Don Carter	308.02–307.25	Bill Lillard	Chicago
1955	Steve Nagy	307.17–303.34	Ed Lubanski	Chicago
1956	Bill Lillard	304.30–304.22	Joe Wilman	Chicago
1957	Don Carter	308.49–305.45	Dick Weber	Chicago
1958	Don Carter	311.03–308.09	Buzz Fazio	Minneapolis
1959	Billy Welu	311.48–310.26	Ray Bluth	Buffalo
1960	Harry Smith	312.24–308.12	Bob Chase	Omaha
1961	Bill Tucker	318.49–309.11	Dick Weber	San Bernardino, CA
1962	Dick Weber	299.34–297.38	Roy Lown	Miami Beach
1963	Dick Weber	642–591	Billy Welu	Kansas City, MO
1964	Bob Strampe	714–616	Tommy Tuttle	Dallas
1965	Dick Weber	608–586	Jim St. John	Philadelphia
1966	Dick Weber	684–681	Nelson Burton Jr.	Lansing, MI
1967	Les Schissler	613–610	Pete Tountas	St. Ann, MO
1968	Jim Stefanich	12,401–12,104	Billy Hardwick	Garden City, NY
1969	Billy Hardwick	12,585–11,463	Dick Weber	Miami
1970	Bobby Cooper	12,936–12,307	Billy Hardwick	Northbrook, IL
1971	Mike Limongello	397 (2 games)	Teata Semiz	St. Paul, MN
1972	Don Johnson	233 (1 game)	George Pappas	New York City
1973	Mike McGrath	712 (3 games)	Earl Anthony	New York City
1974	Larry Laub	749 (3 games)	Dave Davis	New York City
1975	Steve Neff	279 (1 game)	Paul Colwell	Grand Prairie, TX
1976	Paul Moser	226 (1 game)	Jim Frazier	Grand Prairie, TX
1977	Johnny Petraglia	279 (1 game)	Bill Spigner	Greensboro, NC
1978	Nelson Burton Jr.	873 (4 games)	Jeff Mattingly	Greensboro, NC
1979	Joe Berardi	445 (2 games)	Earl Anthony	Windsor Locks, CT
1980	Steve Martin	930 (4 games)	Earl Anthony	Windsor Locks, CT
1981	Marshall Holman	684 (3 games)	Mark Roth	Houston
1982	Dave Husted	1011 (4 games)	Gil Sliker	Houston
1983	Gary Dickinson	214 (1 game)	Steve Neff	Oak Lawn, IL
1984	Mark Roth	244 (1 game)	Guppy Troup	Oak Hill, IL
1985	Marshall Holman	233 (1 game)	Wayne Webb	Venice, FL
1986	Steve Cook	467 (2 games)	Frank Ellenburg	Venice, FL
1987	Del Ballard Jr.	525 (2 games)	Pete Weber	Tacoma, WA
1988	Pete Weber	929 (4 games)	Marshall Holman	Atlantic City, NJ
1989	Mike Aulby	429 (2 games)	Jim Pencak	Edmond, OK
1990	Ron Palombi Jr.	269 (1 game)	Amleto Monacelli	Indianapolis
1991	Pete Weber	956 (4 games)	Mark Thayer	Indianapolis
1992	Robert Lawrence	667 (3 games)	Scott Devers	Canandaigua, NY
1993	Del Ballard Jr.	505 (2 games)	Walter Ray Williams Jr.	Canandaigua, NY
1994	Justin Hromek	267 (1 game)	Parker Bohn III	Troy, MI
1995	Dave Husted	266 (1 game)	Paul Koehler	Troy, MI
1996	Dave Husted	730 (3 games)	George Brooks	Indianapolis, IN
1997	No event—tournament rescheduled to April, beginning in 1998.			
1998	Walter Ray Williams Jr.	466 (2 games)	Tim Criss	Fairfield, CT
1999	Bob Learn Jr.	231 (1 game)	Jason Couch	Uncasville, CT

Note: From 1942 to 1970, the tournament was called the BPAA All-Star. Peterson scoring was used from 1942 through 1962. Under this system, the winner of an individual match game gets one point, plus one point for each 50 pins knocked down. From 1963 through 1967, a three-game championship was held between the two top qualifiers. From 1968 through 1970 total pinfall determined the winner. From 1971 to the present, five qualifiers compete for the championship.

Touring Players Championship

Year	Winner	Score	Runner-Up	Site
1996	Mike Aulby	268 (1 game)	Parker Bohn III	Harmarville, PA
1997	Steve Hoskins	932 (4 games)	Danny Wiseman	Harmarville, PA
1998	Dennis Horan	481 (2 games)	Parker Bohn III	Akron, OH
1999	Steve Hoskins	503 (2 games)	Parker Bohn III	Akron, OH

PBA National Championship

Year	Winner	Score	Runner-Up	Site
1960	Don Carter	6512 (30 games)	Ronnie Gaudern	Memphis
1961	Dave Soutar	5792 (27 games)	Morrie Oppenheim	Cleveland
1962	Carmen Salvino	5369 (25 games)	Don Carter	Philadelphia
1963	Billy Hardwick	13,541 (61 games)	Ray Bluth	Long Island, NY
1964	Bob Strampe	13,979 (61 games)	Ray Bluth	Long Island, NY
1965	Dave Davis	13,895 (61 games)	Jerry McCoy	Detroit
1966	Wayne Zahn	14,006 (61 games)	Nelson Burton Jr.	Long Island, NY
1967	Dave Davis	421 (2 games)	Pete Tountas	New York City
1968	Wayne Zahn	14,182 (60 games)	Nelson Burton Jr.	New York City
1969	Mike McGrath	13,670 (60 games)	Bill Allen	Garden City, NY
1970	Mike McGrath	660 (3 games)	Dave Davis	Garden City, NY
1971	Mike Limongello	911 (4 games)	Dave Davis	Paramus, NJ
1972	Johnny Guenther	12,986 (56 games)	Dick Ritger	Rochester, NY
1973	Earl Anthony	212 (1 game)	Sam Flanagan	Oklahoma City
1974	Earl Anthony	218 (1 game)	Mark Roth	Downey, CA
1975	Earl Anthony	245 (1 game)	Jim Frazier	Downey, CA
1976	Paul Colwell	191 (1 game)	Dave Davis	Seattle
1977	Tommy Hudson	206 (1 game)	Jay Robinson	Seattle
1978	Warren Nelson	453 (2 games)	Joseph Groskind	Reno
1979	Mike Aulby	727 (3 games)	Earl Anthony	Las Vegas
1980	Johnny Petraglia	235 (1 game)	Gary Dickinson	Sterling Heights, MI
1981	Earl Anthony	242 (1 game)	Ernie Schlegel	Toledo, OH
1982	Earl Anthony	233 (1 game)	Charlie Tapp	Toledo, OH
1983	Earl Anthony	210 (1 game)	Mike Durbin	Toledo, OH
1984	Bob Chamberlain	961 (4 games)	Dan Eberl	Toledo, OH
1985	Mike Aulby	476 (2 games)	Steve Cook	Toledo, OH
1986	Tom Crites	190 (1 game)	Mike Aulby	Toledo, OH
1987	Randy Pedersen	759 (3 games)	Amleto Monacelli	Toledo, OH
1988	Brian Voss	246 (1 game)	Todd Thompson	Toledo, OH
1989	Pete Weber	221 (1 game)	Dave Ferraro	Toledo, OH
1990	Jim Pencak	900 (4 games)	Chris Warren	Toledo, OH
1991	Mike Miller	450 (2 games)	Norm Duke	Toledo, OH
1992	Eric Forkel	833 (4 games)	Bob Vespi	Toledo, OH
1993	Ron Palombi Jr.	237 (1 game)	Eugene McCune	Toledo, OH
1994	David Traber	196 (1 game)	Dale Traber	Toledo, OH
1995	Scott Alexander	246 (1 game)	Wayne Webb	Toledo, OH
1996	Butch Soper	442 (2 games)	Walter Ray Williams Jr.	Toledo, OH
1997	Rick Steelsmith	888 (4 games)	Brian Voss	Toledo, OH
1998	Pete Weber	277 (1 game)	David Ozio	Toledo, OH
1999	Tim Criss	238 (1 game)	Dave Arnold	Toledo, OH

Note: Totals from 1963–66, 1968–69 and 1972 include bonus pins.

Tournament of Champions

Year	Winner	Score	Runner-Up	Site
1965	Billy Hardwick	484 (2 games)	Dick Weber	Akron, OH
1966	Wayne Zahn	595 (3 games)	Dick Weber	Akron, OH
1967	Jim Stefanich	227 (1 game)	Don Johnson	Akron, OH
1968	Dave Davis	213 (1 game)	Don Johnson	Akron, OH
1969	Jim Godman	266 (1 game)	Jim Stefanich	Akron, OH
1970	Don Johnson	299 (1 game)	Dick Ritger	Akron, OH
1971	Johnny Petraglia	245 (1 game)	Don Johnson	Akron, OH
1972	Mike Durbin	775 (3 games)	Tim Harahan	Akron, OH
1973	Jim Godman	451 (2 games)	Barry Asher	Akron, OH
1974	Earl Anthony	679 (3 games)	Johnny Petraglia	Akron, OH
1975	Dave Davis	448 (2 games)	Barry Asher	Akron, OH
1976	Marshall Holman	441 (2 games)	Billy Hardwick	Akron, OH
1977	Mike Berlin	434 (2 games)	Mike Durbin	Akron, OH
1978	Earl Anthony	237 (1 game)	Teata Semiz	Akron, OH
1979	George Pappas	224 (1 game)	Dick Ritger	Akron, OH
1980	Wayne Webb	750 (3 games)	Gary Dickinson	Akron, OH
1981	Steve Cook	287 (1 game)	Pete Couture	Akron, OH
1982	Mike Durbin	448 (2 games)	Steve Cook	Akron, OH

Tournament of Champions (Cont.)

Year	Winner	Score	Runner-Up	Site
1983	Joe Berardi	865 (4 games)	Henry Gonzalez	Akron, OH
1984	Mike Durbin	950 (4 games)	Mike Aulby	Akron, OH
1985	Mark Williams	616 (3 games)	Bob Handley	Akron, OH
1986	Marshall Holman	233 (1 game)	Mark Baker	Akron, OH
1987	Pete Weber	928 (4 games)	Jim Murtishaw	Akron, OH
1988	Mark Williams	237 (1 game)	Tony Westlake	Fairlawn, OH
1989	Del Ballard Jr.	490 (2 games)	Walter Ray Williams Jr.	Fairlawn, OH
1990	Dave Ferraro	226 (1 game)	Tony Westlake	Fairlawn, OH
1991	David Ozio	476 (2 games)	Amleto Monacelli	Fairlawn, OH
1992	Marc McDowell	471 (2 games)	Don Genalo	Fairlawn, OH
1993	George Branham III	227 (1 game)	Parker Bohn III	Fairlawn, OH
1994	Norm Duke	422 (2 games)	Eric Forkel	Fairlawn, OH
1995	Mike Aulby	502 (2 games)	Bob Spaulding	Lake Zurich, IL
1996	Dave D'Entremont	971 (4 games)	Dave Arnold	Lake Zurich, IL
1997	John Gant	446 (2 games)	Mike Aulby	Reno, NV
1998	Bryan Goebel	245 (1 game)	Steve Hoskins	Overland Park, KS

ABC Masters Tournament

Year	Winner	Scoring Avg	Runner-Up	Site
1951	Lee Jouglard	201.8	Joe Wilman	St. Paul, MN
1952	Willard Taylor	200.32	Andy Varipapa	Milwaukee
1953	Rudy Habetler	200.13	Ed Brosius	Chicago
1954	Eugene Elkins	205.19	W. Taylor	Seattle
1955	Buzz Fazio	204.13	Joe Kristof	Ft. Wayne, IN
1956	Dick Hoover	209.9	Ray Bluth	Rochester, NY
1957	Dick Hoover	216.39	Bill Lillard	Ft. Worth, TX
1958	Tom Hennessy	209.15	Lou Frantz	Syracuse, NY
1959	Ray Bluth	214.26	Billy Golembiewski	St. Louis, MO
1960	Billy Golembiewski	206.13	Steve Nagy	Toledo, OH
1961	Don Carter	211.18	Dick Hoover	Detroit
1962	Billy Golembiewski	223.12	Ron Winger	Des Moines, IA
1963	Harry Smith	219.3	Bobby Meadows	Buffalo
1964	Billy Welu	227	Harry Smith	Oakland, CA
1965	Billy Welu	202.12	Don Ellis	St. Paul, MN
1966	Bob Strampe	219.80	Al Thompson	Rochester, NY
1967	Lou Scalia	216.9	Bill Johnson	Miami Beach
1968	Pete Tountas	220.15	Buzz Fazio	Cincinnati
1969	Jim Chestney	223.2	Barry Asher	Madison, WI
1970	Don Glover	215.10	Bob Strampe	Knoxville, TN
1971	Jim Godman	229.8	Don Johnson	Detroit
1972	Bill Beach	220.27	Jim Godman	Long Beach, CA
1973	Dave Soutar	218.61	Dick Ritger	Syracuse, NY
1974	Paul Colwell	234.17	Steve Neff	Indianapolis
1975	Eddie Ressler	213.51	Sam Flanagan	Dayton, OH
1976	Nelson Burton Jr.	220.79	Steve Carson	Oklahoma City
1977	Earl Anthony	218.21	Jim Godman	Reno
1978	Frank Ellenburg	200.61	Earl Anthony	St. Louis
1979	Doug Myers	202.9	Bill Spigner	Tampa, FL
1980	Neil Burton	206.69	Mark Roth	Louisville
1981	Randy Lightfoot	218.3	Skip Tucker	Memphis
1982	Joe Berardi	207.12	Ted Hannahs	Baltimore
1983	Mike Lastowski	212.65	Pete Weber	Niagara Falls, NY
1984	Earl Anthony	212.5	Gil Sliker	Reno
1985	Steve Wunderlich	210.4	Tommy Kress	Tulsa, OK
1986	Mark Fahy	206.5	Del Ballard Jr.	Las Vegas
1987	Rick Steelsmith	210.7	Brad Snell	Niagara Falls, NY
1988	Del Ballard Jr.	219.1	Keith Smith	Jacksonville, FL
1989	Mike Aulby	218.5	Mike Edwards	Wichita
1990	Chris Warren	231.6	David Ozio	Reno
1991	Doug Kent	226.8	George Branham III	Toledo, OH
1992	Ken Johnson	230.0	Dave D'Entremont	Corpus Christi, TX
1993	Norm Duke	245.68	Patrick Allen	Tulsa, OK
1994	Steve Fehr	213.09	Steve Anderson	Greenacres, FL
1995	Mike Aulby	230.7	Mark Williams	Reno
1996	Ernie Schlegel	221.2	Mike Aulby	Salt Lake City
1997	Jason Queen	225.5	Eric Forkel	Huntsville, AL
1998	Mike Aulby	224.0	Parker Bohn III	Reno, NV
1999	Brian Boghosian	246.0	Parker Bohn III	Syracuse. NY

Women's Majors

BPAA United States Open

Year	Winner	Score	Runner-Up	Site
1949	Marion Ladewig	113.26–104.26	Catherine Burling	Chicago
1950	Marion Ladewig	151.46–146.06	Stephanie Balogh	Chicago
1951	Marion Ladewig	159.17–148.03	Sylvia Wene	Chicago
1952	Marion Ladewig	154.39–142.05	Shirley Garms	Chicago
1953	Not held			
1954	Marion Ladewig	148.29–143.01	Sylvia Wene	Chicago
1955	Sylvia Wene	142.30–141.11	Sylvia Fanta	Chicago
1955	Anita Cantaline	144.40–144.13	Doris Porter	Chicago
1956	Marion Ladewig	150.16–145.41	Marge Merrick	Chicago
1957	Not held			
1958	Merle Matthews	145.09–143.14	Marion Ladewig	Minneapolis
1959	Marion Ladewig	149.33–143.00	Donna Zimmerman	Buffalo
1960	Sylvia Wene	144.14–143.26	Marion Ladewig	Omaha
1961	Phyllis Notaro	144.13–143.12	Hope Riccilli	San Bernardino, CA
1962	Shirley Garms	138.44–135.49	Joy Abel	Miami Beach
1963	Marion Ladewig	586–578	Bobbie Shaler	Kansas City, MO
1964	LaVerne Carter	683–609	Evelyn Teal	Dallas
1965	Ann Slattery	597–550	Sandy Hooper	Philadelphia
1966	Joy Abel	593–538	Bette Rockwell	Lansing, MI
1967	Gloria Bouvia	578–516	Shirley Garms	St. Ann, MO
1968	Dotty Fothergill	9,000–8,187	Doris Coburn	Garden City, NY
1969	Dotty Fothergill	8,284–8,258	Kayoka Suda	Miami
1970	Mary Baker	8,730–8,465	Judy Cook	Northbrook, IL
1971	Paula Carter	5,660–5,650	June Llewellyn	Kansas City, MO
1972	Lorrie Nichols	5,272–5,189	Mary Baker	Denver
1973	Millie Martorella	5,553–5,294	Patty Costello	Garden City, NY
1974	Patty Costello	219–216	Betty Morris	Irving, TX
1975	Paula Carter	6,500–6,352	Lorrie Nichols	Toledo, OH
1976	Patty Costello	11,341–11,281	Betty Morris	Tulsa, OK
1977	Betty Morris	10,511–10,358	Virginia Norton	Milwaukee
1978	Donna Adamek	236–202	Vesma Grinfelds	Miami
1979	Diana Silva	11,775–11,718	Bev Ortner	Phoenix
1980	Pat Costello	223–199	Shinobu Saitoh	Rockford, IL
1981	Donna Adamek	201–190	Nikki Gianulias	Rockford, IL
1982	Shinobu Saitoh	12,184–12,028	Robin Romeo	Hendersonville, TN
1983	Dana Miller-Mackie	247–200	Aleta Sill	St. Louis
1984	Karen Ellingsworth	236–217	Lorrie Nichols	St. Louis
1985	Pat Mercatani	214–178	Nikki Gianulias	Topeka, KS
1986	Wendy Macpherson	265–179	Lisa Wagner	Topeka, KS
1987	Carol Norman	206–179	Cindy Coburn	Mentor, OH
1988	Lisa Wagner	226–218	Lorrie Nichols	Winston-Salem, NC
1989	Robin Romeo	187–163	Michelle Mullen	Addison, IL
1990	Dana Miller-Mackie	190–189	Tish Johnson	Dearborn Heights, MI
1991	Anne Marie Duggan	196–185	Leanne Barrette	Fountain Valley, CA
1992	Tish Johnson	216–213	Aleta Sill	Fountain Valley, CA
1993	Dede Davidson	213–194	Dana Miller-Mackie	Garland, TX
1994	Aleta Sill	229–170	Anne Marie Duggan	Wichita
1995	Cheryl Daniels	235–180	Tish Johnson	Blaine, MN
1996	Liz Johnson	265–236	Marianne DiRupo	Indianapolis, IN
1997	No event—tournament rescheduled to April, beginning in 1998.			
1998	Aleta Sill	276–151	Tammy Turner	Milford, CT
1999	Kim Adler	213–195	Lynda Barnes	Uncasville, CT

Note: From 1942 to 1970, the tournament was called the BPAA All-Star. Peterson scoring was used from 1949 through 1962. Under this system, the winner of an individual match game gets one point, plus one point for each 50 pins knocked down. From 1963 through 1967, a three-game championship was held between the two top qualifiers. From 1968 through 1973, 1975–77, 1979 and 1982, total pinfall determined the winner. In the other years, five qualifiers competed in a playoff for the championship, with the final match listed above.

AMF Gold Cup

Year	Winner	Score	Runner-Up	Site
1997	Aleta Sill	221–179	C. Gianotti-Block	Richmond, VA
1998	Dana Miller-Mackie	278–170	Dede Davidson	Richmond, VA

WIBC Queens

Year	Winner	Score	Runner-Up	Site
1961	Janet Harman	794–776	Eula Touchette	Fort Wayne, IN
1962	Dorothy Wilkinson	799–794	Marion Ladewig	Phoenix
1963	Irene Monterosso	852–803	Georgette DeRosa	Memphis
1964	D. D. Jacobson	740–682	Shirley Garms	Minneapolis
1965	Betty Kuczynski	772–739	LaVerne Carter	Portland, OR
1966	Judy Lee	771–742	Nancy Peterson	New Orleans
1967	Millie Ignizio	840–809	Phyllis Massey	Rochester, NY
1968	Phyllis Massey	884–853	Marian Spencer	San Antonio
1969	Ann Feigel	832–765	Millie Ignizio	San Diego
1970	Millie Ignizio	807–797	Joan Holm	Tulsa, OK
1971	Millie Ignizio	809–778	Katherine Brown	Atlanta
1972	Dotty Fothergill	890–841	Maureen Harris	Kansas City, MO
1973	Dotty Fothergill	804–791	Judy Soutar	Las Vegas
1974	Judy Soutar	939–705	Betty Morris	Houston
1975	Cindy Powell	758–674	Patty Costello	Indianapolis
1976	Pam Buckner	214–178	Shirley Sjostrom	Denver
1977	Dana Stewart	175–167	Vesma Grinfelds	Milwaukee
1978	Loa Boxberger	197–176	Cora Fiebig	Miami
1979	Donna Adamek	216–181	Shinobu Saitoh	Tucson, AZ
1980	Donna Adamek	213–165	Cheryl Robinson	Seattle
1981	Katsuko Sugimoto	166–158	Virginia Norton	Baltimore
1982	Katsuko Sugimoto	160–137	Nikki Gianulias	St. Louis
1983	Aleta Sill	214–188	Dana Miller-Mackie	Las Vegas
1984	Kazue Inahashi	248–222	Aleta Sill	Niagara Falls, NY
1985	Aleta Sill	279–192	Linda Graham	Toledo, OH
1986	Cora Fiebig	223–177	Barbara Thorberg	Orange County, CA
1987	Cathy Almeida	850–817	Lorrie Nichols	Hartford, CT
1988	Wendy Macpherson	213–199	Leanne Barrette	Reno/Carson City, NV
1989	Carol Gianotti	207–177	Sandra Jo Shiery	Bismarck-Mandan, ND
1990	Patty Ann	207–173	Vesma Grinfelds	Tampa, FL
1991	Dede Davidson	231–159	Jeanne Maiden	Cedar Rapids, IA
1992	Cindy Coburn-Carroll	184–170	Dana Miller-Mackie	Lansing, MI
1993	Jan Schmidt	201–163	Pat Costello	Baton Rouge, LA
1994	Anne Marie Duggan	224–177	Wendy Macpherson-Papanos	Salt Lake City
1995	Sandra Postma	226–187	Carolyn Dorin	Tucson, AZ
1996	Lisa Wagner	231–226	Tammy Turner	Buffalo, NY
1997	S.J. Shiery-Odom	209–185	Audry Allen	Reno, NV
1998	Lynda Norry	213–157	Karen Stroud	Davenport, IA
1999	Leanne Barrette	256–174	Dede Davidson	Indianapolis, IN

Sam's Town Invitational

Year	Winner	Score	Runner-Up	Site
1984	Aleta Sill	238 (1 game)	Cheryl Daniels	Las Vegas
1985	Patty Costello	236 (1 game)	Robin Romeo	Las Vegas
1986	Aleta Sill	238 (1 game)	Dina Wheeler	Las Vegas
1987	Debbie Bennett	880 (4 games)	Lorrie Nichols	Las Vegas
1988	Donna Adamek	634 (3 games)	Robin Romeo	Las Vegas
1989	Tish Johnson	210 (1 game)	Dede Davidson	Las Vegas
1990	Wendy Macpherson	900 (4 games)	Jeanne Maiden	Las Vegas
1991	Lorrie Nichols	469 (2 games)	Dana Miller-Mackie	Las Vegas
1992	Tish Johnson	279 (1 game)	Robin Romeo	Las Vegas
1993	Robin Romeo	194 (1 game)	Tammy Turner	Las Vegas
1994	Tish Johnson	178 (1 game)	Carol Gianotti	Las Vegas
1995	Michelle Mullen	202 (1 game)	Cheryl Daniels	Las Vegas
1996	C. Gianotti-Block	892 (4 games)	Leanne Barrette	Las Vegas
1997	Kim Adler	953 (4 games)	Wendy Macpherson	Las Vegas
1998	Julie Gardner	961 (4 games)	Dede Davidson	Las Vegas

PWBA Championships

1960...Marion Ladewig	1966...Joy Abel	1972...Patty Costello	1978...Toni Gillard
1961...Shirley Garms	1967...Betty Mivalez	1973...Betty Morris	1979...Cindy Coburn
1962...Stephanie Balogh	1968...Dotty Fothergill	1974...Pat Costello	1980...Donna Adamek
1963...Janet Harman	1969...Dotty Fothergill	1975...Pam Buckner	
1964...Betty Kuczynski	1970...Bobbe North	1976...Patty Costello	
1965...Helen Duval	1971...Patty Costello	1977...Vesma Grinfelds	

Men's Awards

BWAA Bowler of the Year

1942...Johnny Crimmins
1943...Ned Day
1944...Ned Day
1945...Buddy Bomar
1946...Joe Wilman
1947...Buddy Bomar
1948...Andy Varipapa
1949...Connie Schwoegler
1950...Junie McMahon
1951...Lee Jouglard
1952...Steve Nagy
1953...Don Carter
1954...Don Carter
1955...Steve Nagy
1956...Bill Lillard
1957...Don Carter

1958...Don Carter
1959...Ed Lubanski
1960...Don Carter
1961...Dick Weber
1962...Don Carter
1963...Dick Weber Billy Hardwick*
1964...Billy Hardwick Bob Strampe*
1965...Dick Weber
1966...Wayne Zahn
1967...Dave Davis
1968...Jim Stefanich
1969...Billy Hardwick
1970...Nelson Burton Jr.
1971...Don Johnson
1972...Don Johnson

1973...Don McCune
1974...Earl Anthony
1975...Earl Anthony
1976...Earl Anthony
1977...Mark Roth
1978...Mark Roth
1979...Mark Roth
1980...Wayne Webb
1981...Earl Anthony
1982...Earl Anthony
1983...Earl Anthony
1984...Mark Roth
1985...Mike Aulby
1986...Walter Ray Williams Jr.
1987...Marshall Holman
1988...Brian Voss

1989...Mike Aulby Amleto Monacelli*
1990...Amleto Monacelli
1991...David Ozio
1992...Dave Ferraro
1993...Walter Ray Williams Jr.
1994...Norm Duke
1995...Mike Aulby
1996...Walter Ray Williams Jr.
1997...Walter Ray Williams Jr.
1998...Walter Ray Williams Jr.

*PBA Bowler of the Year. The PBA began selecting a player of the year in 1963. Its selection has been the same as the BWAA's in all but three years.

Women's Awards

BWAA Bowler of the Year

1948...Val Mikiel
1949...Val Mikiel
1950...Marion Ladewig
1951...Marion Ladewig
1952...Marion Ladewig
1953...Marion Ladewig
1954...Marion Ladewig
1955...Marion Ladewig
1956...Sylvia Martin
1957...Anita Cantaline
1958...Marion Ladewig
1959...Marion Ladewig
1960...Sylvia Martin
1961...Shirley Garms
1962...Shirley Garms

1963...Marion Ladewig
1964...LaVerne Carter
1965...Betty Kuczynski
1966...Joy Abel
1967...Millie Martorella
1968...Dotty Fothergill
1969...Dotty Fothergill
1970...Mary Baker
1971...Paula Sperber Carter
1972...Patty Costello
1973...Judy Soutar
1974...Betty Morris
1975...Judy Soutar
1976...Patty Costello

1977...Betty Morris
1978...Donna Adamek
1979...Donna Adamek
1980...Donna Adamek
1981...Donna Adamek
1982...Nikki Gianulias
1983...Lisa Wagner
1984...Aleta Sill
1985...Aleta Sill Patty Costello*
1986...Lisa Wagner Jeanne Madden*
1987...Betty Morris
1988...Lisa Wagner
1989...Robin Romeo

1990...Tish Johnson Leanne Barrette*
1991...Leanne Barrette
1992...Tish Johnson
1993...Lisa Wagner
1994...Anne Marie Duggan
1995...Tish Johnson
1996...Wendy Macpherson
1997...Wendy Macpherson
1998...Carol Gianotti-Block

*PWBA Bowler of the Year. The PWBA began selecting a player of the year in 1983. Its selection has been the same as the BWAA's in all but three years.

Career Leaders

Earnings

MEN		WOMEN	
Walter Ray Williams Jr.	$2,358,153	Aleta Sill	$998,892
Pete Weber	$2,148,958	Tish Johnson	$914,863
Mike Aulby	$1,956,195	Wendy Macpherson	$829,030
Amleto Monacelli	$1,728,423	Lisa Wagner	$824,076
Parker Bohn III	$1,722,744	Anne Marie Duggan	$773,181

Titles

MEN		WOMEN	
Earl Anthony	41	Aleta Sill	32
Mark Roth	36	Lisa Wagner	30
Walter Ray Williams Jr.	30	Patty Costello	25
Don Johnson	26	Tish Johnson	23
Dick Weber	26	Leanne Barrette	21
Mike Aulby	26		

Note: Men's leaders through August 2, 1999; women's through August 26, 1999.

ROBERT BECK

Soccer

Ladies First

While the U.S. women captivated the nation during the Women's World Cup, their male counterparts quietly improved

BY B.J. SCHECTER

NYTHING YOU can do, I can do better. I can do anything better than you.

As the sound track to a Gatorade commercial pitting Michael Jordan against the most famous women's soccer player in the world, Mia Hamm, those words were broadcast into the homes of millions of Americans preceding, during and following the 1999 Women's World Cup. The spot showed Hamm schooling Jordan on the soccer field, bolting away from the basketball legend on the track and going foil-to-foil with him in a fencing match. The ad was amusing and entertaining, and, in placing Hamm alongside the most famous athlete in the world, it foreshadowed the imprint the U.S. women's national team would leave on the American cultural landscape in summer 1999.

Most Americans knew little or nothing about the team before the World Cup began in June, but during the three-week event the U.S. players captivated the nation. They filled stadiums across the land, starred in a series of funny TV commercials, appeared on *The Late Show* with David Letterman

and, oh yes, won the World Cup with an attractive and skillful style of soccer.

That the team was the nation's best-kept sports secret prior to the tournament had nothing to do with its track record, which was nearly spotless. In 1991 it won the inaugural Women's World Cup (WWC) in China, but the results were buried in most U.S. newspapers and ignored by the electronic media. Four years ago in Sweden the Americans lost to Norway in the semifinals of the second Women's World Cup, but few people on these shores heard much about that, either. In '96 the U.S. won the inaugural gold medal in women's soccer at the Atlanta Olympics, and though the final drew 76,481 fans to Georgia's Sanford Stadium, NBC declined to televise the game. Thus it was that in '99 the Americans hoped to reaffirm their status as the best in the world and—with the tournament taking place in the U.S.—gain some long overdue recognition.

They did both. Compared with the Super Bowl, the NCAA men's basketball tournament, or any other major U.S. sporting

Matt McKeon (14) and the rejuvenated U.S. blanked Germany 2–0 at the Confederations Cup.

THOMAS KIENZLE/AP

event, there was minimal hype leading up to the WWC. But when the tournament kicked off on June 19 at Giants Stadium, with a game between the U.S. and Denmark, we found out two things: The U.S. team was popular (78,972 fans showed up) and could rise to an occasion (it won easily, 3–0).

The excitement surrounding the team snowballed from there. Thousands of kids painted their faces red, white and blue and mobbed the players wherever they went. Newspapers were running stories about them on Page 1, and they were leading nightly newscasts. Letterman, who dubbed the team "Babe City," proclaimed himself its official sponsor. The team was breaking new ground for women in sports and providing young girls with athletes they could look up to. "I grew up watching Magic Johnson and Kareem Abdul-Jabbar, men I could never emulate," said U.S. midfielder Julie Foudy. "Girls need role models."

Despite the suffocating media and public attention, the team never lost sight of its goal. The U.S. reached the final, where a talented Chinese team, winners of two of the last three meetings between the teams, was waiting. With an estimated 40 million viewers, the title game on July 10 was the most watched soccer match in the history of U.S. network television, and the crowd of 90,185 at the Rose Bowl was the largest ever at a women's sporting event.

For 90 minutes the U.S. and China demonstrated beyond doubt that the two best teams in the world were playing for the world title. They attacked continuously, but neither team could solve the other's defense. Michelle Akers, 33, spearheaded the U.S. effort, dominating the game from her central midfield spot. But after a collision late in regulation, Akers, who suffers from chronic fatigue syndrome, left the game with a concussion and a case of dehydration. Without its linchpin the U.S. would go to sudden-death overtime.

In the first of two 15-minute sessions, China nearly ended it as Fan Yunjie headed a corner kick past goalkeeper Briana Scurry. But midfielder Kristine Lilly, stationed at the far post, headed the ball off the line. Overtime saw few other clear chances, and after 120 minutes of scoreless play, the teams went to penalty kicks.

Each side made its first two shots before Scurry provided the Americans with the edge they needed, diving to her left to save Liu Ying's attempt. After every other shooter found the net, U.S. defender Brandi Chastain stepped up in the fifth round, with the chance to win the World Cup. She made no mistake about it. After the ball hit the net, Chastain ripped off her jersey and dropped to her knees before she was mobbed by her teammates.

The moment made a rare media quadruple as it was featured on the covers of *Time*, *Newsweek*, *Sports Illustrated* and *People* that week. The U.S. team had transformed the Women's World Cup into something more than a soccer tournament; it was a cultural event and one that made significant inroads for female athletes.

The men's national team didn't reach the championship level in 1999, but it was perhaps the most improved side in the world this year. Following the disastrous 1998 World Cup, changes were in order. Coach Steve Sampson resigned and was replaced by former Virginia and D.C. United coach Bruce Arena. From the start Arena made it clear that no preferential treatment would be given to veterans and that talented young players with little or no international experience would get the chance to play. Arena demanded and received a four-year contract, which guaranteed that he would coach the U.S. team at the 2002 World Cup should they qualify. "It doesn't help to win games in '98 and '99," Arena said. "You need to start winning games in 2001."

Yet the U.S. started to win almost immediately under Arena. By mid-September 1999 the U.S. had a 7-3-3 record, beating Germany (twice), Argentina and Chile. In late July the Yanks showed how far they have come under their new coach with an impressive third-place finish in the Confederations Cup. After beating New Zealand 2–1 in the opener, the U.S. outplayed Brazil before losing 1–0. Brazilian coach Wanderley Luxemburgo said the U.S. pressured his team better than any opponent Brazil had faced in the '99 Copa America, the championship of South America. In its stunning third match, the U.S. beat Germany 2–0 with its B team. Arena chose to sit nine starters for the game, hoping that the

reserves could get at least a tie, which would put the Yanks in the semifinals. The gamble worked, and although the U.S. fell to host Mexico in the semis two days later, they had gained ground on the world powers. The U.S. closed the event with a 2–0 dismissal of Saudi Arabia to take third place.

Arena took the U.S. job in October '98, after leading D.C. United to its third consecutive MLS Cup final. Joining D.C. in the '98 final was the expansion Chicago Fire, which featured playmaking Polish midfielder Peter Nowak, who became interested in playing for the Fire after logging onto the MLS Web site from his home computer in Munich, Germany. With Nowak, his countryman Roman Kosecki, a cast of hungry young American players, and coach Bob Bradley, a former Arena assistant, the Fire became the first expansion team in modern U.S. pro sports history to win a championship in its first season. Nowak set up both goals in the Chicago's 2–0 win over United.

Late the following season MLS fired commissioner Doug Logan and hired Don Garber, former director of the NFL's international operations, including NFL Europe. It had been Garber's job to sell Europeans on American football; now he was tabbed to sell Americans on European football. On the field in '99, D.C. United appeared ready to reach its fourth consecutive MLS Cup. Even without Arena, United had the league's best record as the playoffs approached.

In Europe, 1999 belonged to another United, Manchester United. The top club in England's Premier League, Man U completed a rare triple by winning its league, the F.A. Cup and the European club championship. United appeared to be on its way to defeat in the waning moments of the European Cup final in May, down 1–0 to Bayern Munich. But Man U scored twice in 3 ½ minutes of stoppage time to pull off an astounding 2–1 victory and send supporters of the 121-year-old club, not to mention the British media (see page 552), into a frenzy.

Whatever your allegiance, there was no denying that Man U's triumph was the high point of a memorable year for the world's most popular sport.

Women's World Cup 1999

Group Standings

GROUP A

Country	GP	W	L	T	GF	GA	Pts
*United States	3	3	0	0	13	1	9
*Nigeria	3	2	1	0	5	8	6
North Korea	3	1	2	0	4	6	3
Denmark	3	0	3	0	1	8	0

GROUP C

Country	GP	W	L	T	GF	GA	Pts
*Norway	3	3	0	0	13	2	9
*Russia	3	2	1	0	10	3	6
Canada	3	0	2	1	3	12	1
Japan	3	0	1	2	1	10	1

GROUP B

Country	GP	W	L	T	GF	GA	Pts
*Brazil	3	2	0	1	12	4	7
*Germany	3	1	0	2	10	4	5
Italy	3	1	1	1	3	3	4
Mexico	3	0	3	0	1	15	0

GROUP D

Country	GP	W	L	T	GF	GA	Pts
*China	3	3	0	0	12	2	9
*Sweden	3	2	1	0	6	3	6
Australia	3	0	2	1	1	6	1
Ghana	3	0	2	1	1	9	1

*Advanced to second round.

Note: In group play, teams are awarded three points for a victory, one for a tie. The top two in each group advance to the quarterfinals.

Group Play Scores

GROUP A
U.S. 3, Denmark 0
Nigeria 2, N Korea 1
U.S. 7, Nigeria 1
N Korea 3, Denmark 1
U.S. 3, N Korea 0
Nigeria 2, Denmark 0

GROUP B
Germany 1, Italy 1
Brazil 7, Mexico 1
Germany 6, Mexico 0
Brazil 2, Italy 0
Germany 3, Brazil 3
Italy 2, Mexico 0

GROUP C
Norway 2, Russia 1
Japan 1, Canada 1
Norway 7, Canada 1
Russia 5, Japan 0
Norway 4, Japan 0
Russia 4, Canada 1

GROUP D
China 2, Sweden 1
Australia 1, Ghana 1
China 7, Ghana 0
Sweden 3, Australia 1
China 3, Australia 1
Sweden 2, Ghana 0

1999 Women's World Cup—Quarterfinals

WORLD CUP FINAL

USA / Germany → USA (3-2)

Norway / Sweden → Norway (3-1)

Brazil / Nigeria → Brazil (4-3) ot

China / Russia → China (2-0)

USA (2-0) → *United States (0-0) ← China (5-0)

* United States won penalty-kick shootout 5–4.

Major League Soccer

1998 Final Standings

Team	Won	Lost	Pts	GF	GA	SOW	Team	Won	Lost	Pts	GF	GA	SOW
WESTERN CONFERENCE							**EASTERN CONFERENCE**						
y-D.C. United..24	8	58	74	48	7		y-Los Angeles..24	8	68	85	44	2	
x-Columbus....15	17	45	67	56	0		x-Chicago 20	12	56	62	45	2	
x-MetroStars...15	17	39	54	63	3		x-Colorado 16	16	44	62	69	2	
x-Miami 15	17	35	46	68	5		x-Dallas 15	17	37	43	59	4	
Tampa Bay.....12	20	34	46	57	1		San Jose 13	19	33	48	60	3	
New England ..11	21	29	53	66	2		Kansas City....12	20	32	45	50	2	

Note: Three points for a win. One point for a shootout win. Win and loss columns include shootout wins and losses.

SCORING LEADERS

Player, Team	GP	G	A	Pts
Stern John, Columbus 27	26	5	57	
Cobi Jones, Los Angeles ...24	19	13	51	
Welton, Los Angeles 31	17	11	45	
Raul Diaz Arce, NE 32	18	8	44	
Roy Lassiter, D.C. 31	18	8	44	

ASSISTS LEADERS

Player, Team	GP	A
Marco Etcheverry, D.C. United 29	19	
Mauricio Cienfuegos, Los Angeles 30	16	
Joe-Max Moore, New England...........21	15	
Eduardo Hurtado, NY/NJ 29	15	

GOALS LEADERS

Player, Team	GP	G
Stern John, Columbus.......................27	26	
Cobi Jones, Los Angeles 24	19	
Roy Lassiter, D.C. United....................31	18	
Raul Diaz Arce, New England.............32	18	
Welton, Los Angeles 31	17	

GOALS-AGAINST-AVERAGE LEADERS

Player, Team	GAA
Zach Thornton, Chicago.....................................1.17	
Kevin Hartman, Los Angeles..............................1.38	
Scott Garlick, D.C...1.43	
Mike Ammann, Kansas City 1.56	
David Kramer, San Jose.....................................1.65	

1998 PLAYOFFS

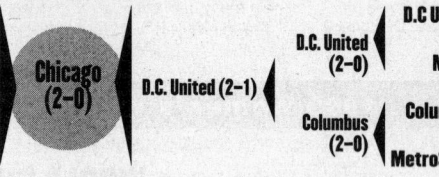

Note: Except for the final, which was a single game, scores are the result of a best-of-three series.

MLS Cup '98

LOS ANGELES, OCTOBER 25, 1998

Chicago................................1	1	—2	
D.C. United............................0	0	—0	

Goals: Podbrozny (Nowak, Razov) 29, Gutierrez (Nowak) 45.

Chicago—Thornton, Brown, Kubik, Okaroh, Gutierrez, Armas, Marsch, Podbrozny, Nowak (Wolff 79), Kosecki (Klopas 56), Razov (Soehn 74).
D.C. United—Presthus, Pope, Agoos, Llamosa (Slivinski 81), Sanneh (Wood 70), Etcheverry, Harkes, Williams, Olsen, Lassiter, Moreno.

Att: 51,350.

International Competition

1998–99 U.S. Men's National Team Results

Date	Opponent	Site	Result	U.S. Goals
Nov 6, 1998	Australia	San Jose, CA	0–0 T	—
Jan 24, 1999	Bolivia	Santa Cruz, Bolivia	0–0 T	
Feb 6	Germany	Jacksonville, FL	3–0 W	Kirovski, Sanneh, Reyna
Feb 21	Chile	Fort Lauderdale, FL	2–1 W	Olsen, Lewis
Mar 11	Guatemala*	Los Angeles	3–1 W	Moore, McBride, Hejduk
Mar 13	Mexico*	San Diego	1–2 L	Hejduk
June 13	Argentina	Washington, D.C.	1–0 W	Moore
July 17	Derby County#	Denver	2–1 W	Lewis, Olsen
July 24	New Zealand†	Guadalajara	2–1 W	McBride, Kirovski
July 28	Brazil†	Guadalajara	0–1 L	—
July 30	Germany†	Guadalajara	2–0 W	Olsen, Moore
Aug 1	Mexico†	Mexico City	0–1 L	—
Aug 3	Saudi Arabia	Mexico City	2–0 W	Bravo, McBride
Sept 8	Jamaica	Kingston	2–2 T	Kreis, Albright

*U.S. Cup '99. # Exhibition. †FIFA Confederations Cup. Record in full internationals from Nov 6, 1998, through Sept 20, 1999: 7-3-3.

1998–99 U.S. Women's National Team Results

Date	Opponent	Site	Result	U.S. Goals
Dec 16, 1998	Ukraine	Los Angeles	2–1 W	Neaton, Baumgardt
Dec 20	Ukraine	Fresno, CA	5–0 W	Milbrett, Foudy (3), Keller
Jan 27, 1999	Portugal	Orlando, FL	7–0 W	Chastain, Lilly (3), Akers, Hamm, MacMillan
Jan 30	Portugal	Fort Lauderdale, FL	6–0 W	Lilly (2), Akers, Fotopoulos, Hamm, MacMillan
Feb 14	FIFA World Stars	San Jose, CA	1–2 L	Foudy
Feb 24	Finland	Orlando, FL	3–1 W	Grubb, Baggett, B. Keller
Feb 27	Finland	Tampa, FL	2–0 W	Fawcett, Hamm
March 14	Sweden	Silves, Portugal	1–1 T	Milbrett
March 16	Finland	Quarteira, Portugal	4–0 W	Milbrett (2), Parlow, Chastain
March 18	Norway	Albufeira, Portugal	2–1 W	Foudy, Lilly
March 20	China	Loulé, Portugal	1–2 L	Milbrett
March 28	Mexico	Los Angeles	3–0 W	Foudy, Lilly (2)
April 22	China	Hershey, PA	2–1 W	Akers, Venturini
April 25	China	East Rutherford, NJ	1–2 L	Foudy
April 29	Japan	Charlotte, NC	9–0 W	Akers, Lilly, Parlow, Milbrett (4), Wagner, Venturini
May 2	Japan	Atlanta	7–0 W	MacMillan (2), Hamm, Fotopoulos (2), Whalen, Venturini
May 13	Holland	Milwaukee	5–0 W	Milbrett, Parlow, Lilly, Hamm, MacMillan
May 18	Holland	Chicago	3–0 W	Chastain (2), Hamm
May 22	Brazil	Orlando, FL	3–0 W	Hamm, Lilly, Milbrett
June 3	Australia	Portland, OR	4–0 W	Fotopoulos, Parlow, Lilly, Milbrett
June 6	Canada	Portland, OR	4–2 W	Hamm, Milbrett, Lilly, Parlow
June 19	Denmark*	East Rutherford, NJ	3–0 W	Hamm, Foudy, Lilly
June 24	Nigeria*	Chicago	7–1 W	own goal, Hamm, Milbrett (2), Lilly, Akers, Parlow
June 27	N Korea*	Foxboro, MA	3–0 W	MacMillan, Venturini (2)
July 1	Germany*	Landover, MD	3–2 W	Milbrett, Chastain, Fawcett
July 4	Brazil*	Palo Alto, CA	2–0 W	Parlow, Akers
July 10	China*	Pasadena, CA	0–0 W (5–4 PKs)	—
Sept 4	Ireland	Foxboro, MA	5–0 W	Milbrett (2), Foudy, Fawcett, Lilly

Record from Sept 30, 1998, through Sept 21, 1999: 23-2-1. *Women's World Cup.

International Club Competition

Intercontinental Cup

Competition between winners of European Cup and Libertadores Cup.

TOKYO: DEC 1, 1998

Real Madrid (Spain) 1   1 —2
Vasco da Gama (Brazil) .. 0   1 —1

Goals: own goal (Nasa 25), Juninho (56), Raúl (83).
Att: 51,000.

Real Madrid: Illgner, Panucci, Sanchís, Sanz, Roberto Carlos, Hierro, Redondo, Seedorf, Sávio (Suker, 89), Raúl, Mijatovic (Jarni, 86).
Vasco da Gama: Carlos Germano, Wágner (Vítor, 75), Odvan, Mauro Galvao, Felipe, Nasa, Luizinho (Guilherme, 85), Juninho, Ramón, (Válber 88), Donizete, Luizao.

European Cup-Winners' Cup

Cup winners of countries belonging to UEFA.

BIRMINGHAM, ENGLAND: MAY 19, 1999

Lazio (Italy) 1   1 —2
Real Mallorca (Spain) 1   0 —1

Goals: Vieri (7), Dani (11), Nedved (81).
Att: 33,021.

Lazio: Marchegiani, Favalli, Salas, Mancini (Couto 90), Mihajlovic, Nesta, Pancaro, Nedved (Lombardo 83), D. Stankovic (Conceicao 56), Almeyda, Vieri.
Real Mallorca: Marcelino, Dani, Ibagaza, J. Stankovic, Lauren, Olaizola, Biagini (Paunovic 73), Engonga.

UEFA Cup

Competition between teams other than league champions and cup-winners from UEFA.

MOSCOW: MAY 12, 1999

Parma (Italy) 2   1 —3
Marseilles (France) 0   0 —0

Goals: Crespo (25), Vanoli (36), Chiesa (55).
Att: 61,000

Parma: Buffon, Thuram, Sensini, Cannavaro, Fuser, D. Baggio; Boghossian, Vanoli, Veron (Fiore 76), Chiesa (Balbo 72), Crespo (Asprilla 84).
Marseilles: Porato, Blondeau, Blanc, Domoraud, Edson (Camara 46), Pires, Brando, Issa, Bravo, Gourvennec, Maurice.

European Cup

League champions of the countries belonging to UEFA (Union of European Football Associations).

BARCELONA: MAY 26, 1999

Manchester United (Eng) .. 0   2 —2
Bayern Munich (Ger) 1   0 —1

Goals: Basler (6), Sheringham (91+), Solskjær (93+).
Att: 90,000.

Manchester United: Schmeichel, G. Neville, Johnsen, Stam, Irwin, Giggs, Beckham, Butt, Blomqvist (Sheringham 67), Cole (Solskjær 81), Yorke.
Bayern Munich: Kahn, Linke, Matthaus (Fink 80), Kuffour, Babbel, Jeremies, Effenberg, Tarnat, Basler (Salihamidzic 88), Jancker, Zickler (Scholl 71).

Libertadores Cup

Competition between champion clubs and runners-up of 10 South American National Associations.

(2ND LEG) SAO PAULO: JUNE 16, 1999

Palmeiras (Brazil) 0   2 —2
Deportivo Cali (Col) 0   1 —1

Goals: Evair (pk, 64), Zapata (pk 69), Oseas (77).
(Aggregate: 2–2; Palmeiras won shootout, 4–3).
Att: 32,000.

Palmeiras: Marcos, Arce (Evair, 57), Baiano, Roque Junior, Rogerio, Sampaio, Alex (Euller, 75), Zinho, Oseas, Nunes.
Deportivo Cali: Dudamel, Perez (Gaviria, 84), Mosquera, Yepez, Bedoya, Zapata, Viveros, Betancourt, Candelo (Hurtado, 62), Cordoba, (Valencia, 81), Bonilla.

Fleet Street Frenzy

HUNBELIEVABLE read one. SUPER SUBS SINK KRAUTS roared another. Faded accounts of the World War I Battle of Jutland? No, those are English tabloid headlines celebrating Manchester United's 2–1 victory over Bayern Munich for the Champion's League title. Man U, winner of England's Premier league and F.A. Cup, trailed 1–0 at the end of 90 minutes but stole the May 26 game during 3 1/2 minutes of stoppage time on goals by late replacements Teddy Sheringham and Ole Gunnar Solskjær. That made manager Alex Ferguson's lads the first English team to achieve soccer's triple—a league title, a national cup and the world's most prized club trophy. Fleet Streeters reacted with typical reserve. The *Daily Mail* proclaimed the evening THE MOST DRAMATIC NIGHT EVER FOR BRITISH FOOTBALL. *The Sun* called the triumph the BEST OF ALL TIME! *The Mirror* deemed the finale THE GREATEST TWO MINUTES IN THE HISTORY OF SPORT. On the continent, Munich's *Süddeutsche Zeitung* lamented THE MOTHER OF ALL DEFEATS.

Lest there be any doubt about the importance of Man U's feat, consider the *Mirror* headline ARISE, SIR ALEX. That's an allusion to the reward Ferguson might get: a knighthood.

1998–99 Club Champions—Europe

Country	League Champion	League Scoring Leader, Club	Cup Winner
Albania	SK Tirana	Bano, FK Lushnja	SK Tirana
Andorra	CE Principat	n/a	CE Principat
Armenia	Tsement Ararat*	Akopyan, Dvin	Tsement Ararat*
Austria	Sturm Graz	Glieder, Austria Salzburg	Sturm Graz
Belarus	Dnepr Transmash*	n/a	Lokomotiv Vitebsk*
Belgium	KRC Genk	Kseller, KSC Lokeren	K Lierse SK
Bulgaria	Litex Lovetch	Beljakov, Litex Lovetch	CSKA Sofia
Croatia	Croatia Zagreb	Musa, Rijeka	Osijek
		Sztipanovics, Rijeka	
Cyprus	Anorthosis	n/a	APOEL Nicosia
Czech Republic	Sparta Prague	Siegl, Sparta Prague	Slavia Prague
Denmark	Aab Aalborg	Fernandez, Viborg	AB
England	Manchester United	Hasselbaink, Leeds	Manchester United
		Owen, Liverpool	
		Yorke, Manchester United	
Estonia	Flora Tallinn*	Kolbasenko, Tallinna Sadam	Flora Tallinn*
Faroe Islands	HB Torshavn*	Borg, B36 Torshavn	HB Torshavn*
Finland	Haka Valkeakoski*	Papovits, Haka Valkeakoski	HJK Helsinki*
France	Bordeaux	Wiltord, Bordeaux	FC Nantes
Georgia	Dinamo Tblisi	Ashvetia, Dinamo Tblisi	Torpedo Kutaisi
Germany	Bayern Munich	Preetz, Hertha Berlin	Werder Bremen
Greece	Olympiakos	n/a	Olympiakos
Hungary	MTK Budapest	n/a	DVSC Epona
Iceland	IBV Vestmannaeyjar*	Johannesson, IBV	IBV Vestmannaeyjar*
Ireland	St. Patrick's Athletic	Molloy, St. Patrick's Athletic	Bray Wanderers
Israel	Hapoel Haifa	Kovaczek, Maccabi Tel-Aviv	Hapoel Tel-Aviv
Italy	AC Milan	Amoroso, Udinese	Lazio
Latvia	Skonto Riga*	n/a	Skonto Riga*
Lithuania	Zalgiris Vilnius	Fomenka, Kareda Siauliai	Kareda Siauliai
Luxembourg	Jeunesse d'Esch	n/a	Jeunesse d'Esch
Macedonia	Sloga Skopje	Oliveira, Pobeda	Vardar Skopje
Malta	FC Valetta	n/a	FC Valetta
Moldova	Zimbru Chisinau	Rogaciov, Serif Tiraspol	Serif Tiraspol
Netherlands	Feyenoord	Van Nistelrooy, PSV	Ajax
Northern Ireland	Glentoran	Kirk, Glentoran	Portadown
Norway	Rosenborg*	Rushfeldt, Rosenborg*	Stabæk*
Poland	Wisla Krakow	Frankowski, Wisla Krakow	Amica Wronki
Portugal	FC Porto	Jardel, FC Porto	Beira Mar
Romania	Rapid Bucharest	Ganea, Rapid Bucharest	Steaua Bucharest
Russia	Spartak Moscow*	Veretennikov, Rotor Volgograd*	Spartak Moscow*
San Marino	Faetano	Renzi, Tre Penne	Cosmos
Scotland	Glasgow Rangers	Marco Negri, Glasgow Rangers	Glasgow Rangers
Slovakia	Slovan Bratislava	n/a	Slovan Bratislava
Slovenia	Maribor Branik	Nikcevic, Nova Gorica	Maribor Branik
Spain	FC Barcelona	Raúl, Real Madrid	Valencia
Sweden	AIK*	Stavrum, Helsingborg*	Helsingborg*
Switzerland	Servette FC	Rey, Servette FC	Lausanne Sports
Turkey	Galatasaray	Sukur, Galatasaray	Galatasaray
Ukraine	Dinamo Kiev	Shevchenko, Dinamo Kiev	Dinamo Kiev
Wales	Barry Town	Williams, Barry Town	ICT Cardiff
Yugoslavia	Partizan Belgrade	Osmanovic, Hajduk Kula	Crvena Belgrade

Note: Results are from 1999 unless followed by *.

The World Cup

Results

Year	Champion	Score	Runner-Up	Winning Coach
1930	Uruguay	4–2	Argentina	Alberto Supicci
1934	Italy	2–1	Czechoslovakia	Vittorio Pozzo
1938	Italy	4–2	Hungary	Vittorio Pozzo
1950	Uruguay	2–1	Brazil	Juan Lopez
1954	West Germany	3–2	Hungary	Sepp Herberger
1958	Brazil	5–2	Sweden	Vicente Feola
1962	Brazil	3–1	Czechoslovakia	Aymore Moreira
1966	England	4–2	West Germany	Alf Ramsey
1970	Brazil	4–1	Italy	Mario Zagalo
1974	West Germany	2–1	Netherlands	Helmut Schoen
1978	Argentina	3–1	Netherlands	César Menotti
1982	Italy	3–1	West Germany	Enzo Bearzot
1986	Argentina	3–2	West Germany	Carlos Bilardo
1990	West Germany	1–0	Argentina	Franz Beckenbauer
1994	Brazil	0–0 (3–2)	Italy	Carlos Alberto Parreira
1998	France	3–0	Brazil	Aime Jacquet

Alltime World Cup Participation

Of the 62 nations which have taken part in the World Cup Finals, only Brazil has competed in each of the 16 tournaments held to date. West Germany or an undivided Germany (1934, '38, '94 and '98) has played in 15 World Cups.

	Matches	W	T	L	Goals For	Goals Against		Matches	W	T	L	Goals For	Goals Against
Brazil	80	53	14	13	173	78	Bulgaria	25	3	8	14	22	49
*Germany	78	45	17	16	162	103	Costa Rica	4	2	0	2	4	6
Italy	66	38	16	12	105	62	Algeria	6	2	1	3	6	10
Argentina	57	29	10	18	100	68	East Germany	6	2	2	2	5	5
France	41	21	6	14	86	58	Saudi Arabia	7	2	1	4	7	13
England	45	20	13	12	62	42	Norway	8	2	3	3	7	8
Yugoslavia	37	17	6	14	60	46	Morocco	10	2	4	4	10	13
†Russia	34	16	6	12	60	40	Wales	5	1	3	1	4	4
Spain	40	16	10	14	61	48	Republic of Ireland	9	1	5	3	4	7
Uruguay	37	15	8	14	61	52	Tunisia	6	1	2	3	4	6
Hungary	32	15	3	14	87	57	North Korea	4	1	1	2	5	9
Netherlands	31	14	9	8	55	34	Cuba	3	1	1	1	5	12
Poland	25	13	5	7	39	29	Turkey	3	1	0	2	10	11
Sweden	37	13	7	17	62	60	Israel	3	1	0	2	1	3
Austria	29	12	4	13	42	48	Jamaica	3	1	0	2	3	9
Czechoslovakia	30	11	5	14	44	45	Iran	6	1	1	4	4	12
Belgium	32	9	7	16	40	56	Honduras	3	0	2	1	2	3
Romania	21	8	5	8	30	32	Egypt	4	0	2	2	3	6
Mexico	37	8	10	19	39	75	Kuwait	3	0	1	2	2	6
Chile	25	7	6	12	31	40	Australia	3	0	1	2	0	5
Portugal	9	6	0	3	19	12	South Korea	14	0	4	10	11	43
Switzerland	22	6	3	13	33	51	Dutch East Indies	1	0	0	1	0	6
Denmark	9	5	1	3	19	13	Iraq	3	0	0	3	1	4
Croatia	6	4	0	2	9	4	Canada	3	0	0	3	0	5
Nigeria	8	4	0	4	13	13	United Arab Emirates	3	0	0	3	2	11
Peru	15	4	3	8	19	31	New Zealand	3	0	0	3	2	12
Paraguay	15	4	6	5	19	27	Haiti	3	0	0	3	2	14
United States	17	4	1	12	18	38	Zaire	3	0	0	3	0	14
Scotland	23	4	7	12	25	41	Bolivia	6	0	1	5	1	20
Northern Ireland	13	3	5	5	13	23	El Salvador	6	0	0	6	1	22
Colombia	13	3	2	8	14	23	Japan	3	0	0	3	1	4
Cameroon	14	3	6	5	14	25	Greece	3	0	0	3	0	8

*Includes West Germany 1950–90. †Includes USSR 1930–1990.
Note: Matches decided by penalty kicks are shown as drawn games.

World Cup Final Box Scores

URUGUAY 1930

| Uruguay...........1 | 3 —— 4 |
| Argentina........2 | 0 —— 2 |

FIRST HALF

Scoring: 1, Uruguay, Dorado (12); 2, Argentina, Peucelle (20); 3, Argentina, Stabile (37).

SECOND HALF

Scoring: 4, Uruguay, Cea (57); 5, Uruguay, Iriarte (68); 6, Uruguay, Castro (89).

Argentina: Botosso, Della Toree, Paternoster, Evaristo, J., Monti, Suarez, Peucelle, Varallo, Stabile, Ferreira, Evaristo, M.

Uruguay: Ballesteros, Nasazzi, Mascheroni, Andrade, Fernandez, Gestido, Dorado, Scarone, Castro, Cea, Iriarte.

Referee: Langenus (Belgium).

FRANCE 1938

| Italy.................3 | 1 —— 4 |
| Hungary...........1 | 1 —— 2 |

FIRST HALF

Scoring: 1, Italy, Colaussi (5); 2, Hungary, Titkos (7); 3, Italy, Piola (16); 4, Italy, Piola (35).

SECOND HALF

Scoring: 5, Hungary, Sarosi (70); 6, Italy, Colaussi (82).

Italy: Olivieri, Foni, Rava, Serantoni, Andreolo, Locatelli, Biavati, Meazza, Piola, Ferrari, Colaussi.

Hungary: Szabo; Polger, Biro, Szalay, Szucs, Lazar, Sas, Vincze, Sarosi, Zsengeller, Titkos.

Referee: Capdeville (France).

SWITZERLAND 1954

| W Germany......2 | 1 —— 3 |
| Hungary...........2 | 0 —— 2 |

FIRST HALF

Scoring: 1, Hungary, Puskas (6); 2, Hungary, Czibor (8); 3, W Germ., Morlock (10); 4, W Germ., Rahn (18).

SECOND HALF

Scoring: 5, W Germ., Rahn (84).

West Germany: Turek; Posipal, Kohlmeyer, Eckel, Liebrich, Mai, Rahn, Morlock, Walter, O., Walter, F., Schaefer.

Hungary: Grosics; Buzansky, Lantos, Bozsik, Lorant, Zakarias, Czibor, Kocsis, Hidegkuti, Puskas, Toth.

Referee: Ling (England).

ITALY 1934

| Italy..................0 | 1 | 1—— 2 |
| Czechoslovakia ..0 | 1 | 0—— 1 |

SECOND HALF

Scoring: 1, Czech., Puc (70); 2, Italy, Orsi (80).

OVERTIME

Scoring: 3, Italy, Schiavio (95).

Italy: Combi, Monzeglio, Allemandi, Ferraris Monti, Monti, Bertolini, Guaita, Meazza, Schiavio, Ferrari, Orsi.

Czechoslovakia: Planicka, Zenisek, Ctyroky, Kostalek, Cambal, Cambal, Krcil, Junek, Svoboda, Sobotka, Nejedly, Puc.

Referee: Eklind (Sweden).

BRAZIL 1950

| Uruguay ....0 | 2 —— 2 |
| Brazil................0 | 1 —— 1 |

SECOND HALF

Scoring: 1, Brazil, Friaca (47); 2, Uruguay, Schiaffino (66); 3, Uruguay, Ghiggia (79).

Uruguay: Maspoli, Gonzales, Tejera, Gambretta, Varela, Andrade, Ghiggia, Perez, Miguez, Schiffiano, Moran.

Brazil: Barbosa, Augusto, Juvenal, Bauer, Banilo, Bigode, Friaca, Zizinho, Ademir, Jair, Chico.

Referee: Reader (England).

SWEDEN 1958

| Brazil................2 | 3 —— 5 |
| Sweden ....1 | 1 —— 2 |

FIRST HALF

Scoring:1, Sweden, Liedholm (3); 2, Brazil, Vava (9); 3, Brazil, Vava (32).

SECOND HALF

Scoring: 4, Brazil, Pelé (55); 5, Brazil, Zagalo (68); 6, Sweden Simonsson (80); 7, Brazil, Pelé (90).

Brazil: Glymar, Santos, D., Santos, N., Zito, Bellini, Orlando, Garrincha, Didi, Vava, Pelé, Zagalo.

Sweden: Svensson, Bergmark, Axbom, Boerjesson, Gustavsson, Parling, Hamrin, Gren, Simonsson, Liedholm, Skoglund.

Referee: Guigue (France).

CHILE 1962

| Brazil...........................1 | 2 —— 3 |
| Czechoslovakia ....1 | 0 —— 1 |

FIRST HALF

Scoring: 1, Czech., Masopust (15); 2, Brazil, Amarildo (17).

SECOND HALF

Scoring: 3, Brazil, Zito (68); 4, Brazil, Vava (77).

Brazil: Glymar, Santos, D., Santos, N., Zito, Mauro, Zozimo, Garrincha, Didi, Vava, Amarildo, Zagalo.

Czechoslovakia: Schroiff, Tichy, Novak, Pluskal, Popluhar, Masopust, Pospichal, Scherer, Kvasnak, Kadraba, Jelinek.

Referee: Latychev (USSR).

World Cup Final Box Scores *(Cont.)*

ENGLAND 1966

England............1	1	2——4
W. Germany 1	1	0——2

FIRST HALF

Scoring: 1, W. Germany, Haller (12); 2, England, Hurst (18).

SECOND HALF

Scoring: 3, England, Peters (78); 4, W. Germany, Weber (90).

OVERTIME

Scoring: 5, England, Hurst (101); 6, England, Hurst (120).

England: Banks, Cohen, Wilson, Stiles, Charlton, J., Moore, Ball, Hurst, Hunt, Charlton, R., Peters.

W. Germany: Tilkowski, Hottges, Schmellinger, Beckenbauer, Schulz, Weber, Held, Haller, Seeler, Overath, Emmerich.

Referee: Dienst (Switzerland).

W. GERMANY 1974

W. Germany 2	0 —2
Netherlands.....1	0 —1

FIRST HALF

Scoring: 1, Netherlands, Neeskens, PK (1); 2, W. Germany, Breitner, PK (26); 3, W. Germany, Müller (44).

W. Germany: Maier, Vogts, Beckenbauer, Schwarzenbeck, Breitner, Hoeness, Bonhof, Overath, Grabowski, Müller, Holzenbein.

Netherlands: Jongbloed, Suurbier, Rijsbergen (de Jong), Haan, Krol, Jansen, Neeskens, van Hanagem, Cruyff, Rensenbrink (van der Kerkhof).

Referee: Taylor (England).

ITALY 1982

Italy...................0	3 —3
W. Germany 0	1 —1

SECOND HALF

Scoring: 1, Italy, Rossi (57); 2, Italy, Tardelli (68); 3, Italy, Altobelli (81); 4, Germany, Breitner (83).

Italy: Zoff, Bergomi, Scirea, Collovati, Cabrini, Oriali, Gentile, Tardelli, Conti, Rossi, Graziani (Altobelli, Causio).

W. Germany: Schumacher, Kaltz, Stielike, Foerster, K., Foerster, B., Dremmler (Hrubesch), Breitner, Briegel, Rummenigge (Müller), Fishcher (Littbrarski).

Referee: Coelho (Brazil).

MEXICO 1986 *(CONT.)*

Argentina: Pumpido, Brown, Cuciuffo, Ruggeri, Olarticoecha, Batista, Giusti, Burruchaga (Trobbiani 90), Enrique, Maradona, Valdona.

W. Germany: Schumacher, Jakobs, Forster, Eder, Brehme, Matthaus, Berthold, Magath (Hoeness 62), Briegel, Rummenigge, Allofs (Voller 46).

Referee: Filho (Brazil).

MEXICO 1970

Brazil.................1	3 —4
Italy..................1	0 —1

FIRST HALF

Scoring: 1, Brazil, Pelé (18); 2, Italy, Boninsegna (32).

SECOND HALF

Scoring: 3, Brazil, Gerson (65); 4, Brazil, Jairzinho (70); 5, Brazil, Alberto (86).

Brazil: Feliz, Alberto, Brito, Wilson, Piazza, Everaldo, Clodoaldo, Gerson, Jairzinho, Tostao, Pelé, Rivelino.

Italy: Albertosi, Burgnich, Cera, Rosato, Facchetti, Bertini (Juliano), Mazzola, De Sisti, Domenghini, Boninsegna (Rivera), Riva.

Referee: Glockner (E. Germany).

ARGENTINA 1978

Argentina 1	0	2——3
Netherlands 0	1	0——1

FIRST HALF

Scoring: 1, Argentina, Kempes (38).

SECOND HALF

Scoring: 2, Netherlands, Nanninga (81).

OVERTIME

Scoring: 3, Arg., Kempes (104); 4, Arg., Bertoni (114).

Argentina: Fillol, Olguin, Galvan, Passarella, Tarantini, Ardiles (Larrosa), Gallego, Kempes, Bertoni, Luque, Ortiz (Houseman).

Netherlands: Jongbloed, Jansen (Suurbier), Krol, Brandts, Poortvliet, Neeskens, Haan, van der Kerkhoff, W., van der Kerkhoff, R., Rep (Nanninga), Rensenbrink.

Referee: Gonella (Italy).

MEXICO 1986

Argentina 1	2 —3
W. Germany 0	2 —2

FIRST HALF

Scoring: 1, Argentina, Brown (22).

SECOND HALF

Scoring: 2, Arg., Valdano (55); 3, W. Germ., Rummenigge (73); 4, W. Germ., Voller (81); 5, Arg., Burruchaga (83).

ITALY 1990

W. Germany 0	1—1
Argentina 0	0—0

SECOND HALF

Scoring: 1, W. Germany, Brehme, PK (84).

W. Germany: Illgner, Brehme, Kohler, Augenthaler, Buchwald, Berthold (Reuter), Littbarski, Haessler, Mattaeus, Voeller, Klinsmann.

Argentina: Goychoechea, Lorenzo, Serrizuela, Sensini, Ruggeri (Monzon), Simon, Basualdo, Burruchag (Calderon), Maradona, Troglio, Dezottir.

Referee: Coelho (Brazil).

World Cup Final Box Scores *(Cont.)*

UNITED STATES 1994

Italy...................0	0	0——0
Brazil 0	0	0——0

Scoring: None. Shootout goals: Italy—2: Albertini, Evani; Brazil—3: Romario, Branco, Dunga.

Italy: Pagliuca, Benarrivo, Maldini, Baresi, Mussi (Apolloni 35), Albertini, D. Baggio (Evani 95), Berti, Donadoni, Baggio, Massaro.

Brazil: Taffarel, Jorginho (Cafu 21), Branco, Aldair, Santos, Silva, Dunga, Zinho (Viola 106), Mazinho, Bebeto, Romario.

Referee: Sandor Puhl (Hungary).

FRANCE 1998

Brazil 0	0——0
France 2	1——3

FIRST HALF
Scoring: 1, France, Zidane (27); 2, France, Zidane (45).

SECOND HALF
Scoring: 3, France, Petit (90).

Brazil: Taffarel, Cafu, Aldair, Baiano, Carlos, Sampaio (Edmundo 74), Dunga, Rivaldo, Leonardo, (Denilson 46), Bebeto, Ronaldo.

France: Barthez, Lizarazu, Desailly, Thuram, Leboeuf, Djorkaeff (Vieira 75) Deschamps, Zidane, Petit, Karembeu (Boghossian 57), Guivarc'h (Dugarry 66).

Referee: Belqola (Morocco).

Alltime Leaders

GOALS

Player, Nation	Tournaments	Goals	Player, Nation	Tournaments	Goals
Gerd Müller, West Germany	1970, '74	14	Ademir, Brazil	1950	9
Just Fontaine, France	1958	13	Eusebio, Portugal	1966	9
Pelé, Brazil	1958, '62, '66, '70	12	Jairzinho, Brazil	1970, '74	9
Sandor Kocsis, Hungary	1954	11	Paolo Rossi, Italy	1982, '86	9
Teofilo Cubillas, Peru	1970, '78	10	Karl-Heinz Rummenigge,		
Gregorz Lato, Poland	1974, '78, '82	10	W. Germany	1978, '82, '86	9
Helmut Rahn, West Germany	1954, '58	10	Uwe Seeler, West Germany	1958, '62, '66, '70	9
Gary Lineker, England	1986, '90	10	Vava, Brazil	1958, '62	9

LEADING SCORER, CUP BY CUP

Year	Player, Nation	Goals	Year	Player, Nation	Goals
1930	Guillermo Stabile, Argentina	8	1966	Eusebio Ferreira, Portugal	9
1934	Oldrich Nejedly, Czechoslovakia	5	1970	Gerd Müller, West Germany	10
1938	Leonidas da Silva, Brazil	8	1974	Gregorz Lato, Poland	7
1950	Ademir de Menezes, Brazil	9	1978	Mario Kempes, Argentina	6
1954	Sandor Kocsis, Hungary	11	1982	Paolo Rossi, Italy	6
1958	Just Fontaine, France	13	1986	Gary Lineker, England	6
1962	Florian Albert, Hungary	4	1990	Salvatore Schillaci, Italy	6
	Valentin Ivanov, USSR		1994	Hristo Stoichkov, Bulgaria	6
	Garrincha, Brazil			Oleg Salenko, Russia	
	Drazan Jerkovic, Yugoslavia		1998	Davor Suker, Croatia	6
	Leonel Sanchez, Chile				
	Vava, Brazil				

Most Goals, Individual, One Game

Goals	Player, Nation	Score	Date
5	Oleg Salenko, Russia	Russia–Cameroon, 6–1	6-28-94
4	Leonidas, Brazil	Brazil–Poland, 6–5	6-5-38
4	Ernest Willimowski, Poland	Brazil–Poland, 6–5	6-5-38
4	Gustav Wetterstrîm, Sweden	Sweden–Cuba, 8–0	6-12-38
4	Juan Alberto Schiaffino, Uruguay	Uruguay–Bolivia, 8–0	7-2-50
4	Ademir, Brazil	Brazil–Sweden, 7–1	7-9-50
4	Sandor Kocsis, Hungary	Hungary–West Germany, 8–3	6-20-54
4	Just Fontaine, France	France–West Germany, 6–3	6-28-58
4	Eusebio, Portugal	Portugal–North Korea, 5–3	7-23-66
4	Emilio Butragueño, Spain	Spain–Denmark, 5–1	6-18-86

Note: 30 players have scored 31 World Cup hat tricks. Gerd Müller of West Germany is the only man to have two World Cup hat tricks, both in 1970. The last hat tricks were 6-21-98, Gabriel Batistuta (Arg) vs. Jamaica; 6-23-90, Tomas Skuhravy (Czech) vs. Costa Rica; 6-17-90, Michel (Spain) vs. South Korea; and.

Attendance and Goal Scoring, Year by Year

Year	Site	No. of Games	Goals	Goals/Game	Attendance	Avg Att
1930 ....Uruguay		18	70	3.89	434,500	24,139
1934 ....Italy		17	70	4.12	395,000	23,235
1938 ....France		18	84	4.67	483,000	26,833
1950 ....Brazil		22	88	4.00	1,337,000	60,773
1954 ....Switzerland		26	140	5.38	943,000	36,269
1958 ....Sweden		35	126	3.60	868,000	24,800
1962 ....Chile		32	89	2.78	776,000	24,250
1966 ....England		32	89	2.78	1,614,677	50,459
1970 ....Mexico		32	95	2.97	1,673,975	52,312
1974 ....West Germany		38	97	2.55	1,774,022	46,685
1978 ....Argentina		38	102	2.68	1,610,215	42,374
1982 ....Spain		52	146	2.80	1,856,277	35,698
1986 ....Mexico		52	132	2.54	2,441,731	46,956
1990 ....Italy		52	115	2.21	2,514,443	48,354
1994 ....United States		52	140	2.69	3,567,415	68,604
1998 ....France		64	171	2.67	2,775,400	43,366
Totals		580	1754	3.02	25,064,655	43,215

The United States in the World Cup

URUGUAY 1930: FINAL COMPETITION

Date	Opponent	Result	Scoring
7-13-30 ..Belgium		3–0 W	US: McGhee 2, Patenaude
7-17-30 ..Paraguay		3–0 W	US: Patenaude 2, Florie
7-26-30 ..Argentina		1–6 L	ARG: Monti 2, Scopelli 2, Stabile 2 US: Brown.

ITALY 1934: FINAL COMPETITION

Date	Opponent	Result	Scoring
5-27-34 ..Italy		1–7 L	US: Donelli ITA: Schiavio 3, Orsi 2, Meazza, Ferrari

BRAZIL 1950: FINAL COMPETITION

Date	Opponent	Result	Scoring
6-25-50 ..Spain		1–3 L	US: Pariani SPN: Igoa, Basora, Zarra
6-29-50 ..England		1–0 W	US: Gaetjens.
7-2-50 ....Chile		2–5 L	US: Wallace, Maca CHL: Robledo, Cremaschi 3, Prieto

ITALY 1990: FINAL COMPETITION

Date	Opponent	Result	Scoring
6-10-90 ..Czechoslovakia		1–5 L	US: Caligiuri Czech: Skuhravy 2, Hasek, Bilek, Luhovy
6-14-90 ..Italy		0–1 L	Italy: Giannini
6-19-90 ..Austria		1–2 L	US: Murray Austria: Rodax, Ogris

UNITED STATES 1994: FINAL COMPETITION

Date	Opponent	Result	Scoring
6-18-94 ..Switzerland		1–1 T	US: Wynalda Sui: Bregy
6-22-94 ..Colombia		2–1 W	US: Escobar (own goal), Stewart Colombia: Valencia
6-26-94 ..Romania		1–0 L	Romania: Petrescu
7-4-94 ....Brazil		1–0 L	Brazil: Bebeto

FRANCE 1998: FINAL COMPETITION

Date	Opponent	Result	Scoring
6-15-98 ..Germany		2–0 L	Ger: Möller, Klinsmann
6-21-98 ..Iran		2–1 L	US: McBride Iran: Estili, Mahdavikia
6-25-98 ..Yugoslavia		1–0 L	Yugoslavia: Komljenovic

International Competition

European Championship

Official name: the European Football Championship. Held every four years since 1960.

Year	Champion	Score	Runner-up	Year	Champion	Score	Runner-up
1960 ......USSR		2–1	Yugoslavia	1980 ......West Germany		2–1	Belgium
1964 ......Spain		2–1	USSR	1984 ......France		2–0	Spain
1968 ......Italy		2–0	Yugoslavia	1988 ......Holland		2–0	USSR
1972 ......West Germany		3–0	USSR	1992 ......Denmark		2–0	Germany
1976 ......Czechoslovakia*		2–2	West Germany	1996 ......Germany†		2–1	Czech Republic

*Won on penalty kicks. †Won in sudden-death overtime.

Under-20 World Championship

Year	Host	Champion	Runner-Up
1977	Tunisia	USSR	Mexico
1979	Japan	Argentina	USSR
1981	Australia	W. Germany	Qatar
1983	Mexico	Brazil	Argentina
1985	USSR	Brazil	Spain
1987	Chile	Yugoslavia	W. Germany
1989	Saudi Arabia	Portugal	Nigeria
1991	Portugal	Portugal	Brazil
1993	Australia	Brazil	Ghana
1995	Qatar	Argentina	Brazil
1997	Malaysia	Argentina	Uruguay
1999	Nigeria	Spain	Japan

Under-17 World Championship

Year	Champion
1985	Nigeria
1987	USSR
1989	Saudi Arabia
1991	Ghana
1993	Nigeria

Under-17 *(Cont.)*

Year	Champion
1995	Ghana
1997	Brazil

Pan American Games

Year	Champion
1951	Argentina
1955	Argentina
1959	Argentina
1963	Brazil
1967	Mexico
1971	Argentina
1975	Brazil/Mexico (tie)
1979	Brazil
1983	Uruguay
1987	Brazil
1991	United States
1995	Argentina
1999	Mexico

South American Championship (Copa America)

Year	Champion	Host	Year	Champion	Host
1916	Uruguay	Argentina	1949	Brazil	Brazil
1917	Uruguay	Uruguay	1953	Paraguay	Peru
1919	Brazil	Brazil	1955	Argentina	Chile
1920	Uruguay	Chile	1956	Uruguay	Uruguay
1921	Argentina	Argentina	1957	Argentina	Peru
1922	Brazil	Brazil	1958	Argentina	Argentina
1923	Uruguay	Uruguay	1959	Uruguay	Ecuador
1924	Uruguay	Uruguay	1963	Bolivia	Bolivia
1925	Argentina	Argentina	1967	Uruguay	Uruguay
1926	Uruguay	Chile	1975	Peru	Various sites
1927	Argentina	Peru	1979	Paraguay	Various sites
1929	Argentina	Argentina	1983	Uruguay	Various sites
1935	Uruguay	Peru	1987	Uruguay	Argentina
1937	Argentina	Argentina	1989	Brazil	Brazil
1939	Peru	Peru	1990	Brazil	Argentina
1941	Argentina	Chile	1991	Argentina	Chile
1942	Uruguay	Uruguay	1993	Argentina	Ecuador
1945	Argentina	Chile	1995	Uruguay	Uruguay
1946	Argentina	Argentina	1997	Brazil	Bolivia
1947	Argentina	Ecuador	1999	Brazil	Paraguay

Awards

European Footballer of the Year

Year	Player	Club	Year	Player	Club
1956	Stanley Matthews	Blackpool	1974	Johan Cruyff	Barcelona
1957	Alfredo Di Stefano	Real Madrid	1975	Oleg Blokhin	Dynamo Kiev
1958	Raymond Kopa	Real Madrid	1976	Franz Beckenbauer	Bayern Munich
1959	Alfredo Di Stefano	Real Madrid	1977	Allan Simonsen	Borussia M'gladbach
1960	Luis Suarez	Barcelona	1978	Kevin Keegan	SV Hamburg
1961	Omar Sivori	Juventus	1979	Kevin Keegan	SV Hamburg
1962	Josef Masopust	Dukla Prague	1980	Karl-Heinz Rummenigge	Bayern Munich
1963	Lev Yashin	Moscow Dynamo	1981	Karl-Heinz Rummenigge	Bayern Munich
1964	Denis Law	Manchester United	1982	Paolo Rossi	Juventus
1965	Eusebio	Benfica	1983	Michel Platini	Juventus
1966	Bobby Charlton	Manchester United	1984	Michel Platini	Juventus
1967	Florian Albert	Ferencvaros	1985	Michel Platini	Juventus
1968	George Best	Manchester United	1986	Igor Belanov	Dynamo Kiev
1969	Gianni Rivera	AC Milan	1987	Ruud Gullit	AC Milan
1970	Gerd Mueller	Bayern Munich	1988	Marco Van Basten	AC Milan
1971	Johan Cruyff	Ajax	1989	Marco Van Basten	AC Milan
1972	Franz Beckenbauer	Bayern Munich	1990	Lothar Matthaeus	Inter Milan
1973	Johan Cruyff	Barcelona	1991	Jean-Pierre Papin	Olympique Marseille

European Footballer of the Year (Cont.)

Year	Player	Club	Year	Player	Club
1992	Marco Van Basten	AC Milan	1996	Matthias Sammer	Borussia Dortmund
1993	Roberto Baggio	Juventus	1997	Ronaldo	Inter Milan
1994	Hristo Stoichkov	Barcelona	1998	Zinedine Zidane	Juventus
1995	George Weah	AC Milan			

African Footballer of the Year

Year	Player	Nation	Year	Player	Nation
1970	Salif Keita	Mali	1985	Mohamed Timoumi	Morocco
1971	Ibrahim Sunday	Ghana	1986	Badou Zaki	Morocco
1972	Chérif Souleyman	Guinea	1987	Rabah Madjer	Algeria
1973	Tshimimu Bwanga	Zaire	1988	Kalusha Bwalya	Zambia
1974	Paul Moukila	Congo	1989	George Weah	Liberia
1975	Ahmed Faras	Morocco	1990	Roger Milla	Cameroon
1976	Roger Milla	Cameroon	1991	Abedi Pele	Ghana
1977	Dhiab Tarak	Tunisia	1992	Abedi Pele	Ghana
1978	Abdul Razak	Ghana	1993	Rashidi Yekini	Nigeria
1979	Thomas Nkono	Cameroon	1994	George Weah	Liberia
1980	Jean Manga Onguene	Cameroon	1995	George Weah	Liberia
1981	Lakhdar Belloumi	Algeria	1996	Nwankwo Kanu	Nigeria
1982	Thomas Nkono	Cameroon	1997	Victor Ikpeba	Nigeria
1983	Mahmoud Al-Khatib	Egypt	1998	Mustapha Hadji	Morocco
1984	ThÇophile Abega	Cameroon			

South American Player of the Year

Year	Player	Team	Year	Player	Team
1971	Tostao	Cruzeiro	1986	Antonio Alzamendi	River Plate
1972	Teofilo Cubillas	Alianza Lima	1987	Carlos Valderrama	Deportivo Cali
1973	Pelé	Santos	1988	Ruben Paz	Racing Buenos Aires
1974	Elias Figueroa	Internacional	1989	Bebeto	Vasco da Gama
1975	Elias Figueroa	Internacional	1990	Raul Amarilla	Olimpia
1976	Elias Figueroa	Internacional	1991	Oscar Ruggeri	Velez Sarsfield
1977	Zico	Flamengo	1992	Rai	São Paulo
1978	Mario Kempes	Valencia	1993	Carlos Valderrama	Junior Barranquilla
1979	Diego Maradona	Argentinos Juniors	1994	Cafu	São Paulo
1980	Diego Maradona	Boca Juniors	1995	Enzo Francescoli	River Plate
1981	Zico	Flamengo	1996	Jose-Luis Chilavert	Velez Sarsfield
1982	Zico	Flamengo	1997	Marcelo Salas	River Plate
1983	Socrates	Corinthians	1998	Martin Palermo	Boca Juniors
1984	Enzo Francescoli	River Plate			
1985	Julio Cesar Romero	Fluminense			

International Club Competition

Intercontinental Cup

Competition between winners of European Champion Clubs' Cup and Libertadores Cup.

1960...Real Madrid, Spain	1974...Atletico de Madrid, Spain	1988...Nacional, Uruguay
1961...Penarol, Uruguay	1975...No tournament	1989...Milan, Italy
1962...Santos, Brazil	1976...Bayern Munich	1990...Milan, Italy
1963...Santos, Brazil	1977...Boca Juniors, Argentina	1991...Red Star Belgrade, Yugos.
1964...Inter, Italy	1978...No tournament	1992...São Paulo, Brazil
1965...Inter, Italy	1979...Olimpia, Paraguay	1993...São Paulo, Brazil
1966...Penarol, Uruguay	1980...Nacional, Uruguay	1994...Velez Sarsfield, Argentina
1967...Racing Club, Argentina	1981...Flamengo, Brazil	1995...Ajax Amsterdam, Netherlands
1968...Estudiantes, Argentina	1982...Penarol, Uruguay	1996...Juventus, Italy
1969...Milan, Italy	1983...Gremio, Brazil	1997...Borussia Dortmund, Ger.
1970...Feyenoord, Netherlands	1984...Independiente, Argentina	1998...Real Madrid, Spain
1971...Nacional, Uruguay	1985...Juventus, Italy	
1972...Ajax, Holland	1986...River Plate, Argentina	
1973...Independiente, Argentina	1987...Porto, Portugal	

Note: Until 1968 a best-of-three-games format decided the winner. After that a two-game/total-goal format was used until Toyota became the sponsor in 1980, moved the game to Tokyo, and switched the format to a one-game championship. The European Cup runner-up substituted for the winner in 1971, 1973, 1974, and 1979.

European Cup

1956...Real Madrid, Spain
1957...Real Madrid, Spain
1958...Real Madrid, Spain
1959...Real Madrid, Spain
1960...Real Madrid, Spain
1961...Benfica, Portugal
1962...Benfica, Portugal
1963...AC Milan, Italy
1964...Inter-Milan, Italy
1965...Inter-Milan, Italy
1966...Real Madrid, Spain
1967...Celtic, Scotland
1968...Manchester United, England
1969...AC Milan, Italy
1970...Feyenoord, Netherlands
1956...Real Madrid, Spain
1957...Real Madrid, Spain
1958...Real Madrid, Spain
1959...Real Madrid, Spain
1960...Real Madrid, Spain
1961...Benfica, Portugal
1962...Benfica, Portugal
1963...AC Milan, Italy
1964...Inter-Milan, Italy

1965...Inter-Milan, Italy
1966...Real Madrid, Spain
1967...Celtic, Scotland
1968...Manchester United, England
1969...AC Milan, Italy
1970...Feyenoord, Netherlands
1971...Ajax Amsterdam,
        Netherlands
1972...Ajax Amsterdam,
        Netherlands
1973...Ajax Amsterdam,
        Netherlands
1974...Bayern Munich,
        West Germany
1975...Bayern Munich,
        West Germany
1976...Bayern Munich,
        West Germany
1977...Liverpool, England
1978...Liverpool, England
1979...Nottingham Forest,
        England
1980...Nottingham Forest,
        England

1981...Liverpool, England
1982...Aston Villa, England
1983...SV Hamburg,
        West Germany
1984...Liverpool, England
1985...Juventus, Italy
1986...Steaua Bucharest,
        Romania
1987...Porto, Portugal
1988...P.S.V. Eindhoven,
        Netherlands
1989...AC Milan, Italy
1990...AC Milan, Italy
1991...Red Star Belgrade, Yugoslav.
1992...Barcelona, Spain
1993...Olympique Marseille, France
1994...AC Milan, Italy
1995...Ajax Amsterdam, Netherlands
1996...Juventus, Italy
1997...Borussia Dortmund, Ger.
1998...Real Madrid, Spain
1999...Manchester United,
        England

Note: On four occasions the European Cup winner has refused to play in the Intercontinental Cup and has been replaced by the runner-up: Panathinaikos (Greece) in 1971, Juventus (Italy) in 1973, Atletico Madrid (Spain) in 1974, and Malmo (Sweden) in 1979.

Libertadores Cup

Competition between champion clubs and runners-up of 10 South American National Associations.

1960...Penarol, Uruguay
1961...Penarol, Uruguay
1962...Santos, Brazil
1963...Santos, Brazil
1964...Independiente, Argentina
1965...Independiente, Argentina
1966...Penarol, Uruguay
1967...Racing Club, Argentina
1968...Estudiantes, Argentina
1969...Estudiantes, Argentina
1970...Estudiantes, Argentina
1971...Nacional, Uruguay
1972...Independiente, Argentina
1973...Independiente, Argentina

1974...Independiente, Argentina
1975...Independiente, Argentina
1976...Cruzeiro, Brazil
1977...Boca Juniors, Argentina
1978...Boca Juniors, Argentina
1979...Olimpia, Paraguay
1980...Nacional, Uruguay
1981...Flamengo, Brazil
1982...Penarol, Uruguay
1983...Gremio, Brazil
1984...Independiente, Argentina
1985...Argentinos Juniors, Arg
1986...River Plate, Argentina
1987...Penarol, Uruguay

1988...Nacional, Uruguay
1989...Atletico Nacional,
        Colombia
1990...Olimpia, Paraguay
1991...Colo Colo, Chile
1992...São Paulo, Brazil
1993...São Paulo, Brazil
1994...Velez Sarsfield, Argentina
1995...Gremio, Brazil
1996...River Plate, Argentina
1997...Cruzeiro, Brazil
1998...Vasco da Gama, Brazil
1999...Palmeiras, Brazil

UEFA Cup

Competition between teams other than league champions and cup winners from the Union of European Football Associations.

1958...Barcelona, Spain
1959...No tournament
1960...Barcelona, Spain
1961...AS Roma, Italy
1962...Valencia, Spain
1963...Valencia, Spain
1964...Real Zaragoza, Spain
1965...Ferencvaros, Hungary
1966...Barcelona, Spain
1967...Dynamo Zagreb, Yugoslav.
1968...Leeds United, England
1969...Newcastle United, England
1970...Arsenal, England
1971...Leeds United, England
1972...Tottenham Hotspur, England
1973...Liverpool, England

1974...Feyenoord, Netherlands
1975...Borussia Monchengladbach,
        West Germany
1976...Liverpool, England
1977...Juventus, Italy
1978...P.S.V. Eindhoven, Netherl.
1979...Borussia Monchengladbach,
        West Germany
1980...Eintracht Frankfurt,
        West Germany
1981...Ipswich Town, England
1982...I.F.K. Gothenburg, Sweden
1983...Anderlecht, Belgium
1984...Tottenham Hotspur, England
1985...Real Madrid, Spain
1986...Real Madrid, Spain

1987...I.F.K. Gothenburg, Sweden
1988...Bayer Leverkusen,
        West Germany
1989...Naples, Italy
1990...Juventus, Italy
1991...Inter-Milan, Italy
1992...Torino, Italy
1993...Juventus, Italy
1994...Internazionale, Italy
1995...Parma, Italy
1996...Bayern Munich, Germany
1997...Schalke 04, Germany
1998...Inter Milan, Italy
1999...Parma, Italy

European Cup-Winners' Cup

Competition between cup winners of countries belonging to UEFA.

1961...A.C. Fiorentina, Italy
1962...Atletico Madrid, Spain
1963...Tottenham Hotspur, England
1964...Sporting Lisbon, Portugal
1965...West Ham United, England
1966...Borussia Dortmund,
    West Germany
1967...Bayern Munich, W. Germ.
1968...A.C. Milan, Italy
1969...Slovan Bratislava, Czech.
1970...Manchester City, England
1971...Chelsea, England
1972...Glasgow Rangers, Scotland
1973...A.C. Milan, Italy

1974...Magdeburg, East Germany
1975...Dynamo Kiev, USSR
1976...Anderlecht, Belgium
1977...S.V. Hamburg, W. Germ.
1978...Anderlecht, Belgium
1979...Barcelona, Spain
1980...Valencia, Spain
1981...Dynamo Tbilisi, USSR
1982...Barcelona, Spain
1983...Aberdeen, Scotland
1984...Juventus, Italy
1985...Everton, England
1986...Dynamo Kiev, USSR
1987...Ajax Amsterdam, Netherlands

1988...Mechelen, Belgium
1989...Barcelona, Spain
1990...Sampdoria, Italy
1991...Manchester United, England
1992...Werder Bremen, Germany
1993...Parma, Italy
1994...Arsenal, England
1995...Real Zaragoza, Spain
1996...Paris St. Germain, France
1997...Barcelona, Spain
1998...Chelsea, England
1999...Lazio, Italy

Major League Soccer

Results

Year	Champion	Score	Runner-up	Regular Season MVP
1996	D.C. United	3–2	Los Angeles	Carlos Valderrama, TB
1997	D.C. United	2–1	Colorado	Preki, Kansas City
1998	Chicago	2–0	D.C. United	Marco Etcheverry, D.C.

Purple Heart

Forget Margaret Thatcher. If there was ever a woman deserving of the nickname Iron Lady, it's U.S. midfielder Michelle Akers. In her 14 years with the national team, Akers, 33, has been the Lenny Dykstra of women's soccer, crashing into defenders, hurtling headlong for the good of the team—and the bad of her body. The damage? Double-digit knee surgeries ("Twelve or 13, I forget," she says), a couple of concussions and, in February 1999, three fractured bones below her left eye. "People are sick of seeing me get hurt," Akers says, "but that's who I am. I take big risks. Sometimes I fall flat on my face, but I also get some mountaintop moments."

Some? Try a few dozen. Talking about team history with Akers is like discussing the Constitution with James Madison. She scored the Americans' first goal, in 1985; had both goals in the U.S. victory in the 1991 Women's World Cup final in China; and drilled the crucial game-tying penalty kick with 13 minutes left in the '96 Olympic semi-final against Norway....

For more than four years Akers has waged a Sisyphean battle with chronic fatigue syndrome, which caused her to sit out almost all of 1997 with debilitating symptoms. "There's the fatigue, but you also have migraines, you don't sleep, your balance and short-term memory are gone," Akers says, "I've gotten lost going to the grocery store."

Unable to run hard for 30 minutes, much less 90, Akers has transformed herself from the world's best striker into merely the world's best defensive midfielder, a feat not unlike Michael Jordan's transition from slasher to fadeaway jump shooter. The opponent's penalty area, where Akers once roamed freely, is now foreign territory to her, except on set plays. She follows a simple dictum:"Walk when you don't have to run, jog when you don't have to sprint," she says. "I've learned to be a lot more efficient with my touches, too."

...The physical side of the game, however, will always be a problem for her. In spring 1999 Akers developed high blood pressure as a result of her chronic fatigue. Because the medication used to treat her condition is banned by the U.S. Olympic Committee, she has been searching for home remedies, to no avail. In mid-April 1999 she suffered heat stroke at practice, and on April 22, when the U.S. played China in a World Cup tuneup in Hershey, Pa., she pulled herself from the game at halftime—but not before scoring the Americans' first goal, on a penalty kick. The U.S. went on to win 2–1.

A-League

Year	Champion	Score	Runner-Up	Regular Season MVP
1991	San Francisco	1–3, 2–0 (1–0 on penalty kicks)	Albany	Jean Harbor, Maryland
1992	Colorado	1–0	Tampa Bay	Taifour Diane, Colorado
1993	Colorado	3–1 (OT)	Los Angeles	Taifour Diane, Colorado
1994	Montreal	1–0	Colorado	Paulinho, Los Angeles
1995	Seattle	1–2 (SO), 3–0, 2–1 (SO)	Atlanta	Peter Hattrup, Seattle
1996	Seattle	2–0	Rochester	Wolde Harris, Colorado
1997	Milwaukee	2–1 (SO)	Carolina	Doug Miller, Rochester
1998	Rochester	3–1	Minnesota	Mark Baena, Seattle

U.S. Open Cup

Open to all amateur and professional teams in the United States, the annual U.S. Open Cup is the oldest cup competition in the country and among the oldest in the world. The tournament is a single-elimination event running concurrent to the MLS season. The winner advances to the CONCACAF Cup, a tournament of the top club teams from North and Central America.

Year	Champion	Year	Champion
1914	Brooklyn Field Club (NYC)	1960	Ukrainian Nationals (Philadelphia)
1915	Bethlehem Steel FC (PA)	1961	Ukrainian Nationals (Philadelphia)
1916	Bethlehem Steel FC (PA)	1962	New York Hungaria (NYC)
1917	Fall River Rovers (MA)	1963	Ukrainian Nationals (Philadelphia)
1918	Bethlehem Steel FC (PA)	1964	Los Angeles Kickers (CA)
1919	Bethlehem Steel FC (PA)	1965	New York Hungaria (NYC)
1920	Ben Miller FC (St. Louis)	1966	Ukrainian Nationals (Philadelphia)
1921	Robbins Dry Dock FC (Brooklyn)	1967	Greek American AA (NYC)
1922	Scullin Steel FC (St. Louis)	1968	Greek American AA (NYC)
1923	Paterson FC (NJ)	1969	Greek American AA (NYC)
1924	Fall River FC (MA)	1970	Elizabeth SC (Union, NJ)
1925	Shawsheen FC (Andover, MA)	1971	Hota SC (NYC)
1926	Bethlehem Steel FC (PA)	1972	Elizabeth SC (Union, NJ)
1927	Fall River FC (MA)	1973	Maccabee SC (Los Angeles)
1928	New York National FC (NYC)	1974	Greek American AA (NYC)
1929	Hakoah All Star SC (NYC)	1975	Maccabee SC (Los Angeles)
1930	Fall River FC (MA)	1976	San Francisco AC (CA)
1931	Fall River FC (MA)	1977	Maccabee SC (Los Angeles)
1932	New Bedford FC (MA)	1978	Maccabee SC (Los Angeles)
1933	Stix, Baer and Fuller FC (St. Louis)	1979	Brooklyn Dodgers SC (NYC)
1934	Stix, Baer and Fuller FC (St. Louis)	1980	NY Pancyprian-Freedoms (NYC)
1935	Central Breweries FC (Chicago)	1981	Maccabee SC (Los Angeles)
1936	German-Americans (Philadelphia)	1982	NY Pancyprian-Freedoms (NYC)
1937	New York American FC (NYC)	1983	NY Pancyprian-Freedoms (NYC)
1938	Sparta A and B.A. (Chicago)	1984	A.O. Krete (NYC)
1939	St. Mary's Celtic SC (Brooklyn)	1985	Greek American AC (San Francisco)
1940	—	1986	Kutis SC (St. Louis)
1941	Pawtucket FC (RI)	1987	Club Espana (Washington, D.C.)
1942	Gallatin SC (PA)	1988	Busch SC (St. Louis)
1943	Brooklyn Hispano SC (NYC)	1989	HRC Kickers (St. Petersburg, FL)
1944	Brooklyn Hispano SC (NYC)	1990	AAC Eagles (Chicago)
1945	Brookhattan FC (NYC)	1991	Brooklyn Italians SC (East NY)
1946	Chicago Viking FC (IL)	1992	San Jose Oaks (CA)
1947	Ponta Delgada SC (Fall River, MA)	1993	Club Deportivo Mexico (San Francisco)
1948	Simpkins-Ford SC (St. Louis)	1994	Greek American AC (San Francisco)
1949	Morgan SC (PA)		
1950	Simpkins-Ford SC (St. Louis)	1995	Richmond Kickers (VA)
1951	German Hungarian SC (NYC)	1996	D.C. United (MLS)
1952	Harmarville SC (PA)	1997	Dallas Burn (MLS)
1953	Falcons SC (Chicago)	1998	Chicago Fire (MLS)
1954	New York Americans (NYC)	1999	Rochester Rhinos (A-League)
1955	Eintracht Sport Club (NYC)		
1956	Harmarville SC (PA)		
1957	Kutis SC (St. Louis)		
1958	Los Angeles Kickers (CA)		
1959	McIlvaine Canvasbacks (Los Angeles)		

North American Soccer League

Formed in 1968 by the merger of the National Professional Soccer League and the USA League, both of which had begun operations a year earlier. The NPSL's lone champion was the Oakland Clippers. The USA League, which brought entire teams in from Europe, was won in 1967 by the LA Wolves, who were the English League's Wolverhampton Wanderers.

Year	Champion	Score	Runner-Up	Regular Season MVP
1968	Atlanta	0–0, 3–0	San Diego	John Kowalik, Chi
1969	Kansas City	No game	Atlanta	Cirilio Fernandez, KC
1970	Rochester	3–0,1–3	Washington	Carlos Metidieri, Roch
1971	Dallas	1–2, 4–1, 2–0	Atlanta	Carlos Metidieri, Roch
1972	NY	2–1	St. Louis	Randy Horton, NY
1973	Philadelphia	2–0	Dallas	Warren Archibald, Mia
1974	Los Angeles	4–3*	Miami	Peter Silvester, Balt
1975	Tampa Bay	2–0	Portland	Steve David, Mia
1976	Toronto	3–0	Minnesota	Pelé, NY
1977	NY	2–1	Seattle	Franz Beckenbauer, NY
1978	NY	3–1	Tampa Bay	Mike Flanagan, NE
1979	Vancouver	2–1	Tampa Bay	Johan Cruyff, LA
1980	NY	3–0	Ft. Lauderdale	Roger Davies, Sea
1981	Chicago	1–0*	NY	Giorgio Chinaglia, NY
1982	NY	1–0	Seattle	Peter Ward, Sea
1983	Tulsa	2–0	Toronto	Roberto Cabanas, NY
1984	Chicago	2–1, 3–2	Toronto	Steve Zungul, SJ

*Shootout.

Championship Format: 1968 & 1970: Two games/total goals. 1971 & 1984: Best-of-three series. 1972–1983: One-game championship. Title in 1969 went to the regular-season champion.

Statistical Leaders

SCORING

Year	Player/Team	Pts	Year	Player/Team	Pts
1968	John Kowalik, Chi	69	1977	Steven David, LA	58
1969	Kaiser Motaung, Atl	36	1978	Giorgio Chinaglia, NY	79
1970	Kirk Apostolidis, Dall	35	1979	Oscar Fabbiani, Tampa Bay	58
1971	Carlos Metidieri, Roch	46	1980	Giorgio Chinaglia, NY	77
1972	Randy Horton, NY	22	1981	Giorgio Chinaglia, NY	74
1973	Kyle Rote, Dall	30	1982	Giorgio Chinaglia, NY	55
1974	Paul Child, San Jose	36	1983	Roberto Cabanas, NY	66
1975	Steven David, Miami	52	1984	Slavisa Zungul, Golden Bay	50
1976	Giorgio Chinaglia, NY	49			

And at the Mike, Wolf Blitzer!	We howled when we heard this one: There's a soccer team in Germany's elite Bundesliga from the town of Wolfsburg (ex-Virginia Cavalier Claudio Reyna is a former member). And it's coached by—we're not making this up—Wolfgang Wolf.

NCAA Sports

DAMIAN STROHMEYER

NCAA baseball
champions Miami

Second Chances

The champions in soccer, hockey and baseball made certain to answer when opportunity came calling again

BY DAVID FLEMING

THE NIGHTMARISH sequence plays over and over in the mind's screening room. A crushing home run, a missed opportunity, a critical error in judgment—the championship-game-turning moment can't be undone, yet the mind returns to it obsessively. There is only one way to erase the torturous memory and banish the demon of self-doubt it summons, and that is to create a second chance, and make the most of it. In 1998–99 three champions did just that.

MEN'S SOCCER

To inspire him during the 1998 season, Indiana forward Dema Kovalenko kept a photo of his most disappointing moment on a soccer field taped to the wall of his apartment. The shot showed Kovalenko, a native of Kiev, lying on the soccer field crying after the Hoosiers' heartbreaking triple-overtime loss to UCLA in the 1997 NCAA semifinal. The Hoosiers were the only undefeated team in the country before they lost to the Bruins 1–0 that day. It was some-

thing Kovalenko didn't want to forget. "The picture motivated me," he said.

So much so that Kovalenko turned down overtures from Major League Soccer to stay in school and take another shot at an NCAA title. Sure enough, the Hoosiers made it past the semis this year, and in the final, played in a steady downpour in front of 15,202 fans at the University of Richmond Stadium, Kovalenko did not let his second chance slip away. He scored a goal and had an assist in the first half and led the Hoosiers to a 3–1 victory over Stanford. It was the school's fourth national title and capped a two-year run powered by Kovalenko and fellow Ukrainians Yuri Lavrinenko and Aleksey Korol. The trio guided Indiana to a 46–3 record during that span.

The Hoosiers' toughest test in '98 actually came in the NCAA quarterfinals against No. 1–ranked Clemson (22–1), at Clemson. Korol, a forward who led Indiana with 17 goals, scored in each half as the Hoosiers slipped past the Tigers 2–1. "This is the

With a goal and an assist in the first half, Kovalenko got the Hoosiers off on the right foot in the NCAA final.

finest victory I can remember at Indiana," said coach Jerry Yeagley. The Hoosiers then rolled past Santa Clara 4–0 in the semis. "What I like most about this team is their passion for the game," Yeagley said. "They take pride in playing a beautiful, entertaining game. These guys can make music when things go right."

With the Ukrainian trio leading the way, they often did. The Hoosiers, who outscored their opponents 65–11 in 1998, scored seven goals in the Final Four—the most by a winning team in 35 years—with the Ukrainians accounting for six of the seven. (The three hit the books as hard as they do the net: They were each named to the 1998 Big Ten All-Academic team.) Not that Indiana needed quite so much offense. Led by U.S. under-20 national team defender Nick Garcia and goalkeeper T.J. Hannig, who had 16.5 shutouts, the Hoosiers' defense allowed an NCAA-best .417 goals per game.

"We felt the pain of the last year for a very long time," said Yeagley, who has 12 Final Four appearances and a 456-80-37 record in 26 years at Indiana. "To come back and get the job done makes this win very, very special. We have exorcised some demons."

MEN'S HOCKEY

National champions in 1993, Maine began the 1998–99 hockey season still shadowed by an NCAA investigation that had uncovered recruiting violations and banned the Black Bears from the postseason in 1996 and '97. They were close to escaping that shadow with their fine play when on Feb. 23, just two weeks before the NCAA final, a darker and longer one fell across their lives: Maine equipment manager Rich Britt

SIMON BRUTY

was killed in a car accident. Reeling from the loss, the Black Bears split their last four games before refocusing and honoring Britt in the tournament by keeping a jersey on the bench for him during every game.

Steadying the team during these rocky times was the cool and brilliant goaltending of junior Alfie Michaud, who won an NCAA-best 28 games in 1998–99. In the Frozen Four, as the NCAA hockey semifinals are known, Michaud had a .964 save percentage, fourth best in the 52-year history of the event. "He's quiet, but he gives us confidence," said Black Bears wing Steve Kariya, the younger brother of NHL star Paul Kariya. "He was our MVP all year."

Tournament officials seconded that motion, naming Michaud, who stopped 35 shots in a 2–1 win over Boston College in the semis, MVP of the event. He turned back 46 more against New Hampshire in a physical and frenetic final in front of 14,447 fans at the Arrowhead Pond in Anaheim. Michaud's biggest save came on a tipped shot in overtime. Minutes later the Black Bears scored the game-winner when left wing Marcus Gustafsson pounced on his own rebound and fired the puck into the right side of the net. Maine had won the NCAA championship 3–2.

"When we won our first title we dedicated it to the state of Maine," said coach Shawn Walsh. "This time we're dedicating it to a great group of players. I also want to pay tribute to the seniors; they showed great character and loyalty to our program." Those players could have transferred when the Black Bears were put on NCAA probation, much as the team could have lost focus after Britt's death. Instead, they stuck with it, yearning for redemption.

BASEBALL

The nightmare was always the same. Miami baseball coach Jim Morris was back at Omaha's Rosenblatt Stadium, site of the College World Series, only he wasn't in the stands enjoying the games. No, Morris's dream had him trapped under the bleachers, unable to escape. These night terrors took root three years ago, when the Hurricanes were one out from winning the national championship—players were even poised on the top step of the dugout waiting to celebrate. But then Louisiana State's Warren Morris blasted a two-out, two-run, game-winning homer to steal Miami's title and Jim Morris's peace of mind.

Morris still chokes up at the memory, but at least now the nightmares are gone. His 1999 team gave him the best therapy possible: On June 19 the scrappy Hurricanes fought past injuries and graduation losses to win the NCAA title with a 6–5 win over Florida State. In one of the year's best collegiate rivalries, Miami beat Florida State in six out of seven meetings, five times by just one run. The championship was Miami's first baseball title in 14 years and helps bring Morris out of the shadow of his legendary predecessor at Miami, Ron Fraser.

The pressure to win it all is intense at Miami, where they, quite literally, use NCAA runner-up trophies as bathroom doorstops inside Mark Light Stadium. "[The '96 loss] was crushing," said Morris. "I don't think anyone understands how difficult it was to handle." If you had to choose a year for the Hurricanes to erase that painful memory, 1999 would not have been your first pick. Miami had lost its three best hitters from the 1998 team, and six players suffered season-ending injuries, including catcher and cleanup hitter Russ Jacobson. But Morris, who espouses the good old-fashioned values of defense, pitching and strategic hitting, coaxed the Hurricanes to a 41–13 regular-season record. Walk-on Greg Lovelady replaced Jacobson and hit .358 over the final 26 games of the regular season; Morris converted juco transfer Mike Neu into a closer, and he led the nation with 14.9 strikeouts per nine innings; pitcher Alex Santos turned down a $350,000 offer from the Los Angeles Dodgers and went 13–3 for Miami instead; and third baseman Lale Esquivel returned to Coral Gables after stints at Alabama and North East Texas Community College and hit .354 with 13 homers and 58 RBIs.

"This year we've been through so much adversity and so many injuries," said Lovelady. "But we've hung together as a team."

In the second inning of the CWS final, first baseman Kevin Brown belted his 22nd homer of the year to make it 1–1 and then drove in three more runs in the fifth with a bases-loaded double. Miami led 6–2. But Florida State, which had used seven pitchers to survive an exhausting, 13-inning 14–11 win over Stanford the day before, would not go quietly. The Seminoles scored three runs to make it 6–5 and once again the Hurricanes found themselves one out away from a national title, clinging to a one-run lead in the ninth. With the count at 3–2 and thoughts of 1996 clouding his head, Neu reared back and spun a curveball past Florida State's Kevin Cash to end the game and start the healing.

"I've thought about that homer thousands and thousands of times," said Jim Morris after the game. "This is a huge monkey off my back."

NCAA Team Champions

Fall 1998

Cross-Country

MEN

	Champion	Runner-Up
Division I:	Arkansas	Stanford
Division II:	Adams St (CO)	Western St (CO)
Division III:	N Central	Calvin

WOMEN

	Champion	Runner-Up
Division I:	Villanova	BYU
Division II:	Adams St	Western St (CO)
Division III:	Calvin	College of New Jersey

Field Hockey

WOMEN

	Champion	Runner-Up
Division I:	Old Dominion	Princeton
Division II	Bloomsburg	Lock Haven
Division III:	Middlebury	William Smith

Football

MEN

	Champion	Runner-Up
Division I-AA:	Massachusetts	Georgia Southern
Division II:	NW Missouri St	Carson-Newman
Division III:	Mount Union	Rowan

Soccer

MEN

	Champion	Runner-Up
Division I:	Indiana	Stanford
Division II:	Southern Connecticut St	S Carolina-Spartanburg
Division III:	Ohio Wesleyan	Greensboro

WOMEN

	Champion	Runner-Up
Division I:	Florida	N Carolina
Division II:	Lynn	Sonoma St
Division III:	Macalaster	College of New Jersey

Volleyball

WOMEN

	Champion	Runner-Up
Division I:	Long Beach St	Penn St
Division II:	Hawaii Pacific	N Dakota St
Division III:	Central (IA)	UC-San Diego

Water Polo

MEN

Champion	Runner-Up
Southern Cal	Stanford

Winter 1998–1999

Basketball

MEN

	Champion	Runner-Up
Division I:	Connecticut	Duke
Division II:	Kentucky Wesleyan	Metropolitan St
Division III:	WI-Platteville	Hampden-Sydney

WOMEN

	Champion	Runner-Up
Division I:	Purdue	Duke
Division II:	N Dakota	Arkansas Tech
Division III:	Washington (MO)	St. Benedict

Fencing

Champion	Runner-Up
Penn St	Notre Dame

Gymnastics

MEN

Champion	Runner-Up
Michigan	Ohio St

WOMEN

Champion	Runner-Up
Georgia	Michigan

Ice Hockey

MEN

	Champion	Runner-Up
Division I:	Maine	New Hampshire
Division II:	St. Michael's (VT)	New Hampshire College
Division III:	Middlebury	WI-Superior

Rifle

Champion	Runner-Up
AK-Fairbanks	Navy

Skiing

Champion	Runner-Up
Colorado	Denver

Swimming and Diving

MEN

	Champion	Runner-Up
Division I:	Auburn	Stanford
Division II:	Drury	Cal St Bakersfield
Division III:	Kenyon	Denison

WOMEN

	Champion	Runner-Up
Division I:	Georgia	Stanford
Division II:	Drury	N Dakota
Division III:	Kenyon	Denison

Wrestling

MEN

	Champion	Runner-Up
Division I:	Iowa	Minnesota
Division II:	Pittsburgh-Johnstown	NE-Omaha
Division III:	Wartburg	Augsburg

Winter 1998–1999 (Cont.)

Indoor Track and Field

MEN

	Champion	Runner-Up
Division I:	Arkansas	Stanford
Division II:	Abilene Christian	St. Augustine's
Division III:	Lincoln (PA)	WI-Oshkosh

WOMEN

	Champion	Runner-Up
Division I:	Texas	Louisiana St
Division II:	Abilene Christian	St. Augustine's
Division III:	Wheaton (MA)	WI-La Crosse

Spring 1999

Baseball

	Champion	Runner-Up
Division I:	Miami	Florida St
Division II:	Cal St-Chico	Kennesaw
Division III:	N Carolina Wesleyan	St. Thomas (MN)

Golf

MEN

	Champion	Runner-Up
Division I:	Georgia	Oklahoma St
Division II:	Florida Southern	S Carolina-Aiken
Division III:	Methodist (NC)	UC-San Diego

WOMEN

	Champion	Runner-Up
Division I:	Duke	Arizona St/ Georgia
Divisions II and III:	Methodist (NC)	Florida Southern

Lacrosse

MEN

	Champion	Runner-Up
Division I:	Virginia	Syracuse
Division II:	Adelphi	LIU-C.W. Post
Division III:	Salisbury St	Middlebury

WOMEN

	Champion	Runner-Up
Divisions I and II:	Maryland	Virginia
Division III:	Middlebury	Amherst

Rowing

WOMEN

Champion	Runner-Up
Brown	Virginia

Softball

	Champion	Runner-Up
Division I:	UCLA	Washington
Division II:	Humboldt St	NE-Kearney
Division III:	Simpson (IA)	Chapman (CA)

Tennis

MEN

	Champion	Runner-Up
Division I:	Georgia	UCLA
Division II:	Lander	Barry
Division III:	Williams	Kalamazoo

NCAA Team Champions (Cont.)

Spring 1999 (Cont.)

Tennis (Cont.)

WOMEN

	Champion	Runner-Up
Division I:	Stanford	Florida
Division II:	BYU-Hawaii	Armstrong Atlantic St
Division III:	Amherst	Williams

Outdoor Track and Field

MEN

	Champion	Runner-Up
Division I:	Arkansas	Stanford
Division II:	Abilene Christian	St. Augustine's
Division III:	Lincoln (PA)	Pacific Lutheran

WOMEN

	Champion	Runner-Up
Division I:	Texas	UCLA
Division II:	Abilene Christian	St. Augustine's
Division III:	Lincoln (PA)	Wheaton (MA)

Volleyball

MEN

Champion	Runner-Up
Brigham Young	Long Beach St

NCAA Division I Individual Champions

Fall 1998

Cross Country

MEN

Champion	Runner-Up
Adam Goucher, Colorado	Abdi Abdirahman, Arizona

WOMEN

Champion	Runner-Up
Katie McGregor, Michigan	Amy Skieresz, Arizona

Winter 1998–1999

Fencing

MEN

	Champion	Runner-Up
Sabre	Keeth Smart, St. John's	Gabor Szelle, Notre Dame
Foil	Felix Reichling, Stanford	Peter Devine, Yale
Épée	Alex Roytblat, St. John's	Thomas Peng, Penn St

WOMEN

	Champion	Runner-Up
Foil	Monique DeBruin, Stanford	Erinn Smart, Columbia
Épée	Felicia Zimmerman, Stanford	Stephanie Eim, Penn St

Gymnastics

MEN

	Champion	Runner-Up
All-around	Jason Hardabura, Nebraska	Justin Toman, Michigan
Vault	Guard Young, Brigham Young	Eddie Seng, Penn St
Parallel bars	Justin Toman, Michigan	Todd Bishop, Oklahoma
		Doug Stibel, Ohio St
Horizontal bar	Todd Bishop, Oklahoma	Blake Bukacek, Nebraska
Floor exercise	Jason Hardabura, Nebraska	Guard Young, Brigham Young
Pommel horse	Brandon Stefaniak, Penn St	Jason Krob, Minnesota
		Jamie Natalie, Ohio St
Rings	Cortney Bramwell, Brigham Young	Ron Roeder, Penn St

Winter 1998–1999 (Cont.)
Gymnastics (Cont.)

WOMEN

	Champion	Runner-Up
All-around	Theresa Kulikowski, Utah	Karin Lichey, Georgia
Balance beam	Theresa Kulikowski, Utah	
	Kiralee Hayashi, UCLA	
	Andree Pickens, Alabama	
Uneven bars	Angie Leonard, Utah	Nikki Peters, Michigan
		Sarah Cain, Michigan
Floor exercise	Marny Oestreng, Bowling Green	Theresa Kulikowski, Utah
Vault	Heidi Moneymaker, UCLA	Theresa Kulikowski, Utah

Skiing

MEN

	Champion	Runner-Up
Slalom	Jayme Smithers, Denver	Stefan Lanziner, New Mexico
Giant slalom	David Viele, Dartmouth	Stefan Lanziner, New Mexico
10-kilometer freestyle	Rune Kollerud, Utah	Frode Kollerud, Utah
20-kilometer classical	Ove Erik Tronvoll, Colorado	Mangus Ericksson, Colorado

WOMEN

	Champion	Runner-Up
Slalom	Linda Wikstrom, Colorado	Jennifer Collins, Dartmouth
Giant slalom	Aimee-Noel Hartlee, Colorado	Erica MacConnell, Vermont
5-kilometer freestyle	Ekaterina Ivanova, Vermont	Steffi Kindt, AK-Anchorage
15-kilometer classical	Britta Wienand, Denver	Ekaterina Ivanova, Vermont

Wrestling

	Champion	Runner-Up
125 lb	Stephan Abas, Fresno St	Jeremy Hunter, Penn St
133 lb	Eric Guerrero, Oklahoma St	Cody Sanderson, Iowa St
141 lb	Doug Schwab, Iowa	Michael Lightner, Oklahoma
149 lb	T.J. Williams, Iowa	Tony Davis, Northern Iowa
157 lb	Casey Cunningham, Cent. Michigan	Clint Musser, Penn St
165 lb	Kirk White, Boise St	Rodney Jones, Oklahoma
174 lb	Glenn Pritzlaff, Penn St	Otto Olson, Michigan
184 lb	Cael Sanderson, Ohio St	Brandon Eggum, Minnesota
197 lb	Tim Hartung, Minnesota	Lee Fullhart, Iowa
285 lb	Stephen Neal, Cal St-Bakersfield	Brock Lesner, Minnesota

Swimming and Diving

MEN

	Champion	Time	Runner-Up	Time
50-yard freestyle	Aaron Ciarla, Auburn	19.36	Brendon Dedekind, Florida St	19.48
100-yard freestyle	Bart Kizierowski, California	42.70	Roland Schoeman, Arizona	42.88
200-yard freestyle	Ryk Neethling, Arizona	1:33.59	Bela Szabados, Southern Cal	1:33.87
500-yard freestyle	Ryk Neethling, Arizona	4:13.80	Bela Szabados, Southern Cal	4:15.69
1650-yard freestyle	Ryk Neethling, Arizona	14:35.57	Chris Thompson, Michigan	14:38.96
100-yard backstroke	Michael Gilliam, Tennessee	47.12	Dan Schultz, Stanford	47.20
200-yard backstroke	Tate Blahnik, Stanford	1:41.42	Matthew Cole, Florida	1:42.21
100-yard breaststroke	Brendon Dedekind, Florida St	53.16	Edward Moses, Virginia	53.50
200-yard breaststroke	Dave Denniston, Auburn	1:55.51	Edward Moses, Virginia	1:57.06
100-yard butterfly	Dod Wales, Stanford	45.89	Adam Pine, Nebraska	46.37
200-yard butterfly	Shamek Pietucha, Virginia	1:43.50	Tom Malchow, Michigan	1:43.58
200-yard IM	Lionel Moreau, Auburn	1:45.24	Nate Dusing, Texas	1:46.65
400-yard IM	Tim Siciliano, Michigan	3:43.54	Beau Wiebel, Georgia	3:46.02

	Champion	Pts	Runner-Up	Pts
1-meter diving†	Rio Ramirez, Miami (FL)	643.10	Troy Dumais, Texas	634.10
3-meter diving†	Troy Dumais, Texas	688.70	Rio Ramirez, Miami (FL)	666.95
Platform#	Rio Ramirez, Miami (FL)	901.60	Troy Dumais, Texas	841.00

*Meet record. †Scoring based on 17 dives. #Scoring based on 14 dives.

Winter 1998–1999 *(Cont.)*
Swimming and Diving *(Cont.)*

WOMEN

	Champion	Time	Runner-Up	Time
50-yard freestyle	Catherine Fox, Stanford	22.13	Courtney Allen, Northwestern	22.47
100-yard freestyle	Martina Moravcova, SMU	48.05	Courtney Shealy, Georgia	48.49
200-yard freestyle	Martina Moravcova, SMU	1:43.84	Sarah Tolar, Arizona	1:45.71
500-yard freestyle	Lindsay Benko, Southern Cal	4:40.22	Ellen Stonebraker, Wisconsin	4:41.26
1650-yard freestyle	Julie Varozza, Georgia	15:59.66	Rachel Komisarz, Kentucky	16:04.42
100-yard backstroke	Marylyn Chiang, California	52.36*	Catherine Fox, Stanford	52.77
200-yard backstroke	Keegan Walkley, Georgia	1:53.63	Misty Hyman, Stanford	1:54.10
100-yard breaststroke	Kristy Kowal, Georgia	59.25	Danica Wizniuk, Virginia	1:00.45
200-yard breaststroke	Kristy Kowal, Georgia	2:07.66*	Elin Austevoll, Stanford	2:09.99
100-yard butterfly	Misty Hyman, Stanford	51.77	Limin Liu, Nevada	51.96
200-yard butterfly	Limin Liu, Nevada	1:53.36*	Misty Hyman, Stanford	1:53.60
200-yard IM	Martina Moravcova, SMU	1:55.64	Marylyn Chiang, California	1:57.83
400-yard IM	Madeleine Crippen, Villanova	4:06.76	Keegan Walkley, Georgia	4:07.06

	Champion	Pts	Runner-Up	Pts
1-meter diving††	Jenny Lingamfelter, SMU	444.40	Lang Rao, Nevada	439.05
3-meter diving#†	Jenny Keim, Miami (FL)	576.90	Laura Wilkinson, Texas	567.55
Platform‡	Laura Wilkinson, Texas	664.75	Jenny Keim, Miami	635.10

*Meet record. †Scoring based on 15 dives. #Scoring based on 17 dives. ‡Scoring based on 12 dives.

Indoor Track and Field

MEN

	Champion	Mark	Runner-Up	Mark
60-meter dash	Leonard Scott, Tennessee	6.58	Marcus Brunson, Arizona St	6.62
60-meter hurdles	Terrance Trammell, S Carolina	7.52	Aubrey Herring, Indiana St	7.75
200-meter dash	Coby Miller, Auburn	20.68	Clement Chukwu, Eastern Michigan	20.73
400-meter dash	Ato Modibo, Clemson	46.11	Robert Wilson, Southern	46.34
800-meter run	Derrick Peterson, Missouri	1:45.88	Trinity Gray, Brown	1:46.05
Mile run	Bernard Lagat, Washington St	3:55.65	Bryan Berryhill, Colorado St	3:56.73
3,000-meter run	Bernard Lagat, Washington St	7:54.92	Mike Power, Arkansas	7:55.36
5,000-meter run	Brad Hauser, Stanford	13:52.79	Brent Houser, Stanford	13:53.44
High jump	Mark Boswell, Texas	7 ft 7 in	Kenny Evans, Arkansas	7 ft 6 in
Pole vault	Jacob Davis, Texas	19 ft 2 ¼ in*	Russ Buller, Louisiana St	18 ft 6 ½ in
Long jump	Maurice Wignall, George Mason	26 ft 1 ½ in	Dwight Phillips, Arizona St	25 ft 3 ½ in
Triple jump	Melvin Lister, Arkansas	55 ft ¾ in	Levar Anderson, Louisiana St	54 ft 3 ¼ in
Shot put	Brad Snyder, S Carolina	64 ft 11 ½ in	Jamie Beyer, Iowa St	64 ft 1 in
35-pound wt throw	Libor Charfreitag, SMU	72 ft 3 ½ in	Kevin Mannon, Wyoming	72 ft 2 ¼ in

WOMEN

	Champion		Runner-Up	
60-meter dash	Debbie Ferguson, Georgia	7.24	LaKeisha Backus, Texas	7.31
60-meter hurdles	Joyce Bates, Louisiana St	8.02	Andria King, Georgia Tech	8.03
200-meter dash	Nanceen Perry, Texas	23.10	Latasha Jenkins, Ball St	23.25
400-meter dash	Suziann Reid, Texas	51.68	Yulanda Nelson, Baylor	52.39
800-meter run	Hazel Clark, Florida	2:01.77*	Claudine Williams, Louisiana St	2:03.38
Mile run	Kate Vermeulen, W Virginia	4:39.07	Mary Jayne Harrelson, Appal'ian St	4:39.53
3,000-meter run	Carrie Tollefson, Villanova	9:15.05	Amy Yoder, Arkansas	9:17.83
5,000-meter run	Leigh Daniel, Texas Tech	16:01.11	Erica Palmer, Wisconsin	16:03.24
High jump	Erin Aldrich, Texas	6 ft 3 ½ in	Dora Gyorffy, Harvard	6 ft 2 ¼ in
Pole vault	Melissa Price, Fresno St	13 ft 11 ¼ in*	Paula Serrano, Cal Poly SLO	13 ft 3 ½ in
Long jump	Trecia Smith, Pittsburgh	21 ft 5 ¼ in	Nicole Gamble, N Carolina	20 ft 10 ¾ in
Triple jump	Nicole Gamble, N Carolina	46 ft 1 ¼ in	Trecia Smith, Pittsburgh	46 ft
Shot put	Marika Tuliniemi, SMU	54 ft 11 ¼ in	Aubrey Schmitt, Minnesota	54 ft 4 ¾ in
20-pound wt throw	Toyinda Smith, Purdue	68 ft 9 in	Florence Ezeh, SMU	68 ft 5 ¾ in

*Meet record.

Rifle

	Champion	Pts	Runner-Up	Pts
Smallbore	Kelly Mansfield, AK-Fairbanks	1185	Jonah Lindberg, AK-Fairbanks	1172
Air rifle	Kelly Mansfield, AK-Fairbanks	396	Emily Caruson, Norwich	395

Spring 1999
Golf
MEN

Champion	Score	Runner-Up	Score
Luke Donald, Northwestern	284	Ryuji Imada, Georgia	287
		Troy Kelly, Washington	

WOMEN

Champion	Score	Runner-Up	Score
Grace Park, Arizona St	212	Candy Hannemann, Duke	213

Outdoor Track and Field
MEN

	Champion	Mark	Runner-Up	Mark
100-meter dash	Leonard Myles-Mills, Brigham Young	9.98 w	John Caple, Florida	10.03 w
200-meter dash	John Caple, Florida	19.87 w	Coby Miller, Auburn	20.04 w
400-meter dash	Clement Chukwu, Eastern Mich	44.79	Derrick Brew, Louisiana St	45.04
800-meter run	Derrick Peterson, Missouri	1:46.97	Patrick Nduwimana, Arizona	1:47.22
1,500-meter run	Clyde Colenso, SMU	3:47.54	Seneca Lassiter, Arkansas	3:47.67
3,000-met. steeple	Matt Kerr, Arkansas	8:44.29	Carlos Suarez-Gonzales, UTEP	8:45.14
5,000-meter run	Bernard Lagat, Washington St	14:01.09	Brad Hauser, Stanford	14:01.82
10,000-meter run	Nathan Nutter, Stanford	29:11.96	Jason Balkman, Stanford	29:12.91
110-meter hurdles	Terrence Trammell, S Carolina	13.45 w	Dawayne Wallace, Tennessee	13.57 w
400-meter hurdles	Bayano Kamani, Baylor	48.68	Corey Murdock, Utah St	49.34
High jump	Mark Boswell, Texas	7 ft 7¾ in	Steffan Strand, Minnesota	7 ft 6½ in
Pole vault	Jacob Davis, Texas	18 ft 2¾ in	Toby Stevenson, Stanford	17 ft 10½ in
Long jump	Melvin Lister, Arkansas	26 ft 10 in	Frankie Young, Indiana St	26 ft 10 in w
Triple jump	Levar Anderson, Louisiana St	56 ft 2 in w	Demetrius Murray, Washington St	54 ft w
Shot put	Janus Robberts, SMU	65 ft 11½ in	Brad Snyder, S Carolina	64 ft 10½ in
Discus throw	Gabor Mate, Auburn	202 ft 1 in	Janus Robberts, SMU	198 ft 11 in
Hammer throw	Andras Haklits, NE Louisiana	243 ft.1 in	Norbert Horvath, Southern Cal	241 ft 11 in
Javelin throw	Matt Narhi, UTEP	261 ft 7 in	Esko Mikkola, Arizona	252 ft
Decathlon	Tom Pappas, Tennessee	4265 pts	Attila Zsivoczky, Kansas St	4187 pts

WOMEN

	Champion	Mark	Runner-Up	Mark
100-meter dash	Angela Williams, Southern Cal	11.04 w	Debbie Ferguson, Georgia	11.10 w
200-meter dash	LaTasha Jenkins, Ball St	22.29 w	Debbie Ferguson, Georgia	22.53 w
400-meter dash	Suziann Reid, Texas	51.08	Mikele Barber, S Carolina	51.66
800-meter run	Claudine Williams, Louisiana St	2:03.38	Liz Diaz, Texas	2:03.44
1,500-meter run	Mary Jayne Harrelson, Appal. St	4:21.06	Grazyna Penc, Southern Cal	4:22.61
3,000-meter run	Carrie Tollefson, Villanova	9:26.51	Kara Wheeler, Colorado	9:29.89
5,000-meter run	Carrie Tollefson, Villanova	16:09.51	Leigh Daniel, Texas Tech	16:12.72
10,000-meter run	Leigh Daniel, Texas Tech	34:01.63	Tara Rohatinsky, Brigham Young	34:04.02
100-meter hurdles	Yolanda McCray, Miami (FL)	12.85 w	Andria King, Georgia Tech	12.87 w
400-meter hurdles	Joanna Hayes, UCLA	55.16	Tanya Jarrett, Texas	55.80
High jump	Kajsa Bergqvist, SMU	6 ft 2¾ in	Dora Gyorffy, Harvard	6 ft 2¾ in
Pole vault	Paula Serrano, Cal Poly-SLO	13 ft 5¼ in*	Tracy O'Hara, UCLA	13 ft 1½ in
Long jump	Trecia Smith, Pittsburgh	21 ft 8¼ in	Angela Brown, George Mason	21 ft 2¾ in
Triple jump	Stacey Bowers, Baylor	45 ft 10 in	Trecia Smith, Pittsburgh	45 ft 7¾ in
Shot put	Seilala Sua, UCLA	57 ft 9 in	Leslie Vidmar, Kent St	55 ft ¼ in
Discus throw	Seilala Sua, UCLA	210 ft 10 in*	Shelly Borrman, Colorado St	191 ft 9 in
Hammer throw	Florence Ezeh, SMU	207 ft 2 in	Michelle Fournier, S Carolina	206 ft 5 in
Javelin throw	Vigdis Gudjonsdottir, Georgia	182 ft 3 in	Olivia McKoy, Louisiana Tech	177 ft 10 in
Heptathlon	Tracye Lawyer, Stanford	5855 pts	Christi Smith, Akron	5773 pts

*Meet record. w=wind-aided.

Tennis
MEN

	Champion	Score	Runner-Up
Singles	Jeff Morrison, Florida	7-6 (7-2), 2-6, 6-4	James Blake, Harvard
Doubles	Ryan Wolters & K.J. Hippensteel, Stanford	6-3, 6-2	Nenad Toroman & Garreth Williams, Tulsa

WOMEN

	Champion	Score	Runner-Up
Singles	Zuzana Lesenarova, UC-San Diego	4-6, 6-3, 7-6 (3)	Marissa Irvin, Stanford
Doubles	Amanda Augustus & Amy Jensen, California	4-6, 7-5, 6-1	Vanessa Castellano & Marissa Catlin, Georgia

FOR THE RECORD·Year by Year

CHAMPIONSHIP RESULTS

Baseball

DIVISION I

Year	Champion	Coach	Score	Runner-Up	Most Outstanding Player
1947	California*	Clint Evans	8–7	Yale	No award
1948	Southern Cal	Sam Barry	9–2	Yale	No award
1949	Texas*	Bibb Falk	10–3	Wake Forest	Charles Teague, Wake Forest, 2B
1950	Texas	Bibb Falk	3–0	Washington St	Ray VanCleef, Rutgers, CF
1951	Oklahoma*	Jack Baer	3–2	Tennnessee	Sidney Hatfield, Tennessee, P-1B
1952	Holy Cross	Jack Barry	8–4	Missouri	James O'Neill, Holy Cross, P
1953	Michigan	Ray Fisher	7–5	Texas	J.L. Smith, Texas, P
1954	Missouri	John (Hi) Simmons	4–1	Rollins	Tom Yewcic, Michigan St, C
1955	Wake Forest	Taylor Sanford	7–6	Western Michigan	Tom Borland, Oklahoma St, P
1956	Minnesota	Dick Siebert	12–1	Arizona	Jerry Thomas, Minnesota, P
1957	California*	George Wolfman	1–0	Penn St	Cal Emery, Penn St, P-1B
1958	Southern Cal	Rod Dedeaux	8–7†	Missouri	Bill Thom, Southern Cal, P
1959	Oklahoma St	Toby Greene	5–3	Arizona	Jim Dobson, Oklahoma St, 3B
1960	Minnesota	Dick Siebert	2–1‡	Southern Cal	John Erickson, Minnesota, 2B
1961	Southern Cal*	Rod Dedeaux	1–0	Oklahoma St	Littleton Fowler, Oklahoma St, P
1962	Michigan	Don Lund	5–4	Santa Clara	Bob Garibaldi, Santa Clara, P
1963	Southern Cal	Rod Dedeaux	5–2	Arizona	Bud Hollowell, Southern Cal, C
1964	Minnesota	Dick Siebert	5–1	Missouri	Joe Ferris, Maine, P
1965	Arizona St	Bobby Winkles	2–1#	Ohio St	Sal Bando, Arizona St, 3B
1966	Ohio St	Marty Karow	8–2	Oklahoma St	Steve Arlin, Ohio St, P
1967	Arizona St	Bobby Winkles	11–2	Houston	Ron Davini, Arizona St, C
1968	Southern Cal*	Rod Dedeaux	4–3	Southern Illinois	Bill Seinsoth, Southern Cal, 1B
1969	Arizona St	Bobby Winkles	10–1	Tulsa	John Dolinsek, Arizona St, LF
1970	Southern Cal	Rod Dedeaux	2–1	Florida St	Gene Ammann, Florida St, P
1971	Southern Cal	Rod Dedeaux	7–2	Southern Illinois	Jerry Tabb, Tulsa, 1B
1972	Southern Cal	Rod Dedeaux	1–0	Arizona St	Russ McQueen, Southern Cal, P
1973	Southern Cal*	Rod Dedeaux	4–3	Arizona St	Dave Winfield, Minnesota, P-OF
1974	Southern Cal	Rod Dedeaux	7–3	Miami (FL)	George Milke, Southern Cal, P
1975	Texas	Cliff Gustafson	5–1	S Carolina	Mickey Reichenbach, Texas, 1B
1976	Arizona	Jerry Kindall	7–1	Eastern Michigan	Steve Powers, Arizona, P-DH
1977	Arizona St	Jim Brock	2–1	S Carolina	Bob Horner, Arizona St, 3B
1978	Southern Cal*	Rod Dedeaux	10–3	Arizona St	Rod Boxberger, Southern Cal, P
1979	Cal St-Fullerton	Augie Garrido	2–1	Arkansas	Tony Hudson, Cal St-Fullerton, P
1980	Arizona	Jerry Kindall	5–3	Hawaii	Terry Francona, Arizona, LF
1981	Arizona St	Jim Brock	7–4	Oklahoma St	Stan Holmes, Arizona St, LF
1982	Miami (FL)*	Ron Fraser	9–3	Wichita St	Dan Smith, Miami (FL), P
1983	Texas*	Cliff Gustafson	4–3	Alabama	Calvin Schiraldi, Texas, P
1984	Cal St-Fullerton	Augie Garrido	3–1	Texas	John Fishel, Cal St-Fullerton, LF
1985	Miami (FL)	Ron Fraser	10–6	Texas	Greg Ellena, Miami (FL), DH
1986	Arizona	Jerry Kindall	10–2	Florida St	Mike Senne, Arizona, LF
1987	Stanford	Mark Marquess	9–5	Oklahoma St	Paul Carey, Stanford, RF
1988	Stanford	Mark Marquess	9–4	Arizona St	Lee Plemel, Stanford, P
1989	Wichita St	Gene Stephenson	5–3	Texas	Greg Brummett, Wichita St, P
1990	Georgia	Steve Webber	2–1	Oklahoma St	Mike Rebhan, Georgia, P
1991	Louisiana St	Skip Bertman	6–3	Wichita St	Gary Hymel, Louisiana St, C
1992	Pepperdine	Andy Lopez	3–2	Cal St-Fullerton	Phil Nevin, Cal St-Fullerton, 3B
1993	Louisiana St	Skip Bertman	8–0	Wichita St	Todd Walker, Louisiana St, 2B
1994	Oklahoma	Larry Cochell	13–5	Georgia Tech	Chip Glass, Oklahoma, CF
1995	Cal St-Fullerton*	Augie Garrido	11–5	Southern Cal	Mark Kotsay, Cal St-Fullerton, CF-P
1996	Louisiana St*	Skip Bertman	9–8	Miami (FL)	Pat Burrell, Miami (FL), 3B
1997	Louisiana St*	Skip Bertman	13–6	Alabama	Brandon Larson, Louisiana St, SS
1998	Southern Cal	Mike Gillespie	21–14	Arizona St	Wes Rachels, Southern Cal, 2B
1999	Miami (FL)	Jim Morris	6–5	Florida St	Marshall McDougall, FSU 3B/2B

*Undefeated teams in College World Series play. †12 innings. ‡10 innings. #15 innings.

DIVISION II

Year	Champion	Year	Champion	Year	Champion
1968	Chapman*	1973	UC-Irvine*	1978	Florida Southern
1969	Illinois St*	1974	UC-Irvine*	1979	Valdosta St
1970	Cal St-Northridge	1975	Florida Southern	1980	Cal Poly-Pomona*
1971	Florida Southern	1976	Cal Poly-Pomona	1981	Florida Southern*
1972	Florida Southern	1977	UC-Riverside	1982	UC-Riverside*

DIVISION II (Cont.)

Year	Champion	Year	Champion	Year	Champion
1983	Cal Poly-Pomona*	1989	Cal Poly-SLO	1995	Florida Southern*
1984	Cal St-Northridge	1990	Jacksonville St	1996	Kennesaw St*
1985	Florida Southern*	1991	Jacksonville St	1997	Cal St-Chico*
1986	Troy St	1992	Tampa*	1998	Tampa*
1987	Troy St*	1993	Tampa	1999	Cal St-Chico
1988	Florida Southern*	1994	Central Missouri St		

DIVISION III

Year	Champion	Year	Champion	Year	Champion
1976	Cal St-Stanislaus	1984	Ramapo	1992	William Paterson
1977	Cal St-Stanislaus	1985	WI-Oshkosh	1993	Montclair St
1978	Glassboro St	1986	Marietta	1994	WI-Oshkosh
1979	Glassboro St	1987	Montclair St	1995	La Verne
1980	Ithaca	1988	Ithaca	1996	William Paterson
1981	Marietta	1989	NC Wesleyan	1997	Southern Maine
1982	Eastern Connecticut St	1990	Eastern Connecticut St	1998	Eastern Connecticut St
1983	Marietta	1991	Southern Maine	1999	N Carolina Wesleyan

*Undefeated teams in final series.

Cross-Country

Men

DIVISION I

Year	Champion	Coach	Pts	Runner-Up	Pts	Individual Champion	Time
1938	Indiana	Earle Hayes	51	Notre Dame	61	Greg Rice, Notre Dame	20:12.9
1939	Michigan St	Lauren Brown	54	Wisconsin	57	Walter Mehl, Wisconsin	20:30.9
1940	Indiana	Earle Hayes	65	Eastern Michigan	68	Gilbert Dodds, Ashland	20:30.2
1941	Rhode Island	Fred Tootell	83	Penn St	110	Fred Wilt, Indiana	20:30.1
1942	Indiana	Earle Hayes	57			Oliver Hunter, Notre Dame	20:18.0
	Penn St	Charles Werner	57				
1943	No meet						
1944	Drake	Bill Easton	25	Notre Dame	64	Fred Feiler, Drake	21:04.2
1945	Drake	Bill Easton	50	Notre Dame	65	Fred Feiler, Drake	21:14.2
1946	Drake	Bill Easton	42	NYU	98	Quentin Brelsford, Ohio Wesleyan	20:22.9
1947	Penn St	Charles Werner	60	Syracuse	72	Jack Milne, N Carolina	20:41.1
1948	Michigan St	Karl Schlademan	41	Wisconsin	69	Robert Black, Rhode Island	19:52.3
1949	Michigan St	Karl Schlademan	59	Syracuse	81	Robert Black, Rhode Island	20:25.7
1950	Penn St	Charles Werner	53	Michigan St	55	Herb Semper Jr, Kansas	20:31.7
1951	Syracuse	Robert Grieve	80	Kansas	118	Herb Semper Jr, Kansas	20:09.5
1952	Michigan St	Karl Schlademan	65	Indiana	68	Charles Capozzoli, Georgetown	19:36.7
1953	Kansas	Bill Easton	70	Indiana	82	Wes Santee, Kansas	19:43.5
1954	Oklahoma St	Ralph Higgins	61	Syracuse	118	Allen Frame, Kansas	19:54.2
1955	Michigan St	Karl Schlademan	46	Kansas	68	Charles Jones, Iowa	19:57.4
1956	Michigan St	Karl Schlademan	28	Kansas	88	Walter McNew, Texas	19:55.7
1957	Notre Dame	Alex Wilson	121	Michigan St	127	Max Truex, Southern Cal	19:12.3
1958	Michigan St	Francis Dittrich	79	Western Michigan	104	Crawford Kennedy, Michigan State	20:07.1
1959	Michigan St	Francis Dittrich	44	Houston	120	Al Lawrence, Houston	20:35.7
1960	Houston	John Morriss	54	Michigan St	80	Al Lawrence, Houston	19:28.2
1961	Oregon St	Sam Bell	68	San Jose St	82	Dale Story, Oregon St	19:46.6
1962	San Jose St	Dean Miller	58	Villanova	69	Tom O'Hara, Loyola (IL)	19:20.3
1963	San Jose St	Dean Miller	53	Oregon	68	Victor Zwolak, Villanova	19:35.0
1964	W Michigan	George Dales	86	Oregon	116	Elmore Banton, Ohio	20:07.5
1965	W Michigan	George Dales	81	Northwestern	114	John Lawson, Kansas	29:24.0
1966	Villanova	James Elliott	79	Kansas St	155	Gerry Lindgren, Washington St	29:01.4
1967	Villanova	James Elliott	91	Air Force	96	Gerry Lindgren, Washington St	30:45.6
1968	Villanova	James Elliott	78	Stanford	100	Michael Ryan, Air Force	29:16.8
1969	UTEP	Wayne Vandenburg	74	Villanova	88	Gerry Lindgren, Wash St	28:59.2
1970	Villanova	James Elliott	85	Oregon	86	Steve Prefontaine, Oregon	28:00.2
1971	Oregon	Bill Dellinger	83	Washington St	122	Steve Prefontaine, Oregon	29:14.0

Men (Cont.)

DIVISION I (Cont.)

Year	Champion	Coach	Pts	Runner-Up	Pts	Individual Champion	Time
1972	Tennessee	Stan Huntsman	134	E Tennessee St	148	Neil Cusack, E Tenn St	28:23.0
1973	Oregon	Bill Dellinger	89	UTEP	157	Steve Prefontaine, Oregon	28:14.0
1974	Oregon	Bill Dellinger	77	Western Kentucky	110	Nick Rose, W Kentucky	29:22.0
1975	UTEP	Ted Banks	88	Washington St	92	Craig Virgin, Illinois	28:23.3
1976	UTEP	Ted Banks	62	Oregon	117	Henry Rono, Washington St	28:06.6
1977	Oregon	Bill Dellinger	100	UTEP	105	Henry Rono, Washington St	28:33.5
1978	UTEP	Ted Banks	56	Oregon	72	Alberto Salazar, Oregon	29:29.7
1979	UTEP	Ted Banks	86	Oregon	93	Henry Rono, Washington St	28:19.6
1980	UTEP	Ted Banks	58	Arkansas	152	Suleiman Nyambui, UTEP	29:04.0
1981	UTEP	Ted Banks	17	Providence	109	Mathews Motshwarateu, UTEP	28:45.6
1982	Wisconsin	Dan McClimon	59	Providence	138	Mark Scrutton, Colorado	30:12.6
1983	Vacated			Wisconsin	164	Zakarie Barie, UTEP	29:20.0
1984	Arkansas	John McDonnell	101	Arizona	111	Ed Eyestone, Brigham Young	29:28.8
1985	Wisconsin	Martin Smith	67	Arkansas	104	Timothy Hacker, Wisconsin	29:17.88
1986	Arkansas	John McDonnell	69	Dartmouth	141	Aaron Ramirez, Arizona	30:27.53
1987	Arkansas	John McDonnell	87	Dartmouth	119	Joe Falcon, Arkansas	29:14.97
1988	Wisconsin	Martin Smith	105	Northern Arizona	160	Robert Kennedy, Indiana	29:20.0
1989	Iowa St	Bill Bergan	54	Oregon	72	John Nuttall, Iowa St	29:30.55
1990	Arkansas	John McDonnell	68	Iowa St	96	Jonah Koech, Iowa St	29:05.0
1991	Arkansas	John McDonnell	52	Iowa St	114	Sean Dollman, Western Ky	30:17.1
1992	Arkansas	John McDonnell	46	Wisconsin	87	Bob Kennedy, Indiana	30:15.3
1993	Arkansas	John McDonnell	31	Brigham Young	153	Josephat Kapkory, Wash St	29:32.4
1994	Iowa St	Bill Bergan	65	Colorado	88	Martin Keino, Arizona	30:08.7
1995	Arkansas	John McDonnell	100	Northern Arizona	142	Godfrey Siamusiye, Arkansas	30:09
1996	Stanford	Vin Lananna	46	Arkansas	74	Godfrey Siamusiye, Arkansas	29:49
1997	Stanford	Vin Lananna	53	Arkansas	56	Mebrahtom Keflezighi, UCLA	28:54
1998	Arkansas	John McDonnell	97	Stanford	114	Adam Goucher, Colorado	29:26

DIVISION II

Year	Champion	Year	Champion	Year	Champion
1958	Northern Illinois	1972	N Dakota St	1986	Edinboro
1959	S Dakota St	1973	S Dakota St	1987	Edinboro
1960	Central St (OH)	1974	SW Missouri St	1988	Edinboro/ Mankato St
1961	Southern Illinois	1975	UC-Irvine	1989	S Dakota St
1962	Central St (OH)	1976	UC-Irvine	1990	Edinboro
1963	Emporia St	1977	Eastern Illinois	1991	MA-Lowell
1964	Kentucky St	1978	Cal Poly-SLO	1992	Adams St
1965	San Diego St	1979	Cal Poly-SLO	1993	Adams St
1966	San Diego St	1980	Humboldt St	1994	Adams St
1967	San Diego St	1981	Millersville	1995	Western St
1968	Eastern Illinois	1982	Eastern Washington	1996	S Dakota St
1969	Eastern Illinois	1983	Cal Poly-Pomona	1997	S Dakota
1970	Eastern Michigan	1984	SE Missouri St	1998	Adams St
1971	Cal St-Fullerton	1985	S Dakota St		

DIVISION III

Year	Champion	Year	Champion	Year	Champion
1973	Ashland	1982	N Central	1991	Rochester
1974	Mount Union	1983	Brandeis	1992	N Central
1975	North Central	1984	St. Thomas (MN)	1993	N Central
1976	North Central	1985	Luther	1994	Williams
1977	Occidental	1986	St. Thomas (MN)	1995	Williams
1978	N Central	1987	N Central	1996	WI-La Crosse
1979	N Central	1988	WI-Oshkosh	1997	N Central
1980	Carleton	1989	WI-Oshkosh	1998	N Central
1981	N Central	1990	WI-Oshkosh		

Women

DIVISION I

Year	Champion	Coach	Pts	Runner-Up	Pts	Individual Champion	Time
1981	Virginia	John Vasvary	36	Oregon	83	Betty Springs, N Carolina St	16:19.0
1982	Virginia	Martin Smith	48	Stanford	91	Lesley Welch, Virginia	16:39.7
1983	Oregon	Tom Heinonen	95	Stanford	98	Betty Springs, N Carolina St	16:30.7
1984	Wisconsin	Peter Tegen	63	Stanford	89	Cathy Branta, Wisconsin	16:15.6
1985	Wisconsin	Peter Tegen	58	Iowa St	98	Suzie Tuffey, N Carolina St	16:22.5

Women (Cont.)
DIVISION I (Cont.)

Year	Champion	Coach	Pts	Runner-Up	Pts	Individual Champion	Time
1986	Texas	Terry Crawford	62	Wisconsin	64	Angela Chalmers, N Arizona	16:55.49
1987	Oregon	Tom Heinonen	97	N Carolina St	99	Kimberly Betz, Indiana	16:10.85
1988	Kentucky	Don Weber	75	Oregon	128	Michelle Dekkers, Indiana	16:30.0
1989	Villanova	Marty Stern	99	Kentucky	168	Vicki Huber, Villanova	15:59.86
1990	Villanova	Marty Stern	82	Providence	172	Sonia O'Sullivan, Villanova	16:06.0
1991	Villanova	Marty Stern	85	Arkansas	168	Sonia O'Sullivan, Villanova	16:30.3
1992	Villanova	Marty Stern	123	Arkansas	130	Carole Zajac, Villanova	17:01.9
1993	Villanova	Marty Stern	66	Arkansas	71	Carole Zajac, Villanova	16:40.3
1994	Villanova	John Marshall	75	Michigan	108	Jennifer Rhines, Villanova	16:31.2
1995	Providence	Ray Treacy	88	Colorado	123	Kathy Butler, Wisconsin	16:51
1996	Stanford	Beth Alford-Sullivan	101	Villanova	106	Amy Skieresz, Arizona	17:04
1997	BYU	Patrick Shane	100	Stanford	102	Carrie Tollefson, Villanova	16:58
1998	Villanova	Marcus O'Sullivan	106	BYU	110	Katie McGregor, Michigan	16:47.21

DIVISION II

Year	Champion	Year	Champion	Year	Champion
1981	S Dakota St	1987	Cal Poly-SLO	1993	Adams St
1982	Cal Poly-SLO	1988	Cal Poly-SLO	1994	Adams St
1983	Cal Poly-SLO	1989	Cal Poly-SLO	1995	Adams St
1984	Cal Poly-SLO	1990	Cal Poly-SLO	1996	Adams St
1985	Cal Poly-SLO	1991	Cal Poly-SLO	1997	Adams St
1986	Cal Poly-SLO	1992	Adams St	1998	Adams St

DIVISION III

Year	Champion	Year	Champion	Year	Champion
1981	Central (IA)	1987	St. Thomas (MN)	1993	Cortland St
1982	St. Thomas (MN)		WI-Oshkosh	1994	Cortland St
1983	WI-La Crosse	1988	WI-Oshkosh	1995	Cortland St
1984	St. Thomas (MN)	1989	Cortland St	1996	WI-Oshkosh
1985	Franklin & Marshall	1990	Cortland St	1997	Cortland St
1986	St. Thomas (MN)	1991	WI-Oshkosh	1998	Calvin
		1992	Cortland St		

Fencing

Men's and Women's Combined
TEAM CHAMPIONS

Year	Champion	Coach	Pts	Runner-Up	Pts
1990	Penn St	Emmanuil Kaidanov	36	Columbia-Barnard	35
1991	Penn St	Emmanuil Kaidanov	4700	Columbia-Barnard	4200
1992	Columbia-Barnard	George Kolombatovich Aladar Kogler	4150	Penn St	3646
1993	Columbia-Barnard	George Kolumbatovich Aladar Kogler	4525	Penn St	4500
1994	Notre Dame	Michael DeCicco	4350	Penn St	4075
1995	Penn St	Emmanuil Kaidanov	440	St. John's (NY)	413
1996	Penn St	Emmanuil Kaidanov	1500	Notre Dame	1190
1997	Penn St	Emmanuil Kaidanov	1530	Notre Dame	1470
1998	Penn St	Emmanuil Kaidanov	149	Notre Dame	147
1999	Penn St	Emmanuil Kaidanov	171	Notre Dame	139

Men
TEAM CHAMPIONS

Year	Champion	Coach	Pts	Runner-Up	Pts
1941	Northwestern	Henry Zettleman	28½	Illinois	27
1942	Ohio St	Frank Riebel	34	St. John's (NY)	33½
1943–46	No tournament				
1947	NYU	Martinez Castello	72	Chicago	50½
1948	CCNY	James Montague	30	Navy	28
1949	Army/ Rutgers	S. Velarde/D. Cetrulo	63		
1950	Navy	Joseph Fiems	67½	NYU/ Rutgers	66½
1951	Columbia	Servando Velarde	69	Pennsylvania	64
1952	Columbia	Servando Velarde	71	NYU	69
1953	Pennsylvania	Lajos Csiszar	94	Navy	86

Men (Cont.)
TEAM CHAMPIONS (Cont.)

Year	Champion	Coach	Pts	Runner-Up	Pts
1954	Columbia	Irving DeKoff	61		
	NYU	Hugo Castello	61		
1955	Columbia	Irving DeKoff	62	Cornell	57
1956	Illinois	Maxwell Garret	90	Columbia	88
1957	NYU	Hugo Castello	65	Columbia	64
1958	Illinois	Maxwell Garret	47	Columbia	43
1959	Navy	Andre Deladrier	72	NYU	65
1960	NYU	Hugo Castello	65	Navy	57
1961	NYU	Hugo Castello	79	Princeton	68
1962	Navy	Andre Deladrier	76	NYU	74
1963	Columbia	Irving DeKoff	55	Navy	50
1964	Princeton	Stan Sieja	81	NYU	79
1965	Columbia	Irving DeKoff	76	NYU	74
1966	NYU	Hugo Castello	5–0	Army	5–2
1967	NYU	Hugo Castello	72	Pennsylvania	64
1968	Columbia	Louis Bankuti	92	NYU	87
1969	Pennsylvania	Lajos Csiszar	54	Harvard	43
1970	NYU	Hugo Castello	71	Columbia	63
1971	NYU/ Columbia	Hugo Castello/ Louis Bankuti	68		
1972	Detroit	Richard Perry	73	NYU	70
1973	NYU	Hugo Castello	76	Pennsylvania	71
1974	NYU	Hugo Castello	92	Wayne St (MI)	87
1975	Wayne St (MI)	Istvan Danosi	89	Cornell	83
1976	NYU	Herbert Cohen	79	Wayne St (MI)	77
1977	Notre Dame	Michael DeCicco	114*	NYU	114
1978	Notre Dame	Michael DeCicco	121	Pennsylvania	110
1979	Wayne St (MI)	Istvan Danosi	119	Notre Dame	108
1980	Wayne St (MI)	Istvan Danosi	111	Pennsylvania/ MIT	106
1981	Pennsylvania	Dave Micahnik	113	Wayne St (MI)	111
1982	Wayne St (MI)	Istvan Danosi	85	Clemson	77
1983	Wayne St (MI)	Aladar Kogler	86	Notre Dame	80
1984	Wayne St (MI)	Gil Pezza	69	Penn St	50
1985	Wayne St (MI)	Gil Pezza	141	Notre Dame	140
1986	Notre Dame	Michael DeCicco	151	Columbia	141
1987	Columbia	George Kolombatovich	86	Pennsylvania	78
1988	Columbia	George Kolombatovich Aladar Kogler	90	Notre Dame	83
1989	Columbia	George Kolombatovich Aladar Kogler	88	Penn St	85

*Tie broken by a fence-off. Note: Beginning in 1990, men's and women's combined teams competed for the national championship.

INDIVIDUAL CHAMPIONS

	Foil	Sabre	Épée
1941	Edward McNamara, Northwestern	William Meyer, Dartmouth	G.H. Boland, Illinois
1942	Byron Kreiger, Wayne St (MI)	Andre Deladrier, St. John's (NY)	Ben Burtt, Ohio St
1943–46	No tournament		
1947	Abraham Balk, NYU	Oscar Parsons, Temple	Abraham Balk, NYU
1948	Albert Axelrod, CCNY	James Day, Navy	William Bryan, Navy
1949	Ralph Tedeschi, Rutgers	Alex Treves, Rutgers	Richard C. Bowman, Army
1950	Robert Nielsen, Columbia	Alex Treves, Rutgers	Thomas Stuart, Navy
1951	Robert Nielsen, Columbia	Chamberless Johnston, Princeton	Daniel Chafetz, Columbia
1952	Harold Goldsmith, CCNY	Frank Zimolzak, Navy	James Wallner, NYU
1953	Ed Nober, Brooklyn	Robert Parmacek, Pennsylvania	Jack Tori, Pennsylvania
1954	Robert Goldman, Pennsylvania	Steve Sobel, Columbia	Henry Kolowrat, Princeton
1955	Herman Velasco, Illinois	Barry Pariser, Columbia	Donald Tadrawski, Notre Dame
1956	Ralph DeMarco, Columbia	Gerald Kaufman, Columbia	Kinmont Hoitsma, Princeton
1957	Bruce Davis, Wayne St (MI)	Bernie Balaban, NYU	James Margolis, Columbia
1958	Bruce Davis, Wayne St (MI)	Art Schankin, Illinois	Roland Wommack, Navy
1959	Joe Paletta, Navy	Al Morales, Navy	Roland Wommack, Navy
1960	Gene Glazer, NYU	Mike Desaro, NYU	Gil Eisner, NYU
1961	Herbert Cohen, NYU	Israel Colon, NYU	Jerry Halpern, NYU
1962	Herbert Cohen, NYU	Barton Nisonson, Columbia	Thane Hawkins, Navy

Men (Cont.)
INDIVIDUAL CHAMPIONS (Cont.)

	Foil	Sabre	Épée
1963	Jay Lustig, Columbia	Bela Szentivanyi, Wayne St (MI)	Larry Crum, Navy
1964	Bill Hicks, Princeton	Craig Bell, Illinois	Paul Pesthy, Rutgers
1965	Joe Nalven, Columbia	Howard Goodman, NYU	Paul Pesthy, Rutgers
1966	Al Davis, NYU	Paul Apostol, NYU	Bernhardt Hermann, Iowa
1967	Mike Gaylor, NYU	Todd Makler, Pennsylvania	George Masin, NYU
1968	Gerard Esponda, San Francisco	Todd Makler, Pennsylvania	Don Sieja, Cornell
1969	Anthony Kestler, Columbia	Norman Braslow, Penn	James Wetzler, Pennsylvania
1970	Walter Krause, NYU	Bruce Soriano, Columbia	John Nadas, Case Reserve
1971	Tyrone Simmons, Detroit	Bruce Soriano, Columbia	George Szunyogh, NYU
1972	Tyrone Simmons, Detroit	Bruce Soriano, Columbia	Ernesto Fernandez, Penn
1973	Brooke Makler, Pennsylvania	Peter Westbrock, NYU	Risto Hurme, NYU
1974	Greg Benko, Wayne St (MI)	Steve Danosi, Wayne St (MI)	Risto Hurme, NYU
1975	Greg Benko, Wayne St (MI)	Yuri Rabinovich, Wayne St (MI)	Risto Hurme, NYU
1976	Greg Benko, Wayne St (MI)	Brian Smith, Columbia	Randy Eggleton, Pennsylvania
1977	Pat Gerard, Notre Dame	Mike Sullivan, Notre Dame	Hans Wieselgren, NYU
1978	Ernest Simon, Wayne St (MI)	Mike Sullivan, Notre Dame	Bjorne Vaggo, Notre Dame
1979	Andrew Bonk, Notre Dame	Yuri Rabinovich, Wayne St (MI)	Carlos Songini, Cleveland St
1980	Ernest Simon, Wayne St (MI)	Paul Friedberg, Pennsylvania	Gil Pezza, Wayne St (MI)
1981	Ernest Simon, Wayne St (MI)	Paul Friedberg, Pennsylvania	Gil Pezza, Wayne St (MI)
1982	Alexander Flom, George Mason	Neil Hick, Wayne St (MI)	Peter Schifrin, San Jose St
1983	Demetrios Valsamis, NYU	John Friedberg, N Carolina	Ola Harstrom, Notre Dame
1984	Charles Higgs-Coulthard, Notre Dame	Michael Lofton, NYU	Ettore Bianchi, Wayne St (MI)
1985	Stephan Chauvel, Wayne St (MI)	Michael Lofton, NYU	Ettore Bianchi, Wayne St (MI)
1986	Adam Feldman, Penn St	Michael Lofton, NYU	Chris O'Loughlin, Pennsylvania
1987	William Mindel, Columbia	Michael Lofton, NYU	James O'Neill, Harvard
1988	Marc Kent, Columbia	Robert Cottingham, Columbia	Jon Normile, Columbia
1989	Edward Mufel, Penn St	Peter Cox, Penn St	Jon Normile, Columbia
1990	Nick Bravin, Stanford	David Mandell, Columbia	Jubba Beshin, Notre Dame
1991	Ben Atkins, Columbia	Vitali Nazlimov, Penn St	Marc Oshima, Columbia
1992	Nick Bravin, Stanford	Tom Strzalkowski, Penn St	Harald Bauder, Wayne St
1993	Nick Bravin, Stanford	Tom Strzalkowski, Penn St	Ben Atkins, Columbia
1994	Kwame van Leeuwen, Harvard	Tom Strzalkowski, Penn St	Harald Winkman, Princeton
1995	Sean McClain, Stanford	Paul Palestis, NYU	Mike Gattner, Lawrence
1996	Thorstein Becker, Wayne St (MI)	Maxim Pekarev, Princeton	Jeremy Kahn, Duke
1997	Cliff Bayer, Pennsylvania	Keith Smart, St. John's (NY)	Alden Clarke, Stanford
1998	Ayo Griffin, Yale	Luke LaValle, Notre Dame	George Hentea, St. John's (NY)
1999	Felix Reichling, Stanford	Keeth Smart, St. John's (NY)	Alex Roytblat St. John's (NY)

Women
TEAM CHAMPIONS

Year	Champion	Coach	Rec	Runner-Up	Rec
1982	Wayne St (MI)	Istvan Danosi	7–0	San Jose St	6–1
1983	Penn St	Beth Alphin	5–0	Wayne St (MI)	3–2
1984	Yale	Henry Harutunian	3–0	Penn St	2–1
1985	Yale	Henry Harutunian	3–0	Pennsylvania	2–1
1986	Pennsylvania	David Micahnik	3–0	Notre Dame	2–1
1987	Notre Dame	Yves Auriol	3–0	Temple	2–1
1988	Wayne St (MI)	Gil Pezza	3–0	Notre Dame	2–1
1989	Wayne St (MI)	Gil Pezza	3–0	Columbia-Barnard	2–1

Note: Beginning in 1990, men's and women's combined teams competed for the national championship.

INDIVIDUAL CHAMPIONS

	Foil
1982	Joy Ellingson, San Jose St
1983	Jana Angelakis, Penn St
1984	Mary Jane O'Neill, Pennsylvania
1985	Caitlin Bilodeaux, Columbia-Barnard
1986	Molly Sullivan, Notre Dame
1987	Caitlin Bilodeaux, Columbia-Barnard
1988	Molly Sullivan, Notre Dame
1989	Yasemin Topcu, Wayne St (MI)
1990	Tzu Moy, Columbia-Barnard
1991	Heidi Piper, Notre Dame
1992	Olga Cheryak, Penn St
1993	Olga Kalinovskaya, Penn St
1994	Olga Kalinovskaya, Penn St

	Foil (Cont.)
1995	Olga Kalinovskaya, Penn St
1996	Olga Kalinovskaya, Penn St
1997	Yelena Kalkina, Ohio St
1998	Felicia Zimmermann, Stanford
1999	Monique DeBruin, Stanford

	Épée
1995	Tina Loven, St. John's (NY)
1996	Nicole Dygert, St. John's (NY)
1997	Magda Krol, Notre Dame
1998	Charlotte Walker, Penn St
1999	Felicia Zimmermann, Stanford

Field Hockey

DIVISION I

Year	Champion	Coach	Score	Runner-Up
1981	Connecticut	Diane Wright	4–1	Massachusetts
1982	Old Dominion	Beth Anders	3–2	Connecticut
1983	Old Dominion	Beth Anders	3–1 (3 OT)	Connecticut
1984	Old Dominion	Beth Anders	5–1	Iowa
1985	Connecticut	Diane Wright	3–2	Old Dominion
1986	Iowa	Judith Davidson	2–1 (2 OT)	New Hampshire
1987	Maryland	Sue Tyler	2–1 (OT)	N Carolina
1988	Old Dominion	Beth Anders	2–1	Iowa
1989	N Carolina	Karen Shelton	2–1 (3 OT)*	Old Dominion
1990	Old Dominion	Beth Anders	5–0	N Carolina
1991	Old Dominion	Beth Anders	2–0	N Carolina
1992	Old Dominion	Beth Anders	4–0	Iowa
1993	Maryland	Missy Meharg	2–1 (3 OT)*	N Carolina
1994	James Madison	Christy Morgan	2–1 (3 OT)*	N Carolina
1995	N Carolina	Karen Shelton-Scroggs	5–1	Maryland
1996	N Carolina	Karen Shelton-Scroggs	3–0	Princeton
1997	N Carolina	Karen Shelton	3–2	Old Dominion
1998	Old Dominion	Beth Anders	3–2	Princeton

*Penalty strokes.

DIVISION II (DISCONTINUED, THEN RENEWED)

Year	Champion	Coach	Score	Runner-Up
1981	Pfeiffer	Ellen Briggs	5–3	Bentley
1982	Lock Haven	Sharon E. Taylor	4–1	Bloomsburg
1983	Bloomsburg	Jan Hutchinson	1–0	Lock Haven
1992	Lock Haven	Sharon E. Taylor	3–1	Bloomsburg
1993	Bloomsburg	Jan Hutchinson	2–1 (2 OT)	Lock Haven
1994	Lock Haven	Sharon E. Taylor	2–1	Bloomsburg
1995	Lock Haven	Sharon E. Taylor	1–0	Bloomsburg
1996	Bloomsburg	Jan Hutchinson	1–0	Lock Haven
1997	Bloomsburg	Jan Hutchinson	2–0	Kutztown
1998	Bloomsburg	Jan Hutchinson	4–3 (OT)	Lock Haven

DIVISION III

Year	Champion	Year	Champion	Year	Champion
1981	Trenton St	1988	Trenton St	1995	Trenton St
1982	Ithaca	1989	Lock Haven	1996	College of New Jersey*
1983	Trenton St	1990	Trenton St	1997	William Smith
1984	Bloomsburg	1991	Trenton St	1998	Middelbury
1985	Trenton St	1992	William Smith		*Formerly Trenton St.
1986	Salisbury St	1993	Cortland St		
1987	Bloomsburg	1994	Cortland St		

Golf

Men

DIVISION I

Results, 1897–1938

Year	Champion	Site	Individual Champion
1897	Yale	Ardsley Casino	Louis Bayard Jr, Princeton
1898	Harvard (spring)		John Reid Jr, Yale
1898	Yale (fall)		James Curtis, Harvard
1899	Harvard		Percy Pyne, Princeton
1900	No tournament		
1901	Harvard	Atlantic City	H. Lindsley, Harvard
1902	Yale (spring)	Garden City	Charles Hitchcock Jr, Yale
1902	Harvard (fall)	Morris County	Chandler Egan, Harvard
1903	Harvard	Garden City	F.O. Reinhart, Princeton
1904	Harvard	Myopia	A.L. White, Harvard
1905	Yale	Garden City	Robert Abbott, Yale
1906	Yale	Garden City	W.E. Clow Jr, Yale
1907	Yale	Nassau	Ellis Knowles, Yale
1908	Yale	Brae Burn	H.H. Wilder, Harvard
1909	Yale	Apawamis	Albert Seckel, Princeton
1910	Yale	Essex County	Robert Hunter, Yale
1911	Yale	Baltusrol	George Stanley, Yale
1912	Yale	Ekwanok	F.C. Davison, Harvard
1913	Yale	Huntingdon Valley	Nathaniel Wheeler, Yale

Men (Cont.)

DIVISION I (Cont.)
Results, 1897–1938 (Cont.)

Year	Champion	Site	Individual Champion
1914	Princeton	Garden City	Edward Allis, Harvard
1915	Yale	Greenwich	Francis Blossom, Yale
1916	Princeton	Oakmont	J.W. Hubbell, Harvard
1917–18	No tournament		
1919	Princeton	Merion	A.L. Walker Jr, Columbia
1920	Princeton	Nassau	Jess Sweetster, Yale
1921	Dartmouth	Greenwich	Simpson Dean, Princeton
1922	Princeton	Garden City	Pollack Boyd, Dartmouth
1923	Princeton	Siwanoy	Dexter Cummings, Yale
1924	Yale	Greenwich	Dexter Cummings, Yale
1925	Yale	Montclair	Fred Lamprecht, Tulane
1926	Yale	Merion	Fred Lamprecht, Tulane
1927	Princeton	Garden City	Watts Gunn, Georgia Tech
1928	Princeton	Apawamis	Maurice McCarthy, Georgetown
1929	Princeton	Hollywood	Tom Aycock, Yale
1930	Princeton	Oakmont	G.T. Dunlap Jr, Princeton
1931	Yale	Olympia Fields	G.T. Dunlap Jr, Princeton
1932	Yale	Hot Springs	J.W. Fischer, Michigan
1933	Yale	Buffalo	Walter Emery, Oklahoma
1934	Michigan	Cleveland	Charles Yates, Georgia Tech
1935	Michigan	Congressional	Ed White, Texas
1936	Yale	North Shore	Charles Kocsis, Michigan
1937	Princeton	Oakmont	Fred Haas Jr, Louisiana St
1938	Stanford	Louisville	John Burke, Georgetown

Results, 1939–1999

Year	Champion	Coach	Score	Runner-Up	Score	Host or Site	Individual Champion
1939	Stanford	Eddie Twiggs	612	Northwestern	614	Wakonda	Vincent D'Antoni, Tulane
				Princeton	614		
1940	Princeton	Walter Bourne	601			Ekwanok	Dixon Brooke, Virginia
	Louisiana St	Mike Donahue	601				
1941	Stanford	Eddie Twiggs	580	Louisiana St	599	Ohio St	Earl Stewart, Louisiana St
1942	Louisiana St	Mike Donahue	590			Notre Dame	Frank Tatum Jr, Stanford
	Stanford	Eddie Twiggs	590				
1943	Yale	William Neale Jr	614	Michigan	618	Olympia Fields	Wallace Ulrich, Carleton
1944	Notre Dame	George Holderith	311	Minnesota	312	Inverness	Louis Lick, Minnesota
1945	Ohio St	Robert Kepler	602	Northwestern	621	Ohio St	John Lorms, Ohio St
1946	Stanford	Eddie Twiggs	619	Michigan	624	Princeton	George Hamer, Georgia
1947	Louisiana St	T. P. Heard	606	Duke	614	Michigan	Dave Barclay, Michigan
1948	San Jose St	Wilbur Hubbard	579	Louisiana St	588	Stanford	Bob Harris, San Jose St
1949	N Texas	Fred Cobb	590	Purdue	600	Iowa St	Harvie Ward, N Carolina
				Texas	600		
1950	N Texas	Fred Cobb	573	Purdue	577	New Mexico	Fred Wampler, Purdue
1951	N Texas	Fred Cobb	588	Ohio St	589	Ohio St	Tom Nieporte, Ohio St
1952	N Texas	Fred Cobb	587	Michigan	593	Purdue	Jim Vickers, Oklahoma
1953	Stanford	Charles Finger	578	N Carolina	580	Broadmoor	Earl Moeller, Oklahoma St
1954	SMU	Graham Ross	572	N Texas	573	Houston, Rice	Hillman Robbins, Memphis St
1955	Louisiana St	Mike Barbato	574	N Texas	583	Tennessee	Joe Campbell, Purdue
1956	Houston	Dave Williams	601	N Texas	602	Ohio St	Rick Jones, Ohio St
				Purdue	602		

Men (Cont.)

DIVISION I (Cont.)

Results, 1939–1999 (Cont.)

Year	Champion	Coach	Score	Runner-Up	Score	Host or Site	Individual Champion
1957	Houston	Dave Williams	602	Stanford	603	Broadmoor	Rex Baxter Jr, Houston
1958	Houston	Dave Williams	570	Oklahoma St	582	Williams	Phil Rodgers, Houston
1959	Houston	Dave Williams	561	Purdue	571	Oregon	Dick Crawford, Houston
1960	Houston	Dave Williams	603	Purdue	607	Broadmoor	Dick Crawford, Houston
				Oklahoma St	607		
1961	Purdue	Sam Voinoff	584	Arizona St	595	Lafayette	Jack Nicklaus, Ohio St
1962	Houston	Dave Williams	588	Oklahoma St	598	Duke	Kermit Zarley, Houston
1963	Oklahoma St	Labron Harris	581	Houston	582	Wichita St	R. H. Sikes, Ark
1964	Houston	Dave Williams	580	Oklahoma St	587	Broadmoor	Terry Small, San Jose St
1965	Houston	Dave Williams	577	Cal St-LA	587	Tennessee	Marty Fleckman, Houston
1966	Houston	Dave Williams	582	San Jose St	586	Stanford	Bob Murphy, Florida
1967	Houston	Dave Williams	585	Florida	588	Shawnee, PA	Hale Irwin, Colorado
1968	Florida	Buster Bishop	1154	Houston	1156	New Mexico St	Grier Jones, Oklahoma St
1969	Houston	Dave Williams	1223	Wake Forest	1232	Broadmoor	Bob Clark, Cal St-LA
1970	Houston	Dave Williams	1172	Wake Forest	1182	Ohio St	John Mahaffey, Houston
1971	Texas	George Hannon	1144	Houston	1151	Arizona	Ben Crenshaw, Texas
1972	Texas	George Hannon	1146	Houston	1159	Cape Coral	Ben Crenshaw, Texas
							Tom Kite, Texas
1973	Florida	Buster Bishop	1149	Oklahoma St	1159	Oklahoma St	Ben Crenshaw, Texas
1974	Wake Forest	Jess Haddock	1158	Florida	1160	San Diego St	Curtis Strange, Wake Forest
1975	Wake Forest	Jess Haddock	1156	Oklahoma St	1189	Ohio St	Jay Haas, Wake Forest
1976	Oklahoma St	Mike Holder	1166	Brigham Young	1173	New Mexico	Scott Simpson, Southern Cal
1977	Houston	Dave Williams	1197	Oklahoma St	1205	Colgate	Scott Simpson, Southern Cal
1978	Oklahoma St	Mike Holder	1140	Georgia	1157	Oregon	David Edwards, Oklahoma St
1979	Ohio St	James Brown	1189	Oklahoma St	1191	Wake Forest	Gary Hallberg, Wake Forest
1980	Oklahoma St	Mike Holder	1173	Brigham Young	1177	Ohio St	Jay Don Blake, Utah St
1981	Brigham Young	Karl Tucker	1161	Oral Roberts	1163	Stanford	Ron Commans, Southern Cal
1982	Houston	Dave Williams	1141	Oklahoma St	1151	Pinehurst	Billy Ray Brown, Houston
1983	Oklahoma St	Mike Holder	1161	Texas	1168	Fresno St	Jim Carter, Arizona St
1984	Houston	Dave Williams	1145	Oklahoma St	1146	Houston	John Inman, N Carolina
1985	Houston	Dave Williams	1172	Oklahoma St	1175	Florida	Clark Burroughs, Ohio St
1986	Wake Forest	Jess Haddock	1156	Oklahoma St	1160	Wake Forest	Scott Verplank, Oklahoma St
1987	Oklahoma St	Mike Holder	1160	Wake Forest	1176	Ohio St	Brian Watts, Oklahoma St
1988	UCLA	Eddie Merrins	1176	UTEP	1179	Southern Cal	E.J. Pfister, Oklahoma St
				Oklahoma	1179		
				Oklahoma St	1179		
1989	Oklahoma	Gregg Grost	1139	Texas	1158	Oklahoma Oklahoma St	Phil Mickelson, Arizona St

Men (Cont.)

DIVISION I (Cont.)

Results, 1939–1999 (Cont.)

Year	Champion	Coach	Score	Runner-Up	Score	Host or Site	Individual Champion
1990	....Arizona St	Steve Loy	1155	Florida	1157	Florida	Phil Mickelson, Arizona St
1991	....Oklahoma St	Mike Holder	1161	N Carolina	1168	San Jose St	Warren Schutte, UNLV
1992	....Arizona	Rick LaRose	1129	Arizona St	1136	New Mexico	Phil Mickelson, Arizona St
1993	....Florida	Buddy Alexander	1145	Georgia Tech	1146	Kentucky	Todd Demsey, Arizona St
1994	....Stanford	Wally Goodwin	1129	Texas	1133	McKinney, TX	Justin Leonard, Texas
1995	....Oklahoma St*	Mike Holder	1156	Stanford	1156	Ohio St	Chip Spratlin, Auburn
1996	....Arizona St	Randy Lein	1186	UNLV	1189	TN-Chattanooga	Tiger Woods, Stanford
1997	....Pepperdine	John Geiberger	1148	Wake Forest	1151	Evanston, Ill.	Charles Warren, Clemson
1998	....UNLV	Dwaine Knight	1118	Clemson	1121	Albuquerque	James McLean, Minnesota
1999	....Georgia	Chris Haack	1180	Oklahoma St	1183	Chaska, MN	Donald Luke, Northwestern

*Won sudden death playoff. Notes: Match play, 1897–1964; par-70 tournaments held in 1969, 1973 and 1989; par-71 tournaments held in 1968, 1981 and 1988; all other championships par-72 tournaments. Scores are based on 4 rounds instead of 2 after 1967.

DIVISION II

Year	Champion	Year	Champion	Year	Champion
1963	.........SW Missouri St	1976	.........Troy St	1989	.........Columbus St
1964	.........Southern Illinois	1977	.........Troy St	1990	.........Florida Southern
1965	.........Middle Tennessee St	1978	.........Columbus St	1991	.........Florida Southern
1966	.........Cal St-Chico	1979	.........UC-Davis	1992	.........Columbus St
1967	.........Lamar	1980	.........Columbus St	1993	.........Abilene Christian
1968	.........Lamar	1981	.........Florida Southern	1994	.........Columbus St
1969	.........Cal St-Northridge	1982	.........Florida Southern	1995	.........Florida Southern
1970	.........Rollins	1983	.........SW Texas St	1996	.........Florida Southern
1971	.........New Orleans	1984	.........Troy St	1997	.........Columbus St
1972	.........New Orleans	1985	.........Florida Southern	1998	.........Florida Southern
1973	.........Cal St-Northridge	1986	.........Florida Southern	1999	.........Florida Southern
1974	.........Cal St-Northridge	1987	.........Tampa		
1975	.........UC-Irvine	1988	.........Tampa		

Note: Par-71 tournaments held in 1967,1970, 1976-78, 1985 and 1988; par-70 tournament held in 1996; and all other championships par-72 tournaments.

DIVISION III

Year	Champion	Year	Champion	Year	Champion
1975	.........Wooster	1984	.........Cal St-Stanislaus	1993	.........UC-San Diego
1976	.........Cal St-Stanislaus	1985	.........Cal St-Stanislaus	1994	.........Methodist (NC)
1977	.........Cal St-Stanislaus	1986	.........Cal St-Stanislaus	1995	.........Methodist (NC)
1978	.........Cal St-Stanislaus	1987	.........Cal St-Stanislaus	1996	.........Methodist (NC)
1979	.........Cal St-Stanislaus	1988	.........Cal St-Stanislaus	1997	.........Methodist (NC)
1980	.........Cal St-Stanislaus	1989	.........Cal St-Stanislaus	1998	.........Methodist (NC)
1981	.........Cal St-Stanislaus	1990	.........Methodist (NC)	1999	.........Methodist (NC)
1982	.........Rampano	1991	.........Methodist (NC)		
1983	.........Allegheny	1992	.........Methodist (NC)		

Note: All championships par-72 except for 1986 and 1988, which were par-71; fourth round of 1975 championships canceled as a result of bad weather, first round of 1988 championships canceled as a result of rain.

Women

DIVISION I

Year	Champion	Coach	Score	Runner-Up	Score	Individual Champion
1982	.....Tulsa	Dale McNamara	1191	Texas Christian	1227	Kathy Baker, Tulsa
1983	.....Texas Christian	Fred Warren	1193	Tulsa	1196	Penny Hammel, Miami (FL)
1984	.....Miami (FL)	Lela Cannon	1214	Arizona St	1221	Cindy Schreyer, Georgia
1985	.....Florida	Mimi Ryan	1218	Tulsa	1233	Danielle Ammaccapane, Arizona St

Women (Cont.)

DIVISION I (Cont.)

Year	Champion	Coach	Score	Runner-Up	Score	Individual Champion
1986	Florida	Mimi Ryan	1180	Miami (FL)	1188	Page Dunlap, Florida
1987	San Jose St	Mark Gale	1187	Furman	1188	Caroline Keggi, New Mexico
1988	Tulsa	Dale McNamara	1175	Georgia	1182	Melissa McNamara, Tulsa
				Arizona	1182	
1989	San Jose St	Mark Gale	1208	Tulsa	1209	Pat Hurst, San Jose St
1990	Arizona St	Linda Vollstedt	1206	UCLA	1222	Susan Slaughter, Arizona
1991	UCLA*	Jackie Steinmann	1197	San Jose St	1197	Annika Sorenstam, Arizona
1992	San Jose St	Mark Gale	1171	Arizona	1175	Vicki Goetze, Georgia
1993	Arizona St	Linda Vollstedt	1187	Texas	1189	Charlotta Sorenstam, Texas
1994	Arizona St	Linda Vollstedt	1189	Southern Cal	1205	Emilee Klein, Arizona St
1995	Arizona St	Linda Vollstedt	1155	San Jose St	1181	Kristel Mourgue d'Algue, Arizona St
1996	Arizona*	Rick LaRose	1240	San Jose St	1240	Marisa Baena, Arizona
1997	Arizona St	Linda Vollstedt	1178	San Jose St	1180	Heather Bowie, Texas
1998	Arizona St	Linda Vollstedt	1155	Florida	1173	Jennifer Rosales, USC
1999	Duke	Dan Brooks	895	Arizona St/Georgia	903	Grace Park, Arizona St

*Won sudden death playoff. Note: Par-74 tournaments held in 1983 and 1988; par-72 tournament held in 1990; all other championships par-73 tournaments.

DIVISIONS II AND III

Year	Champion	Year	Champion
1996	Methodist (NC)	1998	Methodist (NC)
1997	Lynn	1999	Methodist (NC)

Gymnastics

Men

TEAM CHAMPIONS

Year	Champion	Coach	Pts	Runner-Up	Pts
1938	Chicago	Dan Hoffer	22	Illinois	18
1939	Illinois	Hartley Price	21	Army	17
1940	Illinois	Hartley Price	20	Navy	17
1941	Illinois	Hartley Price	68.5	Minnesota	52.5
1942	Illinois	Hartley Price	39	Penn St	30
1943–47	No tournament				
1948	Penn St	Gene Wettstone	55	Temple	34.5
1949	Temple	Max Younger	28	Minnesota	18
1950	Illinois	Charley Pond	26	Temple	25
1951	Florida St	Hartley Price	26	Illinois	23.5
				Southern Cal	23.5
1952	Florida St	Hartley Price	89.5	Southern Cal	75
1953	Penn St	Gene Wettstone	91.5	Illinois	68
1954	Penn St	Gene Wettstone	137	Illinois	68
1955	Illinois	Charley Pond	82	Penn St	69
1956	Illinois	Charley Pond	123.5	Penn St	67.5
1957	Penn St	Gene Wettstone	88.5	Illinois	80
1958	Michigan St	George Szypula	79		
	Illinois	Charley Pond	79		
1959	Penn St	Gene Wettstone	152	Illinois	87.5
1960	Penn St	Gene Wettstone	112.5	Southern Cal	65.5
1961	Penn St	Gene Wettstone	88.5	Southern Illinois	80.5
1962	Southern Cal	Jack Beckner	95.5	Southern Illinois	75
1963	Michigan	Newton Loken	129	Southern Illinois	73
1964	Southern Illinois	Bill Meade	84.5	Southern Cal	69.5
1965	Penn St	Gene Wettstone	68.5	Washington	51.5
1966	Southern Illinois	Bill Meade	187.200	California	185.100
1967	Southern Illinois	Bill Meade	189.550	Michigan	187.400
1968	California	Hal Frey	188.250	Southern Illinois	188.150
1969	Iowa	Mike Jacobson	161.175	Penn St	160.450
	Michigan*	Newton Loken		Colorado St	
1970	Michigan	Newton Loken	164.150	Iowa St	164.050
				New Mexico St	
1971	Iowa St	Ed Gagnier	319.075	Southern Illinois	316.650

*Trampoline.

Men *(Cont.)*

TEAM CHAMPIONS *(Cont.)*

Year	Champion	Coach	Pts	Runner-Up	Pts
1972	Southern Illinois	Bill Meade	315.925	Iowa St	312.325
1973	Iowa St	Ed Gagnier	325.150	Penn St	323.025
1974	Iowa St	Ed Gagnier	326.100	Arizona St	322.050
1975	California	Hal Frey	437.325	Louisiana St	433.700
1976	Penn St	Gene Wettstone	432.075	Louisiana St	425.125
1977	Indiana St	Roger Counsil	434.475		
	Oklahoma	Paul Ziert	434.475		
1978	Oklahoma	Paul Ziert	439.350	Arizona St	437.075
1979	Nebraska	Francis Allen	448.275	Oklahoma	446.625
1980	Nebraska	Francis Allen	563.300	Iowa St	557.650
1981	Nebraska	Francis Allen	284.600	Oklahoma	281.950
1982	Nebraska	Francis Allen	285.500	UCLA	281.050
1983	Nebraska	Francis Allen	287.800	UCLA	283.900
1984	UCLA	Art Shurlock	287.300	Penn St	281.250
1985	Ohio St	Michael Willson	285.350	Nebraska	284.550
1986	Arizona St	Don Robinson	283.900	Nebraska	283.600
1987	UCLA	Art Shurlock	285.300	Nebraska	284.750
1988	Nebraska	Francis Allen	288.150	Illinois	287.150
1989	Illinois	Yoshi Hayasaki	283.400	Nebraska	282.300
1990	Nebraska	Francis Allen	287.400	Minnesota	287.300
1991	Oklahoma	Greg Buwick	288.025	Penn St	285.500
1992	Stanford	Sadao Hamada	289.575	Nebraska	288.950
1993	Stanford	Sadao Hamada	276.500	Nebraska	275.500
1994	Nebraska	Francis Allen	288.250	Stanford	285.925
1995	Stanford	Sadao Hamada	232.400	Nebraska	231.525
1996	Ohio St	Peter Kormann	232.150	California	231.775
1997	California	Barry Weiner	233.825	Oklahoma	232.725
1998	Caliornia	Barry Weiner	231.200	Iowa	229.675
1999	Michigan	Kurt Golder	232.550	Ohio St	230.850

INDIVIDUAL CHAMPIONS

ALL-AROUND

1938.....Joe Giallombardo, Illinois
1939.....Joe Giallombardo, Illinois
1940.....Joe Giallombardo, Illinois
Paul Fina, Illinois
1941.....Courtney Shanken, Chicago
1942.....Newt Loken, Minnesota
1948.....Ray Sorenson, Penn St
1949.....Joe Kotys, Kent
1950.....Joe Kotys, Kent
1951.....Bill Roetzheim, Florida St
1952.....Jack Beckner, Southern Cal
1953.....Jean Cronstedt, Penn St
1954.....Jean Cronstedt, Penn St
1955.....Karl Schwenzfeier, Penn St
1956.....Don Tonry, Illinois
1957.....Armando Vega, Penn St
1958.....Abie Grossfeld, Illinois
1959.....Armando Vega, Penn St
1960.....Jay Werner, Penn St
1961.....Gregor Weiss, Penn St
1962.....Robert Lynn, Southern Cal
1963.....Gil Larose, Michigan
1964.....Ron Barak, Southern Cal
1965.....Mike Jacobson, Penn St
1966.....Steve Cohen, Penn St
1967.....Steve Cohen, Penn St
1968.....Makoto Sakamoto, USC
1969.....Mauno Nissinen, Wash
1970.....Yoshi Hayasaki, Wash
1971.....Yoshi Hayasaki, Wash

1972.....Steve Hug, Stanford
1973.....Steve Hug, Stanford
Marshall Avener, Penn St
1974.....Steve Hug, Stanford
1975.....Wayne Young, BYU
1976.....Peter Kormann, Southern Conn St
1977.....Kurt Thomas, Indiana St
1978.....Bart Conner, Oklahoma
1979.....Kurt Thomas, Indiana St
1980.....Jim Hartung, Nebraska
1981.....Jim Hartung, Nebraska
1982.....Peter Vidmar, UCLA
1983.....Peter Vidmar, UCLA
1984.....Mitch Gaylord, UCLA
1985.....Wes Suter, Nebraska
1986.....Jon Louis, Stanford
1987.....Tom Schlesinger, Nebraska
1988.....Vacated†
1989.....Patrick Kirsey, Nebraska
1990.....Mike Racanelli, Ohio St
1991.....John Roethlisberger, Minn
1992.....John Roethlisberger, Minn
1993.....John Roethlisberger, Minn
1994.....Dennis Harrison, Nebraska
1995.....Richard Grace, Nebraska
1996.....Blaine Wilson, Ohio St
1997.....Blaine Wilson, Ohio St
1998.....Travis Romagnoli, Illinois
1999......Justin Hardabura, Nebraska

HORIZONTAL BAR

1938.....Bob Sears, Army
1939.....Adam Walters, Temple
1940.....Norm Boardman, Temple
1941.....Newt Loken, Minnesota
1942.....Norm Boardman, Temple
1948.....Joe Calvetti, Illinois
1949.....Bob Stout, Temple
1950.....Joe Kotys, Kent
1951.....Bill Roetzheim, Florida St
1952.....Charles Simms, USC
1953.....Hal Lewis, Navy
1954.....Jean Cronstedt, Penn St
1955.....Carlton Rintz, Michigan St
1956.....Ronnie Amster, Florida St
1957.....Abie Grossfeld, Illinois
1958.....Abie Grossfeld, Illinois
1959.....Stanley Tarshis, Mich St
1960.....Stanley Tarshis, Mich St
1961.....Bruno Klaus, Southern Ill
1962.....Robert Lynn, USC
1963.....Gil Larose, Michigan
1964.....Ron Barak, USC
1965.....Jim Curzi, Michigan St
Mike Jacobsen, Penn St
1966.....Rusty Rock, Cal St-Northridge
1967.....Rich Grigsby, Cal St-Northridge
1968.....Makoto Sakamoto, USC
1969.....Bob Manna, New Mexico

Men (Cont.)
INDIVIDUAL CHAMPIONS (Cont.)

HORIZONTAL BAR (Cont.)
1970.....Yoshi Hayasaki, Wash
1971.....Brent Simmons, Iowa St
1972.....Tom Lindner, Souhern Ill
1973.....Jon Aitken, New Mexico
1974.....Rick Banley, Indiana St
1975.....Rich Larsen, Iowa St
1976.....Tom Beach, California
1977.....John Hart, UCLA
1978.....Mel Cooley, Washington
1979.....Kurt Thomas, Indiana St
1980.....Philip Cahoy, Nebraska
1981.....Philip Cahoy, Nebraska
1982.....Peter Vidmar, UCLA
1983.....Scott Johnson, Nebraska
1984.....Charles Lakes, Illinois
1985.....Dan Hayden, Arizona St
          Wes Suter, Nebraska
1986.....Dan Hayden, Arizona St
1987.....David Moriel, UCLA
1988.....Vacated†
1989.....Vacated†
1990.....Chris Waller, UCLA
1991.....Luis Lopez, New Mexico
1992.....Jair Lynch, Stanford
1993.....Steve McCain, UCLA
1994.....Jim Foody, UCLA
1995.....Rick Kieffer, Nebraska
1996.....Carl Imhauser, Temple
1997.....Marshall Nelson,Nebraska
1998.....Todd Bishop, Oklahoma
1999.....Todd Bishop, Oklahoma

PARALLEL BARS
1938.....Erwin Beyer, Chicago
1939.....Bob Sears, Army
1940.....Bob Hanning, Minnesota
1941.....Caton Cobb, Illinois
1942.....Hal Zimmerman, Penn St
1948.....Ray Sorenson, Penn St
1949.....Joe Kotys, Kent
          Mel Stout, Michigan St
1950.....Joe Kotys, Kent
1951.....Jack Beckner, USC
1952.....Jack Beckner, USC
1953.....Jean Cronstedt, Penn St
1954.....Jean Cronstedt, Penn St
1955.....Carlton Rintz, Michigan St
1956.....Armando Vega, Penn St
1957.....Armando Vega, Penn St
1958.....Tad Muzyczko, Mich St
1959.....Armando Vega, Penn St
1960.....Robert Lynn, Southern Cal
1961.....Fred Tijerina, Southern Ill
          Jeff Cardinalli, Springfield
1962.....Robert Lynn, Southern Cal
1963.....Arno Lascari, Michigan
1964.....Ron Barak, Southern Cal
1965.....Jim Curzi, Michigan St
1966.....Jim Curzi, Michigan St
1967.....Makoto Sakamoto, USC
1968.....Makoto Sakamoto, USC
1969.....Ron Rapper, Michigan
1970.....Ron Rapper, Michigan
1971.....Brent Simmons, Iowa St
          Tom Dunn, Penn St

1972.....Dennis Mazur, Iowa St
1973.....Steve Hug, Stanford
1974.....Steve Hug, Stanford
1975.....Yoichi Tomita, Long
          Beach St
1976.....Gene Whelan, Penn St
1977.....Kurt Thomas, Indiana St
1978.....John Corritore, Michigan
1979.....Kurt Thomas, Indiana St
1980.....Philip Cahoy, Nebraska
1981.....Philip Cahoy, Nebraska
          Peter Vidmar, UCLA
          Jim Hartung, Nebraska
1982.....Jim Hartung, Nebraska
1983.....Scott Johnson, Nebraska
1984.....Tim Daggett, UCLA
1985.....Dan Hayden, Arizona St
          Noah Riskin, Ohio St
          Seth Riskin, Ohio St
1986.....Dan Hayden, Arizona St
1987.....Kevin Davis, Nebraska
          Tom Schlesinger, Nebraska
1988.....Kevin Davis, Nebraska
1989.....Vacated†
1990.....Patrick Kirksey, Nebraska
1991.....Scott Keswick, UCLA
          John Roethlisberger, Minn
1992.....Dom Minicucci, Temple
1993.....Jair Lynch, Stanford
1994.....Richard Grace, Nebraska
1995.....Richard Grace, Nebraska
1996.....Jamie Ellis, Stanford
          Blaine Wilson, Ohio St
1997.....Marshall Nelson, Nebraska
1998.....Marshall Nelson, Nebraska
1999.....Justin Toman, Michigan

VAULT
1938.....Erwin Beyer, Chicago
1939.....Marv Forman, Illinois
1940.....Earl Shanken, Chicago
1941.....Earl Shanken, Chicago
1942.....Earl Shanken, Chicago
1948.....Jim Peterson, Minnesota
1962.....Bruno Klaus, Southern Ill
1963.....Gil Larose, Michigan
1964......Sidney Oglesby, Syracuse
1965.....Dan Millman, California
1966.....Frank Schmitz, S Illinois
1967.....Paul Mayer, S Illinois
1968.....Bruce Colter, Cal St-Los
          Angeles
1969.....Dan Bowles, California
          Jack McCarthy, Illinois
1970.....Doug Boger, Arizona
1971.....Pat Mahoney, Cal St-
          Northridge
1972.....Gary Morava, Southern Ill
1973.....John Crosby, S Conn St
1974.....Greg Goodhue, Oklahoma
1975.....Tom Beach, California
1976.....Sam Shaw, Cal St-
          Fullerton
1977.....Steve Wejmar, Wash
1978.....Ron Galimore, Louisiana St
1979.....Leslie Moore, Oklahoma
1980.....Ron Galimore, Iowa St

1981.....Ron Galimore, Iowa St
1982.....Randall Wickstrom, Cal
          Steve Elliott, Nebraska
1983.....Chris Riegel, Nebraska
          Mark Oates, Oklahoma
1984.....Chris Riegel, Nebraska
1985.....Derrick Cornelius,
          Cortland St
1986.....Chad Fox, New Mexico
1987.....Chad Fox, New Mexico
1988.....Chad Fox, New Mexico
1989.....Chad Fox, New Mexico
1990.....Brad Hayashi, UCLA
1991.....Adam Carton, Penn St
1992.....Jason Hebert, Syracuse
1993.....Steve Wiegel, N Mexico
1994.....Steve McCain, UCLA
1995.....Ian Bachrach, Stanford
1996.....Jay Thornton, Iowa
1997.....Blaine Wilson, Ohio St
1998.....Travis Romagnoli, Illinois
1999.....Guard Young, BYU

POMMEL HORSE
1938.....Erwin Beyer, Chicago
1939.....Erwin Beyer, Chicago
1940.....Harry Koehnemann, Illinois
1941.....Caton Cobb, Illinois
1942.....Caton Cobb, Illinois
1948.....Steve Greene, Penn St
1949.....Joe Berenato, Temple
1950.....Gene Rabbitt, Syracuse
1951.....Joe Kotys, Kent
1952.....Frank Bare, Illinois
1953.....Carlton Rintz, Michigan St
1954.....Robert Lawrence, Penn St
1955.....Carlton Rintz, Michigan St
1956.....James Brown, Cal St-
          Los Angeles
1957.....John Davis, Illinois
1958.....Bill Buck, Iowa
1959.....Art Shurlock, California
1960.....James Fairchild, California
1961.....James Fairchild, California
1962.....Mike Aufrecht, Illinois
1963.....Russ Mills, Yale
1964.....Russ Mills, Yale
1965.....Bob Elsinger, Springfield
1966.....Gary Hoskins, Cal St-
          Los Angeles
1967.....Keith McCanless, Iowa
1968.....Jack Ryan, Colorado
1969.....Keith McCanless, Iowa
1970.....Russ Hoffman, Iowa St
          John Russo, Wisconsin
1971.....Russ Hoffman, Iowa St
1972.....Russ Hoffman, Iowa St
1973.....Ed Slezak, Indiana St
1974.....Ted Marcy, Stanford
1975.....Ted Marcy, Stanford
1976.....Ted Marcy, Stanford
1977.....Chuck Walter, Northern Ill
1978.....Mike Burke, Northern Ill
1979.....Mike Burke, Northern Ill
1980.....David Stoldt, Illinois
1981.....Mark Bergman, California
          Steve Jennings, New Mexico

Men *(Cont.)*
INDIVIDUAL CHAMPIONS *(Cont.)*

POMMEL HORSE *(Cont.)*

1982 .....Peter Vidmar, UCLA
     Steve Jennings, New Mexico
1983 .....Doug Kieso, Northern Ill
1984 .....Tim Daggett, UCLA
1985 .....Tony Pineda, UCLA
1986 .....Curtis Holdsworth, UCLA
1987 .....Li Xiao Ping, Cal St-
     Fullerton
1988 .....Vacated†
     Mark Sohn, Penn St
1989 .....Mark Sohn, Penn St
     Chris Waller, UCLA
1990 .....Mark Sohn, Penn St
1991 .....Mark Sohn, Penn St
1992 .....Che Bowers, Nebraska
1993 .....John Roethlisberger, Minn
1994 .....Jason Bertram, California
1995 .....Drew Durbin, Ohio St
1996 .....Drew Durbin, Ohio St
1997 .....Drew Durbin, Ohio St
1998 .....Josh Birckelbaw, California
1999 ......Brandon Stefaniak, Penn St

FLOOR EXERCISE

1941 .....Lou Fina, Illinois
1953 .....Bob Sullivan, Illinois
1954 .....Jean Cronstedt, Penn St
1955 .....Don Faber, UCLA
1956 .....Jamile Ashmore, Florida St
1957 .....Norman Marks, Cal St-
     Los Angeles
1958 .....Abie Grossfeld, Illinois
1959 .....Don Tonry, Illinois
1960 .....Ray Hadley, Illinois
1961 .....Robert Lynn, Southern Cal
1962 .....Robert Lynn, Southern Cal
1963 .....Tom Seward, Penn St
     Mike Henderson, Michigan
1964 .....Rusty Mitchell, S Illinois
1965 .....Frank Schmitz, S Illinois

1966 .....Frank Schmitz, S Illinois
1967 .....Dave Jacobs, Michigan
1968 .....Toby Towson, Michigan St
1969 .....Toby Towson, Michigan St
1970 .....Tom Proulx, Colorado St
1971 .....Stormy Eaton, New Mexico
1972 .....Odessa Lovin, Oklahoma
1973 .....Odessa Lovin, Oklahoma
1974 .....Doug Fitzjarrell, Iowa St
1975 .....Kent Brown, Arizona St
1976 .....Bob Robbins, Colorado St
1977 .....Ron Galimore, Louisiana St
1978 .....Curt Austin, Iowa St
1979 .....Mike Wilson, Oklahoma
     Bart Conner, Oklahoma
1980 .....Steve Elliott, Nebraska
1981 .....James Yuhashi, Oregon
1982 .....Steve Elliott, Nebraska
1983 .....Scott Johnson, Nebraska
     David Branch, Arizona St
     Donnie Hinton, Arizona St
1984 .....Kevin Ekburg, Northern Ill
1985 .....Wes Suter, Nebraska
1986 .....Jerry Burrell, Arizona St
     Brian Ginsberg, UCLA
1987 .....Chad Fox, New Mexico
1988 .....Chris Wyatt, Temple
1989 .....Jody Newman, Arizona St
1990 .....Mike Racanelli, Ohio St
1991 .....Brad Hayashi, UCLA
1992 .....Brian Winkler, Michigan
1993 .....Richard Grace, Nebraska
1994 .....Mark Booth, Stanford
1995 .....Jay Thornton, Iowa
1996 .....Ian Bachrach, Stanford
1997 .....Jeremy Killen, Oklahoma
1998 .....Darin Gerlach, Temple
1999 ....Jason Hardabura, Nebraska

RINGS

1959 .....Armando Vega, Penn St
1960 .....Sam Garcia, Southern Cal

1961 .....Fred Orlofsky, Southern Ill
1962 .....Dale Cooper, Michigan St
1963 .....Dale Cooper, Michigan St
1964 .....Chris Evans, Arizona St
1965 .....Glenn Gailis, Iowa
1966 .....Ed Gunny, Michigan St
1967 .....Josh Robison, California
1968 .....Pat Arnold, Arizona
1969 .....Paul Vexler, Penn St
     Ward Maythaler, Iowa St
1970 .....Dave Seal, Indiana St
1971 .....Charles Ropiequet, S Illinois
1972 .....Dave Seal, Indiana St
1973 .....Bob Mahorney, Indiana St
1974 .....Keith Heaver, Iowa St
1975 .....Keith Heaver, Iowa St
1976 .....Doug Wood, Iowa St
1977 .....Doug Wood, Iowa St
1978 .....Scott McEldowney, Oregon
1979 .....Kirk Mango, Northern Ill
1980 .....Jim Hartung, Nebraska
1981 .....Jim Hartung, Nebraska
1982 .....Jim Hartung, Nebraska
1983 .....Alex Schwartz, UCLA
1984 .....Tim Daggett, UCLA
1985 .....Mark Diab, Iowa St
1986 .....Mark Diab, Iowa St
1987 .....Paul O'Neill, Hou. Baptist
1988 .....Paul O'Neill, New Mexico
1989 .....Vacated†
     Paul O'Neill, New Mexico
1990 .....Wayne Cowden, Penn St
1991 .....Adam Carton, Penn St
1992 .....Scott Keswick, UCLA
1993 .....Chris LaMorte, N Mexico
1994 .....Chris LaMorte, N Mexico
1995 .....Dave Frank, Temple
1996 .....Scott McCall, Will. & Mary
     Blaine Wilson, Ohio St
1997 .....Blaine Wilson, Ohio St
1998 .....Dan Fink, Oklahoma
1999 .....Cortney Bramwell, BYU

† Championships won by Miguel Rubio (All Around, 1988; Horizontal Bar, 1988-89) and Alfonso Rodriguez (Pommel Horse, 1988; Rings, 1989; Parallel Bars, 1989) were vacated by action of the NCAA Committee on Infractions.

A Purpose Pitch

As he warmed up to work the first inning of an April 23, 1999, game, Wichita State pitcher Ben Christensen threw a ball at Evansville leadoff man Anthony Molina while Molina was still about 30 feet from the plate. The ball hit Molina in his left eye, fracturing the socket in three places and leaving his baseball future in doubt.

Christensen, a junior fireballer for the nationally ranked Shockers, had a chilling explanation. He said he thought Molina was trying to time his pitches. So Christensen threw at him—a tactic he says pitching coach Brent Kemnitz taught the team's hurlers.

Molina, who wasn't looking at Christensen when the ball was thrown, was rushed to Wichita's Wesley Medical Center, where he received 23 stitches to close a one-inch gash. He filed assault charges against the pitcher. On April 30 the Missouri Valley Con-

ference suspended Christensen and Kemnitz for the rest of the season. Christensen, who had a 21–1 career record and was expected to be a first- or second-round pick in the '99 major league draft, was also suspended from postseason play.

But his future remains brighter than Molina's. After four days Molina had regained some vision. "But there are still a lot of ifs," he said. If five different eyedrops and a daily pill fail to lower the pressure in his eye, he will need laser surgery. The vision in his left eye was reduced from 20/10 before the beaning to 20/160.

One echo of the incident might survive as the dumb quote of the year. "Nobody intentionally hit someone else," said Wichita State coach Gene Stephenson, who went on to say of losing his star pitcher, "Hey we're the ones who got hurt out of the deal."

Men (Cont.)
DIVISION II (DISCONTINUED)

Year	Champion	Coach	Pts	Runner-Up	Pts
1968	Cal St-Northridge	Bill Vincent	179.400	Springfield	178.050
1969	Cal St-Northridge	Bill Vincent	151.800	Southern Connecticut St	145.075
1970	Northwestern Louisiana	Armando Vega	160.250	Southern Connecticut St	159.300
1971	Cal St-Fullerton	Dick Wolfe	158.150	Springfield	156.987
1972	Cal St-Fullerton	Dick Wolfe	160.550	Southern Connecticut St	153.050
1973	Southern Connecticut St	Abe Grossfeld	160.750	Cal St-Northridge	158.700
1974	Cal St-Fullerton	Dick Wolfe	309.800	Southern Connecticut St	309.400
1975	Southern Connecticut St	Abe Grossfeld	411.650	IL-Chicago	398.800
1976	Southern Connecticut St	Abe Grossfeld	419.200	IL-Chicago	388.850
1977	Springfield	Frank Wolcott	395.950	Cal St-Northridge	381.250
1978	IL-Chicago	C. Johnson/A. Gentile	406.850	Cal St-Northridge	400.400
1979	IL-Chicago	Clarence Johnson	418.550	WI-Oshkosh	385.650
1980	WI-Oshkosh	Ken Allen	260.550	Cal St-Chico	256.050
1981	WI-Oshkosh	Ken Allen	209.500	Springfield	201.550
1982	WI-Oshkosh	Ken Allen	216.050	E Stroudsburg	211.200
1983	East Stroudsburg	Bruno Klaus	258.650	WI-Oshkosh	257.850
1984	East Stroudsburg	Bruno Klaus	270.800	Cortland St	246.350

Women
TEAM CHAMPIONS

Year	Champion	Coach	Pts	Runner-Up	Pts
1982	Utah	Greg Marsden	148.60	Cal St-Fullerton	144.10
1983	Utah	Greg Marsden	184.65	Arizona St	183.30
1984	Utah	Greg Marsden	186.05	UCLA	185.55
1985	Utah	Greg Marsden	188.35	Arizona St	186.60
1986	Utah	Greg Marsden	186.95	Arizona St	186.70
1987	Georgia	Suzanne Yoculan	187.90	Utah	187.55
1988	Alabama	Sarah Patterson	190.05	Utah	189.50
1989	Georgia	Suzanne Yoculan	192.65	UCLA	192.60
1990	Utah	Greg Marsden	194.900	Alabama	194.575
1991	Alabama	Sarah Patterson	195.125	Utah	194.375
1992	Utah	Greg Marsden	195.650	Georgia	194.600
1993	Georgia	Suzanne Yoculan	198.000	Alabama	196.825
1994	Utah	Greg Marsden	196.400	Alabama	196.350
1995	Utah	Greg Marsden	196.650	Alabama	196.425
				Michigan	196.425
1996	Alabama	Sarah Patterson	198.025	UCLA	197.475
1997	UCLA	Valorie Kondos	197.150	Arizona St	196.850
1998	Georgia	Suzanne Yoculan	197.725	Florida	196.350
1999	Georgia	Suzanne Yoculan	196.85	Michigan	196.55

INDIVIDUAL CHAMPIONS

ALL-AROUND
1982 .....Sue Stednitz, Utah
1983 .....Megan McCunniff, Utah
1984 ......Megan McCunniff-Marsden, Utah
1985 ......Penney Hauschild, Alabama
1986 ......Penney Hauschild, Alabama
Jackie Brummer, Arizona St
1987 .....Kelly Garrison-Steves, Oklahoma
1988 .....Kelly Garrison-Steves, Oklahoma
1989 .....Corrinne Wright, Georgia
1990 .....Dee Dee Foster, Alabama
1991 .....Hope Spivey, Georgia
1992 .....Missy Marlowe, Utah
1993 .....Jenny Hansen, Kentucky
1994 .....Jenny Hansen, Kentucky
1995 .....Jenny Hansen, Kentucky
1996 .....Meredith Willard, Alabama
1997 .....Kim Arnold, Georgia
1998 .....Kim Arnold, Georgia

1999 .....Theresa Kulikowski, Utah

VAULT
19782...Elaine Alfano, Utah
1983 .....Elaine Alfano, Utah
1984 .....Megan Marsden, Utah
1985 .....Elaine Alfano, Utah
1986 .....Kim Neal, Arizona St
Pam Loree, Penn St
1987 .....Yumi Mordre, Washington
1988 .....Jill Andrews, UCLA
1989 .....Kim Hamilton, UCLA
1990 .....Michele Bryant, Nebraska
1991 .....Anna Basaldva, Arizona
1992 .....Tammy Marshall, Mass.
Heather Stepp, Georgia
Kristein Kenoyer, Utah
1993 .....Heather Stepp, Georgia
1994 .....Jenny Hansen, Kentucky
1995 .....Jenny Hansen, Kentucky
1996 .....Leah Brown, Georgia
1997 .....Susan Hines, Florida

1998.....Susan Hines, Florida
1999.....Heidi Moneymaker, UCLA

BALANCE BEAM
1982 .....Sue Stednitz, Utah
1983 .....Julie Goewey, Cal St-Fullerton
1984 .....Heidi Anderson, Oregon St
1985 .....Lisa Zeis, Arizona St
1986 .....Jackie Brummer, Arizona St
1987 .....Yumi Mordre, Washington
1988 .....Kelly Garrison-Steves, Oklahoma
1989 .....Jill Andrews, UCLA
Joy Selig, Oregon St
1990 .....Joy Selig, Oregon St
1991 .....Missy Marlowe, Utah
1992 .....Missy Marlowe, Utah
Dana Dobransky, Alabama
1993 .....Dana Dobransky, Alabama
1994 .....Jenny Hansen, Kentucky

Women (Cont.)

INDIVIDUAL CHAMPIONS (Cont.)

BALANCE BEAM (Cont.)
1995.....Jenny Hansen, Kentucky
1996.....Summer Reid, UUtah
1997.....Summer Reid, Utah
　　　　Elizabeth Reid, Arizona St
1998.....Larissa Fontaine, Stanford
　　　　Susan Hines, Florida
1999.....Theresa Kulikowski, Utah

FLOOR EXERCISE
1982.....Mary Ayotte-Law,
　　　　Oregon St
1983.....Kim Neal, Arizona St
1984.....Maria Anz, Florida
1985.....Lisa Mitzel, Utah
1986.....Lisa Zeis, Arizona St
　　　　Penney Hauschild,
　　　　Alabama
1987.....Kim Hamilton, UCLA
1988.....Kim Hamilton, UCLA
1989.....Corrinne Wright, Georgia
　　　　Kim Hamilton, UCLA

1990.....Joy Selig, Oregon St
1991.....Hope Spivey, Georgia
1992.....Missy Marlowe, Utah
1993.....Heather Stepp, Georgia
　　　　Tammy Marshall, Mass.
　　　　Amy Durham, Oregon St
1994......Hope Spivey-Sheeley, UGA
1995.....Jenny Hansen, Kentucky
　　　　Stella Umeh, UCLA
　　　　Leslie Angeles, Georgia
1996.....Heidi Hornbeek, Arizona
　　　　Kim Kelly, Alabama
1997.....Leah Brown, Georgia
1998.....Kim Arnold, Georgia
　　　　Jenni Beathard, Georgia
　　　　Betsy Hamm, Florida
1999.....Marny Oestreng, BGU

UNEVEN BARS
1982.....Lisa Shirk, Pittsburgh
1983.....Jeri Cameron, Arizona St
1984.....Jackie Brummer,
　　　　Arizona St

1985.....Penney Hauschild,
　　　　Alabama
1986.....Lucy Wener, Georgia
1987.....Lucy Wener, Georgia
1988.....Kelly Garrison-Steves,
　　　　Oklahoma
1989.....Lucy Wener, Georgia
1990.....Marie Roethlisberger,
　　　　Minnesota
1991.....Kelly Macy, Georgia
1992.....Missy Marlowe, Utah
1993.....Agina Simpkins, Georgia
　　　　Beth Wymer, Michigan
1994.....Sandy Woolsey, Utah
　　　　Beth Wymer, Michigan
　　　　Lori Strong, Georgia
1995.....Beth Wymer, Michigan
1996.....Stephanie Woods, Alabama
1997.....Jenni Beathard, Georgia
1998.....Karin Lichey, Georgia
　　　　Stella Umeh, UCLA
1999.....Angie Leionard, Utah

DIVISION II (DISCONTINUED)

Year	Champion	Coach	Pts	Runner-Up	Pts
1982	Cal St-Northridge	Donna Stuart	138.10	Jacksonville St	134.05
1983	Denver	Dan Garcia	174.80	Cal St-Northridge	174.35
1984	Jacksonville St	Robert Dillard	173.40	SE Missouri St	171.45
1985	Jacksonville St	Robert Dillard	176.85	SE Missouri St	173.95
1986	Seattle Pacific	Laurel Tindall	175.80	Jacksonville St	175.15

Ice Hockey

DIVISION I

Year	Champion	Coach	Score	Runner-Up	Most Outstanding Player
1948	Michigan	Vic Heyliger	8–4	Dartmouth	Joe Riley, Dartmouth, F
1949	Boston Coll.	John Kelley	4–3	Dartmouth	Dick Desmond, Dartmouth, G
1950	Colorado Coll.	Cheddy Thompson	13–4	Boston U	Ralph Bevins, Boston U, G
1951	Michigan	Vic Heyliger	7–1	Brown	Ed Whiston, Brown, G
1952	Michigan	Vic Heyliger	4–1	Colorado Coll.	Kenneth Kinsley, Colorado Coll., G
1953	Michigan	Vic Heyliger	7–3	Minnesota	John Matchefts, Michigan, F
1954	Rensselaer	Ned Harkness	5–4 (OT)	Minnesota	Abbie Moore, Rensselaer, F
1955	Michigan	Vic Heyliger	5–3	Colorado Coll.	Philip Hilton, Colorado Coll., D
1956	Michigan	Vic Heyliger	7–5	Michigan Tech	Lorne Howes, Michigan, G
1957	Colorado Coll.	Thomas Bedecki	13–6	Michigan	Bob McCusker, Colorado Coll., F
1958	Denver	Murray Armstrong	6–2	N Dakota	Murray Massier, Denver, F
1959	N Dakota	Bob May	4–3 (OT)	Michigan St	Reg Morelli, N Dakota, F
1960	Denver	Murray Armstrong	5–3	Michigan Tech	Bob Marquis, Boston U, F
1961	Denver	Murray Armstrong	12–2	St. Lawrence	Barry Urbanski, Boston U, G
1962	Michigan Tech	John MacInnes	7–1	Clarkson	Louis Angotti, Michigan Tech, F
1963	N Dakota	Barney Thorndycraft	6–5	Denver	Al McLean, N Dakota, F
1964	Michigan	Allen Renfrew	6–3	Denver	Bob Gray, Michigan, G
1965	Michigan Tech	John MacInnes	8–2	Boston Coll.	Gary Milroy, Michigan Tech, F
1966	Michigan St	Amo Bessone	6–1	Clarkson	Gaye Cooley, Michigan St, G
1967	Cornell	Ned Harkness	4–1	Boston U	Walt Stanowski, Cornell, D
1968	Denver	Murray Armstrong	4–0	N Dakota	Gerry Powers, Denver, G
1969	Denver	Murray Armstrong	4–3	Cornell	Keith Magnuson, Denver, D
1970	Cornell	Ned Harkness	6–4	Clarkson	Daniel Lodboa, Cornell, D
1971	Boston U	Jack Kelley	4–2	Minnesota	Dan Brady, Boston U, G
1972	Boston U	Jack Kelley	4–0	Cornell	Tim Regan, Boston U, G
1973	Wisconsin	Bob Johnson	4–2	Vacated	Dean Talafous, Wisconsin, F
1974	Minnesota	Herb Brooks	4–2	Michigan Tech	Brad Shelstad, Minnesota, G
1975	Michigan Tech	John MacInnes	6–1	Minnesota	Jim Warden, Michigan Tech, G
1976	Minnesota	Herb Brooks	6–4	Michigan Tech	Tom Vanelli, Minnesota, F

DIVISION I (CONT.)

Year	Champion	Coach	Score	Runner-Up	Most Outstanding Player
1977	Wisconsin	Bob Johnson	6–5 (OT)	Michigan	Julian Baretta, Wisconsin, G
1978	Boston U	Jack Parker	5–3	Boston Coll.	Jack O'Callahan, Boston U, D
1979	Minnesota	Herb Brooks	4–3	N Dakota	Steve Janaszak, Minnesota, G
1980	N Dakota	John Gasparini	5–2	Northern Michigan	Doug Smail, N Dakota, F
1981	Wisconsin	Bob Johnson	6–3	Minnesota	Marc Behrend, Wisconsin, G
1982	N Dakota	John Gasparini	5–2	Wisconsin	Phil Sykes, N Dakota, F
1983	Wisconsin	Jeff Sauer	6–2	Harvard	Marc Behrend, Wisconsin, G
1984	Bowling Green	Jerry York	5–4 (OT)	MN-Duluth	Gary Kruzich, Bowling Green, G
1985	Rensselaer	Mike Addesa	2–1	Providence	Chris Terreri, Providence, G
1986	Michigan St	Ron Mason	6–5	Harvard	Mike Donnelly, Michigan St, F
1987	N Dakota	John Gasparini	5–3	Michigan St	Tony Hrkac, N Dakota, F
1988	Lake Superior St	Frank Anzalone	4–3 (OT)	St. Lawrence	Bruce Hoffort, Lake Superior St, G
1989	Harvard	Bill Cleary	4–3 (OT)	Minnesota	Ted Donato, Harvard, F
1990	Wisconsin	Jeff Sauer	7–3	Colgate	Chris Tancill, Wisconsin, F
1991	N Michigan	Rick Comley	8–7 (3OT)	Boston U	Scott Beattie, N Michigan, F
1992	Lake Superior St	Jeff Jackson	4–2	Wisconsin	Paul Constantin, Lake Superior St, F
1993	Maine	Shawn Walsh	5–4	Lake Superior St	Jim Montgomery, Maine, F
1994	Lake Superior St	Jeff Jackson	9–1	Boston U	Sean Tallaire, Lake Superior St, F
1995	Boston U	Jack Parker	6–2	Maine	Chris O'Sullivan, Boston U, F
1996	Michigan	Red Berenson	3–2 (OT)	Colorado Coll.	Brendan Morrison, Michigan, F
1997	N Dakota	Dean Blais	6–4	Boston U	Matt Henderson, N Dakota, F
1998	Michigan	Red Berenson	3–2 (OT)	Boston Coll.	Marty Turco, Michigan, G
1999	Maine	Shawn Walsh	3–2 (OT)	New Hampshire	Alfie Michaud, Maine, G

DIVISION II (DISCONTINUED, THEN RENEWED)

Year	Champion	Coach	Score	Runner-Up
1978	Merrimack	Thom Lawler	12–2	Lake Forest
1979	Lowell	Bill Riley Jr	6–4	Mankato St
1980	Mankato St	Don Brose	5–2	Elmira
1981	Lowell	Bill Riley Jr	5–4	Plattsburgh St
1982	Lowell	Bill Riley Jr	6–1	Plattsburgh St
1983	RIT	Brian Mason	4–2	Bemidji St
1984	Bemidji St	R.H. (Bob) Peters	14–4*	Merrimack
1993	Bemidji St	R.H. (Bob) Peters	15–6*	Mercyhurst
1994	Bemidji St	R.H. (Bob) Peters	7–6*	AL-Huntsville
1995	Bemidji St	R.H. (Bob) Peters	11–6*	Mercyhurst
1996	AL-Huntsville	Doug Ross	10–1*	Bemidji St
1997	Bemidji St	R.H. (Bob) Peters	7–4*	AL-Huntsville
1998	AL-Huntsville	Doug Ross	11–4*	Bemidji St
1999	St. Michael's (VT)	Lou DiMasi	12–9*	New Hampshire

*Two-game, total-goal series.

DIVISION III

Year	Champion	Coach	Score	Runner-Up
1984	Babson	Bob Riley	8–0	Union (NY)
1985	Rochester Inst	Bruce Delventhal	5–1	Bemidji St
1986	Bemidji St	R.H. (Bob) Peters	8–5	Vacated
1987	Vacated			Oswego St
1988	WI-River Falls	Rick Kozuback	7–1, 3–5, 3–0	Elmira
1989	WI-Stevens Point	Mark Mazzoleni	3–3, 3–2	RIT
1990	WI-Stevens Point	Mark Mazzoleni	10–1, 3–6, 1–0	Plattsburgh St
1991	WI-Stevens Point	Mark Mazzoleni	6–2	Mankato St
1992	Plattsburgh St	Bob Emery	7–3	WI-Stevens Point
1993	WI-Stevens Point	Joe Baldarotta	4–3	WI-River Falls
1994	WI-River Falls	Dean Talafous	6–4	WI-Superior
1995	Middlebury	Bill Beaney	1–0	Fredonia St
1996	Middlebury	Bill Beaney	3–2	RIT
1997	Middlebury	Bill Beaney	3–2	WI-Superior
1998	Middlebury	Bill Beaney	2–1	WI-Stevens Point
1999	Middlebury	Bill Beaney	5–0	WI-Superior

Lacrosse

Men

DIVISION I

Year	Champion	Coach	Score	Runner-Up
1971	Cornell	Richie Moran	12–6	Maryland
1972	Virginia	Glenn Thiel	13–12	Johns Hopkins
1973	Maryland	Bud Beardmore	10–9 (2 OT)	Johns Hopkins
1974	Johns Hopkins	Bob Scott	17–12	Maryland
1975	Maryland	Bud Beardmore	20–13	Navy
1976	Cornell	Richie Moran	16–13 (OT)	Maryland
1977	Cornell	Richie Moran	16–8	Johns Hopkins
1978	Johns Hopkins	Henry Ciccarone	13–8	Cornell
1979	Johns Hopkins	Henry Ciccarone	15–9	Maryland
1980	Johns Hopkins	Henry Ciccarone	9–8 (2 OT)	Virginia
1981	N Carolina	Willie Scroggs	14–13	Johns Hopkins
1982	N Carolina	Willie Scroggs	7–5	Johns Hopkins
1983	Syracuse	Roy Simmons Jr	17–16	Johns Hopkins
1984	Johns Hopkins	Don Zimmerman	13–10	Syracuse
1985	Johns Hopkins	Don Zimmerman	11–4	Syracuse
1986	N Carolina	Willie Scroggs	10–9 (OT)	Virginia
1987	Johns Hopkins	Don Zimmerman	11–10	Cornell
1988	Syracuse	Roy Simmons Jr	13–8	Cornell
1989	Syracuse	Roy Simmons Jr	13–12	Johns Hopkins
1990	Syracuse	Roy Simmons Jr	21–9	Loyola (MD)
1991	N Carolina	Dave Klarmann	18–13	Towson St
1992	Princeton	Bill Tierney	10–9	Syracuse
1993	Syracuse	Roy Simmons Jr	13–12	N Carolina
1994	Princeton	Bill Tierney	9–8 (OT)	Virginia
1995	Syracuse	Roy Simmons Jr	13–9	Maryland
1996	Princeton	Bill Tierney	13–12 (OT)	Virginia
1997	Princeton	Bill Tierney	19–7	Maryland
1998	Princeton	Bill Tierney	15–5	Maryland
1999	Virginia	Dom Starsia	12–10	Syracuse

DIVISION II *(DISCONTINUED, THEN RENEWED)*

Year	Champion	Coach	Score	Runner-Up
1974	Towson St	Carl Runk	18–17 (OT)	Hobart
1975	Cortland St	Chuck Winters	12–11	Hobart
1976	Hobart	Jerry Schmidt	18–9	Adelphi
1977	Hobart	Jerry Schmidt	23–13	Washington (MD)
1978	Roanoke	Paul Griffin	14–13	Hobart
1979	Adelphi	Paul Doherty	17–12	MD-Baltimore County
1980	MD-Baltimore County	Dick Watts	23–14	Adelphi
1981	Adelphi	Paul Doherty	17–14	Loyola (MD)
1993	Adelphi	Kevin Sheehan	11–7	LIU-C.W. Post
1994	Springfield	Keith Bugbee	15–12	New York Tech
1995	Adelphi	Sandy Kapatos	12–10	Springfield
1996	LIU-C.W. Post	Tom Postel	15–10	Adelphi
1997	New York Tech	Jack Kaley	18–11	Adelphi
1998	Adelphi	Sandy Kapatos	18–6	LIU-C.W. Post
1999	Adelphi	Sandy Kapatos	11–8	LIU-C.W. Post

DIVISION III

Year	Champion	Coach	Score	Runner-Up
1980	Hobart	Dave Urick	11–8	Cortland St
1981	Hobart	Dave Urick	10–8	Cortland St
1982	Hobart	Dave Urick	9–8 (OT)	Washington (MD)
1983	Hobart	Dave Urick	13–9	Roanoke
1984	Hobart	Dave Urick	12–5	Washington (MD)
1985	Hobart	Dave Urick	15–8	Washington (MD)
1986	Hobart	Dave Urick	13–10	Washington (MD)
1987	Hobart	Dave Urick	9–5	Ohio Wesleyan
1988	Hobart	Dave Urick	18–9	Ohio Wesleyan
1989	Hobart	Dave Urick	11–8	Ohio Wesleyan
1990	Hobart	B.J. O'Hara	18–6	Washington (MD)
1991	Hobart	B.J. O'Hara	12–11	Salisbury St
1992	Nazareth (NY)	Scott Nelson	13–12	Hobart
1993	Hobart	B.J. O'Hara	16–10	Ohio Wesleyan
1994	Salisbury St	Jim Berkman	15–9	Hobart

DIVISION III (Cont.)

1995 ....Salisbury St	Jim Berkman	22–13	Nazareth
1996 ....Nazareth	Scott Nelson	11–10 (OT)	Washington (MD)
1997 ....Nazareth	Scott Nelson	15–14 (OT)	Washington (MD)
1998 ....Washington (MD)	John Haus	16–10	Nazareth
1999 ....Salisbury St	Jim Berkman	13–6	Middlebury

Women

DIVISIONS I AND II

Year	Champion	Coach	Score	Runner-Up
1982 ....Massachusetts		Pamela Hixon	9–6	Trenton St
1983 ....Delaware		Janet Smith	10–7	Temple
1984 ....Temple		Tina Sloan Green	6–4	Maryland
1985 ....New Hampshire		Marisa Didio	6–5	Maryland
1986 ....Maryland		Sue Tyler	11–10	Penn St
1987 ....Penn St		Susan Scheetz	7–6	Temple
1988 ....Temple		Tina Sloan Green	15–7	Penn St
1989 ....Penn St		Susan Scheetz	7–6	Harvard
1990 ....Harvard		Carole Kleinfelder	8–7	Maryland
1991 ....Virginia		Jane Miller	8–6	Maryland
1992 ....Maryland		Cindy Timchal	11–10	Harvard
1993 ....Virginia		Jane Miller	8–6 (OT)	Princeton
1994 ....Princeton		Chris Sailer	10–7	Virginia
1995 ....Maryland		Cindy Timchal	13–5	Princeton
1996 ....Maryland		Cindy Timchal	10–5	Virginia
1997 ....Maryland		Cindy Timchal	8–7	Loyola (MD)
1998 ....Maryland		Cindy Timchal	11–5	Virginia
1999 ....Maryland		Cindy Timchal	16–6	Virginia

DIVISION III

Year	Champion	Score	Runner-Up	Year	Champion	Score	Runner-Up
1985...............Trenton St		7–4	Ursinus	1992...............Trenton St		5–3	William Smith
1986...............Ursinus		12–10	Trenton St	1993...............Trenton St		10–9	William Smith
1987...............Trenton St		8–7 (OT)	Ursinus	1994...............Trenton St		29–11	William Smith
1988...............Trenton St		14–11	William Smith	1995...............Trenton St		14–13	William Smith
1989...............Ursinus		8–6	Trenton St	1996...............Trenton St		15–8	Middlebury
1990...............Ursinus		7–6	St. Lawrence	1997...............Middlebury		14–9	College of NJ*
1991...............Trenton St		7–6	Ursinus	1998...............Coll. of NJ*		14–9	Williams
				1999...............Middlebury		10–9	Amherst

*Formerly Trenton St.

Men's and Women's Combined

Year	Champion	Coach	Score	Runner-Up	Score	Individual Champions Air Rifle	Smallbore
1980 ...Tennessee Tech	James Newkirk	6201	W Virginia	6150	Rod Fitz-Randolph, Tennessee Tech	Rod Fitz-Randolph, Tennessee Tech
1981 ...Tennessee Tech	James Newkirk	6139	W Virginia	6136	John Rost, W Virginia	Kurt Fitz-Randolph, Tennessee Tech
1982 ...Tennessee Tech	James Newkirk	6138	W Virginia	6136	John Rost, W Virginia	Kurt Fitz-Randolph, Tennessee Tech
1983 ...W Virginia	Edward Etzel	6166	Tennessee Tech	6148	Ray Slonena, Tennessee Tech	David Johnson, W Virginia
1984 ...W Virginia	Edward Etzel	6206	E Tennessee St	6142	Pat Spurgin, Murray St	Bob Broughton, W Virginia
1985 ...Murray St	Elvis Green	6150	W Virginia	6149	Christian Heller, W Virginia	Pat Spurgin, Murray St
1986 ...W Virginia	Edward Etzel	6229	Murray St	6163	Marianne Wallace, Murray St	Mike Anti, W Virginia
1987 ...Murray St	Elvis Green	6205	W Virginia	6203	Rob Harbison, TN-Martin	Web Wright, W Virginia

Rifle (Cont.)

Individual Champions

Year	Champion	Coach	Score	Runner-Up	Score	Air Rifle	Smallbore
1988	W Virginia	Greg Perrine	6192	Murray St	6183	Deena Wigger, Murray St	Web Wright, W Virginia
1989	W Virginia	Edward Etzel	6234	S Florida	6180	Michelle Scarborough, S Florida	Deb Sinclair, AK-Fairbanks
1990	W Virginia	Marsha Beasley	6205	Navy	6101	Gary Hardy, W Virginia	Michelle Scarborough, S Florida
1991	W Virginia	Marsha Beasley	6171	AK-Fairbanks	6110	Ann Pfiffner, W Virginia	Soma Dutta, UTEP
1992	W Virginia	Marsha Beasley	6214	AK-Fairbanks	6166	Ann Pfiffner, W Virginia	Tim Manges, W Virginia
1993	W Virginia	Marsha Beasley	6179	AK-Fairbanks	6169	Trevor Gathman, W Virginia	Eric Uptagrafft, W Virginia
1994	AK-Fairbanks	Randy Pitney	6194	W Virginia	6187	Nancy Napolski, Kentucky	Cory Brunetti, AK-Fairbanks
1995	W Virginia	Marsha Beasley	6241	Air Force	6187	Benji Belden, Murray St	Oleg Selezner, AK-Fairbanks
1996	W Virginia	Marsha Beasley	6179	Air Force	6168	Trevor Gathman, W Virginia	Joe Johnson, Navy
1997	W Virginia	Marsha Beasley	6223	Kentucky	6175	Marra Hastings, Murray St	Marcos Scrivner, W Virginia
1998	W Virginia	Marsha Beasley	6214	AK-Fairbanks	6175	Emily Caruso, Norwich	Karen Juzinuk, Xavier
1999	AK-Fairbanks	Randy Pitney	6276	Navy	6168	Kelly Mansfield, AK-Fairbanks	Kelly Mansfield, AK-Fairbanks

Skiing

Men's and Women's Combined

Year	Champion	Coach	Pts	Runner-Up	Pts	Host or Site
1954	Denver	Willy Schaeffler	384.0	Seattle	349.6	NV-Reno
1955	Denver	Willy Schaeffler	567.05	Dartmouth	558.935	Norwich
1956	Denver	Willy Schaeffler	582.01	Dartmouth	541.77	Winter Park
1957	Denver	Willy Schaeffler	577.95	Colorado	545.29	Ogden Snow Basin
1958	Dartmouth	Al Merrill	561.2	Denver	550.6	Dartmouth
1959	Colorado	Bob Beattie	549.4	Denver	543.6	Winter Park
1960	Colorado	Bob Beattie	571.4	Denver	568.6	Bridger Bowl
1961	Denver	Willy Schaeffler	376.19	Middlebury	366.94	Middlebury
1962	Denver	Willy Schaeffler	390.08	Colorado	374.30	Squaw Valley
1963	Denver	Willy Schaeffler	384.6	Colorado	381.6	Solitude
1964	Denver	Willy Schaeffler	370.2	Dartmouth	368.8	Franconia Notch
1965	Denver	Willy Schaeffler	380.5	Utah	378.4	Crystal Mountain
1966	Denver	Willy Schaeffler	381.02	Western Colorado	365.92	Crested Butte
1967	Denver	Willy Schaeffler	376.7	Wyoming	375.9	Sugarloaf Mountain
1968	Wyoming	John Cress	383.9	Denver	376.2	Mount Werner
1969	Denver	Willy Schaeffler	388.6	Dartmouth	372.0	Mount Werner
1970	Denver	Willy Schaeffler	386.6	Dartmouth	378.8	Cannon Mountain
1971	Denver	Peder Pytte	394.7	Colorado	373.1	Terry Peak
1972	Colorado	Bill Marolt	385.3	Denver	380.1	Winter Park
1973	Colorado	Bill Marolt	381.89	Wyoming	377.83	Middlebury
1974	Colorado	Bill Marolt	176	Wyoming	162	Jackson Hole
1975	Colorado	Bill Marolt	183	Vermont	115	Fort Lewis
1976	Colorado	Bill Marolt	112			Bates
	Dartmouth	Jim Page	112			
1977	Colorado	Bill Marolt	179	Wyoming	154.5	Winter Park
1978	Colorado	Bill Marolt	152.5	Wyoming	121.5	Cannon Mountain
1979	Colorado	Tim Hinderman	153	Utah	130	Steamboat Springs
1980	Vermont	Chip LaCasse	171	Utah	151	Lake Placid and Stowe
1981	Utah	Pat Miller	183	Vermont	172	Park City
1982	Colorado	Tim Hinderman	461	Vermont	436.5	Lake Placid
1983	Utah	Pat Miller	696	Vermont	650	Bozeman
1984	Utah	Pat Miller	750.5	Vermont	684	New Hampshire
1985	Wyoming	Tim Ameel	764	Utah	744	Bozeman
1986	Utah	Pat Miller	612	Vermont	602	Vermont

Year	Champion	Coach	Pts	Runner-Up	Pts	Host or Site
1987 .....Utah	Pat Miller	710	Vermont	627	Anchorage
1988 .....Utah	Pat Miller	651	Vermont	614	Middlebury
1989 .....Vermont	Chip LaCasse	672	Utah	668	Jackson Hole
1990 .....Vermont	Chip LaCasse	671	Utah	571	Vermont
1991 .....Colorado	Richard Rokos	713	Vermont	682	Park City
1992 .....Vermont	Chip LaCasse	693.5	New Mexico	642.5	New Hampshire
1993 .....Utah	Pat Miller	783	Vermont	700.5	Steamboat Springs
1994 .....Vermont	Chip LaCasse	688	Utah	667	Sugarloaf, ME
1995 .....Colorado	Richard Rokos	720.5	Utah	711	New Hampshire
1996 .....Utah	Pat Miller	719	Denver	635.5	Montana St
1997 .....Utah	Pat Miller	686	Vermont	646.5	Vermont
1998 .....Colorado	Richard Rokos	654	Utah	651.5	Montana St
1999 .....Colorado	Richard Rokos	650	Denver	636	Bates College

Soccer

Men

DIVISION I

Year	Champion	Coach	Score	Runner-Up
1959 ....St. Louis	Bob Guelker	5–2	Bridgeport
1960 ....St. Louis	Bob Guelker	3–2	Maryland
1961 ....West Chester	Mel Lorback	2–0	St. Louis
1962 ....St. Louis	Bob Guelker	4–3	Maryland
1963 ....St. Louis	Bob Guelker	3–0	Navy
1964 ....Navy	F.H. Warner	1–0	Michigan St
1965 ....St. Louis	Bob Guelker	1–0	Michigan St
1966 ....San Francisco	Steve Negoesco	5–2	LIU-Brooklyn
1967 ....Michigan St	Gene Kenney	0–0	Game called
St. Louis	Harry Keough		due to inclement weather
1968 ....Maryland	Doyle Royal	2–2 (2 OT)	
Michigan St	Gene Kenney		
1969 ....St. Louis	Harry Keough	4–0	San Francisco
1970 ....St. Louis	Harry Keough	1–0	UCLA
1971 ....Vacated		3–2	St. Louis
1972 ....St. Louis	Harry Keough	4–2	UCLA
1973 ....St. Louis	Harry Keough	2–1 (OT)	UCLA
1974 ....Howard	Lincoln Phillips	2–1 (4 OT)	St. Louis
1975 ....San Francisco	Steve Negoesco	4–0	SIU-Edwardsville
1976 ....San Francisco	Steve Negoesco	1–0	Indiana
1977 ....Hartwick	Jim Lennox	2–1	San Francisco
1978 ....Vacated		2–0	Indiana
1979 ....SIU-Edwardsville	Bob Guelker	3–2	Clemson
1980 ....San Francisco	Steve Negoesco	4–3 (OT)	Indiana
1981 ....Connecticut	Joe Morrone	2–1 (OT)	Alabama A&M
1982 ....Indiana	Jerry Yeagley	2–1 (8 OT)	Duke
1983 ....Indiana	Jerry Yeagley	1–0 (2 OT)	Columbia
1984 ....Clemson	I.M. Ibrahim	2–1	Indiana
1985 ....UCLA	Sigi Schmid	1–0 (8 OT)	American
1986 ....Duke	John Rennie	1–0	Akron
1987 ....Clemson	I.M. Ibrahim	2–0	San Diego St
1988 ....Indiana	Jerry Yeagley	1–0	Howard
1989 ....Santa Clara	Steve Sampson	1–1 (2 OT)	
Virginia	Bruce Arena		
1990 ....UCLA	Sigi Schmid	1–0 (OT)	Rutgers
1991 ....Virginia	Bruce Arena	0–0*	Santa Clara
1992 ....Virginia	Bruce Arena	2–0	San Diego
1993 ....Virginia	Bruce Arena	2–0	S Carolina
1994 ....Virginia	Bruce Arena	1–0	Indiana
1995 ....Wisconsin	Jim Launder	2–0	Duke
1996 ....St. John's (NY)	Dave Masur	4–1	Florida International
1997 ....UCLA	Sigi Schmid	2–1	Virginia
1998 ....Indiana	Jerry Yeagley	3–1	Stanford

*Under a rule passed in 1991, the NCAA determined that when a score is tied after regulation and overtime, and the championship is determined by penalty kicks, the official score will be 0–0.

Soccer (Cont.)

Men (Cont.)

DIVISION II

Year	Champion	Year	Champion	Year	Champion
1972	SIU-Edwardsville	1982	Florida Int'l	1992	Southern Connecticut St
1973	MO-St. Louis	1983	Seattle Pacific	1993	Seattle Pacific
1974	Adelphi	1984	Florida Int'l	1994	Tampa
1975	Baltimore	1985	Seattle Pacific	1995	Southern Connecticut St
1976	Loyola (MD)	1986	Seattle Pacific	1996	Grand Canyon
1977	Alabama A&M	1987	Southern Connecticut St	1997	Cal St-Bakersfield
1978	Seattle Pacific	1988	Florida Tech	1998	Southern Connecticut St
1979	Alabama A&M	1989	New Hampshire Col		
1980	Lock Haven	1990	Southern Connecticut St		
1981	Tampa	1991	Florida Tech		

DIVISION III

Year	Champion	Year	Champion	Year	Champion
1974	Brockport St	1983	NC-Greensboro	1992	Kean
1975	Babson	1984	Wheaton (IL)	1993	UC-San Diego
1976	Brandeis	1985	NC-Greensboro	1994	Bethany (WV)
1977	Lock Haven	1986	NC-Greensboro	1995	Williams
1978	Lock Haven	1987	NC-Greensboro	1996	College of New Jersey
1979	Babson	1988	UC-San Diego	1997	Wheaton (IL)
1980	Babson	1989	Elizabethtown	1998	Ohio Wesleyan
1981	Glassboro St	1990	Glassboro St		
1982	NC-Greensboro	1991	UC-San Diego		

Women

DIVISION I

Year	Champion	Coach	Score	Runner-Up
1982	N Carolina	Anson Dorrance	2–0	Central Florida
1983	N Carolina	Anson Dorrance	4–0	George Mason
1984	N Carolina	Anson Dorrance	2–0	Connecticut
1985	George Mason	Hank Leung	2–0	North Carolina
1986	N Carolina	Anson Dorrance	2–0	Colorado Col
1987	N Carolina	Anson Dorrance	1–0	Massachusetts
1988	N Carolina	Anson Dorrance	4–1	North Carolina St
1989	N Carolina	Anson Dorrance	2–0	Colorado Col
1990	N Carolina	Anson Dorrance	6–0	Connecticut
1991	N Carolina	Anson Dorrance	3–1	Wisconsin
1992	N Carolina	Anson Dorrance	9–1	Duke
1993	N Carolina	Anson Dorrance	6–0	George Mason
1994	N Carolina	Anson Dorrance	5–0	Notre Dame
1995	Notre Dame	Chris Petrucelli	1–0	Portland
1996	N Carolina	Anson Dorrance	1–0	Notre Dame
1997	N Carolina	Anson Dorrance	2–0	Connecticut
1998	Florida	Becky Burleigh	1–0	N Carolina

DIVISION II

Year	Champion
1988	Cal St-Hayward
1989	Barry
1990	Sonoma St
1991	Cal St-Dominguez Hills
1992	Barry
1993	Barry
1994	Franklin Pierce
1995	Franklin Pierce
1996	Franklin Pierce
1997	Franklin Pierce
1998	Lynn

DIVISION III

Year	Champion
1986	Rochester
1987	Rochester
1988	William Smith
1989	UC-San Diego
1990	Ithaca
1991	Ithaca
1992	Cortland St
1993	Trenton St
1994	Trenton St
1995	UC-San Diego
1996	UC-San Diego
1997	UC-San Diego
1998	Macalester

Softball

DIVISION I

Year	Champion	Coach	Score	Runner-Up
1982	UCLA*	Sharron Backus	2–0†	Fresno St
1983	Texas A&M	Bob Brock	2–0‡	Cal St-Fullerton
1984	UCLA	Sharron Backus	1–0#	Texas A&M
1985	UCLA	Sharron Backus	2–1**	Nebraska
1986	Cal St-Fullerton*	Judi Garman	3–0	Texas A&M
1987	Texas A&M	Bob Brock	4–1	UCLA
1988	UCLA	Sharron Backus	3–0	Fresno St
1989	UCLA*	Sharron Backus	1–0	Fresno St
1990	UCLA	Sharron Backus	2–0	Fresno St
1991	Arizona	Mike Candrea	5–1	UCLA
1992	UCLA*	Sharron Backus	2–0	Arizona
1993	Arizona	Mike Candrea	1–0	UCLA
1994	Arizona	Mike Candrea	4–0	Cal St-Northridge
1995	Vacated	—		Arizona
1996	Arizona*	Mike Candrea	6–4	Washington
1997	Arizona	Mike Candrea	10–2***	UCLA
1998	Fresno St	Margie Wright	1–0	Arizona
1999	UCLA	Sue Enquist	3–2	Washington

*Undefeated teams in final series. †Eight innings. ‡12 innings. #13 innings. **Nine innings. ***Five innings.

DIVISION II

Year	Champion	Year	Champion	Year	Champion
1982	Sam Houston St	1989	Cal St-Bakersfield	1996	Kennesaw St
1983	Cal St-Northridge	1990	Cal St-Bakersfield	1997	California (PA)*
1984	Cal St-Northridge	1991	Augustana (SD)	1998	California (PA)
1985	Cal St-Northridge	1992	Missouri Southern	1999	Humboldt St
1986	SF Austin St	1993	Florida Southern		
1987	Cal St-Northridge	1994	Merrimack		
1988	Cal St-Bakersfield	1995	Kennesaw St		

DIVISION III

Year	Champion	Year	Champion	Year	Champion
1982	Sam Houston St	1988	Central (IA)	1995	Chapman
1982	Eastern Connecticut St*	1989	Trenton St*	1996	Trenton St*
1983	Trenton St	1990	Eastern Connecticut St	1997	Simpson*
1984	Buena Vista*	1991	Central (IA)	1998	WI-Stevens Point
1985	Eastern Connecticut St	1992	Trenton St	1999	Simpson (IA)
1986	Eastern Connecticut St	1993	Central (IA)		
1987	Trenton St*	1994	Trenton St		

*Undefeated teams in final series.

Swimming and Diving

Men

DIVISION I

Year	Champion	Coach	Pts	Runner-Up	Pts
1937	Michigan	Matt Mann	75	Ohio St	39
1938	Michigan	Matt Mann	46	Ohio St	45
1939	Michigan	Matt Mann	65	Ohio St	58
1940	Michigan	Matt Mann	45	Yale	42
1941	Michigan	Matt Mann	61	Yale	58
1942	Yale	Robert J. H. Kiphuth	71	Michigan	39
1943	Ohio St	Mike Peppe	81	Michigan	47
1944	Yale	Robert J. H. Kiphuth	39	Michigan	38
1945	Ohio St	Mike Peppe	56	Michigan	48
1946	Ohio St	Mike Peppe	61	Michigan	37
1947	Ohio St	Mike Peppe	66	Michigan	39
1948	Michigan	Matt Mann	44	Ohio St	41
1949	Ohio St	Mike Peppe	49	Iowa	35
1950	Ohio St	Mike Peppe	64	Yale	43
1951	Yale	Robert J. H. Kiphuth	81	Michigan St	60
1952	Ohio St	Mike Peppe	94	Yale	81
1953	Yale	Robert J. H. Kiphuth	96½	Ohio St	73½

Men (Cont.)
DIVISION I (Cont.)

Year	Champion	Coach	Pts	Runner-Up	Pts
1954	Ohio St	Mike Peppe	94	Michigan	67
1955	Ohio St	Mike Peppe	90	Yale	51
				Michigan	51
1956	Ohio St	Mike Peppe	68	Yale	54
1957	Michigan	Gus Stager	69	Yale	61
1958	Michigan	Gus Stager	72	Yale	63
1959	Michigan	Gus Stager	137½	Ohio St	44
1960	Southern Cal	Peter Daland	87	Michigan	73
1961	Michigan	Gus Stager	85	Southern Cal	62
1962	Ohio St	Mike Peppe	92	Southern Cal	46
1963	Southern Cal	Peter Daland	81	Yale	77
1964	Southern Cal	Peter Daland	96	Indiana	91
1965	Southern Cal	Peter Daland	285	Indiana	278½
1966	Southern Cal	Peter Daland	302	Indiana	286
1967	Stanford	Jim Gaughran	275	Southern Cal	260
1968	Indiana	James Counsilman	346	Yale	253
1969	Indiana	James Counsilman	427	Southern Cal	306
1970	Indiana	James Counsilman	332	Southern Cal	235
1971	Indiana	James Counsilman	351	Southern Cal	260
1972	Indiana	James Counsilman	390	Southern Cal	371
1973	Indiana	James Counsilman	358	Tennessee	294
1974	Southern Cal	Peter Daland	339	Indiana	338
1975	Southern Cal	Peter Daland	344	Indiana	274
1976	Southern Cal	Peter Daland	398	Tennessee	237
1977	Southern Cal	Peter Daland	385	Alabama	204
1978	Tennessee	Ray Bussard	307	Auburn	185
1979	California	Nort Thornton	287	Southern Cal	227
1980	California	Nort Thornton	234	Texas	220
1981	Texas	Eddie Reese	259	UCLA	189
1982	UCLA	Ron Ballatore	219	Texas	210
1983	Florida	Randy Reese	238	Southern Meth	227
1984	Florida	Randy Reese	287½	Texas	277
1985	Stanford	Skip Kenney	403½	Florida	302
1986	Stanford	Skip Kenney	404	California	335
1987	Stanford	Skip Kenney	374	Southern Cal	296
1988	Texas	Eddie Reese	424	Southern Cal	369½
1989	Texas	Eddie Reese	475	Stanford	396
1990	Texas	Eddie Reese	506	Southern Cal	423
1991	Texas	Eddie Reese	476	Stanford	420
1992	Stanford	Skip Kenney	632	Texas	356
1993	Stanford	Skip Kenney	520½	Michigan	396
1994	Stanford	Skip Kenney	566½	Texas	445
1995	Michigan	Jon Urbanchek	561	Stanford	475
1996	Texas	Eddie Reese	479	Auburn	443½
1997	Auburn	David Marsh	496½	Stanford	340
1998	Stanford	Skip Kenney	594	Auburn	394½
1999	Auburn	David Marsh	467½	Stanford	414½

DIVISION II

Year	Champion	Year	Champion	Year	Champion
1963	SW Missouri St	1976	Cal St-Chico	1989	Cal St-Bakersfield
1964	Bucknell	1977	Cal St-Northridge	1990	Cal St-Bakersfield
1965	San Diego St	1978	Cal St-Northridge	1991	Cal St-Bakersfield
1966	San Diego St	1979	Cal St-Northridge	1992	Cal St-Bakersfield
1967	UC-Santa Barbara	1980	Oakland (MI)	1993	Cal St-Bakersfield
1968	Long Beach St	1981	Cal St-Northridge	1994	Oakland (MI)
1969	UC-Irvine	1982	Cal St-Northridge	1995	Oakland (MI)
1970	UC-Irvine	1983	Cal St-Northridge	1996	Oakland (MI)
1971	UC-Irvine	1984	Cal St-Northridge	1997	Oakland (MI)
1972	Eastern Michigan	1985	Cal St-Northridge	1998	Cal St-Bakersfield
1973	Cal St-Chico	1986	Cal St-Bakersfield	1999	Drury
1974	Cal St-Chico	1987	Cal St-Bakersfield		
1975	Cal St-Northridge	1988	Cal St-Bakersfield		

DIVISION III

Year	Champion	Year	Champion	Year	Champion
1975	Cal St-Chico	1984	Kenyon	1993	Kenyon
1976	St. Lawrence	1985	Kenyon	1994	Kenyon
1977	Johns Hopkins	1986	Kenyon	1995	Kenyon
1978	Johns Hopkins	1987	Kenyon	1996	Kenyon
1979	Johns Hopkins	1988	Kenyon	1997	Kenyon
1980	Kenyon	1989	Kenyon	1998	Kenyon
1981	Kenyon	1990	Kenyon	1999	Kenyon
1982	Kenyon	1991	Kenyon		
1983	Kenyon	1992	Kenyon		

Women

DIVISION I

Year	Champion	Coach	Pts	Runner-Up	Pts
1982	Florida	Randy Reese	505	Stanford	383
1983	Stanford	George Haines	418½	Florida	389½
1984	Texas	Richard Quick	392	Stanford	324
1985	Texas	Richard Quick	643	Florida	400
1986	Texas	Richard Quick	633	Florida	586
1987	Texas	Richard Quick	648½	Stanford	631½
1988	Texas	Richard Quick	661	Florida	542½
1989	Stanford	Richard Quick	610½	Texas	547
1990	Texas	Mark Schubert	632	Stanford	622½
1991	Texas	Mark Schubert	746	Stanford	653
1992	Stanford	Richard Quick	735½	Texas	651
1993	Stanford	Richard Quick	649½	Florida	421
1994	Stanford	Richard Quick	512	Texas	421
1995	Stanford	Richard Quick	497½	Michigan	478½
1996	Stanford	Richard Quick	478	SMU	397
1997	Southern Cal	Mark Schubert	406	Stanford	395
1998	Stanford	Richard Quick	422	Arizona	378
1999	Georgia	Jack Bauerle	504½	Stanford	441

DIVISION II

Year	Champion	Year	Champion	Year	Champion
1982	Cal St-Northridge	1988	Cal St-Northridge	1994	Oakland (MI)
1983	Clarion	1989	Cal St-Northridge	1995	Air Force
1984	Clarion	1990	Oakland (MI)	1996	Air Force
1985	S Florida	1991	Oakland (MI)	1997	Drury
1986	Clarion	1992	Oakland (MI)	1998	Drury
1987	Cal St-Northridge	1993	Oakland (MI)	1999	Drury

DIVISION III

Year	Champion	Year	Champion	Year	Champion
1982	Williams	1989	Kenyon	1996	Kenyon
1983	Williams	1990	Kenyon	1997	Kenyon
1984	Kenyon	1991	Kenyon	1998	Kenyon
1985	Kenyon	1992	Kenyon	1999	Kenyon
1986	Kenyon	1993	Kenyon		
1987	Kenyon	1994	Kenyon		
1988	Kenyon	1995	Kenyon		

Tennis

Men

INDIVIDUAL CHAMPIONS 1883–1945

Year	Champion	Year	Champion
1883	Joseph Clark, Harvard (spring)	1914	George Church, Princeton
1883	Howard Taylor, Harvard (fall)	1915	Richard Williams II, Harvard
1884	W.P. Knapp, Yale	1916	G. Colket Caner, Harvard
1885	W.P. Knapp, Yale	1917–18	No tournament
1886	G.M. Brinley, Trinity (CT)	1919	Charles Garland, Yale
1887	P.S. Sears, Harvard	1920	Lascelles Banks, Yale
1888	P.S. Sears, Harvard	1921	Philip Neer, Stanford
1889	R.P. Huntington Jr, Yale	1922	Lucien Williams, Yale
1890	Fred Hovey, Harvard	1923	Carl Fischer, Philadelphia Osteo
1891	Fred Hovey, Harvard	1924	Wallace Scott, Washington
1892	William Larned, Cornell	1925	Edward Chandler, California
1893	Malcolm Chace, Brown	1926	Edward Chandler, California
1894	Malcolm Chace, Yale	1927	Wilmer Allison, Texas
1895	Malcolm Chace, Yale	1928	Julius Seligson, Lehigh
1896	Malcolm Whitman, Harvard	1929	Berkeley Bell, Texas
1897	S.G. Thompson, Princeton	1930	Clifford Sutter, Tulane
1898	Leo Ware, Harvard	1931	Keith Gledhill, Stanford
1899	Dwight Davis, Harvard	1932	Clifford Sutter, Tulane
1900	Raymond Little, Princeton	1933	Jack Tidball, UCLA
1901	Fred Alexander, Princeton	1934	Gene Mako, Southern Cal
1902	William Clothier, Harvard	1935	Wilbur Hess, Rice
1903	E.B. Dewhurst, Pennsylvania	1936	Ernest Sutter, Tulane
1904	Robert LeRoy, Columbia	1937	Ernest Sutter, Tulane
1905	E.B. Dewhurst, Pennsylvania	1938	Frank Guernsey, Rice
1906	Robert LeRoy, Columbia	1939	Frank Guernsey, Rice
1907	G. Peabody Gardner Jr, Harvard	1940	Donald McNeil, Kenyon
1908	Nat Niles, Harvard	1941	Joseph Hunt, Navy
1909	Wallace Johnson, Pennsylvania	1942	Frederick Schroeder Jr, Stanford
1910	R.A. Holden Jr, Yale	1943	Pancho Segura, Miami (FL)
1911	E.H. Whitney, Harvard	1944	Pancho Segura, Miami (FL)
1912	George Church, Princeton	1945	Pancho Segura, Miami (FL)
1913	Richard Williams II, Harvard		

DIVISION I

Year	Champion	Coach	Pts	Runner-Up	Pts	Individual Champion
1946	Southern Cal	William Moyle	9	William & Mary	6	Robert Falkenburg, Southern Cal
1947	William & Mary	Sharvey G. Umbeck	10	Rice	4	Gardner Larned, William & Mary
1948	William & Mary	Sharvey G. Umbeck	6	San Francisco	5	Harry Likas, San Francisco
1949	San Francisco	Norman Brooks	7	Rollins/Tulane/ Washington	4	Jack Tuero, Tulane
1950	UCLA	William Ackerman	11	California	5	Herbert Flam, UCLA
				Southern Cal	5	
1951	Southern Cal	Louis Wheeler	9	Cincinnati	7	Tony Trabert, Cincinnati
1952	UCLA	J.D. Morgan	11	California	5	Hugh Stewart, Southern Cal
				Southern Cal	5	
1953	UCLA	J.D. Morgan	11	California	6	Hamilton Richardson, Tulane
1954	UCLA	J.D. Morgan	15	Southern Cal	10	Hamilton Richardson, Tulane
1955	Southern Cal	George Toley	12	Texas	7	Jose Aguero, Tulane
1956	UCLA	J.D. Morgan	15	Southern Cal	14	Alejandro Olmedo, Southern Cal
1957	Michigan	William Murphy	10	Tulane	9	Barry MacKay, Michigan
1958	Southern Cal	George Toley	13	Stanford	9	Alejandro Olmedo, Southern Cal
1959	Notre Dame	Thomas Fallon	8			Whitney Reed, San Jose St
	Tulane	Emmet Pare	8			
1960	UCLA	J.D. Morgan	18	Southern Cal	8	Larry Nagler, UCLA
1961	UCLA	J.D. Morgan	17	Southern Cal	16	Allen Fox, UCLA
1962	Southern Cal	George Toley	22	UCLA	12	Rafael Osuna, Southern Cal
1963	Southern Cal	George Toley	27	UCLA	19	Dennis Ralston, Southern Cal
1964	Southern Cal	George Toley	26	UCLA	25	Dennis Ralston, Southern Cal
1965	UCLA	J.D. Morgan	31	Miami (FL)	13	Arthur Ashe, UCLA
1966	Southern Cal	George Toley	27	UCLA	23	Charles Pasarell, UCLA
1967	Southern Cal	George Toley	28	UCLA	23	Bob Lutz, Southern Cal
1968	Southern Cal	George Toley	31	Rice	23	Stan Smith, Southern Cal
1969	Southern Cal	George Toley	35	UCLA	23	Joaquin Loyo-Mayo, Southern Cal
1970	UCLA	Glenn Bassett	26	Trinity (TX)	22	Jeff Borowiak, UCLA
				Rice	22	

Men (Cont.)

DIVISION I (Cont.)

Year	Champion	Coach		Runner-Up		Individual Champion
1971	UCLA	Glenn Bassett	35	Trinity (TX)	27	Jimmy Connors, UCLA
1972	Trinity (TX)	Clarence Mabry	36	Stanford	30	Dick Stockton, Trinity (TX)
1973	Stanford	Dick Gould	33	Southern Cal	28	Alex Mayer, Stanford
1974	Stanford	Dick Gould	30	Southern Cal	25	John Whitlinger, Stanford
1975	UCLA	Glenn Bassett	27	Miami (FL)	20	Bill Martin, UCLA
1976	Southern Cal	George Toley	21			Bill Scanlon, Trinity (TX)
	UCLA	Glenn Bassett	21			
1977	Stanford	Dick Gould		Trinity (TX)		Matt Mitchell, Stanford
1978	Stanford	Dick Gould		UCLA		John McEnroe, Stanford
1979	UCLA	Glenn Bassett		Trinity (TX)		Kevin Curren, Texas
1980	Stanford	Dick Gould		California		Robert Van't Hof, Southern Cal
1981	Stanford	Dick Gould		UCLA		Tim Mayotte, Stanford
1982	UCLA	Glenn Bassett		Pepperdine		Mike Leach, Michigan
1983	Stanford	Dick Gould		SMU		Greg Holmes, Utah
1984	UCLA	Glenn Bassett		Stanford		Mikael Pernfors, Georgia
1985	Georgia	Dan Magill		UCLA		Mikael Pernfors, Georgia
1986	Stanford	Dick Gould		Pepperdine		Dan Goldie, Stanford
1987	Georgia	Dan Magill		UCLA		Andrew Burrow, Miami (FL)
1988	Stanford	Dick Gould		Louisiana St		Robby Weiss, Pepperdine
1989	Stanford	Dick Gould		Georgia		Donni Leaycraft, Louisiana St
1990	Stanford	Dick Gould		Tennessee		Steve Bryan, Texas
1991	Southern Cal	Dick Leach		Georgia		Jared Palmer, Stanford
1992	Stanford	Dick Gould		Notre Dame		Alex O'Brien, Stanford
1993	Southern Cal	Dick Leach		Georgia		Chris Woodruff, Tennessee
1994	Southern Cal	Dick Leach		Stanford		Mark Merklein, Florida
1995	Stanford	Dick Gould		Mississippi		Sargis Sargsian, Arizona St
1996	Stanford	Dick Gould		UCLA		Cecil Mamiit, Southern Cal
1997	Stanford	Dick Gould		Georgia		Luke Smith, UNLV
1998	Stanford	Dick Gould		Georgia		Bob Bryan, Stanford
1999	Georgia	Manuel Diaz		UCLA		Jeff Morrison, Florida

Note: Prior to 1977, individual wins counted in the team's total points. In 1977, a dual-match single-elimination team championship was initiated, eliminating the point system.

DIVISION II

Year	Champion	Year	Champion	Year	Champion
1963	Cal St-LA	1976	Hampton	1989	Hampton
1964	Cal St-LA/S Illinois	1977	UC-Irvine	1990	Cal Poly-SLO
1965	Cal St-LA	1978	SIU-Edwardsville	1991	Rollins
1966	Rollins	1979	SIU-Edwardsville	1992	UC-Davis
1967	Long Beach St	1980	SIU-Edwardsville	1993	Lander
1968	Fresno St	1981	SIU-Edwardsville	1994	Lander
1969	Cal St-Northridge	1982	SIU-Edwardsville	1995	Lander
1970	UC-Irvine	1983	SIU-Edwardsville	1996	Lander
1971	UC-Irvine	1984	SIU-Edwardsville	1997	Lander
1972	UC-Irvine/ Rollins	1985	Chapman	1998	Lander
1973	UC-Irvine	1986	Cal Poly-SLO	1999	Lander
1974	San Diego	1987	Chapman		
1975	UC-Irvine/San Diego	1988	Chapman		

DIVISION III

Year	Champion	Year	Champion	Year	Champion
1976	Kalamazoo	1984	Redlands	1993	Kalamazoo
1977	Swarthmore	1985	Swarthmore	1994	Washington (MD)
1978	Kalamazoo	1986	Kalamazoo	1995	UC-Santa Cruz
1979	Redlands	1987	Kalamazoo	1996	UC-Santa Cruz
1980	Gustavus Adolphus	1988	Washington & Lee	1997	Washington (MD)
1981	Claremont-M-S	1989	UC-Santa Cruz	1998	UC-Santa Cruz
	Swarthmore	1990	Swarthmore	1999	Williams
1982	Gustavus Adolphus	1991	Kalamazoo		
1983	Redlands	1992	Kalamazoo		

Women

DIVISION I

Year	Champion	Coach	Runner-Up	Individual Champion
1982	Stanford	Frank Brennan	UCLA	Alycia Moulton, Stanford
1983	Southern Cal	Dave Borelli	Trinity (TX)	Beth Herr, Southern Cal
1984	Stanford	Frank Brennan	Southern Cal	Lisa Spain, Georgia
1985	Southern Cal	Dave Borelli	Miami (FL)	Linda Gates, Stanford
1986	Stanford	Frank Brennan	Southern Cal	Patty Fendick, Stanford
1987	Stanford	Frank Brennan	Georgia	Patty Fendick, Stanford
1988	Stanford	Frank Brennan	Florida	Shaun Stafford, Florida
1989	Stanford	Frank Brennan	UCLA	Sandra Birch, Stanford
1990	Stanford	Frank Brennan	Florida	Debbie Graham, Stanford
1991	Stanford	Frank Brennan	UCLA	Sandra Birch, Stanford
1992	Florida	Andy Brandi	Texas	Lisa Raymond, Florida
1993	Texas	Jeff Moore	Stanford	Lisa Raymond, Florida
1994	Georgia	Jeff Wallace	Stanford	Angela Lettiere, Georgia
1995	Texas	Jeff Moore	Florida	Keri Phebus, UCLA
1996	Florida	Andy Brandi	Stanford	Jill Craybas, Florida
1997	Stanford	Frank Brennan	Florida	Lilia Osterloh, Stanford
1998	Florida	Andy Brandi	Duke	Vanessa Webb, Duke
1999	Stanford	Frank Brennan	Florida	Zuzana Lesenarova, UC-SD

DIVISION II

Year	Champion	Year	Champion	Year	Champion
1982	Cal St-Northridge	1989	SIU-Edwardsville	1996	Armstrong St
1983	TN-Chattanooga	1990	UC-Davis	1997	Lynn
1984	TN-Chattanooga	1991	Cal Poly-Pomona	1998	Lynn
1985	TN-Chattanooga	1992	Cal Poly-Pomona	1999	BYU-Hawaii
1986	SIU-Edwardsville	1993	UC-Davis		
1987	SIU-Edwardsville	1994	N Florida		
1988	SIU-Edwardsville	1995	Armstrong St		

DIVISION III

Year	Champion	Year	Champion	Year	Champion
1982	Occidental	1989	UC-San Diego	1996	Emory
1983	Principia	1990	Gustavus Adolphus	1997	Kenyon
1984	Davidson	1991	Mary Washington	1998	Kenyon
1985	UC-San Diego	1992	Pomona-Pitzer	1999	Amherst
1986	Trenton St	1993	Kenyon		
1987	UC-San Diego	1994	UC-San Diego		
1988	Mary Washington	1995	Kenyon		

Indoor Track and Field

Men

DIVISION I

Year	Champion	Coach	Pts	Runner-Up	Pts
1965	Missouri	Tom Botts	14	Oklahoma St	12
1966	Kansas	Bob Timmons	14	Southern Cal	13
1967	Southern Cal	Vern Wolfe	26	Oklahoma	17
1968	Villanova	Jim Elliott	35	Southern Cal	25
1969	Kansas	Bob Timmons	41½	Villanova	33
1970	Kansas	Bob Timmons	27½	Villanova	26
1971	Villanova	Jim Elliott	22	UTEP	19¼
1972	Southern Cal	Vern Wolfe	19	Bowling Green/ Mich St	18
1973	Manhattan	Fred Dwyer	18	Kansas/Kent St/UTEP	12
1974	UTEP	Ted Banks	19	Colorado	18
1975	UTEP	Ted Banks	36	Kansas	17½
1976	UTEP	Ted Banks	23	Villanova	15
1977	Washington St	John Chaplin	25½	UTEP	25
1978	UTEP	Ted Banks	44	Auburn	38
1979	Villanova	Jim Elliott	52	UTEP	51
1980	UTEP	Ted Banks	76	Villanova	42
1981	UTEP	Ted Banks	76	SMU	51

Men (Cont.)

DIVISION I (Cont.)

Year	Champion	Coach	Pts	Runner-Up	Pts
1982	UTEP	John Wedel	67	Arkansas	30
1983	SMU	Ted McLaughlin	43	Villanova	32
1984	Arkansas	John McDonnell	38	Washington St	28
1985	Arkansas	John McDonnell	70	Tennessee	29
1986	Arkansas	John McDonnell	49	Villanova	22
1987	Arkansas	John McDonnell	39	SMU	31
1988	Arkansas	John McDonnell	34	Illinois	29
1989	Arkansas	John McDonnell	34	Florida	31
1990	Arkansas	John McDonnell	44	Texas A&M	36
1991	Arkansas	John McDonnell	34	Georgetown	27
1992	Arkansas	John McDonnell	53	Clemson	46
1993	Arkansas	John McDonnell	66	Clemson	30
1994	Arkansas	John McDonnell	83	UTEP	45
1995	Arkansas	John McDonnell	59	GMU/Tennessee	26
1996	George Mason	John Cook	39	Nebraska	31½
1997	Arkansas	John McDonnell	59	Auburn	27
1998	Arkansas	John McDonnell	56	Stanford	36½
1999	Arkansas	John McDonnell	65	Stanford	42½

DIVISION II

Year	Champion	Year	Champion	Year	Champion
1985	SE Missouri St	1990	St. Augustine's	1995	St. Augustine's
1986	not held	1991	St. Augustine's	1996	Abilene Christian
1987	St. Augustine's	1992	St. Augustine's	1997	Abilene Christian
1988	Abil. Christian/ St. August.	1993	Abilene Christian	1998	Abilene Christian
1989	St. Augustine's	1994	Abilene Christian	1999	Abilene Christian

DIVISION III

Year	Champion	Year	Champion	Year	Champion
1985	St. Thomas (MN)	1991	WI-La Crosse	1997	WI-La Crosse
1986	Frostburg St	1992	WI-La Crosse	1998	Lincoln (PA)
1987	WI-La Crosse	1993	WI-La Crosse	1999	Lincoln (PA)
1988	WI-La Crosse	1994	WI-La Crosse		
1989	N Central	1995	Lincoln (PA)		
1990	Lincoln (PA)	1996	Lincoln (PA)		

Women

DIVISION I

Year	Champion	Coach	Pts	Runner-Up	Pts
1983	Nebraska	Gary Pepin	47	Tennessee	44
1984	Nebraska	Gary Pepin	59	Tennessee	48
1985	Florida St	Gary Winckler	34	Texas	32
1986	Texas	Terry Crawford	31	Southern Cal	26
1987	Louisiana St	Loren Seagrave	49	Tennessee	30
1988	Texas	Terry Crawford	71	Villanova	52
1989	Louisiana St	Pat Henry	61	Villanova	34
1990	Texas	Terry Crawford	50	Wisconsin	26
1991	Louisiana St	Pat Henry	48	Texas	39
1992	Florida	Bev Kearney	50	Stanford	26
1993	Louisiana St	Pat Henry	49	Wisconsin	44
1994	Louisiana St	Pat Henry	48	Alabama	29
1995	Louisiana St	Pat Henry	40	UCLA	37
1996	Louisiana St	Pat Henry	52	Georgia	34
1997	Louisiana St	Pat Henry	49	Texas/ Wisconsin	39
1998	Texas	Bev Kearney	60	Louisiana St	30
1999	Texas	Bev Kearney	61	Louisiana St	57

Women (Cont.)

DIVISION II

Year	Champion	Year	Champion	Year	Champion
1985	St. Augustine's	1991	Abilene Christian	1997	Abilene Christian
1986	not held	1992	Alabama A&M	1998	Abilene Christian
1987	St. Augustine's	1993	Abilene Christian	1999	Abilene Christian
1988	Abilene Christian	1994	Abilene Christian		
1989	Abilene Christian	1995	Abilene Christian		
1990	Abilene Christian	1996	Abilene Christian		

DIVISION III

Year	Champion	Year	Champion	Year	Champion
1985	MA-Boston	1991	Cortland St	1997	Christopher Newport
1986	MA-Boston	1992	Christopher Newport	1998	Christopher Newport
1987	MA-Boston	1993	Lincoln (PA)	1999	Wheaton (MA)
1988	Christopher Newport	1994	WI-Oshkosh		
1989	Christopher Newport	1995	WI-Oshkosh		
1990	Christopher Newport	1996	WI-Oshkosh		

Outdoor Track and Field

Men

DIVISION I

Year	Champion	Coach	Pts	Runner-Up	Pts
1921	Illinois	Harry Gill	20†	Notre Dame	16†
1922	California	Walter Christie	28†	Penn St	19†
1923	Michigan	Stephen Farrell	29†	Mississippi St	16
1924	No meet				
1925	Stanford*	R. L. Templeton	31†		
1926	Southern Cal*	Dean Cromwell	27†		
1927	Illinois*	Harry Gill	35†		
1928	Stanford	R. L. Templeton	72	Ohio St	31
1929	Ohio St	Frank Castleman	50	Washington	42
1930	Southern Cal	Dean Cromwell	55†	Washington	40
1931	Southern Cal	Dean Cromwell	77†	Ohio St	31†
1932	Indiana	Billy Hayes	56	Ohio St	49†
1933	Louisiana St	Bernie Moore	58	Southern Cal	54
1934	Stanford	R. L. Templeton	63	Southern Cal	54†
1935	Southern Cal	Dean Cromwell	74†	Ohio St	40†
1936	Southern Cal	Dean Cromwell	103†	Ohio St	73
1937	Southern Cal	Dean Cromwell	62	Stanford	50
1938	Southern Cal	Dean Cromwell	67†	Stanford	38
1939	Southern Cal	Dean Cromwell	86	Stanford	44†
1940	Southern Cal	Dean Cromwell	47	Stanford	28†
1941	Southern Cal	Dean Cromwell	81†	Indiana	50
1942	Southern Cal	Dean Cromwell	85†	Ohio St	44†
1943	Southern Cal	Dean Cromwell	46	California	39
1944	Illinois	Leo Johnson	79	Notre Dame	43
1945	Navy	E.J. Thomson	62	Illinois	48†
1946	Illinois	Leo Johnson	78	Southern Cal	42†
1947	Illinois	Leo Johnson	59†	Southern Cal	34†
1948	Minnesota	James Kelly	46	Southern Cal	41†
1949	Southern Cal	Jess Hill	55†	UCLA	31
1950	Southern Cal	Jess Hill	49†	Stanford	28
1951	Southern Cal	Jess Mortenson	56	Cornell	40
1952	Southern Cal	Jess Mortenson	66†	San Jose St	24†
1953	Southern Cal	Jess Mortenson	80	Illinois	41
1954	Southern Cal	Jess Mortenson	66†	Illinois	31†
1955	Southern Cal	Jess Mortenson	42	UCLA	34
1956	UCLA	Elvin Drake	55†	Kansas	51
1957	Villanova	James Elliott	47	California	32
1958	Southern Cal	Jess Mortenson	48†	Kansas	40†
1959	Kansas	Bill Easton	73	San Jose St	48
1960	Kansas	Bill Easton	50	Southern Cal	37

Men (*Cont.*)

DIVISION I (*Cont.*)

Year	Champion	Coach	Pts	Runner-Up	Pts
1961	Southern Cal	Jess Mortenson	65	Oregon	47
1962	Oregon	William Bowerman	85	Villanova	40†
1963	Southern Cal	Vern Wolfe	61	Stanford	42
1964	Oregon	William Bowerman	70	San Jose St	40
1965	Oregon	William Bowerman	32		
	Southern Cal	Vern Wolfe	32		
1966	UCLA	Jim Bush	81	Brigham Young	33
1967	Southern Cal	Vern Wolfe	86	Oregon	40
1968	Southern Cal	Vern Wolfe	58	Washington St	57
1969	San Jose St	Bud Winter	48	Kansas	45
1970	Brigham Young	Clarence Robison	35		
	Kansas	Bob Timmons	35		
	Oregon	William Bowerman	35		
1971	UCLA	Jim Bush	52	Southern Cal	41
1972	UCLA	Jim Bush	82	Southern Cal	49
1973	UCLA	Jim Bush	56	Oregon	31
1974	Tennessee	Stan Huntsman	60	UCLA	56
1975	UTEP	Ted Banks	55	UCLA	42
1976	Southern Cal	Vern Wolfe	64	UTEP	44
1977	Arizona St	Senon Castillo	64	UTEP	50
1978	UCLA/UTEP	Jim Bush/Ted Banks	50		
1979	UTEP	Ted Banks	64	Villanova	48
1980	UTEP	Ted Banks	69	UCLA	46
1981	UTEP	Ted Banks	70	SMU	57
1982	UTEP	John Wedel	105	Tennessee	94
1983	SMU	Ted McLaughlin	104	Tennessee	102
1984	Oregon	Bill Dellinger	113	Washington St	94½
1985	Arkansas	John McDonnell	61	Washington St	46
1986	SMU	Ted McLaughlin	53	Washington St	52
1987	UCLA	Bob Larsen	81	Texas	28
1988	UCLA	Bob Larsen	82	Texas	41
1989	Louisiana St	Pat Henry	53	Texas A&M	51
1990	Louisiana St	Pat Henry	44	Arkansas	36
1991	Tennessee	Doug Brown	51	Washington St	42
1992	Arkansas	John McDonnell	60	Tennessee	46½
1993	Arkansas	John McDonnell	69	LSU/Ohio St	45
1994	Arkansas	John McDonnell	83	UTEP	45
1995	Arkansas	John McDonnell	61½	UCLA	55
1996	Arkansas	John McDonnell	55	George Mason	40
1997	Arkansas	John McDonnell	55	Texas	42½
1998	Arkansas	John McDonnell	58½	Stanford	51
1999	Arkansas	John McDonnell	59	Stanford	52

*Unofficial championship. †Fraction of a point.

DIVISION II

Year	Champion	Year	Champion	Year	Champion
1963	MD-Eastern Shore	1976	UC-Irvine	1990	St. Augustine's
1964	Fresno St	1977	Cal St-Hayward	1991	St. Augustine's
1965	San Diego St	1978	Cal St-LA	1992	St. Augustine's
1966	San Diego St	1979	Cal Poly-SLO	1993	St. Augustine's
1967	Long Beach St	1980	Cal Poly-SLO	1994	St. Augustine's
1968	Cal Poly-SLO	1981	Cal Poly-SLO	1995	St. Augustine's
1969	Cal Poly-SLO	1982	Abilene Christian	1996	Abilene Christian
1970	Cal Poly-SLO	1983	Abilene Christian	1997	Abilene Christian
1971	Kentucky St	1984	Abilene Christian	1998	St. Augustine's
1972	Eastern Michigan	1985	Abilene Christian	1999	Abilene Christian
1973	Norfolk St	1986	Abilene Christian		
1974	Eastern Illinois	1987	Abilene Christian		
	Norfolk St	1988	Abilene Christian		
1975	Cal St-Northridge	1989	St. Augustine's		

Men (Cont.)

DIVISION III

Year	Champion	Year	Champion	Year	Champion
1974	Ashland	1983	Glassboro St	1992	WI-La Crosse
1975	Southern-N Orleans	1984	Glassboro St	1993	WI-La Crosse
1976	Southern-N Orleans	1985	Lincoln (PA)	1994	N Central
1977	Southern-N Orleans	1986	Frostburg St	1995	Lincoln (PA)
1978	Occidental	1987	Frostburg St	1996	Lincoln (PA)
1979	Slippery Rock	1988	WI-La Crosse	1997	WI-La Crosse
1980	Glassboro St	1989	N Central	1998	N Central
1981	Glassboro St	1990	Lincoln (PA)	1999	Lincoln (PA)
1982	Glassboro St	1991	WI-La Crosse		

Women

DIVISION I

Year	Champion	Coach	Pts	Runner-Up	Pts
1982	UCLA	Scott Chisam	153	Tennessee	126
1983	UCLA	Scott Chisam	116½	Florida St	108
1984	Florida St	Gary Winckler	145	Tennessee	124
1985	Oregon	Tom Heinonen	52	Florida St/LSU	46
1986	Texas	Terry Crawford	65	Alabama	55
1987	Louisiana St	Loren Seagrave	62	Alabama	53
1988	Louisiana St	Loren Seagrave	61	UCLA	58
1989	Louisiana St	Pat Henry	86	UCLA	47
1990	Louisiana St	Pat Henry	53	UCLA	46
1991	Louisiana St	Pat Henry	78	Texas	67
1992	Louisiana St	Pat Henry	87	Florida	81
1993	Louisiana St	Pat Henry	93	Wisconsin	44
1994	Louisiana St	Pat Henry	86	Texas	43
1995	Louisiana St	Pat Henry	69	UCLA	58
1996	Louisiana St	Pat Henry	81	Texas	52
1997	Louisiana St	Pat Henry	63	Texas	62
1998	Texas	Bev Kearney	60	UCLA	55
1999	Texas	Bev Kearney	62	UCLA	60

DIVISION II

Year	Champion	Year	Champion	Year	Champion
1982	Cal Poly-SLO	1989	Cal Poly-SLO	1996	Abilene Christian
1983	Cal Poly-SLO	1990	Cal Poly-SLO	1997	St. Augustine's
1984	Cal Poly-SLO	1991	Cal Poly-SLO	1998	Abilene Christian
1985	Abilene Christian	1992	Alabama A&M	1999	Abilene Christian
1986	Abilene Christian	1993	Alabama A&M		
1987	Abilene Christian	1994	Alabama A&M		
1988	Abilene Christian	1995	Abilene Christian		

DIVISION III

Year	Champion	Year	Champion	Year	Champion
1982	Central (IA)	1989	Chris. Newport	1996	WI-Oshkosh
1983	WI-La Crosse	1990	WI-Oshkosh	1997	WI-Oshkosh
1984	WI-La Crosse	1991	WI-Oshkosh	1998	Chris. Newport
1985	Cortland St	1992	Chris. Newport	1999	Lincoln (PA)
1986	MA-Boston	1993	Lincoln (PA)		
1987	Chris. Newport	1994	Chris. Newport		
1988	Chris. Newport	1995	WI-Oshkosh		

Volleyball

Men

Year	Champion	Coach	Score	Runner-Up	Most Outstanding Player
1970	UCLA	Al Scates	3–0	Long Beach St	Dane Holtzman, UCLA
1971	UCLA	Al Scates	3–0	UC-Santa Barbara	Kirk Kilgore, UCLA
					Tim Bonynge, UC-Santa Barbara
1972	UCLA	Al Scates	3–2	San Diego St	Dick Irvin, UCLA

Men (Cont.)

Year	Champion	Coach	Score	Runner-Up	Most Outstanding Player
1973	San Diego St	Jack Henn	3–1	Long Beach St	Duncan McFarland, San Diego St
1974	UCLA	Al Scates	3–2	UC-Santa Barbara	Bob Leonard, UCLA
1975	UCLA	Al Scates	3–1	UC-Santa Barbara	John Bekins, UCLA
1976	UCLA	Al Scates	3–0	Pepperdine	Joe Mika, UCLA
1977	Southern Cal	Ernie Hix	3–1	Ohio St	Celso Kalache, Southern Cal
1978	Pepperdine	Marv Dunphy	3–2	UCLA	Mike Blanchard, Pepperdine
1979	UCLA	Al Scates	3–1	Southern Cal	Sinjin Smith, UCLA
1980	Southern Cal	Ernie Hix	3–1	UCLA	Dusty Dvorak, Southern Cal
1981	UCLA	Al Scates	3–2	Southern Cal	Karch Kiraly, UCLA
1982	UCLA	Al Scates	3–0	Penn St	Karch Kiraly, UCLA
1983	UCLA	Al Scates	3–0	Pepperdine	Ricci Luyties, UCLA
1984	UCLA	Al Scates	3–1	Pepperdine	Ricci Luyties, UCLA
1985	Pepperdine	Marv Dunphy	3–1	Southern Cal	Bob Ctvrtlik, Pepperdine
1986	Pepperdine	Rod Wilde	3–2	Southern Cal	Steve Friedman, Pepperdine
1987	UCLA	Al Scates	3–0	Southern Cal	Ozzie Volstad, UCLA
1988	Southern Cal	Bob Yoder	3–2	UC-Santa Barbara	Jen-Kai Liu, Southern Cal
1989	UCLA	Al Scates	3–1	Stanford	Matt Sonnichsen, UCLA
1990	Southern Cal	Jim McLaughlin	3–1	Long Beach St	Bryan Ivie, Southern Cal
1991	Long Beach St	Ray Ratelle	3–1	Southern Cal	Brent Hilliard, Long Beach St
1992	Pepperdine	Marv Dunphy	3–0	Stanford	Alon Grinberg, Pepperdine
1993	UCLA	Al Scates	3–0	Cal St-Northridge	Mike Sealy/Jeff Nygaard, UCLA
1994	Penn St	Tom Peterson	3–2	UCLA	Ramon Hernandez, Penn St
1995	UCLA	Al Scates	3–0	Penn St	Jeff Nygaard, UCLA
1996	UCLA	Al Scates	3–2	Hawaii	Yuval Katz, Hawaii
1997	Stanford	Ruben Nieves	3–2	UCLA	Mike Lambert, Stanford
1998	UCLA	Al Scates	3–2	Pepperdine	George Roumain, Pepperdine
1999	Brigham Young	Carl McGown	3–0	Long Beach St	Ossie Antonetti, Brigham Young

Women

DIVISION I

Year	Champion	Coach	Score	Runner-Up
1981	Southern Cal	Chuck Erbe	3–2	UCLA
1982	Hawaii	Dave Shoji	3–2	Southern Cal
1983	Hawaii	Dave Shoji	3–0	UCLA
1984	UCLA	Andy Banachowski	3–2	Stanford
1985	Pacific	John Dunning	3–1	Stanford
1986	Pacific	John Dunning	3–0	Nebraska
1987	Hawaii	Dave Shoji	3–1	Stanford
1988	Texas	Mick Haley	3–0	Hawaii
1989	Long Beach St	Brian Gimmillaro	3–0	Nebraska
1990	UCLA	Andy Banachowski	3–0	Pacific
1991	UCLA	Andy Banachowski	3–2	Long Beach St
1992	Stanford	Don Shaw	3–1	UCLA
1993	Long Beach St	Brian Gimmillaro	3–1	Penn St
1994	Stanford	Don Shaw	3–1	UCLA
1995	Nebraska	Terry Pettit	3–1	Texas
1996	Stanford	Don Shaw	3–0	Hawaii
1997	Stanford	Don Shaw	3–2	Penn St
1998	Long Beach St	Brian Gimmillaro	3–2	Penn St

DIVISION II

Year	Champion	Year	Champion	Year	Champion
1981	Cal St-Sacramento	1987	Cal St-Northridge	1993	Northern Michigan
1982	UC-Riverside	1988	Portland St	1994	Northern Michigan
1983	Cal St-Northridge	1989	Cal St-Bakersfield	1995	Barry
1984	Portland St	1990	West Texas A&M	1996	Nebraska-Omaha
1985	Portland St	1991	West Texas A&M	1997	West Texas A&M
1986	UC-Riverside	1992	Portland St	1998	Hawaii Pacific

DIVISION III

Year	Champion	Year	Champion	Year	Champion
1981	UC-San Diego	1987	UC-San Diego	1993	Washington (MO)
1982	La Verne	1988	UC-San Diego	1994	Washington (MO)
1983	Elmhurst	1989	Washington (MO)	1995	Washington (MO)
1984	UC-San Diego	1990	UC-San Diego	1996	Washington (MO)
1985	Elmhurst	1991	Washington (MO)	1997	UC-San Diego
1986	UC-San Diego	1992	Washington (MO)	1998	Central (IA)

Water Polo

Year	Champion	Coach	Score	Runner-Up
1969	UCLA	Bob Horn	5–2	California
1970	UC-Irvine	Ed Newland	7–6 (3 OT)	UCLA
1971	UCLA	Bob Horn	5–3	San Jose St
1972	UCLA	Bob Horn	10–5	UC-Irvine
1973	California	Pete Cutino	8–4	UC-Irvine
1974	California	Pete Cutino	7–6	UC-Irvine
1975	California	Pete Cutino	9–8	UC-Irvine
1976	Stanford	Art Lambert	13–12	UCLA
1977	California	Pete Cutino	8–6	UC-Irvine
1978	Stanford	Dante Dettamanti	7–6 (3 OT)	California
1979	UC-Santa Barbara	Pete Snyder	11–3	UCLA
1980	Stanford	Dante Dettamanti	8–6	California
1981	Stanford	Dante Dettamanti	17–6	Long Beach St
1982	UC-Irvine	Ed Newland	7–4	Stanford
1983	California	Pete Cutino	10–7	Southern Cal
1984	California	Pete Cutino	9–8	Stanford
1985	Stanford	Dante Dettamanti	12–11 (2 OT)	UC-Irvine
1986	Stanford	Dante Dettamanti	9–6	California
1987	California	Pete Cutino	9–8 (OT)	Southern Cal
1988	California	Pete Cutino	14–11	UCLA
1989	UC-Irvine	Ed Newland	9–8	California
1990	California	Steve Heaston	8–7	Stanford
1991	California	Steve Heaston	7–6	UCLA
1992	California	Steve Heaston	12–11	Stanford
1993	Stanford	Dante Dettamanti	11–9	Southern Cal
1994	Stanford	Dante Dettamanti	14–10	Southern Cal
1995	UCLA	Guy Baker	10–8	California
1996	UCLA	Guy Baker	8–7	Southern Cal
1997	Pepperdine	Terry Schroeder	8–7 (OT)	Southern Cal
1998	Southern Cal	John Williams	9–8 (2 OT)	Stanford

Wrestling

DIVISION I

Year	Champion	Coach	Pts	Runner-Up	Pts	Most Outstanding Wrestler
1928	Oklahoma St*	E.C. Gallagher				
1929	Oklahoma St	E.C. Gallagher	26	Michigan	18	
1930	Oklahoma St*	E.C. Gallagher	27	Illinois	14	
1931	Oklahoma St*	E.C. Gallagher		Michigan		
1932	Indiana*	W.H. Thom		Oklahoma St		Edwin Belshaw, Indiana
1933	Oklahoma St*	E.C. Gallagher				Allan Kelley, Oklahoma St
	Iowa St*	Hugo Otopalik				Pat Johnson, Harvard
1934	Oklahoma St	E.C. Gallagher	29	Indiana	19	Ben Bishop, Lehigh
1935	Oklahoma St	E.C. Gallagher	36	Oklahoma	18	Ross Flood, Oklahoma St
1936	Oklahoma	Paul Keen	14	Central St (OK)	10	Wayne Martin, Oklahoma
				Oklahoma St	10	
1937	Oklahoma St	E.C. Gallagher	31	Oklahoma	13	Stanley Henson, Oklahoma St
1938	Oklahoma St	E.C. Gallagher	19	Illinois	15	Joe McDaniels, Oklahoma St
1939	Oklahoma St	E.C. Gallagher	33	Lehigh	12	Dale Hanson, Minnesota
1940	Oklahoma St	E.C. Gallagher	24	Indiana	14	Don Nichols, Michigan
1941	Oklahoma St	Art Griffith	37	Michigan St	26	Al Whitehurst, Oklahoma St
1942	Oklahoma St	Art Griffith	31	Michigan St	26	David Arndt, Oklahoma St
1943–45	No tournament					
1946	Oklahoma St	Art Griffith	25	Northern Iowa	24	Gerald Leeman, Northern Iowa
1947	Cornell	Paul Scott	32	Northern Iowa	19	William Koll, Northern Iowa
1948	Oklahoma St	Art Griffith	33	Michigan St	28	William Koll, Northern Iowa
1949	Oklahoma St	Art Griffith	32	Northern Iowa	27	Charles Hetrick, Oklahoma St
1950	Northern Iowa	David McCuskey	30	Purdue	16	Anthony Gizoni, Waynesburg
1951	Oklahoma	Port Robertson	24	Oklahoma St	23	Walter Romanowski, Cornell
1952	Oklahoma	Port Robertson	22	Northern Iowa	21	Tommy Evans, Oklahoma
1953	Penn St	Charles Speidel	21	Oklahoma	15	Frank Bettucci, Cornell
1954	Oklahoma St	Art Griffith	32	Pittsburgh	17	Tommy Evans, Oklahoma
1955	Oklahoma St	Art Griffith	40	Penn St	31	Edward Eichelberger, Lehigh
1956	Oklahoma St	Art Griffith	65	Oklahoma	62	Dan Hodge, Oklahoma
1957	Oklahoma	Port Robertson	73	Pittsburgh	66	Dan Hodge, Oklahoma
1958	Oklahoma St	Myron Roderick	77	Iowa St	62	Dick Delgado, Oklahoma
1959	Oklahoma St	Myron Roderick	73	Iowa St	51	Ron Gray, Iowa St
1960	Oklahoma	Thomas Evans	59	Iowa St	40	Dave Auble, Cornell

DIVISION I (Cont.)

Year	Champion	Coach	Pts	Runner-Up	Pts	Most Outstanding Wrestler
1961	Oklahoma St	Myron Roderick	82	Oklahoma	63	E. Gray Simons, Lock Haven
1962	Oklahoma St	Myron Roderick	82	Oklahoma	45	E. Gray Simons, Lock Haven
1963	Oklahoma	Thomas Evans	48	Iowa St	45	Mickey Martin, Oklahoma
1964	Oklahoma St	Myron Roderick	87	Oklahoma	58	Dean Lahr, Colorado
1965	Iowa St	Harold Nichols	87	Oklahoma St	86	Yojiro Uetake, Oklahoma St
1966	Oklahoma St	Myron Roderick	79	Iowa St	70	Yojiro Uetake, Oklahoma St
1967	Michigan St	Grady Peninger	74	Michigan	63	Rich Sanders, Portland St
1968	Oklahoma St	Myron Roderick	81	Iowa St	78	Dwayne Keller, Oklahoma St
1969	Iowa St	Harold Nichols	104	Oklahoma	69	Dan Gable, Iowa St
1970	Iowa St	Harold Nichols	99	Michigan St	84	Larry Owings, Washington
1971	Oklahoma St	Tommy Chesbro	94	Iowa St	66	Darrell Keller, Iowa St
1972	Iowa St	Harold Nichols	103	Michigan St	72½	Wade Schalles, Clarion
1973	Iowa St	Harold Nichols	85	Oregon St	72½	Greg Strobel, Oregon St
1974	Oklahoma	Stan Abel	69½	Michigan	67	Floyd Hitchcock, Bloomsburg
1975	Iowa	Gary Kurdelmeier	102	Oklahoma	77	Mike Frick, Lehigh
1976	Iowa	Gary Kurdelmeier	123½	Iowa St	85¾	Chuch Yagla, Iowa
1977	Iowa St	Harold Nichols	95½	Oklahoma St	88¾	Nick Gallo, Hofstra
1978	Iowa	Dan Gable	94½	Iowa St	94	Mark Churella, Michigan
1979	Iowa	Dan Gable	122½	Iowa St	88	Bruce Kinseth, Iowa
1980	Iowa	Dan Gable	110¾	Oklahoma St	87	Howard Harris, Oregon St
1981	Iowa	Dan Gable	129¾	Oklahoma	100¼	Gene Mills, Syracuse
1982	Iowa	Dan Gable	131¾	Iowa St	111	Mark Schultz, Oklahoma
1983	Iowa	Dan Gable	155	Oklahoma St	102	Mike Sheets, Oklahoma St
1984	Iowa	Dan Gable	123¾	Oklahoma St	98	Jim Zalesky, Iowa
1985	Iowa	Dan Gable	145¼	Oklahoma	98½	Barry Davis, Iowa
1986	Iowa	Dan Gable	158	Oklahoma	84¼	Marty Kistler, Iowa
1987	Iowa St	Jim Gibbons	133	Iowa	108	John Smith, Oklahoma St
1988	Arizona St	Bobby Douglas	93	Iowa	85½	Scott Turner, N Carolina St
1989	Oklahoma St	Joe Seay	91¼	Arizona St	70½	Tim Krieger, Iowa St
1990	Oklahoma St	Joe Seay	117¾	Arizona St	104¾	Chris Barnes, Oklahoma St
1991	Iowa	Dan Gable	157	Oklahoma St	108¾	Jeff Prescott, Penn St
1992	Iowa	Dan Gable	149	Oklahoma St	100½	Tom Brands, Iowa
1993	Iowa	Dan Gable	123¾	Penn St	87½	Terry Steiner, Iowa
1994	Oklahoma St	John Smith	94¾	Iowa	76½	Pat Smith, Oklahoma St
1995	Iowa	Dan Gable	134	Oregon St	77½	T.J. Jaworsky, N Carolina
1996	Iowa	Dan Gable	122½	Iowa St	78½	Les Gutches, Oregon St
1997	Iowa	Dan Gable	170	Oklahoma St	113½	Lincoln McIlravy, Iowa
1998	Iowa	Jim Zalesky	115	Minnesota	102	Joe Williams, Iowa
1999	Iowa	Jim Zalesky	100½	Minnesota	98½	Cael Sanderson, Iowa St

*Unofficial champions.

DIVISION II

Year	Champion	Year	Champion	Year	Champion
1963	Western St (CO)	1975	Northern Iowa	1988	N Dakota St
1964	Western St (CO)	1976	Cal St-Bakersfield	1989	Portland St
1965	Mankato St	1977	Cal St-Bakersfield	1990	Portland St
1966	Cal Poly-SLO	1978	Northern Iowa	1991	NE-Omaha
1967	Portland St	1979	Cal St-Bakersfield	1992	Central Oklahoma
1968	Cal Poly-SLO	1980	Cal St-Bakersfield	1993	Central Oklahoma
1969	Cal Poly-SLO	1981	Cal St-Bakersfield	1994	Central Oklahoma
1970	Cal Poly-SLO	1982	Cal St-Bakersfield	1995	Central Oklahoma
1971	Cal Poly-SLO	1983	Cal St-Bakersfield	1996	Pittsburgh-Johnstown
1972	Cal Poly-SLO	1984	SIU-Edwardsville	1997	San Francisco St
1973	Cal Poly-SLO	1985	SIU-Edwardsville	1998	N Dakota St
1974	Cal Poly-SLO	1986	SIU-Edwardsville	1999	Pittsburgh-Johnstown
		1987	Cal St-Bakersfield		

DIVISION III

Year	Champion	Year	Champion	Year	Champion
1974	Wilkes	1983	Brockport St	1992	Brockport
1975	John Carroll	1984	Trenton St	1993	Augsburg
1976	Montclair St	1985	Trenton St	1994	Ithaca
1977	Brockport St	1986	Montclair St	1995	Augsburg
1978	Buffalo	1987	Trenton St	1996	Wartburg
1979	Trenton St	1988	St. Lawrence	1997	Augsburg
1980	Brockport St	1989	Ithaca	1998	Augsburg
1981	Trenton St	1990	Ithaca	1999	Wartburg
1982	Brockport St	1991	Augsburg		

Swimming

Men

Event	Time	Record Holder	Date
50-yard freestyle	19.14	David Fox, N Carolina St	3-25-93
100-yard freestyle	41.80	Matt Biondi, California	4-4-87
200-yard freestyle	1:33.03	Matt Biondi, California	4-3-87
500-yard freestyle	4:08.75	Tom Dolan, Michigan	3-23-95
1650-yard freestyle	14:29.31	Tom Dolan, Michigan	3-25-95
100-yard backstroke	45.25	Neil Walker, Texas	3-28-97
200-yard backstroke	1:40.64	Jeff Rouse, Stanford	3-28-92
100-yard breaststroke	52.32	Jeremy Linn, Tennessee	3-28-97
200-yard breaststroke	1:53.77	Mike Barrowman, Michigan	3-24-90
100-yard butterfly	45.59	Lars Frolander, Southern Methodist	3-28-98
200-yard butterfly	1:41.78	Melvin Stewart, Tennessee	3-30-91
200-yard individual medley	1:43.52	Greg Burgess, Florida	3-25-93
400-yard individual medley	3:38.18	Tom Dolan, Michigan	3-24-95

Women

Event	Time	Record Holder	Date
50-yard freestyle	21.77	Amy Van Dyken, Colorado St	3-18-94
100-yard freestyle	47.61	Jenny Thompson, Stanford	3-21-92
200-yard freestyle	1:43.08	Martina Moravcova, SMU	3-28-97
500-yard freestyle	4:34.39	Janet Evans, Stanford	3-15-90
1650-yard freestyle	15:39.14	Janet Evans, Stanford	3-17-90
100-yard backstroke	52.36	Marylyn Chiang, California	3-19-99
200-yard backstroke	1:52.98	Whitney Hedgepeth, Texas	3-21-87
100-yard breaststroke	59.71	Beata Kaszuba, Arizona St	3-17-95
200-yard breaststroke	2:09.71	Beata Kaszuba, Arizona St	3-18-95
100-yard butterfly	51.34	Misty Hyman, Stanford	3-21-98
200-yard butterfly	1:53.36	Limin Liu, Nevada	3-20-99
200-yard individual medley	1:55.54	Summer Sanders, Stanford	3-19-92
400-yard individual medley	4:02.28	Summer Sanders, Stanford	3-20-92

Indoor Track and Field

Men

Event	Mark	Record Holder	Date
55-meter dash	6.00	Lee McRae, Pittsburgh	3-14-86
55-meter hurdles	7.07	Allen Johnson, N Carolina	3-13-92
200-meter dash	20.36	Obadele Thompson, UTEP	3-8-96
400-meter dash	45.69	Roxbert Martin, Oklahoma	3-8-97
800-meter run	1:45.80	Einars Tupuritis, Wichita St	3-9-96
Mile run	3:55.33	Kevin Sullivan, Michigan	3-11-95
3,000-meter run	7:46.03	Adam Goucher, Colorado	3-14-98
5,000-meter run	13:37.94	Jonah Koech, Iowa St	3-9-90
High jump	7 ft 9¼ in	Hollis Conway, SW Louisiana	3-11-89
Pole vault	19 ft 2¼ in	Jacob Davis, Texas	3-6-99
Long jump	27 ft 10 in	Carl Lewis, Houston	3-13-81
Triple jump	56 ft 9½ in	Keith Connor, SMU	3-13-81
Shot put	69 ft 8½ in	Michael Carter, SMU	3-13-81
		Soren Tallhem, Brigham Young	3-9-85
35-pound weight throw	76 ft 5½ in	Robert Weir, SMU	3-11-83

Women

Event	Mark	Record Holder	Date
55-meter dash	6.56	Gwen Torrence, Georgia	3-14-87
55-meter hurdles	7.41	Michelle Freeman	3-13-92
		Angie Vaughn, Texas	3-14-98
200-meter dash	22.90	Holly Hyche, Indiana St	3-11-94
400-meter dash	51.05	Maicel Malone, Arizona St	3-9-91
800-meter run	2:01.77	Hazel Clark, Florida	3-5-99
Mile run	4:30.63	Suzy Favor, Wisconsin	3-11-89
3,000-meter run	8:54.98	Stephanie Herbst, Wisconsin	3-15-86
5,000-meter run	15:39.75	Amy Skieresz, Arizona	3-7-97
High jump	6 ft 5½ in	Amy Acuff, UCLA	3-11-95
Pole vault	13 ft 11¼ in	Melissa Price, Fresno St	3-6-99
Long jump	22 ft 1 in	Daphne Saunders, Louisiana St	3-12-94
Triple jump	46 ft 9 in	Suzette Lee, Louisiana St	3-8-97
Shot put	60 ft 5¼ in	Teri Tunks, SMU	3-14-98
20-point weight throw	71 ft 8¾ in	Dawn Ellerbe, S Carolina	3-7-97

Outdoor Track and Field

Men

Event	Mark	Record Holder	Date
100-meter dash	9.92	Ato Bolden, UCLA	6-1-96
200-meter dash	19.87	Lorenzo Daniel, Mississippi St	6-3-88
400-meter dash	44.00	Quincy Watts, Southern Cal	6-6-92
800-meter run	1:44.70	Mark Everett, Florida	6-1-90
1,500-meter run	3:35.30	Sydney Maree, Villanova	6-6-81
3,000-meter steeplechase	8:12.39	Henry Rono, Washington St	6-1-78
5,000-meter run	13:20.63	Sydney Maree, Villanova	6-2-79
10,000-meter run	28:01.30	Suleiman Nyambui, UTEP	6-1-79
110-meter high hurdles	13.22	Greg Foster, UCLA	6-2-78
400-meter intermediate hurdles	47.85	Kevin Young, UCLA	6-3-88
High jump	7 ft 9¾ in	Hollis Conway, SW Louisiana	6-3-89
Pole vault	19 ft 1 in	Lawrence Johnson, Tennessee	5-29-96
Long jump	28 ft	Erick Walder, Arkansas	6-3-93
Triple jump	57 ft 7¾ in	Keith Connor, SMU	6-5-82
Shot put	72 ft 2¼ in	John Godina, UCLA	6-3-95
Discus throw	220 ft	Kamy Keshmiri, Nevada	6-5-92
Hammer throw	265 ft 3 in	Balazs Kiss, Southern Cal	5-31-96
Javelin throw	266 ft 9 in	Todd Riech, Fresno St	6-3-94
Decathlon	8279 pts	Tito Steiner, Brigham Young	6-2/3-81

Women

Event	Mark	Record Holder	Date
100-meter dash	10.78	Dawn Sowell, Louisiana St	6-3-89
200-meter dash	22.04	Dawn Sowell, Louisiana St	6-2-89
400-meter dash	50.18	Pauline Davis, Alabama	6-3-89
800-meter run	1:59.11	Suzy Favor, Wisconsin	6-1-90
1,500-meter run	4:08.26	Suzy Favor, Wisconsin	6-2-90
3,000-meter run	8:47.35	Vicki Huber, Villanova	6-3-88
5,000-meter run	15:37.77	Amy Skieresz, Arizona	6-5-98
10,000-meter run	32:28.57	Sylvia Mosqueda, Cal St-Los Angeles	6-1-88
100-meter hurdles	12.70	Tananjalyn Stanley, Louisiana St	6-3-89
400-meter hurdles	54.54	Ryan Tolbert, Vanderbilt	6-6-97
High jump	6 ft 5 in	Amy Acuff, UCLA	6-3-95
Pole vault	13 ft 5¼ in	Paula Serrano, Cal Poly-San Luis Obispo	6-6-99
Long jump	22 ft 9¼ in	Sheila Echols, Louisiana St	6-5-87
Triple jump	46 ft ¾ in	Sheila Hudson, California	6-2-90
Shot put	61 ft 2¼ in	Tressa Thompson, Nebraska	6-4-98
Discus throw	210 ft 10 in	Seilala Sua, UCLA	6-6-99
Hammer throw	209 ft 4 in	Lisa Misipeka, S Carolina	6-6-98
Javelin throw	206 ft 9 in	Karin Smith, Cal Poly-SLO	6-4-82
Heptathlon	6527 pts	Diane Guthrie-Gresham, George Mason	6-2/3-95

Olympics

Sydney prepares to take the plunge

Racket Games

With corruption in its ranks spinning out of control, the IOC needs to change the way it conducts business

BY MERRELL NODEN

THE OLYMPIC GAMES have probably never been the gleaming temple of nobility and lofty ideals we so desperately want them to be. Over the years they have been bloodied by terrorists, exploited for corporate profit, boycotted for political gain and tarnished by drug use and other forms of cheating.

Never before, though, has the Olympic movement looked as tawdry and venal as it did in December 1998 and the early months of '99, as week after week brought further proof of the greed and staggering sense of entitlement that characterized IOC members' response to the Salt Lake Organizing Committee's (SLOC) bid for the 2002 Games. With SLOC members determined not to let these Games get away, as they had on four previous occasions, the courtship process came to resemble an anything-goes grabfest, with cash, trips to the Super Bowl and Disneyland, college tuition, fur coats, cosmetic surgery, antique pistols and even a position in Brigham Young University's history department among the things being offered in exchange for IOC members' votes.

And, as the folks from Salt Lake City quickly came to realize, there was no shortage of IOC members eager to play *Let's Make a Deal*—indeed, who looked on the palm-greasing as business as usual. As one member of the SLOC board of directors put it, "Despite what the IOC says, putting on the Games isn't about the athletes. It's about money."

By the time the scandal had blown up to its full, ugly proportions, it had spread far beyond Salt Lake City and given rise to at least five separate investigations—of the SLOC, of the IOC and of Olympic organizing committees around the world, many of whom were found to have employed the same corrupt methods as the SLOC. Many top SLOC executives, including its president, Frank Joklik, resigned in disgrace, and 10 (of 115) IOC members either resigned or were pushed out (though better connected members escaped with severe reprimands).

It is too early to tell whether lasting damage has been done to the Games' prestige. But it cannot have been a good sign that a number of major Olympic sponsors expressed outrage at the revelations and that one, Johnson & Johnson, cancelled its $30 million sponsorship deal of the 2002 Games. John Hancock Financial Services announced it would end its commitment to the IOC after the 2000 Games. "It's hard to step up in a boardroom now and say we're paying millions for a new Olympic sponsorship," said John Hancock president David D'Alessandro. In April the U.S. Senate conducted hearings on whether to end the IOC's tax exempt status, a change which, if implemented, could have grave consequences for Olympic finances. There was even talk of removing the 2002 Games from Salt Lake City, but nothing came of it.

Andrew Thomson, a former Australian sports minister and son of five-time British Open golf champion Peter Thomson, went furthest of all, calling for an end to the Games. "If you're going to organize sport on a global level, I would have thought the

The Olympics may have been permanently besmirched under Samaranch's stewardship.

first requirement woud be that it be ethically clean and that there be no suggestion of any financial taint at all," Thomson told the Australian Broadcasting Corporation. "Why can't we organize a global competition in some other form where the franchises are not handed out by this extraordinary, bizarre group of men?"

Of course, the most extraordinary of the bunch is longtime IOC president Juan Antonio Samaranch, a former Franco foot soldier who now insists on being addressed as His Excellency. The one measure that would surely have gone a long way towards restoring confidence in the Olympics was for the IOC to get rid of Samaranch. But Samaranch quickly made it plain that he was going nowhere. "I am sincerely disappointed that IOC members were involved in the events revealed in this investigation and am deeply saddened by their conduct," he said piously, as he announced the formation of an ethics

DOUGLAS C. PIZAC/AP

lack of transparency and accountability within the IOC...has brought a dark cloud over the integrity of the Olympics."

The direct catalyst for the most embarrassing scandal in Olympic history was a 1996 letter from the SLOC's Dave Johnson to the daughter of Rene Essomba, a since-deceased IOC member from Cameroon, in which Johnson informed her that the accompanying check for $10,000 would be her last. The letter, which was leaked to KTVX, the ABC affiliate in Salt Lake City, in November 1998, turned out to be a fake, but the information in it was true. SLOC officials admitted that between 1991 and '95 they had provided a total of $400,000 in what they termed "humanitarian aid" to not only Essomba's daughter but also to 12 other students, six of whom were relatives of IOC members.

commission to investigate the whole mess.

One needn't be a cynic to feel that any leader truly "saddened" by the whole mess would have had the good grace to resign promptly. Not Samaranch, who apparently felt no shame in accepting two rifles and a shotgun worth more than $2,000—well above the $150 maximum permitted by IOC by-laws—from the SLOC. Either Samaranch still didn't get it, or he got it all too well, knowing from past experience that he would be allowed to ride out this storm. Far from resigning, he announced that he would be staying on to finish his fifth term, which ends in 2001, and he turned down an invitation to testify before the Senate Commerce Committee, a decision that clearly troubled committee chairman John McCain, who said, "The

As one might expect in a city that prides itself on its strong moral character, many Salt Lake City residents and officials were deeply offended to learn of the payments and were hardly placated when they were assured that the money had come from a private fund. "You hear stories about the wining and dining of IOC members," said Randy Horiuchi, a Utah county commissioner, as he called for an audit of the SLOC's budget. "It may not be right, but you expect that. But giving them cash? In Utah, we call that a bribe."

That's what you call it just about everywhere except at gatherings of certain IOC members. Though in the end it was estimated that only 5% to 7% of the IOC's membership was corrupt, others had to have known what was going on. At IOC meetings in December 1998, Marc Hodler of Switzerland called for an investigation. At 80, Hodler is the second most senior IOC member. To Samaranch, his defection must have felt like a betrayal, since the two are old friends. Once the scent of scandal was in the air, there was no stopping the torrent of damning revelations. By February the five investigations were under way, and virtually every recent bidding city was soon found to have engaged in bribery.

There should have been something funny about the specific instances of greed that emerged day after day, paraded out like the wishes granted in fairy tales. Among the many gaudy "benefits" lavished on IOC members in exchange for their fealty—even while acknowledging their impropriety, Richard Pound, the Montreal-based lawyer who headed up the IOC commission, refused to call them bribes—were a mind-boggling litany of gifts, from jobs to Stetson hats, from the use of Parisian apartments to tours of the Loire Valley castles. To lock up Mongolia's vote, the Sydney bid committee promised to ship seven rare horses to the Gobi desert, a project which in the end cost $160,000. The chairman of the Manchester, England, bid committee admitted knowing the shoe size of one IOC member's second daughter.

To understand how the better judgment of so many people seems to have shorted out simultaneously, one must realize that Salt Lake City had been trying without avail to lure the Olympics to Utah as far back as 1966. It had watched with mounting disappointment as the IOC awarded its prestigious—and lucrative—prize to cities that did not necessarily offer a better venue but were better at playing the game.

Salt Lake City's bid for the 1972 Games had been submitted in a three-ring looseleaf binder. By 1991, when the IOC's then 94 members gathered at the Hyatt Regency in Birmingham, England, to choose the host city for the 1998 Winter Olympics, the SLOC showed it was getting the hang of things by delivering its bid bound in luxurious saddlebag leather scented with pine needles. Nice touch, but unbeknownst to the innocents from squeaky clean Salt Lake

City, larger forces were at work to make this anything but a fair fight. For one thing, rumor had it that Samaranch did not want the Games returning to the U.S. so soon after the 1996 Games in Atlanta. Equally important, a consortium of Japanese businessmen had promised to donate $20 million toward the Olympic Museum Samaranch hoped to build in Lausanne.

Hovering constantly at Samaranch's side throughout the proceedings in Birmingham was a stocky, white-haired Yugoslav businessman named Artur Takacs who, though not an IOC member, was somehow permitted seemingly unlimited access to the delegates. Takacs's role, it turned out, was to ensure that the bid went to Nagano, an outcome sure to be celebrated not only by his patron in the Olympic family, Samaranch, but also by his own family, since his son, Goran, was a paid lobbyist for the Japanese city. If Nagano won the bid, Goran was slated to receive a bonus on top of a guaranteed payment of $363,000.

Never mind that to anyone with even the slightest sense of honor this constituted a breech of ethics. That is the way business is conducted in the clubby confines of the IOC. Nagano triumphed over Salt Lake City by four votes. "We were passing out boxes of saltwater taffy," lamented one SLOC member, "while Nagano was giving them Hondas."

SLOC members were determined not to let this happen again. Between 1991 and '95 they played the game well, dispensing an estimated $700,000 in gifts to IOC members. When their dealings were exposed, the toll in Salt Lake City was tremendous. On Jan. 8, 1999, the SLOC's two top officials, Joklik and Johnson, both resigned, and they were followed by Alfredo La Mont, who had worked in USOC international relations for 14 years. Salt Lake City mayor Deedee Corradini, who was also a member of the SLOC, announced that she would not seek another term.

The scandal continued to mushroom, spreading across oceans and continents. On Jan. 24 six IOC members were expelled, including Augustin Arroyo of Ecuador;

DeFrantz questioned the effectiveness of the IOC's disciplinary actions.

Zein El Abdin Ahmed Abdel Gadir of Sudan; Charles Mukora of Kenya; Sergio Santander of Chile; Lamine Keita of Mali; and Jean-Claude Ganga of Congo, who was accused of accepting more than $200,000 worth of gifts.

The purge did little to silence critics. "What's the new IOC?" asked IOC vice president Anita DeFrantz, a former U.S. Olympic rower. "The IOC without 10 members." Many found it suspicious that of the 10 members who were expelled or who resigned, nine were from developing countries: "When [IOC leaders] were looking for someone to blame, it must have been easy to say, 'Throw the Samoan out,'" said Samoa's Paul Wallwork, expelled because his wife had accepted a $30,000 loan—later repaid—from Tom Welch, the former president of the SLOC bid committee, who resigned in 1997 following allegations of spousal abuse.

The bigger players escaped with warnings. Un Yong Kim of South Korea, a member of the IOC's executive board who stood accused of arranging for his son to work at a local broadcasting company, was given a stinging rebuke. Phil Coles, a former Olympic canoeist and the IOC member from Australia for 17 years, was slapped with the IOC's "most severe warning" for accepting excessive hospitality—some $60,000 worth—from SLOC officials. Later Coles was accused of accepting jewelry worth $6,700 from the Athens bid committee. Indeed, he seems to have been a strategic ally for other bid committees since he appears to have kept dossiers detailing the penchants of other IOC members and

to have shared them with other bid hopefuls. In June a tearful Coles resigned from the Sydney organizing committee.

One by one the various panels submitted their reports. In July the IOC's own reform panel offered a number of proposals: term limits for IOC members, who currently are elected for life; lowering the mandatory retirement age 10 years, to 70; and democratic elections for members. They recommended further the inclusion of 10 active athletes, to be elected by their peers.

One wonders, though, if the recommendations were enough to restore the Olympics to their lofty place in world culture. Many observers expressed the belief that the IOC could not be cleansed while Samaranch was still in power. Or were the people who vandalized the Olympic sculpture garden in Lausanne speaking for the rest of us, when, in June, after it was announced that Turin, Italy, had upset Sion, Switzerland, to win the 2006 Winter Games, they spray-painted the letters M-A-F-I-A, on a statue, one in each of the five Olympic rings?

FOR THE RECORD·1996–98 Games

1996 Summer Games

TRACK AND FIELD
Men

100 METERS
1. ..Donovan Bailey, Canada — 9.84 WR
2. ..Frankie Fredericks, Namibia — 9.89
3. ..Ato Boldon, Trinidad and Tobago — 9.90

200 METERS
1. ..Michael Johnson, United States — 19.32 WR
2. ..Frankie Fredericks, Namibia — 19.68
3. ..Ato Boldon, Trinidad and Tobago — 19.80

400 METERS
1. ..Michael Johnson, United States — 43.49 OR
2. ..Roger Black, Great Britain — 44.41
3. ..Davis Kamoga, Uganda — 44.53

800 METERS
1. ..Vebjoern Rodal, Norway — 1:42.58 OR
2. ..Hezekiel Sepeng, South Africa — 1:42.74
3. ..Fred Onyancha, Kenya — 1:42.79

1500 METERS
1. ..Noureddine Morceli, Algeria — 3:35.78
2. ..Fermin Cacho, Spain — 3:36.40
3. ..Stephen Kipkorir, Kenya — 3:36.72

5000 METERS
1. ..Venuste Niyongabo, Burundi — 13:07.96
2. ..Paul Bitok, Kenya — 13:08.16
3. ..Khalid Boulami, Morocco — 13:08.37

10,000 METERS
1. ..Haile Gebrselassie, Ethiopia — 27:07.34 OR
2. ..Paul Tergat, Kenya — 27:08.17
3. ..Salah Hissou, Morocco — 27:24.67

MARATHON
1. ..Josia Thugwane, South Africa — 2:12:36
2. ..Bong-Ju Lee, South Korea — 2:12:39
3. ..Eric Wainaina, Kenya — 2:12:44

110-METER HURDLES
1. ..Allen Johnson, United States — 12.95 OR
2. ..Mark Crear, United States — 13.09
3. ..Florian Schwarthoff, Germany — 13.17

400-METER HURDLES
1. ..Derrick Adkins, United States — 47.54
2. ..Samuel Matete, Zambia — 47.78
3. ..Calvin Davis, United States — 47.96

3000-METER STEEPLECHASE
1. ..Joseph Keter, Kenya — 8:07.12
2. ..Moses Kiptanui, Kenya — 8:08.33
3. ..Alessandro Lambruschini, Italy — 8:11.28

4 X 100 METER RELAY
1. ..Canada: Donovan Bailey, Robert Esmie, Glenroy Gilbert, Bruny Surin — 37.69
2. ..United States — 38.05
3. ..Brazil — 38.41

4 X 400 METER RELAY
1. ..United States: Alvin Harrison, Anthuan Maybank, Derek Mills, LaMont Smith — 2:55.99
2. ..Great Britain — 2:56.60
3. ..Jamaica — 2:59.42

20-KILOMETER WALK
1. ..Jefferson Pérez, Ecuador — 1:20:07
2. ..Ilya Markov, Russia — 1:20:16
3. ..Bernardo Segura, Mexico — 1:20:23

50-KILOMETER WALK
1. ..Robert Korzeniowski, Poland — 3:43:30
2. ..Mikhail Shchennikov, Russia — 3:43:46
3. ..Valentin Massana, Spain — 3:44:19

HIGH JUMP
1. ..Charles Austin, United States — 7 ft 10 in OR
2. ..Artur Partyka, Poland — 7 ft 9¼ in
3. ..Steve Smith, Great Britain — 7 ft 8½ in

POLE VAULT
1. ..Jean Galfione, France — 19 ft 5¼ in OR
2. ..Igor Trandenkov, Russia — 19 ft 5¼ in
3. ..Andrei Tivontchik, Germany — 19 ft 5¼ in

LONG JUMP
1. ..Carl Lewis, United States — 27 ft 10¾ in
2. ..James Beckford, Jamaica — 27 ft 2½ in
3. ..Joe Greene, United States — 27 ft ½ in

TRIPLE JUMP
1. ..Kenny Harrison, United States — 59 ft 4¼ in OR
2. ..Jonathan Edwards, Great Britain — 58 ft 8 in
3. ..Yoelvis Quesada, Cuba — 57 ft 2¾ in

SHOT PUT
1. ..Randy Barnes, United States — 70 ft 11 in
2. ..John Godina, United States — 68 ft 2½ in
3. ..Oleksandr Bagach, Ukraine — 68 ft ½ in

DISCUS THROW
1. ..Lars Riedel, Germany — 227 ft 8 in OR
2. ..Vladimir Dubrovshchik, Belarus — 218 ft 6 in
3. ..Vasiliy Kaptyukh, Belarus — 215 ft 10 in

HAMMER THROW
1. ..Balazs Kiss, Hungary — 266 ft 6 in
2. ..Lance Deal, United States — 266 ft 2 in
3. ..Oleksiy Krykun, Ukraine — 262 ft 6 in

JAVELIN
1. ..Jan Zelezny, Czech Republic — 289 ft 3 in
2. ..Steve Backley, Great Britain — 286 ft 10 in
3. ..Seppo Raty, Finland — 285 ft 4 in

DECATHLON
Pts
1. ..Dan O'Brien, United States — 8824 OR
2. ..Frank Busemann, Germany — 8706
3. ..Tomás Dvorák, Czech Republic — 8664

Note: OR=Olympic record. WR=world record. EOR=equals Olympic record. EWR=equals world record.

TRACK AND FIELD (Cont.)
Women

100 METERS
1. ..Gail Devers, United States — 10.94
2. ..Merlene Ottey, Jamaica — 10.94
3. ..Gwen Torrence, United States — 10.96

200 METERS
1. ..Marie-José Pérec, France — 22.12
2. ..Merlene Ottey, Jamaica — 22.24
3. ..Mary Onyali, Nigeria — 22.38

400 METERS
1. ..Marie-José Pérec, France — 48.25 OR
2. ..Cathy Freeman, Australia — 48.63
3. ..Falilat Ogunkoya, Nigeria — 49.10

800 METERS
1. ..Svetlana Masterkova, Russia — 1:57.73
2. ..Ana Fidelia Quirot, Cuba — 1:58.11
3. ..Maria Mutola, Mozambique — 1:58.71

1500 METERS
1. ..Svetlana Masterkova, Russia — 4:00.83
2. ..Gabriela Szabo, Russia — 4:01.54
3. ..Theresia Kiesl, Austria — 4:03.02

5000 METERS
1. ..Wang Junxia, China — 14:59.88
2. ..Pauline Konga, Kenya — 15:03.49
3. ..Roberta Brunet, Italy — 15:07.52

10,000 METERS
1. ..Fernanda Ribeiro, Portugal — 31:01.63 OR
2. ..Wang Junxia, China — 31:02.58
3. ..Gete Wami, Ethiopia — 31:06.68

MARATHON
1. ..Fatuma Roba, Ethiopia — 2:26:05
2 ...Valentina Yegorova, Russia — 2:28:05
3. ..Yuko Arimori, Japan — 2:28:39

100-METER HURDLES
1. ..Lyudmila Engqvist, Sweden — 12.58
2. ..Brigita Bukovec, Slovenia — 12.59
3. ..Patricia Girard-Leno, France — 12.65

400-METER HURDLES
1. ..Deon Hemmings, Jamaica — 52.82 OR
2. ..Kim Batten, United States — 53.08
3. ..Tonja Buford-Bailey, United States — 53.22

4 X 100 METER RELAY
1. ..United States: Chryste Gaines, Gail Devers, Inger Miller, Gwen Torrence — 41.95
2. ..Bahamas — 42.14
3. ..Jamaica — 42.24

4 X 400 METER RELAY
1. ..United States: Rochelle Stevens, Maicel Malone, Kim Graham, Jearl Miles — 3:20.91
2. ..Nigeria — 3:21.04
3. ..Germany — 3:21.41

10-KILOMETER WALK
1. ..Elena Nikolayeva, Russia — 41:49 OR
2. ..Elisabetta Perrone, Italy — 42:12
3. ..Wang Yan, China — 42:19

HIGH JUMP
1. ..Stefka Kostadinova, Bulgaria — 6 ft 8¾ in OR
2. ..Niki Bakogianni, Greece — 6 ft 8 in
3. ..Inga Babakova, Ukraine — 6 ft 7 in

LONG JUMP
1. ..Chioma Ajunwa, Nigeria — 23 ft 4½ in
2. ..Fiona May, Italy — 23 ft ½ in
3. ..Jackie Joyner-Kersee, United States — 22 ft 11¾ in

TRIPLE JUMP
1. ..Inessa Kravets, Ukraine — 50 ft 3½ in
2. ..Inna Lasovskaya, Russia — 49 ft 1¾ in
3. ..Sarka Kasparkova, Czech Republic — 49 ft 1¾ in

SHOT PUT
1. ..Astrid Kumbernuss, Germany — 67 ft 5½ in
2. ..Sui Xinmei, China — 65 ft 2¾ in
3. ..Irina Khudorozhkina, Russia — 63 ft 6 in

DISCUS THROW
1. ..Ilke Wyludda, Germany — 228 ft 6 in
2. ..Natalya Sadova, Russia — 218 ft 1 in
3. ..Ellina Zvereva, Belarus — 215 ft 4 in

JAVELIN
1. ..Heli Rantanen, Finland — 222 ft 11 in
2. ..Louise McPaul, Australia — 215 ft
3. ..Trine Hattestad, Norway — 213 ft 2 in

HEPTATHLON
	Pts
1. ..Ghada Shouaa, Syria	6780
2. ..Natasha Sazanovich, Belarus	6563
3. ..Denise Lewis, Great Britain	6489

BADMINTON

Men
SINGLES
1. ..Poul-Erik Hoyer-Larsen, Denmark
2. ..Dong Jiong, China
3. ..Rashid Sidek, Malaysia

DOUBLES
1. ..Rexy Mainaky & Ricky Subagja, Indonesia
2. ..Cheah Soon Kit & Yap Kim Hock, Malaysia
3. ..S. Antonius & Denny Kantono, Indonesia

Women
SINGLES
1. ..Bang Soo Hyun, South Korea
2. ..Mia Audina, Indonesia
3. ..Susi Susanti, Indonesia

DOUBLES
1. ...Ge Fei & Gu Jun, China
2. ..Gil Young Ah & Jang Hye Ock, South Korea
3. ..Qin Yiyuan & Tang Yongshu, China

Note: OR=Olympic record. WR=world record. EOR=equals Olympic record. EWR=equals world record.

BADMINTON *(Cont.)*

MIXED DOUBLES

1. ....Gil Young Ah & Kim Dong Moon, South Korea
2. ....Park Joo Bong & Ra Kyung Min, South Korea
3. ....Liu Jianjun & Sun Man, China

BASEBALL

1. ....Cuba
2. ....Japan
3. ....United States

CANOE/KAYAK

Men

C-1 FLATWATER 500 METERS

1.	Martin Doktor, Czech Republic	1:49.93
2.	Slavomir Knazovicky, Slovakia	1:50.51
3.	Imre Pulai, Hungary	1:50.75

C-1 FLATWATER 1000 METERS

1.	Martin Doktor, Czech Republic	3:54.41
2.	Ivan Klementiev, Latvia	3:54.95
3.	Gyorgy Zala, Hungary	3:56.36

C-2 FLATWATER 500 METERS

1.	C. Horváth & G. Kolonics, Hungary	1:40.42
2.	N. Shuravski & V. Reneischi, Moldova	1:40.45
3.	G. Andriev & G. Obreja, Romania	1:41.33

C-2 FLATWATER 1000 METERS

1.	A. Dittmer & G. Kirchbach, Germany	3:31.87
2.	A. Borsan & M. Glavan, Romania	3:32.29
3.	C. Horváth & G. Kolonics, Hungary	3:32.51

C-1 WHITEWATER SLALOM

		Pts
1.	Michal Martikan, Slovakia	151.03
2.	Lukas Pollert, Czech Republic	151.17
3.	Patrice Estanguet, France	152.84

C-2 WHITEWATER SLALOM

		Pts
1.	F. Adisson & W. Forgues, France	158.82
2.	J. Rohan & M. Simek, Czech Republic	160.16
3.	A. Ehrenberg & M. Senft, Germany	163.72

K-1 FLATWATER 500 METERS

1.	Antonio Rossi, Italy	1:37.42
2.	Knut Holmann, Norway	1:38.33
3.	Piotr Markiewicz, Poland	1:38.61

K-1 FLATWATER 1000 METERS

1.	Knut Holmann, Norway	3:25.78
2.	Beniamino Bonomi, Italy	3:27.07
3.	Clint Robinson, Australia	3:29.71

Men *(Cont.)*

K-2 FLATWATER 500 METERS

1.	K. Bluhm & T. Gutsche, Germany	1:28.69
2.	B. Bonomi & D. Scarpa, Italy	1:28.72
3.	D. Collins & A. Trim, Australia	1:29.40

K-2 FLATWATER 1000 METERS

1.	A. Rossi & D. Scarpa, Italy	3:09.19
2.	K. Bluhm & T. Gutsche, Germany	3:10.51
3.	M. Kazanov & A. Dushev, Bulgaria	3:11.20

K-4 FLATWATER 1000 METERS

1.	Germany	2:51.52
2.	Hungary	2:53.18
3.	Russia	2:53.99

K-1 WHITEWATER SLALOM

		Pts
1.	Oliver Fix, Germany	141.22
2.	Andraz Vehovar, Slovenia	141.65
3.	Thomas Becker, Germany	142.79

Women

K-1 FLATWATER 500 METERS

1.	Rita Kóbán, Hungary	1:47.65
2.	Caroline Brunet, Canada	1:47.89
3.	Josefa Idem, Italy	1:48.73

K-2 FLATWATER 500 METERS

1.	A. Andersson & S. Gunnarsson, Sweden	1:39.32
2.	R. Portwich & B. Fischer, Germany	1:39.68
3.	K. Borshert & A. Wood, Australia	1:40.64

K-4 FLATWATER 500 METERS

1.	Germany	1:31.07
2.	Switzerland	1:32.70
3.	Sweden	1:32.91

K-1 WHITEWATER SLALOM

		Pts
1.	Stepanka Hilgertova, Czech Republic	169.49
2.	Dana Chladek, United States	169.49
3.	Myriam Fox-Jerusalmi, France	171.00

BASKETBALL

Men

Final: United States 95, Yugoslavia 69
Lithuania (3rd)
United States: Charles Barkley, Anfernee Hardaway, Grant Hill, Karl Malone, Reggie Miller, Hakeem Olajuwon, Shaquille O'Neal, Scottie Pippen, Mitch Richmond, John Stockton, David Robinson, Gary Payton

Women

Final: United States 111, Brazil 87
Australia (3rd)
United States: Jennifer Azzi, Ruthie Bolton, Teresa Edwards, Lisa Leslie, Rebecca Lobo, Katrina McClain, Nikki McCray, Carla McGhee, Dawn Staley, Katy Steding, Sheryl Swoopes, Venus Lacey

BOXING

LIGHT FLYWEIGHT (106 LB)
1. ....Daniel Petrov, Bulgaria
2. ....Mansueto Velasco, Philippines
3. ....Oleg Kiryukhin, Ukraine
3. ....Rafael Lozano, Spain

FLYWEIGHT (112 LB)
1. ....Maikro Romero, Cuba
2. ....Bolat Zhumadilov, Kazakhstan
3. ....Zoltan Lunka, Germany
3. ....Albert Pakeev, Russia

BANTAMWEIGHT (119 LB)
1. ....István Kovács, Hungary
2. ....Arnaldo Mesa, Cuba
3. ....Vichairachanon Khadpo, Thailand
3. ....Raimkul Malakhbekov, Russia

FEATHERWEIGHT (125 LB)
1. ....Somluck Kamsing, Thailand
2. ....Serafim Todorov, Bulgaria
3. ....Pablo Chacon, Argentina
3. ....Floyd Mayweather, United States

LIGHTWEIGHT (132 LB)
1. ....Hocine Soltani, Algeria
2. ....Tontcho Tontchev, Bulgaria
3. ....Terrance Cauthen, United States
3. ....Leonard Doroftei, Romania

LIGHT WELTERWEIGHT (139 LB)
1. ....Hector Vinent, Cuba
2. ....Oktay Urkal, Germany
3. ....Fathi Missaoui, Tunisia
3. ....Bolat Niyazymbetov, Kazakhstan

WELTERWEIGHT (147 LB)
1. ....Oleg Saitov, Russia
2. ....Juan Hernández, Cuba
3. ....Daniel Santos, Puerto Rico
3. ....Marian Simion, Romania

LIGHT MIDDLEWEIGHT (156 LB)
1. ....David Reid, United States
2. ....Alfredo Duvergel, Cuba
3. ....Ermakhan Ibraimov, Kazakhstan
3. ....Karim Tulaganov, Uzbekistan

MIDDLEWEIGHT (165 LB)
1. ....Ariel Hernández, Cuba
2. ....Malik Beyleroglu, Turkey
3. ....Mohamed Bahari, Algeria
3. ....Rhoshii Wells, United States

LIGHT HEAVYWEIGHT (178 LB)
1. ....Vassili Jirov, Kazakhstan
2. ....Lee Seung Bao, South Korea
3. ....Antonio Tarver, United States
3. ....Thomas Ulrich, Germany

HEAVYWEIGHT (201 LB)
1. ....Félix Sávon, Cuba
2. ....David Defiagbon, Canada
3. ....Nate Jones, United States
3. ....Luan Krasniqi, Germany

SUPERHEAVYWEIGHT (201+ LB)
1. ....Vladimir Klitchko, Ukraine
2. ....Paea Wolfgram, Tonga
3. ....Duncan Dokiwari, Nigeria
3. ....Alexei Lezin, Russia

GYMNASTICS

Men

ALL-AROUND
		Pts
1.	Li Xiaoshuang, China	58.423
2.	Alexei Nemov, Russia	58.374
3.	Vitaly Scherbo, Belarus	58.197

HORIZONTAL BAR
		Pts
1.	Andreas Wecker, Germany	9.850
2.	Krasimir Dounev, Bulgaria	9.825
3.	Vitaly Scherbo, Belarus	9.800
3.	Fan Bin, China	9.800
3.	Alexei Nemov, Russia	9.800

PARALLEL BARS
		Pts
1.	Rustam Sharipov, Ukraine	9.837
2.	Jair Lynch, United States	9.825
3.	Vitaly Scherbo, Belarus	9.800

VAULT
		Pts
1.	Alexei Nemov, Russia	9.787
2.	Yeo Hong-Chul, South Korea	9.756
3.	Vitaly Scherbo, Belarus	9.724

POMMEL HORSE
		Pts
1.	Donghua Li, Switzerland	9.875
2.	Marius Urzica, Romania	9.825
3.	Alexei Nemov, Russia	9.787

Women

ALL-AROUND
		Pts
1.	Lilia Podkopayeva, Ukraine	39.255
2.	Gina Gogean, Romania	39.075
3.	Simona Amanar, Romania	39.067
3.	Lavinia Milosovici, Romania	39.067

VAULT
		Pts
1.	Simona Amanar, Romania	9.825
2.	Mo Huilan, China	9.768
3.	Gina Gogean, Romania	9.750

UNEVEN BARS
		Pts
1.	Svetlana Chorkina, Russia	9.850
2.	Bi Wenjing, China	9.837
2.	Amy Chow, United States	9.837

BALANCE BEAM
		Pts
1.	Shannon Miller, United States	9.862
2.	Lilia Podkopayeva, Ukraine	9.825
3.	Gina Gogean, Romania	9.787

FLOOR EXERCISE
		Pts
1.	Lilia Podkopayeva, Ukraine	9.887
2.	Simona Amanar, Romania	9.850
3.	Dominique Dawes, United States	9.837

GYMNASTICS (Cont.)

Men

RINGS

	Pts
1. ....Yuri Chechi, Italy	9.887
2. ....Szilveszter Csollany, Hungary	9.812
2. ....Dan Burinca, Romania	9.812

FLOOR EXERCISE

	Pts
1. ....Ioannis Melissanidis, Greece	9.850
2. ....Li Xiaoshuang, China	9.837
3. ....Alexei Nemov, Russia	9.800

TEAM COMBINED EXERCISES

	Pts
1. ....Russia	576.778
2. ....China	575.539
3. ....Ukraine	571.541

Women

TEAM COMBINED EXERCISES

	Pts
1. ....United States: Amanda Borden, Amy Chow, Dominique Dawes, Shannon Miller, Dominique Moceanu, Jaycie Phelps, Kerri Strug	389.225
2. ....Russia	388.404
3. ....Romania	388.246

RHYTHMIC ALL-AROUND

	Pts
1. ....Ekaterina Serebrianskaya, Ukraine	39.683
2. ....Janna Batyrchina, Russia	39.382
3. ....Elena Vitrichenko, Ukraine	39.331

RHYTHMIC TEAM COMBINED EXERCISES

	Pts
1. ....Spain	38.933
2. ....Bulgaria	38.866
3. ....Russia	38.365

SWIMMING

Men

50-METER FREESTYLE

1. ..Aleksandr Popov, Russia	22.13
2. ..Gary Hall Jr, United States	22.26
3. ..Fernando Scherer, Brazil	22.29

100-METER FREESTYLE

1. ..Aleksandr Popov, Russia	48.74
2. ..Gary Hall Jr, United States	48.81
3. ..Gustavo Borges, Brazil	49.02

200-METER FREESTYLE

1. ..Danyon Loader, New Zealand	1:47.63
2. ..Gustavo Borges, Brazil	1:48.08
3. ..Daniel Kowalski, Australia	1:48.25

400-METER FREESTYLE

1. ..Danyon Loader, New Zealand	3:47.97
2. ..Paul Palmer, Great Britain	3:49.00
3. ..Daniel Kowalski, Australia	3:49.39

1500-METER FREESTYLE

1. ..Kieren Perkins, Australia	14:56.40
2. ..Daniel Kowalski, Australia	15:02.43
3. ..Graeme Smith, Great Britain	15:02.48

100-METER BACKSTROKE

1. ..Jeff Rouse, United States	54.10
2. ..Rodolfo Falcon Cabrera, Cuba	54.98
3. ..Neisser Bent, Cuba	55.02

200-METER BACKSTROKE

1. ..Brad Bridgewater, United States	1:58.54
2. ..Tripp Schwenk, United States	1:58.99
3. ..Emanuele Merisi, Italy	1:59.18

100-METER BREASTSTROKE

1. ..Fred DeBurghgraeve, Belgium	1:00.65
2. ..Jeremy Linn, United States	1:00.77
3. ..Mark Warnecke, Germany	1:01.33

200-METER BREASTSTROKE

1. ..Norbert Rózsa, Hungary	2:12.57
2. ..Károly Güttler, Hungary	2:13.03
3. ..Andrei Korneyev, Russia	2:13.17

100-METER BUTTERFLY

1. ..Denis Pankratov, Russia	52.27 WR
2. ..Scott Miller, Australia	52.53
3. ..Vladislav Kulikov, Russia	53.13

200-METER BUTTERFLY

1. ..Denis Pankratov, Russia	1:56.51
2. ..Tom Malchow, United States	1:57.44
3. ..Scott Goodman, Australia	1:57.48

200-METER INDIVIDUAL MEDLEY

1. ..Attila Czene, Hungary	1:59.91 OR
2. ..Jani Sievinen, Finland	2:00.13
3. ..Curtis Myden, Canada	2:01.13

400-METER INDIVIDUAL MEDLEY

1. ..Tom Dolan, United States	4:14.90
2. ..Eric Namesnik, United States	4:15.25
3. ..Curtis Myden, Canada	4:16.28

4 X 100 METER MEDLEY RELAY

1. ..United States: Jeff Rouse, Mark Henderson, Gary Hall Jr., Jeremy Linn	3:34.84 WR
2. ..Russia	3:37.55
3. ..Australia	3:39.56

4 X 100 METER FREESTYLE RELAY

1. ..United States: Jon Olsen, Josh Davis, Bradley Schumacher, Gary Hall Jr.	3:15.41 OR
2. ..Russia	3:17.06
3. ..Germany	3:17.20

4 X 200 METER FREESTYLE RELAY

1. ..United States: Ryan Berube, Joe Hudepohl, Bradley Schumacher, Jon Olsen	7:14.84
2. ..Sweden	7:17.56
3. ..Germany	7:17.71

Note: OR=Olympic record. WR=world record. EOR=equals Olympic record. EWR=equals world record.

SWIMMING *(Cont.)*
Women

50-METER FREESTYLE
1. ..Amy Van Dyken, United States   24.87
2. ..Le Jingyi, China   24.90
3. ..Sandra Volker, Germany   25.14

100-METER FREESTYLE
1. ..Le Jingyi, China   54.50 OR
2. ..Sandra Volker, Germany   54.88
3. ..Angel Martino, United States   54.93

200-METER FREESTYLE
1. ..Claudia Poll, Costa Rica   1:58.16
2. ..Franziska van Almsick, Germany   1:58.57
3. ..Dagmar Hase, Germany   1:59.56

400-METER FREESTYLE
1. ..Michelle Smith, Ireland   4:07.25
2. ..Dagmar Hase, Germany   4:08.30
3. ..Kirsten Vlieghuis, Netherlands   4:08.70

800-METER FREESTYLE
1. ..Brooke Bennett, United States   8:27.89
2. ..Dagmar Hase, Germany   8:29.91
3. ..Kirsten Vlieghuis, Netherlands   8:30.84

100-METER BACKSTROKE
1. ..Beth Botsford, United States   1:01.19
2. ..Whitney Hedgepeth, United States   1:01.47
3. ..Marianne Kriel, South Africa   1:02.12

200-METER BACKSTROKE
1. ..Krisztina Egerszegi, Hungary   2:07.83
2. ..Whitney Hedgepeth, United States   2:11.98
3. ..Cathleen Rund, Germany   2:12.06

100-METER BREASTSTROKE
1. ..Penelope Heyns, South Africa   1:07.73
2. ..Amanda Beard, United States   1:08.09
3. ..Samantha Riley, Australia   1:09.18

200-METER BREASTSTROKE
1. ..Penelope Heyns, South Africa   2:25.41 OR
2. ..Amanda Beard, United States   2:25.75
3. ..Agnes Kovacs, Hungary   2:26.57

100-METER BUTTERFLY
1. ..Amy Van Dyken, United States   59.13
2. ..Liu Limin, China   59.14
3. ..Angel Martino, United States   59.23

200-METER BUTTERFLY
1. ..Susan O'Neill, Australia   2:07.76
2. ..Petria Thomas, Australia   2:09.82
3. ..Michelle Smith, Ireland   2:09.91

200-METER INDIVIDUAL MEDLEY
1. ..Michelle Smith, Ireland   2:13.93
2. ..Marianne Limpert, Canada   2:14.35
3. ..Lin Li, China   2:14.74

400-METER INDIVIDUAL MEDLEY
1. ..Michelle Smith, Ireland   4:39.18
2. ..Allison Wagner, United States   4:42.03
3. ..Krisztina Egerszegi, Hungary   4:42.53

4 X 100 METER MEDLEY RELAY
1. ..United States: Beth Botsford,   4:02.88
   Amanda Beard, Angel Martino,
   Amy Van Dyken
2. ..Australia   4:05.08
3. ..China   4:07.34

4 X 100 METER FREESTYLE RELAY
1. ..United States: Jenny Thompson,   3:39.29 OR
   Catherine Fox, Angel Martino,
   Amy Van Dyken
2. ..China   3:40.48
3. ..Germany   3:41.48

4 X 200 METER FREESTYLE RELAY
1. ..United States: Trina Jackson,   7:59.87
   Sheila Taormina, Cristina Teuscher,
   Jenny Thompson
2. ..Germany   8:01.55
3. ..Australia   8:05.47

DIVING

Men
SPRINGBOARD
		Pts
1.	..........Xiong Ni, China	701.46
2.	..........Yu Zhuocheng, China	690.93
3.	..........Mark Lenzi, United States	686.49

PLATFORM
		Pts
1.	..........Dmitri Sautin, Russia	692.34
2.	..........Jan Hempel, Germany	663.27
3.	..........Xiao Hailiang, China	658.20

Women
SPRINGBOARD
		Pts
1.	..........Fu Mingxia, China	547.68
2.	..........Irina Lashko, Russia	512.19
3.	..........Annie Pelletier, Canada	509.64

PLATFORM
		Pts
1.	..........Fu Mingxia, China	521.58
2.	..........Annika Walter, Germany	479.22
3.	...........Mary Ellen Clark, United States	472.95

INDIVIDUAL ARCHERY

Men
1. ....Justin Huish, United States
2. ....Magnus Petersson, Sweden
3. ....Oh Kyo Moon, South Korea

Women
1. ....Kim Kyung Wook, South Korea
2. ....He Ying, China
3. ....Olena Sadovnycha, Ukraine

Note: OR=Olympic record. WR=world record. EOR=equals Olympic record. EWR=equals world record.

TEAM ARCHERY

Men

1. ....United States
2. ....South Korea
3. ....Italy

Women

1. ....South Korea
2. ....Germany
3. ....Poland

CYCLING

Men

ROAD RACE

1. ..Pascal Richard, Switzerland	4:53:56
2. ..Rolf Sorensen, Denmark	4:53:56
3. ..Maximilian Sciandri, Great Britain	4:53:58

INDIVIDUAL TIME TRIAL

1. ..Miguel Indurain, Spain	1:04:05
2. ..Abraham Olano, Spain	1:04:17
3. ..Chris Boardman, Great Britain	1:04:36

1 KM TIME TRIAL

1. ..Florian Rousseau, France	1:02.712 OR
2. ..Erin Hartwell, United States	1:02.940
3. ..Takanobu Jumonji, Japan	1:03.261

4000 METER INDIVIDUAL PURSUIT

1. ..Andrea Collinelli, Italy	4:20.893
2. ..Philippe Ermenault, France	4:22.714
3. ..Bradley McGee, Australia	4:26.121

4000 METER TEAM PURSUIT

1. ..France: Christophe Capelle, Philippe Ermenault, Jean-Michel Monin, Francis Moreau, Herve Thuet	4:05.930
2. ..Russia	4:07.730
3. ..Australia	4:07.570

SPRINT

1. ..Jens Fiedler, Germany	10.664
2. ..Marty Nothstein, United States	11.074
3. ..Curt Harnett, Canada	10.947

Men (Cont.)

40 KM POINTS RACE

1. ..Silvio Martinello, Italy	37
2. ..Brian Walton, Canada	29
3. ..Stuart O'Grady, Australia	27

Women

ROAD RACE

1. ..Jeannie Longo-Ciprelli, France	2:36:13
2. ..Imelda Chiappa, Italy	2:36.38
3. ..Clara Hughes, Canada	2:36.44

INDIVIDUAL TIME TRIAL

1. ..Zulfiya Zabirova, Russia	36:40
2. ..Jeannie Longo-Ciprelli, France	37:00
3. ..Clara Hughes, Canada	37:13

3000 METER INDIVIDUAL PURSUIT

1. ..Antonella Bellutti, Italy	3:33.595
2. ..Marion Clignet, France	3:38.571
3. ..Judith Arndt, Germany	3:38.744

SPRINT

1. ..Felicia Ballanger, France	11.903
2. ..Michelle Ferris, Australia	12.096
3. ..Ingrid Haringa, Netherlands	12.074

24 KM POINTS RACE

1. ..Nathalie Lancien, France	24
2. ..Ingrid Haringa, Netherlands	23
3. ..Lucy Tyler Sharman, Australia	17

MOUNTAIN BIKING

Men

1. ......Bart Jan Brentjens, Netherlands	2:17:38
2. ......Thomas Frischknecht, Switzerland	2:20:14
3. ......Miguel Martinez, France	2:20:36

Women

1. ......Paola Pezzo, Italy	1:50:51
2. ......Alison Sydor, Canada	1:51:58
3. ......Susan DeMattei, United States	1:52:36

EQUESTRIAN

3-DAY TEAM

1. ......Australia: Wendy Schaeffer, Phillip Dutton, Andrew Hoy, Darien Powers	203.850
2. ......United States	261.100
3. ......New Zealand	268.550

3-DAY INDIVIDUAL

1. ......Blyth Tait, New Zealand	56.80
2. ......Sally Clark, New Zealand	60.40
3. ......Kerry Millikin, United States	73.70

TEAM DRESSAGE

1. ......Germany: Isabell Werth, Monica Theòdorescu, Martin Schaudt, Klaus Balkenhol	5553
2. ......The Netherlands	5437
3. ......United States	5309

INDIVIDUAL DRESSAGE

1. ......Isabell Werth, Germany	235.09
2. ......Anky van Grunsven, Netherlands	233.02
3. ......Sven Rothenberger, Netherlands	224.94

TEAM JUMPING

1. ......Germany: Ulrich Kirchoff, Lars Nieberg, Franke Sloothaak, Ludger Beerbaum	1.25
2. ......United States	12.00
3. ......Brazil	17.25

INDIVIDUAL JUMPING

1. ......Ulrich Kirchoff, Germany	1.00
2. ......Willi Melliger, Switzerland	4.00
3. ......Alexandra Ledermann, France	4.00

Note: OR=Olympic record. WR=world record. EOR=equals Olympic record. EWR=equals world record.

FENCING

Men

FOIL
1. ....Alessandro Puccini, Italy
2. ....Lionel Plumenail, France
3. ....Franck Boidin, France

SABRE
1. ....Stanislav Pozdniakov, Russia
2. ....Sergei Sharikov, Russia
3. ....Damien Touya, France

ÉPÉE
1. ....Aleksandr Beketov, Russia
2. ....Ivan Trevejo Perez, Cuba
3. ....Geza Imre, Hungary

TEAM FOIL
1. ....Russia
2. ....Poland
3. ....Cuba

TEAM SABRE
1. ....Russia
2. ....Hungary
3. ....Italy

Men (Cont.)

TEAM ÉPÉE
1. ....Italy
2. ....Russia
3. ....France

Women

FOIL
1. ....Laura Badea, Romania
2. ....Valentina Vezzali, Italy
3. ....Giovanna Trillini, Italy

ÉPÉE
1. ....Laura Flessel, France
2. ....Valerie Barlois, France
3. ....Gyöngyi Szalay, Hungary

TEAM FOIL
1. ....Italy
2. ....Romania
3. ....Germany

TEAM ÉPÉE
1. ....France
2. ....Italy
3. ....Russia

FIELD HOCKEY

Men
1. ....The Netherlands
2. ....Spain
3. ....Australia

Women
1. ....Australia
2. ....South Korea
3. ....The Netherlands

TEAM HANDBALL

Men
1. ....Croatia
2. ....Sweden
3. ....Spain

Women
1. ....Denmark
2. ....South Korea
3. ....Hungary

JUDO

Men

EXTRA-LIGHTWEIGHT
1. ....Tadahiro Nomura, Japan
2. ....Girolamo Giovinazzo, Italy
3. ....Dorjpalam Narmandakh, Mongolia
3. ....Richard Trautmann, Germany

HALF-LIGHTWEIGHT
1. ....Udo Quellmalz, Germany
2. ....Yukimasa Nakamura, Japan
3. ....Henrique Guimares, Brazil
3. ....Israel Hernandez Plana, Cuba

LIGHTWEIGHT
1. ....Kenzo Nakamura, Japan
2. ....Kwak Dae Sung, South Korea
3. ....Christophe Gagliano, France
3. ....James Pedro, United States

HALF-MIDDLEWEIGHT
1. ....Djamel Bouras, France
2. ....Toshihiko Koga, Japan
3. ....Cho In Chul, South Korea
3. ....Soso Liparteliani, Georgia

Women

EXTRA-LIGHTWEIGHT
1. ....Kye Sun Hi, North Korea
2. ....Ryoko Tamura, Japan
3. ....Amarilis Savón, Cuba
3. ....Yolanda Soler, Spain

HALF-LIGHTWEIGHT
1. ....Marie-Claire Restoux, France
2. ....Hyun Sook Hee, South Korea
3. ....Noriko Sugawara, Japan
3. ....Legna Verdecia, Cuba

LIGHTWEIGHT
1. ....Driulis González, Cuba
2. ....Jung Sun Yong, South Korea
3. ....Isabel Fernández, Spain
3. ....Marisbel Lomba, Belgium

HALF-MIDDLEWEIGHT
1. ....Yuko Emoto, Japan
2. ....Gella Vandecaveye, Belgium
3. ....Jenny Gal, Netherlands
3. ....Jung Sung Sook, South Korea

JUDO

Men *(Cont.)*

MIDDLEWEIGHT
1. ....Jeon Ki Young, South Korea
2. ....Armen Bagdasarov, Uzbekistan
3. ....Mark Huizinga, Netherlands
3. ....Marko Spittka, Germany

HALF-HEAVYWEIGHT
1. ....Pawel Nastula, Poland
2. ....Kim Min Soo, South Korea
3. ....Miguel Fernandes, Brazil
3. ....Stéphane Traineau, France

HEAVYWEIGHT
1. ....David Douillet, France
2. ....Ernesto Perez, Spain
3. ....Harry van Barneveld, Belgium
3. ....Frank Möller, Germany

Women *(Cont.)*

MIDDLEWEIGHT
1. ....Cho Min Sun, South Korea
2. ....Aneta Szczepanska, Poland
3. ....Wang Xianbo, China
3. ....Claudia Zwiers, Netherlands

HALF-HEAVYWEIGHT
1. ....Ulla Werbrouck, Belgium
2. ....Yoko Tanabe, Japan
3. ....Ylenia Scapin, Italy
3. ....Diadenis Luna, Cuba

HEAVYWEIGHT
1. ....Sun Fuming, China
2. ....Estela Rodriguez, Cuba
3. ....Christine Cicot, France
3. ....Johanna Hagn, Germany

MODERN PENTATHLON

1. ....Aleksandr Parygin, Kazakhstan
2. ....Eduard Zenovka, Russia
3. ....Janos Martinek, Hungary

ROWING

Men

SINGLE SCULLS
1. ..Xeno Mueller, Switzerland — 6:44.85
2. ..Derek Porter, Canada — 6:47.45
3. ..Thomas Lange, Germany — 6:47.72

DOUBLE SCULLS
1. ..D. Tizzano & A. Abbagnale, Italy — 6:16.98
2. ..K. Undset & S. Stoerseth, Norway — 6:18.42
3. ..F. Kowal & S. Barathay, France — 6:19.85

LIGHTWEIGHT DOUBLE SCULLS
1. ..M. Gier & M. Gier, Switzerland — 6:23.47
2. ..Van Der Linden & Aardewijn, Netherlands — 6:26.48
3. ..A. Edwards & B. Hick, Australia — 6:26.69

QUADRUPLE SCULLS
1. ..Germany — 5:56.93
2. ..United States — 5:59.10
3. ..Australia — 6:01.65

COXLESS PAIR
1. ..S. Redgrave & M. Pinsent, Great Britain — 6:20.09
2. ..D. Weightman & R. Scott, Australia — 6:21.02
3. ..M. Andrieux & J. Rolland, France — 6:22.15

COXLESS FOUR
1. ..Australia — 6:06.37
2. ..France — 6:07.03
3. ..Britain — 6:07.28

LIGHTWEIGHT COXLESS FOUR
1. ..Denmark — 6:09.58
2. ..Canada — 6:10.13
3. ..United States — 6:12.29

EIGHT-OARS
1. ..The Netherlands — 5:42.74
2. ..Germany — 5:44.58
3. ..Russia — 5:45.77

Women

SINGLE SCULLS
1. ..Ekaterina Khodotovich, Belarus — 7:32.21
2. ..Silken Laumann, Canada — 7:35.15
3. ..Trine Hansen, Denmark — 7:37.20

DOUBLE SCULLS
1. ..M. McBean & K. Heddle, Canada — 6:56.84
2. ..Cao Mianying & Zhang Xiuyun, China — 6:58.35
3. ..I. Eijs & E. Van Nes, Netherlands — 6:58.72

LIGHTWEIGHT DOUBLE SCULLS
1. ..C. Burcica & C. Macoviciuc, Romania — 7:12.78
2. ..T. Bell & L. Burns, United States — 7:14.65
3. ..R. Joyce & V. Lee, Australia — 7:16.56

QUADRUPLE SCULLS
1. ..Germany — 6:27.44
2. ..Ukraine — 6:30.36
3. ..Canada — 6:30.38

COXLESS PAIR
1. ..M. Still & K. Slatter, Australia — 7:01.39
2. ..M. Schwen & K. Kraft, United States — 7:01.78
3. ..C. Gosse & H. Cortin, France — 7:03.82

EIGHT-OARS
1. ..Romania — 6:19.73
2. ..Canada — 6:24.05
3. ..Belarus — 6:24.44

SOCCER

Men
1. ....Nigeria
2. ....Argentina
3. ....Brazil

Women
1. ....United States
2. ....China
3. ....Norway

SOFTBALL

1. ....United States
2. ....China
3. ....Australia

SYNCHRONIZED SWIMMING

1. ....United States
2. ....Canada
3. ....Japan

SHOOTING

Men

RAPID-FIRE PISTOL

	Pts
1......Ralf Schumann, Germany	698
2......Emil Milev, Bulgaria	692.1
3......Vladimir Vokhmianin, Kazakhstan	691.5

FREE PISTOL

	Pts
1......Boris Kokorev, Russia	666.4
2......Igor Basinski, Belarus	662.0
3......Roberto Di Donna, Italy	661.8

AIR PISTOL

	Pts
1......Roberto Di Donna, Italy	684
2......Wang Yifu, China	684
3......Tanu Kiriakov, Bulgaria	683

RUNNING TARGET

	Pts
1......Yang Ling, China	685.8
2......Xiao Jun, China	679.8
3......Miroslav Janus, Czech Republic	678.4

SMALL-BORE RIFLE, THREE-POSITION

	Pts
1......Jean-Pierre Amat, France	1273.9
2......Sergei Beliaev, Kazakhstan	1272.3
3......Wolfram Waibel Jr, Austria	1269.6

SMALL-BORE RIFLE, PRONE

	Pts
1......Christian Klees, Germany	704.8
2......Sergei Beliaev, Kazakhstan	703.3
3......Jozef Gonci, Slovakia	701.9

AIR RIFLE

	Pts
1......Artem Khadzhibekov, Russia	695.7
2......Wolfram Waibel Jr, Austria	695.2
3......Jean-Pierre Amat, France	693.1

TRAP

	Pts
1......Michael Diamond, Australia	149
2......Josh Lakatos, United States	147
3......Lance Bade, United States	147

DOUBLE TRAP

	Pts
1......Russell Mark, Australia	189.0
2......Albano Pera, Italy	183.0
3......Zhang Bing, China	183.0

SKEET

	Pts
1......Ennio Falco, Italy	149.0
2......Miroslaw Rzepkowski, Poland	148.0
3......Andrea Benelli, Italy	147.0

Women

SPORT PISTOL

	Pts
1......Li Duihong, China	687.9
2......Diana Yorgova, Bulgaria	684.8
3......Marina Logvinenko, Russia	684.2

AIR PISTOL

	Pts
1......Olga Klochneva, Russia	490.1
2......Marina Logvinenko, Russia	488.5
3......Maria Grozdeva, Bulgaria	488.5

SMALL-BORE RIFLE, THREE-POSITION

	Pts
1......Aleksandra Ivosev, Yugoslavia	686.1
2......Irina Gerasimenok, Russia	680.1
3......Renata Mauer, Poland	679.8

AIR RIFLE

	Pts
1......Renata Mauer, Poland	497.6
2......Petra Horneber, Germany	497.4
3......Aleksandra Ivosev, Yugoslavia	497.2

DOUBLE TRAP

	Pts
1......Kim Rhode, United States	141.0
2......Susanne Kiermayer, Germany	139.0
3......Deserie Huddleston, Australia	139.0

TABLE TENNIS

Men

SINGLES

1. ....Liu Guoliang, China
2. ....Wang Tao, China
3. ....Joerg Rosskopf, Germany

DOUBLES

1. ....Kong Linghui & Liu Guoliang, China
2. ....Lu Lin & Wang Tao, China
3. ....Lee Chul Seung & Yoo Nam Kyu, South Korea

Women

SINGLES

1. ....Deng Yaping, China
2. ....Chen Jing, Taiwan
3. ....Qiao Hong, China

DOUBLES

1. ....Deng Yaping & Qiao Hong, China
2. ....Liu Wei & Qiao Yunping, China
3. ....Park Hae Jung & Ryu Ji Hae, South Korea

TENNIS

Men	Women
SINGLES	**SINGLES**
1. ....Andre Agassi, United States	1. ....Lindsay Davenport, United States
2. ....Sergi Bruguera, Spain	2. ....Arantxa Sánchez Vicario, Spain
3. ....Leander Paes, India	3. ....Jana Novotna, Czech Republic
DOUBLES	**DOUBLES**
1. ....Todd Woodbridge & Mark Woodforde, Australia	1. ....Gigi Fernandez & Mary Joe Fernandez, United States
2. ....Neil Broad & Tim Henman, Great Britain	2. ....Jana Novotna & Helena Sukova, Czech Republic
3. ....Marc-Kevin Goellner & David Prinosil, Germany	3. ....Conchita Martinez & Arantxa Sánchez Vicario, Spain

VOLLEYBALL

Men	Women
1. ....The Netherlands	1. ....Cuba
2. ....Italy	2. ....China
3. ....Yugoslavia	3. ....Brazil

BEACH VOLLEYBALL

Men	Women
1. ....Karch Kiraly & Kent Steffes, United States	1. ....S. Pires Tavares & J. Silva Cruz, Brazil
2. ....Michael Dodd & M. Whitmarsh, United States	2. ....Monica Rodrigues & A. Samuel Ramos, Brazil
3. ....John Child & Mark Heese, Canada	3. ....Natalie Cook & Kerri Ann Pottharst, Australia

WATER POLO

1. ....Spain
2. ....Croatia
3. ....Italy

WEIGHTLIFTING

119 POUNDS		183 POUNDS	
1. ....Halil Mutlu, Turkey	633 lb OR	1. ....Pyrros Dimas, Greece	864 lb OR
2. ....Zhang Xiangsen, China	616 lb	2. ....Marc Huster, Germany	842 lb
3. ....Sevdalin Minchev, Bulgaria	611 lb	3. ....Andrzej Cofalik, Poland	820 lb
130 POUNDS		**200.5 POUNDS**	
1. ....Tang Ningsheng, China	678 lb OR	1. ....Alexei Petrov, Russia	886 lb
2. ....Leonidas Sabanis, Greece	672 lb	2. ....Leonidas Kokas, Greece	860 lb
3. ....Nikolai Pechalov, Bulgaria	667 lb	3. ....Oliver Caruso, Germany	860 lb
141 POUNDS		**218 POUNDS**	
1. ....Naim Suleymanoglu, Turkey	739 lb OR	1. ....:.Kakhi Kakhiasvili, Greece	926 lb OR
2. ....Valerios Leonidis, Greece	733 lb	2. ....Anatoli Khrapati, Kazakhstan	904 lb
3. ....Xiao Jiangang, China	711 lb	3. ....Denis Gotfrid, Ukraine	886 lb
154 POUNDS		**238 POUNDS**	
1. ....Zhan Xugang, China	787 lb OR	1. ....Timur Taimazov, Ukraine	948 lb
2. ....Kim Myong Nam, North Korea	761 lb	2. ....Sergey Syrtsov, Russia	926 lb
3. ....Attila Feri, Hungary	750 lb	3. ....Nicu Vlad, Romania	926 lb
167.5 POUNDS		**238+ POUNDS**	
1. ....Pablo Lara, Cuba	809 lb	1. ....Andrei Chemerkin, Russia	1008 lb OR
2. ....Yoto Yotov, Bulgaria	794 lb	2. ....Ronny Weller, Germany	1003 lb
3. ....Jon Chol, North Korea	787 lb	3. ....Stefan Botev, Australia	992 lb

FREESTYLE WRESTLING

105.5 POUNDS	125.5 POUNDS
1. ....Kim Il, North Korea	1. ....Kendall Cross, United States
2. ....Armen Mkrchyan, Armenia	2. ....Guivi Sissaouri, Canada
3. ....Alexis Vila, Cuba	3. ....Ri Yong Sam, North Korea
114.5 POUNDS	**136.5 POUNDS**
1. ....Valentin Yordanov, Bulgaria	1. ....Tom Brands, United States
2. ....Namik Abdullayev, Azerbaijan	2. ....Jang Jae Sung, South Korea
3. ....Maulen Mamyrov, Kazakhstan	3. ....Elbrus Tedeyev, Ukraine

Note: OR=Olympic Record. WR=World Record. EOR=Equals Olympic Record. EWR=Equals World Record.

FREESTYLE WRESTLING *(Cont.)*

149.5 POUNDS
1. ....Vadim Bogiev, Russia
2. ....Townsend Saunders, United States
3. ....Zaza Zazirov, Ukraine

163 POUNDS
1. ....Buvaysa Saytyev, Russia
2. ....Park Jang Soon, South Korea
3. ....Takuya Ota, Japan

180.5 POUNDS
1. ....Khadzhimurad Magomedov, Russia
2. ....Yang Hyun Mo, South Korea
3. ....Amir Reza Khadem Azghadi, Iran

198 POUNDS
1. ....Rasul Khadem, Iran
2. ....Makharbek Khadartsev, Russia
3. ....Eldari Kurtanidze, Georgia

220 POUNDS
1. ....Kurt Angle, United States
2. ....Abbas Jadidi, Iran
3. ....Arawat Sabejew, Germany

286 POUNDS
1. ....Mahmut Demir, Turkey
2. ....Alexei Medvedev, Belarus
3. ....Bruce Baumgartner, United States

GRECO-ROMAN WRESTLING

105.5 POUNDS
1. ....Sim Kwon Ho, South Korea
2. ....Aleksandr Pavlov, Belarus
3. ....Zafar Gouliev, Russia

114.5 POUNDS
1. ....Armen Nazarian, Armenia
2. ....Brandon Paulson, United States
3. ....Andrei Kalashnikov, Ukraine

125.5 POUNDS
1. ....Yuri Melnichenko, Kazakhstan
2. ....Dennis Hall, United States
3. ....Sheng Zetian, China

136.5 POUNDS
1. ....Wlodzimierz Zawadzki, Poland
2. ....Juan Luis Maren, Cuba
3. ....Mahmet Pirim, Turkey

149.5 POUNDS
1. ....Ryszard Wolny, Poland
2. ....Ghani Yalouz, France
3. ....Aleksandr Tretyakov, Russia

163 POUNDS
1. ....Filberto Azcuy, Cuba
2. ....Marko Asell, Finland
3. ....Jozef Tracz, Poland

180.5 POUNDS
1. ....Hamza Yerlikaya, Turkey
2. ....Thomas Zander, Germany
3. ....Valery Tsilent, Belarus

198 POUNDS
1. ....Vyacheslav Oleynyk, Ukraine
2. ....Jacek Fafinski, Poland
3. ....Maik Bullmann, Germany

220 POUNDS
1. ....Andrzej Wronski, Poland
2. ....Sergei Lishtvan, Belarus
3. ....Mikael Ljungberg, Sweden

286 POUNDS
1. ....Aleksandr Karelin, Russia
2. ....Matt Ghaffari, United States
3. ....Sergei Mureiko, Moldova

YACHTING

MEN'S 470
1. ....Ukraine
2. ....Great Britain
3. ....Portugal

MEN'S FINN
1. ....Mateusz Kusznierewicz, Poland
2. ....Sebastien Godefroid, Belgium
3. ....Roy Heiner, Netherlands

MEN'S BOARD
1. ....Nikolas Kaklamanakis, Greece
2. ....Carlos Espinola, Argentina
3. ....Gal Fridman, Israel

WOMEN'S 470
1. ....Spain
2. ....Japan
3. ....Ukraine

WOMEN'S EUROPE
1. ....Kristine Roug, Denmark
2. ....Margriet Matthijsse, Netherlands
3. ....Courtenay Becker-Dey, United States

WOMEN'S BOARD
1. ....Lee Lai Shan, Hong Kong
2. ....Barbara Kendall, New Zealand
3. ....Alessandra Sensini, Italy

SOLING
1. ....Germany
2. ....Russia
3. ....United States

STAR
1. ....Torben Grael & Marcelo Ferreira, Brazil
2. ....Hans Wallen & Bobbie Lohse, Sweden
3. ....Colin Beashel & David Giles, Australia

TORNADO
1. ....J. Luis Ballester & Fernando Leon, Spain
2. ....M. Booth & A. Landenberger, Australia
3. ....Lars Grael & Kiko Pellicano, Brazil

LASER
1. ....Robert Scheidt, Brazil
2. ....Ben Ainslie, Great Britain
3. ....Peer Moberg, Norway

BIATHLON

Men
10 KILOMETERS
1. ..Ole Einar Bjorndalen, Norway	27:16.2
2. ..Frode Andresen, Norway	28:17.8
3. ..Ville Raikkonen, FInland	28:21.7

20 KILOMETERS
1. ..Halvard Hanevold, Norway	56:16.4
2. ..Pier Alberto Carrara, Italy	56:21.9
3. ..Aleksei Aidarov, Belarus	56:45.5

4 X 7.5 KILOMETER RELAY
1. ....Germany	1:19:43.3
2. ....Norway	1:20:03.4
3. ....Russia	1:20:19.4

Women
7.5 KILOMETERS
1. ..Galina Koukleva, Russia	23:08.0
2. ..Ursula Disl, Germany	23:08.7
3. ..Katrin Apel, Germany	23:32.4

15 KILOMETERS
1. ..Ekaterina Dofovska, Bulgaria	54:52.0
2. ..Elena Petrova, Ukraine	55:09.8
3. ..Ursula Disl, Germany	55:17.9

3 X 7.5 KILOMETER RELAY
1. ....Germany	1:40:13.6
2. ....Russia	1:40:25.2
3. ....Norway	1:40:37.3

BOBSLED

2-MAN BOB
1. ..Pierre Lueders & Dave MacEachern, Canada	3:37.24
1. ..Guenther Huber & Antonio Tartaglia, Italy	3:37.24
3. ..Christoph Langen & Markus Zimmerman, Germany	3:37.89

4-MAN BOB
1. ....Germany II	2:39.41
2. ....Switzerland I	2:40.01
3. ....Britain I	2:40.06
3. ....France I	2:40.06

CURLING

Men
1. ....Switzerland
2. ....Canada
3. ....Norway

Women
1. ....Canada
2. ....Denmark
3 ....Sweden

ICE HOCKEY

Men
1. ....Czech Republic
2. ....Russia
3. ....Finland

Women
1. ....United States
2. ....Canada
3. ....Finland

LUGE

Men
SINGLES
1. ..Georg Hackl, Germany	3:18.44
2. ..Armin Zoeggeler, Italy	3:18.94
3. ..Jens Mueller, Germany	3:19.09

DOUBLES
1. ..Stefan Krausse & Jan Behrendt, Germany	1:41.105
1. ..Chris Thorpe & Gordy Sheer, United States	1:41.127
3. ..Mark Grimmette & Brian Martin United States	1:41.217

Women
SINGLES
1. ..Silke Kraushaar, Germany	3:23.779
2. ...Barbara Niedernhuber, Germany	3:23.781
3. ...Angelika Neuner, Austria	3:24.253

FIGURE SKATING

Men
1. ....Ilia Kulik, Russia
2. ....Elvis Stojko, Canada
3. ....Philippe Candeloro, France

Women
1. ....Tara Lipinski, United States
2. ....Michelle Kwan, United States
3. ....Lu Chen, China

Pairs
1. ..Oksana Kazakova & Artur Dmitriev, Russia
2. ..Elena Berezhnaya & Anton Sikharulidze, Russia
3. ..Mandy Wötzel & Ingo Steuer, Germany

Ice Dancing
1. ..Pasha Grishuk & Evgeny Platov, Russia
2. ..Anjelika Krylova & Oleg Ovsyannikov, Russia
3. ..Marina Anissina & Gwendal Peizerat, France

SPEED SKATING

Men

500 METERS

1. ...Hiroyasu Shimizu, Japan — 1:11.35*
2. ...Jeremy Wotherspoon, Canada — 1:11.84
3. ...Kevin Overland, Canada — 1:11.86

1000 METERS

1. ...Ids Postma, Netherlands — 1:10.64 OR
2. ...Jan Bos, Netherlands — 1:10.71
3. ...Hiroyasu Shimizu, Japan — 1:11.00

1500 METERS

1. ...Aadne Sondral, Norway — 1:47.87 WR
2. ...Ids Postma, Netherlands — 1:48.13
3. ...Rintje Ritsma, Netherlands — 1:48.52

5000 METERS

1. ...Gianni Romme, Netherlands — 6:22.20 WR
2. ...Rintje Ritsma, Netherlands — 6:28.24
3. ...Bart Veldkamp, Belgium — 6:28.31

10,000 METERS

1. ...Gianni Romme, Netherlands — 13:15.33 WR
2. ...Bob de Jong, Netherlands — 13:25.76
3. ...Rintje Ritsma, Netherlands — 13:28.19

500 METERS SHORT TRACK

1. ...Takafumi Nishitani, Japan — 42.862
2. ...An Yulong, China — 43.022
3. ...Hitoshi Uematsu, Japan — 43.713

1000 METERS SHORT TRACK

1. ...Kim Dong Sung, South Korea — 1:32.375
2. ...Li Jiajun, China — 1:32.428
3. ...Eric Bedard, Canada — 1:32.661

5000-METER SHORT TRACK RELAY

1. ...Canada — 7:06.075
2. ...South Korea — 7:06.776
3. ...China — 7:11.559

Women

500 METERS

1. ...Catriona LeMay Doan, Canada — 1:16.60*
2. ...Susan Auch, Canada — 1:16.93
3. ...Tomoni Okazaki, Japan — 1:17.10

1000 METERS

1. ...Marianne Timmer, Netherlands — 1:16.51 OR
2. ...Chris Witty, United States — 1:16.79
3. ...Catriona LeMay Doan, Canada — 1:17.37

1500 METERS

1. ...Marianne Timmer, Netherlands — 1:57.58 WR
2. ...Gunda Niemann-Stirnemann, Ger — 1:58.66
3. ...Chris Witty, United States — 1:58.97

3000 METERS

1. ...Gunda Niemann-Stirnemann, Ger — 4:07.29 OR
2. ...Claudia Pechstein, Germany — 4:08.47
3. ...Anna Friesinger, Germany — 4:09.44

5000 METERS

1. ...Claudia Pechstein, Germany — 6:59.61 WR
2. ...Gunda Niemann-Stirnemann, Ger — 6:59.65
3. ...Lyudmila Prokasheva, Kazakhstan — 7:11.14

500 METERS SHORT TRACK

1. ...Annie Perreault, Canada — 46.568
2. ...Yang Yang, China — 46.627
3. ...Chun Lee Kyung, South Korea — 46.335

1000 METERS SHORT TRACK

1. ...Chun Lee Kyung, South Korea — 1:42.776
2. ...Yang Yang, China — 1:43.343
3. ...Hye Kyung Won, South Korea — 1:43.361

3000-METER SHORT TRACK RELAY

1. ...South Korea — 4:16.260
2. ...China — 4:16.383
3. ...Canada — 4:21.205

ALPINE SKIING

Men

DOWNHILL

1. ...Jean-Luc Crétier, France — 1:50.11
2. ...Lasse Kjus, Norway — 1:50.51
3. ...Hannes Trinkl, Austria — 1:50.63

SLALOM

1. ...Hans-Petter Buraas, Norway — 1:49.31
2. ...Ole Christian Furuseth, Norway — 1:50.64
3. ...Thomas Sykora, Austria — 1:50.68

GIANT SLALOM

1. ...Hermann Maier, Austria — 2:38.51
2. ...Stefan Eberharter, Austria — 2:39.36
3. ...Michael von Grünigen, Switzerland — 2:39.69

SUPER GIANT SLALOM

1. ...Hermann Maier, Austria — 1:34.82
2. ...Didier Cucher, Switzerland — 1:35.43
3. ...Hans Knauss, Austria — 1:35.43

COMBINED

1. ...Mario Reiter, Austria — 3:08.06
2. ...Lasse Kjus, Norway — 3:08.65
3. ...Christian Mayer, Austria — 3:10.11

Women

DOWNHILL

1. ...Katja Seizinger, Germany — 1:28.89
2. ...Pernilla Wiberg, Sweden — 1:29.18
3. ...Florence Masnada, France — 1:29.37

SLALOM

1. ...Hilde Gerg, Germany — 1:32.40
2. ...Deborah Compagnoni, Italy — 1:32.46
3. ...Zali Steggall, Australia — 1:32.67

GIANT SLALOM

1. ...Deborah Compagnoni, Italy — 2:50.59
2. ...Alexandra Meissnitzer, Austria — 2:52.39
3. ...Katja Seizinger, Germany — 2:52.61

SUPER GIANT SLALOM

1. ...Picabo Street, United States — 1:18.02
2. ...Michaela Dorfmeister, Austria — 1:18.03
3. ...Alexandra Meissnitzer, Austria — 1:18.09

COMBINED

1. ...Katja Seizinger, Germany — 2:40.74
2. ...Martina Ertl, Germany — 2:40.92
3. ...Hilde Gerg, Germany — 2:41.50

Note: OR=Olympic Record. WR=World Record. EOR=Equals Olympic Record. EWR=Equals World Record. WB=World Best.
* Final standings based on the combined time of two 500-meter runs. Shimizu set an Olympic record with his second-run time of 35.59 seconds, and LeMay Doan set an Olympic record with her second-run time of 38.21 seconds.

FREESTYLE SKIING

Men

MOGULS	Pts
1. ..Jonny Moseley, United States	26.93
2. ..Janne Lahtela, Finland	26.00
3. ..Sami Mustonen, Finland	25.76

AERIALS	Pts
1. ..Eric Bergoust, United States	255.64
2. ..Sebastien Foucras, France	248.79
3. ..Dmitri Dashchinsky, Belarus	240.79

Women

MOGULS	Pts
1. ..Tae Satoya, Japan	25.06
2. ..Tatjana Mittermayer, Germany	24.62
3. ..Kari Traa, Norway	24.09

AERIALS	Pts
1. ..Nikki Stone, United States	193.00
2. ..Nannan Xu, China	186.97
3. ..Colette Brand, Switzerland	171.83

NORDIC SKIING

Men

10 KILOMETERS CLASSICAL STYLE	
1. ..Bjørn Dæhlie, Norway	27:24.5
2. ..Markus Gandler, Austria	27:32.5
3. ..Mika Myllylae, Finland	27:40.1

15 KILOMETERS PURSUIT FREESTYLE	
1. ..Thomas Alsgaard, Norway	1:07:01.7
2. ..Bjørn Dæhlie, Norway	1:07:02.8
3. ..Vladimir Smirnov, Kazakhstan	1:07:31.5

30 KILOMETERS CLASSICAL STYLE	
1. ..Mika Myllylae, Finland	1:33:55.8
2. ..Erling Jevne, Norway	1:35:27.1
3. ..Silvio Fauner, Italy	1:36:08.5

50 KILOMETERS FREESTYLE	
1. ..Bjørn Dæhlie, Norway	2:05:08.2
2. ..Niklas Jonsson, Sweden	2:05:16.3
3. ..Christian Hoffmann, Austria	2:06:01.8

4 X 10 KILOMETER RELAY MIXED STYLE	
1. ....Norway	1:40:55.7
2. ....Italy	1:40:55.9
3. ....Finland	1:42:15.5

90-METER HILL SKI JUMPING	Pts
1. ..Jani Soininen, Finland	234.5
2. ..Kazuyoshi Funaki, Japan	233.5
3. ..Andreas Widhoelzl, Austria	232.5

120-METER HILL SKI JUMPING	Pts
1. ..Kazuyoshi Funaki, Japan	272.3
2. ..Jani Soininen, Finland	260.8
3. ..Masahiko Harada, Japan	258.3

120-METER HILL TEAM SKI JUMPING	Pts
1. ....Japan	933.0
2. ....Germany	897.4
3. ....Austria	881.5

INDIVIDUAL COMBINED	Time behind
1. ..Bjarte Engen Vik, Norway	—
2. ..Samppa Lajunen, Finland	27.5
3. ..Valery Stoljarov, Russia	28.2

TEAM COMBINED	Time behind
1. ....Norway	—
2. ....Finland	1:18.9
3. ....France	1:41.9

Women

5 KILOMETERS CLASSICAL STYLE	
1. ..Larissa Lazhutina, Russia	17:37.9
2. ..Katerina Neumannova, Czech Rep	17:42.7
3. ..Bente Martinsen, Norway	17:49.4

10 KILOMETERS PURSUIT FREESTYLE	
1. ..Larissa Lazhutina, Russia	46:06.9
2. ..Olga Danilova, Russia	46:13.4
3. ..Katerina Neumannova, Czech Rep	46:14.2

15 KILOMETERS CLASSICAL STYLE	
1. ..Olga Danilova, Russia	46:55.04
2. ..Larissa Lazhutina, Russia	47:01.00
3. ..Anita Moen-Guidon, Norway	47:52.06

30 KILOMETERS FREESTYLE	
1. ..Julija Tchepalova, Russia	1:22:01.5
2. ..Stefania Belmondo, Italy	1:22:11.7
3. ..Larissa Lazhutina, Russia	1:23:15.7

4 X 5 KILOMETER RELAY MIXED STYLE	
1. ....Russia	55:13.5
2. ....Norway	55:38.0
3. ....Italy	56:53.3

SNOWBOARDING

Men

GIANT SLALOM	
1. ..Ross Rebagliati, Canada	2:03.96
2. ..Thomas Prugger, Italy	2:03.98
3. ..Ueli Kestenholz, Switzerland	2:04.08

HALF-PIPE	Pts
1. ..Gian Simmen, Switzerland	85.2
2. ..Daniel Franck, Norway	82.4
3. ..Ross Powers, United States	82.1

Women

GIANT SLALOM	
1. ..Karine Ruby, France	2:17.34
2. ..Heidi Renoth, Germany	2:19.17
3. ..Brigitte Koeck, Austria	2:19.42

HALF-PIPE	Pts
1. ..Nicola Thost, Germany	74.6
2. ..Stine Brun Kjeldaas, Norway	74.2
3. ..Shannon Dunn, United States	72.8

Olympic Games Locations and Dates

Summer

	Year	Site	Dates	Men	Women	Nations	Most Medals	US Medals
I	1896	Athens, Greece	Apr 6–15	311	0	13	Greece (10-19-18—47)	11-6-2—19 (2nd)
II	1900	Paris, France	May 20–Oct 28	1319	11	22	France (29-41-32—102)	20-14-19—53 (2nd)
III	1904	St Louis, United States	July 1–Nov 23	681	6	12	United States (80-86-72—238)	
—	1906	Athens, Greece	Apr 22–May 28	77	7	20	France (15-9-16—40)	12-6-5—23 (4th)
IV	1908	London, Great Britain	Apr 27–Oct 31	1999	36	23	Britain (56-50-39—145)	23-12-12—47 (2nd)
V	1912	Stockholm, Sweden	May 5–July 22	2490	57	28	Sweden (24-24-17—65)	23-19-19—61 (2nd)
VI	1916	Berlin, Germany	Canceled because of war					
VII	1920	Antwerp, Belgium	Apr 20–Sep 12	2543	64	29	United States (41-27-28—96)	
VIII	1924	Paris, France	May 4–July 27	2956	136	44	United States (45-27-27—99)	
IX	1928	Amsterdam, Netherlands	May 17–Aug 12	2724	290	46	United States (22-18-16—56)	
X	1932	Los Angeles, United States	July 30–Aug 14	1281	127	37	United States (41-32-31—104)	
XI	1936	Berlin, Germany	Aug 1–16	3738	328	49	Germany (33-26-30—89)	24-20-12—56 (2nd)
XII	1940	Tokyo, Japan	Canceled because of war					
XIII	1944	London, Great Britain	Canceled because of war					
XIV	1948	London, Great Britain	July 29–Aug 14	3714	385	59	United States (38-27-19—84)	
XV	1952	Helsinki, Finland	July 19–Aug 3	4407	518	69	United States (40-19-17—76)	
XVI	1956	Melbourne, Australia*	Nov 22–Dec 8	2958	384	67	USSR (37-29-32—98)	32-25-17—74 (2nd)
XVII	1960	Rome, Italy	Aug 25–Sep 11	4738	610	83	USSR (43-29-31—103)	34-21-16—71 (2nd)
XVIII	1964	Tokyo, Japan	Oct 10–24	4457	683	93	United States (36-26-28—90)	
XIX	1968	Mexico City, Mexico	Oct 12–27	4750	781	112	United States (45-28-34—107)	
XX	1972	Munich, West Germany	Aug 26–Sep 10	5848	1299	122	USSR (50-27-22—99)	33-31-30—94 (2nd)
XXI	1976	Montreal, Canada	July 17–Aug 1	4834	1251	92†	USSR (49-41-35—125)	34-35-25—94 (3rd)
XXII	1980	Moscow, USSR	July 19–Aug 3	4265	1088	81‡	USSR (80-69-46—195)	Did not compete
XXIII	1984	Los Angeles, United States	July 28–Aug 12	5458	1620	141#	United States (83-61-30—174)	
XXIV	1988	Seoul, South Korea	Sep 17–Oct 2	7105	2476	160	USSR (55-31-46—132)	36-31-27—94 (3rd)
XXV	1992	Barcelona, Spain	July 25–Aug. 9	7555	3008	172	Unified Team (45-38-29—112)	37-34-37—108 (2nd)
XXVI	1996	Atlanta, United States	July 19–Aug 4	6984	3766	197	United States (44-32-25—101)	

*The equestrian events were held in Stockholm, Sweden, June 10–17, 1956.

†This figure includes Cameroon, Egypt, Morocco, and Tunisia, countries that boycotted the 1976 Olympics after some of their athletes had already competed.

‡The U.S. was among 65 countries that did not participate in the 1980 Summer Games in Moscow.

#The USSR, East Germany, and 14 other countries did not participate in the 1984 Summer Games in Los Angeles.

Winter

	Year	Site	Dates	Men	Women	Nations	Most Medals	US Medals
I	1924	Chamonix, France	Jan 25–Feb 4	281	13	16	Norway (4-7-6—17)	1-2-1—4 (3rd)
II	1928	St Moritz, Switzerland	Feb 11–19	366	27	25	Norway (6-4-5—15)	2-2-2—6 (2nd)
III	1932	Lake Placid, United States	Feb 4–13	277	30	17	United States (6-4-2—12)	
IV	1936	Garmisch-Partenkirchen, Germany	Feb 6–16	680	76	28	Norway (7-5-3—15)	1-0-3—4 (T-5th)
—	1940	Garmisch-Partenkirchen, Germany	Canceled because of war					
—	1944	Cortina d'Ampezzo, Italy	Canceled because of war					
V	1948	St Moritz, Switzerland	Jan 30–Feb 8	636	77	28	Norway (4-3-3—10) Sweden (4-3-3—10) Switzerland (3-4-3—10)	3-4-2—9 (4th)
VI	1952	Oslo, Norway	Feb 14–25	624	108	30	Norway (7-3-6—16)	4-6-1—11 (2nd)
VII	1956	Cortina d'Ampezzo, Italy	Jan 26–Feb 5	687	132	32	USSR (7-3-6—16)	2-3-2—7 (T-4th)
VIII	1960	Squaw Valley, United States	Feb 18–28	502	146	30	USSR (7-5-9—21)	3-4-3—10 (2nd)
IX	1964	Innsbruck, Austria	Jan 29–Feb 9	758	175	36	USSR (11-8-6—25)	1-2-3—6 (7th)
X	1968	Grenoble, France	Feb 6–18	1063	230	37	Norway (6-6-2—14)	1-5-1—7 (T-7th)
XI	1972	Sapporo, Japan	Feb 3–13	927	218	35	USSR (8-5-3—16)	3-2-3—8 (6th)
XII	1976	Innsbruck, Austria	Feb 4–15	1013	248	37	USSR (13-6-8—27)	3-3-4—10 (T-3rd)
XIII	1980	Lake Placid, United States	Feb 13–24	1012	271	37	East Germany (9-7-7—23)	6-4-2—12 (3rd)
XIV	1984	Sarajevo, Yugoslavia	Feb 8–19	1127	283	49	USSR (6-10-9—25)	4-4-0—8 (T-5th)
XV	1988	Calgary, Canada	Feb 13–28	1270	364	57	USSR (11-9-9—29)	2-1-3—6 (6th)
XVI	1992	Albertville, France	Feb 8–23	1313	488	65	Germany (10-10-6—26)	5-4-2—11 (6th)
XVII	1994	Lillehammer, Norway	Feb 12–27	1302	542	67	Norway (10-11-5—26)	6-5-2—13 (T-5th)
XVIII	1998	Nagano, Japan	Feb 7–22	2302 (total)		72	Germany (12-9-8—29)	6-3-4—13 (6th)

Alltime Olympic Medal Winners

Summary

NATIONS

Nation	Gold	Silver	Bronze	Total	Nation	Gold	Silver	Bronze	Total
United States	832	634	553	2019	Australia	86	85	121	292
Soviet Union (1952–88)	395	319	296	1010	Japan	92	89	97	278
Great Britain	169	223	218	610	Romania	63	77	99	239
France	175	179	206	560	Poland	50	67	110	227
Sweden	132	151	174	457	Canada	48	78	90	216
Italy	166	135	144	445	The Netherlands	49	58	81	188
East Germany (1956–88)	159	150	136	445	Bulgaria	43	76	63	182
Hungary	142	129	155	426	Switzerland	46	69	59	174
Germany (1896–1936, 1992–)	124	121	134	379	China	52	63	49	164
					Denmark	38	60	57	155
West Germany (1952–88)	77	104	120	301	Czechoslovakia (1924–92)	49	49	44	142
Finland	99	80	113	292	Belgium	37	49	49	135

Summer *(Cont.)*

INDIVIDUALS — OVERALL

Men					
Athlete, Nation	Sport	G	S	B	Tot
Nikolai Andrianov, USSR	Gym	7	5	3	15
Boris Shakhlin, USSR	Gym	7	4	2	13
Edoardo Mangiarotti, Italy	Fen	6	5	2	13
Takashi Ono, Japan	Gym	5	4	4	13
Paavo Nurmi, Finland	Track	9	3	0	12
Sawao Kato, Japan	Gym	8	3	1	12
Mark Spitz, United States	Swim	9	1	1	11
Matt Biondi, United States	Swim	8	2	1	11
Viktor Chukarin, USSR	Gym	7	3	1	11
Carl Osburn, United States	Shoot	5	4	2	11
Ray Ewry, United States	Track	10	0	0	10
Carl Lewis, United States	Track	9	1	0	10
Aladár Gerevich, Hungary	Fen	7	1	2	10
Akinori Nakayama, Japan	Gym	6	2	2	10
Vitaly Scherbo, UT/Belarus	Gym	6	0	4	10
Aleksandr Dityatin, USSR	Gym	3	6	1	10

Women					
Athlete, Nation	Sport	G	S	B	Tot
Larissa Latynina, USSR	Gym	9	5	4	18
Vera Cáslavská, Czech.	Gym	7	4	0	11
Agnes Keleti, Hungary	Gym	5	3	2	10
Polina Astaknova, USSR	Gym	5	2	3	10
Nadia Comaneci, Romania	Gym	5	3	1	9
Lyudmila Tourischeva, USSR	Gym	4	3	2	9
Kornelia Ender, E Germany	Swim	4	4	0	8
Dawn Fraser, Australia	Swim	4	4	0	8
Shirley Babashoff, United States	Swim	2	6	0	8
Sofia Muratova, USSR	Gym	2	2	4	8

Eight tied with seven.

INDIVIDUALS — GOLD

Men

Ray Ewry, United States	10	Sawao Kato, Japan ... 8	Viktor Chukarin, USSR ... 7

Ray Ewry, United States 10   Sawao Kato, Japan 8   Viktor Chukarin, USSR...............7
Paavo Nurmi, Finland 9   Matt Biondi, United States.........8   Aladár Gerevich, Hungary..........7
Carl Lewis, United States 9   Nikolai Andrianov, USSR 7
Mark Spitz, United States 9   Boris Shakhlin, USSR 7

Women

Larissa Latynina, USSR 9   Krisztina Egerszegi, Hun 5   Janet Evans, United States........4
Vera Cáslavská, Czech 7   Jenny Thompson, United States ..5   Fanny Blankers-Koen, Neth.......4
Kristin Otto, E Germany.............6   Kornelia Ender, E Germany 4   Betty Cuthbert, Australia............4
Agnes Keleti, Hungary 5   Dawn Fraser, Australia..............4   Pat McCormick, United States....4
Nadia Comaneci, Romania 5   Lyudmila Tourischeva, USSR 4   Bärbel Eckert Wöckel, E Ger 4
Polina Astaknova, USSR 5   Evelyn Ashford, United States 4   Amy Van Dyken, United States...4

Winter

NATIONS

Nation	Gold	Silver	Bronze	Total	Nation	Gold	Silver	Bronze	Total
Norway	83	85	68	236	East Germany (1956–88)	39	36	35	110
Soviet Union (1956–88)	78	57	59	194	Sweden	36	26	34	96
United States	59	58	40	157	Switzerland	29	31	31	91
Austria	39	53	53	145	Germany (1928–36, '92–)	34	29	25	88
Finland	37	49	48	134	Canada	24	25	29	78

INDIVIDUALS — OVERALL

Men					
Athlete, Nation	Sport	G	S	B	Tot
Bjørn Dæhlie, Norway	N Ski	8	4	0	12
Sixten Jernberg, Sweden	N Ski	4	3	2	9
A. Clas Thunberg, Finland	S Skat	5	1	1	7
Ivar Ballangrud, Norway	S Skat	4	2	1	7
Veikko Hakulinen, Finland	N Ski	3	3	1	7
Eero Mäntyranta, Finland	N Ski	3	2	2	7
Bogdan Musiol, E Ger/Ger	Bob	1	5	1	7

Women					
Athlete, Nation	Sport	G	S	B	Tot
Raisa Smetanina, USSR/UT	N Ski	4	5	1	10
Lyubov Egorova, UT/Russia	N Ski	6	3	0	9
Galina Kulakova, USSR	N Ski	4	2	2	8
Karin (Enke) Kania, E Germany	S Skat	3	4	1	8
Gunda Niemann Stimemann, Ger.	S Skat	3	4	1	8
Larissa Lazutina, UT/Russia	N Ski	5	1	1	7
Marja-Liisa Kirvesniemi, Fin	N Ski	3	0	4	7
Andrea Ehrig, E Germany	S Skat	1	5	1	7

INDIVIDUALS — GOLD

Men

Bjørn Dæhlie, Nor 8   Matti Nykänen, Fin 4
A. Clas Thunberg, Fin...5   A. Tikhonov, USSR......4
Eric Heiden, U.S. 5   N. Zimyatov, USSR......4
Sixten Jernberg, Swe...4   Ivar Ballangrud, Nor ...4
Evgeny Grishin, USSR..4   Gunde Svan, Swe 4
J. Olav Koss, Norway...4   T. Wassberg, Swe.......4

Women

Lyubov Egorova,   Raisa Smetanina,
UT/Russia 6   USSR/UT.....................4
L. Skoblikova, USSR ...6   G. Kulakova, USSR.....4
Larissa Lazutina,   Chun Lee Kyung, Kor...4
UT/Russia 5
Bonnie Blair, U.S.........5

TRACK AND FIELD

Men

100 METERS

1896	Thomas Burke, United States	12.0
1900	Frank Jarvis, United States	11.0
1904	Archie Hahn, United States	11.0
1906	Archie Hahn, United States	11.2
1908	Reginald Walker, South Africa	10.8 OR
1912	Ralph Craig, United States	10.8
1920	Charles Paddock, United States	10.8
1924	Harold Abrahams, Great Britain	10.6 OR
1928	Percy Williams, Canada	10.8
1932	Eddie Tolan, United States	10.3 OR
1936	Jesse Owens, United States	10.3
1948	Harrison Dillard, United States	10.3
1952	Lindy Remigino, United States	10.4
1956	Bobby Morrow, United States	10.5
1960	Armin Hary, West Germany	10.2 OR
1964	Bob Hayes, United States	10.0 EWR
1968	Jim Hines, United States	9.95 WR
1972	Valery Borzov, USSR	10.14
1976	Hasely Crawford, Trinidad	10.06
1980	Allan Wells, Great Britain	10.25
1984	Carl Lewis, United States	9.99
1988	Carl Lewis, United States*	9.92 WR
1992	Linford Christie, Great Britain	9.96
1996	Donovan Bailey, Canada	9.84 WR

*Ben Johnson, Canada, disqualified.

200 METERS

1900	John Walter Tewksbury, United States	22.2
1904	Archie Hahn, United States	21.6 OR
1906	Not held	
1908	Robert Kerr, Canada	22.6
1912	Ralph Craig, United States	21.7
1920	Allen Woodring, United States	22.0
1924	Jackson Scholz, United States	21.6
1928	Percy Williams, Canada	21.8
1932	Eddie Tolan, United States	21.2 OR
1936	Jesse Owens, United States	20.7 OR
1948	Mel Patton, United States	21.1
1952	Andrew Stanfield, United States	20.7
1956	Bobby Morrow, United States	20.6 OR
1960	Livio Berruti, Italy	20.5 EWR
1964	Henry Carr, United States	20.3 OR
1968	Tommie Smith, United States	19.83 WR
1972	Valery Borzov, USSR	20.00
1976	Donald Quarrie, Jamaica	20.23
1980	Pietro Mennea, Italy	20.19
1984	Carl Lewis, United States	19.80 OR
1988	Joe DeLoach, United States	19.75 OR
1992	Mike Marsh, United States	20.01
1996	Michael Johnson, United States	19.32 WR

400 METERS

1896	Thomas Burke, United States	54.2
1900	Maxey Long, United States	49.4 OR
1904	Harry Hillman, United States	49.2 OR
1906	Paul Pilgrim, United States	53.2
1908	Wyndham Halswelle, Great Britain	50.0
1912	Charles Reidpath, United States	48.2 OR
1920	Bevil Rudd, South Africa	49.6
1924	Eric Liddell, Great Britain	47.6 OR
1928	Ray Barbuti, United States	47.8
1932	William Carr, United States	46.2 WR

400 METERS *(Cont.)*

1936	Archie Williams, United States	46.5
1948	Arthur Wint, Jamaica	46.2
1952	George Rhoden, Jamaica	45.9
1956	Charles Jenkins, United States	46.7
1960	Otis Davis, United States	44.9 WR
1964	Michael Larrabee, United States	45.1
1968	Lee Evans, United States	43.86 WR
1972	Vincent Matthews, United States	44.66
1976	Alberto Juantorena, Cuba	44.26
1980	Viktor Markin, USSR	44.60
1984	Alonzo Babers, United States	44.27
1988	Steve Lewis, United States	43.87
1992	Quincy Watts, United States	43.50 OR
1996	Michael Johnson, United States	43.49 OR

800 METERS

1896	Edwin Flack, Australia	2:11
1900	Alfred Tysoe, Great Britain	2:01.2
1904	James Lightbody, United States	1:56 OR
1906	Paul Pilgrim, United States	2:01.5
1908	Mel Sheppard, United States	1:52.8 WR
1912	James Meredith, United States	1:51.9 WR
1920	Albert Hill, Great Britain	1:53.4
1924	Douglas Lowe, Great Britain	1:52.4
1928	Douglas Lowe, Great Britain	1:51.8 OR
1932	Thomas Hampson, Great Britain	1:49.8 WR
1936	John Woodruff, United States	1:52.9
1948	Mal Whitfield, United States	1:49.2 OR
1952	Mal Whitfield, United States	1:49.2 EOR
1956	Thomas Courtney, United States	1:47.7 OR
1960	Peter Snell, New Zealand	1:46.3 OR
1964	Peter Snell, New Zealand	1:45.1 OR
1968	Ralph Doubell, Australia	1:44.3 EWR
1972	Dave Wottle, United States	1:45.9
1976	Alberto Juantorena, Cuba	1:43.50 WR
1980	Steve Ovett, Great Britain	1:45.40
1984	Joaquim Cruz, Brazil	1:43.00 OR
1988	Paul Ereng, Kenya	1:43.45
1992	William Tanui, Kenya	1:43.66
1996	Vebjoern Rodal, Norway	1:42.58 OR

1500 METERS

1896	Edwin Flack, Australia	4:33.2
1900	Charles Bennett, Great Britain	4:06.2 WR
1904	James Lightbody, United States	4:05.4 WR
1906	James Lightbody, United States	4:12.0
1908	Mel Sheppard, United States	4:03.4 OR
1912	Arnold Jackson, Great Britain	3:56.8 OR
1920	Albert Hill, Great Britain	4:01.8
1924	Paavo Nurmi, Finland	3:53.6 OR
1928	Harry Larva, Finland	3:53.2 OR
1932	Luigi Beccali, Italy	3:51.2 OR
1936	Jack Lovelock, New Zealand	3:47.8 WR
1948	Henri Eriksson, Sweden	3:49.8
1952	Josef Barthel, Luxemburg	3:45.1 OR
1956	Ron Delany, Ireland	3:41.2 OR
1960	Herb Elliott, Australia	3:35.6 WR
1964	Peter Snell, New Zealand	3:38.1
1968	Kipchoge Keino, Kenya	3:34.9 OR
1972	Pekkha Vasala, Finland	3:36.3
1976	John Walker, New Zealand	3:39.17
1980	Sebastian Coe, Great Britain	3:38.4
1984	Sebastian Coe, Great Britain	3:32.53 OR

Note: OR=Olympic Record. WR=World Record. EOR=Equals Olympic Record. EWR=Equals World Record. WB=World Best.

TRACK AND FIELD *(Cont.)*

Men *(Cont.)*

1500 METERS *(Cont.)*

1988....Peter Rono, Kenya	3:35.96
1992....Fermin Cacho, Spain	3:40.12
1996....Noureddine Morceli, Algeria	3:35.78

5000 METERS

1912....Hannes Kolehmainen, Finland	14:36.6 WR
1920....Joseph Guillemot, France	14:55.6
1924....Paavo Nurmi, Finland	14:31.2 OR
1928....Villie Ritola, Finland	14:38
1932....Lauri Lehtinen, Finland	14:30 OR
1936....Gunnar Hīckert, Finland	14:22.2 OR
1948....Gaston Reiff, Belgium	14:17.6 OR
1952....Emil Zatopek, Czechoslovakia	14:06.6 OR
1956....Vladimir Kuts, USSR	13:39.6 OR
1960....Murray Halberg, New Zealand	13:43.4
1964....Bob Schul, United States	13:48.8
1968....Mohamed Gammoudi, Tunisia	14:05.0
1972....Lasse Viren, Finland	13:26.4 OR
1976....Lasse Viren, Finland	13:24.76
1980....Miruts Yifter, Ethiopia	13:21.0
1984....Said Aouita, Morocco	13:05.59 OR
1988....John Ngugi, Kenya	13:11.70
1992....Dieter Baumann, Germany	13:12.52
1996....Venuste Niyongabo, Burundi	13:07.96

10,000 METERS

1912....Hannes Kolehmainen, Finland	31:20.8
1920....Paavo Nurmi, Finland	31:45.8
1924....Vilho (Ville) Ritola, Finland	30:23.2 WR
1928....Paavo Nurmi, Finland	30:18.8 OR
1932....Janusz Kusocinski, Poland	30:11.4 OR
1936....Ilmari Salminen, Finland	30:15.4
1948....Emil Zatopek, Czechoslovakia	29:59.6 OR
1952....Emil Zatopek, Czechoslovakia	29:17.0 OR
1956....Vladimir Kuts, USSR	28:45.6 OR
1960....Pyotr Bolotnikov, USSR	28:32.2 OR
1964....Billy Mills, United States	28:24.4 OR
1968....Naftali Temu, Kenya	29:27.4
1972....Lasse Viren, Finland	27:38.4 WR
1976....Lasse Viren, Finland	27:40.38
1980....Miruts Yifter, Ethiopia	27:42.7
1984....Alberto Cova, Italy	27:47.54
1988....Brahim Boutaib, Morocco	27:21.46 OR
1992....Khalid Skah, Morocco	27:46.70
1996....Haile Gebrselassie, Ethiopia	27:07.34 OR

MARATHON

1896....Spiridon Louis, Greece	2:58:50
1900....Michel Theato, France	2:59:45
1904....Thomas Hicks, United States	3:28:53
1906....William Sherring, Canada	2:51:23.6
1908....John Hayes, United States	2:55:18.4 OR
1912....Kenneth McArthur, South Africa	2:36:54.8
1920....Hannes Kolehmainen, Finland	2:32:35.8 WB
1924....Albin Stenroos, Finland	2:41:22.6
1928....Boughera El Ouafi, France	2:32:57
1932....Juan Zabala, Argentina	2:31:36 OR
1936....Kijung Son, Japan (Korea)	2:29:19.2 OR
1948....Delfo Cabrera, Argentina	2:34:51.6
1952....Emil Zatopek, Czechoslovakia	2:23:03.2 OR
1956....Alain Mimoun O'Kacha, France	2:25:00.0
1960....Abebe Bikila, Ethiopia	2:15:16.2 WB
1964....Abebe Bikila, Ethiopia	2:12:11.2 WB
1968....Mamo Wolde, Ethiopia	2:20:26.4
1972....Frank Shorter, United States	2:12:19.8

MARATHON *(Cont.)*

1976....Waldemar Cierpinski, East Germany	2:09:55 OR
1980....Waldemar Cierpinski, East Germany	2:11:03.0
1984....Carlos Lopes, Portugal	2:09:21.0 OR
1988....Gelindo Bordin, Italy	2:10:32
1992....Hwang Young-Cho, S Korea	2:13:23
1996....Josia Thugwane, South Africa	2:12:36

Note: Marathon distances: 1896, 1904—40,000 meters; 1900—40,260 meters; 1906—41,860 meters; 1912—40,200 meters; 1920—42,750 meters; 1908 and since 1924—42,195 meters (26 miles, 385 yards).

110-METER HURDLES

1896....Thomas Curtis, United States	17.6
1900....Alvin Kraenzlein, United States	15.4 OR
1904....Frederick Schule, United States	16.0
1906....Robert Leavitt, United States	16.2
1908....Forrest Smithson, United States	15.0 WR
1912....Frederick Kelly, United States	15.1
1920....Earl Thomson, Canada	14.8 WR
1924....Daniel Kinsey, United States	15.0
1928....Sydney Atkinson, South Africa	14.8
1932....George Saling, United States	14.6
1936....Forrest Towns, United States	14.2
1948....William Porter, United States	13.9 OR
1952....Harrison Dillard, United States	13.7 OR
1956....Lee Calhoun, United States	13.5 OR
1960....Lee Calhoun, United States	13.8
1964....Hayes Jones, United States	13.6
1968....Willie Davenport, United States	13.3 OR
1972....Rod Milburn, United States	13.24 EWR
1976....Guy Drut, France	13.30
1980....Thomas Munkelt, East Germany	13.39
1984....Roger Kingdom, United States	13.20 OR
1988....Roger Kingdom, United States	12.98 OR
1992....Mark McKoy, Canada	13.12
1996....Allen Johnson, United States	12.95 OR

400-METER HURDLES

1900....John Walter Tewksbury, United States	57.6
1904....Harry Hillman, United States	53.0
1906....Not held	
1908....Charles Bacon, United States	55.0 WR
1912....Not held	
1920....Frank Loomis, United States	54.0 WR
1924....F. Morgan Taylor, United States	52.6
1928....David Burghley, Great Britain	53.4 OR
1932....Robert Tisdall, Ireland	51.7
1936....Glenn Hardin, United States	52.4
1948....Roy Cochran, United States	51.1 OR
1952....Charles Moore, United States	50.8 OR
1956....Glenn Davis, United States	50.1 EOR
1960....Glenn Davis, United States	49.3 EOR
1964....Rex Cawley, United States	49.6
1968....Dave Hemery, Great Britain	48.12 WR
1972....John Akii-Bua, Uganda	47.82 WR
1976....Edwin Moses, United States	47.64 WR
1980....Volker Beck, East Germany	48.70
1984....Edwin Moses, United States	47.75
1988....Andre Phillips, United States	47.19 OR
1992....Kevin Young, United States	46.78 WR
1996....Derrick Adkins, United States	47.54

TRACK AND FIELD *(Cont.)*
Men *(Cont.)*

3000-METER STEEPLECHASE

1920	Percy Hodge, Great Britain	10:00.4 OR
1924	Vilho (Ville) Ritola, Finland	9:33.6 OR
1928	Toivo Loukola, Finland	9:21.8 WR
1932	Volmari Iso-Hollo, Finland	10:33.4*
1936	Volmari Iso-Hollo, Finland	9:03.8 WR
1948	Thore Sjöstrand, Sweden	9:04.6
1952	Horace Ashenfelter, United States	8:45.4 WR
1956	Chris Brasher, Great Britain	8:41.2 OR
1960	Zdzislaw Krzyszkowiak, Poland	8:34.2 OR
1964	Gaston Roelants, Belgium	8:30.8 OR
1968	Amos Biwott, Kenya	8:51
1972	Kipchoge Keino, Kenya	8:23.6 OR
1976	Anders Gärderud, Sweden	8:08.2 WR
1980	Bronislaw Malinowski, Poland	8:09.7
1984	Julius Korir, Kenya	8:11.8
1988	Julius Kariuki, Kenya	8:05.51 OR
1992	Matthew Birir, Kenya	8:08.84
1996	Joseph Keter, Kenya	8:07.12

*About 3450 meters; extra lap by error.

4 X 100-METER RELAY

1912	Great Britain	42.4 OR
1920	United States	42.2 WR
1924	United States	41.0 EWR
1928	United States	41.0 EWR
1932	United States	40.0 EWR
1936	United States	39.8 WR
1948	United States	40.6
1952	United States	40.1
1956	United States	39.5 WR
1960	West Germany	39.5 EWR
1964	United States	39.0 WR
1968	United States	38.2 WR
1972	United States	38.19 EWR
1976	United States	38.33
1980	USSR	38.26
1984	United States	37.83 WR
1988	USSR	38.19
1992	United States	37.40 WR
1996	Canada	37.69

4 X 400-METER RELAY

1908	United States	3:29.4
1912	United States	3:16.6 WR
1920	Great Britain	3:22.2
1924	United States	3:16.0 WR
1928	United States	3:14.2 WR
1932	United States	3:08.2 WR
1936	Great Britain	3:09.0
1948	United States	3:10.4 WR
1952	Jamaica	3:03.9 WR
1956	United States	3:04.8
1960	United States	3:02.2 WR
1964	United States	3:00.7 WR
1968	United States	2:56.16 WR
1972	Kenya	2:59.8
1976	United States	2:58.65
1980	USSR	3:01.1
1984	United States	2:57.91
1988	United States	2:56.16 EWR
1992	United States	2:55.74 WR
1996	United States	2:55.99

20-KILOMETER WALK

1956	Leonid Spirin, USSR	1:31:27.4
1960	Vladimir Golubnichiy, USSR	1:33:07.2
1964	Kenneth Mathews, Great Britain	1:29:34.0 OR
1968	Vladimir Golubnichiy, USSR	1:33:58.4
1972	Peter Frenkel, East Germany	1:26:42.4 OR
1976	Daniel Bautista, Mexico	1:24:40.6 OR
1980	Maurizio Damilano, Italy	1:23:35.5 OR
1984	Ernesto Canto, Mexico	1:23:13.0 OR
1988	Jozef Pribilinec, Czechoslovakia	1:19:57.0 OR
1992	Daniel Plaza, Spain	1:21:45.0
1996	Jefferson Pérez, Ecuador	1:20:07

50-KILOMETER WALK

1932	Thomas Green, Great Britain	4:50:10
1936	Harold Whitlock, Great Britain	4:30:41.4 OR
1948	John Ljunggren, Sweden	4:41:52
1952	Giuseppe Dordoni, Italy	4:28:07.8 OR
1956	Norman Read, New Zealand	4:30:42.8
1960	Donald Thompson, Great Britain	4:25:30 OR
1964	Abdon Parnich, Italy	4:11:12.4 OR
1968	Christoph Höhne, East Germany	4:20:13.6
1972	Bernd Kannenberg, West Germany	3:56:11.6 OR
1980	Hartwig Gauder, East Germany	3:49:24.0 OR
1984	Raul Gonzalez, Mexico	3:47:26.0 OR
1988	Viacheslav Ivanenko, USSR	3:38:29.0 OR
1992	Andrey Perlov, Unified Team	3:50:13
1996	Robert Korzeniowski, Poland	3:43:30

HIGH JUMP

1896	Ellery Clark, United States	5 ft 11¼ in
1900	Irving Baxter, United States	6 ft 2¾ in OR
1904	Samuel Jones, United States	5 ft 11 in
1906	Cornelius Leahy, Great Britain/Ireland	5 ft 10 in
1908	Harry Porter, United States	6 ft 3 in OR
1912	Alma Richards, United States	6 ft 4 in OR
1920	Richmond Landon, United States	6 ft 4 in OR
1924	Harold Osborn, United States	6 ft 6 in OR
1928	Robert W. King, United States	6 ft 4½ in
1932	Duncan McNaughton, Canada	6 ft 5½ in
1936	Cornelius Johnson, United States	6 ft 8 in OR
1948	John L. Winter, Australia	6 ft 6 in
1952	Walter Davis, United States	6 ft 8½ in OR
1956	Charles Dumas, United States	6 ft 11½ in OR
1960	Robert Shavlakadze, USSR	7 ft 1 in OR
1964	Valery Brumel, USSR	7 ft 1¾ in OR
1968	Dick Fosbury, United States	7 ft 4¼ in OR
1972	Yuri Tarmak, USSR	7 ft 3¾ in
1976	Jacek Wszola, Poland	7 ft 4½ in OR
1980	Gerd Wessig, East Germany	7 ft 8¾ in WR
1984	Dietmar Mögenburg, West Germany	7 ft 8½ in
1988	Gennadiy Avdeyenko, USSR	7 ft 9¾ in OR
1992	Javier Sotomayor, Cuba	7 ft 8 in.
1996	Charles Austin, United States	7 ft 10 in OR

POLE VAULT

1896	William Hoyt, United States	10 ft 10 in
1900	Irving Baxter, United States	10 ft 10 in
1904	Charles Dvorak, United States	11 ft 5¾ in
1906	Fernand Gonder, France	11 ft 5¾ in

Note: OR=Olympic Record. WR=World Record. EOR=Equals Olympic Record. EWR=Equals World Record. WB=World Best.

TRACK AND FIELD *(Cont.)*
Men *(Cont.)*

POLE VAULT *(Cont.)*

1908...	Alfred Gilbert, United States Edward Cooke Jr, United States	12 ft 2 in OR
1912...	Harry Babcock, United States	12 ft 11½ in OR
1920...	Frank Foss, United States	13 ft 5 in WR
1924...	Lee Barnes, United States	12 ft 11½ in
1928...	Sabin Carr, United States	13 ft 9¼ in OR
1932...	William Miller, United States	14 ft 1¾ in OR
1936...	Earle Meadows, United States	14 ft 3¼ in OR
1948...	Guinn Smith, United States	14 ft 1¼ in
1952...	Robert Richards, United States	14 ft 11 in OR
1956...	Robert Richards, United States	14 ft 11½ in OR
1960...	Don Bragg, United States	15 ft 5 in OR
1964...	Fred Hansen, United States	16 ft 8¾ in OR
1968...	Bob Seagren, United States	17 ft 8½ in OR
1972...	Wolfgang Nordwig, East Germany	18 ft ½ in OR
1976...	Tadeusz Slusarski, Poland	18 ft ½ in EOR
1980...	Wladyslaw Kozakiewicz, Poland	18 ft 11½ in WR
1984...	Pierre Quinon, France	18 ft 10¼ in
1988...	Sergei Bubka, USSR	19 ft 4¼ in OR
1992...	Maksim Tarasov, Unified Team	19 ft ¼ in
1996...	Jean Galfione, France	19 ft 5 ¼ in OR

LONG JUMP

1896...	Ellery Clark, United States	20 ft 10 in
1900...	Alvin Kraenzlein, United States	23 ft 6¾ in OR
1904...	Meyer Prinstein, United States	24 ft 1 in OR
1906...	Meyer Prinstein, United States	23 ft 7½ in
1908...	Frank Irons, United States	24 ft 6½ in OR
1912...	Albert Gutterson, United States	24 ft 11¼ in OR
1920...	William Petersson, Sweden	23 ft 5½ in
1924...	DeHart Hubbard, United States	24 ft 5 in
1928...	Edward B. Hamm, United States	25 ft 4½ in OR
1932...	Edward Gordon, United States	25 ft ¾ in
1936...	Jesse Owens, United States	26 ft 5½ in OR
1948...	William Steele, United States	25 ft 8 in
1952...	Jerome Biffle, United States	24 ft 10 in
1956...	Gregory Bell, United States	25 ft 8¼ in
1960...	Ralph Boston, United States	26 ft 7¾ in OR
1964...	Lynn Davies, Great Britain	26 ft 5¾ in
1968...	Bob Beamon, United States	29 ft 2½ in WR
1972...	Randy Williams, United States	27 ft ½ in
1976...	Arnie Robinson, United States	27 ft 4¾ in
1980...	Lutz Dombrowski, East Germany	28 ft ¼ in
1984...	Carl Lewis, United States	28 ft ¼ in
1988...	Carl Lewis, United States	28 ft 7½ in
1992...	Carl Lewis, United States	28 ft 5½ in
1996...	Carl Lewis, United States	27 ft 10¾ in

TRIPLE JUMP

1896...	James Connolly, United States	44 ft 11¾ in
1900...	Meyer Prinstein, United States	47 ft 5¾ in OR
1904...	Meyer Prinstein, United States	47 ft 1 in
1906...	Peter O'Connor, Great Britain/Ireland	46 ft 2¼ in
1908...	Timothy Ahearne, Great Britain/Ireland	48 ft 11¼ in OR
1912...	Gustaf Lindblom, Sweden	48 ft 5¼ in
1920...	Vilho Tuulos, Finland	47 ft 7 in
1924...	Anthony Winter, Australia	50 ft 11¼ in WR
1928...	Mikio Oda, Japan	49 ft 11 in
1932...	Chuhei Nambu, Japan	51 ft 7 in WR

TRIPLE JUMP *(Cont.)*

1936...	Naoto Tajima, Japan	52 ft 6 in WR
1948...	Arne Ahman, Sweden	50 ft 6¼ in
1952...	Adhemar da Silva, Brazil	53 ft 2¾ in WR
1956...	Adhemar da Silva, Brazil	53 ft 7¾ in OR
1960...	Jozef Schmidt, Poland	55 ft 2 in
1964...	Jozef Schmidt, Poland	55 ft 3½ in OR
1968...	Viktor Saneyev, USSR	57 ft ¾ in WR
1972...	Viktor Saneyev, USSR	56 ft 11¾ in
1976...	Viktor Saneyev, USSR	56 ft 8¾ in
1980...	Jaak Uudmae, USSR	56 ft 11¼ in
1984...	Al Joyner, United States	56 ft 7½ in
1988...	Khristo Markov, Bulgaria	57 ft 9½ in OR
1992...	Mike Conley, United States	59 ft 7½ in (w)
1996...	Kenny Harrison, United States	59 ft 4¼ in OR

SHOT PUT

1896...	Robert Garrett, United States	36 ft 9¾ in
1900...	Richard Sheldon, United States	46 ft 3¼ in OR
1904...	Ralph Rose, United States	48 ft 7 in WR
1906...	Martin Sheridan, United States	40 ft 5¼ in
1908...	Ralph Rose, United States	46 ft 7½ in
1912...	Pat McDonald, United States	50 ft 4 in OR
1920...	Ville Porhola, Finland	48 ft 7¼ in
1924...	Clarence Houser, United States	49 ft 2¼ in
1928...	John Kuck, United States	52 ft ¾ in WR
1932...	Leo Sexton, United States	52 ft 6 in OR
1936...	Hans Woellke, Germany	53 ft 1¾ in OR
1948...	Wilbur Thompson, United States	56 ft 2 in OR
1952...	Parry O'Brien, United States	57 ft ½ in OR
1956...	Parry O'Brien, United States	60 ft 11¼ in OR
1960...	William Nieder, United States	64 ft 6¾ in OR
1964...	Dallas Long, United States	66 ft 8½ in OR
1968...	Randy Matson, United States	67 ft 4¾ in
1972...	Wladyslaw Komar, Poland	69 ft 6 in OR
1976...	Udo Beyer, East Germany	69 ft ¾ in
1980...	Vladimir Kiselyov, USSR	70 ft ½ in OR
1984...	Alessandro Andrei, Italy	69 ft 9 in
1988...	Ulf Timmermann, East Germany	73 ft 8¾ in OR
1992...	Mike Stulce, United States	71 ft 2½ in
1996...	Randy Barnes, United States	70 ft 11 in

DISCUS THROW

1896...	Robert Garrett, United States	95 ft 7½ in
1900...	Rudolf Bauer, Hungary	118 ft 3 in OR
1904...	Martin Sheridan, United States	128 ft 10½ in OR
1906...	Martin Sheridan, United States	136 ft
1908...	Martin Sheridan, United States	134 ft 2 in OR
1912...	Armas Taipele, Finland	148 ft 3 in OR
1920...	Elmer Niklander, Finland	146 ft 7 in
1924...	Clarence Houser, United States	151 ft 4 in OR
1928...	Clarence Houser, United States	155 ft 3 in OR
1932...	John Anderson, United States	162 ft 4 in OR
1936...	Ken Carpenter, United States	165 ft 7 in OR
1948...	Adolfo Consolini, Italy	173 ft 2 in OR
1952...	Sim Iness, United States	180 ft 6 in OR
1956...	Al Oerter, United States	184 ft 11 in OR
1960...	Al Oerter, United States	194 ft 2 in OR
1964...	Al Oerter, United States	200 ft 1 in OR
1968...	Al Oerter, United States	212 ft 6 in OR
1972...	Ludvik Danek, Czechoslovakia	211 ft 3 in
1976...	Mac Wilkins, United States	221 ft 5 in OR
1980...	Viktor Rashchupkin, USSR	218 ft 8 in

TRACK AND FIELD (Cont.)

Men (Cont.)

DISCUS THROW (Cont.)

1984	Rolf Dannenberg, West Germany	218 ft 6 in
1988	Jürgen Schult, East Germany	225 ft 9 in OR
1992	Romas Ubartas, Lithuania	213 ft 8 in
1996	Lars Riedel, Germany	227 ft 8 in OR

HAMMER THROW

1900	John Flanagan, United States	163 ft 1 in
1904	John Flanagan, United States	168 ft 1 in OR
1906	Not held	
1908	John Flanagan, United States	170 ft 4 in OR
1912	Matt McGrath, United States	179 ft 7 in OR
1920	Pat Ryan, United States	173 ft 5 in
1924	Fred Tootell, United States	174 ft 10 in
1928	Patrick O'Callaghan, Ireland	168 ft 7 in
1932	Patrick O'Callaghan, Ireland	176 ft 11 in
1936	Karl Hein, Germany	185 ft 4 in OR
1948	Imre Nemeth, Hungary	183 ft 11 in
1952	Jozsef Csermak, Hungary	197 ft 11 in WR
1956	Harold Connolly, United States	207 ft 3 in OR
1960	Vasily Rudenkov, USSR	220 ft 2 in OR
1964	Romuald Klim, USSR	228 ft 10 in OR
1968	Gyula Zsivotsky, Hungary	240 ft 8 in OR
1972	Anatoli Bondarchuk, USSR	247 ft 8 in OR
1976	Yuri Sedykh, USSR	254 ft 4 in OR
1980	Yuri Sedykh, USSR	268 ft 4 in WR
1984	Juha Tiainen, Finland	256 ft 2 in
1988	Sergei Litvinov, USSR	278 ft 2 in OR
1992	Andrey Abduvaliyev, Unified Team	270 ft 9 in
1996	Balazs Kiss, Hungary	266 ft 6 in

JAVELIN

1908	Erik Lemming, Sweden	179 ft 10 in
1912	Erik Lemming, Sweden	198 ft 11 in WR
1920	Jonni Myyrä, Finland	215 ft 10 in OR
1924	Jonni Myyrä, Finland	206 ft 6 in
1928	Eric Lundkvist, Sweden	218 ft 6 in OR
1932	Matti Jarvinen, Finland	238 ft 6 in OR
1936	Gerhard Stöck, Germany	235 ft 8 in
1948	Kai Rautavaara, Finland	228 ft 10½ in

JAVELIN (Cont.)

1952	Cy Young, United States	242 ft 1 in OR
1956	Egil Danielson, Norway	281 ft 2¼ in WR
1960	Viktor Tsibulenko, USSR	277 ft 8 in
1964	Pauli Nevala, Finland	271 ft 2 in
1968	Janis Lusis, USSR	295 ft 7 in OR
1972	Klaus Wolfermann, West Germany	296 ft 10 in OR
1976	Miklos Nemeth, Hungary	310 ft 4 in WR
1980	Dainis Kuta, USSR	299 ft 2⅜ in
1984	Arto Härkönen, Finland	284 ft 8 in
1988	Tapio Korjus, Finland	276 ft 6 in
1992	Jan Zelezny, Czechoslovakia	294 ft 2 in OR
1996	Jan Zelezny, Czech Rep.	289 ft 3 in

DECATHLON

		Pts
1904	Thomas Kiely, Ireland	6036
1912	Jim Thorpe, United States*	8412 WR
1920	Helge Lövland, Norway	6803
1924	Harold Osborn, United States	7711 WR
1928	Paavo Yrjölä, Finland	8053.29 WR
1932	James Bausch, United States	8462 WR
1936	Glenn Morris, United States	7900 WR
1948	Robert Mathias, United States	7139
1952	Robert Mathias, United States	7887 WR
1956	Milton Campbell, United States	7937 OR
1960	Rafer Johnson, United States	8392 OR
1964	Willi Holdorf, West Germany	7887
1968	Bill Toomey, United States	8193 OR
1972	Nikolai Avilov, USSR	8454 WR
1976	Bruce Jenner, United States	8617 WR
1980	Daley Thompson, Great Britain	8495
1984	Daley Thompson, Great Britain	8798 EWR
1988	Christian Schenk, East Germany	8488
1992	Robert Zmelik, Czechoslovakia	8611
1996	Dan O'Brien, United States	8824 OR

*In 1913, Thorpe was disqualified for having played professional baseball in 1910. His record was restored in 1982.

Women

100 METERS

1928	Elizabeth Robinson, United States	12.2 EWR
1932	Stella Walsh, Poland	11.9 EWR
1936	Helen Stephens, United States	11.5
1948	Francina Blankers-Koen, Netherlands	11.9
1952	Marjorie Jackson, Australia	11.5 EWR
1956	Betty Cuthbert, Australia	11.5 EWR
1960	Wilma Rudolph, United States	11.0
1964	Wyomia Tyus, United States	11.4
1968	Wyomia Tyus, United States	11.0 WR
1972	Renate Stecher, East Germany	11.07
1976	Annegret Richter, West Germany	11.08
1980	Lyudmila Kondratyeva, USSR	11.06
1984	Evelyn Ashford, United States	10.97 OR
1988	Florence Griffith Joyner, United States	10.54 (w)
1992	Gail Devers, United States	10.82
1996	Gail Devers, United States	10.94

200 METERS

1948	Francina Blankers-Koen, Netherlands	24.4
1952	Marjorie Jackson, Australia	23.7
1956	Betty Cuthbert, Australia	23.4 EOR
1960	Wilma Rudolph, United States	24.0
1964	Edith McGuire, United States	23.0 OR
1968	Irena Szewinska, Poland	22.5 WR
1972	Renate Stecher, East Germany	22.40 EWR
1976	Bärbel Eckert, East Germany	22.37 OR
1980	Bärbel Wöckel (Eckert), East Germany	22.03 OR
1984	Valerie Brisco-Hooks, United States	21.81 OR
1988	Florence Griffith Joyner, United States	21.34 WR
1992	Gwen Torrence, United States	21.81
1996	Marie-José Pérec, France	22.12

Note: OR=Olympic Record. WR=World Record. EOR=Equals Olympic Record. EWR=Equals World Record. WB=World Best.

TRACK AND FIELD *(Cont.)*
Women *(Cont.)*

400 METERS

1964	Betty Cuthbert, Australia	52.0 OR
1968	Colette Besson, France	52.0 EOR
1972	Monika Zehrt, East Germany	51.08 OR
1976	Irena Szewinska, Poland	49.29 WR
1980	Marita Koch, East Germany	48.88 OR
1984	Valerie Brisco-Hooks, United States	48.83 OR
1988	Olga Bryzgina, USSR	48.65 OR
1992	Marie-José Pérec, France	48.83
1996	Marie-José Pérec, France	48.25 OR

800 METERS

1928	Lina Radke, Germany	2:16.8 WR
1932	Not held 1932–1956	
1960	Lyudmila Shevtsova, USSR	2:04.3 EWR
1964	Ann Packer, Great Britain	2:01.1 OR
1968	Madeline Manning, United States	2:00.9 OR
1972	Hildegard Falck, West Germany	1:58.55 OR
1976	Tatyana Kazankina, USSR	1:54.94 WR
1980	Nadezhda Olizarenko, USSR	1:53.42 WR
1984	Doina Melinte, Romania	1:57.6
1988	Sigrun Wodars, East Germany	1:56.10
1992	Ellen Van Langen, Netherlands	1:55.54
1996	Svetlana Masterkova, Russia	1:57.73

1500 METERS

1972	Lyudmila Bragina, USSR	4:01.4 WR
1976	Tatyana Kazankina, USSR	4:05.48
1980	Tatyana Kazankina, USSR	3:56.6 OR
1984	Gabriella Dorio, Italy	4:03.25
1988	Paula Ivan, Romania	3:53.96 OR
1992	Hassiba Boulmerka, Algeria	3:55.30
1996	Svetlana Masterkova, Russia	4:00.83

3000 METERS

1984	Maricica Puica, Romania	8:35.96 OR
1988	Tatyana Samolenko, USSR	8:26.53 OR
1992	Elena Romanova, Unified Team	8:46.04

5000 METERS

1996	Wang Junxia, China	14:57.88

10,000 METERS

1988	Olga Bondarenko, USSR	31:05.21 OR
1992	Derartu Tulu, Ethiopia	31:06.02
1996	Fernanda Ribeiro, Portugal	31:01.63 OR

MARATHON

1984	Joan Benoit, United States	2:24:52 OR
1988	Rosa Mota, Portugal	2:25:40
1992	Valentin Yegorova, Unified Team	2:32:41
1996	Fatuma Roba, Ethiopia	2:26:05

80-METER HURDLES

1932	Babe Didrikson, United States	11.7 WR
1936	Trebisonda Valla, Italy	11.7
1948	Francina Blankers-Koen, Netherlands	11.2 OR
1952	Shirley Strickland, Australia	10.9 WR
1956	Shirley Strickland, Australia	10.7 OR
1960	Irina Press, USSR	10.8
1964	Karin Balzer, East Germany	10.5
1968	Maureen Caird, Australia	10.3 OR

100-METER HURDLES

1972	Annelie Ehrhardt, East Germany	12.59 WR
1976	Johanna Schaller, East Germany	12.77
1980	Vera Komisova, USSR	12.56 OR
1984	Benita Fitzgerald-Brown, United States	12.84
1988	Yordanka Donkova, Bulgaria	12.38 OR
1992	Paraskevi Patoulidou, Greece	12.64
1996	Lyudmila Engqvist, Sweden	12.58

400-METER HURDLES

1984	Nawal el Moutawakel, Morocco	54.61 OR
1988	Debra Flintoff-King, Australia	53.17 OR
1992	Sally Gunnell, Great Britain	53.23
1996	Deon Hemmings, Jamaica	52.82 OR

4 X 100-METER RELAY

1928	Canada	48.4 WR
1932	United States	46.9 WR
1936	United States	46.9
1948	Netherlands	47.5
1952	United States	45.9 WR
1956	Australia	44.5 WR
1960	United States	44.5
1964	Poland	43.6
1968	United States	42.8 WR
1972	West Germany	42.81 EWR
1976	East Germany	42.55 OR
1980	East Germany	41.60 WR
1984	United States	41.65
1988	United States	41.98
1992	United States	42.11
1996	United States	41.95

4 X 400-METER RELAY

1972	East Germany	3:23 WR
1976	East Germany	3:19.23 WR
1980	USSR	3:20.02
1984	United States	3:18.29 OR
1988	USSR	3:15.18 WR
1992	Unified Team	3:20.20
1996	United States	3:20.91

10-KILOMETER WALK

1992	Chen Yueling, China	44:32
1996	Elena Nikolayeva, Russia	41:49 OR

HIGH JUMP

1928	Ethel Catherwood, Canada	5 ft 2½ in
1932	Jean Shiley, United States	5 ft 5¼ in WR
1936	Ibolya Csak, Hungary	5 ft 3 in
1948	Alice Coachman, United States	5 ft 6 in OR
1952	Esther Brand, South Africa	5 ft 5¾ in
1956	Mildred L. McDaniel, United States	5 ft 9¼ in WR
1960	Iolanda Balas, Romania	6 ft ¾ in OR
1964	Iolanda Balas, Romania	6 ft 2¾ in OR
1968	Miloslava Reskova, Czechoslovakia	5 ft 11½ in
1972	Ulrike Meyfarth, West Germany	6 ft 3½ in EWR
1976	Rosemarie Ackermann, East Germany	6 ft 4 in OR

TRACK AND FIELD *(Cont.)*
Women *(Cont.)*

HIGH JUMP *(Cont.)*

1980...Sara Simeoni, Italy	6 ft 5½ in OR
1984...Ulrike Meyfarth, West Germany	6 ft 7½ in OR
1988...Louise Ritter, United States	6 ft 8 in OR
1992...Heike Henkel, Germany	6 ft 7½ in
1996...Stefka Kostadinova, Bulgaria	6 ft 8¾ in OR

LONG JUMP

1948...Olga Gyarmati, Hungary	18 ft 8¼ in
1952...Yvette Williams, New Zealand	20 ft 5¾ in OR
1956...Elzbieta Krzeskinska, Poland	20 ft 10 in EWR
1960...Vyera Krepkina, USSR	20 ft 10¾ in OR
1964...Mary Rand, Great Britain	22 ft 2¼ in WR
1968...Viorica Viscopoleanu, Romania	22 ft 4½ in WR
1972...Heidemarie Rosendahl, West Germany	22 ft 3 in
1976...Angela Voigt, East Germany	22 ft ¾ in
1980...Tatyana Kolpakova, USSR	23 ft 2 in OR
1984...Anisoara Stanciu, Romania	22 ft 10 in
1988...Jackie Joyner-Kersee, United States	24 ft 3½ in OR
1992...Heike Drechsler, Germany	23 ft 5¼ in
1996...Chioma Ajunwa, Nigeria	23 ft 4½ in

TRIPLE JUMP

1996...Inessa Kravets, Ukraine	50 ft 3½ in

SHOT PUT

1948...Micheline Ostermeyer, France	45 ft 1½ in
1952...Galina Zybina, USSR	50 ft 1¾ in WR
1956...Tamara Tyshkevich, USSR	54 ft 5 in OR
1960...Tamara Press, USSR	56 ft 10 in OR
1964...Tamara Press, USSR	59 ft 6¼ in OR
1968...Margitta Gummel, East Germany	64 ft 4 in WR
1972...Nadezhda Chizhova, USSR	69 ft WR
1976...Ivanka Hristova, Bulgaria	69 ft 5¼ in OR
1980...Ilona Slupianek, E Germany	73 ft 6¼ in
1984...Claudia Losch, West Germany	67 ft 2¼ in
1988...Natalya Lisovskaya, USSR	72 ft 11¾ in
1992...Svetlana Kriveleva, Unified Team	69 ft 1¼ in
1996...Astrid Kumbernuss, Germany	67 ft 5½ in

DISCUS THROW

1928...Helena Konopacka, Poland	129 ft 11¾ in WR
1932...Lillian Copeland, United States	133 ft 2 in OR
1936...Gisela Mauermayer, Germany	156 ft 3 in OR
1948...Micheline Ostermeyer, France	137 ft 6 in
1952...Nina Romaschkova, USSR	168 ft 8 in OR

DISCUS THROW *(Cont.)*

1956...Olga Fikotova, Czechoslovakia	176 ft 1 in OR
1960...Nina Ponomaryeva, USSR	180 ft 9 in OR
1964...Tamara Press, USSR	187 ft 10 in OR
1968...Lia Manoliu, Romania	191 ft 2 in OR
1972...Faina Melnik, USSR	218 ft 7 in OR
1976...Evelin Schlaak, East Germany	226 ft 4 in OR
1980...Evelin Jahl (Schlaak), East Germany	229 ft 6 in OR
1984...Ria Stalman, Netherlands	214 ft 5 in
1988...Martina Hellmann, East Germany	237 ft 2 in OR
1992...Maritza Martén, Cuba	229 ft 10 in
1996...Ilke Wyludda, Germany	228 ft 6 in

JAVELIN THROW

1932...Babe Didrikson, United States	143 ft 4 in OR
1936...Tilly Fleischer, Germany	148 ft 3 in OR
1948...Herma Bauma, Austria	149 ft 6 in
1952...Dana Zatopkova, Czechoslovakia	165 ft 7 in
1956...Inese Jaunzeme, USSR	176 ft 8 in
1960...Elvira Ozolina, USSR	183 ft 8 in OR
1964...Mihaela Penes, Romania	198 ft 7 in
1968...Angela Nemeth, Hungary	198 ft
1972...Ruth Fuchs, East Germany	209 ft 7 in OR
1976...Ruth Fuchs, East Germany	216 ft 4 in OR
1980...Maria Colon, Cuba	224 ft 5 in OR
1984...Tessa Sanderson, Great Britain	228 ft 2 in OR
1988...Petra Felke, East Germany	245 ft OR
1992...Silke Renk, Germany	224 ft 2 in
1996...Heli Rantanen, Finland	222 ft 11 in

PENTATHLON

	Pts
1964 ...Irina Press, USSR	5246 WR
1968 ...Ingrid Becker, West Germany	5098
1972 ...Mary Peters, Great Britain	4801 WR*
1976 ...Siegrun Siegl, East Germany	4745
1980 ...Nadezhda Tkachenko, USSR	5083 WR

HEPTATHLON

	Pts
1984 ...Glynis Nunn, Australia	6390 OR
1988 ...Jackie Joyner-Kersee, United States	7291 WR
1992 ...Jackie Joyner-Kersee, United States	7044
1996 ...Ghada Shouaa, Syria	6780

Note: OR=Olympic Record; WR=World Record; EOR=Equals Olympic Record; EWR=Equals World Record; WB=World Best.

BASKETBALL

Men

1936
Final: United States 19, Canada 8
United States: Ralph Bishop, Joe Fortenberry, Carl Knowles, Jack Ragland, Carl Shy, William Wheatley, Francis Johnson, Samuel Balter, John Gibbons, Frank Lubin, Arthur Mollner, Donald Piper, Duane Swanson, Willard Schmidt

1948
Final: United States 65, France 21
United States: Cliff Barker, Don Barksdale, Ralph Beard, Lewis Beck, Vince Boryla, Gordon Carpenter, Alex Groza, Wallace Jones, Bob Kurland, Ray Lumpp, Robert Pitts, Jesse Renick, Bob Robinson, Ken Rollins

1952
Final: United States 36, USSR 25
United States: Charles Hoag, Bill Hougland, Melvin Dean Kelley, Bob Kenney, Clyde Lovellette, Marcus Freiberger, Victor Wayne Glasgow, Frank McCabe, Daniel Pippen, Howard Williams, Ronald Bontemps, Bob Kurland, William Lienhard, John Keller

1956
Final: United States 89, USSR 55
United States: Carl Cain, Bill Hougland, K. C. Jones, Bill Russell, James Walsh, William Evans, Burdette Haldorson, Ron Tomsic, Dick Boushka, Gilbert Ford, Bob Jeangerard, Charles Darling

1960
Final: United States 90, Brazil 63
United States: Jay Arnette, Walt Bellamy, Bob Boozer, Terry Dischinger, Jerry Lucas, Oscar Robertson, Adrian Smith, Burdette Haldorson, Darrall Imhoff, Allen Kelley, Lester Lane, Jerry West

1964
Final: United States 73, USSR 59
United States: Jim Barnes, Bill Bradley, Larry Brown, Joe Caldwell, Mel Counts, Richard Davies, Walt Hazzard, Lucius Jackson, John McCaffrey, Jeff Mullins, Jerry Shipp, George Wilson

1968
Final: United States 65, Yugoslavia 50
United States: John Clawson, Ken Spain, Jo-Jo White, Michael Barrett, Spencer Haywood, Charles Scott, William Hosket, Calvin Fowler, Michael Silliman, Glynn Saulters, James King, Donald Dee

1972
Final: USSR 51, United States 50
United States: Kenneth Davis, Doug Collins, Thomas Henderson, Mike Bantom, Bobby Jones, Dwight Jones, James Forbes, James Brewer, Tom Burleson, Tom McMillen, Kevin Joyce, Ed Ratleff

1976
Final: United States 95, Yugoslavia 74
United States: Phil Ford, Steve Sheppard, Adrian Dantley, Walter Davis, Quinn Buckner, Ernie Grunfield, Kenny Carr, Scott May, Michel Armstrong, Tom La Garde, Phil Hubbard, Mitch Kupchak

Men

1980
Final: Yugoslavia 86, Italy 77
U.S. participated in boycott.

1984
Final: United States 96, Spain 65
United States: Steve Alford, Leon Wood, Patrick Ewing, Vern Fleming, Alvin Robertson, Michael Jordan, Joe Kleine, Jon Koncak, Wayman Tisdale, Chris Mullin, Sam Perkins, Jeff Turner

1988
Final: USSR 76, Yugoslavia 63
United States (3rd): Mitch Richmond, Charles E. Smith IV, Vernell Coles, Hersey Hawkins, Jeff Grayer, Charles D. Smith, Willie Anderson, Stacey Augmon, Dan Majerle, Danny Manning, J. R. Reid, David Robinson

1992
Final: United States 117, Croatia 85
United States: David Robinson, Christian Laettner, Patrick Ewing, Larry Bird, Scottie Pippen, Michael Jordan, Clyde Drexler, Karl Malone, John Stockton, Chris Mullin, Charles Barkley, Earvin Johnson

1996
Final: United States 95, Yugoslavia 69
United States: Charles Barkley, Anfernee Hardaway, Grant Hill, Karl Malone, Reggie Miller, Hakeem Olajuwon, Shaquille O'Neal, Scottie Pippen, Mitch Richmond, John Stockton, David Robinson, Gary Payton

Women

1976
Gold, USSR; Silver, United States*
United States: Cindy Brogdon, Susan Rojcewicz, Ann Meyers, Lusia Harris, Nancy Dunkle, Charlotte Lewis, Nancy Lieberman, Gail Marquis, Patricia Roberts, Mary Anne O'Connor, Patricia Head, Julienne Simpson

*In 1976 the women played a round-robin tournament, with the gold medal going to the team with the best record. The USSR won with a 5-0 record, and the USA, with a 3-2 record, was given the silver by virtue of a 95-79 victory over Bulgaria, which was also 3-2.

1980
Final: USSR 104, Bulgaria 73
U.S. participated in boycott.

1984
Final: United States 85, Korea 55
United States: Teresa Edwards, Lea Henry, Lynette Woodard, Anne Donovan, Cathy Boswell, Cheryl Miller, Janice Lawrence, Cindy Noble, Kim Mulkey, Denise Curry, Pamela McGee, Carol Menken-Schaudt

1988
Final: United States 77, Yugoslavia 70
United States: Teresa Edwards, Mary Ethridge, Cynthia Brown, Anne Donovan, Teresa Weatherspoon, Bridgette Gordon, Victoria Bullett, Andrea Lloyd, Katrina McClain, Jennifer Gillom, Cynthia Cooper, Suzanne McConnell

BASKETBALL *(Cont.)*
Women *(Cont.)*

1992

Final: Unified Team 76, China 66
United States (3rd): Teresa Edwards, Teresa Weatherspoon, Victoria Bullett, Katrina McClain, Cynthia Cooper, Suzanne McConnell, Daedra Charles, Clarissa Davis, Tammy Jackson, Vickie Orr, Carolyn Jones, Medina Dixon

1996

Final: United States 111, Brazil 87
United States: Jennifer Azzi, Ruthie Bolton, Teresa Edwards, Lisa Leslie, Rebecca Lobo, Katrina McClain, Nikki McCray, Carla McGhee, Dawn Staley, Katy Steding, Sheryl Swoopes, Venus Lacey

BOXING

LIGHT FLYWEIGHT (106 LB)

1968	Francisco Rodriguez, Venezuela
1972	Gyorgy Gedo, Hungary
1976	Jorge Hernandez, Cuba
1980	Shamil Sabyrov, USSR
1984	Paul Gonzalez, United States
1988	Ivailo Hristov, Bulgaria
1992	Rogelio Marcelo, Cuba
1996	Daniel Petrov, Bulgaria

FLYWEIGHT (112 LB)

1904	George Finnegan, United States
1906-1912	Not held
1920	Frank Di Gennara, United States
1924	Fidel LaBarba, United States
1928	Antal Kocsis, Hungary
1932	Istvan Enekes, Hungary
1936	Willi Kaiser, Germany
1948	Pascual Perez, Argentina
1952	Nathan Brooks, United States
1956	Terence Spinks, Great Britain
1960	Gyula Torok, Hungary
1964	Fernando Atzori, Italy
1968	Ricardo Delgado, Mexico
1972	Georgi Kostadinov, Bulgaria
1976	Leo Randolph, United States
1980	Peter Lessov, Bulgaria
1984	Steve McCrory, United States
1988	Kim Kwang Sun, South Korea
1992	Su Choi Chol, North Korea
1996	Maikro Romero, Cuba

BANTAMWEIGHT (119 LB)

1904	Oliver Kirk, United States
1906	Not held
1908	A. Henry Thomas, Great Britain
1912	Not held
1920	Clarence Walker, South Africa
1924	William Smith, South Africa
1928	Vittorio Tamagnini, Italy
1932	Horace Gwynne, Canada
1936	Ulderico Sergo, Italy
1948	Tibor Csik, Hungary
1952	Pentti Hamalainen, Finland
1956	Wolfgang Behrendt, East Germany
1960	Oleg Grigoryev, USSR
1964	Takao Sakurai, Japan
1968	Valery Sokolov, USSR
1972	Orlando Martinez, Cuba
1976	Yong Jo Gu, North Korea
1980	Juan Hernandez, Cuba
1984	Maurizio Stecca, Italy
1988	Kennedy McKinney, United States
1992	Joel Casamayor, Cuba
1996	István Kovács, Hungary

FEATHERWEIGHT (125 LB)

1904	Oliver Kirk, United States
1906	Not held
1908	Richard Gunn, Great Britain
1912	Not held
1920	Paul Fritsch, France
1924	John Fields, United States
1928	Lambertus van Klaveren, Netherlands
1932	Carmelo Robledo, Argentina
1936	Oscar Casanovas, Argentina
1948	Ernesto Formenti, Italy
1952	Jan Zachara, Czechoslovakia
1956	Vladimir Safronov, USSR
1960	Francesco Musso, Italy
1964	Stanislav Stephashkin, USSR
1968	Antonio Roldan, Mexico
1972	Boris Kousnetsov, USSR
1976	Angel Herrera, Cuba
1980	Rudi Fink, East Germany
1984	Meldrick Taylor, United States
1988	Giovanni Parisi, Italy
1992	Andreas Tews, Germany
1996	Somluck Kamsing, Thailand

LIGHTWEIGHT (132 LB)

1904	Harry Spanger, United States
1906	Not held
1908	Frederick Grace, Great Britain
1912	Not held
1920	Samuel Mosberg, United States
1924	Hans Nielsen, Denmark
1928	Carlo Orlandi, Italy
1932	Lawrence Stevens, South Africa
1936	Imre Harangi, Hungary
1948	Gerald Dreyer, South Africa
1952	Aureliano Bolognesi, Italy
1956	Richard McTaggart, Great Britain
1960	Kazimierz Pazdzior, Poland
1964	Jozef Grudzien, Poland
1968	Ronald Harris, United States
1972	Jan Szczepanski, Poland
1976	Howard Davis, United States
1980	Angel Herrera, Cuba
1984	Pernell Whitaker, United States
1988	Andreas Zuelow, East Germany
1992	Oscar De La Hoya, United States
1996	Hocine Soltani, Algeria

LIGHT WELTERWEIGHT (139 LB)

1952	Charles Adkins, United States
1956	Vladimir Yengibaryan, USSR
1960	Bohumil Nemecek, Czechoslovakia
1964	Jerzy Kulej, Poland
1968	Jerzy Kulej, Poland
1972	Ray Seales, United States
1976	Ray Leonard, United States

BOXING (Cont.)

LIGHT WELTERWEIGHT (Cont.)

1980	Patrizio Oliva, Italy
1984	Jerry Page, United States
1988	Viatcheslav Janovski, USSR
1992	Hector Vinent, Cuba
1996	Hector Vinent, Cuba

WELTERWEIGHT (147 LB)

1904	Albert Young, United States
1906-1912	Not held
1920	Albert Schneider, Canada
1924	Jean Delarge, Belgium
1928	Edward Morgan, New Zealand
1932	Edward Flynn, United States
1936	Sten Suvio, Finland
1948	Julius Torma, Czechoslovakia
1952	Zygmunt Chychla, Poland
1956	Nicolae Linca, Romania
1960	Giovanni Benvenuti, Italy
1964	Marian Kasprzyk, Poland
1968	Manfred Wolke, East Germany
1972	Emilio Correa, Cuba
1976	Jochen Bachfeld, East Germany
1980	Andres Aldama, Cuba
1984	Mark Breland, United States
1988	Robert Wangila, Kenya
1992	Michael Carruth, Ireland
1996	Oleg Saitov, Russia

LIGHT MIDDLEWEIGHT (156 LB)

1952	Laszlo Papp, Hungary
1956	Laszlo Papp, Hungary
1960	Wilbert McClure, United States
1964	Boris Lagutin, USSR
1968	Boris Lagutin, USSR
1972	Dieter Kottysch, West Germany
1976	Jerzy Rybicki, Poland
1980	Armando Martinez, Cuba
1984	Frank Tate, United States
1988	Park Si-Hun, South Korea
1992	Juan Lemus, Cuba
1996	David Reid, United States

MIDDLEWEIGHT (165 LB)

1904	Charles Mayer, United States
1908	John Douglas, Great Britain
1912	Not held
1920	Harry Mallin, Great Britain
1924	Harry Mallin, Great Britain
1928	Piero Toscani, Italy
1932	Carmen Barth, United States
1936	Jean Despeaux, France
1948	Laszlo Papp, Hungary
1952	Floyd Patterson, United States
1956	Gennady Schatkov, USSR
1960	Edward Crook, United States
1964	Valery Popenchenko, USSR
1968	Christopher Finnegan, Great Britain
1972	Vyacheslav Lemechev, USSR
1976	Michael Spinks, United States

MIDDLEWEIGHT (Cont.)

1980	Jose Gomez, Cuba
1984	Shin Joon Sup, South Korea
1988	Henry Maske, East Germany
1992	Ariel Hernandez, Cuba
1996	Ariel Hernandez, Cuba

LIGHT HEAVYWEIGHT (178 LB)

1920	Edward Eagan, United States
1924	Harry Mitchell, Great Britain
1928	Victor Avendano, Argentina
1932	David Carstens, South Africa
1936	Roger Michelot, France
1948	George Hunter, South Africa
1952	Norvel Lee, United States
1956	James Boyd, United States
1960	Cassius Clay, United States
1964	Cosimo Pinto, Italy
1968	Dan Poznyak, USSR
1972	Mate Parlov, Yugoslavia
1976	Leon Spinks, United States
1980	Slobodan Kacer, Yugoslavia
1984	Anton Josipovic, Yugoslavia
1988	Andrew Maynard, United States
1992	Torsten May, Germany
1996	Vassili Jirov, Kazakhstan

HEAVYWEIGHT (OVER 201 LB)

1904	Samuel Berger, United States
1906	Not held
1908	Albert Oldham, Great Britain
1912	Not held
1920	Ronald Rawson, Great Britain
1924	Otto von Porat, Norway
1928	Arturo Rodriguez Jurado, Argentina
1932	Santiago Lovell, Argentina
1936	Herbert Runge, Germany
1948	Rafael Inglesias, Argentina
1952	H. Edward Sanders, United States
1956	T. Peter Rademacher, United States
1960	Franco De Piccoli, Italy
1964	Joe Frazier, United States
1968	George Foreman, United States
1972	Teofilo Stevenson, Cuba
1976	Teofilo Stevenson, Cuba
1980	Teofilo Stevenson, Cuba

HEAVYWEIGHT (201* LB)

1984	Henry Tillman, United States
1988	Ray Mercer, United States
1992	Félix Sávon, Cuba
1996	Félix Sávon, Cuba

SUPER HEAVYWEIGHT (UNLIMITED)

1984	Tyrell Biggs, United States
1988	Lennox Lewis, Canada
1992	Roberto Balado, Cuba
1996	Vladimir Klitchko, Ukraine

*Until 1984 the heavyweight division was unlimited. With the addition of the super heavyweight division, a limit of 201 pounds was imposed.

SWIMMING
Men

50-METER FREESTYLE

1904	Zoltan Halmay, Hungary (50 yds)	28.0
1988	Matt Biondi, United States	22.14 WR
1992	Aleksandr Popov, Unified Team	22.30
1996	Aleksandr Popov, Russia	22.13

100-METER FREESTLYE

1896	Alfred Hajos, Hungary	1:22.2 OR
1904	Zoltan Halmay, Hungary (100 yds)	1:02.8
1906	Charles Daniels, United States	1:13.4
1908	Charles Daniels, United States	1:05.6 WR
1912	Duke Kahanamoku, United States	1:03.4
1920	Duke Kahanamoku, United States	1:00.4 WR
1924	John Weissmuller, United States	59.0 OR
1928	John Weissmuller, United States	58.6 OR
1932	Yasuji Miyazaki, Japan	58.2
1936	Ferenc Csik, Hungary	57.6
1948	Wally Ris, United States	57.3 OR
1952	Clarke Scholes, United States	57.4
1956	Jon Henricks, Australia	55.4 OR
1960	John Devitt, Australia	55.2 OR
1964	Don Schollander, United States	53.4 OR
1968	Mike Wenden, Australia	52.2 WR
1972	Mark Spitz, United States	51.22 WR
1976	Jim Montgomery, United States	49.99 WR
1980	Jörg Woithe, East Germany	50.40
1984	Rowdy Gaines, United States	49.80 OR
1988	Matt Biondi, United States	48.63 OR
1992	Aleksandr Popov, Unified Team	49.02
1996	Aleksandr Popov, Russia	48.74

200-METER FREESTYLE

1900	Frederick Lane, Australia	2:25.2 OR
1904	Charles Daniels, United States	2:44.2
1906	Not held 1906-1964	
1968	Michael Wenden, Australia	1:55.2 OR
1972	Mark Spitz, United States	1:52.78 WR
1976	Bruce Furniss, United States	1:50.29 WR
1980	Sergei Kopliakov, USSR	1:49.81 OR
1984	Michael Gross, West Germany	1:47.44 WR
1988	Duncan Armstrong, Australia	1:47.25 WR
1992	Evgueni Sadovyi, Unified Team	1:46.70 OR
1996	Danyon Loader, New Zealand	1:47.63

400-METER FREESTYLE

1896	Paul Neumann, Austria (500 yds)	8:12.6
1904	Charles Daniels, U.S. (440 yds)	6:16.2
1906	Otto Scheff, Austria (440 yds)	6:23.8
1908	Henry Taylor, Great Britain	5:36.8
1912	George Hodgson, Canada	5:24.4
1920	Norman Ross, United States	5:26.8
1924	John Weissmuller, United States	5:04.2 OR
1928	Albert Zorilla, Argentina	5:01.6 OR
1932	Buster Crabbe, United States	4:48.4 OR
1936	Jack Medica, United States	4:44.5 OR
1948	William Smith, United States	4:41.0 OR
1952	Jean Boiteux, France	4:30.7 OR
1956	Murray Rose, Australia	4:27.3 OR
1960	Murray Rose, Australia	4:18.3 OR
1964	Don Schollander, United States	4:12.2 WR
1968	Mike Burton, United States	4:09.0 OR
1972	Brad Cooper, Australia	4:00.27 OR

400-METER FREESTYLE (Cont.)

1976	Brian Goodell, United States	3:51.93 WR
1980	Vladimir Salnikov, USSR	3:51.31 OR
1984	George DiCarlo, United States	3:51.23 OR
1988	Uwe Dassler, East Germany	3:46.95 WR
1992	Evgueni Sadovyi, Unified Team	3:45.00 WR
1996	Danyon Loader, New Zealand	3:47.97

1500-METER FREESTYLE

1908	Henry Taylor, Great Britain	22:48.4 WR
1912	George Hodgson, Canada	22:00.0 WR
1920	Norman Ross, United States	22:23.2
1924	Andrew Charlton, Australia	20:06.6 WR
1928	Arne Borg, Sweden	19:51.8 OR
1932	Kusuo Kitamura, Japan	19:12.4 OR
1936	Noboru Terada, Japan	19:13.7
1948	James McLane, United States	19:18.5
1952	Ford Konno, United States	18:30.3 OR
1956	Murray Rose, Australia	17:58.9
1960	John Konrads, Australia	17:19.6 OR
1964	Robert Windle, Australia	17:01.7 OR
1968	Mike Burton, United States	16:38.9 OR
1972	Mike Burton, United States	15:52.58 OR
1976	Brian Goodell, United States	15:02.40 WR
1980	Vladimir Salnikov, USSR	14:58.27 WR
1984	Michael O'Brien, United States	15:05.20
1988	Vladimir Salnikov, USSR	15:00.40
1992	Kieren Perkins, Australia	14:43.48 WR
1996	Kieren Perkins, Australia	14:56.40

100-METER BACKSTROKE

1904	Walter Brack, Germany (100 yds)	1:16.8
1908	Arno Bieberstein, Germany	1:24.6 WR
1912	Harry Hebner, United States	1:21.2
1920	Warren Kealoha, United States	1:15.2
1924	Warren Kealoha, United States	1:13.2 OR
1928	George Kojac, United States	1:08.2 WR
1932	Masaji Kiyokawa, Japan	1:08.6
1936	Adolph Kiefer, United States	1:05.9 OR
1948	Allen Stack, United States	1:06.4
1952	Yoshi Oyakawa, United States	1:05.4 OR
1956	David Thiele, Australia	1:02.2 OR
1960	David Thiele, Australia	1:01.9 OR
1964	Not held	
1968	Roland Matthes, East Germany	58.7 OR
1972	Roland Matthes, East Germany	56.58 OR
1976	John Naber, United States	55.49 WR
1980	Bengt Baron, Sweden	56.33
1984	Rick Carey, United States	55.79
1988	Daichi Suzuki, Japan	55.05
1992	Mark Tewksbury, Canada	53.98 WR
1996	Jeff Rouse, United States	54.10

200-METER BACKSTROKE

1900	Ernst Hoppenberg, Germany	2:47.0
1904	Not held 1904-1960	
1964	Jed Graef, United States	2:10.3 WR
1968	Roland Matthes, East Germany	2:09.6 OR
1972	Roland Matthes, East Germany	2:02.82 EWR
1976	John Naber, United States	1:59.19 WR
1980	Sandor Wladar, Hungary	2:01.93
1984	Rick Carey, United States	2:00.23

Note: OR=Olympic Record. WR=World Record. EOR=Equals Olympic Record. EWR=Equals World Record. WB=World Best.

SWIMMING *(Cont.)*

Men *(Cont.)*

200-METER BACKSTROKE *(Cont.)*

1988	Igor Polianski, USSR	1:59.37
1992	Martin Lopez-Zubero, Spain	1:58.47 OR
1996	Brad Bridgewater, United States	1:58.54

100-METER BREASTSTROKE

1968	Don McKenzie, United States	1:07.7 OR
1972	Nobutaka Taguchi, Japan	1:04.94 WR
1976	John Hencken, United States	1:03.11 WR
1980	Duncan Goodhew, Great Britain	1:03.44
1984	Steve Lundquist, United States	1:01.65 WR
1988	Adrian Moorhouse, Great Britain	1:02.04
1992	Nelson Diebel, United States	1:01.50 OR
1996	Fred DeBurghgraeve, Belgium	1:00.65

200-METER BREASTSTROKE

1908	Frederick Holman, Great Britain	3:09.2 WR
1912	Walter Bathe, Germany	3:01.8 OR
1920	Haken Malmroth, Sweden	3:04.4
1924	Robert Skelton, United States	2:56.6
1928	Yoshiyuki Tsuruta, Japan	2:48.8 OR
1932	Yoshiyuki Tsuruta, Japan	2:45.4
1936	Tetsuo Hamuro, Japan	2:41.5 OR
1948	Joseph Verdeur, United States	2:39.3 OR
1952	John Davies, Australia	2:34.4 OR
1956	Masura Furukawa, Japan	2:34.7 OR
1960	William Mulliken, United States	2:37.4
1964	Ian O'Brien, Australia	2:27.8 WR
1968	Felipe Munoz, Mexico	2:28.7
1972	John Hencken, United States	2:21.55 WR
1976	David Wilkie, Great Britain	2:15.11 WR
1980	Robertas Zhulpa, USSR	2:15.85
1984	Victor Davis, Canada	2:13.34 WR
1988	Jozsef Szabo, Hungary	2:13.52
1992	Mike Barrowman, United States	2:10.16 WR
1996	Norbert Rózsa, Hungary	2:12.57

100-METER BUTTERFLY

1968	Doug Russell, United States	55.9 OR
1972	Mark Spitz, United States	54.27 WR
1976	Matt Vogel, United States	54.35
1980	Pär Arvidsson, Sweden	54.92
1984	Michael Gross, West Germany	53.08 WR
1988	Anthony Nesty, Suriname	53.00 OR
1992	Pablo Morales, United States	53.32
1996	Denis Pankratov, Russia	52.27 WR

200-METER BUTTERFLY

1956	William Yorzyk, United States	2:19.3 OR
1960	Michael Troy, United States	2:12.8 WR
1964	Kevin Berry, Australia	2:06.6 WR
1968	Carl Robie, United States	2:08.7
1972	Mark Spitz, United States	2:00.70 WR
1976	Mike Bruner, United States	1:59.23 WR
1980	Sergei Fesenko, USSR	1:59.76
1984	Jon Sieben, Australia	1:57.04 WR
1988	Michael Gross, West Germany	1:56.94 OR
1992	Melvin Stewart, United States	1:56.26 OR
1996	Denis Pankratov, Russia	1:56.51

200-METER INDIVIDUAL MEDLEY

1968	Charles Hickcox, United States	2:12.0 OR
1972	Gunnar Larsson, Sweden	2:07.17 WR
1984	Alex Baumann, Canada	2:01.42 WR
1988	Tamas Darnyi, Hungary	2:00.17 WR
1992	Tamas Darnyi, Hungary	2:00.76
1996	Attila Czene, Hungary	1:59.91 OR

400-METER INDIVIDUAL MEDLEY

1964	Richard Roth, United States	4:45.4 WR
1968	Charles Hickcox, United States	4:48.4
1972	Gunnar Larsson, Sweden	4:31.98 OR
1976	Rod Strachan, United States	4:23.68 WR
1980	Aleksandr Sidorenko, USSR	4:22.89 OR
1984	Alex Baumann, Canada	4:17.41 WR
1988	Tamas Darnyi, Hungary	4:14.75 WR
1992	Tamas Darnyi, Hungary	4:14.23 OR
1996	Tom Dolan United States	4:14.90

4 X 100-METER MEDLEY RELAY

1960	United States	4:05.4 WR
1964	United States	3:58.4 WR
1968	United States	3:54.9 WR
1972	United States	3:48.16 WR
1976	United States	3:42.22 WR
1980	Australia	3:45.70
1984	United States	3:39.30 WR
1988	United States	3:36.93 WR
1992	United States	3:36.93 EWR
1996	United States	3:34.84 WR

4 X 100-METER FREESTYLE RELAY

1964	United States	3:32.2 WR
1968	United States	3:31.7 WR
1972	United States	3:26.42 WR
1976-1980	Not held	
1984	United States	3:19.03 WR
1988	United States	3:16.53 WR
1992	United States	3:16.74
1996	United States	3:15.41 WR

4 X 200-METER FREESTYLE RELAY

1906	Hungary (1000 m)	16:52.4
1908	Great Britain	10:55.6
1912	Australia/New Zealand	10:11.6 WR
1920	United States	10:04.4 WR
1924	United States	9:53.4 WR
1928	United States	9:36.2 WR
1932	Japan	8:58.4 WR
1936	Japan	8:51.5 WR
1948	United States	8:46.0 WR
1952	United States	8:31.1 OR
1956	Australia	8:23.6 WR
1960	United States	8:10.2 WR
1964	United States	7:52.1 WR
1968	United States	7:52.33
1972	United States	7:35.78 WR
1976	United States	7:23.22 WR
1980	USSR	7:23.50
1984	United States	7:15.69 WR
1988	United States	7:12.51 WR
1992	Unified Team	7:11.95 WR
1996	United States	7:14.84

Note: OR=Olympic Record. WR=World Record. EOR=Equals Olympic Record. EWR=Equals World Record. WB=World Best.

SWIMMING (Cont.)
Women

50-METER FREESTYLE
1988	Kristin Otto, East Germany	25.49 OR
1992	Yang Wenyi, China	24.79 WR
1996	Amy Van Dyken, United States	24.87

100-METER FREESTYLE
1912	Fanny Durack, Australia	1:22.2
1920	Ethelda Bleibtrey, United States	1:13.6 WR
1924	Ethel Lackie, United States	1:12.4
1928	Albina Osipowich, United States	1:11.0 OR
1932	Helene Madison, United States	1:06.8 OR
1936	Hendrika Mastenbroek, Netherlands	1:05.9 WR
1948	Greta Andersen, Denmark	1:06.3
1952	Katalin Szöke, Hungary	1:06.8
1956	Dawn Fraser, Australia	1:02.0 WR
1960	Dawn Fraser, Australia	1:01.2 OR
1964	Dawn Fraser, Australia	59.5 OR
1968	Jan Henne, United States	1:00.0
1972	Sandra Neilson, United States	58.59 OR
1976	Kornelia Ender, East Germany	55.65 WR
1980	Barbara Krause, East Germany	54.79 WR
1984	Carrie Steinseifer, United States	55.92
	Nancy Hogshead, United States	55.92
1988	Kristin Otto, East Germany	54.93
1992	Zhuang Yong, China	54.64 OR
1996	Le Jingyi, China	54.50 OR

200-METER FREESTYLE
1968	Debbie Meyer, United States	2:10.5 OR
1972	Shane Gould, Australia	2:03.56 WR
1976	Kornelia Ender, East Germany	1:59.26 WR
1980	Barbara Krause, East Germany	1:58.33 OR
1984	Mary Wayte, United States	1:59.23
1988	Heike Friedrich, East Germany	1:57.65 OR
1992	Nicole Haislett, United States	1:57.90
1996	Claudia Poll, Costa Rica	1:58.16

400-METER FREESTYLE
1924	Martha Norelius, United States	6:02.2 OR
1928	Martha Norelius, United States	5:42.8 WR
1932	Helene Madison, United States	5:28.5 WR
1936	Hendrika Mastenbroek, Netherlands	5:26.4 OR
1948	Ann Curtis, United States	5:17.8 OR
1952	Valeria Gyenge, Hungary	5:12.1 OR
1956	Lorraine Crapp, Australia	4:54.6 OR
1960	Chris von Saltza, United States	4:50.6 OR
1964	Virginia Duenkel, United States	4:43.3 OR
1968	Debbie Meyer, United States	4:31.8 OR
1972	Shane Gould, Australia	4:19.44 WR
1976	Petra Thümer, East Germany	4:09.89 WR
1980	Ines Diers, East Germany	4:08.76 WR
1984	Tiffany Cohen, United States	4:07.10 OR
1988	Janet Evans, United States	4:03.85 WR
1992	Dagmar Hase, Germany	4:07.18
1996	Michelle Smith, Ireland	4:07.25

800-METER FREESTYLE
1968	Debbie Meyer, United States	9:24.0 OR
1972	Keena Rothhammer, United States	8:53.68 WR
1976	Petra Thümer, East Germany	8:37.14 WR
1980	Michelle Ford, Australia	8:28.90 OR
1984	Tiffany Cohen, United States	8:24.95 OR
1988	Janet Evans, United States	8:20.20 OR
1992	Janet Evans, United States	8:25.52
1996	Brooke Bennett, United States	8:27.89

100-METER BACKSTROKE
1924	Sybil Bauer, United States	1:23.2 OR
1928	Marie Braun, Netherlands	1:22.0
1932	Eleanor Holm, United States	1:19.4
1936	Dina Senff, Netherlands	1:18.9
1948	Karen Harup, Denmark	1:14.4 OR
1952	Joan Harrison, South Africa	1:14.3
1956	Judy Grinham, Great Britain	1:12.9 OR
1960	Lynn Burke, United States	1:09.3 OR
1964	Cathy Ferguson, United States	1:07.7 WR
1968	Kaye Hall, United States	1:06.2 WR
1972	Melissa Belote, United States	1:05.78 OR
1976	Ulrike Richter, East Germany	1:01.83 OR
1980	Rica Reinisch, East Germany	1:00.86 WR
1984	Theresa Andrews, United States	1:02.55
1988	Kristin Otto, East Germany	1:00.89
1992	Krisztina Egerszegi, Hungary	1:00.68 OR
1996	Beth Botsford, United States	1:01.19

200-METER BACKSTROKE
1968	Pokey Watson, United States	2:24.8 OR
1972	Melissa Belote, United States	2:19.19 WR
1976	Ulrike Richter, East Germany	2:13.43 OR
1980	Rica Reinisch, East Germany	2:11.77 WR
1984	Jolanda De Rover, Netherlands	2:12.38
1988	Krisztina Egerszegi, Hungary	2:09.29 OR
1992	Krisztina Egerszegi, Hungary	2:07.06 OR
1996	Krisztina Egerszegi, Hungary	2:07.83

100-METER BREASTSTROKE
1968	Djurdjica Bjedov, Yugoslavia	1:15.8 OR
1972	Catherine Carr, United States	1:13.58 WR
1976	Hannelore Anke, East Germany	1:11.16
1980	Ute Geweniger, East Germany	1:10.22
1984	Petra Van Staveren, Netherlands	1:09.88 OR
1988	Tania Dangalakova, Bulgaria	1:07.95 OR
1992	Elena Roudkovskaia, Unified Team	1:08.00
1996	Penelope Heyns, South Africa	1:07.73

200-METER BREASTSTROKE
1924	Lucy Morton, Great Britain	3:33.2 OR
1928	Hilde Schrader, Germany	3:12.6
1932	Clare Dennis, Australia	3:06.3 OR
1936	Hideko Maehata, Japan	3:03.6
1948	Petronella Van Vliet, Netherlands	2:57.2
1952	Eva Szekely, Hungary	2:51.7 OR
1956	Ursula Happe, West Germany	2:53.1 OR
1960	Anita Lonsbrough, Great Britain	2:49.5 WR
1964	Galina Prozumenshikova, USSR	2:46.4 OR
1968	Sharon Wichman, United States	2:44.4 OR
1972	Beverly Whitfield, Australia	2:41.71 OR

Note: OR=Olympic Record. WR=World Record. EOR=Equals Olympic Record. EWR=Equals World Record. WB=World Best.

SWIMMING (Cont.)
Women (Cont.)

200-METER BREASTSTROKE (Cont.)
1976	Marina Koshevaia, USSR	2:33.35 WR
1980	Lina Kaciusyte, USSR	2:29.54 OR
1984	Anne Ottenbrite, Canada	2:30.38
1988	Silke Hoerner, East Germany	2:26.71 WR
1992	Kyoko Iwasaki, Japan	2:26.65 OR
1996	Penelope Heyns, South Africa	2:25.41 OR

100-METER BUTTERFLY
1956	Shelley Mann, United States	1:11.0 OR
1960	Carolyn Schuler, United States	1:09.5 OR
1964	Sharon Stouder, United States	1:04.7 WR
1968	Lynn McClements, Australia	1:05.5
1972	Mayumi Aoki, Japan	1:03.34 WR
1976	Kornelia Ender, East Germany	1:00.13 EWR
1980	Caren Metschuck, East Germany	1:00.42
1984	Mary T. Meagher, United States	59.26
1988	Kristin Otto, East Germany	59.00 OR
1992	Qian Hong, China	58.62 OR
1996	Amy Van Dyken, United States	59.13

200-METER BUTTERFLY
1968	Ada Kok, Netherlands	2:24.7 OR
1972	Karen Moe, United States	2:15.57 WR
1976	Andrea Pollack, East Germany	2:11.41 OR
1980	Ines Geissler, East Germany	2:10.44 OR
1984	Mary T. Meagher, United States	2:06.90 OR
1988	Kathleen Nord, East Germany	2:09.51
1992	Summer Sanders, United States	2:08.67
1996	Susan O'Neill, Australia	2:07.76

200-METER INDIVIDUAL MEDLEY
1968	Claudia Kolb, United States	2:24.7 OR
1972	Shane Gould, Australia	2:23.07 WR
1976	Not held 1976-1980	
1984	Tracy Caulkins, United States	2:12.64 OR
1988	Daniela Hunger, East Germany	2:12.59 OR
1992	Lin Li, China	2:11.65 WR
1996	Michelle Smith, Ireland	2:13.93

400-METER INDIVIDUAL MEDLEY
1964	Donna de Varona, United States	5:18.7 OR
1968	Claudia Kolb, United States	5:08.5 OR
1972	Gail Neall, Australia	5:02.97 WR
1976	Ulrike Tauber, East Germany	4:42.77 WR
1980	Petra Schneider, East Germany	4:36.29 WR

400-METER INDIVIDUAL MEDLEY (Cont.)
1984	Tracy Caulkins, United States	4:39.24
1988	Janet Evans, United States	4:37.76
1992	Krisztina Egerszegi, Hungary	4:36.54
1996	Michelle Smith, Ireland	4:39.18

4 X 100-METER MEDLEY RELAY
1960	United States	4:41.1 WR
1964	United States	4:33.9 WR
1968	United States	4:28.3 OR
1972	United States	4:20.75 WR
1976	East Germany	4:07.95 WR
1980	East Germany	4:06.67 WR
1984	United States	4:08.34
1988	East Germany	4:03.74 OR
1992	United States	4:02.54 WR
1996	United States	4:02.88

4 X 100-METER FREESTYLE RELAY
1912	Great Britain	5:52.8 WR
1920	United States	5:11.6 WR
1924	United States	4:58.8 WR
1928	United States	4:47.6 WR
1932	United States	4:38.0 WR
1936	Netherlands	4:36.0 OR
1948	United States	4:29.2 OR
1952	Hungary	4:24.4 WR
1956	Australia	4:17.1 WR
1960	United States	4:08.9 WR
1964	United States	4:03.8 WR
1968	United States	4:02.5 OR
1972	United States	3:55.19 WR
1976	United States	3:44.82 WR
1980	East Germany	3:42.71 WR
1984	United States	3:43.43
1988	East Germany	3:40.63 OR
1992	United States	3:39.46 WR
1996	United States	3:39.29 OR

4 X 200-METER FREESTYLE RELAY
1996	United States	7:59.87

Note: OR=Olympic Record. WR=World Record. EOR=Equals Olympic Record. EWR=Equals World Record. WB=World Best.

DIVING
Men

SPRINGBOARD
		Pts
1908	Albert Zürner, Germany	85.5
1912	Paul Günther, Germany	79.23
1920	Louis Kuehn, United States	675.40
1924	Albert White, United States	97.46
1928	Pete DesJardins, United States	185.04
1932	Michael Galitzen, United States	161.38
1936	Richard Degener, United States	163.57
1948	Bruce Harlan, United States	163.64
1952	David Browning, United States	205.29
1956	Robert Clotworthy, United States	159.56

SPRINGBOARD (CONT.)
		Pts
1960	Gary Tobian, United States	170.00
1964	Kenneth Sitzberger, United States	159.90
1968	Bernie Wrightson, United States	170.15
1972	Vladimir Vasin, USSR	594.09
1976	Phil Boggs, United States	619.05
1980	Aleksandr Portnov, USSR	905.02
1984	Greg Louganis, United States	754.41
1988	Greg Louganis, United States	730.80
1992	Mark Lenzi, United States	676.53
1996	Xiong Ni, China	701.46

DIVING (Cont.)

Men (Cont.)

PLATFORM		Pts		PLATFORM (Cont.)		Pts
1904	George Sheldon, United States	12.66		1956	Joaquin Capilla, Mexico	152.44
1906	Gottlob Walz, Germany	156.0		1960	Robert Webster, United States	165.56
1908	Hjalmar Johansson, Sweden	83.75		1964	Robert Webster, United States	148.58
1912	Erik Adlerz, Sweden	73.94		1968	Klaus Dibiasi, Italy	164.18
1920	Clarence Pinkston, United States	100.67		1972	Klaus Dibiasi, Italy	504.12
1924	Albert White, United States	97.46		1976	Klaus Dibiasi, Italy	600.51
1928	Pete DesJardins, United States	98.74		1980	Falk Hoffmann, East Germany	835.65
1932	Harold Smith, United States	124.80		1984	Greg Louganis, United States	710.91
1936	Marshall Wayne, United States	113.58		1988	Greg Louganis, United States	638.61
1948	Sammy Lee, United States	130.05		1992	Sun Shuwei, China	677.31
1952	Sammy Lee, United States	156.28		1996	Dmitri Sautin, Russia	692.34

Women

SPRINGBOARD		Pts		PLATFORM		Pts
1920	Aileen Riggin, United States	539.90		1912	Greta Johansson, Sweden	39.90
1924	Elizabeth Becker, United States	474.50		1920	Stefani Fryland-Clausen, Denmark	34.60
1928	Helen Meany, United States	78.62		1924	Caroline Smith, United States	33.20
1932	Georgia Coleman, United States	87.52		1928	Elizabeth B. Pinkston, United States	31.60
1936	Marjorie Gestring, United States	89.27		1932	Dorothy Poynton, United States	40.26
1948	Victoria Draves, United States	108.74		1936	Dorothy Poynton Hill, United States	33.93
1952	Patricia McCormick, United States	147.30		1948	Victoria Draves, United States	68.87
1956	Patricia McCormick, United States	142.36		1952	Patricia McCormick, United States	79.37
1960	Ingrid Krämer, East Germany	155.81		1956	Patricia McCormick, United States	84.85
1964	Ingrid Engel Krämer, East Germany	145.00		1960	Ingrid Krämer, East Germany	91.28
				1964	Lesley Bush, United States	99.80
1968	Sue Gossick, United States	150.77		1968	Milena Duchkova, Czechoslovakia	109.59
1972	Micki King, United States	450.03		1972	Ulrika Knape, Sweden	390.00
1976	Jennifer Chandler, United States	506.19		1976	Elena Vaytsekhovskaya, USSR	406.59
1980	Irina Kalinina, USSR	725.91		1980	Martina Jäschke, East Germany	596.25
1984	Sylvie Bernier, Canada	530.70		1984	Zhou Jihong, China	435.51
1988	Gao Min, China	580.23		1988	Xu Yanmei, China	445.20
1992	Gao Min, China	572.40		1992	Fu Mingxia, China	461.43
1996	Fu Mingxia, China	547.68		1996	Fu Mingxia, China	521.58

A Golden Girl's Meltdown

Unsung 26-year-old Michelle Smith de Bruin of Ireland shocked the swimming world by racing to three gold medals at the Atlanta Olympics. When critics said Smith de Bruin might be using illicit drugs, she and her husband—discus thrower and shot-putter Erik de Bruin, who'd been banned for failing a drug test—shot back that Michelle had never tested positive for anything illegal.

In 1998, however, Smith de Bruin was hit with a four-year ban by FINA, international swimming's governing body, for spiking a urine sample (taken in a surprise test at her home in January '98) with alcohol. She appealed, but in June 1999 the Court of Arbitration for Sport (CAS) in Lausanne, Switzerland, upheld the ban, and she promptly retired from swimming.

Smith de Bruin has insisted she never used banned drugs. At the CAS hearing, for the first time, there was hard evidence to the contrary. Earlier tests had failed to identify any forbidden substance in her spiked sample, but new results disclosed at the hearing indicated that she had used androstenedione.

A 1999 study reported in the *Journal of the American Medical Association* cast doubt on the value of andro—which is legal in major league baseball but not in most other sports—as a muscle builder for men. But if Smith de Bruin was on andro when she sped through the pool in Atlanta, there's reason to think the stuff might have powerful effects on women.

GYMNASTICS
Men

ALL-AROUND

	Pts
1900 .....Gustave Sandras, France	302
1904 .....Julius Lenhart, Austria	69.80
1906 .....Pierre Paysse, France	97
1908 .....Alberto Braglia, Italy	317.0
1912 .....Alberto Braglia, Italy	135.0
1920 .....Giorgio Zampori, Italy	88.35
1924 .....Leon Stukelj, Yugoslavia	110.340
1928 .....Georges Miez, Switzerland	247.500
1932 .....Romeo Neri, Italy	140.625
1936 .....Alfred Schwarzmann, Germany	113.100
1948 .....Veikko Huhtanen, Finland	229.70
1952 .....Viktor Chukarin, USSR	115.70
1956 .....Viktor Chukarin, USSR	114.25
1960 .....Boris Shakhlin, USSR	115.95
1964 .....Yukio Endo, Japan	115.95
1968 .....Sawao Kato, Japan	115.90
1972 .....Sawao Kato, Japan	114.65
1976 .....Nikolai Andrianov, USSR	116.65
1980 .....Aleksandr Dityatin, USSR	118.65
1984 .....Koji Gushiken, Japan	118.70
1988 .....Vladimir Artemov, USSR	119.125
1992 .....Vitaly Scherbo, Unified Team	59.025
1996 .....Li Xiaoshuang, China	58.423

HORIZONTAL BAR

	Pts
1896 .....Hermann Weingärtner, Germany	—
1900 .....Not held	
1904 .....Anton Heida, United States	40
1908 .....Not held 1908–1920	
1924 .....Leon Stukelj, Yugoslavia	19.73
1928 .....Georges Miez, Switzerland	19.17
1932 .....Dallas Bixler, United States	18.33
1936 .....Aleksanteri Saarvala, Finland	19.367
1948 .....Josef Stalder, Switzerland	19.85
1952 .....Jack Günthard, Switzerland	19.55
1956 .....Takashi Ono, Japan	19.60
1960 .....Takashi Ono, Japan	19.60
1964 .....Boris Shakhlin, USSR	19.625
1968 .....Akinori Nakayama, Japan	19.55
1972 .....Mitsuo Tsukahara, Japan	19.725
1976 .....Mitsuo Tsukahara, Japan	19.675
1980 .....Stoyan Deltchev, Bulgaria	19.825
1984 .....Shinji Morisue, Japan	20.00
1988 .....Vladimir Artemov, USSR	19.90
1992 .....Trent Dimas, United States	9.875
1996 .....Andreas Wecker, Germany	9.850

PARALLEL BARS

	Pts
1896 .....Alfred Flatow, Germany	—
1900 .....Not held	
1904 .....George Eyser, United States	44
1908 .....Not held 1908–1920	
1924 .....August Güttinger, Switzerland	21.63
1928 .....Ladislav Vacha, Czechoslovakia	18.83
1932 .....Romeo Neri, Italy	18.97
1936 .....Konrad Frey, Germany	19.067
1948 .....Michael Reusch, Switzerland	19.75
1952 .....Hans Eugster, Switzerland	19.65

PARALLEL BARS *(Cont.)*

	Pts
1956 .....Viktor Chukarin, USSR	19.20
1960 .....Boris Shakhlin, USSR	19.40
1964 .....Yukio Endo, Japan	19.675
1968 .....Akinori Nakayama, Japan	19.475
1972 .....Sawao Kato, Japan	19.475
1976 ...Sawao Kato, Japan	19.675
1980 .....Aleksandr Tkachyov, USSR	19.775
1984 .....Bart Conner, United States	19.95
1988 .....Vladimir Artemov, USSR	19.925
1992 .....Vitaly Scherbo, Unified Team	9.900
1996 .....Rustan Sharipov, Ukraine	9.837

VAULT

	Pts
1896 .....Karl Schumann, Germany	—
1900 .....Not held	
1904 .....George Eyser, United States	36
1908 .....Not held 1908–1920	
1924 .....Frank Kriz, United States	9.98
1928 .....Eugen Mack, Switzerland	9.58
1932 .....Savino Guglielmetti, Italy	18.03
1936 .....Alfred Schwarzmann, Germany	19.20
1948 .....Paavo Aaltonen, Finland	19.55
1952 .....Viktor Chukarin, USSR	19.20
1956 .....Helmut Bantz, Germany	18.85
1960 .....Takashi Ono, Japan	19.35
1964 .....Haruhiro Yamashita, Japan	19.60
1968 .....Mikhail Voronin, USSR	19.00
1972 .....Klaus Köste, East Germany	18.85
1976 .....Nikolai Andrianov, USSR	19.45
1980 .....Nikolai Andrianov, USSR	19.825
1984 .....Lou Yun, China	19.95
1988 .....Lou Yun, China	19.875
1992 .....Vitaly Scherbo, Unified Team	9.856
1996 .....Alexei Nemov, Russia	9.787

POMMEL HORSE

	Pts
1896 .....Louis Zutter, Switzerland	—
1900 .....Not held	
1904 .....Anton Heida, United States	42
1908 .....Not held 1908–1920	
1924 .....Josef Wilhelm, Switzerland	21.23
1928 .....Hermann Hänggi, Switzerland	19.75
1932 .....Istvan Pelle, Hungary	19.07
1936 .....Konrad Frey, Germany	19.333
1948 .....Paavo Aaltonen, Finland	19.35
1952 .....Viktor Chukarin, USSR	19.50
1956 .....Boris Shakhlin, USSR	19.25
1960 .....Eugen Ekman, Finland	19.375
1964 .....Miroslav Cerar, Yugoslavia	19.525
1968 .....Miroslav Cerar, Yugoslavia	19.325
1972 .....Viktor Klimenko, USSR	19.125
1976 .....Zoltan Magyar, Hungary	19.70
1980 .....Zoltan Magyar, Hungary	19.925
1984 .....Li Ning, China	19.95
1988 .....Dmitri Bilozerchev, USSR	19.95
1992 .....Vitaly Scherbo, Unified Team	9.925
1996 .....Donghua Li, Switzerland	9.875

GYMNASTICS (Cont.)

Men (Cont.)

RINGS

	Pts
1896 .....Ioannis Mitropoulos, Greece	—
1900 .....Not held	
1904 .....Hermann Glass, United States	45
1908 .....Not held 1908–1920	
1924 .....Francesco Martino, Italy	21.553
1928 .....Leon Stukelj, Yugoslavia	19.25
1932 .....George Gulack, United States	18.97
1936 .....Alois Hudec, Czechoslovakia	19.433
1948 .....Karl Frei, Switzerland	19.80
1952 .....Grant Shaginyan, USSR	19.75
1956 .....Albert Azaryan, USSR	19.35
1960 .....Albert Azaryan, USSR	19.725
1964 .....Takuji Haytta, Japan	19.475
1968 .....Akinori Nakayama, Japan	19.45
1972 .....Akinori Nakayama, Japan	19.35
1976 .....Nikolai Andrianov, USSR	19.65
1980 .....Aleksandr Dityatin, USSR	19.875
1984 .....Koji Gushiken, Japan	19.85
1988 .....Holger Behrendt, East Germany	19.925
1992 .....Vitaly Scherbo, Unified Team	9.937
1996 .....Yuri Chechi, Italy	9.887

FLOOR EXERCISE

	Pts
1932 .....Istvan Pelle, Hungary	9.60
1936 .....Georges Miez, Switzerland	18.666
1948 .....Ferenc Pataki, Hungary	19.35
1952 .....K. William Thoresson, Sweden	19.25
1956 .....Valentin Muratov, USSR	19.20
1960 .....Nobuyuki Aihara, Japan	19.45
1964 .....Franco Menichelli, Italy	19.45
1968 .....Sawao Kato, Japan	19.475
1972 .....Nikolai Andrianov, USSR	19.175

FLOOR EXERCISE (Cont.)

	Pts
1976 .....Nikolai Andrianov, USSR	19.45
1980 .....Roland Brückner, East Germany	19.75
1984 .....Li Ning, China	19.925
1988 .....Sergei Kharkov, USSR	19.925
1992 .....Li Xiaoshuang, China	9.925
1996 .....Ioannis Melissanidis, Greece	9.850

TEAM COMBINED EXERCISES

		Pts
1904 ....Turngemeinde Philadelphia		374.43
1906 ....Norway		19.00
1908 ....Sweden		438
1912 ....Italy		265.75
1920 ....Italy		359.855
1924 ....Italy		839.058
1928 ....Switzerland		1718.625
1932 ....Italy		541.850
1936 ....Germany		657.430
1948 ....Finland		1358.30
1952 ....USSR		574.40
1956 ....USSR		568.25
1960 ....Japan		575.20
1964 ....Japan		577.95
1968 ....Japan		575.90
1972 ....Japan		571.25
1976 ....Japan		576.85
1980 ....USSR		598.60
1984 ....United States		591.40
1988 ....USSR		593.35
1992 ....Unified Team		585.45
1996 ....Russia		576.778

GYMNASTICS

Women

ALL-AROUND

	Pts
1952 .....Maria Gorokhovskaya, USSR	76.78
1956 .....Larissa Latynina, USSR	74.933
1960 .....Larissa Latynina, USSR	77.031
1964 .....Vera Caslavska, Czechoslovakia	77.564
1968 .....Vera Caslavska, Czechoslovakia	78.25
1972 .....Lyudmila Tousischeva, USSR	77.025
1976 .....Nadia Comaneci, Romania	79.275
1980 .....Yelena Davydova, USSR	79.15
1984 .....Mary Lou Retton, United States	79.175
1988 .....Yelena Shushunova, USSR	79.662
1992 .....Tatiana Gutsu, Unified Team	39.737
1996 .....Lilia Podkopayeva, Ukraine	39.255

VAULT

	Pts
1952 .....Yekaterina Kalinchuk, USSR	19.20
1956 .....Larissa Latynina, USSR	18.833
1960 .....Margarita Nikolayeva, USSR	19.316
1964 .....Vera Caslavska, Czechoslovakia	19.483
1968 .....Vera Caslavska, Czechoslovakia	19.775
1972 .....Karin Janz, East Germany	19.525
1976 .....Nelli Kim, USSR	19.80
1980 .....Natalya Shaposhnikova, USSR	19.725
1984 .....Ecaterina Szabo, Romania	19.875
1988 .....Svetlana Boginskaya, USSR	19.905
1992 .....Henrietta Onodi, Hungary	9.925
..............Lavinia Milosovici, Romania	9.925
1996 .....Simona Amanar, Romania	9.825

GYMNASTICS *(Cont.)*
Women *(Cont.)*

UNEVEN BARS

	Pts
1952 .....Margit Korondi, Hungary	19.40
1956 .....Agnes Keleti, Hungary	18.966
1960 .....Polina Astakhova, USSR	19.616
1964 .....Polina Astakhova, USSR	19.332
1968 .....Vera Caslavska, Czechoslovakia	19.65
1972 .....Karin Janz, East Germany	19.675
1976 .....Nadia Comaneci, Romania	20.00
1980 .....Maxi Gnauck, East Germany	19.875
1984 .....Ma Yanhong, China	19.95
1988 .....Daniela Silivas, Romania	20.00
1992 .....Lu Li, China	10.00
1996 .....Svetlana Chorkina, Russia	9.850

BALANCE BEAM

	Pts
1952 .....Nina Bocharova, USSR	19.22
1956 .....Agnes Keleti, Hungary	18.80
1960 .....Eva Bosakova, Czechoslovakia	19.283
1964 .....Vera Caslavska, Czechoslovakia	19.449
1968 .....Natalya Kuchinskaya, USSR	19.65
1972 .....Olga Korbut, USSR	19.40
1976 .....Nadia Comaneci, Romania	19.95
1980 .....Nadia Comaneci, Romania	19.80
1984 .....Simona Pauca, Romania	19.80
1988 .....Daniela Silivas, Romania	19.924
1992 .....Tatiana Lisenko, Unified Team	9.975
1996 .....Shannon Miller, United States	9.862

FLOOR EXERCISE

	Pts
1952 .....Agnes Keleti, Hungary	19.36
1956 .....Agnes Keleti, Hungary	18.733
1960 .....Larissa Latynina, USSR	19.583
1964 .....Larissa Latynina, USSR	19.599
1968 .....Vera Caslavska, Czechoslovakia	19.675
1972 .....Olga Korbut, USSR	19.575

FLOOR EXERCISE *(Cont.)*

	Pts
1976 .....Nelli Kim, USSR	19.85
1980 .....Nadia Comaneci, Romania	19.875
1984 .....Ecaterina Szabo, Romania	19.975
1988 .....Daniela Silivas, Romania	19.937
1992 .....Lavinia Milosovici, Romania	10.00
1996 .....Lilia Podkopayeva, Ukraine	9.887

TEAM COMBINED EXERCISES

	Pts
1928 ....The Netherlands	316.75
1932 ....Not held	
1936 ....Germany	506.50
1948 ....Czechoslovakia	445.45
1952 ....USSR	527.03
1956 ....USSR	444.800
1960 ....USSR	382.320
1964 ....USSR	280.890
1968 ....USSR	382.85
1972 ....USSR	380.50
1976 ....USSR	466.00
1980 ....USSR	394.90
1984 ....Romania	392.02
1988 ....USSR	395.475
1992 ....Unified Team	395.666
1996 ....United States	389.225

RHYTHMIC ALL-AROUND

	Pts
1984 .....Lori Fung, Canada	57.95
1988 .....Marina Lobach, USSR	60.00
1992 .....Aleksandra Timoshenko, UTeam	59.037
1996 .....Ekaterina Serebrianskaya, Ukr	39.683

RHYTHMIC TEAM COMBINED EXERCISES

	Pts
1996 .....Spain	38.933

SOCCER
Men

1900 .....Great Britain	1928 .....Uruguay	1964 .....Hungary	1988 .....Soviet Union
1904 .....Canada	1936 .....Italy	1968 .....Hungary	1992 .....Spain
1908 .....Great Britain	1948 .....Sweden	1972 .....Poland	1996 .....Nigeria
1912 .....Great Britain	1952 .....Hungary	1976 .....East Germany	
1920 .....Belgium	1956 .....Soviet Union	1980 .....Czechoslovakia	
1924 .....Uruguay	1960 .....Yugoslavia	1984 .....France	

Women

1996 ....United States

BIATHLON

Men

10 KILOMETERS

1980	Frank Ullrich, East Germany	32:10.69
1984	Eirik Kvalfoss, Norway	30:53.8
1988	Frank-Peter Rötsch, W Germany	25:08.1
1992	Mark Kirchner, Germany	26:02.3
1994	Sergei Tchepikov, Russia	28:07.0
1998	Ole Einar Bjorndalen, Norway	27:16.2

20 KILOMETERS

1960	Klas Lestander, Sweden	1:33:21.6
1964	Vladimir Melyanin, Soviet Union	1:20:26.8
1968	Magnar Solberg, Norway	1:13:45.9
1972	Magnar Solberg, Norway	1:15:55.5
1976	Nikolay Kruglov, Soviet Union	1:14:12.26
1980	Anatoliy Alyabiev, Soviet Union	1:08:16.31
1984	Peter Angerer, W Germany	1:11:52.7

20 KILOMETERS (Cont.)

1988	Frank-Peter Rötsch, W Germany	56:33.3
1992	Evgueni Redkine, Unified Team	57:34.4
1994	Sergei Tarasov, Russia	57:25.3
1998	Halvard Hanevold, Norway	56:16.4

4 X 7.5-KILOMETER RELAY

1968	Soviet Union	2:13:02.4
1972	Soviet Union	1:51:44.92
1976	Soviet Union	1:57:55.64
1980	Soviet Union	1:34:03.27
1984	Soviet Union	1:38:51.7
1988	Soviet Union	1:22:30.0
1992	Germany	1:24:43.5
1994	Germany	1:30:22.1
1998	Germany	1:19:43.3

Women

7.5 KILOMETERS

1992	Antissa Restzova, Unified Team	24:29.2
1994	Myriam Bedard, Canada	26:08.8
1998	Galina Koukleva, Russia	23:08.0

15 KILOMETERS

1992	Antje Misersky, Germany	51:47.2
1994	Myriam Bedard, Canada	52:06.6
1998	Ekaterina Dofovska, Bulgaria	54:52.0

3 X 7.5-KILOMETER RELAY

1992	France	1:15:55.6
1994	Russia	1:47:19.5
1998	Germany	1:40:13.6

BOBSLED

4-MAN BOB

1924	Switzerland (Eduard Scherrer)	5:45.54
1928	United States (William Fiske) (5-man)	3:20.50
1932	United States (William Fiske)	7:53.68
1936	Switzerland (Pierre Musy)	5:19.85
1948	United States (Francis Tyler)	5:20.10
1952	Germany (Andreas Ostler)	5:07.84
1956	Switzerland (Franz Kapus)	5:10.44
1960	Not held	
1964	Canada (Victor Emery)	4:14.46
1968	Italy (Eugenio Monti) (2 runs)	2:17.39
1972	Switzerland (Jean Wicki)	4:43.07
1976	East Germany (Meinhard Nehmer)	3:40.43
1980	East Germany (Meinhard Nehmer)	3:59.92
1984	East Germany (Wolfgang Hoppe)	3:20.22
1988	Switzerland (Ekkehard Fasser)	3:47.51
1992	Austria (Ingo Appelt)	3:53.90
1994	Germany (Harold Czudaj)	3:27.78
1998	Germany (Christoph Langen)	2:39.41

Note: Driver in parentheses.

2-MAN BOB

1932	United States (Hubert Stevens)	8:14.74
1936	United States (Ivan Brown)	5:29.29
1948	Switzerland (Felix Endrich)	5:29.20
1952	Germany (Andreas Ostler)	5:24.54
1956	Italy (Lamberto Dalla Costa)	5:30.14
1960	Not held	
1964	Great Britain (Anthony Nash)	4:21.90
1968	Italy (Eugenio Monti)	4:41.54
1972	West Germany (Wolfgang Zimmerer)	4:57.07
1976	East Germany (Meinhard Nehmer)	3:44.42
1980	Switzerland (Erich Schärer)	4:09.36
1984	East Germany (Wolfgang Hoppe)	3:25.56
1988	USSR (Janis Kipours)	3:53.48
1992	Switzerland (Gustav Weder)	4:03.26
1994	Switzerland (Gustav Weder)	3:30.81
1998	Canada (Pierre Lueders)	3:37.24
	Italy (Guenther Huber)	3:37.24

Note: Driver in parentheses.

CURLING

Men

1998 .....Switzerland, Canada, Norway
Note: Gold, silver, and bronze medals.

Women

1998 .....Canada, Denmark, Sweden
Note: Gold, silver, and bronze medals.

ICE HOCKEY

Men

1920* ....Canada, United States, Czechoslovakia
1924 .....Canada, United States, Great Britain
1928 .....Canada, Sweden, Switzerland
1932 .....Canada, United States, Germany
1936 .....Great Britain, Canada, United States
1948 .....Canada, Czechoslovakia, Switzerland
1952 .....Canada, United States, Sweden
1956 .....USSR, United States, Canada
1960 .....United States, Canada, USSR
1964 .....USSR, Sweden, Czechoslovakia
1968 .....USSR, Czechoslovakia, Canada

1972 .....USSR, United States, Czechoslovakia
1976 .....USSR, Czechoslovakia, West Germany
1980 .....United States, USSR, Sweden
1984 .....USSR, Czechoslovakia, Sweden
1988 .....USSR, Finland, Sweden
1992 .....Unified Team, Canada, Czechoslovakia
1994 .....Sweden, Canada, Finland
1998 .....Czech Republic, Russia, Finland
*Competition held at summer games in Antwerp.
Note: Gold, silver, and bronze medals.

Women

1998 .....United States, Canada, Finland

Note: Gold, silver, and bronze medals.

LUGE

Men

SINGLES			DOUBLES		
1964 .....Thomas Köhler, East Germany	3:26.77		1964 ....Austria	1:41.62	
1968 .....Manfred Schmid, Austria	2:52.48		1968 ....East Germany	1:35.85	
1972 .....Wolfgang Scheidel, W Germany	3:27.58		1972 ....East Germany	1:28.35	
1976 .....Detlef Guenther, West Germany	3:27.688		1976 ....East Germany	1:25.604	
1980 .....Bernhard Glass, West Germany	2:54.796		1980 ....East Germany	1:19.331	
1984 .....Paul Hildgartner, Italy	3:04.258		1984 ....West Germany	1:23.620	
1988 .....Jens Müller, West Germany	3:05.548		1988 ....East Germany	1:31.940	
1992 .....Georg Hackl, Germany	3:02.363		1992 ....Germany	1:32.053	
1994 .....Georg Hackl, Germany	3:21.571		1994 ....Italy	1:36.720	
1998 .....Georg Hackl, Germany	3:18.44		1998 ....Germany	1:41.105	

Women

SINGLES			SINGLES (Cont.)		
1964 .....Ortrun Enderlein, Germany	3:24.67		1984 .....Steffi Martin, East Germany	2:46.570	
1968 .....Erica Lechner, Italy	2:28.66		1988 .....Steffi Walter (Martin) E Germany	3:03.973	
1972 .....Anna-Maria Müller, East Germany	2:59.18		1992 .....Doris Neuner, Austria	3:06.696	
1976 .....Margit Schumann, East Germany	2:50.621		1994 .....Gerda Weissensteiner, Italy	3:15.517	
1980 .....Vera Zozulya, USSR	2:36.537		1998 .....Silke Kraushaar, Germany	3:23.779	

ONE MORE SIGN THAT THE APOCALYPSE IS UPON US

In the summer of 1999 the Salt Lake Organizing Committee unveiled the official manhole cover of the 2002 Olympics.

FIGURE SKATING

Men

1908* ....Ulrich Salchow, Sweden
1920† ....Gillis Grafström, Sweden
1924 ....Gillis Grafström, Sweden
1928 ....Gillis Grafström, Sweden
1932 ....Karl Schäfer, Austria
1936 ....Karl Schäfer, Austria
1948 ....Dick Button, United States
1952 ....Dick Button, United States
1956 ....Hayes Alan Jenkins, United States
1960 ....David Jenkins, United States
1964 ....Manfred Schnelldorfer, West Germany
1968 ....Wolfgang Schwarz, Austria
1972 ....Ondrej Nepela, Czechoslovakia
1976 ....John Curry, Great Britain
1980 ....Robin Cousins, Great Britain
1984 ....Scott Hamilton, United States
1988 ....Brian Boitano, United States
1992 ....Victor Petrenko, Unified Team
1994 ....Alexei Urmanov, Russia
1998 ....Ilia Kulik, Russia

*Competition held at summer games in London.
†Competition held at summer games in Antwerp.

Women

1908* ....Madge Syers, Great Britain
1920† ....Magda Julin, Sweden
1924 ....Herma Szabo-Planck, Austria
1928 ....Sonja Henie, Norway
1932 ....Sonja Henie, Norway
1936 ....Sonja Henie, Norway
1948 ....Barbara Ann Scott, Canada
1952 ....Jeanette Altwegg, Great Britain
1956 ....Tenley Albright, United States
1960 ....Carol Heiss, United States
1964 ....Sjoukje Dijkstra, Netherlands
1968 ....Peggy Fleming, United States
1972 ....Beatrix Schuba, Austria
1976 ....Dorothy Hamill, United States
1980 ....Anett Pötzsch, East Germany
1984 ....Katarina Witt, East Germany
1988 ....Katarina Witt, East Germany
1992 ....Kristi Yamaguchi, United States
1994 ....Oksana Baiul, Ukraine
1998 ....Tara Lipinski, United States

Mixed

PAIRS

1908* ..Anna Hübler & Heinrich Burger, Germany
1920† ..Ludovika & Walter Jakobsson, Finland
1924 ...Helene Engelmann & Alfred Berger, Austria
1928 ....Andree Joly & Pierre Brunet, France
1932 ....Andree Brunet (Joly) & Pierre Brunet, France
1936 ....Maxi Herber & Ernst Baier, Germany
1948 ....Micheline Lannoy & Pierre Baugniet, Belgium
1952 ....Ria Falk and Paul Falk, West Germany
1956 ....Elisabeth Schwartz & Kurt Oppelt, Austria
1960 ....Barbara Wagner & Robert Paul, Canada
1964 ....Lyudmila Beloussova & Oleg Protopopov, USSR
1968 ....Lyudmila Beloussova & Oleg Protopopov, USSR
1972 ....Irina Rodnina & Alexei Ulanov, USSR
1976 ....Irina Rodnina & Aleksandr Zaitzev, USSR
1980 ....Irina Rodnina & Aleksandr Zaitzev, USSR
1984 ....Elena Valova & Oleg Vasiliev, USSR
1988 ....Ekaterina Gordeeva & Sergei Grinkov, USSR
1992 ....Natalia Michkouteniok & Artour Dmitriev, Unified Team

PAIRS (Cont.)

1994 ....Ekaterina Gordeeva & Sergei Grinkov, Russia
1998 ....Oksana Kazakova & Artur Dmitriev, Russia

DANCE

1976 ....Lyudmila Pakhomova & Aleksandr Gorshkov, USSR
1980 ....Natalia Linichuk & Gennadi Karponosov, USSR
1984 ....Jayne Torvill & Christopher Dean, Great Britain
1988 ....Natalia Bestemianova & Andrei Bukin, USSR
1992 ....Marina Klimova & Sergei Ponomarenko, Unified Team
1994 ....Oksana Grishuk and Evgeny Platov, Russia
1998 ....Pasha Grishuk and Evgeny Platov, Russia

*Competition held at summer games in London.
†Competition held at summer games in Antwerp.

Next: Reilly on Death and Taxes

In February 1999, SPORTS ILLUSTRATED's Rick Reilly called on Olympic sponsors, including Time Inc., SI's parent company, to close their checkbooks until the IOC addressed the rampant corruption in its ranks (THE LIFE OF REILLY, Feb. 22, 1999).One reader, U.S. Representative Henry Waxman, took Reilly's column to heart. In April '99 Waxman (D., Calif.) introduced a bill with Representative Rick Lazio (R., N.Y.) that would ban payments from American corporations and individuals to the IOC unless the organization adopts reforms drafted by a commission chaired by former U.S. Senator George Mitchell. "What crystallized this idea was Rick Reilly's column in SPORTS ILLUSTRATED," said Waxman. "Unless we put pressure on the IOC, they won't enact the reforms necessary to show they are dedicated to changing their ways."

Said Reilly, "That's fine and all, but when is Congress going to do something about John Tesh?"

SPEED SKATING

Men

500 METERS

1924	Charles Jewtraw, United States	44.0
1928	Clas Thunberg, Finland	43.4 OR
	Bernt Evensen, Norway	43.4 OR
1932	John Shea, United States	43.4 EOR
1936	Ivar Ballangrud, Norway	43.4 EOR
1948	Finn Helgesen, Norway	43.1 OR
1952	Kenneth Henry, United States	43.2
1956	Yevgeny Grishin, USSR	40.2 EWR
1960	Yevgeny Grishin, USSR	40.2 EWR
1964	Terry McDermott, United States	40.1 OR
1968	Erhard Keller, West Germany	40.3
1972	Erhard Keller, West Germany	39.44 OR
1976	Yevgeny Kulikov, USSR	39.17 OR
1980	Eric Heiden, United States	38.03 OR
1984	Sergei Fokichev, USSR	38.19
1988	Uwe-Jens Mey, East Germany	36.45 WR
1992	Uwe-Jens Mey, East Germany	37.14
1994	Aleksandr Golubev, Russia	36.33
1998	Hiroyasu Shimizu, Japan (second run)	35.59 OR

1000 METERS

1976	Peter Mueller, United States	1:19.32
1980	Eric Heiden, United States	1:15.18 OR
1984	Gaetan Boucher, Canada	1:15.80
1988	Nikolai Gulyaev, USSR	1:13.03 OR
1992	Olaf Zinke, Germany	1:14.85
1994	Dan Jansen, United States	1:12.43 WR
1998	Ids Postma, Netherlands	1:10.64 OR

1500 METERS

1924	Clas Thunberg, Finland	2:20.8
1928	Clas Thunberg, Finland	2:21.1
1932	John Shea, United States	2:57.5
1936	Charles Mathisen, Norway	2:19.2 OR
1948	Sverre Farstad, Norway	2:17.6 OR
1952	Hjalmar Andersen, Norway	2:20.4
1956	Yevgeny Grishin, USSR	2:08.6 WR
	Yuri Mikhailov, USSR	2:08.6 WR
1960	Roald Aas, Norway	2:10.4
	Yevgeny Grishin, USSR	2:10.4
1964	Ants Anston, USSR	2:10.3
1968	Cornelis Verkerk, Netherlands	2:03.4 OR
1972	Ard Schenk, Netherlands	2:02.96 OR
1976	Jan Egil Storholt, Norway	1:59.38 OR
1980	Eric Heiden, United States	1:55.44 OR
1984	Gaetan Boucher, Canada	1:58.36

1500 METERS *(Cont.)*

1988	Andre Hoffmann, East Germany	1:52.06 WR
1992	Johann Olav Koss, Norway	1:54.81
1994	Johann Olav Koss, Norway	1:51.29 WR
1998	Aadne Sondral, Norway	1:47.87 WR

5000 METERS

1924	Clas Thunberg, Finland	8:39.0
1928	Ivar Ballangrud, Norway	8:50.5
1932	Irving Jaffee, United States	9:40.8
1936	Ivar Ballangrud, Norway	8:19.6 OR
1948	Reidar Liaklev, Norway	8:29.4
1952	Hjalmar Andersen, Norway	8:10.6 OR
1956	Boris Shilkov, USSR	7:48.7 OR
1960	Viktor Kosichkin, USSR	7:51.3
1964	Knut Johannesen, Norway	7:38.4 OR
1968	Fred Anton Maier, Norway	7:22.4 WR
1972	Ard Schenk, Netherlands	7:23.61
1976	Sten Stensen, Norway	7:24.48
1980	Eric Heiden, United States	7:02.29 OR
1984	Sven Tomas Gustafson, Sweden	7:12.28
1988	Tomas Gustafson, Sweden	6:44.63 WR
1992	Geir Karlstad, Norway	6:59.97
1994	Johann Olav Koss, Norway	6:34.96 WR
1998	Gianni Romme, Netherlands	6:22.20 WR

10,000 METERS

1924	Julius Skutnabb, Finland	18:04.8
1928	Not held, thawing of ice	
1932	Irving Jaffee, United States	19:13.6
1936	Ivar Ballangrud, Norway	17:24.3 OR
1948	Ake Seyffarth, Sweden	17:26.3
1952	Hjalmar Andersen, Norway	16:45.8 OR
1956	Sigvard Ericsson, Sweden	16:35.9 OR
1960	Knut Johannesen, Norway	15:46.6 WR
1964	Jonny Nilsson, Sweden	15:50.1
1968	Johnny Höglin, Sweden	15:23.6 OR
1972	Ard Schenk, Netherlands	15:01.35 OR
1976	Piet Kleine, Netherlands	14:50.59 OR
1980	Eric Heiden, United States	14:28.13 WR
1984	Igor Malkov, USSR	14:39.90
1988	Tomas Gustafson, Sweden	13:48.20 WR
1992	Bart Veldkamp, Netherlands	14:12.12
1994	Johann Olav Koss, Norway	13:30.55 WR
1998	Gianni Romme, Netherlands	13:15.33 WR

Women

500 METERS

1960	Helga Haase, East Germany	45.9
1964	Lydia Skoblikova, USSR	45.0 OR
1968	Lyudmila Titova, USSR	46.1
1972	Anne Henning, United States	43.33 OR
1976	Sheila Young, United States	42.76 OR
1980	Karin Enke, East Germany	41.78 OR
1984	Christa Rothenburger, East Germany	41.02 OR

500 METERS *(Cont.)*

1988	Bonnie Blair, United States	39.10 WR
1992	Bonnie Blair, United States	40.33
1994	Bonnie Blair, United States	39.25
1998	Catriona LeMay Doan, Canada (second run)	38.21 OR

Note: OR=Olympic Record; WR=World Record; EOR=Equals Olympic Record; EWR=Equals World Record; WB=World Best.

SPEED SKATING (Cont.)

Women (Cont.)

1000 METERS

1960	Klara Guseva, USSR	1:34.1
1964	Lydia Skoblikova, USSR	1:33.2 OR
1968	Carolina Geijssen, Netherlands	1:32.6 OR
1972	Monika Pflug, West Germany	1:31.40 OR
1976	Tatiana Averina, USSR	1:28.43 OR
1980	Natalya Petruseva, USSR	1:24.10 OR
1984	Karin Enke, East Germany	1:21.61 OR
1988	Christa Rothenburger, East Germany	1:17.65 WR
1992	Bonnie Blair, United States	1:21.90
1994	Bonnie Blair, United States	1:18.74
1998	Marianne Timmer, Netherlands	1:16.51 OR

1500 METERS

1960	Lydia Skoblikova, USSR	2:25.2 WR
1964	Lydia Skoblikova, USSR	2:22.6 OR
1968	Kaija Mustonen, Finland	2:22.4 OR
1972	Dianne Holum, United States	2:20.85 OR
1976	Galina Stepanskaya, USSR	2:16.58 OR
1980	Anne Borckink, Netherlands	2:10.95 OR
1984	Karin Enke, East Germany	2:03.42 WR
1988	Yvonne van Gennip, Netherlands	2:00.68 OR
1992	Jacqueline Boerner, Germany	2:05.87

1500 METERS (Cont.)

1994	Emese Hunyady, Austria	2:02.19
1998	Marianne Timmer, Netherlands	1:57.58 WR

3000 METERS

1960	Lydia Skoblikova, USSR	5:14.3
1964	Lydia Skoblikova, USSR	5:14.9
1968	Johanna Schut, Netherlands	4:56.2 OR
1972	Christina Baas-Kaiser, Netherlands	4:52.14 OR
1976	Tatiana Averina, USSR	4:45.19 OR
1980	Bjorg Eva Jensen, Norway	4:32.13 OR
1984	Andrea Schöne, East Germany	4:24.79 OR
1988	Yvonne van Gennip, Netherlands	4:11.94 WR
1992	Gunda Niemann, Germany	4:19.90
1994	Svetlana Bazhanova, Russia	4:17.43
1998	Gunda Niemann-Stirnemann, Germany	4:07.29 OR

5000 METERS

1988	Yvonne van Gennip, Netherlands	7:14.13 WR
1992	Gunda Niemann, Germany	7:31.57
1994	Claudia Pechstein, Germany	7:14.37
1998	Claudia Pechstein, Germany	6:59.61 WR

SHORT TRACK SPEED SKATING

Men

500 METERS

1994	Chae Ji-Hoon, South Korea	43.54
1998	Takafumi Nishitani, Japan	42.862

1000 METERS

1992	Kim Ki-Hoon, South Korea	1:30.76
1994	Kim Ki-Hoon, South Korea	1:34.57
1998	Kim Dong Sung, South Korea	1:32.375

5000-METER RELAY

1992	Korea	7:14.02
1994	Italy	7:11.74
1998	Canada	7:06.075

Women

500 METERS

1992	Cathy Turner, United States	47.04
1994	Cathy Turner, United States	45.98
1998	Annie Perreault, Canada	46.568

1000 METERS

1994	Chun Lee Kyung, South Korea	1:36.87
1998	Chun Lee Kyung, South Korea	1:42.776

3000-METER RELAY

1992	Canada	4:36.62
1994	South Korea	4:26.64
1998	South Korea	4:16.260

ALPINE SKIING

Men

DOWNHILL

1948	Henri Oreiller, France	2:55.0
1952	Zeno Colo, Italy	2:30.8
1956	Anton Sailer, Austria	2:52.2
1960	Jean Vuarnet, France	2:06.0
1964	Egon Zimmermann, Austria	2:18.16
1968	Jean-Claude Killy, France	1:59.85
1972	Bernhard Russi, Switzerland	1:51.43
1976	Franz Klammer, Austria	1:45.73
1980	Leonhard Stock, Austria	1:45.50
1984	Bill Johnson, United States	1:45.59
1988	Pirmin Zurbriggen, Switzerland	1:59.63
1992	Patrick Ortlieb, Austria	1:50.37
1994	Tommy Moe, United States	1:45.75
1998	Jean-Luc Crétier, France	1:50.11

SLALOM

1948	Edi Reinalter, Switzerland	2:10.3
1952	Othmar Schneider, Austria	2:00.0
1956	Anton Sailer, Austria	3:14.7
1960	Ernst Hinterseer, Austria	2:08.9
1964	Josef Stiegler, Austria	2:11.13
1968	Jean-Claude Killy, France	1:39.73
1972	Francisco Fernandez Ochoa, Spain	1:49.27
1976	Piero Gros, Italy	2:03.29
1980	Ingemar Stenmark, Sweden	1:44.26
1984	Phil Mahre, United States	1:39.41
1988	Alberto Tomba, Italy	1:39.47
1992	Finn Christian Jagge, Norway	1:44.39
1994	Thomas Stangassinger, Austria	2:02.02
1998	Hans-Petter Buraas, Norway	1:49.31

ALPINE SKIING
Men (Cont.)

GIANT SLALOM

1952	Stein Eriksen, Norway	2:25.0
1956	Anton Sailer, Austria	3:00.1
1960	Roger Staub, Switzerland	1:48.3
1964	Francois Bonlieu, France	1:46.71
1968	Jean-Claude Killy, France	3:29.28
1972	Gustav Thöni, Italy	3:09.62
1976	Heini Hemmi, Switzerland	3:26.97
1980	Ingemar Stenmark, Sweden	2:40.74
1984	Max Julen, Switzerland	2:41.18
1988	Alberto Tomba, Italy	2:06.37
1992	Alberto Tomba, Italy	2:06.98
1994	Markus Wasmeier, Germany	2:52.46
1998	Hermann Maier, Austria	2:38.51

SUPER GIANT SLALOM

1988	Franck Piccard, France	1:39.66
1992	Kjetil Andre Aamodt, Norway	1:13.04
1994	Markus Wasmeier, Germany	1:32.53
1998	Hermann Maier, Austria	1:34.82

COMBINED*

		Pts
1936	Franz Pfnür, Germany	99.25
1948	Henri Oreiller, France	3.27
1988	Hubert Strolz, Austria	36.55
1992	Josef Polig, Italy	14.58
1994	Lasse Kjus, Norway	3:17.53
1998	Mario Reiter, Austria	3:08.06

Women

DOWNHILL

1948	Hedy Schlunegger, Switzerland	2:28.3
1952	Trude Jochum-Beiser, Austria	1:47.1
1956	Madeleine Berthod, Switzerland	1:40.7
1960	Heidi Biebl, West Germany	1:37.6
1964	Christl Haas, Austria	1:55.39
1968	Olga Pall, Austria	1:40.87
1972	Marie-Theres Nadig, Switzerland	1:36.68
1976	Rosi Mittermaier, West Germany	1:46.16
1980	Annemarie Moser-Pröll, Austria	1:37.52
1984	Michela Figini, Switzerland	1:13.36
1988	Marina Kiehl, West Germany	1:25.86
1992	Kerrin Lee-Gartner, Canada	1:52.55
1994	Katja Seizinger, Germany	1:35.93
1998	Katja Seizinger, Germany	1:28.89

SLALOM

1948	Gretchen Fraser, United States	1:57.2
1952	Andrea Mead Lawrence, United States	2:10.6
1956	Renee Colliard, Switzerland	1:52.3
1960	Anne Heggtveigt, Canada	1:49.6
1964	Christine Goitschel, France	1:29.86
1968	Marielle Goitschel, France	1:25.86
1972	Barbara Cochran, United States	1:31.24
1976	Rosi Mittermaier, West Germany	1:30.54
1980	Hanni Wenzel, Liechtenstein	1:25.09
1984	Paoletta Magoni, Italy	1:36.47
1988	Vreni Schneider, Switzerland	1:36.69
1992	Petra Kronberger, Austria	1:32.68
1994	Vreni Schneider, Switzerland	1:56.01
1998	Hilde Gerg, Germany	1:32.40

GIANT SLALOM

1952	Andrea Mead Lawrence, U.S.	2:06.8
1956	Ossi Reichert, West Germany	1:56.5
1960	Yvonne Rüegg, Switzerland	1:39.9
1964	Marielle Goitschel, France	1:52.24
1968	Nancy Greene, Canada	1:51.97
1972	Marie-Theres Nadig, Switzerland	1:29.90
1976	Kathy Kreiner, Canada	1:29.13
1980	Hanni Wenzel, Liechtenstein (2 runs)	2:41.66
1984	Debbie Armstrong, United States	2:20.98
1988	Vreni Schneider, Switzerland	2:06.49
1992	Pernilla Wiberg, Sweden	2:12.74
1994	Deborah Compagnoni, Italy	2:30.97
1998	Deborah Compagnoni, Italy	2:50.59

SUPER GIANT SLALOM

1988	Sigrid Wolf, Austria	1:19.03
1992	Deborah Compagnoni, Italy	1:21.22
1994	Diann Roffe-Steinrotter, U.S.	1:22.15
1998	Picabo Street, United States	1:18.02

COMBINED*

		Pts
1988	Anita Wachter, Austria	29.25
1992	Petra Kronberger, Austria	2.55
1994	Pernilla Wiberg, Sweden	3:05.16
1998	Katja Seizinger, Germany	2:40.74

*Beginning in 1994, scoring was based on time.

FREESTYLE SKIING

Men
MOGULS

		Pts
1992	Edgar Grospiron, France	25.81
1994	Jean-Luc Brassard, Canada	27.24
1998	Jonny Moseley, United States	26.93

AERIALS

		Pts
1994	Andreas Schoenbaechler, Switz	234.67
1998	Eric Bergoust, United States	255.64

Women
MOGULS

		Pts
1992	Donna Weinbrecht, United States	23.69
1994	Stine Lise Hattestad, Norway	25.97
1998	Tae Satoya, Japan	25.06

AERIALS

		Pts
1994	Lina Cherjazova, Uzbekistan	166.84
1998	Nikki Stone, United States	193.00

NORDIC SKIING
Men

10 KILOMETERS CLASSICAL STYLE

1992....Vegard Ulvang, Norway   27:36.0
1994....Bjørn Dæhlie, Norway   24:20.1
1998....Bjørn Dæhlie, Norway   27:24.5

15 KILOMETERS CLASSICAL STYLE

1924....Thorlief Haug, Norway   1:14:31.0*
1928....Johan Gröttumsbraaten, Norway   1:37:01.0†
1932....Sven Utterström, Sweden   1:23:07.0‡
1936....Erik-August Larsson, Sweden   1:14:38.0*
1948....Martin Lundström, Sweden   1:13:50.0*
1952....Hallgeir Brenden, Norway   1:01:34.0*
1956....Hallgeir Brenden, Norway   49:39.0
1960....Haakon Brusveen, Norway   51:55.5
1964....Eero Mantyränta, Finland   50:54.1
1968....Harald Grönningen, Norway   47:54.2
1972....Sven-Ake Lundback, Sweden   45:28.24
1976....Nikolay Bajukov, Unified Team   43:58.47
1980....Thomas Wassberg, Sweden   41:57.63
1984....Gunde Swan, Sweden   41:25.6
1988....Michael Deviatyarov, USSR   41:18.9

*Distance was 18 km; †Distance was 19.7 km;
‡Distance was 18.2 km.

15 KILOMETERS PURSUIT FREESTYLE

1992....Bjørn Dæhlie, Norway   1:05:37.9
1994....Bjørn Dæhlie, Norway   1:00:08.8
1998....Thomas Alsgaard, Norway   1:07:01.7

30 KILOMETERS CLASSICAL STYLE

1956....Veikko Hakulinen, Finland   1:44:06.0
1960....Sixten Jernberg, Sweden   1:51:03.9
1964....Eero Mantyränta, Finland   1:30:50.7
1968....Franco Nones, Italy   1:35:39.2
1972....Viaceslav Vedenine, USSR   1:36:31.2
1976....Sergei Savelyev, USSR   1:30:29.38
1980....Nikolai Simyatov, USSR   1:27:02.80
1984....Nikolai Simyatov, USSR   1:28:56.3
1988....Alexey Prokororov, USSR   1:24:26.3
1992....Vegard Ulvang, Norway   1:22:27.8
1994....Thomas Alsgaard, Norway   1:12:26.4
1998....Mika Myllylae, Finland   1:33:55.8

50 KILOMETERS FREESTYLE

1924....Thorleif Haug, Norway   3:44:32.0
1928....Per Erik Hedlund, Sweden   4:52:03.0
1932....Veli Saarinen, Finland   4:28:00.0
1936....Elis Wiklund, Sweden   3:30:11.0
1948....Nils Karlsson, Sweden   3:47:48.0
1952....Veikko Hakulinen, Finland   3:33:33.0
1956....Sixten Jernberg, Sweden   2:50:27.0
1960....Kalevi Hämäläinen, Finland   2:59:06.3
1964....Sixten Jernberg, Sweden   2:43:52.6
1968....Olle Ellefsaeter, Norway   2:28:45.8
1972....Paal Tyldrum, Norway   2:43:14.75
1976....Ivar Formo, Norway   2:37:30.50
1980....Nikolai Simyatov, USSR   2:27:24.60
1984....Thomas Wassberg, Sweden   2:15:55.8
1988....Gunde Swan, Sweden   2:04:30.9
1992....Bjørn Dæhlie, Norway   2:03:41.5
1994....Vladimir Smirnov, Kazakhstan   2:07:20.3
1998....Bjørn Dæhlie, Norway   2:05:08.2

4 X 10 KILOMETER RELAY MIXED STYLE

1936 ....Finland   2:41:33.0
1948 ....Sweden   2:32:80.0
1952 ....Finland   2:20:16.0
1956 ....USSR   2:15:30.0
1960 ....Finland   2:18:45.6
1964 ....Sweden   2:18:34.6
1968 ....Norway   2:08:33.5
1972 ....USSR   2:04:47.94
1976 ....Finland   2:07:59.72
1980 ....USSR   1:57:03.46
1984 ....Sweden   1:55:06.3
1988 ....Sweden   1:43:58.6
1992 ....Norway   1:39:26.0
1994 ....Italy   1:41:15.0
1998 ....Norway   1:40:55.7

SKI JUMPING (NORMAL HILL)

		Pts
1964	Veikko Kankkonen, Finland	229.90
1968	Jiri Raska, Czechoslovakia	216.5
1972	Yukio Kasaya, Japan	244.2
1976	Hans-Georg Aschenbach, East Germany	252.0
1980	Toni Innauer, Austria	266.3
1984	Jens Weissflog, East Germany	215.2
1988	Matti Nykänen, Finland	229.1
1992	Ernst Vettori, Austria	222.8
1994	Espen Bredesen, Norway	282.0
1998	Jani Soininen, Finland	234.5

SKI JUMPING (LARGE HILL)

		Pts
1924	Jacob Tullin Thams, Norway	18.960
1928	Alf Andersen, Norway	19.208
1932	Birger Ruud, Norway	228.1
1936	Birger Ruud, Norway	232.0
1948	Petter Hugsted, Norway	228.1
1952	Arnfinn Bergmann, Norway	226.0
1956	Antti Hyvärinen, Finland	227.0
1960	Helmut Recknagel, East Germany	227.2
1964	Toralf Engan, Norway	230.70
1968	Vladimir Beloussov, USSR	231.3
1972	Wojciech Fortuna, Poland	219.9
1976	Karl Schnabl, Austria	234.8
1980	Jouko Tormanen, Finland	271.0
1984	Matti Nykänen, Finland	231.2
1988	Matti Nykänen, Finland	224.0
1992	Toni Nieminen, Finland	239.5
1994	Jens Weissflog, Germany	274.5
1998	Kazuyoshi Funaki, Japan	272.3

TEAM SKI JUMPING

		Pts
1988	Finland	634.4
1992	Finland	644.4
1994	Germany	970.1
1998	Japan	933.0

NORDIC SKIING (Cont.)

Men (Cont.)

NORDIC COMBINED

	Pts
1924....Thorleif Haug, Norway	18.906*
1928....Johan Gröttumsbraaten, Norway	17.833*
1932....Johan Gröttumsbraaten, Norway	446.0
1936....Oddbjörn Hagen, Norway	430.30
1948....Heikki Hasu, Finland	448.80
1952....Simon Slattvik, Norway	451.621
1956....Sverre Stenersen, Norway	455.0
1960....Georg Thoma, West Germany	457.952
1964....Tormod Knutsen, Norway	469.28
1968....Frantz Keller, West Germany	449.04
1972....Ulrich Wehling, East Germany	413.34
1976....Ulrich Wehling, East Germany	423.39

NORDIC COMBINED (Cont.)

	Pts
1980....Ulrich Wehling, East Germany	432.20
1984....Tom Sandberg, Norway	422.595
1988....Hippolyt Kempf, Switzerland	432.230
1992....Fabrice Guy, France	426.47
1994....Fred B. Lundberg, Norway	457.970
1998....Bjarte Engen Vik, Norway	41:21.1†

TEAM NORDIC COMBINED

1988....West Germany
1992....Japan
1994....Japan
1998....Norway

* Different scoring system; 1924–1952 distance was 18 km; 1952–present, 15 km.

† Times in the cross country race were not converted into points. According to the Gundersen Method, used since 1988, starting times in the race are staggered in proportion to points earned in the ski jumping segment of the event.

Women

5 KILOMETERS CLASSICAL STYLE

1964....Klaudia Boyarskikh, USSR	17:50.5
1968....Toini Gustafsson, Sweden	16:45.2
1972....Galina Kulakova, USSR	17:00.50
1976....Helena Takalo, Finland	15:48.69
1980....Raisa Smetanina, USSR	15:06.92
1984....Marja-Liisa Hamalainen, Finland	17:04.0
1988....Marjo Matikainen, Finland	15:04.0
1992....Marjut Lukkarinen, Finland	14:13.8
1994....Lyubova Egorova, Russia	14:08.8
1998....Larissa Lazhutina, Russia	17:37.9

10 KILOMETERS CLASSICAL STYLE

1952....Lydia Widemen, Finland	41:40.0
1956....Lyubov Kosyryeva, USSR	38:11.0
1960....Maria Gusakova, USSR	39:46.6
1964....Klaudia Boyarskikh, USSR	40:24.3
1968....Toini Gustafsson, Sweden	36:46.5
1972....Galina Kulakova, USSR	34:17.8
1976....Raisa Smetanina, USSR	30:13.41
1980....Barbara Petzold, East Germany	30:31.54
1984....Marja-Lissa Hamalainen, Finland	31:44.2
1988....Vida Ventsene, USSR	30:08.3

10 KILOMETERS PURSUIT FREESTYLE

1992....Lyubov Egorova, Unified Team	40:07.7
1994....Lyubov Egorova, Russia	41:38.1
1998....Larissa Lazhutina, Russia	46:06.9

15 KILOMETERS CLASSICAL STYLE

1992....Lyubov Egorova, Unified Team	42:20.8
1994....Manuela Di Centa, Italy	39:44.5
1998....Olga Danilova, Russia	46:55.04

20 KILOMETERS FREESTYLE

1984....Marja-Liisa Hamalainen, Finland	1:01:45.0
1988....Tamara Tikhonova, USSR	55:53.6

30 KILOMETERS FREESTYLE

1992....Stefania Belmondo, Italy	1:22:30.1
1994....Manuela Di Centa, Italy	1:25:41.6
1998....Julija Tchepalova, Russia	1:22:01.5

4 X 5-KILOMETER RELAY MIXED STYLE

1956....Finland	1:9:01.0
1960....Sweden	1:4:21.4
1964....USSR	59:20.0
1968....Norway	57:30.0
1972....USSR	48:46.15
1976....USSR	1:07:49.75
1980....East Germany	1:02:11.10
1984....Norway	1:06:49.7
1988....USSR	59:51.1
1992....Unified Team	59:34.8
1994....Russia	57:12.5
1998....Russia	55:13.5

SNOWBOARDING

Men

GIANT SLALOM

1998....Ross Rebagliati, Canada	2:03.96

HALF-PIPE

	Pts
1998....Gian Simmen, Switzerland	85.2

Women

GIANT SLALOM

1998....Karine Ruby, France	2:17.34

HALF-PIPE

	Pts
1998....Nicola Thost, Germany	74.6

PRE CLASSIC
9

Track & Field

PETER READ MILLER

Smashing!

Controversy took a back seat to an amazing string of shattered records in 1999

BY MERRELL NODEN

Wow! What a year it was in track and field! In one blinding flash of brilliance after another, we were reminded that just when it seems we've seen it all and that our species must be closing in on its physical limits, there's more to come, perhaps a lot more. Revered records fell in what are arguably the sport's most glamorous events, the 100, 400, mile and decathlon. So impressive were those new marks—and the entire world championships in Seville—that they succeeded in overshadowing a slew of positive drug tests involving some of the sport's most beloved athletes. For those who love track and field, the summer of 1999 truly offered the best and worst of times.

The first flash of brilliance came in Athens, on June 16, when Maurice Greene of the U.S. blew away Donovan Bailey's world record in the 100, equalling Ben Johnson's disallowed, stanozolol-fueled mark of 9.79. With his two main rivals, Ato Boldon and Bailey, sidelined much of the year with injuries, Greene was left to concentrate on running fast, which he did again and again, making the once-rare 10-second barrier look pedestrian. The 9.80 he ran at the world championships was especially awesome since he got a mediocre start and had to pull away from Bruny Surin of Canada over the final 30 meters. Greene went on to become the first man to complete a 100-200 double at the world championships and also anchored the winning U.S. 4 x 100 relay team. Believe him when he says he will go faster yet.

More jaw-dropping performances came in early July. Tomás Dvorák of the Czech Republic ruined Dan O'Brien's Fourth of July by breaking his world record in the decathlon, scoring 8,994 points in Prague. Dvorak might well have become the first man to reach 9,000 but for poor pacing in the 1500. Three days later, slender, impossibly smooth Hicham El Guerrouj of Morocco lowered Algerian Noureddine Morceli's world mile record by running 3:43.13 in Rome. "I believed I could do 3:41 or 3:42," said the 24-year-old, "but 300 meters from the end I looked up at the screen and saw [Noah] Ngeny on my shoulder and that distracted me." El Guerrouj wasn't the only one caught off guard by the precocious Kenyan, who ran 3:43.40: Ngeny is only 20 and had never previously broken 3:50.

But the news was not all good. Shortly before the world championships, it was announced that seven-time Olympic medalist Merlene Ottey of Jamaica had tested positive for the steroid nandrolone. That distressing announcement came hard on the heels of the news that Javier

Sotomayor of Cuba, probably the greatest high jumper of all time, had tested positive for cocaine at the Pan American Games. Linford Christie, supposedly semiretired, also tested positive, for nandrolone, and Dennis Mitchell's old suspension was upheld by the IAAF panel. Christie, Sotomayor and Mitchell were all vindicated by their own federations, creating an awkward—and legally perplexing—situation for the sport.

The big story at the world championships was supposed to be Marion Jones, who was conducting a dry run for Sydney in 2000, when she plans to attempt an unprecedented Olympic quintuple (100, 200, long jump, 4 x 100 relay and 4 x 400 relay). But Jones had looked shaky all year in the long jump and after winning the 100 in 10.70, she finished third in the long jump, then pulled up with back spasms in the semis of the 200, ending her season. Jones's injuries appeared not to be serious and she stated that she still plans to go for five gold medals in Sydney.

Even without Jones, there were female stars aplenty in Seville. Gail Devers, who like Jones had had a difficult buildup to the meet, set a new American record in the 100 hurdles, running 12.37. The bronze medal in the hurdles went to Lyudmila Engquist of Sweden who had had a mastectomy in April and competed in Seville between her fourth and fifth chemotherapy treatments. Stacy Dragila of the U.S. won the first world outdoor title in the women's pole vault, tying the world record by clearing 15' 1".

For the first time in the history of this meet, Sergei Bubka did not win the pole vault, which went to Maksim Tarasov of Russia. Other notable champions were Kenyan-born Dane Wilson Kipketer and Haile Gebrselassie of Ethiopia, who won their third and fourth straight world titles, in the 800 and 10,000, respectively, and El Guerrouj, who won the 1500 in 3:27.65, by far the fastest time ever run in a championship final, despite running the final 20 meters while blowing kisses to the crowd. He closed his season by setting a second world record,

GARY M. PRIOR/ALLSPORT

Devers thrilled Seville with an American record in the 100 hurdles.

over 2,000 meters, in Berlin, in 4:44.79.

And finally, there was Michael Johnson. Dogged by injuries and stung by accusations that he had ducked Greene at the national championships, the exceedingly proud Johnson chose to focus on running fast in the Seville 400. By running a seemingly untroubled 43.95 in the semis, he made it clear that Butch Reynolds's 11-year-old world record of 43.29 was in jeopardy. In the final, Johnson pulled away from the field in the third 100, and finished a full 15 meters clear, in 43.18. "He just ran away from us," marveled Antonio Pettigrew, who finished fifth. "It was the most incredible thing I've ever seen."

Indeed, the sport's dominant athlete of the last decade was pointing the way to the future. If 1999 proves to have been merely an appetizer, bring on the first Olympics of the new millenium!

1999 IAAF World Championships

Seville, August 20–29, 1999

Men

100 METERS
1. Maurice Greene, United States — 9.80†
2. Bruny Surin, Canada — 9.84
3. Dwain Chambers, Great Britain — 9.97

200 METERS
1. Maurice Green, United States — 19.90
2. Claudinei Da Sliva, Brazil — 20.00
3. Francis Obikwelu, Nigeria — 20.11

400 METERS
1. Michael Johnson, United States — 43.18WR
2. Claro Sanderlei Parrela, Brazil — 44.29
3. Alejandro Cárdenas, Mexico — 44.31

800 METERS
1. Wilson Kipketer, Denmark — 1:43.30
2. Hezekiél Sepeng, South Africa — 1:43.32
3. Djabir Saïd-Guerni, Algeria — 1:44.18

1500 METERS
1. Hicham El Guerrouj, Morocco — 3:27.65†
2. Noah Ngeny, Kenya — 3:28.73
3. Reyes Estévez, Spain — 3:30.57

3000 M STEEPLECHASE
1. Christopher Koskei, Kenya — 8:11.76
2. Wilson Boit Kipketer, Kenya — 8:12.09
3. Ali Ezzine, Morocco — 8:12.73

5000 METERS
1. Salah Hissou, Morocco — 12:58.13†
2. Benjamin Limo, Kenya — 12:58.72
3. Mohammed Mourhit, Belgium — 12:58.80

10,000 METERS
1. Haile Gebrselassie, Ethiopia — 27:57.27
2. Paul Tergat, Kenya — 27:58.56
3. Assefa Mezgebu, Ethiopia — 27:59.15

MARATHON
1. Abel Antón, Spain — 2:13.36
2. Vincenzo Modica, Italy — 2:14.03
3. Nobuyuki Sato, Japan — 2:14.07

110-METER HURDLES
1. Colin Jackson, Great Britain — 13.04
2. Anier Garcia, Cuba — 13.07
3. Duane Ross, United States — 13.12

400-METER HURDLES
1. Fabrizio Mori, Italy — 47.72
2. Stéphane Diagana, France — 48.12
3. Marcel Schelbert, Switzerland — 48.13

20-KILOMETER WALK
1. Ilya Markov, Russia — 1:23:34
2. Jefferson Pérez, Ecuador — 1:24.19
3. Daniel Garcia, Mexico — 1:24.31

50-KILOMETER WALK
1. German Skurygin, Russia — 3:44.23
2. Ivano Brugnetti, Italy — 3:47.54
3. Nikolay Matyukhin, Russia — 3:48.18

4 X 100 METER RELAY
1. United States — 37.59
2. Great Britain/Northern Ireland — 37.73
3. Nigeria — 37.91

4 X 400 METER RELAY
1. United States — 2:56.45
2. Poland — 2:58.91
3. Jamaica — 2:59.34

HIGH JUMP
1. Vyacheslav Voronin, Russia — 7 ft 9¼ in
2. Mark Boswell, Canada — 7 ft 8½ in
3. Martin Buss, Germany — 7 ft 7¼ in

POLE VAULT
1. Maksim Tarasov, Russia — 19 ft 9 in†
2. Dmitriy Markov, Australia — 19 ft 4¼ in
3. Aleksandr Averbukh, Israel — 19 ft ¼ in

LONG JUMP
1. Iván Pedroso, Cuba — 28 ft 1 in
2. Yago Lamela, Spain — 27 ft 6¾ in
3. Gregor Cankor, Slovakia — 27 ft 5¼ in

TRIPLE JUMP
1. Charles Michael Friedek, Ger — 57 ft 8½ in
2. Rostislav Dimitrov, Bulgaria — 57 ft 4¾ in
3. Jonathan Edwards, Great Britain — 57 ft 4¼ in

SHOT PUT
1. C.J. Hunter, United States — 71 ft 6 in
2. Oliver-Sven Buder, Germany — 70 ft 3½ in
3. Aleksandr Bagach, Ukraine — 69 ft 9 in

DISCUS THROW
1. Anthony Washington, U.S. — 226 ft 8 in†
2. Jürgen Schult, Germany — 223 ft 8 in
3. Lars Riedel, Germany — 223 ft 4 in

HAMMER THROW
1. Karsten Kobs, Germany — 263 ft 3 in
2. Zsolt Németh, Hungary — 259 ft 4 in
3. Vladislav Piskunov, Ukraine — 259 ft 3 in

JAVELIN THROW
1. Aki Parviainen, Finland — 293 ft 8 in
2. Kostas Gatsioudis, Greece — 292 ft 7 in
3. Jan Zelezny, Czech Republic — 287 ft 7 in

DECATHLON
1. Tomás Dvorák, Czech Rep — 8,744 pts.
2. Dean Macy, Great Britain — 8,556 pts.
3. Chris Huffins, United States — 8,547 pts.

Women

100 METERS

1. ......Marion Jones, United States .... 10.70†
2. ......Inger Miller, United States 10.79
3. ......Ekaterini Thánou, Greece 10.84

200 METERS

1. ......Inger Miller, United States 21.77
2. ......Beverly McDonald, Jamaica 22.22
3. ......Merlene Frazer, Jamaica 22.26

400 METERS

1. ......Cathy Freeman, Australia 49.67
2. ......Anja Rücker, Germany 49.74
3. ......Lorraine Graham, Jamaica 49.92

800 METERS

1. ......Ludmila Formanová, Czech Rep ... 1:56.68
2. ......Maria Mutola, Mozambique 1:56.72
3. ......Svetlana Masterkova, Russia 1:56.93

1500 METERS

1. ......Svetlana Masterkova, Russia 3:59.53
2. ......Regina Jacobs, United States 4:00.35
3. ......Kutre Dulecha, Ethiopia 4:00.96

5,000 METERS

1. ......Gabriela Szabo, Romania .... 14:41.82†
2. ......Zahra Ouaziz, Morocco 14:43.15
3. ......Ayelech Worku, Ethiopia 14:44.22

10,000 METERS

1. ......Gete Wami, Ethiopia .... 30:24.56†
2. ......Paula Radcliffe, Great Britain 30:27.13
3. ......Tegla Loroupe, Kenya 30:32.03

MARATHON

1. ......Jong Song-Ok, North Korea 2:26:59
2. ......Ari Ichihaski, Japan 2:27:02
3. ......Lidia Slavuteanu-Simon, Romania 2:27:41

100-METER HURDLES

1. ......Gail Devers, United States 12.37
2. ......Glory Alozie, Nigeria 12.44
3. ......Lyudmila Engquist, Sweden 12.47

400-METER HURDLES

1. ......Daimi Pernia, Cuba 52.89
2. ......Nezha Bidouane, Morocco 52.90
3. ......Deon Hemmings, Jamaica 53.16

20-KILOMETER WALK

1. ......Hongyu Liu, China 1:30:50
2. ......Yan Wang, China 1:30:52
3. ......Kerry Saxby-Junna, Australia 1:31:18

4 X 100 METER RELAY

1. ......Bahamas 41.92
2. ......France 42.06
3. ......Jamaica 42.15

4 X 400 METER RELAY

1. ......Russia 3:21.98
2. ......United States 3:22.09
3. ......Germany 3:22.43

HIGH JUMP

1. ......Inga Babakova, Ukraine .... 6 ft 6¼ in
2. ......Yelena Yelesina, Russia .... 6 ft 6¼ in
3. ......Svetlana Lapina, Russia .... 6 ft 6¼ in

POLE VAULT

1. ......Stacy Dragila, U.S. .... 15 ft 1 in EWR
2. ......Anzhela Balakhonova, Ukraine ... 14 ft 11 in
3. ......Tatiana Grigorieva, Australia .... 14 ft 7¼ in

LONG JUMP

1. ......Niurka Montalvo, Spain .... 23 ft 2 in
2. ......Fiona May, Italy .... 22 ft 9¼ in
3. ......Marion Jones, United States ..... 22 ft 5 in

TRIPLE JUMP

1. ......Paraskevi Tsiamita, Greece ...... 48 ft 10 in
2. ......Yamilé Aldama, Cuba .... 47 ft 11¼ in
3. ......Ólga-Anastasia Vasdéki, Greece 47 ft 11¼ in

SHOT PUT

1. ......Astrid Kumbernuss, Germany .... 65 ft 1½ in
2. ......Nadine Kleinert, Germany .... 64 ft 4 in
3. ......Svetlana Krivelyova, Russia ..... 63 ft 9 in

DISCUS THROW

1. ......Franka Dietzsch, Germany .... 223 ft 7 in
2. ......Anastasia Kelesidou, Greece .... 216 ft 8 in
3. ......Nicoleta Grasu, Romania .... 214 ft 5 in

HAMMER THROW

1. ......Mihaela Melinte, Romania .... 246 ft 9 in
2. ......Olga Kuzenkova, Russia .... 238 ft 1 in
3. ......Lisa Misipeka, American Samoa 216 ft 9 in

JAVELIN

1. ......Mirela Manjani-Tzelili, Greece ... 220 ft 1 in
2. ......Tatyana Shikolenko, Russia ...... 217 ft 9 in
3. ......Trine Solber-Hattestad, Norway .. 216 ft 9 in

HEPTATHLON

1. ......Eunice Barber, France .... 6,861 pts.
2. ......Denise Lewis, Great Britain ...... 6,724 pts.
3. ......Ghada Shouaa, Syria .... 6,500 pts.

†Meet record. WR=world record. EWR=equals world record.

Eugene, Oregon, June 24–27, 1999

Men

100 METERS

1.	Dennis Mitchell, unattached	9.97w
2.	Brian Lewis, Reebok	10.00w
3.	Tim Montgomery, ASICS	10.00w

200 METERS

1.	Maurice Greene, Nike	19.93w
2.	Rohsaan Griffin, ASICS	19.98w
3.	Kevin Little, Team US West	20.19w

400 METERS

1.	Jerome Young, adidas	44.24
2.	Antonio Pettigrew, adidas	44.59
3.	Jerome Davis, unattached	44.91

800 METERS

1.	Khadevis Robinson, S. Monica TC	1:45.92
2.	Bryan Woodward, Reebok Enc	1:46.06
3.	Rich Kenah, ASICS	1:46.13

1500 METERS

1.	Steve Holman, Nike Int'l	3:39.21
2.	Seneca Lassiter, Nike Int'l	3:39.23
3.	Matt Holthaus, Reebok Enc	3:39.57

STEEPLECHASE

1.	Pascal Dobert, Nike Int'l	8:21.48
2.	Robert Gary, adidas	8:22.19
3.	Francis O'Neill, ASICS	8:22.51

5000 METERS

1.	Adam Goucher, Team Fila	13:25.59
2.	Bob Kennedy, Nike Int'l	13:26.85
3.	Daniel Browne, Army	13:36.64

10,000 METERS

1.	Alan Culpepper, adidas	28:22.46
2.	Brad Hauser, unattached	28:24.32
3.	Abdi Abdirahman, Arizona	28:28.26

110-METER HURDLES

1.	Mark Crear, God Speed TC	13.09w
2.	Allen Johnson, Nike	13.15w
3.	Tony Dees, unattached	13.19w

400-METER HURDLES

1.	Angelo Taylor, Nike	48.49
2.	Joey Woody, Reebok	48.61
3.	Torrance Zellner, adidas	48.79

20-KILOMETER WALK

1.	Curt Clausen, NYAC	1:23:34†
2.	Tim Seaman, NYAC	1:23:42
3.	Jonathan Matthews, New Balance	1:24:50

HIGH JUMP

1.	Charles Austin, unattached	7 ft 5¾ in
2.	Henry Patterson, unattached	7 ft 4½ in
3.	Charles Clinger, Weber St	7 ft 4½ in

POLE VAULT

1.	Jeff Hartwig, Nike Int'l	19 ft 9 in†
2.	Nick Hysong, Nike	18 ft 6½ in
3.	Pat Manson, Team US West	18 ft 6½ in

LONG JUMP

1.	Kevin Dilworth, adidas	26 ft 7¾ inw
2.	Erick Walder, adidas	26 ft 6¼ inw
3.	Savante Stringfellow, Mississippi	26 ft ¾ inw

TRIPLE JUMP

1.	LaMark Carter, Nike	56 ft 3¼ inw
2.	Desmond Hunt, unattached	53 ft 7¾ in
3.	Von Ware, unattached	53 ft 5¾ in

SHOT PUT

1.	John Godina, Reebok–Bruin	72 ft 3 in
2.	C.J. Hunter, Nike	69 ft 2½ in
3.	Kevin Toth, Nike Int'l	66 ft 11¼ in

DISCUS THROW

1.	Anthony Washington, US West	222 ft 11 in
2.	John Godina, Reebok–Bruin	218 ft 7 in
3.	Andrew Bloom, Nike	214 ft 2 in

HAMMER THROW

1.	Lance Deal, NYAC	263 ft 7 in
2.	Kevin McMahon, Reebok Enc	246 ft
3.	Jud Logan, M-F Athletic	239 ft 10 in

JAVELIN THROW

1.	Tom Pukstys, adidas	256 ft
2.	Tom Petranoff, M-F Athletic	246 ft 9 in
3.	Oscar Duncan, unattached	242 ft 10 in

DECATHLON

1.	Chris Huffins, Oakley	8,350 pts.
2.	Tom Pappas, Tennessee	8,187 pts.
3.	Dan Steele, US Army	7,938 pts.

Women

100 METERS

1. Inger Miller, Nike — 10.96w
2. Gail Devers, Nike — 10.97w
3. Angela Williams, SoCal Cheet — 11.03w

200 METERS

1. Marion Jones, Nike — 22.10
2. Latasha Jenkins, Ball St — 22.36
3. Inger Miller, Nike — 22.46

400 METERS

1. Maicel Malone-Wallace, New Bal — 51.29
2. Suziann Reid, Texas — 51.38
3. Michelle Collins, Nike Int'l — 51.45

800 METERS

1. Jearl Miles-Clark, Reebok — 1:59.47
2. Meredith Rainey-Valmon, Reeb Enc — 2:00.36
3. Kathleen Rounds, unattached — 2:00.71

1500 METERS

1. Regina Jacobs, Mizuno — 4:02.41†
2. Stephanie Best, ASICS — 4:08.53
3. Shayne Culpepper, adidas — 4:08.69

STEEPLECHASE

1. Elizabeth Jackson, BYU — 10:07.23
2. Lisa Nye, Nike-Portland — 10:12.66
3. Joan Nesbit, New Balance — 10:18.55

5000 METERS

1. Regina Jacobs, Mizuno — 15:24.80†
2. Cheri Kenah, Reebok Enc — 15:26.60
3. Elva Dryer, Nike Int'l — 15:27.26

10,000 METERS

1. Libbie Hickman, Nike Int'l — 31:41.33†
2. Anne-Marie Lauck, Nike Int'l — 31:43.50
3. Deena Drossin, Reebok — 32:00.72

100-METER HURDLES

1. Gail Devers, Nike — 12.54w
2. Miesha McKelvey, San Diego St — 12.67w
3. Andria King, Georgia Tech — 12.73w

400-METER HURDLES

1. Sandra Glover, unattached — 54.95
2. Michelle Johnson, Team Fila — 55.43
3. Joanna Hayes, Gold Medal — 55.76

w=wind aided. †Meet record.

20,000-METER WALK

1. Michelle Rohl, Moving Comf — 1:33:17†
2. Joanne Dow, adidas — 1:35:01
3. Susan Armenta, SoCal Walker — 1:37:04

HIGH JUMP

1. Tisha Walker, HSI — 6 ft 6¼ in
2. Amy Acuff, Nike — 6 ft 4 in
3. Karol Jenkins, Chattanooga TC — 6 ft 4 in

POLE VAULT

1. Stacy Dragila, Reebok — 14 ft 7¼ in†
2. Kellie Suttle, Nike Int'l — 14 ft 1¼ in
3. Melissa Price, Fresno St — 13 ft 9¼ in

LONG JUMP

1. Dawn Burrell, US Army — 22 ft 10 in
2. Marion Jones, Nike — 22 ft 3 in
3. Shana Williams, adidas — 22 ft ¼ inw

TRIPLE JUMP

1. Stacey Bowers, Baylor — 44 ft 9¾ in
2. Tiombe Hurd, Nike — 44 ft 4¼ in
3. Cynthea Rhodes, Reebok — 43 ft 9 in

SHOT PUT

1. Connie Price-Smith, IN Invaders — 61 ft 10½ in
2. Teri Tunks, Nike — 61 ft 8¼ in
3. Tressa Thompson, Nike — 61 ft 5 in

DISCUS THROW

1. Seiala Sua, Reebok-Bruin — 203 ft 8 in
2. Kristin Kuehl, unattached — 199 ft 9 in
3. Aretha Hill, unattached — 193 ft 10 in

HAMMER THROW

1. Dawn Ellerbe, NYAC — 212 ft 5 in†
2. Tamika Powell, Reebok Enc — 210 ft 10 in
3. Windy Dean, NYAC — 210 ft 1 in

JAVELIN THROW

1. Linda Bluetrich, M-F Athletic — 182 ft 2 in
2. Cass Morelock, Nebraska — 175 ft 1 in
3. Ann Crouse, unattached — 173 ft 8 in

HEPTATHLON

1. Shelia Burrell, unattached — 6,101 pts.
2. Tiffany Lott-Hogan, Neways — 6,026 pts.
3. Nicole Haynes, unattached — 5,720 pts.

IAAF World Cross-Country Championships

Belfast, March 27–28, 1999

MEN (12,000 METERS; 7.5 MILES)

1. ....Paul Tergat, Kenya — 38:28
2. ....Patrick Ivuti, Kenya — 38:32
3. ....Paulo Guerra, Portugal — 38:46

WOMEN (4,000 METERS; 2.5 MILES)

1. ....Jackline Maranga, Kenya — 15:09
2. ....Yamna Oubouhou-Belkacem, France — 15:16
3. ....Annemari Sandell, Finland — 15:17

Major Marathons

New York City: November 1, 1998

MEN

1. ....John Kagwe, Kenya — 2:08:45
2. ....Joseph Chebet, Kenya — 2:08:48
3. ....Zebedayo Bayo, Tanzania — 2:08:51

WOMEN

1. ....Franca Fiacconi, Italy — 2:25:17
2. ....Adriana Fernandez, Mexico — 2:26:33
3. ....Tegla Loroupe, Kenya — 2:30:28

Tokyo: November 15, 1998

WOMEN ONLY

1. ....Junko Asari, Japan — 2:28:29
2. ....Ari Ichihashi, Japan — 2:28:29
3. ....Azumi Miyazaki, Japan — 2:30:06

Fukuoka, Japan: December 6, 1998

MEN ONLY

1. ....Jackson Kabiga, Kenya — 2:08:42
2. ....Nobuyuki Sato, Japan — 2:08:48
3. ....Tadayuki Ojima, Japan — 2:09:10

Honolulu: December 13, 1998

MEN

1. ....Mbarak Hussein, Kenya — 2:14:53
2. ....Erick Kimaiyo, Kenya — 2:14:53
3. ....Jimmy Muindi, Kenya — 2:15:26

WOMEN

1. ....Irina Bogacheva, Kyrgyzstan — 2:33:27
2. ....Svetlana Zakharova, Russia — 2:36:44
3. ....Elena Razdroguina, Russia — 2:38:36

Los Angeles: March 14, 1999

MEN

1. ....Simon Bor, Kenya — 2:09:25
2. ....James Bungei, Kenya — 2:10:43
3. ....Christopher Cheboiboch, Kenya — 2:13:49

WOMEN

1. ....Irina Bogacheva, Kyrgyzstan — 2:30:32
2. ....Svetlana Zakharova, Russia — 2:32:54
3. ....Alla Zhilayeva, Russia — 2:33:41

London: April 18, 1999

MEN

1. ....Abdelkader El Mouaziz, Morocco — 2:07:57
2. ....Antonio Pinto, Portugal — 2:09:00
3 ....Abel Anton, Spain — 2:09:41

WOMEN

1. ....Joyce Chepchumba, Kenya — 2:23:22
2. ....Adriana Fernandez, Mexico — 2:24:06
3. ....Manuela Machado, Portugal — 2:25:09

Rotterdam: April 18, 1999

MEN

1. ....Japhet Kosgei, Kenya — 2:07:11
2. ....Fabian Roncero, Spain — 2:07:24
3. ....Julio Rey, Spain — 2:07:38

WOMEN

1. ....Tegla Loroupe, Kenya — 2:22:50
2. ....Susan Chepkemei, Kenya — 2:26:40
3. ....Ana Isabel Alonso, Spain — 2:29:56

Boston: April 19, 1999

MEN

1. ....Joseph Chebet, Kenya — 2:09:52
2 ....Silvio Guerra, Ecuador — 2:10:19
3. ....Frank Pooe, South Africa — 2:11:37

WOMEN

1. ....Fatuma Roba, Ethiopia — 2:23:25
2. ....Franziska Rochat-Moser, Switz — 2:25:51
3. ....Yuko Arimori, Japan — 2:26:39

WR=world record.

FOR THE RECORD·Year by Year

TRACK AND FIELD

World Records

As of September 9, 1999. World outdoor records are recognized by the International Amateur Athletics Federation (IAAF).

Men

Event	Mark	Record Holder	Date	Site
100 meters	9.79	Maurice Greene, United States	6-16-99	Athens
200 meters	19.32	Michael Johnson, United States	8-1-96	Atlanta
400 meters	43.18	Michael Johnson, United States	8-26-99	Seville
800 meters	1:41.11	Wilson Kipketer, Denmark	8-24-97	Cologne
1,000 meters	2:11.96	Noah Ngeny, Kenya	9-5-99	Rieti, Italy
1,500 meters	3:26.00	Hicham El Guerrouj, Morocco	7-14-98	Rome
Mile	3:43.13	Hicham El Guerrouj, Morocco	7-7-99	Rome
2,000 meters	4:44.79	Hicham El Guerrouj, Morocco	9-8-99	Berlin
3,000 meters	7:20.67	Daniel Komen, Kenya	9-1-96	Rieti, Italy
Steeplechase	7:55.72	Bernard Bermasai	8-24-97	Cologne
5,000 meters	12:39.36	Haile Gebrselassie, Ethiopia	6-13-98	Helsinki
10,000 meters	26:22.75	Haile Gebrselassie, Ethiopia	6-1-98	Hengelo, Netherlands
20,000 meters	56:55.6	Arturo Barrios, Mexico	3-30-91	La Flâche, France
Hour	21,101 meters	Arturo Barrios, Mexico	3-30-91	La Flâche, France
25,000 meters	1:13:55.8	Toshihiko Seko, Japan	3-22-81	Christchurch, New Zealand
30,000 meters	1:29:18.8	Toshihiko Seko, Japan	3-22-81	Christchurch, New Zealand
Marathon	2:06:05	Ronaldo da Costa, Brazil	9-20-98	Berlin
110-meter hurdles	12.91	Colin Jackson, Great Britain	8-20-93	Stuttgart, Germany
400-meter hurdles	46.78	Kevin Young, United States	8-6-92	Barcelona
20-kilometer walk	1:17:25.6	Bernardo Segura, Mexico	5-7-94	Bergen, Norway
30-kilometer walk	2:01:44.1	Maurizio Damilano, Italy	10-3-92	Cuneo, Italy
50-kilometer walk	3:40:57.9	Thierry Toutain, France	9-29-96	Héricourt
4x100-meter relay	37.40	United States (Mike Marsh, Leroy Burrell, Dennis Mitchell, Carl Lewis)	8-8-92	Barcelona
		United States (Jon Drummond, Andre Cason, Dennis Mitchell, Leroy Burrell)	8-21-93	Stuttgart, Germany
4x200-meter relay	1:18.68	Santa Monica TC (Mike Marsh, Leroy Burrell, Floyd Heard, Carl Lewis)	4-17-94	Walnut, CA
4x400-meter relay	2:54.20	United States (Jerome Young, Antonio Pettigrew, Tyree Washington, Michael Johnson)	7-22-98	New York City
4x800-meter relay	7:03.89	Great Britain (Peter Elliott, Garry Cook, Steve Cram, Sebastian Coe)	8-30-82	London
4x1500-meter relay	14:38.8	West Germany (Thomas Wessinghage, Harald Hudak, Michael Lederer, Karl Fleschen)	8-17-77	Cologne
High jump	8 ft ½ in	Javier Sotomayor, Cuba	7-27-93	Salamanca, Spain
Pole vault	20 ft 1¾ in	Sergei Bubka, Ukraine	7-31-94	Sestriere, Italy
Long jump	29 ft 4½ in	Mike Powell, United States	8-30-91	Tokyo
Triple jump	60 ft ¼ in	Jonathan Edwards, Great Britain	8-7-95	Göteborg, Sweden
Shot put	75 ft 10¼ in	Randy Barnes, United States	5-20-90	Westwood, CA
Discus throw	243 ft 0 in	Jürgen Schult, East Germany	6-6-86	Neubrandenburg, Germany
Hammer throw	284 ft 7 in	Yuri Syedikh, USSR	8-30-86	Stuttgart, Germany
Javelin throw	323 ft 1 in	Jan Zelezny, Czech Republic	5-25-96	Jena, Germany
Decathlon	8994 pts	Tomás Dvorák, Czech Republic	7-4-99	Prague

Note: The decathlon consists of 10 events—the 100 meters, long jump, shot put, high jump and 400 meters on the first day; the 110-meter hurdles, discus, pole vault, javelin and 1500 meters on the second.

Women

Event	Mark	Record Holder	Date	Site
100 meters	10.49	Florence Griffith Joyner, United States	7-16-88	Indianapolis
200 meters	21.34	Florence Griffith Joyner, United States	9-29-88	Seoul
400 meters	47.60	Marita Koch, East Germany	10-6-85	Canberra, Australia
800 meters	1:53.28	Jarmila Kratochvílová, Czechoslovakia	7-26-83	Munich
1,000 meters	2:28.98	Svetlana Masterkova, Russia	8-23-96	Brussels
1,500 meters	3:50.46	Qu Yunxia, China	9-11-93	Beijing
Mile	4:12.56	Svetlana Masterkova, Russia	8-14-96	Zurich
2,000 meters	5:25.36	Sonia O'Sullivan, Ireland	7-8-94	Edinburgh
3,000 meters	8:06.11	Wang Junxia, China	9-13-93	Beijing
5,000 meters	14:28.09	Jiang Bo, China	10-23-97	Shanghai
10,000 meters	29:31.78	Wang Junxia, China	9-8-93	Beijing
Hour	18,340 meters	Tegla Loroupe, Kenya	8-8-98	Borgholzhausen, Germany
20,000 meters	1:06:48.8	Izumi Maki, Japan	9-19-93	Amagasaki
25,000 meters	1:29:2.9	Karolina Szabó, Hungary	4-22-88	Budapest
30,000 meters	1:47:05.6	Karolina Szabó, Hungary	4-22-88	Budapest
Marathon	2:20:47	Tegla Loroupe, Kenya	4-19-98	Rotterdam
100-meter hurdles	12.21	Yordanka Donkova, Bulgaria	8-20-88	Stara Zagora, Bulgaria
400-meter hurdles	52.61	Kim Batten, United States	8-11-95	Göteborg, Sweden
5-kilometer walk	20:13.26	Kerry Saxby, Australia	2-25-96	Hobart, Australia
10-kilometer walk	41:04	Yelena Nikolayeva, Russia	4-20-96	Sochi
4x100-meter relay	41.37	East Germany (Silke Gladisch, Sabine Reiger, Ingrid Auerswald, Marlies Göhr)	10-6-85	Canberra, Australia
4x200-meter relay	1:28.15	East Germany (Marlies Göhr, Romy Müller, Bärbel Wöckel, Marita Koch)	8-9-80	Jena, East Germany
4x400-meter relay	3:15.17	USSR (Tatyana Ledovskaya, Olga Nazarova, Maria Pinigina, Olga Bryzgina)	10-1-88	Seoul
4x800-meter relay	7:50.17	USSR (Nadezhda Olizarenko, Lyubov Gurina, Lyudmila Borisova, Irina Podyalovskaya)	8-5-84	Moscow
High jump	6 ft 10¼ in	Stefka Kostadinova, Bulgaria	8-30-87	Rome
Pole vault	15 ft 1 in	Emma George, Australia	2-20-99	Sydney, Australia
		Stacy Dragila, United States	8-21-99	Seville
Long jump	24 ft 8¼ in	Galina Chistyakova, USSR	6-11-88	Leningrad
Triple jump	50 ft 10¼ in	Inessa Kravets, Ukraine	8-10-95	Göteborg, Sweden
Shot put	74 ft 3 in	Natalya Lisovskaya, USSR	6-7-87	Moscow
Discus throw	252 ft 0 in	Gabriele Reinsch, East Germany	7-9-88	Neubrandenburg, Germany
Hammer throw	247 ft 3 in	Mihaela Melinte, Romania	8-29-99	Rüdlingen, Switzerland
Javelin throw	262 ft 5 in	Petra Felke, East Germany	9-9-88	Potsdam, East Germany
Heptathlon	7291 pts	Jackie Joyner-Kersee, U.S.	9-23/24-88	Seoul

Note: The heptathlon consists of 7 events—the 100-meter hurdles, high jump, shot put and 200 meters on the first day; the long jump, javelin and 800 meters on the second.

As of September 8, 1999. American outdoor records are recognized by USA Track and Field (USATF). WR=world record. EWR=equals world record.

Men

Event	Mark	Record Holder	Date	Site
100 meters	9.79 WR	Maurice Greene	6-16-99	Athens
200 meters	19.32 WR	Michael Johnson	8-1-96	Atlanta
400 meters	43.18 WR	Michael Johnson	8-26-99	Seville, Spain
800 meters	1:42.60	Johnny Gray	8-28-85	Koblenz, Germany
1,000 meters	2:13.9	Rick Wohlhuter	7-30-74	Oslo
1,500 meters	3:29.77	Sydney Maree	8-25-85	Cologne
Mile	3:47.69	Steve Scott	7-7-82	Oslo
2,000 meters	4:52.44	Jim Spivey	9-15-87	Lausanne
3,000 meters	7:30.84	Bob Kennedy	8-8-98	Monte Carlo
Steeplechase	8:09.17	Henry Marsh	8-28-85	Koblenz, Germany
5,000 meters	12:58.21	Bob Kennedy	8-14-96	Zurich
10,000 meters	27:20.56	Mark Nenow	9-5-86	Brussels
20,000 meters	58:25.0	Bill Rodgers	8-9-77	Boston
Hour	20,547 meters	Bill Rodgers	8-9-77	Boston
25,000 meters	1:14:11.8	Bill Rodgers	2-21-79	Saratoga, CA
30,000 meters	1:31:49	Bill Rodgers	2-21-79	Saratoga, CA
Marathon	2:09:35	Jerry Lawson	10-1-97	Chicago
110-meter hurdles	12.92	Roger Kingdom	8-16-89	Zurich
		Allen Johnson	6-23-96	Atlanta
		Allen Johnson	8-23-96	Brussels
400-meter hurdles	46.78 WR	Kevin Young	8-6-92	Barcelona
20-kilometer walk	1:24:26.9	Allen James	5-7-94	Fana, Norway
30-kilometer walk	2:21:40	Herm Nelson	9-7-91	Bellevue, WA
50-kilometer walk	3:59:41.2	Herm Nelson	6-9-96	Seattle
4x100-meter relay	37.40 WR	United States (Mike Marsh, Leroy Burrell, Dennis Mitchell, Carl Lewis)	8-8-92	Barcelona
		United States (Jon Drummond, Andre Cason, Dennis Mitchell, Leroy Burrell)	8-21-93	Stuttgart, Germany
4x200-meter relay	1:18.68 WR	Santa Monica Track Club (Mike Marsh, Leroy Burrell, Floyd Heard, Carl Lewis)	4-17-94	Walnut, CA
4x400-meter relay	2:54.20 WR	United States (Jerome Young, Antonio Pettigrew, Tyree Washington, Michael Johnson)	7-22-98	New York City
4x800-meter relay	7:06.5	Santa Monica Track Club (James Robinson, David Mack, Earl Jones, Johnny Gray)	4-26-86	Walnut, CA
4x1,500-meter relay	14:46.3	National Team (Dan Aldredge, Andy Clifford, Todd Harbour, Tom Duits)	6-24-79	Bourges, France
High jump	7 ft 10½ in	Charles Austin	8-17-91	Zurich
Pole vault	19 ft 9 in	Jeff Hartwig	7-27-99	Eugene, OR
Long jump	29 ft 4½ in WR	Mike Powell	8-30-91	Tokyo
Triple jump	59 ft 4¼ in	Kenny Harrison	7-27-96	Atlanta
Shot put	75 ft 10¼ in WR	Randy Barnes	5-20-90	Westwood, CA
Discus throw	237 ft 4 in	Ben Plucknett	7-7-81	Stockholm
Hammer throw	270 ft 9 in	Lance Deal	9-7-96	Milan
Javelin throw	285 ft 10 in	Tom Pukstys	5-25-97	Jena, Germany
Decathlon	8891 pts	Dan O'Brien	9-4/5-92	Talence, France

Women

Event	Mark	Record Holder	Date	Site
100 meters	10.49 WR	Florence Griffith Joyner	7-16-88	Indianapolis
200 meters	21.34 WR	Florence Griffith Joyner	9-29-88	Seoul
400 meters	48.83	Valerie Brisco-Hooks	8-6-84	Los Angeles
800 meters	1:56.40	Jearl Miles-Clark	8-11-99	Zurich
1,500 meters	3:57.12	Mary Slaney	7-26-83	Stockholm
Mile	4:16.71	Mary Slaney	8-21-85	Zurich
2,000 meters	5:32.7	Mary Slaney	8-3-84	Eugene, OR
3,000 meters	8:25.83	Mary Slaney	9-7-85	Rome
5,000 meters	14:52.49	Regina Jacobs	7-4-98	Brunswick, ME
10,000 meters	31:19.89	Lynn Jennings	8-7-92	Barcelona
Marathon	2:21:21	Joan Samuelson	10-20-85	Chicago
100-meter hurdles	12.37	Gail Devers	8-28-99	Seville
400-meter hurdles	52.61 WR	Kim Batten	8-11-95	Göteborg, Sweden
5,000-meter walk	20:56.88	Michelle Rohl	4-27-96	Philadelphia
10,000-meter walk	44:41.87	Michelle Rohl	7-26-94	St. Petersburg
4x100-meter relay	41.47	National Team (Chryste Gaines, Marion Jones, Inger Miller, Gail Devers)	8-9-97	Athens
4x200-meter relay	1:29.64	Nike International (Tamika Roberts, Inger Miller, Nicole Green, Marion Jones)	4-25-98	Philadelphia
4x400-meter relay	3:15.51	Olympic Team (Denean Howard, Diane Dixon, Valerie Brisco, Florence Griffith Joyner)	10-1-88	Seoul
4x800-meter relay	8:17.09	Athletics West (Sue Addison, Lee Arbogast, Mary Decker, Chris Mullen)	4-24-83	Walnut, CA
High jump	6 ft 8 in	Louise Ritter	7-9-88	Austin, TX
		Louise Ritter	9-30-88	Seoul
Pole vault	15 ft 1 in EWR	Stacy Dragila	8-21-99	Seville
Long jump	24 ft 7 in	Jackie Joyner-Kersee	5-22-94	New York City
			7-31-94	Sestriere, Italy
Triple jump	47 ft 3½ in	Sheila Hudson	7-8-96	Stockholm
Shot put	66 ft 2½ in	Ramona Pagel	6-25-88	San Diego
Discus throw	216 ft 10 in	Carol Cady	5-31-86	San Jose
Hammer throw	230 ft 2 in	Dawn Ellerbee	5-25-99	Laramie, WY
Javelin throw	227 ft 5 in	Kate Schmidt	9-10-77	Fürth, West Germany
Heptathlon	7291 pts WR	Jackie Joyner-Kersee	9-23/24-88	Seoul

World and American Indoor Records

As of September 8, 1999. American indoor records are recognized by USA Track and Field. World Indoor records are recognized by the International Amateur Athletics Federation (IAAF).

Men

Event	Mark	Record Holder	Date	Site
50 meters	5.56	Donovan Bailey, Canada (W)	2-9-96	Reno
	5.56	Maurice Greene (W, A)	2-13-99	Los Angeles
55 meters*	5.99	Obadele Thompson, Barbados (W)	2-22-97	Colorado Springs
	6.00	Lee McRae (A)	3-14-86	Oklahoma City
60 meters	6.39	Maurice Greene (W, A)	3-1-98	Madrid
200 meters	19.92	Frankie Fredericks, Namibia (W)	2-18-96	Liévin, France
	20.32	Rohsaan Griffin (A)	2-27-99	Atlanta
		Kevin Little (A)	3-5-99	Maebashi, Japan
400 meters	44.63	Michael Johnson (W, A)	3-4-95	Atlanta
800 meters	1:42.67	Wilson Kipketer, Denmark (W)	3-9-97	Paris
	1:45.00	Johnny Gray (A)	3-8-92	Sindelfingen, Germany
1,000 meters	2:15.26	Noureddine Morceli, Algeria (W)	2-22-92	Birmingham, England
	2:18.19	Ocky Clark (A)	2-12-89	Stuttgart, Germany
1,500 meters	3:31.17	Hicham El Guerrouj, Morocco (W)	2-02-97	Stuttgart, Germany
	3:38.12	Jeff Atkinson (A)	3-5-89	Budapest

Men *(Cont.)*

Event	Mark	Record Holder	Date	Site
Mile	3:48.45	Hicham El Guerrouj, Morocco (W)	2-12-97	Ghent, Belgium
	3:51.8	Steve Scott (A)	2-20-81	San Diego
3,000 meters	7:24.90	Daniel Komen, Kenya (W)	2-6-98	Budapest
	7:39.94	Steve Scott (A)	2-10-89	East Rutherford, NJ
5,000 meters	12:50.38	Haile Gebrselassie, Ethiopia (W)	2-14-99	Birmingham, England
	13:20.55	Doug Padilla (A)	2-12-82	New York City
50-meter hurdles	6.25	Mark McKoy, Canada (W)	3-5-86	Kobe, Japan
	6.35	Greg Foster (A)	1-27-85	Rosemont, Illinois
	6.35	Greg Foster (A)	1-31-87	Ottawa, Ontario
55-meter hurdles*	6.89	Renaldo Nehemiah (A)	1-20-79	New York City
60-meter hurdles	7.30	Colin Jackson, Great Britain (W)	3-6-94	Sindelfingen, Germany
	7.36	Greg Foster (A)	1-16-87	Los Angeles
5,000-meter walk	18:07.08	Mikhail Shchennikov, Russia (W)	2-14-95	Moscow
	19:18.40	Tim Lewis (A)	3-7-87	Indianapolis
4x200-meter relay	1:22.11	Great Britain (W) (Linford Christie, Darren Braithwaite, Ade Mafe, John Regis)	3-3-91	Glasgow
	1:22.71	National Team (A) (Thomas Jefferson, Raymond Pierre, Antonio McKay Kevin Little)	3-3-91	Glasgow
4x400-meter relay	3:03.05	Germany (W) (Rico Lieder, Jens Carlowitz, Klaus Just, Thomas Schönlebe)	3-10-91	Seville
	3:02.83	National Team (A) (Andre Morris, Dameon Johnson, Deon Minor, Milt Campbell)	3-7-99	Maebashi, Japan
4x800-meter relay	7:17.8	Soviet Union (W) (Valeriy Taratynov, Stanislav Meshcherskikh, Aleksey Taranov, Viktor Semyashkin)	3-14-71	Sofia, Bulgaria
	7:18.23	University of Florida (A) (Dedric Jones, Lewis Lacy, Stephen Adderly, Scott Peters)	3-14-92	Indianapolis
High jump	7 ft 11½ in	Javier Sotomayor, Cuba (W)	3-4-89	Budapest
	7 ft 10½ in	Hollis Conway (A)	3-10-91	Seville
Pole vault	20 ft 2 in	Sergei Bubka, Ukraine (W)	2-21-93	Donetsk, Ukraine
	19 ft 3¾ in	Billy Olsen (A)	1-25-86	Albuquerque
Long jump	28 ft 10¼ in	Carl Lewis (W, A)	1-27-84	New York City
Triple jump	58 ft 6 in	Alicier Urrutia, Cuba (W)	3-1-97	Sindelfingen, Germany
	58 ft 3¼ in	Mike Conley (A)	2-27-87	New York City
Shot put	74 ft 4¼ in	Randy Barnes (W, A)	1-20-89	Los Angeles
Weight throw	84 ft 10¼ in	Lance Deal (W, A)	3-4-95	Atlanta
Pentathlon	4478 pts	Steve Fritz (W, A)	1-14-95	Lawrence, KS
Heptathlon	6476 pts	Dan O'Brien (W, A)	3-13/14-93	Toronto

*No recognized world record.

To Catch a Thief, In Record Time

To the list of life's verities—you can't fool Mother Nature, you can't beat city hall—we add another: You can't outrun the world's fastest human. Especially when you're carrying luggage.

In late August 1999 at the airport in Seville, 100-meter world-record holder Maurice Greene was being interviewed by Spanish television as fellow American Larry Wade, who ran the second fastest 110-meter hurdles in the world that year, sat close by. In an episode caught on tape by the camera crew, a man sneaked behind Wade, took his duffel bag and dashed across the arrivals hall.

Wade yelled, Greene broke off the interview, and the two sprinters sped off in what proved to be a predictably short pursuit—about 30 yards. They nabbed the unidentified bandit at a baggage carousel, whereupon he was turned over to Spain's Civil Guard.

"It was a great way to start the world championships," said Greene, who, apparently unwinded by his exertions, stole off with the gold medal in the 100 meters six days later.

Women

Event	Mark	Record Holder	Date	Site
50 meters	5.96	Irina Privolova, Russia (W)	2-9-95	Madrid
	6.02	Gwen Torrence (A)	2-9-96	Reno, NV
55 meters*	6.56	Gwen Torrence (A)	3-14-87	Oklahoma City
60 meters	6.92	Irina Privolova, Russia (W)	2-11-93	Madrid
	6.92	Irina Privalova, Russia (W)	2-9-95	Madrid
	6.95	Gail Devers (A)	3-12-93	Toronto
	6.95	Marion Jones (A)	3-7-98	Maebashi, Japan
200 meters	21.87	Merlene Ottey, Jamaica (W)	2-13-93	Liévin, France
	22.33	Gwen Torrence (A)	3-2-96	Atlanta
400 meters	49.59	Jarmila Kratochvílová, Czech (W)	3-7-82	Milan
	50.64	Diane Dixon (A)	3-10-91	Seville
800 meters	1:56.36	Maria Mutola, Mozambique (W)	2-22-98	Liévin, France
	1:58.9	Mary Slaney (A)	2-22-80	San Diego
	1:58.92	Suzy Hamilton (A)	3-7-99	Boston
1,000 meters	2:30.94	Maria Mutola, Mozambique (W)	2-25-99	Stockholm
	2:37.60	Mary Slaney (A)	1-21-89	Portland
1,500 meters	4:00.27	Doina Melinte, Romania (W)	2-9-90	East Rutherford, NJ
	4:00.80	Mary Slaney (A)	2-8-80	New York City
Mile	4:17.14	Doina Melinte, Romania (W)	2-9-90	East Rutherford, NJ
	4:20.5	Mary Slaney (A)	2-19-82	San Diego
3,000 meters	8:33.82	Elly van Hulst, Netherlands (W)	3-4-89	Budapest
	8:39.14	Regina Jacobs (A)	3-7-99	Maebashi, Japan
5,000 meters	14:47.35	Gabriela Szabo, Romania (W)	2-13-99	Dortmund, Germany
	15:22.64	Lynn Jennings (A)	1-7-90	Hanover, NH
50-meter hurdles	6.58	Cornelia Oschkenat, E Germany (W)	2-20-88	Berlin
	6.67	Jackie Joyner-Kersee (A)	2-10-95	Reno, NV
55-meter hurdles*	7.30	Tiffany Lott (A)	2-20-97	Air Force Academy, CO
60-meter hurdles	7.69	Lyudmila Narozhilenko, Russia (W)	2-4-90	Chelyabinsk, Russia
	7.81	Jackie Joyner-Kersee (A)	2-5-89	Fairfax, VA
3,000-meter walk	11:44.00	Yelena Ivanova, CIS (W)	2-7-92	Moscow
	12:20.79	Debbi Lawrence (A)	3-12-93	Toronto
4x200-meter relay	1:32.55	SC Eintracht Hamm, W Gemany (W) (Helga Arendt, Silke-Beate Knoll, Mechthild Kluth, Gisela Kinzel)	2-20-88	Dortmund, W Germany
	1:33.24	National Team (A) (Flirtisha Harris, Chryste Gaines, Terri Dendy, Michele Collins)	2-12-94	Glasgow
4x400-meter relay	3:24.25	Russia (W) (Tatyanna Chebykina, Svetlana Goncharenko, Olga Kotlyarova, Natalya Nazarova)	3-7-99	Maebashi, Japan
	3:27.59	National Team (A) (Michelle Collins, Monique Hennagan, Zundra Feagin-Alexander, Shanelle Porter)	3-7-99	Maebashi, Japan
4x800-meter relay	8:18.71	Russia (W) (Natalya Zaytseva, Olga Kuvnetsova, Yelena Afanasyeva, Yekaterina Podkopayeva)	2-4-94	Moscow
	8:25.50	Villanova (A) (Gina Procaccio, Debbie Grant, Michelle DiMuro, Celeste Halliday)	2-7-87	Gainesville, FL
High jump	6 ft 9½ in	Heike Henkel, Germany (W)	2-8-92	Karlsruhe, Germany
	6 ft 7 in	Tisha Walker (A)	2-28-98	Atlanta
Pole vault	14 ft 11 in	Emma George, Australia (W)	3-26-98	Adelaide, Australia
	14 ft 8¼ in	Stacy Draglia (A)	3-8-98	Sindelfinden, Germany
Long jump	24 ft 2¼ in	Heike Drechsler, E Germany (W)	2-13-88	Vienna
	23 ft 4¾ in	Jackie Joyner-Kersee (A)	3-5-94	Atlanta
Triple jump	49 ft 9 in	Ashia Hansen, Great Britain (W)	2-28-95	Valencia, Spain
	46 ft 8¼ in	Sheila Hudson-Strudwick (A)	3-4-95	Atlanta
Shot put	73 ft 10 in	Helena Fibingerová, Czech. (W)	2-19-77	Jablonec, Czech.
	65 ft ¾ in	Ramona Pagel (A)	2-20-87	Inglewood, CA
Weight throw*	75 ft 2½ in	Dawn Ellerbe (W, A)	1-16-98	Laramie, WY
Pentathlon	4991 pts	Irina Byelova, CIS (W)	2-14/15-92	Berlin
	4632 pts	Kym Carter (A)	3-10-95	Barcelona

*No recognized world record.

World Track and Field Championships

Historically, the Olympics have served as the outdoor world championships for track and field. In 1983 the International Amateur Athletic Federation (IAAF) instituted a separate World Championship meet, to be held every 4 years between the Olympics. The first was held in Helsinki in 1983, the second in Rome in 1987, the third in Tokyo in 1991, the fourth in Stuttgart, Germany, in 1993, the fifth in Göteborg, Sweden, in 1995, the sixth in Athens in 1997, and the seventh in Seville in 1999. In 1993 the IAAF began to hold the meet on a biennial basis.

Men

100 METERS

1983	Carl Lewis, United States	10.07
1987*	Carl Lewis, United States	9.93 WR
1991	Carl Lewis, United States	9.86 WR
1993	Linford Christie, Great Britain	9.87
1995	Donovan Bailey, Canada	9.97
1997	Maurice Greene, United States	9.86
1999	Maurice Greene, United States	9.80

200 METERS

1983	Calvin Smith, United States	20.14
1987	Calvin Smith United States	20.16
1991	Michael Johnson, United States	20.01
1993	Frank Fredericks, Namibia	19.85
1995	Michael Johnson, United States	19.79
1997	Ato Boldon, Trinidad	20.04
1999	Maurice Greene, United States	19.90

400 METERS

1983	Bert Cameron, Jamaica	45.05
1987	Thomas Schoenlebe, E Germany	44.33
1991	Antonio Pettigrew, United States	44.57
1993	Michael Johnson, United States	43.65
1995	Michael Johnson, United States	43.39
1997	Michael Johnson, United States	44.12
1999	Michael Johnson, U.S.	43.18WR

800 METERS

1983	Willi Wulbeck, W Germany	1:43.65
1987	Billy Konchellah, Kenya	1:43.06
1991	Billy Konchellah, Kenya	1:43.99
1993	Paul Ruto, Kenya	1:44.71
1995	Wilson Kipketer, Denmark	1:45.08
1997	Wilson Kipketer, Denmark	1:43.38
1999	Wilson Kipketer, Denmark	1:43.30

1500 METERS

1983	Steve Cram, Great Britain	3:41.59
1987	Abdi Bile, Somalia	3:36.80
1991	Noureddine Morceli, Algeria	3:32.84
1993	Noureddine Morceli, Algeria	3:34.24
1995	Noureddine Morceli, Algeria	3:33.73
1997	Hicham El Guerrouj, Morocco	3:35.83
1999	Hicham El Guerrouj, Morocco	3:27.65

STEEPLECHASE

1983	Patriz Ilg, W Germany	8:15.06
1987	Francesco Panetta, Italy	8:08.57
1991	Moses Kiptanui, Kenya	8:12.59
1993	Moses Kiptanui, Kenya	8:06.36
1995	Moses Kiptanui, Kenya	8:04.16
1997	Wilson Boit Kipketer, Kenya	8:05.84
1999	Christopher Koskei, Kenya	8:11.76

5000 METERS

1983	Eamonn Coghlan, Ireland	13:28.53
1987	Said Aouita, Morocco	13:26.44
1991	Yobes Ondieki, Kenya	13:14.45
1993	Ismael Kirui, Kenya	13:02.75
1995	Ismael Kirui, Kenya	13:16.77
1997	Daniel Komen, Kenya	13:07.38
1999	Salah Hissou, Morocco	12:58.13

10,000 METERS

1983	Alberto Cova, Italy	28:01.04
1987	Paul Kipkoech, Kenya	27:38.63
1991	Moses Tanui, Kenya	27:38.74
1993	Haile Gebrselassie, Ethiopia	27:46.02
1995	Haile Gebrselassie, Ethiopia	27:12.95
1997	Haile Gebrselassie, Ethiopia	27:24.58
1999	Haile Gebrselassie, Ethiopia	27:57.27

MARATHON

1983	Rob de Castella, Australia	2:10:03
1987	Douglas Wakiihuri, Kenya	2:11:48
1991	Hiromi Taniguchi, Japan	2:14:57
1993	Mark Plaatjes, United States	2:13:57
1995	Martín Fiz, Spain	2:11:41
1997	Abel Anton, Spain	2:13:16
1999	Abel Anton, Spain	2:13:36

110-METER HURDLES

1983	Greg Foster, United States	13.42
1987	Greg Foster, United States	13.21
1991	Greg Foster, United States	13.06
1993	Colin Jackson, Great Britain	12.91 WR
1995	Allen Johnson, United States	13.00
1997	Allen Johnson, United States	12.93
1999	Colin Jackson, Great Britain	13.04

400-METER HURDLES

1983	Edwin Moses, United States	47.50
1987	Edwin Moses, United States	47.46
1991	Samuel Matete, Zambia	47.64
1993	Kevin Young, United States	47.18
1995	Derrick Adkins, United States	47.98
1997	Stéphane Diagana, France	47.70
1999	Fabrizio Mori, Italy	47.72

20-KILOMETER WALK

1983	Ernesto Canto, Mexico	1:20:49
1987	Maurizio Damilano, Italy	1:20:45
1991	Maurizio Damilano, Italy	1:19:37
1993	Valentin Massana, Spain	1:22:31
1995	Michele Didoni, Italy	1:19:59
1997	Daniel Garcia, Mexico	1:21:43
1999	Ilya Markov, Russia	1:23:34

50-KILOMETER WALK

1983	Ronald Weigel, E Germany	3:43:08
1987	Hartwig Gauder, E Germany	3:40:53
1991	Aleksandr Potashov, USSR	3:53:09
1993	Jesus Angel Garcia, Spain	3:41:41
1995	Valentin Kononen, Finland	3:43:42
1997	Robert Korzeniowski, Poland	3:44:46
1999	German Skurygin, Russia	3:44:23

4 X 100 METER RELAY

1983	United States (Emmit King, Willie Gault, Calvin Smith, Carl Lewis)	37.86
1987	United States (Lee McRae, Lee McNeil, Harvey Glance, Carl Lewis)	37.90

WR=World record. *Ben Johnson, Canada, disqualified.

Men (Cont.)

4 X 100 METER RELAY (CONT.)

1991..............United States (Andre Cason 37.50 WR
Leroy Burrell, Dennis Mitchell
Carl Lewis)
1993..............United States (Jon Drummond,   37.48
Andre Cason, Dennis Mitchell,
Leroy Burrell)
1995..............Canada (Robert Esmie,   38.31
Glenroy Gilbert, Bruny Surin,
Donovan Bailey)
1997..............Canada (Robert Esmie,   37.86
Glenroy Gilbert, Bruny Surin,
Donovan Bailey)
1999..............United States (Jon Drummond,   37.59
Tim Montgomery, Brian Lewis,
Maurice Greene)

4 X 400 METER RELAY

1983..............USSR (Sergei Lovachev,   3:00.79
Alecksandr Troschilo,
Nikolay Chernyetski, Viktor Markin)
1987..............United States (Danny Everett 2:57.29
Rod Haley, Antonio McKay,
Butch Reynolds)
1991..............Great Britain (Roger Black   2:57.53
Derek Redmond, John Regis,
Kriss Akabusi)
1993..............United States (Andrew   2:54.29 WR
Valmon, Quincy Watts, Butch
Reynolds, Michael Johnson)
1995..............United States (Marlon Ramsey, 2:57.32
Derek Mills, Butch Reynolds,
Michael Johnson)
1997..............United States (Jerome Young, 2:56.47
Antonio Pettigrew, Chris Jones,
Tyree Washington)
1999..............United States (Jerome Davis, 2:56.45
Antonio Pettigrew, Angelo
Taylor, Michael Johnson)

HIGH JUMP

1983..............Gennadi Avdeyenko, USSR   7 ft 7¼ in
1987..............Patrik Sjoberg, Sweden   7 ft 9¾ in
1991..............Charles Austin, United States 7 ft 9¾ in
1993..............Javier Sotomayor, Cuba   7 ft 10½ in
1995..............Troy Kemp, Bahamas   7 ft 9¼ in
1997..............Javier Sotomayor, Cuba   7 ft 9¼ in
1999..............Vyacheslav Voronin, Russia   7 ft 9¼ in

POLE VAULT

1983..............Sergei Bubka, USSR   18 ft 8¼ in
1987..............Sergei Bubka, USSR   19 ft 2¼ in
1991..............Sergei Bubka, USSR   19 ft 6¼ in
1993..............Sergei Bubka, Ukraine   19 ft 8¼ in
1995..............Sergei Bubka, Ukraine   19 ft 5 in
1997..............Sergei Bubka, Ukraine   19 ft 8½ in
1999..............Maksim Tarasov, Russia   19 ft 9 in

WR=World record.

LONG JUMP

1983..............Carl Lewis, United States   28 ft ¾ in
1987..............Carl Lewis, United States   28 ft 5¼ in
1991..............Mike Powell, U.S.   29 ft 4½ in WR
1993..............Mike Powell, United States   28 ft 2¼ in
1995..............Ivan Pedroso, Cuba   28 ft 6½ in
1997..............Ivan Pedroso, Cuba   27 ft 7½ in
1999..............Ivan Pedroso, Cuba   28 ft 1 in

TRIPLE JUMP

1983..............Zdzislaw Hoffmann, Poland   57 ft 2 in
1987..............Khristo Markov, Bulgaria   58 ft 9 ½ in
1991..............Kenny Harrison, United States 58 ft 4 in
1993..............Mike Conley, United States   58 ft 7¼ in
1995..............Jonathan Edwards, G.B.   60 ft ¼ in WR
1997..............Yoelvis Quesada, Cuba   58 ft 6¾ in
1999..............Charle Michael Friedek, Ger 57 ft 8½ in

SHOT PUT

1983..............Edward Sarul, Poland   70 ft 2¼ in
1987..............Werner Günthör, Switz   72 ft 11¼ in
1991..............Werner Günthör, Switz   71 ft 1¼ in
1993..............Werner Günthör, Switz   72 ft 1 in
1995..............John Godina, United States   70 ft 5¼ in
1997..............John Godina, United States   70 ft 4¼ in
1999..............C.J. Hunter, United States   71 ft 6 in

DISCUS THROW

1983..............Imrich Bugar, Czechoslovakia 222 ft 2 in
1987..............Juergen Schult, E Germany   225 ft 6 in
1991..............Lars Riedel, Germany   217 ft 2 in
1993..............Lars Riedel, Germany   222 ft 2 in
1995..............Lars Riedel, Germany   225 ft 7 in
1997..............Lars Riedel, Germany   224 ft 10 in
1999..............Anthony Washington, U.S.   226 ft 8 in

HAMMER THROW

1983..............Sergei Litvinov, USSR   271 ft 3 in
1987..............Sergei Litvinov, USSR   272 ft 6 in
1991..............Yuriy Sedykh, USSR   268 ft
1993..............Andrey Abduvaliyev, Tajikistan 267 ft 10 in
1995..............Andrey Abduvaliyev, Tajikistan 267 ft 7 in
1997..............Heinz Weis, Germany   268 ft 4 in
1999..............Karsten Kobs, Germany   263 ft 3 in

JAVELIN

1983..............Detlef Michel, E Germany   293 ft 7 in
1987..............Seppo Räty, Finland   274 ft 1 in
1991..............Kimmo Kinnunen, Finland   297 ft 11 in
1993..............Jan Zelezny, Czech Republic   282 ft 1 in
1995..............Jan Zelezny, Czech Republic 293 ft 11 in
1997..............Marius Corbett, South Africa 290 ft 0 in
1999..............Aki Parviainen, Finland   293 ft 8 in

DECATHLON

1983..............Daley Thompson, G Britain   8666 pts
1987..............Torsten Voss, E Germany   8680 pts
1991..............Dan O'Brien, United States   8812 pts
1993..............Dan O'Brien, United States   8817 pts
1995..............Dan O'Brien, United States   8695 pts
1997..............Tomás Dvorák, Czech Rep.   8837 pts
1999..............Tomás Dvorák, Czech Rep.   8744 pts

Women

100 METERS

1983	Marlies Gohr, E Germany	10.97
1987	Silke Gladisch, E Germany	10.90
1991	Katrin Krabbe, Germany	10.99
1993	Gail Devers, United States	10.82
1995	Gwen Torrence, United States	10.85
1997	Marion Jones, United States	10.83
1999	Marion Jones, United States	10.70

200 METERS

1983	Marita Koch, E Germany	22.13
1987	Silke Gladisch, E Germany	21.74
1991	Katrin Krabbe, Germany	22.09
1993	Merlene Ottey, Jamaica	21.98
1995	Merlene Ottey, Jamaica	22.12
1997	Zhanna Pintusevich, Ukraine	22.32
1999	Inger Miller, United States	21.77

400 METERS

1983	Jarmila Kratochvilova, Czech.	47.99
1987	Olga Bryzgina, USSR	49.38
1991	Marie-José Pérec, France	49.13
1993	Jearl Miles, United States	49.82
1995	Marie-José Pérec, France	49.28
1997	Cathy Freeman, Australia	49.77
1999	Cathy Freeman, Australia	49.67

800 METERS

1983	Jarmila Kratochvilova, Czech	1:54.68
1987	Sigrun Wodars, E Germany	1:55.26
1991	Lilia Nurutdinova, USSR	1:57.50
1993	Maria Mutola, Mozambique	1:55.43
1995	Ana Quirot, Cuba	1:56.11
1997	Ana Quirot, Cuba	1:57.14
1999	Ludmila Formanová, Czech Rep	1:56.68

1500 METERS

1983	Mary Slaney, United States	4:00.90
1987	Tatyana Samolenko, USSR	3:58.56
1991	Hassiba Boulmerka, Algeria	4:02.21
1993	Dong Liu, China	4:00.50
1995	Hassiba Boulmerka, Algeria	4:02.42
1997	Carla Sacramento, Portugal	4:04.24
1999	Svetlana Masterkova, Russia	3:59.53

3000 METERS

1983	Mary Slaney, United States	8:34.62
1987	Tatyana Samolenko, USSR	8:38.73
1991	Tatyana Dorovskikh, USSR	8:35.82
1993	Qu Yunxia, China	8:28.71

5000 METERS

1995	Sonia O'Sullivan, Ireland	14:46.47
1997	Gabriela Szabo, Romania	14:57.68
1999	Gabriela Szabo, Romania	14:41.82

10,000 METERS

1987	Ingrid Kristiansen, Norway	31:05.85
1991	Liz McColgan, Great Britain	31:14.31
1993	Wang Junxia, China	30:49:30
1995	Fernanda Ribeiro, Portugal	31:04.99
1997	Sally Barsosio, Kenya	31:32.92
1999	Gete Wami, Ethiopia	30:24.56

MARATHON

1983	Grete Waitz, Norway	2:28:09
1987	Rosa Mota, Portugal	2:25:17
1991	Wanda Panfil, Poland	2:29:53
1993	Junko Asari, Japan	2:30:03

*400 meters short.

MARATHON *(CONT.)*

1995	Manuela Machado, Portugal	2:25:39*
1997	Hiromi Suzuki, Japan	2:29.48
1999	Jong Song-Ok, North Korea	2:26:59

100-METER HURDLES

1983	Bettine Jahn, E Germany	12.35
1987	Ginka Zagorcheva, Bulgaria	12.34
1991	Lyudmila Narozhilenko, USSR	12.59
1993	Gail Devers, United States	12.46
1995	Gail Devers, United States	12.68
1997	Ludmila Engquist, Sweden	12.50
1999	Gail Devers, United States	12.37

400-METER HURDLES

1983	Yekaterina Fesenko, USSR	54.14
1987	Sabine Busch, E Germany	53.62
1991	Tatyana Ledovskaya, USSR	53.11
1993	Sally Gunnell, Great Britain	52.74 WR
1995	Kim Batten, United States	52.61
1997	Nezha Bidouane, Morocco	52.97
1999	Daimi Pernia, Cuba	52.89

10-KILOMETER WALK

1987	Irina Strakhova, USSR	44:12
1991	Alina Ivanova, USSR	42:57
1993	Sari Essayah, Finland	42:59
1995	Irina Stankina, Russia	42:13
1997	Annarita Sidoti, Italy	42:56

20-KILOMETER WALK

1999	Hongyu Liu, China	1:30:50

4 X 100 METER RELAY

1983	East Germany (Silke Gladisch, Marita Koch, Ingrid Auerswald, Marlies Gohr)	41.76
1987	United States (Alice Brown, Diane Williams, Florence Griffith, Pam Marshall)	41.58
1991	Jamaica (Dalia Duhaney, Juliet Cuthbert, Beverley McDonald, Merlene Ottey)	41.94
1993	Russia (Olga Bogoslovskaya, Galina Malchugina, Natalya Voronova, Irina Privalova)	41.49
1995	United States (Celena Mondie-Milner, Carlette Guidry, Chryste Gaines, Gwen Torrence)	42.12
1997	United States (Chryste Gaines, Marion Jones, Inger Miller, Gail Devers)	41.47
1999	Bahamas (Sevatheda Fynes, Chandra Sturrup, Pauline Davis-Thompson, Debbie Ferguson)	41.92

4 X 400 METER RELAY

1983	East Germany (Kerstin Walther, Sabine Busch, Marita Koch, Dagmar Rubsam)	3:19.73
1987	E Germany (Dagmar Neubauer, Kirsten Emmelmann, Petra Müller, Sabine Busch)	3:18.63
1991	USSR (Tatyana Ledovskaya, Lyudmila Dzhigalova, Olga Nazarova, Olga Bryzgina)	3:18.43
1993	United States (Gwen Torrence, Maicel Malone, Natasha Kaiser-Brown, Jearl Miles)	3:16.71

Women (Cont.)

4 X 400 METER RELAY (CONT.)

1995	United States (Kim Graham, Rochelle Stevens, Camara Jones, Jearl Miles)	3:22.39
1997	Germany (Anke Feller, Uta Rohlander, Anja Rucker, Grit Breuer)	3:20.92
1999	Russia (Tatyana Chebykina, Svetlana Goncharenko, Olga Kotylarova, Natalya Nazarova)	3:21.98

HIGH JUMP

1983	Tamara Bykova, USSR	6 ft 7 in
1987	Stefka Kostadinova, Bulgaria	6 ft 10¼ in
1991	Heike Henkel, Germany	6 ft 8¾ in
1993	Ioamnet Quintero, Cuba	6 ft 6¼ in
1995	Stefka Kostadinova, Bulgaria	6 ft 7 in
1997	Hanne Haugland, Norway	6 ft 6¼ in
1999	Inga Babakova, Ukraine	6 ft 6¼ in

POLE VAULT

1999	Stacy Dragila, U.S.	15 ft 1 in EWR

LONG JUMP

1983	Heike Daute, E Germany	23 ft 10¼ in
1987	Jackie Joyner-Kersee, U.S.	24 ft 1¾ in
1991	Jackie Joyner-Kersee, U.S.	24 ft ¼ in
1993	Heike Drechsler, Germany	23 ft 4 in
1995	Fiona May, Italy	22 ft 10¾ in w
1997	Lyudmila Galkina, Russia	23 ft 1¾ in
1999	Niurka Montalvo, Spain	23 ft 2 in

TRIPLE JUMP

1993	Ana Biryukova, Russia	49 ft 6 ¼ in WR
1995	Inessa Kravets, Ukraine	50 ft 10¼ in WR
1997	S. Kasparkova, Czech Rep.	49 ft 10½ in
1999	Paraskevi Tsiamita, Greece	48 ft 10 in

WR=World record. EWR=equals world record.

SHOT PUT

1983	Helena Fibingerova, Czech.	69 ft ¾ in
1987	Natalya Lisovskaya, USSR	69 ft 8¼ in
1991	Zhihong Huang, China	68 ft 4¼ in
1993	Zhihong Huang, China	67 ft 6 in
1995	Astrid Kumbernuss, Germany	69 ft 7½ in
1997	Astrid Kumbernuss, Germany	67 ft 11½ in
1999	Astrid Kumbernuss, Germany	65 ft 1½ in

HAMMER THROW

1999	Mihaela Melinte, Romania	246 ft 9 in

DISCUS THROW

1983	Martina Opitz, E Germany	226 ft 2 in
1987	Martina Hellmann, E Germany	235 ft
1991	Tsvetanka Khristova, Bulgaria	233 ft
1993	Olga Burova, Russia	221 ft 1 in
1995	Ellina Zvereva, Belarus	225 ft 2 in
1997	Beatrice Faumuina, New Zeal.	219 ft 3 in
1999	Franka Dietzsch, Germany	223 ft 7 in

JAVELIN

1983	Tiina Lillak, Finland	232 ft 4 in
1987	Fatima Whitbread, G Britain	251 ft 5 in
1991	Demei Xu, China	225 ft 8 in
1993	Trine Hattestad, Finland	227 ft
1995	Natalya Shikolenko, Belarus	221 ft 8 in
1997	Trine Hattestad, Norway	225 ft 8 in
1999	Mirela Manjani-Tzelili, Greece	220 ft 1 in

HEPTATHLON

1983	Ramona Neubert, E Germany	6714 pts
1987	Jackie Joyner-Kersee, U.S.	7128 pts
1991	Sabine Braun, Germany	6672 pts
1993	Jackie Joyner-Kersee, U.S.	6837 pts
1995	Ghada Shouaa, Syria	6651 pts
1997	Sabine Braun, Germany	6739 pts
1999	Eunice Barber, France	6861 pts

Track and Field News Athlete of the Year

Each year (since 1959 for men and since 1974 for women) Track & Field News has chosen the outstanding athlete in the sport.

Men

Year	Athlete	Event	Year	Athlete	Event
1959	Martin Lauer, West Germany	110H/Decath	1979	Sebastian Coe, Great Britain	800/1500
1960	Rafer Johnson, United States	Decathlon	1980	Edwin Moses, United States	400H
1961	Ralph Boston, United States	Long jump	1981	Sebastian Coe, Great Britain	800/1500
1962	Peter Snell, New Zealand	800/1500	1982	Carl Lewis, United States	100/200/LJ
1963	C. K. Yang, Taiwan	Decath/PV	1983	Carl Lewis, United States	100/200/LJ
1964	Peter Snell, New Zealand	800/1500	1984	Carl Lewis, United States	100/200/LJ
1965	Ron Clarke, Australia	5K/10K	1985	Said Aouita, Morocco	1500/5000
1966	Jim Ryun, United States	800/1500	1986	Yuri Syedikh, USSR	Hammer
1967	Jim Ryun, United States	1500	1987	Ben Johnson, Canada	100
1968	Bob Beamon, United States	Long jump	1988	Sergei Bubka, USSR	Pole vault
1969	Bill Toomey, United States	Decathlon	1989	Roger Kingdom, United States	110H
1970	Randy Matson, United States	Shot put	1990	Michael Johnson, United States	200/400
1971	Rod Milburn, United States	110H	1991	Sergei Bubka, CIS	Pole vault
1972	Lasse Viren, Finland	5K/10K	1992	Kevin Young, United States	400H
1973	Ben Jipcho, Kenya	1500/5K/ST	1993	Noureddine Morceli, Algeria	1500/mile/3K
1974	Rick Wohlhuter, United States	800/1500	1994	Noureddine Morceli, Algeria	1500/mile/3K
1975	John Walker, New Zealand	800/1500	1995	Haile Gebrselassie, Ethiopia	5K/10K
1976	Alberto Juantorena, Cuba	400/800	1996	Michael Johnson, United States	200/400
1977	Alberto Juantorena, Cuba	400/800	1997	Wilson Kipketer, Denmark	800
1978	Henry Rono, Kenya	5K/10K/ST	1998	Haile Gebrselassie, Ethiopia	5K/10K

Women

Year	Athlete	Event	Year	Athlete	Event
1974	Irena Szewinska, Poland	100/200/400	1987	Jackie Joyner-Kersee, U.S	100H/LJ/Hept
1975	Faina Melnik, USSR	Shot/Discus	1988	Florence Griffith Joyner, U.S.	100/200
1976	Tatyana Kazankina, USSR	800/1500	1989	Ana Quirot, Cuba	400/800
1977	R. Ackermann, East Germany	High jump	1990	Merlene Ottey, Jamaica	100/200
1978	Marita Koch, East Germany	100/200/400	1991	Heike Henkel, Germany	High jump
1979	Marita Koch, East Germany	100/200/400	1992	Heike Drechsler, Germany	Long Jump
1980	Ilona Briesenick, East Germany	Shot put	1993	Wang Junxia, China	1.5K/3K/10K
1981	Evelyn Ashford, United States	100/200	1994	Jackie Joyner-Kersee, U.S.	100H/LJ/Hept
1982	Marita Koch, East Germany	100/200/400	1995	Sonia O'Sullivan, Ireland	1500/3K/5K
1983	J. Kratochvilova, Czechoslovakia	200/400/800	1996	Svetlana Masterkova, Russia	800/1500
1984	Evelyn Ashford, United States	100	1997	Marion Jones, United States	100/200/LJ
1985	Marita Koch, East Germany	100/200/400	1998	Marion Jones, United States	100/200/LJ
1986	Jackie Joyner-Kersee, U.S.	LJ/Hept			

Marathon World Record Progression

Men

Record Holder	Time	Date	Site
John Hayes, United States	2:55:18.4	7-24-08	Shepherd's Bush, London
Robert Fowler, United States	2:52:45.4	1-1-09	Yonkers, NY
James Clark, United States	2:46:52.6	2-12-09	New York City
Albert Raines, United States	2:46:04.6	5-8-09	New York City
Frederick Barrett, Great Britain	2:42:31	5-26-09	Shepherd's Bush, London
Harry Green, Great Britain	2:38:16.2	5-12-13	Shepherd's Bush, London
Alexis Ahlgren, Sweden	2:36:06.6	5-31-13	Shepherd's Bush, London
Johannes Kolehmainen, Finland	2:32:35.8	8-22-20	Antwerp, Belgium
Albert Michelsen, United States	2:29:01.8	10-12-25	Port Chester, NY
Fusashige Suzuki, Japan	2:27:49	3-31-35	Tokyo
Yasuo Ikenaka, Japan	2:26:44	4-3-35	Tokyo
Kitei Son, Japan	2:26:42	11-3-35	Tokyo
Yun Bok Suh, Korea	2:25:39	4-19-47	Boston
James Peters, Great Britain	2:20:42.2	6-14-52	Chiswick, England
James Peters, Great Britain	2:18:40.2	6-13-53	Chiswick, England
James Peters, Great Britain	2:18:34.8	10-4-53	Turku, Finland
James Peters, Great Britain	2:17:39.4	6-26-54	Chiswick, England
Sergei Popov, USSR	2:15:17	8-24-58	Stockholm
Abebe Bikila, Ethiopia	2:15:16.2	9-10-60	Rome
Toru Terasawa, Japan	2:15:15.8	2-17-63	Beppu, Japan
Leonard Edelen, United States	2:14:28	6-15-63	Chiswick, England
Basil Heatley, Great Britain	2:13:55	6-13-64	Chiswick, England
Abebe Bikila, Ethiopia	2:12:11.2	6-21-64	Tokyo
Morio Shigematsu, Japan	2:12:00	6-12-65	Chiswick, England
Derek Clayton, Australia	2:09:36.4	12-3-67	Fukuoka, Japan
Derek Clayton, Australia	2:08:33.6	5-30-69	Antwerp, Belgium
Rob de Castella, Australia	2:08:18	12-6-81	Fukuoka, Japan
Steve Jones, Great Britain	2:08:05	10-21-84	Chicago
Carlos Lopes, Portugal	2:07:12	4-20-85	Rotterdam, Netherlands
Belayneh Dinsamo, Ethiopia	2:06:50	4-17-88	Rotterdam, Netherlands
Ronaldo Da Costa, Brazil	2:06:05	9-20-98	Berlin, Germany

Women

Record Holder	Time	Date	Site
Dale Greig, Great Britain	3:27:45	5-23-64	Ryde, England
Mildred Simpson, New Zealand	3:19:33	7-21-64	Auckland, New Zealand
Maureen Wilton, Canada	3:15:22	5-6-67	Toronto
Anni Pede-Erdkamp, West Germany	3:07:26	9-16-67	Waldniel, West Germany
Caroline Walker, United States	3:02:53	2-28-70	Seaside, OR
Elizabeth Bonner, United States	3:01:42	5-9-71	Philadelphia
Adrienne Beames, Australia	2:46:30	8-31-71	Werribee, Australia
Chantal Langlace, France	2:46:24	10-27-74	Neuf Brisach, France
Jacqueline Hansen, United States	2:43:54.5	12-1-74	Culver City, CA
Liane Winter, West Germany	2:42:24	4-21-75	Boston
Christa Vahlensieck, West Germany	2:40:15.8	5-3-75	Dülmen, West Germany

Women (Cont.)

Record Holder	Time	Date	Site
Jacqueline Hansen, United States	2:38:19	10-12-75	Eugene, OR
Chantal Langlace, France	2:35:15.4	5-1-77	Oyarzun, France
Christa Vahlensieck, West Germany	2:34:47.5	9-10-77	West Berlin, West Germany
Grete Waitz, Norway	2:32:29.9	10-22-78	New York City
Grete Waitz, Norway	2:27:32.6	10-21-79	New York City
Grete Waitz, Norway	2:25:41.3	10-26-80	New York City
Grete Waitz,*Norway	2:25:29	4-17-83	London
Joan Benoit Samuelson, United States	2:22:43	4-18-83	Boston
Ingrid Kristiansen, Norway	2:21:06	4-21-85	London
Tegla Loroupe, Kenya	2:20:47	4-19-98	Rotterdam, Netherlands

Boston Marathon

The Boston Marathon began in 1897 as a local Patriot's Day event. Run every year but 1918 since then, it has grown into one of the world's premier marathons.

Men

Year	Winner	Time	Year	Winner	Time
1897	John J. McDermott, United States	2:55:10	1946	Stylianos Kyriakides, Greece	2:29:27
*1898	Ronald J. McDonald, United States	2:42:00	1947	Yun Bok Suh, Korea	2:25:39
1899	Lawrence J. Brignolia, United States	2:54:38	1948	Gerard Cote, Canada	2:31:02
1900	James J. Caffrey, Canada	2:39:44	1949	Karl Gosta Leandersson, Sweden	2:31:50
1901	James J. Caffrey, Canada	2:29:23	1950	Kee Yong Ham, Korea	2:32:39
1902	Sammy Mellor, United States	2:43:12	1951	Shigeki Tanaka, Japan	2:27:45
1903	John C. Lorden, United States	2:41:29	1952	Doroteo Flores, Guatemala	2:31:53
1904	Michael Spring, United States	2:38:04	1953	Keizo Yamada, Japan	2:18:51
1905	Fred Lorz, United States	2:38:25	1954	Veikko Karvonen, Finland	2:20:39
1906	Timothy Ford, United States	2:45:45	1955	Hideo Hamamura, Japan	2:18:22
1907	Tom Longboat, Canada	2:24:24	1956	Antti Viskari, Finland	2:14:14
1908	Thomas Morrissey, United States	2:25:43	1957	John J. Kelley, United States	2:20:05
1909	Henri Renaud, United States	2:53:36	1958	Franjo Mihalic, Yugoslavia	2:25:54
1910	Fred Cameron, Canada	2:28:52	1959	Eino Oksanen, Finland	2:22:42
1911	Clarence H. DeMar, United States	2:21:39	1960	Paavo Kotila, Finland	2:20:54
1912	Mike Ryan, United States	2:21:18	1961	Eino Oksanen, Finland	2:23:39
1913	Fritz Carlson, United States	2:25:14	1962	Eino Oksanen, Finland	2:23:48
1914	James Duffy, Canada	2:25:01	1963	Aurele Vandendriessche, Belgium	2:18:58
1915	Edouard Fabre, Canada	2:31:41	1964	Aurele Vandendriessche, Belgium	2:19:59
1916	Arthur Roth, United States	2:27:16	1965	Morio Shigematsu, Japan	2:16:33
1917	Bill Kennedy, United States	2:28:37	1966	Kenji Kimihara, Japan	2:17:11
1918	No race		1967	David McKenzie, New Zealand	2:15:45
1919	Carl Linder, United States	2:29:13	1968	Amby Burfoot, United States	2:22:17
1920	Peter Trivoulidas, Greece	2:29:31	1969	Yoshiaki Unetani, Japan	2:13:49
1921	Frank Zuna, United States	2:18:57	1970	Ron Hill, England	2:10:30
1922	Clarence H. DeMar, United States	2:18:10	1971	Alvaro Mejia, Colombia	2:18:45
1923	Clarence H. DeMar, United States	2:23:37	1972	Olavi Suomalainen, Finland	2:15:39
1924	Clarence H. DeMar, United States	2:29:40	1973	Jon Anderson, United States	2:16:03
1925	Chuck Mellor, United States	2:33:00	1974	Neil Cusack, Ireland	2:13:39
1926	John C. Miles, Canada	2:25:40	1975	Bill Rodgers, United States	2:09:55
1927	Clarence H. DeMar, United States	2:40:22	1976	Jack Fultz, United States	2:20:19
1928	Clarence H. DeMar, United States	2:37:07	1977	Jerome Drayton, Canada	2:14:46
1929	John C. Miles, Canada	2:33:08	1978	Bill Rodgers, United States	2:10:13
1930	Clarence H. DeMar, United States	2:34:48	1979	Bill Rodgers, United States	2:09:27
1931	James (Hinky) Henigan, United States	2:46:45	1980	Bill Rodgers, United States	2:12:11
1932	Paul de Bruyn, Germany	2:33:36	1981	Toshihiko Seko, Japan	2:09:26
1933	Leslie Pawson, United States	2:31:01	1982	Alberto Salazar, United States	2:08:52
1934	Dave Komonen, Canada	2:32:53	1983	Gregory A. Meyer, United States	2:09:00
1935	John A. Kelley, United States	2:32:07	1984	Geoff Smith, England	2:10:34
1936	Ellison M. (Tarzan) Brown, United States	2:33:40	1985	Geoff Smith, England	2:14:05
1937	Walter Young, Canada	2:33:20	1986	Rob de Castella, Australia	2:07:51
1938	Leslie Pawson, United States	2:35:34	1987	Toshihiko Seko, Japan	2:11:50
1939	Ellison M. (Tarzan) Brown, United States	2:28:51	1988	Ibrahim Hussein, Kenya	2:08:43
1940	Gerard Cote, Canada	2:28:28	1989	Abebe Mekonnen, Ethiopia	2:09:06
1941	Leslie Pawson, United States	2:30:38	1990	Gelindo Bordin, Italy	2:08:19
1942	Bernard Joseph Smith, United States	2:26:51	1991	Ibrahim Hussein, Kenya	2:11:06
1943	Gerard Cote, Canada	2:28:25	1992	Ibrahim Hussein, Kenya	2:08:14
1944	Gerard Cote, Canada	2:31:50	1993	Cosmas N'Deti, Kenya	2:09:33
1945	John A. Kelley, United States	2:30:40	1994	Cosmas N'Deti, Kenya	2:07:15

Year	Winner	Time	Year	Winner	Time
1995	Cosmas N'Deti, Kenya	2:09:22	1980	Jacqueline Gareau, Canada	2:34:28
1996	Moses Tanui, Kenya	2:09:16	1981	Allison Roe, New Zealand	2:26:46
1997	Lameck Aguta, Kenya	2:10:34	1982	Charlotte Teske, West Germany	2:29:33
1998	Moses Tanui, Kenya	2:07:34	1983	Joan Benoit, United States	2:22:43
1999	Joseph Chebet, Kenya	2:09:52	1984	Lorraine Moller, New Zealand	2:29:28

Women

Year	Winner	Time	Year	Winner	Time
			1985	Lisa Larsen Weidenbach, United States	2:34:06
			1986	Ingrid Kristiansen, Norway	2:24:55
1966	Roberta Gibb, United States	3:21:40*	1987	Rosa Mota, Portugal	2:25:21
1967	Roberta Gibb, United States	3:27:17*	1988	Rosa Mota, Portugal	2:24:30
1968	Roberta Gibb, United States	3:30:00*	1989	Ingrid Kristiansen, Norway	2:24:33
1969	Sara Mae Berman, United States	3:22:46*	1990	Rosa Mota, Portugal	2:25:24
1970	Sara Mae Berman, United States	3:05:07*	1991	Wanda Panfil, Poland	2:24:18
1971	Sara Mae Berman, United States	3:08:30*	1992	Olga Markova, Russia	2:23:43
1972	Nina Kuscsik, United States	3:10:36	1993	Olga Markova, Russia	2:25:27
1973	Jacqueline A. Hansen, United States	3:05:59	1994	Uta Pippig, Germany	2:21:45
1974	Miki Gorman, United States	2:47:11	1995	Uta Pippig, Germany	2:25:11
1975	Liane Winter, West Germany	2:42:24	1996	Uta Pippig, Germany	2:27:12
1976	Kim Merritt, United States	2:47:10	1997	Fatuma Roba, Ethiopia	2:26:23
1977	Miki Gorman, United States	2:48:33	1998	Fatuma Roba, Ethiopia	2:23:21
1978	Gayle Barron, United States	2:44:52	1999	Fatuma Roba, Ethiopia	2:23:25
1979	Joan Benoit, United States	2:35:15	*Unofficial.		

Note: Over the years the Boston course has varied in length. The distances have been 24 miles, 1232 yards (1897–1923); 26 miles, 209 yards (1924–1926); 26 miles 385 yards (1927–1952); and 25 miles, 958 yards (1953–1956). Since 1957, the course has been certified to be the standard marathon distance of 26 miles, 385 yards.

New York City Marathon

From 1970 through 1975 the New York City Marathon was a small local race run in the city's Central Park. In 1976 it was moved to the streets of New York's five boroughs. It has since become one of the biggest and most prestigious marathons in the world.

Men

Year	Winner	Time	Year	Winner	Time
1970	Gary Muhrcke, United States	2:31:38	1985	Orlando Pizzolato, Italy	2:11:34
1971	Norman Higgins, United States	2:22:54	1986	Gianni Poli, Italy	2:11:06
1972	Sheldon Karlin, United States	2:27:52	1987	Ibrahim Hussein, Kenya	2:11:01
1973	Tom Fleming, United States	2:21:54	1988	Steve Jones, Great Britain	2:08:20
1974	Norbert Sander, United States	2:26:30	1989	Juma Ikangaa, Tanzania	2:08:01
1975	Tom Fleming, United States	2:19:27	1990	Douglas Wakiihuri, Kenya	2:12:39
1976	Bill Rodgers, United States	2:10:10	1991	Salvador Garcia, Mexico	2:09:28
1977	Bill Rodgers, United States	2:11:28	1992	Willie Mtolo, South Africa	2:09:29
1978	Bill Rodgers, United States	2:12:12	1993	Andres Espinosa, Mexico	2:10:04
1979	Bill Rodgers, United States	2:11:42	1994	German Silva, Mexico	2:11:21
1980	Alberto Salazar, United States	2:09:41	1995	German Silva, Mexico	2:11:00
1981	Alberto Salazar, United States	2:08:13	1996	Giacomo Leone, Italy	2:09:54
1982	Alberto Salazar, United States	2:09:29	1997	John Kagwe, Kenya	2:08:12
1983	Rod Dixon, New Zealand	2:08:59	1998	John Kagwe, Kenya	2:08:45
1984	Orlando Pizzolato, Italy	2:14:53			

Women

Year	Winner	Time	Year	Winner	Time
1970	No finisher		1985	Grete Waitz, Norway	2:28:34
1971	Beth Bonner, United States	2:55:22	1986	Grete Waitz, Norway	2:28:06
1972	Nina Kuscsik, United States	3:08:41	1987	Priscilla Welch, Great Britain	2:30:17
1973	Nina Kuscsik, United States	2:57:07	1988	Grete Waitz, Norway	2:28:07
1974	Katherine Switzer, United States	3:07:29	1989	Ingrid Kristiansen, Norway	2:25:30
1975	Kim Merritt, United States	2:46:14	1990	Wanda Panfiil, Poland	2:30:45
1976	Miki Gorman, United States	2:39:11	1991	Liz McColgan, Scotland	2:27:23
1977	Miki Gorman, United States	2:43:10	1992	Lisa Ondieki, Australia	2:24:40
1978	Grete Waitz, Norway	2:32:30	1993	Uta Pippig, Germany	2:26:24
1979	Grete Waitz, Norway	2:27:33	1994	Tegla Loroupe, Kenya	2:27:37
1980	Grete Waitz, Norway	2:25:41	1995	Tegla Loroupe, Kenya	2:28:06
1981	Allison Roe, New Zealand	2:25:29	1996	Anuta Catuna, Romania	2:28:18
1982	Grete Waitz, Norway	2:27:14	1997	Franziska Rochat-Moser, Switzerland	2:28:43
1983	Grete Waitz, Norway	2:27:00	1998	Franca Fiacconi, Italy	2:25:17
1984	Grete Waitz, Norway	2:29:30			

World Cross-Country Championships

Conducted by the International Amateur Athletic Federation (IAAF), this meet annually brings together the best runners in the world at every distance from the mile to the marathon to compete in the same cross-country race.

Men

Year	Winner	Winning Team	Year	Winner	Winning Team
1973	Pekka Paivarinta, Finland	Belgium	1987	John Ngugi, Kenya	Kenya
1974	Eric DeBeck, Belgium	Belgium	1988	John Ngugi, Kenya	Kenya
1975	Ian Stewart, Scotland	New Zealand	1989	John Ngugi, Kenya	Kenya
1976	Carlos Lopes, Portugal	England	1990	Khalid Skah, Morocco	Kenya
1977	Leon Schots, Belgium	Belgium	1991	Khalid Skah, Morocco	Kenya
1978	John Treacy, Ireland	France	1992	John Ngugi, Kenya	Kenya
1979	John Treacy, Ireland	England	1993	William Sigei, Kenya	Kenya
1980	Craig Virgin, United States	England	1994	William Sigei, Kenya	Kenya
1981	Craig Virgin, United States	Ethiopia	1995	Paul Tergat, Kenya	Kenya
1982	Mohammed Kedir, Ethiopia	Ethiopia	1996	Paul Tergat, Kenya	Kenya
1983	Bekele Debele, Ethiopia	Ethiopia	1997	Paul Tergat, Kenya	Kenya
1984	Carlos Lopes, Portugal	Ethiopia	1998	Paul Tergat, Kenya	Kenya
1985	Carlos Lopes, Portugal	Ethiopia	1999	Paul Tergat, Kenya	Kenya

Women

Year	Winner	Winning Team	Year	Winner	Winning Team
1973	Paola Cacchi, Italy	England	1987	Annette Sergent, France	United States
1974	Paola Cacchi, Italy	England	1988	Ingrid Kristiansen, Norway	USSR
1975	Julie Brown, United States	United States	1989	Annette Sergent, France	USSR
1976	Carmen Valero, Spain	USSR	1990	Lynn Jennings, United States	USSR
1977	Carmen Valero, Spain	USSR	1991	Lynn Jennings, United States	Kenya
1978	Grete Waitz, Norway	Romania	1992	Lynn Jennings, United States	Kenya
1979	Grete Waitz, Norway	United States	1993	Albertina Dias, Portugal	Kenya
1980	Grete Waitz, Norway	USSR	1994	Helen Chepngeno, Kenya	Portugal
1981	Grete Waitz, Norway	USSR	1995	Derartu Tulu, Ethiopia	Kenya
1982	Maricica Puica, Romania	USSR	1996	Gete Wami, Ethiopia	Kenya
1983	Grete Waitz, Norway	United States	1997	Derartu Tulu, Ethiopia	Ethiopia
1984	Maricica Puica, Romania	United States	1998	Sonia O'Sullivan, Ireland	Kenya
1985	Zola Budd, England	United States	1999	Jackline Maranga, Kenya	France
1986	Zola Budd, England	England			

Notable Achievements

Longest Winning Streaks

MEN

Event	Name and Nationality	Streak	Years
100-meter dash	Bob Hayes, United States	49	1962–64
200-meter dash	Manfred Gemar, Germany	41	1956–60
400-meter run	Michael Johnson, United States	58	1989–97
800-meter run	Mal Whitfield, United States	40	1951–54
1,500-meter run	Josy Barthel, Luxembourg	17	1952
1,500-meter run/mile	Steve Ovett, Great Britain	45	1977–80
Mile	Herb Elliott, Australia	35	1957–60
Steeplechase	Gaston Roelants, Belgium	45	1961–66
5,000-meter run	Emil Zátopek, Czechoslovakia	48	1949–52
10,000-meter run	Emil Zátopek, Czechoslovakia	38	1948–54
Marathon	Frank Shorter, United States	6	1971–73
110-meter hurdles	Jack Davis, United States	44	1952–55
400-meter hurdles	Edwin Moses, United States	107	1977–87
High jump	Ernie Shelton, United States	46	1953–55
Pole vault	Bob Richards, United States	50	1950–52
Long jump	Carl Lewis, United States	65	1981–91
Triple jump	Adhemar da Silva, Brazil	60	1950–56
Shot put	Parry O'Brien, United States	116	1952–56
Discus throw	Ricky Bruch, Sweden	54	1972–73
Hammer throw	Imre Nemeth, Hungary	73	1946–50
Javelin throw	Janis Lusis, USSR	41	1967–70
Decathlon	Bob Mathias, United States	11	1948–56

Longest Winning Streaks (Cont.)

WOMEN

Event	Name and Nationality	Streak	Years
100-meter dash	Merlene Ottey, Jamaica	56	1987–91
200-meter dash	Irena Szewinska, Poland	38	1973–75
400-meter run	Irena Szewinska, Poland	36	1973–78
800-meter run	Ana Fidelia Quirot, Cuba	36	1987–90
1,500-meter run	Paula Ivan, Romania	15	1988–91
1,500-meter run/mile	Paula Ivan, Romania	19	1988–90
3,000-meter run	Mary Slaney, United States	10	1982–84
10,000-meter run	Ingrid Kristiansen, Norway	5	1985–87
Marathon	Katrin Dörre, East Germany	10	1982–86
100-meter hurdles	Annelie Ernhardt, East Germany	44	1972–75
400-meter hurdles	Ann-Louise Skoglund, Sweden	18	1981–83
High jump	Iolanda Balas, Romania	140	1956–67
Long jump	Tatyana Shchelkanova, USSR	19	1964–66
Shot put	Nadezhda Chizhova, USSR	57	1969–73
Discus throw	Gisela Mauermeyer, Germany	65	1935–42
Javelin throw	Ruth Fuchs, East Germany	30	1972–73
Multi	Heide Rosendahl, West Germany	15	1969–72

Most Consecutive Years Ranked No. 1 in the World

MEN

No.	Name and Nationality	Event	Years
11	Sergei Bubka, Ukraine	Pole vault	1984–94
9	Viktor Saneyev, USSR	Triple jump	1968–76
8	Bob Richards, United States	Pole vault	1949–56
8	Ralph Boston, United States	Long jump	1960–67

WOMEN

No.	Name and Nationality	Event	Years
9	Iolanda Balas, Romania	High jump	1958–66
8	Ruth Fuchs, East Germany	Javelin	1972–79
7	Faina Melnick, USSR	Discus throw	1971–77

Major Barrier Breakers

MEN

Event	Mark	Name and Nationality	Date	Site
sub 10-second 100-meter dash	9.95	Jim Hines, United States	Oct. 14, 1968	Mexico City
sub 20-second 200-meter dash	19.83	Tommie Smith, United States	Oct. 16, 1968	Mexico City
sub 45-second 400-meter run	44.9	Otis Davis, United States	Sept. 6, 1960	Rome
sub 1:45 800-meter run	1:44.3	Peter Snell, New Zealand	Feb. 3, 1962	Christchurch, New Zealand
sub four minute mile	3:59.4	Roger Bannister, Great Britain	May 6, 1954	Oxford
sub 3:50 mile	3:49.4	John Walker, New Zealand	Aug. 12, 1975	Göteborg
sub 13-minute 5,000-meter run	12:58.39	Said Aouita, Morocco	July 22, 1986	Rome
sub 27:00 10,000-meter run	26:58.38	Yobes Ondieki, Kenya	July 10, 1993	Oslo
sub 13-second 110-meter hurdles	12.93	Renaldo Nehemiah, United States	Aug. 19, 1981	Zurich
sub 50-second 400-meter hurdles	49.5	Glenn Davis, United States	June 29, 1956	Los Angeles
7' high jump	7' ⅝"	Charles Dumas, United States	June 29, 1956	Los Angeles
8' high jump	8'	Javier Sotomayor, Cuba	July 29, 1989	San Juan
60' triple jump	60' ¼"	Jonathan Edwards, Great Britain	Aug. 7, 1995	Göteborg
20' pole vault	20'	Sergei Bubka, USSR	March 15, 1991	San Sebastian, Spain
70' shot put	70' 7¼"	Randy Matson, United States	May 5, 1965	College Station, Texas
200' discus throw	200' 5"	Al Oerter, United States	May 18, 1962	Los Angeles
300' (new) javelin	300' 1"	Steve Backley, Great Britain	Jan. 25, 1992	Auckland, New Zealand

Major Barrier Breakers *(Cont.)*

WOMEN

Event	Mark	Name and Nationality	Date	Site
sub 11-second 100-meter dash	10.88	Marlies Oelsner, East Germany	July 1, 1977	Dresden
sub 22-second 200-meter dash	21.71	Marita Koch, East Germany	June 10, 1979	Karl Marx Stadt
sub 50-second 400-meter run	49.9	Irena Szewinska, Poland	June 22, 1974	Warsaw
sub 2:00 800-meter run	1:59.1	Shin Geum Dan, North Korea	Nov. 12, 1963	Djakarta
sub 4:00 1,500-meter run	3:56.0	Tatyana Kazankina, USSR	June 28, 1976	Podolsk, USSR
sub 4:20 mile	4:17.55	Mary Decker, United States	Feb. 16, 1980	Houston
sub 15:00 5,000-meter run	14:58.89	Ingrid Kristiansen, Norway	June 28, 1984	Oslo
sub 30:00 10,000-meter run	29:31.78	Wang Junxia, China	Sept. 8, 1993	Beijing
sub 2:30 marathon	2:27:33	Grete Waitz, Norway	Oct. 21, 1979	New York City
sub 13-second 100-meter hurdles	12.9	Karin Balzer, East Germany	Sept. 5, 1969	Berlin
6' high jump	6'	Iolanda Balas, Romania	Oct. 18, 1958	Budapest
70' shot put	70' 4½"	Nadyezhda Chizhova, USSR	Sept. 29, 1973	Varna, Bulgaria
200' discus throw	201'	Liesel Westermann, West Germany	Nov. 5, 1967	Sao Paulo
200' javelin throw	201' 4"	Elvira Ozolina, USSR	Aug. 27, 1964	Kiev
first 7,000-point heptathlon	7,148	Jackie Joyner-Kersee, U.S.	July 6–7, 1986	Moscow

Olympic Accomplishments

Oldest Olympic gold medalist—Patrick (Babe) McDonald, United States, 42 years, 26 days, 56-pound weight throw, 1920.
Oldest Olympic medalist—Tebbs Lloyd Johnson, Great Britain, 48 years, 115 days, 1948 (bronze), 50K walk.
Youngest Olympic gold medalist—Barbara Jones, United States, 15 years 123 days, 1952, 4 x 100 relay.
Youngest gold medalist in individual event—Ulrike Meyfarth, West Germany, 16 years, 123 days, 1972, high jump.

World Record Accomplishments*

Most world records equaled or set in a day—6, Jesse Owens, United States, 5/25/35, (9.4 100-yard dash; 26' 8¼" long jump; 20.3 200-meter dash and 220-yard dash; and 22.6 220-yard hurdles and 200-meter hurdles.
Most records in a year—10, Gunder Hägg, Sweden, 1941–42, 1,500 to 5,000 meters.
Most records in a career—35, Sergei Bubka, 1983–94, pole vault indoors and out.
Longest span of record setting—11 years, 20 days, Irena Szewinska, Poland, 1965–76, 200-meter dash.
Youngest person to set a set world record—Carolina Gisolf, Holland, 15 years, 5 days, 1928, high jump , 5' 3⅜".
Youngest man to set a world record—John Thomas, United States, 17 years, 355 days, 1959, high jump, 7' 1¼".
Oldest person to set world record—Carlos Lopes, Portugal, 38 years, 59 days, marathon, 2:07:12.
Greatest percentage improvement—6.59, Bob Beamon, United States, 1968, long jump.
Longest lasting record—long jump, 26' 8¼", Jesse Owens, United States, 25 years, 79 days (1935-60).
Highest clearance over head, men—23¼", Franklin Jacobs, United States (5' 8"), 1978.
Highest clearance over head, woman—12¾", Yolanda Henry, United States (5' 6"), 1990.

*Marks sanctioned by the IAAF.

Swimming

**World record breaker
Jenny Thompson**

A Jewel of A Pool

The record-filled Pan Pacs dispelled any doubts about the Olympic-readiness of Sydney's International Aquatic Centre

BY MARK BECHTEL

THE LAST thing the good people of Sydney wanted to hear in 1999 was that their state-of-the-art pool, which will host the swimming competition at the Olympics next summer, is, well, boring. But heading into the August 1999 dry run for the Olympics, the Pan Pacific Championships, that's the way things looked. In the nearly five years the Sydney International Aquatic Centre (SIAC) had been open, not a single long-course world record had been set there.

Fears of an Olympic swimming yawnfest were allayed—and then some—at the Pan Pacs, a competition that saw 12 world records set in eight days and made one wonder if the Australians, hoping to generate a little excitement, had sneaked in under the cover of night and shortened the length of the pool.

Of the dozen records to fall, the most venerable was Mary T. Meagher's mark of 57.93 seconds in the 100-meter butterfly, a record that survived for 18 years. While shaving .05 of a second off Meagher's time, Jenny Thompson, of the U.S., sent a mes-sage that come 2000, she'll be a good bet to replace the albatross around her neck with an individual gold medal. The 26-year-old Thompson shares the record for the most Olympic gold medals won by a U.S. woman (5) with speed skater Bonnie Blair, but due largely to a horrible showing in the 1996 Olympic trials, she has never won an individual gold medal at the Games. All of Thompson's triumphs have been as a member of a relay team. In Sydney, she won gold in the 50- and 100-meter freestyles in addition to the 100-meter but-terfly, a performance made even more impressive by the schedule she raced. The Pan Pacs showcased a new format, which will also be used at the Olympics, that required semifinals in all events up to 200 meters, meaning that Thompson had to hit the water 13 times for her four individual and three relay events. "I'm swimming the maximum number of events my body can possibly take so I can see what I'm capable of doing," Thompson said. "Semis definite-ly make it a test of endurance and much more of a strategy game."

The next wave: the 16-year-old Thorpe impressed mightily at the Pan Pacs.

SIMON ALEKNA/AP

Thompson wasn't the only woman keeping the record book editors busy. Penny Heyns, of South Africa, set four records, the most impressive of which was her 2:23.64 in the 200-meter breaststroke finals. "I'm shocked," she said after clipping .78 of a second off her own record. "As much as I tried to convince myself I was relaxed before the race, I was a little nervous." Heyns got off to a tremendous start in the race, which she credited to her modesty and her swimsuit. "It slipped off my bum a little," she said. "I think that scared me. Maybe that's what it was."

Meagher has one record none of the women could touch, however, and that is her 200-meter butterfly mark, which remained standing after the Pan Pacs, and is two years older than the undisputed star of the men's competition in Sydney, Ian Thorpe of Australia. Propelling himself with his size-16 flippers—er, feet—the 16-year-old knocked almost two seconds off the 400-meter freestyle world record with a race that had poolside tongues wagging. "I've been around swimming for 25 years, and I have never seen a swim like that," said former Olympic champ Rowdy Gaines, who is now a TV commentator. "When Thorpe accelerated away at the 250-meter mark, it was like an out-of-body experience."

Thorpe, who also shattered the 200 free world record, gave a performance that will certainly go down as the best by a failed cricket player. His father, Ken, coached a club team and hoped to turn his son into a star. The problem, in the words of Thorpe's sister, Christina, was that "he lacked coordination. He was a fish out of water."

While Thorpe's performance in the 400 generated the loudest buzz, his accomplishment that most pleased his coach came less than an hour later, when he anchored the Aussie's stunning gold medal performance in the 4 x 100 freestyle relay. Thorpe touched the wall .73 of a second ahead of America's Jason Lezak, sending the U.S. to its first-ever defeat in the event in a major competition. "While you recognize the 400 world record as being great," said Australian coach Don Talbot, "to win the relay and topple the Americans is better."

As the pool settled, the SIAC drew rave reviews from the competitors, who praised its ozone-treated water, angled starting blocks, antiwave lane ropes and turbulence-reducing water depth of three meters. "It's an exciting venue to swim at, especially when the crowd gets going," said Thorpe.

Chances are, next time he swims there against a top international field, Thorpe is going to give them even more to cheer about. "The really scary thing about Ian Thorpe is that we all know he's only just starting to scratch the surface," said U.S. men's Olympic coach Mark Schubert. "What we saw here is just the beginning."

1998-99 Major Competitions

Men

U.S. SPRING CHAMPIONSHIPS
Long Island, NY, March 28–April 1, 1999

50 free	Bill Pilczuk, Auburn Aquatics	22.58
100 free	Scott Tucker, Auburn Aquatics	49.69
200 free	Josh Davis, Texas Aquatics	1:49.45
400 free	Chad Carvin, Mission Viejo	3:52.58
800 free	Brendan Neligan, Nassau L.I.	8:11.12
1500 free	Chris Thompson, Michigan	15:14.11
100 back	Lenny Krayzelburg, Trojan S.C.	54.77
200 back	Lenny Krayzelburg, Trojan S.C.	1:56.95*†
100 breast	Ed Moses, Curl-Burke	1:02.28
200 breast	Tom Wilkens, Santa Clara	2:14.54
100 fly	Adam Pine, Nebraska	53.73
200 fly	Ugur Taner, Hillenbrand	1:59.86
200 IM	Tom Wilkens, Santa Clara	2:02.43
400 IM	Tom Wilkens, Santa Clara	4:17.12
400 m relay	Auburn University	3:47.11
400 f relay	Auburn University	3:26.07
800 f relay	Southern Cal A	7:32.25

1-m spgbd	Mark Ruiz, Team Orlando	415.77
3-m spgbd	Mark Ruiz, Team Orlando	649.47
Platform	Mark Ruiz, Team Orlando	642.51
3-m sync dv	Chris Devine/P.J. Bogart	321.78
10-m sync plt	Mark Ruiz/Justin Dumais	319.08

Diving competitions held in Orlando, FL, April 15-18.

FINA SHORT COURSE WORLD CHAMPIONSHIPS
Hong Kong, China, April 1–4, 1999

50 free	Mark Foster, Great Britain	21.81
100 free	Lars Frolander, Sweden	47.05†
200 free	Ian Thorpe, Australia	1:43.28 WR
400 free	Grant Hackett, Australia	3:35.01 WR
1500 free	Grant Hackett, Australia	14:32.87†
50 back	Rodolfo Falcon, Cuba	24.34†
100 back	Rodolfo Falcon, Cuba	52.44†
200 back	Josh Watson, Australia	1:54.67
50 breast	Dmytro Kraevskyy, Ukraine	27.40
100 breast	Patrik Isaksson, Sweden	59.69
200 breast	Philip Rogers, Australia	2:08.72
50 fly	Mark Foster, Great Britain	23.61†
100 fly	Lars Frolander, Sweden	51.45†
200 fly	James Hickman, Great Britain	1:52.71†
100 IM	Jani Sievinen, Finland	54.18†
200 IM	Matthew Dunn, Australia	1:55.81†
400 IM	Matthew Dunn, Australia	4:06.05†
400 m relay	Australia	3:29.88 WR
400 f relay	Australia	3:11.21†
800 f relay	Netherlands	7:04.48

U.S. NATIONAL CHAMPIONSHIPS
Minneapolis, MN, August 6–10, 1999

50 free	Gary Hall Jr	22.13
100 free	Jason Lezak	49.34
200 free	Ugur Taner	1:49.19
400 free	Chad Carvin	3:49.68
800 free	Ryk Neethling	7:59.41
1500 free	Chad Carvin	15:22.85

100 back	Lenny Krayzelburg	54.00†
200 back	Lenny Krayzelburg	1:56.68*
100 breast	Ed Moses	1:01.21†
200 breast	Brendan Hansen	2:16.07
100 fly	Bryan Jones	53.05
200 fly	Ugur Taner	1:58.82
200 IM	Tom Wilkens	2:02.03
400 IM	Robert Margalis	4:19.70
400 m relay	Texas Aquatics	3:41.65
400 f relay	Texas Aquatics	3:17.65
800 f relay	Texas Aquatics	7:26.99

PAN AMERICAN GAMES
Winnipeg, Canada, August 2–7, 1999

50 free	Fernando Scherer, Brazil	22.24
100 free	Fernando Scherer, Brazil	49.19†
200 free	Gustavo Borges, Brazil	1:49.41
400 free	Luiz Limas, Brazil	3:52.25
1500 free	Timothy Siciliano, United States	15:14.94
100 back	Rodolfo Falcon, Cuba	54.93
200 back	Leonardo Costa, Brazil	1:59.33†
100 breast	Ed Moses, United States	1:00.99†
200 breast	Morgan Knabe, Canada	2:14.73†
100 fly	Francisco Sanchez, Venezuela	53.33†
200 fly	Shamek Pietucha, Canada	1:59.10
200 IM	Curtis Myden, Canada	2:02.38
400 IM	Curtis Myden, Canada	4:15.52†
400 m relay	Brazil	3:40.27†
400 f relay	Brazil	3:17.18†
800 f relay	United States	7:22.29
3-m spgbd	Mark Ruiz, United States	675.21
Platform	Fernando Platas, Mexico	649.74

PAN PACIFIC CHAMPIONSHIPS
Sydney, Australia, August 22–29, 1999

50 free	Brendon Dedekind, South Africa	22.06
100 free	Michael Klim, Australia	48.98
200 free	Ian Thorpe, Australia	1:46.00 WR
400 free	Ian Thorpe, Australia	3:41.83 WR
1500 free	Grant Hackett, Australia	14:45.60
100 back	Lenny Krayzelburg, U.S.	53.60 WR
200 back	Lenny Krayzelburg, U.S.	1:55.87 WR
100 breast	Simon Cowley, Australia	1:02.06
200 breast	Simon Cowley, Australia	2:12.98
100 fly	Michael Klim, Australia	52.49
200 fly	Tom Malchow, United States	1:55.41*
200 IM	Tom Wilkins, United States	2:01.01
400 IM	Matthew Dunn, Australia	4:16.54
400 m relay	United States	3:36.37
400 f relay	Australia	3:16.08
800 f relay	Australia	7:08.79 WR

FINA/USA DIVING GRAND PRIX
Ft. Lauderdale, FL, May 6–9, 1999

3-m spgbd	Dmitry Sautin, Russia	702.63
Platform	Huange Qiang, China	698.67
3-m sync dv	Justin Dumais/Troy Dumais, U.S.	315.27
10-m sync plt	Hu Jia/Huang Qiang, China	342.00

*American record. †Meet record. WR World Record

Women

U.S. SPRING CHAMPIONSHIPS
Long Island, NY, March 28–April 1, 1999

50 free	Tammie Spatz, Texas Aquatics	25.60
100 free	Liesl Kolbisen, Hillenbrand	56.28
200 free	Lindsay Benko, Southern Cal	1:59.72
400 free	Diana Munz, Silver Dolphins	4:10.67
800 free	Diana Munz, Silver Dolphins	8:33.03
1500 free	Diana Munz, Silver Dolphins	16:17.96
100 back	Barbara Bedford, Colorado Springs	1:02.07
200 back	Linda Riker, Club Wolverine	2:13.97
100 breast	Megan Quann, Puyallup	1:10.25
200 breast	Madeleine Crippen, Villanova	2:29.73
100 fly	Misty Hyman, unattached	59.63
200 fly	Misty Hyman, unattached	2:10.49
200 IM	Laura Davis, Terrapins	2:16.55
400 IM	Kaitlin Sandeno, NGSV Gators	4:43.37
400 m relay	Southern Cal A	4:14.30
400 f relay	Southern Cal A	3:50.59
800 f relay	Florida A	8:19.84

1-m spgbd	Michelle Rojohn, Ft. Lauderdale	265.65
3-m spgbd	Erica Sorgi, Mission Viejo	530.52
Platform	Erica Sorgi, Mission Viejo	478.92
3-m sync dv	Kathy Pesec/Tracy Bonner	279.57
10-m sync plt.	Kristin Link/Lindsay Long	288.48

Diving competitions held in Orlando, FL, April 15-18.

FINA SHORT COURSE WORLD CHAMPIONSHIPS
Hong Kong, China, April 1–4, 1999

50 free	Inge de Bruijn, Netherlands	24.35
100 free	Jenny Thompson, United States	53.24
200 free	Martina Moravcova, Slovakia	1:56.11
400 free	Nadejda Chemezova, Russia	4:05.23
800 free	Hua Chen, China	8:20.13†
50 back	Sandra Voelker, Germany	27.63
100 back	Mai Nakamura, Japan	58.67
200 back	Mai Nakamura, Japan	2:06.49
50 breast	Masami Tanaka, Japan	30.80
100 breast	Masami Tanaka, Japan	1:06.38
200 breast	Masami Tanaka, Japan	2:24.15 WR
50 fly	Jenny Thompson, United States	21.18
100 fly	Jenny Thompson, United States	57.65†
200 fly	Mette Jacobsen, Denmark	2:06.52
100 IM	Martina Moravcova, Slovakia	1:00.20
200 IM	Martina Moravcova, Slovakia	2:08.55
400 IM	Yana Klochkova, Ukraine	4:32.32
400 m relay	Japan	3:57.62 WR
400 f relay	Great Britain	3:36.88
800 f relay	Sweden	7:51.70 WR

U.S. NATIONAL CHAMPIONSHIPS
Minneapolis, MN, August 6–10, 1999

50 free	Amy Van Dyken	25.13
100 free	Jenny Thompson	54.66
200 free	Jenny Thompson	2:00.19
400 free	Lindsay Benko	4:11.31
800 free	Cristina Teuscher	8:38.68
1500 free	Brooke Bennett	16:14.77
100 back	B.J. Bedford	1:01.89

200 back	Lindsay Benko	2:12.26
100 breast	Megan Quann	1:08.70†
200 breast	Kristen Caverly	2:30.11
100 fly	Jenny Thompson	58.15
200 fly	Misty Hyman	2:10.14
200 IM	Kristine Quance-Julian	2:16.06
400 IM	Kaitlin Sandeno	4:42.92
400 m relay	Irvine Nova	4:12.33
400 f relay	Hillenbrand A	3:47.53
800 f relay	Trojan A	8:13.39

PAN AMERICAN GAMES
Winnipeg, Canada, August 2–7, 1999

50 free	Tammie Spatz, United States	25.50
100 free	Laura Nichols, Canada	56.25
200 free	Jessica DeGlau, Canada	2:00.65
400 free	Kaitlin Sandeno, United States	4:10.74
800 free	Kaitlin Sandeno, United States	8:34.65†
100 back	Kelly Stefanyshyn, Canada	1:02.14
200 back	Denali Knapp, United States	2:12.48†
100 breast	Stacianna Stitts, United States	1:09.16†
200 breast	Lauren Van Oosten, Canada	2:30.36
100 fly	Karen Campbell, United States	1:00.05
200 fly	Jessica Deglau, Canada	2:09.64†
200 IM	Joanne Malar, Canada	2:14.18†
400 IM	Joanne Malar, Canada	4:38.46†
400 m relay	United States	4:06.08†
400 f relay	Canada	3:45.07
800 f relay	Canada	8:05.56†
3-m spgbd	Eryn Bulmer, Canada	530.22
Platform	Emilie Heymans, Canada	550.98

PAN PACIFIC CHAMPIONSHIPS
Sydney, Australia, August 22–29, 1999

50 free	Jenny Thompson, United States	25.51
100 free	Jenny Thompson, United States	54.89
200 free	Susan O'Neill, Australia	1:58.17
400 free	Brooke Bennett, United States	4:08.39
800 free	Brooke Bennett, United States	8:25.06
100 back	Dyana Calub, Australia	1:01.51
	Mai Kakamura, Japan	1:01.51
200 back	Tomoko Hagiwara, Japan	2:11.36
100 breast	Penny Heyns, South Africa	1:07.08
200 breast	Penny Heyns, South Africa	2:23.64 WR
100 fly	Jenny Thompson, U.S.	57.88 WR
200 fly	Susan O'Neill, Australia	2:06.60
200 IM	Joanne Malar, Canada	2:13.63
400 IM	Joanne Malar, Canada	4:40.23
400 m relay	United States	4:03.09
400 f relay	United States	3:41.86
800 f relay	United States	7:57.61*

FINA/USA DIVING GRAND PRIX
Ft. Lauderdale, FL, May 6–9, 1999

3-m spgbd	Fu Mingxia, China	541.05
Platform	Cai Yuyan, China	528.93
3-m sync dv	Liang Xiao Qiao/ Guo Jingjing, China	291.27
10-m sync plt.	Cai Yuyan/Li Na, China	290.01

*American record. †Meet record.

World and American Records Set in 1999

Men

Event	Mark	Record Holder	Date	Site
200 free	1:46.00	Ian Thorpe, Australia (W)	8-24-99	Sydney
400 free	3:41.83	Ian Thorpe, Australia (W)	8-22-99	Sydney
50 back	24.99	Lenny Krayzelburg (W,A)	8-28-99	Sydney
100 back	53.60	Lenny Krayzelburg (W,A)	8-24-99	Sydney
200 back	1:55.87	Lenny Krayzelburg (W,A)	8-27-99	Sydney
200 fly	1:55.41	Tom Malchow (A)	8-25-99	Sydney
800 free relay	7:08.79	Australia (Ian Thorpe, Bill Kirby, Grant Hackett, Michael Klim) (W)	8-25-99	Sydney

Women

Event	Mark	Record Holder	Date	Site
50 back	28.78	Sandra Volker, Germany (W)	6-12-99	Monte Carlo
100 fly	57.88	Jenny Thompson (W,A)	8-23-99	Sydney
50 breast	30.83	Penelope Heyns, South Africa (W)	8-28-99	Sydney
100 breast	1:06.95	Penelope Heyns, South Africa (W)	7-18-99	Los Angeles
200 breast	2:23.64	Penelope Heyns, South Africa (W)	8-27-99	Sydney
800 free relay	7:57.61	United States (Lindsay Benko, Ellen Stonebraker, Jenny Thompson, Cristina Teuscher) (A)	8-26-99	Sydney

The Thorpedo

Australian swimmer Ian Thorpe was bred to be a star athlete on land, not in water. "I had the backyard all laid out and the [practice] nets from where I used to coach," said Thorpe's father, Ken, a former cricketer and club team coach with Bankstown. Ken spoke shortly after Ian had destroyed the world record in the 400-meter freestyle at the Pan Pacific Championships in Sydney in August. "He was going to be a crickey player."

Ian didn't become one, but cricket's loss has been swimming's gain. Thorpe, a 6'4", 212-pound water baby who didn't turn 17 until October, blew the competition out at the Pan Pacific. He followed his 400-meter stunner by motoring through a 200-meter freestyle semifinal in 1:46.34 on Monday, shaving a third of a second off teammate Grant Hackett's five-month-old world mark. In between, less than an hour after he won the 400, he anchored the Aussies' gold medal performance in the 4x100 freestyle relay. It was the first loss ever by a U.S. men's 4x100 free relay team at a major meet.

And Thorpe's 400 performance drew raves as one of the most impressive swims in history. Australian coach Don Talbot, among others, believes that the Thorpedo, as Aussies call Thorpe, could become the best swimmer ever. Midway through the 400, Thorpe was in second place behind Hackett, then he pulled away over the final 200 meters. Thorpe finished in 3:41.83, paring 1.97 seconds off teammate Kieren Perkins's five-year-old record, the largest reduction in the 400 mark since 1980. "The thing I see in Ian that nobody else has is his tremendous acceleration," says Talbot. "He's a Ferrari when he decides he's going to take off."

Though Thorpe is barely old enough to drive, this wasn't his coming-out party. He became the youngest male member of Australia's national team in 41 years when he made the 1997 Pan Pacific squad as a 14-year-old. A year later he became the youngest male world champion when he won the 400 free at the worlds in Perth.

Thorpe pocketed $16,000 after the Pan Pac 400 final for setting the first world record in Sydney's new Olympic pool and immediately donated the money to a local children's cancer charity and a Sydney-based crisis hotline. "I don't need the money," said Thorpe, who already has enough from his Australian sponsors, which include a major bank.

FOR THE RECORD·Year by Year

World and American Records

MEN
Freestyle

Event	Time	Record Holder	Date	Site
50 meters	21.81	Tom Jager (W, A)	3-24-90	Nashville
100 meters	48.21	Aleksandr Popov, Russia (W)	6-18-94	Monte Carlo
	48.42	Matt Biondi (A)	8-8-88	Austin, TX
200 meters	1:46.00	Ian Thorpe, Australia (W)	8-24-99	Sydney
	1:47.72	Matt Biondi (A)	8-8-88	Austin, TX
400 meters	3:41.83	Ian Thorpe, Australia (W)	8-22-99	Sydney
	3:48.06	Matt Cetlinski (A)	8-11-88	Austin, TX
800 meters	7:46.00	Kieran Perkins, Australia (W)	8-24-94	Vancouver, B.C.
	7:52.45	Sean Killion (A)	7-27-87	Clovis, CA
1,500 meters	14:41.66	Kieran Perkins, Australia (W)	8-24-94	Vancouver, B.C.
	15:01.51	George DiCarlo (A)	6-30-84	Indianapolis

Backstroke

Event	Time	Record Holder	Date	Site
50 meters	24.99	Lenny Krayzelburg (W,A)	8-28-99	Sydney
100 meters	53.60	Lenny Krayzelburg (W,A)	8-24-99	Sydney
200 meters	1:55.87	Lenny Krayzelburg (W,A)	8-27-99	Sydney

Breaststroke

Event	Time	Record Holder	Date	Site
100 meters	1:00.60	F. Deburghgraeve, Belgium (W)	7-20-96	Atlanta
	1:00.77	Jeremy Linn (A)	7-20-96	Atlanta
200 meters	2:10.16	Mike Barrowman (W,A)	7-29-92	Barcelona

Butterfly

Event	Time	Record Holder	Date	Site
100 meters	52.15	Michael Klim, Australia (W)	10-9-97	Brisbane, Australia
	52.76	Neil Walker (A)	8-12-97	Fukuoka, Japan
200 meters	1:55.22	Denis Pankratov, Russia (W)	6-14-95	Canet, France
	1:55.41	Tom Malchow (A)	8-25-99	Sydney

Individual Medley

Event	Time	Record Holder	Date	Site
200 meters	1:59.36	Jani Sievinen, Finland (W)	9-11-94	Rome
	2:00.11	Dave Wharton (A)	8-20-89	Tokyo
400 meters	4:12.30	Tom Dolan (W, A)	9-6-94	Rome

Relays

Event	Time	Record Holder	Date	Site
400 meter medley	3:34.84	United States (W, A) (Jeff Rouse, Jeremy Linn, Mark Henderson, Gary Hall Jr)	7-26-96	Atlanta
400 meter freestyle	3:15.11	United States (W, A) (David Fox, Joe Hudepohl, Jon Olsen, Gary Hall Jr)	8-12-95	Atlanta
800 meter freestyle	7:08.79	Australia (W) (Ian Thorpe, Bill Kirby, Grant Hackett, Michael Klim)	8-25-99	Sydney
	7:12.51	United States (A) (Troy Dalbey, Matt Cetlinski, Doug Gjertsen, Matt Biondi)	9-21-88	Seoul

Note: Records through Sept. 15, 1999.

WOMEN

Freestyle

Event	Time	Record Holder	Date	Site
50 meters	24.51	Li Jingyi, China (W)	9-11-94	Rome
	24.87	Amy Van Dyken (A)	7-26-96	Atlanta
100 meters	54.01	Li Jingyi, China (W)	9-5-94	Rome
	54.48	Jenny Thompson (A)	3-1-92	Indianapolis
200 meters	1:56.78	Franziska van Almsick, Germany (W)	9-5-94	Rome
	1:57.90	Nicole Haislett (A)	7-27-90	Barcelona
400 meters	4:03.85	Janet Evans (W, A)	9-22-88	Seoul
800 meters	8:16.22	Janet Evans (W, A)	8-20-89	Tokyo
1500 meters	15:52.10	Janet Evans (W, A)	3-26-88	Orlando, FL

Backstroke

Event	Time	Record Holder	Date	Site
50 meters	28.78	Sandra Volker, Germany (W)	6-12-99	Monte Carlo
100 meters	1:00.16	Cihong He, China (W)	9-10-94	Rome
	1:00.77	Lea Maurer (A)	1-14-98	Perth, Australia
200 meters	2:06.62	Krisztina Egerszegi, Hungary (W)	8-26-91	Athens, Greece
	2:08.60	Betsy Mitchell (A)	6-27-86	Orlando, FL

Breaststroke

Event	Time	Record Holder	Date	Site
50 meters	30.83	Penelope Heyns, South Africa (W)	8-28-99	Sydney
100 meters	1:06.95	Penelope Heyns, South Africa (W)	7-19-99	Los Angeles
	1:08.09	Amanda Beard (A)	7-21-96	Atlanta
200 meters	2:23.64	Penelope Heyns, South Africa (W)	8-27-99	Sydney
	2:25.35	Anita Nall (A)	3-2-92	Indianapolis

Butterfly

Event	Time	Record Holder	Date	Site
50 meters	26.54	Inge de Bruin, Netherlands (W)	6-18-99	Amersfoort, Neth
100 meters	57.88	Jenny Thompson (W,A)	8-23-99	Sydney
200 meters	2:05.96	Mary T. Meagher (W, A)	8-13-81	Brown Deer, WI

Individual Medley

Event	Time	Record Holder	Date	Site
200 meters	2:09.72	Yanyan Wu, China (W)	10-17-97	Shanghai
	2:11.91	Summer Sanders (A)	7-30-92	Barcelona
400 meters	4:34.79	Yan Chen, China (W)	10-17-97	Shanghai
	4:37.58	Summer Sanders (A)	7-26-92	Barcelona

Relays

Event	Time	Record Holder	Date	Site
400 meter medley	4:01.67	China (W) (He Cihong, Dai Guohong, Liu Limin, Le Jingyi)	9-10-94	Rome
	4:01.93	United States (A) (Lea Maurer, Kristy Kowal, Jenny Thompson Amy Van Dyken)	1-16-98	Perth, Australia
400 meter freestyle	3:37.91	China (W) (Le Jingyi, Ying Shan, Le Ying, Lu Bin)	9-7-94	Rome
	3:39.29	United States (A) (Angel Martino, Amy Van Dyken, Catherine Fox, Jenny Thompson)	7-22-96	Atlanta
800 meter freestyle	7:55.47	East Germany (W) (Manuela Stellmach, Astrid Strauss, Anke Mohring, Heike Friedrich)	8-18-87	Strasbourg, France
	7:57.61	United States (A) (Lindsay Benko, Ellen Stonebraker, Jenny Thompson, Cristina Teuscher)	8-26-99	Sydney

World Championships

Venues: Belgrade, Sept 4–9, 1973; Cali, Colombia, July 18–27, 1975; West Berlin, Aug 20–28, 1978; Guayaquil, Equador, Aug 1–7, 1982; Madrid, Aug 17–22, 1986; Perth, Australia, Jan 7–13, 1991; Rome, Sept 1–11, 1994; Perth, Australia, Jan 8–18, 1998.

MEN

50-meter Freestyle

1986	Tom Jager, United States	22.49‡
1991	Tom Jager, United States	22.16‡
1994	Aleksandr Popov, Russia	22.17
1998	Bill Pilczuk, United States	22.29

100-meter Freestyle

1973	Jim Montgomery, United States	51.70
1975	Andy Coan, United States	51.25
1978	David McCagg, United States	50.24
1982	Jorg Woithe, East Germany	50.18
1986	Matt Biondi, United States	48.94
1991	Matt Biondi, United States	49.18
1994	Aleksandr Popov, Russia	49.12
1998	Aleksandr Popov, Russia	48.93‡

200-meter Freestyle

1973	Jim Montgomery, United States	1:53.02
1975	Tim Shaw, United States	1:52.04‡
1978	Billy Forrester, United States	1:51.02‡
1982	Michael Gross, West Germany	1:49.84
1986	Michael Gross, West Germany	1:47.92
1991	Giorgio Lamberti, Italy	1:47.27‡
1994	Antti Kasvio, Finland	1:47.32
1998	Michael Klim, Australia	1:47.41

400-meter Freestyle

1973	Rick DeMont, United States	3:58.18‡
1975	Tim Shaw, United States	3:54.88‡
1978	Vladimir Salnikov, USSR	3:51.94‡
1982	Vladimir Salnikov, USSR	3:51.30‡
1986	Rainer Henkel, West Germany	3:50.05
1991	Joerg Hoffman, Germany	3:48.04‡
1994	Kieran Perkins, Australia	3:43.80*
1998	Ian Thorpe, Australia	3:46.29

1500-meter Freestyle

1973	Stephen Holland, Australia	15:31.85
1975	Tim Shaw, United States	15:28.92‡
1978	Vladimir Salnikov, USSR	15:03.99‡
1982	Vladimir Salnikov, USSR	15:01.77‡
1986	Rainer Henkel, West Germany	15:05.31
1991	Joerg Hoffman, Germany	14:50.36*
1994	Kieran Perkins, Australia	14:50.52
1998	Grant Hackett, Australia	14:51.70

100-meter Backstroke

1973	Roland Matthes, East Germany	57.47
1975	Roland Matthes, East Germany	58.15
1978	Bob Jackson, United States	56.36‡
1982	Dirk Richter, East Germany	55.95
1986	Igor Polianski, USSR	55.58‡
1991	Jeff Rouse, United States	55.23‡
1994	Martin Lopez Zubero, Spain	55.17‡
1998	Lanny Krayzelburg, United States	55.00‡

200-meter Backstroke

1973	Roland Matthes, East Germany	2:01.87‡
1975	Zoltan Varraszto, Hungary	2:05.05
1978	Jesse Vassallo, United States	2:02.16
1982	Rick Carey, United States	2:00.82‡
1986	Igor Polianski, USSR	1:58.78‡
1991	Martin Zubero, Spain	1:59.52
1994	Vladimir Selkov, Russia	1:57.42‡
1998	Lenny Krayzelburg, United States	1:58.84

100-meter Breaststroke

1973	John Hencken, United States	1:04.02‡
1975	David Wilkie, Great Britain	1:04.26‡
1978	Walter Kusch, West Germany	1:03.56‡
1982	Steve Lundquist, United States	1:02.75‡
1986	Victor Davis, Canada	1:02.71
1991	Norbert Rozsa, Hungary	1:01.45*
1994	Norbert Rozsa, Hungary	1:01.24‡
1998	Frederik Deburghgraeve, Belgium	1:01.34

200-meter Breaststroke

1973	David Wilkie, Great Britain	2:19.28‡
1975	David Wilkie, Great Britain	2:18.23‡
1978	Nick Nevid, United States	2:18.37
1982	Victor Davis, Canada	2:14.77*
1986	Jozsef Szabo, Hungary	2:14.27‡
1991	Mike Barrowman, United States	2:11.23*
1994	Norbert Rozsa, Hungary	2:12.81
1998	Kurt Grote, United States	2:13.40

100-meter Butterfly

1973	Bruce Robertson, Canada	55.69
1975	Greg Jagenburg, United States	55.63
1978	Joe Bottom, United States	54.30
1982	Matt Gribble, United States	53.88‡
1986	Pablo Morales, United States	53.54‡
1991	Anthony Nesty, Suriname	53.29‡
1994	Rafal Szukala, Poland	53.51
1998	Michael Klim, Australia	52.25‡

200-meter Butterfly

1973	Robin Backhaus, United States	2:03.32
1975	Bill Forrester, United States	2:01.95‡
1978	Mike Bruner, United States	1:59.38‡
1982	Michael Gross, East Germany	1:58.85‡
1986	Michael Gross, East Germany	1:56.53‡
1991	Melvin Stewart, United States	1:55.69*
1994	Denis Pankratov, Russia	1:56.54
1998	Denys Sylantyev, Ukraine	1:56.61

200-meter Individual Medley

1973	Gunnar Larsson, Sweden	2:08.36
1975	Andras Hargitay, Hungary	2:07.72
1978	Graham Smith, Canada	2:03.65*
1982	Aleksandr Sidorenko, USSR	2:03.30‡
1986	Tamás Darnyi, Hungary	2:01.57‡
1991	Tamás Darnyi, Hungary	1:59.36*
1994	Jani Sievin, Finland	1:58.16*
1998	Marcel Wouda, Netherlands	2:01.18

400-meter Individual Medley

1973	Andras Hargitay, Hungary	4:31.11
1975	Andras Hargitay, Hungary	4:32.57
1978	Jesse Vassallo, United States	4:20.05*
1982	Ricardo Prado, Brazil	4:19.78*
1986	Tamás Darnyi, Hungary	4:18.98‡
1991	Tamás Darnyi, Hungary	4:12.36*
1994	Tom Dolan, United States	4:12.30*
1998	Tom Dolan, United States	4:14.95

* World record. ‡Meet record.

MEN *(Cont.)*

400-meter Medley Relay

1973	United States (Mike Stamm, John Hencken, Joe Bottom, Jim Montgomery)	3:49.49
1975	United States (John Murphy, Rick Colella, Greg Jagenburg, Andy Coan)	3:49.00
1978	United States (Robert Jackson, Nick Nevid, Joe Bottom, David McCagg)	3:44.63
1982	United States (Rick Carey, Steve Lundquist, Matt Gribble, Rowdy Gaines)	3:40.84*
1986	United States (Dan Veatch, David Lundberg, Pablo Morales, Matt Biondi)	3:41.25
1991	United States (Jeff Rouse, Eric Wunderlich, Mark Henderson Matt Biondi)	3:39.66‡
1994	United States (Jeff Rouse, Eric Wunderlich, Mark Henderson, Gary Hall)	3:37.74‡
1998	Australia (Matt Welsh, Phil Rogers, Robin Backhaus, Rick Klatt, Jim Montgomery)	3:37.98

400-meter Freestyle Relay

1973	United States (Mel Nash, Joe Bottom, Jim Montgomery, John Murphy)	3:27.18
1975	United States (Bruce Furniss, Jim Montgomery, Andy Coan, John Murphy)	3:24.85
1978	United States (Jack Babashoff, Rowdy Gaines, Jim Montgomery, David McCagg)	3:19.74
1982	United States (Chris Cavanaugh, Robin Leamy, David McCagg, Rowdy Gaines)	3:19.26*
1986	United States (Tom Jager, Mike Heath, Paul Wallace, Matt Biondi)	3:19.89
1991	United States (Tom Jager, Brent Lang, Doug Gjertsen, Matt Biondi)	3:17.15‡
1994	United States (Jon Olsen, Josh Davis, Ugur Taner, Gary Hall)	3:16.90‡
1998	United States (Bryan Jones, Jon Olsen, Bradley Schumacher, Gary Wayne Jr.)	3:16.69†

800-meter Freestyle Relay

1973	United States (Kurt Krumpholz, Robin Backhaus, Rick Klatt, Jim Montgomery)	7:33.22*
1975	West Germany (Klaus Steinbach, Werner Lampe, Hans Joachim Geisler, Peter Nocke)	7:39.44
1978	United States (Bruce Furniss, Billy Forrester, Bobby Hackett, Rowdy Gaines)	7:20.82
1982	United States (Rich Saeger, Jeff Float, Kyle Miller, Rowdy Gaines)	7:21.09
1986	East Germany (Lars Hinneburg, Thomas Flemming, Dirk Richter, Sven Lodziewski)	7:15.91‡
1991	Germany (Peter Sitt, Steffan Zesner, Stefan Pfeiffer, Michael Gross)	7:13.50‡
1994	Sweden (Christer Waller, Tommy Werner, Lars Frolander, Anders Holmertz)	7:17.34
1998	Australia (Daniel Kowalski, Grant Hackett, Ian Thorpe, Anthony Rogis)	7:12.48†

WOMEN

50-meter Freestyle

1986	Tamara Costache, Romania	25.28*
1991	Zhuang Yong, China	25.47
1994	Le Jingyi, China	24.51*
1998	Amy Van Dyken, United States	25.15

100-meter Freestyle

1973	Kornelia Ender, East Germany	57.54
1975	Kornelia Ender, East Germany	56.50
1978	Barbara Krause, East Germany	55.68‡
1982	Birgit Meineke, East Germany	55.79
1986	Kristin Otto, East Germany	55.05‡
1991	Nicole Haislett, United States	55.17
1994	Le Jingyi, China	54.01*
1998	Jenny Thompson, United States	54.95

200-meter Freestyle

1973	Keena Rothhammer, United States	2:04.99
1975	Shirley Babashoff, United States	2:02.50
1978	Cynthia Woodhead, United States	1:58.53*
1982	Annemarie Verstappen, Netherlands	1:59.53‡
1986	Heike Friedrich, East Germany	1:58.26‡
1991	Hayley Lewis, Australia	2:00.48
1994	Franziska Van Almsick, Germany	1:56.78*
1998	Claudia Poll, Costa Rica	1:58.90

400-meter Freestyle

1973	Heather Greenwood, United States	4:20.28
1975	Shirley Babashoff, United States	4:22.70
1978	Tracey Wickham, Australia	4:06.28*
1982	Carmela Schmidt, East Germany	4:08.98
1986	Heike Friedrich, East Germany	4:07.45
1991	Janet Evans, United States	4:08.63
1994	Yang Aihua, China	4:09.64
1998	Chen Yan, China	4:06.72

* World record; ‡ Meet record.

WOMEN (Cont.)

800-meter Freestyle

1973	Novella Calligaris, Italy	8:52.97
1975	Jenny Turrall, Australia	8:44.75‡
1978	Tracey Wickham, Australia	8:24.94‡
1982	Kim Linehan, United States	8:27.48
1986	Astrid Strauss, East Germany	8:28.24
1991	Janet Evans, United States	8:24.05‡
1994	Janet Evans, United States	8:29.85
1998	Brooke Bennett, United States	8.28.71

100-meter Backstroke

1973	Ulrike Richter, East Germany	1:05.42
1975	Ulrike Richter, East Germany	1:03.30‡
1978	Linda Jezek, United States	1:02.55‡
1982	Kristin Otto, East Germany	1:01.30‡
1986	Betsy Mitchell, United States	1:01.74
1991	Krisztina Egerszegi, Hungary	1:01.78
1994	He Cihong, China	1:00.57
1998	Lea Maurer, United States	1:01.16

200-meter Backstroke

1973	Melissa Belote, United States	2:20.52
1975	Birgit Treiber, East Germany	2:15.46*
1978	Linda Jezek, United States	2:11.93*
1982	Cornelia Sirch, East Germany	2:09.91*
1986	Cornelia Sirch, East Germany	2:11.37
1991	Krisztina Egerszegi, Hungary	2:09.15‡
1994	He Cihong, China	2:07.40
1998	Roxanna Maracineanu, France	2:11.26

100-meter Breaststroke

1973	Renate Vogel, East Germany	1:13.74
1975	Hannalore Anke, East Germany	1:12.72
1978	Julia Bogdanova, USSR	1:10.31*
1982	Ute Geweniger, East Germany	1:09.14‡
1986	Sylvia Gerasch, East Germany	1:08.11*
1991	Linley Frame, Australia	1:08.81
1994	Samantha Riley, Australia	1:07.96*
1998	Kristy Kowal, United States	1:08.42

200-meter Breaststroke

1973	Renate Vogel, East Germany	2:40.01
1975	Hannalore Anke, East Germany	2:37.25‡
1978	Lina Kachushite, USSR	2:31.42*
1982	Svetlana Varganova, USSR	2:28.82‡
1986	Silke Hoerner, East Germany	2:27.40*
1991	Elena Volkova, USSR	2:29.53
1994	Samantha Riley, Australia	2:26.87‡
1998	Agnes Kovacs, Hungary	2:25.45†

100-meter Butterfly

1973	Kornelia Ender, East Germany	1:02.53
1975	Kornelia Ender, East Germany	1:01.24*
1978	Joan Pennington, United States	1:00.20‡
1982	Mary T. Meagher, United States	59.41‡
1986	Kornelia Gressler, East Germany	59.51
1991	Qian Hong, China	59.68
1994	Liu Limin, China	58.98‡
1998	Jenny Thompson, United States	58.46†

200-meter Butterfly

1973	Rosemarie Kother, East Germany	2:13.76‡
1975	Rosemarie Kother, East Germany	2:15.92
1978	Tracy Caulkins, United States	2:09.87*
1982	Ines Geissler, East Germany	2:08.66‡
1986	Mary T. Meagher, United States	2:08.41‡
1991	Summer Sanders, United States	2:09.24
1994	Liu Limin, China	2:07.25‡
1998	Susie O'Neill, Australia	2:07.93†

200-meter Individual Medley

1973	Andrea Huebner, East Germany	2:20.51
1975	Kathy Heddy, United States	2:19.80
1978	Tracy Caulkins, United States	2:14.07*
1982	Petra Schneider, East Germany	2:11.79
1986	Kristin Otto, East Germany	2:15.56
1991	Li Lin, China	2:13.40
1994	Lu Bin, China	2:12.34‡
1998	Wu Yanyan, China	2:10.88

400-meter Individual Medley

1973	Gudrun Wegner, East Germany	4:57.71
1975	Ulrike Tauber, East Germany	4:52.76‡
1978	Tracy Caulkins, United States	4:40.83*
1982	Petra Schneider, East Germany	4:36.10*
1986	Kathleen Nord, East Germany	4:43.75
1991	Lin Li, China	4:41.45
1994	Dai Guohong, China	4:39.14
1998	Chen Yan, China	4:36.66

400-meter Medley Relay

1973	East Germany (Ulrike Richter, Renate Vogel, Rosemarie Kother, Kornelia Ender)	4:16.84
1975	East Germany (Ulrike Richter, Hannelore Anke, Rosemarie Kother, Kornelia Ender)	4:14.74
1978	United States (Linda Jezek, Tracy Caulkins, Joan Pennington, Cynthia Woodhead)	4:08.21‡
1982	East Germany (Kristin Otto, Ute Gewinger, Ines Geissler, Birgit Meineke)	4:05.8*
1986	East Germany (Kathrin Zimmermann, Sylvia Gerasch, Kornelia Gressler, Kristin Otto)	4:04.82
1991	United States (Janie Wagstaff, Tracey McFarlane, Crissy Ahmann-Leighton, Nicole Haislett)	4:06.51
1994	China (He Cihong, Dai Guohong, Liu Limin, Lu Bin)	4:01.67*
1998	United States (Kristy Kowal, Lea Maurer, Jenny Thompson, Amy Van Dyken)	4:01.93

400-meter Freestyle Relay

1973	East Germany (Kornelia Ender, Andrea Eife, Andrea Huebner, Sylvia Eichner)	3:52.45
1975	East Germany (Kornelia Ender, Barbara Krause, Claudia Hempel, Ute Bruckner)	3:49.37
1978	United States (Tracy Caulkins, Stephanie Elkins, Joan Pennington, Cynthia Woodhead)	3:43.43*

WOMEN (Cont.)

400-meter Freestyle Relay (Cont.)

1982....East Germany (Birgit Meineke, 3:43.97
Susanne Link, Kristin Otto,
Caren Metschuk)

1986....East Germany (Kristin Otto, 3:40.57*
Manuela Stellmach, Sabine
Schulze, Heike Friedrich)

1991....United States (Nicole Haislett, 3:43.26
Julie Cooper, Whitney Hedgepeth,
Jenny Thompson)

1994....China (Le Jingyi, Ying Shan, 3:37.91*
Le Ying, Lu Bin)

1998....United States (Catherine Fox, 3:42.11
Lindsey Farella, Melanie Valerio,
B.J. Bedford)

800-meter Freestyle Relay

1986....East Germany (Manuela 7:59.33*
Stellmach, Astrid Strauss,
Nadja Bergknecht, Heike Friedrich)

1991....Germany (Kerstin Kielgass, 8:02.56
Manuela Stellmach, Dagmar Hase,
Stephanie Ortwig)

1994....China (Le Ying, Yang Alhua, 7:57.96
Zhou Guabin, Lu Bin)

1998....Germany (Silvia Szalai, Antje 8:02.56
Buschschulte, Janina Goetz,
Franziska Van Almsick)

* World record; ‡Meet record.

World Diving Championships

MEN

1-meter Springboard

		Pts
1991	Edwin Jongejans, Netherlands	588.51
1994	Evan Stewart, Zimbabwe	382.14
1998	Yu Zhuocheng, China	417.54

3-meter Springboard

		Pts
1973	Phil Boggs, United States	618.57
1975	Phil Boggs, United States	597.12
1978	Phil Boggs, United States	913.95
1982	Greg Louganis, United States	752.67
1986	Greg Louganis, United States	750.06
1991	Kent Ferguson, United States	650.25
1994	Wu Zhuocheng, China	655.44
1998	Dmitry Sautin, Russia	746.79

Platform

		Pts
1973	Klaus Dibiasi, Italy	559.53
1975	Klaus Dibiasi, Italy	547.98
1978	Greg Louganis, United States	844.11
1982	Greg Louganis, United States	634.26
1986	Greg Louganis, United States	668.58
1991	Sun Shuwei, China	626.79
1994	Dmitry Sautin, Russia	634.71
1998	Dmitry Sautin, Russia	750.90

3-meter Synchronized

		Pts
1998	China (Sun Shuwei, Tian Liang)	313.50

10-meter Synchronized

		Pts
1998	China (Xu Hao, Yu Zhuocheng)	326.34

WOMEN

1-meter Springboard

		Pts
1991	Gao Min, China	478.26
1994	Chen Lixia, China	279.30
1998	Irina Lashko, Russia	296.07

3-meter Springboard

		Pts
1973	Christa Koehler, East Germany	442.17
1975	Irina Kalinina, USSR	489.81
1978	Irina Kalinina, USSR	691.43
1982	Megan Neyer, United States	501.03
1986	Gao Min, China	582.90
1991	Gao Min, China	539.01
1994	Tan Shuping, China	548.49
1998	Yulia Pakhalina, Russia	544.62

Platform

		Pts
1973	Ulrike Knape, Sweden	406.77
1975	Janet Ely, United States	403.89
1978	Irina Kalinina, USSR	412.71
1982	Wendy Wyland, United States	438.79
1986	Chen Lin, China	449.67
1991	Fu Mingxia, China	426.51
1994	Fu Mingxia, China	434.04
1998	Olena Zhupyna, Ukraine	550.41

3-meter Synchronized

		Pts
1998	Russia (Irina Lashko, Yulia Pakhalina)	282.30

10-meter Synchronized

		Pts
1998	Ukraine (Olena Zhupyna, Svitlana Serbina)	278.28

U.S. Olympic Champions

Men

50-METER FREESTYLE

1988	Matt Biondi	22.14*

100-METER FREESTLYE

1906	Charles Daniels	1:13.4
1908	Charles Daniels	1:05.6*
1912	Duke Kahanamoku	1:03.4
1920	Duke Kahanamoku	1:00.4
1924	John Weissmuller	59.0‡
1928	John Weissmuller	58.6‡
1948	Wally Ris	57.3‡
1952	Clarke Scholes	57.4
1964	Don Schollander	53.4‡
1972	Mark Spitz	51.22*
1976	Jim Montgomery	49.99*
1984	Rowdy Gaines	49.80‡
1988	Matt Biondi	48.63‡

200-METER FREESTYLE

1904	Charles Daniels	2:44.2
1906	Not held 1906–1964	
1972	Mark Spitz	1:52.78*
1976	Bruce Furniss	1:50.29*

400-METER FREESTYLE

1904	Charles Daniels (440 yds)	6:16.2
1920	Norman Ross	5:26.8
1924	John Weissmuller	5:04.2‡
1932	Buster Crabbe	4:48.4‡
1936	Jack Medica	4:44.5‡
1948	William Smith	4:41.0‡
1964	Don Schollander	4:12.2*
1968	Mike Burton	4:09.0‡
1976	Brian Goodell	3:51.93*
1984	George DiCarlo	3:51.23‡

1500-METER FREESTYLE

1920	Norman Ross	22:23.2
1948	James McLane	19:18.5
1952	Ford Konno	18:30.3‡
1968	Mike Burton	16:38.9‡
1972	Mike Burton	15:52.58‡
1976	Brian Goodell	15:02.40*
1984	Michael O'Brien	15:05.20

100-METER BACKSTROKE

1912	Harry Hebner	1:21.2
1920	Warren Kealoha	1:15.2
1924	Warren Kealoha	1:13.2‡
1928	George Kojac	1:08.2*
1936	Adolph Kiefer	1:05.9‡
1948	Allen Stack	1:06.4
1952	Yoshi Oyakawa	1:05.4‡
1976	John Naber	55.49*
1984	Rick Carey	55.79
1996	Jeff Rouse	54.10

200-METER BACKSTROKE

1964	Jed Graef	2:10.3*
1976	John Naber	1:59.19*
1984	Rick Carey	2:00.23
1996	Brad Bridgewater	1:58.54

100-METER BREASTSTROKE

1968	Donald McKenzie	1:07.7‡
1976	John Hencken	1:03.11*
1984	Steve Lundquist	1:01.65 *
1992	Nelson Diebel	1:01.50‡

200-METER BREASTSTROKE

1924	Robert Skelton	2:56.6
1948	Joseph Verdeur	2:39.3‡
1960	William Mulliken	2:37.4
1972	John Hencken	2:21.55
1992	Mike Barrowman	2:10.16*

100-METER BUTTERFLY

1968	Douglas Russell	55.9‡
1972	Mark Spitz	54.27*
1976	Matt Vogel	54.35
1992	Pablo Morales	53.32

200-METER BUTTERFLY

1956	William Yorzyk	2:19.3‡
1960	Michael Troy	2:12.8*
1968	Carl Robie	2:08.7
1972	Mark Spitz	2:00.70*
1976	Mike Bruner	1:59.23*
1992	Melvin Stewart	1:56.26

200-METER INDIVIDUAL MEDLEY

1968	Charles Hickcox	2:12.0‡

400-METER INDIVIDUAL MEDLEY

1964	Richard Roth	4:45.4*
1968	Charles Hickcox	4:48.4
1976	Rod Strachan	4:23.68*
1996	Tom Dolan	4.:14.90

3-METER SPRINGBOARD DIVING

1920	Louis Kuehn	675.4 points
1924	Albert White	696.4
1928	Pete Desjardins	185.04
1932	Michael Galitzen	161.38
1936	Richard Degener	163.57
1948	Bruce Harlan	163.64
1952	David Browning	205.29
1956	Robert Clotworthy	159.56
1960	Gary Tobian	170.00
1964	Kenneth Sitzberger	159.90
1968	Bernard Wrightson	170.15
1976	Philip Boggs	619.05
1984	Greg Louganis	754.41
1988	Greg Louganis	730.80

PLATFORM DIVING

1904	George Sheldon	12.66 points
1920	Clarence Pinkston	100.67
1924	Albert White	97.46
1928	Pete Desjardins	98.74
1932	Harold Smith	124.80
1936	Marshall Wayne	113.58
1948	Sammy Lee	130.05
1952	Sammy Lee	156.28
1960	Robert Webster	165.56
1964	Robert Webster	148.58
1984	Greg Louganis	576.99
1988	Greg Louganis	638.61

* World record. ‡ Meet (Olympic) record.

Women

50-METER FREESTYLE

1996	Amy Van Dyken	24.87

100-METER FREESTLYE

1920	Ethelda Bleibtrey	1:13.6*
1924	Ethel Lackie	1:12.4
1928	Albina Osipowich	1:11.0‡
1932	Helene Madison	1:06.8‡
1968	Jan Henne	1:00.0
1972	Sandra Neilson	58.59‡
1984	Carrie Steinseifer	55.92
	Nancy Hogshead	55.92

200-METER FREESTYLE

1968	Debbie Meyer	2:10.5‡
1984	Mary Wayte	1:59.23
1992	Nicole Haislett	1:57.90

400-METER FREESTYLE

1924	Martha Norelius	6:02.2‡
1928	Martha Norelius	5:42.8*
1932	Helene Madison	5:28.5*
1948	Ann Curtis	5:17.8‡
1960	Chris von Saltza	4:50.6
1964	Virginia Duenkel	4:43.3‡
1968	Debbie Meyer	4:31.8‡
1984	Tiffany Cohen	4:07.10‡
1988	Janet Evans	4:03.85*

800-METER FREESTYLE

1968	Debbie Meyer	9:24.0‡
1972	Keena Rothhammer	8:53.86*
1984	Tiffany Cohen	8:24.95‡
1988	Janet Evans	8:20.20‡
1992	Janet Evans	8:25.52
1996	Brooke Bennett	8:27.89

100-METER BACKSTROKE

1924	Sybil Bauer	1:23.2‡
1932	Eleanor Holm	1:19.4
1960	Lynn Burke	1:09.3‡
1964	Cathy Ferguson	1:07.7*
1968	Kaye Hall	1:06.2*
1972	Melissa Belote	1:05.78‡
1984	Theresa Andrews	1:02.55
1996	Beth Botsford	1:01.19

200-METER BACKSTROKE

1968	Pokey Watson	2:24.8‡
1972	Melissa Belote	2:19.19*

* World record; ‡Meet (Olympic) record.

100-METER BREASTSTROKE

1972	Catherine Carr	1:13.58*

200-METER BREASTSTROKE

1968	Sharon Wichman	2:44.4‡

100-METER BUTTERFLY

1956	Shelley Mann	1:11.0‡
1960	Carolyn Schuler	1:09.5‡
1964	Sharon Stouder	1:04.7*
1984	Mary T. Meagher	59.26
1996	Amy Van Dyken	59.13

200-METER BUTTERFLY

1972	Karen Moe	2:15.57*
1984	Mary T. Meagher	2:06.90‡
1992	Summer Sanders	2:08.67

200-METER INDIVIDUAL MEDLEY

1968	Sharon Wichman	2:44.4‡
1984	Tracy Caulkins	2:12.64‡

400-METER INDIVIDUAL MEDLEY

1964	Donna De Varona	5:18.7‡
1968	Claudia Kolb	5:08.5‡
1984	Tracy Caulkins	4:39.24
1988	Janet Evans	4:37.76

3-METER SPRINGBOARD DIVING

1920	Aileen Riggin	539.9 points
1924	Elizabeth Becker	474.5
1928	Helen Meany	78.62
1932	Georgia Coleman	87.52
1936	Marjorie Gestring	89.27
1948	Victoria Draves	108.74
1952	Patricia McCormick	147.30
1956	Patricia McCormick	142.36
1968	Sue Gossick	150.77
1972	Micki King	450.03
1976	Jennifer Chandler	506.19

PLATFORM DIVING

1924	Caroline Smith	33.2 points
1928	Elizabeth Becker Pinkston	31.6
1932	Dorothy Poynton	40.26
1936	Dorothy Poynton Hill	33.93
1948	Victoria Draves	68.87
1952	Patricia McCormick	79.37
1956	Patricia McCormick	84.85
1964	Lesley Bush	99.80

Notable Achievements

Barrier Breakers

MEN

Event	Barrier	Athlete and Nation	Time	Date
100 Freestyle	1:00	Johnny Weissmuller, United States	58.6	7-9-22
100 Freestyle	:50	James Montgomery, United States	49.99	7-25-76
200 Freestyle	2:00	Don Schollander, United States	1:58.8	7-27-63
200 Freestyle	1:50	Sergei Kopliakov, USSR	1:49.83	4-7-79
400 Freestyle	4:00	Rick DeMont, United States	3:58.18	9-6-73
400 Freestyle	3:50	Vladimir Salnikov, USSR	3:49.57	3-12-82
800 Freestyle	8:00	Vladimir Salnikov, USSR	7:56.49	3-23-79
1500 Freestyle	15:00	Vladimir Salnikov, USSR	14:58.27	7-22-80
100 Backstroke	1:00	Thompson Mann, United States	59.6	10-16-64
200 Backstroke	2:00	John Naber, United States	1:59.19	7-24-76
200 Breaststroke	2:30	Chester Jastremski, United States	2:29.6	8-19-61
100 Butterfly	1:00	Lance Larson, United States	59.0	6-29-60
200 Butterfly	2:00	Roger Pyttel, East Germany	1:59.63	6-3-76

WOMEN

Event	Barrier	Athlete and Nation	Time	Date
100 Freestyle	1:00	Dawn Fraser, Australia	59.9	10-27-62
200 Freestyle	2:00	Kornelia Ender, East Germany	1:59.78	6-2-76
400 Freestyle	4:30	Debbie Meyer, United States	4:29.0	8-18-67
800 Freestyle	10:00	Jane Cederqvist, Sweden	9:55.6	8-17-60
800 Freestyle	9:00	Ann Simmons, United States	8:59.4	9-10-71
1500 Freestyle	20:00	Ilsa Konrads, Australia	19:25.7	1-14-60
	16:00	Janet Evans, United States	15:52.10	3-26-88
200 Backstroke	2:30	Satoko Tanaka, Japan	2:29.6	2-10-63
100 Butterfly	1:00	Christiane Knacke, East Germany	59.78	8-28-77
400 Individual Medley	5:00	Gudrun Wegner, East Germany	4:57.51	9-6-73

Olympic Achievements

MOST INDIVIDUAL GOLDS IN SINGLE OLYMPICS

MEN

No.	Athlete and Nation	Olympic Year	Events
4	Mark Spitz, United States	1972	100, 200 Free; 100, 200 Fly

WOMEN

No.	Athlete and Nation	Olympic Year	Events
4	Kristin Otto, East Germany	1988	50, 100 Free; 100 Back; 100 Fly
3	Debbie Meyer, United States	1968	200, 400, 800 Free
3	Shane Gould, Australia	1972	200, 400 Free; 200 IM
3	Kornelia Ender, East Germany	1976	100, 200 Free; 100 Fly
3	Janet Evans, United States	1988	400, 800 Free; 400 IM
3	Krisztina Egerszegi, Hungary	1992	100, 200 Back; 400 IM
3	Michelle Smith, Ireland	1996	400 Free; 200, 400 IM

Olympic Achievements *(Cont.)*

MOST INDIVIDUAL OLYMPIC GOLD MEDALS, CAREER

MEN

No.	Athlete and Nation	Olympic Years and Events
4	Charles Meldrum Daniels, United States	1904 (220, 440 Free); 1906 (100 Free) 1908 (100 Free)
4	Roland Matthes, East Germany	1968 (100, 200 Back); 1972 (100, 200 Back)
4	Mark Spitz, United States	1972 (100, 200 Free; 100, 200 Fly)

WOMEN

No.		
4	Kristin Otto, East Germany	1988 (50 Free; 100 Free, Back and Fly)
4	Janet Evans, United States	1988 (400, 800 Free; 400 IM); 1992 (800 Free)
4	Krisztina Egerszegi, Hungary	1992 (100, 200 Back; 400 IM); 1996 (200 Back)

Most Olympic Gold Medals in a Single Olympics, Men—7, Mark Spitz, United States, 1972: 100, 200 Free; 100, 200 Fly; 4 x 100, 4 x 200 Free Relays; 4 x 100 Medley Relay.
Most Olympic Gold Medals in a Single Olympics, Women—6, Kristin Otto, East Germany, 1988: 50, 100 Free; 100 Back; 100 Fly; 4 x 100 Free Relay; 4 x 100 Medley Relay.
Most Olympic Medals in a Career, Men—11, Matt Biondi, United States: 1984 (one gold), '88 (five gold, one silver, one bronze), '92 (two gold, one silver); 11, Mark Spitz, United States: 1968 (two gold, one silver, one bronze), '72 (seven gold).
Most Olympic Medals in a Career, Women—8, Dawn Fraser, Australia: 1956 (two gold, one silver), '60 (one gold, two silver), '64 (one gold, one silver) 8, Kornelia Ender, East Germany: 1972 (three silver), '76 (four gold, one silver); 8, Shirley Babashoff, United States: 1972 (one gold, two silver); '76 (one gold, four silver).
Winner, Same Event, Three Consecutive Olympics—Dawn Fraser, Australia, 100 Freestyle, 1956, '60, '64; Krisztina Egerszegi, Hungary, 200 Back, 1988, '92, '96.
Youngest Person to Win an Olympic Diving Gold—Marjorie Gestring, United States, 1936, 13 years, 9 months, springboard diving.
Youngest Person to Win an Olympic Swimming Gold—Krisztina Egerszegi, Hungary, 1988, 14 years, one month, 200 backstroke.
Most World Records, Career, Women—42, Ragnhild Hveger, Denmark, 1936–42.

World Record Achievements

Most World Records, Career, Men—32, Arne Borg, Sweden, 1921–29.
Most Freestyle Records Held Concurrently—5, Helene Madison, United States, 1931–33; 5, Shane Gould, Australia, 1972.
Most Consecutive Lowerings of a Record—10, Kornelia Ender, East Germany, 100 Freestyle, 7-13-73 to 7-19-76.
Longest Duration of World Record—19 years, 359 days, 1:04.6 in 100 Free, Willy den Ouden, Netherlands.

Skiing

World downhill
champion Hermann
Maier of Austria

High and Tight

The men's overall title came down to the last race of the year, atop Sierra Nevada

BY MARK BECHTEL

IF ONE RACE neatly summed up the 1999 men's World Cup season it was the Super G at the world championships in early February. Under a sunny, bright-blue Colorado sky, Hermann Maier of Austria stood at the bottom of the Birds of Prey course in Beaver Creek and watched Norwegian Lasse Kjus come barreling down the hill. On one occasion Kjus nearly lost it, yet when he crossed the finish line a "1" popped up next to his name. When Maier, who had turned in the day's fastest time on his run, saw the result, he kicked the snow and let out a snort of disgust. Then he took a closer look at Kjus's time—1:14.53—and realized that it looked awfully familiar. In fact, it was identical to his own time, meaning that for the first time in the 75-year history of the International Ski Federation, two skiers would share the gold medal podium at a world championships.

As the season wound down, the race for the World Cup overall championship remained as tight as that Super G. Kjus, who won an unprecedented five medals at the worlds, nursed a slim lead over countryman Kjetil Andre Aamodt and Maier, the 1998 World Cup overall champ. Maier would win the Super G season title but was eliminated from contention in the overall when he finished 16th in the season's penultimate race. Aamodt came in second, which pulled him within a scant 32 points of Kjus as the pair prepared for the final event of the season, the giant slalom in Sierra Nevada, Spain.

That Kjus and Aamodt would be the last men standing was something of a surprise. Each had won a World Cup overall title before, but Aamodt had won his back in 1994 and Kjus had finished no better than 10th in the overall standings since winning the '96 championship—a victory that had been overshadowed by Alberto Tomba's Olympic heroics. The smart money coming into the season was on the upstart Maier, who despite being born the year after the 28-year-old Norwegians, had six fewer years of World Cup experience. In 1998 the late

To everyone's surprise, three-time Olympic champ Seizinger called it quits.

bloomer won 10 races and two Olympic gold medals, was dubbed "The Hermannator" and coasted to the overall title—a crown that looked to be his for years to come.

But the '99 championship race would finally come down to Kjus and Aamodt, who were as close in life as they were in the standings. For 10 years they were roommates on the World Cup circuit, and they had been best friends since childhood. Aamodt's father was Kjus's first coach. Even in the tensest of situations, the two could joke with each other. Kjus said that his strategy was "to pay someone to bang all night on Kjetil's door" the night before the race, and after each skier's first trip down the hill, it looked like that wouldn't have been a bad idea. Aamodt was in fifth place, while Kjus languished in 15th, in danger of not receiving any points for the race.

On the second leg, though, Kjus produced a brilliant run when he needed it most. His time of 59.82 was the second fastest of the day and vaulted him into seventh place, good enough to hold off Aamodt by 23 points. "This has been a dream winter," Kjus said. "It has been a tough week. Kjetil put great pressure on me. I hope we remain friends for many more years."

While the men's circuit had one of its tightest races ever, the women's tour was dominated by Alexandra Meissnitzer of Austria, who won the giant slalom and Super G championships in addition to taking the overall crown by a whopping 477 points. Meissnitzer had won two medals at Nagano in '98 and looked primed to challenge

defending world overall champ Katja Seizinger in '99, but in the off-season Seizinger tore ligaments in her knee while training and missed the entire season. In late April the 26-year-old German shocked the skiing community by announcing that she would abandon her comeback and hang up her skis for good. "My decision has nothing to do with my injury," Seizinger said. "I have no problems with my knees anymore. It's just that I've got other goals for myself now."

Seizinger wasn't the only big name absent from the women's circuit. America's Picabo Street sat out the year to recover from a horrific crash in the last downhill of '98, and in her absence the U.S. team struggled. Its only bona fide medal contender at the world championships, Kristina Koznick, straddled a gate 16 seconds into her run in the slalom, her best event. American Chad Fleischer finished second in the season's final downhill, but on the whole it was a forgettable season for the U.S. "What we are missing with this generation of athletes is confidence," said U.S. women's coach Marjan Cernigoj. "They train well, but they seem to be scared of the race." With Meissnitzer, Kjus, Aamodt and Maier on the slopes, it's hard to blame them.

World Cup Alpine Racing Season Results

Men

Date	Event	Site	Winner
10-25-98	Giant Slalom	Sölden, Austria	Hermann Maier, Austria
11-20-98	Giant Slalom	Park City, Utah	Stefan Eberharter, Austria
11-22-98	Slalom	Park City, Utah	Pierrick Bourgeat, France
11-27-98	Super G	Aspen, Colorado	Stefan Eberharter, Austria
11-28-98	Slalom	Aspen, Colorado	Thomas Stangassinger, Austria
12-12-98	Downhill	Val d'Isère, France	Lasse Kjus, Norway
12-14-98	Super G	Val d'Isère, France	Hermann Maier, Austria
12-14-98	Night Slalom	Sestriere, Italy	Finn Christian Jagge, Norway
12-18-98	Downhill	Val Gardena, Italy	Lasse Kjus, Norway
12-19-98	Downhill	Val Gardena, Italy	Kristian Ghedina, Italy
12-20-98	Giant Slalom	Alta Badia, Italy	Michael von Grünigen, Switz
12-21-98	Super G	Innsbruck, Austria	Hermann Maier, Austria
12-29-98	Downhill	Bormio, Italy	Hermann Maier, Austria
1-5-99	Giant Slalom	Kranjska Gora, Slovenia	Patrick Holzer, Italy
1-6-99	Slalom	Kranjska Gora, Slovenia	Jure Kosir, Slovenia
1-7-99	Night Slalom	Schladming, Austria	Benjamin Raich, Austria
1-9-99	Super G	Schladming, Austria	Hermann Maier, Austria
1-10-99	Giant Slalom	Flachau, Austria	Benjamin Raich, Austria
1-12-99	Giant Slalom	Adelboden, Switzerland	Hermann Maier, Austria
1-16-99	Downhill	Wengen, Switzerland	Lasse Kjus, Norway
1-17-99	Slalom	Wengen, Switzerland	Benjamin Raich, Austria
1-16/17-99	Combined	Wengen, Switzerland	Lasse Kjus, Norway
1-22-99	Sprint Downhill	Kitzbühel, Austria	Lasse Kjus, Norway
1-23-99	Downhill	Kitzbühel, Austria	Hans Knauss, Austria
1-24-99	Slalom	Kitzbühel, Austria	Jure Kosir, Slovenia
1-23/24-99	Combined	Kitzbühel, Austria	Kjetil André Aamodt, Norway
2-27-99	Giant Slalom	Ofterschwang, Germany	Stefan Eberharter, Austria
2-28-99	Slalom	Ofterschwang, Germany	Finn Christian Jagge, Norway
3-6-99	Downhill	Kvitfjell, Norway	Andreas Schifferer, Austria
3-7-99	Super G	Kvitfjell, Norway	Hermann Maier, Austria
3-10-99	Downhill	Sierra Nevada, Spain	Lasse Kjus, Norway
3-11-99	Super G	Sierra Nevada, Spain	Christian Mayer, Austria
3-13-99	Slalom	Sierra Nevada, Spain	Thomas Stangassinger, Austria
3-14-99	Giant Slalom	Sierra Nevada, Spain	Michael von Grünigen, Switz

Women

Date	Event	Site	Winner
10-24-98	Giant Slalom	Sölden, Austria	Andrine Flemmen, Norway
11-19-98	Giant Slalom	Park City, Utah	Alexandra Meissnitzer, Austria
11-21-98	Slalom	Park City, Utah	Urska Hrovat, Slovenia
11-27-98	Downhill	Lake Louise, Alberta	Renate Götschl, Austria
11-28-98	Downhill	Lake Louise, Alberta	Renate Götschl, Austria
11-29-98	Super G	Lake Louise, Alberta	Alexandra Meissnitzer, Austria
12-3-98	Slalom	Mammoth Mountain, California	Anja Paerson, Sweden
12-4-98	Super G	Mammoth Mountain, California	Christiane Mitterwallner, Austria
12-10-98	Super G	Val d'Isère, France	Alexandra Meissnitzer, Austria
12-11-98	Giant Slalom	Val d'Isère, France	Alexandra Meissnitzer, Austria
12-18-98	Downhill	Veysonnaz, Switzerland	Hilde Gerg, Germany
12-19-98	Downhill	Veysonnaz, Switzerland	Alexandra Meissnitzer, Austria
12-20-98	Slalom	Veysonnaz, Switzerland	Karin Roten, Switzerland
12-27-98	Giant Slalom	Semmering, Austria	Anita Wachter, Austria
12-28-98	Slalom	Semmering, Austria	Kristina Koznick, United States
1-1-99	Super G	Maribor, Slovenia	Hilde Gerg, Germany
1-2-99	Giant Slalom	Maribor, Slovenia	Anita Wachter, Austria
1-3-99	Slalom	Maribor, Slovenia	Pernilla Wiberg, Sweden
1-8-99	Slalom	Berchtesgaden, Germany	Sabine Egger, Austria
1-15-99	Downhill	St. Anton, Austria	Corinne Rey Bellet, Switzerland
1-16-99	Super G	St. Anton, Austria	Corinne Rey Bellet, Switzerland
1-17-99	Slalom	St. Anton, Austria	Trine Bakke, Norway
1-21-99	Downhill	Cortina d'Ampezzo, Italy	Regine Cavagnoud, France
1-22-99	Super G	Cortina d'Ampezzo, Italy	Renate Götschl, Austria

Women *(Cont.)*

Date	Event	Site	Winner
1-23-99	Super G	Cortina d'Ampezzo, Italy	Regine Cavagnoud, France
1-24-99	Giant Slalom	Cortina d'Ampezzo, Italy	Alexandra Meissnitzer, Austria
2-22-99	Giant Slalom	Are, Sweden	Alexandra Meissnitzer, Austria
2-23-99	Slalom	Are, Sweden	Spela Pretnar, Slovenia
2-24-99	Giant Slalom	Are, Sweden	Anita Wachter, Austria
2-27-99	Downhill	Are, Sweden	Renate Götschl, Austria
3-5-99	Downhill	St. Moritz, Switzerland	Renate Götschl, Austria
3-6-99	Super G	St. Moritz, Switzerland	Michaela Dorfmeister, Austria
3-10-99	Downhill	Sierra Nevada, Spain	Alexandra Meissnitzer, Austria
3-13-99	Giant Slalom	Sierra Nevada, Spain	Anita Wachter, Austria

World Cup Alpine Racing Final Standings

Men

OVERALL

	Pts
Lasse Kjus, Norway	1465
Kjetil André Aamodt, Norway	1442
Hermann Maier, Austria	1307
Stefan Eberharter, Austria	1079
Hans Knauss, Austria	913
Andreas Schifferer, Austria	901
Christian Mayer, Austria	766
Michael von Grünigen, Switz.	705
Werner Franz, Austria	614
Benjamin Raich, Austria	575

SLALOM

	Pts
Thomas Stangassinger, Aust.	466
Jure Kosir, Slovenia	391
Pierrick Bourgeat, France	366
Finn Christian Jagge, Norway	360
Kjetil André Aamodt, Norway	283
Sebastien Amiez, France	283
Benjamin Raich, Austria	260
Michael von Grünigen, Switz.	222
Tom Stiansen, Norway	187
Didier Plaschy, Switzerland	182

SUPER G

	Pts
Hermann Maier, Austria	480
Stefan Eberharter, Austria	310
Rainer Salzgeber, Austria	212
Hans Knauss, Austria	211
Andreas Schifferer, Austria	182
Kjetil André Aamodt, Norway	167
Lasse Kjus, Norway	158
Fritz Strobl, Austria	152
Christian Mayer, Austria	152
Paul Accola, Switzerland	139

DOWNHILL

	Pts
Lasse Kjus, Norway	760
Andreas Schifferer, Austria	438
Werner Franz, Austria	427
Hans Knauss, Austria	399
Kjetil André Aamodt, Norway	397
Hermann Maier, Austria	360
Stefan Eberharter, Austria	339
Kristian Ghedina, Italy	296
Hannes Trinkl, Austria	274
Fritz Strobl, Austria	231

GIANT SLALOM

	Pts
Michael von Grünigen, Switz.	483
Stefan Eberharter, Austria	410
Hermann Maier, Austria	371
Kjetil André Aamodt, Norway	335
Christian Mayer, Austria	297
Benjamin Raich, Austria	286
Hans Knauss, Austria	281
Patrick Holzer, Italy	276
Marco Büchel, Lichtenstein	218
Steve Locher, Switzerland	217

Women

OVERALL

	Pts
Alexandra Meissnitzer, Austria	1640
Hilde Gerg, Germany	1163
Renate Götschl, Austria	1035
Martina Ertl, Germany	987
Pernilla Wiberg, Sweden	924
Michaela Dorfmeister, Austria	920
Regine Cavagnoud, France	764
Corinne Rey Bellet, Switz.	680
Andrine Flemmen, Norway	668
Anita Wachter, Austria	656

SLALOM

	Pts
Sabine Egger, Austria	425
Pernilla Wiberg, Sweden	415
Anja Paerson, Sweden	374
Trine Bakke, Norway	335
Ingrid Salvenmoser, Austria	292
Kristina Koznick, United States	265
Spela Pretnar, Slovenia	253
Karin Roten, Switzerland	242
Ylva Nowen, Sweden	218
Urska Hrovat, Slovenia	207

SUPER G

	Pts
Alexandra Meissnitzer, Aust.	459
Michaela Dorfmeister, Austria	373
Martina Ertl, Germany	340
Regine Cavagnoud, France	335
Renate Götschl, Austria	308
Hilde Gerg, Germany	300
Corinne Rey Bellet, Switz.	272
Pernilla Wiberg, Sweden	262
Sylviane Berthod, Switz.	232
Regina Haeusl, Germany	203

DOWNHILL

	Pts
Renate Götschl, Austria	610
Alexandra Meissnitzer, Austria	468
Michaela Dorfmeister, Austria	454
Hilde Gerg, Germany	431
Isolde Kostner, Italy	371
Regina Haeusl, Germany	330
Florence Masnada, France	316
Regine Cavagnoud, France	295
Corinne Rey Bellet, Switz.	251
Ingeborg Helen Marken, Nor.	247

GIANT SLALOM

	Pts
Alexandra Meissnitzer, Austria	620
Anita Wachter, Austria	536
Andrine Flemmen, Norway	458
Sonja Nef, Switzerland	303
Birgit Heeb, Lichtenstein	303
Martina Ertl, Germany	270
Anna Ottosson, Sweden	233
Leila Piccard, France	229
Janica Kostelic, Croatia	225
Deborah Compagnoni, Italy	220

Event Descriptions

Downhill: A speed event entailing a single run on a course with a minimum vertical drop of 500 meters (800 for Men's World Cup) and very few control gates.
Slalom: A technical event in which times for runs on two courses are totaled to determine the winner. Skiers must make many quick, short turns through a combination of gates (55-75 gates for men, 40-60 for women) over a short course (140-220–meter vertical drop for men, 120-180 for women).
Combined: An event in which scores from designated slalom and downhill races are combined to determine finish order.

Giant Slalom: A faster technical event with fewer, more broadly spaced gates than in the slalom. Times for runs on two courses with vertical drops of 250-400 meters for men and 250-300 meters for women are combined to determine the winner.
Super Giant Slalom: A speed event that is a cross between the downhill and the giant slalom.
Parallel Slalom: A technical event that combines slalom and giant slalom turns.

FIS World Championships

Sites

1931	Mürren, Switzerland
1932	Cortina d'Ampezzo, Italy
1933	Innsbruck, Austria
1934	St Moritz, Switzerland
1935	Mürren, Switzerland
1936	Innsbruck, Austria
1937	Chamonix, France
1938	Engelberg, Switzerland
1939	Zakopane, Poland

Men

DOWNHILL

1931	Walter Prager, Switzerland
1932	Gustav Lantschner, Austria
1933	Walter Prager, Switzerland
1934	David Zogg, Switzerland
1935	Franz Zingerle, Austria
1936	Rudolf Rominger, Switzerland
1937	Émile Allais, France
1938	James Couttet, France
1939	Hans Lantschner, Germany

SLALOM

1931	David Zogg, Switzerland
1932	Friedrich Dauber, Germany
1933	Anton Seelos, Austria
1934	Franz Pfnür, Germany
1935	Anton Seelos, Austria
1936	Rudi Matt, Austria
1937	Émile Allais, France
1938	Rudolf Rominger, Switzerland
1939	Rudolf Rominger, Switzerland

Women

DOWNHILL

1931	Esme Mackinnon, Great Britain
1932	Paola Wiesinger, Italy
1933	Inge Wersin-Lantschner, Austria
1934	Anni Rüegg, Switzerland
1935	Christel Cranz, Germany
1936	Evie Pinching, Great Britain
1937	Christel Cranz, Germany
1938	Lisa Resch, Germany
1939	Christel Cranz, Germany

SLALOM

1931	Esme Mackinnon, Great Britain
1932	Rösli Streiff, Switzerland
1933	Inge Wersin-Lantschner, Austria
1934	Christel Cranz, Germany
1935	Anni Rüegg, Switzerland
1936	Gerda Paumgarten, Austria
1937	Christel Cranz, Germany
1938	Christel Cranz, Germany
1939	Christel Cranz, Germany

FIS World Alpine Ski Championships

Sites

1950	Aspen, Colorado
1954	Are, Sweden
1958	Badgastein, Austria
1962	Chamonix, France
1966	Portillo, Chile
1970	Val Gardena, Italy
1974	St Moritz, Switzerland
1978	Garmisch-Partenkirchen, West Germany
1982	Schladming, Austria
1985	Bormio, Italy
1987	Crans-Montana, Switzerland
1989	Vail, Colorado
1991	Saalbach-Hinterglemm, Austria
1993	Morioka-Shizukuishi, Japan
1996	Sierra Nevada, Spain
1997	Sestriere, Italy
1999	Vail, Colorado

Men

DOWNHILL

1950.............Zeno Colo, Italy	1985.............Pirmin Zurbriggen, Switzerland
1954.............Christian Pravda, Austria	1987.............Peter Müller, Switzerland
1958.............Toni Sailer, Austria	1989.............Hansjörg Tauscher, West Germany
1962.............Karl Schranz, Austria	1991.............Franz Heinzer, Switzerland
1966.............Jean-Claude Killy, France	1993.............Urs Lehmann, Switzerland
1970.............Bernard Russi, Switzerland	1996.............Patrick Ortlieb, Austria
1974.............David Zwilling, Austria	1997.............Bruno Kernen, Switzerland
1978.............Josef Walcher, Austria	1999.............Hermann Maier, Austria
1982.............Harti Weirather, Austria	

SLALOM

1950.............Georges Schneider, Switzerland	1985.............Jonas Nilsson, Sweden
1954.............Stein Eriksen, Norway	1987.............Frank Wörndl, West Germany
1958.............Josl Rieder, Austria	1989.............Rudolf Nierlich, Austria
1962.............Charles Bozon, France	1991.............Marc Girardelli, Luxembourg
1966.............Carlo Senoner, Italy	1993.............Kjetil André Aamodt, Norway
1970.............Jean-Noël Augert, France	1996.............Alberto Tomba, Italy
1974.............Gustavo Thoeni, Italy	1997.............Tom Stiansen, Norway
1978.............Ingemar Stenmark, Sweden	1999.............Lasse Kjus, Norway
1982.............Ingemar Stenmark, Sweden	

GIANT SLALOM

1950.............Zeno Colo, Italy	1985.............Markus Wasmaier, West Germany
1954.............Stein Eriksen, Norway	1987.............Pirmin Zurbriggen, Switzerland
1958.............Toni Sailer, Austria	1989.............Rudolf Nierlich, Austria
1962.............Egon Zimmermann, Austria	1991.............Rudolf Nierlich, Austria
1966.............Guy Périllat, France	1993.............Kjetil André Aamodt, Norway
1970.............Karl Schranz, Austria	1996.............Alberto Tomba, Italy
1974.............Gustavo Thoeni, Italy	1997.............Michael von Grünigen, Switzerland
1978.............Ingemar Stenmark, Sweden	1999.............Marco Büchel, Lichtecnstein
1982.............Steve Mahre, United States	

COMBINED

1982.............Michel Vion, France	1993.............Lasse Kjus, Norway
1985.............Pirmin Zurbriggen, Switzerland	1996.............Marc Girardelli, Luxembourg
1987.............Marc Girardelli, Luxembourg	1997.............Kjetil André Aamodt, Norway
1989.............Marc Girardelli, Luxembourg	1999.............Not contested
1991.............Stefan Eberharter, Austria	

SUPER G

1987.............Pirmin Zurbriggen, Switzerland	1996.............Atle Skaardal, Norway
1989.............Martin Hangl, Switzerland	1997.............Atle Skaardal, Norway
1991.............Stefan Eberharter, Austria	1999.............Hermann Maier, Austria
1993.............Cancelled due to weather	Lasse Kjus, Norway

Women

DOWNHILL

1950.............Trude Beiser-Jochum, Austria	1985.............Michela Figini, Switzerland
1954.............Ida Schopfer, Switzerland	1987.............Maria Walliser, Switzerland
1958.............Lucile Wheeler, Canada	1989.............Maria Walliser, Switzerland
1962.............Christl Haas, Austria	1991.............Petra Kronberger, Austria
1966.............Erika Schinegger, Austria	1993.............Kate Pace, Canada
1970.............Annerösli Zryd, Switzerland	1996.............Picabo Street, United States
1974.............Annemarie Moser-Pröll, Austria	1997.............Hilary Lindh, United States
1978.............Annemarie Moser-Pröll, Austria	1999.............Renate Götschl, Austria
1982.............Gerry Sorensen, Canada	

Women (Cont.)

SLALOM

1950.............Dagmar Rom, Austria	1985.............Perrine Pelen, France
1954.............Trude Klecker, Austria	1987.............Erika Hess, Switzerland
1958.............Inger Bjornbakken, Norway	1989.............Mateja Svet, Yugoslavia
1962.............Marianne Jahn, Austria	1991.............Vreni Schneider, Switzerland
1966.............Annie Famose, France	1993.............Karin Buder, Austria
1970.............Ingrid Lafforgue, France	1996.............Pernilla Wiberg, Sweden
1974.............Hanni Wenzel, Liechtenstein	1997.............Deborah Compagnoni, Italy
1978.............Lea Sölkner, Austria	1999.............Trine Bakke, Norway
1982.............Erika Hess, Switzerland	

GIANT SLALOM

1950.............Dagmar Rom, Austria	1985 ....Diann Roffe, United States
1954.............Lucienne Schmith-Couttet, France	1987 ....Vreni Schneider, Switzerland
1958.............Lucile Wheeler, Canada	1989 ....Vreni Schneider, Switzerland
1962.............Marianne Jahn, Austria	1991 ....Pernilla Wiberg, Sweden
1966.............Marielle Goitschel, France	1993 ....Carole Merle, France
1970.............Betsy Clifford, Canada	1996 ....Deborah Compagnoni, Italy
1974.............Fabienne Serrat, France	1997 ....Deborah Compagnoni, Italy
1978.............Maria Epple, West Germany	1999 ....Anita Wachter, Austria
1982.............Erika Hess, Switzerland	

COMBINED

1982 ....Erika Hess, Switzerland	1993 ....Miriam Vogt, Germany
1985 ....Erika Hess, Switzerland	1996 ....Pernilla Wiberg, Sweden
1987 ....Erika Hess, Switzerland	1997 ....Renate Götschl, Austria
1989 ....Tamara McKinney, United States	1999 ....Not contested
1991 ....Chantal Bournissen, Switzerland	

SUPER G

1987 ....Maria Walliser, Switzerland	1996 ....Isolde Kostner, Italy
1989 ....Ulrike Maier, Austria	1997 ....Isolde Kostner, Italy
1991 ....Ulrike Maier, Austria	1999 ....Alexandra Meissnitzer
1993 ....Katja Seizinger, Germany	

Note: The 1995 FIS World Alpine Ski Championships were postponed to 1996 due to lack of snow.

The Whole Nine

After having swept the top five positions in a Nov. 27, 1998, Super G in Aspen, Colo., the Austrian men's ski team topped itself and set a World Cup record on Dec. 21 by taking the top *nine* spots in a Super G at Innsbruck. The previous best showing had been by the French team, which seized the first six positions in a World Cup downhill in Abetone, Italy, in 1968.

The Austrians, who would go on to win 18 World Cup races during the 1998–99 season, were led at the Innsbruck Super G by two-time Nagano Olympics champion Hermann Maier. Maier clocked 1:23.52 to claim his third win of the season and edge countrymen Christian Mayer and Fritz Strobel ... and Stefan Eberharter, Rainer Salzgeber, Hans Knauss, Patrick Wirth, Andreas Schifferer and Werner Franz. Lasse Paulsen of Norway finished 10th.

"It was a sensational race for me, and for the team," said Maier. "We need more races like this." Maybe so, but they already have one that's held every year—it's called the Austrian national championships.

World Cup Season Title Holders

Men

OVERALL

1967 ....Jean-Claude Killy, France	1984 ....Pirmin Zurbriggen, Switzerland
1968 ....Jean-Claude Killy, France	1985 ....Marc Girardelli, Luxembourg
1969 ....Karl Schranz, Austria	1986 ....Marc Girardelli, Luxembourg
1970 ....Karl Schranz, Austria	1987 ....Pirmin Zurbriggen, Switzerland
1971 ....Gustavo Thoeni, Italy	1988 ....Pirmin Zurbriggen, Switzerland
1972 ....Gustavo Thoeni, Italy	1989 ....Marc Girardelli, Luxembourg
1973 ....Gustavo Thoeni, Italy	1990 ....Pirmin Zurbriggen, Switzerland
1974 ....Piero Gros, Italy	1991 ....Marc Girardelli, Luxembourg
1975 ....Gustavo Thoeni, Italy	1992 ....Paul Accola, Switzerland
1976 ....Ingemar Stenmark, Sweden	1993 ....Marc Girardelli, Luxembourg
1977 ....Ingemar Stenmark, Sweden	1994 ....Kjetil André Aamodt, Norway
1978 ....Ingemar Stenmark, Sweden	1995 ....Alberto Tomba, Italy
1979 ....Peter Lüscher, Switzerland	1996 ....Lasse Kjus, Norway
1980 ....Andreas Wenzel, Liechtenstein	1997 ....Luc Alphand, France
1981 ....Phil Mahre, United States	1998 ....Hermann Maier, Austria
1982 ....Phil Mahre, United States	1999 ....Lasse Kjus, Norway
1983 ....Phil Mahre, United States	

DOWNHILL

1967 ....Jean-Claude Killy, France	1983 ....Franz Klammer, Austria
1968 ....Gerhard Nenning, Austria	1984 ....Urs Raber, Switzerland
1969 ....Karl Schranz, Austria	1985 ....Helmut Höflehner, Austria
1970 ....Karl Schranz, Austria	1986 ....Peter Wirnsberger, Austria
Karl Cordin, Austria	1987 ....Pirmin Zurbriggen, Switzerland
1971 ....Bernhard Russi, Switzerland	1988 ....Pirmin Zurbriggen, Switzerland
1972 ....Bernhard Russi, Switzerland	1989 ....Marc Girardelli, Luxembourg
1973 ....Roland Collumbin, Switzerland	1990 ....Helmut Höflehner, Austria
1974 ....Roland Collumbin, Switzerland	1991 ....Franz Heinzer, Switzerland
1975 ....Franz Klammer, Austria	1992 ....Franz Heinzer, Switzerland
1976 ....Franz Klammer, Austria	1993 ....Franz Heinzer, Switzerland
1977 ....Franz Klammer, Austria	1994 ....Marc Girardelli, Luxembourg
1978 ....Franz Klammer, Austria	1995 ....Luc Alphand, France
1979 ....Peter Müller, Switzerland	1996 ....Luc Alphand, France
1980 ....Peter Müller, Switzerland	1997 ....Luc Alphand, France
1981 ....Harti Weirather, Austria	1998 ....Andreas Schifferer, Austria
1982 ....Steve Podborski, Canada	1999 ....Lasse Kjus, Norway
Peter Müller, Switzerland	

SLALOM

1967 ....Jean-Claude Killy, France	1984 ....Marc Girardelli, Luxembourg
1968 ....Domeng Giovanoli, Switzerland	1985 ....Marc Girardelli, Luxembourg
1969 ....Jean-Noël Augert, France	1986 ....Rok Petrovic, Yugoslavia
1970 ....Patrick Russel, France	1987 ....Bojan Krizaj, Yugoslavia
....................Alain Penz, France	1988 ....Alberto Tomba, Italy
1971 ....Jean-Noël Augert, France	1989 ....Armin Bittner, West Germany
1972 ....Jean-Noël Augert, France	1990 ....Armin Bittner, West Germany
1973 ....Gustavo Thoeni, Italy	1991 ....Marc Girardelli, Luxembourg
1974 ....Gustavo Thoeni, Italy	1992 ....Alberto Tomba, Italy
1975 ....Ingemar Stenmark, Sweden	1993 ....Tomas Fogdof, Sweden
1976 ....Ingemar Stenmark, Sweden	1994 ....Alberto Tomba, Italy
1977 ....Ingemar Stenmark, Sweden	1995 ....Alberto Tomba, Italy
1978 ....Ingemar Stenmark, Sweden	1996 ....Sebastien Amiez, France
1979 ....Ingemar Stenmark, Sweden	1997 ....Thomas Sykora, Austria
1980 ....Ingemar Stenmark, Sweden	1998 ....Thomas Sykora, Austria
1981 ....Ingemar Stenmark, Sweden	1999 ....Thomas Stangassinger, Austria
1982 ....Phil Mahre, United States	
1983 ....Ingemar Stenmark, Sweden	

Men (Cont.)

GIANT SLALOM

1967 ....Jean-Claude Killy, France	Pirmin Zurbriggen, Switzerland
1968 ....Jean-Claude Killy, France	1985 ....Marc Girardelli, Luxembourg
1969 ....Karl Schranz, Austria	1986 ....Joël Gaspoz, Switzerland
1970 ....Gustavo Thoeni, Italy	1987 ....Joël Gaspoz, Switzerland
1971 ....Patrick Russel, France	Pirmin Zurbriggen, Switzerland
1972 ....Gustavo Thoeni, Italy	1988 ....Alberto Tomba, Italy
1973 ....Hans Hinterseer, Austria	1989 ....Pirmin Zurbriggen, Switzerland
1974 ....Piero Gros, Italy	1990 ....Ole-Cristian Furuseth, Norway
1975 ....Ingemar Stenmark, Sweden	Günther Mader, Austria
1976 ....Ingemar Stenmark, Sweden	1991 ....Alberto Tomba, Italy
1977 ....Heini Hemmi, Switzerland	1992 ....Alberto Tomba, Italy
Ingemar Stenmark, Sweden	1993 ....Kjetil André Aamodt, Norway
1978 ....Ingemar Stenmark, Sweden	1994 ....Christian Mayer, Austria
1979 ....Ingemar Stenmark, Sweden	1995 ....Alberto Tomba, Italy
1980 ....Ingemar Stenmark, Sweden	1996 ....Michael von Grünigen, Switzerland
1981 ....Ingemar Stenmark, Sweden	1997 ....Michael von Grünigen, Switzerland
1982 ....Phil Mahre, United States	1998 ....Hermann Maier, Austria
1983 ....Phil Mahre, United States	1999 ....Michael von Grünigen, Switzerland
1984 ....Ingemar Stenmark, Sweden	

SUPER G

1986 ....Markus Wasmeier, West Germany	1993 ....Kjetil André Aamodt, Norway
1987 ....Pirmin Zurbriggen, Switzerland	1994 ....Jan Einar Thorsen, Norway
1988 ....Pirmin Zurbriggen, Switzerland	1995 ....Peter Runggaldier, Italy
1989 ....Pirmin Zurbriggen, Switzerland	1996 ....Atle Skaardal, Norway
1990 ....Pirmin Zurbriggen, Switzerland	1997 ....Luc Alphand, France
1991 ....Franz Heinzer, Switzerland	1998 ....Hermann Maier, Austria
1992 ....Paul Accola, Switzerland	1999 ....Hermann Maier, Austria

COMBINED

1979 ....Andreas Wenzel, Liechtenstein	1989 ....Marc Girardelli, Luxembourg
1980 ....Andreas Wenzel, Liechtenstein	1990 ....Pirmin Zurbriggen, Switzerland
1981 ....Phil Mahre, United States	1991 ....Marc Girardelli, Luxembourg
1982 ....Phil Mahre, United States	1992 ....Paul Accola, Switzerland
1983 ....Phil Mahre, United States	1993 ....Marc Girardelli, Luxembourg
1984 ....Andreas Wenzel, Liechtenstein	1994 ....Kjetil André Aamodt, Norway
1985 ....Andreas Wenzel, Liechtenstein	1995 ....Marc Girardelli, Luxembourg
1986 ....Markus Wasmeier, West Germany	1996 ....Günther Mader, Austria
1987 ....Pirmin Zurbriggen, Switzerland	1997–99..........Not awarded
1988 ....Hubert Strolz, Austria	

Women

OVERALL

1967 ....Nancy Greene, Canada	1984 ....Erika Hess, Switzerland
1968 ....Nancy Greene, Canada	1985 ....Michela Figini, Switzerland
1969 ....Gertrud Gabl, Austria	1986 ....Maria Walliser, Switzerland
1970 ....Michèle Jacot, France	1987 ....Maria Walliser, Switzerland
1971 ....Annemarie Pröll, Austria	1988 ....Michela Figini, Switzerland
1972 ....Annemarie Pröll, Austria	1989 ....Vreni Schneider, Switzerland
1973 ....Annemarie Pröll, Austria	1990 ....Petra Kronberger, Austria
1974 ....Annemarie Moser-Pröll, Austria	1991 ....Petra Kronberger, Austria
1975 ....Annemarie Moser-Pröll, Austria	1992 ....Petra Kronberger, Austria
1976 ....Rosi Mitermaier, West Germany	1993 ....Anita Wachter, Austria
1977 ....Lise-Marie Morerod, Switzerland	1994 ....Vreni Schneider, Switzerland
1978 ....Hanni Wenzel, Liechtenstein	1995 ....Vreni Schneider, Switzerland
1979 ....Annemarie Moser-Pröll, Austria	1996 ....Katja Seizinger, Germany
1980 ....Hanni Wenzel, Liechtenstein	1997 ....Pernilla Wiberg, Sweden
1981 ....Marie-Thérèse Nadig, Switzerland	1998 ....Katja Seizinger, Germany
1982 ....Erika Hess, Switzerland	1999 ....Alexandra Meissnitzer, Austria
1983 ....Tamara McKinney, United States	

Women (Cont.)

DOWNHILL

1967 ....Marielle Goitschel, France	1984 ....Maria Walliser, Switzerland
1968 ....Isabelle Mir, France & Olga Pall, Austria	1985 ....Michela Figini, Switzerland
1969 ....Wiltrud Drexel, Austria	1986 ....Maria Walliser, Switzerland
1970 ....Isabelle Mir, France	1987 ....Michela Figini, Switzerland
1971 ....Annemarie Pröll, Austria	1988 ....Michela Figini, Switzerland
1972 ....Annemarie Pröll, Austria	1989 ....Michela Figini, Switzerland
1973 ....Annemarie Pröll, Austria	1990 ....Katrin Gutensohn-Knopf, Germany
1974 ....Annemarie Moser-Pröll, Austria	1991 ....Chantal Bournissen, Switzerland
1975 ....Annemarie Moser-Pröll, Austria	1992 ....Katja Seizinger, Germany
1976 ....Brigitte Totschnig, Austria	1993 ....Katja Seizinger, Germany
1977 ....Brigitte Totschnig-Habersatter, Austria	1994 ....Katja Seizinger, Germany
1978 ....Annemarie Moser-Pröll, Austria	1995 ....Picabo Street, United States
1979 ....Annemarie Moser-Pröll, Austria	1996 ....Picabo Street, United States
1980 ....Marie-Thérèse Nadig, Switzerland	1997 ....Renate Götschl, Austria
1981 ....Marie-Thérèse Nadig, Switzerland	1998 ....Katja Seizinger, Germany
1982 ....Marie-Cecile Gros-Gaudenier, France	1999 ....Renate Götschl, Austria
1983 ....Doris De Agostini, Switzerland	

SLALOM

1967 ....Marielle Goitschel, France	1985 ....Erika Hess, Switzerland
1968 ....Marielle Goitschel, France	1986 ....Roswitha Steiner, Austria
1969 ....Gertrud Gabl, Austria	Erika Hess, Switzerland
1970 ....Ingrid Lafforgue, France	1987 ....Corrine Schmidhauser, Switzerland
1971 ....Britt Lafforgue, France	1988 ....Roswitha Steiner, Austria
1972 ....Britt Lafforgue, France	1989 ....Vreni Schneider, Switzerland
1973 ....Patricia Emonet, France	1990 ....Vreni Schneider, Switzerland
1974 ....Christa Zechmeister, West Germany	1991 ....Petra Kronberger, Austria
1975 ....Lise-Marie Morerod, Switzerland	1992 ....Vreni Schneider, Switzerland
1976 ....Rosi Mittermaier, West Germany	1993 ....Vreni Schneider, Switzerland
1977 ....Lise-Marie Morerod, Switzerland	1994 ....Vreni Schneider, Switzerland
1978 ....Hanni Wenzel, Liechtenstein	1995 ....Vreni Schneider, Switzerland
1979 ....Regina Sackl, Austria	1996 ....Elfi Eder, Austria
1980 ....Perrine Pelen, France	1997 ....Pernilla Wiberg, Sweden
1981 ....Erika Hess, Switzerland	1998 ....Ylva Nowen, Sweden
1982 ....Erika Hess, Switzerland	1999 ....Sabine Egger, Austria
1983 ....Erika Hess, Switzerland	
1984 ....Tamara McKinney, United States	

GIANT SLALOM

1967 ....Nancy Greene, Canada	1984 ....Erika Hess, Switzerland
1968 ....Nancy Greene, Canada	1985 ....Maria Keihl, West Germany
1969 ....Marilyn Cochran, United States	Michela Figini, Switzerland
1970 ....Michèle Jacot, France	1986 ....Vreni Schneider, Switzerland
Françoise Macchi, France	1987 ....Vreni Schneider, Switzerland
1971 ....Annemarie Pröll, Austria	Maria Walliser, Switzerland
1972 ....Annemarie Pröll, Austria	1988 ....Mateja Svet, Yugoslavia
1973 ....Monika Kaserer, Austria	1989 ....Vreni Schneider, Switzerland
1974 ....Hanni Wenzel, Liechtenstein	1990 ....Anita Wachter, Austria
1975 ....Annemarie Moser-Pröll, Austria	1991 ....Vreni Schneider, Switzerland
1976 ....Lise-Marie Morerod, France	1992 ....Carole Merle, France
1977 ....Lise-Marie Morerod, France	1993 ....Carole Merle, France
1978 ....Lise-Marie Morerod, France	1994 ....Anita Wachter, Austria
1979 ....Christa Kinshofer, West Germany	1995 ....Vreni Schneider, Switzerland
1980 ....Hanni Wenzel, Liechtenstein	1996 ....Martina Ertl, Germany
1981 ....Marie-Thérèse Nadig, Switzerland	1997 ....Deborah Compagnoni, Italy
1982 ....Irene Epple, West Germany	1998 ....Martina Ertl, Germany
1983 ....Tamara McKinney, United States	1999 ....Alexandra Meissnitzer, Austria

Women *(Cont.)*

SUPER G

1986 ....Maria Kiehl, West Germany	1993 ....Katja Seizinger, Germany
1987 ....Maria Walliser, Switzerland	1994 ....Katja Seizinger, Germany
1988 ....Michela Figini, Switzerland	1995 ....Katja Seizinger, Germany
1989 ....Carole Merle, France	1996 ....Katja Seizinger, Germany
1990 ....Carole Merle, France	1997 ....Hilde Gerg, Germany
1991 ....Carole Merle, France	1998 ....Katja Seizinger, Germany
1992 ....Carole Merle, France	1999 ....Alexandra Meissnitzer, Austria

COMBINED

1979 ....Annemarie Moser-Pröll, Austria	1989 ....Brigitte Oertli, Switzerland
Hanni Wenzel, Liechtenstein	1990 ....Anita Wachter, Austria
1980 ....Hanni Wenzel, Liechtenstein	1991 ....Sabine Ginther, Austria
1981 ....Marie-Thérèse Nadig, Switzerland	1992 ....Sabine Ginther, Austria
1982 ....Irene Epple, West Germany	1993 ....Anita Wachter, Austria
1983 ....Hanni Wenzel, Liechtenstein	1994 ....Pernilla Wiberg, Sweden
1984 ....Erika Hess, Switzerland	1995 ....Pernilla Wiberg, Sweden
1985 ....Brigitte Oertli, Switzerland	1996 ....Anita Wachter, Austria
1986 ....Maria Walliser, Switzerland	1997–99.........Not awarded
1987 ....Brigitte Oertli, Switzerland	
1988 ....Brigitte Oertli, Switzerland	

World Cup Career Victories

Men

DOWNHILL

25..........................Franz Klammer, Austria
19..........................Peter Müller, Switzerland
15..........................Franz Heinzer, Switzerland

SLALOM

40..........................Ingemar Stenmark, Sweden
35..........................Alberto Tomba, Italy
16..........................Marc Girardelli, Luxembourg

GIANT SLALOM

46..........................Ingemar Stenmark, Sweden
16..........................*Michael von Grünigen, Switz
15..........................Alberto Tomba, Italy

SUPER G

10..........................Pirmin Zurbriggen, Switzerland
7............................Marc Girardelli, Luxembourg
6............................Markus Wasmeier, Germany

COMBINED

11..........................Phil Mahre, United States
Pirmin Zurbriggen, Switzerland
Marc Girardelli, Luxembourg

Women

DOWNHILL

36..........................Annemarie Moser-Pröll, Austria
17..........................Michela Figini, Switzerland
16..........................Katja Seizinger, Germany

SLALOM

33..........................Vreni Schneider, Switzerland
21..........................Erika Hess, Switzerland
15..........................Perrine Pelen, France

GIANT SLALOM

21..........................Vreni Schneider, Switzerland
16..........................Annemarie Moser-Pröll, Austria
15..........................*Deborah Compagnoni, Italy

SUPER G

16..........................Katja Seizinger, Germany
12..........................Carole Merle, France
3............................Maria Kiehl, Germany
Maria Walliser, Switzerland
Sigrid Wolf, Austria

COMBINED

8............................Hanni Wenzel, Lichtenstein
7............................Annemarie Moser-Pröll, Austria
Brigitte Oertli, Switzerland

*still active

U.S. Olympic Gold Medalists

Men

Year	Winner	Event
1980 ....Phil Mahre	Combined
1984 ....Bill Johnson	Downhill
1984 ....Phil Mahre	Slalom
1994 ....Tommy Moe	Downhill

Women

Year	Winner	Event
1948 ....Gretchen Fraser	Slalom
1952 ....Andrea Mead Lawrence	Slalom
1952 ....Andrea Mead Lawrence	Giant Slalom
1972 ....Barbara Ann Cochran	Slalom
1984 ....Debbie Armstrong	Giant Slalom
1994 ....Diann Roffe-Steinrotter	Super G
1998 ....Picabo Street	Super G

Figure Skating

PAUL CHIASSON

World champion Maria
Butyrskaya of Russia

Youth Will Be Served

But not just yet, said a pair of veterans who refused to be crowded out by the next wave

BY MERRELL NODEN

IF ANY woman stands a chance of aging gracefully in the Barbie doll world of figure skating, it is surely Michelle Kwan, at 18 a paragon of womanly beauty and grace. Last year, at the Nagano Olympics, Kwan was upset by Tara Lipinski, a bubbly 15-year-old who threw caution to the wind and skated a long program that was more exuberant, more energetic and more difficult than the one performed by the suddenly conservative Kwan. Lipinski became the youngest athlete to win an individual Winter Olympic gold medal, while Kwan had to settle for silver. Lipinski then skipped off to claim all the rewards that come with winning one of the Olympics' most glamorous gold medals.

Surely Lipinski's departure left the ice to Kwan, but not so. In figure skating, as in the movie *Gremlins*, the real killers attack from below, conquering before they've even appeared on radar. In a year that featured an impressive sweep of world championship golds by Russian skaters and an ugly judging scandal, Kwan's struggle to maintain her intensity and fight off the challenge of yet another tiny foe was a moving spectacle. Battling burnout and saddled with all the worries of an average 18-year-old—like getting into college—she chose not to skate a full schedule of International Skating Union (ISU) events and even mused about taking a year off to recharge her batteries.

Still, Kwan is the class of the field, at least domestically. At the U.S. Figure Skating Championships, held Feb. 7–14 in Salt Lake City, she convincingly won her third title in four years, as all nine judges awarded her first place. But the skater who generated the most excitement at the nationals was Naomi Nari Nam, a 4'8" eighth grader from Irvine, Calif., whose long program included an array of breathtaking spins and five triple jumps. "Turn on the spotlight," said Dick Button, "there's a 13-year-old who was born to be in it!"

Nari Nam finished second and proved she was more than just a brightly smiling cutie-pie when, in her short program, she launched a triple jump and wiped out, banging her head hard on the ice. After sitting dazed for a moment she got up and thrust herself right into a death-drop spin. "Man, can she spin!"

MANNY MILLAN

Ukraine and Sviatoslav Babenko of Russia, were caught on tape during the pairs competition exchanging glances and making gestures to each other, behavior strictly forbidden under ISU rules. Korytek and Babenko, who placed the top seven pairs in precisely the same order, were later banned for two and three years, respectively. While it could not be determined whether collusion affected the outcome, the crowd certainly questioned it, booing loudly when Russia's Elena Berezhnaya and Anton Sikharulidze beat China's Shen Xue and Zhao Hongbo for the gold.

The other Russian skaters needed no outside assistance in Helsinki. Alexei Yagudin, 19, successfully defended his men's title, avenging his loss at the Russian national championships to 16-year-old Evgeni Plushenko. Weiss used a strong long program to move from fourth place to a bronze. In the women's competition, Kwan, who'd looked vulnerable from the start, also stood fourth after the short program. "I've never seen Michelle fall in practice," said Elena Tchaikovskaya, coach of Russian skater Maria Butyrskaya. "But here in practice she had many mistakes. Even falls after jumps.... I think this is because she didn't compete all year."

Kwan was out of contention for the gold even before she took the ice, but she didn't know it, having remained cloistered in her dressing room while Butyrskaya shed her reputation for folding under pressure and clinched the title with her long program. Kwan skated well and took the silver. Butyrskaya thereby became, at 26, the oldest woman to win the worlds, and then she dismissed age as a factor. "I'm skating like a woman on the ice," she said. "Today I proved I'm the best skater in the world and age is not important."

Kwan, no doubt, hopes to prove her right again. "If I still have that flame burning inside me and my legs are healthy," she vowed in Salt Lake City, "I'll be out there."

said Kwan, an unfailingly good sport who has helped Nari Nam with her jumps on weekends, when the younger skater joins her in Lake Arrowhead, Calif.

But even had Nari Nam beaten Kwan, she still could not have competed in the worlds, since the ISU's rules bar skaters younger than 15 unless they've medaled at the previous world junior championships. "It's a deplorable instance of age discrimination," said Nari Nam's coach, John Nicks. "She's been discriminated against all year by the rule." Another concern for Nari Nam is that figure skating judges, with their notoriously quirky vision, frequently require a few looks at a skater before taking her seriously.

The men's championship in Salt Lake City went to Michael Weiss, 22, of Fairfax, Va., who had narrowly missed winning the previous two titles. Though he fell on his quadruple toe loop, Weiss recovered nicely to hit eight triple jumps, four in combination.

A month later, at the world championships in Helsinki, Russia became the first country to win all four disciplines. But doubts were raised about precisely how they had achieved this sweep. Two judges, Alfred Korytek of

FOR THE RECORD · 1999

World Champions

Helsinki, March 23–28

Women

1.......Maria Butyrskaya, Russia
2.......Michelle Kwan, United States
3.......Julia Soldatova, Russia

Men

1.........Alexei Yagudin, Russia
2.........Evgeni Plushenko, Russia
3.........Michael Weiss, United States

Pairs

1.......Elena Berezhnaya and Anton Sikharulidze, Russia
2.......Shen Xue and Zhao Hongbo, China
3.......Dorota Zagorska and Mariusz Siudek, Poland

Dance

1.........Anjelika Krylova and Oleg Ovsyannikov, Russia
2.........Marina Anissina and Gwendal Peizer, France
3.........Shae-Lynn Bourne and Victor Kraatz, Canada

World Figure Skating Championships Medal Table

Country	Gold	Silver	Bronze	Total
Russia	4	1	1	6
United States	0	1	1	2
China	0	1	0	1
France	0	1	0	1
Canada	0	0	1	1
Poland	0	0	1	1

Champions of the United States

Salt Lake City, February 7–14

Women

1.....................Michelle Kwan, Los Angeles FSC.
2.....................Naomi Nari Nam, All Year FSC
3.....................Angela Nikodinov, All Year FSC

Men

1.....................Michael Weiss, Washington FSC
2.....................Trifun Zivanovic, All Year FSC
3.....................Timothy Goebel, Winterhurst FSC

Pairs

1. ....Danielle Hartsell and Steve Hartsell, Detroit SC
2.....................Kyoko Ina and John Zimmedrman, SC of New York/ Birmingham FSC
3.....................Laura Handy and J. Paul Binnebose, University of Delaware FSC

Dance

1. ....Naomi Lang and Peter Tchernyshev, Detroit SC
2.....................Eve Chalom and Mathew Gates, Lone Star FSC
3.....................Debbie Koegel and Oleg Fediukov, Ice Works FSC

Quadruple Goebel

He may have finished 12th in the men's competition, but 18-year-old Timothy Goebel of Lakewood, Ohio, made figure skating history at the world championships in Helsinki in March 1999. During the qualifying round, in the early part of his routine, Goebel launched himself from the back inside edge of his right foot, turned four revolutions in the air and landed on the back outside edge of his left foot, thereby successfully landing the first quadruple salchow jump in the 103-year history of the world championships. "The triple salchow was always the easiest triple jump for me," said Goebel. "I was able to do the quad salchow before I could do a triple axel." By landing that quad in the presitigious competition, the up-and-coming Goebel, who finished third in the '99 U.S. nationals, made his first world championship an event he'll never forget.

Skating Terminology*

Basic Skating Terms

Edges: The two sides of the skating blade, on either side of the grooved center. There is an inside edge, on the inner side of the leg; and an outside edge, on the outer side of the leg.

Free Foot, Hip, Knee, Side, Etc.: The foot a skater is not skating on at any one time is the free foot; everything on that side of the body is then called "free." (See also "skating foot.")

Free Skating (Freestyle): A 4- or 5-minute competition program of free-skating components, choreographed to music, with no set elements. Skating moves include jumps, spins, steps and other linking movements.

Skating Foot, Hip, Knee, Side, Etc.: Opposite of the free foot, hip, knee, side, etc. The foot a skater is skating on at any one time is the skating foot; everything on that side of the body is then called "skating."

Toe Picks (Toe Rakes): The teeth at the front of the skate blade, used primarily for certain jumps and spins.

Trace, Tracing: The line left on the ice by the skater's blade.

Jumps

Waltz: A beginner's jump, involving half a revolution in the air, taken from a forward outside edge and landed on the back outside edge of the other foot.

Toe Loop: A one-revolution jump taken off from and landed on the same back outside edge. This jump is similar to the loop jump except that the skater kicks the toe pick of the free leg into the ice upon takeoff, providing added power.

Toe Walley: A jump similar to the toe loop, except that the takeoff is from the inside edge.

Flip: A jump taken off with the toe pick of the free leg from a back inside edge and landed on a back outside edge, with one in-air revolution.

Lutz: A toe jump similar to the flip, taken off with the toe pick of the free leg from a backward outside edge. The skater enters the jump skating in one direction, and concludes the jump skating in the opposite direction. Usually performed in the corners of the rink. Named after inventor Alois Lutz, who first completed the jump in Vienna, 1918.

Salchow: A one-, two- or three-revolution jump. The skater takes off from the back inside edge of one foot and lands backwards on the outside edge of the right foot, the opposite foot from which the skater took off. Named for its originator and first Olympic champion (1908), Sweden's Ulrich Salchow.

Axel: A combination of the waltz and loop jumps, including one-and-a-half revolutions. The only jump begun from a forward outside edge, the axel is landed on the back outside edge of the opposite foot. Named for its inventor, Norway's Axel Paulsen.

Spins

Spin: The rotation of the body in one place on the ice. Various spins are the back, fast or scratch, sit, camel, butterfly and layback.

Camel Spin: A spin with the skater in an arabesque position (the free leg at right angles to the leg on the ice).

Flying Camel Spin: A jump spin ending in the camel-spin position.

Flying Sit Spin: A jump spin in which the skater leaps off the ice, assumes a sitting position at the peak of the jump, lands and spins in a similar sitting position.

Pair Movements/Techniques

Death Spiral: One of the most dramatic moves in figure skating. The man, acting as the center of a circle, holds tightly to the hand of his partner and pulls her around him. The woman, gliding on one foot, achieves a position almost horizontal to the ice.

Lifts: The most spectacular moves in pairs skating. They involve any maneuver in which the man lifts the woman off the ice. The man often holds his partner above his head with one hand.

Throws: The man lifts the woman into the air and throws her away from him. She spins in the air and lands on one foot.

Twist: The man throws the woman into the air. She spins in the air (either a double- or triple-twist), and he catches her at the landing.

*Compiled by the United States Figure Skating Association.

World Champions

Women

1906	Madge Sayers-Cave, Great Britain
1907	Madge Sayers-Cave, Great Britain
1908	Lily Kronberger, Hungary
1909	Lily Kronberger, Hungary
1910	Lily Kronberger, Hungary
1911	Lily Kronberger, Hungary
1912	Opika von Meray Horvath, Hungary
1913	Opika von Meray Horvath, Hungary
1914	Opika von Meray Horvath, Hungary
1915-21	No competition
1922	Herma Plank-Szabo, Austria
1923	Herma Plank-Szabo, Austria
1924	Herma Plank-Szabo, Austria
1925	Herma Jaross-Szabo, Austria
1926	Herma Jaross-Szabo, Austria
1927	Sonja Henie, Norway
1928	Sonja Henie, Norway
1929	Sonja Henie, Norway
1930	Sonja Henie, Norway
1931	Sonja Henie, Norway
1932	Sonja Henie, Norway
1933	Sonja Henie, Norway
1934	Sonja Henie, Norway
1935	Sonja Henie, Norway
1936	Sonja Henie, Norway
1937	Cecilia Colledge, Great Britain
1938	Megan Taylor, Great Britain
1939	Megan Taylor, Great Britain
1940-46	No competition
1947	Barbara Ann Scott, Canada
1948	Barbara Ann Scott, Canada
1949	Alena Vrzanova, Czechoslovakia
1950	Alena Vrzanova, Czechoslovakia
1951	Jeannette Altwegg, Great Britain
1952	Jacqueline duBief, France
1953	Tenley Albright, United States
1954	Gundi Busch, West Germany
1955	Tenley Albright, United States
1956	Carol Heiss, United States
1957	Carol Heiss, United States

Women (Cont.)

1958	Carol Heiss, United States
1959	Carol Heiss, United States
1960	Carol Heiss, United States
1961	No competition
1962	Sjoukje Dijkstra, Netherlands
1963	Sjoukje Dijkstra, Netherlands
1964	Sjoukje Dijkstra, Netherlands
1965	Petra Burka, Canada
1966	Peggy Fleming, United States
1967	Peggy Fleming, United States
1968	Peggy Fleming, United States
1969	Gabriele Seyfert, East Germany
1970	Gabriele Seyfert, East Germany
1971	Beatrix Schuba, Austria
1972	Beatrix Schuba, Austria
1973	Karen Magnussen, Canada
1974	Christine Errath, East Germany
1975	Dianne DeLeeuw, Netherlands
1976	Dorothy Hamill, United States
1977	Linda Fratianne, United States
1978	Annett Poetzsch, East Germany
1979	Linda Fratianne, United States
1980	Annett Poetzsch, East Germany
1981	Denise Biellmann, Switzerland
1982	Elaine Zayak, United States
1983	Rosalynn Sumners, United States
1984	Katarina Witt, East Germany
1985	Katarina Witt, East Germany
1986	Debi Thomas, United States
1987	Katarina Witt, East Germany
1988	Katarina Witt, East Germany
1989	Midori Ito, Japan
1990	Jill Trenary, United States
1991	Kristi Yamaguchi, United States
1992	Kristi Yamaguchi, United States
1993	Oksana Baiul, Ukraine
1994	Yuka Sato, Japan
1995	Chen Lu, China
1996	Michelle Kwan, United States
1997	Tara Lipinski, United States
1998	Michelle Kwan, United States
1999	Maria Butyrskaya, Russia

Men

1896	Gilbert Fuchs, Germany
1897	Gustav Hugel, Austria
1898	Henning Grenander, Sweden
1899	Gustav Hugel, Austria
1900	Gustav Hugel, Austria
1901	Ulrich Salchow, Sweden
1902	Ulrich Salchow, Sweden
1903	Ulrich Salchow, Sweden
1904	Ulrich Salchow, Sweden
1905	Ulrich Salchow, Sweden
1906	Gilbert Fuchs, Germany
1907	Ulrich Salchow, Sweden
1908	Ulrich Salchow, Sweden
1909	Ulrich Salchow, Sweden
1910	Ulrich Salchow, Sweden
1911	Ulrich Salchow, Sweden
1912	Fritz Kachler, Austria
1913	Fritz Kachler, Austria
1914	Gosta Sandhal, Sweden
1915-21	No competition
1922	Gillis Grafstrom, Sweden
1923	Fritz Kachler, Austria
1924	Gillis Grafstrom, Sweden
1925	Willy Bockl, Austria
1926	Willy Bockl, Austria
1927	Willy Bockl, Austria
1928	Willy Bockl, Austria
1929	Gillis Grafstrom, Sweden
1930	Karl Schafer, Austria
1931	Karl Schafer, Austria
1932	Karl Schafer, Austria
1933	Karl Schafer, Austria
1934	Karl Schafer, Austria
1935	Karl Schafer, Austria
1936	Karl Schafer, Austria
1937	Felix Kaspar, Austria
1938	Felix Kaspar, Austria
1939	Graham Sharp, Great Britain
1940-46	No competition
1947	Hans Gerschwiler, Switzerland
1948	Dick Button, United States
1949	Dick Button, United States
1950	Dick Button, United States
1951	Dick Button, United States
1952	Dick Button, United States
1953	Hayes Alan Jenkins, United States
1954	Hayes Alan Jenkins, United States
1955	Hayes Alan Jenkins, United States
1956	Hayes Alan Jenkins, United States
1957	David W. Jenkins, United States
1958	David W. Jenkins, United States
1959	David W. Jenkins, United States
1960	Alan Giletti, France
1961	No competition
1962	Donald Jackson, Canada
1963	Donald McPherson, Canada
1964	Manfred Schneldorfer, W Germany
1965	Alain Calmat, France
1966	Emmerich Danzer, Austria
1967	Emmerich Danzer, Austria
1968	Emmerich Danzer, Austria
1969	Tim Wood, United States
1970	Tim Wood, United States
1971	Andrej Nepela, Czechoslovakia
1972	Andrej Nepela, Czechoslovakia
1973	Andrej Nepela, Czechoslovakia
1974	Jan Hoffmann, East Germany
1975	Sergei Volkov, USSR
1976	John Curry, Great Britain
1977	Vladimir Kovalev, USSR
1978	Charles Tickner, United States
1979	Vladimir Kovalev, USSR
1980	Jan Hoffmann, East Germany
1981	Scott Hamilton, United States
1982	Scott Hamilton, United States
1983	Scott Hamilton, United States
1984	Scott Hamilton, United States
1985	Aleksandr Fadeev, USSR
1986	Brian Boitano, United States
1987	Brian Orser, Canada
1988	Brian Boitano, United States
1989	Kurt Browning, Canada
1990	Kurt Browning, Canada
1991	Kurt Browning, Canada
1992	Viktor Petrenko, CIS
1993	Kurt Browning, Canada

Men (Cont.)

1994 ....Elvis Stojko, Canada
1995 ....Elvis Stojko, Canada
1996 ....Todd Eldredge, United States
1997 ....Elvis Stojko, Canada

1998 ....Alexi Yagudin, Russia
1999 ....Alexi Yagudin, Russia

Pairs

1908 ....Anna Hubler, Heinrich Burger, Germany
1909 ....Phyllis Johnson, James H. Johnson,
            Great Britain
1910 ....Anna Hubler, Heinrich Burger, Germany
1911 ....Ludowika Eilers, Walter Jakobsson,
            Germany/Finland
1912 ....Phyllis Johnson, James H. Johnson,
            Great Britain
1913 ....Helene Engelmann, Karl Majstrik,
            Germany
1914 ....Ludowika Jakobsson-Eilers, Walter
            Jakobsson-Eilers, Finland
1915-21 ......No competition
1922 ....Helene Engelmann, Alfred Berger,
            Germany
1923 ....Ludowika Jakobsson-Eilers, Walter
            Jakobsson-Eilers, Finland
1924 ....Helene Engelmann, Alfred Berger,
            Germany
1925 ....Herma Jaross-Szabo, Ludwig Wrede,
            Austria
1926 ....Andree Joly, Pierre Brunet, France
1927 ....Herma Jaross-Szabo, Ludwig Wrede,
            Austria
1928 ....Andree Joly, Pierre Brunet, France
1929 ....Lilly Scholz, Otto Kaiser, Austria
1930 ....Andree Brunet-Joly, Pierre Brunet-Joly,
            France
1931 ....Emilie Rotter, Laszlo Szollas, Hungary
1932 ....Andree Brunet-Joly, Pierre Brunet-Joly,
            France
1933 ....Emilie Rotter, Laszlo Szollas, Hungary
1934 ....Emilie Rotter, Laszlo Szollas, Hungary
1935 ....Emilie Rotter, Laszlo Szollas, Hungary
1936 ....Maxi Herber, Ernst Bajer, Germany
1937 ....Maxi Herber, Ernst Bajer, Germany
1938 ....Maxi Herber, Ernst Bajer, Germany
1939 ....Maxi Herber, Ernst Bajer, Germany
1940-46 ......No competition
1947 ....Micheline Lannoy, Pierre Baugniet,
            Belgium
1948 ....Micheline Lannoy, Pierre Baugniet,
            Belgium
1949 ....Andrea Kekessy, Ede Kiraly, Hungary
1950 ....Karol Kennedy, Peter Kennedy,
            United States
1951 ....Ria Baran, Paul Falk, West Germany
1952 ....Ria Baran Falk, Paul Falk, W Germany
1953 ....Jennifer Nicks, John Nicks, Great Britain
1954 ....Frances Dafoe, Norris Bowden, Canada
1955 ....Frances Dafoe, Norris Bowden, Canada
1956 ....Sissy Schwarz, Kurt Oppelt, Austria
1957 ....Barbara Wagner, Robert Paul, Canada
1958 ....Barbara Wagner, Robert Paul, Canada
1959 ....Barbara Wagner, Robert Paul, Canada
1960 ....Barbara Wagner, Robert Paul, Canada
1961 ....No competition
1962 ....Maria Jelinek, Otto Jelinek, Canada

1963 ....Marika Kilius, Hans-Jurgen Baumler,
            West Germany
1964 ....Marika Kilius, Hans-Jurgen Baumler,
            West Germany
1965 ....Ljudmila Protopopov, Oleg Protopopov,
            USSR
1966 ....Ljudmila Protopopov, Oleg Protopopov,
            USSR
1967 ....Ljudmila Protopopov, Oleg Protopopov,
            USSR
1968 ....Ljudmila Protopopov, Oleg Protopopov,
            USSR
1969 ....Irina Rodnina, Alexsei Ulanov, USSR
1970 ....Irina Rodnina, Alexsei Ulanov, USSR
1971 ....Irina Rodnina, Sergei Ulanov, USSR
1972 ....Irina Rodnina, Sergei Ulanov, USSR
1973 ....Irina Rodnina, Aleksandr Zaitsev, USSR
1974 ....Irina Rodnina, Aleksandr Zaitsev, USSR
1975 ....Irina Rodnina, Aleksandr Zaitsev, USSR
1976 ....Irina Rodnina, Aleksandr Zaitsev, USSR
1977 ....Irina Rodnina, Aleksandr Zaitsev, USSR
1978 ....Irina Rodnina, Aleksandr Zaitsev, USSR
1979 ....Tai Babilonia, Randy Gardner,
            United States
1980 ....Maria Cherkasova, Sergei Shakhrai,
            USSR
1981 ....Irina Vorobieva, Igor Lisovsky, USSR
1982 ....Sabine Baess, Tassilio Thierbach,
            East Germany
1983 ....Elena Valova, Oleg Vasiliev, USSR
1984 ....Barbara Underhill, Paul Martini, Canada
1985 ....Elena Valova, Oleg Vasiliev, USSR
1986 ....Ekaterina Gordeeva, Sergei Grinkov, USSR
1987 ....Ekaterina Gordeeva, Sergei Grinkov, USSR
1988 ....Elena Valova, Oleg Vasiliev, USSR
1989 ....Ekaterina Gordeeva, Sergei Grinkov, USSR
1990 ....Ekaterina Gordeeva, Sergei Grinkov, USSR
1991 ....Natalia Mishkutienok, Artur Dmitriev,
            USSR
1992 ....Natalia Mishkutienok, Artur Dmitriev, CIS
1993 ....Isabelle Brasseur, Lloyd Eisler, Canada
1994 ....Evgenia Shishkova, Vadim Naumov,
            Russia
1995 ....Radka Kovarikova, Rene Novotny,
            Czech Republic
1996 ....Marina Eltsova, Andrey Buskhov,
            Russia
1997 ....Mandy Wötzel, Ingo Steuer, Germany
1998 ....Jenni Meno, Todd Sand, United States
1999 ....Elena Berezhnaya, Anton Sikharulidze,
            Russia

Dance

1950 ....Lois Waring, Michael McGean, United States	1972 ....Ljudmila Pakhomova, Aleksandr Gorshkov, USSR
1951 ....Jean Westwood, Lawrence Demmy, Great Britain	1973 ....Ljudmila Pakhomova, Aleksandr Gorshkov, USSR
1952 ....Jean Westwood, Lawrence Demmy, Great Britain	1974 ....Ljudmila Pakhomova, Aleksandr Gorshkov, USSR
1953 ....Jean Westwood, Lawrence Demmy, Great Britain	1975 ....Irina Moiseeva, Andreij Minenkov, USSR
1954 ....Jean Westwood, Lawrence Demmy, Great Britain	1976 ....Ljudmila Pakhomova, Aleksandr Gorshkov, USSR
1955 ....Jean Westwood, Lawrence Demmy, Great Britain	1977 ....Irina Moiseeva, Andreij Minenkov, USSR
1956 ....Pamela Wieght, Paul Thomas, Great Britain	1978 ....Natalia Linichuk, Gennadi Karponosov, USSR
1957 ....June Markham, Courtney Jones, Great Britain	1979 ....Natalia Linichuk, Gennadi Karponosov, USSR
1958 ....June Markham, Courtney Jones, Great Britain	1980 ....Krisztina Regoeczy, Andras Sallai, Hungary
1959 ....Doreen D. Denny, Courtney Jones, Great Britain	1981 ....Jayne Torvill, Christopher Dean, Great Britain
1960 ....Doreen D. Denny, Courtney Jones, Great Britain	1982 ....Jayne Torvill, Christopher Dean, Great Britain
1961 ....No competition	1983 ....Jayne Torvill, Christopher Dean, Great Britain
1962 ....Eva Romanova, Pavel Roman, Czechoslovakia	1984 ....Jayne Torvill, Christopher Dean, Great Britain
1963 ....Eva Romanova, Pavel Roman, Czechoslovakia	1985............Natalia Bestemianova, Andrei Bukin, USSR
1964 ....Eva Romanova, Pavel Roman, Czechoslovakia	1986............Natalia Bestemianova, Andrei Bukin, USSR
1965 ....Eva Romanova, Pavel Roman, Czechoslovakia	1987............Natalia Bestemianova, Andrei Bukin, USSR
1966 ....Diane Towler, Bernard Ford, Great Britain	1988............Natalia Bestemianova, Andrei Bukin, USSR
1967 ....Diane Towler, Bernard Ford, Great Britain	1989............Marina Klimova, Sergei Ponomarenko, USSR
1968 ....Diane Towler, Bernard Ford, Great Britain	1990............Marina Klimova, Sergei Ponomarenko, USSR
1969 ....Diane Towler, Bernard Ford, Great Britain	1991..............Isabelle Duchesnay, Paul Duchesnay, France
1970 ....Ljudmila Pakhomova, Aleksandr Gorshkov, USSR	1992 ....Marina Klimova, Sergei Ponomarenko, CIS
1971 ....Ljudmila Pakhomova, Aleksandr Gorshkov, USSR	1993 ....Renee Roca, Gorsha Sur, United States
	1994 ....Oksana Grishuk, Evgeny Platov, Russia
	1995 ....Oksana Grishuk, Evgeny Platov, Russia
	1996 ....Oksana Grishuk, Evgeny Platov, Russia
	1997 ....Oksana Grishuk, Evgeny Platov, Russia
	1998 ....Anjelika Krylova and Oleg Ovsyannikov, Russia
	1999 ....Anjelika Krylova and Oleg Ovsyannikov, Russia

Champions of the United States

The championships held in 1914, 1918, 1920 and 1921 under the auspices of the International Skating Union of America were open to Canadians, although they were considered to be United States championships. Beginning in 1922, the championships have been held under the auspices of the United States Figure Skating Association.

Women

1914 ....Theresa Weld, SC of Boston	1931 ....Maribel Y. Vinson, SC of Boston
1915-17 ......No competition	1932 ....Maribel Y. Vinson, SC of Boston
1918............Rosemary S. Beresford, New York SC	1933 ....Maribel Y. Vinson, SC of Boston
1919 ....No competition	1934 ....Suzanne Davis, SC of Boston
1920 ....Theresa Weld, SC of Boston	1935 ....Maribel Y. Vinson, SC of Boston
1921 ....Theresa Weld Blanchard, SC of Boston	1936 ....Maribel Y. Vinson, SC of Boston
1922 ....Theresa Weld Blanchard, SC of Boston	1937 ....Maribel Y. Vinson, SC of Boston
1923 ....Theresa Weld Blanchard, SC of Boston	1938 ....Joan Tozzer, SC of Boston
1924 ....Theresa Weld Blanchard, SC of Boston	1939 ....Joan Tozzer, SC of Boston
1925 ....Beatrix Loughran, New York SC	1940 ....Joan Tozzer, SC of Boston
1926 ....Beatrix Loughran, New York SC	1941 ....Jane Vaughn, Philadelphia SC & HS
1927 ....Beatrix Loughran, New York SC	1942 ....Jane Vaughn Sullivan, Philadelphia SC & HS
1928 ....Maribel Y. Vinson, SC of Boston	1943............Gretchen Van Zandt Merrill, SC of Boston
1929 ....Maribel Y. Vinson, SC of Boston	1944............Gretchen Van Zandt Merrill, SC of Boston
1930 ....Maribel Y. Vinson, SC of Boston	

Women (Cont.)

1945............Gretchen Van Zandt Merrill, SC of Boston
1946............Gretchen Van Zandt Merrill, SC of Boston
1947............Gretchen Van Zandt Merrill, SC of Boston
1948............Gretchen Van Zandt Merrill, SC of Boston
1949 ....Yvonne Claire Sherman, SC of New York
1950 ....Yvonne Claire Sherman, SC of New York
1951 ....Sonya Klopfer, Junior SC of New York
1952 ....Tenley E. Albright, SC of Boston
1953 ....Tenley E. Albright, SC of Boston
1954 ....Tenley E. Albright, SC of Boston
1955 ....Tenley E. Albright, SC of Boston
1956 ....Tenley E. Albright, SC of Boston
1957 ....Carol E. Heiss, SC of New York
1958 ....Carol E. Heiss, SC of New York
1959 ....Carol E. Heiss, SC of New York
1960 ....Carol E. Heiss, SC of New York
1961 ....Laurence R. Owen, SC of Boston
1962 ....Barbara Roles Pursley, Arctic Blades FSC
1963 ....Lorraine G. Hanlon, SC of Boston
1964 ....Peggy Fleming, Arctic Blades FSC
1965 ....Peggy Fleming, Arctic Blades FSC
1966 ....Peggy Fleming, City of Colorado Springs
1967 ....Peggy Fleming, Broadmoor SC
1968 ....Peggy Fleming, Broadmoor SC
1969 ....Janet Lynn, Wagon Wheel FSC
1970 ....Janet Lynn, Wagon Wheel FSC
1971 ....Janet Lynn, Wagon Wheel FSC
1972 ....Janet Lynn, Wagon Wheel FSC

1973 ....Janet Lynn, Wagon Wheel FSC
1974 ....Dorothy Hamill, SC of New York
1975 ....Dorothy Hamill, SC of New York
1976 ....Dorothy Hamill, SC of New York
1977 ....Linda Fratianne, Los Angeles FSC
1978 ....Linda Fratianne, Los Angeles FSC
1979 ....Linda Fratianne, Los Angeles FSC
1980 ....Linda Fratianne, Los Angeles FSC
1981 ....Elaine Zayak, SC of New York
1982 ....Rosalynn Sumners, Seattle SC
1983 ....Rosalynn Sumners, Seattle SC
1984 ....Rosalynn Sumners, Seattle SC
1985 ....Tiffany Chin, San Diego FSC
1986 ....Debi Thomas, Los Angeles FSC
1987 ....Jill Trenary, Broadmoor SC
1988 ....Debi Thomas, Los Angeles FSC
1989 ....Jill Trenary, Broadmoor SC
1990 ....Jill Trenary, Broadmoor SC
1991 ....Tonya Harding, Carousel FSC
1992 ....Kristi Yamaguchi, St Moritz ISC
1993 ....Nancy Kerrigan, Colonial FSC
1994 ....Tonya Harding, Portland FSC
1995 ....Nicole Bobek, Los Angeles FSC
1996 ....Michelle Kwan, Los Angeles FSC
1997 ....Tara Lipinski, Detroit SC
1998 ....Michelle Kwan, Los Angeles FSC
1999 ....Michelle Kwan, Los Angeles FSC

Men

1914 ....Norman M. Scott, WC of Montreal
1915-17 ......No competition
1918 ....Nathaniel W. Niles, SC of Boston
1919 ....No competition
1920 ....Sherwin C. Badger, SC of Boston
1921 ....Sherwin C. Badger, SC of Boston
1922 ....Sherwin C. Badger, SC of Boston
1923 ....Sherwin C. Badger, SC of Boston
1924 ....Sherwin C. Badger, SC of Boston
1925 ....Nathaniel W. Niles, SC of Boston
1926 ....Chris I. Christenson, Twin City FSC
1927 ....Nathaniel W. Niles, SC of Boston
1928 ....Roger F. Turner, SC of Boston
1929 ....Roger F. Turner, SC of Boston
1930 ....Roger F. Turner, SC of Boston
1931 ....Roger F. Turner, SC of Boston
1932 ....Roger F. Turner, SC of Boston
1933 ....Roger F. Turner, SC of Boston
1934 ....Roger F. Turner, SC of Boston
1935 ....Robin H. Lee, SC of New York
1936 ....Robin H. Lee, SC of New York
1937 ....Robin H. Lee, SC of New York
1938 ....Robin H. Lee, Chicago FSC
1939 ....Robin H. Lee, St Paul FSC
1940 ....Eugene Turner, Los Angeles FSC
1941 ....Eugene Turner, Los Angeles FSC
1942 ....Robert Specht, Chicago FSC
1943 ....Arthur R. Vaughn, Jr,
              Philadelphia SC & HS
1944-45 ......No competition
1946 ....Dick Button, Philadelphia SC & HS
1947 ....Dick Button, Philadelphia SC & HS
1948 ....Dick Button, Philadelphia SC & HS
1949 ....Dick Button, Philadelphia SC & HS
1950 ....Dick Button, SC of Boston
1951 ....Dick Button, SC of Boston

1952 ....Dick Button, SC of Boston
1953 ....Hayes Alan Jenkins, Cleveland SC
1954 ....Hayes Alan Jenkins, Broadmoor SC
1955 ....Hayes Alan Jenkins, Broadmoor SC
1956 ....Hayes Alan Jenkins, Broadmoor SC
1957 ....David Jenkins, Broadmoor SC
1958 ....David Jenkins, Broadmoor SC
1959 ....David Jenkins, Broadmoor SC
1960 ....David Jenkins, Broadmoor SC
1961 ....Bradley R. Lord, SC of Boston
1962 ....Monty Hoyt, Broadmoor SC
1963 ....Thomas Litz, Hershey FSC
1964 ....Scott Ethan Allen, SC of New York
1965 ....Gary C. Visconti, Detroit SC
1966 ....Scott Ethan Allen, SC of New York
1967 ....Gary C. Visconti, Detroit SC
1968 ....Tim Wood, Detroit SC
1969 ....Tim Wood, Detroit SC
1970 ....Tim Wood, City of Colorado Springs
1971 ....John Misha Petkevich, Great Falls FSC
1972 ....Kenneth Shelley, Arctic Blades FSC
1973 ....Gordon McKellen, Jr, SC of Lake Placid
1974 ....Gordon McKellen, Jr, SC of Lake Placid
1975 ....Gordon McKellen, Jr, SC of Lake Placid
1976 ....Terry Kubicka, Arctic Blades FSC
1977 ....Charles Tickner, Denver FSC
1978 ....Charles Tickner, Denver FSC
1979 ....Charles Tickner, Denver FSC
1980 ....Charles Tickner, Denver FSC
1981 ....Scott Hamilton, Philadelphia SC & HS
1982 ....Scott Hamilton, Philadelphia SC & HS
1983 ....Scott Hamilton, Philadelphia SC & HS
1984 ....Scott Hamilton, Philadelphia SC & HS
1985 ....Brian Boitano, Peninsula FSC
1986 ....Brian Boitano, Peninsula FSC
1987 ....Brian Boitano, Peninsula FSC

Men *(cont.)*

1988 ....Brian Boitano, Peninsula FSC
1989 ....Christopher Bowman, Los Angeles FSC
1990 ....Todd Eldredge, Los Angeles FSC
1991 ....Todd Eldredge, Los Angeles FSC
1992 ....Christopher Bowman, Los Angeles FSC
1993 ....Scott Davis, Broadmoor SC

1994 ....Scott Davis, Broadmoor SC
1995 ....Todd Eldredge, Detroit SC
1996 ....Rudy Galindo, St Moritz ISC
1997 ....Todd Eldredge, Detroit SC
1998 ....Todd Eldredge, Detroit SC
1999 ....Michael Weiss, Washington FSC

Pairs

1914 ......Jeanne Chevalier, Norman M. Scott,
        WC of Montreal
1915-17..No competition
1918 ......Theresa Weld, Nathaniel W. Niles,
        SC of Boston
1919 ......No competition
1920 ......Theresa Weld, Nathaniel W. Niles,
        SC of Boston
1921 ......Theresa Weld Blanchard, Nathaniel W.
        Niles, SC of Boston
1922 ......Theresa Weld Blanchard, Nathaniel W.
        Niles, SC of Boston
1923 ......Theresa Weld Blanchard, Nathaniel W.
        Niles, SC of Boston
1924 ......Theresa Weld Blanchard, Nathaniel W.
        Niles, SC of Boston
1925 ......Theresa Weld Blanchard, Nathaniel W.
        Niles, SC of Boston
1926 ......Theresa Weld Blanchard, Nathaniel W.
        Niles, SC of Boston
1927 ......Theresa Weld Blanchard, Nathaniel W.
        Niles, SC of Boston
1928 ......Maribel Y. Vinson, Thornton L. Coolidge,
        SC of Boston
1929 ......Maribel Y. Vinson, Thornton L. Coolidge,
        SC of Boston
1930 ......Beatrix Loughran, Sherwin C. Badger,
        SC of New York
1931 ......Beatrix Loughran, Sherwin C. Badger,
        SC of New York
1932 ......Beatrix Loughran, Sherwin C. Badger,
        SC of New York
1933 ......Maribel Y. Vinson, George E. B. Hill,
        SC of Boston
1934 ......Grace E. Madden, James L. Madden,
        SC of Boston
1935 ......Maribel Y. Vinson, George E. B. Hill,
        SC of Boston
1936 ......Maribel Y. Vinson, George E. B. Hill,
        SC of Boston
1937 ......Maribel Y. Vinson, George E. B. Hill,
        SC of Boston
1938 ......Joan Tozzer, M. Bernard Fox, SC of Boston
1939 ......Joan Tozzer, M. Bernard Fox, SC of Boston
1940 ......Joan Tozzer, M. Bernard Fox, SC of Boston
1941 ......Donna Atwood, Eugene Turner, Mercury
        FSC/Los Angeles FSC
1942 ......Doris Schubach, Walter Noffke,
        Springfield Ice Birds
1943 ......Doris Schubach, Walter Noffke,
        Springfield Ice Birds
1944 ......Doris Schubach, Walter Noffke,
        Springfield Ice Birds
1945 ......Donna Jeanne Pospisil, Jean-Pierre Brunet,
        SC of New York
1946 ......Donna Jeanne Pospisil, Jean-Pierre Brunet,
        SC of New York
1947 ......Yvonne Claire Sherman, Robert J.
        Swenning, SC of New York

1948 ......Karol Kennedy, Peter Kennedy, Seattle SC
1949 ......Karol Kennedy, Peter Kennedy, Seattle SC
1950 ......Karol Kennedy, Peter Kennedy,
        Broadmoor SC
1951 ......Karol Kennedy, Peter Kennedy,
        Broadmoor SC
1952 ......Karol Kennedy, Peter Kennedy,
        Broadmoor SC
1953 ......Carole Ann Ormaca, Robin Greiner,
        SC of Fresno
1954 ......Carole Ann Ormaca, Robin Greiner,
        SC of Fresno
1955 ......Carole Ann Ormaca, Robin Greiner,
        St Moritz ISC
1956 ......Carole Ann Ormaca, Robin Greiner,
        St Moritz ISC
1957 ......Nancy Rouillard Ludington, Ronald
        Ludington, Commonwealth FSC/
        SC of Boston
1958 ......Nancy Rouillard Ludington, Ronald
        Ludington, Commonwealth FSC/
        SC of Boston
1959 ......Nancy Rouillard Ludington, Ronald
        Ludington, Commonwealth FSC
1960 ......Nancy Rouillard Ludington, Ronald
        Ludington, Commonwealth FSC
1961 ......Maribel Y. Owen, Dudley S. Richards,
        SC of Boston
1962 ......Dorothyann Nelson, Pieter Kollen,
        Village of Lake Placid
1963 ......Judianne Fotheringill, Jerry J. Fotheringill,
        Broadmoor SC
1964 ......Judianne Fotheringill, Jerry J. Fotheringill,
        Broadmoor SC
1965 ......Vivian Joseph, Ronald Joseph,
        Chicago FSC
1966 ......Cynthia Kauffman, Ronald Kauffman,
        Seattle SC
1967 ......Cynthia Kauffman, Ronald Kauffman,
        Seattle SC
1968 ......Cynthia Kauffman, Ronald Kauffman,
        Seattle SC
1969 ......Cynthia Kauffman, Ronald Kauffman,
        Seattle SC
1970 ......Jo Jo Starbuck, Kenneth Shelley,
        Arctic Blades FSC
1971 ......Jo Jo Starbuck, Kenneth Shelley,
        Arctic Blades FSC
1972 ......Jo Jo Starbuck, Kenneth Shelley,
        Arctic Blades FSC
1973 ......Melissa Militano, Mark Militano,
        SC of New York
1974 ......Melissa Militano, Johnny Johns,
        SC of New York/Detroit SC
1975 ......Melissa Militano, Johnny Johns,
        SC of New York/Detroit SC
1976 ......Tai Babilonia, Randy Gardner,
        Los Angeles FSC
1977 ......Tai Babilonia, Randy Gardner, LA FSC

Pairs *(Cont.)*

1978 ......Tai Babilonia, Randy Gardner,
　　　　Los Angeles FSC/Santa Monica FSC
1979 ......Tai Babilonia, Randy Gardner,
　　　　Los Angeles FSC/Santa Monica FSC
1980 ......Tai Babilonia, Randy Gardner,
　　　　Los Angeles FSC/Santa Monica FSC
1981 ......Caitlin Carruthers, Peter Carruthers,
　　　　SC of Wilmington
1982 ......Caitlin Carruthers, Peter Carruthers,
　　　　SC of Wilmington
1983 ......Caitlin Carruthers, Peter Carruthers,
　　　　SC of Wilmington
1984 ......Caitlin Carruthers, Peter Carruthers,
　　　　SC of Wilmington
1985 ......Jill Watson, Peter Oppegard,
　　　　Los Angeles FSC
1986 ......Gillian Wachsman, Todd Waggoner,
　　　　SC of Wilmington
1987 ......Jill Watson, Peter Oppegard,
　　　　Los Angeles FSC

1988 ......Jill Watson, Peter Oppegard,
　　　　Los Angeles FSC
1989 ......Kristi Yamaguchi, Rudy Galindo, St Mortiz ISC
1990 ......Kristi Yamaguchi, Rudy Galindo, St Mortiz ISC
1991 ......Natasha Kuchiki, Todd Sand,
　　　　Los Angeles FSC
1992 ......Calla Urbanski, Rocky Marval,
　　　　U of Delaware FSC/SC of New York
1993 ......Calla Urbanski, Rocky Marval,
　　　　U of Delaware FSC/SC of New York
1994 ......Jenni Meno, Todd Sand,
　　　　Winterhurst FSC/Los Angeles FSC
1995 ......Jenni Meno, Todd Sand,
　　　　Winterhurst FSC/Los Angeles FSC
1996 ......Jenni Meno, Todd Sand,
　　　　Winterhurst FSC/Los Angeles FSC
1997 ......Kyoko Ina, Jason Dungjen, SC of New York
1998 ......Kyoko Ina, Jason Dungjen, SC of New York
1999 ......Danielle Hartsell, Steve Hartsell, Detroit SC

Dance

1914 ......Waltz: Theresa Weld, Nathaniel W. Niles,
　　　　SC of Boston
1915-19...No competition
1920 ......Waltz: Theresa Weld, Nathaniel W. Niles,
　　　　SC of Boston
　　　　Fourteenstep: Gertrude Cheever Porter,
　　　　Irving Brokaw, New York SC
1921 ......Waltz and Fourteenstep: Theresa Weld
　　　　Blanchard, Nathaniel W. Niles, SC of Boston
1922 ......Waltz: Beatrix Loughran, Edward M.
　　　　Howland, New York SC/SC of Boston
　　　　Fourteenstep: Theresa Weld Blanchard,
　　　　Nathaniel W. Niles, SC of Boston
1923 ......Waltz: Mr. & Mrs. Henry W. Howe,
　　　　New York SC
　　　　Fourteenstep: Sydney Goode, James B.
　　　　Greene, New York SC
1924 ......Waltz: Rosaline Dunn, Frederick Gabel,
　　　　New York SC
　　　　Fourteenstep: Sydney Goode, James B.
　　　　Greene, New York SC
1925 ......Waltz and Fourteenstep: Virginia Slattery,
　　　　Ferrier T. Martin, New York SC
1926 ......Waltz: Rosaline Dunn, Joseph K. Savage,
　　　　New York SC
　　　　Fourteenstep: Sydney Goode, James B.
　　　　Greene, New York SC
1927 ......Waltz and Fourteenstep: Rosaline Dunn,
　　　　Joseph K. Savage, New York SC
1928 ......Waltz: Rosaline Dunn, Joseph K. Savage,
　　　　New York SC
　　　　Fourteenstep: Ada Bauman Kelly, George T.
　　　　Braakman, New York SC
1929 ......Waltz and Original Dance combined:
　　　　Edith C. Secord, Joseph K. Savage,
　　　　SC of New York
1930 ......Waltz: Edith C. Secord, Joseph K. Savage,
　　　　SC of New York
　　　　Original: Clara Rotch Frothingham, George
　　　　E. B. Hill, SC of Boston
1931 ......Waltz: Edith C. Secord, Ferrier T. Martin,
　　　　SC of New York
　　　　Original: Theresa Weld Blanchard, Nathaniel
　　　　W. Niles, SC of Boston

1932 ......Waltz: Edith C. Secord, Joseph K. Savage,
　　　　SC of New York
　　　　Original: Clara Rotch Frothingham, George
　　　　E. B. Hill, SC of Boston
1933 ......Waltz: Ilse Twaroschk, Frederick F.
　　　　Fleishmann, Brooklyn FSC
　　　　Original: Suzanne Davis, Frederick
　　　　Goodridge, SC of Boston
1934 ......Waltz: Nettie C. Prantel, Roy Hunt, SC of
　　　　New York
　　　　Original: Suzanne Davis, Frederick
　　　　Goodridge, SC of Boston
1935 ......Waltz: Nettie C. Prantel, Roy Hunt,
　　　　SC of New York
1936 ......Marjorie Parker, Joseph K. Savage,
　　　　SC of New York
1937 ......Nettie C. Prantel, Harold Hartshorne,
　　　　SC of New York
1938 ......Nettie C. Prantel, Harold Hartshorne,
　　　　SC of New York
1939 ......Sandy Macdonald, Harold Hartshorne,
　　　　SC of New York
1940 ......Sandy Macdonald, Harold Hartshorne,
　　　　SC of New York
1941 ......Sandy Macdonald, Harold Hartshorne, SCNY
1942 ......Edith B. Whetstone, Alfred N. Richards, Jr,
　　　　Philadelphia SC & HS
1943 ......Marcella May, James Lochead, Jr,
　　　　Skate & Ski Club
1944 ......Marcella May, James Lochead, Jr,
　　　　Skate & Ski Club
1945 ......Kathe Mehl Williams, Robert J. Swenning,
　　　　SC of New York
1946 ......Anne Davies, Carleton C. Hoffner, Jr,
　　　　Washington FSC
1947 ......Lois Waring, Walter H. Bainbridge, Jr,
　　　　Baltimore FSC/Washigton FSC
1948 ......Lois Waring, Walter H. Bainbridge, Jr,
　　　　Baltimore FSC/Washington FSC
1949 ......Lois Waring, Walter H. Bainbridge, Jr,
　　　　Baltimore FSC/Washington FSC
1950 ......Lois Waring, Michael McGean, Baltimore FSC
1951 ......Carmel Bodel, Edward L. Bodel,
　　　　St Moritz ISC

Dance *(Cont.)*

1952 ......Lois Waring, Michael McGean,
      Baltimore FSC
1953 ......Carol Ann Peters, Daniel C. Ryan,
      Washington FSC
1954 ......Carmel Bodel, Edward L. Bodel, St Moritz ISC
1955 ......Carmel Bodel, Edward L. Bodel,
      St Moritz ISC
1956 ......Joan Zamboni, Roland Junso,
      Arctic Blades FSC
1957 ......Sharon McKenzie, Bert Wright,
      Los Angeles FSC
1958 ......Andree Anderson, Donald Jacoby, Buffalo SC
1959 ......Andree Anderson Jacoby, Donald Jacoby,
      Buffalo SC
1960 ......Margie Ackles, Charles W. Phillips, Jr,
      Los Angeles FSC/Arctic Blades FSC
1961 ......Diane C. Sherbloom, Larry Pierce,
      Los Angeles FSC/WC of Indianapolis
1962 ......Yvonne N. Littlefield, Peter F. Betts,
      Arctic Blades FSC/ Paramount, CA
1963 ......Sally Schantz, Stanley Urban,
      SC of Boston/Buffalo SC
1964 ......Darlene Streich, Charles D. Fetter, Jr,
      WC of Indianapolis
1965 ......Kristin Fortune, Dennis Sveum,
      Los Angeles FSC
1966 ......Kristin Fortune, Dennis Sveum,
      Los Angeles FSC
1967 ......Lorna Dyer, John Carrell, Broadmoor SC
1968 ......Judy Schwomeyer, James Sladky,
      WC of Indianapolis/Genesee FSC
1969 ......Judy Schwomeyer, James Sladky,
      WC of Indianapolis/Genesee FSC
1970 ......Judy Schwomeyer, James Sladky,
      WC of Indianapolis/Genesee FSC
1971 ......Judy Schwomeyer, James Sladky,
      WC of Indianapolis/Genesee FSC
1972 ......Judy Schwomeyer, James Sladky,
      WC of Indianapolis/Genesee FSC
1973 ......Mary Karen Campbell, Johnny Johns,
      Lansing SC/Detroit SC
1974 ......Colleen O'Connor, Jim Millns,
      Broadmoor SC/City of Colorado Springs

1975 ......Colleen O'Connor, Jim Millns,
      Broadmoor SC
1976 ......Colleen O'Connor, Jim Millns,
      Broadmoor SC
1977 ......Judy Genovesi, Kent Weigle,
      SC of Hartford/Charter Oak FSC
1978 ......Stacey Smith, John Summers,
      SC of Wilmington
1979 ......Stacey Smith, John Summers,
      SC of Wilmington
1980 ......Stacey Smith, John Summers,
      SC of Wilmington
1981 ......Judy Blumberg, Michael Seibert,
      Broadmoor SC/ISC of Indianapolis
1982 ......Judy Blumberg, Michael Seibert,
      Broadmoor SC/ISC of Indianapolis
1983 ......Judy Blumberg, Michael Seibert,
      Pittsburgh FSC
1984 ......Judy Blumberg, Michael Seibert,
      Pittsburgh FSC
1985 ......Judy Blumberg, Michael Seibert,
      Pittsburgh FSC
1986 ......Renee Roca, Donald Adair,
      Genesee FSC/Academy FSC
1987 ......Suzanne Semanick, Scott Gregory,
      U of Delaware SC
1988 ......Suzanne Semanick, Scott Gregory,
      U of Delaware SC
1989 ......Susan Wynne, Joseph Druar,
      Broadmoor SC/Seattle SC
1990 ......Susan Wynne, Joseph Druar,
      Broadmoor SC/Seattle SC
1991 ......Elizabeth Punsalan, Jerod Swallow,
      Broadmoor SC
1992 ......April Sargent, Russ Witherby,
      Ogdensburg FSC/U of Delaware FSC
1993 ......Renee Roca, Gorsha Sur, Broadmoor SC
1994 ......Elizabeth Punsalan, Jerod Swallow,
      Broadmoor SC/Detroit SC
1995 ......Renee Roca, Gorsha Sur, Broadmoor SC
1996 ......Elizabeth Punsalan, Jerod Swallow, Detroit SC
1997 ......Elizabeth Punsalan, Jerod Swallow, Detroit SC
1998 ......Elizabeth Punsalan, Jerod Swallow, Detroit SC
1999 ......Naomi Lang, Peter Tchernyshev, Detroit SC

U.S. Olympic Gold Medalists

Women

1956	Tenley Albright	1976	Dorothy Hamill
1960	Carol Heiss	1992	Kristi Yamaguchi
1968	Peggy Fleming	1998	Tara Lipinski

Men

1948	Richard Button	1960	David W. Jenkins
1952	Richard Button	1984	Scott Hamilton
1956	Hayes Alan Jenkins	1988	Brian Boitano

Special Achievements

Women successfully landing a triple axel in competition:
    Midori Ito, Japan, 1988 free-skating competition at Aichi, Japan.
    Tonya Harding, United States, 1991 U.S. Figure Skating Championship.

Tour de France winner Lance Armstrong

Tour de Lance

With an amazing return to form after battling cancer, Lance Armstrong won cycling's greatest race

BY B.J. SCHECTER

IT WAS A story of will. A stirring drama of a man's battle against a deadly disease that had spread throughout much of his body. An uplifting epic that ended with two astonishing victories and sounded almost too good to be true.

Indeed, the French refused to believe it, and during the 23 days in which the greatest comeback in 1999 occurred, many Americans were oblivious to it. The miracle that unfolded in the streets and mountains of France in the summer of 1999 had its beginnings slightly less than three years earlier, when doctors told cyclist Lance Armstrong of the U.S., a two-time world champion, that he had cancer. Horrified, scared and confused, Armstrong thought he was going to die.

Who could have imagined that such a short time later he'd be pedaling down the Champs-Elysées, about to win the most grueling event in sports, the exhausting 2,287-mile test of desire and endurance known as the Tour de France? For a long time the answer was no one, not even Armstrong. Even as he stood on a podium in the middle of the most famous avenue in the French capital, his yellow jersey signifying the race leader glowing in the midday sun, and was

simultaneously kissed by his mother and his wife, Armstrong could not completely comprehend what he had accomplished. It wasn't until the French army started to play *The Star-Spangled Banner* that it finally hit him. He began to cry.

"I was prepared to forget the sport," Armstrong said. "There was a real possibility that I would have to forget a lot of things. I just wanted to keep living. It was scary. Now my victory is going to give inspiration to those who never had it. The disease was a good thing for me. I would not change anything. I came back with a new perspective. If I never had cancer I never would have won the Tour de France. I'm convinced of that."

Tour organizers could hardly have wished for a better story to lift the event out of the doldrums. The 1998 race was tainted by a drug scandal that drove seven teams from the race and called into question the future and foundation of cycling. Just before the '99 Tour began, SPORTS ILLUSTRATED ran a lengthy investigative piece on French trainer Willy Voet, who claimed he had provided performance-enhancing drugs to hundreds of top riders over the years. The 86th riding of the Tour began under a cloud of suspicion and doubt.

And Armstrong—as he regained the yellow jersey for good on July 11 and steamed up the mountains and plowed through freezing rain and hail to become the first American to win the Tour since Greg LeMond in 1990—also came under suspicion in some quarters. Speculation ran rampant. A man may beat cancer, and he may defeat the world-class field at the Tour, but he will not, skeptics said, knock off both within 36 months of one another. Armstrong passed several random drug tests, but that didn't stop reporters from hounding him with questions for much of the 23-day race.

Armstrong regained the yellow jersey on July 11 and wore it all the way to the Champs-Elysées.

The French press in particular refused to believe that Armstrong's meteoric rise from extensive chemotherapy to the ranks of cycling's elite was unaided by drugs. *L'Equipe*, a French sports daily, ran several stories on the subject, including one inquisitive piece with a headline that, when translated, read, ARMSTRONG IS FROM ANOTHER PLANET.

When you consider the level of courage and determination Armstrong displayed during his comeback, that sounds like an apt description. On Oct. 2, 1996, Armstrong's doctor told him that he had testicular cancer. Worse, the disease had spread to other parts of his body. Armstrong had experienced pain in his testicles for some time but had dismissed it as part of a cyclist's normal aches and pains. Now there were tumors in his lungs, and the cancer had spread to his brain. Twenty years ago Armstrong's prognosis would have been bleak indeed, but thanks to advances in cancer research his chances of surviving were about 50–50. "The chemo works or it doesn't work," said oncologist Lawrence Einhorn, who treated Armstrong. "If it works, the patient will live a normal, cancer-free life. If it doesn't, and the cancer comes back, he will usually be dead three to four months later."

Armstrong had one of his testicles removed, underwent brain surgery and chose an aggressive form of chemotherapy, which was administered in three separate five-day stretches. Armstrong would fly from his home in Austin to Indianapolis for the treatments, go home for 2½ weeks and come back for more. His hair fell out, he was frequently nauseated, and he lost 10 to 15 pounds from his already slender frame. But Armstrong never lost sight of his ultimate goal to return to cycling, and during his recovery time in Austin he would go on 30-mile bike rides.

In October 1997—one year after his first round of chemotherapy—Armstrong was declared cancer-free. With a new sense of life's urgency, he set his sights on cycling's ultimate event. For the first time in his career, Armstrong trained in Europe on the same courses he would ride in the race. He trained with ferocious commitment, and on July 3 he won the opening stage of the Tour. He lost the yellow jersey briefly but won it back six days later and kept it for good, stretching his lead in the grueling mountain stages, which had previously given him trouble. He finished the Tour seven minutes, 37 seconds ahead of his nearest competitor. "It was a long road to get to the Tour," he said, "and a longer one to get through it." He was asked if winning the Tour was his greatest accomplishment. "Not really," he said.

It probably pales in comparison to winning a second chance at life.

Archery

National Men's Champions

1879...Will H. Thompson	1909...George Bryant	1941...Larry Hughes	1975...Darrell Pace
1880...L.L. Pedinghaus	1910...Henry Richardson	1946...Wayne Thompson	1976...Darrell Pace
1881...F.H. Walworth	1911...Dr. Robert Elmer	1947...Jack Wilson	1977...Rick McKinney
1882...D.H. Nash	1912...George Bryant	1948...Larry Hughes	1978...Darrell Pace
1883...Col. Robert Williams	1913...George Bryant	1949...Russ Reynolds	1979...Rick McKinney
1884...Col. Robert Williams	1914...Dr. Robert Elmer	1950...Stan Overby	1980...Rick McKinney
1885...Col. Robert Williams	1915...Dr. Robert Elmer	1951...Russ Reynolds	1981...Rick McKinney
1886...W.A. Clark	1916...Dr. Robert Elmer	1952...Robert Larson	1982...Rick McKinney
1887...W.A. Clark	1919...Dr. Robert Elmer	1953...Bill Glackin	1983...Rick McKinney
1888...Lewis Maxson	1920...Dr. Robert Elmer	1954...Robert Rhode	1984...Darrell Pace
1889...Lewis Maxson	1921...James Jiles	1955...Joe Fries	1985...Rick McKinney
1890...Lewis Maxson	1922...Dr. Robert Elmer	1956...Joe Fries	1986...Rick McKinney
1891...Lewis Maxson	1923...Bill Palmer	1957...Joe Fries	1987...Rick McKinney
1892...Lewis Maxson	1924...James Jiles	1958...Robert Bitner	1988...Jay Barrs
1893...Lewis Maxson	1925...Dr. Paul Crouch	1959...Wilbert Vetrovsky	1989...Ed Eliason
1894...Lewis Maxson	1926...Stanley Spencer	1960...Robert Kadlec	1990...Ed Eliason
1895...W.B. Robinson	1927...Dr. Paul Crouch	1961...Clayton Sherman	1991...Ed Eliason
1896...Lewis Maxson	1928...Bill Palmer	1962...Charles Sandlin	1992...Alan Rasor
1897...W.A. Clark	1929...Dr. E.K. Roberts	1963...Dave Keaggy Jr.	1993...Jay Barrs
1898...Lewis Maxson	1930...Russ Hoogerhyde	1964...Dave Keaggy Jr.	1994...Jay Barrs
1899...M.C. Howell	1931...Russ Hoogerhyde	1965...George Slinzer	1995...Justin Huish
1900...A.R. Clark	1932...Russ Hoogerhyde	1966...Hardy Ward	1996...Richard (Butch)
1901...Will H. Thompson	1933...Ralph Miller	1967...Ray Rogers	Johnson
1902...Will H. Thompson	1934...Russ Hoogerhyde	1968...Hardy Ward	1997...Richard (Butch)
1903...Will H. Thompson	1935...Gilman Keasey	1969...Ray Rogers	Johnson
1904...George Bryant	1936...Gilman Keasey	1970...Joe Thornton	1998...Victor Wunderle
1905...George Bryant	1937...Russ Hoogerhyde	1971...John Williams	1999...Victor Wunderle
1906...Henry Richardson	1938...Pat Chambers	1972...Kevin Erlandson	
1907...Henry Richardson	1939...Pat Chambers	1973...Darrell Pace	
1908...Will H. Thompson	1940...Russ Hoogerhyde	1974...Darrell Pace	

National Women's Champions

1879...Mrs. S. Brown	1909...Harriet Case	1939...Belvia Carter	1972...Ruth Rowe
1880...Mrs. T. Davies	1910...J.V. Sullivan	1940...Ann Weber	1973...Doreen Wilber
1881...Mrs. A.H. Gibbes	1911...Mrs. J.S. Taylor	1941...Ree Dillinger	1974...Doreen Wilber
1882...Mrs. A.H. Gibbes	1912...Mrs. Witwer	1946...Ann Weber	1975...Irene Lorensen
1883...Mrs. M.C. Howell	Tayler	1947...Ann Weber	1976...Luann Ryon
1884...Mrs. H. Hall	1913...Mrs. P. Fletcher	1948...Jean Lee	1977...Luann Ryon
1885...Mrs. M.C. Howell	1914...Mrs. B.P. Gray	1949...Jean Lee	1978...Luann Ryon
1886...Mrs. M.C. Howell	1915...Cynthia Wesson	1950...Jean Lee	1979...Lynette Johnson
1887...Mrs. A.M. Phillips	1916...Cynthia Wesson	1951...Jean Lee	1980...Judi Adams
1888...Mrs. A.M. Phillips	1919...Dorothy Smith	1952...Ann Weber	1981...Debra Metzger
1889...Mrs. A.M. Phillips	1920...Cynthia Wesson	1953...Ann Weber	1982...Luann Ryon
1890...Mrs. M.C. Howell	1921...Mrs. L.C. Smith	1954...Luarette Young	1983...Nancy Myrick
1891...Mrs. M.C. Howell	1922...Dorothy Smith	1955...Ann Clark	1984...Ruth Rowe
1892...Mrs. M.C. Howell	1923...Norma Pierce	1956...Carole Meinhart	1985...Terri Pesho
1893...Mrs. M.C. Howell	1924...Dorothy Smith	1957...Carole Meinhart	1986...Debra Ochs
1894...Mrs. Albert Kern	1925...Dorothy Smith	1958...Carole Meinhart	1987...Terry Quinn
1895...Mrs. M.C. Howell	1926...Dorothy Smith	1959...Carole Meinhart	1988...Debra Ochs
1896...Mrs. M.C. Howell	1927...Mrs. R. Johnson	1960...Ann Clark	1989...Debra Ochs
1897...Mrs. J.S. Baker	1928...Beatrice	1961...Victoria Cook	1990...Denise Parker
1898...Mrs. M.C. Howell	Hodgson	1962...Nancy	1991...Denise Parker
1899...Mrs. M.C. Howell	1929...Audrey Grubbs	Vonderheide	1992...Sherry Block
1900...Mrs. M.C. Howell	1930...Audrey Grubbs	1963...Nancy	1993...Denise Parker
1901...Mrs. C.E.	1931...Dorothy	Vonderheide	1994...Judy Adams
Woodruff	Cummings	1964...Victoria Cook	1995...Jessica Carlson
1902...Mrs. M.C. Howell	1932...Ilda Hanchette	1965...Nancy Pfeiffer	1996...Janet Dykman
1903...Mrs. M.C. Howell	1933...Madelaine Taylor	1966...Helen Thornton	1997...Janet Dykman
1904...Mrs. M.C. Howell	1934...Desales Mudd	1967...Ardelle Mills	1998...Janet Dykman
1905...Mrs. M.C. Howell	1935...Ruth Hodgert	1968...Victoria Cook	1999...Denise Parker
1906...Mrs. E.C. Cook	1936...Gladys Hammer	1969...Doreen Wilber	
1907...Mrs. M.C. Howell	1937...Gladys Hammer	1970...Nancy Myrick	
1908...Harriet Case	1938...Jean Tenney	1971...Doreen Wilber	

Chess

World Champions

FIDE

1866–94	Wilhelm Steinitz, Austria
1894–1921	Emanuel Lasker, Germany
1921–27	Jose Capablanca, Cuba
1927–35	Alexander Alekhine, France
1935–37	Max Euwe, Holland
1937–47	Alexander Alekhine, France
1948–57	Mikhail Botvinnik, USSR
1957–58	Vassily Smyslov, USSR
1958–59	Mikhail Botvinnik, USSR
1960–61	Mikhail Tal, USSR
1961–63	Mikhail Botvinnik, USSR

FIDE (Cont.)

1963–69	Tigran Petrosian, USSR
1969–72	Boris Spassky, USSR
1972–75	Bobby Fischer, United States
1975–85	Anatoly Karpov, USSR
1985–93	*Garry Kasparov, USSR
1994–98	Anatoly Karpov, Russia
1999–	Alexander Khalifman

*Kasparov stripped of title by FIDE in 1993; title vacant until '94.

Professional Chess Association

1993–	Garry Kasparov

United States Champions

1857–71	Paul Morphy	1957–61	Bobby Fischer	1987	Joel Benjamin
1871–76	George Mackenzie	1961–62	Larry Evans		Nick DeFirmian
1876–80	James Mason	1962–68	Bobby Fischer	1988	Michael Wilder
1880–89	George Mackenzie	1968–69	Larry Evans	1989	Roman
1889–90	Samuel Lipschutz	1969–72	Samuel Reshevsky		Dzindzichashvili
1890	Jackson Showalter	1972–73	Robert Byrne		Stuart Rachels
1890–91	Max Judd	1973–74	Lubomir Kavale		Yasser Seirawan
1891–92	Jackson Showalter		John Grefe	1990	Lev Alburt
1892–94	Samuel Lipschutz	1974–77	Walter Browne	1991	Gata Kamski
1894	Jackson Showalter	1978–80	Lubomir Kavalek	1992	Patrick Wolff
1894–95	Albert Hodges	1980–81	Larry Evans	1993	Alex Yermolinsky
1895–97	Jackson Showalter		Larry Christiansen		A. Shabalov
1897–1906	Harry Pillsbury		Walter Browne	1994	Boris Gulko
1906–09	Vacant	1981–83	Walter Browne	1995	Patrick Wolff
1909–36	Frank Marshall		Yasser Seirawan		Nick DeFirmian
1936–44	Samuel Reshevsky	1983	Roman		Alexander Ivanov
1944–46	Arnold Denker		Dzindzichashvili	1996	Alex Yermolinsky
1946–48	Samuel Reshevsky	1983	Larry Christiansen	1997	Alex Yermolinsky
1948–51	Herman Steiner		Walter Browne	1998	Alex Yermolinsky
1951–54	Larry Evans	1984–85	Lev Alburt	1999	Boris Gulko
1954–57	Arthur Bisguier	1986	Yasser Seirawan		

Curling

World Men's Champions

Year	Country, Skip	Year	Country, Skip	Year	Country, Skip
1972	Canada, Crest Melesnuk	1982	Canada, Al Hackner	1992	Switzerland, Markus Eggler
1973	Sweden, Kjell Oscarius	1983	Canada, Ed Werenich	1993	Canada, Russ Howard
1974	U.S., Bud Somerville	1984	Norway, Eigil Ramsfjell	1994	Canada, Rick Folk
1975	Switzerland, Otto Danieli	1985	Canada, Al Hackner	1995	Canada, Kerry Burtnyk
1976	U.S., Bruce Roberts	1986	Canada, Ed Luckowich	1996	Canada, Jeff Stoughton
1977	Sweden, Ragnar Kamp	1987	Canada, Russ Howard	1997	Sweden, Peter Lindholm
1978	U.S., Bob Nichols	1988	Norway, Eigil Ramsfjell	1998	Canada, Wayne Middaugh
1979	Norway, Kristian Soerum	1989	Canada, Pat Ryan	1999	Scotland, Hammy McMillan
1980	Canada, Rich Folk	1990	Canada, Ed Werenich		
1981	Switzerland, Jurg Tanner	1991	Scotland, David Smith		

World Women's Champions

Year	Country, Skip	Year	Country, Skip	Year	Country, Skip
1979	Switzerland, Gaby Casanova	1985	Canada, Linda Moore	1993	Canada, Sandra Peterson
1980	Canada, Marj Mitchell	1986	Canada, Marilyn Darte	1994	Canada, Sandra Peterson
1981	Sweden, Elisabeth Hogstrom	1987	Canada, Pat Sanders	1995	Sweden, Elisabet Gustafson
1982	Denmark, Marianne Jorgenson	1988	Germany, Andrea Schopp	1996	Canada, Marilyn Bodogh
1983	Switzerland, Erika Mueller	1989	Canada, Heather Houston	1997	Canada, Sandra Schmirler
1984	Canada, Connie Lallberte	1990	Norway, Dordi Nordby	1998	Sweden, Elisabet Gustafson
		1991	Norway, Dordi Nordby	1999	Sweden, Elisabet Gustafson
		1992	Sweden, Elisabet Johanssen		

U.S. Men's Champions

Year	Site	Winning Club	Skip
1957	Chicago, IL	Hibbing, MN	Harold Lauber
1958	Milwaukee, WI	Detroit, MI	Douglas Fisk
1959	Green Bay, WI	Hibbing, MN	Fran Kleffman
1960	Chicago, IL	Grafton, ND	Orvil Gilleshammer
1961	Grand Forks, ND	Seattle, WA	Frank Crealock
1962	Detroit, MI	Hibbing, MN	Fran Kleffman
1963	Duluth, MN	Detroit, MI	Mike Slyziuk
1964	Utica, NY	Duluth, MN	Robert Magle Jr.
1965	Seattle, WA	Superior, WI	Bud Somerville
1966	Hibbing, MN	Fargo, ND	Joe Zbacnik
1967	Winchester, MA	Seattle, WA	Bruce Roberts
1968	Madison, WI	Superior, WI	Bud Somerville
1969	Grand Forks, ND	Superior, WI	Bud Somerville
1970	Ardsley, NY	Grafton, ND	Art Tallackson
1971	Duluth, MN	Edmore, ND	Dale Dalziel
1972	Wilmette, IL	Grafton, ND	Robert Labonte
1973	Colorado Springs, CO	Winchester, MA	Charles Reeves
1974	Schenectady, NY	Superior, WI	Bud Somerville
1975	Detroit, MI	Seattle, WA	Ed Risling
1976	Wausau, WI	Hibbing, MN	Bruce Roberts
1977	Northbrook, IL	Hibbing, MN	Bruce Roberts
1978	Utica, NY	Superior, WI	Bob Nichols
1979	Superior, WI	Bemidji, MN	Scott Baird
1980	Bemidji, MN	Hibbing, MN	Paul Pustovar
1981	Fairbanks, AK	Superior, WI	Bob Nichols
1982	Brookline, MA	Madison, WI	Steve Brown
1983	Colorado Springs, CO	Colorado Springs, CO	Don Cooper
1984	Hibbing, MN	Hibbing, MN	Bruce Roberts
1985	Mequon, WI	Wilmette, IL	Tim Wright
1986	Seattle, WA	Madison, WI	Steve Brown
1987	Lake Placid, NY	Seattle, WA	Jim Vukich
1988	St. Paul, MN	Seattle, WA	Doug Jones
1989	Detroit, MI	Seattle, WA	Jim Vukich
1990	Superior, WI	Seattle, WA	Doug Jones
1991	Utica, NY	Madison, WI	Steve Brown
1992	Grafton, ND	Seattle, WA	Doug Jones
1993	St. Paul, MN	Bemidji, MN	Scott Baird
1994	Duluth, MN	Bemidji, MN	Scott Baird
1995	Appleton, WI	Superior, WI	Tim Somerville
1996	Bemidji, MN	Superior, WI	Tim Somerville
1997	Seattle, WA	Langdon, ND	Craig Disher
1998	Bismarck, SD	Stevens Pt., WI	Paul Pustovar
1999	Duluth, MN	Superior, WI	Tim Somerville

U.S. Women's Champions

Year	Site	Winning Club	Skip
1977	Wilmette, IL	Hastings, NY	Margaret Smith
1978	Duluth, MN	Wausau, WI	Sandy Robarge
1979	Winchester, MA	Seattle, WA	Nancy Langley
1980	Seattle, WA	Seattle, WA	Sharon Kozal
1981	Kettle Moraine, WI	Seattle, WA	Nancy Langley
1982	Bowling Green, OH	Oak Park, IL	Ruth Schwenker
1983	Grafton, ND	Seattle, WA	Nancy Langley
1984	Wauwatosa, WI	Duluth, MN	Amy Hatten
1985	Hershey, PA	Fairbanks, AK	Bev Birklid
1986	Chicago, IL	St Paul, MN	Gerri Tilden
1987	St Paul, MN	Seattle, WA	Sharon Good
1988	Darien, CT	Seattle, WA	Nancy Langley
1989	Detroit, MI	Rolla, ND	Jan Lagasse
1990	Superior, WI	Denver, CO	Bev Behnke
1991	Utica, NY	Houston, TX	Maymar Gemmell
1992	Grafton, ND	Madison, WI	Lisa Schoeneberg
1993	St Paul, MN	Denver, CO	Bev Behnke
1994	Duluth, MN	Denver, CO	Bev Behnke
1995	Appleton, WI	Madison, WI	Lisa Schoeneberg

U.S. Women's Champions *(Cont.)*

Year	Site	Winning Club	Skip
1996	Bemidji, MN	Madison, WI	Lisa Schoeneberg
1997	Seattle, WA	Arlington, WI	Patti Lank
1998	Bismarck, SD	Wilmette, IL	Kari Erickson
1999	Duluth, MN	Madison, WI	Patti Lank

Cycling

Professional Road Race World Champions

1927 ....Alfred Binda, Italy
1928 ....George Ronsse, Belgium
1929 ....George Ronsse, Belgium
1930 ....Alfred Binda, Italy
1931 ....Learco Guerra, Italy
1932 ....Alfred Binda, Italy
1933 ....George Speicher, France
1934 ....Karel Kaers, Belgium
1935 ....Jean Aerts, Belgium
1936 ....Antonio Magne, France
1937 ....Elio Meulenberg, Belgium
1938 ....Marcel Kint, Belgium
No competition 1939–45
1946 ....Hans Knecht, Switzerland
1947 ....Theo. Middelkamp, Holland
1948 ....Alberic Schotte, Belgium
1949 ....Henri Van Steenbergen, Belgium
1950 ....Alberic Schotte, Belgium
1951 ....Ferdinand Kubler, Switzerland
1952 ....Heinz Mueller, Germany
1953 ....Fausto Coppi, Italy
1954 ....Louison Bobet, France
1955 ....Stan Ockers, Belgium

1956 ....Rik Van Steenbergen, Belgium
1957 ....Rik Van Steenbergen, Belgium
1958 ....Ercole Baldini, Italy
1959 ....Andre Darrigade, France
1960 ....Rik van Looy, Belgium
1961 ....Rik van Looy, Belgium
1962 ....Jean Stablenski, France
1963 ....Bennoni Beheyt, Belgium
1964 ....Jan Janssen, Holland
1965 ....Tommy Simpson, England
1966 ....Rudi Altig, West Germany
1967 ....Eddy Merckx, Belgium
1968 ....Vittorio Adorni, Italy
1969 ....Harm Ottenbros, Netherlands
1970 ....J.P. Monseré, Belgium
1971 ....Eddy Merckx, Belgium
1972 ....Marino Basso, Italy
1973 ....Felice Gimondi, Italy
1974 ....Eddy Merckx, Belgium
1975 ....Hennie Kuiper, Holland
1976 ....Freddy Maertens, Belgium
1977 ....Francesco Moser, Italy

1978 ....Gerri Knetemann, Holland
1979 ....Jan Raas, Holland
1980 ....Bernard Hinault, France
1981 ....Freddy Maertens, Belgium
1982 ....Giuseppe Saronni, Italy
1983 ....Greg LeMond, United States
1984 ....Claude Criquielion, Belgium
1985 ....Joop Zoetemelk, Holland
1986 ....Moreno Argentin, Italy
1987 ....Stephen Roche, Ireland
1988 ....Maurizio Fondriest, Italy
1989 ....Greg LeMond, United States
1990 ....Rudy Dhaenene, Belgium
1991 ....Gianni Bugno, Italy
1992 ....Gianni Bugno, Italy
1993 ....Lance Armstrong, United States
1994 ....Luc LeBlanc, France
1995 ....Abraham Olano, Spain
1996 ....Johan Museeuw, Belgium
1997 ....Laurent Brochard, France
1998 ....Oskar Camenzind, Switz
1999 .....Oscar Gomez Freire, Spain

Tour DuPont Winners

Year	Winner	Time
1989	Dag Otto Lauritzen, Norway	33 hrs, 28 min, 48 sec
1990	Raul Alcala, Mexico	45 hrs, 20 min, 9 sec
1991	Erik Breukink, Holland	48 hrs, 56 min, 53 sec
1992	Greg LeMond, United States	44 hrs, 27 min, 43 sec
1993	Raul Alcala, Mexico	46 hrs, 42 min, 52 sec
1994	Viatcheslav Ekimov, Russia	47 hrs, 14 min, 29 sec
1995	Lance Armstrong, United States	46 hrs, 31 min, 16 sec
1996	Lance Armstrong, United States	48 hrs, 20 min, 5 sec

Note: Race not held since 1996.

Tour de France Winners

Year	Winner	Time
1903	Maurice Garin, France	94 hrs, 33 min
1904	Henry Cornet, France	96 hrs, 5 min, 56 sec
1905	Louis Trousselier, France	110 hrs, 26 min, 58 sec
1906	Rene Pottier, France	Not available
1907	Lucien Petit-Breton, France	158 hrs, 54 min, 5 sec
1908	Lucien Petit-Breton, France	Not available
1909	Francois Faber, Luxembourg	157 hrs, 1 min, 22 sec
1910	Octave Lapize, France	162 hrs, 41 min, 30 sec
1911	Gustave Garrigou, France	195 hrs, 37 min
1912	Odile Defraye, Belgium	190 hrs, 30 min, 28 sec
1913	Philippe Thys, Belgium	197 hrs, 54 min
1914	Philippe Thys, Belgium	200 hrs, 28 min, 48 sec
1915–18	No race	
1919	Firmin Lambot, Belgium	231 hrs, 7 min, 15 sec
1920	Philippe Thys, Belgium	228 hrs, 36 min, 13 sec

Tour de France Winners (Cont.)

Year	Winner	Time
1921	Leon Scieur, Belgium	221 hrs, 50 min, 26 sec
1922	Firmin Lambot, Belgium	222 hrs, 8 min, 6 sec
1923	Henri Pelissier, France	222 hrs, 15 min, 30 sec
1924	Ottavio Bottechia, Italy	226 hrs, 18 min, 21 sec
1925	Ottavio Bottechia, Italy	219 hrs, 10 min, 18 sec
1926	Lucien Buysse, Belgium	238 hrs, 44 min, 25 sec
1927	Nicolas Frantz, Luxembourg	198 hrs, 16 min, 42 sec
1928	Nicolas Frantz, Luxembourg	192 hrs, 48 min, 58 sec
1929	Maurice Dewaele, Belgium	186 hrs, 39 min, 16 sec
1930	Andre Leducq, France	172 hrs, 12 min, 16 sec
1931	Antonin Magne, France	177 hrs, 10 min, 3 sec
1932	Andre Leducq, France	154 hrs, 12 min, 49 sec
1933	Georges Speicher, France	147 hrs, 51 min, 37 sec
1934	Antonin Magne, France	147 hrs, 13 min, 58 sec
1935	Romain Maes, Belgium	141 hrs, 32 min
1936	Sylvere Maes, Belgium	142 hrs, 47 min, 32 sec
1937	Roger Lapebie, France	138 hrs, 58 min, 31 sec
1938	Gino Bartali, Italy	148 hrs, 29 min, 12 sec
1939	Sylvere Maes, Belgium	132 hrs, 3 min, 17 sec
1940–46	No race	
1947	Jean Robic, France	148 hrs, 11 min, 25 sec
1948	Gino Bartali, Italy	147 hrs, 10 min, 36 sec
1949	Fausto Coppi, Italy	149 hrs, 40 min, 49 sec
1950	Ferdi Kubler, Switzerland	145 hrs, 36 min, 56 sec
1951	Hugo Koblet, Switzerland	142 hrs, 20 min, 14 sec
1952	Fausto Coppi, Italy	151 hrs, 57 min, 20 sec
1953	Louison Bobet, France	129 hrs, 23 min, 25 sec
1954	Louison Bobet, France	140 hrs, 6 min, 5 sec
1955	Louison Bobet, France	130 hrs, 29 min, 26 sec
1956	Roger Walkowiak, France	124 hrs, 1 min, 16 sec
1957	Jacques Anquetil, France	129 hrs, 46 min, 11 sec
1958	Charly Gaul, Luxembourg	116 hrs, 59 min, 5 sec
1959	Federico Bahamontes, Spain	123 hrs, 46 min, 45 sec
1960	Gastone Nencini, Italy	112 hrs, 8 min, 42 sec
1961	Jacques Anquetil, France	122 hrs, 1 min, 33 sec
1962	Jacques Anquetil, France	114 hrs, 31 min, 54 sec
1963	Jacques Anquetil, France	113 hrs, 30 min, 5 sec
1964	Jacques Anquetil, France	127 hrs, 9 min, 44 sec
1965	Felice Gimondi, Italy	116 hrs, 42 min, 6 sec
1966	Lucien Aimar, France	117 hrs, 34 min, 21 sec
1967	Roger Pingeon, France	136 hrs, 53 min, 50 sec
1968	Jan Janssen, Netherlands	133 hrs, 49 min, 32 sec
1969	Eddy Merckx, Belgium	116 hrs, 16 min, 2 sec
1970	Eddy Merckx, Belgium	119 hrs, 31 min, 49 sec
1971	Eddy Merckx, Belgium	96 hrs, 45 min, 14 sec
1972	Eddy Merckx, Belgium	108 hrs, 17 min, 18 sec
1973	Luis Ocana, Spain	122 hrs, 25 min, 34 sec
1974	Eddy Merckx, Belgium	116 hrs, 16 min, 58 sec
1975	Bernard Thevenet, France	114 hrs, 35 min, 31 sec
1976	Lucien Van Impe, Belgium	116 hrs, 22 min, 23 sec
1977	Bernard Thevenet, France	115 hrs, 38 min, 30 sec
1978	Bernard Hinault, France	108 hrs, 18 min
1979	Bernard Hinault, France	103 hrs, 6 min, 50 sec
1980	Joop Zoetemelk, Netherlands	109 hrs, 19 min, 14 sec
1981	Bernard Hinault, France	96 hrs, 19 min, 38 sec
1982	Bernard Hinault, France	92 hrs, 8 min, 46 sec
1983	Laurent Fignon, France	105 hrs, 7 min, 52 sec
1984	Laurent Fignon, France	112 hrs, 3 min, 40 sec
1985	Bernard Hinault, France	113 hrs, 24 min, 23 sec
1986	Greg LeMond, United States	110 hrs, 35 min, 19 sec
1987	Stephen Roche, Ireland	115 hrs, 27 min, 42 sec
1988	Pedro Delgado, Spain	84 hrs, 27 min, 53 sec
1989	Greg LeMond, United States	87 hrs, 38 min, 35 sec
1990	Greg LeMond, United States	90 hrs, 43 min, 20 sec
1991	Miguel Induráin, Spain	101 hrs, 1 min, 20 sec

Tour de France Winners (Cont.)

Year	Winner	Time
1992	Miguel Induráin, Spain	100 hrs, 49 min, 30 sec
1993	Miguel Induráin, Spain	95 hrs, 57 min, 9 sec
1994	Miguel Induráin, Spain	103 hrs, 38 min, 38 sec
1995	Miguel Induráin, Spain	92 hrs, 44 min, 59 sec
1996	Bjarne Riis, Denmark	95 hrs, 57 min, 16 sec
1997	Jan Ullrich, Germany	100 hrs, 30 min, 35 sec
1998	Marco Pantani, Italy	92 hrs, 49 min, 46 sec
1999	Lance Armstrong, United States	91 hrs, 32 min, 16 sec

Sled Dog Racing

Iditarod

Year	Winner	Time	Year	Winner	Time
1973	Dick Wilmarth	20 days, 00:49:41	1987	Susan Butcher	11 days, 02:05:13
1974	Carl Huntington	20 days, 15:02:07	1988	Susan Butcher	11 days, 11:41:40
1975	Emmitt Peters	14 days, 14:43:45	1989	Joe Runyan	11 days, 05:24:34
1976	Gerald Riley	18 days, 22:58:17	1990	Susan Butcher	11 days, 01:53:23
1977	Rick Swenson	16 days, 16:27:13	1991	Rick Swenson	12 days, 16:34:39
1978	Dick Mackey	14 days, 18:52:24	1992	Martin Buser	10 days, 19:17:15
1979	Rick Swenson	15 days, 10:37:47	1993	Jeff King	10 days, 15:38:15
1980	Joe May	14 days, 07:11:51	1994	Martin Buser	10 days, 13:02:39
1981	Rick Swenson	12 days, 08:45:02	1995	Doug Swingley	9 days, 02:42:19
1982	Rick Swenson	16 days, 04:40:10	1996	Jeff King	9 days, 05:43:13
1983	Dick Mackey	12 days, 14:10:44	1997	Martin Buser	9 days, 08:30:45
1984	Dean Osmar	12 days, 15:07:33	1998	Jeff King	9 days, 05:52:26
1985	Libby Riddles	18 days, 00:20:17	1999	Doug Swingley	9 days, 14:31:19
1986	Susan Butcher	11 days, 15:06:00			

Fishing

Saltwater Fishing Records

Species	Weight	Where Caught	Date	Angler
Albacore	88 lb 2 oz	Gran Canaria, Canary Islands	Nov 19, 1977	Siegfried Dickemann
Amberjack, greater	155 lb 10 oz	Challenger Bank, Bermuda	June 24, 1981	Joseph Dawson
Amberjack, Pacific	104 lb	Baja California, Mexico	July 4, 1984	Richard Cresswell
Angler	126 lb 12 oz	Sagnefiorden Hoyanger, Nor	July 4, 1996	Gunnar Thorsteinsen
Barracuda, great	85 lb	Christmas Island, Kiribati	April 11, 1992	John W. Helfrich
Barracuda, Mexican	21 lb	Phantom Isle, Costa Rica	Mar 27, 1987	E. Greg Kent
Barracuda, pickhandle	25 lb 5 oz	Scottburgh, Natal, South Africa	July 3, 1996	Demetrios Stamatis
Bass, barred sand	13 lb 3 oz	Huntington Beach, CA	Aug 29, 1988	Robert Halal
Bass, black sea	9 lb 8 oz	Virginia Beach, VA	Jan 9, 1987	Joe Mizelle Jr.
Bass, European	20 lb 11 oz	Stes Maries de la Mer, France	May 6, 1986	Jean Baptiste Bayle
Bass, giant sea	563 lb 8 oz	Anacapa Island, CA	Aug 20, 1968	James D. McAdam Jr.
Bass, redeye	8 lb 12 oz	Apalatchicola River, FL	Jan 28, 1995	Carl W. Davis
Bass, striped	78 lb 8 oz	Atlantic City, NJ	Sep 21, 1982	Albert R. McReynolds
Bluefish	31 lb 12 oz	Hatteras Inlet, NC	Jan 30, 1972	James M. Hussey
Bonefish	19 lb	Zululand, South Africa	May 26, 1962	Brian W. Batchelor
Bonito, Atlantic	18 lb 4 oz	Faial Island, Azores	July 8, 1953	D.G. Higgs
Bonito, Pacific	14 lb 12 oz	Baja California, Mexico	Oct. 12, 1980	Jerome H. Rilling
Cabezon	23 lb	Juan De Fuca Strait, WA	Aug 4, 1990	Wesley Hunter
Cobia	135 lb 9 oz	Shark Bay, Australia	July 9, 1985	Peter W. Goulding
Cod, Atlantic	98 lb 12 oz	Isle of Shoals, NH	June 8, 1969	Alphonse Bielevich
Cod, Pacific	32 lb	Unalaska Bay, AK	June 29, 1997	Donald Boston
Conger	133 lb 4 oz	South Devon, England	June 5, 1995	Vic Evans
Dolphin	87 lb	Papagallo Gulf, Costa Rica	Sep 25, 1976	Manuel Salazar
Drum, black	113 lb 1 oz	Lewes, DE	Sep 15, 1975	Gerald M. Townsend
Drum, red	94 lb 2 oz	Avon, NC	Nov 7, 1984	David Deuel
Eel, American	9 lb 4 oz	Cape May, NJ	Nov 9, 1995	Jeff Pennick
Eel, marbled	36 lb 1 oz	Durban, South Africa	June 10, 1984	Ferdie van Nooten

Saltwater Fishing Records *(Cont.)*

Species	Weight	Where Caught	Date	Angler
Flounder, southern	20 lb 9 oz	Nassau Sound, FL	Dec 23, 1983	Larenza W. Mungin
Flounder, summer	22 lb 7 oz	Montauk, NY	Sep 15, 1975	Charles Nappi
Grouper, warsaw	436 lb 12 oz	Destin, FL	Dec 22, 1985	Steve Haeusler
Halibut, Atlantic	255 lb 4 oz	Gloucester, MA	July 28, 1989	Sonny Manley
Halibut, California	53 lb 4 oz	Santa Rosa Island, CA	July 7, 1988	Russell J. Harmon
Halibut, Pacific	459 lb	Dutch Harbor, AK	June 11, 1996	Jack Tragis
Jack, crevalle	57 lb 14 oz	Southwest Pass, LA	Aug 15, 1997	Leon Richard
Jack, horse-eye	24 lb 8 oz	Miami, FL	Dec 20, 1982	Tito Schnau
Jack, Pacific crevalle	31 lb	Playa Zancudo, Costa Rica	Dec 17, 1997	Roy Roig
Jewfish	680 lb	Fernandina Beach, FL	May 20, 1961	Lynn Joyner
Kawakawa	29 lb	Isla Clarion, Mexico	Dec 17, 1986	Ronald Nakamura
Lingcod	69 lb	Langara Island, B.C.	June 16, 1992	Murray M. Romer
Mackerel, cero	17 lb 2 oz	Islamorada, FL	Apr 5, 1986	G. Michael Mills
Mackerel, king	90 lb	Key West, FL	Feb 16, 1976	Norton I. Thomton
Mackerel, narrowbarred	99 lb	Natal, South Africa	Mar 14, 1982	Michael J. Wilkinson
Mackerel, Spanish	13 lb	Ocracoke Inlet, NC	Nov 4, 1987	Robert Cranton
Marlin, Atlantic blue	1402 lb 2 oz	Vitoria, Brazil	Feb 29, 1992	Paulo R.A. Amorim
Marlin, black	1560 lb	Cabo Blanco, Peru	Aug 4, 1953	A.C. Glassell Jr.
Marlin, Pacific blue	1376 lb	Kaaiwi Point, HI	May 31, 1982	J.W. de Beaubien
Marlin, striped	494 lb	Tutukaka, New Zealand	Jan 16, 1986	Bill Boniface
Marlin, white	181 lb 14 oz	Vitoria, Brazil	Dec 8, 1979	Evandro Luiz Caser
Permit	56 lb 2 oz	Fort Lauderdale, FL	June 30, 1997	Thomas Sebestyen
Pollock	50 lb	Salstraumen, Norway	Nov 30, 1995	Thor Magnus-Lekang
Pompano, African	50 lb 8 oz	Daytona Beach, FL	Apr 21, 1990	Tom Sargent
Roosterfish	114 lb	La Paz, Mexico	June 1, 1960	Abe Sackheim
Runner, blue	11 lb 2 oz	Dauphin Island, AL	June 28, 1997	Stacey M. Moiren
Runner, rainbow	37 lb 9 oz	Isla Clarion, Mexico	Nov 21, 1991	Tom Pfleger
Sailfish, Atlantic	141 lb 1 oz	Luanda, Angola	Feb 19, 1994	Alfredo de Sousa Neves
Sailfish, Pacific	221 lb	Santa Cruz Island, Ecuador	Feb 12, 1947	C.W. Stewart
Seabass, white	83 lb 12 oz	San Felipe, Mexico	Mar 31, 1953	L.C. Baumgardner
Seatrout, spotted	17 lb 7 oz	Ft. Pierce, FL	May 11, 1995	Craig F. Carson
Shark, bigeye thresher	802 lb	Tutukaka, New Zealand	Feb 8, 1981	Dianne North
Shark, blue	454 lb	Martha's Vineyard, MA	July 19, 1996	Pete Bergin
Shark, grter hammrhd	991 lb	Sarasota, FL	May 30, 1982	Allen Ogle
Shark, Greenland	1708 lb 9 oz	Trondheimsfjord, Norway	Oct 18, 1987	Terje Nordtvedt
Shark, porbeagle	507 lb	Caithness, Scotland	Mar 9, 1993	Christopher Bennet
Shark, shortfin mako	1115 lb	Black River, Mauritius	Nov 16, 1988	Patrick Guillanton
Shark, tiger	1780 lb	Cherry Grove, SC	June 14, 1964	Walter Maxwell
Shark, tope	98 lb 8 oz	Santa Monica, CA	Oct 20, 1994	Freed Oakley
Shark, white	2664 lb	Ceduna, Australia	Apr 21, 1959	Alfred Dean
Skipjack, black	26 lb	Baja California, Mexico	Oct 23, 1991	Clifford K. Hamaishi
Snapper, cubera	121 lb 8 oz	Cameron, LA	July 5, 1982	Mike Hebert
Snook	53 lb 10 oz	Parismina Ranch, Costa Rica	Oct 18, 1978	Gilbert Ponzi
Spearfish	90 lb 13 oz	Madeira Island, Portugal	June 2, 1980	Joseph Larkin
Swordfish	1182 lb	Iquique, Chile	May 7, 1953	L. Marron
Tarpon	283 lb 4 oz	Sherbro Island, Sierra Leone	Apr 16, 1991	Yvon Victor Sebag
Tautog	25 lb	Ocean City, NJ	Jan 20, 1998	Anthony Monica
Tilapia, mozambique	2 lb 8 oz	Delray Beach, FL	Nov 10, 1997	Nick Cardella
Trevally, bigeye	31 lb 8 oz	Poivre Island, Seychelles	Apr 23, 1997	Les Sampson
Trevally, giant	145 lb 8 oz	Maui, HI	Mar 28, 1991	Russell Mori
Tuna, Atlantic bigeye	392 lb 6 oz	Puerto Rico, Gran Caneria, Spain	July 25, 1996	Dieter Vogel
Tuna, blackfin	45 lb 8 oz	Key West, FL	May 4, 1996	Sam J. Burnett
Tuna, bluefin	1496 lb	Aulds Cove, Nova Scotia	Oct 26, 1979	Ken Fraser
Tuna, longtail	79 lb 2 oz	Montague Island, NSW, Australia	Apr 12, 1982	Tim Simpson
Tuna, Pacific bigeye	435 lb	Cabo Blanco, Peru	Apr 17, 1957	Russel Lee
Tuna, skipjack	45 lb 4 oz	Baja California, Mexico	Nov 16, 1996	Brian Evans
Tuna, southern bluefin	348 lb 5 oz	Whakatane, New Zealand	Jan 16, 1981	Rex Wood
Tuna, yellowfin	388 lb 12 oz	San Benedicto Is, Mexico	Apr 1, 1977	Curt Wiesenhutter
Tunny, little	35 lb 2 oz	Cape de Garde, Algeria	Dec 14, 1988	Jean Yves Chatard
Wahoo	158 lb 8 oz	Loreto, Baja California, Mexico	June 10, 1996	Keith Winter
Weakfish	19 lb 2 oz	Jones Beach Inlet, NY	Oct 11, 1984	Dennis Rooney
		Delaware Bay, Delaware	May 20, 1989	William E. Thomas
Yellowtail, California	79 lb 4 oz	Baja California, Mexico	July 2, 1991	Robert I. Welker
Yellowtail, southern	114 lb 10 oz	Tauranga, New Zealand	Feb 5, 1984	Mike Godfrey

Fishing (Cont.)

Freshwater Fishing Records

Species	Weight	Where Caught	Date	Angler
Barramundi	63 lb 2 oz	Queensland, Australia	April 28, 1991	Scott Barnsley
Bass, largemouth	22 lb 4 oz	Montgomery Lake, GA	June 2, 1932	George W. Perry
Bass, rock	3 lb	York River, Ontario	Aug 1, 1974	Peter Gulgin
Bass, smallmouth	10 lb 14 oz	Dale Hollow, TN	April 24, 1969	John T. Gorman
Bass, Suwannee	3 lb 14 oz	Suwannee River, FL	Mar 2, 1985	Ronnie Everett
Bass, white	6 lb 13 oz	Orange, VA	July 31, 1989	Ronald Sprouse
Bass, whiterock	27 lb 5 oz	Greers Ferry Lake, AR	Apr 24, 1997	Jerald Shaum
Bass, yellow	2 lb 9 oz	Waverly, TN	Feb 27, 1998	John Chappell
Bluegill	4 lb 12 oz	Ketona Lake, AL	Apr 9, 1950	T.S. Hudson
Bowfin	21 lb 8 oz	Florence, SC	Jan 29, 1980	Robert Harmon
Buffalo, bigmouth	70 lb 5 oz	Bastrop, LA	Apr 21, 1980	Delbert Sisk
Buffalo, black	55 lb 8 oz	Cherokee Lake, TN	May 3, 1984	Edward McLain
Buffalo, smallmouth	82 lb 3 oz	Athens Lake, GA	June 6, 1993	Randy Collins
Bullhead, brown	5 lb 11oz	Cedar Creek, FL	Mar 28, 1995	Robert Bengis
Bullhead, yellow	4 lb 4 oz	Mormon Lake, AZ	May 11, 1984	Emily Williams
Burbot	18 lb 11 oz	Angenmanalren, Sweden	Oct 22, 1996	Margit Agren
Carp	75 lb 11 oz	Lac de St Cassien, France	May 21, 1987	Leo van der Gugten
Catfish, blue	111 lb	Tennesee River, AL	July 5, 1996	William P. McKinley
Catfish, channel	58 lb	Santee-Cooper Reservoir, SC	July 7, 1964	W.B. Whaley
Catfish, flathead	91 lb 4 oz	Lake Lewisville, TX	Mar 28, 1982	Mike Rogers
Catfish, white	18 lb 14 oz	Inverness, FL	Sep 21, 1991	Jim Miller
Char, Arctic	32 lb 9 oz	Tree River, Canada	July 30, 1981	Jeffrey Ward
Crappie, white	5 lb 3 oz	Enid Dam, MS	July 31, 1957	Fred L. Bright
Dolly Varden	18 lb 9 oz	Mashutuk River, AK	July 13, 1993	Richard B. Evans
Dorado	51 lb 5 oz	Corrientes, Argentina	Sep 27, 1984	Armando Giudice
Drum, freshwater	54 lb 8 oz	Nickajack Lake, TN	Apr 20, 1972	Benny E. Hull
Gar, alligator	279 lb	Rio Grande River, TX	Dec 2, 1951	Bill Valverde
Gar, Florida	21 lb 3 oz	Boca Raton, FL	June 3, 1981	Jeff Sabol
Gar, longnose	50 lb 5 oz	Trinity River, TX	July 30, 1954	Townsend Miller
Gar, shortnose	5 lb 12 oz	Rend Lake, IL	July 16, 1995	Donna K. Willmert
Gar, spotted	9 lb 12 oz	Lake Mexia, TX	Apr 7, 1994	Rick Rivard
Grayling, Arctic	5 lb 15 oz	Katseyedie River, Northwest Territories	Aug 16, 1967	Jeanne P. Branson
Inconnu	53 lb	Pah River, AK	Aug 20, 1986	Lawrence Hudnall
Kokanee	9 lb 6 oz	Okanagan Lake, Vernon, BC	June 18, 1988	Norm Kuhn
Muskellunge	67 lb 8 oz	Hayward, WI	July 24, 1949	Cal Johnson
Muskellunge, tiger	51 lb 3 oz	Lac Vieux-Desert, WI, MI	July 16, 1919	John Knobla
Peacock, speckled	27 lb	Rio Negro, Brazil	Dec 4, 1994	Gerald (Doc) Lawson
Perch, Nile	213 lb	Lake Nasser, Egypt	Dec 18, 1997	Adrian Brayshaw
Perch, white	4 lb 12 oz	Messalonskee Lake, ME	June 4, 1949	Mrs. Earl Small
Perch, yellow	4 lb 3 oz	Bordentown, NJ	May 1865	C.C. Abbot
Pickerel, chain	9 lb 6 oz	Homerville, GA	Feb 17, 1961	Baxley McQuaig Jr.
Pike, northern	55 lb 1 oz	Lake of Grefeern, West Germany	Oct 16, 1986	Lothar Louis
Redhorse, greater	9 lb 3 oz	Salmon River, Pulaski, NY	May 11, 1985	Jason Wilson
Redhorse, silver	11 lb 7 oz	Plum Creek, WI	May 29, 1985	Neal Long
Salmon, Atlantic	79 lb 2 oz	Tana River, Norway	1928	Henrik Henriksen
Salmon, chinook	97 lb 4 oz	Kenai River, AK	May 17, 1985	Les Anderson
Salmon, chum	35 lb	Edye Pass, Canada	July 11, 1995	Todd A. Johansson
Salmon, coho	33 lb 4 oz	Pulaski, NY	Sep 27, 1989	Jerry Lifton
Salmon, pink	13 lb 1 oz	Ontario, Canada	Sep 23, 1992	Ray Higaki
Salmon, sockeye	15 lb 3 oz	Kenai River, AK	Aug 9, 1987	Stan Roach
Sauger	8 lb 12 oz	Lake Sakakawea, ND	Oct 6, 1971	Mike Fischer
Shad, American	11 lb 4 oz	Connecticut River, MA	May 19, 1986	Bob Thibodo
Sturgeon, white	468 lb	Benicia, CA	July 9, 1983	Joey Pallotta III
Sunfish, green	2 lb 2 oz	Stockton Lake, MO	June 18, 1971	Paul M. Dilley
Sunfish, redbreast	1 lb 12 oz	Suwannee River, FL	May 29, 1984	Alvin Buchanan
Sunfish, redear	5 lb 3 oz	Sacramento, CA	June 27, 1994	Anthony H. White Sr.
Tigerfish, giant	97 lb	Zaire River, Kinshasa, Zaire	July 9, 1988	Raymond Houtmans
Trout, Apache	5 lb 3 oz	Apache Reservation, AZ	May 29, 1991	John Baldwin
Trout, brook	14 lb 8 oz	Nipigon River, Ontario	July 1916	W.J. Cook
Trout, brown	40 lb 4 oz	Heber Springs, AR	May 9, 1992	Howard L. Collins
Trout, bull	32 lb	Lake Pond Oreille, ID	Oct 27, 1949	N.L. Higgins
Trout, cutthroat	41 lb	Pyramid Lake, NV	Dec 1925	John Skimmerhorn
Trout, golden	11 lb	Cook's Lake, WY	Aug 5, 1948	Charles S. Reed

Freshwater Fishing Records (Cont.)

Species	Weight	Where Caught	Date	Angler
Trout, lake	72 lb	Great Bear Lake, Northwest Territories	Aug 19, 1995	Lloyd Bull
Trout, rainbow	42 lb 2 oz	Bell Island, AK	June 22, 1970	David Robert White
Trout, tiger	20 lb 13 oz	Lake Michigan, WI	Aug 12, 1978	Pete M. Friedland
Walleye	25 lb	Old Hickory Lake, TN	Aug 2, 1960	Mabry Harper
Warmouth	2 lb 7 oz	Yellow River, Holt, FL	Oct 19, 1985	Tony D. Dempsey
Whitefish, lake	14 lb 6 oz	Meaford, Ontario	May 21, 1984	Dennis Laycock
Whitefish, mountain	5 lb 8 oz	Elbow River, Calgary, Alberta, Canada	Aug, 1, 1995	Randy G. Woo
Whitefish, broad	9 lb	Tozitna River, AK	July 17, 1989	Al Mathews
Whitefish, round	6 lb	Putahow River, Manitoba	June 14, 1984	Allan J. Ristori
Zander	25 lb 2 oz	Trosa, Sweden	June 12, 1986	Harry Lee Tennison

Greyhound Racing

Annual Greyhound Race of Champions Winners*

Year	Winner (Sex)	Affiliation/Owner
1982	DD's Jackie (F)	Wonderland Park/ R.H.Walters Jr.
1983	Comin' Attraction (F)	Rocky Mt Greyhound Park/ Bob Riggin
1984	Fallon (F)	Tampa Greyhound Track/ E.J. Alderson
1985	Lady Delight (F)	Lincoln Greyhound Park/ Julian A. Gay
1986	Ben G Speedboat (M)	Multnomah Kennel Club/ Louis Bennett
1987	ET's Pesky (F)	Supplemental (Flagler)/ Emil Tanis
1988	BB's Old Yellow (M)	Supplemental (Southland)/ Margie Bonita Hyers
1989	Osh Kosh Juliet (F)	Tampa Greyhound Track/ William F. Pollard
1990	Daring Don (M)	Interstate Kennel Club/ Perry Padrta
1991	Mo Kick (M)	Flagler Greyhound Track/ Eric M. Kennon
1992	Dicky Vallie (M)	Dairyland Greyhound Track/ George Benjamin
1993	Mega Morris (M)	Jacksonville Kennel Club/ Ferrell's Kennel

* The Greyhound Race of Champions has not been held since 1993.

Gymnastics

World Champions
MEN

All-Around

Year	Champion and Nation
1903	Joseph Martinez, France
1905	Marcel Lalue, France
1907	Joseph Czada, Czechoslovakia
1909	Marcos Torres, France
1911	Ferdinand Steiner, Czechoslovakia
1913	Marcos Torres, France
1922	Peter Sumi, Yugoslavia F. Pechacek, Czechoslovakia
1926	Peter Sumi, Yugoslavia
1930	Josip Primozic, Yugoslavia
1934	Eugene Mack, Switzerland
1938	Jan Gajdos, Czechoslovakia
1950	Walter Lehmann, Switzerland
1954	Valentin Mouratov, USSR Victor Chukarin, USSR
1958	Boris Shaklin, USSR
1962	Yuri Titov, USSR
1966	Mikhail Voronin, USSR
1970	Eizo Kenmotsu, Japan
1974	Shigeru Kasamatsu, Japan
1978	Nikolai Andrianov, USSR
1979	Alexander Ditiatin, USSR
1981	Yuri Korolev, USSR
1983	Dimitri Bilozertchev, USSR
1985	Yuri Korolev, USSR
1987	Dimitri Bilozertchev, USSR
1989	Igor Korobchinsky, USSR
1991	Grigori Misutin, CIS
1993	Vitaly Scherbo, Belarus
1994	Ivan Ivankov, Belarus
1995	Li Xiaoshuang, China
1997	Ivan Ivankov, Belarus
1999	Nicolae Krukov, Russia

Pommel Horse

Year	Champion and Nation
1930	Josip Primozic, Yugoslavia
1934	Eugene Mack, Switzerland
1938	Michael Reusch, Switzerland
1950	Josef Stalder, Switzerland
1954	Grant Chaguinjan, USSR
1958	Boris Shaklin, USSR
1962	Miroslav Cerar, Yugoslavia
1966	Miroslav Cerar, Yugoslavia
1970	Miroslav Cerar, Yugoslavia
1974	Zoltan Magyar, Hungary
1978	Zoltan Magyar, Hungary
1979	Zoltan Magyar, Hungary
1981	Michael Mikolai, East Germany Li Xiaoping, China

World Champions (Cont.)

MEN (Cont.)

Pommel Horse (Cont.)

Year	Champion and Nation	Year	Champion and Nation	Year	Champion and Nation
1983	Dmitri Bilozertchev, USSR	1991	Valeri Belenki, USSR	1994	Marius Urzica, Romania
1985	Valentin Moguilny, USSR	1992	Pae Gil Su, North Korea	1995	Li Donghua, Switzerland
1987	Zsolt Borkai, Hungary		Vitaly Scherbo, CIS	1996	Pae Gil Su, North Korea
	Dmitri Bilozertchev, USSR		Li Jing, China	1997	Valeri Belenki, Germany
1989	Valentin Moguilny, USSR	1993	Pae Gil Su, North Korea	1999	Alexei Nemov, Russia

Floor Exercise

Year	Champion and Nation	Year	Champion and Nation	Year	Champion and Nation
1930	Josip Primozic, Yugoslavia	1970	Akinori Nakayama, Japan	1989	Igor Korobchinsky, USSR
1934	Georges Miesz, Switzerland	1974	Shigeru Kasamatsu, Japan	1991	Igor Korobchinsky, USSR
1938	Jan Gajdos, Czechoslovakia	1978	Kurt Thomas, United States	1993	Grigori Misutin, Ukraine
1950	Josef Stalder, Switzerland	1979	Kurt Thomas, United States	1994	Vitaly Scherbo, Belarus
1954	Valentin Mouratov, USSR		Roland Brucker, GDR	1995	Vitaly Scherbo, Belarus
	Masao Takemoto, Japan	1981	Yuri Korolev, USSR	1996	Vitaly Scherbo, Belarus
1958	Masao Takemoto, Japan		Li Yuejui, Chi	1997	Alexei Nemov, Russia
1962	Nobuyuki Aihara, Japan	1983	Tong Fei, China	1999	Alexei Nemov, Russia
	Yukio Endo, Japan	1985	Tong Fei, China		
1966	Akinori Nakayama, Japan	1987	Lou Yun, China		

Rings

Year	Champion and Nation	Year	Champion and Nation	Year	Champion and Nation
1930	Emanuel Loffler, Czechoslovakia	1970	Akinori Nakayama, Japan	1989	Andreas Aguilar, West Germany
1934	Alois Hudec, Czechoslovakia	1974	N. Andrianov, USSR	1991	Grigory Misutin, USSR
1938	Alois Hudec, Czechoslovakia		D. Grecu, Rom.	1992	Vitaly Scherbo, CIS
1950	Walter Lehmann, Switzerland	1978	Nikolai Andrianov, USSR	1993	Yuri Chechi, Italy
1954	Albert Azarian, USSR	1979	Alexander Ditiatin, USSR	1994	Yuri Chechi, Italy
1958	Albert Azarian, USSR	1981	Alexander Ditiatin, USSR	1995	Yuri Chechi, Italy
1962	Yuri Titov, USSR	1983	Dimitri Bilozertchev, USSR	1996	Yuri Chechi, Italy
1966	Mikhail Voronin, USSR	1985	Li Ning, China	1997	Yuri Chechi, Italy
			Yuri Korolev, USSR	1999	Zhen Dong, China
		1987	Yuri Korolev, USSR		

Parallel Bars

Year	Champion and Nation	Year	Champion and Nation	Year	Champion and Nation
1930	Josip Primozic, Yugoslavia	1979	Bart Conner, United States	1992	Li Jin, China
1934	Eugene Mack, Switzerland	1981	Koji Gushiken, Japan		Alexei Voropaev, CIS
1938	Michael Reusch, Switzerland		Alexandr Ditiatin, USSR	1993	Vitaly Scherbo, Belarus
1950	Hans Eugster, Switzerland	1983	Vladimir Artemov, USSR	1994	Huang Liping, China
1954	Victor Chukarin, USSR		Lou Yun, China	1995	Vitaly Scherbo, Belarus
1958	Boris Shaklin, USSR	1985	Sylvio Kroll, East Germany	1996	Rustam Sharipov, Ukraine
1962	Miroslav Cerar, Yugoslavia		Valentin Moguilny, USSR	1997	Zhang Jinjing, China
1966	Sergei Diamidov, USSR	1987	Vladimir Artemov, USSR	1999	Joo-Hyung Lee, S Korea
1970	Akinori Nakayama, Japan	1989	Li Jing, China		
1974	Eizo Kenmotsu, Japan		Vladimir Artemov, USSR		
1978	Eizo Kenmotsu, Japan	1991	Li Jing, China		

High Bar

Year	Champion and Nation	Year	Champion and Nation	Year	Champion and Nation
1930	Istvan Pelle, Hungary	1978	Shigeru Kasamatsu, Japan	1994	Vitaly Scherbo, Belarus
1934	Ernst Winter, Germany	1979	Kurt Thomas, United States	1995	Andreas Wecker, Germany
1938	Michael Reusch, Switzerland	1981	Alexander Takchev, USSR	1996	Jesús Carballo, Spain
1950	Paavo Aaltonen, Finland	1983	Dimitri Bilozertchev, USSR	1997	Jani Tanskanen, Finland
1954	Valentin Mouratov, USSR	1985	Tong Fei, China	1999	Jesus Carballo, Spain
1958	Boris Shaklin, USSR	1987	Dimitri Bilozertchev, USSR		
1962	Takashi Ono, USSR	1989	Li Chunyang, China		
1966	Akinori Nakayama, Japan	1991	Li Chunyang, China		
1970	Eizo Kenmotsu, Japan		R. Buechner, Germ		
1974	Eberhard Gienger, West Germany	1992	Grigori Misutin, CIS		
		1993	Sergei Kharkov, Russia		

World Champions (Cont.)
MEN (Cont.)

Vault

Year	Champion and Nation	Year	Champion and Nation	Year	Champion and Nation
1934	Eugene Mack, Switzerland	1978	Junichi Shimizu, Japan	1992	Yoo Ok Youl, South Korea
1938	Eugene Mack, Switzerland	1979	Alexander Ditiatin, USSR	1993	Vitaly Scherbo, Belarus
1950	Ernst Gebendinger, Switzerland	1981	Ralf-Peter Hemmann, East Germany	1994	Vitaly Scherbo, Belarus
1954	Leo Sotornik, Czechoslovakia	1983	Arthur Akopian, USSR	1995	G. Misutin, Ukraine A. Nemov, Russia
1958	Yuri Titov, USSR	1985	Yuri Korolev, USSR	1996	Alexei Nemov, Russia
1962	Premysel Krbec, Czechoslovakia	1987	Lou Yun, China Sylvio Kroll, East Germany	1997	Sergei Fedorchenko, Kazakhstan
1966	Haruhiro Yamashita, Japan	1989	Joreg Behrend, East Germany	1999	Xiaopeng Li, China
1970	Mitsuo Tsukahara, Japan	1991	Yoo Ok Youl, South Korea		
1974	Shigeru Kasamatsu, Japan				

WOMEN

All-Around

Year	Champion and Nation	Year	Champion and Nation	Year	Champion and Nation
1934	Vlasta Dekanova, Czechoslovakia	1970	Ludmilla Tourischeva, USSR	1991	Kim Zmeskal, United States
1938	Vlasta Dekanova, Czechoslovakia	1974	Ludmilla Tourischeva, USSR	1993	Shannon Miller, United States
1950	Helena Rakoczy, Poland	1978	Elena Mukhina, USSR	1994	Shannon Miller, United States
1954	Galina Roudiko, USSR	1979	Nelli Kim, USSR	1995	Lilia Podkopayeva, Ukraine
1958	Larissa Latynina, USSR	1981	Olga Bicherova, USSR	1997	Svetlana Chorkina, Russia
1962	Larissa Latynina, USSR	1983	Natalia Yurchenko, USSR	1999	Maria Olaru, Romania
1966	Vera Caslavska, Czechoslovakia	1985	Elena Shoushounova, USSR Oksana Omeliantchik, USSR		
		1987	Aurelia Dobre, Romania		
		1989	Svetlana Bouguinskaia, USSR		

Floor Exercise

Year	Champion and Nation	Year	Champion and Nation	Year	Champion and Nation
1950	Helena Rakoczy, Poland	1979	Emilia Eberle, Romania	1992	Kim Zmeskal, United States
1954	Tamara Manina, USSR	1981	Natalia Ilenko, USSR	1993	Shannon Miller, United States
1958	Eva Bosakava, Czechoslovakia	1983	Ecaterina Szabo, Romania	1994	Dina Kochetkova, Russia
1962	Larissa Latynina, USSR	1985	Oksana Omeliantchik, USSR	1995	Gina Gogean, Romania
1966	Natalia Kuchinskaya, USSR	1987	Elena Shoushounova, USSR Daniela Silivas, Romania	1996	Gina Gogean, Romania
1970	Ludmilla Tourischeva, USSR	1989	Svetlana Bouguinskaia, USSR Daniela Silivas, Romania	1997	Gina Gogean, Romania
1974	Ludmilla Tourischeva, USSR	1991	Cristina Bontas, Romania Oksana Tchusovitina, USSR	1999	Andreea Raducan, Romania
1978	Nelli Kim, USSR Elena Mukhina, USSR				

Uneven Bars

Year	Champion and Nation	Year	Champion and Nation	Year	Champion and Nation
1950	Gertchen Kolar, Austria Anna Pettersson, Sweden	1979	Ma Yanhong, China Maxi Gnauck, East Germany	1991	Gwang Suk Kim, North Korea
1954	Agnes Keleti, Hungary	1981	Maxi Gnauck, East Germany	1992	Lavinia Milosivici, Romania
1958	Larissa Latynina, USSR	1983	Maxi Gnauck, East Germany	1993	Shannon Miller, United States
1962	Irina Pervuschina, USSR	1985	Gabriele Fahnrich, East Germany	1994	Luo Li, China
1966	Natalia Kuchinskaya, USSR	1987	Daniela Silivas, Romania Doerte Thuemmler, East Germany	1995	Svetlana Chorkina, Russia
1970	Karin Janz, East Germany	1989	Fan Di, China Daniela Silivas, Romania	1996	Svetlana Chorkina, Russia
1974	Annelore Zinke, East Germany			1997	Svetlana Chorkina, Russia
1978	Marcia Frederick, United States			1999	Svetlana Chorkina, Russia

World Champions (Cont.)
WOMEN (Cont.)
Balance Beam

Year	Champion and Nation	Year	Champion and Nation	Year	Champion and Nation
1950	Helena Rakoczy, Poland	1978	Nadia Comaneci, Romania	1992	Kim Zmeskal, United States
1954	Keiko Tanaka, Japan	1979	Vera Cerna, Czechoslovakia	1993	Lavinia Milosovici, Romania
1958	Larissa Latynina, USSR	1981	Maxi Gnauck, East Germany	1994	Shannon Miller, United States
1962	Eva Bosakova, Czechoslovakia	1983	Olga Mostepanova, USSR	1995	Mo Huilan, China
1966	Natalia Kuchinskaya, USSR	1985	Daniela Silivas, Romania	1996	Dina Kochetkova, Russia
1970	Erika Zuchold, East Germany	1987	Aurelia Dobre, Romania	1997	Gina Gogean, Romania
1974	Ludmilla Tourischeva, USSR	1989	Daniela Silivas, Romania	1999	Elena Zamolodchikova, Russia
		1991	Svetlana Boguinskaia, USSR		

Vault

Year	Champion and Nation	Year	Champion and Nation	Year	Champion and Nation
1950	Helena Rakoczy, Poland	1974	Olga Korbut, USSR	1992	Henrietta Onodi, Hungary
1954	T. Manina, USSR	1978	Nelli Kim, USSR	1993	Elena Piskun, Belarus
	Anna Pettersson, Sweden	1979	Dumitrita Turner, Romania	1994	Gina Gogean, Romania
1958	Larissa Latynina, USSR	1981	Maxi Gnauck, East Germany	1995	L. Podkopayeva, Ukraine
1962	Vera Caslavska, Czechoslovakia	1983	Boriana Stoyanova, Bulgaria		Simona Amanar, Rom.
1966	Vera Caslavska, Czechoslovakia	1985	Elena Shoushounova, USSR	1996	Gina Gogean, Romania
		1987	Elena Shoushounova, USSR	1997	Simona Amanar, Romania
1970	Erika Zuchold, East Germany	1989	Olesia Durnik, USSR	1999	Jie Ling, China
		1991	Lavinia Milosovici, Romania		

National Champions
MEN
All-Around

Year	Champion	Year	Champion	Year	Champion
1963	Art Shurlock	1975	Tom Beach	1987	Scott Johnson
1964	Rusty Mitchell		Bart Conner	1988	Dan Hayden
1965	Rusty Mitchell	1976	Kurt Thomas	1989	Tim Ryan
1966	Rusty Mitchell	1977	Kurt Thomas	1990	John Roethlisberger
1967	Katsuzoki Kanzaki	1978	Kurt Thomas	1991	Chris Waller
1968	Yoshi Hayasaki	1979	Bart Conner	1992	John Roethlisberger
1969	Steve Hug	1980	Peter Vidmar	1993	John Roethlisberger
1970	Makoto Sakamoto	1981	Jim Hartung	1994	Scott Keswick
	Mas Watanabe	1982	Peter Vidmar	1995	John Roethlisberger
1971	Yoshi Takei	1983	Mitch Gaylord	1996	Blaine Wilson
1972	Yoshi Takei	1984	Mitch Gaylord	1997	Blaine Wilson
1973	Marshall Avener	1985	Brian Babcock	1998	Blaine Wilson
1974	John Crosby	1986	Tim Daggett	1999	Blaine Wilson

Floor Exercise

Year	Champion	Year	Champion	Year	Champion
1963	Tom Seward	1974	John Crosby	1988	Mark Oates
1964	Rusty Mitchell	1975	Peter Korman		Charles Lakes
1965	Rusty Mitchell	1977	Ron Galimore	1989	Mike Racanelli
1966	Dan Millman	1978	Kurt Thomas	1990	Bob Stelter
1967	Katsuzoki Kanzaki	1979	Ron Galimore	1991	Mike Racanelli
	Ron Aure	1980	Ron Galimore	1992	Gregg Curtis
1968	Katsuzoki Kanzaki	1981	Jim Hartung	1993	Kerry Huston
1969	Steve Hug	1982	Jim Hartung	1994	Jeremy Killen
	Dave Thor	1983	Mitch Gaylord	1995	Daniel Stover
1970	Makoto Sakamoto	1984	Peter Vidmar	1996	Jay Thornton
1971	John Crosby	1985	Mark Oates	1997	Jason Gatson
1972	Yoshi Takei	1986	Robert Sundstrom	1998	Jason Gatson
1973	John Crosby	1987	John Sweeney	1999	Jason Gatson

National Champions (Cont.)
MEN (Cont.)

Pommel Horse

Year	Champion	Year	Champion	Year	Champion
1963	Larry Spiegel	1975	Bart Conner	1988	Kevin Davis
1964	Sam Bailie	1977	Gene Whelan	1989	Kevin Davis
1965	Jack Ryan	1978	Jim Hartung	1990	Patrick Kirksey
1966	Jack Ryan	1979	Bart Conner	1991	Chris Waller
1967	Paul Mayer/Dave Doty	1980	Jim Hartung	1992	Chris Waller
1968	Katsuoki Kanzaki	1981	Jim Hartung	1993	Chris Waller
1969	Dave Thor	1982	Jim Hartung	1994	Mihai Begiu
1970	Mas Watanabe	1983	Bart Conner	1995	Mark Sohn
1971	Leonard Caling	1984	Tim Daggett	1996	Josh Stein
1972	Sadao Hamada	1985	Phil Cahoy	1997	John Roethlisberger
1973	Marshall Avener	1986	Phil Cahoy	1998	John Roethlisberger
1974	Marshall Avener	1987	Tim Daggett	1999	John Roethlisberger

Rings

Year	Champion	Year	Champion	Year	Champion
1963	Art Shurlock	1974	Tom Weeder	1987	Scott Johnson
1964	Glen Gailis	1975	Tom Beach	1988	Dan Hayden
1965	Glen Gailis	1977	Kurt Thomas	1989	Scott Keswick
1966	Glen Gailis	1978	Mike Silverstein	1990	Scott Keswick
1967	Fred Dennis	1979	Bart Conner	1991	Scott Keswick
	Don Hatch	1980	Jim Hartung	1992	Tim Ryan
1968	Yoshi Hayasaki	1981	Jim Hartung	1993	John Roethlisberger
1969	Fred Dennis	1982	Jim Hartung	1994	Scott Keswick
	Bob Emery		Peter Vidmar	1995	Paul O'Neill
1970	Makoto Sakamoto	1983	Mitch Gaylord	1996	Kip Simons
1971	Yoshi Takei	1984	Jim Hartung	1997	Blaine Wilson
1972	Yoshi Takei	1985	Dan Hayden	1998	Jeff Johnson
1973	Jim Ivicek	1986	Dan Hayden	1999	Blaine Wilson

Vault

Year	Champion	Year	Champion	Year	Champion
1963	Art Shurlock	1975	Tom Beach	1987	John Sweeney
1964	Gary Hery	1977	Ron Galimore	1988	John Sweeney/Bill Paul
1965	Brent Williams	1978	Jim Hartung	1989	Bill Roth
1966	Dan Millman	1979	Ron Galimore	1990	Lance Ringnald
1967	Jack Kenan	1980	Ron Galimore	1991	Scott Keswick
	Sid Jensen	1981	Ron Galimore	1992	Trent Dimas
1968	Rich Scorza	1982	Jim Hartung	1993	Bill Roth
1969	Dave Butzman		Jim Mikus	1994	Keith Wiley
1970	Makoto Sakamoto	1983	Chris Reigel	1995	David St. Pierre
1971	Gary Morava	1984	Chris Reigel	1996	Blaine Wilson
1972	Mike Kelley	1985	Scott Johnson	1997	Blaine Wilson
1973	Gary Morava		Mark Oates	1998	Brent Klaus
1974	John Crosby	1986	Scott Wilbanks	1999	Guard Young

Parallel Bars

Year	Champion	Year	Champion	Year	Champion
1963	Tom Seward	1977	Kurt Thomas	1988	D. Hayden/K. Davis
1964	Rusty Mitchell	1978	Bart Conner	1989	Conrad Voorsanger
1965	Glen Gailis	1979	Bart Conner	1990	Trent Dimas
1966	Ray Hadley	1980	Phil Cahoy	1991	Scott Keswick
1967	Katsuoki Kanzaki		Larry Gerard	1992	Jair Lynch
	Tom Goldsborough	1981	Bart Conner	1993	Chainey Umphrey
1968	Yoshi Hayasaki	1982	Peter Vidmar	1994	Steve McCain
1969	Steve Hug	1983	Mitch Gaylord	1995	John Roethlisberger
1970	Makoto Sakamoto	1984	Peter Vidmar	1996	Jair Lynch
1971	Brent Simmons		Mitch Gaylord	1997	Blaine Wilson
1972	Yoshi Takei		Tim Daggett	1998	Blaine Wilson
1973	Marshall Avener	1985	Tim Daggett	1999	Jason Gatson
1974	Jim Ivicek	1986	Tim Daggett		
1975	Bart Conner	1987	Scott Johnson		

National Champions *(Cont.)*
MEN *(Cont.)*

High Bars

Year	Champion	Year	Champion	Year	Champion
1963	Art Shurlock	1975	Tom Beach	1987	David Moriel
1964	Glen Gailis	1977	Kurt Thomas	1988	Dan Hayden
1965	Rusty Mitchell	1978	Kurt Thomas	1989	Tim Ryan
1966	Katsuzoki Kanzaki	1979	Yoichi Tomita	1990	Trent Dimas
1967	Katsuzoki Kanzaki	1980	Jim Hartung		Lance Ringnald
	Jerry Fontana	1981	Bart Conner	1991	Lance Ringnald
1968	Yoshi Hayasaki	1982	Mitch Gaylord	1992	Jair Lynch
1969	Rich Grisby	1983	Mario McCutcheon	1993	Steve McCain
1970	Makoto Sakamoto	1984	Peter Vidmar	1994	Scott Keswick
1971	Yoshi Takei		Tim Daggett	1995	John Roethlisberger
1972	Tom Lindner		Mitch Gaylord	1996	Bill Roth
1973	John Crosby	1985	Dan Hayden	1997	Douglas Stibel
1974	Brent Simmons	1986	D. Hayden/D. Moriel	1998	Jason Gatson
				1999	Jamie Natalie

WOMEN

All-Around

Year	Champion	Year	Champion	Year	Champion
1963	Donna Schanezer	1975	Tammy Manville	1989	Brandy Johnson
1965	Gail Daley	1976	Denise Cheshire	1990	Kim Zmeskal
1966	Donna Schanezer	1977	Donna Turnbow	1991	Kim Zmeskal
1968	Linda Scott	1978	Kathy Johnson	1992	Kim Zmeskal
1969	Joyce Tanac	1979	Leslie Pyfer	1993	Shannon Miller
	Schroeder	1980	Julianne McNamara	1994	Dominique Dawes
1970	Cathy Rigby McCoy	1981	Tracee Talavera	1995	Dominique Moceanu
1971	Joan Moore Gnat	1982	Tracee Talavera	1996	Shannon Miller
	Linda Metheny	1983	Dianne Durham	1997	Vanessa Adler
	Mulvihill	1984	Mary Lou Retton		Kristy Powell
1972	Joan Moore Gnat	1985	Sabrina Mar	1998	Kristen Maloney
	Cathy Rigby McCoy	1986	Jennifer Sey	1999	Kristen Maloney
1973	Joan Moore Gnat	1987	Kristie Phillips		
1974	Joan Moore Gnat	1988	Phoebe Mills		

Vault

Year	Champion	Year	Champion	Year	Champion
1963	Donna Schanezer	1975	Kolleen Casey	1988	Rhonda Faehn
1965	Gail Daley	1976	Debbie Wilcox	1989	Brandy Johnson
1966	Donna Schanezer	1977	Lisa Cawthron	1990	Brandy Johnson
1968	Terry Spencer	1978	Rhonda Schwandt	1991	Kerri Strug
1969	Joyce Tanac		Sharon Shapiro	1992	Kerri Strug
	Schroeder	1979	Christa Canary	1993	Dominique Dawes
	Cleo Carver	1980	J. McNamara/B. Kline	1994	Dominique Dawes
1970	Cathy Rigby McCoy	1981	Kim Neal	1995	Shannon Miller
1971	Joan Moore Gnat	1982	Yumi Mordre	1996	Dominique Dawes
	Adele Gleaves	1983	Dianne Durham	1997	Vanessa Atler
1972	Cindy Eastwood	1984	Mary Lou Retton	1998	Dominique Moceanu
1973	Roxanne Pierce	1985	Yolanda Mavity	1999	Vanessa Atler
	Mancha	1986	Joyce Wilborn		
1974	Dianne Dunbar	1987	Rhonda Faehn		

Uneven Bars

Year	Champion	Year	Champion	Year	Champion
1963	Donna Schanezer	1970	Roxanne Pierce	1976	Leslie Wolfsberger
1965	Irene Haworth		Mancha	1977	Donna Turnbow
1966	Donna Schanezer	1971	Joan Moore Gnat	1978	Marcia Frederick
1968	Linda Scott	1972	Cathy Rigby McCoy	1979	Marcia Frederick
1969	Joyce Tanac	1973	Roxanne Pierce	1980	Marcia Frederick
	Schroeder		Mancha	1981	Julianne McNamara
	Lisa Nelson	1974	Diane Dunbar	1982	Marie Roethlisberger
		1975	Leslie Wolfsberger	1983	Julianne McNamara

National Champions (Cont.)
WOMEN (Cont.)

Uneven Bars (Cont.)

Year	Champion	Year	Champion	Year	Champion
1984	Julianne McNamara	1990	Sandy Woolsey	1996	Dominique Dawes
1985	Sabrina Mar	1991	Elisabeth Crandall	1997	Kristy Powell
1986	Marie Roethlisberger	1992	Dominique Dawes	1998	Elise Ray
1987	Melissa Marlowe	1993	Shannon Miller	1999	Jamie Dantzscher/
1988	Chelle Stack	1994	Dominique Dawes		Jennie Thompson
1989	Chelle Stack	1995	Dominique Dawes		

Balance Beam

Year	Champion	Year	Champion	Year	Champion
1963	Leissa Krol	1976	Carrie Englert	1989	Brandy Johnson
1965	Gail Daley	1977	Donna Turnbow	1990	Betty Okino
1966	Irene Haworth	1978	Christa Canary	1991	Shannon Miller
	Linda Scott	1979	Heidi Anderson	1992	K. Strug/K. Zmeskal
1968	Linda Scott	1980	Kelly Garrison-Steves	1993	Dominique Dawes
1969	Lonna Woodward	1981	Tracee Talavera	1994	Dominique Dawes
1970	Joyce Tanac	1982	Julianne McNamara	1995	Doni Thompson
	Schroeder	1983	Dianne Durham		Monica Flammer
1971	Linda Metheny	1984	Pam Bileck	1996	Dominique Dawes
	Mulvihill		Tracee Talavera	1997	Kendall Beck
1972	Kim Chace	1986	Angie Denkins	1998	Dominique Moceanu
1973	Nancy Thies Marshall	1987	Kristie Phillips	1999	Vanessa Atler
1974	Joan Moore Gnat	1985	Kelly Garrison-Steves		
1975	Kyle Gayner	1988	Kelly Garrison-Steves		

Floor Exercise

Year	Champion	Year	Champion	Year	Champion
1963	Donna Schanezer	1977	Kathy Johnson	1990	Brandy Johnson
1965	Gail Daley	1978	Kathy Johnson	1991	Kim Zmeskal
1966	Donna Schanezer	1979	Heidi Anderson		Dominique Dawes
1968	Linda Scott	1980	Beth Kline	1992	Kim Zmeskal
1970	Cathy Rigby McCoy	1981	Michelle Goodwin	1993	Shannon Miller
1971	Joan Moore Gnat	1982	Amy Koopman	1994	Dominique Dawes
	Linda Metheny	1983	Dianne Durham	1995	Dominique Dawes
	Mulvihill	1984	Mary Lou Retton	1996	Dominique Dawes
1972	Joan Moore Gnat	1985	Sabrina Mar	1997	Lindsay Wing
1973	Joan Moore Gnat	1986	Yolanda Mavity	1998	Vanessa Atler
1974	Joan Moore Gnat	1987	Kristie Phillips	1999	Elise Ray
1975	Kathy Howard	1988	Phoebe Mills		
1976	Carrie Englert	1989	Brandy Johnson		

Handball

National Four-Wall Champions
MEN

Year	Champion	Year	Champion	Year	Champion	Year	Champion
1919	Bill Ranft	1933	Sam Atcheson	1947	Gus Lewis	1961	John Sloan
1920	Max Gold	1934	Sam Atcheson	1948	Gus Lewis	1962	Oscar Obert
1921	Carl Haedge	1935	Joe Platak	1949	Vic Hershkowitz	1963	Oscar Obert
1922	Art Shinners	1936	Joe Platak	1950	Ken Schneider	1964	Jimmy Jacobs
1923	Joe Murray	1937	Joe Platak	1951	Walter Plakan	1965	Jimmy Jacobs
1924	Maynard Laswe	1938	Joe Platak	1952	Vic Hershkowitz	1966	Paul Haber
1925	Maynard Laswe	1939	Joe Platak	1953	Bob Brady	1967	Paul Haber
1926	Maynard Laswe	1940	Joe Platak	1954	Vic Hershkowitz	1968	Stuffy Singer
1927	George Nelson	1941	Joe Platak	1955	Jimmy Jacobs	1969	Paul Haber
1928	Joe Griffin	1942	Jack Clemente	1956	Jimmy Jacobs	1970	Paul Haber
1929	Al Banuet	1943	Joe Platak	1957	Jimmy Jacobs	1971	Paul Haber
1930	Al Banuet	1944	Frank Coyle	1958	John Sloan	1972	Fred Lewis
1931	Al Banuet	1945	Joe Platak	1959	John Sloan	1973	Terry Muck
1932	Angelo Trutio	1946	Angelo Trutio	1960	Jimmy Jacobs	1974	Fred Lewis

National Four-Wall Champions *(Cont.)*

MEN *(Cont.)*

1975 .....Fred Lewis	1982 .....Naty Alvarado	1989 .....Poncho Monreal	1996 .....David Chapman
1976 .....Fred Lewis	1983 .....Naty Alvarado	1990 .....Naty Alvarado	1997 ....Octavio Silveyra
1977 .....Naty Alvarado	1984 .....Naty Alvarado	1991 .....John Bike	1998 .....David Chapman
1978 .....Fred Lewis	1985 .....Naty Alvarado	1992 .....Octavio Silveyra	1999 .....David Chapman
1979 .....Naty Alvarado	1986 .....Naty Alvarado	1993 .....David Chapman	
1980 .....Naty Alvarado	1987 .....Naty Alvarado	1994 .....Octavio Silveyra	
1981 .....Fred Lewis	1988 .....Naty Alvarado	1995 .....David Chapman	

WOMEN

1980 .....Rosemary Bellini	1985 .....Peanut Motal	1990 .....Anna Engele	1995 .....Anna Engele
1981 .....Rosemary Bellini	1986 .....Peanut Motal	1991 .....Anna Engele	1996 .....Anna Engele
1982 .....Rosemary Bellini	1987 .....Rosemary Bellini	1992 .....Lisa Fraser	1997 .....Lisa Fraser
1983 .....Diane Harmon	1988 .....Rosemary Bellini	1993 .....Anna Engele	1998 .....Lisa Fraser
1984 .....Rosemary Bellini	1989 .....Anna Engele	1994 .....Anna Engele	1999 .....Anna Christoff

National Three-Wall Champions

MEN

1950 .....Vic Hershkowitz	1963 .....Marty Decatur	1976 .....Lou Russo	1989 .....John Bike
1951 .....Vic Hershkowitz	1964 .....Marty Decatur	1977 .....Fred Lewis	1990 .....Vince Munoz
1952 .....Vic Hershkowitz	1965 .....Carl Obert	1978 .....Fred Lewis	1991 .....John Bike
1953 .....Vic Herskkowitz	1966 .....Marty Decatur	1979 .....Naty Alvarado	1992 .....John Bike
1954 .....Vic Hershkowitz	1967 .....Carl Obert	1980 .....Lou Russo	1993 .....Eric Klarman
1955 .....Vic Hershkowitz	1968 .....Marty Decatur	1981 .....Naty Alvarado	1994 .....David Chapman
1956 .....Vic Hershkowitz	1969 .....Marty Decatur	1982 .....Naty Alvarado	1995 .....David Chapman
1957 .....Vic Hershkowitz	1970 .....Steve August	1983 .....Naty Alvarado	1996 .....Vince Munoz
1958 .....Vic Hershkowitz	1971 .....Lou Russo	1984 .....Naty Alvarado	1997 .....Vince Munoz
1959 .....Jimmy Jacobs	1972 .....Lou Russo	1985 .....Vern Roberts	1998 .....Vince Munoz
1960 .....Jimmy Jacobs	1973 .....Paul Haber	1986 .....Vern Roberts	1999 .....Vince Munoz
1961 .....Jimmy Jacobs	1974 .....Fred Lewis	1987 .....Vern Roberts	
1962 .....Oscar Obert	1975 .....Lou Russo	1988 .....Jon Kendler	

WOMEN

1981 .....Allison Roberts	1986 .....Rosemary Bellini	1991 .....Rosemary Bellini	1996 .....Anna Engele
1982 ....Allison Roberts	1987 .....Rosemary Bellini	1992 ....Anna Engele	1997 ....Allison Roberts
1983 ....Allison Roberts	1988 .....Rosemary Bellini	1993 .....Anna Engele	1998 .....Anna Christoff
1984 ....Rosemary Bellini	1989 .....Rosemary Bellini	1994 .....Anna Engele	1999 .....Allison Roberts
1985 .....Rosemary Bellini	1990 .....Rosemary Bellini	1995 .....Allison Roberts	

World Four-Wall Champions

1984 ....Merv Deckert, Canada	1991 ....Pancho Monreal, United States
1986 ....Vern Roberts, United States	1994 ....David Chapman, United States
1988 ....Naty Alvarado, United States	1997 ....John Bike Jr., United States

Lacrosse

United States Club Lacrosse Association Champions

1960 ......Mt Washington Club	1974 ......Long Island Athletic Club	1988 ......Maryland Lacrosse Club
1961 ......Baltimore Lacrosse Club	1975 ......Mt Washington Club	1989 ......LI-Hofstra Lacrosse Club
1962 ......Mt Washington Club	1976 ......Mt Washington Club	1990 ......Mt Washington Club
1963 ......University Club	1977 ......Mt Washington Club	1991 ......Mt Washington Club
1964 ......Mt Washington Club	1978 ......Long Island Athletic Club	1992 ......Maryland Lacrosse Club
1965 ......Mt Washington Club	1979 ......Maryland Lacrosse Club	1993 ......Mt Washington Club
1966 ......Mt Washington Club	1980 ......Long Island Athletic Club	1994 ......LI-Hofstra Lacrosse Club
1967 ......Mt Washington Club	1981 ......Long Island Athletic Club	1995 ......Mt Washington Club
1968 .....Long Island Athletic Club	1982 ......Maryland Lacrosse Club	1996 ......LI-Hofstra Lacrosse Club
1969 ......Long Island Athletic Club	1983 ......Maryland Lacrosse Club	1997 ......LI-Hofstra Lacrosse Club
1970 ......Long Island Athletic Club	1984 ......Maryland Lacrosse Club	1998 ......LI-Hofstra Lacrosse Club
1971 ......Long Island Athletic Club	1985 ......LI-Hofstra Lacrosse Club	1999 ......New York Athletic Club
1972 ......Carling	1986 ......LI-Hofstra Lacrosse Club	
1973 ......Long Island Athletic Club	1987 ......LI-Hofstra Lacrosse Club	

Little League Baseball

Little League World Series Champions

Year	Champion	Runner-Up	Score	Year	Champion	Runner-Up	Score
1947	Williamsport, PA	Lock Haven, PA	16–7	1974	Kao-Hsuing, Taiwan	El Cajun, CA	7–2
1948	Lock Haven, PA	St. Petersburg, FL	6–5	1975	Lakewood, NJ	Tampa, FL	4–3
1949	Hammonton, NJ	Pensacola, FL	5–0	1976	Tokyo, Japan	Campbell, CA	10–3
1950	Houston, TX	Bridgeport, CT	2–1	1977	Kao-Hsuing, Taiwan	El Cajun, CA	7–2
1951	Stamford, CT	Austin, TX	3–0	1978	Pin-Tung, Taiwan	Danville, CA	11–1
1952	Norwalk, CT	Monongahela, PA	4–3	1979	Hsien, Taiwan	Campbell, CA	2–1
1953	Birmingham, AL	Schenectady, NY	1–0	1980	Hua Lian, Taiwan	Tampa, FL	4–3
1954	Schenectady, NY	Colton, CA	7–5	1981	Tai-Chung, Taiwan	Tampa, FL	4–2
1955	Morrisville, PA	Merchantville, NJ	4–3	1982	Kirkland, WA	Hsien, Taiwan	6–0
1956	Roswell, NM	Merchantville, NJ	3–1	1983	Marietta, GA	Barahona, D.Rep.	3–1
1957	Monterrey, Mex.	LaMesa, CA	4–0	1984	Seoul, S. Korea	Altamonte Sgs, FL	6–2
1958	Monterrey, Mex.	Kankakee, IL	10–1	1985	Seoul, S. Korea	Mexicali, Mex.	7–1
1959	Hamtramck, MI	Auburn, CA	12–0	1986	Tainan Park, Taiwan	Tucson, AZ	12–0
1960	Levittown, PA	Ft. Worth, TX	5–0	1987	Hua Lian, Taiwan	Irvine, CA	21–1
1961	El Cajon, CA	El Campo, TX	4–2	1988	Tai-Chung, Taiwan	Pearl City, HI	10–0
1962	San Jose, CA	Kankakee, IL	3–0	1989	Trumbull, CT	Kaohsiung, Taiwan	5–2
1963	Granada Hills, CA	Stratford, CT	2–1	1990	Taipei, Taiwan	Shippensburg, PA	9–0
1964	Staten Island, NY	Monterrey, Mex.	4–0	1991	Tai-Chung, Taiwan	San Ramon Vly, CA	11–0
1965	Windsor Locks, CT	Stoney Creek, Can.	3–1	1992*	Long Beach, CA	Zamboanga, Phil.	6–0
1966	Houston, TX	W. New York, NJ	8–2	1993	Long Beach, CA	David Chiriqui, Pan.	3–2
1967	West Tokyo, Japan	Chicago, IL	4–1	1994	Maracaibo, Venez.	Northridge, CA	4–3
1968	Osaka, Japan	Richmond, VA	1–0	1995	Tainan, Taiwan	Sprint, TX	17–3
1969	Taipei, Taiwan	Santa Clara, CA	5–0	1996	Kao-Hsuing, Taiwan	Cranston, RI	13–3
1970	Wayne, NJ	Campbell, CA	2–0	1997	Guadalupe, Mex.	Mission Viejo, CA	5–4
1971	Tainan, Taiwan	Gary, IN	12–3	1998	Toms River, NJ	Kashima, Japan	12–9
1972	Taipei, Taiwan	Hammond, IN	6–0	1999	Osaka, Japan	Phenix City, AL	5–0
1973	Tainan City, Taiwan	Tucson, AZ	12–0				

*Long Beach declared a 6–0 winner after the international tournament committee determined that Zamboanga City had used players that were not within its city limits.

Motor Boat Racing

American Power Boat Association Gold Cup Champions

Year	Boat	Driver	Avg MPH	Year	Boat	Driver	Avg MPH
1904	Standard (June)	Carl Riotte	23.160	1927	Greenwich Folly	George Townsend	47.662
1904	Vingt-et-Un II (Sep)	W. Sharpe Kilmer	24.900				
1905	Chip I	J. Wainwright	15.000	1928	No race		
1906	Chip II	J. Wainwright	25.000	1929	Imp	Richard Hoyt	48.662
1907	Chip II	J. Wainwright	23.903	1930	Hotsy Totsy	Vic Kliesrath	52.673
1908	Dixie II	E. J. Schroeder	29.938	1931	Hotsy Totsy	Vic Kliesrath	53.602
1909	Dixie II	E. J. Schroeder	29.590	1932	Delphine IV	Bill Horn	57.775
1910	Dixie III	F. K. Burnham	32.473	1933	El Lagarto	George Reis	56.260
1911	MIT II	J. H. Hayden	37.000	1934	El Lagarto	George Reis	55.000
1912	P.D.Q. II	A. G. Miles	39.462	1935	El Lagarto	George Reis	55.056
1913	Ankle Deep	Cas Mankowski	42.779	1936	Impshi	Kaye Don	45.735
1914	Baby Speed Demon II	Jim Blackton & Bob Edgren	48.458	1937	Notre Dame	Clell Perry	63.675
				1938	Alagi	Theo Rossi	64.340
1915	Miss Detroit	Johnny Milot & Jack Beebe	37.656	1939	My Sin	Z. G. Simmons, Jr	66.133
				1940	Hotsy Totsy III	Sidney Allen	48.295
1916	Miss Minneapolis	Bernard Smith	48.860	1941	My Sin	Z. G. Simmons, Jr	52.509
1917	Miss Detroit II	Gar Wood	54.410	1942-45	No race		
1918	Miss Detroit II	Gar Wood	51.619	1946	Tempo VI	Guy Lombardo	68.132
1919	Miss Detroit III	Gar Wood	42.748	1947	Miss Peps V	Danny Foster	57.000
1920	Miss America I	Gar Wood	62.022	1948	Miss Great Lakes	Danny Foster	46.845
1921	Miss America I	Gar Wood	52.825	1949	My Sweetie	Bill Cantrell	73.612
1922	Packard Chriscraft	J. G. Vincent	40.253	1950	Slo-Mo-Shun IV	Ted Jones	78.216
1923	Packard Chriscraft	Caleb Bragg	43.867	1951	Slo-Mo-Shun V	Lou Fageol	90.871
1924	Baby Bootlegger	Caleb Bragg	45.302	1952	Slo-Mo-Shun IV	Stan Dollar	79.923
1925	Baby Bootlegger	Caleb Bragg	47.240	1953	Slo-Mo-Shun IV	Joe Taggart & Lou Fageol	99.108
1926	Greenwich Folly	George Townsend	47.984	1954	Slo-Mo-Shun IV	Joe Taggart & Lou Fageol	92.613

American Power Boat Association Gold Cup Champions (Cont.)

Year	Boat	Driver	Avg MPH	Year	Boat	Driver	Avg MPH
1955	Gale V	Lee Schoenith	99.552	1978	Atlas Van Lines	Bill Muncey	111.412
1956	Miss Thriftaway	Bill Muncey	96.552	1979	Atlas Van Lines	Bill Muncey	100.765
1957	Miss Thriftaway	Bill Muncey	101.787	1980	Miss Budweiser	Dean Chenoweth	106.932
1958	Hawaii Kai III	Jack Regas	103.000				
1959	Maverick	Bill Stead	104.481	1981	Miss Budweiser	Dean Chenoweth	116.932
1960		No race					
1961	Miss Century 21	Bill Muncey	99.678	1982	Atlas Van Lines	Chip Hanauer	120.050
1962	Miss Century 21	Bill Muncey	100.710	1983	Atlas Van Lines	Chip Hanauer	118.507
1963	Miss Bardahl	Ron Musson	105.124	1984	Atlas Van Lines	Chip Hanauer	130.175
1964	Miss Bardahl	Ron Musson	103.433	1985	Miller American	Chip Hanauer	120.643
1965	Miss Bardahl	Ron Musson	103.132	1986	Miller American	Chip Hanauer	116.523
1966	Tahoe Miss	Mira Slovak	93.019	1987	Miller American	Chip Hanauer	127.620
1967	Miss Bardahl	Bill Shumacher	101.484	1988	Miss Circus Circus	Chip Hanauer & Jim Prevost	123.756
1968	Miss Bardahl	Bill Shumacher	108.173				
1969	Miss Budweiser	Bill Sterett	98.504	1989	Miss Budweiser	Tom D'Eath	131.209
1970	Miss Budweiser	Dean Chenoweth	99.562	1990	Miss Budweiser	Tom D'Eath	143.176
				1991	Winston Eagle	Mark Tate	137.771
1971	Miss Madison	Jim McCormick	98.043	1992	Miss Budweiser	Chip Hanauer	136.282
1972	Atlas Van Lines	Bill Muncey	104.277	1993	Miss Budweiser	Chip Hanauer	141.195
1973	Miss Budweiser	Dean Chenoweth	99.043	1994	Smokin' Joe Camel	Mark Tate	145.260
				1995	Miss Budweiser	Chip Hanauer	149.160
1974	Pay 'n Pak	George Henley	104.428	1996	PICO American Dream	Dave Villwock	149.328
1975	Pay 'n Pak	George Henley	108.921	1997	Miss Budweiser	Dave Villwock	129.366
1976	Miss U.S.	Tom D'Eath	100.412	1998	Miss Budweiser	Dave Villwock	140.309
1977	Atlas Van Lines	Bill Muncey	111.822	1999	Miss PICO	Chip Hanauer	152.591

Unlimited Hydroplane Racing Association Annual Champion Drivers

Year	Driver	Boat	Wins	Year	Driver	Boat	Wins
1947	Danny Foster	Miss Peps V	6	1974	George Henley	Pay 'n Pack	7
1948	Dan Arena	Such Crust	2	1975	Billy Schumacher	Weisfleld's	2
1949	Bill Cantrell	My Sweetie	7	1976	Bill Muncey	Atlas Van Lines	5
1950	Dan Foster	Such Crust/DaphneX	2	1977	Mickey Remund	Miss Budweiser	3
1951	Chuck Thompson	Miss Pepsi	5	1978	Bill Muncey	Atlas Van Lines	6
1952	Chuck Thompson	Miss Pepsi	3	1979	Bill Muncey	Atlas Van Lines	7
1953	Lee Schoenith	Gale II	1	1980	Dean Chenoweth	Miss Budweiser	5
1954	Lee Schoenith	Gale V	4	1981	Dean Chenoweth	Miss Budweiser	6
1955	Lee Schoenith	Gale V/Wha Hoppen	1	1982	Chip Hanauer	Atlas Van Lines	5
1956	Russ Schleeh	Shanty I	3	1983	Chip Hanauer	Atlas Van Lines	3
1957	Jack Regas	Hawaii Kai III	5	1984	Jim Kropfeld	Miss Budweiser	6
1958	Mira Slovak	Bardah/Miss Buren	3	1985	Chip Hanauer	Miller American	5
1959	Bill Stead	Maverick	5	1986	Jim Kropfeld	Miss Budweiser	3
1960	Bill Muncey	Miss Thriftway	4	1987	Jim Kropfeld	Miss Budweiser	5
1961	Bill Muncey	Miss Century 21	4	1988	Tom D'Eath	Miss Budweiser	4
1962	Bill Muncey	Miss Century 21	5	1989	Chip Hanauer	Miss Circus Circus	3
1963	Bill Cantrell	Gale V	0	1990	Chip Hanauer	Miss Circus Circus	6
1964	Ron Musson	Miss Bardahl	4	1991	Mark Tate	Winston/Oberto	3
1965	Ron Musson	Miss Bardahl	4	1992	Chip Hanauer	Miss Budweiser	7
1966	Mira Slovak	Tahoe Miss	4	1993	Chip Hanauer	Miss Budweiser	7
1967	Bill Schumacher	Miss Bardahl	6	1994	Mark Tate	Smokin' Joe Camel	2
1968	Bill Schumacher	Miss Bardahl	4	1995	Mark Tate	Smokin' Joe Camel	4
1969	Bill Sterett, Sr	Miss Budweiser	4	1996	Dave Villwock	PICO American Dream	6
1970	Dean Chenoweth	Miss Budweiser	4	1997	Mark Tate	Close Call	1
1971	Dean Chenoweth	Miss Budweiser	2	1998	Dave Villwock	Miss Budweiser	8
1972	Bill Muncey	Atlas Van Lines	6	1999	Dave Villwock	Miss Budweiser	8
1973	Mickey Remund	Pay 'n Pack	4				

Unlimited Hydroplane Racing Association Annual Champion Boats

Year	Boat	Owner	Wins	Year	Boat	Owner	Wins
1970	Miss Budweiser	Little-Friedkin	4	1985	Miller American	Muncey-Lucero	5
1971	Miss Budweiser	Little-Friedkin	2	1986	Miss Budweiser	Bernie Little	3
1972	Atlas Van Lines	Joe Schoenith	6	1987	Miss Budweiser	Bernie Little	5
1973	Pay 'n Pak	Dave Heerensperger	4	1988	Miss Budweiser	Bernie Little	4
1974	Pay 'n Pak	Dave Heerensperger	7	1989	Miss Budweiser	Bernie Little	4
1975	Pay 'n Pak	Dave Heerensperger	5	1990	Circus Circus	Bill Bennett	6
1976	Atlas Van Lines	Bill Muncey	5	1991	Miss Budweiser	Bernie Little	4
1977	Miss Budweiser	Bernie Little	3	1992	Miss Budweiser	Bernie Little	7
1978	Atlas Van Lines	Bill Muncey	6	1993	Miss Budweiser	Bernie Little	7
1979	Atlas Van Lines	Bill Muncey	7	1994	Miss Budweiser	Bernie Little	4
1980	Miss Budweiser	Bernie Little	5	1995	Miss Budweiser	Bernie Little	5
1981	Miss Budweiser	Bernie Little	6	1996	PICO Amer. Dream	Fred Leland	6
1982	Atlas Van Lines	Fran Muncey	5	1997	Miss Budweiser	Bernie Little	5
1983	Atlas Van Lines	Muncey-Lucero	3	1998	Miss Budweiser	Bernie Little	8
1984	Miss Budweiser	Bernie Little	6	1999	Miss Budweiser	Bernie Little	8

Polo

United States Open Polo Champions

Year	Champion
1904	Wanderers
1905–09	Not contested
1910	Ranelagh
1911	Not contested
1912	Cooperstown
1913	Cooperstown
1914	Meadow Brook Magpies
1915	Not contested
1916	Meadow Brook
1917–18	Not contested
1919	Meadow Brook
1920	Meadow Brook
1921	Great Neck
1922	Argentine
1923	Meadow Brook
1924	Midwick
1925	Orange County
1926	Hurricanes
1927	Sands Point
1928	Meadow Brook
1929	Hurricanes
1930	Hurricanes
1931	Santa Paula
1932	Templeton
1933	Aurora
1934	Templeton
1935	Greentree
1936	Greentree
1937	Old Westbury
1938	Old Westbury
1939	Bostwick Field
1940	Aknusti
1941	Gulf Stream
1942–45	Not contested
1946	Mexico
1947	Old Westbury
1948	Hurricanes
1949	Hurricanes
1950	Bostwick
1951	Milwaukee
1952	Beverly Hills
1953	Meadow Brook
1954	C.C.C.– Meadow Brook
1955	C.C.C.
1956	Brandywine
1957	Detroit
1958	Dallas
1959	Circle F
1960	Oak Brook– C.C.C.
1961	Milwaukee
1962	Santa Barbara
1963	Tulsa
1964	Concar Oak Brook
1965	Oak Brook– Santa Barbara
1966	Tulsa
1967	Bunntyco– Oak Brook
1968	Midland
1969	Tulsa Greenhill
1970	Tulsa Greenhill
1971	Oak Brook
1972	Milwaukee
1973	Oak Brook
1974	Milwaukee
1975	Milwaukee
1976	Willow Bend
1977	Retama
1978	Abercrombie & Kent
1979	Retama
1980	Southern Hills
1981	Rolex A & K
1982	Retama
1983	Ft. Lauderdale
1984	Retama
1985	Carter Ranch
1986	Retama II
1987	Aloha
1988	Les Diables Bleus
1989	Les Diables Bleus
1990	Les Diables Bleus
1991	Grant's Farm Manor
1992	Hanalei Bay
1993	Gehache
1994	Aspen
1995	Outback
1996	Outback
1997	Isla Carroll
1998	Esque
1999	Outback

Top-Ranked Players

The United States Polo Association ranks its registered players from minus 2 to plus 10 goals, with 10 Goal players being the game's best. At present, the USPA recognizes six 10-Goal and nine 9-Goal players:

10-GOAL	9-GOAL
Mariano Aguerre (Greenwich)	Javier Novill Astrada (Palm Beach)
Michael Azzaro (San Antonio)	Miguel Novill Astrada (Palm Beach)
Adolfo Cambiaso (Palm Beach)	Francisco Bensadon (Palm Beach)
Bartolome Castagnolo (Palm Beach)	Christian LaPrida (Palm Beach)
Carlos Gracida (Palm Beach)	Tomas Llorente (Palm Beach)
Guillermo Gracida, Jr (Palm Beach)	Owen R. Rinehart (Langdon Road)
Bautista Heguy (Palm Beach)	Adam Snow (Langdon Road/
Gonzalo Heguy (Palm Beach)	Palm Beach)
Ignacio Heguy (Palm Beach)	
Sebastian Merlos (Aiken)	

Professional Rodeo Cowboys Association World Champions

All-Around

1929....Earl Thode	1949....Jim Shoulders	1967....Larry Mahan	1985....Lewis Feild
1930....Clay Carr	1950....Bill Linderman	1968....Larry Mahan	1986....Lewis Feild
1931....John Schneider	1951....Casey Tibbs	1969....Larry Mahan	1987....Lewis Feild
1932....Donald Nesbit	1952....Harry Tompkins	1970....Larry Mahan	1988....Dave Appleton
1933....Clay Carr	1953....Bill Linderman	1971...:.Phil Lyne	1989....Ty Murray
1934....Leonard Ward	1954....Buck Rutherford	1972....Phil Lyne	1990....Ty Murray
1935....Everett Bowman	1955....Casey Tibbs	1973....Larry Mahan	1991....Ty Murray
1936....John Bowman	1956....Jim Shoulders	1974....Tom Ferguson	1992....Ty Murray
1937....Everett Bowman	1957....Jim Shoulders	1975....Tom Ferguson	1993....Ty Murray
1938....Burel Mulkey	1958....Jim Shoulders	1976....Tom Ferguson	1994....Ty Murray
1939....Paul Carney	1959....Jim Shoulders	1977....Tom Ferguson	1995....Joe Beaver
1940....Fritz Truan	1960....Harry Tompkins	1978....Tom Ferguson	1996....Joe Beaver
1941....Homer Pettigrew	1961....Benny Reynolds	1979....Tom Ferguson	1997....Dan Mortensen
1942....Gerald Roberts	1962....Tom Nesmith	1980....Paul Tierney	1998....Ty Murray
1943....Louis Brooks	1963....Dean Oliver	1981....Jimmie Cooper	
1944....Louis Brooks	1964....Dean Oliver	1982....Chris Lybbert	
1947....Todd Whatley	1965....Dean Oliver	1983....Roy Cooper	
1948....Gerald Roberts	1966....Larry Mahan	1984....Dee Picket	

Saddle Bronc Riding

1929....Earl Thode	1948....Gene Pruett	1965....Shawn Davis	1982....Monty Henson
1930....Clay Carr	1949....Casey Tibbs	1966....Marty Wood	1983....B. Gjermundson
1931....Earl Thode	1950....Bill Linderman	1967....Shawn Davis	1984....B. Gjermundson
1932....Peter Knight	1951....Casey Tibbs	1968....Shawn Davis	1985....B. Gjermundson
1933....Peter Knight	1952....Casey Tibbs	1969....Bill Smith	1986....Bud Munroe
1934....Leonard Ward	1953....Casey Tibbs	1970....Dennis Reiners	1987....Clint Johnson
1935....Peter Knight	1954....Casey Tibbs	1971....Bill Smith	1988....Clint Johnson
1936....Peter Knight	1955....DebCopenhaver	1972....Mel Hyland	1989....Clint Johnson
1937....Burel Mulkey	1956....DebCopenhaver	1973....Bill Smith	1990....Robert Etbauer
1938....Burel Mulkey	1957....Alvin Nelson	1974....John McBeth	1991....Robert Etbauer
1939....Fritz Truan	1958....Marty Wood	1975....Monty Henson	1992....Billy Etbauer
1940....Fritz Truan	1959....Casey Tibbs	1976....Monty Henson	1993....Dan Mortensen
1941....Doff Aber	1960....Enoch Walker	1977....Bobby Berger	1994....Dan Mortensen
1942....Doff Aber	1961....Winston Bruce	1978....Joe Marvel	1995....Dan Mortensen
1943....Louis Brooks	1962....Kenny McLean	1979....Bobby Berger	1996....Billy Etbauer
1944....Louis Brooks	1963....Guy Weeks	1980....Clint Johnson	1997....Dan Mortensen
1947....Carl Olson	1964....Marty Wood	1981....B. Gjermundson	1998....Dan Mortensen

Bareback Riding

1932....Smoky Snyder	1951....Casey Tibbs	1968....Clyde Vamvoras	1985....Lewis Feild
1933....Nate Waldrum	1952....Harry Tompkins	1969....Gary Tucker	1986....Lewis Feild
1934....Leonard Ward	1953....Eddy Akridge	1970....Paul Mayo	1987....Bruce Ford
1935....Frank Schneider	1954....Eddy Akridge	1971....Joe Alexander	1988....Marvin Garrett
1936....Smoky Snyder	1955....Eddy Akridge	1972....Joe Alexander	1989....Marvin Garrett
1937....Paul Carney	1956....Jim Shoulders	1973....Joe Alexander	1990....Chuck Logue
1938....Pete Grubb	1957....Jim Shoulders	1974....Joe Alexander	1991....Clint Corey
1939....Paul Carney	1958....Jim Shoulders	1975....Joe Alexander	1992....Wayne Herman
1940....Carl Dossey	1959....Jack Buschbom	1976....Joe Alexander	1993....Deb Greenough
1941....George Mills	1960....Jack Buschbom	1977....Joe Alexander	1994....Marvin Garrett
1942....Louis Brooks	1961....Eddy Akridge	1978....Bruce Ford	1995....Marvin Garrett
1943....Bill Linderman	1962....Ralph Buell	1979....Bruce Ford	1996....Mark Garrett
1944....Louis Brooks	1963....John Hawkins	1980....Bruce Ford	1997....Eric Mouton
1947....Larry Finley	1964....Jim Houston	1981....J.C. Trujillo	1998....Mark Gomes
1948....Sonny Tureman	1965....Jim Houston	1982....Bruce Ford	
1949....Jack Buschbom	1966....Paul Mayo	1983....Bruce Ford	
1950....Jim Shoulders	1967 ....Clyde Vamvoras	1984....Larry Peabody	

Bull Riding

1929....John Schneider	1933....Frank Schneider	1939....Dick Griffith	1947....Wag Blessing
1930....John Schneider	1934....Frank Schneider	1940....Dick Griffith	1948....Harry Tompkins
1931....Smokey Snyder	1935....Smokey Snyder	1941....Dick Griffith	1949....Harry Tompkins
1932....John Schneider	1936....Smokey Snyder	1942....Dick Griffith	1950....Harry Tompkins
1932....Smokey Snyder	1937....Smokey Snyder	1943....Ken Roberts	1951....Jim Shoulders
John Schneider	1938....Kid Fletcher	1944....Ken Roberts	1952....Harry Tompkins

Professional Rodeo Cowboys Association World Champions *(Cont.)*
Bull Riding *(Cont.)*

1953....Todd Whatley	1965....Larry Mahan	1977....Don Gay	1989....Tuff Hedeman
1954....Jim Shoulders	1966....Ronnie Rossen	1978....Don Gay	1990....Jim Sharp
1955....Jim Shoulders	1967....Larry Mahan	1979....Don Gay	1991....Tuff Hedeman
1956....Jim Shoulders	1968....George Paul	1980....Don Gay	1992....Cody Custer
1957....Jim Shoulders	1969....Doug Brown	1981....Don Gay	1993....Ty Murray
1958....Jim Shoulders	1970....Gary Leffew	1982....Charles Sampson	1994....Daryl Mills
1959....Jim Shoulders	1971....Bill Nelson	1983....Cody Snyder	1995....Jerome Davis
1960....Harry Tompkins	1972....John Quintana	1984....Don Gay	1996....Terry West
1961....Ronnie Rossen	1973....Bobby Steiner	1985....Ted Nuce	1997....Scott Mendes
1962....Freckles Brown	1974....Don Gay	1986....Tuff Hedeman	1998....Ty Murray
1963....Bill Kornell	1975....Don Gay	1987....Lane Frost	
1964....Bob Wegner	1976....Don Gay	1988....Jim Sharp	

Calf Roping

1929....Everett Bowman	1948....Toots Mansfield	1965....Glen Franklin	1982....Roy Cooper
1930....Jake McClure	1949....Troy Fort	1966....Junior Garrison	1983....Roy Cooper
1931....Herb Meyers	1950....Toots Mansfield	1967....Glen Franklin	1984....Roy Cooper
1932....Richard Merchant	1951....Don McLaughlin	1968....Glen Franklin	1985....Joe Beaver
1933....Bill McFarlane	1952....Don McLaughlin	1969....Dean Oliver	1986....Chris Lybbert
1934....Irby Mundy	1953....Don McLaughlin	1970....Junior Garrison	1987....Joe Beaver
1935....Everett Bowman	1954....Don McLaughlin	1971....Phil Lyne	1988....Joe Beaver
1936....Clyde Burk	1955....Dean Oliver	1972....Phil Lyne	1989....Rabe Rabon
1937....Everett Bowman	1956....Ray Wharton	1973....Ernie Taylor	1990....Troy Pruitt
1938....Burel Mulkey	1957....Don McLaughlin	1974....Tom Ferguson	1991....Fred Whitfield
1939....Toots Mansfield	1958....Dean Oliver	1975....Jeff Copenhaver	1992....Joe Beaver
1940....Toots Mansfield	1959....Jim Bob Altizer	1976....Roy Cooper	1993....Joe Beaver
1941....Toots Mansfield	1960....Dean Oliver	1977....Roy Cooper	1994....Herbert Theriot
1942....Clyde Burk	1961....Dean Oliver	1978....Roy Cooper	1995....Fred Whitfield
1943....Toots Mansfield	1962....Dean Oliver	1979....Paul Tierney	1996....Fred Whitfield
1944....Clyde Burk	1963....Dean Oliver	1980....Roy Cooper	1997....Cody Ohl
1947....Troy Fort	1964....Dean Oliver	1981....Roy Cooper	1998....Cody Ohl

Steer Wrestling

1929....Gene Ross	1948....Homer Pettigrew	1965....Harley May	1982....Stan Williamson
1930....Everett Bowman	1949....Bill McGuire	1966....Jack Roddy	1983....Joel Edmondson
1931....Gene Ross	1950....Bill Linderman	1967....Roy Duvall	1984....John W. Jones
1932....Hugh Bennett	1951....Dub Phillips	1968....Jack Roddy	1985....Ote Berry
1933....Everett Bowman	1952....Harley May	1969....Roy Duvall	1986....Steve Duhon
1934....Shorty Ricker	1953....Ross Dollarhide	1970....John W. Jones	1987....Steve Duhon
1935....Everett Bowman	1954....James Bynum	1971....Billy Hale	1988....John W. Jones
1936....Jack Kerschner	1955....Benny Combs	1972....Roy Duvall	1989....John W. Jones
1937....Gene Ross	1956....Harley May	1973....Bob Marshall	1990....Ote Berry
1938....Everett Bowman	1957....Clark McEntire	1974....Tommy Puryear	1991....Ote Berry
1939....Harry Hart	1958....James Bynum	1975....F. Shepperson	1992....Mark Roy
1940....Homer Pettigrew	1959....Harry Charters	1976....Tom Ferguson	1993....Steve Duhon
1941....Hub Whiteman	1960....Bob A. Robinson	1977....Larry Ferguson	1994....Blaine Pederson
1942....Homer Pettigrew	1961....Jim Bynum	1978....Byron Walker	1995....Ote Berry
1943....Homer Pettigrew	1962....Tom Nesmith	1979....Stan Williamson	1996....Chad Bedell
1944....Homer Pettigrew	1963....Jim Bynum	1980....Butch Myers	1997....Brad Gleason
1947....Todd Whatley	1964....C.R. Boucher	1981....Byron Walker	1998....Mike Smith

Team Roping

1929....Charles Maggini	1941....Jim Hudson	1953....Ben Johnson	1965....Jim Rodriguez Jr.
1930....Norman Cowan	1942....Verne Castro	1954....Eddie Schell	1966....Ken Luman
1931....Arthur Beloat	Vic Castro	1955....Vern Castro	1967....Joe Glenn
1932....Ace Gardner	1943....Mark Hull	1956....Dale Smith	1968....Art Arnold
1933....Roy Adams	Leonard Block	1957....Dale Smith	1969....Jerold Camarillo
1934....Andy Jauregui	1944....Murphy Chaney	1958....Ted Ashworth	1970....John Miller
1935....Lawrence Conltk	1947....Jim Brister	1959....Jim Rodriguez Jr.	1971....John Miller
1936....John Rhodes	1948....Joe Glenn	1960....Jim Rodriguez Jr.	1972....Leo Camarillo
1937....Asbury Schell	1949....Ed Yanez	1961....Al Hooper	1973....Leo Camarillo
1938....John Rhodes	1950....Buck Sorrels	1962....Jim Rodriguez Jr.	1974....H.P. Evetts
1939....Asbury Schell	1951....Olan Sims	1963....Les Hirdes	1975....Leo Camarillo
1940....Pete Grubb	1952....Asbury Schell	1964....Bill Hamilton	1976....Leo Camarillo

Team Roping (Cont.)

1977....Jerold Camarillo	1984....Dee Pickett	1991....Bob Harris	1996....Steve Purcella
1978....Doyle Gellerman	1985....Jake Barnes	1992....Clay O. Cooper	Steve Northcott
1979....Allen Bach	1986....Clay O. Cooper	1993....Bobby Hurley	1997....Speed Williams
1980....Tee Woolman	1987....Clay O. Cooper	1994....Jake Barnes	Rich Skelton
1981....Walt Woodard	1988....Jake Barnes	Clay O. Cooper	1998....Speed Williams
1982....Tee Woolman	1989....Jake Barnes	1995....Bobby Hurley	Rich Skelton
1983....Leo Camarillo	1990....Allen Bach	Allen Bach	

Steer Roping

1929....Charles Maggini	1947....Ike Rude	1965....Sonney Wright	1983....Roy Cooper
1930....Clay Carr	1948....Everett Shaw	1966....Sonny Davis	1984....Guy Allen
1931....Andy Jauregui	1949....Shoat Webster	1967....Jim Bob Altizer	1985....Jim Davis
1932....George Weir	1950....Shoat Webster	1968....Sonny Davis	1986....Jim Davis
1933....John Bowman	1951....Everett Shaw	1969....Walter Arnold	1987....Shaun Burchett
1934....John McEntire	1952....Buddy Neal	1970....Don McLaughlin	1988....Shaun Burchett
1935....Richard Merchant	1953....Ike Rude	1971....Olin Young	1989....Guy Allen
1936....John Bowman	1954....Shoat Webster	1972....Allen Keller	1990....Phil Lyne
1937....Everett Bowman	1955....Shoat Webster	1973....Roy Thompson	1991....Guy Allen
1938....Hugh Bennett	1956....Jim Snively	1974....Olin Young	1992....Guy Allen
1939....Dick Truitt	1957....Clark McEntire	1975....Roy Thompson	1993....Guy Allen
1940....Clay Carr	1958....Clark McEntire	1976....Marvin Cantrell	1994....Guy Allen
1941....Ike Rude	1959....Everett Shaw	1977....Buddy Cockrell	1995....Guy Allen
1942....King Merrit	1960....Don McLaughlin	1978....Sonny Worrell	1996....Guy Allen
1943....Tom Rhodes	1961....Clark McEntire	1979....Gary Good	1997....Guy Allen
1944....Tom Rhodes	1962....Everett Shaw	1980....Guy Allen	1998....Guy Allen
1945....Everett Shaw	1963....Don McLaughlin	1981....Arnold Felts	
1946....Everett Shaw	1964....Sonny Davis	1982....Guy Allen	

Note: In 1945–46 champions were crowned only in Steer Roping.

Rowing

National Collegiate Rowing Champions

MEN'S EIGHT

1985 ....Harvard	1990 ....Wisconsin	1995 ....Brown
1986 ....Wisconsin	1991 ....Pennsylvania	1996 ....Princeton
1987 ....Harvard	1992 ....Harvard	1997 ....Washington
1988 ....Harvard	1993 ....Brown	1998 ....Princeton
1989 ....Harvard	1994 ....Brown	1999 ....California

WOMEN'S EIGHT

1979 ....Yale	1986 ....Wisconsin	1993 ....Princeton
1980 ....California	1987 ....Washington	1994 ....Princeton
1981 ....Washington	1988 ....Washington	1995 ....Princeton
1982 ....Washington	1989 ....Cornell	1996 ....Brown
1983 ....Washington	1990 ....Princeton	1997 ....Washington
1984 ....Washington	1991 ....Boston University	1998 ....Washington
1985 ....Washington	1992 ....Boston University	1999 ....Brown

Rugby*

National Men's Club Championship

Year	Winner	Runner-Up	Year	Winner	Runner-Up
1979	Old Blues (CA)	St Louis Falcons	1990	Denver Barbos	Old Blues (CA)
1980	Old Blues (CA)	St. Louis Falcons	1991	Old Mission Beach AC	Washington
1981	Old Blues (CA)	Old Blue (NY)	1992	Old Blues (CA)	Mystic River (MA)
1982	Old Blues (CA)	Denver Barbos	1993	Old Mission Beach AC	Milwaukee
1983	Old Blues (CA)	Dallas Harlequins	1994	Old Mission Beach AC	Life College (GA)
1984	Dallas Harlequins	Los Angeles	1995	Potomac Athletic Club	Old Mission Beach
1985	Milwaukee	Denver Barbos	1996	Old Mission Beach AC	Old Blues (CA)
1986	Old Blues (CA)	Old Blue (NY)	1997	Gentlemen of Aspen	Old Blue (NY)
1987	Old Blues (CA)	Pittsburgh	1998	Gentlemen of Aspen	Old Blue (NY)
1988	Old Mission Beach AC	Milwaukee	1999	Gentlemen of Aspen	Golden Gate (CA)
1989	Old Mission Beach AC	Philly/Whitemarsh			

National Men's Collegiate Championship

Year	Winner	Runner-Up	Year	Winner	Runner-Up
1980	California	Air Force	1990	Air Force	Army
1981	California	Harvard	1991	California	Army
1982	California	Life College	1992	California	Army
1983	California	Air Force	1993	California	Air Force
1984	Harvard	Colorado	1994	California	Navy
1985	California	Maryland	1995	California	Air Force
1986	California	Dartmouth	1996	California	Penn St
1987	San Diego State	Air Force	1997	California	Penn St
1988	California	Dartmouth	1998	California	Stanford
1989	Air Force	Long Beach	1999	California	Penn St

World Cup Championship

Year	Winner	Runner-Up	Year	Winner	Runner-Up
1987	New Zealand	France	1995	South Africa	New Zealand
1991	Australia	England			

*Results are for rugby union competition only.

Sailing

America's Cup Champions

SCHOONERS AND J-CLASS BOATS

Year	Winner	Skipper	Series	Loser	Skipper
1851	America	Richard Brown			
1870	Magic	Andrew Comstock	1–0	Cambria, Great Britain	J. Tannock
1871	Columbia (2–1)	Nelson Comstock	4–1	Livonia, Great Britain	J. R. Woods
	Sappho (2–0)	Sam Greenwood			
1876	Madeleine	Josephus Williams	2–0	Countess of Dufferin, Canada	J. E. Ellsworth
1881	Mischief	Nathanael Clock	2–0	Atalanta, Canada	Alexander Cuthbert
1885	Puritan	Aubrey Crocker	2–0	Genesta, Great Britain	John Carter
1886	Mayflower	Martin Stone	2–0	Galatea, Great Britain	Dan Bradford
1887	Volunteer	Henry Haff	2–0	Thistle, Great Britain	John Barr
1893	Vigilant	William Hansen	3–0	Valkyrie II, Great Britain	William Granfield
1895	Defender	Henry Haff	3–0	Valkyrie III, Great Britain	William Granfield
1899	Columbia	Charles Barr	3–0	Shamrock I, Great Britain	Archie Hogarth
1901	Columbia	Charles Barr	3–0	Shamrock II, Great Britain	E. A. Sycamore
1903	Reliance	Charles Barr	3–0	Shamrock III, Great Britain	Bob Wringe
1920	Resolute	Charles F. Adams	3–2	Shamrock IV, Great Britain	William Burton
1930	Enterprise	Harold Vanderbilt	4–0	Shamrock V, Great Britain	Ned Heard
1934	Rainbow	Harold Vanderbilt	4–2	Endeavour, Great Britain	T. O. M. Sopwith
1937	Ranger	Harold Vanderbilt	4–0	Endeavour II, Great Britain	T. O. M. Sopwith

12-METER BOATS

Year	Winner	Skipper	Series	Loser	Skipper
1958	Columbia	Briggs Cunningham	4–0	Sceptre, Great Britain	Graham Mann
1962	Weatherly	Bus Mosbacher	4–1	Gretel, Australia	Jock Sturrock
1964	Constellation	Bob Bavier & Eric Ridder	4–0	Sovereign, Australia	Peter Scott
1967	Intrepid	Bus Mosbacher	4–0	Dame Pattie, Australia	Jock Sturrock
1970	Intrepid	Bill Ficker	4–1	Gretel II, Australia	Jim Hardy
1974	Courageous	Ted Hood	4–0	Southern Cross, Australia	John Cuneo
1977	Courageous	Ted Turner	4–0	Australia	Noel Robins
1980	Freedom	Dennis Conner	4–1	Australia	Jim Hardy
1983	Australia II	John Bertrand	4–3	Liberty, United States	Dennis Conner
1987	Stars & Stripes	Dennis Conner	4–0	Kookaburra III, Australia	Iain Murray

60-FOOT CATAMARAN VS 133-FOOT MONOHULL

Year	Winner	Skipper	Series	Loser	Skipper
1988	Stars & Stripes	Dennis Conner	2–0	New Zealand	David Barnes

75-FOOT MONOHULL (IACC)

Year	Winner	Skipper	Series	Loser	Skipper
1992	America[3]	Bill Koch	4–1	Il Moro di Vinezia, Italy	Paul Cayard
1995	Black Magic I	Russell Coutts	5–0	Young America, United States	Dennis Conner

Note: Winning entries have been from the United States every year but two; in 1983 an Australian vessel won, and in 1995 a vessel from New Zealand won.

Shooting World Champions

Men

50M FREE RIFLE PRONE

1947 .....O. Sannes, Norway
1949 .....A.C. Jackson,
    United States
1952 .....A.C. Jackson,
    United States
1954 .....G. Boa, Canada
1958 .....M. Nordquist
1962 .....K. Wenk, West Germany
1966 .....D. Boyd, United States
1970 .....M. Fiess, S. Africa
1974 .....K. Bulan, Czech.
1978 .....A. Allan, Great Britain
1982 .....V. Danilschenko, USSR
1986 .....S. Bereczky, Hungary
1990 .....V. Bochkarev, USSR
1994 .....Venjie Li, China
1998 .....Thomas Tamas, U.S.

AIR RIFLE

1966 .....G. Kümmet, W. Germany
1970 .....G. Kusterman, W. Germ.
1974 .....E. Pedzisz, Poland
1978 .....O. Schlipf, W. Germany
1979 .....K. Hillenbrand
1981 .....F. Bessy, France
1982 .....F. Rettkowski, E. Germ.
1983 .....P. Heberle, France
1985 .....P. Heberle, France
1986 .....H. Riederer, W. Germany
1987 .....K. Ivanov, USSR
1989 .....J. P. Amet, France
1990 .....H. Riederer, W. Germany
1994 .....Boris Polak, Israel
1998 .....Artem Khadjibekov, Russia

MEN'S TRAP

1929 .....De Lumniczer, Hungary
1930 .....M. Arie, United States
1931 .....Kiszkurno, Poland
1933 .....De Lumniczer, Hungary
1934 .....A. Montagh, Hungary
1935 .....R. Sack, W. Germany
1936 .....Kiszkurno, Poland
1937 .....K. Huber, Finland
1938 .....I. Strassburger, Hungary
1939 .....De Lumniczer, Hungary
1947 .....H. Liljedahl, Sweden
1949 .....F. Rocchi, Argentina
1950 .....C. Sala, Italy
1952 .....P.J. Grossi, Argentina
1954 .....C. Merlo, Italy
1958 .....F. Eisenlauer,
    United States
1959 .....H. Badravi, Egypt
1961 .....E. Mattarelli, Italy
1962 .....W. Zimenko, USSR
1965 .....J.E. Lire, Chile
1966 .....K. Jones, United States
1967 .....G. Rennard, Belgium
1969 .....E. Mattarelli, Italy
1970 .....M. Carrega, France
1971 .....M. Carrega, France
1973 .....A. Andrushkin, USSR
1974 .....M. Carrega, France
1975 .....J. Primrose, Canada
1977 .....E. Azkue, Spain
1978 .....E. Vallduvi, Spain
1979 .....M. Carrega, France
1981 .....A. Asanov, USSR
1982 .....L. Giovonnetti, Italy

MEN'S TRAP (Cont.)

1983 .....J. Primrose, Canada
1985 .....M. Bednarik, Czech.
1986 .....M. Benarik, Czech.
1987 .....D. Monakov, USSR
1989 .....M. Venturini, Italy
1990 .....J. Damne, E. Germany
1994 .....Dmitriy Monakov, Ukraine
1995 .....Giovanni Pellielo, Italy
1998 .....Giovanni Pellielo, Italy

THREE POSITION RIFLE

1929 .....O. Ericsson, Sweden
1930 .....Petersen, Denmark
1931 .....Amundson, Norway
1933 .....De Lisle, France
1935 .....Leskinnen, Finland
1937 .....Mazoyer, France
1939 .....Steigelmann, Germany
1947 .....I. H. Erben, Sweden
1949 .....P. Janhonen, Finland
1952 .....Kongshaug, Norway
1954 .....A. Bugdanov, USSR
1958 .....Itkis, USSR
1962 .....G. Anderson,
    United States
1966 .....G. Anderson,
    United States
1970 .....Parkhimovitch, USSR
1974 .....L. Wigger, United States
1978 .....E. Svensson, Sweden
1982 .....K. Ivanov, USSR
1986 .....P. Heinz, W. Germany
1990 .....E. C. Lee, S. Korea
1994 .....P. Kurka, Czech Republic
1998 .....Jozef Gonci, Slovakia

Women

THREE POSITION RIFLE

1966 .....M. Thompson,
    United States
1970 .....M. Thompson Murdock,
    United States
1974 .....A. Pelova, Bulgaria
1978 .....W. Oliver, United States
1982 .....M. Helbig, E. Germany
1986 .....V. Letcheva, Bulgaria
1990 .....V. Letcheva, Bulgaria
1994 .....A. Maloukhina, Russia
1998 .....Sonja Pfeilschifter, Germany

AIR RIFLE

1970 .....V. Cherkasque, USSR
1974 .....T. Ratkinova, USSR
1978 .....W. Oliver, United States
1979 .....K. Monez, United States
1981 .....S. Romaristova, USSR
1982 .....S. Lang, W. Germany
1983 .....M. Helbig, E. Germany

AIR RIFLE (Cont.)

1985 .....E. Forian, Hungary
1986 .....V. Letcheva, Bulgaria
1987 .....V. Letcheva, Bulgaria
1989 .....V. Letcheva, Bulgaria
1990 .....E. Joc, Hungary
1994 .....Sonja Pfeilschifter, Germany
1998 .....Sonja Pfeilschifter, Germany

SPORT PISTOL

1966 .....N. Rasskazova, USSR
1970 .....N. Stoljarova, USSR
1974 .....N. Stoljarova, USSR
1978 .....K. Dyer, United States
1982 .....P. Balogh, Hungary
1986 .....M. Dobrantcheva, USSR
1990 .....M. Logvinenko, Sov Union
1994 .....Soon Hee Boo, S. Korea
1998 .....Yieqing Cai, China

AIR PISTOL

1970 .....S. Carroll, United States
1974 .....Z. Simonian, USSR
1978 .....K. Hansson, Sweden
1979 .....R. Fox, United States
1981 .....N. Kalinina, USSR
1982 .....M. Dobrantcheva, USSR
1983 .....K. Bodin, Sweden
1985 .....M. Dobrantcheva, USSR
1986 .....A. Völker, E. Germany
1987 .....J. Brajkovic, Yugoslavia
1989 .....N. Salukvadse, USSR
1990 .....Jasna Sekaric, Yugoslavia
1994 .....Jasna Sekaric, IOP
1998 .....Dorisuren Munkhbayar,
    Mongolia

Softball

Men
MAJOR FAST PITCH

1933.........J. L. Gill Boosters, Chicago	1967.........Sealmasters, Aurora, IL
1934.........Ke-Nash-A, Kenosha, WI	1968.........Clearwater (FL) Bombers
1935.........Crimson Coaches, Toledo, OH	1969.........Raybestos Cardinals, Stratford, CT
1936.........Kodak Park, Rochester, NY	1970.........Raybestos Cardinals, Stratford, CT
1937.........Briggs Body Team, Detroit	1971.........Welty Way, Cedar Rapids, IA
1938.........The Pohlers, Cincinnati	1972.........Raybestos Cardinals, Stratford, CT
1939.........Carr's Boosters, Covington, KY	1973.........Clearwater (FL) Bombers
1940.........Kodak Park, Rochester, NY	1974.........Gianella Bros, Santa Rosa, CA
1941.........Bendix Brakes, South Bend, IN	1975.........Rising Sun Hotel, Reading, PA
1942.........Deep Rock Oilers, Tulsa	1976.........Raybestos Cardinals, Stratford, CT
1943.........Hammer Air Field, Fresno	1977.........Billard Barbell, Reading, PA
1944.........Hammer Air Field, Fresno	1978.........Billard Barbell, Reading, PA
1945.........Zollner Pistons, Fort Wayne, IN	1979.........McArdle Pontiac/Cadillac, Midland, MI
1946.........Zollner Pistons, Fort Wayne, IN	1980.........Peterbilt Western, Seattle
1947.........Zollner Pistons, Fort Wayne, IN	1981.........Archer Daniels Midland, Decatur, IL
1948.........Briggs Beautyware, Detroit	1982.........Peterbilt Western, Seattle
1949.........Tip Top Tailors, Toronto	1983.........Franklin Cardinals, Stratford, CT
1950.........Clearwater (FL) Bombers	1984.........California Kings, Merced, CA
1951.........Dow Chemical, Midland, MI	1985.........Pay'n Pak, Seattle
1952.........Briggs Beautyware, Detroit	1986.........Pay'n Pak, Seattle
1953.........Briggs Beautyware, Detroit	1987.........Pay'n Pak, Seattle
1954.........Clearwater (FL) Bombers	1988.........TransAire, Elkhart, IN
1955.........Raybestos Cardinals, Stratford, CT	1989.........Penn Corp, Sioux City, IA
1956.........Clearwater (FL) Bombers	1990.........Penn Corp, Sioux City, IA
1957.........Clearwater (FL) Bombers	1991.........Guanella Brothers, Rohnert Park, CA
1958.........Raybestos Cardinals, Stratford, CT	1992.........Natl Health Care Disc, Sioux City, IA
1959.........Sealmasters, Aurora, IL	1993.........Natl Health Care Disc, Sioux City, IA
1960.........Clearwater (FL) Bombers	1994.........Decatur Pride, Decatur, IL
1961.........Sealmasters, Aurora, IL	1995.........Decatur Pride, Decatur, IL
1962.........Clearwater (FL) Bombers	1996.........Green Bay All-Car, Green Bay, WI
1963.........Clearwater (FL) Bombers	1997.........Green Bay All-Car, Green Bay, WI
1964.........Burch Tool, Detroit	1998.........Meierhoffer-Fleeman, St. Joseph, MO
1965.........Sealmasters, Aurora, IL	1999.........Decatur Pride, Decatur, IL
1966.........Clearwater (FL) Bombers	

SUPER SLOW PITCH

1981.........Howard's/Western Steer, Denver, NC	1991.........Sunbelt/Worth, Centerville, GA
1982.........Jerry's Catering, Miami, Fla.	1992.........Ritch's Superior, Windsor Locks, CT
1983.........Howard's/Western Steer, Denver, NC	1993.........Ritch's Superior, Windsor Locks, CT
1984.........Howard's/Western Steer, Denver, NC	1994.........Bell Corp, Tampa, Fla.
1985.........Steele's Sports, Grafton, OH	1995.........Lighthouse/Worth, Stone Mt., GA
1986.........Steele's Sports, Grafton, OH	1996.........Ritch's Superior, Windsor Locks, CT
1987.........Steele's Sports, Grafton, OH	1997.........Ritch's Superior, Winsor Locks, CT
1988.........Starpath, Monticello, KY	1998.........Lighthouse/Worth, Stone Mt., GA
1989.........Ritch's Salvage, Harrisburg, NC	1999.........Team Easton, Wilmington, NC
1990.........Steele's Silver Bullets, Grafton, OH	

MAJOR SLOW PITCH

1953.........Shields Construction, Newport, KY	1970.........Little Caesar's, Southgate, MI
1954.........Waldneck's Tavern, Cincinnati	1971.........Pile Drivers, Virginia Beach, VA
1955.........Lang Pet Shop, Covington, KY	1972.........Jiffy Club, Louisville, KY
1956.........Gatliff Auto Sales, Newport, KY	1973.........Howard's Furniture, Denver, NC
1957.........Gatliff Auto Sales, Newport, KY	1974.........Howard's Furniture, Denver, NC
1958.........East Side Sports, Detroit	1975.........Pyramid Cafe, Lakewood, OH
1959.........Yorkshire Restaurant, Newport, KY	1976.........Warren Motors, Jacksonville, FL
1960.........Hamilton Tailoring, Cincinnati	1977.........Nelson Painting, Oklahoma City
1961.........Hamilton Tailoring, Cincinnati	1978.........Campbell Carpets, Concord, CA
1962.........Skip Hogan A.C., Pittsburgh	1979.........Nelco Mfg Co, Oklahoma City
1963.........Gatliff Auto Sales, Newport, KY	1980.........Campbell Carpets, Concord, CA
1964.........Skip Hogan A.C., Pittsburgh	1981.........Elite Coating, Gordon, CA
1965.........Skip Hogan A.C., Pittsburgh	1982.........Triangle Sports, Minneapolis
1966.........Michael's Lounge, Detroit	1983.........No. 1 Electric & Heating, Gastonia, NC
1967.........Jim's Sport Shop, Pittsburgh	1984.........Lilly Air Systems, Chicago
1968.........County Sports, Levittown, NY	1985.........Blanton's, Fayetteville, NC
1969.........Copper Hearth, Milwaukee	1986.........Non-Ferrous Metals, Cleveland

Men *(Cont.)*

MAJOR SLOW PITCH *(Cont.)*

1987..........Starpath, Monticello, KY
1988..........Bell Corp/FAF, Tampa, FL
1989..........Ritch's Salvage, Harrisburg, NC
1990..........New Construction, Shelbyville, IN
1991..........Riverside Paving, Louisville, KY
1992..........Vernon's, Jacksonville, FL
1993..........Back Porch/Destin Roofing, Destin, FL

1994..........Riverside RAM/Taylor Bros., Louisville, KY
1995..........Riverside/RAM/Taylor/TPS, Louisville, KY
1996..........Bell 2/Robert's/Easton, Orlando, FL
1997..........Long Haul/TPS, Albertville, Minnesota
1998..........Chase Mortgage/Easton, Wilmington, NC
1999..........Gasoline Heaven/Worth, Commack, NY

Women

MAJOR FAST PITCH

1933..........Great Northerns, Chicago
1934..........Hart Motors, Chicago
1935..........Bloomer Girls, Cleveland
1936..........Nat'l Screw & Mfg, Cleveland
1937..........Nat'l Screw & Mfg, Cleveland
1938..........J. J. Krieg's, Alameda, CA
1939..........J. J. Krieg's, Alameda, CA
1940..........Arizona Ramblers, Phoenix
1941..........Higgins Midgets, Tulsa
1942..........Jax Maids, New Orleans
1943..........Jax Maids, New Orleans
1944..........Lind & Pomeroy, Portland, OR
1945..........Jax Maids, New Orleans
1946..........Jax Maids, New Orleans
1947..........Jax Maids, New Orleans
1948..........Arizona Ramblers, Phoenix
1949..........Arizona Ramblers, Phoenix
1950..........Orange (CA) Lionettes
1951..........Orange (CA) Lionettes
1952..........Orange (CA) Lionettes
1953..........Betsy Ross Rockets, Fresno
1954..........Leach Motor Rockets, Fresno
1955..........Orange (CA) Lionettes
1956..........Orange (CA) Lionettes
1957..........Hacienda Rockets, Fresno
1958..........Raybestos Brakettes, Stratford, CT
1959..........Raybestos Brakettes, Stratford, CT
1960..........Raybestos Brakettes, Stratford, CT
1961..........Gold Sox, Whittier, CA
1962..........Orange (CA) Lionettes
1963..........Raybestos Brakettes, Stratford, CT
1964..........Erv Lind Florists, Portland, OR
1965..........Orange (CA) Lionettes
1966..........Raybestos Brakettes, Stratford, CT

1967..........Raybestos Brakettes, Stratford, CT
1968..........Raybestos Brakettes, Stratford, CT
1969..........Orange (CA) Lionettes
1970..........Orange (CA) Lionettes
1971..........Raybestos Brakettes, Stratford, CT
1972..........Raybestos Brakettes, Stratford, CT
1973..........Raybestos Brakettes, Stratford, CT
1974..........Raybestos Brakettes, Stratford, CT
1975..........Raybestos Brakettes, Stratford, CT
1976..........Raybestos Brakettes, Stratford, CT
1977..........Raybestos Brakettes, Stratford, CT
1978..........Raybestos Brakettes, Stratford, CT
1979..........Sun City (AZ) Saints
1980..........Raybestos Brakettes, Stratford, CT
1981..........Orlando (FL) Rebels
1982..........Raybestos Brakettes, Stratford, CT
1983..........Raybestos Brakettes, Stratford, CT
1984..........Los Angeles Diamonds
1985..........Hi-Ho Brakettes, Stratford, CT
1986..........Southern California Invasion, Los Angeles
1987..........Orange County Majestics, Anaheim, CA
1988..........Hi-Ho Brakettes, Stratford, CT
1989..........Whittier (CA) Raiders
1990..........Raybestos Brakettes, Stratford, CT
1991..........Raybestos Brakettes, Stratford, CT
1992..........Raybestos Brakettes, Stratford, CT
1993..........Redding Rebels, Redding, CA
1994..........Redding Rebels, Redding, CA
1995..........Redding Rebels, Redding, CA
1996..........California Commotion, Woodland Hills, CA
1997..........California Commotion, Woodland Hills, CA
1998..........California Commotion, Woodland Hills, CA
1999..........California Commotion, Woodland Hills, CA

MAJOR SLOW PITCH

1959..........Pearl Laundry, Richmond, VA
1960..........Carolina Rockets, High Pt, NC
1961..........Dairy Cottage, Covington, KY
1962..........Dana Gardens, Cincinnati
1963..........Dana Gardens, Cincinnati
1964..........Dana Gardens, Cincinnati
1965..........Art's Acres, Omaha
1966..........Dana Gardens, Cincinnati
1967..........Ridge Maintenance, Cleveland
1968..........Escue Pontiac, Cincinnati
1969..........Converse Dots, Hialeah, FL
1970..........Rutenschruder Floral, Cincinnati
1971..........Gators, Ft Lauderdale, FL
1972..........Riverside Ford, Cincinnati
1973..........Sweeney Chevrolet, Cincinnati
1974..........Marks Brothers Dots, Miami
1975..........Marks Brothers Dots, Miami
1976..........Sorrento's Pizza, Cincinnati
1977..........Fox Valley Lassies, St Charles, IL
1978..........Bob Hoffman's Dots, Miami
1979..........Bob Hoffman's Dots, Miami

1980..........Howard's Rubi-Otts, Graham, NC
1981..........Tifton (GA) Tomboys
1982..........Richmond (VA) Stompers
1983..........Spooks, Anoka, MN
1984..........Spooks, Anoka, MN
1985..........Key Ford Mustangs, Pensacola, FL
1986..........Sur-Way Tomboys, Tifton, GA
1987..........Key Ford Mustangs, Pensacola, FL
1988..........Spooks, Anoka, MN
1989..........Canaan's Illusions, Houston
1990..........Spooks, Anoka, MN
1991..........Kannan's Illusions, San Antonio, TX
1992..........Universal Plastics, Cookeville, TN
1993..........Universal Plastics, Cookeville, TN
1994..........Universal Plastics, Cookeville, TN
1995..........Armed Forces, Sacramento, CA
1996..........Spooks, Anoka, MN
1997..........Taylor's Major Slow Pitch, Glendale, MD
1998..........Lakerettes, Conneaut Lake, PA
1999..........Lakerettes, Conneaut Lake, PA

All-Around World Champions
MEN

1891.....Joseph F. Donoghue, U.S.	1934.....Bernt Evensen, Norway	1971.....Ard Schenk, Netherlands
1893.....Jaap Eden, Netherlands	1935.....Michael Staksrud, Nor.	1972.....Ard Schenk, Netherlands
1895.....Jaap Eden, Netherlands	1936.....Ivar Ballangrud, Norway	1973.....Göran Claeson, Sweden
1896.....Jaap Eden, Netherlands	1937.....Michael Staksrud, Nor.	1974.....Sten Stensen, Norway
1897.....Jack K. McCulloch, Can.	1938.....Ivar Ballangrud, Norway	1975.....Harm Kuipers, Netherlands
1898.....Peder Ostlund, Norway	1939.....Birger Wasenius, Finland	1976.....Piet Kleine, Neth.
1899.....Peder Ostlund, Norway	1947.....Lassi Parkkinen, Finland	1977.....Eric Heiden, U.S.
1900.....Edvard Engelsaas, Nor.	1948.....Odd Lundberg, Norway	1978.....Eric Heiden, U.S.
1901.....Franz F. Wathan, Finland	1949.....Kornel Pajor, Hungary	1979.....Eric Heiden, U.S.
1904.....Sigurd Mathisen, Norway	1950.....Hjalmar Andersen, Nor.	1980.....Hilbert van der Duin, Neth.
1905.....C. Coen de Koning, Neth.	1951.....Hjalmar Andersen, Nor.	1981.....Amund Sjobrand, Norway
1908.....Oscar Mathisen, Norway	1952.....Hjalmar Andersen, Nor.	1982.....Hilbert van der Duin, Neth.
1909.....Oscar Mathisen, Norway	1953.....Oleg Goncharenko, USSR	1983.....Rolf Falk-Larssen, Nor.
1910.....Nikolai Strunnikov, Russia	1954.....Boris Shilkov, USSR	1984.....Oleg Bozhev, USSR
1911.....Nikolai Strunnikov, Russia	1955.....Sigvard Ericsson, Swe.	1985.....Hein Vergeer, Neth.
1912.....Oscar Mathisen, Norway	1956.....Oleg Goncharenko, USSR	1986.....Hein Vergeer, Neth.
1913.....Oscar Mathisen, Norway	1957.....Knut Johannesen, Nor.	1987.....Nikolai Guliaev, USSR
1914.....Oscar Mathisen, Norway	1958.....Oleg Goncharenko, USSR	1988.....Eric Flaim, U.S.
1922.....Harald Strom, Norway	1959.....Juhani Järvinen, Finland	1989.....Leo Visser, Netherlands
1923.....Klas Thunberg, Finland	1960.....Boris Stenin, USSR	1990.....Johann Olav Koss, Nor.
1924.....Roald Larsen, Norway	1961.....Henk van der Grift, Neth.	1991.....Johann Olav Koss, Nor.
1925.....Klas Thunberg, Finland	1962.....Viktor Kosichkin, USSR	1992.....Roberto Sighel, Italy
1926.....Ivar Ballangrud, Norway	1963.....Jonny Nilsson, Sweden	1993.....Falko Zandstra, Neth.
1927.....Bernt Evensen, Norway	1964.....Knut Johannesen, Nor.	1994.....Johann Olav Koss, Nor.
1928.....Klas Thunberg, Finland	1965.....Per Ivar Moe, Norway	1995.....Rintje Ritsma, Netherlands
1929.....Klas Thunberg, Finland	1966.....Kees Verkerk, Neth.	1996.....Rintje Ritsma, Netherlands
1930.....Michael Staksrud, Nor.	1967.....Kees Verkerk, Neth.	1997.....Ids Postma, Netherlands
1931.....Klas Thunberg, Finland	1968.....Fred Anton Maier, Nor.	1998.....Ids Postma, Netherlands
1932.....Ivar Ballangrud, Norway	1969.....Dag Fornaes, Norway	1999.....Rintje Ritsma, Netherlands
1933.....Hans Engnestangen, Nor.	1970.....Ard Schenk, Netherlands	

WOMEN

1936.....Kit Klein, U.S.	1962.....Inga Artamonova, USSR	1982.....Karin Busch, GDR
1937.....Laila Schou Nilsen, Nor.	1963.....Lidia Skoblikova, USSR	1983.....Andrea Schöne, GDR
1938.....Laila Schou Nilsen, Nor.	1964.....Lidia Skoblikova, USSR	1984.....Karin Enke-Busch, GDR
1939.....Verné Lesche, Finland	1965.....Inga Artamonova, USSR	1985.....Andrea Schöne, GDR
1947.....Verné Lesche, Finland	1966.....Valentina Stenina, USSR	1986.....Karin Kania-Enke, GDR
1948.....Maria Isakova, USSR	1967.....Stien Kaiser, Neth.	1987.....Karin Kania, GDR
1949.....Maria Isakova, USSR	1968.....Stien Kaiser, Neth.	1988.....Karin Kania, GDR
1950.....Maria Isakova, USSR	1969.....Lasma Kauniste, USSR	1989.....Constanze Moser, GDR
1951.....Eevi Huttunen, Finland	1970.....Atje Keulen-Deelstra, Neth.	1990.....Jacqueline Börner, GDR
1952.....Lidia Selikhova, USSR	1971.....Nina Statkevich, USSR	1991.....Gunda Kleemann, Ger.
1953.....Khalida Shchegoleeva, USSR	1972.....Atje Keulen-Deelstra, Neth.	1992.....Gunda Niemann-Kleemann, Germany
1954.....Lidia Selikhova, USSR	1973.....Atje Keulen-Deelstra, Neth.	
1955.....Rimma Zhukova, USSR	1974.....Atje Keulen-Deelstra, Neth.	1993.....Gunda Niemann, Germany
1956.....Sofia Kondakova, USSR	1975,.....Karin Kessow, GDR	1994.....Emese Hunyady, Austria
1957.....Inga Artamonova, USSR	1976.....Sylvia Burka, Canada	1995.....Gunda Niemann, Germany
1958.....Inga Artamonova, USSR	1977.....Vera Bryndzej, USSR	1996.....Gunda Niemann, Germany
1959.....Tamara Rylova, USSR	1978.....Tatiana Averina, USSR	1997.....Gunda Niemann, Germany
1960.....Valentina Stenina, USSR	1979.....Beth Heiden, U.S.	1997.....Gunda Niemann, Germany
1961.....Valentina Stenina, USSR	1980.....Natalia Petruseva, USSR	1998.....Gunda Niemann, Germany
	1981.....Natalia Petruseva, USSR	1999.....Gunda Niemann, Germany

National Men's Champions

HARD BALL		HARD BALL (Cont.)		HARD BALL (Cont.)	
Year	Champion	Year	Champion	Year	Champion
1907	John A. Miskey	1913	Morton L. Newhall	1920	Charles C. Peabody
1908	John A. Miskey	1914	Constantine Hutchins	1921	Stanley W. Pearson
1909	William L. Freeland	1915	Stanley W. Pearson	1922	Stanley W. Pearson
1910	John A. Miskey	1916	Stanley W. Pearson	1923	Stanley W. Pearson
1911	Francis S. White	1917	Stanley W. Pearson	1924	Gerald Roberts
1912	Constantine Hutchins	1918–19	No tournament	1925	W. Palmer Dixon

National Men's Champions (Cont.)

HARD BALL (Cont.)

Year	Champion
1926	W. Palmer Dixon
1927	Myles Baker
1928	Herbert N. Rawlins Jr.
1929	J. Lawrence Pool
1930	Herbert N. Rawlins Jr.
1931	J. Lawrence Pool
1932	Beckman H. Pool
1933	Beckman H. Pool
1934	Neil J. Sullivan II
1935	Donald Strachan
1936	Germain G. Glidden
1937	Germain G. Glidden
1938	Germain G. Glidden
1939	Donald Strachan
1940	A. Willing Patterson
1941	Charles M. P. Britton
1942	Charles M. P. Britton
1943–45	No tournament
1946	Charles M. P. Britton
1947	Charles M. P. Britton
1948	Stanley W. Pearson Jr.
1949	H. Hunter Lott Jr.
1950	Edward J. Hahn
1951	Edward J. Hahn
1952	Harry B. Conlon
1953	Ernest Howard
1954	G. Diehl Mateer Jr.
1955	Henri R. Salaun
1956	G. Diehl Mateer Jr.
1957	Henri R. Salaun
1958	Henri R. Salaun

HARD BALL (Cont.)

Year	Champion
1959	Benjamin H. Heckscher
1960	G. Diehl Mateer Jr.
1961	Henri R. Salaun
1962	Samuel P. Howe III
1963	Benjamin H. Heckscher
1964	Ralph E. Howe
1965	Stephen T. Vehslage
1966	Victor Niederhoffer
1967	Samuel P. Howe III
1968	Colin Adair
1969	Anil Nayar
1970	Anil Nayar
1971	Colin Adair
1972	Victor Niederhoffer
1973	Victor Niederhoffer
1974	Victor Niederhoffer
1975	Victor Niederhoffer
1976	Peter Briggs
1977	Thomas E. Page
1978	Michael Desaulniers
1979	Mario Sanchez
1980	Michael Desaulniers
1981	Mark Alger
1982	John Nimick
1983	Kenton Jernigan
1984	Kenton Jernigan
1987	Frank J. Stanley IV
1988	Scott Dulmage
1989	Rodolfo Rodriquez
1990	Hector Barragan

HARD BALL (Cont.)

Year	Champion
1991	Hector Barragan
1992	Hector Barragan
1985	Kenton Jernigan
1986	Hugh LaBossier
1993	Hector Barragan
1994	Hector Barragan
1995	W. Keen Butcher
1996	W. Keen Butcher
1997	Rob Hill
1998	Rob Hill
1999	Rob Hill

SOFT BALL

Year	Champion
1983	Kenton Jernigan
1984	Kenton Jernigan
1985	Kenton Jernigan
1986	Darius Pandole
1987	Richard Hashim
1988	John Phelan
1989	Will Carlin
1990	Syed Jafry
1991	Hector Barragan
1992	Phil Yarrow
1993	Phil Yarrow
1994	Roberto Rosales
1995	A. Martin Clark
1996	Mohsen Mir
1997	A. Martin Clark
1998	A. Martin Clark
1999	David McNeely

National Women's Champions

HARD BALL

Year	Champion
1928	Eleanora Sears
1929	Margaret Howe
1930	Hazel Wightman
1931	Ruth Banks
1932	Margaret Howe
1933	Susan Noel
1934	Margaret Howe
1935	Margot Lumb
1936	Anne Page
1937	Anne Page
1938	Cecile Bowes
1939	Anne Page
1940	Cecile Bowes
1941	Cecile Bowes
1942–46	No tournament
1947	Anne Page Homer
1948	Cecile Bowes
1949	Janet Morgan
1950	Betty Howe
1951	Jane Austin
1952	Margaret Howe
1953	Margaret Howe
1954	Lois Dilks
1955	Janet Morgan
1956	Betty Howe Constable
1957	Betty Howe Constable
1958	Betty Howe Constable
1959	Betty Howe Constable
1960	Margaret Varner

HARD BALL (Cont.)

Year	Champion
1961	Margaret Varner
1962	Margaret Varner
1963	Margaret Varner
1964	Ann Wetzel
1965	Joyce Davenport
1966	Betty Meade
1967	Betty Meade
1968	Betty Meade
1969	Joyce Davenport
1970	Nina Moyer
1971	Carol Thesieres
1972	Nina Moyer
1973	Gretchen Spruance
1974	Gretchen Spruance
1975	Ginny Akabane
1976	Gretchen Spruance
1977	Gretchen Spruance
1978	Gretchen Spruance
1979	Heather McKay
1980	Barbara Maltby
1981	Barbara Maltby
1982	Alicia McConnell
1983	Alicia McConnell
1984	Alicia McConnell
1985	Alicia McConnell
1986	Alicia McConnell
1987	Alicia McConnell
1988	Alicia McConnell
1986	Alicia McConnell

HARD BALL (Cont.)

Year	Champion
1987	Alicia McConnell
1988	Alicia McConnell
1989	Demer Holleran
1990	Demer Holleran
1991	Demer Holleran
1992	Demer Holleran
1993	Demer Holleran
1994	Demer Holleran

Note: Tournament not held since 1994.

SOFT BALL

Year	Champion
1983	Alicia McConnell
1984	Julie Harris
1985	Sue Clinch
1986	Julie Harris
1987	Diana Staley
1988	Sara Luther
1989	Nancy Gengler
1990	Joyce Maycock
1991	Ellie Pierce
1992	Demer Holleran
1993	Demer Holleran
1994	Demer Holleran
1995	Ellie Pierce
1996	Demer Holleran
1997	Demer Holleran
1998	Latasha Khan
1999	Demer Holleran

Ironman Championship

Date	MEN Winner	Time	Date	WOMEN Winner	Time
1978	Gordon Haller	11:46	1978	No finishers	
1979	Tom Warren	11:15:56	1979	Lyn Lemaire	12:55
1980	Dave Scott	9:24:33	1980	Robin Beck	11:21:24
1981	John Howard	9:38:29	1981	Linda Sweeney	12:00:32
1982	Scott Tinley	9:19:41	1982	Kathleen McCartney	11:09:40
1982	Dave Scott	9:08:23	1982	Julie Leach	10:54:08
1983	Dave Scott	9:05:57	1983	Sylviane Puntous	10:43:36
1984	Dave Scott	8:54:20	1984	Sylviane Puntous	10:25:13
1985	Scott Tinley	8:50:54	1985	Joanne Ernst	10:25:22
1986	Dave Scott	8:28:37	1986	Paula Newby-Fraser	9:49:14
1987	Dave Scott	8:34:13	1987	Erin Baker	9:35:25
1988	Scott Molina	8:31:00	1988	Paula Newby-Fraser	9:01:01
1989	Mark Allen	8:09:15	1989	Paula Newby-Fraser	9:00:56
1990	Mark Allen	8:28:17	1990	Erin Baker	9:13:42
1991	Mark Allen	8:18:32	1991	Paula Newby-Fraser	9:07:52
1992	Mark Allen	8:09:09	1992	Paula Newby-Fraser	8:55:29
1993	Mark Allen	8:07:46	1993	Paula Newby-Fraser	8:58:23
1994	Greg Welch	8:20:27	1994	Paula Newby-Fraser	9:20:14
1995	Mark Allen	8:20:34	1995	Karen Smyers	9:16:46
1996	Luc Van Lierde	8:04:08	1996	Paula Newby-Fraser	9:06:49
1997	Thomas Hellriegel	8:33:01	1997	Heather Fuhr	9:31:43
1998	Peter Reid	8:24:20	1998	Natascha Badmann	9:24:16

Note:The Ironman Championship was contested twice in 1982.
Sites: Waikiki Beach (1978–79); Ala Moana Park (1980) ; Kailua-Kona (since 1981).

All Guts No Glory

In the world of extreme fitness, there are Iron Men and there are Tough Guys. The former compete in Hawaii. The latter go to an unkempt part of central England, where they claw their way through eight bramble-choked, mud-caked miles on one of the world's most grueling assault courses—all in hopes of earning a hot shower, a cup of tea and a souvenir T-shirt.

On July 25, 1999, about 25,000 people—having paid the £50 entry fee and signed a "death warrant" stating that a fatal injury to any contestant is his "own bloody fault"—converged upon the Wolverhampton countryside to compete in the second annual summer version of the 14-year-old Tough Guy Challenge, a winter event that was expected to draw 7,000 entrants on January 30, 2000. Event founder Billy Wilson, a former Grenadier Guard in the British army, devised the summer Challenge as a way to test new obstacles on his 700-acre property. Though fair-weather racers did not have to endure the Polar Ice Cap obstacle (overcome by climbing with the aid of only a pocketknife or by swimming through a tunnel of near-freezing water), they did encounter such typical Tough Guy venues as the Viet Cong Tunnels of Terror (a pitch-black underground maze), the Tiger (a rope ladder laced with live electrical wires) and the Fire Zone (flame filled passageways), not to mention a crocodile-and-piranha pool (over which they had to shinny on a rope bridge) and beds of stinging nettles.

By Wilson's definition, Tough Guys are not only physically but also emotionally superior to their fellow man. "It is only after your mind has passed through the portal of death,"said Wilson, "that you are suddenly faced with a better world." According to Tough Gal Zelah Morrall, 30, who has been the first woman finisher three times, the only sensation she feels upon rising from the ice-capped underwater tunnels is "the worst ice-cream headache imaginable." Women—"the pretties," Wilson calls them—made up 10% of the field. That's a far cry from 1986, when the first Challenge was run by only a handful of men. Today, Wilson said, "magistrates, prison guards, criminals, Oxford-versus-Cambridge-boat-race people and City of London financial people" help make up the field. The course record is one hour, 42 minutes.

While Tough Guys from the U.S. must travel to England to challenge themselves, Wilson said that he is negotiating to build assault courses "in every one of the United States," starting with California, where his daughter, Tracie, the wife of ex–Duran Duran guitarist Andy Taylor, once lived. "From what I understand, Americans are fat, flabby and full of hamburgers," said Wilson, who (insisting his age is between 21 and 70) claimed he runs on his course every morning. "A challenge is just what they need."

—Kelley King

Volleyball

World Champions
MEN

Year	Winner	Runnerup	Site
1949	Soviet Union	Czechoslovakia	Prague
1952	Soviet Union	Czechoslovakia	Moscow
1956	Czechoslovakia	Soviet Union	Paris
1960	Soviet Union	Czechoslovakia	Rio de Janeiro
1962	Soviet Union	Czechoslovakia	Moscow
1966	Czechoslovakia	Romania	Prague
1970	East Germany	Bulgaria	Sofia, Bulgaria
1974	Poland	Soviet Union	Mexico City
1978	Soviet Union	Italy	Rome
1982	Soviet Union	Brazil	Buenos Aires
1986	United States	Soviet Union	Paris
1990	Italy	Cuba	Rio de Janeiro
1994	Italy	Netherlands	Athens
1998	Italy	Yugoslavia	Tokyo

WOMEN

Year	Winner	Runnerup	Site
1952	Soviet Union	Poland	Moscow
1956	Soviet Union	Romania	Paris
1960	Soviet Union	Japan	Rio de Janeiro
1962	Japan	Soviet Union	Moscow
1966	Japan	United States	Prague
1970	Soviet Union	Japan	Sofia, Bulgaria
1974	Japan	Soviet Union	Mexico City
1978	Cuba	Japan	Rome
1982	China	Peru	Lima, Peru
1986	China	Cuba	Prague
1990	Soviet Union	China	Beijing
1994	Cuba	Brazil	Sao Paulo, Brazil
1998	Cuba	China	Osaka, Japan

Black Knight

Unlike many top chess players, Maurice Ashley wasn't a prodigy. The Brooklynite didn't pick up a pawn until he was 14, but once he started playing, he was hooked. "It was like falling in love," he said. "It was electrifying." Ashley sought to carry his passion to kids in the inner city. "The great thing about chess is the more you play, the more you develop critical thinking skills," he said. "You set goals, solve problems and strategize. These translate into real life." For six years Ashley coached youth teams with names like the Dark Knights and the Raging Rooks before deciding to focus on his own game. In March 1999 at a Manhattan Chess Club tournament he beat Romania's Adrian Negulescu to become the first African-American grandmaster. "The community is so happy and proud," said Ashley, 33, "and I'm happy to make other people happy."

U.S. Men's Open Champions—Gold Division

1928	Germantown, PA YMCA	1965	Westside JCC, CA
1929	Hyde Park YMCA, IL	1966	Sand & Sea Club, CA
1930	Hyde Park YMCA, IL	1967	Fresno, CA VBC
1931	San Antonio, TX YMCA	1968	Westside JCC, Los Angeles, CA
1932	San Antonio, TX YMCA	1969	Los Angeles, CA YMCA
1933	Houston, TX YMCA	1970	Chart House, San Diego
1934	Houston, TX YMCA	1971	Santa Monica, CA YMCA
1935	Houston, TX YMCA	1972	Chart House, San Diego
1936	Houston, TX YMCA	1973	Chuck's Steak, Los Angeles
1937	Duncan YMCA, IL	1974	UC Santa Barbara, CA
1938	Houston, TX YMCA	1975	Chart House, San Diego
1939	Houston, TX YMCA	1976	Maliabu, Los Angeles
1940	Los Angeles AC, CA	1977	Chuck's, Santa Barbara
1941	North Ave. YMCA, IL	1978	Chuck's, Los Angeles
1942	North Ave. YMCA, IL	1979	Nautilus, Long Beach CA
1943–44	No championships	1980	Olympic Club, San Francisco
1945	North Ave. YMCA, IL	1981	Nautilus, Long Beach CA
1946	Pasadena, CA YMCA	1982	Chuck's, Los Angeles
1947	North Ave. YMCA, IL	1983	Nautilus Pacifica, CA
1948	Hollywood, CA YMCA	1984	Nautilus Pacifica, CA
1949	Downtown YMCA, CA	1985	Molten/SSI Torrance, CA
1950	Long Beach, CA YMCA	1986	Molten, Torrance, CA
1951	Hollywood, CA YMCA	1987	Molten, Torrance, CA
1952	Hollywood, CA YMCA	1988	Molten, Torrance, CA
1953	Hollywood, CA YMCA	1989	Not held
1954	Stockton, CA YMCA	1990	Nike, Carson, CA
1955	Stockton, CA YMCA	1991	Offshore, Woodland Hills, CA
1956	Hollywood, CA YMCA Stars	1992	Creole Six Pack, Elmhurst, NY
1957	Hollywood, CA YMCA Stars	1993	Asics, Huntington Beach, CA
1958	Hollywood, CA YMCA Stars	1994	Asics/Paul Mitchell, Hunt. Beach, CA
1959	Hollywood, CA YMCA Stars	1995	Shakter, Belagarad, Ukraine
1960	Westside JCC, CA	1996	POL-AM-VBC, Brooklyn, NY
1961	Hollywood, CA YMCA	1997	Canuck Stuff VBC, Calgary
1962	Hollywood, CA YMCA	1998	T-Town, Tulsa, OK
1963	Hollywood, CA YMCA	1999	LAAC, Los Angeles
1964	Hollywood, CA YMCA Stars		

U.S. Women's Open Champions—Gold Division

1949	Eagles, Houston	1975	Adidas, Norwalk, CA
1950	Voit #1, Santa Monica, CA	1976	Pasadena, TX
1951	Eagles, Houston	1977	Spoilers, Hermosa, CA
1952	Voit #1, Santa Monica, CA	1978	Nick's, Los Angeles
1953	Voit #1, Los Angeles	1979	Mavericks, Los Angeles
1954	Houstonettes, Houston, TX	1980	NAVA, Fountain Valley, CA
1955	Mariners, Santa Monica, CA	1981	Utah State, Logan, UT
1956	Mariners, Santa Monica, CA	1982	Monarchs, Hilo, HI
1957	Mariners, Santa Monica, CA	1983	Syntex, Stockton, CA
1958	Mariners, Santa Monica, CA	1984	Chrysler, Palo Alto, CA
1959	Mariners, Santa Monica, CA	1985	Merrill Lynch, Arizona
1960	Mariners, Santa Monica, CA	1986	Merrill Lynch, Arizona
1961	Breakers, Long Beach, CA	1987	Chrysler, Pleasanton, CA
1962	Shamrocks, Long Beach, CA	1988	Chrysler, Hayward, CA
1963	Shamrocks, Long Beach, CA	1989	Plymouth, Hayward, CA
1964	Shamrocks, Long Beach, CA	1990	Plymouth, Hayward, CA
1965	Shamrocks, Long Beach, CA	1991	Fitness, Champaign, IL
1966	Renegades, Los Angeles	1992	Nick's Kronies, Chicago
1967	Shamrocks, Long Beach, CA	1993	Nick's Fishmarket, Chicago
1968	Shamrocks, Long Beach, CA	1994	Nick's Fishmarket, Chicago
1969	Shamrocks, Long Beach, CA	1995	Kittleman/Branfield's/Nick's, Chi.
1970	Shamrocks, Long Beach, CA	1996	Pure Texas Nuts, Austin, TX
1971	Renegades, Los Angeles	1997	Kittleman/Branfield's/Nick's, Chi.
1972	E Pluribus Unum, Houston	1998	The Exterminators, Barrington, IL
1973	E Pluribus Unum, Houston	1999	Dominican Dream Team, Santo Domingo, D.R.
1974	Renegades, Los Angeles		

United States National Champions

1983

FREESTYLE
105.5 ....Rich Salamone
114.5 ....Joe Gonzales
125.5 ....Joe Corso
136.5 ....Rich Dellagatta*
149.5 ....Bill Hugent
163 ....Lee Kemp
180.5 ....Chris Campbell
198 ....Pete Bush

FREESTYLE *(Cont.)*
220 ....Greg Gibson
Hvy ....Bruce Baumgartner
Team ....Sunkist Kids

GRECO-ROMAN
105.5 ....T. J. Jones
114.5 ....Mark Fuller
125.5 ....Rob Hermann

GRECO-ROMAN *(Cont.)*
136.5 ....Dan Mello
149.5 ....Jim Martinez
163 ....James Andre
180.5 ....Steve Goss
198 ....Steve Fraser*
220 ....Dennis Koslowski
Hvy ....No champion
Team ....Minn. Wrestling Club

1984

FREESTYLE
105.5 ....Rich Salamone
114.5 ....Charlie Heard
125.5 ....Joe Corso
136.5 ....Rich Dellagatta*
149.5 ....Andre Metzger
163 ....Dave Schultz*
180.5 ....Mark Schultz
198 ....Steve Fraser

FREESTYLE *(Cont.)*
220 ....Harold Smith
Hvy ....Bruce Baumgartner
Team ....Sunkist Kids

GRECO-ROMAN
105.5 ....T. J. Jones
114.5 ....Mark Fuller
136.5 ....Dan Mello

GRECO-ROMAN *(Cont.)*
149.5 ....Jim Martinez*
163 ....John Matthews
180.5 ....Tom Press
198 ....Mike Houck
220 ....No champion
Hvy ....No champion
Team ....Adirondack 3-Style, WA

1985

FREESTYLE
105.5 ....Tim Vanni
114.5 ....Jim Martin
125.5 ....Charlie Heard
136.5 ....Darryl Burley
149.5 ....Bill Nugent*
163 ....Kenny Monday
180.5 ....Mike Sheets
198 ....Mark Schultz

FREESTYLE *(Cont.)*
220 ....Greg Gibson
286 ....Bruce Baumgartner
Team ....Sunkist Kids

GRECO-ROMAN
105.5 ....T. J. Jones
114.5 ....Mark Fuller
125.5 ....Eric Seward*

GRECO-ROMAN *(Cont.)*
136.5 ....Buddy Lee
149.5 ....Jim Martinez
163 ....David Butler
180.5 ....Chris Catallo
198 ....Mike Houck
220 ....Greg Gibson
286 ....Dennis Koslowski
Team .......U.S. Marine Corps

1986

FREESTYLE
105.5 ....Rich Salamone
114.5 ....Joe Gonzales
125.5 ....Kevin Darkus
136.5 ....John Smith
149.5 ....Andre Metzger*
163 ....Dave Schultz
180.5 ....Mark Schultz
198 ....Jim Scherr
220 ....Dan Severn

FREESTYLE *(Cont.)*
286 ....Bruce Baumgartner
Team ....Sunkist Kids (Div. I)
            Hawkeye Wrestling
            Club (Div. II)

GRECO-ROMAN
105.5 ....Eric Wetzel
114.5 ....Shawn Sheldon
125.5 ....Anthony Amado

GRECO-ROMAN *(Cont.)*
136.5 ....Frank Famiano
149.5 ....Jim Martinez
163 ....David Butler*
180.5 ....Darryl Gholar
198 ....Derrick Waldroup
220 ....Dennis Koslowski
286 ....Duane Koslowski
Team .......U.S. Marine Corps (Div. I)
            U.S. Navy (Div. II)

1987

FREESTYLE
105.5 ....Takashi Irie
114.5 ....Mitsuru Sato
125.5 ....Barry Davis
136.5 ....Takumi Adachi
149.5 ....Andre Metzger
163 ....Dave Schultz*
180.5 ....Mark Schultz
198 ....Jim Scherr
220 ....Bill Scherr

FREESTYLE *(Cont.)*
286 ....Bruce Baumgartner
Team ....Sunkist Kids (Div. I)
            Team Foxcatcher (Div. II)

GRECO-ROMAN
105.5 ....Eric Wetzel
114.5 ....Shawn Sheldon
125.5 ....Eric Seward
136.5 ....Frank Famiano

GRECO-ROMAN *(Cont.)*
149.5 ....Jim Martinez
163 ....David Butler
180.5 ....Chris Catallo
198 ....Derrick Waldroup*
220 ....Dennis Koslowski
286 ....Duane Koslowski
Team.......U.S. Marine Corp (Div. I)
            U.S. Army (Div. II)

United States National Champions *(Cont.)*

1988

FREESTYLE
105.5 ....Tim Vanni
114.5 ....Joe Gonzales
125.5 ....Kevin Darkus
136.5 ....John Smith*
149.5 ....Nate Carr
163 ....Kenny Monday
180.5 ....Dave Schultz
198 ....Melvin Douglas III
220 ....Bill Scherr

FREESTYLE *(Cont.)*
286 ....Bruce Baumgartner
Team ....Sunkist Kids (Div. I)
Team Foxcatcher (Div. II)

GRECO-ROMAN
105.5 ....T. J. Jones
114.5 ....Shawn Sheldon
125.5 ....Gogi Parseghian*
136.5 ....Dalen Wasmund

GRECO-ROMAN *(Cont.)*
149.5 ....Craig Pollard
163 ....Tony Thomas
180.5 ....Darryl Gholar
198 ....Mike Carolan
220 ....Dennis Koslowski
286 ....Duane Koslowski
Team .......U.S. Marine Corps (Div. I)
Sunkist Kids (Div. II)

1989

FREESTYLE
105.5 ....Tim Vanni
114.5 ....Zeke Jones
125.5 ....Brad Penrith
136.5 ....John Smith
149.5 ....Nate Carr
163 ....Rob Koll
180.5 ....Rico Chiapparelli
198 ....Jim Scherr*
220 ....Bill Scherr

FREESTYLE *(Cont.)*
286 ....Bruce Baumgartner
Team ....Sunkist Kids (Div. I)
Team Foxcatcher (Div. II)

GRECO-ROMAN
105.5 ....Lew Dorrance
114.5 ....Mark Fuller
125.5 ....Gogi Parseghian
136.5 ....Isaac Anderson

GRECO-ROMAN *(Cont.)*
149.5 ....Andy Seras*
163 ....David Butler
180.5 ....John Morgan
198 ....Michial Foy
220 ....Steve Lawson
286 ....Craig Pittman
Team .......U.S. Marine Corps (Div. I)
Jets USA (Div. II)

1990

FREESTYLE
105.5 ....Rob Eiter
114.5 ....Zeke Jones
125.5 ....Joe Melchiore
136.5 ....John Smith
149.5 ....Nate Carr
163 ....Rob Koll
180.5 ....Royce Alger
198 ....Chris Campbell*
220 ....Bill Scherr

FREESTYLE *(Cont.)*
286 ....Bruce Baumgartner
Team ....Sunkist Kids (Div. I)
Team Foxcatcher (Div. II)

GRECO-ROMAN
105.5 ....Lew Dorrance
114.5 ....Sam Henson
125.5 ....Mark Pustelnik
136.5 ....Isaac Anderson

GRECO-ROMAN *(Cont.)*
149.5 ....Andy Seras
163 ....David Butler
180.5 ....Derrick Waldroup
198 ....Randy Couture*
220 ....Chris Tironi
286 ....Matt Ghaffari
Team ....Jets USA (Div. I)
California Jets (Div. II)

1991

FREESTYLE
105.5 ....Tim Vanni
114.5 ....Zeke Jones
125.5 ....Brad Penrith
136.5 ....John Smith*
149.5 ....Townsend Saunders
163 ....Kenny Monday
180.5 ....Kevin Jackson
198 ....Chris Campbell
220 ....Mark Coleman

FREESTYLE *(Cont.)*
286 ....Bruce Baumgartner
Team ....Sunkist Kids (Div. I)
Jets USA (Div. II)

GRECO-ROMAN
105.5 ....Eric Wetzel
114.5 ....Shawn Sheldon
125.5 ....Frank Famiano
136.5 ....Buddy Lee

GRECO-ROMAN *(Cont.)*
149.5 ....Andy Seras
163 ....Gordy Morgan
180.5 ....John Morgan*
198 ....Michial Foy
220 ....Dennis Koslowski
286 ....Craig Pittman
Team ....Jets USA (Div. I)
Sunkist Kids (Div. II)

1992

FREESTYLE
105.5 ....Rob Eiter
114.5 ....Jack Griffin
125.5 ....Kendall Cross*
136.5 ....John Fisher
149.5 ....Matt Demaray
163 ....Greg Elinsky
180.5 ....Royce Alger
198 ....Dan Chaid
220 ....Bill Scherr

FREESTYLE *(Cont.)*
286 ....Bruce Baumgartner
Team ....Sunkist Kids (Div. I)
Team Foxcatcher (Div. II)

GRECO-ROMAN
105.5 ....Eric Wetzel
114.5 ....Mark Fuller
125.5 ....Dennis Hall
136.5 ....Buddy Lee*

GRECO-ROMAN *(Cont.)*
149.5 ....Rodney Smith
163 ....Travis West
180.5 ....John Morgan
198 ....Michial Foy
220 ....Dennis Koslowski
286 ....Matt Ghaffari
Team ....NY Athletic Club (Div. I)
Sunkist Kids (Div. II)

*Outstanding wrestler.

United States National Champions (Cont.)

1993

FREESTYLE

105.5 ......Rob Eiter
114.5 ......Zeke Jones
125.5 ......Brad Penrith
136.5 ......Tom Brands
149.5 ......Matt Demaray
163 ....Dave Schultz*
180.5 ......Kevin Jackson
198 ....Melvin Douglas
220 ....Kirk Trost

FREESTYLE (Cont.)

286 ....Bruce Baumgartner
Team ......Sunkist Kids (Div. I)
              Team Foxcatcher (Div. II)

GRECO-ROMAN

105.5 ......Eric Wetzel
114.5 ......Shawn Sheldon
125.5 ......Dennis Hall*
136.5 ......Shon Lewis

GRECO-ROMAN (Cont.)

149.5 ......Andy Seras
163 ....Gordy Morgan
180.5 ......Dan Henderson
198 ....Randy Couture
220 ....James Johnson
286 ....Matt Ghaffari
Team ......NY Athletic Club (Div. I)
              Sunkist Kids (Div. II)

1994

FREESTYLE

105.5 ......Tim Vanni
114.5 ......Zeke Jones
125.5 ......Terry Brands
136.5 ......Tom Brands
149.5 ......Matt Demaray
163 ....Dave Schultz
180.5 ......Royce Alger
198 ....Melvin Douglas
220 ....Mark Kerr

FREESTYLE (Cont.)

286 ....Bruce Baumgartner*
Team ......Sunkist Kids (Div. I)
              Team Foxcatcher (Div. II)

GRECO-ROMAN

105.5 ......Isaac Ramaswamy
114.5 ......Shawn Sheldon
125.5 ......Dennis Hall
136.5 ......Shon Lewis

GRECO-ROMAN (Cont.)

149.5 ......Andy Seras*
163 ....Gordy Morgan
180.5 ......Dan Henderson
198 ....Derrick Waldroup

GRECO-ROMAN (Cont.)

220 ....James Johnson
286 ....Matt Ghaffari
Team ......Armed Forces (Div. I)
              NY Athletic Club (Div. II)

1995

FREESTYLE

105.5 ......Rob Eiter
114.5 ......Lou Rosselli
125.5 ......Kendall Cross*
136.5 ......Tom Brands
149.5 ......Matt Demaray
163 ....Dave Schultz
180.5 ......Kevin Jackson
198 ....Melvin Douglas
220 ....Kurt Angle

FREESTYLE (Cont.)

286 ....Bruce Baumgartner
Team ......Sunkist Kids (Div. I)
              Team Foxcatcher (Div. II)

GRECO-ROMAN

105.5 ......Isaac Ramaswamy
114.5 ......Shawn Sheldon
125.5 ......Dennis Hall*
136.5 ......Van Fronhofer

GRECO-ROMAN (Cont.)

149.5 ......Heath Sims
163 ....Matt Lindland
180.5 ......Marty Morgan
198 ....Michial Foy
220 ....James Johnson
286 ....Rulon Gardner
Team ......Armed Forces (Div. I)
              Sunkist Kids (Div. II)

1996

FREESTYLE

105.5 ......Rob Eiter
114.5 ......Lou Rosselli
125.5 ......Kendall Cross
136.5 ......Tom Brands
149.5 ......Townsend Saunders
163 ....Kenny Monday
180.5 ......Les Gutches*
198 ....Melvin Douglas
220 ....Kurt Angle

FREESTYLE (Cont.)

286 ....Bruce Baumgartner
Team ......Sunkist Kids (Div. I)
              NY Athletic Club (Div. II)

GRECO-ROMAN

105.5 ......Mujaahid Maynard
114.5 ......Shawn Sheldon
125.5 ......Dennis Hall*
136.5 ......Shon Lewis

GRECO-ROMAN (Cont.)

149.5 ......Rodney Smith
163 ....Keith Sieracki
180.5 ......Marty Morgan
198 ....Michial Foy
220 ....John Oostendrop
286 ....Matt Ghaffari
Team ......Armed Forces (Div. I)
              Sunkist Kids (Div. II)

1997

FREESTYLE

110 ....Kanamti Soloman
119 ....Zeke Jones
127.75 ....Terry Brands
138.75 ....Carl Kolat
152 ....Lincoln McIlravy*
167.5 ......Dan St. John
187.25 ....Les Gutches
213.75 ....Melvin Douglas

FREESTYLE (Cont.)

275.5 ......Tom Erikson
Team ......Sunkist Kids (Div. I)
              NY Athletic Club (Div. II)

GRECO-ROMAN

110 ....Mark Yanagihara
119 ....Broderick Lee
127.75 ....Dennis Hall

GRECO-ROMAN (Cont.)

138.75 ....Kevin Bracken
152 ....Chris Saba
167.5 ......Miguel Spencer
187.25 ....Dan Henderson
213.75 ....Randy Couture*
275.5 ......Rulon Gardiner
Team ......Armed Forces (Div. I)
              NY Athletic Club (Div. II)

*Outstanding wrestler.

United States National Champions *(Cont.)*

1998

FREESTYLE	FREESTYLE *(Cont.)*	GRECO-ROMAN *(Cont.)*
119 ....Sam Henson	286 ....Tolly Thompson	152 ....Chris Saba
127.75 .....Tony Purler	Team ....Sunkist Kids (Div. I)	167.5 ....Matt Lindland
138.75 .....Shawn Charles	NY Athletic Club (Div. II)	187.25 .....Dan Niebuhr*
152 ....Lincoln McIlravy	**GRECO-ROMAN**	213.75 .....Jason Klohs
167.5 ....Steve Marianetti	119 ....Shawn Sheldon	286 ....Matt Ghaffari
187.25 .....Les Gutches*	127.75 .....Dennis Hall	Team ....Armed Forces (Div. I)
213.75 .....Melvin Douglas	138.75 .....Shon Lewis	Sunkist Kids (Div. II)

1999

FREESTYLE	FREESTYLE *(Cont.)*	GRECO-ROMAN *(Cont.)*
119 ....Lou Rosselli	286 ....Stephen Neal*	152 ....David Zuniga
127.75 .....Terry Brands	Team ....Sunkist Kids (Div. I)	167.5 ....Matt Lindland
138.75 .....Cary Kolat	NY Athletic Club (Div. II)	187.25 .....Quincey Clark
152 ....Lincoln McIlravy	**GRECO-ROMAN**	213.75 .....Randy Couture
167.5 ....Joe Williams	119 ....Steven Mays	286 ....Dremiel Byers*
187.25 .....Les Gutches	127.75 .....Dennis Hall	Team ....Minnesota Storm (Div. I)
213.75 .....Dominic Black	138.75 .....Glen Nieradka	Sunkist Kids (Div. II)

*Outstanding wrestler.

Ski-Joring, Bog Snorkeling and Cow Pies

The Fightas with Arthritis geezerama featuring George Foreman and Larry Holmes may have been canceled in early January, but there was no shortage of strange sports events in 1999. February brought the Shrovetide Pancake Race in Liberal, Kans., an illiberal competition in which women sprinted while wearing aprons and flipping flapjacks on handheld griddles. Then came the U.S. Ski-Joring Finals on March 13 and 14 in Red Lodge, Mont. Ski-joring is like cross-country skiing except that each skier is pulled by a horse. After a March 19 visit to Virginia Beach, Va., for the Shamrock Sportsfest, with its Irish pasta party and children's marathon, it was possible to hit Springfield, Mo., for the April 22 Typewriter Toss, in which secretaries heaved Olivettis and Selectrics at a bull's eye from a platform 50 feet high.

On July 3, Wetton, England was host to the World Championships of Toe Wrestling, an upside-down version of arm wrestling in which contestants lie on their backs, lock big toes and try to pin their foes' feet. On Aug. 30, Llanwrtyd Wells, Wales, was the scene of more Union Jacking around, at the World Bog Snorkeling Championships. Boggymen including 1997 champ Pete (Peat) Beaumont donned flippers and tried to snorkel 120 yards through thick muck in less time than Beaumont's record 1:44, a clip of nearly 2.4 mph.

More fastidious racers could head to Nome, Alaska, for the Sept. 6 Great Bathtub Race, the Indy 500 of porcelain pushers. Competitors rolled wheeled tubs brimming with bathers and bubble baths while carrying soap, towels, and bath mats. The following week in Stanley, Idaho, golfers faced hazards including heifers and cow pies in the Sawtooth Cow Pasture Open.

New Year's Eve '99? There wasn't much on tap but a few Bowl games. Maybe George and Larry could have squared off in Times Square. Call that bout Really Auld Lang Syne.

Multimillionaire Kevin Garnett of the Minnesota Timberwolves

WALTER IOOSS JR

The Sports Market

Everybody's Doing It

Investors continued to pour money into sports despite some heavy losses, prompting the question: How long can it last?

BY MERRELL NODEN

I GUESS WE'D be like walking billboards, huh?" mused Albert Belle in the spring of 1999, when someone told him that Major League Baseball was looking into the possibility of selling advertising space on players' uniforms. "Isn't everybody making enough [money] already?"

One does not usually expect to hear such pearls of wisdom and restraint coming from the Orioles' surly slugger, but in this case Belle was, in every sense, right on the money. Bewildered fans spent much of the year wondering how millionaires fortunate enough to play in the NBA or the Ryder Cup could have the bad manners to grouse about their compensation. Boston Celtics point guard Kenny Anderson became the poster child for spoiled, out-of-touch athletes when he joked that because of the NBA work stoppage he might have to sell one of his eight luxury cars.

In a year that saw labor strife in women's basketball and in major league baseball, and an NBA season that came within hours of not taking place at all—a season that all but screamed caveat emptor—there was still no shortage of rich men, women and corporations determined to throw hard-earned money into the risky business of sports. Funnyman Bill Cosby bought a no-joke portion of the New Jersey Nets. Michael Jordan shopped around for a basketball team but didn't buy one. Isiah Thomas couldn't find an NBA team to his liking, so he bought an entire league, the CBA. General Motors agreed to bail out beach volleyball by sponsoring the nine-tournament Alero Beach Volleyball Series. Rumor had it that Rupert Murdoch was thinking about launching a pro rugby league—in the U.S., no less—and before she died, Linda McCartney made a four-year, $3.2 million investment in an all-vegetarian cycling team. Real estate mogul Howard Milstein bid $800 million for the Washington Redskins. Milstein's offer, a record for an American sports franchise,

NICK WASS/AP

was accepted by Redskins trustees in January, then withdrawn on April 7 when some owners, concerned over what they perceived as Milstein's mishandling of the New York Islanders hockey team and the fact that his bid included only $50 million in cash, made it clear he was not welcome.

In a world lusting for any connection to sports, and ready to spend big bucks for it, little one-inch-square patches of advertising on players' uniforms hardly seemed excessive or tacky, as Gene Orza, a lawyer for the baseball players' union, was kind enough to point out. "Selling ads is not what it's about," he said. "What we've been discussing in a very preliminary way are logo patches, very discreet and not obtrusive." You will be forgiven if you laugh out loud at the thought of hard-nosed corporate honchos being content for long to shell out good money, stockholders' money, for something that's "discreet and not obtrusive."

Though as it turned out, not everyone was making all that much money—some were actually losing it. Yet that small worry hardly put a dent in the mad stampede to buy teams and to affix corporate names to anything linked to professional sports. At the start of the 1990s just four teams boasted corporate names on their venues; in '99 at least 68 franchises played in venues bearing corporate names. What lucky baseball team is about to play in Comerica Park? (The Detroit Tigers.) And ignoring completely the fact that the company is Dutch and that many Americans might be hard-pressed to identify the products it makes, Philips Electronics paid Turner Broadcasting $181.9 million for the right to place its name on the new arena in Atlanta, home to the NBA Hawks and the NHL expansion Thrashers, for 20 years.

Don't scoff: Joyce Julius & Associates, which tracks and evaluates sponsor exposure and compares it to conventional advertising, calculated that getting a corporation's name on an arena in Los Angeles would be worth

$251 million in publicity over five years. So Staples, the office-supply company, got quite a deal when it paid just $100 million to put its name on the new home of the Lakers, Clippers and the Kings for 20 years. And, by the way: who do you think is going to win this year's Suzuki Heisman Trophy? That mellifluous name change to college football's most prestigious award brought a desperately needed $1.5 million to the coffers of the bankrupt Downtown Athletic Club.

Television revenues also continued to climb, as networks saw sports programming as cornerstones of larger marketing schemes. Though its eight-year, $1.725 billion contract for NCAA men's basketball won't expire until 2002, CBS is renegotiating its deal with the NCAA. This despite the fact that the network's ratings for the '99 championship game fell to 17.2, the lowest national rating since the 1972 title tilt, an afternoon game (ratings for the entire NCAA tournament fell 7%). With ABC/ESPN, Fox and CBS as its suitors, the NCAA was talking about a 10-year deal worth perhaps as much as $4 billion for marketing, TV, radio and Internet rights.

What was most amazing about this bidding frenzy was the fact that otherwise shrewd businessmen continue to view sports as a smart investment. As we've been learning for years, the professional sports market is a volatile one, as likely to embarrass and bankrupt its owners as to boost them. This year even the Olympics were badly tarnished by charges of bribery, a scandal that caused longtime corporate sponsors like John Hancock to hastily sever their ties to the Games.

You'd think that owning a sports team meant sure, easy bucks, but not so. A study by *Forbes* magazine found that of the 30 big league baseball teams, nearly half (14) lost money in 1998, including the San Diego Padres, who made it to the World Series yet still managed to lose $8 million. The biggest losers of all were the Los Angeles Dodgers, whose losses for 1998 *Forbes* placed at $11.7 million. *Forbes* valued the Dodgers franchise at $270 million, yet so coveted have franchises become, so integral a part of larger marketing plans, that Murdoch paid $350 million for the team in 1998. Conspicuously absent from the list of losers were the Montreal Expos, whose team payroll of $17.6 million was the lowest in baseball, less than the combined salaries of the starting Orioles outfield.

Also in Canada, where hockey has been a kind of national religion for years, the government announced in June that it was looking into ways to help the six National Hockey League franchises based north of the border, which together lost more than $100 million from 1996 to '98.

Still, this year's best argument against investing in pro sports was made by the formerly gold-plated NBA, which endured 191 days of labor strife that ended just 29 hours before the deadline that commissioner David Stern had set for canceling the entire season. Even then it took a marathon bargaining session between Stern and players union head Billy Hunter to finally settle. In the end the players' union voted 179–5 to accept the six-year, collective bargaining agreement that raised the league's minimum salary (to $287,500 for rookies and $350,000 to $1 million for veterans, depending on their years of experience).

Otherwise the deal was a disaster for the players, who seemed to need this season more than management did. The NBA is now the only one of the major pro leagues to have a maximum salary ($14 million). Another concession Stern wrung from the players was a franchise's right to hold on to its draft picks for five years, two years longer than under the previous agreement. Say goodbye to the sort of megacontracts that were becoming common in the NBA, such as the $126 million over six years that the Minnesota Timberwolves paid the then 21-year-old Kevin Garnett in 1997. With salary limits so clearly defined, the great losers were probably agents, who can no longer play team against team in desperate bidding wars.

Knowing that he needed the players to help woo disgruntled fans back, Stern refrained from crowing over what was a tremendous victory for management. Dur-

Stern had reason to smile about the NBA's new labor agreement.

ing an abbreviated NBA preseason in which many games were free to the public, players literally greeted fans at arena doors and signed autographs until their hands cramped. The 50-game NBA season finally began on Feb. 5. With the specter of this labor dispute fresh in their minds, the WNBA players were in no position to win concessions from the league. By agreeing to an increase in the minimum salary (from $15,000 in 1998 to $30,000 for veterans and $25,000 for rookies) and increased benefits, commissioner Val Ackerman wisely brought their dispute to an end without imperiling the season.

On July 14, 57 major league umpires followed the advice of union chief Richie Phillips and tendered their resignations in hopes of leveraging a new collective bargaining agreement. Unfortunately for them, it turned out that their employers weren't as distraught by this maneuver as the umps had expected them to be, and after giving them a week to come to their senses, they accepted the resignations of 22. Wait, shrieked the umps, we didn't mean it; we were just trying to put pressure on you! With the Sept. 2 date of resignation looming, the umps went to U.S. District Court on Sept. 1 seeking an immediate injunction barring baseball from accepting those resignations. The judge mediated a settlement between the league and the umpires' union, but could not save the jobs of the 22 umps whose resignations had been accepted. Their fate would be decided by an arbitrator in Philadelphia, who would determine whether or not Major League Baseball violated the collective bargaining agreement by accepting the 22 resignations.

One wondered how much longer sports could continue to lure investors, which on a grass roots level includes fans. The price of a 30-second ad during the Super Bowl climbed $400,000, to an average of $2 million for Super Bowl XXXIV, while tickets for the game jumped from $275 and $350 in '98 to $325 and $400 in '99. The average ticket for a major league baseball game went up 7% in '99, to $15.26. Something's got to give: Wanna bet it won't be the owners?

Major League Baseball
Address: 245 Park Avenue
             New York, NY 10167
Telephone: (212) 931-7800
Commissioner: Bud Selig
President: Paul Beeston
Executive Director, Public Relations: Richard Levin

Major League Baseball Players Association
Address: 12 East 49th Street, 24th Floor
             New York, NY 10017
Telephone: (212) 826-0808
Executive Director: Donald Fehr
Director of Communications: Greg Bouris
Director of Licensing: Judy Heeter

American League

American League Office
Address: 245 Park Avenue
             New York, NY 10167
Telephone: (212) 931-7600
President: Dr. Gene Budig
Senior Vice President: Phyllis Merhige

Baltimore Orioles
Address: Oriole Park at Camden Yards
             333 W Camden Street
             Baltimore, MD 21201
Telephone: (410) 685-9800
Stadium (Capacity): Camden Yards (48,876)
Managing Partner and Owner: Peter G. Angelos
Vice Chairman/CEO: Joseph Foss
Manager: TBA
Assistant Director of Public Relations: Bill Stetka

Boston Red Sox
Address: 4 Yawkey Way
             Fenway Park
             Boston, MA 02215
Telephone: (617) 267-9440
Stadium (Capacity): Fenway Park (33,871)
CEO: John Harrington
Executive VP and GM: Daniel F. Duquette
Manager: Jimy Williams
Vice President, Public Affairs: Dick Bresciani

Anaheim Angels
Address: P.O. Box 2000
             Anaheim, CA 92803
Telephone: (714) 940-2000
Stadium (Capacity): Edison International Field of
Anaheim (45,050)
Owner: Walt Disney Company
General Manager: Bill Bavasi
Manager: TBA
Vice President of Communications: Tim Mead

Chicago White Sox
Address: Comiskey Park
             333 West 35th Street
             Chicago, IL 60616
Telephone: (312) 674-1000
Stadium (Capacity): Comiskey Park (44,321)
Chairman: Jerry Reinsdorf
General Manager: Ron Schueler
Manager: Jerry Manuel
Director of Publc Relations: Scott Reifert

Cleveland Indians
Address: Jacobs Field
             2401 Ontario Street
             Cleveland, OH 44115-4003
Telephone: (216) 420-4200
Stadium (Capacity): Jacobs Field (43,368)
Chairman of the Board and CEO: Richard Jacobs
Executive VP and General Manager: John Hart
Manager: TBA
Vice President, Public Relations: Bob DiBiasio

Detroit Tigers
Address: 2121 Trumbull Ave.(new add. TBA)
             Tiger Stadium
             Detroit, MI 48216
Telephone: (313) 962-4000
Stadium (Capacity): Comerica Park (TBA)
Owner: Mike Ilitch
Chief Executive Officer and President: John McHale
Manager: Phil Garner
Director of Public Relations: Tyler Barnes

Kansas City Royals
Address: P.O. Box 419969
             Kansas City, MO 64141
Telephone: (816) 921-8000
Stadium (Capacity): Kauffman Stadium (40,529)
Chairman of the Board and CEO: David D. Glass
General Manager: Herk Robinson
Manager: Tony Muser
Vice President, Communications: Mike Levy

Milwaukee Brewers
Address: P.O. Box 3099
             Milwaukee, WI 53201-3099
Telephone: (414) 933-4114
Stadium (Capacity): Milwaukee County Stadium (53,192)
President and CEO: Wendy Selig-Prieb
Senior VPand GM: Dean Taylor
Manager: TBA
Media Relations: Jon Greenberg

Minnesota Twins
Address: 34 Kirby Puckett Place
             Minneapolis, MN 55415
Telephone: (612) 375-1366
Stadium (Capacity): Hubert H. Humphrey
Metrodome (48,678)
Owner: Carl Pohlad
General Manager: Terry Ryan
Manager: Tom Kelly
Manager of Media Relations: Sean Harlin

New York Yankees
Address: Yankee Stadium
             Bronx, NY 10451
Telephone: (718) 293-4300
Stadium (Capacity): Yankee Stadium (57,746)
Principal Owner: George Steinbrenner
Vice President and Executive Consul: Lonn Trost
General Manager: Brian Cashman
Manager: Joe Torre
Director of Media Relations: Rick Cerone

American League *(Cont.)*

Oakland Athletics
Address: 7677 Oakport St., 2nd floor
Oakland, CA 94621
Telephone: (510) 638-4900
Stadium (Capacity): Network Associates
Coliseum (43,662)
Owners: Steve Schott and Ken Hofmann
President: Michael Crowley
General Manager: Billy Beane
Manager: Art Howe
Baseball Information Manager: Mike Selleck

Seattle Mariners
Address: P.O. Box 4100
Seattle, WA 98104
Telephone: (206) 346-4000
Stadium (Capacity): SAFECO Field (47,155)
Chairman: Howard Lincoln
General Manager: TBA
Manager: Lou Piniella
Director of Baseball Information: Tim Hevly

Tampa Bay Devil Rays
Address: One Tropicana Drive
St. Petersburg, FL 33705
Telephone: (727) 825-3137
Stadium (Capacity): Tropicana Field (45,369)
Managing General Partner and CEO: Vincent Naimoli
Senior VP and General Manager: Chuck Lamar
Manager: Larry Rothschild
Vice President, Public Relations: Rick Vaughn

Texas Rangers
Address: P.O. Box 90111
Arlington, TX 76004
Telephone: (817) 273-5222
Stadium (Capacity): The Ballpark in Arlington (49,166)
Owner: Thomas O. Hicks
General Manager: Doug Melvin
Manager: Johnny Oates
Vice President, Public Relations: John Blake

Toronto Blue Jays
Address: SkyDome
1 Blue Jays Way, Suite 3200
Toronto, Ontario, Canada M5V 1J1
Telephone: (416) 341-1000
Stadium (Capacity): SkyDome (50,516)
Senior Chairman: Sam Pollock
President of Baseball Operations/GM: Gord Ash
Manager: Jim Fregosi
Vice President, Media Relations: Howard Starkman

National League

National League Office
Address: 245 Park Avenue
New York, NY 10167
Telephone: (212) 931-7700
President: Leonard Coleman
Vice President of Public Relations: Ricky Clemons

Arizona Diamondbacks
Address: 401 East Jefferson Street
Phoenix, AZ 85004
Telephone: (602) 462-6500
Stadium (Capacity): Bank One Ballpark (49,000)
Managing General Partner: Jerry Colangelo
General Manager: Joe Garagiola Jr.
Manager: Buck Showalter
Director of Public Relations: Mike Swanson

Atlanta Braves
Address: P.O. Box 4064
Atlanta, GA 30302
Telephone: (404) 522-7630
Stadium (Capacity): Turner Field (49,714)
Owner: Ted Turner
Executive VP & General Manager: John Schuerholz
Manager: Bobby Cox
Director of Public Relations: Jim Schultz

Chicago Cubs
Address: Wrigley Field
1060 West Addison
Chicago, IL 60613
Telephone: (773) 404-2827
Stadium (Capacity): Wrigley Field (38,957)
President and CEO: Andrew B. MacPhail
Executive VP of Business Operations: Mark McGuire
VP/General Manager: Ed Lynch
Manager: TBA
Director of Media Relations: Sharon Panozzo

Cincinnati Reds
Address: 100 Cinergy Field
Cincinnati, OH 45202
Telephone: (513) 421-4510
Stadium (Capacity): Cinergy Field (52,953)
CEO/General Partner: Carl Lindner
General Manager: James G. Bowden
Managing Executive: John L. Allen
Manager: Jack McKeon
Director of Media Relations: Rob Butcher

Colorado Rockies
Address: 2001 Blake Street
Denver, CO 80205
Telephone: (303) 292-0200
Stadium (Capacity): Coors Field (50,381)
Chairman, President and CEO: Jerry McMorris
Senior VP of Business Operations: Keli McGregor
General Manager and Executive VP: Bob Gebhard
Manager: Buddy Bell
Director of Public Relations: Jay Alves

Florida Marlins
Address: 2267 N.W. 199th Street
Miami, FL 33056
Telephone: (305) 626-7400
Stadium (Capacity): Pro Player Stadium (42,531
Owner: John W. Henry
General Manager: Dave Dombrowski
Manager: John Boles
Vice President of Communications/Broadcasting: Ron
Colangelo

National League *(Cont.)*

Houston Astros
Address: P.O. Box 288
    Houston, TX 77001
Telephone: (713) 799-9500
Stadium (Capacity): Astrodome (54,313)
Chairman: Drayton McLane
General Manager: Gerry Hunsicker
Manager: Larry Dierker
Director of Media Relations: Warren Miller

Los Angeles Dodgers
Address: 1000 Elysian Park Avenue
    Los Angeles, CA 90012-1199
Telephone: (323) 224-1500
Stadium (Capacity): Dodger Stadium (56,000)
President: TBA
General Manager: Kevin Malone
Manager: Davey Johnson
Director of Publicity: Brent Shyer

Montreal Expos
Address: P.O. Box 500
    Station M
    Montreal
    Quebec, Canada H1V 3P2
Telephone: (514) 253-3434
Stadium (Capacity): Olympic Stadium (46,500)
President: TBA
Vice President and General Manager: Jim Beattie
Manager: Felipe Alou
Director, Media Relations: Peter Loyello

New York Mets
Address: Shea Stadium
    123-01 Roosevelt Ave.
    Flushing, NY 11368
Telephone: (718) 507-6387
Stadium (Capacity): Shea Stadium (55,775)
Chairman: Nelson Doubleday
President and Chief Executive Officer: Fred Wilpon
Senior VP and General Manager: Steve Phillips
Manager: Bobby Valentine
Director of Media Relations: Jay Horwitz

Philadelphia Phillies
Address: P.O. Box 7575
    Philadelphia, PA 19101-7575
Telephone: (215) 463-6000
Stadium (Capacity): Veterans Stadium (62,411)
Chairman: Bill Giles
President: David T. Montgomery
General Manager: Ed Wade
Manager: Terry Francona
Vice President, Public Relations: Larry Shenk

Pittsburgh Pirates
Address: P.O. Box 7000
    Pittsburgh, PA 15212
Telephone: (412) 323-5000
Stadium (Capacity): Three Rivers Stadium (47,687)
CEO and Managing General Partner: Kevin McClatchy
General Manager: Cam Bonifay
Manager: Gene Lamont
Director of Media Relations: Jim Trdinich

St. Louis Cardinals
Address: Busch Stadium
    250 Stadium Plaza
    St. Louis, MO 63102
Telephone: (314) 421-3060
Stadium (Capacity): Busch Stadium (49,738)
President and CEO: Mark Lamping
General Manager: Walt Jocketty
Manager: Tony LaRussa
Director of Media Relations: Brian Bartow

San Diego Padres
Address: P.O. Box 122000
    San Diego, CA 92112
Telephone: (619) 283-4494
Stadium (Capacity): Qualcomm Stadium (66,307)
Chairman: John Moores
General Manager: Kevin Towers
Manager: Bruce Bochy
Director of Media Relations: Glenn Geffner

San Francisco Giants
Address: 24 Willie Mays Plaza
    San Francisco, CA 94107
Telephone: (415) 468-3700
Stadium (Capacity): Pacific Bell Park (40,000 approx)
President/Managing General Partner: Peter Magowan
General Manager: Brian Sabean
Manager: Dusty Baker
Vice President, Communications: Bob Rose

Pro Football Directory

National Football League
Address: 280 Park Avenue
               New York, NY 10017
Telephone: (212) 450-2000
Commissioner: Paul Tagliabue

NFL Players Association
Address: 2021 L Street, N.W.
             Washington, D.C. 20036
Telephone: (202) 463-2200
Executive Director: Gene Upshaw
Director, Public Relations: Frank Woschitz

National Conference

Arizona Cardinals
Address: P.O. Box 888
             Phoenix, AZ 85001
Telephone: (602) 379-0101
Stadium (Capacity): Sun Devil Stadium (73,377)
President and Owner: Bill Bidwill
Vice President: Larry Wilson
General Manager: Bob Ferguson
Head Coach: Vince Tobin
Director of Public Relations: Paul Jensen

Atlanta Falcons
Address: 1 Falcon Place
             Suwanee, GA 30024
Telephone: (770) 945-1111
Stadium (Capacity): Georgia Dome (71,228)
President: Taylor W. Smith
Director of Player Personnel: Ron Hill
Coach: Dan Reeves
Publicity Director: Aaron Salkin

Carolina Panthers
Address: Ericsson Stadium
             800 South Mint St.
             Charlotte, NC 28202
Telephone: (704) 358-7000
Stadium (Capacity): Ericsson Stadium (73,248)
Founder and Owner: Jerry Richardson
President: Mark Richardson
Coach: George Seifert
Director of Communications: Charlie Dayton

Chicago Bears
Address: 1000 Football Drive
             Lake Forest, IL 60045
Telephone: (847) 295-6600
Stadium (Capacity): Soldier Field (66,944)
President: Michael McCaskey
Coach: Dick Jauron
Director of Public Relations: Bryan Harlan

Dallas Cowboys
Address: One Cowboys Parkway
             Irving, TX 75063
Telephone: (972) 556-9900
Stadium (Capacity): Texas Stadium (65,675)
Owner, President and General Manager: Jerry Jones
Coach: Chan Gailey
Public Relations Director: Rich Dalrymple

Detroit Lions
Address: 1200 Featherstone Road
             Pontiac, MI 48342
Telephone: (248) 335-4131
Stadium (Capacity): Pontiac Silverdome (80,311)
Chairman and President: William Clay Ford
Executive Vice President and CEO: Chuck Schmidt
Vice Chairman: Willliam Clayford
Coach: Bobby Ross
Director of Media Relations: Steve Reaven

Green Bay Packers
Address: 1265 Lombardi Avenue
             Green Bay, WI 54304
Telephone: (920) 496-5700
Stadium (Capacity): Lambeau Field (60,890)
President: Bob Harlan
General Manager: Ron Wolf
Coach: Ray Rhodes
Public Relations Director: Lee Remmel

Minnesota Vikings
Address: 9520 Viking Drive
             Eden Prairie, MN 55344
Telephone: (612) 828-6500
Stadium (Capacity): HHH Metrodome (64,000)
Owner: Red McCombs
President: Gary Woods
Coach: Dennis Green
Public Relations Director: Bob Hagan

New Orleans Saints
Address: 5800 Airline Highway
             Metairie, LA 70003
Telephone: (504) 733-0255
Stadium (Capacity): Louisiana Superdome (70,054)
Owner: Tom Benson
President, General Manager and CEO: Bill Kuharich
Head Coach: Mike Ditka
Director of Media Relations: Greg Bensel

New York Giants
Address: Giants Stadium
             East Rutherford, NJ 07073
Telephone: (201) 935-8111
Stadium (Capacity): Giants Stadium (79,469)
President and co-CEO: Wellington T. Mara
Chairman and co-CEO: Preston Robert Tisch
Senior VP and General Manager: Ernie Accorsi
Coach: Jim Fassel
Vice President of Communications: Pat Hanlon

National Conference (Cont.)

Philadelphia Eagles
Address: Veterans Stadium
           3501 South Broad Street
           Philadelphia, PA 19148
Telephone: (215) 463-2500
Stadium (Capacity): Veterans Stadium (65,352)
Owner & Chief Executive Officer: Jeffrey Lurie
Executive Vice President: Joe Banner
Director of Football Operations: Tom Modrak
Coach: Andy Reid
Director of Public Relations: Ron Howard

St. Louis Rams
Address: One Rams Way
           St. Louis, MO 63045
Telephone: (314) 982-7267
Stadium (Capacity): Trans World Dome (66,000)
Owner and Chairman: Georgia Frontiere
Vice Chairman and Owner: Stan Kroenke
President: John Shaw
Coach: Dick Vermeil
Director of Public Relations: Rick Smith

San Francisco 49ers
Address: 4949 Centennial Boulevard
           Santa Clara, CA 95054
Telephone: (408) 562-4949
Stadium (Capacity): 3Com Park (70,207)
Owner: Edward J. DeBartolo Corporation
Edward J. DeBartolo Jr., Denise DeBartolo-York
General Manager: Bill Walsh
Coach: Steve Mariucci
Public Relations Director: Kirk Reynolds

Tampa Bay Buccaneers
Address: One Buccaneer Place
           Tampa, FL 33607
Telephone: (813) 870-2700
Stadium (Capacity): Raymond James Stadium
(66,321)
Owner: Malcolm Glazer
General Manager: Rich McKay
Coach: Tony Dungy
Director of Communications: Reggie Roberts

Washington Redskins
Address: 21300 Redskin Park Drive
           Ashburn, VA 20147
Telephone: (703) 478-8900
Stadium (Capacity): Jack Kent Cooke Stadium
(80,116)
Owner: Daniel M. Snyder
Director of Player Personnel: Vinny Cerrato
Coach: Norv Turner
Vice President of Public Relations: John Maroon

American Conference

Buffalo Bills
Address: One Bills Drive
           Orchard Park, NY 14127
Telephone: (716) 648-1800
Stadium (Capacity): Ralph Wilson Stadium (73,840)
President: Ralph C. Wilson Jr.
Executive VP and General Manager: John Butler
Coach: Wade Phillips
Vice President of Communications: Scott Berchtold

Baltimore Ravens
Address: 11001 Owings Mills Blvd.
           Owings Mills, MD 21117
Telephone: (410) 654-6200
Stadium (Capacity): PSINet Stadium (69,084)
Owner/CEO: Art Modell
President/COO: David Modell
Coach: Brian Billick
VP of Public Relations/Marketing: Kevin Byrne

Cincinnati Bengals
Address: One Bengals Drive
           Cincinnati, OH 45204
Telephone: (513) 621-3550
Stadium (Capacity): Cinergy Field (60,398)
President: Mike Brown
Executive Vice President: Katherine Blackburn
Coach: Bruce Coslet
Director of Public Relations: Jack Brennan

Denver Broncos
Address: 13655 Broncos Parkway
           Englewood, CO 80112
Telephone: (303) 649-9000
Stadium (Capacity): Mile High Stadium (76,082)
President and Chief Executive Officer: Pat Bowlen
General Manager: John Beake
Coach: Mike Shanahan
Director of Media Relations: Jim Saccomano

Indianapolis Colts
Address: P.O. Box 535000
           Indianapolis, IN 46253
Telephone: (317) 297-2658
Stadium (Capacity): RCA Dome (56,127)
Owner and Chief Executive Officer: Jim Irsay
President: Bill Polian
Vice Chairman and COO: Michael Schernoff
Coach: Jim Mora
Vice President of Public Relations: Craig Kelley

Jacksonville Jaguars
Address: One Alltel Stadium Place
           Jacksonville, FL 32202
Telephone: (904) 633-6000
Stadium (Capacity): Alltel Stadium (73,000)
Owner: J. Wayne Weaver
Vice President and CFO: Bill Prescott
Senior VP of Football Operations: Michael Huyghue
Coach: Tom Coughlin
Executive Director of Communications: Dan Edwards

American Conference (Cont.)

Kansas City Chiefs
Address: One Arrowhead Drive
             Kansas City, MO 64129
Telephone: (816) 920-9300
Stadium (Capacity): Arrowhead Stadium (79,451)
Founder: Lamar Hunt
CEO, President and General Manager: Carl Peterson
Coach: Gunther Cunningham
Public Relations Director: Bob Moore

Miami Dolphins
Address: 7500 S.W. 30th Street
             Davie, FL 33314
Telephone: (954) 452-7000
Stadium (Capacity): Pro Player Stadium (75,192)
Chairman of the Board/Owner: H. Wayne Huizenga
President and COO: Eddie J. Jones
General Manager and Head Coach: Jimmy Johnson
VP Media Relations: Harvey Greene

New England Patriots
Address: Foxboro Stadium
             60 Washington St.
             Foxboro, MA 02035
Telephone: (508) 543-8200
Stadium (Capacity): Foxboro Stadium (60,292)
President and Chief Executive Officer: Robert K. Kraft
VP Owners Representative: Jonathan Kraft
VP Business Operations: Andy Wasynczuk
Coach: Pete Carroll
VP of Public and Community Relations: Donald Lowery

New York Jets
Address: 1000 Fulton Avenue
             Hempstead, NY 11550
Telephone: (516) 560-8100
Stadium (Capacity): Giants Stadium (78,739)
Chairman of the Board: Leon Hess
Director of Player Personnel: Dick Haley
Coach: Bill Parcells
Director of Public Relations: Frank Ramos

Oakland Raiders
Address: 1220 Harbor Bay Parkway
             Alameda, CA 94502
Telephone: (510) 864-5000
Stadium (Capacity): Oakland-Alameda County
Coliseum (62,500)
President of the General Partner: Al Davis
Coach: Jon Gruden
Executive Assistant: Al LoCasale
Director of Public Relations: Mike Taylor

Pittsburgh Steelers
Address: Three Rivers Stadium
             300 Stadium Circle
             Pittsburgh, PA 15212
Telephone: (412) 323-1200
Stadium (Capacity): Three Rivers Stadium (59,600)
President: Dan Rooney
Director of Football Operations: Tom Donahoe
Coach: Bill Cowher
Director of Communications: Ron Wahl

San Diego Chargers
Address: Qualcomm Stadium
             4020 Murphy Canyon Road
             San Diego, CA 92123
Telephone: (619) 874-4500
Stadium (Capacity): Qualcomm Stadium (71,400)
Chairman: Alex G. Spanos
President/Vice Chairman: Dean A. Spanos
General Manager: Bobby Beathard
Coach: Mike Riley
Director of Public Relations: Bill Johnston

Seattle Seahawks
Address: 11220 N.E. 53rd Street
             Kirkland, WA 98033
Telephone: (425) 827-9777
Stadium (Capacity): The Kingdome (66,400)
Owner: Paul Allen
President: Bob Whitsitt
Coach/GM: Mike Holmgren
VP of Administration and Communications: Gary Wright
Director of Public Relations: Dave Pearson

Tennessee Titans
Address: Baptist Sports Park
             460 Great Circle Road
             Nashville, TN 37228
Telephone: 615-565-4000
Stadium (Capacity): Adelphia Coliseum (67,000)
President: Jeff Diamond
General Manager: Floyd Reese
Coach: Jeff Fisher
Director of Media Relations: Tony Wyllie

Other Leagues

Canadian Football League
Address: 110 Eglinton Avenue West, 5th floor
             Toronto, Ontario M4R1A3, Canada
Telephone: (416) 322-9650
Commissioner: John Tory
President/Chief Operating Officer: Jeff Giles
Director of Communications: Jim Neish

NFL EUROPE
Address: 280 Park Avenue
             New York, NY 10017
Telephone: (212) 450-2000
President: Oliver Luck (Frankfurt)
Chief Operating Officer: Ken Saunders (London)
Director of Communications: David Tossel

National Basketball Association

National Basketball Association
Address: 645 Fifth Avenue
New York, NY 10022
Telephone: (212) 826-7000
Commissioner: David Stern
Deputy Commissioner: Russell Granik
Sr. VP of Communications: Brian McIntyre

National Basketball Association Players Association
Address: 1700 Broadway
Suite 1400
New York, NY 10019
Telephone: (212) 655-0880
Executive Director: William Hunter

Atlanta Hawks
Address: One CNN Center, South Tower
Suite 405
Atlanta, GA 30303
Telephone: (404) 827-3800
Arena (Capacity): Philips Arena (20,000)
Owner: Ted Turner
President: Stan Kasten
General Manager: Pete Babcock
Coach: Lenny Wilkens
VP of Communications: Arthur Triche

Boston Celtics
Address: 151 Merrimac Street
Boston, MA 02114
Telephone: (617) 523-6050
Arena (Capacity): FleetCenter (18,624)
Owner and Chairman of the Board: Paul Gaston
President and Head Coach: Rick Pitino
General Manager: Chris Wallace
Director of Media Relations: R. Jeffrey Twiss

Charlotte Hornets
Address: 100 Hive Drive
Charlotte, NC 28217
Telephone: (704) 357-0252
Arena (Capacity): Charlotte Coliseum (23,799)
Owners: George Shinn and Ray Wooldridge
Coach: Paul Silas
VP of Public Relations: Harold Kaufman

Chicago Bulls
Address: 1901 W. Madison Street
Chicago, IL 60612
Telephone: (312) 455-4000
Arena (Capacity): United Center (21,711)
Chairman: Jerry Reinsdorf
GM and VP of Basketball Operations: Jerry Krause
Coach: Tim Floyd
Senior Director of Media Services: Tim Hallam

Cleveland Cavaliers
Address: One Center Court
Cleveland, OH 44115
Telephone: (216) 420-2000
Arena (Capacity): Gund Arena (20,562)
Chairman: Gordon Gund
President and COO, Team Division: Wayne Embry
Coach: Randy Wittman
Sr. Director of Communications/Public Relations: Bob Price

Dallas Mavericks
Address: Reunion Arena
777 Sports Street
Dallas, TX 75207
Telephone: (214) 748-1808
Arena (Capacity): Reunion Arena (18,187)
Owners: Ross Perot Jr.
Director of Player Personnel: Donn Nelson
General Manager and Head Coach: Don Nelson
VP of Marketing/Communications: Greg Anderson

Denver Nuggets
Address: Pepsi Center
1000 Chopper Place
Denver, CO 80204
Telephone: (303) 405-1100
Arena (Capacity): Pepsi Center (19,307)
Owner: Donald Sturm
President/Coach: Dan Issel
Media Relations Director: Tommy Sheppard

Detroit Pistons
Address: The Palace of Auburn Hills
Two Championship Drive
Auburn Hills, MI 48326
Telephone: (248) 377-0100
Arena (Capacity): The Palace of Auburn Hills (22,076)
Owner: William M. Davidson
VP of Basketball Operations: Rick Sund
Coach: Alvin Gentry
VP of Public Relations: Matt Dobek

Golden State Warriors
Address: 1011 Broadway
Oakland, CA 94607-4019
Telephone: (510) 986-2200
Arena (Capacity): The Arena in Oakland (19,596)
Owner and CEO: Christopher Cohan
General Manager: Garry St. Jean
Coach: P.J. Carlesimo
Director of Public Relations: Raymond Ridder

Houston Rockets
Address: Two Greenway Plaza, Suite 400
Houston, TX 77046
Telephone: (713) 627-3865
Arena (Capacity): Compaq Center (16,285)
Owner: Leslie Alexander
Chief Operating Officer: George Postolos
Executive VP of Basketball Affairs: Carroll Dawson
Coach: Rudy Tomjanovich
Director of Media Services: Tim Frank

Indiana Pacers
Address: 125 S. Pennsylvania Street
Indianapolis, IN 46204
Telephone: (317) 917-2500
Arena (Capacity): Conseco Fieldhouse (18,500)
Owners: Melvin Simon and Herbert Simon
General Manager: David Kahn
President: Donnie Walsh
Executive VP and Head Coach: Larry Bird
Media Relations Director: David Benner

National Basketball Association (Cont.)

Los Angeles Clippers
Address: The Staples Center
             1111 S. Figueroa Street
             Los Angeles, CA 90037
Telephone: (213) 745-0500
Arena (Capacity): The Staples Center (20,000)
Owner: Donald T. Sterling
Vice President of Basketball Operations: Elgin Baylor
Coach: Chris Ford
Vice President of Communications: Joe Safety

Los Angeles Lakers
Address: 555 Nash Street
             El Segundo, CA 90503
Telephone: (310) 426-600
Arena (Capacity): The Staples Center (17,505)
Owner: Dr. Jerry Buss
Executive VP of Basketball Operations: Jerry West
General Manager: Mitch Kupchak
Coach: Phil Jackson
Director of Public Relations: John Black

Miami Heat
Address: Sun Trust International Center
             One SE 3rd Ave., Suite 2300
             Miami, FL 33131
Telephone: (305) 577-4328
Arena (Capacity): American Airlines Arena (19,600)
Managing General Partner: Mickey Arison
Executive Emeritus: Pauline Winick
President and Coach: Pat Riley
President/GM of Basketball Operations: Randy Pfund
President of Business Operations: Jay Cross
Director of Sports Media Relations: Tim Donovan

Milwaukee Bucks
Address: The Bradley Center
             1001 N. Fourth Street
             Milwaukee, WI 53203
Telephone: (414) 227-0500
Arena (Capacity): The Bradley Center (18,717)
Owner: Herb Kohl
General Manager: Ernie Grunfeld
Coach: George Karl
Public Relations Director: Cheri Hanson

Minnesota Timberwolves
Address: 600 First Avenue North
             Minneapolis, MN 55403
Telephone: (612) 673-1602
Arena (Capacity): Target Center (19,006)
Owner: Glen Taylor
VP of Basketball Operations: Kevin McHale
General Manager and Coach: Phil (Flip) Saunders
Manager of PR and Communications: Kent Wipf

New Jersey Nets
Address: Nets Champion Center
             390 Murray Hill Parkway
             East Rutherford, NJ 07073
Telephone: (201) 935-8888
Arena (Capacity): Continental Airlines Arena (20,049)
Chairman of the Board/Principal Owner: Lewis Katz
Vice Chairman: David Gerstein
President and COO: Michael Rowe
General Manager: John Nash
Coach: Don Casey
Director of Public Relations: John Mertz

New York Knickerbockers
Address: Madison Square Garden
             Two Pennsylvania Plaza
             New York, NY 10121
Telephone: (212) 465-5867
Arena (Capacity): Madison Square Garden (19,763)
Owner: ITT/Sheraton and Cablevision
Governor/CEO of MSG: David W. Checketts
Executive VP and General Manager: Scott Layden
Coach: Jeff Van Gundy
Director of Public Relations: Lori Hamamoto

Orlando Magic
Address: P.O. Box 76
             Orlando, FL 32802
Telephone: (407) 649-3200
Arena (Capacity): Orlando Arena (17,248)
Owner: Rich DeVos
Senior Executive Vice President: Pat Williams
General Manager: John Gabriel
Coach: Glenn "Doc" Rivers
Director of Communications: Joel Glass

Philadelphia 76ers
Address: First Union Center
             3601 South Broad Street
             Philadelphia, PA 19148
Telephone: (215) 339-7600
Arena (Capacity): First Union Center (20,444)
Owner and President: Pat Croce
Head Coach and Vice President of Basketball
  Operations: Larry Brown
General Manager: Billy King
Director of Media Relations: Karen Frascona

Phoenix Suns
Address: P.O. Box 1369
             Phoenix, AZ 85001
Telephone: (602) 379-7916
Arena (Capacity): America West Arena (19,023)
Owner, President & CEO: Jerry Colangelo
Coach: Danny Ainge
VP of Basketball Communications: Julie Fie

Portland Trail Blazers
Address: One Center Court
             Suite 200
             Portland, OR 97227
Telephone: (503) 234-9291
Arena (Capacity): Rose Garden Arena (19,980)
Chairman of the Board: Paul Allen
President and General Manager: Bob Whitsitt
Coach: Mike Dunleavy
Director of Sports Communications: Sue Carpenter

Sacramento Kings
Address: One Sports Parkway
             Sacramento, CA 95834
Telephone: (916) 928-0000
Arena (Capacity): ARCO Arena (17,317)
Owners: Joe and Gavin Maloof
Vice President of Basketball Operations: Geoff Petrie
Coach: Rick Adelman
Director of Media Relations: Troy Hanson

National Basketball Association *(Cont.)*

San Antonio Spurs
Address: Alamodome
100 Montana
San Antonio, TX 78203
Telephone: (210) 554-7787
Arena (Capacity): Alamodome (34,215)
Chairman: Peter Holt
Head Coach and General Manager: Gregg Popovich
Director of Media Services: Tom James

Seattle SuperSonics
Address: 190 Queen Anne Avenue North
Suite 200
Seattle, WA 98109
Telephone: (206) 281-5847
Arena (Capacity): KeyArena (17,100)
Owner: Barry Ackerley
President and General Manager: Wally Walker
Coach: Paul Westphal
Director of Media Relations: Mare Moquin

Toronto Raptors
Address: 40 Bay Street, Suite 400
Toronto, Ontario, Canada M5J 2X2
Telephone: (416) 815-5600
Arena (Capacity): Air Canada Centre (19,800)
Owner: Maple Leaf Sports and Entertainment, Ltd.
VP and General Manager: Glen Grunwald
Coach: Butch Carter
Manager of Media Relations: Dave Haggith

Utah Jazz
Address: 301 West So. Temple
Salt Lake City, UT 84101
Telephone: (801) 575-7800
Arena (Capacity): Delta Center (19,911)
Owner: Larry H. Miller
General Manager: R. Tim Howells
Coach: Jerry Sloan
Director of Media Relations: Kim Turner

Vancouver Grizzlies
Address: General Motors Place
800 Griffiths Way
Vancouver, B.C., Canada V6B 6G1
Telephone: (604) 899-4666
Arena (Capacity): General Motors Place (19,193)
Owner: Orca Bay Sports and Entertainment
President & General Manager: Stu Jackson
Coach: Brian Hill
Director of Media Relations: Steve Frost

Washington Wizards
Address: 601 F Street NW
Washington D.C. 20004
Telephone: (202) 661-5000
Arena (Capacity): MCI Center (20,674)
Owner: Abe Pollin
General Manager and Vice President: Wes Unseld
Coach: Gar Heard
Director of Public Relations: Maureen Lewis

Women's National Basketball Association

Women's National Basketball Association
Address: 645 Fifth Avenue
New York, NY 10022
Telephone: (212) 688-9622
President: Valerie B. Ackerman
Director of Communications: Mark Pray

Charlotte Sting
Address: 3308 Oak Lake Boulevard
Suite B
Charlotte, NC 28208
Telephone: (704) 357-0252
Arena (Capacity): Charlotte Coliseum (8,333)
Executive Vice President: Sam Russo
Coach and General Manager: Marynell Meadors
Director of Public Relations: John Maxwell

Cleveland Rockers
Address: Gund Arena
One Center Court
Cleveland, OH 44115
Telephone: (216) 420-2000
Arena (Capacity): Gund Arena (20,500)
Chairman: Gordon Gund
President, CEO and COO: James C. Boland
Coach: Linda Hill-McDonald
Director of Media Relations: Lori Montgomery

Detroit Shock
Address: 2 Championship Drive
Auburn Hills, MI 48326
Telephone: (248) 377-0100

Detroit Shock *(Cont.)*
Arena (Capacity): The Palace of Auburn Hills (19,000)
Managing Partner: William Davidson
President: Tom Wilson
General Manager/Head Coach: Nancy Lieberman-Cline
Director of Media Relations: Dennis Sampier

Houston Comets
Address: Two Greenway Plaza, Suite 400
Houston, TX 77046-3865
Telephone: (713) 627-9622
Arena (Capacity): The Compaq Center (16,000)
President: Leslie L. Alexander
Coach and General Manager: Van Chancellor
Manager, Media Services: Megan Bonifas

Los Angeles Sparks
Address: Great Western Arena
3900 W. Manchester Boulevard
Inglewood, CA 90306
Telephone: (310) 330-2434
Arena (Capacity): Great Western Forum (17,005)
Chairman: Dr. Jerry Buss
President and General Manager: Johnny Buss
Coach: Orlando Woolridge
Media Relations Director: Laura Reid

Minnesota Lynx
Address: Target Center
600 First Avenue North
Minneapolis, MN 55403
Telephone: (612) 673-8400
Arena (Capacity): Target Center (19,006)

Women's National Basketball Association *(Cont.)*

Minnesota Lynx *(Cont.)*
Chief Operating Officer: Roger Griffith
Head Coach/General Manager: Brian Agler
Coach: Brian Hill
Public Relations Manager: Caryn Fine

New York Liberty
Address: Two Penn Plaza
           New York, NY 10121
Telephone: (212) 465-5867
Arena (Capacity): Madison Square Garden (19,763)
General Manager and Vice President: Carol
 Blazejowski
Coach: Richie Adubato
Director, Public Relations: Maureen Coyle

Orlando Miracle
Address: Two Magic Place
           8701 Maitland Summit Boulevard
           Orlando, FL 32810
Telephone: (407) 916-2400
Arena (Capacity): Orlando Arena (17,000)
Chairman: Rich DeVos
President: Bob Vander Weide
General Manager/Head Coach: Carolyn Peck
Director of Media Relations: Katherine Wu

Phoenix Mercury
Address: 201 East Jefferson Street
           Phoenix, AZ 85004
Telephone: (602) 514-8333
Arena (Capacity): America West Arena (17,623)
Owner, Phoenix Arena Sports: Jerry Colangelo
Chief Executive Officer: Bryan Colangelo
General Manager and Head Coach: Cheryl Miller
Media Relations Director: Neda Kia

Sacremento Monarchs
Address: One Sports Parkway
           Sacramento, CA 95834
Telephone: (916) 455-4647
Arena (Capacity): ARCO Arena (17,317)

Sacremento Monarchs *(Cont.)*
Managing General Partner: Jim Thomas
President: Rick Benner
General Manager: Jerry Reynolds
Head Coach: TBD
Director, Media Relations: Andrea Lepore

Utah Starzz
Address: 301 W. South Temple
           Salt Lake City, UT 84101
Telephone: (801) 325-7827
Arena (Capacity): Delta Center (8,915)
Owner: Larry H. Miller
President and Head Coach: Frank Layden
General Manager: R. Tim Howells
Media Relations Manager: Tami Scott

Washington Mystics
Address: MCI Center
           601 F Street, NW
           Washington, DC 20004
Telephone: (202) 661-5000
Arena (Capacity): MCI Center (20,674)
Chairman: Abe Pollin
President: Susan O'Malley
Coach: Nancy Darsch
Director, Public Relations: Julie Demeo

Other Leagues

Continental Basketball Association
Address: Two Arizona Center
           400 North 5th Street, Suite 1425
           Phoenix, AZ 85004
Telephone: (602) 254-6677
Chairman/CEO: Isiah Thomas
VP of Basketball Operations: Wade Morehead

Hockey Directory

National Hockey League
Address: 1251 Avenue of the Americas
           47th floor
           New York, NY 10020-1198
Telephone: (212) 789-2000
Commissioner: Gary Bettman
President of NHL Enterprises: Richie Woodworth
Senior VP and Dir. of Hockey Operations: Colin Cambell
Director of Public Relations: Frank Brown

National Hockey League Players Association
Address: 777 Bay Street, Suite 2400
           Toronto, Ontario, Canada M5G 2C8
Telephone: (416) 408-4040
Executive Director: Bob Goodenow

Mighty Ducks of Anaheim
Address: Arrowhead Pond of Anaheim
           2695 Katella Avenue
           Anaheim, CA 92806
Telephone: (714) 940-2900
Arena (Capacity): Arrowhead Pond of Anaheim (17,174)
Chairman and Governor: Tony Tavares
President and General Manager: Pierre Gauthier

Mighty Ducks of Anaheim *(Cont.)*
Coach: Craig Hartsburg
Manager of Communications: Rob Scichili

Atlanta Thrashers
Address: 1 CNN Center
           P.O. Box 15538
           Atlanta, GA 30348
Telephone: (404) 827-5300
Arena (Capacity): Philips Arena (18,500)
Owner: Time Warner
President: Dr. Harvey Schiller
General Manager: Don Waddell
Coach Curt Fraser
Director of Media Relations: Tom Hughes

Boston Bruins
Address: One FleetCenter, Suite 250
           Boston, MA 02114-1303
Telephone: (617) 624-1900
Arena (Capacity): FleetCenter (17,565)
Owner and Governor: Jeremy M. Jacobs
Alternative Governor, President and General
 Manager: Harry Sinden
Coach: Pat Burns
Director of Media Relations: Heidi Holland

Buffalo Sabres
Address: Marine Midland Arena
             One Seymour H. Knox III Plaza
             Buffalo, NY 14203
Telephone: (716) 855-4100
Arena (Capacity): Marine Midland Arena (18,690)
Chairman of the Board: John J. Rigas
CEO: Tim J. Rigas
General Manager: Darcy Regier
Coach: Lindy Ruff
VP of Communications: Michael Gilbert

Calgary Flames
Address: Canadian Airlines Saddledome
             555 Saddledome Rise, SE
             Calgary, Alberta T2G 2W1
Telephone: (403) 777-2177
Arena (Capacity): Canadian Airlines Saddledome
(17,139)
Owners: Grant A. Bartlett, Harley N. Hotchkiss, N.
Murray Edwards, Ronald V. Joyce, Alvin G. Libin,
Allan P. Markin, J.R. "Bud" McCaig, Byron J.
Seaman, Daryl K. Seaman
President: Ron Bremner
Executive VP/General Manager: Al Coates
Director of Hockey Operations: Al MacNeil
Coach: Brian Sutter
Director of Communications: Peter Hanlon

Carolina Hurricanes
Address: 5000 Aerial Center, Suite 100
             Morrisville, NC 27560
Telephone: (919) 467-7825
Arena (Capacity): Entertainment and Sports Arena
(18,711)
Owner: Peter Karmanos
President and General Manager: Jim Rutherford
Assistant General Manager: Jason Karmanos
Coach: Paul Maurice
Director of Public Relations: Chris Brown

Chicago Blackhawks
Address: United Center
             1901 W. Madison Street
             Chicago, IL 60612
Telephone: (312) 455-7000
Arena (Capacity): United Center (20,500)
President: William W. Wirtz
Senior Vice President: Robert Pulford
General Manager: Bob Murray
Coach: Lorne Molleken
Public Relations Director: Jim DeMaria

Colorado Avalanche
Address: Pepsi Center
             100 Chopper Place
             Denver, CO 80204
Telephone: (303) 405-1100
Arena (Capacity): McNichols Sports Arena (18,007)
Owner: Donald L. Sturm
President and General Manager: Pierre Lacroix
Coach: Bob Hartley
VP of Communications and Team Services:
Jean Martineau

Dallas Stars
Address: 211 Cowboys Parkway
             Irving, TX 75063
Telephone: (972) 868-2890
Arena (Capacity): Reunion Arena (17,001)
Owner: Thomas O. Hicks
General Manager: Bob Gainey
Coach: Ken Hitchcock
Director of Media Relations: Larry Kelly

Detroit Red Wings
Address: Joe Louis Sports Arena
             600 Civic Center Drive
             Detroit, MI 48226
Telephone: (313) 396-7544
Arena (Capacity): Joe Louis Sports Arena (19,983)
Senior Vice President: Jim Devellano
Head Coach: Scott Bowman
General Manager: Ken Holland
Director of Media Relations: John Hahn

Edmonton Oilers
Address: 11230 110th Street
             Edmonton, Alberta T5G 3H7
Telephone: (780) 414-4000
Arena (Capacity): Skyreach Centre (17,100)
Owner: Edmonton Investors Group
Governor: Jim Hole
Alt. Governor, President and GM: Glen Sather
Coach: Kevin Lowe
VP of Public Relations: Bill Tuele

Florida Panthers
Address: 1 Panther Parkway
             Sunrise, FL 33323
Telephone: (954) 835-7000
Arena (Capacity): Nationall Car Rental Center
(19,250)
Owner: H. Wayne Huizenga
General Manager: Bryan Murray
Coach: Terry Murray
Director of Media Relations: Mike Hanson

Los Angeles Kings
Address: The Staples Center
             1111 South Figueroa Street
             Los Angeles, CA 90037
Telephone: (213) 742-7100
Arena (Capacity): The Staples Center (18,500)
President: Tim Leiweke
General Manager: Dave Taylor
Coach: Larry Robinson
Director of Communications: Michael Roth

Montreal Canadiens
Address: Molson Centre
             1260 de la Gauchetiere West
             Montreal, Quebec H3B 5E8
Telephone: (514) 932-2582
Arena (Capacity): Molson Centre (21,273)
President and Governor: Pierre Boivin
General Manager: Regean Houle
Coach: Alain Vigneault
Director of Communications: Donald Beauchamp

New Jersey Devils
Address: Continental Airlines Arena, PO Box 504
             East Rutherford, NJ 07073
Telephone: (201) 935-6050
Arena (Capacity): Continental Airlines Arena (19,040)
Chairman: John J. McMullen
President and General Manager: Lou Lamoriello
Coach: Robbie Ftorek
VP of Communications: Rick Minch

New York Islanders
Address: Nassau Veterans Memorial Coliseum
             Uniondale, NY 11553
Telephone: (516) 794-4100
Arena (Capacity): Nassau Coliseum (16,297)
Co-Chairman and Governor: Steven M. Gluckstern
Co-Chairman and Alt. Governor: Edward Milstein
General Manager: Mike Milbury
Coach: Butch Goring
VP of Communications: Chris Botta

New York Rangers
Address: Madison Square Garden
             2 Pennsylvania Plaza
             New York, NY 10121
Telephone: (212) 465-6000
Arena (Capacity): Madison Square Garden (18,200)
Owner: Cablevision
President and General Manager: Neil Smith
Coach: John Muckler
VP of Public Relations: John Rosasco

Ottawa Senators
Address: The Corel Center
             1000 Palladium Drive
             Kanata, Ontario K2V 1A5
Telephone: (613) 599-0250
Arena (Capacity): The Corel Centre (18,500)
Founder: Bruce M. Firestone
Chairman and Governor: Rod Bryden
President and Chief Executive Officer: Roy Mlakar
General Manager: Marshall Johnston
Coach: Jacques Martin
Director of Media Relations: Morgan Quarry

Philadelphia Flyers
Address: First Union Center
             3601 South Broad Street
             Philadelphia, PA 19148
Telephone: (215) 465-4500
Arena (Capacity): First Union Center (19,541)
Majority Owner: Comcast Spectacor
Chairman: Ed Snider
President and General Manager: Bob Clarke
Coach: Roger Neilson
Director of Public Relations: Zack Hill

Phoenix Coyotes
Address: Cellular One Ice Den
             9375 East Belle Road
             Scottsdale, AZ 85260
Telephone: (602) 473-5600
Arena (Capacity): America West Arena (16,210)
Chief Executive Officer and Governor: Richard Burke
Owner, CEO and Governor: Richard Burke
GM and Alternate Governor: Bobby Smith
Coach: Bob Francis
VP of Media and Player Relations: Richard Nairn

Pittsburgh Penguins
Address: Civic Arena
             66 Mario Lemieux Place
             Pittsburgh, PA 15219
Telephone: (412) 642-1300
Arena (Capacity): Civic Arena (16,958)
Owner: Mario Lemieux (Lemieux Ownership Group)
General Manager: Craig Patrick
Coach: Kevin Constantine
Director of Media Relations: Steve Bovino

St. Louis Blues
Address: Kiel Center
             1401 Clark Avenue
             St. Louis, MO 63103
Telephone: (314) 622-2500
Arena (Capacity): Kiel Center (19,260)
President and Chief Executive Officer: Mark Sauer
Coach: Joel Quenneville
General Manager: Larry Pleau
Director of Public Relations: Jeff Trammel

San Jose Sharks
Address: San Jose Arena
             525 West Santa Clara Street
             San Jose, CA 95113
Telephone: (408) 287-7070
Arena (Capacity): San Jose Arena (17,483)
Owners: George and Gordon Gund
Executive VP and General Manager: Dean Lombardi
Coach: Darryl Sutter
Director of Media Relations: Ken Arnold

Tampa Bay Lightning
Address: 401 Channelside Drive
             Tampa, FL 33602
Telephone: (813) 229-2658
Arena (Capacity): Ice Palace (19,758)
Owner: Palace Sports & Entertainment/Bill Davidson,
  David Hermelin, Robert Sosnick
President, CEO and Governor: Ron Campbell
Senior VP & General Manager: Rick Dudley
Coach: Steve Ludzik
VP of Public Relations: Bill Wickett

Toronto Maple Leafs
Address: Air Canada Centre
             40 Bay Street - St. 400
             Toronto, Ontario M5J 2X2
Telephone: (416) 815-5500
Arena (Capacity): Air Canada Centre (15,726)
Chairman of the Board: Steve A. Stavro
President: Ken Dryden
Coach/GM: Pat Quinn
Director of Media Relations: Pat Park

Vancouver Canucks
Address: General Motors Place
             800 Griffiths Way
             Vancouver, B.C. V6B 6G1
Telephone: (604) 899-4600
Arena (Capacity): General Motors Place (18,422)
Chairman and Governor: John E. McCaw Jr.
Deputy Chairman, Orca Bay Sports and
  Entertainment: Stanley McCammon
President, CEO and Alternate Governor: Stephen T.
  Bellringer
General Manager: Brian Burke
Coach: Marc Crawford
Manager of Media Relations: Chris Brunwell
Media Relations Coordinator: Reid Mitchell

Washington Capitals
Address: MCI Center
             601 F Street, NW
             Washington, D.C. 20004
Telephone: (202) 628-3200
Arena (Capacity): MCI Center (19,740)
Owners: Ted Leonsis and John Ledecky
Owner and Governor: Richard M. Patrick
Chairman of the Board: Abe Pollin
VP and General Manager: George McPhee
Coach: Ron Wilson
Senior VP of Business Operations: Declan J. Bolger

College Sports Directory

NATIONAL COLLEGIATE ATHLETIC ASSOCIATION (NCAA)
Address: P.O. Box 6222
Indianapolis, IN 46206-622
Telephone: (317) 917-6222
President: Cedric Dempsey
Director of Public Relations: Wallace I. Renfro

ATLANTIC COAST CONFERENCE
Address: P.O. Drawer ACC
Greensboro, NC 27417-6724
Telephone: (336) 854-8787
Commissioner: John Swofford
Director of Media Relations: Brian Morrison

Clemson University
Address: Clemson, SC 29633
Nickname: Tigers
Telephone: (864) 656-2114
Football Stadium (Capacity): Clemson Memorial Stadium (81,474)
Basketball Arena (Capacity): Littlejohn Coliseum (11,020)
President: Dr. James F. Barker
Athletic Director: Bobby Robinson
Football Coach: Tommy Bowden
Basketball Coach: Larry Shyatt
Sports Information Director: Tim Bourret

Duke University
Address: Durham, NC 27708
Nickname: Blue Devils
Telephone: (919) 684-2633
Football Stadium (Capacity): Wallace Wade Stadium (33,941)
Basketball Arena (Capacity): Cameron Indoor Stadium (9,314)
President: Nan Keohane
Athletic Director: Joe Alleva
Football Coach: Carl Franks
Basketball Coach: Mike Krzyzewski
Sports Information Director: Mike Cragg

Florida State University
Address: P.O. Box 2195
Tallahassee, FL 32316
Nickname: Seminoles
Telephone: (850) 644-1403
Football Stadium (Capacity): Doak S. Campbell Stadium (80,000)
Basketball Arena (Capacity): Leon County Civic Center (12,200)
President: Sandy D'Alemberte
Athletic Director: Dave Hart
Football Coach: Bobby Bowden
Basketball Coach: Steve Robinson
Sports Information Director: Rob Wilson

Georgia Tech
Address: 150 Bobby Dodd Way
Atlanta, GA 30332
Nickname: Yellow Jackets
Telephone: (404) 894-5445
Football Stadium (Capacity): Bobby Dodd Stadium at Grant Field (46,000)
Basketball Arena (Capacity): Alexander Memorial Coliseum at McDonald's Center (10,000)
President: G. Wayne Clough
Athletic Director: David Braine
Football Coach: George O'Leary
Basketball Coach: Bobby Cremins
Director of Communications: Mike Finn

University of Maryland
Address: P.O. Box 295
College Park, MD 20742
Nickname: Terrapins
Telephone: (301) 314-7064
Football Stadium (Capacity): Byrd Stadium (48,055)
Basketball Arena (Capacity): Cole Fieldhouse (14,500)
President: Dr. C.D. Mote, Jr.
Athletic Director: Deborah A. Yow
Football Coach: Ron Vanderlinden
Basketball Coach: Gary Williams
Sports Information Director: David Haglund

University of North Carolina
Address: P.O. Box 2126
Chapel Hill, NC 27515
Nickname: Tar Heels
Telephone: (919) 962-2123
Football Stadium (Capacity): Kenan Memorial Stadium (60,000)
Basketball Arena (Capacity): Dean E. Smith Center (21,572)
Interim Chancellor: William McCoy
Athletic Director: Dick Baddour
Football Coach: Carl Torbush
Men's Basketball Coach: Bill Guthridge
Women's Basketball Coach: Sylvia Hatchell
Sports Information Director: Rick Brewer

North Carolina State University
Address: Box 8501
Raleigh, NC 27695
Nickname: Wolfpack
Telephone: (919) 515-2102
Football Stadium (Capacity): Carter-Finley Stadium (51,500)
Basketball Arena (Capacity): Entertainment and Sports Arena (20,000)
Chancellor: Dr. Marye Anne Fox
Athletic Director: Les Robinson
Football Coach: Mike O'Cain
Basketball Coach: Herb Sendex
Sports Information Director: Anabelle Vaughan

University of Virginia
Address: P.O. Box 3785
Charlottesville, VA 22903
Nickname: Cavaliers
Telephone: (804) 982-5500
Football Stadium (Capacity): Carl Smith Center, Home of David A. Harrison III Field at Scott Stadium (44,000)
Basketball Arena (Capacity): University Hall (8,457)
President: John Casteen III
Athletic Director: Terry Holland
Football Coach: George Welsh
Men's Basketball Coach: Pete Gillen
Women's Basketball Coach: Debbie Ryan
Sports Information Director: Rich Murray

Wake Forest University
Address: P.O. Box 7426
Winston-Salem, NC 27109
Nickname: Demon Deacons
Telephone: (336) 758-5640
Football Stadium (Capacity): Groves Stadium (31,500)
Basketball Arena (Capacity): Lawrence Joel Memorial Coliseum (14,407)
President: Dr. Thomas K. Hearn Jr.
Athletic Director: Ron Wellman
Football Coach: Jim Caldwell

Wake Forest University *(Cont.)*
Basketball Coach: Dave Odom
Interim Sports Information Director: Jen Hoover

BIG EAST CONFERENCE
Address: 56 Exchange Terrace, 5th floor
Providence, RI 02903
Telephone: (401) 272-9108
Commissioner: Michael A. Tranghese
Associate Commissioner for Public Relations: John Paquette

Boston College
Address: Chestnut Hill, MA 02467
Nickname: Eagles
Telephone: (617) 552-3004
Football Stadium (Capacity): Alumni Stadium (44,500)
Basketball Arena (Capacity): Silvio O. Conte Forum (8,606)
President: Rev. William P. Leahy, S.J.
Athletic Director: Gene DeFilippo
Football Coach: Tom O'Brien
Basketball Coach: Al Skinner
Sports Information Director: Chris Cameron

University of Connecticut
Address: 2095 Hillside Road
Storrs, CT 06269-3078
Nickname: Huskies
Telephone: (860) 486-3531
Football Stadium (Capacity): Memorial Stadium (16,200)
Basketball Arena (Capacity): Harry A. Gampel Pavilion (10,027)
President: Philip E. Austin
Athletic Director: Lew Perkins
Football Coach: Randy Edsall
Men's Basketball Coach: Jim Calhoun
Women's Basketball Coach: Geno Auriemma
Sports Information Director: Tim Tolokan
Note: Division I-AA football.

Georgetown University
Address: McDonough Arena
Box 571124
Washington, DC 20057-1124
Nickname: Hoyas
Telephone: (202) 687-2492
Football Stadium (Capacity): Kehoe Field (2,400)
Basketball Arena (Capacity): MCI Center (26,000)
President: Rev. Leo J. O'Donovan S.J.
Athletic Director Emeritus: Francis X. Rienzo
Senior Associate Director of Athletics: Dennis Kanach
Athletic Director: Joseph Lang
Football Coach: Robert Benson
Basketball Coach: Craig Esherick
Sports Information Director: Mike Tuberosa, (Men's basketball) Bill Shapland
Note: Division I-AA football.

University of Miami
Address: 5821 San Amaro Drive
Coral Gables, FL 33146
Nickname: Hurricanes
Telephone: (305) 284-3244
Football Stadium (Capacity): Orange Bowl (72,319)
Basketball Arena (Capacity): Miami Arena (15,388)
President: Edward T. Foote II
Athletic Director: Paul Dee
Football Coach: Butch Davis
Basketball Coach: Leonard Hamilton
Sports Information Director: Phil de Montmollin

University of Pittsburgh
Address: Dept. of Athletics
P.O. Box 7436
Pittsburgh, PA 15213-0436
Nickname: Panthers
Telephone: (412) 648-8240
Football Stadium (Capacity): Pitt Stadium (56,150)
Basketball Arena (Capacity): Fitzgerald Field House (6,798), Pittsburgh Civic Arena (17,159)
Chancellor: Mark A. Nordenberg
Athletic Director: Steven Pederson
Football Coach: Walt Harris
Basketball Coach: Ralph Willard
Sports Information Director: E.J. Borghetti

Providence College
Address: 549 River Avenue
Providence, RI 02918
Nickname: Friars
Telephone: (401) 865-2265
Basketball Arena (Capacity): Providence Civic Center (13,410)
President: Rev. Philip A. Smith, O.P.
Assistant VP for Athletics: John Marinatto
Basketball Coach: Tim Welsh
Sports Information Director: Tim Connor
Note: No football program.

Rutgers University
Address: 83 Rockefeller Road
Piscataway, NJ 08854-7005
Nickname: Scarlet Knights
Telephone: (732) 445-4200
Football Stadium (Capacity): Rutgers Stadium (42,000)
Basketball Arena (Capacity): Louis Brown Athletic Center (8,500)
President: Dr. Francis L. Lawrence
Athletic Director: Bob Mulcahy III
Football Coach: Terry Shea
Basketball Coach: Kevin Bannon
Sports Information Director: John Wooding

St. John's University
Address: 8000 Utopia Parkway
Jamaica, NY 11439
Nickname: Red Storm
Telephone: (718) 990-6367
Football Stadium (Capacity): DaSilva Memorial Field (3,000)
Basketball Arena (Capacity): Alumni Hall (6,008), Madison Square Garden (19,876)
President: Rev. Donald J. Harrington, C.M.
Athletic Director: Edward J. Manetta Jr.
Football Coach: Bob Ricca
Basketball Coach: Mike Jarvis
Sports Information Director: Dominic Scianna
Note: Division I-AA football.

Seton Hall University
Address: 400 South Orange Avenue
South Orange, NJ 07079
Nickname: Pirates
Telephone: (973) 761-9497
Basketball Arena (Capacity): Walsh Auditorium (3,200), The Meadowlands (20,029)
President: Monsignor Robert T. Sheeran
Athletic Director: Jeff Fogelson
Basketball Coach: Tommy Amaker
Sports Information Director: Marie Wozniak
Note: No football program.

College Sports Directory *(Cont.)*

Syracuse University
Address: Manley Field House
Syracuse, NY 13244-5020
Nickname: Orangemen
Telephone: (315) 443-2608
Football Stadium (Capacity): Carrier Dome (49,550)
Basketball Arena (Capacity): Carrier Dome (33,000)
Chancellor: Dr. Kenneth Shaw
Athletic Director: Jake Crouthamel
Football Coach: Paul Pasqualoni
Basketball Coach: Jim Boeheim
Sports Information Director: Sue Cornelius Edson

Temple University
Address: Vivacqua Hall, 4th Floor
1700 North Broad Street
Philadelphia, PA 19121-0842
Nickname: Owls
Telephone: (215) 204-7445
Football Stadium (Capacity): Veterans Stadium (66,592)
Basketball Arena (Capacity): Apollo of Temple (10,224)
President: Peter J. Liacouras
Athletic Director: Dave O'Brien
Football Coach: Bobby Wallace
Basketball Coach: John Chaney
Sports Information Director: Brian Kirschner
Note: Plays football in Big East, basketball in Atlantic 10 Conference.

Villanova University
Address: 800 Lancaster Avenue
Villanova, PA 19085
Nickname: Wildcats
Telephone: (610) 519-4110
Football Stadium (Capacity): Villanova Stadium (12,000)
Basketball Arena (Capacity): The Pavilion (6,500), First Union Spectrum (18,060), First Union Center (22,000)
President: Rev. Edmund Dobbin, O.S.A.
Athletic Director: Tim Hofferth
Football Coach: Andy Talley
Basketball Coach: Steve Lappas
Sports Information Director: Dean Kenefick
Note: Division I-AA football.

Virginia Tech
Address: Jamerson Athletic Center
Blacksburg, VA 24061
Nickname: Hokies
Telephone: (540) 231-6726
Football Stadium (Capacity): Lane Stadium/Worsham Field (51,907)
Basketball Arena (Capacity): Cassell Coliseum (10,052)
President: Dr. Paul Torgersen
Athletic Director: Jim Weaver
Football Coach: Frank Beamer
Basketball Coach: Ricky Stokes
Sports Information Director: Dave Smith
Note: Plays football in Big East, basketball in Atlantic 10.

West Virginia University
Address: P.O. Box 0877
Morgantown, WV 26507-0877
Nickname: Mountaineers
Telephone: (304) 293-2821
Football Stadium (Capacity): Mountaineer Field (63,500)
Basketball Arena (Capacity): WVU Coliseum (14,000)
President: David Hardesty
Athletic Director: Ed Pastilong
Football Coach: Don Nehlen
Basketball Coach: Gale Catlett
Sports Information Director: Shelley Poe

BIG TEN CONFERENCE
Address: 1500 West Higgins Road
Park Ridge, IL 60068
Telephone: (847) 696-1010
Commissioner: James E. Delany
Associate Commissioner: Mark Rudner

University of Illinois
Address: 1700 S 4th Street
Champaign, IL 61820
Nickname: Fighting Illini
Telephone: (217) 333-1390
Football Stadium (Capacity): Memorial Stadium (70,904)
Basketball Arena (Capacity): Assembly Hall (16,450)
President: James Stukel
Athletic Director: Ronald Guenther
Football Coach: Ron Turner
Men's Basketball Coach: Lon Kruger
Women's Basketball Coach: Theresa Grentz
Sports Information Director: Barbara Butler

Indiana University
Address: Assembly Hall
1001 E. 17th Street
Bloomington, IN 47408-1590
Nickname: Hoosiers
Telephone: (812) 855-2421
Football Stadium (Capacity): Memorial Stadium (52,354)
Basketball Arena (Capacity): Assembly Hall (17,357)
President: Myles Brand
Athletic Director: Clarence Doninger
Football Coach: Cam Cameron
Basketball Coach: Bob Knight
Sports Information Director: Kit Klingelhoffer

University of Iowa
Address: 157 Carver-Hawkeye Arena
Iowa City, IA 52242
Nickname: Hawkeyes
Telephone: (319) 335-9411
Football Stadium (Capacity): Kinnick Stadium (70,397)
Basketball Arena (Capacity): Carver-Hawkeye Arena (15,500)
President: Mary Sue Coleman
Athletic Director: Robert Bowlsby
Football Coach: Kirk Ferentz
Men's Basketball Coach: Steve Alford
Women's Basketball Coach: Angie Lee
Sports Information Director: Phil Haddy (Men's), Jen Foley (Women's)

University of Michigan
Address: 1000 S. State Street
Ann Arbor, MI 48109
Nickname: Wolverines
Telephone: (734) 763-4423
Football Stadium (Capacity): Michigan Stadium (107,501)
Basketball Arena (Capacity): Crisler Arena (13,562)
President: Lee Bollinger
Athletic Director: Tom Goss
Football Coach: Lloyd Carr
Basketball Coach: Brian Ellerbe
Sports Information Director: Bruce Madej

Michigan State University
Address: 401 Olds Hall
East Lansing, MI 48824
Nickname: Spartans
Telephone: (517) 355-2271
Football Stadium (Capacity): Spartan Stadium (72,027)

Michigan State University *(Cont.)*
Basketball Arena (Capacity): Jack Breslin Student
  Events Center (15,138)
President: M. Peter McPherson
Athletic Director: Clarence Underwood
Football Coach: Nick Saban
Basketball Coach: Tom Izzo
Sports Information Director: John Lewandowski

University of Minnesota
Address: 208 Bierman Athletic Building
                  Minneapolis, MN 55455
Nickname: Golden Gophers
Telephone: (612) 625-4090
Football Stadium (Capacity): Hubert H. Humphrey
  Metrodome (63,669)
Basketball Arena (Capacity): Williams Arena (14,625)
President: Mark Yudof
Athletic Director: Dr. Mark Dienhart
Football Coach: Len Mason
Basketball Coach: Dan Monson
Sports Information Director: Marc Ryan

Northwestern University
Address: 1501 Central Street
                  Evanston, IL 60208
Nickname: Wildcats
Telephone: (847) 491-3205
Football Stadium (Capacity): Ryan Field (47,130)
Basketball Arena (Capacity): Welsh-Ryan Arena (8,117)
President: Henry S. Bienen
Athletic Director: Rick Taylor
Football Coach: Randy Walker
Basketball Coach: Kevin O'Neill
Director of Media Services: Brad Hurlbut

Ohio State University
Address: 410 Woody Hayes Drive
                  St. John Arena, Room 124
                  Columbus, OH 43210
Nickname: Buckeyes
Telephone: (614) 292-6861
Football Stadium (Capacity): Ohio Stadium (91,470)
Basketball Arena (Capacity): Jerome Schottenstein
Center (19,000)
President: William Kirwin
Athletic Director: Andy Geiger
Football Coach: John Cooper
Basketball Coach: Jim O'Brien
Sports Information Director: Gerry Emig

Penn State University
Address: 101D Bryce Jordan Center
                  University Park, PA 16802
Nickname: Nittany Lions
Telephone: (814) 865-1757
Football Stadium (Capacity): Beaver Stadium (93,967)
Basketball Arena (Capacity): Bryce Jordan Center
  (15,000)
President: Dr. Graham Spanier
Athletic Director: Tim Curley
Football Coach: Joe Paterno
Men's Basketball Coach: Jerry Dunn
Women's Basketball Coach: Rene Portland
Sports Information Director: Jeff Nelson

Purdue University
Address: Mackey Arena, Room 15
                  West Lafayette, IN 47907
Nickname: Boilermakers
Telephone: (765) 494-3200

Purdue University *(Cont.)*
Football Stadium (Capacity): Ross-Ade Stadium
  (67,861)
Basketball Arena (Capacity): Mackey Arena (14,123)
President: Dr. Steven C. Beering
Athletic Director: Morgan Burke
Football Coach: Joe Tiller
Basketball Coach: Gene Keady
Sports Information Director: Jim Vruggink

University of Wisconsin
Address: 1440 Monroe Street
                  Madison, WI 53711
Nickname: Badgers
Telephone: (608) 262-1811
Football Stadium (Capacity): Camp Randall
  Stadium (76,129)
Basketball Arena (Capacity): Kohl Center (17,142)
Chancellor: David Ward
Athletic Director: Pat Richter
Football Coach: Barry Alvarez
Basketball Coach: Dick Bennett
Sports Information Director: Steve Malchow

BIG 12 CONFERENCE
Address: 2201 Stemmons Freeway, 28th floor
                  Dallas, TX 75207-2805
Telephone: (214) 742-1212
Commissioner: Kevin Weiberg
Director of Media Relations: Bo Carter

Baylor University
Address: 150 Bear Run
                  Waco, TX 76711
Nickname: Bears
Telephone: (254) 710-2743
Football Stadium (Capacity): Floyd Casey
  Stadium (50,000)
Basketball Arena (Capacity): Ferrell Center (10,078)
President: Robert Sloan
Athletic Director: Tom Stanton
Football Coach: Kevin Steele
Basketball Coach: Dave Bliss
Sports Information Directors: Scott Stricklin

University of Colorado
Address: Campus Box 357
                  Boulder, CO 80309
Nickname: Buffaloes
Telephone: (303) 492-5626
Football Stadium (Capacity): Folsom Field (51,808)
Basketball Arena (Capacity): Coors Event
  Center (11,198)
President: John Buechner
Athletic Director: Dick Tharpe
Football Coach: Gary Barnett
Men's Basketball Coach: Ricardo Patton
Women's Basketball Coach: Ceal Barry
Sports Information Director: David Plati

Iowa State University
Address: 1800 S. Fourth Street
                  Jacobson Building
                  Ames, IA 50011
Nickname: Cyclones
Telephone: (515) 294-3372
Football Stadium (Capacity): Jack Trice Stadium
  (43,000)
Basketball Arena (Capacity): James H. Hilton
Coliseum (14,044)
President: Dr. Martin C. Jischke

Iowa State University (Cont.)
Athletic Director: Gene Smith
Football Coach: Dan McCarney
Men's Basketball Coach: Larry Eustachy
Women's Basketball Coach: Bill Fennelly
Sports Information Director: Tom Kroeschell

University of Kansas
Address: Allen Field House, Room 104
Lawrence, KS 66045
Nickname: Jayhawks
Telephone: (785) 864-3417
Football Stadium (Capacity): Memorial
Stadium (50,250)
Basketball Arena (Capacity): Allen Field
House (16,300)
Chancellor: Robert Hemenway
Athletic Director: Dr. Bob Fredrick
Football Coach: Terry Allen
Men's Basketball Coach: Roy Williams
Women's Basketball Coach: Marian Washington
Sports Information Director: Doug Vance

Kansas State University
Address: 1800 College Ave., Suite 144
Manhattan, KS 66502
Nickname: Wildcats
Telephone: (785) 532-6735
Football Stadium (Capacity): KSU Stadium-Wagner
Field (50,000)
Basketball Arena (Capacity): Bramlage Coliseum
(13,500)
President: Dr. Jon Wefald
Athletic Director: Max Urick
Football Coach: Bill Snyder
Basketball Coach: Tom Asbury
Sports Information Director: Kent Brown

University of Missouri
Address: P.O. Box 677
Columbia, MO 65205
Nickname: Tigers
Telephone: (573) 882-3241
Football Stadium (Capacity): Faurot Field/Memorial
Stadium (62,000)
Basketball Arena (Capacity): Hearnes Center (13,300)
Chancellor: Dr. Richard Wallace
Athletic Director: Michael F. Alden
Football Coach: Larry Smith
Basketball Coach: Quin Snyder
Sports Information Director: Bob Brendel

University of Nebraska
Address: 116 South Stadium
Lincoln, NE 68588
Nickname: Cornhuskers
Telephone: (402) 472-2263
Football Stadium (Capacity): Memorial
Stadium (72,700)
Basketball Arena (Capacity): Bob Devaney Sports
Center (13,500)
President: L. Dennis Smith
Athletic Director: Bill Byrne
Football Coach: Frank Solich
Basketball Coach: Danny Nee
Sports Information Director: Chris Anderson

University of Oklahoma
Address: 180 W. Brooks, Room 235
Norman, OK 73019
Nickname: Sooners
Telephone: (405) 325-8231
Football Stadium (Capacity): Memorial Stadium/Owen
Field (75,004)
Basketball Arena (Capacity): Lloyd Noble
Center (11,100)
President: David Boren
Athletic Director: Joe Castiglione
Football Coach: Bob Stoops
Basketball Coach: Kelvin Sampson
Sports Information Director: Mike Prusinski

Oklahoma State University
Address: 424 Squires Street
Stillwater, OK 74078
Nickname: Cowboys
Telephone: (405) 707-7830
Football Stadium (Capacity): Lewis Field (50,614)
Basketball Arena (Capacity): Gallagher-Iba
Arena (6,381)
President: Dr. James Halligan
Athletic Director: Terry Don Phillips
Football Coach: Bob Simmons
Basketball Coach: Eddie Sutton
Sports Information Director: Steve Buzzard

University of Texas
Address: P.O. Box 7399
Austin, TX 78713
Nickname: Longhorns
Telephone: (512) 471-7437
Football Stadium (Capacity): Darrell K. Royal/Texas
Memorial Stadium (80,216)
Basketball Arena (Capacity): Erwin Special Events
Center (16,231)
Chancellor: Dr. William Cunningham
Athletic Director: DeLoss Dodds
Football Coach: Mack Brown
Basketball Coach: Rick Barnes
Sports Information Director: John Bianco

Texas A&M University
Address: John Koldus Building, Room 222
College Station, TX 77843-1228
Nickname: Aggies
Telephone: (409) 845-5725
Football Stadium (Capacity): Kyle Field (80,200)
Basketball Arena (Capacity): Reed Arena (12,500)
President: Dr. Ray Bowen
Athletic Director: Wally Groff
Football Coach: R.C. Slocum
Basketball Coach: Melvin Watkins
Sports Information Director: Alan Cannon

Texas Tech University
Address: Box 43021
Lubbock, TX 79409
Nickname: Red Raiders
Telephone: (806) 742-2770
Football Stadium (Capacity): Jones Stadium (50,500)
Basketball Arena (Capacity): United Spirit Arena
(15,000)
President: Donald Harragan
Athletic Director: Gerald Myers
Football Coach: Spike Dykes
Men's Basketball Coach: James Dickey
Women's Basketball Coach: Marsha Sharp
Sports Information Director: Kent Partridge

BIG WEST CONFERENCE
Address: 2 Corporate Park, Suite 206
          Irvine, CA 92606
Telephone: (949) 261-2525
Commissioner: Dennis Farrell
Publicity Director: Mike Daniels

Boise State University
Address: 1910 University Drive
          Boise, ID 83725
Nickname: Broncos
Telephone: (208) 426-1288
Football Stadium (Capacity) Lyle Smith Field (30,000)
Basketball Arena (Capacity): BSU Pavilion (13,000)
President: Dr. Charles Ruch
Athletic Director: Gene Bleymaier
Football Coach: Dirk Koetter
Basketball Coach: Rod Jensen
Sports Information Director: Max Corbet

Cal Poly
Address: One Grand Avenue
          San Luis Obispo, CA 93407
Nickname: Mustangs
Telephone: (805) 756-6531
Football Stadium (Capacity): Mustang Stadium (8,500)
Basketball Arena (Capacity): Mott Gym (3,200)
President: Dr. Warren J. Baker
Athletic Director: John McCutcheon
Football Coach: Larry Welsh
Basketball Coach: Jeff Schneider
Sports Information Director: Jason Sullivan

University of California–Irvine
Address: Intercollegiate Athletics, Crawford Hall
          Irvine, CA 92697
Nickname: Anteaters
Telephone: (949) 824-6931
Basketball Arena (Capacity): Bren Event Center (5,000)
Chancellor: Ralph Cicerone
Athletic Director: Dan Guerrero
Basketball Coach: Pat Douglass
Sports Information Director: Bob Olson
Note: No football program.

University of California–Santa Barbara
Address: Department of Athletics
          1000 Robertson Gymnasium
          Santa Barbara, CA 93106-7211
Nickname: Gauchos
Telephone: (805) 893-3428
Basketball Arena (Capacity): Thunderdome (6,000)
Chancellor: Henry Yang
Athletic Director: Gary Cunningham
Basketball Coach: Bob Williams
Sports Information Director: Bill Mahoney
Note: No football program.

California State University–Fullerton
Address: 800 North State College Boulevard
          P.O. Box 6810
          Fullerton, CA 92834-6810
Nickname: Titans
Telephone: (714) 278-3970
Basketball Arena (Capacity): Titan Gym (3,500)
President: Dr. Milton A. Gordon
Athletic Director: John Easterbrook
Basketball Coach: Bob Hawking
Sports Information Director: Mel Franks
Note: No football program.

University of Idaho
Address: Kibbie Activities Center
          P.O. Box 442302
          Moscow, ID 83844-2302
Nickname: Vandals
Telephone: (208) 885-0211
Football Stadium (Capacity): Martin Stadium(37,600)
Basketball Arena (Capacity): Kibbie Dome (10,000)
President: Dr. Robert Hoover
Athletic Director: Mike Bohn
Football Coach: Chris Tormey
Basketball Coach: David Farrar
Sports Information Director: Becky Paull

Long Beach State University
Address: 1250 Bellflower Boulevard
          Long Beach, CA 90840-7701
Nicknames: 49ers, The Beach
Telephone: (562) 985-7565
Basketball Arena (Capacity): The Pyramid (5,000)
President: Dr. Robert C. Maxson
Athletic Director: Bill Shumard
Basketball Coach: Wayne Morgan
Sports Information Director: Steve Janisch
Note: No football program.

University of Nevada–Reno
Address: Legacy Hall
          Athletic Department Room 232
          Reno, NV 89557-0110
Nickname: Wolf Pack
Telephone: (775) 784-6900
Football Stadium (Capacity): Mackay Stadium
  (31,545)
Basketball Arena (Capacity): Lawlor Event Center
  (11,200)
President: Dr. Joe Crowley
Athletic Director: Chris Ault
Football Coach: Jeff Tisdel
Basketball Coach: Trent Johnson
Interim Sports Information Director: Jason Houston

New Mexico State University
Address: Department of Athletics, MSC 3145
          P.O. Box 30001
          Las Cruces, NM 88003
Nickname: Aggies
Telephone: (505) 646-4126
Football Stadium (Capacity): Aggie Memorial
  Stadium (30,343)
Basketball Arena (Capacity): Pan American
  Center (13,071)
President: Dr. William Conroy
Athletic Director: Brian Faison
Football Coach: Tony Samuel
Basketball Coach: Lou Henson
Sports Information Director: Heath Nielsen

University of North Texas
Address: P.O. Box 311397
          Denton, TX 76203-1397
Nickname: Eagles, Mean Green
Telephone: (940) 565-2664
Football Stadium (Capacity): Fouts Field (30,500)
Basketball Arena (Capacity): Super Pit (10,032)
President: Dr. Alfred F. Hurley
Athletic Director: Craig Helwig
Football Coach: Darrell Dickey
Basketball Coach: Vic Trilly
Sports Information Director: Sean Johnson

University of the Pacific
Address: 3601 Pacific Avenue
            Stockton, CA 95211
Nickname: Tigers
Telephone: (209) 946-2472
Football Stadium (Capacity): Amos Alonzo Stagg
  Memorial Stadium (30,000)
Basketball Arena (Capacity): Alex G. Spanos
  Center (6,150)
President: Dr. Donald DeRosa
Interim Athletic Director: John Dunning
Basketball Coach: Bob Thomason
Sports Information Director: Mike Millerick
Note: No football program.

Utah State University
Address: 7400 Old Main Hill
           Logan, UT 84322-7400
Nickname: Aggies
Telephone: (435) 797-1850
Football Stadium (Capacity): Romney Stadium
  (30,000)
Basketball Arena (Capacity): The Smith
  Spectrum (11,000)
President: Dr. George H. Emert
Athletic Director: Rance Pugmire
Football Coach: Dave Arslanian
Basketball Coach: Stew Morrill
Sports Information Director: Mike Strauss

CONFERENCE USA
Address: 35 East Wacker Drive, Suite 650
           Chicago, IL 60601
Telephone: (312) 553-0483
Comissioner: Michael Slive
Media Relations Director: Brian Teter

University of Alabama–Birmingham
Address: Bartow Arena
           617 13th Street South
           Birmingham, AL 35294
Nickname: Blazers
Telephone: (205) 934-7252
Football Stadium (Capacity): Legion Field (83,091)
Basketball Arena (Capacity): Bartow Arena (8,500)
President: Dr. Ann Reynolds
Athletic Director: Gene Bartow
Football Coach: Watson Brown
Basketball Coach: Murray Bartow
Sports Information Director: Grant Shingleton

University of Cincinnati
Address: 309 Lawrence Hall
           Cincinnati, OH 45221-0021
Nickname: Bearcats
Telephone: (513) 556-5191
Football Stadium (Capacity): Nippert Stadium (35,000)
Basketball Arena (Capacity): Myrl Shoemaker
  Center (13,176)
President: Dr. Joseph A. Steger
Athletic Director: Bob Goin
Football Coach: Rick Minter
Basketball Coach: Bob Huggins
Assistant Athletic Director/Media Relations: Tom
  Hathaway

DePaul University
Address: 1011 West Belden Avenue
           Chicago, IL 60614
Nickname: Blue Demons
Telephone: (773) 325-7526
Basketball Arena (Capacity): Rosemont Horizon (18,000)

DePaul University (Cont.)
President: Rev. John P. Minogue, C.M.
Athletic Director: Bill Bradshaw
Basketball Coach: Pat Kennedy
Sports Information Director: John Lanctot
Note: No football program.

University of Houston
Address: 3100 Cullen Boulevard
           Houston, TX 77204
Nickname: Cougars
Telephone: (713) 743-9370
Football Stadium (Capacity): Robertson Stadium
(33,000)
Basketball Arena (Capacity): Hofheinz Pavilion
(8,479)
Chancellor and President: Dr. Arthur Smith
Athletic Director: Chet Gladchuk
Football Coach: Kim Helton
Basketball Coach: Clyde Drexler
Sports Information Director: Chris Burkhalter

University of Louisville
Address: Athletic Department,
           Student Activities Center
           Louisville, KY 40292
Nickname: Cardinals
Telephone: (502) 852-5732
Football Stadium (Capacity): Papa John's Cardinal
  Stadium (42,000)
Basketball Arena (Capacity): Freedom Hall (18,865)
President: Dr. John Schumaker
Athletic Director: Tom Jurich
Football Coach: John L. Smith
Basketball Coach: Denny Crum
Sports Information Director: Kenny Klein

Marquette University
Address: P.O. Box 1881
           Milwaukee, WI 53201-1881
Nickname: Golden Eagles
Telephone: (414) 288-7447
Basketball Arena (Capacity): Bradley Center (19,150)
President: Rev. Robert A. Wild, S.J.
Athletic Director: Bill Cords
Basketball Coach: Tom Crean
Sports Information Director: Kathleen Hohl
Note: No football program.

University of Memphis
Address: 570 Normal Street, Room 203
           Memphis, TN 38152
Nickname: Tigers
Telephone: (901) 678-2337
Football Stadium (Capacity): Liberty Bowl Memorial
  Stadium/Rex Dockery Field (62,380)
Basketball Arena (Capacity): The Pyramid (20,142)
President: Dr. V. Lane Rawlins
Athletic Director: R.C. Johnson
Football Coach: Rip Scherer
Basketball Coach: Tic Price
Sports Information Director: Bob Winn

University of North Carolina–Charlotte
Address: 9201 University City Boulevard
           UNC–Charlotte
           Student Activity Center
           Charlotte, NC 28223-0001
Nickname: 49ers
Telephone: (704) 547-4937
Basketball Arena (Capacity): Dale F. Halton Arena (9,100)

University of North Carolina–Charlotte *(Cont.)*
Chancellor: James H. Woodward
Athletic Director: Judy W. Rose
Basketball Coach: Bobby Lute
Sports Information Director: Tom Whitestone
Note: No football program.

Saint Louis University
Address: 221 North Grand Boulevard, Room 38
            St. Louis, MO 63103-2097
Nickname: Billikens
Telephone: (314) 977-3462
Basketball Arena (Capacity): Kiel Center (20,000)
President: Rev. Lawrence Biondi, S.J.
Athletic Director: Doug Woolard
Basketball Coach: Lorenzo Romar
Sports Information Director: Doug McIlhagga
Note: No football program.

University of South Florida
Address: 4202 East Fowler Ave., PED 214
            Tampa, FL 33620
Nickname: Bulls
Telephone: (813) 974-2125
Football Stadium (Capacity): Raymond James
  Stadium (46,500)
Basketball Arena (Capacity): Sun Dome (10,411)
Interim President: Richard E. Peck
Athletic Director: Paul Griffin
Football Coach: Jim Leavitt
Basketball Coach: Seth Greenberg
Sports Information Director: John Gerdes
Note: The football program began with the 1997 season.

University of Southern Mississippi
Address: P.O. Box 5161
            Hattiesburg, MS 39406
Nickname: Golden Eagles
Telephone: (601) 266-4503
Football Stadium (Capacity): M.M. Roberts
  Stadium (33,000)
Basketball Arena (Capacity): Reed Green
  Coliseum (8,095)
President: Dr. Horace Fleming
Athletic Director: Richard Giannini
Football Coach: Jeff Bower
Basketball Coach: James Green
Sports Information Director: Regiel Napier

Tulane University
Address: James Wilson Jr. Center for
            Intercollegiate Athletics
            New Orleans, LA 70118
Nickname: Green Wave
Telephone: (504) 865-5501
Football Stadium (Capacity): Louisiana Superdome
  (69,767)
Basketball Arena (Capacity): Fogelman Arena (3,600)
President: Scott Cowen
Athletic Director: Scott Devine
Football Coach: Chris Scelfo
Basketball Coach: Perry Clark
Interim Sports Information Director: Rich Paige

IVY LEAGUE
Address: 330 Alexander Street
            Princeton, NJ 08544
Telephone: (609) 258-6426
Executive Director: Jeff Orleans
Publicity Director: Chuck Yrigoyen

Brown University
Address: 235 Hope Street, Providence, RI 02912
Nickname: Bears
Telephone: (401) 863-2219
Football Stadium (Capacity): Brown Stadium (20,000)
Basketball Arena (Capacity): Paul Bailey Pizzitola
  Memorial Sports Center (3,100)
President: E. Gordon Gee
Athletic Director: David Roach
Football Coach: Phil Estes
Basketball Coach: Glen Miller
Sports Information Director: Christopher Humm

Columbia University
Address: Dodge Physical Fitness Center
            3030 Broadway
            New York, NY 10027
Nickname: Lions
Telephone: (212) 854-2534
Football Stadium (Capacity): Lawrence A. Wien
  Stadium at Baker Field (17,000)
Basketball Arena (Capacity): Levien Gymnasium (3,400)
President: Dr. George Rupp
Athletic Director: Dr. John Reeves
Football Coach: Ray Tellier
Basketball Coach: Armond Hill
Director of Athletic Communications: Al Langer

Cornell University
Address: Teagle Hall, Campus Road
            Ithaca, NY 14853-6701
Nickname: Big Red
Telephone: (607) 255-5220
Football Stadium (Capacity): Schoellkopf Field (25,597)
Basketball Arena (Capacity): Newman Arena (4,473)
President: Hunter R. Rawlings III
Athletic Director: J. Andrew Noel Jr.
Football Coach: Pete Mangurian
Basketball Coach: Scott Thompson
Sports Information Director: Patrick Gillespie

Dartmouth College
Address: 6083 Alumni Gym
            Hanover, NH 03755-3512
Nickname: Big Green
Telephone: (603) 646-2465
Football Stadium (Capacity): Memorial Field (20,416)
Basketball Arena (Capacity): Leede Arena (2,100)
President: James Wright
Athletic Director: Richard G. Jaeger
Football Coach: John Lyons
Basketball Coach: Dave Faucher
Sports Information Director: Kathy Slattery

Harvard University
Address: 65 North Harvard St.
            Murr Center
            Boston, MA 02163
Nickname: Crimson
Telephone: (617) 495-2206
Football Stadium (Capacity): Harvard Stadium (30,898)
Basketball Arena (Capacity): Lavietes Pavilion (2,198)
President: Neil L. Rudenstine
Athletic Director: William J. Cleary Jr.
Football Coach: Tim Murphy
Basketball Coach: Frank Sullivan
Sports Information Director: John Veneziano

University of Pennsylvania
Address: Weightman Hall South
            235 South 33rd Street
            Philadelphia, PA 19104-6322
Nickname: Quakers

University of Pennsylvania *(Cont.)*
Telephone: (215) 898-6128
Football Stadium (Capacity): Franklin Field (52,593)
Basketball Arena (Capacity): The Palestra (8,700)
President: Dr. Judith Rodin
Athletic Director: Steven Bilsky
Football Coach: Al Bagnoli
Basketball Coach: Fran Dunphy
Director, Athletic Communications: Shaun May

Princeton University
Address:　　P.O. Box 71
　　　　　　Jadwin Gym
　　　　　　Princeton, NJ 08544
Nickname: Tigers
Telephone: (609) 258-3568
Football Stadium (Capacity): Princeton Stadium
　(30,000),
Basketball Arena (Capacity): Jadwin Gym (7,230)
President: Harold Shapiro
Athletic Director: Gary D. Walters
Football Coach: Steve Tosches
Basketball Coach: Bill Carmody
Sports Information Director: Jerry Price

Yale University
Address:　　Box 208216
　　　　　　New Haven, CT 06520
Nickname: Bulldogs, Elis
Telephone: (203) 432-1456
Football Stadium (Capacity): Yale Bowl (64,269)
Basketball Arena (Capacity): John J. Lee
　Amphitheater (3,100)
President: Richard C. Levin
Athletic Director: Tom Beckett
Football Coach: Jack Siedlecki
Basketball Coach: James Jones
Sports Information Director: Steve Conn

MID-AMERICAN CONFERENCE
Address:　　24 Public Square 15th floor
　　　　　　Cleveland, OH 44113
Telephone: (216) 566-4622
Commissioner: Rick Chryst
Director of Communications: Gary Richter

Ball State University
Address:　　2000 University Avenue
　　　　　　Muncie, IN 47306
Nickname: Cardinals
Telephone: (765) 285-2242
Football Stadium (Capacity): Ball State University
　Stadium (21,581)
Basketball Arena (Capacity): University Arena
　(11,500)
President: Dr. John E. Worthen
Athletic Director: Andrea Seger
Football Coach: Bill Lynch
Basketball Coach: Ray McCallum
Athletic Communications Director: Joe Hernandez

Bowling Green University
Address:　　Perry Stadium East
　　　　　　Bowling Green, OH 43403
Nickname: Falcons
Telephone: (419) 372-2401
Football Stadium (Capacity): Doyt L. Perry Stadium
　(30,599)
Basketball Arena (Capacity): Anderson Arena (5,000)
President: Dr. Sidney A. Ribeau
Athletic Director: Paul Krebs
Football Coach: Gary Blackney
Basketball Coach: Dan Dakich
Sports Information Director: Steve Barr

Central Michigan University
Address:　　West Hall
　　　　　　Mount Pleasant, MI 48859
Nickname: Chippewas
Telephone: (517) 774-3277
Football Stadium (Capacity): Kelly/Shorts
　Stadium (30,199)
Basketball Arena (Capacity): Rose Arena (5,200)
President: Leonard Plachta
Athletic Director: Herb Deromedi
Football Coach: Dick Flynn
Basketball Coach: Jay Smith
Sports Information Director: Fred Stabley, Jr.

Eastern Michigan University
Address:　　371 Convocation Center
　　　　　　Ypsilanti, MI 48197
Nickname: Eagles
Telephone: (734) 487-1050
Football Stadium (Capacity): Rynearson
　Stadium (30,200)
Basketball Arena (Capacity): Convocation Center
　(8,857)
President: Dr. William Shelton
Athletic Director: Dr. David L. Diles
Football Coach: Rick Rasnick
Basketball Coach: Milton Barnes
Sports Information Director: Jim Streeter

Kent State University
Address:　　P.O. Box 5190
　　　　　　Kent, OH 44242
Nickname: Golden Flashes
Telephone: (330) 672-2110
Football Stadium (Capacity): Dix Stadium (30,520)
Basketball Arena (Capacity): Memorial Athletic and
　Convocation Center (6,327)
President: Dr. Carol A. Cartwright
Athletic Director: Laing Kennedy
Football Coach: Dan Pees
Basketball Coach: Gary Waters
Sports Information Director: Will Roleson

Miami University
Address:　　230 Millett Hall
　　　　　　Oxford, OH 45056
Nickname: Red Hawks
Telephone: (513) 529-3113
Football Stadium (Capacity): Yager Stadium (30,012)
Basketball Arena (Capacity): Millett Hall (9,200)
President: Dr. James Garland
Athletic Director: Joel Maturi
Football Coach: Terry Hoeppner
Basketball Coach: Charlie Coles
Sports Information Director: Mike Wolf

Ohio University
Address:　　P.O. Box 689
　　　　　　Convocation Center
　　　　　　Athens, OH 45701-2979
Nickname: Bobcats
Telephone: (740) 593-1174
Football Stadium (Capacity): Don Peden
　Stadium (20,000)
Basketball Arena (Capacity): Convocation
　Center (13,000)
President: Dr. Robert Glidden
Athletic Director: Thomas Boeh
Football Coach: Jim Grobe
Basketball Coach: Larry Hunter
Director of Sports Media Services: Heather CzeCzok

University of Toledo
Address: 2801 W. Bancroft St.
Toledo, OH 43606
Nickname: Rockets
Telephone: (419) 530-3790
Football Stadium (Capacity): Glass Bowl (26,248)
Basketball Arena (Capacity): Savage Hall (9,000)
President: Vik J. Kapoor
Athletic Director: Pete Liske
Football Coach: Gary Pinkel
Basketball Coach: Stan Joplin
Sports Information Director: Paul Helgren

Western Michigan University
Address: Kalamazoo, MI 49008
Nickname: Broncos
Telephone: (616) 387-4138
Football Stadium (Capacity): Waldo Stadium (30,200)
Basketball Arena (Capacity): University Arena (5,800)
President: Dr. Elson Floyd
Athletic Director: Kathy Beauregard
Football Coach: Gary Darnell
Basketball Coach: Bob Donewald
Sports Information Director: John Beatty

PACIFIC-10 CONFERENCE
Address: 800 S. Broadway, Suite 400
Walnut Creek, CA 94596
Telephone: (925) 932-4411
Commissioner: Thomas C. Hansen
Publicity Director: Jim Muldoon

University of Arizona
Address: 106 McHale Center
Tuscon, AZ 85721
Nickname: Wildcats
Telephone: (520) 621-4163
Football Stadium (Capacity): Arizona Stadium (57,803)
Basketball Arena (Capacity): McHale Center (14,489)
President: Dr. Peter Likins
Athletic Director: Jim Livengood
Football Coach: Dick Tomey
Basketball Coach: Lute Olson
Sports Information Director: Tom Duddleston

Arizona State University
Address: ICA Building, Room 105
Tempe, AZ 85287-2505
Nickname: Sun Devils
Telephone: (602) 965-6592
Football Stadium (Capacity): Sun Devil Stadium (74,186)
Basketball Arena (Capacity): Wells Fargo Arena (14,198)
President: Lattie Coor
Athletic Director: Dr. Kevin White
Football Coach: Bruce Snyder
Basketball Coach: Rob Evans
Sports Information Director: Mark Brand

University of California at Berkeley
Address: 210 Memorial Stadium
Berkeley, CA 94720
Nickname: Golden Bears
Telephone: (510) 642-5363
Football Stadium (Capacity): Memorial Stadium (75,028)
Basketball Arena (Capacity): Haas Pavilion (12,300)
Chancellor: Robert Berdahl
Athletic Director: John Kasser
Football Coach: Tom Holmoe
Basketball Coach: Ben Braun
Sports Information Director: Herb Benenson

University of California at Los Angeles
Address: P.O. Box 24044
Los Angeles, CA 90024-0044
Nickname: Bruins
Telephone: (310) 206-6831
Football Stadium (Capacity): Rose Bowl (102,083)
Basketball Arena (Capacity): Pauley Pavilion (12,819)
Chancellor: Albert Carnesale
Athletic Director: Peter T. Dalis
Football Coach: Bob Toledo
Basketball Coach: Steve Lavin
Sports Information Director: Marc Dellins

University of Oregon
Address: Len Casanova Athletic Center
2727 Leo Harris Parkway
Eugene, OR 97401
Nickname: Ducks
Telephone: (541) 346-4481
Football Stadium (Capacity): Autzen Stadium (41,698)
Basketball Arena (Capacity): McArthur Court (9,738)
President: David Frohnmayer
Athletic Director: Bill Moos
Football Coach: Mike Bellotti
Basketball Coach: Ernie Kent
Director of Media Services: David Williford

Oregon State University
Address: Gill Coliseum
Corvallis, OR 97331
Nickname: Beavers
Telephone: (541) 737-3720
Football Stadium (Capacity): Reser Stadium (35,362)
Basketball Arena (Capacity): Gill Coliseum (10,400)
President: Dr. Paul Risser
Athletic Director: Mitch Barnhart
Football Coach: Dennis Erickson
Basketball Coach: Eddie Payne
Sports Information Director: Hal Cowan

University of Southern California
Address: Los Angeles, CA 90089-0602
Nickname: Trojans
Telephone: (213) 740-8480
Football Stadium (Capacity): Los Angeles Memorial Coliseum (94,159)
Basketball Arena (Capacity): Los Angeles Sports Arena (15,509)
President: Dr. Steven Sample
Athletic Director: Mike Garrett
Football Coach: Paul Hackett
Basketball Coach: Henry Bibby
Sports Information Director: Tim Tessalone

Stanford University
Address: Arrillaga Family Sports Center
Stanford, CA 94305
Nickname: Cardinal
Telephone: (650) 723-4418
Football Stadium (Capacity): Stanford Stadium (85,500)
Basketball Arena (Capacity): Maples Pavilion (7,391)
President: Dr. Gerhard Casper
Athletic Director: Dr. Ted Leland
Football Coach: Tyrone Willingham
Men's Basketball Coach: Mike Montgomery
Women's Basketball Coach: Tara Van Derveer
Sports Information Director: Gary Migdol

University of Washington
Address: UW Media Relations
Graves Building, Box 354070
Seattle, WA 98195-4070
Nickname: Huskies
Telephone: (206) 543-2230
Football Stadium (Capacity): Husky Stadium (72,500)
Basketball Arena (Capacity): Key Arena (17,072)
President: Richard L. McCormick
Athletic Director: Barbara Hedges
Football Coach: Rick Neuheisel
Basketball Coach: Bob Bender
Sports Information Director: Jim Daves

Washington State University
Address: P.O. Box 641602
Pullman, WA 99164-1602
Nickname: Cougars
Telephone: (509) 335-2684
Football Stadium (Capacity): Martin Stadium (37,600)
Basketball Arena (Capacity): Friel Court (12,058)
President: Samuel H. Smith
Athletic Director: Rick Dickson
Football Coach: Paul Graham
Basketball Coach: Kevin Eastman
Sports Information Director: Rod Commons

SOUTHEASTERN CONFERENCE
Address: 2201 Richard Arrington Boulevard
Birmingham, AL 35203
Telephone: (205) 458-3000
Commissioner: Roy Kramer
Publicity Director: Charles Bloom

University of Alabama
Address: P.O. Box 870391
323 Paul Bryant Drive
Tuscaloosa, AL 35487
Nickname: Crimson Tide
Telephone: (205) 348-6084
Football Stadium (Capacity): Bryant-Denny
Stadium (83,818)
Basketball Arena (Capacity): Coleman
Coliseum (15,043)
President: Dr. Andrew Sorensen
Interim Athletic Director: Finus Gaston
Football Coach: Mike DuBose
Men's Basketball Coach: Mark Gottfried
Women's Basketball Coach: Rick Moody
Sports Information Director: Larry White

University of Arkansas
Address: Broyles Athletic Center
Fayetteville, AR 72701
Nickname: Razorbacks
Telephone: (501) 575-2751
Football Stadium (Capacity): Razorback Stadium
(50,000); War Memorial Stadium (53,727)
Basketball Arena (Capacity): Bud Walton
Arena (19,200)
Chancellor: Dr. John White
Athletic Director: Frank Broyles
Football Coach: Nutt Houston
Basketball Coach: Nolan Richardson
Sports Information Director: Rick Schaeffer

Auburn University
Address: P.O. Box 351
Auburn, AL 36831-0351
Nickname: Tigers
Telephone: (334) 844-9800
Football Stadium (Capacity): Jordan Hare
Stadium (85,214)
Basketball Arena (Capacity): Beard-Eaves Memorial
Coliseum (13,500)
President: Dr. William V. Muse
Athletic Director: David Housel
Football Coach: Tommy Tuberville
Men's Basketball Coach: Cliff Ellis
Women's Basketball Coach: Joe Ciampi
Interim Sports Information Director: Meredith Jenkins

University of Florida
Address: P.O. Box 14485
Gainesville, FL 32604
Nickname: Gators
Telephone: (352) 375-4683
Football Stadium (Capacity): Ben Hill Griffin Stadium
at Florida Field (83,000)
Basketball Arena (Capacity): Stephen C. O'Connell
Center (12,000)
Interim President: Dr. Charles Young
Athletic Director: Jeremy Foley
Football Coach: Steve Spurrier
Men's Basketball Coach: Billy Donovan
Women's Basketball Coach: Carol Ross
Sports Information Director: John Humenik

University of Georgia
Address: P.O. Box 1472
Athens, GA 30603-1472
Nickname: Bulldogs
Telephone: (706) 542-1621
Football Stadium (Capacity): Sanford Stadium (86,117)
Basketball Arena (Capacity): Stegman Coliseum
(10,523)
President: Dr. Michael F. Adams
Athletic Director: Vince Dooley
Football Coach: Jim Donnan
Men's Basketball Coach: Jim Harrick
Women's Basketball Coach: Andy Landers
Sports Information Director: Claude Felton

University of Kentucky
Address: 23 Memorial Coliseum
Lexington, KY 40506-0019
Nickname: Wildcats
Telephone: (606) 257-3838
Football Stadium (Capacity): Commonwealth
Stadium (68,000)
Basketball Arena (Capacity): Rupp Arena (24,000)
President: Dr. Charles Wethington Jr.
Athletic Director: C. M. Newton
Football Coach: Hal Mumme
Basketball Coach: Orlando (Tubby) Smith
Sports Information Director: Rena Vicini

Louisiana State University

Address: P.O. Box 25095
Baton Rouge, LA 70894
Nickname: Fighting Tigers
Telephone: (225) 388-8226
Football Stadium (Capacity): Tiger Stadium (80,000)
Basketball Arena (Capacity): Pete Maravich
Assembly Center (14,164)
Chancellor: Dr. Mark Emmert
Athletic Director: Joe Dean
Football Coach: Gerry DiNardo
Men's Basketball Coach: John Brady
Women's Basketball Coach: Sue Gunther
Sports Information Director: Herb Vincent

University of Mississippi

Address: P.O. Box 217
University, MS 38677
Nickname: Rebels
Telephone: (601) 232-7522
Football Stadium (Capacity): Vaught-Hemingway
Stadium/Hollingsworth Field (50,577)
Basketball Arena (Capacity): C.M. (Tad) Smith
Coliseum (8,135)
Chancellor: Dr. Robert C. Khayat
Athletic Director: John Schafer
Football Coach: David Cutcliffe
Basketball Coach: Rod Barnes
Sports Information Director: Langston Rogers

Mississippi State University

Address: P.O. Box 5308
Mississippi St., MS 39762
Nickname: Bulldogs
Telephone: (601) 325-2703
Football Stadium (Capacity): Scott Field (40,656)
Basketball Arena (Capacity): Humphrey
Coliseum (10,500)
President: Malcolm Portera
Athletic Director: Larry Templeton
Football Coach: Jackie Sherrill
Basketball Coach: Rick Stansbury
Sports Information Director: Mike Nemeth

University of South Carolina

Address: Rex Enright Athletic Center
1300 Rosewood Drive
Columbia, SC 29208
Nickname: Gamecocks
Telephone: (803) 777-5204
Football Stadium (Capacity): Williams-Brice
Stadium (80,250)
Basketball Arena (Capacity): Frank McGuire
Arena (12,401)
President: Dr. John Palms
Athletic Director: Dr. Mike McGee
Football Coach: Lou Holtz
Basketball Coach: Eddie Fogler
Sports Information Director: Kerry Tharp

University of Tennessee

Address: P.O. Box 15016
Knoxville, TN 37901
Nickname: Volunteers
Telephone: (423) 974-1212
Football Stadium (Capacity): Neyland Stadium (102,854)
Basketball Arena (Capacity): Thompson-Boling Arena
and Assembly Center (24,535)
President: J. Wade Gilley
Athletic Director: Doug Dickey
Football Coach: Phillip Fulmer

University of Tennessee *(Cont.)*

Men's Basketball Coach: Jerry Green
Women's Basketball Coach: Pat Summitt
Sports Information Directors: Bud Ford (Men's),
Debby Jennings (Women's)

Vanderbilt University

Address: P.O. Box 120158
Nashville, TN 37212
Nickname: Commodores
Telephone: (615) 322-4121
Football Stadium (Capacity): Vanderbilt Stadium
(41,600)
Basketball Arena (Capacity): Memorial Gym (14,100)
Chancellor: Joe B. Wyatt
Athletic Director: Todd Turner
Football Coach: Woody Widenhofer
Men's Basketball Coach: Kevin Stallings
Women's Basketball Coach: Jen Foster
Sports Information Director: Rod Williamson

WESTERN ATHLETIC CONFERENCE

Address: 9250 East Costilla Avenue, Suite 300
Englewood, CO 80112
Telephone: (303) 799-9221
Commissioner: Karl Benson
Publicity Director: Jeff Hurd

Air Force

Address: 2169 Field House Drive
USAF Academy, CO 80840-9500
Nickname: Falcons
Telephone: (719) 333-2313
Football Stadium (Capacity): Falcon Stadium (52,480)
Basketball Arena (Capacity): Clune Arena (6,002)
President: Lt. Gen. Tad Oelstrom
Athletic Director: Col. Randall W. Spetman
Football Coach: Fisher DeBerry
Basketball Coach: Reggie Minton
Sports Information Director: David Kellogg

Brigham Young University

Address: 30 Smith Field House
Provo, UT 84602
Nickname: Cougars
Telephone: (801) 378-4911
Football Stadium (Capacity): Cougar Stadium (65,000)
Basketball Arena (Capacity): Marriott Center (23,000)
President: Merrill J. Bateman
Athletic Director: Val Hale
Football Coach: LaVell Edwards
Basketball Coach: Steve Cleveland
Sports Information Directors: Brett Pyne and
Jeff Reynolds

Colorado State University

Address: McGraw Athletic Center
Moby Arena
Fort Collins, CO 80523
Nickname: Rams
Telephone: (970) 491-5300
Football Stadium (Capacity): Hughes Stadium (30,000)
Basketball Arena (Capacity): Moby Arena (8,745)
President: Dr. Albert C. Yates
Athletic Director: Tim Weiser
Football Coach: Sonny Lubick
Basketball Coach: Ritchie McKay
Sports Information Director: Gary Ozello

Fresno State University
Address: 5305 N. Campus Drive, Room 153
              Fresno, CA 93740-8020
Nickname: Bulldogs
Telephone: (559) 278-5091
Football Stadium (Capacity): Bulldog
  Stadium (41,031)
Basketball Arena (Capacity): Selland Arena (10,220)
President: Dr. John Welty
Athletic Director: Dr. Al Bohl
Football Coach: Pat Hill
Basketball Coach: Jerry Tarkanian
Sports Information Director: Steve Weakland

University of Hawaii
Address: 1337 Lower Campus Road
              Honolulu, HI 96822-2370
Nickname: Rainbow Warriors
Telephone: (808) 956-7523
Football Stadium (Capacity): Aloha Stadium (50,000)
Basketball Arena (Capacity): Stan Sheriff Center
  (10,225)
President: Dr. Kenneth Mortimer
Athletic Director: Hugh Yoshida
Football Coach: June Jones
Basketball Coach: Riley Wallace
Sports Information Director: Lois Manin

University of Nevada at Las Vegas
Address: 4505 Maryland Parkway
              Las Vegas, NV 89154-0004
Nickname: Rebels
Telephone: (702) 895-3207
Football Stadium (Capacity): Sam Boyd
  Stadium (36,800)
Basketball Arena (Capacity): Thomas and Mack
  Center (18,500)
President: Dr. Carol C. Harter
Athletic Director: Charles Cavagnaro
Football Coach: John Robinson
Basketball Coach: Bill Bayno
Sports Information Director: Jim Gemma

University of New Mexico
Address: UNM South Complex
              Albuquerque, NM 87131-0041
Nickname: Lobos
Telephone: (505) 925-5500
Football Stadium (Capacity): University Stadium (33,218)
Basketball Arena (Capacity): University Arena—The
  Pit (18,018)
President: Dr. William Gordon
Athletic Director: Rudy Davalos
Football Coach: Rocky Long
Basketball Coach: Fran Fraschilla
Sports Information Director: Greg Remington

Rice University
Address: 6100 Main, MS548
              Houston, TX 77005-1892
Nickname: Owls
Telephone: (713) 527-4034
Football Stadium (Capacity): Rice Stadium (70,000)
Basketball Arena (Capacity): Autry Court (5,000)
President: Malcolm Gillis
Athletic Director: Bobby May
Football Coach: Ken Hatfield
Basketball Coach: Willis Wilson
Sports Information Director: Bill Cousins

San Diego State University
Address: San Diego, CA 92182-4309
Nickname: Aztecs
Telephone: (619) 594-5547
Football Stadium (Capacity): Qualcomm
  Stadium (71,400)
Basketball Arena (Capacity): Cox Arena (12,414)
President: Dr. Stephen Weber
Athletic Director: Rick Bay
Football Coach: Ted Tollner
Basketball Coach: Steve Fisher
Sports Information Director: John Rosenthal

San Jose State University
Address: One Washington Square
              San Jose, CA 95192-0062
Nickname: Spartans
Telephone: (408) 924-1217
Football Stadium (Capacity): Spartan Stadium
  (30,578)
Basketball Arena (Capacity): Event Center (5,000)
President: Dr. Robert L. Caret
Athletic Director: Chuck Bell
Football Coach: Dave Baldwin
Basketball Coach: Steve Barnes
Sports Information Director: Lawrence Fan

Southern Methodist University
Address: SMU Box 216
              Dallas, TX 75275
Nickname: Mustangs
Telephone: (214) 768-2883
Football Stadium (Capacity): Cotton Bowl (68,252)
Basketball Arena (Capacity): Moody Coliseum (8,998)
President: R. Gerald Turner
Athletic Director: Jim Copeland
Football Coach: Mike Cavan
Basketball Coach: Mike Dement
Sports Information Director: Jon Jackson

University of Texas at El Paso
Address: 201 Baltimore
              El Paso, TX 79968
Nickname: Miners
Telephone: (915) 747-5330
Football Stadium (Capacity): Sun Bowl (52,000)
Basketball Arena (Capacity): Don Haskins Center
  (12,222)
President: Dr. Diana Natalicio
Athletic Director: Bob Stull
Football Coach: Charlie Bailey
Basketball Coach: Jason Rabedeaux
Sports Information Director: Jeff Darby

Texas Christian University
Address: Box 297600
              Fort Worth, TX 76129
Nickname: Horned Frogs
Telephone: (817) 257-7969
Football Stadium (Capacity): Amon G. Carter
  Stadium (44,617)
Basketball Arena (Capacity): Daniel-Meyer
  Coliseum (7,166)
Chancellor: Dr. Michael R. Ferrari
Athletic Director: Eric Hyman
Football Coach: Dennis Frachione
Basketball Coach: Billy Tubbs
Sports Information Director: Rick Covington

University of Tulsa
Address: 600 S. College
            Tulsa, OK 74104-3189
Nickname: Golden Hurricane
Telephone: (918) 631-2395
Football Stadium (Capacity): Skelly Stadium (40,385)
Basketball Arena (Capacity): Donald W. Reynolds
 Center (8,300)
President: Dr. Robert Lawless
Athletic Director: Judy MacLeod
Football Coach: Dave Rader
Basketball Coach: Bill Self
Sports Information Director: Don Tomkalski

University of Utah
Address: 1825 E. South Campus Drive, Front
            Salt Lake City, UT 84112-0900
Nickname: Utes
Telephone: (801) 581-8171
Football Stadium (Capacity): Rice-Eccles Stadium
 (46,500)
Basketball Arena (Capacity): Jon M. Huntsman
 Center (15,000)
President: Dr. Bernie Machen
Athletic Director: Dr. Chris Hill
Football Coach: Ron McBride
Basketball Coach: Rick Majerus
Sports Information Director: Liz Abel

University of Wyoming
Address: P.O. Box 3414
            Laramie, WY 82071-3414
Nickname: Cowboys
Telephone: (307) 766-2256
Football Stadium (Capacity): War Memorial Stadium
 (33,500)
Basketball Arena (Capacity): Arena-Auditorium (15,028)
President: Dr. Philip Dubois
Athletic Director: Lee Moon
Football Coach: Dana Dimel
Basketball Coach: Steve McClain
Sports Information Director: Kevin McKinney

INDEPENDENTS

Army
Address: Howard Road Building 639
            West Point, NY 10996
Nickname: Cadets/Black Knights
Telephone: (914) 938-3303
Football Stadium (Capacity): Michie Stadium (39,929)
Basketball Arena (Capacity): Christl Arena (5,043)
Superintendent: Lt. Gen. Daniel W. Christman
Athletic Director: Rick Greenspan
Football Coach: Bob Sutton
Basketball Coach: Pat Harris
Sports Information Director: Bob Beretta
Note: Plays football in Conference USA, basketball in
Patriot League.

East Carolina University
Address: Ward Sports Medicine Building
            Greenville, NC 27858-4353
Nickname: Pirates
Telephone: (252) 328-4600
Football Stadium (Capacity): Dowdy-Ficklen
 Stadium (43,000)
Basketball Arena (Capacity): Williams Arena (7,500)
Chancellor: Dr. Richard R. Eakin
Athletic Director: Michael A. Hamrick
Football Coach: Steve Logan
Basketball Coach: Bill Herrion
Sports Information Director: Norm Reilly

Navy
Address: 566 Brownson Road, Ricketts Hall
            Annapolis, MD 21402
Nickname: Midshipmen
Telephone: (410) 293-2340
Football Stadium (Capacity): Navy-Marine Corps
 Memorial Stadium (30,000)
Basketball Arena (Capacity): Alumni Hall (5,700)
Superintendent: John Ryan, USN
Athletic Director: Jack Lengyel
Football Coach: Charlie Weatherby
Basketball Coach: Don DeVoe
Sports Information Director: Scott Strasemeier
Note: Plays football as independent, basketball in Patriot
League.

University of Notre Dame
Address: Joyce Center
            Notre Dame, IN 46556
Nickname: Fighting Irish
Telephone: (219) 631-6107
Football Stadium (Capacity): Notre Dame
 Stadium (80,012)
Basketball Arena (Capacity): Joyce Athletic and
 Convocation Center (11,418)
President: Rev. Edward A. Malloy, CSC
Athletic Director: Michael Wadsworth
Football Coach: Bob Davie
Men's Basketball Coach: Matt Doherty
Women's Basketball Coach: Muffet McGraw
Sports Information Director: John Heisler

United States Olympic Committee
Address: Olympic House
             1 Olympic Plaza
             Colorado Springs, CO 80909
Telephone: (719) 632-5551
Executive Director: Dick Schultz
Assistant Executive Director for Media and Public
  Affairs: Mike Moran

U.S. Olympic Training Centers
Address: 1 Olympic Plaza
             Colorado Springs, CO 80909
Telephone: (719) 578-4500 extension-5500
Director: Benita Fitzgerald Mosley

Address: 421 Old Military Road
             Lake Placid, NY 12946
Telephone: (518) 523-2600
Director: Jack Favro

U.S. Olympic Training Centers (Cont.)
Address: 2800 Olympic Parkway
             Chula Vista, CA 91915
Telephone: (619) 656-1500
Director: Patrice Milkovich

International Olympic Committee
Address: Chateau de Vidy
             Case Postale 356
             CH-1007 Lausanne, Switzerland
Telephone: 41-21-621-6111
President: Juan Antonio Samaranch
Director General: Francois Carrard
Public Information Contact: Fekrou Kidane

Sydney Olympic Organizing Committee
Address: GPO Box 2000
             Sydney, NSW 2001, Austraila
Telephone: 61-29-297-2000
President: Hon. Michael Knight, MP
GM of Media: Milton Cockburn
(XXVIIth Summer Games; Sept. 15–Oct. 1, 2000)

U.S. Olympic Organizations

National Archery Association (NAA)
Address: 1 Olympic Plaza
             Colorado Springs, CO 80909
Telephone: (719) 578-4576
President: Norm Graham
Executive Director: George Greenway
Media Relations: Bill Kellick

USA Badminton
Address: 1 Olympic Plaza
             Colorado Springs, CO 80909
Telephone: (719) 578-4808
President: Steve Kearney
Executive Director: Dan Cloppas
Media Contact: Chris Trenholme

USA Baseball
Address: Hi Corbett Field
             3400 East Camino Campestre
             Tucson, AZ 85716
Telephone: (520) 327-9700
President: Neil Lantz
Executive Director/CEO: Paul V. Seiler
Director of Media Relations: Jim Street

USA Basketball
Address: 5465 Mark Dabling Blvd.
             Colorado Springs, CO 80918
Telephone: (719) 590-4800
President: Russ Granik
Executive Director: Warren Brown
Assistant Executive Director for Public Relations:
  Craig Miller

U.S. Biathlon Association (USBA)
Address: 29 Ethan Allen Avenue
             Colchester, VT 05446
Telephone: 1 (800) 242-8456
President: Lyle Nelson
Executive Director: Stephen R. Sands
Media Contat: Mary Grace

U.S. Bobsled and Skeleton Federation
Address: P.O. Box 828
             Lake Placid, NY 12946
Telephone: (518) 523-1842
President: Jim Morris
Executive Director: Matt Roy
Communications Director: Becky Metanic

USA Bowling
Address: 5301 South 76th Street
             Greendale, WI 53129
Telephone: (414) 421-9008
President: Elaine Hagin
Executive Director: Gerald Koenig
Communications Directors: Mark Miller and Marc
Whitney

USA Boxing, Inc.
Address: 1 Olympic Plaza
             Colorado Springs, CO 80909
Telephone: (719) 578-4506
President: Gary Toney
Executive Director: Chris Campbell
Director of PR and Media: Shilpa Bakre

U.S. Canoe and Kayak Team
Address: P.O. Box 789
             Lake Placid, NY 12946
Telephone: (518) 523-1855
Chairman of the Board: Helen Collins
Executive Director: Terry Kent
Director of Communications: Lisa Fish

USA Cycling
Address: 1 Olympic Plaza
             Colorado Springs, CO 80909
Telephone: (719) 578-4581
President: Mike Plant
Executive Director and Chief Executive Officer:
  Lisa Voight
Director of Communications: Richard Wanninger

United States Diving, Inc. (USD)
Address: Pan American Plaza, Suite 430
             201 South Capitol Avenue
             Indianapolis, IN 46225
Telephone: (317) 237-5252
President: Steve McFarland
Executive Director: Todd Smith
Director of Communications: Seth Pederson

U.S. Equestrian Team (USET)
Address: Pottersville Rd.
             Gladstone, NJ 07934
Telephone: (908) 234-1251
Executive Director: Robert C. Standish
Director of Public Relations: Marty Bauman

U.S. Fencing Association (USFA)
Address: 1 Olympic Plaza
             Colorado Springs, CO 80909
Telephone: (719) 578-4511
President: Don Alperstein
Executive Director: Michael Massik
Media Relations Director: Colleen Walker-Mar

U.S. Field Hockey Association (USFHA)
Address: 1 Olympic Plaza
             Colorado Springs, CO 80909-5773
Telephone: (719) 578-4567
President: Jenepher Shillingford
Executive Director: Jane Betts
Sport and Public Information Director:
  Howard Thomas

U.S. Figure Skating Association (USFSA)
Address: 20 First Street
             Colorado Springs, CO 80906
Telephone: (719) 635-5200
President: James Disbrow
Executive Director: John LeFevre
Director of Development: Kristin Matta
Communications Coordinator: Bob Dunlop

USA Gymnastics
Address: Pan American Plaza, Suite 300
             201 South Capitol Avenue
             Indianapolis, IN 46225
Telephone: (317) 237-5050
Chairman of the Board: Sandy Knapp
President: Robert Colarossi
Director of Public Relations: Craig Bohnert

USA Hockey
Address: 1775 Bob Johnson Drive
             Colorado Springs, CO 80906
Telephone: (719) 576-8724
President: Walter L. Bush, Jr.
Executive Director: Doug Palazzari
Coordinator, Media Relations: Darryl Seibel

United States Judo, Inc. (USJ)
Address: 1 Olympic Plaza Suite 202
             Colorado Springs, CO 80909
Telephone: (719) 578-4730
President: Yoshihiro Uchida
Executive Director: William Rosenberg

U.S. Luge Association (USLA)
Address: 35 Church Street
             Lake Placid, NY 12946
Telephone: (518) 523-2071
President: Doug Bateman
Executive Director: Ron Rossi
Public Relations Manager: Sandy Caligiore

U.S. Modern Pentathlon Association (USMPA)
Address: 7330 San Pedro, Box 10
             San Antonio, TX 78216
Telephone: (210) 528-2999
President: Dr. Risto Hurme
Executive Director: Rob Stull

U.S. Racquetball Association
Address: 1685 West Uintah
             Colorado Springs, CO 80904
Telephone: (719) 635-5396
President: Otto Dietrich
Executive Director: Luke St. Onge
Public Relations Coordinator: Christie Hyde

USA Roller Skating
Address: 4730 South Street
             P.O. Box 6579
             Lincoln, NE 68506
Telephone: (402) 483-7551
President: Sue Dooley
Executive Director: George H. Pickard
Sports Information Director: Jean Stanek

U.S. Rowing
Address: Pan American Plaza, Suite 400
             201 South Capitol Avenue
             Indianapolis, IN 46225
Telephone: (317) 237-5656
President: Dave Vogel
Executive Director: Frank J. Coyle
Press Contact: Brett Johnson

U.S. Sailing Association
Address: P.O. Box 1260
             Portsmouth, RI 02871
Telephone: (401) 683-0800
President: James P. Muldoon
Executive Director: Terry Harper
Marketing Director: Walt Green
Olympic Yachting Director: Jonathan R. Harley

USA Shooting
Address: 1 Olympic Plaza
             Colorado Springs, CO 80909
Telephone: (719) 578-4670
President of the Board: Stevan B. Richards
Executive Director: Robert L. Jursnick
Director of Marketing: Bob Groate

U.S. Ski and Snowboard Association
Address: P.O. Box 100
             Park City, UT 84060
Telephone: (435) 649-9090
Chairman: Jim McCarthy
President and CEO: Bill Marolt
Vice President of Communications and Media:
  Tom Kelly
Media Services Coordinator: Scott Flanders

U.S. Soccer Federation (USSF)
Address: 1801-1811 South Prairie Avenue
             Chicago, IL 60616
Telephone: (312) 808-1300
President: Robert Contiguglia
Executive Director: Hank Steinbrecher
Media Relations Contact: Brian McCall

Amateur Softball Association (ASA)
Address: 2801 N.E. 50th Street
             Oklahoma City, OK 73111
Telephone: (405) 424-5266
President: Bill Humphrey
Executive Director: Ron Radigonda
Director of Communications: Ron Babb

U.S. Speed Skating
Address: P.O. Box 450639
             Westlake OH 44145
Telephone: (440) 899-0128
President: Bill Cushman
Executive Director: Katie Marquard
Public Relations Director: Kathleen Lynn
Publicity telephone: (719) 578-4543

U.S. Swimming, Inc. (USS)
Address: 1 Olympic Plaza
             Colorado Springs, CO 80909
Telephone: (719) 578-4578
President: Carol Zaleski
Executive Director: Chuck Wielgus
Communications Director: Charlie Snyder

U.S. Synchronized Swimming, Inc. (USSS)
Address: Pan American Plaza, Suite 901
             201 South Capitol Avenue
             Indianapolis, IN 46225
Telephone: (317) 237-5700
President: Laurette Longmire
Executive Director: Debbie Hesse
Media Relations: Brian Eaton

U.S. Table Tennis Association (USTTA)
Address: 1 Olympic Plaza
             Colorado Springs, CO 80909
Telephone: (719) 578-4583
Executive Director: Ben Nisbet
President: Sheri Pittman

U.S. Taekwondo Union (USTU)
Address: 1 Olympic Plaza, Suite 405
             Colorado Springs, CO 80909
Telephone: (719) 578-4632
President: Sang Lee
Executive Director: R. Jay Warwick

USA Team Handball
Address: 1903 Powers Ferry Road, Suite 230
             Atlanta, GA 30339
Telephone: (770) 956-7660
President: Dennis Berkholtz
Executive Director: TBA

U.S. Tennis Association
Address: 70 West Red Oak Lane
             White Plains, NY 10604
Telephone: (914) 696-7000
President: Dr. Harry Marmion
Executive Director: Richard D. Ferman
Director of Communications: Page Crosland

USA Track & Field (formerly TAC)
Address: P.O. Box 120
             Indianapolis, IN 46206-0120
Telephone: (317) 261-0500
President: Patricia F. Rico
Chief Executive Officer: Craig A. Masback
Media Information Coordinator: Tom Surber

U.S. Volleyball Association (USVBA)
Address: 3595 East Fountain Boulevard, Suite I-2
             Colorado Springs, CO 80910-1740
Telephone: (719) 637-8300
President: Rebecca Howard
Executive Director: Kerry Klostermann
Director of Marketing and Communications: Lorene
  Graves

United States Water Polo (USWP)
Address: 1685 West Uintah
             Colorado Springs, CO 80904
Telephone: (719) 634-0699
President: Brett Bernard
Executive Director: Bruce J. Wigo
Scoreboard Editor: Kyle Utsumi

USA Weightlifting
Address: 1 Olympic Plaza
             Colorado Springs, CO 80909
Telephone: (719) 578-4508
President: Brian Derwin
Executive Director and Media Contact: Jim Fox

USA Wrestling
Address: 6155 Lehman Drive
             Colorado Springs, CO 80918
Telephone: (719) 598-8181
President: Larry Sciacchetano
Executive Director: Jim Scherr
Director of Communications: Gary Abbott

Affiliated Sports Organizations

Amateur Athletic Union (AAU)
Address: Walt Disney World Resort
            P.O. Box 10000
            Lake Buena Vista, FL 32830-1000
Telephone: (407) 934-7200
President: Bobby Dodd
Media and Public Relations Director: Melissa Wilson

U.S. Curling Association (USCA)
Address: 1100 Center Point Drive
            P.O. Box 866
            Stevens Point, WI 54481
Telephone: (715) 344-1199
President: Leland Rich
Executive Director: David Garber
Communications Director: Rick Patzke

USA Karate Federation
Address: 1300 Kenmore Boulevard
            Akron, OH 44314
Telephone: (330) 753-6888
President: George Anderson

U.S. Orienteering Federation
Address: P.O. Box 1444
            Forest Park, GA 30298
Telephone: (404) 363-2110
President: Chuck Ferguson
Executive Director: Robin Shannonhouse
Marketing and Public Relations VP: Liz Kotowski
Publicity telephone: (978) 263-9704

U.S. Squash Racquets Association
Address: 23 Cynwyd Road
            P.O. Box 1216
            Bala Cynwyd, PA 19004
Telephone: (610) 667-4006
President: Eben Hardie III
Vice President: Kevin Jernigan

USA Trampoline and Tumbling
Address: 400 West Broadway, Suite 207
            or P.O. Box 306
            Brownfield, TX 79316-0306
Telephone: (806) 637-8670
President: Paul Parilla
Executive Director: Ann Sims

USA Triathlon
Address: 3595 East Fountain Boulevard, Suite F-1
            Colorado Springs, CO 80910
Telephone: (719) 597-9090
President: Jonathan Grinder
Executive Director: Steve Locke
Media Relations Coordinator: Mike McCarley

Underwater Society of America
Address: P.O. Box 628
            Daly City, CA 94017
Telephone: (650) 583-8492
President and Public Relations Manager: Carol Rose

USA Waterski
Address: 799 Overlook Drive, S.E.
            Winter Haven, FL 33884
Telephone: (863) 324-4341
President: Sherm Schrast
Executive Director: Steve McDermeit
Public Relations Manager: Greg Nixon

Miscellaneous Sports Directory

Championship Auto Racing Teams (CART)
Address: 755 West Big Beaver Road, Suite 800
            Troy, MI 48084
Telephone: (248) 362-8800
President and CEO: Andrew Craig
Director of Publicity: Ron Richards

Indy Racing League
Address: 4565 West 16th Street
            Indianapolis, IN 46222
Telephone: (317) 484-6526
President and Founder: Tony George
Executive Director: Leo Mehl
Director of Public Relations: Mai Lindstrom

Professional Sports Car Racing, Inc.
Address: 3502 Henderson Boulevard 2nd floor
            Tampa, FL 33609
Telephone: (813) 877-4672
President: Michael Gue
Communications Director: Bob Holland

National Association for Stock Car Auto Racing (NASCAR)
Address: 1801 W International Speedway Blvd.
            Daytona Beach, FL 32114
Telephone: (904) 253-0611
President: Bill France Jr.
Director of Communications Worldwide: John Griffin

National Hot Rod Association
Address: 2035 East Financial Way
            Glendora, CA 91741
Telephone: (626) 914-4761
President: Dallas Gardner
Director of Communications: Denny Darnell

Bowling, Inc.
Address: 5301 South 76th Street
            Greendale, WI 53129-1191
Telephone: (414) 421-0900
President & COO: David Patrick
Public Relations Manager: Barbara Weitzer
Women's International Bowling Congress Executive
  Director: Roseann Kuhn
American Bowling Congress Executive Director:
  Roger Dalkin

Professional Women's Bowling Association
Address: 7171 Cherryvale Boulevard
        Rockford, IL 61112
Telephone: (815) 332-5756
Tournament Director: Rick Ramsey
Media Director: Dan Leary

Professional Bowlers Association
Address: P.O. Box 5118
        1720 Merriman Road
        Akron, OH 44334-0118
Telephone: (330) 836-5568
Commissioner: Mark Gerberich
Public Relations Director: Dave Schroeder

U.S. Chess Federation
Address: 3054 NYS Route 9 W
        New Windsor, NY 12553
Telephone: (914) 562-8350
Executive Director: Mike Cavallo
Associate Director: Glenn Petersen

International Game Fish Association
Address: 300 Golf Stream Way
        Dania, FL 33004
Telephone: (954) 927-2628
President: Mike Leech

Ladies Professional Golf Association
Address: 100 International Golf Drive
        Daytona Beach, FL 32124
Telephone: (904) 274-6200
Commissioner: Jim Ritts
Director of Communications: Leslie King

PGA Tour
Address: 112 PGA Tour Boulevard
        Ponte Vedra Beach, FL 32082
Telephone: (904) 285-3700
Commissioner: Timothy W. Finchem
Senior Vice President of Communications:
  Bob Combs

Professional Golfers' Association of America
Address: 100 Avenue of the Champions
        Box 109601
        Palm Beach Gardens, FL 33410-9601
Telephone: (561) 624-8400
President: Ken Lindsay
Director of Public Relations: Julius Mason

United States Golf Association
Address: P.O. Box 708, Golf House
        Liberty Corner Road
        Far Hills, NJ 07931-0708
Telephone: (908) 234-2300
President: F. Morgan Taylor
Director of Communications: Marty Parkes

American Greyhound Track Operators Association
Address: Seminole Greyhound Park
        2000 Seminola Blvd
        Cassekberry, FL 32707
Telephone: (407) 699-4286
President: Roy Berger
Secretary and Managing Coordinator: Rob Christmas

U.S. Handball Association
Address: 2333 North Tucson Boulevard
        Tucson, AZ 85716
Telephone: (520) 795-0434
Executive Director: Vern Roberts
Director of Public Relations: Ron Carpenter

Breeders' Cup Limited
Address: 2525 Harrodsburg Road
        PO Box 4230
        Lexington, KY 40504
Telephone: (606) 223-5444
President: D. G. Van Clief Jr.
Media Relations Directors: Dan Metzger and James
  Gluckson

The Jockeys' Guild, Inc.
Address: 250 West Main Street, Suite 1820
        Lexington, KY 40507
Telephone: (606) 259-3211
President: Gary Stevens
National Manager and Secretary: John Giovanni

Thoroughbred Racing Associations of America
Address: 420 Fair Hill Drive, Suite 1
        Elkton, MD 21921
Telephone: (410) 392-9200
President: Harold G. Handel

National Thoroughbred Racing Association
Address: 444 Madison Avenue, Suite 503
        New York, NY 10022
Telephone: (212) 907-9280
VP of NTRA Communications: Chip Tuttle

United States Trotting Association
Address: 750 Michigan Avenue
        Columbus, OH 43215
Telephone: (614) 224-2291
Executive Vice President: Fred J. Noe
Director of Publicity: John Pawlak

Iditarod Trail Committee
Address: P.O. Box 870800
        Wasilla, AK 99687
Telephone: (907) 376-5155
Executive Director: Stan Hooley
Race Director: Joanne Potts

U.S. Lacrosse
Address: 113 W University Parkway
        Baltimore, MD 21210
Telephone: (410) 235-6882
Executive Director: Steven B. Stenersen

Little League Baseball, Inc.
Address: P.O. Box 3485
        Williamsport, PA 17701
Telephone: (570) 326-1921
President & CEO: Stephen D. Keener
Communications Director: Dennis Sullivan

U.S. Polo Association
Address: 4059 Iron Works Parkway
             Lexington, KY 40511
Telephone: (606) 255-0593
Executive Director: Daniel M. Scheraga
Media Contact: Merle Jenkins

American Powerboating Association
Address: P.O. Box 377
             Eastpointe, MI 48021
Telephone: (810) 773-9700
Executive Administrator: Gloria Urbin

Professional Rodeo Cowboys Association
Address: 101 Pro Rodeo Drive
             Colorado Springs, CO 80919
Telephone: (719) 593-8840
Commissioner: Steve Hatchell
Director of Communications: Steve Fleming

U.S.A. Rugby Football Union
Address: 3595 East Fountain Boulevard
             Colorado Springs, CO 80910
Telephone: (719) 637-1022
President: Anne Barry
Chair, Communications Committee: Paul Mabry
Chair, Collegiate and Membership Committee: Bill
 Sexton

The United Systems of Independent Soccer Leagues
Address: 14497 North Dale Mabry Highway,
             Suite 201
             Tampa, FL 33618
Telephone: (813) 963-3909
President and A-League Commissioner: Francisco
 Marcos
Associate Directors of Media Relations: Scott
Creighton and Gerald Barnhart

Major League Soccer
Address: 110 East 42nd Street, Suite 1000
             New York, NY 10017
Telephone: (212) 687-1400
Commissioner: Don Garber
Director of Communications: Dan Courtemanche

National Professional Soccer League
Address: 115 Dewalt Avenue NW, 5th floor
             Canton, OH 44702
Telephone: (330) 455-4625
Commissioner: Steve Paxos
Director of Media Relations: Bob Young

Association of Tennis Professionals Tour
Address: 201 ATP Tour Boulevard
             Ponte Vedra Beach, FL 32082
Telephone: (904) 285-8000
Chief Executive Officer: Mark Miles
Vice President of Communications: Fran Michaelman

COREL WTA Tour (Women's Tennis)
Address: 1266 East Main Street, 4th floor
             Stamford, CT 06902-3546
Telephone: (203) 978-1740; (813) 895-5000
Chief Executive Officer: Bart McGuire
Director of Communications: Joe Favorito

Association of Volleyball Professionals
Address: 330 Washington Blvd., Suite 600
             Marina Del Rey, CA 90292
Telephone: (310) 577-0775
Chief Executive Officer: Harry Usher
Vice President of Sales and Marketing:
 Tom Yamaguchi

MINOR LEAGUES

Baseball (AAA)

National Association of Professional Baseball Leagues
Address: 201 Bayshore Drive S.E.
             St. Petersburg, FL 33701
Telephone: (727) 822-6937
President: Mike Moore
Director of Media Relations: Jim Ferguson

International League
Address: 55 South High Street, Suite 202
             Dublin, OH 43017
Telephone: (614) 791-9300
President: Randy Mobley

Pacific Coast League
Address: 1631 Mesa Avenue
             Colorado Springs, CO 80906
Telephone: (719) 636-3399
President: Branch Rickey

Mexican League
Address: Angela Pola #16
             Col. Periodista, C.P. 11220
             Mexico D.F.
Telephone: 011-525-577-10-07
President: Pedro Cisneros

Hockey

American Hockey League
Address: 1 Monarch Place Ste 2400
             Springfield, MA 01144
Telephone: (413) 781-2030
President, CEO & Treasurer: David A. Andrews
Director of Hockey Operations: Jim Mill
Director of Communications and Media Relations:
 Bret Stothart

International Hockey League
Address: 1395 East 12-Mile Road
             Madison Heights, MI 48071
Telephone: (248) 546-3230
President: Douglas Moss
Director of Communications: Jim Anderson

Halls of Fame Directory

National Baseball Hall of Fame and Museum
Address: P.O. Box 590/25 Main Street
             Cooperstown, NY 13326
Telephone: (607) 547-7200
President: Dale Petroskey
Vice President: Frank Simio
Vice President of Communications and Education:
 Jeff Idelson

Naismith Memorial Basketball Hall of Fame
Address: 1150 West Columbus Avenue
             Springfield, MA 01105
Telephone: (413) 781-6500
CEO: Don E.N. Gibson
Director of Public Relations: Robin Deutsch

National Bowling Hall of Fame and Museum
Address: 111 Stadium Plaza
             St. Louis, MO 63102
Telephone: (314) 231-6340
Executive Director: Gerald Baltz
Communications Director: Jim Baer

National Boxing Hall of Fame
Address: 1 Hall of Fame Drive
             Canastota, NY 13032
Telephone: (315) 697-7095
President: Donald Ackerman
Executive Director: Edward Brophy

Professional Football Hall of Fame
Address: 2121 George Halas Drive NW
             Canton, OH 44708
Telephone: (330) 456-8207
Executive Director: John Bankert
Vice President of Public Relations: Joe Horrigan

LPGA Hall of Fame
Address: 100 International Golf Drive
             Daytona Beach, FL 32124
Telephone: (904) 274-6200
Commissioner: Jim Ritts
Communications Director: Leslie King

Hockey Hall of Fame
Address: 30 Young Street BCE Place
             Toronto, Ontario Canada M5E 1X8
Telephone: (416) 360-7735
Chairman: William Hay
President & COO: Jeff Denomme
VP of Marketing and Communications: Bryan Black

National Museum of Racing and Hall of Fame
Address: 191 Union Avenue
             Saratoga Springs, NY 12866
Telephone: (518) 584-0400
Executive Director: Peter Hammell
Assistant Director: Catherine Maguire
Communications Officer: Richard Hamilton

National Soccer Hall of Fame
Address: Wright Soccer Campus
             18 Stadium Circle
             Oneonta, NY 13820
Telephone: (607) 432-3351
President: Will Lunn

International Swimming Hall of Fame
Address: 1 Hall of Fame Drive
             Fort Lauderdale, FL 33316
Telephone: (954) 462-6536
President: Dr. Samuel J. Freas
Director of Public Relations: Colleen Wilson

International Tennis Hall of Fame
Address: 194 Bellevue Avenue
             Newport, RI 02840
Telephone: (401) 849-3990
Executive Vice President and Chief Operating
 Officer: Mark Stenning
Marketing Manager: TBA

National Track & Field Hall of Fame
Address: 1 RCA Dome, Suite 140
             Indianapolis, IN 46225
Telephone: (317) 261-0500
Chief Executive Officer: Craig Masback
Director of Media Relations: Pete Cava

SPORTSMEN OF THE YEAR

MARK McGWIRE *and* SAMMY SOSA

Sports Illustrated

WALTER IOOSS JR.

DECEMBER 21, 1998
www.cnnsi.com

Awards

Athlete Awards

Sports Illustrated Sportsman of the Year

Year	Recipient
1954	Roger Bannister, Track and Field
1955	Johnny Podres, Baseball
1956	Bobby Morrow, Track and Field
1957	Stan Musial, Baseball
1958	Rafer Johnson, Track and Field
1959	Ingemar Johansson, Boxing
1960	Arnold Palmer, Golf
1961	Jerry Lucas, Basketball
1962	Terry Baker, Football
1963	Pete Rozelle, Pro Football
1964	Ken Venturi, Golf
1965	Sandy Koufax, Baseball
1966	Jim Ryun, Track and Field
1967	Carl Yastrzemski, Baseball
1968	Bill Russell, Pro Basketball
1969	Tom Seaver, Baseball
1970	Bobby Orr, Hockey
1971	Lee Trevino, Golf
1972	Billie Jean King, Tennis
	John Wooden, Basketball
1973	Jackie Stewart, Auto Racing
1974	Muhammad Ali, Boxing
1975	Pete Rose, Baseball
1976	Chris Evert, Tennis
1977	Steve Cauthen, Horse Racing
1978	Jack Nicklaus, Golf
1979	Terry Bradshaw, Pro Football
	Willie Stargell, Baseball
1980	U.S. Olympic Hockey Team
1981	Sugar Ray Leonard, Boxing
1982	Wayne Gretzky, Hockey
1983	Mary Decker, Track and Field
1984	Mary Lou Retton, Gymnastics
	Edwin Moses, Track and Field
1985	Kareem Abdul-Jabbar, Pro Basketball
1986	Joe Paterno, Football
1987	Athletes Who Care:
	Bob Bourne, Hockey
	Kip Keino, Track and Field
	Judi Brown King, Track and Field
	Dale Murphy, Baseball
	Chip Rives, Football
	Patty Sheehan, Golf
	Rory Sparrow, Pro Basketball
	Reggie Williams, Pro Football
1988	Orel Hershiser, Baseball
1989	Greg LeMond, Cycling
1990	Joe Montana, Pro Football
1991	Michael Jordan, Pro Basketball
1992	Arthur Ashe, Tennis
1993	Don Shula, Pro Football
1994	Bonnie Blair, Speed Skating
	Johann Olav Koss, Speed Skating
1995	Cal Ripken Jr, Baseball
1996	Tiger Woods, Golf
1997	Dean Smith, College Basketball Coach
1998	Mark McGwire, Baseball
	Sammy Sosa, Baseball

Associated Press Athletes of the Year

Year	MEN	WOMEN
1931	Pepper Martin, Baseball	Helene Madison, Swimming
1932	Gene Sarazen, Golf	Babe Didrikson, Track and Field
1933	Carl Hubbell, Baseball	Helen Jacobs, Tennis
1934	Dizzy Dean, Baseball	Virginia Van Wie, Golf
1935	Joe Louis, Boxing	Helen Wills Moody, Tennis
1936	Jesse Owens, Track and Field	Helen Stephens, Track and Field
1937	Don Budge, Tennis	Katherine Rawls, Swimming
1938	Don Budge, Tennis	Patty Berg, Golf
1939	Nile Kinnick, Football	Alice Marble, Tennis
1940	Tom Harmon, Football	Alice Marble, Tennis
1941	Joe DiMaggio, Baseball	Betty Hicks Newell, Golf
1942	Frank Sinkwich, Football	Gloria Callen, Swimming
1943	Gunder Haegg, Track and Field	Patty Berg, Golf
1944	Byron Nelson, Golf	Ann Curtis, Swimming
1945	Bryon Nelson, Golf	Babe Didrikson Zaharias, Golf
1946	Glenn Davis, Football	Babe Didrikson Zaharias, Golf
1947	Johnny Lujack, Football	Babe Didrikson Zaharias, Golf
1948	Lou Boudreau, Baseball	Fanny Blankers-Koen, Track and Field
1949	Leon Hart, Football	Marlene Bauer, Golf
1950	Jim Konstanty, Baseball	Babe Didrikson Zaharias, Golf
1951	Dick Kazmaier, Football	Maureen Connolly, Tennis
1952	Bob Mathias, Track and Field	Maureen Connolly, Tennis
1953	Ben Hogan, Golf	Maureen Connolly, Tennis
1954	Willie Mays, Baseball	Babe Didrikson Zaharias, Golf
1955	Hopalong Cassidy, Football	Patty Berg, Golf
1956	Mickey Mantle, Baseball	Pat McCormick, Diving
1957	Ted Williams, Baseball	Althea Gibson, Tennis
1958	Herb Elliott, Track and Field	Althea Gibson, Tennis
1959	Ingemar Johansson, Boxing	Maria Bueno, Tennis
1960	Rafer Johnson, Track and Field	Wilma Rudolph, Track and Field
1961	Roger Maris, Baseball	Wilma Rudolph, Track and Field
1962	Maury Wills, Baseball	Dawn Fraser, Swimming
1963	Sandy Koufax, Baseball	Mickey Wright, Golf
1964	Don Schollander, Swimming	Mickey Wright, Golf

Associated Press Athletes of the Year (Cont.)

	MEN	WOMEN
1965	Sandy Koufax, Baseball	Kathy Whitworth, Golf
1966	Frank Robinson, Baseball	Kathy Whitworth, Golf
1967	Carl Yastrzemski, Baseball	Billie Jean King, Tennis
1968	Denny McLain, Baseball	Peggy Fleming, Skating
1969	Tom Seaver, Baseball	Debbie Meyer, Swimming
1970	George Blanda, Pro Football	Chi Cheng, Track and Field
1971	Lee Trevino, Golf	Evonne Goolagong, Tennis
1972	Mark Spitz, Swimming	Olga Korbut, Gymnastics
1973	O.J. Simpson, Pro Football	Billie Jean King, Tennis
1974	Muhammad Ali, Boxing	Chris Evert, Tennis
1975	Fred Lynn, Baseball	Chris Evert, Tennis
1976	Bruce Jenner, Track and Field	Nadia Comaneci, Gymnastics
1977	Steve Cauthen, Horse Racing	Chris Evert, Tennis
1978	Ron Guidry, Baseball	Nancy Lopez, Golf
1979	Willie Stargell, Baseball	Tracy Austin, Tennis
1980	U.S. Olympic Hockey Team	Chris Evert Lloyd, Tennis
1981	John McEnroe, Tennis	Tracy Austin, Tennis
1982	Wayne Gretzky, Hockey	Mary Decker, Track and Field
1983	Carl Lewis, Track and Field	Martina Navratilova, Tennis
1984	Carl Lewis, Track and Field	Mary Lou Retton, Gymnastics
1985	Dwight Gooden, Baseball	Nancy Lopez, Golf
1986	Larry Bird, Pro Basketball	Martina Navratilova, Tennis
1987	Ben Johnson, Track and Field	Jackie Joyner-Kersee, Track and Field
1988	Orel Hershiser, Baseball	Florence Griffith Joyner, Track and Field
1989	Joe Montana, Pro Football	Steffi Graf, Tennis
1990	Joe Montana, Pro Football	Beth Daniel, Golf
1991	Michael Jordan, Pro Basketball	Monica Seles, Tennis
1992	Michael Jordan, Pro Basketball	Monica Seles, Tennis
1993	Michael Jordan, Pro Basketball	Sheryl Swoopes, Basketball
1994	George Foreman, Boxing	Bonnie Blair, Speed Skating
1995	Cal Ripken Jr, Baseball	Rebecca Lobo, Basketball
1996	Michael Johnson, Track and Field	Amy Van Dyken, Swimming
1997	Tiger Woods, Golf	Martina Hingis, Tennis
1998	Mark McGwire, Baseball	Se Ri Pak, Golf

James E. Sullivan Award

Presented annually by the AAU to the athlete who "by his or her performance, example and influence as an amateur, has done the most during the year to advance the cause of sportsmanship."

1930	Bobby Jones, Golf	1962	Jim Beatty, Track and Field
1931	Barney Berlinger, Track and Field	1963	John Pennel, Track and Field
1932	Jim Bausch, Track and Field	1964	Don Schollander, Swimming
1933	Glenn Cunningham, Track and Field	1965	Bill Bradley, Basketball
1934	Bill Bonthron, Track and Field	1966	Jim Ryun, Track and Field
1935	Lawson Little, Golf	1967	Randy Matson, Track and Field
1936	Glenn Morris, Track and Field	1968	Debbie Meyer, Swimming
1937	Don Budge, Tennis	1969	Bill Toomey, Track and Field
1938	Don Lash, Track and Field	1970	John Kinsella, Swimming
1939	Joe Burk, Rowing	1971	Mark Spitz, Swimming
1940	Greg Rice, Track and Field	1972	Frank Shorter, Track and Field
1941	Leslie MacMitchell, Track and Field	1973	Bill Walton, Basketball
1942	Cornelius Warmerdam, Track	1974	Rich Wohlhuter, Track and Field
1943	Gilbert Dodds, Track and Field	1975	Tim Shaw, Swimming
1944	Ann Curtis, Swimming	1976	Bruce Jenner, Track and Field
1945	Doc Blanchard, Football	1977	John Naber, Swimming
1946	Arnold Tucker, Football	1978	Tracy Caulkins, Swimming
1947	John B. Kelly Jr, Rowing	1979	Kurt Thomas, Gymnastics
1948	Bob Mathias, Track and Field	1980	Eric Heiden, Speed Skating
1949	Dick Button, Skating	1981	Carl Lewis, Track and Field
1950	Fred Wilt, Track and Field	1982	Mary Decker, Track and Field
1951	Bob Richards, Track and Field	1983	Edwin Moses, Track and Field
1952	Horace Ashenfelter, Track and Field	1984	Greg Louganis, Diving
1953	Sammy Lee, Diving	1985	Joan B. Samuelson, Track and Field
1954	Mal Whitfield, Track and Field	1986	Jackie Joyner-Kersee, Track and Field
1955	Harrison Dillard, Track and Field	1987	Jim Abbott, Baseball
1956	Pat McCormick, Diving	1988	Florence Griffith Joyner, Track
1957	Bobby Morrow, Track and Field	1989	Janet Evans, Swimming
1958	Glenn Davis, Track and Field	1990	John Smith, Wrestling
1959	Parry O'Brien, Track and Field	1991	Mike Powell, Track and Field
1960	Rafer Johnson, Track and Field	1992	Bonnie Blair, Speed Skating
1961	Wilma Rudolph, Track and Field	1993	Charlie Ward, Football, Basketball

James E. Sullivan Award *(Cont.)*

1994	Dan Jansen, Speed Skating	1997	Peyton Manning, Football
1995	Bruce Baumgartner, Wrestling	1998	Chamique Holdsclaw, Basketball
1996	Michael Johnson, Track and Field		

The Sporting News Man of the Year

1968	Denny McLain, Baseball	1984	Peter Ueberroth, LA Olympics
1969	Tom Seaver, Baseball	1985	Pete Rose, Baseball
1970	John Wooden, Basketball	1986	Larry Bird, Pro Basketball
1971	Lee Trevino, Golf	1987	No award
1972	Charles O. Finley, Baseball	1988	Jackie Joyner-Kersee, Track and Field
1973	O.J. Simpson, Pro Football	1989	Joe Montana, Pro Football
1974	Lou Brock, Baseball	1990	Nolan Ryan, Baseball
1975	Archie Griffin, Football	1991	Michael Jordan, Pro Basketball
1976	Larry O'Brien, Pro Basketball	1992	Mike Krzyzewski, Basketball
1977	Steve Cauthen, Horse Racing	1993	Pat Gillick and Cito Gaston, Baseball
1978	Ron Guidry, Baseball	1994	Emmitt Smith, Pro Football
1979	Willie Stargell, Baseball	1995	Cal Ripken Jr, Baseball
1980	George Brett, Baseball	1996	Joe Torre, Baseball
1981	Wayne Gretzky, Hockey	1997	Michael Jordan, Basketball
1982	Whitey Herzog, Baseball	1998	Mark McGwire, Baseball
1983	Bowie Kuhn, Baseball		

United Press International Male and Female Athlete of the Year

	MEN	WOMEN
1974	Muhammad Ali, Boxing	Irena Szewinska, Track and Field
1975	Joao Oliveira, Track and Field	Nadia Comaneci, Gymnastics
1976	Alberto Juantorena, Track and Field	Nadia Comaneci, Gymnastics
1977	Alberto Juantorena, Track and Field	Rosie Ackermann, Track and Field
1978	Henry Rono, Track and Field	Tracy Caulkins, Swimming
1979	Sebastian Coe, Track and Field	Marita Koch, Track and Field
1980	Eric Heiden, Speed Skating	Hanni Wenzel, Alpine Skiing
1981	Sebastian Coe, Track and Field	Chris Evert Lloyd, Tennis
1982	Daley Thompson, Track and Field	Marita Koch, Track and Field
1983	Carl Lewis, Track and Field	Jarmila Kratochvilova, Track and Field
1984	Carl Lewis, Track and Field	Martina Navratilova, Tennis
1985	Steve Cram, Track and Field	Mary Decker Slaney, Track and Field
1986	Diego Maradona, Soccer	Heike Drechsler, Track and Field
1987	Ben Johnson, Track and Field	Steffi Graf, Tennis
1988	Matt Biondi, Swimming	Florence Griffith Joyner, Track and Field
1989	Boris Becker, Tennis	Steffi Graf, Tennis
1990	Stefan Edberg, Tennis	Merlene Ottey, Track and Field
1991	Michael Jordan, Pro Basketball	Monica Seles, Tennis
1992	Mario Lemieux, Hockey	Monica Seles, Tennis
1993	Michael Jordan, Pro Basketball	Steffi Graf, Tennis
1994	Nick Price, Golf	Bonnie Blair, Speed Skating
1995	Cal Ripken Jr, Baseball	Steffi Graf, Tennis

Note: Award not given since 1995.

Dial Award

Presented by the Dial Corporation to the male and female national high school athlete/scholar of the year.

	BOYS	GIRLS
1979	Herschel Walker, Football	No award
1980	Bill Fralic, Football	Carol Lewis, Track and Field
1981	Kevin Willhite, Football	Cheryl Miller, Basketball
1982	Mike Smith, Basketball	Elaine Zayak, Skating
1983	Chris Spielman, Football	Melanie Buddemeyer, Swimming
1984	Hart Lee Dykes, Football	Nora Lewis, Basketball
1985	Jeff George, Football	Gea Johnson, Track and Field
1986	Scott Schaffner, Football	Mya Johnson, Track and Field
1987	Todd Marinovich, Football	Kristi Overton, Water Skiing
1988	Carlton Gray, Football	Courtney Cox, Basketball
1989	Robert Smith, Football	Lisa Leslie, Basketball
1990	Derrick Brooks, Football	Vicki Goetze, Golf
1991	Jeff Buckey, Football, Track and Field	Katie Smith, Basketball, Volleyball, Track
1992	Jacque Vaughn, Basketball	Amanda White, Track and Field, Swimming
1993	Tiger Woods, Golf	Kristin Folkl, Basketball
1994	Taymon Domzalski, Basketball	Shannon Miller, Gymnastics
1995	Brent Abernathy, Baseball	Shea Ralph, Basketball
1996	Grant Irons, Football	Grace Park, Golf
1997	Ronald Curry, Football	Michelle Kwan, Figure Skating

Note: Award not given since 1997.

Profiles

DAVID E. KLUTHO

Henry Aaron (b. 2-5-34): Baseball OF. "Hammerin' Hank." Alltime leader in HR (755) and RBI (2,297); third in hits (3,771). 1957 MVP. Led league in HR and RBIs four times each, runs scored three times, hits and batting average twice. No. 44, he had 44 homers four times. Had 40+ HR eight times; 100+ RBI 11 times; .300+ average 14 times. All-Star 24 times . Career span 1954–76; jersey number retired by Atlanta and Milwaukee.

Kareem Abdul-Jabbar (b. 4-16-47): Born Lew Alcindor. Basketball C. Alltime leader points scored (38,387), field goals attempted (28,307), field goals made (15,837); 'second alltime blocked shots (3,189); third alltime rebounds (17,440). Won six MVP awards (1971–72, 1974, 1976–77, 1980). Career scoring average was 24.6, rebounding average 11.2. Ten-time All-Star, All-Defensive team five times. 1970 Rookie of the Year. Played on six championship teams; was playoff MVP in 1971, 1985. Career span 1969–88 with Milwaukee, Los Angeles. Also played on three NCAA championship teams with UCLA; tournament MVP 1967–69; Player of the Year two times.

Affirmed (b. 2-21-75): Thoroughbred race horse. Triple Crown winner in 1978 with jockey Steve Cauthen aboard. Trained by Laz Barrera.

Andre Agassi (b. 4-29-70): Tennis player. Won 1999 French Open to become one of five players in history who have won all four Grand Slams. Won '92 Wimbledon, '94 and '99 U.S. Opens and '95 Australian Open. Ranked No. 1 in 1995 and again in '99.

Troy Aikman (b. 11-21-66): Football QB. MVP of Super Bowl XXVII, in which he completed 22 of 30 passes for 273 yards and four TDs with no interceptions. Led Cowboys to victory in Super Bowls XXVIII and XXX. Career span since 1989 with Dallas Cowboys.

Michelle Akers (b. 2-1-66): Soccer player. Charter member of U.S. women's national team. Scored first goal ever for U.S. women's team on 8-21-85 against Denmark. Second alltime leading scorer in U.S. women's national team history. Member of Women's World Cup champion team in 1991, '99, and third-place team in '95. Member of Olympic champion team in 1996. Battles Chronic Fatigue Syndrome.

Tenley Albright (b. 7-18-35): Figure skater. Gold medalist at 1956 Olympics, silver medalist at 1952 Olympics. World champion two times (1953, 1955) and U.S. champion five consecutive years (1952–56).

Grover Cleveland Alexander (b. 2-26-1887, d. 11-4-50): Baseball RHP. Tied for third alltime most wins (373), second most shutouts (90). Won 30+ wins three times, 20+ games six other times. Set rookie record with 28 wins in 1911. Career span 1911–30 with Philadelphia (NL), Chicago (NL), St. Louis (NL).

Vasili Alexeyev (b. 1942): Soviet weightlifter. Gold medalist at two consecutive Olympics in 1972, 1976. World champion eight times.

Muhammad Ali (b. 1-17-42): Born Cassius Clay. Boxer. Heavyweight champion three times (1964–67, 1974–78, 1978–79). Stripped of title in 1967 because he refused to serve in the Vietnam War. Career record 56–5 with 37 KOs. Defended title 19 times. Also light heavyweight gold medalist at 1960 Olympics.

Phog Allen (b. 11-18-1885, d. 9-16-74): College basketball coach. Fifth alltime most wins (746); .739 career winning percentage. Won 1952 NCAA

championship. Most of career, 1920–56, with Kansas.

Bobby Allison (b. 12-3-37): Auto racer. Third all-time in NASCAR victories (84) at the time of his retirement. Won Daytona 500 three times (1978, 1982, 1988). Also NASCAR champion in 1983.

Naty Alvarado (b. 7-25-55): Mexican-born handball player. "El Gato (The Cat)." Won a record 11 U.S. pro four-wall handball titles starting in 1977.

Lance Alworth (b. 8-3-40): Football WR. "Bambi" led AFL in receiving in 1966, '68 and '69. 200+ yards in a game five times in career, a record. Gained 100+ yards in game 41 times. In 1965 gained 1,602 yards receiving. Career span 1962–70 with San Diego and 1971–72 with Dallas. Elected to Pro Football Hall of Fame 1978.

Gary Anderson (b. 7-16-59): Football K. Four-time Pro Bowl kicker (1983, '85, '93, '98), was second on alltime NFL scoring list entering 1999 season. Made league record 40 consecutive FGs during 1997–98.

Sparky Anderson (b. 2-22-34): Baseball manager. Only manager to win World Series in both leagues (Cincinnati, 1975–76, Detroit, 1984); only manager to win 100 games in both leagues.

Willie Anderson (b. 1880, d. 1910): Scottish golfer. Won U.S. Open four times (1901 and an unmatched three straight, 1903–05). Also won 4 Western Opens between 1902 and 1909.

Mario Andretti (b. 2-28-40): Auto racer. The only driver in history to win Daytona 500 (1967), Indy 500 (1969) and Formula One world championship (1978). Second alltime in CART victories (52) as of retirement in Oct. 1994. Also 12 career Formula One victories. USAC/CART champion 4 times (consecutively 1965–66, 1969, 1984).

Earl Anthony (b. 4-27-38): Bowler. Won PBA National Championship six times, more than any other bowler (consecutively 1973–75, 1981–83) and Tournament of Champions two times (1974, 1978). First bowler to top $1 million in career earnings. Bowler of the Year six times (consecutively 1974–76, 1981–83). Has won 41 career PBA titles since 1970.

Said Aouita (b. 11-2-60): Track and field. Moroccan set world records in 2,000 meters (4:50.81 in 1987), and 5,000 meters (12:58.39 in 1987). 1984 Olympic champion in 5,000; 1988 Olympic third place in 800.

Al Arbour (b. 11-1-32): Hockey D-coach. Led NY Islanders to four consecutive Stanley Cup championships (1980–83). Also played on three Stanley Cup champions: Detroit, Chicago and Toronto, from 1953 to 1971.

Eddie Arcaro (b. 2-19-16, d. 11-14-97): Horse racing jockey. The only jockey to win the Triple Crown two times (aboard Whirlaway in 1941, Citation in 1948). Rode Preakness Stakes winner (1941, 1948, consecutively 1950–51, 1955, 1957) and Belmont Stakes winner (consecutively 1941–42, 1945, 1948, 1952, 1955) 6 times each and Kentucky Derby winner five times (1938, 1941, 1945, 1948, 1952). 4,779 career wins.

Nate Archibald (b. 9-2-48): Basketball player. "Tiny" only by NBA standards at 6' 1", 160 pounds. Drafted by Cincinnati in 1970. Led NBA in scoring (34.0) and assists (11.4) in 1972–73. First team, all-NBA in 1973, '75 and '76. MVP of NBA All Star game in 1981. Retired in 1984.

Alexis Arguello (b. 4-19-52): Nicaraguan boxer.

Won world titles in three weight classes, featherweight, super featherweight and lightweight. Won first title, WBA featherweight, on 11-23-74 when he KO'd Ruben Olivares in 13. Career record: 88 bouts; won 64 by KO, 16 by decision; lost eight.

Henry Armstrong (b. 12-12-12, d. 10-24-88): Boxer. Champion in three different weight classes: featherweight (1937–relinquished 1938), welterweight (1938–40) and lightweight (1938–39). Career record 145-20-9 with 98 KOs (27 consecutively, 1937–38) from 1931 to 1945.

Lance Armstrong (b. 9-18-71): Cyclist. Two-time winner of Tour DuPont (1995, '96). Won 1993 world championships. Recovered from testicular cancer to win 1999 Tour de France title.

Arthur Ashe (b. 7-10-43, d. 2-6-93): Tennis player. First black man to win U.S. Open (1968, as an amateur), Australian Open (1970) and Wimbledon singles titles (1975). 33 career tournament victories. Member of Davis Cup team 1963–78; captain 1980–85.

Assault (b. 1943, d. 1971): Thoroughbred race horse. Horse of the Year for 1946; won Triple Crown that year. Won Kentucky Derby by 8 lengths; Preakness by a neck over Lord Boswell; and the Belmont by three lengths from Natchez. Trained by Max Hirsch.

Red Auerbach (b. 9-20-17): Basketball coach-executive. 938 career wins. Coached Boston from 1946 to 1965, winning nine championships, eight consecutively. Had .662 career winning percentage, with 50+ wins eight consecutive seasons. Also won seven championships as general manager.

Hobey Baker (b. 1-15-1892, d. 12-21-18): Sportsman. Member of both college football and hockey Halls of Fame. College hockey and football star at Princeton, 1911–14. Fighter pilot in World War I, died in plane crash. College hockey Player of the Year award named in his honor.

Seve Ballesteros (b. 4-9-57): Spanish golfer. Notorious scrambler. Won British Opens in 1979, '84 and '88. Won Masters in 1980 and '83.

Ernie Banks (b. 1-31-31): Baseball SS-1B. "Mr. Cub." Won two consecutive MVP awards, in 1958–59. 512 career HR. League leader in HR, RBIs two times each; career batting average of .274; 40+ HR five times; 100+ RBIs eight times. Most HR by a shortstop with 47 in 1958. Career span 1953–71 with Chicago.

Roger Bannister (b. 3-23-29): Track and field. British runner broke the four-minute mile barrier, running 3:59.4 on 5-6-54.

Red Barber (b. 2-17-08, d. 10-22-92): Sportscaster. TV-radio baseball announcer was the voice of Cincinnati, Brooklyn and NY Yankees. His expressions, such as "sitting in the catbird seat," "pea patch" and "rhubarb" captivated audiences from 1934 to 1966.

Charles Barkley (b. 2-20-63): Basketball F. All-Rookie team, 1985. Led NBA in rebounding, 1987. Averaged 20+ points in seven of eight seasons with Philadelphia. 1992 Olympic team leading scorer. Traded to Phoenix before 1992–93 season, then to Houston before '96–97 season. League MVP for 1992–93 season.

Rick Barry (b. 3-28-44): Basketball F. Only player in history to win scoring titles in NBA (San Francisco, 1967) and ABA (Oakland, 1969). Second alltime highest free throw percentage (.900). Career scoring average 23.2. Led league in free throw percentage six times, steals and scoring one time each. Averaged 30+

points 2 times, 20+ points 6 other times. Five-time All-Star. 1975 playoff MVP with Golden State. 1966 Rookie of the Year. Career span 1967–79.

Carmen Basilio (b. 4-2-27): Boxer. Won titles in two weight classes, welter and middle. Won world welter title by TKO of Tony DeMarco in 12 rounds on 6-10-55. Won and then lost middleweight title in two 15-round fights with Ray Robinson. Made three unsuccessful bids to regain middle title. *The Ring* Fighter of the Year for 1957. Career record: 78 bouts; won 26 by KO and 29 by decision; drew seven; lost 16, two by KO.

Sammy Baugh (b. 3-17-14): Football QB-P. Led league in passing six times and punting four times, a record. Also holds record for highest career punting average (45.1) and highest season average (51.0 in 1940). Career span 1937–52 with Washington. Also All-America with Texas Christian three consecutive seasons.

Elgin Baylor (b. 9-16-34): Basketball F. Third alltime highest scoring average (27.4), scored 23,149 points. Averaged 30+ points three consecutive seasons, 20+ points eight other times. Ten-time All-Star. 1959 Rookie of the Year. Played in 8 finals without winning championship. Career span 1958–71 with Los Angeles. Also 1958 MVP in NCAA tournament with Seattle.

Bob Beamon (b. 8-29-46): Track and field. Gold medalist in long jump at 1968 Olympics with world record jump of 29' 2½" that stood until 1991.

Franz Beckenbauer (b. 9-11-45): West German soccer player. Captain of 1974 World Cup champions and coach of 1990 champions. Also played for NY Cosmos from 1977 to 1980.

Boris Becker (b. 11-22-67): German tennis player. The youngest male player to win a Wimbledon singles title at age 17 in 1985. Won three Wimbledon titles (consecutively 1985–86, 1989), one U.S. Open (1989) and one Australian Open title (1991). Led West Germany to two consecutive Davis Cup victories (1988–89).

Chuck Bednarik (b. 5-1-25): Football C-LB. Last of the great two-way players, was named All-Pro at both center and linebacker. Missed only three games in 14 seasons with Philadelphia from 1949–62. Also All-America two times at Pennsylvania.

Clair Bee (b. 3-2-1896, d. 5-20-83): Basketball coach. Originated 1-3-1 defense, helped develop three-second rule, 24-second clock. Won 82.7 percent of games as coach for Rider College and Long Island University. Coach, Baltimore Bullets, 1952–54. Author, 23-volume Chip Hilton series for children, 21 nonfiction sports books.

Jean Beliveau (b. 8-31-31): Hockey C. Won MVP award two times (1956, 1964), playoff MVP in 1965. Led league in assists three times, goals two times and points once. 507 career goals, 712 assists. All-Star six times. Played on 10 Stanley Cup champions with Montreal from 1950 to 1971.

Bert Bell (b. 2-25-1895, d. 10-11-59): Football executive. Second NFL commissioner (1946–59). Also owner of Philadelphia (1933–40) and Pittsburgh (1941–46). Proposed the first college draft in 1936.

James (Cool Papa) Bell (b. 5-17-03, d. 3-7-91): Baseball OF. Legendary foot speed—according to Satchel Paige could flip light switch and be in bed before room was dark. Hit .392 in games against white major leaguers. Career span 1922–46 with many teams of the Negro Leagues, including the Pittsburgh

Crawfords and the Homestead Grays. Inducted in the Hall of Fame in 1974.

Lyudmila Belousova/Oleg Protopov (no dates of birth available): Soviet figure skaters. Won Olympic gold medal in pairs competition in 1964 and 1968. Won four consecutive World and European championships (1965–68) and eight consecutive Soviet titles (1961–68).

Deane Beman (b. 4-22-38): Commissioner of the PGA Tour 1974–94. Won British Amateur title in 1959 and U.S. Amateur titles in 1960 and 1963.

Johnny Bench (b. 12-7-47): Baseball C. MVP in 1970, 1972; World Series MVP in 1976; Rookie of the Year in 1968. 389 career HR. League leader in HR two times, RBI three times. Career span 1967–83 with Cincinnati. Elected to Hall of Fame in 1989.

Patty Berg (b. 2-13-18): Golfer. Alltime women's leader in major championships (16), third alltime in career wins (57). Won Titleholders Championship and Western Open 7 times each, the most of any golfer. Also won U.S. Women's Amateur (1938) and U.S. Women's Open (1946).

Yogi Berra (b. 5-12-25): Baseball C. Played on 10 World Series winners. Alltime Series leader in games, at bats, hits and doubles. MVP in 1951 and consecutively 1954–55. 358 career HR. Career span 1946–63, '65. Also managed pennant-winning Yankees (1964) and Mets (1973).

Jay Berwanger (b. 3-19-14): College football RB. Won the first Heisman Trophy and named All-America with Chicago in 1935.

Raymond Berry (b. 2-27-33): Football E. Led NFL in receiving 1958–60. In 13-season career, caught 631 passes, 68 for TDs. Career span 1955–67, all with Baltimore Colts. Later coached New England Patriots from 1984–89 with 51–41 record.

George Best (b. 5-22-46): Northern Ireland soccer player. Led Manchester United to European Cup title in 1968. Named England's and Europe's Player of the Year in 1968. Played in North American Soccer League for Los Angeles (1976–78), Fort Lauderdale (1978–79) and San Jose (1980–81). Frequent troubles with alcohol and gambling shadowed career.

Abebe Bikila (b. 8-7-32, d. 10-25-73): Track and field. Ethiopian barefoot runner won consecutive gold medals in the marathon at Olympics, in 1960 and 1964.

Fred Biletnikoff (b. 2-23-43): Football WR. In 14 pro seasons caught 589 passes for 8,974 yards and 76 TDs. In 1971 led NFL receivers with 61 catches; in '72 led AFC with 58. Career span 1965–78, all with Raiders. Elected to Pro Football Hall of Fame in 1988.

Dmitri Bilozerchev (b. 12-22-66): Soviet gymnast. Won three gold medals at 1988 Olympics. Made comeback after shattering his left leg into 44 pieces in 1985. Two-time world champion (1983, '87). At 16, became youngest to win all-around world championship title in 1983.

Dave Bing (b. 11-24-43): Basketball G. Averaged 24.8 points a game in four years at Syracuse. NBA Rookie of Year in 1967. Led NBA in scoring (27.1) in 1968. MVP NBA All Star game in 1976. In 12-year career from 1967–78, most of it with Detroit Pistons, averaged 20.3 points.

Matt Biondi (b. 10-8-65): Swimmer. Winner of five gold medals, one silver medal and one bronze medal at 1988 Olympics. Won one gold and one silver at 1992 Olympics.

Larry Bird (b. 12-7-56): Basketball F. Won three consecutive MVP awards (1984–86) and two playoff MVP awards (1984, 1986). Also Rookie of the Year (1980) and All-Star nine consecutive seasons. Led league in free throw percentage four times. Averaged 20+ points 10 times. Career span 1979–92 with Boston. Named College Player of the Year in 1979 with Indiana State. 1997–98 NBA Coach of the Year in first year as coach of Indiana Pacers.

Bonnie Blair (b. 3-18-64): Speed skater. Won gold medal in 500 meters and bronze medal in 1,000 meters at 1988 Olympics and gold medals in both events in 1992 and '94. Also 1989 World Sprint champion. Winner of 1992 Sullivan Award. *Sports Illustrated* Sportswoman of the Year, 1994.

Toe Blake (b. 8-21-12, d. 5-17-95): Hockey LW and coach. Second alltime highest winning percentage (.634) and sixth in wins (500). Led Montreal to eight Stanley Cup championships from 1955 to 1968 (consecutively 1956–60, 1965–66, '68). Also MVP and scoring leader in 1939. Played on two Stanley Cup champions with Montreal from 1932 to 1948.

Doc Blanchard (b. 12-11-24): College football FB. "Mr. Inside." Teamed with Glenn Davis to lead Army to three consecutive undefeated seasons (1944–46) and two consecutive national championships (1944–45). Won Heisman Trophy and Sullivan Award in 1945. Also All-America three times.

George Blanda (b. 9-17-27): Football QB-K. Alltime leader in seasons played (26), games played (340), points scored (2,002) and points after touchdown (943); kicked 335 field goals. Also passed for 26,920 career yards and 236 touchdowns. Tied record with 7 touchdown passes on Nov. 19, 1961. Player of the Year two times (1961, 1970). Retired at age 48, the oldest to ever play. Career span 1949–75 with Chicago, Houston, Oakland.

Fanny Blankers-Koen (b. 4-26-18): Track and field. Dutch athlete won four gold medals at 1948 Olympics, in 100-meters; 200 meters; 80-meter hurdles; and 400-meter relay. Versatile, she also set world records in high jump (5' 7¼" in 1943), long jump (20' 6" in 1943) and pentathlon (4,692 points in 1951).

Wade Boggs (b. 6-15-58): Baseball 3B. Won five batting titles (1983, consecutively 1985–88); has had .350+ average five times, 200+ hits 7 times. Won World Series with 1996 Yankees. Career span 1982–92 with Boston, 1993–97 with New York Yankees, 1998– with Tampa Bay.

Nick Bolletieri (b. 7-31-31): Tennis coach. Since 1976, has run Nick Bolletieri Tennis Academy in Bradenton, Fla. Former residents of the academy include Andre Agassi, Monica Seles and Jim Courier.

Barry Bonds (b. 7-24-64): Baseball OF. One of three players to top 40 homers (42) and 40 steals (40) in same season (1996). Three-time National League MVP (1990, '92, '93); Career span 1986–92 with Pirates; 1993– with Giants. Father Bobby had solid 14-year MLB career, mostly with Giants.

Bjorn Borg (b. 6-6-56): Swedish tennis player. Third alltime in Grand Slam singles titles (11—tied with Rod Laver). Set modern record by winning five consecutive Wimbledon titles (1976–80). Won six French Open titles (consecutively 1974–75, 1978–81). Reached U.S. Open final four times, but title eluded him. 65 career tournament victories. Led Sweden to Davis Cup win in 1975.

Julius Boros (b. 3-3-20): Golfer. Won U.S. Opens in 1952 at Northwood CC in Dallas and in 1963 at The Country Club in Brookline, Mass. Also won 1968 PGA Championship at Pecan Valley CC, San Antonio, when 48 years old, making him oldest winner of a major ever. Led PGA money list in 1952 and '55.

Mike Bossy (b. 1-22-57): Hockey RW. In 1978 set NHL rookie scoring record of 54 goals, broken in 1993. Scored 50 or more each of first nine seasons, totaling 573 goals and 1,126 points in 10 seasons (1977–78 through 1986–87) with New York Islanders. Elected to Hall of Fame in 1991.

Ralph Boston (b. 5-9-39): Track and field. Long jumper won medals at three consecutive Olympics: gold in 1960, silver in '64, bronze in '68.

Ray Bourque (b. 12-28-60): Hockey D. Won Norris Trophy as NHL's top defenseman five times. Career span since1979 with Boston Bruins.

Scotty Bowman (b. 9-18-33): Hockey coach. Ended 1997–98 season as alltime leader in regular season wins (1,057) and in regular season winning percentage (.658). Also alltime leader in playoff wins (194). Has won eight Stanley Cups; coached Montreal, St. Louis, Buffalo, and Detroit. Won Jack Adams Award, Coach of the Year, 1976–77.

Bill Bradley (b. 7-28-43): Basketball F. Played on two NBA championship teams with New York from 1967 to '77. Player of the Year and NCAA tournament MVP in 1965 with Princeton; All-America three times; Sullivan Award winner in 1965. Rhodes scholar. U.S. Senator (D-NJ) 1979–96.

Terry Bradshaw (b. 9-2-48): Football QB. Played on four Super Bowl champions (consecutively 1974–75, 1978–79); named Super Bowl MVP two consecutive seasons (1978–79). 212 career touchdown passes; 27,989 yards passing. Player of the Year in 1978. Career span 1970–83 with Pittsburgh.

George Brett (b. 5-15-53): Baseball 3B-1B. MVP in 1980 with .390 batting average; three batting titles, in 1976, '80, '90; and .300+ average 11 times. Led league in hits and triples three times. Reached 3,000-hit mark in 1992. Career span 1973–93, with Kansas City. Career totals: 3,153 hits; 317 HR; 1,595 RBIs; batting average .305. Elected to Hall of Fame in 1999.

Bret Hanover (b. 1962, d. 1993): Horse. Son of Adios. Won 62 of 68 harness races and earned $922,616. Undefeated as two-year-old. From total of 1,694 foals, he sired winners of $61 million and 511 horses which have recorded sub-2:00 performances.

Lou Brock (b. 6-18-39): Baseball OF. Second alltime most stolen bases (938); second most season steals in modern era (118). Led league in steals eight times, with 50+ steals 12 consecutive seasons. Alltime World Series leader in steals (14—tied with Eddie Collins); hit .391 in World Series play. 3,023 career hits. Career span 1961–64 Chicago (NL), 1964–79 St. Louis.

Jim Brown (b. 2-17-36): Football FB. 126 career touchdowns; 12,312 career rushing yards. Led league in rushing a record eight times. His 5.2 yards per carry average is the best ever. Player of the Year four times (consecutively 1957–58, '63, '65) and Rookie of the Year in 1957. Rushed for 1,000+ yards in seven seasons, 200+ yards in four games, 100+ yards in 54 other games. Career span 1957–65 with Cleveland; never missed a game. All-America in both football and lacrosse at Syracuse.

Paul Brown (b. 9-7-08, d. 8-5-91): Football coach. Led Cleveland to 10 consecutive championship games. Won four consecutive AAFC titles (1946–49) and three NFL titles (1950, consecutively 1954–55). Coached Cleveland from 1946 to 1962; became first coach of Cincinnati, 1968–75, and then general manager. Career coaching record 222-113-9. Also won national championship with Ohio State in 1942.

Avery Brundage (b. 9-28-1887, d. 5-5-75): Amateur sports executive. President of International Olympic Committee 1952–72. Served as president of U.S. Olympic Committee 1929–53. Also president of Amateur Athletic Union 1928–35. Member of 1912 U.S. Olympic track and field team.

Paul (Bear) Bryant (b. 9-11-13, d. 1-26-83): College football coach. Alltime Division I-A leader in wins (323). Won six national championships (1961, consecutively 1964–65, 1973, consecutively 1978–79) with Alabama. Career record 323–85–17, including four undefeated seasons. Also won 15 bowl games. Career span 1945–82 with Maryland, Kentucky, Texas A&M, Alabama.

Sergei Bubka (b. 12-4-63): Track and field. Ukrainian pole vaulter was gold medalist at 1988 Olympics. Only five-time world outdoor champion in any event (1983, '87, '91, '93, '95). First man to vault 20 feet, set world indoor record of 20' 2" on 2-21-93 and world outdoor record of 20' 1½", set on 9-20-92.

Buck Buchanan (b. 9-10-40): Football DT. Career span 1963–75 with Kansas City Chiefs. Elected to Pro Football Hall of Fame 1990.

Don Budge (b. 6-13-15): Tennis player. First player to achieve the Grand Slam, in 1938. Won two consecutive Wimbledon and U.S. singles titles (1937–38), one French and one Australian title (1938).

Dick Butkus (b. 12-9-42): Football LB. Recovered 25 opponents' fumbles, third most in history. Selected for Pro Bowl eight times. Career span 1965–73 with Chicago. Also All-America two times with Illinois. Award recognizing the outstanding college linebacker named in his honor.

Dick Button (b. 7-18-29): Figure skater. Gold medalist at two consecutive Olympics in 1948, 1952. World champion five consecutive years (1948–52) and U.S. champion seven consecutive years (1946–52). Sullivan Award winner in 1949.

Walter Byers (b. 3-13-22): Amateur sports executive. First executive director of NCAA, served from 1952 to 1987.

Frank Calder (b. 11-17-1877, d. 2-4-43): Hockey executive. First commissioner of NHL, served from 1917 to 1943. Rookie of the Year award named in his honor.

Walter Camp (b. 4-7-1859, d. 3-14-25): Football pioneer. Played for Yale in its first football game vs. Harvard on Nov. 17, 1876. Proposed rules such as 11 men per side, scrimmage line, center snap, yards and downs. Founded the All-America selections in 1889.

Roy Campanella (b. 11-19-21; d. 6-26-93): Baseball C. Career span 1948–57, ended when paralyzed in car crash. MVP in 1951, 1953, 1955. Played on five pennant winners; 1955 World Series winner with Brooklyn Dodgers.

Earl Campbell (b. 3-29-55): Football RB. 9,407 career rushing yards; gained 1,934 yards rushing in 1980; 19 TDs rushing in 1979. Led league in rushing three consecutive seasons. Rushed for 1,000+ yards in five seasons. Scored 74 career touchdowns. Player of the Year two consecutive seasons (1978–79). Rookie of the Year in 1978. Career span 1978–85 with Houston, New Orleans. Won Heisman Trophy with Texas in 1977.

John Campbell (b. 4-8-55): Canadian harness racing driver. Alltime leading money winner with over $100 million in earnings. Leading money winner each year 1986–90.

Billy Cannon (b. 2-8-37): Football RB. Led Louisiana State to national championship in 1958 and won Heisman Trophy in 1959. Signed contract in both NFL (Los Angeles) and AFL (Houston). Houston won lawsuit for his services. Played in six AFL championship games with Houston, Oakland, Kansas City. Career span 1960–70. Served three-year jail term for 1983 conviction on counterfeiting charges.

Jose Canseco (b. 7-2-64): Baseball OF. One of three players to top 40 homers (42) and 40 steals (40) in same season (1988). AL MVP in 1988, when he also batted .307 with 124 RBIs. Career span 1985–1992 and 1997 with Oakland; 1993–94 with Texas; 1995–96 with Boston; 1998 with Toronto; 1999– with Tampa Bay.

Harry Caray (b. 3-1-17, d. 2-18-98): Sportscaster. TV-radio baseball announcer 1945–97 with St. Louis (NL), Oakland, Chicago (AL) and Chicago (NL). Achieved celebrity status on Cubs' superstation WGN by singing "Take Me Out to the Ballgame" with Wrigley Field fans.

Rod Carew (b. 10-1-45): Baseball 2B-1B. Won 7 batting titles (1969, consecutively 1972–75, 1977–78). Had .328 career average, 3,053 career hits, and .300+ average 15 times. 1977 MVP; 1967 Rookie of the Year. Career span 1967–85; jersey number (29) retired by Minnesota and Anaheim.

Steve Carlton (b. 12-22-44): Baseball LHP. Second alltime most strikeouts (4,136). Four Cy Young awards (1972, '77, '80, '82). 329 career wins; won 20+ games six times. League leader in wins four times, innings pitched and strikeouts five times each. Struck out 19 batters in one game in 1969. Career span 1965–88 with St. Louis, Philadelphia and four other teams in last two years.

JoAnne Carner (b. 4-21-39): Golfer. Won 42 titles, including U.S. Women's Opens in 1971 and '76 and du Maurier Classic in 1975 and '78. LPGA top earner in 1974 and 1982–83. LPGA Player of the Year in 1974 and 1981–82. Won five Vare Trophies (1974–75 and 1981–83).

Joe Carr (b. 10-22-1880; d. 5-20-39): Football administrator. Instrumental in forming American Professional Football Association in 1920. President of AAFA from 1922 to '39.

Don Carter (b. 7-29-26): Bowler. Won All-Star Tournament 4 times (1952, 1954, 1956, 1958) and PBA National Championship in 1960. Voted Bowler of the Year six times (consecutively 1953–54, 1957–58, 1960, 1962).

Alexander Cartwright (b. 4-17-1820, d. 7-12-1892): Baseball pioneer. Credited with setting the basic rules of baseball: bases 90 feet apart, nine men per side, 3 strikes per out and 3 outs per inning. On June 19, 1846, in what is often cited as the first baseball game, his New York Knickerbockers lost to the New York Nine 23–1 at Elysian Fields in Hoboken, NJ.

Billy Casper (b. 6-24-31): Golfer. Famed putter. Won 51 PGA tournaments. PGA Player of Year in both 1966 and '70. Won Vardon Trophy in 1960, '63, '64, '65 and '68. Won the U.S. Open twice, in 1959 at Winged Foot in Mamaronek, New York, and in 1966 in 18-hole playoff over Arnold Palmer at Olympic Club, San Francisco. Beat Gene Littler in 18 hole playoff to win 1970 Masters.

Tracy Caulkins (b. 1-11-63): Swimmer. Won 3 gold medals at 1984 Olympics. Won 48 U.S. national titles, more than any other swimmer, from 1978 to 1984. Also won Sullivan Award in 1978.

Steve Cauthen (b. 5-1-60): Jockey. In 1978 became youngest jockey to win Triple Crown, aboard Affirmed. First jockey to top $6 million in season earnings (1977). *Sports Illustrated* Sportsman of Year for 1977. Moved to England in 1979; rode Epsom Derby winners Slip Anchor (1985) and Reference Point (1987).

Evonne Goolagong Cawley (b. 7-31-51): Tennis. Won four Australian Open titles from 1974 through '77; won '71 French Open; Wimbledon in 1971 and '80, Runnerup four straight years at U.S. Open (1973–76), which she never won.

Bill Chadwick (b. 10-10-15): Hockey referee. Spent 16 years as a referee despite vision in only one eye. Developed hand signals to signify penalties. Also former television announcer for the New York Rangers.

Wilt Chamberlain (b. 8-21-36, d. 10-12-99): Basketball C. Alltime leader in rebounds (23,924) and rebounding average (22.9). Alltime season leader in points scored (4,029 in 1962), scoring average (50.4 in 1962), rebounding average (27.2 in 1961) and field goal percentage (.727 in 1973). Alltime single-game most points scored (100 in 1962) and most rebounds (55 in 1960). Second alltime most points scored (31,419) and most field goals made (12,681). Four MVP awards (1960, consecutively 1966–68); playoff MVP in 1972 and 1960 Rookie of the Year. Seven-time All-Star. 30.1 career scoring average. Career span 1959–72 with Philadelphia, Los Angeles. College Player of the Year in 1957 at Kansas.

Colin Chapman (b. 1928, d. 12-16-83): Auto racing engineer. Founded Lotus race and street cars, designing the first Lotus racer in 1948. Introduced the monocoque design for Formula One cars in 1962 and ground effects in 1978.

Julio Cesar Chavez (b. 7-12-62): Boxer. Career record through 6-22-98: 101-3-2. Held titles as junior welterweight, welterweight and super featherweight.

Gerry Cheevers (b. 12-7-40): Hockey goalie. Goaltender for Stanley Cup-winning Boston Bruins teams of 1970 and '72. In 12 seasons with Boston had 230-94-74 record with a goals against average of 2.89. Also coached Bruins from 1980–84, with 204-126-46 record. Elected to Hall of Fame 1985.

Cigar (b. 1990): Thoroughbred race horse. Tied Citation's American-record 16-race winning streak with a win on 7-13-96. Won $4 million Dubai World Cup on 3-27-96.

Citation (b. 4-11-45, d. 8-8-70): Thoroughbred race horse. Triple Crown winner in 1948 with jockey Eddie Arcaro aboard. Trained by Ben A. Jones.

King Clancy (b. 2-25-03, d. 11-6-86): Hockey D. Four-time All-Star. Coach, Montreal Maroons, Toronto. Also referee. Trophy named in his honor, recognizing leadership qualities and contribution to community.

Jim Clark (b. 3-4-36, d. 4-7-68): Scottish auto racer. Twenty-five career Formula 1 victories. Formula 1 champion two times (1963, 1965). Won Indy 500 in 1965. Named Indy 500 Rookie of the Year in 1963. Killed during competition in 1968 at age 32.

Bobby Clarke (b. 8-13-49): Hockey C. Won MVP award three times (1973, consecutively 1975–76). 358 career goals, 852 assists. Scored 100+ points 3 times. Played on 2 consecutive Stanley Cup champions (1974–75) with Philadelphia. Career span 1969 to 1984. Also general manager with Philadelphia 1984–90, Minnesota 1991–92, Florida 1993–94, and Philadelphia since 1994.

Roger Clemens (b. 8-4-62): Baseball RHP. Has struck out a record 20 batters in one game on two occasions. Won five Cy Young awards (1986, '87, '91, '97, '98), most by any pitcher. Also 1986 MVP. League leader in ERA six times, wins and strikeouts four times each. Won Triple Crown of pitching in 1997 and '98. Career span 1984–96 with Boston, 1997–98 with Toronto; 1999– with Yankees.

Roberto Clemente (b. 8-18-34, d. 12-31-72): Baseball OF. Killed in plane crash while still an active player. Had 3,000 career hits and .317 career average. four batting titles; .300+ average 13 times. 1966 MVP; 1971 World Series MVP. Twelve consecutive Gold Gloves; led league in assists five times. Career span 1955–72 with Pittsburgh.

Ty Cobb (b. 12-18-1886, d. 7-17-61): Baseball OF. Alltime leader in batting average (.366) and runs scored (2,245); second most hits (4,189); fourth most stolen bases (892). 1911 MVP and 1909 Triple Crown winner. Twelve batting titles. Had .400+ average three times, .350+ average 13 other times; 200+ hits nine times. Led league in hits seven times, steals six times and runs scored five times. Career span 1905–28 with Detroit.

Mickey Cochrane (b. 4-6-03, d. 6-28-62): Baseball C. Alltime highest career batting average among catchers (.320). MVP in 1928, 1934. Had .300+ average eight times. Career span 1925–37 with Philadelphia, Detroit.

Sebastian Coe (b. 9-29-56): Track and field. British runner was gold medalist in 1,500 meters and silver medalist in 800 meters at two consecutive Olympics in 1980, 1984. Set world record in 800 meters (1:41.73 in 1981) and 1,000 meters (2:12.18 in 1981). Served in Parliament after his running career.

Eddie Collins (b. 5-2-1887, d. 3-25-51): Baseball 2B. Alltime leader among second basemen in games, chances and assists; led league in fielding nine times. 3,311 career hits; .333 career average; .330+ average 12 times. 743 career stolen bases; alltime most World Series steals (14—tied with Lou Brock); alltime leader in single-game steals (6, twice). 1914 MVP. Career span 1906–30 with Philadelphia, Chicago.

Nadia Comaneci (b. 11-12-61): Romanian gymnast. First ever to score a perfect 10 at Olympics (on uneven parallel bars in 1976). Won three gold, two silver and one bronze medal at 1976 Olympics. Also won two gold and two silver medals at 1980 Olympics.

David Cone (b. 1-2-63): Baseball P. Won 20 games in 1988 and again in '98 to set ML-record for longest stretch between 20-win seasons. On Yogi Berra Day at Yankee Stadium, 7-18-99, with Berra and Don Larsen in attendance, pitched perfect game against Montreal Expos, 14th in modern major league history. Won 1994 AL Cy Young award. Career span since 1986 with Kansas City, NY Mets, Toronto and NY Yankees.

Dennis Conner (b. 9-16-42): Sailing. Captain of America's Cup winner three times (1980, '87,'88).

Maureen Connolly (b. 9-17-34, d. 6-21-69): Tennis player. "Little Mo" first woman to achieve the Grand Slam, in 1953. Won the U.S. singles title in 1951 at age 16. Thereafter lost only four matches before retiring in 1954 because of a broken leg caused by a riding accident. Was never beaten in singles at Wimbledon, winning 3 consecutive titles (1952–54). Won three consecutive U.S. singles titles (1951–53) and two consecutive French titles (1953–54). Also won Australian title (1953).

Jimmy Connors (b. 9-2-52): Tennis player. Alltime men's leader in tournament victories (109). Held men's #1 ranking a record 160 consecutive weeks, July 29, 1974 through Aug. 16, 1977. Won five U.S. Open singles titles on three different surfaces (grass 1974, clay 1976, hard 1978, consecutively 1982–83). Won two Wimbledon singles titles (1974, '82) further apart than anyone since Bill Tilden. Also won 1974 Australian Open title. Reached Grand Slam final seven other times.

Jim Corbett (b. 9-1-1866; d. 2-18-33): Boxer. "Gentleman Jim." Invented jab. Fight with Australian Peter Jackson on 5-21-1891 ruled no contest when neither could continue into 62nd round. Won heavyweight title on 9-7-1892 with a KO of John Sullivan in 21 rounds; it was first heavyweight title fight using gloves. Lost title when KO'd by Bob Fitzsimmons in 14 on 3-17-1897, then lost two bids to regain it against Jim Jeffries. Career record: 19 fights; won seven by KO and four by decision; drew two; lost four; two no decision.

Angel Cordero (b. 11-8-42): Jockey. Through October 1999, fifth alltime in wins (7,057) and seventh in earnings ($164,561,227). Led yearly earnings three times, in 1976 and 1982–83, winning Eclipse Awards in the last two years.

Howard Cosell (b. 3-25-18, d. 4-23-95): Sportscaster. Lawyer–turned–TV-radio sports commentator in 1953. Best known for his work on "Monday Night Football." His nasal voice and "tell it like it is" approach made him a controversial figure.

James (Doc) Counsilman (b. 12-28-20): Swimming coach. Coached Indiana from 1957 to 1990. Won six consecutive NCAA championships (1968–73). Career record 287-36-1. Coached U.S. men's team at Olympics in 1964, '76. Also oldest person to swim English Channel (58 in 1979).

Count Fleet (b. 3-24-40, d. 12-3-73): Thoroughbred race horse. Triple Crown winner in 1943 with jockey Johnny Longden aboard. Trained by Don Cameron.

Yvan Cournoyer (b. 11-22-43): Hockey RW. "The Roadrunner" had 428 goals and 435 assists during his 15-season career with the Montreal Canadiens. Had 25 or more goals in 12 straight seasons. Played on 10 Stanley Cup championship teams. Elected to Hall of Fame in 1982.

Margaret Smith Court (b. 7-16-42): Australian tennis player. Alltime leader in Grand Slam singles titles (24) and total Grand Slam titles (62). Achieved Grand Slam in 1970 and mixed doubles Grand Slam in 1963 with Ken Fletcher. Won 11 Australian singles titles (consecutively 1960–66, 1969–71, '73), five French titles (1962, '64, consecutively 1969–70, '73), 5 U.S. titles (1962, '65, consecutively 1969–70, '73) and three Wimbledon titles ('63, '65, '70). Also won 19 Grand Slam doubles titles and 19 mixed doubles titles.

Bob Cousy (b. 8-9-28): Basketball G. Finished career with 6,955 assists; in 1958 had 28 assists in a single game. League leader in assists eight consecutive seasons. Averaged 18+ points and named to All-Star team 10 consecutive seasons. 1957 MVP. Played on six championship teams with Boston from 1950 to 1969. Also played on NCAA championship team in 1947 with Holy Cross.

Dave Cowens (b. 10-25-48): Basketball C. After college career at Florida State, NBA co-Rookie of Year in 1971. NBA MVP for 1973. All-Star game MVP in 1973. Career span 1970–71 through 1982–83, all but the last year with the Boston Celtics. Coach of Charlotte Hornets 1996–99. Elected to Hall of Fame in 1991.

Ben Crenshaw (b. 1-11-52): Golfer. Legendary putter. Won Masters in 1984 and '95.

Johan Cruyff (b. 4-25-47): Dutch soccer player. Led Ajax Amsterdam to three European Cup titles, and guided the Netherlands to the 1974 World Cup final, a 2–1 loss to Germany.

Larry Csonka (b. 12-25-46): Football RB. In 11 seasons rushed 1,891 times for 8,081 yards (4.3 per carry) and 64 TDs. MVP of Super Bowl VIII, when he rushed 33 times for a then Super Bowl record 145 yards in Miami's 24–7 defeat of Minnesota. Career span 1968–74, '79 with Miami Dolphins; 1976–78 with New York Giants. Elected to Hall of Fame in 1987.

Billy Cunningham (b. 6-3-43): Basketball player and coach. Averaged 24.8 points a game at North Carolina. In nine seasons (1965–66 through 1975–76) with Philadelphia 76ers, averaged 20.8 points per game. All NBA first team 1969, '70 and '71. In eight seasons as Sixers coach went 454–196 in regular season, 66–39 in playoffs and won NBA title in 1983. Elected to Hall of Fame in 1985.

Bjørn Dæhlie (b.6-19-67): Norwegian skier. Legendary cross-country skier won a Winter Olympics–record eight gold medals over three Games from 1992 to '98. Won a total of 12 Olympic medals and more than 40 World Cup races.

Chuck Daly (b. 7-20-30): Basketball coach. Won two consecutive championships with Detroit (1989–90). Won 50+ games four consecutive seasons. Coach of 1992 Olympic team. Career span as pro coach 1983–92 with Pistons; 1992–94 with New Jersey; 1997–99 with Orlando.

Damascus (b. 1964, d. 1995): Thoroughbred race horse. After finishing third in 1967 Kentucky Derby, won the Preakness, the Belmont, the Dwyer, the American Derby, the Travers, the Woodward and others—12 of 16 starts. Unanimous Horse of the Year in 1967.

Stanley Dancer (b. 7-25-27): Harness racing driver. Only driver to win the Trotting Triple Crown two times (Nevele Pride in 1968, Super Bowl in 1972). Also won Pacing Triple Crown driving Most Happy Fella in 1970. Won The Hambletonian 4 times (1968, '72, '75, '83). Driver of the Year in 1968.

Tamas Darnyi (b. 6-3-67): Hungarian swimmer. Gold medalist in 200-meter and 400-meter individual medleys at 1988 and '92 Olympics. Also won both events at World Championships in 1986 and '91. Set world records in these events at 1991 Championships (1:59.36 and 4:12.36).

Al Davis (b. 7-4-29): Football executive. Owner and general manager of Oakland-LA Raiders since 1963. Built winningest franchise in sports history (332-221-11—a .598 winning percentage entering the 1999 season). Team has won three Super Bowl championships (1976, '80, '83). Also served as AFL commissioner in 1966, helped negotiate AFL–NFL merger.

Ernie Davis (b. 12-14-39, d. 5-18-63): Football RB. Won Heisman Trophy in 1961, the first black man to win the award. All-America three times at Syracuse. First selection in 1962 NFL draft, but became fatally ill with leukemia and never played professionally.

Glenn Davis (b. 12-26-24): College football HB. "Mr. Outside." Teamed with Doc Blanchard to lead Army to three consecutive undefeated seasons (1944–46) and two consecutive national championships (1944–45). Won Heisman Trophy in 1946. Also named All-America three times.

John Davis (b. 1-12-21, d. 7-13-84): Weightlifter. Gold medalist at two consecutive Olympics, 1948, '52. World champion six times.

Terrell Davis (b. 10-28-72): Football RB. Selected in the sixth round of '95 NFL draft, rushed for over 1,000 yards in each of his first four seasons, including a league-leading 2,008 yards in '98 to become the fourth back to break 2,000-yard barrier. Led Denver to back-to-back Super Bowl wins (1998–99) and won Super Bowl MVP award in '98.

Pete Dawkins (b. 3-8-38): Football RB. Starred at Army 1956–58. Won Heisman Trophy 1958. Was first captain of cadets, class president, top five percent of class academically and football team captain; first man to do all four at West Point. Did not play pro football. Attended Oxford on Rhodes scholarship, won two Bronze Stars in Vietnam, rose to brigadier general before leaving Army to become investment banker. Made unsuccessful run for Senate from New Jersey in 1988.

Len Dawson (b. 6-20-35): Football QB. Completed 2,136 of 3,741 pass attempts with 239 TDs. In Super Bowl I threw for one TD in 35–10 loss to Green Bay. MVP of Super Bowl IV. Career span 1957–75, the last 13 seasons with Kansas City Chiefs. Elected to Hall of Fame in 1987.

Dizzy Dean (b. 1-16-11, d. 7-17-74): Baseball RHP. 1934 MVP with 30 wins. League leader in strikeouts, complete games four times each. 150 career wins. Arm trouble shortened career after 134 wins by age 26. Career span 1930–41 and 1947 with St. Louis and Chicago Cubs.

Dave DeBusschere (b. 10-16-40): Basketball F. NBA First Team Defense six straight seasons, 1969–74. Member of NBA champion New York Knicks in 1970 and '73. Career span 1962–63 through middle of 1968–69 season with Detroit Pistons; through 1973–74 with Knicks. Youngest coach (24) in NBA history. Elected to NBA Hall of Fame in 1982.

Pierre de Coubertin (b. 1-1-1863, d. 9-2-37): Frenchman called the father of the Modern Olympics. President of International Olympic Committee from 1896 to 1925.

Oscar De La Hoya (b. 2-4-73): Boxer. Won lightweight gold medal at 1992 Olympics in Barcelona. Won lightweight, super lightweight and welterweight titles as a professional.

Jack Dempsey (b. 6-24-1895, d. 5-31-83): Boxer. Heavyweight champion (1919–26), lost title to Gene Tunney and rematch in the famous "long count" bout in 1927. Career record 62-6-10 with 49 KOs from 1914 to 1928.

Gail Devers (b. 11-19-66): Track and field sprinter/hurdler. Won 100 at 1992 and '96 Olympics; leading 100 hurdles in '92 when she tripped over final hurdle and finished fifth. Successfully completed 100m/100h double at 1993 World Championships, winning 100 in 10.82 and 100 hurdles in American record 12.46. Also won '93 world indoor title in 60 (6.95). Battled Graves Disease.

Klaus Dibiasi (b. 10-6-47): Italian diver. Gold medalist in platform at 3 consecutive Olympics (1968, '72, '76) and silver medalist at 1964 Olympics.

Eric Dickerson (b. 9-2-60): Football RB. Alltime season leader in yards rushing (2,105 in 1984), third alltime most career yards rushing (13,259). Rushed for 1,000+ yards in seven consecutive seasons; 100+ yards in 61 games, including 12 times in 1984. Led league in rushing four times. Rookie of the Year in 1983. Career span 1983–93 with Los Angeles Rams, Indianapolis, L.A. Raiders and Atlanta Falcons.

Bill Dickey (b. 6-6-07 d. 11-12-93): Baseball C. Lifetime average .313. Hit 202 career home runs. Played on 11 AL All-Star teams. In eight World Series, hit five homers and 24 RBIs. Career span 1928–43 and 1946, all with the New York Yankees. Inducted into Hall of Fame 1954.

Harrison Dillard (b. 7-8-23): Track and field. Only man to win Olympic gold medal in sprint (100 meters in 1948) and hurdles (110 meters in 1952). Sullivan Award winner in 1955.

Joe DiMaggio (b. 11-25-14 d. 3-8-99): Baseball OF. "The Yankee Clipper." Tremendous all-around talent. Record 56-game hitting streak in 1941. MVP in 1939, 1941, 1947. Had .325 career batting average; .300+ average 11 times; 100+ RBI nine times. League leader in batting average, HR, and RBI two times each. Played on 10 World Series winners with NY Yankees. Career span 1936–51.

Mike Ditka (b. 10-18-39): Football TE-Coach. NFL Rookie of the Year in 1961. Named to Pro Bowl five times. Made 427 catches for 5,812 yards and 43 TDs. Career span 1961 to '72 with Bears, Eagles and Cowboys. Coach of Bears from 1982–92 with 112–68 overall record. Coach of Bears team that won Super Bowl XX, 46–10 over New England. Coach of New Orleans 1997–. Elected to Hall of Fame 1988.

Tony Dorsett (b. 4-7-54): Football RB. Rushed for 12,739 yards on 2,936 career attempts. Rushed for 1,000+ yards in eight seasons. Set record for longest run from scrimmage with 99-yard touchdown run on Jan. 3, 1983. Scored 91 career touchdowns. Named Rookie of the Year in 1977. Career span 1977–88 with Dallas, Denver. Also won Heisman Trophy in 1976, leading Pittsburgh to national championship. Graduated as alltime NCAA leader in yards rushing and was first man to break 6,000-yard barrier (6,082).

Abner Doubleday (b. 6-26-1819, d. 1-26-1893): Civil War hero incorrectly credited as the inventor of baseball in Cooperstown, NY, in 1839.

Clyde Drexler (b. 6-22-62): Basketball G. Nicknamed "The Glide" for his smooth play. Member of U.S. "Dream Team" that won 1992 Olympic gold medal. Career span 1984–1994 with Portland Trail Blazers and 1995–98 with Houston Rockets, with whom he won his first NBA title in 1995. Became head coach at University of Houston in 1998.

Ken Dryden (b. 8-8-47): Hockey G. Goaltender of the Year five times (1973, consecutively 1976–79). Playoff MVP as a rookie in 1971, maintained rookie status and

named Rookie of the Year in 1972. Led league in goals against average five times. Career record 258-57-74, including 46 shutouts. Career 2.24 goals against average is the modern record. Four playoff shutouts in 1977. Played on six Stanley Cup champions with Montreal from 1970 to 1979.

Don Drysdale (b. 7-23-36, d. 7-3-93): Baseball RHP. Led NL three times in strikeouts (1959, '60, '62) and once in wins (1962). Won 1962 Cy Young Award with 25–9 mark. In 1968 pitched six straight shutouts en route to major league record—broken in 1988 by Orel Hershiser—of 58 consecutive scoreless innings. Career record 209–166, with 2,484 K's and ERA of 2.95. Career span 1956–69, all with Dodgers. Inducted into Hall of Fame 1984.

Tim Duncan (b. 4-25-76): Basketball C. Won 1998 rookie of the year award and named first-team All-NBA, only ninth rookie in league history to be so honored. First-team All-NBA and first-team All-Defensive NBA in '99, when he led Spurs to NBA title and was named Finals MVP. Career span since 1997 with San Antonio.

Roberto Duran (b. 6-16-51): Panamanian boxer. Champion in 3 different weight classes: lightweight (1972–79), welterweight (1980, lost rematch to Sugar Ray Leonard in famous "no más" bout) and junior middleweight (1983–84).

Leo Durocher (b. 7-27-05, d. 10-7-91): Baseball manager. "Leo the Lip." Said "Nice guys finish last." Managed three pennant winners and 1954 World Series winner. Won 2,008 games in 24 years. Led Brooklyn 1939–48; New York 1948–55; Chicago 1966–72; and Houston 1972–73.

David Duval (b. 11-9-71): Golfer. Set record for tour earnings in a single season with $2.6 million in 1998, when he also won Vardon Trophy for lowest scoring average (69.13). Won 1997 Tour Championship, four tournaments in 1998. Four-time all-America at Georgia Tech.

Tomás Dvorák (b. 5-11-72): Czech decathlete. Broke Dan O'Brien's seven-year-old decathlon world record by 103 points on 7-4-99 in Prague, amassing 8,994 points. Won decathlon bronze medal at Atlanta in '96.

Eddie Eagan (b. 4-26-1898, d. 6-14-67): Only American athlete to win gold medal at Summer and Winter Olympic Games (boxing 1920, bobsled '32).

Alan Eagleson (b. 4-24-33): Hockey labor leader. Founder of NHL Players' Association and its executive director from 1967–92. Pleaded guilty on 1-6-98 to three counts of fraud and theft involving players' insurance premiums; served six months of an 18-month jail sentence. Resigned from Hall of Fame 3-25-98.

Dale Earnhardt (b. 4-29-52): Auto racer. NASCAR champion 7 times (1980, 1986–87, 1990–91, 1993–94). Won 1998 Daytona 500.

Stefan Edberg (b. 1-19-66): Swedish tennis player. Won two Wimbledon singles titles (1988, '90), two Australian Open titles (1985, '87) and two U.S. Open titles (1991, '92). Led Sweden to three Davis Cup victories (consecutively 1984–85, '87).

Gertrude Ederle (b. 10-23-06): Swimmer. First woman to swim the English Channel, in 1926. Swam 21 miles from France to England in 14:39. Also won three medals at the 1924 Olympics.

Jason Elam (b. 3-8-70): Football K. Tied Tom Dempsey's 28-year-old NFL record for the longest field goal with a 63-yard boot on 10-25-98 against Jacksonville.

Hicham El Gerrouj (b. 9-14-74): Track and field. Morrocan runner broke world record in mile on 7-7-99, clocking 3:43.13 to trim 1.26 seconds from six-year-old previous record. Performance gave him four world records as of late '99: indoor mile, indoor 1,500 and outdoor 1,500.

Herb Elliott (b. 2-25-38): Track and field. Australian runner was gold medalist in 1960 Olympic 1,500 meters in world record 3:35.6. Also set world mile record of 3:54.5 in 1958. Undefeated at 1500 meters/mile in international competition. Retired at 22.

Ernie Els (b.10-17-69): South African golfer. Two-time U.S. Open winner (1994, '97); first foreign-born player to win the event twice since Alex Smith in 1910. Second at '96 British Open.

John Elway (b. 6-28-60): Football QB. First player taken in 1983 NFL draft. Topped 3,000 yards passing every season from 1985–91. One of two NFL QBs with more than 50,000 passing yards (51,475); 300 career TD passes. Famous for last-minute drives. Won back-to-back Super Bowls (XXXII and XXXII) after three previous Super Bowl losses. Career span 1983–99 with Denver Broncos.

Roy Emerson (b. 11-3-36): Australian tennis player. Alltime men's leader, along with Pete Sampras, in Grand Slam singles titles (12). Won six Australian titles, five consecutively (1961, 1963–67), two consecutive Wimbledon titles (1964–65), two U.S. titles (1961, '64) and 2 French titles (1963, '67). Also won 13 Grand Slam doubles titles.

Kornelia Ender (b. 10-25-58): East German swimmer. Won 4 gold medals at 1976 Olympics and 3 silver medals at 1972 Olympics.

Julius Erving (b. 2-22-50): "Dr. J." Basketball F. Third alltime most points scored for combined ABA and NBA career (30,026). 24.2 scoring average. Averaged 20+ points 14 consecutive seasons. 4 MVP awards, consecutively 1974–76, '81; playoff MVP 1974, '76. All-Star 9 times. Led league in scoring three times. Played on 3 championship teams, with New York (ABA) and Philadelphia (NBA). Career span 1971 to 1986. Executive VP of Orlando 1997–. Elected to Hall of Fame in 1993.

Phil Esposito (b. 2-20-42): Hockey C. "Espo." First to break the 100-point barrier (126 in 1969). 1,590 career points, 717 goals, and 873 assists. Led league in goals six consecutive seasons, points five times and assists three times. Won MVP award two times (1969, 1974). Scored 30+ goals 13 consecutive seasons and 100+ points six times. All-Star 6 times. Career span 1963–81 with Chicago, Boston, NY Rangers. General manager of NY Rangers from 1986–89.

Tony Esposito (b. 4-23-43): Hockey goalie. Brother of Phil. A five-time All Star during 16-season NHL career, almost all of it with the Chicago Blackhawks. In 886 games gave up 2,563 goals, an average of 2.92 per game. Won or shared Vezina Trophy three times. Elected to Hall of Fame in 1988.

Janet Evans (b. 8-28-71): Swimmer. Competed in 1988, '92 and '96 Olympics, winning three gold medals in '88 and one in '92. Set world record in 400-meter freestyle (4:03.85 in 1988); 800-meter freestyle (8:16.22 in 1989) and 1,500-meter freestyle (15:52.10 in 1988). Sullivan Award winner in 1989.

Lee Evans (b. 2-25-47): Track and field. Gold medalist in 400 meters at 1968 Olympics with world record time of 43.86 that stood until 1988.

Chris Evert (b. 12-21-54): Also Chris Evert Lloyd. Tennis player. Second alltime in tournament victories (157). Tied for fourth alltime in women's Grand Slam singles titles (18). Won at least one Grand Slam singles title every year from 1974 to '86. Won seven French Open titles (1974–75; 1979–80, '83, 1985–86), 6 U.S. Open titles (1975–77, 1978, 1980, 1982), three Wimbledon titles (1974, 1976, 1981) and two Australian Open titles (1982, 1984). Reached Grand Slam finals 16 other times. Reached semifinals at 52 of her last 56 Grand Slams.

Weeb Ewbank (b. 5-6-07, d. 11-17-98): Football coach. Only coach to win titles in both the NFL and AFL. Coached Baltimore Colts to classic overtime defeat of New York Giants in 1958 and New York Jets to their stunning 16–7 win over Baltimore in Super Bowl III. Career record of 134-130-7. Career span 1954–62 with Colts and 1963–73 with Jets. Elected to Hall of Fame in 1978.

Patrick Ewing (b. 8-5-62): Basketball C. 1986 Rookie of the Year with New York. 20+ points per game average in 13 of 14 seasons with Knicks. All-NBA first team 1990. Played on 3 NCAA final teams with Georgetown (1982, 1984–85); tournament MVP in 1984. All-America 3 times.

Nick Faldo (b. 7-18-57): British golfer. Three-time winner of Masters (1989–90, consecutively, 1996) and British Open 3 times (1987, 1990, 1992).

Juan Manuel Fangio (b. 6-24-11, d. 7-17-95): Argentine auto racer. 24 Formula 1 victories in just 51 starts. Formula 1 champion 5 times, the most of any driver (1951, consecutively 1954–57). Retired in 1958.

Brett Favre (b.10-10-69): Football QB. Sixth quarterback in NFL history to throw for more than 3,000 yards in five consecutive seasons. Won NFL MVP award three years in a row (1995–97). Led Packers to victory in Super Bowl XXXI. Career span 1991 with Atlanta, since '92 with Green Bay.

Bob Feller (b. 11-3-18): Baseball RHP. League leader in wins 6 times, strikeouts 7 times, innings pitched 5 times. Pitched 3 no-hitters and 12 one-hitters. 266 career wins; 2,581 career strikeouts. Won 20+ games 6 times. Served 4 years in military during career. Career span 1936–41, 1945–56 with Cleveland.

Tom Ferguson (b. 12-20-50): Rodeo. First to top $1 million in career earnings. All-Around champion 6 consecutive years (1974–79).

Enzo Ferrari (b. 2-8-1898, d. 8-14-88): Auto racing engineer. Team owner since 1929, he built first Ferrari race car in Italy in 1947 and continued to preside over Ferrari race and street cars until his death. In 68 years of competition, Ferrari's cars have won over 5,000 races.

Mark Fidrych (b. 8-14-54): Baseball RHP. "The Bird." Rookie of the Year in 1976 with Detroit. Had 19–9 record with league-best 2.39 ERA and 24 complete games. Habit of talking to the ball on the mound made him a cult hero. Arm injuries curtailed career.

Herve Filion (b. 2-1-40): Harness racing driver. Alltime leader in career wins (more than 13,000). Driver of the Year 10 times, more than any other driver (consecutively 1969–74, 1978, 1981, 1989).

Rollie Fingers (b. 8-25-46): Baseball RHP. Won 107 games in relief in his career; 341 career saves; 944

appearances. 1981 Cy Young and MVP winner; 1974 World Series MVP. Alltime Series leader in saves (6). Career span 1968–85 with Oakland, San Diego, Milwaukee.

Bobby Fischer (b. 3-9-43): Chess. World champion from 1972 to 1975, the only American to hold title. Never played competitive chess during his reign. Forfeited title to Anatoly Karpov by refusing to play him.

Carlton Fisk (b. 12-26-47): Baseball C. Alltime HR leader among catchers (352) and second in games caught (2,226). 376 career HR, including a record 75 after age 40. Rookie of the Year in 1972 and All-Star 11 times. Hit dramatic 12th-inning HR to win Game 6 of 1975 World Series. Career span 1969–93 with Boston, Chicago (AL).

Emerson Fittipaldi (b. 12-12-46): Brazilian auto racer. Won Indy 500 in 1989 and '93. Won CART championship in 1989. Formula 1 champion 2 times (1972, 1974).

James Fitzsimmons (b. 7-23-1874, d. 3-11-66): Horse racing trainer. "Sunny Jim." Trained Triple Crown winner 2 times (Gallant Fox in 1930, Omaha in 1935). Trained Belmont Stakes winner 6 times (1930, 1932, consecutively 1935–36, 1939, 1955), Preakness Stakes winner 4 times (1930, 1935, 1955, 1957) and Kentucky Derby winner 3 times (1930, 1935, 1939).

Peggy Fleming (b. 7-27-48): Figure skater. Olympic champion 1968. World champion (1966–68) and U.S. champion (1964–68).

Curt Flood (b. 1-18-38, d. 1-20-97): Baseball OF. Won 7 consecutive Gold Gloves from 1963 to 1969. Career batting average of .293. Refused to be traded after 1969 season, challenging baseball's reserve clause. Supreme Court rejected his plea, but baseball was eventually forced to adopt free agency system. Career span 1956–69 with St. Louis.

Whitey Ford (b. 10-21-26): Baseball LHP. Alltime World Series leader in wins, losses, games started, innings pitched, hits allowed, walks and strikeouts. 236 career wins, 2.75 ERA. Alltime leader career winning percentage (.690—tied with Dave Foutz). Led league in wins and winning percentage 3 times each; ERA, shutouts, innings pitched 2 times each. 1961 Cy Young winner and World Series MVP. Career span 1950, 1953–67 with New York Yankees.

Forego (b. 1970, d. 8-27-97): Thoroughbred race horse. Horse of the Year in 1974 (won 8 of 13 starts); '75 (won 6 of 9); and '76 (won 6 of 8). Finished fourth in 1973 Kentucky Derby. Over six years won 34 of 57 starts and $1,938,957.

George Foreman (b. 1-22-48): Boxer. Heavyweight champion (1973–74). Retired in 1977, but returned to the ring in 1987. Lost 12–round decision to champion Evander Holyfield in 1991. Retired after losing to Tommy Morrison 6-7-93; returned again in 1994 at age 45 to KO Michael Moorer for heavyweight title. Also heavyweight gold medalist at 1968 Olympics.

Dick Fosbury (b. 3-6-47): Track and field. Gold medalist in high jump at 1968 Olympics. Introduced back-to-the-bar style of high jumping, called the "Fosbury Flop."

Jimmie Foxx (b. 10-22-07, d. 7-21-67): Baseball 1B. Won 3 MVP awards, consecutively 1932–33, 1938. Fourth alltime highest slugging average (.609), with 534 career HR; hit 30+ HR 12 consecutive seasons, 100+ RBI 13 consecutive seasons. Won Triple Crown in

1933. Led league in HR 4 times, batting average 2 times. Career span 1925–45 with Philadelphia, Boston.

A.J. Foyt (b. 1-16-35): Auto racer. Alltime leader in Indy Car victories (67). Won Indy 500 4 times (1961, 1964, 1967, 1977), Daytona 500 1 time (1972), 24 Hours of Daytona 2 times (1983, 1985) and 24 Hours of LeMans 1 time (1967). USAC champion 7 times, more than any other driver (consecutively 1960–61, 1963–64, 1967, 1975, 1979).

William H.G. France (b. 9-26-09, d. 6-7-92): Auto racing executive. Founder of NASCAR and president from 1948 to 1972, succeeded by his son Bill Jr. Builder of Daytona and Talladega speedways.

Dawn Fraser (b. 9-4-37): Australian swimmer. First swimmer to win gold medal in same event at 3 consecutive Olympics (100-meter freestyle in 1956, 1960, 1964). First woman to break the 1-minute barrier at 100 meters (59.9 in 1962).

Joe Frazier (b. 1-12-44): Boxer. "Smokin' Joe." Heavyweight champion (1970–73). Best known for his 3 epic bouts with Muhammad Ali. Career record 32-4-1 with 27 KOs from 1965 to 1976. Also heavyweight gold medalist at 1964 Olympics.

Walt Frazier (b. 3-29-45): Basketball G. Point guard on championship Knick teams of 1970 and '73. First team All Star in 1970, '72, '74 and '75. First team All Defense every year from 1969–1975. Averaged 18.9 points per game in 13-season NBA career. Elected to Hall of Fame in 1986.

Frankie Frisch (b. 9-9-1898, d. 3-12-73): Baseball IF. "The Fordham Flash." Led NL in hits in 1923 (223). Hit over .300 13 seasons. Scored 100+ runs 7 times. Drove in 100+ runs three times. Career .316 batting average. Career span 1919–26 with New York Giants and 1927–37 with St. Louis Cardinals' "Gashouse Gang." NL MVP in 1931. Elected to Hall of Fame in 1947.

Dan Gable (b. 10-25-48): Wrestler. Gold medalist in 149–pound division at 1972 Olympics. Also NCAA champion 2 times (in 1968 at 130 pounds, in 1969 at 137 pounds). Coached Iowa to NCAA championship 15 times (consecutively 1978–86, 1991–93 and 1995–97).

Clarence Gaines (b. 5-21-23): College basketball coach. "Bighouse." Retired after 1992–93 season with 828 career wins in 46 seasons at Division II Winston-Salem State since 1947.

John Galbreath (b. 8-10-1897, d. 7-20-88): Horse racing owner. Owner of Darby Dan Farms from 1935 until his death and of baseball's Pittsburgh Pirates from 1946 to 1985. Only man to breed and own winners of both the Kentucky Derby (Chateaugay in 1963 and Proud Clarion in 1967) and the Epsom Derby (Roberto in 1972).

Gallant Fox (b. 3-23-27, d. 11-13-54): Thoroughbred race horse. Triple Crown winner in 1930 with jockey Earle Sande aboard. Trained by James Fitzsimmons. The only Triple Crown winner to sire another Triple Crown winner (Omaha in 1935).

Don Garlits (b. 1-14-32): Auto racer. "Big Daddy." Has won 35 National Hot Rod Association top fuel events. Won 3 NHRA top fuel points titles (1975, 1985–86). First top fuel driver to surpass 190 mph (1963), 200 mph (1964), 240 mph (1973), 250 mph (1975) and 270 mph (1986). Credited with developing rear engine dragster.

Haile Gebrselassie (b. 4-18-73): Track and field. Ethiopian distance runner reclaimed the world record in the 10,000 meters on 6-1-98 in Hengelo, Neth., clocking 26:22.75, and in the 5,000, running 12:39.36 in Helsinki on 6-13-98. Won 10,000 meter gold medal in 1996 Games at Atlanta.

Lou Gehrig (b. 6-19-03, d. 6-2-41): Baseball 1B. "The Iron Horse." Second alltime in consecutive games played (2,130), leader in grand slam HR (23), third in RBI (1,995) and slugging average (.632). MVP in 1927, 1936; won Triple Crown in 1934. .340 career average; 493 career HR. 100+ RBI 13 consecutive seasons. Led league in RBI 5 times and HR 3 times. Played on 7 World Series winners with New York Yankees. Died of disease since named for him. Career span 1923–39.

Bernie Geoffrion (b. 2-16-31): Hockey RW. "Boom Boom" for his powerful slapshot. Won Hart Memorial Trophy for 1960–61. Scored 393 goals and 429 assists in 16 seasons (1950–51 through 1967–68), the first 14 with the Montreal Canadiens, the final two with the New York Rangers. Elected to Hall of Fame 1972.

Eddie Giacomin (b. 6-6-39): Hockey goalie. "Fast Eddie" led NHL goalies in games won for three straight seasons. Shared Vezina Trophy for 1970–71. In 610 games gave up 1,675 goals, a goals against average of 2.82. Career span 1965–75 with the New York Rangers and 1975–78 with Detroit Red Wings.

Althea Gibson (b. 8-25-27): Tennis player. Won 2 consecutive Wimbledon and U.S. singles titles (1957–58), the first black player to win these tournaments. Also won 1 French title (1956).

Bob Gibson (b. 11-9-35): Baseball RHP. 1968 Cy Young and MVP award winner with modern National League best ERA (1.12) and second most shutouts (13). Also 1970 Cy Young award winner. Record holder for most strikeouts in a World Series game (17); Series MVP in 1964, 1967. Won 20+ games 5 times. 251 career wins; 3,117 strikeouts. Pitched no-hitter in 1971. Career span 1959–75 with St. Louis.

Josh Gibson (b. 12-21-11, d. 1-20-47): Baseball C in Negro leagues. "The Black Babe Ruth." Couldn't play in major leagues because of skin color. Credited with 950 HR (75 in 1931, 69 in 1934) and .350 batting average. Had .400+ average 2 times. Career span 1930–46 with Homestead Grays, Pittsburgh Crawfords.

Kirk Gibson (b. 5-28-57): Baseball OF. Played on 2 World Series champions (Detroit in 1984 and Los Angeles in 1988). Hit dramatic pinch-hit HR in 9th inning to win Game 1 of 1988 series. MVP in 1988. Career span 1979–94 with Detroit, LA, KC, Pitt. Also starred in baseball and football at Michigan State.

Frank Gifford (b. 8-16-30): Football RB. NFL Player of Year in 1956 when he rushed for 819 yards and caught 51 passes. Played in seven Pro Bowls. Retired for one season after ferocious hit by Chuck Bednarik. Career span 1952–60 and 1962–64, all with New York Giants. Elected to Hall of Fame in 1977.

Rod Gilbert (b. 7-1-41): Hockey RW. Played 16 seasons, all with the New York Rangers (1960–61 through 1977–78), and had 406 goals and 615 assists. Elected to Hall of Fame 1982.

Sid Gillman (b. 10-26-11): Football coach. Developed wide-open, pass-oriented style of offense, introduced techniques for situational player substitutions and the study of game films. Won one division title with Los Angeles Rams and five division titles and one AFL championship (1963) with Los Angeles/San Diego Chargers. Career span 1955–59 Los Angeles Rams; 1960 Los Angeles Chargers; 1961–69 San Diego; 1973–74 Houston. Lifetime record 124-101-7. Also general manager in San Diego and Houston.

Pancho Gonzales (b. 5-9-28, d. 7-3-95): Tennis player. Won 2 consecutive U.S. singles titles (1948–49). In 1969, at age 41, beat Charlie Pasarell 22–24, 1–6, 16–14, 6–3, 11–9 in longest Wimbledon match ever (5:12).

Jeff Gordon (b. 8-4-71): Auto racer. Began racing go-carts and quarter midgets at age five. Youngest NASCAR Winston Cup Series champion in the modern era, having won the title at age 24 in 1995. Won at least 10 times in three straight seasons (1996–98), and won 13 times in 1998, both modern records.

Shane Gould (b. 11-23-56): Australian swimmer. Won three gold medals, one silver and one bronze at 1972 Olympics. Set 11 world records over 23-month period beginning in 1971. Held world record in five freestyle distances ranging from 100 meters to 1,500 meters in late 1971 and 1972. Retired at age 16.

Steffi Graf (b. 6-14-69): German tennis player. Achieved the Grand Slam in 1988. Has won 4 Australian Open singles titles (1988–90, '94), 7 Wimbledon titles (1988–89, 1991–93, '95–96), 6 French Open titles (1987, '88, '93, '95, '96 and '99) and 5 U.S. Open titles (1988–89, '93 and '95–96). Held the No. 1 ranking a record 186 weeks; Aug. 17, 1987 through March 10, 1991. Gold medalist at 1988 Olympics. Second in alltime Grand Slam singles titles (22).

Otto Graham (b. 12-6-21): Football QB. Led Cleveland to 10 championship games in his 10-year career. Played on 4 consecutive AAFC champions (1946–49) and 3 NFL champions (1950, consecutively 1954–55). Combined league totals: 23,584 yards passing, 174 touchdown passes. Player of the Year 2 times (1953, 1955). Led league in passing 6 times. Career span 1946–55.

Red Grange (b. 6-13-03, d. 1-28-91): Football HB. "The Galloping Ghost." All-America 3 consecutive seasons with Illinois (1923–25), scoring 31 touchdowns in 20-game collegiate career. Signed by George Halas of Chicago in 1925, attracted sellout crowds across the country. Established the first AFL with manager C.C. Pyle in 1926, but league folded after 1 year. Career span 1925–34 with Chicago, New York.

Rocky Graziano (b. 6-7-22, d. 5-22-90): Boxer. Middleweight champion from 1947 to 1948. Career record 67–13. Endured 3 brutal title fights against Tony Zale, with Zale winning by KO in 1946 and 1948, and Graziano winning by KO in 1947.

Hank Greenberg (b. 1-1-11, d. 9-4-86): Baseball 1B. 331 career HR (58 in 1938). MVP in 1935, 1940. League leader in HR and RBI 4 times each. Fifth alltime highest slugging average (.605). 100+ RBI 7 times. Career span 1933-41, 1945-47 with Detroit, Pittsburgh.

Joe Greene (b. 9-24-46): Football DT. "Mean Joe." Anchored Pittsburgh's famed "Steel Curtain" defense. Selected for Pro Bowl 10 times. Played on 4 Super Bowl champions (consecutively 1974–75, 1978–79). Career span 1969 to 1981.

Maurice Greene (b. 7-23-74): Track and field. Set world record for 100 meters (9.79) on 6-16-99 in Athens.

Forrest Gregg (b. 10-18-33): Football OT/G. Played in then-record 188 straight games from 1956 through 1971. Named all-NFL eight straight years starting in 1960. Career span 1956–71, most of it with Green Bay Packers. Played on winning Packer team in first two Super Bowls. Inducted into Hall of Fame in 1977.

Wayne Gretzky (b. 1-26-61): Hockey C. "The Great One." Most dominant player in history. Alltime scoring leader in points (2,795), assists (1,910), and goals (885). Alltime single-season scoring leader in points (215 in 1986), goals (92 in 1982) and assists (163 in 1986). Has won MVP award 9 times, more than any other player (consecutively 1980-87, 1989). Led league in assists 16 times, scoring 11 times, goals 5 times. Scored 200+ points 4 times, 100+ points 10 other times; 70+ goals 4 consecutive seasons, 50+ goals 5 other times; 100+ assists 11 consecutive seasons. Playoff MVP 2 times (1985, 1988). Played on 4 Stanley Cup champions with Edmonton from 1978 to 1988. Traded to Los Angeles on Aug. 9, 1988, then to St. Louis Feb. 1996. Moved as a free agent to NY Rangers before 1996–97 season. Wore uniform No. 99, which NHL retired when Gretzky ended career after '99 season.

Bob Griese (b. 2-3-45): Football QB. Career span 1967–80 with Miami Dolphins. Played in three straight Super Bowls, 1971–73. Quarterback of 1972 Dolphin team that went 17–0. Won Super Bowl VII and VIII. In 14 seasons completed 1,926 passes for 25,092 yards and 192 TDs. Elected to Hall of Fame in 1990.

Ken Griffey Jr. (b. 11-21-69): Baseball OF. Hit 56 home runs in back-to-back seasons (1997–98). Hit career home run No. 300 on 4-13-98 to become, at 28 years 143 days, the second youngest to reach the milestone. Won AL MVP award in 1997, when he hit .304 with 56 HRs and 147 RBI. Father Ken Sr. starred with Cincinnati Reds in 1970s.

Archie Griffin (b. 8-21-54): College football RB. Only player to win the Heisman Trophy 2 times (consecutively 1974-75), with Ohio State. Fifth alltime NCAA most yards rushing (5,177), his 6.13 yards per carry is the collegiate record. Professional career span 1976-83 with Cincinnati; totaled 2,808 yards rushing and 192 receptions.

Lefty Grove (b. 3-6-00, d. 5-22-75): Baseball LHP. 300 career wins and fourth alltime highest winning percentage (.680). League leader in ERA 9 times, strikeouts 7 consecutive seasons. Won 20+ games 8 times. 1931 MVP. Career span 1925-41 with Philadelphia, Boston.

Tony Gwynn (b. 5-9-60): Baseball OF. 8 batting titles (1984, consecutively 1987–89, 1994–97). League leader in hits 6 times, with .300+ average 15 times, 200+ hits 5 times. Career span since 1982 with San Diego.

Walter Hagen (b. 12-21-1892, d. 10-5-69): Golfer. Third alltime leader in major championships (11). Won PGA Championship 5 times (1921, consecutively 1924-27), British Open 4 times (1922, 1924, consecutively 1928-29) and U.S. Open 2 times (1914, 1919). Won 40 career tournaments.

Marvin Hagler (b. 5-23-54): Boxer. "Marvelous." Middleweight champion (1980-87). Career record 62-3-2 with 52 KOs from 1973 to 1987. Defended title 13 times.

George Halas (b. 2-2-1895, d. 10-31-83): Football owner and coach. "Papa Bear." Alltime leader in seasons coaching (40) and second in wins (324).

Career record 324-151-31 intermittently from 1920 to 1967. Remained as owner until his death. Chicago won a record 7 NFL championships during his tenure.

Glenn Hall (b. 10-3-31): Hockey goalie. "Mr. Goalie" was an All-Star goalie in 11 of his 18 seasons. Set record for consecutive games by a goaltender, with 502, and ended career with goals against average of 2.51. Won or shared Vezina Trophy three times. Career span 1952-53 through 1970–71.

Charles Haley (b. 1-6-64): Football DE. Only player in NFL history to be a member of five Super Bowl champions, two with San Francisco (1989, '90) and three with Dallas (1993, '94 and '96). Career span 1986–91 with 49ers; 1992–96 with Dallas ; 1999– 49ers.

Mia Hamm (b. 3-17-72): Soccer player. Alltime leading scorer in U.S. women's national team history. Member of Women's World Cup champion team in 1991, '99, and third-place team in '95. Member of Olympic champion team in 1996. Debuted with national team against China on 8-3-87 as its youngest player ever, at age 15.

Arthur B. (Bull) Hancock (b. 1-24-10, d. 9-14-72): Horse racing owner. Owner of Claiborne Farm and arguably the greatest breeder in history. For 15 straight years, from 1955 to 1969, a Claiborne stallion led the sire list. Foaled at Claiborne Farm were 4 Horses of the Year (Kelso, Round Table, Bold Ruler and Nashua).

Tom Harmon (b. 9-28-19, d. 3-17-90): Football RB. Won Heisman Trophy in 1940 with Michigan. Triple-threat back led nation in scoring and named All-America 2 consecutive seasons (1939-40). Awarded Silver Star and Purple Heart in World War II. Played in NFL with Los Angeles (1946-47).

Franco Harris (b. 3-7-50): Football RB. Rushed for 12,120 yards and 91 touchdowns. Gained 1,000+ yards in 8 seasons, 100+ yards in 47 games. Scored 100 career touchdowns. Selected to Pro Bowl 9 times. Rookie of the Year in 1972. Played on 4 Super Bowl champions (consecutively 1974–75, 1978–79) with Pittsburgh. Super Bowl MVP in 1974. Holds Super Bowl record for most career rushing yards (354). Made the "Immaculate Reception" to win 1972 playoff game against Oakland. Career span 1972–83 with Pittsburgh. Elected to the Hall of Fame in 1990.

Leon Hart (b. 11-2-28): Football DE. Won Heisman Trophy in 1949, the last lineman to win the award. Played on 3 national champions with Notre Dame (consecutively 1946–47, 1949) and the Irish went undefeated during his 4 years (36.0-2). Also played on 3 NFL champions with Detroit. Career span 1950-57.

Bill Hartack (b. 12-9-32): Horse racing jockey. Rode Kentucky Derby winner 5 times (1957, 1960, 1962, 1964, 1969), Preakness Stakes winner 3 times (1956, 1964, 1969) and Belmont Stakes winner 1 time (1960).

Doug Harvey (b. 12-19-24, d. 12-26-90): Hockey D. Defensive Player of the Year 7 times (consecutively 1954-57, 1959-61). Led league in assists in 1954. All-Star 10 times. Played on 6 Stanley Cup champions with Montreal from 1947 to 1968.

Dominik Hasek (b. 1-29-65): Czech hockey G. Two-time NHL MVP (1997, 98) with Buffalo; five-time Vezina Trophy winner (1994–95, 1997–99) as top goalie in league. Led NHL with a 1.95 goals-against average in 1993–94, the first sub-2.00 GAA since Bernie Parent in 1974. Topped that with 1.87 GAA in 1998–99. Guided Czech Republic to Olympic gold medal in 1998 at

Nagano. Career span 1990–92 with Chicago, since '92 with Buffalo.

Billy Haughton (b. 11-2-23, d. 7-15-86): Harness racing driver. Won the Pacing Triple Crown driving Rum Customer in 1968. Won The Hambletonian 4 times (1974, consecutively 1976-77, 1980).

John Havlicek (b. 4-8-40): Basketball F/G. Member of Ohio State team that won 1960 NCAA title. "Hondo" averaged 20.8 points per game over 16-season NBA career, all with Boston. First team NBA All Star in 1971, '72, '73 and '74. Member of eight Celtic teams that won NBA title. Playoff MVP 1974. Elected to Hall of Fame in 1983.

Elvin Hayes (b. 11-17-45): Basketball C. 1968 *Sporting News* College Player of Year as Houston senior. Averaged 21.0 points per game over 16-season NBA career. Led NBA in scoring (28.4) in 1969 and in rebounding in 1970 (16.9 per game) and '74 (18.1). First team All-NBA in 1975, '77 and '79. Elected to Hall of Fame in 1989.

Woody Hayes (b. 2-14-13, d. 3-12-87): College football coach. Won national championship 3 times (1954, 1957, 1968) and Rose Bowl 4 times. Career record 238-72-10, including 4 undefeated seasons, with Ohio State from 1951 to 1978. Forced to resign after striking an opposing player during 1978 Gator Bowl.

Marques Haynes (b. 10-3-26): Basketball G. Known as "The World's Greatest Dribbler." Beginning in 1946 barnstormed more than 4 million miles throughout 97 countries for the Harlem Globetrotters, Harlem Magicians, Meadowlark Lemon's Bucketeers, Harlem Wizards.

Thomas Hearns (b. 10-18-58): Boxer. "Hit Man." Champion in four weight classes: welterweight, super welterweight, middleweight and light heavyweight.

Eric Heiden (b. 6-14-58): Speed skater. Won 5 gold medals at 1980 Olympics. World champion 3 consecutive years (1977-79). Also won Sullivan Award in 1980.

Carol Heiss (b. 1-20-40): Figure skater. Gold medalist at 1960 Olympics, silver medalist at 1956 Olympics. World champion 5 consecutive years (1956-60) and U.S. champion 4 consecutive years (1957-60). Married 1956 gold medalist Hayes Jenkins.

Rickey Henderson (b. 12-25-57): Baseball OF. Alltime career stolen base leader (1,334 through 1999); modern season stolen base record holder in 1982 (130). Led league in steals 11 times. 1990 MVP. Alltime most HR leading off game. Career span since 1979 with Oakland, NY Yankees, Toronto, San Diego and NY Mets.

Sonja Henie (b. 4-8-12, d. 10-12-69): Norwegian figure skater. Gold medalist at 3 consecutive Olympics (1928, 1932, 1936). World champion 10 consecutive years (1927-36).

Orel Hershiser (b. 9-16-58): Baseball RHP. Alltime leader most consecutive scoreless innings pitched (59 in 1988). Cy Young Award winner in 1988 and World Series MVP. Career span 1983–94, Los Angeles; 1995–97, Cleveland; 1998, San Francisco; 1999– NY Mets.

Foster Hewitt (b. 11-21-02, d. 4-22-85): Hockey sportscaster. In 1923, aired one of hockey's first radio broadcasts. Became the voice of hockey in Canada on radio and later television. Famous for the phrase, "He shoots ... he scores!"

Tommy Hitchcock (b. 2-11-00, d. 4-19-44): Polo. 10-goal rating 18 times in his 19-year career from 1922 to 1940. Killed in plane crash in World War II.

Lew Hoad (b. 11-23-34): Australian tennis player. Won 2 consecutive Wimbledon singles titles (1956-57). Also won French title and Australian title in 1956, but failed to achieve the Grand Slam when defeated at Forest Hills by countryman Ken Rosewall.

Ben Hogan (b. 8-13-12, d. 7-25-97): Golfer. Third alltime in career wins (63). Won U.S. Open 4 times (1948, consecutively 1950–51, 1953), the Masters (1951, 1953) and PGA Championship (1946, 1948) 2 times each and British Open once (1953). PGA Player of the Year 4 times (1948, consecutively 1950-51, 1953).

Marshall Holman (b. 9-29-54): Bowler. Won 21 PBA titles between 1975 and 1988. Had leading average in 1987 (213.54) and was named PBA Bowler of the Year.

Nat Holman (b. 10-18-1896, d. 2-12-95): College basketball coach. Only coach in history to win NCAA and NIT championships in same season in 1950 with CCNY. 423 career wins, a .689 winning percentage.

Larry Holmes (b. 11-3-49): Boxer. Heavyweight champion (1978–85). Career record 53–3 with 37 KOs from 1973 to 1991. Defended title 21 times. Fought periodically after 1991, twice for a title, both losses.

Lou Holtz (b. 1-6-37): Football coach. Coached Notre Dame to national championship in 1988 with 12–0 record and a 34–21 win over West Virginia in Fiesta Bowl. Retired after 1996 season with a 216-95-7 career record. 10-8-2 career record in bowl games. Career span 1969–71 at William & Mary (13–20); 1972–75 at N.C. State (33-12-3); 1977–83 at Arkansas (60-21-2); 1984–85 at Minnesota (10–12); 1986–96 at Notre Dame (100-30-2); and 1999– S Carolina.

Evander Holyfield (b. 10-19-62): Boxer. Won heavyweight crown Oct. 25, 1990 when he beat James (Buster) Douglas in Las Vegas. Lost title to Riddick Bowe in Las Vegas on 11-13-92, regained it from Bowe one year later, then lost to Michael Moorer on 4-22-94. Defeated Mike Tyson for WBA crown on 11-9-96 to join Muhammad Ali as the only men to win the heavyweight title three times. Won rematch on 6-28-97 when Tyson was disqualified for biting Holyfield's ears.

Red Holzman (b. 8-10-20; d. 11-13-98): Basketball coach. Led New York Knicks to NBA title in 1970 and '73. NBA Coach of the Year in 1970. Member of Rochester team that won NBA title in both 1946 (in NBL) and '51. After two-year coaching stints with Milwaukee and St. Louis, coached New York Knicks from 1968–82. Elected to Hall of Fame in 1985.

Harry Hopman (b. 8-12-06, d. 12-27-85): Australian tennis coach. As nonplaying captain, led Australia to 15 Davis Cup titles between 1950 and 1969. Mentor to Lew Hoad, Ken Rosewall, Rod Laver and John Newcombe.

Willie Hoppe (b. 10-11-1887, d. 2-1-59): Billiards. Won 51 world championship matches from 1904 to 1952.

Rogers Hornsby (b. 4-27-1896, d. 1-5-63): Baseball 2B. Second alltime in career batting average (.358), won 7 batting titles, including with .424 average in 1924. 200+ hits seven times; .400+ average three times and .300+ average 12 other times. Led league in slugging average 9 times. Triple Crown winner in 1922, 1925; MVP award winner in 1925, 1929. Career span 1915–37 with St. Louis (NL), New York (NL), Boston, Chicago (NL).

Paul Hornung (b. 12-23-35): Football RB-K. Led league in scoring 3 consecutive seasons, including a record 176 points in 1960 (15 touchdowns, 15 field goals, 41 extra points). Player of the Year in 1961. Career span 1957–66 with Green Bay. Suspended for 1963 season by Pete Rozelle for gambling. Also won Heisman Trophy in 1956 with Notre Dame.

Gordie Howe (b. 3-31-28): Hockey RW. Second alltime in goals (801), first in years played (26) and games (1,767). Finished career with 1,850 points and 1,049 assists. Won MVP award 6 times (consecutively 1952–53, 1957–58, 1960, 1963). Led league in scoring 6 times, goals 5 times and assists 3 times. Scored 40+ goals 5 times, 30+ goals 13 other times, 100+ points 3 times. All-Star 12 times. Played on 4 Stanley Cup champions with Detroit from 1946 to 1971. Teamed with sons Mark and Marty in the WHA with Houston and New England from 1973 to 1979, in NHL with Hartford in 1980.

Carl Hubbell (b. 6-22-03, d. 11-21-88): Baseball LHP. 253 career wins. MVP in 1933, 1936. League leader in wins and ERA 3 times each. Won 24 consecutive games from 1936 to 1937. Struck out Ruth, Gehrig, Foxx, Simmons and Cronin consecutively in 1934 All-Star game. Pitched no-hitter in 1929. Career span 1928–43 with New York.

Sam Huff (b. 10-4-34): Football LB. Made 30 interceptions. Career span 1956–69 with New York Giants and Washington Redskins. Elected to Hall of Fame in 1982.

Bobby Hull (b. 1-3-39): Hockey LW. "The Golden Jet." Led league in goals 7 times and points 3 times. 610 career goals. Scored 50+ goals 5 times, 30+ goals 8 other times. Won MVP award 2 consecutive seasons (1965–66). Son Brett won MVP award in 1991, the only father and son to be so honored. All-Star 10 times. Career span 1957–72 with Chicago, 1973–80 with Winnipeg of WHA.

Brett Hull (b. 8-9-64): Hockey RW. Son of Bobby Hull. Won Hart Memorial Trophy for 1990–91 season. Scored Stanley Cup–winning goal for Dallas in third overtime of Game 6 against Buffalo in 1999. Career span 1986–87 with Calgary Flames; 1987–98 with St. Louis Blues; since 1998 with Dallas Stars.

Jim (Catfish) Hunter (b. 4-8-46, d. 9-9-99): Baseball RHP. 1974 Cy Young award winner. Won 20+ games 5 consecutive seasons. Led league in wins and winning percentage 2 times each, ERA 1 time. 250+ innings pitched 8 times. Pitched perfect game in 1968. Member of 5 World Series champions for Oakland and New York Yankees. Career span 1965–79.

Don Hutson (b. 1-31-13, d. 6-26-97): Football WR. Fourth alltime in touchdown receptions (99). Led league in pass receptions 8 times, receiving yards 7 times and scoring 5 consecutive seasons. Caught at least 1 pass in 95 consecutive games. Player of the Year 2 consecutive seasons (1941–42). Career span 1935–45 with Green Bay.

Hank Iba (b. 8-6-04; d. 1-15-93): College basketball coach. Coached Oklahoma A&M (which became Oklahoma State) from 1934 to 1970. Team won NCAA titles in 1945 and '46. 767 career wins is third alltime behind Dean Smith and Adolph Rupp.

Jackie Ickx (b. 1-1-45): Belgian auto racer. Won the 24 Hours of LeMans a record six times (1969, consecutively 1975–77, 1981–82) before retiring in 1985.

Punch Imlach (b. 3-15-18, d. 12-1-87): Hockey coach. 467 wins. With Toronto from 1958 to 1969. Won 4 Stanley Cup championships (consecutively 1962–64, 1967).

Miguel Induráin (b. 7-16-64): Cyclist. Won an unprecedented five consecutive Tours de France (1991–95).

Juli Inkster (b.6-24-60): Golfer. Became only the second woman ever to win all four of the LPGA's modern majors when she won the LPGA Championship on 6-27-99. Finished eagle-birdie-birdie for a 6-under 65 and a four-stroke victory. Inducted to LPGA Hall of Fame in 1999.

Bo Jackson (b. 11-30-62): Baseball OF and Football RB. Only person in history to be named to baseball All-Star game and football Pro Bowl game. 1985 Heisman Trophy winner at Auburn. First pick in 1986 NFL draft by Tampa Bay, but opted to play baseball at Kansas City. 1989 All-Star game MVP. Signed with football's LA Raiders in 1988. Retired 1994 following hip replacement surgery.

Joe Jackson (b. 7-16-1889, d. 12-5-51): Baseball OF. "Shoeless Joe." Third alltime highest career batting average (.356), with .300+ average 11 times. One of the "8 men out" banned from baseball for throwing 1919 World Series. Career span 1908–20 with Cleveland, Chicago.

Reggie Jackson (b. 5-18-46): Baseball OF. "Mr. October." Alltime leader in World Series slugging average (.755). 1977 Series MVP, hit 3 HR in final game on 3 consecutive pitches. 563 career HR total is sixth best alltime. Led league in HR 4 times. 1973 MVP. Alltime strikeout leader (2,597). In a 12-year period played on 10 first-place teams, 5 World Series winners. Career span 1967–87 with Oakland, Baltimore, New York and California. Inducted to baseball Hall of Fame in 1993.

Bruce Jenner (b. 10-28-49): Track and Field. Set then-world decathlon record (8,634) in winning gold medal at 1976 Olympics. Sullivan Award winner in 1976.

John Henry (b. 1975): Thoroughbred race horse. Sold as yearling for $1,100, the gelding was Horse of the Year in 1981 and 1984 and retired with then-record $6,597,947 in winnings.

Ben Johnson (b. 12-30-61): Track and field. Canadian sprinter set world record in 100 meters (9.83 in 1987). Won event at 1988 Olympics in 9.79, but gold medal revoked for failing drug test. Both world records revoked for steroid usage. Suspended for life after testing positive for elevated testosterone level at an indoor meet in Montreal on 1-17-93.

Earvin (Magic) Johnson (b. 8-14-59): Basketball G. Retired Nov. 7, 1991 after being diagnosed with HIV, the virus that causes AIDS. Returned to Lakers Feb '96 at age 36. Finished career second alltime in assists (10,141); alltime playoff leader in assists (2,346) and steals (358). MVP award 3 times (1987, consecutively 1989–90) and playoff MVP in 1980, '82 and '87. Played on 5 championship teams with Los Angeles since 1979. All-Star 8 consecutive seasons. League leader in assists 4 times, steals 2 times, free throw percentage once. Also won NCAA championship and named tournament MVP in 1979 with Michigan State.

Jack Johnson (b. 3-31-1878, d. 6-10-46): Boxer. First black heavyweight champion (1908-15). Career record 78-8-12 with 45 KOs from 1897 to 1928.

Jimmy Johnson (b. 7-16-43): Football coach. Led the Cowboys from 1–15 in 1989, his first season in Dallas, to a 52–17 win over the Buffalo Bills in the Super Bowl XXVII just four seasons later. Also coached Super Bowl XXVIII champion Cowboys. Head coach at Oklahoma State from 1979–83 and Univ. of Miami 1984–88. Johnson's Hurricanes won national championship in 1987. Succeeded Don Shula as Miami Dolphins coach, Jan. '96.

Michael Johnson (b. 9-13-67): Track and field sprinter. First man to win gold medals in both the 200 and 400 at the Olympics (1996). Broke 17-year-old 200-meter world record (from 19.72 to 19.66) in '96 U.S. Olympic trials, then further lowered mark to 19.32 at Atlanta. Won 200 at 1991 World Championships, 400 at '93 worlds and both events at the '95 worlds. Anchored U.S. 4x400 team at 1993 World Championship to world record of 2:54.29 with fastest ever relay carry of 42.97.

Walter Johnson (b. 11-6-1887, d. 12-10-46): Baseball RHP. "Big Train." Alltime leader in shutouts (110), second in wins (416), fourth in losses (279) and third in innings pitched (5,914). His 2.17 career ERA and 3,509 career strikeouts are seventh best alltime. MVP in 1913, 1924. Won 20+ games 12 times. League leader in strikeouts 12 times, ERA 5 times, wins 6 times. Pitched no-hitter in 1920. Career span 1907–27 with Washington.

Ben A. Jones (b. 12-31-1882, d. 6-13-61): Horse racing trainer. Trained Triple Crown winner (Whirlaway in 1941). Trained Kentucky Derby winner 6 times, more than any other trainer (1938, 1941, 1944, consecutively 1948-49, 1952), Preakness Stakes winner 2 times (1941, 1944) and Belmont Stakes winner 1 time (1941).

Bobby Jones (b. 3-17-02, d. 12-18-71): Golfer. Achieved golf's only recognized Grand Slam in 1930. Second alltime in major championships (13). Won U.S. Amateur 5 times, more than any golfer (consecutively 1924-25, 1927-28, 1930), U.S. Open 4 times (1923, 1926, consecutively 1929-30), British Open 3 times (consecutively 1926-27, 1930) and British Amateur (1930). Also designed Augusta National course, site of the Masters, and founded the tournament. Winner of Sullivan Award in 1930.

K.C. Jones (b. 5-25-32): Basketball G-coach. Member of 8 straight NBA-championship Boston Celtic teams in his nine season career from 1958–59 through 1966–67. Averaged 7.4 points and 4.3 assists per game. Coached Celtics from 1983–84 through 1987–88, with 308–102 regular season record and 65–37 playoff record with NBA titles in 1984 and '86.

Robert Trent Jones (b. 6-20-06): English-born golf course architect designed or remodeled over 400 courses, including Baltusrol, Hazeltine, Oak Hill and Winged Foot. In the mid-60s five straight U.S. Opens were played on courses designed or remodeled by Jones.

Roy Jones Jr. (b.1-16-69): Boxer. Won silver medal at the 1988 Olympics in Seoul despite dominating his South Korean opponent in the final. Decision commonly called worst in Olympic boxing history. Awarded Val Barker Trophy as outstanding boxer of '88 Games. Won titles at middleweight, super middleweight and light heavyweight as a professional.

Sam Jones (b. 6-24-33): Basketball G. Played 12 seasons with Boston Celtics (1958–69) which won NBA title every year from 1959–66, plus 1968 and '69. Averaged 17.7 points per game. Elected to Hall of Fame in 1983.

Michael Jordan (b. 2-17-63): Basketball G. "Air." Arguably greatest player of all time. Led Bulls to six NBA titles (consecutively, 1991–93; 1996–98). Retired after 1997–98 season with alltime highest regular season scoring average (31.5) and most points scored in a playoff game (63 in 1986). Guided Bulls to an NBA-record 72 wins in 1995–96. Led league in scoring a record 10 seasons; led in steals 3 times. League MVP in 1988, 1991–92,'96 and '98; Finals MVP in 1991–93 and 1996–98; Rookie of the Year in 1985. All-Star team 6 consecutive seasons, All-Defensive team 5 consecutive seasons. Career span 1984–93, 1995–98 with Chicago. Announced retirement on 10-6-93, returned in March 1995. Also College Player of the Year in 1984. Played on NCAA championship team with North Carolina in 1982. Member of gold medal-winning 1984 and '92 Olympic teams.

Florence Griffith Joyner (b. 12-21-59, d. 9-21-98): Track and field. Won 3 gold medals (100 meters, 200 meters, 4x100-meter relay) at 1988 Olympics; Set world record in 100 (10.49) in 1988 and in 200 (21.34) at the 1988 Olympics. Sullivan Award winner in 1988.

Jackie Joyner-Kersee (b. 3-3-62): Track and field. Gold medalist in heptathlon and long jump at 1988 Olympics and in the former at the 1992 Olympics. Set heptathlon world record (7,291 points) at 1988 Olympics. Also won silver medal in heptathlon at 1984 Olympics and bronze in long jump at 1992 and '96 Olympics. Sullivan Award winner in 1986.

Alberto Juantorena (b. 3-12-51): Track and field. Cuban was gold medalist in 400 meters and 800 meters at 1976 Olympics.

Wang Junxia (b. 1963): Chinese distance runner. Broke four existing world records over six days in Sept. 1993. Broke 10,000 (29:31.78) on 9-8; ran 1500 in 3:51.92 in finishing second to countrywoman Qu Yunxia's world record of 3:50.46 on 9-11; ran 3,000 record of 8:12.19 in heats on 9-12 and lowered it to 8:06.11 on 9-13. Won gold in 5,000 and silver in 10,000 at 1996 Olympics.

Sonny Jurgensen (b. 8-23-34): Football QB. In 18 seasons completed 2,433 of 4,262 pass attempts for 32,224 yards and 255 TDs. Led NFL in passing both 1967 and '69. Career span 1957–1974 with Philadelphia Eagles and Washington Redskins. Elected to Hall of Fame in 1983.

Duke Kahanamoku (b. 8-24-1890, d. 1-22-68): Swimmer. Won a total of 5 medals (3 gold and 2 silver) at 3 Olympics in 1912, 1920, 1924. Introduced the crawl stroke to America. Surfing pioneer and water polo player. Later sheriff of Honolulu.

Al Kaline (b. 12-19-34): Baseball OF. 3,007 career hits and 399 career HR. As a 20-year-old in 1955, became youngest player to win batting title, with .340 average. Had .300+ average 9 times. Played in 18 All-Star games. Career span 1953–74 with Detroit.

Anatoly Karpov (b. 5-23-61): Soviet chess player. First world champion to receive title by default, in 1975, when Bobby Fischer chose not to defend his crown. Champion until 1985 when beaten by Garry Kasparov. Recognized by FIDE as champion in 1994.

Garry Kasparov (b. 4-13-63): Born Harry Weinstein. Chess player. World champion from 1985 to 1993 when stripped of title by FIDE. Won six-game series against IBM computer, Deep Blue, in 1996. Lost to Deep Blue in 1997.

Kip Keino (b. 1-17-40): Track and field. Kenyan was gold medalist in 1,500 meters at 1968 Olympics and in steeplechase at 1972 Olympics.

Jim Kelly (b. 2-14-60): Football QB. Led NFL in passing in 1990 (219 of 346 for 2,829 yards and 24 TDs). Led AFC in passing in 1991. In 11 seasons completed 2,874 of 4,779 attempts for 35,467 yards and 237 TDs. Career span 1983–85 with Houston Gamblers (USFL), 1986–96 with Buffalo Bills. Led Bills to four straight Super Bowls, all losses.

Kelso (b. 1957, d. 1983): Thoroughbred race horse. Gelding was Horse of the Year 5 straight years (1960-64). Finished in the money in 53 of 63 races. Career earnings $1,977,896.

Harmon Killebrew (b. 6-29-36): Baseball 3B-1B. 573 career HR total is fifth most alltime. 100+ RBI 9 times, 40+ HR 8 times. League leader in HR 6 times and RBI 4 times. 1969 MVP. 100+ walks and strikeouts 7 times each. Career span 1954-75 with Washington, Minnesota.

Jean Claude Killy (b. 8-30-43): French skier. Won 3 gold medals at 1968 Olympics. World Cup overall champion 2 consecutive years (1967-68).

Ralph Kiner (b. 10-27-22): Baseball OF. Third to Babe Ruth in alltime HR frequency (7.1 HR every 100 at bats). 369 career HR. Led league in HR 7 consecutive seasons, with 50+ HR 2 times; 100+ RBI and runs scored in same season 6 times; 100+ walks 6 times. Career span 1946–55 with Pittsburgh, Chicago (NL), and Cleveland.

Billie Jean King (b. 11-22-43): Tennis player. Won a record 20 Wimbledon titles, including 6 singles titles (consecutively 1966-68, 1972-73, 1975). Won 4 U.S. singles titles (1967, consecutively 1971-72, 1974), and singles titles at Australian Open (1968) and French Open (1972). Won 27 Grand Slam doubles titles—total of 39 Grand Slam titles is third alltime. Helped found the women's pro tour in 1970, serving as president of the Women's Tennis Association 2 times. Helped form Team Tennis.

Nile Kinnick (b. 7-9-18, d. 6-2-43): College football RB. Won the Heisman Trophy in 1939 with Iowa. Premier runner, passer and punter was killed in plane crash during routine Navy training flight. Stadium in Iowa City named in his honor.

Tom Kite (b. 12-9-49): Golfer. Second alltime PGA money leader. Led PGA in scoring average in 1981 (69.80) and '82 (70.21). PGA Player of Year in 1989, when he won a then-record $1,395,278. Shook reputation for failing to win the big ones by winning 1992 U.S. Open at windy Pebble Beach.

Franz Klammer (b. 12-3-54): Austrian alpine skier. Greatest downhiller ever. Gold medalist in downhill at 1976 Olympics. Also won four World Cup downhill titles (1975-78).

Bob Knight (b. 10-25-40): College basketball coach. Won 3 NCAA championships with Indiana in 1976, 1981, 1987. Coached U.S. Olympic team to gold medal in 1984. 720 career wins and .727 career winning percentage entering 1998–99 season. Career span since 1966 with Army, Indiana.

Olga Korbut (b. 5-16-55): Soviet gymnast. First ever to complete backward somersault on balance beam. Won 3 gold medals at 1972 Olympics.

Johann Olav Koss (b.10-29-68): Speed Skater. Norwegian won three gold medals at 1994 Olympics in Lillehammer, with world records in the 1,500, 5,000 and 10,000 meters. Won 1,500 meter gold medal and 10,000 meter silver medal in 1992 Games at Albertville.

Sandy Koufax (b. 12-30-35): Baseball LHP. Cy Young Award winner 3 times (1963, consecutively 1965-66); and MVP in 1963; World Series MVP in 1963, 1965. Pitched 1 perfect game, 3 no-hitters. League leader in ERA 5 consecutive seasons, strikeouts 4 times. Won 25+ games 3 times. Career record 165-87, with 2.76 ERA. Career span 1955-66 with Brooklyn/Los Angeles.

Jack Kramer (b. 8-1-21): Tennis player. Won 2 consecutive U.S. singles titles (1946-47) and 1 Wimbledon title (1947). Also won 6 Grand Slam doubles titles. Served as executive director of Association of Tennis Professionals from 1972 to 1975.

Ingrid Kristiansen (b. 3-21-56): Track and field. Norwegian runner is only person—male or female—to hold world records in 5,000 meters (14:37.33 set in 1986), 10,000 meters (30:13.74 set in 1986) and marathon (2:21:06 set in 1985, a record that still stands). Also won Boston Marathon 2 times (1986, 1989) and New York City Marathon once (1989).

Bob Kurland (b. 12-23-24): College basketball player. 6' 10¼" center on Oklahoma A&M teams that won NCAA titles in 1945 and '46. Consensus All America and NCAA tournament MVP in both 1945 and '46. Led nation in scoring in '46. His habit of swatting shots off rim led to creation of goaltending rule in 1945. Won gold medals in both 1948 and '52 Olympics. Turned down lucrative pro offers, playing instead for Phillips 66 Oilers AAU team.

Michelle Kwan (b. 7-7-80): Figure skater. Three-time U.S. champion (1996, '98, '99), two-time world champion (1996, '98); silver medalist in 1998 Olympics at Nagano.

Rene Lacoste (b. 7-2-05, d. 10-12-96): French tennis player. "The Crocodile." One of France's "Four Musketeers" of the 1920s. Won 3 French singles titles (1925, 1927, 1929), 2 consecutive U.S. titles (1926–27) and 2 Wimbledon titles (1925, 1928). Also designed casual shirt with embroidered crocodile that bears his name.

Marion Ladewig (b. 10-30-14): Bowler. Won All-Star Tournament 8 times (consecutively 1949–52, 1954, 1956, 1959, 1963) and WPBA National Championship once (1960). Also voted Bowler of the Year 9 times (consecutively 1950–54, 1957–59, 1963).

Guy Lafleur (b. 9-20-51): Hockey RW. Won MVP award 2 consecutive seasons (1977–78), playoff MVP in 1977. Scored 50+ goals and 100+ points 6 consecutive seasons. Led league in points scored 3 consecutive seasons, goals and assists 1 time each. 560 career goals, 793 assists. Played on 5 Stanley Cup champions with Montreal from 1971 to 1985.

Curly Lambeau (b. 4-9-1898; d. 6-1-65): Football QB and coach. Quarterback for Packers team in early 20's. Record 212-106-21 in his 29 seasons (1921–49) as Packer coach, winning three NFL titles in 1929–31.

Jack Lambert (b. 7-8-52): Football LB. Anchored Pittsburgh's famed "Steel Curtain" defense. Selected for Pro Bowl 9 times. Played on four Super Bowl champions (consecutively 1974–75, 1978–79) with Pittsburgh from 1974 to 1984. Elected to Hall of Fame 1990.

Jake LaMotta (b. 7-10-21): Boxer. "The Bronx Bull." Subject of *Raging Bull*, movie by Martin Scorsese, starring Robert DeNiro. Won middleweight title by knocking out Marcel Cerdan in 10 on 6-16-49. Lost title to Ray Robinson, who KO'd him in 13 on 2-13-51. Career record: 106 bouts; won 30 by KO and 53 by decision; drew 4; and lost 19, 4 by KO.

Kenesaw Mountain Landis (b. 11-20-1866, d. 11-25-44): Baseball's first and most powerful commissioner from 1920 to 1944. By banning the 8 "Black Sox" involved in the fixing of the 1919 World Series, he restored public confidence in the integrity of baseball.

Tom Landry (b. 9-11-24): Football coach. Third alltime in wins (270). The first coach in Dallas history, from 1960 to 1988. Led team to 13 division titles, 7 championship games and 5 Super Bowls. Won 2 Super Bowl championships (1971, 1977). Career record 270-178-6.

Dick (Night Train) Lane (b. 4-16-28): Football DB. Third alltime in interceptions (68) and second in interception yardage (1,207). Set record with 14 interceptions as a rookie in 1952. Career span 1952–65 with Los Angeles, Chicago Cardinals, Detroit.

Joe Lapchick (b. 4-12-00, d. 8-10-70): Basketball C-coach. One of the first big men in basketball, member of New York's Original Celtics. Coached St. John's (1936–47, 1956–65) winning four NIT Tournaments. Coached New York Knicks, 1947–56.

Steve Largent (b. 9-28-54): Football WR. Retired as alltime leader in pass receptions (819), and TD receptions (100). 177 consecutive games with reception, 10 seasons with 50+ receptions and 8 seasons with 1,000+ yards receiving. Career span 1976–89 with Seattle. Oklahoma congressman since 1994.

Don Larsen (b. 8-7-29): Baseball RHP. Pitched only perfect game in World Series history for the NY Yankees on Oct. 8, 1956, beating the Dodgers 2–0; named World Series MVP. Career span 1953–67 for many teams.

Tommy Lasorda (b. 9-22-27): Baseball manager. Spent nearly his entire minor and major league career in Dodgers organization as a pitcher, coach and manager. Managed Dodgers since 1977, winning 4 pennants and 2 World Series (1981, 1988). Retired July 1996, citing health concerns. Only three men managed one baseball team longer.

Rod Laver (b. 8-9-38): Australian tennis player. "Rocket." Only player to achieve the Grand Slam twice (as an amateur in 1962 and as a pro in 1969). Third alltime in men's Grand Slam singles titles (11—tied with Bjorn Borg). Won 4 Wimbledon titles (consecutively 1961-62, 1968-69), 3 Australian titles (1960, 1962, 1969), 2 U.S. titles (1962, 69) and 2 French titles (1962, 1969). Also won 8 Grand Slam doubles titles. First player to earn $1 million in prize money. 47 career tournament victories. Member of undefeated Australian Davis Cup team from 1959 to 1962.

Andrea Mead Lawrence (b. 4-19-32): Skier. Gold medalist in slalom and giant slalom at 1952 Olympics.

Bobby Layne (b. 12-19-26; d. 12-1-86): Football QB. Led Detroit Lions to NFL championships in both 1952 and '53. In 1952 led NFL in every passing category. Career span 1948–62, most with the Detroit Lions. Elected to Hall of Fame in 1967.

Sammy Lee (b. 8-1-20): Diver. Gold medalist at 2 consecutive Olympics (highboard in 1948, 1952); bronze medalist in springboard at 1948 Olympics. Won the 1953 Sullivan Award. Also 1960 U.S. Olympic diving coach.

Jacques Lemaire (b. 9-7-45): Hockey C-Coach. As center for Montreal Canadiens from 1967–68 through 1978–79 was part of eight Stanley Cup winning teams. Over 12 seasons, all with Montreal, scored 366 goals and had 469 assists. Elected to Hall of Fame in 1984. Coached Canadiens 1983-85 and N.J. Devils 1993–98.

Mario Lemieux (b. 10-5-65): Hockey C. Won MVP award in 1988, '93, '96. Playoff MVP in 1991. Led league in points 5 seasons and goals scored 3 seasons, assists 1 season. Scored 40+ goals and 100+ points 6 consecutive seasons, including 85 goals and 199 points in 1989. Rookie of the Year in 1985. Won 1992–93 scoring title despite sitting out six weeks to receive treatment for Hodgkin's disease, a form of cancer. Sat out 1994–95 season, returned in '95–96 to lead league in scoring and become second fastest player to score 500 career goals. Career span 1984–94, 1995–97 with Pittsburgh.

Greg LeMond (b. 6-26-61): Cyclist. First American to win Tour de France; won event 3 times (1986, consecutively 1989–90). Recovered from hunting accident to win in 1989.

Ivan Lendl (b. 3-7-60): Tennis player. Second alltime men's most career tournament victories (94). Won 3 consecutive U.S. Open singles titles (1985–87) and 3 French Open titles (1984, consecutively 1985–86). Also won 2 consecutive Australian Open titles (1989–90). Reached Grand Slam final 9 other times.

Suzanne Lenglen (b. 5-24-1899, d. 7-4-38): French tennis player. Lost only 1 match from 1919 to her retirement in 1926. Won 6 Wimbledon singles and doubles titles (consecutively 1919–23, 1925). Won 6 French singles and doubles titles (consecutively 1920–23, 1925–26).

Sugar Ray Leonard (b. 5-17-56): Boxer. Champion in five weight classes: welterweight, junior middleweight, middleweight, super middleweight and light heavyweight. Career record 36-3-1 with 25 KOs from 1977 to 1997, including comeback loss to Hector Camacho at the age of 41. Also light welterweight gold medalist at 1976 Olympics.

Carl Lewis (b. 7-1-61): Track and field. Held world record for 100 meters 9.86; set on 8-25-91 at World Championships in Tokyo. Duplicated Jesse Owens's feat by winning 4 gold medals at 1984 Olympics (100 and 200 meters, 4x100-meter relay and long jump). Also won 2 gold medals (100 meters, long jump) and 1 silver (200 meters) at 1988 Olympics and two gold medals (long jump, 4x100 relay) at 1992 Olympics. Sullivan Award winner in 1981. Won 1996 Olympic long jump gold at age 35, giving him nine career gold medals and making him just the second track and field athlete (along with Al Oerter) to win four golds in a single event.

Nancy Lieberman-Cline (b. 7-1-58): Basketball G. Three-time All-America at Old Dominion. Player of the Year (1979, 1980). Olympian, 1976, and selected for 1980 team, but quit because of Moscow boycott. Promoter of women's basketball, played in WPBL, WABA. First woman to play basketball in a men's professional league (USBL), in 1986. Joined WNBA in 1997, retired in '98 to become GM/coach of the Detroit Shock.

Bob Lilly (b. 7-26-39): Football DT. Dallas Cowboys' first ever draft pick, first Pro Bowl player and first all-NFL choice. Made all-NFL eight times. Career span 1961–74, all with Cowboys. Elected to Hall of Fame in 1980.

Tara Lipinski (b. 6-10-82): Figure skater. In 1998 at Nagano eclipsed Sonja Henie as the youngest individual Winter Olympic champion in history when, at 15, she won the women's figure skating gold medal. Also won U.S. and world championships in 1997.

Sonny Liston (b. 5-8-32, d. 12-30-70): Boxer. Heavyweight champion from 1962 to 1964. Won title by KO of Floyd Patterson on 9-25-62. Lost title when TKO'd by Cassius Clay (Muhammad Ali) on 2-25-64 and then lost rematch on 5-25-65 when KO'd in first round. Career record: 54 fights; won 39 by KO and 11 by decision; lost 4, three by KO.

Vince Lombardi (b. 6-11-13, d. 9-3-70): Football coach. Second highest alltime winning percentage (.740). Career record 105-35-6. Won 5 NFL championships and 2 consecutive Super Bowl titles with Green Bay from 1959 to 1967. Coached Washington in 1969. Super Bowl trophy named in his honor.

Johnny Longden (b. 2-14-07): Horse racing jockey. Rode Triple Crown winner Count Fleet in 1943. 6,032 wins.

Nancy Lopez (b. 1-6-57): Golfer. LPGA Player of the Year 4 times (consecutively 1978-79, 1985, 1988). Winner of LPGA Championship 3 times (1978, 1985, 1989). Member of the LPGA Hall of Fame.

Greg Louganis (b. 1-29-60): Diver. Gold medalist in platform and springboard at 2 consecutive Olympics in 1984, 1988. World champion 5 times (platform in 1978, 1982, 1986; springboard in 1982, 1986). Also Sullivan Award winner in 1984.

Joe Louis (b. 5-13-14, d. 4-12-81): Boxer. "The Brown Bomber." Longest title reign of any heavyweight champion (11 years, 9 months) from June 1937 through March 1949. Career record 63-3 with 49 KOs from 1934 to 1951. Defended title 25 times.

Jerry Lucas (b. 3-30-40): Basketball F. Star at Ohio State. *Sporting News* College Player of Year in both 1961 and '62. In 1960 member of both NCAA championship team and gold-medal winning U.S. Olympic team. Averaged over 20 points and 20 rebounds a game for college career. NBA Rookie of Year in 1964. In 11 NBA seasons averaged 17 points a game. Elected to Hall of Fame in 1979.

Sid Luckman (b. 11-21-16, d. 7-5-98): Football QB. Played on 4 NFL champions (consecutively 1940-41, 1943, 1946) with Chicago. Player of the Year in 1943. Tied record with 7 touchdown passes on Nov. 14, 1943. All-Pro 6 times. 137 career touchdown passes. Career span 1939-50. Also All-America with Columbia.

Jon Lugbill (b. 5-27-61): Whitewater canoe racer. Won 5 world singles titles from 1979 to 1989.

Hank Luisetti (b. 6-16-16): Basketball F. The first player to use the one-handed shot. All-America at Stanford 3 consecutive years from 1936-38.

D. Wayne Lukas (b. 9-2-35): Horse racing trainer. Former college basketball coach and quarter horse trainer. Trained two Horses of the Year, Lady's Secret in 1986 and Criminal Type in 1990. Won 1988 Kentucky Derby with a filly, Winning Colors. Won 1994 Preakness and Belmont with Tabasco Cat. Won all three Triple Crown races in 1995, with Thunder Gulch (Kentucky Derby and Belmont) and Timber Country (Preakness). Won 1999 Derby and Preakness with Charismatic. Six-race Triple Crown winning streak ended at '96 Preakness.

Connie Mack (b. 2-22-1862, d. 2-8-56): Born Cornelius McGillicuddy. Baseball manager. Managed Philadelphia for 50 years (1901-50) until age 87. Alltime leader in games (7,755), wins (3,731) and losses (3,948). Won 9 pennants and 5 World Series (1910-11, 1913, 1929-30).

Greg Maddux (b. 4-14-66): Baseball P. Won unprecedented fourth consecutive Cy Young Award in 1995, when he was 19-2 with a 1.63 ERA and led the Atlanta Braves to their first World Series title. Career span 1986-92 Chicago (NL), 1993- Atlanta.

Larry Mahan (b. 11-21-43): Rodeo. All-Around champion 6 times (consecutively 1966-70, 1973).

Frank Mahovlich (b. 1-10-38): Hockey LW. Winner of Calder Trophy for top rookie for 1957-58 season. In 18 NHL seasons with Toronto Maple Leafs, Detroit Red Wings and Montreal Canadiens, had 533 goals and 570 assists. Played for six Stanley Cup winners. Elected to Hall of Fame 1981.

Phil Mahre (b. 5-10-57): Skier. Gold medalist in slalom at 1984 Olympics (twin brother Steve won silver medal). World Cup champion 3 consecutive years (1981-83).

Joe Malone (b. 2-28-1890, d. 5-15-69): Hockey F. "Phantom Joe." Led the NHL in its first season, 1917-18, with 44 goals in 20 games with Montreal. Led league in scoring 2 times (1918, 1920). Holds NHL record with most goals scored, single game (7) in 1920.

Karl Malone (b. 7-24-63): Basketball F. "The Mailman." Eight-time first-team All-Star. All-Star MVP, 1989, 1993 (shared with John Stockton). All-Rookie team, 1986. League MVP in 1997 when he led Jazz to NBA Finals. Won a second MVP award in '99. Member of 1992 and '96 Olympic teams. Career span since 1985 with Utah.

Moses Malone (b. 3-23-55): Basketball C. Alltime leader free throws made (8,531), fifth in rebounds (16,212) and third in points scored (27,409). 3 MVP awards in 1979, consecutively 1982-83; playoff MVP in 1983. 4-time All-Star. Led league in rebounding 6 times, 5 consecutively. Career span 1976-95 with Houston, Philadelphia, Washington, Atlanta, Milwaukee, San Antonio.

Hermann Maier (b.12-7-72): Austrian skier. Recovered from spectacular crash in the downhill to win two gold medals at 1998 Olympics in Nagano. Won 1998 Super G, Giant Slalom and overall World Cup season titles.

Man o' War (b. 1917, d. 1947): Thoroughbred race horse. Won 20 of 21 races 1919-20. Only loss was in 1919 in Sanford Stakes to Upset. Passed up Derby but won both Preakness and Belmont. Winner of $249,465. Sire of War Admiral, 1937 Triple Crown winner.

Mickey Mantle (b. 10-20-31, d. 8-13-95): Baseball OF. Won 3 MVP awards, consecutively 1956-57 and 1962; won Triple Crown in 1956. 536 career HR. Greatest switch hitter in history. Played in 20 All-Star games. Alltime World Series leader in HR (18), RBI (40) and runs scored (42). No. 7 was a member of 7 World Series winners with NY Yankees. Career span 1951-68.

Diego Maradona (b. 10-30-60): Argentine soccer player. Led Argentina to 1986 World Cup victory and to 1990 World Cup finals. Led Naples to Italian League titles (1987, 1990), Italian Cup (1987) and to European Cham-pions' Cup title (1989). Throughout 1980s often acknowledged as best player in the world. Tested positive for cocaine and suspended by FIFA and Italian Soccer Federation for 15 months in March 1991. Failed drug test in 1994 World Cup and suspended before second round.

Pete Maravich (b. 6-22-47, d. 1-5-88): Basketball G. "Pistol Pete." Alltime NCAA leader in points scored (3,667), scoring average (44.2) and games scoring 50+ points (28, including then Division I record 69 points in 1970). Alltime season leader in points scored (1,381) and scoring average (44.5) in 1970. College Player of the Year in 1970. NCAA scoring leader and All-America 3 consecutive seasons from 1968 to 1970 with Louisiana State. Also led NBA in scoring in 1977. Averaged 20+ points 8 times. All-Star 2 times. Career span 1970–79 with Atlanta, New Orleans/Utah, Boston.

Gino Marchetti (b. 1-2-27): Football DE. Played in Pro Bowl every year from 1955 to '65, except 1958 when he broke right ankle tackling Frank Gifford in Colts' 23–17 win over the Giants. Career span 1952–66, almost all with Baltimore Colts. Inducted into Hall of Fame in 1972.

Rocky Marciano (b. 9-1-23, d. 8-31-69): Boxer. Heavyweight champion (1952–56). Career record 49–0 with 43 KOs from 1947 to 1956. Only heavyweight to retire as undefeated champion.

Juan Marichal (b. 10-24-37): Baseball RHP. 243 career wins, 2.89 career ERA. Won 20+ games 6 times; 250+ innings pitched 8 times; 200+ strikeouts 6 times. Pitched no-hitter in 1963. Career span 1960–75, mostly with San Francisco. Elected to Hall of Fame in 1983.

Dan Marino (b. 9-15-61): Football QB. Set alltime season record for yards passing (5,084) and touchdown passes (48) in 1984. Has passed for 4,000+ yards 5 other seasons. Player of the Year in 1984. Career totals through 1998–99 season: 58,913 yards passing, 408 touchdown passes, first alltime in both categories. Career span since 1983 with Miami.

Roger Maris (b. 9-10-34, d. 12-14-85): Baseball OF. Broke Babe Ruth's alltime season HR record with 61 in 1961. Won consecutive MVP awards and led league in RBIs 1960–61. Career span 1957–68 with Kansas City, New York (AL), St. Louis.

Billy Martin (b. 5-16-28, d. 12-25-89): Baseball 2B-manager. Volatile manager was hired and fired by Minnesota, Detroit, Texas, New York Yankees (five times!) and Oakland from 1969 to 1988. Won World Series with Yankees as manager in 1977 and as player four times.

Pedro Martinez (b. 10-25-71): Baseball P. Dominican righthander went 17–8 with a 1.90 ERA and 305 strikeouts for Montreal in 1997 to win Cy Young award. First pitcher in 25 years to have more than 300 Ks and ERA below 2.00. Was 23–4 with 2.07 ERA for Boston in '99. Started '99 All-Star Game and was named MVP after striking out first four batters.

Eddie Mathews (b. 10-13-31): Baseball 3B. 512 career HR and 30+ HR 9 consecutive seasons. League leader in HR 2 times, walks 4 times. Career span 1952–68 with Milwaukee.

Christy Mathewson (b. 8-12-1880, d. 10-7-25): Baseball RHP. Third alltime most wins (373, tied with Grover Alexander) and shutouts (79); career ERA 2.13. Led league in wins 5 times; won 30+ games 4 times and 20+ games 9 other times. Led league in ERA and strikeouts 5 times each. Pitched two no-hitters. Pitched three shutouts in 1905 World Series. Career span 1900–16 with New York. Played one game for Reds in 1916.

Bob Mathias (b. 11-17-30): Track and field. At age 17, youngest to win gold medal in decathlon at 1948 Olympics. First decathlete to win gold medal at consecutive Olympics (1948, 1952). Also won Sullivan Award in 1948.

Ollie Matson (b. 5-1-30): Football RB. Versatile runner totalled 12,884 combined yards rushing, receiving and kick returning. Scored 73 career touchdowns, including a 105-yard kickoff return on Oct. 14, 1956, the second longest ever. Career span 1952–66 with Chicago Cardinals, Los Angeles, Detroit, Philadelphia. Also won bronze medal in 400-meters at 1952 Olympics. Elected to Hall of Fame in 1972.

Roland Matthes (b. 11-17-50): German swimmer. Gold medalist in 100-meter and 200-meter backstroke at 2 consecutive Olympics (1968, 1972). Set 16 world records from 1967 to 1973.

Don Maynard (b. 1-25-37): Football WR. Retired in 1973 as the NFL's alltime leading receiver. In 15 seasons, 10 with the New York Jets, caught 633 passes for 11,834 yards and 88 TDs. Averaged 18.7 yards per catch for career. In 1967 and '68 led AFL with average of 20.2 and 22.8 yards per catch. Elected to Hall of Fame in 1987.

Willie Mays (b. 5-6-31): Baseball OF. "Say Hey Kid." MVP in 1954, 1965; Rookie of the Year in 1951. Third alltime most HR (660), with 50+ HR 2 times, 30+ HR 9 other times. Led league in HR 4 times. 100+ RBI 10 times; 100+ runs scored 12 consecutive seasons. 3,283 career hits. Led league in stolen bases 4 consecutive seasons. 30 HR and 30 steals in same season 2 times and first man in history to hit 300+ HR and steal 300+ bases. Won 11 consecutive Gold Gloves; set record for career putouts by an outfielder and league record for total chances. His catch in the 1954 World Series off the bat of Vic Wertz called the greatest ever. Career span 1951–73 with New York and San Francisco Giants, New York Mets.

Bill Mazeroski (b. 9-5-36): Baseball 2B. Hit dramatic 9th-inning home run in Game 7 to win 1960 World Series, first of only two Series' to end on a home run. Also a great fielder, won Gold Glove 8 times. Led league in assists 9 times, double plays 8 times and putouts 5 times.

Joe McCarthy (b. 4-21-1887, d. 1-3-78): Baseball manager. Alltime highest winning percentage among managers for regular season (.615) and World Series (.763). First manager to win pennants in both leagues (Chicago (NL), 1929, New York (AL), 1932). From 1926 to 1950 his teams won 7 World Series and 9 pennants.

Mark McCormack (b. 11-6-30): Sports marketing agent. Founded International Management Group in 1962. Also author of best-selling business advice books.

Pat McCormick (b. 5-12-30): Diver. Gold medalist in platform and springboard at 2 consecutive Olympics (1952, 1956). Also won Sullivan Award in 1956.

Willie McCovey (b. 1-10-38): Baseball 1B. Led NL in homers three times (1963, '68, '69) and in RBIs twice (1968–69). 521 career homers. .270 career batting average. Hit 18 grand slams. Rookie of Year 1959. NL MVP in 1969. Career span 1959–73 and 1977–80 with San Francisco Giants, 1974–76 with San Diego Padres and 1976 with Oakland A's. Elected to Hall of Fame in 1986.

John McEnroe (b. 2-26-59): Tennis player. Won 4 U.S. Open singles titles (consecutively 1979–81, 1984) and 3 Wimbledon titles (1981, consecutively 1983–84).

Also won 8 Grand Slam doubles titles. Third alltime men's most career tournament victories (77). Led U.S. to 5 Davis Cup victories (1978–79, 1981–82, 1992).

John McGraw (b. 4-7-1873, d. 2-25-34): Baseball manager. Second alltime most games (4,801) and wins (2,784). Guided New York Giants to three World Series titles and 10 pennants from 1902 to 1932.

Mark McGwire (b. 10-1-63): Baseball 1B. Broke Roger Maris's 37-year-old single-season HR record with 70 in 155 games in 1998; season also included 162 walks—tied for second most alltime—and seventh alltime best slugging pct of .752. Rookie of the Year in 1987, when he hit rookie record 49 HR. Hit 30+ HR 10 times, 40+ HR five times, 50+ HR three straight years (1996–98). Member of 1984 U.S. Olympic baseball team. Career span 1986–97 Oakland; since 1997 with St. Louis.

Denny McLain (b. 3-29-44): Baseball RHP. Last pitcher to win 30+ games in a season (Detroit, 1968); won 20+ games two other times. Won two consecutive Cy Young Awards (1968–69). Led league in innings pitched two times. Served 2½-year jail term for 1985 conviction of extortion, racketeering and drug possession. Re-entered prison in 1997 on fraud conviction. Career span 1963–72.

Mary T. Meagher (b. 10-27-64): Swimmer. "Madame Butterfly." Won three gold medals at 1984 Olympics (100-meter butterfly, 200-meter butterfly and 400-medley relay). In 1981 set world records in 100-meter butterfly (57.93) and 200-meter butterfly (2:05.96).

Rick Mears (b. 12-3-51): Auto racer. Has won Indy 500 four times (1979, '84, '88, '91) and been CART champion three times (1979, consecutively 1981-82). Named Indy 500 Rookie of the Year in 1978.

Eddy Merckx (b. 1945): Belgian cyclist. Won five Tours de France, including four in a row (1969–72).

Mark Messier (b. 1-18-61): Hockey C. Two-time Hart Trophy (MVP) winner; won Stanley Cups with Edmonton (1984, '85, '87, '88 and '90) and NY Rangers (1994). Among top five alltime in points, top ten in goals, assists. Career span 1979–91 Edmonton, 1991–96 NY Rangers, 1997– Vancouver.

Cary Middlecoff (b. 1-6-21): Golfer. Also a dentist. Won 40 PGA tournaments, including 1955 Masters and U.S. Opens in 1949 and '56. Won 1956 Vardon Trophy.

George Mikan (b. 6-18-24): Basketball C. Averaged 20+ points per game and named to All-Star team six consecutive seasons. Led league in scoring three times, rebounding once. Played on five championship teams in six years (1949–54) with Minneapolis. Also played on 1945 NIT championship team with DePaul. All-America three times. Served as ABA Commissioner from 1968 to 1969.

Stan Mikita (b. 5-20-40): Hockey C. Won MVP award two consecutive seasons (1967–68). 926 career assists, 1,467 career points. Led league in assists four straight seasons and points four times. 541 career goals. All-Star six times. Career span 1958–80 with Chicago.

Del Miller (b. 7-5-13; d. 8-19-96): Harness racing driver. Raced in eight decades, beginning in 1929, the longest career of any athlete. Won The Hambletonian in 1950.

Marvin Miller (b. 4-14-17): Labor negotiator. Union chief of MLB Players Association from 1966 to 1984. Led strikes in 1972 and '81. Negotiated five labor contracts

that increased minimum salary and pension fund, allowed for agents and arbitration, and brought about the end of the reserve clause and the start of free agency.

Art Monk (b. 12-5-57): Football WR. Second alltime in pass receptions (940 for 12,721 and 68 TDs through end of 1995–96 season). 106 catches in 1984 was then NFL single season record. Career span 1980–93 with Redskins, 1993–95 with New York Jets, 1995 with Eagles.

Earl Monroe (b. 11-21-44): Basketball G. "The Pearl" played 13 seasons (1968–80) with the Baltimore Bullets and New York Knicks. NBA Rookie of Year in 1968. Member of 1973 NBA championship Knicks team. Averaged 18.8 points a game. Elected to Hall of Fame 1989.

Joe Montana (b. 6-11-56): Football QB. Second alltime highest-rated passer (92.3); third in completions (3,409); retired with 40,551 passing yards and 273 touchdown passes. Won 4 Super Bowl championships (1981, 1984, consecutively 1988–89) with San Francisco. Named Super Bowl MVP three times (1981, 1984, 1989). Player of the Year in 1989. Also led Notre Dame to national championship in 1977. Career span 1979–92 with San Francisco, 1993–94 Kansas City.

Carlos Monzon (b. 8-7-42, d. 1-8-95): Argentine boxer. Longest title reign of any middleweight champion (6 years, 9 months) from Nov. 1970 through Aug. 1977. Career record 89-3-9 with 61 KOs from 1963 to 1977. Won 82 consecutive bouts from 1964 to 1977. Defended title 14 times. Retired as champion.

Helen Wills Moody (b. 10-6-05, d. 1-1-98): Tennis player. Third alltime most women's Grand Slam singles titles (19). Her eight Wimbledon titles are second most alltime (consecutively 1927–30, 1932–33, 1935, 1938). Won seven U.S. titles (consecutively 1923–25, 1927–29, 1931) and four French titles (consecutively 1928–30, 1932). Also won 12 Grand Slam doubles titles.

Archie Moore (b. 12-13-16 d. 12-9-98): Boxer. Longest title reign of any half heavyweight champion (9 years, 1 month) from Dec. 1952 through Feb. 1962. Career record 199-26-8 with an alltime record 145 KOs from 1935 to 1965. Retired at age 52.

Davey Moore (b. 11-1-33; d. 3-23-63): Boxer. Won featherweight title by KO of Kid Bassey in 13 on 3-18-59. Five successful defenses of title, before losing it on 3-21-63 to Sugar Ramos who KO'd him in 10. Died two days after fight of brain damage suffered during fight. Career record: 67 bouts; won 30 by KO, 28 by decision, 1 because of foul; drew 1; lost 7, two by KO.

Noureddine Morceli (b. 2-20-70). Algerian track and field middle distance runner. Set world record for mile (3:44.39) in Rieti, Italy, on 9-5-93. Set world record for 1,500 (3:28.86) on 9-5-92. World champion at 1,500 in both 1991 and '93. Finished a shocking seventh at 1992 Olympics, but won gold medal in '96 at Atlanta. Only man ever to rank first in the world at 1,500/mile four straight years (1990–93).

Joe Morgan (b. 9-19-43): Baseball 2B. Won two consecutive MVP awards in 1975-76. Third alltime most walks (1,865). 689 stolen bases. Led league in walks four times. 100+ walks and runs scored eight times each; 40+ stolen bases nine times. Won five Gold Gloves. Second alltime most games played by 2nd baseman (2,527). Career span 1963–84 with Houston, Cincinnati, San Francisco, Philadelphia and Oakland.

Willie Mosconi (b. 6-27-13; d. 9-16-93): Pocket

billiards player. Won world title a record 15 straight times between 1941 and 1957. Once pocketed 526 balls without a miss.

Edwin Moses (b. 8-31-55): Track and field. Gold medalist in 400-meter hurdles at two Olympics, in 1976, '84 (U.S. boycotted '80 Games); bronze medalist at '88 Olympics. Set four world records in 400-meter hurdles (best of 47.02 set on 8-31-83). Won 122 consecutive races from 1977 to 1987. Won Sullivan Award in 1983.

Marion Motley (b. 6-5-20 d. 6-27-99): Football FB. All-time AAFC leader in yards rushing (3,024). Also led NFL in rushing once. Combined league totals: 4,712 yards rushing, 39 touchdowns. Played with four consecutive AAFC champions (1946–49) and one NFL champion (1950). Career span with Cleveland 1946–1953.

Shirley Muldowney (b. 6-19-40): Drag racer. First woman to win the Top Fuel championship, which she won three times (1977, 1980, 1982).

Anthony Munoz (b. 8-19-58): Football OT. Probably the greatest tackle ever. Made Pro Bowl a record-tying 11 times. Career span 1980–92 with the Cincinnati Bengals. Elected to Hall of Fame 1998.

Isaac Murphy (b. 4-16-1861, d. 2-12-1896): Horse racing jockey. Top jockey of his era, Murphy, who was black, won three Kentucky Derbys (aboard Buchanan in 1884, Riley in 1890 and Kingman in 1891).

Eddie Murray (b. 2-24-56): Baseball 1B. 100+ RBIs six seasons and 30+ HRs five seasons. Retired with 3,255 hits, 504 HRs and 1,917 RBI. Alltime leader in RBI by switch hitter. Career span 1977–88, '96 with Baltimore Orioles; 1989–91, '97 with Los Angeles; 1992–93 with New York Mets, 1994–96 with Cleveland; 1997 with Anaheim.

Jim Murray (b. 12-29-19; d. 8-16-98): Sportswriter. Won Pulitzer Prize in 1990. Named Sportswriter of the Year 14 times. Columnist for *Los Angeles Times* 1961–98.

Ty Murray (b. 10-11-69): Rodeo cowboy. All-Around world champion, 1989–94. Set single-season earnings record, 1990 ($213,771). Rookie of the Year, 1988. At 20 in 1989, became youngest man ever to win national all-around title.

Stan Musial (b. 11-21-20): Baseball OF-1B. "Stan the Man." Had .331 career batting average and 475 career HR. MVP award winner 1943, 1946, 1948. Fourth alltime in hits (3,630) and third in doubles (725). Won seven batting titles. Led league in hits six times, slugging average five times, doubles eight times. Had .300+ batting average 17 times, 200+ hits six times, 100+ RBI 10 times, and 100+ runs scored 11 times. 24-time All-Star. Career span 1941-63 with St. Louis.

John Naber (b. 1-20-56): Swimmer. Won four gold medals and one silver medal at 1976 Olympics. Sullivan Award winner in 1977.

Bronko Nagurski (b. 11-3-08, d. 1-7-90): Football FB. Punishing runner played on three NFL champions (1932, '33, '43) with Bears. 2,778 career yards, 1930–37 and 1943 with Chicago.

James Naismith (b. 11-6-1861, d. 11-28-39): Invented basketball in 1891 while an instructor at YMCA Training School in Springfield, Mass. Refined the game while a professor at Kansas from 1898 to 1937. Hall of Fame is named in his honor.

Joe Namath (b. 5-31-43): Football QB. "Broadway Joe." Super Bowl MVP in 1968 after he guaranteed victory for AFL. 173 career touchdown passes. Led league in yards passing 3 times, including 4,007 yards in 1967. Player of the Year in 1968, Rookie of the Year in 1965. Career span 1965–77 with NY Jets, LA Rams.

Ilie Nastase (b. 7-19-46): Romanian tennis player. "Nasty" for his unruly deportment on court. Beat Arthur Ashe to win 1972 U.S. Open title. Won 1973 French Open. Twice Wimbledon runnerup (to Stan Smith 1972 and Bjorn Borg in '76).

Martina Navratilova (b. 10-18-56): Tennis player. Fourth alltime most women's Grand Slam singles titles (18—tied with Chris Evert). Won a record nine Wimbledon titles, including six consecutively (1978–79, 1982–87, '90). Won four U.S. Open titles (consecutively 1983–84, 1986–87), three Australian Open titles (1981, '83, '85) and two French Open titles (1982, '84). Reached Grand Slam final 13 other times. Also won 38 Grand Slam doubles titles. Her total of 56 Grand Slam titles is second alltime to Margaret Court's. Set mark for longest winning streak with 74 matches in 1984. Also won the doubles Grand Slam in 1984 with Pam Shriver. Won 109 consecutive matches with Shriver from 1983–85. Retired after 1994 season.

Byron Nelson (b. 2-14-12): Golfer. Won the Masters (1937, 1942) and PGA Championship (1940, 1945) two times each and U.S. Open once (1939). Won 52 career tournaments, including 11 consecutively in 1945.

Ernie Nevers (b. 6-11-03, d. 5-3-76): Football FB. Set alltime pro single game record for points scored (40) and touchdowns (6) on Nov. 28, 1929. Career span 1926–31 with Duluth, Chicago. Also a pitcher with St. Louis, surrendered two of Babe Ruth's 60 home runs in 1927. All-America at Stanford, earned 11 letters in four sports.

John Newcombe (b. 5-23-44): Australian tennis player. Won 3 Wimbledon singles titles (1967, consecutively 1970–71), two U.S. titles (1967, 1973) and two Australian Open titles (1973, 1975). Also won 17 Grand Slam doubles titles.

Pete Newell (b. 8-31-15): College basketball coach. Despite coaching only 13 seasons, 1947 through 1960, was first coach to win NIT, NCAA and Olympic crowns. Led Univ. of San Francisco to 1949 NIT title, Cal to 1959 NCAA title, and the 1960 U.S. Olympic basketball team that included Jerry Lucas, Oscar Robertson and Jerry West to gold medal. Overall collegiate coaching record of 234–123.

Jack Nicklaus (b. 1-21-40): Golfer. "The Golden Bear." Alltime leader in major championships (20). Second alltime in career wins (70). Won Masters six times, more than any golfer (1963, consecutively 1965-66, '72, '75, '86—at age 46, the oldest player to win event), PGA Championship five times (1963, '71, '73, '75, '80), U.S. Open 4 times (1962, '67, '72, '80), British Open 3 times (1966, '70, '78) and U.S. Amateur twice (1959, '61). PGA Player of the Year five times (1967, consecutively 1972–73, 1975–76). Also NCAA champion with Ohio State in 1961.

Ray Nitschke (b. 12-29-36 d. 3-8-98): Football LB. Defensive signal caller for the great Packer teams of the '60s. Voted Packer MVP by teammates after 1967 season. MVP of the 1962 NFL title game. Career span 1958–72 with Green Bay Packers.

Chuck Noll (b. 1-5-32): Football coach. Led Pittsburgh to four Super Bowl victories in six years

(1975, '76, '79, '80). Retired in 1991 after 23 years and 209 victories.

Greg Norman (b. 2-10-55): Golfer. "The Shark" led PGA in winnings in 1986, '90, 1995–96. Won Vardon Trophy twice, 1989–90. Won two British Opens (1986, '93) but is almost as famous for his heartbreaking misses. Beaten at the 1986 PGA when Bob Tway holed out a sand shot and '87 Masters when Larry Mize chipped in from a downhill lie. Blew a six-stroke, third-round lead to lose to Nick Faldo by five shots at 1996 Masters. PGA Player of the Year 1996.

James D. Norris (b. 11-6-06, d. 2-25-66): Hockey executive. Owner of Detroit from 1933 to 1943 and Chicago from 1946 to 1966. Teams won four Stanley Cup championships (consecutively 1936–37, '43, '61). Defensive Player of the Year award named in his honor. Also a boxing promoter, operated International Boxing Club from 1949 to 1958.

Paavo Nurmi (b. 6-13-1897, d. 10-2-73): Track and field. Finnish middle- and long-distance runner won a total of nine gold medals at 3 Olympics in 1920, '24, '28.

Matti Nykänen (b. 7-17-63): Finnish ski jumper. Three-time Olympic gold medalist. Won 90-meter jump (1984, '88) and 70-meter jump (1988). World champion on 90-meter jump in 1982. Won four World Cups (1983, '85, 86, '88).

Dan O'Brien (b. 7-18-66): Track and field decathlete. Won world decathlon title in 1991, '93 and '95. Set world decathlon record of 8,891 in Talence, France, on 9-4/5-92, that stood for seven years. Heavily favored to win 1992 Olympic decathlon but missed making U.S. team when he no-heighted in pole vault at U.S. Olympic Trials. Won gold medal at 1996 Olympics in Atlanta.

Parry O'Brien (b. 1-28-32): Track and field. Shot putter who revolutionized the event with his "glide" technique and won Olympic gold medals in 1952 and '56, silver in '60. Set 10 world records from 1953 to 1959, topped by a put of 63' 4" in '59. Sullivan Award winner in 1959.

Al Oerter (b. 8-19-36): Track and field. Gold medalist in discus at 4 consecutive Olympics (1956, '60, '64, '68), setting Olympic record each time. First to break the 200-foot barrier, throwing 200' 5" in 1962.

Sadaharu Oh (b. 5-20-40): Baseball 1B in Japanese league. 868 career HR in 22 seasons for the Tokyo Giants. Led league in HR 15 times, RBIs 13 times, batting five times and runs 13 consecutive seasons. Awarded MVP nine times; won two consecutive Triple Crowns and nine Gold Gloves.

Hakeem Olajuwon (b. 1-21-63): Basketball C. From Nigeria. Led NCAA in field goal percentage, rebounding and blocked shots in 1984 at Houston. Alltime NBA career leader in blocked shots (3,459 through 1997–98). All-NBA First Team 1987–89, '93–94. League MVP in 1994 as he led Houston to NBA title (repeated in '95). Career span since 1985 with the Rockets. Member of 1996 U.S. Olympic team.

Merlin Olsen (b. 9-15-40): Fooball DT. Part of LA Rams "Fearsome Foursome" defensive line. Named to Pro Bowl 14 straight times. Career span 1962–76, all with LA Rams. Elected to Hall of Fame 1982.

Omaha (b. 1932, d. 1959): Thoroughbred race horse. Won Triple Crown in 1935. Trained by Sunny Jim Fitzsimmons.

Mark O'Meara (b. 1-13-57): Golfer. Won Masters and British Open in 1998. Tour rookie of the year in 1981; won 1979 U.S. Amateur.

Shaquille O'Neal (b. 3-6-72): Basketball C. Led NCAA in blocked shots in 1992, with 5.23 a game; averaged 4.58 over his 90-game, three-year career. Top pick of Orlando Magic in 1992 NBA draft. Almost unanimous NBA Rookie of the Year 1993. Averaged 23.4 points, 13.9 rebounds and 3.5 blocked shots in first NBA season. Led league in scoring with 29.3 average in 1994–95. Member of 1996 U.S. Olympic team. Moved to LA Lakers as free agent in July 1996.

Bobby Orr (b. 3-20-48): Hockey D. Defensive Player of the Year more than any other player, eight consecutive seasons (1968-75). Won MVP award three consecutive seasons (1970-72), playoff MVP two times (1970, '72). Also Rookie of the Year in 1967. Led league in assists five times and scoring two times. Career span 1966–77 with Boston.

Mel Ott (b. 3-2-09, d. 11-21-58): Baseball OF. 511 career HR, 1,861 RBI, .304 batting average. League leader in HR and walks six times each. 100+ RBI 9 times and 100+ walks ten times. Career span 1926–47 with New York Giants.

Jim Otto (b. 1-5-38): Football C. Number 00 started every game (308) in his 15-year career (1960–74) with the Oakland Raiders. Inducted into Hall of Fame in 1980.

Kristin Otto (b. 1966): German swimmer. Won six gold medals for East Germany at 1988 Olympics.

Jesse Owens (b. 9-12-13, d. 3-31-80): Track and field. Gold medalist in four events (100 meters and 200 meters; 4x100-meter relay and long jump) at 1936 Olympics. At the 1935 Big 10 championship set or equaled 4 world record in 70 minutes, including 100 yards, long jump, 220-yard low hurdles and 220 dash.

Alan Page (b. 8-7-45): Football DT. First defensive player to be named NFL Player of the Year, in 1972. Career span 1967–78 with Minnesota Vikings and 1978–81 with Chicago Bears. Now sits on Minnesota Supreme Court.

Satchel Paige (b. 7-7-06, d. 6-8-82): Baseball RHP. Alltime greatest black pitcher, didn't pitch in major leagues until 1948 at age 42 with Cleveland. Oldest pitcher in major league history at age 59 with Kansas City in 1965. Pitched in the Negro leagues from 1926 to 1950 with Birmingham Black Barons, Pittsburgh Crawfords and Kansas City Monarchs. Estimated career record is 2,000 wins, 250 shutouts, 30,000 strikeouts, 45 no-hitters. Said "Don't look back. Something may be gaining on you."

Se Ri Pak (b. 9-28-77): South Korean golfer. Named 1998 LPGA Rookie of the Year for a season in which she won both the first major she entered, the LPGA Championships, and the U.S. Open.

Arnold Palmer (b. 9-10-29): Golfer. Fourth alltime in career wins (60). Won the Masters four times (1958, 1960, 1962, 1964), British Open two consecutive years (1961–62) and U.S. Open (1960) and U.S. Amateur (1954) once each. PGA Player of the Year two times (1960, 1962). The first golfer to surpass $1 million in career earnings. Also won Seniors Championship two times (1980, 1984) and U.S. Senior Open once (1981).

Jim Palmer (b. 10-15-45): Baseball RHP. 268 career wins, 2.86 ERA. Won three Cy Young Awards (1973, consecutively 1975–76). Won 20+ games eight times. Led league in wins three times, innings pitched four times, ERA two times. Never allowed a grand slam HR. Pitched on six World Series teams with Baltimore, including shutout at age 20. Pitched no-hitter in 1969. Career span 1965–84.

Bernie Parent (b. 4-3-45): Hockey G. Alltime leader for wins in a season (47 in 1974). Goaltender of the Year, playoff MVP, league leader in wins, goals against average and shutouts two consecutive seasons (1974–75). Career record 270-197-121, including 55 shutouts. Career 2.55 goals against average. Tied record of four playoff shutouts in 1975. Played on two consecutive Stanley Cup champions (1974–75). Career span 1965–79 with Philadelphia.

Brad Park (b. 7-6-48): Hockey, D. Seven-time All Star. In 17 seasons with the New York Rangers, Boston Bruins and Detroit Red Wings (1968–69 through 1984–85) scored 213 goals and had 683 assists. Elected to Hall of Fame 1988.

Jim Parker (b. 4-3-34): Football T/G. Winner of 1956 Outland Trophy as Ohio State senior. Blocked for Johnny Unitas. All-NFL four times at guard, four times at tackle. Career span 1957–67, all with Baltimore Colts. Inducted to Hall of Fame in 1973.

Joe Paterno (b. 12-21-26): College football coach. Fourth alltime in wins in Division I-A (307 through 1998—the most of any active coach at that level). Has won two national championships (1982, 1986) with Penn State since 1966. Career record 298-77-3, including five undefeated seasons. Has also won 18 bowl games.

Lester Patrick (b. 12-30-1883, d. 6-1-60): Hockey coach. Led NY Rangers to three Stanley Cup championships (1928, '33, '40). Originated the NHL's farm system and developed playoff format.

Floyd Patterson (b. 1-4-35): Boxer. Heavyweight champion two times (1956-59, 1960-62). First heavyweight to regain title, in rematch with Ingemar Johansson. Career record 55-8-1 with 40 KOs from 1952 to 1972. Also middleweight gold medalist at 1952 Olympics.

Walter Payton (b. 7-25-54): Football RB. Alltime leader in yards rushing (16,726). Gained 1,000+ yards rushing in 10 seasons. Third alltime in rushing touchdowns (110). 125 career touchdowns. Gained a record 275 yards on Nov. 20, 1977, against Minnesota. Selected for Pro Bowl nine times. Player of the Year two times (1977, 1985). Led league in rushing five consecutive seasons. Career span 1975–87 with Chicago.

Pelé (b. 10-23-40): Born Edson Arantes do Nascimento. Brazilian soccer player. Soccer's great ambassador. Played on three World Cup winners with Brazil (1958, 1962, 1970). Helped promote soccer in U.S. by playing with NY Cosmos from 1975 to 1977. Scored 1,281 goals in 22 years.

Willie Pep (b. 9-19-22): Boxer. Featherweight champion two times (1942-48, 1949-50). Lost title to Sandy Saddler, won it back in rematch, then lost it to Saddler again. Career record 230-11-1 with 65 KOs from 1940 to 1966. Won 73 consecutive bouts from 1940 to 1943. Defended title nine times.

Gil Perreault (b. 11-13-50): Hockey C. Won Calder Trophy as NHL's top rookie for 1970–71 season. Played 17 seasons (1970–71 through 1986–87), all with Buffalo Sabres. Scored 512 goals and had 814 assists in career. Elected to Hall of Fame in 1990.

Fred Perry (b. 5-18-09, d. 2-2-95): British tennis player. Won three consecutive Wimbledon singles titles (1934–36), the last British man to win the tournament. Also won three U.S. titles (consecutively 1933–34, '36), French title (1935) and Australian title (1934).

Gaylord Perry (b. 9-15-38): Baseball RHP. Only pitcher to win Cy Young Award in both leagues (Cleveland 1972, San Diego 1978). 314 career wins, 3,534 strikeouts. 20+ wins five times; 200+ strikeouts eight times; 250+ innings pitched 12 times. Pitched no-hitter in 1968. Admitted to throwing a spitter. Career span 1962–83 with eight teams.

Bob Pettit (b. 12-12-32): Basketball F. First player in history to break 20,000-point barrier (20,880 career points scored). 26.4 career scoring average; 16.2 rebound avg. MVP in 1956, 1959; Rookie of the Year in 1955. All-Star 10 consecutive seasons. Led league in scoring two times, rebounding once. Career span 1954–64 with St. Louis.

Richard Petty (b. 7-2-37): Auto racer. Alltime leader in NASCAR victories (200). Daytona 500 winner (1964, '66, '71, consecutively 1973–74, '79, '81) and NASCAR champion (1964, 1967, consecutively 1971–72, 1974–75, '79) seven times each, the most of any driver. First stock car racer to reach $1 million in earnings. Son of Lee Petty, three-time NASCAR champion (1954, consecutively 1958–59). Retired after 1992 season.

Laffit Pincay Jr. (b. 12-29-46): Jockey. Second only to Bill Shoemaker in wins. Among the top money-winners of all time, approaching $200,000,000 in career earnings. Won five Eclipse Awards as outstanding jockey. Rode three Kentucky Derby winners; two Preakness winners; and one Belmont winner.

Scottie Pippen (b. 9-25-65): Basketball F. Won six NBA titles with Chicago Bulls (consecutively 1991–1993, and 1996–1998). Tied NBA record with seven three-pointers against Utah in Game 3 of '97 Finals. Member of 1992 and '96 gold medal–winning U.S. Olympic basketball teams. Career span 1987–99 with Chicago, 1999 Houston, since 1999 with Portland.

Jacques Plante (b. 1-17-29, d. 2-27-86): Hockey G. First goalie to wear a mask. Second alltime in wins (434) and second lowest modern goals against average (2.38). Goaltender of the Year 7 times, more than any other goalie (consecutively 1955-59, 1961, 1968). Won MVP award in 1961. Led league in goals against average eight times, wins six times and shutouts four times. Was on six Stanley Cup champions with Montreal from 1952 to 1962 and played for four other teams until retirement in 1972.

Gary Player (b. 11-1-35): South African golfer. Won the Masters (1961, '74, '78) and British Open (1959, '68, '74) three times each, PGA Championship two times (1962, '72) and U.S. Open (1965). Also won Seniors Championship three times (1986, '88, '90) and U.S. Senior Open two consecutive years (1987–88).

Sam Pollock (b. 12-15-25): Hockey executive. As general manager of Montreal from 1964 to 1978 won nine Stanley Cup championships (1965–66, 1968–69, '71, '73, 1976–78).

Denis Potvin (b. 10-29-53): Hockey D. Seven-time All Star during 15-season career (1973–74 through 1987–88), all with New York Islanders. Won Calder Trophy for 1973–74 season. Won Norris Trophy three times. Captained Islanders to four Stanley Cup championships. Elected to Hall of Fame in 1991.

Mike Powell (b. 11-10-63): Track and field. Long jumper broke Bob Beamon's 23-year-old world record at 1991 World Championships in Tokyo with a jump of 29' 4½". Won silver in 1992 Olympics.

Steve Prefontaine (b. 1-25-51, d. 5-30-75): Track and field. Distance runner killed in car accident at age 24. Held every American record from 2,000 meters to 10,000 meters at the time of his death. At age 21, finished fourth in the 5,000 at the 1972 Olympics in Munich after holding lead with less than 600 meters to go.

Annemarie Moser-Pröll (b. 3-27-53): Austrian skier. Gold medalist in downhill at 1980 Olympics. World Cup overall champion six times, more than any other skier (consecutively 1971–75, '79).

Alain Prost (b. 2-24-55): French auto racer. Alltime leader in Formula 1 victories (51). Formula 1 champion four times (consecutively 1985–86, '89, '93).

Jack Ramsay (b. 2-21-25): Basketball coach. Coached 11 seasons at St. Joseph's University, with 234–72 record. Overall record of 864–783 as NBA coach. Coach of NBA champion 1977 Portland Trail Blazers. Elected to Hall of Fame 1992.

Jean Ratelle (b. 10-3-40): Hockey C. In 21-season career (1960–61 through 1980–81) with the New York Rangers and Boston Bruins, scored 491 goals and had 776 assists. Twice won Lady Byng Trophy. Elected to Hall of Fame in 1985.

Willis Reed (b. 6-25-42): Basketball C. Played 10 seasons (1965–74), all with the New York Knicks. Career average of 18.7 points a game. NBA Rookie of Year in 1965. Playoff MVP of both Knick championship teams, in 1970 and '73. NBA MVP in 1970. Elected to Hall of Fame in 1981.

Harold Henry (Pee Wee) Reese (b. 7-23-18 d. 8-14-99): Baseball SS. Played for six pennant-winning Dodger teams. Led NL in runs scored in 1949, with 132. Elected to Hall of Fame in 1984.

Mary Lou Retton (b. 1-24-68): Gymnast. Won one gold, one silver and two bronze medals at 1984 Olympics.

Grantland Rice (b. 11-1-1880, d. 7-13-54): Sportswriter. Legendary figure during sport's Golden Age of the 1920s. Wrote "When the Last Great Scorer comes/ To mark against your name,/ He'll write not 'won' or 'lost'/ But how you played the game." Also named the 1924–25 Notre Dame backfield the "Four Horsemen."

Jerry Rice (b. 10-13-62): Football WR. Entering 1999 season, alltime leader in touchdowns (175), touchdown receptions (164) and in consecutive games with a TD reception (13 in 1988). Player of the Year in 1987 and led league in scoring (138 points on 23 touchdowns). Super Bowl MVP in 1989 with record 215 receiving yards on 11 catches. Also set Super Bowl record with three touchdown receptions in 1990 and in 1995. Career span since 1985 with San Francisco 49ers.

Henri Richard (b. 2-29-36): Hockey C. "The Pocket Rocket." Won 11 Stanley Cup championships with Montreal. Four-time All-Star. Career span 1955–75.

Maurice Richard (b. 8-4-21): Hockey RW. "The Rocket." First player ever to score 50 goals in a season, in 1945. Led league in goals five times. 544 career goals. Won MVP award in 1947. All-Star eight times. Tied playoff game record for most goals (five on March 23, 1944). Won eight Stanley Cup championships with Montreal 1942–59.

Bob Richards (b. 2-2-26): Track and field. The only pole vaulter to win gold medal at two consecutive Olympics (1952, 1956). Also won Sullivan Award in 1951.

Branch Rickey (b. 12-20-1881, d. 12-9-65): Baseball executive. Integrated major league baseball in 1947 by signing Jackie Robinson to contract with Brooklyn Dodgers. Conceived minor league farm system in 1919 at St. Louis; instituted batting cage and sliding pit.

Pat Riley (b. 3-20-45): Basketball coach. Going into 1998–99 season most playoff wins (147). Coached Los Angeles to four championships, two consecutively, from 1981 to 1989. 60+ wins seven times (four times consecutively), 50+ wins four other times. Coach of the Year in 1990, '93 and '97. Led New York Knicks to NBA Finals in 1994, then left three weeks later to become coach and part owner of Miami Heat.

Cal Ripken Jr (b. 8-24-60): Baseball SS-3B. Broke Lou Gehrig's record for most consecutive games played (2,131) on Sept. 5, 1995; streak ended at 2,632 games on Sept. 20, 1998. Set record for consecutive errorless games by a shortstop (95 in 1990). MVP in 1983 and '91. Rookie of the Year in 1982. Hit 20+ HRs in 10 consecutive seasons; 15-time All Star.

Glenn (Fireball) Roberts (b. 1-20-31, d. 7-2-64): Auto racer. Won 34 NASCAR races. Died as a result of fiery accident in World 600 at Charlotte Motor Speedway in May 1964. At time of his death had won more major races than any other driver in NASCAR history.

Oscar Robertson (b. 11-24-38): Basketball G. "The Big O." 9,887 career assists; 26,710 points, 25.7 ppg. MVP in 1964, All-Star nine consecutive seasons and 1961 Rookie of the Year. Led league in assists six times, free throw percentage two times. Averaged 30+ points six times in seven seasons, 20+ points four other times. Only player in history to average a season triple-double (1961). Career span 1960–72 with Cincinnati, Milwaukee. Also College Player of the Year, All-America and NCAA scoring leader three consecutive seasons from 1958 to 1960 with Cincinnati. Third all-time NCAA highest scoring average (33.8); seventh most points scored (2,973).

Brooks Robinson (b. 5-18-37): Baseball 3B. Alltime leader in assists, putouts, double plays and fielding average among 3rd basemen. Won 16 consecutive Gold Gloves. Led league in fielding average a record 11 times. MVP in 1964—led league in RBI—and MVP in 1970 World Series. Career span 1955–77 with Baltimore.

David Robinson (b. 8-6-65): Basketball C. *Sporting News* Player of the Year in 1987. Led college players in 1986 in both rebounding (13.0) and blocked shots (5.91). 1990 NBA Rookie of the Year. Led NBA in rebounding 1991 (13.0), in scoring in '94 (29.8) and in blocked shots in '92, when he was named Defensive Player of the Year. Named NBA MVP in 1995. Member of 1988, '92 and '96 Olympic teams. Career span since 1989 with San Antonio. Won NBA title with Spurs in '99.

Eddie Robinson (b. 2-13-19): College football coach. Retired with alltime college record 408 career wins through 1941–97 at Division I-AA Grambling State.

Frank Robinson (b. 8-31-35): Baseball OF-manager. Only player to win MVP awards in both leagues (Cincinnati, 1961, Baltimore, 1966). Won Triple Crown and World Series MVP in 1966. Rookie of the Year in 1956. Fourth alltime most HR (586). 30+ HR 11 times; 100+ RBI 6 times; 100+ runs scored 8 times (led league 3 times). Had .300+ batting average 9 times. Became first black manager in major leagues, with Cleveland in

1975. Career span as player 1956–76. Career span as manager 1975–77 with Cleveland; 1981–84 with San Francisco; 1988–91 with Baltimore.

Jackie Robinson (b. 1-13-19, d. 10-24-72): Baseball 2B. Broke the color barrier as first black player in major leagues in 1947 with Brooklyn Dodgers. 1947 Rookie of the Year; 1949 MVP with .342 batting average to lead league. Had .311 career batting average. Led league in stolen bases 2 times; stole home 19 times. Played on six pennant winners in 10 years with Brooklyn. Elected to Hall of Fame in 1962.

Larry Robinson (b. 6-2-51): Hockey D. Twice won Norris Trophy as NHL's top defenseman. Career span 1972–73 through 1991–92, all but the last three with the Montreal Canadiens. Member of six Montreal teams that won Stanley Cup. Awarded Conn Smythe Trophy as MVP of 1978 Stanley Cup.

Sugar Ray Robinson (b. 5-3-21, d. 4-12-89): Born Walker Smith, Jr. Boxer. Called best pound-for-pound boxer ever. Welterweight champ (1946–51) and middleweight champ five times. Career record: 174-19-6 with 109 KOs from 1940–65. Won 91 consecutive bouts from 1943–51. Fifteen losses came after age 35.

Knute Rockne (b. 3-4-1888, d. 3-31-31): College football coach. Won national championship three times (1924, consecutively 1929–30). Alltime highest winning percentage (.881). Career record 105-12-5, including five undefeated seasons, with Notre Dame from 1918 to 1930.

Bill Rodgers (b. 12-23-47): Track and field. Won the Boston and New York City marathons four times each between 1975 and 1980.

Dennis Rodman (b. 5-13-61): Basketball F. NBA Defensive Player of the Year 1990, '91. First player to win seven consecutive rebounding titles; won NBA titles with Detroit 1989 and '90 and Chicago 1996–98. Career span 1986–93 with Detroit, '93–95 with San Antonio, '95–98 with Chicago and 23 G in '99 with LA.

Chi Chi Rodriguez (b. 10-23-35): Golfer. Led senior money list for 1987 ($509,145). Won eight events during PGA career that began in 1960.

Art Rooney (b. 1-27-01; d. 8-25-88): Owner of Pittsburgh Steelers. Bought team in 1933 and ran it until his death in 1988. Elected to Hall of Fame in 1964.

Murray Rose (b. 1-6-39) Australian swimmer. Won three gold medals (including 400- and 1500-meter freestyle) at 1956 Olympics. Also won one gold, one silver and one bronze medal at 1960 Olympics.

Pete Rose (b. 4-14-41): Baseball OF-IF. "Charlie Hustle." Alltime leader in hits (4,256), games played (3,562) and at bats (14,053); second in doubles (746); fourth in runs scored (2,165). Had .303 career average and won three batting titles. Averaged .300+ 15 times, 200+ hits and 100+ runs scored each 10 times. Led league in hits seven times, runs scored four times, doubles five times. 1963 Rookie of the Year; 1973 MVP; 1975 World Series MVP. Had 44-game hitting streak in 1978. Played in 17 All-Star games, starting at five different positions. Career span 1963–86 with Cincinnati, Philadelphia and Montreal. Manager of Cincinnati from 1984 to 1989. Banned from baseball for life by Commissioner Bart Giamatti in 1989 for betting activities. Served five-month jail term for tax evasion in 1990. Ineligible for Hall of Fame.

Ken Rosewall (b. 11-2-34): Australian tennis player. Won Grand Slam singles titles at ages 18 and 35. Won four Australian titles (1953, '55, consecutively 1971–72), two French titles (1953, '68) and two U.S. titles (1956, '70). Reached four Wimbledon finals, but title eluded him.

Art Ross (b. 1-13-1886, d. 8-5-64): Hockey D-coach. Improved design of puck and goal net. Manager-coach of Boston, 1924–45, won Stanley Cup, 1938–39. The Art Ross Trophy is awarded to the NHL scoring champion.

Donald Ross (b. 1873, d. 4-26-48): Scottish-born golf course architect. Trained at St. Andrews under Old Tom Morris. Designed over 500 courses, including Pinehurst No. 2 course and Oakland Hills.

Patrick Roy (b. 10-5-65): Hockey G. Won Vezina Trophy three times. Won Conn Smythe Trophy twice (1986, '93). Career span 1984–95 Montreal, '95–Colorado. Traded to Colorado by Montreal in Dec. '95, won '96 Stanley Cup with Avalanche. Second-youngest goalie to reach 300 career wins.

Pete Rozelle (b. 3-1-26, d. 12-6-96): Football executive. Fourth NFL commissioner, served from 1960 to 1989. During his term, league expanded from 12 to 28 teams. Created Super Bowl in 1966 and negotiated merger with AFL. Devised plan for revenue sharing of lucrative TV monies among owners. Presided during players' strikes of 1982, '87.

Wilma Rudolph (b. 6-23-40, d. 11-12-94): Track and field. Gold medalist in 3 events (100-, 200- and 4x100-meter relay) at 1960 Olympics. Also won Sullivan Award in 1961.

Adolph Rupp (b. 9-2-01, d. 12-10-77): College basketball coach. Second alltime in NCAA wins (876) and third highest winning percentage (.822). Won four NCAA championships: consecutively 1948–49, '51, '58. Career span 1930–72 with Kentucky.

Amos Rusie (b. 5-3-1871, d. 12-6-42): Baseball RHP. Fastball was so intimidating that in 1893 the pitching mound was moved back 5' 6" to its present distance of 60' 6". Led league in strikeouts and walks five times each. Career record 246–174, 3.07 ERA with New York (NL) from 1889–1901.

Bill Russell (b. 2-12-34): Basketball C. Won MVP award five times (1958, consecutively 1961–63, '65). Played on 11 championship teams, eight consecutively, with Boston (1957, 1959–66, 1968–69). Player-coach 1968–69 (league's first black coach). Second alltime most rebounds (21,620) and second highest rebounding average (22.5); second most rebounds in a game (51 in 1960). Led league in rebounding four times. Also played on two consecutive NCAA championship teams with San Francisco in 1955–56; tournament MVP in 1955. Member of gold medal-winning 1956 Olympic team.

Babe Ruth (b. 2-6-1895, d. 8-16-48): Born George Herman Ruth. Baseball P-OF. Most dominant player in history. Alltime leader in slugging average (.690), HR frequency (8.5 HR every 100 at bats) and walks (2,056); second alltime most HR (714), RBI (2,211) and runs scored (2,174). Holds season record highest slugging average (.847 in 1920). 1923 MVP. Had .342 career batting average and 2,873 hits. 60 HR in 1927; 50+ HR 3 other times and 40+ HR seven other times; 100+ RBI and 100+ walks 13 times each; 100+ runs scored 12 times. Second alltime most World Series HR (15), including his "called shot" off Charlie Root in 1932. Began career as a pitcher for Boston Red Sox: 94 career wins and 2.28 ERA. Won 20+ games 2 times; ERA leader in 1916. Played on 10 pennant winners, seven World Series winners (three with Boston, four with New York). Sold to Yankees in 1920 (Boston hasn't won World Series since). Career span 1914–35.

Nolan Ryan (b. 1-31-47): Baseball RHP. Pitched record 7th no-hitter on May 1, 1991. Alltime leader in strikeouts (5,714), walks (2,795). League leader in strikeouts 11 times, walks eight times, shutouts three times, ERA two times. 300+ strikeouts six times, including season record of 383 in 1973. 324 career wins. Career span 1966–93 with New York (NL), California, Houston, Texas. Elected to Hall of Fame 1999.

Jim Ryun (b. 4-29-47): Track and field. Youngest ever to run under four minutes for the mile (3:59.0 at 17 years, 37 days). Set two world records in mile (3:51.3 in 1966 and 3:51.1 in 1967) and one in 1,500 (3:33.1 in 1967). Plagued by bad luck at Olympics; won silver medal in 1968 1,500 meters despite mononucleosis; was bumped and fell in 1972. Won Sullivan Award in 1967.

Toni Sailer (b. 11-17-35): Austrian skier. Won gold medals in 1956 Olympics in slalom, giant slalom and downhill, the first skier to accomplish the feat.

Juan Antonio Samaranch (b. 7-17-20): Amateur sports executive. Since 1980, Spaniard has served as president of International Olympic Committee.

Pete Sampras (b. 8-12-71): Tennis player. First player in ATP rankings history to hold No. 1 ranking for six consecutive years. Won sixth Wimbledon title in 1999 to equal Roy Emerson's record of 12 Grand Slam singles titles.

Joan Benoit Samuelson (b. 5-16-57): Track and field. Gold medalist in first ever women's Olympic marathon (1984). Won Boston Marathon 2 times (1979, 1983). Sullivan Award winner in 1985.

Barry Sanders (b. 7-16-68): Football RB. Alltime NCAA season leader in yards rushing (2,628 in 1988). Won Heisman Trophy in 1988 at Oklahoma State. Entered NFL in 1989 with Detroit and named Rookie of the Year. Gained 1,000+ yards rushing in each of his first 10 seasons. Ended 1998–99 season second alltime in career rushing yards (15,269). Third player to rush for over 2,000 yards (2,053 in 1997). Led league in rushing in 1990, '94 and 1996–97.

Gene Sarazen (b. 2-27-02 d. 5-13-99): Golfer. Won PGA Championship 3 times (consecutively 1922-23, 1933), U.S. Open 2 times (1922, 1932), British Open once (1932) and the Masters once (1935). His win at the Masters included golf's most famous shot, a double eagle on the 15th hole of the final round to tie Craig Wood (Sarazen then won the playoff). Won 38 career tournaments. Also won Seniors Championship 2 times (1954, 1958). Pioneered the sand wedge in 1930.

Glen Sather (b. 9-2-43): Hockey coach and general manager. As coach, third alltime highest winning percentage (.616). 464 regular season wins. Led Edmonton to 4 Stanley Cup championships (consecutively 1984–85, 1987–88) from 1979 to 1989 and 1993–94. Also played for 6 teams from 1966 to 1976.

Terry Sawchuk (b. 12-28-29): Hockey G. Alltime leader in wins (447) and shutouts (103). Career 2.52 goals against average. Goaltender of the Year 4 times (consecutively 1951–52, 1954, 1964). Led league in wins and shutouts 3 times and goals against average 2 times. Rookie of the Year in 1950. Set record of 4 playoff shutouts in 1952. Played on 4 Stanley Cup champions with Detroit and Toronto from 1949 to 1969.

Gale Sayers (b. 5-30-43): Football RB. Alltime leader in kickoff return average (30.6). Scored 56 career

touchdowns, including a rookie record 22 in 1965. Led league in rushing and gained 1,000+ yards rushing 2 times. Averaged 5 yards per carry. Rookie of the Year in 1965. Tied record with 6 rushing touchdowns on Dec. 12, 1965. Career span 1965–71 with Chicago cut short due to knee injury. Also All-America 2 times with Kansas.

Dolph Schayes (b. 5-19-28): Basketball player. College star at NYU. In 1960 became first NBA player to reach 15,000 career points. Also first NBA player to play in 1,000 games. Led NBA in free throw percentage three times, and averaged .843 for his career. Over stretch of 10 years played in 706 consecutive games. Elected to Hall of Fame 1972.

Bo Schembechler (b. 4-1-29): Football coach. In 21 seasons at Michigan from 1969–89, had a 194-48-5 record. Overall college coaching record 234-65-8.

Mike Schmidt (b. 9-27-49): Baseball 3B. Won 3 MVP awards (1980, '81, '86). 548 career HR, seventh alltime. Led league in HR 8 times, slugging average 5 times and RBI, walks and strikeouts 4 times each. 40+ HR 3 times, 30+ HR 10 other times; 100+ RBI 9 times, 100+ runs scored 7 times, 100+ strikeouts 12 times and third alltime most strikeouts (1,883). 100+ walks 7 times. Won 10 Gold Gloves. Career span 1972–89 with Philadelphia. Elected to the Hall of Fame in 1995.

Don Schollander (b. 4-30-46): Swimmer. Won 4 gold medals (including 100- and 400-meter freestyle) at 1964 Olympics; won 1 gold and 1 silver medal at 1968 Olympics. Also won Sullivan Award in 1964.

Dick Schultz (b. 9-5-29): Amateur sports executive. Second executive director of the NCAA, served from 1987 to '93. Also served as athletic director at Cornell (1976–81) and Virginia (1981–87).

Seattle Slew (b. 1974): Thoroughbred race horse. Horse of the Year for 1977, when he won the Triple Crown, winning the Kentucky Derby by 1¾ lengths; the Preakness by 1½; and the Belmont by 4. In three-year career from 1976–78, won 14 of 17 starts.

Tom Seaver (b. 11-17-44): Baseball RHP. "Tom Terrific." 311 career wins. 2.86 ERA. Cy Young Award winner 3 times (1969, 1973, 1975) and Rookie of the Year 1967. Fourth alltime most strikeouts (3,640). Led league in strikeouts 5 times, winning percentage 4 times and wins and ERA 3 times each. Won 20+ games 5 times; 200+ strikeouts 10 times. Struck out 19 batters in 1 game in 1970, including the final 10 in succession. Pitched no-hitter in 1978. Career span 1967–86 with New York Mets, Cincinnati, Chicago White Sox, Boston.

Secretariat (b. 3-30-70, d. 10-4-89): Thoroughbred race horse. Triple Crown winner in 1973 with jockey Ron Turcotte aboard. Trained by Lucien Laurin.

Katja Seizinger (b. 5-10-72): German skier. Won downhill gold medals in 1994 at Lillehammer and '98 at Nagano. Won Giant Slalom bronze medal at Nagano. 1998 World Cup champion in downhill, Super G and overall. 32 World Cup victories in downhill and Super G.

Monica Seles (b. 12-2-73): Tennis player. Has won 3 consecutive French Open singles titles (1990-92), 4 Australian Open titles (1991-93, '96) and 2 U.S. Open titles (1991-92). Seles' 1993 season ended on 4-30 when she was stabbed in the back by Gunther Parche while seated during a changeover in a tournament in Hamburg, Germany; also missed 1994 season. Returned to tennis in 1995, reached U.S. Open final.

Bill Sharman (b. 5-25-26): Basketball G. First team All Star four straight years 1956–59. Led NBA in free throw percentage every year from 1953–57, and in 1959 and '61. All Star Game MVP in 1955. NBA Coach of the Year in 1972, when his Lakers won NBA title. Elected to Hall of Fame in 1974.

Wilbur Shaw (b. 10-31-02, d. 10-30-54): Auto racer. Won Indy 500 3 times in 4 years (1937, consecutively 1939-40). AAA champion 2 times (1937, 1939). Also pioneered the use of the crash helmet after suffering skull fracture in 1923 crash.

Patty Sheehan (b. 10-27-56): Golfer. Won back-to-back LPGA championships, 1983–84. Won 1992 and '94 U.S. Women's Opens, '93 LPGA title. 1983 LPGA Player of Year. Vare Trophy winner in 1984. Qualified for Hall of Fame in 1993.

Fred Shero (b. 10-23-25, d. 11-24-90): Hockey coach. Fourth alltime highest winning percentage (.612, regular season). Led Philadelphia to 2 Stanley Cup championships (1974-75). Also coached NY Rangers. Played defense for NY Rangers, 1947–50.

Bill Shoemaker (b. 8-19-31): Horse racing jockey. Alltime leader in wins (8,833). Rode Belmont Stakes winner 5 times (1957, 1959, 1962, 1967, 1975), Kentucky Derby winner 4 times (1955, 1959, 1965, 1986—at age 54, the oldest jockey to win Derby) and Preakness Stakes winner 2 times (1963, 1967). Also won Eclipse Award in 1981.

Eddie Shore (b. 11-25-02, d. 3-16-85): Hockey D. Won MVP award 4 times (1933, consecutively 1935–36, 1938). All-Star 7 times. Played on 2 Stanley Cup champions with Boston from 1926 to 1940.

Frank Shorter (b. 10-31-47): Track and field. Gold medalist in marathon at 1972 Olympics, the first American to win the event since 1908. Olympic silver medalist in 1976 marathon. Sullivan Award winner in 1972.

Jim Shoulders (b. 5-13-28): Rodeo. Sixteen career titles. All-Around champion 5 times (1949, consecutively 1956–59).

Don Shula (b. 1-4-30): Football coach. Alltime leader in wins (347). Won 2 consecutive Super Bowl championships (1972–73) with Miami, including NFL's only undefeated season in 1972. Also reached Super Bowl 4 other times. Career span 1963–70 with Baltimore, 1970–95 Miami.

Al Simmons (b. 5-22-02; d. 5-26-56): Baseball OF. "Bucketfoot Al" for hitting stance. Named AL MVP for 1929, when he led league with 157 RBIs. Led league in batting average in 1930 (.381) and '31 (.390). Lifetime average of .334 with 307 homers. Career span 1924–44 with a variety of teams, but mostly Philadelphia A's. Elected to Hall of Fame in 1953.

O.J. Simpson (b. 7-9-47): Given name Orenthal James. Football RB. 11,236 career yards rushing. Gained 1,000+ yards rushing 5 consecutive seasons, including then-record 2,003 yards in 1973. Player of the Year 3 times (consecutively 1972–73, 1975). Led league in rushing 4 times. Gained 200+ yards rushing in a game a record 6 times, including 273 yards on Nov. 25, 1976. Scored 61 career touchdowns, including 23 in 1975. Also won Heisman Trophy with USC in 1968.

Sir Barton (b. 1916, d. 1937): Thoroughbred race horse. In 1919, before they were linked as the Triple Crown, became first horse to win the Kentucky Derby, the Preakness and the Belmont Stakes. Won 8 of 13 starts as 3-year-old.

George Sisler (b. 3-24-1893, d. 3-26-73): Baseball 1B. His 257 hits in 1920 season are alltime major league record. League leader in hits two times, banged out 200+ hits six times. Won two batting titles, including with .420 average in 1922; averaged .400+ 2 times and .300+ 11 other times. Had 2,812 career hits and a .340 lifetime batting average. Career span 1915–30 with St. Louis.

Mary Decker Slaney (b. 8-4-58): Track and field. American record holder in 5 events ranging from 800 to 3,000 meters. Won 1,500 and 3,000 meters at World Championships in 1983. Lost chance for medal at 1984 Olympics when she tripped and fell after contact with Zola Budd. Won Sullivan Award in 1982. Competed in 1996 Olympics at age 37.

Bruce Smith (b. 6-18-63): Football DE. Second alltime in NFL sacks. Played in four consecutive Super Bowls with the Bills (1991–94), all losses. Career span since 1985 with Buffalo.

Dean Smith (b. 2-28-31): College basketball coach. Alltime leader in wins (879); fifth alltime highest winning percentage (.776). Alltime most NCAA tournament appearances (27), reached Final Four 11 times. Won NCAA championship in 1982 and '93. Coached 1976 Olympic team to gold medal. Career span 1962–97 with North Carolina. 1997 *Sports Illustrated* Sportsman of the Year.

Emmitt Smith (b. 5-15-69): Football RB. Led NFL in rushing in 1991 (1,563 yards), '92 (1,713 and 18 TDs), and '95 (1,773). Record 25 TDs in 1995. Rushed for 108 yards in 52–17 Cowboys win over Bills in Super Bowl XXVII. Rushed for 132 yards and named MVP of Super Bowl XXVIII, a 30–13 Dallas victory over Buffalo. Career span since 1990 with Cowboys.

Ozzie Smith (b. 12-26-54): Baseball SS. "The Wizard of Oz." May be the best defensive shortstop in history. Holds alltime record for most assists in a season among shortstops (621 in 1980). Career double-play and assist leader among shortstops. 14-time All-Star. Won 13 consecutive Gold Gloves. Career span 1978–96 with San Diego, St. Louis.

Red Smith (b. 9-25-05, d. 1-15-82): Sportswriter. Won Pulitzer Prize in 1976. After Grantland Rice, the most widely syndicated sports columnist. His literate essays appeared in the *NY Herald Tribune* from 1945 to 1971 and the *NY Times* from 1971 to 1982.

Stan Smith (b. 12-14-46): Tennis. Won 39 tournaments in career, including 1972 Wimbledon in 5 sets over Ilie Nastase. Won 1971 U.S. Open over Jan Kodes and amateur version of U.S. Open in 1969. 1970 won inaugural Grand Prix Masters. Inducted to Tennis Hall of Fame in 1987.

Tommie Smith (b. 6-5-44): Track and field. Sprinter won 1968 Olympic 200 meters in world record of 19.83, then was expelled from Olympic Village, along with bronze medalist John Carlos, for raising black-gloved fist and bowing head during playing of national anthem to protest racism in U.S.

Conn Smythe (b. 2-1-1895, d. 11-18-80): Hockey executive. As general manager with Toronto from 1929 to 1961 won seven Stanley Cup championships (1932, '42, '45, consecutively 1947–49, '51). Award for playoff MVP named in his honor.

Sam Snead (b. 5-27-12): Golfer. Alltime leader in career wins (81). Won the Masters (1949, '52, '54) and PGA Championship (1942, '49, '51) three times each and British Open (1946). Runner-up at U.S. Open four times, but title eluded him. PGA Player of the Year in

1949. Won Seniors Championship six times, more than any golfer (1964–65, '67, '70, 1972–73).

Peter Snell (b. 12-17-38): Track and field. New Zealand runner was gold medalist in 800 meters at two consecutive Olympics in 1960, '64. Also gold medalist in 1,500 meters at 1964 Olympics. Twice broke world mile record; broke world 800 record once.

Duke Snider (b. 9-19-26): Baseball OF. Career .295 average, 407 HR and 1,333 RBIs. Hit 40+ HR five consecutive seasons and 100+ RBIs six times. Also led league in runs scored three consecutive seasons. Played on six pennant winners with the Brooklyn Dodgers. World Series total of 11 HR and 26 RBIs are NL best. Career span from 1947–64.

Sammy Sosa (b. 11-12-68): Baseball RF. Followed Mark McGwire in eclipsing Roger Maris's single-season HR mark in 1998. Lost HR race to McGwire that season but won MVP with .308 average, 66 HR, 134 runs, 158 RBIs. Career span 1989 with Texas; 1989–91 with Chicago White Sox; 1992– with Chicago Cubs.

Javier Sotomayor (b. 10-13-67): Track and field. Cuban high jumper broke the 8-foot barrier with world record jump of 8' 0" in 1989. Set current record of 8' ½" in 7-27-93 in Salamanca, Spain.

Warren Spahn (b. 4-23-21): Baseball LHP. Alltime leader in games won for a lefthander (363): 20+ wins 13 times. League leader in wins eight times (five seasons consecutively), complete games nine times (seven seasons consecutively), strikeouts four consecutive seasons, innings pitched four times and ERA three times. 1957 Cy Young award. 63 career shutouts. Pitched two no-hitters after age 39. Career span 1942–65, all but last year with Boston Braves, Milwaukee.

Tris Speaker (b. 4-4-1888, d. 12-8-58): Baseball OF. Alltime leader in doubles (792), fifth in hits (3,514) and fifth in batting average (.345). One batting title (.386 in 1916), but .375+ average six times and .300+ average 12 other times. League leader in doubles eight times, hits two times and HR and RBI one time each. 200+ hits four times, 40+ doubles 10 times and 100+ runs scored seven times. MVP in 1912. Career span 1907–28 with Boston, Cleveland.

Michael Spinks (b. 7-13-56): Boxer. 1976 Olympic middleweight champion. Brother Leon was heavyweight gold medalist. Won world light heavyweight title on 7-18-81. Defended it five times and consolidated light heavy titles with decision over Dwight Braxton on 3-18-83. Defended four more times. Won heavyweight title on 9-22-85 in decision over Larry Holmes. Lost title to Mike Tyson in 91 seconds on 6-27-88.

Mark Spitz (b. 2-10-50): Swimmer. Won a record seven gold medals (two in freestyle, two in butterfly, three in relays) at 1972 Olympics, setting world record in each event. Also won two gold medals and one silver and one bronze medal at 1968 Olympics. Sullivan Award winner in 1971.

Amos Alonzo Stagg (b. 8-16-1862, d. 3-17-65): College football coach. Third alltime in wins (314). Won national championship with Chicago in 1905. Coach of the Year with Pacific in 1943 at age 81. Career record 314-199-35, including five undefeated seasons, from 1892 to 1946. Only person elected to both college football and basketball Halls of Fame. Played in the first basketball game in 1891.

Willie Stargell (b. 3-6-40): Baseball OF/1B. "Pops" achieved a 1979 MVP triple crown, winning NL regular season, playoff and World Series MVP awards. Led NL in homers in 1971 and '73. Hit 475 career homers. Drove in 1,540 runs. Had .282 career batting average. Played all 21 seasons with the Pirates. Elected to Hall of Fame in 1988.

Bart Starr (b. 1-9-34): Football QB. Played on three NFL champions (consecutively 1961–62, '65) and first two Super Bowl champions (1966–67) with Green Bay. Also named MVP of first two Super Bowls. Player of the Year in 1966. Led league in passing three times. Also coached Green Bay to 53-77-3 record from 1975 to 1983.

Roger Staubach (b. 2-5-42): Football QB. Won Heisman Trophy with Navy as a junior in 1963. Served four-year military obligation before turning pro. Led Dallas to six NFC Championships, four Super Bowls and two Super Bowl titles (1971, '77). Player of the Year and Super Bowl MVP in 1971. Also led league in passing four times. Career span 1969–79.

Jan Stenerud (b. 11-26-42): Football K. Scored 1,699 career NFL points. Converted 373 field goals in 558 attempts. Career span 1967–79 with Kansas City Chiefs, 1980–83 with Green Bay Packers and 1984–85 with Minnesota Vikings. First pure kicker inducted to Hall of Fame, 1991.

Casey Stengel (b. 7-30-1890, d. 9-29-75): Baseball manager. "The Ol' Perfesser." Managed New York Yankees to 10 pennants and seven World Series titles (5 consecutively) in 12 years from 1949 to 1960. Alltime leader in World Series games (63), wins (37) and losses (26). Platoon system was his trademark strategy, Stengelese his trademark language ("You could look it up"). Managed New York Mets from 1962 to 1965. Jersey number (37) retired by Yankees and Mets.

Ingemar Stenmark (b. 3-18-56): Swedish skier. Gold medalist in slalom and giant slalom at 1980 Olympics. World Cup overall champion three consecutive years (1976–78).

Woody Stephens (b. 9-1-13 d. 8-22-98): Horse racing trainer. Trained two Kentucky Derby winners (Cannonade, who won the 100th Derby in 1974 and Swale in 1984) and five straight Belmont winners from 1982–86, starting with 1982 Horse of the Year Conquistador Cielo.

David Stern (b. 9-22-42): Fourth NBA commissioner. Served since 1984. Oversaw unprecedented growth of league. Owners rewarded him with five-year, $40-million contract extension in 1996.

Jackie Stewart (b. 6-11-39): Scottish auto racer. Fourth alltime in Formula 1 victories (27); Formula 1 champion three times (1969, '71, '73). Also Indy 500 Rookie of the Year in 1966. Retired in 1973.

Payne Stewart (b. 1-3-57, d. 10-25-99): Golfer. Two-time U.S. Open champion (1991, '99), also won 1989 PGA Championship. Killed in plane crash.

John Stockton (b. 3-26-62): Basketball G. Alltime leader in assists (13,087) and steals (2,701). Set single-season assist record of 1,164 in 1990–91. Led NBA in assists a record nine consecutive times, 1988–96. Nine-time All-Star, consecutively 1989–97. Co-MVP (with Karl Malone) of 1993 All-Star Game. Member of 1992 and '96 Olympic teams. Career span since 1984 with Utah.

Picabo Street (b. 4-3-71): Skier. Won silver medal in downhill at 1994 Olympics in Lillehammer and gold in Super G at '98 Games in Nagano. World Cup downhill champion in 1995 and '96. Nine career World Cup victories.

John L. Sullivan (b. 10-15-1858, d. 2-2-18): Boxer. Last bareknuckle champion. Heavyweight title holder (1882–92), lost to Jim Corbett. Career record 38-1-3 with 33 KOs from 1878 to 1892.

Paul Tagliabue (b. 11-24-40): Football executive. Fifth NFL commissioner, has served since 1989.

Anatoli Tarasov (b. 1918): Hockey coach. Orchestrated Soviet Union's emergence as a hockey power. Won nine consecutive world amateur championships (1963–71) and three Olympic gold medals in 1964, '68, '72.

Fran Tarkenton (b. 2-3-40): Football QB. Hall of Famer retired with 342 touchdown passes, 47,003 yards passing, 6,467 pass attempts and 3,686 pass completions. Player of the Year in 1975. Career span 1961–78 with Minnesota, NY Giants.

Lawrence Taylor (b. 2-4-59): Football LB. Revolutionized the linebacker position. Ended 1993 season as the alltime leader in sacks. Also named to Pro Bowl a record 10 consecutive seasons. Player of the Year in 1986. Has played on two Super Bowl champions with New York Giants (1986, '90). Career span 1981–93 with Giants. Elected to Hall of Fame 1999.

Isiah Thomas (b. 4-30-61): Basketball G. Member of Indiana University team that won 1981 NCAA title. Point guard for Detroit Pistons 1982–94. All-NBA First Team 1984, '85 and '86. NBA All Star Game MVP both 1984 and '86. Led NBA in assists (13.9) in 1984–85. Fourth alltime in assists (9,061). Member of Pistons team that won NBA title in both 1989 and '90. GM of Toronto Raptors 1995–97.

Thurman Thomas (b. 5-16-66): Football RB. Led AFC in rushing both 1990 (1,297 yards) and '91 (1,407). Career span since 1988 with Buffalo Bills.

Daley Thompson (b. 7-30-58): Track and field. British decathlete was gold medalist at two consecutive Olympics in 1980, '84. At 1984 Olympics set world record (8,847 points) that lasted eight years.

John Thompson (b. 9-2-41): College basketball coach. Head coach at Georgetown (1973–99), where he coached Patrick Ewing, Alonzo Mourning and Dikembe Mutombo. Won NCAA title in 1984, runnerup in '82 and '85.

Bobby Thomson (b. 10-25-23): Baseball OF. Hit dramatic 9th-inning playoff home run to win NL pennant for New York Giants on Oct. 3, 1951. The Giants came from 13½ games behind the Brooklyn Dodgers on Aug. 11 to win the pennant on Thomson's three-run homer off Ralph Branca in the final game of the three-game playoff.

Jim Thorpe (b. 5-28-1888, d. 3-28-53): Sportsman. Gold medalist in decathlon and pentathlon at 1912 Olympics. Played pro baseball with New York (NL) and Cincinnati 1913–19, and pro football with several teams 1919–26. Also All-America two times with Carlisle.

Dick Tiger (b. 8-14-29; d. 12-14-71): Nigerian boxer. Born Richard Ihetu. Two-time middleweight champ, also won light heavyweight title Fighter of the Year for 1962 and '65. Elected to Boxing Hall of Fame 1974.

Bill Tilden (b. 2-10-1893, d. 6-5-53): Tennis player. "Big Bill." Won seven U.S. singles titles, six consecutively (1920–25, '29) and three Wimbledon titles (consecutively 1920–21, '30). Also won six Grand Slam doubles titles. Led U.S. to seven consecutive Davis Cup victories (1920–26).

Ted Tinling (b. 6-23-10, d. 5-23-90): British tennis couturier. The premier source on women's tennis from Suzanne Lenglen to Steffi Graf. Also designed tennis clothes, most notably the frilled lace panties worn by Gorgeous Gussy Moran at Wimbledon in 1949.

Y.A. Tittle (b. 10-24-26): Football QB. Threw 33 TD passes in 1962 and in '63 led league in passing, completing 221 of 367 attempts for 3,145 yards and 36 TDs. Career span 1948–64, mostly with San Francisco 49ers and New York Giants. Inducted into Hall of Fame 1971.

Jayne Torvill/Christopher Dean (b. 10-7-57/ b. 7-27-58): British figure skaters. Won 4 consecutive ice dancing world championships (1981–84) and Olympic ice dancing gold medal (1984). Won world professional championships in 1985. Won Olympic ice dancing bronze in 1994.

Vladislav Tretiak (b. 4-25-52): Hockey G. Led USSR to gold medals at Olympics in 1972, '76, '84. Played on 13 world amateur champions from 1970 to 1984.

Lee Trevino (b. 12-1-39): Golfer. Won U.S. Open (1968, '71), British Open (consecutively 1971–72) and PGA Championship (1974, '84) two times each. PGA Player of the Year in 1971. Also won U.S. Senior Open in 1990. First Senior $1 million season.

Emlen Tunnell (b. 3-29-25, d. 7-23-75): Football S. Alltime leader in interception return yardage with 1,282 and second in interceptions (79). All-Pro nine times. Career span 1948–61 with New York Giants and Green Bay.

Gene Tunney (b. 5-25-1897, d. 11-7-78): Boxer. Heavyweight champion (1926–28). Defeated Jack Dempsey two times, including famous "long count" bout. Career record 65-2-1 with 43 KOs from 1915 to 1928. Retired as champion.

Ted Turner (b. 11-19-38): Sportsman. Skipper who successfully defended the America's Cup in 1977. Also owner of the Atlanta Braves since 1976 and Hawks since '77. Founded the Goodwill Games in 1986.

Mike Tyson (b. 6-30-66): Boxer. Youngest heavyweight champion at 19 years old in 1986. Held title until knocked out by James (Buster) Douglas on 2-10-90. Convicted of rape in 1992, released from prison in 1995. Lost WBA title to Evander Holyfield on 11-9-96. In one of boxing's more bizarre episodes, disqualified from rematch on 6-28-97 for biting Holyfield's ears.

Johnny Unitas (b. 5-7-33): Football QB. 47 consecutive games throwing touchdown pass (1956–60); 290 career touchdown passes; 40,239 career passing yards. Led league in touchdown passes four consecutive seasons. Player of the Year three times (1959, '64, '67). Career span 1956–72 with Baltimore, San Diego.

Al Unser Sr. (b. 5-29-39): Auto racer. Won Indy 500 four times (1970, '71, '78, '87). Retired with 39 career CART victories. USAC/CART champion 3 times (1970, '83, '85). Brother of Bobby.

Bobby Unser (b. 2-20-34): Auto racer. Won Indy 500 three times (1968, '75, '81). Retired with 35 career victories. USAC champion two times (1968, '74). Brother of Al Sr.

Harold S. Vanderbilt (b. 7-6-1884, d. 7-4-70): Sailor. Owner and skipper who successfully defended the

America's Cup three consecutive times (1930, '34, '37).

Glenna Collett Vare (b. 6-20-03, d. 2-2-89): Golfer. Won U.S. Women's Amateur six times, more than any golfer (1922, '25, consecutively 1928–30, '35).

Bill Veeck (b. 2-9-14, d. 1-2-86): Baseball owner. From 1946 to 1980, owned ballclubs in Cleveland, St. Louis (AL), Chicago (AL). In 1948, Cleveland became baseball's first team to draw two million in attendance. That year Veeck integrated AL by signing Larry Doby and then Satchel Paige. A brilliant promoter, Veeck sent midget Eddie Gaedel up to bat for St. Louis in 1951.

Guillermo Vilas (b. 8-17-52): Tennis. Argentine won 50 straight matches in 1977. In '77 won French Open, where he beat Brian Gottfried, and the U.S. Open, where he beat Jimmy Connors. Also won Australian Open twice, 1978–79.

Lasse Viren (b. 7-22-49): Track and field. Finnish runner was gold medalist in 5,000 and 10,000 meters at two consecutive Olympics (1972, '76).

Virginia Wade (b. 7-10-45): Tennis. Beloved in Britain, Wade won three major titles, most notably Wimbledon in 1977, its centenary year, where she triumphed over Betty Stove. Also won 1968 U.S. Open, '72 Australian Open, and doubles titles in '73 at the Australian, French and U.S. Opens, all with Margaret Smith Court.

Honus Wagner (b. 2-24-1874, d. 12-6-55): Baseball SS. Had .327 career batting average, 3,415 hits and eight batting titles. Averaged .300+ 15 consecutive seasons. Led league in RBI four times, with 100+ RBI nine times. Third alltime in triples (252) and league leader in doubles eight times. 703 career stolen bases, league leader in steals five times. Career span 1897–1917 with Pittsburgh.

Grete Waitz (b. 10-1-53): Track and field. Norwegian runner has won New York City Marathon a record nine times (consecutively 1978–80, 1982–86, '88). Won the women's marathon at the 1983 World Championship.

Jersey Joe Walcott (b. 10-31-14, d. 2-25-94): Boxer. Heavyweight champion from 1951 to 1952. Won title at age 37 on fifth attempt before surrendering it to Rocky Marciano. Later became sheriff of Camden, NJ.

Doak Walker (b. 1-1-27, d. 9-27-98): Football HB. Led league in scoring two times, his first and final seasons. All-Pro five times. Played on two consecutive NFL champions (1952–53) with Detroit. Career span 1950 to 1955. Also won Heisman Trophy as a junior in 1948. All-America three consecutive seasons with SMU.

Herschel Walker (b. 3-3-62): Football RB. Won Heisman Trophy in 1982 with Georgia. Turned pro by entering USFL with New Jersey. Gained 7,000+ rushing yards and scored 61 touchdowns in three seasons before league folded. Entered NFL in 1986 with Dallas and led league in rushing yards in 1988 (1,514).

Bill Walsh (b. 11-30-31): Football coach. Led San Francisco to three Super Bowl wins, after the 1981, '84, '88 seasons. Career record with 49ers 102-63-1. Developed short-passing game. Returned to Stanford University for 1992 season.

Bill Walton (b. 11-5-52): Basketball C. College Player of the Year three consecutive seasons (1972–74). Played on two NCAA championship teams (1972–73) with UCLA; tournament MVP twice (1972–73). Sullivan Award winner in 1973. NBA MVP in 1978, playoff MVP in '77. Led league in rebounding and blocks in 1977. Career span 1974–86 with Portland, San Diego, Boston.

War Admiral (b. 1934, d. 1959): Thoroughbred race horse. A son of Man o' War, won Triple Crown and Horse of the Year honors in 1937.

Paul Warfield (b. 11-28-42): Football WR. Caught 427 passes for 8,565 yards and 85 TDs. Played on two Super Bowl-winning Miami Dolphins teams. Career span 1964–77, all with Cleveland Browns except for 1970–74 with Miami Dolphins. Inducted to Hall of Fame 1983.

Glenn (Pop) Warner (b. 4-5-1871, d. 9-7-54): College football coach. Second alltime in wins (319). Won three national championships with Pittsburgh (1916, '18) and Stanford (1926). Career record 319-106-32 with 6 teams from 1896 to 1938.

Tom Watson (b. 9-4-49): Golfer. Winner of British Open five times (1975, '77, '80, consecutively 1982–83), the Masters two times (1977, '81) and U.S. Open once (1982). PGA Player of the Year six times, more than any golfer (consecutively 1977–80, '82, '84).

Dick Weber (b. 12-23-29): Bowler. Won All-Star Tournament four times (consecutively 1962–63, 1965–66). Voted Bowler of the Year three times (1961, '63, '65). Won 31 career PBA titles.

Johnny Weismuller (b. 6-2-04, d. 1-21-84): Swimmer. Won 3 gold medals (including 100- and 400-meter freestyle) at 1924 Olympics and two gold medals at '28 Olympics. Also played Tarzan in the movies.

Jerry West (b. 5-28-38): Basketball G. 10 time All-Star; All-Defensive Team four times; 1969 playoff MVP. Led league in assists and scoring one time each. Career span 1960–72 with Los Angeles. Currently executive vice president of Lakers. Also NCAA tournament MVP in 1959. All-America two times with West Virginia. Played on 1960 gold medal-winning Olympic team.

Whirlaway (b. 4-2-38, d. 4-6-53): Thoroughbred race horse. Triple Crown winner in 1941 with jockey Eddie Arcaro aboard. Trained by Ben A. Jones.

Byron (Whizzer) White (b. 6-8-17): Football RB. Led NFL in rushing 2 times (Pittsburgh in 1938, Detroit in '40). Led NCAA in scoring and rushing with Colorado in 1937; named All-America. Supreme Court justice 1962–93.

Reggie White (b. 12-19-62): Football DE. Alltime leader in sacks. Signed with Green Bay in 1993 for $17 million over four years. Career span: 1984 with Memphis Showboats (USFL), 1985–92 with Philadelphia, 1993–99 with Packers. Member of Green Bay's 1997 Super Bowl championship team.

Charles Whittingham (b. 4-13-13 d. 4-20-99): Thoroughbred race horse trainer. "Bald Eagle" after losing hair to tropical disease in World War II. Led yearly earnings list for trainers from 1970–73 consecutively; in 1975; and in 1981–82 consecutively. Won three Eclipse Awards and trained two Horses of the Year (Ack Ack in 1971 and Ferdinand in '87).

Kathy Whitworth (b. 9-27-39): Golfer. Alltime LPGA leader with 88 tour victories, including six majors. Won LPGA Championship in 1967, '71 and '75. Won Titleholders Championship (extinct major) in 1965 and '66. Won Western Open (extinct major) in 1967. Won Vare Trophy every year from 1965–72, except '68. LPGA Player of Year from 1966–69 and 1971–73.

Hoyt Wilhelm (b. 7-26-23): Baseball RHP. Hall of Famer. Threw knuckleball until age 48. Alltime pitching leader in games (1,070). Career 2.52 ERA, 227 saves. Hit home run in his first at bat (never hit another) and pitched no-hitter in 1958. Career span 1952–72 with 9 teams.

Bud Wilkinson (b. 4-23-15 d. 2-9-94): Football coach. Alltime NCAA leader in consecutive wins (47, 1953–57). Won three national championships (1950, consecutively 1955–56) with Oklahoma, where he coached from 1947 to 1963. Won Orange Bowl 4 times and Sugar Bowl two times. Career record 145-29-4, including four undefeated seasons. Also coached with St. Louis of NFL in 1978–79.

Billy Williams (b. 6-15-38): Baseball OF. "Sweet Swinging." NL Rookie of the Year for 1961. Hit 426 career home runs. Drove in 1,475 runs. Lifetime average of .290. Named to six NL All Star teams. Career span 1959–74 with Chicago Cubs, 1975–76 with Oakland A's. Elected to Hall of Fame in 1987.

Ted Williams (b. 8-30-18): Baseball OF. "The Splendid Splinter." Last player to hit .400 (.406 in 1941). MVP in 1946, '49 and Triple Crown winner in 1942, '47. Sixth alltime highest batting average (.344), second most walks (2,019) and second highest slugging average (.634). 521 career HR. League leader in batting average and runs scored six times each, RBI and HR four times each. Had .300+ average 15 consecutive seasons; 100+ RBI and runs scored nine times each; 30+ HR eight times; and 100+ walks 11 times. Lost nearly five seasons to military service. Career span 1939–42 and 1946–60 with Boston.

Hack Wilson (b. 4-26-1900; d. 11-23-48): Baseball OF. Stood 5' 6" but weighed 210. Had five incredible seasons 1926–30. Best was 1930 when he hit .356, scored 146 runs, hit a NL record 56 homers and drove in 190, which is still the major league record. Career span 1923–34 with several teams. Elected to Hall of Fame in 1979.

Dave Winfield (b. 10-3-51): Baseball OF. Drafted out of Univ. of Minnesota for both pro basketball and football. Led NL in RBIs in 1979 (118). In 1992, first 40-year-old to get 100+ RBIs, with 108. Hit clutch double to win 1992 World Series. Got 3,000th hit, off Dennis Eckersley, on 9-16-93. Career span 1973–80 with San Diego; 1981–90 with Yankees; 1990–91 with California; 1992 with Toronto; 1993–94 with Minnesota; and 1995 with Cleveland.

Major W.C. Wingfield (b. 10-16-1833, d. 4-18-12): British tennis pioneer. Credited with inventing the game of tennis, which he called "Sphairistike" or "sticky" and patented in February 1874.

Colonel Matt Winn (b. 6-30-1861, d. 10-6-49): General manager of Churchill Downs from 1904 until his death; made Kentucky Derby premier U.S. race.

Katarina Witt (b. 12-3-65): East German figure skater. Gold medalist at 1984 and '88 Olympics. Also world champion four times (consecutively 1984–85, 1987–88).

John Wooden (b. 10-14-10): College basketball coach. First member of basketball Hall of Fame as coach and player. Coached UCLA to 10 NCAA championships in 12 years (consecutively 1964–65, 1967–73, 1975). Alltime winning streak 88 games (1971–74). 664 career wins and fourth alltime highest winning percentage (.804). Career span 1949–75 with UCLA.1932 College Player of the Year at Purdue.

Tiger Woods (b. 12-30-75): Golfer. Won three straight U.S. Junior Amateur titles (1991–93), three straight U.S. Amateur titles (1994–96), then took the PGA tour by storm, winning six of his first 21 tournaments, including the 1997 Masters. There he was the youngest winner ever, scoring a record low 270, and winning by the widest margin in tournament history, 12 strokes. 1996 *Sports Illustrated* Sportsman of the Year.

Mickey Wright (b. 2-14-35): Golfer. Second alltime in career wins (82) and major championships (13— tied with Louise Suggs). Won U.S. Open four times (consecutively 1958-59, 1961, 1964), LPGA Championship four times (1958, consecutively 1960–61, '63), Western Open three times (consecutively 1962–63, '66).

Kristi Yamaguchi (b.7-12-71): Figure skater. Olympic champion in 1992. Back-to-back world champion (1991–92).

Cale Yarborough (b. 3-27-40): Auto racer. Won Daytona 500 four times (1968, '77, consecutively 1983–84). 83 career victories. Also NASCAR champion three consecutive years (1976–78).

Carl Yastrzemski (b. 8-22-39): Baseball OF. "Yaz." 3,419 career hits, 452 HR. 1967 MVP and Triple Crown winner. Three batting titles, including .301 in 1968, the lowest ever to win. Second alltime in games played (3,308) and fourth in walks (1,845). Career span 1961–83 with Boston.

Cy Young (b. 3-29-1867, d. 11-4-55): Baseball RHP. Alltime leader in wins (511), losses (315), innings pitched (7,354⅔) and complete games (749); fourth in shutouts (76). Had 2.63 career ERA. Pitched three no-hitters, including a perfect game in 1904. Pitching award named in his honor. Career span 1890–1911 with Cleveland, Boston.

Steve Young (b. 10-11-61): Football QB. Highest rated passer in NFL history, with 97.5 rating entering 1999 season. Led 49ers to victory in Super Bowl XXIX and was named MVP of game. Two-time NFL MVP (1992 and '94). Career span 1984 with LA Express of the USFL, 1985–86 with Tampa Bay, since '87 with San Francisco.

Robin Yount (b. 9-16-55): Baseball OF/SS. Became Brewers shortstop at 18. Won 1982 AL MVP when he hit .331 with 29 homers. 3,142 career hits. Shoulder injury caused move to outfield in 1984. Career span 1974–93, all with the Brewers. Elected to Hall of Fame 1999.

Steve Yzerman (b. 5-9-65): Hockey C. Won back-to-back Stanley Cups with Red Wings (1997, '98). Won Conn Smythe trophy in 1998. Scored 100+ points six consecutive seasons (1987–88 through 1992–93). Career span since 1983 with Detroit.

Babe Didrikson Zaharias (b. 6-26-14, d. 9-27-56): Sportswoman. Gold medalist in 80-meter hurdles and javelin throw at 1932 Olympics; also won silver medal in high jump (her gold medal jump was disallowed for using the then-illegal western roll). Became a golfer in 1935 and won 12 major titles, including U.S. Open three times (1948, 1950, 1954—a year after cancer surgery). Also helped found the LPGA in 1949.

Tony Zale (b. 5-29-13, d. 3-20-97): Boxer. Born Anthony Zaleski. "The Man of Steel." Two-time middleweight champ. Fought Rocky Graziano for title three times in 21 months, winning twice. 67-18-2 with 44 KOs. Elected to Boxing Hall of Fame 1958.

Emil Zatopek (b. 9-19-22): Track and field. Czech runner became only athlete to win gold medal in 5,000 and 10,000 meters and marathon, at 1952 Olympics. Also gold medalist in 10,000 meters at '48 Olympics.

Zinedine Zidane (b. 6-23-72): French soccer player. "Zizou." Led France to 1998 World Cup title; scored two goals in 3–0 win over Brazil in the final. Led Juventus to 1998 Italian League title and to '98 European Cup final. Named '98 FIFA World Player of the Year.

Obituaries

Baseball legend
Joe DiMaggio

Joe Adcock, 71, baseball player. In his 17-year major league career, the former Milwaukee Braves star hit 336 homers and held a .277 lifetime batting average. But it wasn't his numbers that made Adcock so memorable as much as the timing and distance of his clouts.

SI's Ron Fimrite writes:

"Consider these Homeric feats: On April 29, 1953, Adcock became the first major league player to hit a ball into the centerfield bleachers at New York's Polo Grounds since the distance had been increased to a virtually unreachable 483 feet in 1923. On July 31, 1954, he became only the seventh player (there are 12 now) to hit four home runs in one game. He hit them at Ebbets Field off four Brooklyn Dodgers pitchers while using a borrowed bat. In his only other at bat that day, he doubled, giving him 18 total bases, still the single-game record. On June 17, 1956, he became the only player to hit a ball out of Brooklyn's Ebbets Field in leftfield, his drive clearing the 83-foot high roof above the 350-foot sign at ground level.

"On May 26, 1959, Adcock made history again by breaking up the best-pitched game ever with a homer that wasn't a homer. For 12 innings the Pittsburgh Pirates' Harvey Haddix had pitched a perfect game against the Braves in County Stadium. Then in the 13th, Felix Mantilla reached base on an error and advanced to second on a sacrifice by Eddie Mathews, and Haddix walked Henry Aaron intentionally. The perfect game was gone, but the marathon no-hitter was intact. At which point Adcock hit one over the right centerfield fence for an apparent 3–0 Braves win. But after Mantilla crossed the plate, Aaron, who didn't realize Adcock's ball had gone over the fence, touched second and started heading to the dugout, thinking the game was over. Adcock, happily into his home run trot, passed Aaron on his way to the plate and was called out. His homer was scored as a double. The final score went into the books as 1–0."

In Coushatta, LA, of Alzheimer's disease, May 3, 1999.

Dick Beaty, 74, auto racing official. Beaty was NASCAR's Winston Cup director from 1980 to '92. Before being promoted to this top position, Beaty served for years as a NASCAR official and inspector. In the early 50s, Beaty also made 38 Winston Cup starts. In Charlotte, NC, of undisclosed causes, November 22, 1998.

Tom Binford, 74, auto racing official. Binford served as chief steward of the Indianapolis 500 from 1974 to '95. For two decades, his trademark gravelly voice was a mainstay of the nation's most famous race. In 1981, Binford changed the Indy 500 winner from Bobby Unser to Mario Andretti after an all-night review of timing and scoring tapes indicated that Unser had passed several cars under a yellow flag. This ruling was in turn reversed. In Indianapolis, of a brain hemorrhage, January 14, 1999.

Frankie Brimsek, 85, hockey player. During an era when Canadians ruled hockey, Brimsek was a rare American-born star. Brimsek became the Boston Bruins' No. 1 goalie during the 1938–39 season when the team sold future Hall of Famer Cecil (Tiny) Thompson to the Red Wings. After shutting out the Blackhawks in Chicago, Brimsek made his debut at Boston Garden in front of fans stunned by Thompson's departure. He blanked Chicago again, 2–0, then shut out the Rangers 3–0 in his next game. He was scored on in the game after that, ending his scoreless streak at 231 minutes 54 seconds, which broke Thompson's record by more than seven minutes.

After that, he reeled off three more consecutive shutouts, including one against Thompson and the Red Wings. After this feat—six shutouts in seven games—Brimsek became known as Mr. Zero. That season Brimsek led the Bruins to the Stanley Cup title and was awarded the Calder Trophy (rookie of the year) and Vezina Trophy (top goaltender), which he also won in 1942. He led the Bruins to another cup in 1941. A member of the Hockey Hall of Fame, he was an All-Star eight times during his 10-year career. In Virginia, MN., of undisclosed causes, November 11, 1998.

Ricky Byrdsong, 43, basketball coach. Byrdsong was the men's basketball coach at Northwestern from 1993 to '97. While jogging with his children in suburban Illinois, he was gunned down by a white supremacist named Benjamin Smith Besides killing Byrdsong and a Korean man, Smith wounded another nine people in a three-day shooting spree. In Skokie, IL, from gunshot wounds, July 3, 1999.

Randie Carver, 24, boxer. A super middleweight boxer who billed himself as "The Natural," Carver was a former Golden Gloves champion. He won the NABF super middleweight title in 1998 and entered his fight against Kabary Salem with a 23–0–1 record. Tragically, the bout would be his last as he suffered fatal blows to the head in the 10th round. In North Kansas City, MO, from head injuries sustained in a fight, September 14, 1999.

Wilt Chamberlain, 63, basketball player. During a 14-year NBA career with Philadelphia, San Francisco and Los Angeles, Chamberlain, who was also known as the Big Dipper and Wilt the Stilt, compiled such legendary statistics—including a 100-point game against the New York Knicks on March 2, 1962, a 27.2 rebounds per game average in 1960–61, and a 50.4 points per game average the following year—that he has often been called the Babe Ruth of basketball.

SI's Frank Deford writes:

"Seven feet, one and one-sixteenth inches tall was Wilton Norman Chamberlain. No one, however, believed him…To almost everyone he encountered, Wilt appeared simply larger than life, a human optical illusion. He loomed. It was as if he blocked out the sun.

"Were it only that. Were it only everyone else's perception. But the irony was that Wilt Chamberlain, who died of a heart attack last week at 63, was never quite big enough even for himself. Especially in his prime, he constantly felt compelled to do more, to be better, to go higher. For someone so curious and sensitive, he was too influenced—seduced, even—by his own physical preeminence. In a world where he knew he was the Most Man, he never would allow himself the legal dictum *res ipsa loquitur*: the thing speaks for itself. No, Wilt needed numbers to validate himself. If the most points were not enough, then he would get the most rebounds, then the most assists. Never take a rest. Never foul out. Alas, near the end, when he crowed of having had assignations with 20,000 women, that numbing statistical braggadocio made him a figure of fun. Always before he had been controversial, often even villainous, but never foolish.

"There's no doubt that he could do, by himself, almost anything he ordained. I learned that myself, just as the centers he toyed with under the hoop did. In 1969 I wrote a cover story on Chamberlain for *Sports Illustrated*. He was 32 then, his great scoring days were behind him, and I ventured this memorable line: 'There is a growing school of thought that he no longer possesses sufficient moves to make him a bona fide high-scoring threat.' It had, in fact, been more than a year since he had made 50 in any game. So the very next game he played after the magazine came out, Wilt went for 60. Yet in the seventh game of the NBA Finals that year, Russell's swan song, the man who never missed a moment of any importance on the court took himself out of the game, sore-kneed, when the Lakers fell behind the Boston Celtics. Only when Los Angeles rallied without him did Chamberlain petition to go back in, but coach Butch van Breda Kolff refused. It cost van Breda Koff his job. It cost Wilt more, his image.

"His defenders—and it almost defined what sort of person you were, whether you fell into the Chamberlain or the Russell camp—always maintained that Chamberlain would have won as many championships as Russell did if he had been lucky enough to be surrounded by the deep Celtic green. 'No,' Bob Cousy said not long ago. 'To play with Wilt you had to go down, set up and wait for him. We couldn't have played that way.'

"It was not, really, that Chamberlain wasn't a team player. That's simplistic. In his great cathedral house in Los Angeles he kept not a single trophy attesting to his individual achievements, except for his Hall of Fame certificate. He gave all the others away. 'They make other people happier,' he told me matter-of-factly. Rather, I think, he was just so dominating a presence that he overwhelmed his own team. He was, ultimately, primarily an opposing force. Whereas players like Russell made their teammates better, it was Chamberlain's fate to bring out the best in the opposition. Finally he awoke one summer's morning on vacation on an island somewhere in the Adriatic and understood that. 'There was always so much more pain to my losing than there ever was to gain by my winning,' he explained. It was time to quit basketball.

"The rest of his life was much happier. He went barefoot and could play at being Wilt more than having to be him all the time. And if there is a heaven, my man, it's a place where nobody has to shoot free throws."

In Los Angeles, of a heart attack, October 12, 1999.

Steve Chiasson, 32, hockey player. Before joining the Carolina Hurricanes in 1997–98, defenseman Chiasson, who entered the NHL in 1986, played with the Detroit Red Wings, the Calgary Flames and the Hartford Whalers. A capable defender who could also go forward and contribute to the offense, (he scored 62 points for Detroit in 1992–93) Chiasson was remembered by his peers as a "real team leader" who played hard on and off the ice. In Raleigh, NC, from injuries sustained in an automobile accident, May 3, 1999.

Joe DiMaggio, 84, baseball player. A son of Italian immigrants, the Yankee Clipper was revered for his elegant and offhand excellence as a ball player. His statistics speak for themselves: 1,736 major league games played, a batting average of .325 with 2,214 hits, 389 doubles, 131 triples, 361 homers, 1,390 runs scored, 1,537 runs batted in and a 56-game hitting streak. But the numbers alone do not reflect the unique place DiMaggio held in the American consciousness. Long after he retired from his 13 seasons between 1936 and 1951 (missing three seasons during WWII), DiMaggio remains an American icon. His stature was further enhanced when he married Marilyn Monroe in 1954 (they were divorced nine months later). Songwriter Paul Simon paid tribute to DiMaggio in "Mrs. Robinson", an ode to lost heroes from the 1967 film *The Graduate*:

"*Where have you gone Joe DiMaggio?/ A nation turns its lonely eyes to you./ What's that you say, Mrs. Robinson?/ Joltin' Joe has left and gone away.*"

Appearing in *SI*, Robert W. Creamer writes:
"Unlike so many of baseball's stars, DiMaggio wan't flamboyant, bad-tempered, colorful, talkative or explosive. He was quiet and efficient and marvelously skillful in all aspects of the game: hitting, fielding, throwing, running the bases. Ted Williams was a better hitter, but that was the only thing the Boston Red Sox outfielder did superlatively. DiMaggio did everything superlatively, without fuss. At the plate he locked himself into his wide-legged stance, cocked his bat and waited without moving, watching the pitcher, waiting for him to throw. When DiMaggio swung, strength surged from his big thighs and muscular back into his arms and wrists and bat. It was a beautiful swing, rich with power, yet controlled. You almost never saw him strike out. When he hit the ball a long way, as he so often did, he didn't pause to watch it but rather took off running hard for first, looking for an edge that would give him an extra base or two if the ball didn't reach the seats. No wonder he hit so many triples.

"DiMaggio's austere style was defined in a game I saw in the late 1940s between the Yankees and the St. Louis Browns at Yankee Stadium. The Browns, losing by two runs, filled the bases in the ninth inning with one out. The next batter hit a little looping fly ball into right center, too far out for the second baseman to reach and too far in for the outfielders. It seemed a certain base hit, and the St. Louis base runners took off, the tying runs racing toward home from third and second, the winning run heading around second toward third. DiMaggio came loping across from centerfield, and you wondered if, with his powerful arm, he could get the ball on the bounce and throw to the plate in time to cut down the tying run. However, I was astonished, as were the Browns, when without breaking stride, DiMaggio leaned forward, stuck out that long arm of his and caught the ball no more than a foot off the ground. It was a startling catch, but what he did next was prototypically DiMaggio. Still in full stride, he straightened up, threw the ball to the first baseman for the game-ending double play and without stopping, without saying anything, without showing any emotion, continued across the rightfield foul line, into the Yankees' dugout and out of sight, as though it were routine, just the end of another day's work."

In Hollywood, FL, of lung cancer, March 8, 1999.

Chris Dundee, 91, boxing promoter. The older brother of trainer Angelo Dundee, Chris Dundee (born Cristofo Mirena) promoted hundreds of fights, including the Miami Beach bout in which Muhammad Ali, then known as Cassius Clay, knocked out Sonny Liston to win the heavyweight title on Feb. 25, 1964. Other fights he promoted involved such boxers as Sugar Ray Robinson, Jake LaMotta, Archie Moore, George Foreman and Sugar Ray Leonard. Ali trained at Dundee's Miami Beach gym during the three and a half years the heavyweight was banned from boxing for refusing to register for the draft. In Miami, of complications from a stroke, November 16, 1998.

Eddie Elias, 69, bowling pioneer. Elias founded the Professional Bowlers Association in 1958 and was also a television pioneer and sports and celebrity agent. His marketing efforts made bowling television's second-longest-running professional sport behind college football. In Naples, FL, of pneumonia, November 15, 1998.

Larry Ellis, 70, track coach. The first African American head coach in any sport in the Ivy League, Ellis led the Princeton University track team from 1970 to '92. He was coach of the 1984 U.S. Olympic men's track team and a former president of USA Track &

Field. Ellis also coached for 13 years at Jamaica (NY) High, where his athletes included long jumper Bob Beamon, who set a world record at the 1968 Summer Games. In Skillman, NJ, of undisclosed causes, November 3, 1998.

Weeb Ewbank, 91, football coach.

Ewbank coached the Baltimore Colts from 1954–1962 and the New York Jets from 1963–1973 and held a 130–129–7 pro football coaching record. He is best remembered for being the winning coach in two of the most famous games in NFL history—the 1958 NFL championship (his Colts beat the Giants in overtime) and Super Bowl III, (in a surprise upset his Jets clobbered the Colts)

SI senior writer Paul Zimmerman writes:

"The first time I met Weeb Ewbank was in the spring of 1963, right after he had been named general manager and coach of the Jets. I was playing rugby in Van Cortlandt Park in the Bronx. The ball from the game I was in bounced into some bushes, and when some of the other players and I went to retrieve it, we came upon a group of naked and half-naked young men. We were stunned. Then I spotted a little round guy with a crew cut. I recognized him immediately. It was Ewbank, coach of the 1958 and '59 NFL champion Colts. 'Just changing clothes,' he said. 'Just be a minute.' Ewbank was holding open tryouts for the Jets, but the Polo Grounds wasn't available, and Van Cortlandt Park had no locker facilities, so his players were changing behind the shrubbery. 'Don't mind us,' Weeb said merrily. 'Go on with your game.'

"Three years later I became a beat writer for the *New York Post*, and I covered Ewbank's Jets through his retirement in 1973. When I started on the beat, I thought all coaches were like Weeb. I was wrong.

"Pro football players, coaches and writers were a big family back then, and we would go out together on the road. Once before a game in San Diego, I was walking with Weeb and a few others down the main drag in Tijuana, and some guy approached us with a package. 'Films?' he said. 'Filthy films?' 'Christ, no,' Weeb said without breaking stride. 'I've been looking at films all week.'

"Watching Weeb work with Joe Namath was like watching the creation of a great painting. Joe Willie arrived from Alabama as Sonny Werblin's guy, the Jets owner's personal choice. He was an unbroken stallion, able to put up huge numbers—and interceptions in bunches. Weeb tamed him, and by the time Namath led the Jets to their Super Bowl triumph, he had done a 180. To the outside world he was still Joe Willie the wild flinger, but the guys on the beat saw his transformation into one of the game's most meticulous passers.

"Ewbank won't go down with the Lombardis and Halases because he didn't often have the players to win with. When he did, though, he produced. Few coaches ever understood their players or their times as well as Ewbank did. I once asked Weeb how he developed Namath and John Unitas with the Colts. 'Everything was there,' he said. 'I just fine-tuned it. You know the greatest thing about having a Namath or a Unitas? They keep you from making an ass of yourself for 10 years.'"

In Oxford, OH, of natural causes, November 17, 1998.

Jack Gelineau, 74, hockey player.

Gelineau broke into the NHL in the 1948–49 season with the Boston Bruins, playing only four games. He captured the Calder Trophy as the National Hockey League's Rookie of the Year the following season after compiling a 3.28 goals-against average in 67 games. During World War II, he was awarded the British Empire Medal for gallantry after rescuing an injured crewman from a burning plane loaded with ammunition. In Montreal, of cancer, November 12, 1998.

M. Donald Grant, 94, baseball executive.

Chairman of the board of the New York Mets from the team's inception in 1962 until his ouster after the 1978 season, Grant was notorious for orchestrating the "Midnight Massacre" on June 15, 1977. Grant traded away Tom Seaver and Dave Kingman, both of whom were in contract disputes, on that night. After the Mets' second straight last-place finish, the team's eight-man board pushed Grant aside on Nov. 8, 1978, announcing that he was stepping down as of Jan. 1 to allow late founding owner Joan Payson's daughter, Lorinda de Roulet, to run the team. In Hobe Sound, FL, after a long illness, November 28, 1998.

Gene Hart, 68, sports broadcaster.
Known as the first voice of the Philadelphia Flyers, Hart was inducted into the Hall of Fame in 1997. He called Flyers games on radio and television from 1967 to '95, including their Stanley Cup title runs in 1974 and 1975. In Philadelphia, of multiple cystic organ failure, July 14, 1999.

Leon Hess, 85, owner of the NY Jets.
Hess, an oil industry magnate, became the partial owner of the team in 1963 (they were then known as the New York Titans). He gained full control of the franchise when the AFL merged with the NFL and became known as an extremely loyal and supportive "hands-off" manager. In the words of the Baltimore Ravens owner, Art Modell, "[Hess] loved the Jets. He didn't own them for business reasons or to make money." In New York City, from complications of a blood disease, May 7, 1999.

Fred Hobdy, 75, basketball coach.
Hobdy was the Grambling State basketball coach from 1956 to '86 and was a Louisiana Sports and Southwestern Athletic Conference Hall-of-Famer. The winningest coach in Louisiana collegiate basketball history, Hobdy had a 572–288 career record and was renowned for his disciplinarian style. Hobdy also played on his friend Eddie Robinson's 1942 football team at Grambling, before fighting in WWII. The legendary coach Robinson had this to say about Hobdy, "I cherish the fact that I coached him in basketball and football. He was a great leader in basketball, but most of all he was a great leader in life." In Grambling, LA, of cancer, December 8, 1998.

Red Holzman, 78, basketball coach.
When Holzman retired in 1982, he had coached the New York Knicks for 12 ½ years, won 694 games and two NBA titles.

SI writes:

"Red Auerbach doesn't remember the year, other than that it 'was a long time ago, around 1939,' but he does remember the kid. 'I was helping out coaching at George Washington, and this name, Holzman, kept coming up,' Auerbach syas. 'He had played for Franklin Lane High in Brooklyn and [while at the University of Baltimore] was looking for a new college, so I went to check him out. He was a real good defender and a decent shooter. He ended up at CCNY and proved to be what I said he was—a helluva player.'

"William (Red) Holzman turned out to be much more than that. Holzman…made his biggest mark on basketball after retiring as a player in 1954. He coached the New York Knicks to their only NBA titles, in '70 and '73, and was a mentor to several coaches, most notably Phil Jackson.

"After Auerbach took over as coach of the Celtics in 1950, Holzman, dubbed Red by his wife, Selma, for his fiery hair, frequently found himself playing against the other Red's team, and then, during his own early years on the bench with the Milwaukee and St. Louis Hawks, coaching against the Celtics. By the time Holzman took over the Knicks in 1967, however, Auerbach had moved to the Boston front office. That didn't stop one Red from admiring the other.

"'Red had the Knicks moving all the time,' Auerbach says. 'They didn't break like we did, but they were always cutting, passing, moving. I never had much use for the Knicks, but Red Holzman was different. I respected him.'

"Auerbach learned of Holzman's death from a reporter who called him at home. 'I told the guy Red was an honorable man. He was part of my era. He loved the game, just like me. I look around, and I don't know who the hell is left.'"

In New York City, of leukemia, November 13, 1998.

John Hunt, 88, mountain climber. As leader of the 1953 expedition that enabled Sir Edmund Hillary and Tenzing Norgay to conquer Mount Everest, Hunt decided it was his responsibility to remain at base camp while Hillary and Norgay climbed the remaining 400 feet to the summit of the world's highest peak. Hunt said it was the greatest moment of his life, even though there was a sense of personal disappointment because he was not among the first to reach the top. In Henley-on-Thames, England, of undisclosed causes, November 7, 1998.

Jim (Catfish) Hunter, 53, baseball player. A first-ballot Hall of Famer, Hunter was one of baseball's most dominant pitchers during his 15-year career. He pitched a perfect game, won a Cy Young Award, and strung together five straight 20-victory seasons. Pitching for the Oakland Athletics and the Yankees, he won five World Series rings. When Hunter was freed on a technicality from his contract with the Oakland Athletics in 1974, he was one of baseball's first free agents, and ushered in a new era of big money when he signed a five-year $3.75 million contract with the Yankees.

SI's Steve Rushin writes,

"Jim (Catfish) Hunter spent one of his last days on Earth with me—on the 20th anniversary of Thurman Munson's death, no less—and several times on that hot afternoon last month, in the presence of this dying man, I was powerless to contain my tears. He was that funny.

'The first time I pitched to Munson,' Hunter said of his Yankees batterymate while sitting on a porch swing outside his house in Hertford, N.C., 'I was windin' up when he was just startin' to give the sign. He called timeout and ran out to the mound and said, 'What are you on?' I said, 'Whaddya mean, what am I on? I'm not on anythang.'"

'But I haven't gave the sign yet, and you're windin' up.'

'As long as you give the sign before my hand gets over the top of my head, I'm gonna throw whatever you call.'

'How in the hell you gonna do that?'

'I throw every pitch the same way.'

'You don't like to waste time, do you?'

'That's right—give me the damn ball and let me throw it.'

"Hunter, who died of amyotrophic lateral sclerosis—Lou Gehrig's disease—stuffed 20 pounds of life into a five-pound sack. He married his high school sweetheart, skipped the minors, went to the big leagues at 19, threw a perfect game at 22, won five World Series in seven years in the 1970s, retired at 33, was inducted into the Hall of Fame at 41 and died at 53."

In Hertford, NC, of Lou Gehrig's disease, September 9, 1999.

Ken Katagiri, 28, boxer. Since turning pro in 1991, Katagiri a super bantamweight from Japan, had a 5-6-2 record. In the ninth round of a scheduled 10-round bout at Tokyo's Korakuen boxing hall, Katagiri was knocked down by Fusaaki Takenaga, and later died from his inuries. He was the 28th boxing fatality in Japan since the Japan Boxing Commission was created in 1952. In Tokyo, of brain injuries, October 26, 1998.

Lord Killanin, 84, president of the International Olympic Committee (IOC). President of the IOC from 1972 to '80, Killanin succeeded Avery Brundage just after the massacre of Israeli athletes at the 1972 Games in Munich. He presided over some of the most turbulent Olympic games: the 1976 African nations' boycott of the Montreal Games and the 1980 U.S.-led boycott of the Moscow Olympics. In Dublin, Ireland, of undisclosed causes, April 25, 1999.

Archie Moore, 84, boxer. The Mongoose, as Moore was known, has a record that speaks for itself: 183–24–10 with a knockout total ranging from 129 to 145. Moore held the light heavyweight title for 11 of his 27 fighting years before finally retiring at the age of 49. Often called the "Goodwill Ambassador of Boxing", Moore was characterized by ESPN fight analyst Teddy Atlas as " the definition of what being a champion is. His loss is to boxing what Joe DiMaggio's willl be for baseball." In San Diego, CA, of natural causes, December, 9, 1998.

Richard D. (Dick) Moroso, 59, drag racer. Named by *Hot Rod Magazine* as one of the 100 most influential people in drag-racing history, Moroso was a champion drag-racer who was best known as the founder of Moroso Performance Products and as the owner of the Moroso Motorsports Park, a 2.2-mile raceway in Palm Beach Gardens. He retired from competition in 1971 to concentrate on his business. In 1990 his 22-year-old son, Robbie, was killed in a drunken-driving accident shortly after signing a NASCAR sponsorship deal. In Branford, CT, of brain cancer, November 7, 1998.

Marion Motley, 79, football player. Motley was one of two black players to sign with the Cleveland Browns in1946, becoming pro football's first African American players since the 1920s. The bruising fullback and Hall of Famer played 9 seasons, rushing for 4,720 yards. He helped the Browns win all four All-America Football Conference titles from 1946 to '49 and another in the NFL in 1950. He also caught 85 passes for 1,107 yards and seven touchdowns.

SI senior writer Paul Zimmerman writes:

"Most of the world never saw the real Marion Motley. What it saw when the Cleveland Browns entered the NFL in 1950 was a 30-year old fullback with two bad knees. He was still fuctional, still capable of running with speed and power and catching Otto Graham's swing passes—and of picking up pass rushers who wandered through the wall. 'He takes the romance out of the blitz,' said Weeb Ewbank, a Browns assistant in those days.

"The real Marion Motley was the 232-pound monster who burst onto the All-America Football Conference scene in 1946 and terrorized the new league. That's the man who fascinated me as a youngster. When he carried the ball, he was a gathering force. I can close my eyes and see him running right at me in my seat at Yankee Stadium in the 1947 title game, going 51 yards with Harmon Rowe riding his back and punching him in the face. 'Smile Marion,' the photographers said afterward. 'I can't,' he said. 'They knocked out my front teeth.' "

In Cleveland, of prostrate cancer, June 27, 1999.

Chip Myers, 53, football player and coach. Myers was a wide receiver for San Francisco and Cincinnati from 1967 to '76. He also coached with Tampa Bay, Indianapolis, the New York Jets and the New Orleans Saints before his final position as an offensive coordinator with the Minnesota Vikings. In Minneapolis, of a heart attack, February 22, 1999.

Hal Newhouser, 77, baseball player. The only pitcher to win consecutive MVP awards, Newhouser pitched for his hometown Detroit Tigers from 1939 to '53, leading them to the 1945 World Series title with a complete-game victory over the Cubs in Game 7. He was named AL MVP in 1944 after going 29–9, and again in 1945, when he was 25–9 with eight shutouts. A seven-time All-Star who led the AL in wins four times, Newhouser retired with a 207–150 record and a 3.02 ERA, and was elected to the Baseball Hall of Fame by the Veterans Committee in 1992. In Detroit, after a long illness, November 10, 1998.

Joao Carlos de Oliveira, 45, triple jumper. Oliveira was also called Jumping John in Portugese. From 1975 to '85, he held the world triple jump record and was one of Brazil's most popular sports heroes.

SI writes,

"Oliveira, then an army corporal, set his record in Mexico City, leaping 58' 8¼" to break the existing mark by a foot and a half. When he returned to Brazil, he received a trophy from the mayor of São Paulo, and his footprints were cast in cement outside his barracks. Oliveira went on to win bronze medals at the 1976 and 1980 Olympics. Then one night in 1981 the car in which he was riding was hit head-on by a drunk driver near Campinas, Brazil. Oliveira's right leg had to be amputated below the knee. His athletic career was over.

"Last year it seemed Jumping John might be bouncing back. He announced plans to train for the long jump at the 2000 Paralympic Games—'if not to win,' he said, 'to set an example.' His health problems cut short that dream, but many Brazilians would say Oliveira had already set his example."

In São Paulo, of cirrhosis of the liver, June 5, 1999.

Antonio Ordonez, 66, bullfighter. Ordonez was one of Spain's most famous and revered bullfighters. His career spanned more than 30 years (beginning in 1951) during which he faced some 2,000 bulls with his disciplined and classical style of bullfighting. Hemingway immortalized Ordonez and his rivalry with his bullfighting brother-in-law, Luis Miguel Dominguin in the book *The Dangerous Summer*. After retiring his red cape in the 1970s, Ordonez bred bulls for the fight. In Seville, after a long illness, December 19, 1999.

Kim Perrot, 32, basketball player. Perrot was the Houston Comets' point guard during their first two of three consecutive WNBA championship seasons (1997 and '98).The Comets' star averaged 7.2 points and 3.9 assists per game in her career. Though initially signed as a developmental player, Perrot quickly became, in the words of a teammate, "the glue to this team. She held us together."

SI writes:

"Even as she struggled against the cancer that had spread from her lungs to her brain, Houston Comets star Kim Perrot worked to find a way to ease the suffering of others. 'When I first started spending time at the hospital, I noticed families and children hanging around with nothing to do,' she wrote in May in her regular column in the *Houston Chronicle*. Soon after her cancer was diagnosed last February, the feisty 5'5" point guard, the heart of Houston's 1997 and 1998 WNBA championship teams, began raising money to build Kim's Place—a recreational facility that would be open to children with long-term illnesses and their families. To help Perrot reach her goal, in April the Comets and their NBA counterparts, the Rockets, held a fundraiser that took in almost $400,000, which will go toward the $600,000 construction cost."

In Houston, of brain cancer, August 19, 1999.

Katrina Price, 23, basketball player. Price was a 5'10" guard with a promising future when she was found dead at 23 of a presumably self-inflicted gunshot wound.

SI writes:

"Price graduated from Stephen F. Austin in Nacog-doches, TX, in 1998 as the Ladyjacks' alltime leading scorer, with 2,278 points. A two-time Southland Conference Player of the Year and a 1997–98 academic All-America, she joined the Philadelphia Rage of the ABL only to return to Nacogdoches in December '98 when the league folded. Price talked about becoming a coach but was staying in shape to try out for the WNBA in April.

In Nacogdoches, TX, of gunshot wounds, January 18, 1999.

Jerry Quarry, 53, boxer. As a heavyweight contender in the 1960s and '70s, Quarry earned roughly $2.1 million in purses. He earned $338,000 for fighting Muhammad Ali in 1970. Quarry suffered from dementia pugilistica (severe brain damage caused by repeated blows to the head) during the last 15 years of his life.

SI writes:

It would be a shame if Jerry Quarry were remembered only as another Great White Hope, a crowd-pleasing pug who took high-profile beatings from Muhammad Ali and Joe Frazier. Quarry was surprisingly fast, a hard hitter and a brilliant counterpuncher. His 53-9-4 record over 27 years as a pro included victories over Floyd Patterson and Earnie Shavers. In another era he might have worn a championship belt. He was also a warrior of tremendous heart—a quality that contributed to the darker side of his legacy."

In Templeton, CA, of pneumonia and cardiac arrest , January 3, 1999.

Bob Randolph, 92, football player. A starting fullback on the unbeaten 1929 Georgia Tech team, Randolph was also the last surviving player from the 1929 Rose Bowl. Randolph later coached at Furman University. In Spring Hill, GA, of kidney failure, January 20, 1999.

Harold (Pee Wee) Reese, 81, baseball player. A Hall of Fame shortstop who got his nickname from his childhood stint as a champion marble (pee-wee) competitor, Reese played 16 seasons for the Dodgers from 1940 to '58 (missing from 1943 to '45 due to WWII). He served as captain and was on seven of the Brooklyn teams that won National League pennants, including the 1955 World Series winners.

Appearing in *SI*, Robert W. Creamer writes:

"At Ebbets Field his locker stood in the center of the small, crowded clubhouse, along with an old wooden rocking chair someone had put there as a nod to Reese's leadership. The 5'10", 160-pound Reese was an excellent fielder—so good that in 1948, after the Dodgers acquired shortstop Billy Cox, a brilliant glove man, they made him a third baseman, and a capable hitter. His offensive statistics are sometimes dismissed as ordinary, but from '46 through '56, a span during which Brooklyn won six pennants, Reese averaged 40 extra-base hits a year, 97 runs and 65 RBIs. Eight times in his career he finished among the top 10 in the National League MVP vote.

"Still, Reese is best remembered for the role he played in helping Jackie Robinson break baseball's color barrier during the 1947 season. In spring training, when Robinson was still in Brooklyn's minor league system, Reese was asked to sign a petition drawn up by the Dodgers outfielder Dixie Walker stating that the undersigned would not play for Brooklyn if Robinson was brought up. Reese refused to sign, the rebellion was quashed, and Robinson was promoted. During the season Robinson took terrible verbal abuse from rival fans and ballplayers, and was even shunned by some of his teammates. Reese, a white Southerner, played cards with Robinson and before large crowds displayed friendship toward him on the field. On one famous occasion he put an arm around Robinson's shoulders. 'There were times when I went over to talk to him on the field,' Reese told Roger Kahn, 'thinking that people would see this and figure we were friends and this might help Jack.' Robinson never forgot the gesture. In sports to say someone has class is in many ways the highest compliment. Pee Wee Reese was the epitome of class."

In Louisville, of lung cancer, August 14, 1999.

Cal Ripken Sr., 63, baseball coach. Ripken Sr. signed on with the Baltimore Orioles organization as a catcher and worked with the franchise for 36 years. Though he never played in the big leagues, Ripken Sr., managed 14 seasons in the minor leagues before becoming a coach for the Orioles in 1976. He served as the third-base coach in two World Series ('79 and '83) and became the Orioles' manager in 1987. After the Orioles lost their first 6 games of '88, Ripken was fired, but was rehired as a coach in 1989. Ripken Sr., was the first father to manage two sons in the big leagues (Cal Jr. played shortstop and Bill second base). In 1994 Cal Jr.broke Lou Gehrig's record of 2,130 consecutive games played.

SI's Tom Verducci writes about Ripken and his part in Orioles' general manager Paul Richards's informal manuscript, *The Oriole Way*:

"Cal Ripken Sr., a loyal player, coach, manager and scout in the organization for 36 years, added his own colloquies to Richards's doctrine until his retirement in 1992. While in the final days of his fight with lung cancer, Ripken committed his accumulated wisdom to paper. When one of his good days would interrupt the run of bad ones, Ripken would press on with the writing of the book from his deathbed, telling his co-author, SI senior editor Larry Burke, 'Let's get on with it.'

"It was that book, published posthumously as *The Ripken Way*, that Cal Ripken Jr. read on the Orioles' flight from New York to Toronto one early Friday morning in March. 'It's amazing,' the son said. 'I thought I knew my father really well. But there are things in the book about him—what he felt about the game—that I never knew.'"

In Baltimore, of lung cancer, March 25, 1999.

Lou Rymkus, 78, football coach. First coach of the Houston Oilers, Rymkus coached the team to their first AFL championship in 1960 but was fired in 1961 when the team lost three of the season's first five games. He went on to serve as an offensive line coach for the Baltimore Colts when they won Super Bowl V. Rymkus also played tackle for Notre Dame before playing for the NFL Washington Redskins and the Cleveland Browns. In San Felipe, TX, of unknown causes.

Gene Sarazen, 97, golfer. Sarazen has been called one of golf's greatest ambassadors and in 1935 became the first man to win the modern grand slam: The Masters, U.S. Open, British Open and PGA Championship.

SI writes:

"He won the 1922 U.S. Open at age 20, beat Walter Hagen in an epic 38-hole playoff at the '23 PGA and in '35 hit golf's most famous shot, a 235-yard four-wood over a pond at Augusta's par-5 15th hole that rolled into the cup for a double-eagle 2. The natty gent called the Squire won seven major titles before retiring from tournament golf in '73. His wife of 62 years, Mary Catherine, died in '86, but the Squire soldiered on, joining Byron Nelson and Sam Snead to plink a ceremonial first ball off Augusta's 1st tee every April. When he died of pneumonia at 97, golf historians noted his status as one of only four players to win all four majors, and Mark O'Meara called him 'class personified.' But for millions of weekend golfers, Sarazen's greatness boiled down to five worlds: He invented the sand wedge. Without him, we might never reach the 19th hole."

In Naples, FL, of pneumonia, May 13, 1999.

Fritz Shurmur, 67, football coach. Shurmur's coaching career spanned two decades with five teams (the Green Bay Packers and the Seattle Seahawks among them). He was considered one of the league's top defensive coordinators and helped design the Green Bay Packers' defense during their Super Bowl championship season of 1996. In Green Bay, WI, of cancer, August 30, 1999.

Dick Sisler, 78, baseball player. Sisler hit the pennant-winning homer for the 1950 Philadelphia Phillies' "Whiz Kids" team. On the final Sunday of the season, the Phils faced the Brooklyn Dodgers at Ebbets Field, seeking their first pennant since 1915. The team had their large lead whittled to one game in the final two weeks and faced a playoff game if they lost to the Dodgers that Sunday. In the top of the 10th, with the score tied 1–1, Sisler faced Don Newcombe with two men on and one out. Sisler, who had already hit three singles and scored the Phils' only run, hit a three-run homer on a 1–2 fastball. Robin Roberts retired the Dodgers in order to seal the victory. Sitting behind the Brooklyn dugout was Sisler's father, George, a Hall of Famer and Dodgers executive. The Whiz Kids were swept by the Yankees in the World Series but the pennant-winning game would long be remembered. Sisler batted .276 with 55 home runs during his eight-year career, and served as Reds manager for part of 1964 and all of 1965. In Nashville, from pneumonia, November 20, 1998.

Samuel D. Solomon, 82, boxing trainer. Solomon trained Muhammad Ali, Sonny Liston, Leon Spinks, Michael Spinks and Trevor Berbick before they became world champions. Before becoming a trainer in 1950, Solomon fought 300 bouts as both a welterweight and a lightweight and was a catcher in baseball's Negro Leagues. In West Philadelphia, of heart failure, December 13, 1998.

Eddie Stanky, 83, baseball player. Stanky was a fiery second baseman who played with the pennant-winning 1947 Brooklyn Dodgers, '48 Boston Braves, and '51 New York Giants. He finished his 11-year career with a .268 batting average. Stanky went on to become a manager with St. Louis, Chicago (AL) and Texas. He finished his career with a 14-year coaching stint at South Alabama where he was 488–193. In Fairhope, AL, of a heart attack, June 6, 1999.

Payne Stewart, 42, golfer. A two-time U.S. Open champion (1991 and '99), Stewart was famous for the plus fours and tam-o'-shanter he always wore on the course. Also won the 1989 PGA Championship. In Ipswich, SD, in a plane accident, October 25, 1999.

Bob Thurman, 81, baseball player. Thurman signed with the Negro Leagues in 1946 and played as a pitcher and outfielder for the Homestead Grays and the Kansas City Monarchs, playing alongside Satchel Paige and Josh Gibson. In 1949, as black stars started to follow Jackie Robinson into the major leagues, Thurman signed a contract with the New York Yankees, but he never played for them—"It was a publicity stunt," his wife said. Instead, the Yankees sold his contract to the Chicago Cubs, who kept him in the minors. He later spent five seasons with the Reds, mostly as a pinch hitter and reserve outfielder. At age 40, Thurman hit 16 home runs in 199 at bats, a pace of one every 11.9 at bats. Thurman also played 11 winter seasons with the Santruce Crabs of the Puerto Rican League, and was voted into the Puerto Rico Baseball Hall of Fame in 1992. He later became one of the first black scouts in baseball. In Wichita, KS, after battling Alzheimer's disease, October 31, 1998.

Mark Tuinei, 39, football player. An offensive lineman Tuinei spent 15 seasons with the Dallas Cowboys. Voted to the Pro Bowl in 1994 and 1995, the 6'5", 320 pound Tuinei was described by his offensive line coach as a "warrior" who never gave up. His signature phrase was "I will crush you like a grape." In Plano, TX, of a drug overdose, May 6, 1999.

Clyde (Bulldog) Turner, 79, football player. To create an aura of fierceness when he tried out for the football team at Hardin-Simmons University in Abilene, TX, Clyde Turner called himself Bulldog. The Chicago Bears liked the play of the 6'2", 232-pounder enough to make him their No. 1 draft pick in 1940. During his 13-year career with the Monsters of the Midway, as the Bears of George Halas were known, Turner was the center, blocking in the then-new T formation directed by quarterback Sid Luckman. Also a linebacker, he had a league-leading eight interceptions in 1942. He carried the football from scrimmage one time—and ran 48 yards for a touchdown. Turner served as head coach of the New York Titans, the Jets' forerunners, in 1962. A six-time All-Pro, he was elected to the Pro Football Hall of Fame in 1966 and his No. 66 was retired by the Bears. In Gatesville, TX, of lung cancer, October 6, 1998.

Jim Turner, 95, pitching coach. Turner, a longtime New York Yankees pitching coach who was nicknamed the Milkman because of his offseason job delivering milk, spent a record 51 consecutive years in professional baseball and played or coached in 13 World Series. (Turner's record 51 years in uniform are being challenged by Yankees coach Don Zimmer, who completed his 50th season in 1999.) Turner was 19 when he broke into the minor leagues in 1922, playing for Paris, Tenn., for $150 a month. After 12 years in the minors, he made it to the major leagues

as a pitcher with the Boston Bees. Turner won 20 games and led the National League with a 2.38 ERA. He was traded to Cincinnati in 1939 and appeared in the 1940 World Series. He also was in the 1942 World Series for the Yankees, and was the Yankees' pitching coach from 1949 to '59 under manager Casey Stengel. Turner was Cincinnati's pitching coach from 1961 to '65, then returned to the Yankees as pitching coach under Ralph Houk from 1966 to '73, when he retired. In Nashville, after a long illness, November 29, 1998.

Harry (the Hat) Walker, 80, baseball player. Walker, whose nickname came from his habit of adjusting his hat between pitches, was a major league outfielder and manager. He had a career .296 batting average in 11 major seasons and led the National League in hitting (.363) in 1947. He played for St. Louis, Philadelphia, Chicago (NL) and Cincinnati. Walker later started the baseball program at the University of Alabama–Birmingham and became its first coach. In Birmingham, AL, of complications from a stroke, August 8, 1999.

Cleveland (Big Cat) Williams, 66, boxer. Williams was shot in the stomach by a Texas state trooper in 1965. He fought Muhammad Ali for the heavyweight title 18 months later in the Astrodome, battling valiantly, but losing in a third-round knockout. He was inducted into the Boxing Hall of Fame in 1998. In Houston, after being struck by a car, September 10, 1999.

Charlie Whittingham, 86, horse trainer. Whittingham trained 11 national champions and was inducted into thoroughbred racing's Hall of Fame in 1974. He guided Ferdinand to a 1986 Kentucky Derby victory and Sunday Silence to a 1989 Derby triumph. The "Bald Eagle" dominated California horse racing for more than 50 years, earning more than $110 million during his career. Whittingham and Hall of Fame jockey Bill Shoemaker won more than 200 stakes races together, with their most famous victory coming at the 1986 Kentucky Derby, when Shoemaker was the oldest jockey ever at 54 and Whittingham was a spry 73. In Los Angeles, April 20, 1999.

Early Wynn, 79, baseball player. Wynn was a Hall of Fame pitcher (inducted in 1972) who won the Cy Young Award at 39 in 1959. A 300-game winner, the right handed Wynn was known for being a fierce competitor. He pitched from 1939 to '63 for Cleveland, Chicago (AL) and the Washington Senators. He had four 20-win seasons for the Indians. Wynn was also a pinch hitter, with 17 career home runs. After retiring, Wynn served as a pitching coach for the Indians and the Minnesota Twins. In Venice, FL, of complications from a stroke, April 4, 1999.

Norm Zauchin, 69, baseball player. Zauchin was a first baseman for the Boston Red Sox. In one stunning May 27, 1955 game, he drove in 10 runs in five innings. He had three home runs and a double in the first five innings of a 16–0 victory against Washington. In Birmingham, AL, after a long illness, January 31, 1999.

Stanislav Zhuk, 63, figure skating coach. An accomplished skater himself (he finished sixth in the pairs with his wife Nina at the 1960 Olympics), Zhuk was best known for coaching some of Russia's top pairs skaters such as Ekaterina Gordeeva and Sergei Grinkov, and Irina Rodnina and Alexander Zaitzev. In Moscow, of undisclosed causes, November 2, 1998.

2000 Major Events

JANUARY

Major College Bowl Games	Jan. 1 & 2
Sugar Bowl/National Championship	Jan 4
NFL Wild Card Weekend	Jan. 8 & 9
NFL Divisional Playoffs	Jan. 15 & 16
NFL Conference Championships	Jan. 23
Australlan Open	Jan. 24–30
Super Bowl XXXIV	Jan. 30

FEBRUARY

Millrose Games	Feb. 4
AFC-NFC Pro Bowl	Feb. 6
NHL All-Star Game	Feb. 6
U.S. Figure Skating Championships	Feb. 6–13
NBA All-Star Game	Feb. 13
PBA National Championship	Feb 13–19
Daytona 500	Feb. 20

MARCH

Major League Soccer Season Begins	March 18
The Players Championship	March 23–26
World Figure Skating Championships	March 26–Apr 2
Baseball Opening Day	March 29

APRIL

NCAA Final Four	April 1–3
Masters Tournament	April6–9
Stanley Cup Playoffs Begin	April 12
Boston Marathon	April 17
NBA Playoffs Begin	April 22

MAY

Kentucky Derby	May 6
Preakness	May 20
Indianapolis 500	May 28
Stanley Cup Finals Begin	May 30

JUNE

NBA Finals Begin	June 2
French Open Tennis	June 5–11
Belmont Stakes	June 10
U.S. Open Golf	June 15–18

JULY

Wimbledon Tennis	July 3–9
Baseball All-Star Game	July 11
British Open Golf	July 20–23

AUGUST

PGA Championship	Aug. 17–20
College Football Season Begins	Aug. 26

SEPTEMBER

NFL Season Begins	Sept. 3
U.S. Open Tennis	Sept. 4–10
Summer Olympics, Sydney, Australia	Sept.15–Oct. 1

OCTOBER

NHL Season Begins	Oct. 4
MLS Cup	Oct. 14
World Series	Oct. 21
NBA Regular Season Begins	Oct. 31

NOVEMBER

Breeders' Cup	Nov.4
New York Marathon	Nov. 6
Chase Championships	Nov. 13–20
ATP World Tour Championships	Nov. 27–Dec. 3

DECEMBER

Heisman Trophy Presentation	Dec. 9
Major College Bowl Games Begin	Dec. 16